Everyman's Encyclopaedia

VOLUME 11

Everyman, I will go with thee, and be thy guide,
In thy most need to go by thy side.

Everyman's Encyclopaedia

SIXTH EDITION IN TWELVE VOLUMES
EDITED BY D. A. GIRLING

11

SEXTANT–TRACHEID

J M Dent & Sons Ltd

LONDON   MELBOURNE   TORONTO   1978

*Made in Great Britain
Data capture by Computer Data Processing Ltd, London
Computer typeset by Computaprint Ltd, London
Printed and bound by Jarrold & Sons Ltd, Norwich
for
J M Dent & Sons Ltd
Aldine House, Albemarle Street, London*

*First published 1913 − 14
Second edition 1931 − 33
Third edition 1949 − 50
Fourth edition 1958
Fifth edition 1967
Sixth edition 1978*

© *J M Dent & Sons Ltd 1958, 1967, 1978*

ISBN 0 460 04023 5 (this volume)
ISBN 0 460 04098 7 (complete set)

British Library Cataloguing in Publication Data

Everyman's encyclopaedia.– 6th ed
  1. Encyclopedias and dictionaries
  I. Girling, D A
  032   A E5

ISBN 0-460-04098-7

Sextant, an instrument for measuring the angle between two directions. The name, which implies that it incorporates a graduated arc extending over one-sixth (Latin *sextus*) of a circle, is now confined to instruments employing reflection but it was originally introduced by Tycho Brahe to describe an instrument similar to the QUADRANT but graduated for only 60°. The idea of employing a double reflection so that a single observer can look in two directions at once seems to have occurred to several people but the first application to a nautical instrument appears to have been made by Thomas Godfrey of Philadelphia in November 1730. Quite independently in May 1731 John Hadley described to the Royal Society an 'octant' having all the essential features of the modern marine sextant but capable of measuring angles only up to 90°. It was quickly brought into use, and in 1757 at the suggestion of Captain John Campbell the octant was extended into a sextant. In 1752 Lacaille named the southern constellation OCTANS in honour of Hadley's invention just as about one hundred years earlier Hevelius had named SEXTANS after the astronomical instrument used by Tycho Brahe and himself.

Sextant.

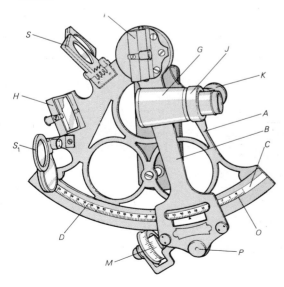

The figure shows a typical modern marine sextant. The metal frame *A* has a graduated circular arc *CD* and carries a movable arm, the 'index bar' *B*, which rotates in a bearing at the centre of the arc *CD*. Mounted on *B* is a small rectangular mirror, the 'index glass' *I*. The frame *A* also carries a bracket *J* to hold the viewing telescope *G*, and, directly in front of *G*, the 'horizon glass' *H*. This is a rectangular piece of glass the right half of which has been made into a mirror and the left half left clear. To find the altitude of a celestial object the observer points the telescope so that he can see the horizon through the clear part of *H* and moves the arm *B* until he sees the celestial object apparently in contact with it. He is, of course, seeing it by light reflected first from the index glass *I* and then from the mirror portion of the horizon glass *H*, and thus deflected by twice the angle between these two mirrors. The instrument is so adjusted that the zero point *O* on the scale *CD* corresponds to the position of the arm *B* when the index glass and the horizon glass are exactly parallel. The arm *B* is positioned by the worm of the micrometer *M* which engages in a rack of constant thread cut accurately in the periphery of the arc *CD*. Its position is read off by taking the whole degrees from the scale *CD*, and the minutes and fractions of a minute from the micrometer head *M*. For rapid movement of the arm, the worm can be disengaged by means of the clutch *P*. Neutral shades, *S* and S_1, can be introduced into one or both of the optical paths when bright objects are being observed. The relative brilliance of the horizon and reflected beams can be adjusted by the screw *K* which moves the viewing telescope and its mount up and down. In use the sextant is held with its plane vertical by means of the wooden handle which is screwed to the opposite side of the frame shown in the figure. On this reverse side there are also three short metal legs on which the instrument can be safely rested when not in immediate use. Sextants usually have two telescopes, one being a high-power 'inverting telescope' fitted with cross wires and the other a bell-shaped low-power 'star telescope' which because of its Galilean arrangement gives an erect image.

A marine sextant is of little use for air navigation since the horizon is usually obscured by haze or cloud. This difficulty is overcome by using a 'bubble' sextant in which the vertical direction is defined by a bubble moving under a spherical surface as in an ordinary spirit level. When observing the zenith distance of a celestial object its image is set in the middle of that of the bubble. In modern high speed planes on which the excrescence of an astrodome cannot be tolerated, sextant observations have to be made through a periscopic system so that only a small retractable window has to project through the aircraft skin. A small, compact, and simplified version of the marine sextant is sometimes known as a 'box' sextant. A model popular with Victorian explorers was completely contained within a strong cylindrical brass box about 10 cm in diameter and 6 cm deep.

Bibliography: O. M. Watts (Ed.), *Sextant Simplified: A Practical Explanation of the Use of the Sextant at Sea*, 5th ed. 1973.

Sexton, a contraction of SACRISTAN. After the Reformation the sacristan's duties in the Church of England largely disappeared, and the sexton has declined into a person who prepares the graves, cares for the churchyard, sweeps the church, and performs similar offices.

Sextus Empiricus (fl. 2nd century AD), Greek philosopher, principal and most impartial historian of SCEPTICISM. Three of his works are extant, all remarkable for their erudition and acumen: *Outlines of Pyrrhonism*; *Against the Dogmatists*; and *Against School Masters*. There is a Loeb Library edition, with translations by R. G. Bury, in four volumes.

Sexual Deviation, see SEXUALITY, HUMAN.

Sexual Intercourse, see SEXUALITY, HUMAN.

Sexual Selection, the term used by Darwin to account for the existence of secondary sex characters. The two methods of sexual selection are combat among the males, and preferential mating where the female chooses her mate. It is really an extension of the theory of natural selection. In the first of the two methods the result is clearly in aid of selection; for if the weaker males are killed, expelled or otherwise left unmated, then the offspring will be more vigorous. The case for preferential mating is not so easy. Darwin, on the one hand, maintained that the female often does choose from among her suitors, not deliberately, but because attracted or excited by their display. Wallace, on the other hand, denied that there is any great evidence of choice, and still less that it is because of any excellence in the male. Thus Darwin held that the colouring, song, etc., of birds and insects are due to persistent choice by the female of mates who are most beautiful, or are the sweetest songsters. Wallace, however, held that the plain plumage of the female, or its lack of song, is a result of natural selection, and is necessary for the preservation of the race, the colouring and lack of song being protective. The role of plumage displays and of song in mating is now held to be part of a very complex instinctive pattern necessary to mating; in any case, it may be seriously doubted if females have any 'appreciation' of beauty in song or appearance, since crude models will frequently evoke the necessary reactions. See also ANIMAL BEHAVIOUR; BIOLOGY; EVOLUTION.

Sexuality, Human. The part sex plays in human relations, in love, and in our image of ourselves as effective men or women, gives it an importance in human terms far beyond its essential purpose of ensuring the continuation of the species. To see human sexuality in perspective, however, it is good first to have some background understanding of the role of sex in evolution and in the reproductive behaviour of other species.

Biological Background. Sexual reproduction is not the only way in which plants and animals reproduce themselves, but it is a major method found throughout the living world, even in one-celled organisms. As a generalisation, an organism that reproduces itself alone can only transmit its own genetic inheritance and all its offspring will resemble it exactly. When two organisms unite to reproduce, that is, reproduce sexually, their inherited characteristics are mixed in the offspring, so that each

Human Sexuality. The anatomy of the female genitals and associated pelvic organs.

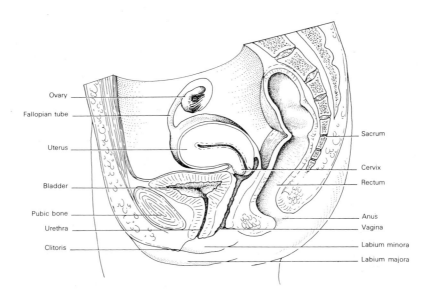

new individual partly resembles each parent, yet is unique. This genetic variety in the new generation ensures that members of the species will differ in their ability to withstand environmental changes that may have detrimental effects, for example, on their food supply or their interaction with other species, and while the average organism may succumb, a few may survive to reproduce and pass on the genes that enable them to cope with the change. (See EVOLUTION; GENETICS; HEREDITY.)

Sexuality in Animals. For sexual reproduction to take place, the male must find the female at the time her eggs are ready to be fertilised. In some species, the female chooses among the available males. In others, the male attracts his chosen female by elaborate courtship rituals. Flashing lights, as in the firefly, scent in many animals, colours in birds and monkeys, attract animals to each other. In the deep ocean, where the population is so sparse that males and females might not meet by chance, the male is sometimes a small parasite on the female, so that, when her eggs are ready, he is there to fertilise them.

For animals the timing of mating is important, as the young must be born when food is plentiful, and when there is time to mature before winter comes. Most animals, in temperate regions, are born in the spring or summer. Mating must take place some time before, depending on the length of gestation, which may be a few weeks for a small animal or many months for the largest species. Birds and mice, for example, mate in the spring and their young are born in the summer. Large animals, with long gestation periods, mate the year before; horses in the spring, deer in the summer, and sheep in the autumn. To control this, the female comes into heat only at certain times, and there is a definite mating season. In a few species, mating takes place when convenient for the adults, and the female stores the sperm until the time is right for the eggs to begin their development.

To fertilise the egg, the sperm must first find it then penetrate it. This is fairly simple for aquatic animals. The female fish or amphibian usually ejects masses of eggs into the water, and the male sprays his sperm over them. In the harsh, dry environment on land, the egg must be protected, and is either covered by a shell, or develops within the mother's body. Land animals copulate, that is, the male inserts his sperm into a special opening in the female's body. The sperm then fertilises the egg before it is encased in its shell, or before it becomes implanted in the womb (uterus) where it develops. Different animal species have different structures and methods for holding the male and female together and inserting the sperm into the female's body.

Sexuality in Humans. The biological basis of sexuality in humans is the same as in animals. In the female, each ovary produces one egg (ovum) each month, which travels down one Fallopian tube to the uterus. If it is not fertilised, it passes out in the menstrual flow through the vagina. The male makes sperm in his testes, and the seminal fluid to carry them in the prostate and other glands. This sperm-containing semen is ejaculated through the penis into the vagina during coitus (copulation or sexual intercourse), the sperm swim to the ovum, and one penetrates it, starting the development of a new individual. Unlike animals, humans have no special season for birth, hence no mating season. Attempts to attract the opposite sex and mating behaviour go on all the time, whether there is an egg ready for fertilisation or not, or even, for many couples, preferably when there is not. Thus in humans, the pleasures of sexuality have taken on a significance largely disconnected from the essential reproductive purpose.

Masculinity and Femininity. Every society has an image of the ideal behaviour for men and women, and tries to make individuals fit into certain patterns, according

Human Sexuality. The anatomy of the male genitals and associated pelvic organs.

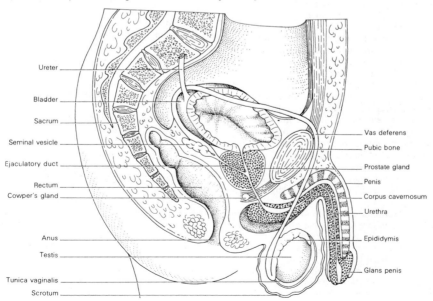

Ureter
Bladder
Sacrum
Seminal vesicle
Ejaculatory duct
Rectum
Cowper's gland
Anus
Testis
Tunica vaginalis
Scrotum

Vas deferens
Pubic bone
Prostate gland
Penis
Corpus cavernosum
Urethra
Epididymis
Glans penis

to their sex. This stereotyping ignores the overlap of characteristics between the sexes. The male and female sexual organs develop from the same rudimentary organs in the embryo, differentiating gradually, for example, into an ovary or a testis, a clitoris or a penis, under the influence of the sex hormones. But every person has the same sex hormones, only the proportions differ in men and women. Studies of mistaken sex, due either to malformation of the external genital organs at birth, or to psychological influences, have shown that one is aware of oneself as a little boy or a little girl by the age of two years. This self-image comes from the way parents and other adults relate to the baby, and need not correspond to its genetic sex. Usually the parents and family of the infant encourage it to behave and see itself in the role assigned to that sex in that society; only the few cases of mistaken sexual identity show that 'masculine' or 'feminine' behaviour is learned, not innate. Another indication of this superficiality of assigned sexual roles comes from anthropological studies, which have found that the attributes, such as gentleness or aggression, that may assigned to one sex, differ from one society to another. Although psychologists have designed tests that place a person along a scale from extreme femininity to extreme masculinity, the tests apply only in the society for which they are designed, and even there most people come somewhere in the middle. Inevitably, each person has genetically controlled attributes of each sex and must also have some learned traits of each sex, for the growing child identifies with aspects of each parent and imitates some habits and attitudes of both its mother and its father.

Psychosexual Development. Sexuality in humans brings us great bodily pleasure, centred in adults in the genitals, but contributed to by the skin, and the mucous membranes of the bodily openings. From earliest infancy, the infant experiences pleasure and pain as he feels and explores his body, and is caressed and handled. Infants seem to develop through phases of awareness and concern with certain aspects of the body, classifed by psychologists as oral, anal and genital. The oral phase centres on the pleasures of sucking, and the relationship to the mother's breast. The anal phase involves the pleasures and discomfort of defecating, and eventually the ability to produce or withhold, perhaps the infant's first experience of power. The greatest pleasure is discovered in normal exploration and play with the genitals. Genital preoccupation becomes latent during the years from about age 6–11, then reawakens around puberty to continue during adult life. The child's feelings and fears about the sensations his body enjoys, mixed with phantasies of power, with anger, and with real frustration when his mother ignores or does not understand his needs, or deliberately restricts his touching or messing activities, influence his sexual behaviour, and indeed, his relations to other people, throughout his life.

A little more distant than internal feelings about sexual identity and bodily pleasure, are the controls exerted by society on individual behaviour. Every society, first through the parents, later through customs and even laws, attempts to control sexual behaviour. Among the major religions, Christianity is the most prohibitive of free sexual expression. Politically, totalitarian states tend to be more concerned than other political regimes with limiting sex-

ual freedom and encouraging such puritan principles as that work and sacrifice come before pleasure. Every society has its own marriage and divorce laws and incest taboos. What is defined as incest differs, however, in various societies and often has little connection with the genetic relationship of the two individuals concerned.

An individual's awareness of sexuality, therefore, is a mixture that includes pleasure, but sometimes also frustration and guilt, and internal feelings and external controls, some from forgotten infancy, and some consciously imposed by his society. His sexuality is a part of his personality, determines to some extent his social and economic opportunities—his chances for education, the jobs open to him, his interests and conversation—and affects his awareness of self and others and his interaction with the men and women he meets.

Homosexuality may result from distortion of normal psychosexual development. Although the person may feel secure in his own sex, he or she is attracted to members of his own sex more than the other. This may be limited to feelings, or may be expressed in sexual acts and falling in love with persons of the same sex. The normal bisexuality—the presence in all individuals of traits, feelings and abilities more common in his society to the other sex—may sometimes be expressed in the ability to love and perform sexual acts with both sexes.

A different problem is transsexuality, in which the person is convinced, even though his body and chromosomes indicate that he is male or female, that he or she is really a member of the other sex. Previously transsexuals only dressed and acted as persons of the other sex. Today they may take sex hormones to deepen the voice and make a beard grow, or to eliminate the beard and produce breasts, and may have surgical operations to change the external genital organs.

Sexual Pleasure. Sexual arousal in the male causes the penis to become engorged with blood, making it hard and erect. The friction of intercourse increases this pleasurable tension until, at the climax (orgasm), the seminal fluid is ejaculated, followed by a softening of the penis and general relaxation. Sexual arousal in the female causes secretions to flow in the vagina, lubricating the tissues to facilitate entry of the penis. The clitoris, a similar structure to the penis, becomes hard and erect, and as excitement increases, tension and intensely pleasurable feelings build up until, at orgasm, the uterus and vagina contract rhythmically, then all the organs relax. The female's secretion corresponds to the male's erection in that both make penetration possible.

In children, and often between adults, sex acts are aimed only at erotic pleasure, although the interweaving of sexual pleasure with love, using touch as a form of communication, and the climax as a sharing and giving each to the other in mutual abandonment, is held up as the ideal. Children start with masturbation, which is caressing the external genital organs to produce sexual excitement and usually orgasm. In males from about the time of puberty, orgasm is accompanied by ejaculation of seminal fluid containing sperm. In females the muscular spasms are internal, and there is no ejaculation. Masturbation is also resorted to by adults for various reasons. Sex play between children, and petting or mutual caressing by adolescents, whether engaged in out of curiosity or for pleasure, is part of learning about sex and the feelings and human relations connected with it.

The female often, especially in restrictive western cultures, needs a more stimulatory atmosphere and more foreplay than does the male, in order to become aroused to the point of orgasm. While both men and women enjoy caressing and being caressed, this is usually essential to the woman, but only an added pleasure to the man. However, once the male has ejaculated, he usually must rest for a while before beginning again, but the female can commonly reach several orgasms, one after the other. The woman can also get great pleasure from a sexual act that does not achieve orgasm, although to the man such an act would be unsatisfying.

Sexual Problems. The basic problems that interfere with the sexual act are frigidity in the woman and impotence in the man. Frigidity is the inability of the woman to become sexually aroused. It is commonly used to refer to her inability to reach orgasm, but this is incorrect, for many women are sexually responsive yet do not reach the climax. Frigidity may result from the man's poor sexual technique, the woman's not being in love with the man, or from a deep belief that sex is bad. Such causes can be treated by sexual counsellors. Frigidity may also be due to a deep fear of giving, or of letting go and losing self-control. Such deeper problems can often be treated by psychotherapy. Advanced types of frigidity include vaginismus, in which the muscles of the vagina resist the entrance of the penis, and dyspareunia, painful intercourse. Women with these problems should see a gynaecologist, who may recommend medical, surgical or psychological treatment.

Impotence is a temporary or permanent interference with normal sexual functioning in the male. It may take the form of failure to produce or to sustain an erection, or the inability to ejaculate at orgasm. Temporary impotence may occur when the man is depressed, tired, drunk, or ill. Persistent impotence is a symptom of deeper problems in the man's personality, such as unconscious fears of women, fear of castration, or of damaging the woman. It is similar psychologically to frigidity, but much more obvious and crippling. It can often be helped by sexual counselling or psychotherapy.

Premature ejaculation is another common male problem. This is a disturbance of potency characterised by premature emission of semen before or immediately after the penis is inserted into the vagina. It may have roots in unconscious phantasies, such as a desire to wet or soil the woman or to cheat her of sexual gratification. Techniques can be learned to enable the man to hold on longer, and psychotherapy or sexual counselling can help.

Insatiable preoccupation with sex and the compulsive need for sexual intercourse is called nymphomania in women and satyriasis in men. It may mask a form of impotence or frigidity, in which the act is never found satisfying, so must be tried again and again with other partners. It may be a form of greed or an attempt to solve feelings of inadequacy. The concept of how often and with how many partners it is normal to have sexual intercourse differs in different societies and times.

Sexual Deviations. Sexual deviations are repetitive, compulsive acts that bring sexual excitement by means other than normal coitus (that is, the insertion of the penis into the vagina during sexual intercourse between willing partners). The normal act is here considered the one that procreates the species. The deviant prefers his chosen method of genital excitement to the ordinary one, and may not be able to reach a climax in any other way.

By this strict definition, homosexuality is a deviation. Minor deviations are a normal part of foreplay and experimentation, but usually lead up to coitus, and are not compulsive or preferred to coitus. Such sex play includes stimulation of the genitals with the mouth, which is called fellatio if it is the penis that is stimulated, and cunnilingus if it is the clitoris and vulva. Buggery, anal intercourse, and mild, playful imitations of the more serious deviations may also occur during foreplay.

Serious deviant behaviour is marked by its compulsive repetition. It is more common in men than in women, and the man does not normally change from one form of deviant behaviour to another. Voyeurism involves watching women undress or couples making love, becoming excited and often masturbating while watching. Exhibitionism is displaying one's penis in public. Fetishism occurs when the man invests some part of the body, such as the foot or hair, or an object or article of clothing, such as underclothes or shoes, with magically exciting qualities. He often can only be aroused by this fetish, and may use it for masturbation. Bestiality, a rare deviation, is coitus with an animal, usually due to lack of a human partner, not by free choice. Paedophilia is sexual play or intercourse with a child, and may vary from a willing or at least docile compliance by the child in return for attention, in which case it is usually some form of caressing, to the use of force or violence on a child victim. Sadism, obtaining sexual excitement from inflicting pain or humiliation on another person, and masochism, being excited by being hurt or humiliated, are related deviations. Usually the person is either sadistic or masochistic, but the roles may be interchangeable. Common sado-masochistic acts include whipping, spanking, or tying up. Sadism and masochism may be life styles that affect all aspects of the person's personality and behaviour, showing up as compulsive domination or being a continual martyr or victim. A few sadists get sexual excitement from mutilating, raping, or killing their victims.

The motive behind deviant needs is rooted in the infant's relation to its parents, brothers, and sisters. It is usually either an overwhelming feeling of inadequacy and fear of adult human relationships, or revenge for rejection and humiliation, especially by powerful women such as the mother, when the person was still too young and helpless to defend himself. In some cases psychotherapy or behaviour therapy are successful in inducing more normal behaviour. It should always be remembered, however, that 'normal' and 'deviant' are in no way synonymous with 'right' and 'wrong'; in man sexual activity is largely divorced from procreation, and the definition of 'normal' adopted here is a matter of convenience, excluding as it does a great deal of both individually and socially harmless, everyday human behaviour.

Bibliography: N. J. Berrill, *Sex and Nature of Things*, 1953; R. von Krafft-Ebing, *Psychopathia Sexualis*, new ed. 1965; T. H. van de Velde, *The Ideal Marriage*, 2nd ed. 1965; W. H. Masters and V. E. Johnson, *Human Sexual Response*, 1966; *Human Sexual Inadequacy*, 1970; K. Horney, *Feminine Psychology*, 1967; R. J. Stoller, *Sex and Gender*, 1968; A. Storr, *Sexual Deviation*, 1970; E. Chesser, *Human Aspects of Sexual Deviation*, 1971; A. Comfort (Ed.) *The Joy of Sex*, 1974.

Seychelles

Seychelles, archipelago of 86 islands in the INDIAN OCEAN, with a land area of 277 km². Some 37 of the islands are granitic and the remainder coralline. Situated 1000 km north-east of the Malagasy Republic, between 3°38′ and 5°45′S and 52°55′ and 53°50′E. MAHÉ, with an area of 184 km², is the largest island, followed by Praslin with 41 km², Silhouette with 16 km², and La Digue with 10 km² (see ATLAS 3).

Geography. Almost all the granite islands are dominated by mountains which rise sharply from the sea to heights of 610 and 910 m. Mahé, 8 km across at its widest, has a chain of peaks, the highest, Morne Seychellois, reaching 905 m. In contrast to other oceanic islands, volcanic or coral in origin, the Seychelles' granites and gneisses are CAMBRIAN or pre-Cambrian and therefore older than any other oceanic island in the world. Temperatures reach a maximum of 29 °C and a minimum of 25 °C. Rainfall averages 2337 mm annually, although in the mountainous rain forests it often reaches 5000 mm. The population was estimated at 59,200 in 1976; 86 per cent is concentrated on Mahé. Victoria, the capital and chief town, has a population of 14,500. Aldabra, Farquhar, and Desroches in the western Indian Ocean are islands attached to the Seychelles. The Aldabra group of islands is the habitat of gigantic land tortoises; many specimens are also to be found on Mahé.

Economy. About half the total land area of the Seychelles is under tree or shrub crops, the remaining land

Seychelles. A typical Seychellois house amid coconut palms, on La Digue. *(Camera Press/M. Kuh)*

being unsuitable for agriculture, or under forestry. Coconut palms and cinnamon trees have been the two mainstay crops and in 1975 accounted for 90 per cent of island exports which were worth Rs35 million; imports were worth Rs191,400,000.

There are 108 km of paved and 14 km of earth roads on Mahé. Praslin has 6 km of paved and 32 km of earth roads; La Digue has 13 km of earth roads. There is an international airport at Mahé which dealt with 37,320 tourists in 1975. Between 110 and 170 merchant ships have called annually at Victoria since 1971, carrying over 80,000 t of import cargo. There is no television, but an extensive radio service operates on the islands.

Government. Since the *coup d'état* of 5 June 1977 Seychelles has been ruled by a president and seven ministers appointed by him; there is no prime minister. Government is at present by decree. Political parties are not permitted for the time being.

In 1975 there were 36 primary and 15 secondary schools providing educational facilities for 12,977 pupils. There is a teacher training college on Mahé.

The new national flag is comprised of two diagonal white stripes which intersect and provide borders for alternating red and navy blue triangles, the blue being at top and bottom.

History. The islands are supposed to have been discovered by a Portuguese, Pedro Mascarenhas, in 1505, but the discovery was not followed by any attempt at colonisation. They were explored by the French in 1742 and 1744 and finally ceded to Britain by the Treaty of Paris, 1814. Before the French occupation they were the resort of pirates, some of whose names are borne by descendants on Mahé today. The French set up their 'Stone of Possession' on Mahé in 1756; later the group was named Seychelles in honour of Viscomte Morau de Seychelles, controller-general of finance under Louis XV. During the

Seychelles. The clock-tower in the centre of the capital, Victoria, is a reminder of British colonial rule, now past. *(Camera Press/N. Watt)*

French Revolution Mahé was used by French ships as a place of refuge and refitment, but on 17 May 1794 it was captured by Captain Newcome of HMS *Orpheus*. The last French governor, de Quincy, eventually became the first *agent civil* under the British government. After the capture of Mauritius in 1810, Seychelles was formally incorporated as a dependency of that colony. In 1897 the administrator was given full powers as governor, and Seychelles was practically separated from Mauritius. The separation was completed in 1903 by an Order in Council constituting Seychelles a separate colony under its own governor. During the French occupation settlers, mostly from Mauritius, were placed on Mahé, and the descendants of these form the majority of the European and mixed element of the population, whose language is French. African slaves were also brought in from Mauritius, and the African community was much increased by the fact of Seychelles being chosen as a refuge for African slaves freed by the British navy. Their descendants today form the large majority of the population. Almost all profess Christianity, being mostly Roman Catholics. The colony has at various times been chosen as a place of deportation, in 1897 for Prempeh, King of Ashanti, in 1901 for Mwanga, King of Buganda, and Kabarega, King of Bunyoro, in 1937 for the leaders of the Arab revolt in Palestine, and in 1956 for Archbishop Makarios of Cyprus.

An elected government was introduced in the late 1960s. After eight years as a self-governing colony, the Seychelles finally established independence, almost the last British colony to do so. In 1976, the year of independence, the Seychelles demanded, and achieved, the return of three islands, Aldabra, Farquhar, and Desroches, formerly detached from the Seychelles administrative area to form the BRITISH INDIAN OCEAN TERRITORY for military purposes. The Seychelles have joined the Commonwealth.

Up to the *coup d'état* of 5 June 1977, government of Seychelles was by a prime minister (J. R. Mancham) and a cabinet of 12 ministers, all elected members of the House of Assembly. There were two political parties. The *coup* took place while the prime minister was in London. The office of prime minister was replaced by that of president, the first president being R. A. René. Seven ministers were nominated by him, and government by decree was introduced.

Bibliography: HMSO, *People of the Seychelles*, 1970; G. Lionnet, *The Seychelles*, 1972; Sir Campbell White (Ed.), *Laws of the Seychelles*, 1973.

Seydlitz, Friedrich Wilhelm von (1721–73), Prussian cavalry general, born at Calcar, near Kleve. Seydlitz became a cornet in the Margrave of Schwedt's cuirassiers, 1740, and was captain of hussars, 1743. He commanded the Württemberg dragoons, 1752, and the Rochow cuirassiers, 1753, becoming colonel in 1755. He was the most brilliant cavalryman of the Seven Years' War. In 1760 Seydlitz took part in the defence of Berlin against the Russians. In 1762 he again distinguished himself at Freiberg. After the making of peace he was transferred to the Silesian cavalry-inspection, and in 1767 made general.

Seymour Family, see BEAUCHAMP; SOMERSET, EARLS AND DUKES OF.

Seymour, Lord Hugh (Hugh Seymour Conway Seymour) (1759–1801), British vice-admiral, in command of the *Latona* at the relief of Gibraltar in 1782. During the three days fighting ending in what is known as the 'Glorious First of June' in 1794 he greatly distinguished himself. He took part in the fighting off L'Orient under Bridport, and held the post of lord of the Admiralty from 1795 to 1798.

Seymour, Lady Jane (c. 1509–37), Queen of England, third wife of HENRY VIII, and mother of Edward VI, born at Wolf Hall, Savernake, Wiltshire. She was a lady-in-waiting first to Catherine of Aragon and then to Anne Boleyn. She married Henry a few days after Anne's execution in 1536. She died in 1537, a few days after giving birth to her son.

Seymour, Lynn (1939–), Canadian-born ballerina of the Royal Ballet. Seymour, who excels not only in classical works but also in intensely dramatic roles and in the broadest of broad comedy, has been fortunate in having throughout her career a choreographer to exploit her great gifts—Kenneth MACMILLAN has done for her what Ashton did for Fonteyn. Apart from the classical ballets—her Giselle is one of the finest in our time—she can give intensely moving performances as Juliet or Anastasia, while in Robbins' *The Concert* she is wildly funny. Mother of three children, she made a fantastic 'come back' in 1975 and was hailed by many as the natural successor to Fonteyn.

Seyss-Inquart, Arthur (1892–1946), Austrian lawyer and politician, born in Moravia, joined the Nazi party

Lady Jane Seymour, from an engraving after the original by Holbein. *(Mansell Collection)*

in 1928. Minister of the interior and security in the Schuschnigg Cabinet from February to March 1938, he became governor of Austria in 1938, and deputy-governor general of Poland in 1939. As Reich commissioner for the Netherlands he became notorious for his cruelty, and after the war was executed as a war criminal.

Sfax, seaport city on the Gulf of Gabès, TUNISIA, 130 km south of Sousse. Its chief articles of trade are cotton and woollen goods, olive oil, fruit, phosphates, and sponges. Population (1974) 100,000.

Sforza, famous Italian ducal family descended from Giacomuzzo, or Muzio, Attendolo (1369–1424), a peasant *condottiere* who adopted the name of Sforza.

Francesco Sforza (1401–66) succeeded his father in command of the *condottiere*. He served Filippo Maria Visconti, Duke of Milan, and in 1441 married his only daughter, Bianca. On Filippo's death in 1447, Francesco defeated the Venetians, hereditary enemies of Milan, and was acknowledged duke of Milan in 1450. His rule was most beneficent.

Galeazzo Maria Sforza (1444–76), succeeded Francesco Sforza as duke of Milan on the latter's death in 1466. He was a cruel and dissolute despot, and was assassinated.

Sforza. Ludovico Sforza, his wife, Beatrice d'Este, and children. Painting in the Pinacoteca, Milan, by Bernardino dei Conti. (*Alinari*)

Gian Galeazzo Sforza (1468–94), son of Galeazzo Maria, succeeded to the Duchy under his mother's regency.

Ludovico Sforza, surnamed il Moro (the Moor) (1451–1508), husband of Beatrice d'Este (see ESTE), supplanted, and probably poisoned, his nephew, Gian Galeazzo. He was betrayed by his own mercenaries in 1500 to Louis XII of France, who kept him in captivity until his death.

Other prominent members of the family were Cardinal Ascagnio, son of Francesco; Bona Sforza (1493–1557), daughter of Gian Galeazzo and wife of the king of Poland; Francesco (d. 1511), son of Gian Galeazzo and Abbot of Marmoutiers; Massimiliano (1490–1530), son of Ludovico, restored to the Duchy in 1512, and his brother, Francesco Maria (1492–1535), made duke by Charles V in 1532.

Bibliography: C. M. Aoly, *A History of Milan under the Sforza*, 1907.

Sforza, Count Carlo (1873–1952), Italian diplomat and statesman, born at Montignoso, near Massa. He had a distinguished diplomatic career at Constantinople, Peking, Paris, Madrid, and London. In 1919 he became under-secretary of state; in 1920 foreign minister under Giolitti. He was ambassador to France in 1922; after Mussolini's March on Rome he resigned and returned to Italy, where he was an active opponent of fascism. By 1928 he was forced into exile, first in Belgium, and later in America. He returned to Italy in 1943, and made a dramatic re-entry into European diplomacy at the Paris Conference of 1947, being once more Italy's foreign minister. His efforts to restore Italian influence in world politics and to bring Italy into the Western alliance occupied the last years of his life. By the time he resigned, owing to ill-health, in 1951, he had seen his policies brought to a successful fruition. Among his publications are: *Fifty Years of War and Diplomacy in the Balkans*, 1941; *Machiavelli: Latin and Italian*, 1942; *The Real Italians*, 1942; *Totalitarian War and After*, 1942; *Contemporary Italy: its Intellectual and Moral Origins*, 1946; and *Italy and the Italians*, 1948.

Sgraffiato, see SLIPWARE.

Sgraffito (Italian, scratched work), form of pottery and house decoration which was very general in prehistoric times throughout the Mediterranean area, and which has been revived in central Italy and Switzerland since the 15th century. The wall is coloured black or dark brown, and then receives a coat of light plaster on which a design is traced so that the dark paint shows through. The modern practice in commercial art of executing black-and-white drawings by 'scraper-board' is based on the same principle, except that the scratching is performed on black over a base of white, producing an effect similar to reproductions from wood engravings.

Bibliography: E. Berger, *Fresko- und Sgraffito-technik*, 1909.

's Gravenhage, see HAGUE, THE.

Shaabi, Qahtan al- (1920–), Southern Yemeni politician, born in Lahej, and educated at Aden College and Khartoum University. After government service he helped organise the National Liberation Front, becoming the country's first president on independence. He was ousted by Salem Rubai Ali in June 1969.

Shaba, formerly Katanga, province of south-eastern ZAIRE bordering on Zambia. It is one of the most important mining districts in the world and in 1973 produced 500,000 t of copper; 90,000 t of zinc concentrates; and 15,000 t of cobalt. LUBUMBASHI is the provincial capital, and Likasi and Kolwezi are important mining centres. The surrounding rural areas are in general thinly populated.

The region played a major role in the civil war which broke out in the Congo after Belgian colonial rule ended in June 1960. It was the most politically and economically advanced of all the provinces and in July 1960, under TSHOMBE, it seceded from the new republic, calling itself the republic of Katanga until forcibly reintegrated into the Congo, with UN assistance, in January 1962. Subsequently Katanga again exercised a dominant influence when Tshombe became premier of the Congo, 1964–65. Area 497,000 km²; population (1974) 3,072,600.

Shabani, town of Rhodesia, 98 km west of Fort Victoria, and centre of the important asbestos-mining area. Population (1974) 17,000, of whom 1600 are whites.

Shabbi, Abu'l-Qasim al- (1909–34), Tunisian poet, a contributor to *Apollo* (see APOLLO POETS). He is recognised as one of the finest Arabic poets writing between the world wars, in spite of his tragically short life, for his single volume of verse, *Songs of Life*, published in 1955. Usually described as a Romantic poet (see ROMANTIC MOVEMENT), the intensity of his vision transcends his own experience and problems to those of his society and humanity at large.

Bibliography: M. M. Badawi, *A Critical Introduction to Modern Arabic Poetry*, 1975.

Shackleton, Sir Ernest Henry (1874–1922), British explorer, born at Kilkee, County Clare, Ireland. He was educated at Dulwich College, and was third lieutenant in the National Antarctic Expedition, 1901. He commanded the British ANTARCTIC expedition, 1908–09. On 1 January 1908 his expedition left New Zealand in the *Nimrod*. He established a base near Mount EREBUS, whence, on 20 October 1908, he started over the ice with sledges and in company with Lieutenant Adams, Dr Eric Marshall and Frank Wild, with provisions for 91 days. On 9 January 1909 they reached 88° 23′S, 156 km from the South Pole,

a record far surpassing that established on Scott's first expedition. Mount Erebus was climbed and the magnetic pole reached by Sir T. W. Edgeworth David and Sir D. Mawson. Shackleton was presented with the special gold medal of the Royal Geographical Society and was knighted in the same year. In 1914–16 he intended to cross Antarctica from Coats Land to McMurdo Sound; but the ship *Endurance* was crushed in ice and abandoned; and the party were rescued only after Shackleton and five others had voyaged to South Georgia in a 7-metre boat. In September 1921 Shackleton left London in the ship *Quest*, for a three-year tour in Antarctica. He died on board, and in accordance with his wish, was buried in South Georgia. Shackleton published accounts of his journeys in *The Heart of the Antarctic*, 1909, and *South: The Story of Shackleton's Last Expedition, 1914–17*, 1919.

Bibliography: F. Wild, *Shackleton's Last Voyage*, 1923; M. and J. Fisher, *Shackleton*, 1957.

Shad, alose, or allice, *Alosa*, a genus of fishes of the herring family Clupeidae, order Clupeiformes, found on both sides of the North Atlantic. They enter rivers to spawn. The British species are the allis shad (*A. alosa*) and the twaite shad (*A. finta*).

Shaddock, see CITRUS FRUITS.

Shaded-pole Motors, see SPECIAL PURPOSE MACHINES.

Shadi, Ahmad Zaki Abu, see APOLLO POETS.

Shadow Clock. The earliest surviving time-measuring devices provided with actual time scales were shadow clocks, the oldest known example being an Egyptian one of about the 10th to 8th centuries BC. In appearance something like a T-square, this instrument comprised a longish base with a shorter cross-piece standing up on a short arm at right angles to it. It was placed in the morning so that the cross-piece lay north and south, with the base pointing towards the west. The shadow from the cross-piece would thus fall on the base—in the early hours near the end, and gradually creeping nearer to the cross-piece itself, until the sun was at its zenith. As soon as noon had been registered the instrument was reversed in order to measure the afternoon hours in similar manner, morning and afternoon being divided into six hours each on a scale along the base. See also SUNDIAL.

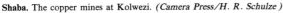

Shaba. The copper mines at Kolwezi. *(Camera Press/H. R. Schulze)*

Shadow Puppets

Shadow Puppets, flat figures held between a light and a translucent screen. Puppets of this kind have been developed mainly in oriental countries, where various traditions have been established. In China the figures are made from translucent fish skins, and are delicately coloured and cut out, creating a coloured shadow upon the screen; the manipulation is by rods from below and the stories are drawn from traditional sources. In Java, Bali and parts of Malaysia the figures are cut from opaque leather but are brightly coloured; only a black shadow is cast on the screen but some members of the audience may sit behind the operator so that they watch the actual puppets rather than their shadows on the screen; an extensive repertory is based upon the stories in the Hindu epic poems of the *Ramayana* and the *Mahabharata*. In Thailand there is a unique Siamese tradition of the *Nang*, very large leather figures or groups of figures which are static in the sense that they do not posses articulated hands or feet but are given expressive movement in a kind of whirling dance by their manipulators. In India there is a regional form of shadow theatre in the Andhra province,

Shadow Puppets. Javanese puppet, 18th or 19th century. *(Topham/Fotogram)*

using very large figures of thin translucent leather, in plays also based on the Hindu epic legends.

The tradition of shadow theatre seems to have spread across Asia to Turkey, where an indigenous form of puppet show developed with a hunchbacked character called Karaguesi as its chief clown; the figures in this show are cut from opaque leather but, unlike the oriental types, are manipulated by rods held at right angles to the screen. Although the Turkish shadow show is now almost extinct, the tradition still survives in a lively and nationalistic form in Greece in the Karaguez theatre.

A shadow show is featured in Ben Jonson's comedy, *A Tale of a Tub*, 1633, but it was not until towards the end of the 18th century that this form of puppet theatre played any large part in Europe. In the 1770s it was featured in Paris as the *Ombres chinoises* and in this form it enjoyed considerable popularity in England for a few decades. The *Ombres chinoises* were, in fact, very unlike Chinese shadow puppets, as they were presented in black silhouettes cut from tin and manipulated by rods and levers from the side of the screen. The most popular piece was a little song called *The Broken Bridge*.

The shadow theatre is an art form capable of great fantasy, and has attracted a number of contemporary puppeteers, notably Lotte Reiniger who exploited this medium in films.

Bibliography: O. Blackman, *Shadow Puppets*, 1960; H. Schönewolf, *Play with Light and Shadow*, 1968.

Shadows. According to geometrical optics, the shadow of an object formed by an extended light source is divided into two regions, as in the figure. No light rays reach the umbra, or shadow proper, so that this is in principle completely dark, but light from some parts of the source reaches the penumbra. For example, in a solar eclipse we see a total eclipse from regions traversed by the umbra of the shadow of the moon but a partial eclipse is seen from the penumbra.

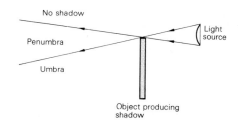

Shadwell, Thomas (c. 1642–92), English poet laureate and dramatist, born at Weeting, Norfolk. He studied at Cambridge University and his first play, *The Sullen Lovers*, based on MOLIÈRE's *Les Fâcheux*, was produced at the theatre in Lincoln's Inn Fields in 1668. After other adaptations he wrote *Epsom Wells*, a coarse but well constructed comedy, which was successful at Dorset Garden in 1672. *The Squire of Alsatia* was presented in 1688 and *Bury Fair* in 1689. Among his other comedies, which show comic power, based on JONSON's theory of 'humours', are *Royal Shepherdess*, 1669, *The Humorists*, 1671, and *The Miser*, 1672.

Shadwell supported the cause of the middle-class Whigs, and when DRYDEN attacked them in *Absalom and*

Achitophel and *The Medal*, Shadwell scurrilously assailed him in *The Medal of John Bayes*, 1682. The punishment which this evoked in Dryden's *MacFlecknoe* and the second part of *Absalom and Achitophel*, in which Shadwell figures as 'Og', gave him an unenviable immortality. However, at the Revolution, he replaced Dryden as poet laureate. Owing to his feud with Dryden, Shadwell has been consistently underrated. He had comic powers of a high order, if counterbalanced by a certain heaviness.

Bibliography: M. Summers (Ed.), *The Complete Works of Thomas Shadwell*, 1927; A. S. Borgman, *Thomas Shadwell: his Life and Comedies*, 1928; H. W. Alssid, *Shadwell*, 1967.

Shaffer, Peter Levin (1926–), English dramatist and novelist. Shaffer came to prominence with *Five Finger Exercise*, 1958, a domestic drama set in a rich middle-class home. This was followed by *The Private Ear and the Public Eye*, 1962, and *The Royal Hunt of the Sun*, 1964, an epic play about the Spanish conquest of Peru which exploits dance, mime and stylised acting techniques. The highly successful farce, *Black Comedy*, 1965, was followed by a philosophical play, *The Battle of Shrivings*, 1970, and by *Equus*, *1973*, a psychological study of a boy who deliberately blinds horses. As the differences in genre indicate, Shaffer is a dramatist of wide interests and range. His work has been as successful in New York as in London. He has written television and screen plays (including *Lord of the Flies*, with Peter BROOK), and novels with his twin brother Anthony Shaffer, who is chiefly known for his highly successful stage thriller, *Sleuth*, 1970, which was later filmed.

Shaftesbury, Anthony Ashley Cooper, 1st Earl of (1621–83), English politician, son of Sir John Cooper, born at Wimborne St Giles, Dorset, and educated at Exeter College, Oxford. In 1638 he became a student at Lincoln's Inn. At the age of 19 he was returned as one of the members for Tewkesbury to the Parliament which met in April 1640. He adhered to the royal interest till he was refused, in 1643, the governorship of Weymouth, promised him by the Marquess of Hertford. Shaftesbury's attitude then changed completely, and he went over to the Parliamentarians; whether motives other than the refusal of the governorship determined this action is obscure.

Shaftesbury sat as one of the members for Wiltshire in the first (Barebones) Parliament, and was appointed one of the Protector's council of state. From 1655 he was in constant opposition to Cromwell. In the Convention Parliament, which met in April 1660, Sir Anthony Cooper (as he now was) was one of the select committee appointed to draw up the invitation to the new King, and one of the commissioners sent over to Breda. At the restoration of Charles, Sir Anthony was made lord-lieutenant of the county of Dorset, chancellor of the Exchequer, and a privy councillor, and in 1661 he was raised to the peerage as Baron Ashley of Wimborne St Giles. After the fall of Clarendon, Lord Ashley formed one of the Cabal ministry. In April 1672 he was created earl of Shaftesbury, and in November following was raised to the office of lord chancellor. In 1673, however, he supported the Test Bill, an action which had the result of breaking up the Cabal, and was dismissed from office. Shaftesbury now openly joined the ranks of opposition as a champion of toleration for dissenters and national liberties. He opposed Danby's Non-resistance Bill (1675), and

in 1677 was sent to the Tower for his protest against prorogation, but was quickly released on making full submission. Though the 'Popish Plot' was not inspired by Shaftesbury, he made use of the two years' terror of 1678–80 most ruthlessly, and even the Habeas Corpus Act, for long known as Shaftesbury's Act, is little extenuation of the execution of Lord Stafford, his personal enemy.

After the fall of Danby, Shaftesbury was made president of Temple's new Privy Council (1679), and he now tried to exclude James, Duke of York, from the succession in favour of Monmouth by presenting an indictment of the former as a Popish recusant (26 June 1680). In the following year he was again sent to the Tower on a charge of treason, but when an indictment was preferred against him at the Old Bailey, the grand jury ignored it. When Monmouth and Lord William Russell refrained from the open rebellion advocated by Shaftesbury, the latter, evidently feeling that there was no safety for him in England, fled to Holland on 18 November 1682, and died there a few months later.

Extremely able and eloquent, despite his self-interest and lack of scruples, Shaftesbury may be regarded as an originator of party government, though he was always prone to score party advantages from plots, intrigues, perjuries, and, especially, religious conflict.

Bibliography: L. F. Brown, *The First Earl of Shaftesbury*, 1934; J. R. Jones, *The First Whigs*, 1961.

Shaftesbury, Anthony Ashley Cooper, 3rd Earl of (1671–1713), English politician and philosopher, grandson of the first Earl of Shaftesbury, born at Exeter House, London. In 1693 he entered Parliament, but he resigned his seat in 1698 and went over to Holland, where he made the acquaintance of Bayle, Le Clerc, and other notable persons. His father dying the following year, he returned home and distinguished himself in the House of Lords; but after the accession of Anne he never took any part in public life. In 1708 he published *A Letter on Enthusiasm*; in 1709 his *Moralists, a Philosophical Rhapsody* and *Sensus Communis: an Essay on the Freedom of Wit and Humour*, in which he announced his doctrine of ridicule being the test of truth; in 1710 his *Soliloquy, or Advice to an Author*; and in 1711 a collected edition of all these works, *Characteristicks of Men, Manners, Opinions, Times*.

Shaftesbury's *Characteristicks* reveal his religious scepticism, and he was attacked as a Deist by Berkeley and others. Other works suggest his sympathy with the CAMBRIDGE PLATONISTS, and with the teaching of Cumberland. His genuinely lofty sentiment gives value to his ethical speculation, the best account of which is in his *Inquiry concerning Virtue in two Discourses*, 1699, a work which shows the influence of Plato. He attacked egoistic hedonism, but it has been suggested that his criterion of morality is so nebulous as to be no more than a matter of taste. His aesthetic speculations are to be found in *Notion of the Historical Draught or Tablature of the Judgment of Hercules*. Shaftesbury's influence on the continent was great. Diderot translated his *Inquiry concerning Virtue* and in 1746 developed Shaftesbury's scepticism in his *Pensées philosophiques*. The *Characteristicks* strongly attracted Lessing, Wieland, and Leibnitz;

Shah Jahan out riding with one of his sons and an escort. (*Victoria and Albert Museum, London*)

Lessing's *Laokoön*, 1766, reveals the influence of Shaftesbury's aesthetic thought.

Bibliography: Life by his son, 1734, and Studies by R. L. Brett, 1951, and F. H. Heinemann, 1952.

Shaftesbury, Anthony Ashley Cooper, 7th Earl of (1801–85), British politician, educated at Harrow and Christ Church, Oxford. He entered Parliament as member for Woodstock in 1826. In 1834 he was made lord of the Admiralty. Reform in poor law, the treatment of lunatics, and the condition of factory operatives were subjects with which he was connected. Largely through his efforts a Ten Hours Bill was passed in 1847. He was the champion in Parliament of the movement for RAGGED SCHOOLS and for nearly 40 years was chairman of the Ragged School Union. His was the influence behind Lord Palmerston's bill for the care and reformation of juvenile offenders. The Lodging House Act, which he piloted through the Upper House (he had succeeded to the

earldom in 1851), was designed to improve the dwellings of the people; it was described by Charles Dickens as the best piece of legislation that ever issued from Parliament.

Shaftesbury, or Shaston, market town in DORSET, England, 30 km south-west of Salisbury and 161 km from London. There is evidence of continuous occupation at Shaftesbury for more than 1000 years. The town was rebuilt c. 880 by Alfred, who founded a Benedictine abbey there, his daughter Ethelgiva being the first abbess. In 981 the remains of Edward the Martyr were re-interred at the abbey, and the shrine became so famous that the town was known for a time as St Edwardstowe. Now only the excavated foundations of the abbey remain; it was demolished soon after its dissolution in 1539. Shaftesbury is mentioned as a borough in the Domesday Book, being then more important than Exeter or Dorchester. The town received its first charter in 1252; two others followed (in 1604 and 1664). Places of interest include St Peter's church, dating largely from the 15th century with some earlier work; and the Gold Hill Wall, a portion of the old town wall, built in Saxon times and later buttressed. The grammar school was founded in 1718 and reorganised in 1872. The Westminster Memorial Hospital was opened in 1874. Population (1971) 3976.

Shag, *Phalacrocorax aristoclis*, a bird, related to the cormorant, in the order Pelecaniformes. It is smaller than the cormorant, with a green tinge to its plumage and in the breeding season has a crest. Its food consists mainly of sand eels for which it dives, staying underwater for up to 54 seconds. It breeds on deeply fissured cliffs, and on rocky parts of isolated islands.

Shagreen, name used, at different periods, for various materials with rough or patterned surfaces made from animal or fish skins. The Persian word, *sāgharī*, was used for a LEATHER made from asses' skins and given a surface decoration by trampling seeds into the dampened skin, leaving it to dry and then shaking out the seeds. The resulting leather with numerous small indentations was much used for sword scabbards. In Western Europe in the 17th and 18th centuries, the French version, *chagrin*, of the Persian *sāgharī* was used for sharkskin, which has a surface pattern of spined scales, and for the skins of various rays, which have calcified papillae; both these materials were used as abrasives (hence the use of *chagrin* in French and later in English to mean a discomfort). In the 18th century, shark and ray skins were made into decorative materials by grinding away the scales or papillae, leaving only a surface pattern which showed up particularly well when the material was dyed green. In England the word *chagrin* for this material became respelled as 'shagreen'.

Shah, word meaning ruler or prince, now applied particularly to the ruler of Iran. In his own land he is also called shahinshah (king of kings).

Shah Jahan (1592–1666), fifth of the Mogul emperors of India, in whose reign Mogul power reached its height; he lost Kandahar in 1653, but added parts of the Deccan in 1636 and 1655. Although able and artistic, Shah Jahan was ruthless; he executed all his male collaterals during the wars of succession, at his instigation Portuguese traders who settled at Hughli were massacred on account of the cruelties of their slave trade, and, a zealous Muslim, he persecuted Hindus in the early part of his reign. Prodigal court expenditure created terrible famines for his people. His age was the golden period for Muslim architecture in India; he built the TAJ MAHAL at Agra as a mausoleum for his favourite wife, Mumtaz Mahall; the palace and Great Mosque at Delhi; and the celebrated Peacock Throne. He founded the modern city of Delhi between 1639 and 1648. In 1657, while Shah Jahan lay dangerously ill, civil war broke out between his four sons. AURANGZEB, the victor, confined his father in the citadel of Agra, where he died in December 1666.

See also INDIA, *Architecture*.

Bibliography: B. P. Saksena, *History of Shah Jahan of Dihli*, 1932; F. Bernier (ed. A. Constable), *Travels in the Mogul Empire, 1656–1668*, 1970.

Shah of Iran, see MOHAMMED RIZA SHAH PAHLAVI.

Shahn, Ben (1898–1969), US painter, born at Kaunas, Lithuania; he was taken to the USA in 1906. Shahn was apprenticed to a lithographer but also attended New York University, the City College of New York, and the National Academy of Design. Many of his paintings and graphic works reflect Shahn's involvement in social issues, for example his famous Sacco and Vanzetti series of paintings.

Shahnama, see FIRDAUSI.

Shahrazad, Scheherazade, see ARABIAN NIGHTS.

Shake, in music, see under ORNAMENTS.

Shakers, popular name of the United Society of Believers in Christ's Second Appearing, founded about 1747 in England by James and Jane Wardley. They were joined by

Shakers wore a common uniform, rose at the same hour, and took their meals together. They made plain-styled furniture which was much sought after by people outside the community. (*Mansell Collection*)

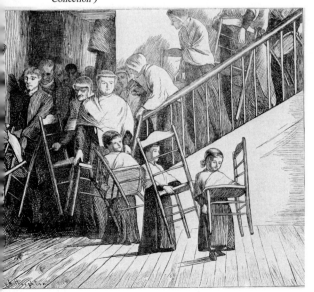

Ann Lee (1736–84) of Manchester, who claimed to be Jesus Christ in his second appearance. In 1774 the sect moved to America, and three years after the death of Ann Lee the society was established on a communistic basis. It was thus the first communistic settlement in the USA.

Bibliography: E. D. Andrews, *The People Called Shakers*, 1953.

Shakespeare, William (1564–1616), English dramatist and poet, born at Stratford-upon-Avon. His father, John Shakespeare, a leading citizen of the town, was a glover and general businessman. His mother was Mary Arden, the daughter of a prosperous landowner (some of whose property she inherited), who married John shortly after 1556. John Shakespeare became an alderman of Stratford in 1565 and in 1568 high bailiff (i.e. mayor), but sometime in the 1570s he apparently had financial difficulties and lost some of his status in Stratford society. The register of Stratford Church records the baptism of seven other Shakespeare children apart from William, three of whom died in childhood.

The young Shakespeare almost certainly attended Stratford Grammar School, where he would have received instruction in the Latin language and literary classics, rhetoric and ancient history. He married, at the age of 18, Anne Hathaway, who was then aged 26. A daughter Susanna was baptised on 26 May 1583, and on 2 February 1585, the twins Hamnet and Judith were christened at Holy Trinity, Stratford. Hamnet died in 1596 at the age of 11.

It is not known what Shakespeare did between this period and 1592, by which time he was established in the London theatrical world. Numerous traditions concerning these years have sprung up: there is the legend that Shakespeare was an habitual deer poacher on the estate of Sir Thomas Lucy; that he was a schoolmaster, a soldier, a sailor, a servant in a great household. None of these speculations, however, has any solid basis in fact. By 1592, at any rate, he was considered an important enough theatrical figure for a rival dramatist, Robert Greene, to attack him in his *Groatsworth of Wit, Bought with a Million of Repentance*. Greene warns his fellow 'University' playwrights that

> 'There is an upstart crow, beautified with our feathers, that with his *Tygers heart wrapt in a Players hide*, supposes he is as well able to bombast out a blank verse as the best of you: and being an absolute *Johannes fac totum*, is in his own conceit the only Shake-scene in a country.'

A few months later Henry Chettle included in the preface to his *Kind Heart's Dream* a rejoinder to Greene's invective, remarking on Shakespeare's 'honesty, and his facetious (i.e. polished) grace in writing, that approves his art'. The fact that Shakespeare dedicated his first published poems, *Venus and Adonis*, 1593, and *The Rape of Lucrece*, 1594, to Henry Wriothesley, Earl of Southampton, indicates that he was by then becoming acquainted with important patrons. Much has been made of the alleged association of the two men, and some scholars have speculated that Southampton is the Fair Youth of the Sonnets. However, no reliable evidence has been found to support the theory.

From 1594 onward Shakespeare was an important

member of the Lord Chamberlain's Company of actors. In 1598 the Company tore down their regular playhouse, the Theatre, and used the timber to build the GLOBE in Southwark. Shakespeare became a 'sharer' in the venture, which entitled him to a percentage of the profits. In 1603 the Company became the King's Men, so that Shakespeare (with some of his colleagues) became a groom of the King's chamber, and entitled to walk in James's coronation procession. In addition to being the leading playwright of the Company and one of its business directors, we know that he continued to act—for example, in 1598, in Jonson's *Every Man in His Humour*, and, in 1603, in his *Sejanus*. An unreliable tradition has it that he was Adam in *As You Like It* and the Ghost in *Hamlet*.

By 1597 Shakespeare was prosperous enough to purchase New Place, the second largest house in Stratford. In the previous year John Shakespeare had been granted a coat of arms, no doubt as a result of his son's eminence and his willingness to pay the necessary fees. He also bought properties in London and in Stratford, and by various business deals ensured his prominence in his native town. He seems to have spent almost all his time in London, visiting Stratford—according to Aubrey—about once a year. In London he lived for a time in St Helen's, Bishopsgate, a short distance away from the Theatre. By October 1599 he had moved to the Liberty of the Clink on the Bankside, near where the Globe now stood. The evidence of a lawsuit in which Shakespeare was a witness indicates that some time before 1604 he lodged with a French Huguenot family in Silver Street, near St Olave's Church.

By 1613, when the Globe was burned out during a performance of *Henry VIII*, Shakespeare had apparently retired permanently to Stratford. On 25 March 1616, he

William Shakespeare, engraving by Martin Droeshout on the title-page of the First Folio, 1623. *(Victoria and Albert Museum, London)*

drew up a will in which he left New Place and most of his property to Susanna, who was now married to a Stratford physician, Dr John Hall. His other daughter, Judith, who had married a neighbour, Thomas Quiney, received a sum of money. His wife Anne received 'my second best bed with the furniture' (i.e. bed-hangings, linen, etc.). This clause has led many to believe that relations between the dramatist and his wife were cool, but it should be remembered that a widow was legally entitled to one third of her husband's estate, which did not need to be stated in the will. Shakespeare died on 23 April 1616, and was buried in the chancel of Holy Trinity, Stratford; within a few years a monument, still extant, was erected over his grave. His widow died in August 1623, a few months before the publication of the first collected edition of his plays by John Heminge and Henry Condell. Two authentic pictures of Shakespeare exist: the portrait by Martin Droeshout on the title page of the First Folio, and the half-length bust on his monument at Stratford. Ben Jonson, Shakespeare's friend and occasional critic, apparently reflects the general opinion of his friends and acquaintances when he described the dramatist in *Discoveries* as 'indeed honest, and of an open and free nature; had an excellent fancy, brave notions, and gentle expression'.

The Plays. The dates of composition of the plays are partly conjectural, but the general chronology has been widely agreed by scholars. In the years immediately following his arrival in London till about 1594–95 Shakespeare may be regarded as a young writer learning the techniques of his art and trying one experiment after another. These years witnessed Shakespeare's first attempts at the chronicle-history (*Henry VI*, 1, 2 and 3, and *Richard III*); at farce based on a classical model (*The Comedy of Errors*); at romantic comedy of character (*The Two Gentlemen of Verona*, *The Taming of the Shrew*); at sensational Senecan revenge tragedy (*Titus Andronicus*); at sophisticated wit-comedy (*Love's Labour's Lost*); and at romantic tragedy (*Romeo and Juliet*). Although they can all be faulted, the striking feature of the early plays is the imaginative power Shakespeare brings to his experiments with established forms and conventions. In spite of his relative immaturity, it is remarkable, for example, how Shakespeare already endows his romantic comedies with a vigour which Robert Greene, who had largely developed the form, never managed. Perhaps the best of these early efforts are *Love's Labour's Lost*, with its brilliant exploitation of language, and *Romeo and Juliet*, with its powerful depiction of a divided society as the background to the lovers' tragedy. The plays written between 1595 and 1600 reveal Shakespeare's development towards full maturity as an imaginative artist and dramatic craftsman. The period includes a group of histories in which the general concerns of the *Henry VI* sequence and *Richard III* are developed with a remarkable insight into psychological subtleties and a sharp but passionate eye for the ironies and ambiguities of political life. *Richard II* far surpasses anything previously done in the chronicle-history genre by exploring the relationship between the private man and the public life of the state. *King John* marks another advance, particularly in the characterisation of Faulconbridge, who contrasts with the weak-minded royal protagonist. Again, the ironies and problems of politics are explored, to the point where every allegiance and belief seems built on shifting sands. In *Henry IV* 1 and 2 the comic world of the tavern, dominated by Shakespeare's greatest comic creation Falstaff, is juxtaposed with the dilemmas and responsibilities attending kingship and political ambition. *Henry V* brings the group to a close, with Shakespeare's portrait of Prince Hal as the ideal soldier-king. In spite of the strongly patriotic note of the play Shakespeare does not shirk the facts of war and the fate of lowly individuals in it, and the audience is reminded by the final chorus that the cycle of peace and war, victory and defeat, national triumph and disaster will unfold again and bring the civil war of Henry VI's reign.

In this same period Shakespeare wrote a number of comedies centring on love and sexual relations, and often featuring the resourceful good-sense of the heroines. These include *A Midsummer Night's Dream*, where the tribulations of youthful sexuality are explored within a lyrical and comic framework; *The Merchant of Venice*, in which comedy hardly subdues the tragic potentiality of Shylock; *Much Ado About Nothing*, with its witty lovers Beatrice and Benedick; and *The Merry Wives of Windsor*, supposedly written at the Queen's request to show Falstaff in love. *As You Like It* and *Twelfth Night* are his masterpieces in the genre of romantic comedy. In all of these plays Shakespeare gains his effects by combining, with apparently effortless skill, ingredients which at first sight seem incompatible. In *Much Ado About Nothing* there is tragic feeling, high comedy and the farce of Dogberry and Verges. In *Twelfth Night*, satire is blended with slapstick, and romance with a sadness that permeates the play. And in *As You Like It* Shakespeare reveals his ability to give fresh life and meaning to already hoary conventions: it was common enough for the heroine to disguise herself as a boy, but at one point in the play Rosalind is no less than a boy actor playing a girl who has disguised 'herself' as a boy and now pretends to be a girl!

The sadness and bitterness which run as undercurrents through *Twelfth Night* and *As You Like It* come to the surface in the so-called 'dark comedies' or 'problem plays' which Shakespeare wrote between c. 1601 and c. 1605. *Troilus and Cressida* is a sardonic exploration of the concept of chivalric honour in relation to sexual conduct and the war between Greece and Troy; and since an element of national mythology was the founding of Britain by Trojan Brutus, the play was perhaps not without topical relevance. *All's Well That Ends Well* and *Measure for Measure* have similarities in plot, since both deal with women deceived by faithless men who are won back through the disguise or substitution of another woman in the act of love. In both, also, benevolent father-figures stage-manage from a distance the unravelling of the complications; in *Measure for Measure* the mysterious Duke seems to be the agent of an ordering Providence, which has led some scholars to read the play as a religious allegory. In any event, there is no doubt that in these plays Shakespeare was scrutinising the baser side of human nature; and though it would be wrong to believe that his conclusions were cynical or pessimistic, the emphasis is certainly on the suffering and evil in which we all share.

Between c. 1601 and c. 1605 Shakespeare produced the four great tragedies which are usually regarded as being his most remarkable achievement. *Hamlet*, the first of them, is perhaps the single best-known play ever written, and its hero has fascinated several centuries of audiences and readers, although some critics (notably T. S. Eliot) have thought the play a failure, even if an undeniably impressive one. This view has not, however, won general acceptance. At the centre of the play is Hamlet's alienation from the life going on, apparently normally, around him, for only he knows the truth about his father's murder. It is a world in which outward fairness masks inward corruption and decay, and in which all appearances are deceptive. Hamlet himself is unable to act, for if he does he must commit murder. Ultimately, it is Providence that contrives a resolution of the prince's dilemma. *Othello* continues Shakespeare's preoccupation with truth and its deceptive simulacrum. The Moor is deceived by Iago, and allows impulsive emotion to get the better of his cool reason. His jealousy leads him to murder Desdemona, and his contrition to commit suicide. One of the most interesting features of the play is Iago's character; he is a complex man and a player of many roles, whose nature and function are deeply imbedded in the long tradition of the morality Vice figure. *King Lear*, the ending of which even the tough-minded Dr Johnson found unbearably moving, is perhaps the most emotionally powerful of all his plays. It embodies, and brings to a new level, many of Shakespeare's previous concerns: the difference between the real and the fake (between Cordelia and her two sisters); the conflict between the passions and the reason; the need to find a larger meaning to our existence; most of all, the necessity of enduring our afflictions patiently. Finally, there is *Macbeth*, which may have been intended to have a topical political relevance in relation to the 'Gunpowder Plot' of November 1605, in which the Scottish-born James narrowly escaped death. It is above all a story of crime and punishment, of the corruption of a noble nature and the torments it brings upon itself through its own evil in killing the king.

Antony and Cleopatra and *Coriolanus*, which immediately followed the great tragedies, may be considered with *Julius Caesar* (which was written just before them) and to some extent with the early *Titus Andronicus* as comprising a distinct group of 'Roman' plays. *Julius Caesar* is based, like the later Roman tragedies, on Shakespeare's reading of North's *Plutarch*. It anticipates to some degree the great tragedies in its concentration on a central theme and plot: the conspiracy to assassinate Caesar, and the confrontation between political rivals, in which the more ruthless win. In *Antony and Cleopatra* the frame of reference is extended to embrace the Roman world empire. The honourable virtues of Rome are contrasted with the love and sensuality of Egypt. Antony is defeated in battle by the calculating Octavius, but paradoxically finds fulfilment in his passionate love-affair with Cleopatra. The play has some of Shakespeare's most beautiful poetry, as befits the crowning achievement of romantic tragedy. The subject of honour is once more to the fore in *Coriolanus*, the hero of which comes into disastrous conflict with the Roman people through his overriding sense of personal honour. It is worth remembering, in relation to this play, that only a few years earlier the English had witnessed the abortive rebellion against Elizabeth's rightful authority by that noble but headstrong young soldier, the Earl of Essex.

Timon of Athens, written at roughly the same time as

Coriolanus, is very uneven in quality, perhaps because it was a pirated text, or because it was written with, or completed by, an inferior dramatist, or—and this is perhaps the best explanation—because it represents an early, unrevised stage of composition. In any case, there is no doubt about the force of the more polished episodes, and especially of the condemnation of the alienating power of money (quoted approvingly by Karl Marx). Experimental features are especially evident in *Pericles*, which initiates the final period of Shakespeare's work, and which includes *Cymbeline*, *The Winter's Tale*, *The Tempest*, and *Henry VIII*. (*The Two Noble Kinsmen* is generally believed to have been written by Shakespeare in collaboration with John Fletcher, who was probably responsible for Acts II, III and IV.)

Certain similarities in theme and technique link these plays closely together. They characteristically present some tragic or poignant complication which is ultimately resolved—in the form of the reconciliation and reunion of antagonists—as a result of repentance and forgiveness. Young people play a prominent role in these plays, for they are the means to a new and hopeful life free of the conflicts of the past. Moreover, the plays have a frankly theatrical, 'make-believe' element, which keeps us at a distance emotionally even as it charms us. *Pericles*, which Ben Jonson labelled 'a mouldy tale', survives in an imperfect text, but it nevertheless establishes the main dramatic elements of this entire period. *Cymbeline* is set in ancient Britain, when Augustus Caesar rules in Rome and Christ is being born in Palestine. It is a remarkable *coup de théâtre*, in which Shakespeare sets in motion several plots and exploits numerous conventions, resolving them all with consummate skill in the final scene. *The Winter's Tale*, a refashioning of a romance by Shakespeare's old rival, Robert Greene, and *The Tempest*, which exploits contemporary interest in newly-discovered lands (e.g. the Bermudas), both feature attractive heroines who are finally won, in spite of difficulties, by the sons of their father's enemies. Perhaps Shakespeare was inspired to write these 'romances' because of the popularity of BEAUMONT and FLETCHER's work and/or because the King's Men acquired a new private indoor theatre, the Blackfriars, where plays which experimented with new techniques and staging conventions could be performed. Whether or not this is so, it seems highly likely that *Cymbeline*, *The Winter's Tale* and *The Tempest* were connected in some way with royal events, notably the marriage of Princess Elizabeth. Finally, in *Henry VIII* (on which Shakespeare collaborated), the theme of reconciliation and regeneration after strife is played out in historical terms, so that the young child who represents hope for the future is none other than Elizabeth I.

Shakespeare's excellence as a dramatist has been recognised since his own times. Francis Meres, in his literary survey, *Palladis Tamia*, 1598, ranked him as the best of English playwrights. John Dryden, in his *Of Dramatic Poesy*, esteemed him as 'the man who of all modern, and perhaps ancient poets, had the largest and most comprehensive soul'; and Dr Johnson, always a severe critic, wrote: 'The stream of time, which is continually washing the dissoluble fabricks of other poets, passes without injury by the adamant of Shakespeare'. For Coleridge, the plays exhibit a mind that was 'most profound, energetic, and philosophical'. Nineteenth-century critics praised Shakespeare to an extent that now seems indiscriminate and idolatrous. Partly as a reaction, appreciation of his plays in the present century has been more analytic, examining in detail such aspects as language, structure, contemporary theatrical conditions, and the social and intellectual context of his work. More reasoned criticism has in no way, however, diminished Shakespeare's reputation, but rather has produced an even greater appreciation of his achievement. No better evidence of this can be adduced than the fact that his plays continue to engage the enthusiastic response of actors, directors and audiences throughout the world.

Textual History. Shakespeare's plays were collected and edited in 1623 by John Heminge and Henry Condell, two of the playwright's former colleagues in the King's Men. This edition, which was prepared with considerable care, is known as the First Folio. It contained 36 plays, of which 18 appeared for the first time in print. Later editions were published in 1632, 1664 and 1685 (known as the Second, Third and Fourth Folios, respectively). Of the plays in the First Folio there is a good case for believing that *Henry VIII* was written in collaboration with John Fletcher; *The Two Noble Kinsmen* was published as their joint work in 1634. The Third Folio (1664) included *Pericles* and six other plays, none of which has a serious claim to Shakespearean authorship: these are *Locrine*, 1595; *Sir John Oldcastle*, 1600; *Thomas Lord Cromwell*, 1602; *The London Prodigal*, 1605; *The Puritan*, 1607; and *A Yorkshire Tragedy*, 1608. It is possible that Shakespeare had a hand in the anonymous *Edward III*, 1596, though the relevant passages could be the work of an imitator. There is more certainty about his part in the writing of the collaborative *Sir Thomas More*, for 147 lines of the play seem to be in Shakespeare's handwriting. None of his other work has survived in autograph manuscript.

Eighteenth-century editors like Nicholas Rowe and Alexander Pope attempted to correct errors in the first editions. While they were often successful, they also made many changes which modern editors do not now accept. In this respect it should be remembered that Shakespeare was understood in this period as being 'wild' and 'uncultivated', even if a genius, and his plays were commonly subjected to ruthless adaptation on stage, to the extent that *King Lear* was given a happy ending in Nahum Tate's version of 1681. An important landmark in textual study of Shakespeare was the publication in 1871 of the first of the 'New Variorum Edition', which brought together all previous variant readings of the texts. In the present century much has been learnt about Elizabethan manuscript and printing practices, and computers are being used to analyse data.

Numerous plays have been ascribed to Shakespeare which he certainly did not write. On the other hand, some people have insisted that Shakespeare did not write any plays at all, and that the Shakespeare canon is actually the work of someone else. The chief 'pretender' to Shakespeare's throne has been Francis Bacon, though the claims of Edward de Vere, Earl of Oxford, William Stanley, Earl of Derby, Roger Manners, Earl of Rutland, and Christopher MARLOWE have all at one time or another been advanced. However, no substantial evidence has ever been produced to reinforce any of these theories.

The Narrative Poems and Sonnets. *Venus and Adonis*, which Shakespeare described as 'the first heir of my invention', was published in 1593, and was followed in the next year by *The Rape of Lucrece*. It was in these years that the London playhouses were closed by a severe outbreak of plague. The outline of *Venus and Adonis* was taken from a tale in Ovid's *Metamorphoses*, and Shakespeare borrowed details from other stories in that work. He blends the Arcadian landscape of Ovid's work with images drawn from the native English countryside, and combines romance with comedy, eroticism with a sense of the transitoriness of human life and passions which anticipates much in the plays and sonnets. In *The Rape of Lucrece* the outline was again Ovidian, but here Shakespeare was concerned to develop the darker side of his vision by examining a story of crime, suffering and retribution in terms which had universal implications. The poems were extremely popular with contemporary readers and went through many editions. In addition to the narrative poems and the sonnets, two other poems are attributed to Shakespeare: 'A Lovers Complaint', which was included in the editions of the sonnets printed in 1609 (the authenticity of which has been debated); and 'The Phoenix and the Turtle', which was included in Robert Chester's *Loves Martyr* in 1601. The latter is very obscure in meaning, for it contains many topical references which are now difficult to identify.

It is for the sonnets (published in 1609) that Shakespeare is chiefly remembered as a poet. These have been variously dated but the consensus of scholarly opinion is that they were mostly written during the earlier part of Shakespeare's career. Nos 58 and 144 appeared in an anthology, *The Passionate Pilgrime*, in 1599, and Francis Meres referred to the sonnets in 1598. It is possible that they were written over a long period of time, as their range and variety of mood and attitude would suggest. We do not know if the sequence of sonnets in the 1609 edition was as Shakespeare intended them. Certainly, the narrative (which in other sonnet-sequences was usually fairly orderly) is difficult to follow, though attempts at rearrangement have not contrived anything better. The first 126 sonnets are centred on a handsome youth, presented as a friend of the poet, and their relationship is dramatised in relation to other persons (especially the poet's woman, whom the youth seduces), to a variety of emotions, and, more generally, to the limitations imposed on human relationships and experience imposed by Time. The remaining sonnets are chiefly concerned with the poet's relations with a dark lady, who, though unfaithful to him, nevertheless continues to inspire his passion.

There has been much speculation as to the identities of Mr W. H. (to whom the sonnets are dedicated), the dark lady, the fair youth and the rival poet, but even though much heat has been generated very little light has been cast on these enigmatic persons. Indeed, there is much in the sonnets that remains unexplained for, in addition to the difficulties of topical allusion, Shakespeare's language is often dense to the point of obscurity, and the feeling and mood impenetrably personal. But certain things at least are clear. The main preoccupation of the sequence is the effect of inexorable time, with its natural movement towards decay and chaos, on personal experience and relationships, especially those of love and friendship. Equally clear is Shakespeare's ability to transcend the restricted conventions with which he was working, and to create a vivid poetic language reflecting the dramatic shifts and movements of his thought and emotion. It is noteworthy that the concerns of many of Shakespeare's mature plays are anticipated (if the early dating is correct) in the sonnets, and it is likely that his experience in writing the sonnets helped develop his mastery of stage poetry.

Chronology of the Plays. Since there is much doubt about the exact dates of many of Shakespeare's plays the following gives the probable years of composition as generally agreed by recent scholars:

1589–92	*1 Henry VI, 2 Henry VI, 3 Henry VI, Richard III, The Comedy of Errors.*
1593–94	*The Taming of the Shrew, Titus Andronicus, The Two Gentlemen of Verona, Love's Labour's Lost.*
1594–95	*A Midsummer Night's Dream.*
1595–96	*Richard II, King John, Romeo and Juliet.*
1596–97	*The Merchant of Venice, 1 Henry IV, 2 Henry IV, The Merry Wives of Windsor.*
1598	*Much Ado About Nothing.*
1599	*Henry V, Julius Caesar.*
1599–1600	*As You Like It.*
1600–2	*Hamlet, Twelfth Night, Troilus and Cressida.*
1602–3	*All's Well That Ends Well.*
1604	*Measure for Measure, Othello.*
1605–6	*King Lear, Macbeth.*
1606–7	*Antony and Cleopatra, Timon of Athens.*
1607–8	*Coriolanus, Pericles.*
1609–10	*Cymbeline.*
1611	*The Winter's Tale, The Tempest.*
1612–13	*Henry VIII.*
1613	*The Two Noble Kinsmen.*

Bibliography: There is a vast critical and scholarly literature about Shakespeare and only a very limited selection can be listed here. Several of the works cited offer much fuller bibliographies.

Editions. The *New Variorum Edition* (begun by H. H. Furness in 1871 and still in progress); J. D. Wilson (Gen. Ed.), *The New Shakespeare* (one play per vol.), 1921–66; G. B. Harrison (Ed.), *The Penguin Shakespeare* (one play per vol.), 1937–59; H. F. Brooks and H. Jenkins (Gen. Eds), *The Arden Shakespeare* (one play per vol.), 1951–; J. T. B. Spencer (Ed.), *The New Penguin Shakespeare* (one play per vol.), 1972–; A. Harbage (Gen. Ed.), *The Pelican Shakespeare* (one play per vol.), rev. ed. 1969. Among one-volume editions of the complete plays are those by Hardin Craig, 1951, and Peter Alexander, 1954.

F. T. Prince (Ed.), *The Poems*, 1960; J. C. Maxwell (Ed.), *The Poems*, 1966; J. D. Wilson (Ed.), *The Sonnets*, 1966.

Textual. A. Walker, *Textual Problems of the First Folio*, 1953; W. W. Greg, *The Editorial Problems in Shakespeare*, 3rd ed. 1954; C. Hinman, *The Printing and Proof-Reading of the First Folio of Shakespeare* (2 vols), 1963.

Biographical. E. K. Chambers, *William Shakespeare: A Study of Facts and Problems* (2 vols), 1930; P. Alexander, *Shakepeare's Life and Art*, 1939; G. E. Bentley, *Shakespeare: A Biographical Handbook*, 1961; A. L. Rowse, *William Shakespeare*, 1963.

Staging, Acting and Stage-History. E. K. Chambers, *The Elizabethan Stage* (4 vols), 1923; M. C. Bradbrook, *Elizabethan Stage Conditions*, 1932; G. E. Bentley, *The Jacobean and Caroline Stage* (7 vols), 1941–68; A. Harbage, *Shakespeare's Audience*, 1941; B. Joseph, *Elizabethan Acting*, 1964; C. B. Hogan, *Shakespeare in the Theatre* (2 vols), 1952–57; G. Wickham, *Early English Stages, 1300 to 1660* (2 vols), 1959–72.

Studies of the Plays. A. C. Bradley, *Shakespearean Tragedy*,

1904; D. N. Smith (Ed.), *Shakespeare Criticism, 1623–1840*, 1916; L. L. Schucking, *Character Problems in Shakespeare's Plays*, 1922; E. E. Stoll, *Art and Artifice in Shakespeare*, 1933; C. Spurgeon, *Shakespeare's Imagery*, 1935; E. M. W. Tillyard, *Shakespeare's Last Plays*, 1938; G. W. Knight, *The Wheel of Fire*, rev. ed. 1949; J. F. Danby, *Shakespeare's Doctrine of Nature*, 1949; W. H. Clemen, *The Development of Shakespeare's Imagery*, 1951; L. C. Knights, *Some Shakespeare Themes*, 1959; W. K. Wimsatt (Ed.), *Samuel Johnson on Shakespeare*, 1960; A. Righter, *Shakespeare and the Idea of the Play*, 1962; H. Granville-Barker, *Prefaces to Shakespeare* (4 vols), 1963; J. Kott, *Shakespeare, Our Contemporary*, 1964; T. Hawkes (Ed.), *Coleridge on Shakespeare*, 1969.

General. C. T. Onions, *A Shakespeare Glossary*, 2nd ed. 1919; K. Muir and S. Schoenbaum (Eds), *A New Companion to Shakespeare Studies*, 1971.

Studies of the Poetry. L. C. Knights, *Explorations*, 1946; T. W. Baldwin, *On The Literary Genetics of Shakespeare's Poems and Sonnets*, 1950; E. Hubler, *The Sense of Shakespeare's Sonnets*, 1952; J. W. Lever, *The Elizabethan Love Sonnet*, 1956.

Shakhty (formerly *Aleksandrovsk Grushevski*), city in ROSTOV *oblast* of the RSFSR, USSR, in the DONETS BASIN 60 km north-east of Rostov-on-Don. It is a centre of coal-mining (anthracite) and electricity production of the East Donbas, and was founded as a coal-mining settlement in 1839. Population (1974) 217,000.

Shale, a rock showing a fissility along bedding planes formed by the compaction and consolidation of CLAY or fine sediments from which the water has been expelled by the weight of overlying sediments.

Shale Oil is the oil obtained by the destructive distillation of oil shale. It is sometimes called synthetic crude oil or syncrude, once it is extracted. Oil shale is a stratified sedimentary rock in which are found numerous fragments of fossil plants and animals. The shale, although containing as much as 35 per cent organic matter, does not contain any oil. The organic material, kerogen, is similar to a precursor of oil, and may be removed from the rock by heating, which decomposes it and forms a complex oily liquid (shale oil) which differs from both crude oil and asphalt. Shale oil is distilled from the shale, and is processed in a similar way to PETROLEUM. One tonne of shale produces about 100 l of shale oil together with large amounts of ammonia, water, and hydrocarbon gases. The shale may be mined in a similar way to coal, but in-situ distillation by underground heating has been attempted, and may be the most satisfactory way of extracting shale oil in the future. The world reserves of shale oil are very large, probably larger than those of crude oil. The largest reserves are in the USA (Colorado, Utah, and Wyoming in particular) and the USSR, but workable amounts are avalable in many parts of the world. In Britain deposits occur in Dorset and in Scotland. The former contain too much sulphur, but in Scotland oil shale was mined and processed from 1861 to 1964. In 1953 the production of shale oil at Bathgate in Scotland was almost 100,000 t, more than half the world's production that year (see BOGHEAD COAL). Oil shale is now considered to be a likely large-scale source of energy in the future as petroleum becomes scarce.

Shaliapin, Feodor Ivanovich (1873–1938), Russian bass singer, born at Kazan, where he sang in the Bishop's choir. He made his operatic debut at Tiflis in Glinka's *Life for the Tsar*. Later he sang at St Petersburg as Ivan the Terrible in Rimsky-Korsakov's *Maid of Pskov*, and gained valuable experience with Mamontov's company (1894–95), singing a variety of bass parts. In 1899 he appeared at the Imperial Opera, Moscow. Two of his favourite roles were Don Basilio in *The Barber of Seville* and Leporello in *Don Giovanni*; his performances were as remarkable for the power of his acting as for the magnificence of his voice. In 1907 he made his New York debut at the Metropolitan in Boito's *Mefistofele*, and in 1913 he first appeared in London at Drury Lane in Mussorgsky's *Boris Godounov* and *Khovanshchina*. He published *Pages from My Life*, 1927, and *Man and Mask*, 1932.

Shallot, a plant allied to the onion. It was long considered to be a different species from the onion, *Allium cepa*, but is now considered to be a variety of it. It is grown in a light soil, in a warm position, and should be planted in January or February. The crop ripens in July. There are two types, the true shallot, the bulb of which grows to the size of a walnut and is used for pickling, and the Jersey shallot, which has a larger, rounder bulb used in cooking and with a sweeter flavour than the onion.

Shalmaneser I, Assyrian king. He founded NIMRUD c. 1250 BC. See ASSYRIA.

Shalmaneser II, Assyrian king. He reigned 1030–1019 BC. See ASSYRIA.

Shalmaneser III, Assyrian king, 859–824 BC. He led numerous expeditions against BABYLONIA, to the borders of URARTU (Armenia), and the west. According to his Black Obelisk (British Museum), the Israelite, Jehu, paid him tribute during his campaign against Damascus. See ASSYRIA.

Shalmaneser IV, Assyrian king, 781–771 BC. He con-

Feodor Ivanovich Shaliapin in the title role of Mussorgsky's opera Boris Godounov. *(Bisonte)*

ducted a number of unsuccessful campaigns against URARTU. See ASSYRIA.

Shalmaneser V, Assyrian king, 727–722 BC. He unsuccessfully besieged Luli of TYRE, and later SAMARIA, the capital of the kingdom of Israel, which fell in the year of his death (2 Kings xvii). See ASSYRIA.

Shama, *Copsychus macrura*, a bird of the family Muscicapidae, order Passeriformes, found in India and sometimes seen as a cage-bird in Britain.

Shamal, see STORM.

Shamanism, name which loosely embraces the main religious beliefs and practices of the indigenous peoples of North Asia, the Eskimoes and the Lapps. The shaman, mistakenly called medicine-man, is believed to make contact with Divinity during trances in ecstatic RITUALS, to converse with spiritual beings, and thus ward off evil influences, cure sickness, bring rain, foretell the future, etc. This ability often places the shaman in an ambiguous situation in his society, since he may be believed to use his abilities to practise black magic and harm his personal enemies. The shaman usually becomes aware of his abilities during childhood or puberty, as a result of severe illness; subsequently he has to abstain from certain foods, activities, and social roles lest he fall seriously ill once more. His position in society and his powers to heal have sometimes been seen to parallel those of psychotherapists in Western society. Though some Westerners have sought to show that shamans are psychotics or epileptics, it would seem, however, that cultural factors far outweigh purely biological dispositions.

See also ECSTASY; PALEO-ASIATICS; TABOO; WITCHCRAFT; YAKUTS.
Bibliography, M. Eliade, *Shamanism,* 1964; A. Balikci, *The Netsilik Eskimoes,* 1970.

Shamash, sun god of the Babylonians and Assyrians, son of SIN and brother of ISHTAR. Shamash had the usual attributes of a sun god; beneficent, healing, life-giving and inimical to all darkness and wickedness, he was the great judge of the universe. Together with the god Adad, he was concerned with oracles. His chief temples were at Larsa in South and Sippar in North Babylonia. In the Sun God Tablet in the British Museum, King Hammurabi is seen receiving his laws from the hands of Shamash. His consort was Aya.

Shamil (1797–1871), religious and political leader of the Muslim mountain peoples of the northern Caucasus in their struggle against Russian conquest. In 1859 he surrendered to the Russians at Gunib and was taken to Central Russia. He died in Mecca.

Shamo, see GOBI.

Shamrock, several trifoliate plants, one of which Saint Patrick is said to have used to illustrate the doctrine of the Trinity. The shamrock has been made the national badge of Ireland. The name is usually given to yellow-flowered species of *Trifolium* and related genera of Leguminosae. The leaves of the yellow-flowered *Trifolium dubium,* the white *T. repens* and of *Medicago lupulina* are the most common kinds. Wood-sorrel, *Oxatis acetosella,* is sometimes also known as shamrock.

Shan, state of BURMA, composed mainly of plateaus and, in the north, high mountains bordering on China, Laos, and Thailand. It is crossed by the River SALWEEN. The state is administered through 52 townships. The northern and eastern parts have been a refuge for anti-government groups, including Chinese nationalists, Burma Communist Party rebels, and disaffected SHANS. It has been a centre of the opium trade.

The former Shan States were semi-independent states under the British sphere of influence, to the north of Burma. They were annexed to the province of Burma after the third Burmese War, in 1885, but the administration was left in the hands of local chiefs (*sawbwas*), under the superintendence of the commissioner of the Federated Shan States. After 1922 this was replaced by a council of the chiefs. Under the 1947 constitution of the Burma Union, the Shan and Wa States were combined. Area 153,997 km²; population 3,178,214.

Shandon, see CORK.

Shang Yang, see CHINESE LITERATURE.

Shan. Village market scene. Fondness for trading and political independence are continuing Shan characteristics. (*Barnaby's Picture Library*)

Shanghai. The city, port, and Huang Pu river. *(Anglo-Chinese Educational Institute)*

Shanghai, the largest city in CHINA, situated on the Huang Pu river in the YANGTZE delta. Formerly a place of only minor significance, in 1842, in accordance with the Treaty of Nanking, Shanghai was chosen as a treaty port to be opened to international trade.

The city is divided into two parts: the old city and the more modern one built during the days when Shanghai was an international settlement. The so-called 'international settlement' was a foreign enclave within Shanghai established by the Western powers. It was here that China's first urbanised labouring class grew up after the First World War, and it was the scene of much political unrest. The city was attacked by Japanese forces in 1932 and, though stubbornly defended, eventually the Chinese government conceded to the Japanese the right to station troops there. During the Second World War Shanghai suffered much less destruction than other large cities in the Far East. It was occupied by the Japanese in 1938 and returned to Chinese control in 1945. During the Chinese Civil War, Shanghai was attacked by Communist forces early in 1949 and fell into their hands at the end of May.

As a treaty port, Shanghai developed rapidly during the second half of the 19th century as the commercial outlet for the whole of the vast Yangtze basin. It grew into a large international port and also a considerable light-manufacturing centre, particularly in textiles and other consumer goods. An important shipbuilding and ship-repairing trade developed. The harbour is equipped with many wharves and large vessels can pass through the harbour at any state of the tide. There are several dry docks for the repairing of ships. Shanghai is politically independent of the province of KIANGSU in which it is located and comes directly under the jurisdiction of the central government. Although it has been official policy to restrict its growth, the urban area and population of Shanghai have grown steadily during recent years. Its industrialisation has continued and its light industries have lost ground to the growth of heavy industries on the outskirts of the city. In particular, Shanghai has now become China's second-largest iron and steel producer after ANSHAN in Manchuria. Most of this new industry is situated at Woosung. Shanghai has also become a major refining centre for copper, lead, and zinc. Chemicals, plastics, synthetic fibres, and fertilisers are other industries now represented there. There is also an oil refinery which processes crude oil from the T'aching field in Manchuria. The population of the city is estimated (1970) to be about 11,000,000.

Shankar, Ravi (1920–), Indian sitar player who studied under Ustad Allauddin Khan of Maihar; outstanding as an exponent and teacher; founder of music schools in Bombay and Los Angeles. During 1949–56 he was musical director of All-India Radio and founded the *Vadya Vrinda* or national orchestra. He has composed music for many films, numbered among which are Satyajit RAY's *Apu* trilogy. His experimental work includes the *Sitar*

Concerto, premièred by the LSO under André Previn. Widely honoured in India and abroad, Shankar has toured the world many times. He is the author of *My Music, My Life*, published in 1968.

Shanklin, seaside resort on the south-eastern coast of the Isle of Wight, England, sheltered by high downs. Ventnor is 6 km to the south by a cliff walk which passes Shanklin Chine. Population (1971) 7496.

Shannon, longest river of Ireland; it rises in the Cuilcagh Mountains, County Cavan, 105 m above sea-level. It flows through Loughs Allen, Boderg, Forbes, Ree, and Derg, past Limerick into the Atlantic. It is 350 km long, and its estuary is 110 km long and 3–16 km wide, navigable by large vessels as far as LIMERICK. Salmon have long been prolific along the river's course. One of the main routeways of ancient Ireland, it now has a hydro-electric plant and an airport named after it.

'Shannon', name of the English frigate which took part in the famous 'ocean duel' with the US *Chesapeake* off Boston Harbour in 1813. After an engagement lasting only 15 minutes the *Chesapeake* was disabled and captured.

Shannon Airport, famous customs-free airport for transatlantic flights, 26 km south-west of Ennis in County CLARE, Republic of Ireland. A large industrial estate and a planned new town have been developed beside the airport since 1958. The estate, in the customs-free area, employs over 4000 and includes over 20 firms. The new town has a population of about 4000.

Shans, a large group of people living in east Burma, north-west Thailand, and north Laos, speaking a variety of different languages. They are closely related to the Thai, Lao, Kachin, Yi, and other groups. They are settled in fertile valleys where they grow wet rice, opium, and raise cattle. They are stratified into commoners, aristocrats, and princes. The latter receive tribute from their people, taxes on trade-goods, and act as war-lords. Feuding is frequent, especially in connection with the opium trade, their only source of foreign income. Their religious beliefs incorporate both Buddhism and non-Buddhist elements. The Shans have a long history. In 1948 the Shan States were given a degree of autonomy within the Burmese Union, but relations with the central authorities broke down and they have been fighting for independence ever since. Many areas are *de facto* independent.
   Bibliography: E. R. Leach, *Political Systems of Highland Burma*, 2nd ed., 1964; J. Friedman, *System, Structure and Contradiction in the Evolution of Asiatic State Formations*, 1975.

Shansi, an inland province of northern CHINA, bounded on the west and south by the Hwang Ho (see YELLOW RIVER), on the north by the Great Wall of China which separates Shansi from Inner Mongolia, and on the east by the Taiheng Shan (mountains) which run between Shansi and Hopeh provinces. Together with neighbouring SHENSI province to the west, Shansi consists of a dissected plateau between 500 and 2000 m in height covered by wind-blown superficial deposits known as LOESS. The source of the loess is the Ordos Desert of Inner Mongolia to the north of Shansi. The principal tributary of the Hwang Ho in Shansi province is the FEN HO which follows a line of faulting. This valley is the major area of

settlement and within it is the city of T'AI-YÜAN, the capital of the province. Agriculture in the valley is largely dependent upon irrigation, the principal crops being winter wheat, kaoliang, and millet. Cotton and hemp are also grown. Further west in Shansi the agriculture becomes poorer, mainly because of the dryness of the climate. In recent years increased geological prospecting in China has shown that Shansi is rich in both coal and iron-ore. Large coal-mines have been developed at Tatung in the north of the province, at Hsi-shan west of T'ai-yüan, at Fen-hsi, and at Itang. T'ai-yüan has grown rapidly in recent years. It is a food-processing and textile centre and has also become important for heavy industry because of the Communist government's industrial dispersal policy. T'ai-yüan is now one of China's most important iron- and steel-producing centres and its population exceeds one million. Tatung is a major railway junction and coal-mining centre. It also has cement industries and heavy engineering works. Shansi has many places of historical interest, being one of the earliest settled regions of China. These include the Yunkang grottoes near Tatung which are famous for their Buddhist sculptures. Area 157,000 km²; population (1972) about 20,000,000.

Shantarski Islands, archipelago of 15 islands in the Sea of OKHOTSK in the KHABAROVSK *krai* of the RSFSR, USSR. Area about 2500 km².

Shantung, maritime province of north-east CHINA whose eastern half forms a peninsula separating the Gulf of CHIHLI from the YELLOW SEA. Its relief consists of two upland areas separated by a central depression about 80 km wide. The central upland contains the sacred mountain of T'ai Shan. Fishing has always been a major industry, and a wide variety of crops are grown including wheat, maize, cotton, tobacco, peanuts, and fruit. The province is famous for its silks and its wines. Its rural areas

Shansi. Loess landscape around Sian. (*Werner Forman Archive*)

are densely populated; it is the second most populous province of China (after Szechwan), and its density is only exceeded by Kiangsu. The Hwang Ho (see YELLOW RIVER) crosses the province and enters the sea in the north. Over the centuries the mouths of this river have changed a great deal, causing widespread flooding and destruction in the province; in the 12th century the river reached the sea to the south of the peninsula. In recent years the province's mineral resources, chiefly coal and iron-ore, have been intensively developed, and an oil-field has been discovered at Shengli in the Hwang Ho delta. The capital of the province, TSINAN, is the major manufacturing centre. TSINGTAO and Chefoo are the largest ports. Ch'u-fou, the birthplace of CONFUCIUS, lies in the south-west of the province. Tsingtao, Chefoo, and Weihaiwei were all former treaty ports. Area 153,300 km²; population (1972) about 60,000,000.

Shap Fells, granitic upland in Cumbria, England, crossed by the main railway line to Scotland and the M6 motorway. The old quarrying and railway village of Shap has lost much of its casual transport trade since the motorway was constructed. There is a ruined 12th-century abbey nearby. Height 422 m.

Shapinsay, one of the ORKNEY ISLANDS, Scotland, 7 km north-east of Kirkwall. Length 8 km; width 7 km. It contains many Norse and pre-Norse antiquities. Population 353.

Shapiro, Karl Jay (1913–), US poet, born in Baltimore. Educated at the universities of Virginia and Johns Hopkins, he was always deeply interested in poetry, and in 1935 published his first volume. During the Second World War, while serving on the Pacific front, he wrote *Person, Place and Thing*, 1942, and *V-Letter*, 1944, which won the Pulitzer Prize. In 1945 appeared his *Essay on Rime*, a blank-verse critique of modern poetry, and in the same year he received the Shelley Memorial Prize.

In 1947 he was Consultant in Poetry to the Library of Congress, and in 1950 became editor of *Poetry*. Appointed professor of writing at the University of Nebraska in 1956, he is the editor of *Prairie Schooner*. *Beyond Criticism*, a prose elaboration of his poetical theories, and *Poems 1940–1953* both appeared in 1953. Other books include: *Poems of a Jew*, 1958; *In Defence of Ignorance*, 1960, *The Bourgeois Poet*, 1964, and *White-Haired Love*, 1968.

Shapley, Harlow (1885–1972), US astronomer, born at Nashville, Missouri, and educated at Missouri and Princeton. He worked at Mount Wilson Observatory (1914–21) and Harvard, where he was professor and director of the observatory (1921–52). At Mount Wilson Shapley worked on globular clusters and from their distribution showed that the Sun was some 50,000 light years from the centre of the Milky Way, not near it as had hitherto been supposed. At Harvard he built up the observatory and established a large and very active graduate school of astronomy.

Sharebroker, see STOCK EXCHANGE.

Shareholder, see COMPANY AND COMPANY LAW.

Shares, see STOCK; STOCK EXCHANGE.

Shariah (Arabic, road leading to a water-hole), Islamic religious law, incorporating all the practical aspects of Mohammed's religious and social teachings. The Shariah is drawn from four sources: the KORAN, the Sunna or traditional life of Mohammed, *ijma* or the consensus of opinion of the ULEMA on any question, and *qiyas* or analogy, the last being sought only when none of the first three criteria was applicable. These in turn may be interpreted by four different schools (*madhahib*) of jurists, all founded in the 8th and 9th centuries, the Hanifi, the Maliki, the Shafii, and the Hanbali, each differing according to its attitude to speculative opinion as opposed to adherence to the letter of the law. The various schools predominate in different parts of the Muslim world. The Hanifis hold sway in India and Central Asia and in the lands of the defunct Ottoman empire, while the Malikis are found in North Africa and eastern Arabia. The Shafiis in turn are the major influence in lower Egypt, East Africa, and parts of Palestine, Arabia, and India. Finally, the Hanbali school has no great influence outside Wahabi territory. Although in the main the various schools do not differ in essentials, an individual who fears a judgment from his own favoured school on a particular matter may appeal to a court of one of the other schools.

The Shariah is administered by CADIS who hold their own courts. Historically these courts have been totally independent of the secular authorities, who were nevertheless bound to recognise their judgments in Muslim countries, although secular or *mazalim* courts were also held. Today, where their jurisdiction still prevails, the Shariah courts are mostly restricted to cases concerning marriage, the family, inheritance, and the like. In most Muslim countries nowadays, the Shariah is being adapted to, or incorporated into, a western body of law. Formerly, summaries of important cases were submitted to a mufti (jurist) for an opinion and his reply was known as a *fatwa*. There is an extensive body of legal literature concerned with these *fatwas*. In the Ottoman empire the chief mufti of Istanbul was called the *Shaykh al-Islām* (see SHEIKH), and he was regarded as the highest religious and legal authority in the empire.

Bibliography: N. J. Coulson, *A History of Islamic Law*, 1964.

Sharing of Profits, see PROFIT SHARING.

Sharjah, see UNITED ARAB EMIRATES.

Shark, fish in the order Selachii, of subclass ELASMOBRANCHII in class CHONDRICHTHYES, the FISH that have a cartilaginous instead of a bony skeleton. Subclass Elasmobranchii includes the sharks and rays (Batoidei). Both have five to seven pairs of gill slits, but in the sharks these open on the side, which in the rays they open underneath the flattened body. The pectoral fins of rays join the body in front of the gills, forming a wide flap, but in the sharks the forward edge is free and attached behind the gills. Sharks and rays are living fossils, as many genera today closely resemble fossil sharks of the Jurassic period. There are over 200 living species of shark and over 300 species of ray.

All sharks are carnivorous, but two species, the basking shark, *Cetorhinus maximus*, and the whale shark, *Rhincodon typus*, filter plankton from the seawater, living entirely on these microscopic organisms and, perhaps, small fish. Others eat crustacea, fish, squid, sea birds,

Shark. A carcharinid, probably *Carcharinus leucas*, the bullshark, common in all tropical seas and frequently attacking man. *(Barnaby's Picture Library)*

rubbish from ships and carrion. The sharks most dangerous to man are the white shark, *Carcharodon carcharias*, the blue sharks, *Prionace*, the sand sharks, *Odontaspis*, the tiger sharks, *Galeocerdo*, and the hammerheads, *Sphyrna*.

Male sharks have specially adapted fins, called claspers, with which they insert sperm into the females. Pregnant females ready to give birth congregate in preferred nursery areas. These vary from shallow bays to the deep ocean, according to species. Some species are oviparous, that is, they lay eggs. Others are ovoviviparous, and retain the egg within the mother, often giving the embryo more nourishment after it has eaten all the yolk. A few species are viviparous, nourishing the young through special tissues until they are ready for birth. Some species of shark live over 20 years. Although the classification of sharks is not definitively fixed, the order Selachii may conveniently be divided into seven suborders.

Suborder Notidanoidei has existed from the Lower Jurassic period to the present. These sharks have six or seven gill openings and an anal fin. They are widely distributed. Modern species are about 5 m long and include the cow sharks and the seven gilled sharks, such as *Notorhynchus*.

Suborder Chlamydoselachoidei has existed from the Miocene period, but there is only one modern species, *Chlamydoseclachus*, the rather rare frilled shark, which is up to 2 m long. .

Suborder Heterodontoidei has existed from the Upper Devonian period. These sharks have five gill openings, an anal fin and are up to 1·5 m long. They are bottom-dwellers. Examples are the horned sharks, bullhead shark and the Port Jackson shark.

Suborder Squaloidei has existed from the Upper Cretaceous period. The anal fin is missing. The body is nearly cylindrical in shape and not so dorso-ventrally flattened as in the typical sharks. This suborder contains the spiny dogfishes, prickly dogfish and the sleeper sharks. The suborder as a whole has a wide distribution. The length of species varies from a pygmy shark (*Euprotimicrus*) which may be up to 26 cm long to the Greenland sleeper shark which may be over 6 m long.

Suborder Pristiophoroidei has existed from the Cretaceous period. They are the SAW SHARKS. The group is distinguished from the SAWFISHES (which are classed as rays, not sharks) in having gill openings at the side of the head, not underneath it. There are two genera, *Pristiophorus* and *Pliotrema*.

Suborder Squatinoidei has existed from the Jurassic period. These are the angel sharks. They have a flattened body with eyes on the upper surface, no anal fin, and may be up to 2·4 m long. There is one genus, *Squatina*, with possibly 11 different species.

Suborder Galeoidei has survived from the Jurassic period. This suborder is the largest of the Selachii as it contains the typical sharks. The notochord is replaced in the adults by vertebrae with a calcified cartilaginous centre. They have two dorsal fins, a heterocercal tail (unsymmetrical with the dorsal lobe smaller than the ventral), pelvic claspers, and five gill openings. There are approximately fifteen living families most of which are marine predators, although a few freshwater forms exist (*Carchinius* is known to ascend rivers for considerable distances). They may be up to 20 m long. The white shark, *Carcharodon carcharias*, is probably the most dangerous shark known to man. It grows to 12 m. Other sharks in this suborder are the sand, mackerel, mako, basking, whale, blue, and hammerhead sharks, and the porbeagle.

Small sharks, which are found in several suborders, are called dogfishes.

Bibliography: P. W. Gilbert and others (Eds.), *Sharks and*

Survival, 1963; *Sharks, Skates and Rays*, 1967; P. Budker, *The Life of Sharks*, 1971.

Sharon, plain on the coast of Palestine (now ISRAEL), which stretches from JAFFA to CAESAREA PHILIPPI, about 65 km long. The 'roses' for which it was famous in ancient times are supposed to have been narcissi. The present-day ROSE OF SHARON is a *Hypericum*.

Sharp, Cecil (1859–1924), musical researcher, born in London, famous for his collections and arrangements of folk-songs, country dances, morris dances, etc. He founded a school of music at Adelaide, Australia, in 1889, and the English Folk Dance Society in 1911 (renamed English Folk Dance and Song Society, 1932). His publications include *A Book of British Song*, 1902, *Folk Song Collected in the Appalachian Mountains*, 1917, and *English Folk Songs: Some Conclusions*, 1907 (fourth edition, 1965).
   Bibliography: W. Shuldham-Shaw, *Cecil Sharp and English Folk Dances*, 1929; A. H. Fox Strangways and M. Karpeles, *Cecil Sharp*, 2nd ed. 1955.

Sharp, Granville (1735–1813), British philanthropist and scholar, born at Durham, and educated at the grammar school there. Sharp became closely involved in the struggle for the liberation of slaves and his litigation on the matter resulted in the formulation of the principle that 'as soon as any slave sets foot upon English territory he becomes free'. He took a leading part in founding a society for the abolition of slavery and in establishing the settlement for freed slaves in Sierra Leone. He is described as the patriarch of the famous CLAPHAM SECT.

Sharp, William (1855–1905), Scottish novelist, born at Paisley; he also used the pseudonym Fiona Macleod. Educated at Glasgow Academy and University, he studied law, but preferred reading Gaelic folklore. In 1884 he became art critic of the *Glasgow Herald* and also edited the Canterbury Poets. He settled in London in 1877 but travelled widely, ending his days in Sicily. *The Human Inheritance*, a volume of his verse, appeared in 1882; he also wrote the novels *Wives in Exile*, 1896, and *Silence Farm*, 1899, and edited *Lyra Celtica*, 1896, an anthology of Celtic poetry.

However, he is most famous for the romantic tales published under the pseudonym Fiona Macleod. Overwritten and spurious in their Celticism, reminiscent of OSSIAN, they played an important part in the Celtic revival. They include *Pharias, a Romance of the Isles*, 1893, *The Mountain Lovers*, 1895, *The Sin Eater*, 1895, *The Washer of the Ford*, 1896, *The Dominion of Dreams*, 1899, *The Divine Adventure*, 1900, and *Winged Destiny*, 1904. He is a symbolist and has a curious feminine quality. His *Letters* were published in 1907.
   Bibliography: E. A. Sharp, *William Sharp, a Memoir,* 1912; F. Alaya, *William Sharp—"Fiona Macleod", 1855–1905*, 1970.

Sharp (♯), character in musical notation which indicates that a note is to be sung or played a semitone higher than its natural pitch. The sharp sign always occurs before the note to be sharpened in the case of an accidental, for example where the sharp comes in temporarily in the course of a piece of music, outside the prescribed key, and the effect then does not extend beyond the bar in which the sharp is put. But the sharps occurring regularly in the key chosen by the composer are placed in the key-signature at the beginning of each stave, and apply throughout unless contradicted by another accidental. A double sharp (✕) is a sign placed before a natural note, to show that the pitch is to be raised by a whole tone.

Sharpness, seaport in Gloucestershire, England, on the eastern bank of the River SEVERN, 25 km south of Gloucester. A 1268-metre-long railway bridge across the river collapsed in 1960 and was not rebuilt. At Sharpness there is one of the world's highest tidal ranges (up to 16 m). Population (1971) 2000.

Sharqiya, province of Lower Egypt, in the eastern Nile Delta. It contains part of Lake Manzala, a large coastal lagoon, in the north-west and it is through this province that many invading forces have come. The capital is Zigazig (population 173,000). Area 4180 km². Population 2,344,000.

Shasta, Mount, peak and extinct volcano of the CASCADE RANGE in Siskiyou county, California, and one of the highest peaks in the USA. Altitude 4316 m.

Shaston, see SHAFTESBURY.

Shastri, Lal Bahadur (1904–66), Prime Minister of India (1964–66), educated at Kashi Vidyapith, Benares. He was active for the Indian National Congress from 1921 and served a time in prison in 1930. He was general secretary, UPCC, 1935–38; minister of police and transport UP, 1947; general secretary of the Indian National Congress, 1951; minister for transport and communications in the Indian government, 1957–58; commerce and industry, 1958–61; home affairs, 1961–63; minister without portfolio, 1964; and became prime minister on 12 June 1964, on the death of Nehru. He died in Tashkent in the USSR on 11 January 1966.

Two things became clear during Shastri's short term of office. One was that he typified the highest qualities of the Hindu mind, the search for synthesis in agreement in the face of disagreement. The other was that peace remained his constant purpose, however much circumstances embroiled him at the centre of strife.

Shatt, see CHOTT.

Shatt-al-Arab, see EUPHRATES.

Shaving Soap, see SOAP.

Shavuot, see PENTECOST.

Shaw, George Bernard (1856–1950), English playwright, born in Dublin, of a genteel but poor Protestant family. He had little formal education but when he went to London in 1876 he studied voraciously. By 1883 he had written several novels, none of which were published. He became a socialist and in 1884 joined the newly-created Fabian Society, which included the Webbs (see PASSFIELD, BARON; WEBB, BEATRICE) and H.G. WELLS. He was an effective orator and remained a passionate socialist reformer throughout his life, acting as a borough councillor for St Pancras, London, as well as writing such popular propaganda as *The Intelligent Woman's Guide to Socialism and Capitalism*, 1928.

He wrote reviews, pamphlets and music and art criticism for a number of papers during the 1880s and 1890s. More significant, however, was his drama criticism for *The Saturday Review*, which he wrote between 1895 and

George Bernard Shaw setting out on his visit to Russia in July 1931. *(Popperfoto)*

on brilliantly witty serio-comic dialogue and playfully ironic inversion of audience expectations about character and situation to sugar the pill of his didacticism. He was skilful also in exploiting popular tastes for his own ends, as in *The Devil's Disciple*, where the conventions of melodrama are used in a sardonic and vigorous manner. Moreover, Shaw continued to invite implicit comparison with Shakespeare, most notably in *Caesar and Cleopatra*, which in spite of its comic contrasts with the tragedy, succeeds in communicating some of the same thoughtful expansiveness characteristic of Shakespeare's best work. As a result, Shaw contrived to be at once a leader of the intellectually serious and progressive English theatre and a successful popular playwright.

The years before the First World War produced a number of lightweight but popular comedies, including *Misalliance*, 1910, *Androcles and the Lion*, 1912, and *Pygmalion*, 1913, a great commercial success at the time which has since been many times revived, and was, under the title *My Fair Lady*, turned into a long-running musical and film. *Heartbreak House*, written during the war, combines lyricism and farce in depicting the decline of Edwardian England, and is regarded by some critics as his finest play. It was followed in 1921 by *Back to Methusaleh*, an ambitious cycle of plays in which Shaw offers his view of history from Adam to the distant future. In *St Joan*, 1923, the chronicle-history which is—with *Pygmalion*—his best-known and most revived play, Shaw again examined the implications of religious belief. The play mainly explores the contrast between the version of Christianity practised by Joan—the 'outsider' motivated by the 'Life Force'—and that upheld by the established Church. Although by now in his seventies Shaw's creative energy remained unflagging, and with *The Apple Cart*, 1929, he began to write a number of 'political extravaganzas', including *Too True to be Good*, 1932, *On the Rocks*, 1933, *The Six of Calais*, 1934, *The Millionairess*, 1936, *Geneva*, 1938, and *'In Good King Charles's Golden Days'*, 1939. In these plays Shaw presented his views on the need for morality in both domestic and international politics in the context of topical European developments and personalities. The postwar *Buoyant Billions*, 1948, and *Far-Fetched Fables*, 1950, do not come up to the standard of his mature plays.

The basis of Shaw's achievement is the combination of an adventurous and lucid intellect with a remarkable flair for theatrical comedy. These qualities, which helped several later or contemporary dramatists to find a comic form for treatment of serious issues, are evident also in the numerous prefaces with which Shaw introduced his plays to the reading public. These not only explain the ideas presented in his work but often also develop arguments not immediately connected with specific plays, either in relation to minor subjects which interested him at the time, or the major concerns of the intellectual disciplines. They are often as long, or longer, than the actual plays, and frequently as, or more, entertaining. Had Shaw never written a word for the stage, his reputation as a polemical essayist would have been assured on the basis of his prefaces, reviews, and propaganda works.

Shaw was as unorthodox and as vigorous in his personal life as he was in his creative work. He was a dedicated vegetarian, and regarded much orthodox medical treatment with grave suspicion. He married in 1898 Charlotte

1898 (reprinted subsequently as *Our Theatre in the Nineties*, 1932). It was at this time that he began to champion Henrik IBSEN, whose work he saw as combining outright didacticism and art (see *The Quintessence of Ibsenism*, 1891, enlarged edition 1913). Shaw took Shakespeare as the model—with Ibsen— for a new drama which would be in vital contact with contemporary life and problems, though with characteristically perverse exaggeration, he claimed his own superiority over Shakespeare.

During the 1890s Shaw began to supply the public with the didactic 'problem' plays he believed were needed. *Widowers' Houses*, which attacked slum landlords, reached the stage in 1892, and was followed by the popular success, *Arms and the Man*, 1894, a satire on romantic attitudes towards war. *Mrs Warren's Profession* was written in 1893 but was banned by the Lord Chamberlain and not produced (and then only privately) till 1902. Here, Shaw examined the social nature and implications of prostitution, without any of the romantic melodrama of previous 'women with a past' plays. *The Philanderer*, an Ibsenite play about the 'new woman', was written in 1893. Other works of this early period are *Candida*, 1895, *The Devil's Disciple*, 1897, *Caesar and Cleopatra*, 1898, *John Bull's Other Island*, 1904, *Man and Superman*, 1905, *Major Barbara*, 1905, and *The Doctor's Dilemma*, 1906. These are vehicles for Shaw's criticisms of, and feelings about, such various subjects as religion, the ethics of the medical profession, Anglo-Irish relations, puritanism and sex. *Man and Superman*, perhaps the most impressive of them, presents the first full working-out of Shaw's idea of the Life Force—'the struggle of Life to become divinely conscious of itself'—in terms of the battle of the sexes.

The serious implications of the issues Shaw treated, and the evangelical attitude he adopted towards them, do not, however, detract from the entertainment value of these plays. For Shaw developed a comic technique which relied

Shaw, Henry Wheeler

Payne-Townshend, a wealthy Irish lady, when he was almost 42. From 1906 he lived at Ayot St Lawrence, Hertfordshire, where he died on 2 November 1950. He had refused all honours except the Nobel Prize for literature, which he was awarded in 1925. His *Sixteen Self Sketches*, 1949, contains important biographical information.

Bibliography: Works (36 vols), 1930–50; *The Complete Plays*, 1934; *The Complete Prefaces*, 1934; *Collected Letters*, 1953; Eric Bentley, *Bernard Shaw*, 1950; St John Ervine, *Bernard Shaw: His Life, Work, and Friends*, 1956; A. Henderson, *George Bernard Shaw: Man of the Century*, 1956; G. K. Chesterton, *George Bernard Shaw*, 1909; R. Mander and J. Mitchenson, *A Theatrical Companion to Shaw*, 1955; M. Meisel, *Shaw and the Nineteenth Century Theater*, 1963; C. B. Purdom, *A Guide to the Plays of Bernard Shaw*, 1963; L. Crompton, *Shaw the Dramatist*, 1969; G. E. Brown, *George Bernard Shaw*, 1970; M. M. Morgan, *The Shavian Playground*, 1972.

Shaw, Henry Wheeler, see BILLINGS, JOSH.

Shaw, Richard Norman (1831–1912), British architect, born in Edinburgh. His family moved in 1845 to London, where he entered the office of William Burn and studied in the Royal Academy Schools, winning the Gold Medal and Travelling Studentship, 1854. After travelling abroad, he became assistant in 1858 to G. E. STREET, and began practice in 1862, working as partner with W. E. Nesfield until 1868. He then created an immense practice, which included many country mansions, such as Cragside, Northumberland; Adcote, Salop; Bryanston, Dorset; town-houses such as Lowther Lodge, Kensington (1873); 180 and 196 Queen's Gate, London; Swan House, Chelsea (1876); churches at Bedford Park and Ilkley; Albert Hall Mansions, the first large block of flats in London (1879); the Gaiety Theatre; New Scotland Yard (1888); and the Piccadilly Hotel (1905). His work, which at first was picturesque, with an abundance of ornament, half-timber, gables and bold chimneys, became progressively more classical based on 17th-century Dutch brick houses in England. He had great influence on late 19th-century English architecture.

Bibliography: N. Pevsner, *Studies in Art, Architecture and Design* (vol. 2: *Victorian and After*), 1968.

Shaw, Robert Archibald (1927–), British actor, novel-

Robert Shaw as Henry VIII in the film of Robert Bolt's *A Man for All Seasons*. (Popperfoto)

ist and dramatist. Shaw is best known as an actor who has appeared in classical roles with the Royal Shakespeare Company and in major parts in modern plays in both London and New York. Examples of the latter are Blackmouth in *Live Like Pigs* by John ARDEN and Aston in *The Caretaker* by Harold PINTER. He has also achieved fame as a film actor, appearing as Henry VIII in *A Man for All Seasons*, 1966, *The Birthday Party*, 1968, *Battle of Britain*, 1969, and *Figures in a Landscape*, 1969, for which he also wrote the screenplay. His novels include *The Hiding Place*, 1959, for which he won the Hawthornden prize; *The Sun Doctor*, 1961; and *The Man in the Glass Booth*, 1967. He dramatised the latter, which is a study of Nazi persecution of the Jews, and it was successfully staged in London and New York in 1967–68. His first play, *Off the Mainland*, 1956, was a melodrama about the Cold War. *Cato Street*, presented by the Young Vic in 1971, deals with the famous conspiracy to murder the British Cabinet. Shaw has also regularly appeared in, and written plays for, television. He was married to the actress Mary Ure, who died in 1975.

Shawl, article of dress worn over the shoulders, or head and shoulders, as a wrapping. For many centuries this simple garment remained in constant use among women of almost all nationalities and classes, both for themselves and for their babies. It is an essential feature of dress in certain parts of India and Iran, etc., but even in the East it is much less worn than formerly, and in Europe it is now rarely seen. The decline in its use for adult wear coincided with the advent of cheap, machine-made clothing and the invention of weather- and water-proof coats. In the world of fashion, the shawl undergoes periodic revivals, reappearing sometimes for evening wear, sometimes diminished to a fringed head-wrap, sometimes developing into the 'stole', worn loosely over the shoulders and often matching the skirt. The Paisley shawl was a favourite adornment for the piano-top in Edwardian times. As baby-wear, the shawl is still popular.

Shawm (German *Schalmei*, *Pommer*), woodwind instrument, the forerunner of the OBOE, with a double-reed mouthpiece and a wide bell. The largest sizes had a curved crook similar to that of the BASSOON. The shawm of the Psalms in Coverdale's translation is a misrendering of SHOFAR.

Shawnee, North American Indian people, belonging to the Iroquoian linguistic group. They are renowned for their extensive migrations through most of the east and south of the USA. Today they number about 5000, and most of them live in Oklahoma.

Shawqi, Ahmad (1868–1932), Egyptian poet, one of the greatest of the modern period, usually known as *Amir al-Shu'ara'*, Prince of Poets. His early career was spent at the court of the Khedive 'Abbas II, much as a court poet in the old Arabic tradition and this is reflected in the style and themes of his work from the period. He was exiled from Egypt during the First World War, and returned an enthusiastic supporter of Egyptian nationalism. Although bitterly attacked by some for his associations with the Khedive, his literary reputation is safeguarded by the quality of his poetry, collected into four volumes and known as the *Shawqiyyat*. He also wrote some of the earliest drama in literary Arabic.

Shawm.

Bibliography: M. A. Khouri, *Poetry and the Making of Modern Egypt,* 1971; M. M. Badawi, *A Critical Introduction to Modern Arabic Poetry,* 1975.

Shays' Rebellion took place in 1787 in Massachusetts. The leaders, Daniel Shays and Eli Parsons, were defeated by Gen. Shepard and Maj.-Gen. Lincoln, and fled to Vermont. The following year they were pardoned. The insurrection expressed itself in attempted obstruction of the courts with a view to preventing the collection of debts and taxes, but its immediate efffect was to strengthen the desire for an efficient federal government.

Shchedrin, N., see SALTYKOV, MIKHAIL YEV-GRAFOVICH.

Shcheglovsk, see KEMEROVO.

Shcherbakov, see RYBINSK.

She-oak, see CASUARINACEAE.

Shear. When a body or a section of a body is subjected to equal and opposite parallel forces it is said to be in a state of shear and the forces are called shear forces. There is a tendency for adjacent elements in the body to slide relative to one another; for instance a rectangle subjected to shear would tend to become a parallelogram. The force per unit surface area is called the shear stress. A common practical case of shear is found in a riveted joint between two steel plates. If an attempt is made to slide one plate relative to the other the rivet is subjected to a shear stress equal to the applied force divided by its cross-sectional area. Shear stresses also occur in a beam which is supported at the two ends and loaded at the centre. If the beam were not solid but made up of a number of flat plates lying one above the other, then as the beam deflected under load the plates would slide relative to each other.

In a solid beam the elements of the beam do not slide but there are shear forces exerted within its fabric.

Shear Legs, or shears, machines used for lifting and moving heavy weights a short distance horizontally. They are often constructed temporarily of stout poles for building works and quarries, but are also constructed of tubular steel for dockyard work, when they lift as much as 200 t. Two legs form an isosceles triangle capable of some rotation on its base; a third leg from the apex reaches the ground well behind the middle of the isosceles base, and its forward or backward movement raises and lowers the apex as well as moving it to and fro. To increase the lift a hand- or steam-operated winch and pulley tackle may be used. In dockyards, shear legs are often mounted on floating platforms.

Shearwater, about 15 species of family Procellariidae, in order Procellariiformes. All the species are oceanic, and either dark above and white below or all dark. They are related to the albatrosses and petrels which they resemble in having long wings. They get their name from their habit of skimming low over the sea on still wings. Shearwaters breed colonially in burrows, often in huge numbers. The Manx shearwater, *Puffinus puffinus puffinus,* is a common breeding bird in parts of Britain. *P. tenuirostris,* the muttonbird or whalebird, breeds in Australia but for the rest of the year moves over the Pacific; it is killed for meat and oil.

Sheba, the name given in the Bible to a state (modern Yemen) in southern Arabia (see SABAEANS) which was rich because it controlled the trade route, especially for incense. The story of Solomon and the Queen of Sheba occurs in 1 Kings x and in the Koran and is well known to Arab writers, who call her Bilqis. The royal house of Ethiopia claimed descent from this union.

Sheboygan, port city, capital of Sheboygan county, Wisconsin, USA, on Lake Michigan, in a dairying and cheese-making area 80 km north of Milwaukee. It manufactures furniture, enamelware, iron and steel, and wood products. Population 48,484.

Shechem, see NABLUS.

Shechinah, see SHEKINAH.

Sheehan, Patrick Augustine (1852–1913), Irish novelist and priest, born at Mallow, County Cork. Ordained in 1875, he began his pastoral work in England, but in 1877 returned to Ireland, and from 1895 was priest at Doneraile in Cork, being made a canon of Cork Cathedral in 1905. In 1895 he published his first novel, *Geoffrey Austin,* a story of student life, a sequel to which, *The Triumph of Failure,* appeared in 1899. In 1898 Sheehan published his best-known work, *My New Curate,* sketches of the life of a typical Irish priest. Other novels are *Glenanaar,* 1905, *Lisheen,* 1907, *The Blindness of Dr Gray,* 1909, *Miriam Lucas,* 1912, and *The Graves at Kilmorna,* 1915.

Sheeler, Charles (1883–), US painter, born in Philadelphia, noted for views of American industrial works and architecture in a highly finished, precise manner influenced by photography. Pictures made at the Ford works at Detroit are examples of his pictorial comment on modern technology.

Sheep

Sheep, a ruminant animal of the genus *Ovis*, family Bovidae (the cud-chewing animals) of order Artiodactyla (the cloven-hoofed mammals), which has been domesticated from a very remote period. Wild sheep occur in various parts of the world, and the moufflon is still in a semi-wild state in the islands of Sardinia and Corsica, but the origin of the various domesticated breeds is uncertain.

Breeds. Britain has long been one of the chief sheep countries of the world, and its breeds have been valued highly. Nowadays more imports into Britain occur, notably the Finnish Landrace, and the Ile de France. The two most notable breeds of sheep which owe nothing to British blood are the Merino, bred almost exclusively for its great quantity of fine wool, and the Astrakhan or Karakul, the lambs of which yield the valuable fur. Mention should also be made of the milk-yielding sheep of France, the most notable breed of which is the Larzac; its milk is used chiefly in the production of Roquefort cheese. The British breeds of sheep are considerably less numerous than they were a century ago, all but the best of them having been incorporated in more modern breeds suited to present-day requirements.

Existing breeds are usually classified as (1) mountain and moorland and (2) lowland, the latter class being subdivided into longwools and shortwools, into which last category the Down breeds fall. The chief mountain and moorland breeds are Blackface, Welsh Mountain, Rough Fell, Lonk, Derbyshire Gritstone, Swaledale, Exmoor Horn, Dartmoor, Cheviot and Herdwick. These are hardy, good foragers which thrive on poor food; slow-maturing in their natural habitat, but when kept under good lowland conditions producing lambs which fatten readily. Most of the lowland longwool breeds have been improved in the past by crossing with the Leicester, which was originally a large, heavy-fleeced, slow-maturing animal. About 1750, Robert Bakewell of Dishley began to breed for an early-maturing, moderate-sized animal by rigid selection and inbreeding, and was rewarded with enormous success, the Dishley Leicesters becoming world famous. Other longwools are the Border Leicester, the Lincoln (the largest and heaviest breed of domesticated sheep), Kent or Romney Marsh, Teeswater, South Devon, Devon Longwool, Blue-faced Leicester and Roscommon (the only Irish pure breed). They are all characterised by absence of horns, a heavy fleece of long, lustrous wool, and whitish face and legs, and are associated with districts where food is plentiful. The mutton is not generally considered of the finest quality. In the shortwool category the Down (Southdown, Hampshire, Dorset, Shropshire, Oxford, Suffolk) breeds all owe much to the Southdown, which was used in their formation. The Southdown has long been famous for the quality of its mutton, and it is unsurpassed for rapidity of both feeding and early maturity, while the close fine wool realises very high prices. The Down breeds were originally associated with Down districts of somewhat high elevation, with dry soils, but are now widely distributed. Other shortwool breeds of note are Dorset Horn, Ryeland, Kerry Hill, and Clun Forest, which last has found favour in recent years for ability to thrive on grass and arable land, standing up well to winter folding. The Dorset Horn deserves mention as being the only British breed to come into season most of the year round, and is thus capable of producing three crops of lambs in two years.

Every breed has its distinct characteristics, which, as a rule, are preserved only when the sheep are bred in the district of their origin. Elsewhere they soon become modified, and it seems likely, therefore, that British breeds will long continue to be of importance as sources of fresh and improving blood for stock of the great sheep-pasturing countries. Sheep breeders have long appreciated the value of hybrid vigour from first-class animals, and three notable crosses which are commonly kept in flocks are: (1) the Scotch half-bred (Border Leicester × Cheviot); (2) the Masham (Wensleydale or Teeswater male × Swaledale female); (3) the Greyface (Border Leicester × Blackface). The trend of sheep-keeping in Britain during the last half century has been that, with rising costs, the arable land sheep gave way largely to grassland flocks with a steady decrease in total numbers. This decrease was greatly accentuated during the war years as more and more grassland was ploughed out.

After a marked decline in popularity the sheep is re-establishing itself as an important source of food. Intensive, indoor keeping of sheep is being studied as well as the improvement of hill pastures. New breeds (Finnish) which can produce three to four lambs a year are coming into use in conjunction with the rearing of the surplus ones by artificial means.

Diseases. Anthrax is a notifiable disease. (See DISEASES OF ANIMALS ACTS.) *Black disease* is a blood infection (septicaemia) associated with wounds in the liver caused by the immature forms of the LIVER FLUKE. Protective vaccination is available in flocks where the disease occurs. *Blackquarter*, *blackleg*, or *quarter evil*, is caused by bacillary spores present on certain lands. Sudden deaths are common, and the shoulder or thick part of the hind leg is swollen and crackles on pressure. Preventive inoculations are available. *Blow fly, fly strike, maggots* are names for conditions caused by the green bottle fly (*Lucilia sericata*), which attacks the parts of sheep soiled with liquids, such as droppings of lambs with diarrhoea. Lambs are docked as a precautionary measure against fly strike, which is more common in lowland than in hill sheep. Crutching, i.e. clipping of wool from hind parts, is also a preventive, as is dipping in modern parasiticides. *Braxy* is a term applied to a condition characterised by gastro-intestinal symptoms which may be due to either local or general infection. The condition usually occurs during cold weather amongst animals kept on old grazings or those that have been moved from hills to lowlands. Vaccination is a preventive. *Contagious pustular dermatitis* is an eruptive pox-like condition caused by a virus which affects the udders of ewes, and the mouths, faces and feet of sucking lambs. Mild cases may, on occasion, recover without treatment, but applications of antiseptic lotions and, in severe cases, the use of antibiotics, assist recovery. Preventive vaccination is possible. The disease is communicable to man, and is not uncommon in shepherds. *Contagious ophthalmia*, heather blindness, is a very infectious disease which may lead to temporary blindness. In many flocks it attacks the lambs every year, the older sheep having acquired immunity. Eye lotions assist recovery, which, fortunately, usually occurs spontaneously after a lapse of time.

Entero-toxaemias are a group of diseases caused by

Sheep. TOP LEFT Kent. TOP RIGHT Île de France. ABOVE LEFT Blackface. ABOVE CENTRE Kent/Southdown cross. ABOVE RIGHT Dorset Horn ram. LEFT Merino ram. BELOW LEFT Finnish Landrace. BELOW RIGHT Spraying sheep to eliminate external parasites. *(Topham)*

toxins of the bacterium *Clostridium welchii*. Type-D *welchii* infection occurs in ewes on good keep, especially after being moved from poorer pastures. *Pulpy kidney* of lambs is caused by the same organism. It attacks lambs mostly between the ages of 6 and 16 weeks. It is common in lambs of the smaller breeds, and deaths from this infection are often erroneously thought to be due to wool ball. Early fat lambs are mostly victims, especially when put on to better keep. Castration and docking, by checking the growth, will help to reduce incidence. Type-C toxin is responsible for losses in sheep on permanent grazings in certain valleys in northern Wales and on the Kent Romney marshes. *Lamb dysentery*, caused by type B, is probably the best known of this class of infection. Diarrhoea may occur as early as 12 hours after birth. The disease is common in lambs from one to three weeks old. Old permanent lambing pens, in which infection becomes concentrated, are a frequent source of infection in newborn lambs. All diseases of the *C. welchii* group can be controlled by the appropriate hyperimmune serum or by a combined polyvalent vaccine. The antibodies in the milk of vaccinated ewes give passive immunity to sucking lambs. *Foot rot*, a disease of the horny and soft parts of the feet due to the combined actions of two microorganisms, is the most common cause of lameness, and probably the most widespread of all sheep diseases. Although usually associated with wet pastures, it cannot arise unless the causal organisms are present. Antibiotic sprays offer the easiest and most speedy forms of treatment and a vaccine is now available for prevention. The organisms cannot live more than a few weeks (probably only a fortnight) on land in the absence of infected sheep, and thus, with efficient treatment and adequate precautions, eradication of the disease is practicable. *Foot and mouth disease* is a notifiable disease. *Joint-ill* in lambs is a septic infection of the joints due to infection which enters through the navel of the newborn animal. *Liver fluke disease* is still widespread, although the life history of the liver fluke is well known and there are efficient drugs for treatment of infected animals. The secondary host can be killed by spraying its habitat with copper sulphate. The fluke also attacks man. Affected sheep waste and become dropsical and, in the later stages of the disease, 'razor-backed, bottle-jawed and pot-bellied'. The liver is enlarged, with distended bile ducts engorged with the flukes. Much illness is brought about by internal worms which live in the digestive or respiratory tracts. *Parasitic gastroenteritis*, with symptoms of diarrhoea and wasting, is caused by stomach worms; and *parasitic bronchitis*, or *husk*, is invasion of the lungs by nematode worms. The disease can be controlled by vaccination. Over-crowding of sheep on the land appreciably increases the risk of illness from both these types of worms. Eggs and larvae of the worms may survive for long periods on the land, but resting the land, even for a few months, will materially reduce the worm burden. Although modern drugs are a marked advance on the older forms of treatment, stomach worms are still a serious cause of losses to the sheep farmer. Improvement of pastures and temporary leys has tended to increase the severity of these parasitic diseases in many cases, since this improved grazing has led to more animals per acre, and risk of parasitic infestation increases geometrically with heavier stocking. *Pregnancy toxaemia*, or twin-lamb disease, is a fatal disease of pregnant ewes. Ewes which live long enough to lamb recover spontaneously. Prevention is achieved by scientific feeding to ensure that the ewe is kept in top condition. *Scab*, caused by mange parasites, was formerly common in certain parts of Great Britain, and compulsory dipping of sheep in an endeavour to limit this disease was enforced under the Diseases of Animals Acts. Whilst scab was, and remains, a notifiable disease, the introduction of dips containing BHC (gammexane) quickly solved the problem, and scab is no longer important in Great Britain, although sporadic outbreaks do occur. *Wool ball*: fits, attacks of colic and, rarely, deaths in lambs may occur through impaction of the digestive tract with balls of wool which the lambs have licked off their own or their mothers' bodies. *Trembles* or *louping ill* is a virus disease that cattle, horses, pigs, and man may also catch. It affects the nervous system. Affected sheep carry the head high and take short jumpy steps; finally they become paralysed and die. The causal virus is transmitted by the blood-sucking tick, *Ixodes ricinus*, which is found in large numbers on rough grazings in bracken, heather and gorse bushes. It may be controlled by vaccination. Preventive measures include dipping of sheep and the elimination of herbage which harbours the ticks.

Bibliography: J. Russell Greig, *The Shepherd's Guide*, 1958; C. R. W. Spedding, *Sheep Production and Grazing Management*, 1970.

Sheep Dip, see SHEEP, *Diseases*.

Sheep Ked, *Melophagus ovinus*, insect belonging to the family Hippoboscidae (suborder Cyclorrhapha) in order DIPTERA. They are ectoparasites of SHEEP, and feed on their blood. Adult keds are particularly well-adapted to clinging to their hosts; they are flattened dorso-ventrally and their legs bear terminal claws. The female fly, which lacks wings, deposits 10–15 larvae which she cements to the sheep's fleece. The oval-shaped, non-motile larvae pupate almost instantaneously while still attached to the host. The newly-emerged adults suck the sheep's blood. The sheep react to these irritations by scratching and thus damage their wool. In addition the keds defecate on the wool, which lowers its quality. Dipping the sheep regularly removes the keds.

Sheepdog, see OLD ENGLISH SHEEPDOG; SHEEPDOG TRIALS; SHETLAND SHEEPDOG.

Sheepdog Society, International, see SHEEPDOG TRIALS.

Sheepdog Trials and demonstrations are now very popular events at agricultural shows and the National Trials have entries in excess of 150 dogs in three days. The International Sheepdog Society holds annual trials in England, Scotland, Wales, Ireland and the Isle of Man to select a team from each country to compete at the International Trials held in England, Scotland and Wales in turn. Twelve dogs with the highest points are selected in England, Scotland and Wales and four in Ireland and the Isle of Man. These dogs are run on the national course which is the same as the qualifying course at the International Trials. Shepherd classes are also competed for, and there are contests for 'brace' or double dogs and a driving championship at the International Trials.

The Qualifying Course. For this event five sheep (two

of which are marked) are released about 366 m from the competitor. On command the dog should do a wide, fast 'outrun' slowing down behind the sheep to 'lift' (start) them gently and 'fetch' them quietly but firmly in as straight a line as possible between two hurdles, about 6 m apart, up to and around the handler. At this point the drive starts in a triangular fashion to left or right as the contour of the field allows. About 140 m away are two more hurdles about 6 m apart. Once through these the dog must guide the sheep into a quick turn in front of the handler, through another pair of gates and back to the handler. During these tests the handler remains beside a post marking the starting position but at this point he proceeds to the shedding ring 37 m in diameter which is marked with sawdust. Within this ring he must 'shed' (separate) two of the three unmarked sheep and keep them in control. After this they are united and taken to a pen with a 2 m length of rope on the gate for the handler to hold. The dog must work the sheep into the pen and, once inside, the gate is closed. Only one task remains to complete the event. This is known as 'singling' and it is performed in the shedding ring. One of the two marked sheep must be 'singled' off from the remainder and kept apart from the others until the judges are satisfied that the dog is in control. There is a time limit of 15 minutes and judges award points as follows: outrun 20, lifting 10, fetching 20, driving 20, shedding 10, penning 10, single 10; maximum 100.

Sheerness, former naval base, seaside resort, and industrial port on the Isle of SHEPPEY, Swale District, Kent. The dockyard was formerly a naval base, but was handed over to a trading estate in 1960 and now there are several large berths, two of which were opened in 1972 to handle vessels up to 200 m long. Containerisation and a roll-on/roll-off system operate. The boatstore (1859) in the dockyard is the earliest known multi-storey iron-framed building. See also QUEENBOROUGH.

Sheffield, John, see BUCKINGHAM AND NORMANBY, JOHN SHEFFIELD, 1ST DUKE OF.

Sheffield, John Baker Holroyd, 1st Earl of (1735–1821), British politician, who achieved notoriety for his part in suppressing the Gordon Riots of 1780. He was made Baron Sheffield in 1781 and Earl Sheffield in 1816. He was a friend of Gibbon and edited Gibbon's *Miscellaneous Works* in 1796.

Sheffield, city, municipal district, and six parliamentary boroughs of South YORKSHIRE, England. Its importance is due to its industry, particularly the production of special steels and steel products. It is noted for its cutlery and hand tools.

Situated on the coal measures, with workable seams, including the famous Silkstone seam within the city boundary, Sheffield is bisected by the Don and its tributaries, the Loxley, Rivelin, Porter, and Sheaf, flowing from the millstone grit to the west. Sheffield is flanked to the west and south by moorlands, including the Peak District National Park, and the southern PENNINES. Thomas de Furnival granted it a charter in 1297. Under the Talbot Earls of Shrewsbury, it was closely connected with one of the foremost noble families until 1616. The Talbot Earls often resided in the town, and in the early 16th century built the Manor Lodge and the Shrewsbury

chapel in the parish church. In 1616 the manor passed to the Howard family; the present Duke of Norfolk retains considerable interests in the city as ground landlord.

Mary Queen of Scots languished in the manor and castle, 1569–83, her custodian being the sixth Earl of Shrewsbury. The parish church of St Peter and St Paul, a 12th-century foundation, became the cathedral in 1914 when the diocese of Sheffield was created from part of that of YORK. Enlargement of the cathedral, begun in 1937, was partially completed in 1942 and further building began in 1963. A few old grinding mills still stand beside the streams; one, Shepherds Wheel in Whiteley Woods, has been completely restored. On the Sheaf the Abbeydale Industrial Hamlet is a restored industrial complex with its millponds, water-wheels, and numerous workshops for a wide variety of old craft industries. The remains of Beauchief Abbey are within the city boundary. Public buildings include the town hall, opened in 1897 and extended in 1923, with sites now being developed for a civic centre; the Cutlers' Hall, erected in 1832 on the site of previous buildings; the city hall, opened in 1932, with six halls including the magnificent oval hall seating 2500; the Castle Market Building completed in 1959; and the Central Library and Graves Art Gallery, opened in 1934. Here are the Fitzwilliam muniments from Wentworth Woodhouse, the Arundel Castle muniments, and the Crewe muniments. In addition to an extensive green belt, over 1375 ha of the city are publicly owned parks and open space. Over 240 ha of the Peak District National Park are within the city boundary. The city museum in Weston Park has unique collections of cutlery and old Sheffield plate and an important collection of British antiquities particularly rich in Bronze Age specimens. The 'Grice' collection of Chinese ivories is displayed in the Graves Art Gallery. Municipal services include the water supply with its fine reservoirs in the Loxley, Rivelin, and Ewden valleys, transport and public works, and printing departments. The city has an international reputation in the field of municipal housing. Park Hill and Hyde Park developments, Gleadless Valley and neighbourhood unit redevelopment are of special interest. Redevelopment of the central area has made Sheffield a regional shopping centre; numerous departmental stores and more than 200 shops having been built since the Second World War. The university obtained its charter in 1905 (see SHEFFIELD, UNIVERSITY OF). 'The Master, Wardens, Searchers, Assistants and Commonalty of the Company of Cutlers in Hallamshire in the County of York' was incorporated in 1624. The Company owns the trademark 'Sheffield', and elects a Master Cutler annually. This office is regarded in the city as second only to that of Lord Mayor. The Cutlers' Feast, Forfeit Feast, and installation of the Master are important events in the calendar of the Cutlers' Company.

Sheffield has a long industrial history. Iron was worked in the vicinity in the 12th century, and Sheffield was famed for its knives by the time of Chaucer. Cutlery long remained the industry of the 'little mester', but the 18th century saw many industrial changes. The invention by Boulsover in 1742 of the method of coating copper with silver to form the well-known 'old Sheffield plate', established an industry which flourished until it was superseded by electroplating in the 1850s. In 1740 Huntsman invented the process for making crucible steel and later established his works at Attercliffe. At the same time coke began to be widely used for smelting. Even more important was Bessemer's converter of 1856. At the same time there arose a demand for steel for railways, armaments, and constructional purposes. Little steel for general purposes is produced today. Sheffield's unique position depends on its production of alloy and special steels made to withstand high pressures or temperatures, to be acid-resistant, or possess other unusual qualities. Most were invented in Sheffield laboratories and works (including stainless steel). Much emphasis is placed on the importance of research in the industry. Sheffield has a high reputation for craftsmanship, apparent also in its heavy engineering industry. Melting shops, heavy forges, rolling mills, plate and wire mills make up the industrial conurbation of Sheffield. Its cutlery industry includes knives, razors, scissors, surgical instruments, agricultural and other machine knives, joiners', carvers', mechanics', and garden tools, and coal-cutting and boring tools. The production of silver and electroplated goods, with silver and gold refining, forms another group of industries. There are important subsidiary industries including type-founding, snuff, confectionery, food, refractory materials, and cardboard-box making.

In 1843 Sheffield was incorporated as a borough, and made a city 50 years later. It was first represented in Parliament in 1832. Sheffield is now the centre of the metropolitan district extending north to STOCKSBRIDGE and PENISTONE. Population (1971) 520,327.

Bibliography: D. L. Linton (Ed.), *Sheffield and Its Region*, 1956; S. Pollard, *History of Labour in Sheffield, 1850–1939*, 1959; W. Hampton, *Democracy and Community: A Study of Politics in Sheffield*, 1970; A. Hilton, *Sheffield History*, 1973; J. E. Vickers, *Sheffield Old and New*, 1973; B. E. Coates and others, *Census Atlas of South Yorkshire*, 1974; B. Hinchcliffe (Ed.), *Sheffield as It Was*, new ed. 1974.

Sheffield, University of, founded 1905, originated in three previous institutions. In 1897 the Sheffield School of Medicine (founded 1828), Firth College of Arts and Science (founded 1879), and Sheffield Technical School (opened 1886) were combined to form University College, Sheffield. A royal charter of 1905 established the college as the University of Sheffield. There are faculties of arts, social sciences, materials, architecture, law, pure science, medicine, engineering, and a training department for teachers, a postgraduate school of librarianship, and a centre of Japanese studies. Students number approximately 7000.

Sheffield Plate, see SILVERSMITHING.

'Sheffield Telegraph', one of the oldest daily morning papers in Britain to be published outside London, incorporating the *Daily Independent*, 1819, and the *Sheffield Telegraph*, 1855. Re-titled the *Sheffield Daily Telegraph and Daily Independent* in 1938, its name changed to the *Telegraph and Independent* in 1939 and to the *Sheffield Telegraph* in 1942. It is politically independent.

Shefford, small town in BEDFORDSHIRE, England, on the River Ivel, 15 km south-east of Bedford, with the remains of an ancient priory. Local industries include the manufacture of insulating tapes and laundering. St Francis'

Catholic Orphanage for Boys is in Shefford. Population (1971) 2585.

Shefket Pasha, Mahmud (1857–1913), Turkish soldier and politician, born in Baghdad. He was appointed, in 1907, commander of the Third Army Corps stationed at Salonika. Here he joined the 'Young Turks', and from here, when the counter-revolution of 13 April 1909 broke out, he marched on Constantinople with his army and deposed the Sultan, Abdul-Hamid. From then till 9 July 1912 he was minister for war, and was grand vizier, until his murder in 1913.

Sheikh (Arabic *shaikh*), Arabian and Muslim title, used to designate chieftains, lesser magistrates, and scholars. The word literally means an elder, and denotes a dignity that has no very precise significance. Basically it is little more than *primus inter pares*; thus chiefs of tribes and heads of villages are both called sheikhs. Particularly important, however, was the *Shaikh al-Islam*. Originally a title of honour granted to theologians, under the Ottoman Empire it became the prerogative of the MUFTI of Istanbul, especially when in the 16th century he became head of the *Ilmiye*, a council of ULEMA, concerned with religious, legal, and educational matters. In prestige and ceremony he stood second only to the Grand VIZIER, and his political and religious influence was massive. His chief duty was to ensure that the state was run in accordance with the SHARIAH, and his advice was sought as a matter of course on all important matters of state.

Shekel, a Babylonian unit of weight, and the name used in the Bible for silver coins of approximately the same weight circulating in ancient Israel. These coins were four DRACHMA pieces minted mostly in Phoenicia and Syria. The shekel was only struck by the Jews themselves during their first and second revolts against Rome (AD 66–70 and 132–35).

Shekinah, or Shechinah (Hebrew, dwelling or presence), expression frequently occuring in the Targums and Talmud to denote the divine presence, the idea being developed in Jewish Rabbinical thought after Old Testament times. The original conception grew from the description of the presence of the Lord in the holy of holies in the tabernacle, indicated by the cloud enveloping it as the manifestation of God, which was thought of as the light behind the cloud.

Bibliography: Abelson, *The Immanence of God*, 1912.

Shelburne, William Petty, Earl of, see LANSDOWNE, WILLIAM PETTY, 1ST MARQUESS OF.

Sheldon, Charles Monroe (1857–1946), US clergyman and writer, born at Wellesville, New York state. Educated at Phillips Academy, Andover, Massachusetts and Brown University, he became a Congregational minister. From 1920 to 1925 he was editor of the *Christian Herald*. He is remembered for his religious novel *In His Steps*, 1896, which was one of America's greatest best-sellers of all time. No such success was achieved by Sheldon's other books, which include *His Brother's Keeper*, 1895, and *The Heart of the World*, 1905. He published an autobiography in 1925.

Sheldon, Edward Brewster (1886–1946), US dramatist, born in Chicago, educated at Harvard. *Salvation*

Nell, 1908, his first play, was followed by *The Nigger*, 1909, and *Romance*, 1913, which was one of the most famous hits of its time. Others of his plays are *The Princess Zim-Zim*, 1911, and *The High Road*, 1912. In 1918 he contracted arthritis, which eventually made him a complete invalid, and later he became blind, but continued to work, carry on correspondence and exert an importance influence on the New York theatre. Later plays, in which he collaborated with others, are *Bewitched*, 1924; *Lulu Belle*, 1926; *Jenny*, 1929; and *Dishonored Lady*, 1930.

Bibliography: E. W. Barnes, *The Man Who Lived Twice*, 1956.

Sheldon, Gilbert (1598–1677), English prelate, born at Stanton, Staffordshire. He was warden of All Souls College, Oxford, for some years, and became chancellor of the university in 1667. He held various preferments in the Church and became archbishop of Canterbury in 1663. He was an active and liberal promoter of the rebuilding of St Paul's Cathedral, and he endowed and erected at his own expense the Sheldonian Theatre at Oxford, which was designed by Wren and completed in 1669.

Bibliography: Life by V. Staley, 1913; N. Sykes, *From Sheldon to Secker*, 1959.

Shelduck, *Tadorna tadorna*, handsome, brilliantly plumaged member of the duck family, Anatidae, in the order Anseriformes. It is found naturally on European coasts and in central and eastern Asia, but is often kept on ornamental waters. The name refers to a shield-like patch on the breast. Its nest is often made in old rabbit holes, and in it 10–12 white eggs are laid. The drake is about 60 cm long, the head and neck are glossy green and the rest of the plumage is chiefly black and white, with rich chestnut breast and a bronze patch on the wing.

Shell, see AMMUNITION.

Shell, the hard covering of an animal, including the carapace of a tortoise, crab or lobster; more correctly confined to the calcareous structures characteristic of phylum MOLLUSCA. A typical mollusc shell is composed of

Shelduck. *(Topham/Coleman)*

carbonate of lime mixed with conchiolin, an animal substance similar to chitin. The shell is secreted by the mantle, a fold of skin which envelops the mollusc's body. Additions to the shell are formed only by the edge of the mantle and, since growth is discontinuous, lines of growth are shown on the exterior surface. Typically there are three layers in a snail's shell, an outer one which, on empty, sea-washed sea shells thrown up on the beach, is often worn off, a middle prismatic layer, and an inner nacreous layer.

The nature of a shell is determined largely by the conditions in which its builder lives. In species which live in still water or float at the surface it is usually thin, light and smooth. Molluscs that adhere to rocks exposed to the buffeting of the waves, or on sandy or gravelly bottoms, where they are likely to be rolled about by the action of tides, have thick tough shells which are often strengthened by ridges, spines or knobs. Shells are also modified according to the degree of protection necessary to guard their inmates from predatory enemies. Freshwater shells are light and thin and, though the shells of some land snails are strong and hard, none is as heavy or thick as are many marine forms.

Shells are divided into two main groups, univalves, which are all in one piece, as in the whelk and snail, and bivalves, which consist of two distinct portions, as in oysters and mussels. Both types show wide diversity in shape, colour and surface conformation. A simple univalve shell is represented by the limpet, the shape being that of a low broad-based pyramid with the internal chamber undivided. In the great majority of shells of this group the pyramid is twisted into a spiral about a central column, the visceral mass of the mollusc being lodged in the lowest and largest whorl. Much of the great variation in shape shown by univalve shells is due to differences in the height of the spiral, the number of its whorls and the form assumed by the opening. The general shape may remain similar to that of the limpet, as in the abalone, *Haliotis*, in which the lowest whorl is very broad and the spiral almost flat. Periwinkles and top shells represent a further step from the primitive form. Though the base is still broad and almost flat, the whorled pyramid is higher, with a well-marked peak. The whelk shows a taller spiral, with more strongly defined whorls; while shells like the augers, *Turritella*, have high narrow spirals of many gradually diminishing whorls. At the other extreme is the shell of the fresh-water snail *Planorbis*, which is coiled in the horizontal plane, and the cowry, which must be broken if its spiral structure is to be revealed.

In bivalves the shell valves may be similar, as in the cockle, or dissimilar, as in the scallop, in which one is strongly convex, while the other is flat. The valves are hinged at the top by an elastic ligament or membrane, which exerts a pull on the areas to which it is attached. This pull is countered by the contraction of muscle bands that stretch between the valves. An empty shell shows distinctive scars at the points of attachment of these muscles. The muscle scars are usually connected by a curved line which indicates where the mantle was fixed to the shell. This line may form a simple curve, as in the cockle, or be deeply indented, as in the piddock and venus shells. Accurate closing of the valves is often ensured by the development of interlocking teeth or ridges at the top margins. The course taken by the line and the detailed

Shell

arrangement of the hinging devices are important in classifying and identifying bivalve shells.

The only cephalopod that builds a true shell is the pearly NAUTILUS. Though similar in general form to a coiled univalve shell it is wholly different in structure, for the interior is partitioned into a number of separate compartments, of which only the last is occupied. The others represent chambers which have formed the home of the builder at previous stages of growth and take on the function of a bouyancy mechanism when it moves into a new, larger compartment. The female paper nautilus, *Argonauta*, also secretes a shell of sorts, but this serves as a floating cradle for the reception and transport of her eggs and young rather than as a dwelling. It is unchambered, very thin, light, buoyant and semi-transparent, and is formed, not by the mantle as are true shells, but by two flat plates on two of the mollusc's eight arms.

Both univalve and bivalve shells are abundantly represented in Britain. Univalves, like limpets, winkles, top shells, necklace shells, whelks, screw shells, spindles and conelets, are among the most common of seashore objects. British fresh-water and land snails also build shells of very diverse form, from the flat coil of the ram's horn (*Planorbis*) to the tall spiral of the pond snails (*Lymnaea*) and the door snails. In size they vary from the dwarf snail, barely 0.3 cm in diameter, to the Roman snail measuring 5 cm across. The whelks provide the largest univalve shells found in Britain, but they are dwarfed by such exotic species as the spindle-shaped tulip shells of the shores of South Carolina, which may be 60 cm long, and the West Indian pink conch, or fountain shell, weighing up to 1.8 kg. Univalves include many tropical and sub-tropical forms of great beauty. Special mention may be made of the volutes, olives, harp-snails, cones and wing-snails. The last-named are allied to the pelican's foot, often found on British shores and so called from the shape assumed by the expanded mouth of the shell.

Shells.

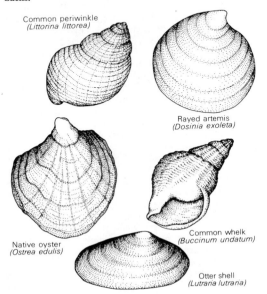

Common periwinkle
(*Littorina littorea*)

Rayed artemis
(*Dosinia exoleta*)

Native oyster
(*Ostrea edulis*)

Common whelk
(*Buccinum undatum*)

Otter shell
(*Lutraria lutraria*)

The most generally distributed British bivalves include oysters, mussels, scallops, cockles, trough shells, gapers (in which the hind edges of the valves do not meet, but 'gape' more or less widely), the attractively marked venus, carpet, tellin and sunset shells, the white file-edged piddocks, and the long narrow razor-shells (of a shape especially adapted for burrowing quickly in sand and mud). Among the many large and interesting bivalves of tropical and subtropical waters are the pearl mussels, the brightly coloured thorny oysters and the clams, in some species of which a single valve may weigh over 90 kg.

Bibliography: N. Tebble *British Bivalve Shells*, 1966; N. F. McMillan, *British Shells*, 1968.

'Shell' Transport and Trading Company Limited, The, is an English company which owns 40 per cent of the Royal Dutch/Shell group of companies. The other 60 per cent is owned by the Royal Dutch Petroleum Company (Naamloze Vennootschap Koninklijke Nederlandsche Petroleum Maatschappij). Royal Dutch was established in the Netherlands in 1890 and Shell was established in 1897. The two companies joined forces in 1907. The Royal Dutch/Shell group now includes over 500 companies in 100 countries. The main business of the group is exploring for, extracting, refining, and distributing petroleum, but it also has substantial interests in natural gas, chemicals, metals, coal, and nuclear energy. The total net income of the group in 1973 was £730 million and it employed 168,000 people.

Shell Heaps, or mounds, see KITCHEN MIDDENS.

Shell-shock, a term for traumatic neurosis that was widely used during the First World War to describe various neurotic syndromes which are now recognised as anxiety states and anxiety hysterias. Its invention and adoption may well have been facilitated by the preoccupation of the public mind at that time with the recently learned effects of high explosive. While it is true that the onset of symptoms was, in some cases, associated with some specific incident, such as proximity to a shell-burst, many more occurred in areas remote from shell-fire. The suggestion, seemingly implicit in such a term, that an important, or even essential, causal part was played by concussive trauma was as inaccurate as the picture which it tended to convey of a previously perfectly healthy individual being stricken down with dramatic suddenness. In the majority of cases the appearance of symptoms merely marked the point where the breaking stress had been reached after a prolonged period of tension, even if the latter had been unsuspected. The role played by any special incident was merely precipitant, and the true cause lay in conflict between the individual's instinct of self-preservation and the demands of patriotic duty, loyalty and self-respect. The heavy emotional charge investing such a conflict finally become too strong, was dissociated from it, and erupted into consciousness as 'free' anxiety. The latter, or its somatic 'attachments', accounted for a variety of signs and symptoms, such as tremor, inability to talk, paralysis, insomnia, and amnesia. These rendered the individual unfit for further service in the danger zone, revealing thereby their unconscious purposive aspect. Thus the original conflict had been solved in a manner involving no conscious guilt or loss of honour. See PSYCHONEUROSIS; PSYCHOPATHOLOGY.

Bibliography: I. R. C. Batchelor, *Henderson and Gillespie's Textbook of Psychiatry*, 10th ed. 1969.

Shelley, Mary Wollstonecraft (1797–1851), English novelist, born in London, the daughter of the philosopher William GODWIN and Mary Wollstonecraft, and second wife of the poet Percy Bysshe SHELLEY. Shelley was a friend and correspondent of Godwin and met Mary when she was about 17; shortly afterwards the couple eloped, finally settling in Italy. After the suicide of Shelley's wife, Harriet, they were married (1816) and had a son, Percy Florence.

Mary Shelley is best known as the author of the weird and brilliant tale of horror *Frankenstein: or, The Modern Prometheus*, 1818, which of all novels written in the 'gothic' style has had the most striking influence. It originated in a ghost story, told by Mary in competition with Shelley and BYRON, and its basic idea, that science can give life to inanimate matter, has fascinated writers ever since. Her other novels include *Valperga*, 1823; *The Last Man* (probably her best work), 1826; and *The Fortunes of Perkin Warbeck*, 1830. After Shelley's death she published his *Posthumous Poems*, 1824, and edited his *Poetical Works*, 1839. Her *Journal*, letters, and travel books, such as *History of a Six Weeks' Tour*, 1817, give many valuable insights into Shelley's work and their life together.

Bibliography: Lives by R. Church, 1928, R. G. Grylls, 1923, and S. Norman, 1938; E. Bigland, *Mary Shelley*, 1959; K. N. Cameron and D. H. Reiman (Eds), *Shelley and His Circle: 1773–1822*, 1961–74.

Shelley, Percy Bysshe (1792–1822), English poet, born at Field Place, near Horsham, Sussex. He was educated at Sion House School, Isleworth, and at Eton, where he speedily earned a reputation for eccentricity but

Percy Bysshe Shelley, portrait by Amelia Curran painted at Rome in 1819. (*National Portrait Gallery, London*)

also showed himself an apt scholar, learning Greek and Latin, and reading omnivorously. Before his schooldays were over he had published two prose romances and, in collaboration with his sister Elizabeth, a book of verse, *Original Poetry, by Victor and Cazire*, 1810. In 1810 he entered University College, Oxford, but soon after matriculating he joined Thomas Jefferson HOGG, the future biographer, in the production of a pamphlet, *The Necessity of Atheism*, 1811, which gave so much offence that he was sent down. Forbidden by his father to come home, he went instead to London. Here he met (characteristically, through trying to rescue her from her father's oppression) Harriet Westbrook, two years younger than himself, with whom he eloped to Edinburgh in 1811.

For a while the couple lived at Keswick, Shelley meanwhile showing himself an ardent revolutionary in politics, championing the various radical movements in Britain and more especially in Ireland (1812). In the following year he published privately *Queen Mab*, and came under the influence of the radical William GODWIN. At this time he and his wife drifted apart, and in spring 1814 Shelley eloped again—to Switzerland with Godwin's daughter Mary. This action accorded with his view of marriage as an artificial and degrading restraint, and he appeared surprised when like-minded friends nevertheless condemned his conduct. In 1816 Harriet drowned herself. Shelley then married Mary Godwin, issued the memorable *Alastor*, and also travelled in Switzerland and France. Returning to England, he became reconciled to his father, who settled on him a small but adequate income; and after living for some time at Marlow, and then near Windsor, Shelley and his wife proceeded to Italy. Here they led a wandering life, saddened by the death of an infant son and daughter; but in 1820 they finally settled at Pisa.

His contact with Italy was a landmark in Shelley's intellectual development. Here he composed *The Cenci*, 1819, 'Ode to the West Wind', 1819, *Rosalind and Helen*, 1819, and *Prometheus Unbound*, 1820; while at Pisa he wrote many of his finest short lyrics, and also *Epipsychidion*, 1821, *Adonais*, 1821, his elegy on the death of KEATS, and *Hellas*, 1822. He continued to champion the cause of freedom in England and Italy, while he read Greek literature incessantly, mastered Spanish, Italian, and German, and translated CALDERÓN, DANTE, and GOETHE. From Pisa he went to Ravenna to stay with BYRON, whose acquaintance he had made some years before. In July 1822, while sailing to Spezia, his boat foundered in a storm and he was drowned. After many days his body was found by his friend Edward TRELAWNY, who cremated it on the seashore, with Byron among the mourners. The ashes were taken to Rome and interred in the Protestant cemetery which Shelley himself had described as a place so lovely that 'it might make one in love with death'.

Shelley is often pictured as an ethereal visionary. This view fails to take account of his development from the over-simplified theories of his youth, his great learning, or his readiness to risk involvement with the pain and injustice of the world. In *A Defence of Poetry*, written in 1821, but unpublished until 1840, Shelley declared his belief in poetry as a moral force: 'The greatest instrument of moral good is the imagination; and poetry administers to the effect by acting upon the cause'. Many of his poems were radical and reforming in aim; but, though these excited much contemporary interest and contain stirring passages (such as his eulogies on freedom in *Hellas*), Shelley is chiefly remembered as one of the greatest lyric poets. His experiments in poetic drama (apart from *The Cenci*) and his political hymns are insignificant beside such masterpieces as the 'Ode to the West Wind', 'The Cloud', and 'To a Skylark'.

His sensitive descriptions of natural beauty concentrate always on the play of movement and light rather than on solid or sensuous qualities. His poetry shares the qualities of the world which it describes: a world in a state of flux ('Nought may endure but Mutability') and moral struggle. Other poets have written some of the most sympathetic studies of him, including SWINBURNE, Francis THOMPSON, Arthur SYMONS, and W. B. YEATS, on whom he was a strong influence. An edition of the *Prose* was edited by D. L. Clark, 1954; and *Letters* by F. L. Jones, 1964.

Bibliography: R. Ingpen and W. E. Peek (Eds), *Complete Works* (10 vols), 1926–30, 1965; T. Hutchinson (Ed.), *Complete Poetical Works*, 1934, rev. G. M. Matthews, 1970; E. Blunden, *Shelley: A Life Story*, 1946; C. Baker, *Shelley's Major Poetry*, 1948; K. N. Cameron, *The Young Shelley*, 1950, and *Shelley: The Golden Years*, 1974; H. Bloom, *Shelley's Mythmaking*, 1959, and *The Visionary Company*, 1961; E. R. Wasserman, *Shelley: A Critical Reading*, 1971; R. Holmes, *Shelley: The Pursuit*, 1974.

Shellfish, popular unscientific name which includes edible molluscs (phylum MOLLUSCA) such as the whelk, periwinkle, oyster and mussel, as well as such crustaceans (phylum ARTHROPODA, class CRUSTACEA) as the crab, lobster, prawn and shrimp.

Shelta, or Shelter, Shelterox, Sheldru, Sheltru, is apparently a corruption of Irish *bēlra* or *bērla* (or *bēarla*), meaning speech, language, jargon. It is a mysterious form of speech, of uncertain origin, used by Irish gypsies, although it seems not to be connected with ROMANY. It draws on English as well as Irish for its vocabulary. See also IRELAND, *Language*.

Bibliography: A. A. S. Macalister, *The Secret Languages of Ireland*, 1937.

Shema, central prayer of Judaism (Deut. vi. 4–9). It is the affirmation of the One God, to be loved and taught to all, prominent in all public and private prayer of Jews, and recited at the death bed.

Shemiran, northern suburb of TEHRAN, Iran, at the foot of the ELBURZ MOUNTAINS. It is the site of the National University of Iran. Population (1966) 157,000.

Shen Nung, Chinese deity of medicine and agriculture. The immediate predecessor of the mythical Yellow Emperor, Shen Nung is known as the Agricultural Emperor for his invention of the cart and other agricultural implements. Legend gives him a miraculous childhood in which he could both walk and talk at the age of five days and had all his teeth at seven days, while at the age of three years he was tilling the fields. When grown he measured 8 ft 7 in (2·62 m) in height. He is revered and loved for his study of plants and their uses in curing disease and is said to have classified 365 species of medicinal plants. He died at the age of 168 and became an Immortal.

Shen-yang, see MUKDEN.

Shenandoah, river of Virginia and West Virginia, USA, a tributary of the POTOMAC, which joins it at its passage through the Blue Ridge, after a course north-east for 325 km. The valley, which is fertile and noted for its apples and dairying, is overlooked on the south side by the mountains of the Shenandoah National Park.

Shenandoah Valley Campaign. The valley of the River Shenandoah in north-west Virginia, scene of many conflicts during the Civil War in the USA, became especially famous in the summer of 1864. Gen. U. S. Grant, with 150,000 Federal troops, was confronting Gen. Robert E. Lee, with 75,000 Confederates, in a campaign whose object was to capture Petersburg and then Richmond, the capital of the Confederacy. In the hope of relieving those cities, Lee sent Gen. Jubal A. Early with 15,000 picked troops to threaten the national capital of Washington. By mid-July Washington was within Early's grasp, but he hesitated, and the next day his chance was gone, because Grant had sent two veteran army corps to defend the city. Early turned up the valley and sent troops into Chambersburg, Pennsylvania, which was burned down. Grant now sent his best cavalry general, Phil Sheridan, to attack Early. He also instructed him to lay the whole valley waste, so that it could not afford a field for Confederate operations. Sheridan attacked Early in the first battle of Winchester. No decisive result was obtained. On 19 September a second battle was fought there and Sheridan won. He again defeated Early at Fisher's Hill. On 5 October Sheridan began his famous raid down the Shenandoah Valley. Pursuant to orders, he destroyed everything the enemy might use. Early, now reinforced, crept upon the sleeping Confederate troops at Cedar Creek, and in a short time defeated and almost put them to rout. Sheridan himself was at Winchester, some 32 km away. Hearing the sound of heavy cannonading, he hastened to the battlefield and routed his enemy. The devastation of the valley prevented further movements there by either side.

Bibliography: E. Stackpole, *Sheridan in the Shenandoah*, 1961.

Shenshin, see FET, AFANASI AFANASIEVICH.

Shensi, an inland province of northern CHINA to the west of Shansi. It is bounded on the north by the Ordos Desert of Inner Mongolia and on the south by the Tapa Shan. Most of the province lies north of the Tsinling Shan (mountains) and, like neighbouring SHANSI province, consists of a dissected upland covered by deposits of wind-blown LOESS, a superficial deposit derived from the deserts of Inner Mongolia to the north. The height of the plateau of northern Shensi is about 1000 m above sea-level. It is a rather remote area with a hard climate and relatively short growing periods for crops. Spring wheat and millet are the major crops and as the Ordos Desert approaches, grazing for animals becomes more important than arable cultivation because of lack of rainfall. The most populated part of Shensi is the Wei Ho valley, a tributary of the Hwang Ho, flowing eastwards at the foot of the Tsinling Shan. The valley is well watered and extensively irrigated, with winter wheat, tobacco, and cotton being the major crops. In the extreme south of the province the Han valley, sheltered by the Tsinling Shan to the north and the Tapa Shan to the south, has an almost subtropical climate similar to that of the Szechwan and besides wheat, corn, and rice, fruit crops such as apples, pears, apricots, and grapes are produced. The capital of Shensi province is SIAN in the Wei valley. Sian is an ancient capital of China but more recently it has been developed into a major industrial city in accordance with the Communist government's industrial dispersal policies. Several factories, including a sewing machine and watch factory, have been moved to Sian from Shanghai, and it has also become an important textile centre. In the north of Shensi province is YENAN, which became the base for the Communist forces at the end of their 'Long March' from Kiangsi province in 1937. Area 195,800 km²; population (1972) about 22,000,000.

Shenstone, William (1714–63), English poet, born at Halesowen, Worcestershire. He studied at Pembroke College, Oxford, where he was a contemporary of Dr JOHNSON. *Poems upon Various Occasions* was published in 1737, and this was followed by *The Judgement of Horatio*, 1741, and *The Schoolmistress*, 1742, a humorous imitation of SPENSER. After 1745 Shenstone took up landscape gardening which earned him a wider reputation than his poetry. His works were published in three volumes, 1764–69, edited by R. DODSLEY, and his letters were edited by M. Williams in 1939.

Bibliography: Life by R. Graves, 1788; I. A. Williams, *Seven Eighteenth Century Bibliographies*, 1924; A. R. Humphreys, *William Shenstone*, 1937.

Sheōl, see HELL.

Shepard, Alan (1923–), US astronaut, born at East Derry, New Hampshire. On 5 May 1961 he became the second man to enter space. His space capsule was fired from Cape Canaveral (later Cape Kennedy) 180 km into space, and Shepard maintained communication with the ground throughout his 15-minute flight. In 1971 he made a lunar landing in *Apollo 14*, and during a 33½-hour exploration gathered samples from the Moon's surface and set up scientific equipment.

Shepard, Ernest Howard (1879–1976), British artist and cartoonist, born in London, and educated at Heatherley's and the Royal Academy schools. During the First World War he was commissioned with the Royal Artillery and awarded the MC. He was elected to the *Punch* Table in 1921. Shepard produced illustrations for A. A. Milne's *Winnie-the-Pooh*, 1926, Kenneth Grahame's *The Golden Age*, 1928, and *The Wind in the Willows*, 1931, which continue to be the standard versions even in modern editions. He published an autobiography, *Drawn from Memory*, 1957.

Shepherd Kings, see EGYPT; HYKSOS.

Shepherd of Hermas, The (Pastor Hermae), early Christian allegorical and hortatory treatise in three parts: 'Visions', 'Mandates', and 'Similitudes'. The author is usually classed among the APOSTOLIC FATHERS, but there is much discussion as to his identity. The Muratorian canon makes him brother of Pius I, Bishop of Rome (c. 140–54). The work is prized as a record of 2nd-century Christianity in Rome. Its date is given by modern scholars as between AD 140 and 155. Its offer of an exceptional absolution for serious sins is important in the development of penitential discipline. Irenaeus, Clement of Alexandria, and Origen highly esteemed the work, and it was publicly read in churches at one time, but excluded from the sacred canon by the 4th century. There is a translation by K. Lake in *The Apostolic Fathers* (Loeb Classical Library), 1912.

Bibliography: P. Carrington, 'Hermas and His Angel' in *The Early Christian Church*, vol. 1, 1957.

Shepherdia argentea, rabbit berry or buffalo berry, deciduous shrub of North America, in family Elaeagnaceae, with silvery leaves and yellow flowers in spring, which are succeeded by scarlet edible berries.

Shepherd's Bush, see HAMMERSMITH.

Shepherd's Dog, see OLD ENGLISH SHEEPDOG; SHETLAND SHEEPDOG.

Shepherd's Purse, *Capsella bursa-pastoris*, a common plant belonging to the Cruciferae (cabbage family) and characterised by its two-valved fruits. The plant is extraordinarily adaptable, and, being self-fertilised, is able to flower and seed the whole year round.

Sheppard, David Stuart (1929–), English cricketer and churchman, educated at Sherborne and Trinity Hall, Cambridge. He first achieved prominence as an outstanding cricketer, winning a blue at Cambridge and playing for England while still an undergraduate in 1950. He played in 22 Test matches before his retirement in 1963, and captained England in 1954. He played for Sussex, 1947–62.

He was ordained into the Church of England in 1955 and spent most of his early ministry in inner London, as assistant curate at Islington, 1955–57, and as warden of the Mayflower Family Centre in Canning Town, 1957–69. He succeeded Dr John ROBINSON as suffragan bishop of Woolwich in 1969, and in 1975 was appointed bishop of

David Sheppard, while working as a curate in Islington, 1956. *(Popperfoto)*

Sheppard, Hugh Richard Lawrie

Liverpool. His publications include *Parson's Pitch*, 1964, and *Built as a City*, 1974.

Sheppard, Hugh Richard Lawrie, known as Dick (1883–1937), English churchman, educated at Marlborough and Cambridge. In 1914 he served as a chaplain in France, and became, in the same year, vicar of St Martin-in-the-Fields, London, where his progressive methods soon made his name known everywhere. He resigned in 1927, and in 1929 became dean of Canterbury. He was prominent in forming the Peace Pledge Union. He wrote *The Human Parson*, 1924, *The Impatience of a Parson*, 1927, and *My Hopes and Fears for the Church*, 1930.
  Bibliography: R. Ellis Roberts, *H. R. L. Sheppard. Life and Letters*, 1942; C. H. S. Matthews, *Dick Sheppard*, 1948.

Sheppard, Jack (1702–24), English criminal, born at Spitalfields, London. In April 1724 he was committed to St Giles's roundhouse, but escaped, and, captured again in May, broke out of New Prison, Clerkenwell. In July he was again caught, and in the following month was tried and condemned to death. He escaped twice more, but was caught drunk, and watched day and night until his execution at Tyburn on 16 November. He was a popular hero, and Harrison Ainsworth made him the subject of a novel, *Jack Sheppard*. He figures also in Henry Fielding's *Jonathan Wild*.
  Bibliography: C. Hibbert, *The Road to Tyburn*, 1957.

Shepparton, town of Victoria, Australia, centre of the fruit-growing area in Goulburn valley, 182 km north of Melbourne, in one of the main irrigation districts. Dairying and fruit-growing are the chief occupations and there are industries, including engineering, sawmilling, metal casting, ham and bacon curing, and fruit canning for export. Population 19,110.

Shepperton, village in Spelthorne District of Surrey,

England, on the north bank of the THAMES and famous for its film studios. The church has 13th-century elements. Population (1971) 10,585.

Sheppey, Isle of, an island off the North KENT coast, England, at the mouth of the THAMES, joined to the mainland by a bridge over the River Swale since 1959. Both arable farming in the north and grassland farming in the south on reclaimed marshes are important; the latter still grazes many sheep. Sheppey, Anglo-Saxon in origin, means Sheep Island. SHEERNESS is the main town.

Shepstone, Sir Theophilus (1817–93), South African statesman, born at Westbury, near Bristol, but went to South Africa as a child. He was African interpreter at Cape Town, 1835, and British resident among the Pondo and Fingo tribes in 1839. Having held the position of agent for the African peoples of Natal in 1845, he was made secretary for native affairs in 1856. He initiated the idea of 'Reserves' for Africans. He is chiefly remembered, however, as the administrator of the Transvaal, which he annexed in 1877 and governed until 1879. He was knighted in 1876.

Shepton Mallet, market town near WELLS, Somerset, England, with stone quarries, breweries, perry making, and shoe manufacturing. The 12th-century parish church has a unique carved oak roof, containing 350 panels and 350 bosses all carved with different designs. Shepton Mallet has a market cross (1500). Population (1971) 5920.

Sheraton, Thomas (1751–1806), English furniture maker and designer, born at Stockton-on-Tees. Although trained as a cabinet maker he was primarily a furniture designer. His fame rests on his published works, the *Cabinet-Maker and Upholsterer's Drawing Book*, 1791–94, and *The Cabinet Dictionary*, 1803. His name

Sheraton design for a 'Grecian dining table' from his *Cabinet Directory*, 1803. *(Victoria and Albert Museum, London)*

has been associated with the style of furniture fashionable during the 1790s and at the beginning of the 19th century. Its appeal today rests on its simplicity, its restrained ornament and its fine tapering legs. His designs were often adapted from French patterns. Whether Sheraton himself made furniture is unclear.

Bibliography: R. Fastnedge, *Sheraton Furniture*, 1962.

Sherborne, town in DORSET, England, 10 km east of Yeovil. It possesses the superb abbey church of St Mary the Virgin, which, founded by Saint Aldhelm in the 8th century, still contains traces of Saxon work. Early in the 12th century the Saxon building was replaced by a Norman church, and much of this structure is still standing. In the 15th century the Norman choir was demolished and replaced by the perpendicular choir with its beautiful fan vaulting. The nave was also rebuilt in this period. The old castle is a Norman structure, now in ruins, and Sherborne Castle was built by Sir Walter Raleigh. A silk-weaving mill was built at Sherborne in 1740 by Huguenot refugees. Public schools for both boys and girls exist in the town. Population (1971) 7272.

Sherbrooke, Robert Lowe, 1st Viscount (1811–92), British statesman, born at Bingham, Nottinghamshire; he was educated at Winchester and Oxford, and was called to the Bar in 1842. He went to Sydney, becoming a leading advocate there, and was elected a member of the legislative council of New South Wales. In 1850 he returned to England, where he became a leader-writer on *The Times*. In 1868, the year in which he sat as the first member for London University, he became chancellor of the Exchequer under Gladstone, and held office until 1873, when he went for a short time to the Home Office. In 1879 failing health compelled his retirement, and he was made a viscount the following year. Lowe was a brilliant and epigrammatic speaker, and an admirable debater.

Sherbrooke, town of Quebec, Canada, at the junction of the Magog and St Francis rivers, 160 km east of Montreal. Sherbrooke is in the heart of an agricultural and dairying area, and mining and lumbering are carried on nearby. It has cellulose, asbestos, paper, machinery, and cloth-making industries. Sherbrooke is the seat of a Roman Catholic bishop, and has a Roman Catholic university, founded in 1955. Population 80,700.

Sherburn-in-Elmet, parish in the SELBY District, North YORKSHIRE, England, with a church dating back to 1215. It is engaged in gypsum mining, agriculture, food processing, and light industry. Population (1971) 3449.

Shereef, see SHERIF.

Sheridan, Richard Brinsley (1751–1816), English dramatist and politician, born in Dublin, son of Thomas A. Sheridan, an actor; educated at Harrow. In 1770 his family moved to Bath. Here, after an unsuccessful attempt at literary collaboration with Nathaniel Halhed, he married his first wife, Elizabeth Linley. The couple settled in London at Orchard Street, and were soon accepted in society. Sheridan now turned his hand to play-writing, and in 1775 *The Rivals* was produced at Covent Garden, establishing his reputation. The following year he acquired a share in Drury Lane Theatre, and in 1777 produced there *The Duenna*, an opera with music by his father-in-law, Thomas Linley, and *The School for*

Scandal. The latter play is regarded by many as the most brilliant comedy of manners in the language. It was followed by *The Critic*, 1779.

Social success had come easily to Sheridan and his young wife; their position was precarious, but fortunately Sheridan had won the acquaintanceship of Burke and Fox through Dr Johnson and the members of the Literary Club. From writing political essays, Sheridan soon diverged into politics proper. Through the interest of Fox he entered Parliament in 1780, supporting the Whigs, and was under-secretary for foreign affairs in 1782 and secretary to the Treasury in the coalition ministry of 1783. He was at this time very close to the Prince of Wales. He was treasurer of the Navy in the 'All the Talents' administration, 1806–07, and in his last years was receiver of the Duchy of Cornwall. In 1792 Mrs Sheridan died, and three years later Sheridan married Esther Jane Ogle, daughter of the dean of Winchester, sold his shares in Drury Lane, and settled at Polesden in Surrey. In 1799 his last play, *Pizarro*, was produced; it was an adaptation of Kotzebue's *Spaniards in Peru*. George III was right when he described it as 'a very poor composition'; but it was a success. The end of Sheridan's life was darkened by financial difficulties and by sickness. He was buried in Westminster Abbey.

In politics Sheridan distinguished himself as an orator during the impeachment of Warren Hastings (1787). As a dramatist his fame rests chiefly upon *The Rivals* and *The School for Scandal*. *The Critic*, though very witty, is scarcely more than a parody. *The School for Scandal* is a compromise between the new sentimental drama, which followed the Restoration drama, and the comedy of manners. Technically, it is most effective, particularly in the ingenious 'screen' scene, and shows a real social insight. Both it, and *The Rivals*, have been much revived in modern times.

Bibliography: Lives by W. A. Darlington, repr. of 1933 ed., 1973, and L. Gibbs, repr. of 1974 ed., 1973; O. Sherwin, *Uncorking Old Sherry: Richard Brinsley Sheridan*, 1961; M. Bingham, *Sheridan: The Track of a Comet*, 1972; R. C. Rhodes, *Some Aspects of Sheridan Bibliography*, 1928, and *Harlequin Sheridan: the Man and the Legends*, 1933.

Sherif, or Shereef (Arabic *sharif*, noble), in Islam, a title given sometimes to descendants of the family to which MOHAMMED belonged, but usually confined to his direct descendants, of whom there are two branches: the offspring of HASAN and HUSAIN. Though the majority are unimportant, sherifs have ruled in many places. But only Jordan and Morocco now have sherifian kings. The sherifs (or properly, *ashraf*) are to be found in all groups of Islamic society, and until recent times had considerable personal prestige. In Mecca the Hasanis were called sherifs and the Husainis, sayyids. In Hadramaut both branches were called sayyids and most did not carry arms (the few who did were thought of as acting improperly); in fact, they presented an influence for peace among the warring tribes. In Morocco reverence for sherifs is strong and they are apt to regard the sultan as only one of themselves. Many are believed to be special channels of God's goodness so that their every action prospers; to live near them or even to touch them brings a blessing.

Sheriff and Sheriff Courts. In the Norman judicial and financial administrative system in England the sheriff

Sheriff and Sheriff Courts

(from the Old English for shire-reeve) was the accredited representative of the central authority and the special nominee of the king. The rise of the sheriff probably dates from the end of the 10th century, and the office reached the zenith of its influence under the Norman kings. There were sheriffs for every county, and in each the sheriff was civil president of the shire-moot, executor of the law, captain of the fyrd, and steward of the royal demesne (Langmead). The sheriff also kept a COURT LEET called the sheriff's tourn, the object of which court was to relieve the shire-moot or county court of a part of the great number of small criminal cases annually tried there. The office of sheriff was open to grave abuses. Although the sheriff was the means of exerting the royal authority, he could still impede it, especially if he was a powerful baron. Henry I abolished these baron-sheriffs and substituted some officials of the royal household, to hold office for one year subject to good behaviour. Moreover, the sheriff's activities were made subject to careful scrutiny by the Exchequer. By the Provisions of Oxford (1258) the yearly tenure of office was confirmed. With the elaboration of administrative machinery the importance of the sheriff continued to decline. From the mid-16th century the office of sheriff was purely civil, and it was in 1557 that the lord-lieutenant was first appointed to act as the chief military officer of the county.

The chief duties of the sheriff today are: (1) to act as returning officer for county elections if approved by the county council, and to publish election petitions; (2) to suppress riots, with power in that connection to call out the *posse comitatus*; (3) to carry out sentences of death; (4) to summon juries for the High Court; (5) to attend judges on circuits and provide them with suitable police and escort; and (6) to execute all writs and processes of the High Court. The appointment of sheriffs is regulated by the Sheriffs Act 1887, which made the mode of appointment uniform throughout England and Wales. The chancellor of the Exchequer together with the judges of the High Court, attend usually in the Lord Chief Justice's court each November to consider the excuses of those substantial county landowners who have been previously selected by the circuit judge as fit for the office of sheriff. Three are selected by the above tribunal for each county, and the list is then submitted to the Queen for approval. No person may be chosen twice in three years if there is any other qualified person in his county. All sheriffs appoint under-sheriffs to act as their deputies.

In Scotland, although the office of sheriff had the same origin as in England, its judicial functions developed separately. The sheriff principal is now the chief local judicial officer; his jurisdiction extends in most cases to an area comprising two or more counties. The sheriff principal is primarily an appellate judge but has also many administrative duties which include acting as returning officer for the parliamentary constituencies within his sheriffdom. There are at present 12 sheriff principals in Scotland. With the exception of the sheriff principals of Midlothian and Lanarkshire, they are not full-time resident judges, but usually reside in Edinburgh and continue to practise at the Bar, visiting their sheriffdoms when necessary. The resident judge of first instance is called the sheriff. He is a full-time professional judge roughly corresponding to the English COUNTY COURT judge, but with much wider civil jurisdiction and, in addition, commissary

(or PROBATE), and extensive criminal jurisdiction. In civil cases there are certain rights of appeal from the sheriff to the sheriff principal or the COURT OF SESSION, and from the sheriff principal to the Court of Session. In criminal cases there are certain rights of appeal from the sheriff principal or sheriff to the High Court of Justiciary (see JUSTICIARY, HIGH COURT OF). The qualification for the office of sheriff principal or sheriff is ten years' standing as an advocate or solicitor. Honorary sheriffs may be appointed by the sheriff principal. They hold office during the pleasure of the sheriff principal, are unpaid, and require no legal qualification.

In the USA the sheriff is a county official, generally popularly elected, and a resident of the county. His duties can be compared with those of the police in England. The sheriff is responsible for guarding prisoners and juries, attending the local sessions, serving their processes and executing their judgments. His chief judicial function lies in the determining of writs of inquiry or damages.

Sheriff Courts. From the institution of the county courts in 1846 the sheriff's civil jurisdiction in England has declined. His court still exists, but as a court distinct from the modern county court. The main matters dealt with in the sheriff court are elections and execution of writs.

The sheriff courts in Scotland are the equivalent of the English county courts, but, in addition, they possess wide-ranging criminal jurisdiction. The sheriff has exclusive jurisdiction in all civil cases where the sum in issue is not more than £250, and can hear almost any civil action, with the notable exception of divorce and some company cases. In criminal matters, the sheriff may try almost any crime except rape and murder, although in more serious cases he may remit to the High Court for sentencing. The sheriff clerk is the clerk of the sheriff court, and his duties correspond to those of a REGISTRAR in the English county court.

See also HIGH SHERIFF; LOCAL GOVERNMENT.

Bibliography: G. R. Y. Radcliffe and Lord Cross, *The English Legal System*, 5th ed. 1971.

Sheriffmuir, location in STIRLING DISTRICT, Central Region of Scotland, scene of an indecisive battle in 1715 between the Jacobites under the Earl of Mar and the Hanoverians under the Duke of Argyll. It is on the northern slope of the Ochils, about 5 km from DUNBLANE.

Sherman, John (1823–1900), US financier and politician, born at Lancaster, Ohio, and admitted to the Bar in 1844. He entered Congress in 1855 as a Republican, and in 1859 was chairman of the Committee on Ways and Means. From 1861 to 1877 he was senator from Ohio, and again from 1881 to 1897. Under President Hayes (1877–81) he was secretary of the Treasury, and under President McKinley (1897–98) secretary of state. The silver law of 1890 was named after him, and also the Anti-Trust Act of the same year (see SHERMAN ANTI-TRUST ACT). He wrote *Recollections of Forty Years in the House, Senate, and Cabinet: An Autobiography*, 1895.

Sherman, Roger (1721–93), American patriot, one of the signatories of the Declaration of Independence, born in Newton, Massachusetts. He was delegate from Connecticut to Congress, 1774–81, and 1783–84; one of the committee of five who drafted the declaration. A member of the Constitutional Convention of 1787, where he introduced the famous 'Connecticut Compromise', and of the Connecticut ratifying convention. He was a US senator from 1791 to 1793.

Sherman, William Tecumseh (1820–91), US general, born at Lancaster, Ohio, and educated there and at West Point. He served in Florida against the Seminole Indians, and in the war with Mexico (1846–48), but resigned from the army in 1853 to conduct a banking business at San Francisco. He joined the North on the outbreak of the Civil War, and after taking part in the battles of Bull Run (1861) and Shiloh (1862), was, in 1863, made head of the army of the Tennessee, and in 1864 commander in the West. He took Atlanta on 1 September 1864, and later in the same year abandoned his base and marched 483 km across Georgia to the sea. In 1865 he again abandoned his base and marched to Richmond, defeating Johnston and co-operating with Grant. Johnston surrendered to Sherman in April 1865, thus bringing the war to an end. Sherman published his *Memoirs* in 1875.

Bibliography: W. T. Sherman, *Memoirs*, 2 vols, 1875; H. Hitchcock, *Marching With Sherman*, ed. M. A. de Wolfe, 1927; L. Lewis, *Sherman: Fighting Prophet*, 1932; E. LeConte, *When The World Ended*, ed. E. S. Miers, 1957.

Sherman Anti-Trust Act (1890), passed by the Congress of the USA with the intention of breaking up the monopolies of the day. The act was named after John SHERMAN, American financier and Republican statesman,

General Sherman. *(Mary Evans Picture Library)*

who was largely concerned in the enactment of the Anti-Trust Bill during the presidency of Benjamin Harrison. The act forbade 'every contract, combination in the form of trust or otherwise, or conspiracy, in restraint of trade or commerce among the several states, or with foreign nations', and declared it to be an offence to 'establish or attempt to establish a monopoly, or to combine or conspire . . . to establish a monopoly of commerce between the several states or in the foreign nations'. It offered several modes of enforcement with severe penalties, but accomplished little. At the outset the courts had a difficulty in interpretation (whether the act applied to all contracts in restraint of trade or only to those 'in unreasonable restraint of trade'), and they therefore tended to liberality of interpretation. Successive presidents, too, failed to enforce the act; several states passed enactments which helped the trusts to evade it; and in 1895 the Supreme Court, in a decision in favour of the 'sugar trust', gave the anti-monopoly forces a stinging defeat. In 1914 Congress passed the Clayton Anti-Trust Act in an attempt to remedy the defects of the Sherman Act. Anti-trust action was renewed under President Franklin D. Roosevelt, and is now a prime feature of US economic policy.

See also COMPETITION; MONOPOLY.

Bibliography: H. U. Faulkner, *American Economic History*, 8th ed. 1960.

Sherpa (feminine *Sherpari*), Mongolian people who originally migrated from Tibet to Solo Khombu, in northeast Nepal. The word 'Sherpa' means 'man from the east'. The Sherpas have earned fame as mountain porters on Himalayan expeditions. TENZING NORGAY, who climbed Everest in 1953, is a Sherpa. Many Sherpas have emigrated to Darjeeling in India where porters are recruited by expedition leaders. Solo Khombu comprises two areas on the southern side of the Everest massif. The lower, more southerly, is Solo (1219 m to 2438 m); the higher, northerly, is Khombu, with villages up to 3962 m. From Khombu have come most of the high-climbing Sherpas. Wheat is grown in Solo; barley and potatoes in Khombu. The potato is the stable food. Sheep, goats, and yaks are bred. Until recently a great deal of trading was done with Tibet, over Nangpa La (5791 m) and with Nepal, in salt, rice, wool, spices, yaks, and small manufactured goods from India. The Sherpas are estimated to number 85,000. They are Buddhists of the Red Hat sect (see BUDDHISM).

Bibliography: C. von Furer-Haimendorf, *The Sherpas of Nepal*, 1964.

Sherriff, R(obert) C(edric) (1896–1975), English playwright and novelist, born at Kingston-upon-Thames. He went into the insurance business, to which he returned after service in the First World War, but in 1929 his play *Journey's End*, which had grown out of his own war letters home from the front, was produced and immediately made him famous. After studying at Oxford for two years he went to Hollywood. His later plays, none of which approached his first success, include *Badger's Green*, 1930, *Dark Evening*, 1949, *Home at Seven*, 1950, and *A Shred of Evidence*, 1960. He also wrote several successful screenplays, such as *The Invisible Man*, 1933. His novels include *The Fortnight in September* 1931, *Greengates*, 1936, *The Hopkins Manuscript*, 1939,

Another Year, 1946, *King John's Treasure*, 1954, and *The Wells of St Mary's*, 1961. *No Leading Lady*, 1968, is an autobiography.

Sherrington, Sir Charles Scott (1857–1952), British physiologist of the nervous system, born in London and educated at Caius College, Cambridge, and St Thomas's Hospital, London. He qualified in medicine in 1885 and during the next thirty years produced more than 300 papers recording experimental studies of the nervous system. After lecturing on physiology at St Thomas's Hospital and receiving the Royal and Copley medals of the Royal Society, he was professor of physiology at Liverpool University, 1895–1913. In 1913 he was appointed Waynflete professor of physiology in the University of Oxford. He was Fullerian professor at the Royal Institution, 1914–17. He was a member of the Medical Research Council, president of the Royal Society in 1920, and of the British Association in 1922. Sherrington was created GBE in 1922, received the Order of Merit in 1924, and in 1932 was awarded the Nobel Prize for medicine jointly with E. D. Adrian. His greatest contribution to physiology lay in his study of the physical basis of mind; he anticipated PAVLOV in the discovery of the nervous phenomenon labelled by the latter 'conditioned reflex' (see BEHAVIOURISM).

Publications include *The Integrative Action of the Nervous System*, 1906, *Mammalian Physiology*, 1916, various papers to the Royal and other scientific societies, especially on the brain and nervous system, *Selected Writings*, 1929, and *Man on his Nature*, 1940, being the Gifford Lectures delivered at Edinburgh in 1937–38.

Bibliography: Lord Cohen, *Physiologist, Philosopher and Poet*, 1958.

Sherry, wine from the region which centres round Jerez de la Frontera in Andalusia; Puerto de Santa Maria is associated with the type of wine known as Fino, and Sanlucar, on the estuary of the Guadalquivir, is the home of Manzanillas. Called SACK in the time of Shakespeare (and much enjoyed by his Falstaff), its name passed from Sherris-Sack, distinguishing it from Sacks (export wines) made elsewhere, to sherry, Xeres, or Jerez in its English form. Sherry is remarkable for the variety of types into which wines, apparently identical, develop of their own accord. It owes its character to a secondary fermentation or *flowering* which would be disastrous in the case of other wines, though it gives to the wines grown in the Jerez region their inimitable nutty flavour. When the flowering of the wine is over, it is introduced into the solera, a complicated system of blending and maturing which keeps uniform the type and standard of the sherries of the various types shipped to the consumer. There are two main categories of sherry. First the clean, dry wines which are apéritifs; manzanillas, very dry indeed; finos, very nearly as dry, and usually fuller-flavoured; and amontillados, so-called from their likeness to the Montilla wine grown near Córdoba, into which the best finos develop with time. The second category, the olorosos, are fuller and rounder wines, very rich in flavour and scent, which when very old become so velvety that they seem to be sweet, though they have no trace of sugar. The best sherry when sweetened owes its sugar to wine made from the Pedro Ximénez grape or *vino de color* composed of one-third of fresh grape juice and two-thirds of boiled-down must. Sherry is not fortified until its fermentation is complete, and it is naturally one of the driest of wines. See SPANISH WINES.

Bibliography: G. Rainbird, *Sherry and the Wines of Spain*, 1966; J. Jeffs, *Sherry*, rev. ed. 1971; G. M. Gonzales, *Sherry: The Noble Wine*, 1972.

's Hertogenbosch (French *Bois le-Duc*), capital of the province of North Brabant, Netherlands, situated at the confluence of the Aa and Dommel, 45 km south-east of Utrecht. It has an important cattle market. St John's church (founded in the early 14th century) is one of the finest medieval churches in the Netherlands. 's Hertogenbosch had its origins as a hunting-lodge of the dukes of Brabant. In 1184 it was raised to the status of a town and fortified with walls. In the mid-15th century it was considerably enlarged. Numerous abortive attempts were made by the Netherlands to get possession of the town in the 16th and 17th centuries, but in 1629 it was taken after a five-months' siege. It fell to France in 1794 and to the Prussians in 1814. Population 84,700.

Sherwood, Mary Martha (1775–1851), English writer, born at Stanford, Worcestershire. She married an army officer, and spent some time in India. Her best-known work is *The History of the Fairchild Family: or, The Child's Manual*, 1818, which became a children's classic. She wrote over 300 books, now rarely read, many of them novels; others, such as *Sabbaths on the Continent*, 1835, record her reactions to other people's religious views.

Bibliography: J. W. Darton, *The Life and Times of Mrs Sherwood*, 1910; N. Royde Smith, *The State of Mind of Mrs Sherwood*, 1946.

Sherwood, Robert Emmet (1896–1955), US playwright, born in New Rochelle, New York state. Educated at Harvard, he was editor of *Life* from 1924 to 1928, and dramatic critic to that periodical and to *Scribner's Magazine*. His first play, *The Road to Rome*, 1927, is a satire on Hannibal and war. *Reunion in Vienna*, 1931, is on the motif of the exiled Hapsburgs. In 1934 he produced *The Petrified Forest*, a melodrama of frustrated lives; and in 1936 *Idiot's Delight*, on the theme of world peace. For this last-named play he was awarded a Pulitzer prize, and won it again in 1938 with *Abe Lincoln in Illinois*, and for a third time with *There Shall be No Night*, 1940, dramatising the Russian invasion of Finland. He was awarded the gold medal for drama of the American Academy of Arts and Letters (1940), and he also received awards for the best screenplay of 1947, *The Best Years of our Lives*, from the Motion Picture Academy and the International Film Festival (Brussels). Other works include: *Unending Crusade*, 1932, *Acropolis* and *Roosevelt and Hopkins*, 1948.

Sherwood Forest, ancient royal forest, extending from Nottingham to Worksop, and long associated with stories of ROBIN HOOD.

Sherwood Foresters (Nottinghamshire and Derbyshire Regiment), The, a British regiment. The 1st Battalion was the old 45th Regiment of Foot, and its records before 1740 are those of the 56th Foot, or 'Green Marines', raised in the reign of George II. After that time the 45th Foot was mainly recruited from Nottinghamshire and was confirmed in its title of the 45th Foot. It received its present designation of Sherwood Foresters in 1881. On the army reorganisation of 1881 the 45th was listed with the 95th (Derbyshire) Regiment, which had been formed in 1824. It fought at Louisburg, in most of the great battles of the Peninsular War (its sobriquet of 'the Old Stubborns' is due to its bravery at Talavera) and the chief battles of the Crimea; and its other pre-1914 battle honours also include central India, Egypt (1882), Tirah, and the South African War (1899–1902). In the First World War the Sherwood Foresters expanded to 30 battalions and fought in France and Flanders, Italy, Gallipoli, and Egypt. In the Second World War units of the regiment served in Norway, north-western Europe, Africa, Italy, and Singapore. In February 1970 the regiment amalgamated with the Worcestershire Regiment to form The Worcestershire and Sherwood Foresters Regiment (29th/45th Foot). The new regiment is part of the Prince of Wales's division.

Bibliography: C. N. Barclay, *The History of the Sherwood Foresters (Nottinghamshire and Derbyshire Regiment) 1919–1957,* 1959.

Sheshonq, or Shishak, name of five kings of Libyan origin, who ruled Egypt in the 22nd and 23rd Dynasties, beginning in 945 BC. Sheshonq I invaded Palestine and sacked Jerusalem. He stripped the Temple of gold and silver; and gave a daughter in marriage to Jeroboam, King of Judah. The mummy of Sheshonq III in a silver coffin was found at TANIS in 1939.

Shetland (from Old Norse *Hjaltland,* 'high land' or 'Hjalte's land') or Zetland, archipelago off the north coast of Scotland. The archipelago, which was formerly a county and is now administered by the Shetland Isles Islands Council, contains over 100 islands, of which 17 are inhabited. It lies some 80 km north-east of the ORKNEY ISLANDS. The largest island is Mainland, and others include Yell, Unst, Fetlar, Bressay, Papa Stour, and Whalsay. The islands form a group 110 km long, and have a total area of over 1400 km². They are for the most part bleak, hilly, and clad in moorland. The climate is moist, cool and windy. In summer there is almost perpetual daylight, but the winter days are very short.

Shetland is rich in archaeological sites, the best known of which are Jarlshof, Mousa, and Clickhimin. The archipelago was under Norse domination from the 9th to the 15th centuries, and a strong Scandinavian flavour is retained. Crofting and fishing are the traditional occupations, the former concentrating on sheep, and locally, on ponies, while the latter supports a fish-processing industry. Shetland woollens are well known, and the hosiery industry is an important source of income. Recently, oil discoveries off the north-east of Shetland have resulted in the growth of an oil exploration support industry, and oil is to be piped ashore to Sullom Voe, 35 km north of LERWICK where a massive oil storage and transhipment complex is under construction. Population 17,327.

See also map under ORKNEY ISLANDS.

Bibliography: A. C. O'Dell, *Historical Geography of the Shetland Isles,* 1935; A. T. Cluness, *The Shetland Islands,* 1951; H. Heineberg, *Changes in the Economic-Geographical Structure of the Shetland Isles,* 1973.

Shetland Pony, see HORSE.

Shetland Sheepdog, breed of dog which originated

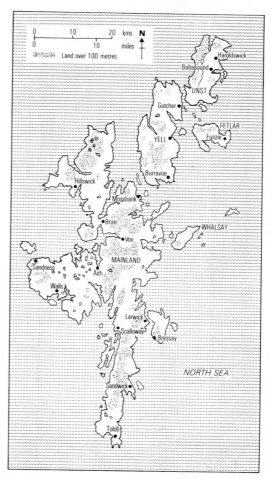

Shetland.

among the crofters of the Shetlands. It was of varied size and appearance, until definite rules of breeding were laid down. It is similar to a collie, but does not stand higher than 37 cm at the shoulder. The coat is sable, sable and white tricolour, black and tan, or blue merle. It weighs about 6 kg.

Shevchenko, Taras Hryhorovych (1814–61), Russian writer, the most celebrated Ukrainian poet. Born a serf, he was bought out of serfdom by a group of Russian and Ukrainian intellectuals. For participation in the Brotherhood of Saints Cyril and Methodius, a secret Pan-Slav society, he was banished in 1847 for ten years and forbidden to write or paint. His most famous work is *Kobzar,* 1840, a collection of poems in popular romantic style. Shevchenko exercised great influence on the Ukrainian literary and national movement.

Bibliography: V. Rich (Trans.), *Song Out of Darkness,* 1961; V. Mijakovskij and G. Y. Shevelov (Eds), *Taras Sevcenko 1814–61. A Symposium,* 1962; C. Andryushen and W. Kirkconnell, *The Poetical Works of Taras Shevchenko. The Kobzar,* 1964.

Shewa

Shewa, or Shoa, province of southern ETHIOPIA, formerly an independent kingdom until its conquest by Theodore of Ethiopia in 1855. It is traversed by the Blue Nile, is partly mountainous, and produces oranges, bananas and citrons, as well as gold and iron ore. The capital, ADDIS ABABA, is the seat of government for the whole province and the country as a whole. Area 85,400 km²; population density 62·9 per km²; population (1972) 5,369,500.

Shiah, see SHIITE.

Shidzuoka, see SHIZUOKA.

Shiel, Loch, lake (27 km long, 0·8 km wide) of Scotland, on the boundary between the former counties of Inverness and Argyll. There is a monument at Glenfinnan marking the place where Prince Charles Edward raised his standard on 19 August 1745.

Shield, William (1748–1829), English composer, born at Swalwell, County Durham. An orphan at the age of nine, he was apprenticed to a shipbuilder, but studied music with Avison in Newcastle. He led the subscription concerts there, but eventually migrated to London in 1772 to play in the Opera orchestra. He became composer to Covent Garden theatre, 1778–91 and 1792–1807, and in 1817 was appointed Master of the King's Music. His many stage works included *The Flitch of Bacon*, *Rosina* and *Robin Hood*, and he also wrote instrumental music, songs, glees and two treatises.

Shield, an article of defensive armour of great antiquity. It was usually carried on the left arm, leaving the right arm free for striking. The Greek shield of Homeric times was of great size, generally circular or oval, covered with bronze and embossed. The shield in Greek and Etruscan times was smaller, and the Roman legionary's shield was usually rectangular and longitudinally curved to the body. The shield carried by the Normans at the time of the battle of Hastings was long and kite-shaped. In the course of the next two centuries, shields were shortened into a triangle with curved sides. The broad surfaces of shields have always offered a field for decoration, and in the later Middle Ages they were used to display the heraldic arms of the owner. The smaller shield was the buckler or fist shield, which was used in England in the swordplay of broadsword and buckler. In the organised armies of the 16th century, targeteers with shields were used. Otherwise shields disappeared from the battlefield with the introduction of plate armour for the man-at-arms.

Most primitive peoples have some form of shield. The long shield of most African peoples is made of piebald cowhide. The smaller circular shields of Persia and India are often damascened with designs in precious metal. A specialised form of shield was the pavis, a tall rectangular object supported on the ground by a prop, used for sheltering an archer when shooting. Shields were generally carried by straps on the inside, one for the hand, a second through which the arm was passed, and (in the Middle Ages) a third to pass over the head and round the neck. The smaller shields generally have a central boss with a cross-strap on the inside for holding by the hand. The shield has been revived from time to time, for instance the shield carried by troops and police to protect them from the missiles of rioters. The shield had a long history in the tournament and became incorporated as an integral part of tournament armour.

See ARMOUR; HERALDRY, *The Shield and its Parts*.
Bibliography: G. Grazebroke, *Dates of Shields*, 1890.

Shield Fern, see POLYSTICHUM.

Shields, North, see NORTH TYNESIDE.

Shields, South, see SOUTH TYNESIDE.

Shifnal, market town in Salop, England, between Wolverhampton and Telford. It has an ancient church. Light engineering is carried on. The local agricultural land is of high quality and the town occupies a strategic position in the Green Belt separating Telford from the Black Country. Population (1971) 3896.

Shigatse, second largest city of TIBET, on the south bank of the Brahmaputra, 225 km west of Lhasa. It stands 3596 m above sea-level. The Tashilumpo monastery with

Shield.

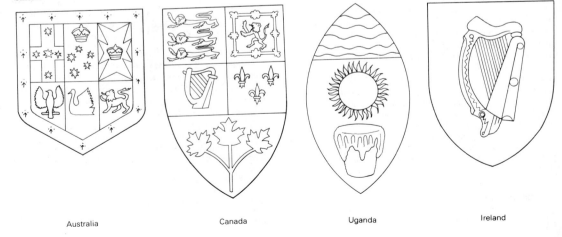

Australia   Canada   Uganda   Ireland

its 3500 priests was the palace of the Pachen Lama (see TIBET; LHASA), who was second to the DALAI LAMA in temporal power but superior in spiritual power before China took control over Tibet in 1951. The monastery is situated just to the south-west of the city, and between it and the city is the *thom* or bazaar, which is an important trading centre. A trunk road between it and Lhasa and a hydro-electric power station were built by the Chinese in 1955.

Shih Chi, see CHINESE LITERATURE.

Shih Tzu (Chinese, lion dog), an ancient Tibetan dog similar to the PEKINGESE. The head is broad and round with hair falling well over the eyes, which are large, round and dark but not prominent. The legs are short and muscular. The tail is heavily plumed and carried over the back. The coat is long and dense. All colours are allowed; a white blaze and tip of tail is desirable. The weight may be up to 8·5 kg.

Shihkiachwang, city in HOPEH province of China, situated to the east of T'ai-yüan at the foot of the Taiheng Shan. Its growth has been due to it being a road and rail focus on the main national routes and it has become a commercial centre and a collecting point for the region's agricultural produce. Its industrialisation began after 1949. Its first industries were textiles and food processing, followed in the 1960s by chemicals and light engineering. Local coal-mines provide power. The city's transport rôle has been increased by the construction of an airport. Population (1970) 950,000.

Shiite, or Shiah, a member of that division of ISLAM which follows ALI, the son of Abu Talib as the first legitimate successor of Mohammed; they called themselves the party (Arabic *shia*) of Ali. The slaughter of Husain (see HASAN) gave a martyr to the cause, and ideas of the divine rights of kings and Persian discontent with Arab rule may have added strength. The head of the state, whom they prefer to call IMAM, must be a descendant of Ali. As imam he is without sin and endowed with special knowledge which makes him the infallible interpreter of God's will; the imam is the only guarantee of salvation, and he who knows not the imam dies a heathen death. The orthodox Shiites recognise a series of 12 imams, the last of whom disappeared, 'went into occultation', from which he will return to fill the earth with righteousness as it is now filled with injustice. The government of Persia is still conducted in the name of the Hidden Imam. (None of these 12 ever held temporal power.) The Shiites observe the five daily prayers but add to the call, 'Come to the best of work'; they have developed their own system of law, which differs only in small points. One peculiarity is that they allow temporary marriage; a man gives a woman money and they separate on the agreed date. Besides the usual Muslim festivals they have their own special ones; they celebrate Mohammad's adoption of Ali as his successor and, in particular, the death of Husain; a sort of passion play reproduces the final scenes of his life and death amid general lamentation. They have their own collections of 'traditions', reports of what Mohammad said and did. It is a general ambition to be buried at Karbala or Najaf, as near as possible to Husain or Ali. The Shiites divided into many sects, but

Shikoku. Landscape near Matsuyama. *(Barnaby's Picture Library)*

only two need be named. The Zaidis allow any member of Mohammad's family to be imam if he can make good his claim; they allow two imams to exist at one time in different lands. A Zaidi state was formed in Yemen in the 10th century and survived till recently. The ISMAILIS admit only six of the imams recognised by the orthodox Shiites. Shiah became the state religion of Persia about 1500, under the Safawid Dynasty; it is common in Iraq, North India, and East Africa.

Bibliography: D. M. Donaldson, *The Shi'ite Religion*, 1933; J. N. Hollister, *The Shi'a of India*, 1953.

Shikarpur, town of Pakistan, on the right bank of the Indus. It stands on the old trade route to Afghanistan and Central Asia, and has a large covered bazaar where silk, indigo, grains, and spices are sold. Population (1969) 62,500.

Shikoku, island of Japan. With an area of 18,787 km², it is the smallest of the four main islands, and is separated from Honshū by the narrow INLAND SEA. Population is largely concentrated in the small coastal plains which front the Inland Sea, and its largest cities are MATSUYAMA and TAKAMATSU. Population 3,948,000.

Shildon, town in SEDGEFIELD District of County DURHAM, England, 16 km south-west of Durham, with silk, fur, and clothing factories, railway wagon, brick, and concrete works. Population (1971) 15,000.

Shillelagh, village of County WICKLOW, Republic of Ireland, 26 km from Arklow. The oak wood of Shillelagh gives its name to the Irish bludgeon. Population 246.

Shillibeer, George (1797–1866), British coachbuilder, born in London. Having studied his trade in Long Acre, Covent Garden, he set up business in Paris, where he was commissioned to build two omnibuses, and in 1829 introduced that type of vehicle into London. He later invented a patent funeral carriage which killed the use of the popular term 'Shillibeer' for an OMNIBUS.

Shilling, English silver or cupro-nickel coin, equal in value to one-twentieth of a pound or to 12d. The first shilling issued by Henry VII in 1504 was the first English coin to bear a realistic portrait of the sovereign. The shilling is still in use today as the decimal 5p piece.

Shillong

Shillong, capital of MEGHALAYA state and a temporary capital of ASSAM state, India, situated on the Brahmaputra river at 1593 m above sea-level. Rebuilt since the 1897 earthquake destroyed most of the town, Shillong is a local trade centre and an important military base. Population (1971) 73,529.

Shilluk, Nilotic people living in the Sudan. The Shilluk country is the flat grassland on both sides of the Nile; cattle are their wealth and, although much millet is grown, not enough is harvested to meet the demands of a relatively dense population. The Shilluk live in hamlets under the authority of a headman. They are an example of a society with a divine kingship, the king, or *Reth*, being regarded as a reincarnation of Nyikang, the Shilluk culture-hero, who is closely connected to the Christian concept of god, and whose spirit is everlasting. The king is responsible for the well-being of his people, moral and material, and is, by tradition, put to death if he grows weak or senile.
    Bibliography: E. E. Evans-Pritchard, *The Divine Kingship of the Shilluk of the Nilotic Sudan*, 1948; C. G. Seligman, *Pagan Tribes of the Nilotic Sudan*, 1965.

Shiloh, Ephraimite city, JOSHUA's headquarters and place of the first sanctuary of Israel in which the ark was kept. SAMUEL was brought up there by ELI under whom the ark was captured by the Philistines at Ebenezer, about the middle of the 11th century BC, and Shiloh destroyed by fire (1 Sam. iv). This has been confirmed by excavation. Previously unwalled, the city was walled and became populous during the early Iron Age, which suggests the date of the conquest under Joshua as c. 1200 BC.

Shiloh. In Gen. xlix. 10 occurs the phrase 'till Shiloh come'. This was taken by the rabbis as a name for the Messiah. The versions and the Samaritan text, however, render the vowels of the Hebrew uncertain, and it is likely that the Septuagint's 'that which is his', and the Syriac 'he whose it is', indicate the correct Hebrew as *selloh*, i.e. 'till he comes whose it is'. The reference is still Messianic.

Shiloh, Battle of, two days' conflict in the American Civil War, 6–7 April 1862, between the Confederates under Johnston and the Federals under Grant. The latter were worsted on the first day and had to retire, but reinforcements coming to their aid, they won a great victory on the second day. The battlefield was near the Tennessee River at Pittsburg Landing.

Shimizu, seaport city on the coast of Shizuoka-ken, Japan, with an export trade in plywood, fish products, and tea. Industries include canning, aluminium smelting, and shipbuilding. Population (1974) 243,800.

Shimonoseki, seaport city of Yamaguchi-ken, Japan, on the Inland Sea. It was bombarded in 1864 by the fleets of Britain, America, France and Holland, in retaliation against the local DAIMYO. It was opened to foreign commerce in 1890, and is an important commercial centre with a good harbour. By the treaty signed between China and Japan in 1895, the Sino-Japanese War was ended (see CHINA, *History*). It is one of the largest fishing ports in Japan, and is noted for its tinned marine products. Industries include shipbuilding, chemicals, and metals manufacturing. Population (1974) 266,000.

46

Shin, a school of Buddhism in Japan, founded by Shinran Shonin (1173–1262). It is the culmination of the Pure Land teaching (see PURE LAND SCHOOL), and is one of the two largest Buddhist schools in Japan today, the other being Zen. See BUDDHISM; MAHĀYĀNA; ZEN.

Shin, Loch, lake (27 km long, 1·5 km wide) of Highland Region, Scotland, lying across the northern Highlands in a north-west to south-east direction and drained by the River Shin, which flows into the River Oykell. Its waters have been harnessed for hydroelectricity.

Shingles, *Herpes zoster*, an inflammatory skin affection, characterised by the formation of vesicles along the course of a cutaneous nerve. The skin eruption usually disappears in a few weeks, but the accompanying neuralgic pain may persist for months, especially in older people. Shingles is caused by a virus infection, the virus being identical to that which causes chicken-pox. It is not unusual for a person who has been in contact with a case of chicken-pox to develop *Herpes zoster*, but cross-infection in the opposite direction does not seem to occur, nor does shingles seem to be infectious from one person to another.

Shinosite, see PICRIC ACID.

Shinran Shonin (1173–1262), founder of the Shin School of Buddhism in Japan. See SHIN; PURE LAND SCHOOL.

Shinto (the way of the gods) is the indigenous religion of Japan. Unlike major world religions, basic Shinto does not affirm a timeless Absolute as the ground of phenomena, nor any universal law. Rather, it puts its faith in the possibilities inherent in all concrete forms of existence, seeing man's nature as infinite and eternal through his interrelatedness with all life. Thus a Shintoist, knowing himself to be expressing one form of existence (namely the human) among countless others, feels at one with all phenomena and experiences this oneness directly in his contact with ancestors, family, descendants, work, local and national communities, the human race generally, and all the myriad forms of nature. A Shintoist reveres reality as it reveals itself in form, rather than in any ultimate principle or cause. His apprehension of the numinous is

Shinto. The floating *torii* at the shrine of Itsukushima, Miyajima, Japan. Such ceremonial gateways mark the entrance to the sacred precincts of a Shinto temple, and also define certain sacred spots. (*Barnaby's Picture Library*)

Shinto. Selichiro-Tani, High Priest of the Shinto faith, in the grounds of the shrine of Fushimi Inari near Kyōto. *(Camera Press/Nick de Morgoli)*

related wholly to circumstance. Nature in particular creates for a Shintoist a spiritual sense of communion and he imbues trees, mountains, lakes and rivers and all other forms of nature with spiritual essences called *kami* (a term both singular and plural).

Kami are at the heart of Shinto and are not so much 'beings' as the 'beingness' of an outstanding and awe-inspiring place, person, animal or object. The word itself means 'great' and it applies to harmful as well as benign influences. In simple Folk Shinto the *Kami* are regarded as deities, and shrines abound everywhere for their worship and appeasement. Human goodness and creativity are regarded in two ways, first as being in accordance with the will of the highest *Kami* who have brought the land of Japan into being, and, second, as the fulfilment of human existence. In return, the *Kami* are revered according to their contributions to human well-being and thus there is a hierarchy of deities with Amaterasu the great sun-goddess at the top and unenshrined *Kami* at the bottom.

Intellectual Shintoists regard the *Kami* as a form of life-giving myth which enriches and harmonises the Japanese people. The elaborate rituals practised at the shrines emphasise the oneness of matter and spirit, for Shintoists believe that all material objects are expressions of spiritual powers.

The origins of Shinto lie in Japanese pre-history. In course of time it was influenced by Buddhism, Confucianism (particularly with regard to ritual and decorum) and Christianity, but it continued to retain its most vital beliefs. At present it is expressed in four main ways: Imperial Shinto, Sect Shinto, Shrine Shinto and Folk Shinto. (State Shinto, which many Westerners still think of as basic Shinto, was started as a political movement in 1869 when the newly formed Meiji government felt that

a discontented populace would be drawn together by a sense of national identity. Consequently they revived the ancient Department of Shinto affairs, disestablished Buddhism, and invested Shinto priests and institutions with official support. This led to a state religion which was authoritarian and ethical rather than spiritual and in 1945–46 the law was repealed and State Shinto ceased to exist.)

Imperial Shinto is forbidden to the general public and is centred round the rites performed by the Emperor of Japan, who is believed to be a direct descendant of Amaterasu, the sun goddess.

Sect Shinto is a term used for 13 groups formed during the 19th and 20th centuries. Each sect eventually received government recognition as a branch of Shinto and all but two, the Konkokyo and Tenrikyo, revere the same high trinity of Kami as basic Shinto, namely Amaterasu, Izanagi and Izanami.

The Association of Shinto Shrines came into existence following the abolition of State Shinto. Now known as Shrine Shinto it is perhaps the most representative and the most religious of all the Shinto groups. Its priests lay great emphasis on rituals and mystical rites which they perform in the thousands of shrines dedicated to the different Kami. The main rituals are concerned with purification of body and heart (the body symbolises the spirit in such a way that physical purification, such as starvation, is accepted as spiritual). These rituals follow three main courses: physical purification such as lengthy journeys on foot followed by near starvation, or immersion of the body for lengthy periods in icy water; exorcism performed by a priest who passes a purification wand over the worshippers; dedication to the Kami through shrine offerings of harvest foods and music, dance and prayers.

Folk Shinto is a general term which covers the many superstitious and semi-shamanistic customs of the remote country people of Japan.

Bibliography: G. Kato, *What is Shinto?*, 1935; D. C. Holtom, *The National Faith of Japan*, 1938; D. T. Suzuki, *Zen and Japanese Culture*, 1959; Agency for Cultural Affairs, *Japanese Religion*, 1972; (for Folk Shinto) C. Blacker, *The Catalpa Bow*, 1976.

Shinty (Gaelic *camanachd*), a ball and stick game, once played as a mass struggle of opposing Scottish Highland clans. It was codified towards the end of the 19th century by the Camanachd Association; the similar Irish game also became codified and known as HURLING. Shinty is played 12 a side, 45 minutes each way on a field 132 to 183 m long by 64 to 91 m wide, with sidelines and hail (goal) lines marked. In front of each hail a line 3·65 m long, parallel to the hail line and joined to it by quarter-circles, forms the 9-m area. The hail is 3·65 m wide and 3 m high. There is a centre circle of 4·5 m radius.

The caman (stick) is shorter than a hockey stick, with a heavier blade, and is made of one piece of wood. The ball is leather-covered cork and worsted, 6·4 cm in diameter. Shinty is a game with more violence than hockey, played often at greater speed, for combat is aerial as well as at ground level. Over 40 clubs are affiliated to the Camanachd Association, whose Challenge Cup is competed for by teams which are grouped by area.

Shinwell, Emanuel Shinwell, Baron (1884–), British

politician, born in London but passed his early years in Glasgow. He was responsible for the national organisation of the Marine Workers' Union. He was elected Labour MP for Linlithgow (1922–24) and (1928–31), for Seaham (1935–50), and for Easington (1950–70). As minister of fuel and power from 1945 to 1947 he carried through the nationalisation of the coal-mines. He was war minister in 1947 and minister of defence, 1950–51. He was created a life peer in 1970. His publications include: *The Britain I Want*, 1943; *Conflict Without Malice*, 1955; *The Labour Story*, 1973; and *I've Lived Through It All*, 1973.

Ship, The, constellation, see ARGO.

Ship-money, tax imposed by the British Crown upon seaports and trading towns which compelled them to provide and furnish warships to combat piracy or to pay money for that purpose. It was first levied about 1007 to form a navy to oppose the Danes, but appears after this to have fallen into disuse. Although forbidden by the Petition of Right in 1628, it was levied by Charles I between 1634 and 1638 without the consent of Parliament and was extended to inland shires and towns.

In 1637 John HAMPDEN refused to pay ship-money and, in a test case before the Exchequer of Pleas, 7 out of 12 judges decided that Charles was entitled to levy the tax. It was a source of great discontent in the pre-Civil War period and was abolished in 1641 by the Long Parliament.

Ship Worm, see TEREDO.

Shipbuilding, see SHIPS AND SHIPBUILDING.

Shipley, town in BRADFORD District, West YORKSHIRE, England, on the River Aire, with woollen and engineering industries. Population (1971: urban district) 28,492.

Shipping, Ministry of, formed in Britain in 1916 to control Allied shipping resources and secure the most economic use of tonnage. The tonnage shortage (see SHIPPING LOSSES) became acute towards the close of Asquith's premiership, and the Advisory Committee of the Transport Department of the Admiralty presented the Premier and the Secretary of the Admiralty with a memorandum urging that the Shipping Control Committee or some other central authority should be entrusted with full powers to survey the tonnage situation as a whole and to transfer any vessel or any service to such other employment as might seem expedient. When Lloyd George took office he at once appointed Sir Joseph (afterwards Lord) Maclay shipping controller with ministerial rank. Executive duties were carried out by a director of transport and shipping. The Ministry was wound up after the cessation of hostilities. In the Second World War merchant-ship construction came within the province of the Ministry of Shipping, but, in the interests of co-ordination, was later transferred to the Admiralty, the department responsible for the building of warships. The types and design of the merchant ships were, however, decided in co-operation with the Ministry of Shipping, later merged in the Ministry of War Transport.

Bibliography: C. E. Fayle, *Seaborne Trade* (*History of the Great War in Offical Documents*), 1923.

Shipping, Registration of, see LOAD LINE; MERCHANT SHIPPING ACTS.

Shipping Forecasts, see WEATHER FORECAST.

Shipping Losses in the World Wars. In August 1914 the UK possessed 19,195,160 tonnes of steam vessels, and about 370,850 tonnes of sailing ships and non-propelled craft; the German Empire, 5,546,600 tonnes; the USA, 5,408,400; Norway, 2,545,200; France, 2,356,200; Japan, 1,735,400; Italy, 1,694,760; Holland, 1,520,000; Sweden, 1,735,400; and Russia possessed (as far as could be ascertained) more than 1,016,000 tonnes.

During the First World War the UK's losses in shipping totalled 7,925,100 tonnes, a very large part of which was due to submarine warfare; yet although nearly half of the mercantile marine was lost during the struggle, the gross metric tonnage in December 1918 was only 2,500,000 below the 1914 figures. Captured enemy ships and purchases from other nations accounted for part of the new tonnage added, but even so, the output of the British shipbuilding yards was remarkable.

During the Second World War, between 3 September 1939 and 31 August 1945, 5150 British, Allied and neutral merchant ships, totalling 21,916,860 tonnes, were lost by enemy action. Of these 2627 belonged to the British Empire, totalling 11,579,780 tonnes. Allied and neutral countries lost 2523 ships (10,337,080 tonnes). During the worst period, the nine months from June 1940, the losses averaged 592,125 tonnes a month. With the entry of Japan into the war shipping losses in the early part of 1942 were again heavy.

See also SHIPS AND SHIPBUILDING, *Shipbuilding Methods in the World Wars*.

Shipping Routes. The shipping routes of the Roman Empire lay principally in the Mediterranean, linking Rome with Gades, Tarraco, Massilia, Carthage, Alexandria, etc. In the Middle Ages the centre of the Mediterranean shipping routes shifted from Rome to Venice, while in the northern seas the shipping routes radiated from the Hanse towns. Columbus opened the route to America in 1492, while the shipping routes to the Far East were for a long time in the hands of the Portuguese, following Vasco da Gama's voyage in 1498. The shortest trans-ocean routes are the east–west great circle tracks, which give the greatest saving of distance in the higher latitudes. On the other hand, heavy weather, usually coming from the west, is more prevalent in higher latitudes and the seasonal variations in winds, currents, and ice movements have to be taken into account.

From a shipping point of view, the most dangerous ice area is in the North-West Atlantic, where an International Ice Patrol Service is maintained. Facilities are available on many ocean routes for shore-based advice on the optimum route taking all considerations into account and for facsimile broadcasts of weather and ice maps. Admiralty routeing charts show the normal weather and current patterns for each month and give a variety of other information. *Ocean Passages for the World*, published by the Hydrographer of the Navy, together with Admiralty Distance Tables, contain comprehensive information on the factors which affect routeing and advise on the best routes. The most direct routes between European ports and Australia or New Zealand are through either the Suez Canal (opened in 1869) or the Panama Canal (opened in 1915). Alternative routes, best taken east-bound owing to climatic conditions, are round the Cape of Good Hope and Cape Horn. There are no regular routes north of the American and Asiatic continents. From 1898 to 1968 the North Atlantic Lane Agreement required that ships of the participating companies keep to laid-down routes when crossing the North Atlantic. In the 1960 Safety of Life at Sea conference the idea of traffic-separation schemes in congested areas was advanced. By 1964 some owners were observing separation schemes on a voluntary basis. It is now mandatory for UK ships to observe separation schemes, but complete compliance by all ships will not occur until the 1970 Collision Regulations come into force.

Ships and Shipbuilding.

History of Sailing Ships. Shipbuilding is one of the most ancient of crafts. By way of a raft or catamaran, and certainly by means of a hollowed tree-trunk, canoes and coracles were naturally evolved. Many dug-out canoes of prehistoric date have been found in Britain in marshes or old river courses; they were probably hollowed out by wedges and by fire. The building of ships must have begun at a very early date. Paintings and sculptures of ancient Egypt show that the Egyptians built ships apparently constructed of planks, and propelled by oars and sails. The Phoenicians, according to Herodotus, set out from the Red Sea, passed by way of Ophir round the Cape of Good Hope, and entering the Mediterranean again through the Pillars of Hercules or Strait of Gibraltar, arrived in Egypt after three years. They also traded with India and Britain, and reached the mouth of the Rhine. Either the Phoenicians or the Egyptians invented the bireme and trireme war-galley, thus increasing the vessel's speed (oar power) without having to increase its length. The Chinese were known as seafarers at the same time.

The Greeks were great navigators and fought many naval battles with the Persians and the Phoenicians. The greatest development, however, resulted from rivalry between the Carthaginians and Romans. Then the great fighting galleys were evolved. The Attic trireme carried a

Ships and Shipbuilding. An Elizabethan man-of-war. *(Barnaby's Picture Library)*

crew of 200–225 men, 170 being rowers, the rest being seamen and marines. The trireme, or three-banked galley, was generally open amidships, where the rowers sat, with decks fore and aft for the soldiers. Sometimes the fighting deck extended the whole length of the ship, and this appears to have been always the case with vessels greater than the triremes. These galleys were built higher aft than forward, and generally had a beak or ram at the prow for cutting into opposing ships. They usually carried one mast amidships, bearing one large square sail. The Romans appear to have had three classes of ship: (1) warships; (2) merchant ships; and (3) ships built for great speed, to carry passengers and dispatches. They were built of pine or cedar, with the bows made of oak clamped with brass. Copper was introduced in the time of Nero, because of its non-corrosion, and the caulking in those days seems to have been flax.

The earliest known boat outside the Mediterranean was found at Alø (Denmark). It dates from about 300 BC and was about 13 m long. Two boats of around 200 BC–AD 100 were found at North Ferriby (Yorkshire). The Vikings used both oars and sails. The clinker-built ship in which the Sutton Hoo burial was found was about 25 m long and 4·5 m in maximum beam. A famous Viking ship, built about AD 250, found in a Schleswig peat-bog at Nydam, is preserved at Kiel. Both these ships were steered by stern-paddles. Another Viking ship was excavated from a tumulus at Gokstad in the Oslo Fjord. It is exhibited at Bygdöy; it is 23·5 m long, 5·3 m in beam, and 1·8 m deep. The keel is 17·4 m long and 0·36 m deep. It had one pine mast 12 m high, and 16 oars a side, each from 7·5 to 12 m long and projecting through ports in the sides. Along the bulwarks was a row of shields to protect the rowers. Alfred the Great's navy with 80–120 oared galleys was successful against the Danes. The galleys were twice as long, quicker, easier to manage, and rolled less than the Danish ships. On the other hand, they set back the evolution of sailing ships, and long voyages became infrequent, until Richard Cœur de Lion in AD 1190 sent a fleet of 9 large ships, 150 smaller ones, and only 38 galleys to the Holy Land. About this time the stern rudder was invented, probably in the Netherlands. In the Mediterranean the ships had been developing in size, and the use of sails was beginning to supersede oars, for it is on record that Richard's fleet was increased by over 100 large sailing ships at Marseilles and Sicily.

With the beginning of the 14th century, however, both the theory and practice of shipbuilding began to evolve rapidly. This was because at that time the mariner's compass was invented by Flavio Giolo. This, of course, rendered 'coasting' more or less unnecessary, and from then on the introduction of sails and other appliances became general and rapid. England lagged behind at first in the new era, but Henry V, at the beginning of the 15th century, had several large vessels built which equalled and surpassed anything then existing. One of these was 50 m long and 14 m in beam.

Henry VIII built what was really the first ship in the British navy. This was the *Henry Grâce à Dieu*, 42 m long, 12 m in beam, of 1000 t burden. She carried 120 guns and cost £8700 to build. He organised the navy as a distinct service by setting up the Admiralty, Trinity House, and dockyards at Deptford, Woolwich, and Portsmouth. Great progress was made in shipbuilding through-

Ships and Shipbuilding

out Tudor times, and among technical improvements were striking topmasts, use of chain pumps, introduction of studding, topgallant, sprit and topsails, and weighing anchor by capstan and long cable.

The ships of the 16th century were built very short and beamy, with high ends, especially at the stern. This high stern undoubtedly completed the disaster to the Spanish Armada, by rendering the ships unmanageable in the storm which overtook them. The 17th century is notable, because at that time lived Phineas Pett, who reputedly introduced the FRIGATE into the British navy, and also designed and caused to be constructed (in the face of heavy opposition) the *Sovereign of the Seas*, which was the first three-decker. She cost £300,000 to build, and was 1640 t burden, being 51 m long, 15 m in beam, and carrying 100 guns. The 17th century also saw the foundation of the Shipwright's Company (1612), its first president being Phineas Pett.

The science of naval architecture did not develop quickly in Britain. Ship carpentry was very skilled, and Pett and his son and Sir A. Deane did much to raise the level of the science. But France, Spain, Sweden, and Denmark at this time possessed much finer and bigger ships than Britain, though in the latter part of the 18th century British ships became supreme. In the beginning of the 19th century Robert Leppings made a departure completely from the stereotyped methods of construction. He introduced diagonal inner ties and riders, which, in conjunction with the old transverse framing, prevented 'hogging', or the dropping of the ends of a ship relative to the middle. Other improvements, such as the introduction of 'filling pieces', which occupied the space between the frames up to the bilges, so strengthening the ship against hogging and at the same time forming a safeguard in case of accident to the ship's bottom; lessening of the long beak

Ships and Shipbuilding. *The Rising Star*, 1821, built for the War of Independence in Spanish South America, 'upon the principle of navigating either by sails or by steam, the impelling apparatus being placed in the hold and caused to operate through apertures in the bottom of the vessel'. It was the first steam-driven vessel to cross the Atlantic, and the first to enter the Pacific. *(Science Museum, London)*

heads; and the abolition of the high, square sterns, are all directly attributable to Leppings's régime as surveyor of the navy.

By 1820 England, owing to her commercial possessions, had become the chief country as regards sailing ships, and of English shipping concerns the East India Company occupied the foremost position. Iron gradually began to enter more and more into the construction of ships, and by 1840 wood had practically been superseded in shipbuilding, except in the USA and Canada, where large ships were still sometimes built of wood. The fastest sailing ships were of composite build (wooden planking on iron frames). Leppings was succeeded by Sir William Symonds (surveyor of the navy, 1832–87), who brought English sailing men-of-war to their finest pitch. He improved their seaworthiness and speed, evolved the elliptical stern, and invented the system whereby spars were interchangeable not only on one ship, but also between different ships and different classes of ships. By this time differences between merchant vessels and men-of-war had become more apparent than in earlier periods, and the rivalry between US and British owners for the possession of the Chinese and Indian tea trade led to the improvement of the merchant vessel. The first real clipper, the *Ann McKim*, was built in Baltimore in 1832, and Britain soon adopted this fine type of fast-sailing ship. *Sir Launcelot*, one of the finest of the tea clippers, marks the highest development of the sailing ship. She was built in 1865, and was able to complete the passage from Foochow to the Lizard in 85 days. The celebrated sailing ship *Cutty Sark*, built in 1868 of wood and iron construction, and now preserved in a concrete dry-berth at Greenwich, was employed in the wool trade. Fast vessels were also required in the emigrant traffic to Australia. Here US competition was especially keen. US ships varied from 2000 to 2500 t, and one of them, the *Champion of the Seas*, covered 860 km in a day while running to the eastward on a voyage from Liverpool to Melbourne in 1854. This meant that she was driven at the average speed of 20 knots (37 km/h) for a day and a night, a speed which steamships did not reach for many years. By the end of the 19th century ships became larger, and a four-masted barque-rig became the standard type of sailing vessel. These ships were sometimes 120 m long, and carried up to 5000 t.

Types of Sailing Ship. Sailing ships are either square-rigged (fig. 1) or fore-and-aft rigged, or a compromise between these types. The one-masted sprit-rig with a triangular or quadrilateral foresail is probably the oldest type of sailing ship still in use in northern Europe. A miniature of a ship of this type is seen in a Flemish manuscript of AD 1420. The cutter, or sloop, a gaff-sailed one-master, probably developed from the Dutch yachts of the 18th century. Two-masters are either gaff- or sprit-sailed, having a difference in the size of the two masts. The Thames barge was an example of a sprit-sailed vessel, having a big mainsail and small mizzen, while the gaff-sailed two-master may have two sails of equal size, or a large mainsail and small mizzen, as in a yawl or ketch, or a big mainsail and a somewhat smaller mizzen. The last American schooners were particularly fine vessels having four to six masts. The day of the sailing ship for the purposes of trade is past. This was brought about by the introduction of the steamship, although in the beginning

Ships and Shipbuilding. A British two-masted schooner, the *Dispatch*, built at Garmouth, Scotland, 1888. *(National Maritime Museum, Greenwich)*

the steam-tug actually furthered the development of the sailing ship, as it permitted the sailing capacities of ships on the high seas to be considered without regard to their easy management in confined waters.

History of Steamships. The idea of propelling ships independently of the wind obviously first led to the use of manual labour in pulling of oars. It might be assumed from old sculptures that the Egyptians used oxen to turn wheels which propelled the ship. Whether or not this is so, it is certain that minds have been engaged from very early times in endeavouring to conceive some form of mechanical propulsion. The discovery of the use of steam as a means of propulsion of land vehicles soon led naturally to attempts to utilise it on behalf of floating vessels. Many attempts, however, had to be made before success was won, and steamships did not take their place as commercial factors as rapidly as locomotives did. It is claimed that the first attempt at such propulsion was made by Blasco de Garay at Barcelona in 1583. Denis Papin applied his engine (originally proposed as a pump) to a model boat, the *Fulda*, at Cassel in 1707; but the local boatmen destroyed the ship at night, and he himself narrowly escaped with his life. In 1736 Jonathan Hulls took out a patent in England for a steam-engine which was intended to be used in a tug-boat, but it never materialised. In 1770 an American, William Henry, having seen James Watt's engine, constructed model boats at Lancaster, Pennsylvania, and although these were unsuccessful, among those who watched were John Fitch and Robert Fulton, who were two of the first successful steamship designers. At last, in 1786, James Ramsey constructed one which travelled at 6 km/h upstream. In 1790 Fitch constructed one which attained a speed of 11 km/h. So the efforts went on, and it was even claimed that John Stevens, an American, actually ran a twin-screw steamer at 10 km/h on the River Hudson in 1804. In any case, he did build a steamer in 1808, which ran from New York to Philadelphia. In Britain Patrick Miller, a retired banker, together with his son's tutor, James Taylor, and William Symington, an expert mechanic, were working in order to apply the steam-engine to ships, after Miller had spent

years in experimenting with hand-driven mechanism. In 1788 they produced a boat; it was not, however, a commercial success. In 1802 the *Charlotte Dundas* was launched on the Forth and Clyde Canal, having been constructed by Symington. She towed two barges, carrying 70 t each. The paddle-wheel was at the stern. The effort was not persevered with because the wash, it was feared, would seriously injure the banks. Fulton had seen this vessel, and in 1807 he built a steamer, the *Clermont*, which ran from New York to Albany (240 km) in 32 hours and back in 30. This steamer was kept in service, and two others added, and in 1812 was launched the *Comet*, first built in 1804, which was built in Scotland by Bell, Napier, and Robertson. This ship had a paddle on each side, which drove her along at 8 km/h. She also was a commercial success, and two others were then built for service from Glasgow. From this time the steamship-building industry rapidly developed on the banks of the Clyde. In 1814 the *Marjory* was built, and was the first steamer to sail on the Thames. In 1818 a steamer was built by Napier for cross-channel purposes, sailing from Greenock to Belfast. The first steamship to cross the Atlantic was the Dutch vessel *Curaçao*, later renamed *Calpé*. Built at Dover in 1826, she was a wooden paddler of 438 t register. Purchased by the Dutch as a man-of-war, but employed on the mail service to the West Indies, she left Rotterdam on her first passage in April 1827, and took a month to cross. The next transatlantic steamer, the *Royal William*, was built in Canada, one of her owners being Samuel Cunard. Designed to sail between Quebec and Halifax, she crossed from Quebec to London in 17 days in 1833. Britain's entry into the transatlantic efforts began with the *Great Western*, a paddle-steamer 72 m long, 11 m in beam, and with a hold 7 m deep, built for the Great Western Railway Company. Three days before her departure from Bristol on 8 April 1938 the *Sirius*, 52 m long, had left Cork, and both were bound for New York. The *Sirius* arrived in the morning and the *Great Western* in the afternoon of 23 April, the former having taken 18 days and the latter 15 days to cross. The first

Ships and Shipbuilding. The German four-masted barque *Magdalene Vinnen*, built at Kiel, 1921. *(National Maritime Museum, Greenwich)*

Ships and Shipbuilding

great iron steamship built was the *Rainbow*, launched in 1838, which traded from London to Ramsgate and Antwerp. Early steamers still depended partly on sails for auxiliary power, and they were used when possible.

It was only with great difficulty that the prejudice against the use of iron was overcome. Its advantages are now obvious, for it possesses greater strength with lightness. Wood has to be nearly as heavy as its cargo to have sufficient strength, while iron, and steel even more so, can carry twice its own weight. On the other hand, metal bottoms are apt to foul and corrode, so for a while composite vessels were built, i.e., wood planking on iron frames, the planks being caulked and copper sheathed. Today yachts are built in this manner.

The next era in shipbuilding began in 1839, when Pettit Smith designed the *Archimedes*, which was the first steamer propelled by a screw. Brunel, the designer of the *Great Western*, fitted the *Great Britain* with a screw-propeller, and in 1845 she crossed from Liverpool to New York in 14½ days. The year 1858 saw the launch of the famous but ill-fated *Great Eastern*, the work of Brunel and John Scott Russell. This vessel, 50 years in advance of her time, was 211 m long, with one set of engines driving 18-metre paddle-wheels and another driving a 7-metre propeller, five funnels and six masts carrying 5400 m² of sail. A failure as a passenger ship, she was used as a cable-layer before being broken up in 1889. In 1862 the Cunard Company obtained permission to fit the mail steamers with propellers, and subsequently the paddle-wheel was relegated to comparatively smooth water. The reasons for this are that a propeller will suffer less from the rolling of a ship than will paddles, and even with pitching motions it is less affected than paddles if well immersed. Again, it acts on a relatively larger volume of water in any given time, and is less affected by the changes in the draught of a ship, which must inevitably happen with cargo steamers. This, together with the opening of the Suez Canal in 1869, and the simultaneous introduction of the compound engine, raised steamships to superiority over sailing ships, with the result that they became larger and greater in number as sailing ships decreased in importance.

The size of ships is indicated by their gross tonnage, which is a measurement of the internal cubic capacity of the ship reckoned at 100 cubic feet (2·83 m³) to the ton. Port and other dues are levied on a vessel's net tonnage, which is obtained by deducting from the gross tonnage the volume of all those internal spaces which do not contribute to her earning capacity (e.g., machinery space). It is customary, however, to speak of cargo vessels, ore carriers, and tankers in terms of their deadweight carrying capacity, this being the total amount of cargo and stores a vessel can carry without immersing her load line, expressed in tonnes deadweight, that is, of 1000 kg.

The evolution in marine propulsion has consisted rather in the improvement of engines than in any variation in the method of propulsion. Thus in 1902 the turbine engine was employed on passenger steamers on the Clyde, and in 1905 was applied to the transatlantic service. The next step was the provision of INTERNAL COMBUSTION ENGINES. (For the development of internal combustion engines and electrical engines, in relation to ship propulsion, see MOTOR BOAT; MOTOR SHIP.) In the period

following 1914 there was a rapid advance in the motor ship, and its development is shown in table 1.

The great speeds which have been obtained today require an enormous consumption of fuel. This can well be understood by noting that it requires over 10,000 times as great a power to drive the *Queen Elizabeth 2* only 6 times as fast as Bell's *Comet*. Naturally the former ship is of a much greater displacement than the *Comet*, but the 'lines' have been improved.

Year	Number	Gross metric tonnage
1914	297	238,036
1919	912	764,648
1931	4,080	9,582,336
1939	7,551	17,189,385
1948	9,646	17,465,903
1956	15,554	38,103,800
1964	29,413	79,259,035
1975	56,844	217,165,740

Ships and Shipbuilding. Table 1.

The Blue Riband of the Atlantic. In the 20th century the North Atlantic continued to be the scene of intense rivalry between large passenger liners up to the 1950s. The 'Blue Riband' was held for 21 years by the Cunarder *Mauretania*, which raised her original 1909 record of 26·06 knots to 26·85 knots 20 years later (1 knot = 1·85 km/h), before losing the honour to the German liner *Europa* (27·91 knots) the following year (1930). In 1933 the *Europa*'s sister ship *Bremen* put the record up to 28·51 knots, and in the same year the Italian liner *Rex* added another fraction (28·92 knots). A new phase ensued with the building of the rival French and British liners *Normandie* and *Queen Mary*. In June 1935 the *Normandie* took the 'Blue Riband' from the *Rex* with 30·31 knots, losing it to the *Queen Mary* in August 1936 (30·63 knots). In 1937 the *Normandie* made a crossing at 30·99 knots in March, and bettered it in August (31·20 knots). A year later the *Queen Mary* set up a record which was to stand for 14 years (31·69 knots). A new level was attained when in July 1952 the US liner *United States*, equipped with machinery and many other features designed with a view to national-defence possibilities, made her eastbound maiden voyage at an average speed of 35·59 knots. In all these fast high-powered vessels the propelling machinery has consisted of steam turbines; in the *Normandie* the turbines were coupled to electric generators supplying power to the propeller motors.

Tanker Shipping. Not least of the remarkable developments which have taken place in the shipping sphere since 1945 is that in the world's TANKER fleets. Post-war reconstruction and industrial development tended to create an oil-hungry world, but there could be no more oil without more transport to carry bulk supplies from their sources to the areas of consumption. The shipyards of the world were flooded with orders for tankers; and because it is more economic to carry a given volume of oil in one large vessel than in two smaller ones, the size of the tankers ordered became increasingly larger. In 1939 the largest tanker in the world was the *C. O. Stillman*, a vessel with a carrying capacity of 24,000 t deadweight. Vessels of 28,000 t were ordered soon after the Second

World War, and these were followed by the 32,000-tonners. In 1953 the *Tina Onassis*, of 45,930 t, entered service, followed by several vessels of similar size. The draught of all these vessels was such that they were capable of passing through the Suez Canal carrying their full deadweight (or most of it), but in 1956 a tanker of 85,875 t (*Universe Leader*) was completed for service between the Persian Gulf and the Atlantic Coast of the Americas (via the Cape). The Suez Canal crisis in the summer of that year, with its disruption of the free flow of the world's oil supplies, focused general attention on the possibility of working giant tankers over the Cape route, and concurrently orders were placed in the USA for a vessel of 106,500 t. The prolonged closure of the Suez Canal after 1967 and the great increase in oil consumption led to the development of the very large tanker, or 'supertanker'. The *Globtik London*, at 483,930 t deadweight, is currently (1976) the largest British merchant ship. The development of the world's tanker shipping is illustrated by table 2, which is based on Lloyd's Register statistics (figures in millions of tonnes gross).

Year	All shipping	Tanker shipping	Percentage of tankers
1930	69·0	7·7	11·2
1939	69·6	11·8	16·9
1948	81·6	15·8	19·4
1956	106·9	28·7	26·8
1964	155·4	51·4	33·0
1974	316·0	131·6	41·5

Ships and Shipbuilding. Table 2.

Shipbuilding. A ship, and particularly a modern luxury liner, is a monument to the ingenuity and skill of man. It is a floating township carrying everything civilisation demands for personal comfort, in addition to propelling machinery capable of developing a power of thousands of watts and which can drive the vessel at speeds often exceeding 50 km/h. Warships are even more complex structures, owing to the nature of the work required of them; they must be fast, light, and so arranged as to offer as little obstruction to the full use of the armament as possible. The normal procedure is for the shipowner who is ordering a new vessel to give to the naval architect his requirements. These usually include length, breadth, draught, displacement, speed, type of main engines (steam turbines or internal combustion engines), number of passengers to be catered for, type and weight of cargo to be carried, and the classification society (Lloyd's, Bureau Veritas, etc.), if any, in which the ship is to be classed. This information enables the approximate shape of the hull to be determined, and this serves as a datum from which the design can be commenced, modifications being introduced when necessary. The approximate load water-line may be estimated by making use of Archimedes' principle, which states that for a body to float the weight of the body must be equal to the weight of fluid displaced.

When a vessel of a new class is being constructed, there being no similar ship already built which may be used for comparison, it is customary to make a model of the hull in paraffin wax from the drawings of the lines, termed 'sheer drawings'. This model is then towed at various

Ships and Shipbuilding. Construction of an oil tanker in a Japanese shipyard. (*Barnaby's Picture Library*)

speeds in a specially constructed tank containing seawater, and the resistances at the different speeds measured, the lines being modified until the model gives the required performance. There are formulae for translating the data obtained from the model into dimensions relating to the full-size ship; so as a result of these experiments the sheer drawings are altered as may be required and calculations dealing with strength then proceed.

The ship is treated as a girder carrying an irregular load (due to weight of shell, machinery, and cargo), and receiving a distributed support from the water. The dimensions, called scantlings, of its structural members are determined from two standard conditions of loading: (1) the ship being assumed to be at rest on the crest of a

Ships and Shipbuilding. Figure 1.

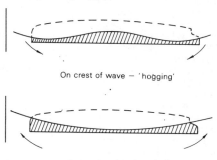

On crest of wave – 'hogging'

Across trough – 'sagging'

Ships and Shipbuilding

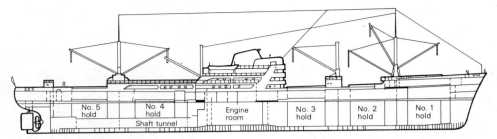

Ships and Shipbuilding. Figure 2. Large cargo vessel. *(Source: Admiralty Manual of Seamanship, vol. 3, HMSO)*

wave equal in length to the length of the vessel and of depth $1/20$ of the length; and (2) the ship being taken at rest across the trough of a wave similar to that assumed in the first case. In case (1) the vessel is said to be 'hogging' and in (2) to be 'sagging' (fig. 1). These are extreme conditions, and the tendency is to cause the structure to bend in the manner suggested by the arrows. To determine the displacement of the ship when on the wave it is convenient at various points, or stations, along the length to draw a curve of sectional areas. If the profile of the wave is traced and put on the profile of the ship, the area of each section up to the surface of the wave may at once be sealed off, and by integrating these areas throughout the length, the displacement and centre of buoyancy are found. As the total weight must be equal to the total buoyancy (i.e., total weight of sea-water displaced) the displacement on the wave is finally fixed after several trials. Next, on a base of ship length, curves for buoyancy for both sagging and hogging conditions and curves of weight are plotted. The difference between the curves of buoyancy and weight, when plotted, gives the loading curve.

In considering the longitudinal strength of a section, account must be taken only of such material as actually contributes to the strength through an appreciable length in the neighbourhood of the section, such as plating of the outer and inner bottom, keel, continuous longitudinals, deck plating, etc. A check of weights and position of centre of gravity is now made, after which stresses under launching conditions are worked out. These stresses are occasionally very high, and call for special attention. Stability calculations follow. The centre of gravity of the ship, with everything she has on board, must be in the same straight vertical line as the centre of gravity of the displaced water, called the centre of buoyancy. When at sea the action of the wind and waves tend to move a ship from her upright position, but she must be so designed that the vessel returns to her correct position, in which case she is said to be stable. A ship is said to be in unstable equilibrium when, on being inclined from her position of rest, she tends to move farther from that position; whilst if she stays inclined without trying to right herself, she is said to be in neutral equilibrium.

With the main dimensions known, work now commences on details in connection with passenger accommodation, etc., within, as well as the various items of the superstructure. Work has already commenced on the construction of the machinery, whilst the shipyard drawing-office is busy preparing drawings and 'moulds' for the vessel herself. The first thing to consider is the slipway.

This is of concrete on a good foundation, with rows of hardwood building blocks forming columns about 2 m high and about 1 m apart, except where special weights are to come, when they are much closer. The heights are adjusted by cast-iron wedges to suit the underside of the keel. The top of the slipway has a slope towards the water of 1 in 200.

In the drawing-office the drawings of the different plates are made at $1/10$ scale, and the lines are faired. The information from these drawings can be fed into a computer, where it is transferred to tapes for the control of cutting machines. Another method of marking plates is to photograph the drawings to $1/10$ scale, then to project the $1/100$-scale photograph on to the actual plates and use a photosensitive powder for marking.

All the larger ships are built on the longitudinal system, in which the bending stresses are taken by fore-and-aft continuous members called longitudinals, stringers, and keelsons. These are braced by 'transverse frames', which are welded into place between the longitudinals and stiffened by heavy angle sections. Smaller ships, down to a flying-boat hull, have the main strength in the transverse frames, which are continuous, whilst the longitudinal members are intercostal, i.e., fitted in between the main frames.

Shipbuilding Methods in the World Wars. During the First World War quite a number of vessels were constructed of reinforced concrete, and one of the following methods was used: (1) ships made monolithically; and (2) ships made in cast portions, which were raised and cemented together. A reinforced-concrete ship is limited in size by its excessive weight, but is cheap to build and was of value in wartime when steel was scarce. Such vessels look clumsy, are inclined to be 'dead' or sluggish in the water, and have small relative cargo capacity. On the other hand, repairs are simple to carry out and the vessel can be made quite watertight, whilst there is, of course, no trouble due to corrosion, such as occurs with steel ships, provided that the concrete is carefully made with a good aggregate cement, and not too much water. The ship is built with particularly robust transverse members tied by long longitudinals, whilst the sides have one or two layers of wire netting or expanded metal for reinforcement. This method has since become popular for building yachts and other small craft.

As early as the spring of 1942 Britain's war losses of shipping totalled one-third of her mercantile marine, and she had begun the Second World War with 2000 fewer sea-going ships than in 1914, and with barely one-third of the workers employed in 1918. On the ability of British and US shipyards to replace losses, naval and mercantile, and to repair damaged vessels and, furthermore, to increase the strength of both these services, depended the very issue of the war. The shipbuilding industry in Britain had languished between the wars, and unemployment in the yards was rife. Yet now the industry was confronted with this tremendous task. The shipyards therefore first concentrated on those types of ships with which they were most familiar, and the policy was helped by the fact that for several years individual shipbuilders had produced semi-standardised ships, e.g., some specialised in tankers, others in refrigerated ships, and on these general types the wartime programme was based, while avoiding over-standardisation. Seven principal types of wartime merchant ships evolved. Chief of these was a tramp ship or cargo vessel, with capacity of 10,000 t deadweight, propelled by steam reciprocating engines. These could be produced in six months by special construction methods involving the system of prefabrication. With prefabrication, sections of different sizes are constructed on the ground, or even at outside engineering works, and then hoisted by crane into place, and joined up to the main structure. Thus there were prefabricated bulkheads, stern sections, double bottom and tank tops, etc. (fig. 2).

A special feature of shipbuilding in the Second World War was the construction of great numbers of elaborate landing-craft, which could discharge quickly upon open beaches, not only the personnel, but also the heavy weapons and equipment, of a large army. Design constantly changed according to experience. Many were built in Britain, particularly for the invasion of Sicily and Normandy, but it is doubtful whether these craft could have been supplied in sufficient numbers or within any useful period but for the remarkable applications of mass-production to shipbuilding, which had been evolved in US shipyards by Henry Kaiser and others in response to the previous demand for replacing merchant tonnage; another interesting feature of wartime construction was the large number of small naval vessels which were built of timber, many of them being prefabricated and assembled inland.

Since the war, the shipyards of the world have largely been modernised to take advantage of the new techniques of prefabrication and welding. The principal object is to secure a smooth flow of steel from the stock-yard to the prefabrication shops, where on raised welding skids large sections are assembled; these are lifted by suitable cranes and welded into place in the hull on the building berth. Formerly ships were built up plate by plate and girder by girder on the building berth, all the joints being riveted. The latest developments turn on the possibility of building a tanker in dry dock in five complete hull sections, which would be joined afterwards; by this

Ships and Shipbuilding. The IHI Kure Shipyard, Japan, is the largest in the world. *(Barnaby's Picture Library)*

method there would be no 'keel-laying', and the time taken to build a tanker of 30,000 t deadweight might be as little as 11 weeks (fig. 3).

Launching. The vessel is launched in its lightest possible condition after all the watertight parts of the structure have been tested and the outside plating given several coats of anti-corrosive and anti-fouling paint. When all is ready for the launch, shores are knocked away and side blocks are removed in sections, thus allowing the whole weight of the vessel to be taken on the groundways and sliding-ways. These launching ways are of pine, big, solid baulks, teak- or oak-faced on the top, about 1·2 m square section for the groundways and similar but smaller blocks for the sliding-ways. Between the latter and the ship's bottom are wedges. The bow and stern are supported in special cradles, called poppets. Between the groundways and sliding-ways some kind of lubricant is introduced, consisting generally of tallow, grease and soft soap, whilst slipping is prevented by cleats and dogshores of African oak. Finally, the dogshores are knocked away and the vessel is held by the launching trigger only, which is actuated electrically. Once started, the ship moves quickly, but to slow it down the surface of the groundways has a slight camber. The dangerous moment is the instant when the stern is 'waterborne' and the fore poppets are taking the only load on the groundways. When the vessel

Ships and Shipbuilding. Figure 3. Tanker. *(Source: Admiralty Manual of Seamanship, vol. 3, HMSO)*

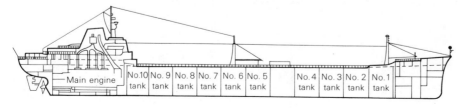

Ships and Shipbuilding

is afloat, anchors and drags are run out to bring her to rest, after which she is towed into dry dock and examined for injury. The final phase is now entered upon, which consists in installing the machinery, funnels, masts, lifeboats, and internal fittings.

Ships have been occasionally launched almost completed, but for a sizeable vessel this is a very risky procedure. In narrow rivers ships are often launched sideways in a cradle, and small ships, e.g., submarines, are sometimes built in a dry dock and floated out when completed. Where very large ships are built in a limited space, they can be constructed in two halves, in some cases in separate yards. The two halves are then launched and are joined up in the water using special welding techniques.

Post-war Machinery Developments. The years since the Second World War have seen the emergence of new types of propelling machinery, in the form of the gas turbine and medium-speed diesels, while steady advances have been made in the design of steam turbines and diesel engines; apart from some specialised uses, the steam reciprocating engine, which in the days of cheap coal was the mainstay of the shipping industry, is now obsolete. The recent trend in the design of marine engines is towards the development of those which give greater power for less weight, space, and fuel consumption. Although large tankers and bulk cargo carriers are being built with geared turbine machinery and boilers employing advanced heating principles, attention is mainly focused on the development of diesel engines, the power of which is steadily increasing. Progress with the development of the gas turbine has been marked in the Royal Navy, where all new warships are powered by this type of engine. In the Merchant Marine progress is slower, because of high fuel costs.

It is, however, in the future possibilities of nuclear power for marine propulsion that the greatest interest is centred. Here the working principle is the use of heat extracted from a reactor to raise steam which is expanded through turbines. The first nuclear-powered vessel to be completed was the US submarine *Nautilus*, which completed her sea trials successfully in January 1955.

Until recent years it has been necessary in the interest of trim to place the propelling machinery of a passenger liner amidships, but if the machinery is placed aft the task of conveniently accommodating the public rooms in the hull is greatly facilitated by the absence of uptakes, etc. The increasing lightness and compactness of modern machinery has enabled naval architects to solve the problem of trim, and in 1952 a French liner with machinery aft (*El Djézaïr*, of 7608 gross tons) was built for service in the Mediterranean. The experiment was repeated on a much larger scale in the British *Southern Cross* and *Northern Star* (20,204 gross tons), which, being entirely without cargo holds, hatches, derricks, etc., represented a point of departure in passenger-liner design. In 1961 the SS *Canberra* (45,000 gross tons) was completed for the P. & O.-Orient line, in which the turbo-electric machinery was sited aft and the two funnels side by side. The cargo holds are forward, but to leave the deck clear of hatches, these are loaded through the ship's side.

The spate of technical development in recent years has been such that forecasting seems hardly profitable. Until nuclear power plants become readily applicable to commercial vessels, the gas turbine and the medium-speed diesel engine may well have important parts to play, and the good power/weight ratio of these prime movers may mean that for both passenger and cargo work vessels will be built with machinery aft in increasing numbers, so that the familiar 'three-island' profile (created by forecastle, midship superstructure and poop) may pass from the seas. Important new developments in shipping have been the container ship, LASH ship, and bulk carrier.

Ships and Shipbuilding. The 'heavy lift' cargo vessel *Adventurer*. (*Barnaby's Picture Library*)

Stabilisers. The need to improve the stability of warships in order to increase the effectiveness of their gunfire was apparent prior to the Second World War and led to the development of the activated fin type stabiliser which was kept on the secret list until after the war. When released this pioneer type, known as the Denny-Brown stabiliser, was fitted in a number of merchant ships where the elimination of rolling was considered to be advantageous. The effect of stabilisation is to decrease the overall hull resistance and allow an increase in the sustained sea speed of the ship due to the absence of bilge keels and the reduction in rolling effected. It also provides increased comfort and enables maintenance and repair work to be carried out at sea under greatly improved conditions.

In 1960, a new anti-rolling device, known as the flume stabilisation system, made its appearance and proved so successful that it has since been fitted in a number of ships of various types ranging from giant tankers to weather ships. The system was developed by the firm of J. McMullen of New York and employs a hydrodynamically controlled flow of liquid in a specially designed tank system. By means of nozzles known as flumes, the liquid ballast is made to lag the roll of the ship by 90°, thus damping the roll of the vessel and also counteracting the tendency to roll past the normal to the slope of the wave. A 75 per cent reduction in roll is claimed for this system, which costs only a fraction of that of the fin type stabiliser. It can be installed without docking the ship and since it is not dependent on speed for its operation, it functions equally well when the ship is stopped, an advantage not shared by the fin type.

See also NAVY AND NAVIES; SAILS AND RIGGING; STEAMSHIP; SUBMARINE.

Bibliography: K. J. Rawson and E. C. Tapper, *Basic Ship Theory,* 1968; R. Carpenter, *Modern Ships,* 1970; D. Lobley, *Ships Through the Ages,* 1972; J. M. Graham, *North Atlantic Run,* 1972.

Ship's Company. The designation of a ship's crew as her 'company' is of ancient origin, but today the term is more used in the navy than in the merchant service, where 'crew' is preferred. The ship's company of a warship, known as her complement, includes both officers and men

Ships and Shipbuilding. Control room of the US nuclear ship *Savannah.* *(Barnaby's Picture Library)*

and varies according to the size of the ship, her armament and equipment. Thus the complement of a modern carrier is between 2000 and 3000, of a cruiser 700, of a frigate 220 to 260. The ship's company includes a proportion of officers and men from the many different specialist branches and categories of which the navy is composed. For example, a frigate carries 7 seaman specialist officers, one of whom is the captain, 2 engineer/electrical officers, 1 supply and secretariat officer, 125 seamen, 50 engineer artificers and mechanics, 12 tactical and radio communication operators, 12 electrical and radio mechanics, 5 electrical and ordnance artificers, 16 supply and secretariat ratings. In each category there is a proportion of senior ratings of the chief and petty officer rates, which include artificers, and also some leading rates. The larger ships also carry a detachment of Royal Marines. The

Ships and Shipbuilding. The British cable ship *Mercury.* *(Popperfoto)*

complement of flagships is enlarged to allow for the admiral, his staff and retinue.

Shipton, Mother (c. 1488–c. 1558), reputed prophetess of Knaresborough in Yorkshire. Said to have been the child of a witch who consorted with the devil, she married, in 1512, Tobias Shipton, a builder, and lived for over 70 years. She is first mentioned in 1641 as having foretold the death of Wolsey; she is also said to have predicted the Civil War, the Fire of London in 1666, and the end of the world in 1881. Mother Shipton's cave can be seen at Knaresborough and the Dropping Well is still associated with her supernatural powers.

Shipwrecks, see WRECKS.

Shiraz, capital city of FARS province, Iran, on the highway from Tehran to Bushire. Grain, rice, pulses, tobacco, gum tragacanth, clarified butter, wool, skins, and carpets are the main products. There are manufactures of cotton goods, glass, attar of roses, and inlaid fancy articles. The city has numerous mosques. The tombs of the poets Sa'di and Hafiz are on the outskirts of the city. A university was established here in 1962. Population (1971) 410,000.

Bibliography: J. I. Clarke, *Iranian City of Shiraz*, 1963.

Shire, see COUNTY; LOCAL GOVERNMENT.

Shire Breed, see HORSE.

Shirley, James (1596–1666), English dramatist and poet, born in London. He was educated at Merchant Taylors' and afterwards at St John's College, Oxford, and also at Catharine Hall, Cambridge. He took orders, but was converted to Roman Catholicism. With the profession of playwright he combined that of schoolmaster. His plays were derivative, and reflected the tastes of the Caroline court. His more interesting comedies, however, anticipated in some respects Restoration Comedy; they included *The Witty Fair One*, 1628, *The Gamester*, 1633, and *The Lady of Pleasure*, 1635. His tragedies, perhaps the best of which were *The Traitor*, 1631, and *The Cardinal*, 1641, were worthy but generally lifeless efforts. Shirley also wrote many tragi-comedies and romantic dramas, as well as masques and poems. He died in the Great Fire.

Bibliography: W. Gifford and A. Dyce (Eds), *Dramatic Works and Poems* (6 vols), repr. of 1833 ed., 1966; R. S. Forsythe, *Shirley's Plays in their Relation to the Elizabethan Drama*, 1914; A. H. Nason, *James Shirley, Dramatist*, 1915; A. Harbage, *Cavalier Drama*, 1936; Study, with bibliography, by S. A. and D. R. Tannenbaum, 1946.

Shirley, Lawrence, see FERRERS, LAWRENCE SHIRLEY, 4TH EARL.

Shitta Wood, or shittim wood, derived from some species of acacia, from which the Tabernacle was largely constructed.

Shiva, see ŚIVA.

Shizuoka, or Shidzuoka, city and capital of Shizuoka-ken, Japan, 150 km south-west of Tokyo. The centre of a tea and mandarin orange trade, it is also noted for the production of tinned food, textiles, and furniture. Population (1974) 444,000.

Shkodër (Italian *Scutari*), town of Albania near the south-east end of Lake SCUTARI, and connected with the Adriatic Sea via the Buenë (Boyana) river. It is also the capital of Shkodër district. It has a large trade in wool, tobacco, maize, and skins, and its manufactures include cement, alcohol, and cigarettes. Adjacent is a hill crowned by an old Venetian citadel. Population (town) 59,100; (district) 178,000.

Shlisselburg, see PETROKREPOST.

Shlonsky, Abraham (1900–73), Israeli poet, born in the Ukraine. He settled in Palestine in 1921 and there edited journals and made translations into Hebrew. One of the first Symbolists in Israel, his poetry is among the most lively in the Hebrew language and concerns the development of his new land and its people's attitudes.

Shmidt, Otto Yul'yevich (1891–1956), Soviet expedition leader, scientist, and administrator. He made his first Arctic expedition to Zemlya Frantsa-Iosifa in 1929 and became, in 1930, director of the Arctic Institute (Leningrad) and head of the newly formed government department to develop the Arctic, the Glavsevmorput (see NORTHERN SEA ROUTE). He held this position for six years, leading many expeditions, notably those in the *Sibiryakov* (1932), *Chelyushkin* (1933–34), and that which established PAPANIN's drifting station (later called SP-1) at the North Pole in 1931. He continued his scientific work after his dismissal (at the time of the GREAT PURGE) in 1939, becoming a professor of mathematics at Moscow University. The strong position held by the USSR in all fields of polar research is in many ways due to his work and influence. His work bears the mark of being much influenced by the philosophy of N. F. FËDOROV.

Bibliography: T. E. Armstrong, *Russians in the Arctic, Soviet Exploration 1937–57*, 1958.

Shoa, see SHEWA.

Shock, a state of collapse following injury. It is the result of a diminution of the effective circulating volume of the blood, due to loss of blood from external haemorrhage, to loss of plasma (as in extensive burns), or to loss of blood through leakage into damaged tissues. In shock there is also a sudden increase in the capacity of the blood vessels, so that the patient 'bleeds' into his own circulatory system, the blood gravitating to the vessels of the abdomen. The degree of shock is affected by reflex nervous influences. A painful injury is likely to cause a greater degree of shock, and an apprehensive person suffers more severely from shock than a phlegmatic one. Often these two factors operate at the same time.

A patient suffering from shock looks pale with a greyish colour, particularly about the lips and ears. The skin is cold and moist, and the hands and feet icy cold. The patient is apathetic but alert, and answers questions readily. The pulse is rapid and weak, and the blood pressure is low.

Treatment of shock consists in measures to restore the circulating volume of blood, and, medically, the principal treatment is blood transfusion. First-aid treatment consists in arresting haemorrhage when present and covering wounds. If the patient complains of being cold or is shivering he should be warmed gently with hot bottles and coverings. A patient who does not complain of cold should not be warmed. Apart from these measures, the patient should be disturbed as little as possible, and should be kept lying down and at rest until medical aid is available.

Shock is sometimes used to describe a condition of acute mental distress, such as occurs upon the sudden death of a close relative or the witnessing of an accident. Fainting may occur under these circumstances and this is due to a reflex nervous reaction.

Shock, Electric, see RESUSCITATION.

Shockley, William Bradford (1910–), Anglo-US physicist, born in London; educated at the California Institute of Technology and the Massachusetts Institute of Technology, where he taught from 1932 to 1936 before joining the staff of the Bell Telephone Laboratories. Working with J. Bardeen and W. H. Brattain, Shockley discovered the junction TRANSISTOR in 1948. The three men shared the Nobel Prize for physics in 1956 for their discovery. Since 1958, Shockley has been at Stanford University, where he became professor of engineering science in 1963.

Shockworkers' Movement, movement among the industrial and building workers, mostly young, in Soviet Russia (1927–35) aimed at speeding up work; it was inspired and controlled by the Communist party. It was later replaced by the STAKHANOV MOVEMENT. See also FIVE-YEAR PLANS.

Shoddy, kind of soft woollen goods made from old woollen rags. Dewsbury is the English centre of the industry. The term is also applied to the waste thrown off during the process of wool manufacture. In common parlance the word has come to refer to any poor material; also used figuratively.

Shoebill, see BALAENICEPS.

Shoeburyness, see SOUTHEND-ON-SEA.

Shoes, see BOOTS AND SHOES.

Shofar, ancient Jewish wind instrument, made of a ram's horn, still used in the synagogue.

Shoghi Effendi (1896–1957), Bahá'í spiritual leader, born in Acre. He was educated at the American University of Beirut, and later went to Balliol College, Oxford, whence he was called in 1921 to succeed his grandfather, 'Abdu'l-Bahá, as head of the BAHÁ'Í faith, returning to Palestine to take up his responsibilities. He beautified the centre of Bahá'í pilgrimage on Mount Carmel.

Shogun, abbreviation of Seiitaishogun, which was the highest rank of the Japanese SAMURAI or warrior class, originally meaning 'Grand General for Conquering Ainus and other Tribes'. From 1192, when Minamoto no Yoritomo was made the first shogun of the Kamakura Shogunate government, until 1867, when Tokugawa Yoshinobu, the 15th shogun of the Tokugawa Shogunate government, restored to the emperor the reins of national government, the shogun was in reality the ruler of Japan, although the emperor retained nominal supremacy.

Shoji, paper sliding or folding panel or screen used in Japanese furnishing as an integral part of the house. The term can also include light wooden panels. Over the centuries shojis have been a vehicle for some of the finest Japanese painting.

Shola, or sola, *Aeschynomene aspera*, a pithy-stemmed, Indian, leguminous swamp plant, used for making light helmets worn by Europeans in the tropics.

Sholapur, town in MAHARASHTRA state, India, 340 km south-east of Bombay, and second largest to BOMBAY as a cotton textile centre in India. Population (1971) 398,000.

Sholokhov, Mikhail Aleksandrovich (1905–), Soviet novelist, born in the Don Cossack region where he spent most of his life. He published several stories about the Don Cossacks in 1925, but became famous in 1928 with the publication of the first volume of his four-volume masterpiece *The Silent Don* (translated by S. Garry, 1942), a realistic historical epic showing the life of the Don Cossacks on the eve of, and during, the First World War, and in the first five years after the October Revolution. It is remarkably objective in its treatment of both sides in the Civil War, and, composed in the colourful language typical of all Sholokhov's works, is regarded as one of the masterpieces of SOCIALIST REALISM. In the 1970s doubts were cast on Sholokhov's authorship of the early volumes by SOLZHENITSYN, among others.

His second novel, *Virgin Soil Upturned*, 1932–60 (translated by S. Garry, 1935; second part translated as *Harvest on the Don* by H. Stevens, 1960), deals with the forced collectivisation of agriculture in the Don Cossack region and the Cossacks' opposition to it. Sholokhov has written little of value since 1940. He was awarded the Nobel Prize for literature in 1965.

Bibliography: D. A. Stewart, *Mikhail Sholokhov. A Critical Introduction*, 1967; C. G. Bearne, *Sholokhov*, 1969.

Shooting. Despite the invention of gun-powder and the resultant use of primitive 'hand-gonnes' in the 14th century, it was not until the latter part of the 17th century that shooting for sport, as we understand the term today, began to emerge. In the previous 300 years fowl and game had certainly been shot, but purely for the larder and with no element of sport; a fowling piece would be manoeuvred into such a position that a shot 'into the brown' at resting birds would show maximum results—the notion of shooting flying birds and the concept of the sporting chance emerged only with an improvement in ignition and weight in fowling pieces. The early match- and wheel-locks were too tardy to allow a shot at a flying bird, but the invention in the early 16th century of the snap-hance and its later refinement as the flintlock, changed all this.

The flintlock principle was simple: a flint held in the jaws of the hammer struck a steel plate when the trigger was pressed, causing a shower of sparks to ignite powder in the pan, thus exploding the main charge.

Nearly instantaneous ignition was then possible, though wind and rain presented hazards. These were overcome in 1805 when the Rev. Alexander John Forsyth invented the first percussion lock, which in its later versions consisted of a cap containing an explosive agent which detonated the main charge on being struck by the hammer. The muzzle-loading system incorporating the percussion cap was to last until about 1856 when the first breechloader, the pin-fire, revolutionised shotgun shooting. Rapid loading was now a fact and by the 1890s the breech loader,

Shooting

seen at its peak in the double 12-bore hammerless sidelock ejector, dominated the sporting world. It is a fact that improvements in the subsequent 90 years have only been marginal—little more could be achieved in the way of balance, speed of loading or practical results.

Until the 1850s and from the early part of the previous century, game had invariably been shot by 'walking-up' over dogs, which were usually setters or pointers. It was a leisurely, pleasant pastime with pauses between shots as each sportsman reloaded his muzzle-loader and the blue smoke rolled away. The countryside was more open but game was, apart from partridges, by no means common. Rabbits were not widespread, though 50 years later their numbers had increased considerably.

The breech loader gave a different emphasis to the sport as it was now possible to achieve a rapid rate of fire. This led to the development of the continental *battue*, an organised shoot in which reared pheasants were driven over the guns by beaters. Initially this method was condemned outright by the more conservative and older school; it was 'murder, slaughter, only for arm-chair sportsmen too idle to seek the game themselves' but the vociferous clamour was gradually quietened as sportsmen came to appreciate what was involved. The pheasants, if properly shown, flew fast and high—testing the skill of the finest shots.

Lowland game shooting. In Britain this comprises pheasant (1 October to 1 February inclusive) and partridge (1 September to 1 February). The methods used are 'driving' in which teams of beaters send pheasants from woodlands or partridges across open ground over guns sited much as for grouse, or 'walking-up' with or without dogs in which birds of either species are flushed from fields of winter fodder or root-crops or from young forestry plantations and are shot going away. In each case the party normally consists of six or eight guns with 20 or more beaters and other helpers. Driven pheasant shooting ranks high in the shooting world, forming the mainstay of the shooting scene in Great Britain. Those tackling their first pheasants will do well to average one bird for six cartridges.

Rough shooting. The shooters have no human assistance and the quarry may be game, woodcock, snipe, wildfowl, hares, rabbits or woodpigeons. Rough-shooters customarily operate in pairs, shooting over dogs, of which spaniels are the most effective, in the manner of shooting general before the introduction of the breech-loading guns. Seldom more than 10 per cent of the bag expected at a formal shoot is taken, but since this form of shooting involves locating the quarry in addition to shooting it, the element of hunting skill added to that of marksmanship is regarded a reward in itself.

Partridges declined in number between 1955 and 1975 due to a combination of bad weather, pesticides and reduction in nesting cover. It appears that now, however, the partridge population might be increasing again in some parts.

Two organisations closely associated with shooting are: the British Field Sports Society, 26 Caxton Street, London, SW1H 0RG, and the Wildfowlers' Association of Great Britain and Ireland, Marford Mill, Chester Road, Rossett, Clwyd, Wales.

The Game Conservancy, Burgate Manor, Fordingbridge, Hampshire, is closely connected with shooting and has a small but highly trained staff involved in research into ways of maintaining and increasing the supply of game and duck, despite pressures from modern society.

See also CLAY PIGEON SHOOTING; CLOSE SEASONS; FIREARMS; GAME LAWS; GROUSE SHOOTING; GUNS; WILDFOWLING.

Bibliography: P. Stanbury and G. L. Carlisle, *Shotgun Marksmanship*, 1962; H. W. Carlton and T. Radcliffe, *Spaniels for Sport*, 1969; C. Coles (Ed.), *The Complete Book of Game Conservation*, 1971; M. Brander (Ed.), *International Encyclopaedia of Shooting*, 1972; T. Jackson (Ed.), *Gundogs in Britain*, 1974.

Shooting Star, see METEOR.

Shop Steward, also known as shop secretary, or works representative, local representative in the UK of the members of a trade union employed in a single place of work, e.g. a factory or 'shop'. They are an important link in the local organisation of a trade union. In some unions, mainly in the engineering and allied industries, they play a larger part than in others. The increasing tendency for wage-bargaining at factory level to supplement national bargaining has strengthened their position in certain industries. Their duties include the inspection of contribution cards and the recruitment of new members. They are also responsible for submitting reports to the district committee of the trade union concerned, and for ensuring that the provisions of any agreement between the trade union and the employer are carried out. As the elected representatives at the place of work, they often act as spokesmen in the presenting of grievances to the employer.

Shops Acts. The Shops Acts 1950–65 control the hours of closing and the hours of employment for retail shops and wholesale warehouses in Britain. Breaches of the acts are punishable by fines. Matters of health, safety, and welfare are dealt with by the Offices, Shops and Railway Premises Act 1963. The following is an outline of the Shops Acts 1950–65.

Hours of Closing. (1) Every shop must close for at least one half-day each week. This day may be chosen by the shopkeeper but may only be altered once in every three months. (2) A local authority may, if the majority of occupiers of any particular class of shop, or of all classes, are in favour, by order exempt a class, or classes, of shops from the requirement to close on one half-day each week. (3) Every shop must close not later than 8 p.m., except for one night a week when it may close at 9 p.m. The local authority may, however, with the consent of two-thirds of the affected shopkeepers, impose an earlier closing hour, which may not be before 7 p.m. There are exemptions for shops selling confectionery and tobacco and for many transactions including meals, drink, newly cooked provisions, medicines, newspapers, and motor supplies needed for immediate use. A customer in the shop before closing time may be served after that time. (4) It is illegal to carry on in any place any retail trade or business at a time when a shop for that trade may not be open. But mobile vans and shops may be open at any time so long as they do not operate from a fixed site. (5) Shops carrying on several trades under one roof (e.g. multiple stores and supermarkets) do not need to close their separate trades at the times and days laid down by the local authority, but must still close for a half-holiday each week. (6) Local authorities at holiday resorts may make special provisions for closing for up to four months each year.

Conditions of Employment. (1) All shop assistants must have one half-day off each week. If they work for more than six hours at a time they must have a 20-minute break. If they work between 11.30 a.m. and 2.30 p.m. they must have a 45-minute break during that time, which is increased to 60 minutes if the meal is taken off the premises, and if they work between 4 p.m. and 7 p.m., a 30-minute break. This does not apply to staff employed in places serving refreshments; but they must not work more than 65 hours in any week, and must have 32 week days and 26 Sundays off each year, and must have up to two hours a day for meals. (2) If a person works on a Sunday for more than four hours he must have a whole day off, and a half day if he works less than four hours, in both cases besides his normal half-day. There are exceptions including places serving refreshments, milk roundsmen, and chemists. (3) Young Persons. (a) Between the ages of 16 and 18 they may not work more than 48 hours in any week. Nor may they do more than 12 hours overtime in any one week, nor more than 50 hours overtime in any year, nor work any overtime in more than six weeks a year. In the catering trade they may not work more than 60 hours in any week, or 96 hours in any fortnight. In the motor trade they may not work more than 54 hours in any week or 144 hours in any three weeks. (b) Under the age of 16 they may not work more than 44 hours in any week, with an extra four hours permitted at Christmas. (c) No one under 18 may be employed between 10 p.m. and 6 a.m., except people over 16 after 5 a.m. for the delivery of newspapers, bread, and milk. (d) There are special provisions for young people employed in hotels and theatres.

Sunday Closing. (1) All shops must close on Sunday except for certain transactions including meals, drink, newly cooked provisions, confectionery, fruit and vegetables (not in tins), milk, medicine, motor supplies, tobacco, and newspapers. Local authorities may authorise shops to sell bread and confectionery, fish and groceries on a Sunday, normally before 10 a.m. only. Local authorities in holiday resorts may authorise shops to sell food and certain tourist requirements on 18 Sundays each year. No butcher shops may open on Sunday. (2) There are special provisions for Jewish shops, which must close on Saturday and may open on Sunday until 2 p.m.

Notices and Records. In a number of cases a shopkeeper must display a notice in his shop, e.g. of the early closing day, of the half-days for his staff, of hours of work in the catering trade, of the hours of work for young people, and of Sunday opening. He must also keep records of Sunday work and of the hours worked by young people.

Shoran, see RADIO BEACONS.

Shore, Jane (d. c. 1527), mistress of EDWARD IV, born in London, was the daughter of a mercer and the wife of a goldsmith. She became Edward's mistress c. 1470. After the King's death she was accused by Richard III of sorcery and compelled to do penance (1483). She died in poverty.

Shore, John, see TEIGNMOUTH, JOHN SHORE, 1ST BARON.

Shore, Peter David (1924–), British politician, educated at Quarry Bank High School, Liverpool, and King's College, Cambridge. He was head of the Research Department of the Labour party from 1959 until his election as Labour MP for Stepney in 1964. Since 1974 he has represented Stepney and Poplar. He was successively parliamentary secretary, Ministry of Technology, 1966–67, and parliamentary secretary, Department of Economic Affairs, 1967, and entered the Cabinet in 1967 as secretary of state for Economic Affairs, a post he held until 1969. He was minister without portfolio and deputy leader of the House of Commons from 1969 to 1970, continuing to be a member of the Cabinet. Between 1970 and 1974 he was Opposition spokesman on European affairs and was a leading opponent of British entry to the European Economic Community. In March 1974 he became secretary of state for Trade, but, following his prominent rôle as an anti-Marketeer in the referendum of 1975, he was appointed secretary of state for Industry. Following the reconstruction of the government by James Callaghan on his appointment as prime minister in 1976, Shore became secretary of state for the Environment.

Shore, see SEASHORE.

Shoreditch, see HACKNEY.

Shoreham-by-Sea, seaport in the Adur District of West SUSSEX, England, with the old town now being joined to New Shoreham. The latter is a thriving port with a shipbuilding, coal, and timber trade. Population (1971) 18,230.

Shorians, Turkic-speaking people living in southern Siberia, in the south of the Kuznetsk basin (Kemerovo Oblast), numbering about 16,000. Traditionally hunters and cedar-nut collectors, they also farm today. They are now a small minority in Shoria, where large iron ore deposits are being exploited.

Jane Shore. (*Popperfoto*)

Shoring

Shoring (from *shore*, a prop, term used for temporary support of a structure). The three main types of shoring are raking, flying or horizontal shoring, and dead shoring (or vertical or needle shoring). Shoring is used mainly to support the loads of a wall or structure during alterations and was used extensively during the Second World War for repairing bomb damage.

Fig. 1 shows an example of raking shores; the timbers are usually placed at angles of 60–75°, and at horizontal distances apart of about 2·5 m. The sole pieces *S* are not quite at right angles to the shore resting on them, but at a slight inclination which facilitates levering for tightening up; on bad ground it is necessary to prepare a foundation for them. Horizontal and flying shores (fig. 2) are used for supporting vertical walls of a structure from bowing when intermediate supports are removed, and also to support forms in reinforced concrete construction.

A dead shore is used for carrying dead weight of a structure whilst part is removed to form additional openings (fig. 3). In this case the weight of the structure is carried by a horizontal needle which in turn bears on dead shores or struts which rest on a solid base.

See also UNDERPINNING.

Short-circuit, a condition when two or more terminals of a source of electrical energy, or two or more conductors between which a potential difference exists, are connected together through a path of negligibly small resistance. Short-circuit of overhead transmission lines may occur as a result of flash-over between lines; short-circuit of cables may occur by failure of insulation. Short-circuit tests, i.e., with output terminals short circuited, are carried out on transformers and rotating electrical machines for the determination of the copper losses. See ELECTRICAL MACHINES; TRANSFORMER.

Short Day Plants, see DAYLENGTH.

Short Sight, see MYOPIA; REFRACTION, ERRORS OF.

Short Story, type of prose fiction, shorter than the NOVEL, characterised by its compact, condensed form. In the history of literature it emerged fairly recently as a separate genre, although the narration of short stories and tales is one of the oldest literary forms.

In the early literature of Asia and the Middle East, FABLES and fairy-tales mark the early short story, which seems to have been a distinct product of the East.

Shoring.

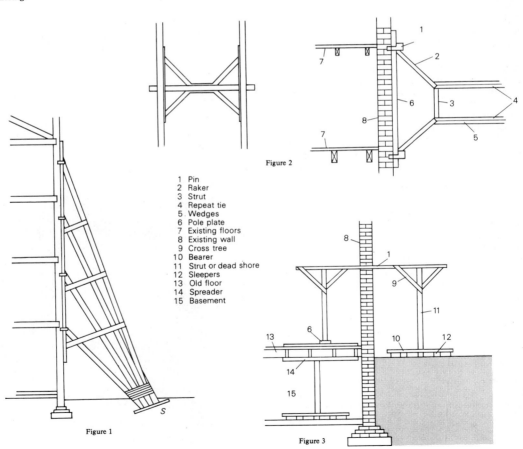

1 Pin
2 Raker
3 Strut
4 Repeat tie
5 Wedges
6 Pole plate
7 Existing floors
8 Existing wall
9 Cross tree
10 Bearer
11 Strut or dead shore
12 Sleepers
13 Old floor
14 Spreader
15 Basement

Figure 1

Figure 2

Figure 3

Although folk-tales exist in all cultures, in northern Europe the folk-themes were incorporated into EPICS and SAGAS, in which there was a tendency to expand an idea and add stories together, rather than to condense them. Eastern stories found their way into Western literature, however; the fables of Aesop, for example, being derived from Eastern sources. Among classical works, simple objective short stories can be found in Apuleius's *Golden Ass*, written in the 2nd century AD, while Ovid's *Metamorphoses* includes a collection of short tales composed into a whole. The Bible incorporates many examples of the short story, such as the story of Ruth; these are among the best-known in the world, and a frequent source of inspiration and literary symbol.

One of the most beautiful of the Eastern collections of short stories is that now called *The Arabian Nights* (see ARABIAN NIGHTS). Its basis is Persian, dating back to the 10th century; but it is probable that the stories are Arabian and were gathered together between the 14th and 16th centuries. Also of Eastern origin are many of the popular tales in the 14th-century didactic collection known as the *Gesta Romanorum* (see GESTA ROMANORUM) written in Latin. They, and similar collections, had great indirect influence upon the Western short story, long before complete translations reached Europe.

BOCCACCIO, whose *Decameron* is one of the landmarks in the history of both the novel and the short story, was from Italy, a country which had a great deal of contact with the East. His short stories closely resemble Eastern collections in form, though his plots were inspired by the chivalric romances. The medieval secular stories in verse, of which GOWER's *Confessio Amantis* and CHAUCER's *Canterbury Tales* (which owe much to Boccaccio and to the *Gesta Romanorum*) are outstanding, were preceded by the French *contes dévots*, religious anecdotes in a style borrowed from the early Christian Greeks (see CONTES). The Christians had been greatly influenced by the New Testament parables, among the most beautiful of early short stories. French poets also produced the *lai*, a Celtic fairy story in verse, and the *fabliau*, a satirical short story in verse (see FABLIAU); several of Chaucer's stories are close analogues of the *fabliaux*. Medieval and Renaissance tales were usually simple in narrative, and almost completely objective. In this rudimentary kind of short story, prose and rhyme were interchangeable.

The conventional short story continued throughout the Renaissance, flourishing especially in Italy, but towards the end of the period, prose displaced verse for the short narrative. Italian short stories of a rather artificial character reached England through William Painter's *The Palace of Pleasure*, 1566–67, and similar collections, but by this time the familiar themes were almost played out. Short stories survived inside many of the early novels, such as those of DEFOE and STERNE, as digressions and anecdotes, and even in later works, such as those of DICKENS. But as a separate entity the short story form temporarily disappeared.

A major factor in the short story's resurgence in the 19th century was the growth of the mass reading public, and the proliferation of MAGAZINES. The writer whose influence was paramount in creating the modern short story was Edgar Allan POE, who followed the tradition of the fable and the medieval tale by employing a direct narrative. Into it he intruded his own personality, adopt-

Short Story. Cover for an edition of Kipling's *In Black and White*, 1889. *(Mansell Collection)*

ing a subjective treatment, often within an objective framework. A typical Poe story is brief and finely constructed; all inessentials are rigorously removed. Later, CHEKHOV concentrated on Poe's liberation of the author-narrator; in his hands, the short story became a vehicle for expressing feeling, a mirror for emotion. This allowed lesser talents to indulge in self-conscious incoherences; and though writers of the quality of D. H. Lawrence, Katherine Mansfield, James Joyce, Sean O'Faolain, and Elizabeth Bowen succeeded with the short story, the form's popularity suffered in consequence. The best short stories are self-conscious only in the sense that the author sets out to write a short story, and not a short novel; they are carefully planned in every detail. Followers of the French writers MAUPASSANT and DAUDET concentrated on producing concise cameos, taking their inspiration from Poe's mastery of form. Their treatment remained, however, severely objective; emotional subjects were dealt with dispassionately, and this is typical of the Franch short story.

The humorous short story, simply narrative in treatment and gaining in effect through the necessary compression, was a peculiarly American development. The acknowledged master is Mark TWAIN, along with O. HENRY and Joel Chandler HARRIS. With the stories of Henry JAMES, the American short story gained new depth, borrowing from Chekhov; the humorous short stories of Theodore DREISER and James THURBER have a certain seriousness which owes something to James. The humorous short story in England, exemplified in the writing of W. W. JACOBS and P. G. WODEHOUSE, generally lacks this depth. In the 19th century there was a revival of interest in the fairy-tale and in fantasy, with writers such as Hans ANDERSEN in Denmark and J. M. BARRIE in Britain. The ghost stories of M. R. JAMES are an example of how the short story form adapted well to certain specialised genres. Adventure and action were particularly developed in the short stories of the American Jack LONDON, while KIPLING demonstrated that the short story could cover a wide range of time and space effectively.

The flowering of the short story in Britain and America in the late 19th and early 20th centuries owed a great deal to the growing number of magazines and newspapers which provided writers with their principal publishing outlets. To this period belong the works of Leonard Merrick and 'SAKI'. After the First World War increased costs led to a decrease in the numbers of such magazines and, with fewer outlets, it became far less easy for the unknown author to make his name through the short story. The gradual disappearance of the magazines which had published the work of leading short story writers such as Sherwood ANDERSON, for example, reduced the importance of the genre. But it did not destroy it as a literary form. In the United States magazines such as the *New Yorker* and *Esquire* continued to publish them.

American populist writers, including Damon RUNYON, maintained a large following. And leading novelists continued to write short stories of distinction—among them Somerset MAUGHAM, Graham GREENE, Scott FITZGERALD, Ernest HEMINGWAY, William SAROYAN, Carson McCULLERS, John Cheever, and Flannery O'Connor. James THURBER and S. J. Perelman were masters of the

humorous short story. Most of the leading writers of science fiction have used the format for much of their work. (See SCIENCE FICTION.)

Although few, if any, contemporary writers have achieved a reputation through short stories alone, contemporary novelists, such as John WAIN, Saul BELLOW, and Bernard MALAMUD, continue to contribute to the short story, and also prominent in the field are A. E. COPPARD, T. F. POWYS, Joyce CARY, Liam O'FLAHERTY, Doris LESSING, Muriel SPARK, H. E. BATES, Frank O'CONNOR, and Flann O'BRIEN.

The Italian neo-realists, such as Alberto MORAVIA, and the Soviet post-revolutionary writers, among them Isaac Babel, are also noted for their short stories. Among the most admired short-story writers of the century are the French author COLETTE and the Argentinian Jorge Luis BORGES.

Bibliography: H. S. Canby, *The Short Story in English*, 1909; F. L. Pattee, *The Development of the American Short Story*, 1932; E. A. Cross, *A Book of the Short Story*, 1934; S. O'Faolain, *The Short Story*, new ed. 1973.

Short Ton, see METROLOGY.

Shorter, Clement King (1857–1926), British journalist and critic, born in London. Educated at Birkbeck Institution, from 1877 to 1890 he worked in Somerset House. As a journalist Shorter had an important influence on the English pictorial press. In 1891 he became editor of the *Illustrated London News*; in 1893 he founded and edited the *Sketch*, and was editor of the *Sphere*, 1900–26.

His critical works include *The Brontës and their Circle*, 1896; *Immortal Memories*, 1907; *The Brontës: Life and Letters*, 1908; *George Borrow and his Circle*, 1913, and two books on Napoleon. *C.K.S.*, 1926, is an unfinished autobiography.

In 1896 he married Dora SIGERSON, the Irish poet.

Shorthand, the art of writing, with the aid of certain signs, more quickly and in less space than by means of longhand. The expressions 'shorthand', 'stenography', and 'longhand' became generally used in England during the 17th century. Man's first attempt at writing consisted

Shorthand.

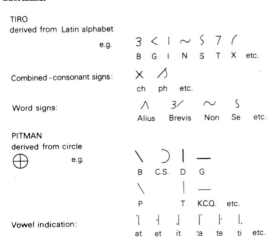

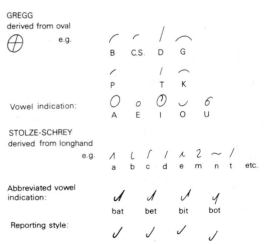

of small sketches. These were eventually simplified into the alphabet. 'M' was derived from the Old Phoenician word *mem* for 'water', depicted by a wavy line. The origin of shorthand is very remote and is bound up with the natural tendency to abbreviate in all systems of writing. In 1883 a marble slab of the 4th century BC was found at the Acropolis, Athens, bearing a syllabic script, which represented consonants and vowels by simplified signs which have a definite shorthand character. CICERO's secretary Tiro devised a shorthand with signs for whole words, roots, prefixes, and suffixes. SENECA was one of the improvers of the system, which was later used in the monasteries, for example by Thomas BECKET and a monk, John of Tilbury. In 1588 Dr Timothy Bright of Cambridge produced the first noteworthy geometrical system consisting of circles, half-circles, and straight lines. Systems derived from the alphabet are called cursive, graphic, or script.

Some systems are light-line; that is to say, the strokes are of even thickness. Others employ some thickening to express certain sounds. Nearly all shorthand systems are phonetic, i.e., a word is spelt as sounded and not as normally written. For instance, F is used for Ph (foto for photo), K for hard C (kat for cat). Consequently many systems have no complete alphabet; but those that do have one allow exact spelling when advisable. British and Irish systems with few exceptions were and are geometrical, and of these the following are the most important inventors:

1. John Willis, born c. 1575, had a complete alphabet, but also used dots, placed near the consonants, as vowels; the dots were placed on a descending scale just as are notes in the internationally accepted Old Notation of music.

2. Thomas Shelton, born 1601, employed signs to express a combination of two or more consonants that often occur together, e.g., NG, SH, TH. He called his system 'tachygraphy'. Pepys used this system in writing his diary.

3. John Byrom, born near Manchester 1692, and author of the Christmas hymn 'Christians, awake'. John and Charles Wesley were among his pupils.

4. Thomas Gurney, whose system, published c. 1750 (based on that of William Mason), was used by Charles Dickens. Gurney's grandson, William Brodie Gurney, became the shorthand writer of both Houses of Parliament in 1806 and the family held that appointment thereafter.

5. Samuel Taylor, born c. 1748, designed and taught the British system which had the greatest influence abroad. The Parisian book-dealer Bertin adapted it to French; Danzer, an Austrian major, to German; and Marti, artist and inventor of the fountain pen, to Spanish.

6. Sir Isaac Pitman, born at Trowbridge 1813, achieved the greatest success, especially in English-speaking countries. Based on the circle and the straight line, his system provides for thickening of certain strokes. Vowels are indicated by dots placed on a descending scale in their alphabetical order. Originally, they were in their musical or natural order. Pitman's is the leading system in Britain today.

7. In France, Emile Duployé (1833–1912), a priest, invented a geometrical system. John Sloan, his friend, adapted this to English under the name of Sloan-Duployan. It is much used in Ireland.

8. Thomas Malone of Dublin (1847–1925), one of Sloan's helpers, and Dr John Gregg (1867–1948), likewise born in Ireland, designed similar geometrical systems, both based on oval slanting to the right. Gregg went to the USA where his system predominates.

9. Reginald Dutton, born in Nottingham 1886, used a system where the letters most often employed are given the most easily written signs.

Cursive systems are found especially on the Continent, east of the Rhine.

1. Franz Gabelsberger, born in Munich 1789, derived his system from longhand. Like Tiro, he sometimes intersected shorthand signs whereby one sign crosses another, producing a third.

2. Heinrich Stolze, born in Berlin 1798, invented and taught an excellent system. He took, for example, a loop of the small longhand M as his shorthand M, used a simplified N like Tiro's, and expressed D, which is related in sound to T, by a downstroke half the size of T. And so, at the same time, the length of the signs generally conforms to their duration of pronunciation. (It requires a little more effort to pronounce, say T than D.) He expressed high-sounding vowels by raising consonants above the line, and low-sounding vowels by lowering consonants beneath it in accordance with musical feeling. Raising and lowering, or increasing the distance between two letters on the line, is called 'positioning' and likewise usually allows for duration of pronunciation. Incidentally, sign-shape and positioning partly imitate the 'feel' and movement of speech.

The cursive systems of Schrey (merged with Stolze's), Arends, formerly much used in countries around the Baltic, and those of Groote (Holland), Melin (Sweden) and Sokolov (Russia) are among those influenced by Gabelsberger and Stolze. In Spain, the recent cursive system of Dalmau of Barcelona should be noted.

Stenotypy (machine shorthand) is a system of recording speech first developed in the late 19th century and now much used in North America for court reporting. Letters (or groups of letters) represent phonetic syllables and words. Keys on the left print initial consonants on the left and keys on the right print final consonants on the right. Four keys below centre print vowels. All the letters of a syllable (or word) are struck at once and printed on a pad, which moves upwards one space after each syllable is struck. The limited keyboard means that missing letters have to be replaced by combinations of other letters, thus PH = initial M, KW = initial Q. The machines are silent and speeds of 250 words per minute have been reached.

Speed is measured in some countries in words; in others, in syllables. Of shorthand libraries, the oldest and largest is the Stenographisches Bibliothek, a department of the Sächsische Landesbibliothek, Landesamt, Dresden. In England, the Carlton Collection at London University can be seen on application.

In the 20th century systems have been developed for rapid note-taking in which ordinary roman characters are used but words are drastically abbreviated. For example, 'Speedwriting', devised by Emma Dearborn (USA) about 1924, 'Dutton Speedwords' and 'Pitman Script'. These systems can be learned more easily than Pitman or Gregg shorthand but are not as rapid in use.

Bibliography: E. H. Butler, *The Story of British Shorthand,*

Shorthorn Breed

1951; J. R. Gregg and others, *Gregg Shorthand Manual Simplified*, 2nd ed. 1955; R. J. G. Dutton, *Dutton Speedwords*, rev. ed. 1971; E. D. Smith, *Pitman Script: Basic Text*, rev. ed. 1974; and various shorthand courses by Pitman Publishing.

Shorthorn Breed, see CATTLE.

Shorthouse, Joseph Henry (1834–1903), English novelist, born in Birmingham, where he became a chemical manufacturer. His first, and by far his best, book, *John Inglesant, A Romance*, 1881, which captured the High Church feeling of the day, and compensated for faulty construction by its charm of style, made him famous. His later novels, *The Little Schoolmaster Mark*, 1883, *Sir Percival*, 1886, *The Countess Eve*, 1888, and others, were much inferior.

Bibliography: S. Shorthouse (Ed.), *Life, Letters, and Literary Remains*, 1905; M. Polak, *The Historical, Philosophical, and Religious Aspects of John Inglesant*, 1934.

Shoshone, North American Indian peoples living in the Basin-Plateau area of Idaho, Utah, and Wyoming. There are many Shoshone peoples, commonly known by the whites as 'Diggers'. They now number about 7600.

Shostakovich, Dimitri (1906–75), Soviet composer, studied at the Petrograd (Leningrad) Conservatoire. He had his first symphony performed before he was 20. One of the finest, most original Soviet composers, he nevertheless came into conflict with the authorities, especially over his realistic and grim opera, *Lady Macbeth of the Mtsensk District*, 1934. This was denounced as 'chaos instead of music' in a *Pravda* article (1936); a revised version (under the title *Katerina Izmaylova*) was staged in 1962. By compromising judiciously he was able to go on expressing his distinct individuality to a great extent. His works include another opera, the satirical *The Nose* (based on Gogol, 1928, performed 1930), three ballets, much incidental and film music, 15 symphonies, chamber and piano music, and songs.

Shoshone. Tendoy, The Climber, chief of the Lemhi Shoshones, photographed in Salmon City, Idaho, about 1883. *(Mansell Collection)*

Shotgun, see FIREARMS.

Shottery, village in Warwickshire, England, 1·5 km west of STRATFORD-UPON-AVON. Here is Anne Hathaway's Cottage, a thatched farmstead, the early home of Anne, wife of the poet Shakespeare. It is the property of Shakespeare's Birthplace Trust and is open to the public.

Shotton, together with Connah's Quay, makes up a straggling industrial settlement of the Alyn and Deeside District of Clwyd, north-east Wales. It contains a major steelworks and other associated industries, and was formerly included in the HAWARDEN rural district which had a population in 1971 of 42,491.

Shotts, town in the MOTHERWELL DISTRICT, Strathclyde Region, Scotland, formerly an important coal-mining town and one of the early iron-making centres of Lanarkshire. The town now has engineering and toy-manufacturing industries. Population 9512.

Shou-hsing, Chinese god of Long Life. He is one of a triad of Gods of Happiness, the other two being the god of Happiness, Fu-hsing, and the god of Salaries, Lu-hsing. Shou-hsing is the best known, for longevity is the greatest blessing in China. His image is well-known to the West for his exceptionally high brow and bald head. He leans on a large stick, or rides a fawn, and holds a peach symbolising immortality. He is the keeper of death records and decides everyone's date of death. His name is identical with the star Canopus, the second brightest star, and it is thought that when it cannot be seen, calamities occur.

Shoulder, region where the arm joins the trunk. The articulation of the humerus (arm-bone) with the scapula or shoulder-blade is an example of a ball-and-socket joint (see JOINTS). The scapula is a flat, triangular bone with a depression called the glenoid cavity into which the head of the humerus fits. The shallowness of the cavity allows great mobility of the shoulder-joint, but renders it liable to dislocation. A certain amount of protection is afforded by the glenoid ligament, which forms a sort of lip about the cavity, increasing its depth, and the acromion, a process of the scapula which forms a protective arch overhanging the shoulder socket.

Shove-halfpenny, a form of the old game of shovel-board. Shovel-board or shove-board is played, especially on ship's deck, by pushing or shoving disks (once pieces of money) with hand or cue along a board marked with transverse lines, the object being to play the disk so that it rests between each set of lines or in one of a number of squares chalked on the deck. It was also called shove-goat, shuffle-board and shove-penny, during the 16th and 17th centuries. A parallelogram was drawn on the middle of a table and divided into numbered compartments. The players then placed in turn a silver groat or smooth halfpenny upon the edge of the table and by a stroke of the palm sent it among the partitions, where it scored according to the number on which it came to rest. In the contemporary game each player in turn strikes five metal discs on a board divided into nine 'beds'. Three discs in a bed fill it, and any disc placed in that bed by the same side afterwards counts for the opponents, except in the case of last point for game. According to some, the game had its origin in Egypt or elsewhere in the Middle East as early as the 11th century and reached England some time after the Crusades.

Shovell, Sir Cloudesley, or Clowdisley (c. 1650–1707), English admiral of the fleet, baptised at Cockthorpe, Norfolk; went to sea in 1664 under the care of Sir Christopher Mynns and later served with Sir John Narborough. In 1692 he played an important part in the defeat of the French at Barfleur, and in 1704 he assisted Sir George Rooke in the storming of Gibraltar. His ship was lost with all hands off the Scilly Isles. In 1967, divers working off the islands began recovering artefacts from the wreck of the *Association*, Sir Cloudesley Shovell's treasure ship.

Shoveller, *Anas clypeata*, species of Anatidae (web-footed birds), order Anseriformes, which has a very wide distribution in all the continents, and is noted for the brilliant coloration of the male. The female is tawny, but the male is dark brown, with bright brown lower surfaces, green head, white neck, black and white wings, greyish bill, and orange feet. The bird is so named because of its bill which is long and spatulate. It is used for filtering out small organisms from sand and mud.

Show Jumping, an equestrian sport dating from the second half of the 19th century when riders, particularly cavalry officers, began to jump their horses competitively over artificial obstacles, as opposed to the natural fences of the hunting field. It quickly became popular and in recent years it has become, largely through television, a major spectator sport.

There are many different types of competition, but basically there are only two kinds of obstacles: uprights, such as walls and gates, and spreads, such as parallel and triple bars. Faults are awarded as follows: a knock down, 4; fall of horse or rider, 8; first refusal, 3; second refusal, 6; third refusal, elimination. Time faults are incurred if the stipulated 'time allowed' is exceeded. When there is equality of faults at the end of a round competitors are usually required to 'jump off'. Time is often used as a final deciding factor.

The Olympic Games include both individual and team events. The courses for such competitions comprise over a dozen fences, including at least two 'combinations'— groups of 2 (a double) or 3 (a treble) obstacles in close succession which test a horse's ability to adjust his stride. The average height of Olympic fences is about 1·50 m, with spreads of up to 2·00 m and a 5·00-m water jump.

Show jumping enjoys world-wide popularity. International competitions at big shows such as Aachen, London, Rome, New York and Dublin are run under the rules of the Fédération Equestre Internationale. National competitions in Britain are run under the rules of the British Show Jumping Association. The most coveted individual trophy outside the Olympics is the King George V Gold Cup which is competed for annually at London's Royal International Horse Show.

There are no hard and fast rules as to what type or size of horse makes the best show jumper. The leading nations since the Second World War have included Germany, Britain, Italy, the USA, France and Canada, who use a wide variety of breeds and types of horse.

See also HORSE TRIALS; RIDING.

Bibliography: P. Smythe, *Show Jumping*, 1967; D. Williams, *Show Jumping—The Great Ones*, 1970; Colonel Sir Mike Ansell, *Riding High*, 1974; P. Macgregor-Morris, *Show Jumping— Officers' Hobby into International Sport*, 1975; M. Clayton and W. Steinkraus (Eds), *The Complete Book of Show Jumping*, 1975.

Show Me State, see MISSOURI.

Showboat, floating theatre found on major American rivers, especially the Mississippi and the Ohio, which travelled downstream, and moored for one or more nights near a town or settlement. The first showboat was built by the English-born actor, William Chapman (1764–1839), and he and his family put on popular dramas and music and dance shows. During the 19th century showboats became extremely elaborate, but because of the Civil War they almost disappeared. They were revived, however, in the 1870s, showing melodramas and vaudeville acts. During the early decades of the 20th century the number of showboats declined, and only a few survive as museum pieces. A film *Showboat* (see MUSICAL COMEDY) was made in 1935, using a genuine showboat built in 1885.

Bibliography: B. Bryant, *Children of Ol' Man River*, 1936; B. L. Burman, *Big River to Cross*, 1938.

Showerproof, see WATERPROOF AND WATER REPELLENCY.

Shrapnel, type of ammunition, consisting, as originally constructed, of a spherical iron shell containing a large number of bullets, sufficient powder being mixed with the bullets to burst the shell when the fuse ignited the charge. It was at first called spherical case-shot, and was designed to attain a longer range than grape-shot or common case-shot. The bursting charge was of just sufficient strength to open the shell and enable the bullets to be propelled forward in a cone-shaped shower covering a large front. The later kind of shrapnel had its bursting charge in a cylinder in the middle of the elongated projectile used with rifled guns. It was invented in 1784 by Henry Shrapnel (1761–1852), an officer of the Royal Artillery, adopted by the British army in 1803, but not used in action until 1808.

Shrapnel ammunition was increasingly used throughout the 19th century, being valued for the 'searching' effect of overhead bursts against entrenched infantry. In the First World War it led to the invention of the 'shrapnel helmet'. Early anti-aircraft guns used shrapnel almost exclusively, but by 1939 the fragmentation effect of high-explosive ammunition had so far improved as almost to render shrapnel obsolete, and though the term was still loosely used, mainly by journalists, to signify splinters from high-explosive shells, the use of shrapnel proper was mainly confined to anti-personnel mines.

Shreveport, city on Red river, in the north-western corner of Louisiana, USA. The city lies close to a rich oil-field also yielding sulphur, and has become the centre of a large refining and chemical industry complex. The agricultural area nearby produces cotton, and there are processing and textile industries. Population 182,064.

Shrew, a small, mouse-like mammal of family Soricidae

in order Insectivora. Five species occur in Britain. The common shrew, *Sorex araneus*, is about 8 cm long, with a long, supple, pointed snout bearing numerous stiff hairs projecting beyond the lower jaw; its fur is reddish-grey above and greyish beneath. It has glands which secrete a strong, unpleasant odour as a means of defence. It feeds on insects, worms, and often on members of its own kind killed after a fight. The pigmy shrew, *S. minutus*, is a rare and beautiful little animal with iridescent fur. The water shrew, *Neomys fodiens*, lives mainly on molluscs, and is essentially aquatic in habit, though only slightly modified for such a life; the feet are fringed with stiff hairs that aid in swimming.

Shrew Mole, *Scalopus aquaticus*, the typical species of a genus of American moles, with a slender and elongated snout, webbed hindtoes, a short tail, and in most features resembling the European mole, *Talpa*. Closely allied is the starnose, *Condylura cristata*, a small brownish-black animal, native to North America, with a similar dentition to that of the European mole, but with a star-like fringe of fleshy tentacles surrounding the nostrils at the tip of the snout.

Shrewsbury, Charles Talbot, 12th Earl and only Duke of (1660–1718), English politician, held various minor positions under Charles II and James II, and was one of those responsible for inviting William of Orange to England. After the accession of William and Mary, he was appointed secretary of state, and in 1694 was made a duke and head of the government. He was charged with negotiating with the Jacobites, and retired from office and went abroad in 1700. Ten years later, however, he returned to public life, and helped to secure the Hanoverian succession.
Bibliography: D. H. Somerville, *The King of Hearts,* 1962.

Shrewsbury, Earl of, see BELLÊME, ROBERT, EARL OF SHREWSBURY.

Shrewsbury, Earldom of. This earldom is one of the oldest in the English peerage. It was first granted to Roger de Montgomery in 1071. His son, Robert Bellême (see BELLÊME, ROBERT, EARL OF SHREWSBURY) or Belesme, forfeited his estates and titles for rebellion in 1102. The title was revived in 1442 for John, 5th Baron Talbot (see SHREWSBURY, JOHN TALBOT, 1ST EARL OF), whose decendants still hold the title, which ranks as the premier earldom in the English peerage. The present holder is the 21st Earl. He was born in 1914 and succeeded his grandfather in 1921. The 12th Earl of Shrewsbury (see SHREWSBURY, CHARLES TALBOT, 12TH EARL AND ONLY DUKE OF) was also the only Duke of Shrewsbury.

Shrewsbury, John Talbot, 1st Earl of (c. 1388–1453), English soldier, a son of the fourth Baron Talbot. He was imprisoned for a time as a suspected Lollard, but was lieutenant of Ireland, 1414–19, and again in 1445. One of the most daring and distinguished warriors of his age, from 1420 onward he fought intermittently in the French wars, defeating the Burgundians at Crotoy (1437), recovering Harfleur (1440), and Bordeaux (1452). He was killed in an attempt to raise the siege of Castillon. He was created earl of Shrewsbury in 1442.

Shrewsbury, borough and county town in SALOP,

England, on the River SEVERN, 244 km north-west of London. Shrewsbury was occupied by a British community, who called it *Pengwern*; later the Saxons renamed the site *Scrobbesbyrig* (alternatively *Salopesberia*, whence *Salop*). Offa made Shrewsbury part of his kingdom of Mercia at the end of the 8th century; in the Saxon and Norman periods it was frequently raided by the Welsh. Early in the 13th century Llewelyn the Great twice captured Shrewsbury; Edward I made it his seat of government (1277–83), and here Dafydd, last Welsh royal prince, was tried and executed (1283). At the battle of Shrewsbury (1403), which took place just outside the modern town, Hotspur was defeated and killed. Charles I set up his headquarters here in 1642, but the town fell to the Parliamentarians in 1645.

The town centre is on a peninsula of rising ground within a horseshoe bend of the Severn; suburbs beyond the river are reached by two principal bridges which from their position on the main east–west highway are known respectively as the English Bridge and the Welsh Bridge. Shrewsbury retains much of its medieval character, particularly in the centre of the town, with its black-and-white timber-frame buildings, which sometimes lean out and almost touch, and its quaint street-names. At the narrowest point of the peninsula stands the castle, founded c. 1070 by Roger de Montgomery; it served as a royal fortress until the time of Charles II, but was rebuilt by Telford. Roger de Montgomery also founded a Benedictine monastery at Shrewsbury in 1083, but at the dissolution the monastic buildings were demolished, together with the east end of the abbey church of SS Peter and Paul, the west end being spared as a parish church. The town was formerly walled, though now only a portion of the original wall can be seen. Substantial remains of a unique 13th-century town house, probably the 'Bennetteshalle' known to have belonged to the abbots of Haughmond, were investigated in 1957, prior to demolition. (The ruins of Haughmond Abbey, founded in 1135 by William Fitz-Alan for Augustinian canons, lie 5 km north-east of the town.) During the time of Elizabeth I many of the timber-framed mansions which survive today were built, for example Ireland's Mansion (1575) and Owen's Mansion (1592). Rowley's House (c. 1595), another 16th-century timber-framed building, houses the museum of Roman antiquities from the city of Viroconium at Wroxeter near Shrewsbury. The beautiful church of St Mary, part Norman and part Early English, possesses some remarkable glass, including a 14th-century Jesse window of English glass, and stained glass from Trier (Trèves).

By the river is Shrewsbury School, originally situated in the town (the 17th-century school buildings are now the borough library and museum). There is also a high school for girls, founded in 1872. Industries include precision engineering, malting, the manufacture of diesel engines, locomotives, machine tools, electrical equipment, and agricultural implements. The main heavy industries are located in the northern suburbs along garden-city lines. The cattle market, one of the busiest in England, has been moved to a new and larger site in the northern suburbs. Shrewsbury, with part of the surrounding rural area, forms a county constituency returning one MP. Population (1971) 56,200.
Bibliography: D. P. H. Wrenn, *Shrewsbury and Shropshire,*

1968; *Some Account of the Ancient and Present State of Shrewsbury* (1808), 1972 ed.

Shrewsbury School, public school for boys, founded by Edward VI in 1552 and described by Camden in 1586 as 'the largest school in all England'. Among its former pupils are Sir Philip Sidney, Fulke Greville, 'The Trimmer' Halifax, Judge Jeffreys, Ambrose Philips, Darwin, Samuel Butler, and Nevil Shute. It owed its advance in the 19th century to three headmasters of unusual ability, Dr Butler, Dr Kennedy, and Dr Moss, who between them spanned 110 years. The School removed to its present site across the Severn in 1882. There are about 600 pupils.

Shrikes, or butcher-birds, as they are sometimes called from the way some of them impale small animals, lizards, frogs and insects on thorns, constitute the passeriform family Laniidae. They have long, sharply clawed feet and hooked beaks. The great grey shrike, *Lanius excubitor*, is a regular winter visitor to Britain. It is about 25 cm long. The lesser grey shrike, *L. minor*, a little smaller, resembles its larger relation and is an occasional visitor. The red-backed shrike, *L. collurio*, was a well-known summer visitor. It has now declined to a handful of breeding pairs in south-east England. The other visiting species is *L. senator*, the woodchat shrike, a black-backed bird about 18 cm long.

Shrimp, *Crangon*, a genus of crustaceans. The common shrimp (*C. vulgaris*) is one of the most abundant crustaceans on British coasts, frequenting shallows in immense shoals, but also visiting deep water. It is greyish-brown dotted with dark brown, which gives it a very close resemblance to sand. It is about 5 cm long, and has a round, articulated carapace with two pairs of antennae; the 'tail' or telson is flat, laminated and hirsute; the eyes are prominent and close together. After boiling the cuticle becomes brown. Large quantities of small PRAWNS, which turn pink on boiling, are sold as shrimps.

Shrinkproofing, see CLOTH SHRINKAGE.

Shriver, Robert Sargent, Jr. (1915–), US politician, born at Westminster, Maryland; educated at Yale University. He married Eunice May Kennedy. Initially a lawyer and journalist, he became general manager of the Chicago Merchandise Mart (1948–60). He played an important rôle in the successful presidential campaign of his brother-in-law John F. KENNEDY (1960). He was director of the Peace Corps (1961–66) and director of the Office of Economic Opportunity (1964-68); he also served as special assistant to President Johnson (1964–68). He became US ambassador to France (1968–70), and was the unsuccessful Democratic vice-presidential candidate in 1972. He remained active in Democratic national politics, and was an announced candidate for the Democratic presidential nomination in 1976.

Shropshire, former English county, since the local government reorganisation of 1974 known as SALOP.

Shropshire Breed, see SHEEP.

Shropshire Light Infantry, The King's, a British regiment, formerly the 53rd and 85th Foot. The 53rd (1st Battalion), raised in 1755, served in Gibraltar, Canada, and in 1793 under the Duke of York in Flanders. Under Wellington it served in the Peninsular War, and went to St Helena, where it gained great praise from Napoleon as a model regiment. It took part in the Sikh war in India (1844) and in the Indian Mutiny. The 85th (2nd Battalion), raised in 1794 by Field Marshal Sir George Nugent, was called 'Bucks Volunteers', having been recruited largely in Buckinghamshire. The regiment was in the Peninsula, and later participated in the battle of Bladensburg and the capture of Washington. Further honours were gained in Afghanistan and South Africa. These regiments linked in 1881 to form the present regiment. During the First World War 13 battalions were raised, which served in France, Flanders, Macedonia, and Palestine. In the Second World War the regiment served in north-western Europe, North Africa, and Italy. The 1st Battalion served in the 28th infantry brigade of the Commonwealth division in Korea. In July 1958 the regiment was amalgamated with three other regiments to form The Light Infantry which is now a part of the Light Division.

Shrove Tuesday, day before Ash Wednesday, and a day of preparation for Lent. The name denotes it as the time for shrift or shriving, i.e. confession before the Easter Communion. The pancakes appropriate to the day are almost the sole widespread survival in England of the merrymakings with which it was once celebrated (see CARNIVAL). In various parts of England a variety of celebrations still occur, e.g. the pancake race at Olney, Buckinghamshire; the tossing of the pancake at Westminster School; the football game at Ashbourne, Derbyshire; the hurling at St Columb, Cornwall, played with a silver-coated ball; and skipping on the foreshore at Scarborough, Yorks. See also MARDI GRAS.

Shrubb, Alfred (1878–1964), British athlete, from 1901 to 1904 winner of ten Amateur Athletic Association Championships at one, four and ten mile distances, and twice International Cross Country Champion. He is said to have discovered his potential as a distance runner aged 20, when racing across Sussex fields to a fire. He upset contemporary theories by running all the year round, training in all weathers. He held world records for every distance from two miles to one hour 'against the clock', all made in 1903 and 1904, most of which stood for over 20 years. He was suspended by the AAA in 1906, but was reinstated 46 years later as a token of his great career. As a professional he ran against horses, and after the 1908 Olympics in a number of marathon races on small indoor tracks.

Shrubs, woody perennials of fairly small size, in which the primary stem usually grows slowly compared with that of a tree, while the lateral branches develop more rapidly and at all levels above the ground without an obvious main trunk. The term is, however, somewhat loosely applied, being largely used in GARDENING. Shrubs are grown in gardens for the ornamental value of their foliage or bloom, or for their massed effect in a 'shrubbery'. This feature of the garden should combine a proportion of both evergreen and deciduous shrubs, so that the whole may be decorative at all seasons. As shrubs usually occupy a position for a lengthy period, careful preparation of the soil by trenching and by adding leaf soil or peat and decayed manure is advisable. Deciduous shrubs are best planted in October or November, and evergreens in either September or May. Most deciduous shrubs bloom on the wood made the previous year, and these should be pruned when they have ceased flowering.

Shu, Egyptian deity personifying the life-giving air, proceeding from Atum, the god of Heliopolis, and father of Geb, the earth, and NUT, the sky. By AKHNATON Shu was assimilated with Ra-Harakht. In the Late Period Shu was also equated with the sun as a youthful ruler, and so with the king.

Shubad, Shub-ad or Pu-abi, Queen of UR, c. 2500 BC. Her stone-built tomb, discovered by Sir Leonard Woolley in 1928, contained about 20 other bodies: her attendants, a harpist, grooms, court-ladies, and guards. The grave-gifts, including elaborate gold and lapis-lazuli head-dresses, a lyre, a harp, and a sledge are now in the British, Iraq, and Philadelphia Museums.

Shudi, Burkat, originally named Burkhardt Tschudi (1702–73), born at Schwanden, Switzerland. He went to England in 1718 and established himself as a harpischord-maker, providing instruments for such famous figures as Handel. He worked with KIRKMAN and BROADWOOD at various times.

Shugborough, a large house 9 km south-east of Stafford, has been the home of the Anson family, later to become Earls of Lichfield, from 1624 until the present day. The present late 17th-century house, with 18th-century alterations, contains plasterwork by Vassali and Joseph Rose. A group of neo-Grecian monuments in the park was built by James 'Athenian' Stuart. Shugborough was acquired by the National Trust, with about 365 ha of land, through the Treasury in 1966.

Shukri, 'Abd al-Rahman, see DIWAN POETS.

Shumen, see KOLAROVGRAD.

Shunt, an electric conductor connected in parallel with a circuit (or part of a circuit) for diverting part of the main current. In shunt motors and generators, the field winding is connected in parallel with the armature. Galvanometers and most other meters depending on the movement of a fine coil of wire can be 'shunted' with a coil which takes the larger part of the current. Multi-range instruments are provided with sets of shunts diverting known fractions of current. See ELECTRICAL MACHINES; ELECTRIC METERS.

Shushtar, town in the province of KHUZESTAN, Iran, on the Karun river at the head of navigation. Below the town is the Shadhirvan dam and bridge, said to have been built by Roman prisoners in the reign of Shapur I. The bridge, called Valerian's bridge, is part of a complex of canals and barrages. Population (1966) 22,000.

Shute, Nevil, pseudonym of Nevil Shute Norway (1899–1960), Australian novelist and engineer, born at Wadebridge, Cornwall, England. Educated at Shrewsbury and Balliol College, Oxford, he served in both world wars and became managing director of an aeroplane factory. Later he settled in Australia, which forms the background of many of his novels, the best-known being *A Town Like Alice*, 1950, and *On the Beach*, 1957. Others are *Marazan*, 1926, *What Happened to the Corbetts*, 1939, *Pastoral*, 1944, *No Highway*, 1948, *The Far Country*, 1952,

Nevil Shute. *(Camera Press)*

In the Wet, 1953, *Slide Rule* (autobiography), 1954, and *Beyond the Black Stump*, 1956.

Shuya, town in the IVANOVO *oblast* of the RSFSR, USSR, 30 km south-east of Ivanovo. It has a big textile industry. Founded in the late 14th century, it had a lively trade with Volga towns and, through Yaroslavl, with England: the first textile manufactures date from 1755. Population (1970) 70,000.

Shwebo, township and town in the Sagaing division of Burma, bounded on the east by the Irrawaddy river, lying 67 km north-west of Mandalay. It was one of Burma's many old capitals. The township is in an agricultural area with extensive irrigation schemes. Township: area 1055 km²; population 166,900.

SI Units, see METROLOGY; PHYSICAL UNITS.

Sialkot, town of Pakistan, some 120 km north of Lahore. It has been identified with the Indo-Greek city of Sagala and is the site of a fort and the mausoleum of the Sikh apostle, Nanak (d. 1538). It is well known for its manufacture of sporting goods and surgical instruments. Population (1972) 212,000.

Siam, see THAILAND.

Siamang, see GIBBON.

Siamese Cat, see CAT.

Siamese Fighting Fish, *Betta splendens*, a beautiful fish noted for its colour and elaborate behavioural displays. One variety, bred in Bankok, is used for sport; two fish are allowed to fight and wagers are made on the outcome. The male builds a nest of bubbles and looks after the eggs. Domesticated fish are available in Britain for tropical fish enthusiasts.

Siamese Twins. The term is usually applied to twins

who are united bodily but possess separate personalities. It includes partners who share various combinations of trunk and limbs. The internal organs may partly or wholly each be a mirror image of the other rather than a replica. It is usually assumed, but not proved, that conjoined twins are monovular (develop from the same ovum) and are due to fission of an embryo. Siamese twins may be joined at the navel, at the sternum (breastbone), at the head or at the pelvis. The place of fusion may include an important internal organ such as the stomach, intestine or liver, or the brains may be joined. The name is derived from Chang and Eng (1811–74), twins fused at the hip, born in Siam. The incidence of conjoined twins is not known exactly, and owing to the difficulties of their birth many are stillborn. Others are so handicapped by their abnormality that they survive only a short time. The treatment is that of surgical division at the place of junction, which is possible only if vital organs are not involved. Cases of successful operation are recorded, and in 1954 Professor Ian Aird in London separated the conjoined twins of Kano. These were joined face to face, at the lower part of the chest and upper abdomen. To a certain extent their livers were joined, but each organ had its own circulation. One of the separated twins died shortly after operation, but the other survived. Other similar cases, varying somewhat in the anatomical details of the fused parts, have been separated since, but not always with survival of both twins. A notable case of survival of both twins after separation occurred in 1959.

Sian, or Ch'angan, capital of SHENSI province on the Lunghai railway in northern China, on the right bank of the Wei Ho, 125 km above its confluence with the Hwang Ho. It was the old imperial capital of the Chou, Ch'in, Han, and T'ang dynasties, and is considered the cradle of Chinese civilisation. Under the T'ang dynasty it was known as Siking and was an international metropolis of over a million people. Its 'Forest of Stone Tablets', containing inscriptions from the 8th century BC until the present, is housed to the south of the city. Since 1950 much industry has been developed in accordance with the Communist government's policy of industrial dispersal. Whole factories have been moved to the city from Shanghai, including textile mills, a sewing-machine factory, and a watch factory. A new university has also been established. Over 300,000 people have been transferred from Shanghai to Sian. Population (1970) 1,900,000.

Sibelius, Jean (christened Johan) (1865–1957), Finnish composer, born at Hämeenlinna (Tavastehus). When 20 he abandoned law studies at Helsinki University to become a pupil of Wegelius at the Conservatoire. He also studied in Berlin under Albert Becker from 1889 to 1890, and in Vienna with Goldmark and Robert Fuchs from 1890 to 1891. At the age of 32 the State made him an annual grant for life, to free him for composition; much later (1930) the State sponsored gramophone recordings of some of his major works. As the composer of nationalistic music banned in Finland by the tsarist police, Sibelius had his house at Järvenpää searched during the Finnish Civil War (February 1918) by Red Guards and, with his family, took refuge in Lappviken Asylum. In the Second World War he lived unmolested at Järvenpää, where he remained until his death.

Sibelius himself said that nature was the book that inspired him. Certainly the brooding vigour of his music evidences exceptional sensitivity to the natural harmonies and rhythms of nature. His reputation has been built and rests mainly upon his seven symphonies, which are triumphs of organic musical thought whose progressive concentration resulted at last in the single-movement seventh symphony. No less mastery is shown in symphonic poems such as *Pohjola's Daughter*, *The Oceanides* and *Tapiola*. Sibelius also wrote much light music and theatre scores, a violin concerto, choral music, chamber music, piano works and some magnificent songs. His country's greatest creative artist, he was perhaps overvalued, or valued for the wrong reasons, in his lifetime; but his achievement is massive and indestructible.

Bibliography: G. Abraham (Ed.), *Sibelius: a Symposium*, 1947; N.-E. Ringbom, *Jean Sibelius: a Master and his Work*, 1954; H. Johnson, *Jean Sibelius*, 1959; R. Layton, *Sibelius*, 1965.

Šibenik, town in Croatia, Yugoslavia. It is on the Dalmatian coast, on the Gulf of Šibenik, near the mouth of the River Krka. An old citadel overlooks the town which has a 15th-century cathedral. It is a naval station, has hydroelectric works, and exports bauxite, wood, wines, and marble. Population 30,000.

Siberia, area comprising the Asiatic part of the USSR, excluding Central Asia. The term is not very specific; physical geographers use it to denote the whole territory between the URALS and the Pacific Ocean, but in economic and political geography, the Urals, the SOVIET FAR EAST, and KAZAKH SSR are usually excluded. The main natural regions of Siberia are the West Siberian lowland between the Ural Mountains and the YENISEI river, the Central Siberian plateau between the Yenisei and LENA, and the mountainous regions of southern Siberia (see ALTAI; SAYAN MOUNTAINS). The climate is almost wholly continental, the degree of continentality increasing from west to east, with very cold winters particularly in the north-east where the 'Cold Pole' lies (see VERKHOYANSK; OIMYAKON). The Pacific coast differs in having a monsoonal climate. Large parts of Siberia are affected by PERMAFROST, especially east of the Yenisei. All but one of the main rivers cross Siberia meridionally, originating in the mountains of the south and flowing into the Arctic Ocean; the exception, the AMUR, flows west to

Siberia. The village of Makovskoe has celebrated the 350th anniversary of its foundation. *(Novosti Press Agency)*

east into the Sea of OKHOTSK. Lakes are numerous in the west, but the largest is BAIKAL in the south-east. Vegetation follows latitudinal zones, with TUNDRA along the Arctic coast, coniferous forest (the most typical Siberian landscape), wooded steppe, and steppe in the extreme south (see ISHIM; TOBOL). Vegetation changes with altitude in the mountains. See ATLAS 28–29.

Siberia is very sparsely populated: the population in 1970 was (economic region, i.e. excluding TYUMEN and KURGAN *oblasti*, YAKUTSK ASSR, the Far East, and North Kazakhstan) about 21,000,000. Over half the population is urban; the chief cities are NOVOSIBIRSK, OMSK, NOVOKUZNETSK, KRASNOYARSK, IRKUTSK, PROKOPYEVSK, BARNAUL, KEMEROVO, and TOMSK. The overwhelming majority of the population are Russian and other settlers from European Russia who have colonised the region since the 16th century. The indigenous population totals about one million, and nowhere does it form a majority. The most numerous are the Turkic-speaking group with KAZAKHS in the south-west (North Kazakhstan), TATARS in the west, YAKUTS in the north-east, and the peoples of the southern mountains, followed by the BURYATS in the south-east who belong to the Mongol group, the Finno-Ugrian group in the north-west (see KHANTY-MANSI NATIONAL OKRUG; EVENKI), and the Tungus group scattered throughout the east.

Siberia has great natural resources—coal (see KUZNETSK BASIN), iron ore (see ALDAN; ANGARA; MINUSINSK BASIN), non-ferrous metals (see ALTAI; NORILSK; TRANSBAIKALIA), gold (see ALDAN; KEMEROVO; TOMSK), and diamonds (see YAKUTSK ASSR); recently, numerous deposits of oil and natural gas have been discovered in the West Siberian plain (see KHANTY-MANSI NATIONAL OKRUG). There are also vast forests (pulp-quality conifers in the north, lumber-quality in the south and the Far East) and fertile black earth soil in the south-west. The water-power potential of its great rivers, where some of the USSR's largest hydro-electric power stations have been built is enormous. The exploitation of these resources started after the Russian conquest of Siberia which began in the 1580s, and was completed in the early 19th century when North Kazakhstan was annexed. At first fur was the main attraction, metallurgy started in the 18th century, and gold-mining in the 19th. Modern industrial development began during the First World War, and has been particularly intensive since the 1930s (see FIVE-YEAR PLANS; URAL-KUZNETSK COMBINE). Agricultural colonisation was greatly facilitated by the building of the TRANS-SIBERIAN RAILWAY, and STOLYPIN's agrarian reforms. Siberia, which never knew serfdom, developed a very prosperous farming community which at the beginning of the century specialised in dairy products and exported considerable quantities to Britain. This was ruined, however, by the First World War, Russian Civil War, and COLLECTIVISATION OF AGRICULTURE. The VIRGIN LAND CAMPAIGN of 1953–56 was aimed at the expansion of grain production in Siberia. In the late 19th and early 20th centuries, a political trend developed known as Siberian Regionalism, which advocated a kind of dominion status for Siberia within Russia. An ephemeral Siberian government was set up in 1918 (see CIVIL WAR, RUSSIAN). It was a place of banishment for criminals and political prisoners from the 18th century and from the 1830s to the mid-1950s was the main region of CORRECTIVE LABOUR CAMPS, some of which may still exist. It was the main area of new industrial development during the Seven-Year Plan (1958–65) and a large-scale expansion of scientific research was facilitated by the establishment in 1956 of the Siberian division of the USSR Academy of Sciences in Novosibirsk, and the subsequent construction of a new academic town (see AKADEMGORODOK).

Bibliography: M. G. Levin and L. P. Potapov (Ed.), *Peoples of Siberia*, 1964; G. St George, *Siberia*, 1970; T. Armstrong, *Russians in the Arctic: Aspects of Soviet Exploration and Exploitation of the Far North, 1937–57*, 1972; P. Dibb, *Siberia and the Pacific: A Study of Economic Development and Trade Prospects*, 1972; G. Markov (trans. by C. Cook), *Siberia*, 1972; H. Portisch (trans. from German by H. Fox and E. Osers), *I Saw Siberia*, 1972.

Siberian Khanate, Tatar state formed in western Siberia after the break-up of the GOLDEN HORDE in the 15th century. It was conquered by COSSACKS under YERMAK in 1582 and annexed to Muscovy.

Siberian Runes, see ORKHON INSCRIPTIONS.

Sibi, town of Pakistan, near the entrance to the Bolan Pass, the route to QUETTA. One of the largest natural gas fields in the world was discovered in the Sibi district in 1952. It has a reserve of 141,585 m^3 which is expected to last over 350 years. Population 20,000.

Sibiu (formerly German *Hermannstadt*), town of central Romania, on the River Cibin, capital of the province of the same name about 217 km north-west of Bucharest. The Roman town of *Cibinium* was sited there, but the present-day town was founded by the Saxons as *Hermannstadt* in the 12th century. In the 15th century Sibiu grew to be a major centre for TRANSYLVANIA, and much later (1703–91 and 1849–65) was capital of the state. Parts of the medieval town, with narrow streets connected by alleys, are still preserved. Remnants of the old fortifications remain, and the Brukenthal museum, founded by the governor of Transylvania (1777–87), contains an art gallery and ethnographical material. There is a 14th- to 15th-century Lutheran church, an Orthodox cathedral (finished in 1906, modelled on the Hagia Sofia in Istanbul), and an 18th-century Roman Catholic cathedral. The town is now a major industrial centre, producing machine tools, textiles machinery, tanning, textiles, paper, and foodstuffs. Population (1975) 149,607.

Sibthorp, John (1758–96), British botanist, born at Oxford; succeeded his father as professor of botany at Oxford (1784), and before his early death made two journeys to Greece. *Flora Oxoniensis*, 1794, was his work, and *Flora Graeca*, 1806–40, was based on his collection of 3000 species.

Sibthorpia, a genus of trailing plants of the Scrophulariaceae (foxglove family), named after Dr Humphrey Sibthorp (1713–97). *S. europaea*, the Cornish moneywort, the only British species, is an elegant little plant with small round notched leaves and minute pale pink and yellow flowers. This and *S. peregrina*, from Madeira, are commonly grown in greenhouses and indoors.

Sibyl, name of certain priestesses of Apollo, who prophesied under his direct inspiration. The most famous, the Cumaean Sibyl (see CUMAE), guided AENEAS to Hades

ULTIMA CVMÆI VENIT IAM
CARMINIS AETAS MAGNVS
AB INTEGRO SAECLORVM
NASCITVR ORDO IAM RE
DIT ET VIRGO REDEVNT
SATVRNIA REGNA IAM
NOVA PROGENIES CÆLO
DEMITTITVR ALTO

Sibyl of Cumae, detail of pavement mosaic with marble inlay by Master Stefano in Siena Cathedral. *(Alinari)*

(Virgil, *Aeneid*, book vi). She sold the Sibylline books to Tarquinius Priscus, offering him first nine books, then six, and finally three for the same price. These were preserved in the Capitol, and might be consulted only by order of the Senate. The Sibylline Books were destroyed in the fire which burned the Capitol in 83 BC. A new collection was assembled, and was preserved until AD 405. During that time additions were made from Jewish and Christian sources.

Bibliography: H. Diels, *The Sibylline Oracles* (trans. M. S. Terry), 1890.

Sicani, people who, with the Elymi (founders of Segesta and Eryx), were the first recorded inhabitants of SICILY. Originally they occupied most of the island, but were gradually driven by the SICULI into the centre and north-west. Among their cities was Hyccara.

Siceli, see SICULI.

Siceliots, see SICILY, *History*.

Sicilian Vespers, see SICILY, *History*.

Sicilies, Kingdom of the Two, see NAPLES, KINGDOM OF; SICILY, *History*.

Sicily (Italian *Sicilia*), the largest and most populous island in the MEDITERRANEAN SEA, situated between latitude 36°38′ and 38°18′N, and between longitude 12°25′ and 15°40′E. It forms an administrative region of ITALY (from which it is divided by the narrow Strait of MESSINA), and consists of nine provinces: Agrigento, Caltanissetta, Catania, Enna, Messina, Palermo, Ragusa, Syracuse, and Trapani. The island has regional autonomy within the constitutional unity of the Italian state; it has wide legislative powers in such matters as industry, com-

merce, agriculture, mining, and fisheries, and may also make laws pertaining to communications, health, education, banking, labour, and food; it may, in addition, levy taxes and raise loans. There are universities at Palermo, CATANIA, and Messina. Area 25,735 km². Population (1975) 4,861,230. The chief city is PALERMO.

Geography. Climate, Resources, and *Industry.* Eighty per cent of Sicily is hilly or mountainous terrain averaging 150 m above sea-level over much of the interior, even higher along the north coast. The great volcano of ETNA is the highest point. The longest plain is that of Catania in the east, but there are also coastal plains in the south and west. The largest rivers are the Simeto, Cantara, Platani, and Salso, none of which is navigable. See ATLAS 22.

The climate is equable, particularly on the northern and eastern coasts. The mean temperature ranges from 8 °C in winter to 27 °C in summer; the Sirocco (see WIND) sometimes sends the temperature up to more than 38 °C, mostly in early summer. Most of the interior is devoted to poor crops of wheat with sheep and goats on the meagre pasture. The coastal plains are fertile and intensively cultivated producing vegetables (artichokes, tomatoes, cabbages), citrus fruits, and wines—the major exports of the island. The lack of industry has not eased the problems of poverty and emigration. The most industrialised areas are around Palermo and SYRACUSE (the wealthiest part of the island).

Minerals found include sulphur, rock-salt, and petroleum. The fisheries (tunny, sardines, coral, and sponges) are important. In ancient times the fertile soil produced wheat in such abundance that the island came under Greek influence, to be held sacred to DEMETER, and was later the chief source of Roman corn supplies before the conquest of Africa. Other valuable products are wine, saffron, honey (see HYBLA), almonds, and fruit.

Bibliography: M. Guido, *Archaeological Guide to Sicily*, 1967; F. M. Guercio, *Sicily: Garden of the Mediterranean*, 1968; D. M. Smith, *Latifundia in Modern Sicilian History*, 1968; J. Galtung, *Development Study of Three Villages in Western Sicily*, 1972; R. King, *Sicily*, 1973; A. Pereira, *Discovering Sicily*, 1974.

History. The earliest recorded inhabitants of Sicily were the Elymi and the SICANI, who were driven by the SICULI into the central and western parts of the island. The first settlers from overseas were the Phoenicians, who estab-

Sicily. Traditional farming methods used on the island. *(Topham/Fotogram)*

Sicily

lished a number of trading stations; but they too were gradually confined to the north-west by the advent of Greek colonists, who came to be called Siceliotae (Siceliots), to distinguish them from the native Siceli.

In 409–408 BC the Carthaginians, who had long been overlords of the few remaining Phoenician settlements, established a firm foothold in Sicily by the destruction of Selinus and Himera. Their capture of Acragas (Agrigento) in 405 made them masters of the western part of the island, and they soon came into conflict with Syracuse and other Greek city-states.

At the end of the First Punic War in 241 BC (see PUNIC WARS) the Carthaginians were obliged to evacuate Sicily, the western half of which was made a Roman province, while the eastern half continued under the rule of Hieron II of Syracuse as an ally of Rome. But after the revolt of Syracuse during the Second Punic War (216 BC) and its capture by M. Claudius Marcellus (211 BC), the whole island was included in the province of Sicily and administered by a praetor. Sicily was the first Roman territory to be cultivated by slave-gangs (see SERVILE WARS). Later history under Roman rule was uneventful. In AD 440 the island was conquered by the GOTHS, who had overrun Italy. In 535 BELISARIUS took possession of it, and annexed it to the Byzantine Empire. A Saracen invasion in 827 followed, and by 878 the Saracens became possessors of the entire island. Sicily flourished during the Muslim rule, recovering from the effects of the decay of the Roman Empire. But the Saracens in turn were driven out by the Normans under Robert and Roger Guiscard, (see GUISCARD, ROBERT), who ruled in the island from 1072 to 1194.

After 1194 the island passed under the domination of the German emperors. At the court of FREDERICK II (crowned at Palermo in 1198), a major political figure and a poet in his own right, a new school of poetry was developed, using the Italian language proper for the first time, and exercising great influence on the formation of Italian language and literature. After Frederick's death in 1250, Hohenstaufen power waned in Sicily and in 1265 Pope Clement IV invested Charles of Anjou with the Sicilian kingdom. Angevin rule ended in 1282 in Sicily with a popular revolution, known, because it broke out at the hour of vespers, as the Sicilian Vespers. Peter III of Aragon was invited to become king of Sicily, and Naples and Sicily were reunited in 1442 when Alfonso V, King of Sicily, won control of Naples. Throughout the second half of the 15th century, the 16th, 17th, and 18th centuries Sicily remained loyal to Spain, the House of Savoy (1713–18), the Austrian Hapsburgs (1718–34), and then to the Spanish Bourbons.

When the French occupied Naples in 1799, the Bourbon court fled to Sicily which was under the protection of the British navy and occupied by British forces. With the encouragement of the British commander, Lord George Bentinck, a form of constitutional assembly was created to satisfy the separatist demands of the Sicilian nobles. On the restoration of the Bourbons in 1815,

Sicily. The town of Cefalù. *(Topham/Fotogram)*

Sicilians were deeply affronted by the abrogation of the island's former separate status in the new Kingdom of the Two Sicilies. The island's political, economic, and administrative subordination to Naples accounted for subsequent discontent and the growth of autonomist aspirations. Sicilians played an active rôle in the struggles for Italian unification, but the principal target of the revolutions on the island in 1820 and 1848—the first in that year of European revolutions—and again in 1860, was Naples and Neapolitan rule.

The risings of 1860 in western Sicily provided GARIBALDI with his opportunity to invade the south, and on 11 May 1860 he landed at Marsala with his Thousand volunteers, rallied the peasants to his cause, and defeated the Bourbon forces. Having established himself as governor (dictator), Garibaldi delayed in handing over control of the island to Piedmont, but annexation to the northern state finally occurred after a favourable plebiscite had been arranged. Sicilians were again bitterly disappointed by the annexation, and this together with the discontent arising from poverty gave Sicily a violent and unhappy history in the late-19th century. Annexation was followed by widespread brigandage, and in 1866 by open revolt. Conditions in Sicily increasingly attracted attention throughout the peninsula, leading to a parliamentary inquiry and an outstanding private inquiry carried out in 1876 by SONNINO and Franchetti, neither of which, however, resulted in legislative measures. The island was quickly integrated into the national political system due to the opportunities for electoral corruption which the island's social structure offered (see MAFIA), and Sicily's tradition of contributing a high number of the nation's politicians was quickly established. This also acted as a further obstacle to reform, and together with rapidly deteriorating economic conditions, stemming principally from the collapse of the island's prime industry, sulphur mining, contributed to the socialist and revolutionary aspects of the risings in 1893–94 known as the Sicilian *fasci*. Sicily was at once placed under martial law, the risings crushed, and the socialist unions destroyed. Thereafter emigration, especially to North America, provided the main solution to the island's problems. The decade before the First World War witnessed a major cultural revival on the island in the work of Giovanni Verga, Luigi Capuana, and the young Pirandello.

Sicily was again the theatre of social discontent after the First World War, but showed little enthusiasm for fascism before Mussolini came to power. Beyond a rigorous attack on the Mafia the Fascist régime did little to tackle the island's problems. The Allied landings in July 1943 and the subsequent liberation of the island caused heavy damage, and were followed by the appearance of a new separatist movement in response to which Sicily was granted a degree of regional autonomy in 1946. Thereafter the Christian Democrats again followed a policy of eliciting support from conservative forces on the island, including the Mafia, which blocked reform and frustrated the activities of the *Cassa del Mezzogiorno*. In 1953 oil was discovered off-shore near Ragusa and Gela, and the establishment of a refining industry gave the economy of eastern Sicily a firmer base. The island's problems continued to be publicised by a group of writers of very high literary merit, including Tomasi di LAMPEDUSA (author of *The Leopard*), Leonardo SCIASCIA, and the sociologist Danilo DOLCI. Crime and emigration continue to provide sad indices of the island's social conditions, and in 1962 a parliamentary inquiry into the Mafia was set up which has still to make its findings public.

See also ITALY, *Modern History*.

Bibliography: M. Finlay, *Ancient Sicily*, 1968; D. Mack Smith, *Medieval Sicily*, 1968; *Modern Sicily*, 1968.

Art and Architecture. Sicily's art has been moulded by the peoples who invaded her. There are substantial Greek ruins at Agrigentum, Selinus and Segesta and the Greek theatre at Syracuse, hewn out of the solid rock, is one of the finest in the world. Greek plays are still performed there occasionally. At Taormina there are a number of Roman remains, including that of a Roman theatre. The mosaics of the Imperial villa at Piazza Armerina are among the finest surviving from the late Roman world. But the most beautiful examples of Sicilian art belong to the era of Norman domination. In buildings to be seen at Palermo, Monreale, Catania and Trapani the Norman style is perfectly blended with styles showing Byzantine and Saracen influence. At Palermo there is a fine 12th-century Norman cathedral, the Palatine Chapel (1129–43), and a short distance away are the cathedral and cloisters of Monreale, built in 1174, possessing some of the most beautiful glass mosaics in the world. Many now unimportant towns have remains of Norman or Saracen castles. Antonello da MESSINA and Pietro Novelli de Monreale were both natives of Sicily. There are some good examples of Italian baroque at Palermo, Noto, Catania and the south-east.

See also ITALIAN ART; ITALIAN ARCHITECTURE.

Sicily. Monreale Cathedral, built in the 12th century by William the Good, shows a mixture of Arabic, Norman and other styles. This watercolour is of the mosaic decoration on the walls of the Deaconry. (*Victoria and Albert Museum, London*)

Sickert, Walter Richard

Bibliography: O. Demus, *The Mosaics of Norman Sicily*, 1950.

Sickert, Walter Richard (1860–1942), painter and etcher, born in Munich, the eldest son of Oswald Adalbert Sickert, a Danish painter; he became a naturalised British subject. After a short period as an actor, Sickert studied art at the Slade School and then under Whistler at Chelsea; he was also a pupil of Degas. It was not until he was over 60 that his merit as an artist was recognised in England, although he was well-known in the rest of Europe, and he had a strong influence on younger British painters. In his work he was an individualist, and in his outlook a rebel against convention. Sickert was one of the first British painters to appreciate the significance of IMPRESSIONISM. In all his paintings he sought light, colour, and tone more than anything else. He is noted for his pictures of Dieppe, Venice, and London streets, for scenes of the theatre and music-hall, and the more intimate aspects of domestic life; all treated with great verve and wit. Among his earlier works are a number of portraits, including the *George Moore* (Tate Gallery), *Charles Bradlaugh at the Bar of the House of Commons* (Manchester), and *Miss Hilda Spring as Imogen Parrot in 'Trelawny of the Wells'*. Elected an ARA in 1924, Sickert was president of the Royal Society of British Artists for a short time after 1928. Other of Sickert's works include *The Camden Town Murder*, 1906, *Sinn Fein*, 1915, *Pulteney Bridge*, 1918; examples are to be found in the British Museum, Tate Gallery, and Bibliothèque Nationale.

Bibliography: Study by L. Browse, 1960; Sir O. Sitwell (Ed.), *A Free House*, 1947 (life, with Sickert's own writings); W. Baron, *Sickert*, 1973.

Sickingen, Franz von (1481–1523), German knight, born at Ebernburg, near Worms. He took part in several wars and feuds and became a popular hero. Having embraced the Reformation, he led the knights of southwest Germany against the ecclesiastical princes. With the help of the Swabian League, the rulers of Trier, Hesse, and the Palatinate marched on his castle near Kaiserlautern, and forced Sickingen, after a short siege in which he was mortally wounded, to capitulate.

Sickle-cell Anaemia, see ANAEMIA.

Sickness and Unemployment Benefit, see NATIONAL INSURANCE.

Siculi, or Siceli, a people who, coming from central Italy in prehistoric times, entered Sicily (which derived its name from them) and drove the SICANI from much of the island. Their main towns were Agyrium, Centuripae, Henna, and three named Hybla. The agricultural pursuits of the Siculi and the volcanic nature of the island led them to worship gods of the underworld.

Siculum Fretum, see MESSINA, STRAIT OF.

Sicyon, ancient Greek city-state in northern Peloponnesus between Corinth and Achaea. Its territory, though small, was fertile, producing olives and fruit; there were also important fisheries. From the end of the 6th century BC until shortly before the mid-4th century, Sicyon was largely dominated by Sparta or Corinth. Before that period it was under a tyranny (665–c. 565). A new succession of tyrants followed one another from 369 until

Walter Sickert. *Ennui*, c. 1913. (*Ashmolean Museum, Oxford*)

251, when Sicyon was freed by ARATUS and made a member of the ACHAEAN LEAGUE. The glory of Sicyon, however, lay in the field of art. The school of painting established by Eupompus included Pamphilus and APELLES; and a long line of sculptors, beginning with Canachus, reached its climax in LYSIPPUS.

Bibliography: C. Skalet, *Ancient Sicyon*, 1928; A. Andrewes, *The Greek Tyrants*, 1956.

Sidcup, see BROMLEY.

Siddhi (attainment), in Hindu philosophy the attainment of supernormal powers. These are generally believed to be acquired through the practice of YOGA, although PATAÑJALI has stated that they can be inherited or obtained through drugs. Eight main categories of siddhis are said to be available to man. They are: (1) shrinking, so that one is able to see into the smallest object; (2) expanding to cosmic dimensions so that the heavens can be observed intimately; (3) levitation, the ability to be weightless; (4) immovableness, the power to be as heavy as a mountain; (5) space travel, to touch the moon; (6) will-power, enabling one to have anything one wants; (7) control over everything; (8) the power to be a god and to create or destroy the world.

Bibliography: Louis Renon, *Religions of Ancient India*, 1953; Ernest Wood, *Yoga*, 1970.

Siddons, Mrs Sarah (1755–1831), British actress, born at Brecon, Wales, the daughter of the provincial actor Roger Kemble and sister of John Philip and Charles KEMBLE. She married the actor, William Siddons, when 18 years of age. Garrick engaged her in 1775 to play at Drury Lane as Portia, but she was not successful in this and other parts. She went into the provinces and did not return to London until 1782, after which she was a favourite with the public until her retirement in 1812. In tragic roles she was at her best, her dignified presence and splendid voice being especially suited to those parts. Among her famous roles were Lady Macbeth, Constance in *King John*, Jane Shore in Rowe's tragedy, and Zara in Congreve's *The Mourning Bride*. There are portraits of her by Gainsborough, Reynolds (*The Tragic Muse*) and many others, and a statue by Chantrey in Westminster Abbey.

Bibliography: Lives by N. Royde-Smith, 1933, and Y. ffrench, 1936; R. Manwell, *Sarah Siddons: Portrait of an Actress*, 1971.

Side-Saddle Flower, see SARRACENIA.

Sideboard, see FURNITURE.

Sidereal Time, see TIME.

Siderite, see IRON ORES.

Siderostat, Heliostat, Coelostat. These three instruments all have a plane mirror which is rotated round a polar axis at such a speed that the reflection of a star or of the Sun can be observed continuously by a fixed telescope. In the case of the first two the mirror is driven at the normal diurnal rate, i.e., one revolution in one

Mrs Siddons as Elvira in *Pizarro* at the Theatre Royal, Drury Lane, 24 May 1799. *(Victoria and Albert Museum, London)*

sidereal day for the siderostat, in one solar day for the heliostat, and the reflected field rotates about the central fixed direction. In the coelostat the mirror is driven at half the appropriate diurnal rate and the reflected field does not rotate, a fact which makes this instrument of greater practical utility. For all three instruments the fixed reflected beam can be diverted into any other desired direction by a second plane mirror.

Sidesmen, properly synodsman, Anglican church officers, elected by the incumbent of a benefice and the parochial church meeting, whose duty it is to assist the churchwardens in their various duties, especially in the conduct of public worship. In early times they took an oath to present all offenders before the ecclesiastical courts.

Sidgwick, Henry (1838–1900), British philosopher, born at Skipton, Yorkshire, and educated at Rugby and Trinity College, Cambridge. He occupied many academic posts. His theory of ethics is presented in his most important book, *Methods of Ethics*, 1874. The basic moral principle (which is not reducible to non-moral terms) rests on our intuitive grasp that we ought to aim at pleasure. However, the pleasure of others is as important as one's own, which gives Sidgwick's account a utilitarian complexion. The problem then is to reconcile the conflicting demands of one's own and other people's pleasure.

Bibliography: W. C. Harvard, *Henry Sidgwick and Later Utilitarian Political Philosophy*, 1959.

Sidi-bel-Abbes, a walled town 75 km by rail south of the city of Oran, Algeria; it occupies a most important strategical position, and trades in wheat, tobacco, and alfalfa. It was the headquarters of the French Foreign Legion until the French withdrawal in 1962 after independence. Population (1966) 105,000.

Sidky, Ismail (1875–1950), Egyptian statesman, educated at the Collège des Frères, Cairo, and at the Khedival Law School. He entered politics, and joined Zaghlul Pasha and the Wafd in the struggle for Egyptian independence. With Zaghlul and others he was deported by the British to Malta, but released at Allenby's insistence in April 1919. Subsequently Sidky broke with Zaghlul, and, with the British, soon became the Wafd's most formidable enemy. In 1924 he was appointed prime minister. He held ruthless sway for three years, but in January 1933 became seriously ill. After his recovery, in 1936, he joined the national delegation which negotiated the Anglo-Egyptian treaty with the British. He opposed every suggestion that Egypt should declare war on the Axis, and in the war period shed the last remnants of his reputation as a British puppet. He was recalled to office again in 1946.

Sidlaw Hills, in TAYSIDE REGION, Scotland, extending from Kinnoul Hill near Perth, in a north-easterly direction, to the North Sea at Red Head in Angus District, and to STONEHAVEN in the east. The highest points are Craigow Hill (455 m) and King's Seat (377 m).

Sidmouth, Henry Addington, Viscount (1757–1844), British politician, born in London and educated at Winchester and Oxford. He entered Parliament in 1784. He was appointed Speaker (1789–1801), and, on the retirement of Pitt in 1801, became prime minister. Addington

Sidmouth

was a weak prime minister and his ministry came to an end in 1804, when he was created Viscount Sidmouth, although he subsequently held lesser posts.

Bibliography: P. Zeigler, *Addington,* 1962.

Sidmouth, seaside resort in Devon, England, on Lyme Bay, at the mouth of the Sid, 20 km south-east of Exeter. Population (1971) 12,076.

Sidney, Algernon (1622–83), English politician, born at Penshurst, Kent, entered the Parliamentary army, and fought against Charles I at Marston Moor, where he was severely wounded. He later held several parliamentary posts, but retired from public life, 1653–59. After the Restoration he went abroad, returning to England in 1677. He was tried for treason for his alleged involvement in the Rye House Plot in November 1683 before Jeffreys, was found guilty and executed. His *Discourses Concerning Government* was published in 1698.

Sidney, Sir Philip (1554–86), English soldier, statesman, and poet, born at Penshurst, Kent, a nephew of the Earl of Leicester. He was educated at Shrewsbury, where he formed a friendship with Fulke GREVILLE, and at Christ Church, Oxford. In Paris in 1572 he took refuge at the English embassy during the massacre of St Bartholomew. After travelling in Europe he returned to England in 1575 and met Penelope Devereux, the 'Stella' of his sonnets. He was entrusted with missions to the Emperor and William the Silent, and in 1578 became known as a poet; SPENSER dedicated the *Shepheardes Calender* to him. In 1581 he lost Elizabeth I's favour for a time, but in 1583 he was knighted and in the same year married Frances Walsingham. He was made governor of Flushing in 1585, became involved in war, and while leading a charge at ZUTPHEN received a fatal wound. The story of his passing a cup of water to a dying soldier with the words 'Thy need is greater than mine' is probably authentic. Liked and admired by all as the pattern of chivalric virtue and nobility, Sidney is the most attractive of the great Elizabethan figures.

His literary work, all written between 1581 and 1584 but not published until after his death, is of the first importance. The *Apologie for Poetrie,* later renamed *Defence of poesy,* is the first example of literary criticism in English. His *Astrophel and Stella* started the vogue in England of the sonnet sequence; and his pastoral medley, *Arcadia,* written for his sister Mary, Countess of PEMBROKE, is the greatest of all the Elizabethan prose romances.

Bibliography: A. Feuillerat (Ed.), *The Complete Works* (4 vols), 1912–26 (*The Prose Works* re-issued, 4 vols, 1962); W. A. Ringler (Ed.), *The Poems,* 1962; F. Greville, *The Life of Sidney,* 1652; E. J. Buxton, *Sir Philip Sidney and the English Renaissance,* 1964; K. O. Myrick, *Sidney as Literary Craftsman,* reissued 1965; N. L. Rudenstine, *Sidney's Poetic Development,* 1967; R. Howell, *Sidney, the shepherd knight,* 1968; R. Kimbrough, *Sidney,* 1970.

Sidney Sussex College, Cambridge, founded in 1596 on the site of a monastery of Grey Friars under the will of Lady Frances Sidney, countess dowager of Sussex. The chapel and library were rebuilt in 1780. The library includes a notable collection of theological works, and possesses a fine collection of mathematical and scientific

Sir Philip Sidney. (*National Portrait Gallery, London*)

works known as the Taylor Library. Among its eminent members have been Oliver Cromwell, Sir Roger L'Estrange, and Thomas Fuller. There are some 300 undergraduate and 60 postgraduate students, and 36 fellows.

Sidon (modern Arabic *Saidā*), chief city of ancient PHOENICIA, on the coast of LEBANON, 40 km south of Beirut. In the earliest times Sidon was the leading city of the Phoenicians, whence the latter's alternative name, 'Sidonians'. It was celebrated for its glass, purple dye, and wines; other activities were ornamental metal-working and the weaving of fabrics. Sidon is first mentioned in the Tel-el-Amarna tablets for the joint resistance of its prince Zimrida and the Amorites to the attempt of Egypt to conquer the seaboard. It later became a satellite of the Assyrian monarchs, one of whom, Esarhaddon, in subduing a revolt, utterly destroyed the city and built a new city on another site, calling it by his own name, *Is-esarhaddon,* but the name Sidon persists to this day. The subsequent history of Sidon follows that of Phoenicia, but it remained throughout an important trading centre. Its later history was scarcely less chequered. It suffered heavily during the Crusades, but once more experienced prosperity under the Druze prince, Fakr ed-Din (1595–1634), and again under Mohammed 'Ali (1832–40). There is abundant evidence of Sidon's ancient greatness: the squared blocks used in building the harbour, the rock-cut reservoirs, the traces of walls, columns, etc. (For biblical references see Genesis x. 19; Matthew xi. 21, 22; and Acts xxvii. 3.) The gardens and orange groves are extensive, and oranges and lemons are an important export. Fishing provides some employment, but the largest employer is the oil refinery, linked by pipeline to Saudi Arabia. The population are mostly Sunni Muslims. Population (1970) 34,000.

Bibliography: N. Jidejian, *Sidon through the Ages,* 1972.

Sidonius Apollinaris (c. AD 431–c. 488), born at Lugdunum (Lyons). He was made a senator by Avitus, Emperor of the West, whose daughter he had married.

After living in retirement for some years he came to Rome on an embassy from the Arverni to Anthemius (467), who raised him to patrician rank. In 469 he returned to Gaul and was appointed bishop of Clermont-Ferrand. After his death he was canonised.

His extant writings include 24 poems and nine books of valuable letters. There is an edition with translation by W. B. Anderson (Loeb Library, 1965).

Siebengebirge (seven hills), range of hills in West Germany, on the right bank of the Rhine some 10 km north of Bonn. The best-known peak is the DRACHENFELS, but Ölberg (464 m) is higher. The area was designated a nature park in 1958.

Siedlce, town of Poland, in Warsaw province, 90 km east of Warsaw. It dates from the 16th century. It is the centre of a cattle-breeding and agricultural district, and manufactures machinery, cement, and glass. Population (1974) 42,512.

Siegbahn, Karl Manne Georg (1886–), Swedish physicist, born at Örebro. He studied at Lund, and was professor at Lund from 1920 to 1923, at Uppsala, 1923–37, and has been professor at Stockholm since 1937. He was director of the Nobel Institute of Physics, 1939–64. He is famous for accurate measurements in connection with X-rays, for which he received the Nobel Prize in 1924. He was elected foreign member of the Royal Society and was awarded the Hughes Medal, 1934, and the Rumford Medal, 1940.

Siege (Old French *sege*, siege; modern *siège*, seat: from *sedere*, to sit), the 'sitting down' of an army or military force before a fortified place for the purpose of taking it either by direct military operations or by starving it into submission. The science of siege warfare reached its most complicated development in the 17th and 18th centuries. Fortresses were first blockaded, so as to cut off all intercourse from without, the besieging force encamping just beyond reach of the enemy's guns. Detached works, if any, had to be captured before the opening of the trenches began. These were laid out in zigzag form, the prolongations of which were directed so as to clear the works of the fronts attacked; and when a direct advance became necessary they were provided with traverses at short intervals, or blind saps were used, i.e. trenches covered in with timber and earth. These, when two or three of such lines of approach were used, were termed parallels, and it was by the aid of these parallels that the batteries, dispersed over a wide area, concentrated their fire upon the revetments. Not only were those parallels formed to approach the walls of the fortress, but the resources in men and ammunition were, by the nature of the case, largely in favour of the besiegers, who were constantly harassed by the artillery of the besieged. Therefore a line of circumvallation or a covering field army was employed. The former mode of protection provided for the surrounding of the place attacked with a high bank of earth, while the latter, by virtue of its greater mobility, was able to meet the relieving army many kilometres from the line of action.

This mode of warfare gave rise to an immense technical literature from the reign of Louis XIV to the end of the 18th century, probably because the warfare of position was suited to the politics of alternating aggression and diplomacy, and also to the tactics of small, professional, non-national armies of the 17th and 18th centuries. The possession of this or that fortress could be used as a counter for diplomatic bargains, and its capture or denial to the enemy was a more satisfying objective for a mercenary general than the destruction of the enemy main force, which might mean an untimely end to the war, the disbanding of the victors, and the unemployment of their commander. Hence the need for an elaborate technique whose fine points would not be intelligible to the monarch or minister who employed such commanders.

When a more realistic and ruthless mode of warfare was adopted by the armies of the French revolutionary period, siege warfare receded to a position of lesser importance, and as the 19th century progressed the power of artillery to destroy rapidly outstripped the skill of military engineers to protect fortresses. Though money and labour were still lavishly expended on fortifications, only two protracted sieges of military importance occurred in that century—at Sevastopol and Paris. On the outbreak of war in 1914 the forts of the French and Belgian frontiers proved as little effective as in 1870, and when the defensive finally asserted itself over the offensive the war in western Europe was stabilised about a system not of fortresses, but of field works.

In the Second World War, while it was demonstrated that under modern conditions no purely military fortress could stand a siege of any length, a large fortified town could do so, and though it could not continue to function as a town could yet maintain a kind of life devoted to purely military ends. Tobruk was twice besieged and so were all the Atlantic and many of the Channel ports of France. Stalingrad was the scene of two successive sieges, first of the Soviet garrison by the Germans and then vice versa. Leningrad sustained the longest siege, and was also the most expensive. Despite the ingenuity of defensive military engineers, the only effective obstacle *in depth* to tanks is a large built-up area, and only the very largest built-up areas can provide cover for the rearward services as well as for the fighting troops of major formations as now organised.

A state of siege provides for the suspension of civil law, which is made subordinate to military law. A fortress, city, or district is thus put under MARTIAL LAW, i.e. under the authority of the military power. This may occur in the case of: (1) the presence of an enemy, as at a siege; (2) the failure of the civil power in cases of domestic insurrection; and (3) the occupation of a conquered district by the military.

Bibliography: R. Hargreaves, *The Enemy at the Gate: a book of famous sieges,* 1946; C. Duffy, *Fire and Stone: The Science of Fortress Warfare 1660–1860,* 1975; I. V. Hogg, *Fortress: A History of Military Defence,* 1975.

Siegen, Ludwig von (1609–c. 1680), German artist, born at Utrecht. He became a soldier in the service of the landgrave of Hesse. In 1642 he produced the first reputed MEZZOTINT, a portrait of the landgrave's mother. In 1654 he showed his method to Prince Rupert, who introduced it into England (with prints dated 1657–59).

Siegen, city in NORTH RHINE-WESTPHALIA, West Germany, on the Sieg, 93 km south-east of Düsseldorf. It was once a seat of the princes of Nassau-Oranien. There is a 13th-century hexagonal church, and a castle (now a museum). It was the centre of an iron-mining district, but now has office equipment and computer manufacturers. RUBENS was born here. Population 58,500.

Siegfried, André (1875–1959), French writer and economist, born at Le Havre. His works include *Tableau politique de la France de l'Ouest sous la Troisième République*, 1913; *L'Angleterre d'aujourd'hui*, 1924; *Les États-Unis d'aujourd'hui*, 1927; *La Crise britannique au XXe siècle*, 1931; *Tableau des partis en France*, 1931; *La Crise de l'Europe*, 1935; *Le Canada, puissance internationale*, 1937; *Mon père et son temps*, 1946; *L'âme des peuples*, 1949; *La Géographie politique des cinq continents*, 1953; and *Les Voies d'Israël*, 1958.

Siegfried, see NIBELUNGS.

Siegfried Line, name given by the Germans to the line of defence taken up by their armies in France in September 1918. The name was also given by the British to the WEST WALL in the Second World War (see WESTERN FRONT IN THE SECOND WORLD WAR).

Siem Reap, town and province in north-west CAMBODIA, situated just to the north of TONLE SAP. To the north of the town lie the 105 km² ruins of ANGKOR Thom and Wat and this has greatly contributed to its importance. Population (1962) 10,232.

Siemens, Ernst Werner von (1816–92), German electrical engineer, born at Lenthe, Hanover. He became superintendent of the artillery workshops in Berlin (1844), and laid the first telegraph line in Germany between Berlin and Frankfurt am Main (1848). He founded the firm of Siemens & Halske, and was associated with the London firm of Siemens Brothers. He founded the Physikalisch-Technische Reichsanstalt at Charlottenburg (1886), and published many scientific and technical articles.

Siemens, Sir William (Karl Wilhelm) (1823–83), British electrical engineer, brother of Ernst Werner von Siemens, born at Lenthe, Hanover. He settled in England in 1844 and was naturalised in 1859. His inventions were chiefly concerned with the application of heat and in the field of metallurgy, and, as manager of the firm of Siemens Brothers, he constructed the Portrush electric tramway (1883) and many overland and submarine telegraphs. He was elected Fellow of the Royal Society in 1862, and president of the British Association in 1882.

Siemens-Martin Process, see IRON AND STEEL, *Production of Steel*.

Siemianowice Śląskie (German *Laurahütte*), town of Poland, in Katowice province, 5 km north of Katowice. It has coal-mines and iron works. Population 68,000.

Siena, province of Italy, in south TUSCANY. Area 3820 km². Population (1974) 257,000.

Siena (ancient *Saena Julia*), Italian city and capital of the above province, some 50 km south of Florence. It is built on three hills, 305 m above sea-level. The city was originally Etruscan (see ETRURIA) and became a Roman colony in the time of Augustus. In the 12th century it became a free city adhering to the Ghibelline faction (see GUELPHS AND GHIBELLINES). In 1399 it came into the hands of the VISCONTI. It later recovered its freedom, but was subjected by Pandolfo Petrucci in 1487. In 1555 the city was taken by the army of the Emperor Charles V, and four years later was annexed to the Duchy of TUSCANY. It has many splendid buildings and a genuine medieval atmosphere with its narrow winding streets and the famous 'Palio' held every August; the 17 divisions of the city (*contrade*) parade in medieval costume and compete in a horse race round the city's streets. The magnificent 12th–14th-century archiepiscopal cathedral contains a pulpit by Niccolò PISANO, and sculptures by MICHELANGELO, DONATELLO, and BERNINI. There is also a huge unfinished church called the 'new cathedral', on which work was stopped by a plague of 1348. The famous Gothic brick *Palazzo Pubblico* has a tower 100 m high, and contains many notable paintings. There are numerous palaces and mansions, interesting fountains, a university (1247), and a gallery containing a collection of paintings of the Sienese School (see ITALIAN ART). The medieval banking traditions of Siena survive to the present day in the Monte dei Paschi (founded 1625). Population (1974) 56,500.

Sienkiewicz, Henryk (1846–1916), Polish novelist, born at Wola Okrzejska, author of *Quo vadis?*, 1896 (English translation 1898), a novel about Nero's Rome, popularised by several film versions. He received the Nobel Prize for literature in 1905. Probably the best-known Polish writer abroad, and the most translated (often badly), he began his career as a journalist, literary critic, and short-story writer. In 1876–78 he visited the United States where he travelled and witnessed the Polish actress MODJESKA's first successes. He was constantly on the move and most of his writing was done outside Poland.

Starting in 1883, when it first began as a serial, he achieved unparalleled success and lasting popularity with his war trilogy, set in 17th-century Poland: *Ogniem i mieczem* (*With Fire and Sword*, 1891–93), *Potop*, 1886 (*The Deluge*, 1891), *Pan Wołodyjowski*, 1888 (*Pan Michael*, 1893). The work blends a colourful plot, vivid narrative, memorable characters, adventure, and romance. His other prominent novels include: *Krzyżacy*, 1900 (*The Teutonic Knights*, 1943); a book for children *W pustyni i puszczy*, 1911 (*In Desert and Wilderness*, 1945); and *Bez dogmatu*, 1891 (*Without Dogma*, 1893), a novel in the form of a diary. His letters were translated as *Portrait of America*, 1959.

Bibliography: M. M. Gardener (Ed.), *Tales from Sienkiewicz*, 1946; M. Kosko, *Un 'best-seller' 1900, Quo Vadis?*, 1960; W. Lednicki, *Henryk Sienkiewicz*, 1960.

Sienna, pigment consisting of hydrated ferric oxide, manganese dioxide, and earthy matter. It derives its name from Siena in Italy, where an earth is found containing the oxides of iron and manganese. There are two varieties, 'raw' and 'burnt', the former being dull brown in colour and the latter formed, as its name implies, by heating the 'raw' sienna when it deepens to a reddish brown. Both varieties are used as PIGMENTS.

Sierra, Gregorio Martinez (1881–1947), Spanish playwright and novelist, born in Madrid. His first real success was *Canción de Cuna*, produced in 1911. Among his other plays are farcical comedies, such as *Sueño de una noche de Agosto*, *Madame Pepita*, and carefully fashioned studies of character reflecting the

Sierra Leone. Freetown. *(Camera Press/S. Harrison)*

worth of homely virtues, such as *El Reiño de Dios*, 1916, and *Navidad*, 1916. Sierra lived in voluntary exile in South America during the civil war, only returning to Spain in the year of his death. Perhaps his most important contribution to the Spanish stage was, however, his managership of the Teatro Eslava between 1917 and 1925, when he introduced contemporary foreign plays to the Spanish public, as well as staging LORCA's first play.

Bibliography: J. G. Underhill, *The Cradle Song and Other Plays*, 1922; F. W. Chandler, *Modern Continental Playwrights*, 1931.

Sierra de Guadarrama, range of mountains in Spain, separating the provinces of Madrid and Segovia, and lying between the Duero and the Tajo rivers. The Pico de Peñalara reaches 2405 m.

Sierra Leone, Republic of, formerly a British colony and protectorate on the coast of WEST AFRICA, lying between 6°55′ and 10°N latitude. The sea coast, 336 km in length, extends from the border of the Republic of GUINEA to the Mano river, on the border with LIBERIA. It is bounded on the west by the Atlantic, north and east by the Republic of Guinea, and south by Liberia. The former colony, comprising the Sierra Leone peninsula, Tasso, Banana, and York Island, and the township of Bonthe on Sherbro Island has been renamed West Area; the remainder, representing the former protectorate, is divided into the east, north, and south provinces, known collectively as the 'provinces'. Area 71,488 km².

Geography. Relief. Sierra Leone is a country of varied relief. In the north-east lie two granite massifs, the Loma Mountains and the Tîngi Hills rising above 1800 m; Loma Mansa, the highest peak in West Africa, rises to 1948 m. Southwards and westwards from these mountains extends the main plateau of Sierra Leone; formed over the gneisses and schists of the Pre-Cambrian basement, it seldom rises much above 500 m. Along its western edge the Sula Mountains form a range of hills rising to 700 m, and on their eastern side the land declines below 100 m towards a broad lowland extending from the north-west to the south-east of the country. The major rivers, such as the

Sierra Leone, Republic of

Mano, Bafi, Seli, and Rokel, drain the hills, forming wide floodplains across this zone, much of which is inundated during the wet season and is known as the 'bolilands'. Beyond these lowlands, the rivers have formed extensive deltas that have been partly drowned to form ria-like estuaries fringed by islands and lagoons. The former importance of the rivers and lagoons for trade and transport led to the rise of early ports (such as BONTHE, on Sherbro Island), which today have only little economic significance. The Freetown peninsula, in marked contrast with the rest of the coastal zone of Sierra Leone and most of West Africa, forms an area of highland, rising to nearly 1000 m. The hills are formed of a dark intrusive rock and remain forested over large areas. They induce very high rainfall over the peninsula and in FREETOWN, which has developed on the lower slopes, thus taking advantage of the best natural deep-water harbour in West Africa. See ATLAS 40.

Climate. Sierra Leone lies in one of the wettest parts of West Africa, but is far enough north of the equator to experience a severe dry season from November to April. Freetown receives nearly 3500 mm of rain annually, with more than 750 mm in the wettest months of July, August, and September. Inland, rainfall declines from 2500 mm to a little below 2000 mm in the drier north and east, although high rainfall occurs over all the major hill masses, feeding the many large rivers. Temperatures are characteristic of the West African tropics with the mean around 30 °C and daytime maxima varying from 27 °C during the rainy months of July and August to 36 °C in the hottest month (April). Night minima vary from 23 °C during much of the year to less than 17 °C during the dry season when the dusty 'Harmattan' wind blows from the Sahara.

Vegetation and Soils. Most of Sierra Leone lies in the rain forest zone, but the intensity of the dry season leads to seasonal leaf shedding which has encouraged clearance of the forest by fire over large areas. Much of the country is now covered by a degraded secondary bush, but forest survives on the lower hills and mountains and is widespread in the south-east of the country. Grasslands occur in the extensive swamps of the 'Bolilands', and in swampy depressions elsewhere.

Soils in Sierra Leone tend to be severely leached of plant nutrients by the heavy rainfall, and few areas have a high inherent fertility. The better soils tend to occur in the alluvial plains and deltas, and the drier north is more favoured than the centre of the country. Swamp soils are capable of supporting paddy rice cultivation, but swamp management is not traditional and is being extended only gradually.

Population. The total population in 1974 was 3,002,426. Except for Freetown, the capital, the development of large towns has only occurred since the Second World War. Provincial capitals are Makeni (north), Bo (south), and Kenema (east). The average population density is one of the highest in Africa; it is at its densest in areas of diamond mining and around the capital.

Bibliography: K. G. Dalton, *Geography of Sierra Leone*, 1965; J. I. Clarke, *Sierra Leone in Maps*, 1970; G. B. Collier, *Sierra Leone*, 1970; R. J. Harrison Church, *West Africa*, 1974.

Economy. Agriculture. Agriculture is the main economic activity with most of the population producing their own food on small farms. Rice is the major staple

Sierra Leone, Republic of

crop, with traditional upland rice increasingly supplemented by swamp rice. Cassava, sweet potatoes, maize, and sorghum are also widely grown, primarily for subsistence. Oil-palms are also important in most areas, and once provided the main exports, while cocoa and coffee provide sources of cash in the south-east. Cattle are largely confined to the north while some fishing is undertaken along the coast.

Industry. Mining now provides the chief exports, with diamonds of paramount importance. Large-scale mining began in 1935 at Yengema; small-scale alluvial mining was encouraged elsewhere from 1956, and illegal mining on the company lease forms a third substantial element. Another company has mined iron ore at Marampa since 1933, and bauxite mining in the Mokanji Hills began in 1963. Manufacturing is very poorly developed and is largely confined to a few consumer goods industries in Freetown. Electricity is produced from imported oil, but a hydro-electric scheme at Bumbuna is planned.

Communications. Internal communications depended at first on bush paths and small north–south flowing rivers, and then on the railway built eastwards from Freetown, but now roads are all important and the railway has been closed (the iron-ore line remains open). External links depend mainly on ships using the excellent Freetown harbour, and the international airport at Lungi across the harbour from Freetown.

Trade. The balance of external trade normally shows a deficit, and dependence on diamonds for over 60 per cent of export earnings is a source of insecurity. Foodstuffs form about 20 per cent of imports and inflation is a growing problem. Britain is the main destination for diamonds and other exports, but its share in imports has fallen to 25 per cent. The Mano River Union aims at eventual economic union between Sierra Leone and Liberia.

Finance. The currency unit is the *leone*, tied to the £ sterling at 2 *leone* to £1.

Government. *Constitution.* Sierra Leone acquired its first constitution in 1961, but the opposition of the military created political uncertainty in the 1960s. In 1968 there was a return to civilian rule, consolidated by the introduction of a republican constitution in April 1971; one which created the post of Executive President, the

Sierra Leone. A piassava crop being brought in for grading. *(Camera Press/S. Harrison)*

first to be appointed being the former Prime Minister, Dr Siaka STEVENS. Although the 1961 constitution had stipulated that a general election was required to approve any fundamental constitutional change, the government considered the 1967 election to have provided the requisite approval. In August 1975, parliament approved in principle a one-party constitution, provided for under the 1971 constitution, subject to popular approval in a referendum. The Executive President is elected for five years by the House of Representatives, and serves a maximum of two terms, sharing executive power with a Cabinet headed by a Prime Minister who, since 1975, no longer doubles as vice-president. The legislature is represented by a House of Representatives, dominated by the one official party, the All People's Congress (APC). The constitution safeguards the office of Paramount Chief.

Legislature. The House of Representatives has a total of 85 members elected by universal suffrage, as well as 12 Paramount Chiefs, who have no party affiliations, and three members nominated by the President. In the election of May 1977 the APC won 62 seats and the opposition party, the Sierra Leone People's Party (SLPP), won 15. Elections for the remaining eight seats, which were in the Bo district, were postponed because of violence on polling day.

The country is in two distinct parts: the western area, which is the former crown colony of Sierra Leone and contains the capital, Freetown, and on the other side, the three provinces, the former protectorate of Sierra Leone. Each of the three provinces is under the political control of a resident minister, and the provinces are sub-divided into a total of twelve districts, with each district being administered by a district officer. Each of the districts is further sub-divided into over 140 chiefdoms, governed by Paramount Chiefs and chiefdom councillors, although district councils may over-ride the decisions of the chiefs.

Justice. The judicial code of Sierra Leone is based largely on English 19th-century statutes and common law and equity, although native courts do operate according to native law and custom in matters between natives and are outside the jurisdiction of other courts. The formal structure is headed by a supreme court, below this a court of appeal for all subordinate courts (the high courts and the magistrates' courts); the latter being limited in criminal cases to preliminary investigations.

Armed Forces. In 1976 Sierra Leone had an army of 2675, a navy of 100, and an air force of 25. The strength of the police force was about 4000 men.

Education. In the mid-1960s, literacy (of the over 10s) was only 7·7 per cent of the population. In 1973 there were 182,000 pupils in primary education, 45,000 in secondary, 1000 in vocational, 1000 student teachers, and 2000 in higher education. The University of Sierra Leone was formed from Fourah Bay College and Njala University College.

Welfare. There is no comprehensive state welfare scheme, although the Division of Social Welfare is involved in community welfare to the extent of providing youth clubs and maternity centres. Government provision of health facilities is to be supplemented by an agreement with China to provide medical personnel. In 1973 there were 112 doctors, 14 dentists, and 630 nurses. Every interior district has at least one hospital, and in 1972 there was a total of 28 hospitals, with specialist facilities located in Freetown and Bo. The total number of hospital beds then numbered 2837. There is a growing awareness of the need to develop preventative medicine, and the public health section and the endemic diseases control unit are involved in the fight against such diseases as leprosy and sleeping sickness.

Religion. Although there are Christian and Muslim minorities, the overwhelming majority of the people follow animist beliefs.

Language. The official language is English, but the indigenous tribal languages of Mende and Temne are widespread.

National Flag. Three horizontal bands of green, white, and blue.

Bibliography: M. Kilson, *Sierra Leone: Political Change in a West African State*, 1967; J. R. Cartwright, *Politics of Sierra Leone 1947–67*, 1971.

History. Discovered in 1462 by the Portuguese navigator, Pedro de Sintra, the colony of Sierra Leone originated in the sale and cession in 1788 of a piece of land by 'King' Nembana and his subordinate chiefs to Capt. John Taylor of HM brig *Miro* on behalf of the 'free community of settlers, lately arrived from England'; this piece of land was called Frenchman's Bay, later changed to St George's Bay. The main purpose of the colony in its inception was to secure a home in Africa for freed slaves and homeless Africans from England. The enterprise of 1788 proved a failure, and in 1791 a new settlement was formed, the promoters being Alexander Falconbridge, Sir R. Carr Glynn, Granville Sharp, and William Wilberforce. These pioneers obtained a charter of incorporation as the Sierra Leone Company, but the company in 1807 transferred its rights to the Crown. The territory received additions from time to time by various concessions from the native chiefs. It became a Crown Colony in 1808. The Protectorate, forming the hinterland of the colony, was formed in 1896. In 1898, when the first attempts were made to collect house-tax, many chiefs in the Protectorate came out in revolt, and about 1000 British subjects, both African and European, were killed, together with some American missionaries.

Sierra Leone's first constitution, introduced in 1951, was a unitary constitution, and removed the political component from the privileged status of the Creoles of the Colony, by giving power to the majority, i.e. the peoples of the Protectorate. In 1958 a new constitution prepared the way for independence. This was established on 27 April 1961, when Sierra Leone became an independent member of the Commonwealth. When its first premier, Sir Milton MARGAI, died in 1964 he was succeeded by his brother, Sir Albert Margai, who, in January 1966, played a leading part in the Commonwealth prime ministers' conference held in Lagos. Although the government party, the Sierra Leone People's party (SLPP), which had won power in 1951, was a Protectorate-based and, therefore, more popular party, it did depend very much on the support of the traditional chiefs. During the 1960s resentment against these allegedly parochial interests began to find a forum in the All People's Congress (APC), led by Dr Siaka STEVENS, and the opposition was given strength by fears that Sir Albert Margai prepared to create a one-party state. The popular base of approval had begun to shift away from the APC and towards the SLPP.

In March 1967 there was a great deal of dispute over alleged malpractices in the general elections which saw the All People's Congress (APC) gain power, with Dr Siaka Stevens as prime minister, the upshot being that the army officers were able to gain control of the country and establish the National Reformation Council, under the chairmanship of Col. A. T. Juxton-Smith. But in April 1968 a second, countervailing army revolt, largely of the lower ranks, opened the way for a return to civilian rule, and Dr Siaka Stevens was able to take office.

Political instability became more acute and government intransigence more apparent when the Sierra Leone People's party (SLPP) was joined in opposition by a new opposition party, the United Democratic party (UDP), which included two former government ministers. In 1970 the UDP was banned, and most of its leaders arrested.

The government claimed to have forestalled an attempted coup by arresting three army officers in 1970; and in March 1971 the army commander, Brig. Bangura led two assassination attempts on Dr Stevens's life, prompting the Premier to sign a defence agreement with President Sékou Touré of Guinea. The latter was able to reciprocate by sending Guinean troops to assist the loyal sections of the Sierra Leone army in protecting Dr Stevens and restoring law and order.

Guinean troops remained in Sierra Leone for another two years, as a safeguard against possible opposition to the introduction of the republican constitution, introduced in Parliament in April 1971, under which Dr Stevens became executive president, and the post of prime minister was held by Sorie I. Koroma. The victory of the All People's Congress was consolidated in May 1973, when the Sierra Leone People's party was prevented from presenting candidates in the general election. But the APC has been cautious in victory, and has not sought to formalise the de facto position of a one-party state. Fears of opposition were seemingly justified when, in July 1974, there was an abortive coup while President Stevens was out of the country. The upshot was that 15 civilians and 7 soldiers were later executed for treason. In August 1975 the House of Representatives unanimously approved a motion calling for a one-party system of government and the introduction of a new republican constitution.

Bibliography: C. Fyfe, *A History of Sierra Leone*, 1962; A. Porter, *Creoldom*, 1963; C. Fyfe, *Sierra Leone Inheritance*, 1964; R. G. Saylor, *The Economic System of Sierra Leone*, 1967; C. Fyfe and E. Jones, *Freetown—A Symposium*, 1968; J. Peterson, *Province of Freedom*, 1969.

Sierra Madre, name of the three principal mountain ranges of MEXICO. The Sierra Madre Occidental runs along the west coast to join the Sierra Madre Oriental, which runs along the east coast, at about the 19th parallel in the centre of Mexico. From about this junction the mountain range continues southwards under the name of Sierra Madre del Sur to the Isthmus of Tehuantepec. The Sierra Madre Occidental is the most formidable range of the three, being about 1280 km long, 320 km wide, with elevations mostly over 1800 m rising to over 3000 m.

Sierra Maestra, mountain range running along the extreme south-east coast of CUBA, extending from Cape Cruz to Guantánamo; the Pico Turquino (1974 m) is the highest point in Cuba.

Sierra Morena, mountain range in southern Spain,

extending east to west between the GUADIANA and GUADALQUIVIR rivers.

Sierra Nevada, mountain range in southern Spain, mainly in the province of GRENADA, but also extending into ALMERIA. Mulhacén (3477 m), its highest peak, is also the highest mountain in Europe outside the ALPS and the CAUCASUS. The snowline is at 3000 m. Winter sports facilities have been developed in recent years.

Sierra Nevada, mountain range in the USA, lying mainly in California, and forming the southern part of the chain of the mountains of the Pacific. The northern section of this chain is formed by the CASCADE RANGE, and the dividing point in the chain is conventionally taken as being Lassen Peak (3186 m) in northern California. The Sierra Nevada forms the eastern wall of the Central Valley of California. It has a general ridge line at over 2500 m, above which protrude individual peaks, the highest of them being Mount Whitney (4418 m). There are no easy passes; the Donner Pass, by which the main road and rail routes cross, is at 2150 m, and the mountains formed a formidable last barrier to the early overland travellers to California. The western side of the Sierra is scored by some of America's deepest valleys, partially ice-carved, and these include the Yosemite Valley and King's Canyon, both of them now national parks. The eastern side is faulted and very steep, and provides one of the swiftest natural transitions in North America, from snow-covered peak, through dense forest, to scrub and down to desert, the lowest point on the continent, DEATH VALLEY being little more than 100 km east of Mount Whitney. On the western slopes are groves of SEQUOIAS, the famous California giant redwoods.

Sierra Nevada de Mérida, 480-km long mountain range of western VENEZUELA, a north-eastern extension of the eastern Cordillera, dividing Zamora and Mérida provinces. Concha and Columna, both 4800 m high, are the main peaks.

Sierra Nevada de Santa Marta, mountain group in the north-east of the department of Magdalena, Colombia, near the Caribbean Sea, rising to over 5400 m.

Sieve of Eratosthenes, a routine for compiling a table of PRIME NUMBERS devised by the Greek mathematician ERATOSTHENES. In order to determine all prime numbers less than a given number N, all numbers less than N (except 1) are written down. The first prime is 2, so cross out 2 and every second number, starting with $2^2 = 4$. The next prime is 3, so cross out every third number (if not deleted already), starting with $3^2 = 9$. All the numbers left less than 9 will then be prime numbers; they are 5 and 7. Cross out every fifth number, starting with $5^2 = 25$, and every seventh number, starting with $7^2 = 49$. All numbers left less than 49 will then be prime. Continue the process as long as necessary (that is, as far as the last prime before $\sqrt{N}$).

Sieyès, Emmanuel Joseph, Comte (1748–1836), French cleric and politician, born at Fréjus. He was one of the chief theorists of the revolutionary and Napoleonic eras. He became vicar-general and chancellor of the diocese of Chartres. His famous pamphlet, *What is the Third Estate?*, 1788, secured for him a place as one of the deputies of Paris to the States-General. He produced a plan for a new French constitution in 1789. Later he voted for the death of Louis XVI. He was, with Napoleon, one of the three consuls, but exercised little influence on practical politics. He was exiled as a regicide until 1830.

Sigebert, Saint (d. 635), King of East Anglia. Baptised in France, he introduced Christianity into his kingdom, with the help of SS Felix and Fursey. He entered a monastery, which he was compelled to leave to lead his subjects against the pagan King Penda of Mercia, in which conflict Sigebert was killed. His feast is on 27 September.

Sigerson, Dora (1866–1918), Irish poet, born in Dublin. In 1896 she married Clement SHORTER and settled in London, but at the Irish Easter Rising of 1916 she worked on behalf of the accused rebels. Her *Collected Poems*, 1907, were followed by *New Poems*, 1912, *Love of Ireland*, 1916, *The Sad Years*, 1918, and *Sixteen Dead Men and Other Ballads of Easter Week*, 1919.

Sigfrid, Saint (d. c. 1045), English priest and monk, probably of Glastonbury. He visited Norway at the invitation of its king, and achieved great success as a missionary. Among his converts was Olaf, King of Sweden. His feast is on 15 February.

Sighişoara (German *Schässburg*; Hungarian *Segesvár*), town in Transylvania, Romania, 72 km north of Sibiu. It was founded by German colonists in the 13th century. The Russians defeated the Hungarians there in 1849. Population 30,000.

Sight, see BLINDNESS; COLOUR-BLINDNESS; EYE; OPTICS; REFRACTION, ERRORS OF; VISION.

Sight, Bill of, see BILL OF SIGHT.

Sight, Short, see MYOPIA; REFRACTION, ERRORS OF.

Sighthound, see GREYHOUND.

Sights for Shooting. RIFLE sights are derived from those used on the cross-bow. The first known rifle (c. 1495) had an aperture rearsight, by which aim was taken through a hole in line with the eye. This particular sight was fixed but other examples made during the same period had elaborate arrangements for both elevation and lateral movement. The aperture was generally 5–15 cm away from the eye when firing. Over the next 300 years the open sight almost completely replaced the 'peep' (or aperture). This sight consisted of a notch in a horizontal bar 38–46 cm from the eye when firing. The foresights in both cases were of the blade, bead, or barleycorn style. A fixed sight was used for both sporting and military rifles until the mid-19th century. The shooter took a 'fine', 'normal', or 'full' sight for short, medium, or long ranges, respectively. The adjustable military sights following this were the 'tangent', in which a bar was slid vertically upwards or downwards in a frame, and so called because the distances are marked so that the range could be varied. During the same period, target shooters rediscovered the advantages of the 'peep' and also found that the 'ring' (or hollow bead) foresight gave excellent results on bulls eye aiming marks, and these are in use today together with blade (or 'post') foresights. More sophisticated rearsights are graduated in minutes of angle which make them universally applicable. For sporting rifles, variations of the open sight, the v, the u, the bar, the express, the buckhorn and others have been widely used, but are not often used now, except for shooting dangerous game at short range. At present, most military rifles have aperture rearsights with large peep holes on the Lyman principle, together with blade foresights. Luminous elements may be used together with the foresight for night use. The 'Sniper Scope' working on infrared rays, and the light intensifier have been used with considerable success for special applications. Although telescopic sights are reputed to have been used in the American War of Independence, Colonel Davidson's patent of 1834 was one of the first modern short-type telescopes of the kind used today for military and sporting purposes. Improved manufacturing methods made them reliable enough for service use and the German army, in 1944, planned to equip every soldier with a four-power telescopic-sighted rifle. The development of the long-tube telescopes used on target rifles was already advanced by the mid-19th century, and the design has changed very little since then. Aiming reticles are generally of the cross hair or post type. Short-tube telescopes use internal adjustments, whilst long-tube models usually have external adjustment by means of micrometer thimbles. Most modern sporting rifles are equipped with telescopic sights. Most PISTOLS are supplied with open sights with square rear-notch and blade foresight. Some sporting weapons have aperture or telescopic sights but these are not very popular. The sights of MACHINE-GUNS for infantry use are of a similar design to rifles. Heavy machine-guns for anti-aircraft use are generally mounted in batteries and controlled by radar. The 'cartwheel' pattern, once popular, was rendered obsolete by the high speed of present-day aircraft. ARTILLERY guns used for direct fire as for tank and anti-tank applications use a spotting rifle of smaller calibre mounted co-axially, with laser, infrared, radar, or other advanced types of sights. For indirect fire the traditional system of establishing a base line with surveying instruments so that map references can be used, is still followed. For horizontal control, the recently developed paralleloscope is widely used. For vertical control, modifications of the traditional Gunner's quadrant are still the universal method followed. Modern improvements in measuring and aiming devices have increased accuracy of fire to a marked degree.

Bibliography: C. C. Trench, *A History of Marksmanship*, 1972.

Sighvatr Thórdarson (c. 995–c. 1045), Icelandic court poet, one of the most competent practitioners of SKALDIC POETRY. He became the poet of St OLAF about 1015 and remained so until the king's fall in 1030. Sighvatr's poem *Austrfararvísur*, which colourfully and wittily describes a mission to the king of Sweden, is perhaps his best poem. Much of his work commemorates the life and deeds of his master.

Sigismund (1368–1437), Holy Roman Emperor from 1410, a son of Emperor Charles IV. He succeeded his father as margrave of Brandenburg (1378), and on the death of his father-in-law, Louis the Great, became King of Hungary (1387), and in 1410, on the death of Rupert III, was elected Holy Roman Emperor, and was crowned in 1414. Sigismund was a prominent member of the Council of Constance (1414), which brought the Great Schism to an end, and was involved in the death of John HUSS, an event which roused the Bohemians against him so that it was only after 17 years of war that Sigismund was able to enter their capital as king. Sigismund's character is still disputed by historians. It is hard to decide whether he was the better Catholic or Imperialist. His support made possible the Council of Constance; yet the overriding consideration he gave to Imperial diplomacy wrecked it, and in sanctioning the condemnation of Huss, Sigismund would seem to have used a religious instrument to crush a movement which was most repugnant to him because of its nationalist tendencies. This dualism of character and ambition prevented him, in spite of his intelligence and capability, from achieving very much of endurance in either church or state.

Sigismund, name of three kings of Poland.

Sigismund I (1467–1548), the son of Casimir IV, became king in 1506. He waged war against the Teutonic knights (1519–21) and against Muscovy in support of Lithuania. Though himself a Catholic, he protected Protestants and Jews from persecution.

Sigismund II Augustus (1520–72), the son of Sigismund I, whom he succeeded. He was a tactful diplomatist, and through him the Union of Lublin with Lithuania was achieved. He was the last of the JAGELLONS.

Sigismund III (1566–1632), the nephew of Sigismund II and son of John III, King of Sweden. He was elected to the Polish throne in 1587, and succeeded his father in Sweden in 1592, although he was dethroned there in 1604. His reign was disturbed by risings of the nobles, by wars with the Turks, and by the persecutions of the Protestants.

Sigmaringen, town in BADEN-WÜRTTEMBERG, West Germany, on the Danube, 75 km south of Stuttgart. It was once the capital of the duchy of Hohenzollern-Sigmaringen (see HOHENZOLLERN). The castle here has several valuable art collections. Population 12,000.

Sign, in mathematics, either of the symbols $+$ or $-$ which indicate whether a number is positive or negative. See also SYMBOLS.

Sign-manual, signature or mark made by a person upon any legal instrument to show his concurrence in it. It now denotes specifically the signature of a reigning sovereign. In Britain a warrant under the royal sign-manual (see SIGNET) has been, since 1884, a sufficient authority for passing any instrument under the Great Seal of the UK. The authenticity of the royal sign-manual is admitted in courts of law upon production of the instrument to which it is attached.

Signac, Paul (1863–1935), French painter, born in Paris, associated with SEURAT in the development of 'Neo-Impressionist' painting—the scientific use of spectrum colour. He painted with mosaic-like blocks of pure colour in many landscapes and seascapes of the Normandy, Brittany, and Mediterranean coasts. His theoretic aims are set out in his book, *D'Eugène Delacroix au Néo-Impressionisme*, 1899.

Bibliography: F. Cachin, *Paul Signac*, 1972.

Signal-to-noise Ratio, in radio receivers, the ratio of the output to the noise arising in the receiver itself through thermal agitation in the transistors and other causes.

Signals, Traffic

Signals, Traffic, see MOTOR LAW.

Signals and Signalling. Success in military operations is largely dependent upon the rapid distribution of essential intelligence among one's own forces and the interruption or prevention of a like distribution among the enemy's forces. The competition among nations for improved means of communication ensures the maintenance and development of interest in the scientific aspect of the subject.

Military. As the mobility and complexity of modern warfare increase, the military commander at all levels, from the theatre commander-in-chief down to the commander of every tank and infantry platoon, depends more and more on rapid and efficient communications to obtain and exploit success on the field of battle. The principal purposes for which such communications are required can be divided broadly into four categories: (1) to give commanders and their staffs a constant supply of information on the dispositions, movements and activities of their own and enemy troops; (2) to enable commanders to issue operational and administrative orders; (3) to establish the most direct contact possible between forces requiring special liaison facilities, e.g., the air arm in support of ground forces, and those involved in normal close support functions such as artillery support of infantry or armoured units, and armoured support of infantry; and (4) to keep other formations in the area of battle fully supplied with information on all matters detailed in the categories listed above.

Development. Up to and including the beginning of the 19th century musketry was comparatively poor in quality of weapons and ammunition and in the range at which much effect could be achieved; the cavalry had a considerable degree of mobility, but their weapon range was limited to the length of their lances or swords; the main support-arm, the artillery, had a strictly limited range and limited killing power, as the exploding missile, or shell, had not yet been introduced on any great scale. At this time, therefore, the trumpet and bugle sufficed as short-range control signals in battle, and mounted dispatch riders and runners served to pass orders and messages over longer distances. During the 19th century musketry improved in range, reliability, and accuracy, mobile and more effective artillery came into service, the machine-gun was introduced, and the tactics of the normal battle changed substantially. Signals now had to pass over greater distances faster and with greater security—denial of signals to the enemy. Artillery developments were the greatest single factor. Once the range had become so great that the fall of shot could not be observed from the gun-lines, instantaneous communication between the observation post and the gun-position officer with the battery became necessary. Signalling by lamp, flag, Morse (see TELEGRAPHY) or SEMAPHORE, and heliograph from defiladed positions was therefore adopted. These methods were introduced before the First World War, but towards the end they were used to a lesser degree as line telegraphy and line telephony (LT) came into general service. During that war wireless (telegraphy) was first used for military purposes, mainly between higher formations. Between 1918 and 1939 all signalling equipment became lighter, much more efficient, and less fragile. During this period radio telephony (RT) was introduced throughout field forces; and as wireless and line fulfilled all normal field requirements, visual signals became obsolete.

Naval. The origin of naval signalling is probably as old as ships themselves. At the battle of Salamis in 480 BC a red cloak raised aloft was used as a signal for the Greek fleet to bear down on their Persian adversaries. The earliest record of signals in the British navy is contained in the Black Book of Admiralty, 1338. For many years a small number of large flags and pennants were used, their significance depending on the mast on which they were hoisted. In 1660 the French introduced coloured flags to indicate each letter of the alphabet, but in the British navy numeral flags only continued to be used for many years. At the battle of Trafalgar, 32 flags comprising 12 groups of numbers were needed to make Nelson's famous signal. It was not until after the battle that Sir Home Popham altered the system he had introduced in 1800 to include alphabetical flags used in combination with numeral flags to provide some 500 different two-flag hoists, and laid the foundation of a system of naval signalling which is still used. In 1817 Captain Marryat modified Popham's code and 40 years later this was adopted for commercial use, becoming in 1887 what is known today as the International Code. The present code was adopted in 1969 and is translated into a number of languages to enable ships' crews speaking different languages to communicate. Meanwhile navies had developed flag codes of their own, but after the Second World War the need to evolve a common signal book for use among the NATO navies and to reduce the number of signal flags carried, led to the adoption of the international alphabet (the US Navy had already done so), and use of the same numeral flags as the US Navy. In addition, there are certain special flags and pennants for naval use. The Royal Navy retains its own code, groups of flags meaning one thing in the naval and another in the international code. Other forms of visual signalling include semaphore and searchlight signalling projectors or flashing lamps. Radio telegraphy and telephony are also in constant and growing use, requiring a complicated organisation of frequencies for various purposes. The Morse code is still used for lamp, sound signalling by siren, and radio telegraphy, but for the last named the five-unit code is preferred when making automatic transmissions, as this allows the rate of transmission to be doubled. The employment of a particular method and frequency is governed by the circumstances of the moment, but the communications organisation in the Navy today is recognised as one of vital importance. Upon the accurate and rapid receipt of enemy reports (e.g., from outlying air or surface or submarine units) will depend the success of any subsequent action. New developments are the use of satellites to improve radio communications between the UK and ships abroad. The US Navy has developed a very low-frequency world-wide radio system to communicate with submerged submarines.

Military and Civil Aviation. The conduct of air operations, particularly air defence, the movement, control and navigation of military and civil aircraft, are today entirely dependent upon highly developed radio, radar, and landline combined communications systems. Efficient communications are so essential to its operations that there is a special signals command in the RAF and the Ministry of Aviation operates a National Air Traffic

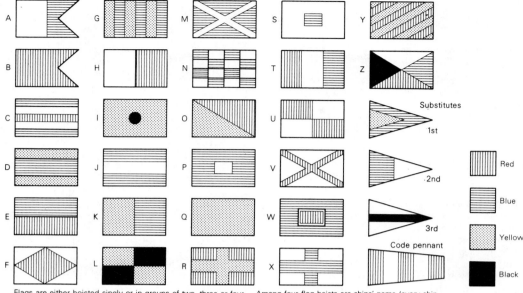

Flags are either hoisted singly or in groups of two, three or four. Among four-flag hoists are ships' name (every ship is allocated four signal letters) and geographical positions. Special meanings of some flags are

A, 'Am on speed trials'
C, 'Yes'
D, 'Keep clear of me'
F, 'I am disabled'

G, 'I want a pilot, '
K, 'Stop your ship'
L 'You should stop. I have something important to communicate'

N, 'No'
O, 'Man overboard'
P, 'Repair on board. Am proceeding to sea'

Q, 'Quarantine'
S, 'Am going full speed astern'
U, 'You are standing into danger'
V, 'I require assistance'

Signals and Signalling.

Control Service for the combined control of military and civil air traffic.

Signals of Distress, etc. The code signal of distress is NC, but the 'distant signal', a square flag with a ball, is used, or a reversed ensign, or the firing of the minute gun. At night the minute gun, flames from any burning material, or single rockets or shells fired at intervals, are signs of distress. Aircraft distress signals consist of red lights fired into the sky, and the international distress call 'mayday' by means of RT. Other special signals have become customary. Thus *P*, a blue-and-white flag, signifies that the vessel is about to put to sea; *G* is the call for a pilot; quarantine is denoted by *Q*, a plain yellow flag; three black balls in the daytime, or three red lights at night, shown vertically, are the sign of a breakdown. In foggy or obscure weather anchored vessels ring a bell; sailing vessels make one, two, or three blasts on a foghorn; fishing vessels sound the bell and foghorn alternately; steam vessels give long blasts on the siren with intervals of not more than two minutes.

Coastguard. At coastguard stations there is a system of signals to give warning of gales and their probable direction. By day a cone is hoisted: with the apex upwards it indicates a northerly gale and with the apex downwards a southerly gale. By night three lights in the form of a triangle are used on the same principle.

Bibliography: Navy Department, *Admiralty Manual of Navigation* (vol. 1), new ed. 1971.

Signature, see DEED.

Signature, in music, is applied to key, which is described by the tonic of the scale in which a composition is written, and can be either major or minor, the sharps or flats of the key being written at the beginning of each stave; or to time, indicating the rhythmic structure, written on the stave at the beginning of the work, e.g. ¾, 3 crotchets to a bar, ⅜, 3 quavers to a bar, and so on.

Signature Tune, a term originally used by dance bands for a popular tune of their own choice to identify them at the beginning and end of their acts; now extended to cover the tunes which identify particular series of programmes on radio and television.

Signatures, The Doctrine of, an ancient theory that the external aspects of plants and minerals are intended to indicate the diseases which they will remedy; for example that nature suggests by the black pupil-like spot in the corolla that *Euphrasia*, or eyebright, is good for the eyes, and similarly, by its saffron hue, that yellow turmeric cures jaundice, or that trefoil is good for heart disease.

Signet, or Privy Signet, one of the three legally recognised British royal seals for authenticating documents, the other two being the Great Seal and the Privy Seal (see SEAL). The Privy Seal was used for letters patent before they passed the Great Seal, but by the Great Seal Act 1884 a SIGN-MANUAL warrant, countersigned either by the chancellor, a secretary of state, the first lord of the Treasury, or any two Treasury commissioners, is sufficient for affixing the Great Seal, and no future documents are to have the Privy Seal affixed thereto. The only function of the Signet was to authenticate the sign-manual; but as grants under the sign-manual are sufficiently authenticated either by counter-signature under the foregoing act or in some cases by one of the secretarial seals (e.g. warrants appointing colonial governors), there is now no further use for the Signet.

Signet, Writer to the, member of a society of legal practitioners in Edinburgh who formerly had important privileges, now nearly all abolished. They are so named because they were originally clerks to the office of the king's secretary, their duties being to prepare all warrants or charters for sealing with the king's signet. Writers to the signet now form a society under the presidency of the keeper of the signet, who is a Crown appointee. The writers to the signet were recognised as members of the College of Justice in 1687.

Signorelli, Luca (c. 1441–1524), Italian painter, born at Cortona. He was the pupil of PIERO DELLA FRANCESCA, but less serene in style and one of the first to paint figures in violent action. Today his finest work will be found in the chapel of S. Brizio, a part of the cathedral of Orvieto.
Bibliography: Study by L. Dussler, 1927.

Sigurdsson, Jón (1811–79), Icelandic statesman and scholar; spent his life in fighting for the commercial and political freedom of Iceland and the cultural and economic advancement of his people. The abolition of the Danish trade monopoly was achieved in 1854 and a certain measure of home rule in 1874.
Bibliography: T. Ó. Johnson, *Jón Sigurdsson, the Icelandic Patriot,* 1887.

Sigurjónsson, Jóhann (1880–1919), Icelandic dramatist, born at Laxamýri, who for a while enjoyed a considerable reputation in Scandinavia. His most important dramas are *Fjalla-Eyvindur*, 1912, concerning an outlaw, and *Galdra-Loftur*, 1915, about a magician.

Sihanouk, King Norodom (1922–), former King and Prime Minister of CAMBODIA (now Kampuchea), noted for his unconventional political behaviour. As King of Cambodia he proclaimed his country independent in 1945; he was a member of the Cambodian royal family whom the French excluded in 1904 but, in fact, was himself chosen by them to be king in 1941. While on a visit to the USA in 1953 he made a forthright public speech demanding independence for Cambodia. On his return he left his capital to live in Thailand until Cambodia was independent. Asked by the Thai government to leave, he returned, not to PHNOM PENH, but to SIEM REAP. He abdicated in favour of his father, Norodom Sumarit, who became king in March 1955, whilst he himself became Prime Minister. In 1960 his father died, so he became head-of-state as well. During the 1960s he managed to maintain a neutral stance between China and the US and kept the country uninvolved in the Vietnam conflict. Whilst on a diplomatic visit abroad in 1970, General Lon Nol staged a military coup to depose Sihanouk, thus allowing US forces to attack Viet Cong strongholds in Cambodia. Sihanouk went to Peking and formed a royal government in exile supporting any anti-US movements. There he became the figurehead of the Khmer Rouge guerrillas against Lon Nol, and resumed his position of

Norodom Sihanouk. *(Camera Press)*

head-of-state after the victory of the guerrillas in 1975. After one year as a Communist figurehead he resigned all his posts saying that he wanted to retire from political life. Perhaps his biggest achievement was to keep Cambodia intact and relatively united during the post-Second World War troubles in South-East Asia.

Sikang, former western province of China, lying between SZECHWAN and TIBET, and watered by the Yangtze. It embraces almost all of eastern Tibet; the western parts are entirely mountainous. There is no railway; main roads link it with Szechwan and Tsinghai. The Ch'eng-tu–Lhasa highway built in 1955 traverses its whole breadth from east to west. The province was merged partly with Szechwan and partly with the Tibetan Autonomous Region in 1955. Its former area was 451,520 km².

Sikelianos, Angelos (1884–1951), Greek poet, born in Lefkas, where he was educated before studying at Athens University. His first mature poem *The Light-Shadowed*, written in 1907, shows his identification with nature. Ten years later, *Mother of God* and *Easter of the Greeks* reveal a deepening mysticism and the development of a concept of a universal religious myth which gave the impulse to his organisation of the Delphic festivals of 1927 and 1930. Later in life he turned to writing tragedies, but many of his best poems are less ambitious short lyrics, contained in the three volumes of *Lyric Lite*, 1946.
Bibliography: P. Sherrard, *The Marble Threshing Floor,* 1956.

Sikhs (Sanskrit *S'ishya*, disciple), community in the Punjab (India) State, which was divided between India and West Pakistan in 1947, and again in 1966, numbering 10 million today. They are the probable descendants of the original inhabitants of the Indus valley. Originally a small religious community, gathering round their founder, NANAK (1469–1539), they gradually grew into a nation because of their proselytising powers. Nanak was succeeded by the nine *gurus* or teachers, the last and most famous of whom was Govind Singh. Nanak, a humanitarian, aimed at combining Hindus and Muslims into one brotherhood by a unique blend of Hindu and Sufi beliefs. To the Hindu's ancient and highly-evolved concept of God as formless, timeless, and beyond all human comprehension he conjoined the Sufi emphasis upon the revelation of God as light within the human heart, and the suffering involved in separation from the Beloved. The climax of his thought was to be found in the concept of ineffable union with God, the Formless One, and his teaching about the path to this union is still the mystical heart of Sikhism, followed to this day by orthodox Sikhs. Nanak's mission was a dynamic one and brought him a devoted following who practised the chief doctrines as preached by Nanak, which are: 'The unity of God, brotherhood of man, rejection of caste and the futility of idol worship.' He appointed a disciple to follow him and the line of prophetic succession continued until the Tenth Guru, Govind Singh. The Sikh community thus gained their character from ten leaders, each of whom emphasised a particular aspect of the teaching, exemplified in his own life. Of these ten, the fifth, Arjun Mal, compiled the sacred book of the Sikhs, the Adi-Granth, and had built the holy city of Amritsar, before he was tortured to death for his religious beliefs by the Mogul Emperor, Jahangir. His willing martyrdom generated a new strand of sacrifice and acceptance of suffering which came to aid the Sikhs in the warfare they engaged on under the sixth guru, Hargovind. The tenth guru, Govind Singh, combated the Muslim power and religion, while he also repudiated the caste system of Hinduism. He taught that God could be found only in humility and sincerity, and wrote the second volume of the Scriptures, which teaches the Sikhs to worship one God, reject superstitions, be

strictly moral, and live by the sword. As a result of his teaching the Sikhs ultimately aspired and obtained political independence in 1764. They continued to wage wars in order to retain independence but were defeated by the British in 1849.

Sikh Union. The India-Pakistan frontier was drawn through the Sikh area, and there was a mass migration into the East Punjab. A Sikh state was created in 1948 when seven Punjab states were merged into a union known as the Patiala and East Punjab States Union.

Sikhs are divided into non-Jat Sikhs and Jats. The non-Jat Sikhs are strict followers of their religion and wear the five Sikh symbols: a steel dagger, a bangle, a comb, uncut hair, and short breeches. The Jats are less strict. A considerable number of Sikhs came to the British Isles. Their outer characteristics of turban to contain long hair, beard, and strong physique, as well as their inner qualities of diligence and courage are now familiar to many Westerners.

Bibliography: H. Singh, *The Heritage of the Sikhs*, 1963; K. Singh, *A History of the Sikhs* (2 vols), 1963–66; W. H. Macleod, *The Sikhs of the Punjab*, 1970.

Si Kiang (West River), longest river in South China. See CHINA, *Geography*.

Sikkim, state of INDIA, strategically located south of China, east of Nepal, and west of Bhutan. It lies on the southern slopes of the Himalayas and its Singalila range contains the third highest mountain in the world, Kanchenjunga (8578 m). Its environments range from subtropical lowlands to above the snowline. Its forests are extensive and many rare species of orchid continue to survive there. The population totals 204,750, 65 per cent of whom are recently immigrated Nepalese Hindu, 30 per cent Buddhist; 80 per cent are illiterate. The chief crops are maize, rice, millet, cardomom, and tea. A road network is being developed primarily for Indian defence needs. Area 7107 km². The capital is Gangtok.

History. Sikkim was absorbed into British India in 1935, and after independence it became an Indian protectorate. This status was finally abolished in 1975, after a long period of strain between the two countries, when India admitted Sikkim as the 22nd state of the republic. Its hereditary *chogyal* (ruler) was deposed; Palden Thondup Namgyal had succeeded to the throne in 1963 as the 12th monarch of the Namgyal dynasty, said to descend from the ancient Yarlung dynasty of TIBET. Throughout its history Sikkim maintained close religious, commercial, and personal ties with Tibet, and its royal family had inter-married with the aristocracy of Lhasa. The border with Tibet was sealed at the outbreak of hostilities between India and China in 1961. Several incidents involving Indian and Chinese troops took place there, especially on the strategic pass of Matu La, Sikkim's principal access point to the Chumbi Valley.

Bibliography: B. Olschak, *Sikkim*, 1965; B. S. K. Grover, *Sikkim India*, 1976.

Sikorski, Władysław (1881–1943), Polish statesman and soldier, born in Galicia. He studied in Cracow and at the Lvov Technical College. In the First World War he supported the policy of the restoration of Poland by the Central Powers, and later commanded an army in the Polish-Soviet War (1919–20). In 1921 he was chief of the general staff and in 1922 prime minister, restoring order

Sikhs. Ranjit Singh, ruler of the Sikh empire 1799–1839 with its capital at Lahore. Tempera painting, c. 1830. *(Victoria and Albert Museum, London)*

and obtaining general recognition of the Russo-Polish line of demarcation. But after PIŁSUDSKI's coup in 1926 he retired and for ten years lived in Paris. In 1939, he left Poland to build up a Polish army abroad and on 30 September was nominated premier of the exiled Polish government and commander-in-chief of all the Polish forces abroad. In 1940 he established his quarters in London as chief of the Polish general staff. The following year he signed a treaty in Moscow, restoring diplomatic relations between the USSR and Poland and annulling the Nazi-Soviet partition of Poland. Sikorski was killed in an aeroplane crash at Gibraltar.

Sikorsky, Igor Ivan (1889–1972), Russian aeronautical engineer, born in Kiev, educated at the naval academy, St Petersburg, and at the Polytechnic Institute, Kiev. He emigrated to the USA in 1919 and was naturalised there in 1928. Early interested in aeroplane design, he constructed and flew the first successful four-engined aeroplane in 1913. Sikorsky produced several four-engined bombers for the Russian Government (1914–17). He made the first successful and practical helicopter in the Western Hemisphere (1939), and became one of the leading designers of helicopters.

Sila, La, Italian plateau in northern CALABRIA. A thinly populated area of lakes, meadows, and pine and beech forest over 1000 m above sea-level, it is divided into three parts (from north to south: Sila Greca, Sila Grande, and Sila Piccola) by rivers that have been dammed. It is a holiday area but also produces hydro-electricity and dairy products.

Silage, see HAY AND SILAGE.

Silay, city in the province of Negros Occidental on the north-west coast of NEGROS Island in the Philippines, 16 km north of Bacolod. Sulphur is mined nearby and it has a large sugar mill, but its main function is as a commercial and fishing port. Population (1970) 65,600.

Silbermann, Gottfried (1683–1753), south German manufacturer of organs, clavichords, pianos, etc., born at Klein-Bobritzsch (Saxony) and settled at Freiburg in 1710; he provided instruments for C. P. E. Bach among others.

Silbury Hill, the largest ancient man-made mound in

La Sila. (*Camera Press/March Penney*)

Europe, situated 1·5 km south of AVEBURY, Wiltshire, and probably contemporary with the Late Neolithic sanctuary there. It is about 40 m high and has a ditch surrounding it about 6 m deep which was used as the quarry for the building of the mound. Six known attempts have been made to find out its constructional details and purpose. They have revealed that the sides were originally terraced, that it may have been about a third higher, and that the main mound was built over a primary mound about 25 m in diameter in a series of horizontal layers. Local legends of a life-size statue of King Sil and his horse contained in the interior have been disproved, however, as no burial or any significant finds have ever been made. Its purpose is still unclear, but it may have been a cenotaph. See also BARROW.
  Bibliography: R. J. C. Atkinson, *Silbury Hill* (BBC pamphlet), 1968.

Silchester, village in HAMPSHIRE, England, 11 km north of Basingstoke, the site of *Calleva Atrebatum*, cantonal capital of the Atrebates, a Belgic tribe which inhabited a large district south of the middle Thames from Surrey to north-east Wiltshire. The stone walls, enclosing some 40 ha, were added around AD 200 as a facing to a previously existing earthwork, which was itself a contraction of a larger enclosure, possibly 150 years older. Outside the walls are the remains of an amphitheatre. The town plan was recovered by extensive excavation in 1890–1909, when the sites of the forum, basilica, inns, a bath-house, a building (probably a Christian church), etc., were found; the excavations were filled in, and most of the area is now under cultivation, but occasional excavations have been made more recently. There is a small museum near the present rectory, but the great Silchester collection is in Reading Museum.
  Bibliography: G. Boon, *Silchester: The Roman Town of Calleva,* 1974.

Silene, see CAMPION; CATCHFLY.

Silent Spirit, distilled spirit, without flavour or odour, prepared from potatoes, damaged grain, molasses, etc. It contains over 90 per cent of absolute alcohol, and is used in the manufacture of liqueurs and scents.

Silenus, in Greek mythology, son of Hermes or Pan, an aged woodland deity or satyr (see SATYRS), with a reputation for song, prophecy, drunkenness, and lechery. With other aged satyrs (collectively called *Sileni*), he was the companion of DIONYSUS, and always carried a wine-skin. He is represented commonly as a jovial old man, bald and puck-nosed, fat and intoxicated. Unable to trust his own legs, he is generally shown riding on an ass or supported by other satyrs. When in a drunken sleep, mortals might compel him to prophesy and sing by girding him with chains of flowers.

Silesia (German *Schlesien*; Polish *Śląsk*; Czech *Slezsko*), region of Eastern Europe, lying in the middle and the upper Oder basin and bordered in the south by the Sudeten mountains. Since 1945 most of Silesia has been within the frontiers of Poland. It has a total area of about 50,165 km². Silesia is mainly lowland, but Schneekoppe (Polish *Śnieżka*) in the Riesengebirge (Polish *Karkonosze*) rises to 1603 m. It is extremely fertile, especially in the south and south-west, but its mineral deposits are of prime importance: its coalfields are among the most important in Europe, and there are rich deposits of iron, lead, and zinc. The metallurgical industries of the area are highly developed, and there are also manufactures of machinery, textiles, chemicals, glass, and paper. The principal towns are (in Poland) Wrocław (German *Breslau*), Opole (*Oppeln*), Katowice (*Kattowitz*), Bytom (*Beuthen*), Chorzów (*Königshutte*), and (in Czechoslovakia) Opava (German *Troppau*).

Silesia belonged to the Czechs in the 10th century, and to Poland from 990. It was contested between Poland, Bohemia, and Germany. From 1138 onwards Silesia was politically divided and in the 13th century consisted of 30 small duchies. Despite strong links with Poland, the duchies of Silesia recognised Czech suzerainty which Poland accepted in 1339. A few duchies returned to Poland in the 15th century. Much of Lower Silesia was settled and developed in the Middle Ages by the Germans, and the German language spread widely. In 1525 Silesia came under Hapsburg rule and in 1742 under Prussian rule, except for the south-east which remained Austrian. In the 19th century Upper Silesia, which had a mixed German-Polish population, became one of the leading industrial areas of Germany.

By a plebiscite in 1921, following the First World War, Poland received the south-east part of Silesia with the city of Katowice. Most of Austrian Silesia was taken by Czechoslovakia in 1919. In 1939 the Germans annexed Polish Upper Silesia. In 1945 the Soviet army conquered Silesia. After the end of the Second World War, under the Potsdam Agreement, Prussian Silesia passed entirely to Poland (with the exception of a small part west of the Neisse), most of the German population having been deported west of the Neisse.

Silesian War, Third, see SEVEN YEARS' WAR.

Silesius, Angelus, see ANGELUS SILESIUS.

Silica, silicon dioxide (SiO_2), occurs in nature as five distinct minerals: quartz, tridymite, cristobalite, opal, and lechatelierite.

Quartz, silicon dioxide, SiO_2, one of the most abundant minerals in the crust of the earth. It crystallises in the trigonal system, commonly forming prismatic hexagonal crystals terminated by two sets of rhombohedrons. It has a vitreous lustre, hardness of 7, and specific gravity of 2·65. It has a conchoidal fracture. Quartz may also occur in massive cryptocrystalline form. Quartz is stable over a wide range of geological conditions, and is an essential constituent of silica-rich igneous rocks and many metamorphic rocks. As it is hard and very resistant to chemical weathering it is the most abundant mineral in SEDIMENTARY ROCKS, and forms the bulk of most sandstones. It also makes up a large part of hydrothermal vein deposits and granite pegmatites.

Quartz occurs in two distinct varieties, macrocrystalline and cryptocrystalline (the latter often classed as chalcedony). Macrocrystalline varieties include *milky quartz*: milk-white and almost opaque, due to the presence of many small air bubbles. It often occurs in large quantities in veins. *Amethyst*: transparent, purple quartz. The colour is related to the presence of small amounts of iron. Amethyst is widely used as an ornamental and semi-precious stone. It generally occurs lining cavities in volcanic rocks. *Rose quartz*: pale pink quartz, rarely occurring as crystals. The colour is due to the presence of small amounts of manganese, titanium, or lithium. *Citrine*: transparent yellow quartz, the colour being due to the presence of small amounts of ferric hydroxide. It is used as a semi-precious stone and resembles TOPAZ. *Smoky quartz*: transparent brown to black quartz, sometimes known as Cairngorm Stone, and used as an ornamental stone. Similar colour changes can be produced in colourless quartz by subjecting it to radiation. *Cat's eye*: quartz which contains small fibrous inclusions, causing the reflection of light in a narrow beam, as in a cat's eye. *Aventurine quartz*: transparent quartz containing spangles of mica, used as an ornamental stone. *Ferruginous quartz*: quartz containing iron oxides, imparting a red or brown colour.

Cryptocrystalline varieties (chalcedony): chalcedony is a group name for the compact varieties of silica composed of minute crystals of quartz with submicroscopic pores. They occur in massive form, often filling cavities in rocks or as nodules in sedimentary rocks. Varieties include *Agate*: a banded form of chalcedony. The banding is caused by intermittent deposition in cavities and the bands are subparallel to the cavity walls. Some agates show natural colour banding but frequently artificial stains are used to enhance the appearance of a specimen. *Onyx*: a plane-banded alternately light and dark agate. *Carnelian* and *sard*: red and reddish-brown chalcedony, frequently used for signet rings. *Heliotrope* and *bloodstone*: green chalcedony containing red spots of jaspar. *Moss agate* (Mocha stone): white or cream chalcedony enclosing brown or black dendritic moss-like aggregates of manganese oxides. *Jaspar*: opaque chalcedony, usually red to brown, the colour being due to colloidal particles of iron oxides. *Chert*: massive dull-coloured opaque chalcedony, occurring in stratified form in sedimentary rocks. The silica is derived from the remains of sponges and radiolaria deposited in the SEDIMENTARY ENVIRONMENT. *Flint*: grey or black chalcedony, occurring in nodular form in a sedimentary rock matrix, commonly in the chalk of southern England. It has a characteristically conchoidal fracture which, combined with its hardness and durability, made it a common material for tools fashioned by primitive man. It was used for lighting tinder before the advent of the match, as it generates sparks when struck by steel. It has also been used as a building stone and roadstone. *Plasma*: sub-translucent bright green chalcedony, sometimes dotted with white. *Prase*: translucent, dull green chalcedony. *Chrysoprase*: apple-green chalcedony, used as a semi-precious stone. *Tiger eyes*: chalcedony which has replaced asbestos, retaining its fibrous structure. It is yellow, brown, or blue in colour and used as a semi-precious stone.

Tridymite, a high-temperature polymorph of silica, SiO_2. It is composed of about 95 per cent silica with some aluminium and alkalis. It occurs as crystals in the form of small hexagonal plates, white or colourless, with a vitreous lustre. It is a high-temperature form of quartz, being stable at temperatures between 870° and 1470°C. It occurs in cavities in volcanic rocks formed at high temperature, such as rhyolite, trachyte, and andesite.

Cristobalite, the polymorph of silica stable at temperatures above 1470°C. It occurs as small white octahedral crystals, often twinned and aggregated in clusters, in volcanic rocks formed at high temperatures. It is found in obsidian, rhyolite, and trachyte, often in association with tridymite.

Opal, composed of a solidified colloidal gel of silica, usually containing a small percentage of water in submicroscopic pores. Water content varies from 1 to 21 per cent; in precious opal it is around 6 to 10 per cent. Opal has a hardness of 5½ to 6½. It may be colourless, white, yellow, red, green, blue, or black. Precious opal exhibits a delicate play of colours. Opal is deposited at low temperatures from silica-bearing waters, and may occur in fissures and cavities in any rock. Extensive deposits are formed around hot springs (geyserite). Precious opal is found in Mexico and South and East Australia. Fire opal has a yellow or orange-red colour, while black opal is dark blue, dark green, grey, or black in colour. Opal is brittle and not very hard as a gemstone, and for this reason is usually mounted with some form of metal backing. DIATOMITE, a form of opal, is a deposit formed from the remains of siliceous organisms. It occurs in extensive beds and is mined for use as a filtering agent, an insulating medium, and a mild abrasive.

Lechatelierite, silica glass, unstable at temperatures below 1713 °C. It is formed when lightning strikes in sand, fusing small amounts to glass; tubes of glass (FULGURITES) several metres long may be formed in this way.

Silica Glass, or quartz GLASS, is fused vitreous quartz. It can be made either translucent or transparent to visible light. Unlike ordinary glasses it will also transmit much ultraviolet and infrared radiation. It has a small thermal expansion coefficient and may therefore be cooled and heated rapidly without breaking. It also has a much higher melting-point than either soda or borosilicate glasses. For these reasons it is used in scientific apparatus and in special lamp bulbs (e.g., quartz-iodine lamps).

Silicates, alkali metal salts formed when alkali metal carbonates are fused with silica at high temperatures. Carbon dioxide is driven off, and a complex mixture of silicates is left. A few silicates contain simple orthosilicate (SiO_4^{4-}) ions, but most are complex polymeric structures. See also ZEOLITES.

Silicic Acid, see SILICON.

Silicon, non-metallic chemical element, symbol Si, atomic number 14, atomic weight 28·086. It does not occur in the uncombined state, but in combination with other elements it is, with the exception of oxygen, the most abundantly distributed of all the elements, present to the extent of 28 per cent by weight in the earth's crust. As the dioxide, silica, it occurs both free, and combined with various bases, as flint, felspar, sand, quartz, opal, chalcedony, etc. In combination with oxygen, and metals such as aluminium and magnesium, it occurs in clays and marls, and constitutes a large number of rocks. As prepared by heating fine sand and magnesium together, or by heating sodium in a stream of silicon tetrachloride, silicon is in the form of an amorphous brown powder (relative density 2·15). Amorphous silicon is soluble in alkalis with evolution of hydrogen, and burns in air and chlorine forming the dioxide and tetrachloride respectively. When prepared in the presence of zinc or aluminium, silicon forms long needle-shaped crystals (relative density 2·4), which do not burn in oxygen, are very hard and are used for scratching

glass. Silica, or silicon dioxide, occurs in nature in the amorphous form as an opal, and in the diatomaceous deposits or 'kieselguhr' of Germany. It is formed when silicic acid is heated or by the action of an acid on sodium silicate. In the crystalline condition as quartz, silica forms prismatic crystals of the hexagonal system. As rock crystal, silica is occasionally cut and polished, and substituted as a gem for diamond. Tridymite is crystalline silica, which frequently forms twin crystals in trachytic rocks. At the temperature of the oxy-hydrogen flame, silica melts to a transparent viscous liquid, which can be drawn out into fine threads that are extremely elastic and resistant, and are used by physicists in delicate instruments of precision. Silica is also used in the manufacture of silica-glass, quartz-glass, Vitreosil, etc. Articles made of this glass will withstand sudden and extreme changes of temperature without cracking, owing to the very low coefficient of expansion of the substance. Silicon dioxide forms silicic acids of more or less definite constitution, which are difficult to obtain pure. If hydrochloric acid is added to a solution of an alkaline silicate, a gelatinous precipitate is obtained of the dibasic acid, $SiO(OH)_2$ or H_2SiO_3. If, however, the alkaline silicate is cautiously added to the acid, the silicic acid remains in solution probably as the orthosilicic acid, $Si(OH)_4$ or H_4SiO_4. The sodium chloride in the solution may be removed by DIALYSIS, but on standing the acid solution solidifies to a jelly of the approximate composition, H_2SiO_3. The acid may be looked upon as the parent substance from which the silicates are derived. Silicon forms a fluoride which is decomposed on passing into water. Water-glass is a concentrated solution of sodium silicate; in preserving eggs it acts by clogging up the pores in the shells, thus keeping out putrefactive bacteria. Silicon also forms a series of spontaneously inflammable hydrides, analogous to the alkane HYDROCARBONS. These run from silane (SiH_4) to silico-hexane (Si_6H_{14}). It seems however, that though silicon chemistry is in many ways similar to CARBON chemistry, the ability to form long chains, characteristic of carbon compounds, is shown by silicon only to a limited extent. Investigations into the preparation of high polymers combining carbon and silicon units in the molecule have resulted in a new class of compounds, the siloxanes or silicones. They are non-conductors of electricity, and thus find use as insulators, and as they are insoluble in water, chemically very inert and able to withstand extremes of temperature, they find many very important practical uses as greases, oils, elastomers (silicon rubber), and water-repellent films. The silicates, originally thought to be derivatives of the silicic acids, have recently been shown to be formed of giant chain molecules, where each silicon atom is linked to four oxygen atoms. They form fibrous structures, as in asbestos, and thin leaves or sheets, as in mica and talc. The insolubility and high melting points of silicates are a result of these structures. Silicon is also an important ingredient of steel, and silicon carbide is widely used as an abrasive and refractory material under the name of carborundum. Pure crystals of silicon have immensely valuable applications as semiconductor materials in the manufacture of transistors, solar cells, and other solid-state devices. See FERRO-SILICON; GLASS; IRON AND STEEL.

Silicon Bronze, alloy of silicon and copper, containing

3–5 per cent of the former, with small quantities of zinc, iron, and manganese. Where zinc is present in large quantity the more correct term is silicon brass. The alloys have a much greater strength than gunmetal, but casting is a more difficult operation.

Silicon Steel, see IRON AND STEEL, *Alloy Steels*.

Silicones, see SILICON.

Silicosis, see PNEUMOCONIOSES.

Siliqua, see FRUIT.

Silistra (Roman *Durostorum*), town and province of Bulgaria, on the Danube facing Romania. It was founded as a Roman camp in the 1st century AD and was an important town of Moesia. The Turks captured it in the early 15th century and made it into a fortress. The present town is modern and its port ships a large volume of grain. Population 38,400.

Silius Italicus, Tiberius Catius Asconius (c. AD 25–c. 101), Latin epic poet, consul in 68 and governor of Asia in 77. He was the author of *Punica*, on the second Punic War, which was rediscovered by Poggio BRACCI-OLINI in 1416; it is by common consent the longest and worst poem in the whole range of Latin literature. Suffering from an incurable illness, Silius Italicus starved himself to death.
Bibliography: J. D. Duff (Trans.), *Punica* (2 vols), 'Loeb Classical Library', 1934.

Silk and Sericulture. Silk is a textile fibre obtained from the cocoon of the silkworm, of which *Bombyx mori* is the most important, but also from the silkmoths *Antheraea mylitta* of India and *A. pernyi* of China. Some silk has been obtained in the past from various spiders but such products have found no textile uses, although they have

Silk and Sericulture. Silkworms feeding on mulberry leaves at Lullingstone Castle, Kent. *(Popperfoto)*

been used for cross-wires in optical instruments such as telescopes and bomb-aimers. According to legend, silk culture, or sericulture, started in China in 2640 BC and spread via Korea to Japan by AD 300 and to Constantinople under Justinian in AD 555. Attempts were made to introduce silk culture to the UK and USA but without success.

The larvae eat mulberry leaves and in about 5 weeks grow to about 8 cm in length and start to spin their cocoons. Most of the larvae are killed in their cocoons, only a few being required for egg production. A disease of the silk worm, *pébrine*, is of importance; it was investigated in France by Pasteur, who found that bacteria were responsible and that control was possible if strict hygiene was observed.

The cocoon consists of about 900 m of continuous fibre, two parallel filaments being stuck together by a gum called seracin. To obtain the fibre the cocoons are softened in hot water, the ends found, and the cocoons unwound, care being taken that as the thickness of the individual fibres varies the overall thickness of the yarn is kept constant by adding or removing cocoons. The original yarns are twisted and the yarns then combined by a further twisting operation to produce 'thrown' silk, These yarns have names such as tram, organzine, crepe, grenadine, and compenzine. Embroidery and sewing silks are also made by similar processes.

The silk from damaged cocoons, cocoons in which the larva has hatched out, and the wild silks are spun into a yarn by processes similar to the worsted process. These yarns are known as spun silk or schappe silk.

Silk is made of protein; it is very strong, stretches and recovers easily, and absorbs water readily. In processing, the gum (seracin) is removed but the silk is treated with tin salts or with other gums to increase its weight and reduce its price. It is used for very fine (thin) cloths and as a luxury fibre where its strength, lustre, softness, and water absorption are called for. Production has dropped greatly since the Second World War and many of its uses have been almost completely taken over by other fibres, particularly nylon.

Raw silk production in 1974 was 49,000 t (19,000 from Japan and 500 from Europe), 0·15 per cent of world textile production.
Bibliography: J. G. Cook, *Handbook of Textile Fibres*, vol. 1: *Natural Fibres*, 4th ed. 1968.

Silk Screen, see SCREEN PROCESS PRINTING; SERIGRAPHY.

Silkin, Jon (1930–), English poet, born in London; educated at Leeds University. He taught in the Army Education Corps, at several British and United States universities, and worked for six years as a manual labourer. In 1952 he founded the magazine *Stand*, and in 1954 published his first collection of verse, *The Peaceable Kingdom*. He achieved his true poetic voice in *The Re-ordering of the Stones*, 1961, and *Nature With Man*, 1965. His mature style is marked by a self-reflective voice, and slow, rhythmic movements, alternating with sharp, dramatic statements, as in the collection *The Principle of Water*, 1974. He has also written a study of the poetry of the First World War, *Out of Battle*, 1972, and edited *Poetry of the Committed Individual*, 1973.

Silkworm, see SILK AND SERICULTURE.

Sill

Sill, an igneous intrusion of sheet-like form, showing a conformable relationship with the bedding of the country rocks. Intrusion takes place by MAGMA forcing its way between beds of rock and uplifting the overlying rocks. Sills vary in thickness from a few centimetres to tens of metres, and may extend laterally for tens of square kilometres.

The rocks of sills are generally fine-grained, except in the larger sills where they range from fine-grained at the margin to coarse-grained at the centre. At the interface with the country rock, sills show a very fine-grained texture, forming a chilled margin, and the country rock shows signs of heating. Both features are characteristic of an igneous intrusion. The Whin Sill of Northern England is an example of a very large sill.

Sillanpää, Frans Eemil (1888–1964), Finnish novelist, born at Hämeenkyrö, which provided the scene for most of his novels. After studying biology at Helsinki University he devoted himself completely to writing. He published his first novel, a love story, in 1916, but it was in 1919 that he began to attract public attention with *Hurskas kurjuus* (*Meek Heritage*, 1938), a novel that dealt with the events leading to the brutal civil war of 1918. Other novels, in which he developed ideas of 'biological fatalism', include *Nuorena nukkunut*, 1931 (*Fallen Asleep While Young*, 1933), and *Miehen tie*, 1932. Sillanpää was awarded the Nobel Prize for literature in 1939. His reputation as the foremost Finnish author continued to grow, and the novel written during the Second World War, *Ihmiselon ihanuus ja kurjuus*, 1945, is considered by some his best work.
Bibliography: R. Koskimies, *Kirjallisia näköaloja*, 1948; E. H. Linkomies, *F. E. Sillanpää. Eräitä peruspiirteitä*, 1948.

Sillein, see ŽILINA.

Silliman, Benjamin, name of two US chemists, father and son. The father (1779–1864), born at North Stratford, Connecticut, served from 1802 to 1853 as professor of chemistry and mineralogy at Yale. He was the founder and, from 1818 to 1838, the editor of the *American Journal of Science and Arts*. He wrote *Elements of Chemistry*, 1830–31. The son (1816–85), born at New Haven, Connecticut, was a chief founder of the Sheffield School of Science (Yale), and taught chemistry in its precursor from 1847. In 1854 he succeeded his father as professor of chemistry in Yale. A co-editor of the *American Journal of Science*, he did original work in mineralogy and applied chemistry.

Sillitoe, Alan (1928–), English novelist, born in Nottingham, and educated at secondary modern school. He served as a radio operator in the Royal Air Force,

Frans Sillanpää. *(Popperfoto)*

1946–49, until he was found to have tuberculosis and given a pension. He travelled in France, Spain, and Italy, 1952–58. At first he thought of himself primarily as a poet, and published several collections of verse, including *Rats and Other Poems*, 1960, and *Storm and Other Poems*, 1974. However, he is most widely acclaimed for his novels and stories about working-class life, notably *Saturday Night and Sunday Morning*, 1958, and *The Loneliness of the Long Distance Runner*, 1959, both of which have been filmed from his own screenplays. His later novels deal with characters from other sections of society, but always view the plight of individuals trapped in a stifling social environment. Among his other works are *The Ragman's Daughter* (short stories), 1963, and the novels *A Start in Life*, 1970, and *Raw Material*, 1972.

Silloth, small port and holiday resort on the SOLWAY FIRTH, in the Allerdale district of Cumbria, England, west of Carlisle. Population (1971) 2662.

Silo, see HAY AND SILAGE.

Siloam (Old Testament Shiloah), the lower pool close to Jerusalem, to which a tunnel was built by Hezekiah, bringing the water of Jerusalem's only spring the Gihon ('Gusher') or 'Virgin's Fountain' on the western side of the KIDRON from the upper pool into the city. An inscrip-

Sill. Section across the northern Pennines of the Great Whin Sill. *(Source: A. Holmes, Principles of Physical Geology, 1965)*

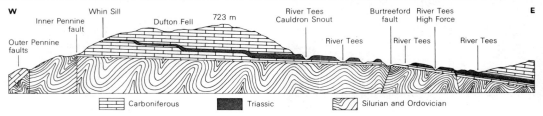

tion in the tunnel was found in 1880 recording this (see 2 Chron. xxxii. 3).

Silone, Ignazio, pseudonym of Secondo Tranquilli (1900–), Italian novelist, born at Pescina dei Marsi. He joined the newly founded Italian Communist party in 1921, but left it in 1930. Because of his anti-fascist activities he had to leave for Switzerland, where he lived from 1930 to 1944. He then returned to Italy and, as a socialist, edited the paper *Avanti*.

Silone's knowledge and understanding of peasant life are shown in his novel *Fontamara*, 1930. This is bitterly anti-clerical; but the conflict between Christian and revolutionary ideals is portrayed with greater sympathy in *Pane e vino*, 1937 (*Bread and Wine*, 1964). Silone's writing is distinguished by human understanding and sympathetic irony in the handling of his subjects. His later works include *Il seme sotto la neve*, 1941 (*The Seed Beneath the Snow*, 1943), *Una manciata di more*, 1952 (*A Handful of Blackberries*, 1954), *Il segreto di Luca*, 1956 (*The Secret of Luca*, 1959), *La volpe e le camelie*, 1960 (*The Fox and the Camellias*, 1960), and *Uscita di Sicurezza*, 1965.

Bibliography: R. W. B. Lewis, *The Picaresque Saint*, 1959; L. d'Eramo, *L'Opera di Ignazio Silone*, 1972.

Silphium, compass plant or pilot weed, a hardy perennial, belonging to the Compositae (daisy family). *S. laciniatum*, which grows 2 m high and has yellow flowers in summer, has the peculiarity while young of turning its leaf-edges north and south to avoid mid-day heat, and hence is called the compass plant. Other species are *S. perfoliatum* (*connatum*) and *S. terebinthinaceum*, prairie dock.

Silt, the mineral fraction of SOILS which is between 20 and 2 μm (0·02 to 0·002 mm) in size on the International Texture Scale (50 and 2 μm on the US Department of Agriculture scale). The particles are small, irregular fragments, essentially micro-sands, with quartz as the dominant mineral. They add little to the nutrient content of soils and because of their small size may give rise to cultivation problems unless supplemented by clay, sand, and organic material.

Siltstone, an ARGILLACEOUS ROCK composed of grains ranging in diameter from 0·004 to 0·06 mm.

Silures, ancient British people who inhabited what are now the counties of Gwent, the three Glamorgans, and the southern part of Powys. They opposed the Roman conquest, but were subdued by SCAPULA and his successors (48–78). Their chief town was Venta Silurum (modern Caerwent) about 9 km west of Chepstow, where excavations have been made.

Silurian System, geological name of the third of the Paleozoic systems of strata occurring above the ORDOVICIAN and below the DEVONIAN SYSTEMS. The Silurian began between 435 and 460 million years ago and ended about 405 million years ago. Rocks of Silurian age outcrop in Wales, the Southern Uplands of Scotland, the Lake District, and in numerous small inliers; they also occur in the west of Ireland. The Silurian is divided into the Llandovery series, at the base, followed by the Wenlock and Ludlow series. The Downtonian series, which occurs above the Ludlow, is classified by some authors as

Silurian and by others as Devonian. As it represents the final phase of Silurian sedimentation it will be described with the Silurian.

The Silurian rocks as a whole are characterised by two contrasted FACIES; the 'shelf' facies, shallow water fossiliferous sediments laid down on the continental shelf, and the 'basin' facies, graptolitic shales and greywackes deposited towards the centre of the basin of deposition. The Silurian is divided into a number of zones based on the graptolite faunas. The Llandovery series in Wales consists of shales, mudstones, and greywackes containing brachiopods, trilobites, and graptolites. In the Welsh Borders the Llandovery strata are thinner and represent near-shore deposition. Further north in the Lake District there are black graptolitic shales and mudstones of Llandovery age, deposited in the same basin as the Welsh rocks. In the Southern Uplands the Llandovery consists of fine-grained black graptolitic shales at the base, passing up into coarse grits, greywackes, and conglomerates. The Wenlock series in the Welsh Borders contains the Wenlock limestone, a highly fossiliferous limestone containing brachiopods, corals, stromatoporoids, trilobites, and many other shelly fossils typical of the 'shelf' facies rocks. Towards the west they pass laterally into greywackes and graptolitic shales of the 'basin' facies. The Ludlow series shows the same pattern of facies distribution between the Welsh Borders and central Wales; in the Welsh Borders it consists of shales and a limestone horizon, the Aymestry limestone, again highly fossiliferous. In the Lake District the Wenlock consists of flags, while the Ludlow is a very thick sequence of sandy mudstones, flags, and grits. Further north in the Southern Uplands the Wenlock consists of thick greywackes. The Downtonian occurs in the Welsh Borders and includes red and purple marls and sandstones, with a very well-known bone bed, the Ludlow bone bed, at its base. This contains fish scales, spines, and fragmental fish remains. The Downtonian contains occasional fish remains and the oldest known land plants.

The first jawed fishes appeared in the Silurian, but the bulk of the fauna is made up of brachiopods, trilobites, crinoids, cephalopods, lamellibranchs, and gasteropods. The graptolites died out in the British area before the end of the Silurian, but are found at higher horizons in continental Europe.

The Silurian marks the last episode in the filling of the Lower PALAEOZOIC basins of deposition, and the thick greywackes which become more pronounced and thicker towards the top of the Silurian are the precursors of the CALEDONIAN OROGENY; they represent the thick 'flysch' type deposits indicative of an increased mobility in the crust. They can be related to ridges and basins formed early in the history of the Caledonian mountain chain. The major late-Caledonian orogenic episode occurred in late Silurian and early Devonian times, and caused low-grade regional metamorphism and granite intrusion.

Bibliography: L. M. Cocks, *Correlation of Silurian Rocks in the British Isles*, 1971.

Silva, António José da (1705–39), Portuguese dramatist, born in Rio de Janeiro; he was tortured by the Inquisition during his college days at Coimbra because he was a Jew, and finally suffered martyrdom. His comedies, the best of which is *Guerras do Alecrim e da Mangerona*,

1737, are notable for their vigorous verbal and situational comedy, and for their mordant social satire.

Silvanus, ancient Italian deity, originally of uncultivated fields and of forests, especially as protector of their boundaries. Later his patronage was extended to cattle, and he was identified with PAN and FAUNUS.

Silver, metallic chemical element, symbol Ag, atomic number 47, atomic weight 107·868; occurs in nature in the free state and in combination. Natural silver generally contains gold, copper, and other metals. Important ores are argentite (Ag_2S), pyrargyrite (ruby silver ore, Ag_3SbS_3), stephanite (Ag_5SbS_4), and horn silver (AgCl). Lead ores (galena) constitute one of the main supplies of silver. Mexico and the USA are the two great silver-producing countries, and yield about one-third of the world's output. The metallurgical processes for the extraction of the metal from its ores may be classified as: (1) amalgamation methods, (2) cyanide process, (3) smelting methods.

1. Amalgamation methods depend on the fact that mercury reduces certain compounds of silver and forms an amalgam with the liberated metal. The amalgam formed is collected, washed, and filtered and the silver obtained by distilling off the mercury. This method has been replaced by the cyanide process.

2. In the cyanide process the ore is mixed with water and ground into a slime, which is then mixed with sodium cyanide solution. Air oxidation follows, to convert any sodium sulphide to sulphate. Finally, the sodium argentocyanide in solution is reduced to silver with zinc dust. The metal is removed and purified.

3. With smelting methods the argentiferous ores are smelted with lead ores, and an alloy of silver and lead is obtained. If the alloy is rich in silver it is subjected to cupellation in a special cupel or furnace, the bed of which is composed of bone ash and pearl ash. During cupellation lead oxide (PbO) forms a scum on the surface of the molten metal and is blown off, while some of it is absorbed by the furnace bed. If too poor in silver to be directly cupelled, the alloy is concentrated by Parkes's process. This process depends upon the fact that when zinc is added to a melted alloy of lead and silver the zinc forms an alloy with the silver, rises to the surface, and can be readily removed as it solidifies before the molten lead. The operation is carried out in iron pots, and the zinc-silver alloy is skimmed off with a ladle, liquated and finally distilled, and the residue of silver and lead is cupelled.

A relatively large proportion of the new silver produced is obtained during the refining of other metals, such as copper and lead. Owing to its high value, silver-bearing scrap is carefully conserved, and greatly contributes to available supplies of the metal. Such silver is usually refined electrolytically.

Silver is a lustrous white metal (relative density 10·5, melting point 961·5 °C), and is extremely malleable and ductile, being second only to gold. It has the highest conductivity for heat and electricity of all the metals. Two oxides of silver are known, the monoxide, argentic oxide (AgO), and a suboxide, argentous oxide (Ag_2O). The monoxide is the most important, and is formed by addition of sodium, potassium or barium hydroxide to a solution of a silver salt. It is a brown amorphous powder,

soluble in strong ammonia, and is formed also when a soluble chloride is added to silver nitrate. The bromide and iodide are formed similarly by addition of soluble bromides and iodides to silver nitrate. These halogen salts are largely used in photography, since they blacken on exposure to light. The most important salt of silver is the nitrate, which is formed by dissolving the metal in nitric acid.

Silver is a semi-noble metal because of its considerable resistance to corrosion, and is also of especially pleasing appearance and high reflectivity. It is unattacked by foodstuffs and fruit juices. For these reasons it has been used from ancient times for coinage and for domestic and ornamental articles. Pure silver alone being somewhat too soft for these purposes, an alloy containing 92·5 per cent silver and 7·5 per cent copper is used, and is known as 'sterling' from Old English *steorra*, star, with which some early Norman coins were marked. It is illegal to offer for sale articles which have not been assayed and 'hall-marked' (see HALLMARKS) to confirm that the silver content is at least of this quality.

Silver is also used as an electroplated coating on decorative and domestic articles, which are often made from 'nickel silver', also called 'German silver', an alloy of copper, nickel and zinc which does not in fact contain silver, hence EPNS (electroplated nickel silver). Silver is widely employed in the electrical and chemical engineering industries and is a constituent of silver solders.

Silver in Manufacturing. In the silverware trade the metal is used chiefly for ornamental table pieces, presentation ware, and trophies.

Silver Tarnish. Experiments have been conducted for many years in an effort to produce a silver alloy of the required standard which will be resistant to tarnish. Although this has not been achieved, research has produced cleaning preparations which readily remove tarnish, and there is now an impregnated paper which effectively wards off tarnish when used as a shelf lining or a wrapping.

Silver Coinage. The British silver coinage, which originated in the 7th century was of sterling standard until 1921 (except for the debasements of the Tudor period). In that year it was debased to 50 per cent silver. The British Government in 1946 introduced a new Coinage Bill, which provided that coins formerly struck in silver (with the exception of Maundy money) could thenceforth be struck in cupro-nickel. Technically the Bill did not abolish silver as coinage, but for all practical purposes meant that all coins were to be replaced by cupro-nickel. The Bill received the royal assent 6 November 1946. The government's decision was founded on sound practical grounds, silver having become too expensive, especially as it had to be paid for in dollars. The domestic demand for silver had risen too, partly because of war-time requirements for coinage, and partly because of the greatly increased use of silver for industrial purposes, especially in the electrical and photographic trades. Almost all the pre-1946 silver coins have disappeared from circulation although they are still legal tender; this is due to the Royal Mint systematically withdrawing them and melting them down, together with a degree of private collecting and illicit melting to remove the silver.

Silver-fish, see APTERYGOTA; THYSANURA.

Silver Fox, see FUR.

Silver State, see NEVADA.

Silver Thaw, American popular term for hoar frost, rime, and glazed frost. See PRECIPITATION.

Silver War Badge, British decoration approved, in 1916, for issue to officers and men of the British, Indian, and Overseas Forces who had served at home or abroad since 4 August 1914, and who, on account of age or from physical infirmity arising from wounds or sickness caused by military service, had, in the case of officers, retired or relinquished their commissions, or, in the case of men, been discharged from the army. In view of the provisions of the Military Service (Review of Exceptions) Act 1917 the conditions of the grant of the Silver War Badge were modified and various terms used in the original grant were defined. The Silver War Badge has a brooch attachment. A similar device, but of much less elaborate design, was instituted for the Second World War. Named the King's Badge, it was issued by the Ministry of Pensions.

Silverpoint drawing by Leonardo da Vinci, Bust of a Warrior. (British Museum, London)

Silverpoint, technique of drawing with an instrument pointed with silver on paper prepared with a gesso ground. It was used for the most exquisite work by LEONARDO DA VINCI, DÜRER and early Flemish masters. It is little used today because modern paintings rarely demand intricate preparatory studies or favour the delicacy of touch achieved with this medium.

Silversmithing. Among ancient races the art of working gold or silver (see also GOLDSMITHING), either by hammering or by casting, reached a remarkably high degree of skill. The attractive colour of these metals; their resistance to corrosion, by which they outlast other metals, their readiness to take shape under the hammer (malleability), or when cast, their ductility when drawn into wire, coupled with the high polish obtainable—these qualities commended them to craftsmanship, and Egyptian tombs have revealed an equal skill in gold and silversmithing, though silver was then the greater rarity. The gold cups of Vaphio, found in Crete, speak of the Mycenaean civilisation, 1800–1100 BC, and the command they show of modelling animals or the human figure in low relief continued through Greek and Roman times. The Mildenhall treasure, found in 1942 in Suffolk and judged to be Roman work of AD 300–400, comprised trays, dishes, goblets, spoons and bowls. Silversmiths in the Byzantine era imparted colour to their gold and silver by enamelling, and the art, carried westwards, reached Britain through France.

In England, as in the rest of Europe, the Church was the chief patron in the early Middle Ages, but from the 14th century onwards, the extent of domestic patronage increased dramatically, as the inventories of kings and noblemen show. Much of the grandest silver was decorated with enamels (e.g. the Royal Gold Cup in the British Museum). Tudor plate is strongly influenced by German and Netherlandish craftsmen who settled in England during the Reformation, bringing with them Renaissance and Mannerist forms and decoration. The Civil War saw the melting down of much plate, and the silver which was made is characterised by its simplicity and provincialism. Most English plate now surviving dates from the Restoration onwards. The dominant stylistic influence in this period is Dutch and most pieces are heavily embossed with floral ornament, sometimes combined with animals: CHINOISERIE made its first appearance usually as engraved ornament. With the arrival of the Huguenot refugees from 1685 onwards French influence also made itself felt. They brought with them the ornate classical designs current in France and combined them with the severe outlines of the 'William and Mary' style to produce an idiosyncratic effect which lasted until the 1730s. The asymmetrical, scrolling lines of the Rococo preponderated until the 1760s when the Roman silver unearthed at HERCULANEUM contributed to a revival of classicism which thrived in varying forms until the 1820s. Victorian silver is characterised by the same eclecticism and historicism as the other branches of the arts.

The silversmith, for the last six hundred years, has been rigidly controlled in the quality of his metal (see HALL-MARKS). Sterling silver has throughout been the standard, except when an alloy of higher silver content (Britannia silver) was enforced. The first systematic use of a substitute for silver was the invention of Sheffield plate, by

Silversmithing

Silversmithing. TOP LEFT Silver anklet of chain pattern from Ajmir, India, 19th century. CENTRE LEFT Cup from the silver treasure found at Boscoreale, Pompeii. The inscriptions exhort enjoyment of life while it lasts. BOTTOM LEFT Sheffield plate cup and cover, 1760. BELOW Knife and spoon by Antonio Gentile da Faenza, late 16th century, Italian. FACING PAGE Fruit plate, English Tudor, c. 1573. (CENTRE LEFT *Louvre, Paris/Bisonte;* BELOW *Metropolitan Museum of Art, New York, Rogers Fund, 1947;* OTHERS *Victoria and Albert Museum, London*)

Thomas Boulsover in 1742; upon a sheet of copper he fused a thin sheet of silver, at first on one side only, then on both. This sheet was then worked into the forms current in silverware. Since the copper showed at the edges, special mouldings called mounts were soldered on. Both in cost and through being largely struck from dies, Sheffield Plate offered serious competition to silversmiths. The subsequent invention of electro-plating (1840), for the same reasons, enables many more people to purchase 'silver' domestic ware, the centres for this manufacture being Birmingham and Sheffield. The same factories produce silverware, and, in addition, London silversmiths have retained the hand methods of tradition and produce the higher grade of article.

Bibliography: C. C. Oman, *English Domestic Silver*, 1934, 1947; Victoria and Albert Museum, *Charles II Domestic Silver, Tudor Domestic Silver, English Silver from Charles II to the Regency;* G. S. Gibb, *The Whitesmiths of Taunton*, 1946; J. M. Phillips, *American Silver*, 1949; G. Grimwade, *The Queen's Silver*, 1953, and *Rococo Silver 1727–65*, 1974; J. F. Hayward, *Huguenot Silver in England 1688–1727*, 1959; M. Clayton, *The Collector's Dictionary of Silver and Gold*, 1971.

Silvertown, see NEWHAM.

Silves, town of Portugal, in Faro district 50 km northwest of Faro. It was the capital of ALGARVE under the MOORS, from whom it was taken in 1242. There is a Gothic cathedral and a ruined Moorish castle. The region produces figs, olives, vines, and almonds. Population 27,000.

Silvester (popes), see SYLVESTER.

Silvester Gozzolini, Saint (1177–1267), Italian religious founder, born at Osimo. In 1231, after receiving a vision of St Benedict, he instituted a new congregation of Benedictines, known as Blue Benedictines, from the colour of their habit. It was approved by the pope in 1247. Silvester represents the new growth of Benedictinism in Italy, which coincided with the foundation of the new orders of friars. Canonised in 1598, his feast is on 26 November.

Silviculture, or sylviculture (Latin *sylva*, *silva*, a wood; *cultura*, cultivation), the theory and practice of cultivating (growing and tending) forest crops (see ARBORICULTURE; FORESTRY). The silviculture of naturally-occurring forests of mixed species is much more complex than that of even-aged plantations of a single species, and has perhaps reached its highest form in the management of the 'selection' forests in Switzerland.
Bibliography: D. M. Smith, *The Practice of Silviculture*, 7th ed. 1962.

Sim, Alastair (1900–76), British actor, born in Edinburgh. He was a lecturer in elocution at Edinburgh, 1925–30, and Rector of Edinburgh University, 1948–51. His first stage appearance was in 1930; subsequently he was associated as actor or producer with several of James Bridie's plays, including *Mr Bolfry*, *Dr Angelus* and *Mr Gillie*. He made his film debut in 1934, and among his films were the *Inspector Hornleigh* series, *Cottage to Let*, *Let the People Sing*, *Green for Danger*, *Hue and Cry*, *Happiest Days of your Life*, *Laughter in Paradise*, *Scrooge*, *The Belles of St Trinian's* and *Geordie*. He specialised in the portrayal of comic, rather eccentric characters. In 1953 he was made a CBE.

Simancas, town of Spain in the province of Valladolid, on the River Pisuerga. The national archives have been kept in its citadel since 1563. Population 1100.

Simaroubaceae, family of 20 genera and 120 species of dicotyledonous shrubs and trees, mainly tropical and subtropical, although a number of species are hardy in Britain. The bark usually contains bitter compounds which have been used medicinally (see QUASSIA) and the leaves are generally pinnately compound. The flowers are often borne in much-branched clusters; the sepals number three to seven and the petals are of equal number. The stamens are generally twice as many as the sepals; the carpels are three to five, joined together, ripening generally to a dry fruit, sometimes breaking when ripe into winged, wind-dispersed parts. The main genera are AILANTHUS (tree of heaven), *Picrasma*, *Quassia* and *Simarouba*.

Simbirsk, see ULYANOVSK.

Simcoe, Lake, in Ontario, Canada, between Lake Ontario and Georgian Bay. It is 50 km long by 29 km wide, and discharges itself into Lake Huron through the Severn river. This lake, along with many others in this part of Canada, has become an important recreation focus. It is surrounded by holiday cabins and second homes belonging to families living in the cities of southern Ontario. Area 700 km².

Simenon, Georges (1903–), Belgian novelist, born at Liège. A prolific writer of fiction, including ambitious psychological novels like *La Neige était sale*, 1948 (*The Stain on the Snow*, 1953), he is internationally famous for his detective stories. His name is inseparably linked with that of Maigret, the *commissaire de police*, who figures in more than 70 of his tales.
Bibliography: T. Narcejac, *The Art of Simenon*, 1952.

Simeon, one of the tribes of Israel, descended from Simeon, the second son of Jacob and Leah. It played an important part in the conquest of Canaan, and it received the territory to the south of Judah, but was almost extinguished in wars against the PHILISTINES, and absorbed into Judah, perhaps in the days of Samuel. This was the fulfilment of the curse on Simeon uttered in the Blessing of Jacob (Gen. xlix. 5–7), for the slaughter of the Shechemites (Gen. xxxiv. 1–31).

Simeon, a devout Jew in Jerusalem awaiting the Messiah. On seeing the infant Jesus brought into the Temple he uttered the hymn of praise, now know as *Nunc Dimittis* (Luke ii. 29–35).

Simeon I, the Great (d. 927), Tsar of the Bulgars, succeeded Prince Vladimir in 893. Under Simeon Bulgar power reached its zenith. He twice captured Adrianople, and in 923 forced the Byzantine Emperor to a humiliating peace.
Bibliography: D. Obolensky, *The Byzantine Commonwealth*, 1971.

Simeon II (1937–), former King of Bulgaria, son of Boris III and Giovanna of Italy. He succeeded to the throne on his father's death in 1943, but in 1946 Bulgaria became a republic, and Simeon has since lived in exile abroad.

Simeon, Charles (1759–1836), English cleric, born at Reading, educated at Eton and King's College, Cambridge. After being elected a fellow of King's he was ordained, and in 1783 became perpetual curate of Holy Trinity, Cambridge. He was one of the leaders of the evangelical party in the Church of England, and exercised great influence at his university. He was one of the founders of the CHURCH MISSIONARY SOCIETY, and established the Simeon Trust to provide livings for evangelical clergy.

Simeon, Song of, see NUNC DIMITTIS.

Simeon of Durham (c. 1070–c. 1130), English chronicler, precentor of Durham. He was the author of *Historia Ecclesiae Dunelmensis* (first printed in 1732), the manuscript of which is preserved in the library of Bishop Cosin, and of *Historia Regum Anglorum et Danorum*.

Simeon Stylites, Saint (from the Greek *stulos*, pillar) (390–459), Christian monk of Syria in the 5th century. He is reputed to have spent the last 37 years of his life on a pillar, 20 m high and 1 m wide at the top, erected near Antioch. He preached by day, and crowds of pilgrims flocked to receive his exhortations. His feast is on 5 January.

Simferopol, capital city and cultural centre of the Crimean *oblast* (see CRIMEA) of the Ukrainian SSR, USSR, and the centre of a fruit-growing district. It has varied engineering and food industries, and is the site of the Crimean branch of the Ukrainian Academy of Sciences. Excavations of prehistoric and Scythian settlements have been made here. Founded in 1784 on the site of the Tatar settlement of Ak Mechet, it was the capital of the Tatar nationalist government in 1918, of General Wrangel's government in 1920, and of the Crimean Autonomous Republic 1921–46. Population (1974) 275,000.

Simile (Latin *similis*, like), a comparison, definitely expressed, between two things of different kinds. It is therefore not a simile to say that a girl looks like Cleopatra, but it is to say 'My love is like a red, red rose'. Usually a simile is introduced by the words 'like' or 'as' (Kipling's 'He trod the ling like a buck in spring and he looked like a lance in rest', for example).

A simile is especially effective when an abstract thought is illustrated by a concrete comparison, as in Keats's lines:

Then felt I like some watcher of the skies
When a new planet swims into his ken.

The simile is closely related to METAPHOR, but is explicit, whereas the metaphor's comparison is implicit. See also FIGURE OF SPEECH.

Simla, capital of HIMACHAL PRADESH state, India, situated on a ridge in the foothills of the Himalayas 2200 m above sea-level. A hill resort with sanatoria, it was a favourite summer resort for the British rulers and Indian government until independence. Population (1971) 47,000.

Simmel, Georg (1858–1918), German philosopher and sociologist who held university posts at Berlin and Strasbourg. His essays have been influential in the development of sociology, particularly those concerning forms of social interaction, for instance reciprocal relations in dyadic and triadic groups (groups with two or three members respectively).

Bibliography: K. Wolff (Ed.), *The Sociology of Georg Simmel*, 1950.

Simms, William Gilmore (1806–70), US man of letters, born at Charleston, South Carolina. He studied law there and was admitted to the Bar in 1827. Simms was the author of a poem, *Atalantis*, and several historical romances including *The Yemassee*, 1835, *Mellichampe*, 1836, and *Beauchampe*, 1842. Of these *The Yemassee* is the most important, giving an account of a campaign which is otherwise virtually unknown, and dealing largely with Indian character and nature. His revolutionary romances depict social life at Charleston, and their action extends over the whole revolutionary period, with faithful portraits of the political and military leaders of the time.

Bibliography: Life by Joseph Ridgely, 1962.

Simnel, Lambert (fl. 1477–1534), English impostor, son of an Oxford joiner. As a tool in the hands of an Oxford priest, Richard Symonds, he was put forward to impersonate Edward, the young Earl of Warwick, son of George, Duke of Clarence, who was a prisoner in the Tower. Symonds secured the support of MARGARET, DUCHESS OF BURGUNDY and other Yorkist leaders for his protegé and Simnel was taken to Ireland where Yorkist sympathies were strong. In 1487 Simnel was crowned Edward VI in Dublin Cathedral.

When the conspiracy was discovered by Henry VII, Warwick was shown to the London public; meanwhile an armed force from Ireland, under the command of Sir Thomas Fitzgerald, landed in Lancashire, and marching upon the royal army, attacked it near Stoke-on-Trent (16 June 1487), where the battle took place in which the King's forces were victorious, and Simnel and the priest made prisoners. It is traditionally said that Simnel was then made a scullion in the King's kitchens.

Simon, Claude (1913–), French novelist, born in Tananarive, Madagascar. His early novels were conventional and include *Le Tricheur*, 1945, *La Corde raide*, 1947, *Gulliver*, 1952, and *Le Sacre du printemps*, 1954. It was with *Le Vent*, 1957, *L'Herbe*, 1958, *La Route des Flandres*, 1960, and *Le Palace*, 1962, that he came to the notice of the public and was, misleadingly, classified as a 'new novelist'. The later novels (*Histoire*, 1967, *La Bataille de Pharsale*, 1969, *Les Corps conducteurs*, 1971, and *Triptyque*, 1973) have confirmed his reputation as among the most gifted novelists of his age. In 1970 he published an autobiographical work, *Orion aveugle*. He has written little criticism and remains outside the polemics surrounding the 'New Novel'.

Bibliography: J. Loubère, *Claude Simon*, 1975.

Simon, Sir John (1816–1904), British surgeon and sanitary reformer, born in London. In 1847 he became surgeon and lecturer on pathology at St Thomas's Hospital, and the following year he was appointed the first medical officer of health to the City of London. He held this appointment until 1855, when he was appointed medical officer to the Central Board of Health, and in 1858 he became medical officer to the Privy Council, which had taken over the duties of the Board. On the formation of the Local Government Board in 1871 he became its first medical officer, but in 1876 he resigned after disagreements with the administrative staff, after seeing the passing of the Public Health Act, 1875. He was also largely responsible for the Medical Act of 1858, introduced 'to regulate the qualifications of practitioners in medicine and surgery', and for the formation of the General Medical Council, which was created by that Act. His work in sanitary science directed its whole development. His principal works were *Public Health Reports*, 1887, and *English Sanitary Institutions*, 1890. He was created KCB in 1897.

Bibliography: R. Lambert, *Sir John Simon and English Social Administration*, 1963.

Simon, Jules François (1814–96), French statesman and philosopher, born at Lorient, became professor of philosophy at the Sorbonne in 1839. He was later deprived of his chair because of his political opinions. After the fall of the Empire, Simon was made minister of public instruction by the provisional government, and later minister of the interior, and put down the resistance of Gambetta to the peace concluded with Germany. In 1875 he was elected a member of the Academy and a life senator. On the resignation of Dufaure he became premier, but his policy of conciliation and the hostility of the Republicans alarmed MACMAHON, who virtually invited him to resign.

Simon Maccabaeus, Jewish high priest, one of the five brothers who fought against Syria for the freedom of

Palestine. From the first year of his pontificate (141 BC) a new era was counted. See also JEWS.

Simon Magus (fl. c. AD 37), a magician (Magus) who became a Christian and offered St Peter money in exchange for the power of bestowing the Holy Spirit by laying on of hands; hence 'simony'. Acts viii. 5–24 tells that he had proclaimed himself as 'some great one', and had a large following. Second-century Christian literature contains much legendary matter about him, in which the only certain fact seems to be that his teaching incorporated Christian elements. The inevitable hostility of such commentators as Justin Martyr, *Apology* I, xxvi and lvi, and Irenaeus, *Against the Heretics* I, xxiii, makes it impossible to distinguish truth from fiction.

Simon of Stackpole Elidor, John Allsebrook Simon, 1st Viscount (1873–1954), British statesman, born at Bath and educated at Fettes and Wadham College, Oxford. He became a fellow of All Souls College, Oxford, in 1897, was called to the Bar in 1899, and rapidly became an extremely successful advocate. He entered Parliament as a Liberal in 1906 and was appointed solicitor-general in 1910. In 1913 he became attorney-general with a seat in the Cabinet. When the Coalition Government was formed in May 1915 he was appointed home secretary, but resigned in 1916 as he was opposed to conscription. A period of 15 years out of office followed during which Simon devoted himself to his career as a back-bench MP and at the Bar. (He lost his Parliamentary seat in 1918, but was returned as Independent (Asquith) MP for Spen Valley in 1922, a seat he continued to hold until 1940.) Simon was appointed chairman of the statutory commission which was to investigate the development of government in India, in 1927, but his report was shelved.

In 1930 he formed and led the National Liberal party with the object of supporting the newly formed government of Ramsay MacDonald and in 1931 took office as foreign secretary where he was particularly criticised for failing to take a stronger line over Japanese aggression in Manchuria. In 1935 he was transferred to the Home Office and in 1937 to the chancellorship of the Exchequer. From 1935 to 1940 he was deputy leader of the House of Commons. He became lord chancellor in the National Government of 1940 and in that year was created viscount. He played little part in politics after Churchill's defeat in 1945. His publications include the autobiographical *Retrospect*, 1952.

Simon of Wythenshawe, Ernest Emil Darwin Simon, 1st Baron (1879–1960), British industrialist and social reformer, born in Manchester and educated at Rugby and Cambridge. Involved initially in local government, he became a member of Manchester City Council in 1912 and was mayor in 1921. He spent two periods in Parliament, as a Liberal, from 1923 to 1924 and 1929 to 1931 and, briefly, served in 1931 as parliamentary secretary to the Minister of Health. An authority on housing the working classes and slum clearance and improvement schemes, he was also a member of the departmental committee on the valuation of dwelling houses in 1938. In 1946 he joined the Labour party and in 1947 was raised to the peerage. He was keenly interested in education and had begun in 1916 an association with Manchester University which led to his being chairman of Manchester University Council from 1941 to 1957. He was also chairman of the BBC from 1947 to 1952.

Bibliography: M. Stocks, *Ernest Simon of Manchester*, 1963.

Simon Stock, Saint (c. 1165–1265), English friar, born at Aylesford, Kent. He became a Carmelite and, in 1247, sixth general of the order. In this position he established houses in the chief university cities of Europe (Cambridge, 1248; Oxford, 1253; Paris, 1260; Bologna, 1260) and modified the rule, making the Carmelites an order of mendicant friars, instead of hermits. His feast is on 6 May.

Simone Martini, see MARTINI, SIMONE.

Simonides of Ceos (c. 556–468 BC), Greek lyric poet, born at Iulis, in Ceos. Having visited Hipparchus at Athens, he stayed for a time with Scopas in Thessaly, and returned to Athens at the beginning of the Persian wars. He moved to the court of Hieron at Syracuse about 476. The most famous of Simonides's surviving fragments is the epitaph on the Spartan dead at Thermopylae.

Bibliography: J. M. Edmonds (Trans.), *Lyra Graeca*, 1922; C. M. Bowra, *Greek Lyric Poetry from Alcman to Simonides*, 1936.

Simonoseki, see SHIMONOSEKI.

Simonstown, naval base in CAPE PROVINCE, South Africa, on False Bay, 37 km south of Cape Town; it derives its name from Simon Van der Stel, an early governor of the Cape of Good Hope. In 1741 it was occupied by the Netherlands government as a naval and military base. In 1814 the British Admiralty made Simonstown the main base for the South Atlantic Naval Squadron, and thus the most important strategic Royal Navy base in the southern hemisphere. There are extensive dry-docks and harbour works. In 1922 the Union government agreed to take responsibility for the maintenance and manning of the forts commanding them. Under an agreement signed in 1955 Simonstown was transferred to South Africa, but Britain was guaranteed the fullest facilities in both peace and war. The strategic importance of Simonstown was highlighted when the Suez Canal was closed and most shipping from Far East and Australasia had to use the Cape route. This caused embarrassment to British Labour governments in the 1960s which were compelled to honour the Simonstown Agreement entailing the continued supply of certain armaments to South Africa. In 1975 another Labour government ended the agreement, although the facilities of Simonstown remain open to Britain, as to other countries.

Simony (derived from SIMON MAGUS), the purchase or sale of spiritual things. Early conciliar decrees prove that simony became common in the Church after the ages of persecution. The Council of Chalcedon (451) forbade ordination for money, and St Gregory the Great later denounced the same evil. Simony became widespread in the Middle Ages, especially by way of traffic in ecclesiastical preferment, which was repeatedly forbidden by such popes as Gregory VII as well as by the third Lateran Council (1179). Simony was treated in great detail by St Thomas Aquinas, and was vigorously condemned three centuries later by the Council of Trent. The present

Roman Catholic legislation is contained in canons 728, 2372, 2392 and 2371 of the *Codex Juris Canonici*. The Anglican canons of 1604 included provision against simony in the reception of benefices. The system of ecclesiastical patronage gave rise to simony in many cases, an abuse remedied by the English Benefices Act of 1898.

Simoum, see STORM; WIND.

Simple Harmonic Motion (SHM), general name given to motion of natural vibration and oscillation. It is the motion of a body under the influence of an opposing force that is directly proportional to the displacement of the body from a point in its line of motion. Thus it includes the oscillation about the position of equilibrium of a weight supported by a spring or an elastic string, the small oscillations of the bob of a pendulum, the vibration of any point on the string of a musical instrument, and finally wave motion in general, of which the last example is a particular case. Thus, if a series of waves moves regularly over a surface, any point on the surface will move up and down with SHM. If equal and opposite waves move in opposite directions, a standing wave will be formed, and certain points called *nodes* will remain fixed; and this is the case with the strings of a musical instrument fixed at both ends which are nodes. If a pencil is moved up and down with SHM in contact with a piece of paper which is moved sideways at a uniform rate, a characteristic tracing is obtained. The curve produced (fig. 1) can be obtained by plotting the graph of sin *x*.

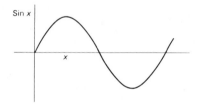

Simple Harmonic Motion. Figure 1. Sine curve.

A point moves with SHM when its acceleration at any instant is proportional, and opposite in sign, to its displacement from a given point. The motion represented in fig. 1 can be shown to agree with this definition as follows.

Simple Harmonic Motion. Figure 2.

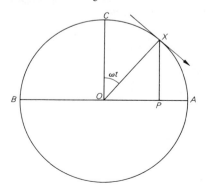

Let a point *X* (fig. 2) move with uniform speed along the circumference of a circle, and let *XP* be the perpendicular on any fixed diameter *AB*. Then *P* will move with SHM. It will be seen that *P* moves continually backwards and forwards along *AB*, coming to rest instantaneously and turning back again at *A* and at *B*, and having its highest velocity when passing through the centre *O*. The time taken over one complete journey backwards and forwards (*OAOBO*) is termed the *period* of oscillation. The time to any position since last passing through the middle point *O* going in a direction previously fixed as positive is called the *phase*, and $a = OA$ is the *amplitude*. If ω is the constant angular velocity of *OX* (in radians per second), and *t* the time (in seconds) from *C*, the end of the perpendicular diameter to *AB*, to the point *X*, then the angle *COX* is ωt. *OP* is the projection of *OX* on *AB* and equals $a \sin \omega t$. This displacement of *P* from *O* varies with time in the manner shown in fig. 1. The period is the time for *X* to go once completely round the circumference i.e., $2\pi/\omega$, and is independent of the amplitude *a*. Since *X* has a velocity $a\omega$ along the tangent to the circle, and by virtue of its circular motion an acceleration $a\omega^2$ along *XO*, it will be seen that *P* has a velocity $a\omega\cos\omega t$ along *OA* and an acceleration towards *O*, $a\omega^2\sin\omega t$, i.e., $\omega^2 OP$. Thus the point *P* has an acceleration directed towards *O* which is proportional to its displacement from *O*. Therefore *P* moves with SHM about *O*. As the point *P* passes through *O* on its backwards journey, the acceleration becomes a retardation proportional to the distance from *O*. More complicated forms of SHM may be obtained by compounding two or more SHMs. The compounding of two SHMs of equal periods, but different amplitudes *a* and *b*, along axes *Ox* and *Oy* produces a motion given by the ellipse $x^2/a^2 + y^2/b^2 = 1$.

Simplified Spelling. The primary purpose of an alphabetic script is to represent in a visible form the sounds of the spoken language (see ALPHABET). It is sometimes maintained that the ideal of such a script would be that each sound should be represented by one character only, and that each character should have only one sound. However, this ideal is not fully realised in the spelling of any modern European language, although some—German, Italian, and Spanish among the major ones—approach it. However, the written form of the two main cultural languages of western Europe, English and French, is very far removed from the spoken form. English, for example, has innumerable anomalies such as: (1) the different sound of *-ough* in *bough*, *though*, *through*, *thorough*, *cough*, *rough*, and (2) the different representations of the same diphthong in *vain*, *vein*, *way*, *whey*, *weight*, *game*, and so on.

The main reason for this state of affairs is that the spelling of English, which was reasonably close to the spoken language in the medieval period, has not kept pace with the changing pronunciation; for example, the *-gh* in words like *light*, *brought*, is a relic of a sound—the *ch* of *loch*—that had already disappeared 400 years ago. Further, the situation has been aggravated by the introduction of 'silent' letters under the influence of ETYMOLOGY, for example, the *b* of *debt* and the *p* of *receipt* recall the Latin *debitum* and *receptum*; some such additions are mistaken, for example, the *s* of *isle* (Old

Simplified Spelling

French *isle* from Latin *insula*) has been carried over into the unrelated word *island* (earlier *iland* from Old English *igland*).

While the difficulties presented by the archaic spelling of English are sometimes exaggerated, they are nevertheless real, and suggestions and schemes for reform are frequently put forward. Different aims and methods are possible. One may attempt either: (1) to rationalise the existing orthography by a number of limited reforms—one could, for example, cut out 'silent' letters which have no rôle in pronunciation and write *det*, *lam*, *thru*, and so on; replace *ph* by *f*; distinguish between the two values of *th* and write, for instance, *dhey*, *dhen*; and change the spelling of a few individual words, replacing *rough* and *cough*, for example, by *ruf* and *cof*; or (2) to introduce a far-reaching reform, basically phonetic, using either (a) the existing alphabet with a number of additional characters or (b) a completely new alphabet. But orthographies are meant primarily for the eye, and silent letters in words like 'phlegm' and 'paradigm' provide a visual link with associated forms in which the letters are pronounced, as in 'phlegmatic' and 'paradigmatic'.

One of the earliest advocates of spelling reform in England was Isaac PITMAN, who, having been inspired by the complexity of English orthography to launch his SHORTHAND in 1837, went on to introduce in 1843 in his *Phonotypic Journal* a new alphabet of 40 characters, those of the Roman alphabet and modifications thereof, suitable for the printing of English. One advantage claimed for this system was that it made learning to read much easier, while at the same time not departing too far from traditional orthography, so that existing books would still be legible to those who might wish to continue to read them, just as Chaucer's spelling is still fairly accessible to the modern reader. A. J. Ellis's *A Plea for Phonetic Spelling*, 1848, is an illustration of contemporary ideas on the issue.

In recent years Pitman's ideas have been introduced by teachers through the Initial Teaching Alphabet (i.t.a.), used in some reading primers for the primary school system in Britain. It is probably the most successful of the teaching alphabets because its closeness to the Roman alphabet facilitates the ultimate move into the generally-used orthography.

In the 20th century spelling reform has been advocated by various bodies, including the Simplified Spelling Society (founded 1908), which in 1932 petitioned the Board of Education to inquire into the problem. The Augmented Roman Alphabet was introduced experimentally into a number of British schools in 1961, designed purely to make learning to read easier for children. There were no capital letters, and 19 new characters represented two-lettered or confusingly symbolised elements of English spelling. However, the experiment met with very limited acceptance.

In his will George Bernard SHAW provided for the design and publication of a completely new and phonetic non-Roman alphabet, and in 1962 an edition of *Androcles and the Lion* in the 'Shaw Alphabet', with introduction, key, and parallel text in the normal alphabet, was published. The 48-character alphabet was designed by Kingsley Read.

The difficulties involved in any substantial reform of English spelling are so great that any major change seems unlikely in the foreseeable future. However, the alphabet of the International Phonetic Association aims to eliminate the inequalities and redundancies of ordinary alphabets. See also PHONETICS.

Bibliography: W. A. Craigie, *Problems of Spelling Reform*, 1944; J. A. Downing, *The New Augmented Roman Alphabet*, 1962; W. Haas, *Alphabets for English*, 1969.

Simplon Pass, Swiss Alpine pass between Brig in canton VALAIS and Iselle in Italy. The road over the pass was built between 1800–07 on Napoleon's orders. There are as many as 600 bridges and rock tunnels along the route. The road (length 47 km) is less used since the opening of the 20 km long railway tunnel (the longest in the world) in 1906. Altitude 2008 m.

Simpson, Sir George Clarke (1878–1965), British meteorologist, born in Derby, educated at the Diocesan school there and at Göttingen University; he was Imperial Meteorologist in India from 1906 to 1920, and was meteorologist to the British Antarctic expedition, 1910–12, and wrote on atmospheric electricity, terrestrial radiation, and ice ages. Simpson was director of the Meteorological Office from 1920 to 1938.

Simpson, Sir James Young (1811–70), British physician who introduced chloroform anaesthesia. Born at Bathgate, Scotland, he graduated MD at Edinburgh in 1832, where he was appointed professor of midwifery eight years later. In 1847 he discovered the anaesthetic value of chloroform and its advantages over ether. He introduced it into his obstetric practice immediately finding himself in conflict with the Calvinists, who opposed the use of anaesthesia in childbirth. It was not until 1853 when Queen Victoria accepted the use of chloroform for the birth of Prince Leopold that criticism of Simpson died down. He published books and papers on gynaecology, obstetrics, anaesthesia, and homeopathy, and was also distinguished for his writings on general literature and archaeology. He was made a baronet in 1866. A bust was erected in his honour in Westminster Abbey.

Bibliography: Life by E. B. Simpson, 1896; J. A. Shepherd, *Simpson and Syme of Edinburgh*, 1969; M. Simpson, *Simpson the Obstetrician*, 1972; R. S. Atkinson, *James Simpson*, 1973.

Simpson, N(orman) F(rederick) (1919–), English dramatist, educated at Emmanuel School and London University. He first achieved success with *A Resounding Tinkle*, 1957, which won the *Observer* play competition in 1956, and which was later performed at the Royal Court Theatre, London. His next full-length play was *One Way Pendulum*, 1959, 'a farce in a new dimension', which continued the vein of satirical comic fantasy of his first play. This was a success in the West End and later in repertory, and was also made into a film, 1964, scripted by Simpson. A later full-length play was *The Cresta Run*, a farcical study of espionage. Simpson has also written short plays and revue sketches, and television and radio plays. He has clear affinities with some of the dramatists of the THEATRE OF THE ABSURD, especially Eugène IONESCO: he specialises in making intricate and bizarre speculations and creating events based on absurd logical premises.

Bibliography: M. Esslin, *The Theatre of the Absurd*, rev. ed. 1968.

Simpson, Robert (1921–), British composer and writer

on music, born at Leamington, Warwickshire; studied with Howells and took a Mus D at Durham, 1952. In the same year his book *Carl Nielsen, Symphonist* appeared. He has worked for the BBC since 1951. His most important works are his five symphonies, heavily influenced by Nielsen and Bruckner. His 50th birthday Symposium was edited by E. Johnson, 1971.

Simpson, Tommy, see CYCLE RACING.

Simpson's Rule, a method for finding the approximate value of the area under a curve. Simpson's rule gives an approximation to the area enclosed by three straight lines and a curve as in fig. 1. AC and BD are parallel. $A\hat{C}D$ and $C\hat{D}B$ are right angles. (The area enclosed by a more complicated curve can be found by dividing it up into pieces to which Simpson's rule can be applied individually.) Draw an odd number $(2n - 1)$ of equidistant lines parallel to AC (see fig. 2). Denote the lengths of the lines by $y_0 \ (= AC)$, $y_1, ..., y_{2n-1}$, $y_{2n} \ (= BD)$. Then Simpson's rule is that the area $ABCD$ is approximately

$$CD(y_0 + 4y_1 + 2y_2 + 4y_3 + 2y_4 + ... + 2y_{2n-2} + 4y_{2n-1} + y_{2n})/6n.$$

In fact the rule adds together approximations to the n areas shaded in fig. 3. The approximation is arrived at by assuming the curves at the tops of these areas are PARABOLAS. The rule was stated by Thomas Simpson (1710–61).

Sims, James Marion (1813–83), US gynaecologist, born in Lancaster district, South Carolina, and educated at Jefferson Medical College, where he qualified in 1835. He is remembered for his operation for the repair of a vesico-vaginal fistula (an abnormal opening from the bladder to the vagina, due to injury). For this he invented the 'duck-billed' vaginal speculum (originally a bent spoon) named after him, which permitted an unobstructed view of the vaginal wall. He also devised a method for the amputation of the cervix uteri (neck of the womb). In 1853 he established the State Hospital for Women, New York, where, at Bryant Park, a statue to his memory was erected in 1894.

Simson, Robert (1687–1768), British mathematician, born at Kirktonhall, Ayrshire. Having studied in Glasgow and London, he was, in 1711, appointed by Glasgow University to the professorship of mathematics and held this post until 1761. His great work was his restoration of EUCLID's lost treatise on *Porisms*, 1776, and he also published *The Elements of Euclid*, 1756, which was for a long time the standard text of Euclid in Britain.

Simulator, Flight. Because of the high cost of flying modern aircraft, flight simulators are used for most types of aircraft to simulate actual flying conditions and thus economise in the cost of flying training and flight development work by enabling much of it to be done on the ground. Flight simulators are an extension of the LINK TRAINER principle.

Simuliidae, a family of the order DIPTERA, class Insecta. These are the blackflies or (USA) buffalo gnats. They are small but stoutly built flies with short antennae. They have broad wings with all the obvious veins in the anterior part of the wing. The family is widely distributed, the adults often occurring in such large numbers as to make them a nuisance, quite apart from the blood-sucking habit of the females. There are six larval stages that are found in running water, including cascades and waterfalls; they have a well capsulated head, a solitary thoracic proleg and a posterior sucker composed of small hooks by which they anchor themselves against the current. They are found on stones, reeds and crabs, mayfly larvae, and other aquatic forms. The pupae usually rest in a tent of silk in similar situations to the larvae. *Simulium* species are the vectors of ONCHOCERCIASIS in Central and South America, Africa, and the Yemen. They also transmit other filarial worms to cattle and to ducks. Simuliids are vectors of a large number of avian malarias to many birds including domestic stock, turkeys, ducks, and geese in North America and Canada. In addition, number of blackflies attacking livestock can be so great and the attacks so fierce as to kill the livestock, and human deaths have also occurred. Simuliidae are most abundant in north temperate and subarctic regions.

Simpson's Rule.

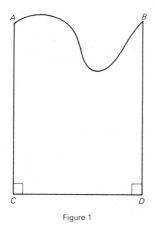

Figure 1

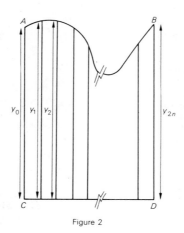

Figure 2

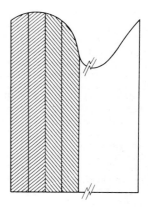

Figure 3

Sin

Sin, in Christian theology, is any word, deed, or thought contrary to the will of God (cf. St Augustine, *Contra Faustum* 22, 27; St Thomas, *Summa Theologica* i, 2, q. 71). It may be variously analysed. There is ORIGINAL SIN and Actual Sin, the sins we actually commit as distinct from an inherited infirmity and liability to do so. There is Material Sin and Formal Sin. Material Sin is a transgression of the Divine Will or Law regarded in itself, and apart from the knowledge and consent of the transgressor. Material Sins become Formal when they are deliberately and knowingly committed. Only Formal Sins involve guilt, because only they are the acts of a responsible person; but where the ignorance or lack of volition is culpable, responsibility, and so guilt, cannot be altogether avoided. There are degrees of gravity in sin and from this fact arises the further distinction between Venial Sin and Mortal Sin. Mortal Sin is a sin so grave that it completely cuts the soul off from God and Grace, and makes it liable to eternal damnation. Venial Sin is a sin of lesser degree that offends God, or displeases Him in some measure, without interrupting the soul's relations with Him.

Wycliffe, Luther, Calvin, and certain Jansenists following Baius, denied that there was such a thing as a venial sin making all sins, however small, mortal and deserving of Hell.

See also BAPTISM; GRACE; HELL; PENANCE.

Sin, or Zu'en (Sumerian *Nanna*), 'lord of wisdom', Babylonian moon god, chief of the second divine triad, composed of Sin, Shamash and Adad, or SHAMASH and ISHTAR. The Babylonian or Sumerian calendar was regulated by the moon, whence the high place held by this god in the national pantheon. Sin was the first-born of ENLIL, the Bel of Nippur, father of Shamash, the sun, and of Ishtar. Probably the most ancient seat of worship of Sin was at Ur; another was at Harran. He held a less exalted position in the Assyrian pantheon, being overshadowed by Ashur (see ASSUR).

Sin Eaters, men who, by partaking of food and drink (often a crust of bread and a pot of ale, or a piece of bread upon a plate of salt) laid upon the coffin or breast of a corpse, lift the burden of sin from the departed spirit and thus assure to it 'ease and rest' hereafter. This superstition was especially practised in Wales and bordering counties.

Sinai, province of EGYPT, a triangular peninsula at the head of the Red Sea. Area 62,000 km². The capital is El Arish (population 15,000). Minerals known to exist are manganese at Um Bogma and petroleum at Abu Durba. Sinai is the ancient source of turquoise. The inscribed monuments and the stone inscriptions and writings which were found in the Sinai peninsula fall into two groups: (1) the inscriptions known as Palaeo-Sinaitic, belonging probably to the 15th century BC. These, found in 1904–05 and 1928, in Serābit el Khādem, are written in a script which Albright has claimed to have deciphered; (2) the Neo-Sinaitic inscriptions and writings belonging to the 1st–3rd centuries AD and written in a script (Neo-Sinaitic) which may be considered as the link between the Nabataean and the Arabic alphabets. The peninsula is largely desert, occupied by a sparse nomadic population.

The modern significance of Sinai rests on its strategic importance as a buffer zone between Israel and Egypt, and the production of oil, begun in 1946, at Abu Rudeís,. The peninsula was occupied by Israeli forces in the June War of 1967, but Egyptian forces re-established themselves east of the Suez Canal in the war of 1973 (see ARAB-ISRAELI RELATIONS).

Bibliography: R. Samuel, *Negev and Sinai*, 1974.

Sinai, mountain also known as *Horeb*, upon which the law was delivered to Moses. Its identity is not absolutely certain, but the weight of opinion favours Jebel Mūsā ('Mountain of Moses'), 2500 m. In the 6th century AD many Anchorites inhabited the region; but today there is only one monastery, the Orthodox Convent of St Catherine, which is believed to possess her relics. Here were discovered the great Codex Sinaiticus and the Syriac Codex of the Gospels.

Sinaiticus, Codex, with the Vaticanus, one of the two earliest Greek vellum codices extant. Originally it probably had at least 730 leaves; now there are only 390, of which 242 contain a great part of the Old Testament and 148 leaves contain the whole New Testament with the Epistle of Barnabas and part of the 'Shepherd' of Hermas. Forty-three leaves (all of the Old Testament) are at Leipzig, three fragments at Leningrad; all the remaining leaves are in the British Museum, acquired in 1933 from the Soviet government for £100,000. Codex Sinaiticus was discovered in 1844 and 1859 by Constantine

Sinai. View from the top of Mount Sinai. *(Camera Press/Sam Waagenaar)*

Codex Sinaiticus. *(British Library, London)*

Tischendorf (1815–74) in the monastery of St Catherine at Mount SINAI (hence Sinaiticus). The leaves, which are of fine vellum, measure c. 40 x 35 cm, and are admirably preserved. The text is written in four columns to the page (two in the poetical books), with 48 lines to the column. Codex Sinaiticus seems to have been written by three scribes, and there are many corrections. The words are written continuously without separation, but high and middle points as well as the colon are used for punctuation. There are no accents or breathings. Sacred names are abbreviated. The place where Codex Sinaiticus was written is uncertain: Egypt is probable and Palestine (especially Caesarea) possible. The probable date is the middle of the 4th century. Codex Sinaiticus was published in full by Tischendorf in facsimile type in 1862; a photographic facsimile was published by the Oxford University Press: New Testament, 1911; Old Testament, 1922.

Bibliography: Codex Sinaiticus (8th ed.), 1934; H. J. M. Milne and T. C. Skeat, *The Codex Sinaiticus and the Codex Alexandrinus*, 1938.

Sinaloa, state of MEXICO, with its western coastline on the Gulf of California and the Pacific. Much of the state, particularly in the north, lies in the coastal plain with the foothills of the Sierra Madre Occidental rising in the east. The climate is hot and dry and cultivation is only possible with artificial irrigation or in the numerous small valleys carrying streams from the mountains to the sea. Essentially an agricultural state, the main crops being maize, beans, rice, sugar cane, vegetables, wheat, and cotton. Cattle raising is important in the hills to the east. It is an important mining area, the chief minerals being iron, lead, copper, and zinc, but poor communications have hampered development. All along the coast fishing plays a significant part in the economy. CULIACÁN is the capital and other major towns are the port of MAZATLÁN (population 174,000) and Los Mochis (45,000). Area 58,092 km². Population (1975) 1,642,000.

Sinatra, Frank, real name Francis Albert (1917–), US singer and actor. He began in radio in 1936 and became a band singer. He made his first appearance in films in 1943 and won an Oscar for the best supporting actor in *From Here to Eternity* (1953). Other films include *High Society, Guys and Dolls, None But the Brave* and *Von Ryan's Express*. Sinatra is the owner of music publishing companies and has composed a number of popular songs.

Sinclair, May (1870–1946), English writer, born at Rocky Ferry, near Birkenhead; educated at the Ladies' College, Cheltenham. She published some verse in 1887 and 1890 and her first novel, *Audrey Craven*, in 1896, but it was only with *The Divine Fire*, 1904, that she began to make a reputation for realism comparable with that of Gissing. With *The Creators*, 1910, and other works, she earned by about 1916 the general reputation of being one of the leading women writers. She served in the First World War with a field ambulance, recording her experiences under the title *Journal of Impressions in Belgium*, 1915; she also wrote two metaphysical essays, *A Defence of Idealism*, 1917, and *The New Idealism*, 1922; a late novel is *A Cure of Souls*, 1924.

Sinclair, Upton Beall (1878–1968), US novelist, born in Baltimore, Maryland. He was educated at the College of the City of New York and Columbia University. *Manassas*, 1904, was a brilliant novel of the Civil War. A socialist, he turned his attention to capitalistic abuses, and in 1906 gained world-wide fame by his powerful novel, *The Jungle*. This was a bitter exposure of the methods existing in the stockyards and meat-packing plants of Chicago, and led to Congress passing the first national pure food law.

In 1913 Sinclair investigated the abuses in the coalfields of Colorado, exposed them, and once more caused Congress to act. Out of his studies grew his novel *King Coal*, 1917. *The Profits of Religion*, 1918, is a bitter attack on the alleged coalition of religion with capitalism; *The Brass Check*, 1919, seeks to prove the alliance between big business and American newspapers; *The Goose Step*, 1923, seeks to show how rich men, by endowing universities, influence the economic and political beliefs of the students. *Money Writes*, 1927, shows what he sincerely believed to be the influence of capitalism upon those who produce the country's literature.

Sinclair founded the American Civil Liberties Union in California. He won the Pulitzer Prize in 1943 for *Dragon's Teeth*, 1942, which formed one of the Lanny Budd series (so named from its hero), a fictional account of world history from 1913 onwards in some ten books, beginning with *World's End*, 1940, and going on to *The Return of Lanny Budd*, 1953. *American Outpost*, 1932, is an autobiography.

Sind, or Sindhu (indigenous name for the River INDUS), former autonomous province of PAKISTAN consisting mainly of the Indus Valley for the last 480 km of the river's course. The eastern part of the region is mostly the Thar Desert as far as the Indian frontier. The whole region is one of scanty rainfall, beyond the range of the monsoon, and dependent for water on canal irrigation. The Lloyd Barrage at Sukkur provides water to 2,025,000 ha of

Sindbad the Sailor

wheat and rice; lower down, near Kotri, a second barrage has been built across the Indus by Pakistan to irrigate 1,100,000 ha. Rice, cotton, wheat, barley, oilseeds, and vegetables are grown in the district. Of the livestock, the red Sindhi cattle are famous, and buffaloes and camels are plentiful. Salt is the main mineral product. Modern industries are making their appearance with the development of hydro-electric and natural gas power sources. KARACHI has a shipyard and modern industries, and there are cement works, textile mills, foundries, and other modern plant in various parts of the province. Through HYDERABAD Sind has a rail link with India.

History. From 2300 to 1750 BC Sind is known to have been part of the Indus civilisation. The old site of MOHENJO-DARO goes back to pre-Aryan times. Its earliest recorded history began with its annexation to the Persian Empire under Darius I. It was later under the domination, successively, of the empires of Alexander the Great, Seleucus, Chandragupta Maurya, the Indo-Greeks and Parthians, and the Scythians and Kusans. Sind became Buddhist in the 1st century AD, but was brought under Brahmin rule until the Arab conquest in 711 and the spread of Islam. Sind was an administrative province of the Ummayad and Abbasid empires from 711 to 900. As the central authority weakened in Baghdad, the Arab governors established their own dynastic rule in Sind during the 10th century. The area passed into the control of the Moguls from 1591 to 1700, who were followed by two independent Sind dynasties from whom Sind was taken by the British, under Sir Charles Napier, in 1843. Napier's punning one-word dispatch 'Peccavi' ('I have sinned') is said to be the shortest in military history.

Sind was part of the Bombay Presidency until 1937 when it was established as a separate province. After partition, in 1947, it became part of the province of West Pakistan from 1955 to 1970, when it was re-established as a separate province.

Bibliography: H. T. Lambrick, *History of Sind*, 2 vols, 1965–74.

Sindbad the Sailor, one of the characters in the ARABIAN NIGHTS. He is described as a wealthy citizen of Baghdad, who makes seven voyages, discovering, among other wonders, a ROC's egg and the valley of diamonds.

Sindelfingen, town in BADEN-WÜRTTEMBERG, West Germany, 12 km south-west of Stuttgart. It has a very distinctive modern RATHAUS, and is notable for the modern industries found in the town. Daimler Benz has had a factory here since 1915. Electronic equipment, computers (IBM), watches, shoes, and textiles are important industries here. Population 57,000.

Sindhi, Indo-Aryan language, spoken in the province of Sind, Pakistan, and in north-west India by some 7,000,000 people. Vicholi is the most common dialect. Persian and Arabic influences derive from historic Muslim influence, and the alphabet used is a Persian form of the Arabic. Hindu speakers use a DEVANAGARI script. There is little written literature in Sindhi.

Sinding, Christian (1856–1941), Norwegian composer, born at Kongsberg. He studied at Christiania (Oslo) and later, with the Norwegian Government's support, in Germany, where he spent many years of his life. For a time he was professor of composition at Rochester, New York. He wrote a great deal of music, but is chiefly remembered for the popular salon piece, *The Rustle of Spring*.

Sine, see TRIGONOMETRY.

Sinecure, properly a benefice without cure of souls (*sine cura animarum*), i.e., (1) where a rector and vicar are instituted to the same church, the former is excused from duty and the rectory is called a sinecure benefice; (2) where the benefice, being donative, is committed to the incumbent by the patron expressly without cure of souls, the cure not existing; (3) where a parish is destitute of parishioners (called also depopulation). Certain cathedral offices, viz. canonries and prebends, are also called sinecures.

By extension 'sinecure' is used in everyday speech to describe a post of profit which involves no work.

Sinew, see TENDON.

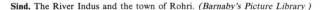

Sind. The River Indus and the town of Rohri. *(Barnaby's Picture Library)*

Singapore, island republic of 610 km², situated about 1°30′N of the equator, linked by a causeway to the southern tip of Malaya to which it previously belonged.

Geography. Relief. A granitic core rises to 177 m at one point and is surrounded by low-lying, often marshy land, much of which has been reclaimed. Land is Singapore's only appreciable resource: 16 per cent of the total area of 597 km² is cultivated, 5 per cent under forest, and 35 per cent in urban use. See ATLAS 34.

Climate. Its climate is tropical, with temperatures ranging from 24 °C to 35 °C; rainfall (averaging 2438 mm annually) occurs throughout the year, but is heaviest during the north-east MONSOON (October–March).

Population. In 1976 it totalled 2·3 million: 76 per cent Chinese, 15 per cent Malays, 7 per cent Indians and Pakistanis. Overall population density averages 3760 per km², but urban density exceeds 15,450 per km². Through strong government measures the population growth rate declined from 2·9 per cent a year in 1967 to 1·5 per cent in 1974. Despite marked anglicisation in social life and education, Chinese, Malay, and Tamil are still widely spoken, and many traditional celebrations are maintained.

Economy. Agriculture is highly intensive and supplies all local needs of pork, poultry, and eggs; 60 per cent of vegetable needs and all cereals are imported. Agriculture accounts for 2·8 per cent of the GDP.

Industry. Manufacturing accounts for a further 25 per cent of the GDP, compared with 10·7 per cent in 1966. Electronics, oil refining, and transport equipment (including shipbuilding and repair) are the main industries. With nine oil refineries (capacity over one million barrels/day), Singapore is the world's third largest refinery complex; while 60 shipyards build everything from oil rigs to tankers and have dry-dock facilities of up to 400,000 t capacity. The main industrial site is the 2835-ha Jurong Industrial Estate, with its own deep-water harbour and rail link, 450 factories, and a new town. It is the regional headquarters, and a complete support base, for 400 companies involved in mineral exploration and extraction in South-East Asia: total foreign investment was over US-$1700 million in 1975 (between 1965–75, US investment alone increased from US$50 million to US$500 million).

Communications. Port facilities comprise nearly 6 km of deep-water wharves (9145 m containerised) with berths for 40 ships, in addition to coastal facilities. The state shipping line, Neptune Orient (established 1968) owns 24 vessels, and operates liner, tanker, and dry cargo services; while Singapore International Airlines (established 1972) runs a fleet of 19 Boeings serving 20 countries.

Trade. Strategically located on a major sea route and near resource-rich Malaysia and Indonesia, and with deep-water harbours and container facilities, Singapore is the fourth largest port in the world in terms of tonnage handled (60·5 million t in 1974). Foreign trade amounted to about S$36,000 million in 1974: 20 per cent was 'colonial' trade with Brunei, Malaysia, and Indonesia; other major trading partners were the Middle East (13·4 per cent, mainly oil), the United States (13·5 per cent), and Japan (14·6 per cent). There was a 1975 surplus in overall balance of payments of S$6512 million. Total trade accounted for 25 per cent of the GDP.

Planning. Official economic strategy emphasises devel-opment of export-oriented manufacturing and complete servicing facilities for foreign investment in regional extractive industry: this has meant providing a suitable industrial and financial infrastructure, fiscal incentives for investment, technical, managerial, and marketing know-how, and a trained, disciplined, and cheap labour force. A basic social objective of mass planned resettlement is being met by the Housing and Development Board. There is no firm national plan, but statutory bodies operate their own five-year plans, financed by annual ordinary and development budgets.

Labour. Despite strict control over the entry of foreign workers, rapid industrialisation during the early 1970s meant the admission of 120,000 short-contract Malaysian workers. In 1975 there were 90 employees' unions (membership over 203,560); about 80 per cent of the unionised labour force (27 per cent of the total labour force) were in unions affiliated to the government-party-controlled National Trades Union Congress. Strict labour legislation controls workers' rights, and factory wages are about 20 per cent the Japanese level.

Finance. The unit of currency is the Singapore dollar, of 100 cents. Singapore changed its intervention currency from sterling to the US dollar in June 1972 after the floating of the £ sterling.

Singapore is a major financial centre, with 64 commercial banks and 21 merchant banks (compared to 33 banks in 1963) and an ASIAN DOLLAR MARKET whose funds have grown from US$33 million in 1968 to US$10,000 million in 1975. The island has recently developed as a

Singapore. Chinese street scene. The colonial-style Central Fire Station is in the background. *(Barnaby's Picture Library)*

Singapore

tourist centre, from which it derived receipts of S$450 million in 1974 (S$193 million in 1968).

Government. Constitution. In December 1965 Singapore became an independent republic, with a president, a 12-member cabinet led by the prime minister, and a 51-seat (now 69 seats) parliament whose members are elected by compulsory universal suffrage.

Legislature. With political opposition legally circumscribed, Singapore has a one-party parliament composed of the People's Action Party (PAP). An advisory 21-member presidential council exists to determine if legislation is discriminatory on racial or religious grounds or inconsistent with basic individual liberties, but has no authority to examine any bill certified by the prime minister as affecting 'the defence or security of Singapore or relating to public safety, peace, or good order'.

Following the general election held on 23 December 1976 the PAP won 53 contested seats and was returned unopposed in the other 16.

Justice. The judiciary consists of a Supreme Court (including a high court, a court of appeal, and a court of criminal appeal) and three lower courts (magistrates' courts, criminal district courts, and civil district courts). It is theoretically independent of the executive, but extensive legislation governing internal security, freedom of speech and assembly, election procedure, and union activities (e.g. the Internal Security Act 1960, Control of Publications legislation, and the Employment Act 1968) clouds the separation of powers: publications are licensed annually, detention without trial may be indefinite, and there is no trial by jury; capital offences are tried by two high court judges. There exist two industrial arbitration courts with limited powers, and a Shariah court concerned with Muslim law regarding marriage, divorce, and maintenance. Abortion was legalised under the Abortion and Voluntary Sterilisation Act 1970.

Armed Forces. Apart from an armed police force of some 11,000 men and one Gurkha unit equipped to deal with civil unrest, Singapore's armed forces comprise 30,000 men (with 35,000 reservists). Equipment included 120 aircraft (mainly Hawker Hunter and Skyhawk fighter-bombers), AMX tanks, and 75 Bloodhound surface-to-air missiles. Regular troops are supported by a volunteer People's Defence Force, which assists the police in internal security duties. All military and para-military units (such as the Vigilante Corps and Special Constabulary) are closely coordinated by the Ministries of Defence and Home Affairs. Military training begins at school, with national service compulsory.

Education. In 1975, Singapore had 391 primary schools (328,401 students), 114 secondary schools (153,029 students), and 15 institutions of higher education including five universities and colleges (21,150 students). Of the 700,000 children of school age, 75 per cent attend school. The medium of instruction is English, Chinese, Malay, or Tamil, with emphasis on bilingualism and English as first language.

Welfare. By 1975 the public sector (through the Housing and Development Board and Jurong Town Corporation) housed over 1 million people. Environmental health measures have been vigorously enforced, and a high rate of birth control achieved through the Family Planning and Population Board (established 1966) and legislation against large families. There is a modest public assistance scheme, and the Central Provident Fund (a form of compulsory saving scheme) covers most workers under contract of service. There are 15 government hospitals, with 7000 beds.

Religion. Religious diversity persists: the Chinese are mainly Buddhist, Taoist, and Confucianist; Malays and Pakistanis are Muslim; and Indians mainly Hindu. Some Chinese and Indians, and most Eurasians, are Christian.

Official Languages. English, Chinese, Malay, and

Singapore. *(Topham/Fotogram)*

Tamil—of which English is the main language of education, administration, and commerce.

National Anthem. Majullah Singapura (traditional).

National Flag. One red and one white horizontal band, with a white crescent and five five-pointed stars on the red band near the staff.

History. In the 14th century, Singapura (the Lion City) is mentioned as being a Malay capital, destroyed about 1391. In 1819, Stamford RAFFLES of the EAST INDIA COMPANY concluded a treaty with the nominal rulers of Singapore, Sultan Hussein and the Temenggong Abdul Rahman, allowing the company to establish a trading base near the Rochor river. In 1824 a treaty was signed ceding the entire island and most offshore islands to the company, and in 1832 Singapore was incorporated in the STRAITS SETTLEMENTS. The island rapidly developed as an entrepôt centre, with its population growing from 120 in 1819 to 40,000 in 1840. It was from their political and commercial base in Singapore that the British intervened in the Malay Straits during the 1870s. Between the two World Wars the building of a great naval base at Singapore stressed the colony's strategic importance, and in consideration of this Singapore was made into a separate Crown Colony when the Straits Settlements were disbanded in 1946. The strategic concept upon which Singapore developed was that of a protected naval base from which a powerful fleet could operate, and it was therefore defended against sea attack by fixed coastal defences. Plans for defence along the Malay peninsula were worked out when the base was completed, but these proved useless during the Second World War. The Japanese pushed the British forces down into Singapore in 1942 and on 15 February the British commander surrendered. The British retook the island on 5 September 1945.

Progress towards internal self-government was rapid after 1945, with political agitation led by David Marshall, leader of the Labour Front. The legislative council inaugurated in 1948 under the new constitution of 1946 had elected only nine members; in 1951 this was increased to 12. In 1953 the governor appointed a commission under Sir George Rendel to review Singapore's constitutional position, and its recommendations were accepted in 1955 by the British government as the new constitution, which came into force in 1959. The first elections under the Rendel constitution resulted in victory for the Labour Front, and Marshall became chief minister. He resigned in 1956 after disagreeing with the British government on the question of greater local control over internal security; his successor, Lim Yew Hock, reached agreement with Britain on the self-government issue, the internal security aspect being covered by the proposed establishment of an internal security council within the projected new constitution. This came into force in 1959, when Singapore was granted self-government.

In 1963 Singapore joined the new Federation of MALAYSIA, but the existence of a large Chinese majority in the state, many of whom were hostile to central control by a predominantly Malay government, exacerbated racial and political tensions which led to Singapore's secession from Malaysia on 9 August 1965. Singapore became a republic in December 1965. From 1966, the People's Action Party (PAP) government under the Prime Minister, LEE KUAN YEW, embarked on a policy of making Singapore a tightly disciplined 'garrison state' on the Israeli model. Lee established a national army, extended the police force, para-military bodies, and party community organisations, brought the trade unions under PAP control, and legislated against political opposition. One justification for the policy of strict regimentation and militarisation was that Singapore—as a wealthy, largely Chinese city-state surrounded by a hostile Malay population—needed to protect itself, another was the need to achieve the political stability necessary for foreign investment, a third was the rundown of the British military presence announced in the British government's 1967 White Paper on defence. After 1966, with the re-opening of Indonesia to foreign investment, Singapore's servicing role in regional development—and its 'colonial city' character—were greatly enhanced.

In 1967 the British military presence contributed 20 per cent to Singapore's GDP; by 1971 this presence was minimal and gradually the complex of military bases passed into local control. The British Far East Command ceased in 1971 and the British naval base was formally closed. In 1971 a consultative pact on the coordination of external defence was signed by Singapore, Malaysia, Australia, New Zealand, and Britain, creating the joint ANZUK force. This force was officially disbanded on 1 January 1975, but there remains a token British contribution to the area's integrated air defence system and a commitment to consult with other members of the five-power defence agreement. The Singapore government now provides servicing facilities for foreign naval vessels, but official policy is against the establishment of a naval base on the island by any power.

Bibliography: I. Buchanan, *Singapore in South East Asia,* 1972; P. P. Courtenay, *A Geography of Trade and Development in Malaya,* 1972; T. J. S. George, *Lee Kuan Yew's Singapore,* 1973; Singapore Ministry of Culture, *Singapore 1974;* EUROPA, *The Far East and Australasia,* annual.

Singara, see SINJAR.

Singer, Isaac Merrit, see SEWING-MACHINE; SINGER COMPANY, THE.

Singer Company, The, manufacturers of the SEWING-MACHINE invented by Isaac Merritt Singer (1811–75) in 1851. The business began in Boston, Massachusetts in that year by the formation of a partnership between Isaac Singer and Edward Clark. Demand for the new appliance became so great that arrangements had to be made to cope with rapidly increasing business and the Singer Manufacturing Company was incorporated in the state of New Jersey. The Singer Company is now a multi-national diversified corporation. Its products include industrial and domestic sewing machines; business machines and systems; education and training products; information systems and products; aerospace and marine systems products; and various consumer products. The company's operations in the UK are conducted by The Singer Company (UK) Limited. Isaac Singer was the first to initiate a system of credit terms, later familiarly known as HIRE-PURCHASE.

Singing, see FOLK-MUSIC AND FOLK-SONG; MUSIC; OPERA; ORATORIO; SOLMISATION; SONG; SOUND; VOICE; also ALTO; BASS; SOPRANO; TENOR; TREBLE.

Singkep, island in the Riau-Lingga archipelago, Indo-

Single-phase Induction Motors

nesia. One of the three 'tin' islands (see BANGKA and BELITUNG), which together produce almost all of Indonesia's tin. Singkep is the smallest producer. The Singkep Tin Company was founded in 1889, but little was achieved in the early years of exploitation; the state tin company, P. N. Timah, now controls mining.

Single-phase Induction Motors, as the name implies, are induction motors designed to operate from single-phase supplies, the usual supply available in most homes. The number of single-phase induction motors in use is greater than all the other types of motors taken together. They are usually small (less than 300 W although some larger motors can produce up to 4 kW of power) and are not very efficient. They also operate at low power factor, but are cheap, robust, and simple to operate. However, the theory of operation is not so simple and will not be described here (but see ELECTRICAL MACHINES). It is sufficient to state that unlike three-phase induction motors where the supply produces a rotating field in the air gap, a single-phase supply produces a pulsating field. This does not produce a starting torque. By providing a second auxiliary winding in which the current differs in phase from the current in the main winding, a starting torque can be obtained. The phase difference can be achieved by using extra elements in the auxiliary winding circuit, resistors, inductors, or capacitors; the last named is the most common. A centrifugal switch is often used to disconnect the starting winding after the motor has reached a certain speed, and it can also be used to re-connect the capacitor to improve the power factor. Other methods of starting which are used instead of the auxiliary winding include variable reluctance in the air gap and shading ring. Single-phase motors are used extensively in domestic equipment.

Bibliography: J. Hindmarsh, *Electrical Machines and Their Application,* 1970.

Single-stick, see FENCING.

Single Tax, a tax on land, replacing all other taxes. In the 18th century in France the PHYSIOCRATIC SCHOOL held that all taxes ultimately fall on the land, increase of wealth (*produit net*) being due to agriculture and not to industry. They accordingly proposed their *impôt unique* (single tax) on the net income from land. The idea made great headway, but was ridiculed by Voltaire. The later exponent and populariser of the single tax, Henry George, had a different approach, arguing that only work should be rewarded and not the mere possession of land which no one has made. The landowner should be paid for his improvements: a single tax—sufficient, he argued, for all revenue purposes—should confiscate the values due to nature and society.

Singleton, village on the South DOWNS in Chichester District of West Sussex, England. Here is the Weald and Downland Open Air Museum, with exhibits of farmhouses, smithy, barns, charcoal burners' hut, and much more historical material being constantly added. Population 500.

Singspiel, see GERMAN AND AUSTRIAN MUSIC.

Singular Point. In complex ANALYSIS, singular point is an alternative term for singularity of an ANALYTIC FUNCTION. In ANALYTICAL GEOMETRY, a singular point of a curve is a point at which it does not have a unique TANGENT. There are the following types of singular point (illustrated in the figure):

1. An isolated point (or acnode) (P_1), which is a point that satisfies the equation of a curve, but is not in every neighbourhood of any other point of the curve. For example, the point $(0, 0)$ satisfies the equation $y^2 = x^3 - x^2$ but no nearby point satisfies the equation (because the right-hand side is negative when $x < 1$).

2. A multiple point (or crunode) (P_2) at which the curve has more than one distinct tangent because several branches of the curve intersect there.

3. A cusp (or spinode) in which two branches of the curve meet and their tangents coincide. In a cusp of the first kind (P_3), the two branches are on opposite sides of the common tangent (for example, the point $(0, 0)$ on the curve $y^2 = x^3$). In a cusp of the second kind (P_4) they are

Singular Point.

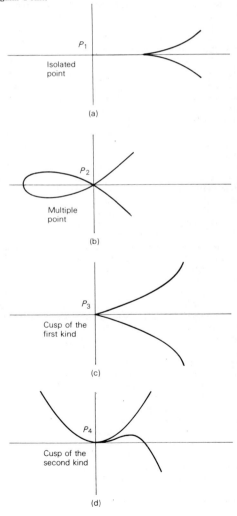

(a)

(b)

(c)

(d)

on the same side (for example the point $(0, 0)$ on the curve $y = x^2 \pm x^{5/2}$).

Sinhala, see SRI LANKA.

Sinhalese, an Indo-Aryan language, the official language and script of Sri Lanka (Ceylon). It is the mother tongue of over 9,000,000 people (1972), three-quarters of the population of the island. Sinhalese literature is attested since the 10th century.

Sining, see HSINING.

Sinister, in heraldry, denotes the left side of a shield considered from the bearer's side. For the bend sinister, see HERALDRY, *Ordinaries* (5).

Sinjar (ancient *Singara*), town and hilly district in North Iraq, west of Mosul. In the wars between Persia and the Byzantine Empire it was the scene of much fighting. The present town is much smaller than the ancient city. It and the district are inhabited by Yezidi Kurds. The Christians of northern Iraq still speak Syriac among themselves.

Sink-hole, a depression characteristic of KARST areas which enables water to percolate into an underground drainage system. The form of a sink-hole ranges from a shallow saucer-like depression to a cylindrical pipe. Various local terms used to describe this feature include swallow-hole or *ponor* (Serbo-Croat) where the stream actually disappears into the depression, and pothole where it leads into a cave system. See also DOLINE; POLJE.

Sinkiang Uighur, autonomous region in western CHINA, and its largest administrative unit. Sinkiang became an autonomous region in 1955 and consists of two basins separated from each other and encircled by high mountains. From north to south these are: the ALTAI Mountains (separating Sinkiang from the Mongolian People's Republic), DZUNGARIA, the TIEN SHAN (with peaks to over 6100 m), the TARIM Basin (containing the TAKLA MAKAN Desert, LOP NOR, and the Turfan Depression— c. 275 m below sea-level), and the Kunlun Mountains separating Sinkiang from Tibet. Sinkiang has a frontier (some 2900 km) with the Soviet Union, and a 65-km frontier with Afghanistan (the PAMIRS). The latter, with the western Kunlun (Karakoram), also separates Sinkiang from the Indian sub-continent. The main approach to the region from the rest of China is from Kansu across the GOBI Desert. Its external boundaries have all been fixed by international treaties, agreements, and protocols except for a length of about 240 km in the Pamirs facing the Soviet Union.

The population is mainly of Turkish stock (hence 'Chinese Turkestan'), and Islamic by religion and culture. The main racial group are the Uighurs. In recent years official policy has resulted in increasing Chinese (Han) colonisation here and the Chinese proportion of the population is probably approaching 40 per cent—a much higher proportion than formerly. The climate (especially of that portion north of the Tien Shan) is extreme. The main occupations are animal husbandry (by Kazakhs, Kirghiz, and Mongols) and farming (wheat, rice, maize, cotton, and fruit) on rich oases where streams from the mountains reach the plains. The mineral resources include petroleum, gold, coal, and iron-ore. Prior to 1954 the

Soviet Union participated with China in three joint companies to exploit the petroleum, non-ferrous and rare metals, and to operate air services (see CHINA, *History*).

Since the middle 1950s the oil industry has grown rapidly, particularly around the Karamai oil-field in the Dzungarian Basin. Commercial production began in 1958 with the field being linked to refineries at Tushantze. Coal for local use is mined near URUMCHI (the capital of the province), which is also an engineering and cement-industry centre. Education has progressed under the present régime and Urumchi is the seat of a university. Sinkiang has always been a turbulent area. Racial tensions and proximity to the Soviet Union affect its political stability. China has greatly improved its communications with the region by the construction of the Lanchow–Sinkiang railway. Its dispute with the Soviet Union has resulted in the extension of this line to link up with the Soviet railway system being deferred. The deserts here afford China the space in which to pursue her nuclear experiments, Lop Nor being the principal testing area. Area 1,642,000 km². Population (1972) about 10 million.

Sinking, operation of excavating and lining shafts to reach mineral deposits at depth. A complete geological exploration of the area is a necessary preliminary to fix the most favourable position for sinking. This is usually done by trial boreholes. The size of shaft is also important, and the trend is towards large shafts; in Britain shafts up to 7·5 m in diameter have been sunk. The modern practice is to erect the permanent headgear and winding engine at the outset, and use a giant power-driven crane, with a swinging jib, as a temporary arrangement for winding the initial debris from the shaft.

The sinking is commenced by digging out the overburden, and as the shaft sides are laid bare temporary supports are put in. These consist of iron rings, made in segments, and bolted together. The first ring is suspended from a strong wooden framing at the shaft top. The second ring is suspended from the first by iron hangers or hooks. The rings are set at 1·2 or 1·5-metre vertical intervals in the shaft, and lagging-boards are fixed behind and against the rocksides. Every fourth ring or so is supported on steel pegs driven into the shaft side. These temporary supports are inserted for depths of 20 m or so before the permanent brick lining is put in. On reaching a firm bed of rock a foundation is prepared to receive a curb on which the brick wall is constructed. When sinking is resumed sufficient ground is left to act as a temporary support under the curb. The shaft is then opened out to its full diameter, and temporary rings put in as before. Having excavated about another 20 m the second curb is laid down, and the second length of walling is built upwards to join the first section. A scaffold or staging is suspended in the shaft to enable the masons to construct the walling.

When sinking through hard rock, drills and explosives are necessary to break it. Pneumatic drills are normally employed, mounted on steel frames, which enable several drills to operate simultaneously. An explosive of the nitroglycerine class, having a strong shattering effect, may be used. The modern tendency is to adopt delay action firing in shaft sinking. The debris at the shaft bottom is

Sinking

loaded by shovels into large-capacity buckets or kibbles, which are hoisted to the surface and discharged.

When sinking through rocks yielding moderate to large quantities of water, a special shaft lining, such as brick coffering, concrete, or tubbing, is employed to seal off the water. Coffering, which is not often employed nowadays, consists of a thick brick wall, with the space behind well rammed with puddled clay. A concrete lining may be constructed from solid blocks, moulded to the radius of the shaft, and laid in good-quality cement. Liquid concrete is also used, in which case forms or shutterings are necessary to retain the plastic concrete in position until it sets firmly. In many sinkings the concrete is reinforced by steel. Cast-iron tubbing consists of a series of rings, each being made up of several segments. In the British system the flanges are next to the rock sides, in the German system the flanges face the shaft space. The tubbing is built upwards, ring after ring, and all joints are made with strips of yellow pine or sheet lead. In the British system each ring is kept in position by tight wedging and the interlocking of the flanges. In the German method the ring segments are bolted together.

The cementation process of sinking through heavily watered ground was introduced into Britain in 1911 by the François Cementation Company. Liquid cement is injected, at high pressure, into the water-bearing fissures. When the cement has set the water is completely sealed off, and the sinking can then proceed in the ordinary way. A second length is then cemented, excavated, lined, and the process is repeated until the water-bearing strata have been passed. Pile sinking is sometimes adopted to penetrate loose sand or gravel of limited thickness. A strong timber frame is fixed at the shaft top, and piles, made of pine wood, are driven down all round the frame. The piles are 0·6–0·9 m long, pointed and shod with iron to prevent them splitting. Excavation of the sand is then commenced, and after digging 0·6 m or so a fresh frame is placed inside the piles to support them. Another round of piles is forced down, and the process repeated until the hard rock is reached, when the shaft is lined with brick or cast iron rings. In drop shaft sinking a plain cast-iron cylinder may be used. The lower ring has a cutting shoe, and weights are added on top to force it through the sand. The sand may then be loaded out by a Priestman grab, which can remove a tonne of material at each scoop.

The freezing process of sinking through water-bearing measures was introduced in the early 1900s by Poetsch. A number of boreholes, fitted with tubes, are put down in the ground around the shaft, through which is circulated a freezing mixture consisting of cold brine. A wall of frozen ground is thus formed around a soft central core. Sinking is then carried down in the usual way and a water-tight lining put in. The freezing method was applied successfully at Boulby Potash mine in Cleveland in the early 1970s. This is an expensive process, and shafts may cost more than £1000 per metre to sink and line. The Goberts and Koch systems are modifications of the Poetsch freezing process. Another method formerly applied in hard, heavily watered rocks is the Kind-Chaudron, in which the shaft is bored out in two stages. A small shaft is first bored by a boring tool called a trepan, and afterwards enlarged by a larger trepan. The shaft is then lined with tubbing, all operations being performed while the water is still in the shaft. Several shafts in the Netherlands and Germany

were sunk by this method. In the Pattberg method the shaft is bored out in one operation and large pumps employed to force the muddy debris to the surface.

Under normal dry conditions a sinking rate of from 20 to 30 m per month can be obtained, although rates up to 300 m per month and more have been achieved in South Africa.

See also COAL-MINING; MINING.

Bibliography: Mining Society of South Africa, *Symposium on Shafts and Shaft Sinking*, 1949; I. C. F. Statham, *Coal Mining Practice*, 1958; B. Boky, *Mining*, 1967.

Sinking Fund, fund formed to pay off public debt, or company debt, or to replace capital equipment. The first public sinking fund was established in 1716 by Sir Robert Walpole; it was made up of the excess from the South Sea Aggregate and General Funds. The fund was increased in 1727 by further reductions of the interest on the public debt, which added a sum of £400,000 to the sinking fund. For a time the sinking fund was regularly applied to its ostensible purpose, but soon the ministry began to take money from the sinking fund for the services of the year. Sir Robert Walpole's sinking fund terminated in 1786, when William Pitt constituted a new fund by appropriating £1 million per annum to it, the public debt then amounting to £238 million.

In 1792 a novel sinking fund was constituted in the shape of a fund of 1 per cent on the capital stock created by every loan, raised by a tax, over and above the provision for the interest of the loan; the idea was that no relief should be afforded to the public from the taxes which constituted the 1 per cent sinking fund until a capital stock equal to that created by the loan had been purchased by it. This really introduced the principle of the true sinking fund as it is now understood, viz. that in raising further loans, besides interest, provision should be made for gradual redemption. Modifications of Pitt's scheme were introduced by Lord Sidmouth and Lord Henry Petty, the latter by a complicated arrangement to lessen the burden of taxation; but in 1813 Nicholas Vansittart, then chancellor of the Exchequer, proposed to revert to Pitt's act of 1792 with the object of restoring to the stockholder all the advantages of that act.

The net result of the financial jugglery of the chancellors up to 1828, as shown in the report of the Parliamentary Finance Committee of 1828, was that over £1 million million of fresh loans had been raised to redeem, nominally, some £500 million of the public debt. The different acts relating to the sinking fund were repealed in 1866. In 1875 the 'new sinking fund' was established; a permanent annual charge on the consolidated funds of £28 million was to be applied to the payment of the debt; and out of the permanent annual charge certain specified annual charges were to be paid (such as perpetual or terminable annuities on the consolidated funds, interest on Exchequer bonds or bills, and interest on Bank of England advances).

The new sinking fund was included in the expenditure of the current financial year, while the old sinking fund was merely the surplus of revenue, if any, after all the expenditure had been met; the new sinking fund must by statute be applied to no other purpose than the reduction of the national debt, but the old sinking fund might be applied to any other purposes. Lloyd George, as chancellor of the Exchequer, in introducing the celebrated Budget of 1909, made proposals for 'raiding' the new sinking fund to the extent of £6 million; in 1910 the payment of that part of the permanent annual charge for the national debt which was not required for the annual charges (see above), or for the reduction of Exchequer bonds, was suspended.

In 1923 another 'new' sinking fund was set up by Baldwin. This gave place to that of Winston Churchill, who in the Budget of 1928–29 established a new permanent debt charge. This was originally fixed at £338 million and later increased to £500 million. Debt reduction was made by means of terminable annuities, the capital value of which was deducted from the debt upon the expiration of the term for which the annuities were payable, and by means of a number of specific sinking funds, viz. 4 per cent Funding Loan Sinking Fund, 3 per cent Funding Loan Sinking Fund, Victory Bonds Sinking Funds. Payments for these funds and annuities were met from the permanent debt charge in years with a surplus of ordinary expenditure; in years with a deficit 'above the line', they appeared 'below the line'. The permanent debt charge was suspended in 1940 and abolished in 1954. With the exception of those attached to particular stocks, all sinking funds relating to the national debt ceased when the National Loans Fund was established in 1968.

See also PUBLIC DEBT; BUDGET.

Sinn Féin (We Ourselves), name of an Irish republican movement which, in the period before 1922, aimed at economic and political separation from Britain. It took its name from the watchword of the organisation *Cumann na Gaedhal*, which advocated the policy suggested by Arthur GRIFFITH in the journal *The United Irishman* that Irish MPs elected to the Imperial Parliament should not take their seats at Westminster, but should form a government in Ireland. On the outbreak of the First World War, John REDMOND, the leader of the Irish Nationalist party (see NATIONALIST PARTY) in the House of Commons, pledged the loyalty of Ireland to the Crown, and great numbers of Irishmen joined the forces. The war, however, provided an opportunity for those who believed that the union between Britain and Ireland could be dissolved only by force to increase their strength; in 1916 there was a rebellion in Dublin, the 'Easter Rising', which took Augustine BIRRELL, the chief secretary, and the authorities by surprise. The 'Rising' was soon suppressed, and 14 of the leaders were executed (see CONNOLLY, JAMES; PEARSE, PATRICK HENRY). The execution of the Easter week leaders (who had had hitherto the sympathy of only a minority), and the attempt to apply conscription to Ireland in 1918, caused a change in the temper of the country and the Sinn Féin movement gained more and more popular support.

The result of the general election of 1918 showed how bitter feeling against England had become, for the Sinn Féin party (half of whose candidates were in prison) overwhelmed the old Irish Nationalist party, only seven of whose candidates were returned to Westminster; John DILLON, who had succeeded Redmond, lost his seat. The elected members of the Sinn Féin party set up an independent parliament (*Dáil Éireann*) in Dublin, and organised a complete, and effective, system of administration for the country; the whole machinery of British adminis-

tration in Ireland had, in fact, broken down. Then followed a period of guerrilla warfare between the Crown forces in Ireland and the forces of the new Republican government. In 1920 the ineffective Home Rule Act of 1914 was replaced by the Government of Ireland Act 1920 (of the Parliament of Westminster), which provided for separate parliaments for the six counties of Northern Ireland (see IRELAND, NORTHERN, *History*) and for the other 26 counties. On 26 December 1921, after a conference between the British government and the Sinn Féin leaders—of whom the principal spokesmen were Griffith and Michael Collins—a treaty was signed, which led to the setting-up of the Irish Free State (see IRELAND, REPUBLIC OF, *History*). British forces evacuated the 26 counties of the new state, but the refusal of a section of Sinn Féin, led by Eamonn DE VALERA, to accept the terms of the treaty led to armed conflict until 1923 between his followers and the forces of the new Free State. Sinn Féin declined rapidly in importance after de Valera resigned its presidency in 1926 to form Fianna Fáil. It continues, however, as the political representative of the IRISH REPUBLICAN ARMY, and seeks, by force, the end of Irish partition.

Sinneh, see SANANDAJ.

Sinningia, a genus of hairy herbs, native to Brazil, in family Gesneriaceae, with showy, bell-shaped flowers; *S. speciosa* is a parent of the greenhouse plant known as GLOXINIA.

Sino-Japanese War (1894–95). Keen competition between Japan and China for markets in Korea was the real cause of this war. Its immediate cause, however, was the violation of an agreement made between LI HUNG-CHANG and Count Ito for maintaining the *status quo* by the dispatch of Chinese troops to Korea without notice to the Japanese government.

The resulting and thorough defeat of the Chinese was a startling revelation of the rise of Japanese power in the Far East. Japan's first opportunity to interfere in Korean affairs came as a result of disorders in Korea, of which China was the nominal suzerain. Japan then secured a treaty with China involving the independence of the principality. The Chinese government sought to retrieve the position by intrigue, which soon brought the two countries to the brink of war, troops from both being already in Korea. Then followed a number of incidents, which compelled Li Hung-chang to arrange a *modus vivendi* with Count Ito, under which the troops on both sides were withdrawn; but the agreement was broken in the manner indicated above, and war was declared by Japan on 1 August 1894, actual hostilities having begun a week previously with the sinking of the transport *Kowshing*, a British vessel carrying Chinese troops.

In the battle of Pyong-yang (15 September), a Chinese army was routed with heavy loss, Chinese methods of generalship being archaic in the extreme. On 17 September, however, the Chinese navy fought stoutly, and the most important naval action of the war took place off the island of Hai-yang, when the Chinese fleet was defeated. Late in October a Japanese army under Count Oyama invaded Manchuria. The fortress of Port Arthur was taken by storm on 21 November with only slight loss to the Japanese.

Sinop

In February 1895, at the decisive battle of Wei-hai, the Chinese land and sea forces were utterly defeated, the Chinese admiral, Ting, committing suicide in his ship. The Japanese, continuing to advance, now closed on Peking, with the result that Li Hung-chang himself departed for Japan to conclude peace. A treaty was signed at Shimonoseki in April and ratified in May at Chifu, under which Korean independence was recognised, and Liao-tung, Formosa (Taiwan), and the Pescadores were ceded to Japan. Other terms included the opening of ports in Szechwan, Hupeh, and other provinces, and a large indemnity to Japan. Later, however, Japan was induced by France, Germany, and Russia to give back Liaotung in exchange for an increased indemnity. This interference by Western powers aroused the indignation of Japan, especially against Russia, and formed a remote cause of the RUSSO-JAPANESE WAR (1904–05). As the result of the Sino-Japanese War, Japan established its position in Asia and expanded its markets. The revelation of China's weakness rendered it more than ever liable to invasion by the Western powers, and eventually caused the revolution which overthrew the imperial régime.

See also CHINA, *Modern History*; JAPAN, *Modern History*; KOREA, *Modern History*.

Sinop (ancient Greek *Sinope*), town and minor port on the Black Sea coast and capital of Sinop province, Turkey. It was founded in 630 BC by settlers from MILETUS and became the greatest Greek commercial city on the Black Sea, as it was the terminus of a caravan route from the Euphrates. Among its exports was red sulphate of arsenic from CAPPADOCIA, commonly called Sinopic red earth. In the 5th century BC Sinop received a colony from Athens and over the next 100 years it grew more powerful until its fleet controlled half the Black Sea. In 183 BC Sinop was captured by PHARNACES of Pontus, who made it the capital of his kingdom. MITHRADATES had brought it to great commercial prosperity when it was taken by LUCULLUS in 70 BC and partly destroyed. Julius CAESAR established a Roman colony there in about 45 BC, but the port was already losing its trade to Ephesus, which was more favourably situated for Roman shipping. It was taken by the Turks in the 15th century. Population (town) 15,100; (province) 265,700.

Sint-Niklaas (French *St-Nicolas*), town in the province of East Flanders, Belgium, 19 km west of Antwerp. It is the capital of the former Waasland. Its manufactures are woollen, cotton, and linen goods, carpets, pottery, bricks, and furniture. The market place, the *Groote Markt*, is the largest in the country. There is a very interesting archae-ological museum. Population 48,900.

Sint-Truiden (French *St-Trond*), town in the province of Limbourg, Belgium, 17 km south-west of Hasselt. It has various manufacturing industries and is situated in a region covered by extensive orchards. Population 21,300.

Sinter, see TRAVERTINE.

Sintra, town of Portugal, 24 km north-west of Lisbon. It is known for its palaces, gardens, and Moorish remains. In 1808 the Convention of Sintra between England and France provided for the evacuation of Portugal by the French. It is now a holiday resort. Population 20,320.

Sinus, see PARANASAL SINUSES.

Sinus Aelanticus, see AQABA, GULF OF.

Sinus Aquitanicus, or Cantabricus, see BISCAY, BAY OF.

Sinyavski, Andrei Donatevich (1925–), Soviet writer and critic. He has published articles on Soviet poets which display considerable originality and sensitivity, and a study, *On Socialist Realism*, translated by G. Dennis, 1961. The latter, and all Sinyavski's fiction, has been published only abroad, under the name of Avram Tertz (*The Trial Begins*, translated by M. Hayward, 1960; *The Icicle and other stories*, translated by M. Hayward and R. Hingley, 1963; *The Makepeace Experiment*, translated by M. Harari, 1965). His original works reveal and examine the psychological characteristics of people living under the Soviet régime, often through the use of fantasy. His writings were considered to be anti-Soviet and in 1966 he was sentenced to seven years hard labour. In 1973 he was allowed to leave the USSR and has since published an essay *On the Literary Process in Russia*, 1974, and a book *In the Shadow of Gogol*, 1975.

Sion (German *Sitten*), capital of the canton of VALAIS, Switzerland, lying in the valley of the RHÔNE south-east of Lake Geneva. It has three ruined castles, a 15th-century cathedral, and a 13th-century church. A market centre for the canton's vegetables, fruit, and wine. Population (1974) 23,900; mainly French-speaking and Roman Catholic.

Sion College, Victoria Embankment, London, established in 1630 by the will of the Rev. Dr Thomas White, died 1624, as a College (i.e. Society) for the City clergy, with an almshouse. The original site was on London Wall. The buildings were sold in 1884 and the present building was opened in 1886. The College contains a fine theological library.

Sioux, North American Indians, properly called DAKOTA.

Sioux City, city and county seat of Woodbury county, Iowa, USA, on the Missouri river where the Big Sioux and the Floyd enter it, 250 km north-west of Des Moines. It is a rail and highway centre with large stockyards, and a major livestock and grain market; it does much meat packing and manufactures dairy products, flour, feed, and animal serums. It has an annual stock show, and is the seat of Morningside College and Briar Cliff College. Population 85,925.

Sioux Falls, city and county seat of Minnehaha county, South Dakota, USA, on the Big Sioux river. The river here falls 30 m and supplied water power for early industries. The city is a great wheat and livestock centre; it has important stockyards and fairgrounds. Population 72,488.

Siphon, bent tube with arms of unequal length used for drawing off liquid from one vessel into another. In use, the tube is first filled with liquid and placed so that the shorter arm dips into the vessel to be emptied. The pressure on the short-arm side of the bend is then equal to the pressure of the atmosphere minus that of a column of liquid of the height of the short arm, measured vertically; the pressure

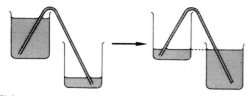

Siphon.

on the long-arm side of the bend is equal to the pressure of the atmosphere minus that of a column of liquid of the height of the long arm. Consequently there is a movement of liquid from the short-arm side of the bend to the long-arm side, and this continues until the mass of liquid becomes discontinuous or until the heights of the columns in the two arms are equal.

A soda siphon does not work by siphon action, but rather relies on the pressure of undissolved gas (carbon dioxide) to force the liquid out of the tube.

Siphonaptera, an order of the class Insecta, subclass Pterygota. These are the fleas. They are small, wingless, laterally-compressed insects that are usually heavily chitinised (have a hard cuticle). The antennae are in grooves, and the mouthparts piercing and sucking. The adults are ectoparasites of birds and mammals living mainly in their nests, burrows, or body covering. Most species are host-specific, that is, they are confined to a particular host species. The hindlegs are often especially large and long as an adaptation for jumping.

Metamorphosis is complete with, usually, three larval stages. The larva is small, white, hairy, legless, and maggot-like. It scavenges on dried blood, faecal matter from the adults, and other organic matter in the nests or clothing of the host. The pupal stage is in a cocoon formed of silk coated with debris that camouflages it. The adult often remains within the cocoon until it detects the presence of a host. The adults are active animals, commonly changing from one host individual to another. They spend a considerable time off the host, and leave the host to lay their eggs, which develop on the ground or in the host nest.

There are over 1800 species, only a few of which are important to man as vectors of disease, although many are

Siphonaptera. An X-ray photograph of the dog flea. (*Popperfoto*)

indirectly important as they maintain the reservoir of disease among wild animals. Fleas are vectors of bubonic PLAGUE, murine TYPHUS, and tularaemia, and they are also known to transmit myxomatosis virus to rabbits, and *Salmonella* food poisoning in mammals, but they are not thought to be important in the latter two cases. The most important vectors belong to the genera *Leptopsylla*, *Nosopsyllus*, and *Xenopsylla*. The last is important in plague transmission as the bacteria block the flea's gut and the starving flea may infect many hosts in attempting to feed. All three genera are important in the transmission of murine typhus. They are also intermediate hosts of *Dipylidium caninum*, the dog and cat tapeworm (see CESTODA), which is occasionally picked up by children when the animal licks their faces after nipping a flea in its teeth. Fleas are intermediate hosts of *Hymenolepis diminuator* of rats and mice also. Two genera, *Echidnophaga* and *Tunga*, are endoparasites, the adults burrowing into the skin of the host animals. *Echidnophaga* mainly infests chickens and other fowl. The eggs are laid on the soil, and the larvae hatch and pupate there. *Tunga*, commonly known as the jigger flea, infests man, mainly on the feet between the toes, and is important as a route for secondary infection as well as causing intense discomfort. It also infests other animals.

The bites of several species cause allergic reactions with intense itching. Unfortunately, these species tend to be the most common household fleas. *Ctenocephalides canis*, the dog flea, and *C. felis*, the cat flea, are very annoying in this respect, and appear to be on the increase owing to wall-to-wall carpeting and central heating, which provide an ideal environment for these species. Although the adults bite man readily, it seems that the eggs only develop on their normal hosts. The bite of the human flea, *Pulex irritans*, also causes a severe reaction, but it is rare in the UK. Other fleas may attempt to bite individuals who handle their host animals, but contact with them is uncommon.

Siphonophora, see HYDROZOA; PORTUGUESE MAN-OF-WAR.

Sipunculida, a phylum of approximately 250 species of marine worms, also known as peanut worms. They have a cylindrical body divided into two parts and range in size from 2 mm to 70 cm long. There is a crown of short, hollow ciliated tentacles or lobes around the mouth. They live in sand, mud, rock crevices, or empty shells. Common species are *Golfingia* and *Sipunculus*.

Siqueiros, David Alfaro (1896–), Mexican painter and graphic artist, inspired in aim by the Mexican revolution. Principal works are mural paintings in Mexico City, dynamic and strongly proletarian in sentiment, of which *March of Humanity* (4600 m²) expresses most clearly his message. He has also painted many portraits.

Sir (French *sire*, a variant of *seigneur*, from Latin *senior*), official title of baronets and knights, which is prefixed to the Christian name of the bearer, e.g. Sir Francis Laking, Bart., Sir George Alexander. Long applied loosely in addressing any person of position or seniority, it is now rarely used in this sense.

Sirach, see ECCLESIASTICUS.

Siracusa, see SYRACUSE.

Siraj-ud-daula

Siraj-ud-daula (1728?–57), Nawab of Bengal, captured the fort connected with the British factory at Calcutta in 1757, and shut up 146 prisoners in the military prison, afterwards known as 'the BLACK HOLE OF CALCUTTA'. Calcutta was retaken by Robert Clive in 1757, and Siraj-ud-daula was finally defeated in June of the same year. He was killed at his capital, Murshidabad.

Sirat, al- (*al-sirat*, the path, Latin *strata*), a bridge over hell, thinner than a hair and sharper than a sword along which all must pass to reach paradise. This bridge is not mentioned in the Koran but is an accepted dogma of Islamic theology. The concept is a direct borrowing from the AVESTA.

Siren, sound signalling apparatus. As used for fire warnings, air-raids, etc., the siren consists of three parts, viz., motor, rotor, and stator. The rotor is fixed to the motor spindle and spins inside the stator, which is fitted to the motor frame. Whilst the motor is running, air is drawn through a large hole in the end of the rotor, and is then driven out through a number of openings in the rotor and stator. As the openings in the rotor pass the openings in the stator the air is able to pass freely, but as the openings in the rotor pass the closed part of the stator the air is obstructed. The pitch of the note emitted depends upon the number of openings in the rotor and the speed of the motor, e.g., 10 openings give 512 vibrations per second (one octave above middle C) with the motor running at approximately 3000 revolutions per minute. The volume of sound depends upon the amount of air passed through the rotors.

Another type is especially used in lighthouses and lightships, and also in factories. It has the advantages of a steady and immediate note, great volume of sound, and the ability to produce precise blast sequences, and has a characteristic 'grunt' at the end of each blast. This is the 'diaphone', of which several sizes are produced. It operates by compressed air fed to the instrument from an air storage tank. When the driving valve is opened air is admitted to the back of a piston, causing it to oscillate rapidly and exhaust air through ports. Once the piston is in motion a sounding valve is opened, allowing a much larger volume of air to reach the chamber, and pass through the annular slots in the cylinder bore. The piston, which is cut with identical annular slots, oscillates so that during each movement the slots in the piston match with the slots in the cylinder. When this happens air passes from the chamber through the cylinder wall and piston to a resonator with a large puff. Due to the reciprocating action, the puffs of air occur rapidly at about 180 per second, and are of considerable volume; this results in a very powerful sound being produced. The note emitted is pitched at approximately F in the bass clef.

Siren, the typical genus of tailed eel-like amphibians in the family Sirenidae. The species are characterised by having four-fingered forelimbs, three external gills on each side, no hind limbs and no eyelids. *S. lacertina* is the mud-eel, over 60 cm long, and occurs in North America. It resembles PROTEUS, except that teeth and hind limbs are absent in *Siren*.

Sirenia, the order of mammals which contains the sea-cows; many fossil forms have been found as well as the living species of the genera *Dugong* (or dugongs) and

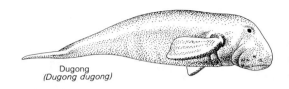

Dugong
(Dugong dugong)

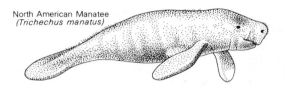

North American Manatee
(Trichechus manatus)

Sirenia. Examples of the two families in the order.

Trichechus (or manatees). *Hydrodamalis stelleri*, or Steller's sea-cow, which attained a length of 10 m, became extinct due to depredations of man within 50 years of its discovery in 1741. Sirenia inhabit various seashores and are purely vegetarian in diet. The mammary glands are pectoral in position, so that Sirenia may have been mistaken for mermaids.

Sirens, nymphs whose songs irresistibly lured sailors to destruction. ODYSSEUS plugged his men's ears with wax and tied himself to the mast, and so passed them in safety (*Odyssey* xii). When the ARGONAUTS sailed by, Orpheus outsang the sirens, after which they threw themselves into the sea and became rocks.

Siricius, Saint (b. c. 334), Pope (bishop of Rome), 384–99, born in Rome. An epoch in papal history is marked by his letter to Archbishop Himerius of Tarragona, which has been called the first papal decretal and is among those considered genuine (see ISIDORIAN DECRETALS). His pontificate has some slight importance in the development of the primacy for that reason, but the influence which he and his successor St Anastasius I (399–401) exercised upon Western Christianity cannot compare with that of their contemporary St AMBROSE, Bishop of Milan.

Sirius, Alpha Canis Majoris or 'the DOG STAR', a first magnitude STAR in CANIS MAJOR. The name Sirius is derived from the Greek word for 'sparkling', a description it fully warrants since, after the Sun, it is the brightest star in the sky. In ancient Egypt, where its hieroglyph was a dog, its reappearance in the early morning sky heralded the annual rising of the Nile. Sirius is double with an orbital period of 50 years. The eighth magnitude companion is sometimes known as 'the Dark Companion' since it was first detected by BESSEL in 1850 from its gravitational effect on the observed proper motion of Sirius. It was seen for the first time in 1862 by Alvan Clark but it was not till the 1920s that it was recognised as a white dwarf, the first known example of such stars which have mean densities of the order of 100,000 times that of water. See ASTRONOMY; STARS.

Sirk, Douglas (1900–), Danish-born film director who worked in Germany (1935–37), France (1939), Holland

(1939), and the USA (1942–58). Sirk has a great familiarity with the avant-garde theatre of Europe and with other arts (he studied art history under Erwin PANOFSKY), which gave his American melodramas a rare brilliance: *Magnificent Obsession* (1953), *All That Heaven Allows* (1955), *Written on the Wind* (1956), *The Tarnished Angels* (1957), *A Time to Love and a Time to Die* (1957), *Imitation of Life* (1958).

Sirocco, see WIND.

Sisal, a textile fibre obtained from the leaf of *Agave sisalana*, which is indigenous to Mexico but is now also grown in Tanzania and Brazil. It is used for twine, especially for baler and binder machines, for floor coverings, and in millinery. In 1974 production was 759,000 t (300,000 from Brazil, 157,000 from Tanzania, and 80,000 from Kenya). This is 2·2 per cent of world fibre production.
Bibliography: J. G. Cook, *Handbook of Textile Fibres*, vol. 1: *Natural Fibres*, 4th ed. 1968.

Siskin, *Carduelis spinus*, a bird species of the family Fringillidae, order Passeriformes, related to the goldfinch. Its colour is a greenish-yellow, and it is frequently seen in Britain where it breeds, mainly in coniferous woods. In winter it is often to be seen in company with the redpoll, *Acanthis flammea*, in deciduous woods especially alder. It has recently taken to visiting bird tables.

Sisley, Alfred (1839–99), landscape painter of English parentage, born in Paris. He became acquainted with Monet and Renoir in the studio of the classical painter Gleyre. Sisley was a member of the Impressionist group (see IMPRESSIONISM), and his work shows the influence of the light-effects of Monet. He settled in Moret-sur-Loing but visited England in 1871 and 1874. He is known as one of the purest Impressionists. Well-known works include *The Square at Argenteuil* 1872 (Louvre) and *The Canal*, 1872 (Louvre).
Bibliography: J. Rewald, *History of Impressionism*, 2nd ed. 1961.

Sistan, see BALUCHISTAN.

Sistine Chapel, principal chapel of the VATICAN at Rome. It was begun by Pope Sixtus IV in 1473, and is famous for the paintings which cover its walls and vault, notably those by MICHELANGELO including *The Creation*, *The Deluge* and *The Last Judgment*, and also masterpieces by Botticelli, Perugino and Pinturicchio. The voting of the cardinals at the election of a new pope takes place in the Sistine Chapel. (See also CONCLAVE.)

Sistova, see SVISHTOV.

Sisymbrium, see HEDGE MUSTARD.

Sisyphus, legendary son of Aeolus and Enarete, and king of Corinth. He promoted navigation and commerce, but lived an evil life, for which he was punished in TARTARUS, forever rolling a huge stone up a hill, which, at the top, always rolled back. See *Iliad*, vi. 153; *Odyssey*, xi. 593.

Sitar, fretted Indian lute which has existed in its present form for 700 years. It has 6 or 7 main strings, and from 11 to 19 sympathetic strings. The main strings are plucked with a plectrum, *mizrab*, worn on the index finger of the right hand.

Sithole, Ndabaningi (1920–), Rhodesian leader who founded the Zimbabwe African National Union (ZANU), the members of which originally formed the core of the Rhodesian guerrilla movement. He studied in the USA and is a pastor of the Methodist Church. In 1959 he published *African Nationalism* and in 1964 was arrested for alleged incitement to violence, and later accused of plotting political assassinations. On 12 December 1974 he was conditionally released in order to participate in talks about Rhodesia's (Zimbabwe's) future. In 1975 he sought refuge abroad, returning in July 1977 to help bring about a Rhodesian settlement.

Sitka, town and former capital of Alaska, USA, situated on the west coast of Baranov Island, facing Sitka Sound, 160 km south-west of Juneau. Between 1804–67 it was the Russian capital, and then became the capital of the unorganised territory. In 1900 Juneau supported it as capital of Alaska. A feature of interest is the Russo-Greek church dating from 1816. Since 1940 Sitka has been an important naval base; it is also a trading and commercial centre. Its fishing, lumbering, canning, and cold-storage operations are important. Population 3370.

Sitsang, see TIBET.

Sittang, river of Burma. It flows southward to debouch into the Gulf of Martaban. The Sittang, which is nearly 400 km long, is only navigable for a short distance by large craft, but is extensively used for floating logs down to the coast.

Sitten, see SION.

Alfred Sisley. *A Road at Louveciennes*, 1876. *(Musées de Nice/Lauros-Giraudon)*

Sitting Bull

Sitting Bull (1835–90), famous chief of the Dakota Sioux Indians, son of Jumping Bull. During the American Civil War he led bands which attacked white settlers in Iowa and Minnesota. He finally made peace with the government, but broke his word and refused to retire to the reservation. This led to a campaign in which Gen. G. A. Custer and his entire command were massacred. Sitting Bull fled to Canada, but returned in 1881 and lived at Standing Rock. When the Sioux refused to sell their lands, he encouraged them. An attempt was made to arrest Sitting Bull in 1890, during which he was shot.

Sittingbourne, town in the Swale District of KENT, England. It is an important fruit-growing area and has local industries including the manufacture of paper, cement, bricks, and clothing; also fruit packing and preserving. The large agricultural research station here was opened in the 1940s and a considerable complex has since developed. Population (1971) 30,600.

Sittwe, formerly Akyab, township and town in Arakan state, Burma. After the cession of Arakan in 1826 Sittwe was made the seat of government and grew rapidly from a small fishing village into a leading port. Its chief export is rice. Township: area 228 km²; population 143,200.

Sitting Bull. *(Mansell Collection)*

Sitwell, Dame Edith Louise (1887–1964), English poet and critic, born at Scarborough, Yorkshire, sister of Osbert and Sacheverell SITWELL. Edith Sitwell began her career as a poet modestly with *The Mother and Other Poems,* 1915, a volume which showed French influence, especially that of Baudelaire. In 1916 the first volume of *Wheels* appeared, an annual anthology of verse, which she edited until it was discontinued in 1921; it served as a showcase for her work and that of other young poets who were fighting an artistic revolt against the Georgians. Her verse was notable for its visual imagery and verbal music, and was an influence on T. S. Eliot and W. B. Yeats. An early series of poems called *Façade* was first recited by her at a public performance, accompanied by music composed by William Walton, in 1923. Her *Collected Poems* appeared in 1930. Later work, especially *Street Songs,* 1942, and *Song of the Cold,* 1945, is more preoccupied with religious themes and symbolism.

Other books of verse were *Clown's Houses,* 1918, *The Sleeping Beauty,* 1924, *Gold Coast Customs,* 1929, *The Canticle of the Rose,* 1948, and *Gardeners and Astronomers,* 1953. Her prose works include *Poetry and Criticism, an Essay,* 1925, *Alexander Pope,* 1930, *The English Eccentrics,* 1933, *Aspects of Modern Poetry,* 1934, *Victoria of England,* 1936, and *Fanfare for Elizabeth,* 1946. In 1933 she was awarded the medal of the Royal Society of London, and in 1954 was made a Dame Grand Cross of the Order of the British Empire; in the same year she became a Roman Catholic. Her autobiography, *Taken Care Of,* was published in 1965.

Bibliography: Studies by C. M. Bowra, 1947; J. Lehmann, 1952.

Sitwell, Sir Osbert (1892–1969), English poet and novelist, born in London, the brother of Edith and Sacheverell SITWELL; educated at Eton. He entered the Sherwood Rangers, a yeomanry regiment, in 1911, was transferred to the Grenadier Guards in 1912, and served with them in the First World War. The war and subsequent peace excited Osbert Sitwell to bitter satire, both in prose and verse. His first volume of satires, *Argonaut and Juggernaut,* 1919, was followed by *The Winstonburg Line,* 1919, an attack on Winston Churchill's projected campaign in north Russia.

In his two novels, *Before the Bombardment,* 1926, and *The Man Who Lost Himself,* 1929, he claimed to have originated the 'novel of reasoned action', which seeks to discover a balance between the reason, unreason, and previous history 'in which each action, event and thought is founded'. His verse, some of which appears in *Selected Poems,* 1943, is often caustic and mocking; however, his reputation chiefly rests on a series of autobiographical memoirs, *Left Hand, Right Hand!,* 1944, *The Scarlet Tree,* 1945, *Great Morning,* 1947, *Laughter in the Next Room,* 1948, and *Noble Essences,* 1950. In 1956 he was made a CBE, and in 1958 a Companion of Honour.

Sitwell, Sir Sacheverell (1897–), English poet and essayist, younger brother of Edith and Osbert SITWELL, born at Scarborough; educated at Eton and Balliol College, Oxford. In the First World War he served with the Grenadier Guards. His poetry is traditional in form and style, and reveals his preoccupations with art and music. It includes *The Hundred and One Harlequins,* 1922,

Edith Sitwell, portrait by Wyndham Lewis. *(Tate Gallery, London)*

The Thirteenth Caesar, 1924, *Exalt the Eglantine,* 1926, *The Cyder Feast,* 1927, and the complete version of *Dr Donne and Gargantua,* 1930. His prose works consist of the seminal study *Southern Baroque Art,* 1924, *All Summer in a Day* (an autobiographical fantasia), 1926, *German Baroque Art,* 1927, the three volumes that comprise *The Gothick North,* 1929, *Spanish Baroque Art,* and a volume of short stories, *Far from My Home,* 1931.

Sacheverell Sitwell was the founder and secretary of the Magnasco Society, which exists to further the appreciation of 17th- and 18th-century Italian art. Later works are *Conversation Pieces,* 1936, *La Vie Parisienne,* 1937, *Roumanian Journey,* 1938, *Sacred and Profane Love,* 1940, *Primitive Scenes and Festivals,* 1942, *The Homing of the Winds,* 1942, *Splendours and Miseries,* 1943, *British Architects and Craftsmen,* 1954, *Spain,* 1950, and *Portugal and Madeira,* 1954.

Sir Osbert Sitwell. *(Popperfoto)*

Śiva

Śiva (the Lord of Sleep), one of the creator deities belonging to the trinity of BRAHMĀ, VISHNU and Śiva. Profound Hindu understanding has embodied in Śiva the power of universal disintegration and dispersion. All that is born must die, is a law of the universe. Hindus add that BRAHMAN, the Source, is changeless, timeless and beyond birth and death. Hence the death of the body enables the transmigrating soul to return to its Source, which is birthless and deathless, before it is born again. Thus Śiva, as the power of disintegration and death, is also the merciful redeemer who enables the weary soul to rest in its Source.

Śiva alone remains at the end of one phase and the beginning of the next. He is pictured as a fathomless void, comparable to the silence and stillness of dreamless sleep.

'Beyond this darkness there is neither day nor night, neither existence nor non-existence, but Śiva alone, the indestructible. Even the sun lies prostrate before him. From him springs forth the ageless wisdom.' (Svetasvatara Upanishad).

In images he is represented in either of two ways. In one he is a fearful destroyer, the embodiment of death: in the other he is the beginning of all creation, mysteriously dancing through the forests and scattering his seed to create unknown new worlds and beings. As new life, his symbol is the LINGAM and his vehicle the bull.

Bibliography: Swami Prabhavananda and Frederick Manchester, *The Upanishads*, 1957; Alain Daniélou, *Hindu Polytheism*, 1964; A. K. Rāmānujan, *Speaking of Śiva*, 1973.

Sivaji (1627–80), founder of Mahratta power, and a great Hindu hero and rebel. He revolted against the Bijapur rulers in 1646, and spent the rest of his life more or less continuously in a state of war. As a military leader he showed daring and resource; as a religious leader, he

Śiva as Lord of the Dance, 11th-century bronze from Madras state. (*Victoria and Albert Museum, London*)

pointed the way to a Hindu revival while showing toleration towards Christians and Muslims.

Sivas, town and capital of Sivas province, Asiatic Turkey, situated on the Kizil Irmak river and the railway and road from Ankara to Erzurum. The town is a major agricultural market centre and has food-processing industries. There are important 13th-century Seljuk monuments. The Sivas Conference, 1919, confirmed Kemal ATATÜRK as leader of the new Turkey. Population (town) 157,000; (province) 732,000.

Sivash Sea, see AZOV, SEA OF.

Siwa, oasis in MATRUH province, Egypt. It lies below sea-level and contains several artesian wells. The celebrated temple and oracle of Zeus Ammon, in the oasis, was visited by Alexander the Great.

Six Acts, series of statutes passed in 1819 after the 'massacre of Peterloo' (see PETERLOO MASSACRE) to clarify the law on public meetings and prevent further popular disturbances—which ministers at the time considered presaged revolution. They prohibited meetings for military training, authorised the issue of warrants for the seizure of arms, limited meetings to draw up public petitions to not more than 50 people living in the parish where the meeting was to be held, allowed magistrates to seize seditious and blasphemous literature, dealt with procedure for bringing cases to trial, and imposed stamp duty on certain periodical pamphlets.

Six Articles, Statute of, see ARTICLES, SIX.

Six Counties, see IRELAND, NORTHERN.

Six Nations, see IROQUOIS.

Sixth Form College, school or college for sixth-form pupils. The nature of the college may be defined by age, e.g. pupils aged 16–19, or by qualification—passes at 'O' level, and therefore by nature of work—post 'O' level standard. If only defined by age then both academic and non-academic courses are offered: if minimum entry qualifications are demanded then the college is essentially selective and academic, and its minimum economic size for efficient operation is thought to be about 400 pupils. It is claimed by its supporters that more pupils will continue their education in the adult atmosphere of the sixth-form college, and that much better academic provision could be made for them there. Although the sixth form college is a common pattern of organisation in Europe, there has been much opposition to it, particularly from teachers' organisations, in England. As a result there are comparatively few examples—Mexborough, in South Yorkshire, being a famous one—although their numbers are now increasing. Others include Atlantic College, Wales—an international school—Luton, and those run by the boroughs of Southampton and Exeter.

Bibliography: R. W. King, *The English Sixth Form College*, 1968; A. D. Edwards, *The Changing Sixth Forms in the 20th Century*, 1970; A. D. C. Peterson, *The Future of the Sixth Form*, 1973.

Sixtus IV, Francesco della Rovere (b. 1414), Pope, 1471–84, a Franciscan, born near Savona; he succeeded Paul II. He encouraged the spread of learning, began the Sistine Chapel and the Sistine Bridge, and was a patron of

Sixtus IV, fresco (anonymous) showing the Pope giving an audience in the Palatine. *(Bisonte)*

all the arts. He was involved in a conspiracy against the Medici which resulted in a war with Florence (1478) and urged the Venetians to attack Ferrara and then abandoned them.

Sixtus V, Felice Peretti, Pope, 1585–90, Franciscan preacher, and professor of theology at Rimini and Siena. His rule was characterised by a number of reforms. He brought order to the Papal States. He also built the Vatican library, and published a new edition of the Septuagint and of the Vulgate. He fixed the number of cardinals at 70.

Size, see GLUE.

Sizergh Castle, 5 km south of Kendal, Cumbria. The 14th-century pele tower was built for defence against Border raids, but the castle is largely Tudor, containing fine panelling, old English furniture and Stuart and Jacobite relics. The castle was given to the National Trust with 1562 acres by the Hornyold-Strickland family in 1950.

Sjælland (English, Zealand; German *Seeland*), largest island of DENMARK, bounded by the Kattegat, the Great Belt, the Sound (ØRESUND), and the Baltic. It has a greatly indented coast, the Roskilde fjord being the longest fjord. The surface of the island is undulating and the soil fertile. Agriculture, dairy farming, cattle breeding, and fishing are carried on. The chief town is COPENHAGEN. Area 7225 km². Population 1,900,000.

Skagerrak, arm of the sea situated between Norway and Jutland, connecting the Baltic and North Seas by means of the KATTEGAT. It varies between 112 and 145 km in width, and is about 250 km long.

Skagway, town of south-east Alaska, USA, at the head of Chilkoot Inlet of Lynn Canal. It is a trade and shipping centre for an interior mining area and the coastal terminus of the White Pass and Yukon railway; it is also a seaport and has an airport. It was founded about 1897. Population 675.

Skaldic Poetry. *Skald* or *skáld* is the Old Icelandic word for poet and, used in a technical sense, it refers to the court poets of medieval Scandinavia. The earliest of

these were Norwegian, but after the late 10th century, they were, without exception, Icelandic. The central theme of the skalds' poetry was praise of the kings or princes to whom they were attached. Later, their style was adopted by poets other than court poets and the term skaldic poetry is used of works composed in this style. Much of the corpus of skaldic poetry was composed in the pre-literary period and is preserved in Icelandic prose works of the 13th and 14th centuries, particularly in the *Snorra Edda* and *Heimskringla* of SNORRI STURLUSON and in sagas about poets such as EGILS SAGA SKALLA-GRÍMSSONAR.

Skaldic poetry differs markedly from Eddic poetry (see EDDA) which continues and develops the traditional Germanic verse-form. Five-sixths of it is in the metre called *dróttkvætt*, the main features of which are that there are six syllables to each line; each line ends in a trochee; there are eight lines to a stanza; and even lines contain full-rhyme, odd lines half-rhyme. In addition, skaldic poetry makes lavish use of kennings, or poetical circumlocutions (for example, 'the whale's land' for 'the sea'; 'waster of gold' for 'generous prince').

The origin of skaldic poetry is uncertain. Bragi Boddason (9th century) is probably the oldest skaldic poet whose fragments of poetry are preserved. In his *Ragnarsdrápa*, the *dróttkvætt* technique is seen at an advanced stage of perfection. Egill Skalla-Grímsson (10th century) is an important skald, as is SIGHVATR THÓRDARSON (11th century). The subject matter often describes battle and sea-voyages, but *dróttkvætt* is later used for religious subjects. The corpus of skaldic poetry is edited by Finnur Jónsson in *Den norsk-islandske skjaldedigtning*, 1912–15.

Bibliography: L. M. Hollander, *The Skalds*, 1945.

Skalkottas, Nikos (1904–49), Greek composer, born at Chalkis in Euboea. He was intended for a career as a concert violinist and in 1921 began to study in Berlin, where, however, he became a composition pupil of Weill and Schoenberg. In 1933 he returned to Greece and spent the remainder of his life as an obscure orchestral player, composing in his spare time. Only after his death did his vast output begin to be performed. Skalkottas was Greece's first composer of international stature. His works, mostly orchestral and chamber music, include 36 *Greek Dances*, 19 concerti for various instruments, and the symphony *The Return of Ulysses*.

Skanderborg, town in Århus county, Denmark, a tourist centre near lakes Mosso and Silkeborg. Population 11,000.

Skåne, or Scania, old province in the south of Sweden, now included in the counties of MALMÖHUS and KRISTIANSTAD.

Skaraborg, southern county of Sweden, lying between Lakes VÄNERN and VÄTTERN. It is chiefly a farming area, but there are munition works at Karlsborg. Area 8468 km²; population (1974) 262,400.

Skat, German card game, invented towards the beginning of the 19th century. It still has a great vogue in Central and North Germany, and is essentially a German game, played with special German cards. These number 32, and are of different colours; each of the colours has a different

Skate

value, and the cards are counted according to their colours and numerical value. The game consists of obtaining 61 points for a single game, 89 for a double, and 120 for the full game.

Skate, fish of the elasmobranch family Rajidae, suborder Rajoidei, which occurs in all temperate seas. The body of the fish is in the shape of a flattened disk, formed by its union with the greatly developed, fleshy pectoral fins; the tail is slender and usually bears two dorsal fins. The egg cases are oblong, and are commonly known as mermaid's purses. Several well-known species are *Raja radiata*, the starry skate; *R. oxyrhynchus*, the long-nosed skate; and *R. laevis*, the barn-door skate.

Skating, see ICE SKATING; ROLLER SKATING.

Skean-dhu, or sgean-dhu (Gaelic, black knife), short knife, usually worn with Highland dress and carried in the right stocking.

Skeat, Walter William (1835–1912), British philologist, born in London. He became professor of Anglo-Saxon at Cambridge in 1878. Founder of the Early English Text Society (with FURNIVALL) in 1864, in 1873 he also founded the English Dialect Society. Of the works he edited, those of especial importance were *Piers Plowman*, 1867, reprinted 1954, and *The Complete Works of Geoffrey Chaucer*, 1894–97. He also wrote a pioneering *Etymological Dictionary of the English Language*, 1882, revised edition 1910.

Skegby, village in Nottinghamshire, England, 25 km from Nottingham, part of the SUTTON-IN-ASHFIELD district, and in the heart of a coal-mining area.

Skegness, largest seaside resort of Lincolnshire, England. It has 9 km of sandy beaches. Butlin established his first holiday camp at Skegness. Population (1971) 13,500.

Skeleton, a rigid structure for the support or protection of the softer tissues of a plant or animal. When the skeleton is external, as in the shells of insects or crabs, it is called an exoskeleton; when it forms an interior framework for the support of surrounding tissues, it is known as an endoskeleton. In man, the medial supporting structure is the VERTEBRAL COLUMN (spine); it consists, in the infant, of 33 *vertebrae*, of which the upper seven are *cervical*, or neck vertebrae; the next 12 are *thoracic*, or chest vertebrae; the next five are *lumbar*, or loin vertebrae; the next five *sacral*, or pelvic vertebrae; and the last four *coccygeal*, or caudal vertebrae. In the adult the sacral vertebrae unite to form the *sacrum*, and the coccygeal vertebrae unite to form the *coccyx*. The spine supports the skull, which consists of 22 bones, eight cranial and 14 facial, of which only the jaw-bone is movable. The organs of the chest are protected by the ribs, which articulate with the vertebrae behind; seven of them on each side unite with the *sternum*, or breastbone, in front; the next four do not unite directly with the sternum, and are called false ribs; while the last has a free extremity in front, and is called a floating rib.

The upper limbs hang from the shoulder-girdle, which consists of the *clavicle*, or collar-bone, in front, and a flat, triangular bone called the *scapula*, or shoulder-blade, behind. Articulating in the glenoid cavity of the scapula

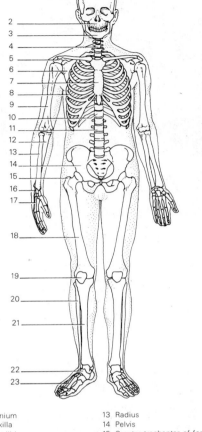

1 Cranium	13 Radius
2 Maxilla	14 Pelvis
3 Mandible	15 Greater trochanter of femur
4 Cervical vertebra	16 Carpal bones
5 Clavicle	17 Metacarpal bones
6 Scapula	18 Femur
7 Sternum	19 Patella
8 Ribs	20 Fibula
9 Humerus	21 Tibia
10 Thoracic vertebra	22 Tarsal bones
11 Lumbar vertebra	23 Metatarsal bones
12 Ulna	

Skeleton. The human skeleton.

is the *humerus*, or bone of the upper arm; at its lower extremity the humerus possesses a *trochlea* or pulley for the *ulna*, and a small head for articulating with the *radius*. The ulna and radius, the bones of the forearm, articulate with the wrist or *carpus*, which consists of eight bones in two rows. Then come five *metacarpal* bones, which articulate with the *phalanges* of the fingers.

The lower limbs articulate with the pelvic girdle, each half of which consists of three bones, the ilium, ischium and pubis, fused together and firmly attached to the sacrum, and supporting the viscera. The arrangement of bones in the legs is somewhat similar to that of the arm bones. The *femur*, or thigh bone, is the longest bone in the body. The bones of the lower leg are the *tibia*, or shin bone, and the slenderer *fibula*. These articulate with the femur and the sesamoid *patella*, or knee-cap, above, and with the bones of the *tarsus*, or ankle, below. The foot also possesses five *metatarsal* bones and the *phalanges* of the toes. See BONE; JOINTS.

Skelleftea, town in the county of VÄSTERBOTTEN, Sweden, standing on the River Skellefte, 16 km from the sea. Since the discovery of the Boliden mines with their rich variety of ores (including gold), the town has grown considerably. Population (1974) 72,000.

Skelligs, The, three islets off the coast of County KERRY, Republic of Ireland, 15 km south-west of Valentia Island. The Little Skellig is the most southerly of breeding places for the gannet in the area. Great Skellig has ruins of a monastery in the main enclosure amidst its twin peaks which rise to 218 m and 198 m above sea-level.

Skelmersdale, town in the new West Lancashire borough of LANCASHIRE, England, lying to the west of Wigan. It was designated a New Town in 1961, mainly for overspill from Liverpool. Since then it has attracted a number of industries and by 1971, its population had increased to 30,582; this is eventually expected to be around 80,000.

Skelmorlie, village in Inverclyde District, Strathclyde Region, Scotland, on the coast 8 km north of Largs. Adjacent to Skelmorlie is Wemyss Bay, a rail terminal and centre for pleasure steamer sailings on the CLYDE, especially to ROTHESAY. Here also are Skelmorlie and Wemyss Castles. Population 1535.

Skelton, John (1460–1529), English poet, born in Norfolk; educated at both Oxford and Cambridge. His first recorded verses were composed on the death of Edward IV (1483). He was appointed tutor to the Duke of York (afterwards Henry VIII), and, taking holy orders in 1498, was given the living of Diss, Norfolk.

He achieved a European reputation as a poet and man of letters, and under Henry VIII became in effect (if not name) poet laureate. Most of his poetry is satirical, on political and religious matters, and in an idiosyncratic style of short rhyming lines. *Phyllyp Sparrowe* is a parody of the liturgical office for the dead, delivered upon a young lady's pet; *A Ballade of the Scottish Kynge* is an attack on Henry's enemies, written after FLODDEN (1513); *Speke Parrot*, 1521, *Collyn Clout*, 1522, and *Why Come Ye Not to Court?*, 1522, all combine attacks on the growing influence of Cardinal WOLSEY with criticism of humanist learning.

Skelton also wrote *Magnyfycence*, 1516, the first secular MORALITY play in English, and *The Tunnyng of Elynour Rummynge*, an energetic and realistic depiction of the drunken Elynour in an ale-house, which has been instrumental in creating an apocryphal account of his own life as dissolute. Skelton's reputation was completely eclipsed after the Reformation and his status as a major poet was only re-established in the 20th century. His *Poems* are edited by R. S. Kinsman, 1970; and *Magnyfycence* by R. L. Ramsey, 1958.

Bibliography: P. Henderson, *The Complete Poems*, 1949; P. Green, *John Skelton*, 1960; A. R. Heiserman, *Skelton and Satire*, 1962; W. O. Harris, *Skelton's 'Magnyfycence' and the Cardinal Virtue Tradition*, 1966; M. Pollet, *John Skelton, Poet of Tudor England* (trans.), 1971.

Skelton and Brotton, town in CLEVELAND, England, 16 km east of MIDDLESBROUGH. Agriculture is the principal industry. Population (1971) 15,122.

Skene, William Forbes (1809–92), British historian, born at Inverie, Inverness-shire. He was educated at Edinburgh, in Germany, and at St Andrews University. In 1881 he was appointed Historiographer-Royal for Scotland. His chief works are *The Highlanders of Scotland: their Origin, History and Antiquities*, 1837; *Celtic Scotland: a History of Ancient Alban*, 1876–80, and as editor, *The Chronicles of the Picts and Scots*, 1867. His work, though much criticised, has never been replaced by better.

Skerries, seaside resort and fishing port 29 km north of DUBLIN, Republic of Ireland. Population 3044.

Skerries, several groups of rocky islets around the coast of Great Britain and Ireland. The name is specially applied to a group of islets off the north-west coast of ANGLESEY, in the Irish Sea.

Skerryvore, rock in the Inner Hebrides, Scotland, 19 km south-west of Tiree, long a menace to mariners. A lighthouse designed by Alan Stevenson (son of Robert Stevenson) was erected in 1844.

Skewen, a suburb of NEATH in West Glamorgan, South Wales, situated on Swansea Bay. Its industries include oil refining (Llandarcy), manufacture of pressed steel components, and other light industries.

Ski-bobbing, sport best described as cycling on snow, the rider sitting on a kind of bicycle frame fitted with short skis instead of wheels. The rider wears miniature foot-skis, not much longer than his boots. The foot-skis are fitted with metal claws at the heels to assist braking. One attraction is that it is easier to learn than ordinary skiing. Recreational ski-bobbers can easily attain speeds around 100 kmph. Leading racers have exceeded 160 kmph.

An early 'ski-bike' for transport purposes was patented by an American, Stevens, in 1892 in Hartford, Connecticut. As a competitive sport, ski-bobbing evolved in the 1950s after an Austrian, Englebert Brenter, developed a more suitable machine. The International Ski-Bob Federation was founded in 1961, subsequently swelling to more than 20 member nations. World championships began in 1967. Combined titles are contested for the best overall performances in downhill and slalom events.

Ski-jöring, a recreational snow sport on skis, the participant being towed behind horse, motor-cycle or other vehicle. See also WINTER SPORTS.

Skibbereen, market town and seaport in County CORK, Republic of Ireland, on the River Ilen, 29 km south-west of Bantry. It is the cathedral town of the Ross diocese. Population 2104.

Skiddaw, mountain in the Cumbrian LAKE DISTRICT NATIONAL PARK, England, and the highest point (930 m) of the area north of Keswick, which also includes SADDLEBACK.

Skidmore, Owings and Merrill, US architectural partnership, founded in 1935, which has pioneered modern office design. The Lever Building, Park Avenue, New

Skiing. Rosi Mittermaier, women's downhill champion at the 1976 Winter Olympics. *(Popperfoto)*

York (1952), was an INTERNATIONAL STYLE building designed by one of the partners, Gordon Bunshaft; this tasteful yet austerely geometrical block was widely imitated in the USA and other parts of the world. In recent years, however, the firm's architects have favoured a more expressive style. The Sean Tower, Chicago (1971–73) is another exercise in the direct manner of the Lever Building.

Skiing, moving across snow with feet attached to shaped runners; skis originated in Scandinavia about 5000 years ago. The oldest known ski, at least 4500 years old, was found in a peat bog at Höting, Sweden. A Stone Age rock carving at Rödey, Norway, of two skiers hunting elks, has been dated around 2000 BC. Ski scouts were used by King Sverre of Norway at the battle of Ilsen, near Oslo, in 1200. Skis were originally made from large animal bones and fixed to the feet by leather thongs. Modern skiing evolved from 1880 after Sondre Nordheim invented ski bindings at Morgedal, Norway, and Norwegians introduced skiing to most parts of the world which had snow during the latter half of the 19th century.

As a holiday recreation, skiing developed after 1896, when an Austrian, Mathias Zdarsky, designed the first skis and bindings with turning specifically in mind. An Englishman, E. C. Richardson, first devised proficiency tests in 1903, when he helped found the Ski Club of Great Britain, the sport's first national administration.

Alpine ski racing, so called because it originated on the ideal terrain of the European Alps, is now practised in more than 40 countries. The competitive sport comprises downhill, slalom and giant slalom events, with contestants individually timed and usually starting at one-minute intervals, the winner being the fastest to complete a course correctly. Combined titles are won by the best all-round performers in the three events.

Downhill courses, designed to test courage and fitness, are set with length, steepness and degree of difficulty appropriate to the standard of competitors. The length of a senior course varies from 2·4 to 4·8 km, with a vertical descent between 750 and 900 m. A winner's average speed is usually between 65 and 80 kmph.

Slalom courses, shorter than downhill, comprise a series of pairs of poles with flags, called 'gates', positioned at angles designed to test skill in turning and pace-checking, as distinct from the sheer speed in downhill events. A racer who misses a gate is disqualified unless he climbs back to pass through it. Senior courses can have 50 to 75 gates and a vertical drop between 200 and 300 m. The distance between the two poles of each gate should be at least 3 m and the distance between gates must be not less than 75 cm. The flags are 1·8 m above the snow and each pair is distinguished by red, yellow and blue colours.

Giant slalom courses blend characteristics of the downhill and slalom in one event. The trail is longer than the slalom, with wider gates set farther apart.

The world's first downhill race, instigated by an Englishman, Sir Arnold Lunn, took place in 1911 at Montana, Switzerland. The first slalom, invented by Lunn, was held in 1922 at Mürren, Switzerland. World alpine ski championships date from 1931. Alpine ski racing gained Olympic status in 1936. World Alpine Ski Cup awards, inaugurated in 1967, are based on consistency of form in selected international events at different venues spread over a season. A German girl, Christel Cranz, won 12 world titles. An Austrian, Toni Sailer, won seven men's world titles. He and Jean-Claude Killy, of France, each won three Olympic gold medals. Annemarie Moser-Proell (Austria) won five consecutive World Cup awards and Gustavo Thoeni (Italy) won four times in five years.

Nordic ski racing comprises long-distance cross-country running on undulating terrain of a kind which abounds in Scandinavia. Senior men's races are contested over 15, 30 and 50 km, and women's over 5 and 10 km. There are also team relay races, 4×10 km for men and 3×5 km for women. The course is roughly circular, starting and ending at the same point. A good racer can achieve an average speed around 16 kmph. Although more strenuous and fatiguing, it is less hazardous than alpine racing. Long rhythmic strides with energy-economising movement are characteristic. Competitors are individually timed, starting at half-minute intervals. World and Olympic championships date from 1924 (1952 for women). Sixten Jernberg (Sweden) was the first man to win eight world titles and four Olympic gold medals. Alevtina Koltjina (USSR) was the first woman to win eight world titles.

Ski jumping, a highly specialised branch of nordic skiing, originated at Iverslokka, Norway, in 1866. Major events start from heights of 90 m and 70 m, competitors skiing in turn down a ramp, reaching up to 120 kmph before take-off. The longest recorded jumps have exceeded 150 m, but the winner is not necessarily the one who jumps farthest. A panel of five judges award marks for style and technique, which are assessed in conjunction with the distance cleared. World and Olympic ski jumping championships began in 1924. One of the most successful jumpers has been Birger Ruud (Norway), with five world and two Olympic titles. Separate world ski-flying championships began in 1972, with emphasis on distance cleared and using higher take-offs.

The nordic combination is an event to test the overall ability of skiers in jumping and in 15 km nordic cross-country ski racing, winners being determined on a points basis.

Skiing. Jacky Flash competing in a slalom event. *(Topham/Fotogram)*

Both alpine and nordic disciplines of skiing are governed by the International Ski Federation (FIS), founded in 1924. It had 47 members by its 50th anniversary.

Recreational skiing expanded rapidly after the Second World War, aided by the growth of mechanical mountain uplift, artificial snow-making machines to augment the natural falls, and plastic slopes for off-snow practice. The main concentration of holiday skiing takes place in the European Alps, Scandinavia, and the North American Rocky Mountains, Appalachians, Sierra Nevada and Laurentians.

Skis are not perfectly straight but slightly arched. The most suitable length for general use should equal, approximately, the height from the ground to one's palm when the hand is stretched directly above the head. The average width of the upturned pointed tip is fractionally under 9 cm, and at the squared tail 8 cm. All skis, whether of wood, metal or plastic, are covered with a waterproof top surface and finished with steel edges. Most skis nowadays are made mainly of epoxy-fibreglass materials.

Ski poles, reaching about the height of the armpit, are used to balance and to assist in turning, stopping or climbing. The shafts are usually made of tonkin or fibreglass. Small, disc-shaped 'baskets', about 4 cm from the pointed ends, prevent the poles from sinking into the snow.

Ski boots with rigid soles and squarish toes are fastened by clips or laces and attached to the skis by sophisticated mechanical bindings with safety devices adjusted to release the foot in emergency to reduce injury risk. While the recreational skier uses an all-purpose ski, the senior racer requires a different, highly specialised type of blade for each of the downhill, slalom and giant slalom events. The nordic skier's skis are lighter, longer and narrower than those used for the alpine style and the poles are longer. The ski jumper does not use poles.

Bibliography: A. Lunn, *The Story of Skiing*, 1952; H. Bass, *The Magic of Skiing*, 1959; M. Milne and M. Heller, *The Book of European Skiing*, 1966; H. Evans, B. Jackman and M. Ottaway, *We Learned to Ski*, 1974.

Skikda, formerly Philippeville, Mediterranean port of CONSTANTINE department, Algeria. It occupies the site of ancient *Rusicade*, which was the port for Cirta (now Constantine), and has the remains of a large Roman theatre. The port exports the agricultural and mineral products (iron ore, marble) of its hinterland and is an important sardine fishing port. A natural gas pipeline from the Sahara has its terminus here. Population (1966) 88,000.

Skimmer, or scissor-bill, *Rhynchops,* genus of birds with bills in which the lower mandible is longer and flatter than the upper, and fits into it like a penknife blade into its handle. There are three species found on inland and coastal waters in the tropics. They are related to the gulls and terns. They feed on small fish and other aquatic life taken from just below the surface of the water by skimming it with the beak, hence their name.

Skimmia, a genus of evergreen shrubs belonging to the Rutaceae (citrus family). They are found in China and Japan. There are eight species. *S. japonica,* its varieties and hybrids, are grown in gardens for their clusters of bright berries.

Skin

Skin, the outer, protective covering of the animal body. In human beings, it consists of two layers, the epidermis (cuticle or scarf-skin) above, and the true skin, the dermis (or corium), beneath. Both arise from the epithelium of the embryo. The *epidermis* consists of layers of epithelial cells, the outermost of which are dead horny scales or keratin, which are continually shed, while the lower layers actively multiply to replace them. The skin, in man, is renewed continually and imperceptibly, but in some animals, such as the snake, it is cast in large portions or all at once. The epidermis has no blood vessels, but is nourished by lymph (see LYMPHATIC SYSTEM). It is thickest on the palms of the hands and soles of the feet. Horns, hoofs, nails, hairs and feathers are all epidermal outgrowths. There are minute folds on the skin of the fingertips and larger ones at the joints.

The colour of the skin, and its darkening upon exposure to sunlight, is due to the pigment melanin, contained in special cells, the melanocytes, in the epidermis. The number of melanocytes is the same in all races of man, but in the darker races they produce melanin more actively. The purpose of melanin is to protect the cells of the skin from the ultraviolet rays of the sun, thus in people of any skin colour, the melanocytes become more active upon exposure to sunlight.

The *dermis* is a layer of fibrous tissue merging gradually into the looser subcutaneous connective tissue underneath. It has an irregular junction with the epidermis, with conical papillae, arranged in rows, jutting into the upper layer. The papillae contain loops of blood capillaries and nerve endings, the tactile corpuscles. The hair follicles, in which the hairs grow, are embedded in the dermis. Each has an associated muscle, the arrector pili, which makes the hair stand on end and causes gooseflesh.

The *sebaceous glands* in the dermis excrete sebum into the hair follicles. They also occur on hairless skin, where they secrete directly onto the skin surface. Sebaceous glands line the margin of the eyelid and secrete ear-wax, cerumen, in the ear. Smegma is a mixture of sebum and cellular debris that collects in the skin folds of the penis and around the clitoris. Vernix caseosa (Latin, a cheese-like coating) is a fatty covering over the skin of the foetus during the final three months of pregnancy. It is formed from the epidermal cells and also contains sebaceous secretion.

The *sweat glands* are of two types; eccrine sweat glands are found all over the body and apocrine sweat glands in the arm-pits, around the genitals and the nipples. Their bases are deep within the dermis, where the coiled end is surrounded by blood capillaries. Only a thin lining separates the sweat from the lymph and blood plasma bathing the gland. Sweat evaporates all the time as insensible perspiration, and it is only when it flows copiously that it forms visible drops. It is usually alkaline, colourless, odourless and contains salts, including urea, one of the body's main waste products. The occasional unpleasant odour of sweat is due to the action of bacteria upon it, especially in the apocrine areas.

Functions. The skin is an excretory organ, via the agency of the sweat glands, which pick up waste products from the blood and excrete them to the outside. It helps regulate the body temperature, through the evaporation of sweat which cools the body. Goose-flesh, when it is cold, is the result of the skin contracting, which is accompanied by shivering to create heat, and by the contraction of the superficial blood vessels to keep the heat deep within the body. When the body is hot, the skin relaxes, and the superficial blood vessels dilate allowing the blood to give off more of its heat through the skin. Some exchange of gases is possible through the skin. In many fish, amphibia such as the frog, and some other animals, the skin is the major excretory and respiratory organ, but in human beings its function as such is much less, for instance, its gaseous exchange is about 0·5 per cent that of the lungs. It is almost impermeable to water from the outside, but oils can enter, and some drugs or poisons can be administered by rubbing them on the skin. The skin is a major organ of sensation, with special receptors for pressure and pain. It protects the body from infection, both by providing an intact covering and by its active role in fighting invading organisms. (See IMMUNOLOGY.) It also supplies much of the body's vitamin D requirements, as the epidermis contains a precursor which changes to vitamin D upon exposure to sunlight.

Wear. The skin gets dry or chapped after exposure to cold weather or too assiduous use of soap. In these conditions, water that is normally bound in the horny layers of the epidermis is rapidly lost. The skin becomes rough, loses its pliability and may crack. The condition can be corrected by using moisturisers to diminish water loss and emollient creams to soften the skin. If the

Skin. A section of human skin showing the layers and the structures associated with the skin.

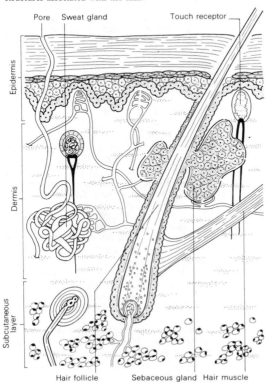

Pore Sweat gland Touch receptor

Epidermis

Dermis

Subcutaneous layer

Hair follicle Sebaceous gland Hair muscle

skin is stretched over a long period, as over the abdomen during pregnancy or on very obese individuals, stretch marks or striae appear. These are pearly white streaks from a few millimetres to several centimetres long, and are due to loss of elasticity in the connective tissue of the dermis, resulting in small tears. The wrinkles that appear with age also reflect the loss of elasticity in the dermal connective tissue, accompanied by the loss of subcutaneous fat deposits.

Diseases. The skin may reflect a diseased condition of the body or be diseased itself. Any inflammation of the skin can be called a dermatitis. *Rashes* occur in diseases such as scarlet fever and measles, or during teething, or accompany digestive disorders. Although irritation can be allayed by treatment with ointments, the more remote causes must be combated. *Eczema* is an eruption peculiar to a hypersensitive skin, the hypersensitivity being inherited or acquired. The skin is red and the lesions consist of grouped, small vesicles which tend to exude, or 'weep', and form a crust. The factor which causes the sensitive skin to erupt may be constitutional (as it most often is in infantile eczema), it may be an ALLERGY or it may result from some pathological process damaging some other part of the body. The sulphonamide drugs and some of the antibiotics may produce sensitivity when applied to the skin. Sunlight in certain cases may do the same. Eczema may also be caused by the toxins of a bacterial infection. Nervous factors may cause an attack and always play a part in prolonging its course. Apart from local applications, the treatment consists where possible in treating the cause. The patient's psychological reactions to the disease, and, in the case of a child, the parent's reactions, must also be treated. *Erysipelas* (St Anthony's fire) commences with painful swelling of the skin, redness and fever, giving place to vesication and shedding of the epidermis, and to deeper suppuration. It is caused by the bacterium, *Streptococcus pyogenes*. The site of infection is usually near the eye, ear, nostril or mouth, and the lymph glands then become enlarged with the spread of inflammation. Good results are obtained by the use of sulphonamides or penicillin. Erysipelas tends to be epidemic. Many other bacterial, parasite, viral, and fungal diseases also affect the skin.

Birth-marks, such as a mole or soft naevus, grow from the epidermis; hard moles originate in the malpighian layer at the base of the epidermis. *Drug eruptions* are skin eruptions following the use of certain drugs. They are due to the efforts of the skin to eliminate the poison, and pass away when the drug is discontinued. The skin is subject to *malignant growths*, such as epithelioma, rodent ulcer and malignant melanoma. This latter is a highly malignant growth which starts in a pigmented mole or naevus.

Skin-grafting consists in transplanting skin from one part of the body to some part where the skin has been removed by injury—such as a burn—or disease. The thickness of skin transplanted varies, but it must be healthy and contain the living cells. The surface of the wound is carefully cleaned and prepared, and the new skin takes root and covers the wound more quickly than would be done by natural healing. Skin grafting is successful because the person's own skin is used, so there is little danger of TRANSPLANTATION REJECTION, as there is in transplanting organs from another person.

Bibliography: S. Rothman, *Physiology and Biochemistry of the Skin*, 1954; R. T. Tregear, *Physical Functions of Skin*, 1966.

Skin Effect, the non-uniform distribution of alternating current intensity over the cross-section of a solid conductor. The current at the surface is linked with a magnetic field in the adjacent layer, the current in this layer with a field in the next, etc. Thus the reactance of the conductor increases towards the axis. The penetration of the current towards the axis becomes less with increasing frequency.

Skink, a LIZARD of the family Scincidae, the members of which live in Europe, Africa, Asia, and Australia. The common skink (*Scincus scincus*), which grows to a length of 23 cm, is found in the Sahara and along the shores of the Red Sea.

Skinner, Burrhus Frederic (1904–), US psychologist, born in Susquehanna, Pennsylvania. Professor of psychology at Harvard, 1948–57, and Edgar Pierce professor since 1958, Skinner has become famous as the most assertive of behaviourist psychologists, holding that his experiments with pigeons and other animals prove the existence of a reward principle governing all behaviour, including that of human beings. In *Walden Two*, 1948, reissued 1962, *Beyond Freedom and Dignity*, 1973, and other books, he has described a Utopia of beneficent control and manipulation which, however, many commentators find unconvincing and unpleasant.

Skinner Box, a device used to investigate 'conditioned' animal behaviour. It consists of a living-box with an object that an animal in the box can manipulate. The form of the object varies for different animals; for rats it is a lever which can be pressed, for pigeons a disc which can be pecked. When the animal moves the object sufficiently, a pellet of food may be delivered to it, thus reinforcing the action undertaken. This makes the animal more likely to repeat it. The lever/disc can initiate other stimuli such as opening a door, delivering water, giving electric shocks.

Skinners' Company, one of the 12 chief livery companies of the City of London. In the 13th century there were two brotherhoods of Skinners, and in 1327 Edward III incorporated them by charter; in 1395 Richard II, himself a Skinner, united these two brotherhoods as the Guild or Fraternity of Corpus Christi. The company's hall, rebuilt after the Great Fire of 1666 and restored after minor damage in the Second World War, still stands on its original site, 8 Dowgate Hill. Though no longer exercising its right to control the use, manufacture, and sale of furs, the company continues to administer its schools, estates, almshouses, and charitable trusts. See also MERCHANT TAYLORS; CITY COMPANIES.

Skins, see FUR.

Skipton, market town in the CRAVEN District, North YORKSHIRE, England, 32 km north-west of BRADFORD. Manufactured products include cotton and rayon goods. The grammar school was founded in 1548 by William Ermysted. The castle, dating partly from the 11th century, was a Civil War stronghold. Population (1971: urban district) 12,437.

Skirret, *Sium sisarum*, a species of the Umbelliferae

Skirt

(carrot family) related to the British waterparsnip (*S. latifolium*). Its roots are tuberous, and are edible when boiled.

Skirt, popular garment covering the figure from the waist down, to varying lengths; during the 1960s it reached its shortest ever with the mini-skirt. See DRESS.

Skittles, game dating from the 14th century which was originally introduced into Great Britain from Germany and became a popular public-house game. The rules varied considerably between areas, the game also commonly being known as 'kails' or 'ninepins'. The basic principle is to bowl a ball or flat wooden 'cheese', weighing from 4·5 kg to 6·35 kg, down a lane or alley at the nine skittles evenly spaced in a diamond-shaped frame (see diagram). The skittles are roughly cigar-shaped, about 30 cm high and weigh from 3 kg to 4 kg.

The game is played between two opponents or two opposing sides. The simplest game consists in throwing at the pins with the ball and scoring in the following manner: if all the pins are floored with the first throw 3 points are scored; if with two throws 2 points are scored; with three throws 1 point; and with more, none. Often, however, a game consists of three sets of throws, a point scored for each pin downed. The maximum score in a single set of throws is 27.

Responsibility for the game in Great Britain has now been assumed by the Amateur Skittle Association.

Dutch skittles differ in that the ball is bowled down a groove and has a slight bias. Enfield skittles is a parlour game, played on a table with miniature skittles and usually an ivory ball.

See also TENPIN BOWLING.

Skłodowska, Marja, see CURIE, MARIE.

Skobolev, see FERGANA.

Skokholm, small island, 5 km off the west coast of the Preseli District of South Wales, where R. M. Lockley established the first migratory bird-marking station in Great Britain in 1927. The island is leased by the West Wales Field Society; in 1946 it was established as Skokholm Bird Observatory, and is now administered by the Council for the Promotion of Field Studies.

Skomer, small island just off the southern arm of St Bride's Bay in the Preseli District of South Wales, noted for its many hut-circles.

Skopje (Turkish *Üsküb*), capital of the republic of MACEDONIA, Yugoslavia, on the Vardar river, in the north-west of the great plain of Skopje. In pre-Roman times it was the capital of ILLYRIA, and in the 10th and 11th centuries it was the capital of an independent Macedonian kingdom. It suffered in the various Turkish wars, and in the 17th century its population was greatly reduced by fires and plague. It was extensively damaged by an earthquake in July 1963 but it has been rebuilt with the aid of gifts from 78 countries. The old town, on the right bank, has a medieval citadel, and numerous old churches and mosques. Nearby is a Roman aqueduct with 55 arches. Skopje has a university, and has metallurgical and foodstuff industries. Population (1971) 389,000.

Skram, Amalie (1847–1905), Norwegian novelist, born in Bergen. One of the main Norwegian writers of the Naturalist movement, she depicts in many novels the oppression of women in contemporary society. Her central work, *Hellemyrsfolket*, four volumes, 1887–98, is a realistic and pessimistic study of four generations of a family which demonstrates the impossibility of overcoming inherited weaknesses.

Bibliography: B. Krane, *Amalie Skrams diktning*, 1961.

Skryabin, Aleksandr Nikolaevich, see SCRIABIN, ALEXANDER.

Skuas, birds of family Stercorariidae, in the order Charadriiformes, suborder Lari, the latter including the gulls and terns. Skuas are entirely marine, and very widely distributed, although their chief breeding grounds are on the islands of the north Atlantic, from the coast of Labrador to the Shetlands, and on the islands of the Antarctic. Several of the species may also be found on British coasts. They average about 50 cm long, with long, well-developed wings and short, stout legs, and in colour are greyish above, white below; in character they are fierce, and will attack smaller birds to make them disgorge the fish they have captured. There are seven species. *Catharacta skua*, the great skua, and *Stercorarius parasiticus*, the Arctic skua or parasitic jaeger, are well-known species.

Skull, the skeleton of the head and face. It consists of the cranial cavity, or brain case, plus the bones of the face, which include the walls of the orbits (eye-sockets) and nasal cavity and form the roof of the mouth (hard palate), and a separate lower jaw or mandible. There are 21 bones forming the bulk of the skull, and in adult life they are united by immobile fibrous joints called sutures. In addition there are several bones that develop separately from the phalangeal arches (rudimentary structures in the embryo resembling gills), such as the mandible, which articulates by a synovial joint with the temporal bones of

Skittle alley.

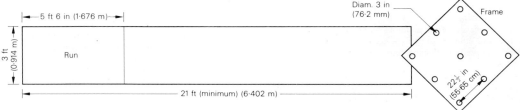

the cranium, and the ossicles of the middle ear within the temporal bone. The bones of the skull base develop in cartilage whereas the skull vault develops in membrane. At birth this ossification of the skull vault is not complete, leaving small membranous areas, notably the anterior and posterior fontanelles, which only close during the second year of life. This incomplete ossification and imperfect interlocking of the bones means that the skull is less rigid at birth and the slight mobility facilitates delivery of the baby. The face at birth is smaller in proportion to the brain case than in the adult (although the skull is large relative to the body). The small face is due to the teeth not being fully formed and paranasal sinuses being undeveloped.

The shape and size of the skull are used as means of classification by anthropologists and biologists. Thus the pre-human *Homo habilis* who lived about two million years ago had a skull (and therefore brain) volume of about 510 ml whilst that of modern *Homo sapiens* has an average volume of 1400 ml, reflecting a great increase in intellectual capacity. The notable features of the human skull are the large size of the brain case, the small size of the face (even in the adult the apparatus of mastication is reduced), and the way the skull is poised on the vertebral column.

Skunk, an American carnivorous mammal in family Mustelidae of order CARNIVORA, with remarkably developed anal glands from which, when provoked, it ejects a foetid secretion. The common skunk (*Mephitis mephitis*) is about 70 cm long, including the tail, and black or dark brown in colour with white markings on the head and back. Its head is small, long and conical, and the ears short and rounded; the legs are short, and the animal burrows in the earth. Its food consists largely of small rodents and insects, but fruit and poultry eggs are often stolen. It is daring and fierce, and can inflict a nasty wound with its teeth, but its intolerable secretion is more feared. Its furry skin is purified and largely used by furriers.

Sky, see ATMOSPHERE; DUST; METEOROLOGY; STAR; VISIBILITY.

Sky-diving, see PARACHUTE.

Skye, large and beautiful island in HIGHLAND REGION, Scotland. Much of the island is underlain by Tertiary volcanic rocks and the scenery of the central part is very mountainous, rising to over 1000 m. The coastline is deeply indented by numerous sea-lochs, and most of the

Skunk. Striped skunk, *Mephitis mephitis*. (*Topham/Lee Rue III*)

Skye. The Cuillins and Sligachan Burn. (*Topham/Scowen*)

settlements are coastal. Crofting and tourism are the main sources of income, and large areas have been afforested in recent years. The island is 75 km long by 25 km wide and extends to 171,520 ha in area. Population (1971) 7183.

Bibliography: O. F. Swire, *Skye: The Island and Its Legends*, 1972; K. C. Sillar and R. Meyler, *Skye*, 1973.

Skye and Lochalsh District, one of eight districts of HIGHLAND REGION, Scotland. It consists of the islands of Skye (see above) and RAASAY and part of the adjacent mainland area. PORTREE is the administrative centre. Area 245,200 ha. Population (1971) 10,000.

Skye Terrier, bred in the Isle of Skye as a vermin dog. Though often kept as a lapdog it is still a courageous animal, keen for sport. The modern type has a long head with a powerful jaw. The skull is wide at the front of the brow, narrow between the ears, and tapering towards the muzzle. The eyes are dark and rather close, the nose is black. The body is long and low, the shoulders broad, chest deep, legs short, straight and muscular, and feet small. The coat is long and straight, with a soft woolly undercoat, the colours dark or light blue or grey or fawn with black points. There are two varieties: the prick-eared and the drop-eared.

Skylark, see LARK.

Skyros (Greek *Skíros*), island of Greece in the Aegean Sea, the largest of the Northern SPORADES group, 40 km

131

north-east of Euboea. The land is mountainous; sheep and goats are reared, but its mineral ores (chrome, iron, manganese, copper, gypsum, and lignite) are more important economically. Marble is also exported. Rupert BROOKE is buried there. Area 207 km²; population 2800.

Sla, see SALÉ.

Slade, Felix (1790–1868), British art collector, born at Lambeth. He bequeathed his collections of engravings, glass and pottery to the British Museum. Slade was also a noted book-collector, and left £35,000 for the endowment of art (Slade) professorships at Oxford, Cambridge and University College, London, the Slade School of art being called after him.

Slade School of Fine Art, University College, London, opened in 1871, the oldest and best known university art school. Under the first Slade professor, Sir Edward Poynter, training was based on drawing directly from the model as in France. Many noted painters, including Augustus John, McEvoy, Orpen, and Wyndham Lewis, and later Gilman, Gove, and Stanley Spencer, passed through the Slade, a record maintained under later professors, Henry Tonks (1919–30) and Sir William Coldstream (1949–75) among them.

Sládkovič, Andrej (1820–72), Slovak poet, born at Krupina, a leading writer in the STÚR school. His greatest work, *Marína*, 1846, is a long, beautiful, lyrical and contemplative poem, in which he combines love for a peasant girl with love for his country. Equally well known is *The Detvan*, 1853, the story of an idealised peasant in the reign of MATTHIUS CORVINUS, but this epic lacks unity and its verse is less successful.

Slag, mixture of silicate, chiefly of lime and alumina, produced in many metallurgical operations. Blast furnace slag is chiefly calcium and aluminium silicate, and varies in character from a glass to a stony type. Some 20 million t of blast furnace slag are produced annually. Some kinds of slag are made into bricks and paving setts. Cement is made from slag containing much lime, while the phosphoric slag from the basic-steel process and from the Cleveland iron is used as a manure. Slag-wool, which is sound and heat proof, and used for covering boilers and steam-pipes, is prepared by blowing steam through molten slag.

Slalom, see SKIING; WATER SKIING.

Slane, village of County MEATH, Republic of Ireland, 13 km north-east of Navan. On Slane Hill (152 m) St Patrick kindled the Paschal fire in 433, proclaiming Christianity throughout the land. Slane is the birthplace of the poet Francis Ledwidge, 1891–1917. Population 483.

Slaney, picturesque river of Ireland, rising in the WICKLOW Mountains and flowing through CARLOW and WEXFORD to the sea at Wexford harbour. Length 100 km.

Slang, often used to describe colloquial language in general, more specifically describes the colloquial speech peculiar to certain groups. Slang is usually esoteric, understood within the group, but less intelligible to those outside. Slang may be humorous, obscene, witty, and both imaginative and repetitive.

Argot, meaning slang current among criminals, is a French term of unknown origin, though some authorities hold that argot originated with the associations formed by Parisian vagabonds in the 14th and 15th centuries and termed the 'Courts of Miracles'. The English word 'cant' originally referred to the cryptic slang of the 'vagrom men', or vagrants, of the 17th and 18th centuries. It is now used to mean vague and high-sounding language, with the additional force of 'hypocrisy'. By jargon is meant technical or professional terminology.

Thieves, tramps, and gypsies developed slang as a group language. But it was commonly assimilated into common speech. That this readily occurs can be seen from the example of the French word for head, *tête*, which derives, not from the Roman *caput* (head) but from Roman slang, *testa*, an earthenware pot. The slang of the underworld and the street passes equally readily into literature. Shakespeare and other Elizabethan writers recognised the characteristic racy metaphorical pungency of contemporary slang, and made use of it. Later writers, seeking greater naturalism and realism, have introduced slang as an antidote to the refinements of 'literary' language.

Combined with local dialects, such as the colloquial speech of the London COCKNEY, and the specialised lingo of soldiers, sailors, and adventurers, the 18th century in England saw a lively use of underworld slang. For example, 'To dance the Paddington frisk' meant to be hanged (at Tyburn). Some slang words, such as 'mob' (from the Latin *mobile vulgus*), attained complete respectability. Other slang words, such as 'booze' for example, though used in English for 400 years, have failed to become respectable. Underworld slang, popularised by films, books, and television, remains current. The police, formerly 'peelers' or 'bobbies' (after Sir Robert PEEL) are now more commonly 'coppers', 'bogies', 'Old Bill', or 'the fuzz'.

Although much slang is accidental in origin, it may also reflect changing social patterns. Young people, in particular, adopt slang as a means of identity; it serves both as a bond between them, and as a barrier against outsiders, often of their parents' generation. Youthful slang serves to emphasise the generation gap; it therefore dates rapidly, as generations (and slang fashions) succeed each other. Faced with new youthful phenomena, the older generation turns to new words to identify them; hence 'teddy boys', 'mods', 'rockers', 'skinheads', and 'hippies'.

Slang words are formed in several ways. Some may be borrowed from other languages, as with the Anglo-Indian 'char'. Existing words are combined to form new ones, as in 'snazzy', formed by a blend of 'snappy' and 'jazzy', themselves slang terms. Other formations include the invention of new compounds, such as 'stag night', 'blind date', or 'hen party'; and abbreviation, as in 'bus' from 'omnibus'. Distortion of existing words so as to alter their meaning is a common slang device, as in 'lay off', 'do in', and 'drop out'. ONOMATOPOEIA gives 'jabber', 'blubber', and so on. A word may be appropriated by a group and endowed with a new meaning, for example, 'gay' as applied to homosexuals.

Military slang often serves to maintain morale by minimising danger and discomfort. Both world wars provide many examples, including 'prang', 'flap', 'crate', 'kite', 'glasshouse', 'whizzbang', 'Blighty', 'doodlebug'. In the 20th century the mass media have popularised the use of abbreviated, metaphoric terms such as 'to axe', 'to liquidate', 'demo', 'skyjacker', 'whizzkid', 'VIP', 'Eurocrat', 'petrodollar', 'ecodoom', and others. (See ABBREVIATIONS.) The effect of high speed air travel is described as 'jet lag'; those able to afford it as the 'jet set'. Broadcasting has provided its own slang, including 'anchor man', 'newscaster', 'sitcom', 'phone-in', 'chat-show', 'peak hour'. Sport has proved another fertile breeding ground for slang, originated both by sportsmen and sportswriters. Cricket is notable for words like 'googly', 'Chinaman', 'duck', 'yorker', and 'maiden'; and 'stumped' has been adopted for wider use.

The re-use of existing words, or combinations of words, with new meanings has largely replaced such older forms of slang as Cockney rhyming slang. Examples of rhyming slang are legion; common are 'plates' (plates of meat) for 'feet', 'apples and pears' for 'stairs', 'rosie lee' for 'tea', and 'titfer' (tit for tat) for 'hat'. Back slang, formed by reversing an existing word, has virtually died out. One of the few examples surviving is 'yob' from 'boy'.

EUPHEMISM is a frequent hallmark of slang, as in 'to go west', 'to kick the bucket'. Some slang words are derived from the names of real people. 'Bunk' or 'bunkum' comes from a US politician of that name, whose lengthy address to Congress consisted of nothing at all. 'Limey' is said to derive from Americans' amused reactions to lime-eating English sailors, who were following instructions to avoid scurvy. 'Yank' or 'Yankee', now used of any American, was originally used for a New Englander, then of the Federal forces during the Civil War. The word's derivation is unknown, though several theories have been advanced.

Slang frequently serves to enhance the language, adding fresh vigour and liveliness. But modern slang, in particular, depends on novelty for its force and is often short-lived in consequence. The United States, with its varied ethnic background, has been and remains a major source of new words in English. (See AMERICANISM.)

Bibliography: J. S. Farmer and W. E. Henley, *Dictionary of Slang and Colloquial English*, 1905; E. E. Partridge, *A Dictionary of the Underworld*, 1950, and *A Dictionary of Slang and Unconventional English*, 1970; G. W. Turner, *The English Language in Australia and New Zealand*, 1966.

Slater, see WOOD-LICE.

Slates are fine-grained, low-grade metamorphic rocks with a highly developed CLEAVAGE due to parallel alignment of their constituent minerals, as a result of directed stress during METAMORPHISM. The almost perfect cleavage enables slates to be split into thin laminae with great ease, thus enabling them to be used for roofing, for which purpose their durability and light weight make them eminently suitable.

The colour of slate varies from area to area, ranging between grey, blue, black, red, and green. The areas where slates have been worked in Britain are North Cornwall, North Wales, the Lake District, and West Scotland. The slate is extracted by quarrying using wedges or wire saws and more rarely by carefully controlled explosives. The rough blocks thus obtained are trimmed using large diamond saws and the individual slates split off by hand with a hammer and wedge. The slates are finally trimmed to size, again manually, the sizes being popularly called after aristocratic titles, for example, duchesses, countesses,

etc.—the larger the slate, the higher the aristocratic rank. The essentially labour intensive working of the slate industry led to its decline at the beginning of the 20th century in the face of more mechanised tile production, and more recently with changing building techniques. Slate is now used mainly for repair work to roofing or to maintain architectural continuity in an area of existing slate roofs; it also has specialised uses such as for the better grades of billiard tables.

Slaughter of Animals Acts. These Acts govern the conditions under which animals in slaughterhouses and knackers' yards are to be treated prior to and during slaughter. Animals must be suitably housed and fed and must be rendered unconscious by a mechanically operated instrument before being bled, unless slaughtered in accordance with the Jewish or Muslim rites. Slaughtermen are required to be licensed annually by the local authority, but the licence is valid anywhere in England and Wales, except for the slaughter of horses, asses and mules, which is restricted to the area of the licensing authority. A similar Act is applicable to Scotland. These acts are now incorporated in the DISEASES OF ANIMALS ACTS.

Slaughterhouse, premises licensed by the local authority for the slaughter of animals for meat for sale for human consumption. The term abattoir, of French origin, means a public slaughterhouse. By the Public Health Act, 1875, councils of both municipal boroughs and urban district councils had power to provide slaughterhouses and knackers' yards; but rural district councils had first to obtain the authorisation of the Local Government Board. Private slaughterhouses or knackers' yards which existed before 1848 required only to be registered with the local council; but all other private slaughterhouses or yards required an annual licence, and had to be managed in accordance with the by-laws of the local authority. Such by-laws were subject to confirmation by the Ministry of Health. Legislation relating to the licensing of slaughterhouses and knackers' yards and the responsibilities of local authorities is now contained in the Food and Drugs Act, 1955, under which new ones may not be licensed except with the consent of the Minister of Agriculture, Fisheries and Food. Regulations made under the Slaughter of Animals Acts are designed to ensure the humane treatment of animals in slaughterhouses. Local Authorities are empowered by the Food and Drugs Act to make by-laws (which are subject to confirmation by the Minister of Agriculture, Fisheries and Food) for securing the proper management and the maintenance of sanitary conditions. As far as practicable, meat is inspected by a qualified officer of the local authority before distribution. Carcasses which are not fit for human consumption are disposed of for other purposes. Modern slaughtering practice has a number of highly skilled operations and many by-products: sausages, canned meats, intestines for sausage casings and surgical gut, glands for medicinal purposes, edible fats, technical greases, glue, animal feeding meals, fertilisers, hide and skins, hair for brushes, and several other uses.

Slave Coast, name formerly applied to that part of the coast of West Africa which lies between Ghana and the

133

Slavery

River Benin, now comprising the People's Republic of Benin and part of Nigeria.

Slavery, the condition of a human being who is the property of another. It may vary from the extreme 'rightlessness' of the Roman *servus*, whose labour could be exploited and his life taken by his master with impunity (although later, in the Christian era, this constituted murder), to the mitigated rigour of the *ascripti glebae*, or serfs of the soil of the later empire and the Middle Ages, who, though they passed with the soil and were bound to remain on it, had some of the position of freemen. Slavery may be a status to which a man was born, or be thrust upon him by debt, capture in war, or his own crimes; or, as in America, it may be rather the condition of having to perform compulsory labour at the will of a conquering people. In Rome the sentiments against slavery inspired by the Christian teaching, or expressed in language borrowed from the Stoic philosophy, produced penalties for ill-treatment of slaves rather than a tendency to abolish the status itself. The Greeks of the pre-Stoic period were so habituated to slavery that their philosophers never objected to it, and seemed to suppose that it was founded on diversities in the races of mankind. Slavery appears to have been from the earliest ages the natural or normal condition of a large proportion of mankind in almost every country until comparatively recent times. It probably still exists in parts of the Middle East.

The practice among all ancient nations was to enslave prisoners of war. Another ancient source of slaves was kidnapping, especially among maritime peoples, such as the Phoenicians, Cretans, and Cilicians; and Herodotus states that some of the Thracian tribes sold their children to foreign dealers. Among the Greeks slavery existed from the heroic times. Agricultural labour was in some instances performed by poor freemen for hire, but in most places, especially in the Doric states, by a class of bondmen, the descendants of the older inhabitants, who lived upon and cultivated the lands appropriated by the conquering race. Sometimes indeed these bondmen paid rent; in Europe the evolution of the land-serf into the free agricultural tenant probably followed much the same lines. Athens, Corinth, and other commercial states had a large number of purchased slaves, mostly natives of barbarous countries. In Attica there were private slaves belonging to families, and public slaves belonging to the state, who were employed in the fleet and on public buildings and roads. The number of slaves, domestic and rustic, possessed by the wealthy Romans was enormous; some had up to 10,000. The Roman slave had no rights, and was regarded as a chattel; he could acquire no property, and all the produce of his labour accrued to his master. He could not contract a Roman marriage; union with a person of his own rank was styled 'contubernium'. Public slaves in Rome belonged to the state or to public bodies, such as municipia and collegia, or to the emperor in his sovereign capacity; some were employed in public duties of a highly honourable nature, for example as keepers of public buildings, prisons, or other state property, while others were employed as road repairers, watchmen, lictors, and scavengers. Private slaves were either urban or rustic according to whether they served in town or on country estates. The *servi terrae* of the later period of the empire reveal strong points of resemblance to the serfs and villeins of the Middle Ages, but there appears to be no evidence of any historical connection between the *coloni*, *rustici*, or *ascripti glebae* and the *villani* of the feudal system.

The English villein or depressed ceorl must not be confused with the bondman or serf. The English serfs (*thralls*, *theows*, or *slaves*) were either hereditary slaves, i.e. descendants of the old Britons, or wite theows, persons reduced to servitude for crime or neglect to pay a fine, or by voluntary sale. They soon disappeared as a class after the Conquest. The *villani* were the cultivators of the land; each had a house and a certain quantity of arable land lying in scattered strips in the common fields of the village, and there were many ways by which a villein could buy his freedom, for example by residing in a town as a burgage tenant for a year and a day. When the traffic in slaves ceased among the Christian nations of Europe it continued to be carried on in the age of the crusades by the Venetians, who supplied the markets of the Saracens with slaves purchased from the Slavonian tribes along the Adriatic. Christian captives taken by Muslims were sold in Asiatic and North African markets, and continued to be sold till the beginning of the 20th century, when the interference of the Christian powers, the conquest of Algiers by France, and the emancipation of Greece resulted in the abolition of the practice in Barbary, Egypt, and the Ottoman Empire.

With the discovery of America, a new description of slavery arose. Christian nations purchased African Negroes for employment in mines and plantations of the New World, in substitution for the native Indians, who were too weak to perform the work exacted by their

Slavery. The loading plan for an 18th-century slave ship in which Africans were conveyed to America. (*Bisonte*)

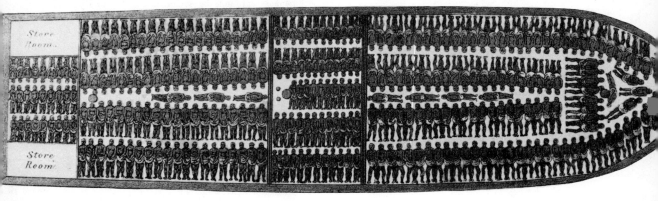

$150 REWARD

RANAWAY from the subscriber, on the night of the 2d instant, a negro man, who calls himself *Henry May*, about 22 years old, 5 feet 6 or 8 inches high, ordinary color, rather chunky built, bushy head, and has it divided mostly on one side, and keeps it very nicely combed; has been raised in the house, and is a first rate dining-room servant, and was in a tavern in Louisville for 18 months. I expect he is now in Louisville trying to make his escape to a free state, (in all probability to Cincinnati, Ohio.) Perhaps he may try to get employment on a steamboat. He is a good cook, and is handy in any capacity as a house servant. Had on when he left, a dark cassinett coatee, and dark striped cassinett pantaloons, new—he had other clothing. I will give $50 reward if taken in Louisvill: 100 dollars if taken one hundred miles from Louisville in this State, and 150 dollars if taken out of this State, and delivered to me, or secured in any jail so that I can get him again.

WILLIAM BURKE.

Bardstown, Ky., September 3d, 1838.

Slavery. An American broadsheet advertising for a runaway slave. *(Bisonte)*

Spanish taskmasters. Again, the Portuguese, who were early possessed of a great part of the coast of Africa, obtained by force or barter a considerable number of slaves; and the demand for slaves by the Portuguese in the Atlantic harbours soon induced the native chiefs to make predatory incursions into each other's territories to take captives for the European market. In the British colonies in the latter part of the 18th and the beginning of the 19th century much was done by Parliament. Courts were established to hear the complaints of the slaves, flogging of females was forbidden, and the condition generally of the slave population was greatly ameliorated. Thomas Clarkson and the Quakers prepared the ground for William WILBERFORCE, who brought the subject before Parliament in 1788. Owing to the lucrative nature of the slave trade opened up by the conquest of Dutch colonies, the traffic was not abolished by Parliament until 1807. In 1811 Brougham carried a bill for making slave trading a felony, punishable by transportation or hard labour, and in 1824 the slave trade was declared to be piracy and capitally punishable. The consequence of agitation by Britain after the Napoleonic wars was that long before the middle of the 19th century most of the European and American powers had passed similar laws, or entered into treaties for the prohibition of the traffic. For long, however, a considerable internal slave trade continued to flourish in the USA; and Negroes continued to be bred and sold in Maryland and Virginia, and some other of the slave-holding states, and carried to the more fertile lands of Alabama, Louisiana, and other southern states. The slavery question was a predominant cause of the American Civil War of 1861–65. The victory of the Union over the Southern Confederate States ended slavery for ever in the USA.

In the 20th century forced-labour camps and concentration camps, particularly in Nazi Germany, reduced their inhabitants to conditions of slavery and it would be unwise to consider slavery as entirely a thing of the past.

Bibliography: C. W. W. Greenidge, *Slavery*, 1958; M. I. Finlay (Ed.), *Slavery in Classical Antiquity*, 1960; T. F. Buxton, *African Slave Trade and its Remedy*, reprint of 1839–40 ed., 1968; L.

Filler, *Slavery in the United States*, 1972; H. Marsh, *Slavery and Race*, 1974.

Slaveykov, Pencho Petko (1866–1912), Bulgarian poet, essayist, and leading man of letters, son of Petko Rachev SLAVEYKOV. He studied in Leipzig, reading widely in German literature, before returning to Bulgaria to become director of the National Library and of the National Theatre, and to edit, with his great friend the literary critic Dr K. Krustev, the review *Misul* (Thought). He died in Italy, driven there by political intrigue.

Slaveykov's poetry marks the beginning of a new epoch in Bulgarian literature, which until then had always been predominantly committed to causes (religious, or, in modern times, national, political, and social). For the first time a Bulgarian writer opened up man's inner world; he was interested in the individual, in suffering, and in efforts to rise to the level of the superman. His Epic Songs present Bulgarian national themes and portraits of figures of European genius (Prometheus, Michelangelo, Beethoven, Lenau, Shelley). Remarkable, too, is his partly autobiographical anthology of imaginary poets *Isles of the Blessed*, 1910. His essay on Bulgarian folk poetry appeared in English in H. Baerlein's *The Shade of the Balkans*, 1904.

Slaveykov, Petko Rachev (1827–95), Bulgarian poet and statesman; he was for some years a schoolmaster. In 1861 he took part in the discussion in Constantinople on the independence of the Bulgarian Church. From 1863 he mainly worked in Constantinople, editing a succession of Bulgarian journals. After the liberation of 1878 he served for a time as Bulgarian minister of education and of internal affairs.

Slaveykov was a prolific and many-sided author. He knew his country well, and collected and published valuable collections of folk-literature. Influenced at first by Greek, then Russian models, he laid the foundations of Bulgarian poetry, showing that Bulgarian was a suitable poetic instrument by successfully adopting a tonic prosody (based on stressed syllables), and by bringing the literary language close to spoken Bulgarian.

Slavici, Ion (1848–1925), Romanian writer, born at Șiria, Arad. After studies at Budapest and Vienna, where he befriended EMINESCU, he founded the journal *Tribuna* which advocated a literature based on peasant life, and his stories, collected in the volumes *Nuvele din popor*, 1881, and *Pădureanca*, 1884, are examples of this. *Mara*, 1894, a love drama set in a provincial town, is his most successful novel.

Bibliography: P. Marcea, *Ion Slavici*, 1967; D. Vatamaniuc, *Ion Slavici*, 1968; O. Manning (Ed.), *Romanian Short Stories*, 1971.

Slavkov, Czechoslovak town in southern Moravia. Under its German name, Austerlitz, it is famous as the scene of NAPOLEON's great victory over the Austrians and the Russians on 2 December 1805.

Slavonia (Serbo-Croatian *Slavonija*), district of the Balkan peninsula, extending from the River Sava to the River Drava. For a long while it formed part of the province of Croatia-Slavonia, and it now forms part of the republic of CROATIA, Yugoslavia. The principal town is OSIJEK.

Slavonic and East European Studies, School of, London University, established in 1915 as part of King's College London and became an institute of London University in 1928. The School is concerned with the study of these languages and literatures: Bulgarian, Czech, Finnish, Hungarian, Polish, Romanian, Russian, Serbo-Croat, Slovak; and with the political and economic history and the politics of the countries in which those languages are spoken, and of Albania, East Germany, and Greece. The academic staff numbers 50 and there are 160 undergraduate and 40 postgraduate students. The Library contains 120,000 volumes.

Slavonic Languages, or Slavic, branch of the INDO-EUROPEAN LANGUAGES. There are three main groups of Slavonic languages: (1) the Eastern group, consisting of Russian (Great Russian), Belorussian (White Russian), and Ukrainian (Ruthenian, Little Russian); (2) the Western group, including Polish, Czech (and its close relative, Slovak), and Lusatian (or Wendish); another West Slavonic dialect, Polabian, spoken along the lower Elbe in the region of Lüchow and known only from a few short texts, became extinct in the 18th century; (3) the Southern group, including Serbo-Croat, Slovene, Bulgarian, and Macedonian (this group is now separated geographically from the other Slavonic languages by a Hungarian- and Romanian-speaking area).

Slavonic is first attested in the 9th century in the form of Old Church Slavonic, a Macedonian dialect which became the liturgical language of the Orthodox Slavs and Romanians. The foundations of the comparative grammar of the Slavonic languages were laid in F. Miklosich's *Vergleichende Grammatik der slavischen Sprachen* (4 vols), 1874–79.

Bibliography: W. J. Entwistle and W. A. Morison, *Russian and the Slavonic Languages*, 1949; R. G. A. de Bray, *Guide to the Slavonic Languages*, rev. ed. 1969.

Slavonski Brod, town in Croatia, Yugoslavia, on the left bank of the River Sava. It has a Turkish citadel, is an important rail and road junction, has oil and engineering works, and a trade in wine and cereals. Across the river is the twin town of Bosanski Brod. Population 38,000.

Slavophiles, members of a philosophic and political movement in 19th-century Russia which stressed its national peculiarities, tended to idealise the Russian past, and opposed Westernisation; politically the Slavophiles were liberal but not democratic, putting their faith in the virtues of the peasant communes (see MIR). Parts of their programme were realised in Alexander II's reforms. From the 1860s Slavophilism largely merged with PAN-SLAVISM. The Slavophile leaders were Khomyakov and Kireevsky and the Aksakov brothers.

Bibliography: P. Christoff, *An Introduction to Nineteenth Century Russian Slavophilism*, 1961; S. Lukashevich, *Ivan Aksakov*, 1965.

Slavs, or Slavonians (native name *Slowene*, or *Slowane*, derived by some from *Slawa*, fame, but better from *Slowo*, a word, thus meaning 'speaking' or 'articulate', as distinguished from other nations, whom they called *Niemetz*, or 'Mutes'), general name of an ethnic and linguistic group of Indo-Europeans, whose settlements extend from the Elbe to the Kamchatka, and from the Arctic Sea to Ragusa on the Adriatic, the whole of east and south-east

Europe being occupied by them. They were known to the ancient writers under the designations of Sarmatians and Scythians. The original names of the Slávic peoples seem to have been Wins or Wens (*Venedi*) and Serbs. The earliest historical notices extant represent the Slavs as having their chief settlements about the Carpathians, from which they spread northward to the Baltic, westward as far as the Elbe and the Saal, and later, after the overthrow of the kingdom of the Huns, southward beyond the Danube and over the whole peninsula between the Adriatic and the Black Sea. These migrations ceased in the 7th century.

The Slavs may be divided into three groups: the eastern, western, and southern Slavs. The first comprehends Russians, Ukrainians, Belorussians; the second Poles, Czechs, Moravians, Slovaks, and Wends; the third Serbs, Croats, Slovenes, and Macedonians. They speak Slavonic languages, some written in the Cyrillic, and some in the Roman alphabet.

The Slavs are represented by ancient writers as an industrious race, living by agriculture and the rearing of flocks and herds, as hospitable and peaceful. The government had a patriarchal basis, and chiefs or princes were chosen by assemblies. The religion of the early Slavs seems to have been a kind of nature-worship. The chief deity was Swiatowit, with whom were associated, on a nearer footing of equality than the other gods, Perun and Radegast. Christianity was introduced among the eastern Slavs in the 9th century by SS Cyril and Methodius. Today the eastern Slavs are members of the Eastern Orthodox Church, while the western and southern Slavs belong to the Roman Catholic Church. Historically the western Slavs have been differentiated from the eastern and southern Slavs. The western Slavs took part in the European historical experience, and the eastern and southern Slavs had little contact with Europe, were subject to Mongol and Turkish rule, and consequently to a political pattern of bureaucratic, militarised autocracies. There was a short-lived and politically unsuccessful Pan-Slavic movement initiated by intellectuals in the 19th century. Today national politics and identities prevail.

Bibliography: F. Dvornik, *The Slavs in European History and Civilisation*, 1962; Hembold of Bosan (trans. F. J. Tschan), *The Chronicle of the Slavs*, 1968; M. Gimbùtas, *The Slavs*, 1971.

Slavyansk, town in the DONETSK *oblast* of the Ukrainian SSR, USSR, in the Don Basin. There are salt mines (since the 17th century), with soda-works, an engineering industry, and saline and mud baths nearby. It was founded in 1676 as a fortress town. Population (1970) 124,000.

Sleaford, market town in LINCOLNSHIRE, England, 27 km south of Lincoln. The original settlement was to the east of the modern town, and objects found on the site give evidence of Iron Age as well as Roman, Anglo-Saxon, and later occupation. Notable features include the parish church, 12th–15th centuries, and its half-timbered vicarage; Carre's Hospital (a group of almshouses); and Carre's Grammar School, founded in 1604. CRANWELL is 6 km to the north-west. Population (1971) 8050.

Sleat, Sound of, narrow strait dividing the Isle of Skye from the mainland of Scotland. It is about 32 km long and varies in width from less than 1 to 12 km.

Sledmere, village of HUMBERSIDE, England, 13 km from

Driffield. Sledmere Hall, for long the seat of the Sykes family, is noted for its stud of horses established by Sir Mark Masterman Sykes in 1804. Population (1971) 280.

Sleeman, Sir William Henry (1788–1856), British soldier and administrator, born at Stratton, Cornwall. He served with the Bengal army, which he joined in 1809 and in the Nepalese war (1814–16). His great work in India was the suppression of Thuggi. As resident in Oudh during the era of scandalous misrule by the king's favourites, Sleeman himself advised against extreme measures, but in the event Oudh was annexed by the British in 1856.
Bibliography: F. Tuker, *The Yellow Scarf*, 1961.

Sleep, a recurrent state of inertia and unresponsiveness; the eyelids close, the pupils become very small, secretion of saliva, digestive juices and urine falls, and respiratory exchange and heat rate diminish. Electrically recorded brain waves, ELECTROENCEPHALOGRAMS, undergo changes reflecting those of the electrical activity of the brain. Consciousness is lost, but only temporarily, for any sufficient new stimulus will cause the return of wakefulness.

Sleep is usually, in man, the concomitant of fatigue, whether physical or mental; less commonly it results from a monotonous repetition of a stimulus. Sleep may be induced by a variety of chemical agents such as barbiturates or anaesthetics. Various disease processes and certain forms of trauma will produce unconsciousness to the depth of coma. There is indeed a disease, narcolepsy, in which the afflicted person cannot help passing into brief periods of sleep.

Study of the EEG tracings and physiological changes in sleepers has shown that sleep is a far more complex state than had previously been thought. There are for example five different phases or stages of sleep, falling into two main categories: orthodox or non-rapid eye movement (NREM) sleep and paradoxical or rapid eye movement (REM) sleep. NREM sleep is characterised by large-amplitude, slow-frequency EEG tracings, a tense musculature, a regular heart beat, very few eye movements and a relative lack of reported dreams. REM sleep is characterised by small-amplitude, faster-frequency tracings, a relaxed musculature, an irregular heart beat and is rich in reported dreams. During these periods eye movements occur (hence the name) and apparently correspond to the movements that the eyes of the dreamer make as he follows the scenario of his dream. Persons blind from birth and incapable of visualisation show all the features of REM sleep except the eye movements. 'Action' dreams are accompanied by more eye movements than 'static' or sedentary dreams.

Both types of sleep are essential. Selective deprivation of either state by monitoring the brain waves and waking the sleeper at the onset of a particular sleep state results in depression of measured performance, personality changes and a rebound swing in favour of the deprived state in the uninterrupted sleep which follows the nights of experiment, as if to make up the deficit. During a normal night, a sleeper will pass initially into NREM sleep and, after approximately 90 minutes, his sleep pattern becomes REM with all its accompanying phenomena. This REM period has a variable duration and may often be terminated by a brief awakening before NREM sleep supervenes. This cycle is followed through the night. Various drugs, such as tranquillisers, antidepressants, hypnotics and stimulants, have been shown to affect sleep patterns in different ways. Hypnotics, tranquillisers and stimulants initially depress REM sleep, whereas antidepressants may actually increase the time spent in the REM state. Withdrawal of the drugs is followed by the rebound phenomenon mentioned earlier. The therapeutic significance of these changes is still a subject of experimentation but may help to elucidate the mechanisms of certain mental disorders.

Mechanism of Sleep. Animal experiments, observations of patients with brain lesions, and sophisticated testing of human volunteers have established some knowledge of the mechanism of sleep and have led to much speculation as to its function.

There exists in the mammalian brain stem, the phylogenetically primitive part of the brain, a complex of neuronal centres, known collectively as the reticular-activating system, which has extensive connections, both excitatory and inhibitory, with almost every other part of the nervous system, central, peripheral and automatic. It plays an integral part in collating stimulus, response and awareness into a regular pattern of alertness, wakefulness and sleep. Some parts of it act as an arousal mechanism to increase wakefulness, and others, lying more posteriorly, result in sleep when stimulated. Interestingly, sleep can be induced by stimulating almost any part of the brain, including the waking system, the result depending less upon the location of the stimulus than upon its frequency. It may be supposed that specific excitation of these areas induces a 'damp-down' effect on the waking system, allowing the hypnogenic centres to predominate and produce sleep. Different areas of the reticular-activating system are involved in the production of REM and NREM sleep and different chemicals appear to be present in these regions.

Function of Sleep. This is in part physiologically restorative, allowing spent energies to be recovered, but far more complex roles have been suggested for REM sleep. In psychoanalytic theory, sleeping and dreaming are essential for processing repressed material so that it can be integrated into the person's thoughts, feelings and memories, thus maintaining a healthy personality. REM sleep may act as a mechanism for controlling innate drive and maintaining a periodic state of alertness in an otherwise defenceless animal during its most vulnerable state.

Others postulate REM sleep as analogous to the periodic clearing out of computer data storage banks, when material is scanned and either returned for storage or eliminated; or as a period during which experiences are reviewed and long term memory is laid down for 'permanent storage' in the electro-chemical matrix of the brain cells. These two states are in part functionally complementary.

Bibliography: I. O. Oswald, *Sleep*, 1968; W. B. Webb (Ed.), *Sleep: An Active Process*, 1973; G. C. Lairy and P. Salzarulo (Eds), *The Experimental Study of Human Sleep*, 1975.

Sleep-walking, see SOMNAMBULISM.

Sleeper Shark, see SHARK.

Sleeping Sickness, see TRYPANOSOMIASIS.

Sleepy Sickness

Sleepy Sickness, see ENCEPHALITIS.

Sleet, see PRECIPITATION.

Slessor, Kenneth (1901–71), Australian poet, born at Orange, New South Wales. Educated at Sydney Grammar School, he became a reporter and co-editor of *Vision*, 1923–24; he also worked on the Sydney *Sun* and *Smith's Weekly*, later becoming its editor. Almost all Slessor's surviving poetry was written before the Second World War, when he was official war correspondent in the Middle East and New Guinea. As literary editor of the *Sun*, editor of the Sydney *Telegraph*, and finally as editor of *Southerly* (1956–61), he became a benevolent elder statesman of poetry and journalism in Sydney. His poetry relies heavily on picturesque visual imagery and a self-conscious wit, but in his most admired work, including the triple sonnet 'Out of Time' and the long poems *Five Visions of Captain Cook* and *Five Bells*, he can convey the sense of the flux and richness of passing life. *Poems*, 1957, contains his small, influential collection.

Slesvig, see SCHLESWIG.

Sleuth Hound, see BLOODHOUND.

Slickensides, grooved or ridged structures, or scratches, formed on rock surfaces by friction during earth movements. The surfaces of fault planes are often slickensided, and the orientation of the slickenside is parallel to the direction of movement on the fault plane.

Slide Rule. An instrument invented about 1621 and widely used for making rapid approximate calculations until the appearance of cheap pocket-sized electronic calculators in the early 1970s. A slide rule has two pieces of equal length. One piece (the stock) forms a channel in which the other piece (the slide) can be moved. The working of the common slide rule is based on LOGARITHMS. The stock has two scales, upper and lower. The slide moves between these and has also two scales, identical with the former. The scales are divided by lines marked 1, 2, 3, 4, ..., 9, 10, such that the distance 1–2 is 0·3010, 1–3 is 0·4771, 1–4 is 0·6021, ... these distances being log 2, log 3, log 4, ...(these logarithms being to the base 10). The divisions 1–2, 2–3, ... are also subdivided, giving log 1·1, log 1·2, ... Addition of two logarithms gives the logarithm of the product of the two numbers, thus log 2 + log 3 brings the slide to log 6, the number 6 being read off the scale. Continued multiplication (and division) is facilitated by the cursor, a frame with a hair

line on glass, sliding over the slide rule, which can be placed over any intermediate result. The divisions on the lower scales are twice those on the upper, i.e., 2log 2, 2log 3, ... so that the numbers on the upper scales are the squares of numbers on the lower; 2 is below 4, 3 below 9, etc. The readings give only the mantissae of the logarithms. The common form of slide rule has logarithmic sines and tangents on the reverse as well as a simple log-scale. Numerous special-purpose slide rules have been devised.

Bibliography: J. N. Arnold, *The Complete Slide Rule Handbook: Principles and Applications*, 1954; I. Asimov, *An Easy Introduction to the Slide Rule*, 1965; B. Snodgrass, *The Slide Rule*, 2nd ed. 1971.

Slieve Donard, see MOURNE MOUNTAINS.

Sligo, maritime county in the Republic of IRELAND, bounded on the north by the Atlantic, south-west and west by Mayo, east by Leitrim, and south-east by Roscommon. The bays of KILLALA and Sligo indent the shore, while the surface near the sea is flat and boggy. The Ox Mountains and Benbulben Range rise behind the coastal plain. The highest point is Truskmore (641 m) on the eastern boundary. The rivers are unimportant, but Loughs Gill, Glencar, Arrow, Easky, Talt, and Gara are picturesque. Dairying and cattle grazing are the chief agricultural activities. There is some mineral wealth, including barytes, coal, lead, and copper. W. B. Yeats wrote much of his poetry about Sligo, where he lived for many years. Area 1839 km²; population 50,275.

Sligo, municipal borough and market town, seaport and county town of County SLIGO, Republic of Ireland, situated on the Garavogue river, between Lough Gill and the sea. It is one of the chief western ports of Ireland, the exports being barytes, lead and zinc concentrates, eggs, potatoes, and cattle; the imports include coal, timber, tar, motor spirit and oils, salt, manures, and provisions. The main industries are nylon and hospital products. It possesses a fine ruin, the Dominican abbey founded by Maurice Fitzgerald, lord justice, in 1252; and 5 km away at Carrowmore is a remarkable collection of megalithic remains. Drumcliff is 8 km to the north. In Lough Gill, 8 km by 2 km, 3 km to the south, is the tiny isle of Inishfree immortalised by W. B. Yeats. Population 14,456.

Slim of Yarralumba and Bishopston, William Joseph Slim, 1st Viscount (1891–1970), British sol-

---

Slide Rule.

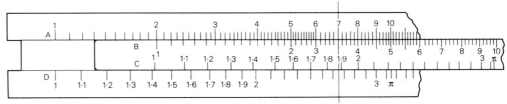

The hair line on the movable cursor shows that twice 3·5 (on scale B) is 7 (on scale A). Scales C and D are twice as big as scale A, and from them squares and square roots can be calculated. Numbers are spaced at distances proportional to their logarithms.

dier, born at Bristol. After active service in Belgium, France, Iraq, and the Dardenelles during the First World War, he was granted a regular commission and transferred to the Indian army. In 1940 he commanded the 10th infantry division of the 5th Indian division in north-east Africa and Eritrea and the 10th Indian division in Iraq and Iran. In 1942 he commanded the 1st Burma Corps, directing its fighting withdrawal to India and, later, as commander of the FOURTEENTH ARMY, his operations during 1944 marked the turning point of the Burma campaign and inflicted a crushing defeat on the Japanese. In September 1945 Slim was appointed commander of the Allied land forces, South-East Asia. In 1946 he became commandant of the Imperial Defence College and in 1948 chief of the Imperial General Staff, in succession to Field Marshal Lord Montgomery. He was knighted in 1944 and became field marshal in 1949. He was governor-general and commander-in-chief of Australia from 1953 to 1960 and was created viscount in 1960.

See also BURMA, SECOND WORLD WAR CAMPAIGNS IN.

Bibliography: G. Evans, *Slim as a military commander*, 1969; W. Slim, *Defeat into victory*, 3rd ed. 1972.

Slime-eel, see HAGFISH.

Slime Mould, see MYXOMYCOTA.

Slindon Estate, West Sussex. This 1420-hectare estate of farm and woodland includes Bignor and Coldharbour Hills, Glatting Beacon and most of Slindon village, with its 17th-century flint cottages. Much of the estate was acquired by the National Trust in 1950, the remainder in 1970.

Slip, in induction machines, is the synchronous speed minus the rotor speed, divided by synchronous speed. See ELECTRICAL MACHINES.

Slipware, name applied to objects of earthenware decorated with a semi-liquid clay mixture, known in England as 'slip'. Slip-covered earthenware is older than Chinese porcelain, for example the Romano-British specimens from Castor, England.

The two basic methods of slipware decoration are *sgraffiato*, in which the slip, usually of a contrasting colour with the base such as white pipe-clay over red earthenware, is scratched, so revealing a design. The second method is where the slip is trailed or piped across the body ('slip-trailing'). Among the outstanding early examples of *sgraffiato* slipware are the Gabi wares of Persia as early as the 8th or 9th century. Medieval Byzantine earthenware and similar wares from Cyprus led on to the superb creations of Bologna and Venice in the 15th century. In Egypt during the Mameluke period (13th and 14th centuries) the use of slip decoration was richly developed, especially 'slip-trailing'. It was this technique also that was so popular in the 17th and 18th centuries in Europe, especially in the Balkans and particularly in England at Wrotham, Staffordshire, and in the West Country.

Slipway, or slip, sloping rails running into the water of a river, dock, etc., carrying a cradle, used to draw vessels out of the water for inspection or repair. To minimise land use, the lower end may be enclosed by walls and a gate which can be shut to exclude the tide. This modification makes it a slip-dock. Slipways are used mostly for vessels of not more than 10,000 t instead of dry docks (see figure in DOCK). In the USA the docks used for the rapid ferryboat services are aptly called slips. Here the floating platform is shaped to fit exactly the rounded end of the boat, while two semi-flexible wings composed of lashed piles extend into the water. The boat glides in between the wings and meets the platform with ease and precision.

Sliven, town of eastern Bulgaria, capital of Sliven province, situated on the south-east slopes of the Balkan Mountains 64 km north-east of Stara Zagora. It is an agricultural centre, and manufactures textiles and carpets. There are coal mines nearby, and there is a spa some 11 km to the south-east. Population 84,000.

Sloan, Tod, properly James Forman (1874–1933), US jockey, who, by adopting a crouching seat almost on the horse's neck, revolutionised horse racing in England, to which he came in 1897. He rode 20 winners in that year; in 1898, 43 winners and 21 seconds out of 98 mounts. He won on 31·7 per cent of his mounts in England, but was barred from race riding at the end of 1900 for betting.

Sloane, Sir Hans (1660–1753), Irish physician and naturalist, born at Killyleagh, County Down, and educated in Paris and Montpellier. It could be said that he introduced the scientific method into medicine. He was a great believer in the importance of diet; and also helped establish the practice of inoculation for smallpox. He attended Queen Anne, was created baronet in 1716, and was president of the Royal Society (1727–40) and of the Royal College of Physicians (1719–35). He founded the Botanical Gardens in 1721. He was a great collector of natural history specimens and books and manuscripts, and he left his collections to the nation. They formed the nucleus of the British Museum. Sloane in 1712 purchased the manor of Chelsea, and his ownership is indicated in Sloane Square, Sloane Street, Hans Crescent, and other roads. He also has the distinction of inventing a recipe for chocolate mixed with milk ('Sir Hans Sloane's Milk Chocolate') which was used by Cadbury's until 1885. He wrote *Voyage to the Islands of Madera, Barbadoes*, etc., 1707–25.

Bibliography: Life by G. R. de Beer, 1953.

Slocum, Joshua (1844–?1909), Canadian sailor, born in Nova Scotia. In 1869 he became captain of a trading schooner carrying grain and coal between San Francisco and Seattle. In 1892 Slocum was offered the remains of the *Spray*, and on 4 April 1895, after completely rebuilding her, he sailed from Boston on his voyage round the world alone. He anchored at Newport three years later, having completed his voyage. In 1909 he set off from Bristol, Rhode Island, in the *Spray*, for the Orinoco River and was never seen again. Slocum wrote *Voyage of the 'Liberdade'*, 1894, and *Sailing Alone Round the World*, 1900.

Bibliography: W. M. Teller, *The Search for Captain Slocum*, 1959.

Sloe, see BLACKTHORN.

Sloop, small one-masted fore-and-aft rigged vessel, differing from a cutter in having a jib-stay and standing bowsprit. The name was also applied from 1676 to relatively small warships carrying guns on the upper deck only; then

Slope Wall

to a small corvette and, since the days of steam, to minor warships on trade-defence duties. In June 1947 the term sloop was abolished in the Royal Navy.

Slope Wall, name given to a wall, built of rubble or rough stone, which is erected on the side of a sloping earthen bank in order to prevent erosion.

Sloth, any of several tree-dwelling mammals that hang upside down from branches and move extremely slowly. They belong to the family Bradypodidae in the order Edentata. There are six living species in two genera. *Bradypus* has four species of three-toed sloths, called ais. They have nine vertebrae in their necks instead of the usual mammalian seven, and can turn their heads almost completely around to see behind them. *Choloepus*, the unaus, includes two species of two-toed sloths. They all live in tropical America.

Sloths have rounded faces, small ears and rudimentary tails. The body is about 70 cm long. The forelegs are longer than the hindlegs, and on the ground the animals cannot walk, but drag themselves along. The hair is brown, long, coarse and shaggy. An alga lives in the hair, and in damp weather turns it green so that it looks like grass, which helps the animal to blend in with its leafy background. Sloths are nocturnal animals. They usually live alone in the treetops, eating the leaves, and give birth to one young at a time, which spends its first few weeks clinging to its mother's hair.

Sloth Bear, *Melursus*, a large animal with a shaggy coat and a large white V on its chest. It feeds on termites, which it obtains by tearing their nest to pieces with its long claws. It devours the insects by scooping them up with a long tongue and protruding lower lip. It also eats fruits and honey. The young are carried on the mother's back when she is moving. The sloth bear inhabits the wooded parts of India and Ceylon. This animal is a bear, a member of family URSIDAE, order CARNIVORA, not an ant-eater.

Slough, town, since 1974 in BERKSHIRE, England, 32 km west of London. Formerly a small market town, it has grown since the beginning of the 20th century into a large residential and industrial area, which is still rapidly expanding, being granted a borough charter in 1938. It was the scene of many of Sir William Herschel's astronomical discoveries. During the First World War a government mechanical transport depot was established at Slough, which was afterwards converted into a trading estate of 280 ha, containing some 290 factories. Other factories in the town bring the total to approximately 400. There are numerous light and precision engineering works, and motor-car, pharmaceutical, confectionery, and paint plants. The Slough community centre is on a scale never previously attempted in Britain. Population (1971) 87,075.

Slough, a mass of necrotic tissue which becomes detached from surrounding healthy tissues. When a portion of tissue has become so far destroyed that the circulation is not adequate, a layer of cells tends to be formed separating the healthy from the diseased flesh, and this ultimately leads to its detachment. (See NECROSIS.)

Slovak Socialist Republic, constituent division of the federal republic of Czechoslovakia since 1969. The capi-

Slovenia. The lake and castle of Bled. *(Barnaby's Picture Library)*

tal is BRATISLAVA. Area 127,877 km²; population (1975) 14,738,311.

See CZECH SOCIALIST REPUBLIC; CZECHOSLOVAKIA, *Government*; SLOVAKIA.

Slovakia (Czech *Slovensko*; German *Slowakei*), territory of CZECHOSLOVAKIA, the most easterly part of the republic, bounded on the west by MORAVIA and on the east by RUTHENIA. Until 1948 it was a province (area 48,955 km²; capital Bratislava), but it is now divided into three administrative regions (*kraju*): West, Central and East Slovakia. The greater part lies in the western CARPATHIANS, but in the south-west is the fertile land of the DANUBE valley, and in the east is a plain of the River Tisza. It is mainly agricultural; the plains produce cereals, wine, fruit, and tobacco.

The SLOVAKS were conquered by the MAGYARS in the 10th century, and remained subject to the Hungarian sovereign until the collapse of Austria-Hungary in 1918 (see HUNGARY, *History* and AUSTRIA, *History*). By the treaties of Trianon and St-Germain-en-Laye, Slovakia then became part of the new republic of Czechoslovakia. During the 19th century there had been a resurgence of nationalist feeling in Slovakia, which had been suppressed by the government in favour of the Magyars, and after the formation of Czechoslovakia there was still a nationalist party (founded by Andrew Hlinka) which opposed the centralisation of government at Prague. In 1938, after the MUNICH PACT, Slovakia secured a measure of autonomy, though losing territory to Hungary and Poland. The new Slovak government, led by Josef Tiso, abolished all political parties except the nationalist party. In March 1939 the Prague government, fearing that a declaration of Slovak independence was imminent, attempted to replace Tiso and his ministers by others friendly to Prague. This event provided Germany with a pretext for annexing BOHEMIA and MORAVIA, and Slovakia was declared an independent state under German protection, with Tiso as president. Later Slovakia was occupied by German troops, and was forced to aid the invasion of Poland.

After the outbreak of the Second World War, Slovaks abroad co-operated with the Czechs on the side of the Allies, and took part in the formation of a provisional Czechoslovak government under BENEŠ in London. In 1944 there was an anti-German rising in Slovakia, which was suppressed by the Germans and the para-military 'Hlinka Guard'. At the end of the war Slovakia was incorporated with Czechoslovakia.

See CZECHOSLOVAKIA, *History*.
Bibliography: E. Steiner, *Slovak Dilemma*, 1973.

Slovaks, Slavic (see SLAVS) people inhabiting the eastern region of Czechoslovakia, where they number about 4·5 million. From the 10th century until 1918 they were under the dominance of the MAGYARS. Until the 18th century the written language was a form of Czech, but it was then supplanted by the Slovak dialect. The Slovaks are independent peasants with a long standing and rich tradition of which they are proud. The majority are Roman Catholics. See also CZECHOSLOVAKIA, *History*.

Slovene Language, see YUGOSLAVIA, *Language*.

Slovenes, branch of the southern SLAVS, living in north-west Yugoslavia, the provinces of Styria and Carinthia in Austria, Gorizia and Carniola in Italy, and adjacent areas of Hungary. They were formerly under Hapsburg rule, but after the First World War they united with the Serbs and Croats to form the state of Yugoslavia. Today they are members of the Autonomous People's Republic of SLOVENIA in north-west Yugoslavia.

Like Serbian and Croat, Slovene is one of the southern Slav group of Indo-European languages; it is an official language of Yugoslavia and is written exclusively in Roman characters. The Slovenes possess some literary reputation, and the poets France Preseren and Valentine Vodnik are the best known of their writers. The Slovenes number about 1·75 million and the majority are Roman Catholic.

Slovenia (Serbo-Croatian *Slovenija*), constituent republic of YUGOSLAVIA, bounded by Italy, Hungary, Austria, and Croatia. The greater part of it was under Hapsburg rule from the 14th century until 1918, except for the period of the Napoleonic conquest 1809–13. At the end of the First World War it was incorporated in the new kingdom of the Serbs, Croats and Slovenes, later renamed Yugoslavia (see CARNIOLA). During the Second World War it was portioned out between Germany, Italy, and Hungary.

Slovenia is mountainous, containing parts of the Julian, Savinje, and Karawanken Alps. The Julian Alps form the watershed for its rivers, of which the Sava and its tributaries, the Savinja and Krka, the Drava and the Mura

belong to the Black Sea system, while the Soča belongs to the Adriatic system. Slovenia is rich in coal, mercury, and zinc. There is much stock raising. Vines and cereals are grown, but potatoes are the chief crop. The principal towns are LJUBLJANA (the capital), MARIBOR, and CELJE. Area 20,250 km^2; population (1971) 1,697,500.

Slovensko, see SLOVAKIA.

Slow-worm, *Anguis fragilis*, a wormlike reptile usually about 30 cm long, of which half is tail. Internal traces of limbs indicate that it is a LIZARD. Its nostrils are provided with shields, while its eyes are protected by scaly and movable eyelids. It possesses long pointed teeth which incline backwards. The colour varies a great deal, but usually the adult is brown above and black underneath, while its young are white with a black stripe running along the centre of the back. They inhabit bushes and feed upon earthworms and slugs. Their bite is harmless. They are timid creatures, and when frightened their muscles contract so rigidly that endeavours to bend the creature often cause breakage. They hibernate during winter in groups of about twenty.

Słowacki, Juliusz (1809–49), Polish Romantic poet and dramatist, born in Kremenets; educated at the University of Vilnius. After the outbreak of the November 1830 rising he left Poland, stayed in England and Switzerland, then toured Italy, Greece, and the Middle East, before settling among the émigrés in Paris, where he died. He received little attention, unlike his rival MICKIEWICZ, until the end of the 19th century. His plays, which he never saw acted, established a tradition of Polish poetic drama, close to the spirit of Shakespeare and CALDERÓN. His major work includes three volumes of verse, *Poezye*, 1832–33, the longer poems *Beniowski*, 1840, and the great tour de force conceived in the spirit of messianic mysticism *Król-Duch* (unfinished), 1847; the plays, *Kordian*, 1834, *Balladyna*, 1839, *Lilla Weneda*, 1840, *Mazepa*, 1840 (English translation, 1930), and *Sen srebrny Salomei*, 1844. His letters to his mother are classics of Polish prose.

Bibliography: M. Kridl, *The Lyric Poems of Juliusz Slowacki*, 1958; J. Peterkiewicz and B. Singer (Eds), *Five Centuries of Polish Poetry*, 2nd ed. 1970.

Slowakei, see SLOVAKIA.

Slow-worm. *Anguis fragilis*, with young. *(Topham/Coleman)*

141

Slowpitch

Slowpitch, see SOFTBALL.

Sloy, Loch, small loch in Dumbarton District, Strathclyde Region, Scotland, 5 km west of Loch Lomond. A hydro-electric power station opened in 1950 operates at its outlet to Loch Lomond.

Sludge, see SEWAGE.

Slug, air-breathing molluscs (class GASTROPODA, subclass PULMONATA in which an external shell is either lacking or greatly reduced). Those belonging to the family Limacidae are without external shells, though most of them possess a small internal shelly plate or a few calcareous granules under the skin of the back. Like snails, they have a mouth composed of external fleshy lips and, within, a ribbon-like mass of teeth. They are mostly plant-feeders. They move by means of a flattened muscular part of the body called the foot. Slugs are hermaphrodites but cross-fertilising. Numerous eggs are laid in decaying vegetation. The commonest and most destructive British one is the grey field slug *Limax agrestis*. Other species include the bulb- or root-eating slug, the black slug, and the yellow or household slug. Another group of slugs, characterised by the small shell being external, hunt and destroy earthworms and insects, and are almost as beneficial as the others are injurious to cultivated crops.
Bibliography: N. W. Runham and P. J. Hunter, *Terrestrial Slugs*, 1970.

Slug, mass, see METROLOGY.

Slumping, term used in geology to describe the collapse or flowage of soft or unconsolidated rock material under the influence of gravity. Slumping on land is associated with landslides and SOLIFLUCTION. Beneath the surface of the sea, sediment brought in by rivers may accumulate in such great thicknesses that it becomes unstable, and the stimulus of EARTHQUAKE shocks may make the surface layer slump, or slide down into deeper water. By this means, great sheets of sediment become disturbed and crumpled.

Slums and Slum-clearance, see CLEARANCE AND REDEVELOPMENT (HOUSING); HOUSING; OVERCROWDING, ABATEMENT OF.

Słupsk (German *Stolp*), town of Poland, in Koszalin province, 61 km north-east of Koszalin on the River Slupia. Until 1945 it was in POMERANIA. There are timber, chemical, and engineering industries. Population (1974) 74,825.

Sluter, Claus (d. 1406), Flemish sculptor, probably born in Haarlem. He was employed by Duke Philip the Bold of Burgundy. He sculpted the Moses Well and the figures on the Chapel Portal at the Carthusian monastery at Champmol, outside Dijon, and the tomb of the Duke (now in the Dijon Museum). Sluter was a master of portraiture, capable of bestowing extreme actuality also on imaginary figures, such as the prophets around the Moses Well, yet retaining a grandeur of conception, even in figures of the smallest proportions, as in the 'weepers' on the Duke's tomb.
Bibliography: T. Müller, *Sculpture in the Netherlands, Germany, France and Spain 1400–1500*, 1966.

142

Sluyters, Jan (1881–1957), Dutch painter, and a leading Post-Impressionist, who experimented in various styles, for example FAUVISM and CUBISM, and finally settled on a highly colourful EXPRESSIONISM, as in his nude studies, portraits, and still-lifes.

Smack, a sailing vessel, having auxiliary steam or motor power, sometimes used for fishing, with a hold amidships. The term smack is also used for a small-decked or half-decked vessel.

Smailholm Tower, tower in Roxburgh District, Borders Region of Scotland, 9 km north-west of KELSO, dating from the 16th century. Near it is Sandyknowe Farm, where Sir Walter Scott stayed for some time as a child.

Small Holdings. The Agriculture Act 1970 Part III contains the statutory provisions relating to small holdings. The upper size limit for small holdings is defined as such that the holding should provide full-time employment for not more than two men. The small-holding authorities are the GLC and county councils in England and Wales. A small-holding authority may acquire land for small holdings by agreement but no longer has powers of compulsory purchase or hiring. The minister of Agriculture has a general power to provide small holdings and also power to do so on default of a small-holding authority. Land acquired for small holdings may be let to a person who has or will soon have sufficient agricultural experience. The minister has made regulations concerning the method of selecting tenants and the qualifications which they should possess.

Smalley, Roger (1944–), British composer and writer on music, born at Swinton, Manchester; studied at the Royal College of Music under Fricker from 1961, at Morley College under Goehr, and (1965) at Cologne under Stockhausen, of whose ideas, as of the avant-garde stance in general, he is an important and uncompromising exponent. Since 1967 he has lived in Cambridge, where he has held a fellowship at King's College. His group Intermodulation has given important performances of electronic music. Of his own works, several, including the *Missa Brevis* (1967), are based on 16th-century models by William Blitheman.

Smallhythe, hamlet, 2 km south of TENTERDEN, in Ashford District of Kent, England. This was a thriving medieval shipbuilding port which declined with the silting of the River Rother. The actress Ellen Terry lived at the early 16th-century Smallhythe Place, which is now a theatre museum.

Smallpox, or variola, a contagious infectious disease due to a virus and characterised by a skin eruption. Smallpox starts with headache, backache and febrile symptoms, followed in two or three days by a papular eruption mainly on the trunk, face and head. The eruption quickly becomes vesicular and then pustular, and after about a fortnight the pustules dry into crusts. When these separate the skin is usually left pitted, and the scars, or 'pockmarks', remain permanently. In mild cases the eruptions are scanty and discrete, but in more severe cases the eruptions are so numerous that they join together in a confluent mass. In an even more severe type of the disease, known as haemorrhagic smallpox, the vesicles become filled with blood. Fever and toxaemia are most severe in the immediate pre-eruption and in the pustular stages of the illness. The incubation period is from 12 to 14 days. In its most virulent form smallpox is a lethal disease. Even the less virulent forms have claimed victims among the unvaccinated, and on all occasions smallpox must be regarded as potentially dangerous.

Smallpox used to be endemic in Asia where it was difficult to eradicate because of overcrowding and low standards of living. It was most probably first introduced into Europe by the returning crusaders, and as sea communications developed it was carried to the new world by explorers and settlers. The introduction of compulsory vaccination in 1853, together with improved preventive health measures, the introduction of port health inspection of immigrants and seafarers, and increasing medical knowledge of the nature of infections led gradually to the virtual stamping out of smallpox in the UK and there has been no major epidemic during this century. Vaccination ceased to be compulsory in 1948, and as a result fewer children are now immunised. The speed of modern travel enables people to move across the world well within the incubation period of smallpox, and it is possible for a traveller infected in one country to develop the disease several days after he has arrived in another country and mixed freely with the community. At least one recent outbreak in England was started by the arrival of an air passenger who was in the symptomless incubation stage of the complaint. Vaccination of known contacts within a day or two of their exposure to infection will modify the severity of any attack that subsequently develops.

Vaccination confers immediate and complete immunity for about two or three years, and a lesser degree of immunity for many years, if not for life. It is rare for anyone who has been vaccinated in infancy to suffer from a severe attack of smallpox if infected later on in life. Isolation of victims, tracing, segregating and vaccinating immediate contacts, vaccination of the population exposed to risk, and disinfection of infected houses and contagious material, are the epidemiological measures used for stopping an outbreak. There is as yet no proven specific treatment but in 1963 a new drug, N-methylisatin B-thiosemicarbazone was tried on 1000 persons in Madras who had been in intimate contact with infection. Only three mild cases of smallpox occurred among them whereas 78 cases occurred in a similar number of contacts who did not receive the drug but most of whom had been vaccinated.

Since the Second World War a huge World Health Organisation programme has been in operation to eradicate smallpox altogether. The programme has been extremely successful, eradication from the Indian subcontinent being apparently achieved by 1975. Constant surveillance in the future is a condition of continuing success, however.

Smalt, silicate of cobalt and potassium prepared by fusing roasted cobalt ore with quartz sand and pearl ash. The fused mass of blue glass is ground beneath water, and is extensively used as a PIGMENT.

Smart, Christopher (1722–71), English poet, born at Shipbourne, Kent. Helped by the Duchess of Cleveland, he was sent to Cambridge where he became a fellow of Pembroke Hall in 1745. On leaving the University he went to London and lived by writing for periodicals.

Christopher Smart, portrait painted about 1745. (*National Portrait Gallery, London*)

His *Poems on Several Occasions*, which contains 'The Hop Garden', was issued in 1752, and in the following year *The Hilliad* appeared, satirising John Hill, a personal enemy.

Smart eventually developed a form of religious mania and it was in confinement that he produced some of his best work, including *Rejoice in the Lamb* (*Jubilate Agno*) and his most famous poem, *A Song to David*, 1763. A hymn to the author of the Psalms, its mastery of technique, direct style, and brilliant imagery make it one of the most remarkable poems of the 18th century. Unfortunate to the last, he died in the King's Bench prison, to which he had been committed for debt. Although it created no great impression at the time, more recent studies have placed a high regard on Smart's work. His *Collected Poems* were edited by N. Callan, 1949, and *A Song to David* by E. Blunden, 1924.

Bibliography: E. G. Ainsworth and C. E. Noyes, *Christopher Smart*, 1943; C. Devlin, *Poor Kit Smart*, 1961; A. Sherbo, *Christopher Smart: Scholar of the University*, 1967; P. M. Spacks, *Poetry of Vision*, 1967.

Smart, Sir George (1776–1867), English musician, born in London. He was a choirboy and later an organist at the Chapel Royal, and studied composition under Arnold. He was knighted in 1811, and became a favourite festival conductor. He wrote many church anthems and chants, and also taught. Some of his glees were long popular. Jenny LIND was his most famous pupil; in 1826 he gave hospitality to Carl WEBER, who died at his house.

Smear Dab, see LEMON SOLE.

Smeaton, John (1724–92), British civil engineer, born at Austhorpe, near Leeds. Although intended for the law, he became an instrument maker and later turned to civil engineering. His greatest work was the building of the third Eddystone Lighthouse after the second was burnt down in 1755. He was surveyor and engineer of the Forth and Clyde Canal and built several bridges in Scotland.

Smectymnuus, pseudonym (formed from the first letters of their names) of Stephen Marshall, Edmond Calamy, Thomas Young, Matthew Newcomen, and William Spurstow. They were joint authors of an attack on episcopacy called *An Answer to a Booke* (by J. HALL, Bishop of Norwich) *entituled, an Humble Remonstrance. In which the originall of Liturgy (and) Episcopacy is discussed ...*, 1641. Both the *Booke* and the *Answer* gave rise to considerable controversy, in which, among others, MILTON took part.

Smell, see NOSE.

Smellie, William (1697–1763), British obstetrician, born in Lanark, Scotland. He studied medicine at Glasgow and began to practise as a surgeon and apothecary in Lanark in 1720. He settled in London in 1739, and two years later began to teach midwifery at his house. He owed much to William HUNTER, who went to live with him. He was MD Glasgow, 1745. Smellie wrote a *Treatise on the Theory and Practice of Midwifery*, 1752, in which he described the mechanism of childbirth more accurately than anyone previously; he laid down safe rules regarding the use of forceps (of which he introduced several types); he also wrote two supplementary volumes of case reports, 1754 and 1764. All these works were revised by Tobias Smollett, his friend. Smellie was the dominating figure among the obstetricians of his period.
Bibliography: Life by R. W. Johnstone, 1952.

Smellie, William (1740–95), British printer and scientist, born in Edinburgh. One of his first literary undertakings was the first edition of the *Encyclopaedia Britannica*, entirely planned and compiled by him. He translated Buffon's *Natural History, 1781*, and wrote the *Philosophy of Natural History*, 1790–99.
Bibliography: Life by R. Kerr, 1811.

Smelling Salts, a mixture of compounds usually containing ammonia which, when inhaled, acts as a stimulant and is used as a restorative.

Smelt, fishes of genus *Osmerus*, order Salmoniformes, found in Europe and North America. They bear close resemblance to the salmon in habit and appearance, but they are of smaller size, and their natural habitat is the sea, although they frequently enter rivers for spawning and thrive in fresh water. *O. eperlanus*, the common smelt, is considered a delicacy when fresh, and *O. mordax*, an American species, is also eaten.

Smelting, see METALLURGY.

Smetana, Bedřich (1824–84), Czech composer, born at Litomyšl, showed early gifts which his father discouraged, but was able to learn the piano and theory at school at Plzeň and at Proksch's Music School in Prague. After holding a post in the household of Count Thun he ran into difficulties by adhering to the revolutionary movement against Austrian rule, and went to Sweden as conductor in 1856. He returned to Prague in 1861, became conductor of the Hlahol choral society, and in 1866 of the provisional national theatre, where his first two operas, *The Brandenburgers in Bohemia* and *The Bartered Bride*, were produced that year. All the later ones were also produced there, six of them complete, and the last, the unfinished *Viola* (on Shakespeare's *Twelfth Night*), long after his death, in 1924. He became deaf in 1874 and resigned, but remained creatively active until he became insane in 1883. The later finished operas were *Dalibor*, 1868, *Two Widows*, 1874, *The Kiss*, 1876, *The Secret*, 1878, *Libuše*, 1881, and *The Devil's Wall*, 1882, but none had the overall success of *The Bartered Bride*, which has remained the outstanding Czech national opera and at the same time a repertory comic opera everywhere. Smetana also created the Czech national symphonic poem with his cycle of six, *My Country*, 1874–79, and wrote choral and other orchestral works, two string quartets, a piano trio, piano pieces and songs.
Bibliography: B. Large, *Smetana*, 1970.

Smethwick, town in WEST MIDLANDS METROPOLITAN COUNTY, England, 5 km north-west of Birmingham, of which it is now effectively a suburb, although administratively part of the borough of Sandwell since 1974. Smethwick is the home of the epoch-making inventions of BOULTON, WATT, and MURDOCK. Its principal industries are engineering, brewing, and the manufacture of weighing machines, metals, screws, nuts and bolts, and optical, technical, and domestic glass. There are also foundries. Population (1971) 68,400.

Smew, *Mergellus albellus*, species of duck, family Anatidae, order Anseriformes. The male bird is chiefly white with black markings, the female is white with reddish markings, and both have a handsome appearance. They inhabit northern Asia and Europe from Kamchatka to Lapland, and frequently winter in Britain, but do not touch North America.

Smigły-Rydz, Edward (1886–1941), Polish soldier and politician, born in Galicia. He fought with PIŁSUDSKI on the Austrian side in the First World War. In 1919 he was Piłsudski's coadjutor in setting up the Polish state, and commanded an army during the Polish-Soviet War (1919–20). Smigły-Rydz again helped Piłsudski in the coup of 1926. On Piłsudski's death in 1935 Smigły-Rydz was made marshal and inspector-general of the forces. On Poland's defeat in 1939 he fled to Romania but returned secretly to Warsaw in 1941 where he died.

Smiles, Samuel (1812–1904), British biographer and social reformer, born at Haddington, Scotland, and trained for the medical profession, graduating from Edinburgh University. He practised for some time at Leeds, but, abandoning medicine, became editor of the *Leeds Times* and an active social reformer. His writings include *Life of George Stephenson*, 1857; the phenomenally popular *Self-Help*, 1859; and *Lives of the Engineers*, 1861.
Bibliography: S. Smiles (ed. A. Briggs), *Self-Help*, 1958.

Smirke, Sir Robert (1781–1867), the leading Greek Revival architect in England, born in London. He was trained by Sir J. SOANE, then travelled in Italy and Greece. Starting practice about 1807, he designed Covent Garden Theatre, London's first Greek Doric building (1808–09; burnt down 1856); the British Museum (1823–47); the General Post Office (1824–29; demolished 1913); and the east wing of Somerset House (1830–31).

Smith, Adam (1723–90), Scottish political economist, born at Kirkcaldy, Fife. After studying at Glasgow University and Balliol College, Oxford, he was in 1751

Adam Smith. *(Mary Evans Picture Library)*

appointed to the chair of moral philosophy at Glasgow. He was friendly with David Hume and many leading English and French literary figures of the day. He published in 1759 his *Theory of the Moral Sentiments*, and in 1776 issued *The Wealth of Nations*, the foundation of all works on political economy. This is the first work in which the principles of political economy are set forth scientifically, and has had incalculable influence. It has passed through innumerable editions and been translated into many languages. His *Lectures on Rhetoric and Belles Lettres* were published in 1963 with an introduction by J. M. Lothian.

See also CLASSICAL ECONOMISTS; ECONOMIC THOUGHT, HISTORY OF.

Bibliography: E. Ginsberg, *The House of Adam Smith*, 1934; R. L. Heilbroner, *The Great Economists*, 1955; A. Smith, *Wealth of Nations* (ed. A. S. Skinner), 1970; S. Hollander, *The Economics of Adam Smith*, 1973.

Smith, Alexander (1830–67), Scottish poet and essayist, born at Kilmarnock. He was a pattern-designer in Glasgow, but, having become known as a promising poet, in 1854 he was appointed secretary of Edinburgh University. After contributing to the *Glasgow Citizen* he published *A Life Drama*, 1853, which was much admired. In prose he wrote *Dreamthorp* (essays), 1863, *A Summer in Skye*, 1865, his most attractive and lasting work, and two novels. He belonged to the so-called 'spasmodic' school of poetry.

Bibliography: T. Brisbane, *The Early Years of Alexander Smith*, 1869; M. A. Weinstein, *W. E. Aytoun and the Spasmodic Controversy*, 1968.

Smith, Arnold Cantwell (1915–), Canadian diplomat, educated at Toronto, Grenoble, and Oxford universities and Gray's Inn. He joined the Canadian diplomatic service in 1939 and held posts in several parts of the world. Smith was Canadian ambassador to the United Arab Republic, 1958–61, and to the USSR, 1961–63. From

1965 to 1975 he was secretary-general of the newly-formed Commonwealth Secretariat. He then went to Carleton University, Ottawa, as professor of international affairs.

Smith, Arthur James Marshall (1902–), Canadian poet, critic, and anthologist, born in Montreal; educated at the universities of McGill and Edinburgh, he was professor of English at Michigan State University until 1972. As editor and anthologist he brought many Canadian poets to an international audience, and his critical influence encouraged them to recognise their cosmopolitan kinship with YEATS, POUND, or AUDEN.

Smith's poetry is small in quantity; his first two books are included in *Collected Poems*, 1962, and this in turn appears in *Poems, New and Collected*, 1967. The humour, wit, and assurance which control his many styles and themes make him an excellent example, as well as advocate, of formal lyric poetry. His most significant criticism is in *Towards a View of Canadian Letters: Selected Essays, 1928–72*, 1973, and anthologies of Canadian critics, *Masks of Fiction*, 1961, and *Masks of Poetry*, 1962. His anthologies of Canadian poets since *New Provinces*, 1936, were made with F. R. SCOTT; most important are *The Book of Canadian Poetry*, 1943, revised 1948, 1957; *The Oxford Book of Canadian Verse: In English and French*, 1960 (with an excellent introduction); *Modern Canadian Verse: In English and French*, 1967; *The Book of Canadian Prose: Volume I*, 1965 (up to Confederation), *Volume II*, 1973; and *The Blasted Pine*, 1967, a collection of satiric poetry.

Smith, Bessie (c. 1895–1937), one of the greatest US blues singers, born at Chattanooga, Tennessee. In 1923 at the start of the classic blues period she began an extensive recording career, when most blues artists used jazz accompaniment—for example instrumentalists such as Louis ARMSTRONG and Fletcher Henderson. By the early 1930s she went into a decline, partly because of changing styles but also because of her temperament and heavy drinking. Following a car accident, she died as a result of being refused hospital treatment because she was black. She starred in a film, *St Louis Blues*, 1929, her recording of that song being among her best known, along with 'Nobody knows you when you're down and out', 1929 and 'Do your duty', 1933.

Bibliography: P. Oliver, *Bessie Smith*, 1959; R. Hadlock, *Jazz Masters of the Twenties*, 1965.

Smith, David (1906–65), US sculptor, born at Indiana, died at Vermont. He began as a painter but in 1932 started making welded metal sculpture under the influence of PICASSO and GONZALEZ. In 1940 he exhibited the *Medals for Dishonour*, bitterly satirising the establishment. After the war his sculpture became more abstract and reached its culminating point in the stainless steel *Cubi* series, begun in 1961, in which massive geometric forms are assembled with great virtuosity and expressive power.

Bibliography: G. McCoy (Ed.), *David Smith*, 1973.

Smith, George (1831–95), British philanthropist, born near Tunstall, Staffordshire, son of a brickmaker. He discovered clay at Coalville and organised a large brick-making business there. An earnest social worker, he wrote *The Cry of the Children*, 1871, which resulted in legislation controlling the employment of child-workers in brickfields. He later devoted his attention to improving the condition of gypsy children.

Smith, Sir George Adam (1856–1942), Scottish biblical scholar and minister, born in Calcutta, India, educated at Edinburgh, Tübingen, and Leipzig. He became professor of Old Testament languages, literature, and theology at the United Free Church College, Glasgow in 1892. He was principal of Aberdeen University from 1909 to 1935, and was knighted in 1916. He was moderator of the United Free Church General Assembly, 1916–17, and chaplain to the king from 1933 until his death. He travelled extensively in Egypt, Syria, and Palestine. His writings include *Historical Geography of the Holy Land*, 1894 (25th ed. 1931); *The Twelve Prophets*, 1896–97; *Jerusalem*, 1907; *The Early Poetry of Israel*, 1912; and *Jeremiah*, 1923.

Smith, George Murray (1824–1901), British publisher, born in London. In 1838 he joined the firm of Smith Elder, of which his father was part-founder, and in 1845 became head of the publishing department. Energetic, bold, and astute, he soon secured the work of such authors as Charlotte Brontë, Thackeray, and Ruskin. He founded the *Cornhill Magazine* in 1860, and put Thackeray in the editorial chair. Five years later he brought out the *Pall Mall Gazette*. He made a fortune outside publishing, and used some of his capital to produce the *Dictionary of National Biography*, 1885–1912, edited first by Sir Leslie Stephen and then by Sir Sidney Lee. The firm of Smith Elder was absorbed by the house of JOHN MURRAY in 1917. A memoir by Sir Sidney Lee appeared in 1901.

Smith, Herbert (1862–1938), British trade union leader and Socialist, born at Barnsley, Yorkshire. At the age of ten he started work in the mines. In 1904 he was vice-president of the Yorkshire Miners' Association, and in 1906 president. He succeeded Robert Smillie as president of the Miners' Federation of Great Britain in 1922, holding this office until 1929. In the coal dispute which resulted in the General Strike of 1926 Smith and Arthur Cook were the miners' leaders.
Bibliography: M. Morris, *The General Strike*, 1976.

Smith, Horatio (1779–1849), English novelist and parodist, born in London, commonly known as Horace Smith. He published several novels and contributed to various periodicals before, in 1812, he and his elder brother, James (1775–1839), produced their joint work, *Rejected Addresses: or, the New Theatrum Poetarum*, a series of parodies of popular contemporary writers. This pretended to contain entries sent in to win the prize offered by the managers of Drury Lane for the best address to be delivered at the reopening of the theatre.
Bibliography: A. H. Beavan, *James and Horace Smith*, 1899.

Smith, Iain Crichton (1928–), Scottish writer, born at Lewis and educated at Aberdeen University, he became a teacher. His poetry is written in English: *The Long River*, 1955; *Thistles and Roses*, 1961; *Deer in the High Hills*, 1962; *The Law and the Grace*, 1965; *From Bourgeois Land* and a translation of Donnachadh Ban's *Ben Dorain*, 1969 (see MACINTYRE, DUNCAN); as are two novels, *Consider the Lilies*, 1968; *The Last Summer*, 1969; and

a volume of short stories, *Survival without Error*, 1970, together with some plays. He also writes in Gaelic, and in both languages his work expresses with clarity and rhetorical force man's loneliness in a dehumanised world.

Smith, Ian Douglas (1919–), Rhodesian politician, born at Selukwe, Rhodesia; educated at Selukwe School, Chaplin School, Gwelo, and Rhodes University, South Africa. He had a distinguished career in the RAF, 1941–46, and after the Second World War became a farmer. From 1948–53 Smith was a member of the Southern Rhodesia Legislative Assembly, and a member of the Federal Parliament, 1953–61. A former chief whip of the United Federal party, Smith resigned from it in 1961, and was a founder of the Rhodesian Front in 1962. When the Rhodesian Front came to power in Southern Rhodesia in 1962, Smith was returned to the Legislative Assembly and appointed deputy premier and minister of the Treasury. He became premier and minister of external affairs and defence in April 1964. Smith represented the wing of his party which demanded immediate independence for Southern Rhodesia: when negotiations with Britain broke down, Smith made a unilateral declaration of independence in November 1965, which Britain considered illegal. In 1976, after ten years of 'illegal independence' Smith found himself under heavy pressure to reach an accommodation with the moderate wing of the African National Council on procedures to achieve black majority rule in Rhodesia. He agreed to participate in talks held at Geneva in the autumn of 1976 aimed at creating a constitutional settlement. This, however, proved to be abortive though further attempts were made, and an election held among the minority white electorate in August 1977 resulted in a clear win for Smith's Rhodesian Front.
See also RHODESIA, *History*.

Smith, James, see SMITH, HORATIO.

Smith, John (1580–1631), English adventurer and effective founder of Virginia, born at Willoughby, Lincolnshire. He fought in France and Italy, and then in the Austrian army against the Turks. Left for dead on a battlefield, he was discovered by the Turks, carried to Constantinople, and sold into slavery. He killed his master, made good his escape, and reached England in 1605. The following year he joined an emigrant party destined

Ian Smith. *(Popperfoto)*

for what is now the state of Virginia. The whole colony would have perished but for the energy and resourcefulness of Smith, who assumed a natural leadership. While exploring the Chickahominy River he was taken captive by the Indians, his life being spared, according to his account, only when the Indian princess POCAHONTAS, interceded on his behalf. Smith later became governor of the colony, succeeded in making the settlers work, and, in the meantime, saved them from starving by trading with the Indians and securing much-needed food. Later he explored and mapped the coast of the territory, which he named New England. He returned to England in 1609, continued to encourage colonisation, wrote books, and made maps.

Bibliography: P. L. Barbour, *The Three Worlds of Captain John Smith*, 1964.

Smith, Joseph, see MORMON CHURCH.

Smith, Sir Keith Macpherson (1890–1955), Australian airman, born in Adelaide. He served in the Royal Flying Corps in the First World War, and with his brother Ross was the first to fly from England to Australia in 1919. They were knighted for this achievement in the same year.

Smith, Logan Pearsall (1865–1946), US critic and essayist, born at Millville, New Jersey. He was educated at the Penn Charter School, Haverford College, Harvard, and Balliol College, Oxford. His ancestors were Quakers, and his father combined prosperous management of a glass-bottle factory with equally prosperous evangelism. His autobiographical *Unforgotten Years*, 1938, gives an account of his ancestry. Smith's years at Oxford confirmed his desire to devote his life to 'the delicate torture of trying to express in words what he felt and saw', or, more concisely, to the study of the English language and the writing of English prose. His easy mastery of words and language is displayed at its best in his collections of *Trivia*, 1918, *More Trivia*, 1921, and *All Trivia*, 1933, which were thoughts and comments longer than epigrams, shorter than Baconian essays, but combining the wit and wisdom of each. His book, *The English Language*, 1912, embodied the first fruits of the new science of SEMANTICS or the meaning of words. He wrote on, and edited, the works of authors as different as Donne, Milton, and Santayana. Smith's works include *Sir Henry Wotton*, 1907, and *On Reading Shakespeare*, 1933.

Bibliography: R. Gathorne–Hardy, *Recollections of Logan Pearsall Smith*, 1949.

Smith, Maggie (1931–), British actress who first appeared at Oxford in 1952 as Viola in *Twelfth Night*. She has since made numerous appearances in plays by Shakespeare, Ibsen, Strindberg and others, taking both comic and tragic roles. Of her films *The Prime of Miss Jean Brodie*, 1968, is her best known, for which she was awarded an Oscar. She has also made numerous television appearances.

Smith, Sir Matthew Arnold Bracy (1879–1959), British painter, born at Halifax in Yorkshire. He studied at the Slade School and in Paris, being much influenced by the colour of MATISSE although his handling of paint was far more vigorous. Subsequently, in a series of nudes, landscapes, flower, and still-life paintings, he showed a sense of colour unrivalled in the work of modern British artists. He was knighted in 1954.

Smith, Richard (1931–), British artist, born at Letchworth and educated at Luton and St Albans schools of art before going to the Royal College of Art. Smith has spent long periods in the USA and exercised considerable influence on the development of POP ART, though it can be argued that he himself has never been a Pop Artist. His painting alludes to the scale and colour of commercial imagery but does not quote from or parody it. Major exhibitions of his work were held at the Whitechapel Gallery in 1966 and the Tate Gallery in 1975.

Smith, Robert (1689–1768), British mathematician, born near Gainsborough and educated at Trinity College, Cambridge, becoming Plumian Professor of astronomy in 1716. He was the founder of the prizes called after him, competed for by Cambridge wranglers. He published his *Opticks* in 1738 and *Harmonics* in 1760.

Smith, Rodney ('Gypsy') (1860–1947), English evangelist, born at Woodford, Essex. A gypsy, he taught himself to read and write. At 17 he met General William Booth at a Salvation Army meeting in Whitechapel Road, London, and became one of the most remarkable evangelists of modern times. He published an autobiography in 1902, and several volumes of addresses.

Smith, Sir Ross Macpherson (1892–1922), Australian airman, born in Adelaide, who with his brother Keith was the first to fly from England to Australia in 1919. He was killed in an aeroplane accident.

Smith, Samuel (1802–92), British early documentary photographer, born at Tydd St Giles, Isle of Ely. From 1852 to 1864, using a variation of the CALOTYPE process, he made a detailed record of the changes taking place in his home town of Wisbech.

Bibliography: M. Millward and B. W. Coe, *Victorian Townscape, the Work of Samuel Smith*, 1974.

Smith, Samuel Francis (1808–95), US clergyman and poet, born in Boston. Educated at the Latin School, Boston, and Harvard, he studied for the ministry at Andover Theological Seminary. While there he was asked to provide verses for a song book, and wrote 'My Country, 'tis of Thee'. With the title 'America' it was adopted as the national hymn of the United States in 1832. Smith's *Poems of Home and Country* were published in 1895.

Smith, Sarah, see STRETTON, HESBA.

Smith, Sir Sidney, see SMITH, SIR WILLIAM SIDNEY.

Smith, Stevie, pseudonym of Florence Margaret Smith (1902–71), English poet, born at Hull; educated at Palmers Green High School and the North London Collegiate School. For many years she worked in a publishing house. Her poetry—*A Good Time Was Had By All*, 1937, *Not Waving But Drowning*, 1957, *The Best Beast*, 1969, and many other collections—tackles serious themes through a calculated scattiness and seemingly casual manner. Her *Collected Poems* appeared in 1976. Among her novels are *Novel on Yellow Paper*, 1936, and *The Holiday*, 1948; *Some Are More Human Than Others*, 1958, is a book of drawings.

Smith, Sydney (1771–1845), British cleric, author, and

wit, born at Woodford, Essex. He was educated at Winchester and New College, Oxford. He took holy orders in 1794, and later, while residing at Edinburgh, founded, with Jeffrey and Brougham, the *Edinburgh Review* in 1802. He came to London in 1803, and in the following year attracted attention by his lectures. He became a popular figure in society, and was a member of the Holland House set. In 1807 he wrote the *Plymley Letters* in favour of Catholic emancipation. He was rector of Foxton from 1806, and appointed a canon of St Paul's in 1831. He was one of the wittiest men of his day, and a sparkling conversationalist.

Bibliography: Memoir, with a selection from his correspondence, by his daughter, Lady Holland, 1855; Lives by S. J. Reid, 1884; G. Russell, 1905; O. Saint-Clair, 1913; H. Pearson, 1945.

Smith, Sydney Goodsir (1915–75), Scottish poet and critic, born in Wellington, New Zealand. Moving to Scotland, he was educated at Edinburgh and Oxford universities and became one of the leaders of the modern Scottish renaissance, showing strong medieval influence in his version of Lallans (see SCOTLAND, *Language*). His *Selected Poems* appeared in 1947, followed by *Under the Eildon Tree*, 1948, *So Late into the Night*, 1952, *Figs and Thistles*, 1959, and *Cokkils*, 1954. He also wrote *A Short Introduction to Scottish Literature*, 1951.

He is a lyric poet whose main themes are love, nationalism, and Edinburgh low life analysed with intense feeling. His play, *The Wallace*, had considerable success at the Edinburgh Festival, 1960.

Smith, Theobald (1859–1934), US pathologist, born at Albany, New York. He was educated at Cornell University, and appointed director of the pathological laboratory of the Bureau of Animal Industry, US Department of Agriculture. Here he specialised in the study of infectious diseases, particularly in farm animals. From 1915 until his death he was director of animal pathology at the Rockefeller Institute for Medical Research. He first differentiated bovine from human tuberculosis.

Smith, W. H., & Son Ltd, British firm of wholesale and retail newsagents, booksellers, and stationers. The business was begun about 1792 by Henry Walton Smith and his wife Anna. Their younger son, William Henry, by his enterprise in dispatching the London newspapers to the country on the morning coaches instead of on the night mail-coaches, became the pioneer of rapid newspaper distribution. He built up a great wholesale newspaper trade, and was among the first to use the railways to further his business. His son, also William Henry, statesman and philanthropist, established the firm's bookstalls, advertising agency, and circulating library. In 1905, when two railway contracts had to be relinquished, his son, later the 2nd Viscount Hambleden, opened 173 shops to replace the lost bookstalls, and extended their trade into stationery, printing, and book-binding. By 1939 there were 1500 retail branches. The firm became a private limited company in 1929, with the 3rd Viscount Hambleden as governing director, and a public limited company in 1949, with his brother, the Hon. David Smith, as chairman.

Later years saw great diversification, modernisation, and reorganisation. A Canadian subsidiary, founded in 1949, has 30 branches stretching from coast to coast. In England and Wales, retail outlets have been concentrated in 300 shops and 65 main bookstalls; there are also 130 wholesale houses. The headquarters, Strand House, moved from Portugal Street to New Fetter Lane in 1976, the distribution of newspapers and magazines hitherto associated with it having been decentralised within London. The main warehouse for other supplies moved from London to Swindon in 1967.

Smith, William (1769–1839), often called 'the father of English geology'. He was a civil engineer, but during his extensive travels surveying the routes to be used for canals he recognised the use of fossils in the correlation and ordering of strata. The information gathered on his travels was utilised in his classic geological map of the British Isles, published in 1815. His achievements are remarkable in that they were products solely of his own genius, since he received neither finance nor encouragement in their execution.

Smith, William Henry (1825–91), British politician and newsagent, born in London. He developed his father's newspaper agency into the prosperous business it is today, opening the firm's first railway bookstall at Euston in 1848. He entered Parliament in 1868, and nine years later became first lord of the Admiralty under Disraeli. When Salisbury became prime minister Smith was appointed first lord of the Treasury and leader of the House of Commons. *Punch* bestowed upon him the nickname 'Old Morality'.

Bibliography: Viscount Chilston, *W. H. Smith*, 1965.

Smith, Sir William Sidney, commonly known as Sir Sidney Smith (1764–1840), British admiral, born in London; entered the navy in 1777, and was present at the action off Cape St Vincent in 1780 and Dominica in 1782. His most famous exploit was the defence of St Jean d'Acre in 1799.

Smithfield, situated a short distance north-west of St Paul's Cathedral, London, was originally a tournament ground and cattle market outside the city wall, and from 1868 has been the site of the principal London meat market. It has also been a fairground (see BARTHOLOMEW FAIR), a place of trial, and a place of martyrdom, mostly of Protestants under Mary I.

Smithson, name of two British architects, Alison (1928–) and Peter (1923–), husband and wife. The term 'new brutalism' stems from them and epitomises their intention to present the structure and materials of their buildings without concealment by decoration. Hunstanton School, Norfolk (1954), is the first example. Other buildings are the Economist Building in London (1964), Robin Hood Gardens, Tower Hamlets (1970), and the Garden Building at St Hilda's College, Oxford (1970).

Smithson, James Macie (1765–1829), British founder of the SMITHSONIAN INSTITUTION in Washington DC, USA. Born in France, he devoted his life to scientific work, mainly chemistry and mineralogy. He was admitted a fellow of the Royal Society in 1787. As a mineralogist he identified a new ore known as smithsonite. Smithson's will written in 1826 left the bulk of his estate to his nephew and any heirs he might have, but provided that if his nephew died childless, the money should go to the United States to found an institution bearing the Smithson name.

His nephew died in 1835 without children and Smithson's money—105 bags containing some 100,000 gold sovereigns, a great fortune in those days—was brought to America in 1838. The Smithsonian Institution on the Mall in Washington DC was established in 1846.

Smithson died in Genoa, Italy, but in 1904 his remains were escorted from Italy by Alexander Graham Bell, inventor of the telephone and a Regent of the Institution, and were ceremonially reinterred in a specially built room in the original Smithsonian building, where they have been viewed by millions of visitors to Washington.

Bibliography: L. Carmichael and J. C. Long, *James Smithson and the Smithsonian Story*, 1965; M. G. Grosvenor, 'How James Smithson came to rest in the institution he never knew', in *Smithsonian* magazine, January 1976.

Smithsonian Institution, Washington DC, USA, owes its origin to the generosity of an Englishman, James M. SMITHSON, who in 1826 bequeathed £100,000 to the US government to found an institution for 'the increase and diffusion of knowledge among men'. The Institution was formally organised in 1846 and the first building completed in 1855. From time to time various funds have been added to the original bequest. The US Congress has vested responsibility for administering the Institution in the Smithsonian Board of Regents, composed of the Chief Justice, the Vice President, three members of the Senate, three members of the House of Representatives, and nine citizen members. The Secretary (S. Dillon Ripley has held this position since 1964) is the executive officer and director of the Institution's activities.

Throughout its history, the Institution has carried on important scientific investigations and has conducted explorations in all parts of the world. It has administered the national collections and performed other educational public service functions. Some 4000 employees, including a staff of more than 500 professional scholars and scientists, work for the Institution. The Smithsonian operates three major history and science museums (the National Museum of Natural History, the National Museum of History and Technology, and the National Air and Space Museum); and six art museums (the Freer Gallery of Art, the National Collection of Fine Arts, the National Portrait Gallery, the Renwick Gallery, the Hirshhorn Museum and Sculpture Garden, and the Cooper-Hewitt Museum of Decorative Arts and Design). All are located in Washington DC except the Cooper-Hewitt in New York City.

Technically part of the Smithsonian but with their own autonomous boards of trustees are the National Gallery of Art, the John F. Kennedy Center for the Performing Arts, and the Woodrow Wilson International Center for Scholars, all in Washington. The Anacostia Neighbourhood Museum in south-east Washington is operated in cooperation with the local community.

Besides museums, major Smithsonian components include the National Zoological Park in Washington, a Radiation Biology Laboratory in Maryland, where the effects of solar radiation are studied, an Oceanographic Sorting Center in Washington, the Belmont Conference Center in Maryland, the Chesapeake Bay Center for Environmental Studies in Maryland, the Smithsonian Astrophysical Observatory in Massachusetts, and a Tropical Research Institute in Panama.

The Smithsonian also carries on a wide range of programmes in co-operation with other institutions, universities, and government agencies on every continent, and offers its scientific facilities and intellectual resources for research from elementary to postgraduate level. It circulates research publications throughout the world, and is engaged in varying aspects of publication, distribution, exchange, and information-retrieval services. Its communication activities include radio, television, and motion-picture programmes. The Smithsonian Associates has more than 1 million national members throughout the US who receive the monthly illustrated magazine, *Smithsonian*, founded in 1970.

Smock Mills, see WINDMILL.

Smoke, see AIR POLLUTION.

Smoke Detectors. These devices are in general confined to places where the presence of smoke and visible vapours is unusual, e.g., ships' holds or aircraft. Three systems are in general use: (1) a system where a suction fan is used to draw air from the protected spaces to a centrally placed observation cabinet where a hidden light beam reveals the presence of smoke; (2) a system in which a beam of light (or infrared ray) is directed across the protected space to fall on a detector unit which utilises the photoelectric cell as a means of completing an electrical circuit to sound an alarm; and (3) a system which is governed by the effect of smoke upon the electrical conductivity of the atmosphere.

Smoke Weapons. The tactical use of smoke, both defensively to conceal the movement and disposition of troops and offensively to blind the enemy, is a practice of great antiquity. It is probable that the Byzantine *syphonistai* used chemical smoke, as well as incendiary arms. In medieval times large siege engines were employed to shoot 'carcasses' or bundles of rags and tow impregnated with pitch and sulphur to form a dense smoke.

Tanks carry one or more smoke mortars fixed outside the turret which project a small smoke bomb for a maximum range of 90 m on a fixed trajectory. This weapon can only be roughly aimed by alignment of the tank itself. Special smoke-generating ammunition can be fired from most types of modern field artillery, both for effect and to facilitate spotting by the observer. Mortars can fire similar ammunition. The greatest exponents of the offensive use of smoke in the Second World War were the Germans, and many weapons subsequently used to fire high explosive were originally designed to fire smoke or gas projectiles. They were served by a special arm of the service called *Nebeltruppen*, and the best known of such weapons was the *Nebelwerfer*, a multi-barrelled rocket weapon. The primary use of defensive smoke is to cloak preparations for an attack. It was so used by the Allies just before and in the final Battle of Cassino. A permanent smoke screen was later maintained across the upper part of the Apennine-Reno valley to deny to the enemy observation of an otherwise untenable position. Allied preparations for the crossing of the lower Rhine in the spring of 1945 were similarly covered by the extensive use of smoke. Aircraft were also used to lay smoke screens to cover military operations.

In the navy, smoke is used as a defence weapon and is of particular value in enabling ships to break off in action with superior forces, and for protecting convoys and damaged ships from attack. Such smoke is normally generated through the funnels by the incomplete combustion of oil fuel. During the second Battle of Sirte (22 March 1942) in the Mediterranean, Admiral Vian used smoke to prevent a greatly superior Italian force from sighting the convoy it was trying to attack, and to cover his ships while withdrawing after delivering torpedo attacks on the enemy.

Smoke floats, dropped over the side, were first used during the First World War, and were planned to provide cover for the blockships entering Zeebrugge on St George's Day, 1918; but on this occasion the wind changed at the wrong moment and the smoke did not provide all the protection required. Smoke floats were supplied to certain independently routed ships in the Second World War to enable them to escape when attacked by submarines or surface ships. Smoke-shells, fired from guns, are now used in the navy only to provide targets for anti-aircraft practice. See also CHEMICAL WARFARE.

Smokeless Powder is a propellent explosive which replaced blackpowder (i.e., gunpowder) and which did not emit the smoke and flash of early gunpowders. The basic ingredients of all smokeless powders are nitrocellulose with either nitroglycerine or dinitroglycerol, and a number of additives. BALLISTITE and CORDITE are examples of such products developed by NOBEL (1888), and Abel and Dewar (1889). In manufacture a paste is made of the components which is rolled into sheets, dried, and the gelatinised product cut into granules. Alternatively, the paste may be extruded into filaments, dried, and cut into short lengths or granules. These products are finished off to a great variety of small arms or sporting powders. See EXPLOSIVES.

Smoking. For some time it has been known that the inhalation of CIGARETTE smoke causes cessation of ciliary action in the respiratory tract. This results in an increased number of dust particles, together with tar from the cigarette, entering the bronchioles. These particles are not swept upwards towards the trachea to be got rid of by swallowing but accumulate, eventually causing irritation leading to the familiar unproductive smokers' cough.

TOBACCO smoke also causes acute constriction of the large airways, but it seems to have very little effect on the size or function of the small airways.

A new smoking material undergoing tests in 1975 showed that a 70 per cent mixture of tobacco to 30 per cent new smoking material also showed these effects, although a 100 per cent new smoking material did not produce such changes. The mixture, however, yielded a similar concentration of carbon monoxide in the smoke as did a conventional cigarette. Cigarettes containing this material were first marketed in Britain in 1977. Carbon monoxide attacks the HAEMOGLOBIN of the red blood cell, forming carboxyhaemoglobin which prevents oxygen uptake. Even when inhalation of neat smoke is stopped, it is about 112 days before the damaged red cells are replaced by fresh red cells from the bone marrow.

Carcinoma of the lung arises in the bronchus, and heavy smokers have been shown to have a death rate from carcinoma of the lung 30 times that of non-smokers.

Causes of carcinoma of other tissues or parts of the body are not so clear cut, see CANCER.

It is not the nicotine content of the cigarette that is carcinogenic, this merely causes the craving for another cigarette, but the tar content which is inhaled, that causes the problem; thus CIGAR and pipe smokers do not suffer to the same extent, although they are more liable to carcinoma of the mouth and lips.

It is now believed that some people are more susceptible to cancer of the lung because they do not synthesise a sufficient quantity of an enzyme that renders this inhaled tar harmless before it has chance to stimulate the cells to divide abnormally.

Smoky Mountains, see APPALACHIAN MOUNTAINS.

Smolensk, *oblast* in the RSFSR, USSR, west of Moscow, situated on the Smolensk-Moscow uplands, which are largely composed of morainic material, fairly well dissected, and rise to over 300 m. The climate is continental, although not extreme. Mixed forests cover 30 per cent of the area and there are peat and lignite (MOSCOW COAL BASIN) deposits. The area is predominantly agricultural with flax growing, dairy-farming, food (mainly dairy products), and textile industries, and large-scale peat extraction. It belonged to the medieval Kievan state, became an independent principality in 1127, Lithuanian in 1404, and Muscovite in 1514. The major urban centres are Smolensk (see below), Roslavl, and Vyazma. Area 49,800 km². Population (1975) 1,087,000 (48 per cent urban).

Smolensk, capital city, economic and cultural centre of Smolensk *oblast* (see above), USSR, on the DNIEPER. It has textile, food, instrument-making, and metal-working industries, and is an important transportation centre. There are many outstanding churches and other architectural monuments of the 12th–19th centuries. Known since the 9th century, it was the capital of the Krivichi tribe and of Smolensk principality; it was Lithuanian, 1404–1514, then Muscovy's key western fortress, and an important commercial and administrative centre. It was the scene of bitter fighting in 1812 and 1941, and was largely destroyed, 1941–43. Population (1974) 242,000.

Smollett, Tobias George (1721–71), Scottish novelist, born at Dalquhurn, Dumbartonshire. He was educated at Dumbarton Grammar School and Glasgow University. He was for a short time a ship's doctor, but after 1743 he settled as a surgeon in London, where he had gone in 1739 hoping to have his tragedy, *The Regicide*, staged. Disappointed, he went to serve as a surgeon's mate, and, on returning from the Cartagena expedition of 1741, devoted himself to literature.

In 1748 he published his first novel, *Roderick Random*, partly autobiographical, which stirred public concern about medical conditions in the navy, and then in quick succession came *The History of an Atom*, 1749, a skit on British politics, *Peregrine Pickle*, 1751, with vivid pictures of low life abroad, and *Ferdinand, Count Fathom*, 1753. *Sir Launcelot Greaves* appeared in 1762 and *Humphrey Clinker*, the most genial of his novels, about a Welsh family's tour of Scotland, in 1771. Among his other works were a *History of England*, 1757, in continuation of HUME's, an *Ode to Independence* (published posthumously, 1773), a translation of VOLTAIRE, and *Travels through France and Italy*, 1766.

Tobias Smollett. *(National Portrait Gallery, London)*

Smollett is one of the leading figures among the novelists of the 18th century. Himself inspired by LESAGE, his influence on his successors has been very great, especially on SCOTT, Herman MELVILLE, and DICKENS. His work was uneven in quality, but he had genuine, rather broad humour, an excellent breezy style, unquenchable high spirits, and a great gift for characterisation, particularly for caricature which is both violent and grotesque. As a novelist in the picaresque manner (see PICARESQUE NOVEL), he set a constantly recurring fashion, while for buoyancy and in depicting the odd in life he is not inferior to Dickens. His sea stories, if highly melodramatic, are full of life and endless invention. Frequently involved in bitter controversy, extremely egoistical, and often recklessly malicious, he was, on one occasion, imprisoned for libel, an event which embittered him for the rest of his life. His *Letters* were edited by E. S. Noyes in 1926.

Bibliography: G. Saintsbury (Ed.), *Complete Works* (12 vols), 1928; L. M. Knapp, *Tobias Smollett: Doctor of Men and Manners*, 1949; R. Giddings, *The Tradition of Smollett*, 1967; R. Paulson, *Satire and the Novel in Eighteenth-century England*, 1968; G. S. Rousseau and P. G. Bouce (Eds), *Tobias Smollett: Bicentennial Essays*, 1972.

Smolt, see SALMON.

Smoo, Cave of, double-chambered cave (the second cavern is always under water) in the cliffs to the east of Durness village on the north coast of Highland Region, Scotland.

Smooth-coated Collie, see COLLIE.

Smooth-haired Dachshund, see DACHSHUND.

Smooth-haired Fox-terrier, see FOX-TERRIER.

Smooth Snake, *Coronella austriaca*, a common SNAKE in southern and central Europe and, in Britain, found principally in Dorset and Hampshire. It grows to a length of 60 cm, and it is brownish-red or grey in colour, with dark-brown spots along its back. It is ovoviviparous, producing live young. It is not venomous.

Smuggling includes offences of importing or exporting either goods on which duty and tax have not been paid or goods liable to prohibition. The Customs and Excise Act 1952 provides penalties for the evasion of duties or prohibitions and for the making of false declarations in connection therewith. The Finance Act 1968 also provides penalties for the non-declaration of goods in excess of statutory personal allowances. These enactments provide for the forfeiture of goods not declared or improperly declared, and for the forfeiture of vessels, vehicles, or containers used in their conveyance. Other provisions are made for the control and prevention of smuggling. On average, some 10,000 seizures of smuggled goods are made annually in Britain and some £300,000 is collected in court fines and compounded penalties. See also BOOTLEG-GING; PROHIBITION.

Smut, a plant disease caused by a fungus of the order Ustilaginales. When the spores remain for a time within the sorus, the disease is known as covered smut; that of barley being caused by *Ustilago hordei*; of oats by *U. kolleri*. Stinking smut or bunt of wheat is caused by *Tilletia foetida* and *T. caries*. Loose smut describes an infection when the spores are in an uncovered powder mass, freed by wind and rain; that of barley is caused by *U. nuda*; of oats by *U. avenae*; of wheat by *U. tritici*. A striped smut of rye is caused by *Urocystis occulta*, and of grasses by *Ustilago striaeformis*. See also PLANT DIS-EASES; RUST FUNGI.

Smuts, Jan Christian (1870–1950), South African soldier and statesman; born in Bovenplaats, Riebeek West, Cape Colony. In 1886 Smuts entered Victoria College, Stellenbosch. Having graduated at the Cape University, he went to England in 1891 as Ebden scholar. At Cambridge he took a double first in the law tripos in 1892, and graduated LLB from Christ's College in 1894. In 1895 he began practice at the Cape Town Bar. The Jameson Raid of 1895 made him a Republican; he was admitted to the Bar of the Transvaal the same year, and began practice at Johannesburg. In 1898 he became state attorney under President KRUGER. In 1899 he published a statement of the Boer case against the British, entitled *A Century of Wrong*. In 1901 he was given supreme command of the Boer forces in Cape Colony, and proved a daring and able commando leader. Under British rule he became col-

Jan Christian Smuts. *(Popperfoto)*

onial secretary of the Transvaal in 1907. With Botha, Smuts worked untiringly to restore prosperity to the Transvaal, and following the formation of the Union of South Africa in 1910, to promote good feeling and solidarity between the various white groups within the Union. He was minister of the interior and minister of mines for South Africa, 1910–12; minister of defence, 1910–20; minister of finance, 1912–13. He commanded the troops in British East Africa, 1917–18. Throughout the First World War Smuts was instrumental in quelling the pro-German separatist groups within the Union, and continued to work for Anglo-Boer co-operation. Following BOTHA he became prime minister and minister for native affairs, Union of South Africa, in 1919, and he and Botha were plenipotentiaries at the peace conference in Paris. His government lasted until 1924, when he was heavily defeated by a combination of Nationalists and Labour.

Smuts now had time to set down his own philosophy in *Holism and Evolution*, 1926. Holism was the name he gave to his doctrine that an organism is more than its parts by an ineffable essence of its whole, and that the emergence of new and larger wholes constitutes a real progress in the universe. In 1929 Smuts gave the Rhodes memorial lectures at Oxford, published the following year as *Africa and Some World Problems*. He became a Fellow of the Royal Society in 1930.

In 1933 HERTZOG formed a coalition government, with Smuts as deputy prime minister. Some Nationalists, under MALAN, seceded, forming an extreme Afrikaner opposition. In 1934 the coalition was strengthened when Smuts's moderate Nationalist, pro-empire South African party merged with Hertzog's, the United South African National party being the result. On the outbreak of the Second World War Smuts advocated the co-operation of South Africa with the Allies, while Hertzog and Malan urged neutrality. In the debate which ensued Smuts prevailed with a vote of 80 against 67. Hertzog resigned, and Smuts formed a War Cabinet (5 September). At the election in July 1943, when the main issue was inevitably South Africa's continued participation in the war, Smuts achieved his greatest triumph, having a clear majority of 67 in the House, and a popular vote more than double that of all his opponents combined. Smuts had become supreme commander of the Union defence forces in 1940: he was made a field-marshal in 1941, being the first dominion soldier to hold this rank. Smuts helped to draft the UN charter in 1945, and in 1946 was the leader of the South African delegation to the UN Assembly in New York. He received the Order of Merit from King George VI during the royal visit to South Africa in 1947. But in the general election in 1948 Smuts was defeated by 79 to 75, Malan gaining his victory on domestic issues. Smuts became the leader of an Anglo-Afrikaner opposition once again, protesting vehemently against the government's racial policy of segregation. He was elected chancellor of Cambridge University in 1948. In June 1950 Smuts resigned the leadership of the United party, and died soon afterwards.

Bibliography: F. S. Crafford, *Jan Smuts: A Biography*, 1943; J. C. Smuts, *Jan Christian Smuts: A Biography*, 1952; W. C. Hancock, *Smuts Vol I: The Sanguine Years*, 1962; *Smuts Vol II: The Fields of Force*, 1968.

Smyrna, see İZMIR.

Smyrnaeus, see QUINTUS SMYRNAEUS.

Smyslov, Vasily (1921–), Soviet world chess champion 1957–58; born in Moscow, he became an international grandmaster in 1941 at which time he was the youngest holder of this title in the world. First attempt at the world title resulted in a draw with BOTVINNIK in 1954, but in 1957 he beat his old rival to become world champion.

Smyth, Charles Piazzi (1819–1900), British astronomer, born at Naples, and educated at Bedford where his father, Admiral Smyth, had retired and had a private observatory. In 1835 Piazzi Smyth joined Maclear at the Cape of Good Hope and served as his chief assistant till his appointment as astronomer royal for Scotland in 1845, a post he held until his retirement in 1888. At the Cape, Smyth was for the first three years in close contact with Sir John Herschel and later took a leading part in resurveying Lacaille's arc of the meridian, a job which involved observations from the tops of several high mountains. In Edinburgh he was a pioneer in spectroscopy and photography; he also went on various expeditions, including one in 1856 to Tenerife to demonstrate the advantages of observing from a high mountain. He made a detailed survey of the Great Pyramid of Gizeh but his accounts of this work are so interspersed with mystical speculations that his scientific reputation suffered.

Smyth, Dame Ethel (1858–1944), British composer, born in London. She studied in Leipzig, first at the Conservatory, and then privately with Herzogenberg. She had some works performed there, and after her return to England one or two appeared in London, including the Mass in D major, in 1893. Her earlier operas were produced in Germany. She lived much abroad, but in 1910 received the Hon Mus D degree from Durham University, and about that time joined actively in the movement for women's suffrage. In her later years she suffered from deafness and, regarding herself as neglected on account of her sex, composed less and less, but wrote a number of brilliant autobiographical books. She received the DBE in 1922, and an honorary degree at Oxford in 1926. Her works include the operas *Fantasio* (after Musset), 1898, *The Forest*, 1901, *The Wreckers*, 1906, *The Boatswain's Mate* (after W. W. Jacobs), 1916, *Fête galante*, 1923, *Entente cordiale*, 1925, *The Prison*, for solo voices, chorus and orchestra, the Mass in D major, choral and chamber music, etc. Her publications include *Impressions that Remained*, 1919, *Streaks of Life*, 1921, *As Time Went On*, 1936, *What Happened Next*, 1940.

Bibliography: C. St John, *Ethel Smyth: a Biography*, 1959.

Snaefell, the highest point on the Isle of Man (see MAN, ISLE OF), 9 km south-west of Ramsey. The mountains are composed mainly of slate rocks comparable to those of the English LAKE DISTRICT. Height 620 m.

Snail, air-breathing shelled molluscs of class GASTROPODA forming a great number of species, some of which themselves include many varieties. With the SLUGS they are divided into two groups. One of these is characterised by a single pair of non-retractile tentacles, with the eyes at the base; a familiar example is the British pond snail (*Limnaea stagnalis*). The members of the other group have two pairs of retractile tentacles, with the eyes at the summit of the upper pair. Snails are almost exclusively vegetable feeders, and are provided with cutting upper jaws and a rasping ribbon or radula in the mouth. Sea, land and water snails are found in all parts of the world, some land snails living at great altitudes. The sexes may be distinct, but snails are often hermaphrodite, cross fertilisation still being necessary. Many possess a structure not found in other molluscs: it is a beautiful crystalline body (Cupid's dart), which is ejected during copulation from a sac specially constructed for the purpose. Each snail shoots its dart at the other and each receives sperm from the other. *Achatina eulica* is the largest snail, being 15–22 cm from head to tail. It has been found recently in America, but originates from Africa; it was introduced to California in equipment salvaged from the Pacific area during the Second World War. The Roman snail (*Helix pomatia*) is also large and occurs on chalk downs in Britain. It is a favourite table delicacy in France. The garden snail (*H. aspersa*) is common in Britain. The garlic snail (*Vitica alliaria*) emits a peculiar odour when disturbed.

Snails are well equipped with varied sense organs, especially those of balance and smell. Many snails hibernate in the winter, in the ground or beneath leaves, and secrete a mucous plug to seal the aperture.

Bibliography: A. E. Ellis, *British Snails*, 2nd ed. 1969.

Snake, formerly Lewis, river of the USA, and biggest tributary (1670 km long) of the COLUMBIA river. It rises as the South Fork in a lake 2375 m high in the YELLOWSTONE NATIONAL PARK, Wyoming, and flows south-west through Idaho and then north to form the boundary between Idaho and Oregon and between Idaho and Washington. Navigation is hindered by rapids and falls, of which the chief are the Shoshone Falls (60 m). The river valley in Idaho receives irrigation from the river, and there are hydro-electricity plants. Elsewhere the river runs in canyons, of which the longest and deepest is Hell's Canyon (maximum depth 2400 m). The canyon and lower sections of the river's course have been extensively dammed, and have been a political battleground between public and private power development interests.

Snake, the suborder Serpentes or Ophidia of order Squamata of class REPTILIA. All have a long and vermiform body, and most are covered with scales. They

Snake. *Opheodrys aestivus*, rough grass snake. (*Topham/Coleman*)

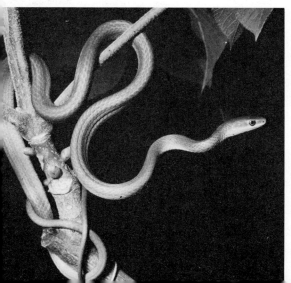

differ from the lizards, the other suborder of order Squamata, in their lack of a shoulder girdle, movable eyelids, covering of the tympanum (eardrum) and bladder. Traces of limbs are present in the boas and pythons, while, on the other hand, many lizards, notably the blind-worm, are without limbs. A marked characteristic of snakes is the distensible jaw, which enables the prey to be swallowed whole. Many snakes possess fangs (modified teeth) in the upper jaw, having grooves for the venom which runs from modified salivary glands where it is produced; the forked tongue is harmless. A popular classification is that of poisonous or non-poisonous; however, of the important families, the Boidae include only non-poisonous snakes while the Viperidae are all poisonous, but the Colubridae, to which more than three-quarters of all snakes belong, contain both poisonous and non-poisonous forms. No external characteristics are known by which it is possible to distinguish at a glance those that are, and those that are not, venomous. With few exceptions all snakes are covered with scales, which are skin folds, and the whole skin is frequently shed; on the heads of some are plates similar to those of lizards. A snake's skeleton is composed of a great number of vertebrae and ribs; locomotion is effected partly by the passage of a lateral wave away from the head, and partly by the action of large scales on the under-surface of the body, each being attached to a pair of movable ribs. The gripping action and slight movement of the scales help locomotion. Most snakes are oviparous (lay eggs), but some, including the viper (adder), bring forth their young alive (viviparous). The hypnotic power of snakes' eyes is universally credited, but careful observation in captivity suggests that the power is exaggerated. Snakes are of comparatively recent geological age, and are most numerous in the tropical countries. Some are only a few centimetres in length, while the anaconda is reputed to exceed 9 m. In Britain there are three species only: the grass snake, the viper, and the rare smooth snake. The majority of snakes are terrestrial, but there are also many species of amphibious water snakes (e.g. genus *Natrix* of family Colubridae, non-venomous, all continents except South America) and of SEA SNAKES.

Bibliography: J. Stidworthy, *Snakes of the World*, 1969; L. G. Appleby, *British Snakes*, 1971.

Snake-bird, or darter, water birds of genus *Anhinga*, related to the cormorant and pelican, forming the family Anhingidae, in the order Pelecaniformes. They swim in lakes, rivers or seas with only the head on the long neck showing above water, moving sinuously, then darting forward to seize a fish, the neck vertebrae being specially adapted for flexibility. The snake-birds are widely distributed throughout Central and South America, southern Asia and Australia, and vary little in colour. *A. anhinga*, the American snake-bird, inhabits tropical regions; its general colour is greenish-black, the tail is tipped with brown, the wings marked with silvery-grey, and the feathers are small and soft. It is about 90 cm high. It nests in a tree, and lays four chalky-white eggs.

Snake-bite. Snake venom is very toxic saliva containing a mixture of poisonous proteins; the bite of venomous snakes varies considerably in its effects due to the amount and potency of the particular venom, the condition of the snake (if it has recently bitten, less poison will be injected), and the health of the person bitten. In general, viper venoms cause local swelling and pain and possibly haemorrhagic shock, whereas the venoms of elapids (cobras, mambas, kraits and the Australian taipan snake) cause paralysis of the muscles concerned with seeing, breathing and swallowing. Venomous snakes have two types of bite; one to paralyse the prey, in which case a large amount is injected and the prey rapidly dies; and the other to act as a defence in order for the snake to escape, only a small amount of venom being then injected. Fortunately, the second type of bite is generally used against humans, and the majority of victims have minimal poisoning. For treatment, reassurance is of prime importance since fright will exaggerate the effects of the poison and a *placebo* drug is often effective (alcohol or aspirin can also be given). The bite should be washed, and only if a large amount of venom has been injected and hospital treatment cannot be obtained within 30 minutes should a firm (but not tight) tourniquet be applied just above the bite (shoelaces, cloth or grass can be used). Immobilisation of the affected part is generally recommended, since movement tends to disseminate the poison more quickly through the body. The patient should be taken to hospital, and if the snake has been killed it should also be taken so that it can be identified. Anti-venom is available for some snakes, but should only be used by doctors in emergencies and must never be given for the bite of a different snake. In Britain the only naturally occurring venomous snake is the adder *Vipera berus*, but the bite is rarely fatal.

Snake-charming. This has been practised in Egypt and throughout the East from the earliest times. It is still common in Egypt and in India, where the cobra is generally used. Snake-charming is usually an hereditary calling, and the success of the handler in making the snake perform rhythmic movements seems to depend upon a knowledge of the nature and peculiarities of the reptile. The fangs are usually first removed.

Snake-Eyes, game with dice, in which players in turn cast two dice from a cup. A player scores the total pips cast, and may elect to throw again as many times as he likes, adding to his score with each additional throw. But if he throws a '1' spot with either die he forfeits his score for the 'round', and if at any time he throws 'snake-eyes' (1-1) he loses his accumulated score during the whole of the game (just as at bar-billiards, the whole score is lost if the black skittle is knocked down). The winner of the kitty is the first player to reach 101 points. See also CRAPS; DICE.

Snake Fly, any member of the insect family Raphidiidae, in suborder Megaloptera of order NEUROPTERA, but now commonly treated as comprising a distinct insect order, Raphidioptera. Members of this family are very specialised, entirely land-dwelling, and are generally included within two genera: *Raphidia* and *Inocellia*. The adult insects have an unusually long prothorax (region immediately behind the head) which forms a kind of 'neck' and the entire body is elongate, ending in a drawn out slender egg-laying apparatus (ovipositor), hence the name 'snake flies'. More than 80 species are known, of which four, in the genera *Agulla* and *Raphidia*, have been found in Britain.

Snake flies are found in wooded regions, among flowers or tree-trunks. The female inserts the eggs, with its long ovipositor, into slits in the bark, especially of conifers. The larva forages under the loose bark, preying on soft-bodied insects.

Snake Indians, see SHOSHONE.

Snake Worship, or ophiolatry, is a feature of many primitive cultures. The reptile is sometimes worshipped as the shrine of a deity, e.g. the rattlesnake in the Natchez temple of the sun, the snake associated with Aesculapius and that associated with Quetzacoatl. The serpent is a symbol of craft and cunning, as in the case of the serpent of Eden, the Apophis serpent of the Egyptians and the awesome Azhi Dahâka of the Zoroastrians. The Sanskrit *nâga*, snake, signifies also snake worshippers, descended from a reptile deity, thus linking snake worship with TOTEMISM. Snakes are often associated with Earth deities as seems to have been the case in Minoan Crete. In Africa the Zulus, accepting the change of skin as an emblem of immortality, believe, like the Maravi, that the spirits of the dead transmigrate into serpents.

Bibliography: J. P. Vogel, *Indian Serpent Lore*, 1926; W. D. Hambly, *Serpent-worship in Africa*, 1931; J. J. Williams, *Voodoos and obeas*, 1933; L. Cottrell, *The Bull of Minos*, 1955.

Snakes and Ladders, popular board game where players throw dice to enable their men to travel a journey of 100 squares to finish. At various points men alighting on a square containing the foot of a ladder can climb to the top. At other points the mouth of a snake requires the man to descend to the square occupied by the snake's tail.

Snakesbeard, *Ophiopogon*, a genus of 20 perennials in family Liliaceae, with long narrow variegated leaves and racemes of white or lilac flowers. *O. jaburan*, Japan, and *O. intermedius*, China, are nearly hardy. *O. japonicus* has edible starchy rhizomes (underground stems).

Snakewood, see CECROPIA.

Snapdragon, see ANTIRRHINUM.

Snapper, several fishes in the family Lutjanidae of order Perciformes in the bony, ray-finned fish class Actinopterygii. They are tropical, carnivorous fishes, about 60 cm or more long. Many are red, but the species come in many colours. They are valuable edible fishes, especially one of the red species, *Lutjanus blackfordi*, the red snapper.

Sneek, town in the province of Friesland, Netherlands, 21 km south-west of Leeuwarden. It is a butter and cheese market and has tobacco manufactures. Large regattas are held each summer on the Sneekermeer to the east of the town. Population 27,700.

Sneem, village in County KERRY, Republic of Ireland, 26 km west of KENMARE, a beauty spot and centre for artists. Michael Walsh ('Father O'Flynn', 1828–66) is buried here. Sub-tropical Parknasilla is 3 km to the south. Population 283.

Sneezewort, *Achillea ptarmica*, a perennial herb of the Compositae (daisy family), found in Britain, elsewhere in Europe, in Asia Minor and Siberia. The plant has a strong pungent odour. Its root-stock is long and creeping, and when reduced to a dry powder may be used as a substitute for snuff. See ACHILLEA.

Sneezing, violent expiration of air from the nose and mouth. It is caused by irritation of the nerve endings of the mucous membrane, either by nasal catarrh or by foreign substances, as in taking snuff. It is an involuntary reflex respiratory act, the stimulus being carried by the trigeminal nerve to the medulla, where it induces a reflex action. A quick inspiration occurs, followed by a violent expiration in which most of the air is driven through the nose. Sneezing may also be induced by a bright light. Paroxysmal sneezing occurs in HAY FEVER.

Sneferu, see EGYPT, *History*.

Snell, Hannah (1723–92), British female soldier, born at Worcester. In 1745 she enlisted in the army of Carlisle, but later deserted and joined the marines as 'James Gray'. She served in the East Indies, and was wounded at Pondicherry, but her sex was not discovered. Her adventures were published in 1750.

Snellius, Willebrord, or Snell (1591–1626), Dutch physicist, astronomer and mathematician, born at Leiden; in 1613 he succeeded his father as professor of mathematics in the university of Leiden. In 1615 he attempted the measurement of the earth by triangulation, publishing the results in *Eratosthenes Batavus* ('The Batavian [i. e. Dutch] Eratosthenes', referring to the 2nd-century-BC Greek philosopher who measured the earth), 1617. Unfortunately, faulty instruments rendered the results inaccurate. He also discovered the law of the refraction of light in 1621 (see REFLECTION AND REFRACTION OF LIGHT).

Snellmann, Johan Vilhelm (1806–81), Finnish politician, philosopher, and writer, born in Stockholm. Snellmann was an ardent supporter of Finnish nationalism. He fought for the recognition of Finnish as a national language, and used his international reputation as a writer and thinker to publicise the nationalist aspirations of his countrymen.

Snell's Law, see REFLECTION AND REFRACTION OF LIGHT.

Snelus, George James (1837–1906), British metallurgist, born in London. He revolutionised steel manufacture by the purification of pig-iron in a basic lined Bessemer converter.

SNG, see SYNGAS.

Snipe, common name given to certain species of the family Scolopacidae, order Charadriiformes. They are closely related to the woodcocks. The birds inhabit marshes, which they probe with their long, straight bills for the worms, insects and molluscs on which they live. Their nests are made on the grass, and the eggs are four in number. The cry of the birds resembles the sound 'scape-scape', and during the breeding season they make a peculiar drumming or bleating noise in their downward flight. The species found in Britain are the common snipe, *Gallinago gallinago*, about 25 cm long and mottled black and brown; *Lymnocryptes minima*, the slightly smaller jack snipe, and *G. media*, the great or solitary snipe, which reaches 30 cm in length. *G. delicata*, Wilson's snipe, is the commonest American species. The snipe's flight is swift and darting, making it a difficult

target. Perhaps for this reason, especially good marksmen used to despatch enemy soldiers were called snipers.

Snipers, formerly called sharpshooters. Their regular use only became possible with the general adoption of the rifle. The skirmishers organised in fusilier or rifle regiments, whom it was customary to deploy in front of the infantry of the line after the Seven Years' War, were the ancestors of the modern snipers or 'tirailleurs', a title still borne by some French colonial regiments. Nowadays there are no specialised regiments of snipers, but the establishment of an infantry battalion in many armies provides for a section of snipers. Snipers customarily work in pairs of one marksman and one observer, both because sentinel observation wearies the eye of the marksman and because in order to obtain the greatest effect the target must be carefully selected. Sniping is an economical method in static warfare of maintaining an aggressive attitude without great expenditure of ammunition, and was so used by the Boers in South Africa and by both sides during the trench warfare of 1914–18.

Snitterfield, village in Warwickshire, England, 6 km north of STRATFORD-UPON-AVON, and early home of John Shakespeare, father of the poet.

Snodland, an industrial village in Tonbridge and Malling District of Kent, England, on the MEDWAY 10 km southwest of Rochester, with lime, cement, and paper works. Population (1971) 4320.

Snøhetta (Norway), see DOVREFJELL.

Snooker is played by two players, or four players in two partnerships, with 15 red and six coloured balls and the striking ball, white. One of the reds must be potted first, and this entitles the player to pot any coloured ball, which is returned to its specific spot on the table. Potted reds stay down, i.e. in the pocket(s). This procedure is followed, red and coloured alternately, until all reds are potted, leaving on the table only the coloured balls which are then potted in the following order, and with the scoring values shown: yellow (2), green (3), brown (4), blue (5), pink (6), black (7). The same values count for colours potted in the first part of the game, reds gaining one point each. The word 'snooker' applies to the act of 'laying a snooker', an integral feature of the game. A player is said to be snookered with regard to any ball when a direct stroke to the ball he wants to play at is obstructed by one he may not lawfully strike. An English amateur championship of snooker was inaugurated by the Billiards Association in 1916, a world professional championship by the Control Council in 1927, and a world amateur championship in 1963. Since 1970 the professional side of the game has been governed by the World Professional Billiards and Snooker Association. In 1973, the amateur governing body changed its name to the Billiards and Snooker Central Council.

Snooker originated at the Ooty Club, Ootacumund, in the Nilgiri Hills in Southern India in 1875 when Colonel Sir Neville Chamberlain devised a new game for the bored British officers under his command by welding together some of the elements of billiards, pyramids and pool. It is played on a table of similar size and markings to that of English BILLIARDS.

John Roberts, the best player and leading figure of the

day, brought the game back to England in 1885 and by 1887 it was also established in Australia where Frank Smith, Sen., who managed a billiard room in Sydney, did much to regularise the rules.

Frank Smith, Jun. made the first century break, 116, in Sydney, Australia, 1918 (though a century of 112 by George Hargest, an amateur, at Blackwood, Monmouthshire, was recorded in 1915).

Century breaks grew more frequent and E. J. (Murt) O'Donoghue, a New Zealander, made snooker's third century, 102, at Te Aroha in 1919 and achieved the maximum possible break of 147 (15 reds, 15 blacks and all the colours) at Griffiths, New South Wales, in 1934.

Some twenty players have since achieved maximums but the official 147 record for breaks made under championship conditions is jointly held by Joe DAVIS (1955) and Rex Williams (1965). In the 1920s, snooker began to become very popular with amateurs but it was not until the 1930s that the professionals acknowledged that its popularity might outstrip that of billiards and, as it has proved, by a ratio of almost 20 players to one.

Bibliography: J. Davis, *How I Play Snooker*, 1950, and *Advanced Snooker*, 1954; J. Pulman, *Tackle Snooker*, 1974; C. Everton, *Better Billiards and Snooker*, 1975; R. Williams, *Snooker: How to Become a Champion*, 1975; T. Lowe, *Snooker*, 1975; Periodical: *Snooker Scene* (monthly).

Snoring, an abnormal form of respiration that occurs during SLEEP. It is characterised by deep inspirations and a noise of low pitch caused by the vibration of the soft palate and uvula as the current of air passes. It is usually caused by the mouth falling open and may in that case be prevented by lying on the side. It may indicate a partial blockage of the nasal passage, e.g. by adenoids or catarrh, in which case medical treatment may prevent it.

Snorkel, see UNDERWATER SWIMMING.

Snorri Sturluson (1179–1241), Icelandic chieftain, poet, and historian. Snorri was descended from distinguished families on both sides and, from the age of three, was brought up by Iceland's greatest chieftain, Jón Loptsson. After making a rich marriage, he established himself at Reykholt, western Iceland. He was law-speaker of the ALTHING, 1215–18 and 1222–31, and travelled in Norway and Sweden, 1218–20. Though a peaceable man, Snorri became involved in the civil disturbances of his time and in 1237 was forced to flee to Norway to a patron, Earl Skúli. He returned to Iceland in 1239, against the wishes of King HAAKON of Norway, and was killed by Gissur Thorvaldsson in 1241 on Haakon's orders.

Two works can with certainty be ascribed to Snorri; *Snorra Edda* (Snorri's *Edda*) and *Heimskringla*. The former is a treatise in four parts on SKALDIC POETRY, the last part of which, *Háttatal*, was composed first. *Háttatal* (List of Metres) is, in effect, a poem in honour of Earl Skúli and King Haakon consisting of 102 stanzas composed in 100 different metres. The other parts are a prologue, *Gylfaginning*, a treatise of heathen mythology, and *Skáldskaparmál*, which deals with the diction of the skalds. *Heimskringla* (the name is of late origin) is Snorri's greatest work. It is a history of the Norwegian kings from the earliest times down to 1177. The middle section, the life of St OLAF, was written first and is a masterpiece of medieval prose. Snorri used a wide variety

of sources for *Heimskringla*, including much skaldic poetry, and although its basis is historical, it also contains much apocryphal matter. EGILS SAGA SKALLA-GRÍMSSONAR is thought by many to be Snorri's work.

The best edition of *Heimskringla* is by Bjarni Adalbjarnarson, 1951–53 and subsequent reprints. Among English translations is one by S. Laing, 1973.

Snotingaham, see NOTTINGHAM.

Snow, C(harles) P(ercy), Baron of Leicester (1905–), English novelist and scientist, born at Leicester. Educated at Alderman Newton's School and University College, Leicester, he studied physics at Cambridge and was a fellow of Christ's College, 1930–50. During the Second World War he was a government science expert, and in 1945 was appointed a civil service commissioner. During the 1960s, he was a junior cabinet minister. In 1950 he married the novelist Pamela Hansford JOHNSON. Knighted in 1957, he was made a life peer in 1964.

His first novel was a detective story, *Death under Sail*, 1932, followed by *The Search*, 1935. From 1935 to 1971 Snow was occupied in writing the 11-volume novel sequence, 'Strangers and Brothers', about the academic, public, and personal lives of Lewis Eliot, through which Snow analyses the effects and uses of power and bureaucracy in modern English society. Snow's particular domain has always been the world of science. His study, *The Two Cultures*, 1959, was a controversial attempt to argue that scientific and humanistic cultures have become separate and distinct. He has also published *The Two Cultures and a Second Look*, 1964; *Public Affairs*, 1971, a collection of essays; and *Trollope*, 1975, a literary biography.

Snow, John (1813–58), British anaesthetist and epidemiologist, born in York. After serving as an apprentice to a Newcastle upon Tyne surgeon, Snow studied at the Great Windmill Street School, London, and at the Westminster Hospital. He qualified in 1838 and was MD, 1844. He was the first specialist anaesthetist; before the introduction of chloroform he administered ether 152 times, but in the 11 years after 1847 he administered chloroform 4000 times. Queen Victoria received her first anaesthetic from Snow on 7 April 1853, at the birth of Prince Leopold. Snow wrote his distinguished book *On Ether*, in 1847, and his division of the stages of anaesthesia into five degrees was not improved upon for seventy years. His *On Chloroform and other Anaesthetics*, 1858, is a classic of anaesthesiology; it was reprinted in 1950. He invented a chloroform inhaler in 1848. Snow was also interested in public health; by statistical and other investigations he proved in 1849 that cholera was transmitted by water infected with faecal matter. His book *On the Mode of Communication of Cholera* first appeared in that year; its second edition, 1855 (reprinted 1936), is more important, and recorded that the outbreak in Broad Street (now Broadwick Street), Soho, was due to contamination by sewage of the pump there. The site of the pump is now occupied by a public-house, renamed 'The John Snow'.

Bibliography: B. M. Duncum, *Development of Inhalation Anaesthesia*, 1947; T. E. Keys, *History of Surgical Anaesthesia*, 1963.

Snow, see PRECIPITATION.

Snow-blindness. The glare from snow may cause acute conjunctivitis (inflammation of the lining of the eyelids) after long exposure. This condition is accompanied by acute pain and photophobia, and sometimes conjunctival haemorrhages. Those subject to it should wear dark glasses.

Snow-bunting, *Plectrophenax nivalis*, a bird species in the family Emberizidae, order Passeriformes, sometimes found in Britain, a winter visitor from northern Europe and Siberia. Its plumage in winter is white with the upperparts rusty-brown, in summer it is white and black. Breeding takes place in rocky and mountainous situations.

Snow-finch, or snow-bird, species of *Montifringilla*, birds in the family Fringillidae, order Passeriformes, distributed widely over the Ethiopian, Palaearctic and Oriental regions. The birds are about 15 cm in length and mainly white with grey and black markings. Only one species, *M. nivalis*, occurs in Europe.

Snow Leopard or ounce, *Leo uncia*, a species of the cat family Felidae in order CARNIVORA, from the mountains of central and southern Asia where it ranges to an altitude of 4000 m in summer. It is similar in shape and size to the leopard but with longer fur, up to 8 cm long. The snow leopard hunts a variety of small and medium-sized mammals which it traps after stalking them usually at night.

Snow-mobiling, sport on a motorised snow sled, developed since 1960 and most popular in North America, both for racing and as a holiday recreation at winter resorts. See also WINTER SPORTS.

Snow-plough, machine for clearing snow from roads, railways, etc. A simple type is made of timber, a wedge-shaped frame of heavy baulks being dragged apex first, the sides throwing the snow sideways into ridges, leaving a clear path between. For railway work the wedge attached to the front of the engine is a half-pyramid, an edge of which runs from the apex upwards towards the engine. Where a heavy snowfall has to be cleared a rotary plough is used, consisting of a number of cutting vanes arranged in a rapidly rotating wheel. Hot-air blasts from jet engines have also been used to clear drifts.

Snow-shoe, broad flat shoe used to prevent the feet from sinking beneath the snow. The North American shoe, varying in shape, is from 45 to 180 cm long. A hide-webbing is mounted on a strong wooden framework. Special shoes are used by Eskimos in order to cross floating or broken ice surfaces.

Snowberry, *Symphoricarpos rivularis*, in the Caprifoliaceae (honeysuckle family), a shrub bearing soft spongy white berries in autumn, planted and often naturalised in Britain, forming thickets in damp places. The name is also used for *Chiococca racemosa*, in the Rubiaceae (bedstraw family), a West Indian evergreen shrub with fragrant white flowers in elongate groups, and for *Chiogenes hispidula* in the Ericaceae (heather family), a creeping evergreen shrub with bell-shaped flowers followed by white mealy fruits.

Snowden, John, see CECIL, JOHN.

Snowden of Ickornshaw, Philip Snowden, Viscount (1864–1937), British politician, born at Keighley, Yorkshire and educated at the local elementary school. Snowden joined the Independent Labour party and became one of its most devoted propagandists. He was elected a member of its administrative council in 1898, and chairman from 1903 to 1906 and again from 1917 to 1920. From 1906 to 1908 he was MP for Blackburn and from 1922 to 1931 for Colne Valley. He was made a privy councillor in 1924 and was chancellor of the Exchequer during the short Labour administration. In 1929 Snowden was again chancellor. After the 1931 general election he became lord privy seal—a post he resigned in 1932—and was created a viscount. His publications include: *A Socialist Budget*, 1907; *Socialism and Syndicalism*, 1919; *Labour and the New World*, 1921; *The Faith of a Democrat*, 1928; and his *Autobiography*, 1934.

Bibliography: C. Cross, *Philip Snowden*, 1966.

Snowdon, Antony Charles Robert Armstrong-Jones, Earl of (1930–), British photographer, son of R. O. L. Armstrong-Jones and the Countess of Rosse, educated at Eton and Jesus College, Cambridge. On 6 May 1960 he married Princess MARGARET and on 3 October 1961 was created Earl of Snowdon. He and Princess Margaret separated in 1976. He has continued his career as a photographer and designer and since 1962 has been artistic adviser to Sunday Times Publications Ltd. His publications include: *Private View*, 1965; *Venice*, 1972; and *Assignments*, 1972.

Snow Leopard, Leo uncia. The coat is unusually long, as is the tail, which makes up almost half the overall length of about 2 m. (*Topham*)

Snowdon

Snowdon (Welsh *Eryri*), highest mountain mass in England and Wales, 16 km south-east of the Menai Straits, consisting of five main peaks, Y Wyddfa (1085 m), Carnedd Ungain (1065 m), Crib Goch (921 m), Y Lliwedd (898 m), and Llechog (884 m). Shaped roughly like an octopus, the massif extends six tentacles or arms around 12 lakes. It is extremely popular for both family walkers and mountaineers. The only rack railway in Great Britain runs from Llanberis to the summit of Y Wyddfa where there is a restaurant. The Snowdonia National Park was established in 1951 and a national nature reserve of 935 ha in 1964.

Snowdonia, mountainous region of North Wales, comprising three massifs above 1000 m divided by the passes of Llanberis and Nant Ffrancon: SNOWDON, the GLYDERS, and the Carnedds (Carnedd Dafydd, Carnedd Llewelyn, etc.). Snowdonia was designated a National Park in 1951. The park area of 2189 km² dominates the county of GWYNEDD and extends eastwards into Clwyd.

Bibliography: Countryside Commission, *Snowdonia*, 1974; A. Farquharson-Coe, *Wales' Snowdonia*, 1975.

Snowdrop, *Galanthus nivalis*, a perennial garden plant of the Amaryllidaceae (daffodil family), flowering in winter, even in the snow, and early spring. The plant is bulbous and is sometimes seen growing wild in woods and fields. It has two tapering leaves and one pendulous white flower at the top of the stem.

Snowflake, see LEUCOJUM.

Snowline, see PRECIPITATION.

Snowshill Manor, Gloucestershire, 5 km south of Broadway, a Tudor Cotswold manor house with an early 18th-century façade. Snowshill is primarily of interest because it belonged to Charles Paget Wade, an inveterate collector of anything and everything that appealed to him, including clocks, toys, bicycles, orientalia, musical instruments, craft tools and bygones. Mr Wade left Snowshill and its contents to the National Trust in 1951.

Snowy Mountains Hydro-electric Authority, was constituted by Act of the Australian Parliament in 1949, with power to construct and operate works for the storage and diversion of waters and the generation of hydroelectric power in the Snowy Mountains area. Completed in 1972, the project is one of the world's largest engineering undertakings. The objects are to supply electricity to the Commonwealth of Australia for defence purposes and for consumption in the Australian Capital Territory (see CANBERRA) and to increase the supply of water available for irrigation purposes. The Act also provides for the sale of electricity to a state or state authority. The total cost of the scheme was $A782 million. Generating capacity in 1973 was 2·2 million kW out of the projected total of nearly 4 million kW.

Bibliography: L. Wigmore, *Background of the Snowy Mountains Scheme*, 1969.

Snowy River, river of Australia, whose headwaters rise in New South Wales in the Great Dividing Range, the southern portion of which is known as the Snowy Mountains. The Snowy river commences near the north-east slope of Mount Kosciusko and reaches the sea in Bass Strait. The total catchment area is 13,493 km² and the maximum length of the river, 483 km. The headwaters of the Snowy river are now diverted to flow west and north into the upper Murray and Tumut rivers. See SNOWY MOUNTAINS HYDRO-ELECTRIC AUTHORITY.

Snuff, inhalant powder manufactured from ground tobacco leaves and stems (i.e., the mid-rib of the tobacco leaf). Cortes discovered that snuff was used by the Mexicans early in the 16th century, and the general habit of taking snuff in Europe started in Spain about 1620. In Britain, regular manufacture began in the middle of the

Snowdonia. *(Camera Press/Ken Lambert)*

18th century and developed rapidly. In fashionable circles smoking gave way to the new craze, which persisted until ousted by the cigar early in the 19th century. At this time snuff was made by powdering tobacco, which was afterwards coloured and perfumed with various scents. Snuff is manufactured at a great variety of moistures, from dry, as powder, as in the Irish and Welsh 'High Dried' snuff, to the heavier humid 'Rappee' type. It is ground to varying degrees of fineness by methods which differ according to the class of snuff. Alkaline salts are used in the process, and flavour is added as required. All snuffs are sifted in the final stage to ensure obtaining the correct 'grain', or degree of fineness. The introduction of snuff flavoured with menthol and similar substances has proved very popular in recent years.

Fine decorated snuff boxes were made throughout Europe particularly in the 18th century. They were made in every material from gold to wood, and enabled jewellers and miniature painters to produce many very beautiful masterpieces.

Bibliography: C. W. Shepherd, *Snuff, Yesterday and Today*, 1963; B. G. Hughes, *English Snuff Boxes*, 1971; J. Arlott, *Snuff Shop: Fribourg & Treyer*, 1974.

Snyders, Frans (1579–1657), Flemish painter, born in Antwerp. He studied under the younger Pieter BRUEGHEL and Henrick van BALEN, then travelled in Italy for a time, and finally settled at Antwerp. He was one of Ruben's assistants. He excelled as a painter of still-life and animals and executed fine battle-pieces.

Soames, Sir (Arthur) Christopher (John) (1920–), British politician, educated at Eton and Sandhurst. He married a daughter of Sir Winston Churchill. Soames entered Parliament as a Conservative in 1950, and after holding junior office was minister of War, 1958–60, and minister of Agriculture, 1960–64. He lost his parliamentary seat at the 1966 general election. Between 1968 and 1972 he was British ambassador to France. From 1973 to 1977 he was a commissioner of the European Economic Community, one of the first two to be nominated by Britain following its entry into the Community. He was knighted in 1972.

Soane, Sir John (1753–1837), British architect, born at Whitchurch, Goring, Oxfordshire, the son of a bricklayer. He distinguished himself in the Royal Academy Schools; travelled in Italy, 1778–80. He began private practice in London, and in 1788 was appointed architect to the Bank of England which he rebuilt from 1788 to 1833, his most important work. Other buildings include: Pitshanger Manor, Ealing (1800–03; now the public library); Dulwich College Art Gallery (1811–14; restored 1953 after war damage); the Stables, Chelsea Hospital (1814–17); and his own eccentric home, No. 13 Lincoln's Inn Fields (1812–13), which he bequeathed to the nation in 1835, together with his collection of antiques and a number of notable paintings, including Hogarth's two series: *The Rake's Progress*, 1735, and *The Election*, 1755. (The house is known as 'Sir John Soane's Museum'.)

Bibliography: Biographies by J. Summerson, 1952, and D. Stroud, 1961.

Soap, substance which possesses detergent and cleansing properties. Chemically it is the salt of an alkali and fatty acid. Most commonly the alkali is sodium hydroxide (NaOH), but potassium hydroxide (for soft soaps), calcium hydroxide (for lubricant soaps), and other alkalis may be used, as may organic bases, e.g., triethanolamine. The fatty acids are derived from natural animal and vegetable oils and fats. Chemically these are triglycerides. As huge quantities are required, those available in large quantities are most commonly used, e.g., tallow and coconut oil, while lesser amounts of lard, groundnut oil, palm kernel oil, and palm oil are used. For soaps made from a given alkali, e.g., sodium hydroxide, the properties of the soap vary according to the oils and fats used, e.g., coconut soap, which has relatively short fatty acid chains, gives a quick, abundant lather, but dissolves rapidly, while tallow soap, which has longer fatty acid chains, wears away more slowly but gives less lather. Commercial soaps are usually made from blends of fats to give the desired properties, a typical blend for personal use being 80 parts tallow to 20 parts coconut oil.

The blend of fats is usually first bleached by mixing and heating with an absorbent, finely divided clay such as FULLER'S EARTH and filtered. Traditionally SAPONIFICATION takes place in large kettles or pans, by boiling the fat blend with steam in the presence of the alkali. When all the fat has been converted into soap saponification is complete and a solution of sodium chloride (brine) is added to separate the soap in the form of granules ('salting' or 'graining' out) from a lye which settles below. The lye, which contains glycerine liberated in the reaction, is drawn off and the 'salting' process repeated a number of times to recover as much of the valuable glycerine as is economically possible. The remaining soap is then boiled again and 'fitted', i.e., partially grained, and allowed to settle for 24 to 48 hours, when the upper layer of neat soap can be removed from the vessel for further processing into bars, tablets, or flakes. In modern factories the saponification, 'graining', and fitting steps are carried out continuously, using temperatures in excess of 100 °C, and corresponding pressure, to ensure rapid saponification. Glycerine removal by graining is carried out in various forms of counter-current liquid/liquid extraction plant, while the final settling period is eliminated by using continuous centrifuges. In this way the production time for a batch of, say, 25 t of soap is reduced from several days to a few hours.

Soap bars and tablets for household or laundry use can be made from neat soap by simply cooling in presses or in box-like frames, when the soap solidifies and can be cut up. However, for toilet soap the moisture content of the neat soap, at 30 to 31 per cent, is too high and must be reduced to 12 to 15 per cent, by drying the neat soap. The drying can be accomplished by first chilling the neat soap on a water-cooled drum to solidify it, and then passing the particles of solid soap, separated from the drum by a knife, through a drying chamber. The soap is carried on perforated conveyors and subjected to heated air directed by fans to evaporate the moisture. The method preferred nowadays is to heat the neat soap to a temperature in excess of 100 °C by pumping it through a steam-heated heat exchanger. The soap is then discharged as a spray into a cylindrical chamber in which a vacuum is maintained. The water vapour is thus separated from the soap, which in turn is quickly cooled and solidified at the required moisture content for toilet soap, in the chamber.

Soap-berries

The small pieces of solidified soap are then fed into a mixing machine where colour, perfume, and possibly other additives, e.g., superfatting oils, germicidal ingredients, and medicaments as required, are added. The mixing is completed by passing through roller mills where the mixture is homogenised and plasticised, and is then fed into the plodder, which comprises a compression screw rotating in a cylindrical barrel with a tapering cone at the discharge end. The screw compresses the soap in the cone, and it emerges from an orifice at the smaller end as a continuous bar. This is automatically cut into short lengths, stamped to form tablets in familiar shapes, and wrapped. Modern design stampers and wrapping machines can produce about 200 tablets per minute.

The process for the production of soap flakes is similar to that used for toilet soaps except that the fats are selected so as to avoid brittleness in the final flakes to prevent breakdown to dust in the packets. The moisture content is 2 to 3 per cent lower, and instead of the plodding stage the soap is further milled on very finely controlled steel roller mills to produce thin flakes for easy dissolving in lukewarm water. Cutting rollers are mounted on the mills to cut the film of soap into diamond-shaped flakes.

A similar process to that for toilet soaps is used for shaving sticks. Oleic acid, stearic acid, and coconut oil, with a proportion of potassium hydroxide in the alkali are used to give the stable, slow-drying lather which is required.

Shaving cream is usually a type of shaving soap with the additions of glycerine, water, and various oils to render it emollient and creamy.

Many other types of soap used in industry are made to various formulae and specifications, e.g., powders or granules of calcium soaps as lubricants in metal working and metal wire drawing. Other special soaps are used in cosmetics, paints, disinfectants and polishes, while special soaps are sold for the treatment of leather, i.e., saddle soap.

The disadvantage of soap as a detergent (see DETERGENTS) is that it is precipitated by salts present in hard water, forming scum. Extra soap has to be used in proportion to the hardness of the water, to overcome the effect of these salts and leave an excess of soap to function as a detergent, i.e., soap must first soften the water.

Bibliography: C. V. Boys, *Soap Bubbles and the Forces which Mould Them,* 1960; H. R. Edwards, *Competition and Monopoly in British Soap Industry,* 1962; A. E. Musson, *Enterprise in Soap and Chemicals,* 1965; F. Ponge, *Soap* (trans. L. Dunlop), 1969; W. A. Poucher, *Perfumes, Cosmetics and Soaps: Production, Manufacture and Application of Perfumes* (vol 2, 8th ed. G. Howard), 1975.

Soap-berries, fruits of the tree *Sapindus saponaria* in family Sapindaceae. They make a good lather in water due to the chemical saponin they contain, and are therefore used at times instead of soap.

Soapstone, see TALC.

Soapwort, see SAPONARIA.

Soar, river of LEICESTERSHIRE, England, rising just within the Warwickshire borders. It flows through Leicester and Loughborough to Ratcliff, where it joins the TRENT, 14 km south-west of Nottingham and 17 km south-east of Derby. It is navigable as far as Leicester. Length 65 km.

Soares, Mario (1925–), Portuguese lawyer and leader of the Portuguese Socialist party. Having engaged in, and suffered imprisonment for, anti-régime activities during the premierships of SALAZAR and Marcelo Caetano, Soares came to prominence as leader of the Socialist party after the 1974 revolution. During his brief period as foreign minister he was responsible for independence negotiations with Portugal's African colonies. Although his party won the largest share (38 per cent) of the vote in the elections of 1975, Soares and his colleagues were denied substantial government office by the leaders of the ruling Armed Forces Movement. In 1976, however, President Eanes appointed Soares prime minister.

Bibliography: M. Soares, *Portugal's Struggle for Liberty,* 1975.

Sobelsohn, Karl, see RADEK, KARL.

Sobers, Sir Garfield St Aubrun (1936–), West Indian cricketer, born at Bridgetown, Barbados. A left-handed batsman and bowler, he first played for Barbados aged 16 and in his first Test match at 17. The most gifted all-rounder of modern times, he appeared in 93 Tests and scored more Test runs (8032) than any man in history, and also took 235 Test wickets. He captained West Indies a record 39 times between 1964–65 and 1971–72, and when 21 years old made the world record Test score of 365 not out for West Indies v. Pakistan at Kingston in 1957–58. His 26 Test centuries are second only to Sir Donald BRADMAN's 29. He has played also for Nottinghamshire, for South Australia, and extensively in league cricket in England. He is the only man to score six successive sixes in a single over in a first-class match (v. Glamorgan at Swansea, 1968). He was knighted in 1975.

Sobieski, see JOHN, kings of Poland, *John III.*

Sobieski, Brothers, see ALBANY, COUNT.

Socage, see LAND LAWS.

So-che (Turkish *Yarkand*), walled town and oasis in SINKIANG UIGHUR autonomous region of China, on the River Yarkand about 160 km south-east of Kashgar. A very old trade centre with bazaars, caravanserais, and many mosques. Traditional industries like carpets and embroidered silks have been part of its way of life for centuries. It is also the centre of an irrigated agricultural region producing grain, fruit, and oil palm. Population (1970) around 90,000.

Sochi, town in the KRASNODAR *krai* of the RSFSR, USSR, on the BLACK SEA coast at the foot of the main CAUCASUS range. It has become the main Soviet health resort (sea bathing, sulphur springs), and extends along the Black Sea coast for a distance of nearly 40 km. Population (1974) 244,000.

Social and Cultural Ecology, the study of the social and cultural consequences of man's relationship with his physical environment, a subject which has aroused much interest among social anthropologists and cultural geographers in recent years, especially in the United States. Environment may not determine all social and cultural facts, but it nevertheless imposes important constraints on the development of tendencies inherent in these facts. Climatic conditions, for instance, may affect modes of subsistence and the organisation of production, which, in turn, affect trade, political and ritual activities. There has been much effort by anthropologists in recent years to bring together the ecological approach and the structuralist, evolutionist, and Marxist approaches.

See also ANTHROPOLOGY; GEOGRAPHY; HUNTING AND GATHERING; PASTORALISM; PLOUGH AGRICULTURE; SOCIAL EVOLUTION; STRUCTURALISM; SWIDDEN AGRICULTURE.

Bibliography: R. A. Rappaport, *Pigs for Ancestors*, 1967; A. Vayda, *Environment and Cultural Behaviour*, 1969; M. Sahlins, *Stone Age Economics*, 1972; E. Terray, *Marxism and Primitive Societies*, 1972.

Social Anthropology, see ANTHROPOLOGY.

Social Change, a sociological concept which can refer to large-scale or to small-scale phenomena. Societies can over a long period of time or through sudden and successful revolution change their nature. So British society changed from a rural to an urban society, from one that was agricultural to one that was industrial. This change led to, and also expressed, a whole complex of changes in all kinds of social relation from the market and the work-place to the family. Social change can also take place on a much smaller scale. For instance, particular conditions become defined and accepted as social problems whereas at an earlier period they would have been regarded as simply private sorrows that had to be endured. A good example of this would be 'battered wives'. Social change on this small scale is relatively easy to understand. In the example given the factors leading to the changed perception would include the influence of strong campaigners, of ideas connected with the movement of Women's Liberation, and the fact that previously the public had accepted the notion of the 'battered baby'.

Social change on the larger scale is much more difficult to understand and there is no agreement among sociologists about the most crucial factors. Sociologists who emphasise SOCIAL EVOLUTION scarcely offer a theory that explains social change: they describe it under the domination of a master metaphor. Those who see society as built almost exclusively on consensus are hard put to it to explain change, though reference to the unintended consequences of social action and latent as well as manifest functions is to some extent helpful. The most obvious division amongst sociologists concerning the origins of social change is between those who stress the material basis of change and those who see a more crucial rôle for ideas. This division is well illustrated in the different theories of Marx and Weber. Marx argued that the means of production determine the form of society. Weber, in his study of the relationship between capitalism and Protestantism, argued that a particular set of ideas were required in addition to certain material and social changes.

Bibliography: M. Weber (trans. T. Parsons), *The Protestant Ethic and the Spirit of Capitalism*, 1967; W. E. Moore, *Social Change*, 2nd ed., 1974.

Social Conflict, a sociological concept which does not imply that all instances of social antagonism involve social conflict. Competition and bargaining are not forms of

social conflict, but class warfare is. Sociologists do not agree on the part social conflict plays in SOCIAL CHANGE. The early sociologists of the 19th century stressed the slowly evolving patterns of society, and it was Karl Marx who first placed social conflict (in his case it was conflict between classes) at the centre of a systematic attempt to understand society. All social institutions and each social group were on one side of the conflict or the other. Until fairly recently this perspective was not well represented in sociology. Almost exclusive emphasis was placed on what has been described as the consensus view of society, i.e. social institutions are part of an interlocking social system supported by broadly agreed values. Disagreement and difference were possible, of course, but problems in the system could be managed without the breakdown of the system. More recently two main tendencies are visible in the way sociologists treat social conflict, though it should be noted that generally there is now more agreement on its importance. First, there has been a strong revival of interest in the Marxian analysis of society. One form this has taken is the reinterpretation of social deviance which is seen not as the result of individual psychological disturbance but as a form of protest or social sabotage against the domination of the ideas and power of the ruling class. Crime, drug-taking, homosexuality, and so on, are seen as proceeding from, or as being, a fundamental criticism of society.

Consensus view	Coercion or conflict view
1 Every society is a relatively persistent, stable structure of elements.	1 Every society is subject to change at every point.
2 These elements are well integrated.	2 Every point displays dissensus and conflict.
Consensus view	*Coercion or conflict view*
3 Every element makes a contribution to the maintenance of the social system.	3 Every element in a society contributes to social disintegration and change.
4 Every functioning social system is based on a concensus of values among members.	4 Every society is based on the coercion of some by others.

Second, some writers question the extent to which the kinds of social conflict visible in present-day societies will actually lead to the dissolution of particular societies. Some sociologists, therefore, stress the positive functions that social conflict can play in maintaining societies. Social conflict, for those arguing in this way, unites social groups and gives each conflicting group an interest in the coherence of their opponents. The outcome of conflict may be the relief of otherwise unbearable tension, and so on. Another view argues that social conflict is a characteristic of life within any social institution rather than a feature of the life of society across institutions. Ralf Dahrendorf in particular is associated with the view that conflict in industrial institutions is confined to that particular area of society. His summary of the two dominant views of society, that of integration or consensus and that of coercion and conflict, is well known and helps us to see the assumptions involved.

Bibliography: M. Gluckman, *Custom and Conflict in Africa*, 1955; L. A. Coser, *The Functions of Social Conflict*, 1956; R. Dahrendorf, *Class and Class Conflict in an Industrial Society*, 1959; T. Parsons et al, *Theories of Society*, 1965.

Social Contract

Social Contract, general term for a group of theories which attempt to explain the nature of political authority in terms of a contract amongst the citizens, or between the citizens and their governors; this forms the basis for the justification, and terms of exercise of, political power. The contract is often presented as having initiated existing political societies, but it is not necessary to take its historical existence as fact, nor is it usually meant in this way. The contract derives its moral force from being one to which a free individual would reasonably consent, rather than from the fact of his ever having done so.

In HOBBES's version the position of free individuals 'in a state of nature' is presented as so dire that they contract to submit all except their actual lives to the will of the sovereign who thus exercises an almost absolute political authority. The contract in Hobbes is between individuals to give up their natural rights, leaving an all-powerful sovereign in possession of his own, thus unmodified by any promises on his part. In LOCKE's formulation the contract is amongst the individuals in a more orderly state of nature, possessing 'natural law'—a moral force limiting contractors as to what they can promise. The area of 'trust' or discretion allowed to the monarch as chief of the executive is thus limited by the intentions of those entering society ('...the preservation of their lives, liberties and estates' through the establishment of known, binding, and universally applicable laws). The exercise of prerogative power to the detriment of these ends is ipso facto illegal, and, if persisted in, justifies resistance by the citizens. In ROUSSEAU's version the moral justification for the exercise of political power requires constant reaffirmation in the meeting of citizens to endorse the decisions and personnel of the government, as being consistent with the General Will, that is with the persistence of equality and freedom in the society. Social contract theory has survived a period of disrepute during the 1950s and early 1960s, and versions have been incorporated in the work of modern political theorists. The term has been employed in Britain to describe an 'understanding' between the trade unions and the Labour government over prices and wages.

See also POLITICAL THOUGHT.

Bibliography: J. Locke, (ed. P. Laslett), *Two Treatises of Government*, 1967; J. Rawls, *A Theory of Justice*, 1972; T. Hobbes, *Leviathan*, (Everyman's Library), 1973; J. J. Rousseau (ed. J. H. Bumfit and J. C. Hall; trans. G. D. H. Cole), *The Social Contract*, 2nd ed. 1973.

Social Credit, economic doctrine proposed in the 1930s in the USA by Maj. C. H. Douglas. He argued that 'poverty amidst plenty'—the great depression of the 1930s—was due to a flaw in the price system whereby all costs of production were not reflected in equivalent purchasing power. The state should therefore make periodic monetary gifts to its citizens to make good the alleged deficiency. Maj. Douglas also wanted taxation abolished. His theories made a great appeal between the world wars though little is now heard of the movement, except in Canada, where it has had some political success at provincial level for a time, but only by applying methods of financial orthodoxy.

Social Dance. In the 11th and 12th centuries the most civilised courts in Europe were those of Provence in the south of France. The Provençal region was larger than it is today and had strong links with Spain where a high level of artistic accomplishment developed during the Moorish occupation. Some of its features were introduced by various noblemen into the Provençal courts and here they blended with the Greek and Roman traditions of former occupations. Poetry and music were composed by the Provençal TROUBADOURS who were skilled in the arts of verse, dance and song, although the songs were usually written in a dance rhythm.

Medieval castles and houses were dark, smoky and uncomfortable, and social gatherings took place out of doors. The earliest dance was the carole, of which there were two forms, a chain file of dancers, the FARANDOLE, and the closed circle, the branle. Caroles were always danced to songs, usually sung by the dancers themselves. 'Sumer is icumen in' is an example of a farandole. The dances were impersonal; anyone could join in, no partners were required, and they could be danced by nobility and country people alike. The troubadors' approach to life revolved around the duty of each man to the lady of his choice so they evolved the *estampie*, a dance to be performed by a couple, or one man and two ladies. This was the beginning of the couple dance; a presence or front was established and from these the dancers could move forward or back and weave patterns. As the dance changed so did the music, as instruments were introduced. When secular instrumental music ceased to be merely an accompaniment for the voice it developed in interest until it eventually became completely independent.

With the coming of the Albigensian Crusade in 1208, Provençal society was eliminated and the troubadors fled to various European courts. These fugitives were welcomed on account of their songs and dances and in this way the early caroles and estampies were transported to Italy, Sicily, Germany, France, and England. In each country these dances developed very differently except for England where they changed only slightly from the 13th to the 16th century. By the 14th and 15th centuries the central fire had been moved to the side of the great hall which was the centre of activity, thus providing space for dancing indoors. Bows and curtsies were executed before and after the dance to the most important people on the dais. French fashions were popular at this time and the ladies wore heavy and voluminous clothes with elaborate head dresses. Costume has always influenced dance movement and as the dancers found difficulty in moving forward and backwards so couples progressed round the room in an anti-clockwise direction, as they do today.

The 15th century saw the medieval world of France, England, Germany, and the Netherlands nearing its end and society became more formal. The main dance of this period was the basse dance, reflecting the change of manners and custom. Groups of steps changed within each dance and these in turn were subjected to certain fixed rules. In Renaissance Italy dancing flourished together with the other arts. Unhampered by the very elaborate costumes of the French, the dancers were able to use their bodies more freely. The Italian basse dance also developed from the early estampies and farandole, but the dancing masters attached to the great Italian families introduced dances known as balli. These contained a variety of figures, patterns, and numbers of dancers and had specially composed music for each dance. 'Contrary' body movement called *maniera* was used, and there was

162

also much more mobility in the feet resulting in the 'rise and fall' called *aiere*.

By the 16th century the court entertainment and dances had become very elaborate and large scale spectacles or BALLETS were produced. The presentation of ballet at the French court in 1581 began to change the pattern of dance. In England during the reigns of Henry VIII and Elizabeth I, the following dances were extremely popular: PAVANES, GALLIARDS, COURANTES, rounds, measures and *La Volta*. During this period the legend of 'the dancing English' was established and the English COUNTRY DANCE also found favour in many of the European courts. An important development took place in France in 1661, when Louis XIV retired from dancing in the court ballets and the *Académie Royale de Danse* was formed. For the first time professional dancers were trained to appear in court ballets.

Social dancing continued in the form of MINUETS, SARABANDS and GIGUES, but when performed on the stage these dances became very technical. Freed from the professional or entertainment aspect, however, social and ballet dancing developed along independent lines. The COTILLION found great favour but with the coming of the French Revolution, old ideas were swept away and QUADRILLES, LANCERS and set dances became popular. The WALTZ and POLKA soon followed and with the introduction of ragtime and jazz in the early 20th century, the one-step, TANGO, charleston, quickstep and foxtrot set what was to become the English style of ballroom dancing. Continuing the development were the rumba, the samba, the cha-cha-cha, jitterbug, jive, rock and roll and twist, all of which have contributed to the art of social dance.

Bibliography: M. Wood, *Historical Dances*, 1952, *More Historical Dances*, 1956, and *Advanced Historical Dances*, 1960; C. Sachs, *World History of the Dance* repr. 1963; Periodical: *The Dancing Times* (monthly).

Social Evolution.
Nineteenth-century anthropologists and sociologists, inspired by the work of Charles DARWIN in biology, attempted to construct evolutionary schemas to account the differences between Western society and the multitude of societies encountered during the colonial expansion. Western society and its institutions were thought to be the highest and best developments of human society, culture, and civilisation.

The theories were discredited by the structural-functionalists in the 1920s, who saw that such schemas were unscientific conjectures, frequently based on a false assessment of other societies. Interest in social evolution was renewed in the United States during the 1940s with the works of J. Steward and L. A. White, who were more subtle in their approaches. Steward had a considerable influence among archaeologists in the 1950s, and evolutionary studies regained prominence and respectability among the cultural ecologists in the United States, and the structural-Marxists in France. Modern anthropologists have rid themselves of the ethnocentric bias that Western society and culture are the best, and are attempting to use scientific criteria for their analyses.

See also ANTHROPOLOGY; ARCHAEOLOGY; SOCIAL ECOLOGY.

Bibliography: E. Durkheim, *Elementary Forms of the Religious Life*, 1912; J. Frazer, *The Golden Bough*, 1936; A. R. Radcliffe-Brown, *Structure and Function in Primitive Societies*, 1952; S. Streuver, *Prehistoric Agriculture*, 1971; M. Sahlins, *Stone Age Economics*, 1972; E. Terray, *Marxism and Primitive Societies*, 1972; J. Steward, *Theory of Culture Change*, 1973.

Social Forecasting,
attempts to predict the likely future with special reference to the size, age, structure, and distribution of a POPULATION. Less frequently it refers to attempts to predict more qualitative changes, for example in moral values and behaviour. Social forecasting is clearly a very difficult art, but it is playing a larger part in Britain as a basis for social planning, for example in Regional Economic Planning Councils. The registrars-general of England and Wales, Scotland, and Northern Ireland, and the government actuary agree each year on the assumptions that will form the base of the projections for each year published separately and for the United Kingdom. These assumptions are obviously of crucial importance. For example, estimates of the total population at any particular date depend on assumptions concerning mortality, natality, and migration.

Social Insurance,
private or state service for the prevention of individual poverty resulting from hazards of personal fortune over which individuals have little or no control. The question of social insurance was among the first to which the British government attended when, during the Second World War, they began to develop a programme of reconstruction for the future. In June 1941 the government invited Sir William BEVERIDGE to conduct a comprehensive survey of existing schemes, and some 18 months later he presented his report on Social Insurance and Allied Services (Cmd. 6404), an outline policy covering 'all citizens without upper income limit... all-embracing in scope of persons and needs'. It did not purport to be a complete and final scheme, ready for immediate translation into legislative form. Further, the plan was based on three assumptions: (1) the institution of a scheme of children's allowances; (2) the framing of a comprehensive health service; (3) the avoidance of mass unemployment. The government accepted these assumptions as necessary prerequisites to an improved and comprehensive plan of social insurance. The government's own independent proposals for a national health service were then already under consideration, as well as their policy for maintaining a high and stable level of employment after the war. Also, their plan for a scheme of family allowances had been prepared. The government's final proposals, which were published in September 1944 (Cmd. 6550), embodied a great part of the Beveridge plan.

These proposals assumed that there must be both an increased rate of sickness and unemployment benefit and retirement pension, and a system of family allowances which would contribute substantially to the maintenance of growing children. It was decided that the cost of these latter allowances ought to be met from the proceeds of taxation, and therefore that they were outside the scheme of social insurance properly so called. With that one exception the proposals adhered to the underlying principle that freedom from want must be achieved in the first instance by social insurance, i.e. that benefits must be earned by contributions. This principle has long been one of the essential features of British social legislation, and the government's policy assumed that it still reflected the wishes of the people. Contributions from insured persons and their employers, in these proposals, covered only part

Social Philosophy

of the ground. It was calculated, therefore, that towards the whole cost of the services 54 per cent at first and, 20 years later, 64 per cent would have to come from taxation; while as to the narrower field of insurance only 31 per cent at the outset, rising in 20 years to 50 per cent, would come from taxation. It was also decided that the scope of social insurance should be extended in two different senses, i.e. the range and amount of benefits provided and the number of people included. The government's scheme as a whole was planned to embrace the entire population, and the broad principle as to contributions in relation to earnings was that of equal benefits for equal contributions within a specified class or group. Another valuable principle was that the administration of a single comprehensive universal scheme of social insurance must be unified. There was general agreement between the political parties on social insurance until the 1960s. Disagreement then centred on the administration of the graduated retirement pension scheme and on the level and scope of flat-rate benefits. Decline in economic growth has also raised some important questions as to the level of benefits the tax system could provide.

The problem of industrial injury insurance, or what had for the past four decades been known as WORKMEN'S COMPENSATION was dealt with in Cmd. 6551. In view of the special benefits which the government proposed to provide, the industrial injury insurance scheme could not be unified with the general scheme of social insurance, but had to be treated as a separate branch of social insurance. Broadly the benefits provided under the scheme take the place of the cash benefits payable under the general scheme in cases of disability and of the widow's, orphan's, and guardian's benefits in case of death. No funeral benefit is payable under this scheme, but it is provided by the death grant proposed under the general scheme of social insurance.

The Redundancy Payments Act 1965 requires employers to pay compensation, on a scale related to service, to certain employees laid off or put on short time, or dismissed as redundant because the work they are doing is no longer necessary or has ceased to exist. The act also established a central Redundancy Payment Fund, financed by surcharges on the employer's National Insurance contributions.

See also NATIONAL HEALTH SERVICE; NATIONAL INSURANCE; PENSIONS; SOCIAL SECURITY.

Bibliography: V. N. George, *Social Security: Beveridge and After*, 1968.

Social Philosophy, that aspect of philosophy which brings philosophic methods to bear on the larger problems of social life and social history. It is closely related to political philosophy, from which it was scarcely distinguished until the 19th century. Its recognition as a separate aspect of philosophy was due to the growing consciousness of society as being more comprehensive than the state, which also led to the appearance of SOCIOLOGY as a separate study. Social philosophy is intimately and inextricably linked with general philosophy. A materialist interpretation of the universe implies a materialist interpretation of social life; and similarly with an Idealist, a dualist, a spiritual interpretation. The development of social philosophy, however, follows a significant change in the philosopher's point of view. Much of

the thought of the Renaissance and Reformation periods envisages man as an individual face to face with God or with the universe; and this presupposition is still found in some 20th-century thinkers. As against this, since the middle of the 19th century the view that man is a product of material forces has been widely held; to the followers of Karl MARX and many others, man's place in society is determined by his relation to the means of production. All social philosophers envisage the individual as placed in society and, at least in some degree, conditioned by it, and have considered the implications of the existence and activity of this more complex unit in the universe. As a result, the place and value of the individual in the universe have been radically reconsidered. Biology has had much influence on this, and further emphasis has come from the growing consciousness of the disabilities and problems of a mass civilisation. The philosophic alternatives of sinking the individual in the mass or finding scope and value for the individual in other dimensions have been widely discussed.

The social nature of ethics, i.e. duty as a social imperative, has been the subject of vigorous discussion, which has ranged from the view that society in imposing duties expresses the will of God on the way of spiritual progress for the universe, to the view that duty is just what society decides to decree for purely practical ends. Discussion has also arisen on the question whether a moral purpose can be observed in history.

See also PHILOSOPHY.

Bibliography: R. A. Nisbet: *Social Philosophers: Community and Conflict in Western Thought*, 1974.

Social Psychology, a behavioural science that is difficult to define so that its distinctiveness stands out in relation both to individual or general psychology and to sociology. It can be seen as the study of psychological aspects of social interaction, as the study of social influence, or of the psychological processes that accompany, determine, or are determined by, social change. In addition the more psychologically inclined among social psychologists have, until very recently, tended to stress 'the objective', scientific study of observed behaviour, ignoring the extent to which their experiments were themselves part of the social world. More sociologically minded social psychologists have, until recently, tended to study the 'how' rather than the 'what' of social interaction.

Social psychology in a rudimentary form dates from the end of the 19th century partly as a reaction against McDougall's theory of instincts. Of importance in the development of the discipline were Charles Horton Cooley (1864–1929) with his concept of a 'looking-glass self' (or the power to imagine how others will see and judge us) and his distinction between primary and secondary social groups. Of more direct influence were the ideas of George Herbert Mead (in his book *Mind, Self and Society*). Mead believed that man becomes a self through processes of rôle-taking and taking the rôle of the other. Also important were the ideas of the neo-Freudians, like Karen HORNEY (1885–1952) and Erich Fromm (b. 1900), who drew attention to the effects on psychological development of social institutions in general. This theme is evident in what has been termed the culture and personality school (particularly associated with Margaret Mead and Ruth Benedict). This school argues against innate dispositions and in favour of the overwhelming influence of socialisation, particularly in child-rearing.

Since then social psychology has developed in a number of directions. There has been a considerable emphasis on attitudes, particularly of prejudice, and on the study of small groups. After the Second World War social psychological studies of service men (*The American Soldier* by Stouffer et al., 1949) or of the rehabilitation of ex-service personnel (organisational psychiatry) were very influential. Important work has been done in industry particularly in relation to small groups, leadership, and the connections between social behaviour and systems of management and of work. More recently there has been a call to reconstruct the whole subject of social psychology so that it studies human behaviour in a way that is human.

Bibliography: G. Lindzey, *Handbook of Social Psychology*, vols 1 and 2, 1968, 1969; J. A. C. Brown, *The Social Psychology of Industry*, 1970; N. Warren and M. Jahoda (Eds), *Attitudes*, 2nd ed. 1973; N. Armistead (Ed.), *Reconstructing Social Psychology*, 1974.

Social Security. In Britain the first step towards the creation of a system of state social security was taken by the passing of the National Assistance Act 1948, the fundamental purpose of which was to achieve the final replacement of the Poor Law (see POOR LAW, HISTORY OF) by entirely new services founded on new conceptions of social welfare. Under the act a National Assistance Board administered a state scheme of financial aid for all people who fell outside the national insurance scheme (see NATIONAL INSURANCE), or whose requirements were not wholly met from that or any other source. The cost of this service falls on the Exchequer. Provision was made for a local government welfare service, of which an important feature is the provision of residential accommodation for old and infirm people and others requiring care and attention. The sick who need hospital treatment are the responsibility of the NATIONAL HEALTH SERVICE. The local authority welfare service also extends to the blind and other handicapped persons (see DISABILITY AND THE DISABLED).

The Ministry of Social Security Act 1966 provided a new administrative framework by combining the National Assistance Board and the Ministry of Pensions and National Insurance in the Ministry of Social Security. The term 'national assistance' was replaced by 'supplementary benefits' which are administered by a Supplementary Benefits Commission. People in need have now a statutory entitlement to claim benefit. In 1968 the Ministry of Social Security was merged with the Ministry of Health to become the new Department of Health and Social Security. The Supplementary Benefits Commission awards supplementary pensions where income requirements plus a sum for rent are below a guaranteed minimum level, and supplementary allowances which may be claimed by people aged 16 years or more if their resources fall short of income requirements. Those people in full-time work or involved in trade disputes are not eligible, though in the latter case dependants are. Income requirements are set out in Schedule 2, Supplementary Benefits Act 1966.

Under the Families Income Supplements Act 1970, families with at least one dependent child under 16 (or over 16 if still at school), whose total family income is below the 'prescribed amount' if the head of the family is employed, are entitled to a Family Income Supplement. This supplement is calculated as one-half of the amount by which the family's total income falls below the 'prescribed amount', subject to statutory maxima.

The only qualification for eligibility for social security is need according to general standards prescribed in regulations requiring parliamentary approval. Where need is established the assistance will provide for dependants as well as the applicant. Discretionary power is given to deal with special cases. There is no household means test. Resources as well as requirements of applicants and their wives are considered jointly. No account is taken of the income of earning sons and daughters, but they are deemed to be making a reasonable contribution towards the household expenses. The value of the house of an owner occupier is ignored when assessing the treatment of an applicant's capital. Other capital of less than £325 owned by husband, wife, and dependants jointly is ignored. For capital over £325 a weekly income of 5p is assumed for every complete £25 over £300 but up to £800. On each £25 over £800 an income of 12½p is assumed. Applicants are dealt with by local officers of the Commission. There is a right of appeal to an independent Appeal Tribunal. A condition of the allowance may be registration for employment. Men who are unemployed and whose prospects of employment would be improved by a course at a re-establishment centre can attend one of the residential or non-residential centres provided. If a

Social Security. The table shows total expenditure on national assistance/supplementary benefits between 1965/66 and 1974/75. It excludes cost of administration.

Type of benefit	Year and total amount each year									
	1965/66	1966/67	1967/68	1968/69	1968/70	1970/71	1971/72	1972/73	1973/74	1974/75
Supplementary benefits (1):										
Old persons	135	171	200	215	233	253	286	285	288	326
Unemployed persons	28	32	65	79	80	95	155	191	150	200
Sick persons	46	54	65	72	76	81	84	85	95	118
Other persons in need	46	52	70	80	100	115	140	154	181	232
Other non-contributory benefits:										
Old persons pensions	—	—	—	—	—	8	24	28	29	32
Family income supplement	—	—	—	—	—	—	5	11	14	14
Attendance allowance	—	—	—	—	—	—	6	25	38	66
Lump sums to pensioners	—	—	—	—	—	—	—	81	82	93

(1) National Assistance (including non-contributory old-age pensions) ceased after 26 November 1966, when it was replaced by supplementary benefits.

Source: Central Statistical Office, Annual Abstract of Statistics, 1975.

Social Settlements

man unreasonably refuses to go to such a centre his case may be referred to an independent Appeal Tribunal, who can offer a man maintenance at a residential centre in lieu of ordinary benefits, or make attendance at a non-residential centre a condition of the receipt of benefits. The Commission may also take proceedings against a man who neglects or refuses to maintain himself or his family. The 1948 act requires the provision and maintenance of reception centres where 'persons without a settled way of life' can be given temporary board and lodging. Some centres are administered by local authorities as the Commission's agents.

The second group of services come under the control of the local authority, and include residential accommodation for the aged, the infirm, and others, with special welfare services for the handicapped. These services are run by non-metropolitan county councils and metropolitan district councils, in London by the borough councils, and in Scotland by the counties and large burghs. The residential accommodation, board, lodging, and attendance is intended for all who cannot wholly look after themselves. The local authority fixes a standard charge which those who can afford pay in full. By the National Assistance (Charges for Accommodation) Regulations 1965, those who cannot afford it pay according to their resources and commitments, subject always to a minimum of £6.20 a week, and everyone is deemed to need £1.55 a week pocket money. People in financial need are referred to the Supplementary Benefits Commission. Local authorities are also empowered to extend to the deaf, the dumb, and the crippled the same welfare services which are provided for the blind. The authorities may arrange for voluntary organisations to act as their agents in providing residential accommodation and specialised welfare services. Private institutions for the care of the old and disabled must be registered, and local authorities are empowered to inspect and withhold registration in unsatisfactory cases. The Chronically Sick and Disabled Persons Act 1970 extended the services to those whom the local authority assessed as substantially and permanently handicapped.

Social Settlements. The Universities Settlement in East London, widely known as Toynbee Hall, was founded in 1884 to be a house of residence for men from Oxford and Cambridge who wished to take part in the life of East London and to join with their neighbours in working for its betterment. Its example was quickly followed and at one time there were some 50 residential settlements in Britain, several hundred in the USA, and some in Europe. Since they were founded the divide between rich and poor which used to exist has been substantially bridged. Some of the old widespread poverty has disappeared, material conditions have vastly improved, the social services, and especially education, have released individual ability which was masked by ignorance and thwarted by lack of opportunity. For the last 20 years the Settlement movement has been very uncertain of its direction. Recently some life and enthusiasm has been restored through the idea of settlements as centres of community work, a newly developing perspective in social work. Many of the settlements now receive grants from the local authorities in aid of particular branches of work, but all are voluntary institutions, financed mainly from voluntary funds. Both

for the management of activities and for their finance, 'users' from the neighbourhood are increasingly responsible.

Social Stratification, a sociological concept which refers to societies as composed of distinct social strata or relatively permanent levels arranged in some kind of hierarchy. Different societies are stratified in different ways. Pre-industrial societies are not stratified in terms of social classes but of castes and of estates. A caste system is rooted in a religious order and the ranking is not invidious as all members of the society subscribe to the system of allocation of what are basically ritualistic functions. Societies divided into estates, such as early medieval society into King, Nobles, Commoners, and Clergy, likewise rested on commonly held views about the ascription of positions compared to modern industrial societies which emphasise their achievement. Stratification by caste or estate breaks down under modern capitalism which depends on increasing division of labour and specialisation: recruitment to different positions in modern industrial society cannot depend upon the idea of 'my station and its duty'. Such a society is stratified on economic lines and so social class becomes one of the significant terms, if not the most significant, for understanding social divisions.

'Social class' is not an easy concept to grasp. There is a range of meanings attached to normal, every-day use, and also, amongst some people, a feeling that the term should not be used; it is as if the use of 'social class' was itself divisive. In sociology there are difficulties of another kind. These concern the meaning of the term and different theories on the importance of class for understanding contemporary society. For Marx social class was based essentially on economic position: a class in itself was a group objectively united through a common relationship to the means of production, but this objective situation did not lead to class action. This comes about when a class becomes what Marx called 'a class for itself'. Class consciousness requires awareness both of class membership and of class interest plus a will to advance such interests. Weber, on the other hand, saw a class as an aggregate of people with the same life chances. He also distinguished three dimensions in terms of which modern societies were stratified, namely power, privilege, and prestige. He believed that classes were stratified according to their relation to the production and acquisition of goods and that status groups were stratified in terms of their consumption of goods as represented by special life-styles. He instanced more social classes and status groups in society than did Marx, who moved between two or three classes (ruling class and proletariat or these two plus a middle class).

Sociologists also disagree on the extent to which Marx's prediction concerning the increasing polarisation of society has come about and the extent to which social class is a useful notion over and above its value in predicting certain aspects of a person's social life, such as his educational experience and size of family. It certainly seems useful, and studies which use only a subjective definition ('you are the class you think you are') are very limited. The concept is useful even in societies which appear to have abandoned the idea of class as a possible basis of social life. In Soviet society, for example, social stratification continues to be a major factor, but it depends on the exercise of political rather than economic power through the machinery of state control. Such machinery is, on the whole, successfully employed by the political leaders, though some aspects of the status dimension of stratification elude them.

Bibliography: R. Bendix and S. M. Lipset, *Class, Status and Power*, 1953; T. Bottomore, *Classes in Modern Society*, 1965; G. Lenski, *Power and Privilege*, 1966; A. Beteille (Ed.), *Social Inequality*, 1969; D. Lane, *The End of Inequality? Stratification under State Socialism*, 1971; A. Swingewood, *Marx and Modern Social Theory*, 1975.

Social War, in Roman history, a two-year conflict caused by the persistent refusal of Rome to extend its franchise to its Latin allies. It was precipitated in 90 BC by the assassination of M. Livius DRUSUS; all central and southern Italy took to arms, the machinery of a new Italian state was planned and Corfinium, renamed Italica, was to be its capital. The first year's campaigns were on the whole disastrous for Rome; but towards the end of that year and early in 89 some partial concessions did much to satisfy the demands of the allies, who gradually lost interest in the struggle. By the end of 89 only the Lucanians and Samnites were in open revolt, which was quelled by SULLA. He brought the war to a close by capturing Nola in 88 BC.

Social Worker, a very wide term with no settled meaning. In Britain it refers to those professionally trained or untrained who work in statutory or voluntary, permanent or temporary, agencies which operate public programmes of social welfare. Most social workers are now employed in local authority social service departments, and in the probation and after-care service. Training for social work is now well-established in universities and institutions of higher education. At one time social workers undertook specialised tasks (for example, they were medical social workers, psychiatric social workers, and so on) and their training was correspondingly specialised. Since the 1960s, however, the tendency has been towards generic training (training for social work in general) and this has been echoed both in the local authority reorganisation of the previously separate departments of Children, Health, Welfare and also in the formation of a single unified professional association, the British Association of Social Work. The most recent development has been to include residential work as part of social work. The promotion of training in all fields of social work and the responsibility for appraising and reviewing all courses leading to the Certificate of Qualification in Social Work belong to the Central Council for Education and Training in Social Work, established in 1971.

Bibliography: N. Timms, *Social Work: An Outline for the Intending Student*, 1970; J. Haines, *Skills and Methods in Social Work*, 1975.

Socialisation, a sociological concept describing the complex processes whereby a person grows up to become an adult member of a particular society; it refers also to the results of these processes and to ways in which people are 'encouraged' to remain adult after childhood is over. Some writers place exclusive emphasis on psychological factors and on the nuance of relationships within the family. Other writers see that one can only be brought up to be a child/young person/adult in a particular society or even

stratum of a society. Emphasis has recently been placed on the overriding importance of the very early years of life and particularly on the significance of the early mother-child relationship. It has been argued that a baby deprived of consistent and loving care from a stable figure runs the risk of not developing as a human person. Considerable interest has been shown in patterns of child-rearing (for example, the extent of physical punishment, onset and attitudes to toilet training) and in differences in such patterns between social classes.

Our understanding of socialisation is, however, still rudimentary. In particular we need to know more about the concept central to both psychological and sociological understanding, namely internalisation, or the taking in and making one's own, of beliefs, behaviour, and values that are at first experienced as external. We should also develop knowledge of the extent to which processes of socialisation are differentially experienced and have differential results according to sex, age, and membership of particular groups. Another crucial issue concerns the extent to which socialisation is the dominant method of social control.

Bibliography: G. H. Mead, *Mind, Self and Society*, 1934; S. Freud, *An Outline of Psychoanalysis*, 1949; F. Elkin, *The Child and Society: The Process of Socialization*, 1960; J. Klein, *Samples from English Cultures*, vol 2, 1965.

Socialism, political doctrine and movement which advocates the partial or complete abolition of private property, and the establishment of society upon a basis of the common ownership of some or all of the means of production, distribution, and exchange. Sharing some of the sources of COMMUNISM, socialism has evolved along different lines, to the point where it is claimed that it offers an alternative to the faults of unrestricted capitalism on the one hand and of communism on the other. Many parties and states now calling themselves socialist, are committed only to government intervention in the free market, and to egalitarian social welfare and taxation policies. As social democrats, rather than communists, they are also committed to the pursuit of such policies through political means, eschewing insurrection and non-constitutional activity, at least within states allowing freedom of political action and expression.

Criticisms of private property and the advocacy of common ownership are to be found in the works of some of the Greek and Roman thinkers, but amongst the early Christian fathers, and modern socialism arises more directly from the 18th-century critics of capitalism. Attacks upon the oppression of the unpropertied by propertied classes are to be found among the works of Mably, Necker, Rousseau, and others. In the 19th century SAINT SIMON, FOURIER, and Robert OWEN contributed their various solutions to the problem of ensuring a better treatment of the industrial proletariat, and Louis BLANC propounded the scheme of planned production with the assistance of state credits and the common ownership of the means of production. Lassalle and Rodbertus put forward similar theories. Much more significant, however, was the teaching of Karl MARX and Friedrich ENGELS.

The spread of socialism gathered speed, and by 1939 there were 32 nations represented on the Labour and Socialist International (see INTERNATIONAL). Before the First World War the association was known as the

Socialism

International Socialist Bureau. A fundamental cleavage opened between those socialists who wished to achieve socialism by peaceful evolutionary methods, usually within an existing framework of parliamentary democracy, and those, the communists, who believed that the class-war, culminating in revolution, was the only possible and indeed desirable method. Marxian tactics were exemplified by the German Social-Democratic party, which carried its opposition to the bourgeois parties to the length of refusing to vote for the budget for armaments, and have been further demonstrated in the rise to power of communist parties in Eastern Europe, which, though willing to co-operate with opponents for the sake of tactical advantage, never abandon this fundamental antagonism. In Britain the Social Democratic party was the representative of the Marxians; the INDEPENDENT LABOUR PARTY and the FABIAN SOCIETY representing the evolutionary section. The two bodies joined in 1900 with the trade unions to form the Labour Representation Committee, now called the Labour party.

In the second half of the 19th century the standard of living of the working classes showed a general improvement, a development contrary to the prophecies of Marx. This helped to give a wide measure of acceptance in Western Europe to the ideas of the evolutionary socialists, who conceived of the winding-up of capitalism by peaceful reform. Disagreements which existed within the various Internationals also weakened the revolutionary tendency. Ultimately in Soviet Russia was established the most complete system of planned economy under a state machine dominated by the Communist party, whilst in Western Europe socialism set itself the task of reconciling economic planning with the freedoms generally accepted in a democracy.

In Germany, uncompromising socialists under Karl LIEBKNECHT organised the Spartacists League, which engineered the German revolution of November 1918, hastening the end of the war. But when, after the war, the Spartacists developed into communists they were suppressed by the government. The schism in socialism was made permanent by the formation of the Third International in Moscow in 1920, and in sympathy with the Russian Communists large Communist parties broke away from the Socialists in most European countries, while the moderate elements entered the government in many states, concentrating on social legislation and the widening of state influence on economic life. After the First World War moderate socialists became presidents or premiers in many European countries, among them being Ramsay MacDonald in Britain, Ebert in Germany, Adler in Austria, Stauning in Denmark, and Branting in Sweden. Indeed, the growth in numbers and in strength of the Socialist parties in all countries is one of the most marked political phenomena of the early years of this century. In Britain the Labour (or Socialist) party (see LABOUR PARTY) formed a Labour government in 1924 for eight months, although without an independent majority, and again in 1929 Labour was returned to office, holding 288 seats. But in 1931, during the general election in November, the serious condition of British finance, attributed by the opponents of socialism to the government's mismanagement, gave rise to a crisis in national affairs, and the pendulum swung violently back, resulting in a drop in the strength of the parliamentary Labour

party until 1945, when it returned to power for six years. In most countries the acute economic depression of 1931 resulted in a definite set-back to socialism.

Attempts which were made subsequently to heal the breach between Socialists and Communists by the Popular Front Movement (a suggestion for political collaboration of Communists, Socialists, and other left-wing parties against fascism put forward by the Communist International in 1935) had no more than a temporary influence in France and Spain. The progress of fascism in Europe in the period of German-Italian collaboration indirectly paralysed the policies of the Socialist parties in the democratic countries, for in the hope of thwarting the rise of fascism they acquiesced in measures which were inconsistent with their principles, and supported Conservative governments in those countries. The effect of the Second World War was greatly to reduce the importance of the Socialist International.

In 1945 the British Labour party won a sweeping victory at the election of that year, and in the Speech from the Throne at the opening of the first session the new government under Attlee included in their legislative programme proposals for large-scale nationalisation. In 1950 the Labour party was again returned to office but by a greatly reduced majority, with the result that the government temporised on further schemes of nationalisation. In 1951 the Labour party was replaced in office by the Conservatives. It was out of office for 13 years. When it returned to power, in 1964, nationalisation was no longer the cornerstone of its policies, though it was pledged to renationalise steel. The experience of nationalisation in practice educated the country in its possibilities and limitations. By 1964 socialism was being advocated in Britain as the system best able to achieve modernisation, not nationalisation, and its working-class image was fading. In Scandinavia, where it had had striking successes ever since the 1920s, socialism had long before discarded its revolutionary image and achieved a working compromise with capitalism.

In France the French Socialists were usually numerically inferior in parliament, but were the cause of frequent Cabinet downfalls. After the inauguration of the Fifth Republic their influence appeared negligible, the Communists being now the major party of the Left. Socialism in Italy has exercised influence since 1945 through some outstanding individuals rather than on account of its numerical strength, which is small compared with that of the Communists.

In Belgium the Socialist party exerted a powerful influence on the political life of the country from 1930 onwards. After the Second World War it played a prominent part in securing the abdication of Leopold II. Socialism in Holland has increased in influence since the Second World War. In Germany, evolutionary socialism is a powerful force in the Federal Republic. The Socialists in East Germany were fused with the Communists at the establishment of the German Democratic Republic and are now indistinguishable from them.

In the USA before the First World War the socialist vote numbered only about 1 million, and only one member was elected to the House of Representatives. Socialist propaganda was severely curtailed during the First World War on account of its hostility to the war, and a large element subsequently moved to the Communist party. But in the USA neither socialism nor communism has made any headway as a political party, the labour leaders concentrating rather on working within one or other of the two existing parties. In the 1870s German intellectuals, more acquainted with the tenets of Marx and Lassalle than with US labour, tried to establish an American socialism, but they met with little success. The INDUSTRIAL WORKERS OF THE WORLD, formally organised in 1905, was thoroughly indigenous, though it borrowed something from the syndicalist teaching of Sorel. Notwithstanding some success in the lumber and mining camps of the west and in the textile centres of the east, the IWW never had any real numerical strength, and its hostility to US participation in the First World War in 1917–18 put it out of business. The strong US trade unionism which has grown up since the depression of the 1930s is not socialist in its theories, the US worker accepting the capitalist system, and regarding himself as an integral part of it. Socialism in the USA has until recently been a term generally considered virtually synonymous with communism, and branded as anti-American.

Since the Second World War many of the Afro-Asian countries have adopted government forms which they label as 'socialist', e.g. Ghana and Indonesia. With the exception of India, however, these have little in common with socialism as understood in the West.

See also GUILD SOCIALISM; POLITICAL THOUGHT; SYNDICALISM.

Bibliography: R. Owen, *The Book of the New Moral World*, 1836–42; *Socialism, or the Rational System of Society*, 1840; H. Laski, *Karl Marx*, 1924; G. D. H. Cole, *Social Theory*, 1930; *Fabian Socialism*, 1943; M. Cole, *Makers of the Labour Movement*, 1948; G. D. H. Cole, *History of Socialist Thought*, 5 vols, 1953–60; H. Wilson, *The Relevance of British Socialism*, 1964; N. Mackenzie, *Socialism*, 1966; B. Russell, *Roads to Freedom: Socialism, Anarchism and Syndicalism*, 11th ed. 1966; G. Lichtheim, *Origins of Socialism*, 1969; *Short History of Socialism*, 1970; R. Berki, *Socialism*, 1975.

Socialist Realism,

the 'basic method' of literature and art in Soviet Russia, defined as 'truthful, historically concrete representation of reality in its revolutionary development', which 'must be combined with the task of the ideological transformation and education of the working man in the spirit of socialism'. The concept of Socialist Realism was conceived by its creators, STALIN, ZHDANOV, and GORKI, as a further development of Lenin's demand for the harnessing of literature to Party aims. Socialist Realism was first made obligatory for writers in 1932, when all existing writers' associations were dissolved by the Communist party and replaced by a single Soviet Writers' Union.

The combination of conflicting demands contained in the official definition of Socialist Realism could rarely be satisfied in practice, and its enforcement by the authorities has done much to stifle artistic life. Many of the most original works of post-war Soviet literature have been criticised or suppressed because of their pessimistic or 'non-progressive' tone.

See also FADEEV, ALEKSANDR ALEKSANDROVICH; RUSSIAN LITERATURE; SINYAVSKI, ANDREI DONATEVICH.

Bibliography: M. Slonim, *Soviet Russian Literature*, 1967.

Socialist Revolutionaries,

Russian political party, formed in 1902 by adherents of revolutionary POPULISM. Its programme, besides making common radical demands, aimed at a federal structure for the Russian state, self-determination for non-Russian peoples, and socialisation of the land. Assassination of leading government officials was a part of the Socialist Revolutionaries' tactics, and was carried out by an autonomous 'fighting organisation', for many years headed by the *provocateur* Azef. In 1917 a section of the party, Left Socialist Revolutionaries, split off, supported the Bolshevik seizure of power, and participated in the Bolshevik government until the Brest-Litovsk Treaty in 1918. The Socialist Revolutionaries had the majority in the Constituent Assembly which was dispersed by the Bolsheviks. The party was suppressed in Russia in 1922.

Bibliography: O. H. Radkey, *The Agrarian Foes of Bolshevism*, 1958; L. B. Schapiro, *The Origin of the Communist Autocracy*, 1966.

Society for Promoting Christian Knowledge,
see CHRISTIAN KNOWLEDGE, SOCIETY FOR PROMOTING.

Society for the Propagation of the Gospel,
see UNITED SOCIETY.

Society for the Protection of Ancient Buildings,
see PROTECTION OF ANCIENT BUILDINGS, SOCIETY FOR THE.

Society Islands,
main group in FRENCH POLYNESIA, comprise Windward Islands (Tahiti, Mooréa, Mehetia, etc.) and Leeward Islands (Huahune, Raiatea, etc.) The administrative centre of French Polynesia is Papeete in Tahiti. They were named by Captain James Cook when leading Royal Society Expedition to Tahiti in 1769. The islands became successively a protectorate (1847) and a colony (1880) of France, finally opting to be an Overseas Territory within French Community in 1958. Area 1673 km^2; population (1967) 81,424.

Society of Authors.
Founded in London by Walter Besant in 1884, the Society soon attracted the support of leading writers, its objects being to defend the rights and promote the interests of authors, reform domestic copyright, and promote international copyright. These objects are essentially unchanged, but the scope of the Society's work has continuously extended, so that today it caters comprehensively for writers in all the media, and makes special provision for playwrights, radiowriters, educational and children's writers, and other specialists. Members are entitled to legal and business advice in connection with their work, and will be defended at law if the case concerns a matter of principle affecting authorship at large. The Society is controlled by an elected committee of management, and administered by a secretariat. *The Author*, a quarterly, has been published by the Society continuously since 1890.

Society of Friends,
see FRIENDS, SOCIETY OF.

Society of Graphical and Allied Trades (SOGAT),
has approximately 200,000 members embracing roughly three-quarters of the employees in the printing and allied trades. It is the tenth largest trade union in Great Britain and traces its origins back to the 16th century. In its present form it is a combination of 34 previous unions.

Society of Jesus,
see JESUITS.

Socinus

Socinus, Latinised surname of two celebrated heresiarchs, the founders of Socinianism, which is akin to modern UNITARIANISM. Lelio Francisco Maria Sozini, or Loelius Socinus (1525–62), was born at Siena in Tuscany, his father being a jurist. He was keenly interested in theology, and in 1546 joined a secret society for the free discussion of theological matters. After having travelled through Europe where he was received by several Reformers, notably Melanchthon and Calvin, he finally settled at Zürich, where he eventually died. Fausto Paolo Sozini, or Faustus Socinus (1539–1604), nephew of the preceding, had from his youth sympathised with his uncle's views. From 1579 until his death he lived in Poland, where the Minor (Reformed) Church adopted his theological scheme. Here he acquired a very considerable following. After his death his writings exercised considerable influence throughout Western Europe. Socinianism differs from Arianism in its denial of the existence of Jesus before his birth as a man. It differs from Unitarianism in holding that this birth was miraculous, and that Christ was then endowed with certain divine qualities.

Bibliography: E. M. Wilbur, *A History of Unitarianism: Socinianism and its Antecedents*, 1946; J. A. Tedeschi (Ed.), *Italian Reformation Studies in honor of Laelius Socinus*, 1965.

Sociolinguistics, see LINGUISTICS.

Sociology. One of the main difficulties in elucidating the meaning of 'sociology', is that the term is used so very widely. Any investigation, however slight or casual, into people's habits, anything that can be described as 'social' is instantly called 'sociological'. The attempt to remedy this, however, meets the difficulty that sociologists themselves do not agree on a number of crucial issues. Should sociology be persued as a series of value-free investigations or is the sociologist committed to changing, as well as to understanding, society? Is sociology a discipline that approximates in its ways of investigation to the natural sciences (physics, for example) or is it a discipline, rigorous but humanistic, that attempts to understand the views and ideas of members of a particular society? Sociologists spend a great deal of time discussing these and related questions, but we can perhaps advance towards elucidating sociology if we consider some of the main terms sociologists use in the pursuit of understanding society.

First, we can consider *social relations*. Max WEBER talks of a social relation as one where two or more persons are engaged in conduct wherein each takes account of the behaviour of the other in a meaningful way and is therefore orientated in these terms. It is important to note that a social relation in which attitudes are completely and fully orientated to each other is not typical. Second, *social systems* are the organised sets of relationships between social rôles and social organisations and institutions. Third, we can review a number of additional specifically sociological concepts such as ANOMIE, ROLE, and SOCIAL STRATIFICATION. All these terms taken together give some idea of sociological work.

The term 'sociology' was first used by Auguste COMTE (1798–1857) who referred to it in the fourth volume of *Cours de philosophie positive*, 1839. His studies of change between types of society mark a significant and continuing interest in what has been termed 'evolutionary sociology'. The two most important sociologists working in this tradition in England were Herbert SPENCER (1820–1903)

and L. T. HOBHOUSE (1864–1929). The work of Hobhouse (*Morals in Evolution*, 1915; and *Social Development*, 1924) is probably the high-water-mark of this tradition. For much of the period between 1930 and 1950 sociology in Britain was dominated by another tradition, namely that of the straightforward empirical description of social problems and conditions associated with the work of such earlier investigators as Charles BOOTH. There was little interest in the development of specifically sociological theory and the rich European theorising associated with WEBER, MARX, DURKHEIM, SIMMEL, and PARETO (who together can be called the founding fathers of sociology) seemed to have little impact.

Since then, however, the situation has changed dramatically. Sociology has become a very well established feature of education in universities, polytechnics, and other institutions of higher education. Most universities have chairs in sociology and the subject is extremely popular with applicants for undergraduate and postgraduate places. As a response to this there has developed a keen interest in theory (some critics suggest that sociology only consists of detailed and repetitive discussion of the work of the founding fathers), in criticism of the existing social order, and in the development of specialised applications of sociology to particular problems and institutions.

The present state of sociological theory seems rich or chaotic, according to one's point of view. Marx, particularly early Marx, seems to some to be a source of considerable inspiration. Others, such as the so-called Frankfurt School (Habermas, Adorno, and others) build on and adopt a Marxian analysis. Functionalism, which will be discussed below, still enjoys prestige, whilst for sociologists who adopt a phenomenological perspective (attempting to suspend assumptions and examine social interaction as it takes place) the social structure seems to dissolve before a never-ending analysis of common-sense and taken-for-granted meanings. Yet other sociologists leave theoretical discussion and elaboration aside and concentrate on empirical work, on establishing the facts. This viewpoint was uppermost in the USA in the 1950s and early 1960s and was responsible for the quip that a sociologist was a man who spent a great deal of research money finding the way to a brothel. It is still, however, a significant viewpoint and some sociologists equate their discipline not just with empirical research, but with one particular method of conducting such research, namely that of the social survey.

This growth in theoretical positions has had at least two important effects on the developments of sociology. First, it has led to attempts to order the multitude of approaches and to suggestions that there are only two sociologies, one of consensus and the other of conflict; thus one has to choose where allegiance lies. Second, it has led to a steady, if not always steadying, criticism both of the existing social order (as repressive simply through the operations of its day-to-day business) and of sociological theories which are taken to support the repression. Of these the best known is structural functionalism (see STRUCTURALISM).

Functionalism probably owes its origins to Emile Durkheim, who argued that social institutions exist for the purposes of fulfilling social needs. The major developments in the theory, however, are due to anthropologists in the 1920s and 1930s and to US sociologists in the

1930s and 1940s. A. R. RADCLIFFE-BROWN emphasised the importance of the study of society as a whole and of establishing the ways in which each social institution in that society related to other institutions particularly in so far as they contributed to 'the necessary conditions' of existence for that society. In the USA structural-functionalism is associated mainly with the highly influential theories of Talcott Parsons, who stressed the normative order (the basic agreement on values) to be found at the centre of every social system. Merton, another US sociologist who made a distinction between the manifest and latent functions that a particular social institution might serve, argued that functionalism was capable of a conservative or a radical interpretation. However, since the 1960s the former interpretation has been dominant and functionalism has been adversely criticised as a means simply of blessing the status quo and as significantly failing to explain social change. If societies are on-going systems of basic agreements, how can they ever change in any drastic way?

The third recent change referred to above was the development of various specialisations within sociology. The application of sociology to industry developed relatively early, but we now see an increasing number of 'sociologies' concerned with the application of sociology to particular social institutions: for example, the sociology of religion, of education, of social deviance, of science, of sexual behaviour, of social welfare, of the professions, of health. These developments pose at least two problems. First, how useful or otherwise applicable do practitioners in these fields of work find the sociological applications? This in turn raises a central question concerning the extent sociology can be what is called a 'value-free' pursuit. If sociologists study social problems, for instance, are they free from any commitment to the viewpoint of the established order or to 'the underdog'?. Second, how far do these sub-divisions of sociology take on, as it were, an independent life, so that the sociology of deviance, for example, becomes totally disconnected from the study of health or of political sociology? The recent revival of interest in social deviance (as in criminal or sexually abnormal behaviour) has arisen partly from an attempt on the part of sociologists to connect more firmly research in deviance with the mainstream sociological concerns with power, socialisation, and group membership.

Bibliography: D. Martin, *A Sociology of English Religion*, 1967; N. Timms, *A Sociological Approach to Social Problems*, 1967; G. Hurd, *Human Societies*, 1973; J. Rex, *Approaches to Sociology*, 1974; J. Bailey, *Social Theory for Planning*, 1975.

Sociology of Knowledge, study of the social conditions under which various beliefs, especially political, religious, and economic, flourish. Insofar as the sociology of knowledge claims to show that our view of the world is determined by social factors it tends to undermine belief in any objective social truths, and leads to a socially and historically determined philosophical relativism. See also IDEOLOGY.

Bibliography: K. Manheim, *Ideology and Utopia*, 1936.

Sociometry, a field, or survey, technique used in psychology, psychiatry, and social anthropology, which relies on questioning or observing patterns of acceptance, rejection, or indifference between members of a group, for example in schools, industry, or the armed forces. The diagrammatic presentation of the network of relationships is called a sociogram.

Socotra, island in the Indian Ocean, 250 km north-east of Cape Guardafui, East Africa, and near the entrance to the Gulf of Aden. Length east to west, 115 km; greatest breadth, 35 km. It was under British protection as a dependency of Aden, the Mahri sultan of Qishn and Socotra having concluded a treaty with the British government in 1886; it now forms part of the People's Democratic Republic of YEMEN. The island is mainly a lofty tableland, rising to above 1200 m, with a narrow coastal plain. This and the valleys are very fertile. Myrrh, frankincense, incense, aloes, and butter (ghee) are produced; cattle and goats are reared. The main settlement is Tamridah. It possesses a highly strategic submarine base. Area 3580 km²; population c. 1200.

Socrates (469–399 BC), Greek philosopher, born at Athens. He left no writings so that our information about him depends on the records of others, chiefly his pupil PLATO and XENOPHON. Socrates grew to manhood while Athens was at the height of its glory. About 450 he seems to have become interested in the Ionian philosophy recently introduced into Athens by Anaxagoras, and he attached himself to Archelaus, the latter's successor. It seems that this early interest in physical science led to disillusionment, and Socrates determined to strike out on his own. In doing so he was undoubtedly influenced by Pythagorean teaching; at any rate, by 439 he enjoyed a widespread reputation for wisdom. He is next found serving as a hoplite in the army at Potidaea (430), Delium (424), and Amphipolis (422), where he won renown for his valour and powers of endurance. About 423 he was burlesqued in the *Connus* of Ameipsias and the more celebrated *Clouds* of Aristophanes; and it is certain that the cause of this not always good-natured satire

Socrates. Statuette of Roman date from a Greek original of the 4th century. *(British Museum, London)*

Socrates Scholasticus

was Socrates' new asceticism and novel doctrines about the soul. In 406 Socrates allowed himself to be elected to the Council of Five Hundred, where, despite popular clamour, he refused to lend his voice to the condemnation of the victorious admirals after Arginusae. Following the expulsion of the Thirty Tyrants, Socrates was charged with impiety (*asebeia*) and corruption of Athenian youth. The second of these offences meant in effect Socrates' encouragement of the young to criticise the existing order. He was found guilty by a narrow majority, but by his attitude after the verdict he so enraged his judges that he was sentenced to death. The execution was delayed for 30 days, during the Delian festival, and during that time Socrates refused to avail himself of plans for his escape. He drank the hemlock in the spring of 399. The description of his last hours is found in the *Phaedo* of Plato, and is among the masterpieces of European literature.

The value of Socrates' contribution to philosophy is disputed. Some attribute directly to him much of the doctrine of his disciple Plato, but this view is rejected by many scholars, and indeed Socrates himself denied that he had any set of positive doctrines to teach. Nevertheless, it may safely be maintained that Socrates was the founder of the spiritual view of knowledge and conduct. He defined the soul as that in man which has knowledge, and also ignorance, good and bad. Thus for the first time intelligence is distinguished from sensation, and the soul identified with the normal consciousness or character of man. Moreover Socrates declared that the soul was immortal. It was but a step from this conviction to the doctrine that goodness is knowledge (*epistēmē*). The Socratic method of 'examination in arguments' (*skepsis en logois*) or 'Socratic irony' was in itself not new; it had already been employed by Zeno against Pythagorean geometry. What was new was its application by Socrates to questions of ethics and aesthetics. Socrates believed that he had a divine mission to convict men of sin (i.e. ignorance) by question and answer, examining systematically the fundamental assumptions from which discussion of conduct and morality arose, and insisting upon a strict definition of terms. In this, Socrates may be regarded as the founder of formal logic.

Bibliography: R. L. Levin and J. Brewer, *The Question of Socrates*, 1961; G. C. Field, *Plato and His Contemporaries*, 1967; W. K. C. Guthrie, *A History of Greek Philosophy* (vol. 3), 1969.

Socrates Scholasticus (c. 380–c. 450), Christian church historian, born at Constantinople in the reign of the Emperor Theodosius the Younger. He continued the *Ecclesiastical History* of EUSEBIUS, from the beginning of the reign of Constantine (306) to 439.

Soda Water, see SOFT DRINKS.

Soddy, Frederick (1877–1956), British chemist, born at Eastbourne. He was educated at Eastbourne College, the University College of Wales, Merton College, Oxford, and also at McGill University, Montreal, under RUTHERFORD, and in London under Sir William RAMSAY. He was demonstrator in chemistry at McGill University (1900–02), lecturer on chemistry and radioactivity at Glasgow (1904–14), professor of chemistry at Aberdeen (1914–19), and professor of inorganic and physical chemistry at Oxford (1919–36). His chief field of work was that

of radioactivity. In 1913 he elaborated the theory of ISOTOPES and, with Rutherford, stated the displacement law of radioactivity. He was elected FRS in 1910. In 1921 he won the Nobel Prize for chemistry. In later life he wrote on economics. His publications include *The Interpretation of Radium*, 1904; *Chemistry of the Radioactive Elements*, 1912–14; *Matter and Energy*, 1912; *Science and Life*, 1920; *Cartesian Economics*, 1922; *Money versus Man*, 1931; *Interpretation of the Atom*, 1932; *Role of Money*, 1934; *The Arch-Enemy of Economic Freedom*, 1943; and *The Story of Atomic Energy*, 1949.

Söderberg, Hjalmar Emil Fredrik (1869–1941), Swedish writer born in Stockholm. He is famous for the clarity and economy of his style, as shown in short stories, such as *Historietter*, 1898, and novels, including *Martin Bircks ungdom*, 1901 (*Martin Birck's Youth*, 1930), *Doktor Glas*, 1905 (*Doctor Glas*, 1963), and *Den allvarsamma leken*, 1912. He also wrote a highly praised play, *Gertrud*, 1906. His view of life was unremittingly pessimistic and disillusioned: 'I believe in the lust of the flesh and the incurable loneliness of the soul', he wrote, and his works are mainly about the thwarted and disappointed love-affairs of the middle classes.

Söderblom, Nathan (1866–1931), Swedish Protestant theologian, born at Helsingland. After a university education at Uppsala he became rector of the Swedish church in Paris (1894). In 1901 he returned to Uppsala as professor, and was made archbishop in 1914 after two years as professor at Leipzig. He wrote on historical and theological subjects, particularly *The Nature of Revelation*, 1903, *Origin of Belief*, 1914, and his remarkable Luther studies *Humour and Melancholy*, 1919. In 1931 Söderblom gave the Gifford lectures in Edinburgh, published in 1933 as *The Living God*. He was a leading advocate of the unity of the Christian churches. He also did much to promote international understanding and peace, and for this was awarded the Nobel Peace Prize in 1930.

Bibliography: Lives by P. Katz, 1925, and J. M. van Veen, 1940; B. Sundkler, *Nathan Söderblom*, 1968.

Söderhamn, Swedish seaport near the mouth of the Ljusne river, 70 km south of Gävle. There are sawmills and planing works, wood-pulp works, and iron works. The town has a large timber trade. Population 14,000.

Södermanland, county of eastern Sweden, between the Baltic coast and Lake Hjälmaren. There are iron mines and metal-working and engineering industries. The capital is NYKÖPING. Area 5267 km²; population (1974) 250,700.

Södertälje, town in the county of Stockholm, Sweden, a flourishing industrial suburb of the capital, with pharmaceutical, heavy vehicle construction, and engineering plants. Södertälje Canal connects Lake Mälaren with the Baltic. Population (1974) 77,800.

Sodium, metallic chemical element, symbol Na, atomic number 11, atomic weight 22·9898, one of the ALKALI METALS; occurs abundantly in nature as the chloride. Sodium chloride, or common salt, is found in sea-water and some lakes and springs. It is obtained by evaporation of sea-water in pans, or from the great natural deposits or rock salt found in Cheshire and Stassfurt. As the nitrate, sodium is found in Chile and Peru (Chile salt-petre), and as the fluoride (cryolite), $3NaF\cdot AlF_3$, in Greenland. It is also the constituent of many silicates, and is present in animal organisms and in plants. Sodium was first isolated by Sir Humphry DAVY by the electrolysis of sodium hydroxide. It is manufactured by electrolysis of fused sodium chloride, the sodium collecting round the cathode while chlorine is evolved at the anode (see ELECTROCHEMISTRY), or by electrolysis of fused silver hydroxide, which is Davy's original process adapted to modern electrical resources.

Sodium is a soft, silvery-white metal (relative density 0·97) which tarnishes instantly on exposure to air, forming a film of sodium oxide. (Because of this, it must be stored immersed in a liquid containing no oxygen, such as liquid paraffin.) It is so soft that it can easily be cut with a knife, and extruded into wire at room temperature. It melts at 97·5 °C, and boils at 883 °C, forming a purple vapour. Heated in air, the metal forms sodium peroxide (Na_2O_2) and sodium monoxide (Na_2O), and when heated in hydrogen forms the hydride (NaH). It rapidly decomposes water with the formation of the hydroxide and the evolution of hydrogen: $2Na + 2H_2O = 2NaOH + H_2$. Sodium is used either alone or in the form of the mercury amalgam, as a reducing agent for organic compounds, and is also employed in the preparation of the peroxide and cyanide. Its potassium alloy, which is liquid at ordinary temperatures, has been used as a heat-transfer medium in nuclear reactors.

Sodium forms two oxides, the monoxide and the peroxide. The monoxide is a white amorphous compound produced by the partial oxidation of the metal in a limited supply of air. Sodium monoxide reacts with water to form the hydroxide: $Na_2O + H_2O = 2NaOH$. Sodium peroxide is a yellowish-white solid obtained by heating the metal in air in aluminium vessels. It decomposes water and forms sodium hydroxide. Oxygen is also evolved, and on account of this property the peroxide is used as an oxidising agent. With cold dilute hydrochloric acid, the peroxide forms hydrogen peroxide, which is used for bleaching. Sodium hydroxide (caustic soda) is manufactured by the electrolysis of brine, collecting round the cathode while chlorine is evolved at the anode. Sodium chloride is the most important halogen compound of the metal, and is obtained by the evaporation of sea-water or from salt beds. It is the main source of the metal and of chlorine; as an article of food it is of great importance. Sodium nitrate, or Chile saltpetre ($NaNO_3$), occurs in the crude state ('caliche') in Peru and Bolivia. It was formerly largely employed for the manufacture of nitric acid and is of great importance as a fertiliser. Much sodium nitrate is now obtained from synthetic nitric acid. Heated strongly, it evolves oxygen and is converted into the nitrite, which is used for preparing organic dyes. Sodium thiosulphate, ($Na_2S_2O_3$, 'hypo') is employed in photography, as it dissolves the unaltered halogen salts of silver from the film after development, but does not affect the image. The most important of the artificially prepared compounds of sodium is the carbonate, commonly known as 'soda' (Na_2CO_3). The process first adopted in its manufacture was the 'Leblanc' or 'black ash' process. This was superseded by the Solvay or ammonia soda process. Sodium

cyanide is made on the industrial scale from COAL GAS. It is used for the extraction of gold.

Sodium Chloride, common salt, NaCl, occurs in large quantities in sea-water and in extensive deposits of rock salt. It is either extracted by evaporation of brine, or mined, according to circumstances. Sodium chloride crystallises in cubes, is quite soluble in water, but almost insoluble in alcohol. It is used for seasoning and preserving food, for melting snow and ice on roads, and as a starting material in the manufacture of caustic soda and metallic sodium.

Sodium Fusion Test, or Lassaigne test, process used to determine the elements present in an organic liquid or solid. Carbon and hydrogen are normally assumed to be present, and are not involved in this test. The test compound is placed in a small, hard glass test-tube, with a few pellets of sodium. The tube is then heated, gently at first, until no more vapour is produced and the bottom of the tube is red hot. The tube is then plunged immediately into about 10 ml of distilled water. The tube breaks and the sodium and organic material are dissolved. This mixture is then filtered, the filtrate becoming the test solution for separate analyses for the elements nitrogen, chlorine, bromine, iodine, and sulphur.

There is a range of procedures to indicate the presence or absence of these elements and the essence of the procedure described above is to get the organic material into solution.

Bibliography: F. G. Mann and B. C. Saunders, *Practical Organic Chemistry*, 4th ed. 1975.

Sodium Sulphate, or Glauber's salt, $Na_2SO_4\cdot 10H_2O$, compound prepared by heating salt with sulphuric acid, and crystallising the residue from water, from which it separates as colourless prisms. The 10 molecules of water of crystallisation are lost on prolonged exposure to the air. Sodium sulphate has a cooling, bitter and saltish taste, is a mild laxative and diuretic, and is present in the waters of Karlovy Vary, Cheltenham, etc. It is used in large amounts in paper-making processes, and as a constituent of some synthetic detergents.

Sodium Tetraborate, see BORAX.

Sodom and Gomorrah, two of the five 'cities of the plain', which now lie beneath the shallow waters of the southern end of the Dead Sea. Near Sodom LOT took up his residence, but fled before the destruction of the cities recounted in Gen. xix. 24 ff. The region is sulphurous and bituminous, and such places are liable to earthquakes and sudden eruptions of gas and oil, which may ignite spontaneously, giving off clouds of smoke.

Bibliography: G. E. Wright, *Biblical Archaeology*, 1957.

Sodoma, Il, real name Giovanni Antonio Bazzi (1477–1549), Italian painter, born at Vercelli. Going to Milan as a young man he was much influenced by Leonardo da Vinci. He worked in several Italian cities but mainly in Siena where he painted frescoes of religious subjects. He was working in the Vatican until 1508, where Raphael retained his work in the centre of the ceiling fresco in the Stanza della Segnatura. He executed some frescoes of scenes from the *Life of Alexander* in the Villa Farnesina, Rome. *The Vision of St Catherine*, 1526

(Siena, S. Domenica), is one of the principal examples of his graceful and ornate style.

Sodor and Man, title of the Anglican bishop responsible for the Isle of Man (see MAN, ISLE OF). It is a relic of the former Norse kingdom disbanded in 1266 when the Hebrides became part of Scotland.

Soest, city in NORTH RHINE-WESTPHALIA, West Germany, 50 km east of Dortmund. It was an important member of the HANSEATIC LEAGUE. It has several fine medieval churches. It is a tourist centre and has important sugar refineries. Population 43,000.

Sofia, capital of BULGARIA, situated in the west of the country, some 480 km north-west of Istanbul and 320 km south-east of Belgrade. Its situation has made it an important crossroads for trade and communications throughout its history. Neolithic origins have been established. It was a Thracian settlement (see THRACE) from the 8th century BC onwards, until occupied by the Romans in 29 BC. It was sacked by the Huns in 447. The town was developed under the Byzantine empire, when the church of St Sofia was built. In 809 it was captured by Bulgaria and was given the name *Sredets*. In the 11th and 12th centuries it was again Byzantine, but fell to the Turks in 1382. The ruler of RUMELIA was resident there, but by the 19th century Sofia was reduced to a provincial outpost. It was named the capital of independent Bulgaria in 1879. Sofia was an important anti-Fascist resistance centre in the Second World War.

Post-war expansion has been great, and it is largely a modern city. There is an Orthodox cathedral (1924), two old mosques, the University of Sofia (1888), and museums, theatres, and an opera house. Sofia has important international air and rail links. Its main industries are engineering, textiles, chemicals, and electrical goods. Population (1975) 965,728.

Soft Drinks, originally an American term for non-alcoholic beverages to distinguish them from hard (i.e., alcoholic) drinks. The term is still used to denote non-alcoholic drinks, carbonated or still, containing natural or artificial flavouring and usually sweetened. Fruit drinks, soda water, tonic water, ginger beer, etc. are all considered soft drinks, but tea, cofee, cocoa, milk, and vegetable juices are not.

Carbonated or aerated waters and beverages, into which carbon dioxide is introduced under pressure, originated from the desire to imitate the naturally sparkling waters of certain springs. They were first attempted by Thurneysser in 1560, later by Hoffman, 1708, and Geoffroy, 1724. Joseph PRIESTLEY experimented, 1767-72, and proposed several improved methods, including the use of the pressure pump, successfully developed commercially by Paul, Schweppe, and Gosse. The seltzogene for home use derived from an invention by John Nooth in 1774, and the syphon from Charles Plinth's 'fountain' of 1813. More recently, a home syphon was developed to which a capsule of high pressure carbon dioxide was attached and the gas absorbed. The crown cork, the usual small bottle closure, was invented by William Painter in 1892, larger bottles being secured by screw tops.

Carbon dioxide for the manufacture of carbonated soft drinks is purchased either as a solid (dry ice) or as a liquid under pressure. The flavouring syrup is either diluted before carbonation or added to water that is already carbonated. The entire process is almost entirely automated and can be carried out at high speed.

Softball, a condensed version of BASEBALL, is a very popular participant sport in many countries. At the beginning of this century a version of baseball using a larger, softer ball was played indoors. A National Amateur Playground Ball Association of the USA was organised in 1908 to promote outdoor play with the larger ball. In 1933 the Amateur Softball Association of America organised world championships for both men and women, since when softball has been the official title of the sport. An International Softball Federation was formed in 1952 and has a membership of some 30 nations.

The ball is 30·16 cm to 30·79 cm in circumference and weighs 170 g to 184 g; far from being soft, it is as hard as a baseball. The bat must be under 86·36 cm long and 5·39 cm in diameter. The pitching distance is 14 m for men, 11·61 m for women and 18·3 m between the bases for both.

The rules of softball are similar to baseball, the principal differences being that the ball is pitched underhand and must be released below hip level with the wrist not further from the body than the width of a wrist. Seven innings are played. Base runners must remain in contact with a base until the ball leaves the pitcher's hand.

The combination of smaller distances, larger ball and smaller bat, makes softball as fast and skilful as baseball, although the rules of softball have always been geared to the requirements of the amateur player.

A further version of softball called 'Slowpitch' has been developed in recent years and has grown in popularity. It may be played with standard equipment or, if space is limited, on a field with a 15 m square infield and with a larger ball 40·6 cm in circumference, 255 g to 283·5 g in weight. The main difference from softball (fast pitch) is that the ball must describe an arc of not less than 1 m in its flight towards the batsman and must be delivered at moderate speed. The umpire may eject a pitcher for repeatedly pitching the ball too fast or without the required trajectory.

Softwood, see TIMBER.

Sogdiana, see SAMARKAND.

Sogn og Fjordane, county of Norway, bordering on the Atlantic and including SOGNE FJORD. Its wild mountains provide some of Norway's most important water-power resources. Area 18,480 km²; population (1975) 102,600.

Sogne Fjord, inlet running eastward from the sea on the west coast of NORWAY. It is the longest (about 160 km), and also the deepest, in the country. There are no offshoots for the first 80 km from the sea, but after that the fjords of Fjærland, Sogndal, Årdal, Lærdal, and Aurland branch off in various directions. The fjord is popular with tourists because of its magnificent panoramas of mountain scenery.

Soham, parish in CAMBRIDGESHIRE, England, 10 km east of Ely. St Andrew's church is partly of 12th-century construction; there is a grammar school founded in 1687. The parish has orchards and market-gardening; sugar beet and potatoes are grown. Population (1971) 5410.

Sogne Fjord. *(Camera Press)*

Soignies (Flemish *Zinnik*), town in the province of Hainaut, Belgium, 16 km north of Mons. It has important quarries of freestone and limestone. The church of St Vincent is one of the oldest and most remarkable examples of Romanesque architecture in the country. The forest of Soignies which lies south-east of Brussels is a remnant of the once vast and splendid forest of this name. Population 12,100.

Soil may be defined as a naturally occurring body made up of mineral and organic constituents and differentiated into layers or horizons, each horizon having different chemical, physical, and biological properties. It is the end product of the interaction of five factors: parent material, climate, organisms, topography, and time. Some work-

ers have considered these factors as either active (climate and organisms) or passive (topography and parent material). The initial stage of soil is the parent material. This consists of either solid rock and mineral materials (e.g. GRANITE, BASALT, SANDSTONE) or drift deposits (e.g. BOULDER CLAY, river alluviums, glacial outwash sands, and gravels). WEATHERING processes act upon the parent materials to produce a mineral mixture of sands, silts, and clay. Weathering processes may be determined by climatic conditions, and the vegetation colonising the soil will also be responsive to and reflect climatic considerations. The vegetation growing on soil will add organic matter to the mineral parent material, and will also support a diverse animal population, including man, which will add further organic material to the mineral framework as organic waste and other residues. The mineral base thus acquires a biological population. Slope stability will help determine the amount and rate of soil formation, particularly through the water balance in the soil which is again dependent upon slope conditions. Finally all these factors and their related processes such as podsolisation, laterisation, and gleying, like all natural phenomena, combine over a period of time to produce a soil. Thus all five soil forming factors, isolated by Dokuchiaev, the Russian 'father of soil science', in 1883, are interconnected.

The unit of soil study is the *soil profile*, a two-dimensional section of soil. This unit is taken for practical convenience, for although soil exists in three dimensions it is difficult to study in this manner. The profile is composed of several layers or *horizons* each of which is given a letter to display certain characteristics. For example, at the surface in a podsol soil (see PODSOLIC

Soil. Diagram of sand/clay/silt fraction.

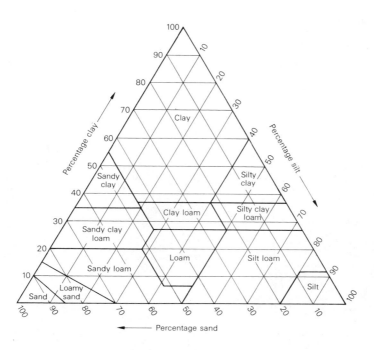

Soil

Soil. Profile of a podsol soil with the pegs marking the different horizons. *(J. A. Soulsby)*

SOILS) the organic debris of dead leaves, twigs, etc. is termed the litter horizon; this litter undergoes chemical and biological breakdown in the fermentation horizon until it becomes HUMUS. These horizons are designated L (litter), F (fermentation), and H (humus) horizons or may be known collectively as the O (organic) horizon and noted as O1, O2, and O3. Below the organic horizons lies the mineral material which is designated A or E showing depletion of certain minerals, which may be redeposited in the horizons below—the B horizons which overlie the C horizon or parent material. Thus the master horizons from the surface downwards are denoted O, A, B, C. Subscripts denote special horizon characteristics, e.g. B2h indicates a horizon rich in redeposited humus, and Ap denotes an upper mineral horizon which has been ploughed. The terms TOPSOIL and SUBSOIL are popular expressions of the horizon concept. Most soils undergo successive waves of development, e.g. with the change from natural woodland to cropland which is later abandoned, and are thus not the result of a single set of interacting processes. Each phase of development produces features which are then inherited by the next phase. The main processes operating in soil formation are hydration, hydrolysis, solution, oxidation reduction, and clay mineral production. These processes can be the result of physical and biological action expressed as a chemical result. Hydrolysis is important in mineral destruction and the release of plant nutrients into solution, and with solution processes, which dissolve minerals, a series of secondary minerals are produced, e.g. aluminium oxides which are then reworked by hydration processes to absorb water. The release of elements into either a dry or moist environment allows oxidation or reduction processes to occur (see PEAT BOGS; GLEY SOILS) and thus soils display a wide variety of properties depending upon their mode of formation. Colour is determined and precisely noted by means of Munsell Soil Color Charts. The colours are indicative of various processes, e.g. blues and greys indicate iron in a reduced ferrous state whilst black colourations may indicate the presence of manganese or humus. Some soils, however, inherit specific colours from

their parent material, e.g. Old Red Sandstone. The elemental particles (SAND, SILT, CLAY) mix together in soil giving the soil a particular textural class, e.g. sandy loam, and join aggregates known as structure units. The main structures recognised are blocky, prismatic, columnar, platy, and massive/single grain, with a wide variety of sub-classes, e.g. fine sub-angular blocky. Structure is a soil condition which can be easily altered by cultivation but structure units are important as controls on moisture and fertility.

In their natural state soils are classified for moisture status on a five-point scale from excessively to very poorly drained. The pH value of soils ranges from three (acid) through seven (neutral) to nine (alkaline). Most agricultural and horticultural plants prefer a slightly acid soil for maximum yields. When soils are examined under field conditions, the slope, altitude, drainage class, parent material and stoniness, topography, and vegetation are noted along with the amount of humus present. The horizon thickness and sequence are described in terms of colour, structure, texture, cohesion, rooting system and

Soil. Vines growing in volcanic soil in the Canary Islands. *(Barnaby's Picture Library)*

stoniness, and samples are taken for quantitative laboratory determination of nutrient state, pH, humus content, etc. Following this, soils are classified at two levels: the great soil group or sub-group level, e.g. peaty podsol, and the local level as a soil series based on local parent material and drainage status. The series distribution can be plotted on a map.

See also individual soil group entries, e.g. CHERNOZEMS, AND CHESTNUT EARTH SOILS.

Bibliography: E. A. Bridges, *World Soils*, 1970; E. A. Fitzpatrick, *Pedology*, 1971, and *An Introduction to Soil Science*, 1974; J. G. Cruickshank, *Soil Geography*, 1972; S. W. Buol, F. D. Hole and R. J. McCracken, *Soil Genesis and Classification*, 1973; N. C. Brady, *The Nature and Properties of Soils*, 1974.

Soil-creep, imperceptible downward migration of soils under the influence of gravity. Its effects may be shown by the tilting of fences on hill slopes, and by the curving of tree-trunks, which change their direction of growth in an effort to remain vertical. Common manifestations of this phenomenon are terracettes about 25 cm wide where sheep have repeatedly used the same track on steep hill slopes causing further downward movement. See also SOLIFLUCTION.

Soil Erosion and Conservation. *Soil erosion* is usually considered to be the removal of soil particles from the earth's surface by wind or water or a combination of both. It is frequently the effect which results from the mismanagement of soil by human agencies. For this reason soil erosion should be distinguished from normal or geological erosion which is the breakdown of rocks by WEATHERING processes and their removal from the weathering site by gravity, water, wind, or ice. This natural process of erosion is slow and barely noticeable over hundreds of years, in contrast to soil erosion, or accelerated erosion, which takes place rapidly in a period of weeks, or even hours. Soil erosion takes place most frequently where vegetation cover is sparse or absent and little protection is afforded to the soil when severe wind or rain storms occur.

Vegetation cover protects the soil in a number of ways: (a) by protecting the soil from the impact of raindrops; (b) by providing a medium for the uptake of water through plant roots; (c) by slowing the speed of run-off across the land surface; and (d) by slowing down the speed of the wind. If a minimal vegetation cover exists, then the amount of erosion will depend upon the intensity of rainfall, the angle of slope for water to run across, the soil characteristics, and the speed of the wind.

Water erosion. Soft rain does little damage to soil, but under thunderstorm conditions raindrops average 2 mm in diameter and fall at a speed of 7 m per second (15 mph) and splash erosion occurs. When the moisture reaching the soil cannot be absorbed, a sheet of water moves across the ground surface removing fine particles and dissolving plant foods. Soils are thus left thinner and less fertile by this sheet erosion. On steeper slopes, or when run-off is heavy, water begins to flow in small channels causing rill erosion. These channels may merge and if the combined channel moves across a steep break in a field the small waterfall created has a much greater erosive power and rapid back cutting occurs. Gullies are formed which proceed to deepen and widen under rainstorm conditions, sometimes to depths of over 50 m. The amount of material removed depends upon soil characteristics; sandy soils can absorb water more easily than soils with a high clay content. Run-off will be greater on clay soils but water erosion can be much more rapid on coarse-grained sands which lack the cohesion of clays. Soil removed in this manner is then dumped where slope gradients lessen and water movement is slowed. Lakes become silted up by deposited material and rivers receiving floodwaters may not be able to remove the extra sediment load. Channels thus become blocked and flooding occurs.

Wind erosion can only begin on bare soils. Particles greater than 3 mm in diameter can only be moved by hurricane force winds. Particles between 3 mm and 0·5 mm are rolled along by the wind. Fine particles, less than 0·1 mm in diameter, can stay in suspension in the wind but

Soil Erosion and Conservation. BELOW Rill erosion at Ducktown, Tennessee. RIGHT Gully erosion in Glen Tilt, Scotland. *(J. A. Soulsby)*

Soil Erosion and Conservation

must be initially moved from the ground surface by impact from larger particles which move across the ground in a series of jumps; for at the ground surface itself, wind speed is zero.

Most erosion is caused by man's activities, as soil erosion only occurs naturally in desert areas where there is little vegetation. When a grassland or forest vegetation cover is removed or altered, soil erosion may begin. Population pressures increase demands for food and cultivation is taken into marginal environments, whilst overstocking of pastures removes grasses leaving the soil open to the elements. Lack of rotation removes essential elements necessary to provide a fertility balance and structure units, which provide soil stability, break down. Continued cultivation of row crops, e.g. cotton, tobacco, raspberries, may lead to erosion especially when these rows run downslope, as the spaces between rows form channels for water movement under heavy rain. The removal of forest cover on steep slopes removes the leaves which break the impact of rainwater and the mass of vegetation which slows down winds. The litter of twigs and dead leaves under trees act as a barrier to rapid run-off which occurs when this barrier is removed. Much soil erosion is caused either by social and economic pressures or the use of unsuitable agricultural practices in an alien environment.

Soil Conservation can be carried out at a variety of scales from local to national. Wind erosion can be overcome by planting wind breaks, but where this is not feasible crops can be planted in strips 60 m apart at right angles to the prevailing wind. A stubble cover or straw mulch will conserve moisture and also protect against wind erosion and water erosion associated with rapid spring snow melt. Dunes can be stabilised by planting with vegetation which binds the sand into place, e.g. mar-

Soil Erosion and Conservation. View at Holkham, Norfolk, Nature Reserve in 1973, showing (left to right) pines planted on dune in 1890; the resulting naturally seeded pine spreading seawards; sand dune; and beach. *(D. F. Ball)*

ram grass. Gullies are the most severe problem in water erosion and if less than 2 m deep can be checked by fencing off and re-seeding or re-planting. In deeper gullies the flow of water must be reduced, therefore earth or brushwood dams are built, slopes are reduced by bulldozer and reseeded immediately or the slopes planted with quick growing vegetation, e.g. loblolly pine or kudzu. Sheet and rill erosion can be combatted by contour ploughing and terracing. This reduces the speed and volume of downslope flow and hence run-off. Managerial practices can also reduce erosion. Mixed farming which allows permanent pasture to be sown is an excellent anti-erosion measure, whilst crop rotation ensures that row crops are not continuously grown on the same area. At the national level most conservation work has been undertaken in the USA. At the time of the establishment of the Department of Agriculture's Soil Conservation Service in 1934, 66 per cent of the total US land area was suffering from soil erosion. The soil bank scheme provided subsidies for land which remained under grass, land capability surveys have been undertaken to determine crop suitability, and hence the risk of erosion is minimised. The most outstanding example of erosion control and land rehabilitation is the multi-purpose rural planning scheme established in 1933 under the TENNESSEE VALLEY AUTHORITY which used the Tennessee river drainage basin as the erosion control unit.

Bibliography: G. V. Jacks and R. V. Whyte, *The Rape of the Earth*, 1939; J. H. Stallings, *Soil Conservation*, 1957; M. Morgan, *Soil Erosion and Conservation*, 1969; D. H. Simms, *The Soil Conservation Service*, 1970; N. Hudson, *Soil Conservation*, 1971. For graphic descriptions of the human misery of soil erosion see J. Steinbeck, *The Grapes of Wrath*, 1965; E. Caldwell, *Tobacco Road* new ed. 1970.

Soil Injection, in building, particularly of civil engineering works, is a protective process applied to form a barrier to GROUNDWATER, which might otherwise jeopardise the stability of a structure. It is particularly useful for ensuring the safety of dams by restricting groundwater movement so that foundations are not scoured out or moved by uplift pressures. Formation of an impervious wall or curtain is usually attained by injecting fluid mixes or suspensions into the adjoining ground through steel tubes. Basically any such injected grout should be of finer mechanical analysis than the strata to be injected so that it penetrates fissures or interstices adequately. For this purpose cement grout is often used (the process may then be called cementation). Where large amounts are needed it is current practice to use up to 50 per cent of fly ash in the grout to reduce the expensive cement content. Other materials used are bitumen emulsions, clay slurries, and proprietory chemicals. Soil injection is carried out by technical specialist firms with wide field experience and can be an expensive process.

Soil Moisture, the principal means by which nutrients and small particles are transferred within a soil. The structure and texture of soils along with the prevailing method and total amount of precipitation will determine the moisture status. Clays and organic soils have the highest water retention capacity whilst silts and organic soils have the highest amount of available moisture, as these fine particles and organic materials can absorb moisture. Soils with well developed structures and coarse sandy textures will allow free entry and flow of water. Rates of movement are largely determined by the volume of water and the pore space. Thus large amounts of water in a soil with large pore spaces will move almost vertically downwards, but in tightly packed clay soils water is retained in the narrow pores and moves upwards during dry periods by capillarity and may be evaporated off at the surface. Pore space is measured as total pore space or soil porosity, and a soil may show pores of various sizes. Macropores are over 75 μm (0·075 mm) wide and allow rapid movement of water, in mesopores, 75 to 30 μm (0·075 to 0·030 mm) in width, water is retained for use by plants whilst in micropores, less than 30 μm wide (0·030 mm), water is not available to plants. Water movement depends upon the action of physical forces within the soil. It is attracted onto the mineral and organic particles by surface tension and the effectiveness of this force depends upon the thickness of the moisture film, with thin films being held much more strongly than a thicker film. Thus in micropores the film is very thin and is very difficult to remove in comparison with the water in a macropore where gravity and plant activity are much more significant forces. Soil moisture can thus be grouped into three categories: (a) gravitational water, held in macropores at less than one-third atmosphere of pressure; this water can move under the influence of gravity; (b) capillary (matric) water, held in mesopores at between 30 and one-third atmospheres of pressure, which can be moved in capillaries by surface evaporation if pressure is greater than 15 atmospheres and by plant roots if between one-third and 15 atmospheres; (c) hygroscopic water, held in the micropores with a tension of up to 10,000 atmospheres; this water cannot be removed in natural conditions. It is thus apparent that water held at over 15 atmospheres is not available, in general, to plants, and thus when water is held in the soil at above 15 atmospheres the wilting point of plants is reached and water only becomes available on subsequent wetting. Wilting point is not fixed, however, and varies with the soils and plants concerned. When all water has drained off by gravitational activity, the state known as field capacity is reached at a pressure of one-third atmospheres. Thus the water generally available to plants is that between field capacity at one-third atmospheres and wilting point at 15 atmospheres. Soil moisture movement as a vapour is also notable, with a tendency for vapour transfer to take place downwards during the day in a soil and upwards at night.

Bibliography: N. C. Brady, *The Nature and Properties of Soils*, ch. 7, 1974.

Soiling, the accidental passage of small amounts of stool into the clothing. Although this often occurs in the aged and in persons with neurological disorders, it is most common in young children between five and ten years of age, who rapidly become social outcasts because of the smell. The most common cause is a severe degree of chronic constipation. The rectum becomes distended with impacted faeces and only liquid stool can escape. This may lead to an erroneous diagnosis of diarrhoea. Severe constipation in children usually results from problems with potty training, emotional problems, or a painful crack in the anus. Medical help is usually needed to deal with the situation.

Soilless Culture, the growing of plants in a compost which does not include soil. The first development of the soilless COMPOST occurred at the University of California where a range of mixtures was recommended, of different levels of sand and peat, all of which included fertilisers and lime. The choice of mixture depends on the purpose for which it will be used, and varies for seeds and seedlings of different ages. Other soilless composts may include grit, perlite or vermiculite. See also HYDROPONICS.

'Soir, Le', Belgian newspaper, published in Brussels and founded in 1887. The country's most popular daily paper, it is independent in political outlook, though its views are often expressed very decidedly, and is owned by the Rossel family.

Soissons, French town in the *département* of Aisne, on the River Aisne. It saw the rise to power of CLOVIS I, and here, in 752, the last of the MEROVINGIANS was ousted by PÉPIN LE BREF. It commands the north-east approaches to Paris, and has been sacked at least 15 times. It has a splendid 13th-century cathedral. Soissons has a large agricultural trade and metallurgical industries. Population 26,000.

Soke, word signifying jurisdiction, and especially the privilege of holding a court. It is thus used in Domesday Book. By extension it came to be used to describe the area under a particular jurisdiction; the word survives in the 'soke of Peterborough'.

Sokolnikov, Grigori Yakovlevich, original surname Brilliant (1888–1939), Soviet politician. He joined the Bolshevik faction of the Russian Social Democratic Workers' Party in 1905. In 1919, as one of the 'party-minded Bolsheviks', he opposed Lenin's intransigence towards the Mensheviks. After the FEBRUARY REVOLUTION in 1917 Sokolnikov became a member of the Bolshevik Central Committee, and after the seizure of power (see OCTOBER REVOLUTION) he was in charge of the nationalisation of the banks. As chairman of the third Soviet delegation he signed the Brest-Litovsk peace treaty in 1918. During the Civil War (see CIVIL WAR, RUSSIAN) he was a high-ranking political commissar in the Red Army. From 1921 to 1926 he was commissar of finance. He participated in the 'new opposition' (see LEFT OPPOSITION), and in 1928–29 was in charge of the Soviet oil industry. From 1929 to 1932 he was ambassador to Britain. At the second show trial of the GREAT PURGE in 1937, Sokolnikov was sentenced to 10 years imprisonment; he probably died in an 'isolator' prison.

Sokolovsky, Vasili Danilovich (1897–1968), Soviet soldier, born at St Petersburg (Leningrad). He was a lieutenant-general in 1940, and in the Second World War commanded the Russian forces in the Vyasma area in the spring and summer of 1942, and in the fighting of March 1943. In September 1943 Smolensk, for long Hitler's headquarters on the Eastern Front, was taken by storm by Sokolovsky. He was chief of staff to the First Ukrainian Army under Marshal KONIEV, which swept through southern Poland in January 1945, and crossed the Oder in the same month. Sokolovsky was promoted to marshal after the war in Europe. In 1946 he was made military governor and commander-in-chief of the Soviet zone of Germany, and Russian representative on the

Sokoto

Allied Control Commission. In 1949 Sokolovsky became a first deputy minister of defence, and from 1952 to 1960 he was chief of the general staff. From 1952 to 1961 he was a full member of the Central Committee of the Communist Party and after 1961 he was a candidate member. He was consistently an unusually outspoken commentator on military subjects, putting forward views reflecting those of military professionals rather than those of the Party's political appointees in the army. He edited an important book, *Military Strategy*, 1963.

Sokoto, province in the north-western corner of northern Nigeria, formerly an independent state. The province is watered by the Rima or Sokoto, which joins the Niger at Gomba, and by other affluents of the Niger. Extensive areas are occupied by rocks of Tertiary age; gold in lode formation has been discovered at Bin Yauri and Mailele. The province is fertile, especially with orchard bush, in the south; but the northern part merges into the sandy conditions of the Sahara. Average rainfall is under 63 cm. The rearing of cattle, almost exclusively owned by the FULANI, is the chief activity, and there is an important trade in hides and skins. Crops for domestic consumption are guinea corn, millet, and some cotton. The district is inhabited by Hausa-speaking tribes, all more or less of negroid type, who are predominantly Muslim. Sokoto was brought under British control in 1903.

Sokoto, capital of North-Western State, NIGERIA. It grew from a small village into a military and administrative centre after the FULANI conquests over the HAUSA states in the early 19th century and has remained an important regional centre for north-western Nigeria. Population 90,000.
Bibliography: S. J. Hogben and A. H. M. Kirke-Greene, *The Emirates of Northern Nigeria*, 1966.

Sola, see SHOLA.

Solan Goose, see GANNET.

Solanaceae, the tomato family, includes about 90 genera and 2000 species of dicotyledons, mainly herbaceous but including some shrubs. The flowers usually have five sepals, joined at their bases to form a tube, and five petals, also forming a tube, to which the stamens are attached. These usually number five, but in some genera such as SCHIZANTHUS with bilaterally symmetrical flowers, only four stamens are present and often only two of these produce pollen. The ovary is attached above the base of the petal tube and consists of two fused carpels; it ripens to give either a dry capsule fruit or a berry. Solanaceae is closely related to Scrophulariaceae (foxglove family) and sometimes can only be distinguished by the presence of PHLOEM both inside and outside the XYLEM in stems of Solanaceae. Many Solanaceae are poisonous plants yielding alkaloids, which are sometimes extracted for medicinal and other purposes; the most important are perhaps atropine, hyoscyamine and nicotine. These are named after the genera *Atropa* (deadly nightshade), *Hyoscyamus* (henbane) and *Nicotiana* (tobacco), but their presence is not exclusively confined to these genera. Other poisonous genera include DATURA (thorn apple) and *Mandragora* (mandrake). The largest genus is *Solanum*, which includes the POTATO, *S. tuberosum*, the green parts of which are toxic. The TOMATO (*Lycopersicum esculentum*) and *Capsicum* (pepper) belong to related genera. A few Solanaceae are grown for their decorative flowers (*Petunia*), or fruits (*Physalis* and some species of *Capsicum*).

Solano, see WIND.

Solanaceae. LEFT Henbane, *Hyoscyamus niger*, yields the drugs atropine, hyoscyamine, and scopolamine. BELOW Deadly nightshade, *Atropa belladonna*, gives belladonna. Henbane and the nightshades are examples of poisonous species of this family, as their extracts are only useful drugs if prepared and used correctly. Other members of the family important to man are *Nicotiana tabacum*, tobacco, and several species, such as *Petunia*, that are cultivated for their flowers. (*Topham/Markham*)

Solanaceae. Edible plants in the family are potato (ABOVE), tomato, aubergine, and bell pepper. *(Topham)*

Solanum, chief genus of SOLANACEAE, consisting of nearly 1700 species, natives of tropical and temperate lands. It contains such important plants as the POTATO, *S. tuberosum* and the AUBERGINE, *S. melongena*. The TOMATO, *S. lycopersicum*, is generally put in a separate genus *Lycopersicum*. Other cultivated members of the genus are the winter cherry (*S. capsicastrum*), Jerusalem cherry (*S. pseudocapsicum*) and the potato vine (*S. jasmimoides*). For the British members, see NIGHT-SHADE.

Solar, in a large Tudor house, a sitting-room or parlour giving the owner's family some privacy from the communal life of the great hall and affording sunlight in summer (see also HALL).

Solar Constant, the total radiant energy received from the Sun by unit area of a surface normal to the Sun and just outside the Earth's atmosphere when the Sun-Earth distance has its mean value. The presently accepted value based on observations made from very high flying aircraft is 1·950 calories per square centimetre per minute, i.e., 136·0 mW cm².

Solar Engines. During the siege of Syracuse, 214 BC, Archimedes is said to have burnt the Roman fleet by concentrating the rays of the sun on the ships by means of mirrors. The possibility of such a feat was tested by Buffon, 1747, who succeeded in setting fire to wood at a distance of 64 m by means of 360 plane mirrors mounted in a frame. At 6·5 m he melted silver with 117 mirrors. In 1755 Hoesen of Dresden constructed parabolic mirrors, with one of which, 1·5 m in diameter, Wolf melted coins almost instantly. De Saussure (1740–99) constructed 'hot boxes', made of half-cubes of glass, fitting one within the other, with air spaces between. The sides and back were wrapped in non-conducting material, and the vessel rested on a blackened non-conducting table. He achieved a temperature of 110 °C in the central box. Sir J. Herschel, carrying out experiments at the Cape of Good Hope, South Africa (1834–38), with a simpler type of box obtained a temperature of 115 °C, and cooked meat and vegetables. From 1860 to 1880 A. Mouchot of Tours constructed parabolic mirrors of large size installed in Algeria for pumping water. With the aid of a simpler machine M. Pifri, 1882, printed the *Soleil Journal*. Ericsson of America drove a 3·5-kilowatt engine by similar means. The Eneas solar engine (1901) was used in California and Arizona. Mirrors were used to focus the sun's rays onto a boiler and a steam pressure of 11 atm was obtained.

One of the drawbacks of solar engines is that if appreciable quantities of energy are to be harnessed, very large reflecting surfaces are required. Some relatively simple units have been constructed using fixed reflectors; in others the reflector is mounted on pivots and is given a continuous motion so as to follow the sun across the sky. In recent years several solar furnaces have been constructed in France. One at Mont Louis uses a mirror with an area of 90 m² and a focal length of 6 m; it has attained temperatures up to 4000 °C and furnaces with a power of 1 MW are considered quite feasible.

Solar generators, usually of the thermoelectric type, have been used in space projects. However, heat exchangers with the very large surface areas required are generally expensive. Nevertheless, the attraction of a practically inexhaustible energy source free from pollution is very great, and efforts are being made to devise economic solar engines. A US group has recently proposed a vapour engine to produce 160 MW of energy operating between the warm (solar-heated) water of the sea's surface and the cooler water some 500 m below the surface.

At present the most likely applications of the solar engine are in places such as Africa or India; by using a thermoelectric generator rather than a conventional heat engine the solar energy can be converted directly into electrical energy.

Solar heating for domestic purposes has been used successfully in the USA, Israel, and Malta. Generally fixed absorbers are used with warm-water circulation. Other applications have been for distillation of sea water, drying of fish, and curing of tobacco in so-called 'solar-barns'.

Bibliography: D. S. Halacy, *Coming Age of Solar Energy*, 1966; B. J. Brinkworth, *Solar Energy for Man*, 1972. Journal: *National Geographic*, March 1976.

Solar 'Flares', see SUN, *Flares*.

Solar System, the region of space dominated by the SUN, a very ordinary star whose nearest stellar neighbours are over four light years away. Around the Sun revolves what is probably the debris of its formation and which includes nine PLANETS, themselves attended by satellites, a host of MINOR PLANETS, innumerable COMETS, METEORS, and an extensive but extremely tenuous cloud of gas and dust, some of which we see as the ZODIACAL LIGHT. Of the total mass of the system, 99·86 per cent is concentrated in the Sun itself and 0·135 per cent in the planets, over two-thirds of it in Jupiter.

The solar system gives every indication of being a strongly unified system having a common origin and development. It is isolated in space; all the planets go round the Sun in orbits that are nearly circular and coplanar, and in the same direction as the Sun itself rotates; moreover this same pattern is continued in the regular system of satellites that accompany Jupiter, Saturn, and Uranus. What the common origin may have been and how the solar system actually developed is, in spite of the many theories that have been advanced, still a mystery. The problem of the formation of the solar system seems to be a particular case of the more general problem of the formation of stars out of pre-existing nebulosity, a phenomenon that appears to be occurring in many nebulous regions. How such condensations start and develop is still far from clear; in the case of the solar system the time at which the condensation took place seems to be fairly definite since the age of the system is the same as that of the Earth, the Moon, and the meteorites, viz., about 5×10^9 years.

If this general hypothesis is correct, the solar system is no more likely to be unique than the Sun is to be a unique star. Many other planetary systems are likely to exist and to contain bodies on which conditions are similar to those on the Earth, and thus favourable for the development of life as we know it.

Bibliography: R. Jastrow and A. G. W. Cameron (Eds), *Origin of the Solar System*, 1963; Scientific American, *The Solar System*, 1976.

Solario, Andrea da (c. 1460–c. 1520), Italian painter, probably born in Milan and influenced by Leonardo da Vinci. He travelled in Italy and went to France in 1507, possibly visiting Flanders before his return in 1515 which would account for the Flemish influence discernible in his later work. Several works are preserved in Milan and in Italian galleries elsewhere, and two portraits and a *Madonna and Child* are in the National Gallery, London.

Solario, Antonio de, also known as Lo Zingaro (active 1502–c. 1518), Italian painter and, though his work is signed 'a Venetian', a gypsy by origin. There are some fine frescoes of his in the convent of San Severino, Naples, depicting the life of St Benedict.

Solarium (from Latin *sol*, sun), a glazed veranda or sun-parlour, acting as a sun-trap, especially in a sanatorium.

Solatium. In Scots law when a person has died through a wrongful or negligent act of another, the deceased's relatives, if they have a title to sue, may claim not only damages but also *solatium* or recompense for injury to their feelings. English law, however, does not recognise any claim for solatium of this kind.

Solatium is also used to mean that part of a claim in DELICT intended to compensate the pursuer (the plaintiff) for the pain and suffering which he has undergone.

Solbad Hall, town in the Austrian TIROL, on the Inn to the east of Innsbruck. A spa with mineral springs, its nearby salt mines are still worked. Brewing is a major industry here. Population (1971) 12,300.

Solder and Soldering. Soldering and its counterpart, brazing, are joining processes applied mainly to metals but used also for joining metals to non-metals such as ceramics. The essential features of the processes are that a molten filler wets the surfaces to be joined, bridges gaps between them, and solidifies to form a joint. The filler may be either pure metal or an alloy but its melting point must be significantly below that of the parts being joined, so that (unlike welding) they are not fused during brazing. The distinction between soldering and brazing is one of temperature, soldering being carried out below an arbitrary temperature level and brazing above. This arbitrary temperature is normally taken as being about 500 °C, which is slightly below the minimum melting point for fillers based on silver-copper alloys. The term 'soft soldering' is normally applied to soldering with a filler based on the lead-tin alloy system, while silver soldering and hard soldering are colloquial names given to brazing when a silver based filler is used. A solder is the filler used for soldering.

Soldered joints are relatively weak, but they are often used to ensure a continuous path for electrical currents (as in radio or television sets) or to seal vessels and prevent leaks (as in the construction of tin cans), rather than to transmit high stresses. Brazed joints can be much stronger and frequently transmit high stresses. Soldered and brazed joints are usually weak when stressed in tension, but strong when stressed in shear. Thus butt joints, e.g., a joint between the abutting ends of two bars, are normally avoided, while lap joints, e.g., where the edge of one strip overlaps another, are preferred. Strictly speaking, there should be a small gap (about 0·1 mm) between the faces to be joined, so that surface tension forces can act between the molten filler and these faces to draw the filler through the joint and ensure that the joint is properly filled and sound. To a large degree, strength or soundness in soldered or brazed joints depends on achieving good wetting of the surfaces to be joined by the filler. Assuming that the correct filler is being used, to ensure wetting it is necessary to clean the parts prior to soldering or brazing to protect them from contamination and oxidation during heating and to provide means of reducing surface oxides left after the previous cleaning operation. For low-quality work mechanical cleaning (abrading with emery paper or scraping) can be used for cleaning prior to brazing, but for high-quality work chemical cleaning or degreasing is preferred. With soldering, reduction of surface oxide and protection during heating is achieved by using a chemical flux, usually in the form of a liquid, jelly, or paste, applied to the joint before and during heating. For small-scale electrical work (radio and television sets) the flux is normally incorporated in the filler wire, in the form of cores. Chemical fluxes are also used for brazing, but because of the higher temperatures involved gaseous (e.g., hydrogen) and vacuum environments can be used to protect the parts and reduce surface oxides. Fluxes for brazing are usually based on inorganic chemicals active at the brazing temperature, such as borax, while fluxes for soldering may have an inorganic or organic base. Most fluxes and flux residues are corrosive and joints should therefore be cleaned (normally by scrubbing in hot water) after soldering or brazing. The main exceptions to this general rule are a range of specially prepared inorganic soldering fluxes used mainly for electronic work (where post-solder cleaning is impractical).

For most common metals simple solders based on lead-tin alloys are satisfactory, although more complex solders may be required for soldering at very low temperatures or where high service temperatures are expected. For aluminium and its alloys special solders based on zinc have to be used. There is a very wide range of alloys that can be used as fillers for brazing, the best known and the most commonly used of which are based on copper and/or silver. Alloys mainly based on nickel, gold, or aluminium are used for special materials, and where particular joint properties are required or special service requirements have to be met. Solders and fillers are available in many forms, the most common of which is the rod, which is usually about 1·5 to 3 mm thick. It is used mainly for hand soldering or brazing, although for some soldering operations, typically tinsmithing, much thicker rods are used. Alternative forms include powders, pastes, creams, shims and preforms for preplacement in or at the joint prior to heating, and a bath of molten metal. Probably the best known soldering technique is that of using a soldering iron, as for the repair of radio and television sets. Here heat is provided by the hot tip of the soldering iron (usually electrically heated), which is held against the parts being joined while they reach soldering temperature. The solder is applied to the iron or the joint, the iron being removed from the joint after the solder has flowed and wetted the parts being joined. A second common soldering technique used for tinsmithing and other large joints employs a blowlamp or a gas torch for heating. Other soldering techniques are named after the heating process used, e.g., induction, resistance, oven (furnace), or the method of applying filler, e.g., dip, wave, jet, cascade, all of which employ molten filler. Wave soldering is very important in modern electronics, where it is used for soldering printed circuit boards, these boards being passed through the top of a wave of molten solder so that many joints are effected in one operation lasting only two or three seconds.

The most common brazing technique employs a gas torch for heating; other techniques are named after the heating method, e.g., furnace, induction, or resistance, or after a particular feature of the process, e.g., vacuum, salt-bath, or dip. Vacuum brazing is particularly important for brazing aero-engine parts, where joint integrity is of great importance, while a special form of salt-bath brazing, where the molten salt is a flux as well as a heating medium, is very important for joining aluminium parts.

Wiping or plumbing used to join pipes and cable sheaths is a process using solder but not strictly soldering, since the joint configuration does not give a narrow gap between the parts through which the molten solder is drawn by surface tension forces. It is in essence a casting-together process since the molten or semi-molten solder is poured over the joint to heat it and is moulded on to the joint using wiping pads. The pads are impregnated with tallow, which acts as a flux and helps the solder wet the parts

being joined. This process, which is manual, requires skill and experience since the operator has not only to push the solidifying solder against the parts being joined so that it wets them, but also to smooth and shape the joint as final solidification occurs.

Soldier Beetle, insect belonging to the family Cantharidae, of order COLEOPTERA. This is a large family containing about 3500 species of which 41 are represented in the British Isles. The two genera that are commonly encountered are *Cantharis* and *Rhagonycha*. The common soldier beetle, *C. fusca*, is a British species. It has soft, black elytra; a reddish pronotum (shield) with a black patch and black legs. It reaches a length of 15 mm and can be found in the daytime during the months of April to July on field, garden, and forest plants. It feeds particularly on aphids. Its larvae are black, and are to be found in the soil or among moss.

Soldier-bird, or blood-bird, *Myzomela sanguineolenta*, a species of the honey-eater family, Meliphagidae, order Passeriformes. It occurs in Australia, and its plumage is of brilliant scarlet and black.

Soldiers', Sailors', and Airmen's Families Association, British voluntary organisation that exists to be of use to the families of Service and ex-Service men and women and to provide them with relief when they are in distress. There are 1500 SSAFA branches in the UK and on Service Stations overseas, manned by 12,000 voluntary workers and maintained almost entirely by voluntary subscriptions. The officers' widows branch of the SSAFA provides rent-free flats, rent grants, and emergency help for widows and unmarried daughters of deceased officers. The Association was established in 1885. Its headquarters is at 27 Queen Anne's Gate, London, SW1H 9BZ.

Sole, a FLAT-FISH, belonging to the family Soleidae, order Pleuronectiformes. A related family Cynoglossidae is known as tongue-soles. The best-known species is *Solea solea*, the common sole, which occurs in many parts of Europe. It attains a length of from 25 to 50 cm, and is the most highly valued of all food fishes. Other species are *S. lascaris*, the lemon sole, *S. minuta*, the little sole, and *S. variegata*, the banded sole. The American sole or hog-choker belongs to an allied genus, and is known as *Achirus fasciatus*.

Sole Bay, Battle of, see SOUTHWOLD.

Solenhofen Stone, limestone which is quarried mainly at Solenhofen, near Munich, as a lithographic stone. Owing to its excessively fine grain, it has preserved excellent fossil remains, and is thus the most important member of the German Portlandian stage of the JURASSIC SYSTEM. Skeleton fishes, casts of cephalopods showing their soft parts, and skeletons of pterodactyls are all found, and the beds are famous for containing the remains of the first-known bird, ARCHAEOPTERYX.

Solenodon, either of two species of small West Indian mammals in family Solenodontidae of order Insectivora. They are about 28 cm long, with an almost equally long naked tail. They have shaggy hair, long, pointed snouts, and strong claws. They come out mostly at night, and eat insects, worms and other invertebrate animals. Their saliva is poisonous. The Cuban solenodon is in danger of extinction.

Solenoid, see CURRENT ELECTRICITY.

Solenostemma, see ARGEL.

Solent, The, western part of the strait between the Isle of Wight and the coast of Hampshire, England. It is 27 km long by 1·6–8 km wide, and famous for its yacht racing.

Soler, Antonio (1729–83), Spanish composer and organist who was also a friar, born at Olot in Catalonia. He was *maestro di capilla* at Lérida Cathedral, and organist and choirmaster at the Escurial monastery from 1753. Soler wrote much church music as well as organ concerti and incidental music for plays; but his most celebrated works are probably his many harpsichord sonatas, distinguished successors to those of Domenico SCARLATTI (with whom he probably studied).

Soleure, see SOLOTHURN.

Sol-fa, Tonic, see SOLMISATION.

Solfatara, the name for volcanic activity confined to the emission of superheated steam from fissures. Small quantities of other gases, such as carbon dioxide and hydrogen sulphide are usually present. Solfataric activity is found in all volcanic regions and in some cases sufficient sulphur may be deposited to be commercially worked, for example on White Island, New Zealand.

Solferino, Italian village in LOMBARDY, 30 km northwest of Mantua. The French and Piedmontese defeated the Austrians here on 24 June 1859 (see ITALY, *History*). Population 900. See also CASTIGLIONE DELLE STIVIERE.

Solicitor, member of that branch of the English legal profession consulted directly by the public. BARRISTERS can be consulted only through solicitors. To be admitted to the roll of solicitors it is necessary to pass the law examinations held by the Law Society and serve a period of articles (i.e. apprenticeship) with a practising solicitor. A solicitor's work includes advising his clients on the law, conducting legal transactions on transfer of property (i.e. conveyancing), drafting wills, administration of trusts and estates of deceased persons, drafting commercial contracts, forming companies, conducting civil litigation and criminal cases, and planning and tax appeals. Solicitors can be struck off the roll, suspended from practising, or fined by a statutory disciplinary body for professional misconduct.
Bibliography: T. Lund, *A Guide to the Professional Conduct and Etiquette of Solicitors*, 1960.

Solicitor-General, in England and Wales, is the law officer of the Crown next below the ATTORNEY-GENERAL and acts as his deputy. He is a leading barrister, an MP, and a member of the government. He is not allowed to engage in private practice, and he advises the Crown in the more important cases in court. The Crown is represented in Scotland by the solicitor-general for Scotland.

Solid, geometrically, is a figure with three dimensions (see CURVE). See CONE; CYLINDER; ELLIPSOID; POLYHEDRON; PRISM; SPHERE; SPHEROID.

Solid. Physically a solid differs from a GAS and a LIQUID in the respect that it possesses a definite shape and has a definite volume. In terms of the theory of PHASES OF MATTER, when the molecules of a substance are in a state of aggregation such that the distances between the molecules are relatively large, then the molecular attractions have a negligible influence on the motions of the molecules. This is typical of the gaseous state. The molecules of a liquid, while subject to the attractive forces of their neighbours, are still sufficiently free to be able to wander fortuitously from one point to another. The molecules of a solid, however, are closely packed and the attractive forces exerted on an individual molecule by its immediate neighbours are so great that the molecule has very little freedom of movement and it remains 'attached' to its neighbours. The great elasticity of solids is due to this characteristic of the solid state, i.e., it is difficult to deform a solid, and it has the property of easily recovering its original shape after the deforming stress is removed. Definiteness of shape, density and volume of a solid are similarly explained by the molecular aggregation peculiar to this state. The ultra-microscopic character of solids was revealed by X-ray analysis initiated by W. H. Bragg and his son, W. L. Bragg. They showed that crystalline materials consisted of atoms (or ions) in regular arrays (see CRYSTALLOGRAPHY), and many solids, e.g., metals, that appear to be amorphous are polycrystalline, i.e., made up of many randomly orientated minute crystals.

Solidago, see GOLDENROD.

Solidus, Roman gold coin, first struck by Constantine the Great in 312 at 144 to the kg, also the standard gold coin, the nomisma, of the Byzantine Empire (see BEZANT). The solidus was the source of several medieval coins. It was divided into thirds (*tremisses*), and whilst the gold tremissis was the standard gold coin of western Europe until the 8th century, it was copied in silver by the barbarians. The name solidus survives in French *sou*.

Solifluction, flow, under the influence of gravity, of soil and loose debris on the surface of the earth. It is a phenomenon which generally occurs when the material is saturated with water, and particularly after the thawing of deeply frozen ground. The principal cause of movement is the alternate freezing and thawing of wet unconsolidated materials resulting in soil flow on slopes as low as 3°. See also SOIL-CREEP; SOIL EROSION AND CONSERVATION.

Solihull, town and borough in West Midlands county, England, 11 km south-east of Birmingham. The borough is extensive and, although best known for its high-class residential areas, it includes the large Birmingham overspill estate of Chelmsley Wood, Birmingham Airport, and the National Exhibition Centre, opened in 1975. Population (1971) 108,230.

Solikamsk, town in the PERM *oblast* of the RSFSR, USSR, on the River Kama; probably the first permanent Russian settlement in the URALS. From the 16th–18th centuries the salt-works here was the largest in Russia. In the 17th century it was a major centre on the trade route to Siberia. Large potash deposits were discovered in 1925; production started in 1933, and the town has since developed a big chemical industry. Paper and cellulose are also produced. Population (1970) 89,000.

Soliman, see SULEIMAN THE MAGNIFICENT.

Solimena, Francesco, called l'Abbate Ciccio (1657–1747), Neapolitan painter, shared with his friend, Luca GIORDANO, the highest reputation among contemporary artists, and died a wealthy man. His style was vigorous and exciting if somewhat lacking in depth, and he was very productive throughout his long lifetime. Most of his work is in Naples, much of it in the churches for which it was painted. He had a very large and busy studio, CONCA and Alan RAMSAY being amongst his pupils.

Solingen, city in NORTH RHINE-WESTPHALIA, West Germany, 10 km south-east of Düsseldorf. In the Middle Ages it was well known for its sword blades; it is nowadays the 'Sheffield of Germany' with an important cutlery industry. To the east, the Mugsten Bridge, is the highest railway bridge in West Germany. Population 178,000.

Solinus, Gaius Julius (fl. 3rd century AD), Roman compiler, author of a geographical work entitled *Collectanea Rerum Memorabilium*, commonly known by its second title, *Polyhistor*. Solinus was so obviously indebted to PLINY's *Natural History* for his information, a debt which he nowhere acknowledges, that he has been called 'Pliny's ape'.

Solis, Juan Diaz de (c. 1450–1516), Spanish navigator, born at Lebrija, near Seville. He is said to have discovered HONDURAS and YUCATÁN with Pinzon in 1506. In 1512 he succeeded VESPUCCI as pilot-major of Spain, and in 1515 sailed in search of a south-west passage to India. He discovered the Rio de la PLATA, but was killed there by Indians.

Solis y Rivadeneira, Antonio de (1610–86), Spanish dramatist and historian, born at Alcalá de Henares. In 1654 he became secretary to Philip IV, and took holy orders at the age of 56. He wrote courtly, satirical plays, and a *Historia de la conquista de México*.

Solitaire, *Pezophaps solitarius*, extinct flightless bird of the dodo family, Raphidae, in the pigeon order Columbiformes. It seems to have been restricted to the island of Rodriguez in the Indian Ocean, and was described by the exiled François Leguat in 1708. In height the male was about 83 cm and in weight about 20 kg; the legs were longer and the bill smaller than those of the dodo.

Solitaire, game played by one person with a board and marbles, the object being to remove the latter from hollows in the former by 'jumping', as in draughts, in such a sequence that the last marble is left in the central hollow. The word is also the American name for PATIENCE.

Sollya, the Australian bluebell creeper, a genus of family Pittosporaceae. They are evergreen twining shrubs with deep blue flowers in cymes, introduced into British gardens from Australia. There are only two species: *S. fusiformis* and *S. parviflora*. Both are cultivated.

(i)	(ii)	(iii)
d'	f'	
t	m'	l
l	r'	s
s	DOH'	f
	TE	m
	ta le	
m	LAH	r
	la se	
r	SOH	d
	ba fe	t,
d	FAH	
t,	ME	l,
	ma re	
l,	RAY	s,
	de	
s,	DOH	f,
f,	t,	m,
m,	l,	r,
r,	s,	d₂
d,	f,	t₂
t₂	m,	l₂

Solmisation. Diagram 1.

Solmisation, chiefly represented today by tonic sol-fa, is the system of fitting notes to syllables to indicate their position in the scale. Although an analogous idea seems to have been known to the Greeks, the modern method was introduced during the 11th century, probably by GUIDO D'AREZZO. At that time the hexachord system had superseded the Greek tetrachords, and the syllables *ut*, *re*, *mi*, *fa*, *sol*, *la*, the first in successive lines of a hymn to John the Baptist composed about 770, which began each line one note higher than the previous line, were applied to the notes of the natural hexachord C D E F G A, the hard hexachord G A B C D E, and the soft hexachord F G A B flat C D. A kind of modulation called mutation was employed where a melody exceeded the compass of one hexachord, *ut* being sung instead of *fa* or *sol* when changing from the natural to the soft or hard hexachord respectively. This system was later extended to correspond with the octachord, by the addition of a syllable *si* for the diatonic seventh, and *ut* was replaced by *do*; both changes were derived from the method of solmisation known as bocedisation, advanced by Waelrant (c. 1518–95), who proposed the use of the syllables *bo*, *ce*, *di*, *ga*, *lo*, *ma*, *ni*. The application of numerals to notes, suggested by P. Galin (d. 1821), improved by Aimé Paris (d. 1866), and perfected by Emile Chevé (d. 1884), was in principle the same as the English system of tonic sol-fa.

In modern tonic sol-fa there are two chief systems: (1) fixed *do*, and (2) movable *doh*. The fixed *do* system regards C as *do* in whatever key it occurs. Although

Solmisation. Diagram 2.

Solo

excellent for absolute pitch, this method is weak where, for instance, remote modulations occur in quick succession. Another theoretical objection is that, as with the black keys of a piano, C sharp and D flat, D sharp and E flat, and so on, are necessarily regarded as identical. No satisfactory method of naming these accidentals has yet been devised. The movable *doh* is far preferable, as formulated in the tonic sol-fa system, drafted by Sarah Glover (d. 1867), with anglicised spellings of solmisation syllables, but established and perfected by John Curwen (d. 1880), who opened a tonic sol-fa college in 1863. His method corresponds to the equal temperament principle and is easily assimilated. changes to subdominant or dominant respectively. Minor scales are regarded as variants of the relative, not tonic, major; this practice is justified by the use in ordinary staff-notation of the same key-signature for both. Passages are written out horizontally and divided vertically by lines, colons, stops and commas ('and') into bars, beats and divisions of beats (see Diagram 2).

Solo, see SURAKARTA.

Solo Whist, card game normally played by four players with the full pack of 52 cards. It is also a good game for five, each player in turn standing out for one deal. The game as played by four is here described; as in ordinary WHIST, tricks are to be made. A bare majority of tricks counts for nothing; the object is to make either (1) eight tricks with a partner (*proposition*), or (2) five (*solo*) or nine (*abondance*) tricks from one's own hand against the remaining three players in combination, or (3) so to play one's own hand as to make no tricks at all (*misère*). Each hand constitutes a separate game. Partnerships change round after round, while *misère* is a special call. The cards are dealt three at a time down to the last four, which are then dealt singly, the last being turned up as the trump in the dealer's hand. The player on the dealer's left has the first call. A player, if he does not 'pass', can either (1) *propose*, which, of course, involves asking for a partner, or (2) call a *solo*, or (3) call simple *misère*, the trump suit being discarded, or (4) call simple *abondance*, naming his own trump suit if he pleases before the first card is led, or (5) call *open misère* (*misère ouverte*), i.e. undertake not only to lose all 13 tricks but to show his own cards immediately the first trick is played, or (6) call *abondance déclarée*, i.e. undertake to win all 13 tricks, choosing his own trump suit. The value of these different calls is in the inverse order to that in which they are stated. An *abondance* in trumps is superior to an *abondance* in a plain suit. If the first player elects to 'pass', he, and he only, may accept a proposition made by any of the remaining players, provided such propositions have not been previously accepted or superseded by a higher call. An inferior call is necessarily of no avail if a previous player has made a better one. If the dealer, when it comes to his turn to call, proposes (assuming there be no better call by a previous player), only the player on his immediate left may accept. A player who makes the highest call, viz. *abondance déclarée*, leads, wherever he may be seated in relation to the dealer. A player having once made a call may increase it to any superior call. If all the players pass, the cards are dealt anew by the second player, unless it has been previously arranged in such an event to play general *misère*, when the player who takes the thirteenth trick

pays some agreed stake to the other players. Stakes are proportioned to the value of the calls. Where an *abondance*, proposition or solo succeeds with tricks to spare ('over tricks') these are paid for according to a previously arranged scale. Conversely, 'under tricks', i.e. those short of the number required are paid for by the person failing to fulfil his call. If a card is exposed by one of the opponents of a *misère*-caller, or a card led out of turn against him, or a revoke is made, the *misère*-caller can claim the stakes.

In the case of other exposures, the aggrieved player can demand that the exposed card be played or not played, and this as long as the card remains unplayed. But the offender can always throw away the exposed card if he cannot follow suit, or he can lead it, except against a solo or *abondance*. The penalty of 'cutting a suit' is enacted when a player leads out of his turn. In this case, if the other players do not choose to regard the card so led as exposed, they may call a suit from the offender or his partner when it comes to the turn of either of these next to lead, and this demand must be complied with under penalty of a revoke. The penalty for a revoke is the loss of three tricks. If the offender suceeds, notwithstanding the subtraction of three tricks, in making enough to win his declaration, he loses the declaration and pays into the stakes the agreed price of his call to each of his adversaries (or, if he have a partner, the two pay the penalty jointly). If both sides or all the players revoke, the deal is null and void.

In solo for three, one complete suit is removed, leaving a pack of 39 cards dealt out (in threes) in the ordinary way. The order of calls is solo, *abondance*, *abondance* in trumps, *misère*, *abondance déclarée* and *misère ouverte*.

Solo whist differs from CONTRACT BRIDGE in that there is no universally accepted code of rules.
Bibliography: A. S. Wilks, *Solo Whist and Auction Solo*, 1923.

Soloist, in music, instrumental or vocal performer of a work with piano, chamber or orchestral accompaniment. The solo part in a concerto is often particularly virtuosic, especially in 19th-century works such as the Liszt piano concertos. A soloist in vocal works takes the part of a particular character, for example in the Bach Passions, or is employed to sing arias and recitatives in contrast to the chorus, as in Handel's *Messiah*.

Solomon, third King of Israel, son and successor of DAVID, reigning c. 970–931 BC. Solomon has become a symbol of wisdom, pomp and magnificence. Although an autocrat, with vast numbers of oppressed slaves and a large harem of foreign women who introduced pagan cults into Israel, he did much to increase the prosperity of his kingdom by ruthlessly destroying his enemies and by greatly increasing international trade especially with Hiram of Tyre. He was a great builder particularly in Jerusalem and constructed the First TEMPLE. He is reputed to have written the biblical books of Proverbs and the Song of Solomon and to have been visited by the Queen of SHEBA. His wisdom is illustrated by the story of two women who each claimed to be the mother of a living baby. Solomon swiftly discovered who was the true mother by suggesting they divided the baby in half. The real mother immediately gave up her claim to the child thus exposing the false mother. His age was certainly one of the most flourishing in the history of Israel; archaeology corroborates the biblical record (e.g. at MEGIDDO). Possibly owing to his harsh treatment of the northern tribes of Israel, after his death the land was split into the separate kingdoms of ISRAEL and Judah. His name is frequently mentioned in Muslim literature especially in the *Thousand and One Nights*.

Bibliography: F. Thieberger, *King Solomon*, 1947.

Solomon, name used by Solomon Cutner (1902–), British pianist of Jewish descent, born in London. He first appeared in public at the age of eight, playing a Mozart concerto at the Queen's Hall, London, and made his first tour of British cities at the age of nine, playing with all the leading British orchestras. At 14 he retired for five years' study, and re-embarked on concert work by giving a recital at the Wigmore Hall in 1921. He later gave recitals and played concertos throughout Britain as well as on the Continent. During the Second World War he undertook extensive recital tours for the Forces, notably in Egypt, Palestine, North Africa, Malta and Europe. He was awarded the CBE, 1946.

Solomon, Song of, see CANTICLES.

Solomon, Wisdom of, Vulgate *Liber Sapientiae*, Book of Wisdom. It is in the Apocrypha of the English Bible, but also included in the Roman Catholic canon. Solomon is not actually named in the book, but he is manifestly the speaker in chapters vi–ix, for he is the builder of the Temple in Jerusalem in ix. 7, 8. The Wisdom of Solomon is an exhortation to seek wisdom, first, because it brings salvation to the pious Jews; secondly, because of its divine essence; and thirdly, because the history of Israel shows how wisdom brought blessings to Israel and calamities to the heathen. It was written originally in Greek, by an Alexandrian Jew with a philosophical education; its most probable date is 100–50 BC. The personification of Wisdom (in vii–xii, and xviii.15) prepared the way for the Logos doctrine of Saint John, and for the revelation of the Holy Spirit. The Wisdom of Solomon was used by St Paul (Rom. 1: 18–32; Wis. xiii. 1, 10).

Solomon Islands, archipelago of Melanesia, in the west Pacific, stretching from north-west to south-east for some 965 km between 5° and 11° S and 154°40′ and 162°30′E. The Solomon Islands (until 1975 the British Solomon Islands Protectorate) consists of six large islands (Bougainville is part of the archipelago but falls within the administrative area of Papua New Guinea), Choiseul, Ysabel, and Malaita (the northern chain) and Guadalcanal, New Georgia, and San Cristobal (the southern chain), and countless smaller ones, extending over 1448 km². The capital is Honiara on the island of Guadalcanal.

Geography. Relief. The islands are of volcanic formation, and the coral reefs are only an adjunct to mountain massifs which rise to a height of 26,246 m. They have been little explored and still less economically developed. They are picturesque, with primeval forests of slender palms, coral gardens lining the translucent sea bottom, tiny coral islets everywhere, and lovely lagoons. Stone urns adorned with strange reliefs seem to indicate the existence of a genuine Melanesian culture. See also ATLAS 64.

Climate. The climate is unhealthy: malaria, framboesia, and other tropical diseases are prevalent. North-west and south-east monsoons prevail; torrential rain and storms of freakish violence sweep the group; and the scattered islands are subject to earthquakes.

Economy. Dependent upon primary production mainly, the chief crops being copra, timber, and tuna. Cocoa and chillies are also exported and an oil palm industry is being set up. Cattle raising is a new development and rice is grown for home consumption. Bauxite, copper, and nickel deposits hold out hope of an industrial future in the islands. The building construction industry is fully occupied but there is as yet little manufacturing. Two factories make corrugated iron and biscuits, and boat-building is a traditional occupation.

Government. The 1974 constitution established the office of Governor of the protectorate, with a legislative assembly whose 24 elected members have chosen a chief minister and a council of ministers which is responsible to the legislative assembly for any advice given to the Governor. The Governor is responsible for defence, external affairs, internal security, and the public service. Internal self-government was instituted in Janaury 1976 with independence to follow 12 to 18 months later.

Education. In 1974 24,115 children attended 412 registered primary schools and 1526 attended six secondary schools. There is a teacher training college at Honiara and also a Technical Institute.

History. The first European known to have visited the Solomon Islands was a Spaniard, Alvaro de Mendana, who set out on a voyage of discovery in 1568. The islands were not rediscovered until 1767, when Captain Carteret found the Santa Cruz group and Malaita; Bougainville sighted some of the islands in 1768. Mendana named them 'the Isles of Solomon, to the end that the Spaniards, supposing them to be those islands whence Solomon fetched gold to adorn the Temple of Jerusalem, might be the more desirous to go and inhabit the same'.

The British sphere of influence in the Solomon Islands was recognised in 1886. Three principal factors led to the establishment of a British protectorate over the Solomon group by treaty with Germany in 1893: Australia's fear of German power in the Pacific; the need to put an end to the massacres, of both Europeans and natives, which resulted from the recruiting methods of those seeking labour for plantations in Queensland and Fiji; and the desire to ensure a civilised government and to maintain order. Many other islands were added to the Protectorate in 1898–99, including the Santa Cruz group, Rennell and Bellona; and in 1900 Choiseul, Ysabel, and some islands in the Bougainville Straits were transferred by convention from Germany to Great Britain. After the Solomon Islands became a British protectorate law and order were established and native headmen were appointed to help in the administration of justice. The northern Solomons (Bougainville, Buka, and some other islands) were captured from Germany by Australia in 1914 and mandated to Australia after the First World War. In the Second World War the Solomon Islands were invaded by Japanese forces in 1942, but these were driven out of most of the islands by American and Australian forces by the end of 1943; the Japanese garrison on Bougainville held out until the surrender of Japan in 1945. The Islanders displayed great loyalty to the Allied cause.

The total area of the Solomon Islands (formerly the

protectorate) is 29,785 km² (land area). Population (1973) 178,940, of whom Melanesians numbered 166,640.

Bibliography: Hakluyt Society, *Discovery of the Solomon Islands*, 1901; W. G. Ivens, *Melanesians of the South-East Solomon Islands*, 1927; S. G. C. Knibbs, *The Savage Solomons*, 1929; R. Firth, *We, the Tikopia*, 1936; F. M. Keesing, *The South Seas in the Modern World*, 1941.

Solomon's Seal, *Polygonatum*, a genus of herbaceous perennials in family Liliaceae, with handsome leafy stems and axillary bell-shaped flowers, followed by red or blue-black berries. *P. multiflorum*, *P. odoratum* and *P. verticillatum* are British, and others are grown in gardens in Britain, especially the hybrid between *P. multiflorum* and *P. odoratum* (*P. × hybridum*).

Solomos, Dionysios (1798–1857), Greek poet, born on Zante. Educated in Italy, he wrote first in Italian. Returning home he studied Greek poetry and in his long *Ode to Liberty*, 1823, the source of the Greek national anthem, vindicated the possibilities of the common language. There and in Corfu he wrote *Lambros*, *The Cretan*, and successive drafts of *Missolonghi, or The Free Besieged* but he completed none of them. In him a romantic inspiration is combined with an ever more completely realised purity of form. The maturity of his thought and language was unparalleled in the Greek literary world of his day, and despite its sadly fragmentary nature his poetry still retains its appeal.

Bibliography: R. J. H. Jenkins, *Dionysios Solomos*, 1940; P. Sherrard, *The Marble Threshing Floor*, 1956.

Solon (c. 640–c. 559 BC), Athenian legislator. Having early distinguished himself as a poet, first in a light and amatory vein, then in the gnomic style, Solon took part in the dispute between Athens and Megara (c. 596), and moved a decree initiating the first Sacred War. Such indeed was his reputation that he was called upon to end the civil strife with which Attica was rent.

In 594 he was chief archon, and some time later, during a period of economic distress and conflict, was given unlimited power, which he exercised to cancel all existing debts and to forbid loans on the security of the borrower's person. He likewise encouraged trade by revising the Athenian coinage, and gave fresh impulse to industry by offering citizenship to immigrant craftsmen. So popular were these measures that Solon was invited to reorganise the constitution (see GREECE, ANCIENT). He began by repealing the laws of DRACO, except those relating to homicide. Next, he divided the citizens in classes according to their landed property, thus constituting a limited oligarchy; enlarged the functions of the *Ecclesia* (general assembly); instituted the *Boulē*, a deliberative council; and probably entrusted the guardianship of the laws and public morality to the court of Areopagus.

Having enacted these reforms as well as some other laws, Solon left Athens for a period of ten years, visiting Egypt, Cyprus, and possibly Lydia. Old quarrels were revived during his absence, and shortly after his return to Athens power was seized by PISISTRATUS, to whom Solon is said to have given sage counsel on more than one occasion.

Considerable fragments of Solon's poems have survived.

Bibliography: K. Freeman, *The Work and Life of Solon*, 1926; V. Ehrenberg, *From Solon to Socrates*, 1973.

Solothurn (French *Soleure*), canton in north-west SWITZERLAND, stretching from Basel to Bern and crossed by the foothills of the JURA MOUNTAINS. There are shoe, paper, cement, textile, watch, and engineering industries. Agriculture, forestry, and cattle-rearing are also carried on. The canton is largely agricultural and is drained by the River AAR. About 97 per cent of the land is productive. Area 791 km². Population (1974) 299,600; mainly German-speaking with three-fifths being Roman Catholics.

Solothurn, capital of the canton of the same name (see above), Switzerland, on the River AAR, 30 km north of Bern. It is an important railway junction; industries include electrical engineering and watchmaking. It is on the site of the Roman fortress of Salodurum, and has a notable collection of old weaponry and armour. Population (1974) 16,700.

Solovetski Islands (Russian *Solovetskiye Ostrova*), group of islands in the WHITE SEA, at the entrance to Onega Bay, in the ARKHANGELSK *oblast* of the RSFSR, USSR. On the largest island, Solovetski, a famous monastery (see below) was founded in the 15th century. Several 16th-century buildings remain, including the monastery refectory and the Cathedral of the Transfiguration. Area 347 km².

Solovetsky Monastery, former Russian Orthodox monastery on Solovetsky Island in the White Sea. Founded in 1429, it was for a long time an important religious, cultural, and economic centre of northern Russia. From the late 16th century it was also a fortress and a place of banishment for religious or political offenders. From 1667 to 1676 Solovetsky Monastery defied the authority of the patriarch and the tsar, and it was finally stormed by Muscovite troops. In 1854 it was shelled by British warships. In 1920 the monastery was abolished and transformed into a concentration camp for opponents of the communist regime.

Soloviëv, Sergei Mikhailovich (1820–79), Russian historian, author of the fundamental work *History of Russia from the Earliest Times* in 29 volumes, brought up to 1774.

Soloviëv, Vladimir Sergeevich (1853–1900), Russian philosopher and poet, son of the above. He created the first comprehensive philosophical system in the history of Russian thought: the philosophy of all-unity. Partly by the study of philosophy and partly by personal religious intuition, Soloviëv abandoned his early atheistic materialism and accepted Christianity, believing the ideal essence of the world existed in the mind of God, and naming this essence 'Sophia' (wisdom), conceived of as a feminine entity, of whom he experienced three visions. He tried to revive the Christian humanism of such thinkers as Erasmus, St Thomas More, and St Francis de Sales, supplied a theological and philosophic justification for it, and urged that the principle of holiness should be introduced into every sphere of man's social life. His philosophy influenced BERDYAEV and other Russian thinkers, and also BLOK and the symbolist poets.

Bibliography: S. L. Frank (Ed.), *A Solovyov Anthology*, 1950; V. Zenkovsky, *A History of Russian Philosophy*, 2 vols, 1954.

Solstice, strictly a moment when the Sun is furthest from the equator but often used to refer to the general period of such an occurrence. The Sun is furthest north on 21 or 22 June as it enters the ZODIACal sign of Cancer and is vertically overhead at midday at places on the Tropic of Cancer (latitude 23½° north). This is the time of midsummer and the longest day in the Northern Hemisphere and of midwinter and the shortest day in the Southern Hemisphere. Similarly midwinter/midsummer and the shortest/longest day occur on 21 or 22 December as the Sun enters the sign of Capricorn and is furthest south. See SEASONS.

Solti, Sir George (1912–), British conductor of international repute, born in Budapest, where he studied with Kodály, Bartók and later in Switzerland under Toscanini. He has been musical director of several great opera companies, including Covent Garden, 1961–71. A guest conductor in many European and American cities, he raised the Chicago Symphony to a position among the most acclaimed of world orchestras, especially through his recordings of romantic composers. He was awarded the CBE, 1968; KBE, 1971.

Soluble Glass, or water glass, is prepared by fusing SILICA (sand or flint) with sodium carbonate, or with carbon and sodium sulphate, when the sodium silicates may be dissolved out. It may also be prepared by digestion of silica and caustic soda under pressure. It is thus obtained as a viscous solution from which concentrated acids precipitate the hydroxide; dilute acids with weak solutions retain the silicic acid in solutions, but the mass gradually gelatinises and then solidifies. Soluble glass has been used for preparing artificial stone on buildings as a protection against weathering, for the manufacture of cheap varieties of soap, for preserving eggs and for fireproof cements. See SILICON.

Solutions, in physical chemistry, homogeneous mixtures of two or more substances constituting one phase, the composition of which can be continuously varied between certain limits. The most familiar solution is that of a solid (the solute) dissolved in a liquid (the solvent), but since matter exists in three distinct phases—solid, liquid and gas—and since matter in any state can be mixed with matter in every other state, at least theoretically, the following different classes of solutions are possible: (1) gas in gas; (2) liquid in gas; (3) solid in gas; (4) gas in liquid; (5) liquid in liquid; (6) solid in liquid; (7) gas in solid; (8) liquid in solid; (9) solid in solid; (10) more complicated solutions with the three stages of aggregation represented. Essentially, then, the study of solutions consists in the study of such classes of mixtures. When different substances are brought together they either act chemically on one another or they simply mix. It is this latter class only, where no chemical action takes place, that constitutes true solutions. In terms of the PHASE RULE a solution is a single phase. Such a solution, which is believed to contain only either single molecules or parts of molecules, is called a simple, or true solution. There exists also a class of intimate solid-liquid mixture where the solute particles consist of groups of small numbers of molecules. Such

mixtures are called colloidal solutions (see COLLOID). See also ELECTROLYSIS.

Solway Firth, in part the estuary of the River Esk, and in part an inlet of the Irish Sea. It separates England from Scotland, that is, the north-west of CUMBRIA from the Scottish region of DUMFRIES AND GALLOWAY. At its mouth the firth is over 40 km wide, but at its narrowest point only 3 km wide. There are salmon fisheries. The tides ebb and flow with great rapidity, creating a 'bore' of some 16 km/h.

Solway Moss, district in Cumbria, England, consisting of reclaimed marshland near the Scottish border between the Sark and Esk rivers, where the English defeated James V of Scotland in 1542.

Solyman, see SULEIMAN THE MAGNIFICENT.

Solzhenitsyn, Aleksandr Isaevich (1918–), Soviet writer. He studied at Rostov University, and was an artillery officer in the Second World War until his arrest in 1945 on a trumped-up charge of treason. He was released in 1953 and spent the next three years in exile.

His story of life in a labour camp, *One Day in the Life of Ivan Denisovich* (translated by R. Parker, 1963), appeared in 1962. Subsequently his major work had to be published abroad, including his two best novels, *Cancer Ward*, 1962–66 (translated by N. Bethell and D. Burg, 1968), which, based on personal experience, describes the inmates of a hospital ward for cancer sufferers and is also an allegorical statement about Stalin's Russia, and *The First Circle*, 1955–64 (translated by M. Guybon, 1968), about a research institute staffed by political prisoners. He has also written stories, plays, and the first part of a trilogy about Russia in the 20th century, *August 1914*, 1972 (translated by M. Glenny). Solzhenitsyn was awarded the Nobel Prize for literature in 1970.

In 1973 he wrote an open letter to the Soviet authorities, which perhaps contributed to his expulsion from the USSR. He has since begun publication of a history of Russian labour camps, *Gulag Archipelago*, 1974 (translated by T. P. Whitney), and increasingly engages in political polemic. *Lenin in Zurich* appeared in 1975. Like many earlier Russian writers, Solzhenitsyn sees the writer as the conscience of his country, and, like the SLAVOPHILES, he desires a return to the spiritual values of Orthodoxy.

Bibliography: G. Lukacs, *Solzhenitsyn*, 1969; D. Burg and G. Feifer, *Solzhenitsyn*, 1972; C. Moody, *Solzhenitsyn*, 1973.

Soma, one of the plants from which the ambrosia of the Indian gods is said to be derived; hence it is sacred. The ninth book of the *Rigveda-Samhita* consists of hymns intended to be recited in honour of *soma*. Various plants with milky latex are said to have been the true *soma*, notably *Asclepias acida* and *Periploca aphylla*. In later Vedic literature *soma* is identified as the Moon God.

Somali, Cushitic people concentrated in the Somali Republic, some living also in the Territory of the Afars and Issas, Ethiopia, and Kenya. They are composed of nomadic pastoralists (who preponderate), traders, and some town dwellers. They live in families, grouped in clans, under an elective or hereditary chieftainship. They are mainly Sunni Muslims of the Shafi'i sect. The Somali number about 4 million.

Somalia

Bibliography: I. M. Lewis, *Peoples of the Horn of Africa*, 1955; *A Pastoral Democracy*, 1961.

Somalia, or officially the Somali Democratic Republic, situated in the Horn of Africa (East Africa), bounded by the French Territory of the Afars and Issas in the north, Ethiopia in the west, and Kenya in the south-west. The state is composed of the two former territories of British Somaliland and Italian Somaliland (Somalia). Area 637,657 km².

Geography. Relief. The north is occupied by an extension of the Ethiopian highlands, with peaks rising to 2400 m overlooking the Gulf of Aden; but in the south are lowlands crossed by rivers such as the Webi Shebeli which fall gently to the Indian Ocean. See also ATLAS 41.

Climate. Temperatures are high, and during the monsoon period from April to September the climate is unpleasant. Rainfall along the coast is very low, but on the interior plateau region can reach 500 mm.

Population. The region has long had close links with Arabia, and the present day inhabitants are SOMALI with Arab admixture. The population totalled 2,940,000 in 1972 and the main town is MOGADISHU (the capital).

Economy. Most of the population are pastoralists, depending mainly on their cattle, sheep, goats, and camels for their livelihood. Some undertake no cultivation, but in the south sorghum, millet, or maize are grown by most families. Efforts are being made to expand rice growing in the river valleys, but at present irrigated agriculture consists mainly of plantation production of bananas for export and sugar for local use. Following the decimation of herds and flocks in the drought of the early 1970s, more people have had to turn to cultivation, often in new settlements, and also to offshore fishing.

Few minerals have been found, though much oil prospecting has been undertaken, and the manufacturing sector is extremely small, mainly food processing. Since

Somalia. The sea-front at Mogadishu. (*Camera Press/Alastair Matheson*)

independence, much development expenditure has been directed to communications, so that Mogadishu, Kisimayu, and Berbera all have well-equipped ports and the length of all-weather roads has greatly increased; the road between Belet-Uen and Burao is the second largest Chinese aid project in Africa. There is no railway, nor any area where potential traffic would justify one. As one of the world's poorest countries, Somalia has depended heavily on foreign aid for development spending with Italy, the European Economic Community, the USA, and the USSR all making major contributions. Exports, mainly of live animals to Saudi Arabia and bananas to Italy, have never matched the value of imports of manufactures, food, and fuel, of which Italy remains the chief source. The currency unit is the shilling.

Government. Constitution. A constitution was promulgated in 1960 when the two former colonies of British Somaliland and Italian Somaliland united to form the Republic of Somalia in July 1960. This constitution provided for a President, elected by the National Assembly, who would be head of state; a Prime Minister with extensive executive powers; and a single National Assembly in Mogadishu, formed from the previous northern (British Somaliland) and southern (Italian Somaliland) legislatures. The 1960 constitution was suspended following the bloodless army coup of 21 October 1969, and a Supreme Revolutionary Council (SRC), which consisted of army and police officers, was formed to replace the National Assembly. The SRC claimed that military intervention had been necessary in order to preserve true democracy and justice, and to protect the state, now named the Somali Democratic Republic, against the divisive forces of corruption and tribalism. The President of the Supreme Revolutionary Council, Major-General Muhammad Sid Barre, became the nominal head of state. Although no new constitution has been drawn up, General Barre did state in October 1970, that ideologically Somalia was a 'socialist state'.

Legislature. The National Assembly was dissolved on 21 October 1969, with legislative and executive power then being combined in the 23-member Supreme Revolutionary Council. Subsequently, a subordinate legislative organ, the council of secretaries, has been established. In December 1974, the SRC established five committees which were given the brief of assisting policy planning and formulation. For the purposes of local government, Somalia is now divided into eight regions and 40 districts, and the new revolutionary socialist initiative has seen a reorganisation of local government, aimed at increasing the participation of the people in politics. Although decisions still emanate largely from the centre, everyday administration is through the regional and district revolutionary councils.

Justice. All laws must conform not only to the provisions of the constitution, but must also satisfy the Islamic code. Since the military take-over in 1969, the judicial structure has been augmented by a supreme revolutionary court, having countrywide jurisdiction in civil, penal, administrative, and accounting matters; as well as the national security court, established in 1969, and the military supreme court formed in 1970 to try members of the former government and armed forces respectively. The conventional legal administration has two courts of appeal, at Mogadishu and Horgeisa; eight regional courts;

and 48 district courts. Such matters as marriage and divorce are handled by district courts known as district Qadis according to Islamic and traditional law. In July 1973 a new civil code law, to replace remaining British and Italian laws, was introduced to deal with such matters as house rents, inheritance agreements, trade agreements, and contracts.

Armed Forces. Military service is voluntary, and in 1974 the army had 20,000 men, the air force 2750, and the navy 300. In addition there was a People's Militia of 3000 and a border guard force of 500. Somalia receives considerable military aid and advice from the USSR in return for providing facilities for the Soviet Navy at Berbera.

Education. The literacy rate is of the order of 10 per cent of the total population, and much difficulty has arisen from the problems of arranging agreement, because of religious differences, on a common alphabet. Government schools do provide free elementary education, but do not have, as yet, sufficient capacity to take all children. In 1973 there were 70,000 pupils and 2024 teachers in primary school, 27,000 pupils and 983 teachers in secondary school, 1000 student teachers, and 2000 pupils receiving a vocational education. There is a university institute in Mogadishu, although it is estimated that there are some 1500 Somali students studying abroad. There is an education training programme, aided by the USSR and UNESCO, in operation; in 1973, the Somali Language Commission was founded in order to introduce teachers and civil servants to the new alphabet. A rural development scheme aims at increasing literacy among nomadic groups.

Welfare. Drought causes severe problems, and substantial foreign aid is required to deal with its effects. Otherwise there is no provision by the state in terms of social welfare. Free medical treatment is available at government hospitals and dispensaries. In the mid-1960s there were 24 hospitals and 174 health centres; by 1973 there were a total of 5387 hospital beds available. Medical personnel in 1973 included 106 doctors, 22 pharmacists, 164 midwives, and 836 nurses.

Religion. The population is overwhelmingly Muslim, but there is a small Roman Catholic community.

Language. The national and sole official language is now Somali, which has been introduced in a further attempt to create unity, and combat the hold of Arabic and English in the north and Italian in the south.

National Flag. Pale blue, with a large five-pointed white star in the centre.

History. The Democratic Republic of Somalia, as it is now known, became an independent republic in 1960 when the former colonial territories of British Somaliland and Italian Somaliland united to form the Republic of Somalia. Former Italian Somaliland (Somalia) was secured by a treaty with the Sultan of Zanzibar, who was the suzerain, in 1892 and thereafter the territory was extended by agreement between the Sultan and Britain. In 1905 there was a further cession of the Benadir ports by the Sultan of Zanzibar to Italy in return for the payment of £144,000. In the same year Britain leased to Italy territory near Kismayu. The port of Kismayu and other land in the vicinity was given to Italy by Britain after the First World War. This territory was formerly known as Jubaland. The invasion of Ethiopia headed by Graziani, was launched from Somalia in 1935, and, in 1936, follow-

ing the Italian conquest of Ethiopia, Somalia was incorporated with Eritrea and Ethiopia to become Italian East Africa. In August 1940 Italian forces from Somalia invaded British Somaliland and overran the protectorate, but in 1941 British, South African, and Indian troops wrested Somalia from the Italians and a British military government was established. In 1950 Italian administration was resumed under UN trusteeship.

British Somaliland became a protectorate in 1884, being administered by the Resident of Aden as a dependency of the government of India as Aden then was. In 1898 responsibility was passed to the Foreign Office and in 1905 to the Colonial Office. Between 1901 and 1921 there was spasmodic warfare between the protecting power and the Somalis whose zeal and persistence was kept alive under the inspiration and leadership of Mohamed bin Abdullah Hassan, a religious leader who gave it the character of a 'holy war'. In 1954 Britain, under pressure from Ethiopia, recognised Ethiopian sovereignty over an area known as the Reserved Areas as well as land farther south in the protectorate. 'Safeguards' were made to ensure the rights of the nomadic inhabitants to be allowed to graze their livestock in the area concerned. This transaction continues to be opposed by the Somalis as a breach of faith by the protecting power, and is a serious subject of contention between Ethiopia and Somalia and has led to sporadic military action. Relations with Ethiopia are not helped by the fact that Somalia has declared its support for the Eritrean Liberation Front (ELF). Somalia also considers that the northern province of Kenya should become part of Somalia because the pastoral people who inhabit this part of Kenya are ethnically of the Somalian people and holds that the existing boundaries are arbitrary and of European origin, having no historical justification. Somalia's insistence led to a break in diplomatic relations between Britain and Somalia in 1963.

In the decade before 1960 both Britain and Italy had prepared their respective colonies for independence and negotiations between the politicians of the two colonies were completed in July 1960, when the republic was formed. It was governed by a tripartite coalition government, the two most important political parties of the former British colony uniting with the powerful Somali Youth League (SYL) of the Italian colony to form a government. The greater part of the executive power in the new republic was vested in the Prime Minister, Dr Abdirashid Ali Shermarke, and this established the precedent that the president and premier should belong to different clans. In 1967 Shermarke was elected president by the National Assembly, and Muhammad Haji Ibrahim Egal became prime minister.

By the late 1960s external pressure on the republic, from Ethiopia and Kenya, had decreased significantly, but this allowed internal dissension to come to prominence, and especially the resentment at the de facto one-party rule of the SYL. Events came to a head with the assassination of Shermarke on 15 October 1969; and on 21 October 1969, the army, led by Maj.-Gen. Muhamed Siad BARRE, took control in a bloodless coup. Army and police officers formed the Supreme Revolutionary Council which took over the government functions, with Barre as a supposedly nominal head of State. But Barre soon asserted himself and gained real control of the government, and, acting as president, claims to have set the nation on the proper road to national unity through 'Scientific Socialism', a philosophy which aims at eradicating the divisive forces of tribalism and promoting economic development.

Bibliography: I. M. Lewis, *Peoples of the Horn of Africa: Somali, Afar and Saho,* 1955; *A Pastoral Democracy: a Study of Pastoralism and Politics among the Northern Somali of the Horn of Africa,* 1961; *The Modern History of Somaliland: From Nation to State,* 1965; V. Thompson and R. Adloff, *Djibouti and the Horn of Africa,* 1968.

Sombor, town in Serbia, Yugoslavia, in the autonomous province of VOJVODINA. It is a modern town and is the centre of a rich agricultural district. Population 44,000.

Sombrero, small island of the former British colony of ST KITTS-NEVIS in the West Indies. It was formally transferred from the British VIRGIN ISLANDS as a matter of administrative convenience as from 1 May 1956. It contains a lighthouse and lighthouse keeper and a handful of other residents. Area 5 km².

Somers, Sir George (1554–1610), English adventurer, born Lyme Regis, Dorset. A founder of the Virginia Company in 1606, he was wrecked in 1609 when his ship *Sea Venture* on passage to Virginia grounded on the BERMUDAS, of which Somers took possession and where he established a colony in 1610, but died soon afterwards.

Somers, John, 1st Baron Somers of Evesham (1651–1716), English politician, born at Claines, near Worcester, and educated at Trinity College, Oxford. He took part in the framing of the Declaration of Right in 1689, and became William III's most trusted minister, being in turn solicitor-general, attorney-general, lord keeper of the Great Seal, and in 1697 lord chancellor. He was created Baron Somers the same year. For most of Anne's reign he was out of favour but on the accession of George I he was made a privy councillor.

Somers Island, see BERMUDAS.

Somersby, village 11 km north-west of Spilsby, in Lincolnshire, England. It is the birthplace of Tennyson.

Somerset, Earls and Dukes of, titles held in the late Middle Ages by the BEAUFORT family and, since 1660, by the descendants of Edward Seymour, Duke of Somerset. The 1st Earl was John Beaufort (c. 1371–1410), the eldest of the three sons of John of Gaunt and Catherine Swynford. He was succeeded in turn by his three sons, John (1403–44), the 3rd Earl, being created duke of Somerset in 1443. John, whose daughter, Margaret, was the mother of Henry VII, fought with Henry V in Aquitaine and Normandy, and his dukedom was a reward for his services there. The title was re-created for his younger brother, Edmund Beaufort (d. 1455), in 1448. He was killed at the first battle of St Albans, whereupon his son, Henry (1436–64), succeeded to the dukedom. Henry was a distinguished Lancastrian, and fought at Wakefield (1460) and St Albans (1461), and was finally captured and executed by the Yorkists at Hexham. The family titles were forfeited, although Henry's brother, Edmund (c. 1438–71), was styled 4th Duke until his execution after the battle of Tewkesbury.

The Seymours descend from a Norman family, who came from St Maur in Normandy to England in the 13th century. The 1st Duke of this line was Edward Seymour (c. 1506–52), brother-in-law of Henry VIII and protector of England in the reign of his nephew, Edward VI. Other illustrious members of this family are William Seymour, 2nd Duke (1588–1660), husband of Arabella Stuart; Charles, 6th Duke (1662–1748), a member of the Kit-Kat Club and a Tory favourite of Queen Anne; and Algernon, 7th Duke (1684–1750), governor of Minorca (1737–42), who died without male issue. The 8th Duke, Sir Edward Seymour of Berry Pomeroy (1695–1757), claimed the title by his descent from the 1st Duke by his first marriage and it is from him that the present bearer of the title is descended.

Somerset, Edward Seymour, Duke of (c. 1506–52), English statesman, Lord Protector of England. He served in France as a soldier and diplomat. Henry VIII married his sister, Jane Seymour. On the death of the King in 1547, Somerset became protector during the minority of Edward VI, his nephew. He aimed at peaceful union with Scotland but failed to conciliate the Scots, was drawn into war, and finally defeated them at the battle of Pinkie in 1547. Somerset was a convinced Protestant and by the Act of Uniformity (1549) he tried to enforce the use of the first (and most extreme) Book of Common Prayer. Disagreements in the Privy Council threatened his position, first in 1549 when he was imprisoned in the Tower for a short time and again in 1551 when he was charged with high treason and executed. He enriched himself enormously from confiscated Church lands, but his religious views were sincere and under his administration Protestantism gained a firm foothold in England.

Bibliography: A. F. Pollard, *England under the Protector Somerset,* 1900.

Somerset, Robert Carr, Earl of, and Viscount Rochester (c. 1589–1645), English courtier, favourite of James I, of the family of Ker of Ferniehurst. His good looks won him royal favour: he was given Sir Walter Raleigh's manor of Sherborne in 1609, was created viscount Rochester in 1611 and earl of Somerset in 1613. He married the divorced Countess of Essex in 1613. His influence over the King began to decline after the introduction of George Villiers, later Duke of Buckingham, at court and he finally lost his position when the circumstances surrounding the death of Sir Thomas OVERBURY were revealed. He and his wife were found guilty of murder and condemned to death, but reprieved and imprisoned until 1622.

Bibliography: B. White, *A Cast of Ravens,* 1965.

Somerset, a maritime county in the south-west of ENGLAND, bounded on the south-west by Devon, on the south-east by Dorset, on the east by Wiltshire, and on the north-east by Avon, while the Bristol Channel washes the northern and north-western shores. A large area north of the Mendip Hills was once Somerset but, since 1974, forms part of Avon.

Somerset was originally part of the kingdom of Wessex, and figured largely in King Alfred's struggle with the Danes. During the Civil War a battle was fought at Allermoor in 1645. The Duke of Monmouth was proclaimed king at TAUNTON in 1685 but was taken at SEDGEMOOR soon after. Somerset contains many notable

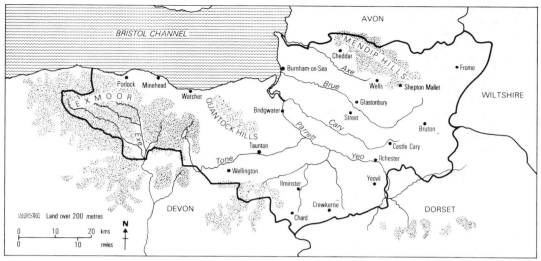

Somerset.

remains of Roman villas, abbeys, and castles, notably at GLASTONBURY and DUNSTER, while there is a celebrated cathedral at Wells (see WELLS CATHEDRAL). Roman remains include a large mosaic pavement near Langport, while the Mendip caves have yielded many relics of prehistoric man. There are many later-Saxon stone carvings in the church at Milborne Port.

Along the northern coast are low cliffs, with long sandy beaches and mud tracts at low tide, more especially in the north-west. The chief inlet is Bridgwater Bay; the only important harbour is at the mouth of the Parret, Somerset's principal river. Other rivers flowing through the county are the AXE, EXE, Brue, and YEO; most of these tend to flow in a north-westerly direction through the county. The most prominent surface features of Somerset are the MENDIP HILLS and the QUANTOCK HILLS, extending from Taunton north-westwards towards the sea and culminating in Willsneck (387 m). Due south are the low-lying moors, the second largest area of fen country in England, which includes Sedgemoor. The wild forest of EXMOOR lies partly in the extreme west of the county and partly in Devon. DUNKERY BEACON (518 m), the highest point in the county, is in this area.

The main occupations are agriculture and dairy-farming, including the manufacture of the famous Cheddar cheese. The chief crops are wheat, barley, oats, turnips, mangolds, etc.; teasels are grown for the woollen industry, and willows and withies for wicker-work. Large numbers of sheep and cattle are reared. Peculiar to the Exmoor district is a breed of hardy ponies; red deer are also found there. The numerous orchards of the county supply the cider- and perry-making industry. The holiday and tourist trade forms another important occupation, and many visitors are attracted both to the seaside resorts and to rural Somerset and its historic monuments. BURNHAM-ON-SEA and MINEHEAD are the principal coastal holiday resorts. Minerals in the area include iron, lead, zinc, slate, and fuller's earth. Peat is cut in the Vale of Avalon. The principal towns are WELLS, Taunton (the

county town superseding the old capital, Somerton), BRIDGWATER, YEOVIL, FROME, and Glastonbury.

Industries of the county include aircraft construction, the making of scientific instruments, chemicals, woollens, worsted and silk goods, gloves, leather goods and shoes, cellophane paper, sail-cloth, linen shirts, brushes, agricultural implements and machinery, and Bath-bricks manufactured at Bridgwater from the sand of the River Parret. There is good river fishing, including salmon fishing, particularly in West Somerset. The county returns four members to Parliament. The county is 345,799 ha in area; population (1971) 395,000.

Bibliography: A. Wickham, *Churches of Somerset*, 1965; A. Mee, *Somerset* (Ed. E. T. Long), 1968; B. Little, *Portrait of Somerset*, 2nd ed., 1974; R. Whitlock, *Somerset*, 1975.

Somerset Herald, an officer of the HERALDS' COLLEGE, historically associated with the dukes of Somerset.

Somerset. Peat fields near Glastonbury. *(Camera Press)*

Somerset House

Somerset House, a government building in the Strand, London, which formerly housed the General Register Office (of births, marriages, deaths), Inland Revenue, Valuation Office, Probate and Divorce Registery, and other public offices. The present building, erected by Sir William Chambers between 1776 and 1786, was built on the site of the old 'Inne of Chancerie' and adjoining buildings, which were pulled down by the Protector Somerset, who began here, in 1549, a palace which was incomplete at the time of his execution. It was later used by Elizabeth I, Henrietta Maria, and Catherine of Braganza, and was demolished in 1775. The east wing of the present Somerset House was built 40 years after the main building, and is used by King's College. There has been some public debate about the use to which Somerset House should be put now that the General Register Office has removed to St Catherine's House, Kingsway.

Somerset Light Infantry (Prince Albert's), The, a British regiment, the old 13th Foot, raised in 1685. In 1706 the Earl of Peterborough converted it into a regiment of dragoons, which saw service in Gibraltar and at Dettingen. It fought at Culloden, with which action the unique practice of the sergeants of the regiment wearing their sashes over the left shoulder is traditionally connected, the officers having all become casualties. For distinguished services at Jellalabad, 1842, the regiment was granted the mural crown superscribed 'Jellalabad'. It was in the Crimean and Afghanistan, and later in the Burmese and

Somerset House. *(Camera Press/L. Wilson)*

South African campaigns. During the First World War it raised 16 battalions, which served in France, Flanders, Palestine, Mesopotamia, and on the North-West Frontier of India. In the Second World War the Somerset Light Infantry fought in Italy, Burma, and on the Western Front. The 1st Battalion of the Somerset Light Infantry were the last British troops to leave the dominion of India; they sailed from Bombay on 29 February 1948. The Somerset and the Duke of Cornwall's Light Infantry were amalgamated in 1959, as the Somerset and Cornwall Light Infantry, in the Light Infantry Brigade. In July 1968 the regiments of the Brigade were amalgamated to form The Light Infantry.
    Bibliography: H. Popham, *The Somerset Light Infantry*, 1968.

Somerton, parish and town in Somerset, England, 8 km north-west of Ilchester. It was a residence of the Saxon kings and once the capital of Somerset. Population (1971) 3267.

Somervell, Sir Arthur (1863–1937), British composer and educationist, born at Windermere. He was educated at Uppingham and King's College, Cambridge, where he studied composition with Stanford, in Berlin, and with Parry. In 1894 he became professor at the Royal College of Music, and in 1901 an inspector of music in schools, this leading to an appointment as official inspector of music to the Board of Education, which he resigned in 1928. His songs, especially settings of lyrics from *Maud* (Tennyson), *A Shropshire Lad* (Housman), and *James Lee's Wife* (Browning), are his best-known works. He also composed two masses, choral works, including a setting of Wordsworth's *Intimations of Immortality*, a symphony, etc., and edited *Songs of the Four Nations* and other folk-songs. He was knighted in 1929.

Somerville, Edith Anna Oenone (1858–1949), Irish novelist and artist, born on Corfu, the daughter of an Irish army officer. She studied art in Paris, Düsseldorf, and London, and later illustrated her own books. The first woman master of foxhounds, she wrote a hunting anthology, *Notes of the Horn*.
    Her other work appeared under the pen names 'E. Œ. Somerville and Martin Ross', the latter being her cousin Violet Martin with whom she collaborated from 1886 until her death in 1915. Among their best-known novels are *An Irish Cousin*, 1889, *Naboth's Vineyard*, 1891, *The Real Charlotte*, 1894, *The Silver Fox*, 1897, *Some Experiences of an Irish R.M.*, 1899, and *Further Experiences of an Irish R.M.*, 1908; they also wrote *Through Connemara in a Governess Cart*, 1893, and *Some Irish Yesterdays*, 1906. Books by Edith Somerville alone include *The Big House at Inver*, 1925, *Irish Memories*, 1917, and *Wheel-Tracks*, 1923.
    Bibliography: Study by G. Cummins, 1952.

Somerville, Mary (1780–1872), British writer on mathematics and physical science, born at Jedburgh, Roxburgh. In 1804 she married her cousin Samuel Greig who died in 1806. In 1812 she married another cousin, Dr William Somerville, and moved to London, where in 1826 she read a paper before the Royal Society on the *Magnetic Rays of the Solar Spectrum*, in consequence of which she was requested by Lord Brougham to translate Laplace's great work, the *Mécanique céleste*. This she published in 1831; *The Connection of Physical Sciences* appeared in 1834; *Physical Geography* in 1848; and *Molecular and Microscopic Science* in 1869. She founded a scholarship at Oxford, and Somerville College was named after her.

Somerville College, Oxford, named after Mary Somerville, created in 1879 as an interdenominational foundation to enable women to enjoy the higher education offered at Oxford University. Long before its degrees were open to women (1920), Somerville numbered among its graduates women distinguished as scholars, writers, scientists, and reformers. The College has now reached what it regards as the right size, with about 300 undergraduates, over 100 graduates reading for higher degrees, nearly 30 tutorial fellows and many lecturers. Its library of over 75,000 books is a particular asset. A history of the College is being written to mark its centenary.

Somme, *département* of northern France, with a short coastline on the English Channel, formed from part of the ancient province of Picardy, and crossed east to west by the Somme river. In general, the surface is level, a great plateau. Somme is an important agricultural area and produces cereals, sugar-beet, apples, and livestock. The principal industries are textiles and chemicals, sugar-refining and distilling. The chief towns are AMIENS (the capital), ABBEVILLE, Montdidier, and Péronne. Area 6175 km²; population (1975) 538,000.

Somme, river of northern France, rising near St Quentin, and flowing by Amiens and Abbeville to the English Channel. It is connected by canal with the Oise and the Scheldt. Length 245 km.

Somme Battles. The first important battle on the Somme during the First World War took place during the late summer and autumn of 1916. The British and French attacked the Germans between Beaumont-Hamel on the

Somme Battles. Working party of British troops in the mine crater at Beaumont Hamel, November 1916. The crater was formed by a British mine which exploded in the area when it was held by the Germans. *(Bisonte)*

north and Chaulnes on the south of the river. The attack was launched on 1 July 1916, and on the extreme left the British were held up, but farther south good progress was made. The French also made good progress towards Péronne. The strength of the German lines was unsuspected, and successive series of trenches were discovered, making a break-through practically impossible. On 14 July Bazentin, High Wood, Longueval, and Delville Wood were captured by the British. Before the end of the month Ovillers and Pozières were taken. During August little headway was made, but during September Guillemont, Le Forest, and Cléry were gained after strong resistance, and later the line was pushed forward through Thiepval, Flers, Combles, east of Cléry, Belloy, and Estrées. Pressure was maintained until November and the

Somme Battles. The front line, Ovillers, July 1916. *(Bisonte)*

line eventually rested on Serre, Le Transloy, west of Péronne, and Chaulnes.

The second battle occured during the last German offensive, in the spring of 1918 when the Germans advanced on both sides of the Somme from St Quentin to Villers-Bretonneux. They maintained pressure until 23 April, on which date their line in this area ran from Albert, north of the Somme, to the west of Moreuil on the Avre.

The third battle took place during the Allied counter-offensive when the Americans and Australians, fighting side by side, captured Hamel on 19 July 1918. The success of the French south of the Somme about Noyon threatened the Germans on the Somme and by 31 August Péronne had fallen to the Allies. The victorious Allies then simply swept on, and soon cleared the Somme area.

There were no comparable battles on the Somme in the Second World War. In 1940 at the end of May Gen. Weygand tried to reorganise the French armies along the line of the Somme and Aisne rivers, but on 7 June the German armour dashed forward from a Somme bridge-head, and two days later had reached Rouen. Similarly when the tables were turned in 1944 there was no battle; the British 21st Army Group broke out in August in the direction of Beauvais, captured Amiens, and crossed the Somme, and a headlong drive then followed along almost the whole front.

Sommerfeld, Arnold Johannes Wilhelm (1868–1951), German physicist, born at Königsberg (now Kaliningrad, USSR), famous for his work on atomic structure and on the conduction of electricity in metals. He was professor of mathematics at Clausthal Mining Academy (1897), of applied mathematics at Aachen Technical High School (1900), and of theoretical physics at Munich from 1906 onwards.

Sommerfelt, Alf Axelsson (1892–1965), Norwegian scholar, born at Trondheim. His books, dealing mainly with the Celtic languages, include *Le breton parlé à Saint-Pol-de-Léon*, 1920, *The Dialect of Torr, Co. Donegal*, 1921, *Studies in Cyfeiliog Welsh*, 1925, and *Munster Vowels and Consonants*, 1927. A selection of his articles on Celtic, Caucasian, and general linguistics was published in *Diachronic and Synchronic Aspects of Language*, 1962.

Somnambulism, sleep-walking, being up and about while asleep. This occurs when there is a wish that is forbidden, which seeks expression during sleep because the conflict between what is wished for and its forbidden nature is too great to bring into consciousness. It occurs in children and adults and is a totally unconscious activity in that the sleepwalker has no awareness of his behaviour. It can be seen as an attempt to solve a conflict without bringing it into consciousness. For example, a child may sleep-walk from one room to another, removing himself from the parent whom he feared and seeking instead the other parent with whom he has a different relationship. Consciously he may be unaware of the difference in his feeling towards both parents.

Somnath, or Patan, ruined town on the Kathiawar Peninsula, Saurashtra, India, 61 km north-west of Diu. The most famous of the Gujarat temples was the Siva shrine at Somnath. This was the special object of MAHMUD OF GHAZNI's zeal when, in 1025, he destroyed the temple.

Sompting, village near Worthing in the Adur District of West Sussex, England, with one of England's oldest churches (c.1000) having a gabled pyramidal cap—a 'Rhenish helm'. Population (1971) 7645.

Sonar, see ECHO SOUNDING.

Sonata, term designating both a type of composition and a musical form. The word is the feminine past participle of the Italian *suonare*, to sound; a sonata is thus originally simply 'a thing sounded', i.e. played, as distinct from a cantata (from *cantare*), 'a thing sung'. In the 17th century the term implied primarily, though not necessarily, a chamber work in several movements for two or more players. A distinction grew up between the *sonata da chiesa*, suitable for performance in church, and the *sonata da camera*, a purely secular work, including dance movements and hence analogous to the suite; but the two categories frequently overlapped.

From about the middle of the 18th century onwards the term sonata came to be generally restricted to a work in several movements for a single instrument or for two different or related instruments (e.g. piano and violin, two pianos, etc.). Sonata form derives from the binary structure of the older dance forms, where the first half ends in a key other than the tonic. In the classical sonata of the 18th and early 19th centuries (and in many later sonatas as well) it is used regularly in a quick first movement, and often in other movements as well.

Composers have never restricted the sonata to a definite number of movements (though three or four are the most usual), nor to any prescribed order of movements. Though the first movement tends to be quick, there are plenty of examples in which it is slow. Similarly, in the 18th-century sonata a minuet may occur as a middle movement or as a final movement or be omitted altogether. The rondo was a favourite choice for the last movement but it was by no means universal. C. P. E. Bach, Haydn, Mozart and Beethoven all showed considerable freedom in writing sonatas; other forms such as variations and fugue were also included. The romantic tendency to link the movements of a work together was vividly illustrated by Liszt, whose Piano Sonata, in a single movement, uses transformation of themes as in a symphonic poem. The most important examples of the genre include the piano sonatas of Haydn, Beethoven and Schubert, the duo sonatas of Brahms, Franck and Fauré, and the chamber sonatas of Debussy.

The typical sonata form (it must be stressed that there are innumerable divergences from the following idealised pattern, *especially* in the work of Haydn, Mozart and Beethoven, on whose practice the theoretical foundations of the form were based) shows the following main outlines: a single movement in two principal sections, the first, called the exposition, ending in another key than that of the tonic. Two main thematic groups make up its material, with room for subsidiary themes and connecting bridge passages, and these groups are not very accurately but conveniently described as first and second subjects. The first is in the tonic key, the second usually in the dominant in a movement in a major key and in the relative major in one in a minor key. The second section begins with a 'development' or working-out which, as its names suggest, develops some of the foregoing material in new ways. This 'development' leads to the 'recapitulation', where the opening of the movement, i.e. the first subject, returns as before, though possibly with new embellishments; the second subject, however, now also appears in the tonic key, major or minor, and in the latter case it is normally in minor, even if in the first section it appeared in major. All this necessitates a new transition between first and second subjects, and it is often here rather than in the working-out that the greatest point of interest or surprise of a sonata movement lies. The movement may end in the tonic exactly as the first section ended in another key; but there may be a coda added, either a very brief tailpiece of a merely ceremonial nature or a more developed section which may further work upon the foregoing material, as often in the case of Beethoven. In modern times the significant key-relationships of sonata form have ceased to have primacy, but composers often use the general configuration of the form, or compose against its background.

Sonata form is naturally not restricted to works called sonatas but occurs equally in trios, quartets, symphonies, etc.

Sonchus, in the family Compositae, a genus of about 50 European annual or perennial herbs, with prickly leaves, milky juice and yellow flowers. *S. arvensis*, field milk-thistle, *S. palustris*, marsh sow-thistle, *S. oleraceus*, milk-or sow-thistle, and *S. asper*, spiny milk or sow-thistle, are natives of Britain.

Sønderborg, Danish seaport on the island of ALS, in Sønderjylland county. It is connected with the mainland by a bridge. The church is medieval and the palace (dating back to the 12th century) contains an important regional museum. Sønderborg has textile mills, machine shops, a margarine factory, and oil refining works. Population 23,000.

Sonderbund Civil War, see SWITZERLAND, *Modern History*.

Sønderjylland, county in DENMARK, on the border with West Germany. As Northern Schleswig it was under German rule from 1864 to 1920, when a plebiscite restored it to Denmark. Various types of farming are carried on. The capital is ÅBENRÅ. Area 3929 km². Population 242,800.

Sondrio, province of Italy, in north LOMBARDY. Area 3215 km². Population (1974) 169,000.

Sondrio, Italian town and capital of the above province, situated on the Adda about 100 km north-east of Milan. It is the centre of the VALTELLINA and its wine trade is the most important activity. Population (1974) 20,000.

Song, an art-form combining poetry and music, usually for vocal solo and accompaniment. The first phase of the modern art of song was the troubadour period (11th–14th centuries), although folk-songs, chants and other forms of intoned declamation of verses had been known from the first (see FOLK-MUSIC AND FOLK-SONG; MUSIC). Composers of the 14th century, in both France and Italy, developed a subtle art of solo song with instrumental accompaniment, and this continued to be a favourite form of

secular music in the 15th century. The popularity of the lute and similar instruments in the 16th century led not only to the transcription of works originally written for a vocal ensemble but also to the composition of original songs in which the singer could provide his own accompaniment. This art reached its peak in Elizabethan and Jacobean times in England, in the work of such lutenist-composers as DOWLAND and CAMPION.

The introduction of OPERA in the 17th century had a profound effect on the development of song, leading as it did to new vocal forms and styles, such as recitative and aria, and to the perfecting of methods of using the voice which were reflected in more elaborate styles of writing for it. By the early 18th century the concert aria was well established; and during that century the ground was prepared for the art-song of the romantic period. Schubert's fertile imagination found an ideal outlet in song, which also appealed strongly to the lyrical instincts of romantic composers such as Schumann and Brahms. These composers tended to cultivate strophic forms, whereas the influence of Wagner encouraged Wolf to free the vocal line from obligatory adherence to the musical structure of a song. His example was followed by many later composers.

In France the outstanding contributions to song have been made by Duparc, Fauré, Debussy, and Ravel. While the romantic *Lied* tradition was carried into the 20th century by (among others) Strauss, Pfitzner, and Schoeck, in the works of Mahler song aspired towards symphonic form, above all in the 'song-cycle-symphony' *Das Lied von der Erde*. In Finland, Sibelius wrote impressive songs; while in Britain a notable tradition of lyric song found exponents in such diverse figures as Warlock, Finzi, Butterworth, Frank Bridge, Havergal Brian and F. G. Scott. Schoenberg, Berg, and Webern all wrote songs, and even today the song shows little sign of being abandoned by serious composers, even though its most traditional forms flourish now rather in the realms of musicals and pop. Gershwin and Kurt Weill are examples of composers who tried to bridge the gap between the two worlds.

See also CANTATA; CAROL; GLEE; MADRIGAL; MEISTERSINGER; MINNESINGERS.

Song Da (Black River), river in South-East Asia that rises in Yunnan (China) and flows south-east parallel to the SONG HUONG before uniting with it near Songtay in North Vietnam. Length 800 km.

Song Huong, or Song Koi, known to the French as the *Fleuve Rouge*, or Red River; it is the main river of North VIETNAM, and in its extensive alluvial delta lives the bulk of the population of the north. Rising in Yunnan (China), it joins the SONG DA (Black River) in Tonkin and enters the Gulf of Tonkin through several mouths. It is 1200 km in length. Its volume is irregular, reaching an average flow at HANOI of 11,250 m³ in August and dropping to 1050 m³ in March, and its waters carry large quantities of reddish sediment. In 1870–71 the French explorer Jean Dupuis discovered a route from the sea to Yunnan along this river. His efforts to open this route to shipping caused a conflict with the Vietnamese government and led to France's establishing a protectorate in TONKIN.

Song of Songs, see CANTICLES.

197

Song Thrush

Song Thrush, or mavis, *Turdus ericetorum*, a bird familiar throughout Europe, with a loud, sustained, richly varied song. It is about 20 cm long; the upper parts are light brown, the wing coverts tipped with reddish-yellow, and the yellowish neck and breast spotted with dark brown. It belongs to the family Muscicapidae of the order Passeriformes.

Songhay, or Songais, farming and fishing people of Mali, living around the northern bend of the Niger, below Tombouctou. The Songhay are skilled craftsmen and are descendants of the great Songhai empire of the Middle Ages which lasted until the end of the 17th century. They number over 300,000.

Sonic Boom, noise produced by shock waves from aircraft travelling at supersonic speeds. The disturbances in the atmosphere generated by a body in motion slower than the speed of sound (subsonic) are propagated away from the body at the speed of sound, and hence travel faster than the body itself. At supersonic speeds, however, the body moves faster than the waves it creates, and the waves are then attached to it. The waves are mostly concentrated at the nose and tail at a reasonable distance below the aircraft, and form an N-wave. These concentrated waves are shock waves and are of finite amplitude, and normally of infinitesimal thickness. As a supersonic aeroplane passes overhead at high altitude the shock wave pattern sweeps over the ground and is heard as one or two distinct bangs or booms. In many cases the sonic boom sounds similar to close thunder. The intensity of the boom at ground level depends on the aircraft size, speed, and altitude. Its character is greatly affected by atmospheric conditions. Manoeuvring aircraft at supersonic speeds and flying at low altitude can create conditions of havoc on the ground. Normally civil and military aircraft do not fly at supersonic speeds over populated areas. Extensive research on the effects of sonic booms was built into the development programme of *Concorde*. This research confirmed that under steady supersonic flight at cruise altitude the damage to property on the ground differed little on average from that caused by normal environmental effects.

Sonnet (Italian, small sound), term originally applied to any short poem. Specifically, it is a poem of 14 lines, with a definite rhyme-scheme. The lines are in the prevailing metre of the language, in Italian, the hendecasyllable, in French, the alexandrine, in English, the decasyllable or five-foot line (see METRE).

The original Italian or Petrarchan sonnet (see PETRARCH) consisted of two parts—the first eight lines called the octave or octet, and the last six lines termed the sestet. The octave was rhymed *abbaabba*, and the sestet usually *cdecde*, though there were other variants. This poetic form is peculiarly well suited to the flowing, musical language of its native country, but when it was adopted by English poets in the 16th century it was found necessary to allow some structural alteration, so that the sonnet might be moulded into a different language.

The early English employers of sonnet form were SUR-REY and WYATT, followed by SPENSER, DRAYTON, and Sir Philip SIDNEY. Spenser tampered with the rhymes in the octave, introducing a third rhyme, which was carried into the sestet. From these altered forms sprang the English sonnet, which was to win fame on its own account. The Shakespearean sonnet broke away entirely from Italian traditions, and produced a poetic form of great beauty. His rhymes were arranged in a new order: *abab, cdcd, efef, gg*, thus doing away with the octave and sestet, and substituting three quatrains and a couplet. Naturally these differed in effect from the Italian sonnet, but the form was so admirably adapted to the expression of the poet's ideas that Shakespeare's sonnets are among the finest ever composed.

With Milton the sonnet was once more written on its original model; the rhymes reverted to their former position, though occasionally Milton changed the order of the rhymes in the sestet to *cd, cd, cd*. Another departure introduced by Milton was the abolition of the pause at the end of the octave. Hitherto there had been a pause not only at this point, but also at the end of each quatrain. Milton's plan of going without interruption from one quatrain to another, or from octave to sestet, gave an effect of grandeur and nobility. From the time of Milton onwards the sonnet received little attention from English poets until Wordsworth and Keats. Again it was the Italian sonnet form which was produced. Rossetti also used the sonnet to good effect, while Elizabeth Browning's *Sonnets from the Portuguese*, 1847, are also notable.

Bibliography: T. W. H. Crosland, *The English Sonnet*, 1926; G. Sterner, *The Sonnet in American Literature*, 1930; E. Hamer, *The English Sonnet*, 1937; L. C. John, *The Elizabethan Sonnet Sequences*, 1938; J. W. Lever, *The Elizabethan Love Sonnet*, 1956; J. Fuller, *The Sonnet*, 1972.

Sonnino, Baron Sidney (1847–1922), Italian politician, born at Pisa. He entered the Italian Chamber in 1880 as a Liberal, and his knowledge of finance and economics made him prominent. As finance minister from 1893 to 1896 he saved Italian credit by drastic fiscal and financial reforms. He became leader of the Opposition, and was prime minister for two short periods. In November 1914 he became foreign secretary, and brought Italy into the First World War on the Allied side. He was chosen to be one of the Italian delegates at the Inter-Allied Peace Conference in Paris (1919).

Sonora, state of MEXICO. Situated in the extreme northwest of the country, it is bordered in the north by the USA, in the east by the state of Chihuahua, in the south by the state of Sinaloa, in the north-west by the beginning of the peninsula of Baja California, and in the west by the Gulf of California. Most of the state—apart from the western parts—is very mountainous, traversed north to south by the Sierra Madre Occidental. Three types of climate are found: hot and dry in the semi-desert of the north-west; warm with light rainfall in the valleys and foothills of the mountains; cold in the high mountains with snowfalls in the north-east. There are numerous rivers flowing west into the Pacific, the El Yaqui being one of the most important, and many have been harnessed by dams for hydro-electric power and irrigation purposes. Irrigation is essential for crop cultivation, the main crops being wheat (the state is one of the chief producers in Mexico), cotton, maize, rice, beans, tobacco, sugar cane, and vegetables. Cattle raising is practised on a large scale particularly in the north. Fishing is important and forms a valuable export to the USA. Gold, silver, and copper are mined, but there are also considerable deposits of other minerals, e.g. iron, which have not been exploited. The capital is HERMOSILLO; other important towns are Obregón (population 153,000), Guaymas (60,000), and NOGALES (45,000). Area 184,934 km²; population (1975) 1,368,300.

Sonsonate, department of El SALVADOR in the western part of the country. It is a rich coffee-growing area and also produces sugar cane, tobacco, tropical fruits, and balsam. It is El Salvador's chief cattle-raising and dairy-farming area. The volcano Izalco, in the north of the department, is one of the most recently formed volcanoes in the world and currently the most active one in Central America. It is known as the 'Beacon of the Pacific', being visible at night from many kilometres out in the Pacific. El Salvador's main port, ACAJUTLA, is in the department. Area 1204 km²; population (1970) 203,000.

Sonsonate, capital of the above department in El Salvador. It is the commercial centre of the region, being connected by road with most parts of the country and lying on the San Salvador–Acajutla railway. Founded in 1552, the city is one of the country's oldest settlements, and despite the development of modern buildings still retains much of its colonial atmosphere. Noteworthy is the beautiful church of El Pilar and the cathedral with its 17 cupolas. Population (1970) 45,634.

Sontius, see ISONZO.

Sony Corporation, Japanese manufacturer of consumer electronic goods, such as televisions and radios with headquarters in Tokyo and subsidiary companies throughout the world. The corporation was founded in 1946 as the Tokyo Tsushin Kogyo and changed its name to Sony in 1958.

Soochow (Chinese *Su-chou*), city in KIANGSU province of eastern China, built on a group of islands east of Lake T'ai-hu. There are silk and cotton mills. Glass, metal, lacquer, embroidery, and carved goods are also produced. A splendid city in the Middle Ages, Soochow, with its dozens of stone bridges, temples, and pagodas, has been regarded as the 'Venice of the East'. In recent years the city's old-established silk industry has been augmented by chemical production and paper making. Population (1970) 1,000,000.

Sooner State, see OKLAHOMA.

Soot, finely divided carbon resulting from incomplete combustion of organic matter, such as bituminous coal, wood, and oil. It contains some quantity of hydrocarbons and ammonium sulphate (when obtained from wood or coal), and has been used as a fertiliser. Soot obtained from resins is used for pigments. See CARBON.

Soper, Donald Oliver, Baron (1903–), British Methodist minister, educated at Aske's School, Hatcham, St Catherine's College, Cambridge, Wesley House, Cambridge, and the London School of Economics. From 1926 to 1929 he was minister of the South London Mission, 1929–36 minister of the Central London Mission, and since 1936 he has been superintendent of the West London Mission, Kingsway Hall. A prominent pacifist and socialist, he is a prolific writer and a frequent speaker at meetings and on radio and television. He was made a life peer in 1965. He is also president of the League against Cruel Sports. His books include *Christianity and its Critics*, *It is Hard to Work for God*, *The Advocacy of the Gospel*, and *Aflame with Faith*.

Sophia (1630–1714), Electress of Hanover, daughter of the Princess Elizabeth of England and Frederick V, Elector Palatine of the Rhine, and granddaughter of James I (VI of Scotland), born at The Hague. She married in 1658 Ernest Augustus, the youngest of the four brothers representing the Lüneburg branch of the house of Brunswick, their eldest son, George Louis, afterwards becoming king of England as George I. Ernest Augustus became elector of Hanover in 1692. An Act of Settlement was proposed in the English Parliament in January 1701, settling the crown at the death of Anne upon the Princess Sophia and her heirs, 'being Protestant', which received the royal assent in June of the same year. In June 1714 the Electress Sophia died suddenly at Herrenhausen, and on the death of Queen Anne, which followed soon after, Sophia's eldest son succeeded to the throne of England.
Bibliography: M. Kroll, *Sophie, Electress of Hanover*, 1973.

Sophia, Saint (Greek *Hagia Sophia*, Holy Wisdom), name of many churches, the most famous being Saint Sophia in Constantinople, built for the Emperor Justinian by Anthemius of Tralles and Isidore of Miletus, and consecrated in 538. The Holy Wisdom or Logos was a term used of Christ, to whom the churches of this name are dedicated. After the Ottoman conquest of Constantinople (now Istanbul) Saint Sophia became a mosque. With the overthrow of the sultanate it became a museum.

Sophists, in ancient Greece, originally teachers of rhetoric and the art of disputation. They were not a school or sect, but a class of popular lecturers who aimed at imparting universal culture. The name implied an element of professional skill over and above the 'wisdom' denoted by its literal meaning; thus Pythagoras and Socrates we. sometimes called Sophists by their contemporaries. After 450 BC the term covered anyone who taught for pay, and because of the repugnance felt for this practice by men such as Plato it began to acquire a derogatory meaning. The subject of the Sophist's teaching really amounted to 'how to get on in the world', whether by the 'virtue' of Protagoras, the oratory of Gorgias, or the memory-training of Hippias. For this reason a sophist came to mean one who merely pretends to knowledge, or who attempts to make the worse appear the better cause.
Bibliography: J. Burnet, *Early Greek Philosophy*, 1963.

Sophocles (496–406 BC), Athenian tragic poet, born at Colonus. He excelled at an early age in both music and gymnastics, being chosen at the age of sixteen to lead the chorus at a victory celebration after Salamis (480). He won the tragic prize for the first time, with *Triptolemus*, in 468. In 440 he was one of the ten *strategoi* appointed to conduct the Samian war. A story is told that in his last years his son Iophon asked the court to declare Sophocles *non compos mentis*. By way of reply the aged dramatist read a passage from *Oedipus Coloneus* (which had been lately written but not yet produced) and the judges immediately dismissed the suit.

Sophocles made three notable innovations in the drama. (1) He raised the number of the chorus from 12 to 15 but gave it a less direct share in the action than hitherto. (2) He introduced a third actor. (3) He produced trilogies the members of which were unconnected in subject. Only seven of his 123 plays are extant: *Ajax* (before 440), *Antigone* (440), *Electra* (between 440 and 412), *Oedipus Tyrannus* (c. 431), *Trachiniae* (between 420 and 415), *Philoctetes* (409), *Oedipus Coloneus* (posthumous, 401). Besides these we possess more than 1100 fragments, including 400 lines of the satyric drama *Ichneutae* found in a papyrus at Oxyrhynchus in 1907.

Bibliography: see text with commentary by R. C. Jebb (7 vols), 1884–96; Oxford Text and Fragments by A. C. Pearson, 1924 and 1917 respectively. *Ichneutae* has been edited (with translation) by R. J. Walker, 1919. There is a verse translation of the tragedies by Sir G. Young in Everyman's Library. See also T. B. L. Webster, *An Introduction to Sophocles*, 1936 (rev. ed. 1969); Sir C. M. Bowra, *Sophoclean Tragedy*, 1944; F. R. Earp. *The Style of Sophocles*, 1944; F. J. Letters, *The Life and Work of Sophocles*, 1953; H. Kitto, *Sophocles*, 1958; W. N. Bates, *Sophocles*, 1964.

Sophonisba (d. c. 204 BC), daughter of the Carthaginian general Hasdrubal, son of Gisco. She married Syphax in order to obtain his support in the second PUNIC WAR. At the capture of Cirta, she fell into the hands of MASINISSA. According to the story (Livy, 30. xii–xv) Masinissa, to whom she had once been betrothed, sent her poison in order to spare her the humiliation of captivity in Rome.

Sophora, a genus, containing about 50 species, of the Leguminosae (pea family), including trees with very hard wood, shrubs and some herbs. The leaves are pinnate, the yellow, white or blue flowers occur in upright groups, and the pod is cylindrical and constricted between the seeds like a string of beads. Well-known species are *S. japonica*, or pagoda tree, *S. davidii*, Chinese shrub, *S. tetraptera*, kowhai, a native of New Zealand, and *S. sericea*, a North American prairie herb.

Sopot, town of Poland, in Gdańsk province, 11 km north of Gdańsk. It has developed since 1820 as a seaside resort. Population 49,000.

Soprano, term in music denoting (1) the highest pitched voice, the usual compass being from C below treble clef to B above; (2) a vocalist with this voice; usually boys and women, also *castrati* in the 17th and 18th centuries; (3) the C clef on first line of stave.

Sopron (German *Odenburg*), town of Hungary, in Győr-Sopron county, 77 km west of Győr. It is near the Austrian border and the Neusiedler See. By origin a Celtic settlement, Sopron was a prosperous town in Roman times (*Scarabantia*) and in the Middle Ages. In 1920, by the Treaty of Trianon, it was given to Austria as part of BURGENLAND, but it was recovered by Hungary after a plebiscite in 1921. The town has many beautiful mansions and old churches, including the fine edifice (13th–15th centuries) called the Goat Church. There is a school of mining (1919), and wine, textile, chemical, and other industries. Population 45,000.

Sopwith, Sir Thomas Octave Murdoch (1888–), British airman, yachtsman, and inventor, born in London. In 1910 he won the Baron de Forest £4000 prize for a flight from England to the Continent. His aircraft company (founded 1911) built several planes used in the First World War, and he assisted in the development of the Hawker Company's machines, the Hurricane, Typhoon and Tempest, in the Second World War. He was knighted in 1953.

Soranus of Ephesus (AD 98-138), Greek obstetrician and gynaecologist, born at Ephesus; he studied at Alexandria and practised at Rome. He was the greatest obstetrician and gynaecologist of antiquity; his work was adopted by later writers and was unsurpassed for 1500 years. His obstetrical and gynaecological writings were published (Greek text) in 1838 and (German translation) 1800. He also wrote on fractures and on acute and chronic diseases.

Sorau, see ŻARY.

Sorb, see SERVICE TREE.

Sorbiodunum, see SARUM, OLD.

Sorbonne, most famous of the colleges in the medieval university of Paris. It was founded in the mid-13th century by Robert de Sorbon (1207–74), chaplain to Louis IX, with the king's consent. The college was devoted entirely to theology and was regulated by the strictest discipline. None could enter it until he had already graduated as bachelor of arts, and the management of the college was in the hands of a body of 36 students, the *Socii*. The course of study, including frequent disputations, was most thorough, and the Sorbonne rapidly rose to the highest position among the theological schools of Europe. Such was its reputation that difficult cases were actually sent from Rome for its decision. The Sorbonne welcomed the introduction of printing, but with the decay of the scholastic philosophy its fame also died away. It clung to the old ideas until the revolution, when its property was all confiscated.

On the reorganisation of the University of Paris in 1808, the Sorbonne became the seat of the three faculties of literature, science, and theology. In 1823 the university library was moved to the Sorbonne. In 1868 the École des Hautes Etudes, and in 1897 the École des Chartes were established there. Reconstruction of the buildings was completed in 1889.

Since 1969 the Sorbonne has lost its academic unity and is just a building shared by various colleges of the Paris University (see PARIS, UNIVERSITY OF). It remains the seat of the Rectorat and of the vice-chancellor of Paris University.

Sorbus, a genus with about 100 species of deciduous trees and shrubs found in Europe, North America and Asia, in family Rosaceae. *S. aria*, WHITEBEAM, *S. aucuparia*, mountain ash or ROWAN, and *S. torminalis*, wild service tree, are native to Britain. The genus is allied to, and used to be included under, *Pyrus*.

Sorcery, see MAGIC; WITCHCRAFT.

Sordello (c. 1200–70), Italian troubadour, born at Goito. He first appeared at Florence in a small company of jugglers. Forced to flee to Provence because of the abduction of Cunizza da Romano, he came under the protection first of Guillaume de Blacatz, and afterwards of Charles d'Anjou. He is credited with having written some 30 love-songs; especially famous in his lament on the death of Blacatz. See also TROUBADOUR.

Bibliography: C. de Lollis, *Vita e poesie di Sordello di Goito*, 1896.

Sore Throat, a term used for many varied conditions characterised by pain in the region of the uvula, tonsils, pharynx, and larynx. Inflammation of the fauces, the region bounded by the soft palate, uvula, and tonsils, is due to micro-organisms. It may be caused by acute infection, either bacterial or viral, when it is often accompanied by other symptoms such as fever, chills, and headache. In young and middle-aged adults a sore throat sometimes persists for months, often with no other symptoms. A sore throat can be due to local irritation due to smoking or drinking.

Sorel, Charles, Sieur de Souvigny (c. 1600–74), French novelist, born in Paris, remembered chiefly for his *Histoire comique de Francion*, 1623–33, a major work in the vein of comic realism, and *Le Berger extravagant*, 1627, which describes the pastoral follies of a young Parisian bourgeois whose head has been turned by reading contemporary fashionable novels.

Bibliography: F. E. Sutcliffe, *Le Réalisme de Charles Sorel*, 1965.

Sorel, Georges (1847–1922), French social philosopher, born at Cherbourg. He became an engineer for the department of bridges and highways, but gave up his post in 1892 and began an intensive self-education. His outlook reflects the Anarchist philosophy of Proudhon and Bakunin, but denies any belief in progress and advocates instead a 'heroic conception of life'. While at first he allied himself with Jaurès in the Dreyfus affair, and later championed the syndicalist cause, in the years immediately preceding the First World War he veered towards the extreme French right-wing nationalists of the 'Action Française' group. In his eyes the war was the 'crusade of democracy' and 'demagogic plutocracy', and he welcomed Russian Communism and Fascism alike, because both movements, in his eyes, stood for an 'imperialism of producers'. Italian, Spanish, and German Fascism borrowed from Sorel's theories the concept of a corporate state and of a heroic myth to sustain popular enthusiasm. Sorel's works include *Le Procès de Socrate*, 1889, *L'Avenir socialiste des syndicats*, 1898, *La Décomposition du Marxisme*, 1908, *Réflexions sur la violence*, 1908, *Les Illusions du progrès*, 1908, *Matériaux d'une théorie du prolétariat*, 1919, *De l'utilité du pragmatisme*, 1921, and *D'Aristote à Marx*, 1935.

Bibliography: J. H. Meisel, *The Genesis of Georges Sorel*, 1966.

Sörensen, Henrik (1882–1962), Norwegian painter and book illustrator. His work includes landscapes and allegorical subjects in an expressionist and vivid style, and he painted one of the largest murals in existence, in Oslo's new town hall.

Sørensen, Villy (1929–), Danish short-story writer and essayist, born in Copenhagen. He introduced Absurdism to Denmark with two volumes of bizarre and fantastic tales, *Sære Historier*, 1953, and *Ufarlige Historier*, 1955. His philosophical essays *Digtere og Dæmoner*, 1959, and *Hverken-eller*, 1961, which develop the line of thought originated by KIERKEGAARD, are highly rated. An intellectual writer, Sørensen's reflections on critical method inspired a whole generation of critics.

Sorghum (Italian *Sorgho*), a genus of annual or perennial grasses, of about 30 species and several cultivated types, in family Gramineae, native to warm countries. *S. vulgare*, probably African in origin, has several varieties, such as *saccharatus*, sweet sorghum, grown for its sugary sap and also for fodder; sorghums grown for their long, stiff, branched panicles (variety *technicus*) are known as broomcorn; those grown for grain include variety *drummondii* (chicken-corn), variety *durra* (surra), variety *caffrorum* (Kaffir corn), and variety *caudatus* (feterita). *S. halepense*, Johnson grass, is a perennial, grown for hay or pasture in mild countries, but is often a troublesome weed. *S. sudanensis*, Sudan-grass, and *S. virgatus*, Tunisgrass, are annuals grown for forage.

MILLET is generally similar to *Sorghum*, but is not very closely related botanically.

See also GRAIN PRODUCTION.

Soria, province of Spain, in CASTILLA LA VIEJA. It is an open, dry, and generally infertile region, crossed by the upper waters of the Duero river. Timber, charcoal, salt, and asphalt are produced. Area 10,318 km²; population 104,000.

Soria, capital of the province of Soria, Spain, on the Duero river. It has a fine Renaissance palace, several old churches, and a museum of objects from nearby NUMANTIA. Foodstuffs and timber are produced. Population 25,030.

Soriano, department of south-western Uruguay, bounded by the Uruguay river and Río Negro. There is agriculture and stock raising. Area 8876 km²; population 115,000 (including Lobos and Vizcaino islands). MERCEDES is the capital.

Sorn, village in Cumnock and Doon District, Strathclyde Region, Scotland, on the north bank of the River Ayr, 6 km east of Mauchline. Here also is Sorn Castle, residence of Lord Sorn.

Sorocaba, town of Brazil, in the state of SÃO PAULO, 90 km west of São Paulo city, on Sorocaba river. One of the leading industrial towns of the country, with electricity supplied by hydro-electric power, it has cotton and silk spinning mills, and manufactures cement, hats, footwear, alcohol, and fertilisers. There are also railway workshops and printing works. It is the centre of a rich agricultural area producing primarily coffee, cotton, sugar cane, and fruit. Population 180,000.

Sorolla y Bastida, Joaquin (1863–1923), Spanish painter, born in Valencia, studied under Pradilla, and in Paris. He was the foremost Spanish Impressionist, producing a large number of works, especially landscapes and marine pieces.

Sororate, institution, found in many societies, by which a wife is replaced by her sister if she dies or is barren, because the husband's family feels that her family has failed to carry out the marriage contract of supplying a woman who will bear children for her husband.

The sororate was practised by Indians of the North American Great Basin. They also practised the levirate, by which a widow married her dead husband's brother.

Sororities, see FRATERNITIES AND SORORITIES.

Sorrel

Sorrel, various plants with a tangy, acid taste. *Rumex acetosa*, British sorrel, and *R. scutatus*, French sorrel, of the Polygonaceae, are sometimes grown as salad vegetables or substitutes for spinach. *Oxyria digyna* (Polygonaceae) is mountain sorrel; *Oxalis acetosella* (Oxalidaceae) is wood sorrel.

Sorrel-tree, *Oxydendrum arboreum*, a species of the Ericaceae (heather family).

Sorrento, Italian town in CAMPANIA, on the Sorrentine Peninsula of the Bay of NAPLES, 30 km south-east of Naples. It has an archiepiscopal cathedral, and there are remains of Roman villas. It is a popular tourist resort on account of its climate, bathing, and beautiful scenery. Wine is produced locally, citrus fruit, fish and red vases; for all of which the town has been known since Roman times. TASSO was born here. Population (1974) 13,100.

Sorsogon, province of southern LUZON in the Philippines. It is traversed by a wooded volcanic mountain range, culminating in the volcano of Bulusan, interspersed with broad level farmlands growing hemp, coconuts, rice, and sweet potatoes. Area 2141 km². Population (1970) 426,842.

Sortes Virgilianae, method of divination in which some sacred book was opened at random, deductions being drawn from the first passage which met the eye. The Romans for long had recourse to the sibylline books (see SIBYL) in this manner, but after the destruction of these in 83 BC, Virgil's *Aeneid* became the most popular book for the purpose, and hence the name of this method of sortilège. Early Christian literature shows that many Christians used the Bible in this way, but the practice was condemned in several councils. Muslims frequently make use of the Koran for *sortes virgilianae*.

See also BIBLIOMANCY.

Sorrel, *Rumex acetosa*, in summer. *(Topham/Markham)*

Sortilège, or casting of lots, a system of DIVINATION. A common method is to use pieces of wood or straw, which are marked and covered up, one or more being then drawn out at random.

Sør-Trøndelag, county of NORWAY, in the north-west, between Sweden and Trondheim Fjord, a generally wooded area. Agriculture and lumbering industries are carried on. The capital is TRONDHEIM. Area 18,750 km². Population (1975) 240,000.

Sorus, see FERNS.

Sosigenes (fl. 1st century BC), Alexandrian astronomer and mathematician. He was employed by Caesar to reform the calendar and it appears from Pliny that he taught that the motion of Mercury is round the Sun. All that remains of his work consists of extracts from his *Revolving Spheres*, preserved in the 6th-century commentary by Simplicius on Aristotle's *De caelo*.

Sosnowiec, town of Poland, in Katowice province, on the River Czarna Przemsza, 10 km east of Katowice. It is a metallurgical centre, and has engineering, chemical, and other industries. Population (1974) 149,700.

Sospiri, Ponte dei, see BRIDGE OF SIGHS.

Sotavento, Islas de, see LEEWARD ISLANDS.

Soteriology (Greek *sōtēria*, salvation), branch of theology which deals with the salvation of mankind by Jesus Christ. See ATONEMENT.

Sotheby's, the biggest firm of fine art auctioneers in the world, founded by Samuel Baker, a Covent Garden bookseller, in 1744. The full title is now Sotheby Parke Bernet and Company and the head office is 34–35 New Bond Street, London, W1. It has auction rooms or offices in 25 cities throughout the world. In 1964 Sotheby's bought Parke Bernet in New York, America's largest fine art auction house, and in 1974 purchased Mak van Waay of Amsterdam, Holland's biggest auction firm. Sales are now held regularly in London in New Bond Street, Belgravia and Chancery Lane, in New York at Madison Avenue and 84th Street, in Los Angeles, Toronto, Zurich, Florence, Monte Carlo, Hong Kong, Johannesburg, Madrid and in Scotland at Edinburgh, Glasgow and Gleneagles Hotel, Perthshire. Impressionist and modern pictures contribute the major portion of the company's annual turnover, which averages between £75 million and £90 million net, but books, works of art, Chinese porcelain and furniture all bring in large amounts each year. Jewels are now sold in London, New York, Los Angeles, Zurich, Hong Kong and Johannesburg and add almost as much to the total turnover as Impressionist pictures. Sotheby's 200 experts in all branches of fine art travel to all parts of the world to advise on fine art and there are regular visits of teams of experts to towns and cities in Britain when local residents are invited to bring fine art for appraisal free of charge and without obligation.

Sothern, Edward Askew (1826–81), British actor, born in Liverpool. He created the role of Dundreary in *Our American Cousin*, 1858, which made that play a remarkable commercial success and initiated a 'Dundreary cult'. In 1864 he played the title role in *David Garrick* with success. He continued to be a highly successful comic actor in both London and New York. Three sons of his went on the stage, of whom Edward Hugh (1859–1933) was the most successful. He ran for many years a Shakespeare repertory company with the American actress Julia Marlowe, who became his second wife. He also revived his father's old part of Dundreary.

Sothic Year, an Egyptian year of 365¼ days defined as the interval between successive heliacal risings of Sirius (Sothis). The Egyptian calendar year was 365 days, and there were no leap years so that its beginning could coincide with that of the Sothic year only once in 1460 (= 365/¼) years, a period which was known as the Sothic Cycle. It has been suggested that the initial date of the continuous 365-day calendar was 2782 BC when its first day would have coincided with that of the Sothic year and with the summer solstice.

Sōtō, one of the two chief schools of Zen Buddhism in Japan, the other being Rinzai.

Soto, Fernando de (1496–1542), Spanish explorer, born at Jérez de los Caballeros, Estremadura, voyaged to Darien in 1519 under Davila, and joined the expedition to Nicaragua in 1527. From the conquest of Peru, in which he seconded Pizarro, he returned home with 180,000 ducats, and as a result the Emperor Charles V permitted de Soto to embark at his own expense on the subjugation of Florida. He set out in 1539 from Tampa Bay in search of El Dorado. In 1541 he discovered the River Mississippi, and crossed over to the Ouachita river, but his companions were decimated by disease and continual skirmishes with the Indians, and all the clues to the source of the treasure proved elusive. In 1542 de Soto died of fever and disappointment, and the remnants of his expedition eventually reached Mexico.
Bibliography: T. Maynard, *De Soto and the Conquistadores,* 1930.

Soubise, name of a famous French Huguenot family, connected with the house of Rohan by the marriage of Catherine de Parthenay to Vicomte René de Rohan (1575). Benjamin de Rohan, Duc de Soubise (1589–1642), a younger son of this marriage, fought under Maurice of Orange-Nassau in the Low Countries, and with his elder brother, Henri, Duc de Rohan, took part in the religious wars in Poitou, Brittany, and Anjou. Benjamin commanded the siege of La Rochelle (1625). The most famous descendant of this house is Charles de Rohan, Prince de Soubise (1715–87), a peer and marshal of France, who served under Louis XV, in the campaigns of 1744–48, and in the Seven Years' War, being defeated at Rossbach (1757).

The Hôtel de Soubise, now part of the Archives National in Paris, is one of the most beautiful buildings of the Marais district.

Soudan, see Sudan.

Soufflot, Jacques Germain (1713–80), French architect, born at Irancy. He studied for several years in Rome. In Lyons he made his reputation with the Hôtel Dieu, 1740. After further study in Rome, he returned to Paris, and in 1755 won the important competition for the church of St Geneviève (see Panthéon).

Soufrière, town and district of St Lucia, an island in the Windward group of the West Indies. Known for its sulphur springs and health baths and for the proximity of two spectacular, forest-clad volcanic cones rising sheer out of the sea, the Gros Piton (798 m) and Petit Piton (750 m). Population 7535 in 1970. The people are mainly dependent on agriculture though a few make their living from fishing.

Soufrière (sulphur), name of several active and inactive volcanoes in the West Indies, among them Grande Soufrière on southern Basse-Terre Island, Guadeloupe, at 1484 m; La Soufrière at the north end of St Vincent in the Windward Islands, at 1234 m, which erupted violently on 7 May 1902 causing 2000 deaths, becoming inactive the following year; and another on southern Montserrat in the Leeward Islands, at 914 m.

Soul (Greek *psyche*, Latin *anima*) religious conception of an immaterial element in man, capable of existence apart from the body, and immortal seat of the personality and of life, physical as well as intellectual, moral, aesthetic, and spiritual, in respect of which last it is sometimes called the Spirit (Greek *pneuma*).

Pre-Christian Concepts. Popular Belief. Belief in a soul with operations that could be distinguished from those of the body goes back to very early times. The experiences of sleep and unconsciousness, of self-awareness, imagination, memory (ranging far beyond the physical present), and the possession of abstract, purely immaterial, and intellectual ideas, all seemed to verify its existence, though it was not necessarily conceived of as separate and immaterial. The soul was rather regarded as a material substance but of a tenuous, rarified, volatile kind, like a scent or breath. Often it was imagined to possess the form of the physical body (cf. the Egyptian *Ka*). It was universally believed, as burial customs show, to survive bodily death, but the nexus between soul and body was generally thought to survive also in some way. Proper burial of the body was thought vital to the soul, whose dwelling is described as below ground, dark, cheerless, cut off from life and love and light and God, and is even called 'the pit' or 'the grave'. Such is the Greek *Hades* and Hebrew *Sheol* (see Hell). Existence there is but a dream-like reflection of life on earth, insubstantial and unsatisfying. In short, man has always been assured of 'survival' but never found much comfort in it (cf. Isa. xxxviii. 18 ff.). A blessed, satisfying hereafter was thought to be only for exceptional persons, deified or assumed to the abode of the gods. Two important developments, however, took place eventually among the Jews. In the time of the Maccabees the promise of a glorious general resurrection of soul and body first appears; at the same time, stimulated by Greek thought, the Jews of the Dispersion began to conceive of the soul as a completely spiritual discarnate entity (see *The Wisdom of Solomon* iii. 1 ff.).

Philosophy. Greek metaphysical thought examined the nature of reality independently of traditional concepts, and acutely aware of the duality between matter and mind, the eternal and the contingent, it formed new ideas about the soul and its relation to the universe, which, like human nature, was held to possess an enduring transcendent reality behind the outward flux of physical events. The earliest theories of the soul were therefore cosmological in character, treating it as a particle of the cosmic substance, whether viewed as fire, as a refined ethereal matter (the world soul), or as (according to Pythagoras) certain mathematical harmonies. Brahman and Buddhist pantheism, with the conception of the soul as part of the entirely immanent divine being, and due to be reabsorbed in it or reincarnated in some other physical vehicle (see METEMPSYCHOSIS; PYTHAGORAS), evidently contributed to these ideas. Plato was the first philosopher to define the soul as a thinking and moral entity with a being of its own, but his views were inconsistent, and never harmonised by himself. He sometimes affirms and sometimes denies personal immortality, or makes it conditional on the divine pleasure. However, he taught that the soul is prior to, independent of, and distinct from the body, and imprisoned and fettered by it. Aristotle on the contrary taught that the soul is the first entelechy (organising principle) of the living body, but he left its distinct and permanent existence uncertain.

Christian and Post-Christian Concepts. Christian. Christianity, insisting that man's main concern in life was the salvation or loss of his soul, and offering all men a blissful hereafter in body and soul, made the soul all-important. Yet no explicit advance was made in the definition of the soul in New Testament times. The Gospels use the two terms *Psychē* and *Pneuma* (used in the Greek Old Testament to translate the Hebrew *Nephesh*, life, and *Ruach*, breath), and use them in the Old Testament way, i.e. unsystematically and indiscriminately to designate the soul. Tertullian wrote the first Christian study of the soul (*De Anima*), notable chiefly as the source of the Traducian heresy (that the soul, like the body, is derived from the parents). But St AUGUSTINE taught (*de Trinitate*) that the soul is distinct from the body, entirely immaterial and spiritual (the will being specially important among its faculties), but that the body is itself good, the soul being its first cause, and also its end, its *summum bonum*. He did not, however, decide between Traducianism and Creationism (see below). St THOMAS AQUINAS completed the orthodox Catholic doctrine of the soul, insisting on the unity of the rational soul with the sensitive and vegetative principles, and declaring that the soul informs (i.e. is the form of) the body, a belief which was declared *de fide* by the Council of Vienna in 1311. He defined the soul as an incomplete substance; while capable of existence without the body, it has an exigence for it. He asserted that the soul is absolutely simple, unextended, and spiritual, in spite of its relation to the body; it is not totally immersed in the body, and though it uses it, it transcends it and is independent in its operations. Finally, he affirmed that the rational soul is created by God directly (Creationism).

Philosophic Theory. After Descartes, philosophic theory was long preoccupied with the problem of knowledge and what seemed the impassable gap between mind and matter. Descartes posited the action of the Deity to account for the interaction of soul and body. The Occasionalists denied that there was any real reaction between mind and matter in the act of knowing, only a correspondence, which Leibniz accounted for as a pre-established harmony. Spinoza declared that there was only one substance, of which thought and extension are both attributes: the soul is the idea of the body. The Idealist Berkeley banished the duality by denying the existence of the material world except in the knowing mind. Hume denied the identity of the knowing mind, reducing experience to a flux of discrete sensations. Kant denied the knowability of the phenomenal world, except as a noumenon, created by the unconscious imposition on it of mental categories. On the other hand, Hobbes and the materialists abolished the great gulf by denying the existence of the mind or soul except as an epiphenomenon of organised matter. This is essentially the position of Marx and his followers, and is the unstated premiss of most social sciences, psychology (especially behaviourist psychology), etc.; all scientific investigations of behaviour, in fact, assume that causation and conditioning will, by themselves, provide adequate explanations that can be embodied in 'laws'. Charles Darwin's theory of evolution contradicted the religious assumption that man was set apart from the rest of nature by virtue of a separate creation and endowment with a soul. Even the conceptual validity of MIND, a term free from the religious associations of soul, has been challenged by philosophers like RYLE, who regard it as a 'category mistake'. The work of brain surgeons, who are able to change a patient's personality by lobotomy, is powerful evidence that the 'soul' has a physical basis; so is the more limited success of aversion therapy and similar conditioning techniques. On the other hand most Existentialists, e.g. J.-P. Sartre, insist that man is 'free', which can be interpreted as a way of saying that he has a soul; and Arthur Koestler and others have claimed that examples of undetermined behaviour can be observed in nature. Whether the traditional doctrine of the soul will survive these debates remains very much in question.

Soult, Nicolas Jean de Dieu (1769–1851), Duke of Dalmatia, French soldier, born at Saint-Amans-la-Bastide (Tarn). He joined the French army as a private (1785). His promotion was rapid. In 1792 he was adjutant-general, and after Fleurus he was made general of a brigade (1794). He fought with great distinction under Masséna in Switzerland, and in 1804 was appointed by Napoleon a marshal of France, and after the Russian campaign (1806–07) was given a dukedom. He then commanded in Spain and Portugal, and after his defeats at La Coruña (1809), Albuera (1811), and Salamanca (1812) he quarrelled with Joseph Bonaparte, who demanded his recall; but Soult reassumed command in 1813, first in Spain and then in southern France, where he displayed brilliant generalship in pitting his raw recruits against Wellington's veterans. During Louis XVIII's brief triumph he turned Royalist, but declared for Napoleon in 1815, and after Waterloo was banished till 1819. He was present as French ambassador at the coronation of Queen Victoria (1838). He was twice minister for war under Louis-Philippe, and was premier in 1832, and from 1840 to 1847. His *Mémoires* appeared in 1854.

Sound, term used to mean both the sensation received via the EARS and the vibrations that cause the sensation. Everything that makes sound, such as a machine, a violin string, a tuning fork, or vocal cords, does so by vibrating. The surrounding medium (air, for example) vibrates and waves of vibration spread out in every direction. If they hit the tympanum (eardrum), it too vibrates and the vibrations are transmitted by small bones to detector cells inside the ear. Here, nerve impulses are set up and register in the brain as a sensation of sound. Fig. 1 shows a

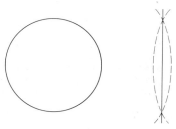

Sound. Figure 1. Sounding plate or gong. LEFT Front view. RIGHT Side view.

sounding plate or gong. When it is struck it vibrates outwards, back again, and outwards on the other side. As it moves outwards the air is compressed; as it moves back inwards it creates a low pressure and so on. Thus alternate waves of high, low, and high pressure are set up by the gong vibrating. Human ears cannot detect vibrations slower than about 30 times a second (30 Hz) which produces a very deep note. Middle C corresponds to a vibration of 261 Hz. Human ears can also not detect frequencies above about 22,000 Hz, which produce very high notes, though some animals' ears, such as those of dogs and bats, can do so. Older people lose their response to the highest frequencies. If (as for example, in outer space or in a vacuum) there is no material to vibrate, sound cannot be conducted. Sound waves are *longitudinal*, i.e., the vibrations of the medium through which the waves are propagated take place in the direction in which the waves are travelling. BOYLE was the first scientist to demonstrate that sound cannot travel through a vacuum, and his experiment may be repeated by suspending a vibrating electric bell inside a vessel from which the air is gradually exhausted by means of an air pump. The sound of the bell ultimately vanishes, but when the air is readmitted the sound is heard again. The velocity with which sound travels in air at ordinary temperatures is about 340 m/s or 1200 km/h while its velocity in water is about 1400 m/s; in solids the velocity with which sound travels is considerably greater than its velocity in air or liquids. LAPLACE first showed that the velocity of sound in a gas is given by the equation $V = \sqrt{(\gamma p/d)}$ where p is the pressure of the gas, d its density, and γ the ratio of the SPECIFIC HEAT of the gas at constant pressure to its specific heat at constant volume. For air and other diatomic gases γ has the value of 1·41; for monatomic gases $\gamma = 1·67$. The velocity of sound in a solid vibrating longitudinally is given by the equation $V = \sqrt{(Y/d)}$ where Y is Young's modulus of elasticity for the solid. Since the pressure of a gas is directly proportional to its density, it follows from the previous equation that the velocity of sound in a gas is independent of the pressure of the gas. For a perfect gas, the velocity varies, however, with the temperature as the square root of its absolute temperature. Thus sound travels faster in warm air than in cold air, and this results in a refraction or bending of the waves in air, whose strata are at different temperatures. Refraction of sound also takes place when there is a wind blowing, and as a result sound carries better with the wind than against it. Fig. 2 explains how this happens. Suppose a person at A is shouting to one at B and that the direction of the wind is as indicated in the figure. The

friction between the air and the ground causes the wind to travel more slowly near the ground than in the layer of air above it. The wave front AC would therefore gradually become bent to A_3C_3. Thus the sound is 'concentrated' by the refraction and B's ear-drum is set vibrating more violently that it would be if the air were still.

Loudness, Pitch, and Quality. Our sensations of sound possess the three characteristics of loudness, pitch, and timbre.

Loudness. Common observation shows that the loudness of a note depends only on the amplitude or extent of the vibration of the sounding body. Thus, for example, the loudness of a note sounded on a piano can be decreased by damping down the vibrations by means of a piece of baize controlled by a pedal. In the same way the apparent loudness of a source of sound diminishes as the observer moves farther away from it.

Pitch. The pitch of a note is governed solely by the frequency with which the sounding body vibrates. This was first demonstrated by Savart by means of a revolving toothed wheel. He pressed a card against the teeth of the wheel, and in this way the card was tapped by each tooth as the wheel revolved. The pitch of the note emitted by the vibrating card was found to rise with the speed of revolution of the wheel. Savart showed further that any two notes form an octave if the ratio of their frequencies is 2 : 1. The musical intervals known as the fifth and third are formed by any two notes whose frequencies are in the ratio of 3 : 2 and 5 : 4, respectively. The eight notes that comprise the *diatonic scale* of modern music are given below with their frequency ratios reduced to their simplest terms.

$$C \quad D \quad E \quad F \quad G \quad A \quad B \quad c$$
$$24 : 27 : 30 : 32 : 36 : 40 : 45 : 48$$

The actual frequency of any note in the scale may be calculated from this table, since the frequency of C is 261 Hz.

Timbre. The timbre of a note depends on the shape of the waves it creates. This shape is governed by the form of the vibrating body, the way in which it is made to vibrate and by the sounding board on which it is mounted. Fig. 3 represents the displacements of the air created by the vibrations of a tuning-fork. This diagram is constructed in the following way. Ox represents the direction in which the sound is travelling. Let a, b, c, ... be the positions of the layers of air when undisturbed. When the waves are propagated the layers will be displaced in the direction in which the sound travels. Draw bB, cC, etc., perpendicular to Ox, to represent the magnitude of the displacements of the respective layers. In this way a

Sound. Figure 2. Effect of wind on sound.

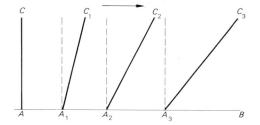

representation of the wave form is obtained. The differences in shape produce the differences in quality or timbre (see below, *Harmonics*).

Sound. Figure 3. Air displacements caused by a tuning-fork.

Vibration of Stretched Strings. Whenever a stretched string is plucked, bowed, or hammered, a wave travels to and fro along the string with a velocity that depends on the tension of the string and the mass per unit length of the string. The frequency of vibration of the string is given by the equation $n = (1/2l)(T/m)$, where l is the length of the string, T its tension, and m its mass per unit length. This equation can be verified experimentally by means of a sonometer that consists of a string mounted on a sounding-board. One end of the string is fixed, and a known weight hung from its other end determines the tension of the string. The effective length of the string can be varied by means of a wooden knife-edged bridge, placed underneath the string. Different tensions are obtained by different weights, and strings of different materials or thicknesses can be used in order to vary the mass per unit length of the string employed. The strings are tuned to the same pitch by moving the bridge until the note emitted by the string when plucked corresponds to that of a tuning-fork or to a fixed comparison string mounted side by side with the experimental string.

The violin has four strings of different masses per unit length, and the violinist is able to adjust the pitch of any string by altering its tension. The effective length of the string is altered by moving the finger along it, and in this way the violinist is able to obtain a wide range of notes. This property of instruments of this type is responsible for a greater delicacy of musical interpretation than that obtained with instruments like the piano, whose range of notes is fixed.

Harmonics. If a string is plucked in the middle it vibrates as in fig. 4a, and the note emitted is called the gravest, lowest, or *fundamental* note of the string. If it is damped at the middle and bowed elsewhere, it vibrates as in fig. 4b, emitting the octave of the fundamental note.

Sound. Figure 4. Harmonics: three forms of vibration.

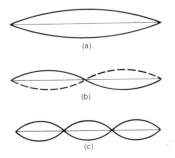

Fig. 4c shows the form of the vibrating string when damped at a point one-third of its length from a fixed end. The note emitted has a frequency three times that of the fundamental note. In general, if a string is damped at a point $1/n$ of its length from a fixed end, the note emitted has a frequency n times that of the fundamental note, where n is any integer. This note is known as the $(n-1)$th overtone or *harmonic* of the fundamental note. It can be shown by a mathematical or geometrical analysis due to FOURIER that the shape of a violin string after it has been plucked can be regarded as a mixture of curves like those in fig. 4a, b, and c. In other words, the note emitted by a violin string is a mixture of simple notes or *tones* whose frequencies are integral multiples of the fundamental tone, i.e., it consists of the fundamental tone and its harmonics. The relative intensities of the different harmonics depend entirely on the method of mounting a string and on the manner in which it is bowed or struck. The timbre, or quality, and the richness (or otherwise) of the note emitted, depend entirely on the mixture of the fundamental tone and its harmonics and this determines the characteristics of the sounds from various stringed instruments.

Pipes. Vibrating columns of air form the source of sound in many musical instruments. In fig. 5, AD is a column of air open at the end A and closed at its lower end by a column of water. The level D can be raised or lowered by means of a flexible pipe BC. If a vibrating tuning-fork is held over A, the air in AD is set into a forced vibration with a period equal to that of the fork. There are certain positions of D for which the natural period of vibration of the air column is equal to that of the fork, or a harmonic of the note emitted by the fork. In this case *resonance* occurs, and the air column emits a loud note. It is found that the length of AD is approximately $\frac{1}{4}\lambda$, $\frac{3}{4}\lambda$ etc., where λ is the wavelength of the note and is related to the frequency (ν) by the equation $V = \nu\lambda$, where V is the velocity of sound in air. The form of the vibrations of the air column in each of these cases is represented on a displacement diagram shown in fig. 6. In fig. 6a the pipe is sounding its fundamental note. Fig. 6b shows the displacement diagram for the first overtone, the frequency being three times that of the fundamental note.

Sound. Figure 5.

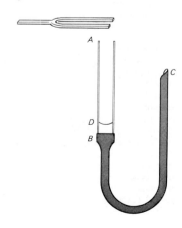

In fig. 6c the pipe is sounding the second overtone, whose frequency is five times that of the fundamental note. In an actual wind instrument that is closed at one end, these overtones are present mixed with the fundamental note, and their relative intensities determine the timbre of the note emitted by the instrument. Fig. 7 represents the displacement diagrams for a pipe open at both ends, a, b, and c being the diagrams for the fundamental note and its first two overtones, whose frequencies are respectively twice and three times that of the fundamental note. It will be noticed that in an open pipe all the harmonics are present, while in the closed pipe only the *odd* harmonics are present.

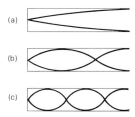

Sound. Figure 6.

The Doppler Effect. When a source of sound is moving towards an observer the frequency of the note heard is greater than that of the note emitted by the source. This phenomenon was first explained by DOPPLER as follows. Suppose the frequency of the note emitted by the source is n, then n vibrations are emitted per second by the source, and, if both the observer and the source are stationary, this number of vibrations will be contained in an air column of length V, where V is the velocity of sound in air. If, however, the source is moving with a velocity v towards the stationary observer, then in 1 second it emits n vibrations, but this number of vibrations is contained in an air column of length $(V - v)$, since the source has moved on a distance v in 1 s. Now the waves travel towards the observer with a velocity V. Hence in 1 s he receives the vibrations contained in an air column of length V. The observer therefore receives not n, but $nV/(V - v)$ vibrations per second, and the pitch of the note therefore seems to be raised. It can be shown in a similar way that when the observer and source are receding from each other the pitch of the note heard by the observer is lower than that emitted by the source. The effect is very striking when an observer is standing on a railway platform and an express train that is sounding its whistle rushes through the station, but the effect can be detected when a motor-cyclist or motorist passes an observer. It must not be confused with the increase and decrease of intensity of the sound as the source approaches and recedes. Doppler's principle also holds good in the case of a moving source of light, and it has enabled astronomers to measure the velocity of recession of stars moving in the line of sight (see SPECTRUM AND SPECTROSCOPE).

Ultrasonics. The human ear is quite insensitive to vibrations of frequency greater than about 20,000 Hz, and vibrations of frequency beyond the audible range are called ultrasonic (the term 'supersonic' is sometimes used as synonymous with 'ultrasonic', but as it is also widely used in connection with speeds greater than that of sound in air, ambiguity is avoided it if is not used to denote high frequencies). Many animals and birds can emit and detect vibrations inaudible to the human ear. For example, it has been shown that the capacity of a bat to avoid obstacles in its flight, without the assistance of vision, is due to its use of pulses of ultrasonic waves of frequency about 50,000 Hz. It emits about 60 of these pulses per second when in flight, and these pulses are reflected back to it even by small objects. The bat is able to assess both the direction from which the reflected waves come, and also the interval between their emission and return; it can thus estimate both the direction and distance of obstacles in its path, by means essentially similar to those used in RADAR except that it uses sound waves instead of electromagnetic radiations. Ultrasonic waves in water are similarly used in one system (Sonar) for the detection of submerged submarines, and for ECHO SOUNDING.

Ultrasonics of much higher frequency (up to many million Hz) can be generated by use of magnetostriction or the piezoelectric effect (see OSCILLATORS). If a bar of ferromagnetic material (see INDUCTION, MAGNETIC) is magnetised (e.g., by passing an electric current through a coil wound round it) its length changes slightly. This is called magnetostriction, and if the bar is immersed in a liquid or gas, and the current is an alternating one, the movements of the ends of the bar produce waves in the fluid having a frequency equal to that of the changes in length, i.e., equal to the frequency of the alternating current. If pressure is applied to a suitably cut piece of quartz or other crystal, causing change in its thickness, electric charges of opposite sign are produced on its faces. Conversely, if charges are applied to its faces, its thickness changes too. These phenomena constitute the piezoelectric effect. If it is arranged that the charges are produced and removed at a frequency equal to that of the natural frequency of vibration of the quartz plate, it is set into intense vibration, and it then produces ultrasonic waves in the surrounding medium.

Because of their high frequency and short wavelength, ultrasonics travel as a beam through matter without much spreading. In other words, they can travel through opaque matter in much the same way as light does through transparent materials, although at a much lower speed. They can therefore be used to detect flaws and cracks in such objects as steel billets, since a crack produces reflection, and sets up sound 'shadows'. This is at present their chief industrial use, but many others have been suggested and put into practice. If sufficiently intense they can break up particles of one liquid suspended in another to produce finely dispersed suspensions (emul-

Sound. Figure 7.

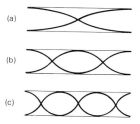

sions). Similarly, they can be used to remove small bubbles of gas trapped in a liquid, and are so used to render clear the molten material from which certain kinds of artificial gems (rubies, sapphires) are made. They also remove dirt and grease in laundering, kill bacteria, and sterilise milk. More recently, ultrasonics have been used to break up cells so that subcellular organelles become separable in a minimally damaged state. See also ACOUSTICS; DECIBEL; NOISE; PHYSICAL CONSTANTS.

Bibliography: Lord Rayleigh, *Theory of Sound* (2 vols), 1926; E. G. Richardson, *Sound*, 1953; C. A. Coulson, *Waves*, 7th ed. 1955; A. B. Wood, *A Textbook of Sound*, rev. ed. 1955; E. G. Richardson and A. E. Brown, *Ultrasonic Physics*, 2nd ed. 1962; Sir J. Jeans, *Science and Music*, new ed. 1969 (original ed. 1937); R. F. Gunstone, *Sound*, 1972; C. Johnson and others, *Sound*, 1972.

Sound, The, see ØRESUND.

Sound Amplification and Reproduction, see AMPLIFIER; MICROPHONE; RECEIVER, RADIO; RECORD PLAYER; TAPE RECORDER; TELEPHONY; TRANSISTOR.

Sound Insulation deals with the reduction or elimination of unwanted sound (see NOISE). ACOUSTICS is concerned with the correction of hearing conditions in auditoria, i.e., the modification of wanted sound.

Sound is an aural sensation produced by vibrations originating from many sources, e.g., voices, radio and television, footsteps, machines, and traffic. These vibrations are transmitted by all forms of matter—solids, liquids, and gases. In buildings they may be airborne, structure-borne, or conducted by service pipes and ducts. Sound may be modified by its surroundings. Music played in an empty room will generate a different apparent volume of sound than if played in a fully furnished room. Sound insulation thus poses considerable problems for the designer and a satisfactory solution may depend on a combination of several methods. Wherever possible noisy areas should be separated from quiet ones. Machinery should be mounted on anti-vibration or shock-absorbing mountings, and where necessary housed in a sound-insulated room. Carpeting will reduce impact sounds, while the provision of a resilient layer within a floor structure will reduce the transmission of sound to a room beneath.

Materials of low density do not effectively reduce the passage of sound through a structure. The role of such materials is mainly of value in effecting acoustical control. Materials of high density, e.g., concrete, stonework, and brick, on the other hand, have good sound energy-absorbing characteristics. Further improvements in sound insulation may be provided by discontinuity of structure as in hollow wall construction. Double windows may be necessary to reduce the effects of high traffic noise. The space between the glazing should be between 150 and 250 mm and the internal edges of the opening lined with sound-absorbing materials. Double glazing, where the panes are close together has little sound-insulation value. Sound insulation may be rendered ineffective unless air gaps, e.g., open windows and space around doors, are eliminated. Requirements concerning standards of sound insulation of parts of buildings are laid down in building regulations.

Bibliography: British Standards Institution, CP 3: Chapter III: 1972 *Sound insulation and noise reduction*.

Sound Ranging first assumed importance during the First World War, when it was employed to detect the positions of enemy gun batteries. A central station was electrically connected to each of three distant stations that were equipped with receiving microphones. The impact on the microphone of the sound waves from a gun set up fluctuations of the current in the electrical circuit connecting it to headquarters. These fluctuations were automatically recorded on a rotating drum by means of separate electromagnetic styluses connected in series with the three microphones, respectively. In this way the intervals that elapsed between the instants at which the sounds reached the three stations were recorded, and from a knowledge of the velocity of sound in air and the exact positions of the three stations, the enemy battery could be located. The principle of sound ranging is used at sea for the accurate fixing of the positions of two ships relative to one another. One ship drops an explosive charge set to fire on reaching a certain depth. The instant of the explosion is transmitted by radio to the other ship which is listening on her hydrophone. The difference in time between the receipt of the radio signal and the arrival of the sound of the explosion enables the distance between the two ships to be calculated within about a kilometre and the direction of the radio signal received gives the bearing. See ECHO; ECHO SOUNDING.

Sound Spectrogram, a device for analysing sounds, e.g. the human voice or bird song. The sound is recorded on a continuous tape and then played back through the sound spectrogram at high speed. A spectrograph is produced which plots time on a horizontal axis, frequency (pitch) on a vertical axis, and amplitude (loudness) as degrees of shading, so that a 'picture' of the sound is produced.

Soup, a liquid food made by boiling vegetables, bones and meat. The nutritional value of soup varies in relation to the proportion of solid food it contains. Its main function in the diet is to stimulate the digestive juices. It is most usually served as a first course to a meal. Soups may be classified as clear soups and broths, thick soups and mixed soups. Clear soups are really well flavoured stock with added garnishes. Broths contain meat and vegetables cut in tiny pieces; they should not be cloudy or thickened. Thick soups may be thickened by a purée, or with a starchy food or egg yolk. Chilled soups and fruit soups are popular in hot climates. There are many forms of partially prepared soups on the market, both canned and packet. They are a popular product, as they are very convenient, quick and easy to prepare. See also COOKERY.

Soupault, Philippe (1897–), French writer, born at Chaville (Seine-et-Oise). A founder of SURREALISM, his works include poems, *Rose des vents*, 1920, *Westwego*, 1922, *Georgia*, 1926, *Il y a un océan*, 1936, *L'Arme secrète*, 1946, *Chansons du jour et de la nuit*, 1949, and *Sans phrases*, 1953, as well as 15 novels, including *Le Bon apôtre*, 1923, *Les Frères Durandeau*, 1924, *En joue*, 1925, *Les Dernières nuits de Paris*, 1928, and *Le Grand homme*, 1929. He also produced plays, such as *Tous ensemble au bout du monde*, 1947, essays and critical works, including *Souvenirs de James Joyce*, 1945, *Profils perdus*, 1963, and studies of Henri Rousseau, Apollinaire, Lautréamont, William Blake, Uccello, Baudelaire, and Labiche.

Sous, see Sus.

Sousa, John Philip (1854–1932), US bandmaster, author and composer, born in Washington, DC, the son of a Portuguese musician. His compositions include numerous marches: *The Washington Post, El Capitan, Stars and Stripes for Ever, Imperial Edward,* etc.; operettas, waltzes and songs. He published *National, Patriotic, and Typical Airs of all Lands,* 1890; two novels, *The Fifth String* and *Pipetown Sandy;* and his reminiscences, *Marching Along,* 1928.

Sousse, seaport and commercial centre of central TUNISIA. It was founded by the Phoenicians and flourished under the Carthaginians and Romans. Fishing, especially sardines, is important, and other industries include textile milling, olive oil manufacture, and food canning. Population (1974) 90,000.

Soustelle, Jacques (1912–), French scholar and politician, born at Montpellier and educated at the École Normale Supérieure. He is an expert on Aztec civilisations. He joined Gen. de Gaulle in London during the Second World War, and became minister for information in 1945. He was the leading Gaullist deputy, and was governor-general in Algeria. He played a leading part in the events of 1958 that led to the establishment of the Fifth Republic. He quarrelled with de Gaulle over Algerian policy, and was exiled from 1962 to 1968. He is a municipal councillor in Lyons.

Soutar, William (1898–1943), Scottish poet, born at Perth. Educated at Edinburgh University, for the last 14 years of his life he was bedridden with a form of paralysis. Writing both in English and in Scots with delicate artistry and rare humour, he was considered one of the most gifted poets of the modern Scottish renaissance. Among his books of verse are *Conflict,* 1931, *Seeds in the Wind,* 1933, *The Solitary Way,* 1934, *A Handful of Earth,* 1936, *Riddles in Scots,* 1937, *In the Time of Tyrants,* 1939, *But the Earth Abideth,* 1943, and *The Expectant Silence,* 1944. His *Diaries of a Dying Man* were published in 1954.

Bibliography: Collected Poems, 1949; A. M. Scott, *William Soutar,* 1958.

Souterrains, or underground dwellings, have a very wide geographical distribution. They are found in China, Korea and Japan, along the northern boundaries of the Old World as far as Scandinavia; they occur in Iceland, Greenland and North America, and in one form or another in most countries of Europe. They vary as much in form as in distribution, and in date range from prehistoric to modern times. Aristotle, Xenophon and Strabo all give some account of such structures.

In modern archaeology, souterrains are small underground caverns lined and roofed with boulders or stone slabs. In the British Isles they are found in Cornwall (where they are known as 'fogous') and Scotland ('weems' or 'earth houses'), but above all in Ireland, where they are numbered in thousands. Similar structures are found in Brittany, dating to the pre-Roman Iron Age. Such a method of building must have recommended itself to more than one group of peoples, prehistoric and historic, for use as grain or food storage cellars, or as refuges, and many varieties are known. In Ireland, souterrains were widely used in the Early Christian period between AD 500 and 1100, and also during later troubled times. A large souterrain formed part of the early Iron Age settlement at Jarlshof, Shetland, in which early iron-smiths lived. Souterrains are also associated with the courtyard type of house exemplified by the Chysauster village near Penzance in Cornwall, which was occupied late in the early Iron Age and in the Roman period, and is now well-preserved and accessible as an ancient monument. In the Orkneys and Outer Hebrides they form part of wheel-type houses and appear to be associated with BROCH cultures of the Bronze Age. It is likely that the souterrain idea spread to the British Isles from Western Gaul.

Other kinds of ancient monument to which the name souterrain has been wrongly applied in the past include pit-dwellings and storage-pits of the early Iron Age, common in the south of England.

See also ARCHAEOLOGY; IRELAND, *Archaeology.*

Bibliography: E. Clark, *Cornish Fogous,* 1961; F. T. Wainwright, *The Souterrains of Southern Pictland,* 1963; C. Thomas, 'Souterrains in the Irish Sea Province' in *The Iron Age in the Irish Sea Province* (ed. C. Thomas), 1972; A. T. Lucas, 'Souterrains, the literary evidence' in *Bealoideas* (vols 39–41), 1971–73.

South, Sir James (1785–1867), British astronomer, born in London. He had a private observatory at Southwark, and was one of the founders of the London (afterwards Royal) Astronomical Society, of which he was elected president in 1829. Between 1821 and 1823 he collaborated with Sir John Frederick William HERSCHEL in a programme of measurements of double stars, and later with Laplace in Paris. He was knighted in 1830.

South Africa, formerly Union of South Africa, now Republic of South Africa (RSA), independent state in the southernmost portion of Africa, comprising the four provinces of CAPE PROVINCE, NATAL, ORANGE FREE STATE, and TRANSVAAL. These were previously British colonies and Boer republics (see BOER WARS). South Africa is bounded on the north-east by Mozambique, on the north by Rhodesia, on the north-west by Botswana, and on the west by South-West Africa. South Africa administers SOUTH-WEST AFRICA (SWA, also known as Namibia) as an integral part of the republic. Area 1,210,600 km².

South Africa. Tent encampment in the Kalahari Desert. *(Camera Press/Pat Smith)*

South Africa

Geography. Relief. Most of South Africa is part of the vast interior plateau of southern Africa, with an average altitude of 1250 m. The lowland belt along the 3000-km long coast varies in width from 5 to 50 km, mainly about 150 m above sea-level. Within the plateau area are several distinct regions: the Little, or Southern, KARROO, is the tableland about 25 km wide separated from the coastal strip by the Langeberg and Outeniqua ranges, with an average height of 600–900 m, and the Highveld of the Orange Free State and Transvaal is between 1250 and 1850 m. There are several great mountain ranges including the DRAKENSBERG, Stormberg, Roggeveld, Bokveld, Nieuveld, and Kamiesberg. The best-known mountain is TABLE MOUNTAIN at Cape Town. South Africa's two most important rivers are the ORANGE, with its tributary, the VAAL, and the LIMPOPO. The Great Escarpment between the interior plateaus and the coastal lowland prevents navigation on South Africa's rivers. See ATLAS 46.

Climate. South Africa's climate is associated particularly with long hours of sunshine. Pretoria receives 74 per cent of the possible maximum, Cape Town and Port Elizabeth 67 per cent, and Durban 54 per cent. The country lies mainly within the temperate zone apart from a small region of the Transvaal and a major part of Natal. The warm Mozambique current, which brings rain, flows down the east coast, and the cold Benguela current up the west coast. Mean annual temperatures vary from 23 °C in the western Orange river valley and 21 °C on the east coast, to 15 °C on the west coast and 13 °C in the higher parts of the Drakensberg. The summer months are December to February, and June to August the winter. The Cape receives its rain in the winter, whereas in the rest of South Africa the winter climate is dry (with frost at higher altitudes) and the rains fall in the summer months. Average rainfall in Johannesburg is 830 mm and 400 in Kimberley; 1150 mm in Durban and 630 in Cape Town. Humidity is highest in summer, especially on the coast of Natal, where it is over 90 per cent for long periods.

Population. The first people the 17th-century Dutch colonisers encountered were BUSHMEN and HOTTENTOTS. The former fled to the interior; the latter with the settlers and East Indian slaves were the ancestors of the present-day Cape coloureds. The Africans originating in the central and eastern parts of South Africa belong to four main groups, all BANTU-speaking: (1) the NGUNI, who include the ZULU, SWAZI, Ndebele, and the many Transkei tribes (XHOSA, Pondo, Bhaca, Bomvana, and MFENGU); (2) the Sotho, including the Basuto, TSWANA, LOVEDU, and Pedi; (3) the Shangaan-Tsonga; (4) the VENDA. These peoples were cultivators and pastoralists and all had strongly patrilineal political systems, with patriarchal chiefs and kings, who were regarded as near-divine. Today between 30 and 60 per cent of the Black population live in the cities. Tribal affiliation is the basis of the HOMELANDS system.

The Dutch, who were later called Boers, and now Afrikaners, and the British who established colonial settlements during the 18th and 19th centuries, form the two distinctive groups of the white population today. The descendants of Indian traders, long established on the east coast of Africa, and Chinese imported as labourers in the last century form an Asian group.

Fundamental to the South African political system is the policy of APARTHEID, or separate development. As a result certain areas of the country are designated 'white', and others Bantu 'homelands'. Within the urban structure districts are similarly designated 'white', 'coloured' or African (these last are frequently separate 'townships'). These zones are strictly controlled, and there is no freedom of movement between them. Nine homelands are designated, occupying under 14 per cent of South Africa. With the emphasis now on multi-national development, the majority have self-governing legislatures. The TRANSKEI became independent in 1976, and BOPHUTHATSWANA in 1977. The homelands contribute about four per cent of South Africa's GNP. In the common or white areas a reduction in the more petty aspects of apartheid is gradually taking place in some of the major towns.

In 1975 there were an estimated 4,240,000 whites, 2,368,000 coloureds, 727,000 Asians, and 18,136,000 blacks in South Africa; the total population was 25,471,000. There are also many immigrant African labourers from outside the republic, e.g. from Lesotho, Swaziland and Rhodesia. The main towns are JOHANNESBURG, CAPE TOWN (legislative capital), PRETORIA (administrative capital), DURBAN and PORT ELIZABETH.

Bibliography: A. Nel, *Geographical Aspects of Apartheid in South Africa*, 1962; C. Seligman, *Races of Africa*, 1963; N. C. Pollock and S. Agnew, *Historical Geography of South Africa*, 1964; M. Cole, *South Africa* (2nd ed.), 1966; D. R. Morris, *The Washing of the Spears*, 1966; D. M. Smith (Ed.), *Separation in South Africa: People and Policies*, 1976.

Economy. South Africa's immense mineral wealth laid the foundation for rapid industrial growth. Economic growth rivalled that of Japan in the 1960s; gross domestic product (GDP) more than doubled. It reached £11,448 million in 1973. GDP per capita (1970) was £296, greater than any other African country except Libya. Although South Africa therefore ranks as semi-developed, income is very unevenly divided. This results from a continuing surplus of African unskilled labour, and a growing shortage of skilled labour, partly an artificial shortage arising from policies of job reservation aimed to protect whites from competition. Income differentials between whites and Africans were 5·1:1 in manufacturing and 14·5:1 in mining in 1973. African wages have grown faster than

South Africa. The black township of Soweto. (*Camera Press/Tom Blau*)

South Africa. The Prieska copper mine in Cape Province. *(Camera Press)*

white wages since 1973, but many Africans are still below the poverty datum line, and the absolute gap continues to widen. The low level of African incomes will have a restrictive effect on industrial growth, which requires expanding local markets as export markets remain limited. Manufacturing overtook mining as the leading sector of the economy during the Second World War. Foreign investment has played a leading rôle in both mining and manufacturing. It amounted to £640·5 million in 1936, or 43 per cent of total foreign investment in Africa at that date. Another large wave of foreign investment occurred after 1945, associated with the Orange Free State goldfields. Subsequently foreign investment slowed down, with a net outflow between 1959 and 1964. In 1972 foreign liabilities stood at £4768 million (£2659 million to the sterling area, mainly Britain), and foreign assets (including gold reserves) were worth £1881 million, mainly in

Rhodesia, Zaire, and Malawi. In 1973 there was a net capital outflow of £72·2 million.

Agriculture. This sector contributed only 8·9 per cent of the gross domestic product in 1972. The biggest export is wool, worth £76·3 million in 1972, followed by maize and maize products, sugar, preserved fruit and jam, citrus fruit, deciduous fruit, and hides and skins. Other agricultural products exported in quantity are mohair and karakul ('Persian' lamb). All these exports were worth £461·7 million in 1972. The wide range of products is made possible by the climatic variations across the country.

Normally South Africa produces enough wheat and other grains to be self-supporting, and has been able to supply surpluses to neighbouring countries in recent years. Cattle thrive, allowing meat and dairy produce to be exported in good years, although severe droughts in northern areas often bring ruin to small farmers. The worst drought in living memory lasted four years in some districts (ended in 1965), but the risks are being lessened by irrigation works; the ORANGE river project is expected to increase the irrigated area by 40 per cent. In the western Cape there is an important wine industry, started over 250 years ago. In the last two decades South Africa has built up a big fishing industry, and in conjunction with the territory of SOUTH-WEST AFRICA (Namibia) now ranks among the six major fishing fleets of the world.

Industry. Mining is one of the bases of the South African economy, but is no longer the chief contributor to the gross domestic product. In 1972 mining contributed 11 per cent, compared with 22·4 per cent for manufacturing. The country is endowed with great mineral resources, and virtually every known mineral is found except oil (now produced from coal at SASOLBURG). South Africa is the world's biggest producer of gold, gem diamonds, and antimony, and ranks as follows as a producer of other minerals: asbestos (3rd); beryl (5th); chromite (2nd); industrial diamonds (3rd); manganese (2nd); platinum

South Africa. The Williamson diamond mine. *(Camera Press/TIO)*

South Africa

(2nd); uranium (3rd); and vanadium (2nd). Over 70 per cent of gold produced outside the Communist Bloc (885,554 kg in 1973, valued at £1083 million) is mined in South Africa, employing 417,197 people, including 37,505 whites. There is no indication that the production of gold will decrease in the near future, for although some mines are rapidly being worked out, new ones are coming into production in the Far West RAND and the Orange Free State. As uranium is a by-product of certain gold mines, it is produced at much less cost than in other countries where it is mined as a main product. There are plentiful deposits of coal and iron ore. Consequently South Africa produces steel very cheaply, as well as cheap thermal electricity.

The total value of South Africa's mineral production in 1973 was £1742 million. Total employment was 735,492, including 85,277 whites; the wage bill was £441 million. Government revenue from mining in the 1973–74 tax year was estimated at £167·8 million. Since 1974 the gold-mining industry has experienced labour shortages, particularly because of a decrease in migrant labour from Malawi and Lesotho.

Secondary industry in South Africa expanded after the Second World War, founded on cheap steel and energy, a super-abundance of unskilled African labour, a growing internal market, and a wide range of domestically-produced raw materials. The vast quantity of coal available enabled a prosperous chemical industry to be developed, worth £428·6 million in 1972. Production is mainly based on the Sasolburg plant in the Orange Free State where oil is manufactured from coal. The many by-products are processed to produce synthetic rubber and nitrogen.

Local raw materials encourage the manufacture of cotton and wool textiles of every type, and there is an important clothing industry. All classes of light engineering are represented, and industries based on wood (furniture, paper, pulp, synthetic fabrics) are well developed. Vehicle assembly plants have been established with fiscal inducements and legal requirements to use local materials. South Africa's aircraft and armaments industries have grown quickly in the past ten years.

Forty per cent of South Africa's manufacturing industries are located in the southern Transvaal, in the so-called Vaal Triangle, and other important areas are at PORT ELIZABETH-UITENHAGE and DURBAN-Pinetown.

Communications. The railways are state owned and have a total length of 22,195 km, of which 9707 km is electrified. The South African railways also operate road transport services over 50,000 km for passengers and goods. Internal and international air services are operated by South African Airways, also state owned. Johannesburg, Durban, and Cape Town have international airports, and a new one is planned for La Mercy, Natal. There are 13,274 km of trunk roads, and 185,000 km of provincial roads. South Africa's telecommunications network is one of the most sophisticated in the world. The South African merchant marine, Safmarine, established in 1946, has 40 vessels ranging from mailships to supertankers.

Trade. Exports totalled £1482 million in 1973, of which gold accounted for 41 per cent. Britain took 29 per cent, Japan 10 per cent, and African countries (mainly Rhodesia and Zambia) 14 per cent of exports. Most other African countries boycott South African goods, although some are known to trade with it clandestinely. Britain supplied 19 per cent of South Africa's imports; more than 90 per cent were manufactures. South Africa successfully resisted the Arab oil embargo imposed in 1973, obtaining oil from other sources, notably Iran, and from its own coal supplies.

Finance. The unit of currency is the *Rand* of 100 cents, introduced in 1961.

Bibliography: L. P. Green and T. J. D. Fair, *Development in Africa*, 1969; D. Hobart Houghton and J. Dagut, *Source Material on the South African Economy 1860–1970* (2 vols), 1972; D. Hobart Houghton, *The South African Economy*, 1973.

Government. *Constitution* and *Legislature.* Set out in the Republic of South Africa Constitution Act of 31 May 1966, which is very similar in content to the South Africa Act of 1909, an Imperial Act of Parliament and the constitutional basis of the former Union of South Africa. The head of state is the State President (in 1977 Nicolaas Diederichs). He has power to dissolve the Senate and House of Assembly, to appoint ministers and deputy ministers, to prorogue Parliament, and so on. He is elected by an electoral college consisting of the members of the Senate and House of Assembly and holds office for seven years. The executive government of the Republic is vested in the State President acting on the advice of the Executive Council which consists of ministers who must not number more than 18. The legislative power is vested in Parliament. The House of Assembly (1978) consists of 171 members, 165 elected in the RSA, and six members elected from SWA (Namibia). The four seats allocated to white representation of coloured interests were abolished in 1969. The Senate consists of 55 members, 44 elected on a provincial basis by electoral colleges (including two from Namibia), and 11 nominated by the State President (two from each province and also Namibia). All male and female Europeans over the age of 18 are entitled to vote. The executive government has its seat in PRETORIA and the seat of legislature is CAPE TOWN, thus the country has two capitals.

Each of the four provinces (Cape, Natal, Orange Free State, and Transvaal) has a Provincial Council, an administrator, and an Executive Committee. The Council is elected on the same franchise as the House of Assembly.

Under its apartheid, or 'separate development' policy, the government has also set up nine 'Homelands' governments, or Bantustans, with the option for independence if they wish. The Transkei became independent on 26 October 1976 (though only recognised as such by South Africa). Bophuthatswana became independent on 6 December 1977.

See also CAPE PROVINCE, *Government*.

Justice. Based on Romano-Dutch law as developed by judicial decisions and legislative enactments. The Department of Justice in Pretoria is responsible for the administration of justice, rendering specific services in regard to combatting subversive activities, and promoting appropriate statutory enactments.

Education. There is separate provision for ethnic groups, and control of education is divided between different government departments and subsidiary bodies.

Whites. Education is compulsory for all Whites between the ages of 7 and 16. The Provincial Councils are

South Africa. The urban Bantu Council in session. *(Camera Press/Tom Blau)*

responsible for primary and secondary education, teacher training, and education of the mentally handicapped. The Department of National Education (DNE) controls all higher education such as universities, colleges of further or technical education, and provides for the physically handicapped. Ninety-five per cent of children attend state schools, divided into four phases of three years each, viz: junior and senior primary, and junior and senior secondary schools. There were (1974) 2565 schools in the RSA attended by 903,489 pupils. There are 10 residential universities for Whites; five conduct lectures in Afrikaans, four in English, and one in both languages. Enrolment in 1974 was over 68,000, and was expected to rise to 80,000 by 1980. There is also the University of South Africa (UNISA) with headquarters in Pretoria, where all study is done externally, and which caters for all population groups.

Coloureds. From 1910 to 1963 the provinces were responsible for Coloured education. In 1964 responsibility was transferred to the Department of Coloured Affairs, and in 1969 to the Administration of Coloured Affairs. The ACA now controls all Coloured Peoples' education programmes except for the University of the Western Cape—a residential university established exclusively for the use of the Coloured community—and the Kromme Rhee Agricultural Training Centre, which are administered by the Department of Coloured and Rehoboth Affairs. Compulsory education from the age of seven was introduced in 1974 and schools follow the White pattern. There were (1974) 1908 schools in the RSA for Coloureds, catering for 619,024 pupils. One thousand, seven hundred and seven Coloureds were enrolled in university and university colleges for full-time courses.

Asians (Indians). All educational facilities are administered and controlled by the Department of Indian Affairs. There are 373 schools mainly in Natal and the Transvaal catering for 176,802 pupils (1974). The exclusively

Indian University of Durban-Westville (2000 students), and the Springfield and Transvaal Colleges of Education provide further education facilities.

Blacks. The Department of Bantu Education, with headquarters in Pretoria, exercises direct control over all primary, secondary, and tertiary education for Blacks outside the HOMELANDS (Bantustans). The system is organised on a regional basis (including Namibia), subdivided into circuits with an inspector of education in charge of each. In 1973 there were 5337 schools (including farm, special, and Roman Catholic schools) in 'White' areas catering for 1,263,316 children; Homeland Education Departments covered 6090 schools and 2,048,967 pupils. Schooling is not compulsory but 72 per cent of children in the 7–15 age group were estimated to be in school in 1973. Children follow an eight-year primary school course where instruction is in the mother tongue of the pupil, followed by a three-year junior secondary course, and a further two-year course leading to Senior Certificate/Matriculation in English or Afrikaans. There are three universities for Blacks, administered by the Department of Bantu Education. Total enrolment (1974) was 4321; a further 277 students enrolled at White universities, and 3765 with UNISA (the total was 1500 in 1956).

Total revenue expenditure (1973–74) was 711,900,000 Rand, of which the provinces spent 371·1 million, and the DNE 123·1 million.

Welfare. The government does not operate a 'welfare state', and such social security provision as there is rests largely with the voluntary agencies, although the government offers certain minimum services varying between the ethnic groups.

Social Security. The Department of Social Welfare and Pensions concerns itself with provisions for Whites. The Department operates through a national welfare board, four specialist commissions, and 10 regional welfare boards, which exercise the powers and perform the duties delegated to them by the central board and also make recommendations to them on matters relating to family life, welfare planning, and social welfare. Through the regional boards, the Department administers schemes for pensions, allowances and grants, the payment of subsidies to registered charitable organisations, and arranges for the care of committed persons. The Social Pensions Act of 1973 consolidated and amended the laws on pensions and allowances for aged, blind, and disabled persons, and war veterans.

At the end of 1973, 122,796 Whites were receiving old age pensions and 24,672 disability pensions. About 94 per cent were receiving the maximum amounts permitted. Family allowances are available to families with three or more children where the father is employed but receives an income less than families receiving assistance under other state social security schemes. In 1972–73 an amount of 1,684,146 Rand was paid to 2125 families. The state provides 65 homes for aged persons who do not qualify for a private home, 233 of which are state-aided. The Children's Act of 1960 provides for the protection of infants and the prevention of their exploitation.

The major welfare acts apply to all races but administration of them is divided for Coloureds, Indians, and Africans as follows:

Coloureds. In 1958 responsibility for Coloured welfare was transferred from the Department of Social Welfare to the Administration of Coloured Affairs. At 31 July 1973, 70,673 Coloureds were in receipt of an old age pension and 30,463 a disability pension, with about 91 per cent receiving the maximum amounts permitted. There were one state and 14 aided homes for the aged.

Indians. In 1963 welfare services, including pensions, allowances, and other social assistance schemes were transferred to the newly-established Department of Indian Affairs. At 31 July 1973 there were 11,513 Indians in receipt of an old age pension and 10,972 a disability pension, with about 96 per cent receiving the maximum amounts permitted. There were two aided homes for the aged.

Africans. Responsibility for African welfare rests with the Social Development Division of the Department of Bantu Administration and Development, although most Homeland governments now administer their own welfare and social benefit schemes as well as the administration of grants and allowances. In 1973, excluding the Homelands, 167,204 Africans were in receipt of an old age pension and 52,727 a disability pension. It was estimated that only 34 per cent were receiving the maximum amounts permitted. There were one state and 22 aided homes for the aged; most of the latter were in the Homelands and run by the churches.

Hospitals and Health. Major hospital and health provision rests with the provincial and local authorities, working in co-operation with the Department of Health and seven regional offices. The Department also liaises with the ethnic departments responsible for the health and welfare of Coloureds, Indians, and Africans. Since 1970 the health services in the Homelands have been controlled by the Department of Bantu Administration and Development with the central Department of Health acting as executive authority. Eventually the control will pass to the Homeland governments. The Transkei established its own

Department of Health in 1973. About one-fifth of provincial expenditure contributes to health provision. Cape Province has 82 hospitals, the OFS 22, Natal 23, and the Transvaal 61, totalling (1973) 61,850 beds. In addition there are about 100 private hospitals in the Republic. In 1974 there were 79,984 hospital beds available for Africans, Coloureds, and Indians in the 'common areas' of the Republic. In the Homelands, 105 mission or other hospitals and 543 clinic centres provided 27,756 beds serviced by 470 White and 70 African medical practitioners.

There is no medical insurance scheme so, unless acknowledged indigent, patients contribute to medical services. The Medical Schemes Act of 1967, however, provides for the establishment of schemes for health insurance, financed by contributions from employer and employee.

Religion. Among the Whites the largest group belongs to the Dutch Reformed Church, 1,487,080 (1970), as well as 573,400 Coloureds. There are 399,950 White adherents of the Anglican church, as well as 333,200 Coloureds, and 937,720 Bantu. Other sects with large memberships are Methodist, Roman Catholic, Lutheran, Presbyterian, Congregational, and Jewish. There are many Bantu separatist churches, and 423,300 Hindus. The 1970 census showed that there were 4·8 million who claimed no religion.

Armed Forces. Since December 1921 the government has undertaken the military defence of the country. Under the South African Defence Act of 1912 (as amended in 1922 and 1932), every citizen between the ages of 17 and 60 is liable to render personal service in time of war, and those between 17 and 25 are liable to undergo a period of peace training for four years, but the Act provides that only half the total number liable to peace training will, in fact, undergo that training unless Parliament makes financial provision for the training of a greater number. Since South Africa left the Commonwealth and became a Republic in 1961, her armed forces can no longer be considered available for Commonwealth defence. The Simonstown Agreement was terminated in June 1975. The South African Navy with a personnel of 5000 (1400 conscripts) includes three submarines, two destroyers, and 10 minesweepers. The South African Army (1976) comprises 7000 regulars, 31,000 conscripts, and a 138,000 active reserve or citizen force (part-time). There is also a part-time para-military commando force of about 90,000 men organised and trained as a home guard. They are highly mobile and include armoured cars, infantry, and an air section. There is a small but highly-efficient air force, equipped with 133 combat aircraft, including Mirage III fighter bombers, Buccaneers for tactical support, a maritime reconnaissance squadron of Shackletons, and four helicopter squadrons. A Coloured Corps now serves with the Defence Forces, and an Indian Battalion has been recently established. Black participation in the Defence Forces is under consideration.

Official Languages. English and Afrikaans.

National Anthem. Die Stem van Suid-Afrika (The Call of South Africa).

National Flag. A horizontal tricolour of orange, white, and blue, with the Union Jack, the old OFS flag, and the old Transvaal Vierkleur in the central white stripe.

Bibliography: P. van den Berghe, *South Africa: A Study in*

Conflict, 1968; H. Adam, *Modernizing Racial Domination: Dynamics of South African Politics*, 1973; J. Barber, *South Africa's Foreign Policy (1945–70)*, 1973; P. Randall (Ed.), *South Africa's Political Alternatives*, 1973.

History. To Independence. The original inhabitants of the Cape when Bartholomeu Dias, the Portuguese navigator, first rounded the Cape of Good Hope in 1488, were the BUSHMEN, a nomad people, and the Khoi-Khoi (HOTTENTOTS) who were pastoralists. The Bantu-speakers were moving down from east and central Africa and in 1652 when Jan van Riebeeck established the first staging post for east-bound ships of the Dutch East India Company, they were still far to the north and east of Table Bay. As the settlement grew the Bushmen fled into the interior; the Khoi-Khoi, deprived of their cattle, occupied menial positions in the settlement and interbred with the settlers, imported slaves and others, to become in time the ancestors of the present Cape Coloured population. It was not until 1770 that the stock farmers or BOERS, moving east, encountered the XHOSA of the NGUNI tribes, at the Great Fish River. This was the beginning of a black/white struggle in South Africa which is not yet resolved.

In 1688 the small white settlement was increased by an influx of Huguenots from France but in 1795 when the British first occupied the Cape the total white population was only about 15,000. The British returned in 1806, following the fall of the Batavian Republic to Napoleon's forces, and the Dutch possessions in South Africa were later ceded to Britain by the Treaty of Amiens, 1814. British governors introduced reforms in Cape Colony, such as equality before the law irrespective of colour, an ordinance in 1828 which freed the Khoi-Khoi from working for unwanted masters and the gradual emancipation of the slaves which, while accepted by many inhabitants of the Cape Peninsula, greatly incensed the stock farmers in the interior. But British insistence on 'anglicising' the Colony and making English rather than Dutch the official language was deeply resented by all. The Great Trek of 1834–38, when about 10,000 men, women, and children left the Colony in their covered ox-wagons, was an attempt to escape from British control and establish independent republics governed by the Boers themselves. Led by men such as Piet Retief and Gert Maritz the Voortrekkers penetrated north of the Vaal and east to Natal establishing several small republics of which only the Orange Free State and the South African Republic (Transvaal) survived. By the Sand River Convention of 1852 and the Bloemfontein Convention of 1854 Britain withdrew all claim to exercise authority north of the Vaal and Orange rivers. Meanwhile Natal, to which the Boers had been forced to withdraw by the British, became a British Colony in 1843 and was granted self-government in 1856.

The discovery of diamonds in Kimberley in 1870 and of gold on the Witwatersrand in 1886 led to the eventual destruction of the independent republics. Foreigners or 'uitlanders' flooded into the small republics which themselves had neither the resources nor the inclination to develop the mines. An attempt by the British to annex the South African Republic was defeated in the first Anglo-Boer War at Majuba Hill in 1881 and under Paul KRUGER (1825–1904), elected president in 1883, the Transvaal tried jealously to maintain undiluted Boer or Afrikaner rule. The Uitlanders were largely denied the franchise and this led to unrest within the Republic (fomented from outside by Cecil RHODES), and the politically dubious Jameson Raid of 1895, when Dr Starr JAMESON invaded the Transvaal and was forced to surrender to the Boers. The German annexation of South-West Africa in 1884 and its other colonial interests in East Africa encouraged Kruger to seek support from that quarter. Such a development would have thwarted Rhodes's and the British government's ambitions in Africa and was an underlying cause, of which the Uitlander problem was the symptom, for the second Anglo-Boer War which started on 11 October 1899. The Orange Free State threw in its lot with the Transvaal and the Boers invaded Natal with initial successes against the British troops. When later defeated in the field they resorted to commando or guerrilla tactics which prolonged the war for three years. The British, in retaliation, introduced a 'scorched earth' policy, so that when the war ended in the Peace of Vereeniging on 31 May 1902 most Boer homesteads and farms had been destroyed. To protect the women and children the British concentrated them in camps (hence concentration camps) where 26,000 died from disease. The tragedy created immense bitterness among Afrikaners and contributed to the later Anglo-Afrikaner political struggle which continues to this day. British casualties

South Africa. The old Kimberley mine photographed in 1872. *(Bisonte)*

South Africa

were nearly 6000 dead and 23,000 wounded. The Boers lost between 4000 and 5000 men and 40,000 were taken prisoner. The outcome of the war led to the Union of South Africa but it also stimulated Afrikaner nationalism.

Britain annexed the South African Republic and the Orange Free State but both were given responsible government in 1906 and 1907. Their constitutions did not mention a non-racial qualified franchise which, though weakly implemented in practice, had been a feature of the earlier constitutions of the Cape and Natal. A National Convention (1908–10) dominated by Lord Milner, SMUTS, and BOTHA, and composed of white representatives of the four colonies, drafted a constitution for the Union of South Africa which deliberately deferred the question of the non-racial franchise, except for the Cape which was allowed to retain its existing constitution in this respect. The British parliament endorsed the proposals of the National Convention, embodied in the South Africa Act 1909, and on 31 May 1910 the Union of South Africa achieved independence within the British Empire, under the premiership of Gen. Louis Botha.

From Independence to the Second World War. Smuts (1870–1950) and Botha (1862–1919) believed that the healing of the breach between Boer and Briton was essential to South Africa's future and did not favour Afrikaner nationalism. In a famous speech at De Wildt, near Pretoria, in 1912 the former Boer general, James Barry Munnik HERTZOG (1866–1942), however, announced that in a conflict of interests between Britain and South Africa he would place the interests of South Africa first. The apparent anti-British tone of the speech caused Botha to resign and reform his government without Hertzog, who in 1914 founded the National party in opposition to the governing South African party (SAP). Also in opposition were the South African Labour party founded in 1910 by Col. F. H. P. Cresswell and the British-orientated Unionist party.

From 1913 to 1922 there were several major strikes in the South African gold and coal-mines—in the earlier period mainly to gain white trade union recognition from the mineowners. In 1922, however, the white miners struck over the use of blacks in jobs previously done by whites; for a brief period a revolutionary council controlled the Rand until Smuts brought in the troops to quell it. Three ringleaders were hanged and others temporarily imprisoned or deported. As a consequence in the 1924 election Smuts' SAP was defeated by a Nationalist-Labour Pact government and Hertzog became prime minister. In five years the government introduced legislation (the Industrial Conciliation Act 1924 and the Wages Act 1925) to protect the white unions and workers from black encroachment; strengthened the economy by an injection of state capital into industry and the creation of semi-public industrial bodies such as the Iron and Steel Industrial Corporation (ISCOR); ensured that English and Afrikaans languages had equal status in education and government; found a compromise solution to the 'flag issue', whereby the orange, white, and blue of 17th-century Holland had a centre-piece of the Union Jack and the flags of the former Boer Republics; and tried to introduce measures to remove blacks from the Cape electoral roll. At the 1929 general election, though the Labour party was split, the Pact held. Hertzog's National

South Africa. A Boer picket group at Spion Kop. *(Bisonte)*

party, however, won enough seats to form a government on its own but in refusing, in the midst of world recession, to go off the gold standard, he nearly brought the country to economic ruin. Pressurised by Tielman Roos, who emerged from political retirement to demand abandonment of the gold standard and the formation of a national government, Hertzog's government succumbed and there was an almost immediate improvement in the country's economic position. In 1933 Hertzog's National party and Smuts' SAP 'fused', eventually to form the United South African National party (United party). Dr D. F. Malan of the Cape National party broke away in 1934 but reunited with Hertzog and some of his followers in 1939 to form the Reunited National party (Herenigde Nasionale party), the forerunner of the Nationalist party in South Africa today.

In 1934 the House of Assembly passed two Status Bills, seen by Hertzog as his crowning constitutional achievement, which confirmed by acts of the Union parliament the understanding (under the 1931 Statute of Westminster) that the Union parliament was independent of legislative control by the British parliament and that the Crown acted solely on the advice of South African ministers in matters concerning South Africa. In 1936 by 169 votes to 11 the South African parliament adopted the Bantu Representation Act, removing Africans in Cape Province from the Voters' Roll. It also passed the Native Land & Trust Act 1936, allocating less than 14 per cent of South Africa's land as African 'reserves'.

Post-Second World War. The Union, despite a brief internal revolt, had fully participated in the First World War when approximately 6700 South Africans were killed. At the outset of the Second World War Hertzog declared that South Africa would remain neutral. He was challenged by Smuts and on 4 September 1939 was defeated in parliament by 80 votes to 67. Hertzog resigned and Smuts became premier. The South African army played an important part in the Ethiopian and Libyan campaigns. Many fell prisoner at Tobruk but Springbok armoured units participated in the Eighth Army advance under Gen. Alexander. At home, however, Afrikaners were deeply divided and by 1941 it was clear that a majority of Afrikaners were against the war effort and in favour of a republic. Hertzog retired from politics in 1940 and a few of his supporters under Havenga, disillusioned with the Reunited National party, formed the Afrikaner party. The Ossewa-Brandwag (Sentinels of the Ox-Wagon) which had been formed as a cultural organisation following the Voortrekker Centenary Celebration of Dingaan's defeat at Blood River in 1838, developed into a strongly pro-Nazi political force and many Afrikaners were interned. At the general election of 1943, however, Smuts won an overwhelming victory with 105 seats to Malan's National party's 43.

South Africa had benefited economically during the war years, but between 1945 and 1948 the Smuts government was condemned at the United Nations for South Africa's racial policies (particularly towards the Indians) and attacked at home for appearing, under the liberal guidance of Jan H. Hofmeyr, to seek to blur racial divisions between black and white. In 1947 Malan and Havenga entered into an electoral pact. At the general election of 1948 the National and Afrikaner parties gained 79 seats and Smuts' United party 74. To many Afrikaners the Nationalist victory atoned for a 'Century of Wrong'.

Up to 1948 the predominant racial struggle in South Africa had been between the English-speakers and the Afrikaners. Since Union in 1910 legislation under successive governments had increasingly restricted the civil rights and movement of Indians and blacks but it was the Malan government that elevated practice into a theory of APARTHEID or 'separate development'. Over 25 years later 'multi-national' rather than 'separate' development is preferred, but the basic policy remains. As the government prepared to put theory into practice it was confronted by the Defiance Campaign of 1952, a non-violent mass movement aimed by blacks at drawing attention to the worst of their grievances. The campaign collapsed and most of its leaders and supporters were exiled or imprisoned, but it brought into the open South Africa's key racial issues. The government's decision to abolish the political rights of the Cape Coloureds was hotly contested by the Torch Commando, initially led by ex-servicemen's organisations, but in 1953 the Nationalist party was returned with an enhanced majority despite an electoral pact between the United and Labour parties which had operated at general elections since 1943. In 1958 the Labour party lost all parliamentary representation and ceased to exist. Meanwhile, in 1953 a small group broke with the United party to form the Liberal party. It was multi-racial and eventually included unqualified universal suffrage among its aims. It never won a parliamentary seat and eventually disbanded in 1968 when the government brought in legislation forbidding mixed political organisations. The only other multiracial political party in South Africa, the Communist party, was disbanded under the Suppression of Communism Act 1950. In 1959 another group broke with the United party to form the Progressive party. Although for many years Helen Suzman was its only MP, in 1974 seven members were returned to parliament.

In 1975 the Progressive party joined with another splinter group from the United party to form the South African Progressive Reform party, with Colin Eglin as leader. The new party had 12 seats in Parliament in 1977 (out of a total of 171) and aims to replace the United party as the official opposition. The basic policy of the party is power-sharing between black and white.

Meanwhile the Nationalist government pressed ahead with apartheid legislation including the Group Areas Act 1949, giving legal status to traditional residential segregation; the Separate Representation of Voters Act 1956, which removed coloureds from the electoral roll and, following the Tomlinson Commission Report of 1955, legislation to implement the Homelands policy of apartheid. Additional legislation banned mixed marriages, limited the number of Africans allowed in urban areas, and denied Africans the right to strike. The effect has been to make anything other than official contact between black and white in South Africa almost impossible. In 1954 J. G. STRIJDOM succeeded Malan as prime minister and Dr H. F. VERWOERD succeeded Strijdom in 1958. A referendum on the Republican issue on 5 October 1960 showed 52 per cent in favour of a republic and 48 per cent against—a numerical majority of 74,580 out of a total vote of 1,626,336. In 1961 Verwoerd attended the Commonwealth Conference to put South Africa's case for remaining a member of the Commonwealth as a republic. The attack on its racial policies made him withdraw his application. The attack was particularly severe because of African unrest and tragic incidents at Sharpeville and Lange which had been followed by penal legislation including the banning of the African National Congress and the Pan Africanist Congress. On 31 May 1961 South Africa became a republic outside the Commonwealth.

At every election the Nationalists maintained their majority. In 1966 Verwoerd was assassinated by a parliamentary messenger and Balthazar Johannes VORSTER became prime minister. While maintaining the apartheid policies of his predecessors he has deliberately sought to improve the Republic's relations with Black Africa and, under strict control, to promote the Bantustans. Meetings with the heads of the Bantustans, if unproductive, were initially a novel event in South Africa and, partly due to the buoyant economy in the 1970s, a shortage of white industrial workers is forcing change in relations with black workers, particularly in their efforts to form trade unions. In 1975, in co-operation with President Kaunda of Zambia, Vorster sought to find a peaceful solution to black control of Rhodesia.

At the United Nations, however, South Africa's racial policies remain condemned both within the Republic and for its refusal, as yet, to relinquish control of South-West Africa (Namibia). Black African states particularly resented South Africa's military intervention in Angola.

Intervention in Angola. South Africa made no move to intervene in Mozambique in June 1975 when the Portuguese handed over power to FRELIMO under Samora Machel. The situation in Angola raised different problems, however, and, in September 1975, the government admitted that, under a former Portuguese agreement, it had troops in Angola to guard a hydro-electric plant on the Cunene River which supplied water to northern Namibia and into which the Republic had put millions of pounds. In November, however, there were reports that

South Africa

UNITA had begun to acquire military equipment which could only have come from South Africa and later it was acknowledged that South African troops were in the battle zone. In January 1976, Dr Botha, the South African Defence Minister, said that 29 soldiers had been lost in battle and 14 killed in accidents.

As the Cuban/MPLA forces swept south (see ANGOLA, History) the South Africans withdrew and temporarily dug themselves in some 40–80 km north of the Angolan border 'from the Atlantic to the Zambian border'. Under heavy pressure from the USA and elsewhere, however, they evacuated part of the border area on 12 March 1976 and totally withdrew on 27 March.

The political repercussions of this intervention, however, were a disaster for South Africa's détente policies with Black Africa. When it became clear that South Africans were in Angola Black African opinion, which had been divided over recognition of the Soviet-backed Popular Liberation Movement (MPLA), swung heavily in its favour, though it later appeared clear that South Africa had entered the country at the request of UNITA's leader, Jonas Savimbi (though he later denied this), and with the tacit approval of the United States and some African countries. On 25 January 1976, Dr Botha said that South Africa was not prepared to fight on behalf of the free world alone, but would defend with determination its own borders and those interests and borders for which it was responsible.

Internally, the government introduced two new security laws; one, expected to supersede the Suppression of Communism Act 1950, gave the government powers to ban any individual or organisation which 'endangers the security of the state'. In addition, early in 1976, the government introduced legislation empowering South African armed forces to cross the country's borders to counteract any threat to security south of the Equator.

The breakdown of the Rhodesian Constitutional talks in March 1976, to the start of which Vorster had made an important contribution, added to the likelihood of increased guerrilla warfare in Rhodesia and the MPLA victory in Angola had greatly heartened the liberation movement in South-West Africa, the South-West African People's Organisation (SWAPO). In retrospect, events in Angola created a watershed in the history of southern Africa, the repercussions of which appear destined to continue for a long time.

Efforts were made late in 1976 and early in 1977 to achieve unity amongst the white opposition parties, and in March 1977 Sir De Villiers Graaff, the UP leader, and Theo Gerdener, the leader of the Democratic Party, expressed their agreement to form a new party called the New Republic Party. Earlier in the year, six members on the right wing of the UP had formed the new South Africa Party. In a general election in November 1977 the National Party won a landslide victory.

The African Struggle. Running parallel with the Afrikaner struggle for power has been the Africans' struggle to gain recognition and status within their own country. From the 1770s on there were continual African battles and wars against the stock farmers, the Voortrekkers, and the British. The Battle of Blood River in 1838 when the Voortrekkers defeated Dingaan's impis is still celebrated in South Africa as DINGAAN'S DAY or the Day of the Covenant. In 1879 Cetewayo's ZULU impis defeated

the British at Isandhlwana, but were later finally defeated themselves at Ulundi. Earlier remnants of tribes had fled to Lesotho (formerly Basutoland) and Rhodesia to found new settlements, but by the end of the 19th century whites, whether British or Afrikaner, were in control south of the Limpopo River. Lesotho, Botswana (Bechuanaland), and Swaziland were designated British protectorates and were never governed by South Africa.

In 1906 the Bambata in Natal rose in rebellion but were quickly crushed. Since then the African struggle has hitherto been essentially a peaceful one though it has had its martyrs through imprisonment, exile, and death. The African National Congress (ANC) was founded in 1912 by Dr Pixley Seme and the Rev. John Dube to develop African unity and existed until 1960 when it was banned, but continues in exile overseas. In the 1920s Clement Kadalie's Industrial and Commercial Union (ICU) with a peak membership of 100,000 temporarily superseded the ANC, but it collapsed in 1929 partly through internal feuding but also through government intervention. In the 1930s an All African Convention campaigned without success against the Hertzog Bill to deprive Cape Africans of the franchise and in the 1940s the Congress Youth League sought to influence the ANC towards more 'Africanist' policies. In the early post-war period ANC leaders, encouraged by UN anti-racial policies and the gaining of independence by former British and other colonies, sought, with the coloureds and Indians peacefully to demonstrate to draw attention to their grievances, such as the Pass Laws and the Group Areas Act. The Defiance

South Africa. Rigid enforcement of apartheid has led to mass evictions of Africans from shanty towns and other settlements. Here, Africans are evicted from Besterspruit, northern Natal, to a site 50 km away, in 1962. *(Camera Press)*

Campaign collapsed in a few months; leaders, including Chief Lutuli, were banned or imprisoned and new legislation introduced to make it almost impossible for such a demonstration to occur again. The Congress Alliance, a body representative of all races, including whites, sought to reorganise the resistance movement and in 1955 a Freedom Charter was adopted at Kliptown. Later, differences led to a breakaway movement, the Pan Africanist Congress, being formed in 1959 with Robert Sobukwe as president. The PAC launched a peaceful demonstration against the Pass Laws at Sharpeville and Lange on 21 March 1960. White police, panicking, fired on the unarmed crowds and killed and wounded about 300. The repercussions were world wide and the flight, of capital and withdrawal of investment temporarily rocked the Republic's economy. The government introduced stronger measures to deal with opponents and many leaders went into exile. Others joined guerrilla forces outside South Africa believing that armed struggle is the answer to the Republic's race problems. In June 1976 rioting in Soweto township near Johannesburg led to the deaths of over 170 people, a number of whom were students demonstrating against the compulsory use of the Afrikaans language as the medium of instruction. Further unrest continued periodically throughout 1977 in Soweto and other townships.

In the 1970s several Homeland leaders such as Chief BUTHELEZI of KwaZulu and Chief Phatudi of Lebowa have emerged as national African leaders urging a common programme of reform. Chief Mantanzima of the TRANSKEI was the first to seek independence for his Homeland in 1976. New African-orientated organisations such as the South African Students' Organisation (SASO) and the Black Peoples' Convention (BPC) have sprung up, backed by Black Community Programmes, an offshoot of the Christian Institute of Southern Africa. All have had their activities circumscribed by the banning of able leaders or limitation of funds. The Durban strikes by African workers in 1972–73, however, resulted in limited amended legislation in favour of the African worker.

Coloureds and Indians also have no representation on white government bodies. The Coloured Persons Representative Council, established in 1969, partly elected, partly nominated, is vested, under the Department of Coloured Relations, with legislative and administrative powers mainly concerned with education and social services on behalf of coloured people.

The South African Indian Council, established under the South African Indian Council Act of 1968, advises the government and makes recommendations to the Department of Indian Affairs on all matters affecting the Indian population.

The bodies are the political equivalent of the Homeland Administrations but, apart from a limited number of appointed 'growth areas', coloureds and Indians have no effective territorial base.

Bibliography: L. Kuper, *Passive Resistance in South Africa*, 1956; S. Patterson, *The Last Trek*, 1957; A. Luthuli, *Let My People Go*, 1962; J. K. Ngubane, *An African Explains Apartheid*, 1963; G. Mbeki, *South Africa: the Peasants' Revolt*, 1964; L. Kuper, *An African Bourgeoisie*, 1965; D. Brown, *Against the World*, 1966; M. Ballinger, *From Union to Apartheid*, 1969; D. R. Morris, *The Washing of the Spears*, 1969; D. W. Kruger, *The Making of a Nation*, 1970; P. Walshe, *The Rise of African Nationalism in South Africa; African National Congress 1912–52*, 1971; L. Thompson and M. Wilson (Eds), *Oxford History of South Africa Vols I & II*, 1971; H. Adam, *Modernizing Racial Domination: Dynamics of South African Politics*, 1973; J. Robertson, *Liberalism in South Africa 1948-63*, 1971; J. Strangwayes-Booth, *A Cricket in the Thorn Tree*, 1976; South African Institute of Race Relations, *Annual Surveys of Race Relations in South Africa*.

Architecture. Dutch colonial architecture in South Africa ('Cape Dutch') is the best surviving evidence for the splendid rural and country-house architecture of Holland itself, most of which was destroyed in the 19th and 20th centuries. The south-west corner of South Africa was settled and producing fine wine as well as grain and fruit for provisioning the trading ships travelling between Europe and the East by the late 17th century; the wealth this produced enabled the construction and embellishment of several thousand fine estate houses and their outbuildings in a northern, gabled version of Palladian style. More than 600 of these homes survive, mostly dating in their present form from the 18th and early 19th centuries, with stucco decorations and furnishings in the Baroque, Rococo and Neoclassical styles. The most admired are 'Groot Constantia' (1692–1794), 'Stellenberg' (c. 1742–95), and 'Ida's Vallei' (1789). Two churches in the Cape Dutch style survive, Paarl (1804) and Tulbach (1743) and the tower of the original Groote

South Africa. The Cape Dutch style official residence of the South African prime minister. *(Bisonte)*

South Africa

Kerke in Cape Town (1704). The façade of the Rococo Government House (c. 1770) has been restored.

In Cape Town a fine urban architecture was developed, which reached its peak at the end of the 18th century in the work of two distinguished immigrants from Europe, Louis Michel Thibault, who had been trained by A.-J. GABRIEL at the Royal Academy in France, and Anton Anreith, a Bavarian sculptor from a family active as architects in the Austrian Empire; their most important surviving works are the Old Supreme Court Building (1807), the Goede Hoop Masons' Lodge (1801), and the wine cellar of 'Groot Constantia' (1792), with a remarkable pediment by Anreith.

Dominated by British influence after the second occupation of 1806, the architecture of South Africa became increasingly Georgian in the 1820s. From this period date the Regency houses 'Newlands' (1819) and Worcester Drostdy (1825). Late Georgian is well represented in the Western Cape, and especially in John Rennie's design for the Observatory (1821), and in many towns and farms of the Eastern Cape, notably Grahamstown, Bathurst, and Somerset East.

The discovery of diamonds at Kimberley, followed soon afterwards by gold at Johannesburg, brought sudden wealth and with it the British Empire style with its ornamented cast-iron verandahs and Renaissance revival façades.

Sir Herbert BAKER made his reputation as Cecil Rhodes' architect in South Africa. Besides numerous houses and office buildings, his work includes the Rhodes Memorial, Cape Town (1905), and the Union Buildings, Pretoria (1910). Sir Edwin LUTYENS was responsible for the Cenotaph (1920) and the Art Gallery (1905), both in Johannesburg.

Modern architects appeared fully-fledged in the early 1930s, under the direct influence of Le Corbusier, acting through his admirer Rex Martienssen. Together with his friends, Gordon McIntosh, N. Hanson, B. Cook and J. Fassler, he executed before the Second World War a remarkable series of projects ranging from the 20th-century theatre, Johannesburg (1936), to small houses. Other architects were influenced by Frank Lloyd Wright and Mies van der Rohe. A later reaction in the direction of Empiricism and British functionalism was resisted only

by Norman Eaton (Barclays Banks, Pretoria and Durban). Recent outstanding buildings are the Johannesburg Standard Bank Building (1966, by the West Germans I. Hentrich and Ove Arup) and the Cape Town Foreshore buildings of Revel Fox (begun 1968).

Bibliography: G. F. Pearse, *Eighteenth Century Architecture in South Africa*, 1957; R. B. Lewcock, *Early Nineteenth Century Architecture in South Africa*, 1963; H. Fransen and M. A. Cook, *The Old Houses of the Cape*, 1965; B. Kearney, *Architecture in Natal*, 1973.

Art. Painting in South Africa extends from rock-sketches by the primitive bushmen to a large and lively number of painters and sculptors, at first mainly European and based particularly in the Cape and Natal, and now increasingly embracing non-European artists. The leading pioneer of the early European painters to settle in South Africa was Thomas Baines (1820–75), who left an amazingly full record with both pen and brush of his expeditions with explorers such as Livingstone and Chapman. Hugo Naudé (1869–1941) is generally regarded as the first important South African artist, painting in an 'Impressionistic' style; his contemporary J. E. A. Volschenk (1853–1936) painted detailed descriptions of the veld and *kopje* under the light of the African sun, while J. H. Pierneef captured on both canvas and wall not only light-filled scenes of the bushveld but also the strange beauty of the Witwatersrand mine-dumps. Gwelo Goodman, a popular Impressionist, painted a wide variety of Cape and Natal landscapes and studies of African flowers.

Moving into the realm of 'modern' art, Pieter WENNING was South Africa's first 'pure painter' who, in spite of a short career, had great influence on a generation of later painters. Prominent among them were Irma Stern (1894–1966), Adolph Jentsch (1888–), Terence McCaw, Gregoire Boonzaaier (1909–) and Cecil Skotnes; Walter Battiss (1906–) based his style on African rock-art and subscribed little to foreign influence. Alexis Preller, his younger contemporary, also showed a peculiarly South African quality in his work, bordering on Surrealism. Hendrik Pierneef (1886–1957) was another who excelled in the depiction of South African subjects, and earned a great reputation at home and abroad. South Africans who worked mainly overseas included Enslin du Plessis, Maud Sumner, Edward Woolfe and the Bantu painter Gerard Sekoto, together with the leading portrait painter, Neville Lewis.

Among the early sculptors Anton van Wouw (1862–1945) was outstanding, especially with his smooth bronze studies of Kruger, Boer types and Bantu tribesmen. Two artists in 20th-century idiom followed, Moses Kottler with his wooden figure studies and Lippy Lipschitz (1903–) who used wood in an Expressionist style; Coert Steynberg became the leading sculptor among a group devoting themselves to the national historical life of the Afrikaner people. Leading non-European sculptors include Louis Maurice and Sydney Kumalo. Among those who tended more to abstraction, Edouardo Villa (1920–) may be counted a leader.

Bibliography: F. L. Alexander, *Art in South Africa: painting, sculpture and graphic work since 1900*, 1962.

Art Museums. The South African National Gallery at Cape Town was founded in 1895 and its present home completed in 1930. In addition to a large collection of

South Africa. The Union Buildings, Pretoria, designed by Sir Herbert Baker. *(Barnaby's Picture Library)*

South Africa. *View of N'tabeni* by J.H. Pierneef. *(National Gallery of South Africa, Cape Town)*

South African art there are representative Dutch, English and French works—the nations that particularly influenced the development of South African art. There is also a collection of indigenous art of Africa, and a large collection of British sporting pictures.

Johannesburg Art Gallery opened in 1915; the building was designed by Sir Edwin LUTYENS. The collections consist mainly of French and British 19th- and 20th-century paintings and sculpture and 17th-century Dutch paintings.

At Pretoria the Art Museum moved into its own building in 1964; the collections represent South African arts from the mid-19th century to the present day, together with a small number of European works.

Language. The official languages of the Republic of South Africa are English and AFRIKAANS. Afrikaans was officially recognised for all purposes by the Official Languages of the Union Act, No. 8, of 1925. It is the language into which 17th-century Netherlandish Dutch had developed among the Dutch-speaking people of South Africa. Its differences from modern European Dutch are mainly due to a different environment and to an importation of Hottentot, Bantu, Malay, and Portuguese words into the vocabulary. Not until the 19th century were efforts made to elevate Afrikaans from a spoken dialect to a written language. After individual attempts a society was founded in 1875, the *Genootskap van Regte Africaners*.

During the South African War the official Netherlandish was dying out as a spoken language, while Afrikaans absorbed English influences. From 1905 to 1914 the

South Africa. *View of the Diamond Diggings on the Vaal River* by Kidger Tucker, 1879. *(Sotheby's Ltd)*

221

South Africa

movement to reintegrate Dutch South Africa by means of a national language gathered strength, and an Afrikaans literature came into existence. In 1914 Afrikaans was officially recognised for use in primary schools, a recognition extended in 1918 and made absolute in 1925. Afrikaans is now the universal form of Dutch used throughout South Africa. It is the home language of 57 per cent of the whites in the Republic.

Literature. Despite its comparatively young tradition of written literature, South Africa has produced many outstanding writers of all races. However, the majority tend to be relatively little known abroad for a variety of reasons, mainly stemming from the complexity of South African political and ethnological structures. Government censorship, and the fact that there are two official languages (English and Afrikaans), as well as numerous African languages, are factors which have generally resulted in a limited readership. As many writers have to choose between writing in accordance with the censorship regulations, or seeking publication outside the country, those who do gain an international reputation frequently achieve this as a result of publicity arising from the official banning of their work in South Africa. In spite of the difficulties, South Africa's literary tradition continues, its vitality fostered by such dedicated individuals as the publisher and writer Lionel Abrahams, and various small presses which provide an outlet for new writers, particularly black and coloured.

English Literature. During the early period travel literature dominated, but it was largely written by visitors to the country, rather than by permanent residents. The tradition of South African poetry can be said to have begun with the British settler, Thomas Pringle (1789–1834), whose collection *Ephemerides*, 1828, was one of the earliest examples of a work using peculiarly South African imagery and description, as well as colloquial terminology. However, it took almost a century for poetry to come into its own as a valid literary form, inherently South African. The 1920s and 1930s witnessed the rise of such poets as Roy CAMPBELL, William PLOMER, and Francis Carey Slater (1876–1958), of whom Campbell and Plomer in particular were important for their work in bringing South African poetry to the attention of the outside world. They were followed by an increasing number of poets of high calibre, among them the white poets, Douglas Livingstone (*The Skull in the Mud* and *Sjambok*), Guy Butler, Anthony Delius, Sheila Fugard, Ruth Miller, and Jeni Couzyn. The work of the coloured poet and political writer, Denis Brutus, who left South Africa in 1966, should also be mentioned.

Not until recently have black poets begun to express themselves in English to any significant extent. Benedict Wallet Vilakazi, with *Inkondlo kaZulu* and *Amal 'Ezulu* (translated as *Zulu Horizons*), and Herbert Dhlomo (*Valley of a Thousand Hills*) are two Zulu poets who have largely contributed to the birth of a written Zulu literature. Mazisi Kunene (*Zulu Poems*) is another. However, during the 1970s there appeared a comparatively large wave of new poets writing in English. A few examples are Mongane Wally Serote, Oswald Mbuyiseni Mtshali, and Sydney Sepamla whose work shows signs of an indomitable creative spirit which, against all odds, insists on expressing itself with a forceful vigour, honesty, and humanism.

Undoubtedly, the first noteworthy South African novelist was Olive SCHREINER, while other early writers of talent included Perceval Gibbon (1879–1926) and Sir Percy Fitzpatrick (1862–1931), whose book, *Jock of the Bushveld*, 1907, about a transport rider and his hunting dog, vividly captured veld life. The 1920s and 1930s produced a wide range of literary talent; besides Roy Campbell and William Plomer there were Laurens VAN DER POST and Sarah Gertrude MILLIN. Other writers who established themselves during this era include Elizabeth Charlotte Webster, whose *Potholes*, 1928, is a fascinating description of a diamond-rush; Pauline Smith, who sensitively portrayed the life of Afrikaans farmers in *The Little Karroo*, 1925; and Deneys Reitz. His *Commando*, 1929, subtitled *A Journal of the Boer War*, supplies a vivid account of that historical period. Also historical in theme, Stuart Cloete's novels (for example, *Turning Wheels*, 1939, and *The Fiercest Heart*, 1961) have achieved a fairly wide popularity. The short-story writer, Herman Charles Bosman (1905–51), author of *Mafeking Road* and *Unto Dust*, who wrote with gentle irony and much humour about a small Afrikaans farming community bordering the Transvaal and Cape Province, deserves a wider readership. Frank Brownlee (1875–1952) is another writer worthy of greater notice for his works about Xhosas living in the Transkei (*Ntsukumbini, Cattle Thief, Lion and Jackal*), understandingly and unpatronisingly written. Modern women novelists of stature are numerous. Among them are Daphne Rooke, Jillian Becker, and Yvonne Burgess, whose second novel, *The Strike*, 1975, was a highly provocative treatment of the socio-political climate in South Africa. Almost certainly, however, the two most widely-known writers, both within their own country and overseas, are Nadine GORDIMER and Alan PATON, while Jack Cope, Dan Jacobson, and the coloured writers, Peter Abrahams and Alex La Guma, are also important for their contributions to the literary scene. Finally, on the basis of their popular entertainment value, Wilbur Smith's novels (such

South Africa. The poet and novelist William Plomer. *(Camera Press/Mark Gerson)*

as *When the Lion Feeds* and *Gold*) require a brief mention.

For many years, the black literary tradition in South Africa was principally an oral one. Within the past few decades, however, more writers have begun to use English as their literary medium, thus making their work more widely accessible. But the growth of such a body of writers has been affected by censorship and banning orders, which were particularly disruptive to development in the mid-1960s. Nat Nakasa, the first black columnist on a white newspaper, was one of the foremost writers of the early 1960s. His descriptions of life as a black intellectual under the laws of apartheid reflect a balanced perspective, self-integrity, compassion, and, despite occasional despair, a never-failing sense of humour. Like his colleague, Lewis Nkosi, another writer of distinction, he left South Africa, and later committed suicide in New York. Dugmore Boetie (d. 1966) also belongs to this period. Other writers of note include Ezekiel Mphahlele, Can Themba, Casey Motsisi, and Todd Matshikiza.

Although not the only dramatist South Africa has so far produced, Athol FUGARD is without doubt the most important, having achieved a reputation both at home and abroad for his plays about apartheid and its effects on individual lives and personal relationships.

Afrikaans Literature. There are examples of Afrikaans writing in the late 19th century, but the language only really became established as a literary medium after the turn of the century. With its roots in the rural tradition, Afrikaans literature for a time concentrated on cementing its own culture and values, and expressed itself solely in 'patriotic' writing. Later, however, its exponents increasingly explored more universal themes; their work reflects a growing awareness of the need to speak for all people and for anyone, and to reflect the problems of South Africans of all races.

Among poets, Eugène N. Marais, with 'Winternag', 1905, first made his fellow Afrikaners conscious of the potential of their language as a valid, indigenous means of literary communication. Other poets of this period are Jan Celliers ('Die Vlakte', 1906); J. D. du Toit, 'Totius' ('By die Monument', 1908); C. Louis Leipoldt (*Oom Gert Vertel en Ander Gedigte*, 1911); and C. J. Langenhoven, at whose instigation Afrikaans was first officially recognised in 1914, and whose 'Die Stem van Suid Afrika' became the South African national anthem.

Two important poets of the 1920s are C. M. van den Heever, whose work reflects a change in focus from patriotism to individual problems of religion and personal conflicts, and A. G. Visser, one of the more penetratingly satirical Afrikaans writers. But it was during the 1930s that Afrikaans poetry flowered into greater profundity and insight. The new direction and power is possibly best exemplified by Nicholaas Petrus van Wyk LOUW, with *Die Dieper Reg* and *Raka*. Other outstanding poets to appear at this time include W. E. G. Louw (*Die Ryke Dwaas*); I. D. du Plessis (*Stryd*); Uys Krige (*Hart sonder Hawe*); and Elisabeth Eybers (*Die Vrou*); followed by D. J. Opperman (*Heilige Beeste*, *Joernal van Jorik*); and Peter Blum (*Enklaves van die Lig*).

The suicide of Ingrid Jonker in 1965 was a tragic loss to the 'new consciousness' movement in Afrikaans poetry and literature in general. Her poems are disturbingly self-searching and share certain similarities with those of Sylvia PLATH. However, many other talented poets have come to the fore in recent years. Among them, Breyten Breytenbach stands out as the best known and the most controversial. His poems relentlessly portray an intense love-hate relationship with the 'vaderland'. The blending of Zen Buddhist elements with biting irony and paradox make him a unique figure on the Afrikaans literary scene.

Another interesting development has been the emergence of a number of coloured poets using Afrikaans as their medium; S. V. Petersen, P. J. Philander, and Adam Small in particular. The Jewish poet, Olga Kirsch, writes about Israel in Afrikaans.

The first Afrikaans prose writer of significance is J. van Melle (1887–1953). Later writers continued the rural traditon he established, comparable to the best produced in the pan-Dutch languages; but it was not until the appearance of the writers of the 1960s (the 'Sestigers') that Afrikaans prose made an important contribution to modern literature. Writers such as Dolf van Niekerk, Jan Rabie, Chris Barnard, and Étienne Leroux belong to this period; Étienne Leroux, particularly, has acquired a reputation as a writer of satirical fantasy in which the dilemma of modern society, specifically within the complexity of the South African setting, is ruthlessly exposed.

But probably more than anyone else, André BRINK has proved himself a writer of significance; his contributions to drama and prose have shaken the foundations of Afrikaans literary conformity. Some of his work's political content has been severely criticised by the establishment, but he is nevertheless regarded by many as having opened the way to universalism for other Afrikaans writers.

Little drama of importance was written before the 1920s. C. Louis Leipoldt's folk dramas are the first significant contribution, his *Die Heks* being performed in 1925. Heroic themes followed, with works by writers such as N. P. van Wyk Louw, Uys Krige, and D. J. Opperman. Absurdist drama appeared with Bartho Smit's *Putsonderwater*, while one of the most successful dramatists is P. G. du Plessis, author of *Nag van Legio* and *Siender in die Suburbs*, who ranks among the most pithy and satirical commentators on the Afrikaans scene.

Bibliography: G. M. Miller and H. Sergeant, *Critical Survey of South African Poetry in English*, 1957; G. F. Butler (Ed.), *Book of South African Verse*, 1959; P. J. Nienaber (Ed.), *Perspektief en Profiel*, 1960; N. Gordimer and L. Abrahams (Eds), *South African Writing Today*, 1967; E. R. Seary (Ed.), *South African Short Stories*, 1969; N. Gordimer, *Black Interpreters*, 1973; R. Royston (Ed.), *To Whom It May Concern: An Anthology of Black South African Poetry*, 1973; E. Patel (Ed.), *The World of Nat Nakasa*, 1975.

Music. South African music falls into three categories—the tribal songs of the Bantu, the *Volksliedjies*, mostly picnic songs, of the Boers, and the modern compositions of South Africans inspired by European feeling and technique. Of the latter an outstanding composer is Arnold van Wyk, whose best symphonies have been played and praised in London.

South Africa Company, see RHODES, CECIL JOHN.

South African War, see BOER WARS; SOUTH AFRICA, *History*.

223

South America. Antuco volcano in southern Chile. (Barnaby's Picture Library)

South America, the southern portion of a continental mass lying between the Pacific and the Atlantic Oceans, joined to the northern portion by the isthmus of Panama. It comprises the ten republics of BRAZIL, ARGENTINA, VENEZUELA, COLOMBIA, ECUADOR, PERU, CHILE, BOLIVIA, PARAGUAY, and URUGUAY, besides GUYANA, SURINAM, and FRENCH GUIANA. Its area is about 18,200,000 km² and the population 205,177 (1974 estimate). The extreme longitudes are Cape Branco, 35°W, and Punta Parina, 81°W, and the extreme latitudes Punta Gallinas, 12°30′N, and Cape Horn, 56°S.

Geography. Relief. South America is a compact land mass and has a fairly regular coastline, save in southern Chile, where sunken valleys have resulted from subsidence which has left mountain peaks as islands. The general relief of the continent consists of three areas of highlands, the ANDES and the plateaus of Guiana and Brazil, which are separated by the three drainage basins of the AMAZON, the PLATA, and the ORINOCO. The highlands of Guiana and Brazil are the oldest part of the continent, and geologically resemble the old plateaus of Africa, India, and Western Australia.

The Brazilian plateau is highest in the east, rising to 3000 m and forming a rugged coastline with many good natural harbours. The highlands descend to the west by terraces to the plains of the Amazon, the Paraná, and the Paraguay rivers. Deep gorge-like valleys have been cut by the rivers, many of which are interrupted by falls, but the Tocantins and the Paraná are navigable for a considerable distance, and provide access far into the interior of the highland country. The Guiana highlands closely resemble those of Brazil, from which they are separated by the Amazon valley. They also rise to a height of 3000 m, and descend gradually to the coast in the north. The Sierra Pacaraima and Roraima are the highest parts, and are formed of red sandstone assuming the shape of a great flat-topped plateau. A further plateau area extends along the eastern side of the southern Andes, part of which forms the GRAN CHACO and reaches the east coast in southern Argentina, where it is called PATAGONIA. Here it is traversed by such rivers as the Colorado, the Negro, and the Chubut. Lakes are formed in some of the valleys by the presence of dams of residual moraines left from the ice age.

The Andes, sometimes known as the Western Cordilleras, from the Spanish word for 'cord', are extensive chains of parallel folded mountains which were formed during the subsidence of the bed of the Pacific Ocean. They are new mountains as distinct from the ancient rocks, and contain limestones which were deposited under deep water later than the older sandstones of the eastern highlands. Unlike the highlands of Brazil, the Andes show little evidence of denudation. They show signs of crustal movement due to earthquake and volcanic action.

The formation of the great plains is due to enormous quantities of silt brought down by the great river systems. Indeed, at one time these plains were the beds of wide sea areas, the sediments of rivers from the highlands having filled them.

The Amazon is one of the great river systems of the world. It is navigable for ocean steamers for upwards of 4000 km. Its chief tributaries are the Tocantins, Xingú, Tapajós, Madeira, Purús, Ucayali, Negro, Yapura, Napo, and Morona. It has a huge estuary from 80 to 320 km wide. The Río de la Plata is the estuary formed by the Paraná, the Paraguay, and the Uruguay rivers. The Paraná is navigable for the greater part of its course, and forms the main stream. The River Orinoco rises in the Guiana highlands and reaches the Atlantic on the north coast, forming a great delta. It is navigable for small boats. See also ATLAS 58–59.

Climate. The distribution of rainfall in South America is affected by three factors: (1) the areas of high pressure over the South Atlantic and the South Pacific between latitudes 20° and 40°; (2) the tropical continental region of low pressure in the Upper Amazon basin; and (3) the direction of the ocean currents which wash both east and west coasts, together with a cold current which clings to the coast along most of the western coast. The summer rainfall of the continent is of a monsoonal type, but differs from that of Asia in that there is no movement outward of high-pressure air owing to the continent being as a whole warmer than the surrounding seas during all seasons.

Geology. The continent of South America can be divided into three major geological provinces. The oldest rocks occur in the east of the continent, in the plateaus of

South America. Reconstruction of an Inca house. (Topham/Fotogram)

the Guyana and Brazilian Shields, separated by the Amazon basin. To the west and north is an area of broad plains, underlain by Palaeozoic rocks, and to the west again is the Andean mobile belt, lying along the length of the Pacific coast and extending along the north Caribbean coast. This belt is of Mesozoic to Tertiary age.

The Guyana Shield. This is a high plateau area of old rocks, occupying Guyana, Surinam, French Guiana, and parts of Venezuela, Colombia, and Brazil. The oldest rocks are highly metamorphosed basement plutonic complexes, mainly of middle to late Pre-Cambrian age, but including some remnants of early Pre-Cambrian complexes, together with a variety of less highly metamorphosed sedimentary and volcanic successions. These represent the remains of mobile belts which reached the final stages of their activity 2000 million years ago. These old assemblages are unconformably overlain by a flat-lying sedimentary formation known as the Roraima Formation. This comprises several thousand metres of sandstones, conglomerates, and shales, some containing detrital diamonds. The sediments are intruded by large masses of basic igneous rock, forming thick sheets of gabbro, sills, and dykes. These were intruded in late Pre-Cambrian times, between 2000 and 1800 million years ago.

The Brazilian Shield. This shield area underlies the whole of Brazil and stretches through Uruguay and into the adjoining states to the west. Although covered in part by younger sediments, the old Pre-Cambrian crystalline basement is well exposed in north-east Brazil. Most of the rocks are of late Pre-Cambrian age, and represent deposits laid down in geosynclinal zones parallel to the present Atlantic coast. A basement of older rocks has been largely reworked during late Pre-Cambrian mobile belt activity. Two major cycles can be seen; during the first cycle the rocks of the Pre-Minas Series were laid down—sediments, volcanics, and some thick ironstone formations. These were folded, metamorphosed, and invaded by granites during an orogenic phase lasting from about 1350 to 1100 million years ago. The second cycle includes the rocks of the Minas Series, and makes up the wide coastal zone known as the Brazilides. The Minas Series consists of psammites, pelites, laminated ironstones, manganiferous beds, and quartzites. These were folded and metamorphosed in the period 650 to 500 million years ago, and late granites were then intruded. This belt in turn was covered by an unconformable series of sediments.

In many parts of the Brazilian Shield the Pre-Cambrian metamorphic rocks are overlain by glacial deposits of very late Pre-Cambrian age, termed Infracambrian. These are similar to glacial deposits of the same age found in other continents.

Palaeozoic Areas. Rocks of Palaeozoic age cover a large area between the old shield areas of the east and the Andean belt to the west. They consist of shallow-water sediments laid down on a platform fringing the ancient shield areas. Deposition appears to have started in the west, where Cambro-Ordovician sediments are seen in Bolivia; elsewhere the sedimentary sequence begins with rocks of Silurian or Devonian age. The Devonian sediments include glacial tillites in a number of areas, indicating a further period of glaciation in Devonian times.

Towards the end of the Upper Palaeozoic, important changes took place in the super-continent of Gondwana-

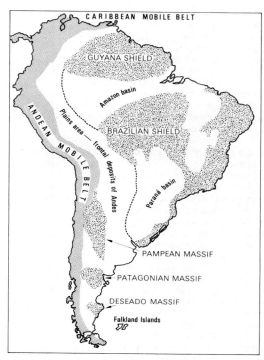

South America. Main geological units. *(Source: H. H. Read & J. V. Watson, Introduction to Geology, 1975)*

land, of which South America was still a part. Beds of a continental facies accumulated in new basins of deposition at the margins of the old shield and within the shield. At the base of this succession are glacial deposits of Permo-Carboniferous age. In the Santa Catarina system of the Paraná basin these terrestrial glacial deposits reach a maximum thickness of 1600 m, and they are followed by coal measures, shales, sandstones, and volcanics, spanning a period from late Carboniferous to late Triassic times. The whole sequence forms a 4 km thick pile of continental sediments.

The first phase in the break-up of Gondwanaland is seen in late Jurassic to early Cretaceous times, when plateau basalts outpoured over much of the Paraná and Amazon basins. Associated with the continental disruption are the marine evaporites and carbonates deposited in mid-Cretaceous times along the Atlantic coast. At the same time the diamond-bearing kimberlite pipes were intruded in the Minas Gerais area of the Brazilian Shield. From late Mesozoic times onwards the southern continents moved apart by a process of SEA-FLOOR SPREADING in the South Atlantic.

The Andean Mobile Belt. This belt at the western margin of the continent was active through most of Phanerozoic time. Thick accumulations of Palaeozoic and Mesozoic rocks built up in a geosynclinal environment, and there were episodes of orogenic activity in mid- and late Palaeozoic times, and again in late Mesozoic times, when huge granite masses were intruded. This was followed by widespread volcanic activity and uplift of the

225

South America

mountain chain of the Andes. The continued westward movement of South America is evident from the deep-seated earthquakes occurring below the Andes, and the deep ocean trench off the coast. Late orogenic volcanic activity continued from late Cretaceous times up to the present day, with the eruption of andesite lavas. Copper deposits are found in Chile associated with granites intruded in Palaeogene to Neogene times. In the late Tertiary, uplift was accompanied by explosive volcanic activity, resulting in vast sheets of ignimbrite and acid pyroclastic rocks, especially in eastern Chile.

Outside the Andean belt, thick continental sandstones and conglomerates were deposited from the rising mountain chain during Tertiary and Quaternary times. In the extreme north, adjoining the Caribbean mobile belt, thick deposits of marine Cretaceous, Tertiary, and recent sediments were laid down in the eastern Venezuela basin. This contains important oil deposits.

Flora. Looking first at tropical Latin America, it has been estimated that some 3000 genera are endemic to tropical America taken as a whole. Certain of these have a wide distribution throughout the area, such as the cocoa genus, *Theobroma*, while others are more localised. The Caribbean region is the cradle of a wide range of valuable plants and, in many ways, it is the neotropical counterpart of peninsular Malaysia in South-East Asia (see ASIA, *Flora*). From the Caribbean region emanate maize (*Zea mays*), vanilla (from the orchid genus *Vanilla*), *Dahlia variabilis*, and the well-loved house plant poinsettia (*Euphorbia pulcherrima*). The Amazon region, with the largest tract of tropical rain forest in the world and in which the endemic species may number as many as 3000, has also provided the world with some important species. Of particular note are the Pará rubber (*Hevea brasiliensis*) and cocoa (*Theobroma cacao*). The region is also famous for one of the world's most majestic plants, the giant water-lily of the Amazon (*Victoria amazonica*), which is named after Queen Victoria. The tropical rain forests of Amazonia, while not so species-rich as those of South-East Asia, are richer than those of Africa. The most characteristic families of the Latin American rain forest formation are the Leguminosae, Meliaceae, Moraceae, Sapotaceae, Euphorbiaceae, Myristicaceae, and Lecythidaceae. The South Brazilian floristic region is exceptionally rich and the home of a number of well-known garden and hot-house plants, including *Bougainvillea spectabilis*, *Passiflora caerulea*, and *Begonia semperflorens*.

The word 'savanna', which is now a technical term for tropical grassland with trees, is, in fact, an Amerindian word, reflecting the wide variety of savanna vegetation in tropical South America.

In Brazil, for example, there are scrubby woodlands known as *campo cerrado* ('closed grassland'), vast expanses of savanna with scattered trees or patches of forest called *campo sujo* ('dirty grassland'), and open grasslands with trees only in the valley bottoms termed *campo limpo* ('clean grassland'). There is also, in the drought-affected north-east, a thorny, deciduous woodland called *caatinga*. A characteristic genus of the Latin American savannas is *Curatella*.

The flora of temperate Latin America comprises at least 1500 genera and over 12,500 species. The Andean region is particularly interesting from a number of points of view.

On the one hand, the more temperate parts have provided some important garden plants, like *Berberis darwinii*, *Buddleia globosa*, and *Tropaeolum* species, while the region in general is the home of an extraordinary number of plants of some economic importance, including the potato (*Solanum tuberosum*), the tomato (*Lycopersicon esculentum*), and tobacco (*Nicotiana tabacum*). On the other hand, the zonation of vegetation in the Andes is highly distinctive, with the *páramos* of the northern Andes (a mountain grassland consisting of tall bunch grasses and shrubs) and the *puna* of the central Andes, a dry mountain grassland of short grass.

The Mediterranean region of Chile possesses some interesting woodland remnants, with species adapted to dry conditions, such as *Lithraea caustica* (a source of rashes and fever if touched) and *Quillaja saponaria*. Near Valparaiso, there is the endemic palm, *Jubaea spectabilis*, and dry rocky habitats carry the large *Puya* species of the Bromeliaceae and cylindrical cacti. Of particular note in southern Chile and Tierra del Fuego are some 50 genera which, while occurring in southern Latin America, are also found in Oceania. Three genera, namely *Acaena*, *Tetragonia*, and *Gunnera*, are also found in South Africa. The southern beech genus, *Nothofagus*, forms beautiful forests in southern Chile, just like those of New Zealand. Southern Chile also boasts some interesting coniferous elements, including species of the genera *Austrocedrus*, *Araucaria* (the monkey-puzzle tree genus), and *Podocarpus*.

The pampas region of Argentina, which is characterised by one of the world's most important grasslands, is not noted for its own distinctive elements, but carries a number of predominant elements of wider distribution, such as *Larrea divaricata*, *Prosopis alba*, and many grasses and members of the Compositae. A number of introduced species have made a real impact on the landscape, especially the milk-thistle (*Silybum marianum*) and the cardoon (*Cynara carduncellus*).

The deserts of Latin America are of great interest. The Sonoran desert of northern Mexico carries a cactus 'forest', dominated by the large candelabra cacti, such as the saguaro (*Carnegiea gigantea*), a giant cactus that can store up to 3000 litres of water and live over a year without water absorption. In contrast, the Peruvian–Chilean coastal desert is famous for the only true 'fog-plant' known among the flowering plants, namely the genus *Tillandsia* (Bromeliaceae), which is able to use water-drops from condensed fog.

Bibliography: H. Walter, *Vegetation of the Earth*, 1973; J. C. Willis (revised ed. H. K. Airy Shaw), *A Dictionary of Flowering Plants and Ferns*, 1973; R. Good, *The Geography of the Flowering Plants*, 1974.

Fauna. The Isthmus of Panama, the tenuous link joining North and South America, has not always been there. For many millions of years the two continents were sundered, creating a situation in which South America, though close to its northern neighbour, was effectively separated from it. This long isolation permitted the archaic South American fauna to evolve without competition from more advanced forms.

The uplifting of the Isthmus of Panama created a land bridge over which a stream of immigrants moved into the southern continent and superimposed themselves upon the native fauna. The traffic was not all one-way: a number of South American forms, among them the porcupine and opossum, emigrated north.

Together with geophysical and other factors, this helps to account for the extraordinary diversity which is perhaps the most remarkable characteristic of the South American fauna. A setting in which equatorial rain forest and Alpine tundra, lowland pampas and highland puna, searing deserts and snow-capped mountain ranges lie in close proximity allows for exceptional diversity.

Though much of the archaic fauna vanished either through inability to compete with the immigrants or in the great Pleistocene extinctions, some survived. The survivors included some of the marsupial fauna—otherwise found only in Oceania—and the edentates—the sloths, armadillos, and ant-eaters. Much of the fauna, both archaic and recent, has diversified to an unusual extent. This holds, in particular, for the rodents, the bats, and the primates, as well as for many of the birds, fishes, and invertebrates. They exhibit adaptive radiation and evolutionary convergence to a degree and on a scale that is unsurpassed. The result is an unequalled profusion of life in all its forms.

Among the mammals are the capybara, largest of living rodents; three species of tapirs, whose nearest relative is found in South-East Asia; and the vicuna and guanaco, descendants of the ancient New World camels. Their relatives the llama and the alpaca are wholly domesticated. The primates, all of which are arboreal, range from the vociferous howlers, the long-limbed spider monkeys, and the tiny marmosets and tamarins, to the douroucoli, or night monkey, the only true monkey that is nocturnal. Specialisation to arboreal life is marked in many species by the development of a prehensile tail, which serves as a fifth limb, and claws. The primates are not alone in evolving prehensile tails: the kinkajou is one of only two carnivores to have a prehensile tail. There is also a prehensile-tailed porcupine.

South America's faunal luxuriance is not confined to terrestrial habitats. The huge slow-flowing Amazon and its great tributary rivers have generated a complex aquatic fauna. The fish include a number of highly specialised forms, among them electric fish, lungfish, the predatory piranha and arapaima, as well as the river dolphin and manatee. The reptiles include the anaconda and the boa constrictor, and the cayman; while seasonally the river turtles assemble along the Amazon and Orinoco in such numbers that they impede the passage of boats.

Offshore, the cold waters of the PERUVIAN (HUMBOLDT) CURRENT give rise to vast shoals of fish, the anchovy in particular, that make it the richest fishery in the world. This biological cornucopia supports seals and sea-lions as well as huge flocks of 'GUANO' birds, cormorants, pelicans, and boobies.

But however remarkable its mammal, fish, and invertebrate faunas, it is the birds that constitute the continent's chief glory. South America is an ornithological paradise. One-quarter of all living bird species are to be found there. Many of the indigenous forms have no counterpart on any other continent. The birds range from the ostrich-like rhea of the treeless pampas to the Andean condor, largest of the living birds of prey, the macaws and grotesquely-billed toucans of the rain forest, and nectar-feeding hummingbirds which flit from flower to flower like jewelled moths.

This proliferation of life is equalled only by the profligate manner of its exploitation. The fur-bearers, above all the marine species, have been particularly severely depleted. The South American fur seals, once numbered in millions, were almost wiped out by commercial hunting. More recently, the hide-hunters have brought the alligator-like cayman close to extinction. Intensive development of the pampas for ranching, exploitation of the rain forest, and remorseless hunting pressure are having a dire effect on the native South American fauna.

Ethnography. The Indians of South America have survived to form a considerable proportion of the present-day population, unlike their equivalents in North America. From a point of view of population constituents, South America can be divided into three groups. In the south, Chile, Argentina, Uruguay, and Paraguay have a majority of people of European origin. In the north and north-west, along the Andes in Colombia, Ecuador, Peru, and Bolivia, the majority of the populations are of indigenous origin. In the east, centre, and north-east, the populations of Brazil, the Guianas, and Venezuela are predominantly non-indigenous. People of African and European origin make up the majorities, although there are considerable proportions of Amerindians, as well as minorities from Asia. Linguistically the Amerindian populations are divided into 14 groups: the ARAWAK, AYMARÁ, Barbacoas, CARIBS, Catuquina, Chibcha, Ge, Guahibo, Guaycuru, Pano, Saliva, Takana, Tucano, and TUPI-GUARANÍ. In all more than 400 peoples have been identified throughout South America, although many of these, particularly along coastal areas, have become culturally and physically assimilated with the predominant culture, where they have not disappeared altogether.

After 20,000 BC, when man entered the New World, HUNTING AND GATHERING activities led to the beginning of farming between 7000 and 5000 BC. Beginning with small-scale plant collection, the cultivation of maize and manioc had developed into the basis of economic activity by the beginning of the 2nd millenium BC. These farming communities resembled present-day chiefdoms, with class divisions, and the importation of luxury raw material for craftsmen to work into articles for the chiefs and priestly rulers. Chavin, in Peru, reached this stage in about 1000 BC, and from this beginning true states developed. The first imperial state in the Andes arose in the city of Tiahuanaco in Bolivia. A religion, based on the worship of figures with feline and condor attributes, was carried, through military force, into Peru where a new centre was founded at Huari. This civilisation, which arose and fell between AD 600 and 1000, spread also to many coastal areas. After the collapse of Huari, Peru and the Central Andes were not unified again until the rise of INCA power in the 15th and 16th centuries. During this period a huge area, from Ecuador through Peru and Bolivia to Chile, was brought under QUÉCHUA control and culture; this was manifested, as in earlier civilisations, in distinctive metal-working, textiles, and pottery styles. With the arrival of the Spaniards, authority in the Andes was transferred to an alien culture. The spread of new diseases, which arrived with the Europeans, is still continuing, with disastrous effects, among the newly discovered tribes of central and north-eastern Amazonia.

Today the Aymará and Quéchua peoples of the Andes are poor small-scale farmers living in much the same way as their ancestors had done before the arrival of the Spaniards. Attempts have been made to return control of more of the land to the Indians. In Bolivia the agrarian reforms of 1953 had their origins in Aymará discontent in the 1940s. In Peru the reforms which began in 1963 were carried out at the instigation of the central government.

In other parts of South America the only peoples still living in a traditional manner are some of the tropical forest peoples, whose population numbers approximately 750,000. These fall into two groups: those living away from the two main rivers, the Orinoco and the Amazon, and their tributaries, who are swidden agriculturalists (see SWIDDEN AGRICULTURE) depending principally on the cultivation of manioc; and those living along rivers who depend on fishing and hunting. However all peoples still hunt and fish to some extent, and many of the riverine tribes grow crops. The position of the tropical forest Indians is deteriorating as people of the dominant Iberian culture spread into their areas to look for land and minerals. In western Colombia, for instance, the main threat comes from the increasing needs of cattle ranchers, while in Brazil the search for minerals and the opening up of the country with new roads produces new dangers from disease, alcohol, and exploitation. This situation is exemplified by the history of Xingu National Park in the state of Mato Grosso, Brazil. This was set up in 1952 by the Villas Boas brothers to encourage and protect a group of nine culturally distinct Indian peoples in order to try and preserve their identity and traditions. However in 1961 and 1968 the area for the park was hugely decreased because of pressure from commercial interests; more recently a road has been built across the park thus allowing unrestricted access to Indians by outsiders. In view of this pattern over much of South America, it is likely that by the end of this century there will be very few tropical Indian groups preserving their own way of life.

Bibliography: J. H. Steward (Ed.), *Handbook of the South American Indians*, 1946; T. O'Leary, *Ethnographic Bibliography of South America*, 1963; G. Willey, *Introduction to American Archaeology*, Vol. III, 1971; R. Hanbury-Tenison, *A Question of Survival*, 1973; P. Caraman, *The Lost Paradise*, 1975.

Archaeology and Ancient Civilisation. Until recently archaeological research in South America has been restricted to areas with good preservation or fine artifacts. Today each country is subject to extensive investigation. For some (e.g. Peru, Bolivia) a great deal was already known, if not fully understood, but for others (e.g. Brazil and Uruguay) prehistoric knowledge was lacking. The new information has changed the overall perspective significantly. Furthermore, in the absence of pre-European documents, ethnohistorical research of Colonial records has added much information concerning socio-political organisation, religion, economy and agriculture of the ancient cultures.

By the 16th century high civilisation had been achieved in the Central Andes (Peru and Bolivia); chiefdoms existed in the North and South Andes whilst in Amazonia and in the Pampas there was an amalgam of primitive agricultural and hunting tribes. There is much controversy over the source of origin of South American civilisation but evidence suggests an independent development initially in Amazonia and flourishing in the mountains.

The earliest record of human occupation

South America. Peruvian red-ware water vessel. (*Victoria and Albert Museum, London*)

(18,250±1050 BC) was discovered by R. MacNeish at Flea Cave in Ayacucho, Peru. It comprises crude stone choppers and scrapers in association with the shattered bones of extinct ground sloth. This suggests that man first entered South America around 30,000 BC. By 13,000 BC new stone hunting tools, such as spearpoints, made from flakes made the killing of game more efficient in both Peru and Venezuela. At the end of the glaciation (9000 BC) new lightweight fishtail, stemmed or leaf spear points increased hunting intensity leading to the extinction of the ground sloths and horse by 7500 BC. After this time economies became more diversified; llama and deer were hunted and there is much evidence of interest in plant collecting. Cultures of this type are known from Venezuela and Brazil to Tierra del Fuego.

Agriculture was invented independently in South America between 8000 and 2000 BC, although no precise origin has been located. The botanist, Pickersgill, suggests that it was invented east of the Andes although the only archaeological evidence comes from the Andes and the coast of Peru. The main crops were the potato, manioc, two species of bean, etc.

Maize and other seed plants were introduced from Mexico around 2500 BC. The only domesticated animals were the llama, alpaca, and guinea pig.

The earliest pottery (3400 BC) has been excavated at Valdivia (Ecuador) and Puerto Hormiga (Colombia) but it does not appear in Peru before 1800 BC. Yet by 2500 BC Peru had developed impressive pyramid and temple complexes in association with fishing and farming villages (e.g. Las Haldas and Kotosh). Between 1000 and 300 BC Peru was dominated by a politico-religious movement, known as the Chavin cult. It was first recognised by Tello as an art style of large carvings, metals and ceramic. It comprised both anthropomorphic and zoomorphic gods characterised by snarling feline mouths with subsidiary mouths representing arms and legs, and snakes the hair. The iconography was basically Amazonian in context, although the main centre, Chavin de Huantar, was in the highlands. Two main deities are suggested by differences in the mouth, Staff God and Smiling God. Much of northern Peru fell under direct influence of the cult via local U-shaped temples with massively carved feline heads (e.g. Huaca de los Reyes at Trujillo), but southern Peru escaped this. There, only the iconography appeared on finely decorated Paracas pottery.

Following the demise of Chavin, Peru entered a thousand years of regional cultures (e.g. Nazca, Mochica, Recuay). During this period art, architecture, pottery and metallurgy all reached a cultural apogee leading some scholars to term it Classic or Florescent. Each area was a small nation state dominated by a theocracy. The pyramid was the major building of the period. On the coast large adobe pyramids were built in each valley, the largest being the Huaca del Sol near Trujillo, which measured 200 × 150 m and over 25 m high. It was built in vertical

South America. Clay figurine of a tribal chief, found near Santarem, Brazil. It is 500–1000 years old. *(Camera Press/D. Botting)*

columns of adobes and took over a hundred years to complete. Mochica pottery is among the finest in South America. It was mass-produced in moulds and painted in scenes of everyday life or mythology or modelled in effigies of important people, deformities, foods and sexual life. The most characteristic shape was the stirrup-spouted bottle. The multicoloured Nazca pottery was even finer. Tello found at Paracas embroidered strands which are the finest textiles from South America.

On the shores of Lake Titicaca another nation developed around the city of Tiahuanaco. It too had a distinctive pottery style and religious iconogral whose god was carved on the Gateway of the Sun in the city. Just after AD 600 the Tiahuanaco state expanded south across the altiplano and north to Huari, where it flourished. From Huari the Gateway God and Tiahuanaco painted pottery spread throughout Peru in another politico-religious movement. City planning altered as the pyramid became less important and secular palaces and storehouses were built (e.g. at Cajarmarquilla and Marca Huamachuco). The temple complex at Pachacamac (north of Lima) was an important pilgrimage and cultural centre. The unification lasted for 500 years and by AD 1200 small nations again emerged (e.g. Chimor, Chincha, Inca, Chucuito etc.). Each had a distinctive art and pottery style (e.g. Chimor—black pottery moulded in Mochica fashion). The Kingdom of Chimor was the largest. It had many large cities, each served by an elaborate canal field system, and containing royal compounds with a tomb and massive storage facilities (e.g. Chan Chan). The kingdom engaged in trade with Amazonia for coca and Ecuador for spondylus shell, both important in ceremony. The Inca conquered Chimor in 1464 and dominated the central Andes for the next 70 years (see INCA).

The archaeology of the northern Andes is less well-known but it has reputedly the best goldwork in the New World (Quimbaya). At San Agustín, Colombia (c. 400 BC) large megalithic anthropomorphic carvings, temples and tombs represent the emergence of chiefdoms. The village federation (c. AD 1500) of the Tairona, Chibcha and Cara, etc., were advanced town-based cultures with fine skills in art and metalwork.

The prehistory of the southern Andes is dominated by the cultural achievements of Tiahuanaco and Inca along its northern frontier and these stimulated urban developments at Turi, Chile. The southern part of the continent remained at a primitive hunting stage.

The Amazon basin was in the past regarded as an archaeological backwater but the investigations of Lathrap have shown otherwise. Pottery-using peoples existed by 2000 BC and several pottery styles common in South America can be linked to cultural beginnings in the jungle. Lathrap has postulated that the spread of these can be related to the diffusion of the Arawakan and Tupi-Guaranian languages.

Bibliography: E. Lanning, *Peru Before the Incas,* 1967; D. Lathrap, *The Upper Amazon,* 1970; G. R. Willey, *An Introduction to American Archaeology* (vol. 2 *South America*), 1971.

Architecture, see LATIN AMERICA, *Architecture.*

History. South America was once a colony of Spain and Portugal. The Spanish conquistadores, after brutally conquering the Indians, AZTECS, INCAS, and Chibchas, exploited the Indian peoples by compelling them to labour as miners and agriculturalists. Because, unlike the British

South America

in North America, the Spaniards and Portuguese took few women with them, the practice of race mixture was established early in the 16th century. Immigration into South America on any appreciable scale was a late development of the 19th century, and the main stream of immigrants flowed into southern Brazil, Argentina, Uruguay, Chile, and Cuba. Spaniards and Portuguese predominated, but there were also large elements of Italians and Germans. Immigration has given an almost European outlook to Argentine society, besides conducing greatly to the material and social welfare of the River Plate countries and southern Brazil. South America lacks racial homogeneity: Bolivia, for example, has a primarily Indian population, Argentina a primarily European one, and Colombia a primarily *mestizo* (half-Indian, half-European) one. The different countries differ widely in wealth and power, and also in social and political development.

Spain's great American empire was more or less completely explored and colonised by the end of the 16th century. It was the first durable and large European overseas empire. Spain's objective, the extraction of minerals, was successfully achieved; but there was no serious attempt to build up a balanced economy. The underprivileged ethnic groups were kept in ruthless subjection, and even Spanish colonists were excluded from posts in government and administration. Economic and administrative reforms were made in the 18th century but came too late to streamline the empire, which collapsed in the beginning of the 19th. The immediate causes of the collapse were Spain's monopolistic myopia and the growing demand of Spanish Americans for self-government. These latter included many great leaders famous in the annals of the Spanish-American struggle for independence, particularly SAN MARTIN and BOLIVAR, liberators respectively of the south and north of Spanish America, revered not only as great leaders in the field but also as statesmen.

But having achieved independence in the Spanish-American revolution, the Spanish Americans were faced with the still greater task of organising their states in their newly won freedom. The independence of Spanish America was assured by British sea-power and by Lord Castlereagh's note to the European chancelleries in 1817 saying that no other power than Spain would be allowed to use force against the Spanish colonies. Some few years later President Monroe of the USA sent his famous message to Congress with has come down to posterity as the MONROE DOCTRINE, seen by some observers as a guarantee of the independence of the new states.

In 1830 twelve new republics and one new empire, Brazil, had been added to the number of independent states. There were 16 new republics, if the five republics of Central America were counted separately. These latter, in 1823, were theoretically united in the confederation of Central America, which survived only until 1838. Cuba did not attain self-government until 1902, and Panama was part of Colombia until 1903. Haiti declared its independence of France in 1804, but the Dominican Republic fell under the dominion of Haiti and later was again incorporated with Spain for a few years. The great republic of Colombia, the creation of Bolívar, split into the three states of Ecuador, Colombia, and Venezuela. Brazil peacefully declared a conservative counter-revolution against a liberal régime in Portugal and by 1822 had established an empire under the house of Braganza. The boundaries of the new Spanish-American countries followed, in the main, the old colonial administrative divisions, but they were ill-defined and the source of innumerable inter-state conflicts. But though independent the states were far from prosperous. The wars of independence left a vicious circle of economic dislocation, poverty, and administrative inexperience. But the eventual independence of South America ranks with the American and French revolutions as one of the chief formative influences on modern history. Capital flowed from Europe into the new states. Already by 1825 more than £20 million had been invested by British capitalists in South America. Foreign immigrants, together with foreign investments in South American shipping, ports, and public utilities, have all played a decisive part in the spectacular rise of some of these states. Poverty and ignorance remain widespread in the midst of great cultivation and wealth. A high percentage of the people in most South American countries are illiterate. Yet the quality of Latin-American literature since 1939 has equalled that anywhere in the world and surpassed that of Spain and Portugal.

Politically, economically, and intellectually the South American republics are playing an increasingly important part in world affairs. The development of the Monroe Doctrine into what once seemed to be an assertion by the USA of sovereignty and supremacy in the Caribbean area roused the greatest resentment in South America, for it was regarded by the republics as a threatened infringement of their equality in international law and of their political independence. But the USA's policy was profoundly modified under Franklin Roosevelt, whose 'good neighbour' policy signalised a distinct change in inter-American relations, as was exemplified in later Pan-American conferences (see PAN-AMERICAN CONFERENCE). Subsequent political developments in inter-American relations included the Declaration of Lima in 1938, which was a striking pronouncement of inter-American solidarity.

In 1948 at the Ninth International Conference of American States held in Bogotá, Colombia, a charter was adopted setting up the ORGANISATION OF AMERICAN STATES (OAS), whose object was to achieve amongst the member states an order of peace and justice, to promote their solidarity and strengthen their collaboration, and to

South America. Cortes and his small army of Spaniards defeat the Aztecs at Otumba, 1520. From a painting by Antonio Gomez, 1853. *(Mansell Collection)*

defend their sovereignty, territorial independence, and integrity. The member states comprised the 20 Latin-American countries plus the USA; but Cuba, following its revolution in 1959, was excluded from the OAS. Further developments on these lines were the Act of Bogotá in 1960 which reaffirmed that economic development and social progress were indissolubly linked; and in 1961 the Alliance for Progress was proposed by John F. Kennedy, President of the USA, initiating a joint venture by the American nations designed to cope with the fundamental needs of the South American people in a ten-year development period. Since the late 1960s the USA, more preoccupied with the Far East and the Middle East, has devoted less attention to South America. A more limited, but important, development was the establishment in 1960, by the Treaty of Montevideo, of the LATIN-AMERICAN FREE TRADE ASSOCIATION (LAFTA) to which Argentina, Brazil, Chile, Mexico, Paraguay, Peru, and Uruguay were signatories.

Conspicuous changes have been wrought in Latin America since the two world wars: civil aviation has revolutionised South American life to an extent greater than in any other part of the world. The second great change is industrialisation. Until the second half of the 20th century South America mainly produced foodstuffs and raw materials, depending for its manufactured goods on Europe and North America. The world wars, by almost paralysing sea-borne trade, and the economic depression of 1929 to 1933, were factors in compelling the Latin American countries to adopt a policy of industrial self-sufficiency. Since then local industries, especially in Argentina, Brazil, and Mexico, have made great advances.

See also PAN-AMERICANISM; PAN-AMERICAN UNION; ATLAS 56.

Bibliography: J. H. Elliott, *Imperial Spain*, 1963; J. Lynch, *Spain and the Hapsburgs*, 2 vols, 1964–69; J. Lambert, *Latin America: Political Institutions and Social Structures*, 1967; M. Morner, *Race Mixture in the History of Latin America*, 1969; G. Pendle, *A History of Latin America*, 1969; S. and B. Stein, *The Colonial Heritage of Latin America*, 1970; J. Lynch, *The Spanish American Revolutions*, 1973; G. Connell-Smith, *The United States and Latin America*, 1973.

Literature, see SPANISH AMERICAN LITERATURE.

South American Native Languages

South American Native Languages fall into four vast linguistic regions. The Chibcha or Muysca (*muhizca cehà*, body of five extremities, man) linguistic family comprises languages spoken in the southern part of Central America and in the north-west of South America, that is, from south Nicaragua through Costa Rica, Panama, Colombia, to north Ecuador. Cuna or Túle, a branch of the Chibcha, has its own ancient picture-writing, and is spoken by some 25,000 people on the Gulf of Darien (Panama). Another branch, Guaymi, is spoken north of the isthmus.

In the Caribbean area various languages and dialects are spoken by peoples inhabiting the tropical forests and grasslands extending from the Cordilleras to the Atlantic and from the River Plate to the Antilles. These languages belong to four main linguistic families: Arawak, Carib, Tapuya or Tabuya, and Tupi or Tupi-Guarani. The latter is the only native language of South America officially used in newspapers and public speeches.

The central Andean plateau, the region of the Inca Empire (see PERU), extending from Ecuador to Chile, was inhabited by Quéchua-speaking peoples. In the northern part of the empire lived the Chimu, speaking a Mochica language not belonging to the Quéchua family. Their descendants, the Yunca, live along the coast, but Quéchua, subdivided into various dialects, is still the main native language, and is spoken by 6,000,000 people.

The native population of the southern grasslands and forests, including the greater part of Uruguay, Argentina, and Chile, belongs to three or four linguistic families, comprising many languages. Of these the principal are Pampean, Tehuel-che or Patagonian, Araucan, Guaycurú, and Fuegian.

See also MEXICAN AND CENTRAL AMERICAN NATIVE LANGUAGES; NORTH AMERICAN NATIVE LANGUAGES.

South Arabia, Federation of, formerly a federation within the Commonwealth, comprising the former colony of ADEN and a number of Arab emirates, sheikhdoms, and sultanates in the western Aden protectorate, with a total area of about 155,400 km^2 and a population of about 750,000. The capital was Al-Ittihad. The federation promoted co-ordination of resources, education, medical services, defence, and communications between the constituent states, and was normally governed by a Federal Council of 94 members. Executive powers were vested in a Supreme Council of Ministers. The nucleus of the federation, calling itself the Federation of Arab Emirates of the South, was formed in 1959 by the six states of Baihan, Dhala, Audhali, Fadhli, Lower Yafa, and Upper Aulaqi. In succeeding years more states joined, including Aden itself (1963). The name was changed to Federation of South Arabia in April 1962, and it included 14 states. The western part of the federation was claimed by the Yemen, and the frontier was the scene during 1964–66 of sporadic fighting, especially in the Jebel Radfan area, 100 km north of Aden, instigated by the United Arab Republic, who infiltrated agents and terrorists into Aden. Failure of the federal government to condemn or take action against terrorism, which was largely directed at British services, resulted in suspension of the constitution in September 1965 and the resumption of direct rule, though plans for eventual independence in 1968 were not abandoned. See below, and YEMEN, PEOPLE'S DEMOCRATIC REPUBLIC OF.

South Arabia, Protectorate of, formerly a protectorate of approximately 287,500 km^2 with an estimated population of 868,000 comprising 21 Arab states of which 17, together with the state of Aden, formed the Federation of South Arabia (see above). Until 1965 the territory was known as Aden Protectorate. The non-federated states were Upper Yafa (including certain small sheikhdoms), the Qu'aiti sultanate of Shihr and Mukalla, the Mahri sultanate of Qishn and Socotra, and the Kathiri sultanate. All enjoyed protective treaty relations with Britain. The protectorate was bounded on the east by the Qara country, part of the territory of the Sultan of Muscat and Oman (now Oman), and on the north and west by the Great Desert and Yemen, whose southern boundary was provisionally fixed by the Treaty of San'a (1934), by which the British government and the Imam Yahia of Yemen agreed to maintain the *status quo* frontier as it was at the date of the treaty.

South Australia

South Australia, state of the Commonwealth of Australia bounded on the south by the Southern Ocean, with Queensland, New South Wales, and Victoria to the east, and West Australia on its western border. All the country from the 26th parallel of latitude to the Indian Ocean was also annexed to South Australia, but in 1911 was taken over by the Commonwealth. This area is now known as the Northern Territory. The total area of South Australia is 984,000 km².

Geography. Most of South Australia is under 600 m in height, and the eastern half of the state is under 150 m. The area around Lake EYRE lies below sea-level and is the lowest elevation of the Australian continent. Much of the state is desert, chiefly the Great Victoria and Simpson deserts, which are covered by sand ridges. There are three ranges of mountains in South Australia; the Mount Lofty Ranges (maximum height 727 m), the Flinders Ranges (maximum height 1165 m), and the Musgrave Ranges (1440 m). There are also wide expanses of flat or undulating land, particularly the Nullabor Plain in the south. Apart from the MURRAY river system, most of South Australia's drainage network operates intermittently, feeding into salt lakes such as lakes Eyre, Torrens, Frome, and Gardner.

The climate is very mild. The rainfall at Adelaide averages 533 mm annually, most of it falling between May and October. The mean temperature is 17 °C, the extreme range being 1 °C to 44 °C. Further inland rainfall decreases considerably to give an arid climate in the interior with very high temperatures.

The population in 1976 was an estimated 1,244,700. ADELAIDE, the capital and main commercial centre, had a population of 899,300. Other important towns of the state are PORT PIRIE, WHYALLA, and PORT AUGUSTA. The number of full-blooded aboriginals is about 7140.

Economy. Agriculture, severely restricted throughout most of the state by unreliable rainfall, is concentrated in the south-east, on the Yorke peninsula and north of Adelaide as far as Peterborough. The total area under crops in 1973–74 was 2,500,000 ha, of which 1,050,000 was under wheat, 800,000 under barley, and 240,000 under hay. Viticulture is extensive: in 1973–74 28,330 ha produced over 181,000,000 litres of wine. These vines, which also yield raisins and currants for export, are grown under irrigation. There are 42,491 ha irrigated along the Murray river between the Victoria border and Morgan. Oranges and peaches are other important crops. Stock-raising is the more traditional type of farming: in 1974 there were over 17,900,000 sheep and 1,400,000 cattle. In 1973–74 the wool-clip weighed some 45,400,000 kg, valued at over \$A70 million.

South Australia has a rapidly growing mining and manufacturing economy. Post-war industrialisation has centred around motor-vehicles, electrical goods, and household appliances, most of which are produced in and around ADELAIDE. Outside Adelaide the two most important industrial undertakings are steel and shipbuilding at WHYALLA and the lead smelters at PORT PIRIE. Other factories are located near their source of supply, such as the sawmills and pulp- and paper-mills of the south-east, the fruit-processing plants of the upper Murray, and the wineries and distilleries of the Barossa Valley. Metal processing employs the largest percentage of the state's 118,000 employees in manufacturing.

The total value of mineral production is about \$A110 million. The iron-ore deposits of the Middleback range are used to supply the steel industry at PORT KEMBLA and NEWCASTLE. South Australia also has the bulk of Australia's gypsum. Because of the arid climate large salt deposits are found around Port Augusta and Whyalla and from here two-thirds of Australia's salt requirements are met. The state has large deposits of oil and natural gas in the Gidgealpa and Moomba fields. Adelaide is supplied with gas from here, and in 1976 a liquefied natural gas and oil pipeline from these fields to PORT AUGUSTA was completed which supplies the raw material for a developing petrochemical complex at nearby Redcliffe. This complex, built with Australian and Japanese funds, will produce caustic soda and ethylene-dichloride. It is hoped that other industries will be generated by this oil-refining and petrochemical industry, and that the area's population will be increased by 100,000 by the 1990s. South Australia also possesses large opal and pyrites deposits. The main overseas exports are wool, lead, wheat, beef, pig iron, iron ore, zinc, and copper. The total exports in 1973/4 were valued at \$A394 million.

Government. The parliament of South Australia consists of a Legislative Council and a House of Assembly. The council consists of 20 members and the assembly 47. Voters must be 18 years of age and have been on the electoral roll 6 months, besides being natural-born or naturalised British subjects. The franchise for both houses was extended to adult women in 1894. Responsible government is carried out by 12 ministers, members of the legislature, who form the Cabinet and are ex-officio members of the Executive Council.

History. South Australia was probably known to the Dutch in the middle of the 16th century, was surveyed by TASMAN in 1644, and was charted by Flinders in 1802. In 1828 Stuart explored the Murray river to its mouth. In 1831 Major Baron suggested the desirability of forming a British settlement in the neighbourhood of the Murray river. The province was founded on Gibbon Wakefield's system of colonisation under an Act of 1834. The first colonists landed at Kangaroo Island but the settlement was almost immediately transferred to the mainland, where the province was proclaimed at Glenelg on 28 December 1836. The discovery of copper at Kapunda in

South Australia. Cooper's Creek entering Lake Eyre. *(Camera Press)*

1842 and at the Burra in 1845 paved the way to prosperity. South Australia became a state of the Australian Commonwealth in 1901.

Bibliography: S. Berekmeri and M. F. Page, *South Australia*, 1972; D. D. Harris and D. A. M. Lee, *Regional Geography of South Australia*, 1973; M. Williams, *Making of the South Australian Landscapes*, 1974; *South Australian Year Book*.

South Bend, city and county seat of St Joseph county, Indiana, USA, on the St Joseph river, in an agricultural area 120 km east of Chicago. It manufactures automobiles, aeroplanes, machinery, foundry products, and has food-processing industries. The University of Notre Dame and St Mary's College are nearby. Population 125,580.

South Carolina (Palmetto State), one of the 13 original states of the USA, with an area of 80,432 km². It is bounded on the north by North Carolina, on the east by the Atlantic Ocean, and on the south-west by Georgia. Along the coast is a belt of low swampy marine terraces of recent uplift, inland lies a series of parallel ridges and vales, while in the far west the surface rises to the rolling upland of the Piedmont plateau. All three divisions of the state carry considerable areas of forest, chiefly pine, poplar, oak, and hickory; there are 5 million ha of commercial forest, half hardwoods and half softwoods. The climate is subtropical at the coast, but winters are more severe inland. The January mean temperature at Charleston is 10 °C, but only 4·1° at Greenville.

In 1969 there were 40,000 farms covering some 2·8 million ha; however, it should be noted that, only 10 years earlier, the number of farms had been double this figure, a statistic which reveals the course of development within

South Carolina. Bayou country. *(Barnaby's Picture Library)*

the state. Traditionally agricultural, South Carolina has experienced in recent decades a rapid industrialisation and this, coupled with mechanisation on the farm (e.g. in cotton growing operations), has had the effect of drawing many small farmers off the land and away from enterprises of marginal profitability. Even today, less than half of the farms remaining have annual sales of more than $2500, so that their numbers are likely to fall much further before a purely commercial agriculture results. There are about 1 million ha under crops, of which 150,000 are under corn, 120,000 under cotton, and 25,000 under tobacco, the leading single source of farm income. South Carolina is the second biggest US producer of peaches after California, and a number of other agricultural specialities have developed, in part through the conversion or exhaustion of old cotton lands. Meanwhile industrialisation has given the state one of the highest percentages in the nation of a workforce employed in industry (39 per cent). South Carolina has a large share in the Southern textile industry, and other principal groups of manufactures are forest-based. Hydro-electric projects (e.g. on the SANTEE river system) provide the necessary power. There are some 3500 industrial plants in the state.

In 1975 the population was 2,818,000, an increase of 20 per cent over the figure for 1960. The density of population was 34 per km², 47 per cent was classed as urban and 30 per cent was Black. These figures mask the fact that, during the 1960s, there was a net white immigration of 44,000 but a net emigration among the Black population of nearly 200,000, as the latter moved out, generally to cities in the north.

The first permanent settlement in South Carolina was made by the English in 1670, and CHARLESTON soon became the chief focus, retaining to this day many relics of its colonial past, as well as serving as principal seaport. The colony remained under a proprietary government with North Carolina until 1729, when it became a separate Crown colony. It was the first state to secede from the Union in 1860 and suffered severe damage in the military struggle that followed in 1861–65. The capital is COLUMBIA, which is also the seat of the University of South Carolina.

Bibliography: D. D. Wallace, *The History of South Carolina*, 1934, and *South Carolina: A Short History*, 1951; D. E. Harless, *South Carolina: An Economic Profile*, 1964.

South Carolina Regiment, see WEST INDIA REGIMENT.

South Dakota (Coyote State), state of the north-central USA, bordered on the north by North Dakota, on the east by Minnesota and Iowa, on the south by Nebraska, and on the west mainly by Wyoming. It has an area of 199,550 km². It was admitted to the Union in 1889 and its capital is PIERRE. Most of the state's surface is made up of the Great Plains, rising gently from east to west and deeply dissected along the lines of the Missouri river and its tributaries to form the so-called 'badlands' topography which, on the White river, becomes so spectacular and castellated that the area has been designated a national monument. In the south-western corner of the state there is a dramatic interruption of this level surface, where the granitic BLACK HILLS form a forested dome rising to over 2200 m in Harney Peak. The Black Hills were

South Dakota

regarded as sacred ground by Indians, but as a source of gold by white men (South Dakota is today the US's largest producer of gold), and inevitably conflict ensued. Today the area is chiefly notable as a tourist attraction; it includes the Mount Rushmore Memorial.

South Dakota is bisected by the MISSOURI river. The section east of the river is on the whole humid (500 mm or more of precipitation), while west of the river there may be as little as 250 mm in the extreme north-west. The eastern half of the state has an economy resembling that of the CORN BELT further east, with intensive livestock raising on fodder crops. West of the river, ranching on the natural range grasses is the dominant activity. The Missouri river and its tributaries have been progressively dammed within the state (Oahe and Fort Randall are the mainstream dams) and water is thus made available for irrigation farming, so that intensification is possible. (In addition, hydro-electric capacity installed at the dams totals 1·4 million kW.) In 1969, 46,000 farms covered 18·5 million ha, an area which had increased since 1959 by 300,000 ha, at a time when most states were registering a decline in their farm areas. Average farm size is over 400 ha, and three-quarters of the value of farm produce sold comes from livestock. There are 1·1 million ha of corn in eastern South Dakota and 900,000 ha of wheat in the central part of the state.

The Dakotas were settled in a series of advances and retreats by farmers who only discovered by trial and error how far into the arid west agriculture could be carried. The state developed no large urban centre; the towns are agricultural markets pure and simple. Today, the population is classed as 56 per cent rural; North and South Dakota have the lowest urban proportions of any states. This has had its impact on recent population trends for, with the general tendency of workers to move out of

South Dakota. Corn Palace, Mitchell—the world's only palace decorated completely on the exterior (and partially inside) with ears of coloured corn (maize). Each year it is redecorated with 3000 bushels. *(Barnaby's Picture Library)*

agriculture and into industry or services in the city, the most rural states suffer loss of population. Between 1960 and 1970, South Dakota underwent a net emigration of 92,000; like North Dakota, it suffered a loss in total population of 2·2 per cent (only one other state, West Virginia, experienced a decline during this period). At the same time, this sparse rural population (3·4 per km²) required the upkeep of nearly 130,000 km of roads to serve it. In 1971 there were only 16,000 jobs in manufacturing in the state (mainly in agriculture-based industries), compared with 56,000 in government. The University of South Dakota is at Vermillion, in the extreme south-east, and there is a state university at Brookings and a school of mines at Rapid City. Population (1975) 683,000.

Bibliography: Federal Writers' Project, *South Dakota: A Guide to the State*, revised ed., 1952; H. S. Schell, *History of South Dakota*, 2nd ed., 1968.

South Downs, see DOWNS, NORTH AND SOUTH.

South-East Asia, a subdivision of the continent of ASIA that is broadly divided into two parts: mainland and insular. Mainland South-East Asia is usually defined as including Vietnam, Burma, Laos, Cambodia, Thailand, Malaysia, and Singapore; it consists in the main of north–south trending mountain ranges and valleys associated with some of the world's largest rivers, e.g. the MEKONG and IRRAWADDY. The insular sector includes Philippines, Brunei, and Indonesia, and either forms an island arc off the coast of Asia or part of the Asian continental shelf. The climate is predominantly tropical and the natural vegetation is forest. The area is very diverse culturally but similar in the type of agriculture that prevails, i.e. rice growing, and thus the economic development of most of the countries has been broadly along the same lines. The political fragmentation of the area and the internal and external struggles of the various states has been a notable feature of the region in the 20th century. See individual country entries.

South-East Asia Collective Defence Treaty, South-East Asian counterpart to the NORTH ATLANTIC TREATY, signed in Manila on 8 September 1954 between Britain, the USA, Australia, New Zealand, Pakistan, France, Thailand, and the Philippines for their 'continuous and effective self-help and mutual aid'. Bangkok was made the political headquarters of the Treaty organisation (SEATO) in February 1955. The organisation was weakened by the refusal of India, Indonesia, and Sri Lanka to join it, changing attitudes in Australia and New Zealand, the collapse of US policy in Indo-China, the resignation of Pakistan from the organisation in 1973, and the refusal of France to participate after 1974. SEATO came to an end on 30 June 1977.

South-East Asian Architecture. Until the early centuries AD, the dominant cultures were the northern Thai and the Dongson culture of the eastern deltas and scattered parts of the archipelago. The architecture was apparently limited to large thatched timber hall-houses and communal granaries. Indian Buddhist and Hindu influences spread into the area, first achieving a sophisticated architecture in Indonesia, for example the great Buddhist STUPA of Borobudur (c. 800) and the Hindu temples of Dieng (c. 700), both in Java. From Indonesia Buddhist and Hindu architecture spread into Indo-

China, replacing the earlier direct Indian influence, and eventually led to the great achievements of the Khmer style in the immense urban complexes of Angkor, Cambodia. Burmese architecture was under direct Indian and Ceylonese Buddhist influence, culminating in the stupas of Pagau. Thailand likewise experienced the same influences, as well as direct contact with Burma. But Thai conquest of the late Angkor civilisation meant that some elements of that architecture survived into modern times, especially in the raised timber palaces and houses.

South-East Asian Literature. Geographically, South-East Asia can be conveniently divided into mainland and maritime areas. The former area comprises Burma, Thailand, Laos, Cambodia, and Vietnam, and the latter the whole island complex of Indonesia, the Philippines, and Malaysia. Strong external political, economic, and cultural influences have affected the region, though no one influence appears in equal strength over the whole of South-East Asia. Early and medieval India influenced literary development in what is now Burma, Thailand, Cambodia, and Laos, west Malaysia, and the western parts of Indonesia, particularly the important islands of Java, Bali and, to some extent, Sumatra.

Buddhist ideas and impulses affected the written literatures, though in the Indonesian and Malaysian areas this was overlaid, after the 15th century, by Islam. Vietnam moved early into the cultural orbit of China while Christianity, through the Spanish colonial conquest, became and remained a strong influence in the Philippines. Hinduism shaped the cultural life of the areas in which it appeared, and South-East Asian versions of Indian tales and legends remain an important property of the literatures to the present day. Thus there is a common feature

South-East Asian Architecture. Part of an outer wall in stone relief at the temple complex of Bayon, Cambodia, built 12th –13th centuries, and once the artistic apex of the Khmer civilisation. *(Luc Ionesco)*

South-East Asian Architecture. Aerial view of Angkor Wat, Cambodia, built at the beginning of the 12th century. *(Luc Ionesco)*

at the core of Indian-influenced literatures; even so the effect of local inspiration must not be ignored.

In modern times the introduction of Western culture and technology, notably the development of printing, has changed the form of literary production and the mode of expression from poetry to prose. In most South-East Asian cultures, prose in pre-modern times had been used for practical purposes; it now became a vehicle for imaginative writing. The varying effect of political and social pressures during the 20th century has produced greatly different developments in detail within the general framework of new prose literature.

Burma. The early centuries of recorded history in Burma were disturbed times of conflict between the Mons, whose cultural centres lay in lower Burma and western Thailand, the Shans, a Thai people from the north-west, and the Burmese themselves. Mon Buddhist influence was strong from the beginning; the literature had a monastic flavour and the monasteries, closely associated at the highest levels with the court, were important centres of literary production. Writing on palm-leaf strips, bound together as a form of book, developed early (see BOOK). This, together with a large body of stone inscriptions, often dedicatory, dating from the 12th century, marked the first stage of Burmese literature. This reached its peak during the 15th and 16th centuries when the country was ruled from Ava, in upper Burma. At this time emerged the long sermon in verse, panegyric poems on rulers and priests commemorating important events. From the establishment of the Taungoo dynasty, about 1540, an uncertain unity was established under Burmese domination and during the next two centuries classical literature developed further with the introduction of short odes of a lyrical nature, less obviously inspired by the religious motive. Historical works in prose, an important branch of Burmese literature, also emerged from the 16th century. Expansionist tendencies, not unknown under Taungoo, became marked in the Konbaung period from 1752. The Thai capital of Ayuthaya was captured in 1767 and one of the sources of Burmese drama was that of the Thai, which was much concerned with Indian-derived dramatic works based on the story of Rāma. The late development of Burmese dramatic literature is a reflection of the strong Buddhist tendencies which have been a constant factor.

During the 19th century a tendency towards secularisation and popularisation arose. Narrative poetry and locally-inspired drama introducing satirical and humorous elements were its vehicles. By this time, however, the Burmese were involved in the protracted struggle with Britain which resulted in the exile of the Burmese rulers in 1886 and the disappearance of the court as an effective focus for the arts. Printing technology began to change the modes of literary production in the 1870s and 1880s and literature moved more into the public domain. Older literature was printed, suggesting an intention to preserve Burmese cultural values in the face of alien pressure. At the same time novelettes and short stories, ranging from the trivial to the serious, began to be produced in large numbers. The development of a modern literature in Burmese was, however, somewhat inhibited by the colonial presence, and Burmese as a vehicle for significant modern literary work came into its own only after independence in 1948. But precursors existed, especially writers of the novel, who, before the Second World War were aided by the establishment of literary clubs and movements. Post-war literature takes into account political and social conflicts and pressures and further exploits the satire and humour which is a characteristic of change from the traditional to the modern.

Thailand, Cambodia, and Laos. The literature of the Khmer who, until the 15th century, occupied not only the territory of the present-day Khmer republic but areas in what are now Vietnam, Thailand, and Laos, formed a base upon which the classical literatures of Thailand and Laos were able to develop. Although Mahāyana and Hinayana Buddhism were known and practised in the old Khmer state, literary works owe much to Brahmanistic tradition. Among the Khmer, as among the Lao and the Thai, important Buddhist literature exists, but religious influence was less dominant than in Burma.

The earliest Khmer writings were in the form of stone inscriptions, used to record information. However, the major imaginative work in verse was the *Reamker*, based, with many local additions and changes, on the *Rāmāyana*. The form of presentation was dramatic, involving shadow play and masked drama (see ORIENTAL DRAMA). Those Khmer works found their way to the Lao states and to Ayuthaya, the Thai capital (1350–1767), where they were further developed. In common with other South-East Asian cultures the first literary presentations in Thailand were lithic inscriptions. The earliest, from the first Thai capital, Sukhothai, dates from the end of the 13th century and demonstrates the existence of a well-formed literary style. The poetic literature which developed during the Ayuthaya period reached its full flowering in the reign of King Norai (1657–88) and appeared mainly in three major forms. The dramatic form used mainly stories of Indian origin and exploited the possibilities of shadow-play, masked drama, and dance-drama which, by the 18th century, had a specialised form played by the ladies of the court. In southern Thailand there developed shadow-play influenced by the Malays, and popular plays performed by strolling troupes, using material drawn from Jātaka or Buddhist birth stories, in general paralleling the use of such material in other South-East Asian Buddhist countries. Another major division of verse literature was the narrative heroic poem. Some of these probably had an oral origin and certainly were recited until recent times. The material used for manuscript was palm-leaf or locally-made paper. These stories, in which the hero performed as lover as well as warrior, differed from the Indian-based

stories in that the hero, capable perhaps of magic, was human and not a divine manifestation. Thirdly, from the 16th century developed long poems with an amatory motif which, in some types, continue to the present day. The most interesting variety is that of the lament of the lover absent from his beloved on a journey.

The Burmese conquest of 1767 produced in due course a strong literary revival. Many poems, known only as play-books or in short versions, were written down in full. This development occurred in the early part of the Bangkok period, from 1782, and most of the works then produced are available today. Traditional literature was strongly maintained throughout the 19th century but gradually, as court-based society became less dominant, began to give way to the prose fiction of modern times. The arrival of the printing press about 1840 was the original stimulus for change, and the printing of traditional literature and official material constituted the first phase. Slowly an interest in imaginative prose writing grew and was assisted by the foundation of literary magazines, though these were often ephemeral. The literary circle of King Vajiravudh (reigned 1810–25) introduced new western-influenced genres with their prose plays and stories. During the 1920s literature in paperback form based on old tales, new novelettish romances, and stories taken from films satisfied the emerging popular market, while newspapers and magazines provided a focus for the development of more serious fiction writing. Many writers were journalists, and this symbolised the change of emphasis from court to people in terms of patronage. Since Thailand was not colonised by Western powers, the change from classical to modern was a natural process. In the 1930s, women writers producing works of good quality became prominent alongside the journalists. The subject-matter of the numerous novels and short stories, whose output was unbroken except briefly during the Second World War, extended beyond romance to deal with important social questions. But the emphasis remained on human relationships and, with some important exceptions, socio-political writing did not develop strongly. However, the emergence of young writers in the aftermath of the 1974 upheavals has begun to change this emphasis towards overt political writing, and to a new interest in the pioneers of such writing of the 1950s. Modern literary developments in Laos and Cambodia have followed similar general lines to those of Thailand, but on a very small scale.

Vietnam. The long domination of China over Vietnam, from the 2nd century BC to the 10th century AD, had profound influences over literary development. Chinese characters, used with specific Vietnamese pronunciation, were employed in writing. After the period of direct Chinese control came to an end, a revised system of writing in characters continued to be used and only in the 19th century was a widespread change made to a roman alphabet based on an earlier invention by Christian missionaries. (See CHINA, *Literature*.) Important early historical works are known from the 14th century, and prose, as well as verse, has been widely employed in Vietnamese literature of the classical period. Narrative verse romances are popular, as are shorter poems of a lyric type, often with patriotic themes. During the 19th century magazines and books printed in roman characters signalled the emergence of modern literature; the poetic tradition was not, however, lost but was adapted to contemporary needs. Political and patriotic themes as well as those of romance have always been popular. Censorship during the colonial period was a limiting factor in literary development and in North Vietnam a committed Communist literature with specific aims and intentions developed, prior to reunification.

Philippines. Literary development in the Philippines has been very strongly influenced by outside forces. The Spanish conquest of 1565, and subsequent occupation, was followed by the American period from 1896. Thus Spanish and English were introduced and inevitably became the media for literary work. Pre-conquest literature was mainly oral and in verse. Tagalog eventually emerged as the most important literary language after writing in a roman script had been introduced during the Spanish occupation. Poetic romances, influenced by the Spanish, were produced in local metres, together with some dramatic work in vernacular languages. The growth of local literature dates from the recent past with the encouragment of the use of vernacular languages, particularly Tagalog (called Filipino since 1959). A tradition of drama and the novel is now well established, common themes being patriotic and nationalistic.

Indonesia and Malaysia. Literary traditions in Indonesia reach back a thousand years to literature in Old Javanese. Indian, particularly Hindu, influences were strong in Old Javanese epic literature and through this medium the heroic poems of India, the *Rāmāyana* and the *Mahābhārata*, were brought to Indonesia. These works, as adapted and subjected to Islamic influence, and many others of Muslim derivation, have given a strong and continuing impulse to the traditional drama in Indonesia. Though later literature in Javanese continued to be produced after the conversion of Java to Islam, Old Javanese literature was preserved in Bali, which did not become Muslim.

Old Malay literature has not survived in the same sense but the Malay language has been used as a trade language throughout the islands for centuries. A literary aspect to Malay developed in the Muslim state of Malacca in the 15th century and became the basis for 'classical' Malay, written in Arabic script, as opposed to the south-Indian based scripts employed for such languages as Javanese and Balinese. Other important centres for Malay in its literary aspect were Acheh in north Sumatra and the Minangkabau region further south. Eventually Malay as used in Indonesia came to be written in roman script during the period of Dutch rule. In British Malaya a more conservative tradition prevailed.

The impulse for a common modern language for Indonesia was political. It was seen as a possible unifying factor among the several hundred different, but mostly related, languages of the islands. In 1928, arising from a conference held by young nationalists in what is now Jakarta, the term Bahasa Indonesia was first used for a language which has developed an important literature of its own. The language evolved from modern Malay, as used in Indonesia since the early part of the 20th century, and a modern literature and outlets for publication already existed when the nationalists encouraged its rapid development during the 1930s. The Japanese occupation of Indonesia, when Dutch was proscribed, furthered its use, and by the war of independence there had developed a group of prose and poetry writers who had strong links with the world of journalism.

The older nationalist writers, the literary and linguistic theoretician T. S. Alijahbana, the novelists the Pane brothers, the poet Amir Hamzah, concerned with the periodical *Pudjangga Baru*, were joined by younger men who later became known as 'the generation of 1945'. Prominent among them was the poet Chairil Anwar, whose work has become widely known through English translation. Literary controversy has always been a feature of the modern Indonesian literary scene and this was particularly bitter during the late 1950s and early 1960s, when modern writers of generally 'humanist' attitudes clashed with the committed writers associated with LEKRA, the Communist cultural organisation. Many writers, such as H. B. Jassin and Mochtar Lubis, suffered at this time, but a change came after the establishment of a new régime in 1965.

A characteristic of modern Indonesia is the co-existence of vital new writing in poetry, in prose fiction, and in the drama. Traditional drama also continues in Java and Bali, and new, important popular forms have developed in east and central Java.

In the Malay states literary interests remained more traditional until independence in 1957, but a new phase developed in the 1970s through writers who sought to serve Malaysia's national aspirations.

See also CHINA, *Literature*; INDIA, *Literature*; JAPAN, *Literature*; OCEANIA, LITERATURE AND FOLKLORE; ORIENTAL DRAMA.

South-Eastern League, ephemeral anti-Communist republic which existed in 1918 in the south-east of European Russia. It was originally formed in October 1917 as a regional organisation of COSSACKS, Caucasian mountain peoples, and the nomadic peoples of the northern Caucasus. After the Bolshevik seizure of power (see OCTOBER REVOLUTION) it proclaimed itself an independent state, but soon disintegrated.

South Foreland, see FORELAND, NORTH AND SOUTH.

South Georgia, island in the South Atlantic Ocean lying between 54°00′ S and 54°55′ S and 35°45′ W and 38°05′ W. It is about 169 km long and 32 km wide with steep glaciated mountains and an indented coastline. It is part of the FALKLAND ISLANDS DEPENDENCIES. South Georgia probably was first sighted in 1675 by Antonio de la Roche sailing in a British merchant ship. James Cook landed here in 1775 and took possession for King George III, after whom the island is named. There is a whaling station at Grytviken.

South Holland, province of the Netherlands, bounded on the north by North Holland, on the east by Utrecht and North Brabant, on the south by Zeeland, and on the west by the North Sea. It lies mostly below sea-level. The chief industry is agriculture, and there is considerable shipping trade. The chief towns are The HAGUE (capital), ROTTERDAM, DORDRECHT, and LEIDEN. Area 3325 km²; population 3,018,000.

South Island, see NEW ZEALAND.

South Kazakhstan, see CHIMKENT.

South Kirkby, town in WAKEFIELD District, West York-

South Korea

shire, England, 15 km south of Wakefield town centre. Coal-mining is a very important industry in South Kirkby and the surrounding area. Population (1971) 11,219.

South Korea, or officially the Republic of Korea, came into being in 1948 when an independent republic was established south of the 38th parallel as a result of the UN-supervised elections. It is bounded on the north by NORTH KOREA, on the west by the Yellow Sea, on the south by the Korea Strait, and on the east by the Sea of Japan. It occupies the major part of the Korean peninsula (see KOREA). Capital, SEOUL. Area 98,000 km². Population (1975) 34,708,500. See ATLAS 37.

Economy. In contrast to North Korea, South Korea has remained very firmly within the orbit of the anti-Communist nations and in particular has been strongly supported by the USA. This support has taken the form of very substantial economic aid and also the stationing of US armed forces in South Korea in order to deter North Korea from aggression. In May 1961 a military régime headed by General PARK Chung Hee took over the government, and although in theory civilian government was restored in 1963 under President Park, who had meanwhile retired from the army, South Korea has remained a very closely controlled one-party state.

The principal areas of agriculture and settlement in South Korea lie on or near the west coast. However, south-east Korea, particularly around the city of PUSAN, is also well populated in parts. Before the partition of Korea, about 60 per cent of the total population lived in the area now occupied by South Korea. After the Korean War, about two million people moved from North Korea into South Korea and in addition many former emigrants returned to South Korea from Japan. The present population of South Korea, at 35 million, is thus considerably larger than that of North Korea. Because of the influx of people, South Korea's difficulties were considerably greater than those of North Korea after the Korean War. The towns became enormously swollen with refugees; there was a great deal of unemployment; all power supplies, which had previously been derived from the north, had been cut off; and the major industrial areas, which were located in the north, were denied to South Korea.

South Korea. The chemical plant at Pusan. *(Barnaby's Picture Library)*

Nevertheless, in recent years economic progress has been substantial, in large part because, as in the case of TAIWAN, the US has been determined to turn South Korea into a showcase for capitalism in an Asian setting.

Agriculture remains the basis of the economy, but industry has grown rapidly during the last decade or so. Winters are much milder than in the north aı.d areas suitable for agriculture more extensive. One important measure has been the carrying out of a partial land reform, under which more land has been distributed to peasant families. In addition, irrigation facilities have been greatly expanded. More marginal land has been brought under cultivation and the application of chemical fertilisers has been significantly increased. The result of these and other measures of agricultural development has been a notable improvement in agricultural output, for example the production of rice rose from 3 million t in 1955 to over 4·6 million t by 1975. In the production of other food crops, such as barley and sweet potatoes, there have been increases of the same order. Nevertheless, because of its dramatic increase in population, South Korea remains a food deficit area and it is debatable whether the cultivated area can be extended very much more.

Apart from some deposits of anthracite in the south-east, South Korea has few mineral resources upon which to base a programme of industrialisation. However, the combination of an abundant labour force, political stability, and a high level of overseas aid and investment, has resulted in significant industrial development in South Korea. Exports of industrial goods have risen markedly in recent years and industrial products now account for over half the total value of all exports. The United States and Japan are South Korea's chief trading partners. A wide variety of light consumer goods is now being produced by South Korea and the first steps have been taken in establishing motor car manufacture. Additionally, the production of steel, fertilisers, and cement have increased markedly. The principal industrial cities are Seoul (the capital city) and Pusan. In all more than half of South Korea's population lives in towns and cities and it will only be through further industrial development that employment problems will be solved. Fortunately, there has been a good deal of international investment in manufacturing in South Korea during the last decade and its future prospects would seem to depend upon whether peace can be maintained with its bellicose northern neighbour.

Bibliography: D. C. Cole and P. N. Lyman, *Korean Development: The Interplay of Politics and Economics*, 1971; G. T. Brown, *Korean Pricing Policies and Economic Development in the 1960s*, 1974; see also under KOREA.

Government. Constitution. The constitution of December 1972 defines the state simply as a 'democratic republic'. An electoral college, the National Conference for Reunification, with 2539 popularly-elected members (banned from having any party affiliation) elects the president of the republic and 73 non-constituency members of the National Assembly.

Legislature. The executive consists of the president, the prime minister, and the State Council of 20 ministers and heads of government agencies. All these are appointed by the president subject to confirmation by the National Assembly. The assembly has 146 constituency members and 73 non-constituency members. Its main function under the constitution is to consider the budget during its one regular annual session of 90 days. As the financial year starts on 1 January, the session is usually called in September. In this session and during special sessions of up to 30 days each, which may be called at any time by any party, as well as in its committees which function continuously, the assembly can question any government policy or appointment, and it also discusses bills, most of which are formulated by the State Council. After assembly approval, laws are promulgated by presidential decree. There is provision in the constitution for local government, but this has not yet been implemented. Local officials are appointed by the Minister of Home Affairs.

Justice. The judges of the Supreme Court are appointed by a panel nominated by the president and the legislature. Judges of lower courts are appointed by the Minister of Justice, usually on the recommendation of the Chief Justice and the Bar Association. Trials are conducted by single judges or panels of judges. The prosecution is under the control of the Ministry of Justice, which also administers the 23 prisons. There is a national police force under the Ministry of Home Affairs.

Armed Forces. The armed forces are directed by the joint chiefs of staff, who are subject to the National Security Council. This consists of the president, the prime minister, and seven members of the State Council. The army has a strength of 600,000 regulars and conscripts, with annual reserve training in the Homeland Reserve Force after discharge. The air force is equipped with US fighter-bombers and the navy with patrol boats and destroyers. South Korea has been pressing the USA for many years for assistance in building up an armaments industry of its own, and in 1975 it made a point of declaring that it has the technical ability to produce nuclear weapons.

Education. Primary education (ages 6–12) is compulsory, and there are about six million children at primary schools. Entry to middle school (ages 12–15) is nonselective, and about 70 per cent of children attend (some two million pupils). Selection for high school is by national examination, for which some 80 per cent of middle school pupils apply, of whom about 85 per cent find places. There are about 400,000 pupils in academic high schools and 350,000 in vocational high schools. Entry to higher education is by national qualifying examination, which some 100,000 sit annually for 60,000 places at 72 universities and 30 or so other institutions. Every large city and every province has a national university, and the remaining 60 are private, but subject to licensing by the Ministry of Education. About 250,000 students are in higher education. A University of the Air was inaugurated in 1972. The latest official illiteracy rate is 11 per cent of the population over age 12 in 1970.

Welfare. There are some welfare services, including a certain amount of municipal housing in the cities, but medical services and housing are generally run on commercial lines and are far from adequate for the poor.

Religion. The religions of South Korea have been animism, Buddhism, and Confucianism, which was the official faith between 1392 and 1910. The ban on Roman Catholics was lifted in 1882 and they now number nearly 4 million.

Official Language. The official language is Korean. It is government policy to encourage spelling in the Korean alphabet only, but the tradition of using Chinese characters to write words of Chinese origin persists strongly, particularly in newspapers.

National Anthem. The East Sea and Mount Paektu, first adopted in the last years of the Yi dynasty, when it was sung to the tune of *Auld Lang Syne.* The author of the words is now established as being Yun Chi-ho (1866–1945). Since 1948 it has been sung to a tune composed in 1904–05.

National Flag. A disc divided horizontally by an S-shaped line, red above and blue below, on a white background with parallel black bars in each corner.

History. The Republic of Korea was established in the southern half of Korea on 15 August 1948. The Korean War (see KOREAN HISTORY), which broke out in June 1950 and ended in a truce signed in July 1953, ruined South Korea. The country lost 226,000 troops. South Korea's economic recovery was hindered under Syngman RHEE and Chang Myon by poor planning and inefficient execution, involving wide corruption. Since 1961 successive economic plans have been more capably worked out and implemented with increasing confidence. Capital has been provided almost entirely by foreign loans, mainly from the USA and Japan. The resumption of diplomatic relations with Japan in 1964 was a major factor in this recovery. Since 1971 industrial growth has been one of the fastest in the world, particularly in international trade. The Saemaul, or 'New Communities' campaign, inaugurated in the spring of 1971, has noticeably spread the benefits of increasing prosperity into the rural areas.

The South seems recently to be more resigned to the division of the country, but it continues to warn the world of the dangers of compromise with Communism, and sternly represses any political movement in the South whose aims coincide in any way with those proclaimed by the North. Syngman Rhee's government was overthrown by popular demonstrations in April 1960, and a Democratic party prime minister, Chang Myon, presided over a year of political confusion, which was ended by a military coup in May 1961. The leader of the military junta, PARK Chung Hee, was elected president, as candidate of a new party, the Democratic 1970s. In February 1977 the USA announced proposals for the phased withdrawal of ground troops from South Korea. party, in October 1963, and re-elected in May 1967, and, after amendment of the constitution, again in April 1971. In October 1972 President Park suspended the South Korean constitution and in November a national referendum approved what was called the Yushin, or 'Revitalisation', constitution. Political and humanitarian talks have been held with North Korea since the early 1970s.

See also NORTH KOREA, *History.*

Bibliography: J. A. Kim, *Divided Korea: The Politics of Development 1945–1972*, 1975.

South Lancashire Regiment, The (The Prince of Wales's Volunteers),

a British regiment formed in Nova Scotia in 1717 as Phillip's Regiment of Foot, becoming 40th Foot in 1751 and bearing the title 'The 40th (2nd Somersetshire Regiment of Foot)' from 1782 to 1881. It served in Canada until 1761. In 1881 it amalgamated with 82nd Foot (The Prince of Wales's Volunteers) to form

The South Lancashire Regiment (Prince of Wales's Volunteers). The regiment's battle honours prior to the First World War include Louisburg, Havana, Montevideo, the Peninsular War, Niagra, Waterloo, Kandahah, Ghuznee, Cabool, Maharajpore, Sevastopol, Lucknow, New Zealand, and the Relief of Ladysmith. The 40th Foot served with distinction at Waterloo, the anniversary of which is a Regimental Day. In the First World War battalions of the regiment fought in every major theatre of the war and won four VCs. In the Second World, battalions of the regiment fought with distinction at Dunkirk, in Madagascar, Burma, and in north-western Europe, the 1st Battalion being one of those to make the initial landing during the Normandy Landings. In 1958 the regiment amalgamated with The East Lancashire Regiment to form The Lancashire Regiment (Prince of Wales's Volunteers). In 1970 The Lancashire Regiment (Prince of Wales's Volunteers) and The Loyal Regiment (North Lancashire) were amalgamated to form The Queen's Lancashire Regiment.

South Molton, a market town in Devon, England, 16 km south-east of Barnstaple, with charters granted by Elizabeth I and Charles II. The church of St Mary Magdalene is largely Perpendicular. South Molton is the centre of an agricultural district; the annual sheep fair is held on the first Wednesday of August. Local industries include shirtmaking, building, tanning, dyeing and cleaning, and woodworking. Population (1971) 2975.

South Orkney Islands, group of mountainous, ice- and snow-covered islands lying in the South Atlantic Ocean between 60°20′ and 60°50′S and 44°20′ and 46°45′W. They were discovered in 1821 by a joint expedition of the British Capt. George Powell and the American Capt. Nathaniel Palmer. The islands lie within the BRITISH ANTARCTIC TERRITORY.

South Ossetian Autonomous Oblast lies in the GEORGIAN SSR, USSR, on the southern slopes of the main CAUCASUS range. The economy is based on sheep and goat breeding, and some handicraft industries. The *oblast* was formed in 1922; capital, TSKHINVALI. Area 3900 km². Population (1975) 103,000 (37 per cent urban).
See also OSSETIANS.

South Pembrokeshire, new district of the county of DYFED, south-west Wales. Area 545 km²; population (1975) 38,060.

South Platte, river of the USA, rising near Mount Lincoln on the eastern slope of the Rocky Mountains, and flowing through South Park northwards to Nebraska, where it unites with the North Platte and forms the PLATTE river. It provides irrigation water for the northern part of the COLORADO Piedmont, and has had to be supplemented by stream diversions across the continental divide.

South Pole, see ANTARCTICA; ANTARCTIC EXPLORATION.

South Sandwich Islands, chain of volcanic islands lying in the South Atlantic Ocean extending from 56°18′ S to 59°27′ S in about 26°30′ W. They were discovered in 1775 by James Cook who called them Sandwich Land for the fourth Earl of Sandwich, First Lord of the Admiralty.

The Traverse Islands, forming the northern end of the chain, were discovered by Bellingshausen in 1819. They are part of the FALKLAND ISLANDS DEPENDENCIES (UK).

South Sea Bubble, name popularly given to a British financial scheme under which the directors of the South Sea Company (incorporated in 1710 by an act which gave to it the monopoly of trading in the Pacific Ocean and along the east coast of South America from the Orinoco to Cape Horn) made an offer to the government in 1720 to pay off the whole National Debt and to buy up the irredeemable annuities, amounting to £800,000 a year, provided the different public securities were consolidated into one fund in their hands and the government gave the company certain exclusive commercial privileges. The Bank of England projected a rival scheme, but Parliament accepted that of the South Sea Company, which had, in spite of the limited privileges conceded to it in the ASSIENTO by Spain, been highly successful in the slave trade. The moot question was whether the fund-holders would convert their stock for shares in the company, for they could not be compelled to do so. The issue, however, was not long in doubt, as the public, inflamed by the brilliant prospects held out by the directors of the gold and silver lands awaiting exploitation in South America, crowded into the rush for shares. £110 shares rose in price to £1000, the public disregarding the high improbability of the company being able to make a profit of 50 per cent in order to pay interest at the rate of 5 per cent. The fever of speculation did not end with the South Sea Company. Numerous other concerns, for the most part of a bogus nature, competed for public favour. The South Sea Company's prosecution of some of these concerns merely served to open the eyes of the public to the recklessness of its own scheme, and its shares dropped to £135, with the result that though the few who had sold out reaped enormous profits, the majority of those who had 'held on' were ruined, and the failure assumed the proportions of a gigantic financial disaster. Sir Robert Walpole did much to restore national credit by arranging to assign £9 million of South Sea stock to the Bank of England, a like amount to the East India Company, and to repay the bonus of £7·5 million which the government had received. By this combined operation the proprietors and subscribers got back about one-third of their money.
Bibliography: L. Melville, *The South Sea Bubble*, 1921; V. Cowles, *The Great Swindle*, 1961.

South Shetland Islands, archipelago of 12 islands lying 1000 km south-east of Cape Horn, between 61°S and 63°S and extending 450 km between 54°W and 63°W. The chief islands are Livingstone, Smith, Clarence, King George I, Elephant, and Deception. They were discovered and named by Capt. William Smith in 1819, and are now part of the BRITISH ANTARCTIC TERRITORY.

South Shields, see SOUTH TYNESIDE.

South Staffordshire Regiment, The, a British regiment, formerly the 38th and 80th Regiments. The 38th, raised in 1705, served in operations in the West Indies, America, Flanders, Cape of Good Hope, Montevideo, the Peninsula, Burma, Crimea, and the Indian Mutiny. The 80th, raised in 1793, served in operations in Flanders (1794), Egypt (1801), the Sikh Wars, Burma, the Indian

Mutiny, and the Zulu Wars. The two regiments were linked in 1881 to form the present regiment, which served in Egypt (1882), the Sudan, and in the South African War. During the First World War it raised 18 battalions, which served in France, Flanders, Italy, Gallipoli, and Egypt. In the Second World War the regiment fought in the Dunkirk campaign, in Normandy, and at Arnhem (1944); in North Africa and Sicily; and in Burma as Chindits. The North and South Staffordshire Regiments were amalgamated in 1959, as The Staffordshire Regiment (The Prince of Wales's).

South Tyneside, district of TYNE AND WEAR, England, occupying an area of 64 km². South Tyneside extends from the south bank of the lower Tyne to the outskirts of SUNDERLAND, including the industrial towns of South Shields, HEBBURN, and JARROW.

A low plateau of magnesian limestone with cliffs up to 30 m high falls eastwards to low undulating country at Jarrow Slake. South Shields was the site of a Roman fort and signal station and of a medieval river port. At Jarrow a 7th-century monastery for a time housed the Venerable BEDE. These settlements took their present form in the 18th and 19th centuries, however. The relatively deep and sheltered reach of the Tyne west of South Shields was used for many centuries by colliers waiting to sail to London. The availability of coal and sand ballast favoured the growth of a glass industry in the 17th century and of chemical manufacture in the 18th century. Coal-mining has taken place within the district for several centuries and two working mines remain. The integrated shipyards at Jarrow closed in the 1930s but heavy electrical industries remained at Hebburn. Subsequent diversification of industry has created employment on trading estates in light engineering, electronics, and food processing. The present population of the district is 12 per cent lower than that of 1921. Population (1971) 172,000.

South Wales Borderers, The, a British regiment, the old 24th Foot, raised in 1689, fought under William III in Ireland and Flanders. It distinguished itself in Marlborough's campaigns, and also in the Peninsula under Wellington. Further honours were gained during the Sikh war (1848–49) in India. Two outstanding events in the regiment's history are connected with the Zulu war of 1877–89; at Isandlwana, the colour was saved by Lts. Melvill and Coghill, both of whom lost their lives while crossing the Buffalo River; and RORKE'S DRIFT was defended heroically, one company withstanding a force of 4000 Zulus. During the First World War the regiment raised 18 battalions, which served in France, Flanders, Macedonia, Gallipoli, Egypt, Mesopotamia, and Tsingtao. In the Second World War units of the regiment served in Norway, north-western Europe, North Africa, and Burma. The Monmouthshire Regiment, a territorial regiment, formed part of the corps of the South Wales Borderers. On 11 June 1969 the regiment amalgamated with The Welsh Regiment to form The Royal Regiment of Wales (24th/41st Foot).

Bibliography: J. Adams, *The South Wales Borderers,* 1968.

South-West Africa, or Namibia, territory on the south-western coast of Africa, bounded on the north by Angola and Zambia, on the east by Botswana, on the south-east by South Africa, and on the west by the Atlantic Ocean.

Once a German colony, South-West Africa has been administered by South Africa since 1920, under increasing hostility from the international community. Area 853,000 km².

Geography. Relief. The country consists of a coastal desert region, the Namib desert, ranging from 100 ʰto 160 km in width, mountainous central highlands, and the eastern KALAHARI region. The Namib lies parallel with the Atlantic Ocean. It is mainly uninhabited, except for a few places such as the diamond workings at the mouth of the Orange river, and the ports of LÜDERITZ, WALVIS BAY (South African), and SWAKOPMUND. The central plateau (average altitude 1100 m) is a watershed between the Namib and the Kalahari. The boundary rivers, such as the ORANGE, CUNENE, OKAVANGO, and Chobi, are the only permanent ones, but these do not rise in South-West Africa. See ATLAS 46.

Climate. In the Namib the annual rainfall is only 20 mm on average, although the coastal area has high humidity. The mean temperature in the central area varies from 22 °C in the centre to 16 °C on the coast, modified by altitude in the first case and by the cold Benguela ocean current in the second. During the summer months parts of the Namib reach 38 °C, and as high as 49 °C has been recorded.

Population. The country is very sparsely populated. The total population was 852,000 in 1974, and 90,583 were whites. Bantu-speaking groups of the indigenous population include the HERERO, Kakovelders, OVAMBO, East Caprivians, Okavango, and a small group of TSWANA; other distinctive groups are the BUSHMEN, NAMA, Rehoboth Basters, and coloureds. The Ovambo and Okavango are closely related and form more than half the population. The white population is almost wholly Afrikaans or German-speaking. The main towns are WALVIS BAY (South African), WINDHOEK (the capital), LÜDERITZ, and SWAKOPMUND.

Bibliography: H. Vedder, L. Fowie and C. H. L. Hahn, *The Native Tribes of South-West Africa,* 1928; J. P. Van S. Bruwer, *South-West Africa: The Disputed Land,* 1969.

Economy. The monetised economy is concentrated in the south (Police Zone), the sector of white settlement. African labour is recruited under contract from the north, and from 'homelands' in the south. Apart from loans and subsidies, South Africa supplies nearly half the capital investment and 90 per cent of total imports, and receives half the exports. Foreign capital controlled 61 per cent of investment in mining and manufacturing in 1966. Over one-third of the gross domestic product accrues to foreign capital as repatriated profits and dividends.

Agriculture. Cattle contribute 60 per cent of commercial agricultural output. White cattle ownership totalled 1·8 million in 1971. There are 4·5 million karakul sheep, and South-West Africa is the leading exporter of pelts. Two-thirds of cattle exports and 40 per cent of the dairy output is sold to South Africa. By 1964 fishing was second to mining as an export earner. Sixty-nine per cent of the catch (760,000 t in 1975) is pilchards. The introduction of fishing by factory ships since 1966 and the danger of over-fishing have prompted measures to control the volume of the catch. Fish meal, fish oil, and canning industries have expanded rapidly. Gross sales of fish products have averaged £33 million to £40 million in recent years.

South-West Africa

Industry. Minerals are the largest single contributor to exports, gross national product, and revenue. Revenue totalled £79·6 million in 1970; production is worth about £150 million per annum. The 18 mining companies are all in the southern sector. Diamonds, mainly from alluvial deposits in the coastal belt, account for just over half the total production. Base minerals, whose share has been increasing, include copper (especially from TSU-MEB), lead, zinc, manganese, tin, vanadium, and others. Five new mines (three for copper) opened between 1969 and 1973. Production at the Rossing uranium mine, the largest in southern Africa, is expected to reach 5,000 t in 1978. No official production statistics have been issued since 1966.

Manufacturing is confined to processing perishable goods, finishing and assembling materials from South Africa, and specialised repair and construction work. Construction industries have boomed with increased road-building since 1960.

Communications. The network serves primarily the southern sector. By the end of 1972 there were 2756 km of tarred roads (none in 1953). The 2326 km of railways are subsidised by South Africa. The system includes links to the ports of WALVIS BAY and LÜDERITZ. WINDHOEK has an international airport.

Trade. Official figures have been incorporated with those of South Africa since 1957. In 1970 exports were valued at £135 million, imports at £92 million.

Bibliography: J. H. Wellington, *South West Africa and its Human Issues*, 1967.

Government. *Administration.* The Republic of SOUTH AFRICA has been responsible for the administration of South-West Africa (Namibia) since 1920, when the then Union accepted a mandate from the League of Nations to administer the territory as an integral part of the Union. With the demise of the League of Nations, South Africa continued to administer the area. The country is represented in the South African Parliament by six members, and in the Senate by two elected and two nominated (by the South African State President) members. There are four self-governing regional administrations: for Whites, the Ovambo, Kavango, and Lozi (Eastern Caprivi), covering 68 per cent of the population. These exercise certain local functions; other functions are exercised by relevant South African departments, mainly through local representatives. There is also the SWA Coloured Council, consisting of six elected members and five appointed by the South African government, which also appoints the chairman of the Council's executive.

Justice. Romano-Dutch law is followed, as administered in the Cape Province of South Africa; certain Acts of the South African Parliament are applicable directly to the territory, e.g. proclamations of the State President or the administrator, ordinances of the Legislative Assembly, portions of the German law specially preserved, and which do not conflict with any of the above.

Education. The pattern of education is similar to that in South Africa in that the Department of National Education and the Department of Bantu Education carry similar responsibilities, the latter in conjunction with the Ovambo and other Homeland Education departments. In 1973 there were 493 schools in Namibia catering for 115,488 African primary and secondary pupils. They were taught by 2522 African and 140 White teachers. There were also 23,000 White children in over 60 schools taught by 1700 teachers. Schooling increased among the Ovambo from 85 schools and 21,010 pupils in 1961 to 259 schools and 70,241 pupils in 1973, and the number of teachers in the same period rose from 445 to 1449. Among the Kavango in 1973 there were 14,635 pupils taught by 245 teachers at 115 schools.

Welfare. The same system applies as in South Africa. In 1974 there were five homes for the aged (one state and four aided), and a home for Afrıcans had been established in Damaraland. There were 27 hospitals and 50 clinical centres in the 'Homelands' providing 3441 beds. In addition 17 hospitals serve all population groups and 21 the White population only, the latter providing 1085 beds. In the year 1972–73 expenditure on health services amounted to 10·1 million Rand compared with 2 million ten years earlier. Other than Whites, patients are entitled to free medical, including specialist, treatment. In 1974 there were 39 White medical practitioners serving the 'Homelands' but no African practitioners.

Armed Forces. The defence of the territory is the responsibility of the Republic of South Africa. There is a small garrison at Windhoek, composed of a battalion of infantry of the citizen force, and artillery units. In addition, since 1974 South African forces (estimated at 40,000) have been increasingly involved in seeking to secure the Namibian–Angolan border against the infiltration of SWAPO guerrillas. Following a border incident in August 1975, when the Chief Minister of Ovamboland was murdered, the security forces decided to carry out 'hot pursuit' tactics which developed into a major offensive against SWAPO bases in Angola.

Official Languages. English, German, and Afrikaans.

History. In the early 1880s F. A. W. Lüderitz, a German merchant, purchased part of the south-west African coast from the NAMA chiefs in the vicinity and placed his acquisition under the protection of the German Empire in 1884, which gradually extended its authority over the whole territory. Following the First World War, South-West Africa came under League of Nations mandate, with South Africa as the administering authority. After the Second World War South Africa sought to incorporate the territory into the Union but, largely because of the Rev. Michael Scott's championship of the HERERO cause, the UN General Assembly proposed that the territory should be placed under the UN Trusteeship System. South Africa refused and since 1946 the United Nations has been trying by persuasion or demand to wrest South-West Africa from South African control. The issue has been continually referred to the International Court of Justice which, between 1949 and 1971, handed down five opinions on various aspects of the case. On 21 June 1971 the Court concluded by 13 votes to 2 that South Africa's presence in South-West Africa was illegal and that it was under obligation to withdraw its administration immediately. This view was endorsed by the Security Council but so far (1976) South Africa has not complied. Various other UN bodies have taken up the Namibian cause; in 1966 the General Assembly terminated the mandate and the following year established a UN Council to administer the territory, which in future was to be called Namibia. Hitherto no member of the Council has been able to enter the territory although the Security Council has asked the secretary-general to report regularly on the position.

The *Odendaal Commission* was appointed by the South African government in 1962 to inquire into the 'moral welfare and social progress' of, particularly, the black inhabitants of the territory and produced a plan for 'separate development' of the various racial groups which the South African government has since set out to implement by the establishment of separate administrations under the general aegis of Pretoria for the OVAMBO, the Kavango, and the LOZI in East Caprivi. Other HOMELANDS are being developed in DAMARALAND, HEREROLAND, and Kaokoveld. Together the homelands will occupy about 25 per cent of the total territory of Namibia. European farmland comprises 48 per cent.

The South West Africa People's Organisation (SWAPO), the Namibian organisation recognised by the African Liberation Committee of the Organisation of African Unity (OAU), refuses to accept an APARTHEID policy in Namibia and since 1966 has engaged in intermittent guerrilla activity in the territory.

Based on Angola, the civil war in that country enabled the guerrillas to take advantage of the confusion on the border to penetrate more deeply into Namibia than before and engage with South African troops, who also took the opportunity to try and track down SWAPO bases north of the Namibian border.

Meanwhile, at the beginning of September 1975, the South African government sponsored a Constitutional Conference in Windhoek, on the future of Namibia. One hundred and fifty six delegates from eleven ethnic groups attended the Conference (including whites and Bushmen) and the Conference produced a 'declaration of intent', envisaging independence by 1978 as a loose confederation of ethnic territories, rather on the Swiss model. The Declaration was sent to the UN General Assembly, but SWAPO and an umbrella organisation, the Namibian National Convention (NNC), which were not invited, attacked and rejected the Conference because of its ethnic basis, and reiterated their goal of a unitary state in Namibia. The Conference, however, resumed its deliberations in March 1976 to try and agree a new constitution for the territory. Final agreement was reached early in March 1977 on the structure of an interim government which was to be formed in order to lead Namibia to full independence by 31 December 1978.

South Yorkshire, see YORKSHIRE, SOUTH.

Southall, see EALING.

Southampton, Henry Wriothesley, 3rd Earl of
(1573–1624), English courtier, Shakespeare's patron. He succeeded his father, the 2nd Earl, in 1581, and studied at Cambridge and Gray's Inn. From 1590 he was prominent at court, and Shakespeare dedicated *Venus and Adonis* and *The Rape of Lucrece* to him. Southampton was involved in Essex's Irish conspiracy, and was sentenced to death. But the sentence was commuted to life imprisonment, and he was later freed and restored to royal favour by James I. He was actively involved in the Virginia and East India companies. Southampton died while serving against the Spaniards in the Netherlands.

Bibliography: A. L. Rowse, *Shakespeare's Southampton*, 1965.

Southampton, district council, parliamentary borough, and seaport in HAMPSHIRE, England, on a peninsula between the Test and Itchen rivers, at the head of Southampton Water, 20 km south-west of Winchester. Southampton was a Roman settlement in AD 43; the Roman *Clausentum* was on the promontory east of the Itchen. Early in the Saxon or Jutish invasion a settlement, Hamwih, was formed on the other side of the Itchen and on the east of the peninsula between Itchen and the Test. After the Teutonic invasions Southampton developed into a port of some standing, but the old walled town was not established until the Conquest. The Bargate still stands in the main street; two other gates remain, and four of the towers. The Norman House and Canute's Palace are among the oldest examples of Norman domestic architecture in Great Britain. The Tudor House (c. 1535) is now a museum. In Winkle Street is the ancient hospital of God's House, founded in 1185 for the entertainment of strangers and of pilgrims going to the shrine of St Swithin at Winchester, or to Canterbury. St Michael's (early Norman, with features of later date) is the oldest church in Southampton; its disproportionately high spire was originally a landmark (built c. 1745) for navigators. A memorial column marks the place of embarkation of the Pilgrim Fathers on the *Mayflower* in August 1620. A charter of incorporation was granted to the town by Henry I. It was created a county by Henry VI. In the reigns of Edward III and Richard II, as today, it was one of the chief ports of embarkation for troops engaged in foreign wars. The university (see SOUTHAMPTON, UNIVERSITY OF) lies to the north of Southampton. Southampton has five grammar schools, including King Edward VI School, founded in 1554, and Taunton's School, founded in 1760, both with additional new buildings, and there is provision for commercial and technical education. The Merchant Navy School of Navigation is at the mouth of the River Hamble. The buildings comprising the new civic centre include the municipal offices and council chamber, the law courts and police offices, and guildhall, the central and dominating feature of the centre. The extensive town parks of Southampton stretch for 800 m through the heart of the business part of the city.

The modern importance of Southampton is due to its magnificent natural harbour, which enjoys a double tide, and to its docks, which can accommodate the largest liners. The building of the modern system of docks was begun in 1838, ownership passing successively to the Southampton Dock Company, the London and South-West Railway, and in 1948 to the British Transport Commission. The Old Docks, covering some 80 ha, contain three large tidal basins, known as the Ocean, Empress, and Outer Docks, with a total quay length of 6·4 km. The New Docks, completed in 1934, facing the River Test, afford 2·4 km of deep water quay dredged to a maximum depth of 12 m at low water ordinary spring tide. The provision of modern quayside accommodation and cargo handling equipment, together with good rail and road communication, enables ships using the docks to make a quick turn-round. At the extreme western end of the New Docks is the King George V graving dock. It is 366 m long and 41 m wide at its entrance; it was built primarily for the *Queen Mary* and can take vessels up to 100,000 t gross. Immediately behind the New Docks 53 ha of reclaimed land have been developed as an industrial estate. The Ocean passenger terminal building, constructed especially for the transatlantic service, is one of the finest in the world. Steamers from the port sail to all parts of the world, although passenger traffic has been reduced drastically due to competition from air travel and most of the large passenger liners have ceased operating. Southampton is the chief passenger port and, after London and Liverpool, the busiest port in the UK. Southampton airport is now under private ownership and has scheduled and charter services. The Royal Pier, 305 m long, is used chiefly in connection with the passenger, motor-car, and cargo traffic to and from the Isle of Wight. There are motor body works at the town's north-eastern suburb of Swaythling. Southampton is growing in importance as a manufacturing centre, many well-known makers of goods having factories in and around the town. There are many shipbuilding and repair yards.

Southampton was frequently bombed during the Second World War; in all there were some 57 air raids. The dock area and many municipal buildings suffered heavily and over 3000 dwellings were destroyed or made totally uninhabitable. Several churches were destroyed; the ancient structure of Holy Rood, though severely damaged, has been preserved as a memorial to the men of the Merchant Navy.

Population (1971) 215,118.

Bibliography: C. Platt, *Medieval Southampton: The Port and Trading Community, AD 1000–1600*, 1973; C. Platt and R. Coleman-Smith (Eds), *Excavations in Medieval Southampton, 1953–69*, 1974.

Southampton, University of, opened as the Hartley Institution in 1862, was incorporated as a college of London University in 1902 and constituted a university by royal charter in 1952. The campus is situated in Highfield, 3 km north of the city centre and now has a theatre, concert hall, two art galleries, and a photographic gallery. There are faculties of arts, science, engineering and applied science, social sciences, educational studies, law, and medicine. There are over 4000 undergraduate and 1000 postgraduate students.

Southampton Water, inlet of the English Channel, stretching from the Solent and Spithead into Hampshire, England, for about 18 km. Its greatest breadth is 3·2 km. Southampton Water forms a first-rate natural harbour, the Isle of Wight forming a natural breakwater, giving the area a double high tide.

Southborough, town in Tunbridge Wells District of Kent, England, largely of 19th-century growth. Population (1971) 9505.

Southcott, Joanna (1750–1814), English religious visionary, born at Gittisham in Devonshire, daughter of a farmer. About 1792 she declared herself to be the woman of Revelation xii, and gave forth prophecies in rhyme, several collections of which were published. Her prescriptions for universal happiness are said to have been sealed in a box which her followers will only allow Anglican bishops to open. When one did so in 1927, it was found to contain nothing of interest or value.

Bibliography: G. R. Balleine, *Past Finding Out*, 1956.

Southend-on-Sea, seaside resort in ESSEX, England, at the mouth of the Thames, 60 km east of London, the second largest seaside town in the British Isles, embracing Westcliff, Leigh, Thorpe Bay, and Shoeburyness, with all the traditional holiday attractions. Southend is one of the driest resorts in England, the annual rainfall being less than 500 mm. Historic buildings include the Cluniac priory of St Mary's at Prittlewell, founded about 1110 by Robert Fitz-Sweyne as a cell of the priory at Lewes, Sussex. Southchurch Hall, a 13th-century building, on the site of an earlier Saxon building, was the residence of Sir Richard de Southchurch, Sheriff of Essex in 1265; it is now used as a public library. St Mary the Virgin, Prittlewell, dates from the 7th century; the present Norman nave was erected in the 11th century, the processional aisle in the 12th century, and the chancel tower and Jesus chapel in the 15th century. The last-named has a beautiful stained-glass window attributed to Albrecht Dürer, and was formerly in the church of St Ouen, Rouen.

Southend has a pier 2 km in length, claimed to be the longest in the world, and 16 public parks, gardens, and pleasure-grounds, including its famous Cliff Gardens, covering over 240 ha.

The Domesday Book contains references to the parishes of Prittlewell, Southchurch, Leigh, Shoeburyness, and Eastwood, which now comprise the area upon which Southend is built. This area has been peopled from remote times. There were successive occupations by Celts, Romans, Saxons, and Danes. The pagan Saxons settled in the area from 500 to 650, and in 894 King Alfred defeated the Danes at Benfleet, driving them across the site of modern Southend to Shoeburyness, where they formed a settlement. The name *Southende*, i.e. the south end of Prittlewell, was first used in a legal document in the reign of Henry VIII. The rise of the town as a health resort dates from about 1794, when it became a fashionable place for sea-bathing. There are several industries, including light engineering, boat-building, brick-making, sea-moss dyeing and processing; plastics, radio components, textiles, furniture, jewellery, paint and varnish are also manufactured. Population (1971) 162,770.

Southern, Richard William (1912–), British medieval historian; educated at the Royal Grammar School, Newcastle upon Tyne, and Balliol College, Oxford. He was fellow and tutor at Balliol, 1937–61; Chichele professor of modern history, University of Oxford, 1961–69; and has been president of St John's College, Oxford since 1969.

Southern's most distinguished work has been concerned with the study of medieval thought and learning and his exceptional gifts of exposition were notably displayed in *The Making of the Middle Ages*, 1953. Others of his publications are: *St Anselm and His Biographer*, 1963; *Western Views of Islam in the Middle Ages*, 1962; *Memorials of St Anselm*, 1969; *Medieval Humanism and other studies*, 1970; and *Western Society and the Church in the Middle Ages*, 1970.

Southern Alps, mountain range of South Island, New Zealand, running 325 km southwards from Arthur's Pass down the west side of the island. The rock is largely a sandstone felspar combination called greywacke. Sixteen mountains rise above 3000 m, all situated near the centre of the range. The highest peaks are Mount Cook (3764 m) and Mount Tasman (3498 m). The range is much more heavily glaciated than the European Alps. The Tasman glacier, on the east side of Mount Cook, is 29 km long and more than 1·5 km wide. The Franz Josef, on the west side, although much shorter, is fed so heavily from its upper snow-fields that it flows to within 180 m of the sea. There are no subalpine passes across the central sector of the main divide. The lowest is Copland Pass, 2118 m, between Hooker and Copland valleys. The weather of the Southern Alps is notoriously unstable. The range lies just 32 km from the Tasman Sea, which brings heavy north-westerly storms to the main ridge. These warm wet winds drop their moisture on the high peaks and lesser ranges eastwards, but are dry when they cross the Canterbury Plains. They seldom deposit snow below 2440 m. Good Alpine weather comes with the cold southerly winds, and these, if prolonged, deposit snow down to 1220 m. The summer climbing season extends from mid-November to early April. February and March are reckoned to be the least unsettled months. Winter weather is much better than summer, making skiing a popular sport.

Bibliography: R. Hewitt and M. Davidson, *Mountains of New Zealand*, 1954; P. Graham, *Mountain Guide* (an autobiography), 1965.

Southern Bug, see BUG, SOUTHERN.

Southern Continent, see TERRA AUSTRALIS INCOGNITA; ANTARCTIC EXPLORATION.

Southern Cross, see CRUX.

Southern Dialect, see ENGLISH LANGUAGE.

Southern Lights, see AURORA.

Southern Railway, see RAILWAYS.

Southern Rhodesia, see RHODESIA.

Southern Yemen, see YEMEN, PEOPLE'S DEMOCRATIC REPUBLIC OF.

Southerne, Thomas (1660–1746), English dramatist, born at Oxmantown near Dublin. Educated at Trinity College there and at Oxford, he studied law at the Middle Temple and served for a time in the army. He became a friend of Dryden and wrote prologues and epilogues for some of his plays. Although his three comedies of manners were popular when first produced, his two best plays, sentimental tragedies based on novels by Aphra BEHN, are *The Fatal Marriage*, 1694, and *Oroonoko*, 1696, which was an attack on the slave trade.

Bibliography: Life by J. W. Dodds, repr. 1970.

Southernwood, see ARTEMISIA.

Southey, Robert (1774–1843), English poet, editor, and biographer, born in Bristol. He is sometimes regarded as one of the 'Lake Poets', more because of his friendship with COLERIDGE and WORDSWORTH and residence in Keswick than for any Romantic influence felt in his work. Educated at Westminster (from which he was expelled for writing against flogging) and Balliol College, Oxford, he was an early admirer of the French Revolution, whose aims he supported in the poem *Joan of Arc*, 1796. In 1794 he became a friend of Coleridge, and in 1795 married Edith Fricker, whose sister Sara married Coleridge. He joined with Coleridge in planning the utopian 'pantisocracy', a scheme for a radical community in the United States, which came to nothing.

In 1796 Southey visited Lisbon and published *Letters written during a Short Residence in Spain and Portugal*, 1797. In 1803 he moved to Keswick, where he lived near Wordsworth. His long epic poems reflect the contempor-

ary fashion for exotic melodrama: *Thalaba the Destroyer*, 1807; *Madoc*, 1805, and *The Curse of Kehama*, 1810, are all in this vein. Southey's youthful radicalism later gave way to conservatism; in 1807 he obtained a small government pension, and in 1813 he became poet laureate, after SCOTT had refused the honour. Southey's *A Vision of Judgement*, 1821, an adulatory estimate of George IV, provoked BYRON into his satirical answer, *The Vision of Judgement*, 1822.

Southey was a prolific, if often uninspired, writer. He wrote a *Life of Nelson*, 1813, and *Life of Wesley*, 1820; edited the works of COWPER and CHATTERTON; published histories of Brazil and the Peninsular War; translated the *Chronicle of the Cid*; and contributed to the *Quarterly Review* in his efforts to maintain his large family. However, his less formal work now seems the most successful; in *The Doctor*, an anecdotal miscellany, 1834–47, he included the famous fairy tale of 'The Three Bears'. Southey is best remembered for short poems such as 'The Battle of Blenheim' and 'The Inchcape Rock'. He declined both the editorship of *The Times* and a baronetcy (1835), and after his wife's death (1837) married Caroline Bowles, herself a minor poet. His letters were edited by the Rev. C. C. Southey, 1849-50, and by M. H. Fitzgerald, 1912.

Bibliography: W. Haller, *Early Life of Southey*, 1917; G. Carnall, *Robert Southey and his Age*, 1960; K. Curry (Ed.), *New Letters of Robert Southey*, 1965.

Southgate, see ENFIELD.

Southhill, Baron, see TORRINGTON, GEORGE BYNG, VISCOUNT.

Southport, town and seaside resort in the Sefton borough of MERSEYSIDE METROPOLITAN COUNTY, England, 24 km south-west of Preston. It acquired its first hotel for seabathing visitors in the 18th century but growth was slow until the railway to Liverpool was built in 1848, and the line to Wigan and Manchester in 1855. Through the wishes of the lord of the manor, Southport was laid out in a rectangular pattern of tree-lined streets. Its main street, Lord Street, resembles a boulevard. Like many seaside towns, Southport has length rather than breadth; 10 km long and less than 2 km inland, it is built mainly on old sand dunes. The peat mosslands away from the coastal belt provide unsuitable foundations for houses and are best used as market gardening land. On the seaward side, hundreds of hectares of land have been reclaimed for gardens, a marine lake, swimming pools and other athletic facilities, and an amusement park. Holiday visitors are essential to Southport's prosperity but most now come only for the day. Southport is a popular residential town; several thousand use the fast electrified rail services to Liverpool daily and over a thousand commute to Manchester. Industries began in workshops of the central artisan area but there has been some expansion since the 1930s, mainly in engineering, clothing, and food. In 1971 the population, which has fluctuated little for 50 years and in 10-year periods normally shows a natural decrease through excess of deaths over births due to the high proportion of elderly residents, was 84,574.

Southsea, seaside resort and yachting centre in Hampshire, England, on the southern side of PORTSMOUTH, of which it is part.

Southwark. The George Inn. *(Camera Press/J. Blau)*

Southwark, which has been known as 'The Borough' since c. 1550, is a London borough which was created on 1 April 1965 and comprises the former metropolitan boroughs of Bermondsey and Camberwell. Southwark's estimated population in 1974 was 241,700.

The name 'Southwark' means 'southern fort'; it was the fortified bridge-head of the City of London, being the point where all roads from the south and south-east converged on London. Intimately connected with the City, Southwark was granted to the latter by a charter of 1327, and in 1550 became the city ward of Bridge Without. It is famous in history for its inns and prisons, which figure extensively in the works of such writers as Chaucer, Shakespeare, and Dickens. Bankside, the area between Southwark and Blackfriars Bridges, was renowned in the 16th and 17th centuries for its theatres, such as the Globe, the Rose, the Swan, and the Fortune, and for bear- and bull-baiting, taverns, and brothels. The George Inn, in Borough High Street, is the last galleried inn left in London. Southwark Cathedral was originally the Augustinian priory church of St Mary Overie ('over the water') founded c. 1106 on the site of an earlier church. Destroyed by fire c. 1212, it was apparently not rebuilt until the end of the 13th century. It was extensively restored between 1838 and 1897, but the chancel is a fine specimen of Early English architecture. The priory was dissolved in 1540, and the church, within a new parish, was renamed St Saviour's. In 1905 it became the cathedral church of the new diocese of Southwark. St George's Roman Catholic Cathedral, built between 1841 and 1848, was damaged in air raids in 1941 but rebuilt between 1951 and 1958. The IMPERIAL WAR MUSEUM was built on the site of the Bethlehem Hospital (see BEDLAM) in Lambeth Road. On the east side is Guy's Hospital (see GUY, Thomas), which was founded in 1722–24. Southwark Bridge, designed by John Rennie, was built between 1815 and 1819. The KING'S BENCH PRISON and the MARSHAL-SEA, notorious debtors' prisons, were both in Southwark.

Bermondsey had a rich Cluniac priory, of which there are very scanty remains, which was founded in 1089 and lasted until the Dissolution. On the riverside in the Middle Ages there were many hostelries and the town houses of the abbots of St Augustine, Canterbury, and of Battle, Sussex, and of the priors of Lewes, Sussex. Many Huguenots settled in Bermondsey after the Massacre of St Bartholomew (1572), and are credited with the foundation there of the leather industry. Rotherhithe (meaning a 'landing-place where cattle are shipped') was originally a separate village to the east of Bermondsey. It contains the now closed Surrey Commercial Docks, which were begun in 1809 and at one time were the largest timber docks in the world. Bermondsey has three tunnels under the Thames: the Thames Tunnel from Rotherhithe to Wapping, the Rotherhithe Tunnel to Shadwell, and a tunnel emerging near the south-west angle of the Tower of London used for water supply only. The old villages of Camberwell and Peckham were extensively developed from c. 1820 onwards. George, Prince of Denmark, consort of Queen Anne, lived on Camberwell Green (Denmark Hill is named after him), and so did Mendelssohn; Ruskin lived on Denmark Hill. The manor of Dulwich once belonged to the abbey of Bermondsey, and was eventually acquired by Edward Alleyn, the founder of DULWICH COLLEGE. Dulwich was a village until developed in the 19th century, and it still retains something of its former character. The Picture Gallery, a small but important collection with a fine representation of the Dutch school, was originally founded by Noel Desenfans, who bequeathed it to Sir Francis Bourgeois; with additional pictures the latter bequeathed it to Dulwich College. Dulwich Park, a fine open space, was presented to the public in 1890. Although the southern part of the borough is heavily residential, there is some light industry in the northern, riverside district.

Bibliography: D. Johnson, *Southwark and the City*, 1967.

Southwell, Robert (c. 1561–95), English Jesuit martyr and poet, born at Horsham St Faith, Norfolk; educated at Douai and Paris. He joined the Society of Jesus in 1578, and returning to England (1587) became chaplain to the countess of Arundel (1589). During his missionary activities he spent most of his time in hiding in London or in Roman Catholic country houses where he wrote many prose pamphlets: *Marie Magdalen's Funerall Teares*, *The Triumphs over Death*, *An Epistle of Comfort*, and *A Humble Supplication to Her Majesty*, all written in 1591. A long poem, *Saint Peter's Complaynt*, 1595, the beautiful *Burning Babe*, 1595, and other pieces were written to encourage Catholics under persecution. In 1592 he was betrayed and arrested by the authorities. After suffering torture and being imprisoned for three years he was hanged at Tyburn for treason.

Bibliography: Prose works (ed. W. J. Walter), 1928; *Poems* (ed. J. M. McDonald and N. P. Brown), 1967; Studies by R. A. Morton, 1929, P. Janelle, 1935, and C. Devlin, 1956.

Southwell, town in Nottinghamshire, England, 24 km north-east of Nottingham. It is claimed that a church was first established here in 630 by Paulinus, second bishop of York. In 1884 the old minster of St Mary was made a cathedral; the minster, begun c. 1110, shows architectural

styles from Norman to Perpendicular; the choir is
Early English work, and the Decorated chapter house has
some beautiful carving. There is a 14th-century screen.
Bishop's Manor is the episcopal residence and there is an
ancient grammar school. From the Saracen's Head Hotel
on 5 May 1647 Charles I went under escort to nearby
Kelham and surrendered to the Scottish army. The main
industries are lace-making, milling, and agriculture.
Population (1971) 4300.

Southwold, former municipal borough (first charter
granted by Henry VII in 1490) and seaside resort in
SUFFOLK, England, 19 km south-west of Lowestoft. The
parish church of St Edmund, largely rebuilt (1460–90), is
noteworthy for its clerestory and aisle windows, and its
great rood screen. In 1672 an indecisive naval battle
between the English and Dutch fleets took place in Sole
or Southwold Bay. During this century much has been
done to protect Southwold from incursions by the sea.
Southwold is the site of a brewery and a lighthouse.
Population (1971) 1998.

Soutine, Chaim (1894–1943), painter, born at Smilo-
vitchi, Lithuania, associated with the School of Paris. He
made his way to Paris after working in an art school at
Vilna, and like his friend MODIGLIANI led a Bohemian life.
His paintings, which include portraits, landscapes, and
still-life, are distinguished by expressive distortions of
form and colour reminiscent of Van GOGH.
   Bibliography: Castaing and Leymarie, *Chaim Soutine*, 1965.

Soutsos, Alexandros, see GREECE, *Literature*.

Soutsos, Panagiotis, see GREECE, *Literature*.

Souvigny, Charles Sorel, Sieur de, see SOREL,
CHARLES.

Sovereign, large gold coin valued at 20s., introduced by
Henry VII in 1489 and issued by the Tudors and Stuarts.
Also a modern British gold coin of the same nominal
value first struck in 1817. The reverse design by Pistrucci
shows St George and the dragon. The sovereign with the
same reverse design is still being struck, although it is
no longer in circulation. The gold sovereigns struck in
1974 were offered for sale by the Bank of England at about
£30 each.

Sovereignty, that relationship of authority which exists
between the supreme (sovereign) legitimate power in a
state and its inhabitants. The existence of such a relationship as a fact can be explained by invoking the political
tradition of a country, into which all inhabitants, wit-
tingly, or unwittingly, are to some extent introduced, and
through which their attitudes to political authority are
formed. In modern political science the term 'political
culture' is often used to refer, in a less historically self-
conscious way, to the fruits of its political tradition.
The existence of a strong sovereign is less likely where the
political tradition is weak through erosion, discontinuity, or where the political culture does not contain
within it the necessary ideals of obedience. Hence the
weakness of sovereignties exercised in states of recent
emergence, or of heterogenous, or undeveloped political
cultures. Various theories of sovereignty have been put
forward to justify the exercise of such power. Amongst
them those deriving from the SOCIAL CONTRACT and the

utilitarian (see UTILITARIANISM) positions are most
important in modern discussions of the issue. In the 19th
century when it was felt that the only limitations properly
imposed on political power were those which were self-
imposed, the assertion of a nation's sovereignty implied
freedom from internal influence by other powers. Since
the Second World War increasing international interde-
pendence and the growth of the influence of multinational
corporations on domestic economies has led to a drastic
reduction in the sphere of autonomous sovereignty.
   Bibliography: S. I. Benn, 'The Uses of Sovereignty' in A.
Quinton (Ed.), *Political Philosophy*, 1967.

Sovereignty of the Sea. 'It has become', wrote W. E.
Hall in *International Law* (1880), 'an uncontested principle of modern international law that the sea, as a general
rule, cannot be subjected to appropriation'. This principle
has, for the most part, been adhered to in its entirety.
Perhaps the only exception to it is the general recognition
of a state's sovereignty over the waters adjacent to its own
coast-line (see TERRITORIAL WATERS). At the beginning
of the 17th century a vague right over all the seas surrounding Europe was set up by the various European
nations, and these rights appear to have been theoretically
based upon services rendered to commerce, although it
is significant that such psuedo-rights were exercised only
by such states as were possessed of strong fleets and were
notable for their maritime prowess.

The present state of international law concerning the
sovereignty of the sea is as follows:

1. International waters, which are under the full sovereignty of the state washed by them, include bays with
mouths not exceeding 24 miles (38·6 km), and certain
'historic' bays, e.g. Hudson Bay. Where the coast-line of
a bay touches a number of states, there is no generally
accepted rule. There is no right of 'innocent passage'
through internal waters.

2. Marginal waters belong to the states bordered by
them, though the permissible width of such 'territorial
seas' is a matter of some dispute. There is a right of
innocent passage through the territorial seas, though it is
unclear to what extent this may lawfully be enjoyed by
warships. The right may on notice be suspended,
except where the waters in question constitute 'international straits'. As to the extent to which a state should
exercise its jurisdiction over the territorial seas, see INTER-
NATIONAL LAW.

3. Certain sovereign rights exist over the continental
shelf adjacent to a state, and perhaps also to the sea above
such a shelf.
   Bibliography: L. Oppenheim, *International Law*, 1928; C. J.
Colombos, *International Law of the Sea*, 6th ed. 1967.

Sovetsk (formerly German *Tilsit*), city in KALININGRAD
oblast of the RSFSR, USSR, on the Neman 100 km
north-east of Kaliningrad. It has a timber and paper
industry. It was founded in 1288 by Teutonic Knights as
a castle, and has been a town since 1552. Napoleon I
concluded treaties here with Russia and Prussia in July
1807, by which Prussia lost her possessions west of the
Elbe, and Westphalia was formed out of West Prussia and
Hanover. Population (1970) 38,000; mostly settlers from
central European RSFSR (before the war wholly German; the population in 1939 was 59,000).

Sovetskaya Gavan

Sovetskaya Gavan, town in the KHABAROVSK *krai* of the RSFSR, USSR, and port on the Tatar Strait in East Siberia. There are timber, fishing, and ship-repair works. The port will be the eastern terminus of the Baikal–Amur railway. Population (1970) 28,000.

Soviet Air Force. At the start of the Second World War the Soviet Air Force was outnumbered and outclassed by the Luftwaffe, but between 1944 and 1955 it was built up into a powerful and efficient force, with a total operational strength of 20,000 aircraft. The Soviet Union had, however, made little study of the wider potentialities of air power and the Soviet Air Force was almost entirely a tactical force operating in support of the army.

After the war it continued to develop on similar lines, but by 1950 Russia had begun to build up a force of strategic bombers. About the same time the USSR started to develop a modern air defence system, equipped with high performance fighters. By 1949 the Soviet Union had developed an atomic bomb, and a hydrogen bomb by 1953. Since then the USSR has made rapid progress and in 1961 alone made 31 tests of nuclear weapons, including the largest explosion yet recorded of about 50 megatons. In all, prior to the signing of the Test Ban Treaty in 1963, it had carried out some 136 tests in the atmosphere. As in the case of the RED ARMY the air force is divided into offensive-defensive functions. The Strategic Rocket Force of about 350,000 men functions separately, and is offensive in character, with most of its missiles grouped in the western USSR. There is also the group of long-range and medium-range fighters and bombers, estimated at some 1000 and 1500 respectively. These planes act within the framework of the Warsaw Pact. The defence forces comprise some 3000 aircraft and a variety of missiles and anti-missiles; the missile systems are, as in the USA, expensive to install. Expansion and sophistication of these systems is something which the Strategic Arms Limitation Talks (SALT) have sought to reduce. A round number of 10,000 rocket launchers is said to have been built in the USSR in the mid-1970s to function together with the anti-aircraft artillery.

As in the USA, air defence is gradually being taken over by the anti-aircraft missile, and a proportion of the fighters will probably be transferred to the tactical role. Russia has developed an anti-missile missile, but cannot hope to intercept more than a proportion of the missiles which could be launched against it. The air transport force includes a separate element capable of lifting several airborne divisions. The aircraft, including civil aircraft which could be used for military purposes, include the TU-114, which can carry 200 men, the Il-62, which is very similar to the British VC-10, and the giant An-24 (Antaeus), which can carry 500–600 men.

Bibliography: A. Lee, *The Soviet Air Force*, 1961; D. W. Wragg, *The Soviet Air Force in World War II*, 1974; International Institute for Strategic Studies, *The Military Balance*, annual.

Soviet Central Asia, see CENTRAL ASIA (SOVIET).

Soviet Far East, territory comprising the PRIMORSKI and KHABAROVSK *krai*, the YAKUTSK ASSR, and the AMUR, MAGADAN, KAMCHATKA, and SAKHALIN *oblasti* of the RSFSR, USSR. It is a region of rich mineral deposits, and was formerly an area of banishment and labour camps. Before 1938–45 there was also a large Japanese, Korean, and Chinese population, now expelled or departed. The territory was gradually annexed by Russia between 1649 and 1875. A part of Sakhalin and the KURIL ISLANDS was subsequently lost temporarily to Japan but restored to the USSR in 1945. In the early 20th century the colonists developed strong regional tendencies which found partial expression in the creation of the FAR EASTERN REPUBLIC (1920–22), used as a buffer state between Soviet Russia and Japan at the time of the CIVIL WAR, (RUSSIAN) and the Far Eastern *krai* (1926–38). Area 6,215,900 km². Population (1975) 6,435,000 (75 per cent urban); mostly Russians, Ukrainians, and Yakuts.

Bibliography: E. S. Kirby, *Soviet Far East*, 1971.

Soviet Navy. Russia has been a sea power since the end of the 17th century, when PETER I, THE GREAT founded the Imperial Navy. The Imperial Navy came to an end with the 1917 OCTOBER REVOLUTION, in which the Red sailors at Kronstadt played a prominent part. For the next 10 years, while Lenin's new economic policy had priority, the Soviet Navy received little attention, but thereafter it began to expand under Stalin's direction. In June 1941, when hostilities began against Germany, the Soviet Navy included 3 battleships, 8 cruisers, 85 destroyers, 250 submarines, and a large number of minor war vessels. With the exception of the battleships and cruisers, some 25 per cent of the navy was stationed in the Far East, the remainder being divided between the Arctic, Baltic and Black Sea fleets. There was also a land-based naval air arm.

The Soviet Navy was not very effective in the Second World War, nor was the quality of training and equipment comparable with that of the leading Western powers. Soviet Russia emerged from the war with a number of newly acquired ice-free naval bases in the russified Baltic States and East Prussia; in the Far East its strategic position was improved by the acquisition of the Kuril Islands and the recovery of the southern half of Sakhalin. For some 10 years after the end of the Second World War, Soviet naval policy was undecided, but in 1955, two years after Stalin's death, a policy was adopted which gave priority to the submarine arm and the building of destroyers and motor torpedo-boats. By the mid-1970s it was estimated that the strength of the fleet had grown to 28 cruisers, over 90 destroyers, and about 300 submarines (of which 35 are nuclear-powered). The many smaller ships included minesweepers and coastal escorts. An aircraft carrier of 40,000 t was launched in 1975 and a second is under construction; most of the bigger ships carry rockets and helicopters. The Soviet Navy has made great progress in the fitting of missiles to surface ships and submarines. The emphasis has been on the development of ship-to-surface (SSM) types. All SSM missiles are believed to carry nuclear warheads. The navy accounts for 15–20 per cent of Soviet defence expenditure.

The personnel is believed to number 475,000 officers and men. A small percentage of the men are employed on a long-service basis; the rest are selected conscripts who serve for four years and then join the reserves, from which the specialists are recalled for periodic training. The Soviet Navy comes under the Minister of Defence, and is headed by an Admiral with the title of Deputy Minister for the Navy.

Geographical circumstances compel the Soviet Union to divide its navy into four main fleets: the Northern, based on the Murmansk coast and the White Sea; the Baltic, based on Kronstadt and ports in the Baltic States; the Black Sea, based on Sevastopol; and the Far East, with bases at Vladivostok and Petropavlovsk. A large nuclear-propelled ice-breaker, *Lenin*, was completed in 1955. As regards logistics, shipbuilding, and maintenance, the four main fleets are entirely self-supporting. In the last 30 years new shipyards have been developed at Severodvinsk near Archangel, and at Khabarovsk and Komsomolsk on the Amur river.

Bibliography: D. Fairhall, *Russia Looks to the Sea*, 1973; D. W. Mitchell, *A History of Russian and Soviet Sea Power*, 1974.

Soviet Russia, see RUSSIAN SOVIET FEDERATED SOCIALIST REPUBLIC; UNION OF SOVIET SOCIALIST REPUBLICS.

Soviet System, see SOVIETS.

Soviets (Russian *sovet*, council), organs of state power in the USSR. According to the STALIN constitution of 1936, 'soviets of toilers' deputies' are the 'political basis' of the state. Local, provincial, and republican soviets, and the Supreme Soviet of the USSR, are formally elected by universal, equal, direct, and secret vote. The elections are in fact fictitious because there is always only one candidate.

Soviets first appeared as soviets of workers' deputies in the 1905 revolution, and they reappeared in 1917 as soviets of workers' and soldiers' deputies. After the Kornilov Affair (see KORNILOV) the main soviet fell under Bolshevik influence. The St Petersburg soviet headed by TROTSKY formed a military revolutionary committee, through which the Bolsheviks seized power (see OCTOBER REVOLUTION). From 1917 to 1936 soviets were considered organs of the DICTATORSHIP OF THE PROLETARIAT. Stalin aptly described soviets as 'transmission belts from the party to the masses'. Non-members of the Communist Party can be 'elected' deputies, but are always in fact selected in advance by the party. There has always been some uncertainty as to exactly how important the soviets are in the political system of the USSR, in spite of their theoretical importance. At the local level their activity includes mobilisation of voluntary labour, maintenance and expansion of communal services, housing, sanitation, and transport. This corresponds fairly closely to local government services in other countries, where centralised politics and finance tend to strongly influence levels of local government activity.

The Supreme Soviet of the USSR, although in theory the supreme legislature, or parliament, meets only twice a year for a few days at a time. It then rubber-stamps a backlog of legislation, much of it already in effect, initiated by the POLITBURO of the party or the Council of Ministers. Its votes have, to date, without exception, been unanimous. It has two chambers, with some 1500 deputies in all. When not in session, its work is carried out by its Praesidium of 33 members, the chairman of which, at present Nikolai Podgorny, is the titular head of state. Historically, the Supreme Soviet is the heir to the All-Russian Congress of Soviets (1917–23) and the All-Union Congress of Soviets (1923–36).

Bibliography: M. Fainsod, *How Russia is Ruled*, 1963; L. Schapiro, *The Government and Politics of the Soviet Union*, 1970.

Sow-thistle, see SONCHUS.

Sowerby Bridge, town in CALDERDALE District, West Yorkshire, England, 6 km south-west of HALIFAX on the River Calder. There are engineering works and bedsteads are manufactured. Chemicals, carpets, and woollen, worsted, and cotton goods are also produced. The pre-industrial town of Sowerby, which was earlier of importance in the woollen trade, is located on higher ground between the rivers Calder and Ryburn. Population (1971: urban district) 16,271.

Soweto, the largest wholly Black urban complex of townships in Southern Africa, a suburb of JOHANNESBURG where most of the inhabitants work. It is divided into tribal areas to prevent inter-tribal strife but has been held up as a prime example of African urbanisation and the acceptance of apartheid. However, African riots in 1976 that left over 100 dead and 1200 injured, and further subsequent unrest, have damaged this image. In 1970 it comprised 26 townships with an area of 6734 ha and a population of about 560,000.

Sowing. The planting of seed, both of garden and of field plants, is an operation on which the success of the future plant greatly depends. The smaller the seed, the shallower should be the covering. The preparation of the seed-bed should depend largely on the habits of the plant, but while in general the soil should never be dust dry, it must not be so wet as to be sticky. Many of the operations of CULTIVATION are to produce reliable seed-beds. Thin sowing is to be recommended in almost every case. Sowing in drills has numerous advantages, the chief of which are that the plants can be hoed with ease, and also that the seed can be evenly covered. The machines in general use are the internal force-feed drill, the external force-feed drill and the cup drill. Others with more limited use are tooth-and-brush pinion drills. Broadcasting seed barrows are often used for sowing grass seeds, though the increasing modern tendency is to drill these seeds with force-feed or cup drills. Combined drills, with separate hoppers from which fertiliser and seeds are sown at the same time, are now fairly widely used. Research on the placement of fertiliser in relation to the seed is leading to adaptations of design which will expedite ideal relative placement of seed and fertiliser for the various crops.

Soxhlet Extraction, process of repeated extraction of a crude product, often of natural origin, by hot solvent. The extractor apparatus used is a complicated, delicate piece of glassware, designed so that solvent vapour can flow continuously through a tube containing the product and back to the bulk of the solvent, taking with it the product that has been dissolved. The extractor is connected to a reflux condenser to stop the escape of solvent (see REFLUX HEATING) and the process carries on until sufficient product has been dissolved and removed by the solvent.

Soya, Carl Erik (1896–), Danish playwright and novelist, born in Copenhagen. His plays are popular, satirical, and experimental, using unexpected stage effects; among the best are *Hvem er jeg?*, 1932; *Chas*, 1938; and *To Traade*, 1943 (*Two Threads*, 1955). His main nov-

Soya Bean

els are *Min Farmors Hus*, 1943 (*Grandmother's House*, 1966), and *Sytten*, 1953–54 (*Seventeen*, 1961).

Soya Bean, or soybean, *Glycine* (*Soja*) *max*, *G. hispida*, and *G. soja*, in the family Leguminosae; thought to have been derived from *G. ussuriensis*, which grows wild throughout much of East Asia. It is an annual plant of great genetic diversity; it varies in height from 20 cm to 2 m; has branching stems which may be stiffly erect, prostrate or of climbing habit; has trifoliate leaves, varying widely in shape, size and colour; and bears clusters of two to five pods at each axil along its stems. The pods vary in length from 3 to 7 cm and contain two or three seeds, which may be almost spherical, elongated or flat, and from 7 mm to 15 mm in length. The ripe seeds may be pale yellow, green, brown or black, or a combination of these colours. The seeds are very rich in protein, about 35 per cent by weight; those of medium size usually contain the most oil, about 18 per cent by weight. The stems, leaves and pods are normally covered with brown or grey hairs.

The earliest written records show that the plant was cultivated in China more than 4800 years ago, but it was not until about 1908 that soya beans were shipped to England and received world-wide attention. Soya beans are now cultivated throughout the world but especially in warm temperate and subtropical regions. World production for 1974 was estimated at nearly 57,000,000 t, of which well over half was produced by the USA, with China being the other main grower. Average world yields were about 1270 kg per hectare; USA yields were 1580 kg per hectare. Soya beans have been a staple food in the Orient for many hundreds of years, and the bulk of production in China, Japan, Korea, Indonesia and Thailand is still used for direct consumption, while the USA exports on a large scale to Canada, Europe and Japan.

Many varieties have been developed and are cultivated in China for special purposes, which include production

Soya Bean.

of flour, soy sauce, curd, milk and sprouts. In the western hemisphere mainly pale yellow beans of medium size are cultivated, and almost the entire crop not retained for seed is processed for oil and flour. The oil is used in edible products and, to a lesser extent, as a technical oil, while the meal residue is a valuable source of protein formerly used chiefly in animal and poultry feed. Relatively small quantities of the meal are used in the production of plywood glues, emulsion paints and washable wallpapers. It is also used as a fertiliser, particularly in Asia.

Soya beans are now recognised as one of the most economical sources of protein for human food. The defatted meal is being increasingly used to produce textured soya protein, having food value comparable with animal protein. Soya meal is made into a dough, which is coagulated by heat treatment; in this form the product is used mainly in conjunction with meat as an extender. It is also possible to produce soya protein in a fibrous condition which, when suitably flavoured, forms an acceptable meat substitute. See SOYA BEAN OIL.

Soya Bean Oil, or soybean oil (iodine value 132 ± 8), is derived from the seed of the leguminous plant of genus *Glycine*, indigenous to eastern Asia, but because it is economically the most important bean in the world it is now cultivated world-wide. The main soya bean producing countries are China, including Manchuria, and the USA. The seed contains about 18 per cent of oil, which is sometimes removed by expression in continuous screw presses but to a much greater extent by extraction with a solvent, on account of the higher yield obtained (see OILSEEDS, PROCESSING OF). Solvent-extracted and particularly expelled soya bean oil, like linseed oil, contains relatively large amounts of nonglyceride material consisting mainly of phosphatides, which slowly precipitates on storage and must be removed before the oil can be processed to finished products. Precipitation may be carried out in the refining process by addition of a suitable quantity of alkali in excess of that required for neutralisation of the free fatty acids, so that the whole of the phosphatides are removed with the soap stock; but it has become common practice to remove first the bulk of the phosphatides by a 'degumming' process, in which they are caused to coagulate by hydration and are separated by centrifugation. Recovered phosphatide sludge is known commercially as 'soya bean lecithin' or simply 'lecithin', and when dried and refined is used in small quantities in many industrial applications. The liquid neutral oil may be bleached with activated earth to a very pale colour and deodorised so that it has neither taste nor odour. Large quantities are also 'hardened' by hydrogenation, before being deodorised, to produce products ranging in consistency from liquid at room temperature to a hard fat melting at about 65 °C. In general, hydrogenation also removes certain colouring matter susceptible to reduction, and retards reversion—development of off-flavour in the oil. Main fatty acid constituents of the oil are: unsaturated, oleic (23–24 per cent) and linoleic (50–60 per cent); saturated, a total of 11–14 per cent. It also contains up to about 8 per cent of linolenic acid, which has an important bearing upon its use as a semi-drying oil. Soya bean oil was originally used only for soap making and as an illuminant, but the bulk is now refined and used in the manufacture of margarine, cooking fats and oils, salad

Wole Soyinka. *(Camera Press)*

oils, mayonnaise, and salad dressings. As a semi-drying oil, it has found limited use as an extender for linseed oil in the surface-coatings industry, but large quantities are now used for the production of non-yellowing alkyd-resins for varnishes and high gloss paints, particularly in the USA. The soapstock from alkali refining and the steam deodoriser distillates are sources of fatty acids, which are recovered for the manufacture of alkyd resins, and sterols, used to a limited extent for the synthesis of some of the sex hormones and adrenal cortical hormones. Lecithin, on account of its antioxidant, emulsifying, colloidal, surface-active and softening properties, has found many important applications in a wide variety of industries, including the margarine, chocolate, confectionery, ice-cream, baking, pharmaceutical, cosmetic, paint, rubber, petroleum, leather, and textile industries.

Soybean, see SOYA BEAN.

Soyinka, Wole (1934–), Nigerian author, born in Abeokuta, Western State, of Yoruba parents; educated at University College, Ibadan, and the University of Leeds. Soyinka was resident playwright at the Royal Court Theatre in 1958, and in 1960 returned to Nigeria to study African dramatic arts. He was twice imprisoned for political acts, in 1965 and again in 1967. When released he resumed his post as director of the school of drama at Ibadan, resigning in 1972.

Soyinka has written a number of plays, all of which draw on Yoruba theatrical traditions as well as European (especially Brechtian) ones. The best-known are *Kongi's Harvest*, 1967, a satire on totalitarian régimes, *The Road*, 1966, which mingles farce and tragedy in its exploration of death, and *Madmen and Specialists*, 1971, forcefully attacking political expediency and greed. He has also published volumes of poetry, *Idanre and Other Poems*, 1967, and poems composed in prison, *The Shuttle and the Crypt*. His novel, *The Interpreters*, set in contemporary Nigeria, was awarded the Jock Campbell Prize for Commonwealth Literature, 1968. A second novel, *Season of Anomie*, and *The Man Died*, an exposé of political corruption in Nigeria, have also been published. Soyinka founded the theatre groups '1960 Masks' and the Orisun Theatre Company and edits *Transition*, a political and cultural magazine.

Bibliography: E. Jones, *The Writings of Wole Soyinka*, 1973.

Spa, town in Belgium, 27 km south-east of Liège in the Ardennes, with mineral springs. It was in the 18th century the most fashionable resort of this kind in Europe. It has a famous casino. In 1918 Spa was the headquarters of the German High Command. Kaiser William II abdicated here on 10 November, and fled to the Netherlands. In 1918–19 it was the seat of the armistice commission, and in 1920 a European conference was held here. A large factory produces every year about 50 million bottles of Spa water. Population 9500.

Spa Treatment, see BALNEOLOGY.

Spaak, Paul-Henri (1899–1972), Belgian statesman and lawyer, born at Schaarbek. He studied at the Free University of Brussels, and then practised at the Bar. In 1932 he entered parliament as a Socialist deputy for Brussels. From 1935 to 1945 he was minister of foreign affairs in PIERLOT's government, which he accompanied to London in 1940. He was foreign minister, 1946–50, and prime minister, 1950–54. During his term of office Spaak played a prominent part in the promotion of the BENELUX customs agreement (1944); the Treaty of Rome, under which the EUROPEAN ECONOMIC COMMUNITY was established; and the negotiations for the NORTH ATLANTIC TREATY.

He was equally conspicuous in the activities of the United Nations and was elected, in January 1946, as first president of the UN Assembly. In August 1949 the European Consultative Assembly at Strasbourg unanimously elected him to preside over their first meeting. Spaak led his party's opposition to the return of LEOPOLD III, which took place in 1950. From 1954 he was foreign minister in van Acker's government. From 1957 to 1961 he was secretary-general of NATO, and he was deputy premier and foreign minister.

Space and Time. The present century has seen remarkable developments in the theory of RELATIVITY which have been responsible for profound modifications in the views of physicists, astronomers, mathematicians, and also to a large extent of philosophers. Not the least among these modifications is a new conception of space and time, though the problem of space and time is not a new one. Nicholas of Cusa (1401–64) held that space and time, being merely products of the mind, are inferior to the mind that created them. Giordano BRUNO (1548–1600) pointed out, what every amateur astronomer now knows, that such words as 'above', 'below', 'at rest', and 'in motion' are meaningless in the universe of revolving suns and planets, for which there is no fixed centre. On the

Space and Time

other hand, NEWTON contrasted the absolute time of the scientist with the less precise common-sense conceptions of space and time. He regarded the material world as a collection of particles, each one of which could be at rest or moving, not merely in relation to the others, but in relation to absolute space. In more recent times, before EINSTEIN advanced his views, POINCARÉ pointed out some of the difficulties in the concepts of absolute space and time. He reminded us that if each dimension of space became a thousand times larger, so that an object which previously measured a metre would now measure a kilometre, no one could know about it because the length of our measuring rods would have changed in the same ratio. The same applies to time, and if all the phenomena of the universe happened a thousand times more slowly, no one would be aware of the change.

Co-ordinate Systems or Frames of Reference. From these two illustrations it is not difficult to approach the point of view of relativity which declares that it is impossible to give a clear definition of an 'absolute' space and time. Only 'relative' space and time exists, in which each observer refers events to his own frame of reference—his map or co-ordinate system against which he notes the places at which events occur, together with synchronised clocks used to time events at different places. Any frame of reference is as good as any other for describing events from, and for experimenting to determine the laws of nature, whether a fixed laboratory, a moving train, or a receding star. The systems of co-ordinates include the three dimensions of space, and that of time also. Hence relativity is concerned with a four-dimensional set of co-ordinates called space-time, and in the transformation of the appearance of events as observed from one frame to show how they will appear when viewed from another frame of reference.

In Einstein's *Relativity: The Special and the General Theory* an illustration is given of the difficulties that arise if space and time are considered in two different co-ordinate systems. A man stands at the window of a railway carriage travelling with uniform velocity, and drops a stone on the embankment. He sees the stone descending in a straight line. Someone standing at the side of the track sees it as a parabola, the well-known curve in which projectiles move (atmospheric friction is ignored in all cases). Expressed in mathematical language, the body described a vertical path with reference to a certain system of co-ordinates and a parabola with reference to another system of co-ordinates, the first system being rigidly attached to the carriage and the second to the ground. This simple example shows quite clearly that there is no such thing as an independently existing trajectory; the trajectory is dependent on the frame of reference.

The Relativity of Time and Simultaneity. For a complete description of its motion we must specify how the body alters its position with *time*. If we want to deal with every point on each curve it is necessary to specify the time at which the body was there. This does not seem a very difficult matter provided each observer possesses a clock of identical construction, so that both can determine positions occupied by the stone at each tick of the clock. It is unnecessary to deal with practical obstacles to extreme accuracy owing to experimental errors etc. We may assume that all measurements are perfectly made by perfect instruments, but even then a serious difficulty arises in connection with the question of simultaneity—determining whether two events take place at the same time or not. Suppose a train is travelling along an embankment with a number of passengers, and lightning strikes the embankment at points A and B simultaneously, as seen by observers on the embankment (after they have allowed for the time taken by light to reach them from A and B, travelling at the velocity $c = 3 \times 10^8$ m/s). Are they also simultaneous with reference to passengers in the train? To answer this question draw a straight line AB and take M as its centre. The light from A and B will reach M on the embankment at the same instant, but now suppose M' is a passenger midway between A and B but on the train which is moving towards B. Remembering that the velocity of light is finite and that in the time required by the light to reach M' the passenger in the train has moved (very little, it is true) towards B, the light from flash B will reach him before the light from A. M' will then argue that light travels at the same velocity c for all observers (see RELATIVITY, *Development of Special Relativity*; MICHELSON-MORLEY EXPERIMENT), and hence to him from both points A and B on the train which were adjacent with A and B on the embankment and also struck by the lightning. Since he observed the flash from B first, and was midway between A and B, he concludes the flash B occurred before the flash A. Thus, observers on the embankment conclude flashes A and B occurred simultaneously; observers on the train say the flash at B occurred before the flash at A. We are, therefore, forced to conclude that there is no single, absolute time common to all observers. Time and our observation of time are relative and depend on our frame of reference.

Relativity of Distance. Measurement of distance also gives different results depending on the motion of the frame of reference of the observer. For instance, if the passenger on the train carries a 1-metre ruler, observers on the embankment may decide to measure its length. To do this, they must simultaneously note the positions of the two ends of the moving ruler against some distance scale marked out on the embankment. They will observe the ruler's length to be less than 1 m (see RELATIVITY, *Development of Special Relativity*). The passenger on the train will not be surprised, because he will say that events which were simultaneous on the embankment (marking the two ends of the ruler) were not simultaneous for him on the train, and that the observers on the embankment marked the front end before the rear end, which moved during the interval to give a shorter reading. However they can only agree to differ, and say their experiences of time and distance are both relative and different.

We shall now consider an observer O, who judges that the world A is moving away from him, say due east, with a velocity $0.8c$. An observer in A's world says that there are two special events, the second occurring six units due east of the first and 10 s later. (For mathematical convenience, we shall take the unit of distance to be the distance travelled by light in 1 s, i.e., 3×10^8 m.) How does O record these time and space intervals? Without showing how the results are attained it may be stated that O says the time interval is 24·67 s and the space interval 23·33 units. Another observer O' says that A's world is moving from him due east with a velocity $0.3c$, which is quite consistent with O's opinion, because both O and O' may have their own velocities independent of A's world. The observations of O' lead him to conclude that the time interval is 12·37 s and the space interval 9·43 units. Now suppose we find the value of $t^2 - s^2$ in each case we have the following results:

$$24\cdot67^2 - 23\cdot33^2 = 64,$$
$$12\cdot37^2 - 9\cdot43^2 = 64,$$

and if we take any number of cases, varying as we please the velocity of A's world, but retaining the second special event six units from the first and 10 s later, the number 64 will always be obtained. The expression $\sqrt{(t^2 - s^2)}$, which equals 8 in the present circumstances, that is $\sqrt{(10^2 - 6^2)}$, is called the *separation* of the two events (a name which is due to Professor A. N. Whitehead, but *interval* is also used), and is a fusion of space and time. It is independent of the world in which the records are made, and represents an intrinsic property connecting the two events, irrespective of the conditions under which they were observed. If we take A's world to be the Earth, and O to represent any of the solar planets or planets of stars in some distant nebulae, then as all these planets have different velocities with reference to the Earth, an observer on each one would make different records of t and s, and each one is entitled to his own view. If, however, an observer on the Earth says that there are two special events, the second occurring six units from the first and 10 s later, although the different observers will not agree with these figures, they will all agree that the separation is eight. If A's time and space intervals between another pair of events were 40 and 24 respectively, the separation for every one would be $\sqrt{(40^2 - 24^2)} = 32$, however much we altered the velocity of A's world relative to the observers, or, which is the same, the velocities of the observers relative to A's world. It will now be seen that if a number of objects are at rest with respect to one another, a three-dimensional continuum can represent their spatial relations, but it cannot do this if the objects are in motion with reference to one another. We then need a four-dimensional continuum of space-time. Moreover, the separation in this case between two events, which is equal to the proper time for that body, that is the time interval measured by a clock in the body's universe, is a maximum. While an infinite number of paths can be drawn joining two points in space-time, one stands out uniquely, and all observers agree that it provides a separation greater than any other. This world line is called a *geodesic*, and is the path followed by bodies which are left to themselves. Bertrand Russell, in *The ABC of Relativity*, calls this tendency to follow a geodesic the law of cosmic laziness. As the Earth moves round the Sun it chooses such a route that the time of any portion of its course, judged by its own clocks, is no longer than the time judged by clocks which move in any other route.

Up to the present the principle of special relativity only has been dealt with; this principle was enunciated by Einstein in 1905, and in simple language it implies that no experiment can detect *uniform* motion through the aether (assuming that the aether of space exists). In 1915 Einstein's General Theory of Relativity was published, and this deals with events moving relatively to one another with *variable* velocity. Far-reaching problems are opened up by the general theory which is more difficult than the special theory. Readers are recommended to study some of the more elementary books in the bibliography at the end of this article and that on relativity (e.g., Born), with particular attention to the description of the observer in a lift with a transparent bottom through which he can view the Earth as he drops towards it after release from an aeroplane. This explains the principle of equivalence (of fundamental importance in the General Theory of Relativity) which may be stated as follows: A gravitational field of force is equivalent to an artificial field of force, or to a frame of reference moving with uniform acceleration in a field where there is no gravitation, so that in any small region it is impossible by any experimental means to distinguish between them. The presence of matter, while responsible for creating a gravitational field, can nevertheless be neutralised by an observer in his immediate neighbourhood, and within this small neighbourhood the principles of the restricted special theory are applicable. If, however, an observer is moving through a space-time domain in which there is matter, although he can neutralise the gravitational field in his immediate vicinity and measure the separation of events by his own clock, other observers in different worlds will not agree with him. They will say that the presence of matter has distorted the space-time in its neighbourhood (and the more matter there is the greater is the distortion), and the geodesic, which is straight in the special theory for all observers, is no longer straight. To them the path for maximum separation is now curved owing to the distortion of space-time. All this eliminates the necessity for an 'attractive force' exercised by the Sun on the planets which causes them to describe ellipses with the Sun in one focus. Each planet simply selects such a path that when the distortion of space-time, owing to the presence of a massive body, the Sun, is allowed for, the separation measured along the path between any two events is a maximum. As an illustration we may take the case of a steep hill on which large boulders or other obstructions such as trees, prevent us from walking in a straight line to the top. Instead of attempting to walk in a straight line, it will often be much easier to take circuitous routes, thus avoiding the obstructions. Newton's law of GRAVITATION has now become a geometrical law that every body pursues the easiest course from one place to another, a course which is beset with obstacles in the tangled domain caused by the presence of a great mass like the Sun or any other body. The paths of the planets or other heavenly bodies, computed on the basis of the Newtonian law of gravitation, fits in so closely with the actual paths as observed that Newton's law was generally accepted until recent times. The movement of the perihelion of the orbit of Mercury, which puzzled astronomers for many years, is inexplicable in terms of Newton's law, but is explained, with only a very small discrepancy, by Einstein's geometrical law.

See also COSMOLOGY.

Bibliography: A. Eddington, *Space, Time, and Gravitation*, 1920; E. Schrödinger, *Space-Time Structure*, 1950; M. Jammer, *Concepts of Force: Study in the Foundations of Dynamics*, 1957; M. Born, *Einstein's Theory of Relativity*, rev. ed. 1962; H. Bondi, *Relativity and Common Sense*, 1965; E. F. Taylor and J. A. Wheeler, *Spacetime Physics*, 1966; W. G. V. Rosser, *Introductory Relativity*, 1967; W. Rindler, *Essential Relativity: Special, General, and Cosmological*, 1969; P. A. Schilpp (Ed.), *Albert Einstein: Philosopher-Scientist* (2 vols), 1973.

Space Heating

Space Heating, see AIR CONDITIONING; GAS SPACE HEATERS; HEATING.

Space Travel. A speed of 40,000 km/h enables a rocket to escape from the Earth's gravitational pull, and to set course for other planets. The five-fold increase in rocket speed, from the German V2, was not headline news, until in October 1957 the breakthrough came and the Soviet *Sputnik I* took the world by surprise. Even rockets launched at 27,000 km/h fall back upon the Earth within an hour, while a launch at 29,000 km/h may place a satellite in orbit for years, or even centuries.

The satellites that have been launched fall into four distinct classes: scientific satellites; manned satellites and satellites leading to manned space travel; satellites having commercial applications to benefit men on Earth; and military satellites.

Scientific Satellites. Scientists have been studying the upper atmosphere for at least a century. Observations from balloons and aircraft are limited to say about 30 km altitude, but rocket probes have carried instruments to higher altitudes, supplemented by scientific satellites for altitudes over 150 km. The International Geophysical Year was convened to make a concerted scientific study of conditions in the atmosphere, and it may be said to have brought about the launching of the first satellites. Measurements have been made of temperature, density, composition of atmosphere, wind velocity, number and type of electrified particles, magnetic field, intensity of sunlight in the radio, infrared, visible, ultraviolet, X-ray, and gamma radiations. Some of these observations have been made with astronomical telescopes in orbit. Many of these phenomena are unable to penetrate the Earth's atmosphere, which filters them out, and thus observations of phenomena are often being made for the first time; astronomers speak of the two 'windows' into space, through which they have been forced to 'look', the familiar one in the visible region, and the other in the UHF radio bands, used by radio astronomers. *Explorer I* enabled Dr J. van Allen, USA, to make a discovery, in 1958, of two rings or belts of very energetic charged particles surrounding the Earth's equatorial regions. The positively charged proton belt lies at 3000 km altitude, and a belt of negatively charged electrons is situated at 30,000 km altitude. By their rapid spiral movement, these charged particles generate a magnetic field which interacts with the Earth's magnetic field so as to toss them from pole to pole indefinitely. There is a rough balance between particles lost by collisions and new particles trapped as they arrive from outer space. These van Allen belts represent a serious hazard to man, transistors, and other types of equipment sensitive to radiation, a hazard not known before the advent of space travel. It has also been found that the Earth and its trapped particles are in a solar wind consisting of charged particles shot out from the Sun. Solar flares occur from time to time, and take 36 hours to reach the Earth. Their prediction will be vital to future manned space travel as radiation concentrations dangerous to human life exist during a solar flare.

Manned Space Travel. The second *Sputnik* contained a live dog Laika and was the first stage towards manned space travel, followed in 1961 by Yuri GAGARIN, who made one complete orbit of the Earth and landed back in the USSR, using a drag-retarded vehicle named

Vostok. This exploit was followed by a 17-orbit flight by Titov, then Glenn (USA) made a 3-orbit trip. Other noteworthy feats have been 'walking in space', which showed the possibility of in-flight vehicle maintenance, and rendezvous between two or more spacecraft in orbit. In December 1968 the first men orbited the Moon, and in July 1969 the US astronauts Neil ARMSTRONG and Edwin Aldrin made the first Moon landing by men. They were followed by several other US crews. Since the end of the *Apollo* flights in 1972 the US space programme has been centred on long-duration flights in a station called *Skylab*, orbiting the Earth. Manned transfer to *Skylab* will be via the *Space Shuttle*, a re-usable vehicle that can be flown back to base like an aeroplane. Recovery in space will be improved by the joint code of practice worked out by the USSR and USA and put into effect in the successful *Apollo-Soyuz* link-up.

Unmanned shots designed to explore conditions by means of instruments are always sent before subjecting humans to the unknown. This category includes the US *Surveyor* and *Lunar Orbiter* craft which respectively soft landed and photographed the Moon from close range to aid selection of the most suitable landing site. In 1971 the Soviet Union landed an automatic car called *Lunokhod* which drove on the Moon's surface. They also collected small samples of Moon rock by automatic probes and brought them back to Earth.

Information from unmanned flights to Venus indicate that it is too hot to permit manned landings. The dense atmosphere consists mostly of carbon dioxide, and the surface pressure is about 100 times as great as Earth's atmospheric pressure. The US *Mariner 4* spacecraft in 1965 sent the first television pictures of Mars, which showed the surface to be covered by circular 'craters' very much like the Moon, with little trace of the straight lines or 'canals' supposed to have been seen by astronomers. The technology involved in taking, transmitting, and receiving these pictures from a planet that never comes within 57 million km of the Earth marked a great step forward in the art of radio communication. Later probes showed that the atmosphere is made of thin, unbreathable carbon dioxide gas. There is no appreciable amount of water on Mars, or on the Moon. Mars may be as lifeless as the Moon, although photographs sent by the *Mariner 9* probe in 1972 show what appear to be active volcanoes on Mars. The 1976 photographs from *Viking I* show the crater structure on Mars exhibits surprising differences from those on the Moon. The *Viking* craft are carrying out experiments to see if the Martian soil contains primitive organisms. *Viking I* landed on Mars in July 1976, and was followed by *Viking 2* in September 1976.

Manned spacecraft design incorporates the well-developed techniques of pressure cabins as in airliners, as well as precautions against other known hazards. The first of these, collision with meteorites and other rapidly moving space debris, was exaggerated in the past, but will remain a peril. A light 'meteor bumper' round the spacecraft will vaporise all but the largest meteors. In addition to the radiation hazard to health mentioned above under scientific satellites, there is the problem of high-energy particles from space called cosmic rays, which may damage an astronaut's brain. The effects of weightlessness are not as severe as had been thought, although astronauts on

Space Travel. ABOVE *Apollo 10* command and service module seen from the lunar module. BELOW *Apollo 11* and Buzz Aldrin on the Moon. *(Popperfoto)*

Space Travel

long missions have to perform exercises to keep their muscles and heart in trim. The fourth new hazard is that experienced when re-entering the Earth's atmosphere. The use of rocket braking in space is expensive; thus if it takes a rocket of 200 t to put 1 t in orbit, it would take an orbiting rocket of 200 t to land 1 t safely back on the Earth by retro-braking, and this would mean a launch rocket of 40,000 t. Fortunately when returning to Earth the atmosphere can be used for braking, changing the kinetic energy of motion into heat, which can be absorbed by the air, and also radiated into space. Manned space capsules employ a bluff front end, which while it absorbs a little of this heat, generates a strong shock wave in the air, which heats the air at a distance from the capsule. Some 95 per cent of the heat can be dissipated in this fashion. A variant of the aerodynamic drag retarded re-entry is to use a triangular aircraft-shaped capsule, and to fly it at a high angle of incidence, so as to produce a single inclined strong shock wave, which not only slows down the capsule, but produces a lift force which can be used to sustain and to steer the vehicle to the best landing site. To replace the costly rockets which are destroyed on use, the United States plans to test the *Space Shuttle*.

Applications Satellites. Foremost among these are communications satellites. With the exception of a few limited frequency bands—the broadcast bands—radio waves travel in straight lines, and distant reception of land-based television stations is impossible on account of the Earth's curvature. This can be overcome by placing the transmitter in orbit, where it can receive a programme from one continent and relay it to another. Telephone and telegraphic messages can also be transmitted. The *Intelsat* series and the Soviet *Molniya* have proved vital to world communications. The latest *Intelsat* designs can relay 6000 telephone conversations, or 12 colour channels. The ground stations at the two ends are giant radio dish aerials some 25 m in diameter, which focus on the satellite, and increase the ratio of signal to noise. There are three general types of orbit which appear to be useful: (1) sunseeking, which gives better service in local daylight (peak) hours; (2) longitude-seeking or stationary, such as *Intelsat*, which is at an altitude of 35,700 km and co-rotates with the Earth, so that the satellite appears to hover above a particular longitude on the equator; and (3) latitude-seeking, such as *Molniya*, which orbits in ellipses and spends most of its time over a particular band of latitudes in the northern hemisphere. These satellites have come to dominate worldwide communications. There are new plans for 'domestic' satellites which will relay local information, such as agricultural or medical information to remote areas of India. Another type of 'applications' satellite is the weather satellite, of which *Nimbus* is a good example. Pictures of cloud cover are relayed back to weather stations enabling forecasts to be made more quickly and accurately. Hurricanes can be detected some three days sooner by this means. The ice formations in the St Lawrence River have also been examined easily by examining weather satellite pictures. Ordnance survey and navigation have also been improved by using a satellite as one apex of a very large triangle. Both manned and automatic missions are now planned to study the location of natural resources on Earth.

Military Satellites. The conquest of space promises to be much more peaceful than the conquest of the air.

Foreign territory is continually photographed by satellites. It is much more economical and reliable to send a bomb by ballistic missile than to re-enter it from a satellite, or fire it from the Moon. Satellites cannot 'drop' bombs, in the simple manner that an aircraft can. Again, bombs exploding in space cannot generate a shock wave in the non-existent air, so their effect is far less. The US 'rainbow' bomb was a nuclear explosion in space, which produced its own radiation belts for some months, but the explosive force was reduced by being let off in space. It is to be hoped that the international agreement that all celestial bodies are international will be observed. Thus the military applications of space seem to be much smaller than is commonly supposed.

Bibliography: A. C. Clarke (Ed.), *Coming of the Space Age*, 1967; House of Commons, *United Kingdom Space Activities: Select Committee on Science and Technology Report*, 1971; R. Turnill, *Observer's Book of Manned Space Flight*, 1972, and *Observer's Book of Unmanned Space Flight*, 1974; M. T. Bizony (Ed.), *New Space Encyclopaedia: Guide to Astronomy and Space Research*, 2nd ed. 1973; B. Lovell, *Origins and International Economics of Space Exploration*, 1973; K. W. Gatland, *Pocket Encyclopaedia of Space Flight*, 1975; A. L. Levine, *Future of the United States Space Program*, 1975; P. Moore, *The Next Fifty Years in Space*, 1976; C. Sarfas, *Space and Space Travel*, 1976.

Spaghetti, see PASTA.

Spahi, name derived from the Persian word *Sipah*, whence the English 'Sepoy', formerly applied to part of the Turkish cavalry before the reorganisation of 1836. From 1326 to that time they formed a formidable part of the sultan's army. The French gave the same name to a body of light cavalry organised in Algeria and Tunisia.

Spahlinger, Henry (1882–1965), Swiss bacteriologist, born in Geneva and educated at the university there. He was director of the Bacteriological Research Institute, Carouge, Geneva. Most of his work was on the study of TUBERCULOSIS, its therapy and prevention. In 1912 he introduced a method of treatment of tuberculosis now named after him and consisting of: (1) the destruction of tuberculous toxins by injection of various bacteriolytic and antitoxic sera; and (2) therapeutic vaccination with a series of tuberculins. He made his method public in 1932.

Spain (Spanish *España*, Latin *Hispania*, Greek *Iberia*), country of south-western Europe, forming with Portugal the Iberian Peninsula. It is separated from France on the north by the PYRENEES, on the east and south by the Mediterranean Sea, in the north-west it has a coast on the Bay of Biscay, and on the west is bounded by the Atlantic Ocean and Portugal. GIBRALTAR lies at its extreme southerly point. Area 489,506 km².

Geography. Relief. Geologically the peninsula is an ancient raised landmass, the *meseta*, situated between high mountains of more recent development, the Pyrenees and the ranges of ANDALUSIA. The *meseta* is drained by a series of parallel rivers, which flow from east to west. The most important of these is the GUADALQUIVIR, which flows through Andalusia to the Atlantic and is navigable as far as SEVILLE. The other rivers, including the Minho, Duero, Tajo, and Guadiana, are too small in volume to be of value as waterways. The EBRO, the longest river in Spain, runs south-eastwards in a tectonic basin to

Spain. Landscape in Castile. *(Topham/Fotogram)*

the Mediterranean, providing irrigation for the plains of ARAGON and CATALONIA. The line of the Pyrenees continues parallel to the south coast of the Bay of Biscay in the CANTABRIAN MOUNTAINS. To the south-east the Cordillera Ibérica forms the watershed between the Duero and the Tajo on the one side and the Ebro on the other. Further south are the Betic cordilleras which end in the rocky promontory of Gibraltar. The country is divided by three parallel ranges: the Sierra Morena separates the valleys of the Guadalquivir and the Guadiana; the mountains of Toledo separate the Guadiana and the Tajo; and the Sierra de Guadarrama separates the Tajo and the Duero. See ATLAS 21.

Climate. The hinterland of the Bay of Biscay and the Atlantic coast has an equable climate. GALICIA has the heaviest rainfall (Santiago de Compostela has 200 mm annually). In the *meseta* long winters are followed by short springs and very hot summers. MADRID has temperatures over 40°C in summer and below freezing in winter; the Guadarrama Mountains, a short distance from the city, are covered with snow during most of the year. The Mediterranean coast has mild, wet winters and hot, dry summers in general, though the region between Valencia and Gibraltar is sub-tropical. ALMERIA is the driest province, with 30 mm of rain a year.

Population. The position of Spain in southern Europe meant that it received influxes of population from the north, including CELTS, from the south, the MOORS, and from eastern Mediterranean lands, in particular Phoenicians, Greeks, and Romans. The Arab and Roman influences left the most lasting imprint. Today the only ethnic minority in Spain is the 200,000 gypsies. The total population (including the Balearic and Canary Islands) is 35,850,000. Madrid is the capital, and other major cities are BARCELONA, VALENCIA, SEVILLE, and SARAGOSSA. Spain is a predominantly industrial country, and since the 1930s there has been a major movement of population away from the countryside to the towns.

Bibliography: E. Allison Peers, *Spain: A Companion to Spanish Travel*, 1930; W. B. Fisher and H. Bowen-Jones, *Spain: An*

Spain. Winter scene in the Sierra Morena. *(Topham/Fotogram)*

Spain

Introductory Geography, 1966; J. A. Michener, *Iberia*, 1968; S. Sitwell, *Spain*, 1975.

Economy. Agriculture. Except in the humid northern coastal region, natural conditions for agriculture are poor over much of Spain because of aridity, thin soils, and abrupt relief. Only 21 million ha can be considered arable out of a total area of over 50 million ha. This situation is complicated by an inequitable property distribution, large estates in the south and south-west contrasting with small fragmented farms in the centre and north. State efforts to remedy these conditions have been directed to irrigation, land settlement, farm consolidation, and reafforestation. More sophisticated consumer tastes and the reduction of the farm labour force from 42 to 27 per cent of the active population over the period 1960–72 have allowed wheat production, often on unsuitable land, to be diminished in exchange for fodder crops, meat, and dairy products. Fresh fruit production has also been expanded. Oranges are an important export, as also are olive products (of which Spain is the world's largest producer) and wines such as Rioja, Valdepeñas, and Jerez.

Industry. Spain is rich in minerals and has played an historic role as an ore producer for Europe. Moreover, as a result of the demand for raw materials for its fast-expanding industries, coupled with a world crisis in the price and supply of minerals, Spanish mining is enjoying a resurgence. Nevertheless, Spain cannot now supply its own raw material and energy requirements; despite expanded domestic production of coal, hydro- and thermal electricity, and atomic energy, and an extensive oil-prospecting campaign, oil imports account for the greater part of Spain's balance of payments deficit. It is through the growth of manufacturing industry that Spain has become the fifth industrial producer in Western Europe. Spanish gross industrial output in 1972 was 13 times greater than in 1960, a rate of growth surpassed only by

Spain. Vineyards in Tarragona. *(Topham/Fotogram)*

Japan among the 22 OECD nations. The most dynamic branches of industry have been the non-traditional ones— vehicles, ships (Spain is the world's fourth shipbuilding nation), machinery, metal products, and chemicals— whereas traditional activities (foodstuffs, woodworking, and textiles) have grown only slowly. The importance of foreign investment in Spanish industry can be seen in that, of the first 500 companies in the country, over 200 have a foreign participation.

Communications. Spain had 13,400 km of railway track in 1975; the Renfe plan (1974–77) called for the electrification of 2750 km. Madrid and Barcelona both have underground systems and these are to be expanded. There are 142,000 km of roads but this includes only 450 km of motorway with another 250 km under construction. Iberia is the national airline.

Trade. Spain's traditional exports used to be agricultural products and raw materials, but these have now been superseded by industrial manufactures (ships, vehicles and vehicle parts, and a wide range of consumer goods), which made up 63 per cent of all exports in 1973. The European Economic Community is Spain's main customer, taking 47·45 per cent of exports in 1974, followed by the United States (12 per cent), Latin America (9 per cent), and growing sales to the OPEC and COMECON countries. Spain's imports consist largely of machinery, manufactured goods, fuel, and raw materials for economic development, and considerably exceed exports. The heavy trade deficit (exports covered only 51 per cent of imports in 1974) is usually compensated by capital inflows, remittances from the 1·1 million Spaniards working abroad ($1414 million in 1973), and earnings from tourism ($3274 million in the same year). Spain has the world's largest surplus from tourism and received 30 million visitors in 1975, a figure nearly equal to the indigenous population. Tourism has been the main motor of economic development, and recognition of Spanish success in this field can be seen in the choice of Madrid as the permanent headquarters of the World Tourist Organisation.

Planning. After a period of comparative stagnation, which lasted from the end of the Spanish Civil War in 1939 until 1959 and which was the product of political isolation, attempts at self-sufficiency and xenophobic attitudes on the part of the government, Spain has undergone

Spain. Cultivating newly-planted Palamino grape vines at a vineyard just outside Jerez. *(Barnaby's Picture Library)*

a rapid economic transformation. Belated assistance to recovery from the civil war was provided by the United States under pacts signed on 26 September 1953, by which America sent non-military aid to Spain in return for strategic bases in that country. The real turning point for the economy, however, was the Stabilisation Plan of July 1959, which was prepared with the assistance of the OEEC (now OECD) and the International Monetary Fund. In exchange for $420 million of aid, the Spanish government forsook economic autarchy and introduced a freer market system, reforming its foreign exchange arrangements, freeing imports, progressively eliminating price and other controls, and above all liberalising legislation on foreign investments.

Since the early 1960s the Spanish economy has been the fastest-growing in Western Europe, because of the low international value of the *peseta*, cheap labour costs, and high increases in productivity brought about by strong foreign capital investment, which reached $934 million in 1972. Since 1964 economic development has been guided by a series of four-year plans. The great volume of imports needed for these development programmes has been paid for by increased exports (made possible by improved productivity and low wage costs) and by large injections of foreign currency from emigrants' remittances and tourism. As a result, Spain has been transformed from an agricultural into an industrial country and living standards have risen rapidly, income per head increasing fourfold between 1963 and 1974, to $2000. There have however been recent manifestations of a pronounced slowing down in economic growth.

Finance. Spain's impressive economic growth and stability have made the *peseta* one of the world's hard currencies. Foreign currency reserves equalled $6000 million at the end of 1974.

Currency, Weights and Measures. The unit of currency is the *peseta*, which has 100 *céntimos*. The *peseta* has in 1976 an exchange rate of 124 pesetas to £1 sterling. The metric system is in general use.

Bibliography: S. G. Payne, *Franco's Spain*, 1968; J. Vincens Vives, *An Economic History of Spain*, 1969; G. Hills, *Spain*, 1970; M. Roman, *The Limits of Economic Growth in Spain*, 1972.

Government. *Constitution.* Spain, except for a republican interlude in 1874, was an hereditary monarchy until ALFONSO XIII left the country in 1931 without formally abdicating. The republic, which then followed, was brought to an end when the present state was established by the victory of General FRANCO in April 1939 at the end of a three-year civil war (see *History* below). The present Spanish constitution is made up of seven fundamental laws promulgated over a period of nearly 30 years, from the first one, the Labour Charter issued in 1938, to the more recent, the Organic Law of the State, dated January 1967. One of these laws, the Succession Law of 1947, turned Spain again into a monarchy, leaving in the hands of General Franco the choice of the future king and the moment of his accession to the throne. In 1969 Franco chose Prince Juan Carlos, grandson of Alfonso XIII, to be his heir, although he did not become king until Franco's death on 20 November 1975. The Spanish monarch enjoys wide constitutional powers in political and administrative matters. He appoints the President of the Government (prime minister) and, on the latter's recommendation,

other members of the Council of the Realm. *Las Cortes*, the Spanish parliament, is bi-cameral. It is made up of a lower house of 350 members, and an upper house (or Senate) consisting of 207 elected members and 41 nominated by the king.

Political Parties. From 1937 to 1977 the National Movement was the only political party permitted in Spain; it was abolished on 1 April 1977. Other political parties were legalised that year, including the Communist party; and 156 parties grouped together in 10 national coalitions and 12 regional alliances contested the general elections held on 15 June 1977.

Justice. Justice is administered by *tribunales* and *juzgados* (tribunals and courts), which together form the *Poder Judicial* (Judicial Power). They consist of a *Tribunal Supremo*, 15 *audiencias territoriales* (divisional high courts), 50 *audiencias provinciales* (provincial high courts), over 570 *juzgados de primera instancia* (courts of first instance), and over 9000 *juzgados municipales, comarcales y de paz* (local magistrates' courts).

Local Administration. The provinces are composed of municipalities presided over by the *ayuntamiento* (municipal council). Each council has a number of *concejales* (councillors) elected by heads of families, trade unions, and other local corporations. The *alcalde* (mayor) is elected by the councillors, except in Madrid and Barcelona where he is appointed by the government. The provinces are administered by the *diputaciones provinciales* (county councils) elected in a way similar to that of the municipal councils. Given the highly centralised nature of Spanish government, municipal and provincial councils enjoy rather limited financial and administrative powers.

Overseas Possessions. Having granted independence to Equatorial Guinea (1968), and handed over Spanish Sahara to Morocco (1976), Spain's only overseas territories are the Canary Islands and two small towns in North Africa: CEUTA and MELILLA.

Armed Forces. Military service is compulsory (18 months). The total strength of the armed forces is 302,300 men, and the defence budget in 1973 was $995 million. The army is 220,000 strong, divided into one armoured division, two mountain divisions, two mechanised infantry divisions, one armoured cavalry brigade, 11 infantry brigades, one high mountain brigade, two parachute brigades, two artillery brigades, two battalions with surface-to-air missiles, and smaller garrisons in the Balearic and Canary Islands, and at Ceuta and Melilla in North Africa. The navy, 46,000 men strong, has eight submarines, 25 destroyers, one cruiser, five corvettes, 23 minesweepers, one helicopter carrier, nine frigates (some with surface-to-air missiles), and a high number of other craft and vessels. The air force, 35,700 strong, has 201 combat aircraft, 11 fighter bomber squadrons, one anti-submarine squadron, and various other transport, auxiliary, and training units. On 26 September 1953 the USA and Spain signed an agreement covering economic aid and the construction and use of military facilities in Spain by the USA; an agreement which included a naval base at Rota, near Cádiz, and several air bases. This agreement has been renewed several times, the most recent and for a period of five years in January 1976.

Education. Elementary education is compulsory and free up to the age of 14. In 1973 there were approximately

Spain

4·5 million pupils attending primary schools, and 1,800,000 in secondary education. A large percentage of the latter attend private and denominational schools. There are 20 state universities including Barcelona (two), Bilbao, Granada, Madrid (two), Murcia, Oviedo, Salamanca, Santiago, Sevilla, Valencia, Valladolid, Zaragoza, and La Laguna (Canary Islands); two independent universities are at Bilbao and Pamplona, plus a number of polytechnics and higher technical schools. There is also a 'university of the air'.

Welfare. There is a fairly wide scheme of national insurance in operation providing cover for all workers and a large number of the self-employed. The scheme covers accident at work, temporary and permanent incapacity, help for dependants, and widows' and old-age pensions. Contributions are paid jointly by employer and employee on a scale dependent on income.

Religion. The great majority of the people are Roman Catholic. The church was disestablished in 1931, but was re-established under the present régime. There are ten metropolitan sees and 64 suffragan sees. The Archbishop of Toledo is primate. A Concordat was signed in Rome on 27 August 1953 to replaced that abrogated in 1931. There are about 35,000 Protestants with some 200 chapels and churches. There are approximately 1000 practising Jews in Spain.

Official Language. Spanish, although Catalan is widely spoken in the north-east, and Basque in the north.

National Anthem. Title: *Marcha Real Española* (author and origin unknown). It was adopted by Charles III in 1770.

National Flag. Three horizontal bands of red, yellow, and red, with the national coat-of-arms.

Bibliography: B. Crozier, *Franco*, 1967; S. G. Payne, *Franco's Spain*, 1968; R. Tamames, *La República: La Era de Franco*, 1973; R. de la Cierva, *Historia básica de la España actual*, 1974; J. Amodia, *Franco's Political Legacy*, 1976.

Prehistory. The prehistory of Spain has attracted a good deal of attention. The distribution and significance of MEGALITHIC CULTURE have an important bearing on the Neolithic culture of Western Europe. The CAVE ART includes impressive cave paintings of great antiquity in the province of Asturias at Altamira, Castilio, Pindal, etc., and many others in different parts of the peninsula; also shelters in Cantabria with drawings depicting men and women as well as animals. The most important sites are Cogul near Lerida, Valltorta and Albarracim. The style is similar to that of some palaeolithic rock drawings in North Africa.

Rock shelter art is also found in the Neolithic and Early Bronze Ages in megalithic tombs. The Iberian settlement of the peninsula may have started c. 3000 BC or the Neolithic era. The first metal workers, called the Millaran culture after the fort of Los Millares, were dominant in the south until ousted by the attacks of beaker-using nomads (see BEAKER PEOPLE) who spread c. 2200 BC over Spain and, later, into most of North Europe.

Late in the Bronze Age the Tartesians settled on the shores of the Guadalquivir River, spread to the south-east of Spain and either absorbed or drove the Iberians to the lands beyond, and to the north of the Alicante. About 600 BC the Celts entered Spain via the Pyrenees and arrived at the West Atlantic coast. Eventually they fused with the Iberians. Greek settlements, notably Ampurias, were founded in the 6th and 5th centuries. In the 4th century the Carthaginians settled in the south.

Bibliography: H. N. Savory, *Spain and Portugal*, 1968.

Early History. The history of Spain begins with the Carthaginian invasion (238 BC). HAMILCAR and HASDRUBAL conquered most of the south-east as far as the Iberus (Ebro), and Carthago Nova (Cartagena) was founded in 228. These successes aroused the jealousy of Rome, and in 226 a treaty was concluded between the two peoples. The capture of Saguntum by Hannibal in 219 was the *casus belli* of the Second Punic War. The Romans drove the Carthaginians from the peninsula, but nearly

Spain. Cave drawing from Canton de la Visera showing herds of oxen, human figures, and a bird. *(Mansell Collection)*

two centuries elapsed before they had mastered the whole country. At the end of the Second Punic War (201 BC) they organised Spain into two provinces: Hispania Citerior, east of the Iberus, and Hispania Ulterior, west of that river; by far the greater part of this latter was only potentially under Roman rule. Augustus completed the conquest of Spain and made a new division of three provinces as follows: (1) Tarraconensis, including the whole of the north-west and centre; (2) Baetica, separated from the former by a line drawn from the Anas (Guadiana) to a point on the Mediterranean about 2°E; and (3) Lusitania, corresponding roughly to modern Portugal. Henceforward Spain was thoroughly Romanised. The emperors Trajan and Hadrian were born at Italica on the River Baetis; while Latin literature of the early Empire is distinguished by the names of Seneca, Lucan, Martial, and Quintilian, all of whom were of Spanish origin.

With the decline of the Roman Empire, the 'barbarians of the north' entered the peninsula (AD 409), and the Visigoths under Euric (Ewaric) established their supremacy and remained rulers of Spain until the beginning of the 8th century. However, the Roman law and Roman system of administration were too firmly ingrained to be swept away by the barbarian invaders. The administration was modelled directly on that of the Roman system. The first four kings of Visigothic Spain, after the death of Amalric, were Arians. In the reign of Reccared (586–601) the Catholic religion was adopted by the kings of Spain and Arianism abandoned. With the reign of Roderic, the Visigothic kingdom came to an end.

Bibliography: C. H. V. Sutherland, *The Romans in Spain, 217 BC–117 AD*, 1939; A. H. M. Jones, *The Later Roman Empire, 284–602*, 1964; E. A. Thompson, *The Goths in Spain*, 1969.

Modern History. The Muslim invasion began in July 711. Tarik, the Muslim general, crossed the straits, landed in the south of Spain, and immediately defeated Roderic. Reinforcements poured in from Africa, and by 718 the Muslims had reached the Pyrenees. Rapidly they overran the south of France and penetrated to the Loire, only to be beaten back here by CHARLES MARTEL at Tours (732). The ease with which the peninsula had been conquered illustrates the anarchy which existed in the country before the invasion. The inhabitants of Spain regarded the Muslims simply as the successors of their previous masters; to them it was a matter of indifference whether they were ruled by Muslims or Visigoths. They retained their religion, they paid their customary dues, and they were far better governed by the representatives of the caliph than they had been by the Visigoths. But the Muslims who conquered Spain were themselves a mixed race. The Arab and the Berber could not live in peace; the struggles of the Ommiads and the Abbasides led to disruption; Arab and Berber fought out their quarrels in Spain, and soon the early anarchy of the Visigothic days returned.

This lack of unity among the Muslims enabled the Christian states in the north to keep their identity. Strongest of the Christian kingdoms was Galicia. As its population increased so did its bounds, and with the increase of Galicia and Asturias (Asturo Galaica) came the beginning of the struggle of León and Castile against the Moors. Gradually Castile became the leading Christian

power, and played the greatest part in the reconquest of the country. From the middle of the 8th to the middle of the 9th century, the rule of the Muslims had been a failure; it had been strong or weak according to the character of the emir. The 10th and the beginning of the 11th centuries, however, saw the revival of the power of the Muslims. This increase corresponded with a decrease in the power of the Christians, due to dissension. The reign of Abd-er-Rahman III was the heyday of Moorish prosperity. He re-established law and order, he gave the country peace, and reduced even the Christian states to his vassalage. From 912 to 961 he ruled the country with a firm hand, and his reign was both magnificent and just. His son continued the good rule (961–76), but later adventurers and puppets were placed on the throne, and the Moorish Empire seemed on the verge of extinction. It was broken up into small states, and, above all, the Christian states began to revive.

Between the years 912 and 1002 the Christian states in the north had been crushed by the power of the caliphs. They had also had internal troubles, and so had been unable to withstand the spread of the strong Moorish power. The Christian states had endured a period of anarchy as bad as that of the Moors, but they emerged from it in a better state than before. When the kingdom of Castile was founded in 1037 it had traditions and laws, and had already granted many of its serfs emancipation, and many of its towns charters. The great model charter of León had been granted by Alfonso V in 1020. Sancho the Great of Navarra and his son FERDINAND I did much to unite the kingdoms of the north. Castile, León, and Galicia were by this time united as one kingdom, whilst the other kingdoms of the north were regarded as dependencies of this larger one. Under Ferdinand the reconquest of Spain began. He advanced as far as the Tagus, threatened Valencia, entered Andalusia, and even penetrated as far as Seville. Ferdinand I died in 1065, and his possessions were divided amongst his three sons; but the greatest share of power passed to his second son, Alfonso VI, whose reign is one of the most important in this period of the history of Spain. He continued the work of his father with conspicuous success, and by his marriage with a Burgundian princess made Castile a power in western Europe. Against the Moors his success was immediate, and he overran the whole of Muslim Spain, and even took the town of Toledo (1085). The fall of Toledo occasioned the invasion of the ALMORAVIDES from Africa, and the conquests of Alfonso were checked by the defeat of Zalaca. Alfonso had to give up some of his conquests, but he kept Toledo, and he had shown that it was possible to defeat the Moors.

The Almoravids were more fanatical and less cultivated than the Spanish Arabs, and did much to alienate their Christian subjects, and also their Muslim predecessors. During the next hundred years the Christian conquest of Spain continued. In 1230 the crowns of León and Castile were finally united, and already the various spheres of expansion had been marked out for Castile and Aragon respectively. Castile was to develop to the south; Murcia and Andalusia were to belong to it, whilst Aragon was to expand by conquering Valencia and the Balearic Islands. By 1248, under FERDINAND III, the Moorish possessions in Spain were reduced to Granada and the ports and hinterland of Almería, Adra, Motril, and

Spain. *The Surrender of Granada* by Pradilla; Ferdinand and Isabella receive the city from the Moors. *(Palacio del Senado, Madrid/Photo MAS)*

Málaga. Alfonso X, the Learned, was succeeded by his son Sancho IV, whose reign was occupied in putting down the revolts of rivals, and was followed by the confusion of two long minorities. The cruelties of PEDRO THE CRUEL were terminated only by his murder. He was succeeded by Henry II, Count of Trastamara, king by election. During his reign the power of the *Cortes* was great, but it could not check the absolute power of the king. He was succeeded by John I, who claimed the succession to the throne of Portugal, but, defeated in battle, had to give up that claim. His son, Henry III, physically weak, was nevertheless able to restore order to Castile, and was succeeded by his son John II. During the minority of this king, Ferdinand, his uncle, was elected king of Aragon (he was Ferdinand II of Aragon and Sicily and III of Naples). The history of Aragon during this period is closely connected with Sicily and Naples. When the throne of Aragon was left vacant, in 1410, Ferdinand, the uncle of the King of Castile, was elected to the vacancy, although the crown should, by strict hereditary rule, have passed to John II of Castile.

The separation between the two kingdoms, however, did not last much longer. In 1474, on the death of Henry IV, his sister Isabella claimed the throne of Castile. In 1426 Ferdinand, the uncle of John of Castile, had died and was succeeded by Alfonso V, whose Spanish possessions were ruled for him by his brother John I, who finally succeeded to the throne in 1458 on the death of Alfonso V. His reign was occupied chiefly in war, and he died in 1479, leaving the throne to his son Ferdinand, who in 1469 had married Isabella of Castile. The union of Spain was at last accomplished.

The reign of the 'Catholic' sovereigns was the beginning of the greatness of Spain. Spain's foreign policy made it one of the great European powers. Whilst many of the later ills of Spain can be traced to mistakes made during this period, most of its glories originated at this time, too. The Moors were finally driven out, and united Spain was able to proclaim itself the leader of Europe. The various kingdoms and provinces were united under one central authority. The peninsula was rounded off by the final cession of Spanish Navarra to the crown of Spain, and gradually the independent *Cortes* of the various provinces, although nominally they still held power, became subservient to the central authority. The discovery of America and the papal division of the sphere of discovery between Spain and Portugal was of vast importance to the new monarchy, whose watchword was 'Catholicism'. The Spanish kings regarded themselves as essentially *the* Catholic sovereigns of Europe. Nor was this unnatural for Spain had vindicated its claim to the title in its long centuries of war with the Muslims, and later when Protestantism became a vital force, no one had more right to champion the Holy See than the Spanish kings.

On the death of Isabella, the crown of Castile passed to her daughter Joanna the Mad, who had married Philip, the son of Maximilian the German emperor. For a time Castile and Aragon were ruled separately, but on the death of Philip, Ferdinand again administered Spain and finally, on his death, left the whole of his kingdom to his daughter and to her son Charles as regent. In 1516 Charles practically succeeded to the throne of Spain as Charles I, and three years later was elected to the throne of Maximilian and ruled as CHARLES V, and by this latter name he is best known. During his reign the history of Spain, or at least of the Spanish king, is the history of Europe. The importance of this reign to Spain itself, however, lies in the fact that during it the royal power was definitely established, the monarchy became wholly despotic, and the constitutions of the various provinces were practically abolished. Trouble arose with the last remnants of the Moors in the Alpujarras mountains where they were severely defeated. Charles also attempted to crush them in north Africa. Here his attempt on Tunis was a success, but he failed to capture Algiers. His love for Flanders, and the number of Flemish favourites whom he appointed to high positions in the Spanish court, was also a cause of internal trouble, and finally, worn out by disease and worry, he abdicated. He failed to obtain the election of his son, Philip, to the Empire; that crown passed to his brother; but his hereditary possessions he left to his son, who reigned as PHILIP II and amongst these were the Netherlands. It was now the policy of Spain to obtain a means of land communication from the Netherlands to the peninsula. To do this the territory of France was threatened, the result being that the possession of the Netherlands meant the continued hostility of France. Philip was a man of tenacious purpose, but lacking political flair, and totally devoid of imagination. He regarded himself as, above all else, the Catholic champion of Europe. This position was the keystone of his life's work, and he died still pursuing this policy and having ruined Spain in its pursuit. He ruled over the empire of Spain at its greatest. His power extended over Spain, the Netherlands, the greater part of Italy, the whole of South America, a large part of North America, possessions in the East Indies and in Africa. He possessed the finest fighting machine in Europe, both military and naval. He won the great victory of Lepanto over the Turks. His position in Europe as the greatest monarch was unquestioned, yet he was broken by his fatal policy in the Netherlands, by which he raised up the hatred of France, by the cruelties of Alva in Flanders, which led to the revolt of the Netherlands, and by his quarrel with England, which led to the destruction of the powerful Spanish fleet (see ARMADA, SPANISH).

The greatest days of Spain passed with Philip's death in 1598. The century which followed saw a rapid decline; the reign of Philip III witnessed the final declaration of the independence of the United Provinces. The military history of the closing stages of the war suggests that Spain finally lost it through lack of resources and not because of military deficiency; almost at the end of the struggle it could still win ephemeral military triumphs, as at Breda. PHILIP IV ruled practically from the beginning to the end of the Thirty Years' War, a war in which Spain took an active part, but from which it received little reward. Its soldiers, however, were still the finest in Europe. By the Peace of Westphalia the independence both of Portugal, which had been incorporated with Spain in 1580, and of the United Provinces was recognised. The power of France had been steadily increasing during the whole of

this period, until finally France, under Louis XIV, had become the dominant power in Europe. In the wars of the reign of Louis XIV Spain had its share, but it gained nothing and lost something after each war.

During the whole of the reign of CHARLES II (1665–1700) Europe waited for the division of the spoils at his death. France, Austria, and Bavaria had claims to the Spanish throne. It was known that Charles II would die childless. Two partition treaties were arranged. The first provided for the accession of the young Elector of Bavaria, and the two other powers were compensated from the still large dominions of Spain. The second gave the throne to Austria and again compensated France from the residue to the empire. The Spanish king and people, however, repudiated both treaties, and by the will of Charles II the whole of the Spanish dominions were left to Philip of Anjou, grandson of Louis XIV, and he was proclaimed King of Spain in May 1700. This led, however, to the War of the Spanish Succession, the beginning of the downfall of the supremacy of France. By the Treaty of Utrecht, 1713, all Spain's Italian possessions, the Netherlands, Minorca, and Gibraltar were taken from it leaving it one of the weakest powers in Europe. Spain's relations with Britain continued to be bad, and again culminated in war in 1738.

The period from the death of Philip V (1746–88) was a golden age of Spanish internal history. Ferdinand VI (1746–59) and Charles III (1759–88) initiated wide reforms, reformed the revenues, and placed Spain again upon a satisfactory financial basis. Roads were improved, commerce encouraged, banks firmly established, and the colonial revenues carefully and wisely superintended.

In 1788 Charles IV became king, and Spain quickly reverted to the state of affairs which had existed in the reign of Charles II. The ministers of Charles III were replaced by the royal favourite GODOY, who was greedy and incompetent. On the outbreak of the French Revolution, Spain at first took no part, but finally, after the execution of the French king, declared war. It was however, in 1796, forced to sign a treaty with France by which it promised aid to the French. The result was that its fleet was defeated at St Vincent and its trade practically annihilated. Finally in 1807 a quarrel between Charles IV and his son Ferdinand culminated in an appeal to Napoleon. Charles and Ferdinand were both summoned to Bayonne, where the crown of Spain was ceded to Napoleon; but the Spanish people recognised only their own chosen king, Ferdinand VII, and the War of Liberation began. Joseph Bonaparte was finally driven out in 1813, together with all the French troops (see PENINSULAR WAR).

A constitution for Spain was drawn up in 1812 at Cádiz, and Ferdinand promised to be faithful to it. In 1814, however, when he returned to Spain he was able to restore the old Spanish absolute monarchy.

In 1833 his daughter Isabella succeeded him, and in 1843 signed the constitution of 1836, which had been modelled on that of Cádiz (1812). But the reign was chaotic, her ministers were weak, and she was not able to keep the country in order. From 1833 to 1839 the country was in a state of civil war (the first Carlist war), when supporters of Don Carlos (1788–1855), Isabella's uncle, sought unsuccessfully to establish their leader's claim to the throne. The administration became increasingly corrupt, and finally, in 1868, Isabella abdicated in favour of

Spain

Alfonso XII.

From 1868 to 1870, a provisional government was set up, and many experiments were tried in order to bring peace to the country, but the only immediate outcome of this was to supply France and Germany with a *casus belli* for the war of 1870. When Napoleon III refused to admit the candidature of the Hohenzollern Prince Leopold for the throne of Spain, Amadeus I of Savoy was finally elected, and he remained in the country for a period of three years; at the end of that time he resigned and withdrew from Spain. For a year Spain became a republic, and at the end of that time Alfonso XII was reinstated as king. In 1872 the second Carlist war had broken out, and in 1876 it ended with the withdrawal of Don Carlos (grandson of the first Carlist claimant) to France. In 1885 Alfonso XII died, and in the following May his son, Alfonso XIII, was born and was recognised as king, his mother, Queen Maria Christina, acting as regent. In 1898 the Cuban question gave rise to the war with the USA. The result of this war was the loss of the whole of the Spanish territory in the West Indies and Philippines; Spain's navy was destroyed, and the huge cost of the war was a very heavy burden on an impoverished country. On 17 May 1902 Alfonso was crowned.

A host of troubles called for a stable government. In Catalonia hatred was developing between the Catalan Nationalists and the Radical Centralists. The Moroccan question, however, was patched up by a Franco-Spanish treaty (1904), recognising Spanish rights. During the 1905 elections antagonism to the military in Catalonia resulted in the Law of Jurisdictions, allowing military tribunals to try offences against military institutions. The power of the military in Spanish politics, in which the King concurred, was thus increased. The Catalan movement was also intensified. From 1905 to 1907 the Liberals held office. By 1910 Canalejas had come to the front as the Liberal leader. Although a Catholic, he curbed the clerical power in Spain, and in Morocco he successfully countered a French military bid for supremacy, against which the Germans also sent the cruiser *Panther* to Agadir. His work towards a settlement of the Catalan question was ended by his assassination in Madrid by an anarchist on 12 November 1912. During the First World War Spain was neutral, being divided between the pro-Ally liberal anticlerical Left and the pro-German reactionary clerical Right.

A military bid for power was brewing, pressure being put upon the government by the secret military committees of defence, organised by army officers. On 10 August 1917 a general strike, aiming at a Socialist Democratic republic, spread over the whole nation. In suppressing it the army became the strongest force in the state. La Cierva, the man responsible for the execution of Francisco FERRER, the extremist anti-clerical and socialist, in 1909, became, as the representative of the military committees, war minister and practical dictator of a new Cabinet, with Garcia Prieto as premier. Cierva's conflict with Spanish syndicalism brought about his downfall. On 3 December 1918 the liberal Romanones returned to power, and secured the entry of Spain to the Council of the League of Nations. Political chaos followed: government succeeded government. A military revolt broke out on 13 September 1923, under PRIMO DE RIVERA. The government resigned. The King was forced by the army to recognise a military directorate, with Primo de Rivera as president.

The functions of the *Cortes* were suspended and the control of departments was left to under-secretaries, later (1925) raised to the status of ministers. Industry and agriculture prospered under the dictatorship; culture not at all. The most commendable policy of the dictator was that of retrenchment in Morocco. In Spain the dictatorship depended on a censorship, and from 1926 to 1927 on martial law. Eventually, the dictatorship brought the throne into such disrepute that the King dismissed Gen. Primo. But when municipal elections in April 1931 resulted in a sweeping Republican victory, the King left the country without, however, renouncing any of his rights.

A provisional Republican government was set up under ALCALÁ-ZAMORA, head of a conservative group within the Republican party. On 14 April a Catalan Republic

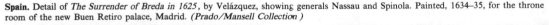

Spain. Detail of *The Surrender of Breda in 1625*, by Velázquez, showing generals Nassau and Spinola. Painted, 1634–35, for the throne room of the new Buen Retiro palace, Madrid. *(Prado/Mansell Collection)*

was proclaimed, with Maciá as president. The provisional Republican government was confirmed by the general elections, held on 28 June 1931. On 14 July the *Cortes* began the task of drawing up the constitution, which was completed by December. There were many strikes and Communist riots, and in October the government was split upon a vote by which the *Cortes* favoured the separation of the Church and the state. Alcalá-Zamora resigned, and a new Cabinet was formed by Azaña. In November ex-King Alfonso was formally outlawed, and in December Alcalá-Zamora was elected president of the Republic.

The Civil War. In the five years between the overthrow of the monarchy and the Civil War the Second Republic was a parody of democracy, attacked by both right (Monarchist) and left (Communist and Anarchist) extremists. A month after the proclamation of the Republic the mob set fire first to the Jesuit church in the centre of Madrid, then to other churches and convents in the city and suburbs. The government took no effective action, being content to attach the blame, not to the mob, but to the Monarchists. This incited the mob to further violence, and soon churches and convents in most of the large cities of Spain were set afire. By a decree in January 1932 the Society of Jesus was 'dissolved on Spanish territory', and its property taken by the state. Between 1934 and 1936 Spain was under a centre-right government in which the Catholics, the largest single group, were inadequately represented. In the general elections of February 1936, the newly formed Popular Front were swept into power. Out of 470 seats they held 260 (166 more than after the 1933 elections), the right and centre 214. The new Cabinet, under Azaña, consisted entirely of Republican Left and Republican Union ministers, and some Socialist, Syndicalists, Anarchists, Marxists, and Communists. Under this government another outburst against the Church took place. Spain was moving towards complete chaos. Right (mainly FALANGISTS) and Left extremists were fighting in the streets. Two opposite para-military formations were being trained: the Falangist clandestinely, Socialists, Communists, and others openly.

The Civil War began in July 1936, immediately after the murder of, first, Lt. Castillo—one of the trainers of the para-military formations the Left—and then of the Monarchist leader, Calvo Sotelo. Alcalá-Zamora had to invoke the very powers of repression for which public opinion had condemned the dictatorship.

The history of the early days of the revolt is obscure; but so carefully prepared was the plan of the insurgents under Gen. FRANCO that it was almost simultaneous in the garrisons of Spanish Morocco, Madrid, Seville, Málaga, Burgos, and Saragossa. The moderate Left leaders were impotent to meet imminent trouble threatening from Right and Left, but the Left Wing under Largo Caballero, the Socialist leader, expected a struggle and prepared for it, while Socialist and Communist youth bodies were organising themselves on para-military lines, as were on their side, but not openly, the young Falangists. Franco aimed at securing an authoritarian, or, as his political opponents saw it, a Fascist régime.

The revolt which heralded the Civil War broke out in Morocco (18 July 1936), and fighting soon spread to Cádiz, Seville, Málaga, and Saragossa. The Spanish Legion held Ceuta and Melilla. Ill-armed government

Spain. Rebel soldiers entering Santander on 27 August 1937. *(Popperfoto)*

forces in the first two days stormed the Montana barracks in Madrid. A few days later Franco set up a provisional government and sent Gen. Mola southward to attack the capital. On the heights of the Guadarrama mountains, which encircle the city to the north, the militiamen held Mola's army, and indeed Madrid. The insurgents, however, soon took Pamplona, Valladolid, Burgos, and Saragossa. Franco brought Moorish troops into southern Spain in German troop-carrying planes and swept up to Badajoz. After a fortnight of war the Republicans held south-east Spain, much of north-east Spain and Madrid, Barcelona, Valencia, and Córdoba; Franco's forces held the rest of the country, including Seville, the area around Gibraltar, and Spanish Morocco. Soon German and Italian planes and troops were sent to aid Franco. The French government under Léon BLUM tended to favour the Republican government but advised neutrality; the USSR favoured the Republicans, and later sent war material and other not very effective aid, demanding payment in gold for every tank and plane. The UK government on 4 August 1936 proposed a five-power pact or declaration of neutrality, and the USSR purported to concur in this policy, which, however, was very unequal in its effects, for while Britain and France held strictly to the bond, Germany and Italy sent every material aid to the insurgents, which the policy of 'non-intervention' denied to the legal government.

Insurgent forces now advanced towards Madrid in the north and at the same time bombarded Irun from the air. Insurgent tanks, aircraft, and infantry on 26 August attacked San Sebastian and Irun. Irun fell on 4 September and San Sebastian on 12 September. Meanwhile in the south and west rebel forces were advancing towards the capital and to the relief of the besieged rebel garrison in Toledo. The historic siege of the Alcázar lasted from 1 August till 27 September, when the rebel troops succeeded in recapturing Toledo, despite the opening of the Alberche River barrages whereby the Republicans hoped to arrest them. The Republican government, under Largo Caballero, who had succeeded Azaña as premier, moved to Valencia, leaving Gen. Miaja in command in Madrid. The government forces were now laying siege to Oviedo, and the siege was not raised till the end of three months. But the real centre of gravity was Madrid. In October the rebels captured several villages within a few miles of the government's strongest defences. On 2 October Navalcarnero, the key town on the road to the capital, fell to the rebels, and a month later they captured the chief airport of Madrid. Franco might now have taken Madrid had he pressed his advantage; but evidently he wished to spare as much of the historic part of the city as possible, while at the same time he was aware that his own forces, which were largely Moroccan, would soon be joined by Italian and German troops. But in the meantime the Republican forces were reinforced with the International Brigades, and so the city was saved from immediate danger. In November the German and Italian governments informed the British government that they had recognised Franco's government, though they did not propose to leave the Non-Intervention Committee. Early in February 1937 the city of Málaga was bombarded by rebel cruisers and it fell on 8 February. This was a heavy blow for the Republicans and one which reduced their hopes for the outcome of the war.

International interest was by now attracted to the naval and military activities in the north. Blockade-running of food ships to Bilbao was often successful, and on 30 April the insurgent battleship *España* was sunk by a mine. Soon after this the rebels sent squadrons of German planes to bomb the old Basque town of Guernica. This notorious attack involved the total destruction of the town, and many civilians were killed, a prelude to methods employed in the Second World War. The loss of Málaga and the pressure on Bilbao led to the fall of Caballero's government. A new Socialist government was formed under Negrín, but the effective head was Prieto, the defence minister. The fact that foreign warships were carrying out the plan of non-intervention patrol in Spanish territorial waters was always liable to lead to 'incidents'. On 29 May the German pocket-battleship *Deutschland* was bombed off the Balearic Islands by Spanish government aircraft, and 31 of her crew were killed. By way of reprisal, on 31 May German naval forces fired 200 shells into Almería, destroying the harbour fortifications and killing 19 inhabitants.

On 25 August Santander was taken by the insurgents, and throughout September and half October the insurgent advance through the northern Spanish provinces continued, until on 21 October Gijón fell, and, but for desultory fighting in the Galician mountains, resistance in the north was at an end. During the first fortnight of December Franco concentrated large forces once more near Guadalajara for a final assault on Madrid. But on 17 December the Republicans stormed and entered Teruel. For a time the long-standing threat to the Mediterranean coast had been removed; but two months later (22 February 1938) the insurgents recaptured the town and swept towards the coast in the most rapid advance made since their abortive drive on Madrid in the autumn of 1936. The insurgents now decided to strike from Aragon to overrun the southern part of Catalonia. Meanwhile German and Italian staffs ordered air raids against Barcelona. After a month the rebel forces drove a wedge between Barcelona province and the rest of Republican Spain; and although the Republicans still held their own on the left bank of the Ebro, they had suffered a serious defeat just at a moment when their chances had seemed to improve.

On 23 April 1938 the rebel army launched a major offensive for the capture of Sagunto and the important towns of Castellón and Valencia, but Castellón only fell after seven weeks, and the attack on Sagunto was repelled. During May and June the bombing of towns and villages in Catalonia and on the coast of Alicante was intensified. On 25 July the government forces relieved the insurgent pressure on Sagunto and Valencia by a surprise crossing of the Ebro over a 161-kilometre front and the recapture of several hundreds of square kilometres of territory. In September heavy fighting continued in Andalusia and Estremadura as well as in Catalonia and on the borders of Teruel–Valencia, but the position generally appeared to be a stalemate. On 23 December after a great artillery barrage supported by the German 'Kondor' air force and Italian 'Legionary Aviation', the rebel army began its assault along a 161-kilometre front. By 21 January 1939 it had reached Tarragona and was well on the way to encircling the Republican eastern army. Government forces began an offensive on the Estremadura and Andalusia fronts as a diversion, but with no success, and by 25 January the Negrín government decided that it must leave Barcelona to its fate and try to carry on the war by guerrilla methods in the mountains and valleys of northern Catalonia. Out of an army of 700,000 in all only 200,000 were engaged in this zone, the bulk of the government forces being in the central-southern zone pivoting on Valencia. But everything depended on keeping open the sea passage to Valencia against the Italian threat by sea and air. It was then that demoralisation set in. The Catalonians were tired of the struggle. Gradually the whole façade of the Republican resistance crumpled. Azaña, President of the Republic, had fled to France and advised surrender. Franco confined his activities to the investment of Catalonia, confident of victory. Then, in March Col. Casado, commander of the Republican central army, seized power in Madrid and set up a council of defence whose task it should be to end a hopeless struggle on the best terms possible and while the government forces were still intact. The British and French governments at once recognised the Franco junta in Burgos. On 23 March Casado's emissaries flew to Burgos to seek terms. Franco demanded unconditional surrender and negotiations were suspended. Madrid was occupied by the Nationalist (as Franco's forces were now styled) forces on 29 March 1939, this final token of Gen. Franco's victory coinciding with the arrival at Cádiz of a further contingent of Italian troops.

The material damage caused by the Civil War, though severe, was not as heavy as might have been expected. The official inventory listed nearly 700 blown bridges and 11 cathedrals partly or totally destroyed, including the late-

Romanesque cathedrals of Sigüenza and Lérida, the Gothic cathedrals of Oviedo and Huesca, and the 14th-century church of Santa Maria del Mar in Barcelona. At Toledo the damage was restricted to the Alcázar and its immediate vicinity.

The new régime soon showed no mercy for its defeated foes. Decrees were promulgated suppressing regional liberties in Catalonia and the Basque provinces; authorising the restoration to ex-King Alfonso and his family of their private property; and reversing the agrarian legislation of the Negrin government. But the Franco régime was itself faction-ridden and held together only by the solidarity of the army leaders. The freedom of worship won in the 19th century was now replaced by the establishment of a state church (Roman Catholic), and there was a distinct tendency to make religion subservient to the political purpose of the state. Franco's efforts to shake off the now unwelcome grip of the Axis powers were unsuccessful, and on 8 May he duly subscribed to the ANTI-COMINTERN PACT but rejected a proposal made by Count Ciano for a formal Spanish-Italian alliance. In most respects, however, Franco's Spain was modelled on Fascist Italy, as a national syndicalist state under himself as El Caudillo (Spanish equivalent of 'Führer'), responsible 'only to God and to history', with power to rule by presidential decree if necessary, but with a Cabinet buttressed by the political junta of the National Council, a body resembling the Fascist Grand Council of Mussolini's Italy.

Spanish History during the Second World War. From the beginning of the war Franco's sympathies, voluntarily or otherwise, were with the Axis powers, yet neutrality up to a point was advantageous to both. But to revive the Spanish empire with German help and so restore the old links with Latin America was the main policy of the Falange (Fascists). The Germans early in the war promised to help Spain in this project, and equally the further Spanish expansion in Morocco and north-west Africa at the expense of France, just as they had falsely promised to help Italy's 'natural claims' in Savoy, Tunis, and Corsica. In return Hitler expected Franco to allow German forces to march through Spain and co-operate with Spanish forces in an attack on Gibraltar. Franco's attitude, however, seems to have been an equivocally neutral one, not because he had no Fascist ambitions but because he was not sure of his own countrymen or of Spain's resources. When, however, Germany attacked the USSR in 1941 Hitler shelved his contradictory promises in the west because his hands were full in the east. Moreover, since he was attacking Russia, Spain was the sole gateway left open for communication between Germany and the outside world, particularly to America, whence the Germans obtained information through Portugal and Spain, while the flood of German propaganda and instructions to their agents in the American continent passed the same way.

In the spring of 1942, when the Allies, although still on the defensive, were planning the invasion of north Africa, Spain's continued neutrality was essential to the success of this operation. Hence the Allies made every effort to counteract powerful Axis pressure and to discourage Franco from making any flank attack from the Spanish peninsula. During 1942 and 1943 Spain was prevailed upon to grant the Allies a gradually increasing number of facilities. By 1944 it was clear to Franco that, as the Allies were winning the war or certainly could not lose it, it was time he heeded their warnings to take stock of Spain's position. It says much for his grip on Spain that the collapse of the German and Italian dictators did not touch off a reaction in Spain that would have resulted in his own overthrow.

Spain since 1945. Immediately after the war the Falange, the army, the Church, and the upper bourgeoisie kept together in support of Franco because they were haunted by the spectre of another revolution. Economically still very weak, as the war had checked its own reconstruction programme, Spain for some years after 1945 suffered political isolation. It was not a member of the United Nations. In December 1946 the UN recommended the withdrawal of all embassies from Spain, a decision complied with by most nations. Anxious to consolidate his internal position, Franco adopted a conciliatory attitude towards some of his former opponents. In 1947 he announced that Spain would become a monarchy, with a regency council and himself as head of state. If the chief of state died the regency council should propose a successor, a king or regent, to be approved by a two-thirds majority of the *Cortes*. A referendum later that year approved this decision. Prince Juan Carlos (see JUAN CARLOS I), the son of Don Juan (the latter named by Alfonso XIII as his successor) has lived most of his life in Spain, close to Franco. This implication of an eventual Bourbon restoration probably consolidated Franco's régime in the country as a whole, but caused considerable misgiving among a section of the Falange. On 15 July 1957 the Spanish parliament was officially informed that the monarchy would be restored in Spain on the death or withdrawal from power of Franco.

By 1948 the Western powers were re-examining their attitude towards Spain in the light of the far greater Communist threat to their stability. The UN removed the ambassadorial ban on Spain, and in 1952 Spain joined UNESCO. In 1951 it received a loan from the Export-Import Bank. In 1953, under a ten-year defence agreement signed with the USA, Spain was to receive arms and economic aid and to allow the Americans the use of naval and air bases in its territory. This agreement has been periodically renewed with the Spanish government driving a harder bargain on each occasion.

Until the end of the 1960s it appeared that Spain stood a good chance of reintegrating itself within the European community and of achieving a smooth political succession. But both predictions were contingent largely upon the willingness and ability of Franco to relinquish office and power, and this failed to happen, except during a few weeks in the summer of 1974 when ill health obliged him to transfer his functions as chief of state to Prince Juan Carlos. Meanwhile troubles of all kinds assailed the régime.

The world-wide economic recession of the mid-1970s exposed the weaknesses of the Spanish economy which depends largely on trade with a Great Britain that is now within the European Economic Community, and on the falling profits of tourism. The government's emphasis on its historic links with the Arab nations and with those of South America (on grounds of Spanish Islam and *hispanidad* respectively) has brought few benefits other than cultural ones at a time when soaring domestic inflation has politicised large sections of the hitherto complacent middle class.

The militant Basque separatist movement, ETA (*Euzkadi Ta Azkatasuna*, Basque Homeland and Liberty) has waged unremitting war in the north, and Catalan nationalism, though less active, is no less well established: thus the two economically most advanced areas of Spain present the most critical political problems for Madrid.

The universities have been in constant turmoil since the late-1960s, as have the industrial workers, whose numbers have grown with the large scale movement away from the land, and who have made numerous attempts to establish authentic trade unions in opposition to the state-controlled syndicates. Both students and workers received aid from increasing numbers of priests whose actions reflect the dissatisfaction of the new generation of Spanish churchmen with the Church's traditionally acquiescent rôle, in response to the social teachings of Pope John XXIII and to their fears for the future after Franco's death. The assassination, allegedly by members of ETA, of Franco's Vice-President, Carrero Blanco, in 1973, and the overthrow of the friendly régime in Portugal in 1974 faced the government with new problems. Franco's age and ill-health exacerbated the struggle for power between the anti-monarchical and anti-liberal old-style Falangists, the more outward-looking members of OPUS DEI, and the cautiously pragmatic politicians represented by the Prime Minister, Carlos Arias Navarro. In 1975 the death of Gen. Franco brought a restoration of the monarchy and the renewal of open political debate and party activity for the first time since the 1930s. A more liberal cabinet was formed, but left-wing discontent continued when the expected amnesty for political prisoners was not granted. Early in 1976 mass rallies were held, and Communist- and Socialist-led groups united in the Democratic Formation. Later, the *Cortes* approved bills lifting restrictions on political meetings, and a revised amendment to the Penal Code was passed; Adolfo Suárez González replaced Navarro as prime minister. A partial amnesty was granted, and the proposal for an elected two-chamber parliament was approved by a popular referendum in December 1976. In February 1977 legislation was enacted legalising most political parties, the Communist party being legalised in April; the National Movement—Spain's state political party under Franco—was abolished on 1 April.

In June 1977 the first general elections since 1936 were held. Pre-election tension had run high in the Basque provinces, with several people losing their lives in demonstrations and kidnappings. The centre-left coalition Union of the Democratic Centre (UCD), headed by González, won 165 of the 350 seats in the Congress of Deputies, and 105 of the 207 elected seats in the Senate. The King subsequently nominated a further 41 senators. The inaugural session of the *Cortes* was opened by the King on 22 July.

Bibliography: S. de Madariaga, *Spain*, 1942; G. Brenan, *The Spanish Labyrinth*, 2nd ed. 1950; R. Heer, *The Eighteenth Century Revolution in Spain*, 1958; S. G. Payne, *Falange*, 1961; H. Thomas, *The Spanish Civil War*, 1961; J. H. Elliot, *Imperial Spain 1469-1716*, 1963; J. Lynch, *Spain under the Habsburgs*, 2 vols, 1964 and 1969; G. Jackson, *The Spanish Republic and the Civil War 1931-9*, 1965; H. Kamen, *The Spanish Inquisition*, 1965; R. Carr, *Spain 1808-1939*, 1966; S. G. Payne, *Politics and the Military in Modern Spain*, 1967; S. G. Payne, *Franco's Spain*, 1968; J. Vicens Vives, *Economic History of Spain*, 1969; S. G. Payne, *The Spanish Revolution*, 1970; J. Vicens Vives, *Approaches to the History of Spain*, 2nd ed. 1970; A Castro, *The Spaniards*, 1971; G. Jackson, *The Making of Medieval Spain*, 1972; M. Gallo, *Spain under Franco*, 1973; P. E. Russell (Ed.), *Spain: A Companion to Spanish Studies*, 1973.

Art, Architecture and Art Museums, see PRADO, MUSEO DEL; SPANISH ART; SPANISH ARCHITECTURE.

Language. Spanish is a Romance language (see ROMANCE LANGUAGES), closely related to Portuguese, Italian, and French. It is today spoken not only in Spain, alongside CATALAN, the BASQUE LANGUAGE, and Galician—a Portuguese dialect—but also in all the countries once contained in the Spanish Empire, that is, all Central and South America, excepting Brazil and the Guyanas, the Philippines (where it has now largely been ousted by English and Tagalog), and in areas settled by Spaniards in Morocco. It is also widely spoken in the USA, notably by immigrant Puerto Ricans, and throughout Europe by migrant workers. The total number of Spanish speakers probably exceeds 140,000,000, and its geographical extension is second only to English.

Castilian, which is the more accurate name for the Spanish language, developed from the Latin spoken in the ancient county of Castile, and as early as the 10th or 11th centuries it was being used in written form, although the earliest documents are 12th century. Early Castilian owes much to the 13th-century king, Alfonso the Wise, and to the 14th-century writers Don Juan Manuel and Juan Ruiz. As the Iberian Peninsula was reconquered from the Arabs, many Arabic words entered the language, and the vocabulary was constantly enriched from Latin and other sources, including the other languages of Spain. In 1492 Antonio de Nebrija published the *Grammar of the Castilian Language* which can be regarded as the first modern grammar of any language. Numerous dialects were spoken in medieval Spain, for example, Asturian, Navarrese, Aragonese, and Mirandese, and these were gradually displaced by Castilian, though they survived to some extent in remote rural areas. By the 16th and 17th centuries the political predominance of Castile was reflected in the triumphant emergence of Castilian as the official national language, and from that time it has gradually encroached upon the remaining non-Castilian languages.

In modern times the best Castilian is reputedly spoken around Valladolid. Andalusian Spanish pronounces 'c' before 'e' and 'i' as 's'—a feature common to all Latin America, the standard pronunciation being 'th' as in 'think'. There is a marked tendency in southern Spanish and that of Latin America to pronounce 'll' as 'y' or 'j' instead of a palatalised 'l', and to aspirate 's' before consonants and at the end of words; thus *está* is commonly pronounced *ehtá* in South America. South American Spanish has been much influenced by English and Amerindian languages, though at no points are the Iberian and American versions of Spanish any more divergent than American and British English. The vocabulary of Iberian Spanish continues to evolve rapidly, the main sources of new words being American English and French. A language academy has been in existence since the 18th century, and strives ineffectually to standardise usage.

See also PORTUGAL, *Language*; LADINO.

Bibliography: C. Smith, *Collins Spanish-English, English-Spanish Dictionary*; W. J. Entwistle, *The Spanish Language*, new ed. 1962.

Literature. The first great work of Spanish literature, a poem concerning the exploits of the CID, is the *Cantar de mio Cid*, written about 1140 (see 'POEMA DI MIO CID'). Few such examples of popular epic poetry were transmitted in written form, however, because of the medieval tradition of public recitation by *juglares*, wandering players. In the 13th and 14th centuries there developed a more learned school of poetry, known as *Mester de Clerecía*, beginning with Gonzalo de BERCEO. An outstanding 14th-century work is the *Libro de buen amor*, an animated miscellany of fables and other poems, in autobiographical form, by Juan RUIZ, better known as the Archpriest of Hita.

Popularly known as the Golden Age of Spanish literature, the 16th and 17th centuries showed great enthusiasm for Italian and classical literature, whose works provided a springboard for much of Spain's literary activity at this time. Following Italian models, GARCILASO DE LA VEGA, writing in metres new to Spain, established serious love poetry. The Salamancan theologian Luis de LEÓN wrote lyric poetry on moral themes, and St JOHN OF THE CROSS, friend and adviser of the mystic St TERESA, reached unprecedented heights of lyricism in his mystical poetry. In the field of secular poetry, familiar themes were re-worked with increasing sophistication and this culminated in the complex imagery and syntax of Luis de GÓNGORA whose *Soledades* was one of the most controversial and influential works of the century.

In prose, the literary giant is CERVANTES, author of *Don Quixote*. Francisco de QUEVEDO was an eminent satirist and Baltasar GRACIÁN a moralist with a pithy style. He was also a literary theorist who codified the principles underlying a contemporary taste for poetic wit, akin to that of the English METAPHYSICAL POETS.

On the stage, 'cloak and dagger' drama predominated with plays by the fecund Lope de VEGA, and TIRSO DE MOLINA, creator of the legendary figure of Don Juan. CALDERÓN added to this tradition a cultured language, and in the field of one-act allegorical religious plays, *autos sacramentales*, far outstripped his rivals.

The 18th century, barren in verse and imaginative prose, though fertile in ideas, produced a notable playwright in Leandro Fernández de Moratín, who wrote *El sí de las niñas*. There were also some fine attempts to disseminate the new scientific and political thought of 18th-century Europe in the works of FEIJÓO and JOVELLANOS. War against Napoleon completed a gradual rejection of French styles and thought in favour of a patriotic, medievalist revival. This culminated in a heady and short-lived ROMANTIC MOVEMENT influenced heavily by SCOTT and BYRON. Its major figures are José de ESPRONCEDA, El Duque de Rivas (1791–1865), M. de la Rosa (1787–1862), and Mariano José de LARRA; the latter's brilliant and despairing analyses of contemporary manners and politics inaugurated a revival of creative prose

Spain. Manuscript, dated 1140, of the Spanish epic poem *Cantar de mio Cid*. (National Library, Madrid/Photo MAS)

Spain. Illustration by Gustave Doré for the frontispiece to Cervantes's *Don Quixote*. *(Bisonte)*

writing. In drama, de Rivas's *Don Álvaro* and ZOR-RILLA's *Don Juan Tenorio* surpass similar French and English Romantic attempts. Excluding bad imitations of Scott's 'archaeological' novels, the first novels dealing with contemporary life are the reactionary and sentimental portrayals of Andalucía by Fernán CABALLERO (Cecilia Böhl von Faber). The genre matured into a perceptive realism with Juan Valera (1824–1905), Pedro ALARCÓN, especially in *El sombrero de tres picos*, and Maria de PEREDA, particularly with *Sotileza* and *Peñas arriba*, who defended fresh, provincial life against 19th-century disbelief and materialism. Urban life was brilliantly analysed by Benito PÉREZ GALDÓS, master of the modern novel, while PARDO BAZÁN and BLASCO IBÁÑEZ wrote naturalist novels in the manner of ZOLA.

Romanticism excepted, the 19th century's lack of poetry is displayed by the bourgeois moralising of Ramón de CAMPOAMOR and Núñez de Arce (1834–1903), though Gustavo BÉCQUER and Rosalía CASTRO began an overdue exploration of subjective fantasy and intimate feeling. Castro's work was often written in Galician dialect. The century ended in decadence and corruption, literary and social, symbolised by America's defeat of Spain in the wars of 1898. This cataclysm prompted the younger generation to a programme of national introspection and historical evaluation, coupled with an iconoclastic determination to abandon a disastrous past. The 'generation of '98' included Pio BAROJA, Miguel de UNAMUNO, 'AZO-RÍN', and Ramiro de Macztu. The Nicaraguan poet Ruben DARÍO offered a new stylistic liberty to younger writers cramped by traditional forms of expression. Among these were Francisco Villaespesa and Ramón de VALLE-INCLÁN. As a result, a period of refined, musical poetry named *modernismo* emerged. Two of the movement's most important poets were Juan Ramón JIMÉNEZ (who won the Nobel Prize in 1956) and Antonio MACHADO. Machado, already reacting against the aloof aestheticism of his contemporaries, wrote indescribably gentle, humane visions of Castile and its history, *Campos de Castilla*, 1912, now commonly considered the best Spanish poetry of the 20th century. In prose, Ramón del Valle-Inclán, 'Azorin', and Gabriel MIRÓ continued the traditions of 'artistic prose', while Miguel de Unamuno tackled the whole problem of Spain, modernity, faith, and disbelief in such works as *La agonía del cristianismo*, 1917, and *Del sentimiento trágico de la vida*, 1913; similar urgent preoccupations inform his novels, such as *Abel Sánchez*, 1917, and *Niebla*, 1914.

The post-First World War period is remarkable for its poetry. The so-called 'generation of 1927' (Pedro Salinas, Jorge GUILLÉN, Vicente ALEIXANDRE, Rafael ALBERTI, Luis CERNUDA, and GARCÍA LORCA), all born after 1890, assimilated into traditional verse diction the 'isms' of the period; vitalism, Freudism, Surrealism, and so on. All are important, though García Lorca's vitalism, coupled with vivid imagery, won him international fame, especially with *Romancero gitano*, 1928, and *Canciones*, 1927. In drama Jacinto BENAVENTE and García Lorca excel. The former studied European drama profitably, winning the Nobel Prize in 1922; the latter broke new ground with *Bodas de Sangre* (*Blood Wedding*) and *Yerma*, 1933–35. Among essayists Gregorio Marañon, Eugenio D'Ors, and ORTEGA Y GASSET must be mentioned. The latter's reputation demonstrates the lack of original socio-philosophical ideas in Spain. Miguel HERNÁNDEZ, who died in one of Franco's prisons, is the finest poet of the Civil War period.

After the war writers found themselves, following the death or exile of most of those authors already mentioned, in a cultural vacuum. In poetry, the early archaising formalism evident in the work of Dionisio Ridruejo and José G. Nieto yielded to a humane subjectivism with Carlos Bousoño and José Luis Hidalgo, and to the leftist revolutionary poetry of Gabriel Celaya, Victoriano Cremer, and especially José Hierro. In the novel Camilo José CELA excels, with *La colmena*, 1951, and *La familia de Pascual Duarte*, 1942, over a number of competent writers of whom Ana Maria Matute, J. and L. GOYTISOLO, Carmen LAFORET, M. Delibes, and J. M. Gironella may be mentioned. Recurrent themes have been a sense of isolation and anguish, revolt against Americanised culture (post-1956), and attempts to discover new means of negotiating the horror of civil war and the emptiness of the resultant society and régime.

See also CATALAN LITERATURE; PORTUGAL, *Literature*; SPANISH-AMERICAN LITERATURE.
Bibliography: A Literary History of Spain (series), 1972.
Music, see SPANISH MUSIC.

Spalding, market town in LINCOLNSHIRE, England, on the Welland, 23 km south-west of Boston. There is a 13th-century parish church, and a grammar school founded in 1567. The town grew up around a priory. Spalding is a horticultural and agricultural centre; tulips and daffodils are grown in great quantity, and there are manufactures of agricultural implements and tractors. The town is a railway junction. The Spalding Gentlemen's Society is the oldest antiquarian society in England. Population (1971) 17,000.

Spandau, German town at the confluence of the rivers Havel and Spree; since 1920 a suburb of West BERLIN. It was one of the oldest towns of Brandenburg and a residence of the electors. It was famous for its state arsenal. Today its fame derives from the prison which housed Nazi war criminals, including the longest-surviving war criminal sentenced at Nürnberg, Rudolf HESS.

Spandrel, in architecture, (1) a near-triangular space between the curve of the arch and an enclosing rectangle; (2) between the curves of two adjacent arches; (3) the wall between two contiguous arches and the sloping string of a staircase or floor-level.

Spaniel, important group of dogs characterised by large, pendulous ears and long, silky hair. The Clumber spaniel takes its name from Clumber, near Worksop, England, a seat of the Dukes of Newcastle, one of whom introduced it from France. It is white, with lemon markings on the head and ears; is massively built, weighing up to 32 kg, with a large head, heavy brows, long body, short and thick legs, and long and dense coat. Though rather slow, it is a good gun-dog, and does not give tongue. The COCKER SPANIEL averages less than half the weight of the Clumber. The American cocker spaniel is, since 1940, a separate breed, but is was originally bred from English cockers in America. It is becoming an increasingly popular pet and show dog. It has a shorter head than the English counterpart, a domed skull and deep stop. The eyes are large and dark and the ears long. The body is short and the coat much more profuse than in other spaniels. The colours are the same as in the English cocker. The weight is 10–12 kg and the height 37–38 cm. The English springer is next to the cocker, the most popular of sporting spaniels. It is larger than the cocker standing 51 cm high and weighing about 22·5 kg and has a longer body; the colours most favoured are liver and white, and black and white. The Welsh springer is smaller than the English variety, and in colour dark, rich red, and white. The field spaniel was formerly only black, but is now bred in other colours, including black and tan, red roan, blue roan, and liver and white. The weight is 16–23 kg and the height 46 cm. The Irish water spaniel is markedly different from the other varieties. It is a rich, dark liver colour and the coat is composed of dense, crisp curls; the ears are long, and set on low. It is a wonderfully intelligent and plucky dog, taking to water readily. The weight is about 27 kg and the height 51–58 cm. The Sussex spaniel, probably the oldest variety, is a rich golden liver colour and the coat is dense and perfectly straight. It is smaller than the Clumber, but has great length of body. It gives tongue and is rather slow, but a very reliable worker. The weight is 18–20 kg and the height 38–40 cm. Toy spaniels have long been kept as pets, and have much to recommend them. Another toy breeds is the Japanese chin (also called Japanese spaniel), white in colour, marked with black or red. The Tibetan spaniel has several features in common with the Pekingese, but belongs to the group.

Spanish-American Literature. The physical conquest of America which began in the 16th century was closely followed by its spiritual domination, initiated by the rapid spread of the conquerors' language. The areas where the new spoken language derived from Romance languages, and therefore Latin, are commonly known as Latin America. In South and Central America the dominant new language was Spanish and, with the exception of Brazil, where Portuguese was adopted, the literature produced in these countries was written in Spanish. (See BRAZIL; CENTRAL AMERICA; MEXICAN AND CENTRAL AMERICAN NATIVE LANGUAGES; PORTUGAL; ROMANCE LANGUAGES; SOUTH AMERICA; SOUTH AMERICAN NATIVE LANGUAGES; SPAIN.)

Early Spanish-American literature includes the *Cartas de Cristóbal Colón* describing the contact of Columbus with a new world. The *Cartas de Relación*, 1519–26, of Hernando CORTES are five reports of his conquest of Mexico; and of great interest to historians, if not so much to men of letters, are the writings of some of the warriors and adventurers who completed the conquest. Among them are Alvar Nuñez Cabeza de VACA, *Naufragios y comentarios*, 1542; Gaspar de Carvajal (1504–84), *Descubrimiento del Río de las Amazonas*, a striking narrative of adventure; Cieza de León (1519–69), *Historia de Perú*, 1533; and Alonso de Góngora Marmolejo, *Historia de Chile*, 1575. Of special literary merit is *Verdadera historia de la conquista de la Nueva España*, 1552, by Bernal DÍAZ DEL CASTILLO. The conquistadors were followed by monks and priests. Fray Bartolomé de las Casas (1475–1566) did not spare the warriors and adventurers, as shown in his notable work *Brevísima relación de la destrucción de las Indias*, 1552, while Cristóbal de Molina (d. 1578), a monk who went with the conquistador Almagro, relates the epic of the discovery of Peru in his *Relación de la conquista y población del Perú*, 1552.

The second generation of Spanish-Americans inherited the literary tendencies of the conquistadors: Creoles, half-breeds, and pure natives became chroniclers of the conquest, mainly from the point of view of the conquered. Hernando de Alvarado, the son of an Aztec emperor, wrote *Crónica Mexicana*, 1598, and Fernando de Alva Ixtlixochitl the *Historia de los chichimecas*. The famous Inca, GARCILASO de la Vega, son of a Spanish conquistador and a princess of the Sun, went to Spain, where he wrote *La florida del Inca o la historia del Adelantado Hernando de Soto*, 1605, and his masterpiece, *Comentarios reales*, 1609, the history of the Inca Empire.

The epic of the *Conquista* inspired poets such as the Spaniard Alonso de ERCILLA, whose *La Araucana*, 1569–89, is based on his adventures in Chile. This is the first work of real literary merit in Spanish produced in America. The Chilean Pedro de Oña imitates Ercilla in his *Arauco Domado*. Dr Martin del Barco Centenera published in Lisbon, 1602, *La Argentina y conquista del Río de la Plata*, a work rich in valuable information. The deeds of Cortes found their epic poet in Antonio Saavedra Guzmán, who wrote *Peregrino Indiano*, 1599. The first native-born poet of Mexico was Francisco de Terrazas, though a few stanzas only are preserved of his *Nuevo Mundo y Conquista*. Gabriel Lasso de la Vega wrote

Spanish-American Literature

Cortés Valeroso, 1588; the Peruvian Pedro de Peralta produced *Lima Fundada o Conquista del Perú*, 1732; and Fray Diego de Ojedo *La Cristiada*, 1611. Sor Juana Inés de la Cruz, a woman poet whose works are collected in *Inundacia Castalida*, 1698, also wrote a religious play, *Auto Sacramental del divino Narciso*. The 18th century is barren in literary work of merit, but in Spanish America there was much scientific investigation in all aspects of natural history and physical geography.

The end of the 18th and the beginning of the 19th century saw the dawn of the movement for independence, which in course of time ended with the creation of 20 independent nations in Latin America. Writers of this period draw inspiration not only from the French revolutionary authors but also from the more liberal-minded Spanish contemporaries. The Ecuadorian, José Joaquin de Olmedo (1780–1874), wrote *La victoria de Junín: Canto a Bolivar*, 1825, and translated into Spanish POPE's *Essay on Man*. The Cuban, José Maria de Heredia (1803–39), left many works of merit, both in Spanish and French; his *En el Teocalli de Cholula*, 1820, anticipated by ten years the appearance of Romanticism in Spain (see ROMANTIC MOVEMENT), and his *Oda al Niágara* has special merit.

Romanticism flourished in Spanish America at the time of the war of independence against Spain. Domingo Faustino SARMIENTO, the vehement Argentinian publicist, advised his compatriots to turn their backs once for all on Spain and seek inspiration in their native land. His main work is *Facundo o civilización y barbarie*, 1845. Esteban Echeverría (1805–51) introduced Romanticism into Argentina with *Elvira o la novia del Plata*, *Los consuelos*, and *Rimas*. José Mármol (1817–71) wrote against the Argentinian tyrant ROSAS; his best work, *Amalia*, is of great historic interest. The masterpiece of this period, however, is *María* by Jorge ISAACS. Juan Zorrilla San Martín (1855–1931), a native of Uruguay and author of a novel in verse, *Tabaré*, 1888, is considered the greatest Romantic poet of Spanish America. The influence of Spanish authors such as Benito PÉREZ GALDÓS and José María de PEREDA is felt in the works of José López Portillo (1850–1923) in *La Parcela*, 1898, and in Rafael Delgado's *La Calandria*, 1891, while the Spanish tendency is dominant in the writing of the Peruvian Ricardo Palma (1833–1919), whose *Tradiciones Peruanas* (ten volumes), 1872–1906, is his chief work.

Towards the end of the 19th century a new modernistic tendency is found in Spanish America and for the first time Spanish-American writers make their contribution to world literature. The book that heralded the transition was *Azul*, a volume of verse by the Nicaraguan Rubén DARÍO, 1888. The Colombian, José Asunción Silva (1865–96), had as models POE, D'ANNUNZIO, and BAUDELAIRE. His most important work is the poem *Nocturno III*. Amado Nervo, a Mexican, left amongst other works *Diafanidad*.

The period of modernism was followed in Spanish America by *el mundonovismo*, that is to say, a period during which the inspiration is the New World itself. The Mexican, Enrique Gonzalez Martínez, wrote *Silenter*, *Los senderos ocultos*, and *La muerte del cisne*, 1915; and the Argentinian, Leopoldo Lugones (1874–1938), *Las montañas del oro*, 1897, *Los crepúsculos del jardín*, 1905, and *Lunario sentimental*, 1909. His verse is ironic. The Peruvian, José Santos Chocano

(1875–1934), a true Romantic, wrote *Los caballos de los conquistadores*, *Alma América*, and *Fiat Lux*. The most notable woman poet the continent has produced is Gabriela MISTRAL. The Uruguayan, José Enrique Rodó (1872–1917), was an outstanding essayist whose best work, *Ariel*, 1900, has had a profound influence on all thinking Latin-Americans.

Realistic novelists of this period include the Chilean, Alberto Blest Gana (1830–1920), author of *Martín Rivas*, 1862, and *Durante la Reconquista*, 1897; the Colombian, Tomás Carrasquilla (1851–1940), with *Frutos de mi tierra* and *La marquesa de Yolombó*, 1928; and the Mexican, Frederico Gamboa, whose *Santa* was published in 1903. As regards the novel of the cities, in general the themes are based on the sordid side of city life. A good example is the Argentinian, Manuel Gálvez (1882–1962), with *La maestra normal*, 1914, while *Nacha Regules*, 1919, describes the miserable life in the brothels of Buenos Aires. Joaquín Edwards Bello (1888–1968) handles in masterly manner the life of the *roto* (down and out under-dog) of Chile in his well-known book *El roto*, 1920. Enrique Larreta (1875–1961), of Argentina, interpreted the Spanish spirit in his famous novel *La gloria de Don Ramiro*, 1908, a story dealing with 18th-century Lima, while the Uruguayan, Carlos Reyles (1868–1938), finds his inspiration in Spain with *El embrujo de Sevilla*, 1921, and wrote *Beba*, 1894, influenced by ZOLA.

One aspect of writing in Spanish America has been the growth of *gauchesca* literature. Writers have interpreted the native folklore mainly around the 'gaucho'—a wide definition of the type being 'a native of the La Plata pampas of Spanish-Indian descent: cattle men who mostly live and work in the country'. Having in mind that La Pampa reaches from the west to the east Atlantic, and from Bolivia, Paraguay, and the Gran Chaco to Tierra del Fuego, it can be understood that the *gauchesca* literature has a vast background and is by no means peculiar to Argentina. But the Argentinian Sarmiento, with his *Facundo*, opened up this interesting field, while Robert CUNNINGHAME GRAHAM and William Henry Hudson followed suit, both in Spanish and in English. In epic verse three poems are noteworthy: *Santos Vega*, by Hilario Ascasubi (1807–75), *Fausto*, by Estanislao del Campo (1834–80), and the great Argentinian classic *Martín Fierro*, by José HERNÁNDEZ. Another Argentinian, Ricardo Guiraldes (1886–1927), produced in *Don Segundo Sombra*, 1926, a nostalgic and poetic farewell to the gaucho, the best *gauchesca* interpretation in novel form.

Poetry in the 20th century followed from the work of the *modernistas* and their leader, Rubén Darío. These poets, although dealing with literary borrowings from French, had broken with the dead Spanish of three centuries' colonial rule and had explored new linguistic and rhythmic possibilities, claiming an independence for Latin American culture. This experimentalism culminated in the 1920s and 1930s with the work of Pablo NERUDA, César VALLEJO, Vicente Huidobro (1893–1948), Oliverio Girondo (1891–1967), and Nicolás Guillén (1902–) among others. In their hands poetry became a powerful instrument against rigid language forms, and reflected two immense influences, SURREALISM and the Spanish Civil War. The most difficult and rewarding of the group is the Peruvian César Vallejo, who crystallised the generation's concerns in intensely private and committed poetry. Pablo Neruda developed in a similar way, from his early nostalgic and introspective poems, *Veinte poemas de amor y una canción desesperada*, 1924, *Residencia en la tierra*, 1933, to his 'awakening' by the Spanish Civil War. Unlike Vallejo, Neruda's was a more sudden, less conscious development and most of his poetry was written before the War.

Political commitment and poetic experimentation were legacies which determined the work of the succeeding generation. The Mexican Octavio Paz (1914–), turned to André BRETON's metaphysical Surrealism, writing a poetry which competed with religion in its claims as an answer to man's predicament. His key works, *Libertad bajo palabra*, 1968, *Salamandra*, 1962, *Ladera este (Configurations)*, 1968, are complemented by his brilliant critical essays, *The Labyrinth of Solitude*, 1967, and the *Bow and the Lyre*, 1973. Paz's dominance in Mexican poetry is such that later writers can be defined as Pazian and anti-Pazian, and this is similarly the case with Neruda. The most successful anti-Nerudean is Nicanor Parra (1914–) of Chile whose *Poemas y antipoemas*, 1954, steer between dogmatic politics, sensual imagery, and Surrealism with a sense of irony, humour, and the absurd. The equally influential Nicaraguan poet, Ernesto Cardenal (1925–), fused politics with his radical Christianity. His long poems criticise capitalist materialism in terms of the Indians and other oppressed peoples, *Antología*, 1972; *The Psalms of Struggle and Liberation*, 1971.

In general, Spanish-American poetry of the 20th century, with its combination of the literary and the colloquial, European models and such native sources as popular songs, Afro-Cuban rhythms, and pre-Columbian myths, is of extreme value and originality.

The weakest aspect of Spanish-American literature is in the theatre, though even here the works of the Mexican Rodolfo Usigli and the Spanish-Argentinian Alejandro Casona are likely to remain in the repertoire.

The 20th-century novel continued to be realistic-descriptive, prolonging the characterisations and plot structures of the 19th century. In spite of such cataclysmic events as the Mexican Revolution, 1910–17, novels still aimed to reveal to unaware readers the truth about their own land. Spanish-American fiction was therefore regressive in the first third of the century; the absence of a literary tradition, and a commitment to supplement this, led to an impoverishment of craft in favour of theme or content. For example, the Mexican Mariano Azuela (1873–1952), a doctor with Pancho Villa's soldiers, saw how the Revolution's ravages completely changed the face of Mexico, and his writings reflect the change. The powerful but crudely written *Los de abajo*, 1915, charts the rise and fall of a guerrilla group exploited by power seekers and intellectuals. It is a bitter novel of the Revolution betrayed (a theme that became constant in Mexican post-Revolutionary literature, as did the atrocious treatment of the Indian) where the horror of the theme submerges the presentation. This happens also in *El mundo es ancho y ajeno* (*Broad and Alien is the World*), 1941, by the Peruvian Ciro Alegría (1909–67), and in *Huasipungo*, 1934, by the Ecuadorian Jorge Icaza (1906–). José Eustasio Rivera (1889–1928) of Colombia wrote *La vorágine*, 1924 (*The Vortex*, 1935), the story of

a wild poet on the run from justice with his mistress, charting their progressive de-civilisation as they cope with the jungle, fever, and murder. It is a protest also against the absence of law, gun rule, and brutal survival of the fittest. The Venezuelan Rómulo Gallegos (1884–1968) came nearest to balancing moral outrage and novelistic craft in a series of novels including *Doña Bárbara*, 1929, dealing with the struggles to civilise the wild plains, and *Canaima*, 1935, with the jungle; and the most successful realist is the Uruguayan Horacio QUIROGA, whose stories pitch weak man against uncompromising nature. The work of Ricardo Guiraldes is an exception to this absence of craft, especially with *Don Segundo Sombra*.

Themes of social injustice continued to occupy succeeding novelists, but by the 1940s experimental European and United States fiction had been read. There had also been an increase in middle-class readership and, as publishing expanded, there was a need for sophistication in novelistic craft. For example, Miguel Angel ASTURIAS deals with the Guatemalan Indian, but from his myths and legends, not from the descriptions of an outsider. The Peruvian José María Arguedas (1911–69) was brought up among Indians and wrote novels about their plight, and from their point of view, translating their speech rhythms into Spanish, as in the haunting *Los ríos profundos*, 1958. Juan Rulfo (1918–) of Mexico provides the best example of this inner view in *Pedro Páramo*, 1955, where the ghost town of Comala is all that has been repressed, ignored, and forgotten in Latin America.

To themes of social oppression and man's insignificance in the face of nature were later added those of urban problems. The rise in population and move from countryside to towns led to a mushrooming of the larger capital cities. The Argentinian Roberto Arlt (1900–42) was a forerunner of novelists tackling such problems, and his *Los siete locos*, 1929, and *Los Lanzallamas*, 1931, deal with the Buenos Aires immigrant subworld of pimps, gangsters, and anarchists determined to change society. Arlt's nightmarish city life is transformed by Julio CORTÁZAR in *Rayuela*, 1963, into a senseless urban world whose metaphors are the circus and the madhouse. Ernesto Sábato (1911–) also exploited madness in his first novel *El túnel*, 1948, narrated by a murderer, and an incestuous relationship in *Sobre héroes y tumbas*, 1961, which dramatises Buenos Aires at the time of PERON's fall (1955) and attempts to grapple with the problem of national identity through psychology. The Uruguayan Juan Carlos Onetti (1909–) centres his fiction on an imaginary town, describing a depressing world of mediocrity and poverty in *La vida breve*, 1950; *El astillero*, 1961; and *Juntacadáveres*, 1968; while the Mexican Carlos Fuentes (1929–) describes Mexico City in his panoramic *La región más transparente*, 1958 (*Where the Air is Clear*, 1960), tracing the failure and cynicism which obscure the vision of a better reality. His *La muerte de Artemio Cruz*, 1962, symbolises Mexico's betrayal of its revolutionary promises. All Fuentes's fiction is concerned with identity, for example *Cambio de piel*, 1967 (*Change of Skin*, 1968). Disenchantment unifies the work of Mario Vargas Llosa (1936–) of Peru, among whose novels are *La ciudad y los perros* (*The Time of the Hero*), 1962, and *La casa verde*, 1966. He is concerned about the absence of morality in his society and this is the theme of *Conversación en la catedral*, 1970. More skilled in verbal and satirical explorations are writers such as Guillermo Cabrera Infante of Cuba, with *Tres tristes tigres*, 1967, and the Argentinian Manuel Puig, with *La traición de Rita Hayworth* (*Betrayed by Rita Hayworth*), 1968, and *Boquitas pintadas* (*Heartbreak Tango*), 1970, which point towards a more complex and morally ambiguous criticism of society.

The mentor of most writers after 1945 is the Argentinian Jorge Luis BORGES. His awareness of the limitations of literature and language, of the pointlessness of good intentions, and of the relativity of points of view, embodied in terse, sad, ironic short stories such as *Ficciones*, 1944, and *El Aleph*, 1949, has been an example of consciousness of craft. Perhaps most representative of 20th-century writers, however, are Alejo CARPENTIER and Gabriel GARCÍA MÁRQUEZ. Their exuberant imaginations have fed on Surrealism and 'fantastic' literature and both incorporate the fusion of a marvellous, mythic nature with downtrodden man. Although their stories, Carpentier's *El reino de este mundo*, 1947, *El siglo de las luces*, 1962; and Márquez's *Cien años de soledad*, 1967, transcend limitations of time and space, they are still intensely Spanish-American and give ironic fictional form to the continent's most potent myth, the New World.

See also BRAZIL, *Literature*; SOUTH AMERICA.

Bibliography: B. Moses, *Spanish Colonial Literature in South America*, 1922; J. R. Spell, *Contemporary Spanish American Fiction*, 1945; S. Carmen Rosenbaum, *Modern Women Poets of Spanish America*, 1945; E. Ballagas, *Mapa de la poesía negra americana*, 1946; F. Alegría, *Breve historia de la novela hispanoamericana*, 1959; L. Harss, *Into the Mainstream*, 1966; J. M. Cohen, *Latin American Writing Today*, 1967; J. Franco, *The Modern Culture of Latin America*, 1967, and *An Introduction to Spanish American Literature*, 1969; J. Loveluck, *La novela hispanoamericana*, 1969; J. Donoso and W. A. Henkin, (Eds), *Contemporary Latin American Literature*, 1969; S. Yurkievich, *Fundadores de la nueva poesía latinoamericana*, 1971; D. Gallagher, *Modern Latin American Literature*, 1973.

Spanish-American War, The, was the outcome of the conditions set up in Cuba by the political discontent in the island throughout the 19th century. War broke out in Cuba in 1868 when Spain refused to accede to demands for limited autonomy, and lasted ten years. It was succeeded by a period of peace, but in 1895 the Cubans again revolted. Under pressure from American commercial and naval interests, the US government urged Spain to terminate the war and establish civil government in Cuba. However, before any action had been taken by Spain, on 15 February 1898, the US battleship *Maine* was destroyed by an explosion in Havana harbour with the loss of 266 lives. US public opinion at once accused the Spanish officials, and a resolution was passed by Congress declaring Cuba independent and empowering the president to make Spain relinquish its claims over the island. An ultimatum to this effect was sent to Spain, fixing 23 April as the last date for submission. Spain declared war formally on 24 April.

On 22 April Rear-Adm. Sampson began the blockade of Havana and the northern coast of Cuba with his North Atlantic squadron. Meanwhile Commodore Dewey, who had been stationed at Hong Kong with the American squadron, was ordered to begin operations, and sailed to Manila Bay in the Philippines. He gained a complete victory, took possession of Cavite, and awaited the arrival of a land force to capture Manila. The town however, did not surrender until 13 August. On 29 April the Spanish admiral, Cervera, had left the Cape Verde Islands *en route* for Santiago, where he arrived on 19 May. Sampson at once instituted a blockade of the harbour. On 19 June Maj.-Gen. Shafter arrived off Santiago, and successfully landed his troops at Balquiri, and three days later the Spaniards were driven back from Sevilla. Gen. Shafter then began his attack on Santiago, whither the Spaniards had retreated, San Juan being captured by the Americans. Operations began on 1 July and on 4 July the city was summoned to surrender, but without success. In the meantime Adm. Cervera's squadron had been ordered to sea by the Madrid government. He accordingly left Santiago harbour, and suffered defeat at the hands of Sampson; his squadron was destroyed, and he himself wounded. After this Santiago surrendered on 17 July, and Spain sued for peace. It was arranged that Spain should evacuate Cuba, should cede Puerto Rico to the USA as well as its island in the Antilles, and one of the Ladrones, and should leave the Philippines in the possession of the USA, after a $20 million payment. In 1899 a treaty was signed, and Spain evacuated Cuba, the Philippines, and other islands.

Bibliography: R. Carr, *Spain*, 1966; H. Thomas, *Cuba or the Pursuit of Freedom*, 1970; L. Gardner et al, *Creation of the American Empire*, 1973.

Spanish Architecture, chiefly because of the Muslim invasion and occupation of much of the land, is more difficult to describe briefly than that of any other European country. Spain possesses many well-preserved remains of Roman buildings, notably in the town of Mérida; but the finest surviving monuments are the great bridge over the Tagus at Alcántara, which has been continuously in use since it was built in AD 105; and the colossal aqueduct at Segovia, over 750 m long, with its

Spanish Architecture. Interior of the Alhambra, Granada, built by the Moors, late 14th century. *(Topham/Fotogram)*

Spanish Architecture. ABOVE The Casa Batlló, Barcelona, designed by Antonio Gaudí, c. 1905. BELOW The nave of Abderrahman I, at the Mosque, Cordoba. RIGHT Renaissance courtyard at the Casa de las Conchas, Salamanca. BELOW RIGHT The Gothic spires of Burgos Cathedral contrast with vernacular house and shop fronts in the Calle de la Llana de Ateuva. (ABOVE *Bisonte;* BELOW AND RIGHT *MAS Barcelona;* BELOW RIGHT *Barnaby's Picture Library*)

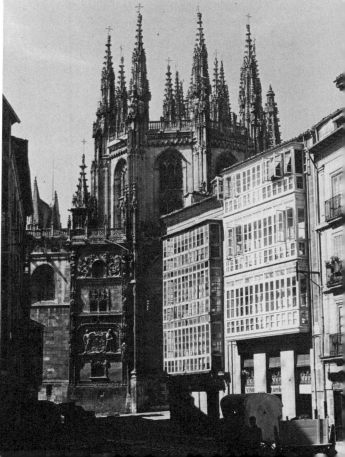

Spanish Architecture

central arches nearly 30 m high. The Visigoths, who invaded Spain in AD 415, were converted to Christianity, and erected a number of small churches; but only a few of those commonly called 'Visigothic' are certainly original. Five remain fairly intact, and are ascribed to the 7th century or thereabouts: among them is S. Juan de Baños near Palencia (661). When the Muslim Arabs invaded Spain from Africa in 711 influences from Syria, Arabia, Egypt and North Africa were introduced. In 786 the construction of the famous mosque at Córdoba was begun, and its building continued for more than two centuries. (In 1236 it became a Christian cathedral and underwent some alteration.) It is very large, intricately designed and richly decorated.

Meanwhile the Christian Visigoths had taken refuge in the mountains of Asturias in the north of Spain, where they built a number of small churches. Of ten still surviving from the period c. 715–c. 915, five are situated near Oviedo, including S. Miguel in that town and S. Julian de los Prados at Santullano. Three more—S. María de Naranco, S. Cristina de Lena and S. Miguel de Lino—apparently by one architect, were built 842–50. They had apses, round arches and stone barrel-vaulting. In the province of León, refugee Christian craftsmen from the south built several 'Mozarabic' (i.e. Christian-Moorish) churches in the 10th century, all small and rather inaccessible; but in these we find the 'round-horseshoe' arch (see ARCH), which is a feature first found in Visigothic architecture. The campaigns of the 11th century drove back the Moors to the south, and then a great boom in church-building began in north Spain. The finest Romanesque example is the cathedral of Santiago de Compostela (1075 onwards); others are S. Isidoro at León (begun

1054) and the Old Cathedral at Salamanca (12th century). Abreast of these, but over a long period, the Moors in the south built the ALHAMBRA at Granada (c. 1377), and the beautiful Giralda tower or minaret at Sevilla (1184–90).

Gothic churches in Spain are derived from French and German sources. They include the cathedrals of Toledo, 1227; Burgos, 1221; León, 1255; Barcelona, 1298; Gerona, 1312; Pamplona, 1317; then, in a florid style showing Moorish influence, Salamanca (New Cathedral), 1509; Segovia, 1522; and Sevilla, 1402.

The arrival of the Renaissance in Spain during the 16th century coincided with the 'Plateresque' style, so called because its intricate decoration suggested the work of a silversmith (platero). There are many examples in Valladolid, Salamanca and Zaragoza. The larger houses of this period focused on a beautiful internal courtyard (patio). The fully developed Italian Renaissance appears in the cathedrals of Granada (1528), Málaga (1528) and Jaén (1540); but most of all in Philip II's immense palace, monastery and church known briefly as 'the Escorial', begun in 1559.

The Baroque style was welcomed with enthusiasm in Spain, where some of its most remarkable and picturesque buildings are to be seen, several of them by the Spanish architect Churriguera, others by Italian architects. They include the façades of the cathedrals of Santiago (1738), Jaén (1667), Granada (1667), Murcia and Valladolid (1676); the royal palaces at Madrid (1738), La Granja (1719), and Aranjuez; and the great Jesuit college at Loyola with a Sanctuary designed by the Italian Carlo FONTANA (1689).

After c. 1750, Spanish architecture experienced the succession of architectural revivals that occurred in other countries. During the past hundred years, its most striking buildings have been those of Antoni GAUDI including the huge and bizarre church of the Holy Family at Barcelona, begun 1883, the Parc Güell (1900) and Casa Milho (1905). New buildings for the University City at Madrid were half-destroyed in the Civil War of 1936–39. Since that date, modern buildings have tended to follow the 'functional' fashions of other parts of Europe, but with respect for vernacular traditions.

Bibliography: B. Bevan, *History of Spanish Architecture*, 1938; G. Kubler and M. Soria, *Art and Architecture in Spain and Portugal*, 1959.

Spanish Armada, see ARMADA, SPANISH.

Spanish Art. The history of art in Spain is an extremely long one. The paintings at Altamira, the most important of the several sites of Paleolithic cave art found in Spain, are about 14,000 years old. This art, however, cannot be thought of as being characteristically Spanish in any way, and the same may be said of the art created there when Spain was culturally influenced by Phoenician, Greek, and Carthaginian colonists. Spain was under Roman dominance from 218 BC to AD 414, and although there are extensive Roman architectural remains, and some mosaics and fragments of mural painting survive, there is no evidence to suggest that Roman art in Spain developed any distinctive regional characteristics. The Iberian peninsula was overrun by the Visigoths in 414 and by the Arabs in 711. The Visigoths contributed little to artistic develop-

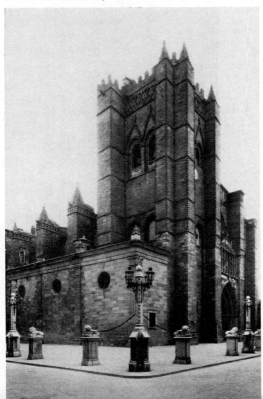

Spanish Architecture. The Gothic cathedral at Avila is incorporated into the 12th-century walls of the city. (*MAS Barcelona*)

ments, crudely carrying on Roman traditions; the Arab civilisation in Spain was brilliant but belongs to the world of Islam. A genuine Spanish national art began to develop with the Mozarabic syle, a blend of Christian and Moorish elements, which began in the 9th century. The Moors were not finally expelled until 1492, but with the advent of the Romanesque style Spain came much more into the mainstream of European artistic development, and drew on a succession of foreign influences. Pilgrimages and the crusading spirit against the Moors helped to prompt these. French and Italian influence predominated in the 12th to 14th centuries, a powerful Flemish influence in the 15th century, and strong Italian influence in the 16th century. Spain in this time grew to be the most powerful nation in the world, and rather belatedly in the 17th century a great national school characterised by realism and religious intensity came into being. A feature of Spanish art is its pronounced regional variations which only became devitalised with the increasing importance of Madrid in the 18th century.

Sculpture. French influence was dominant in Spanish Romanesque an Gothic architecture and sculpture, and Alonso BERRUGUETE is the first great national figure in the latter art. He did much to introduce Italian Renaissance influences, which became dominant in the 16th century. MONTAÑES and Alonso CANO were among the finest sculptors of religious images during the 17th century, the great period of Spanish sculpture when painted wooden statues, expressive of intense religious fervour, were a popular art-form. The 18th century saw incredible elaboration and technical virtuosity in popular religious works of great realism, and in the 19th century Jose ALVAREZ, with his neoclassic style, may be compared with Canova. In the 20th century sculpture has produced nothing of great importance, with the exception of Picasso.

Painting. The origins of painting in Spain are to be traced in illuminated manuscripts and in the remains of mural decoration. Many manuscripts survive from the 9th and 10th centuries, reflecting strong Islamic and Byzantine influence in the style known as Mozarabic. In the Romanesque period Spain was one of the great centres of painting and has more surviving examples of fresco painting from that time than any other country (many are in the Museum of Catalan Art, Barcelona). An important school of manuscript illuminators grew up at the court of Alfonso X of Castile (1221–84), reflecting the French influence which became important in the early Gothic period. Italian influence became dominant in the 14th century and powerfully affected Ferrer Bassa, the first great identifiable Spanish painter, and the founder of the Catalan school. Luis DALMAU, working a century later, reflects the Flemish influence which had become powerful by then. Broadly speaking, painting advanced with the drive of Christian Spain against the Moors, the *Reconquista*, and was most notable in Catalonia and Aragon. By the 15th century a really national type of painting had emerged, with the rise of the Seville school and such masters as Bartolomé BERMEJO. However, Flemish influence was still very strong and Italian influence became a powerful feature in the 16th century, Pedro and Alonso Berrueguete being associated respectively with the introduction of the Renaissance and Mannerist styles into Spain. In the late 16th century Spain could boast her first

Spanish Art. Painting by Pedro Berruguete of *St Dominic and the Albigenses*, c. 1503. *(Prado, Madrid)*

great genius in the art of painting, though a Cretan by birth—EL GRECO. Other important painters of the 16th century are Juan de Juanes (c. 1523–79), Juan de Las ROELAS, Luis de VARGAS and Luis de MORALES (who was strongly influenced by Leonardo da Vinci). The transition from Mannerist to Baroque heralded the great age of Spanish painting and in the 17th century Spain produced a host of important painters in a great creative outpouring—RIBERA, ZURBARÁN, CANO, MURILLO, Valdés Leal (1622–90) and, towering above them all, the supreme genius of VELÁZQUEZ. With the advent of the Bourbons in the 18th century, foreign influence again made itself particularly felt, and a succession of foreign painters were

Spanish Art

Spanish Art. ABOVE LEFT *The Virgin and Child* by Luis de Morales, mid-16th century. ABOVE RIGHT *The Club-foot Boy* by Jusepe de Ribera, 1642. The paper states that he is also dumb—such subjects, depicting human frailties and freaks, are a Spanish tradition. BELOW *The Agony in the Garden* by El Greco, 1605–10. (ABOVE LEFT *Prado, Madrid;* ABOVE RIGHT *Louvre, Paris/Giraudon;* BELOW *National Gallery, London*)

established at Court, while regional characteristics tended to wane as Madrid grew in importance. Spanish individualism asserts itself once more in the exceptional art of GOYA, after whom there comes a long decline, though Esquivel (1806–57), Lopez (1772–1850) and Mariano Fortuny (1838–74) may be mentioned amongst the 19th-century painters. A picturesque and colourful Spain is seen in the work of Zuloaga (1870–1945) and Sorolla (1863–1923), an impressionistic painter who revels in sunlight. The work of modern Spanish painters, particularly Pablo PICASSO, Juan GRIS (Jose Gonzales) and the Catalonian Surrealists, Salvador DALÍ and Joan MIRÓ has been of great general significance in the development of 20th century art, although the most important painters have been largely expatriates. A new school of abstract painting developed in Spain itself in the 1940s, leading figures being Antonio Tapies (1923–) and Modesto Cuizart (1925–).

Spanish Art. Portrait of Pope Innocent X by Velázquez, 1649–51. *(National Gallery of Art, Washington/Andrew Mellon Collection)*

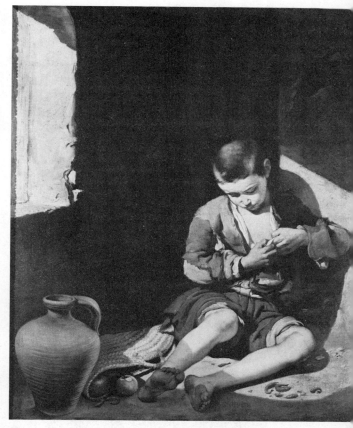

Spanish Art. *The Beggar Boy*, by Murillo, c. 1670. Chiefly renowned as a painter of religious subjects, Murillo also made many paintings of beggar children and rustic scenes. *(Louvre, Paris/Giraudon)*

See also SPAIN, *Art Museums*; SPANISH ARCHITECTURE.
Bibliography: A. F. Calvert, *Sculpture in Spain*, 1912; C. R. Post, *Spanish Painting*, 1930–35; P. Hendy, *Spanish Painting*, 1946; O. Hagen, *Patterns and Principles of Spanish Art*, 1948; G. Kubler and M. Soria, *Art and Architecture in Spain and Portugal and their American Dominions, 1500–1800*, 1959; J. Gudiol, *The Arts of Spain*, 1964; J. Moffitt, *Spanish Painting*, 1973.

Spanish Broom, *Spartium junceum*, resembles the common BROOM but has smoother stems; it is the single species of its genus, which belongs to the Leguminosae (pea family). It flourishes in gardens and round the Mediterranean, and is naturalised in the south of England, especially near London. Its flowers give a yellow dye.

Spanish-fly, see BLISTER-BEETLE.

Spanish Main, name formerly applied to the CARIBBEAN SEA, and to the north coast of South America from the Orinoco to Darien, also to the shores of the Spanish possessions in Central America.

Spanish Moss, see TILLANDSIA.

Spanish Music

Spanish Music. Spain possesses an unusually rich, varied and individual folk-music tradition. The dominance of the Moors in the southern part of the country from the 8th to 15th centuries caused Oriental elements to take deep root in popular song and dance; and the entry of the gypsies into the country during the latter century infused other distinctive elements—the *flamenco* style of singing, dancing and instrumental playing especially shows strong gypsy influence. Moreover the various Spanish regions, with their fierce desire for separate identities, each developed their own unique musical characters—it is possible, for example, to speak of the 'exotic' Andalusian style (which is what the world at large tends to mean when it thinks of 'Spanish music'); the more 'down-to-earth' style of Catalonia, home of street-dances such as the *Sardana;* and the more 'austere' music of Castile. Spain is the home of very many kinds of dance-music, and two dance-types—the PAVANE and SARABAND—became an integral part of European music very early. The PASSACAGLIA also probably has its origins in a Spanish street-dance.

The first important Spanish composers, however,

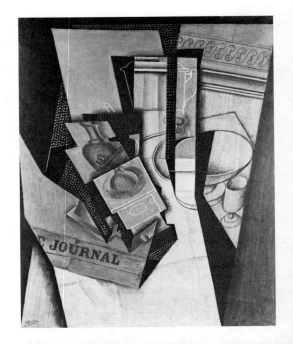

Spanish Art. BELOW Scene from *El Hechizado por Fuerza* (*The Forcibly Bewitched*) by Goya, painted c. 1796, from the comedy by Antonio de Zamora. ABOVE RIGHT *Breakfast* by Juan Gris, 1914, a collage in paper. BELOW RIGHT *Birth of the World* by Joan Miró, oil on canvas, 1925. (BELOW *National Gallery, London;* ABOVE RIGHT *Musée national d'Art Moderne, Paris/Lauros-Giraudon;* BELOW RIGHT *Museum of Modern Art, New York*)

were the 16th-century composers of Church music, whose work naturally reflects little of this popular background. They followed the lead of the great Flemish composers whose *a capella* techniques had become the model for all Europe. Cristobal MORALES was one of the first to compose in this style, and the slightly later Tomas Luis de VICTORIA was one of the great European masters of his time, ranking with Byrd and Palestrina. Also during the 16th century Luis Milan produced a large body of secular songs to the accompaniment of the native *vihuela*, a lute-like instrument that was superseded about 1600 by the guitar. Antonio de CABEZON also wrote for the *vihuela*, but is more celebrated for his organ music—the first significant instrumental music written by a Spaniard.

The tradition of keyboard music persisted through the 17th and 18th centuries: the sonatas of Antonio SOLER influenced those of Domenico Scarlatti (who was himself active in Spain towards the end of his life) and thus the development of European instrumental music generally. The *Zarzuela*, the distinctive national form of comic opera, came into being in the early 17th century and flourished until the 20th—over the years a gigantic repertoire of them has accumulated, though the form did not reach its full flowering until the 19th century, in the works of Franciso BARBIERI. Martin y Soler was an enormously successful operatic composer whose fame in his lifetime

rivalled that of Mozart. But there was little Spanish orchestral music of any note, save for the work of the short-lived Arriaga (1806–25).

Towards the end of the 19th century a 'nationalist' style, drawing on the great store of folk-music, began to take shape, partly under the impetus of the researches of Pedrell (1841–1922) who also composed operas and was a most influential teacher. The pianist-composers Isaac ALBENIZ and Enrique GRANADOS—the latter a pupil of Pedrell—were the harbingers of this national school of composition. Both were active in Paris, where French composers (especially Debussy and Ravel) found great inspiration in their work. It was, paradoxically, Debussy's particularly vital synthesis of 'Spanish' elements in his *Iberia* that showed Manuel de FALLA, another Pedrell pupil, how he could write a truly contemporary Spanish music. Falla's works—especially the ballets *El Amor brujo* and *El sombrero de tres picos*—had great international success and established a colourful and exotic style which he himself developed away from but which, after the Spanish Civil War, was held up by the Nationalist Government as the officially approved musical language. The talented Halffter brothers left the country; and Pedrell's last pupil Roberto Gerhard, the most original figure after Falla, was forced to flee from his native Catalonia and settled in Britain, though the remarkable works he wrote afterwards never entirely lost their Span-

Spanish Music. Frontispiece to Pablo Minguet's treatise on the practice of music. (*Conservatoire de Musique, Paris/Giraudon*)

ish accent. In Spain itself, however, a second-hand Falla-ism occupied the stage in the works of Turina, Joaquin RODRIGO, Mompou and—to a lesser extent—Oscar ESPLA. Only in the last decade or so has there been some move to come abreast of 20th-century trends elsewhere, partly initiated by another Halffter, Christobal (1930–), who teaches at the Madrid Conservatoire. In Xavier Benguerel Spain has at least one respected figure among the European avant-garde.

Bibliography: G. Chase, *The Music of Spain*, 1959; F. Sogeña, *La Historia de la Música española contemporanea*, 1958; M. Valls Gorina, *La Musica española despues Manuel de Falla*, 1962.

Spanish Reformed Church, small body of Protestants founded in Seville in 1871 by an ex-Roman Catholic priest, Francisco Palomares. In 1878 they petitioned the Lambeth Conference for a bishop, and this led in 1894 to the consecration of Bishop Juan B. Cabrera by Lord Plunket, Archbishop of Dublin, and the Anglican bishops of Clogher and Down. The Lusitanian Church, which has similar roots to the Spanish Reformed Church, was founded in Portugal at the same time in the last century. The one bishop serves both churches. The Spanish Reformed Church prayer book is founded on the Anglican Book of Common Prayer, but also contains materials taken from the old Mozarabic rite. In 1963 full communion was established between the Spanish Reformed Church and the Church of England. The Spanish Reformed Church has about a dozen congregations.

Spanish Succession, War of the, 1702–14, fought by France, Bavaria, and Spain against Britain, Austria, Prussia, Denmark, Holland, and Portugal. Savoy fought for France first, but changed sides after 1703.

The war was caused by Charles II of Spain dying in 1700 without direct heirs, leaving his throne to a grandson of Louis XIV of France. Louis immediately claimed his rights, though under partition treaties of 1698 and 1700 he had renounced his family's claims to the Spanish throne forever. The dangers of an ultimate union of France and Spain under one ruler were fully realised by the other major powers, but especially by William III of Britain (though possibly primarily in his rôle as stadholder of the Netherlands), who formed the Grand Alliance, which declared war on France in May 1702.

Three outstanding generals took part in the war: John Churchill, Duke of MARLBOROUGH and EUGÈNE, FRANÇOIS, PRINCE OF SAVOY, on the side of the Alliance, and the Duke of Berwick on the side of France. Marlborough won the battles of Blenheim (1704), Ramillies (1706), Oudenarde (1708), and Malplaquet (1709); Berwick's greatest victory was at Almansa (1707).

After 1710 British interest in the war flagged, and a Franco-British armistice was signed (1712). The Peace of Utrecht (1713) finally ended the war proper, although Charles VI fought on until 1714. The war left the Bourbon Philip of Anjou as king of Spain, but it was agreed that no single person should ever rule both Spain and France. Austria gained considerable territory in Italy, and also the Spanish Netherlands. Britain obtained Gibraltar, Minorca, and land in Canada. Spain and France were both considerably weakened by the war itself, and the resulting territorial settlements left Spain-in-Europe a second-class power.

Bibliography: H. Kamen, *The War of Succession in Spain 1700–15*, 1969.

Spanish Town, town of JAMAICA, on the Rio Cobre, 18 km north-west of Kingston. Founded as Santiago de la Vega in 1525, it was the capital of Jamaica until 1871. Among the main historical buildings are the cathedral and the old house of assembly. It is a railway junction. Population (1970) 41,600.

Spanish Wines. Best known for fortified wines, such as SHERRY and MÁLAGA WINE, and cheap blended wines usually sold under a brand name, Spain does produce, in Rioja, a wine capable of excellence. Around the towns of Haro and Logroño, along the valley of the river Ebro, both red and white Rioja wine is produced. The best wines are the red ones, and the best of these are the *reservas*. Aged for up to ten years in oak barrels, they have a unique velvety, refined quality. The most delicate wines come from the area known as Rioja Alta, the more full-bodied wines from Rioja Alavesa, and the lesser quality wines from Rioja Baja. See also WINE.

Bibliography: G. Rainbird, *Sherry and the Wines of Spain*, 1966; J. Read, *Wines of Spain and Portugal*, 1973; T. A. Layton, *Wines and Castles of Spain*, 1975.

Spar, term applied to some crystalline minerals, e.g. calc-spar (crystalline calcite), a fluorspar of non-metallic aspect (crystalline fluoride of calcium).

Spark, Muriel Sarah (1918–), Scottish writer, born in Edinburgh and educated at the James Gillespie School. She worked at the Foreign Office in London during the Second World War, and lived for a time in Central Africa. From 1947 to 1949 she was editor of *The Poetry Review*. She began by publishing critical biographies, among them *Tribute to Wordsworth*, 1950, *Child of Light*, 1951, on Mary SHELLEY, *The Brontë Letters*, 1954, and helped edit Cardinal NEWMAN's *Letters*, 1957. Her poetry includes

Spanish Music. Andrés Segovia, the celebrated Spanish guitarist. (*Erich Auerbach*)

The Fanfarlo and Other Verse, 1952. However, she is best known as a novelist, her earlier books, such as *The Ballad of Peckham Rye*, 1960, and *Girls of Slender Means*, 1963, being humorous fantasies. Later novels dealt with deeper themes. Among her books are *Memento Mori*, 1959; *The Prime of Miss Jean Brodie*, 1961, perhaps her best-known work; *The Mandelbaum Gate*, 1965; *The Driver's Seat*, 1970; and *Not to Disturb*, 1971. *Collected Poems* and *Collected Stories* appeared in 1967, and *The Abbess of Crewe* in 1973. She is a prolific, far-ranging writer, witty, terse, and incisive.

Bibliography: P. Kemp, *Muriel Spark*, 1974.

Spark Gap, air gap between two, usually spherical, electrodes used as protection against overvoltage on transmission lines. The line is connected to one sphere, the other is connected to earth. When the voltage on the line exceeds a set value, a spark discharge between the spheres releases the high tension. The breakdown strength of air is about 30 kV/cm. Spark gaps are also used for measuring high voltages; the electrodes should then, according to recent research, have a smooth surface providing a uniform field.

Sparking Plug, see MOTOR-CARS, *Ignition*.

Sparrow, a name given loosely to many small birds of various families, but applied particularly to the different members of the genus *Passer* in the family Ploceidae of order Passeriformes. They are natives of almost all parts of the Old World, but not of Australasia, and were introduced into America. There, and in Spain, they are troublesome because of their liking for seeds and grain crops. The common British sparrow, known usually as the house sparrow, is *P. domesticus*, and this species occurs also in North Africa and Europe. It is a strongly built bird that chirps; in diet it is omnivorous, feeding on insects and their larvae in spring and summer, and on grain in winter. *P. montanus*, the tree sparrow, the only other British species, is a smaller bird, found on the west coast of Scotland and in England. The hedge sparrow or dunnock, *Prunella modularis*, is a species of Prunellidae, and is related to the nightingales and thrushes.

Sparrow, Java, see RICE BIRD.

Sparrow-hawk, term applied in Britain to *Accipiter nisus*, in America to several other species of the family Falconidae, order Falconiformes, but especially to *Falco sparverius*, the American kestrel. The former occurs in Europe, Asia and North Africa, and is bluish-grey, with brown and white markings; the latter is reddish, with black and slate-grey markings. Both are handsome birds of active habits. The British sparrow-hawk was formerly used in falconry. Mice, insects and even snakes form the food of *F. sparverius*, but *A. nisus* prefers birds and mice.

Sparta, city and state (as a state more commonly called Lacedaemon) of ancient Greece, situated in a plain on the right bank of the Eurotas, 32 km from the sea. The legendary founder was Lacedaemon, who called the city Sparta after his wife, daughter of Eurotas. Archaeological excavations have shown that Sparta was an important centre of Aegean civilisation (see AEGEAN CULTURE) during the 2nd millenium BC. By the 8th century, one section of the population was reduced to serfdom, and

Sparrow-hawk. *(Topham/Markham)*

these people were thenceforward known as HELOTS; while the provincial population and surrounding villages made tributary to Sparta, became known as *Perioeci*, in whose hands were trade and industry. Neither the helots nor the perioeci had political rights. The state was therefore dominated by a ruling class of less than 10,000 persons (excluding women and children), forming an exclusively warrior caste called 'Spartiates'. The consitution was as follows. There were two kings ruling jointly with limited powers, and a council of elders (the *Gerousia*) consisting of 30 members including the kings. A board of five EPHORS, elected annually, presided over the council and submitted its measures to the popular assembly (*Apella*), of which all Spartiates over the age of 30 were members. In practice, affairs were largely in the hands of the ephors.

The reduction of MESSENIA led to an increase in the number of helots, who, with the perioeci, seem to have amounted to about 100,000 (including women and children). By the time of the Persian invasion in 490 BC, the Spartan hegemony extended over Elis, Arcadia, Argolis, Sicyon, and Corinth; and Sparta was unanimously assigned the chief command. But after the final defeat of the Persians at Plataea (479), the haughtiness of PAUSANIAS disgusted many of the Greek states, who transferred their loyalty to ATHENS. Sparta, however, recovered her supremacy (404) by the overthrow of Athens in the PELOPONNESIAN WAR. She was herself defeated by the Thebans under Epaminondas at Leuctra (371), and the restoration of Messenia two years later completed the humiliation of Sparta. Following the Macedonian conquest of Greece, Sparta retained sufficient independence to refuse participation in the Asiatic campaigns of Alexander; but her power continued to decline. Agis IV (244–241) attempted but failed to restore the 'institutions of Lycurgus' (see LYCURGUS). Cleomenes III (235–222) was more successful; but following

Spartacists

his defeat at Sellasia in the latter year, Sparta was obliged to join the Achaean League, and fell, with the rest of Greece, under Roman power in 146 BC.

The modern town of Sparta (modern Greek *Sparti*) is capital of the department of LACONIA; population (1971) 11,981.

Bibliography: Annual of the British School at Athens, nos. xii–xvi and xxvi–xxx; F. Ollier, *Le Mirage spartiate*, 1933; K. M. T. Chrimes, *Ancient Sparta*, 1949; G. L. Huxley, *Early Sparta*, 1962; A. H. M. Jones, *Sparta*, 1967.

Spartacists (*Spartakusbund*), radical Marxist group founded in Germany in 1917 by Karl LIEBKNECHT and Rosa LUXEMBURG, both of whom met their death after an attempted rising in 1919. The modern German Communist party developed out of the Spartacists.

Spartacus (d. 71 BC), in Roman history, leader of the third slave revolt (see SERVILE WARS). Originally a Thracian shepherd, he later served in the Roman army, but deserted and placed himself at the head of a brigand gang. Taken prisoner, he was sold to a trainer of GLADIATORS. In 73 BC Spartacus belonged to a company owned by one Lentulus at Capua. He persuaded his fellow gladiators to make a bid for freedom; about 70 of them broke out of their barracks and took refuge in the crater of Vesuvius. Chosen as their leader, Spartacus was soon joined by runaway slaves. Having defeated two Roman forces, they rose in number by the end of that year to 90,000, and were in possession of most of southern Italy. In 72 they defeated both consuls and made their way to the foot of the Alps. The slaves, however, would go no farther. Spartacus, obliged to retreat, was defeated and killed on the River Silarus by M. Licinius CRASSUS (71 BC). Those of his followers who were captured were crucified; the remaining fugitives were liquidated by Pompey (see POMPEIUS) on his way home from Spain.

Bibliography: L. G. Gibbon, *Spartacus*, 1970.

Spartanburg, capital of Spartanburg county, South Carolina, USA, 145 km north-west of Columbia. It is an important commercial and transportation centre (rail, air, highway). Industries include cotton and iron production and lumber milling. Population 44,546.

Spartium junceum, see SPANISH BROOM.

Spasm, sudden involuntary contraction of a MUSCLE. There are two varieties of spasm: tonic and clonic. In *tonic* spasm the contraction persists for some time, then relaxation may take place suddenly or gradually. In *clonic* spasm the contraction and relaxation succeed each other regularly. Contraction of muscle is brought about by efferent, or motor, nerve impulses. Spasm, being involuntary, occurs as a result of unpremeditated, uncontrolled nervous impulses which originate either in the motor nervous system itself or in reflex stimuli from the afferent, or sensory, nervous system. Thus muscle spasm occurs automatically in injury or inflammation due to the pain stimuli that travel up the sensory nerves from the affected part, transfer to the motor nerves, and return to the muscles in the affected part. This chain of impulses is known as a reflex action, and is nature's way of guarding the affected part against harmful movement.

Muscle spasm occurs, for instance, in fractures, acute lumbago, and as a result of the inflammation in peritonitis. Colic is a reflex spasm of the involuntary muscle of a hollow organ. Alternatively, spasm may occur as a result of direct stimulation of the motor nerves or motor nerve roots from pressure, as in pregnancy and some orthopaedic conditions, or from inflammation, as in certain diseases of the nervous system, from metabolic toxins, as in uraemia, from bacterial toxins, as in lockjaw (see TETANUS), and from chemical poisons (see STRYCHNINE). An epileptic fit (see EPILEPSY) is characterised by clonic spasm.

A painful tonic spasm of a muscle or a group of muscles

Spartacists demonstrate in Berlin in 1918. (*Bisonte*)

is called *cramp*. It is probably due to a local circulatory failure to remove the metabolic products of the active muscle fibres, and these products act as an irritant to the tissues. It is common experience that cramp occurs in a group of muscles which have been in one position for a long time, an example is *writer's cramp*. *Bather's cramp* is due to muscular exertion in cold surroundings which reduce the circulatory flow to the muscles involved. *Athlete's cramp* may occur in any circumstances where the circulation of blood through the muscles is insufficient to remove the excess waste metabolic products produced in the muscles as a result of their greatly increased contractions. Intermittent CLAUDICATION is a form of cramp that occurs in the leg and calf muscles. This condition occurs mostly in elderly people, whose hardened and narrowed arteries are unable to carry sufficient blood to muscles in a state of activity. Heavy smokers are also subject to intermittent claudication. Typically, the spasm of intermittent claudication comes on after walking a few hundred yards, goes off with rest, and then returns again after resumption of movement. Spasm can also be induced by certain drugs which cause excessive sodium excretion. It can also be the result of calcium deficiency which can occur as a result of various metabolic discorders. Spasm may be relieved by muscle-relaxing drugs.

Spassky, Boris (1937–), Soviet world chess champion, born in Leningrad; he joined the Young Pioneers Chess Club and in 1965 won the Candidates' Matches, making him challenger for the world title. He lost to the champion PETROSIAN but, after a second challenge, became world champion in 1969. Spassky was the first Russian world champion to lose the title to an American when in 1972 Bobby FISCHER took the crown from him by 12½ points to 8½. In Belgrade, 1977–78, Spassky was defeated by Viktor Korchnoi in a match for the right to challenge the reigning world champion, KARPOV.

Spastic, see CEREBRAL PALSY.

Spawn, the extruded egg mass of such oviparous animals as fish, amphibians, and molluscs. It is produced in very variable quantities (e.g. the ling lays about 150,000,000 eggs, and the American oyster 60,000,000 eggs), and is much preyed upon, even, as in the case of the stickleback, by the female herself; a variety of means have been devised for its protection. The name is also given to the mycelium of mushrooms and other fungi, seen as white threads in decaying matter.

In fish *spawning* is the reproductive phase, variously involving aggregation of the fish, courtship, extrusion of eggs and sperm into the water, and fertilisation of the eggs. Large migrations may precede spawning, as in salmon and herring. In some groups the spawn is not released, fertilisation being internal.

Speaker of the House of Commons, see HOUSE OF COMMONS, *The Officers of the House of Commons.*.

Spear, a weapon used by hunters and warriors of most races and ages. Its origin was a sharpened stick, later tipped with a head of worked flint and then bronze and finally iron. The metal heads of spears vary very greatly in size and shape at different periods.

In the Middle Ages the spear was divided into two forms, the spear proper and the lance, the latter being the weapon of the cavalry. With the introduction of the stirrup horsemen were able to couch the lance under the arm and when charging to bring the whole impetus of the impact against the enemy. The lance became heavier in the course of the Middle Ages, and particularly so in the sport of jousting. With the disuse of armour a lighter lance came into use such as that carried by the Polish lancers, who were imitated in all the standing armies of Europe. In modern times experiments have been made with lances of hollow steel. The lance was in the Middle Ages decorated with a pennon which was often decorated with the heraldic arms of the owner, and in modern times a pennon of red and white. In the 16th and 17th centuries pikemen were much used. These were spearmen with a weapon (see PIKE) which was so long that the pikes of the front three ranks formed a defensive wall in front of the main body, which was generally a square. The invention of the bayonet, which could be fixed to the musket, rendered the pike obsolete, since the musketeer armed with a bayonet could both attack the enemy and defend himself.

See also ARMOUR.

Spear Lily, or giant lily (*Doryanthes excelsa*), of the Amaryllidaceae (daffodil family), a magnificent Australian flowering plant with ornamental foliage, sometimes grown in large greenhouses. It bears clusters of scarlet blooms on huge stems, approximately three metres tall, in late summer. Old plants throw off suckers very freely, and the plant is easily propagated.

Spearmint, see MINT.

Special Air Service, The, in the British army, consists of one regular and two TAVR regiments of highly-skilled troops whose main operational rôle is the harassment of the enemy behind his own lines. The regular element of the SAS is selected from all branches of the army thus ensuring the presence of the widest range of military skills in the regiment. Each trooper is also expected to be a specialist in at least one of the four individual skills of

The Special Air Service. Lt-Col. Stirling talking to the officer commanding the SAS Desert Rats patrol, Lt McDonald, on 18 January 1943. (*Bisonte*)

Special Case

linguist, signaller, medic, or explosives expert.

Careful selection and rigorous training test both the physical and mental capacity of each candidate. The would-be trooper must pass an initial selection course lasting three weeks, and then undergo a further eleven weeks of training, followed by three weeks of combat survival training. The volunteers who successfully reach this stage are accepted into the SAS and their training then begins in earnest. The TAVR regiments also have an exacting selection procedure but it is staged over a longer period. The average age of a regular SAS trooper is 27 and during his three-year tour of duty he will spend six to seven months each year on overseas duty.

The concept of a small force of men trained specifically to raid behind enemy lines was put forward early in the Second World War by a Scots Guards subaltern, David Stirling. As a result L Detachment, Special Air Service Brigade, was formed in July 1941, and shortly after an amphibious unit, the Special Boat Service, was raised. By 1944 there were five SAS regiments, the 3rd and 4th being French and the 5th Belgian. In 1945 the 1st and 2nd regiments were disbanded and the 3rd, 4th, and 5th were transferred to their national armies. In 1947 the 21st SAS (Artists) Regiment was formed as a unit of the Territorial Army, to be followed in 1959 by a second TA regiment, the 23rd SAS. The regular 22nd SAS Regiment was raised in 1952 during the Malayan emergency, and it has since served in Borneo, the Radfan, Aden, Malaysia, Dhofar, and Northern Ireland.

A memorial clocktower at Bradbury Lines, Hereford, the home of the 22nd SAS, bears an inscription which encapsulates the regiment's spirit and professionalism: 'We are the pilgrims, master: we shall go always a little further: it may be beyond that last blue mountain barr'd with snow, across that angry or that glimmering sea'.

Special Case, in Scots law, is a case in which the law, but not the facts, are in dispute and which the parties agree to present directly to the Inner House of the COURT OF SESSION.

Special Constabulary, see POLICE.

Special Drawing Rights, a scheme which came into effect in 1970 under the auspices of the INTERNATIONAL MONETARY FUND, to supplement international currency reserves and increase world liquidity. Participants, who must be members of the IMF, must, if asked by the Fund, provide convertible currency for another participant in exchange for SDRs, which are allocated in proportion to IMF quotas. Britain received IMF allocations of SDRs of £171 million in 1970, £125 million in 1971, and £124 million in 1972. These were taken into the official reserves.

Special Education, term used for the provisions made to instruct groups of pupils who are regarded as handicapped (UK) or exceptional (USA). Thus in the USA it includes courses and schools for gifted children (although it is becoming increasingly recognised in Britain that gifted children may require special educational facilities). The provision of special facilities for the physically handicapped dates from the 18th century. In 1760 Thomas Braidwood (1715–1806) opened a school for the deaf and dumb in Edinburgh. Alexander Melville Bell (1819–1905) pioneered a system of 'visual speech', by which deaf mutes could be taught to speak. In England schools for handicapped children were first established in the 19th century and many of them were supported by voluntary associations. The cost of educating such children is high—for a blind child about three times as much as for a normal child. Public opinion in Britain now supports the view that every child, however handicapped, should be trained to the fullest capacity and enabled to enter the adult world and maintain himself in it. The 1944 Education Act laid down that local education authorities should provide special education treatment either within ordinary schools or in special schools or classes. The local education authorities were to ascertain which children were in need of this kind of help, and close links were established between the school health services and local education authorities. A number of categories were defined in regulations in 1953. They are: blind, partially sighted, deaf, partially deaf, educationally sub-normal, epileptic pupils, physically handicapped, pupils suffering from speech defects, and delicate children. There is no reason today why any handicapped child should not receive expert help to overcome his difficulties. There are some 970 schools in Britain, including hospital, day, and boarding schools. Some schools cater for maladjusted pupils. In 1973 some 119,098 pupils were enrolled in special schools. In 1974 a government committee, under the chairmanship of Mrs Mary Warnock, was set up to review the education of handicapped children.

Similar categories exist in the USA; in addition the mentally gifted are frequently grouped with exceptional children. Mentally retarded pupils with IQs from 50 to 75 are classed as educable, those with IQs of 25 to 50 as 'trainable' in institutions for their care and instruction. Somewhat similar groups of children are identified in the USSR. Those with very serious mental defects are cared for by the medical authorities.

Bibliography: R. Gulliford, *Special Educational Needs,* 1971; J. W. Palmer (Ed.), *Special Education in the New Community Services,* 1973; J. S. Payne, *Exceptional Children in Focus: Incidents, Concepts and Issues in Special Education,* 1975.

Special Purpose Machines. Several electrical machines developed for special applications are described below.

Cross-field Machines, also known variously as Amplidyne, Metadyne, Rotadyne, Magnicon, Rototrol, etc., are direct current (d.c.) machines specially designed for use as rotary amplifiers, i.e., causing large changes in the output power by small changes in the input (control) power. In the conventional single-axis d.c. machine (see ELECTRICAL MACHINES) the field winding produces the main magnetic flux in one direction (called the direct axis) and an electromotive force (e.m.f.) is generated in the rotating winding at brushes $Q_1 Q_2$ (fig. 1), which when carrying a current produces a magnetic flux in a direction at right angles to the direct axis (called the quadrature axis). This flux is sometimes also called the cross field because it is assumed to be passing right across the flux in the direct axis. If a pair of brushes are placed on the commutator at $D_1 D_2$ on the direct axis, an e.m.f. will be present there due to the rotation of the rotating winding in the cross field. If an attempt is made to connect a resistance load to the $D_1 D_2$ brushes the field due to the current which will flow will be in a direction opposing the

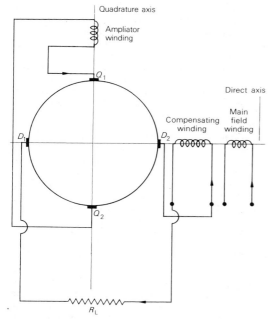

Special Purpose Machines. Figure 1.

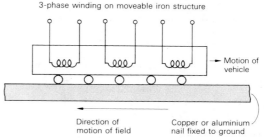

Special Purpose Machines. Figure 2. Linear induction motor.

main flux in the direct axis, causing a collapse of the voltage at Q_1Q_2 and D_1D_2 to low values. This reduction of voltage can be avoided if an additional winding (called the compensating winding) on the direct axis is connected in series with the brushes D_1D_2, and a useful output can be obtained in and a useful output can be obtained in the load R_L. The output can be further improved by connecting the brushes Q_1Q_2 to an extra winding (called the ampliator winding) to provide more flux on the quadrature axis. Hence, a small change of field current on the main field winding can produce a large change in the output at the load. By providing more control windings on the direct axis, this machine can be used to change the output automatically in response to changes in speed, voltage, current, etc. of machines being controlled by the cross-field machine. These machines are manufactured under various trade names like 'Metadyne', which has no compensating winding, giving the machine a characteristic with nearly constant current irrespective of the value of the resistance R_L; and 'Amplidyne', which has full compensating winding, giving a nearly constant voltage across R_L irrespective of changes in its value.

Hysteresis Motors are electric motors designed to run at constant speed at all loads, the speed being related to the frequency of supply as for the synchronous motors, but using specially constructed permanent magnet rotors instead of the d.c.-excited rotors of synchronous motors. They are usually of small power outputs (less than 300 W) and are used for driving record-players, clocks, and similar equipment requiring constant speeds.

Linear Motors are electrical machines designed to produce motion in a straight line, as contrasted with the usual rotary motion of most electric motors. They can be used for running conveyor belts, pumping liquid metals,

catapulting aircraft from short runways, or driving electric trains. Also, when the actual movement is small, they can be used to provide powerful thrusts. In this mode of operation they are called actuators.

The main form of linear motor being considered for use is the linear induction motor. The three-phase winding of the rotating induction motor is wound on a flat, slotted iron structure, and the magnetic field due to the three-phase currents travels in a straight line along the structure. If another metallic structure is nearby, e.m.f.s will be induced in that structure by the travelling field causing electric currents to flow therein; the interaction of the currents and the travelling field will produce forces causing whichever structure is free to move to do so (fig. 2).

Printed-Circuit Motors are small d.c. electric motors with a disk-type rotor on which the conductors of the winding are formed (by a photographic process) in a radial pattern. The disk is placed in a magnetic field and current is fed to the conductors via brushes; a torque is produced as long as current flows. The advantage of this method of construction is that the rotor is very light and has small inertia enabling it to respond quickly to changes in current and torque. These motors are used mainly in control systems.

Pole-amplitude-modulated Motors are specially designed induction motors which can be operated at different speeds. The different speeds are achieved by re-connecting the winding in different ways so as to produce a different number of poles for each method of connection. Usually, the motor is designed for two or

Special Purpose Machines. Figure 3.

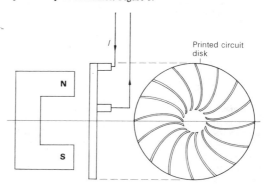

three different speed settings and the changeover is accomplished by using a controller or contactor switch.

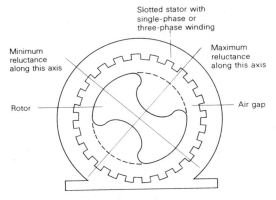

Special Purpose Machines. Figure 4. Reluctance motor.

Reluctance Motors are electric motors designed to run at constant speed at all loads. As in the case of synchronous motors the speed is related to the frequency of the supply. However, unlike synchronous motors, reluctance motors do not require a d.c. supply for the rotor. Reluctance motors are cheap and reliable. Like induction machines they have three-phase stator windings, but the rotor is specially constructed to give saliency effects (fig. 4), showing that the air gap is not uniform around the circumference of the stator. This causes the reluctance of the magnetic circuit to vary as the rotor position changes, hence the name reluctance motor. This motor provides less output than an induction motor of the same frame size, but has advantages because of its constant speed in such applications as rotating stores in computers, and in the plastics industry where several machines driven by different electric motors must all run at the same speed.

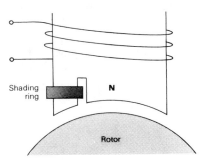

Special Purpose Machines. Figure 5.

Shaded-pole Motors are small electric motors for operation on single-phase supplies. In most single-phase induction motors an auxiliary winding has to be provided for starting, with associated switching circuits. In the shaded-pole motor, the starting torque is produced by having a small band of copper (called the shading ring) round a part of the pole (fig. 5). This has the effect of retarding

the rise and fall of magnetic flux in the 'shaded' part of the pole compared to the flux under the main part of the pole. This distortion of the flux pattern is enough to produce currents in the short-circuited rotor (the squirrel cage rotor) giving rise to forces which will start rotation. The starting torque is small and the motors will only start against low loads. They operate at low power factors and are not very efficient, but they are cheap and robust, and are used for domestic equipment like liquidisers and electric fans.

Stepping Motors, or stepper motors, are electric motors designed to operate in steps of small angular movements instead of continuous rotation. Every time a pulse of voltage is applied to the motor windings, the rotor moves one step, e.g., through an angle of 18°. These motors are used extensively in control systems such as machine tool operation and counters.

Universal Motors are small electrical machines capable of use on both a.c. and d.c. supplies. They are generally of small output (less than 200 W), and are used extensively in domestic equipment such as vacuum cleaners, polishers, and electric drills. The machines have a commutator winding on the rotor, and may have either a permanent magnet or a series-connected field system.

Bibliography: G. S. Brosan and J. T. Hayden, *Advanced Electrical Power and Machines*, 1966; E. R. Laithwaite, *Induction Machines for Special Purposes*, 1966, and *Propulsion Without Wheels*, 2nd ed. 1971; B. V. Jayawant, *Induction Machines*, 1968; P. Alger, *Polyphase Induction Machines*, 1970; J. Hindmarsh, *Electrical Machines and Their Applications*, 2nd ed. 1970.

Special Service Troops, see COMMANDO; SPECIAL AIR SERVICE.

Specialty Debt, one that is evidenced by DEED or instrument under seal. Such a DEBT is called a debt by specialty in order to distinguish it from a simple contract debt (see CONTRACT). Specialty debts enjoy priority in the order of payment of debts out of the assets of a solvent or insolvent estate over all simple contract debts.

Species, chiefly used as a term in biology. In the attempt to study life in its infinite variety, grouping according to similarity is a necessary scientific process. The plant and animal kingdoms are both divided into phyla, each consisting of several classes which are further subdivided into orders, families, genera, species and varieties. For most practical purposes, an organism is referred to by its generic and specific names: thus man is *Homo sapiens* (genus *Homo*; species *sapiens*), the daisy is *Bellis perennis* (genus *Bellis*; species *perennis*). This binomial system of nomenclature was devised by Linnaeus in the 18th century and has stood the test of time.

Although biologists have often argued about the best definition of the species, it does appear to be a natural unit for, if a large collection of plants or animals is assembled, it is generally possible to form groups within which the individual specimens resemble one another strongly and between which there are marked discontinuities. These groups constitute species. Furthermore, if breeding experiments are undertaken, it can generally be shown that members of the same species are fully interfertile with one another whilst matings between members of two different species either fail or produce sterile hybrids. The species can therefore be defined in two different ways.

Traditionally, species are defined by the possession by their members of certain morphological characters not possessed by members of other species. Many modern biologists prefer a so-called 'biological' definition of the species, as a group of interbreeding populations which is reproductively isolated from other such groups. 'Populations', in this sense, are groups of individuals of the same kind living in the same area. Thus the bluebells growing in a wood constitute a population. They interbreed with one another freely and are potentially capable of interbreeding with the bluebell populations in every other wood, if plants from two populations should meet or pollen be carried from one area to another.

Reproductive isolation means the prevention of interbreeding, by internal or external barriers. There are many different types of natural barrier, the commonest being physical incompatibility between markedly different species. In the case of two rather similar species belonging to the same genus or family, mating may be physically possible but interbreeding is prevented by some other barrier. Separation may be geographical, if the two species occur in different parts of the world, or ecological if they occupy different habitats in the same geographical area. Sometimes members of two rather similar species do come into contact with each other but are prevented from mating because, in the case of animals, sexual attraction is lacking between males and females of the different species or, in the case of plants, different insects are needed to carry out pollination. Another situation is found where two species mate or cross-pollinate but the hybrid offspring are inviable, weak or sterile. The mule is a well known example of a sterile hybrid, arising from mating between the ass and horse. The universal occurrence of barriers preventing hybridisation suggests that the reproductive isolation of species has a selective value in evolution. As a result of evolution each species is well adapted to its own particular niche or habitat, but hybrids between two species are intermediate between the parents in most characters and therefore not adapted to live in the habitat of either parental species. Unless a suitable 'hybrid habitat' exists, they will be unable to establish themselves. Evolution has therefore led to mechanisms which prevent the formation of such 'unfit' individuals.

There are some genera in which species are not as clearly separated as usual. This may be because new species are actively evolving at the present time. Examples are the plant genera *Rubus* and *Rosa*. Some biologists (the 'splitters') favour the establishment of many species in these genera whilst others (the 'lumpers') prefer a division into a few species only. The classification of fossils into species presents great difficulties. Fossils are often only small fragments, e.g. a bone or a piece of wood, and the palaeontologist has no idea of the form of the whole animal or plant. In such cases, specific names are given to each small part until such time as further remains are found which show the true relationships of the organism. If a species has evolved gradually over a long period of time it is difficult to decide at what stage a new specific name is warranted. In practice, the fossil record is so incomplete that this difficulty does not often arise. Finally, it should be mentioned that modern man represents only one species as the differences between races are quite superficial and all are fully interfertile.

See EVOLUTION; HYBRID; TAXONOMY.

Bibliography: R. Mayr, *Animal Species and Evolution*, 1963; O. T. Solbrig, *Evolution and Systematics*, 1966; V. Grant, *Plant Speciation*, 1971.

Specific Gravity, see RELATIVE DENSITY.

Specific Heat of any substance, the quantity of heat, measured in CALORIES or JOULES, which will raise the temperature of the substance through 1 °C. Modern methods for the determination of the specific heats of solids and liquids involve the measurement of the rise of temperature produced in them when a known amount of heat energy is provided by an electric current. The specimen is usually suspended on fine threads in a vacuum and the temperature conveniently measured by a resistance thermometer which may also act as the heater. In the case of gases the determination is more difficult. Each gas possesses two specific heats one at constant pressure and the other at constant volume. The apparatus required is described in any text-book on heat. The specific heat of a body is by no means a constant quantity, but varies with the state of the substance, the presence of impurities, and the temperature. Thus the specific heat of ice at 0 °C is 0·504 whereas that of water at 0 °C is 1·000. Again, the specific heat of water varies from 1·00 at 0 °C to 1·03 at 100 °C. Dulong and Petit discovered that the product of the specific heat and the atomic weight is the same for every elementary substance. This law is, however, only approximately true for elements at ordinary temperatures in the solid state. This product is termed the ATOMIC HEAT and its average value is about 6·2.

Specific Performance, see CONTRACT.

Speckle Pattern. When a rough surface is illuminated by laser light it appears to be covered with a random pattern of light and dark patches called a speckle pattern. This is actually an interference pattern consisting of a superposition of a very large number of sets of interference fringes formed by interference between pairs of beams from all the scattering points on the rough surface. The individual fringe patterns have all possible spacings, orientations and contrasts, and the sum of them all appears as completely random.

Bibliography: R. J. Collier and others, *Optical Holography*, 1971.

Spectacles, glass or plastic lenses mounted in frames or half-frames (or rimless mountings) so as to be held before the eyes in cases of defective vision or eye-strain. Roger Bacon (1214–94) is popularly referred to as the inventor of spectacles since he mentions the usefulness of 'the medium of crystal or glass or other transparent substance' for 'old persons and those with weak eyes' in his *Opus Majus* published in 1268. The first mention of the word 'spectacles', however, appears in a Florentine manuscript (author unknown) dated 1299, but there seems little doubt that the Chinese employed lenses ground from quartz or semi-precious stones from early times. Marco Polo records that when he first visited China in 1270 he found the people using lenses to aid their sight.

Aids to vision are now extensively used; convex lenses are used to correct hypermetropia (long sight), concave lenses for myopia (short sight), and cylindrical lenses for ASTIGMATISM. In cases of presbyopia (old sight) convex lenses are added to the distance correction, if any, to compensate for the loss of accommodation (ability to focus near objects), and prismatic lenses to correct muscle imbalance. Glass used in lenses must be colourless and without surface flaws, such as chips, scratches, greyness, waves or small bubbles, which would all interfere with the production of a clear undistorted retinal image. The bulk of spectacle lenses are made of glass, a special hard crown of mean refractive index (in Great Britain) of 1·523 and specific gravity of about 2·6. Tinted lenses may be used to protect over-sensitive eyes from glare or normal eyes from excessive glare. Bifocal or trifocal (multi-focal) lenses are specially ground lenses that give presbyopic people the combined effect of lenses for distance and nearer range in one pair of spectacles. Plastic lenses, too, are manufactured in both bifocal and single-sight prescriptions; they are unsplinterable and much lighter in weight than glass lenses. The surfaces, however, are not so hard as glass, and are therefore more easily scratched. Toughened glass lenses are used by people engaged in hazardous occupations. The frame of the spectacles should fit comfortably, and it is essential that it should bring the optical centre of the lens opposite the centre of the pupil of the eye in front of which it is placed, unless decentration to produce prismatic effect is intentional.

Contact lenses made from glass or plastic, and worn in direct contact with the eye under the eyelids, can be used to correct visual defects for which no spectacles can be designed, and they also have cosmetic advantages. Now made of hard or soft plastic, they have the advantage over glasses in that they can neither be seen—hence their cosmetic value, e.g. to actors—nor readily dislodged; they are therefore of use to sportsmen except swimmers. They are expensive as compared with glasses and, as they are small, are easily lost whence insurers charge high premiums. Unlike glasses, they cannot be worn by everyone who could benefit from them, but the new soft materials have much increased tolerence. Although in theory a replacement for glasses in general, a satisfactory substitute for a presbyopic correction has not so far been evolved. From many points of view they are safer than glasses, but represent a hazard in certain industrial situations; for the normal windscreen-wiping action of the eyelids is ineffective and if a foreign body should get trapped between the lens a corneal abrasion may ensue. This is extremely painful and could cause a serious infection. Ocular hygiene is of much greater importance with contact lenses than with glasses.

'Spectator, The', title shared by two British periodicals. The original *Spectator*, founded by Sir Richard STEELE and Joseph ADDISON, was published daily from 1 March 1711 until 6 December 1712, and was later revived for a short period by Addison alone. Steele had formerly founded and edited the *Tatler*, and the *Spectator* followed many of the ideas he had introduced there. The 'Spectator Club' and its members, including perhaps the most famous, Sir Roger de Coverley, provided the means to comment on various aspects of manners and morals, the articles being written by 'Mr Spectator'. Addison and Steele wrote most of the essays between them, and, in general, the journal's aim was entertainment and moral instruction, with little reference to politics. As well as influencing the popularity of periodicals throughout the 18th century, the *Spectator* also had an effect on the

'The Spectator'. Engraving after a painting by C. R. Leslie shows Sir Roger de Coverley on his way to church, accompanied by Mr Spectator and surrounded by his tenants. *(Mansell Collection)*

development of prose writing generally, including the developing novel.

The modern *Spectator* was founded in 1828 by Robert Stephen Rintoul, who was also its editor. The title was taken from Addison and Steele's periodical, and also, perhaps, the ideal of a non-political 'family journal'. Although non-political in intent, the *Spectator* declared its faith in 1832 by taking a strong stand in favour of the Reform Bill, and its influence, independent of party, was used to support the trade union movement and to further the colonial schemes of Gibbon WAKEFIELD. Today's *Spectator* supplies authoritative comment, both critical and explanatory, on political and public issues of national and international interest. It is usually considered to be on the Right politically.

See also MAGAZINES.

Spectre, see APPARITION.

Spectre of the Brocken, see BROCKEN SPECTRE.

Spectrographic Analysis, the determination of the composition of materials by studying their spectra. The term refers mainly to the determination of the chemical elements, e.g., in the rapid analysis of steels and non-ferrous alloys during manufacture. Large concave grating spectrographs known as polychromators are set up with as many as 30 exit slits, corresponding to the spectrum lines of many different elements. A reasonably accurate determination can be made in a few seconds if a computer is coupled to the instrument, so that continuous process control is possible in steelmaking. The term spectroscopic analysis can also include other techniques, e.g., fluorescence and absorption spectroscopy, which are directed more towards the study of molecular structure. See also SPECTRUM AND SPECTROSCOPE.

Bibliography: M. Slavin, *Emission Spectrochemical Analysis*, 1971.

Spectroheliograph, special photographic spectroscope

suggested by P. J. C. JANSSEN in 1870, applied by G. E. Hale and Deslandres about 1890. A second slit, parallel to the collimator slit, is placed close in front of the sensitive plate; the photographic plate is moved in correspondence with the Sun's movement across the collimator slit (see COLLIMATION) with the result that a photograph is produced by light of only the single wavelength isolated by the second slit. Thus the distribution of a single element, e.g. hydrogen or calcium, across the Sun's disk can be examined. See also SPECTRUM AND SPECTROSCOPE.

Spectrohelioscope, an instrument invented by HALE which permits the visual observation of the Sun in monochromatic light. It is a modification of the spectroheliograph which was developed in the 1890s more or less independently by Deslandres in France, Hale in the USA, and Lockyer in Britain. Its purpose was to photograph the Sun in the light of a single spectral line, usually the red Balmer line of hydrogen or a violet line of ionised calcium. A long-focus telescope was used to form an image of the Sun on the slit jaws of a large spectrograph. The slit allowed light from a narrow strip of the solar image to pass into the spectrograph where it was spread out into a high-dispersion spectrum. A second slit in the image plane of the spectrograph permitted radiation of the selected wavelength to fall on a photographic plate, and record there an image of the narrow strip of the Sun isolated by the first slit. The image of the Sun on the first slit and the photographic plate behind the second were moved across at the same uniform speed so that a picture of the whole Sun was gradually built up. In the spectrohelioscope, Hale replaced the photographic plate by an eye-piece and traversed the image of the Sun rapidly to and fro over the first slit by means of a rotating optical cube. A similar and synchronised rotating optical cube between the second slit and the eye-piece integrated the resulting monochromatic solar image. The instrument has been rendered obsolete by the development by LYOT and others of optical filters having very narrow pass bands.

Spectrophotometer, an instrument which measures the transmission of light by a material, e.g., a glass or a solution, for different wavelengths. Spectrophotometers are used in biological, chemical, and medical laboratories to determine the chemical composition of samples such as blood, other body fluids, polluted water, or plant sap. There are also reflection spectrophotometers, which measure varying reflectivity through the spectrum of, e.g., pigments or coloured ceramics. A spectrophotometer comprises essentially a light source with a continuous spectrum, a monochromator, a device for holding the sample to be measured, and a photoelectric detector, usually coupled to a recording system. The measurement is made with and without the sample in position and a comparison of the readings gives the absorption or transmission curve. Spectrophotometers are made for all regions of the spectrum from the ultraviolet to the very long-wavelength infrared and they can be made to display the results graphically on an oscilloscope or as numerical data printed out by a computer. See also SPECTRUM AND SPECTROSCOPE.

Spectroscopic Binaries are stars whose duplicity is revealed by their spectra. As the two stars revolve about their mutual centre of mass, they alternately approach and recede from the observer, resulting in a periodic Doppler shift in the lines of their spectra. If the orbital motion happens to lie at right angles to the line of sight, there is no approach nor recession so that such a system cannot be detected as a spectroscopic binary. In about one case in six, the component stars are sufficiently similar in brightness for the spectra of *both* to appear; then as one star approaches, the other recedes, so that the spectral lines appear sometimes double, sometimes single, giving a *double-lined* spectroscopic binary.

The line-of-sight velocity of the brighter star, or of each star in a double-lined spectroscopic binary, is measured from the Doppler shift at various stages of the orbital period, resulting in one or two velocity curves. Analysis of these curves gives a lower limit of the combined mass in the case of a single-line binary, or of the lower limit of the mass of each component in the case of a double-line binary.

The first spectroscopic binary to be discovered was the brighter component of MIZAR by E. C. PICKERING in 1889. Many hundreds are now known with orbital periods ranging from 82 minutes to 15 years. Selection effects ensure that the most common period is a few days.

See BINARY STARS.

Spectrum and Spectroscope. When a beam of light is passed through a prism, diffraction grating, or other dispersing agency, it is generally spread out in a fan-wise beam which if made to fall on a white screen produces a coloured band of light known as a spectrum. Study of spectra began when Newton bought a glass prism at Stourbridge Fair, near Cambridge, and performed the celebrated series of experiments described in his *Opticks*. Newton's description of his first experiment runs as follows:

> In a very dark Chamber at a round hole about one third part of an Inch broad made in the Shutter of a Window I placed a Glass Prism, whereby the beam of the Sun's Light which came in at that hole might be refracted upwards towards the opposite Wall of the chamber, and there form a coloured Image of the Sun.

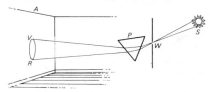

Spectrum and Spectroscope. Figure 1.

Fig. 1 is Newton's diagram explaining the arrangement. Newton observed that the patch of coloured light VR thrown on the paper consisted of overlapping patches of the following colours: violet (V), indigo, blue, green, yellow, orange, red (R), arranged in that order. Newton recognised that white light consists of the wide range of colours seen in the spectrum and in RAINBOWS. The violet light is deviated most and the red least, and to avoid overlapping images of the Sun it is necessary to use a narrow illuminated slit as object and employ lenses to produce focused images of the many colours, as in the modern spectroscope.

Spectrum and Spectroscope

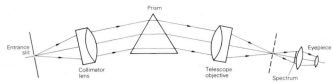

Figure 2. Optics of a simple spectroscope.

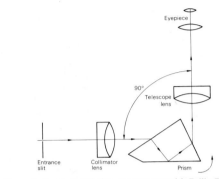

Figure 3. Constant deviation spectroscope with Pellin-Broca prism.

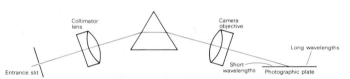

Figure 4. A prism spectrograph.

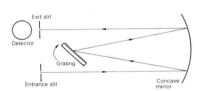

Figure 5. Grating monochromator.

Types of Spectroscope. Fig. 2 shows the principle of a simple prism spectroscope. The light from which the spectrum is to be obtained falls on the entrance slit, which is a slit of adjustable width with metal jaws. The slit is at the focus of the collimator lens (see COLLIMATION), so that each point on the slit produces a beam of parallel light. The prism deviates each wavelength through a different angle, on account of the varying REFRACTIVE INDEX of the glass, but all the rays of one wavelength are deviated through the same angle since they enter the prism parallel to each other. The system so far is in effect forming the spectrum at an infinite distance, since the rays of each wavelength are parallel, but different wavelengths travel in different directions. The telescope is used to view the spectrum at infinity; the telescope objective forms an image of the spectrum in its focal plane and the eyepiece is used to view this image. The collimator and telescope are mounted on rotatable arms and the prism is on a rotating table, so that the three components can be arranged at any angle to each other. In this form the spectroscope could be used for the visual study of spectra but it is not very convenient because the telescope must be moved to bring different parts of the spectrum into view. However, instruments of this kind, called spectrometers, are made with accurate angle calibrations for use in measuring the angles and refractive indices of prisms. The constant deviation spectroscope (fig. 3) is more conveni-

ent for visual use; the collimator and telescope are fixed, usually at right angles to each other, and the dispersing prism is rotated to scan the spectrum across the field of view of the eyepiece. The prism rotation movement is calibrated directly in units of wavelength.

For quantitative scientific work it is usually necessary to record the spectrum photographically or photoelectrically. Fig. 4 shows the optical system of a prism spectrograph for photographing the spectrum; essentially the eyepiece of the spectroscope has been replaced by a photographic plate or film, and the telescope objective becomes the camera objective. The focal surface is usually tilted to the axis as shown because it is unnecessary to correct the lenses for CHROMATIC ABERRATION. All the components are pre-set in fixed positions.

In comparing spectroscopic apparatus we consider DISPERSION, which is the extent to which different wavelengths are spread apart on the plate or film, and RESOLVING POWER, which is concerned with the smallest wavelength difference between neighbouring spectrum lines which can be distinguished. In both these respects better results are obtained by using DIFFRACTION GRATINGS instead of prisms for dispersion. A typical photoelectric grating instrument is shown in fig. 5. The concave mirror collimates the light from the entrance slit and the reflecting diffraction grating disperses the light. A different part of the same mirror focuses the spectrum onto an exit slit and a photoelectric detector is placed behind this slit. An arrangement of this kind is called a monochromator rather than a spectrograph; it can be used, as the name implies, to produce a beam of monochromatic light of chosen wavelength from the exit slit. The wavelength is changed simply by rotating the grating as indicated. Monochromators of this kind, and others with mirrors instead of lenses, have the advantage that they need no refocusing for different wavelengths, so that they can be used over a great range from the ultraviolet to the infrared. Very large grating spectrographs are constructed with a single optical element; a concave diffraction grating, which serves both to disperse the spectrum and to focus it, is shown in fig. 6.

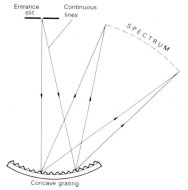

Spectrum and Spectroscope. Figure 6. Large concave grating spectrograph.

Types of Spectra. Visible light comprises a small range of wavelengths from the entire known electromagnetic spectrum. A solid hot body, e.g., a filament lamp, produces a *continuous spectrum* or continuum containing all wavelengths in proportions depending on the temperature of the body. If a single chemical element is obtained in gaseous form, e.g., sodium or mercury vapour, and is heated sufficiently, it will produce light with a *line spectrum*; this consists of a number of sharply defined bright lines as seen in the spectroscope, indicating that only certain discrete wavelengths are emitted; these wavelengths are unique to the element in question and they form an infallible identifying 'signature'. The spectrum lines may be many or few in the visible spectrum: sodium has only two closely spaced yellow-orange lines but iron has many thousands. It is convenient to heat the material by an electrical discharge, arc, or spark, through a tube containing the vapour; the neon signs used in advertising have their characteristic colour because the lines in the neon spectrum are excited in this way. If light with a continuous spectrum is passed through a relatively cool gas or vapour an *absorption spectrum* is obtained: the continuum is crossed by dark lines at the wavelengths corresponding to the emission lines of the gas or vapour. The spectrum of the Sun is of this kind; the dark lines are called Fraunhofer lines after their discoverer and they form the earliest used wavelength standards. If the absorbing medium is a liquid or solid the absorption lines broaden into bands.

Spectra are also classified according to the mechanism which produces them. In all cases a photon of light is emitted with frequency v as a result of a change in energy of the emitting system of amount hv, where h is Planck's constant, 6.6×10^{-34} J s, but there are several possibilities for the emitting system. Photons of visible and ultraviolet light correspond to transitions in the energy states of the outer or valence electrons in individual atoms and these produce *atomic spectra*. In the infrared the transitions are in states of vibration or rotation of molecules *(molecular spectra)*. Atomic spectra may show very fine detail or *fine structure*, corresponding to mixtures of isotopes of the same element and to other refined effects. Also spectrum lines may be broader or narrower according to the temperature and other conditions in the light source. If a spectrum is produced by exciting the atoms very energetically, e.g., by an intense electric spark, many more lines are produced and these are due to energy transitions in ionised atoms. On the other hand gentle excitation as in a low pressure gas discharge produces only the spectrum of the non-ionised or neutral atoms. The narrowest ordinary spectrum lines, i.e., those containing the smallest range of wavelengths, are produced by special discharge tubes containing only a single isotope of the required element; if it is a gas the tube is run at low temperature and pressure, and the spectrum is excited by a radio frequency field from external electrodes (electrodeless discharge). For solids a hollow-cathode discharge tube is used and the cathode contains the element of which the spectrum is to be excited.

LASERS produce even narrower spectrum lines under the right conditions but they are essentially different from ordinary sources of line spectra. Whereas the range of wavelengths from a carefully run discharge tube is given by $\delta\lambda/\lambda = 10^{-6}$ approximately, for a well-stabilised laser the corresponding fraction would be about 10^{-9}. Such narrow lines are beyond the resolving capability of conventional spectroscopes and special interferometric techniques are used.

Interferometric Spectroscopes. For some purposes, in particular very high resolution spectroscopy and infrared spectroscopy, it may be preferable to use an INTERFEROMETER rather than a prism or grating instrument. An interferometer does not produce a visible spectrum which can be thrown on a screen: its mode of action can be understood by considering the Michelson interferometer. If this instrument is illuminated with monochromatic light of wavelength λ and if one of the mirrors is steadily moved at speed v the centre of the field of view of the fringe system will go alternately light and dark at frequency $2v/\lambda$. If the light is not monochromatic all the different wavelengths present will produce a similar alternation of light and dark, or modulation, but each wavelength will have its own different frequency of modulation. Thus the different wavelengths λ are encoded in the output as modulations at frequencies $2v/\lambda$, and to obtain the spectrum we have to decode or demodulate the output. This can be done by the mathematical technique of Fourier analysis and this method of spectroscopy is sometimes called Fourier transform spectroscopy. It was originally used by Michelson in 1892 to establish that the red spectrum line of cadmium vapour was the narrowest known and was therefore the most suitable for the proposed calibration of the metre in terms of the wave-

Spectrum and Spectroscope

length of light. Fourier transform spectroscopy is nowadays a routine method of infrared absorption spectroscopy. The other important interferometric spectroscope is the FABRY-PEROT INTERFEROMETER or etalon. This is a multiple-beam interferometer (see MULTIPLE-BEAM INTERFEROMETRY) and it therefore forms fringes with much narrower bright than dark parts. Thus if the incident light is not exactly monochromatic each wavelength will form its own fringe system, and with appropriate geometry the fringes can be seen as separate. A good Fabry-Perot etalon may have a resolving power approaching 500,000. However, the usable spectral range is very narrow, usually less than 50 times the resolution limit, so that a dispersing prism or grating must be used as an auxiliary system.

Ultraviolet and Infrared Regions of the Spectrum. Light of wavelength less than about 4×10^{-7} m does not produce any sensation of sight when it falls on the human eye; again, light of wavelength greater than c. 8×10^{-7} m produces no response in the eye. The former is known as ultraviolet light, and the latter as infrared light, and particular methods are required for investigation in these regions. When a body such as a piece of metal is heated it first emits infrared light that is detected by its heating effect. Subsequently the body emits the shorter visible red rays, and as it gets hotter still the whole visible spectrum and ultraviolet light are emitted and the body looks white.

Infrared Spectrum. A sensitive thermometer placed in the infrared region is sufficient to detect the presence of an infrared spectrum from a hot body, but in order to measure wavelengths and intensities of the light in this region a more refined technique is required. The spectroscope used for this work has a prism of rock salt that (unlike glass) is transparent to infrared light. Lenses of this material may be used in the spectroscope, but it is more satisfactory to use metallic mirrors in place of lenses for focusing the light. The concave diffraction grating is a most suitable instrument for this region of the spectrum. The radiation is recorded on photographic film or by instruments. The longest infrared waves measured are of the order of 1 mm; longer waves are termed microwaves. Study of the absorption bands in the infrared spectrum have shown that it is possible to associate the latter with the vibrations of specific groups in the molecule being studied and measurements in the infrared have been valuable in the problems of association, complex compounds, hydrogen bonding, etc. For diatomic molecules measurements on the infrared spectra have enabled the moments of inertia, and hence the bond lengths, to be determined.

Automatic spectrophotometers measure the absorption of radiation at particular wavelengths when it is passed through a transparent sample (usually a liquid). The radiation absorbed reveals the composition of the sample, and this has proved a particularly powerful tool for identifying organic compounds, which have important absorption characteristics in the infrared.

Ultraviolet Spectrum. The ultraviolet spectrum extends from wavelengths of 4×10^{-7} m, corresponding to the violet end of the visible spectrum, to wavelengths as short as about 10^{-9} m. Shorter wavelengths are known as X-rays. The existence of the ultraviolet spectrum was discussed as early as 1801, when Ritter found that silver chloride was most rapidly affected when it was placed beyond the extreme violet of the visible spectrum. Stokes in 1852 explained that Ritter's discovery was really the discovery of an invisible spectrum, and by means of the phenomenon of FLUORESCENCE exhibited by such bodies as uranium glass, Stokes revealed the presence of a wealth of bright lines in the ultraviolet spectra of elements. It is now known that the number of bright lines in the ultraviolet region far exceeds the number of such lines in the visible spectrum. Since ultraviolet light is readily absorbed by ordinary glass, the usual form of prism spectroscope is useless for the analysis of the ultraviolet spectrum. Quartz lenses and prisms may be used instead, for these are fairly transparent to a wide range of wavelengths in this region. The concave grating is very suitable, and Féry's spectrograph is often used. Ultraviolet light affects photographic plates, and in mapping spectra in this region such a plate, enclosed in a camera, replaces the visual method adopted for the visible spectrum. Spectra in the ultraviolet region have proved of practical value in that compounds containing the same characteristic groups give analogous spectra. This has led to the elucidation of the structures of a number of compounds, e.g., alkaloids and purines. Furthermore, spectral study has contributed to the elucidation of the question of colour in organic compounds.

The Doppler Effect. The fact that the bright lines in stellar spectra exhibit a shift towards the violet end of the spectrum if the star is moving in the line of sight towards the observer is an example of the Doppler effect explained in the article on SOUND. Similarly, the lines are shifted towards the red end of the spectrum if the star is receding in the line of sight. From measurements of these shifts it is possible to deduce the speed of recession or approach. This has been of particular importance in the study of motions of galaxies in the universe. It is also possible to determine the speed of rotation of the Sun and planets in this way, for the peripheral portions are moving in the line of sight towards or away from the observer. The existence of double stars rotating about their common centre of gravity, and too close together to be resolved by a telescope, is revealed by the Doppler shift of the bright lines in the spectrum. Magnetic fields in stars can be detected by the splitting of spectral lines (see ZEEMAN EFFECT).

Theory of Spectra. By the process of trial and error Balmer discovered in 1885 that the wavelength λ of the bright lines in the spectrum of hydrogen could be expressed by the formula $\lambda = Kp^2/(p^2 - 2^2)$, where K was a constant and p was given the values 3, 4, 5, ... Another way of expressing the formula is $1/\lambda = k = R(1/2^2 - 1/p^2)$ where k is the wave number, i.e., the number of wavelengths per metre, and R is Rydberg's constant, which is 10,967,758 m^{-1}. Balmer conjectured that the spectrum of hydrogen might possibly contain other series of lines given by

$$k = R(1/1^2 - 1/p^2), \text{ and } k = R(1/3^2 - 1/p^2),$$

but the spectroscope in his day was not able to detect such lines in the ultraviolet and infrared. They were actually found later by Lyman and Paschen, respectively, and the series of lines corresponding to the last two formulae are called the Lyman and Paschen series. Balmer's law remained for some time a simple but unexplained empirical law enabling the wavelength of any hydrogen line in the above series to be computed when the wavelength of one of the lines was known.

Then came the QUANTUM THEORY and Rutherford's nuclear theory of the atom (see NUCLEUS). From these Bohr developed a theory of the hydrogen atom. His theory, put concisely, is as follows:

1. The hydrogen atom consists of a positively charged nucleus (the proton) round which an electron describes an orbit under the electrical attraction between the proton and electron. Expressed mathematically, for a circular orbit we have $mv^2/r = e^2/r^2$, where m is the electronic mass, moving with velocity v in an orbit of radius r, under the attractive force e^2/r^2, where e is the charge on the electron and on the proton.

2. Of the infinite variety of orbits that are possible according to the laws of classical dynamics, Bohr asserted that only those orbits are stable for which the angular momentum is an integral multiple of $h/2\pi$, where h is Planck's constant and has the value $6\cdot6 \times 10^{-34}$ J s. This second assumption of Bohr expressed in mathematical form becomes $mvr = nh/2\pi$, where n is an integer. Combining these two equations we obtain the radii of the stable orbits of the electron, viz.,

$$r = n^2h^2/4\pi^2e^2m.$$

3. Bohr's last assumption is that the emission of radiation from the hydrogen atom follows Einstein's photoelectric law (see PHOTOELECTRICITY), $E_p - E_n = h\nu$, i.e., radiation of frequency ν is emitted when the electron jumps from one orbit where the energy of the atom is E_p to another nearer the nucleus, where its energy is E_n. In other words, the quantum of energy radiated is equal to the difference between the energies of the atom in its initial and final states.

Now it may be shown that the energy of the atom when the electron is in the nth orbit is

$$C - 2\pi^2me^4/h^2n^2,$$

where C is a constant. It follows that

$$E_p - E_n = (2\pi^2me^4/h^2)(1/n^2 - 1/p^2).$$

Now $E_p - E_n = h\nu = hc/\lambda$. Hence

$$k = 1/\lambda = R(1/n^2 - 1/p^2),$$

where R is the constant

$$2\pi^2me^4/h^3c.$$

By these bold assumptions, Bohr reached the equation that is identical with that deduced by Balmer from the observed facts. In other words, the formula

$$1/\lambda = R(1/n^2 - 1/p^2)$$

is explained. The different terms inside the brackets correspond to the different energy levels within the atom, and the process of emission of light by an element consists of: (1) atomic excitation in which the electron is thrown out of its original orbit to one farther removed from the nucleus; (2) the return to an inner level or orbit, while the energy corresponding to the difference between these two levels is radiated in accordance with the quantum theory. Bohr's theory, bold as it was, was justified quantitatively. Furthermore, its conclusions were strengthened by its applications not only to the spectra of other elements, but also to the interpretation of X-ray spectra of elements. In spite of the success of the Bohr theory, there were many details in the spectrum of hydrogen which it was unable to explain, but it would exceed the limits of space to deal with these. Since 1925 the Bohr-Sommerfeld model of the atom has been abandoned (Sommerfeld was responsible for various modifications, such as the introduction of elliptical orbits of electrons round the nucleus). Nevertheless, Bohr's theory is still used for many purposes, largely because the model is easily visualised.

Microwave Spectroscopy. A relatively new technique uses the absorption of radio waves by matter, whose wavelengths are between about 1 and 300 mm. The radiations are known as microwaves, and into the corresponding region of the spectrum come many low-energy transitions of atoms and molecules. The radio-frequency currents are generated, and these produce variable electromagnetic fields which are made to influence the material being studied in various ways so as to find its molecular, atomic, or nuclear characteristics. Results of microwave absorption have enabled such quantities as bond lengths, DIPOLE MOMENTS, and atomic masses to be calculated. The absorption of radio waves at precise frequencies has allowed very accurate atomic clocks to be made using these carefully regulated frequencies.

See also MASS SPECTROGRAPH; PHYSICAL CONSTANTS; WAVE MECHANICS.

Bibliography: H. Dingle, *Practical Applications of Spectrum Analysis*, 1950; R. A. Sawyer, *Experimental Spectroscopy*, 1951; C. Candler, *Modern Interferometers*, 1951; S. Tolansky, *High Resolution Spectroscopy*, 1957; R. W. Reid, *The Spectroscope*, 1966; P. Bousquet, *Spectroscopy and Its Instrumentation* (trans. K. M. Greenland), 1971; K. I. Tarasov, *The Spectroscope* (trans. J. H. Dixon), 1974.

Speculum Metal, alloy consisting of 68 parts of copper and 32 parts of tin. It is white in colour and takes a high polish. Formerly used for specula or mirrors of reflecting telescopes, it has now been partly replaced by silvered or aluminised glass. It is used in the manufacture of diffraction gratings.

Speculum Perfectionis, the Mirror of Perfection, a life of St FRANCIS OF ASSISI, written about 1318 and based on the memories of his companion Brother Leo.

Spedding, James (1808–81), English editor, born at Mirehouse, Cumberland. At Trinity College, Cambridge, he was one of the celebrated 'Apostles' group. His great literary achievement was the editing, with R. L. Ellis and D. D. Heath, of the works of Francis BACON (in 7 volumes, 1857–59, with 7 more volumes of *Letters and Life*, 1861–72). *Life and Times of Francis Bacon* appeared in 1878.

Spee, Maximilian, Count von (1861–1914), German admiral, born at Copenhagen. In 1914 he was in command of the Far East squadron, and on the outbreak of the First World War escaped from Chinese waters. On 1 November 1914 he defeated an inferior British squadron commanded by Adm. Cradock at Coronel (see CORONEL, BATTLE OF), but on 8 December his squadron was annihilated at the battle of the Falkland Islands, Spee himself going down with his flagship, the *Scharnhorst*.

Speech, see VOICE AND SPEECH.

Speed Control of Electric Motors

Speed Control of Electric Motors. When mechanical loads are required to operate at different speeds, e.g., fans, trains, steel-rolling mills, or lathes, this can be very easily achieved by using electric motors. In each case the torque required at any particular speed depends on that speed. With a fan, for instance, torque is proportional to N^2, whereas for traction, the required torque is approximately proportional to $1/N$, where N is the speed in revolutions per minute. Thus the motor selected for any drive must be capable of providing the required torque at the specified speed, and must be capable of speed control as required.

Provided the torque-speed characteristic of the motor selected is suitable (see ELECTRICAL MACHINES), the method of speed control may prove a decisive factor in the final choice of the type of motor. Direct current (d.c.) motors (and those designed as universal motors for use on both d.c. and alternating current (a.c.)) are the easiest to control. The speed may be increased by increasing the applied voltage and/or decreasing the field current by inserting extra resistance in the field circuit; the speed may be decreased by reducing the applied voltage or inserting resistance in the armature circuit. The voltage can be raised or lowered by using controlled rectifiers (thyristors) to control the conduction angle if d.c. is obtained by rectification of a.c., or by chopping if the d.c. is obtained from batteries or d.c. generators. Chopping involves switching the d.c. supply on and off using thyristors, and the average voltage is altered by varying the relative periods when the supply is on and off. Another way of effectively changing the applied voltage to a motor is possible when several motors are used to provide the drive as, for example, in electric trains. By connecting all the motors in series, the voltage per motor is lowest (see figure). Such an arrangement as this can be gradually changed to groups of motors in series and parallel until for maximum speed all the motors are in parallel, when the voltage per motor is highest. Each motor must of course be rated for the highest voltage. This changeover is smoothly effected by the use of a CONTROLLER in the driver's cabin. When series motors are connected in parallel, special field interconnections have to be made to ensure that the load is equally shared and that all machines run at the same speed. Induction machines are the cheapest, especially the squirrel-cage type, but they are not suitable for speed control. With a.c., voltage change can easily be achieved by using autotransformers. Voltage change will give a small amount of speed change, although the torque developed by the motor is proportional to V^2, and the change in torque may be too large and unacceptable. Two-phase induction motors used as SERVOMOTORS in control systems do use voltage control but they are not used there for speed variation, rather for small movements only. Another method of speed control would be the use of change of supply frequency. To maintain the torque it is necessary to keep the ratio V/f constant, and this makes the change of frequency a little difficult. Cycloconvertors are used for frequency changing; they incorporate thyristor and transistor circuits operating in the invertor mode (see RECTIFIER). Different iron losses with varying frequencies may require adjustment of the rating of motors not specifically designed for variable speed operation. If discrete steps of speed are required, e.g., ⅓, ½, ¼, it is possible to use a motor with two or three different

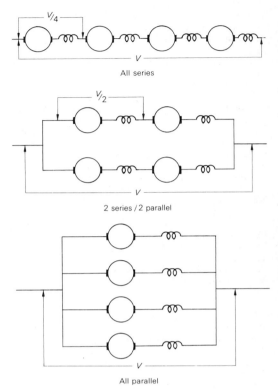

All series

2 series / 2 parallel

All parallel

Speed Control of Electric Motors. Four d.c. series motors connected in different ways to obtain speed control.

windings for different numbers of poles (pole-change motors) or to use a specially wound motor capable of re-connection for different numbers of poles (see SPECIAL PURPOSE MACHINES, *Pole-amplitude-modulated Motors*). If induction motors with wound rotors were available, speed could be controlled by inserting extra resistances in the rotor circuits. Special schemes using additional machines called frequency-changers can also be used in such cases but this is expensive. More expensive machines, such as a.c. commutator motors and Schrage motors, are available, and they are only used in exceptional circumstances. Synchronous motors are constant speed machines. In this respect, reluctance motors and hysteresis motors are also constant speed machines, the value of the speed being given by $N = 60f/p$, where N is the speed in revolutions per minute, f is the frequency of the supply in herz, and p is the number of pairs of poles.

Bibliography: A. T. Dover, *Electric Traction*, 4th ed. 1965; J. Hindmarsh, *Electrical Machines and Their Application*, 2nd. ed. 1970; Institution of Electrical Engineers Conference Publication No. 93, *Variable Speed Drives*, 1973.

Speed Skating, see ICE SKATING; ROLLER SKATING.

Speedway Racing, see MOTOR RACING.

Speedwell, see VERONICA.

Speen, see NEWBURY.

Speenhamland System, method of outdoor poor relief adopted by the Berkshire justices in 1795 in response to widespread unemployment, high prices, and low wages particularly among agricultural workers. The parish was to supplement wages below an absolute minimum set by the justices, in accordance with the price of bread and the size of the man's family. The system spread to much of the south and east of England but its general effect was further to depress wages and greatly to increase the rate burden. The Poor Law Amendment Act of 1834 aimed to end such outdoor relief to the able-bodied poor; relief was only to be provided in workhouses run on draconian lines and outdoor relief to be reserved for the very old or sick.

Speidel, Hans (1897–), German soldier, educated at the universities of Tübingen and Berlin, the Technische Hochschule, Stuttgart, and the Kriegsakademie. Speidel became a regular army officer in 1914. Between the wars he held a number of regimental and staff appointments. In the Second World War he rose to be chief of staff to an army group under ROMMEL and held this appointment when the Allies invaded Normandy. Speidel was charged with participation in the German generals' plot against Hitler. He was tried but was subsequently acquitted. From 1951 to 1955 he was military adviser to the German Federal government. In 1955 he became chief of staff. From 1957 until 1963 he was commander of the NATO land forces. He was made special adviser to the Federal government on military affairs in 1963. He wrote *We Defended Normandy* (English translation, 1951).

Speiss, crude arsenide of cobalt or nickel which is obtained on smelting the arsenical ores of these metals. A naturally occurring arsenide of cobalt with nickel and iron is called speiss-cobalt.

Speke, John Hanning (1827–64), British explorer, born at Jordans, near Ilminster, Somerset. In 1844 he joined the Indian Army and served in the Punjab campaigns. In 1857–58 he took part in an expedition led by Richard BURTON to discover the source of the NILE, by journeying westward from Zanzibar. After Burton fell ill, Speke continued without him, to discover and name Lake VICTORIA, which he claimed to be the source of the great river. Burton challenged him bitterly and publicly over this, but Speke received the approval of the establishment and in 1860 was sent on a second expedition in the region with J. A. Grant. Speke was shot in a hunting accident in England, alleged by Burton to have been suicide.
Bibliography: J. H. Speke, *Journal of the Discovery of the Source of the Nile,* 1863; A. Moorehead, *The White Nile,* 1966.

Speke, see LIVERPOOL.

Speke Hall, Merseyside. The manor of Speke was mentioned in the Domesday Book and was therefore in existence in 1066. The present 16th-century house is a fine example of Tudor half-timbering, and contains fine plasterwork. Speke was given to the National Trust in 1944 and is let to Liverpool Corporation.

Speleology (the study of CAVES) is an interdisciplinary field covering such topics as cave exploration and survey, the biology of cave life, the palaeontology of prehistoric finds in caves, and cave geology and geomorphology. Much of the work in this area is done by amateurs and semi-professionals with publication in such specialist journals as the *Transactions of the British Cave Research Association.*

Spelling Reform, see ORTHOGRAPHY; SIMPLIFIED SPELLING.

Spelt (common wheat), see WHEAT.

Spelter, ingot zinc obtained by the smelter on remelting and casting the condensed zinc vapour. It also denotes an alloy of equal parts of zinc and copper used in brazing.

Spemann, Hans (1869–1941), German zoologist, born at Stuttgart. He was successively professor at Rostock University, a director of the Kaiser Wilhelm institute of biology in Berlin, and professor at and rector of Freiburg University. He did pioneer work in homology and evolutionary mechanics, gaining the Nobel Prize for medicine in 1935. He published *Beiträge zu einer Theorie der Entwicklung,* 1935, and *Forschung und Leben,* 1943.

Spence, Sir Basil Urwin (1907–76), British architect, born in Bombay. He trained in Edinburgh and started private practice in 1930. For nearly 20 years his work comprised houses, factories, theatres and the Scottish Pavilion at the Empire Exhibition, 1938. In 1951 he won the competition for Coventry Cathedral, and in 1952 began the Nuclear Physics Building at Glasgow University. Other work has included university buildings at Edinburgh, Southampton, Nottingham, Durham and Liverpool, 1954–58; the church of St Francis, Wythenshawe, Manchester, 1958; Hampstead Town Hall, 1958; replanning of the slum area of Gorbals at Glasgow with modern multi-storey residential flats; buildings at Sussex University, 1962–63; rebuilding of Knightsbridge Barracks; and the new British Embassy at Rome.

Spence, James Lewis Thomas Chalmers (1874–1955), Scottish poet and mythologist, born in Dundee. Educated at Edinburgh University, he was on the staff first of the *Scotsman* and then of the *British Weekly.* His dialect verse was one of the early influences in the Scottish renaissance, and he was also one of the founders of the Scottish National Party. His books of verse include *Le Roi d'Ys,* 1910, *The Plumes of Time,* 1926, and *Collected Poems,* 1953.

Spence made a special study of the early history of Central America, and published *The Civilisation of Ancient Mexico,* 1911, *Myths of Mexico and Peru,* 1913, and *The Gods of Mexico,* 1923, which is a standard work. Other works are *An Encyclopaedia of Occultism,* 1920, *The Problem of Atlantis,* 1924, *The Fairy Tradition in Britain,* 1948, *The History and Origins of Druidism,* 1950, and *Second Sight,* 1951.

Spencer, family name of the earls of Sunderland, and of some of the dukes of Marlborough. The following were two prominent members of the family.
Dorothy Spencer (1617–84), Countess of Sunderland. Edmund Waller the poet celebrated her in his verses as *Sacharissa.* She was married to Henry Spencer, 1st Earl of Sunderland.
Charles Spencer (1706–58), 5th Earl of Sunderland

Spencer, Herbert

and 3rd Duke of Marlborough. He was a soldier and a politician, and fought at the battle of Dettingen.

Spencer, Herbert (1820–1903), British social philosopher, born at Derby, one of the major pioneers of SOCIOLOGY. A self-educated engineer, Spencer's first published works were letters to *The Nonconformist*, 1842, on social problems. As sub-editor of *The Economist*, 1848–53, he made the acquaintance of Huxley, Tyndall, George Eliot, and J. S. Mill, and wrote his first important work, *Social Statistics*, published in 1851. Thereafter Spencer was absorbed in applying the doctrine of evolution to man in society, first of all in *Principles of Psychology*, 1855. Two years later came *Essays: Scientific, Political and Speculative*, and while preparing these scattered writings for publication he realised that they were characterised by a unity of principle. In 1860, therefore, Spencer announced *A System of Synthetic Philosophy*, a work not completed until 1896. It covers metaphysics, biology, psychology, sociology, and ethics. The preparation of the first volume, *First Principles*, 1862, had serious effects upon Spencer's health, and from this time his life was a struggle against ill health. His last years were clouded with disappointment and 'scientific hypochondria'. His writings include a volume of essays on *Education*, 1861, and an *Autobiography*, 1904. Spencer's attempt to synthesise the sciences, and his scheme of social evolution, have been superseded, but his pioneering importance has probably been underestimated.

Bibliography: D. Duncan, *Life and Letters of Herbert Spencer*, 1908; S. Andreski (Ed.), *Principles of Sociology*, 1969; J. Y. D. Peel, *Herbert Spencer: The Evolution of a Sociologist*, 1971.

Spencer, John Charles Spencer, 3rd Earl (1782–1845), British politician, born in London and educated at Harrow and Trinity College, Cambridge. He is better known as Lord Althorp, a title he held until the death of his father in 1834. Althorp became an MP in 1804 and chancellor of the Exchequer under Lord Grey in 1830. A man of extremely high principles, respected by both friends and opponents, he remained steadfast in his zeal for the Reform Bill and in rallying his followers to support it. After seeing the Bill pass in 1832 he gradually lost influence and interest in political life and retired to his estates on succeeding to the earldom in 1834.

Bibliography: H. W. C. Davis, *The Age of Grey and Peel*, 1929.

Spencer, Sir Stanley (1891–1959), British painter, born at Cookham-on-Thames in Berkshire. He studied at the Slade School from 1910 to 1914, and served in the First World War. His military service produced its effect on his painting, particularly evident in his greatest work, the mural paintings of the Memorial Chapel at Burghclere. The side walls of the chapel depict crowded and active scenes of military life, while the east wall shows the Resurrection and relief from earthly burdens. For most of the remainder of Spencer's work two sources are responsible: Cookham and the Bible, and his pictures are a blend of the real and the imaginary. Among his other major works are *The Resurrection*, 1929 (Tate Gallery); the series *Christ in the Wilderness*, blending the simple realities of nature with Spencer's imaginative portrayal of Christ; and *Sarah Tubb and the Heavenly Visitors*.

Bibliography: Lives by E. Rothenstein, 1945, G. Spencer, 1961, and M. Collis, 1962.

Spender, Stephen (Harold) (1909–), English poet and critic, born in London; educated at University College School and University College, Oxford. He fought in the Spanish Civil War, and served in the London fire service during the Second World War. Spender was closely associated with W. H. AUDEN, Christopher ISHERWOOD, Louis MACNEICE, and C. DAY LEWIS in the late 1920s and 1930s. His verse of that time, including *Poems*, 1933, *Vienna*, 1934, and *The Still Centre*, 1934, shares their concern with socialism, as well as a pervasive influence of Rainer Maria RILKE and Federico GARCIA LORCA.

Later his work became more personal and introspective, and after his *Collected Poems*, 1955, he published only one further collection, *The Generous Days*, 1971. Increasingly his public literary activities have been as an editor and critic: he edited *Horizon*, 1939–41, and *Encounter*, 1953–67, and lectures frequently in the United States. From 1970 to 1976 he was professor of English at University College, London. Among his critical studies are *The Struggle of the Modern*, 1963, *Love-Hate Relations*, 1974, and, as editor, *W. H. Auden: A Tribute*, 1975, and *T. S. Eliot*, 1975. *The Backward Son*, 1940, is a novel, and *World Within World*, 1951, an autobiography.

Stanley Spencer. *Cows at Cookham*, 1936. (*Ashmolean Museum, Oxford*)

298

Spener, Philip Jakob (1635–1705), German theologian, founder of Pietism, born at Rappoltsweiler, Alsace. He studied at Strasbourg, Basel, Tübingen, and Geneva, and in 1663 was appointed preacher and lecturer at Strasbourg, later becoming pastor at Frankfurt-on-Main. From his work here sprang the Pietist movement, strongly attacked by orthodox Lutherans.

Bibliography: Lives and Studies by P. Grünberg, 1893–1906, G. Kertz, 1936 and K. Aland, 1943; H. Daniel-Rops, *The Church in the Eighteenth Century*, 1964.

Spengler, Oswald (1880–1936), German historical philosopher, born at Blankenburg. He studied history and philosophy, finally evolving his own system of historical philosophy. In Munich, working as a schoolteacher, he finished his main work, *Der Untergang des Abendlands*, 1918–23 (*The Decline of the West*, 1926–29), which, appearing immediately after Germany's defeat in the First World War, matched the mood of the hour. This, and the wide-ranging erudition of the author, gave the book an unexpected popularity, and it soon became world-famous. Spengler held that the different cultures of the world came to life, independent of one another, reached maturity, declined, fell, and died in identical cycles. This is essentially the view more recently put forward by Arnold TOYNBEE in his *Study of History*, though there it is expressed in less mystical and grandiose terms than Spengler's. According to Spengler, the civilisation of the West has entered its final phase, characterised by great-power conflicts, artistic sterility, the spread of pacifist and socialist ideas among the masses, etc. Later works, such as *Preussentum und Sozialismus*, 1920, and *Der Mensch und die Technik*, 1931, were less successful. Spengler greeted the rise of Nazism in Germany with some enthusiasm, but soon fell silent.

Bibliography: H. Stuart Hughes, *Oswald Spengler, A Critical Estimate*, 1952.

Spennymoor, industrial town 8 km south of the city of DURHAM, England. Population (1971) 7000.

Spenser, Edmund (c. 1552–99), English poet, born in London, the son of a Lancashire clothmaker who had moved to the capital. The first great modern English poet, Spenser was educated at Merchant Taylors' School, then a grammar school, under Dr Mulcaster. In 1568 he was admitted as sizar at Pembroke Hall, Cambridge. The fierce religious passions of the age had their effect on Spenser and influenced his early compositions and translations of PETRARCH, which are preserved in the treatise *Theatre of Worldlings*, published about 1569 by a Flemish refugee, Fel John Noodt, predicting the ruin of Rome and Antichrist. Spenser seems to have entered those student circles which were wrangling in pedantic disputations over Calvinistic theology. Little is known of his career at Cambridge, but he took his master's degree in 1576, though his Latin composition was apparently poor, and his classical learning copious but inaccurate.

It is known, however, that he formed a lasting friendship with two other Cambridge students, Gabriel HARVEY and Edward Kirke, the latter being the first commentator of Spenser's (at first anonymous) *Shepheardes Calender*. Harvey was a distinguished classical and Italian scholar, who influenced Spenser's ideas, but he was essentially a modernist who had no time for Spenser's interest in medieval chivalry and the ROMANCE tradition. In Spenser's earliest poetry, the PASTORALS, Harvey is among the imaginary rustics as the poet's 'most familiar friend', under the name of Hobbinol, and to him the poet addresses his confidences under the name of Colin Clout, which he borrowed from the satirist SKELTON.

By 1579 Spenser was in London once more, had become acquainted with Sir Philip SIDNEY and his circle, and obtained a post in the household of Sidney's uncle, the Earl of LEICESTER. With Sir Philip Sidney, Dyer, and others, he formed a literary club, the Areopagus. The letters he wrote at this time give glimpses of his character and opinions, and of his belief that English poetry should be shaped on classical models. They also mention other compositions either lost or worked into his later poetry, such as *Slumber*, *Dreams*, *Epithalamion Thamesis*, *Dying Pelican*, and *Comedies*.

In London once again, Spenser had come to realise his powers as a poet. At the age of 27 he had 'not only realised an idea of English poetry far in advance of anything which his age had yet conceived or seen' (Dean Church), but had already in his mind the outlines of his *Faerie Queene*, and may perhaps have written some portion of it. Shortly after moving to Leicester House he published (1579) the *Shepheardes Calender*, which was well received. This consists of twelve ECLOGUES, one for each month of the year. The style fluctuates from idealisation to a more realistic satire, and the work touches covertly on the religious controversies of the day; but in essence the poems are pastorals discussing the themes of time, decay, and the cycle of the seasons. In choosing such a work for his first major publication, Spenser was aligning himself with the major classical tradition, as represented by VIRGIL. In the following year he was appointed secretary to Lord Grey de Wilton, then going as lord deputy to Ireland. Spenser remained in Ireland, holding various posts, until within a month of his death, though he paid occasional visits to England.

In Ireland he was visited by Sir Walter Raleigh, who was his neighbour at Kilcolman, and the visit had important results. For he now renewed the old pastoral form of the *Shepheardes Calender*, and described, under his customary poetic disguise, the circumstances which once more transported him back from Ireland to the court, the goal of all who wished to make their way in the world. This poem, *Colin Clout's Come Home Again*, contains, besides history, criticism, satire, and love passages, the interruption of his retired and 'pastoral' life by the appearance of Raleigh, the 'Shepherd of the Ocean'. At Kilcolman Raleigh became acquainted with Spenser's work on the *Faerie Queene*, and his penetrating judgment told him how far it was in advance of any preceding English poetry. Raleigh's visit thus led directly to the publication of Spenser's masterpiece. Previously Spenser had written an elegy on Sir Philip Sidney (*Astrophel*), who died in 1586. It was three years later that he completed the first three books of the *Faerie Queene*, which had actually been started as early as 1579, and the next three books appeared in 1596.

In 1595 Spenser published *Amoretti* and *Epithalamion*, celebrating his courtship and marriage to his second wife, Elizabeth Boyle. *Amoretti* is one of the most distinguished of the Elizabethan sonnet sequences, with a fine balance of sensuous passion and idealisation, and it is the only one which celebrates a genuine romance culminat-

The Salvage serves Serena well,
Till she Prince Arthure fynd;
Who her together with his Squyre,
With th' Hermit leaves behynd.

Edmund Spenser. Illustration by Walter Crane for an edition of Spenser's *Faerie Queene. (Victoria and Albert Museum, London)*

ing in marriage. The *Epithalamion* is a richly ornate marriage ode in the classical manner, and the finest of its type in the language. Another marriage ode, *Prothalamion*, for the daughters of the Earl of Worcester, appeared in the following year.

Spenser's lasting claim to fame rests on the unfinished *Faerie Queene*. In the *Letter to Sir Walter Ralegh*, published in the 1590 edition of the poem, he explains that the work is 'a continued Allegory, or darke conceit'. (See ALLEGORY.) In the person of Prince Arthur he intends to portray 'the image of a brave knight, perfected in the twelve private moral vertues'. While Arthur was to embody all twelve virtues, each of the planned twelve books was to depict one of Gloriana's knights as the special guardian of a particular virtue. Arthur has a vision of the Faerie Queene, Gloriana, in whom, says Spenser, 'I conceive the most excellent and glorious person of our soveraigne the Queene, and her kingdome in Faery land'. So the allegory comprehends a celebration of Elizabeth and her court, England (and more particularly Protestant England, embattled against Catholic Spain), and at the same time an examination of chivalric virtue and romantic passion.

While the references in certain passages are not always easy to define precisely, the narrative is simple to follow in general terms and the language is richly evocative in its distinctive stanzaic form (nine lines, eight iambic pentameters, closing with an alexandrine, and rhyming ababbcbcc, the Spenserian stanza) of Spenser's own invention. The six completed books of the poem contain the exploits of: The Knight of the Red Crosse (Holinesse); Sir Guyon (Temperaunce); Britomart (Chastitie); Cambel and Triamond (Friendship); Artegall (Justice); and Sir Calidore (Courtesie). There are also 'Two Cantos of Mutabilitie' which were part of a projected 'Legend of Constancie' and were not published until 1609.

Selections of Spenser's works appear in *The Shepherd's Calendar and Other Poems*, edited by P. Henderson, 1932; *The Fairie Queene*, edited by J. Hales, 1910; and *Selected Poetry*, edited by A. C. Hamilton, 1966.

Bibliography: E. Greenlaw (Ed.), *A Variorum Edition* (9 vols), 1932–49; J. C. Smith and E. de Selincourt (Eds), *The Poetical Works* (3 vols), 1909–10; A. C. Judson, *Life* (in the *Variorum Edition*); C. S. Lewis, *The Allegory of Love*, 1936; J. W. Lever, *The Elizabethan Love Sonnet*, 1956; M. P. Parker, *The Allegory of the Faerie Queene*, 1960; A. C. Hamilton, *Allegory in the Faerie Queene*, 1961; G. Hough, *A Preface to the Faerie Queene*, 1961; W. Nelson (Ed.), *Form and Convention in the Poetry of Spenser*, 1961, and *The Poetry of Edmund Spenser*, 1963; A. Fowler, *Spenser and the Numbers of Time*, 1964; K. Williams, *Spenser's Faerie Queene: The World of Glass*, 1966; P. J. Alpers, *The Poetry of the Faerie Queene*, 1968; F. Kermode, *Spenser, Donne, Shakespeare*, 1971.

Speranski, Mikhail Mikhailovich, Count (1772–1839), Russian statesman. In 1808 he became deputy minister of justice. At the request of ALEXANDER I he worked out a plan for the reform of the legislative and administrative system of the state, providing for representative assemblies in local government and for an elected state DUMA. This plan was being carried out when Speranski was disgraced as a result of an intrigue and banished to Nizhny-Novgorod in 1812. In 1819 he was appointed governor-general of Siberia, where he radically reformed the administration. In the reign of NICHOLAS I Speranski

codified (1826–33) the existing Russian laws for the first time since the Code of Alexis Mikhailovich in 1649.

Sperm Oil, or spermaceti oil (iodine value 130 ± 20), is obtained from from the SPERM WHALE or CACHALOT. The crude oil is yellow to dark brown in colour, and has a fishy odour. Spermaceti separates on cooling, and the clear yellow oil which is left is purified by treatment with potassium hydroxide. Sperm oil forms a valuable lubricant for delicate machinery, since it does not readily become rancid or gummy. Spermaceti is used in cosmetics, ointments, candles, and textile dressing.

Sperm Whale, see CACHALOT; WHALE.

Spermatophyta, or Phanerogamia, one of the main divisions of the vegetable kingdom, the seed-bearing plants, which include the ANGIOSPERMS and GYMNOSPERMS.

Spermatozoa, see BIOLOGY; DEVELOPMENTAL BIOLOGY; EMBRYOLOGY; REPRODUCTION.

Sperry, Elmer Ambrose (1860–1930), US inventor, born in New York. As a boy he made electrical experiments and later established a plant in Chicago for the manufacture of electric arc lights. He followed this with electrical mining apparatus and electrical locomotives. Later he developed the high-intensity arc search-light. This search-light became the standard for the principal armies and navies of the world, and has been used for many commercial purposes. The Sperry high-intensity arc was also applied to cinematography, both in the making of films and in their projection. Sperry was the leader in the application of the GYROSCOPE to practical uses (see NAVIGATION). His gyro compass was quickly adopted by the Royal Navy and other leading navies of the world; following the First World War it became standard in the world's merchant fleets. His gyroscope ship stabiliser reduced the roll of vessels at sea. With his son Lawrence he developed a gyroscope aircraft automatic control for safety in flight. This auto-pilot led to the development of such instruments as the artificial horizon, directional gyro, and gyro-magnetic compass.

Sperry Rand Corporation is a US firm with subsidiaries in all parts of the world. It was formed in 1955 by the amalgamation of Remington Rand Incorporated and The Sperry Corporation. The numerous firms which are now part of the group include E. Remington and Sons, which began manufacturing typewriters in 1873, the Sperry Gyroscope Company Incorporated (founded by Elmer Ambrose Sperry in 1910), Rand Systems Corporation (founded by James H. Rand in 1915), and the Vickers Manufacturing Company, which was founded in 1921 by Harry F. Vickers and developed power-steering for automobiles in 1925. The corporation is now organised in six divisions: Sperry Univac (computers and office products); Sperry New Holland (agricultural machinery); Sperry Vickers (fluid-power systems, products and components); Sperry (navigation and guidance systems for marine and aerospace applications); Sperry Flight Systems (compasses and flight-control systems for aircraft and spacecraft); and Sperry Remington (electric shavers).

Spetsai, or Spetse (Greek *Spétsai*), island of Greece, at the entrance to the Gulf of Argolis. In the 1970s it has

Speusippus

developed into a popular tourist resort, particularly for Athenians. Area 18 km²; population 3200.

Speusippus (c. 407–339 BC), Greek philosopher, born at Athens. Educated first in the school of ISOCRATES, he joined the Academy on its foundation and succeeded PLATO as its head. Speusippus was among those who diverted the metaphysical theories of Plato into the realms of vague mathematical speculation and thus alienated ARISTOTLE.

Spey, river of SCOTLAND, one of the swiftest in Britain, and noted for its salmon. It flows from Badenoch, and enters the sea 6 km north of Fochabers. The upper river augments the Lochaber hydro-electric scheme. Whisky is produced in its valley. Length 176 km.

Speyer, or Spires (formerly *Spira*), city in the RHINE-LAND-PALATINATE, West Germany, at the confluence of the Rhine and the Speyer river, 17 km south of Ludwigshafen. Its site has been occupied for some 3000 years; there were Celtic and, later, Roman settlements (*Civitas Nemetum*) here. The present city was founded by the FRANKS and it became the seat of a bishopric in the 7th century. At the end of the 13th century it was made a free city of the empire. Fifty diets have been held in the city, and from 1513 until 1689 it was the seat of the supreme court of the empire. The term 'Protestant' comes from the protest of the reformers against the majority decision of the diet here in 1529 (see PROTESTANTISM). The city was devastated in the Thirty Years' War. The splendid Romanesque cathedral contains the tombs of eight German emperors and kings; it was begun by CONRAD II in 1030 and has been several times ruined and restored. The neo-Gothic *Gedächtniskirche* commemorates the 'protest' of 1529. Electrical engineering, metallurgy, oil refining, and aircraft engineering are the main industries. Population 43,000.

Spezia, La, province of Italy, in eastern LIGURIA. Area 880 km². Population (1974) 244,000.

Spezia, La, Italian seaport and capital of the above province, situated some 80 km south-east of Genoa. It stands on a gulf, called the Gulf of La Spezia (Latin *Portus Lunae*), on the Riviera di Levante. Poets and painters have testified to the beauty of its surroundings since ancient times. The city itself is predominantly modern, with wide avenues and large gardens. It has an ancient cathedral. Since 1861 La Spezia has been the main naval port of Italy, and it has shipyards, munitions and iron works, and oil refining and electrical industries. Shelley was drowned in the gulf here in 1822. Population (1974) 122,750.

SPG (Society for the Propagation of the Gospel), see UNITED SOCIETY.

Sphagnales, a family of MOSSES, which contains one genus, *Sphagnum*. They are found in cold temperate zones, and are popularly known as bog mosses. The plants have erect stems with numerous leaves, and bear male and female organs on separate lateral shoots. The leaves are pierced with minute holes, and are thus moisture-absorbent. As the plants grow upwards the lower parts die without decaying, accumulate, and in time form moss beds, called peat, of increasing thickness. When dry,

Sphagnales. *Sphagnum*, peat moss. *(Topham/Markham)*

sphagnum moss is light, firm and elastic, and is used when moistened for packing plants, growing orchids, and for potting composts; and may even be used for surgical dressings.

Sphagnum, see SPHAGNALES.

Sphalerite (Greek *sphaleros*, treacherous), the principal ore of zinc, usually found associated with GALENA. Sphalerite is zinc sulphide (ZnS), but substitution of iron for zinc occurs. When pure it is colourless, but increased iron content deepens the colour from yellow through yellow-brown to black. The resinous lustre is an aid to identification which may otherwise be difficult with twinned or distorted aggregates (hence its name, also its German derived name, *Blende*, from German *blenden*, to deceive). Sphalerite occurs in hydrothermal veins and replacement bodies associated with galena and silver minerals in Idaho, Utah, British Columbia, and Broken Hill in Australia.

Sphene, or titanite, silicate of titanium and lime, occurring as a common accessory mineral in igneous rocks in which it occurs as tiny disseminated crystals, and also in metamorphic rocks. In colour it is dark brown, crystallises in the monoclinic system, and displays strong double refraction (hardness 5·5; specific gravity 3·5). It takes its name from the Greek word meaning wedge, as this is its characteristic crystal shape.

Sphenodon punctatus, New Zealand lizard, called tuatara by the Maoris, the only living member of the Rhynchocephalia. It has a long, compressed tail, and is up to 60 cm in length. The body is covered on the upper part with small scales and tubercles, a crest of spines running the length of the back; the forelimbs and hindlimbs each bear five clawed and webbed toes. It is amphibious in habit, but usually spends the day in a burrow of its own excavation, hunting for insects, crustaceans, worms, and even small fish by night. The eggs are deposited in sand and usually take more than a year to hatch. This reptile has traces of a median third eye, the PINEAL ORGAN, situated on the roof of the brain, corresponding in its position with that of the pineal gland of vertebrates generally.

Sphenoid Bone, wedge-shaped bone lying across the base of the skull near its middle and taking part in the formation of the cavity of the cranium, the orbits and the posterior nares.

Sphere, a surface on which all points are the same distance (called the radius) from a fixed point called the centre; or the solid body consisting of such a surface and its interior. If the radius of a sphere is r then its volume is $4\pi r^3/3$ and its surface area is $4\pi r^2$ (see PI). Any line segment from the centre to a spherical surface is called a radius. Any CHORD that passes through the centre is called a diameter. All diameters of a sphere have the same length (twice the radius of the sphere) which is called the diameter of the sphere.

If a plane passes through the centre of a sphere its intersection with the surface is called a great circle. The radius of a great circle is the same as the radius of the sphere. Two great circles always intersect; the line of intersection is called an axis and it intersects the surface at two points called poles. The plane through the centre perpendicular to an axis is called an equatorial plane and it intersects the surface in a great circle called an equator.

If two planes are parallel and either both intersect a sphere or one intersects it and the other is tangent to it, then the part of the spherical solid between the planes is called a segment and the part of the spherical surface between them is called a zone (see figure). The distance between the two planes is called the altitude of the zone or segment. The volume of a segment is

$$\pi h(3r_1^2 + 3r_2^2 + h^2)/6.$$

The area of a zone is $2\pi rh$.

Two planes through the centre of a sphere cut off a portion of the solid called a lune. The volume of a lune is $2r^2\alpha$, where α is the dihedral angle between the two planes (α is also the spherical angle between the two great circles defined by the planes). Note that outside of mathematics a lune is called a segment.

In Cartesian co-ordinates the equation of a sphere, centre (a, b, c), radius r is:

$$(x - a)^2 + (y - b)^2 + (z - c)^2 = r^2.$$

In spherical co-ordinates, the equation of a sphere centre

Sphere.

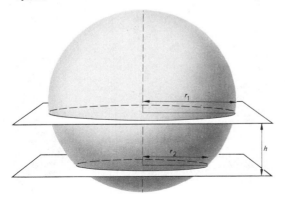

Sphinx. *Oedipus and the Sphinx*, by Ingres. *(National Gallery, London)*

the origin, radius ρ, is $r = \rho$.

See also ANGLE; TRIANGLE, *Spherical Triangles*.

Sphere, the Celestial, see CELESTIAL SPHERE.

Spherical Aberration, see ABERRATIONS OF LENSES.

Spheroid, surface traced out by an ELLIPSE rotating about one of its axes. It is also the solid bounded by such a surface. Rotation about the major axis produces a prolate spheroid with equation

$$(x^2/a^2) + (y^2 + z^2)/b^2 = 1,$$

and rotation about the minor axis produces an oblate spheroid with equation

$$(x^2 + y^2)/a^2 + (z^2/b^2) = 1,$$

where a is the semimajor axis and b is the semiminor axis. The earth is approximately an oblate spheroid, the polar diameter being nearly 43 km shorter than the equatorial diameter.

Sphincter Muscles, ring-like muscles whose action opens or closes certain orifices. The external *sphincter ani* closes the anus; the internal *sphincter ani* constricts the rectum; the *sphincter pyloricus* closes the pyloric orifice of the stomach; the *sphincter vesicae* constricts the urethral orifice of the bladder. The *sphincter pupillae* contracts the pupil in response to bright light.

Sphinx, fabulous monster, of Egyptian origin, figuring also in Greek mythology. In Egypt it was usually represented as a lion with a king's head, but later, as in Greece, it was a winged monster with a human female bust. One of the oldest and most famous examples is the Great Sphinx of Giza, near the group of PYRAMIDS. This was probably worked in the reign of KHAFRE to represent the king with the body of a recumbent lion guarding the royal cemetery and mortuary temples. Subsequently it was often imitated on a smaller scale, and avenues of sphinxes frequently flanked the approaches to

303

Sphinx Moth

temples. The Great Sphinx, which is 73 m long, used to get sanded up, and has been occasionally dug out, as an 18th Dynasty inscription records. Another important early sphinx is the red granite one of King Pepi I, now in the Louvre. In certain religious scenes the king as sphinx makes offerings to deities or tears his enemies to pieces. From Egypt, the idea of the sphinx spread to Assyria and Phoenicia, and representations are common on Persian gems. In Greece, the most famous sphinx, was that of Thebes in Boeotia, with a woman's head, lion's feet and tail, and bird's wings. She set the inhabitants a riddle and devoured all those who could not solve it. When it was at length solved by Oedipus, the sphinx destroyed herself (see THEBAN LEGEND).

Sphinx Moth, see HAWK-MOTH.

Spica, in astronomy, Alpha Virginis, a first magnitude STAR in VIRGO. Spica is Latin for 'Ear of Corn'. It is a spectroscopic binary with a period of 4·01 days.

Spice Islands, see MALUKU.

Spices, certain vegetable products which are used for flavouring foods. They all contain an essential oil which gives an aromatic odour. Their odour and flavour stimulate the flow of gastric enzymes which initiate the digestive process, but their nutritional value is negligible. They are derived from various parts of plants: the fruit, the seed, the stem, the flower-bud, the bark and the root. See also CONDIMENT.

Spiddal, village of County GALWAY, Republic of Ireland, in the heart of the Gaeltacht district, 19 km west of Galway city. Colaiste Chonnacht (Irish College) provides summer courses in the Irish language. Population 120.

Spider-crab, any crab of the family Majidae in class Crustacea. The carapace is much longer than it is wide. The legs are long, and often thick, in proportion to the body. *Macrocheira kaempferi*, the giant crab, is the largest arthropod known. It measures 4 m from one claw tip to the other.

Spider Monkey, see ATELES; BRACHYTELES.

Spiders, Araneae, a large and very varied order in class ARACHNIDA. Their most striking characteristic is the possession of a set of glands secreting a viscid fluid which hardens on exposure to the air to form a silky thread. These glands are numerous, and their secretion is made through many minute tubes on the under-surface of the spinnerets at the end of the abdomen. By means of their silky threads spiders construct their dwellings, some of them highly specialised and many of great beauty. The threads make webs and traps for the capture of prey, they serve for aerial transport, and are used as a safeguard against falling. Not all spiders use webs, however. Spiders are oviparous, and the female encloses her eggs in a silken bag which is sometimes carried about with her, sometimes concealed in the nest, and sometimes attached to solid objects. The young do not undergo metamorphosis. Spiders are predaceous, and bite the prey, then suck out the juices and soft parts.

Over 30,000 species, mostly small, are known, but a few tropical forms attain great size, for example, a body length of 9 cm. Probably the most feared are TARANTULAS, some of which are poisonous; their bite can cause local inflam-

mation but rarely death. The water spider (*Argyroneta aquatica*) is remarkable for constructing a web below water; a bubble of air entangled in the web serves as a 'diving bell'. Wolf-spiders (Lycosidae) are a widely distributed group of predaceous spiders. Many of the species are found in woods and dry commons; others are aquatic.

Bibliography: W. S. Bristow, *The World of Spiders*, 1971.

Spiderwort, see TRADESCANTIA.

'Spiegel, Der', German political weekly magazine, founded in 1947. It achieved a large circulation and probed a number of controversial topics. As the result of one of these, the magazine's offices were raided by the police and its editor, Rudolf Augstein, was imprisoned, 1962. A major government upheaval resulted.

Spiegel, Hendrik Laurensz (1549–1612), Dutch poet and humanist, born in Amsterdam. A stoical moderate, he attacked the extremes of his day and his *Hertspiegel*, 1614, shows affinity with COORNHERT's liberal Christian ethic.

Spielhagen, Friedrich (1829–1911), German novelist, born at Magdeburg; he studied law and literature at Berlin and Bonn. After a period of teaching, he settled in Berlin in 1862 and devoted himself to literature. His novels are topical and deal generally with social questions.

Spielhagen's first great success was *Problematische*

Spiders. A mosquito-catching spider with a white egg sac. *(Popperfoto)*

Spiders. Garden spider on its web. *(Popperfoto)*

Naturen (in four volumes), 1861, followed by its sequel *Durch Nacht zum Licht*, 1862. The best of his later novels are *In Reih' und Glied* (five volumes), 1869, and especially *Sturmflut*, 1877. He also wrote his autobiography in *Finder und Erfinder*, 1890.

Bibliography: V. Klemperer, *Die Zeitromane Spielhagens und ihre Wurzeln*, 1913.

Spigelia, see PINK-ROOT.

Spike Island, island off Cobh in County CORK, Republic of Ireland. Formerly a convict prison, it is now an army coastal-defence station.

Spikenard, see INULA; NARDOSTACHYS.

Spillikins (also called 'sticks'), traditional English game originally played with straws. A similar game has been played elsewhere with strips of bamboo, ivory or bone. Now 49 rounded sticks 10 cm long, rather like knitting-needles sharpened at both ends, and differently coloured to indicate their points value, are used. Nineteen of the sticks are worth two points, 14 are worth three points, ten are worth five, five are worth ten, and one stick is worth 20 points. The first player takes up the sticks, holds them upright on the covered table, forms a fan, and releases them to fall in a confused circular heap. The next player then tries to withdraw one spillikin at a time without disturbing the others. The slightest stir of any stick, other than the one he is engaged with, means his turn is at an end. Only a ten-point spillikin may be used to help

withdraw another. As soon as a player fails he totals up his score and drops for the next man. The player with the highest total after a given number of drops is the winner.

Spilsby, market town in Lincolnshire, England, 23 km south-east of Louth. There is a grammar school and a 14th-century church. The town trades in agricultural produce.

Spina Bifida, failure in embryonic life of the closure of the *neural tube*, which forms the brain and spinal cord and their coverings. One of the commonest severe malformations in the human infant, it occurs in as many as 1 per 400 births in parts of the British Isles. There is a striking regional variation in its incidence throughout the world and major efforts are being made to discover its cause. A woman who has had one child with spina bifida is ten times more likely to have another so affected.

The most severe form of neural tube malformation is *anencephaly*, where the brain and skull are rudimentary. Occasionally the back of the skull fails to close, resulting in a protrusion of the brain, or *encephalocoele*. *Meningocoele* and *meningomyelocoele* result from the failure of closure of the bony arch of the vertebral column, with a varying degree of overlying skin defect. This usually occurs in the lower part of the back, and the terms mean the protrusion, respectively, of MENINGES and of meninges and spinal cord through the defect. Depending on its severity there may be paralysis of the legs, and disturbance of bladder and bowel function ranging from minor to severe. HYDROCEPHALUS is common. Occasionally the defect is so minor that it only affects the bony arch of the vertebrae (*spina bifida occulta*).

It is now possible to diagnose the condition in early pregnancy by examining a sample of AMNIOTIC FLUID from around the foetus for the presence of a substance known as alpha-fetoprotein. This is a major advance, since affected foetuses may be aborted. There is at the moment much controversy about the ethics of attempting to save severely affected children. The Spina Bifida Trust sponsors research into the disorder.

Spinach, *Spinacia oleracea*, a species in the family Chenopodiaceae, which grows wild in Asia. The plant is herbaceous, and the leaves are eaten as a vegetable; they are rich in vitamin C and iron.

Spinae, see NEWBURY.

Spinal Cord, spinal medulla, the main nerve trunk of vertebrate animals. It is part of the central NERVOUS SYSTEM. It develops, like the brain, from the embryonic neural tube. In the adult the spinal cord is approximately 45 cm long; it runs in the vertebral canal, formed by the posterior arches of successive vertebrae, from the bottom of the skull where is is continuous with the medulla oblongata of the BRAIN. The spinal cord runs throughout the length of the VERTEBRAL COLUMN in the foetus, but because of disproportionate growth only extends to the third lumbar vertebra in the newborn and in the adult it terminates at about waist-level, opposite the disc between the first and second lumbar vertebrae. As the spinal cord rises within the vertebral canal, it leaves behind it a thin filament of membranous covering, the *filum terminale*, attached to the coccyx and a great bundle of

Spinal Cord

nerves, the *cauda equina*, descending to their point of exit from the vertebral canal.

The spinal cord, like the brain, consists of NERVE CELLS (grey matter) and their myelinated processes or nerve fibres (white matter). The grey matter is arranged in an H-shape around the central canal of the spinal cord, and it is surrounded in turn by the white matter which contains the ascending and descending tracts (figs. 1 and 2). The ratio of grey to white matter is 1:2 in the sacral (pelvic) region and 1:5 in the cervical (neck) region. Although the cord is cylindrical in shape, decreasing in diameter from above downwards, there are two enlargements, one in the cervical region and one in the lumbar region, at the origin of the nerve supplies to the upper and lower limbs.

Anterior (motor) and posterior (sensory) nerve roots (fig. 1) emerge from the antero-lateral and postero-lateral aspects on both sides of the spinal cord. These anterior and posterior spinal nerve roots unite as they pass between adjacent vertebrae (in the intervertebral foramina) to form SPINAL NERVES. An anterior nerve root is a collection of many nerve fibres (axons) which all have their cells of origin in the *anterior horn* of grey matter at a certain level (segment) in the spinal cord. Since the spinal cord is shorter than the vertebral column, the segment from which a pair of roots arises lies above and not opposite the corresponding vertebra. The motor neuron with its cell body in the anterior horn is known clinically as a *lower motor neuron*; disease or injury to a lower motor neuron leads to a flaccid (limp) paralysis of the MUSCLE fibres it supplies (as in poliomyelitis). Apart from motor fibres destined to supply muscles, some anterior nerve roots also contain preganglionic fibres of the AUTONOMIC NERVOUS SYSTEM.

The posterior sensory nerve roots contain nerve fibres of all diameters which transmit impulses from the periph-

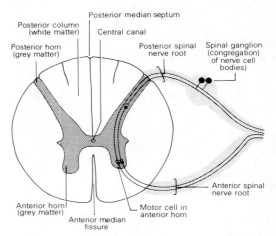

Spinal Cord. Figure 1. Diagrammatic transverse section through a thoracic segment of the spinal cord. One reflex arc (connection between the anterior and posterior nerve roots) is indicated.

ery to the spinal cord. These fibres all have their cells of origin in *spinal ganglia* (dorsal root ganglia) which are oval swellings apparent on all posterior roots. The fibres of a posterior nerve root become segregated according to function on entering the spinal cord, but many of them terminate in the posterior horn of grey matter. There they synapse (make contact) with *interneurons*, which in turn send processes to the cell bodies of anterior nerve roots in the anterior horn. Other posterior sensory fibres make direct contact with an anterior horn cell without any intervening neurons. In this fashion, the spinal cord is built up of segmentally arranged *reflex arcs* which regu-

Spinal Cord. Figure 2. A transverse section through the spinal cord to show the location of important pathways.

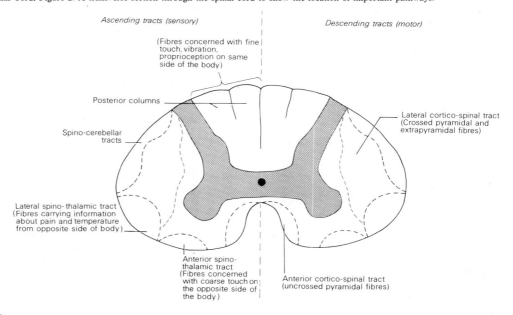

late the activity of muscles, glands, and other tissue. The reflex arc is a functional unit and it depends on an adequate stimulus causing an impulse to be transmitted along a sensory neuron to the spinal cord (or brain). There it influences directly, or via an interneuron, a motor neuron which carries impulses to the appropriate muscle. Reflexes vary in their complexity, but simple stretch reflexes, such as the knee jerk, are constant in healthy individuals. Therefore absence or variation in character of a knee jerk is a simple but valuable diagnostic clue to the clinician.

A simple reflex movement such as the knee jerk is essentially an involuntary act. However, in man all spinal reflex arcs, especially those involving interneurons, are modified by higher centres in the brain. This influence exercised by the brain is dependent amongst other things upon the development of long ascending and descending pathways in the spinal cord (fig. 3). We have already seen in the anatomy of the spinal reflex arc that many fibres of

a posterior nerve root synapse with an interneuron in the posterior horn of grey matter. Whereas those interneurons involved in reflex arcs then send processes to anterior horn motor cells, other posterior horn interneurons send their fibres diagonally across the cord to ascend in the *anterior spinothalamic tract* (figs. 2 and 3). These fibres transmit information which is solely concerned with our sense of touch. They ascend in the anterior spinothalamic tract and then through the brain stem to the thalamus where they synapse with the third and final neuron in the pathway. This neuron sends its nerve fibre to the area of cerebral cortex where the appropriate bodily part, such as the hand or arm, is represented.

The anterior spinothalamic tract only contains about half the neurons concerned with the sensation of touch; the remainder run in the *posterior columns* of the spinal cord. The first neuron in this pathway again has its cell body in a spinal ganglion and its main fibre, or *axon*, enters the spinal cord in a posterior nerve root. Thereafter,

Spinal Cord. LEFT Figure 3(a). The sensory pathways from a part of the body to the brain. RIGHT Figure 3(b). The motor (pyramidal) pathways from the brain to a muscle.

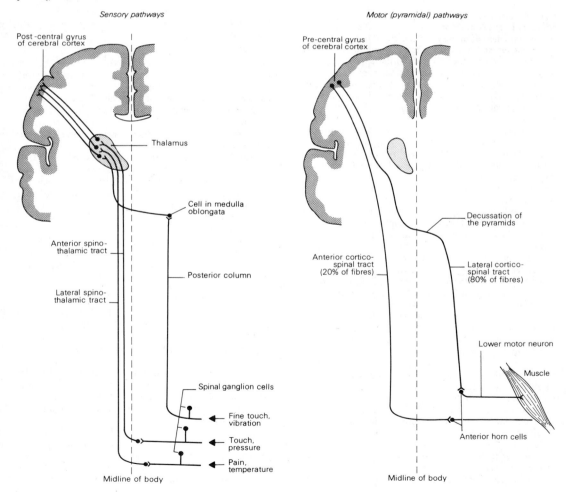

307

Spinal Cord

the axon passes into the posterior column of white matter and runs up the cord without crossing to the other side until it reaches the great *sensory decussation* in the medulla oblongata. These axons terminate in the thalamus, like the secondary neurons of the anterior spinothalamic tract, and a third neuron then transmits the incoming information to the cerebral cortex of the brain. The posterior columns are concerned with sensations of fine touch as well as pressure, vibration, and proprioception (sense of position of one's limbs in space).

The third main ascending pathway serving conscious sensation is the *lateral spinothalamic tract*. This tract is specifically concerned with sensations of pain and temperature. Like the other two spinocortical sensory tracts, the lateral spinothalamic pathway has three neurons between the periphery and the cerebral cortex (the first cell body in a spinal ganglion, the second in the posterior horn of the cord, and the third in the thalamus). Although it is known that the three major ascending pathways are concerned with different sense modalities (e.g., pain, temperature, touch), the mechanism underlying such specificity is not understood. In the skin there are various *end organs* which are excited by a specific form of stimulus such as pressure or vibration. A physical stimulus is transduced by the relevant collection of end organs into nerve impulses which travel along a spinal nerve and enter the cord via a posterior nerve root. A pattern of impulses then ascends in the appropriate sensory tract to be interpreted by the brain so that a conscious sensation is experienced. Apart from neurophysiological considerations, sensory perception depends on hormonal, psychological, and environmental factors.

There are complementary descending motor pathways present in the spinal cord, by which signals can be sent from higher centres to the lower motor neuron cells in the anterior horns of the cord. These tracts are concerned with production of both reflex and voluntary movements. The main pathway for controlling voluntary movement is the *pyramidal tract*, so named because its fibres form a pair of swellings, the pyramids, on the anterior surface of the brain stem. The fibres of the tract have their cells of origin in the cerebral cortex mostly in the motor area in front of the central sulcus of the brain, whence they pass through the depths of the cerebral hemispheres to the brain stem. At the pyramids in the medulla oblongata, about 80 per cent of the fibres decussate (cross to the other side) and then descend as the lateral *corticospinal tract* in the white matter of the spinal cord. At each spinal segment, fibres enter the anterior horn of grey matter and connect up with the lower motor neurons, which in turn stimulate muscles. The remaining 20 per cent of fibres which did not decussate at the pyramids form the smaller *anterior corticospinal tract*. At each spinal segment, some fibres from this tract cross within the spinal cord and pass to anterior horn cells of the opposite side. Thus lower motor neurons, with their cells in the anterior horns of the cord, are subject to control from the cerebral cortex of the opposite side of the brain. This cortical influence is mediated via upper motor neurons of the pyramidal tract which have their cell bodies in the cerebral cortex and extremely long processes or axons which decussate either in the brain stem or in the spinal cord.

In addition to the pyramidal tract fibres which carry voluntary motor impulses, there is a heterogeneous set of pathways which are often collectively termed the *extrapyramidal tracts*. They are fundamentally concerned with bodily posture and to this end are implicated in visual, auditory, and balancing reflexes. The anatomy of the extrapyramidal system is extremely complex, involving multi-neuron chains. These tracts end principally on those anterior horn cells which innervate the trunk and proximal limb muscles, whereas the pyramidal tracts connect mainly with motor cells which innervate the more distal limb muscles. It should be remembered that the distinction between pyramidal and extrapyramidal tracts is an artificial one and in the human body they operate in an entirely complementary fashion.

The importance of the spinal cord for reflex integration and as the trunk of communication to the brain is illustrated when the cord is accidentally transected. This tragic event is followed by a period of *spinal shock* (which lasts for at least two weeks in man), when all spinal reflexes are profoundly depressed. Some reflexes eventually return and then tend to be hyperactive. There is also a permanent and total loss of sensation in the regions below the level of transection because the ascending pathways have been cut, together with muscle paralysis because the descending pathways were cut.

Spinal Nerves, the nerves arising from the SPINAL CORD of a vertebrate animal, which leave it between the vertebrae. They are formed by the union of anterior (motor) and posterior (sensory) spinal nerve roots in the foramina (passages) between adjacent vertebrae. There are 31 pairs of spinal nerves in man (8 cervical, 12 thoracic, 5 lumbar, 5 sacral, and 1 coccygeal nerve). All the spinal nerves have the same basic distribution between the muscular layers of the body wall.

Each spinal nerve is attached to the spinal cord by a posterior (dorsal or sensory) root and an anterior (ventral or motor) root. Every root consists of a number of rootlets, each of which contains many nerve fibres. The anterior roots mainly contain fibres which have their cells of origin in the anterior horn of the spinal cord. These fibres leave the cord from its antero-lateral aspect; they transmit efferent, motor, impulses from the cord to the periphery. The posterior roots only transmit afferent, sensory, impulses to the cord from the periphery, such as muscles or skin. In the intervertebral foramen the posterior root immediately expands into a *spinal ganglion* (dorsal root ganglion), which is a collection of sensory NERVE CELLS. The cells are pseudo-unipolar: they each give rise to one short process which divides into two branches. One branch courses towards the spinal cord, the other branch travels in the spinal nerve to the skin or other peripheral structures.

As the spinal nerve escapes from the interventricular foramen it divides into *dorsal* and *ventral rami*, both of which contain sensory and motor fibres. The dorsal ramus passes posteriorly close to the vertebral column and is distributed to the skin, muscles, and ligaments of the back. The dorsal rami do not supply any limb muscles. The larger ventral ramus, depending on the segmental level of its nerve, may girdle the body in between the layers of thoracic or abdominal muscles giving off branches. Other ventral rami unite to form complicated networks, such as the *brachial plexus*, from which the major nerves supplying the limbs are derived.

The spinal nerves are essentially distributed in a segmental manner so that the skin of the trunk and limbs is innervated in strips of *dermatomes*. There is, in fact, overlap between the territories supplied by adjacent nerves. The overlap is sufficient to prevent total sensory loss in the corresponding dermatome when a single spinal nerve is destroyed, although there is change in sensation. When three consecutive spinal nerves are destroyed there is total sensory loss in the territory supplied by the intermediate nerve.

Spindle Tree, see EUONYMUS.

Spine, see VERTEBRAL COLUMN.

Spined Loach, *Cobitis taenia*, a small fish of the LOACH family, order Cypriniformes. It is rarely found nowadays but occasionally occurs in English waters. It is distinguished from the STONE LOACH by having a movable double spine below each eye.

Spinel, name given to a group of minerals which are double oxides of one or more divalent metals and one or more trivalent metals. They all crystallise in the cubic system. There are three series of spinel minerals, grouped according to their main trivalent metal; they are the spinel series, the magnetite series, and the chromite series. Spinel, $MgAl_2O_4$, is the commonest mineral in the spinel series. The crystals are octahedral and vary in colour from red to blue, green, brown, and black. Hardness is $7\frac{1}{2}-8$, specific gravity 3·58. Red spinel is known as ruby spinel or Balas ruby. The 'Black Prince's Ruby' in the Imperial State Crown is a fine example. Spinels are high temperature minerals, and are found as accessory minerals in basic igneous rocks and in highly aluminous metamorphic rocks. Spinels of gem quality occur in contact metamor-phosed limestone and in alluvium derived from them, and are found in Sri Lanka, Burma, India, and Afghanistan. Gahnite ($ZnAl_2O_4$), a dark bluish-green mineral, belongs to the spinel series; it occurs mainly in granitic pegmatites. Magnetite ($Fe^{2+}Fe_2^{3+}O_4$), the most important member of the magnetite series, is magnetic IRON ORE. It is famous as lodestone (Anglo-Saxon *Lōd*, way). Chromite ($Fe^{2+}Cr_2O_4$) is the chief member of the chromite series and is the chief source of chromium and its compounds. It normally occurs in massive form, black to brown in colour, with a metallic lustre. It occurs as an accessory mineral in ultrabasic igneous rocks, often as segregated masses and lenses. It is mined in Turkey, South Africa, the USSR, and the Philippines (at present the world's largest producer of refractory grade ore).

Spinello, Aretino (active 1373; d. 1410/11), Italian painter, born at Arezzo. In the tradition of Giotto, he executed frescoes illustrating the life of San Niccolò at Arezzo. Spinello painted the principal chapel of Santa Maria Maggiore, Florence, and the frescoes in the monasteries of San Miniato, San Bernardo and Monte Oliveto. In the town hall of Siena are his scenes from the life of Pope Alexander III.

Spinet, stringed keyboard instrument of the harpsichord family but, like the VIRGINALS, smaller; it is distinguished in shape from other members of the family by its leg-of-mutton outline, and probably named from a fancied resemblance of its quill plectra to spines (Italian *spinetta*, diminutive of *spina*, thorn). The strings were placed at an angle of about 45 ° with the keys and, as described by J. C. Scaliger (b. 1484), were sounded by being plucked by quill plectra. The spinet was a favourite instrument in England, Italy, Holland, etc., during the 16th to 18th centuries, and was also manufactured in America during the 18th century. See also HARPSICHORD; PIANOFORTE.

Spinet, built in Venice in 1570 by G. A. Boffo. *(Giraudon)*

Spinning

Spinning, the textile processes leading to the production of yarn. There are two types of yarn, staple and filament; the first are made from relatively short (1–100 cm) fibres, the second from virtually continuous fibres. For man-made fibres, the term 'spinning' is also used to describe the production of textile fibre from the bulk raw material as well as the production and processing of short fibre to yarn. There are many other spinning routes, most of which were first developed for natural fibres, e.g., jute, flax, and spun silk, but some variants have been recently developed for synthetic fibres, semi-worsted spinning for carpet yarns, high-bulk acrylic yarn spinning, etc.

The methods used for the spinning of natural staple yarns were worked out at a very early date and have been modified to cater for the synthetic fibres. The major traditional routes are the worsted, woollen, and cotton systems. Each spinning method is designed to deal with fibres of certain properties, the average length and diameter of the fibres being the most important criteria. The traditional spinning methods can also be used to describe yarns made from synthetics, e.g., within the industry the term 'worsted spun acrylic yarn' is used, but in the UK this type of term is not acceptable as a description when selling or advertising to the general public.

For all fibres and many of the synthetics a preliminary operation is to open out the tightly packed shipping bales and to mix or blend fibre of different origins, so as to preserve the properties of the overall blend despite natural

Spinning. Four stages in the worsted process: Carding (BELOW LEFT) or separating the fibres before the wool can be combed (BELOW RIGHT). This machine extracts the short fibres and lays the longer ones in parallel formation, the key operation of the worsted process. BOTTOM LEFT The wool slivers are then reduced in thickness by drawing (from the cans on the left) and roving (via the reels on the right), before being spun into worsted yarn on a ring spinning machine (BOTTOM RIGHT). *(all photos: International Wool Secretariat)*

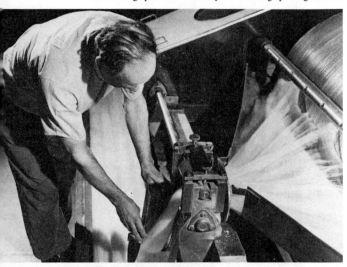

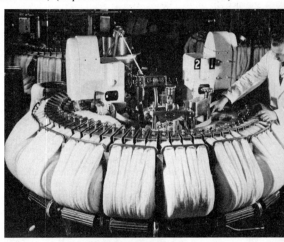

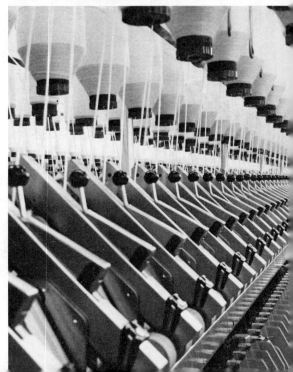

or manufacturing variations or to produce some desirable combination of properties.

Spinning of Staple Fibres. *Cotton.* The first process is carding, in which a loose 'sheet' of cotton fibres from the opening machines is gently separated by the moving spikes of the carding machine, certain impurities are removed by air currents, and the cotton is delivered as a loose rope of fibres, known as a sliver.

These slivers are now stretched or drawn by passing through a series of drawing machines. The drawing machine has two sets of rollers, one set running faster than the other, and the sliver is pulled out as it moves first through the slow rollers, then the faster ones. Several slivers can be fed into each machine, thus ensuring a very thorough mixing of fibres, but the important change is that the slivers gradually become thinner and the fibres more aligned. If the cotton is to be used in high-quality cloth or for very fine yarns, short fibres must be removed as otherwise they tend to form lumps in the slivers and the final yarn. This operation is known as 'combing' and is also a most important means of aligning fibres.

The final operation is the production of yarn from the final sliver by the insertion of twist. This is the spinning process proper and many machines have been used.

In the spinning industry the mule became virtually obsolete following the government-aided reorganisation of the cotton industry after the Second World War, and it was replaced by ring spinning machines. More recently self-twist spinning and open-ended spinning systems have been introduced which further improve the productivity of the operation.

In ring spinning the sliver is fed from rollers through the traveller and onto the spindle. As the spindle rotates, the sliver is twisted; the traveller does not rotate as fast as the spindle, with the result that the yarn is wound onto the spindle.

In open-ended spinning carefully cleaned fibres are fed onto a fast rotating plate where they are rolled up into a twisted yarn and drawn out of the head onto a large bobbin.

Wool. For most wool (certain carpet wools being one of the exceptions) the natural grease or lanolin is removed before processing. After blending, the wool is very gently washed in warm water containing soap or detergent, care being taken to prevent any felting of the wool. The wool is dried and passes to the cards. In woollen spinning the card produces a continuous thin web of fibres which is mechanically split into longitudinal strips, each 1 to 2 cm wide. These strips are carried to a spinning machine and spun into yarn without further processing. Spinning mules are still used but most woollen yarns are now produced on ring spinning machines. Some yarn is twisted to form folded yarns.

In worsted spinning the card produces a single sliver which is drawn to finer slivers in a manner similar to the cotton spinning process, but the fibre is invariably combed to remove short fibre ('noil') and further improve the alignment of the fibres. After further drawing and mixing of slivers the yarn is spun and usually twisted to two- or three-fold yarns, or for double jersey knitting remains as a single yarn.

There are other spinning routes devised originally for the natural fibres, e.g., jute and flax, and some for special new end-uses, e.g., tufted carpet yarns; but they are all similar in principle to one or other of the methods originally used for cotton and wool.

Spinning of Synthetic Fibres. The production of synthetic fibre always leads to a liquid, usually slightly viscous. This liquid is carefully filtered, air bubbles are removed, and it is pumped through a spinneret, which consists of a plate perforated with one or more holes usually of a circular shape. As the liquid or spinning dope leaves the holes in the spinneret it is hardened and becomes the fibre, which is pulled away by driven rollers.

The methods of hardening the fibre indicate the spinning method and include:

1. Melt spinning, where the dope is molten fibre and solidifies as it leaves the spinneret; this method is used for nylon, polyester, polypropylene, and acrylics.

2. Dry spinning, where the dope is a solution of the fibre in a solvent which is evaporated away as the dope leaves the spinneret; the process is used for acetate, triacetate, and acrylics.

3. Wet spinning, where the dope is spun into another liquid and by virtue of some chemical change the hardened fibre is formed, e.g., viscose, in which an alkaline dope is spun into an essentially acidic bath.

Before spinning, solid agents which scatter light can be added to reduce the lustre of the fibre and coloured agents can be added (dope dyeing or spin dyeing) to produce a coloured fibre. The shape of the spinnerets is frequently altered, especially in the melt spinning process, to produce cross-sections other than circular, and the speed of the yarn relative to the rate of pumping the fibre-forming liquid to the spinnerets controls the thickness of the fibres.

After spinning, fibres may be treated chemically; they may be extended several times in length and have various agents applied to their surfaces to improve their processing properties.

Frequently, many single fibres (10 to 200) are produced from a spinneret to form a continuous filament yarn which directly passes into the knitting or weaving operation. In some cases single filaments are used for such non-textile applications as bristles, racquet strings, and fishing lines. Many thousands of fine fibres may be brought together to form a tow, which is taken to a machine that cuts the fibres into short lengths comparable to that of the natural fibres. The operation can be done to produce a random mass of short fibre for carding or to produce a well-oriented sliver or top suitable for directly passing into a spinning system similar to that used for worsted or cotton.

A recently developed spinning route used for some polypropylene is the fibrillation method. A film is extruded which is then slit into ribbons and, at the same time, fine grooves are impressed lengthwise onto the ribbons. As the ribbons are stretched they begin to split along the grooves and form a complex interconnected mass of finer ribbons suitable for rope and cordage or for floor coverings.

Yarns produced from continuous filament have a different character to those from staple yarns, even of the same fibre. Continuous filament yarns are less bulky (and hence less warm), more lustrous, less hairy, and more slippery than staple yarns.

The final operation in all spinning processes may be the

Spinoza, Baruch

folding or twisting together of single yarns. Two or more yarns may be folded together to produce yarns which are more stable, more uniform, or stronger than single yarns of the same thickness; but there is also the opportunity to fold yarns of different colour to produce marl yarns or even to modify the twisting so that a whole range of fancy yarns may be produced. These include the bouclé, gimp, knop, and loop yarns.

The coloration or dyeing operation may be carried out at many points in the spinning operation for man-made fibres: at the fibre-producing stage or at the loose fibre, sliver, singles yarn, or final yarn operation.

See BULKING; DRYING MACHINES; YARN.

Bibliography: Textile Institute, *Manual of Cotton Spinning* (vols 1–5), 1958–73; A. Brearley, *Worsted*, 1964, and *The Woollen Industry*, 1965; H. Spibey (Ed.), *British Wool Manual*, 2nd ed. 1970.

Spinoza, Baruch, from 1656 known as Benedictus (1632–77), Jewish-Dutch philosopher, born in Amsterdam, of Portuguese-Jewish descent, the family name being Espinoza or Despinoza. He was educated in Amsterdam under Manaruch ben Israel and took Dutch nationality. When he was 20 his unorthodox religious views led to his expulsion from the Jewish community in Holland. Spinoza made his living by teaching and grinding optical lenses. He lived near Leiden from 1660 to 1663, and there began to formulate his own philosophy. From 1663 to 1670 he lived near The Hague, removing to the town itself in 1670. He suffered much during the French invasion of Holland in 1672, and developed pulmonary consumption, from which he died. He refused a chair of philosophy at Heidelberg, the better to preserve his leisure and freedom. He lived a solitary and abstemious life but was on good terms with those who shared his intellectual interests; and he was an assiduous correspondent, besides being a Dutch patriot.

Spinoza's Hebrew learning enabled him to become the

Baruch Spinoza. *(Mansell Collection)*

founder of the historical explanation, or 'higher criticism', of the Bible. Spinoza regarded it as literature and not dogma, and as a criticism of life putting forward the view that conduct is the chief thing therein, and that the eternal makes for righteousness. Spinoza's philosophy is contained in his *Ethics*, not published during his lifetime, because of his reputation as an atheist. Set out in axioms and propositions in the pure rationalistic style, it is founded on a rationalised Judaism, the dualism of Descartes reconciled into monism, and the ideas of Hobbes. Spinoza defined the final cause or purposes at work in nature, and denied, in their ordinary sense, immortality of the soul, free will, and moral responsibility. Nature and God are identified, and all things, good or bad in human eyes, are integral parts of the divine being. If the fortunes of a man depend solely on God's will, then all things must necessarily be agents of His will; He is the only power at work, and everything is an expression of His will and nature. Spinoza's political theory may be called Nietzschean; he propounds as an observable truth of natural history that might makes right. Good and evil are relative to finite and particular interests, but in the absolute the distinction is transcended.

Man's reason may be powerful enough to support only those of his habits and passions which are destined to success. This renunciation of the impossible is what Spinoza calls happiness, and it is this knowledge and love of the universe that all his maxims aim to secure. The solid and humble well-being which he promised to those who accepted his teaching exactly reasserts the kind of hope and aspiration which occurs so frequently in the older parts of the Bible. He departed farthest from Jewish ideas and approached, perhaps unawares, those of the Greeks, in his doctrine of human freedom and immortality. In their ordinary acceptance these are excluded from his fatalistic system, since everything that happens is inevitable, preordained, and predictable. For Spinoza freedom meant power; that a man's nature, consistent and unified, should be able to express itself clearly in his thought and work. Immortality means a quality of life produced by the intellectual essence of a man's thought, for a man who understands himself 'under the form of eternity' knows the eternal quality that belongs to him, since when his life is over the truth of his life remains part of the infinite context of facts.

Spinoza's philosophy reaches its highest point in his physics. Natural science could alone reveal what was fundamental and, in his view, divine. The two regions where science could come into contact with nature were mathematical physics and self-consciousness. His detailed scientific speculation is antiquated, but he reached the valuable concept of the absolutely infinite, in which universe man was the merest incident.

The two works published in his lifetime were *Renati des Cartes Principiorum Philosophiae, Mori Geometrico Demonstratae*, 1663, and *Tractatus Theologico-Politicus*, 1670. His works were published the year of his death.

Bibliography: S. Hampshire, *Spinoza*, 1956; L. Roth, *Spinoza, Descartes and Maimonides*, 1963; H. A. Wolfson, *The Philosophy of Spinoza*, 2 vols, repr. 1969; P. Kashap (Ed.), *Studies in Spinoza*, 1972.

Spiny Sharks, see ACANTHODII.

Spira, see SPEYER.

Spiracles, orifices at the ends of the tracheae (air-tubes) in insects. RESPIRATION is carried on by means of the tracheae, which penetrate into all parts of the body, subdividing into smaller tracheoles. The arrangement of the spiracles on the body varies among groups and life-stages. The spiracles are closed by valves actuated by special muscles. When the valves are closed, the air is driven by body contractions into the finer branches of the tracheal system.

Spiraea, in the family Rosaceae, a genus of deciduous shrubs with about 100 species, bearing white or pink to crimson flowers. It is distributed widely in the northern hemisphere. *S. salicifolia*, pink, is cultivated and sometimes naturalised in Britain. Also notable are *S. canescens*, 2–3 m high, white; *S. densiflora* and *S. douglasii*, dwarf, rose; *S. media*, 1–2 m, white; *S. japonica*, 1–2 m, rosy-red; and hybrids such as the white *S.* × *vanhouttei*. Herbaceous spiraea are classed under *Aruncus* and *Filipendula*.

Spiral, name given to curves which wind around a point in successive convolutions, the curve receding more and more from the point which is called the centre. These curves are best represented in polar co-ordinates (see ANALYTICAL GEOMETRY), the centre being taken as the pole.

The simplest equation is of the spiral of Archimedes, $r = a\theta$. The logarithmic spiral, $\log kr = a\theta$, is also known as the equiangular spiral because the angle between a radius vector to a point on the spiral and the tangent at that point is always the same. The hyperbolic (or reciprocal) spiral has the equation $r\theta = a$ and is asymptotic to a line distant a from the initial line. The parabolic spiral (or Fermat's spiral) is $r^2 = a\theta$.

Spiranthes, lady's tresses, a genus of terrestrial orchids with small white flowers. *S. aestivalis*, summer lady's tresses, *S. romanzoffiana*, drooping lady's tresses, and *S. spiralis*, autumn lady's tresses, with their scented, white flowers spirally twisted on a spike, are found in Britain, although the first-named is perhaps now extinct.

Spire (Old English *spir*), in architecture, an elongated pyramidal structure erected on the top of a tower. Though commonly regarded as an ornamental feature, it was originally a normal pyramidal roof (as at Southwell Cathedral); but in Gothic times it was elongated to a much greater height, either for effect or to express medieval religious aspiration—'a finger pointing to Heaven'. Sometimes an octagonal stone spire rises direct from a square tower without a parapet, the transition being made by means of 'broaches' (see BROACH); sometimes the tower has a parapet.

In England there are notable stone spires on Chichester, Norwich and Salisbury Cathedrals; and on the parish churches of Louth, Newark and Patrington; and notable wooden spires at Chesterfield and Harrow.

Spires, see SPEYER.

Spirit, see ALCOHOLS; METHYLATED SPIRIT; PETROLEUM REFINING; PROOF SPIRIT; RECTIFIED SPIRIT.

Spirit (Latin *spiritus*, breath). Breath, apparently identical with life, provided a natural term for an invisible living power. This religious concept covers a variety of

 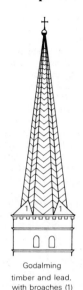

Southwell Cathedral (Romanesque style)
Godalming timber and lead, with broaches (1)

Spire.

usages. Christian theologians from Irenaeus have taught the 'tripartite' nature of man, that he is an amalgam of body, soul, and spirit, the spirit being regarded as that part which is most open to divine influence, and which may survive death. Modern religious thinkers since Kierkegaard have identified man's spirit with his inner psyche or true self.

Spirit is also used to denote a superhuman order of being unlimited by space and time. According to the Bible, God himself is spirit. In Christian theology, the third person of the Trinity is the Holy Spirit, who first came to the disciples at Pentecost.

Spirits, whether good or evil, have played a large part in popular belief and practice, particularly in China where the various fortunes of life are ascribed to gods, spirits of the dead and demons. In the West, popular superstition has sometimes explained mental illness and epilepsy in terms of possession by evil spirits, and exorcisms have been conducted to cast them out. In contemporary Christian circles there has been a revival of the charismatic movement in which the Holy Spirit is invoked and people speak in tongues. Spiritualism is a cult which claims to communicate with the spirits of the dead.

See also ANGEL; DEVIL; GHOST; HOLY SPIRIT; SOUL.

Spirit Healing, see THAUMATURGY.

Spirit of Nitre, a liquid whose chief constituent is ethyl nitrite. It has been used as a DIAPHORETIC since it dilates blood vessels and it also has a mild DIURETIC action.

Spirit of Salt, name given to a solution of hydrochloric acid as prepared from sodium sulphate and common salt by Glauber in 1646.

Spiritualism, or Spiritism, a philosophy or religion, based on a belief in life after death and the possibility of communication between the dead and the living. It originated in America in 1848, and rapidly spread to other

Spirochaete

parts of the world. The movement was widely popularised by Conan Doyle, who in his writings and lectures claimed spiritualism to be 'a religion for those who find themselves outside all religions'.

There are two main groups of spiritualistic phenomena, mental and physical, and there are both mental and physical mediums (persons endowed with psychic awareness). In the presence of such persons, alleged supernormal phenomena take place, often when the medium is in a trance. Movement of objects without contact (telekinesis) is one type of physical phenomenon. Mental phenomena include information given by mediums which they could not have acquired through any normal means (see CLAIRVOYANCE and CLAIRAUDIENCE). Many mediums have been detected producing alleged phenomena fraudulently, but there have been mediums (notably Daniel Douglas HOME, in the 19th century) who have submitted to examination, agreed to stringent control, and have still puzzled investigators.

Materialisation, the alleged building up of a living human form in ECTOPLASM exuded from the medium, is the culmination of spiritualistic physical demonstration. There are, however, few cases of complete materialisation which have satisfied critical observers. Considerably better evidence exists for partial materialisation.

Spiritualistic mental phenomena have been extensively investigated by members of the Society of Psychical Research, and their records include many instances of mental phenomena unaccountable by known laws of nature.

See also PSYCHICAL RESEARCH.

Bibliography: M. Barbanell, *Spiritualism Today*, 1969; R. H. Ashby, *The Guidebook for the Study of Psychical Research*, 1973.

Spirochaete, see BACTERIA.

Spiš (German *Zips*; Hungarian *Szepes*), district in Czechoslovakia, in eastern Slovakia on the south-east slopes of the Tatra Mountains (see CARPATHIANS). It was settled by Germans in the 13th century, and is famous for its German Gothic architecture. There were large-scale deportations of Germans after the Second World War. The chief town is Levoča.

Spit, a depositional feature formed along a coastline with marked longshore drift, often displaying one or more recurved ends. These are produced either by the interaction of different sets of wave trains from varying directions, or by wave refraction. Often the remnants of previous recurved ends can be identified in the form of beach ridges, as at Blakeney Point, Norfolk. In many cases LAGOONS and salt marshes form on the landward side of spits. When a spit links an island to the mainland, the feature is called a tombolo (see COAST).

Spitalfields, see TOWER HAMLETS.

Spithead, roadstead in the ENGLISH CHANNEL, between Portsmouth and the Isle of Wight. Here was fought in 1545 a battle between the English and French fleets, in which the latter was dispersed. More recently Spithead has been the scene of many memorable Royal Navy reviews.

Spitsbergen, Norwegian archipelago in the ARCTIC OCEAN, lying between ZEMLYA FRANTSA IOSIFA and GREENLAND. The main islands are Spitsbergen, Edgeøya, Nordaustlandet, Barentsøya, and Prins Karls Forland. The land area of the group is about 62,050 km². The archipelago is grouped with a number of nearby islands, including Kvitøya, Kong Karls Land, Hopen, and Bjørnøya, under the name Svalbard. They are said to have been discovered by Barents in 1596, but it is probable that the Icelanders and Norwegians visited them in the Middle Ages. All the islands are mountainous; the highest peak is Newtontoppen, 1690 m, in the north-eastern part of Spitsbergen. There is much ice, generally in the form of long valley glaciers. Spitsbergen lies between 76°30' and 80°N, latitude. At this latitude there is total daylight for 122 days; for 128 days there is either full sunlight or twilight only; and for a period of 115 days the sun does not rise above the horizon. The chief mineral is coal, some 850,000 t annually being mined, of which half is extracted by the USSR. Asbestos and copper are also found. Polar bears, foxes, and reindeer are among the land animals; musk-oxen have been introduced. The eiderduck and other wildfowl breed on the islands, and seals and occasionally walruses are found. Whale-hunting was carried on in the 17th century, and possession of the area was then disputed between the Norwegians, Dutch, and English. Whale-hunting ceased in the 18th century, but on the discovery of rich beds of coal, the question of sovereignty was again raised. Norway's sovereignty of the islands was recognised by treaty at the Paris Peace Conference in 1920, and in 1925 Norway officially took possession of the archipelago. All signatory nations were given the same hunting, mining, and fishing rights as Norway. The winter population of the islands is 3000, of whom 2000 are Russian. The main centres of population are on the west coast of Spitsbergen at the capital of Longyearbyen and the Russian mining settlements of Barentsburg and Grumantbyen. The Norwegians maintain weather and radio stations on several of the islands.

Bibliography: T. Mathisen, *Svalbard in the Changing Arctic*, 1954; V. Solokov (Ed.), *Geology of Spitzbergen*, 1970.

Spitteler, Carl Friedrich Georg (1845–1924), Swiss poet and novelist, born at Liestal, near Basel. After studying law and theology he became a teacher in Finland and Russia, and later in Neuveville. Spitteler was an editor in Basel and Zürich, and after 1892 a freelance journalist. He first came into prominence with *Olympischer Frühling*, 1900, a powerful and original epic, depicting the Greek gods in their heroism as well as their mortality. For this and his later work he received the Nobel Prize for literature in 1919.

His two other epics, *Prometheus und Epimetheus*, 1881, and *Prometheus der Dulder*, 1924, also deal with themes from Greek mythology, expressing his belief in the primacy of ethical over aesthetic values. Spitteler set himself against the naturalistic tendencies of his time, approaching them only in his minor works.

Bibliography: G. Bohnenblust, W. Altwegg, and R. Faesi (Eds), *Sämlichte Werke*, 1945; F. Buri, *Prometheus und Christus*, 1945.

Spitz, Mark Andrew (1950–), US swimmer, born at Modesto, California; he can claim to be his sport's most successful competitor ever on the basis of his feat at the Munich (1972) Olympic Games. He won seven gold medals (100 and 200 m freestyle and butterfly, 4 × 100 m and 4 × 200 m freestyle relay; and 4 × 100 m medley relay) all in world record times—a run unlikely to be equalled. He also won two freestyle team golds at the 1968 Games, and between 1967 and 1972 set 27 world records for freestyle and butterfly events.

Spitz, see POMERANIAN.

Splay, see CANT.

Spleen, a lymphoid organ serving a number of functions none of which is essential, for removal of the spleen has no important consequences. Its functions include the formation of leucocytes and antibodies, removal of dead and dying cells, and storage of iron in the form of ferritin and haemosiderin. In some mammals, but not man, it plays a significant role as a reservoir of blood. Any of these functions can be taken up by other lymphoid and reticuloendothelial organs. See also LYMPHOID TISSUE.

Spleenwort, see ASPLENIUM.

Splints, structures made of wood, leather, zinc, aluminium, perspex or other materials so as to fit about a fractured or diseased limb in order to render it immovable. Modern treatment of the fractured limb is initially to immobilise it in an inflatable plastic splint as a first-aid measure, and then later to apply a more permanent and less bulky splint moulded to the shape of the limb. For this purpose plaster of Paris bandages, applied wet and then allowed to harden, are used as a rule, but more recently glass fibre bandages have offered a more waterproof and lighter alternative. Other types of splints are available for treatment of deformities and diseased limbs. Lively splints give support while at the same time allowing movement against tension springs, and are used to restore hand function. Padded splints are used for babies with congenital dislocation of the hips. The legs are held in such a position that the hip joint develops normally.

Bibliography: J. M. Kennedy, *Orthopaedic Splints and Appliances*, 1974.

Split (Latin *Spalatum*), seaport in Croatia, Yugoslavia, the chief town of DALMATIA. The Roman emperor DIOCLETIAN built an immense palace here, to which he retired after his abdication in 305. In the 7th century the nearby town of Salona was destroyed, and the inhabitants began to develop a new settlement around the palace. The palace, greatly altered, remains; a mausoleum within it has been a cathedral since 650, and more than 400 houses are crowded together inside the palace walls. Split has extensive shipyards and docks, textile and engineering industries, and a trade in wines and agricultural produce. It is a tourist resort. Population (1971) 114,000.

Splügen Pass, pass across the Rhaetian Alps between Splügen in canton Graubünden in Switzerland and Chiavenna in Italy, near the head of Lake Como. There are remains of a Roman road; the present road was built 1818–23. Length 40 km. Altitude 2117 m.

Spitsbergen. The coal shipment dock at Longyearbyen. *(Camera Press/Richard Harrington)*

Spock, Benjamin McLane (1903–), US paediatrician, born in New Haven, Connecticut; professor of child development, Western Reserve University School of Medicine, Cleveland, Ohio. He was educated at Yale College and the College of Physicians and Surgeons, Columbia University (MD, 1929). He practised paediatrics in Cornell Medical College, New York Hospital, and New York City Health Department, 1933–47, with interruption for service in the US Navy, 1944–46. He was a member of the staff of the Rochester Child Health Institute, Mayo Clinic, and University of Minnesota, 1947–51. From 1951 to 1955 he organised a teaching programme in child psychiatry and development at Pittsburgh University Medical School. He was appointed to the Chair of Child Development, Western Reserve University, in 1955. Spock is best known as a popular writer and television broadcaster on child psychology and development. His first book, *The Common Sense Book of Baby and Child Care*, reprinted in 1946 as *The Pocket Book of Baby and Child Care*, (new edition 1969), sold millions of copies in America alone and has been translated into 12 languages. Among his later books were *Dr Spock Talks with Mothers*, 1961, and *Problems of Parents*, 1963. He received an honorary doctorate of science from the University of Durham, England, in 1963. Spock is co-chairman of the Committee for a Sane Nuclear Policy. He was amongst those who led opposition to the Vietnam war, the so-called Spock trial (in which Spock was acquitted) being one of the major focusing events of the anti-war movement.

Spode, Josiah (1733–97), British potter, apprenticed to Thomas Whieldon (see WHIELDON WARE), established a pottery factory at Stoke-on-Trent in 1770. His son added porcelain in 1800 and stone-china in 1805 to its productions (see CHINAWARE). In 1833 it became the still existing firm of 'Copelands'.
Bibliography: T. G. Cannon, *Old Spode*, 1924; L. Whiter, *Spode*, 1970.

Spohr, Louis (1784–1859), German composer, conductor and violinist born at Brunswick, studied at the court there and at the age of 14 was ready to go on tour. He was court musician at Gotha (1805), director of the orchestra at the Theater an der Wien (1813–14) and at Frankfurt (1817–19). Finally, he settled at the court of Kassel (1822–57) as musical director. He left ten operas, ten symphonies, oratorios, violin concertos and various other works. His style mixes Classical idioms with experimental chromatic harmonies, producing a lush effect which once made his music very popular but which now seems somewhat jaded. His treatise on violin-playing appeared in 1832, and his autobiography in 1850–61 (English translation, 1865).

Spokane, city in the state of Washington, USA, 370 km east of Seattle. A fur traders' post was the first settlement on the site (1810), which is at the falls of the Spokane river, and the earliest town bore the name of Spokane Falls. It was not until the 1880s, however, after the arrival of the Northern Pacific Railroad, that the advantages of Spokane's location became clear, lying as it did between the wheatlands of the Columbia plain and the minerals and forests of the mountains. By 1900 it had become the largest city between Minneapolis and the Pacific coast, and was served by four transcontinental railways. This enabled it to claim, as it does to this day, to be the capital of the 'inland empire'. It remains a route centre and the seat of Gonzaga University and Whitworth College. Population 170,516.

Spoleto (ancient *Spoletium*), Italian town in UMBRIA, built on a hill 50 km south-east of Perugia. It was once Etruscan (see ETRURIA) and became a Roman colony in 242 BC, and later resisted Hannibal in 217. It was later a LONGOBARD duchy, and from 1247 to 1860 belonged to the PAPAL STATES. It has a fine archiepiscopal cathedral (partly 11th century) containing frescoes by PINTORICCHIO and the tomb of Filippo LIPPI. The town plays host to several cultural gatherings, notably the 'Festival dei Due Mondi' of opera and theatre. Population (1974) 18,000; municipality (1971) 37,400.

Spolia Opima, spoils of honour, arms taken on the field of battle by a victorious Roman general in person from the commander-in-chief of a defeated army. The spoils thus obtained were dedicated to Jupiter Feretrius. Roman history (or legend) affords only three examples of *spolia opima*: those won by ROMULUS from Acro, King of the Caerenses; those won by A. Cornelius Cossus from Tolumnus, King of Veii, 437 BC; those won by M. Claudius Marcellus from Britomartus, King of the Insubrian Gauls, 222 BC.

Sponde, Jean de (1557–95), French poet, born at Mauléon in the Basque country. Having long been a prominent Calvinist, he became a Roman Catholic about the same time as Henry IV (1593).

His poetry, consisting principally of *Les Amours* (sonnets), *Stances*, and *Sonnets de la mort*, and his prose *Méditations sur les Psaumes*, 1588, remained more or less in oblivion until in the 20th century attention was drawn to it by Professor A. M. Boase in various articles and editions.
Bibliography: A. M. Boase and F. Ruchon (Eds), *Œuvres poétiques*, 1949.

Spondee, in prosody, a metrical foot consisting of two stressed syllables, equivalent to a DACTYL or ANAPAEST, and thus met with in these metres (see METRE). Examples are 'moonshine' and 'primrose'.

Spondias, a tropical genus of 10 trees, of the Anacardiaceae (cashew nut family), which contains *S. dulcis*, sweet otaheite apple, and *S. lutea*, golden apple or Jamaica plum; the fruits are edible and fleshy, with a central stone.

Sponge, any of the invertebrate animals that make up phylum Porifera, the 'pore-bearers'. They are the most primitive of the multicellular animals, as they do not have distinct tissues or organs, and the individual cells that make up the organism retain some independence. There are about 5000 species, of which perhaps 150 live in fresh water; the others are all marine, living mostly in shallow water, but a few live at depths of about 5 km. A living sponge looks like a slimy mass from 1 mm to 2 m in diameter, often coloured bright red, orange, yellow, blue, or black. The bath sponge and other sponges used at home and in commerce are the skeletons stripped of the living cells. Sponges are always attached to a firm object, and the organism as a whole does not move.

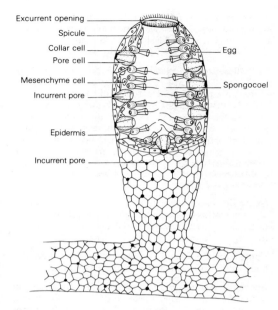

Excurrent opening

Spicule

Collar cell

Pore cell

Mesenchyme cell

Incurrent pore

Egg

Spongocoel

Epidermis

Incurrent pore

Sponge. The internal structure of a simple sponge.

The simplest sponge is a vase-shaped sac. The large opening at the top is the excurrent opening. The sides are perforated with incurrent pores. The outside is protected by a layer of flat covering cells, and the inside is lined with collar cells, each of which has a flagellum which whips back and forth, creating a current of water that flows in through the pores and out the large opening. If particles of ink or charcoal are dropped into the water near a sponge, the current it creates can be seen. As the water flows by the collar cells, suspended food particles stick to the collar that surrounds each flagellum and are taken into the cell. The food may be digested in each cell or engulfed in a vacuole (membrane-covered space) and passed on to a digestive cell. The porous structure allows water, containing oxygen and food, to come into contact with every cell and to carry away the reproductive cells and waste products, so more complex organs and systems are not needed. Probably sponges arose from one-celled Flagellata (Protozoa) that formed a colony and, adapting to a sessile (attached to the bottom) way of life, gave up their independence.

Between the outer covering cells and the collar cells is a layer of gelatinous material containing many amoeboid mesenchyme cells, which move around, digest food, transport wastes, and secrete the skeleton, which is composed, according to species, of calcium carbonate, spongin, which is related to both silk and horn, or a glassy, siliceous material. The skeleton is made up of spicules, small elements shaped differently in each species, that are arranged into the sponge's particular form that may be irregular, goblet-shaped, or an elaborate tubular structure. Pore cells surround the pores and other cells guard them. There may be muscle cells that can narrow the pore openings. There is no nervous system. If something touches or damages the sponge, only cells in that area respond at first, then gradually nearby cells react, but the

animal does not react as a whole. Large sponges have a complicated structure with an elaborate system of canals running throughout the animal.

Sponges reproduce sexually by excreting eggs and sperm, either in the same individual or in neighbouring ones. A free-swimming larva develops, which swims to a new location before settling down to become a sessile adult. Almost any piece of sponge can also grow into a new sponge, and asexual reproduction also occurs by budding and branching.

There are three classes. Calcispongiae includes sponges with a calcium skeleton. They are mostly small, less than 10 cm high, and mostly live in shallow water. *Leucosolenia* and *Scypha*, simple, vase-shaped sponges that may grow in groups, are genera of this class.

Hyalospongiae, the glass sponges, have a siliceous skeleton of six-pointed spicules. They are usually symmetrical, 10 to 30 cm high and shaped like cups or urns. *Euplectella*, the Venus's flowerbasket, is an example. Most live at depths between 450 and 900 m, though some have been found even deeper. A certain species of shrimp lives as a commensal (see COMMENSALISM) with the Venus's flowerbasket; the male and female enter when they are small and once grown, are unable to get out; they live on the food brought in by the current flowing through the sponge.

Demospongiae contains most of the common sponges. They have a siliceous skeleton and are often brilliantly coloured. They may be irregular, goblet- or urn-shaped. The boring sponges belong to this class, and also the freshwater sponges, which are mostly encrusting types, and may contain green algae. *Spongia* and *Hippospongia* are the commercial bath sponges. They are gathered by divers in the Gulf of Mexico, the Caribbean, and the Mediterranean; the living animals are allowed to die, and the cleaned spongin skeleton is sold.

Bibliography: D. Nichols and J. A. L. Cooke, *The Oxford Book of Invertebrates,* 1971; R. Buchsbaum, *Animals Without Backbones,* 2nd ed. 1972.

Sponsors, godparents who present a child for baptism and make the baptismal confession and promises to keep the faith, in its name. According to the rule of the Church of England, every male child must have two godfathers and one godmother, while a female child has two godmothers and one godfather. In the Roman Catholic Church one sponsor, or at most two of different sexes, is required, both at baptism and at confirmation.

Spontaneous Combustion, burning which takes place without the application of any igniting agent. Combustion is generally a form of oxidation in which sufficient heat is produced to render the particles of the material incandescent. The mere contact of atmospheric oxygen with a substance is not usually sufficient to produce chemical combination; a certain temperature or the presence of oxygen in a particularly active form is essential. In cotton-waste impregnated with oil, oxidation may proceed slowly until sufficient heat has been generated to cause it to burst into flame. The temperature necessary to produce flame varies with different substances. Thus carbon bisulphide vapour is ignited if the temperature rises to 150 °C, which is insufficient to produce incandescence in most other bodies. Phosphorus in a finely divided condition combines with oxygen with the evolution of light and heat

Spontaneous Generation

at ordinary temperatures. The conditions necessary for spontaneous combustion are the presence of a substance with a low temperature limit for flame, and a source of heat, such as slow oxidation, which eventually reaches that limit. Thus damp hay may burst into flame through the gradual rise in temperature caused by fermentation.

Spontaneous Generation, see ORIGIN OF LIFE.

Spontini, Gaspare (1774–1851), Italian composer, born at Maiolati, near Jesi. He studied at the Naples Conservatorio dei Turchini from 1791. PICCINNI was among his masters. He produced his first opera in Rome in 1796, and in 1798, when the Neapolitan court took refuge at Palermo, he was appointed its *maestro di cappella*. In 1803 he settled in Paris, and in 1820 he was appointed musical director to the Prussian court in Berlin, whence he visited Dresden, Vienna and Paris (1822–23) and England (1838). He returned to Paris in 1842, became deaf in 1848, and returned to his birthplace, where he died. Of nearly 30 operas the most important is the French *La Vestale*, 1807.

Spoof, game originating in South Africa, in which any number of players each start with three matches. Any number of these from 0 to three are concealed in a clenched fist and all guess in turn how many in all are concealed. Guesses must be different. With each correct guess, one match is eliminated; the correct player has first subsequent guess. The first player to dispose of all the matches is the winner.

Spoonbills, together with the ibises form the family Threskiornithidae, order Ciconiiformes. They are characterised by their curious bills, which are long and flat, and are dilated at the end into the shape of a spoon. Their feet are adapted for wading, and the birds obtain their food, consisting chiefly of fish, frogs, molluscs and crustaceans, from shallow water. The spoonbill is found in Europe and central and southern Asia, and is a visitor to eastern England, where it formerly bred.

Spoonerism, figure of speech comprising an accidental transposition of initial letters or syllables of two or more adjacent words. It owes its name to the Rev. W. A. Spooner (1844–1930), warden of New College, Oxford. Instances are 'Kinkering kongs their tatles tike' for 'Conquering kings their titles take'; 'Will nobody pat my hiccup' for 'Will nobody pick my hat up'; and 'You are occupewing my pie' for 'You are occupying my pew'. While some of the most diverting, including the first cited, may be attributed to Dr Spooner, most are apocryphal.
Bibliography: J. Huxley, *On Living in a Revolution*, 1944.

Spoons, made of pottery, were used in the Windmill Hill culture of the Neolithic period, and bronze spoons occur in the Early Iron Age, but in all probability these were for ritual and not utilitarian use. There are two main types of Roman spoons; those for table use have long tapering points at the end opposite the bowl for the removal of shellfish from the shell, and others with long tapering bowls are for the removal of ointments from slender glass phials. Spoons were commonly in use in antiquity, and many Roman and Saxon examples in metal are known; many others in horn or wood must have perished, and the name spoon, from the Old English *spon*, a chip, is a reminder that early spoons were made of wood. Folding

spoons were in use in medieval times when personal sets were customary. There was considerable variety in metal, decoration, and shape. The form of spoon now in use came into fashion about 1750–60. See also APOSTLE SPOON.

Sporades, group of islands in the Aegean Sea belonging to Greece. The Northern Sporades (Greek *Voríai Sporádhes*) are part of the department of EUBOEA. They are part of a submarine ridge which falls away steeply in the north to the Aegean Sea. The main islands are SKYROS, Skiathos, and Skopelos, where cattle rearing, fruit growing, and shipbuilding are the chief occupations. The Southern Sporades (Greek *Nótiai Sporádhes*) was the name formerly given to the DODECANESE ISLANDS.
Bibliography: H. M. Denham, *The Aegean: A Sea-Guide to its Coasts and Islands*, 1963.

Sporadic, in medicine, term applied to diseases which occur in scattered cases, although their usual incidence is EPIDEMIC. Sporadic cases often differ in a marked manner from epidemic cases.

Sporangium, in plants, a single-celled or multicellular body which comes to contain asexual SPORES.

Spore, a minute, generally single-celled structure by which the lower plants (algae, fungi, ferns, liverworts, mosses) and certain Protozoa characteristically reproduce. The essential feature of a spore is that, whether or not its production is preceded by MEIOSIS, it can germinate and produce a vegetative body without need for fusion with another spore or other structure beforehand. In this sense spores are asexual reproductive bodies. In algae, ferns, liverworts and mosses, for sexual reproduction two kinds of spore are produced which differ in size and in behaviour, microspores and megaspores; these are homologous evolutionarily with the pollen-grains and embryo-sacs respectively of Spermatophyta. In the Fungi a great range of spore types exists; the classification of the group is largely based on spore form. The well-known fruiting-bodies of higher fungi form spores in colossal numbers, well seen when a dry puff-ball is compressed. In Bacteria resting spores, extremely resistant to temperature and chemicals, may be produced in adverse conditions; such spores can retain viability for years.

Sporozoa, a large and important class of microscopic unicellular parasitic animals, PROTOZOA, so called on account of the readiness with which they break themselves up into reproductive spores. The majority of them are minute, but their poisonous products give rise to deadly diseases in man and animals. The principal groups of Sporozoa are the gregarines, the coccidians and the haemosporidians. One of the best-known gregarines is *Monocystis*, which is very common in the white spermatic sacs of the earthworms. In its younger stage, as an oval nucleated body, it penetrates the male spermatic sac. There it comes side by side with another, and when they have adhered they form a glass-like cyst. Gametes are formed inside the cyst; they fuse in pairs, and each zygote forms a boat-shaped sporocyst. The latter divides into eight sporozoids, which remain unchanged until swallowed by another earthworm, when their life-cycle begins again. Gregarines occur only in invertebrates. Coccidians are found in mice, rabbits, frogs, insects, molluscs and lower animals. They reproduce by splitting and by the formation of spores after fertilisation by true spermatozoa. These two distinct processes of multiplication occur also in the haemosporidia, a group of blood parasites, one of which, *Plasmodium*, causes MALARIA.

Sport, see AIKIDO; ANGLING; ARCHERY; ATHLETICS; BADMINTON; BASEBALL; BASKETBALL; BILLIARDS; BOB-SLEDDING; BOXING; BOWLING; BOWLS; BROOMBALL; BULLFIGHT; CANOEING; CRICKET; CROQUET; CURLING; CYCLE RACING; DIVING; DOG-SLEDDING; DRESSAGE; DRIVING; FALCONRY; FENCING; FIVES; FOOTBALL; FOX-HUNTING; GOLF; GRASS-SKIING; GREYHOUND RACING; GYMNASTICS; HANDBALL; HARNESS RACING; HIGH-LAND GAMES; HOCKEY; HORSE RACING; HURDLING; HURLING; ICE HOCKEY; ICE SKATING; ICE YACHTING; J'AI ALAI; JUMPING; KARATE; KENDO; KITE; LACROSSE; LAWN TENNIS; MOTOR RACING; MOUNTAINEERING; NETBALL; OLYMPIC GAMES; ORIENTEERING; PELOTA; POLO; POTHOLING; QUOITS; RACKETS; RIDING; ROCK CLIMBING; RODEO; ROLLER SKATING; ROUNDERS; ROW-ING; RUNNING; SHINTY; SKATING; SKI-BOBBING; SKI-JÖRING; SKIING; SHOOTING; SHOW JUMPING; SNOOKER; SNOW MOBJLING; SOFTBALL; SQUASH RACKETS; STEEPLE-CHASING; STOOLBALL; SURFING; SWIMMING; TABLE TEN-NIS; TAE-KWON-DO; TENNIS, REAL; TENPIN BOWLING; THAI BOXING; THROWING; TOBOGGANING; TRAMPOLIN-ING; TUG-OF-WAR; UNDERWATER SWIMMING; VOL-LEYBALL; WALKING; WATER POLO; WATER SKIING; WEIGHT LIFTING; WRESTLING; YACHTING.

Sporting Pictures. The ancient Greeks' enthusiasm for athletes, which was the incentive behind much of their sculpture, finds some pictorial record on the pottery given as prizes. Roman mosaics and frescoes depict gladiatorial combat, and beasts of the chase and arena. Hawking is illustrated in medieval manuscripts, for example the manual by the Emperor Frederick II of Hohenstaufen. A pair of elegant hunting pictures by UCCELLO are in the Ashmolean Museum, Oxford. A set of horse-portraits frescoed by Giulio ROMANO is in the Palazzo del Tè, Mantua.

Sporting Pictures. *A Hound and a Bitch in a Landscape* by George Stubbs. *(Tate Gallery, London)*

Sporting Pictures. *The Paddock at Longchamps* by Raoul Dufy. *(Stedelijk Museum, Amsterdam)*

English sporting art began with Francis Barlow (1626–1702) and John Wootton (d. 1756). STUBBS is the supreme horse-portraitist and animal painter, his expertise strengthening the tradition through Ben Marshall (1767–1835) and the Herrings in the 19th century, down to Sir Alfred Munnings in the 20th century, and assuring at least a sound regard for anatomy in innumerable hunting prints. GÉRICAULT painted the Derby, and DEGAS found piquant design in racecourse subjects. Bullfighting was a theme of Spanish painting in the 17th century, for example *correros* in the Plaza Mayor, Madrid. In the 18th and 19th centuries GOYA produced, besides paintings, a series of etchings of the bullring (*La Tauromaquia*), as did Picasso in the 20th century.

Rowing scenes were painted by the American, Thomas EAKINS, while another more recent American, George Bellows, did some fine paintings of boxing. Cricket, however, has inspired no great painting, and neither has the mass spectator sport of soccer stirred the imagination of modern artists.

Bibliography: W. Silkey, *Animal Painters of England*, 1900; W. S. Sparrow, *A Book of Sporting Painters*, 1931.

Sports (mutations), see GENETICS; MUTATION; VARI-ATION, IN BIOLOGY.

Sports, Book of, name given to a proclamation of James I in 1618, declaring, much to the fury of the Puritans (see PURITANISM), that certain games could be played after church on Sundays. In 1644 this book was ordered to be publicly burned by decree of the Long Parliament.

Sports Council, The, an independent body in England, established by royal charter in 1972. There are separate Councils in Scotland, Wales, and Northern Ireland. To ensure a consistent approach to common problems the chairman and vice-chairman of the Scottish and Welsh Councils are also members of the Sports Council; and the chairman of the Sports Council for Northern Ireland serves on a UK Affairs Committee.

The main object of the Sports Council is to develop the knowledge and practice of sport in the interests of social welfare and the enjoyment of leisure among the public at large, and the encouragement of the attainment of high standards. To this end, it receives an annual grant from central government, which for the financial year 1976/77 totalled some £10·2 million.

There are 27 members of the Sports Council and it meets six times a year to receive reports and recommendations from its four main committees: facilities, sports development, information (research), and finance. It is also served by administrative and technical staff at headquarters, national centres, and regional offices. The nine regional councils in England act as co-ordinating advisory bodies to local authorities, sports clubs, and organisations, as well as private developers and the general public. They research and identify deficiencies in facilities and follow up with development plans and policies.

Through its grant-aid policy, the Sports Council encourages local authorities to provide projects of a regional and sub-regional nature, and finances experimental and prototype schemes to demonstrate the different ways in which facilities can be provided. Assistance is also given to the governing bodies of sport under four main headings: administration, coaching and preparation training, development, and international events.

Spot-welding, see WELDING.

Spotsylvania Court House, now generally known as Spotsylvania, post village, capital of the county of the same name, in Virginia, 18 km south-west of Fredericksburg, and 88 km north by west of Richmond. In 1864 it was the scene of engagements between the forces of Grant and Lee.

Spottiswood, Alicia Ann, or Spottiswoode (1810–1900), Scottish poetess and composer, born at Lauder, Berwickshire. In 1836 she married Lord John Scott, son of the Duke of Buccleuch, but after his death in 1860 she reverted to her maiden name and became known for her Scottish songs, 'Durisdeer' and others. Among these is the famous 'Annie Laurie', which was written in its original form by William Douglas of Fingland, Kirkcudbright, and published in 1824; she rewrote it and added a third stanza, besides composing the music.

Spottiswoode, John (1565–1639), Scottish archbishop, born at Calder. He was educated at the University of Glasgow. On the death of Archbishop James Beaton, he was appointed to the see of Glasgow. He was moderator of the General Assembly 1610, 1616, 1617, and of the Perth Assembly, 1618, which sanctified the Five Articles. In 1615 he was transferred to the see of St Andrews. He crowned Charles I at Holyrood in 1633. In 1635 he was made chancellor of Scotland. He was buried in Westminster Abbey. The writings of Spottiswood are his well-known *History of the Church of Scotland*, 1655, and a Latin treatise, *Refutatio libelli de regimine ecclesiae Scoticanae*, written in answer to a tract of Calderwood's and published in 1620.

Sprain, wrenching of a joint, causing stretching or laceration of the ligaments. The most commonly sprained joint is the ankle, since it is, of all joints, the one which bears most weight. The immediate effects of sprains are pain and loss of power in the joint. Swelling soon takes place. Where fracture is suspected the joint should be appropriately treated. In ordinary sprains swelling may be lessened by the application of cold water immediately after the injury. After the joint has swollen, however, hot water should be employed to ease the pain. The part should be well bandaged and rested.

Sprat, Thomas (1635–1713), English clergyman, poet, scientist, and wit, born at Beaminster, Dorset. He became bishop of Rochester (1684) and was one of the first fellows of the ROYAL SOCIETY, of which he published a history in 1667 (modern edition, 1966). He also wrote a life of his friend Abraham COWLEY, the poet, 1668.

Sprat, *Clupea sprattus*, a small member of the herring genus, order Clupeiformes, common around the British Isles. It is from 7 to 15 cm long, with smooth scales and a prominent lower jaw. It has a sharp, toothed edge to its belly. The sprat is a favourite food-fish in mid-autumn. Larger sprats are tinned and sold as 'brisling'.

Spray Painting, see PAINTING AND DECORATING.

Spree, river of East Germany, which rises on the borders of Bohemia and the district of Kottbus, and after flowing generally north and north-west joins the River HAVEL at Spandau. It passes through Bautzen, Kottbus, and Berlin. A marshy area in its valley near Kottbus is called the Spreewald. Length 365 km.

Spring, Howard (1889–1965), Welsh novelist, born in Cardiff. He became a journalist, and in 1931 book critic of the *Evening Standard*. His realistic novels, usually describing a wide selection of people, show good description of setting and background, and a feeling for characterisation, particularly of working people. They include *Shabby Tiger*, 1934, and its sequel *Rachel Rosing*, 1936. *O Absalom*, 1938, was republished as *My Son, My Son*; it was filmed and translated into several languages. He also wrote *Fame is the Spur*, 1940, *Hard Facts*, 1944, *Dunkerleys*, 1946, *There is No Armour*, 1948, *The Houses in Between*, 1951, *A Sunset Touch*, 1953, and *All The Day Long*, 1959. *Darkie & Co.*, 1932, *Sampson's Circus*, 1936, and *Tumbledown Dick*, 1939, are children's books.

Spring published the autobiographical *Heaven Lies About Us*, 1939, *In the Meantime*, 1942, and *And Another Thing*, 1946.

Spring, the first of the four SEASONS, defined astronomically as the interval between the vernal equinox and the summer solstice but in popular usage taken to mean the period from mid-February till the end of April in Great Britain and from the beginning of March till the end of May in North America.

Spring, a flow of water rising from the point where the underground water-table reaches the surface. Seasonal movement of the water-table often causes this flow to be intermittent. Under certain geological conditions a line of springs may occur at approximately the same level affording a fairly reliable water supply to a group of settlements, hence the term 'spring-line villages'.

Spring Balance, see BALANCE.

Springbok, *Antidorcas marsupialis*, a beautiful ANTELOPE found in central and southern Africa. It is of a tawny-red general colour with a white under-surface and head, and obtains its name from the long distances it can leap. This animal is the national emblem of the Republic of South Africa.

Springer, Axel (1912–), German publisher, born at Altona, Germany, whose publishing group controls a number of West German newspapers and periodicals. His father owned the *Altonauer Nachtrichen* on which he trained as a journalist before setting up his own company in 1945. The Springer group publishes books, magazines, and newspapers such as *Die Welt, Bild Zeitung, Berliner Morgenpost*, and *Welt am Sonntag*; it also produces programmes for radio and television.

Springer, in architecture, the lowest voussoir of an arch, having its under-surface level with the springing-line (see ARCH).

Springer Spaniel, see SPANIEL.

Springfield, parish in Essex, England, 2 km north-east of Chelmsford, to which the parish in part belongs. Population (1971) 885.

Springfield, city and capital of Illinois, USA, and county seat of Sangamon county, 300 km south-west of Chicago, situated in a farming and coal-mining region. The tomb and monument of Abraham LINCOLN are here in the city where he lived and worked before becoming president, also the centennial building (with Illinois State Historical Library), Illinois State Library and state fairgrounds. New Salem State Park is 25 km to the north-west. Population 91,753. 40,556.

Springfield, city in Massachusetts, USA. It is situated on the Connecticut river in the west of the state, with the centre of the original settlement on the east bank, so that the river lay between the town and the menace of Indian attack. The town was founded in 1635, but its growth dates from the establishment of an arsenal in 1777, since when its connection with small arms, especially the Springfield rifle, has been its best-known feature. But the manufacture of small arms is only one of a number of industries characteristic of the region (see MASSACHUSETTS) in combining small quantities of necessary raw materials with a maximum of skilled labour. In the metropolitan area of Springfield–Chicopee–Holyoke today there are over 1000 industrial plants employing nearly 75,000 workers. Population (city) 163,905; (metropolitan area) 529,922.

Springfield, city of Ohio, lying between Columbus and Dayton on Interstate Highway 70. It is a manufacturing city and the seat of Wittenberg University. Population 81,926.

Springfield, city in the state of Missouri, USA. It is situated in the OZARK MOUNTAINS province, a part of which is known as the Springfield plateau. It is a manufacturing centre in a region which contains few cities, and is the seat of Missouri State College and Drury College. Population 120,096.

Springs, town in the TRANSVAAL, South Africa, 47 km east of Johannesburg, a leading industrial town and also

Spruce. Norway spruce. *(Topham/Markham)*

centre of a number of gold-mines, two of which also produce uranium. Industries include the manufacture of alloy steels and non-ferrous products, paper making, cycles, sheet glass, electrical goods, and mining machinery. There is also a uranium plant. Population 99,047, including 43,721 whites.

Springtail, see COLLEMBOLA.

Sprinting, see RUNNING.

Spruce, trees of the coniferous genus *Picea*, of which there are numerous species in Europe, Asia and North America. The most important European species, *P. abies*, the common or Norway spruce, is sold commercially as European whitewood or deal, and is used for building, construction work, box making and the production of pulp for paper and newsprint. Various North American species are also widely used for these purposes. See also TIMBER.

Spruce Beer, alcoholic beverage used in Canada, and prepared by fermenting sugar solutions and essence of spruce with yeast.

Spur, apparatus fastened to the heel of a horseman's boot for goading the horse, the modern variety usually consisting of small blunt-pointed wheels called rowels. In the days of chivalry the use of the spur was limited to knights. It was among the emblems of knighthood, and still forms part of the British regalia.

Spurge, see EUPHORBIA.

Spurge Laurel, see DAPHNE.

Spurgeon, Charles Haddon (1834–92), British preacher, born at Kelvedon, Essex, joined the Baptists in 1850. He was pastor at Waterbeach, Cambridgeshire, in 1852, but he was soon transferred to Southwark, London. His sermons at Exeter Hall crowded the building, and he became minister of the Metropolitan Tabernacle when it was opened in 1861. He founded a college and an orphanage. His autobiography was published posthumously (1897–1900).

Bibliography: W. Williams, *Personal Reminiscences*, 1895; Lives by W. Y. Fullerton, 1921, J. C. Carlile, 1933, and A. Roth, 1934.

Spurn Head, promontory at the south-east extremity of north Humberside, England, on the estuary of the HUMBER. Since the erection of groynes in 1864 the inroads of the sea have been checked to some extent. There are two lighthouses.

Sputnik, see SATELLITE, ARTIFICIAL.

Sputum, secretions from the lining or mucous membrane of the respiratory canal, usually consisting of saliva mixed with mucus from the nasal passage. If it is clear white in colour, this usually indicates a minor irritation of the respiratory tract. Purulent, yellowish sputum indicates more severe infection. In some diseases of the lung such as BRONCHIECTASIS, lung abcess, tuberculosis and carcinoma of the lung the sputum is purulent, blood-stained and offensive. See CANCER; HAEMOPTYSIS.

Spy, in war, is a person who, in order to obtain information for his own side, operates in enemy-held territory surreptitiously and under various forms of disguise. A spy, if captured, is put to death, but an officer or soldier in uniform must be treated as a prisoner of war. Military law, although distinct in ordering the death of a spy, is not clear in defining what constitutes one. The employment of spies in war is held to be legitimate by all states, but the spy himself is regarded as an outlaw, although spies are of two types, the renegade who sells his own country to the enemy for some reward or to further an ideology, and the spy who operates in the enemy territory to obtain information for his own side. Spies are employed by civil governments in peace-time, for the discovery of armament developments, etc., and are not unknown in the industrial world, in the discovery of trade secrets. See also ESPIONAGE.

Spy, see WARD, SIR LESLIE.

Spyri, Johanna (1829–1901), Swiss author, born at Hirzel. She wrote many children's stories set in the Swiss mountains, among them *Heidi*, which has become one of the most famous children's books and has been translated into many languages.

Squadron. In the Royal Navy the term is applied to administrative groups of warships, either working separately or attached to fleets. In the British army the term is used for a body of horsed cavalry, armoured troops, or engineers forming the sub-division of a regiment. Normally two, three, or four squadrons comprise a regiment, each squadron being under the command of a major. Each squadron is divided into two, three, or four troops. The strength of a squadron varies, but is usually between 50 and 100 men. With minor variations this organisation exists in most other armies. The word is of Italian origin, and means a 'square' battle formation of companies of infantry or troops of cavalry in close order. The squadron is the smallest operational unit of the RAF, and consists of a number of aircraft and flying and ground personnel. The number of aircraft employed and the rank of the commanding officer vary according to the rôle of the squadron. The commanding officer is usually either a squadron-leader or a wing-commander.

Squall, Line. In an isolated THUNDERSTORM the increase in wind and fall in pressure may be short-lived, but often the accompanying drop in temperature lasts longer, setting up a local cold front (see FRONTS). This atmospheric activity can develop into a line squall caused by the sudden aggravation of unstable conditions by warm air being hindered in its path by friction on the ground surface, and being overrun by colder air. The line squall carries with it a characteristic roll cloud. As rain from air high above the front falls through the colder air, it evaporates and cools the air even before absorbing latent heat from it; if this cold air has trapped some warm air, more violent instability is produced, and the down-flowing cold air reaches great speed. This is called the squall wind. The convection may be so fierce that a vortex develops and forms a funnel cloud as in the tornado (see CYCLONE). This funnel cloud or waterspout (over the sea) advances across the area affected with the squall. See WIND.

Squamata, see REPTILIA.

Squarcione, Francesco (1397–1474), Italian painter, born in Padua. He is historically more important as the master of a large workshop and collector of Greek and Roman antiquities. Only two of his works are now known, a polyptych in Padua and a signed *Madonna* in Berlin. His archaeological collection strongly influenced his pupils, the most important of whom were MANTEGNA and TURA.

Square, The, constellation, see NORMA.

Square Dancing, term used for the American style of country dancing when a 'caller' tells the dancers which figure to perform. Originally the name referred to a dance performed by four couples standing in a square formation and was based on the COTILLION and QUADRILLE. The dances, whose movements came from the English COUNTRY DANCES, were taken to the USA by immigrants. Later, Scottish, Irish, Dutch, and other nationalities became absorbed into the American background and the dances developed and changed according to their regions. Contra, the longways set, and the running set in circle formation are all part of square dancing.

Square Measure, see METROLOGY.

Square-rig, rig of a ship whose principal sails are extended on yards, suspended horizontally at the middle, and can be set on either side at a greater or lesser angle with the keel, but not on one side as a fore-and-aft sail. See SAILS AND RIGGING.

Square Root, see ROOT.

Squaring the Circle, see QUADRATURE.

Squash, see CUCURBITACEAE.

Squash Rackets, game for two or four players which evolved from RACKETS, almost certainly at Harrow School in the mid-19th century. There nearly every boarding house had a blank wall running at right angles to another which became used for a popular 'squashed'

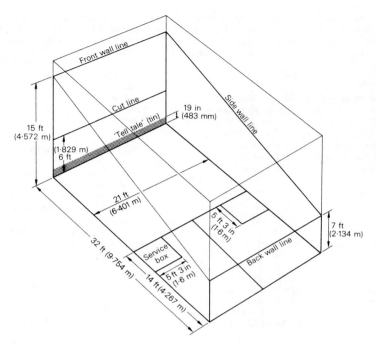

Front wall line

Cut line

Side wall line

19 in
(483 mm)

15 ft
(4·572 m)

'Tell tale' (tin)

(1·829 m)
6 ft

21 ft
(6·401 m)

5 ft 3 in
(1·6 m)

7 ft
(2·134 m)

32 ft (9·754 m)

Service
box

Back wall line

5 ft 3 in
(1·6 m)

14 ft (4·267 m)

Squash Rackets. Diagram of court.

version of rackets using a soft, india-rubber ball. Players gaining in proficiency then proceeded to the hard-ball larger court game of rackets. Based primarily in the public schools up till the 1960s, squash now attracts much wider participation, because of its simplicity and convenience as exercise for office-bound executives, and also because, being an indoor game, it can be played all year round. Its dramatic growth in the 1970s has resulted in a playing population in excess of a million with separate associations for men and women.

The court is only a third of the area of a rackets court, being 9·75 m long and 6·40 m wide; the front wall height (to the boundary line) is 4·57 m. Running along the bottom of the front wall is a board—known as the 'tin'—which serves the same purpose as the net at tennis. The object of the game is to hit a small rubber ball over the tin but under the front boundary line so that it evades an opponent until after it has bounced twice or forced the opponent to make a mistake. After service, the ball can be played off any of the four walls before and/or after hitting the front wall.

The procedure for service is the same as for rackets: the player winning the toss serves on to the front wall from either of the two service boxes so that it rebounds into the opposite half of the court. Only the server can score, the receiver needing first to win a rally in order to become 'in hand' and then to win the next rally to score.

A game is won by the first player to reach a score of nine except when the score reaches eight all. The player who first reached eight then has the option of 'setting' the game to either the first player to reach ten, or of letting the game to the winner of the next scoring rally.

In the USA squash is played on a narrower court (5·6

m wide) and some other dimensions vary; either player can score no matter who is serving. This version has also become popular in Mexico, while the English game has a substantial following in Australia and South Africa. Pakistan and Egypt have consistently produced top flight champions and the Khan family of Pakistan established almost a monopoly of all the world's main championships for almost two decades.

In 1969 Jonah Barrington, a Cornishman, became the first man to make squash a full-time career, and since then commercial sponsorship has escalated. Glass-back courts have made it possible for crowds of up to 450 to watch the game, where before this innovation the largest gallery was that of the Lansdowne Club, London, holding 200.

Control of the game is vested in a number of squash rackets associations. The growth of the world game necessitated wider control and the inaugural meeting of the International Squash Rackets Federation (ISRF) took place in London during January 1967 with seven founder members: Britain, Australia, India, New Zealand, Pakistan, Southern Africa and the United Arab Republic. The first world championships were staged in Australia during 1967, the home country easily winning both the team and individual championships.

Bibliography: L. Hamer and R. Bellamy, *Squash Rackets*, 1968; J. Barrington, *Barrington on Squash*, 1973; R. B. Hawkey, *Starting Squash*, 1975. Periodical: *Squash Rackets Association Handbook* (annual).

Squid, a relative of the cuttlefish and, more distantly, of the octopus. It belongs to the mollusc class CEPHALOPODA (subclass DIBRANCHIA, order DECAPODA). Eight of its ten tentacles are short, and two are long, with suckers on the end for grasping prey. The squid swims by taking in water,

Squill

then squirting it out forcefully, and also by means of its two lateral fins. The fins in the flying squid are strong enough to give it a gliding jump that occasionally lands it on the decks of ships. *Loligo vulgaris*, a common species, is eaten by man.

Squill, see SCILLA.

Squill, the dried, sliced bulb of white, or Mediterranean squill *Urginea maritima*, which contains glycosides with pharmacological activities similar to those of DIGITALIS. It was used by Egyptian physicians in 1500 BC. However, it is less potent and is very poorly absorbed from the intestine. Squill has an irritant effect on the mucosal lining of the stomach when taken orally, and this causes a reflex expectorant action, hence its use in chronic bronchitis, but in larger doses causes vomiting. Red squill is used as a rat poison in the form of a paste; the glycosides responsible are different from those with medicinal action.

Squilla, a genus of burrowing arthropods of class CRUSTACEA that bear a striking resemblance to the praying mantis both in appearance and feeding behaviour. They have large pincers which are projected from the burrow to seize the prey animals. *S. mantis* is common in the Mediterranean, where it is used as food, and is occasionally taken off British coasts. It is about 18 cm long. Some Mediterranean species have a beautiful planktonic LARVA.

Squinch, or squinch-arch, in architecture, a small arch built diagonally across the internal angles of a square structure, to carry a circular or octagonal dome or spire.

Squint, or hagioscope, slanting aperture cut through the walls of the chancel in certain medieval churches, so as to make the elevation of the Host visible from a side chapel.

Squinting, or strabismus. In correct vision the axes of both eyes correspond in direction and turn towards the object looked at. The motor muscles so act that any movement of one eye causes a harmonious movement of the other. Sometimes the axes of the eyes are not parallel and the eyes do not move harmoniously together, and this is known as squinting, or strabismus. It may take place upwards, downwards, inwards or outwards; both eyes may be affected, or it may be confined to one. It usually occurs in childhood, due to a defect in the muscles or nerves of the eye or to a unilateral refractive error leading to cortical malfunction. Excessive fatigue, fever or shock can be precipitating conditions, especially if a latent squint already exists. Another common cause is either short or long sight, and the squint can then be remedied by spectacles alone.

It is important to remember that in squinting binocular vision is lost. When it first occurs in an adult and the eyes look in different directions, double vision (diplopia) results. In the case of a young child, however, whose binocular functions are as yet not fully developed, diplopia is only a fleeting symptom. Mental suppression of the image formed in the squinting eye takes place and there is a definite loss of vision in that eye (AMBLYOPIA). In treating a squint the non-squinting eye may have to be covered, in order to train the squinting eye to function

again. The longer a squint remains untreated, the longer it will take for the squinting eye to recover its vision. A branch of ophthalmic optics known as orthoptics is now correcting many forms of squinting by exercises designed to stimulate weak muscles or nerve reactions in one or both eyes. In some cases operative treatment is necessary. In adult life a form of squint arising from paralysis of one or more of the external eye muscles can occur.

Bibliography: J. Hurtt and others, *Comprehensive Review of Orthoptics and Ocular Motility*, 1972; G. T. W. Cashell and I. M. Durran, *Handbook of Orthoptic Principles*, 3rd ed. 1974.

Squire, Sir John Collings (1884–1958), English poet and critic, born in Plymouth; educated at Blundell's and St John's College, Cambridge, he became a freelance journalist. Squire was one of the leading Georgian poets. In 1913 he was literary editor of the *New Statesman*; from 1919 to 1934 he edited the *London Mercury*, a monthly magazine of literature and the arts to which he contributed under the name of Solomon Eagle. His verse includes *Collected Parodies*, 1921, *Poems in One Volume*, 1926, and *Selected Poems*, 1948. He was knighted in 1933.

Squire, abbreviated form of ESQUIRE. Originally a squire was the armour-bearer of a knight, to whom he was next in rank, and had various privileges and exemptions. The word later became popularly applied to the chief land owner in an English country district.

Squirrel, *Sciurus*, a genus of arboreal rodents in the family Sciuridae. *S. vulgaris*, the European or red squirrel, is widely distributed over Europe and parts of Asia. The British red squirrel is a subspecies, restricted to the British Isles. The body is reddish-brown above and white below; the ears are large and tufted. The body is about 20 cm long, and the bushy tail only a little shorter. It feeds on fruits and shoots, and sometimes eggs and small birds. It has been destroyed in large numbers in Scotland on account of its habit of barking and otherwise damaging forest trees. In the south of England it has been driven away from its haunts by the introduced grey or Canadian squirrel (*S. carolinensis*), which has adapted itself with remarkable swiftness The grey squirrel is far more aggressive than the red one. The African ground or spiny squirrels belong to the genus *Xerus*. The flying-squirrels (*Pteromys*) of Asia have a membrane stretching from the

Squirrel. The grey squirrel. (*Topham/Coleman*)

Sri Lanka. The Mahaweli river is the island's longest and most important. *(Barnaby's Picture Library)*

forelimb to the hindlimb, which enables them to glide for distances up to 80 m.

Squirrel-cage Motor, see ELECTRICAL MACHINES, *Three-phase Induction Machine.*

Squirrel Monkey, monkey of the genus *Saimiri*, in the family CEBIDAE. These are two species, both of which are arboreal, insectivorous and gregarious; the long tail is non-prehensile and the face is small.

Sraffa, Piero (1898–), Italian economist, Fellow of Trinity College, Cambridge, since 1939. His *The Production of Commodities by Means of Commodities*, 1960, constituted a watershed in critical discussion of economic theory and launched a school among the younger generation of economists, which re-established the central importance of the classical theories of David Ricardo and Karl Marx.

Sri Lanka (formerly Ceylon; Sanskrit *Sinhala*), pear-shaped island in the Indian Ocean, crown colony of Great Britain from 1802 until 1948, when it became a self-governing dominion. It is separated from India by the Gulf of Manaar and Palk Strait, but is virtually joined to the mainland by the submerged coral reefs and sandbanks known as ADAM'S (RAMA'S) BRIDGE, and by Rameswaram Island. It lies between 5°55′ and 9°50′N latitude and 79°40′ and 80°53′E longitude. Its length from Dondra Head to Palmyra Point (north to south) is about 428 km, and its width varies from 50 to 225 km. Area 65,610 km².

Geography. Relief. The island is dominated by its mountainous southern half. Its highest peak is Pidurutalagala (2524 m), although Adam's Peak (2243 m) is probably better known. The land slopes gradually down to the coast, except in the north where it forms an undulating plain. The coast is fringed by lagoons and sand bars. Ninety per cent of the country lies below 300 m. The country's rivers radiate from the central highlands like the spokes of a wheel. The main river is the Mahaweli (325 km long) but the majority are less than 150 km long. See ATLAS 33.

Climate. Sri Lanka has an equatorial climate tempered by the surrounding sea and modified by the monsoons. Precipitation forms its most important element, varying

from 1000 mm in the north to over 5000 mm in the highlands. The south-west is generally well watered whilst the north and south-east require irrigation; large 'tanks' are scattered around the island for this purpose. The temperature averages 27 °C for most of the year around the coastal lowlands; this drops to 18 °C in the highlands. Most places have a high relative humidity. The south-west monsoon blows from May to October and the north-east monsoon prevails from December to March. The annual and diurnal temperatures vary only about 4 °C.

Population. The present population of Sri Lanka is around 12,710,000, composed of different races represented by the Sinhalese, Tamils, Moors, and Burghers. The approximate racial distribution is 70 per cent Sinhalese, 20 per cent Tamils, 7 per cent Moors, and the rest are composed of Burghers, Malays, etc. Twenty-five per cent of the population is urban and concentrated in the COLOMBO region. Other major towns are JAFFNA, KANDY, and GALLE.

Bibliography: R. Percival, *Account of the Island of Ceylon*, 1972; O. H. K. Spate and A. T. Learmouth, *India, Pakistan and Ceylon*, 1972.

Economy. Agriculture. The economy of Sri Lanka is almost entirely dependent on agriculture. More specifically it is dependent on three crops: tea, rubber, and coconuts. Of the total cultivated area of 1·9 million ha, over 25 per cent is under rice cultivation and a further 25 per cent under tea and rubber. Of the other food crops cassava is the most important for domestic consumption, covering 78,000 ha. Despite the high annual rainfall the eastern part of the island has a long dry season during which irrigation is essential, and nearly half a million ha are irrigated. Productivity of the major crops has shown little improvement; total rice production has increased from 1 million t in 1963 to 1·15 million in 1975. Tea production remained virtually constant at approximately 220,000 t during this period, although this reflects the rôle of internationally agreed export quotas. Production of natural rubber increased from 105,000 t to 154,000 t during the period. In addition to the major crops, Sri Lanka also grows a number of minor ones, notably spices such as cardamom for which the island has long been famous. Company owned estates were nationalised in 1975.

Sri Lanka. Tea picking is delicate work done mainly by women. *(Barnaby's Picture Library/Kenneth Simmons)*

Sri Lanka

Industry. Industrial activity represents a very small part of Sri Lanka's economic activity. When it became independent from Britain in 1948 there were no large-scale industrial activities. All the required manufactured goods were imported. During the period since it became independent efforts have been made to diversify the economy. Cotton textile manufacturing was introduced, based entirely on imported cotton. Production of woven cotton goods increased from 4 million to 27 million m in 1973. Formerly dependent on imports for many of its modern construction materials, Sri Lanka has now built up its cement industry. From a production of 75,000 t in 1963 the total production reached 460,000 t in 1973.

Energy. With no reserves of coal or oil, Sri Lanka has depended to a large extent on hydro-electricity for its power. Total energy consumption in 1974 stood at 2·11 million metric t of coal equivalent. Of the total electricity generating capacity of 281,000 kW, some 195,000 kW was in the form of hydro-electric capacity.

Communications. Despite its small size and compact shape, the rugged terrain of the centre of the island have always made communications difficult. The railway network now has a track distance of 1535 km of which 1395 km are broad gauge and the remainder narrow gauge. The railways carried over 10,000 million passenger kilometres in 1974 and 7600 million ton kilometres of freight. In the 15 years up to 1975 the road network was developed substantially. The total length of the road network is now over 42,000 km, of which paved roads make up nearly 20,000 km.

Trade. Sri Lanka's trade has been dominated by the need to export tea, rubber, and coconuts in order to buy both manufactured goods and food. The country remains dependent on this pattern of trade today, despite efforts to achieve self-sufficiency. Imports of rice have been reduced from 403,000 t in 1963 to 294,000 t in 1973, but this reduction was more than compensated by the rise in wheat imports from 140,000 to 323,000 t in the same period. Imports of sugar rose from 140,000 to 292,000 t, and thus Sri Lanka's dependence on imports for these essential raw material supplies can be seen to have remained a central feature of the economy. Equally, her exports have been made up almost entirely of tea, rubber, and coconut products, of which the latter make up 25 per cent by value and rubber and tea the remainder between them. There has however been some significant change in Sri Lanka's major trading partners during the period of her independence. China has increased her trade to become Sri Lanka's largest single trading partner, importing 267 million Rupees' worth of commodities in 1975 and exporting 359 million Rupees' worth of commodities. Pakistan has also become a major trading partner, while industrial commodities continue to be imported largely from Europe and Japan.

Bibliography: OECD, *Agriculture in Ceylon*, 1970; A. N. S. Karunatilake, *Economic Development in Ceylon*, 1972.

Government. Constitution and *Legislature*. Sri Lanka became independent from Britain on 4 February 1948 on the implementation of the Ceylon Independence Act passed the previous year. Constituted as a parliamentary democracy on Westminster lines, elections in May 1970 led to the adoption of a new constitution, which came into effect on 22 May 1972. Under the new constitution Sri Lanka was declared to be a 'Free, Sovereign and Indepen-

dent Republic', whose sovereignty was held to rest in the people. It is a unitary state, whose sovereignty is exercised through the national State Assembly. This assembly has three functions: a) legislative power is vested in the assembly; b) it has executive authority, including authority over defence; and c) it controls judicial power through the courts. The assembly comprises 157 members, who are elected by universal suffrage for all over 18 years of age. The head of state is the President, who is nominated by the Prime Minister. Executive power is held by the Prime Minister and Cabinet who are collectively responsible to the assembly.

Justice. The legal system was amended on 1 January 1974, with a new structure being introduced with effect over all the courts. In addition to the Supreme Court, the highest court in the country, there were to be high courts, district courts, and magistrates' courts. District judges and magistrates are appointed by the Cabinet. Judges are appointed by the President.

Education. The earliest Western schools were Catholic, set up by the Portuguese after 1505. From 1656 the Dutch established schools to preach Protestantism. Education is compulsory and free for all children between the ages of 5 and 14. The literacy rate is very high. 2·8 million pupils attend 10,000 primary and secondary schools. The combined enrolment of the University of Sri Lanka (founded in 1942) is over 13,000; it has sites in Colombo and three other towns.

Welfare. There is an island network of hospitals, clinics, and dispensaries where treatment is free. An institute for community development was set up in 1966. The housing problem is being dealt with by new housing estates being built around the major urban centres to reduce overcrowding. Rice is subsidised by the state. The standard of social life is amongst the highest in Asia.

Religion. Over 66 per cent of the population are Buddhist, 18 per cent are Tamil-speaking Hindus, and there are important Muslim and Christian minorities.

Official Language. Sinhalese, spoken by about 70 per cent of the population. Tamil and English are also widely used.

National Anthem. Namō Namō Mathā, written and composed by Ahanda Samarakoon.

National Flag. Dark crimson with a yellow border, in each corner of which a bo-leaf is depicted. In the centre is a gold lion and at the left are two vertical stripes of green and orange.

Bibliography: H. C. Sirr, *Ceylon and Singhalese*, 1972; UNESCO, *Cultural Policy in Sri Lanka*, 1973; A. J. Wilson, *Politics in Sri Lanka*, 1974.

Early History. As recorded in the Buddhist Chronicle the *Mahawansa*, itself a unique document dating back to around the 5th century BC when civilisation was flourishing in the capital city of Anuradhapura situated in the north, Ceylon was originally colonised by settlers of Indo-Aryan origin who came to the island around 1500 BC, contemporary with Indo-Aryan settlements in India. The legendary founder of the early kingdom is believed to be Prince Vijaya from Bengal. Between the 5th century BC and 10th century AD ANURADHAPURA was the capital and centre of civilisation. The turning point was the introduction of Buddhism in the 3rd century BC at the instigation of Emperor ASOKA, who sent his personal emissary Mahinda bearing the message of the Buddha.

King Devanampiyatissa of Ceylon received it with enthusiasm and readily adopted Buddhism as a national faith, since when it has flourished as the premier religion of the island. Buddhism became not only the main religion but the main inspiration to cultural and spiritual life of the early civilisation, expressed in the numerous temples, stupas, and religious monuments which were built by successive kings and which made Anuradhapura one of the greatest cities of ancient times, known particularly for its unique form of Buddhist civilisation. The Buddhist stupas which include the Ruwanweliseya, Thuparamaya, Abaya Giri, and Jetawana Ramaya, are exemplary forms of Buddhist art apart from their monumentality (see *Architecture* below). Anuradhapura was also famous as the 'tank' civilisation for its network of artificial irrigation by which monsoon water, which would otherwise have flowed into the sea, was harnessed by elaborate canals, dykes, and reservoirs and utilised for rice cultivation, thus earning Ceylon the reputation of the 'granary of Asia'. Outstanding rulers at this time were the Kings Mahasen, Datusena, and Aggabodhi.

Politically, Ceylon was subject to sporadic invasion by adventurers from South India and one of its early kings, Dutugamunu, earned regard as a national hero by distinguishing himself in liberating the country from one such invasion. With the growth of expansionist kingdoms in South India and changes in the South Indian policy, the kingdoms of the Pallawas, Pandyas, and Cholas competed for mastery and their impact was felt by the Anuradhapura civilisation; the latter becoming involved in South Indian political conflicts. This led to the Cholyan invasion of the 11th century under Emperor Rajaraja the Great who subjugated the northern part of the country.

The Cholyan invaders were expelled in 1070 by a resistance struggle which was led by Prince Vijayabahu who became king in 1070 and established himself in the new capital, south-east of Anuradhapura, POLON-NARUWA. Being a fortified city, Polonnaruwa was better situated to face recurrent invasions from South India. The Polonnaruwa phase of Ceylon history is notable for two kings, Vijayabahu and Parakramabahu the First, 1151 to 1186. The reign of Parakramabahu is called the Golden Age as it saw the building of religious monuments, 'tanks', and general economic development of the country on a large scale. It was even marked by an aggressive foreign policy on the part of the king, who sent expeditions to Burma and South India. The cumulative effect of South Indian invasion and recurrent turmoil made life in the north intolerable and eroded its irrigation system which was its pride. This led to the withdrawal of Sinhalese kings from Polonnaruwa to other sites, fortified mountain resorts in the south and south-west, until in the 15th century they established themselves at Kotte on the south-west coast near Colombo and in the 16th century in the hill capital of KANDY. The break-up of the centralised monarchy thus led to the establishment of a number of independent kingdoms which vied with each other for supremacy. This state of internal conflicts gave the opportunity for foreign invaders to establish themselves.

Modern History. *European occupation.* The period of European occupation began in 1505 with the landing of the Portuguese in Colombo after their arrival on the Malabar coast. Though initially disinclined to territorial dominion, they involved themselves in the local civil war

Sri Lanka. Standing and reclining Buddhas, 8 m high, at the ruined city of Polonnaruwa. (*Barnaby's Picture Library*)

between Sinhalese rulers and by the end of the 16th century established themselves in the maritime provinces; but their efforts to conquer the hill kingdom of Kandy failed. The Dutch arrived in Asia in continuation of their conflict with Hapsburg Spain and in the middle of the 17th century they replaced the Portuguese in the maritime provinces of Ceylon. The Dutch were mainly interested in the cinnamon trade and developed the maritime provinces commercially, but relations with the kingdom of Kandy were strained and in the 18th century the latter turned to the British East India Company for aid in dislodging the Dutch. The British were at first disinclined, owing to their alliance with the Dutch, but with the outbreak of the revolutionary war in Europe they occupied the maritime provinces and at the Peace of Amiens (1802) these territories were ceded to them. In 1815 they subjugated the Kingdom of Kandy, thus completing the British conquest of Ceylon.

Initially, British interest in Ceylon was a by-product of its continental and colonial rivalry with France; but, following the acquisition of its Indian empire in the 18th century, possession of Ceylon was deemed essential mainly owing to its strategic harbour of TRINCOMALEE.

The British period lasted from 1815 till 1948 and was marked by various significant developments which transformed the economic and social character of the country. In the economic sphere a plantation system was introduced to replace the old rice cultivation economy of ancient times. Cash crops such as coffee and subsequently tea and rubber were introduced, vast plantations were opened up, and the economy of the country made dependent on the commercial proceeds of these commodities. The English language was introduced and taughts in schools, accompanied by efforts to promote Christianity which had already been introduced by the Portuguese. British political and legal institutions and their accompanying

Sri Lanka

socio-political ideas were introduced and a Western type of civilisation fostered in the colony. In the process the ancient traditions, institutions, and cultural forms of the society were progressively eroded. Towards the end of the 19th century the British government took an interest in the ancient heritage in the form of a policy to revive and develop disused irrigation works. They also opened up the country by a network of roads and railways, under the impetus of the plantation economy and the planters, which enabled the political and administrative unification of the island.

Ceylon became a crown colony of Britain in 1802 (unlike India which was ruled by the East India Company until 1857). This basic form of crown colony government remained unchanged till the first decade of the 20th century, except for some modifications in 1833 when a small legislative council was introduced. Under the pressure of the congress movement in India and a general demand for self government within the British Empire (which in Ceylon was championed by the national congress consisting of leading representatives of the people), the Imperial government was considering constitutional changes in colonies. In Ceylon a series of reforms was introduced by Governor Manning between 1922 and 1924, the effect of which was the creation of a partly-elected legislature and an executive council. However, executive authority resided with the governor and the officials. The composition, as well as the manner of appointment, of elected members followed the communal method based on the Morley-Minto reforms of 1911 in India which had introduced Hindu/Muslim representation. The next step in the constitutional development of Ceylon was the report of the Donoughmore Commission which visited the country in 1930 and made some unique and even radical recommendations. These were for the establishment of a state council form of government, providing for a legislature called the State Council, elected on the basis of adult suffrage, which would appoint its own board of ministers. This constitution gave the people a considerable share of responsibility, and one of its unique features was the rejection of communal representation which the Commission described as a canker on the body politic. The Donoughmore Constitution was adopted in 1931 and continued until 1946 when, with the Saulbery Constitution, Ceylon approached independence.

Independence. At the end of the war, under pressure of the universal demand for de-colonisation not confined only to British colonies, the British government appointed the Saulbery Commission in 1946 to frame a new constitution for Ceylon pursuant to a declaration to accord self-government to the island. The Commission recommended autonomy to a greater degree than before but by 1947 the demand for complete independence was conceded by the British government. On 4 February 1948 the transfer of power was effected. The independence constitution saw the appointment of a governor-general, who was the King's representative, and the establishment of a Senate. A defence agreement was signed by the two governments providing for the use of the harbour of Trincomalee under certain circumstances. The new constitution provided for a legislature of 51 and executive power was vested in the Prime Minister and Cabinet. The first Prime Minister was Mr D. S. SENANAYAKE. This constitution remained in

force until 22 May 1972 when a new constitution framed by a constituent assembly specially established for that purpose was adopted. This was the constitution of the Republic of Sri Lanka under which the President replaced the governor-general and the senate was abolished. The new constitution represented the completion of the process of independence as it derived its authority from the Parliament of Sri Lanka. The island was renamed Sri Lanka, its old classical designation.

The history of Sri Lanka since 1948 has been marked by an endeavour to accelerate its economic development and evolve political, economic, and social systems attuned to the needs and abilities of the country. The parliamentary process has worked in a way which has made Ceylon one of the notable democratic systems in Asia. Between 1948 and 1970 six governments were in office. A significant event was the advent to power in 1956 of the government of Mr S. W. R. D. BANDARANAIKE, leader of the Sri Lanka Freedom Party pledged to a philosophy of democratic socialism which expressed itself in a programme of socialistic legislature and a foreign policy of non-alignment. The government of Mr Bandaranaike is credited with ushering in the age of the common man. Following his assassination in September 1959, his widow Mrs Sirima R. D. BANDARANAIKE was elected Prime Minister in July 1960. She held office as Prime Minister until 1977, except for the period 1965–70 when the United National Party was in power under the premiership of Mr Dudley SENANAYAKE. The period of office of Mrs Bandaranaike was a further step in the development of democratic socialism in the country through such measures as land reforms, land distribution, land acquisition, state control of major industries and similar measures which transformed the socio-economic character of the country. In its foreign relations Sri Lanka is a member of the Commonwealth and follows a policy of non-alignment. It is the founder member of non-alignment since its inception in 1961 and has played a prominent part in this movement. A notable contribution made by Mrs Bandaranaike was the proposal for a peace zone in the Indian Ocean, endorsed by the United Nations. In August 1976

Sri Lanka. Buddhist stupa at Polonnaruwa, 3rd to 2nd centuries BC. *(Barnaby's Picture Library)*

Sri Lanka. Gilt bronze Tara, 10th to 11th centuries AD. (*British Museum, London*)

Sri Lanka was the venue for the 5th Summit of Non-Aligned Nations Conference. In July 1977, after a general election marked by much violence and with an aftermath of civil unrest, the United National Party again came into power headed by J. R. Jayawardene.

Bibliography: L. A. Mills, *Ceylon under British Rule 1795–1932*, 1964; E. F. C. Ludowyck, *Modern History of Ceylon*, 1966; W. Knighton, *History of Ceylon*, 1971.

Art and Architecture. Buddhism reached Sri Lanka from northern India in the 3rd century BC, establishing itself first in the ancient north capital of Anuradhapura and rapidly replacing the earlier religious forms throughout the island; the latter, however, re-emerged as part of the local manifestation of the Greater Vehicle (*Mahayana*) after the initial *Hinayana* phase had passed. The earliest surviving Buddhist buildings are the great STUPAS of Mihintale and Anuradhapura. Called *dagobas*, especially in their prolific smaller forms, these were sometimes surrounded by pillared buildings, and even enclosed within timber roofs. During the great expansion of South Indian Hinduism in the 5th to 8th centuries AD, Sri Lanka was repeatedly invaded. But a new flowering of Buddhist culture, focused on the city of Polonnaruwa, took place during the 12th century with the reported assistance of monks from Burma and possibly Thailand, who enriched the architectural vocabulary with imported forms. Chinese influence was briefly felt at various periods, especially in the early 15th century, by which time the power of the island was fragmented between a number of kingdoms, the most conservative of which focused on the central hill capital of Kandy. Surviv-

ing temples and monasteries mostly date from this period or later, but the structural system is ancient. They have low earth or masonry platforms, wooden columns and heavy tile roofs. Embossed tiles decorate the eaves, and columns and doorways are richly carved. The walls are painted with legends and scenes in superimposed friezes. Singhalese houses are focused on a single courtyard; they have only one or two enclosed rooms, the remainder of the house being open, except for a raised rice bin.

The island has a rich heritage of churches dating from the Portuguese and Dutch colonial periods, of fine Dutch town and country houses, and of late Georgian and Victorian British colonial architecture.

Bibliography: S. Bandaranayaka, *Singhalese Monastic Architecture*, 1975.

Language, see SINHALESE; TAMIL.

Srinagar, summer capital of JAMMU AND KASHMIR state, India, beautifully sited on the Jhelum river in the Vale of Kashmir, 1600 m above sea-level. To the north-east, the Dal Lake with its floating gardens and houseboats is an important tourist centre. The town with its canals and

Sri Lanka. Late Sinhalese (Kandy) painting of the 'Vine-flower Sprite', early 19th century. (*Victoria and Albert Museum, London*)

wooden bridges has numerous mosques, public gardens, palaces, museums, and a fortress, and the University of Jammu and Kashmir (1948). Government factories and cottage industries produce carpets, silk, silver, leather, and copperware. Population (1971) 423,250.

Srirangam, town in Tamil Nadu state, India, on an island in the Cauvery river, 3 km north of Tiruchirappalli. Srirangam is the site of one of the great Hindu temples of India, and as a place of pilgrimage can be compared to VARANASI. There are two main temples (17th century), one dedicated to VISHNU and the other to SIVA. Population (1971) 51,000.

SS Troops, see SA AND SS.

Ssu-ma Ch'ien, see CHINESE LITERATURE.

Stabat Mater, medieval Latin hymn on the seven sorrows of the Virgin Mary, so called from its opening words. In the Roman Missal it forms the SEQUENCE for the feast of the Seven Dolours of the Blessed Virgin Mary. The author was probably Jacopone da Todi. There are many musical settings, by composers including Palestrina, Pergolesi, Vivaldi, Verdi, Dvořák, and Szymanowski.

Stabilisation (exchange rates), financial policy of counteracting wide fluctuations in the relative value of monetary units. The world-wide economic depression of 1930–32 brought the subject under discussion at the World Economic Conference in London in 1933, but with no practical results. Stabilisation of exchange rates after the Second World War was the aim of the BRETTON WOODS AGREEMENTS (1946), by which the INTERNATIONAL MONETARY FUND was set up, which began work in 1947. By the agreement, fixed exchange rates of the other currencies (par values) were to be established with the dollar (and thus indirectly with gold, since the dollar had still a fixed value in gold); changes in par values (with certain exceptions) required the approval of the Fund. Real stabilisation requires freedom of exchange restrictions; in recent years British exchange control regulations have been very few. The stabilisation of exchange rates, to be effective without exchange restrictions, is dependent on internal financial stability, i.e. avoidance of inflation. See also EXCHANGE, FOREIGN.

Stabilisers, see SHIPS AND SHIPBUILDING, *Post-war Machinery Developments*.

Stability, property by which a structure tends to maintain its original position, and by which a moving system tends to recover its typical configuration when slightly disturbed. See EQUILIBRIUM.

Stachys, a genus of the Labiatae (deadnettle family), containing over 300 species. These are world-wide in distribution, except for Australasia, and the British species are known as hedge-nettle or woundwort. *S. sylvatica* is the hedge woundwort (with foetid leaves), and *S. palustris* the marsh woundwort. *S. affinis* is the Chinese artichoke which forms edible small white tubers on underground shoots. *S. olympica* is often grown in gardens for its decorative leaves, which are densely covered with white woolly hairs.

Stack, an isolated pinnacle of rock standing in the sea close to the coastline, produced where cliffs have retreated under marine abrasion (see COAST), leaving scattered offshore remnants. Among the most notable stacks in Britain are the NEEDLES at the western end of the Isle of Wight, and the Old Man of Hoy in the Orkney Islands.

Stade, city in LOWER SAXONY, West Germany, 140 km north-west of Hannover. It once stood on the Elbe, but owing to a change in the course of the river now lies 5 km upstream on the Schwinge. It was a member of the HANSEATIC LEAGUE. There are oil refining, atomic power, chemical, and aluminium industries in this industrial growth area. Population 40,300.

Stadholder, or Stadtholder, corrupt form of the Dutch *stad-houder* (stead-holder), a title formerly applied to a royal lieutenant or viceroy of a province, who was also a chief magistrate. It became a hereditary title in the House of Orange (see ORANGE, HOUSE OF).

Stadium, Latin form of Greek word *stadion*, a *stade* being a standard measurement in ancient Greece. This was 600 Greek feet (about 185 m or 20 yds), the length of the first race in the original Olympic Games. The name was applied to the race itself and then to the place where the race was held, the sense in use today.

The White City Stadium in London was built for the 1908 Olympic Games with accommodation for over 70,000. The Municipal Stadium in Rio de Janeiro can hold 200,000 spectators, while the Strahova Stadium in Prague has accommodated over 240,000 for gymnastic displays.

Staël, Madame de (1766–1817), or Anne-Louise-Germaine Necker, Baronne de Staël-Holstein, French novelist and essayist, born in Paris, the daughter of Necker, the celebrated financier. Having published her *Lettres sur Rousseau*, in 1788, in 1792 the Revolution forced her to leave France, and for some years she travelled, visiting Switzerland, England, Germany, and Italy, writing her *Réflexions sur la paix intérieure*, 1795, and *De l'influence des passions*, 1796. A quarrel with

Madame de Staël, from an engraving. *(Mansell Collection)*

Napoleon, against whom she intrigued constantly, led to her exile in 1803.

She moved to Weimar, where she met and studied literature with Schiller and Goethe, and later to Berlin, where she met August SCHLEGEL, who lived at her home on Lake Geneva after 1804. Her two novels, *Delphine*, 1802, and *Corinne*, 1807, are interesting, though excessively long. She was again exiled in 1810, and had to seek refuge in Russia, Sweden, and London, where her masterpiece, *De l'Allemagne*, 1810, gained her access to intellectual circles. In 1814 she was welcomed to Paris by Louis XVIII, but her health gradually gave way under the strain of nursing her delicate second husband.

Before her influence, German literature was unknown to France. Her *De l'Allemagne* overcame French prejudice and abandoned the sensualist point of view of 18th-century philosophy.

Bibliography: C. Herold, *Mme de Staël, Mistress of an Age*, 1958; F. d'Eaubonne, *Une Femme témoin de son siècle*, 1966.

Staël, Nicolas de (1914–55), Russian painter of the modern French school, born in St Petersburg. His family emigrated from Russia in 1919 and he was brought up in Brussels where he studied at the Academy of Fine Arts. He settled in Paris in 1943. He developed an original form of abstract painting in which the suggestion of figure, landscape, or still-life is implicit using the palette knife to create large, flat areas of colours.

Bibliography: D. Cooper, *Nicolas de Staël*, 1961.

Staff, Air, generic term covering the three branches, air, technical, and administrative, into which the RAF staff is organised. The term is also used to describe the operational branch, i.e., the air branch, only. The controlling authority for the RAF, under the secretary of state for Defence and the Defence Council, is the Air Force Board, the chairman being the minister of Defence (RAF). Major defence policy is formulated centrally by the Defence Council but day-to-day management is exercised by the Air Force Board. The air officers commanding-in-chief and commanders-in-chief have at their headquarters their own air, technical, and administrative staffs, and administer smaller headquarters and units (e.g. groups, stations, training establishments). Officers are trained in staff duties at the RAF Staff Colleges, Joint Services Staff College, and Royal College of Defence Studies. They are, however, only employed on staff duties for limited periods—at other times they carry out their normal work of flying, administration, or technical duties.

Staff, Military. The staff exists to assist the military commander in his day-to-day duties and transmit his orders to the troops. Staff officers are provided at all levels; in the British army the highest being at the Ministry of Defence (Army Department) in London, and then down through the various echelons of command to brigades and garrisons at home and abroad. Up to the middle of the 19th century operational staffs were of small size, consisting of a few selected officers who helped the general in non-active periods and acted as mounted messengers in battle. The GENERAL STAFF system, or 'multiple brain', was originated by the Prussians and, in various forms, has been adopted by all other military powers. Today staffs are divided into two main branches—the General Staff (dealing with plans and operations) and the Administrat-

ive Staff (responsible for supplies, non-operational moves, quartering, etc.). At each headquarters—Army, Corps, Division, etc.—the staff is controlled and co-ordinated by the senior staff officer, normally called the 'chief of staff'.

Staff College, RAF, Bracknell, Berkshire, for training officers in staff duties and widening their outlook. It works closely with the other British staff colleges, and officers from the other services and from the Commonwealth and foreign air forces also attend the course, which lasts one year. Graduates have the letters 'psc' placed after their names in the Air Force List.

Staff Colleges. Early in the 19th century the increasing complexity of military operations made it necessary to give officers destined for the staff special training in staff duties. In Britain the army's Staff College at Camberley may be said to be the 'mother' of many similar colleges throughout the Commonwealth. The first course at Camberley opened in April 1858, in buildings of the Royal Military College, and it was not until 1862 that the present building on the London Road was occupied. In July 1905 the Staff College at Quetta, in India (now in Pakistan), was opened for officers of the Indian and British armies serving in India.

At first the curriculum was somewhat antiquated and theoretical; but, as experience was gained, it gradually came to conform with current requirements. Today there are Army Staff Colleges in the Commonwealth as follows:

United Kingdom—Staff College, Camberley.

Canada—Canadian Land Forces Command and Staff College, Kingston.

Australia—Australian Staff College, Queenscliff.

India—Indian Defence Services Staff College, Wellington.

With variations to suit local and service conditions these Staff Colleges all follow the pattern of the original Staff College, Camberley. In most cases the courses last for one year and the aim is to train officers to become staff officers and at the same time give them the general and military background necessary for high command at a later date. At the National Defence College, Latimer (where the course is of nine months duration), the aim is to fit officers for staff work in an integrated headquarters.

It should be noted that all officers before going to the Staff College, Camberley, attend a short course at the Military College of Science at Shrivenham, which aims at giving officers a background knowledge of science applicable to military affairs.

All other countries with modern military forces have establishments for training staff officers, the most notable being the US Command and General Staff College, at Fort Leavenworth. There is also the NATO Defence College, at Paris, where officers of the NATO countries are trained for staff and other duties in an international force.

See also MILITARY EDUCATION AND MILITARY SCHOOLS.

Bibliography: B. Bond, *The Victorian Army and the Staff College 1854–1914*, 1972.

Staffa, small uninhabited island of the Inner HEBRI-

Stafford

DES, Scotland, lying 11 km west of Mull. Its circumference is about 2·5 km. Geologically it is composed of volcanic basalt, and is remarkable for its numerous caves, with prismatic and columnar forms. The most famous are Fingal's Cave (70 m long), Clamshell Cave, McKinnon's or Cormorant's Cave, and Boat Cave.

Stafford, borough, market town, and county town of Staffordshire, England, on the River Sow, in the green belt between Wolverhampton and Stoke-on-Trent. It was mentioned in the Anglo-Saxon Chronicle of AD 913 as Betheney. A royal mint existed on the site in about 940. In Domesday Book the town appears as Stadford. Its first charter was granted by King John in 1206. In 1643 the Parliamentarians destroyed the town walls and Stafford Castle after their victory at Hopton Heath. A later castle built on the same site has now been demolished. Notable buildings include St Mary's Church, containing a bust of Izaak Walton, who was born in Stafford; St Chad's Church; and the High House, said to have been built in 1555. Chetwynd House, now the head post office, has associations with SHERIDAN, who was MP for the town, 1780–1806. Stafford is an important rail centre, and is served by the M6 motorway. Its chief industries include electrical engineering, shoemaking, salt, adhesives, grinding wheels, concrete reinforcement, and other engineering products. There are colleges of further education and art, and North Staffordshire Polytechnic provides degree courses. Population 56,000. As a result of local government reorganisation (1974) a new Stafford borough was created, incorporating STONE and rural districts. Total population (1971) 114,300.

Staffordshire, a midland county of ENGLAND, bounded on the north-east by Derbyshire, the east by Leicestershire, the south-east by Warwickshire, the south by the West Midlands county and Hereford and Worcester, the south-west by Salop, and the north-west by Cheshire. The surface generally is level, rising to hilly regions in the north and south-west. The hills in the north form part of the PEAK district, and in the south include KINVER EDGE; Cannock Chase includes a large open area in the middle of the county. The chief river is the TRENT with its tributaries, the Churnet, Dove, Penk, Sow, and Tame. The county includes the great manufacturing district known as the POTTERIES. Coal was mined in Staffordshire

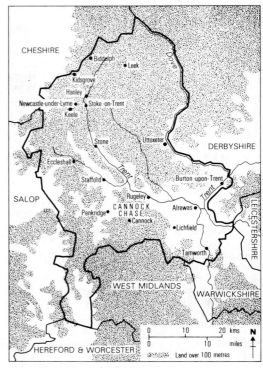

Staffordshire.

by the 13th century, and, as in another long established industry, pottery, great expansion started in the 18th century. Coal is still mined in the Potteries and in Cannock Chase. The Black Country, long famous for its metal industries, is no longer in Staffordshire but forms part of the separate West Midlands metropolitan county. Industries in Staffordshire are the breweries at BURTON UPON TRENT, electrical works, and the manufacture of boots and shoes at STAFFORD. Despite the great importance of its industries, much of the county depends on farming, particularly dairying.

Staffordshire. Bottle kilns. *(Barnaby's Picture Library)*

Railway communication is by both the Midland and the Western regions of British Rail; the Trent and Mersey, the Staffordshire and Worcestershire and other canals serve the county. Stafford is the county town and the county itself is in Lichfield diocese. The University of KEELE, formerly the University College of North Staffordshire, was established near the heavily populated area round STOKE-ON-TRENT. Evidence of pre-Roman and Roman occupation of the county is accumulating, and Wall (*Letocetum*) was a Roman station on Watling Street near Lichfield. In Anglo-Saxon times, Staffordshire formed part of the kingdom of MERCIA, the Mercian kings having their residence at TAMWORTH. Besides the cathedral at Lichfield, there are many beautiful parish churches both in towns such as Stafford and in villages such as Clifton Campville and Gonsall. There are also remains of castles at Chartley, Tamworth, and TUTBURY. David Garrick, Samuel Johnson, Isaak Walton, and Admiral Jervis, Earl of St Vincent, were natives of Staffordshire. Area 2716 km²; population 991,100.

Bibliography: Victoria County History: Staffordshire, vols 1–5, 8, and 17, 1908–76; A. Mee, *Staffordshire* (rev. F. R. Banks), 1971; N. Pevsner, *Staffordshire*, 1974.

Staffordshire Bull Terrier, a dog which differs from the modern BULL TERRIER in several ways, and is a representative of the original fighting breed. Dogs weigh from 12·5 to 17·5 kg; their height is from 35 to 40 cm. The head is short and deep, the neck thick and muscular, the chest wide and deep and the hindquarters light but strong. The coat may be any shade of red, fawn, black or brindle, with or without white markings. The breed is unexcelled as a guard and an increasingly popular companion.

Staffordshire Regiment, The, a British army regiment formed in January 1959 by the amalgamation of the South Staffordshire Regiment and the North Staffordshire Regiment. The regiment forms part of the Prince of Wales's Division.

Stag-beetle, insect belonging to the family Lucanidae of the order COLEOPTERA (superorder Scarabaeoidea). They are so-called because most of the males possess enormous mandibles shaped rather like the antlers of a stag. Very often the length of these mandibles equals the length of the rest of the body. The mandibles appear to be largely ornamental and cannot be moved by the jaw muscles. There are over 900 species within this family; of these only three species are found in Britain, including *Lucanus cervus*, the stag-beetle common to Europe and Asia. The males are much bigger than the females. The adult male *L. cervus* measures up to 80 mm in length. It is dark brown, with chestnut-coloured wing cases which completely cover its abdomen. Another characteristic feature is the smooth appearance of the wing cases, which are devoid of ridges. The larvae inhabit the rotting wood or the roots of trees, such as oak. In the case of *L. cervus* the larval stage spans a period of about four years. Thereafter pupation follows, in a cell made from gnawed wood fragments, for about one year before the adult beetle emerges. The adults are active fliers and are attracted to light.

Stage, see ACTING; COSTUME, THEATRICAL; DRAMA; THEATRE.

Stage Coach, see COACH AND COACHING.

Staghound, foxhound used only for the purpose of hunting either the wild or the 'carted' deer (see FOXHOUND). The DEERHOUND is a quite distinct breed.

Stagira, or Stagirus, ancient town of Macedonia, Greece, in north-east Chalcidice, on the Strymonic Gulf. It was the birthplace of ARISTOTLE, often therefore called the Stagirite. The present village of Stavro occupies the site.

Stahl, Georg Ernst (1660–1734), German chemist, born at Auspach, Bavaria. He studied medicine at Jena, and in 1693 was appointed professor of medicine at the University of Halle, where he also taught chemistry. Influenced by the ideas of Becher and Kunckel on combustion, he developed the theory of phlogiston, a substance which supposedly separated from objects when they burnt. The theory was finally discredited by LAVOISIER.

Staffordshire. Alton Towers. *(Camera Press/A. G. Hutchinson)*

Stained Glass

Stained Glass is pre-eminent among artistic media for its intensity of colour, range of contrast and sparkling transparency. All these are enhanced by the dark meandering pattern of the H-section lead strips used to bind the pieces of glass together. Mentions of stained glass windows in the early centuries of the Christian era probably refer to bull's-eyes of coloured glass set in pierced frames of stone, stucco, metal or wood. Figured windows, with details drawn with iron oxide and fused on to the glass, appear in the 11th century (Augsburg Cathedral), indicating a sound technology for manufacturing glass in a wide range of colours. The output increased enormously in the 12th century with widespread social effect. For example, the enlargement of windows advanced the growth of Gothic architecture; improved heat-conservation enabled assemblies to meet in all weathers; the spectacular presentation of religious subject-matter provided the Church with a major propaganda weapon.

The art of stained glass reached its peak early, perhaps the finest of all windows being that presented to Poitiers Cathedral by Henry II of England in 1162. Superb displays of 12th- and 13th-century stained glass can be seen at Chartres, Bourges, Le Mans, Paris (Notre Dame and Sainte Chapelle), Léon and Canterbury. In the 14th century, stained glass began to yield its primacy as a decorative medium to painting, which increasingly was to affect stained glass design. Fine examples of this middle period are at York, Gloucester, Erfurt, Assisi, Florence (in the Cathedral some 15th-century glass was designed by Donatello, Ghiberti and Uccello), Milan, Seville and Cambridge (King's College Chapel). Renaissance glass in the 16th to 18th centuries used larger panes, often of white glass decorated with filigrees of black and gold ('silver stain') and impermanent enamels. Masterpieces are in Florence (Laurentian Library by Vasari), Auch, Westminster Abbey, and some Parisian churches and Oxford

Stained Glass. *The Annunciation*, said to be from Torcello, Italy, 14th century. *(Victoria and Albert Museum, London)*

Stained Glass. Panel of stained and painted glass of the Arms of the Counts of Kyburg. Swiss, late 15th century. *(Victoria and Albert Museum, London)*

colleges. Figure-subjects in the late period were often painted *en grisaille*, i.e. in tones of grey, though this subtle treatment was used far earlier for the abstract 'Five Sisters' window at York. Flemish roundels of the late period are collectors' pieces. In the 19th century Munich glass was fashionable. Perhaps the best Gothic Revival stained glass was English, especially that of the Burne Jones–Morris circle. In the 20th century, French painters including MATISSE (at Vence) and LÉGER (at Audincourt) introduced 'abstract design', much used in postwar church-building in Germany (especially the Cologne Archdiocese) and England (Coventry Cathedral). Good modern work has appeared in the USA and Scandinavia. A technical incentive has been the development of a fused glass technique and the use of cement and apoxy resin compounds for binding spalled slab glass. Britain, Italy and Spain have also maintained a strong traditional connection. The ART NOUVEAU style in Europe, and Tiffany in the USA, improved the undistinguished use of stained glass for domestic uses. But secular stained glass on any large scale has not yet caught on, though electrical backlighting might encourage a development. A feature of the present time is the increased knowledge of glass conservation (Canterbury and York Cathedrals).

See also ART-FORMS; GLASS ENGRAVING.

Bibliography: G. Manchini, *Italian Stained Glass Windows*, 1957; M. Aubert and others, *Le Vitrail Français*, 1958; L. Armitage, *Stained Glass*, 1959; J. Baker, *English Stained Glass*, 1960; L. Lee, *Stained Glass*, 1967. Also, volumes of *Corpus Vitrearum Medii Aevi*.

Stainer, Jacob (c. 1617–83), Austrian violin-maker, born at Absam, Tyrol. He learned the craft at Innsbruck, and also perhaps with one of the AMATI family or with Vimercati. From 1641 he worked on his own account, with his brother Marcus (b. c. 1625), the latter becoming later an independent craftsman. A highly arched belly and back are characteristic of Stainer's instruments, which were often preferred to those of the Cremonese school until tastes in instrumental sonority changed at the end of the 18th century.

Stainer, Sir John (1840–1901), British organist, composer and theorist, born in London. In 1856 he became organist at St Michael's College, Tenbury, and in 1860 went to Oxford, taking the D Mus degree in 1865. In 1872 he became organist at St Paul's Cathedral. Stainer was knighted in 1888, and became professor of music at Oxford in 1889. Besides compositions for organ, church services and textbooks, he left several cantatas, e.g. *Daughter of Jairus*, 1878, and oratorios, including *Gideon*, 1887, and especially *The Crucifixion*, 1887.

Stainer, Leslie, see HOWARD, LESLIE.

Staines, formerly part of Greater London, now part of Spelthorne District of Surrey, England, growing up from a Thames bridging point. A bridge existed here in the 13th century and a newer bridge was completed in 1962. The town has many factories and Heathrow (London Airport) is nearby. Population (1971) 55,045.

Stainforth, see HATFIELD.

Staining, see PAINTING AND DECORATING.

Stainless Steel, see IRON AND STEEL.

Stair, John Dalrymple, 2nd Earl of (1673–1747), Scottish soldier and diplomat. He was educated at the universities of Leyden and Edinburgh, and in 1701 joined a Scottish foot regiment and served in Marlborough's campaigns. He succeeded to the earldom in 1707, and was made commander-in-chief of the forces of Scotland. He served with distinction at Oudenarde, Malplaquet, Ramillies, and Dettingen.

Stairs, see JOINERY.

Stakes, see HORSE RACING.

Stakhanov Movement, ideological movement among the workers and *kolkhoz* peasants in the USSR, aimed at raising the productivity of labour. It was originated in 1935 by the coal-miner A. Stakhanov on instruction of the Party authorities. Specially favourable conditions were given to selected workers, who, together with several assistants, achieved spectacular production results, which were used as justification for raising production targets for all workers. Since the Second World War this practice has continued under other names; for example, the workers at any place of work are urged by the Party to 'struggle for the title of Brigade of Socialist Labour' (or higher, of Communist Labour).

Stalactites and Stalagmites are the colloquial names for columnar forms of chemical concretions known as speleotherms which occur in natural caves in limestone areas (see KARST). Stalactites hang vertically from a cave roof and are initiated by the development of a single sheath of crystals surrounding a central passage of groundwater. As the water, saturated in carbon dioxide, drops from the roof it partly evaporates and results in a small precipitation of calcium carbonate forming around the edges. Each successive drop causes the deposit to grow

like a quill with later flow down the outer surface precipitating further layers of crystals thereby creating the extended conical form. Stalagmites grow upwards from the cave floor to the source on the roof in forms ranging from simple bosses to slender pillars. Curtain-like structures which form under suitable conditions are often banded with impurities to give white, blue, and red coloration. Marked variation in the rate of growth has been recorded, the average being around 0·25 mm a year.

Stalbridge, town in Dorset, England, 11 km from Sherborne, with a very old church and a fine market cross dating from the 14th century. Population (1971) 1964.

Stalin, Joseph, real name Iosif Vissarionovic Dzhugashvili (1879–1953), dictator of Russia and of the world Communist movement, the most accomplished totalitarian ruler in modern history. A Georgian (or possibly an Ossete) by birth, son of an artisan, he was educated at the theological seminary at Tiflis, but was expelled in 1898 on account of his revolutionary connections. He joined the RUSSIAN SOCIAL DEMOCRATIC WORKERS' PARTY in 1898 and the Bolshevik faction in 1903, and worked underground in Transcaucasia as an active but minor follower of Lenin until 1913, when Lenin and Zinoviev, desperately short of collaborators, co-opted him into the Bolshevik central committee. This did not mean much at the time, but ensured his formal seniority when he returned to St Petersburg from banishment after the FEBRUARY REVOLUTION in 1917 (he had been banished six times, but escaped five). He was then second in the Bolshevik hierarchy in the capital, after Kamenev, and became editor of the party's newspaper 'PRAVDA'. Stalin followed Kamenev's conciliatory policy towards the PROVISIONAL GOVERNMENT, but when Lenin arrived from abroad accepted his plans for the seizure of power by the Bolsheviks. After the OCTOBER REVOLUTION he was commissar for the nationalities' affairs in the Soviet government 1917–23, and commissar for workers and peasants inspectorate, 1919–22. After the crisis over the Brest-Litovsk Treaty (see BREST-LITOVSK, TREATY OF), in which the Left

Stalin with Lenin (seated second and third from the left in the centre row) with a group of delegates to the Eighth Congress of the Russian Communist party (Bolsheviks), Moscow, March 1919. *(Novosti Press Agency)*

Stalin Peak

Communists and Trotsky opposed Lenin, Stalin became, apart from Sverdlov, Lenin's closest collaborator. During the Civil War (see CIVIL WAR, RUSSIAN) he was, like other leading Communists, a senior political commissar in the Red Army. He was a member of the POLITBURO from its foundation and in 1922 became general secretary of the Party's (see COMMUNIST PARTY OF THE SOVIET UNION) Central Committee.

Stalin's rudeness and high-handedness disturbed Lenin, who shortly before his final illness made plans to remove Stalin from his position of power. By the time Lenin died, however, Stalin had consolidated his hold on the party apparatus. In the inner-party struggle that ensued he joined forces with Zinoviev and Kamenev and defeated Trotsky, using the slogan of 'building socialism in one country first' as against Trotsky's 'permanent revolution'. He then, together with Bukharin and Rykov, defeated the 'new opposition' of Zinoviev and Kamenev and the 'combined opposition' of these two with Trotsky (see LEFT OPPOSITION), and finally defeated the RIGHT OPPOSITION of Bukharin and Rykov with the help of his own followers MOLOTOV, VOROSHILOV, KAGANOVICH, ORDZHONIKIDZE, and KIROV, whom he gradually promoted to the Politburo. He ruled together with them as undisputed leader of the victorious clique from 1929 until 1934, launching the FIVE-YEAR PLANS, the COLLECTIVISATION OF AGRICULTURE, and the so-called 'cultural revolution', i.e. large-scale replacement of old intellectuals, whether liberal, technocratic (see INDUSTRIAL PARTY; SHAKHTY), Populist (see NEO-POPULISM) or ex-Menshevik (see MENSHEVIKS), by new ones hastily trained from among uneducated party members. From 1934, when an opposition emerged among his own followers led by Kirov, Stalin abandoned 'collective leadership' and established his personal rule. Constant purging of the party and state apparatus culminated in the GREAT PURGE, aimed at the extermination of all potential and imaginary opponents.

Henceforth Stalin's rule was a reign of terror (see STALINISM). In 1940 Stalin became officially the head of the government, in 1941 chairman of the State Defence Committee, commissar (later minister) of defence and supreme commander-in-chief of the Soviet armed forces. He interfered personally with the work of the military commanders, and assumed the ranks of marshal and, later, generalissimo. The comparative relaxation of the political atmosphere in the war years was followed, from 1946, by the complete restoration of Stalinism as it had developed before the war and its imposition on the satellite countries of Eastern Europe. The last years of Stalin's rule were characterised by extreme obscurantism, xenophobia, chauvinism, and anti-Semitism. His works include *History of the Communist Party of the Soviet Union (Bolsheviks)*, *Short Course* (ed. by Stalin), 1939, *Problems of Leninism* (11th ed.), 1940.

Bibliography: B. D. Wolfe, *Three Who Made a Revolution*, 1966; M. Djilas, *Conversations with Stalin*, 1969; I. Deutscher, *Stalin*, 1970; L. Schapiro, *The Communist Party of the Soviet Union*, 1970; R. Conquest, *The Great Terror*, 1971; A. Ulam, *Stalin*, 1973.

Stalin Peak, see COMMUNISM PEAK.

Stalinabad, see DUSHANBE.

Stalingrad, see VOLGOGRAD.

Stalinir, see TSKHINVALI.

Stalinism, theory and practice of Stalin's near-totalitarian rule in the Soviet Union and the satellite states of Eastern Europe, as well as in the world Communist movement. The existence of Stalinism as a distinct body of theory has always been denied by orthodox Communist propaganda, which has contended that Stalin simply further developed and enriched the teaching of Marx and Lenin. Moreover, since the 20th Congress of the Communist Party of the Soviet Union, when KHRUSHCHEV admitted, in secret session, some of Stalin's mistakes and crimes, discussion of the notion of Stalinism has been avoided by all Communists, except for the Chinese and their allies, who still revere Stalin, and extreme revisionists in countries like Italy, who want to examine the roots of Stalinism objectively.

In fact, Stalinism as a theory is largely a combination of Leninism (see BOLSHEVISM; LENIN, VLADIMIR ILYICH) and NATIONAL BOLSHEVISM. There are also additional elements, some of them contributed by Stalin himself, others by Molotov, Zhdanov, Vyshinsky, etc., such as the doctrines of the possibility of building socialism in a single country first; of the continuing existence of the state even under full communism, if there is still capitalist encirclement; of SOCIALIST REALISM in the arts and literature; of the happy and prosperous life of the Soviet people; of the latter's moral and political unity; of its unbounded love for the Communist party, the security organs, and Stalin personally; of Stalin as a universal genius, source of limitless wisdom and benevolence.

Most of these doctrines are dogmatic postulates in form and fictitious in content, their purpose being to enforce conformity of public behaviour and expression. The practical concomitant was, in Stalin's lifetime, the terror of the security organs (see NKVD; MGB) and the fear of the concentration camp (see CORRECTIVE LABOUR CAMPS) awaiting the non-conformist. The relaxation of terror since Stalin's death and Beriya's fall (see BERIYA, LAVRENTI PAVLOVICH) started the process of disintegration of the Stalinist system, which was greatly accelerated by Khrushchev's secret speech in 1956. The post-Stalin Soviet leaders have all tried to maintain the basic elements of Stalinism, while greatly reducing the level of terror. This has been an almost impossible task, however, as revisionists and anti-Communists in Russia and other Communist countries have naturally taken advantage of the lessened terror to attack fundamental aspects of Stalinism.

Bibliography: R. C. Tucker, *The Soviet Political Mind*, 1963; R. C. Tucker and S. Cohen (Eds), *The Great Purge Trial*, 1965; A. B. Ulam, *Stalin*, 1973.

Stalino, see DONETSK.

Stalinogorsk, see NOVOMOSKOVSK.

Stalinsk, see NOVOKUZNETSK.

Stall, in church architecture, an elevated seat in the choir or chancel of a cathedral or other church. It is wholly or partially enclosed by a high back and sides, and has projecting arms separating it from its neighbour; there is usually a ledge for books. Stalls are generally of wood, though sometimes of stone embellished with sculptured foliage and grotesques; while in some cases the stall is covered with a canopy of tabernacle work. Most of the stalls in English churches and chapter-houses date from pre-Reformation times and were intended for the use of the clergy, chapter or monks. In cathedral and collegiate churches they are occupied by the canons and prebends. Sometimes there is a row of stalls for the choir, because they fulfil part of the duties of the monks; the chanting of the divine office.

Stalowa Wola, town of Poland, in Rzeszów province, 61 km north of Rzeszów, in the valley of the River San. A steel mill was built there in 1938 by the Polish government as part of its policy to establish an industrial region away from Poland's western frontier with Germany. The town has three electricity-generating stations. Population 32,000.

Stalybridge, a former Cheshire town with an industrial tradition dating back 200 years; since 1974 it has been part of the Tameside borough of the Greater MANCHESTER METROPOLITAN COUNTY, England. Situated 12 km north-east of Stockport and originally a cotton town (a cotton mill was built here in 1776), its industries are now more varied and include electrical engineering, metallurgy, paper, rubber, and plastics. Population (1971) 22,805.

Stambolov, Stefan (1854–95), Bulgarian politician and poet, born at Tirnovo. He became leader of the anti-Russian national-liberals and was prime minister from 1887 to 1894.

Bibliography: A. G. H. Beaman, *Stambuloff*, 1895.

Stamboul, see ISTANBUL.

Stamen, the pollen-bearing organ of a FLOWER.

Stamford, borough market town on the River Welland in LINCOLNSHIRE, England. It became a royal borough in 972. Part of the earthworks of a Norman castle may still be seen, and during the Middle Ages a number of monasteries were founded and 17 parish churches built. Of the latter six survive, and St Martin's, St Mary's, All Saints, and St John's are highly interesting. The Benedictine priory of St Leonard retains a Norman arcade and a fine west front. Among the many noteworthy buildings, Browne's Hospital, dating from the time of Edward IV, possesses a chapel with a good screen and some exquisite glass. Burghley House, south of the town, was begun in 1575 by Lord Burghley. The house and grounds are open to the public at certain times. Agriculture, engineering, plastics, and timber and stone trades are important. The *Lincoln, Rutland, and Stamford Mercury* is one of the oldest newspapers in the country, and is said to have been established in 1695. Population (1971) 15,000.

Stamford, city of Fairfield county, Connecticut, USA, on Long Island Sound, about 56 km from New York. It is the commercial centre of an extensive region and an important manufacturing town, while its proximity to New York City, and ease of access by rail and by the Connecticut Turnpike, make it a dormitory town for the metropolis. Population 108,800.

Stamford Bridge, village in HUMBERSIDE, England, on the River Derwent, 13 km north-east of York. It was the scene of the defeat of invading Norwegians under HAROLD III (Hardrada) by the English under HAROLD, on 25 September 1066. Population (1971) 1206.

Stamitz, Johann (1717–57), Bohemian composer, born at Némecký Brod. In 1741 he became a member, and soon afterwards director, of the famous elector's orchestra at Mannheim, and was the founder of the Mannheim school of early symphonists. He wrote some 70 symphonies, which helped to establish the symphonic form later used by HAYDN and MOZART, many concertos and much chamber music.

Stammering and Stuttering, fairly common forms of speech disorder, which are due to the inco-ordinated action of the muscles around the larynx. In stammering there is a hesitation or delay in the pronunciation of a syllable, while in a stutter there is a machine-gun-like repetition of the initial letters of a syllable. Stammering may be divided into two types, depending on whether it originates in childhood or makes its first appearance later in adolescence or adult life. The former is generally regarded as being mainly physiological in origin, i.e. it is believed to be the result of physiological instability in the organisation of the neuromuscular apparatus concerned in speech. It may, however, be provoked or aggravated by emotional factors, and it may arise as an imitation of other children's speech. There may be a family history of stammering or some other form of speech defect. The relatively frequent association of stammering with a family history of left-handedness has given rise to the theory that the condition is basically due to the incomplete dominance of the leading hemisphere of the brain (see CEREBRAL DOMINANCE). This would appear to be confirmed by electroencephalograph records showing the alpha waves of the two hemispheres to be out of phase.

Treatment of the physiological type of stammer usually takes the form of training in breath-control and patient re-education in articulation, coupled with the removal of any aggravating emotional factors, and suggestion aimed at increasing self-confidence. Some childhood stammers, however, especially those appearing in the first few years of speech development, may be mainly psychogenic. It has been shown in some cases that stammering may be due to infantile conflicts even as early as the suckling phase. Any threat to the oral region, at the stage when phantasies are apt to centre around it, may lead to the production of a stammer as a psychoneurotic symptom. Stammering of recent origin in the adolescent or the adult is entirely psychogenic. It can often be cured through treatment of the underlying anxiety state by psychotherapy.

Bibliography: I. R. C. Batchelor, *Henderson and Gillespie's Textbook of Psychiatry*, 10th ed. 1969; J. Hunt, *Stammering and Stuttering: Their Nature and Treatment*, 1968; C. Van Riper, *The Nature of Stuttering*, 1971.

Stamp Act, act passed in Britain in 1765 through the efforts of Grenville, and in spite of the protests of 6 out of the 13 New England colonies of America, by which the British government gave itself the right to levy a tax on all manner of documents, such as legacies, cheques, and receipts, as a means of raising revenue for colonial defence. The colonists, already irritated by Grenville's customs duties of 1764, declined to use the stamped paper, and on the principle of no taxation without representation denied the right of the home government to tax them

Stamp Collecting

at all. The Rockingham Whigs, represented by Burke and Chatham, who succeeded Grenville in office, repealed the act in 1766, but with a saving measure in the shape of an act declaring that England had full legislative and fiscal authority over the colonies.

Stamp Collecting, see PHILATELY.

Stamp Duty is a duty charged in Britain on certain documents. The principal statute is the Stamp Act 1891. It is not charged on transactions but only on instruments effecting transactions. Thus if a transaction can be effected orally, no duty is payable. Nor does an instrument which is ineffective for its intended purpose attract duty. There are two principal kinds of stamp duty. First there are the fixed duties which are fixed sums charged on certain instruments regardless of the value of the property disposed of by the instrument. An example is the duty of 50p charged on a deed. Secondly, there are the *ad valorem* duties, the amount of which depends on the value of the transaction. The most common instruments attracting stamp duty are: (1) conveyances or transfers on the sale of land or other property, such as shares; (2) leases; (3) voluntary dispositions, e.g. conveyances of property into settlement; (4) policies of life assurance. In 1975 no stamp duty other than the 50p fixed duty was payable on conveyances (whether voluntary or on sale) or leases where the CONSIDERATION, value, or premium (under a lease) was £15,000 or less. Reduced rates of duty applied where the consideration, etc., was £30,000 or less.

Examples of instruments which are exempt from all stamp duties include transfers of government stocks, instruments for the sale of ships, instruments of apprenticeship and articles of clerkship, and policies of insurance other than life assurance. Stamps are now always impressed on the instrument, except on contract notes for the sale of shares where a special adhesive stamp may be used. The former practice of stamping contracts and receipts with ordinary postage stamps was abolished completely after February 1971.

An unstamped instrument is inadmissible in evidence (except in criminal proceedings) and renders, for example, the purchaser under a conveyance on sale, the lessee under a lease, or the settlor by a voluntary conveyance, liable to a penalty if the instrument is stamped after execution (although most stamping is done after execution and the practice of the Revenue is to take no objection to stamping within 30 days of execution). The penalty is the unpaid duty, plus £10, plus interest on unpaid duty over £10 at 5 per cent per annum until the interest equals the unpaid duty over £10. In addition there is frequently a fine of £10. The administration of stamp duty is in the charge of the commissioners of Inland Revenue.

Bibliography: B. J. and E. M. E. Sims, *Sergeant on Stamp Duties*, 6th ed., 1972, with supplements; B. Pinson, *Revenue Law*, published annually.

Stamp of Shortlands, Josiah Charles Stamp, 1st Baron (1880–1941), British economist. He entered the civil service in 1896, and in his spare time read for an economics degree. After war broke out in 1939 the government appointed Stamp as 'adviser on economic coordination', to assist the Cabinet committee on economic and financial policy. Of his books the most scholarly was his *British Incomes and Property*, 1916, a critical sifting of the statistics which provided a sounder basis than had previously existed for estimates of the national dividend and its distribution. His *Wealth and Taxable Capacity*, 1922, was a popular exposition of the statistical methods involved in the estimation of the nation's wealth; and *The National Income*, 1927, in collaboration with A. L. Bowley, was a most authoritative calculation of the magnitude of that wealth. In 1929 he published *Taxation During the War*, a first-hand account of the taxation methods of 1914–19.

'Stampa, La', Italian newspaper, founded in 1868 and published in Turin. An independent morning newspaper, there is an evening edition also, *Stampa Sera*. Circulating throughout Italy, *La Stampa* is one of the country's most respected newspapers. It is controlled by Gianni Agnelli, head of the Fiat company.

Stand, see WHITEFIELD.

Standard, the uppermost and largest of the five petals composing the irregular corolla of papilionaceous flowers, such as the sweet pea. It overhangs the lateral wings and the 'keel'. In horticulture a standard tree or shrub is one grown on a single upright stem.

Standard, Royal, popular name of the British sovereign's armorial banner. The earliest royal banner bore only three lions passant. In 1340 these arms were quartered with those of France on account of Edward III's claim to the French crown. These were afterwards removed, and those of Ireland were introduced in 1603. The lion rampant within a tressure represents Scotland. From the time of George I until the accession of Victoria, the Royal Standard also bore the arms of Hanover. Since that time it has remained in its present form. See HERALDRY, *Royal Arms*.

The term standard is correctly applied to a long tapering flag used primarily for the display of the BADGE.

Standard Cell, see CELL, VOLTAIC.

Standard Chartered Bank Limited was founded in 1969 by a merger of The Chartered Bank (incorporated in England by royal charter 1853) and The Standard Bank Limited (established 1862). The Head Office is at 10 Clements Lane, London EC4. The Standard Chartered Bank with its branches, subsidiaries, and associated companies has more than 1500 offices in over 60 countries. See also BANKS AND BANKING.

Standard Deviation, see STATISTICS, *Standard Deviation and other Measures of Dispersion*.

Standard Hill, in North YORKSHIRE, England, near NORTHALLERTON, was the scene of the battle of the Standard, fought in 1138 between DAVID I of Scotland and the northern barons, which resulted in David's defeat. The English fought under the banners of several saints, fastened on a pole, with a cross above; hence the name of the battle.

Standard of Living, a term used to indicate the amount of goods and services (utilities) enjoyed by a community or individually by its members. It can be assessed by investigating or measuring the kinds of, and expenditure on, food, housing, clothing, and other necessities or amenities in any section of the community. The results of such inquiries may be measured against certain 'desirable' or 'minimum' standards in order to assess the adequacy of an existing standard of living, or the results of successive inquiries may be compared in order to assess the changes in the standard of living over a period of time. The results may also be used for the purpose of comparing the standard of living of different countries. International differences in standards of living result from differences in national income, and tend to increase because the accumulation of capital can take place more quickly in countries which already have a certain amount. There can also be differences in the standard of living of people in the same country, due to unequal distribution of the national income. See also COST OF LIVING; PRICE.

Standard Solutions, solutions the concentration of which is known; now expressed as the number of moles of a substance dissolved in 1 litre of solvent (see MOLAR SOLUTION). Standard solutions were formerly expressed in terms of normal solutions. For example, in normal, semi-normal, and decinormal solutions 1 litre of the solution contains 1 gram-equivalent, ½ gram-equivalent, $^1/_{10}$ gram-equivalent, respectively, of the dissolved substance.

Standard Temperature and Pressure are 273·15 K (0 °C) and 101,325 Pa (760 mm Hg), respectively. An earlier term was normal temperature and pressure.

Standard Time, see TIME.

Standard Weights and Measures, see METROLOGY.

Standardisation. Attempts at standardising tokens of value, weights, and measures occurred early in the history of civilisation. The Romans had standardised measures of weight. In the 13th century it was enacted that three barley corns = 1 in, 12 in = 1 ft, 3 ft = 1 ell. Most of such standards came about through a more or less unconscious evolutionary process based on common use and have survived through the centuries. With the introduction of the craft guilds in the Middle Ages, standards of workmanship and the development of technique were taken care of by the guilds, and the marking system (or guild marks) then adopted brought great credit to British workmanship and commerce; in some cases these guild marks have continued to the present day. To meet modern needs, standards of measurement have been set up in other fields—units of temperature, electricity frequencies, atomic weights, etc.

The remarkable expansion of production during the latter half of the 19th century in Great Britain in particular, allied with increasing ease of communication bringing the products of many manufacturers to the consumers, drew attention to the need of simplification and standardisation in order to reduce an unnecessary multiplicity of sizes and ranges, to permit assessment of fitness for purpose, to provide a uniform basis of comparison, to define in uniform terms the correct applications, and to secure accuracy of descriptions. Sir Joseph Whitworth, the inventor of the screw thread bearing his name and of precision machine tools, was the first to advocate standardisation to secure interchangeability, and Great Britain was the first country to put standardisation on an organised basis when, in 1901, the Institutions of Electri-

cal, Mechanical and Civil Engineers, the Iron and Steel Institute, and the Institution of Naval Architects set up a joint committee from which has developed the present BRITISH STANDARDS INSTITUTION (BSI). Standards organisations exist in 76 countries. The International Organisation for Standardisation integrates the vast amount of work undertaken by member countries in order to achieve unification of national standards. The BSI holds the secretariat of many international committees dealing with subjects as varied as steel, aircraft, solid mineral fuels, textiles, and blood-transfusion equipment.

The modern system for all scientific measurement is based on SI units (*Système Internationale d'Unités*). See METROLOGY; PHYSICAL UNITS.

Standardisation, International Organisation for, see STANDARDISATION.

Standards Institution, British, see BRITISH STANDARDS INSTITUTION.

Standing Orders, are, in Britain, the printed rules for regulating the proceedings of both Houses of Parliament, which, unless repealed, remain in force from parliament to parliament. They may be supplemented from time to time by sessional or temporary orders and resolutions. The standing orders which relate to the public business of the House of Commons are by no means a complete code of procedure but require to be more informally supplemented by unwritten precedents, general practice, and specific rulings from the Speaker. No special procedure is involved in the making, suspending, or repeal of a standing order except that adequate notice must normally be given. The majority of the standing orders date from the early 19th century and have been frequently amended since. In the House of Lords the public business standing orders, unlike those in the Commons, exist in the main to declare practice; some modify practice but rarely with the intent of accelerating business as in the Commons. In addition to the public business standing orders each House has elaborate standing orders for the regulation of private bill procedure.

See also HOUSE OF COMMONS; HOUSE OF LORDS; LOCUS STANDI; PARLIAMENT.

Bibliography: T. Erskine May, *Parliamentary Practice*, 19th ed. 1976.

Standing Stones, see GREAT BRITAIN, *Archaeology*; HENGE MONUMENTS; IRELAND, *Archaeology*; MENHIR; MEGALITHIC MONUMENTS; MONOLITH; PREHISTORY; STONE AGE; STONE CIRCLES.

Standish, Myles (c. 1584–1656), American colonist, born in Lancashire, England; died at Duxbury, Massachusetts. He served under the Veres in the Netherlands before 1603, but in 1609 settled at Leyden, from which place he embarked in 1620 for New Plymouth in the *Mayflower*. He was chosen military captain of the colony in 1621, and defended it against the attacks of the Indians, notably at Weymouth, 1623, when he defeated the Indians and broke up their hostile league. His exploits are celebrated in fictional form by Longfellow in the *Courtship of Miles Standish*, and by Lowell in an *Interview with Miles Standish*.

Stanehive, see STONEHAVEN.

Stanfield, William Clarkson

Stanfield, William Clarkson (1793–1867), British marine painter, born at Sunderland. After early experience in the merchant service and navy, he became a theatrical scene painter and friend of David ROBERTS. He was later popular for his pictures of sea and coast, and became known as 'The English van de Velde'. He was made an RA in 1835. William IV commissioned him to paint *The Opening of New London Bridge, 1831*.

Bibliography: C. Wood *Dictionary of 19th century Painters*, 1971; J. Maas, *Victorian Painters*, 1973.

Stanford, Sir Charles Villiers (1852–1924), composer and music teacher, born in Dublin; educated at Cambridge, and studied music at Leipzig and Berlin. Organist of Trinity College, Cambridge, and conductor of Cambridge University Musical Society (1872–93) and of the Leeds Festival (1901–10). He was appointed professor of composition at the Royal College of Music from its opening in 1883, and of music at Cambridge University, 1887, holding both posts till his death. He was knighted in 1901. He was perhaps more influential as a teacher than as a composer. His very numerous compositions include eight published operas, of which the best are *The Canterbury Pilgrims*, 1884, *Shamus O'Brien*, 1896, *Much Ado About Nothing*, 1901, *The Critic*, 1916, and *The Travelling Companion*, produced 1925; incidental and church music; many choral works, including *The Revenge, Phaudrig Crohoore, Songs of the Sea, Stabat Mater*; seven symphonies and five *Irish Rhapsodies* for orchestra; concertos for piano, violin, cello and clarinet; eight string quartets and other chamber music; sonatas; piano pieces; and about 150 songs. He published an autobiography, *Pages from an unwritten diary*, 1914.

Bibliography: Life by H. P. Greene, 1935.

Stanford University, coeducational, nonsectarian, privately owned university at Stanford, California, USA, near San Francisco, with branch undergraduate campuses in Italy, France, Austria, and England, and a marine station at Pacific Grove, California. It was founded in 1885 in memory of their son by Mr and Mrs Leland Stanford; he was a governor of California and a builder of the first transcontinental US railroad. In its libraries are more than 4 million volumes. There are seven schools—business, earth sciences, education, engineering, humanities and sciences, law, and medicine—and among 27 special institutes are the Hoover Institution on War, Revolution, and Peace and the Stanford Linear Accelerator Center. In 1976 there were approximately 11,500 students, 6500 undergraduates and 5000 graduates, from the 50 states of the union and some 70 foreign countries. Competition for admission is highly competitive; approximately half of undergraduates and nearly all graduates receive financial aid. Of the 1100 faculty members, seven are Nobel Laureates and 60 are members of the National Academy of Sciences. The market value of endowment was $364 million in 1975. Outer areas of the 3500-hectare campus in the Santa Clara Valley include a biological preserve, space exploration antennae, faculty homes, agricultural uses, and light industry. The original academic buildings were conceived by Frederick Law Olmsted.

Stanhope, Charles Stanhope, 3rd Earl (1753–1816), British politician and scientist, born in London and educated at Eton and Geneva. He entered Parliament in 1780, and advocated the cessation of the American war and parliamentary reform. He also opposed the Fox-North coalition, and attacked Pitt's proposals for a sinking fund. He succeeded to the peerage in 1786 and became chairman of the 'Revolution Society' in 1788, openly avowing his republican sentiments. Among his many inventions were printing instruments and processes, a microscope lens, calculating machines, and steam vessels. He was interested in canals and published many scientific works on subjects as varied as electricity and musical tones.

Stanhope, Lady Hester Lucy (1776–1839), traveller, daughter of Charles, 3rd Earl of Stanhope. She was housekeeper and trusted confidante of her uncle, William Pitt (1803–06), but after his death and the deaths of her brother and Sir John Moore, with whom she was in love, she left England and went on a pilgrimage to Jerusalem. She lived in a villa near Sidon, among the DRUSE tribe, from 1813 until her death. Her memoirs were published in 1845, edited by C. L. Meryon, and her life and correspondence in 1913, edited by the Duchess of Cleveland.

Stanhope, James Stanhope, 1st Earl (1673–1721), English soldier, born in Paris. Educated at Eton and Trinity College, Oxford, he served first under the Duke of Savoy, and then under William III, in Flanders, in the war against France. He was returned to Parliament in 1702, and was an MP until his elevation to the peerage. He distinguished himself in the campaign in Spain, and in 1707 was made major-general, and in 1708 appointed commander-in-chief of the British forces in Spain. He captured Port Mahon, but was defeated and captured by the French in 1710 at Brihuega. In 1714 he was appointed

Lady Hester Stanhope. *(Mansell Collection)*

Konstantin Stanislavsky with Bernard Shaw in 1931. *(Novosti Press Agency)*

one of the two principal secretaries of state. In July 1717 Stanhope was created Baron Stanhope of Elvaston, and Viscount Stanhope of Mahon in the island of Minorca, and a few weeks later Earl Stanhope.

Bibliography: B. Williams, *Stanhope*, 1932.

Stanhope, Philip Dormer, see CHESTERFIELD, PHILIP DORMER STANHOPE, 4TH EARL OF.

Stanhope Medal, gold medal, instituted in 1873, which is awarded annually by the general court of the ROYAL HUMANE SOCIETY, on the recommendation of its committee, for the outstanding example of gallantry during the year. The award originated in a memorial fund raised to commemorate the services of Captain Chandos Scudamore Stanhope, RN.

Stanislas I Leszczyński, see POLAND, *Modern History.*

Stanislav, see IVANO-FRANKOVSK.

Stanislavsky, Konstantin Sergeevich (1865–1938), Russian actor, producer and teacher. He began his career as an amateur, and by constant study, partly under the elder Kommissarzhevsky, became one of the most versatile actors his country has ever produced. He played in every form of drama, and even prepared for Opera. With NEMIROVICH-DANCHENKO he founded the Moscow Art Theatre and opened a new era in dramatic production and acting. His method was seemingly natural acting as opposed to declamation. He produced many plays by Chekhov and Gorky, and was himself a splendid character actor. He published *An Actor Prepares* (trans. E. Hapgood), 1948.

Stanley, see DERBY, EARLS OF.

Stanley, Arthur Penrhyn (1815–81), British churchman and theologian, born at Alderley, Cheshire. He was educated at Rugby, under Arnold, and at Balliol College, Oxford, and in 1838 was elected a fellow of University College and took orders. In 1856 he was professor of ecclesiastical history and canon of Christ Church, and in 1864 dean of Westminster. He travelled in Palestine and Egypt (1852–53), in Russia (1857 and 1874), accompanied the Prince of Wales on an eastern tour (1862), and visited America (1878). Stanley was well known for his broad church views. He wrote *Life of Arnold*, 1844, *Sermons on the Apostolical Age*, 1847, *Bishop Stanley*, 1851, *Memorials of Canterbury*, 1854, *Sinai and Palestine*, 1856, *Lectures on the Jewish Church*, 1863–76, *Memorials of Westminster Abbey*, 1868, and *Essays on Church and State*, 1870.

Bibliography: R. E. Prothero and G. G. Bradley, *Life and Correspondence*, 1893; H. Bolitho (Ed.), *A Victorian Dean*, 1930.

Stanley, Sir Henry Morton (1841–1904), assumed name of John Rowlands, explorer and author, born in Denbigh, North Wales. At the age of 15 he went to New Orleans, USA, where he met the benefactor whose name he took in preference to that of his natural father's, and in 1861 entered the Confederate army. The years 1863 and 1864 were spent in voyages to the West Indies, Italy, and Spain, and in 1867 he was appointed correspondent for the *New York Herald*, and accompanied Lord NAPIER's Abyssinian expedition. He next visited Spain, the Suez Canal, Palestine, Turkey, Persia, and India, and was sent to find David LIVINGSTONE, reaching Zanzibar in 1871. He came upon him at Ujiji, greeting him with the famous words, 'Dr Livingstone, I presume!' and together they explored the north end of Lake Tanganyika. In 1872 he published *How I found Livingstone*, and in 1874 set off on another expedition, circumnavigated Lake Victoria, passed down the Lualaba to its confluence with the Congo (Zaire) and then traced the course of that river to the sea. Having published *Through the Dark Continent*, 1878, he in 1879 again set out and founded the Congo Free State. He took part in the expedition for the relief of Emin Pasha, governor of the Equatorial Province, Egypt, and met Emin on the shores of Lake Albert. Stanley married Dorothy Tennant in 1890, and was a Liberal Unionist MP between 1895 and 1900 after reassuming his British citizenship. Among other works of his are *The Congo*, 1885; *In Darkest Africa, or The Rescue of Emin*, 1890; and *My Early Travels in America and Asia*, 1895.

Bibliography: Dorothy Stanley (Ed.), *The Autobiography of Henry Morton Stanley*, 1909; F. Hird, *H. M. Stanley: the Authorized Life*, 1935; I. Anstruther, *I Presume*, 1956; B. Farwell, *The Man Who Presumed*, 1957; N. R. Bennett (Ed.), *Stanley's Despatches to the New York Herald 1871–72, 1874–77*, 1970; D. Wilcox, *Explorers*, 1975.

Stanley, John (1713–86), English organist and composer, born in London. He was blind from the age of two, but became a pupil of Maurice Greene, and was later organist at various London churches. In 1779 he succeeded BOYCE as Master of the King's Music. His works included cantatas, songs, six concertos for strings, flute sonatas and organ voluntaries.

Stanley, Wendell Meredith (1904–), US biochemist, who held posts at several American universities. He worked on enzymes and virus proteins, sharing the 1946 Nobel Prize for chemistry.

Stanley, industrial town in County DURHAM, England, 11 km south-west of Newcastle. It has coal-mines, roller-bearing factories, and women's and children's clothing factories. Population (1971) 41,940.

Stanley, village in Derbyshire, England, 8 km north-east of Derby. It has coal-mines.

Stanley, Port, capital of the FALKLAND ISLANDS. It has a memorial commemorating the victory of Admiral Sturdee over von Spee's squadron on 8 December 1914. Port Stanley is the only important settlement of the colony, and is situated on the coast of East Falkland. There is a good harbour and a wireless station. Population (1972) 1081.

Stanleyville, see KISANGANI.

Stanmore, see HARROW.

Stannaries (Latin *stannum*, tin), the Court of the Stannaries of Cornwall and Devon was a court of record (see RECORD, COURT OF), with a special jurisdiction for the administration of justice among the tinners of those counties. The judge of the court was called the vice-warden. The jurisdiction rested on an ancient privilege confirmed by royal charter in 1305, granted to the tin miners to sue and be sued in their own court so as to avoid being drawn from their business to the public detriment. All tinners and labourers in and about the stannaries (a compendious term denoting primarily the tin mines, but also the tinners, and the customs and privileges attached to the mines) during the time of their working in the mines might sue and be sued in this court in all matters arising within the stannaries, excepting real property cases and capital charges. An appeal lay formerly to the lord warden and legal assessors, with a final appeal to the Judicial Committee of the Privy Council, but this appellate jurisdiction was transferred to the Court of Appeal in 1875. The jurisdiction of the court, abolished in 1897, is now exercised by the COUNTY COURTS.

Stannic Acid, see TIN.

Stans, capital of Nidwalden (the eastern demi-canton of UNTERWALDEN), Switzerland, situated to the south-east of Lucerne. Noted as the home of WINKELRIED and for its *Landsgemeinde* (open-air cantonal elections). Mainly a tourist centre in a fruit-growing area. Population (1974) 5800.

Stansfield, Grace, see FIELDS, GRACIE.

Stansted, see LONDON AIRPORT.

Stanton, Elizabeth Cady (1815–1902), US feminist, born at Johnstown, New York. A convention in support of the movement towards securing women's suffrage was held at Seneca Falls in June 1848, and from this resulted Mrs Stanton's Women's Bill of Rights. From 1869 to 1890 she was president of the National American Woman Suffrage Association. She contributed to *The History of Woman Suffrage*, 1887–1902. Her reminiscences, *Eighty Years and More*, were published in 1898; reprinted 1972.

Stanton Drew, village in Avon, England, 10 km south of Bristol. It has a Norman bridge, an old toll house at the approach to the village, and a prehistoric stone circle nearby. There is trout-fishing in the River Chew. Population (1971) 673.

Stanyhurst, Richard (1547–1618), Irish scholar, historian, and poet, born in Dublin. His historical writings include *De vita S. Patricii Hyberniae Apostoli*, 1587, but he is chiefly remembered for his translation of the first four books of Virgil's *Aeneid*, written in quantitative metre and published in Leyden, 1582.

Stanza, in prosody, Italian term meaning a collection of lines arranged in an ordered pattern connected by metre and rhyme to form a regular division of 'verse' of a poem. Among various special forms are the Alcaic stanza and Spenserian stanza.

Staphylea, a genus of 10 hardy deciduous shrubs in family Staphyleaceae, of northern temperate regions. *S. colchica*, from the Caucasus, *S. holocarpa*, from China, and *S. pinnata*, the bladder nut of Asia Minor, are grown in British gardens for their panicles of white flowers and bladder-like fruits.

Staphyloma, a bulging outward of part of the globe of the eye. Anterior staphyloma is a bulging forward of the cornea and sclera (probably caused by a perforating corneal ulcer). Posterior staphyloma is protrusion backward of the sclera at the posterior pole, usually accompanied by inflammation of the choroid (choroiditis), which is the middle or vascular coat of the eyeball.

Staple (Old French *estape*, mart or market-place for wines), once written *estaple*. The term was used to denote those towns called 'staple towns', both in England and in Europe, where the principal products or 'staple commodities' of a country were sold. Instances of important staple towns were London, Calais, Antwerp, Bruges, Canterbury, Newcastle, Bristol, Norwich, Chichester, Carmarthen, Cork, and York. Wool was the product most commonly involved. All merchandise sold for the purpose of export was compelled either to be sold at the staple or afterwards brought there for export. Afterwards the word 'staple' came to be applied to the merchandise itself which was sold at the staple town.

In England the merchants of the staple reached the zenith of their power under Edward II. They had their own court, 'the Court of the Mayor of the Staple', which was of considerable antiquity. Most of the enactments relative to the staple were passed during the reigns of Edward I and II. One object of the Statute of Acton Burnell (see ACTON BURNELL, STATUTE OF), which was passed in 1283, was to remove the staple previously held at Calais to various towns in England, Wales, and Ireland. In 1328 the staple was abolished, though removed by Edward III. In 1353, by the Ordinance of the Staple (see CUSTOMS AND EXCISE DUTIES) the staple was regulated and the privileges of the staple merchants confirmed. The staple declined with the decline of the export of wool and the rise in that of English cloth. It finally disappeared in 1617 when export of English wool was prohibited.

Bibliography: E. E. Power, *The Wool Trade in English Medieval History*, 1941.

Staple Howe, one of the earliest British Iron Age defended settlements to be excavated (6th to 5th centuries BC), situated 12 km east of Malton, Yorkshire. It has an oval palisade on top of a chalk hillock surrounding two or more huts and a granary or watchtower.

Bibliography: T. C. M. Brewster, *The Excavation of Staple Howe*, 1963.

Stapledon, Sir George (1882–1960), British agricultural expert, educated at Westward Ho! and Emmanuel College, Cambridge. He was professor of Agriculture, Aberystwyth, 1919; director of grassland improvement station, Stratford, 1948. He deeply influenced British agriculture by breeding improved strains of grasses and encouraging the use of leys or sown pastures.

Stapledon, William Olaf (1886–1950), English novelist, born near Liverpool; educated at Abbotsholme School and Oxford. He was for a time a schoolmaster and later on the staff of Liverpool University. His successful *Last and First Men*, 1931, an imaginative story of the earth through future aeons, was followed by *Last Men in London*, 1931, *Waking World*, 1934, *Star Maker*, 1937, and *Worlds of Wonder*, 1949.

Stapleford, see BEESTON AND STAPLEFORD.

Stapleton, Walter de (1261–1326), English bishop, born at Annery, Devonshire, and educated at Oxford, becoming professor of canon law. In 1307 he became bishop of Exeter. He was a member of the Privy Council in the reign of Edward II, and undertook several diplomatic missions to France and elsewhere. With his brother he founded Stapleton Hall at Oxford, now Exeter College. Stapleton was murdered by a mob as a confidant of Edward II.

Stapulensis, Jacob, see FABER, JACOBUS.

Star, a celestial body akin in nature to the SUN. This entry is confined to speculations about the constitution and evolution of a star; relevant observations are given in the entry on STARS.

Stars are believed to originate in cool interstellar clouds as the result of chance density fluctuations. These clouds consist mainly of hydrogen and helium but with traces of other elements and a sprinkling of dust grains. A star begins its independent existence as a huge tenuous volume of this INTERSTELLAR MATTER gradually separating from the parent cloud. As it contracts gravitational energy is released in the form of heat, very slowly at first but at an ever increasing rate as the star-to-be grows smaller and denser. At first its temperature scarcely rises since the dust grains are able to radiate away much of the heat as it is produced; the star has begun to shine, feebly at first and then more strongly, as an infrared source.

As the star grows denser a smaller proportion of the heat generated can escape into space and its material gradually warms up. The grains are first vaporised and then later, as the temperature rises still higher, its atoms, along with those of the former interstellar gas, are completely ionised. The star has become a sphere of 'perfect' gas consisting of a neutral mixture of free electrons and bare atomic nuclei. Its further development is a problem that was first treated mathematically by Lane just over a hundred years ago. Lane showed that in a state of quasi-equilibrium in which the inward gravitational pull was everywhere just balanced by the outwards gas pressure, the temperature in the centre would be proportional to M/R, where M is the mass of the gas sphere and R its

radius. The star would, however, be contracting very slowly so as to release just sufficient gravitational energy to replace that being radiated away from the surface. As it contracted, its central temperature would automatically become higher so that its ultimate fate would be to become a very small, exceedingly dense and hot star in which the material no longer behaved like a perfect gas.

For a sphere with the mass and radius of the Sun, this simple theory implies a central temperature of about 24,000,000 K; but such a sphere could maintain the Sun's present power output without appreciable change for a few tens of millions of years only. It was this fact that showed that the simple theory of gravitational contraction was inadequate, for terrestrial fossil evidence makes it seem certain that the Sun has been shining at very much its present strength for well over a thousand million years. Nevertheless, gravitational contraction provides the underlying mechanism of stellar evolution. The principal modern addition to it is the realisation that as soon as the central temperature and density reach the point at which nuclear transformations can take place, enough energy is produced by the transformation of hydrogen into helium to replace that being lost at the surface. The star has therefore no need to contract further until its internal sources of nuclear energy are exhausted.

Until this begins to happen the star remains practically unaltered for a long period of time and its representative point on the H-R diagram remains on or near the main sequence. Where about the star is on the main sequence, how long it takes to contract before it gets there, and how long it remains there, are all determined by the mass of the star; the larger the mass, the shorter these periods and the brighter the star. A star with the mass of the Sun takes a few million years to reach the main sequence, and then remains on it for about ten thousand million years, twice the present age of the Sun. A star a hundred times more massive than the Sun will remain on the main sequence for only a million years, while one a tenth as massive will remain there for a million million years, i.e., longer than the age of the GALAXY.

The nuclear transformations take place near the centre so the star gradually acquires an inert helium core (itself subject to gravitational contraction) surrounded by a thin shell of burning hydrogen. As the core grows the outer layers have to adjust themselves to maintain the mechanical and thermal equilibrium of the star. The star expands, becomes a yellow giant, and consumes its store of nuclear energy ever more quickly. What happens further depends on the mass of the star. If this is less than 1·2 that of the Sun, the core becomes degenerate and the star, having shed its outer layers, becomes a white dwarf (see ASTRONOMY; SIRIUS). If the mass exceeds this Chandrasekhar's limit, the core cannot become degenerate and the further development of the star is more catastrophic. As the core grows increasingly hot other nuclear transformations take place resulting in the helium being converted first into carbon and oxygen and then with them successively into heavier elements until iron, the most stable of all, is reached. Finally there is a supernova (see NOVAE) outburst that may leave behind it a pulsar (see PULSARS) which appears to be a rapidly rotating *neutron star*. But there is also a mass limit for neutron stars; if the central remnant that is left after the supernova explosion has a mass more than twice that of the Sun it cannot collapse into the neutron star state but would have to form a BLACK HOLE.

In a white dwarf the 'gas' formed by the electrons is degenerate, i.e., the electrons are packed together as tightly as they can go so that the ordinary gas laws no longer apply. The atomic ions, mainly protons and alpha particles are, however, still free to move around as a gas. Chandrasekhar was the first to show that the state of a star composed of such material is uniquely determined by its mass, that the higher this mass the smaller the radius which becomes zero for masses of about 1·2 that of the Sun. For masses greater than this, the greater pressure results, as it were, in the electrons and protons being squeezed together to form neutrons. The resulting neutron stars would be only a few tens of kilometres in diameter, far smaller and denser than the white dwarfs.

The possibility of such stars had been pointed out by the Soviet scientist Landau in 1932 but the idea remained dormant until the discovery of the pulsars demonstrated that such stars might really exist. This recognition helped to revive another old idea, that of bodies so massive and dense that the velocity of escape from their surface exceeds that of light. As Laplace pointed out in 1798, such a mass would not be visible from the outside and can rightly be called a black hole.

There is no limit to the mass that a black hole can have provided that its radius is less than the SCHWARZSCHILD limit of $2GM/c^2$, where M is its mass, G the constant of gravitation, and c the velocity of light. For one solar mass the critical radius is 3 km. As a mass in contracting to the critical limit releases an immense amount of energy, black holes have been tentatively suggested as a possible explanation of various high energy processes which are not yet understood, e.g., in QUASARS or in X-ray sources such as Cygnus X-1. Since the mass in a black hole retains its gravitational properties it may be possible to locate the 'ghost' of a former star that has evolved into a black hole by examining spectroscopic binaries for one in which the mass inferred for the invisible companion exceeds twice the solar mass. A systematic search of the appropriate standard catalogue has, however, failed to reveal even one promising case.

Bibliography: M. Schwarzschild, *Structure and Evolution of the Stars*, new ed. 1966; L. H. Aller, *Atoms, Stars and Nebulae*, 1971.

'Star, The', see 'EVENING NEWS'.

Star apple, see CHRYSOPHYLLUM CAINITO.

Star Carr, one of the most important Mesolithic sites in Europe, situated 8 km south-east of Scarborough, Yorkshire. An occupation site of a hunting family, it has provided much evidence of the economy, lifestyles and natural habitat of its inhabitants. Red deer accounted for most of the meat diet, followed by roe deer, elk, wild ox and wild pig. The site may have been occupied on a seasonal basis, and its lakeside location used for fishing, the number of bone harpoons providing ample evidence for this.

Bibliography: J. G. Clark, *Star Carr*, 1954.

Star Chamber, English high court of justice going back at least as far as Edward III's reign, when jurisdiction was exercised in the *Chambre des estoiles*, Westminster, the name being derived, perhaps, from a starry decoration on the ceiling. It originated in the civil and criminal jurisdiction of the Privy Council and was in fact identical with the king's council (see CURIA REGIS) acting in its judicial capacity. After the establishment of the Court of Chancery this jurisdiction declined, but was revived on account of the lawlessness and corruption of juries which followed the Wars of the Roses. In 1487 the Statute 3 Henry VII, c. 1, constituted a committee of the council, a court with considerable judicial powers, for the purpose of suppressing the evils arising from seditious assemblies and from LIVERY AND MAINTENANCE. The members of the court were the lord chancellor, lord treasurer, keeper of the privy seal, a bishop, a lord of the council, and the two chief justices. Under Edward VI the Star Chamber was still a committee of the council, but by the end of Elizabeth I's reign it had become a judicial body distinct from the latter; but it had ceased to remedy the uncertainties and inadequacy of the common law, and under the Stuarts it became merely an instrument for enforcing the claims of the prerogative. The procedure of the court consisted in summoning the accused to appear and then examining him on oath. The court imposed punishments of mutilation and whipping, and used torture to extract evidence or confessions. The court developed the offences of criminal libel and perjury. Its abolition in 1641 deprived the Crown of a formidable weapon for the suppression of free speech and writing and for the enforcement of proclamations which the king had no right to make.

Bibliography: G. R. Y. Radcliffe and Lord Cross, *The English Legal System*, 5th ed. 1971.

Star Clusters are groups of stars which are close together in space, share a common motion, and have a common origin. They may contain very many stars or only a few; their star densities may be as high as 1000 per cubic parsec or less than 1 per 100 cubic parsecs. In the former case their mutual gravitation may be expected to hold the cluster stars together almost indefinitely while in

Star Clusters. Figure 1. Schematic colour (B-V)—apparent magnitude (m) diagram for four clusters of different ages.

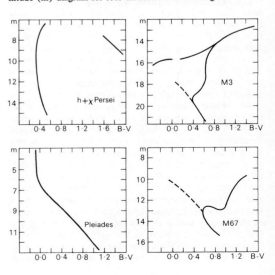

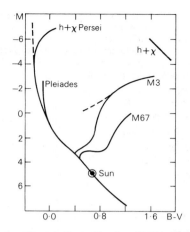

Star Clusters. Figure 2. Composite colour (B-V)—absolute magnitude (M) diagram formed by superimposing the common sections of the four curves in figure 1. This diagram shows how stars evolve away from the 'main sequence' with time.

the latter what few stars there are will quickly dissipate into the general star field. As all the members of a star cluster are at approximately the same distance, the observed relation between their colours and apparent magnitudes (fig. 1) is essentially that between their colours and absolute magnitudes (fig. 2) which can be compared directly with the appropriate portion of the Hertzsprung-Russell diagram to give a measure of the cluster's distance. Differences in the shape of this relationship from cluster to cluster provide a clue to the way in which stars evolve and a method of determining a cluster's age.

The more conspicuous clusters were originally catalogued with the NEBULAE, and are usually known by their number in their Messier or NGC catalogues. A few of the naked-eye clusters like the PLEIADES, HYADES, and PRAESEPE are also known by their traditional names. A comprehensive catalogue of clusters and their associated bibliographies has been prepared by Czechoslovak astronomers. It is printed on loose cards so that extra entries can be easily added and follows the usual practice of dividing the clusters into globular, open, and associations.

The Globular Clusters are the most striking objects in the galactic halo, i.e., away from the Milky Way. About 120 are known, and, allowing for distance, are all rather similar in appearance. They are very nearly spherically symmetrical, and contain an immense number of stars which are concentrated towards the centre where they are so close together that it is impossible to resolve them completely into individual stars even in the biggest telescopes. Their brightest stars are red, and there are usually RR Lyrae VARIABLE STARS from which the distances of the clusters can be estimated. These distances range from 10,000 to 200,000 light years, and it is possible that some of the more distant ones are not really members of our Galaxy but 'inter-galactic tramps'. The diameters of the clusters range from 60 to 300 light years with the number of stars in a cluster varying from about 10,000 to 100,000, their integrated light giving an absolute magnitude in the

range −5 to −9. The colour-magnitude curves indicate that they are very old objects, possibly of the order of 10,000 million years.

The Open Clusters, of which the Pleiades, Hyades, and Praesepe may be taken as typical, are very much smaller than the globulars; they contain very many fewer stars which are more widely scattered, and show little or no concentration towards their own centre. They are relatively young objects and are found in the disk of the Galaxy, i.e., along the Milky Way. About 1000 of them have been identified, but there must be very many times this number hidden by dust clouds or indistinguishable against the rich stellar background. The number of stars in an open cluster varies from a few dozen to over a thousand but on the average they contain a few hundred stars scattered through a volume rather less than 30 light years in diameter. The brightest stars are blue or red depending on the cluster's age; some of the youngest which are usually found immersed in nebulosity contain bright blue supergiant stars which make their integrated absolute magnitude as bright as −10, considerably brighter than that of the brightest globular. On the other hand the integrated absolute magnitude of some of the open clusters can be as faint as 0.

Associations can be regarded as very extended open clusters with few members; as such they must have been recently formed for otherwise they would already have dispersed. Two kinds are recognised though they may co-exist as in Orion. These are the O-associations containing O and B type stars and the T-associations whose members are T Tauri stars which are red eruptive variable stars newly formed from the surrounding interstellar matter. About 100 associations have been recognised in the spiral arms of the Galaxy but there must be many more hidden from view. A typical O-association contains up to 50 O and B type stars scattered irregularly through a volume of space from 100 to 600 light years in diameter. One of the best known associations is that centred on a group of stars in the middle of the Orion nebula.

Star Clusters. The open cluster M67. *(Hale Observatories)*

Star, Delta

Star, Delta, different methods of connecting three-phase circuit elements, as shown in fig. 1 (star) and fig. 2 (delta). For the star (or Tee) connection, the six ends of the three-phase windings of machines (alternator, motor, or transformer) are connected such that three ends form the line terminals, and the other three are joined together to form the star point or neutral point (N.P. in fig. 1). A balanced three-phase system is one in which the three voltages (and currents) have the same peak value, and which are 120° apart in time phase. For a star-connection, the current at the neutral point for a balanced system is zero, and a fourth wire (neutral) is not necessary. In distribution systems, a fourth wire is usually provided. If the voltage *OA* of phase *A* is taken as the reference phasor,

$$OA = \hat{E}\sin\omega t; \text{ then}$$
$$OB = \hat{E}\sin(\omega t - 120°) \text{ and}$$
$$OC = \hat{E}\sin(\omega t - 240°).$$

The line voltage *AB* is the vector difference of *AO* and *OB* or

$$\hat{E}\sin\omega t - \hat{E}\sin(\omega t - 120°)$$
$$= \hat{E}\{\sin\omega t - \sin\omega t \cos 120° + \cos\omega t \sin 120°\}$$
$$= \hat{E}\{\sin\omega t + \tfrac{1}{2}\sin\omega t + (\tfrac{1}{2}\sqrt{3})\cos\omega t\}$$
$$= \sqrt{3}\hat{E}\sin(\omega t + 30°).$$

This shows that the line voltage is $\sqrt{3}$ times the phase voltage. The line current is equal to the phase current. For the delta- (or pi-) connection, the phase windings are connected in series in a mesh, and there is no neutral point. For balanced sinusoidal voltages, the vector sum of the phase voltages *OA*, *OB*, and *OC* is zero, and there is no voltage to produce any circulating current. In this case the line voltage is equal to the phase voltage, and the line current is $\sqrt{3}$ times the phase current. (See also ALTERNATING CURRENT; THREE-PHASE SYSTEM.)

The primary windings of large power transformers are usually connected in delta, while the secondaries are star-connected, feeding the high-voltage transmission lines and providing a neutral point. Star/star connection is used in small high-voltage transformers. Star/delta starting of induction motors is the initial connection of the stator windings in star so that only the (line voltage of the supply)/$\sqrt{3}$ is applied to the phase, switching over to 'delta' when the motor is running.

For solving electrical network problems, it is sometimes convenient to be able to replace a star-connected circuit by a delta-connected circuit and vice-versa. This can be done using the following equations:

$$R_{AB} = R_A + R_B + R_A R_B / R_C$$
$$R_{BC} = R_B + R_C + R_B R_C / R_A$$
$$R_{CA} = R_C + R_A + R_C R_A / R_B$$

for star into delta and

$$R_A = R_{AB} R_{AC} / R_T$$
$$R_B = R_{AB} R_{BC} / R_T$$
$$R_C = R_{AC} R_{BC} / R_T$$
(where $R_T = R_{AB} + R_{BC} + R_{CA}$)

for delta into star.

'Star of Africa', see CULLINAN DIAMOND.

Star of Bethlehem, see ORNITHOGALUM.

Star of India, see ORDERS OF KNIGHTHOOD, *Great Britain and Ireland (6)*.

Star-spangled Banner, see UNITED STATES OF AMERICA, *Government*.

Star Stone, see SAPPHIRE.

Star-stone, see ASTERIA.

Star Tulip, see CALOCHORTUS.

Stara Zagora, town of central Bulgaria, capital of Stara Zagora province, lying south of the Shipka pass through the BALKAN MOUNTAINS. It was founded by the Romans, and was an important market town under the Turks. It was ceded to Bulgaria in 1877. There are technical schools and a teachers' training college. Textiles, chemicals, tobacco, and foodstuffs are manufactured. The province is noted for its roses. Population (1973) 119,246.

Starboard (Old English *steor*, rudder; *bord*, side) means the right-hand side of a ship as one faces forward; it is so named because it was the side on which the steering oar or steerboard was fixed in primitive vessels. The term 'larboard', now obsolete, meant the opposite or left-hand side facing forward; it may be derived from Old English *laere*, 'empty', signifying the side not occupied by the steerboard and therefore the one used for going alongside for loading, hence 'ladeboard'. Because of confusion caused by similarity of sound between 'starboard' and 'larboard' the latter has been replaced by 'port', the term now in use. At night a green light is carried on the starboard and a red light on the port side of a vessel.

Starch, or amylum $(C_6H_{10}O_5)_n$, carbohydrate, widely disseminated throughout the vegetable world. It occurs in rice and all kinds of grain in quantities up to 70 per cent, and also occurs in tubers, such as potatoes and arrowroot. From these substances it is prepared by macerating (potatoes) or fermenting (grain) and then washing with water. The starch settles from the water as a paste, which is washed by decantation. It forms a white powder which is made up of striated granules, is insoluble in cold water, but swells and gelatinises in hot water, and is coloured blue with iodine. Boiled with dilute acids it is converted

Delta Star.

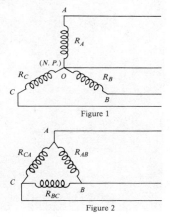

Figure 1

Figure 2

to dextrin and GLUCOSE and heated with diastase it forms dextrin and maltose, which are also formed by the action of saliva and pancreatic juice on starch. In green plants starch is formed from water and atmospheric carbon dioxide by the photosynthetic pigment chlorophyll; the necessary energy is derived from sunlight (see PHOTOSYNTHESIS).

Starch occurs in two forms, α-amylose and amylopectin. α-Amylose consists of long unbranched chains of glucose molecules; the chains vary considerably in size and molecular weight. α-Amylose is not truly soluble in water. Amylopectin consists of a highly branched mass of glucose units, branches occurring every 12th residue. Its molecular weight may be as high as 1 million.

Starch, Animal, see GLYCOGEN.

Starets (Russian, Elder), in the Russian Orthodox Church, a revered monk, spiritual tutor of younger monks. In the 19th century some *startsy* exercised considerable influence on writers and intellectuals, including Dostoevski and Soloviëv (see OPTINA PUSTYN').

Starfish, animals of class Asteroidea in the phylum ECHINODERMATA. They have a star-like shape, the rays of which usually number five; these are movable arms with skeletal structures, consisting of calcareous plates transversely arranged and articulated with one another like vertebrae. The mouth is in the middle of the underside of the central disc. A wide furrow, the ambulacral groove, extends from the mouth to the tip of each arm. These contain the tube feet, which are extensions of the water vascular system involved in locomotion. Movable spines protect these delicate structures. The upper surface bears the anus and the madreporite, a porous structure which allows communication between the water vascular system and the exterior. The precise role of the madreporite, and associated structures such as the stone canal, is poorly understood, but the water vascular system as a whole acts as a hydraulic system during locomotion. Elongation of the tube feet is brought about by forcing water into them. Upon contact with the substratum the

Starfish. The common British starfish, *Asterias rubens. (Barnaby's Picture Library)*

centre of the terminal sucker of the foot is drawn in, causing adhesion by vacuum.

In some starfish, specialised jawed appendages (pedicellariae) are present. These are of several types but all basically function to capture small prey and in defence. Starfish are carnivorous, different species showing marked dietary preferences. *Asterias rubens*, the common British starfish, feeds on bivalve molluscs. The shell is pulled open by pressure applied through the tube feet and the stomach is inserted into the gap, digestion occurring within the molluscan shell. Considerable losses may result in shellfisheries. The eye spots at the tip of each arm are the only specialised sense organs. Starfish show marked regenerative abilities and in some species asexual reproduction by splitting occurs. Most starfish species are dioecious (the animal is either male or female) with the eggs being fertilised outside the female, in the sea. A freeswimming, bipinnaria LARVA develops which settles and metamorphoses to the adult form.

Stargard, town in Poland, in Szczecin province, on the River Ina, 32 km east of Szczecin. Until 1945 it was in POMERANIA. It dates from the 12th century, and was a member of the HANSEATIC LEAGUE. It became part of BRANDENBURG under the Treaty of Westphalia in 1648. Population 46,000.

Starhemberg, Ernst Rudiger, Prince (1899–1956), Austrian politician, born at Eferding. From 1929, as head of the *Heimwehr* (home defence force), he supported the Austrian government, and his name became associated with the savage suppression of the Social Democrats. He was vice-chancellor to Dollfuss and Schuschnigg from 1934 to 1936 and, having broken with the National Socialists, tried to implement a native Austrian brand of fascism. In 1938 he fled to England, and served in the RAF for a short time, and then went to Argentina. He returned to Austria after the Second World War.

Starfish. Sun star, *Crossaster papposus. (Barnaby's Picture Library)*

Staring, Anthony Christiaan Winand

Bibliography: E. R. Starhemberg, *Between Hitler and Mussolini*, 1942.

Staring, Anthony Christiaan Winand (1767–1840), Dutch poet, born at Gendringen. He completed his education at Göttingen University, and became a gentleman farmer in the Gelderland district. His sober style and subtle humour are in marked contrast to the sentimentality and bombast of his contemporaries.

Bibliography: E. Endt, *Keur uit Starings gedichten*, 1955.

Stark, Dame Freya Madeline (1893–), British explorer and writer, educated in Italy, at Bedford College and at the School of Oriental Studies. She worked on the *Baghdad Times* and published *Baghdad Sketches* in 1933. *The Valleys of the Assassins*, 1934, describes journeys in Persia and Luristan. She wrote *The Southern Gates of Arabia*, 1936, after explorations in the HADHRAMAUT. During the Second World War she worked for the Ministry of Information in the Middle East and North America. Other publications include *Seen in the Hadhramaut*, 1938; *A Winter in Arabia*, 1940; *Letters from Syria*, 1942; *East is West*, 1945; *Perseus in the Wind*, 1948; *Ionia*, 1954; *The Lycian Shore*, 1956; *Alexander's Path*, 1958; *Riding to the Tigris*, 1959; *Dust in the Lion's Paw*, 1961; *Journey's Echo*, 1963; *Rome on the Euphrates*, 1966; *Minaret of Djam: An Excursion in Afghanistan*, 1970; *Southern Gates of Arabia*, 1971; *Turkey*, 1971. She was made a DBE in 1972.

Stark Effect, a phenomenon relating to the emission spectra of atoms in an electric field (see SPECTRUM AND SPECTROSCOPE). Atoms that emit light while in a powerful electric field have their spectra changed by the field, and each line of the ordinary spectrum is split into a number of components which may be polarised in various ways. The phenomenon was discovered in 1913 by the German physicist, Johannes Stark (awarded the Nobel prize for physics, 1919), and investigated in detail by him in the following years.

Starling, Ernest Henry (1866–1927), British physiologist, born in Bombay. He studied at Guy's Hospital, London (1882), and became head of the department of physiology. In 1899 he was appointed Jodrell professor of physiology at University College, London, and retired in 1923, having been appointed the first Foulerton research professor of the Royal Society in 1922. At University College he formed a lifelong partnership with Sir W. M. BAYLISS. His investigations covered a wide field, the most important being the secretion of lymph and other body fluids, the discovery of secretin (a hormone of the digestive system) and the laws governing the heart's action. He formulated Starling's law of the heart: the energy of the contraction is a function of the length of the muscle fibres. His many works include *Principles of Human Physiology*, 1912, a standard textbook (11th ed. 1952). He became a Fellow of the Royal Society in 1899 and was awarded its Gold Medal in 1913.

Starling, *Sturnus vulgaris*, a bird of the family Sturnidae, order Passeriformes, common in Europe and Britain. It is about 20 cm long, and the head, neck, back and underparts are a metallic glossy black. The feathers on the upper parts are tipped with buff, and the wings are greyish-black, with a reddish-brown fringe. The female is less glossy and lustrous than the male. Nests are made almost anywhere, and about five pale-blue eggs are laid. The food consists principally of worms, snails and insects, and the birds are therefore beneficial to man, though they often devour orchard fruit, and are sometimes destructive to seed wheat. A number of closely related foreign birds are known as starlings. For the rose-coloured starling see PASTOR.

Star-nosed Mole, see SHREW MOLE.

Stars are self-luminous bodies like the SUN, but so far away that to the naked eye they appear as bright points of light whose positions relative to each other do not alter. To the casual observer they may seem numberless but those visible as separate entities, even on the darkest and clearest of nights, probably do not exceed 3000, though many times this number of fainter stars combine together to give the MILKY WAY its luminous cloud-like appearance. All stars of possible naked-eye visibility are included in the Yale *Bright Star Catalogue* which has just over 9000 entries. At any moment, half of these stars will be below the horizon, and of the others many of the fainter will be reduced to below the limit of visibility by atmospheric extinction which increases quite rapidly towards the horizon.

Table 1 lists the 21 brightest stars in the sky—those known traditionally as 'of the first magnitude'—and also those stars which are known to be closer than 10 light years. The significance of the various columns is explained in detail later; the two most significant are probably those giving the distance expressed in light years (d) and the absolute magnitude (M_v) which measures the star's intrinsic brightness on a logarithmic scale. Two facts stand out clearly: that there is a very big range in the brightness of individual stars; and that intrinsically faint stars are very much more common than brighter ones, at least in our immediate neighbourhood which is the only part of space in which we can observe these fainter stars. It is not possible to give an exact answer to the question which is frequently asked 'How many stars in the Galaxy?'. All that can be said is that the estimated mass of the Galaxy is 200,000 million times that of the Sun. If most of this is condensed into stars, and if the greater number of these are like the stars near the Sun with an average mass of only 0·2 that of the Sun, the number of stars in the Galaxy may well be of the order of a million million.

The successive columns of table 1 give the star's name; its right ascension (RA) and declination ($Dec.$) for AD 2000 which give its position in the sky; its visual magnitude (V); its colour ($B-V$); its distance (d) in light years ($L.Y.$); its proper motion in seconds of arc per year (PM); its radial velocity in kilometres per second (RV); and its absolute visual magnitude (Mv).

Many of the quantities given in table 1 are not known exactly, being subject to 'observational uncertainty' even for the brightest stars. This is particularly true for those distances in excess of 100 light years and of quantities, such as absolute magnitudes, derived from them. Where the individual results may be uncertain, mean values are often reliable. These are given in table 2 for those types of star which are most common in the sky. Successive columns give the type; the absolute visual magnitude (M_v); the colour ($B-V$); the surface temperature (T); the mass expressed in terms of that of the Sun as unit (M);

(a) The brightest stars

Name	RA (2000) (h)	(min)	Dec. (°)	(')	Sp		V	B–V	d l.y.	PM (")	RV (km/s)	M_v
Sun					G2	V	−26·7	+0·63				+4·8
Sirius	06	45	−16	43	A1	V	−1·42	0·00	8·6	1·32	−8	+1·4
Canopus	06	24	−52	41	F0	II	−0·72	+0·16	185	0·02	+21	−4·5
Alpha Centauri	14	40	−60	50	G2	V	−0·28	+0·72	4·3	3·68	−24	+4·7
Arcturus	14	16	+19	11	K2	III	−0·06	+1·24	36	2·28	−5	−0·3
Vega	18	37	+38	47	A0	V	0·00	0·00	26	0·34	−14	+0·5
Capella	05	17	+46	00	G8	III	+0·06	+0·81	32	0·44	+30	+0·1
Rigel	05	15	−08	12	B8	Ia	+0·18	−0·03	680	0·00	+21	−6·4
Procyon	07	39	+05	14	F5	IV	+0·36	+0·42	11	1·25	−3	+2·7
Achernar	01	38	−57	15	B5	IV	+0·48	−0·16	140	0·10	+19	−2·6
Beta Centauri	14	04	−60	22	B1	II	+0·62	−0·24	180	0·04	−11	−3·1
Betelgeuse	05	55	+07	24	M2	Iab	+0·7	+1·86	170	0·03	+21	−2·9
Alpha Crucis	12	27	−63	06	B1		+0·76	−0·25	200	0·04		−3·2
Altair	19	51	+08	52	A7	V	+0·78	+0·22	16	0·66	−26	+2·3
Aldebaran	04	36	+16	30	K5	III	+0·8	+1·55	68	0·20	+54	−0·8
Antares	16	29	−26	26	M1	I	+0·9	+1·83	590	0·03	−3	−5·4
Spica	13	25	−11	09	B1	V	+0·98	−0·23	160	0·05	+1	−2·4
Pollux	07	45	+28	01	K0	III	+1·13	+1·00	35	0·62	+3	+1·0
Fomalhaut	22	58	−29	37	A2	V	+1·16	+0·09	22	0·37	+6	+2·0
Deneb	20	41	+45	16	A2	Ia	+1·25	+0·09	530	0·00	−5	−3·5
Beta Crucis	12	48	−59	42	B0	IV	+1·25	−0·24	290	0·05	+20	−4·8
Regulus	10	08	+11	58	B7	V	+1·35	−0·12	84	0·25	+4	−0·7

(b) The nearest stars

Name	RA (2000) (h)	(min)	Dec. (°)	(')	Sp		V	B–V	d l.y.	PM (")	RV (km/s)	M_v
Sun					G2	V	−26·7					+4·8
Alpha Centauri A	14	40	−60	50	G2	V	+0·1		4·3	3·68		+4·5
Alpha Centauri B	14	40	−60	50	K5	V	+1·5		4·3	3·68		+5·9
Proxima Centauri	14	29	−62	41	M5e	V	+11		4·3	3·68		+15·4
Barnard's Star	17	58	+04	33	M5	V	+9·5		5·9	10·30		+13·2
LFT 750	10	57	+07	03	M6e	V	+13·5		7·6	4·84		+16·7
LFT 756	11	04	+36	02	M2	V	+7·5		8·1	4·78		+10·5
Sirius A	06	45	−16	43	A1	V	−1·5		8·6	1·32		+1·4
Sirius B	06	45	−16	43	wd		+7·2		8·6	1·32		+10·1
UV Ceti A	01	38	−17	58	M6e	V	+12·5		8·9	3·35		+15·3
UV Ceti B	01	38	−17	58	M6e	V	+13·0		8·9	3·35		+15·8
LFT 1437	18	50	−23	50	M5e	V	+10·6		9·4	0·74		+13·3

Stars. Table 1.

and the radius expressed in that of the Sun as unit (R).

Tables 1 and 2 and the Hertzsprung-Russell diagram summarise the observational data derived from the brighter stars and form the basis for the theory of stellar constitution given under STAR. The way in which stars group together in organised systems is indicated in STAR CLUSTERS, galaxy, and GALAXIES.

Traditional ways in which the brighter stars have been identified are described under CONSTELLATION, and that article includes a series of charts indicating the position of several hundred. The modern way of identifying a star is to give its number in some general catalogue or, if it is too faint to appear in one or other of the accepted catalogues, by specifying its right ascension (see CELESTIAL SPHERE) and DECLINATION, or by marking its position on a chart.

The distance of a star is found from its PARALLAX; its motion through space from its PROPER MOTION and RADIAL VELOCITY; its apparent brightness and colour from the MAGNITUDE and colour index, this latter being the difference between its magnitude as measured in two specified spectral ranges, usually in the blue (photographic) and the yellow (visual). The magnitude depends partly on the intrinsic brightness of the star, partly on its distance, and partly on the degree to which the star's light in its journey through space has been dimmed by interstellar matter. The intrinsic brightness is measured by the ABSOLUTE MAGNITUDE, while the intrinsic colour can be found by correcting the observed colour index for the effect of interstellar reddening. An alternative way of gauging a star's intrinsic colour is by examining its spectrum. This, especially if obtained with high dispersion,

Stars. Table 2.

Sp	M_v V	III	B–V V	III	T V	III	M V	III	R V	III
B0	− 3·7		−0·31		38,000 K		17		7·6	
A0	+ 0·7		0·00		15,400		3·5		2·6	
F0	+ 2·8		+0·30		9,000		1·8		1·4	
G0	+ 4·6	+1·8	+0·57	+0·65	6,700	6,000 K	1·1	2·5	1·1	6·3
K0	+ 6·0	+0·8	+0·84	+1·06	5,400	4,400	0·8	4·0	0·9	16
M0	+ 8·9	−0·3	+1·39	+1·65	3,800	3,400	0·5	6·3	0·6	43
M5	+12·0		+1·61		3,000		0·2		0·3	

Stars

differs in detail from star to star but its main features can, in general, be described by giving its type.

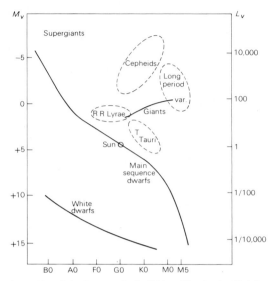

Stars. Plot of absolute magnitude (M_v) and luminosity (L_v) for different classes of stars.

Spectral Classification. When low dispersion stellar spectra were first examined it was found that they could be sorted empirically into a relatively small number of classes. At Harvard, where the Henry Draper Catalogue was prepared, these classes were designated A, B, C,.... With greater experience it was realised that not all of these classes were really necessary and that the logical order for the remainder was O, B, A, F, G, K, and M. This represents a descending order of surface temperature (more strictly, of the degree of ionisation in the stellar atmosphere) from about 50,000 to 3000 K. The rather rare variable stars of classes R, N, and S come towards the end of the sequence. P was reserved for gaseous nebulae, more particularly for planetaries, but is now rarely used.

As the general quality of spectra improved decimal sub-division of the spectral classes was introduced and also luminosity criteria. Though mainly determined by temperature, the degree of ionisation also depends on the pressure which is lower in the extended atmosphere of a giant than in the more concentrated one of a dwarf. This results in subtle differences in the relative strengths of certain spectral lines which can be used to estimate the luminosity class. In the Morgan-Keenan (M-K) system, I following the spectral type denotes a supergiant, III an ordinary giant, and V a normal dwarf; II and IV are reserved for the relatively infrequent stars intermediate between these three main classes, VI for sub-dwarfs, and VII for white dwarfs.

Along with changes of spectrum go conspicuous changes of colour. O and B stars are bluish white (e.g., many of the stars in Orion); A stars are white (Sirius, Vega); G stars are yellow (Capella, the Sun); K stars are orange (Arcturus); M stars are light red (Antares); R and S stars are also red, while N stars look like drops of blood when seen through a telescope (none are visible to the naked eye).

The Henry Draper Catalogue gives the spectral types of approximately 225,000 stars including nearly all those of magnitude 8·5 and brighter. Over 99 per cent of these have types included in the sequence from B0 to M8, the distribution between the main subdivisions being: B 2 per cent, A 29 per cent, F 9 per cent, G 21 per cent, K 33 per cent, and M 6 per cent.

Lines of different chemical elements are prominent at different parts of the spectral sequence: helium in O and B types, hydrogen in A, various metallic elements in F, G, and K, bands of simple molecules in M, R, N, and S. This does not indicate grossly different chemical constitutions for the various types of stars, only different physical conditions in their photospheres. Allowing for these it appears that the chemical constitutions of the different stars are remarkably similar. Hydrogen is by far the most abundant element and accounts for about 70 per cent of the mass. Helium accounts for another 25 per cent and all the other elements together for not more than 5 per cent. It is the percentage of these other elements that varies most, being very low in old stars, such as those in the galactic halo, and rather higher in younger stars.

Diameters. The origin of the term 'giant' and 'dwarf' was the observed fact that stars of the same spectral type can have absolute magnitudes that differ very considerably. As their surface temperatures are the same, each square centimetre of stellar surface will, in accordance with Stefan's Law, be emitting the same amount of radiation. Thus if one of the stars is 100 times brighter than the other, its surface must be 100 times larger, i.e., its diameter is 10 times larger. As the surface temperature of a star can be estimated from its spectrum it is possible, if the star's distance is known, to use Stefan's Law to calculate the area of the star and thus its diameter. The diameters so found vary from about 500 times that of the Sun for a red super-giant to about 0·025 that of the Sun for a white dwarf. As the range in the masses of the stars as found from studies of BINARY STARS is very limited, the range in the mean stellar densities is very large indeed. The tremendous dimensions implied for red super-giants like Antares mean that it should have an apparent diameter of about 0·04 seconds of arc. This has been verified by direct interferometric measurements, and also by observing the time it takes for this star to be completely occulted by the Moon. Diameters deduced from observations of eclipsing binary stars are also of the same order as those deduced from Stefan's Law.

Hertzsprung-Russell (H-R) Diagram. When absolute magnitudes were first plotted against spectral type for stars near the Sun, the only stars at that time for which the distances were known with any certainty, they were found to lie in one or other of two relatively narrow bands which have become known as the 'main sequence' or 'dwarf branch' and the 'yellow giant branch'. The one or two white dwarfs fell well below the main sequence. The diagram has been gradually extended as the distances of other objects have been found by various indirect methods. A major advance in understanding the diagram was made when it was found possible to fit together the colour-magnitude relations for various star clusters with each other and with that observed for the nearby stars. This gave a very clear demonstration of the way in which stars evolve, the intrinsically bright stars very much faster than the faint, and provided a method of estimating the ages of the clusters.

Bibliography: G. O. Abell, *Exploration of the Universe*, abbrev. ed. 1973.

Stars, Military. British designers of military medals have in recent times occasionally adopted the design (and designation) of a star, in place of the more normal round type. The most familiar of these are:

Kabul to Kandahar Star (1880). Given to all troops taking part in Lord Roberts' famous march, 3–13 August 1880. Ribbon (left to right)—red, white, yellow, white, blue (shaded and watered).

Ashanti Star (1896). Awarded to all who took part in the expedition of 1895–96 to suppress slavery and human sacrifices. Ribbon (left to right)—yellow, black, yellow, black, yellow.

1914 Star. Awarded to all who served in France and Belgium between 5 August and midnight 22/23 November 1914. In October 1919 the King approved the issue of a bar to those already awarded the 1914 Star who were actually under fire in France or Belgium during the dates mentioned. Ribbon (left to right)—red, white, blue (shaded and watered). This decoration is often, though incorrectly, called the 'Mons Star'.

1914–15 Star. Similar in design to the 1914 Star with the exception of the date. The ribbon is identical. Awarded to all who served in a theatre of war in 1914–15 and were not eligible for the 1914 Star.

1939–45 Star. Granted for service in operations from 3 September 1939 to 15 August 1945. Ribbon (left to right)—dark blue, red, light blue.

Atlantic Star (1939–45). The general rule, to which there were a few exceptions, was that personnel of the Royal Navy and Merchant Navy qualified with six months' service afloat in the Atlantic or Home Waters between 3 September 1939 and 8 May 1945. Air crews became entitled after two months with an operational unit if they had been in action against the enemy and had also been awarded the 1939–45 Star. Ribbon (left to right)—blue, white, sea green (shaded and watered).

Air-Crew Europe Star (1939–44). Awarded for operational flying from UK bases over Europe (including the UK) for a period of two months between 3 September 1939 and 4 June 1944. Ribbon (left to right)—black, yellow, light blue, yellow, black.

Africa Star (1940–43). Awarded to the armed forces and Merchant Navy for entry into the North Africa operational area between 10 June 1940 and 12 May 1943; also for service in Abyssinia, Sudan, Somaliland, Eritrea, and Malta. Ribbon (left to right)—pale buff, dark blue, red, pale buff, light blue, pale buff. A silver Arabic '8' or '1' on the ribbon indicates service with the Eighth Army between 23 October 1942 and 12 May 1943, or the First Army between 8 November 1942 and 12 May 1943.

Pacific Star (1941–45). Awarded for service in the Pacific theatre of operations from 8 December 1941 to the end of the war against Japan. The land territories included Hong Kong, Malaya, Nauru, Sumatra, Timor, Java, New Guinea, and the smaller Pacific islands. Ribbon (left to right)—red, dark blue, green, yellow, green, light blue, red.

Burma Star (1941–45). Granted for service in the Burma theatre of operations between 11 December 1941 and the end of the war with Japan. Ribbon (left to right)—dark blue, orange, dark blue, red, dark blue, orange, dark blue.

Italy Star (1943–45). Awarded to those who between 11 June 1943 and 8 May 1945 served in the Italian theatre of operations which in addition to Italy and Sicily included Greece, Yugoslavia, the Aegean and Dodecanese, Corsica, Sardinia, Elba, Pantellaria Island, the waters of the Mediterranean, and, in the closing stages of the war, Austria. Ribbon (left to right)—red, white, green, white, red.

France and Germany Star (1944–45). Awarded to those who entered the operational area in France, Belgium, Holland, and Germay from 6 June 1944 to 8 May 1945. Ribbon (left to right)—blue, white, red, white, blue.

Rules existed for the award of Second World War Stars which limited the number which any one individual could receive. These were designed to prevent recipients getting two or more Stars for 'overlapping' campaigns.

A few other countries have adopted stars as decorations, such as the American Silver Star and Bronze Star, and the Egyptian Military Star of Fouad I.

Bibliography: H. Taprell Dorling, *Ribbons and medals— Naval, Military, Air Force and Civil*, 1956; R. W. Gould, *Campaign Medals of the British Army 1815–1972*, 1972.

Stars and Stripes, see UNITED STATES OF AMERICA.

Starshine Camera, or night-sky recorder, a device used in meteorology to give an estimate of the amount of cloud present during the night. A camera is pointed to the region of the sky in which α-Ursae Minoris (the pole star) and δ-Ursae Minoris are seen. On a clear night the light from these stars produces complete circles on the film. When cloud is present the traces are partially or completely obscured.

Starvation, see FAMINE; FASTING; HUNGER.

Starwort, name used sometimes for STITCHWORT but more commonly for *Callitriche* (family CALLITRICHACEAE), a genus of small aquatic plants whose oval leaves, sometimes floating, form a star-like pattern round the stem. Several species occur in ponds in Britain.

Stassfurt, town of East Germany, in the district of Magdeburg, on the River Bode, 29 km south of Magdeburg. It has potash and magnesite deposits, and manufactures chemicals and machinery. Population 26,300.

Staszic, Stanisław (1755–1826), Polish political writer, statesman, scholar, and philosopher, and a leading representative of the Enlightenment in Poland. Staszic was ordained priest in 1778 and studied science in Paris. Being of non-noble origin he could not enter the Polish parliament but supported the movement for political and social reform with his pen. After the Partitions he devoted himself to the economic development of the country; he discovered coal deposits and built the first coal-mine in Poland. Staszic was president of the Warsaw Society of the Friends of Learning from 1808 and called for the improvement of the condition of the peasantry. He held high office in the fields of education and industry in the Duchy of Warsaw from 1807 to 1812 and in the Kingdom of Poland from 1815 to 1824.

State, autonomous system of political control exercised over citizens inhabiting a determinate geographical area. Our modern notion of the state is a product of a particular period of European history and the above definition requires some explication and qualification given modern conditions. Each state exists in a legally independent relationship with other states. Such independence may be modified by treaty, but cannot be wholly relinquished whilst statehood remains. The system of control is derived from a formal structure of law which is backed up by coercive force of which the state has a legal monopoly. Administrative control is embodied in an organised system of rôles and offices. The relationship between the individual citizen and the system of control can take various forms, from one in which the flow of influence is almost totally from authority to citizen (autocracy), to one of almost equal influence (democracy) (see CONSTITUTION). The legal structure of the state will contain definitions of those who are to be included as citizens. The area of competence of a state will be expressed in geographical terms, consequently many of the inhabitants will be excluded from citizenship whilst still coming under the jurisdiction of the state, e.g., resident aliens, paupers, and women, have all at one time or another been excluded from citizenship.

The state is the autonomous authority within its determinate area, but although all legal powers exercised within that area derive from it, this sovereignty is subject to increasing influence from international organisations of various kinds, economic and political. It is the mutual recognition of such legal authority by other states which in practice defines their existence. (Occasionally dual administration of certain areas is exercised by outside powers, but such countries under mandate, like colonies, cannot be considered to possess full statehood. Such dual administration may be granted by international agencies such as the UN.) Conversely each citizen is logically capable of obeying only one state authority. Although the practice of dual citizenship is allowed by some states, what this amounts to is a right to change effective allegiance by taking up residence in the alternative state.

Composite Forms of State. In contra-distinction to simple and unitary states, states which consist of component parts organised like states are called composite states. In these there is a distinction between the power of the collective or chief state and the independence of the separate states or dependencies. Composite states are commonly classified into: (1) FEDERATIONS or federal empires, e.g. the USA. Both the collective and the particular states have a complete organisation and polity, but their constitutions are generally limited by the over-riding power of the organised nation, the constitution of which appropriates to the national legislature and executive exclusive power in regard to certain well-defined spheres of action, more especially in foreign affairs and taxation. (2) CONFEDERATIONS, e.g. the German Confederation of 1815, 'a conglomeration of states, each having its own organisation', and severally independent in all or most matters except external or foreign relations. A confederation insists on the individual independence of

each component, while federation insists on the supremacy of the common government. (3) Suzerainties and PROTECTORATES. The Holy Roman Empire exercised a general dominion over a number of vassal states, while modern examples are furnished by many African protectorates. These may be regarded as inchoate colonial dependencies of the protecting power. (4) States and colonial dependencies in absolute subjection to a mother country.

Relation of the State to Individuals. Membership of a state is usually acquired by birth, marriage, or naturalisation. Most nations recognise nationality as a personal relation, not wholly dependent on place of birth or domicile, but also partly on descent from members of the nation.

A person ceases to belong to a state by marriage (i.e. a wife who acquires the nationality of an alien loses her former nationality) and free renunciation, e.g. by emigration with no *animus revertendi*. Nationality is chiefly of importance in regard to conscription or compulsory service, and restriction on the exercise of certain handicrafts and trades.

See also GOVERNMENT; POLITICAL THOUGHT; SOVEREIGNTY.

Bibliography: L. T. Hobhouse, *Metaphysical Theory of the State*, 1918; H. J. Laski, *The State in Theory and Practice*, 1935; H. Finer, *The Theory and Practice of Modern Government*, 1932; V. I. Lenin, *State and Revolution*, 1933; S. I. Benn and R. S. Peters, *Social Principles and the Democratic State*, 1959; J. Lock (ed. P. Laslett), *Two Treatises on Government*, 1967.

State, Acts of, term used in English law to signify any prerogative act of policy in the field of external affairs. No action in TORT lies in respect of an act injurious to the person or to the property of aliens outside Her Majesty's dominions done by any representative of the Crown and which is either previously sanctioned or subsequently ratified by the Crown. Such an act is an act of state. An act of state is not within the jurisdiction of municipal (i.e. domestic) courts, so that once it is established to the satisfaction of the court that the act has been performed by the Crown or a foreign government, the court will not investigate the matter further. But it is insufficient for a bland assertion of 'act of state' to be made. Act of state cannot be pleaded as a defence in an action in tort against the Crown by a British subject or by a friendly alien if, in the latter case, the tort was committed within Her Majesty's dominions.

Bibliography: S. A. de Smith, *Constitutional and Administrative Law*, 2nd ed. 1973.

State Church, or established church, church established by custom or legislation as the official church of a country. It is used on those occasions when the need of a religious ceremony is felt by the state. In return the Church recognises the head of the state in some way. In England and Scotland there are established churches under the authority of Parliament. The Anglican Church was disestablished in Ireland in 1869 and in Wales in 1919.

State Trading, buying and selling at home or abroad by the state. It plays a great part in the economy of the USSR.

In Britain state trading received a great impetus during the First World War, and a still greater one during the Second World War, when the buying and selling of most industrial raw materials and foodstuffs were undertaken by the government in the interest of the national war effort. In the First World War state trading was gradually extended to most foodstuffs and practically all imports. However, the general opinion was that the war experience had not proved that state trading possessed any permanent advantage over the private capitalist system under normal conditions.

During the Second World War state trading assumed even larger proportions than during the First. Trade in all foodstuffs was concentrated in the hands of the Ministry of Food, and industrial materials were bought and sold by the Ministry of Supply and the Board of Trade. All these departments used the existing private firms as agents, and there is no doubt that the success the ministries achieved during the war was due to the advice they received from traders with long experience.

There are several ways of carrying out state trading. The department concerned may make a contract for an individual lot of a commodity (e.g. oranges), or it may buy in advance at a fixed price the production of a period ahead (e.g. six-month contracts for metals produced in a certain area), or definite quantities of certain goods at prices determined in advance for several years ahead, the so-called long-term contracts; the commonly used expression 'bulk-buying' includes all forms of state-buying except the buying of occasional lots.

The Labour party stated before the end of the Second World War that it intended to continue state trading in times of peace. The Ministry of Food therefore continued to buy most foodstuffs, the Ministry of Supply non-ferrous metals, and the Board of Trade raw materials such as timber and hides. During the shortages of the immediate postwar period long-term contracts permitted Britain to buy more cheaply than it would otherwise have done in a period of rising prices. When, however, goods became more plentiful and world prices began to fall, this advantage had gone. Since 1949 there has been a gradual diminution of state trading. By 1957 it was confined largely to strategic stock-piling, except of course for the nationalised industries, the National Health Service, education services, and roads. Thus while state trading *per se* is not a prominent term in contemporary political discussion its absence from current usage must not disguise the importance of the government's participation in the economy, for it is responsible for the expenditure of approximately 40 per cent of the national income of Great Britain.

See also NATIONALISATION.

Staten Island, see RICHMOND.

Stater, ancient Greek term meaning standard coin. The term normally refers to the gold coins weighing about 8 g which circulated widely during the Hellenistic period. It also indicates the standard silver coins which were issued by the Greek cities and which varied in weight according to the place of issue. Thus the Corinthian stater was a three-drachma piece, while the Athenian was a four-drachma piece.

Copies of the Greek gold stater were struck by the Celtic tribes of western Europe and it was the stater of this type that circulated in Britain at the time of the Roman invasions.

States-General, name given to the various legislative assemblies of France prior to the Revolution: (1) The *États-généraux* of 1314, which established, at least in principle, 'that the free consent of the three orders of the realm is necessary to the levying of taxation'; (2) *États de la langue d'oc* which assembled at Toulouse, and that of *la langue d'oïl*, which met at Paris (1351); (3) *États de 1357*, an extreme radical assembly which demanded the abolition of the inalienability of Crown demesne lands, the extirpation of corruption in the distribution of judicial posts, and the right to create a commission of 36 members to administer the affairs of the whole kingdom; (4) *États de Paris* (1413), convoked by Charles VI ostensibly to reform abuses but in reality to exact subsidies; (5) *États d'Orléans* (1439), which established an annual tallage of £1·2 million for the maintenance of a permanent army; (6) *États de Tours* (1484), notable for the declaration in a remarkable speech by Philippe Pot, a Burgundian deputy, of the principle of popular sovereignty. (7) The *États de Paris* (1614) did not meet again until 1785. These were strictly the last states-general held in France, for in 1789 they were transformed into the NATIONAL ASSEMBLY.

States-General, legislative body of the Netherlands which, in 1814, superseded the National Assembly, which had itself been established in 1795 in place of the old States-General of the United Provinces.

States of Matter, see PHASES OF MATTER.

States of the Church, see PAPAL STATES.

'Statesman, The', see 'HINDU, THE'.

Static, see ATMOSPHERICS.

Statice, see LIMONIUM.

Statics, branch of mechanics which deals with the action of forces in compelling a body to remain at rest or not alter its motion. See EQUILIBRIUM; GRAPHIC STATICS.

Stationery Office, Her Majesty's, see HER MAJESTY'S STATIONERY OFFICE.

Stations (in liturgy, Latin *stationes*), name originally referring to the lengthy services held in the early Christian Church on fast days, namely Wednesday and Friday, during which the faithful 'stood on watch' (*stare*); these came to be known as 'station days'. By a natural development the name was transferred to the church in which the liturgy was held. In the 5th century at Rome, on days when the bishop celebrated the liturgy, a special church was appointed and came to be known as the 'station church'. A procession usually preceded the liturgy, and gave rise to the phrase 'statio ad ...' meaning 'service at ...' the church in question. In this form the direction for Sundays and the older liturgical days survived in the Roman missal.

Stations of the Cross, or Way of the Cross, late medieval devotion originating in the pilgrimages to the Holy Land. In the 15th and 16th centuries in certain cities of Europe an exact topographical reproduction of the points of devotional interest seen by pilgrims in Jerusalem was attempted by means of shrines in various parts of the city. Reproductions subsequently lost all attempt at topographical meaning and, shrinking in size, came to consist

Statistics

of images or pictures showing various scenes from Christ's journey to Calvary. As such they eventually took permanent form, and are found as pictures, each surmounted by a cross, on the walls inside Roman Catholic churches. They are 14 in number, and the devotion consists in going from one to another and saying appropriate prayers at each. Sometimes 14 crosses are erected without pictures, but the devotion is made in the same way.

Statistics is the branch of mathematics that deals with methods of collecting, recording and analysing numerical data. The word is also used (as a plural noun) to describe numerical data acquired by observation, measurement or experiment. The singular noun 'statistic' is used for a number which is derived from collected data and describes or summarises the data, for example, the mean or the standard deviation of the data (see below).

Economic and Demographic Statistics. Much commonly used statistical material consists of simple counts of objects, or monetary transactions, etc., of a defined kind. This material answers such questions as: How many people are there in a country? How many under age 15? What was the value of the country's exports in 1970? Most national governments have departments devoted to collecting and publishing data of this kind. The Statistical Office of the United Nations Department of Economic and Social Affairs has done much to establish uniform standards for collection and preparation of such data and publishes several series of statistics giving international comparisons. In the UK, the Office of Population Censuses and Surveys is responsible for counting the population every ten years and for carrying out numerous other social surveys; the Central Statistical Office collects a vast range of data on the UK economy.

Time Series and Index Numbers. Economic and demographic statistics are usually presented as 'time series'—that is, as sequences of measurements made at regular intervals; for example, the estimated population at 1 July each year, or the value of exports each month. Time series which are recorded at intervals of three months or less are commonly subjected to 'seasonal adjustment'. If, for example, electricity consumption in England is measured monthly then there will naturally be a sharp increase between September and October. From a knowledge of what has happened in previous years it is possible to compute the expected rise between those two months. Subtracting the expected rise from the actual figures gives 'seasonally adjusted' figures which will show up any significant changes in amount of consumption. Often time series are also presented in the form of 'index numbers' instead of actual figures; the value for a chosen time, called the 'base period' (or 'base year' if the time series is an annual one), is designated 100 and figures for other times are expressed as percentages of the figure for the base year. For example, if a time series is:

year	1968	1969	1970	1971	1972	1973
observation	2000	2100	2200	2300	2400	2800

and 1968 is chosen as base year then the index numbers are as follows.

year	1968	1969	1970	1971	1972	1973
index	100	105	110	115	120	140

Index numbers are particularly useful for comparing trends in different time series.

Statistics about Individuals. Economic and demographic statistics are concerned with establishing total values; most of the mathematical theory of statistics is concerned with summarising information about individuals. Three examples are: the heights of adult males in England; the amounts of milk obtained from individual cows; the attitudes of people to aircraft noise. There are two basic problems with statistics of this kind:

1. It is usually impractical to obtain data relating to every individual in the 'population' (every adult male, every cow, every person); is it possible to obtain data for a sample of the population and infer from those data the characteristics of the entire population?

2. How can the data be presented and summarised so as to be of practical use?

Sampling. Luckily, for many purposes samples of a manageable size can be used to provide very accurate information about entire populations. Statistical theory can be used to calculate the minimum size of sample necessary to give any desired degree of accuracy. For practical purposes, the way in which a sample is chosen presents more difficulties than its size. The sample must be truly representative of the population. When sampling a human population, for example, it is important to maintain the balance of sex, age, type of occupation, urban/suburban/rural residence, and so on. A major problem in setting up surveys of human populations is to frame the questions being asked so that they are always intelligible and unambiguous. Because the methods used can greatly affect the validity of the results, statisticians usually publish with their results details of sampling methods and of questionnaires used; this is particularly important in cases of major public interest such as political opinion polls.

Height mm	Number of persons
1525–1575	4
1600–1650	18
1675–1725	42
1750–1800	28
1825–1875	8

Statistics. Table 1. Frequency distribution of heights of 100 adult males (individual heights measured to nearest 25 mm).

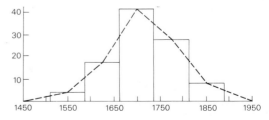

Statistics. Figure 1.

Describing Data. The term 'raw data' is used for collected data which have not been organised or analysed in any way. A simple first step in summarising large amounts of data is to distribute them into classes and determine the number of individuals in each class, called the class frequency. Table 1 illustrates this for the heights of 100 adult males.

This table can be converted into the diagram of rectangles shown in fig. 1, which is called a histogram. The graph obtained in fig. 1 by joining the midpoints of the tops of the rectangles is called a frequency polygon.

Table 1 can be converted into the cumulative frequency distribution shown in table 2, and can be graphed as a cumulative frequency polygon, or ogive, as in fig. 2.

Height mm	Number of persons
Less than 1512·5	0
Less than 1587·5	4
Less than 1662·5	22
Less than 1737·5	64
Less than 1812·5	92
Less than 1887·5	100

Statistics. Table 2. Cumulative frequency distribution derived from Table 1.

Mean, Median, and Mode. The preceding section described some ways of presenting data; this section and the next describe some important 'measures' of data. These are statistics (in the sense of numbers derived from raw data) which are particularly valuable for comparing sets of data. The mean, median and mode are different ways of finding a 'typical' or 'central' value of a set of data. The mean or arithmetic mean is obtained by adding up all the observed values and dividing by the number of values; it is the number which is commonly used as an average value. The median is the middle value, that is, the value which is exceeded by half the items in the sample. The mode is the value which occurs with greatest frequency—the most common value. Fig. 3 shows how mean, median, and mode can differ in a frequency distribution. The mean is the most useful measure for the purposes of statistical theory.

The idea of the median may be extended and a distribution can be divided into four quartiles. The first quartile is the value which is exceeded by three-quarters of the

Statistics. Figure 2.

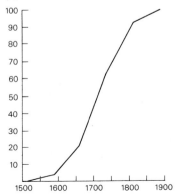

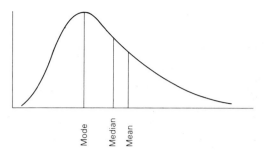

Statistics. Figure 3.

items; the second quartile is the same as the median; the third quartile is the value that is exceeded by one-quarter of the items.

Standard Deviation and other Measures of Dispersion. The mean is a very incomplete summary of a group of observations; it is useful to know also how closely the individual members of a group approach the mean, and this is indicated by various measures of dispersion. The range is the difference between the maximum and minimum values of the group; it is not very satisfactory as a measure of dispersion. The mean deviation is the arithmetic mean of the differences between the mean and the individual values, the differences all being taken as positive. However, the mean deviation also does not convey much useful information about a group of observations. The most useful measure of dispersion is the variance, which is the arithmetic mean of the squares of the deviations from the mean. The positive square root of the variance is called the standard deviation. It is usual to standardise the measurements by working in units of the standard deviation measured from the mean of the distributions, enabling statistical theories to be generalised. A standardised distribution has a mean of zero and a standard deviation of unity. Another useful measure of dispersion is the semi-interquartile range, which is one-half of the distance between the first and third quartiles, and can be considered as the average distance of the quartiles from the median. In many typical distributions the semi-interquartile range is about two-thirds of the standard deviation and the mean deviation is about four-fifths of the standard deviation.

Statistical Inference. One of the most important uses of statistical theory is in testing whether experimental data support hypotheses or not. For example, an agricultural researcher arranges for different groups of cows to be fed different diets and records the milk yields. The milk-yield data are analysed and the means and standard deviations of yields for different groups vary. The researcher can use statistical tests to assess whether the variation is of an amount that should be expected because of the natural variation in cows or whether it is larger than normal and therefore likely to be influenced by the difference in diet.

Correlation. Correlation measures the degree to which two quantities are associated, in the sense that a variation in one quantity is accompanied by a predictable variation in the other. For example, if the pressure on a quantity of gas is increased then its volume decreases. If observations of pressure and volume are taken then statistical correlation analysis can be used to determine whether the volume of a gas can be completely predicted from a knowledge of the pressure on it. An extension of this is regression analysis, which is used to find an equation linking two (or more) correlated quantities.

Bibliography: S. S. Wilks, *Mathematical Statistics*, 1962; D. R. Cox, *Planning of Experiments*, 1966; W. G. Cochran, *Sampling Techniques*, 2nd ed. 1967; P. G. Moore, *Principles of Statistical Techniques*, 2nd ed. 1969; M. J. Moroney, *Facts from Figures*, new ed. 1969; R. Loveday, *A First Course in Statistics*, 3rd ed. 1970, and *Practical Statistics and Probability*, 1974; F. Mosteller and others, *Probability with Statistical Applications*, 2nd ed. 1970; W. J. Reichmann, *Use and Abuse of Statistics*, new ed. 1970; Central Statistical Office, *Facts in Focus*, 1972, and *List of Principal Statistical Series and Publications*, 2nd ed. 1974; M. R. Spiegel, *Schaum's Outline of Theory and Problems of Statistics*, 2nd ed. 1972; J. E. Freund, *Modern Elementary Statistics*, 4th ed. 1973.

Statius, Publius Papinius (c. AD 45–c. 96), Latin poet, born at Naples. His extant works are *Thebais*, 12 books on the strife of Polynices and Eteocles (see THEBAN LEGEND); *Achilleis*, an unfinished epic in two books; and *Silvae*, a collection of 32 occasional poems. JUVENAL speaks of him as bombastic; but although he is often too rhetorical, he had considerable descriptive powers.

Bibliography: J. H. Mozley (Trans.), *Works*, 'Loeb Classical Library', 1928; D. W. T. C. Vessey, *Statius and the Thebaid*, 1973.

Stator, the stationary part of a rotating machine, alternator, motor, or turbine. See ELECTRICAL MACHINES.

Statuary, see SCULPTURE; STONE-CARVING.

Statue of Liberty, see LIBERTY ISLAND.

Statute, see LEGISLATION AND LEGISLATIVE PROCESSES.

Statute of Frauds 1677, see FRAUDS, STATUTE OF, 1677.

Stauffenberg, Claus, Count Schenk von (1907–44), German soldier, born in Bavaria. He was severely wounded in the Second World War, and in 1944 was a colonel on the General Staff. Stauffenberg was one of the leaders of the unsuccessful attempt on Hitler's life on 20 July 1944, and it was he who placed the bomb in Hitler's bunker. He was shot the next day.

Bibliography: R. Manvell and H. Fraenkel, *The July Plot*, 1964.

Staunton, Howard (1810–74), British chess champion between 1841–51; also an actor and Shakespearean scholar of some note. He defeated the strongest French and German chess players of the day but would not meet the brilliant American player, Paul MORPHY. Controversy has raged ever since over whether Staunton was afraid to meet this challenge, though at his best he would almost certainly have won at world championship level. He did not, as is frequently claimed, design the pieces used in club and tournament play today; the original set was named after Staunton by his friend, the designer Nathaniel Cook in 1835. Staunton's books include *The Chess Players' Handbook*, 1847, *The Chess Players' Companion*, 1849.

Staurolite, a mineral composed of iron and aluminium silicate ($FeAl_4Si_2O_{10}[OH]_2$). It crystallises in the monoclinic system forming brown prismatic crystals which are commonly twinned in a characteristically cruciform manner. It has a hardness of 7 and specific gravity 3·7–3·8. Staurolite is a characteristic mineral of medium-grade metamorphic rocks and is found in aluminium-rich schists and gneisses. Many fine perfect crystals are found in Virginia, Georgia, and North Carolina, USA, and the cruciform twins are sold as souvenirs.

Stavanger, city in the county of Rogaland, NORWAY, of which it is the county town. It lies 160 km south of Bergen, and was founded in the 8th or 9th century. Stavanger has a splendid Gothic cathedral, built by Bishop Reinald from Winchester in the 12th century, rebuilt after a fire in 1272, and restored in 1886. It is the centre of a sheep farming area, and has a large fish-canning industry, with more than 100 factories. There is an important shipyard, and much shipping is registered in Stavanger. The city is the centre of Norway's North Sea oil exploration and oil rig construction. Population (1975) 85,600.

Stave, or staff (music), see NOTATION.

Stavisky, Alexandre (1886–1934), naturalised Frenchman, of Russian birth, responsible for a financial scandal in France in 1934. He floated a very large sum in bogus bonds, in the name of the municipal credit establishment of Bayonne. Stavisky committed suicide after a warrant for his arrest had been issued. The scandal caused the fall of two governments, a general strike, and riots in Paris.

Stavropol, *krai* in the RSFSR, USSR, situated in the North CAUCASUS, in the foothills of the main Caucasus Mountains range, and has dry steppe in the north-east. There are very rich deposits of natural gas, and mineral springs. The KARACHAYEVO-CHERKESS Autonomous Oblast lies within the *krai*. Wheat and sunflowers are grown, and cattle and sheep raised for meat, milk, and wool. Natural gas is piped to Moscow and Leningrad, and there are various food industries. The main towns are Stavropol (see below), PYATIGORSK, and KISLOVODSK. Area 80,600 km². Population (1975) 2,421,000 (42 per cent urban).

Stavropol (1935–44, *Voroshilovsk*), capital city, economic and cultural centre of Stavropol *krai* (see above), USSR, with varied food, wool, and leather industries, and is the starting-point of the natural gas pipeline to Moscow. Population (1974) 226,000.

Stavropol, see TOLYATTI.

Stays, on sailing ships, strong ropes which support a mast, in a fore-and-aft direction. The fore stays lead forward and the back stays aft, both being secured to the side of the ship. To be 'in stays' is to be head-to-wind when going about from one tack to another, and to 'miss stays' is to fail in the attempt to go about.

Stays, in BOILERS. As a circular or spherical construction is the only one that will support internal steam pressure without undue distortion, it is necessary for all flat surfaces of a boiler to be stayed. Where there are two flat surfaces opposite each other, with steam between them, the staying consists of a large number of steel or copper rods, screwed into both plates, and rendered steamtight by external nuts, or by riveting over. The flat ends of cylindrical boilers are sometimes stayed with flanged plates riveted inside the boiler.

Stead, Christina (1902–), Australian novelist, born at Rockdale, New South Wales. Educated at Sydney University, she lived in London, Paris, and New York. Subtle yet vigorous in characterisation, Christina Stead excels in the evocation of defeated personalities, as in her one Sydney novel, *Seven Poor Men of Sydney*, 1934, where the counterpoint of the seven lives is handled with alertness and power. Her greatest achievement is perhaps the appallingly perceptive Californian novel *The Man Who Loved Children*, 1940.

Other novels are *House of All Nations*, 1938; *Letty Fox, Her Luck*, 1946; *A Little Tea, A Little Chat*, 1948; *The People with the Dogs*, 1952; *Dark Places of the Heart*, 1966 (in England, *Cotters' England*, 1967). Short stories are in *The Salzburg Tales*, 1934, and novellas in *The Puzzle-Headed Girl*, 1967.

Bibliography: R. G. Geering, *Christina Stead*, 1970.

Stead, William Thomas (1849–1912), British journalist, born at Embleton, Alnwick; educated at Wakefield. In 1871 he became editor of the Darlington *Northern Echo*, and, on moving to London, was appointed assistant editor of the *Pall Mall Gazette* in 1880, succeeding John Morley as editor in 1883. Stead's series of articles 'The Maiden Tribute to Modern Babylon', on the traffic in young girls in London, though it secured the passing of the Criminal Law Amendment Act 1885, resulted in his spending three months in Holloway prison for 'procuring a child for immoral purposes'. He also did much to bring about the dispatch of GORDON to the Sudan.

Stead left the *Pall Mall* in 1889, and subsequently founded the *Review of Reviews*, 1890, the magazine being a new feature in British journalism, and *Borderland*, a spiritualistic journal, 1893–97. His books include *The Truth about Russia*, 1888, *The Pope and the New Era*, 1889, *If Christ came to Chicago*, 1893, and *Mrs Booth*, 1900. He was drowned when the liner *Titanic* sank.

Steady-state Theory, see COSMOLOGY.

Stealing, Going Equipped for. It is an offence, in

Christina Stead. *(Angus and Robertson)*

England, under the Theft Act 1968 for any person, when not at his place of abode, to have with him any article for use in the course of, or in connection with, any BURGLARY, THEFT, or cheat. The offence is punishable with a maximum of three years' imprisonment and is expressly declared to be an arrestable offence. 'Theft' includes taking a conveyance without authority, and 'cheat' means obtaining property by deception.

See also ARREST; DECEPTION, OBTAINING PROPERTY BY.

Bibliography: E. Griew, *The Theft Act 1968*, 2nd ed. 1974.

Steam, a dry, colourless and transparent gaseous substance formed by the evaporation of water at any temperature. The term is often used erroneously for the damp clouds of white water droplets produced by the condensation of warm steam in a cooler atmosphere. Steam, or water vapour, is released by water or ice at all temperatures provided the atmosphere is not already saturated with water vapour, in which case slight cooling or pressure increase will bring about condensation of the vapour to liquid water. The pressure exerted by the evaporating water, the saturated vapour pressure (SVP), increases with temperature as does the quantity of water vapour the atmosphere can hold. When water boils, the SVP of the water equals the pressure of the atmosphere above it and the temperature at which this happens is the boiling-point (b.p.). Physical methods which involve the observation of the b.p. of water (or another liquid) are referred to as 'ebullioscopic'. The b.p. of water is related to the atmospheric pressure above it. At atmospheric pressure (101,325 Pa) the b.p. of water is 100 °C; at a pressure of 1,564,000 Pa, it is 200 °C. At the critical pressure of steam, viz., 22,090,000 Pa, the compressed steam has the same density as water, the relevant b.p. being 374 °C.

As steam leaves the surface of water, there is also some steam condensing back at the water surface to form liquid water again. A state of dynamic equilibrium exists and the atmosphere above the liquid water is said to be *saturated*. In the absence of liquid water, steam becomes *superheated* and behaves more or less like a typical gas in response to temperature and pressure changes.

A change of state from liquid to gas involves the expenditure of energy in overcoming forces which hold water molecules close within the liquid. This energy, known as the 'latent heat of vaporisation', becomes smaller as the water temperature (and hence the separation of the water molecules) increases, finally reaching zero at the critical point, 374 °C.

The production of steam from water is accompanied by a very great expansion in volume: a given mass of steam at 100 °C occupies more than 1600 times the volume of the same mass of water at 100 °C. At the critical point, the specific volumes of steam and water become equal (0·03 m³/kg).

Steam has many uses in engineering and 'Steam Tables' are available which list in full all the variations in the parameters mentioned above. The large latent heat of vaporisation released when steam condenses makes steam a particularly good heating medium. It is of special value as a steriliser (e.g., in autoclaves) and in engineering (such as the Frasch process for the extraction of sulphur) but its principal use is in steam turbines, engines, and hammers.

Steam and Power Hammers

Steam and Power Hammers. Among the many ideas of James Watt in connection with his study of steam engines was one resulting in a patent (1784) for a steam hammer. William Deverell of Surrey also took out a patent in 1806. The first machine in actual use (1842) was constructed by Bourdon, mechanical engineer of the Creusot works in France, after designs sketched by James Nasmyth. The sketch showed an inverted cylinder, mounted in a heavy frame, with a heavy block of iron on the end of the piston rod. The block was raised by admitting steam under the piston and released by an attendant, who allowed the steam to escape. The mass fell under the action of gravity on to the anvil below. In 1843 steam was admitted above the piston to aid gravitation, and continuous automatic operation was tried but abandoned. The next hammer had a weight of 5 t and a fall of 1·5 m. The steam hammer was first used for forging and for pile-driving, a hammer weighing 4 t giving 80 blows to the minute. A more modern development is the self-acting Massey steam hammer, made in weights ranging from 0·5 to 1·2 t. A curved lever is moved automatically by a roller on the hammer during the up-and-down movement of the tup or hammer, admitting steam alternately above and below the hammer piston. A hand-lever, which can be set in any of a range of notches, varies the movement of the valve-rod, and consequently alters the stroke of the hammer. A stop-valve controlled by a hand- or foot-lever regulates the amount of steam admitted and therefore the force of the blows. The steam hammer has now been largely superseded by the pneumatic power hammer although it is still used where ample supplies of steam are available.

Pneumatic power hammers are self-contained, the hammer head being operated by compressed air which is produced by an integral reciprocating compressor driven by an electric motor. A hand- or foot-lever controls the vertical movement of the valve. In the 'not-working'

position air flows freely from one side of the pump piston to the other as the piston reciprocates, without affecting the ram. In the 'full-work' position air passes from above the pump piston to the top of the hammer cylinder and from below the pump piston to the bottom of the hammer cylinder, so that the ram is alternately lifted and thrown down with maximum force in time with the reciprocation of the pump. Intermediate positions of the valve partially close the connecting passages to give a wide variation in the force and nature of the blow. In addition, lower positions of the valve allow air to be transferred from a reservoir to hold the ram up or down with a constant pressure below or above the ram piston. An air-buffer space at the top of the cylinder prevents the piston striking the cylinder cover. Hammers of this type are made up to 2 t falling weight. A light hand-hammer operated by compressed air is used in riveting (see RIVET).

Steam Distillation, process for purifying solids and liquids which are generally water-insoluble. It can be applied to systems in which the substance to be purified is volatile and the impurities non-volatile (see figure).

The mixture to be distilled is contained in *A*, either as a liquid, or mixed with water, if solid. Steam is passed into *A* and volatilises the required product. The steam-product mixture passes into tube *B* where it is condensed and is then collected in *C*. Solid materials usually crystallise in *C*, and can be recovered by filtration, while liquids separate as a distinct layer, if they are not soluble in water.

Steam Engine.

Mechanism. *General.* The mechanism of a simple double-acting steam engine is illustrated in fig. 1. The steam pressure within the cylinder acts on the piston, which is rigidly attached, through the piston rod, to the cross-head. The piston rod passes through the cylinder cover inside a steamtight stuffing box or gland. The connecting rod converts the reciprocating motion of the

Steam Distillation.

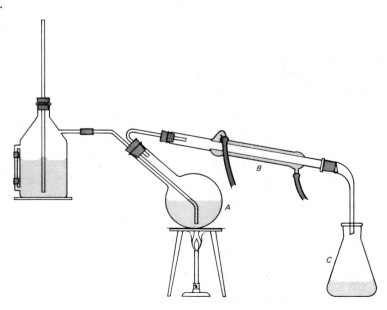

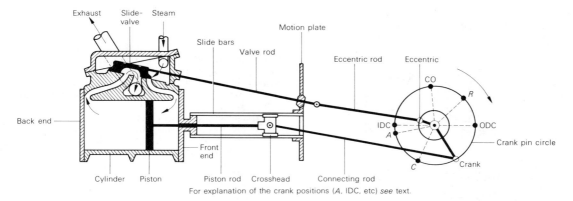

Steam Engine. Figure 1. Mechanism of simple double-acting engine.

cross-head into rotary motion at the crank. The cross-head runs in rigid guides, called slide bars, which take up the side thrust due to the connecting rod. When the piston is at either end of the cylinder the engine is said to be on dead centre. Considering the back end of the cylinder first, steam is admitted slightly before inner dead centre (IDC) when the crank is at the point of admission (A) (fig. 1). This preadmission allows time for the steam to traverse the ports and exert its full pressure before the engine reaches dead centre; preadmission is thus greater in high-speed engines. Admission of steam continues until the point of cut-off (CO), when the valve closes, and the steam begins to expand. When the steam pressure has fallen sufficiently, due to expansion, the exhaust valve opens at the point of release (R); pre-release is necessary, to give the steam time to leave the cylinder before outer dead centre (ODC) is reached, and the return stroke begun. As the pressure drop across the exhaust port is much lower than that across the inlet port, the duration of pre-release is necessarily greater than that of preadmission.

Valves. In the earliest engines steam was controlled by two cocks at each end of the cylinder. The four cocks were soon replaced by a single slide-valve (fig. 2a). This consists of an open box of cast iron, brass, or gunmetal, sliding face-down on a flat surface, in which are two steam ports leading to the two ends of the cylinder, and between them an exhaust port leading to the atmosphere or to a con-

denser. The valve is kept seated on the port face by the pressure of steam outside it. When it is moved to one side (the position shown in fig. 1), one steam port is opened to live steam, and the other to the exhaust port, via the hollow inside of the valve. When it is in its central position, the amount that it overlaps the outside edge of the steam port is called the steam lap (fig. 2b), while the amount that it overlaps the inside edge is called the exhaust lap—the negative exhaust lap is called exhaust clearance. The slide-valve has two main disadvantages: (1) the steam and exhaust events are interdependent; (2) the pressure of steam on the back of the slide-valve is more than enough to keep it steamtight, and the resulting friction causes wear of valve and port face, and absorbs much power. To avoid this, the balanced slide-valve, in which part of the back of the valve is relieved of steam pressure, was invented (fig. 2d). A more modern solution is the piston-valve, consisting of two small pistons on the same spindle, working in a cylindrical steam chest, in which steam and exhaust ports are cut, exactly as in the flat port face on which the slide-valve works. Fig. 3 (a and b) shows the essential resemblance between the slide-valve and the piston-valve. The latter is perfectly balanced, and comparatively frictionless, but depends on piston rings for steamtightness, and so is liable to leak. In the piston-valve the pistons can be well spaced out, and the steam ports correspondingly shortened (fig. 3c) to reduce steam losses. Piston-valves are standard practice on locomotives

Steam Engine. Figure 2. Valves.

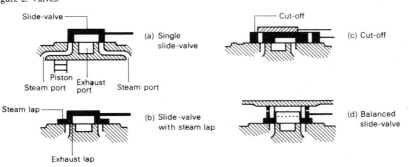

Steam Engine

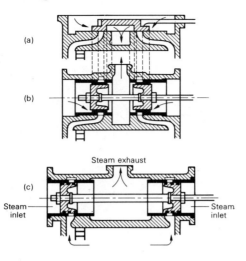

(a)

(b)

Steam exhaust

(c)

Steam inlet — Steam inlet

Comparison of a Slide-valve with cap
　　　　　　 b Piston-valve
　　　　　　 c Piston slide-valve with spaced pistons

Steam Engine. Figure 3. Piston slide valves.

and steam engines using superheated steam. The Corliss engine was a reversion to the original idea of four independent valves per cylinder; it used cylindrical valves, with a rotary motion like plug cocks, but having passages specially shaped to give large port openings. Corliss engines are no longer made, but independent steam- and exhaust-valves nowadays are standard practice on high-efficiency stationary engines; poppet-valves or lift- or drop-valves, which come down on to a seat, as in internal combustion engine practice, are used instead of valves with a sliding or rotating action. Such valves require little force to move them, give a large valve opening with a small lift, are easy to make and maintain steamtight, and by means of cams can be made to open and close exactly as the designer wishes. Single-beat valves are used in steam lorries, but balanced double-beat valves are the general rule in stationary practice (fig. 4). Double beat valves are also used in locomotives.

Valve Gears. The early slide-valves were worked by an eccentric placed so that at dead centre the valve was closing both steam ports. To give preadmission, however, the valve should be open at dead centre by a small amount called the lead; this is done by shifting the eccentric on the shaft relative to the crank. A single eccentric, set in this manner, gives only one direction of rotation, and to make the engine reversible a large number of different valve gears have been invented. It is seen (fig. 1) that the eccentric always leads the crank; to run backwards there must be a second eccentric similarly set on the other side of the crank, and means for driving the valve from it. In the Stephenson gear (fig. 5a), the ends of the two eccentric rods were connected by a curved link, in which worked a slide block and pin attached to the valve rod. The link and eccentric rods were lifted up or down so that the drive to the valve came from either eccentric. It was soon found that, at intermediate positions, the valve gear still functioned, but at an earlier cut-off. Thus the engine could be

adjusted for varying loads by 'notching up', and changing the point of cut-off. Other link gears are the Gooch and the Allan straight link gear. The radial gears depend on the geometrical fact that the motion of the two eccentrics can be represented by: (1) a constant motion in phase with the cross-head or crank; (2) a variable and reversible motion at right angles to the crank. This is clearly shown in the Walschaerts gear (fig. 5b), where the pendulum lever, worked from the cross-head, provides the 'lap and lead' component, while an eccentric at right angles to the crank provides the variable 'travel' component, through a radius rod and reversing link. Poppet-valves on stationary engines are operated by cams on a geared camshaft running alongside the cylinder. The inlet valves usually have a drop mechanism; i.e., the valve is opened by the cam, against a spring, at the point of admission; at the point of cut-off the connection between the valve rod and the valve is abruptly broken, and the valve comes sharply on to its seat under the action of the spring, giving a clear-cut point of cut-off without throttling. The drop-mechanism, and hence the point of cut-off, is controlled by the governor.

Flywheel. The pressure of steam acting on the piston of an engine varies continuously throughout the stroke and would produce a very irregular motion of the engine were it not for the flywheel. The size of the flywheel depends on: (1) the percentage variation in speed allowable throughout the stroke; (2) the variation in engine torque throughout the stroke; (3) the speed of the engine.

Governor. The governor plays a similar part to the flywheel, but over a longer period of time. If the mean power developed by the engine is greater than the power absorbed by the load, the speed gradually increases; the governor has to detect this and reduce the power of the engine until normal speed is regained and vice versa. Most governors depend on the action of centrifugal force. A simple Watt governor is shown in fig. 6. The vertical shaft, carrying two heavy balls at the end of arms, is rotated by some portion of the engine mechanism. Centrifugal force tends to move the balls outward, while the controlling force of gravity tends to move them inward. At any speed an equilibrium is reached; if the speed is increased, or falls short of its normal value, the balls move out or in, thus raising or lowering a collar connected to the throttle-valve through a lever and so controlling the output of the engine. A governor must be very sensitive to small variations in speed; to increase the sensitivity a static load may

Steam Engine. Figure 4. Poppet- (lift-, or drop-) valves.

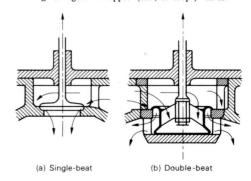

(a) Single-beat　　　　(b) Double-beat

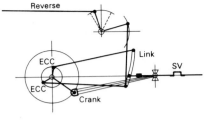

Stephenson (link-motion)

(a)

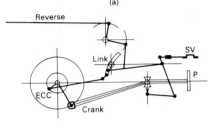

Walschaerts (radial)

(b)

Steam Engine. Figure 5. Valve gears.

be added to the Watt governor, giving a larger controlling force without altering the centrifugal force (Porter's governor), or the arms of the governor may be crossed, so reducing the variation in height h and consequently the speed range of the governor, which means increasing its sensitivity. Modern stationary engines employ a spring as a controlling force (fig. 7). An engine may be controlled either by the throttle or by the cut-off. With the former the governor opens or closes a valve in the steam pipe. This is very simple and requires little power at the governor, but is uneconomical, as the full pressure of steam is rarely used. In cut-off governing the valve gear is

adjusted to give a later or earlier cut-off; with drop-valves the governor controls the point at which the valve is disconnected from the operating gear (see *Valve Gears* above). This method is the more economical, but is generally more complicated. If a governor is made very sensitive, hunting or rhythmic speed variation of the engine may be set up. This is caused by the governor instantly responding to speed variations and overshooting the mark each time; in such a case the governor must be made less rapid acting by means of an oil dash-pot or other damping device.

***Forms of Steam Engine.** The Simple Steam Engine* is a single-cylinder, slow-speed, horizontal machine with a slide-valve, using saturated steam and exhausting to the atmosphere. Another type is the vertical high-speed engine with forced lubrication and a totally enclosed crankcase to keep out dust and to stop oil being thrown about.

Condensing Engines. By exhausting into a closed air-tight vessel, in which steam is condensed to water almost instantaneously, very low back pressures can be attained, with a corresponding increase in efficiency. Condensers are of two types, surface condensers, and jet condensers. The former consists of a chamber traversed by a large number of small tubes, through which passes cold water. The exhaust steam is condensed on the outside of these tubes; the condensate thus formed is extracted from the bottom of the condenser by an 'air pump' and, after being freed from oil, is returned to a hot well in the boiler-house to feed the boilers. Being warm it saves coal; and as it contains no impurities, it does not cause scaling of the boilers as fresh water would (see TURBINE, STEAM). In the jet condenser (fig. 8) the exhaust steam is condensed in a small chamber by direct contact with a jet of cold water; the mixture of condensate and jet water is extracted by means of an 'air pump' and led to the hot well. Jet condensers are more efficient and smaller than surface condensers; but the jet water must be very pure, as any impurities in it are conveyed to the boilers, and deposited as scale; they cannot therefore be used on sea-going

Steam Engine. Figure 6. Principle of governors.

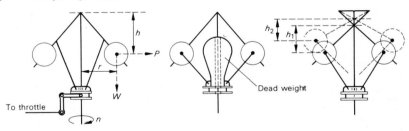

Watt's conical pendulum governor

(a)

Porter's or loaded governor

(b)

Governor with arms crossed

(c)

W = weight of each ball in newtons
W/g = mass of each ball in kilograms
n = speed of rotation of spindle, revolutions per second
r = radius of path in which balls revolve
h = vertical distance of path below point of suspension of rods on spindle axis
P = centrifugal force on each ball = $4\pi^2 n^2 r W/g$

Condition of equilibrium:
$Wr = Ph.$
$\therefore Wr = 4\pi^2 n^2 rh\, W/g.$
$\therefore n^2 h = g/4\pi^2$

Steam Engine

ships. Condensers are used on nearly all stationary and marine engines.

Compound Engines. In compound engines steam is partially expanded in a small high-pressure cylinder, and then passed to a receiver; from here it is admitted to a larger low-pressure cylinder, where the rest of the expansion takes place, finally exhausting to the atmosphere, or a condenser. The range of expansion in each cylinder is thus halved. Engines in which the steam is used in three or four stages are called triple- or quadruple-expansion engines. Advantages of the compound system are: (1) later cut-off in each cylinder, thus simplifying the valve gear (see *Valves* above); (2) the pressure difference between the steam and the cylinder walls in each cylinder is less than in a simple engine so that heat losses are reduced and there is less condensation of the steam. Even with superheated steam a compound engine exhausting to the atmosphere will show a saving of 5–10 per cent.

Uniflow Engines. In a uniflow engine steam is admitted by valves as usual, but exhaust takes place through ports cut in the cylinder wall; when uncovered by the piston on the outward stroke release takes place, and when closed again on the return stroke compression occurs. As these events are interdependent, release must be early to avoid excessive compression. In the uniflow engine steam flows only one way—in at the ends via the valves, and out at the middle via the exhaust ports. Live steam does not have to enter through ports that have been cooled by exhaust steam, thus reducing the 'missing quantity', and wet exhaust steam escapes directly to a cold exhaust port, so that re-evaporation is reduced, giving a free exhaust. Uniflow engines are a comparatively recent development; they are generally fitted with cam-operated drop valves, and are used in mills and collieries where a simple high-efficiency steam engine is required.

Development of the Steam Engine. The first stationary steam engines were designed for pumping water from mines, to enable them to be sunk much deeper than was possible with hand-pumps. The first practical pumping

Steam Engine. Figure 7. Governor controlled by spring.

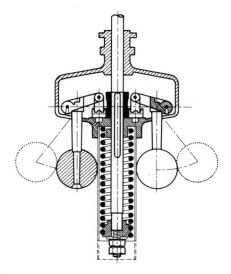

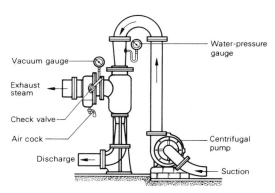

Steam Engine. Figure 8. Jet condenser.

engine was built by Savery in 1698 (fig. 9); on the down stroke the surface of the water in the receiver was used as a piston, the water being forced out by the pressure of steam from the boiler when the steam cock was opened; on the return stroke the steam in the receiver was condensed by pouring water over the outside from the water cock; the resultant vacuum was filled by water from the mine ready for the next down stroke. This engine was very inefficient, as the steam had to heat the receiver at each stroke before it could fill it. Further, the height to which it could be pumped was dependent on the boiler pressure, which in those days was very low. Its successor, Newcomen's engine, 1711, used a piston, piston rod, and beam to actuate a separate pump so that mine water could be forced to heights, depending on the relative sizes of the steam and water cylinders, without requiring a high steam pressure. The cylinder, however, was still used as a condenser (a jet of water being injected each stroke), which meant a very large steam consumption. The idea of keeping the cylinder hot continuously, by using a separate condenser, was due to Watt, who patented a single-acting engine on this system in 1769, and brought out his first double-acting engine in 1782. Watt made a scientific study of the steam engine, and invented the separate condenser, the 'air-pump', expansive working of steam, lagging of the cylinder and steam pipes, the stuffing-box, the governor, the indicator and the parallel motion (of which the modern equivalent is the cross-head and slide bar); the crank was also his invention, but the patent was stolen. The success of his low-pressure condensing engine delayed the coming of the high-pressure non-condensing engine and the compound engine (invented by Hornblower, 1781) for many years. And, as his machines were beam engines, the direct-acting engine was a rarity until after 1825. With the invention of the crank in 1781, the steam engine came into extensive use for power purposes, and was the only power used until the end of the 19th century. Steam engines worked the first electric power stations, where the need for high speeds was met by vertical engines and the later demand for large powers by enormous vertical triple- and quadruple-expansion engines. When alternating-current power stations became the rule, turbines replaced the steam engine. In more recent times internal combustion engines and electric motors have taken the field, and the steam turbine is supreme as prime mover for large installations, and especially where steam ('back-

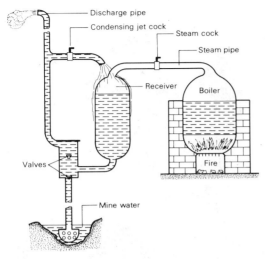

Steam Engine. Figure 9. Savery's stationary pumping engine.

pressure') is needed for other purposes. Steam engines were used in motor cars from about 1890 until 1914, but were then superseded by the petrol engine. For many years after that they continued in use for powering heavy lorries, road rollers and traction engines.

See also INDICATOR, ENGINE; LOCOMOTIVE; THERMO-DYNAMICS.

Bibliography: H. W. Dickinson, *Short History of the Steam Engine*, 2nd ed. 1963; G. Watkins, *Stationary Steam Engine*, 1968; J. Farey, *Treatise on the Steam Engine. Historical, Practical and Descriptive* (2 vols), 1971; R. H. Thurston, *History of the Growth of the Steam Engine*, new ed. 1972.

Steam Turbine, see STEAMSHIP; TURBINE, STEAM.

Steamship. The first practical steamboat was the *Charlotte Dundas*, a tug built by Symington in 1801, and fitted with one of Watt's double-acting condensing engines, driving a stern paddle-wheel. The first naval steamship was the *Lightning*, built at Deptford in 1823. All early steamships were fitted with paddle-wheels so that the main shaft was transverse, at a considerable height above the ship's bottom, and which rotated at a slow speed. The first marine engine (as distinct from a land engine fitted into a ship) was the side-lever engine, a variation of the beam engine that was proving so successful on land. The beam or 'lever' was placed at the side of a vertical cylinder, in the bottom of the boat, and was driven by return rods from the crosshead. It was used on merchant ships almost until the advent of the screw-propeller in 1840; in the Navy, however, direct-acting engines were tried, both of the orthodox type and with oscillating cylinders placed vertically under the crankshaft, working upwards to save space, for until 1869 steam in the Navy was used only as an auxiliary to sails. Successful experiments with the screw-propeller were carried out by Ericson in 1837, and the first ship so fitted was Brunel's enormous passenger steamer *Great Eastern*, 1840; but propellers did not become standard practice in the mercantile marine till about 1860. The propeller did not interfere with the sailing qualities of a ship, and was much

less vulnerable than the paddle-wheel, so it found great favour in the Navy. Marine-engine design was thereby completely changed, as the main shaft was now fore-and-aft, low down in the ship, and rotated at a high speed. The first naval vessel with a propeller, the *Rattler*, 1843, had oscillating cylinders working downwards, geared to the propeller shaft. This expedient was only temporary, as higher-speed engines, direct coupled to the main shaft, were soon developed. Some difficulty was experienced with them, as they had to be entirely below the water-line to avoid damage in action; the vertical marine engine working downwards on to the shaft, as used in merchant ships, could not be employed and there was very little room in the width of the ship for horizontal engines. With the introduction of armoured ships in 1872 the vertical marine engine was adopted, and this proved the final type both for the Navy and the mercantile marine. With the low boiler pressures at first used (70–140 kN/m²), single-expansion engines were adequate, but as pressures rose to 400 and 800 kN/m², compound engines came into use (1870); with a still further rise in pressure to 1000 kN/m² (1885), and to 2000 kN/m² with water-tube boilers in the Navy (1895), triple-expansion engines became general. In the merchant service quadruple-expansion engines were also developed (1900). The early engines had jet condensers, which introduced salt water into the boilers, causing rapid scaling and corrosion; surface condensers had previously been tried and found unsatisfactory, but in 1860 they were reintroduced and improved boiler conditions considerably. Today the reciprocating steam engine is obsolete; for large powers it has given way to the steam turbine and for lower powers it is being replaced by the diesel engine.

As the ship's propeller became very inefficient at speeds above 2000 rev/min direct turbine drive would require a large number of stages to reduce the steam velocity, and very large rotors, and though employed in earlier vessels, it has now given way to reduction-geared drive. Another solution is turbo-electric drive, which has many advantages. The high-speed steam turbine drives an electric generator supplying power to motors driving the shafts. The propelling motors can then be independently started, speed-regulated, and reversed by remote control from a central control board. Electric light is needed in any case, and electric power is convenient for working deck machinery, pumps, ventilators and other auxiliaries, and for refrigerators, cooking, lifts, etc. As compared with the reciprocating engine, the turbine has the advantage of light weight, small size, and greater efficiency. However, its high fuel consumption has prevented wider adoption.

The first turbine-driven ship was the *Turbinia* (1897), a small vessel built by Parsons to demonstrate his marine steam turbine to the Admiralty. It had three units (high pressure, intermediate pressure, and low pressure) driving three propeller shafts, and reached a speed of 34·5 knots (63·8 km/h). The first naval vessel fitted was the destroyer *Viper* (1900), speed 36·5 knots (67·5 km/h) compared with 28 knots for previous destroyers; and since 1905, when the *Dreadnought* (23,000 h.p., or 16,150 kW) was so equipped, naval vessels of all classes have been fitted with steam turbines. The 42,000-tonne battle-cruiser *Hood* (1917) had four geared turbines developing 150,000 h.p. (112,000 kW). The first merchant ships with

Stearic Acid

turbines were the *Victorian* and *Virginian* of the Allan Line, soon followed by the Cunard liner *Carmania* (21,000 h.p., or 15,700 kW, 1905); she proved so satisfactory that the two next Cunard mail steamers the *Lusitania* and *Mauretania* (67,000 h.p., or 50,000 kW, 1907) were equipped in the same way, giving a speed of 26 knots (48 km/h).

Today the main use for the turbine is on the very large tankers and container ships where very high powers, of the order of 30,000 h.p. (22,000 kW) from each shaft, are required. The latest turbines are being designed to operate with steam temperatures of 600 °C and pressures of 14,000 kN/m² and it is claimed that these turbines, although having a slightly higher fuel cost than the diesel, will, because of their greater reliability, offer lower total running costs.

With naval ships, except for the very large aircraft carriers and nuclear submarines, the steam turbine has been replaced by the gas turbine because of the savings in space and manpower requirements. The current generation of nuclear-powered ships, naval and commercial, use the reactor for raising steam and the steam turbine for propulsion. At the present time one of the most powerful turbine installations in the world is on the US aircraft carrier *Enterprise*. It is claimed that she developed more power during her trials than any other ship in history. She has two reactors for each of her four sets of turbines and develops 280,000 h.p. (210,000 kW).

See also PADDLE-STEAMER; SHIPS AND SHIPBUILDING.

Stearic Acid, $CH_3 \cdot (CH_2)_{16} \cdot COOH$, a saturated fatty acid, occurs widely distributed as the glyceride in animal and vegetable fats and oils—usually associated with the glycerides of palmitic and oleic acids. It is most abundant in the more solid fats, particularly animal fats. Pure stearic acid is white, crystalline, insoluble in water but soluble in alcohol and ether, and has a relative density of 0·85 at its melting point 69 °C, whereas commercial stearic acid may be white or slightly yellowish in colour and have a melting point as low as 53 °C. All salts of stearic acid except those of alkali metals are insoluble in water. Commercial stearic acid is obtained chiefly from split and distilled animal fatty acids by hydraulic pressing or fractional crystallisation at low temperature from a solvent. Three grades are usually produced, known as 'single-', 'double-' or 'triple-pressed' stearic acid, but, as these methods merely separate the saturated and unsaturated acids, they are by no means pure compounds. Actually, single- and double-pressed stearic acid contains more palmitic than stearic acid. Production of stearic acid of about 90 per cent purity is usually by fractional distillation of the fatty acid mixture, but small quantities are produced by completely hydrogenating and splitting vegetable oils. Among the more important manufactured products in which stearic acid and its derivatives are used are foods, soaps, detergents, lubricants, protective coatings, gramophone records, polishes, cosmetics, toilet preparations, candles, matches, crayons, rubber compounds, and paper coatings. Commercial stearic acid is often called stearin or stearine; this is a misnomer, as stearin is a glyceride of stearic acid. See FATTY ACIDS.

Stearin, or tristearin, $(C_{17}H_{35} \cdot COO)_3 C_3 H_5$, is a component of the solid fats, and when pure is a colourless, tasteless substance, soluble in ether but insoluble in water.

David Steel. (*Camera Press*)

It is decomposed by water and dilute mineral acids at moderately high temperatures (200 °C), forming GLYCEROL and STEARIC ACID.

Steatornis, see GUACHARO.

Steed, Henry Wickham (1871–1956), British journalist, born at Long Melford, Suffolk. He was educated at Sudbury Grammar School, and at Jena, Berlin, and Paris universities. In 1896 he became foreign correspondent to *The Times* in Berlin, and was the newspaper's foreign editor throughout the First World War. From 1918 to 1922 he was editor of *The Times*, and was proprietor and editor of the *Review of Reviews* from 1923 to 1931. He also lectured on European history at London University, 1925–38. His works include *The Hapsburg Monarchy*, 1913, *Through Thirty Years, 1892–1922*, 1924, *The Antecedents of Post-war Europe*, 1932, *Hitler: Whence and Whither?*, 1934, *The Press*, 1938, *The Fifth Arm*, 1940, *Words on the Air*, 1946.

Steel, David Martin Scott (1938–), British politician and leader of the Liberal party since 1976, educated at the Prince of Wales School, Nairobi, George Watson's College, Edinburgh, and Edinburgh University. He was assistant secretary of the Liberal party, 1962–66, and a BBC TV interviewer, 1964–65. In 1965 he was elected Liberal MP for Roxburgh, Selkirk, and Peebles and was sponsor of the private member's bill to reform the law on abortion, 1966–67. From 1970 to 1975 he was Liberal chief whip. In 1976 he succeeded Jeremy THORPE as leader of the Liberal party and was the first party leader in Britain to be elected by party supporters outside Parliament rather than by MPs.

Steel, see IRON AND STEEL; METALLURGY; ROLLING MILLS; STRUCTURAL STEELWORK.

364

Steel-bow Lease. In old Scots law, steel-bow goods comprised corn, straw, cattle, or instruments of tillage delivered by a landlord to the tenant at entry on the condition that at the end of the tenancy a like quantity of such goods would be redelivered by the tenant. In addition, the tenant paid a steel-bow rent on the value of the stock. Many Scottish farm leases still provide that straw and dung will be steel-bow goods.

Steel Drum, percussion musical instrument invented in the 1940s in Trinidad. Various materials were used initially but nowadays the bottoms of very large oil drums are always used. Small areas on the face of the drum are isolated by hammer and punch and are then tuned by hammering. Steel drums are used in sets, the highest or ping-pong with some 25 small areas, each producing a different pitch, the second pan with about 14, a pair of third pans each with 9 or 10 notes, and usually 4 bass pans with 4 or 5 notes each. The depths of the pans are proportionate to their pitches, the ping-pong being 7 cm to 10 cm deep and the bass pans being the whole oil drum with the top cut out. Steel drums are, apart from electronic instruments, the most recently invented musical instruments but their potential has not been properly explored by composers.

Bibliography: P. Seeger, *Steel Drums*, 1964.

Steele, Sir Richard (1672–1729), English essayist and dramatist, born in Dublin. He was educated at Charterhouse, London, where Joseph ADDISON was a fellow pupil, and at Christ Church and Merton colleges, Oxford. In 1694, he enlisted in the Life Guards, becoming a captain, and led a carefree, dissipated life. Reacting against this, in 1701 he published *The Christian Hero*, a moral work, and in the same year produced his first, and most amusing, comedy, *The Funeral*, at Drury Lane. *The Lying Lover*, produced in 1703, was less successful, although *The Tender Husband*, 1705, was better received. Steele then turned to journalism, and in 1707 was made gazetteer, or official government writer, in charge of producing *The London Gazette* (see 'LONDON GAZETTE'); he also wrote political pamphlets supporting the Whigs. In 1709 he founded *The Tatler* (see 'TATLER, THE') and, as Isaac Bickerstaff, a pseudonym borrowed from Jonathan Swift, contributed two-thirds of its essays. Several of the remainder were written by Addison, but Steele's are characterised by his easy, light style. In *The Tatler*, Steele produced the same mixture of entertainment and moral instruction (avoiding politics) which was later the great feature of *The Spectator*. For this journal, started by both writers in 1711, Steele invented many of the famous characters, such as Sir Roger de Coverley, while Addison, with his more polished writing, concentrated on developing ideas (see 'SPECTATOR, THE'). Steele contributed about 250 of the daily papers, and also invented the 'Spectator Club'. In 1713 he entered Parliament, and in the following year issued *The Crisis*, a paper in favour of the Hanoverian succession; it brought about his expulsion from the House but also the reward of various offices after George I's accession.

Steele also produced other journals, including the *Guardian* and *The Englishman*, which were political, and *Town-Talk* and the *Theatre*, which ran for a short time. His last comedy, *The Conscious Lovers*, produced at Drury Lane in 1722, is one of the best English 'sentimental' comedies. Gradually Steele's health deteriorated; he disagreed with his friend Addison, and later retired to Wales, where he died.

Although a successful dramatist, it is as an essayist that Steele is famous. Unlike Addison, he was not completely a man of his time, some characteristics recalling the Restoration and others foreshadowing the later 18th century; he was a classicist only by opportunity and accident. With clear thought and a gift of delicate treatment, he seeks the ideal of pleasant negligence, his form more spontaneous than painstaking. In *The Tatler*, Steele's individual work, he followed a favourite task, the reform of manners and the victory of culture over excess individualism. His comedies also express beliefs in homely virtues and moral principles, to which are added a gift for fun and lively dialogue. *The Spectator* is edited in five volumes by D. F. Bond, 1965; and *The Englishman*, 1713–15, by R. Blanchard, 1955.

Bibliography: G. A. Aitken, *The Life of Richard Steele*, 1889; A. R. Humphreys, *Steele, Addison and their Periodical Essays*, 1959; W. Connely, *Sir Richard Steele*, 1968; C. Winton, *The Early Career of Richard Steele*, and *Sir Richard Steele M.P.: The Later Career*, 1970; J. Loftis, *Steele at Drury Lane*, 1973.

Steelwork, see STRUCTURAL STEELWORK.

Steelyard, see BALANCE.

Sir Richard Steele, portrait by Sir Godfrey Kneller, painted in 1711 for the Kit-Cat Club. (*National Portrait Gallery, London*)

Steen, Jan

Steen, Jan (1625/6–79), Dutch painter, born at Leiden, probably studied under Nicholas Knupfer (1603–60), Adriaen van Ostade, and his father-in-law Jan van Goyen. He worked mainly in Leiden. In 1672 he received a license to operate a tavern there, and in popular esteem he is associated primarily with merry or riotous drinking scenes. Steen was, however, a painter of great ability, whose humorous view of popular life is accompanied by a real gift of composition and colour and he was more versatile than is generally realised, painting portraits, historical and religious works as well as genre scenes. He was one of the most prolific painters of the period.

Steenbok, see STEINBOK.

Steeple, term applied to a tall tower, usually including its spire; especially applied to the spired towers of Sir Christopher WREN's City churches in London.

Steeplechasing (athletics). This event is now standardised at 3000 m (1 mile 1520 yards). It comprises 28 hurdles (0·91 m high) and a water-jump (3·66 m square) in each of the seven laps. The water is 0·70 m in depth at the foot of the hurdle, sloping to ground level at the end of the jump—competitors go either over or through the water. Originally the water-jump was constructed with a hurdle and hedge so that the competitor could not vault the jump by placing a foot on the hurdle, but had to jump the hedge and land in the water. Since the 1930s, however, it has been possible for competitors to place a foot on the hurdle and so clear the water-jump with comparative ease, so that the event has more or less become a flat race with a few obstacles. The world record stands at 8 minutes 08·0 seconds, nearly 40 seconds faster than the first world record at the 1952 Olympics (cf. Paavo Nurmi's record in 1926 for 3000 m flat was 8 minutes 20·4 seconds).

For horse racing, see POINT-TO-POINT.

Steer, Philip Wilson (1860–1942), British painter,

Jan Steen. *Music Making on a Terrace,* c. 1670. The costumes of the two men are probably based on theatrical types. *(National Gallery, London)*

born at Birkenhead. He studied painting at the Gloucester School of Art and in Paris. His *Chepstow Castle* and *Mrs Raynes*, both in the Tate Gallery, are perhaps his finest achievements in landscape and portraiture respectively. He first exhibited at the Royal Academy in 1883, but was more closely associated with the New English Art Club. A fine early series of paintings at Walberswick were executed in a Neo-Impressionist style, but he will rank primarily as a landscape artist in the tradition of CONSTABLE. His watercolours were noticeable for their atmospheric quality and freedom of style. Steer was awarded the Order of Merit in 1937.

Bibliography: Life by R. Ironside, 1944; B. Laughton (Ed.), *Philip Wilson Steer: Paintings,* 1972.

Steevens, George (1736–1800), English critic, born in London and educated at Eton and Cambridge. He issued various reprints of the quarto edition of Shakespeare, and assisted Dr JOHNSON in his edition, and also in his *Lives of the Poets*. In 1793 he himself brought out a new edition of Shakespeare, dealing rather freely with the text.

Steevens, George Warrington (1869–1900), British journalist, born in London. Educated at the City of London School and Oxford, where he became a fellow of Pembroke, he turned to journalism and was famous as a foreign correspondent of the *Daily Mail*. Among his works were *With Kitchener to Khartoum*, 1898, and *From Cape Town to Ladysmith*, 1900, the latter compiled from dispatches written before his death during the siege. (See LADYSMITH.)

Stefano, Tommaso di, see GIOTTINO.

Stefan's Law, named after Joseph Stefan, Austrian physicist (1835–93), states that the electromagnetic energy radiated from a heated body is proportional to the fourth power of its absolute temperature. Thus, if R is the amount of energy radiated per second from unit surface area of a body at an absolute temperature T, then $R = \sigma T^4$, where σ is Stefan's constant. Strictly the law applies only to 'black bodies' (see RADIATION), but it is frequently a good approximation to the radiation of other objects.

Stefánsson, Davið (1895–1964), Icelandic lyric poet and dramatist, born at Eyjafjörður. His one novel, *Sólon Islandus*, 1940, telling of an Icelandic vagabond and dreamer, and his plays, including *Gullna hliðið*, 1941, are of less importance than his remarkably graceful lyrical poetry.

Stefansson, Vilhjalmur (1879–1962), Canadian explorer, born at Arnes, Manitoba, of Icelandic ancestry; graduated at State University of Iowa. He made three expeditions to the Canadian ARCTIC learning the ESKIMO language and employing their hunting and travelling techniques in his exploration. The first expedition, 1906–07, is described in *Hunters of the Great North*; the second, 1908–12, in *My Life with the Eskimo*; and the third, 1913–18, in *The Friendly Arctic*. Stefansson then began a life as a scholar, lecturer, and author bringing to the attention of the world the potentialities and strategic importance of the Arctic. Among his later writings were: *The Northward Course of Empire*, 1922; *The Adventure of Wrangel Island*, 1925; *The Standardisation of Error*, 1927; *Adventures in Error*, 1937; *Three Voyages of Mar-*

tin Frobisher, 1938; *Unsolved Mysteries of the Arctic*, 1938; *Iceland: The First American Republic*, 1939; *Ultima Thule: Further Mysteries of the Arctic*, 1940; *Greenland*, 1942; *Arctic Manual*, 1944; *Not by Bread Alone*, 1946; *The Fat of the Land*, 1956; *North-west to Fortune*, 1958; *Discovery* (autobiography), 1964.

Stegosaurus, a genus of late Jurassic North American DINOSAURS of the order Ornithischia. They were ungainly quadrupedal herbivores, with very small heads, a double row of triangular plates along the back, and spikes on the tail.

Stegoselachians, a group of extinct skate-like 'armoured sharks' of the Lower Devonian period belonging to the PLACODERMI.

Steier, see STEYR.

Steiermark, see STYRIA.

Stein, Gertrude (1874–1946), US poet and critic, born at Allegheny, Pennsylvania. She was educated at Radcliffe College and Johns Hopkins medical school, where she made a study of brain anatomy. From 1904 she lived in Paris, and in the First World War was decorated for her work for the French wounded.

In her works, influenced by the artists Picasso and Matisse, whose paintings she collected, she developed an abstract, experimental type of prose which in turn had some influence on later writers. Some of the mannerisms of a conscious innovator were abandoned, with profit to intelligibility, in the later volumes. She described her books as fiction or autobiography or children's literature, but neither her own descriptions nor the oddity of her titles give any real clue to their contents, which, however, show much observation and profundity. In Paris she befriended and encouraged several expatriate American writers, including Ernest Hemingway. Her writings include *Three Lives*, 1908, *Making of Americans*, 1925, *Autobiography of Alice B. Toklas*, 1933, continued in *Everybody's Autobiography*, 1937, a study on Picasso, 1938, *Paris France*, 1940, *Wars I Have Seen*, 1945, *Brewsie and Willie*, 1946, and *Four in America*, 1947.
Bibliography: Studies by D. Sutherland, 1951, and E. M. S. Sprigge, 1957.

Stein, Heinrich Friedrich Karl, Freiherr vom und zum (1757–1831), German statesman, born near Nassau. He entered the service of Frederick the Great in 1780. From 1804 to 1807 he was minister for trade. After Tilsit he was recalled and given a free hand as minister of the Interior. His reforms included the abolition of serfdom, the introduction of free trade in land, a reorganisation of the Cabinet system, and the establishment of local self-government in towns. His work was aimed at arousing resistance to the French, and Napoleon on this account secured his dismissal. At the Congress of Vienna Stein pressed for a united Germany with a constitution excluding the princes, but was successfully opposed by METTERNICH. He then retired, studied history, and founded (1819) an historical research society, which published *Monumenta Germaniae historica*.
Bibliography: J. R. Seeley, *Life and Times of Stein*, 1879.

Stein, Sir Marc Aurel (1862–1943), naturalised British explorer, archaeologist, and Asiatic scholar, born in

Budapest. He travelled widely in Kashmir, central Asia (conducting excavations in Khotan), West China (see CAVES OF A THOUSAND BUDDHAS), Persia, Iraq, and Transjordan. His publications include: *Chronicle of Kings of Kashmir* (translated from Sanskrit), 1900; *Ancient Khotan*, 1907; *Ruins of Desert Cathay*, 1912; *Serindia*, 1921; *The Thousand Buddhas*, 1921; *On Alexander's Track to the Indus*, 1929; *Archaeological Reconnaissances in North-Western India and South Eastern Iran*, 1937; and *Old Routes of Western Iran*, 1940.

Steinamanger, see SZOMBATHELY.

Steinbeck, John Ernst (1902–68), US novelist and short-story writer, born at Salinas, California. Educated at Stanford University, he first won attention with the appearance in 1935 of the ironically humorous *Tortilla Flat*, a novel of life among the *paisanos* of Monterey, California. His reputation grew steadily with the publication of the novels *Of Mice and Men*, 1937, dramatised, 1939, and filmed, 1940, and, especially, *The Grapes of Wrath*, 1939, filmed in 1940. This novel, which won the

John Steinbeck. *(Popperfoto)*

Steinbok

Pulitzer Prize, tells of a refugee family from the dust-bowl of America, and is among the foremost of modern realistic fiction. Mostly his books are a blend of realism and romance, and their background and atmosphere are generally rural.

Among Steinbeck's other books are *Cup of Gold*, 1929, *Pastures of Heaven*, 1932, *To a God Unknown*, 1933, *The Moon is Down*, 1942, *Cannery Row*, 1945, *The Wayward Bus*, 1947, *The Pearl*, 1947, *East of Eden*, 1952, *Sweet Thursday*, 1954, *Pippin IV*, 1957, and *The Winter of Our Discontent*, 1961. In 1962, the year in which *Travels with Charley* was published, he was awarded the Nobel Prize for literature.

Bibliography: Studies by H. T. Moore, 1939; J. H. Jackson, 1940; F. W. Watt, *Steinbeck*, 1962; J. Fontenrose, *John Steinbeck*, 1967; R. M. Davis (Ed.), *Steinbeck: A Collection of Critical Essays*, 1972.

Steinbok, or steenbok, *Raphicerus campestris*, a southern African ANTELOPE, reddish-brown in colour and about 60 cm high at the shoulder. It differs from the grysbok (*R. melanotis*) in having no lateral (false) hoofs.

Steiner, George (1929–), English critic and scholar, born in Paris; educated at the universities of Paris, Chicago, Harvard, and Oxford. Steiner worked for the London *Economist*, 1952–56, taught at Princeton and Cambridge, became extraordinary fellow of Churchill College, Cambridge, in 1969, and in 1974, professor of English and comparative literature at the University of Geneva.

Steiner's large-scale studies *Tolstoy or Dostoyevsky*, 1959, and *The Death of Tragedy*, 1961, were followed by a collection of essays, *Language and Silence*, 1967, mainly concerned with the cultural-political crisis of our time as reflected in literature. A later critical study is *After Babel*, 1975, an attempt to integrate linguistic studies into literary criticism. *Anno Domini*, 1964, is a collection of short stories, and *White Knights in Reykjavik*, 1973, an account of the Fischer-Spassky chess match.

Steiner, Jakob (1796–1863), Swiss mathematician, born at Utzenstorf. Until he was 14 he could not write. PESTALOZZI took him into his school, 1813. Steiner went to Heidelberg University in 1818, and became professor of mathematics at Berlin University in 1834. He made numerous contributions to geometry, especially PROJECTIVE GEOMETRY, where he introduced the idea of 'duality': a theorem remains true if throughout its statement the word 'line' is replaced by 'point' and vice versa.

Steiner, Rudolf (1861–1925), Austrian founder of anthroposophy, born at Kraljevic, Croatia; he studied mathematics and natural science, and later worked in the Goethe archives at Weimar. From 1902 he evolved a new study of the 'higher worlds', opposed to traditional occultism. His theories of education, using the arts therapeutically in the treatment of mental deficiency, had much influence, his pioneer school at Stuttgart (established in 1919) inspiring similar experiments in many countries, including Britain. His works include *Welt- und Lebensanschauungen des neunzehnten Jahrhunderts*, 1900–01, *Theosophie*, 1904, *Wie eflangt man Erkenntnisse der höheren Welten*, 1909, and an autobiography, *Mein Lebensgang*, 1925.

Steinitz, Wilhelm (c. 1836–1900), naturalised US world chess champion, champion 1872–92, born in Prague of a large Jewish family. He studied at Vienna but soon decided to devote himself to chess, journalism providing a living while he studied chess theory. In 1866 he played and defeated Adolph Anderssen, then regarded as the world's strongest player. For the next 20 years Steinitz held this position, but in 1894 he was defeated by Emanuel LASKER who then claimed the world title as he did again in a return match two years later. Books include *The Modern Chess Instructor*, Part 1, 1889, Part 2, 1895.

Steinlen, Théophile (1859–1923), French graphic artist, born at Lausanne. He went to Paris, c. 1882, and devoted himself to depicting the popular life of the city, Montmartre in particular. He produced numerous lithographs, drawings, book illustrations, and posters.

Steinway, originally Steinweg, Henry Engelhard (1797–1871), US piano manufacturer of German birth, born at Wolfshagen. He established a firm in New York in 1853, and his pianos maintain a very high reputation.

Stella, Frank (1936–), US painter, born in Massachusetts. In 1960 he made a great impact when he exhibited paintings on a large scale consisting of thin regular white stripes on black. From 1960 to 1962 he worked in metallic paint, again using thin stripes which repeated the non-rectangular shape of the support. Later paintings by Stella employ a wider range of colour, the choice of which emphasises the flatness of the painting which is then contradicted by the use of overlapping shapes.

Bibliography: R. Rosenblum, *Frank Stella*, 1971.

Stellaland, one of two republics (the other being Goshen) which the BOERS from the Transvaal set up in 1882 on land which had been given them by native chiefs in return for help rendered in inter-tribal wars. It was so named on account of the fact that the great comet of 1882 was visible at the time of its formation. It had its capital at Vryburg. Cecil Rhodes saw in these republics, which lay astride the Missionary Road, a threat to vital communications to the north, and accordingly brought pressure on the prime minister of the Cape Colony to have them dissolved. This was done without bloodshed following Sir Charles Warren's arrival in Bechuanaland (now Botswana) in 1884.

Stellar Interferometer, an instrument invented by A. A. Michelson in 1890 for determining the diameters of stars. Atmospheric turbulence disturbs the path of the light reaching ground-based telescopes to an extent which makes it impossible to see detail in stellar objects of angular size less than about 1″ of arc. The stellar interferometer circumvents this difficulty. The angular size of a star, generally less than 0·02″, determines the distance apart on the ground between points which are coherently illuminated, i.e., points such that INTERFERENCE fringes can be obtained between beams of light from the star falling on these two points. Thus by measuring the contrast of the interference for points a different distance apart it is possible to deduce the angular size of the star. Michelson's instrument consisted of a long girder with mirrors mounted on a telescope; the mirrors could be set at different spacings and they sent the light down through the telescope to form interference fringes in the focal plane. See also COHERENCE OF LIGHT; INTERFEROMETER.

Bibliography: A. A. Michelson, *Studies in Optics*, 1927 (repr. 1962); M. Born and E. Wolf, *Principles of Optics*, 5th ed. 1975.

Stellar Magnitudes, see MAGNITUDE.

Stellar Parallaxes, see PARALLAX.

Stellaria, see STITCHWORT.

Stellenbosch, town of Cape Province, South Africa, 48 km east of Cape Town, situated in a vine-growing valley, west of the Drakenstein Mountains. The second oldest town in South Africa, the site of Stellenbosch was selected by Simon Van der Stel, one of the earliest and most progressive governors of the Cape. It has a picturesque Rhenish church, which stands in the *Braak* or village square, with a fine pulpit carved by Anton Anreith. Stellenbosch has a university with (1973) some 8850 students; until 1918 it was called Victoria College and here were educated James Barry Hertzog and Jan Christian Smuts, both prime ministers of South Africa. In the district are fruit farms and vineyards, and Stellenbosch is the wine centre of South Africa. Population 29,728 of whom 13,646 are whites.

Stelvio Pass, Alpine pass leading from Bormio in Italy to Santa Maria in Switzerland. It is the highest motor road over the ALPS (2757 m), and is remarkable for its large number of hairpin bends.

Stem, the aerial leaf-bearing portion of a plant, though many stems also extend underground to form a rhizome, which can be distinguished from a root by the leaves and flowering shoots it produces. The stem supports the leaves and flowers and conveys the food materials. In the first year of growth the stem is usually green, soft and herbaceous, but in the second year and later in a perennial plant or a tree it may become dark, hard and woody. Herbaceous perennials that die down each autumn have persistent underground stems or branches, which, unlike

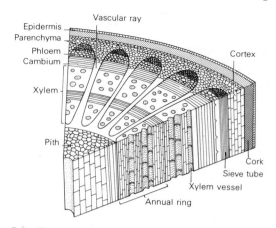

Stem. The internal transport system in a tree trunk.

roots, bear small scale leaves, for example the rhizomes of the iris and Solomon's seal, and the stolons of the lily-of-the-valley and couch grass. Underground storage stems include tubers and corms. Above ground, stems may be erect, ascending, prostrate, creeping, climbing or twining. The zone of the stem from which the leaves diverge is called the node. Stem anatomy is very variable in different plant groups, varying from the soft stems of herbaceous monocotyledons to the thick woody stems of trees.

Stemonaceae (synonym Roxburghiaceae), a family of monocotyledonous herbaceous plants with tuberous roots, of the tropics. *Stemona tuberosa*, a climber, with green bell-shaped flowers, is sometimes grown in warm greenhouses.

Sten Gun, see FIREARMS; SUBMACHINE-GUN.

Stencilling, art of forming letters or ornamental designs by means of a stencil. The required words or pattern are first cut out on a stencil or thin plate, which is then laid flat upon a surface and coloured over with a brush so that

Stem. Electron micrographs of the phloem transport system. LEFT Longitudinal section showing a sieve plate between two sieve-tube elements and a companion cell. RIGHT Cross-section of similar cells. *(Raynor Jones)*

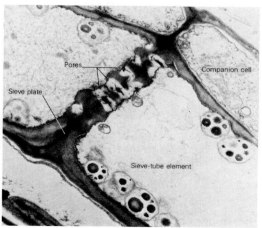

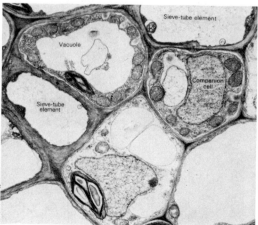

the surface below is marked as required. The advantage of stencilling is that any number of copies can thus be made from one plate. This method is used for colouring prints and decorating furniture, woodwork, cloth, etc. If different colours are required to produce flowers, fruits, etc., the design for one colour only must be made on the stencil, the second colour being imprinted with a new plate after the first colour has been dried. A similar method is the use of masks, in which both the part cut out of the stencil and the hole left in it are used; variations of tone are obtained by the overlap of transparent colours applied by spraying. For office use, when a great number of circulars are required, it is more convenient to use a wax sheet, on which words may be written or typed. The *pochoir* process, developed in France, applies the stencil principle to the reproduction of pictures in flat colour. See also PRINTMAKING.

Stendal, town of East Germany, in the district of Magdeburg, 56 km north-east of Magdeburg. In the second half of the 13th century it was the capital of the BRANDENBURG Mark. The cathedral, begun in 1188, was rebuilt in the 14th century. There are metal, chemical, and foodstuff industries. Population 37,000.

Stendhal, pseudonym of Marie Henri Beyle (1783–1842), French author, born at Grenoble. He was in turn soldier, shopman, and diplomat. After some years spent in the commissariat, he went with Napoleon on the Russian campaign, and was at the retreat from Moscow. After Napoleon's fall he moved to Milan but in 1821 returned to Paris where he soon became known in literary circles. In 1830 he was appointed consul at Trieste and then at Civita Vecchia, a post he held until his death.

His works are remarkable for their fineness of observation and for the extraordinary abundance of ideas. His critical works include *Histoire de la peinture en Italie*, 1817, *Rome, Naples et Florence*, 1817, *Racine et Shakes-*peare, 1823–25, and *Promenades dans Rome*, 1829. His chief novels are *Le Rouge et le noir*, 1831, *La Chartreuse de Parme*, 1839, and the unfinished *Lucien Leuwen*, published 1894. Amongst a variety of miscellaneous works are his *Mémoires d'un touriste*, 1838. The *Journal de Stendhal*, 1888, *Vie de Henri Brulard*, 1890, *Souvenirs d'égotisme*, 1892, and his correspondence, all published posthumously, are valuable as autobiography.

Stendhal had the gift of psychological analysis, and it is for this, rather than for continuity and arrangement of plot, that his novels are so outstanding. Although he shared many of the literary ideas of the Romantics, he remained fiercely independent. His masterpiece, *Le Rouge et le noir*, had an enormous influence on European literature, and with Julien Sorel he created a new type of hero. Stendhal's reputation has risen considerably in modern times, and it has been appreciated that his work was a century in advance of his true era.

Bibliography: G. Blin, *Stendhal et les problèmes du roman*, 1955; F. W. J. Hemmings, *Stendhal: A Study of his Novels*, 1964; M. Wood, *Stendhal*, 1971.

Stenness, on MAINLAND in the Orkney Islands, Scotland, is the site of well-known prehistoric field antiquities. The ring of Brodgar, a stone circle 104 m in diameter, is the largest in Scotland. Maes Howe, a fine chambered tomb with dry stone walling, is allied to the Boyne megalithic culture of Ireland. Both are protected as ancient monuments.

Steno, Nicolaus, or Niels Stensen (1638–86), Danish anatomist, geologist, and priest, born in Copenhagen. He studied medicine there and at Leiden and Amsterdam. He discovered the excretory duct of the paratid, and the ceruminous glands (*Observationes Anatomicae*, 1622). He was professor of anatomy at Copenhagen, 1672–74. Adopting the Roman Catholic faith, he entered the priesthood, becoming a bishop in Germany in 1677.

Stenography, see SHORTHAND.

Stenosis, see STRICTURE.

Stenton, Sir Frank Merry (1880–1967), British historian; educated at Southwell Grammar School, University College, Reading, and Keble College, Oxford. He was professor of modern history at Reading, 1912–46, and vice-chancellor, 1946–50. He was knighted in 1948. A very distinguished scholar of Anglo-Saxon history, Stenton's publications include: *The First Century of English Feudalism, 1066–1166*, 1932; *Anglo-Saxon England*, 1943, 3rd ed. 1971; *The Latin Charters of the Anglo-Saxon Period*, 1955.

Stentor, Homeric herald, who shouted before the walls of Troy as loud as 50 men. Hence the adjective *stentorian*.

Stentor, genus of ciliated Protozoa occurring in fresh water. The unicellular individuals of *S. coeruleus* can be up to 2 mm long and are blue from a pigment in the ectoplasm.

Stepanakert, capital of NAGORNO-KARABAKH AUTONOMOUS OBLAST in the Azerbaijan SSR, USSR, 95 km south-east of Kirovabad. It has a silk industry. Population (1975) 33,000.

Stendhal, portrait in Consul's uniform. *(Mansell/Bulloz)*

Stephanandra, a genus of Japanese deciduous shrubs, in family Rosaceae; *S. incisa* and *S. tanakae* are grown for their elegance and foliage colour in gardens.

Stephanotis, a genus of climbing evergreen hothouse plants with white, waxy, fragrant flowers, also known as Madagascar jasmine. *S. floribunda* is cultivated in British greenhouses. The variety *elvastoni* is a dwarf herb and more free-flowing. There are five members of the genus, which belongs to the Asclepiadaceae (milkweed family).

Stephen, Saint, first Christian martyr, a Jew of Greek culture, one of seven deacons set apart to minister to the Christian community in Jerusalem. He was charged with preaching 'against the Temple and the Law', and made a defence of his belief and conduct before the Sanhedrin, but was stoned by the angry crowd. His dying prayer led to the conversion of Saint Paul, who had taken part in his martyrdom. On 3 August is commemorated the discovery of the reputed relics of St Stephen at Kafr Gamala in 415, and on 7 May their translation to Rome. (See Acts vi and vii.)

Stephen I, Saint, Pope (bishop of Rome), 254–257, born in Rome. He engaged in a prolonged controversy with St Cyprian, Bishop of Carthage, on the question of rebaptising heretics. In 257 an edict of the Emperor Valerian attacked the church organisation and ordered official adherence to the gods of Rome. Stephen was driven into exile where he died.

Stephen II, Pope, 752–57, born in Rome. He sought the aid of Pepin le Bref against Aistulf, King of Lombardy, and by doing so secured for Rome the exarchate of Ravenna. He was of weak character, instrument of every party in turn.

Stephen (István), name of kings of Hungary in the Middle Ages.
Stephen I (c. 970–1038), King of Hungary, instituted Christian monarchy in Hungary. Born a pagan and named Vajk, the son of 'Duke' Geza, he was baptised and became Stephen. He married Gisella, daughter of Henry II of Bavaria, before succeeding his father in 997. With the help of Bavarian knights Stephen defeated his pagan rivals, confiscated their property, and established bishoprics by handing over land confiscated from his opponents to the Church. The Archbishop of Esztergom became the head of the Church hierarchy. Stephen was recognised as king by the Pope Sylvester II and Emperor Otto III and was inaugurated at Christmas in 1000 AD. Hungarian tradition has it that the Pope sent a crown to Stephen for the inauguration (ST STEPHEN'S CROWN); however recent research tends to regard this story as unfounded. Stephen created a new social and political order, based on settled village life, agriculture, and land ownership, which the two sets of laws he issued helped to consolidate. His wars on Bavaria and on Poland were successful. Stephen was canonised in 1083; he was venerated for centuries as the law giver. Had it not been for the achievements of Stephen the Hungarians would have perished as all their nomadic predecessors in the Carpathian Basin had done, disappearing without trace.
Stephen II (ruled 1116–31) waged many unsuccessful wars on his neighbours.

Stephen III (ruled 1162–72) had to fight off claimants who enjoyed the support of the Emperor Manuel of Byzantium and one of them was Stephen IV (ruled 1163–65).
Stephen V (ruled 1270–72) waged war on Ottokar II, King of Bohemia.

Stephen (c. 1097–1154), King of England, son of Stephen, Count of Blois and Adela, daughter of William I. He promised to recognise the claims of MATILDA, daughter of Henry I, to the English throne, but on Henry's death usurped the crown (1135), his brother Henry, Bishop of Winchester, being one of his leading supporters. Though a good soldier, Stephen lacked diplomatic tact: his reign was marked by civil war of an intermittent character. In spite of early concessions he made to the Church Stephen lost ecclesiastical support by his ill-judged attack on the Salisbury family (see ROGER OF SALISBURY). When his son, Eustace, predeceased him Stephen abandoned his attempt to found a new dynasty in England: at the Treaty of Wallingford (1153) he agreed that Henry, Matilda's son, should succeed him. His reign illustrates the immense power exercised by the Church, which, between 1135 and 1153, virtually played the rôle of kingmaker.
Bibliography: A. L. Poole, *From Domesday Book to Magna Carta, 1087–1216*, 2nd ed. 1955; C. Brooke, *The Saxon and Norman Kings*, 1967; R. H. C. Davis, *King Stephen*, 1967; H. A. Cronne, *The Reign of Stephen*, 1970.

Stephen, George, see MOUNT STEPHEN, GEORGE STEPHEN, BARON.

Stephen, Sir Leslie (1832–1904), English biographer and critic, born in London. He was educated at Eton, King's College, London, and Trinity Hall, Cambridge. At the university he distinguished himself at the Union and also as an athlete. A devoted Alpinist he wrote on mountaineering, and collected his papers as *The Playground of Europe*, 1871. He was ordained in 1855, but seven years later found himself unable to remain a Christian, and resigned his tutorship at Cambridge. (He relinquished holy orders in 1875.)
In London he worked for the *Saturday Review* and the *Pall Mall Gazette*, and in 1866 began to contribute to the *Cornhill Magazine* (which he edited from 1871 to 1882) the essays known as *Hours in a Library*, 1874–79. His best book on religion is *An Agnostic's Apology*, 1893. Among his other works are a *History of English Thought in the Eighteenth Century*, 1876, *English Literature and Society in the Eighteenth Century*, 1904, and lives of JOHNSON, POPE, SWIFT, George ELIOT, and HOBBES. He was editor of the *Dictionary of National Biography* from 1886 to 1891, and was knighted in 1902. Virginia WOOLF was his daughter. F. W. Maitland edited *Life and Letters*, 1906.
Bibliography: D. MacCarthy, *Leslie Stephen*, 1937; N. G. Annan, *Leslie Stephen*, 1951.

Stephen Báthory, King of Poland, see BÁTHORY; POLAND, *History*.

Stephen Dushan (d. 1355), Tsar of the Serbs and Greeks, became the ruler of the Serbs in 1331, having already distinguished himself in the battle of Velbuza in 1330, when the Serbians decisively defeated the Bulgarians. A brilliant military leader, he conquered most of

Stephen Harding, Saint

Macedonia, Thessaly, and Albania and was crowned 'Tsar of the Serbs and Romans' (i.e. Greeks) in 1346. He died while planning a campaign to capture Constantinople, and after his death his empire disintegrated following the Turkish victories of Maritza (1371) and Kosovo (1389). The area he had ruled came under Turkish suzerainty. In 1349 he issued a *Zahonik* (law code) which throws much light on the social conditions of the Balkans at that time.

Stephen Harding, Saint (d. 1134), English monk of Sherborne. He became abbot of Cîteaux in 1109, soon after which an increase in numbers at the monastery necessitated new foundations. Stephen drew up the nucleus of the 'Charter of Charity' to protect the original austerity and uniform government of the Cistercian order.

Stephen of Muret, Saint (1054–1124), born at Thiers, Auvergne, France. Though not himself a monk, he founded the Grandmontine branch (now extinct) of the Benedictine order. The mother house was at Grandmont in Normandy; discipline was severe and strict poverty and silence were observed. He was canonised in 1189 at the request of Henry II of England, where there had been three houses.

Stephen of Perm, Saint (1340–96), saint of the Russian Orthodox Church, illuminator of the KOMI people. He invented the Komi alphabet and translated parts of the Bible into Komi.

Stephen the Great (1457–1504), Voivode of Moldavia. He maintained the independence of Moldavia for nearly 50 years when the Turks were pouring into Europe and European countries found it easier to attack each other than to unite against the Turks. He defeated the following invasions: Hungarian under Matthias Corvinus, 1467; Tatar, 1469; Turkish, 1473, 1475, 1476, 1485, 1486; Polish, 1499, 1501. He was a great administrator and also encouraged literature, and church and monastery building.

Stephens, or Stephanus, see ESTIENNE, CHARLES.

Stephens, Alexander Hamilton (1812–83), US statesman, born in Georgia. He was elected to Congress (1843–59), where he urged the annexation of Texas (1845) and secured the passing of the KANSAS-NEBRASKA BILL (1854). He opposed the secession of Georgia in 1860, but afterwards became vice-president of the Confederate states (1861). He again sat in Congress (1873–82), and was elected governor of Georgia (1882).

Stephens, James (1882–1950), Irish poet and novelist, born in Dublin; he was self-educated. An Irish nationalist, his work combines realism with Celtic myth and legend, producing a fantastic art which is both sympathetic to human ills and grotesque. His prose fantasy, *The Crock of Gold*, which received the Polignac prize, was published in 1912, and his collection of *Irish Fairy Tales* in 1923. Collected editions of his poems appeared in 1926 and 1931.

Among Stephens's other works are *The Charwoman's Daughter*, 1912, *The Hill of Vision*, 1912, *Deirdre*, 1923, *In the Land of Youth*, 1924, *Etched in Moonlight*, 1928,

George Stephenson. (*Science Museum*, London)

and *Kings and the Moon*, 1938. His *Letters* were published in 1974.

Bibliography: H. Pyle, *James Stephens*, 1965.

Stephens, John Lloyd (1805–52), US explorer and travel-writer, co-founder of the Panama railway company, born at Shrewsbury, New Jersey; trained as a lawyer. With his friend the English architect and artist Frederick Catherwood, he was one of the first to explore the ruined Maya cities of Central America. He published the famous *Incidents of Travel in Central America, Chiapas and Yucatan*, 1841, and *Incidents of Travel in Yucatan*, 1843, both illustrated by Catherwood.

Bibliography: V. W. Von Hagen, *Search for the Maya: the Story of Stephens and Catherwood*, 1973.

Stephenson, George (1781–1848), British inventor, born in Newcastle upon Tyne; for many years he worked in various mines as an engineer. In 1815 he, simultaneously with Sir Humphry Davy, invented a safety lamp. He designed a locomotive (which he called *My Lord*) which was successfully tried on the tramroads of the Killingworth Colliery in 1814. The projectors of the Stockton and Darlington Railway appointed him their engineer (1822), when their line, the first railway on which passengers and goods were carried by a locomotive, was opened on 27 September 1825. The success of this venture led to the employment of Stephenson in the construction of the Liverpool and Manchester Railway, which he carried successfully through Chat Moss. It was on this line that his improved invention, the *Rocket*, made its trial trip at 47 km/h. Henceforth until his death he was employed as a designer of railways, and during these years greatly improved upon his early locomotive. His work was of the greatest importance in railway development.

Stephenson, Robert (1803–59), British engineer, born near Newcastle upon Tyne, son of George Stephenson. He travelled in South America, and returning to England in 1827 took part in the construction of his father's *Rocket*, and in the laying of the first railways in the country. In 1833 he became chief engineer on the London and Birmingham Railway. He was one of the greatest railway engineering experts of his time, specialising in the building of bridges, including the high-level bridge at Newcastle. He used a novel box girder type of construction in his bridge across the Menai Straits (1850), and that still in original form at Conway (1848), in which the railway tracks were completely enclosed in parallel iron tubes. He was MP for Whitby (1847–59).

Stepney, see TOWER HAMLETS.

Stepniak, Sergei Mikhailovich, see STEPNYAK, SERGEI MIKHAILOVICH.

Stepnoi, see ELISTA.

Stepnyak, Sergei Mikhailovich, pseudonym of Sergei Mikhailovich Kravchinski (1852–95), Russian revolutionary, member of the underground Populist (see POPULISM) organisation 'Land and Freedom'. He assassinated the chief of the gendarmes Mezentsov in 1878; later he lived in Switzerland and England. Among his works are: *Underground Russia*, 1882; *The Russian Storm Cloud*, 1886; and *The Career of a Nihilist*, 1889.

Steppe (Russian *step'*), term applied particularly to the grasslands of the southern USSR, and generally to any similar areas in temperate zones (see PAMPAS; PRAIRIE) where light rainfall, confined to spring and early summer, produces natural grassland with few trees, usually in continental interiors. The soil is deep and often rich in HUMUS content, as in the 'black earth' areas of the Ukraine, though southern Siberia is less fertile. Grain is a major crop, and wild flowers, usually bulbous, abound. See also CHERNOZEMS AND CHESTNUT EARTH SOILS.

Stepping Motors, see SPECIAL PURPOSE MACHINES.

Stereo-comparator, a photogrammetric instrument based on the stereoscope; for measurement of three-dimensional co-ordinates of photographic images. After suitable mathematic transformations, these photograph co-ordinates may be expressed as ground co-ordinates, defining the real positions of the points. They are employed mainly in AERIAL SURVEYING but also in a wide variety of stereoscopic photograph work.

Stereochemistry, branch of chemistry concerned with the spatial relations of the atoms in the molecule. PASTEUR (1850) obtained crystals of sodium ammonium racemate, and found two classes of crystals, the crystals of one class being the mirror-image of the other. Solutions of the separated classes of crystals rotated the plane of polarised light either to the right or to the left, i.e., they were

dextro- and laevo-rotatory. Pasteur's theory on these substances was developed independently by LE BEL and VAN'T HOFF (1874). They concluded that a substance is optically active only when its molecule is asymmetric, the most common form of asymmetry being shown by a molecule that contains at least one carbon atom which is directly united with four different groups. One of the simplest of such optically active compounds is lactic acid, which contains one asymmetric carbon atom:

$$CH_3 \overset{\overset{\displaystyle H}{|}}{\underset{\underset{\displaystyle OH}{|}}{C}} COOH$$

Van't Hoff suggested that the carbon atom was situated at the centre of a regular tetrahedron and the four groups in combination at the four solid angles. The conclusions to be drawn are: (1) a compound of the type CR_2X_2 (where R and X represent any group) can exist in only one form; (2) a compound of the type CR_2XY can exist in only one form (two groups are identical); (3) compounds of the type $CRXYZ$ (carbon atom asymmetric) exist in two different forms, i.e., there are two optical or stereochemical isomers or enantiomorphs. More generally, any substance the molecules of which are asymmetric (whether they contain carbon or not) can exist in three forms, a dextro-rotary form, a form laevo-rotary to the same extent, and an optically inactive form, consisting of a mixture or loose compound of equal weights of the dextro- and laevo-enantiomorphs. This inactive form is said to be 'externally compensated' or 'racemic'. Unless very special methods are followed, synthesis of a substance with asymmetric molecules always yields the externally compensated mixture, and the process of separating this into the two optical enantiomorphs is called 'resolution'. Resolution is difficult since the dextro and laevo forms have identical chemical properties, solubilities, and boiling and melting points, but can be effected by forming derivatives with an optically active substance yielding two products no longer identical in solubility, or other properties; these can be separated by fractional crystallisation.

Other forms of stereoisomerism may not involve optical activity, which, as we have seen, is dependent on asymmetry of the molecule. Thus fumaric acid and maleic acid are stereoisomers, but are not optically active, since their molecules are symmetrical. The spatial arrangements of these two acids are:

$$\begin{array}{ccc} H\!-\!C\!-\!COOH & & H\!-\!C\!-\!COOH \\ \parallel & \text{and} & \parallel \\ H\!-\!C\!-\!COOH & & HOOC\!-\!C\!-\!H \end{array}$$

$$\textit{(maleic acid)} \qquad\qquad \textit{(fumaric acid)}$$

The acid groups are held rigidly on the same (*cis*) or opposite (*trans*) side of the double bond.

Stereographic Projection, see MAPS.

Stereoisomerism, see STEREOCHEMISTRY.

Stereophonic Reproduction, see QUADRAPHONY; RECORD PLAYER; STEREOPHONY; TAPE RECORDER.

Stereophony

Stereophony, an improved method of listening to music, where the sound is produced by two LOUDSPEAKERS, rather than just one. With one speaker ('monophony'), all notes emerge from the same speaker, and all the music appears to come from the same place. With stereophony, even though all notes are coming from only two speakers, the ear is fooled, and receives an impression of a spread between the speakers. The exact apparent location of a particular note depends solely on the relative intensities of the note from each speaker. A note with equal intensity from each speaker will appear to come from halfway between them, while a note with all its intensity from one speaker and none from the other will be heard at the extreme edge of the sound image. With practice, one can listen to a stereophonic recording of an orchestra and hear each instrument in its correct place, as if the orchestra itself were before one. The most effective use of stereophony is made by listening to a stereophonic recording through headphones.

Both records and tapes are now usually issued in stereo (see RECORD PLAYER; TAPE RECORDER). On a stereophonic tape, each channel is in a separate part, and separate playback heads are used for each 'track'. Thus the channels are separate at all times. A stereophonic record has only one groove per side, and thus both channels are coded into the one groove: the groove walls are inclined at 45° to each other, with 'hill and dale' recordings on each wall, one channel on each wall. Thus the stylus of a stereophonic record deck vibrates both

up-and-down and side-to-side. These vibrations are decoded in the stylus, and two signals are passed to the stereophonic amplifier. A stereophonic amplifier is merely two monophonic amplifiers in one unit, with some additional controls. The amplifier feeds signals to two loudspeakers.

Bibliography: W. F. Boyce, *Hi Fi Stereo Handbook*, 2nd ed. 1965; J. L. Bernstein, *Audio Systems*, 1966.

Stereophotogrammetry, a development of the older method of PHOTOGRAMMETRY, in which two photographs taken of each view are such that the plates are in the same vertical plane at the two stations. When the camera is set at one station the 'base' to the next station is set out parallel to the plate by means of a telescope fixed in the correct position on the camera. The base is usually 30–120 m. The base is measured, and after exposure the camera is set at the second station, at the other end of the base, parallel to its previous position, the direction being controlled by means of the telescope. Special instruments, photo-theodolites for field work, and stereoplotters for plotting, have been designed and have greatly facilitated the use of this method. See also MAPS; SURVEYING.

Bibliography: A. R. Hinks, *Maps and Survey*, 1942.

Stereoscope, an optical instrument which permits two separate images representing the views of our two eyes to be combined into a single image with apparent depth and solidity. Sir Charles WHEATSTONE first constructed a stereoscope in 1832, and in 1838 published details of a

Stereophony. The basic stereophonic set-up.

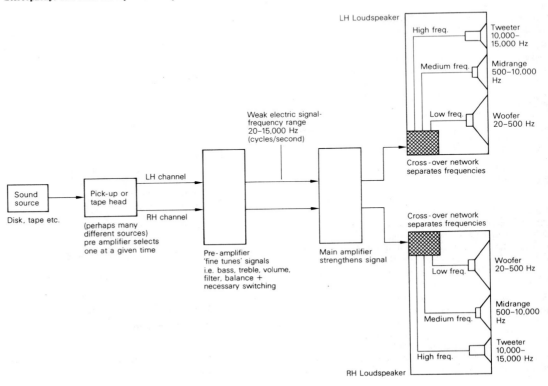

374

Stereoscope. Two Victorian examples. *(Kodak Museum)*

reflecting viewer using mirrors to combine two dissimilar diagrams. Both Calotype and Daguerreotype photographs (see PHOTOGRAPHY) were made for Wheatstone's stereoscope, but it was not until after Sir David Brewster in 1844 published details of a viewer using prismatic lenses that stereoscopy became widely used. A version of Brewster's stereoscope was shown at the Great Exhibition of 1851, where it attracted the attention of Queen Victoria. A craze developed for collecting stereoscopic photographs, easily mass produced by the new wet collodion process, and for two decades the stereoscope was a common feature of the Victorian parlour. These viewers ranged from simple box types held in the hand, through table models carrying fifty or more cards on an endless belt to floorstanding models taking up to three hundred stereographs. By far the most popular stereoscope was the open (American) model designed by Oliver Wendell HOLMES in 1861, which remained on sale until 1939. The stereoscope has enjoyed periodic revivals of popularity since its first appearance, notably at the end of the last century, when the introduction of the rollfilm camera made possible inexpensive stereocameras for amateur use.

Stereophotographs were at first taken with two cameras side by side, or by a single camera moved sideways between two successive exposures. Twin lens cameras, in which the stereoscopic pair of images could be recorded simultaneously date from the early 1850s. More recently, beamsplitting devices have been employed, using mirrors or prisms, attached to the single camera lens. They produce a pair of stereoscopic images side by side on the negative or transparency film.

Other methods of viewing stereoscopic images have been devised. J. C. d'Almeida demonstrated in 1858 that two magic lanterns, fitted with red and green filters, could be used to project two stereoscopic images in superimposition. When viewed through green and red spectacles, the images combined to give an image in depth.

This anaglyph method, as it became known, can also be employed by printing red and blue stereoscopic images in superimposition on paper, a method first described by Ducos du Hauron in 1891. It was used for the projection of stereoscopic motion pictures by C. Grivolas in 1897, and anaglyphs have been used for book illustrations. The projection of stereoscopic photographs through polarising filters permits their being viewed in depth through polarising spectacles. This principle was first demonstrated by J. Anderton in 1891, but did not become fully practical until the invention of a cheap polarising material by Dr E. S. LAND in 1932. The polarised light method permits the projection of stereoscopic films in full colour, and has been used in the cinema for this purpose.

The parallax stereogram is a method of viewing which allows the viewer to see an image in depth without optical aids. The method was suggested by A. Berthier in 1896, and developed by, among others, F. E. IVES in 1907. Two stereoscopic images are printed as interlaced strips behind a grid of parallel lines spaced a short distance away. The bars of the grid obscure for each eye the elements of the image intended for the other, and a picture in depth is seen directly. This principle has been used for motion picture projection in the Soviet Union since 1941, in a method devised by S. M. Ivanov. Parallax stereograms are currently used for advertising and postcard pictures, using interlaced stereoscopic images laminated with a thin plastic film embossed with cylindrical lenses which more efficiently serve the purpose of the earlier grid.

Stereoscopic pictures have applications in science and applied photography. Aerial reconnaissance and surveying make use of stereoscopic techniques, as does PHOTOGRAMMETRY. Stereoscopic radiography permits the accurate location of objects within the body of the object investigated. In astronomy, stereoscopic images have been made of the moon and other astronomical subjects, using the movement of the earth over huge distances to provide a picture separation sufficient to give images in depth. The first men to visit the moon, in 1969, took with them a stereoscopic camera to take close-up photographs of the lunar surface.

Bibliography: A. W. Judge, *Stereoscopic Photography*, 3rd ed. 1950.

Stereotyping (Greek *stereos*, solid), processes used in the production of duplicate plates of type and photoengravings for use in letterpress printing. Originally implying the production of metal plates, the term now includes the making of rubber and plastic duplicates.

In the metal stereotyping process, a mould is made by pressing a sheet of damp 'flong', a faced paper matrix board, into the original printing surface and after setting the impression by drying out the moisture, the mould is used for making casts in 'stereo metal' which is an alloy of tin, antimony, and lead. This method provides a means of rapidly producing multiple sets of printing plates. For newspaper printing, the moulds are made on powerful hydraulic presses and curved plates are cast on mechanised equipment having outputs of up to four plates per minute. Metal stereotyping is also used for the production of multiple sets of moulds or plates for distribution of advertising matter to newspapers and periodicals. In other fields calling for duplicate plates the metal process

Steric Hindrance

is being rapidly replaced by rubber and plastic stereotyping.

In rubber and plastic stereotyping the moulds are made in a heat-setting (thermosetting) phenolic board material. This is softened by heat then pressed into the original printing surface where it is held under heat and pressure until 'cured' into a heat-resisting, rigid condition. Plate-making is then carried out by hydraulically pressing the rubber or plastic into the mould. In the case of rubber and thermosetting plastic platemaking, the material is held in the mould under heat and pressure until curing has taken place, but with thermoplastic materials the mould and plate must be cooled off under pressure by transfer from the hot press to a chilling press. Stereotyping in rubber and plastics, although slower than the metal process, has several important advantages such as low weight, flexibility and, in the case of rubber, a printing life of more than a million impressions. Stereotyping in rubber and plastic produces surfaces which are easy to print from but which do not reproduce such fine details as metal plates.

Steric Hindrance, in organic chemistry, occurs when the size and spatial distribution of the component groups of a molecule prevent or hinder a reagent from approaching the molecule and reacting with it. The presence of bulky groups in a molecule frequently explains why a given reaction proceeds more slowly than for other similar, but more compact, molecules.

Sterilisation, the complete destruction of all forms of life. Certain substances, for example those to be injected into the blood-stream, or surgical instruments, must be sterile. This means that no forms of life—no bacteria, viruses or fungi, nor the cysts or spores by which they hibernate or reproduce—are present in them. Sterilisation may be done by several processes. *Autoclaving,* cooking the material to be sterilised in steam at a high pressure, is effective for surgical instruments, but would ruin more delicate things. *Filtration* is useful for delicate solutions, such as antibiotics. Other methods are *dry heat,* which must be greater and applied longer than the moist heat of the autoclave; *burning* of material to be discarded; *gamma radiation*; and *chemicals*, especially ethylene oxide gas.

Other methods are used where complete sterilisation is not necessary. ANTISEPTICS are chemicals that either prevent micro-organisms from multiplying or kill most of them. Disinfectants are similar to antiseptics, but the term usually refers to chemicals used on table tops and floors. Preservatives in food slow down the growth of harmful micro-organisms. Pasteurisation of milk kills the disease-producing organisms but not the others. Cooking also kills most micro-organisms.

Sterilisation (Surgical) includes several procedures for making a person incapable of reproduction. These include vasectomy, cutting and tying of the vasa deferentia (the ducts leading from the testes to the urethra), in the male, and cutting and tying the Fallopian tubes in the female. Sterilisation in the male is a simple and quick operation and is reversible. In the female, cauterisation of the Fallopian tubes can be performed through the laparoscope, which is also a quick method. Clips are also put on the Fallopian tubes as a method of sterilisation. See also BIRTH CONTROL.

Bibliography: C. Wood, *Vasectomy and Sterilisation*, 1974.

Sterility, see INFERTILITY.

Sterling (silver), see METROLOGY; SILVER.

Sterling (from the old English *steorra*, star, since some of the early Norman coins were marked with a small star), term applied in Britain to all lawful coins of the realm. Weight and fineness determine the *standard* of coins, and only coin of the true standard is called sterling. Formerly all coin had, by the provisions of an act of 1352, to be of sterling metal, but the Crown varied the standard even before that act was repealed. By the Coinage Act 1870 the standard weight and fineness was fixed as follows: (1) for gold coin: fine gold, alloy, or millesimal fineness 916.66; (2) for silver: fine silver, alloy, or millesimal fineness 925; (3) for bronze: mixed metal, copper, tin, and zinc. At the outbreak of the First World War the GOLD STANDARD was suspended (i.e. no new gold coins were issued, and the Bank of England was no longer obliged to redeem its bank-notes in gold). In 1925 the pound was brought back to its old parity and the Bank of England was obliged by the Gold Standard Act 1925 to sell gold at the old fixed price in the form of bars, but bank-notes remained unredeemable into gold coin. The obligation to sell gold in bars was suspended on 21 September 1931, and has not been restored since. See also STERLING AREA.

Sterling Area, term used to describe the free association of countries based on the use of sterling as an international financial medium. The term came into use after Britain abandoned the GOLD STANDARD in 1931 (i.e. when the British government ceased selling gold at a fixed price in exchange for sterling) and was applied to those countries which tied their currencies to sterling rather than to gold and who held their exchange assets (gold and other currency reserves) in London. There was no formal agreement and membership was not clearly defined but the 1937/38 League of Nations *Monetary Review* listed the following 'members': Australia, Denmark, Egypt, Estonia, Finland, India, Iceland, Latvia, New Zealand, Norway, Palestine, Portugal, Siam, Sweden, and South Africa.

During the Second World War exchange controls were imposed by the sterling area countries, as a result of which large sterling balances accumulated in London, and all receipts of scarce currencies were paid into a common pool from which drawings were made for essential needs only.

At the end of the war the Bretton Woods Agreement was reached in 1945 which envisaged a speedy return to freely convertible currencies and stable exchange rates. This was not achieved and because of the great scarcity of hard currencies (mainly the dollar) the UK could not exchange the large sterling balances that had built up. Consequently the Exchange Control Act of 1947 was passed and all members of the sterling area (now defined in the Exchange Control Act as the Scheduled Territories) set up controls to limit the changing of sterling into gold or other 'hard' currencies (i.e. currencies which were in short supply and whose countries' economies were in good health). Sterling became more freely convertible into other currencies at the end of 1958.

During the 1960s many members of the sterling area started to diversify their reserves by holding other currencies as well as sterling. Following the losses on reserves held in sterling as a result of the sterling devaluation in 1967 this tendency received a strong stimulus and Britain found it necessary to negotiate a series of agreements with other sterling area countries under which these countries undertook to maintain an agreed proportion of their reserves in sterling in exchange for a guarantee in terms of the dollar on part of these countries' sterling reserves.

In 1978 the Scheduled Territories consisted of the United Kingdom, the Irish Republic, the Channel Islands, the Isle of Man, and Gibraltar. The sterling area may be said to no longer exist.

See also BALANCE OF PAYMENTS; CONVERTIBILITY; EXCHANGE, FOREIGN; EXCHANGE CONTROL; INTERNATIONAL MONETARY FUND; STERLING BALANCES.

Bibliography: F. Hirsch, *Money International*, 1969.

Sterling Balances are balances held at the Bank of England and other British banks by non-residents or overseas central banks and monetary authorities. Member countries of the STERLING AREA acquiring dollars or other convertible currency usually sell it to the British Treasury and their sterling balances are credited with the appropriate sum. When they wish to buy dollars or other convertible currencies they draw from their balances in the pool. Sterling balances therefore increase when the trade of the sterling area with the rest of the world is favourable (i.e. sterling area countries are in surplus with the rest of the world) and decrease if it is unfavourable.

Sterlitamak, town in BASHKIR ASSR, USSR, on the River Belaya, 120 km south of Ufa. It has chemical, engineering, and food industries, and the Ishimbay oilfields are nearby. It was founded in 1766. Population (1974) 205,000.

Stern, Daniel, see AGOULT, MARIE CATHERINE SOPHIE DE FLAVIGNY, COMTESSE D'.

Stern, Gladys Bronwyn (1890–1973), English novelist, born in London; educated at Notting Hill High School. She studied at the London Academy of Dramatic Art. Her first novel, *Pantomime*, 1914, was followed by *Grand Chain*, 1917. Her 'Matriarch' novels include *Tents of Israel*, 1924, *A Deputy Was King*, 1926, *Mosaic*, 1930, *Shining and Free*, 1935, and *The Young Matriarch*, 1942. *Monogram*, 1936, and *Another Part of the Wood*, 1941, are autobiographical.

Stern, Otto (1888–1969), German-US physicist, born at Sohrau. He held various university posts in Germany until 1933, and was professor of physics at the Carnegie Institute of Technology, Pittsburgh, 1933–45. His chief fields of work were thermodynamics, theories of kinetic gases, and the quantum theory. In 1943 he received the Nobel Prize for his research into atomic physics. Together with Gerlach he showed that atoms have a magnetic moment, and the component in the direction of an applied magnetic field is quantised.

Sterne, Laurence (1713–68), English novelist, born at Clonmel, County Tipperary, Ireland; educated at Jesus College, Cambridge. The son of an army officer, Sterne's early boyhood was spent moving from camp to camp with the regiment, but at the age of ten he was sent to school.

After graduating from Cambridge, he was ordained and became vicar of Sutton-in-the-Forest in 1738 and prebendary of York in 1740. In 1760 he was also appointed perpetual curate of Coxwold, where he lived happily in the house he called Shandy Hall.

In 1741 he married Elizabeth Lumley, but the marriage was not altogether happy; she had a mental breakdown and the couple eventually separated. From 1741 onwards, Sterne wrote various miscellaneous pieces, and in 1759 produced *A Political Romance*, later called *The History of a Good Warm Watch-Coat*, 1769, an allegorical satire on Church dignitaries. At the time of his wife's illness, Sterne began writing *The Life and Opinions of Tristram Shandy*, his masterpiece, which was published between 1760 and 1767. This comic novel, one of the most remarkable in English literature, creates its own world, exploring ideas, thoughts, and action; almost without plot, it unfolds in a meandering, seemingly unplanned style, the usual progression deliberately changed. *Tristram Shandy* was a success, although condemned by some critics for its immorality. To follow, Sterne collected and issued several volumes of sermons, published as *The Sermons of Mr Yorick*, 1760–69.

A decline in health (Sterne was a lifelong sufferer from tuberculosis) led to a tour of France and Italy, 1762–64, which provided much of the material for *A Sentimental Journey*. In 1767 he met Mrs Elizabeth Draper with whom he began a sentimental love affair, and after she returned to her husband in Bombay, Sterne wrote the *Journal to Eliza*, 1775 (*Letters from Yorick to Eliza*, 1773). *A Sentimental Journey Through France and Italy* was published in 1768, shortly before his death.

With Sterne, the extreme limit of the sentimental novel was reached, but his mastery of emotion and humour brought to it self-possession and detachment. *Tristram Shandy* was a revolutionary novel, precursor of the works of James Joyce and Proust in its handling of time and consciousness, though it has also been seen as a comic satire on the well-made novel of the earlier 18th century, and as a satirical reduction of claims made for rationality as the main principle of human order. *A Sentimental Journey* develops Sterne's doctrine of sensibility; it is a journey through Yorick's emotional biography more than an actual itinerary, and has perhaps one of the most famous endings in the English novel.

See also NOVEL.

Bibliography: Complete Works, 1773 and 1774; W. L. Cross (Ed.), *Complete Works*, 1906; the 'Shakespeare Head' edition, 1926–27; W. L. Cross, *The Life and Times of Laurence Sterne*, rev. ed. 1929; T. Yoseloff, *A Fellow of Infinite Jest*, 1945; L. Hartley, *Laurence Sterne in the Twentieth Century*, 1967; D. Thomson, *Wild Excursions*, 1972; A. B. Howes, *Sterne: the Critical Heritage*, 1974.

Sternheim, Carl (1878–1942), German dramatist, born in Leipzig; he studied philosophy and literary history. Sternheim's early romantic tragedies were failures, but then turning a savage, satirical eye on the philistinism and dubious moral standards of his society, he wrote a series of brilliant comedies, *Aus dem bürgerlichen Heldenleben*, 1910–1922. Invariably the centre of scandal and outrage, they attracted the attention of the censor.

Among his most successful works was the loose trilogy *Die Hose*, 1911; *Der Snob*, 1914; and *1913*, 1915, about three generations of a family of social climbers. Sternheim's dispassionate criticism of bourgeois hypocrisy is pursued in *Bürger Schippel*, 1913, although this has rare elements of compassion. *Die Kassette*, 1912, ostensibly exposing greed and vanity, examines the mechanisms of bourgeois convention, while the political comedy *Der Kandidat*, 1914, is based on FLAUBERT.

A growing concern with politics and social and individual responsibility led to *Tabula Rasa*, 1916, where the central character, a self-seeking workers' representative, betrays his class and joins the bourgeoisie. There is no social satire in the powerful and eloquent *Die Marquise von Arcis*, 1919, borrowed from a story by DIDEROT, which pleads against the rigid conventions that condemn individuals to their station in life. In true German Expressionism (see EXPRESSIONISM) manner it demands the emergence of a new man in a new society.

Bibliography: W. Emrich, *Das Gesamtwerk* (9 vols), 1963; H. F. Garten, *Modern German Drama*, 1959; R. Beckley, *German Men of Letters* (vol. 11), 1963; W. Wendler, *Carl Sternheim. Weltvorstellung und Kunstprinzipien*, 1966.

Sternum, or breastbone, a nearly flat bone, 15–20 cm long in the adult, which lies in the midline of the anterior wall of the thorax (chest). It can be felt beneath the skin throughout its whole length, from the root of the neck into the abdominal wall. The sternum has three components—the manubrium, body and xiphoid process—which are united by cartilage. The join between the manubrium and body is an important palpable landmark, the sternal angle, which lies opposite the second ribs.

Steroids, chemical compounds with the basic structure:

This is a large group of naturally occurring compounds, several of which have a profound effect on the body. Many of them can now be made synthetically, and are used in medical treatment. The most important examples of steroid compounds are the precursors of certain VITAMINS, CHOLESTEROL, and HORMONES. The hormones are those made in the adrenal cortex, such as cortisone, and the sex hormones: the female oestrogens, including progesterone, and the male androgens, including testosterone.

Stesichorus (c. 640–c. 555 BC), Greek lyric poet, born at Mataurus; he later lived in Himera, Sicily. He stands with ALCMAN at the head of the Dorian school of choral poetry, and is described by LONGINUS as 'most like Homer'. He took legends for his subjects, often adding innovations and re-shaping them in a lyrical, rather than epic, manner. Only about 30 short fragments of his work survive.

Stethoscope, an instrument used in medical practice as a medium for auscultation (listening to noises made by the body). Respiratory, cardiac, arterial, venous, intestinal, foetal, and other sounds are conveyed to the ear of the examiner. The French physician Laënnec invented the stethoscope in 1819. The earliest form consisted of a straight tube, usually of wood or metal, trumpet-shaped at one end with a cupped ear piece at the other. This was succeeded by the binaural stethoscope in general use today, with two ear pieces connected by flexible tubing to a chest piece.

Stettin, see SZCZECIN.

Stettinger Haff, see ZALEW SZCZECIŃSKI.

Stettinius, Edward Riley (1900–49), US business executive and administrator, born in Chicago, Illinois, and educated at Pomfret School, Connecticut, and Virginia University. In 1926 he joined General Motors and in 1931 became a vice-president of the company. In 1934 he joined the US Steel Corporation, and subsequently became chairman of its board of directors. In the Second World War President Roosevelt appointed him Lease-Lend administrator. He succeeded Sumner Welles in 1943 as under-secretary of state, and a year later succeeded Cordell Hull as secretary of state. He was chief adviser to Roosevelt at the Yalta Conference, 1945. His work at the Inter-American conference at Mexico City confirmed his abilities as a negotiator, and was followed by President Truman appointing him as the first US delegate to the UN Conference at San Francisco. In 1946 he returned to business. He wrote *Lease-Lend: Weapon for Victory*, 1944, and *Roosevelt and the Russians: the Yalta Conference*, 1949.

Steuart, House of, see STEWART.

Steuart, Sir James (1712–80), Scottish man of affairs and mercantilist. In 1767 he published *An Enquiry into the Principles of Political Œconomy*, which had little impact on the development of economic thought because it was overshadowed by Adam Smith's *Wealth of Nations*, which was published nine years later.

Bibliography: R. L. Meek (Ed.), *Precursors of Adam Smith*, 1973.

Steubenville, town and county seat of Jefferson county, Ohio, USA, on the Ohio river, 71 km south-west of Pittsburgh. It occupies the site of Fort Steuben, built in 1786. There are coal-mines, iron and steel works, clay and paper products, and a pottery industry here. Natural gas is found nearby. Population 30,771.

Stevenage, new town in HERTFORDSHIRE, England, 48 km from London. The former parish church, dedicated to St Nicholas, is mainly early English. At the southernmost end of the town the six hills (tumuli) stand on a narrow strip of land alongside the old Great North Road, and many antiquarians incline to the belief that they are of Roman origin. Stevenage has an annual fair dating back to 1280. The boys' grammar school was founded by Thomas Alleyn in 1558. Stevenage was the first new town to be designated under the New Towns Act 1964, and is now a thriving industrial centre. It manufactures aircraft and electrical and plastic goods; together with engineering these form its chief industries. A new town centre with pedestrian shopping precincts has been built—there are many new factories and churches. Population (1971) 67,016.

Stevens, Alfred (1818–75), British sculptor and decorative artist, born at Blandford, Dorset; spent nine years of study in Italy (1833–42) including one year under THORWALDSEN at Rome. His work was influenced in conception by the High Renaissance and is noted for powerful composition and purity of line. His greatest work was the bronze monument to Wellington in St Paul's Cathedral, which was left unfinished at his death and not completed until 1912. Other notable works were designs for mosaics of the Prophets under the dome of St Paul's, a magnificent scheme of decoration for Dorchester House, and the vases and charactarel lions of the British Museum railings. He left a vast number of fine drawings (Tate Gallery) and some portraits of unusual distinction, that of Mrs Collmann (National Portrait Gallery, London) being his masterpiece.
Bibliography: Study by W. Armstrong, 1881.

Stevens, Alfred (1828–1906), Belgian painter, born in Brussels, studied under INGRES at the École des Beaux-Arts, Paris. He settled in that city, and became a constant exhibitor in the salons. In the Brussels gallery are *Lady in Pink* and *The Lady-Bird*. He produced many interior scenes of middle-class life, influenced by COURBET.
Bibliography: Studies by C. Lemonnier, 1906, and P. Lambotte, 1907.

Stevens, Siaka Probyn (1905–), Sierra Leonese politician; his early career was in the police and later the railway administration. A fervent trade unionist, he was active in 1943 in the formation of the miners' union, becoming secretary-general. In 1960 he founded the opposition political party, the All People's Congress; this party won a majority at the legislative elections held in March 1967. Siaka Stevens was appointed prime minister, but, before he could take office, a military coup forced him to flee to Guinea. However, in April 1968 another military coup established the validity of the 1967 elections, and on 27 April 1968 Siaka Stevens became prime minister. On 21 April 1971 he became the first executive president of the Republic of Sierra Leone.

Stevens, Wallace (1897–1955), US poet, born at Redding, Pennsylvania; he became an executive of a Hartford, Connecticut, insurance company. Stevens was one of the leading poets of American modernism. His poetry, collected in two volumes, *Collected Poems*, 1954, and *Opus Posthumous*, 1957, first appeared in *Poetry* (Chicago) in 1912, but he did not publish a volume until *Harmonium* in 1923.

His work, concerned with the status of the imagination and the power of a poetic fiction, evolved from a dandyish flamboyance to a spare, philosophical form; most of it is an examination of the poetic act itself. His criticism is collected in *The Necessary Angel*, 1951; his letters were drawn together in 1967.
Bibliography: F. Kermode, *Wallace Stevens*, 1960; J. J. Enck, *Wallace Stevens: Images and Judgements*, 1964; R. H. Pearce and J. H. Miller (Eds), *The Act of Mind: Essays on the Poetry of Wallace Stevens*, 1965.

Stevenson, Adlai Ewing (1900–65), US politician, born in Los Angeles, California. He graduated from Princeton University, 1922, Northwestern University, 1926, was admitted to the Bar in the same year, and practised law in Chicago. He was assistant to the secretary

Stevenage. The town centre. *(Camera Press/Jeffery W. Whitelaw)*

of the navy, 1941–44. He was one of the US delegates to the UN General Assembly, 1946–47. He was elected governor of Illinois in 1948. Stevenson was Democratic candidate for president in 1952. Though defeated by EISENHOWER he retained his position as leader of his party. He again ran for the presidency in 1956, again being defeated by Eisenhower. Stevenson represented a more reflective trend in the Democratic party, as opposed to the New Deal radicalism of others. From 1961 he was US ambassador to the UN. He died suddenly in London.

Stevenson, Robert (1772–1850), British engineer, born in Glasgow, educated at Glasgow and at Edinburgh University. He supervised the construction of a lighthouse on the island of Little Cumbrae when he was 19, and, as engineer to the Northern Lighthouses Commissioners, constructed the lighthouse on the Bell Rock off Arbroath, Forfarshire (1807–11).

Stevenson, Robert Louis

Stevenson, Robert Louis (1850–94), Scottish poet, novelist, and essayist, born in Edinburgh; his original middle names were Lewis Balfour. His father and grandfather had been lighthouse builders and it was intended that he too should be an engineer, but his weak health made this inadvisable. Educated at Edinburgh Academy and University, he studied law, was called to the Bar in 1875, but never practised. At the age of 15 he published a pamphlet on *The Pentland Rising of 1666* in praise of the COVENANTERS, and in 1876 began contributing to the *Cornhill* and other magazines. This rapidly gained him a reputation in literary circles, and the essays were later collected in *Virginibus Puerisque*, 1881, and *Familiar Studies of Men and Books*, 1882. On account of his delicate health (he suffered from tuberculosis), Stevenson travelled abroad, recounting his experiences in *An Inland Voyage*, 1878, his first book, and *Travels with a Donkey in the Cevennes*, 1879. He went to California in 1879 and married an American, Mrs Fanny Osbourne, 1880. Returning to Scotland, he was reconciled with his disapproving parents and then proceeded to Davos, Switzerland, in search of a cure. To amuse his stepson Lloyd Osbourne, he began an adventure story about pirates and buried treasure which appeared from 1881 as a serial in the boys' paper *Young Folks*. Originally called *The Sea Cook* after its plausibly attractive villain Long John Silver, the tale was published in book form in 1882 as *Treasure Island*. Its great success finally decided Steven-

Robert Louis Stevenson, painting by W. B. Richmond, 1887. *(National Portrait Gallery, London)*

son's profession and his work afterwards showed growing confidence and skill. Other stories include *Kidnapped*, 1886, *The Black Arrow*, 1888, *The Master of Ballantrae*, 1889, and *Catriona*, 1893. In a very different vein was *Prince Otto*, 1885, the year in which he also published *The Dynamiter*, a sequel to *The New Arabian Nights*, 1882, and written in collaboration with his wife. Another collaborator was his stepson, Lloyd Osbourne, who was responsible for much of *The Wrong Box*, 1888, *The Wrecker*, 1892, and *The Ebb Tide*, 1894. Stevenson's poetry in *A Child's Garden of Verses*, 1885, reveals a rare feeling for the remembered emotions and thoughts of childhood and also notable is *Underwoods*, 1887, a book of English and Scots verse. *The Strange Case of Dr Jekyll and Mr Hyde*, 1886, is both a thrilling tale of horror and a study in the duality of human nature. *The Merry Men*, 1887, contains the story 'Thrawn Janet', and other works are *Across the Plains*, 1892, and *Island Nights' Entertainments*, 1893. At his death Stevenson left unfinished *St Ives*, the last six chapters of which were supplied by Sir Arthur QUILLER-COUCH, 1897, and *Weir of Hermiston* which promised to be a masterpiece. His earliest dramatic work was *Deacon Brodie*, 1880, revised 1888, and his later plays were written with W. E. HENLEY. They include *Beau Austin*, 1884, *Admiral Guinea*, 1884, and *Robert Macaire*, 1885.

In 1888 Stevenson sailed for the South Seas and settled in Vailima, Samoa, during the following year. Here his health improved and he worked steadily, interesting himself in the lives of the local people and the atmosphere of the islands. To the Samoans he was Tusitala, 'teller of tales'. He died in 1894 and was buried on Mount Vaea.

Hailed in his lifetime, Stevenson was later considered important only as a writer for children, but critical revaluation has revealed him as a realistic and intelligent craftsman whose clear, exact, smooth style shows influence of the French Symbolists (see SYMBOLISTE, L'ÉCOLE). He brought a high artistic quality to the adventure story, and the essays and studies analyse authors and their work with simplicity and directness. His best work has intensity, imaginative appeal, and a rare sense of place and time, combining skilful plotting with perceptive characterisation, high drama with moral subtlety.

A tireless letter-writer, Stevenson's correspondence has been subjected to much critical scrutiny. His *Vailima Letters* were edited by his friend Sir Sidney Colvin, 1895, who also published letters to his family and friends in 1899 (two volumes) and 1911 (four volumes).

Bibliography: Sir E. Gosse (Ed.), *Works*, 1894–98; L. Osbourne (Ed.), *Works* (with 5 vols of letters), 1923; G. Balfour, *The Life of Robert Louis Stevenson*, 1901; and Lives by W. Raleigh, 1915; J. A. Steuart, 1924; G. K. Chesterton, 1927; D. L. Dalglish, 1937; J. C. Furnas, 1951; D. Daiches, *Robert Louis Stevenson*, 1947; L. Cooper, *Robert Louis Stevenson*, 1947; R. Kiely, *Robert Louis Stevenson and the Fiction of Adventure*, 1964; E. M. Eigner, *Robert Louis Stevenson and Romantic Tradition*, 1966.

Stevenson, Thomas (1818–87), British engineer, born in Edinburgh. He joined with his father, Robert Stevenson, and his brother David in lighthouse construction, making a particular study of lighting methods. He invented the thermometer screen, known by his name. There is a character sketch by his son, Robert Louis Stevenson, in *Memories and Portraits*, 1887.

Stevenston, industrial and residential town in CUNNINGHAME DISTRICT, Strathclyde Region, Scotland, on the Firth of Clyde, 45 km south-west of Glasgow. At nearby Ardeer there is an explosives factory of Imperial Chemical Industries established by Nobel. Population 12,047.

Stevin, Simon, also Stevinus (1548–1620), Dutch mathematician, born at Bruges. In his youth he was a merchant's clerk, travelled widely in Europe and served Prince Maurice of Orange as a civil and military engineer. He appears to have invented a carriage with sails, and to have originated systems of defence by sluices and artillery. His chief success was his small pamphlet on decimal fractions published in Dutch (1585), and entitled (in the French translation) *La disme, enseignant facilement expédier par nombres entiers san rompuz, tous comptes se rencontrans aux affaires des hommes*. Decimal fractions had been used in the extraction of square roots long before his time, but Stevin established their daily use. He also made contributions to hydrostatics.

Steward, Lord High, see HIGH STEWARD OF ENGLAND.

Steward of the Household, Lord, in England, is the chief officer of the ancient court of the Board of Green Cloth, and was originally called the Lord Great Master of the Household. He has power over the finances of the royal household, and controls and selects all officers and servants except those of the chapel, chamber, and stable. He receives his charge from the sovereign and holds it during the sovereign's pleasure.

Stewart, Steuart, or Stuart, Scottish family tracing its descent from a Breton immigrant, Alan Fitzlaald, in the 11th century. His son, Walter (d. 1177), was made steward of Scotland by David I, and founded Paisley Abbey in 1163. The stewardship remained in the family, the various branches of which are descended from the seven sons of John (killed at Falkirk, 1298). The first royal Stewart was the son of Walter, sixth steward, and Marjory, daughter of Robert Bruce, and came to the Scottish throne as Robert II in 1371. The direct royal male line ended at the death of James V in 1542. His daughter, Mary, who adopted the spelling 'Stuart', claimed the throne of England by descent from Margaret Tudor, queen of James IV, and her son, James VI, became James I of England and progenitor of the royal line of Great Britain.

The Stuarts were in exile during the Commonwealth period (1645–60), and after the flight of James II of England the elder male line was permanently debarred. James II was succeeded by his elder daughter, Mary, and her husband, William of Orange, grandson of Charles I, and they were succeeded by Anne, younger daughter of James II. The male line of James II ended with the death of his grandsons, Charles Edward (the Young Pretender) and Henry, known as Cardinal York.

Stewart, Alfred Walter, see CONNINGTON, J. J.

Stewart, David, see ROTHESAY, DAVID STEWART, 1ST DUKE OF.

Stewart, Douglas Alexander (1913–), New Zealand poet, dramatist, and critic, born at Eltham; educated at New Plymouth Boys' High School and Victoria University College. After working as a journalist in New Zealand, Stewart joined the staff of *The Bulletin* in 1938 and was literary editor, 1941–61. His eight volumes of poems are on the whole light hearted and singing, with a delightful spontaneity. He also displays dramatic qualities and an insight into character in his four verse dramas, of which *The Fire on the Snow* and *Ned Kelly* are the more widely respected. His interest in ballads is shown in his own sequence *Glencoe*, 1947, and *Australian Bush Ballads*, 1955, edited with Nancy Keesing. *Collected Poems* appeared in 1967. Also important is *The Flesh and the Spirit: an Outlook on Literature*, 1948, a collection of his influential and stimulating criticisms from *The Bulletin*.

Bibliography: N. Keesing, *Douglas Stewart*, 1969.

Stewart, Dugald (1753–1828), British philosopher, born in Edinburgh, Scotland, educated at the high school and university there. In 1785 he was appointed professor of moral philosophy in Edinburgh. He was one of the Scottish 'common sense' school, and mainly follows REID. His works include *Elements of the Philosophy of the Human Mind*, 1792, *Outlines of Moral Philosophy*, 1794, and *The Philosophy of the Active and Moral Powers*, 1828. His works were collected by Sir William Hamilton, 1854–60.

Bibliography: S. A. Grave, *The Scottish Philosophy of Common Sense*, 1960.

Stewart, Jackie, full name John Young (1939–), British racing driver, born in Dumbarton, Scotland. He began motor racing in Scotland as a hobby (1961) but his immediate success led to Grand Prix racing in 1965, and in that year he won his first Grand Prix in Italy, driving a BRM. In 1966 he had a bad accident at Spa, Belgium, but recovered quickly. Stewart's Matra won seven Grand Prix races in 1969, and in so doing he won the World Championship for the first time. Driving for the Tyrrell team, Stewart repeated this success in 1971 and 1973. In nine seasons of Grand Prix competition, Stewart won 27 Grands Prix, more than any other driver in history. He retired from the sport at the end of the 1973 season. Before taking up motor racing, he had reached Olympic standard at clay-pigeon shooting.

Stewart, James, see MURRAY, JAMES STEWART, 1ST EARL OF.

Stewart, James, see ARRAN, JAMES STEWART, EARL OF.

Stewart, James (1908–), US film actor, tall and seemingly awkward, and with an unusual drawling voice. He has appeared in *Mr Smith Goes to Washington*, *The Philadelphia Story*, *Destry Rides Again*, *Winchester 73*, *Harvey*, *Rear Window*, *The Glenn Miller Story*, *The Man from Laramie*, *Anatomy of a Murder*, and many others.

Stewart, John Innes Mackintosh (1906–), Scottish writer of detective stories and scholar, born near Edinburgh; his pseudonym is Michael Innes. Educated at Edinburgh Academy and Oxford, he was professor of English at Adelaide University, 1939–45. He then returned from Australia, and in 1949 was elected a Student of Christ Church, Oxford. Under the pseudonym Michael Innes he has written erudite crime stories, which include *Death at the President's Lodging*, 1936, *Hamlet*,

Stewart, Michael

Revenge!, 1937, *Lament for a Maker*, 1938, *A Comedy of Terrors*, 1940, *Operation Pax*, 1951, and *The Man from the Sea*, 1955. Among his scholarly works are an edition of FLORIO's translation of Montaigne, 1931, and *Character and Motive in Shakespeare*, 1949.

Stewart, Michael (1906–), British politician, educated at Christ's Hospital and St John's College, Oxford. He became a teacher, and lectured for the WEA, 1931–42. After war service he became a Labour MP in 1945, and held junior office under Clement Attlee. In 1964 he became minister of Education, but succeeded Patrick Gordon Walker as foreign secretary, following Gordon Walker's defeat at Leyton in January 1965. From 1966 to 1967 he was secretary of state for Economic Affairs and from 1968 to 1970 he was again foreign secretary. His publications include *The British Approach to Politics*, 1938, and *Modern Forms of Government*, 1959.

Stewart, Robert, see CASTLEREAGH, ROBERT STEWART, VISCOUNT, AND 2ND MARQUESS OF LONDONDERRY.

Stewart Island, island off the south coast of South Island, New Zealand. The coast is deeply indented, and Paterson Inlet is a good harbour. The principal settlement is at Oban. Stewart Island is mountainous and thickly forested, and is a holiday resort. Its oysters are famous. Area 1735 km²; population 400.

Stewartby, town in BEDFORDSHIRE, England. The world's largest brickworks are here, producing over 11 million bricks weekly, using the fine clay of the blue Oxford clay belt. The model village was built in 1927. Population (1971) 1085.

Stewartia, camellia-like deciduous shrubs in the family Theaceae, having creamy or white flowers. Species grown are *S. malacodendron*, *S. ovata*, *S. pseudo-camellia* and *S. sinensis*. Propagation is by seeds and cuttings.

Stewarton, town in Kilmarnock and Louden District, Strathclyde Region, Scotland, on the River Annick, 8 km north of KILMARNOCK, manufacturing textiles, especially woollens. Population 4492.

Stewartry, administrative district of DUMFRIES AND GALLOWAY REGION in South-West Scotland. It˙ is smaller than the former Kirkcudbrightshire. Area 167,250 ha. Population about 22,000.

Stick Insect, *Carausius morosus*. (*Popperfoto*)

Stewing, see COOKERY.

Steyn, Marthinus Theunis (1857–1916), South African statesman, born in the Orange Free State; educated in Holland and England, being called to the Bar at the Inner Temple in 1882. He was a lawyer and a judge in his native state, of which, in 1896, he became president. He led guerrilla forces in the South African War, but later supported the British government.

Steyning, former seaport on the now silted-up River Adur in Adur District of West Sussex, England. There are remains of a Benedictine house together with a 12th-century church and 17th-century school. Population (1971) 3245.

Steyr, or Steier, Austrian town in the province of Upper Austria, at the confluence of the Enns and the Steyr. There are fine medieval, Renaissance, and Baroque buildings. It manufactures motor cars, bicycles, cutlery, paper, and textiles. Population (1971) 40,578.

Stibnite, chief ore of ANTIMONY; antimony trisulphide, Sb_2S_3. Stibnite is orthorhombic and is often found in prismatic crystals showing vertical striations and spear-shaped terminations. It occurs in low-temperature hydrothermal veins and is mined in China, Mexico, Bolivia, and Algeria.

Stick Insect, insect placed with LEAF INSECTS, in the order PHASMATODEA. Most stick insects belong to the family Phasmatidae. In common with the leaf insects, they mimic parts of plants, usually resembling the twigs of the vegetation on which they are found. The common stick insect, *Carausius morosus*, is a native of India. The adult, which measures about 8·5 cm in length, lacks wings and feeds on rose and privet leaves. The females are parthenogenetic.

Stickleback, the popular name.given to small fishes of the order Gasterosteiformes. They have elongated, compressed slender bodies, always without true scales, but often protected by means of bony scutes (plates). The anterior dorsal fin is represented by isolated spines, and the ventral fin is formed of a strong spine and one or two soft rays. The sticklebacks are noted for their red breast when in season and their nest-building habit, the males constructing nests of leaves, twigs and grass, and binding them together by a mucus which they secrete. Nearly all the species are found in fresh water in Europe, Asia and America, are very pugnacious, and feed on spawn of other fishes. *Gastrosteus aculeatus* (the three-spined stickleback) and *Pygosteus pungitius* (the ten-spined stickleback) can live in either fresh or salt water. *Spinachia spinachia* (the sea stickleback) is a much larger and more slender species; it is entirely marine, attains a length of 17 cm, and is armed with 15 short spines on the back.

Stiernhielm, Georg (1598–1672), Swedish poet, born at Vika. He studied at Uppsala University and in Germany, and from about 1640 was court poet to Queen Christina. He wrote sonnets, lyrics, and idylls, but his greatest achievement was a didactic allegorical poem, *Hercules*, 1647. A man of great learning, he helped to raise poetry in popular esteem and has justly been called 'the father of the Swedish art of poetry', for he did much to harmonise traditional Swedish culture with literary styles adopted from the rest of Europe.

Bibliography: P. Wieselgren, *Georg Stiernhielm*, 1948.

Stifter, Adalbert (1805–68), Austrian novelist and painter, born at Oberplan. He studied law and natural science at Vienna, and from 1860 to 1865 was an inspector of schools in Upper Austria. Stifter committed suicide after a long illness.

A descriptive writer of very great power, he excelled in portraying the harmony between man and nature and his novels reflect his country childhood spent among village craftsmen. His most notable works are the novels *Der Hochwald*, 1842, *Der Nachsommer* (The Indian Summer), 1857, describing the development of a young man, and the historical epic *Witiko*, 1865–67, and his exquisite short stories, *Studien*, 1844–50, and *Bunte Steine*, 1853. His collected works and letters were published in 25 volumes, 1901.

Bibliography: E. Lunding, *Adalbert Stifter*, 1946; Lives and Studies by W. Kosch, 1946, E. A. Blackall, 1948, C. Hohoff, 1949, K. Steffen, 1955.

Stigand (d. 1072), English prelate. In 1047 he became bishop of Winchester, and undertook negotiations between Edward the Confessor and Godwin (1051–52). When the latter re-established his position in England, ROBERT OF JUMIÈGES fled, and Stigand was uncanonically appointed archbishop of Canterbury in his place, in 1052, and was accordingly excommunicated (by five popes successively), but received the pallium from the antipope Benedict X in 1058. A covetous and worldly man, he exemplified many of the weaknesses in the English Church before the Conquest. Nevertheless he retained his position until in 1070 he was charged with various ecclesiastical offences by the papal legate, deprived of his see, and imprisoned. He was succeeded by LANFRANC.

Stigma, see FLOWER.

Stigmatisation (Medieval Latin, from Greek *stigma*, a mark), impression on certain individuals of the 'stigmata' or five wounds (in the hands, feet, and side) which Jesus received on the cross, generally held to be given miraculously as a favour to some of those specially devoted to the Passion. St Paul's words in Gal. vi. 17 do not necessarily state that he bore the stigmata. The first certain instance and the only one generally recognised, is that of St Francis of Assisi. Since that time over 300 instances are claimed, 29 during the 19th century, and Therese Neumann and Padre Pio in the 20th. The cases of Katharina Emmerich (1774–1824) and St Gemma Galgani (1878–1903) attracted considerable attention. Explanations of the phenomenon vary. The Roman Catholic Church does not treat stigmatisation as an incontestable miracle.

Stikker, Dirk Uipko (1897–), Dutch politician and diplomat, educated at Groningen University. He was foreign secretary, 1948–52, and ambassador to Britain, 1952–58. From 1958 to 1962 he was the Dutch permanent representative to NATO and OEEC, and in 1962 succeeded Paul-Henri SPAAK as secretary-general of NATO, resigning for health reasons in 1964.

Stilbite, see ZEOLITES.

Stilicho, Flavius (c. 365–408), Roman general and effective ruler of the Western Empire from 395 until 408. He was half-Roman, half-Vandal, the son of a mercenary captain. THEODOSIUS I made him commander-in-chief of the army and before his death appointed Stilicho guardian of his young son, Honorius, who was to reign in the West. On the accession of Theodosius's elder son, Arcadius, to the Eastern throne Stilicho brought about the downfall and death of the Emperor's adviser, Flavius Rufinus, an old rival. The poet Claudian began to publish poems in praise of Stilicho, an important source of information about the politics of the time.

In 397 Stilicho took an army to Greece in order to defeat the invading Visigoths under Alaric, but failed to bring them to battle. In 401 Alaric invaded Italy and threatened Milan. Stilicho withdrew troops from the Rhine frontier and Britain to strengthen his army and defeated the Visigoths at Pollentia (Pollenzo) and again in 403 at Verona though Alaric was allowed to escape.

In 405 Stilicho annihilated a vast horde of invading Germans, mostly Ostrogoths, led by Radagasius. By 408 his influence had declined. There was strong, though secret, opposition to him in Italy and even among the soldiers his popularity was not so secure. When the Eastern Emperor, Arcadius, died, Stilicho proposed to go to Constantinople. A palace official, Olympius, spread the rumour that Stilicho planned to put his own son, Eucherius, on the throne. Stilicho was imprisoned in Ravenna on Honorius's orders and beheaded later. Eucherius was slain shortly afterwards.

Bibliography: J. B. Bury, *A History of the Later Roman Empire*, 1923; A. Cameron, *Claudian: Poetry and Propaganda at the Court of Honorius*, 1970.

Still, Andrew Taylor (1828–1917), US osteopath, born in Jonesboro, Virginia. He is said to have attended Holston College, Newmarket, Tennessee, and in 1874 he founded OSTEOPATHY as it is known today. He met with a great deal of opposition; his teaching has been considerably modified by his successors. In 1892 he founded the American School of Osteopathy at Kirksville, Missouri. His books include *Philosophy of Osteopathy*, 1899, and *Osteopathy, Research and Practice*, 1910.

Still, see DISTILLATION.

Still-life, an art-form, consisting of inanimate objects grouped decoratively and generally represented illusionistically. It has sometimes been used as an adjunct, for example in the floral borders of medieval manuscripts or the candelabra of Van Eyck's *Arnolfini Wedding* portrait (National Gallery, London). A famous piece of trick *trompe l'oeil* painting is the still-life group in the centre of Holbein's *The Ambassadors* (National Gallery). A favourite theme, used not only in the background of paintings but also in decorative schemes of intarsia woodinlay, was that of an open cupboard door with a picturesque medley within.

In the development of the oil-painting technique, still-life assisted by providing a stringent discipline. Gradually still-life came to be accepted as a picture-format on its own account. In this it was reverting to an ancient precedent, appearing as such in Roman frescoes. Indeed, a prototype of 'successful' still-life is provided by Xeuxis' legendary bunch of grapes, so realistic that it deceived birds. An early example of 'pure' still-life is Jacopo de' Barbari's

Still-life

Still-life. *Still Life with Water Jug*, by Cézanne, c. 1892–93. *(Tate Gallery, London)*

Partridge with Gauntlets and an Archer's Bolt (Munich).

The genre reached a new expertise in the 17th century with painters such as de HEEM and SNYDERS in the Low Countries, ZURBARAN and the *bodegon* (tavern) painters in Spain, and Ruoppolo, the fruit-painter of Naples. Again in the 18th century still-life served painting as a whole by enabling CHARDIN to attain new heights in the study of the pictorial factor of 'tonality' (see TONE), e.g. in *The Attributes of the Arts* (Louvre). In this respect, Chardin was followed in the 19th century by a master of tonal still-life, FANTIN-LATOUR. Yet again still-life served a pioneering role when CÉZANNE used it to attempt modelling with gradations of colour. Finally, in the 20th century, PICASSO and BRAQUE used it for their Cubist experiment with 'synthetic' drawing, which conflated many aspects of the same object so as to produce new flat-pattern effects.

See also FLOWER PAINTING.

Bibliography: A. Gwynne-Jones, *Introduction to Still-Life*, 1954; B. Dunstan, *Starting to Paint Still-Life*, 1969.

Stillborn, see ABORTION; FOETUS; OBSTETRICS.

Stillicide, or eavesdrop, is a SERVITUDE in Scots law whereby a proprietor can build so that the rain-water falling on his house is thrown on to his neighbour's ground. Without this he would not be entitled to do so.

Stillingfleet, Edward (1635–99), English cleric, born at Cranborne, Dorset, became a fellow of St John's College, Cambridge (1653), MA (1656), DD (1668), and was incorporated at Oxford (1677). In 1667 he became prebendary of St Paul's, London, in 1669 canon of Canterbury, in 1677 archdeacon of London, in 1678 dean of St Paul's and in 1689 bishop of Worcester. He was a popular preacher and acted as chaplain to Charles II. His works include *Irenicum*, 1569, *Origines Sacrae*, 1663, *A Rational Account of the Grounds of the Protestant Religion*, 1664, and *Origines Britannicae, or the Antiquities of the British Church*, 1685. An edition of his *Works*, with a life by R. Bentley was published in 1710.

Stilt, *Himantopus himantopus*, a long-legged wader bird of order Charadriiformes. It has a very wide distribution. The name is given to these birds by reason of their very thin, long pink legs which extend far behind the body. It lives in flooded areas and swamps, particularly where there is soft mud. The species is cosmopolitan, with separate subspecies in the USA, South America, Australasia and a wholly black subspecies found only on South Island, New Zealand.

Stilted Arch, see ARCH.

Still-life by the Spanish painter Francisco Zurbaran; he uses a combination of striking realism and stark composition to endow simple objects with a spiritual significance. *(Prado, Madrid)*

Stilton, village in CAMBRIDGESHIRE, England, 11 km north-west of Peterborough and situated on the Great North Road. It gives its name to a slow-maturing, semi-hard, blue cheese made in Cambridgeshire and Leicestershire, which is still sold as Stilton. Population (1971) 910.

Stilts, poles provided with stirrup-like projections for the feet at a certain distance from the ground, at one time used for walking over rough or marshy places. Stilt-walking has long been a form of amusement. Stilts were used regularly in the Landes, a district of Gascony, and the Marquesas and other Pacific islands, and stilt-races remain a favourite feature of festivities in the Landes. Namur in Belgium was famed for its stilt-walkers over many centuries. Stilts also figure in Italian masquerades.

Stilwell, Joseph Warren (1883–1946), US soldier, born in Florida, trained at West Point Academy. He served in the Philippines (1904–06), and was an instructor at West Point (1906–10). Thereafter service in China and study of the language made him one of the foremost authorities in the USA on Chinese life. In the First World War he served in France. When Japan attacked the USA in 1941, Stilwell was chosen as US military representative in China. Chiang Kai-shek appointed him chief of staff and commander of the Fifth and Sixth Chinese armies, co-operating with the British forces in the defence of Burma. Cut off from supplies after the Japanese had captured Mandalay and Lashio (1942), he led the remnants of his troops in a remarkable retreat across the mountains to India, and returned to Chungking by air to resume the struggle from there. From October 1943 Stilwell conducted an advance of over 322 km, pushing the Japanese 18th Division back to their main base, Myitkyina. Stilwell lacked tact and political insight, and disliked the British. He was primarily a fighting soldier. After an open breach with Chiang Kai-shek, Stilwell was given a home command in the USA. Later he commanded the American Tenth Army at Okinawa.

See also BURMA, SECOND WORLD WAR CAMPAIGNS IN.

Bibliography: L. Anders, *Ledo Road: General Joseph W. Stilwell's Highway to China,* 1965; T. H. White (Ed.), *Stilwell Papers, An Iconoclastic Account of America's Adventures in China,* 1972; B. W. Tuchman, *Sand Against the Wind: Stilwell and the American Experience in China, 1911–45,* 1973.

Stimson, Henry Lewis (1867–1950), US statesman, born in New York City, educated at Yale and Harvard universities, and began practice at the Bar of New York City in 1891. He was US attorney for the Southern district of New York state, 1906–09, attacking several trusts and combines. President Taft made him secretary of war (1911–13). During the First World War he served in the army. He was secretary of state, 1929–33, formulating the Stimson Doctrine of nonrecognition of territories and agreements obtained by acts of aggression. He headed the US delegation to the London Naval Conference (1930), and was a member of the Permanent Court of Arbitration at The Hague (1938). In 1940 Stimson was appointed secretary of war, retiring from public life in 1945. His publications include *Democracy and Nationalism in Europe,* 1934, *The Far Eastern Crisis,* 1936, and his memoirs, *On Active Service in Peace and War* (with M. Bundy), 1948.

Stimulants, agents that increase activity. They may be general, exciting the body as a whole to greater activity, or may affect particular organs, such as the heart, kidneys, liver, stomach, or brain. They are distinguished from tonics by their more immediate and transient action. It often happens that while a small dose of a stimulant causes greater intensity of vital processes, a larger dose or repeated small doses tend to cause depression. Thus alcohol is an effective stimulant in moderate doses, but if its use is continued the vital processes become depressed, so that collapse is an important symptom of alchoholic poisoning. The most common stimulants are alcohol, nicotine, ammonia, tea, coffee, various essential oils, strychnine, amphetamine, electricity, and heat and cold under certain conditions.

Stinging Cell, see NEMATOCYST.

Stingray, any individual of the family Urolophidae, suborder Myliobatoidei, for example *Trygon pastinaca,* a ray of the Mediterranean and east Atlantic, and sometimes found around the southern shores of England, in which a serrated poisonous spine is present on the whip-like tail. This spine projects upwards and backwards and may inflict a severe wound. Species of *Pteroplatea,* in the same family, are also able to cause deep and poisoned wounds.

Stinkweed, *Diplotaxis,* a small yellow-flowered plant in family Cruciferae, whose leaves have a foetid smell when crushed. It occurs as a weed on railway embankments and other wastelands in Britain.

Stinkwood, term applied to the wood of numerous plants, used especially in reference to *Gustavia augusta,* a species of Lecythidaceae. The wood has a foetid smell, and the tree occurs in tropical America.

Stinnes, Hugo (1870–1924), German industrial magnate, born at Mülheim. Stinnes became a proprietor of mines, and established depots on the North, Baltic, Mediterranean, and Black Seas. During the First World War he acquired large holdings in iron mines, steamship lines, newspapers, and hotels, and achieved immense power in German economic life, his largest concern being the Siemens-Rheinelbe-Schuckert Union. This, under Hitler, was a principal component of the armament and engineering industries.

Stip (Turkish *Istib*), town in Macedonia, Yugoslavia, on the River Bregalnica. It was Turkish until the First World War. It has an old citadel and is an agricultural centre. Population 18,800.

Stipa, a genus of 300 hardy perennial grasses of family Gramineae. *S. pennata,* feather grass, 75 cm tall, is an ornamental plant of gardens. *S. tenacissima* is the esparto grass of Spain and North Africa, used in paper-making.

Stipend, originally the pay of soldiers, but now the annual allowance or income of an ecclesiastical benefice, and, in a wider sense, any settled pay for services daily, monthly, or annually. In the Roman Catholic Church stipend also denotes the fee a priest is entitled to for saying mass. 'Stipendiary' in a wide sense means one who performs services for a settled income, but specifically a paid magistrate.

Stipple Engraving, a method of engraving which, like AQUATINT and MEZZOTINT, is a 'grain' process, i.e. the grain is formed by a series of dots so arranged as to conform to the planes and modelling of the subject. The first practitioner of stipple engraving was Johann Lutma, a 17th-century German silversmith, several of whose plates are extant. Notable French engravers in stipple were Jean François of Nancy (b. 1717), Louis Bonnet (b. 1743) and Gilles Demarteau (b. 1772), the two last being engravers in the crayon style. The first English stipple engraver was William Wynne Ryland (1732–83), who, after completing his training in Paris, became engraver to King George III. See also ENGRAVING; PRINTMAKING, *Colour Prints*.

Stippling, in interior decorating, the production of a finely granulated surface on paintwork, achieved by beating the wet surface with a flat-faced bristle brush. Use is made of stipplers with rubber plates or cylinders on surfaces of coarse texture. Stippling is used on oil-bound, quick-setting, non-glossy paint. An even change from one colour to another can be obtained by this method. In picture painting, drawing or engraving stippling is a method of obtaining effect by means of dots instead of solid areas of colour or tone, or continuous lines (see STIPPLE ENGRAVING).

Stipule, a leaf-like projection at the base of a leaf and on either side of the stem. It may be a scale serving to protect a bud, a spinous protection against animals (e.g. acacia), or it may be large and green, and augment the photosynthetic capacity of the leaf (e.g. pea). Some stipules, for example on the smilax, are sensitive climbing tendrils.

Stirling, James (1926–), British architect. He designed with James Gowan (1924–) an influential housing estate at Ham Common, Richmond, 1958, and the Department of Engineering building, Leicester University, 1959–63. Alone, or in partnership with others, he subsequently designed the History Faculty building at Cambridge, 1965–68; new buildings for Queen's College, Oxford, 1968–70; student residential buildings for St Andrew's University, 1964– ; and the Olivetti training headquarters, 1969– .

Stirling, William Alexander, Earl of, see ALEXANDER, SIR WILLIAM, EARL OF STIRLING.

Stirling, royal burgh (since 1226) and former county town of Stirlingshire, now in Stirling District, Central Region of Scotland, situated on the River Forth, 43 km north-east of Glasgow. Its strong strategical position has made it the key to the Highlands. The castle was the birthplace and residence of several Scottish kings. The view from the castle walls is remarkable for its interest and beauty, and from there can be seen the field of Bannockburn (1314), Stirling Old Bridge, the Abbey Craig with the Wallace Monument, Cambuskenneth Abbey, and the sinuous reaches of the Forth. At St Ninians there is the site of the 'bore stone' on which Bruce's standard was set up after the Battle of BANNOCKBURN. The main industries are agricultural implements, fertilisers, carpets, textiles, and cigarettes. A new university was established at Stirling in the mid-1960s. Population (1971) 29,776.

Bibliography: J. R. Easter, *Plan for Central Stirling*, 1974.

Stirling, University of, created by royal charter in December 1967. The only campus university in Scotland, it provides courses for degrees in arts, social sciences, and physical sciences. There are about 2100 students. It is the only British university using the semester system.

Stirling District, formerly part of south-west Perthshire, this district is now part of the CENTRAL REGION, Scotland. To the west and south it is bounded by the Strathclyde Region (districts of Argyll and Bute, Dumbarton, Clydebank, Bearsden and Milngavie, Strathkelvin, Cumbernauld and Kilsyth); to the south-east and east by the Central Region (districts of Falkirk and Clackmannan); and to the north-east and north by Tayside Region (Perth and Kinross District). The area of Stirling District is 216,999 ha and at the 1971 census, the population was 76,443.

The district stretches from Breadalbane in the north-west through the Trossachs to the Carse of Forth in the south-east. The north of the district is part of the Grampian mountain system with several peaks over 900 m elevation. Amongst the highest mountains are Ben More (1174 m), Ben Lui (1130 m), and Ben Challum (1022 m). The area has many lochs; amongst the most important are Loch KATRINE (water reservoir for the city of Glasgow), Loch Voil, Loch Vennachar, Loch Ard, and the Lake of MENTEITH. The main rivers are the TAY, Earn, and Forth. Large-scale afforestation has occurred in Breadalbane and the Trossachs, and the attraction of the natural scenery of loch, mountain, and river has led to the development of a considerable tourist industry concentrated on Aberfoyle and Callander. The area has often featured in episodes of Scottish history; there are several notable battlefields such as Stirling Bridge (1297), BANNOCKBURN (1314), and SHERIFFMUIR (1715).

Light engineering and woollen manufacturing industries are located in Stirling and Dunblane. Agriculture is important in the Carse of Forth and along the main river valleys. There are many fine examples of early religious establishments; Dunblane Cathedral (13th century), Cambuskenneth Abbey (1147), and the Church of the Holy Rude in Stirling (15th century). Stirling Castle, whose main buildings date from the 15th and 16th centuries, and Doune Castle dating from the early 15th century, are splendid examples of the castle-building of that period.

Stirling is the regional capital of the Central Region. Other important settlements in the southern part of the district are DUNBLANE, CALLANDER, and ABERFOYLE. In the northern part of the district, although relatively small as regards population, settlements such as Killin, Lochearnhead, Crianlarich, and Tyndrum are important as route centres and tourist resorts.

Bibliography: D. W. G. Timms (Ed.), *Stirling Region*, 1974.

Stitch, a sharp pain in the side. It may be caused by pleurisy, by spasm of the respiratory muscles during violent exercise, or by intercostal neuralgia.

Stitchery, see EMBROIDERY.

Stitchwort, a cosmopolitan genus of 120 species in the Caryophyllaceae (campion family). Their narrow radiating petals, white in colour, give the flower a star-like or stellate appearance. British species are *S. nemorum*, wood stitchwort; *S. media*, the common stitchwort, also called common chickweed; *S. holostea*, the greater stitchwort; *S. palustris*, the glaucous marsh stitchwort; *S. graminea*, the lesser stitchwort; and *S. alsine*, the bog stitchwort. *S. holostea* is from 30 to 60 cm high, and has large white flowers; it is common in copses and hedgegrows, and was occasionally planted in gardens as a border flower.

Stoa, in Greek architecture, a detached portico. Stoas were built round many sanctuaries and AGORAS, and were an essential element of Greek town planning (see GREEK ARCHITECTURE). The Stoa of Attalos at Athens, gift of a Pergamene king (c. 150 BC), has been completely reconstructed.

Stoat, or ermine, *Mustela erminea*, a small carnivorous mammal, native of Europe, with a much elongated body covered with short fur. The stoat generally retains its reddish-brown colour in Britain, but in winter in colder latitudes (including northern Scotland) its fur becomes partially or wholly white and much denser, and is then highly valued by furriers. It is about 25 cm long, with a black-tipped tail about 12 cm long. It destroys enormous numbers of rats and mice, and this service is probably worth the loss the stoat causes by destruction of game. It is closely related to the weasel, both being in family Mustelidae of order CARNIVORA.

Stobaeus, Johannes (fl. 6th century AD), Greek anthologist. His collected fragments of Greek authors on a variety of topics have survived in two works, *Eclogae* and *Florilegium*, in which references to earlier literature are helpful for added knowledge of many authors and works.

Stock, in geology, see PLUTON.

Stock, term usually associated in the public mind with shares and dealings on a stock exchange, though negotiability on a stock exchange is not an essential incident of stock.

 British Government Stock (gilt-edged). The government invites the public to share in a loan. Each subscriber is allotted stock for his accepted contribution, e.g. Treasury Stocks, Exchequer Stock, Funding Loan, Consolidated Stock (Consols). Stock was also issued in exchange for proprietary interests in nationalised industries, e.g. British Transport Stock. Thereafter the stock may be bought or sold through a stock exchange, the price at which it is transferred varying according to the credit conditions prevailing at the time. Interest at an agreed rate is paid, usually half-yearly. The terms of issue state whether the stock shall be redeemed within a certain time or at the option of the government. Most government stock can be transferred from one holder to another in multiples of 1p.

 Dominion Government Stocks are similar to British, except that the revenues of the dominion concerned are alone liable for the service of the loan. These stocks are freely negotiable on the stock exchanges of the world.

 Stock of a Public Authority, such as the Port of London Authority and local government bodies. Such authorities borrow funds to build and equip their docks and other structures, and their revenues provide periodical interest and ultimate repayment of the funds borrowed in accordance with the contract made when the stock is first offered for subscription.

 See also COMPANY AND COMPANY LAW.

Stock, abbreviation of stock gillyflower, *Matthiola incana*. All the garden varieties of the simple-stemmed stock, 10-week stock, Brompton stock, and queen's stock have been derived from *M. incana*. The wallflower-leaved stock, *M. bicornis*, is a small plant, with narrow hoary leaves and dull brown flowers; it grows in Greece, and is the night-scented stock, which is grown in greenhouses for its fragrance by night. Also fragrant is the sub-shrub *M. odoratissima*. *M. fenestralis* is the window-stock. In Britain the sea stock, *M. sinuata*, occurs rarely by the sea coast, mostly in the south-west.

Stock Exchange. The function of a stock exchange is to provide a market in which STOCKS and shares of all descriptions can be freely bought and sold, and in which the provision of new finance for governmental or industrial purposes can be facilitated through the flotation of new issues of capital.

The London Stock Exchange, colloquially termed the 'House', is situated in the triangle formed by Throgmorton Street, Old Broad Street, and Bartholomew Lane in the City of London. In 1973 a new building was completed on this site, comprising a 100-metre tower and a separate public relations block. There are 4000 members and 1300 clerks who are admitted to the dealing floor.

The Stock Exchange in 1976 transacted business to a total of £106,000 million, an average of about £375 million each working day. The total number of transactions in 1976 was 4·8 million. It provides a market for the buying and selling of around 8500 different securities, including over 6700 securities of companies, with a total market value of about £250,000 million, covering the whole field of government, municipal, and commercial finance.

Demand for ordinary (equity) shares has grown, partly because of a belief that such shares will maintain or increase their real value. However, the climate of economic uncertainty in 1973–74 caused large falls in share values. Institutional investors, such as insurance companies, pension funds, and investment and unit trusts, have become increasingly important in recent years. They accounted for over 50 per cent of market holdings of

Stock Exchange. Interior of the London Stock Exchange. *(Popperfoto)*

ordinary shares in 1976, compared with 25 per cent in 1964.

Through the machinery of the Stock Exchange a large proportion of the nation's assets and income is made liquid for collection by the government in the form of capital transfer tax or as income tax. The Stock Exchange is not an isolated organisation that can be considered by itself. It is an essential and inseparable part of the financial machinery of the country, without which neither the government nor the commerce and industry of the nation could function efficiently.

Finance. The capital was originally £720,000 in 20,000 shares, £36 paid, but was altered in 1948 by reducing each share to 1s. fully paid, 40,000 redeemable annuities of £4 per annum being issued *pro rata* to shareholders as compensation. These annuities may be held by non-members, and a considerable proportion of them is now so held.

Constitution. The constitution of the Stock Exchange, which was founded c. 1773, is laid down by a Deed of Settlement of 31 December 1875, which superseded the original Deed of Settlement of 27 March 1802. In 1972 the Constitution was amended to allow the amalgamation of the London Stock Exchange and the other stock exchanges in the United Kingdom and the Irish Republic, which took place in 1973. Control is vested in a council which is elected by members and consists of an executive body of 46 members, including 10 representatives of the country exchanges. No one can be elected to the council unless he is, and has been for the previous five years, a member of the Stock Exchange. The council is responsible for the rules and regulations, which are enforced by strict disciplinary powers, and, supplemented by a traditional integrity among the members based upon the motto 'Dictum meum pactum', ('My word is my bond'), maintains a high standard of honesty and fairness in dealings by members for the public. The disciplinary powers of the council include the power to censure, to suspend a member from entry to the House, and to expel a member from the Stock Exchange. In general, the business of the council is concerned both with the internal management of the Stock Exchange for the members and with external matters relating to the public interest. The granting of quotations to new issues of capital under further safeguards is also an important part of the council's work. Routine business is mainly delegated to standing committees which are responsible to the council, though all major questions of policy are decided by the council itself.

Membership. A candidate for membership, who must be not less than 21 years of age, has to complete three years' training with a Stock Exchange firm or firms prior to admission and be proposed and seconded by existing members. The entrance fee is £1000, payable to a nomination redemption fund, and the annual subscription is £300. Clerks are employed in two categories. 'Authorised' clerks are allowed to carry out dealings, and 'Unauthorised' clerks have the right of entry to the House, but may not deal. There is no entrance fee for clerks but an authorised clerk pays an annual subscription of £240 and an unauthorised clerk pays £75. An authorised clerk must be at least 18 years of age and an unauthorised clerk 16 years.

Brokers and Jobbers. The members are divided into two categories, namely brokers and jobbers, and carry on their business either as individuals or in partnership. A broker may not enter into partnership with a jobber. Brokers act as agents in buying and selling for members of the public, receiving a commission on the business done; they carry out orders in any class of security which the client desires to buy or sell. It is also their business to advise clients on questions of realisation and investment; to make and certify valuations for probate; and from time to time to advise and assist companies in the raising of capital; and in this connection to effect placings or to procure underwriting for new issues. Members of the Stock Exchange are not allowed to advertise or to approach persons other than their own principals.

Jobbers are principals, dealing on their own account. They may not deal with the public, but only with other members of the Stock Exchange. They do not deal in all securities indiscriminately, but specialise in one or more groups of securities, or 'markets' as they are called: e.g. gilt-edged stocks (consisting mainly of British government securities); insurance shares; bank shares; foreign government bonds; the shares of mining, or brewery, or investment trust companies; or in one or more of the many sub-divisions of the great mass of commercial and industrial companies. Other 'markets' are those for oil, rubber, tea, and nitrate shares. The trading floor of the House is divided by custom into these various markets, where the jobbers specialising in those particular securities have their stands, i.e. places where they stand and may always be found. The brokers move all over the floor contacting those jobbers whom they need for the particular business in hand. The jobbing system is peculiar to the London Stock Exchange, and its existence tends to eliminate violent fluctuations in prices.

Dealings on the Stock Exchange. A broker on receiving an order from a client approaches a jobber who specialises in the particular type of security, and if the price made by the jobber is acceptable he deals with that jobber. By the custom of the Stock Exchange a jobber may not ask the broker whether he is a buyer or a seller and therefore, when asked for a quotation, he always names both his buying and his selling price; this is called 'making a price'. He makes his price as far as he can judge by the law of supply and demand; the idea that the jobbers fix or control the prices of securities is a misconception. A jobber may, but is unlikely to, refuse to make a price in active securities. The difference between the buying and selling price varies according to the volume of dealings. Where dealings are frequent and the jobber can 'undo' his bargain without difficulty, he makes a 'close' price, but where dealings are less frequent he has to make a wider price, because he carries the greater risk of being unable to do the reverse bargain and make his profit or cut his loss. In the last resort the prices are fixed by competition.

A jobber who has made a price is bound by custom to deal at that price in a reasonable amount of stock or shares. If the transaction is larger or smaller than normal the amount in which the price is made is decided by discussion between the two parties. For instance, in answer to a broker wanting to deal in a certain government stock, a jobber might make a price of 96½ to 96¾ in £100,000 stock, indicating that he is willing to buy £100,000 at 96½ per cent or sell a like amount at 96¾ per cent. If the broker's order is for £500,000 stock, he would ask the price in that amount and the jobber might either be willing to deal at that price or, because of the greater risk, feel obliged to widen the difference between the buying and selling prices. Further bargaining may then take place before the deal is concluded. A broker after executing an order for a client must send him a contract note duly stamped which, *inter alia*, gives the title of the security, the amount purchased or sold, the relative price and value, and the date by which payment has to be made. It is the broker's duty to see that all bargains are made at the best possible prices for his client and that share or stock transfers are duly registered with the company and the relative document of title obtained for them.

Settlement of Bargains. British funds, corporation and company stocks (Great Britain and Northern Ireland), public boards, dominion, provincial, and Commonwealth government securities are dealt in 'for cash', and the buying broker is liable to pay on the following day in return for delivery of the stock. Other securities, unless dealt in by special arrangement, are bought or sold for 'the account' and bargains are settled on the account days which are fixed annually by the council and normally recur at fortnightly intervals.

Continuation Facilities. A continuation (or *contango*) is an arrangement for carrying forward the settlement of a transaction from one account to the next. The normal arrangement is for the buyer who does not wish to take up his stock to pay a rate of interest to a seller who is willing not to deliver, and who in effect therefore lends to the buyer the money value of the transaction. Continuations form a useful part of the machinery for maintaining free markets. They provide a means of bridging the delays in delivery between London and overseas exchanges, or delays arising from other causes. They also enlarge the scope of the jobbing technique and enable jobbers to be more free and more flexible in their price making, since they can, by means of continuations when they are available, carry over an uncovered position from one account to another instead of being compelled to level their books at the end of each account—a process which may be disadvantageous not only to themselves but to the market in which they operate. Continuations can also be used as a medium for speculation, and were largely so used in the past. Many brokers now will not entertain speculative continuations, and where they are entertained, substantial margins are usually required, as a protection against loss. Continuations, for whatever purpose they are entered into, are transactions in real values which must ultimately be settled.

Option dealing has also a useful function in the maintenance of free markets, but, like continuations, it can also be used for purely speculative purposes.

Dealing Ex & Cum Dividend or Ex & Cum Rights. 'Ex-div.' or 'x.d.', means that if a buyer has bought a security so marked, the current dividend belongs to the seller and the price then no longer includes the value of the dividend. 'Cum div.' means that the buyer has the right to the dividend due to be paid, and should it be sent by the company to the seller the amount must be paid over by him to the buyer. Similarly 'cum rights' means that in a transaction any advantages, perhaps in the form of an offer of new securities on favourable terms or a free issue of shares by means of capitalising reserves (sometimes called bonus shares), passes to the buyer, while 'ex-rights'

means that such advantage remains with the seller. Government and other securities dealt in in the gilt-edged market are quoted 'ex dividend' on and after the day on which the books close or the balance is struck for the payment of dividend; registered securities of, for example, industrial companies are quoted 'ex-dividend' on the making-up day (five days before the account day) preceding the first day on which the transfer books are closed for the payment of the dividend. Bearer securities are quoted 'ex dividend' on the day the dividend is payable.

Arbitrage Dealing. The term ARBITRAGE refers to professional dealings between London and overseas exchanges, and consists in buying in one exchange and selling in another. Either brokers or jobbers can obtain from the council authority to do this type of business.

Securities which may be dealt in. Brokers and jobbers may deal only in securities which have been granted quotation by the council and certain other securities which fall within a narrow classification. To obtain quotation the company or other issuer of the security must comply with stringent regulations imposed by the council in addition to the requirements of the law. Companies are willing to co-operate in fulfilling the regulations in order to obtain a market for their securities. The council, in granting a quotation, express no opinion as to whether or not a company will achieve the success to which it looks forward, but every effort is made to see that the proposition is put fully and fairly before the public, and that no known undesirable persons are connected with it. On the grant of quotation a company must pay a fee calculated on the money value of the security issued.

The Stock Exchange Daily Official List. This list is compiled from securities quoted and the bargains marked. The official 'marking' is made up from the marking slips signed by the broker or jobber recording transactions effected before 2·15 p.m. Transactions after that hour on the same day may be marked on the following morning and will then bear a distinguishing sign to show that they were done on the previous day. Except for the few transactions which owing to special circumstances are effected outside the market price and bear a distinguishing mark, all recorded transactions represent bargains done at the market price at the time of dealing. Fluctuations in prices are sent out by the Exchange Telegraph Company on automatic machines ('tape prices') and by the Stock Exchange over a closed circuit Market Price Display Television Service.

Other official publications of the council are the *Stock Exchange Weekly Official Intelligence* and the *Stock Exchange Official Year Book*, which gives details of some 8500 companies.

In 1953 a visitors' gallery was built in the Stock Exchange, from which the dealings could be watched. This was part of the effort made to publicise the Stock Exchange. The Stock Exchange also undertakes extensive publicity work and provides a wide range of educational material to schools and others.

Scale of Commissions. The minimum scale of commissions varies according to the type and price of the security. The detailed scale may be obtained on application to the secretary of the Stock Exchange. Brokers are allowed to share their commissions with agents who are approved by the council and whose names appear in one

389

or other of the registers of agents kept by the council pursuant to the agency rules.

Provincial and Overseas Exchanges. In addition to the London Stock Exchange there are exchanges in Belfast, Birmingham, Bristol, Cardiff, Dublin, Glasgow, Liverpool, and Manchester. Together they constitute a body called the Associated Stock Exchanges. Stockbroking firms exist also in a large number of smaller towns scattered throughout Britain and Eire. These firms constitute the Provincial Brokers Stock Exchange, the membership of which is approximately 210. Both of these bodies work in co-operation with the London Stock Exchange and have adopted substantially the same rules. Throughout the Commonwealth and the USA, and in many other overseas countries, there are stock exchanges which have business relations with the London Stock Exchange. The New York stock exchange is located in and called Wall Street.

Bibliography: H. D. Berman, *Stock Exchange*, 1971; P. Donaldson, *Guide to the British Economy*, 3rd ed. 1971; H. McRae and F. Cairncross, *Capital City*, 1973.

Stockbridge, small town in Hampshire, England, 14 km south-west of Winchester. Agriculture is the main occupation, and wheat, barley, and oats are the chief crops. Population (1971) 431.

Stockhausen, Karlheinz (1928–), German composer, born at Mödrath. He studied first in Cologne, then in Paris with MESSIAEN and MILHAUD. Since 1953 he has worked at a studio for ELECTRONIC MUSIC at Cologne, and in 1955 founded with Herbert Eimert the periodical *Die Reihe* for the propagation of serial and electronic music. His composition courses at Darmstadt, started in 1957, have become a regular forum for the avant-garde. His works include *Gesang der Jünglinge*, 1956, for treble and electronic tape, *Gruppen* for three orchestras, 1957, and *Für kommenden Zeiten*, '17 texts for intuitive music', 1970.

Bibliography: J. Cott, *Stockhausen: Conversations with the Composer*, 1974; Studies by K. Wörner, trans. 1973, and J. Harvey, 1975.

Stockholm, county of eastern SWEDEN. It surrounds the national capital (see below) but is administratively separate. It is a fertile lowland region with many lakes. Small amounts of iron-ore are mined in the north-east, but its main industries are metallurgical, paper, and electrical equipment manufacture. Area 6503 km². Population (1974) 1,489,000.

Stockholm, capital of SWEDEN, situated where Lake Mälaren joins Saltsjön, an inlet of the Baltic Sea thickly dotted with islands. The oldest part of the city is built on the island that separates the two stretches of water. Here it grew up in the middle of the 13th century round the fortress that had been erected to guard the vital entrance to the trading centres of Lake Mälaren. On the foundations of this old fortress there now stands the imposing royal palace, built to the design of Nicodemus

Stockholm. *(Camera Press)*

Tessin the younger (1697–1754). Its exterior bears the stamp of the Roman Renaissance style, while inside there are many exquisite examples of 18th-century art from home and abroad. Close to the palace is Storkyrkan, Stockholm's episcopal church, the oldest parts of which date from the 13th century. Among other things it contains a famous group, representing St George and the Dragon, executed by the Lübeck sculptor Bernt Notke at the end of the 15th century. To the south of these imposing buildings extends an area of dwelling-houses dating from medieval times, with narrow twisting streets and lanes.

There are a number of official and administrative buildings in *Gamla stan*, the old town, including *Riddarhuset* (the House of the Nobility), *Högsta domstolen* (the supreme court), and *Kanslihuset* (government offices). Others, such as *Riksdagshus* (Houses of Parliament), *Riksbank* (National Bank of Sweden), and *Utrikes-departmentet* (Foreign Office), are not far away. On the little island of Riddarholmen, immediately to the west of *Gamla stan*, is the Franciscans' old church, once the centre of their monastic buildings and later Sweden's pantheon, where former kings are buried. Formerly, the municipal as well as the national government was concentrated around this part, but now both the law courts and the city hall are on the island of Kungsholmen. The *Stadshuset* (city hall), which is Stockholm's best-known building from modern times, was designed by Ragnar Östberg and opened in 1923. It combines southern influences with northern brick architecture, and has an extremely beautiful situation on the shore of Lake Mälaren.

Stockholm extends north and south of the old town across the so-called 'malm' areas—Norrmalm, Östermalm, and Södermalm—which were first built on to any extent during the 17th century, and which are now completely covered by the many blocks of flats and offices that were built here as a result of the 19th-century industrialisation. The turn of the century saw the development of garden suburbs, e.g. Djursholm and Saltsjöbaden, and somewhat later the municipal garden suburbs of Bromma and Brännkyrka, west and south-west of Stockholm, were established. By the 1930s the inner part of the city had been completely built over, and the building of houses is now expanding rapidly in areas which only a few years ago were open country. In these new outer districts, mainly south of the city, there are modern suburban communities in units of about 20–30,000 inhabitants, connected by underground railway (*Tunnelbanan*) to central Stockholm. These communities include Vällingby and Skärholmen. Also outside the city are large residential areas consisting of villas and small cottages with gardens and allotments. Most of those who live in these areas go to work in the centre of the city, which has given rise to serious traffic problems. Numerous large bridges and traffic installations have therefore been built during the last decade, including Västerbron, Tranebergsbron, and Slussen. From the old town a fine old bridge leads northwards past the Houses of Parliament to Gustaf Adolfs Torg and the Royal Opera House. This is the beginning of Norrmalm, where most of the office buildings and banks are concentrated. Here, too, there are numerous theatres, cinemas, and restaurants. The other parts of the city have more the stamp of residential areas. This is particularly the case with Östermalm, which is bordered to the south by the capital's most fashionable thoroughfares, Strandvägen and Birger Jarlsgatan. The former is especially popular with its lime-trees and proximity to the water, and leading as it does out to Stockholm's classical amusement centre, Djurgården, a kind of insular Bois de Boulogne. This is also the site of Skansen, the world-famous open-air museum, which reflects the old Swedish life as it was lived on country estates and farms, and is also a zoo. At Djurgården and the adjacent island of Skeppsholmen the Swedish navy has one of its bases. Besides the ordinary elementary and secondary schools, Stockholm has numerous higher educational institutions, such as the university, embracing all faculties except theology. Stockholm's inner harbour, which gives the city much of its aesthetic appeal, is both large and deep, and is kept open all the year round, sometimes with the help of icebreakers in the winter. In the northern part of Djurgården is Frihamnen, the 'Free Harbour'. There is passenger traffic from Stockholm not only to most of the Swedish coastal towns but also to the USSR and Finland. Commercial traffic is worldwide. The airport of Stockholm for internal traffic is at Bromma. The international airport is at Arlanda, 48 km north of Stockholm. The city has many big industries such as shipbuilding, engineering, iron-founding, sugar refining, brewing, tanning, and the manufacture of silk, cotton, soap, tobacco, cork, and leather. Some of the famous names among the industries of Stockholm are Bolinder, De Laval, Atlas-Diesel, Separator, Elektrolux, Primus, and L. M. Ericsson. Population (1975) 665,202.

Bibliography: H. Calmfors, *Urban Government for Greater Stockholm*, 1968; S. Furness (Ed.), *Stockholm*, 1970; *Stockholm and Cologne: Urban Planning and Land-Use Control*, 1972; D. Pass, *New Community Development Process in Stockholm: Vallingby and Farsta*, 1973.

Stockings, see HOSE.

Stockmar, Christian Friedrich, Baron von (1787–1863), German politician, born at Coburg, educated at the University of Jena. He became the confidential adviser of Leopold I of the Belgians. In 1836 he went to England to act as adviser to the young Princess Victoria, who succeeded to the throne in the following year, and for some time had a good deal of influence at the British court.

Stockport, industrial town on the River MERSEY, 10 km from Manchester, and now part of the Stockport borough of the Greater MANCHESTER METROPOLITAN COUNTY, England. The Mersey is formed here by the confluence of the rivers Tame and Goyt, and their valleys were favourable sites for textile mills. Until recently, Stockport's river banks were lined with mills, but most of these and also the poor-quality houses around them, have now been demolished. The old town, however, was sited on a sandstone ridge around the parish church (dating back to the 12th century). It is a town on two levels, and now has on the lower level a new shopping area with large car parks, actually built partly over the river. The north–south road through the town was built in 1824–26 on an embankment with a bridge above the river, and the massive railway viaduct of 1838–40 is an even more striking feature of the town. To many visitors, Stockport may seem to be a grim town but in fact it has some fine buildings, notably the

Stocks

town hall and the fine large church of St George. The decline of cotton has been offset by the growth of numerous other industries, including chemicals and engineering, with some large works on the west side of the town and also at Reddish, formerly an independent town. The town suburbs stretch southwards towards the Cheshire Plain and northwards across the Mersey. Population (1971) 139,644.

Bibliography: W. Astle (Ed.), *History of Stockport*, 1971.

Stocks, device which was used for the punishment of certain criminal offenders. It consisted of two baulks of timber so padlocked together as to imprison the feet, sometimes also the hands and even the neck, in holes made for the purpose. Stow's *Survey of London*, 1598, describes them as erected in every ward of London for vagabonds and other petty offenders, while set up in the prison in Cornhill, and called the cage, was a pair of stocks for the punishment of night walkers. They were last used in England in the middle of the 19th century. In the USA they survived until before the Civil War as a punishment for slaves, but were in more general use in the 18th century. See also PILLORY.

Stocksbridge, former urban district of South YORKSHIRE, England, 15 km north-west of SHEFFIELD. It manufactures alloy, stainless and other special steels, also vehicle springs and umbrella frames. It is situated partly within the Peak District National Park. Population (1971) 13,404.

Stockton, Frank Richard (1834–1902), US novelist, born in Philadelphia. He worked as a wood engraver, but after the success of *Ting-a-Ling*, 1870, a volume of short stories for young people, he turned from art to writing. Among a dozen volumes of short stories the most outstanding is *The Lady or the Tiger*, which became celebrated. He wrote several humorous novels full of absurdities, the best-known being *Rudder Grange*, 1879, with its two sequels, *The Rudder Grangers Abroad*, 1891, and *Pomona's Travels*, 1894.

Stockton, county seat of San Joaquin county, California, USA, 115 km south-east of San Francisco, on an arm of the San Joaquin river. Its chief industries are the manufacture of agricultural implements, lumber products, flour and food preparations, and there is a trade in the fruit, cattle, and grain of the rich San Joaquin valley. Population 107,644.

Stockton-on-Tees, town and district of CLEVELAND, England, 5 km west of MIDDLESBROUGH. The town is believed to have received its charter of incorporation as a borough between the years 1201 and 1208, and its first market charter was granted in 1310. The chief buildings of interest are the parish church, town hall (1735), the first railway ticket office, sites connected with the first passenger railway from Stockton to Darlington (see STEPHENSON, GEORGE), and new municipal buildings in Church Road. Markets are held twice a week in the High Street, one of the widest in England. John Walker, inventor of the first friction match, and Thomas Sheraton, the famous designer and maker of furniture, were born here. In addition to the old-established heavy industries of iron, steel, chemicals, and engineering, many new industries

have been attracted to the town. Area (district) 195 km²; population (1971) 162,000.

Stockwood, Arthur Mervyn (1913–), English churchman, educated at Kelly College and Christ's College, Cambridge. He was vicar of the University Church, Cambridge, 1955–59, and since 1959 has been bishop of Southwark. His books include *There is a Tide*, 1946, *Whom They Pierced*, 1948, *I Went to Moscow*, 1955, *The Faith Today*, 1959, and *Cambridge Sermons*, 1959.

Stoics, sect of ancient philosophers and moralists opposed to the Epicureans in their views of human life. The founder of the system was ZENO (fl. 3rd century BC) of Citium in Cyprus, who derived his first impulse from Crates the Cynic. He opened his school in a building or porch, called the Stoa Poikile (Painted Porch), at Athens, whence the name of the sect. Zeno and his successors, Cleanthes and CHRYSIPPUS, represent the first period of the system. The second period (200–50 BC) embraces its general promulgation and its introduction to the Romans.

Stoicism is a combination of many elements adapted from earlier philosophies, together with certain peculiar developments of its own. To the Stoic, philosophy is a way of life in which knowledge serves the living of the good life, conceived as the practice of virtue. This is in the Socratic tradition. The Stoic doctrine is a materialist theory with a difference; for matter, the one constituent of the world, is considered as governed by reason, which as a principle of action is itself a tenuous substance permeating the universe. It is as participating in reason that all men are brothers. What animates each individual is a rational material soul, which acquires knowledge. It is to help with this acquisition that the early Stoics laid the foundations of a new branch of logic, namely what we now call the simple propositional calculus. Their general theory enabled the Stoics to take a thoroughly tolerant attitude towards religion, regarding the various practices as symbolic of the truth. Stoicism was thus eminently suitable as a general outlook for a world empire.

A more detailed account of Stoic ethics is best undertaken in connection with the third or Roman period of Stoicism. In this period we have Cato the younger, who invited to his house the philosopher Athenodorus, and, under the Empire, the three Stoic philosophers whose writings have come down to us—the younger Seneca, Epictetus, who began life as a slave, and the Emperor Marcus Aurelius Antoninus. Stoicism prevailed widely in the Roman world, although not to the exclusion of Epicurean views; indeed, both these main philosophical currents of the period have directly in view the same practical end, namely that if there were any good attainable at all, it must be found by each man within himself, and whatever of theoretical interest was implied in either philosophy was subordinate to that end; and, again, although they might be reached by widely divergent roads, there was, superficially at least, a close resemblance between the characteristic *apatheia* (freedom from emotion) of the Stoics and the *ataraxia* (imperturbability) of the Epicureans. The *moral* system is best considered under four heads: the theology, the psychology or theory of mind, the theory of the Good or human happiness, and the scheme of virtue or duty. (1) The Stoics held that the universe is governed by one good and wise God, together with inferior or subordinate deities. God exercises a moral government; under it the good are happy, while misfortunes happen to the wicked. They did not admit that the Deity intermeddled with the minutiae, but they allowed that omens and oracles might be accepted as signs of the foreordained arrangement of God. Like most other ancient schools, the Stoics held God to be corporeal like man; body is the only substance; nothing incorporeal could act on what is corporeal; the First Cause of all, God or Zeus, is the primeval fire, emanating from which is the soul of man in the form of a warm ether. (2) Next, as to the constitution of the mind. We have bodies like animals, but reason or intelligence like the gods. Animals have instinctive principles of action; man alone has a rational intelligent soul. According to Marcus Aurelius, we come into contact with Deity through our intellectual part, and our highest life is thus the divine life. But the most important Stoic doctrine respecting the nature of man is the recognition of reason as a superior power or faculty that subordinates all the rest, the governing intelligence. (3) The Stoic theory of happiness, or rather of the Good, was not identified with happiness in the ordinary sense. The Stoics began by asserting that happiness is not necessary, and may be dispensed with, and that pain is no evil. They disallowed the direct and ostensible pursuit of pleasure as an end (the point of view of Epicurus), but allured their followers partly by promising them the victory over pain, and partly by certain enjoyments of an elevated cast that grew out of their plan of life. Next to the discipline of endurance we must rank the sentiment of pride, which the Stoic might justly feel in his conquest of himself, and in his lofty independence and superiority to the casualties of life. The last and most elevated form of Stoic happiness was the satisfaction of contemplating the Universe and God. (4) The Stoic theory of virtue is implicated in the ideas of the Good above described. The Stoics were the first to preach what is called cosmopolitanism. They said: 'There is no difference between Greeks and barbarians; and the world is our city'. Seneca urges kindness to slaves, for 'are they not men like ourselves, breathing the same air, living and dying like ourselves?' The Epicureans declined, as much as possible, interference in public affairs, but the Stoic philosophers all urged men to the duties of active citizenship, and were the first who pronounced positive beneficence a virtue. They adopted the four Cardinal Virtues (Wisdom, or the Knowledge of Good and Evil; Justice; Fortitude; Temperance) as part of their plan of the virtuous life, the life according to nature. Justice, as the social virtue, was placed above all the rest. But most interesting to us are the indications of the idea of Beneficence. Epictetus is earnest in his exhortations to forgiveness of injuries. Marcus Aurelius often enjoins the same virtue, and suggests considerations in aid of the practice of it; he contends as strongly as Butler and Hume for the existence of a principle of pure, i.e. unselfish, benevolence in the mind, in other words, that we are made to advance each other's happiness. There is also in the Stoic system a recognition of duties to God, and of morality as based on piety. Not only are we all brethren, but also the 'children of one Father'. The extraordinary stress put upon human nature by the full Stoic ideal led to various compromises. The rigid following of the ideal issued

in one of the paradoxes, namely that all the actions of the wise man are equally perfect, and that, short of the standard of perfection, all faults and vices are equal. This has a meaning only when we draw a line between spirituality and morality, and treat the last as worthless in comparison with the first. The later Stoics, however, gave a positive value to practical virtue, irrespective of the ideal. The idea of duty was of Stoic origin, fostered and developed by the Roman spirit and legislation. The early Stoics had two different words for the 'suitable' (*kathēkon*) and the 'right' (*katorthōma*). It was a point with the Stoic to be conscious of 'advance', or improvement. By self-examination he kept himself constantly acquainted with his moral state, and it was both his duty and his satisfaction to be approaching to the ideal of the perfect man. Contentment and apathy were not to permit grief even for the loss of friends. Seneca, on one occasion, admits that he was betrayed by human weakness on this point. The chief ancient authorities on the Stoics are the writings of Epictetus, Marcus Aurelius, and Seneca, themselves Stoic philosophers, together with notices in the works of Cicero, Plutarch, Sextus Empiricus. Diogenes Laërtius, and Stobaeus.

Bibliography: E. Zeller, *Stoics, Epicureans and Skeptics*, rev. ed., 1962; J. Christensen, *An Essay on the Unity of Stoicism*, 1962; L. Edelstein, *The Meaning of Stoicism*, 1966.

Stoke Newington, see HACKNEY.

Stoke-on-Trent, parliamentary borough and city of Staffordshire, England, 23 km north of Stafford on the Trent and Mersey Canal, just off the M6 motorway. It includes the six towns of BURSLEM, HANLEY, LONGTON, FENTON, TUNSTALL, and STOKE-UPON-TRENT, which were incorporated in the county borough of Stoke-upon-Trent in 1910. City status was granted in 1925. Educational institutions include the North Staffordshire Polytechnic (well known for its pottery classes), and the city took a leading part in the establishment of the University of Keele. Stoke-on-Trent is famous for the manufacture of pottery and porcelain, often being referred to as 'The Potteries'. Other major industries are coal-mining, iron and steel production, and rubber tyre manufacture. A considerable number of light engineering works are allied to these major industries. The city is on an electrified rail route from Birmingham to Manchester. Much imaginative restoration of derelict land has taken place in recent years. Population (1971) 258,300.

Stoke Poges, town and parish of BUCKINGHAMSHIRE, England, 3 km north of Slough. The church of St Giles is part Norman and part Early English. The poet Gray is buried in the churchyard, which is identified with the scene of his *Elegy*. Population (1971) 4850.

Stoke-upon-Trent, formerly a borough, since 1910 part of the city of STOKE-ON-TRENT. It contains the main railway station for Stoke-on-Trent, pottery factories, and a large rubber tyre manufactory.

Stoker, Bram (1847–1912), Irish novelist, born in Dublin; educated at Dublin University. An invalid in childhood, he developed into a fine athlete while at university, and also had a brilliant academic career. Afterwards he worked for ten years in the civil service, eventually becoming Inspector of Petty Sessions in Ireland. In 1878 he became Henry IRVING's acting manager at the Lyceum theatre, London, and later wrote *Personal Reminiscences of Henry Irving*, 1906. He published several novels, but is remembered above all for *Dracula*, 1897, one of the most spine-chilling horror stories in English literature. Set in Transylvania, and recounting the tale of the vampire, Count Dracula, Stoker used many features of the gothic novel, incorporating traditional folk material, and occultism. The story has remained very popular, and has formed the basis for several successful films. A sequel, *Dracula's Guest*, was published posthumously in 1914.

    Bibliography: H. Ludlam, *A Biography of Dracula*, 1962.

Stokes, Adrian (1887–1927), British bacteriologist, born in Lausanne; educated at Trinity College, Dublin. In 1919 he became professor of bacteriology and preventive medicine at Dublin University. He moved to London University in 1922 to become the Sir William Dunn professor of pathology. He was a member of the Rockefeller Commission on Yellow Fever in West Africa from 1920 until his death. In 1927 Stokes succeeded for the first time in the experimental infection of the monkey with yellow fever virus. He also showed that an epidemic of jaundice was caused by a spirochaete carried by rats, and studied tetanus and typhoid. He died of yellow fever while studying the disease in Lagos, Nigeria.

Stokes, Sir (Frederick) Wilfrid (1860–1927), British engineer, born in Liverpool, educated at St Francis Xavier's, Liverpool, and Catholic University College, Kensington. He was chief assistant in the London office of Ransomes & Rapier Limited, and later chairman and managing director. He superintended the erection of sluices on the Manchester Ship Canal, and introduced improvements in sluices, cranes, refrigerators, etc. He invented, in 1915, the 'Stokes Gun' or trench mortar—a tube entirely closed at the breech, and fitted with a fixed internal striker which ignites the detonator cap to fire the propellent charge, when the projectile is dropped down the mortar tube.

Stokes, Sir George Gabriel (1819–1903), Irish mathematician and physicist, born at Skreen, County Sligo, educated at Bristol and Pembroke College, Cambridge, where he was appointed Lucasian Professor of mathematics in 1849. He discovered the nature of fluorescence, showed that quartz (but not ordinary glass) is transparent to ultraviolet light, did fundamental work in hydrodynamics (see VISCOSITY), and made important contributions in mathematics, including a basic theorem of vector analysis. He was a firm supporter of the aether theory and used his work on hydrodynamics to investigate the properties of the hypothesised substance. His works include *Mathematical and Physical Papers*, 1880–1905, *On Light*, 1884–87, and *Memoirs and Scientific Correspondence*, 1907.

Stokesay, see CRAVEN ARMS.

Stokesley, market town in the Hambleton District, North YORKSHIRE, England, 15 km south of MIDDLESBROUGH. Population (1971: parish) 3007.

Stokes's Law, see VISCOSITY.

Stokowski, Leopold (1882–1977), US conductor, born in London of Polish and Irish parents. He was appointed

Sir George Gabriel Stokes. *(Mary Evans Picture Library)*

organist of St James's Church, Piccadilly, 1900. From 1912 to 1936 he conducted the Philadelphia Orchestra, and later several other American orchestras. One of the most gifted and colourful performers of the century, he appeared in films, made many orchestral arrangements (notably of Bach), and was a great advocate of modern music throughout his career. He still conducted and recorded at the age of 95.

Stolberg, Christian, Count (1748–1821), German poet, brother of Friedrich Leopold STOLBERG. Both were members of the famous Göttingen Hainbund, of which BÜRGER and Voss were also members. They collaborated in *Gedichte* (a volume of poems edited by H. C. Boie in 1779); *Schauspiele mit Chören*, 1787, designed to reawaken interest in Greek drama; and some patriotic poems, *Vaterländische Gedichte*, 1825. Christian also wrote *Gedichte aus dem Griechischen*, 1782, and a translation of Sophocles, 1782.

    Bibliography: Der Brüder Christian und Friedrich Stolberg gesammelte Werke (20 vols), 1820–25.

Stolberg, Friedrich Leopold, Count (1750–1819), German poet, brother of Christian STOLBERG, with whom he collaborated in works intended to arouse new interest in Greek drama. Leopold was the better poet of the two and wrote *Timoleon* (a tragedy), 1784; translations of the *Iliad*, 1778, of *Plato*, 1796–97, *Aeschylus*, 1802, and OSSIAN, 1806. He also produced a novel, *Die Insel*, 1788; *Geschichte der Religion Jesu Christi*, 1806–18; and a life of Alfred the Great, 1815.

    Bibliography: Der Brüder Christian und Friedrich Stolberg gesammelte Werke (20 vols), 1820–25.

Stole, ecclesiastical vestment consisting of a long band of silk or rich stuff, coloured according to the season, and often embroidered, usually with crosses at the centre and ends (which may be widened for decorative purposes). It is worn over the alb by bishops, priests, and deacons, bishops and priests hanging it round the neck and straight down in front, deacons wearing it over the left shoulder and fastened on the right thigh. Bishops and priests also wear it hanging straight down over the surplice at sacramental functions. A deacon's liturgical vestment in the East from the 4th century, used perhaps as *sudaria* (see SUDARIUM), in lengthened form stoles spread through the Church as scarves of rank for the major orders, and reached the West about the 8th century. The name *stola* was first used in Gaul.

Stolen Goods. Possession of stolen goods recently after their loss is *prima facie* evidence, in English law, that the person in possession stole the goods or received them knowing them to have been stolen; but if many months have elapsed between the loss and the discovery the possessor cannot, in the absence of any other circumstances implicating him in the theft, be called upon to account for the manner in which he came by the goods. This is the doctrine of 'recent possession'.

Under the Theft Act 1968, a person convicted of an offence in relation to the theft of goods may be ordered: (1) to restore the goods to anyone entitled to them; (2) to deliver other goods representing the stolen goods to anyone entitled to them; or (3) to pay not more than the value of the stolen goods out of money in the possession of the convicted offender at the time of his arrest to anyone who, if the goods had been in the offender's possession, would have been entitled to restoration of them. Where a restoration order is made, any person to whom the stolen goods have been sold in good faith, or who has lent money in good faith on the security of the goods, may be paid not more than the loan or purchase price out of the money in the possession of the convicted offender at the time of his arrest.

See HANDLING STOLEN GOODS; THEFT.

Bibliography: E. Griew, *The Theft Act 1968*, 2nd ed. 1974.

Stolon, see VEGETATIVE REPRODUCTION.

Stolp, see SŁUPSK.

Stolypin, Pëtr Arkadevich (1862–1911), Russian statesman. Stolypin's policy was, on the one hand, firm suppression of the revolution (see REVOLUTION OF 1905) and, on the other, reforms designed to remove the causes of discontent. He did not shrink from unpopular measures (dissolution of two DUMAS) or even unconstitutional ones, such as the reform of electoral law in 1907 by imperial decree. Stolypin's agrarian reforms (1906–11) enabled the peasants to leave the village communities (see MIR) and set up separate farms. In 1907–16 over 2 million homesteads left the communities, about one-eighth of the total. Stolypin also facilitated purchase of land by the peasants through the Peasant Bank and colonisation of Siberia and Russian Central Asia by peasants from over-populated provinces of European Russia. A liberal conservative Stolypin was opposed both by the radicals and the extreme Right. He was assassinated by a Socialist Revolutionary terrorist (see SOCIALIST REVOLUTIONARIES) who was also a police agent.

Stoma (plural stomata), a pore in the epidermis of a leaf or a herbaceous stem which allows interchange of gases between the plant and the atmosphere during the processes of respiration and photosynthesis, and the escape of water vapour by transpiration. A stoma is bounded by two guard cells which, by the varying thickness of their walls, alter shape according to the amount of water they contain (depending e.g. on the sugar content of the guard cells), temperature, and light.

Stomach, in man, the pear-shaped digestive sac situated in the upper part of the abdomen, the wider end to the left, the narrower to the right, but with its centre somewhat to the left of the median line. It is entered by the oesophagus at the *cardiac orifice*, where the circular muscle is thickened to form a sphincter. Its opening into the intestine is called the *pylorus*. The innermost coat of the stomach consists of mucous membrane made up of a layer of epithelial cells resting on connective tissue. When the organ is not fully distended the mucous membrane is thrown into folds called *rugae*; when it is distended, the rugae become flattened. Outside the submucous coat of connective tissue are three coats of unstriped muscle, of which the inner is oblique, the next circular, and the outer longitudinal. The whole of the organ is covered by PERITONEUM, the serous membrane which lines the interior of the abdominal cavity and covers the viscera. The mucous coat contains gastric glands which secret GASTRIC JUICE and mucus. Entering the stomach by the cardiac orifice, the food is acted upon by the gastric juice, which contains hydrochloric acid and the enzyme pepsin. The juice is effectively mixed with the salivated food by the movements of the muscular walls of the stomach, the degree of distension of the sac being just sufficient to accommodate the contents. When the food has been rendered acid by the action of the gastric juice and has been propelled by peristalsis to the pyloric canal, the pylorus opens to admit the food to the small intestine. The effect of digestion in the stomach is to convert proteins into polypeptides. The gastric juice has also some bactericidal influence.

Disorders of the Stomach. Gastritis is inflammation of the lining of the stomach. *Acute gastritis* may be caused by indigestible food, chemicals, such as corrosive poisons, alcohol and bacteria and bacterial toxins. Symptoms are pain, vomiting of stomach contents, occasionally streaked with blood, and prostration. The treatment is a medical matter, and consists in treating the cause. First-aid treatment consists in giving small quantities of water with a little sugar in it at frequent intervals. *Chronic gastritis* may follow from repeated acute attacks, and is especially associated with alcoholism. The lining of the stomach is in a state of chronic congestion; the mucous membrane and in some cases the muscular coat become thickened. The activity of the glands is lessened and the patient becomes a chronic dyspeptic. Treatment consists in treating the cause.

Dyspepsia is a symptom of a disturbance in gastric function, and its causes are various. It often presents itself as discomfort, a feeling of fullness over the upper abdomen, flatulence, soreness and heartburn. It may be acute or chronic. When acute it is usually due to acute gastritis, or it may be secondary to disease in one of the other organs of digestion, particularly the liver and gall bladder. Chronic, persisting dyspepsia often results from nervous or emotional stress or physical over-fatigue, or it may result from such continued insults to the stomach as hurried meals, badly cooked food and excessive drinking of alcohol. Heavy smoking, or the constant use of irritant drugs such as aspirin may irritate the gastric mucosa and cause dyspepsia. The over-conscientious, over-anxious, worrying type of person is more liable to dyspepsia than the carefree, lethargic type.

Peptic ulcer is, after the causes listed above, the next most common cause of dyspepsia. Peptic ulcer is a term which includes *gastric ulcer* and *duodenal ulcer*. Although each type of ulcer is distinctive in its site, their symptoms, causes and treatment are similar in many respects. The exact cause of peptic ulcers is not known. They may arise suddenly in persons who have previously been free of all dyspeptic symptoms, and the first sign of these ulcers may be some catastrophe, such as vomiting of blood (haematemesis) or perforation of the stomach or duodenal wall and consequent PERITONITIS. It is possible in some cases that acute ulcers are caused by trauma from some abrasive material in the contents of the alimentary canal, such as a piece of bone. Disturbing though they may be in their mode of onset, acute ulcers usually heal quickly, and often give rise to no further trouble. Most commonly peptic ulcers are the underlying disease of which chronic dyspepsia is the manifestation. It is often difficult to tell in dyspepsia when an ulcer is present, but as a rule the symptoms are more persistent and severe, and, in the case of a duodenal ulcer, pain often wakes the patient at night. Pain which is typical of peptic ulcers is situated in the upper abdomen (the epigastrium), comes on half an hour after a meal, in the case of a gastric ulcer, but whilst the stomach is empty in the case of a duodenal ulcer. X-ray examination with a barium meal is helpful, and in many cases will reveal an ulcer cavity or 'crater'. Duodenal ulcer is associated with an increase in the acid content of the gastric juice, and an analysis of the latter assists in confirming the diagnosis. By means of an instrument called the gastroscope, which is passed down the oesophagus, it is possible to inspect the inside of the stomach by direct vision, and in doubtful cases gastroscopy may reveal an ulcer that failed to show in an X-ray picture. Gastroscopy also enables the physician to get an idea of the nature of the ulcer and to obtain a small cutting from it (biopsy) for pathological examination to exclude malignancy. Peptic ulcers may be treated medically or surgically. Generally speaking, the initial treatment is medical, and consists in rest in bed, strict diet and antacid drugs, and drugs which reduce gastric activity. Most ulcers respond to this régime, but are liable to relapse when the patient resumes his normal habits, which were probably significant in causing the initial ulcer. For instance, people engaged in occupations involving mental strain and responsibility, and irregular hours and meals are more subject to peptic ulcers than others.

In relapsing cases, and in those cases that fail to respond to medical treatment, surgery is necessary. Chronic peptic ulcers cause scarring and fibrosis of the stomach wall with loss of elasticity and, when the ulcer is near the pylorus, contraction (stenosis) of the pylorus, causing obstruction to the outlet. This condition invariably needs surgical relief. Peptic ulcers, especially gastric ulcers, may be malignant (see CANCER), and these must always be treated by surgical removal if feasible. Vomiting of blood is always a matter for medical attention. The first-aid treatment should be absolute rest, and, at the most, the patient may be given a small piece of ice to suck. Nothing else whatever must be given by the mouth. An ulcer which perforates gives rise to acute, intense abdominal pain, together with prostration, and usually vomiting at first. The patient lies still and is apprehensive lest any pressure be applied to the abdomen. Medical aid should be sought.

Congenital pyloric stenosis is a condition at birth in which there is an overgrowth of fibrous tissue in the submucous and muscular coats of the pylorus forming a constricting tumour which prevents the stomach contents from passing on into the duodenum. It is more common in boys than in girls. All but the mildest cases are treated by surgical operation with excellent results, and there is no evidence of any handicap to health or gastric function in later life.

Stone, Sir Benjamin (1838–1914), British documentary photographer and politician, who made a systematic photographic record of British folk customs and Parliamentary ceremonies and personalities.

Bibliography: W. Jay, *Customs and Faces*, 1972.

Stone, Frank (1800–1859), British painter, born in Manchester, went to London in 1831. His subjects, such as *The Tryst*, were in the conventional sentimental genre disliked by the Pre-Raphaelites. His son, Marcus Stone (1840–1921), was also an artist specialising in sentimental historical pieces. He was elected RA in 1887. Both father and son were friends of Dickens, and Marcus illustrated *Great Expectations* and *Our Mutual Friend*.

Bibliography: G. Reynolds, *Victorian Painting*, 1966.

Stone, Marcus, see STONE, FRANK.

Stone, Nicholas (1586–1647), English sculptor, born at Woodsbury, near Exeter. After working in Holland he was appointed master-mason for building the new banqueting-house of Whitehall in 1619, and in 1626 master-mason of Windsor Castle. His tombs include those of Spenser (Westminster Abbey), Donne (St Paul's), and Bodley (Oxford). He designed the porch at St Mary's, Oxford. Stone had three sons, Henry, Nicholas, and John. Henry Stone (d. 1653) was a sculptor and painter. He studied in Italy and the Netherlands, and made many copies of Italian and Flemish pictures. Nicholas Stone (d. 1647), the second son, a sculptor, worked under BERNINI in Rome.

Stone, market town in STAFFORDSHIRE, England, on the Trent, 11 km north of Stafford. There was formerly a priory and a grammar school established in 1558. Brewing, ceramics, and the manufacture of glass and footwear are carried on. The town is now part of the borough of Stafford. Population (1971) 12,000.

Stone, village 3 km east of Dartford, Kent, England, with an impressive Early English church of St Mary's built (c. 1260) by the masons of WESTMINSTER ABBEY with a tall nave and rich carvings. Cement manufacture is the chief industry. Population (1971) 8305.

Stone. For the chief types of stone used in architecture see BUILDING STONE; for dressing stone see MASONRY.

Stone, in medicine, see CALCULUS; GALL-STONES; LITHOTOMY; RENAL CALCULUS.

Stone, see METROLOGY.

Stone Age. The history of man's early progress is best

Stone Age. Remains of Neolithic dwellings on Gozo island, Malta. *(Barnaby's Picture Library)*

understood by its relation to the three technological stages in his development, in the first of which he used stone tools and weapons (see also FLINT IMPLEMENTS). The Stone Age has been divided into the Old Stone Age (Palaeolithic), when stone implements were merely chipped into shape, Middle Stone Age (Mesolithic) and the New Stone Age (Neolithic), when implements of stone were ground and polished. Recent research has been largely directed towards the relationship of the Palaeolithic to geochronology and to the elucidation of an absolute chronology based upon geology; while the economic aspect of the Neolithic cultures have attracted as much attention as the typology of the implements and pottery and the study of chambered tombs.

Palaeolithic men were hunters, and their remains have been found in the caves in which they lived, and in the sedimentary deposits of river gravels. The *Early Palaeolithic* is divided into the cultures of Chelles and St Acheul. (The various cultures are known by Continental names, as French and Belgian workers were first in this systemised study.) Its principal deposits belong to the Riss-Würm interglacial period, when the 'warm' fauna included *Elephas antiquus*, a rhinoceros, and *Hippopotamus major*. The *Middle Palaeolithic* is characterised by the Mousterian flake industry, and in geological time its spread is in the period of the Würm advance. Neanderthal man lived with a 'cold' fauna which included the mammoth, horse, ox and reindeer. The *Upper Palaeolithic* has the cultures named Aurignacian, Solutrean and Magdalenian, and in geological time it covered the retreat of the Würm glaciation and a dry and rather cold subsequent period. The fauna changed when, with the onset of colder conditions, the steppe became a tundra.

The walls of certain caves lived in by Palaeolithic man were decorated with sketches and paintings of magic and religious significance. This remarkable practice is often found in the Magdalenian culture of south-west France and north-west Spain, and its association with hunting is unmistakable. The best-known series of paintings are in a cave at LASCAUX (see also CAVE ART).

There are several distinct cultures in the Mesolithic period, all of them based on a food-gathering economy. The climate had much improved, and hunting and fishing are well represented by the presence of microliths (see

FLINT IMPLEMENTS) and fish-spear barbs. In Britain there seem to be four cultures, one of which has affinities with the Baltic.

The Neolithic, with its colonisation from the mainland of Europe and along the Atlantic coast route, saw a higher civilisation based upon agriculture and stock-raising; there was a wide trade in flint and stone axes, e.g. from Langdale in Westmorland, and the period was also marked by the spread of megalithic tombs (see MEGALITHIC MONUMENTS) and the construction of earthwork camps with causeways or interrupted ditches. There is one kind of domestic pottery which is ultimately based upon vessels of leather and skin. Plants, both cereal and textile, were cultivated. Sheep, oxen, goats and swine were domesticated.

See also BEAKER FOLK; BRONZE AGE; GREAT BRITAIN, *Archaeology*; IRON AGE; PREHISTORY.

Bibliography: V. G. Childe, *The Dawn of European Civilization*, 1957; K. P. Oakley, *Frameworks for dating Fossil Man*, 1964; H. Breuil and R. Lautier, *The Men of the Old Stone Age*, 1965; S. Piggott, *Ancient Europe*, 1965; J. G. D. Clark, *The Stone Age Hunters*, 1967; F. Bordes, *The Old Stone Age*, 1968; C. Renfrew, *Before Civilization*, 1973; J. Waechter, *Man before History*, 1976.

Stone Carving

Stone Carving. Sculpture in hard material, stone or wood, differs from sculpture in plastic material, clay. The former is a paring down of material, the latter is a building

Stone Carving. *Eckehart and Uta*, City Burghers, mid-13th century. Stone figures in the nave of Naumberg Cathedral, Germany. *(Bildarchiv Foto Marburg)*

Stone Circles

up (see MODELLING). A clay model lends itself to reproduction by someone other than the artist (indirect method), whereas the essential point of carving is that it must be carried out by the sculptor's own hand (direct method). The greatest stone carving is that in which the sculptor works direct, sensing the form in the block of stone and making it grow out of the material as he carves it, as did Michelangelo. Stone carving has been associated with architecture in all the great periods of art—Egyptian, Mesopotamian, Greek, Maya, Aztec. In the cathedrals of the European Middle Ages ceilings were intricately carved, and the stone supporting pillars were shaped and carved at base and capital. Images of saints, to fill the niches, effigies and heraldic beasts on tombs, gargoyles, screens, and altarpieces all supplied work for the medieval stone carver. The tradition of architectural stone carving or monumental sculpture, a particular feature of Indian art, has been revived in modern times. In England Eric GILL led the way with architectural and especially religious stone carving, executed as well as designed by the sculptor. A large number of modern sculptors, including Jacob EPSTEIN and Henry MOORE, have since devoted themselves to 'direct' stone carving. See also CARVING; INDIAN SCULPTURE; ROCK SCULPTURES AND ENGRAVINGS; SCULPTURE. Concrete is a medium which may be used plastically in a mould, or it may be carved like stone.

Bibliography: C. Rich, *The Methods and Materials of Sculpture,* 1948.

Stone Circles, rings of standing (or now fallen) stones, usually on level ground, are nearly all religious or astronomical monuments, most of them belonging to the Bronze Age. Some, such as Stonehenge, Avebury, Callanish in the island of Lewis, and Stenness in Orkney, are remarkable for their size and state of preservation. Others, for example 'The Hurlers' and the 'Nine Maidens' in Cornwall, are of lesser size but still imposing. Many stone circles are incomplete, the stones having been removed for building. They are often the basis of legend and folklore. They are virtually unknown on the Continent of Europe.

See AVEBURY; CARNAC; MEGALITHIC MONUMENTS; STONEHENGE.

Bibliography: A. Thorn, *Megalithic Sites in Britain,* 1967, and *Megalithic Lunar Observatories,* 1971; E. Hadingham, *Circles and Standing Stones,* 1975.

Stone-fly, see PLECOPTERA.

Stone Loach, *Nemacheilus barbatulus,* order Cypriniformes, a small, carnivorous, bottom-living fish that frequents clear shallow streams. It is found in Siberia, and parts of Europe, including Britain. Its length never exceeds 12 cm, and the flesh is very delicate. It has six sensitive barbules hanging from the upper lip. See LOACH.

Stone Worship, see FETISHISM; IDOLATRY.

Stonechat, *Saxicola torquata,* a small bird related to the robin and nightingale, in family Muscicapidae, order Passeriformes. The male bird has a black head and throat, dark back and tawny breast, and the female differs from it in that its head is brown. It is frequently seen in Britain, and occurs in Europe, Asia and Africa.

Stonehenge. Aerial photograph of the site. *(Aerofilms)*

Stonecrop, see SEDUM.

Stonehaven, or Stanehive, port, seaside resort, market town, burgh, and main settlement of KINCARDINE AND DEESIDE DISTRICT, Grampian Region, Scotland, on Stonehaven Bay, 24 km south of Aberdeen. Nearby are the ruins of Dunnottar Castle. Stonehaven has a secure harbour, a small fishery, and a distillery. Population 4730.

Stonehenge (from the Old English *hengen,* that which is hung up, the reference being to the horizontal lintel stones), great circles of standing stones on Salisbury Plain, 3 km west of Amesbury, Wiltshire. Stonehenge is a prehistoric site of various periods, and in a limited sense it has sometimes been compared to the architectural development of a cathedral.

The first monument about 2200 BC was a low circular earth bank about 98 m in diameter with a shallow outer ditch, and a single entrance fronted by the Avenue, parallel banks 14 m apart and ditches, part of the course of which has been recovered by aerial photography. It continues in a straight line for 275 m and then divides, one branch curving north and the other east to the Avon at West Amesbury. Within and close to the earthcircle was a circle of 56 large ritual pits, the Aubrey Holes (discovered by John Aubrey in 1666), which contained bone pins, a polished stone mace-head and deposits of human cremated bones, all typical of the Neolithic cultures of Wessex early in the second millennium BC. The Heelstone within its small ditch was also part of this monument.

In the second phase associated with Beaker pottery (see BEAKER FOLK) was erected a double circle of Blue Stones from the Preseli Mountains in Pembrokeshire. It seems that the entrance of this Blue Stone double circle was aligned on the present axis of the monument, that is the orientation on the mid-summer sunrise marked by the Avenue. About 1800 BC this double circle was removed and the stones rearranged to form a horseshoe and a circle within the peristyle of the great upright monoliths of sarsen stone in the third building phase (c. 1500–1400 BC). All the sarsen stones are carefully dressed, and the vertical stones have tenons made to fit mortice holes on the undersides of the lintels, which are curved to meet the circumference of the circle and the whole corrected for perspective. The Y and the Z holes, part of a construction which was never completed, two irregular circles of square socket holes which lie between the sarsen circle and the Aubrey Circle and the resetting of 60 Blue Stones to form a circle inside the sarsen peristyle, and the building of a Blue Stone horseshoe within the sarsen stone trilithons represent the final phases. The earliest Blue Stone monument with carefully finished and trimmed stones may have provided a prototype for the later work on the massive sarsen stones. An important result of recent research has been the recognition of prehistoric carvings which appear to be contemporary with the original working of the stones on two of the sarsen uprights. Copper or bronze flat axes were depicted, and also what may be a hafted dagger. The form has parallels with Early Mycenaean types and has been used as evidence of Wessex–Mycenae trade links. However, differences of date have led to difficulties in accepting these links.

Stonehenge Down, including the Avenue and the Cursus, was purchased by public subscription in 1927 and 1929, and vested in the National Trust in order to preserve the view from Stonehenge, which was a gift to the nation and is in the custody of the Department of the Environment. In 1958 the Department re-erected in their original positions a trilithon and three other stones which fell in 1797 and 1900 respectively. G. S. Hawkins suggested (*Nature* 1963, 1964) that Stonehenge was constructed for astronomical observations and as an eclipse predictor; thus raising possibilities of profound cultural and religious significance.

See also ARCHAEOLOGY; AVEBURY; MEGALITHIC MONUMENTS; STONE AGE; WOODHENGE.

Bibliography: An interesting early account is W. Stukeley, *Stonehenge, A Temple Restored to the British Druids*, 1740; R. J. C. Atkinson, *Stonehenge*, 1956, has references to earlier work; for considerations of its astronomical use see F. Hoyle in *Nature* (no. 5048), 1966, and G. S. Hawkins, *Stonehenge Decoded*, 1965.

Stonehouse, or East Stonehouse, since 1914 a part of PLYMOUTH, Devon, England, situated between Devonport and Plymouth, with which it forms the 'Three Towns'.

Stonehouse, town in GLOUCESTERSHIRE, England, 5 km west of Stroud. Stonehouse was once a centre of the cloth-making industry; now bricks are manufactured, and engineering and other industries are carried on. Wycliffe College, a public school, is situated here. Population (1971) 5893.

Stonehouse, town in Hamilton District, Strathclyde Region, Scotland, 11 km south-east of Hamilton, on Avon Water. The Reformation martyr Patrick Hamilton was

Stonehenge. Chart of the principal Bronze Age barrow cemeteries in the Stonehenge area.

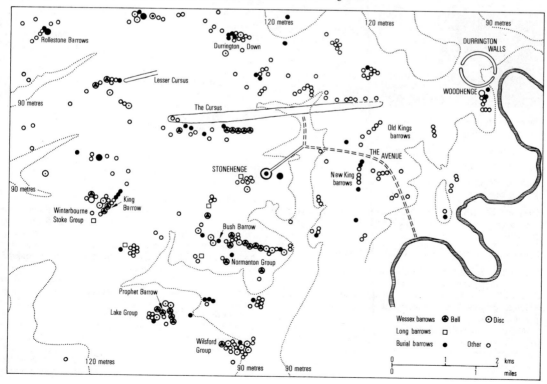

Stoneware vase painted in brown slip under a white glaze; Chinese Sung Dynasty. *(British Museum, London)*

born in Stonehouse. This area was formerly important for coal-mining. Population 4093.

Stones, Precious, see GEM; and separate articles on DIAMOND; EMERALD; SAPPHIRE; RUBY; JADE.

Stones, Standing, see MEGALITHIC MONUMENTS; MONOLITH; PREHISTORY; STANDING STONES; STONE CIRCLES.

'Stonewall' Jackson, see JACKSON, 'STONEWALL'.

Stoneware, name for all objects made of clay and baked in a high-temperature kiln at approximately 1200–1400 °C, so that the body is vitrified and is therefore no longer porous. This term does not include objects made of PORCELAIN.

In Roman times fine-quality stoneware, often decorated with 'diamond-cut' designs, was made. In China a vitrified feldspathic stoneware was the precursor of porcelain and was produced in the 6th century AD. In Europe in post-Roman times it has been a northern product because of the need for a plentiful, cheap supply of wood for its firing. In the late Middle Ages German wares, like the English 'Cistercian' ware, were often thinly potted and fired to stoneware hardness. From the 15th century the Rhineland, Saxony and Bavaria were centres for the production of grey stoneware covered with a salt glaze, and a distinctive English version, very thinly potted, was made in Staffordshire in the 18th century in imitation of porcelain. In the late 17th and early 18th centuries a red stoneware was made in Holland (e.g. by Arij de Milde), in Germany (e.g. by Böttger), and in England (e.g. by Elers, Wedgwood and Dwight). John Dwight's stoneware factory at Fulham, established in 1671, produced a small series of portrait busts and statues in stoneware which ranked among the finest sculpture of the time. Not made from moulds, they are the creation of an unknown sculptor, the finest being the life-size bust of Prince Rupert of the Rhine (British Museum) and the memorials to his daughter Lydia in the Victoria and Albert Museum. WEDGWOOD's researches on stoneware produced fine-quality bodies, 'basaltes' 'jasper', etc., which he used to produce Greek vases, cameo reliefs, etc.

Stonework, see MASONRY.

Stonewort, see CHARACEAE.

Stony Stratford, market town of BUCKINGHAMSHIRE, England, on Watling Street and the River Ouse, 13 km north-east of Buckingham. Stony Stratford is now part of the new town of MILTON KEYNES. Population (1971) 4295.

Stonyhurst College, Roman Catholic independent boarding school for boys, near Whalley, Lancashire, run by the Society of Jesus. It had its origin in the College of St Omer founded in France in 1593 for English Catholic boys. In 1794 the school moved to Lancashire, to a house given them by the Weld family. In 1966 the College was amalgamated with Beaumont College, a sister school of the Society of Jesus in Windsor. It has two dependent preparatory schools, St Mary's Hall, Stonyhurst, and St John's, Beaumont. There are 500 boys at the College and 300 at the two preparatory schools.

Stool of Repentance, seat or pew in churches in Scotland, upon which those who had come under the censure of the ecclesiastical authorities for some sin, such as drunkenness or lying, were made to stand.

Stoolball is an old game, one of the ancestors of cricket, popular in southern England between the 15th and 18th centuries. One player bowled a ball underarm to another defending a stool with his hand, the bowler going in if the ball hit the stool, and the batsman scoring when he hit the ball. The game was revived in a version adapted from cricket by W. W. Grantham as exercise for recuperating soldiers, and the first public match was played in Hove in 1917. The Stoolball Association was formed in 1924.

Two teams of 11 play one innings each, wickets being pitched 14·6 m (16 yds) apart. Each wicket consists of the face and edge of a board 30·4 cm (1 ft) square mounted on a stake projecting 1·42 m (4 ft 8 in) from the ground. Bowlers deliver underarm, a jerked ball or one which bounces before reaching the wicket being considered a 'no-ball'. As in cricket, the striker scores by hitting the ball away across a boundary or far enough to let the batsmen change ends. The batsman can be dismissed bowled, caught, run out, or be adjudged body before wicket, and he is also out if he hits the ball twice. The game is still played in Southern England.

Stools, see FAECES.

Stopes, Marie Carmichael (1880–1958), British advocate of birth control, born in Edinburgh. In 1904 she became instructor in palaeobotany at Manchester University, being the first woman to be appointed to its scientific staff. She was co-founder with her husband, H. V. Roe, of the mothers' clinic for constructive birth control, and became president of the Society for Constructive Birth Control and Racial Progress. She wrote many books on marriage and contraception.

    Bibliography: H. V. Stopes-Roe and I. Scott, *Marie Stopes and Birth Control*, 1974; R. Hall, *Marie Stopes*, 1977.

Stopford, Robert Wright (1901–76), English prelate, educated at Liverpool College and Hertford College, Oxford. He became a teacher of history at Oundle School before being ordained in 1932. From 1935 to 1941 he was principal of Trinity College, Kandy, in Ceylon (now Sri Lanka), and from 1941 to 1945 principal of Achimota College, Gold Coast (now Ghana). He was general secretary of the National Society and secretary of the Church Assocation Schools Council, 1952–55, suffragan bishop of Fulham, 1955–56, and bishop of Peterborough, 1956–61. In the latter year he became bishop of London, holding the office until 1973. In 1967–69 he served as joint chairman of the Anglican-Methodist Unity Commission.

Stoph, Willi (1914–), East German politician, born in Berlin. The leading economist in the ruling party (SED) after the war, he became a member of its central commit-

Marie Stopes. *(Popperfoto)*

tee in 1950 and of East Germany's Politburo in 1953. He also helped develop the police and the army in the German Democratic Republic, and succeeded Otto GROTE-WOHL as its president in 1964. Stoph's meetings with BRANDT in 1970 helped to inaugurate the latter's *Ostpolitik*.

Stoppage in Transitu, right conferred on the unpaid vendor of goods who has parted with the goods to stop them on the insolvency of the buyer, before they have reached the latter's actual or constructive possession, and to resume possession until they are paid for. Stoppage in transitu differs from LIEN in two respects: it can be exercised only when the buyer is insolvent and only when the goods have left the possession of the seller. The effect of stoppage in transitu is not to rescind the sale, and, indeed, the buyer can recover damages if the vendor resells when he ought not. But in some cases the vendor may at once resell against the buyer: (1) where the goods are perishable; (2) where the right of resale was expressly reserved in the contract of sale. Apart from these cases the seller must give notice of his intention to resell, and also give the buyer a reasonable opportunity to pay or TENDER the price.

Stoppard, Tom (1937–), English playwright. He was for some years a journalist in Bristol before becoming a freelance and ultimately a professional writer. *Rosencrantz and Guildenstern are Dead*, 1967, was a great success on both sides of the Atlantic, and was followed by *The Real Inspector Hound*, 1968, *After Magritte*, 1970, *Jumpers*, 1972, *Travesties*, 1974, and *Dirty Linen*, 1976. Stoppard has written plays for radio and television, short stories (*Introduction 2*, 1964), and a novel, *Lord Malaquist and Mr Moon*, 1965.

    Stoppard is a brilliant exponent of a form which is perhaps best described as 'philosophical farce'. He portrays man desperately seeking some ultimate sanction for his existence, but failing to find any rational system which can provide the key to an incomprehensible universe. He does not, however, like BECKETT or PINTER, emphasise the bleakness of this failure, but rather the extraordinary ingenuity and energy with which we construct our logical systems, even though they are built on totally unverifiable, or absurd, premises. The best example of this is the philosophising of George, the professor of moral philosophy who is the central figure of *Jumpers*, perhaps his most intricate and entertaining play to date. Here, the failure of language—a recurrent preoccupation of Absurdist Drama (see THEATRE OF THE ABSURD)—and the relativity of truth are explored in language which is itself brilliantly witty and comic; and the confusion between rôle and identity is presented in a manner which stresses the specifically theatrical nature of the play.

Storace, Stephen (1763–96), English violinist and composer of Italian descent, born in London, studied at Naples; as a boy prodigy he could play the most difficult works of Tartini. Ater touring Italy he reached Vienna, where his sister Ann Selina (Nancy) (1766–1817) appeared at the Italian Opera, and he produced two operas, *Gli sposi malcontenti*, 1785, and *Gli equivoci*, 1786, and some chamber music, meeting Mozart, in the production of whose *Figaro* his sister appeared and who influenced him. He returned to England in 1787, and produced with the greatest success the operas *The Haunted Tower*, 1789, *No Song, No Supper*, 1790, and *The Pirates*, 1792.

Storage Batteries, group of electric accumulators storing energy.

Store, Bill of, see BILL OF STORE.

Storey, David Malcolm (1933–), English novelist and playwright, born in Wakefield. He studied at the Slade School of Fine Art in London, but became known as a novelist with *This Sporting Life*, 1960, dealing with the life and emotional inadequacy of a professional rugby player. *Flight into Camden*, 1960, *Pasmore*, 1972, *A Temporary Life*, 1973, and *Saville*, 1976, followed. Storey wrote his first play, *The Restoration of Arnold Middleton* in 1959, though it was not performed until 1967. It was followed by *In Celebration*, 1969, *The Contractor*, 1969, *Home*, 1970, *The Changing Room*, 1971, *The Farm*, 1973, *Cromwell*, 1973, *Life Class*, 1974, and *Mother's Day*, 1976. His plays concentrate on the various aspects and implications of what Storey believes to be our acutely alienated society.

Stork, any birds of the Ciconiidae, a family of 17 species of wading birds with long conical bills, long three-toed legs and large wings in the order Ciconiiformes. The white or house stork, *Ciconia ciconia*, was formerly plentiful in Britain, but is now only an occasional visitor. It is widely distributed on the Continent, in many parts of which it is strictly protected for its service in destroying reptiles, small mammals and insects, and in devouring offal. Its great, clumsy nest is often to be seen on a house top or church spire. Its plumage is greyish white, its quills and longest feathers on the wing coverts black, and the beak and legs red. It migrates to Africa in winter. In the black stork, *C. nigra*, the upper surface is black and the lower parts are white. This species also is protected, and during migration occasionally strays to Britain. It is widely found in southern and central Europe, Asia and parts of Africa. The adjutant, ibis, heron and spoonbill are related birds.

Storm, Theodor Woldsen (1817–88), German poet and novelist, born at Husum, Schleswig. He studied law at Kiel and Berlin, and spent most of his life as a magistrate and judge in Schleswig-Holstein and Prussia.

He first became known as a lyric poet by his *Gedichte*, 1852, but it was as a writer of *Novellen* that he gained his reputation. His first story, *Immensee*, 1852, gained him general recognition, and was followed by numerous other short stories, including *Psyche*, 1875, *Hans und Heinz Kirch*, 1882, and *Der Schimmelreiter*, 1888. A sense of melancholy pervades many of his poems, which treat of childhood, family, love, and death. It occurs also in his novels, the earlier often romantic, the later true masterpieces of realism and feeling for tragedy. Three of his stories were published as *Drei Novellen* (edited by Dr P. Vrijdaghs and W. Ripman), 1932.

Bibliography: Lives and Studies by G. Storm, 1911–12; E. Steiner, 1921; P. Schütze, 1925; F. Stuckert, 1940; K. Boll, 1940.

Storm, a wind force of 10 on the Beaufort scale (see WIND), i.e. between 24·5 and 28·4 metres/second (m/s). The term is used to cover any strong wind, for example gales, which vary from 17 to 30 m/s, but especially those accompanied by heavy rain, snow, hail, or dust. The *buran* of Central Asia is a violent sandstorm, sometimes accompanied by snow. A group of winds in North Africa, Arabia, Iraq, and Iran all cause dust and sandstorms; the *shamal* is a northerly wind, blowing most of the summer in southern Iran and Iraq. It has a monsoonal origin and transports dust down the Arabian Gulf; the *haboub*, more violent than the *shamal*, is associated with violent sandstorms, thunderstorms, and even tornadoes. This last is caused by and moves with the Intertropical Front (see FRONTS) on its migration from West Africa northwards during late April and early May. In terms of wind intensity and sand-carrying potential the *haboub* is more like the *harmattan* than the *simoom* or *khamsin*.

Storm Surge, a change in the sea-level caused by atmospheric phenomena. They are caused by severe storms and hurricanes. Generally, positive surges, when the sea-level is increased, occur if the winds are onshore and negative if the winds are offshore. There is a gradual change in sea-level several hours before the storm approaches, a sharp rise or fall as the storm passes, followed by periodic oscillations, which last for between one and two tidal cycles, as the water level returns to normal. In the northern hemisphere storm surges can propagate southwards along eastern coasts and northwards along western coasts and can be amplified by longshore winds. They are also higher in an estuary which has a wide entrance, and so surges travelling down the east coast of Britain and entering the Thames estuary pose a considerable flood threat to London. Plans have been made to build a barrage across the river below Tower Bridge.

Storm surges occur whenever there are hurricanes, mainly in the tropics (see CYCLONE), or severe storms in the mid-latitudes. They are frequent in the English Channel and North Sea where they are caused by severe atmospheric depressions. The maximum amplitude in the North Sea is 2–3 m but can be larger, and in 1953 a large surge breached many of the dykes of the Netherlands, flooded 25,000 km² of land, killed 2000 people, and forced 600,000 people from their homes. Less severe flooding also occurred in south-east England. Now regular infor-

Stork. *(Topham/Coleman)*

mation about surges in the North Sea is given by the British Storm Tide Warning Service.

Other severe surges have occurred in the Bay of Bengal due to the monsoon winds and in the Gulf of Mexico due to hurricanes. Strong winds also give rise to water movements in inland waters and lakes; these are called SEICHES.

Bibliography: R. W. Fairbridge, *Encyclopaedia of Oceanography*, 1966; R. Neumann and B. W. Pearson, *Principles of Physical Oceanography*, 1966; G. L. Pickard, *Descriptive Physical Oceanography*, 1975.

Storm Troops (*Sturmabteilung*), see SA AND SS.

Storm Warnings, see WEATHER FORECAST.

Stornoway (Stjarna's Vagr or Bay), seaport and most important town of LEWIS ISLAND (east coast), Outer Hebrides, Scotland. It was made a burgh of barony by James VI. It is the centre of the Harris tweed industry, and a fishing centre. There is also some offshore oil-related industry. Car ferries sail to Ullapool. There is an airport nearby. Population 5152.

Storstrøm, county in DENMARK comprising part of Sjælland and the islands of LOLLAND, FALSTER, and MØN. It is a fertile farming area, and also has fishing and canning industries. The capital is Nykøbing. Area 3396 km². Population 255,400.

Storting (Old Norse *stor*, great; *ting*, assembly), parliament of Norway. See NORWAY, *Government*.

Stoss, Veit (c. 1440–1533), German sculptor, born at Horb. He worked in Cracow, 1477–96, carving a large wooden altarpiece with the *Death of the Virgin*, for St Mary's Church, and the stone tomb of King Casimir IV Jagellio (in the Cathedral). He spent the remainder of his life in Germany, Nuremberg and Bamberg. His style, deriving to a great extent from that of the Netherlands and Upper Rhine, is a dramatic, realistic, and personal version of the late Gothic idiom.

Bibliography: T. Müller, *Sculpture in the Netherlands, Germany, France and Spain, 1400–1500*, 1966.

Stothard, Thomas (1755–1834), British artist, born in London. He entered the Royal Academy schools in 1777, and was made an RA in 1794. He illustrated the novels of Richardson, Fielding, Smollett, and Sterne, as well as *Robinson Crusoe, Gil Blas*, and *The Pilgrim's Progress*. His *Pilgrimage to Canterbury* is his best-known work.

Stoup, stone bowl near the door of a church, containing the holy water with which those who enter make the sign of the cross. The iconoclasts at the Reformation smashed most of the old stoups in England, but many have been restored and are in use. The practice of washing with water before worship goes back to ancient Jewish customs. The disciples washed their hands and feet before the Last Supper. In primitive Christian basilicas there was a pool or fount for the purpose in a courtyard outside the entrance of the church, as at San Clemente, Rome.

Stour, name of several English rivers, including one which forms the boundary between SUFFOLK and ESSEX. This river flows into the estuary of the Orwell at Harwich, and is navigable to Catawade. It is 76 km long. Water is now pumped through a tunnel from the Great Ouse to

flow down the Stour for abstraction as water supply for East Suffolk and Essex.

Stour, a tributary of the Hampshire (England) Avon. The river is 88 km long, rises in Wiltshire and, flowing through Dorset, joins the Avon at Christchurch.

Stour, river rising in the West Midlands county in the borough of Dudley, a tributary of the SEVERN, which it joins at STOURPORT. It was an important source of water power during the earlier part of the Industrial Revolution. Its length is 32 km.

Stour, Great, rises near Lenham in Kent, and flows past ASHFORD, CANTERBURY, and SANDWICH, before entering Pegwell Bay. Length 64 km. It has two tributaries, East Stour and Little Stour.

Stourbridge, market town and borough of WEST MIDLANDS METROPOLITAN COUNTY, England, 19 km west of Birmingham, on the River Stour, including the town of Stourbridge and the districts of Wollaston, Pedmore, Oldswinford, Lye, and Wollescote. Stourbridge was incorporated in Dudley in 1974. The Edward VI Grammar School (1552) was attended by Dr Johnson (1725–26), and there is a blue-coat school (1667). The district has glass manufactures established by Hungarian immigrants c. 1557, brickworks, manufactures of fire clay, leather, and galvanised and enamelled holloware. Population (1971) 56,530.

Stourhead, mansion at Stourton, Wiltshire. The house and its contents, and the estate of 1000 ha, including the gardens and the villages of Stourton and Kilmington, were given to the National Trust by Lord Hoare in 1946. Henry Hoare, the banker, commissioned Colen Campbell to build the house in 1722, and the landscaped gardens were laid out c. 1741–50. The house contains works of art and furniture by Thomas Chippendale the Younger.

Stourport-on-Severn, town in Hereford and Worcester, England, at the junction of the Severn and Stour, the former being crossed here by a handsome bridge. The terminus of the Staffordshire and Worcestershire Canal, it is a centre of inland navigation, formerly for commercial purposes but now entirely for recreation. Like BEWDLEY, Stourport attracts many day tourists during the summer. Carpets, iron and porcelain goods, and wire products are made, and there are petrol storage depots. The town is now part of the Wyre Forest district. Population (1971) 19,440.

Stout, one of the stronger beers, popular in Britain. It is brewed from highly kilned malt with a proportion of roasted malt of barley which gives it a characteristic flavour. It may be strongly or lightly hopped. There are varieties of stout, such as oatmeal and glucose. See also BEER.

Stove, see HEATING.

Stow, Randolph (1935–), Australian novelist and poet, born at Geraldton, Western Australia; educated at Geraldton, Guildford Grammar, and the University of Western Australia. He travelled widely and taught in various universities including Leeds and Dar es Salaam. After *A Haunted Land*, 1956, and *The Bystander*, 1957, Stow's reputation as a novelist was established by *To the*

403

Islands, 1958, and strengthened by *Tourmaline*, 1963; his major novel is generally agreed to be *The Merry-go-round in the Sea*, 1965, a brilliant evocation of Western Australia as seen by a child growing up during the Second World War. Stow's poetry is less widely known, but creates the same stripped, dusty environments with equal power: *A Counterfeit Silence*, 1969, contains much of his best work. His children's novel, *Midnite*, 1967, has become a classic, splendidly mocking the Australian cult figures of bushranger and explorer.

Stow-on-the-Wold, market town in Gloucestershire, England, on the Fosse Way, 32 km north-east of Cheltenham. It is a place of great charm, with an old church and a 14th-century market cross. Population (1971) 1737.

Stowe, Harriet Elizabeth Beecher (1811–96), US novelist and philanthropist, born at Litchfield, Connecticut. Her first publication was *The Mayflower*, 1843. *Uncle Tom's Cabin* appeared in *The National Era*, in serial form, in 1850, and on its appearance in book form two years later attained an almost unequalled popularity. Half a million copies were sold in the United States, and it was translated into 22 foreign languages. It had a great influence in stirring up public opinion in the northern states against slavery. In 1853 Harriet Beecher Stowe visited England to lecture on the slavery question. Among her succeeding novels were *Dred, a tale of the Great Dismal Swamp*, 1856, *The Minister's Wooing*, 1859, and *Oldtown Folks*, 1869.
    Bibliography: Lives by C. E. and L. B. Stowe, 1889; C. Gilbertson, 1937; F. Wilson, 1942; E. Wagenknecht, *Harriet Beecher Stowe*, 1965.

Stowmarket, market town in SUFFOLK, England, on the Gipping, 19 km north-west of Ipswich. Its manufactures include paints and agricultural implements. It is the site of the Suffolk Museum of Rural Life. Population (1971) 8676.

Strabane, market town of County TYRONE, Northern Ireland, on the River Mourne, 32 km north of Omagh. Shirts and underclothing are made here. Population (1971) 9325.

Strabismus, see SQUINTING.

Strabo (c. 63 BC–c. AD 22), Greek geographer and historian, born at Amasia in Pontus. He travelled extensively in Greece, Italy, Egypt, Sardinia, and Ethiopia. His historical memoirs remain only in fragments, but his *Geography*, one of the most important works of antiquity on that subject, is extant.
    Bibliography: H. L. Jones (Trans.), *Geography*, 1923–32; J. O. Thomson, *History of Ancient Geography*, 1945.

Strachey, (Giles) Lytton (1880–1932), English biographer and critic, born in London; educated at Trinity College, Cambridge, where he won the Chancellor's English Medal. He contributed to reviews, and attained prominence with *Landmarks in French Literature*, 1912. Strachey became famous in 1918 with *Eminent Victorians* (lives of Cardinal Manning, Florence Nightingale, Arnold of Rugby, and General Gordon), which was followed in 1921 by his famous life of *Queen Victoria*. Strachey was a leading figure in the revolution in attitude towards the Victorians, mercilessly attacking their moral hypocrisy. His next large biography was *Elizabeth and Essex*, 1928.

He also contributed some 90 full-length reviews to the *Spectator*, 1904–14, then under the editorship of John St Loe Strachey, who was his cousin. His *Literary Essays* were collected in 1948.
    Bibliography: M. Holroyd, *Lytton Strachey: A Critical Biography* (2 vols), 1967–68.

Stradella, Alessandro (1642–82), Italian composer, born at Montefestino. He taught singing in Venice, was apparently active in Turin and Rome, and seems to have been assassinated in Genoa: the circumstances are obscure and entwined with legends of romantic intrigue, which gave FLOTOW the subject of his opera *Stradella*. As he was of noble birth, he was probably educated privately in music. His work includes operas, a prologue for a revival of Cesti's *La Dori*, sacred and secular cantatas, oratorios (e.g. *S. Giovanni Battista*, 1676), madrigals, concertos, etc. Handel borrowed from his serenata *Qual prodigio* for *Israel in Egypt*; the aria *Pietà, Signore*, which is not at all in the style of his time, may be by Rossini.

Stradivari, Antonio (c. 1644–1737), one of the greatest Italian violin-makers associated with Cremona. He was an apprentice under Nicola AMATI, and until 1684 devoted himself chiefly to models in the Amati style. In 1690 he began making 'long Strads', and finally, after 1700, he discarded the Amati style and pursued original lines. Two famous 'Strads' are the Boissier (formerly owned by Sarasate) and the 'Alard', considered his masterpiece. He is famous also as a maker of violas and violoncellos.
    Bibliography: W. H. Hill, *Stradivari*, rev. ed. 1964.

Strafford, Thomas Wentworth, 1st Earl of (1593–1641), English statesman, born in London of an established Yorkshire family. He studied at St John's College, Cambridge, and at the Inner Temple. He entered Parliament as a member for Yorkshire in 1614 but was not active there until the early 1620s when he soon became prominent as a critic of royal policy, opposing the actions of Charles I's ministers. He supported Sir John ELIOT against Buckingham, was imprisoned for refusing to pay the forced loan, and helped to frame the Petition of Right.

Thomas Wentworth, 1st Earl of Strafford, a portrait painted c. 1633, after Van Dyck. *(National Portrait Gallery, London)*

Then, in 1628, he went over to the King's side, eagerly accepting a barony and the presidency of the Council of the North. There he ruled autocratically, and sometimes ruthlessly, for the next five years, firmly upholding the royal prerogative and limiting the power of the northern magnates. Wentworth was concerned less with the principles of government than with its efficiency and efficacy. He believed firmly in the royal prerogative and that King and Parliament should act in partnership, the King and his ministers as the executive and Parliament as an advisory body; his leanings were all towards a benevolent, paternalistic autocracy on the Tudor model.

In 1633 Wentworth was appointed lord deputy of Ireland where he continued the policy of 'Thorough' which he had evolved together with Archbishop LAUD, now his trusted friend. For six years he dominated Ireland: he reorganised the law courts, the financial system, the army and the navy, began new industries, attempted to deal with the complicated land question, extended Laudian ecclesiastical policies into the Irish Church, and greatly increased revenues from customs dues. Ireland had a period of peace and some prosperity; Wentworth enriched himself and made many powerful enemies.

Charles I never gave Wentworth his full support and only gave him his full confidence when, in 1639, it was too late. Then, after the first Bishop's War, he summoned Wentworth to him and created him earl of Strafford. Strafford urged the King to summon Parliament, apparently hoping that national hatred of the Scots would persuade the opposition to vote supplies. But Parliament refused to do so until its grievances had been dealt with. Meanwhile the Scots occupied Northumberland and Durham, Charles was forced to come to terms at Ripon and to summon another Parliament. The first act of this, the Long Parliament, was to move the impeachment of Strafford. It was soon clear that this would not succeed so the Commons proceeded against him by attainder. Charles signed his death warrant in fear of the London mob attacking his wife and family if he failed to do so and Strafford was executed.

Strafford's character remains an enigma. His contemporaries accused him of overwhelming ambition, yet this was not the whole story. He made the wrong choices: he chose the wrong side in the great constitutional battle of his time; he chose to serve a king who did not put his faith in him and was, perhaps, half afraid of him. There was nobility in his vision of government. He wished to spread order, justice, and security but his methods of doing so brought him numerous enemies and the fear of the common people who called him 'Black Tom Tyrant'.

Bibliography: H. F. Kearney, *Strafford in Ireland*, 1961; C. V. Wedgwood, *Thomas Wentworth*, 1961.

Strain and Stress. Strain is the change in size or shape or both of a body under the action of stress; stress is a set of forces in equilibrium maintaining a strain. See ELASTICITY; MATERIALS, STRENGTH OF; METALLURGY; MODULUS; SHEAR.

Straits Settlements, general name before 1946 for the British Crown Colony which comprised SINGAPORE, Penang, and Malacca in Malaya; Labuan, off the northern coast of Borneo; and Christmas Island and the Cocos Islands to the south of Sumatra. It was dissolved by the Straits Settlements (Repeal) Act 1946, Singapore

becoming a separate colony, Penang and Malacca part of the Federation of MALAYSIA, and Labuan part of North Borneo (now SABAH). Christmas Island and the Cocos Islands were administered with Singapore, but were transferred to Australian control in 1958 and 1955 respectively. See also MALAYAN HISTORY.

'Straits Times', Malaysia's national newspaper, established in 1845. Published simultaneously in Singapore and Kuala Lumpur, it circulates throughout the Malaysian area. Associated publications are the *Sunday Times*, *Malay Mail*, *Sunday Mail*, *Berita Harian*, and *Berita minggu* (romanised Malay), *Singapore Trade*, *Her World* (for women), *Straits Times Annual*, *Straits Budget*, and *Directory of Singapore and Malay*.

Stralsund, port of East Germany, in the district of Rostock, 69 km north-east of Rostock. It was an important member of the HANSEATIC LEAGUE. During the Thirty Years' War it withstood a siege by Wallenstein, but in 1678 it was taken by Frederick William of Brandenburg. It fell into the hands of the Prussians in 1715, the French in 1807, and the Danes in 1809. In 1915 it became part of Prussia. Its churches include the fine 14th-century Nikolaikirche; the old town still preserves its medieval appearance. There are boat-building, engineering, and chemical industries. Population 72,000.

Stramonium, the dried leaves and flowering tops of *Datura stramonium* (or thornapple) containing the alkaloid hyoscyamine with smaller amounts of hyoscine and atropine. It has been used in tablets or mixtures to relieve bronchial spasm in asthma and can be smoked or burnt in powders for this purpose, although the inhaled fumes may cause irritation and aggravate bronchitis.

Strand, London thoroughfare between Charing Cross and Fleet Street, originally a trackway along the strand or margin of the river connecting the cities of London and Westminster. It does not appear to have been paved before the time of Richard II. From early times, but especially in the Tudor and Stuart periods, it was lined with the mansions of the rich.

'Strand Magazine', British periodical, founded in 1891 by George (afterwards Sir George) NEWNES, and published until 1950. A pioneer monthly magazine, it featured light popular literature, accompanied by illustrations. Early success was achieved by Sir Arthur Conan DOYLE's *Adventures of Sherlock Holmes*, illustrated by Sidney Paget's imaginative portraits of Holmes and Dr Watson; later issues included the humorous stories of W. W. Jacobs, with their realistic studies of Thames riverside low life, illustrated by Will Owen. It was to the *Strand Magazine* that Kipling contributed *Puck of Pook's Hill*, and H. G. Wells *The First Men in the Moon*. Later interest was sustained by P. G. Wodehouse's stories of 'Jeeves'.

Strandhill, popular seaside resort, 8 km west of SLIGO, Republic of Ireland, picturesquely situated at the foot of Knocknarae (334 m), legendary burial site of Queen Maeve, heroine-queen of Connacht. Population 385.

Strangford Lough, island-dotted inlet in the east of County DOWN, Northern Ireland. The entrance to it lies between Strangford and Portaferry in the south. It is bounded on the east by the Ards peninsula.

Strangles

Strangles, see HORSE, *Diseases*.

Strangulation, a term used to describe constriction of the trachea (windpipe) often causing death from asphyxia; or the constriction of parts of organs resulting in restriction of their blood supply. (See HERNIA.)

Stranraer, seaport and royal burgh of Wigtown District, DUMFRIES AND GALLOWAY REGION of Scotland, on Loch Ryan, 13 km north-east of Port Patrick. Its chief building of interest is the 16th-century castle. Its large tidal harbour is used as the terminus of the shortest cross-channel service with Ireland. It trades in dairy produce, and has oatmeal mills and nurseries. The North-West Castle, now an hotel, was the home of Sir John Ross, the Arctic explorer. Population 9853.

Straparola, Giovanni Francesco (c. 1480–c. 1557), Italian writer, born at Caravaggio. He is chiefly remembered for his *Piacevoli notti*, a series of tales in imitation of BOCCACCIO's *Decameron*, which provided sources for Shakespeare and Molière, among other writers, and also contained stories such as *Beauty and the Beast* and *Puss in Boots*.

Strapwork, in Flemish and Elizabethan architecture, a form of ornament in stone, stucco or wood carving, composed of interlacing bands, resembling straps, with 'rivets' at their intersections.

Strasbourg (German *Strassburg*), French city, capital of the *département* of Bas-Rhin and chief town of the ALSACE planning region. It lies 445 km east of Paris, on the River Ill, 3 km west of the RHINE, near its junction with the Rhine-Rhône and Rhine-Marne canals. The original Celtic village was garrisoned by the Romans until captured in 455 by the FRANKS, who called it *Strateburgum*. In 842 the Frankish kings CHARLES THE BALD and LOUIS the German allied themselves against Lothaire I. In the 13th century Strasbourg became a free city, but was seized by Louis XIV, and formally ceded to France by the Treaty of Rijswijk in 1697. In 1870 the town surrendered to the Prussians after a seven-week siege, and was returned to France only in 1918. It was occupied by Germany (1940–44) during the Second World War.

It was at Strasbourg in the 15th century that GUTENBERG invented his printing press. Much of medieval Strasbourg stood on an island in the Ill, and some is still preserved. The city's most interesting buildings include the cathedral (11th–15th centuries), the church of St Peter (12th–13th centuries, with an 11th-century transept), the church of St Thomas (13th–14th centuries), and the German Renaissance rathaus (1585). The University of Strasbourg was founded in 1538. The town was selected as the headquarters for the COUNCIL OF EUROPE in 1949. Strasbourg has been important from early times as a centre of communications; it is now a railway junction for Paris, the Netherlands, West Germany, and Switzerland. Its river, harbours, and canals make it the chief inland port of France, trading in potash, iron ore, oil, and grain. Its industries include the manufacture of rolling-stock, electrical equipment, river boats, perfumes, soap, chemicals, oil-refining, and textiles, and breweries, flour mills, sugar, and tobacco processing. The long-established printing and publishing trades are still important. The city is famous for its *pâté-de-fois-gras* and *sauerkraut*. Population (1975) 253,384.

Strassburg, Gottfried von, see GOTTFRIED VON STRASSBURG.

Strasser, Gregor (1892–1934), German politician, born at Geisenfeld in Upper Bavaria. He took part in Hitler's putsch of 1923. Later he organised the National Socialist party in the Reichstag. He lost favour for his radically anti-capitalist views. Hitler had him first expelled from the party, then murdered in the 1934 purge.

Strasser, Otto (1897–1974), German politician, born at Windsheim. He joined his brother Gregor in the Nazi party and directed its Berlin publishing house from 1926 to 1930. He then founded the Black Front, suppressed when Hitler came to power in 1933. Strasser fled abroad, returning to Germany in 1955.

Strategy and Tactics. Until the closing years of the 19th century the terms 'strategy' and 'tactics' were easily defined. 'Strategy' meant the movement of troops to the area of conflict, such as the concentration of Wellington's and Blücher's armies before Waterloo. 'Tactics' meant the dispositions and moves of troops when in close combat, or under fire, on the battlefield. Similarly 'naval strategy' implied the preliminary moves to the area of a naval engagement, such as the concentration of the British battle fleet in home waters prior to the outbreak of the First World War. Naval 'tactics' denoted the handling of fleets or squadrons when contact with the enemy had been made.

With increases in the range of weapons, better communications by sea and land, and, later, the introduction of aircraft, these hitherto simple definitions were inadequate. Since the first flight in 1903, aircraft in particular have added a new complication to warfare: the air being common to both land and sea operations there was no longer a clear dividing line. Originally air operations were subsidiary to those of the other services, but because of their ability to operate over enemy territory, a school of thought developed in the 1920s which claimed that aircraft by striking directly at the heartland of a nation could defeat it without the intervention of the other services. However, it was not until the dropping of the atomic bombs on Japan in 1945 that a country was defeated by air power alone. As war tended to become more widespread the term 'grand strategy' was introduced to indicate the global deployment of national manpower (and other resources) for military purposes. Examples are the movement of British and French ships and troops to the Dardanelles in 1915, Hitler's decision in 1940 to send the German Afrika Korps to North Africa and later, in 1941, his decision to attack the USSR. In the air the major strategic decision of the Second World War was the launching of the Allied strategic air offensive against Germany (see AERIAL WARFARE). Because of the flexibility of aircraft and the ease with which they can be switched from one rôle or target to another there has always been controversy as to the best air strategy to adopt. It is common ground, however, that the successful operation of land forces usually depends for its success upon air superiority over the battlefield and that similarly the success of a bombing offensive depends upon the extent to which the enemy air defences can be subdued.

During the Second World War for example the success of the Allied bombing offensive threw Germany increasingly on the defensive in the air and as a result its aircraft production was concentrated latterly almost entirely upon defensive fighters, thus leaving the Allied invasion of Europe largely free from air attack. Since the war, because of the loss of many of its overseas air bases, Britain has had to develop an island strategy for air reinforcement whereby air bases are established on a number of islands, and at the same time the range of aircraft is being constantly extended and increased still further on occasion by air refuelling and the fitting of extra fuel tanks, the strategic aim being to enable any aircraft to reach any part of the world in an emergency.

The simple term 'strategy' was reserved for the movement of forces within a theatre of operations. Whilst simple 'strategy' remains a mainly military affair, 'grand strategy' in a major war now involves practically every human activity—foreign policy, politics, industry, economics, etc. In fact it is synonymous with the national war plan. Tactics underwent a similar transformation. 'Grand tactics' indicates the movement of forces within striking distance of the enemy, such as the movement of a reserve division from one flank of an extensive defensive position to the other flank, or the concentration in the areas of operations of a number of naval squadrons from different commands as in the case of the *Bismarck* victory, or the movement of air forces to North Africa for the campaigns in that area. The term 'minor tactics' is used for the activities, in close combat, of small bodies of troops, such as sections and platoons, which make up a modern battle. The term 'air tactics' is usually applied to the formations and methods adopted by aircraft. For instance, they usually fly in formation by day for mutual support; fighters sometimes escort bombers by day and bombers have developed a low-flying technique whereby they are much less vulnerable to air defences. It will be apparent that it is not always easy to say when one kind of tactic ends and another begins, and sometimes difficult to differentiate between 'strategy' and 'grand tactics'.

Since 1945 the terms 'strategic' and 'tactical' have been applied to weapons, particularly nuclear weapons. Intercontinental and intermediate range missiles (with ranges in excess of 800 km) with a nuclear war-head are frequently referred to as 'strategic missiles'. Those nuclear weapons with lesser ranges, used in direct or indirect support of ground troops, are called 'tactical nuclear weapons'. Similarly long-range bomber aircraft (such as those in the US Strategic Air Command) are known as 'strategic aircraft'; those normally employed in support of land or sea forces as 'tactical aircraft'. Missiles are increasingly taking the place of strategic aircraft and it seems likely that the rôle of aircraft will eventually revert almost entirely to the original one of tactical support for the other services.

Bibliography: B. Liddell Hart, *Strategy, the Indirect Approach,* 1954; S. W. Roskill, *The Strategy of Sea Power,* 1962; K. Von Clausewitz, *On War* (trans. J. J. Graham), 3 vols, 1962; A. Beaufre, *An Introduction to Strategy,* 1965; E. M. Earle, *Makers of Modern Strategy,* 1966; A. Beaufre, *Strategy for Tomorrow,* 1975.

Stratfield Saye House, seat of the Duke of Wellington, near Basingstoke, Hampshire, England. The central portion of the present house was built about 1630. Wellington chose Stratfield Saye when Parliament voted him a country estate, and after 1817 he filled the house with his acquisitions from Paris, Spain and contemporary London. The collection of French and English furniture is notable. There are Roman mosaic pavements from SILCHESTER.

Stratford, town of Ontario, Canada, through which pass six lines of the Canadian National Railway, which has repair shops here. Furniture and agricultural implements are made; other industries include woollen goods and food processing. Since 1952 Stratford has been the scene of an internationally famous annual festival of Shakespearean drama, held from June to August. Population 23,900.

Stratford, town of Fairfield county, Connecticut, USA, 8 km north-east of Bridgeport. An annual Shakespeare festival was inaugurated here in 1955. Population 44,400.

Stratford de Redcliffe, Stratford Canning, 1st Viscount (1786–1880), British diplomat, born in London, educated at Eton and King's College, Cambridge. Through his cousin, George Canning, he became secretary of the embassy at Constantinople in 1808, and minister plenipotentiary in 1810. He negotiated the Treaty of Bucharest between Russia and Turkey in 1812. After service in Switzerland he became minister to the USA (1820–24). He was envoy to St Petersburg (1824), and again to Constantinople (1825), and later entered Parliament. He was at Constantinople again in 1842 as ambassador, and remained there throughout the Crimean War, largely influencing the political reforms and foreign relations of Turkey and earning for himself the title of 'The Great Elchi' (great ambassador). Some of the responsibility for not preventing the Crimean War is undoubtedly Stratford de Redcliffe's.

Stratford-upon-Avon, borough and market town in WARWICKSHIRE, England, 35 km south-south-east of Birmingham, pleasantly situated in the wooded valley of the Avon. The river is crossed by a fine bridge, erected during the reign of Henry VII by Sir Hugh Clopton, Lord Mayor of London. The town is famous as the birthplace of Shakespeare, and is visited every year by travellers from all parts of the world. Here may be seen the reputed birthplace of the poet in Henley Street, purchased for the nation in 1847 for £3000 (it is administered by the Shakespeare Birthplace Trust, which also runs the adjoining library and study centre, opened in 1964, and several

Stratford-upon-Avon. *(Topham/Scowen)*

other Shakespeare-connected buildings); Anne Hathaway's cottage, 1·5 km from the centre of the town; the graves of the poet and his wife in the chancel of Holy Trinity; 'The Cage', which was for 36 years the home of Judith, Shakespeare's younger daughter, wife of Thomas Quiney, vintner; Hall's Croft, old-timbered residence of Susanna, the poet's elder daughter, who married Dr John Hall, his executor, which now houses the offices of the British Council and a Festival Club; Wilmcote, the house of Shakespeare's mother Mary Arden, a fine timbered farmhouse of the Tudor period, 5 km outside the town; Nash's House, restored in 17th-century style, with the adjoining vacant site of Shakespeare's house, New Place, and its Elizabethan garden; and King Edward VI Grammar School, endowed in 1482 by Rev. Thomas Jolyffe, MA, of Stratford, and re-endowed by Edward VI. The original theatre built by public subscription as the Shakespeare Memorial Theatre, a redbrick building which opened in 1879 for annual summer seasons of Shakespeare's plays, was destroyed by fire in 1926. The present building, which changed its name in 1961 to the Royal Shakespeare Theatre, was designed by Elizabeth Scott and opened in 1932. The buildings adjoining the theatre were not seriously damaged by the fire. They include the Library, which, mainly owing to the liberality of C. E. Flower (1830–92) and his wife, contains some 10,000 volumes of Shakespeare editions and dramatic literature, and a number of pictures, including the 'Droeshout' portrait. It can be used by accredited students. The art gallery and museum, containing pictures and exhibits illustrative of the history of the theatre and of Shakespeare productions, can be visited on payment of a small fee. Mason Croft, once the home of Marie Corelli, is now the Institute of Shakespeare Studies, run by the University of Birmingham.

Stratford is a place of great antiquity. The Chapel of the Guild of the Holy Cross dates from the 13th century, Holy Trinity church occupies the site of a Saxon monastery, and dates from the 13th century. The town hall, first erected in 1633, was rebuilt in 1767; it has complete records of the sequence of bailiffs, mayors, and town clerks from 1553 (including the poet's father, John Shakespeare), and of high stewards from 1610. The town trades in cattle and agricultural produce; 6 km east of the town lies Charlecote Park and its 16th-century house which was acquired by the National Trust in 1945. Population (1971) 18,389.

Bibliography: E. I. Fripp, *Shakespeare's Stratford*, 1928; J. C. Trewin, *Portrait of the Shakespeare Country*, 1970; N. Harris, *The Shakespeares*, 1976; official town guide.

Strathaven, market and residential town in East Kilbride District, Strathclyde Region, Scotland, on Avon Water, 22 km south-east of Glasgow. It has a ruined 15th-century castle. In the Middle Ages Strathaven's silk was famous, and the town had considerable importance. Population 5464.

Strathclyde, early British kingdom, c. 560, covering, at its zenith, the western part of the lowlands of Scotland, the greater part of Westmorland, and Cumberland. Its capital was Alclyde, the rock fortress at Dumbarton. It came from time to time under Northumbrian influence, but was not finally absorbed into the Scottish kingdom until the middle of the 10th century.

Strathclyde Region is the largest and most populous of the new (1975) administrative units of SCOTLAND. There are 19 districts: ARGYLL AND BUTE, DUMBARTON, City of GLASGOW, CLYDEBANK, BEARSDEN AND MILNGAVIE, STRATHKELVIN, CUMBERNAULD AND KILSYTH, MONKLANDS, MOTHERWELL, HAMILTON, EAST KILBRIDE, EASTWOOD, LANARK, RENFREW, INVERCLYDE, CUNNINGHAME, KILMARNOCK AND LOUDEN, KYLE AND CARRICK, CUMNOCK AND DOON Valley. The Argyll and Bute District includes most of the Inner HEBRIDES south of Skye. The total population is 2,527,129, i.e. about 50 per cent of Scotland. Its area is 14,000 km². It has subsumed the following counties: Bute, Dunbarton, Lanarkshire, Ayrshire, Argyll, a small part of Stirlingshire and Renfrewshire, and the city of Glasgow.

Strathclyde, University of, amalgamation of the Royal College of Science and Technology (dates back to 1795) and the Scottish College of Commerce, founded in 1964. There are ten schools of study in this mainly scientific and technological institution which cover science, engineering, arts, social studies, business, administration, law, and education. There are about 6000 students, approximately 1100 of them living in university accommodation.

Strathcona and Mount Royal, Donald Alexander Smith, 1st Baron (1820–1914), Canadian politician, born at Archiestown, Morayshire, Scotland, emigrated to Canada, and entered the Hudson's Bay Company's service in 1838. In 1869 he was governor of the company's territories and in 1871 became chief commissioner of the North-West. Smith was special commissioner during the Riel rebellion in the Red River Settlements. He was a member of the first Executive Council of the North-West Territories, MP for Selkirk in the Dominion House of Commons (1871–72, 1874, and 1878), and for Montreal West (1877–96). He was instrumental in the building of the Canadian Pacific railway. He was created a baron in 1897. From 1896 to 1914 he was Canadian high commissioner in Britain.

Strathkelvin District, part of STRATHCLYDE REGION, Scotland, a large area north-east of the city of Glasgow occupying parts of the former counties of Stirlingshire and East Dunbartonshire. The district includes the northern edge of Glasgow but extends through agricultural land with several small towns to the slopes of the volcanic (Carboniferous) plateau of the CAMPSIE FELLS. The River Kelvin, an important right-bank tributary of the lower Clyde, flows through the area. The administrative centre is KIRKINTILLOCH. Population (1971) 80,181.

Strathmore, wide valley of Scotland, bounded on the north by the GRAMPIANS, and on the south by the LENNOX, OCHIL, and SIDLAW HILLS. It runs for some 160 km north-east to south-west across Scotland from the North Sea through KINCARDINE AND DEESIDE DISTRICT (Grampian Region) and Tayside Region.

Strathmore and Kinghorne, Earl of, Scottish title held by the Lyon family, the Strathmore barony since 1445, and the earldom of Kinghorne since 1606. John, the 9th Earl (1737–76), took the additional name of Bowes. Lady Elizabeth, daughter of Claude George (1855–1944), the 14th Earl, married Prince Albert, Duke of York, in 1923, and in 1936 became queen consort when he suc-

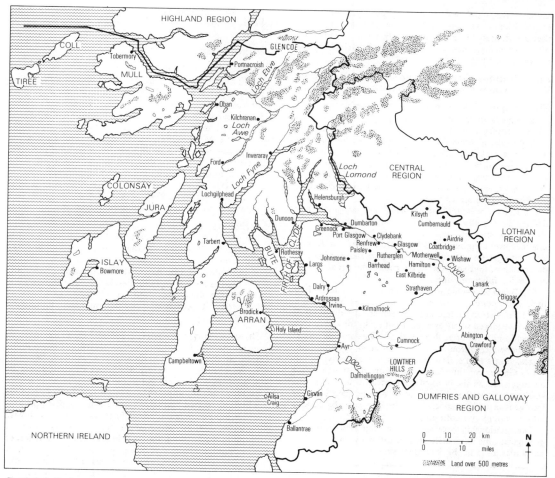

Strathclyde Region.

ceeded to the throne as George VI. The family seat is Glamis Castle, Angus.

Strathnairn, Hugh Henry Rose, 1st Baron (1801–85), British soldier, born and educated in Berlin. He entered the British army in 1820, and was a major-general by 1854. He served in the Crimean War and the Indian Mutiny, in which he played a distinguished part. He was commander-in-chief in India in 1860 and in Ireland in 1865. He was created a baron in 1866; promoted general in 1867, and field-marshal in 1877.

Strathpeffer, village in Ross and Cromarty District, Highland Region, Scotland. It is a tourist centre with several large hotels. Population 874.

Strathspey, see BADENOCH AND STRATHSPEY DISTRICT.

Strathspey, musical term applied to Scottish dance tunes in a slow 4-4 time with much ornamentation. The music was said to have originated in the Spey valley, a region well known for maintaining a high standard of dancing performance. The interesting feature of the strathspey is the introduction of the dotted rhythm or 'snap' (a semi-quaver followed by a dotted quaver). This peculiarity was thought to have developed from the agile fingering of the bagpipe player and the sharp movement of the wrist in the up-bowing of the fiddler. It is also attributed to the inflection found in the Gaelic vocal 'mouth music'. The snap became a feature of Scottish music and was introduced into the compositions of many European musicians such as Handel and Haydn. The strathspey dance steps and style became popular in the 18th century when REELS were performed to this music and called strathspey reels. Later reel and JIG tunes were adapted to this rhythm.

Stratification, geological term used to describe the layered or bedded character of a sequence of rocks. Stratified rocks are made up of a succession of layers, beds, or strata, which were deposited one above the other by such agents as rivers, wind, ice, or the sea. Each bed may be distinguished to a greater or lesser extent from

Stratificational Grammar

those above and below it by differences in colour or composition. Even if all the beds in a series are identical, they are separated by surfaces of contact along which they often part easily. These contact surfaces between beds are known as bedding planes.

Stratificational Grammar, also stratificational linguistics, see GRAMMAR; LAMB, SYDNEY M.; LINGUISTICS.

Stratigraphical Nomenclature, the terminology used by geologists in the description and grouping together of sedimentary rock units. Geologists have always used separate sets of terms for the division of geological time into convenient portions and for the actual rocks belonging to these portions of time. More recently two additional sets of terms have been introduced, so that there are now four fundamental ways in which a rock sequence may be classified. These are as follows:

(1) Rock stratigraphic units, which are recognised and defined by the observable physical characteristics of the rocks. The smallest unit is the bed; beds are grouped together into members, members into formations, formations into groups and super-groups. These units are often diachronous, and so these terms cannot be equated with any of the following ones.

(2) Biostratigraphic units, which are characterised by their fossil content. The smallest unit is the biozone.

(3) Time stratigraphic units, which are sub-divisions of rocks considered solely as a record of rocks formed during a specific interval of geological time. The smallest unit is a chronozone; chronozones are grouped together into stages, stages into series, and series into systems.

(4) Geological time units, which are divisions of time distinguished on the basis of the record of the rocks. The smallest unit is the chron; chrons are grouped together into ages, ages into epochs, epochs into periods, periods into eras, and eras into eons.

The relationship between time stratigraphic units and geological time units is illustrated below by reference to a particular zone in the SILURIAN SYSTEM.

Geological time units	Time stratigraphic units
Eon — Phanerozoic	
Era — Palaeozoic	
Period — Silurian	System — Silurian
Epoch	Series — Ludlow
Age	Stage — Leintwardinian
Chron	Chronozone — zone of *Monograptus leintwardinensis*

Stratigraphy, see GEOLOGY.

Stratosphere, see ATMOSPHERE.

Stratton, Frederick John Marrian (1881–1960), British astronomer, born in Birmingham, and educated at Birmingham and Cambridge, which was his home for the rest of his life and where he was professor of astrophysics, 1928–47. Trained as a classical astronomer, he became interested in spectroscopy, especially of the Sun and of novae. His *Astronomical Physics*, 1925, was the first book to treat the subject in a modern way. He was a man of many and varied activities in his college (Caius) in Cambridge and in the world at large. He was general secretary of the British Association from 1930 to 1935 and of the International Astronomical Union from 1925 to 1935. He

had a distinguished career on active service during the First World War and he also served in the Second World War.

Stratton, see BUDE.

Straub, Jean-Marie (1933–), French film director, who has spent much of his life in a German milieu. One of the most 'difficult' of contemporary film-makers, his intense films repay repeated viewing. A committed Marxist, his early *Machorka-Muff* (1963) and *Nicht Versöhnt* (1965) are more overtly political than his beautiful *The Chronicle of Anna Magdalena Bach* (1968), while the asceticism of both his visual style and his actors' performances recall the films of Robert BRESSON. His more recent films include *The Bridegroom, the Comedienne, and the Pimp* (1968), *Othon* (1970), *The History Lesson* (1972), *Moses and Aaron* (1974). Straub always works in close collaboration with his wife, Danielle Huillet.

Straubing, city in BAVARIA, West Germany, on the Danube 110 km north-east of Munich. Its churches include a 12th-century Romanesque basilica, and the 15th-century Agnes-Bernauer-Kapelle, built in memory of the wife of Duke Albrecht III of Bavaria, who was drowned as a witch in 1435. Besides being an agricultural centre, the town has electrical, clothing, and brewing industries. FRAUNHOFER was born here. Population 44,000.

Strauss, David Friedrich (1808–74), German theologian, born at Ludwigsburg, Württemberg; studied under Baur at Tübingen and Schleiermacher at Berlin. Turning to Hegelianism, he rapidly developed a radical tendency to atheism. He became lecturer in philosophy at Tübingen in 1832. In 1835 appeared his rationalist *Life of Jesus*, in which he treated Christianity as a commonplace pseudo-mythological religion and Christ as a sort of Jewish Socrates. A storm arose, and certain modifications were made in the 1839 edition. But in that year he was forced to resign the chair of philosophy at Zürich, to which he had but recently been appointed; his indignation vented itself in the 1840 edition (English translation by George Eliot, 1840), in which he abandoned Christianity. In 1840–41 he published *Christliche Glaubenslehre*. Other works are *Reimarus*, 1862, *Voltaire*, 1870, and *The Old and New Faith*, 1872. His complete works were edited by E. Zeller and published 1876–78.

Bibliography: Lives and Studies by E. Zeller, 1874; A. Haurath, 1876–78; T. Ziegler, 1908–09; H. Grossmann, 1939.

Strauss, Johann, the elder (1804–48), Austrian dance-composer, born in Vienna. In 1825 he founded his own orchestra with which he became famous abroad. He composed waltzes, marches, quadrilles and polkas.

Bibliography: F. Lange, *Josef Lanner und Johann Strauss*, 2nd ed. 1919.

Strauss, Johann, the younger (1825–99), Austrian composer, born in Vienna, son and pupil of the above. From 1849 he led his father's orchestra, giving it up in 1863 to his brothers Joseph and Eduard, in order to concentrate on composition. He achieved great popularity as the 'waltz king', by his expressive talent, gift for melody and rhythm and apt instrumental technique. *The Blue Danube* is perhaps the most famous of his several hundred waltzes, while the *Tritsch-Tratsch Polka* is among his best-known works in this form. His operettas include *Indigo*, 1871, *Die Fledermaus*, 1874, *A Night in Venice*, 1883, and *The Gypsy Baron*, 1885. He also composed many polkas, galops and other dances which, in conjunction with his waltzes, number over 500.

Bibliography: Lives and Studies by H. E. Jacob, Eng. trans. 1940, and W. Jaspert, 1948; A. Strauss, *Strauss schreibt Briefe*, 1926.

Strauss, Richard (1864–1949), German composer, born in Munich, where he studied and briefly attended the university, completing his musical studies in Berlin. At the age of 21 he became assistant conductor to Bülow at Meiningen, where he met Alexander Ritter, who won him over from classical ideals of style to more modern notions and to programme music. He became chief conductor at Meiningen in 1885, and soon afterwards began to cultivate the symphonic poem, his best examples being *Don Juan*, 1888, *Death and Transfiguration*, 1889, *Till Eulenspiegel*, 1895, *Thus Spake Zarathustra*, 1896, *Don Quixote*, 1897, and *A Hero's Life*, 1898. As an opera composer he came forward a little later, though *Guntram* had been produced at Weimar in 1894. *Feuersnot* scandalised Dresden in 1901 and *Salome* the same city in 1905. Hugo von Hofmannsthal was librettist for his next five operas, *Elektra*, 1909, *Der Rosenkavalier*, 1911—his greatest success—*Ariadne auf Naxos* (first version, as an epilogue to Molière's *Bourgeois gentilhomme*, 1912, full operatic version, 1916), *Die Frau ohne Schatten*, 1919, *Die Aegyptische Helena*, 1928; and these, with *Arabella*, 1933, were soon accepted as among the greatest contributions to German opera. The autobiographical *Intermezzo* was produced in 1924. In *Die schweigsame Frau*, 1935, he collaborated with Stefan Zweig, and in *Friedenstag*, 1938, *Daphne*, 1938, and *Die Liebe der Danae*, 1952, with Josef Gregor. The last opera, *Capriccio*, 1942, had a libretto by himself and Clemens Krauss. After *Ariadne* a certain decline set in: the technique became repetitive and the invention tired; but he continued to take the liveliest interest in the problems of opera as an art. His two ballets, the choral works and the orchestral music apart from the symphonic poems are less important, but his oboe concerto and two horn concertos must be mentioned, and among the chamber music the early piano quartet, the *Metamorphoses* for 23 solo string instruments and two sonatinas for 16 wind instruments; also the *Four Last Songs* with orchestra. Among the more than 120 songs with piano are many that count among the classic examples of the German Lied.

Bibliography: F. Trenner, *Dokumente*, 1954; F. and A. Strauss (Eds), *The Correspondence between Richard Strauss and Hugo von Hofmannsthal*, Eng. trans. 1961; W. Mann, *Richard Strauss*, 1964; R. Myers (Ed.), *Richard Strauss and Romain Rolland: Correspondence, Diary and Essays*, 1968; N. del Mar, *Richard Strauss*, new ed. 1972.

Stravinsky, Igor Fyodorovich (1882–1971), US composer of Russian birth, born in Oranienbaum (now Lomonosov). In 1903 he became a pupil of Rimsky-Korsakov. His first composition, a symphony which was entirely academic, was performed in 1908. After his master's death, a new stimulus came from DIAGHILEV who produced Stravinsky's ballet *The Firebird* in 1910 (his first masterpiece, still in the tradition of the Balakirev school). His second ballet, *Petrushka*, 1911, revealed a new personality, while *The Rite of Spring*, 1913,

proved of revolutionary significance, causing a riot in Paris. *The Wedding* (composed 1914–17, orchestrated and performed 1923) and *The Soldier's Tale*, 1918, demonstrate Stravinsky's continued desire to vary his style, sometimes using older models as a basis—folk-song, Bach, Tchaikovsky, for instance. After the First World War, Stravinsky's work showed a new austerity, as in the one-act opera buffa *Mavra*, 1921–22, or the piano concerto, 1924. He turned to absolute music in the classical manner, as in the octet for wind instruments, 1923, the oratorio *Oedipus Rex*, 1927, and the ballet suite *Apollo Musagetes*, 1928, written in America. *The Fairy's Kiss*, 1928, the *Capriccio* for piano and orchestra and the *Symphony of Psalms*, 1930, filled old forms with new ideas. A movement towards definite classicism was made in the symphony in C.

From 1940 Stravinsky settled in the USA (he became an American citizen in 1945). Later works include a symphony in three movements, 1945. His experiments have had a great effect upon contemporaries. Among his later works should be mentioned the opera *The Rake's Progress*, 1951, in which he reverted, in his own way, to *bel canto* and opera in set numbers; a cantata, 1952, in which, as in the opera, he showed a new interest in English words; a septet for strings, wind and piano, 1952; the cantatas *Threni*, 1958, and *A Sermon, a Narrative and a Prayer*, 1961; *Movements* for piano and orchestra, 1960; and *The Flood*, a musical play for television, 1962. In his last works he used an individual form of 12-note composition. He published *Chronicles of my Life*, 1936, and (with R. Craft) *Conversations with Igor Stravinsky*, 1959, and *Memories and Commentaries*, 1960.

Bibliography: E. W. White, *Stravinsky*, 1966; P. M. Young, *Stravinsky*, 1966; R. Vlad, *Stravinsky*, 1971.

Straw, the stalk or stem of various corn crops such as wheat, barley, oats, rye, maize, leguminous crops, and also flax and hemp. It is put to many uses for litter, thatching, plaiting, and also, when other feeding-stuffs are scarce, as a food for livestock. It varies widely in quality according to species and variety, and considerable attention has been paid in recent years to the production of short-strawed varieties which by the strength or firmness of their straw do not 'lodge' or become knocked down by the wind, due to insufficient light, to overcrowding, or to excess of fertilisers.

Strawberry, various species of the genus *Fragaria* in the family Rosaceae. Botanically, the edible flesh is neither a

Igor Stravinsky. *(Bisonte)*

berry nor even a true FRUIT; the true fruits or achenes are the so-called seeds on the outside of the fleshy receptacle. The fruit of the wood strawberry, *F. vesca*, the only native British species, is small and delicately flavoured. The hautboy strawberry sometimes grows wild, but in such cases it is a garden escape. From it, the Chile strawberry, *F. chiloensis*, and the scarlet strawberry, *F. virginiana*, the cultivated varieties are mostly derived. Strawberries do best on a deeply worked loam enriched with decayed manure. The plants are set out in late summer or early autumn about 50 cm apart, in rows 76 cm apart. When the bloom appears, long clean straw must be spread between the rows, partly as a protection against late frosts, but chiefly to keep the fruit clean. In September the ground should be thoroughly cleared, runners removed, and the soil well stirred, and dressed with ash from the garden-refuse fire. In February or March well-decayed manure should be applied, and dressings of liquid manure are desirable while fruit is being produced. The plants are propagated by allowing runners to root in small pots containing light loamy soil.

Strawberry Hill, see RICHMOND-UPON-THAMES; WALPOLE, HORACE, 4TH EARL OF ORFORD.

Strawberry Tree, see ARBUTUS.

Strawboard, see CARDBOARD.

Strawson, Peter Frederick (1919–), British philosopher, who in 1968 became Wayneflete professor of metaphysical philosophy at Oxford. In his *Introduction to Logical Theory*, 1952, he discusses the character of formal argument and shows how ordinary discourse differs from formal systems. In *Individuals*, 1959, he shows that the basic feature enabling us to recognise different things as individual is location in space and time. Other works include *Logico-Linguistic Papers*, 1971.

Stream, see HYDROLOGY; RIVER.

Stream, Braided, a RIVER whose main channel is wide and shallow and whose flow passes through a series of small interlaced channels separated from each other by bars. This branching is sometimes described as 'anastomising'. Most braided streams occur where the confining banks are ill-defined, e.g. on ALLUVIAL FANS in semi-arid areas, or on glacial outwash plains (see GLACIATION). But they also occur in mountainous areas where the local gradient is steep and the bank material coarse. A close relationship exists between braiding and MEANDERing, the slope/discharge ratio always being higher for the braided stream. Generally a braided stream is much less sinuous in plan than a meandering stream.

Streaming Potential, see ELECTROPHORESIS.

Street, George Edmund (1824–81), British architect, a leader of the Gothic Revival, born at Woodford, Essex. He travelled widely in Europe, worked under Sir George SCOTT, and began practice in London in 1849. He won the great competition for the Law Courts, 1866–68. He was deeply religious and designed a large number of churches including: All Saints, Boyne Hill, Maidenhead (1854–59); St Saviour, Eastbourne (1867–68); All Saints, Clifton, Bristol (1863–68); St John, Torquay (1861–71); and St Mary Magdalen, Paddington, London (1868–78).

He wrote and illustrated *Brick and Marble in North Italy*, 1855, and *Gothic Architecture in Spain*, 1865.

Street, town in Somerset, England, near Glastonbury. Shoes, leather board, and sheepskin goods are made here. Nearby is Millfield School. Population (1971) 8143.

Streicher, Julius (1895–1946), German politician, born at Fleinhausen near Augsburg. After the First World War he began a violent anti-Semitic and nationalistic movement at Nuremberg. Hitler made Streicher gauleiter at Nuremberg. Streicher founded a special weekly paper for 'the struggle for the truth against traitors' entitled *Der Stürmer*, which specialised in Jew-baiting. After Hitler's triumph in 1933 the views of *Der Stürmer* soon prevailed throughout Germany, and when Hitler decided on boycotting Jewish shops Streicher was made Aktionsführer (riot leader). Later he became governor of Franconia. Streicher was sentenced to death at the Nuremberg trial in 1946 and executed.

Strelitzia, a genus of Musaceae (the banana family) which occurs exclusively in Africa, and contains five species. *S. reginae* is known as the queen's flower, bird's-tongue flower, or bird-of-paradise flower, because of its showy and beautiful orange and blue flowers.

Strength of Materials, see MATERIALS, STRENGTH OF.

Strepsiptera, an order of the class Insecta, subclass PTERYGOTA. These are small insects that are endoparasitic on other insects. The males are free-living, with forewings reduced to small club-like structures, but with large hindwings; the females usually remain in a puparium that protrudes slightly from the host insect. A few species have larva-like females that leave the hosts. The larval development is hypermetamorphic, that is with a different form for each of the several stages. There are 300 species. All are parasitic in various insects of the orders Hemiptera and Hymenoptera.

Streptocarpus, a genus of the Gesneriaceae (gloxinia family), found in Africa. It contains 100 species, usually known as Cape primroses, which are downy herbs, bearing beautiful flowers, generally of a purple or blue colour. The genus is much grown as a house plant. The leaves or leaf-cuttings, when placed in potting compost, produce new plants.

Streptococci, see BACTERIA.

Streptomycin, an aminoglycoside ANTIBIOTIC which interferes with the synthesis of proteins. Its most important use is in the treatment of TUBERCULOSIS, when it is often combined with other drugs.

Stresa, Italian town in PIEDMONT, on the western shore of Lake MAGGIORE, a tourist and health resort. Population 4000. Two important international conferences were held here: (1) in September 1932 the representatives of 15 European states met to discuss the economic recovery of Central and Eastern Europe; (2) in April 1935 between Britain, France, and Italy. See FRANCE, *History*.

Stresemann, Gustav (1878–1929), German statesman, born in Berlin. He attended the Andreas Realgymnasium and Leipzig University. At 28, as a National Liberal, he entered the Reichstag. During the First World War he favoured reform at home but annexations abroad. After the revolution of 1918 he led a section of his party that became the German People's party. In August 1923 he became, briefly, chancellor of the Republic, being later succeeded by Wilhelm Marx. He was foreign minister in various governments until his death. In 1925 Stresemann proposed the security pact, which was signed at Locarno in October, and it was largely through his efforts that Germany was admitted to the League of Nations. Stresemann shared the Nobel Peace Prize with Briand in 1926. It is now obvious, however, that Stresemann was more of a nationalist than was once thought, and that he was well aware, and approved, of the efforts made by Germany to evade the military restrictions imposed at Versailles. His essays and speeches were published in English, translated by C. R. Turner, 1930, and his diaries, letters, and papers, edited and translated by E. Sutton, 3 volumes, 1935.

Bibliography: H. A. Turner, *Stresemann and the Politics of the Weimar Republic*, 1963; H. W. Gatzke, *Stresemann and the Rearmament of Germany*, 1969.

Stress, see STRAIN AND STRESS.

Stretford, former municipal borough of Lancashire, England, lying just to the south-west of Manchester's city centre; it now lies within the Trafford borough of the new Greater MANCHESTER METROPOLITAN COUNTY. As a borough it derived great benefit from the inclusion of much of the Trafford Park industrial estate within its boundaries. It contains some 200 factories employing around 50,000 people in a wide variety of industries, and is served by the MANCHESTER SHIP CANAL. An enclosed shopping area has now replaced its former retail trading centre. Within Stretford lies Old Trafford, the home of Manchester United, and the headquarters of the Lancashire Cricket Club. Population (1971) 54,297.

Stretton, Hesba, pseudonym of Sarah Smith (1832–1911), English novelist, born at Wellington, Shropshire. Her most famous works were *Jessica's First Prayer*, 1867, published by the Religious Tract Society and translated into every European language, and *Alone in London*, 1869. She contributed stories to *Household Words* and *All the Year Round* and wrote over 50 books. She also helped to found the London Society for the Prevention of Cruelty to Children, in 1884.

Streuvels, Stijn, pseudonym of Frank Lateur (1871–1969), Flemish novelist, born at Heule. He achieved for Flemish prose what his uncle, Guido GEZELLE, had achieved for poetry. A baker's son, his concern was for the west Flemish proletariat, whose interests and environment are portrayed with sympathy, if pessimistically, in works such as *De Vlaschaard*, 1907, and his masterly novella *Het leven en de dood in den ast*, 1926.

Bibliography: H. Speliers, *Afscheid van Streuvels*, 1971.

Strickland, Agnes (1796–1874), English historical writer, born in London. She wrote in 1833 *Historical Tales of Illustrious British Children* and, also for the young, *Tales and Stories from History*, 1836. Her best-known and more famous work, written with her sister Elizabeth, is the *Lives of the Queens of England*, 1840–48, followed, amongst others, by *Lives of the Queens of Scotland and English Princesses connected with the Regal Succession of Great Britain*, 1850–59, and *Lives of the Last Four Stuart Princesses*, 1872.

Bibliography: U. Pope-Hennessy, *Agnes Strickland: Biographer of the Queens of England*, 1940.

Stricture, or stenosis, narrowing of a tube in the body or of its opening, by inflammatory or other changes in its walls or from outside pressure. The term is most commonly used of urethral stenosis, caused by ulceration due to gonorrhoeal infection (see GONORRHOEA). *Pyloric stenosis* is constriction of the pyloric outlet of the stomach. *Mitral stenosis* is constriction of the mitral orifice of the heart. *Oesophageal stenosis* is constriction of the oesophagus (gullet).

Stridor, a noise caused by obstruction to the passage of air, into or out of the lower respiratory tract. In adults it is often accompanied by other symptoms such as HOARSENESS or shortness of breath, but in young children and babies stridor may be the only symptom of a potentially serious obstruction. Inspiratory stridor in children is known colloquially as 'croup' and it is caused by inflammation in the larynx. Diphtheria occasionally extends into the larynx to produce croup, but immunisation has virtually eliminated this cause. Expiratory stridor (wheezing) is due to bronchial obstruction, whereas noises in both phases of respiration are usually due to obstruction in the trachea.

Strigidae, see OWL.

Strijdom, Johannes Gerhardus (1893–1958), South African politician, born in Willowmore, Cape Province, prime minister of the Union of South Africa and leader in chief of the National party, 1954–58. He was MP for Waterberge, 1929–58.

Strike, see DIP AND STRIKE.

Strike, The General (1926), 'sympathetic' strike by the trade unions of Great Britain, undertaken in support of the Miners' Federation in their dispute with the coal-owners. Because of the bad state of the coal-mining

The General Strike of 1926. Volunteers drove the buses. *(Mansell Collection)*

industry the government had in 1925 granted the owners a year's subsidy and set up a commission of inquiry under Sir Herbert Samuel. The commission recommended (6 March) that a scheme of reorganisation of the industry be put into operation as soon as practicable. The government subsidy was due to expire in May 1926, and the owners posted notices of this and of their intention not to continue to employ the miners thereafter except at lower rates and for longer hours; but they made no definite proposals until after the expiry of the notices, and then did not include any plans for substantial reorganisation. In consequence the Trades Union Congress called a conference of its constituent unions and reported that it could see no alternative to a general sympathetic strike as a means of furthering the miners' cause. The executives resolved that a strike be called as from midnight 3–4 May.

The vast majority of the organised workers ceased work, though the essential services were partially carried on by volunteers acting upon plans outlined by the government in the light of the experience of the railway strike of 1919 and the miners' strike of 1920. In the absence of newspapers the government took control of the radio, and issued a journal of its own, the *British Gazette*, whilst the TUC published the *British Worker*. Sir Herbert Samuel was invited by a negotiating committee (which included miners' representatives) to interpret certain parts of the report of his commission and to act as mediator. The Samuel memorandum was prepared as a basis of settlement and accepted by the TUC in the belief that it would be acceptable to the government, but when it was presented to the executive of the Miners' Federation they refused its terms, notwithstanding that it had the backing of their own representatives on the negotiating committee. The TUC, feeling that the other unions had gone as far as they could in supporting the miners, advised the executives of its constituent bodies to call the strike off, and it ended inconclusively on 13 May. The miners stayed out for another six months but were eventually driven back to work by starvation. They returned on the owners' terms, to longer hours, lower wages, and district agreements—and the owners did nothing to improve conditions.

The legality or illegality of the General Strike was widely discussed, and Sir John Simon in particular put forward a closely reasoned argument for its illegality. This view found no general support amongst lawyers, and the fact that it was considered necessary to make sympathetic strikes illegal by the Trade Disputes Act (repealed in 1946) appears to afford evidence that the General Strike was not contrary to law. The General Strike involved over 2 million employed persons, and caused the loss of about 162 million working days.

Bibliography: R. P. Arnott, *The Miners*, 1953; A. J. P. Taylor, *English History 1914–1945*, 1965; P. Renshaw, *The General Strike*, 1975; G. A. Phillips, *The General Strike*, 1976.

Strike and Lock-out. A strike is not defined in the UK by law, but is generally taken to be a cessation of work by employed persons acting together, or their refusal to continue work in order to compel their employer(s), or to aid other employed persons to compel their employer(s), to accept or not to accept conditions of employment. A lock-out is the refusal of an employer, by means of closing the place of employment, to continue to employ persons in order to compel them, or to aid other employers to compel persons employed by them, to accept conditions of employment. Strike action is criminally prohibited in respect of the armed forces, the police, and merchant seamen at sea.

In Britain, when a strike or lock-out occurs as part of a trade dispute, as defined by the Trade Union and Labour Relations Act 1974, certain protection is given against some of the commoner legal wrongs which may take place, for instance, in PICKETING.

A trade dispute is defined by the act as a dispute between workers and employers about terms and conditions of work, or about rights in connection with trade union membership (including recognition of a union by the employer) and activity. In other words, it may cover any aspect of the individual employment relationship, including those with unions. Workers include employees, people who work without being employed (e.g. self-employed), and civil servants. Official statistics do not differentiate between strikes of work-people and lock-outs by employers.

The official figures relate to stoppages of work due to disputes connected with terms of employment or conditions of labour. They exclude stoppages involving fewer than ten workers, and those lasting less than one day except any in which the aggregate number of working days lost exceeds 100. The average number of stoppages of work recorded as beginning in each year was 1241 for the years 1919–21, 465 for 1922–32, 735 for 1933–39, 1625 for 1940–45, 1804 for 1946–55, 2514 for 1956–65, and 2610 for 1966–71. The average number of workpeople involved in stoppages in progress in each year was 2,108,000 for the years 1919–21, 607,818 for 1922–32, 295,000 for 1933–39, 492,333 for 1940–45, 557,600 for 1946–55, 1,136,600 for 1956–65, and 1,352,666 for 1966–71.

The average number of working days lost each year was 49·1 million for the years 1919–21, 21·6 million for 1922–32, 1·7 million for 1933–39, 2 million for 1940–45, 2·2 million for 1946–55, 3·8 million for 1956–65, and 6·9 million for 1966–71. The averages for the years 1922–32 include figures for the General Strike of 1926. (See STRIKE, THE GENERAL.)

The record year for strikes, however, was 1972, when 23·9 million days were lost, a total boosted by the national stoppage in the coal-mining industry. In 1973 7·2 million days were lost and in 1974 14·7 million, of which 38 per cent were accounted for by a further miners' strike.

See also INDUSTRIAL RELATIONS; LABOUR DISPUTE; LABOUR LEGISLATION; TRADE DISPUTES ACTS; TRADE UNION.

Strindberg, Johann August (1849–1912), Swedish novelist, dramatist, poet and essayist, born in Stockholm. He studied at Uppsala University, interrupting his career there for financial reasons. From 1874 to 1882 he was an assistant at the Stockholm Royal Library.

Strindberg was an extremely prolific author. His novel *The Red Room*, 1879 (trans. 1913), was acclaimed as Scandinavia's first realist-social novel. He was influenced at this time by DICKENS, the GONCOURTS and possibly FLAUBERT; to these he added his own bitter, penetrating observations on humanity. He adopted much of NIETZSCHE's doctrine, being one of the supreme examples of Idealism, distorted by extreme introspective pessimism. Strindberg was thrice married and divorced; his hatred of women and peculiar conception of paternity, seen in embryo in *The Red Room*, and becoming almost maniacal in the collections of short stories, *Marriages*, 1884, 1885, and the plays *The Father*, 1887 (trans. 1907), and *Miss Julie*, 1888 (trans. 1911), had their origin in his own abnormality and acute inferiority complex, and eventually became an obsession. He spent some time in a mental sanatorium. Strindberg never fully recovered from the breakdown he suffered when prosecuted for blasphemy on the publication of *Marriages*. In later years he turned from Nietzschean Idealism to evolve a religious mysticism, which found expression in the dramatic trilogy *To Damascus*, 1898–1904 (trans. 1933-35). He may have been influenced by SWEDENBORGianism, but dramas such as *The Spook Sonata*, 1907 (trans. 1916), show a dabbling in the psychic and the occult.

Strindberg was Sweden's greatest dramatic artist, and possibly its greatest literary figure. There can be no doubt about the emotional power of his plays, or of their remarkable, if distorted, insight into sexual relations. Nor is their any doubt about the influence of his work on later dramatists, especially the Expressionists. He was a very versatile artist; the years which produced his angry masterpiece, *The Father*, produced also the charming tale, *The Dwellers of Hemsö*, 1887, and he wrote several travel sketches and light essays.

Bibliography: Lives by A. Jolivet, 1931; F. Strindberg, 1936; E. Sprigge, 1949; C. E. W. L. Dahlström, *Strindberg's Dramatic Expressionism*, 1930; B. Mortensen and B. W. Downs, *Strindberg, an introduction to his life and work*, 1949; B. G. Madsen, *Strindberg's Naturalistic Theatre*, 1962; F. L. Lucas, *The Drama of Ibsen and Strindberg*, 1962.

String, see ROPE AND ROPE-MAKING.

Stripes and Chevrons. Devices worn on uniform—usually on the sleeve—have been in use from the earliest times to indicate RANK, skill at arms, and good conduct. They were introduced into the British army in 1802, and since then many different designs have been worn to indicate various attainments. The best known stripes are the V-shaped kind for the ranks of non-commissioned officers. Other devices brought into use from time to time and sometimes discarded are crossed rifles (for expert rifle shots), crossed flags (for qualified signallers), a gold stripe (for each wound in the First World War), a red chevron (to indicate operational service in 1914), and similar blue chevrons for each subsequent year's operational service in the First World War (for naval officers the chevrons were silver and gold respectively). These are the most common of the many devices of this kind which have been worn in the British army. The US army has somewhat similar rank emblems for its NCOs except that they are inverted; they also employ various devices to indicate specialist skills and attainments. In the Royal Navy a good conduct stripe or badge is awarded after four years of good conduct, and every four years thereafter up to a maximum of three. Stripes and chevrons are similarly used in the RAF to indicate rank.

Strobilanthes, a large genus of Acanthaceae, with 250 species. *S. cusia*, growing in South-East Asia, yields a blue dye. *S. dyerianus*, cultivated in Britain, is a dwarf evergreen shrub, with long iridescent leaves, purple beneath, and violet flowers in spikes.

Stroboscope, device for causing a moving object to appear stationary, utilising the optical phenomenon of the stroboscopic effect. The stroboscope consists either of a shutter or of a means of illumination by a series of light flashes, so arranged that any given point, when viewed or illuminated, is in the same position at each occurrence. Machinery in motion is examined by this method. The principle is applied in checking the speed of gramophone turntables; the intermittent illumination is provided by room lighting fed from the alternating mains supply. The stroboscope was developed and named by Simon R. von Stampfer in 1832.

Strode, William (c. 1599–1645), English parliamentarian, educated at Exeter College, Oxford. He entered Parliament in 1624 and retained his seat there until his death. He is remembered as one of the FIVE MEMBERS whom Charles I attempted to arrest in the Commons in 1642.

Stroganov, name of a famous merchant family living in northern Russia. Under Ivan the Terrible the Stroganovs were granted the right to establish saltworks in the Urals; they had their own towns there, with Cossack mercenaries as guards. One of the commanders, YERMAK, conquered the Siberian Khanate for Muscovy in the early 1580s.

Stroheim, Erich von (1885–1957), Austro-American film actor and director, born in Vienna. He emigrated to the USA in 1909 and entered films under D. W. GRIFFITH in 1914. Between 1918 and 1928 he directed eight films of great power; but thereafter his uncompromising methods prevented him from obtaining backing and so he concentrated on film acting, often appearing as Prussian villains. His films include, as director: *Blind Husbands* (1918), *Foolish Wives* (1921), *Greed* (1923), *Merry Widow* (1925), *Wedding March* (1927), *Queen Kelly* (1928, unfinished); and as actor: *Blind Husbands*, *Foolish Wives*, *Wedding March*, *La Grande Illusion* (1937), *Five Graves to Cairo* (1943) and *La Danse de Mort* (1947).

Bibliography: T. C. Curtiss, *Von Stroheim*, 1971; T. Quinn, *Von Stroheim*, 1973.

Stroke, see CEREBRAL HAEMORRHAGE.

Stromboli, see LIPARI ISLANDS.

Stromness, small town, service centre, and seaport on the south-west of MAINLAND, Orkney Islands, Scotland, 22 km west of Kirkwall. Population 1646.

Strømø, or Stremoy, largest of the FAEROE ISLANDS. Area 373 km². Population 15,000.

Strong, Leonard Alfred George (1896–1958), English poet and novelist, born at Plympton, Devon; educated at Plymouth, Brighton, and Wadham College, Oxford, where he worked as a schoolmaster for ten years, then moved to London. His volumes of verse include *Dublin Days*, 1921, *The Lowery Road*, 1924, *At Glenan Cross*, 1928, *Northern Light*, 1930, and *Call to the Swans*, 1936. Among his novels are *Dewer Rides*, 1929, *Sea Wall*,

1933, *Corporal Tune*, 1934, *Mr Sheridan's Umbrella*, 1935, *Laughter in the West*, 1937, *The Bay*, 1941, *The Director*, 1944, and *Trevannion*, 1948.

Strongbow, name of Richard de Clare, 2nd Earl of Pembroke (d. 1176), an English noble who joined Dermot, King of Leinster, in the latter's recovery of his kingdom from the King of Connaught, married his daughter, and succeeded him. In 1172 he acknowledged Henry II's overlordship. He did much to increase English power in Ireland.

Stronsay, island in the Orkney group, Scotland. It is 10 km long and up to 8 km wide. Agriculture is the main industry. Population 436.

Strontium, metallic chemical element, symbol Sr, atomic number 38, atomic weight 87·6; one of the ALKALINE EARTHS. It occurs in nature as strontianite ($SrCO_3$) and celestine ($SrSO_4$). The metal is obtained by the electrolysis of the fused chloride. It is a white metal with a low relative density (2·6), chemically similar to, though more reactive than, calcium. It readily oxidises in air and decomposes in water at ordinary temperatures. Heated in hydrogen it forms a hydride (SrH_2) which when heated *in vacuo* yields pure strontium. Two oxides of strontium are known, the monoxide and peroxide. The monoxide, strontia, slakes like lime, forming strontium hydroxide ($Sr(OH)_2$). Excepting the sulphate, carbonate, and phosphate, the salts of strontium are soluble in water. They impart a crimson colour to flame, and are therefore used in pyrotechny. The hydroxide is largely used in the manufacture of beet sugar. The isotope of atomic weight 90 has become of great general importance on account of its toxic effects associated with radioactive fall out. Because of its similarity to calcium, radioactive strontium replaces calcium in animal and human bones, and its radioactive decay causes leukaemia.

Strood, a Medway town in Kent, England. A canal was opened in 1824 but was unsuccessful. The 13th-century Temple Manor House is open to the public. Population (1971) 6145.

Strophanthus, a genus of the Apocynaceae (periwinkle family), the species of which are found from southern Africa to China. There are over 60 of these, and they consist of small trees or shrubs bearing peculiar flowers which have long thread-like lobes on their petals. *S. hispidus* yields the poison strophanthin and the seeds have been used to stimulate the action of the heart. *S. sarmentosus* yields an acid from which CORTISONE may be produced.

Strophe (Greek, turning), section or stanza of a Greek choral ode, sung by the chorus as they moved in one direction, and followed by the ANTISTROPHE when they moved back in the other direction.

Strossmayer, Josef Georg (1815–1905), Austrian Roman Catholic bishop, born at Eszek, educated at Budapest and Vienna. Ordained in 1838, he was shortly afterwards appointed professor at the Diakovar Seminary, and consecrated bishop of Bosnia and Sirmio. He worked for the development of Croatian literature, and established the unity of Agram (1874) and other cultural centres. He opposed the opportuneness of a definition of papal infallibility in the Vatican Council. He wrote *Monumenta Slavorum meridionalium*, 1863.

Stroud, town in GLOUCESTERSHIRE, England, 13 km south-east of Gloucester. For many centuries broadcloth and scarlet-dyed cloth have been made in the neighbourhood. There are also breweries, engineering works, woollen and cloth mills, saw-mills and factories making plastics and fibre board. Population (1971) 19,152.

Structural Formula, in chemistry, a formula expanded in such a way as to represent the relative arrangements of the atoms in a molecule. Thus the structural formula of alcohol, C_2H_6O, is $CH_3 \cdot CH_2 \cdot OH$. Further expansion gives a graphic formula, e.g.

$$\begin{array}{ccccc} & H & & H & \\ & | & & | & \\ H - & C & - & C & - O - H. \\ & | & & | & \\ & H & & H & \end{array}$$

See FORMULA.

Structural Geology, the study of individual structures such as FOLDS, FAULTS, and LINEATIONS within rock units. The structures seen within a rock unit may be of primary or secondary origin; primary structures are those developed during the original formation of the rock, and include depositional textures such as graded bedding and depositional structures such as load casts and worm burrows. These features are classed as sedimentary structures; by far the greater part of structural geology is concerned with the secondary structures, which are those developed when the rock is deformed by forces acting in the earth's crust. Rock structures include the effects of plastic yielding, as in the case of folding, and of fracturing, as in the formation of faults and JOINTS.

Two quite different methods are used to illustrate the various structures that may be present in rocks. Firstly, the major structures such as folds, faults, and joints may be described and plotted on a geological map or illustrated by means of cross-sections and block-diagrams of the strata. Secondly, the geometry of the rock structures may be plotted on a statistical basis; the attitude of such features as joint planes, cleavage, and dip are recorded and plotted on fabric diagrams. A statistical analysis of the fabric of a rock can then be made.

The structural geology of a particular area may be seen as part of the broader framework of the regional structural geology, and this is the study of GEOTECTONICS.

Bibliography: E. H. Whitten, *Structural Geology of Folded Rocks*, 1971; M. K. Hubbert, *Structural Geology*, 1973.

Structural Linguistics, see BLOOMFIELD, LEONARD; GRAMMAR; LINGUISTICS.

Structural Steelwork, a form of construction in which the main strength lies in the steelwork. The advantages of this method include tensile strength and erection speed; the disadvantages include corrosion liability and low resistance to fire damage unless suitably encased. Tall buildings may be constructed from hot rolled Universal columns and beams which are joined by welds or high strength bolts. The British Steel Corporation makes a wide range of mild steel beams with Universal I cross-

Structural Steelwork. A large Nodus roof covering the Alton indoor sports centre, England. *(British Steel Corporation)*

sections proportioned to give adequate bending strength in the flanges of the I with enough thickness of the web to transmit shearing forces to the supports without buckling. Light industrial and farm buildings may be constructed from Universal sections to give pitched portals (two columns with two sloping rafters) with clear unobstructed spans to support the external cladding. The ductility of the steel provides a useful reserve for impact damage from tractors, or for settlement of hastily prepared foundations.

Hot rolled hollow rectangular-section steel members are used where their superior performance under twisting loads and their pleasing appearance compensate for their extra cost. Space frames such as the 54- × 38-metre Nodus roof illustrated achieve lightness and grace by the use of slender tubes. Geodesic and other forms of domed roofs are made from hollow sections to give large-span roofs over markets and sports stadia.

Composite construction may be regarded as a logical development of the practice of encasing steel in concrete for fire protection. This concrete is now regarded as having a structural purpose which utilises its compressive strength. The two materials are made to act compositely by shear connectors on the steel surfaces in contact with the concrete; the shear connectors may be studs welded on by an automatic electric stud-welding process, in which the passage of a very large current fuses the stud to the steel.

Advice on the use of structural steel may be obtained from organisations associated with the steel industry such as the British Constructional Steelwork Association and the Constructional Steelwork Research and Development Association.

Bibliography: British Standards Institution, Code of Practice 117:1965 *Composite construction in structural steel and concrete*; British Standard 449:1969 *The use of structural steel in building*, and Addenda No. 1:1975; British Standard 4:Part I:1972 *Hot-rolled sections*, and Part II:1969 *Hot-rolled hollow sections*; British Standard 4360:1972 *Weldable structural steels*.

Structuralism, a method of analysis used in many disci-

plines, ranging from mathematics and physics to the social sciences, and even to literature and the history of art. It has gained much renown, especially in France, in recent years with the works of the anthropologist, Claude LÉVI-STRAUSS. The term was first used by the Vienna school of linguists in the 1920s, but the works of Karl Marx, Sigmund Freud, and Albert Einstein have much in common with structuralism.

The structuralist does not analyse entities, but the relationship with other atomic particles. Models, or structures, of such relationships are then constructed by logical deduction from first principles. The elements of a structure are of the same kind, hence a structure is a system. Furthermore, structures are not empirical realities, but theoretical constructions which attempt to explain empirical phenomena: no physicist has ever seen an atom, yet this does not prevent his model of the structure of the atom from going a long way to explain atomic phenomena and, when applied to technology, it generates many new developments. By altering some of the elements of the structure, a transformation is obtained. This may account for other phenomena that were not previously considered to be related to the first (see TOTEM-ISM); on the other hand, no empirical example may be found to correspond to the transformation, and the structuralist has then to account for this.

This approach to science is very different from many of the approaches followed in the 18th and 19th centuries, which were empiricist and inductivist. Many practitioners of the social sciences today, however, reject the idea that structuralism can be applied to their disciplines, and seriously doubt whether they can be called 'sciences' in the same way as such sciences as physics and chemistry.

See also ANTHROPOLOGY; EMPIRICISM; LINGUISTICS.

Bibliography: A. Einstein, *Autobiographical Notes* in P. A. Schlipp (Ed.), *Albert Einstein: Philosopher-Scientist*, 1959; F. de Saussure, *General Course in Linguistics*, 1960; N. Chomsky, *Cartesian Linguistics*, 1966; R. Barthes, *Elements of Semiology*, 1967; L. Althusser and E. Balibar, *Reading 'Capital'*, 1970; M. Lane (Ed.), *Structuralism, a reader*, 1970; J. Piaget, *Structuralism*, 1971; C. Lévi-Strauss, *Structural Anthropology*, 1972; M. Godelier, *Horizons, Trajets Marxistes*, 1974.

Struensee, Johann Friedrich, Count (1737–72), German-Danish statesman, born at Halle in Saxony. In 1768 he was appointed physician to CHRISTIAN VII, King of Denmark, whom he accompanied on his tour to Germany, France, and England. In 1771 he became minister of state, and carried out many reforms. His policy, foreign birth, and liaison with Queen CAROLINE MATILDA brought about his downfall, and he was executed for treason.

Struma (Greek *Strymon*), river of Bulgaria and Greece. It rises in the Vitosha Mountains in SOFIA province, and flows south-east for 346 km to the Aegean Sea. It provides Sofia with a natural outlet to the Aegean.

Strumica, town and district in Macedonia, Yugoslavia, in the valley of the River Strumica. It has a trade in agricultural produce and tobacco. Population 16,000.

Strutt, John William, see RAYLEIGH, JOHN WILLIAM STRUTT, 3RD BARON.

Strutt, Robert John, see RAYLEIGH, ROBERT JOHN STRUTT, 4TH BARON.

Struve, family whose members were distinguished astronomers for four generations. Friedrich Georg Wilhelm von Struve (1793–1864), born at Altona, Germany, was director of the observatory at Dorpat in Russia (now Tartu, Estonia, USSR), 1820–39; in 1839 he supervised the construction of the new central observatory at Pulkovo, near St Petersburg, of which he was director until 1861. He is best known for his pioneer work in measuring and cataloguing double stars, and for the measurement of the parallax of Vega, in 1837. One of his 18 children, Otto Wilhelm von Struve (1819–1905), born at Dorpat, was his father's assistant at Pulkovo from 1839, and became director, 1862–90.

Two sons of Otto Wilhelm became astronomers: Karl Hermann von Struve (1854–1920), born at Pulkovo, founded the Berlin-Babelsberg observatory in 1913; Ludvig von Struve (1858–1920), born at Pulkovo, was professor of astronomy at Kharkov University.

A son of Ludvig, Otto Struve (1897–1963), born at Kharkov, fought with the White Russian army, escaped to the USA as a refugee in 1921, and obtained a post at Yerkes Observatory near Chicago. He was director at Yerkes, 1932–39; founded the McDonald Observatory of the University of Texas and was its director, 1939–47; returned to Chicago in 1947; was director of the Leuschner Observatory of the University of California, 1950–59; and was first director of the National Radio Astronomy Observatory, 1959–62. He was most prolific and published over 500 papers on many aspects of stellar spectroscopy, stellar rotation, binary stars, and interstellar gas. He was a great popular writer, an ardent internationalist, and president of the International Astronomical Union, 1952–55. His publications include *Stellar Evolution*, 1950; *The Universe*, 1962; (with B. Lynds and H. Pillans), *Elementary Astronomy*, 1959; and (with V. Zerbergs), *Astronomy of the 20th Century*, 1962.

Struve, Pëtr Berngardovich (1870–1944), Soviet economist, sociologist and politician of German descent. In the 1890s he was the leading Marxist theorist in Russia (see LEGAL MARXISTS), and in 1898 drafted the manifesto of the Russian Social Democratic Workers' party. He soon left Social Democracy and became leader of the constitutional movement of the liberal intelligentsia (see ZEMSTVO), editing, in the years 1902–05, its journal, *Liberation*, which was published abroad. In 1905 he returned to Russia and joined the Constitutional Democratic party (see CONSTITUTIONAL DEMOCRATS). In 1907 he became a member of the Second DUMA. He took a leading part in the VEKHI movement and advocated the co-operation of liberals with the government. During the civil war (see CIVIL WAR, RUSSIAN) he was minister of foreign affairs in Gen. Wrangel's government in the Crimea. Later he emigrated and was prominent in the activities of the moderate Right. Struve's two main works, *Economy and Price*, 2 vols, 1913–16, and *Social and Economic History of Russia*, 1952, are available only in Russian.

Bibliography: P. B. Struve, 'Medieval Agrarian Society in its Prime: Russia' in *The Cambridge Economic History of Europe*, vol. 1, 1941; G. Fischer, *Russian Liberalism*.

Strychnine, an alkaloid occurring in *Strychnos nux-vomica, S. colubrina, S. ignatii, S. icaja* and other trees of the same genus (see below). The alkaloid is contained with brucine in the bark, leaves, seeds and root. Strychnine is a crystalline solid, insoluble in water, but soluble in alcohol and chloroform. It has an alkaline reaction and a bitter taste; optically it is laevo-rotatory. Strychnine, usually in the form of a more soluble salt, has long been used, with or without iron, as a bitter tonic or stimulant, but there is no evidence that it is particularly effective. It has been given as a respiratory stimulant especially in the treatment of poisoning by depressants of the central nervous system. It should not be used as a laxative due to its toxicity.

Strychnine in larger doses acts as a powerful poison. The symptoms of poisoning commence with a stiff neck, then the patient is seized with tetanic convulsions, the muscles being contracted for a minute at a time; often the body is thrown into the form of an arch, the patient resting on his head and heels. A volatile anaesthetic should be rapidly administered until it is possible to give an intravenous dose of a barbiturate and a muscle relaxant such as curare. The patient should be kept in complete darkness. An emetic should not be given. See POISONS.

Strychnos, a genus of 200 tropical plants of the family Strychnaceae. Most are poisonous. *S. nux-vomica* is an Indian tree containing several alkaloids, the chief of which are STRYCHNINE and brucine. *S. toxifera* of South America yields CURARE used as an arrow poison and for relaxing muscles in surgery.

Strydom, Johannes Gerhardus, see STRIJDOM, JOHANNES GERHARDUS.

Stuart, Arabella, or Arbella (1575–1615), only child of Charles Stuart, Duke of Lennox, grandson of Margaret Tudor and younger brother of Henry, Lord Darnley, the father of James I and VI. James and she, therefore, were cousins, and she was, before the birth of his son, Henry, in February 1594, next to James in succession to the English throne. Her name was brought forward in 1603 in the affair of the alleged plot for which Sir Walter RALEIGH was tried. One of the charges against Raleigh was that he

Lady Arabella Stuart, an anonymous portrait. (*National Portrait Gallery, London*)

designed to raise the Lady Arabella to the throne, under the protection of Spain. There is no probability that any such design was ever seriously contemplated. Her situation, however, was difficult and dangerous, particularly after her secret marriage in 1610 to William Seymour. Seymour was the grandson of Lady Catherine Grey and, hence, had a claim to the throne under Henry VIII's will. Seymour escaped and reached Flanders in safety. Arabella also escaped but was recaptured and imprisoned in the Tower, where she died insane.

Bibliography: P. M. Handover, *Arabella Stuart*, 1957.

Stuart, Charles Edward Louis Philip Casimir (1720–88), known as the 'Young Pretender' and 'Bonnie Prince Charlie', the elder son of the Chevalier de St George, the 'Old Pretender', born in Rome. He served in the wars of the Polish and Austrian Succession, distinguishing himself when very young at Gaeta (1734) and Dettingen (1743). In 1743 he headed an unsuccessful French invasion of England, but in 1745 succeeded in landing at Eriskay in the Hebrides. Marching southwards, he entered Edinburgh and held his court at Holyrood. He defeated Cope at Prestonpans. With a troop of 6500 men he invaded England, and marched as far south as Derby, when his advisers, seeing no prospect of success, urged him to retreat to Scotland. There he was again victorious at Falkirk (1746), but was overwhelmed by the Duke of Cumberland at CULLODEN, and for many months hid in

Charles Stuart, the Young Pretender. *(Scottish National Portrait Gallery, Edinburgh)*

the Highlands with a price of £30,000 on his head. Before the end of the year he escaped to France, from where he was expelled in 1748. He spent the remainder of his life wandering in Europe, living for some time in Rome, and became a drunkard. He married Louisa von Stolberg in 1772, but the marriage was extremely unhappy and childless. See also MACDONALD, FLORA; STUART, JAMES FRANCIS EDWARD.

Bibliography: E. R. R. Linklater, *The Prince in the Heather*, 1965; D. Daiches, *Charles Stuart*, 1973; M. Forster, *The Rash Adventurer*, 1973.

Stuart, Francis (1902–), Irish novelist, born in Queensland, Australia, of Irish parents. Educated at Rugby, in England, in 1920 he went to live in Dublin and was converted to Roman Catholicism. He fought in the Irish civil war, was interned in 1922, and afterwards settled in County Wicklow.

Stuart's volume of poems, *We Have Kept the Faith*, 1923, was awarded a prize by the Royal Irish Academy. From 1939 to 1944 he was a lecturer in English at the University of Berlin. His novels include *Women and God*, 1931, *Pigeon Irish*, 1932, *The Coloured Dome*, 1932, *Try the Sky*, 1933, *Glory*, 1933, *In Search of Love*, 1935, *The White Hare*, 1936, *Julie*, 1938, *The Great Squire*, 1939, *The Pillar of Cloud*, 1948, *Redemption*, 1949, *The Flowering Cross*, 1950, *The Chariot*, 1953, *The Pilgrimage*, 1955, *Angels of Providence*, 1959, *Blacklist Section H*, 1972, and *Memorial*, 1973. *Things To Live For*, 1935, is autobiographical.

Stuart, Gilbert (1755–1828), American portrait painter, born in Rhode Island. He went to England in 1775, studying under Benjamin WEST. After working in London and Dublin (1778–93) he returned to America to paint George Washington (several versions existing) and portrayed many other distinguished Americans.

Stuart, Henry Benedict Maria Clement, Cardinal York (1725–1807), last of the Stuarts, the second son of James Stuart, the 'Old Pretender', born in Rome. He went to France in 1745 to support his brother, Charles Edward, and after his return to Italy was created cardinal deacon with the title of York by Pope Benedict XIV. In the following year he was ordained priest and nominated arch-priest of St Peter's. In 1759 he was consecrated as titular Archbishop of Corinth, in 1761 appointed Archbishop of Frascati, and in 1763 vice-chancellor of St Peter's. On the death of his brother in 1788 the Cardinal styled himself 'Henry IX, not by the will of men, but by the Grace of God' but no other ruler, not even the Pope, acknowledged his title. In 1799 he accepted from George III an annual pension of £4000. In 1803, as senior cardinal bishop, he became dean of the Sacred College and Bishop of Ostia and Velletri. He died in Rome and was buried in St Peter's, leaving to the Prince of Wales certain crown jewels.

Bibliography: B. Fothergill, *The Cardinal King*, 1958.

Stuart, House of, see STEWART.

Stuart, James Francis Edward (1688–1766), Prince of Wales, commonly styled the 'Chevalier de St George', and later known as the 'Old Pretender', the son of JAMES II by his second wife, Mary of Modena. His birth precipitated the revolution of 1688. In 1701 James II died and

James Stuart, the 'Old Pretender'. Portrait by F. de Troy. (Scottish National Portrait Gallery, Edinburgh)

his son was accepted by the JACOBITES as king of England and Scotland under the style of James III. He served with distinction in the French army before the Peace of Utrecht, and in 1715 went to Scotland to take part in the unsuccessful Jacobite rising. He married Maria Clementina Sobieski in 1719 and was the father of Charles Edward STUART, the 'Young Pretender'. The rising of 1745 was the last attempt to secure his restoration.

Bibliography: P. Miller, *James: Old Pretender,* 1971.

Stuart, John, see BUTE, JOHN STUART, 3RD EARL OF.

Stuartia, see STEWARTIA.

Stubbs, George (1724–1806), British painter born in Liverpool. He served an artist's apprenticeship, but studied anatomy, and even lectured at York hospital. He is famous for sporting or animal pictures, and scenes of rural life, e.g. *Gimcrack,* c. 1765 (Private Collection); *Mares and Foals,* c. 1763 (Tate Gallery); *The Reapers,* 1784 (Private Collection). He was also in demand as a portrait painter, especially of family groups. Stubbs published *The Anatomy of the Horse,* 1766, illustrated by his own engravings, and experimented in working in enamel on copper, or china plaques provided by the Wedgwood potteries. He became an RA elect in 1780, but never a full member.

Bibliography: B. Taylor, *Stubbs,* 1971.

Stubbs, Philip, or Stubbes (c. 1555–c. 1610), English Puritan pamphleteer. In 1583 he published *The Anatomie of Abuses,* which involved him in the MARPRELATE CONTROVERSY.

Stubbs, William (1825–1901), British historian and churchman, born at Knaresborough, and educated at Ripon Grammar School and Christ Church, Oxford. In 1866 he became regius professor of modern history at Oxford. In 1884 he was consecrated bishop of Chester, and three years later translated to the see of Oxford. His chief publication, *Constitutional History of England,* 1873–78, is a work of monumental scholarship. His *Select Charters and other Illustrations of English Constitutional History from the Earliest Times to the reign of Edward I,* 1870, has been published in many editions and he contributed valuable introductions to the Rolls series of 19 volumes of chronicles. Stubbs's work gave a new direction to the study of medieval English history and continues to have considerable influence, particularly in the teaching of history at Oxford.

Stucco, Italian word applied in most languages to PLASTER of any kind used as a coating for walls to give them a finished appearance. The term now covers smooth lime/sand plastering applied to the exterior face of a wall.

Studites, Greek monks belonging to the reformed order founded at Constantinople by St Theodore of the Studium, who died in 826. The Studites were the first monks to establish themselves on Mount Athos. The Studite reform was comparable in its widespread effects to the later Cluniac reform in the West.

Stuffing, see TAXIDERMY.

Stuhlweissenburg, see SZÉKESFÉHERVÁR.

Stukeley, William (1687–1765), English antiquary, friend of Isaac NEWTON, tutee of Dr Mead, a founder of the Society of Antiquaries and its first secretary. An exponent of neo-Druidism, he published *Stonehenge, a Temple Restor'd to the British Druids,* 1740, and *Abury* (AVEBURY), 1743.

Bibliography: S. Piggott, *William Stukeley, an Eighteenth century Antiquary,* 1950; A. L. Owen, *The Famous Druids: A Survey of Three Centuries of English Literature on the Druids,* 1962.

Stupa (Sanskrit, mound), Buddhist monument erected to commemorate, or enshrine relics of, the Buddha or his disciples. The stupa is usually in the form of a tumulus of masonry shaped like a dome or tower, and often surrounded by an elaborately carved stone railing with lofty gateways at the cardinal points. When intended for the preservation of relics it is called a *dagoba* (see PAGODA). There are numerous examples in India and South-East Asia, which archaeologists date between 200 BC and modern times. The oldest are dome-shaped and are built on cylindrical or polygonal bases which rise in terraces. The most noteworthy is at Sanchi, near Bhopal, but the village of Amaravati in the Krishna district of Madras has one of the finest Buddhist monuments in India. One of the largest of the terraced kind is at Manikyala (Pakistan), a plain hemisphere in form. A number of fine stupas remain in use in Sri Lanka. A feature of the stupa form is the structure of the cone or apex, which is shaped like an open umbrella and called the *chatri* or *tee* (Burmese *hti*).

See also INDIA, *Architecture.*

Bibliography: H. Goetz, *Art of the World* (Vol. 1, *India*), 1959.

Stupor, the state of partial unconsciousness in which the patient can be roused by pain or may respond vaguely to questions. The deeper state of UNCONSCIOUSNESS, in which nothing rouses the patient, is COMA.

Štúr, L'udovit (1815–56), Slovak poet and scholar, who followed the ideas of Slav reciprocity propagated by KOLLÁR. He virtually created the Slovak literary language, a construction based on central Slovak dialects, and published his Slovak grammar in 1846. In the 1848 revolution he led the Slovak armed uprising. Štúr was more a poetic theorist than a poet; he published only one collection, *Songs and Lyrics*, 1853, and wrote more in Czech than Slovak.

Bibliography: H. Tourtzer, *L'udovit Štúr et l'idée de l'indépendance slovaque*, 1913.

Sture, Sten, name of two regents of Sweden.

Sten Sture the Elder (1440–1503) raised levies from the peasants and twice defeated CHRISTIAN I of Denmark, the second time (1471) at the battle of Brunkeberg. He was finally obliged to acknowledge the suzerainty of JOHN II, King of Denmark and Norway (1483).

Sten Sture the Younger (1492–1520) was the son of Svante Nilsson, regent of Sweden (d. 1512). His brief but stormy rule was occupied with the humiliation of his rival, Archbishop Trolle, whom he immured in a monastery after capturing his stronghold of Stäkket (1516), and, further, with two great battles against CHRISTIAN II of Denmark; at Brännkurka (1518) he was victorious, but during the second, fought near Bogesund, he was killed.

Sturgeon, any fish in the family Acipenseridae of the infra-class Chondrostei. They are large and have elongated bodies, bearing five rows of large bony projections; the mouth is small, has no teeth, and in front of it are four barbels. Sturgeon are voracious feeders on small animals and plants. CAVIARE is sturgeon roe (eggs), and ISINGLASS is made from the swimbladders of several Russian and American species. Of the 20 or so species only *Acipenser sturio* is occasionally found off British coasts. The sturgeon is a royal fish; any specimen caught off the British coast must first be offered to the monarch.

Sturla Thórdarson (1214–84), Icelandic historian and poet, nephew of SNORRI STURLUSON. He was the author of one version of *Landnámabók* (see LANDNÁMABÓK), the greater part of *Sturlunga saga*, and other sagas. Several of his poems have been preserved.

Sturluson, Snorri, see SNORRI STURLUSON.

Sturm, Jacques Charles François (1803–55), Swiss mathematician, born in Geneva. He was tutor to the son of Mme de Staël, and in 1823 went to Paris. In 1829 he discovered the theorem which is named after him. This theorem completes the resolution of equations of any degree by an intermediate determination of the number of real roots lying between two given limits. With Colladon he measured the velocity of sound in water by using a bell submerged in Lake Geneva. He became professor at the École polytechnique in 1838. His *Cours d'analyse* (Course on analysis) and *Cours de mécanique* (Course on mechanics) at the École polytechnique were published posthumously in 1857–59 and 1861 and were widely used as textbooks.

Sturm und Drang, see GERMAN LITERATURE.

Sturmius, Saint (d. 779), first German to become a Benedictine, a favourite disciple of St Boniface. He chose the site of Fulda, and became abbot there. He was regarded as second only to St Boniface as apostle of Germany. Sturmius was canonised in 1139; his feast is on 17 December.

Sturt, Charles (1795–1869), Australian explorer, born in India, served in the Peninsular War, and migrated to Australia in 1826. On his first expedition in 1828 he traced the course of the inland rivers of New South Wales. The next year he followed the River MURRUMBIDGEE to its junction with the MURRAY and then the Murray to its mouth in Lake Alexandrina, solving the problem of where the inland rivers flowed. In 1844 he set out from Adelaide and, going north-west, penetrated to the centre of Australia. His contribution to the knowledge of the inland of Australia was of great importance, for it opened the way for rapid expansion of settlement inland.

Bibliography: J. H. L. Cumpston, *Charles Sturt: His Life and Journeys of Exploration*, 1951.

Sturtevant, Edgar Howard (1875–1952), US linguist, born at Jacksonville, Illinois. A student of BUCK, he eventually became professor of linguistics at Yale (1927). He began his career as a classicist, but is perhaps better known for his work in the fields of general linguistics and Hittite studies. He propounded the theory, not now generally accepted, that Hittite was not a branch of Indo-European, but a 'cousin', that is, that Hittite and Indo-European were two branches of an 'Indo-Hittite' group of languages, and contributed to the 'laryngeal theory' in *The Indo-Hittite Laryngeals*, 1942.

Among his books are *Linguistic Change*, 1917, *The Pronunciation of Greek and Latin*, 1920, revised edition 1940, *A Comparative Grammar of the Hittite Language*, 1933, revised edition 1951, and *An Introduction to Linguistic Science*, 1947.

Bibliography: Obituary and bibliography in *Language* 28, 1952.

Stuttering, see STAMMERING AND STUTTERING.

Stuttgart, city of south-west Germany, capital of the *Land* of BADEN-WÜRTTEMBERG. It is situated in a natural basin, open only towards the Neckar, which flows through the suburb of Bad Cannstatt. The surrounding area has numerous orchards and vineyards. The city owes its name to a stud farm which is mentioned as existing here in the 12th century. In 1482 it was made the provincial capital of the counts of Württemberg, but its fortunes declined after the Thirty Years' War. Its modern importance dates from the raising of WÜRTTEMBERG to the status of a kingdom in 1806. The city was heavily bombed during the Second World War. Stuttgart has three Gothic churches, one of which, the Stiftskirche, dates from the 12th–15th centuries. The old palace (13th-century, rebuilt 1553–78) now houses the provincial museum of Württemberg. The *Liederhalle*, and the *rathaus* with its 68-m high tower are two notable modern buildings in the city, which has long been known for its parks and gardens. There are two universities as well as several colleges of the arts and sciences. Stuttgart is one of the leading industrial cities of the country, employing 160,000 people in over 500 firms. Its manufactures include electrical goods (Bosch, Standard, AEG, IBM, Bauknecht), cars (Daimler-Benz, Porsche), metallurgical goods, optical instruments, clothing, and food industries. It is a banking and major exhibition centre. It is also a noted publishing centre. The area exports a large amount of wine and also bottled mineral water. HEGEL was a native of Stuttgart, and SCHILLER was a student in the city. Population (1974) 613,000.

Stuyvesant, Peter (1592–1672), Dutch colonial governor who became director-general of the New Netherlands in 1646, until the surrender of New Amsterdam (New York) to the English in 1644. He spent his later years in New York, and his farm (Bouwerij) gave its name to the Bowery.

Styal, village 2 km north-west of Wilmslow, Greater Manchester. The village and 100-ha estate in the Bollin valley were given to the National Trust in 1939, to preserve as an example of an early industrial community. Quarry Bank Cotton Mill was built in 1784, and the remainder of Styal village shortly after this.

Stye (also sty) or hordeolum, an inflammation of the modified sweat glands between the eyelashes, or of the hair follicles of the eyelashes themselves. Strictly speaking, a hordeolum is an inflammation of the gland and a stye is an inflammation of the hair follicle. It commences with a hardening of the skin about the part, followed by swelling and soreness. Suppuration of the lower layers of the skin follows and the central core subsequently sloughs off. Hot fomentations tend to ease inflammation.

Style, Old and New, of dates, see CALENDAR.

Stylites, see SIMEON STYLITES, SAINT.

Stylobate, see ORDERS OF ARCHITECTURE.

Styrax, a genus of shrubs and trees, chiefly deciduous, in the family Styracaceae, with about 100 species. *S. japonica*, of Japan, is hardy for British gardens; *S. benzoin*, of Sumatra, is the source of benzoin, a drug that forms part of 'Friar's Balsam'.

Styrene, $CH_2:CHC_6H_5$, vinyl benzene, formed by the thermal unsaturation of ethylbenzene. Styrene is the monomer for the plastic polystyrene. Styrene is a colourless liquid with boiling point 145 °C.

$$CH_3CH_2C_6H_5 \xrightarrow{500\,°C} CH_2{=}CHC_6H_5$$

ethylbenzene   *styrene*

Styria (German *Steiermark*), province of south-east AUSTRIA, bordered on the east by Hungary and on the south by Yugoslavia. It was part of the Roman province of NORICUM. In the 6th century there was an influx of Slovenes, and in 1056 the district came into the possession of the Margraves of Steyr. It became Austrian in 1192, ceded to Ottakar II of Bohemia in 1260, and to the HAPSBURGS in 1276. Before the First World War it was a duchy and crown land of Austria. The Styrian districts, occupied by Slovenes, went to Yugoslavia in 1919 (see ST GERMAIN-EN-LAYE, TREATY OF; TRIANON, TREATY OF), and Yugoslavia made further claims after the Second World War. The province is mountainous, containing the outlying ranges of the eastern Alps (Dachstein, 2996 m), and it is bisected west–east by the valleys of the Mur and Mürz. The other main river is the Enns. The Alpine slopes are mainly forested, and forestry is a major industry

although the economy of the province has always been dependent on its minerals, for example iron ore and brown coal. Agriculture employs more than 40 per cent of the working population. There are large iron and steel works at DONAUWITZ-LEOBEN. The capital is GRAZ. Area 16,385 km². Population (1971) 1,192,100.

Styx (Greek, hateful), river of Peloponnesus, rising in the mountains near Nonacris, in northern Arcadia, and falling 185 m sheer down a rock into a ravine. From this point it was supposed by the ancients to flow round the underworld (see CHARON). When the gods swore by Styx they dared not break the oath, under pain of a year's unconsciousness and nine years' exile. To mortal oathbreakers its waters (which, as in the case of immortals, were drunk at the time of swearing) were deadly poison. The tradition originated probably in some form of trial by ordeal. The nymph of Styx was said to dwell at the entrance to Hades, in a grotto supported by silver columns. She was the mother of NIKE.

Suakin, decaying seaport of the Sudan, situated partly on an island in the Red Sea near the coast, with which it is connected by a causeway. It has been superseded by PORT SUDAN, and is now used for the coasting trade only. It has railway communication with Berber, Port Sudan, and Atbara.

Suarès, André, pseudonym of Gélix-André-Yves Scantrel (1868–1948), French writer, born at Vallon-de-l'Oriol (Bouches-du-Rhône). He wrote poetry, *Rêves de l'ombre*, 1937, and plays, in particular *La Tragédie d'Élektre et d'Oreste*, 1905, and *Cressida*, 1914, but most of his work consists of essays and critical writings, including *Images de la grandeur*, 1901, *Voici l'homme*, 1906, *Bouclier du Zodiaque*, 1908, *Sur la vie* (three volumes), 1909–12, *Le Voyage de Condotiere*, in three volumes (*Vers Venise*), 1910, *Fiorenza*, 1932, *Sienne, la bien aimée*, 1932, *Tolstoï vivant*, 1911, and *Trois hommes: Pascal, Ibsen, Dostoievski*, 1912.

Suarez, Francisco (1548–1617), Spanish philosopher and theologian, born at Granada; educated at Salamanca, where he entered the Society of Jesus in 1564. He wrote his first work, *De Verbo Incarnato*, in 1590, noted for its attempts to reconcile the Thomist view of the Redemption as the final cause of the Incarnation with that of DUNS SCOTUS. Suarez was appointed professor of theology at Coimbra in 1597, where he lectured until 1616. He was an adherent of Thomas Aquinas but was opposed by strict Dominican Thomists for tending towards Molinism (see MOLINA, LUIS). His *Defensio fidei* attacked the doctrine of a divine right of kings and the English oath of allegiance in particular. His collected works were published in 26 volumes (1856–61), and a selection by J. B. Scott (1944). Suarez is considered the greatest Jesuit theologian and his opinions on many dogmatic questions continued to have importance in modern theological schools.

Sub-Carpathian Russia, official name of TRANSCARPATHIA from 1919 to 1939 when it was part of Czechoslovakia.

Subiaco, Italian town in LAZIO, overlooking the valley of the Aniene, 50 km east of Rome. The town appears to have grown up since the founding of the first Benedictine monasteries in the vicinity. Of these the most interesting are San Benedetto, founded in 505, which surrounds the cave in which St Benedict took refuge, and Santa Scolastica, founded in 981, which in the 11th century ranked as a principality, and which preserves a book from the first printing press in Italy, established here in 1464. Population (1974) 6800.

Subinfeudation, see LAND LAWS.

Subject and Subjective. *Subject* means the mind as knowing something or as affected by a thing, while *object* is that which is known or which affects the mind in a certain way. Mind may be known in a direct, internal, or subjective way, by directing attention to what is going on in the mind at the time of its occurrence or afterwards. This is known as *introspection*, or the method of internal or *subjective* observation. On the other hand, the mental phenomena of other people can be studied only indirectly by observing their speech or behaviour. This constitutes the external, indirect, or *objective* method of observation. So, for example, a knowledge of others' thoughts may be arrived at by their speech, or conclusions as to their motives by noticing their action. Both methods possess difficulties. To withdraw attention from the more striking events of the external world and to fix it on the more obscure events of the inner world is obviously difficult; and the existence of unconscious motives, posited by psychoanalysis, brings into question the validity of any conclusions. On the other hand, external observation risks serious misinterpretation because of the multiplicity of possible motives, even where no element of evasion or deception is present. The two approaches have a parallel in psychology: the Freudian and other schools of psychoanalysis operate on the basis of introspective material supplied by the patient, while behaviourists and psychiatrists are more concerned with the pattern of his actions.

Subjectivism, in philosophy, is the opposite of objectivism. The latter holds that there is an objective order existing independently of the person who seeks to know it. By contrast, subjectivism denies that there is such an independent order. Moreover, the subjectivist would argue that even if there were such an order, we could never know that there was. The most extreme form of subjectivism is solipsism, the view that a person can assert the existence only of himself. Idealist philosophy may be objective, as in Hegel, or subjective, as in the epistemology of Berkeley.

Subleyras, Pierre (1699–1749), French painter, born in Provence. He studied painting under his father, and under Antoine Rivalz of Toulouse. Subleyras went to Paris in 1724, and in 1726 gained the grand prize given by the French Academy for his *Brazen Serpent*, and in 1728 he was accordingly sent to Rome, with a pension from the government. In 1739 Subleyras married Maria Felice Tibaldi, a distinguished miniature-painter. Patronised by popes, cardinals, and the Roman nobility, he mainly produced religious paintings, but showed his real talent in portraiture.

Sublimation. When a solid, on the application of heat, passes straight to the vapour state without first becoming liquid, it is said to sublime (see PHASES OF MATTER).

On cooling, the vapour becomes solid without first becoming liquid. Sublimation depends on the fact that the boiling-point of the solid substance is lower than its melting-point at atmospheric pressure. Thus by increase of pressure a substance which sublimes can be made to go through a liquid stage before passing into the vapour state. By sublimation, non-volatile impurities which are originally present are left behind, and thus a method of purifying those substances which sublime is established. Arsenious acid, benzoic acid, and sulphur are purified by this means. When calomel (mercurous chloride) is sublimed, dissociation takes place, a certain amount of recombination occurring on cooling. Ammonium chloride dissociates into ammonia and hydrogen chloride gas, which recombine on cooling (see DISSOCIATION; TRIPLE POINT). For the use of the term sublimation in psychology, see FREUD, SIGMUND.

Sublingual Glands, the smallest of the salivary glands, situated one on each side of the floor of the mouth, beneath the tongue. Their ducts open along the sublingual fold in the mucous membrane of the floor of the mouth.

Submachine-gun. Its German name, *Maschinen-pistole*, shows at once its origin and function, i.e., a weapon intended to be to the pistol what the MACHINE-GUN is to the rifle. Developed probably from the Mauser Parabellum, an automatic pistol of heavy calibre with detachable stock and a magazine containing some two dozen rounds, the first submachine-gun to be extensively manufactured was the Thompson (whence 'Tommy gun') under US patent. Ostensibly sold for 'sporting' purposes, its chief users up to 1939 were American criminals and policemen. A similar weapon, the 'Suomi pistol', was used by the Finns in the 'winter war' of 1940–41, and at the same period the German patrols on the western front were armed with Schmeisser submachine-guns. These were all-metal weapons with folding stock and straight vertical magazine. The Suomi pistol inspired the prototype of the Russian submachine-guns, which, like it and the Thompson gun, can be fitted with a vertical drum holding about a hundred rounds, and fires bullets of heavy pistol calibre (about 11·4 mm). Other makes used in the Second World War were the Steyr-Solothurn and the Beretta.

A simple type of submachine-gun, the Sten, was evolved in Great Britain. Its parts were mainly of stamped steel, and especially suited for mass production. It had a simple 'blow-back' open-bolt action, was subject to few stoppages, and was of a calibre which permitted it to fire standard German 9-millimetre pistol ammunition. Thousands of these weapons were dropped to partisans in occupied Europe during the Second World War. It was also used by British airborne troops, commandos, and the Home Guard.

Submachine-guns are 'personal', not support infantry weapons. None is effective over 180 m. They are chiefly used in patrolling and street fighting, and in the final stages of an assault. As a result of experience gained during the Second World War a new weapon, the assault rifle, was developed. Using ammunition of smaller calibre than a rifle it combined the submachine-gun's facility for rapid fire with greater accuracy, and was adopted by many armies as a replacement for the machine pistol.

Submandibular Glands

Submandibular Glands, a pair of salivary glands situated far back beneath the lower jaw on each side. Each gland is about the size of a walnut, and discharges its secretion by the submandibular or Wharton's duct opening on the sublingual papillae on the floor of the mouth. The submandibular glands as well as the parotid glands are often affected in an attack of MUMPS.

Submarine. The true submarine is a vessel designed to operate beneath the surface of the sea, but until the advent of nuclear power, submarines were in fact submersibles, i.e., surface craft capable of limited operations submerged. Although in both world wars submarines were used effectively by the Germans to destroy Allied shipping, in the Second World War they were also much used by the Allies. British submarines made an important contribution to the defeat of the Axis forces in North Africa by their successful attacks on the enemy's supply lines, and in the Pacific, US and British submarines completely eliminated the Japanese merchant marine.

Submarines are submerged by flooding special ballast tanks, and in order to rise again to the surface the water in these tanks is discharged overboard, through valves placed at the bottom of the tanks, by means of compressed air. In addition, certain of the main ballast tanks have connections to electric pumps, which are sufficiently powerful to deliver against the greatest pressure of water ever likely to be met with in practice, and these may be used to empty the tanks in the event of the compressed air failing or some other emergency. These ballast tanks are outside the pressure hull, which must be strong enough to withstand the pressure of water at the depths to which the craft will be required to operate and which nowadays is as much as 300 m. This is achieved by using a hull of circular section, strengthened by transverse frames at regular and close intervals and divided into a number of watertight compartments by bulkheads, each of which is fitted with a rapid-closing watertight hatch. The conning tower or fin of the submarine is built up from the pressure hull and fitted with watertight hatches to allow access to the bridge. It houses the search and attack PERISCOPES, snort or Schnorkel tube, and the radar and radio masts when not in use. These are all raised and lowered by hydraulic rams within the submarine. When fully raised the periscope projects 12 m above the hull and at this depth the vessel is reasonably safe from ramming by a surface ship. In the latest submarines the diving planes are fitted on either side of the conning tower. Conventionally powered submarines, with diesel engines for surface propulsion and battery driven electric motors when submerged, are obsolescent, although because of the high cost of nuclear reactors, some are still being laid down. Nuclear power gives the submarine a greatly enhanced performance and enables higher speeds to be attained submerged than would be possible on the surface, and to maintain such speed indefinitely, so the cost of installation is outweighed by the advantages obtained.

The first reliable practical attempt at building a submarine vessel appears to have been in the 17th century, when a Dutchman, Cornelius Drebbell, successfully navigated a boat, manned by 12 rowers in the Thames.

The first practical submarines were the *Holland* class ordered by the British Admiralty in 1899. These were 19·2 m long, 3·6 m beam, of circular cross-section and shaped somewhat like a fat cigar. When submerged their displacement was 120 t, and they were propelled on the surface by an internal combustion engine of 160 h.p. (117 kW) which gave a speed of 10 knots (18·5 km/h); when under water an electric motor of 70 h.p. (52 kW) propelled the vessel at 7 knots (13·0 km/h). The latter was driven from electric batteries, which could be recharged when on the surface by the petrol engine.

Between 1959 and 1961 eight submarines of the *Porpoise* class (1605 t) were completed; they are designed for continuous submerged patrol using the snort. Between 1960 and 1964 eight submarines of the *Oberon* class (1610 t) were completed; these have a high underwater speed and are fitted with a special high-capacity battery. Britain's first nuclear-powered submarine, *Dreadnought* (3000 t), was completed in 1963 with a reactor supplied by the US navy. Six more British built fleet submarines are in service with four more being built. In addition four submarines are armed with ballistic missiles.

German U-boat building policy, until Allied anti-submarine methods forced them to experiment, was similar in both world wars, i.e., the development and enlargement of a proved type. In 1944 the Germans introduced the Schnorkel or snort, a breathing-tube which allowed the boat to charge batteries without having to surface, and this invention has since been adopted by other navies. They also designed three new types; one large, one small with increased submerged speed, and one type which was fitted with an engine using hydrogen peroxide, enabling prolonged submerged steaming at a speed in excess of 20 knots (37 km/h). The principle is now obsolete due to the introduction of nuclear power. US submarines developed on standard lines from the *Holland* type of 1900, and during the First World War were mainly of the medium-sized patrol type. The construction of a large 1500-tonne type patrol class, with a surface speed of 21 knots (39 km/h) from twin shafts each having two or four engines geared to the shaft, was started in 1940 and formed the main part of the US submarine fleet in the Second World War. These *Fish* class submarines were of a very fine type with powerful armament, big radius of action, and the best living 'accommodation of any submarine in the world. Air-conditioning and air purification have been brought to a high state of efficiency.

The first nuclear-powered submarine in the world, the *Nautilus*, was completed for the US navy in 1955. The *Nautilus* has a water-cooled thermal reactor and geared turbines. Following the successful trials with the *Nautilus*, the US navy embarked on an extensive building programme of nuclear-powered submarines of several different types. By the adoption of a tear-drop form of hull design and fitting one large propeller instead of two as formerly, very high underwater speeds in excess of 30 knots (55 km/h) have been reached. In 1975 the US navy had 41 ballistic missile submarines and 61 patrol submarines with a further 27 being built. The USSR has 48 nuclear ballistic missile submarines, 39 fitted with shorter-range missiles, and 28 patrol submarines, with a rapid building programme.

The use of submarines for unrestricted warfare against all types of shipping which was so condemned during and after the First World War led to attempts to return to the agenda of The Hague Conference of 1899, when the Soviet government proposed the total prohibition of submarines as weapons of war, but a similar proposal found no response in the uneasy peace following the Second World War. Total war at sea, whether by the declaration of 'sink at sight' zones, or the acceptance that any enemy merchant ship sighted is taking part in that country's war effort and is therefore a fighting unit, has no more been questioned than the use of bombers over enemy towns and cities. Submarine development of the future seems, therefore, to be dictated by the amount of money each country is prepared to spend on it rather than by considerations of any illegality of this form of warfare. In fact the introduction of nuclear power points to an expansion of this type of warship at the expense of surface vessels.

Bibliography: A. Mars, *British Submarines at War, 1939–45*, 1971; *Jane's Fighting Ships*, pub. annually.

Submarine Cables, see CABLES, ELECTRIC.

Submarine Forests are evidence of the subsidence (see EPEIROGENY) of the land in recent geological times. They occur along the Firths of Forth and Tay, on the coasts of Devon, Cornwall, Somerset, Lancashire, and at Grimsby on the Humber. Generally, these forests are rarely depressed far below high-water mark, and consist of beds of peat, some 1–2 m thick, abounding in trunks and roots of trees in the lower portion, and in mosses in the lighter-coloured upper portion.

Submarine Mines, see MINES, MILITARY AND NAVAL.

Subotica (Hungarian *Szabadka*; German *Maria-Theresiopol*), town in Serbia, Yugoslavia, in the autonomous province of VOJVODINA. It is near the Hungarian border, has a large Hungarian minority, and is the agricultural centre of the fertile plain between the rivers Danube and Tisza. Electrical machinery, chemicals, textiles, and foodstuffs are manufactured. Subotica is an important rail junction and has a university. Population (1971) 78,000.

Subpoena, in English law, the name of the writ for calling a witness to give evidence (*subpoena ad testificandum*). It is applied for only where it is feared the supposed witness will not voluntarily come forward or is actively hostile to the party calling him. The writ for calling upon any person to bring to court books, deeds, or other documentary evidence is called a *subpoena duces tecum*.

Subsidence, see EPEIROGENY.

Subsidies were taxes in aid formerly granted to the kings of England. They were imposed not immediately on property, but upon persons in respect of their reputed estates. These subsidies were first voted in the reign of Richard I, and later came to be a fixed sum of £70,000. In 1398 a subsidy on wool and leather was granted to Richard II for life. These subsidies were discontinued after 1663, when a land tax was substituted.

Sums of money paid by one state to another under the terms of a treaty were also known as subsidies. They were used to purchase the service of auxiliary troops, or to acquire the aid of a foreign state in a war against an enemy. Thus Britain has at various times paid large subsidies to nations that have been its allies in war, especially against the French in the 18th century.

Modern subsidies take the form of government grants to industries and commercial undertakings, such as those made to shipping and air lines. The best-known subsidies in Britain are the food subsidies, used to keep down the price of essential foods. A government subsidy to avoid an increase in the price of bread was introduced in 1974. The estimated cost of this subsidy was £21 million in its first year. Butter and milk were also included in a food subsidy programme. Although the old system of agricultural subsidies was discontinued when Britain joined the European Economic Community in 1973, Britain benefits from the EEC's common agricultural policy, which also operates a system of subsidies. The other large British government subsidy is that to enable local authorities to let council houses at rents below that which they would fetch if let on the open market.

Subsoil, a term dating from the period when soil was conceived of as two parts, topsoil and subsoil. It refers to the B horizons, which are not penetrated in normal cultivation practices. See also SOIL.

Subspecies represent incipient SPECIES, which can often be recognised by their morphology and distinct distribution, but which still retain some genetic contact with one or more of the other related subspecies.

Substance, in philosophy, that which exists in itself. A created substance is that which exists in itself and arrives as a subject in which attributes (accidents) inhere. Such is the teaching of Aristotle and the Scholastics, who classified substances according to their perfection as complete (e.g. God, angels) and incomplete (e.g. human and animal souls), and according to their degree of unity as single (God, angels, souls) and complex (man, animal, plant). This view was repudiated by Locke and others, who held that every object has some *fundamental* or *essential* quality, which, being present, preserves its identity, and which, being removed, renders it no longer the same substance, but another. According to this system, therefore, substance is unknowable, or at least unknown, for which reason Kant attached to it the name NOUMENON; by contrast, PHENOMENON indicates the exterior knowable quality or group of qualities which shows itself to our senses or is conceived directly by our intelligence. According to Descartes, there are two substances: matter, whose essence is extension, and minds, whose essence is thinking. Spinoza recognised only a single substance, namely the world as a whole, which he identifies with God. Matter and minds are then regarded as aspects of the one substance. Leibniz, on the other hand, held that there were infinitely many substances, which he called monads. The atoms of Democritus in Greek philosophy, as much as those of physical science till the late 19th century, were uncreated substances which, as unchanging elements, were used as principles for explaining change in complex things. A similar function belongs to the atomic propositions used by some modern philosophers of logic such as Russell and the early Wittgenstein.

See BERKELEY; DESCARTES; HUME; KANT; LEIBNIZ; LOCKE; WITTGENSTEIN.

Substitution, in mathematics, is the replacement of one algebraic quantity by another of equal value differently expressed, a device which is particularly useful in integration, where solutions can often be obtained by the introduction of a new independent variable.

Substitution. In orthodox economics the assumption that substitution is possible between the factors of production, i.e. capital and labour, is necessary in order to explain the workings of the price system in a competitive economy. This substitutability is supposed to ensure that it will always be possible to ensure full employment by adjusting the level of wages. Such a theory ignores the fact that the level of employment at any time depends on the amount of machinery in existence and whether it is being used to its full capacity.

See also ELASTICITY; MARGIN; SUPPLY AND DEMAND.

Substitution Reactions, in chemistry, occur when a compound of the type R-X undergoes reaction to become R-Y (i.e., one group has been substituted for another). The study of the various possible mechanisms of substitution, first classified by Ingold (1930s), is of great theoretical interest.

Subways, constructions under the footways of streets used for telegraph wires, electric light and power cables, gas, water, and other pipes. These subways are so constructed that there is room for a man to walk and work in them; inspection entrances are constructed at intervals, thus removing the necessity of breaking up the footways when the pipes underneath have to be repaired. Subways are also a feature in the underground system of railways, connecting different tube railways together. Another feature is the construction of subways at the junction of important thoroughfares in cities to avoid the congestion of pedestrian traffic and lessen the danger to life. In the USA the term is applied to the underground electric railway systems of New York City. Except where they run under the rivers, and at one or two land points owing to the conformation of the terrain, the subways are in no sense 'tubes' like those of London. In the main they are tunnels built at a small distance beneath the surface of the streets. See also TUNNELLING.

Succession. The law of succession is that according to which the succession to the property of deceased individuals is regulated. In English law, this may be: (1) in cases where a deceased party has died intestate (see INTESTACY), when the order of succession follows fixed rules contained in the Administration of Estates Act 1925, as amended by the Intestates' Estates Act 1952; or (2) according to a SETTLEMENT by deed, will, or other instrument, under which land or any interest in land or other property stands for the time being limited to or in trust for any person by way of succession.

See also HEIR; INHERITANCE; PRIMOGENITURE; WILLS AND TESTAMENTS.

Succession, Intestate (Scotland). The law in Scotland has in the past made a distinction between heritable property (i.e. generally land and buildings) and moveable property (i.e. money, furniture, stocks, and shares). See HERITABLE AND MOVEABLE.

Under the old rules, by the rule of primogeniture and preference for males, heritable property passed to the 'heir-at-law', e.g. a man's house went to his eldest son, even if there were older daughters.

All these rules were abolished by the Succession (Scotland) Act 1964, which made significant changes in the law of both testate and intestate succession, and now, on intestate estates, heritable and moveable property alike are governed by the rules which in the past governed the distribution of moveable property, though a number of changes have been made in pursuance of the fact that male and female are treated alike, and the fact that there is now no regard to age.

'Legal rights' may be claimed by the widow and children of the deceased, on both testacy and intestacy. The 1964 act retains three of these rights, namely: (1) JUS RELICTAE—the right of a widow to claim one-third of the husband's moveable estate, though if there is no issue or no surviving issue, then this is increased to one-half. (2) Jus Relicti—an equivalent right given to the widower on his deceased wife's estate. (3) LEGITIM—the right of the children, including adopted and illegitimate children, to claim one-third of the deceased parent's moveable estate, though again, this is increased to one-half if there are no surviving parents.

The 1964 act introduced certain new rights for the widow or widower in cases where there was no will. These are the 'prior rights' of the surviving spouse and are exigible out of the estate after deduction of debts, funeral expenses, and any death duties, but before any legal rights have been met. These 'prior rights' may be summarised as follows: (1) right to the dwellinghouse of the deceased, in which the surviving spouse was normally resident at the time of death, but in certain cases, as where the dwellinghouse is part of business premises, or where it exceeds the value of £15,000 then the value of the house up to £15,000 is given; (2) the furniture and plenishings of the dwellinghouse up to a value of £5000; (3) the sum of £2500, where the deceased left issue, but where no issue, then £5000 can be claimed.

Subject to the above mentioned rights an intestate estate is divisible as follows: Intestate survived by: (1) children—whole estate to the children; (2) parents and brothers and sisters but no prior relative—half of the estate to the parents and half to the brothers and sisters; (3) parents or parent but no prior relative—whole estate to the parents; (4) surviving spouse but no prior relative—whole estate to the surviving spouse; (5) uncles and aunts but no prior relative—whole estate to uncles and aunts; (6) grandparent or grandparents but no prior relative—whole estate to grandparent or grandparents; (7) none of above or their heirs—whole estate to the brothers and sisters of the grandparents, whom failing, to more remote ancestors; (8) no heir—whole estate to the Crown as *ultimus haeres*. 'Prior relative' means any person higher in the table or his or her heir.

In the case of a legally adopted child, the 1964 act falls into line with English law when it gives the adopted child the same rights as the natural child of the adopters. At the same time, the adopted child loses any claim on the estate of his natural parents.

Succession, Plant, term covering the development of plant communities in a given area. Generally there is a definite sequence; usually smaller types of plants are replaced gradually by larger forms. Over long periods of time this natural process tends to generate plant communities in places which were originally either stretches of water or bare earth, and which were first colonised by smaller plants or lichens. See ECOLOGY.

Succession, Royal. Inheritance by heirs male, when applied to the royal office, is the SALIC LAW, which prevailed in France and other countries. Down to 1688 the English succession was regulated by custom, Parliament claiming some right to intervene. In 1700, when it became evident that both William III and his sister-in-law, Anne, would probably die without issue, the ACT OF SETTLEMENT was passed to provide for the succession after their deaths. This is the act under which, as modified by the Act of Abdication of Edward VIII, the Crown is still held. The Act of Settlement: (1) declared that if a Roman Catholic obtains the Crown the subjects of the realm are thereby absolved of their allegiance; (2) settled the Crown on the Electress Sophia and the Protestant heirs of her body; and (3) expressly excludes any person holding communion with the Church of Rome, professing the popish religion, or marrying a Papist. The purpose of the Act of Settlement was to exclude the exiled James II, his descendants, and all other Roman Catholics from the succession, and in order to do so Parliament sought out the nearest Protestant to the old royal line, namely Sophia, Electress of Hanover, granddaughter of James I. No queen before the passage of this act had succeeded with a wholly undisputed title; but under its terms it is placed beyond doubt that a king's daughter succeeds in preference to her father's, though not to her own, younger brother. It was by virtue of this rule that Queen Victoria ascended the throne, instead of her uncle, Ernest, Duke of Cumberland (though he inherited Hanover, which was under the Salic Law), and by the same rule that Queen Elizabeth II, not the Duke of Gloucester, succeeded George VI. Her eldest son, Prince Charles (1948–), follows her and is himself followed by his future descendants of either sex and then by his brother, Prince Andrew (1960–), and his descendants, then by his brother, Prince Edward (1964–), and his descendants, then by his sister, Princess Anne (1950–), and her descendants, all these coming before Princess Margaret and her descendants of either sex.

Succinic Acid, HOOC·CH$_2$·CH$_2$·COOH, occurs widely in nature, and was formerly known as a product of distillation of amber. It can be prepared by reduction of tartaric, malic, or maleic acids, or from ethyl acetoacetate or malonate. It has a melting point of 185 °C and sublimes readily.

Succubus, see DEMONOLOGY.

Succulent Plants, those which have developed very fleshy leaves or stems, or both, capable of retaining moisture in long spells of dry, hot weather. They are native to arid areas in tropical or subtropical regions and include cacti, *Agave, Aloe, Crassula,* and *Mesembryanthemum*. They are popular indoor plants in temperate countries. Plants growing in strongly saline conditions, e.g. *Salicornia* in salt marshes, are also typically succulent, again for water conservation.

Suceava, town and province of northern Romania, situated on the river of the same name. It was historically important as the capital of Moldavia, 1401-1565, and now has textile and lumber industries. Population 45,000.

Sucker, see VEGETATIVE REPRODUCTION.

Sucking-fish, any member of the family Echeneidae, the remoras, in the order Perciformes, so named on account of the suctorial oval disk they bear on the upper part of the head. This sucker is in fact a highly modified dorsal fin. By means of this disk they attach themselves to sharks, and they are to be found in all warm seas. They feed, at least in part, on the external parasites of oceanic sharks. Other sucking-fish are the suckers, which form the family Gobiesocidae, order Gobiesociformes, and the lumpsuckers, which form the Cyclopteridae, order Scorpaeniformes.

Sucking Lice, see ANOPLURA.

Suckling, Sir John (1609–42), English poet, playwright, and prose writer, born at Whitton, Middlesex. Suckling studied at Cambridge, and then entered Gray's Inn. He travelled abroad, and is said to have served for a time under GUSTAVUS Adolphus. He equipped a troop of men for Charles I's campaign against the Scots, but they fled at first sight of the Scots at Duns. Later he became involved in a plot to rescue STRAFFORD from the Tower, and had to flee to France, dying in Paris, probably by his own hand.

Though he wrote in more than one genre, it is as a poet that he is best known. Some of his shorter pieces are incomparable for charm and delicacy, such as his 'Ballad upon a Wedding' and 'Why so pale and wan, fond lover?'. Suckling clearly owes something to DONNE, and wrote in the metaphysical style of the day (see METAPHYSICAL POETS).

The relaxed cynicism and libertine stance of many of his poems must be set against the protestations of high platonic passion in his tragedies (particularly *Aglaura*, 1637) to achieve a balanced impression of one of the most stylish, if tragically flawed, of the Cavaliers. His works were collected posthumously in *Fragmenta Aurea*, 1646.

Bibliography: L. A. Beaurline and T. Clayton (Eds), *Works,* 1971; K. M. Lynch, *The Social Mode of Restoration Comedy,* 1927; J. B. Broadbent, *Poetic Love,* 1964.

Sucre, state of north-east VENEZUELA, on the Caribbean coast and the Gulf of Paria. The capital is CUMANÁ. Coffee and cocoa are the chief products, and there is a large fish-canning industry in Cumaná. Fishing along the coast is an important economic activity. Population (1975) 512,800.

Sir John Suckling, portrait after Van Dyck, painted about 1640. *(National Portrait Gallery, London)*

Sucre

Sucre, capital town of the department of Chuquisaca, BOLIVIA, and legal capital of Bolivia itself (La Paz being the actual seat of government). Its altitude is 3390 m but it has a mild climate. Sucre is the seat of the judiciary and the archbishop. A bishopric since 1552, and the seat of the Archbishop of La Plata and Charcas since 1609, it possesses a cathedral dating back to 1553. The University of San Javier was founded in 1624. The best buildings, besides the cathedral, are the legislative palaces, from which Bolivia's independence was declared in 1825, the palace of justice, and Junin College. It is connected by railway with Potosí, being on a branch line of the Antofagasta–La Paz main line. Population (1974) 88,000.

Sucrose, see SUGAR.

Suda, or Suidas, is the name of a late 10th-century AD lexicon, or literary reference book. Despite many failings of scholarship, it is a valuable source in that it records much of the work of earlier scholars.
Bibliography: A. Adler (Ed.) *Suda* (5 vols), 1928–38.

Sudan, or Soudan, a republic as from 1 January 1956. Formerly the name of a vast tract of equatorial Africa lying south of the Sahara Desert and Egypt, and stretching from Cape Verde on the west coast to Massana on the east, it extended south to the Congo basin and the equatorial lakes, with Ethiopia and British East Africa forming its eastern boundary. It was also known as Negritia, or Bilad-es-Sudan, the 'Land of the Blacks'. Later it was divided into three parts: French Sudan on the west, central Sudan, and the Anglo-Egyptian Sudan on the east.

Sudan is bounded by Egypt on the north; Libya, Chad, and the Central African Empire lie to the west; Zaire, Uganda, and Kenya lie to the south; and Ethiopia and the Red Sea are to the east. The estimated area of Sudan is 2,506,000 km², making it the largest state in Africa.

Geography. Relief. The physiography of the Sudan is dominated by the drainage basin of the River NILE, most of which is below 750 m. There are highlands rising to 2200 m along the shore of the Red Sea in the east, and in the west of DARFUR province the Marra Mountains rise to over 3000 m. The northern Sudan is desert, mostly sandy to the west of the Nile but stony to the east.

Southern Sudan has extensive areas of flat clay plains along the Blue Nile, where the river floods seasonally, and along the White Nile the clay plains are permanently flooded to form the SUDD, a vast area of marshland. The Nile traverses the region from south to north, with a large bend westwards about latitude 20°N, enclosing part of the Nubian Desert, which extends to the Red Sea coast. The LIBYAN DESERT lies to the immediate west. Where the Nile enters the Sudan it is known as the Bahr-al-Jebel (or White Nile), receiving in its course the waters of the Bahr-al-Ghazal and Sobat rivers. At Khartoum it receives the Bahr-al-Azrek (or Blue Nile), an important affluent flowing north-west. From henceforth it flows on as the Nile, taking in the Atbara above Berber. Between Wadi Halfa and Khartoum there are five of the six Nile cataracts. See ATLAS 41.

Climate. Climatic conditions in the Sudan vary considerably. The northern half of the country has a desert continental climate with hot summers and mild winters. The average daily maximum temperature at Wadi Halfa in July is 42 °C, with an average daily minimum of 26 °C; the January mean monthly temperature is 21 °C. There is, however, very little precipitation and this is erratic in any case. In the southern half of the country summer temperatures are reduced to a monthly July mean of 25 °C, but precipitation and humidity increase markedly further south, so that Equatoria province receives very high rainfall in July though there is practically no rain in January.

Population. The total population of Sudan in 1974 was estimated at 17,324,000, partly Arab, partly Negroid, and partly Nubian. The main Arab groups include the Baggara and Igessana tribes; the Negroid peoples include the Shilluk, Dinka Nuer, Azande Beja, and many others. Some 13 per cent of the total population live in urban areas. The main cities are KHARTOUM, OMDURMAN, and PORT SUDAN.
Bibliography: G. Nachtigal, *Sahara and Sudan*, vol. 4, 1971.

Economy. Agriculture. The most fertile regions are those lying east and south of Khartoum watered by the Atbara and the Blue and White Niles. Here there are large areas under dura (the staple native food), millet, sesame, and pulse. In order to ensure a guaranteed water supply, the government brought into existence the Gezira irrigation scheme, for the launching of which the

Sudan. Nubian mudbrick house near Wadi Halfa. *(Barnaby's Picture Library)*

British government guaranteed loans to over 11,500,000 to cover the construction of the dam over the Blue Nile at Sennar and the main canalisation. A strict rotation of crops is observed, and the scheme enables at present an area of 370,000 ha to be cultivated between the Blue and White Niles. One-quarter is under cotton, Sudan's major export crop. Sudan aims at becoming the major agricultural producer for the Arab and African worlds.

Industry. Most of Sudan's limited industrial capacity is centred on Khartoum. The textile industry is the largest single employer of labour, and the annual output is worth over £10 million. Sugar refining is increasing in importance, and by 1973 the Guneid and Khashm El Girba factories were producing 112,000 t. The cement industry is also expanding, although output was only worth £3 million in 1973. Cement and sugar are in the public sector, unlike the textile industry which is privately owned. There are both state-owned and private food processing plants which compete freely with each other. Other industries include tanning, soap manufacture, flour milling, soft drink bottling, and dairying.

Communications. Roads are poor, and river transport remains important. Government passenger and cargo steamers ply along the Nile, and regular services are established over 3700 km. From Rejaf, on the upper White Nile, there is motor transport to the Congo and the Ugandan frontier. Sudan Airways operates internal services between the main centres and external services to neighbouring countries in Africa, and to Europe, carrying some 141,000 passengers in 1973. Some foreign airlines also operate services to and through the Sudan.

Trade. Agricultural commodities account for over 90 per cent of Sudan's export earnings, with cotton exports alone worth an average of £60 million during the 1970–73 period. Receipts vary considerably from year to year, however, due to fluctuations in the world market price of cotton, and this seriously limits Sudan's ability to import, thus making long-term planning difficult. The value of cotton exports, for example, slumped by over 50 per cent between 1972 and 1973. Export earnings from other commodities such as oil seeds, gum, and animal products are usually more stable. Sudan's main import items are manufactured consumer goods, vehicles, petroleum, industrial plant, and agricultural machinery. Despite rising cereal production within the country, over £4 million was spent on food imports in 1973. The chief import suppliers include China, Japan, India, Italy, and West Germany. Trade with the Soviet Union and other East European countries declined dramatically over the 1970–73 period.

Finance and Planning. Customs and excise duties constitute the main source of government revenue, although income tax and profits from state-owned industries are increasing in importance. Government revenue in 1973 amounted to almost £200 million, but the size of the budget deficit has increased in recent years due to rising development spending. Defence expenditure still accounts for almost one-quarter of the total budget, despite the ending of the internal conflict in the south. Increasing amounts have been allocated to education, health, and municipal expenditure. A three-phase, 15-year plan for the textile industry provides for investment of £700 million by 1990, which will include 15 new spinning mills; this will create an additional 45,000 industrial jobs.

Sudan. Landscape in Equatoria province. *(Camera Press/George Rodger)*

Government. Constitution and Legislature. The Sudan is a democratic republic. A new constitution was proclaimed in 1973. Under this the executive authority lies with the President (nominated by the Sudanese Socialist Union - the only recognised political organisation) and his cabinet. The legislature is the 250-member National People's Assembly which sits for four-year terms. In the assembly, 125 of the seats are filled by elected representatives of geographical areas, 25 are appointed by the President, 30 are filled from the administrative units through a process of election and selection, and 70 seats are allotted to the people's working forces alliance.

In 1972 the long civil war in the south came to an end. From 1955 to 1972 the southern rebels had carried out guerrilla operations against the government. In November 1973 there were elections for a southern regional assembly. Under the regional constitution for South Sudan the three southern provinces form a region with its own executive in Juba, headed by a President who is also Vice-President for the country as a whole. The President of South Sudan is appointed by the Regional People's Assembly. This assembly has 60 seats of which 30 are taken by elected members representing geographical constituencies, 21 are filled by the people's working forces alliance, and the remaining nine by representatives of the administrative units.

Under the constitution the assembly may postpone legislation passed in the National Assembly if it considers

Sudan. The battle of Omdurman, fought on 2 September 1898. Chromolithograph after R. A. Sutherland. *(National Army Museum, London)*

it harmful to the south. The regional constitution can only be changed by a four-fifths majority of the National Assembly.

Sudan comprises 15 provinces, each under a commissioner, who is also the provincial secretary of the Sudanese Socialist Union (SSU).

Justice. Criminal justice is applied through the code of criminal procedure. There are major, minor, and magistrates' courts. Appeals go to the high court. Civil justice ordinance governs civil justice through the supreme court, court of appeal, and other courts. The supreme court is also the custodian of the constitution. Islamic Shari'ah law is administered through Shari'ah courts in the areas of marriages, wills, and inheritance.

Armed Forces. In 1976 the armed forces numbered 52,600 with 50,000 of that total represented by the army. There are 2000 men in the air force and 600 in the navy. In South Sudan there are 6000 former Anya Nya rebels organised into the regional militia. Sudan has a defence agreement with the Arab League Unified Military Command.

Education. Education is free at primary level from the ages of 7 to 11. There are also intermediate schools for those aged 11 to 15 and secondary schools for those aged 15 and upwards. Overall it is estimated that 80 per cent of the population remains illiterate, and one of the most urgent national priorities remains the struggle against illiteracy. In 1973–74 there were 37,516 teachers and 1·4 million pupils. There are three universities in the Sudan. The University of Khartoum is the largest, and there is also a branch of the University of Cairo in Khartoum. There is an Islamic University situated at Omdurman.

Welfare. The public health services are organised by the Ministry of Health. In 1975 there were 81 hospitals, 60 health centres, and 1244 dispensaries. There are more than 500 doctors in the Sudan.

Religion. Most Sudanese are Muslims. Animists form the next largest group, and there is also a small Christian community.

Official Language. The language of the Sudan is Arabic in the north and various African dialects in the south.

National Anthem. Nahnu djundul'lah. Words by Ahmed M. Salih, tune by Murgan.

National Flag. The flag is a tricolour of red, white, and black with a green triangle at the hoist.

Bibliography: 'Abd Al-Rahim, *Imperialism and Nationalism in the Sudan: A Study in Constitutional Political Development, 1899–1956,* 1969; G. Morrison, *Southern Sudan and Eritrea,* 1971; Z. Mustafa, *Common Law in the Sudan: An Account of the "Justice, Equity and Good Conscience" Provision,* 1971; C. Eprile, *War and Peace in the Sudan, 1955–72,* 1974.

History. Northern Sudan was anciently known as Kush and from about 1500 to 1200 BC was under Egyptian domination. Kush was an independent kingdom from about 750 BC to AD 350; the capital changed from Napala to Meroë about 300 BC. In the 6th century northern Sudan was converted to Christianity; a century later the Muslims arrived, and eventually Christianity was replaced by Islam, though Christianity lingered on in some areas until the 16th century. Southern Sudan remained untouched by foreign influences until the 19th century; it was entirely cut off by the *sudd*, or barriers of reeds and mud that blocked the Nile. MEHEMET ALI, the Viceroy of Egypt, conquered the Sudan in 1820. Egypt nominally governed the Sudan for the next 65 years; it was in fact governed by nobody. Britain, through the control that it exerted on Egypt, appointed Gen. Charles GORDON as governor-general of the Sudan (1877–79) and attempted its reorganisation. Around 1880 Mohammed Ahmed, a Muslim agitator, proclaimed himself MAHDI and organised a revolt in Egyptian Sudan. He besieged Khartoum and Gen. Gordon was killed. The Mahdi's successor, the Khalifa, held his own for nearly 13 years,

430

desolating the country, and reducing the population from 8·5 million to 2 million. In 1896 Britain decided to reconquer the Sudan and Sir Herbert KITCHENER assembled a strong Anglo-Egyptian force, moved forward out of Egypt into Dongola, and in the following year advanced to Abu Hamad and began building the Sudan railway across the Nubian Desert from Wadi Halfa to Abu Hamad. Then, in 1898, a joint British and Egyptian army marched against the Khalifa's capital, and shattered his power at the battles of Atbara and Omdurman. The Khalifa was killed on 1 November 1899 at Umm Diwaykarat by a force led by Sir Francis Wingate. Late in 1899 Wingate succeeded Kitchener as governor-general of the Sudan, and a period of peace followed in which the country developed rapidly. Under an Anglo-Egyptian agreement signed on 19 January 1899 the two countries governed the Sudan jointly on a condominium basis; tribalism was encouraged during this period, and until 1956 the country was known as the Anglo-Egyptian Sudan.

Proposals for the future of the Anglo-Egyptian Sudan were discussed by the British and Egyptian governments in 1946 during treaty negotiations held in the autumn of that year. It was tentatively agreed that the titular sovereignty should be vested in the Egyptian crown, but that the joint administration should continue for some years and the Sudanese should eventually have the fullest freedom in choosing their own constitutional future. During the following few years Egyptian nationalists demanded immediate annexation of the Sudan. After King Farouk was overthrown in Egypt in 1952, Egypt declared itself willing to grant Sudan self-determination. Ominously in August 1955 the southern rebellion began with a mutiny at Torit. On 19 December 1955 the Sudanese parliament unanimously passed a resolution that a fully independent state should come into immediate existence. Britain and Egypt acceded to this on 31 December, and on 1 January 1956 the Sudan became a sovereign state, and joined the Arab League.

During the period since independence Sudanese politics have been dogged by instability, which can be attributed to divisions between pro-Western and pro-Egyptian factions, splits within the parties, to the economic difficulties in administering Africa's largest country, and to the civil war, which lasted for 17 years, between the north and the non-Muslim, non-Arab south.

These factors became most apparent as soon as independence had been declared and the problems of coping with a newly-independent country had to be tackled. Thus, after it had become clear that divided and manoeuvring politicians were unable to deal with a deteriorating economic situation, Gen. Ibrahim ABBOUD staged a military coup on 17 November 1958, which was greeted with some measure of relief.

Even the politicians initially acquiesced at the suspension of parties, parliament, and the constitution. Schemes for the development of agriculture, trade, and communications were initiated and there was some success in the vital sector of cotton sales. But the domination of the military began to cause resentment, aggravated by rumours of corruption and the feeling that the economy was again being mishandled. An attempt to set up a political movement along the lines of Pakistan's 'basic democracies' caused further friction between the military

and civilians. The military government also mistakenly believed that a military solution could be enforced in the south. In 1963 rebellion broke out there with greater ferocity than before, and by this time the guerrillas had become united under the name Anya-Nya. Abboud's régime was expelled after a general civilian strike in October 1964.

The first move made by the civilian government that followed was to restore civilian politics and then it turned its attention to the southern problem. However, a Round Table Conference convened in March 1965 to consider arrangements for autonomy made no real progress. After elections in June 1965 a coalition of the Umma and National Unionist party was formed with Mohammed MAHGOUB as prime minister. Ismail AZHARI was made president. The clashes in the south worsened, and the political parties themselves split up. Sadiq el-Mahdi became prime minister in July 1966 until Mahgoub returned to power in May 1967. The continuing inability of this government to improve the financial and economic situation contributed directly to the coup led by Col. NUMEIRY on 25 May 1969.

Numeiry's régime was at first closely modelled on the Free Officer's movement led by Nasser in Egypt. Sudan was aligned with the Arab world almost to the point of union with Egypt and Libya. Links with the Eastern bloc were tightened, and firms, both local and foreign, were nationalised. Political parties were banned. In March 1970 the Mahdists were suppressed by a fierce military attack on Aba Island. But the most severe challenge came in July 1971, when for three days Numeiry was ousted by a Communist-led coup. A purge of Communists followed and 14 people were executed. Thereafter Numeiry set up the Sudan Socialist Union as the sole political organisation, and in October was elected president. The orientation of the régime was turned towards the West and the more conservative Arab governments. The private sector was encouraged. In April 1972 Numeiry pulled off a major achievement by concluding an agreement which set up a regional government in the south within a federal and united Sudan. A regional parliament and Higher Executive Parliament (headed by Abel Alier, a national vice-president) were set up. Some instability remained and the Sudanese government witnessed street demonstrations and small scale attempts at coups. The government's usual problems of bad infrastructure and distribution of essential commodities were aggravated by global inflation and the rise in oil prices. The continuing domination of the military has also caused resentment; Numeiry managed to survive, in 1976, a serious attempted coup, which was probably mounted with Libyan assistance, and Sudan subsequently severed diplomatic relations with Libya. Relations with Ethiopia deteriorated early in 1977 following allegations that Sudan was aiding Eritrean secessionists in Ethiopia. In April 1977 Numeiry was re-elected president for a second six-year term.

Bibliography: C. G. and B. Z. Seligman, *Nilotic Tribes of the Anglo-Egyptian Sudan*, 1932; P. M. Holt, *A Modern History of the Sudan*, 1961; K. D. Henderson, *Sudan Republic*, 1966; B. M. Said, *The Sudan*, 1966; O. Albino, *The Sudan: A Southern Viewpoint*, 1970; P. M. Holt, *The Mahdist State in the Sudan 1881–98*, 1970; M. A. Mahgoub, *Democracy on Trial*, 1974.

Sudan, French, see MALI.

Sudanese Languages, see AFRICAN LANGUAGES.

Sudarium (Latin, sweat-cloth), scarf of silk attached to various religious insignia carried by hand, to keep them from being moistened by perspiration, especially in hot climates. In the West the use of the sudarium is less frequent than in the East, but it is still used at times on bishops' and abbots' croziers.

It also refers, in the sequence *Victimae Paschali*, to the linen cloth in which the body of Christ was buried. This, however, is more generally called by the Greek name, *sindon*, or in English the HOLY SHROUD, which is believed to be preserved at Turin.

Sudarium is also the name given to the cloth or towel of St Veronica, with which a relic preserved in St Peter's, Rome, and enshrined in one of the piers of the dome, is identified; and, finally, it is the Latin name for the MANIPLE.

Sudbury, market town in SUFFOLK, England, on the River Stour, 26 km south of Bury St Edmunds. The town consists of three parishes in each of which is an interesting 15th-century church, and there is a 15th-century grammar school. The main industries are flour-milling, malting, and textiles, woollen manufacture being introduced by the Flemings in the 14th century. Population (1971) 8166.

Sudbury, city of north-western Ontario, Canada, 482 km north-west of Toronto on the Canadian Pacific and Canadian National railways. In the district 90 per cent of the world's nickel supply is produced; also a large output of copper. The town is the chief commercial centre of northern Ontario. Population 90,300.

Sudbury Hall, Derbyshire, was begun c. 1613 but not completed until much later in the century. It is built of diaper brick, and contains plaster ceilings painted by Laguerre, a staircase carved by Edward Pierce and an overmantel by Grinling Gibbons. Sudbury Hall was transferred to the National Trust through the Treasury in 1967.

Sudd, swampy lowland region of central SUDAN where the White NILE and BAHR-AL-GHAZAL 'lose themselves'. The river flow is impeded by papyrus and aquatic grass and as much as half their combined volume is lost through evaporation and seepage. A canal has long been proposed to bypass this area, inhabited only by a few Nilotic tribes. Area 128,000 km².

'Süddeutsche Zeitung', West German newspaper, published in Munich. It appeared first in 1945, twice, and later three times, weekly. Since 1949 the paper has been published as a daily. It has a wide circulation in southern Germany and is also read abroad. Independent politically, the paper is one of West Germany's most important and influential.

Sudermann, Hermann (1857–1928), German playwright and novelist, born at Matziken, East Prussia. He began his career as a chemist's apprentice but received further education at Königsberg University and later taught in Berlin. After a short spell of journalism in 1881–82 he began writing novels in the Maupassant style. But it was as a dramatist that he won most of his popularity; his naturalistic plays, notably *Heimat* (or *Magda*), 1892, were highly successful. They resemble HAUPTMANN'S and IBSEN'S plays on social issues, though with none of their profundity. His later plays were critical and commercial failures, and made Sudermann return to prose-writing.

Bibliography: Lives and Studies by J. Leux, 1931, H. F. Garten, 1964.

Sudeten Mountains, mountain system of Central Europe, lying on the north-east frontier of Czechoslovakia. The principal divisions are the RIESENGEBIRGE, Lausitzergebirge, Isergebirge, and Jeschkengebirge. Sněžka is the highest point. See SUDETENLAND.

Sudetenland, land formerly occupied by the German minority in Bohemia, concentrated chiefly near the German frontier formed by the Sudetic Mountains. The Sudetens were mainly descendants of the German colonists invited by the Přemyslid dynasty in the Middle Ages. Before the Second World War they numbered 3,232,000 or about 20 per cent of the population of Czechoslovakia, and controlled 40 per cent of its industries. This German minority was a useful lever in Hitler's hands to force the gateway into Czechoslovakia. To some extent Czech mishandling exacerbated Sudetic grievances. After the German annexation of Austria, their leader, Henlein, called on the Czech government to transfer the Sudetic region to the German Reich. This demand was, of course, rejected, but by the MUNICH PACT 'the orderly taking over of the Sudetenland by Germany' was provided for. On the basis of the Potsdam Conference (see POTSDAM AGREEMENT) some 3,300,000 Germans were evicted from Czechoslovakia after the end of the Second World War.

See also CZECHOSLOVAKIA, *History*.

Sudorifics, agents promoting sweat. See DIAPHORETICS.

Sue, Joseph Marie (1804–57), French novelist, born in Paris; he was known as Eugène Sue. His novels, realistic and ingeniously constructed, were very popular, perhaps the best-known being *Les Mystères de Paris*, 1842, describing the underworld of the capital. *Le Juif errant*, 1844–45, was an attack on the Jesuits, and *Les Mystères du peuple*, 1849–56, was suppressed in 1857. In 1848 Sue, a socialist, was elected a representative of the Assemblé Nationale, but on the election of Napoleon III was expelled from French territory, and he retired to Annecy.

Bibliography: J.-L. Bory, *Eugène Sue*, 1962.

Suebi, see SUEVI.

Suede, any LEATHER finished with a nap on the flesh side.

Suenens, Leon Joseph (1904–), Belgian cardinal. He was educated at the Gregorian University in Rome, and went on to be ordained in 1927. His abilities attracted attention and he was rapidly promoted. During the greater part of the Second World War, 1940–45, he was private chamberlain to the Pope, Pius XII. In 1941, he was appointed auxiliary bishop of Malines, the primatial see of Belgium. In 1945 he succeeded to the archbishopric of Malines (or Mechlen), and primacy of Belgium, an office that he was to hold for 16 years. In 1962, he was elevated to the cardinalate. Suenens is a leading member of the reforming movement in the Roman Catholic Church. He played an important part in the shaping of the policy of the Second Vatican Council, and is a powerful voice for progress in the Curia. He, along with Cardinal Willebrands of the Netherlands, was the personal representative of the Pope at the enthronement of the present Archbishop of Canterbury.

Suess, Edward (1831–1914), Austrian geologist, and Viennese professor famous for his work on EARTHQUAKES and crustal movement; he published *Antlik der Erde* (The Face of the Earth), and *The Origin of the Alps*, both classic works.

Suetonius, full name Gaius Suetonius Tranquillus (c. 70–c. 140), Roman historian. After practising as an advocate he became confidential secretary to the Emperor HADRIAN, but spent his later years in retirement. The most important of his surviving works is the *De Vita Caesarum*, a collection of 12 imperial biographies from Julius Caesar to Domitian. Though often scandalous in content, it is based on good sources. There is an edition with translation by R. Graves in the Penguin Classics series, 1970.

Sueur, Eustache le, see LE SUEUR, EUSTACHE.

Suevi, or Suebi, name given by the Romans to a group of peoples inhabiting central Germany, chief of whom were the Hermanduri, Langobardi, Marcomanni, Quadi, and Semnones. TACITUS, however, uses the name to include all the tribes in the basin of the Elbe, together with all those to the north and east. Others, writing in the 2nd and the 4th centuries AD, apply it almost exclusively to the Quadi.

Suez, seaport town and province of EGYPT, situated at the head of the Gulf of Suez and west of the mouth of the Suez Canal, 120 km east of Cairo. Suez is a refuelling station for ships passing through the canal. Port Ibrahim, 3 km south of Suez, is a fine harbour at the entrance to the canal. The town was largely deserted after the Arab-Israeli War of 1967, and its oil refinery was badly damaged. Following the campaign of 1973 and the re-opening of the canal, Suez is being rebuilt as a new town. Population before the 1967 war was 265,000.

Suez Canal. Ship, with air force escort, sailing up the canal from the point where it widens to become the Great Bitter Lake. *(Camera Press)*

Suez, Gulf of, western arm of the RED SEA after its bifurcation in latitude 28°N, whence it extends north-west for 300 km to latitude 30°N. It lies between Egypt and the Sinai Peninsula. Average breadth, 50 km.

Suez, Isthmus of, neck of land connecting Asia and Africa, having the Gulf of Suez to the south and the Mediterranean to the north, and through which is cut the SUEZ CANAL. Minimum width, 116 km.

Suez Canal. A French businessman, Ferdinand de LESSEPS, founded a company in 1856 to build a canal linking the MEDITERRANEAN SEA at Port Said on the northern coast of Egypt with Suez on the RED SEA. Work was started in 1859 and completed 10 years later. This canal provided a direct link between Europe and the Indian Ocean, as shipping no longer had to circumnavigate the Cape of Good Hope (see ATLAS 30).

Half the shares in the Suez Canal Company were assigned to the Egyptian government in exchange for granting the company a 99-year concession to operate the canal. The remaining shares were held by French subscribers, but Disraeli soon realised the importance of the canal for the British Empire, and especially India. Britain bought shares worth £4 million in 1875, and acquired a controlling interest in the company after occupying Egypt in 1882.

Following the Suez Crisis in 1956, the Egyptian government under NASSER nationalised the Suez Canal Company 12 years before the company's operating concession was due to expire. After heated negotiations, shareholders were awarded £28 million in compensation when an agreement was eventually reached in 1959.

The canal was closed for an eight-year period as a result of the June 1967 six-day war when Israel occupied the Sinai bank. Following the October 1973 war, and the subsequent Interim Peace Agreement signed by Egypt and Israel under the auspices of the United States Secretary of State, Dr Kissinger, the canal was reopened.

Dues from the passage of shipping during the year 1975–76 after reopening are estimated at £200 million, over twice the amount collected in 1966–67. The canal is only 11 m deep however, and therefore cannot accommodate ships of over 70,000 t loaded. Ambitious plans have been drawn up to deepen the canal to over 17 m, which will enable supertankers of up to 150,000 t to pass through. The work is being carried out by a Japanese company, at a cost of £200 million, and should be completed by 1978. This will enable the canal to accommodate over 90 per cent of the world's shipping.

Bibliography: B. Hirschfeld, *Story of the Suez Canal*, 1968; H. Thomas, *Suez Affair*, 1970; UNCTAD, *Economic Effects of the Closure of the Suez Canal*, 1974.

Suffocation, see ASPHYXIA.

Suffolk, Charles Brandon, Duke of (c. 1484–1545), English nobleman and soldier, son of William Brandon who had carried Henry VII's standard at Bosworth. Suffolk was brought up at court. He distinguished himself in the French campaign in 1513, was created viscount Lisle in that year, and duke of Suffolk a year later. In 1515 he secretly married Mary TUDOR, sister of Henry VIII and widow of Louis XII of France. This at first made Henry extremely angry, but Suffolk soon regained his favoured position and later acted for Henry on a number of occasions. Suffolk was the grandfather of Lady Jane GREY.

Suffolk, William de la Pole, 4th Earl and 1st Duke of, see POLE, DE LA.

Suffolk, most easterly, and one of the largest English counties (381,000 ha), bounded by Norfolk to the north, by Cambridgeshire to the west, by Essex to the south, and by the North Sea to the east. The coastline, which is generally low and singularly regular, has been locally encroached upon by the sea, as in the famous cliffs at DUNWICH.

Suffolk derives its name from settlement by the South Folk in the latter part of the 5th century AD. The county suffered much from the later incursions of the Danes. Walton was the scene of the landing of the Earl of Leicester in 1173 when he marched against Henry II. During the 14th century Suffolk became one of the richest counties in England owing to the influx of Flemish weavers from abroad. During the Civil War it was a stronghold of Parliament. Interesting remains of monastic buildings may be seen at BURY ST EDMUNDS (Benedictine), LEISTON (Premonstratensian), Kersey, Butley, and Ixworth (Augustinian), Sibton (Cistercian), and CLARE (Austin Friary). There are castles at FRAMLINGHAM and Orford, and a Roman fort (Burgh Castle) near YARMOUTH; and fortified manor-houses at Mettingham and Wingfield. Many of the numerous churches are of great size and beauty, and they are frequently ornamented with patterns in flint work. Over 40 churches have round towers, many of which date from the 12th century. Because of its early settlement and prosperity, the county is rich in buildings of architectural and historic interest. In particular, LAVENHAM is probably unrivalled in Britain in its wealth of medieval buildings. The domestic architec-

ture is of great interest and Moyses' Hall, Bury St Edmunds (12th century), and Little Wenham Hall (13th century) are the earliest examples. There are fine houses at Hengrave and Long MELFORD. Ickworth Hall (5 km from Bury St Edmunds) is an 18th-century mansion in the classic style. On the coast are the well-known seaside resorts of LOWESTOFT, SOUTHWOLD, ALDEBURGH, and FELIXSTOWE.

The surface of the county is flat on the east and undulating on the south and west. In the extreme north-west, near MILDENHALL, is a small area of fenland, and south-east of Mildenhall, at Rede, is the highest point (128 m) in the county. In the north-east are the BROADS as in Norfolk, and around BRANDON is the BRECKLAND, originally heathland, but now largely afforested or reclaimed for agriculture. Many relics of prehistoric man have been found here. The rivers are generally small, the most important being the WAVENEY (separating Suffolk from Norfolk), Deben, ORWELL, and STOUR (forming the southern boundary of the county). Large sea-going vessels sail up the Orwell to IPSWICH Dock and to Cliff Quay, where there is a large modern power station and extensive wharf facilities. Apart from yachting on the Orwell, Deben, Stour, Alde, and on Oulton Broad, there is little in the way of barge, wherry, or small craft traffic. Nearly all the county is under cultivation, and the soil, though not rich, is extremely varied and fertile. Barley, oats, wheat, and sugar beet are grown on a large scale, and farming, especially since the Second World War, is in a very flourishing condition. Cattle, sheep, and pigs are reared, but the local breed of HORSE, known as Suffolk Punch, once extensively used for agricultural purposes, has been displaced by the tractor and mechanical cultivation. The thriving fishing industry is concentrated at

Suffolk.

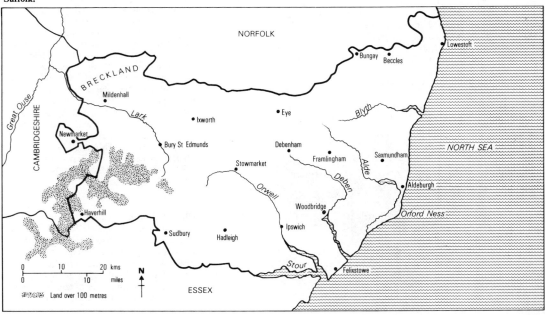

Lowestoft, which handles the bulk of the herring and mackerel catch.

Most manufactured products are agricultural; farm implements are made at Ipswich, Stowmarket, and Bury St Edmunds, and artificial manures at Ipswich, which also has clothing manufactures. In addition, there are chemical works, and factories connected with silk, coconut matting, and horse-hair industries. Ipswich, the county town, Felixstowe, and Lowestoft are ports, and other important towns are Bury St Edmunds (the old shire town of West Suffolk), Aldeburgh, BECCLES, and SUDBURY, and the urban districts of Felixstowe, STOWMARKET, and NEW-MARKET (the world-famous centre of the bloodstock and horse-racing industry). Lesser towns are BUNGAY, HAD-LEIGH, HALESWORTH, HAVERHILL, Saxmundham, Leiston, and WOODBRIDGE. Until 1974 the county was divided into two divisions of East and West Suffolk. There are five parliamentary divisions in the country. Population (1971) 537,000.

Bibliography: C. Strutt and J. Venmore-Rowland, *Setting for a Suffolk Festival*, 1968; E. Sandon, *View into the Village: Study in Suffolk Building*, 1969; J. Burke, *Suffolk*, 1971; J. Fitch, *Churches of Suffolk: Redundancy and a Policy for Conservation*, 1972; N. Scarfe (Ed.), *Suffolk*, 1972; C. Harrison, *Victorian and Edwardian Suffolk*, 1973.

Suffolk Breed, see SHEEP.

Suffolk Punch Breed, see HORSE.

Suffolk Regiment, The, a British regiment, formerly 12th Foot, raised in 1685, which fought under William III in Ireland and Flanders, and under George II at Dettingen. In 1719 it served as Marines in Sir George Byng's fleet, and was present at the defeat of the Spanish fleet off Messina. It is one of the few select 'Minden' regiments, and also took part in the famous defence of Gibraltar (1779–83), going on to India to gain further honours at Seringapatam. The regiment served in the Kaffir War of 1851–53, in the New Zealand War of 1860–66, and in the second Afghan War of 1878–80. It was again in South Africa for the war of 1899–1902. During the First World War it raised 23 battalions, which served in France, Flanders, Macedonia, Gallipoli, Egypt, and Palestine. In the Second World War the 1st Battalion fought in France in 1940, the 4th and 5th were at the defence of Singapore, the 7th was in North Africa and Italy with the Royal

Armoured Corps, and the 2nd served in Burma. In 1959 the regiment amalgamated with the Royal Norfolk Regiment to form the 1st East Anglian Regiment, and in 1964 it was redesignated the 1st Battalion The Royal Anglian Regiment.

Bibliography: G. Moir, *The Suffolk Regiment*, 1969.

Suffrage, Women's, see WOMEN'S SUFFRAGE.

Suffren de Saint Tropez, Pierre André de (1726–88), French admiral, born at Saint Cannat, Provence, and entered the French navy in 1743. He was twice captured by the British, and was made captain in 1772. After serving in Malta he fought five fiercely contested if indecisive battles against the British under Adm. Hughes in 1782 and 1783. He returned to France at the conclusion of the Treaty of Versailles, and was created a vice-admiral of France.

Sufism (a European formation from the Arabic *suf*, wool), the name of the mystical movement in Islam. Mohammed preached the worthlessness of this world as compared with the world to come, and some took his words literally and led an ascetic life. They wore wool, probably in imitation of monks, and the individual was called a Sufi. Some Muslims found the ordinary ritual unsatisfying and turned religion inwards; it became adoration, typified by this prayer: 'If I worship Thee from fear of hell, burn me in it; if I worship Thee from hope of paradise, exclude me from it; if I worship Thee for Thy own sake, withold not from me Thy eternal beauty'. God was the one Being, the infinite moral good and eternal beauty, love for whom relieved the soul of the pain of desire. The need to make a system to co-ordinate such ideas was met by certain tenets of later Greek philosophy which taught that everything is an emanation from God and the goal of life is reunion with its source. In its extreme form this became pantheism. Many described the path (*tariqa*) to God in great detail with its states and stages. *Tariqa* was also the name for the ritual peculiar to each DERVISH order and for the order itself. Sufis used the images of wine and earthly love to describe their relation to God, and it is often impossible to tell whether a Persian poem is to be taken literally or in a religious sense. The aim of the Sufi was to be so absorbed in God that in his ecstasy he could no longer distinguish between 'I' and 'Thou'. See also MEDITATION; MYSTICISM; REINCARNATION.

Bibliography: A. J. Arberry, *Sufism*, 1950.

Sugar, name of a class of sweet-tasting CARBOHYDRATES, which is subdivided into simple sugars or monosaccharides and the compound sugars, di- and trisaccharides, etc. The mono compounds are termed pentose, hexose, heptose, according to the number of carbon atoms in the molecule. They are polyhydroxy derivatives of paraffin hydrocarbons with an aldehyde or ketone group in the molecule (hence termed aldose or ketose sugars) from which their property of reducing Fehling's solution is due. Pentoses have the general formula $C_5H_{10}O_5$ and hexoses $C_6H_{12}O_6$. Examples of the former are arabinose and xylose and of the latter DEXTROSE (glucose or grape-sugar) and LAEVULOSE (fructose or fruit-sugar). The disaccharides have the general formula $C_{12}H_{22}O_{11}$ and include sucrose (cane-sugar, the ordinary sugar of commerce, whether derived from cane or beet), MALTOSE, and LAC-

Suffolk. Flatford Mill. (*Camera Press/A. G. Hutchinson*)

Sugar

TOSE (milk-sugar). Raffinose, $C_{18}H_{32}O_{16}$, is the best-known trisaccharide. Di- and trisaccharides can be split into constituent monosaccharides by heating with dilute acids or by action of ENZYMES. In this reaction one or two molecules of water are absorbed and the change is termed hydrolysis. Sucrose on hydrolysis yields glucose and fructose, the mixture being known as invert sugar because the optical rotation of the solution is changed from the positive to the negative. Invert sugar with a little sucrose constitutes the major part of honey and, with rather more sucrose, golden syrup, the remainder being water and salts. In jam manufacture some inversion of sucrose is due to acidity of the fruit. Maltose on hydrolysis yields two molecules of glucose, and lactose one molecule each of glucose and galactose. Sucrose, the most important sugar, is very soluble in water; it is insoluble in absolute alcohol, but will dissolve in aqueous alcohol. It crystallises from water in monoclinic prisms and melts at 188 °C, giving a glassy mass on cooling (barley-sugar). Prolonged heating causes gradual dehydration, darkening, and production of caramel. See also NUTRITION.

Sugar Manufacturing. Although the term sugar applies to the whole class of compounds, it is frequently used to refer to sucrose in particular. Its sweet taste was palatable to neolithic man, but sugar did not become an important food till the 19th century. Of the present major sources of sugar, sugar cane is believed to have originated in the wetter parts of Asia or the south Pacific. It was not introduced to Europe until the 1st century AD, when the Arabs brought it to the Mediterranean. Sugar beet, also now a major source, was known as a vegetable in the Middle Ages, but was not used for the manufacture of crystalline sugar until late in the 18th century.

Sucrose is commercially extracted from the stem of the sugar cane or from the root of the sugar beet. Smaller quantities are also obtained from sugar palm, sugar maple and sorghum cane.

The sugar cane contains 11–15 per cent sugar and its juice 8–21 per cent. The former is squeezed out in roller crushing mills under great pressure, and the juice, after heating and clarifying, is settled in tanks and the clear juice separated. Steam-heated, quadruple-effect evaporators concentrate it, and it is then boiled in vacuum pans at low temperature to yield massecuite, a mixture of sugar crystals and mother syrup. The latter is separated by spinning the massecuite in high-speed centrifugal machines. The mother syrup is reboiled, yielding a further crop of sugar, and its resultant syrup reboiled a third time, yielding from the centrifugals a third crop of sugar and cane molasses. The latter is economically exhausted of sucrose, although it still contains 35–45 per cent. The mixed sugars constitute the brown raw cane sugar, which is sent to refineries for further purification by the carbonation process (lime and carbon dioxide gas) and the bone charcoal process, after which boiling yields the white refined sugar: granulated, caster, icing and cube.

Sugar beet roots contain on average about 17 per cent sucrose and the juice 12–15 per cent. The roots are washed, sliced and extracted by hot water in diffusion batteries or continuous counter-current vessels and the juice purified by the carbonation process; after filtration follows a procedure identical with that in the cane-sugar industry. Raw beet sugar also needs refining. The molasses from beet sugar contains about 50 per cent sucrose. US and European practice is to treat it by the Steffan lime process or the barium process to recover more sugar, but this is not the custom in the UK. Both cane and beet factories may produce white sugar by further purification of the clarified or the carbonated juice respectively, but the products are rarely of the high purity of refined sugar.

Bibliography: International Sugar Organisation, *Sugar Year Book*, published annually.

Sugar Beet, see BEET; SUGAR.

Sugar Beet Yellows, a virus disease in which the middle and old leaves of an infected plant become yellow and die. The young leaves usually remain green. The disease is caused by at least two viruses, beet yellows virus and the commoner beet mild yellows virus. The viruses are spread by aphids, especially *Myzus persicai*, from overwintering members of the genus *Beta*; beet mild yellow virus also overwinters on some weeds. The beet yellows virus persists in the aphid for only about 24 to 36 hours, but the beet mild yellows virus will persist for 10 days. Systemic insecticides kill the aphid vector and so control the disease.

Sugar Cane, *Saccharum officinarum*, a large tropical grass with shoots reaching 3–4 m in height and having thick solid stems (unlike the hollow ones of most grasses) which yield a sugary juice when crushed. Sugar cane is thought to be native in South-East Asia, but is now cultivated very widely in moist tropical and subtropical regions as an extremely productive crop, being one of the world's main sources of sugar. The cane is generally propagated vegetatively, by planting pieces of the stem.

Suger (c. 1081–1151), French prelate, historian, and statesman. He was abbot of St-Denis, and began the construction of the famous church. Minister and counsellor to Louis VI and Louis VII, he was regent of France during the Second Crusade. He wrote a life of Louis VI and a history of the reign of Louis VII.

Bibliography: R. Fawtier, *The Capetian Kings of France* (trans. L. Butler and R. J. Adam), 1960.

Suggia, Guilhermina (1888–1950), Portuguese cellist, born in Oporto of Italian descent, studied under her father and under Klengel at Leipzig. Following her debut at Gewandhaus concerts there, she toured Europe. In 1912 she toured in Europe and beyond. Later she settled in London, and gained British nationality by marriage.

Suharto (1921–), second president of Indonesia. Born in Java, Suharto served both the Dutch and the Japanese occupation armies during the Second World War, achieving the rank of *chudancho* under the latter. As a result of his military training, he quickly attained high rank during the independence struggle and thereafter. He early befriended both Untung and Latief, who were later involved in the unsuccessful pro-SUKARNO coup of 1965. Having apparently encouraged them to stage the coup, which eliminated his six main army rivals, he turned on them, suppressed the coup, and presided over the slaughter of some million left-wing sympathisers. In 1959 Suharto had been relieved of his post in the Diponegoro Division of the Indonesian army for alleged corruption. Nevertheless, after the fall of Sukarno he was confirmed in power as president by the MPRS (Provisional People's

Consultative Assembly) in 1968. Corruption has, however, continued to flourish under his rule; the bankruptcy of the state oil combine, Pertamina, indicates the trend.

Suhl, district (*Bezirk*) of East Germany, bounded on the north by Erfurt and Gera districts, on the east and south by Bavaria, and on the west by Hessen, West Germany. It contains part of the THURINGIAN FOREST. Area 3856 km²; population (1974) 551,400.

Suhl, town of East Germany, capital of the district of Suhl, in the Thuringian Forest. It dates from the 12th century, but did not receive its charter as a city until 1527. It was later noted for its small-arms; the industry depended on local iron-mines which are now exhausted. There are motor-car, precision instrument, and chemical industries. Population 33,000.

Suhrab, see RUSTAM.

Sui Juris (Latin, in his own right), legal phrase borrowed from the Roman law of emancipation, and used in English law to denote a person who, not being a minor, mental patient or otherwise under any legal disability, is legally capable of managing his own affairs, and of suing and being sued in his own right. In the law of trusts where all the beneficiaries interested in the trust property are *sui juris*, they can together require the trustees to vest the legal estate in the property in them.

Suicide. By the Suicide Act 1961, suicide ceased to be a criminal offence in English law. If, however, two persons agree to commit suicide together and one dies and the other survives, the survivor is criminally liable, but he cannot be prosecuted without the consent of the director of public prosecutions. If the survivor killed the deceased, he will be guilty of MANSLAUGHTER; if the deceased killed himself, he will be guilty of aiding and abetting suicide. The former offence carries a maximum penalty of life imprisonment; the latter fourteen years' imprisonment.

See also HOMICIDE.

Suir, river of the Republic of Ireland, rising in Tipperary in the Devilsbit Hills, and flowing south past Thurles and Cahir, to Waterford, and uniting with the BARROW to form Waterford Harbour. Length 160 km.

Suite, in music, a series of dances put together into a group unified by key. The origin of the suite is to be found in the coupling of two contrasted dances in the 16th century. Then followed the grouping of a number of dance movements of different kinds, sometimes with thematic relations between them, so that they were in effect variations on each other. The wealth of characteristic dances in the French ballet led to the composition of orchestral suites preceded by an overture, for concert performance. German composers such as Kusser, Fischer and Georg Muffat were particularly influenced by Lully's dance style, and produced publications of orchestral dance-suites.

As well as orchestral suites, the keyboard suite developed in Germany, France and England. Froberger established a set order of dances, but in France composers did not adhere to a set pattern in the number and order of dance movements. French composers particularly favoured descriptive titles for their suite-movements, whereas the German suite—finding its apex in Bach—was more abstract in character. Bach established a basic form derived from Froberger, with prelude, allemande, courante, sarabande, followed by a group of optional dances such as gavotte, minuet, bourrée and passepied, and finally a gigue. At the opposite extreme are the 27 *Ordres* (suites) of Couperin, which are very free in form and make considerable use of descriptive, non-dance pieces (such as 'Les petits moulins à vent'). The binary form usual in suite-movements became extended and took on a more organised character with regard to the repetition of material and the key-scheme, so that it contributed towards the new 'sonata-form'. Today the term is used loosely for a collection of short pieces, for example derived from a ballet or film score.

Suk, Josef (1874–1935), Czech composer and viola player, born at Křečovice. He studied at Prague and under Dvořák, whose daughter he married in 1898. In 1922 he became a professor at Prague Conservatoire and rector in 1930. His earlier works are in the style of Dvořák; later he developed a more modern style of his own. His work includes symphonies (particularly *Asrael*, inspired by the memory of his wife), chamber music, choral works and piano pieces. He also wrote incidental music for three plays, but no opera.

Sukarno, Achmed (1901–70), first president of Indonesia. Convinced from the first of a calling to lead the Indonesian people to independence, Sukarno as he grew up devoted himself both to his own education and to familiarising himself with leading figures and currents in the nascent nationalist movement. He graduated as an engineer from Bandung Technical College in 1925. He simultaneously obtained wide introductions by his acquaintanceship with a prominent nationalist, Tjokroaminoto, with whom he lodged. By 1927 he was himself prominent enough to be one of the founders of the Indonesian Nationalist party (PNI). Arrested in 1929, he spent much of the following decade in captivity or exile.

The Japanese, however, gave him free rein, and on the declaration of independence in 1945 there was no challenge to his claim to be Indonesia's first president. For the next two decades, he epitomised in the minds of both Indonesians and others the dearly won independence. His progressively more nationalist and anti-imperialist poli-

President Sukarno. (*Popperfoto*)

cies, particularly during 1957–65, attracted to him the hostility of Western leaders, and he was eased from power in stages from 1965 to 1967–68. His place in both Indonesian and international history is, however, assured; both as a consummately skilful populist and as a figure as representative as one could find of what he himself dubbed the 'newly emerging forces' (NEFOS) of the Third World.

Sukhothai, ancient site in central THAILAND, 322 km north of Bangkok, which survives as a complex of ruined temples with the remains of a city rampart. Together with the very similar city of Si Sachanalai, a little to the north, it was the dominant centre of a Thai kingdom during the 13th and 14th centuries. Its Buddhist temples date mainly from the 14th century, but its most famous king was Ram Khamheng, who in 1292 set up the oldest surviving Thai language inscription. His campaigns extended south to Nakhon Si Thammarat, west to Pegu, and east to Laos. But after c. 1370, Sukhothai declined and was eventually absorbed by the kingdom of PHRA NAKHON SI AYUTTHAYA.

Sukhumi, capital of the ABKHAZIAN ASSR, Georgian SSR, USSR, on the BLACK SEA. The town, which is a popular resort, has fruit canning, tobacco, and leather industries, and a famous botanical garden. Originally it was an ancient Greek colony, then a Turkish fortress town, passing to Russia in 1810. Population (1975) 114,600.

Sukkur, town of Pakistan, on the INDUS, opposite Rohri. The town is the starting-point of the railway traversing the Bolan and Nari passes to QUETTA. Sukkur is principally known for the Sukkur or Lloyd Barrage, a great irrigation project on the Indus, built between 1923 and 1932. It irrigates an area of 2·4 million ha. Population (1972) 159,000.

Sukuma, Bantu farming people, numbering about 1·5 million, living south of Lake Victoria around Mwanza in Tanzania. Composed of many small groups, formerly all politically autonomous, they are today united in the Sukuma Federation.

Sukwo, see MELANESIA.

Sulaimaniya, town and province (*liwa*) in north-east Iraq, part of KURDISTAN on the frontier with Iran. It is a centre of trade with Iran and also of Kurdish nationalism. The province is mountainous but tobacco, fruit, and cereals are grown here. Area (province) 12,000 km². Population (1970) of town 98,000; province (1974) 537,750.

Sulawesi, formerly known as Celebes, island of Indonesia, separated from Kalimantan to the west by the Makasar Strait, with an area of 188,784 km². Sulawesi owes its mountainous topography and spread-eagled form to the convergence of several Tertiary fold lines and extensive uplifting, faulting, and subsidence between the two main continental shelves, the Sunda to the west and Sahul to the east. Most of the island is rugged upland above 450 m, with numerous rift-like lowlands, and soil erosion and leaching are prevalent. However, despite difficult terrain, swamps are absent and the soil (though not rich) supports a relatively productive shifting agricultural system and lowland wet-rice farming. Good agricultural land is concentrated in the south-west peninsula and Minahasa, associated with volcanic soils. The island is rich in nickel, iron, gold, silver, and a variety of other minerals. Seventy per cent of the island is forested; most of the southern forests are tropical deciduous. The presence of such 'Australian' fauna as marsupial lemurs marks Sulawesi as a transitional biogeographical area between the 'Asian' and 'Australian' realms (see WALLACE LINE). Climate is equatorial monsoon (except for the central highlands) with an average annual rainfall of about 2550 mm and a dry season during the east monsoon (June–September) especially marked in the south. See also ATLAS 35.

Total population in 1971 was 8,535,000. Two major groups are the Makasarese and the Bugis, both of Deutero-Malay stock, and related to the Javanese and Sumatran coast Malays. Traditionally traders rather than farmers, these groups now practise mainly wet-rice cultivation in the south-west of the island. The Menadonese (or Minahasans), also of Deutero-Malay stock and akin to the Filipinos, inhabit the eastern half and northern limb of Sulawesi; they are Christian rather than Muslim in religion, and practise sedentary farming. Other coastal peoples include the Gorontalese and Mandarese, who are of Deutero-Malay/Proto-Malay stock, Muslim, and practise wet-rice farming. The Proto-Malay Torajas of interior Sulawesi, on the other hand, are animist-Christian in religion, with a social organisation based on long-house communities and shifting cultivation. Major towns are Makasar (population 500,000) and Menado (185,000).

Sulawesi's main food crops are rice (500,000 ha under wet rice, 121,500 ha under dry rice) and maize. Other food crops include cassava, sweet potatoes, and peanuts. Coconuts are grown over much of lowland Sulawesi, especially in Minahasa; the island provides most of Indonesia's production of 800,000 t of copra and most of the production of coconuts. Sulawesi's main agricultural exports are copra, coconut oil, peanut oil, palm oil, castor oil, and kapok. Timber is a minor export, while almost all Indonesia's nickel production comes from south Sulawesi. Minor mineral exports include sulphur, gold, copper, and kaolin. The island's transport network is concentrated in two regions, the south-west peninsula and the north-east peninsula, around Menado; elsewhere roads are mainly coastal and in poor condition. The main port is Makasar in the south-west.

History. Although Sulawesi had long trading contacts with Muslim ports elsewhere in the archipelago, Muslim control was late in coming, partly because of the population's strong loyalty to local customary law (or *adat*). It was only in 1603 that the ruler of Makasar adopted Islam, somewhat opportunistically, to allow extension of his political control over northern states and islands in the Moluccas (see MALUKU). The interior tribes, however, resisted conversion to Islam. During the 17th century Makasar was a major port for Java-Moluccas trade, site of an important spice factory, and—partly through smuggling—a threat to the Dutch clove monopoly. It remained strongly independent of European control until Dutch conquest in 1667. The subduing of Makasar was followed, during the 18th century, by a period of Bugis ascendancy. After acting as mercenaries for the Dutch, the seafaring Bugis roamed throughout the archipelago, attacking Java and Sumatra, settling in western Malaya, and in 1772 establishing political control over first JOHOR, then the tin states of KEDAH and PERAK. This threat to Dutch influence led, after 1755, to open war between the Dutch and Bugis, and the Dutch gradually contained Bugis influence until the early 19th century, when the British effectively ended Bugis hegemony in the western archipelago and the Malayan peninsula. The Bugis remained in control of Sulawesi, but in 1859 the south-west of the island passed into Dutch hands. By 1880 Sulawesi was effectively under Dutch political control. After Indonesia achieved independence in 1949, regional separatist movements developed into a military revolt on the island, with North Sulawesi (home of the highly literate Menadonese) gaining *de facto* autonomy under military rule in 1958 and linking up with the central Sumatran regional separatists. A state of emergency was declared in 1957, and the rebellion was broken by 1961.

Suleiman the Magnificent (c. 1496–1566), Sultan of Turkey, surnamed 'the Magnificent' by Europeans and 'the Lawgiver' by his compatriots. He became sultan in 1520, seized Belgrade in 1522, captured Rhodes from the Knights of St John in 1523, defeated and killed King Louis of Hungary at Mohacs in 1526, took Armenia and the cities of Tabriz and Baghdad from the Persians in 1534, conquered Croatia in 1537, established a pasha in Buda in 1541, and, in 1560, gained a decisive naval victory over a Christian confederacy at Djerbeh. He was succeeded by SELIM II, his son by a Russian slave; Suleiman murdered his legitimate offspring to further this end.

Sulgrave Manor, Northamptonshire, England, 11 km from Banbury, built by Lawrence Washington, in 1560, on the site of a dissolved priory. A descendant, John Wash-

Suleiman the Magnificent. *(Mansell Collection)*

ington, emigrated to Virginia in 1656, and his great-grandson, George WASHINGTON, became the first President of the USA. The present house, altered and restored, was bought by the British public in 1914 to commemorate the treaty of Ghent, and was later endowed in perpetuity by the Society of the Colonial Dames of America. It is open to the public and contains portraits of Washington and some of his possessions.

Sulla, Lucius Cornelius (138–78 BC), surnamed Felix, Roman general and statesman. He was quaestor in 107 under MARIUS in the Jugurthine War, and it was to him that JUGURTHA surrendered, an event which marked the beginning of his rivalry with Marius. He continued, however, to serve under Marius against the Cimbri and Teutones from 104 until 102, when Marius's undisguised jealousy drove him to take a command under Q. Lutatius CATULUS, with whom he fought at Campi Raudii in the following year. In 93 he was praetor, and in 92 was sent as propraetor to Cilicia with orders from the SENATE to restore Ariobarzanes to the throne of Cappadocia, from which he had been driven by MITHRIDATES. This task fulfilled, he received a Parthian embassy asking alliance with the republic, and returned in 91 to Rome.

Sulla's ability and reputation had led the OPTIMATES to look to him as their leader, and thus political animosity was added to professional jealousy and personal hatred on the part of Marius. At this stage, however, the outbreak of the SOCIAL WAR hushed all private quarrels. Both men took an active part in hostilities against the common foe; nevertheless, whereas Marius was now advancing in years, Sulla gained some brilliant victories, notably his defeat of the Samnites and capture of their chief town Bovianum. Sulla was consul in 88, and ended the war by taking Nola. Meanwhile he had obtained command in the Mithridatic war. Sulla remained at Rome until his year of office had expired, and then set out to oppose Mithridates at the beginning of 87. During the next four years he won a series of amazing victories, and collected a large amount of plunder. Having sacked Athens (86), and driven the enemy from Greece, he crossed the Hellespont in 84 and in the same year concluded peace with Mithridates.

Sulla now prepared to return to Italy, where the Marian party had regained the upper hand. Leaving his legate, L. Licinius Murena, as governor of Asia, and taking with him, among other booty, the library of Apellicon, he set out and landed at Brundisium in the spring of 83. By promises and bribery he won over or neutralised most of the forces which his enemies could bring against him, leaving only a few Samnites. In 82 the struggle was brought to a close, first by the defeat of the younger Marius at Sacriportus near Praeneste, and then by the great victory over the Samnites under Pontius Telesinus before the Colline Gate at Rome.

Sulla was now absolute master of Rome and Italy; he resolved to take revenge upon his enemies and to destroy all potential opposition to the Optimates. The steps he took are known as the 'Sullan proscription'. He was given the office of dictator and drew up a list (*proscriptio*) of men who were said to be outlaws and enemies of the state. The reign of terror spread to the whole peninsula; new lists appeared; no one was safe, for Sulla gratified his friends by including in these fatal documents their personal enemies, or those whose property was coveted by his adherents.

Sullivan, Sir Arthur Seymour

At the beginning of 81 he celebrated a magnificent triumph for his victories in the Mithridatic war, and devoted the following year to the carrying of his constitutional and administrative reforms. These were in effect a restoration of the Senate to its old legislative and executive supremacy. Believing he could ensure the stability of his regime by the constant threat of arms, he established military colonies throughout the length and breadth of Italy. His personal safety was in the hands of a bodyguard created for this purpose by the emancipation of slaves who had belonged to persons proscribed by him. They were known as Cornelii after their patron, and are said to have numbered as many as 10,000.

Convinced by an old prophecy that he had not long to live, he withdrew into private life (79) and devoted his time to literature and the preparation of his memoirs (now lost but used by Plutarch). He died the following year of a long-standing disease.

Sulla's reforms were unsuited to the times; they scarcely survived him, except for the *quaestiones perpetuae* (permanent tribunals), which formed the basis of all future criminal justice.

Sullivan, Sir Arthur Seymour (1842–1900), British composer, born in London, son of an Irish bandmaster at Sandhurst. He entered the Chapel Royal choir in 1854, shortly afterwards studying at the Royal Academy under Sterndale Bennett and Goss. His first important work was an overture written in 1858 during his student days at the Leipzig Conservatory. With W. S. GILBERT as librettist he wrote many light operas: *Thespis, or The Gods Grown Old*, 1871, *Trial by Jury*, 1875, *The Sorcerer*, 1877, *H.M.S. Pinafore*, 1878, *The Pirates of Penzance*, 1879, *Patience*, 1881, *Iolanthe*, 1882, *Princess Ida*, 1884, *The Mikado*, 1885, *Ruddigore*, 1887, *The Yeomen of the Guard*, 1888, *The Gondoliers*, 1889, *Utopia Limited*, 1893, and *The Grand Duke*, 1896. Sullivan also composed choral works: *Light of the World*, 1873, *Martyr of Antioch*, 1880, and *Golden Legend*, 1886; the grand opera *Ivanhoe*, 1891; other operettas such as *Cox and Box*, 1869, and *The Rose of Persia*, 1899; incidental music, orchestral overtures, church music and songs. He was knighted in 1883.

Bibliography: G. Hughes, *The Music of Arthur Sullivan*, 1960; P. Young, *Sir Arthur Sullivan*, 1971.

Sullivan, John L(awrence) (1858–1918), US prizefighter, known as 'the Boston Strong Boy'. He won the bare-knuckle championship of America against Paddy Ryan, 1882, and was undefeated for ten years. A contest with the English champion, Charley Mitchell, at Chantilly, France, resulted in a draw after 39 rounds, preventing him from claiming the world championship. His greatest victory was over Jake Kilrain in 1889, when he knocked out the latter in the 75th round. At a further attempt at world status, he was beaten by James J. CORBETT in a contest with gloves in 21 rounds. His autobiography, *Reminiscences of a 19th Century Gladiator*, was published in 1892.

Sullivan, Louis Henry (1856–1924), US architect, born at Boston; trained in America and at the École des Beaux Arts, Paris; started practice in Chicago, 1880. He designed many commercial and other buildings, generally favouring a variant of the Romanesque style; but in his Wainwright Building at St Louis (1890–91) he adopted a more functional style of design, expressing directly the metal-frame structure, and in his Transportation Building at the World's Fair, Chicago (1893), he made a remarkable attempt to evolve a definitely original and American design, not based on any traditional type. This idea has since been developed by his most distinguished disciple, Frank Lloyd WRIGHT. Other widely admired works are the Guaranty Building, Buffalo (1894), which uses terracotta panels made from moulds sculptured by the architect to clad the steel frame, and the Carson, Pirie, Scott Store, Chicago (1899–1904), which has exposed cast-iron panels with immensely inventive decoration around the shop windows, and tiled cladding over the expressed steel frame of the floors above.

Sullom Voe, long, deep coastal inlet in the northern part of Mainland in the SHETLAND Isles, Scotland. It lies 35 km north of LERWICK. A huge complex for storing and transhipping oil from the northern part of the North Sea is at present under construction. The complex is fed by pipelines from the offshore oil-fields, and is able to take supertankers.

Sully, Maximilien de Béthune, Duc de (1559–1641), French statesman, born at Rosny. In 1572 he entered the service of Henry, the young King of Navarre, and he fought for the Protestants in the religious wars in France. Sully's devotion to Henry was absolute; he was employed by him in many delicate and difficult negotiations, and after the assassination of the French king, Henry III, and until the entry of Henry IV into Paris (March 1594), Sully did much to establish his master's diplomatic position as rightful king of France.

He was appointed a member of the great council of finance (1596). His first step was to obtain the appointment of a commission of inquiry into the state of the revenue and its collection. He was soon afterwards promoted superintendent of finance. Sully decreased taxation and reformed the corrupt system of collection, and greatly improved the finances of the country. His success led to his appointment as grand-master of the artillery, director of the marine, master of works, and director of bridges and highways. He became in fact sole minister of France. In 1606 he was created Duc de Sully and a peer of France. The murder of Henry IV in 1610 terminated the career of Sully as minister, but he retained several lesser offices. He was appointed a marshal of France by Louis XIII in 1634. In his later years he prepared his memoirs 'of the great and royal economies of Henry IV' for publication. These were published between 1634 and 1662.

Bibliography: D. Buisseret, *Sully and the Growth of Centralized Government in France, 1598–1610*, 1968.

Sully-Prudhomme, René-François-Armand (1839–1907), French poet, born in Paris. His works include *Stances et poèmes*, 1865, *Les Épreuves*, 1866, *Les Solitudes*, 1869, *Les Destins*, 1872, *Les Vaines tendresses*, 1875, *La Justice*, 1878, *L'Expression dans les beaux arts*, 1883, *Le Prisme*, 1886, *Le Bonheur*, 1888, *Réflexions sur l'art des vers*, 1892, a metrical translation of the *De rerum natura* of Lucretius, and a study of *Pascal*, 1905. His best work has severe beauty of form and a serene melancholy of thought, while often showing great intellectual power. He was awarded the Nobel Prize for literature in 1901.

Sulmona, Italian town in the region of ABRUZZO, 55 km south-east of L'Aquila in a fertile basin ringed by high, bare mountains. It was an important medieval town and the Annunziate (1320), including a church (1700) and a Renaissance palace, is the chief monument. There are engineering works here today, and OVID was born here. Population (1974) 18,200.

Sulphite Wood Pulp, used in paper manufacture, is prepared from coniferous wood from which the bark and knots have first been removed. The wood is then crushed and boiled in lined boilers of large capacity with bisulphite liquor. Digestion may take 20 hours under 34 kg steam pressure or 80 hours under 20 kg pressure. The earliest patent for the process was taken out in 1867 by Silghman, but it was not commercially successful until Ekman's improvements in 1890. There are large sulphite pulp mills at Corner Brook, Newfoundland. See PAPER.

Sulphonamides. These drugs were discovered in 1935 by Domagk, working for the German firm of Bayer; he showed that the aniline dye prontosil was effective in controlling infection of mice by the lethal bacteria known as haemolytic streptococci. The numerous antiseptics already known to be capable of destroying bacteria were too toxic for use in the body, though Ehrlich had introduced salvarsan (ARSPHENAMINE) in 1909 as a means of combating spirochaetes in syphilis, and mepacrine (ate-brin) was used in 1930 against the malarial parasite. In 1936 Colebrook at Queen Charlotte's Hospital used prontosil clinically for patients suffering from puerperal (childbed) fever, caused by haemolytic streptococci (see OBSTETRICS). In the same year also French workers at the Pasteur Institute were able to show that the active part of the prontosil molecule was sulphanilamide,

$$H_2N \quad \langle \bigcirc \rangle \quad SO_2 NH_2$$

the simplest sulphonamide from which many others have since been prepared by replacing a hydrogen (H) atom in the SO_2NH_2 group with another radical. Sulphapyridine,

$$H_2N \quad \langle \bigcirc \rangle \quad SO_2 —NH— \langle \bigcirc \rangle N$$

for example, contains the pyridine molecule, while sulphaguanidine contains guanidine and is:

$$H_2N \quad \langle \bigcirc \rangle \quad SO_2 —NH —C \begin{smallmatrix} NH_2 \\ \\ NH \end{smallmatrix}$$

The sulphonamides inhibit the synthesis of folic acid (an essential growth factor for some bacteria, e.g. streptococci) from para-aminobenzoic acid. (Man uses preformed folic acid and thus his cells are not affected by sulphonamides.) Sulphonamides have a broad spectrum of antibacterial activity and individually vary in their efficiency of absorption and duration of action. They are used in patients who are sensitive to ANTIBIOTICS and also for infections of the urinary tract and respiratory tract, trachoma, and meningococcal meningitis. Their use has declined due to the development of resistant bacteria which metabolise sulphonamides to an inactive form. However, they are frequently administered with other drugs, e.g. with trimethoprim, which interferes at a later stage in the folic acid pathway, in the drug co-trimoxazole, principal constituent of the proprietary preparations Septrin and Bactrim.

Sulphonamides have certain disadvantages: they may cause nausea and vomiting, anorexia (loss of appetite), drowsiness and reduced mental activity; the less soluble ones are apt to crystallise in the kidneys and impede the flow of urine unless ample fluids are taken; in susceptible persons they cause a rash. They may also cause agranulocytosis, i.e. a shortage of granulocytic white corpuscles in the blood.

Sulphur, non-metallic chemical element, symbol S, atomic number 16, atomic weight 32·06. It occurs in the free state in two forms: a volcanic deposit, found in lava fissures and extinct volcanoes; and in combination with gypsum (from which the sulphur has been thermally reduced). In combination with other elements, sulphur is widely distributed, occurring as sulphides in many important ores, such as those of zinc (blende), lead (galena), mercury (cinnabar), antimony (stibnite), and iron and copper (pyrites). Sulphur is found in the sulphates gypsum ($CaSO_4$), heavy spar ($BaSO_4$), and Epsom salts ($MgSO_4$). Sulphur is present in trace quantities in organic products such as garlic, mustard, hair, eggs, etc. To free natural sulphur from earthy impurities it is stacked in brick kilns having a sloping floor and ignited with burning brushwood. Some sulphur burns, and the heat of its combustion causes the remainder to melt and flow away from the impurities into rough moulds. About one-third of the total sulphur present is wasted by this method. Pyrites is sometimes burned in order to obtain sulphur, but more generally the pyrites is roasted with excess of air to obtain sulphur dioxide for sulphuric acid manufacture. Crude sulphur is purified by distillation from iron retorts into brickwork chambers. In these chambers the sulphur condenses and forms a powdery deposit, the 'flowers of sulphur' of commerce. As the distillation goes on the temperature rises, the powder melting to an amber-coloured liquid which is run out into wooden moulds, forming 'roll sulphur'. Nowadays sulphur is recovered from waste gases from industrial processes. The sulphur dioxide is concentrated, and absorbed in salts to form sulphites and bisulphites. These are acidified and the purer sulphur dioxide is reduced by white-hot coke to produce sulphur which is distilled and condensed. In the Frasch process, used in the USA, superheated water is forced down into the sulphur (*in situ*, below ground). The sulphur melts and is forced to the surface, together with air, by means of special pumps. The process is very efficient, and most of the sulphur of commerce and industry is now obtained in this way.

Sulphur exists in the allotropic forms: rhombic (α), monoclinic (β), and amorphous (γ); also as nacreous (crystalline), plastic and colloidal, whilst there are three forms of liquid sulphur (λ, μ, and π). The vapour

Sulphuric Acid

of sulphur is a mixture of S_8, S_6, S_4, S_2 in varying proportions according to temperature. Native sulphur is octahedral, and is a pale yellow solid, soluble in carbon disulphide and in benzene, turpentine, etc. It is an extremely bad conductor of electricity and heat. At 114·5 °C sulphur melts to an amber-coloured mobile liquid. When the temperature is further raised the liquid darkens in colour and becomes more viscous, until at 230 °C the liquid appears almost black and cannot be poured. Further rise of temperature causes the liquid to regain its mobility, and at 444 °C it boils to a deep red vapour. Sulphur burns easily in air, forming sulphur dioxide. It combines directly with many metals and nonmetals, forming sulphides, e.g., iron and copper burn brightly in sulphur vapour. Sulphur is used as an insulator, in pyrotechnics, in medicine as an aperient, and in vulcanising RUBBER.

A few of the more important simple compounds of sulphur are the following. Hydrogen sulphide (H_2S) is a gas which escapes from volcanoes, and is also found in some mineral waters which are reputed cures for rheumatism and some skin diseases. It is commonly prepared by the action of dilute hydrochloric acid on ferrous sulphide in a Kipp's apparatus ($FeS + 2HCl = H_2S + FeCl_2$). Hydrogen sulphide is a colourless, poisonous gas, with a smell like that of rotten eggs. It burns in air with a lilac flame, forming sulphur dioxide, water, and free sulphur. Its value in the laboratory is as a reducing agent and on account of the fact that it precipitates the sulphides of certain metals from solution. Sulphur dioxide (SO_2) is formed wherever sulphur or its compounds are burned in air. For the manufacture of sulphuric acid, sulphur dioxide is prepared by roasting pyrites in air: $4FeS + 11O_2 = 2Fe_2O_3 + 8SO_2$. The laboratory method of preparation consists in heating copper turnings or sulphur, with sulphuric acid, or by the action of an acid on a sulphite, when the gas is evolved. Sulphur dioxide is a colourless gas, with a suffocating smell, and is very soluble in water, forming an acid solution (see SULPHUROUS ACID). The gas is easily liquefied (at −10 °C under ordinary pressure), and is thus supplied in that condition in syphons. The solution of the gas in water is used as a reducing agent and for bleaching straw and wool. Sulphur dioxide is used as a disinfectant and as an 'antichlor' to remove last traces of chlorine from articles bleached with the latter. Sulphur trioxide (SO_3) is produced when a mixture of oxygen and sulphur dioxide is passed over heated platinised asbestos, or it may be conveniently prepared by gently distilling pyrosulphuric acid. It is a white crystalline solid which fumes in contact with air and combines violently with water to form sulphuric acid.

Sulphuric Acid, hydrogen sulphate, or oil of vitriol, H_2SO_4, acid formed when sulphur trioxide is dissolved in water. Commercially the acid is formed by two processes—the chamber process, which is now virtually obsolete, and the contact process. The principle involved in both processes is that sulphur dioxide and oxygen will combine to form sulphur trioxide in the presence of a suitable catalyst. The trioxide will then combine with water to form sulphuric acid. The chamber process used nitrogen dioxide as the catalyst, but was inefficient, as substantial quantities of it were lost during reaction. In the contact process the catalyst is made of platinised asbestos suspended in layers of vertical steel cylinders. A mixture of sulphur dioxide (from burning sulphur or from roasted pyrites) and air is cooled, thoroughly freed from dust and other impurities by passing through dust chambers, washed with a small amount of alkali, and then, after being heated to about 400–450 °C, subjected to the action of the catalyst. The gases pass up outside these tubes and are then deflected through them. Great care must be taken to ensure that the temperature does not rise too high. The resulting gases, which contain sulphur trioxide, are bubbled through strong sulphuric acid (97–98 per cent), water being added so as to keep pace with the absorption of the trioxide and to maintain the acid at about the same strength. Vanadium pentoxide is also used as a catalyst.

Sulphuric acid is a colourless, oily liquid (relative density 1·84) which has a great affinity for water and is used as a drying agent. The mixing of the acid with water is accompanied by a great evolution of heat, hence care must be taken when mixing, otherwise explosive ebullition takes place. Sulphuric acid is used in the Leblanc process for carbonate of soda, in galvanising, tinplate, explosives, artificial silk, plastics and aerated water industries and many others, and in the production of dyes and many important organic 'intermediates'. The acid is dibasic, forming both normal and acid salts. Of the normal salts, several occur in nature, for example, barytes ($BaSO_4$) and Epsom salts ($MgSO_4$). The sulphates are mostly soluble in water; those of lead, calcium, and strontium are only sparingly soluble, while barium sulphate is insoluble in water and in acids. This last salt is, therefore, used as a test for the presence of the acid. Addition of a soluble barium salt to a sulphate is followed immediately by the precipitation of the insoluble barium sulphate. The acid salts are similar in properties to the normal salts, but have an acid reaction. The alums are a well-known group of double sulphates (see ALUM). Fuming sulphuric acid is obtained by dissolving sulphur trioxide in sulphuric acid. It is a colourless, strongly fuming liquid and solidifies on cooling to a crystalline mass.

Sulphurous Acid, a solution of sulphur dioxide in water ($SO_2 + H_2O = H_2SO_3$). Several hydrates with 6, 10, and 14 molecules of water are known. The solution smells strongly of sulphur dioxide and gradually oxidises in air to sulphuric acid. It is dibasic and forms two series of salts: normal sulphites, prepared by the action of excess of hydroxide or carbonate of the metal on the acid, e.g. sodium sulphite (Na_2SO_3); and acid sulphites, such as potassium hydrogen sulphite ($KHSO_3$), prepared by having excess of acid acting on the hydroxide. The alkaline sulphites are soluble in water, the sulphites of other metals being insoluble or nearly so. The metabisulphites (e.g., $K_2S_2O_5$) and the bisulphites are also derivatives of the acid and are used in photography. Chemically the sulphites, bisulphites, and the acid are mild reducing agents, and the last two are used in bleaching wool.

Sultana, see RAISIN.

Sultanabad, see ARAK.

Sultaniyah, formerly a town of Persia between Abhar and Zanjan, founded in 1305 and made the capital city of the Ilkhan dynasty. It is now in ruins.

Sulu Archipelago, archipelago of the southern PHIL-IPPINES, having the Sulu Sea on the north-west and the Celebes Sea on the south-east. There are about 400 islands, divided into six groups stretching some 270 km. Products include cassava, fruits, coconuts, rice, hemp, sesame, indigo, and cocoa, with shell and pearl fishing, weaving, and cord-making also carried on. The sea provides the mainstay of the economy including pearl beds, coral, and turtle fisheries in addition to commercial fishing. It has no mineral wealth. The province is mainly populated by Muslims (Moros) who are fiercely independent. The islands have become a smuggler's haven as this was their only method of resisting civil authority. It is from here that the claim of jurisdiction over Sabah emanates. Since 1972 opposition to central government has been more open and the archipelago has witnessed fierce exchanges between Muslim separatists and government forces. The capital is Jolo on the island of JOLO. Area 2688 km². Population (1970) 427,386. See also ATLAS 35.

Bibliography: M. O. Ariff, *Philippines' Claim to Sabah,* 1970.

Sulzberger, Arthur Hays (1891–1968), US newspaper proprietor, born in New York; educated at Columbia University, he started work in the cotton goods business in 1914. In 1917 he married the daughter of Adolph Ochs, owner of the *New York Times,* whom he succeeded as publisher in 1935. Between 1935 and his retirement in 1961, Sulzberger spread the circulation of the newspaper first throughout the United States, and then throughout the world. He often declared that he never wanted the paper to become 'too livened up', either in Paris or New York, saying that 'the good grey *Times* is still the best there is and should stay that way'. See also 'NEW YORK TIMES'; NEWSPAPERS.

Sumach, sumac or shumack, see RHUS.

Sumatra (Indonesian *Sumatera*), the largest island of the Indonesian archipelago wholly under Indonesian control. Area 425,092 km². A mountain spine stretches down the west coast from the Aceh highlands, through the Batak plateau and Menangkabau highlands, to the Benkulu Mountains. A major barrier to east-west movement, this area is of considerable recent or active vulcanicity, a factor which has strongly affected the soil pattern, from the acidity of the Batak land to the far more fertile neutral-basic soil of much of the more recent volcanic areas in the Menangkabau and Benkulu highlands. Along the west coast are occasional coastal plains and a continuous belt of steep foothills, heavily forested and with major timber potential (especially teak and ebony); while the east coast is characterised by a wide belt of freshwater and tidal swamp (as wide as 250 km in east-central and south Sumatra) separating the foothill zone of the range's eastern flank from the coast. The swampland is marked by extensive seasonal flooding and large, thick deposits of acid peat, making it both unhealthy and difficult to penetrate; however, the foothills are rich in mineral resources: gold in the Menangkabau Plateau; major oil deposits in the east-central and southern foothills; and brown coal in both Menangkabau country and the eastern Benkulu range. Seventy per cent of the island is forested. Sumatra's climate is tropical monsoonal, with a dry,

hot season from May to September and a rainy season from November to March. See also ATLAS 34.

Total population in 1971 was 20,813,000. There are four main ethnic groups each numbering three million or more: the Acehnese, Menangkabau, Sumatran coast Malays, and BATAKS, who are all of Deutero-Malay stock except the Bataks, who derive from earlier Proto-Malay stock. The Acehnese are a mainly coastal people inhabiting the north Sumatran region of Aceh; they are strongly Muslim with an advanced Islamic culture and social organisation, and use an Arabic script. They have a strong tradition of trading and refined craftsmanship, yet their economy is based on *sawah*, or wet-rice, cultivation. The Menangkabau, occupying the central uplands and adjacent west coast, have a similarly strong and advanced Islamic culture with a fine tradition of trade and craftsmanship, and a highly evolved irrigated rice economy (practised on both lowlands and upland terraces). They are distinctive in their matrilineal social organisation. The Sumatran coast Malays of the east coast have much in common with the peninsular Malays in religion and culture. With a seafaring tradition, their economy is based on shifting cultivation and occasional poor quality wet-rice agriculture. The Bataks have little affinity to the other three major groups: they occupy the uplands of north-central Sumatra around Lake Toba and the neighbouring west coast, practising both terraced *sawah* cultivation and shifting cultivation; those near Menangkabau settlement are predominantly Muslim, but Christianity is predominant in the Toba region, and animism further north; there is considerable local and regional division, with a social organisation of largely autonomous villages based on multi-family dwellings. Other smaller population groups in Sumatra include the Rejong-Lampung peoples of southern Sumatra (nominally Muslim, with Indianised cultures influenced by the Javanese) and many small upland and coastal tribal aborigines such as the Negrito Orang Akit and the Proto-Malay Sakai (peoples either animistic or nominally Muslim, whose economy is based on hunting, fishing, and gathering). Urban centres are nowhere as large as the largest JAVANESE cities: MEDAN, PALEMBANG, and PADANG are the biggest.

Sumatra has long been Indonesia's major source of cash crop exports (other than timber). Since 1870 the *Cultuurgebied* (Plantation District), a swamp-free, fertile lowland area along the north-east coast between the Asahan river and Aceh, has been a principal growing area for tobacco (grown around Medan), rubber, tea, coffee, palm oil, and sisal. As a whole, Sumatra is the main producer of Indonesian rubber, accounting for 75 per cent of smallholder production and 60 per cent of estate production (the main rubber producing province is South Sumatra); it is also the main producer of oil palm (concentrated in the Medan region), coffee (90 per cent of which is grown by smallholders), tea, and pepper (the latter grown mainly on South Sumatran smallholdings). Timber is an important export, mainly from South Sumatra, where half the forest area is under cutting licence. Of the major food crops, Sumatra is the main producer of rice outside Java, with 1·4 million ha under wet rice and 550,000 ha under dry rice (North Sumatra, with 600,000 ha of rice-land, is the island's main rice producing province, exporting a surplus to the rest of the island). Other food crops include maize, cassava, sweet potatoes, peanuts, and soybeans.

Sumatra

Sumatra is the main oil producing region in Indonesia. In spite of considerable offshore and onshore exploration elsewhere, most newer wells outside Sumatra are at early stages of production, while the well-developed fields in the Minas area of east-central Sumatra produce 45 million t of Indonesia's 69·7 million t a year. Since 1967 important new oil and natural gas fields have been developed, mainly off the south-east and north-east coasts. The Arun field off the Aceh coast contains the largest natural gas deposit in East Asia (and one of the largest in the world), with reserves of 425,000,000,000 m³. At present, the Arun field is being linked to a major liquified natural gas plant at nearby Lok Seumawe. Also of major importance in Sumatra's development is the construction of a major hydro-electric and aluminium smelting complex based on the ASAHAN river in north-east Sumatra.

Transport development is concentrated in three key areas of export production and their nearby coastal outlets: although road, rail, and port facilities are in need of rehabilitation, there are concentrations of such facilities in the south (between Palembang and Teluk Betung), on the west-central coast (between Bukit Tinggi and Padang), and in the north-east region of the *Cultuur-gebied* (centred on Medan and linking Kotaraja and Rantauparapat).

History. The earliest Chinese-Indonesian and Indian-Indonesian trading contacts in pre-Christian times appear to have been with Sumatra. Between the 7th and 12th centuries, the Indianised maritime power of Sri Vijaya, based in Palembang, controlled Sumatra's east coast as well as the west coasts of the Malay Peninsula and Kalimantan. While the Java-based Majapahit empire consolidated its hold over south and west Sumatra, before a brief period of ascendancy in the 14th century, the Hindu-Malay Menangkabau kingdom established itself firmly in the north, leaving, after its eclipse, one of the most advanced cultures in Indonesia. From the 15th century, the Muslim influence was dominant, and the pattern of political power in Sumatra changed markedly from one oriented to Java to one marked by the effective successor to Sri Vijaya in the 15th century, and from 1496 onwards the sultanate of Aceh (or Achin) was dominant in the north. Aceh developed as one of the most distinctive Muslim territories in Indonesia, bringing a large body of Mogul culture into Sumatran social and political life. Its sultans resisted both Portuguese and Dutch attempts at domination, but after an expensive war was begun in 1873, the Dutch gained sovereignty over Aceh in 1908, making it the last part of Indonesia to come under formal Dutch control. After Indonesia gained independence in 1949, a separatist movement set up an autonomous military régime in central Sumatra in 1956, and by 1957 South and central Sumatra were under *de facto* autonomous military administration. Sumatra's relative wealth, its historical and cultural distinctiveness from Java, and its resentment against subsidising Java economically without commensurate political power, made the central government's anti-Dutch policies a catalyst of discontent insofar as they discriminated against Sumatra as the major source of exports. The separatists wanted the anti-Communist, and Sumatran, vice-president, Mohammed Hatta, to head the new government. However, the rebellion, like the related rebellion in North SULAWESI, was broken by 1961.

Sumer. Copper figure of a bison, Sumerian work, c. 2300 BC, from Van (eastern Turkey). *(British Museum, London)*

Sumba, formerly Sandalwood Island, island in the province of Nusa Tenggara, Indonesia, 48 km south of Flores. With some stock-raising and cotton growing, and formerly an important source of sandalwood, the island's economy is based on shifting maize cultivation and hunting, fishing, and gathering. The inhabitants are non-Malay Sumbanese, animist and Christian in religion. Area 10,350 km²; population (1971) 310,000.

Sumbawa, island in the province of Nusa Tenggara, Indonesia. The landscape is mountainous, and in the north-east stands the active 2851-m Tambora volcano. In 1815 Tambora erupted, ejecting some 152 km³ of material over a 700-km wide area, reducing the mountain's height by 1250 m, and leaving an 11-km wide crater. The eruption caused NEW ENGLAND's notorious 'year without summer' by blocking off the sun's warmth with dust in the upper atmosphere. The local economy involves both wet-rice farming, and shifting cultivation in the interior, with livestock rearing. Teak, horses, and tamarind are the main exports. Bima is the main port and town. Population (1971) 243,577.

Sumbul, an Indonesian name applied to two plants which have fragrant roots. One of these, known also as musk-root, is *Ferula sumbul*, and is a species of Umbelliferae; the other is *Nardostachys jatamansi*, the spikenard, a species of Valerianaceae.

Sumer, or Sumeria, term which the ancient Semites of AKKAD, Mesopotamia, applied to the country of the lower valley of the Tigris and Euphrates rivers, namely south Babylonia.

Little is known of the early history of Sumer or of the origins of the Sumerians. The term Sumerian describes, strictly speaking, only the language, and from the earliest written texts it is clear that the population of the area contained both linguistically, and probably, ethnically, mixed elements. No kind of social distinction appears to have been made between people with Sumerian or Semitic names, and some of the city names may be derived from yet another language group. For these reasons, the old theory which assumed a conflict between Semites and Sumerians has now been generally abandoned. The Sumerians represented the dominant cultural group of the Near East until c. 2000 BC, strongly influencing such distant places as MARI on the Euphrates, and ASHUR. They invented the earliest known system of writing, first attested about 3100 BC (gradually developed into the CUNEIFORM WRITING), and produced a vast and highly developed literature, consisting of myths, histories, hymns, liturgies, epics, commercial documents, etc. Even after the loss of political independence, the Sumerian cultural supremacy continued for many centuries. The Accadians adopted from them the script, the literary and liturgical language, and a large part of their literature. See BABYLONIA.

Bibliography: J. Oates in *Iraq* (vol. 22), 1960; E. Strommenger and M. Hirmer, *The Art of Mesopotamia*, 1966; S. N. Kramer, *The Sumerians: Their History, Culture and Character*, new ed. 1971.

Sumerian Language (Accadian *lišan šumēri*, language of Sumer), spoken by the Sumerians, who, in the 4th, 3rd, and early 2nd millenniums BC, inhabited southern Mesopotamia. Its affinities (non-Semitic and Indo-European) are still a matter for discussion. Scholars have claimed to have discovered in it resemblances to Basque, Georgian, Chinese, Turkish, Bantu, and other languages, but particularly to Ural-Altaic or Caucasian forms of

Sumer. Reconstructed headdress and jewellery of Queen Shubad, c. 2500 BC, from the royal cemetery at Ur, excavated by Sir Leonard Woolley. *(British Museum, London/Werner Forman Archive)*

speech (see ALTAIC LANGUAGES). Its structure is complicated and not yet fully understood, though it can be translated with a considerable degree of accuracy.

Sumerian was an agglutinative speech, combining into single words various linguistic elements, each having a distinct, fixed connotation and a separate existence; for example, *šag*, heart; *šag-mu*, my heart; *šag-mu-ta*, from my heart. These particles could be attached to whole clauses or sentences as well as to individual words; for example, 'From the terror of God' is *Nig-huš-dingir-a-ta*, where *dingir*, God, *nig-huš*, terror, *-a* (for *-ak*) of, and the ablative particle *-ta* governs the whole preceding phrase. The formation of the verb was extremely complicated. To the simple root were attached prefixes and suffixes whose significance is not always clear, so that a finite verb-form is not a single word but a concatenation. Take the root *du*, to build; *Lugal dingir-ra-ni e mu-na-ni-du*, The king built a temple for his god.

Some scholars suggest that the Sumerian language had a series of vocal 'tones', like Chinese, which distinguished homonyms. For example, *šag*, heart, and *šag*, to be gracious, were probably distinguished in speaking by the pitch of the voice.

Two dialects or literary styles are distinguishable in the Sumerian documents—the *eme-ku* or pure speech and the *eme-sal* or broad speech. The latter is used only in religious documents and is distinguished from the much commoner *eme-ku* by certain differences of orthography and pronunciation; for example, the *eme-ku* for 'god' is *dingir*, the *eme-sal* is *dimmer*. The Sumerian language is preserved in about 250,000 clay tablets, of which more than 95 per cent are economic in character (contracts, wills, receipts, and letters). About 3000 tablets contain literary compositions, and about 600 are building and dedicatory inscriptions, some of them being very important historical sources. All this material indicates that the Sumerians represented the dominant cultural group of the ancient Near East from the last centuries of the 4th millennium BC until the 1st century of the 2nd millennium BC.

Bibliography: C. J. Gadd, *A Sumerian Reading-book*, 1924; L. A. Waddell, *Indo-Sumerian Seals Deciphered*, 1925; *Sumer-Aryan Dictionary*, 1927; C. L. Woolley, *The Sumerians*, 1929; A. Deimel, *Sumerische Grammatik*, 2nd ed. 1939; S. N. Kramer, *Sumerian Mythology*, 1944; J. B. Pritchard and others, *Ancient Near Eastern Texts*, 1950; D. Diringer, *The Alphabet*, 4th impression 1953, and *The Hand-produced Book*, 1953.

Sumgait, town in AZERBAIJAN SSR, USSR, situated on the northern shore of the Apsheron Peninsula, 25 km north-west of Baku. It is the centre of the metallurgical industry (pipe-rolling mill, aluminium plant), and also has a chemical industry (synthetic rubber, superphosphates). It was founded in 1949. Population (1974) 138,000.

Summary Jurisdiction. The summary jurisdiction of JUSTICES OF THE PEACE in England is a power conferred on justices by various acts of Parliament to try certain minor offences without the aid of a jury and to make orders for payment of money on complaint. There is an appeal to the CROWN COURT against conviction, sentence order, or decision of a court of summary jurisdiction. Appeals on questions of law only lie to the divisional court of Queen's

Bench. See also CRIMINAL LAW.
Bibliography: Stone's *Justices Manual*, published annually.

Summational Tones, see COMBINATION TONES.

Summer, the second of the four SEASONS, defined astronomically as the interval between the summer solstice and the autumnal equinox but in popular usage taken to mean the period from the beginning of May to the end of August in Great Britain and from the beginning of June to the end of August in North America. Midsummer Day is 24 June, i.e, two or three days after the actual solstice.

Summer Time, see DAYLIGHT SAVING.

Summerhill, a progressive coeducational primary and secondary school at Leiston, Suffolk, founded in 1921 by A. S. NEILL who was also its headmaster. The school, in which the revolutionary educational theories of its founder are put into practice, is self-governing—the children regulate themselves, direct their own class attendance, and make their own rules in school council. Neill argued that a school must free children from discipline and moral teaching to develop in their own way, work joyfully, and live positively. The school has never been 'recognised' as efficient by the Department of Education and Science, something which Neill never sought, and has not been a commercial success, relying on an influx of American students to keep it on its feet financially.

Summerskill, Edith Summerskill, Baroness (1901–), British politician, born in London, and educated at King's College, qualifying as a doctor in 1924. She entered Parliament as Labour MP for West Fulham in 1938 and represented Warrington, 1955–61. From 1945 to 1950 she was parliamentary secretary to the Ministry of Food; and minister of national insurance (1950–51). A prominent exponent of women's rights, she was made a life peer in 1961.

Summons, in English law, a citation to appear in court. It is a written notification, signed by the proper officer, to be served on a party to an action to warn him to appear on a specified day to answer the claim of the plaintiff. In the High Court procedure a writ of summons is one of the four forms of originating process to commence an action and is usually used where there is a dispute of fact. It contains, *inter alia*, an endorsement of the nature of the claim made, or of the relief or remedy required in the action, so that the defendant may know why he is sued. The plaintiff may state the particulars of his case in full on his writ of summons, which then takes the place of a statement of claim.

An originating summons is another form of originating process and is used where there is a question of law or construction of a document, rather than one of fact, in dispute. It is a customary mode of commencing actions in the Chancery Division of the High Court.

The issue of a summons together with particulars of the claim is the ordinary mode of commencing an action in the county court.

See also POLICE.

Sumner, Charles (1811–74), US politician, born in Boston, and educated at Harvard, being admitted to the Bar in 1834. He was a determined opponent of slavery. In 1851 he was elected to the Senate where he opposed the

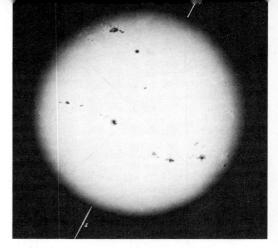

Sun. Very heavily spotted solar disk, 1 April 1958. *(Royal Greenwich Observatory, Herstmonceux)*

KANSAS-NEBRASKA BILL, and in 1856 he was assaulted by Preston Brooks and incapacitated for three years. In 1861 he urged emancipation, and later insisted that Congress and not the president should control Reconstruction. He led Senate opposition to President Andrew JOHNSON and was prominent in urging Johnson's impeachment.

Sumner, James Batcheller (1877–1955), US biochemist. He worked on the chemistry of enzymes and proteins, and shared the 1946 Nobel Prize for chemistry.

Sumperk (German *Schönberg* or *Mährisch-Schönberg*), town of central Czechoslovakia, in north Moravia. It has textile industries and oil-refineries. Population 23,000.

Sumptuary Laws (Latin *sumptuarius*, from *sumptus*, expense) were designed to restrain the expenses of citizens in wearing apparel, equipages, diet, and furniture. Sumptuary laws were promulgated by Solon in Athens, by Sparta, and by Sulla, Caesar, and Augustus in Rome. In England Edward II and later kings issued sumptuary laws. During the Second World War some countries, especially Britain, issued sumptuary laws restricting the shape and trimmings of garments of both men and women in the interests of economy of material and labour.

Sumter, Fort, see FORT SUMTER.

Sumy, *oblast* in the UKRAINIAN SSR, USSR, situated on the south-west border of the central Russian upland, partly in the black earth belt. Fifteen per cent of the area is covered with forests, mainly deciduous. Wheat, maize, sugar-beet, sunflowers, potatoes, and hemp are grown, and pigs and cattle are reared. There are varied food, engineering, and chemical industries. In the Middle Ages the region belonged to Pereyaslavl principality; it became Lithuanian in 1362, and Muscovite in 1503. It was occupied by the Germans in 1941–43. Area 23,800 km². Population (1970) 1,505,000 (44 per cent urban).

Sumy, capital and economic centre of Sumy *oblast* (see above), USSR, north-west of Kharkov. It has varied industries: equipment for the mining and food industries, sugar, fertilisers, and woollens. It was founded in 1652 by Cossack settlers from Polish-held Ukraine; in the 18th and 19th centuries it was an important trade centre. Its industrial development dates from the 19th century. Population (1974) 189,000.

Sun, the centre of our SOLAR SYSTEM. It is a typical medium-sized STAR whose distance from the Earth, as found from observations of its PARALLAX, averages 149,600,000 km. It is the only star to which we are sufficiently close to study its surface details and outer atmosphere.

The material of the Sun is in a gaseous state so that it has no definite boundary but fades gradually into space. However, the Sun appears to have a relatively sharp edge because most of its light that reaches us comes from a layer only a few hundred kilometres thick which is called the 'photosphere', and is regarded as being the surface of the Sun. Above it are the 'chromosphere' and the 'corona' which together form the solar atmosphere. Superimposed on the steady shining of the Sun are short-lived disturbances that occur from time to time in the atmosphere, and constitute a sort of solar weather. These range from cold areas called 'sunspots' and hot areas called 'plages', which may last for weeks or even months, to violent explosions called 'flares' whose life is measured in hours, if not in minutes. The individual events of the solar weather seem to occur at random but their overall frequency reaches a maximum at about 11-year intervals. They seem to be connected with the solar magnetic field, and some of them cause disturbances in the Earth's upper atmosphere. When solar activity is at a minimum, the Sun is said to be 'quiet', and its state at such a period is referred to as the 'Quiet Sun'.

The Interior. The most important property of the Sun is the vast energy it is steadily pouring out into space. A simple calculation based on its distance and the observed value of the SOLAR CONSTANT shows that it is radiating 3.86×10^{26} J/s. Moreover, evidence from terrestrial fossils indicates that there has been no appreciable alteration in this rate for several hundred million years, and probably longer. The age of the Sun, assumed to be much the same as that of the Earth, Moon, and meteorites, is of the order of 4.5×10^9 years. Its mass is 1.99×10^{30} kg

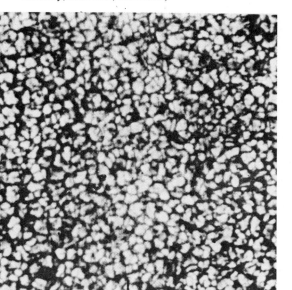

Sun. Photospheric granulation. Enlarged portion of a photo taken with the 12-inch telescope of Project Stratoscope. *(Princeton University, ONR NSF, and NASA)*

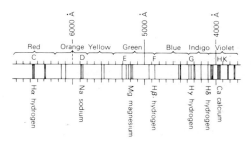

Sun. The solar spectrum in the visual region.

and its diameter 1,392,000 km, giving a mean density of 1.409 g/cm³.

As in other stars, the source of the Sun's energy is thought to be the gradual conversion of hydrogen into helium in the deep interior where the temperature is of the order of 15,000,000 K, and the pressure such that the density is approximately 150 g/cm³. Energy from the centre gradually makes its way outwards by radiative processes until it reaches some layer not far below the surface. From there on, the energy is transported by vast convection currents. The estimated period for which the Sun can maintain its present steady output of energy is another 5×10^9 years, after which it is expected to evolve into a red giant star, burning up the Earth and other inner planets in the process.

The Photosphere. The general appearance of the Sun in the optical region is shown in fig. 1. In the absence of spots, the first thing that attracts attention is the general decrease of brightness towards the edge. This is a consequence of the fact that the photosphere is not a thin surface but a zone in which the opacity, or fogginess, of the solar material is thinning out, and in which the temperature is falling from about 9000 K at the bottom to 4300 K at the top. At the centre of the disk, our line of sight is normal to the solar layers and penetrates to deeper, hotter levels than it does nearer the edges where it is looking obliquely through the layers. Thus, taken as a whole, the photosphere really has no proper 'black-body' temperature, but in the optical region its radiation approximates to that of a black body with a temperature of about 5800 K, and the maximum of its radiant energy distribution is at 4750 Å, in the blue-green region of the spectrum.

If conditions are good and the telescope powerful enough, it will be seen that the photosphere appears granulated (left), and that the pattern of this granulation is continuously changing. The individual granules are the tops of the rising and falling convection currents that transport the solar energy from the interior to the surface.

The spectrum of the photosphere is continuous and crossed by many absorption lines. The strongest ones were noted by Fraunhofer and are often referred to by the letters he assigned to them. These are shown in fig. 3. Since the photosphere is very bright, a high dispersion spectrograph can be used and tens of thousands of absorption lines observed. The work of identifying them all still goes on. So far lines from over 70 of the terrestrial elements have been found. With the exception of hydrogen and helium, the relative abundances of the various elements in the photosphere seem to be very similar to those on Earth.

Sunspots. When present, the most conspicuous features on the face of the Sun are the spots, sometimes large and many, sometimes few and small, very occasionally none at all. They appear to be shallow depressions in the general photospheric level and, in their simplest form, consist of a black centre, the *umbra*, surrounded by a striated grey border, the *penumbra*. The umbra appears black only by contrast for its spectrum shows its temperature to be about 3900 K. The spectrum also shows a Zeeman effect implying the presence of strong local magnetic fields which may be responsible for the formation of the spot through their interference with the rising and falling photospheric convection currents.

Individual spots may be short lived or may last for months. Those that last less than a day are never more than small dark 'pores'; those that endure longer usually grow in size and complexity. Many spots become larger than the Earth, while a few have stretched over 100,000 km. They tend to occur in pairs and in groups with many small pairs clustered round a larger one (fig. 4). The magnetic polarity associated with the following spot of a pair is always the reverse of that of the leader. In the middle of the 19th century Schwabe found that the frequency with which sunspots appear varies in an 11-year cycle. This cycle is not perfectly regular, either as regards the length of the period, or as to the amplitude of the fluctuation. But on average, and starting from a sunspot minimum, the daily number of spots will increase to a maximum in about four years, and then decrease to the next minimum in the next seven. This same period is shared by other forms of solar activity.

Most sunspots are found within two zones at equal distances north and south of the solar equator. The latitude of these zones changes from about 30° at the

Sun. Large sunspot group of 17 May 1951. *(Hale Observatories)*

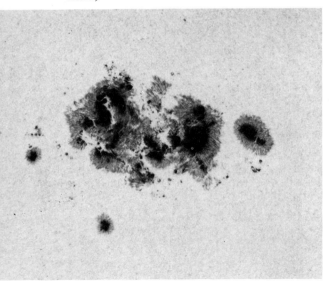

beginning of a cycle to about 18° at the time of maximum and to 0° at the end of the cycle. The magnetic polarity associated with the leading spot changes with each cycle, so that in some ways, the underlying period is 22 years rather than 11.

The slow movement of the spots across the disk shows that the Sun is rotating round an axis that is inclined at 7° 15′ to the normal to the plane of the ecliptic. Near the equator they indicate a sidereal period of rotation of 24·65 days; near latitude 20°, of 25·19 days; in latitude 30°, of 25·85 days; and in latitude 35°, of 26·63 days. At latitude 75°, where the period has to be determined by measuring the Doppler shift of the spectrum lines at the east and west limbs, it is about 33 days. The corresponding synodic periods, i.e., the intervals between successive passages of spots across the central meridian as seen from the Earth, are about two days longer than these. This differential rotation of the Sun is only possible because the Sun is not a solid body. Its relatively slow rotation presents a difficult problem to those who try to formulate a theory of the formation of the solar system since it means that most of the angular momentum of the system comes from the orbital motion of the planets and not from the rotation of the Sun that contains 99·86 per cent of the mass.

The Chromosphere. This is the transition region between the photosphere and the corona. It is the region in which the density of the solar material decreases through eight orders of magnitude; the region in which the processes ensuring the quasi-thermodynamical equilibrium of the photosphere give way to selective mechanisms that bring the solar plasma under the control of the magnetic fields and raise the electron temperature to something over a million degrees It used to be pictured as a layer about 10,000 km thick in which the temperature rose slowly from 4300 K, the minimum in the solar atmosphere, to about 10,000 K, and then increased very rapidly to the coronal value of 1,000,000 K. It is now realised, however, that the picture of a uniform layer applies only to the bottom 1000 km and that higher up the chromosphere is very inhomogeneous. Lumps of relatively cool and dense chromospheric material intermingle with regions that have the very low coronal density and the very high coronal temperature. In particular, spikes of chromospheric material called 'spicules' stick far out into the lower corona.

Normally the feeble light from the chromosphere is completely masked by that scattered from the photosphere. During a total eclipse, however, there are a few moments just before and after totality when the photosphere is covered by the Moon and the chromosphere can be seen as a thin red arc of light. Halley first saw it as a red flash during the total eclipse of 1715. It is to this characteristic redness, arising mainly from hydrogen alpha, that it owes its name of 'coloured sphere'. The spectrum of the chromosphere is almost a complete reversal of the photospheric one, strong emissions replacing strong absorptions. This makes it possible to observe the chromosphere in the light of any one of its stronger emissions by means of a SPECTROHELIOSCOPE or by using an appropriate LYOT filter.

Prominences. These are jets of chromospheric material projected into the corona. Seen at the limb, they look like huge flames rising out of the Sun. They take many forms, e.g., arches, loops, or columns, which are probably

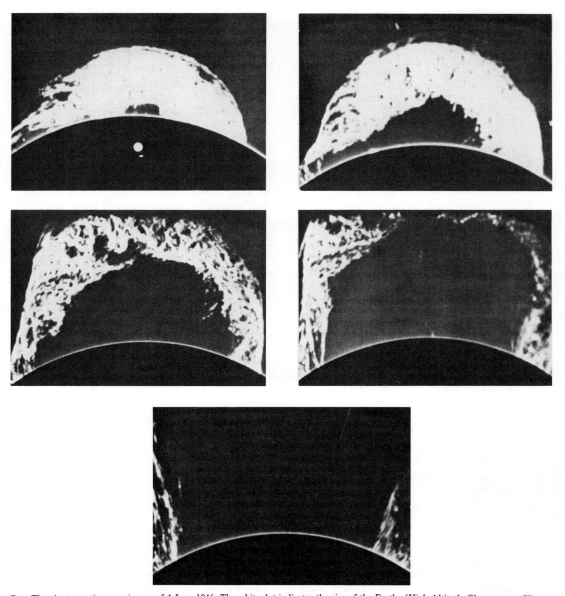

Sun. The giant eruptive prominence of 4 June 1946. The white dot indicates the size of the Earth. *(High Altitude Observatory, Climax, Colorado)*

determined by the local magnetic fields. They may be quiescent, remaining suspended above the chromosphere for days or weeks, or they may be eruptive, moving with speeds up to 300 km/s. The progress of a large eruptive prominence is shown in fig. 5. Seen against the disk of the chromosphere (fig. 6), the prominences show up as dark streaks since they are not intrinsically as bright as the main chromosphere.

Flares. The explosive events in the chromosphere in which large amounts of energy are released in a small volume over a short period of time are known as

'flares'. They are associated with active solar areas and usually occur in the vicinity of a complex sunspot group. The energy released appears in many forms ranging from radio and microwave bursts to visible and X-ray radiation, as well as streams of charged particles which, for very intense flares, may attain cosmic-ray velocities. It is such particles, coming directly or indirectly from solar flares, that produce terrestrial magnetic storms and short-wave radio fade outs. The development of a bright flare is shown in fig. 7. When examining these photographs it must be remembered that the apparently dark background

449

is itself very bright and that the black streaks are luminous prominences.

The Corona. This is a very high-temperature, extremely low-density extension to the solar atmosphere, stretching far out into interplanetary space. It can be seen as a pearly-white halo during a total eclipse and the brighter inner portions can be observed with a CORONAGRAPH. The corona can also be observed at radio wavelengths. The coronal light can be split into two components, that coming from the 'F-corona' which is photospheric light scattered from small dust particles, and that from the 'K-corona', which is the photospheric light scattered by fast moving electrons plus a number of ionic emissions. The F-corona can be regarded as an inner extension of the ZODIACAL LIGHT and has the usual Fraunhofer spectrum, hence the 'F'. The K or inner corona has a continuous spectrum on which are superimposed a number of emission lines arising from forbidden transitions in very highly ionised atoms, the strongest ones being from Fe X, Fe XIV, and Ca XV. The Fraunhofer absorption lines do not appear in the continuous spectrum because they have been blurred out by the very high random velocities of the scattering electrons. The very high temperature conditions in the solar corona combined with the even lower densities of interplanetary space mean that it must be expanding outwards, giving rise to what is called the 'solar wind' which blows continuously out from the Sun with a velocity of about 450 km/s. It was first observed by a Soviet space probe in 1959, but its existence had been surmised earlier from its effects on comet tails and from theoretical considerations. The shape and extent of the corona appears to reflect the state of the Sun's activity, being brighter and more extensive when the Sun is most active.

Sun. The chromosphere photographed with the Lyot Hα heliograph. *(Cape Observatory)*

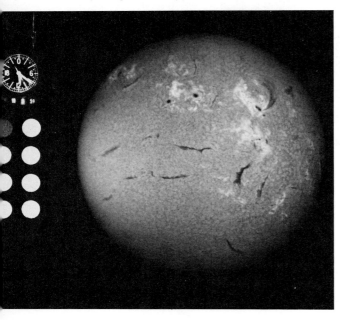

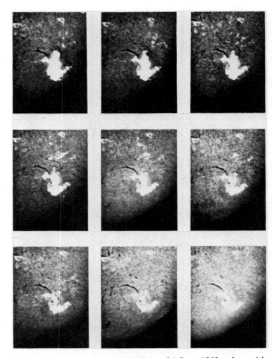

Sun. Development of the bright flare of 1 June 1960, taken with the Lyot Hα heliograph. *(Cape Observatory)*

The Sun should never be observed directly through a telescope or binoculars as this can cause blindness. The Sun's disk may be observed by using a telescope to project its image onto a white card.

See also CALENDAR; ECLIPSES OF THE SUN AND MOON.

Bibliography: D. H. Menzel, *Our Sun*, 2nd ed. 1959; G. Abetti, *The Sun* (trans. Sidgwick), 2nd ed. 1963; G. Gamow, *A Star Called The Sun*, new ed. 1967; J. C. Brandt, *Physics and Astronomy of the Sun and Stars*, 1966; A. G. Smith, *Radio Exploration of the Sun*, 1967.

'Sun, The', British newspaper which first appeared in 1964 as a successor to the *Daily Herald* (see 'DAILY HERALD'), and the first new mass-sale paper in Britain for over 30 years. In 1969 the title was bought by the Australian publisher Rupert MURDOCH, and the paper became a heavily illustrated sensational tabloid, growing rapidly in circulation to challenge the position of the *Daily Mirror* as Britain's largest selling daily newspaper. See also NEWSPAPERS.

Sun Animalcules, see SARCODINA.

Sun-birds, various species of birds in the family Nectariniidae, order Passeriformes. They are inhabitants of tropical parts of the Old World, frequenting Africa, India, and northern Australia. In appearance they are extremely brilliant, shining with metallic colours, and very small.

Sun-bittern, *Eurypya helias,* heron-like bird, the only member of the family Eurypygidae order Gruiformes, which occurs in Central America. It is fairly large, about

42 cm, with a long neck and slender bill. Its plumage is mottled, but the chief shades are brown, black and white. It frequents the marshy banks of large rivers.

Sun Worship has been universally common at all times, the sun being naturally regarded as the source of life. The sun-god was worshipped in Egypt as Ra, in Greece as Apollo, and under other names in Peru, North America, and North Europe. In Egypt the reforming Pharaoh, Akhnaten, husband of Nefertiti, made the solar disk (the Aten) the object of a monotheistic religion.

Sun Yat-sen (1866–1925), Chinese statesman and first president of republican China, a farmer's son born in a farming village in Hsiang-shan in Kwangtung. He was educated at a school in Honolulu (1879–83) and at Queen's College, Hong Kong (1884–86), where he became a Christian. In 1892 he graduated in medicine at Hong Kong.

In 1894, following the outbreak of war between China and Japan, Sun Yat-sen went to Honolulu and founded the Society for the Restoring of China (Hsing Chung Hui). He returned to China the next year and plotted an armed rising, with the projected seizure of Canton as a base of the revolution. But the plot failed, a price was set on his head, and he fled to Europe. He returned to the East and lived in Japan from 1898 to 1900, where he met the leaders of the popular parties. During 1906–11 he took part in, or directed, numerous uprisings, most of them abortive; but that at Wu-ch'ang, on 10 October 1911, was successful, and some 13 of 18 provinces responded to the revolutionary call and declared their independence of the Manchu dynasty. Later in the year the newly formed Senate elected him provisional president of the republic and in 1912 the Nanking Assembly inaugurated him president, but he resigned his office after 14 days in favour of Yüan Shih-k'ai, the Emperor having abdicated, and thereby ended over 260 years of Manchu rule in China.

But Yüan proved to be a reactionary and a traitor to the republic, and in the ensuing few years a bitter struggle went on between Sun Yat-sen's newly organised party, the KUOMINTANG (the Nationalist party), and the reactionaries under Yüan, who died in 1916. In 1917 Sun had himself elected president of a Southern Chinese Republic, at Canton, but he fled before Gen. Ch'en Chiung-ming in 1922. In 1924 he undertook a radical reorganisation of

his party on the model of the Communist party in Soviet Russia. Sun Yat-sen died in Peking of cancer, and a split occurred in the Kuomintang after his death. Later differences arose between the Kuomintang and the Communists. It is clear that Sun Yat-sen's greatest contribution to Chinese nationalism lies in the vigour and force of his personal leadership, which revitalised it and made it an irresistible driving force, first against the alien rule of the Manchu dynasty and later against foreign domination in China. After his death he became greatly venerated in China. His publications include: *The International Development of China*, 1922; *Memoirs of a Chinese Revolutionary*, 1927; and *The Three Principles of the People*.

See also CHINA, *Modern History*.

Bibliography: N. Gangulee, *The Teachings of Sun Yat-sen*, 1945; H. Z. Schriffrin, *Sun Yat-sen and the Origins of the Chinese Revolution*, 1968.

Sunburn, see SUNSTROKE; SUNTAN.

Sunbury-on-Thames, part of Spelthorne District of Surrey, England, which includes Kempton Park and SHEPPERTON. There is a lock and weir on the THAMES here. Population (1971) 39,735.

Sunda Islands, islands of the Indonesian archipelago. The Greater Sunda (or Sunda Raya) group comprises the larger islands of SUMATRA, JAVA, KALIMANTAN, SULAWESI, and adjacent smaller islands, and, with the exception of Sulawesi, corresponds to the Indonesian extension of the Sunda continental shelf. The Lesser Sundas (or NUSA TENGGARA) lie to the south-east and include the smaller islands of BALI, LOMBOK, SUMBAWA, TIMOR, etc. Nusa Tenggara is an administrative province of Indonesia.

Sunday, first day of the week. The word is derived from the Old English *Sunnandæg* (day of the sun). See SABBATH.

'Sunday Express', British Sunday newspaper, founded in 1918 by Lord BEAVERBROOK. The *Sunday Express* is printed simultaneously in London and Manchester. Independent in politics, it often includes contributions from leading national and international figures, dealing with outstanding events, as well as other news and features.

'Sunday Mirror', British Sunday newspaper founded in 1915 by Lord ROTHERMERE as the *Sunday Pictorial*, a week before the establishment of the *Illustrated Sunday Herald*. The *Mirror* never lost this initial advantage. In 1964 it changed its name to the *Sunday Mirror*. Today there is a strong connection between the boards of directors of the *Sunday Mirror* and of the *Daily Mirror*.

'Sunday People', British Sunday newspaper established in 1881. Although independent, politics are not an important feature. Formerly called the *People*, the newspaper features popular columnists and strong true-life stories and is owned by the International Publishing Corporation Limited.

Sunday School, an organisation which gives religious instruction to children and young people on Sundays and is usually attached to a church or chapel.

The catechising of the young was adopted by the Christians from Jewish practice, but varied in scope at

Sun Yat-sen. *(Bisonte)*

different periods and places. The idea of Sunday Schools to rejuvenate religious life was suggested by St Charles Borromeo and by Luther. However, in England the Sunday School movement developed as an effort to combat illiteracy as well as to impart religious instruction. The founder of the movement was Robert RAIKES, who, with his friend Stocks, rector of St John's, set up Sunday Schools in Gloucester in 1780.

The movement grew rapidly. Wesley gave it wholehearted support, and Evangelicals and Dissenters were generally in favour. In 1803 the undenominational Sunday School Union was formed; it is now the National Christian Education Council. Later in the 19th century a number of 'secular Sunday Schools' were organised by trade union and other bodies, which gave entirely secular instruction to children and adults.

Today the term Sunday School is confined to those strictly religious in scope; basic instruction in reading and writing is no longer part of Sunday School, but historically the movement is important in national as well as religious history as having provided one of the links between the charity schools and regular and universal elementary education. The World's Sunday School Association was set up in 1907; in 1947 it became the World Council of Christian Education and Sunday School Association, with headquarters in Geneva.

'Sunday Telegraph', British Sunday newspaper founded in 1961 under the same ownership as the *Daily Telegraph*, but with a largely different editorial staff. Politically it is independent Conservative. Among its features are reviews of books, plays, music, and the theatre; an extensive survey of industry, trade unions, the City, and the Stock Market; and detailed coverage of sport. From 1976 it included a colour magazine, previously issued with the *Daily Telegraph*.

'Sunday Times', British Sunday newspaper, founded in 1822 and at one time owned by Mrs Julius Beer, whose husband owned the *Observer*. It passed to Herman Schmidt, who in 1897 had started the *Sunday Special*, which amalgamated with the *Sunday Times* in 1904. It was bought in 1915 by Viscount CAMROSE and Viscount KEMSLEY and, coming into the sole control of the latter in 1937, entered a period of rapid development. This continued in marked degree after Lord THOMSON of Fleet acquired the paper in 1959; it became the first newspaper in Britain to be printed in separate sections and, in 1962, to include a separate colour magazine. Literary, dramatic, and musical criticism of a high standard has long been a prominent feature of the paper, which is also noted for its regular articles on foreign affairs, politics, economics, finance, art, and women's interests. The newspaper achieved considerable distinction under the editorship of Harold EVANS, who was appointed in 1967.

Sunday Trading, see SHOPS ACT, *Sunday Closing*.

Sunder, Lucas, see CRANACH, LUCAS.

Sunderbunds, see GANGES.

Sunderland, port and district of TYNE AND WEAR, England, occupying an area of 137 km². The population of the town of Sunderland is 217,000. The remainder of the population of the district live in WASHINGTON NEW

TOWN and large mining villages including HOUGHTON-LE-SPRING and HETTON-LE-HOLE.

At Sunderland the River WEAR cuts a 30-metre-deep gorge through the local magnesian limestone plateau to reach the North Sea. Churches were first built at Monkwearmouth on the north bank of the Wear in 674 and at Sunderland on the south bank later in the 7th century. Sunderland developed as a port during the Middle Ages, with a charter dating from 1154. During the Civil War of 1642–49, Sunderland increased coal exports to London, for both towns were held by the Parliamentarians and the Newcastle trade was disrupted. The coal trade grew until 1914, facilitated by wagonways and railways to Sunderland's hinterland in County Durham. The first shipyard was established in 1775 and the wet dock was built in 1840. Records of shipbuilding go back to 1346. During the 19th century several shipyards were built on the restricted river frontage, and Sunderland became one of the leading shipbuilding centres in Britain. Although the industry has declined, three yards remain. Sunderland also has marine and general engineering industries, and manufactures glassware, radio components, and furniture. The trade of the port was 1·3 million t in 1974.

Central Sunderland has been redeveloped as the major shopping centre for the district. It is linked to the north bank of the Wear by a high-level bridge. A four-lane ring road immediately to the west of the town links Sunderland with Teesside, North Tyneside, and Newcastle.

Eight collieries are still in production in Sunderland district. The former mining villages are now largely residential. Population of district (1971) 293,000.

Bibliography: B. T. Robson, *Urban Analysis: A Study of City Structure with Special Reference to Sunderland*, 1969.

Sundew, common name for four genera of insectivorous plants (including VENUS FLY TRAP, *Dionaea*), but generally restricted to genus *Drosera*, which contains nearly 100 species growing in boggy places throughout the

Sundew. *Drosera anglica. (Topham/Markham)*

Sundial at Eyam Church, Derbyshire. *(Barnaby's Picture Library)*

world. The leaves form a rosette and are covered with sticky glandular hairs, whereby insects are trapped and held while they are digested by means of enzymes secreted from the hairs ('tentacles') onto the leaf surface. The flowers, usually white or pink, are borne on a leafless stalk. In the British Isles there are three species, *D. intermedia*, a common bog-plant, *D. anglica*. found chiefly in Ireland and Scotland, and *D. rotundifolia*, the common or round-leaved sundew. The last is an acrid and caustic plant used in Italy in making the liquor called Rossoli. See INSECTIVOROUS PLANTS.

Sundial, an instrument for measuring the TIME from the position of the shadow of a fixed object (the gnomon) cast by the Sun. Now chiefly decorative, sundials were of great importance before the days of cheap reliable mechanical clocks, and very many ingenious forms were developed. A properly constructed and orientated sundial may be expected to give the local apparent solar time to the nearest minute from which the standard time can be easily derived by applying the appropriate corrections for longitude and the equation of time. If the dial has been specially constructed for the locality the longitude correction may have been incorporated in the graduations and the equation of time engraved on the dial in tabular or analemmatic form. In more elaborate dials provision is made for applying this correction semi-automatically by moving an appropriate part.

Sundials may be grouped as 'altitude dials' or 'direction dials' according to whether their calibration is dependent on the changing height or direction of the Sun; they can be further classified as 'particular' if they have been calculated for use in one place only, or as 'universal' if they can be adjusted for use at any latitude. Portable sundials are of this latter type and can be used, as they were in the desert in the Second World War, to replace magnetic compasses which are very unreliable in the neighbourhood of tanks and armoured cars.

The form of sundial most usually encountered in parks and public gardens is a horizontal direction dial with the

edge of its gnomon parallel to the Earth's axis, i.e., the angle of the gnomon equals the latitude of the place, and the gnomon itself is in the north-south vertical plane. Simpler to construct because the graduations are equally spaced are the cylindrical dials in which the shadow of a rod set up parallel to the axis of the Earth falls on to a cylindrical band having the rod as its axis. Direction dials, once set up, work equally well at all seasons of the year. Altitude dials, on the other hand, have to take account of the variation of the Sun's declination throughout the year and, in some cases, need continual adjustment.

History. The early Chinese, Babylonians, and Egyptians all used shadow devices to indicate the passing of time. The shadows of natural objects may have been used at first but later columns were set up for this specific purpose. There is one such giant column that was erected about 3000 BC at Materich near Cairo. A sister of Cleopatra's Needle on the Thames Embankment, it stood before the temple of the Sun and worship is supposed to have commenced when its shadow fell across the temple entrance. There was a steady development of sundials throughout the pre-classical and classical periods of antiquity. The Greeks worked out their geometry and Ptolemy gives a full discussion of the subject in the ALMAGEST. Thereafter sundials came into everyday use and there were convenient portable models for travellers. In 606 the Pope ordered that sundials should be placed on churches, doubtless thus beginning the close association of churches with sundials and later with clocks. The modern division of the day into 24 hours of equal length was adopted in the 15th century. From then till the 18th century sundials were produced in great numbers and in many different forms. Collections of the many that survive are to be found in most of the larger museums.

Bibliography: F. W. Cousins, *Sundials: A Simplified Approach by Means of the Equatorial Dial*, 1969; R. R. J. Rohr, *Sundials: History, Theory and Practice*, 1973; A. E. Waugh, *Sundials: Their Theory and Construction*, new ed. 1973.

Sundman, Per Olof, see SWEDEN, *Literature.*

Sundsvall, Swedish seaport in VÄSTERNORRLAND, on the east coast, on a wide bay of the Baltic Sea. Its harbour is sheltered by Alnö Island. Sundsvall is the regional centre for central Norrland. There is a large concentration of timber processing industries in the vicinity of the town. Population (1974) 93,000.

Sunfish, any fish of the family Centrarchidae, in order Perciformes. They inhabit fresh water in North America. The species, of which about 30 are known, are compressed and have a somewhat oval body and a spot on the operculum (gill cover). Most of them build nests, all are voracious, and many are valued as food. The genus *Micropterus*, the black bass, is found in Europe.

Sunflower. *Helianthus annuus* is the common sunflower, an annual, native to North and Central America, grown in gardens; *H. rigidus* is the perennial sunflower, of running habit; both are in family Compositae. Varieties are grown for their seeds, yielding oil for commerce, and cattle cake.

Sunflower Oil (iodine value 130 ± 5) comes from the seeds of the plant *Helianthus annuus* (common sunflower), indigenous to Mexico but extensively cultivated in the USSR and to a lesser extent in Yugoslavia, Turkey, and South Africa. The seed varies in colour from white to brown or black; it has a hard, fibrous husk constituting about 45 per cent of the whole seed, and contains 22–30 per cent of oil. It may be eaten directly, but by far the greater part of the world crop is crushed in hydraulic or continuous screw presses, or is solvent-extracted, for the production of edible oil. Seed processed in modern mills is usually decorticated before crushing to produce a better yield of oil and a residual cake suitable for animal food-stuffs. Sunflower oil is a clear pale yellow; it is liquid at low temperatures, and resembles olive oil in many respects. Component fatty acids are: saturated, total 5–15 per cent; unsaturated, oleic (25–42 per cent) and linoleic (52–66 per cent). The better qualities of the oil are directly consumed as table or cooking oils or are used in the manufacture of compound cooking fats and margarine. It is also used for making soap, as a lubricant, and, due chiefly to the high linoleic content and absence of linoleic acid, in the production of non-yellowing alkyds and artists' colours.

Sunflower State, see KANSAS.

Sungari, large river of MANCHURIA, rising near the North Korean frontier in the CH'ANG-PAI SHAN. Its upper reaches join the River Nen; it then flows north-east to join the River AMUR south-west of its confluence with the Ussuri. Its total length is about 1850 km.

Sunlight Treatment, see HELIOTHERAPY.

Sunni, or Sunnite, a member of the majority group of Muslims who accept the first three caliphs as legitimate successors of Mohammed. See ISLAM.

Sunrise, see TWILIGHT.

Sunset, see TWILIGHT.

Sunshine Recorders, instruments for recording the duration of bright sunshine. That recommended by the meteorological authorities in Britain is the model devised by J. F. Campbell in 1853 and improved by Professor Sir George G. Stokes in 1879. It has a glass globe which acts as a lens, the sun's image being received on a card in the zodiacal frame. The card is accurately marked in hours and fractions. The concentrated rays of the sun burn a trace as the sun travels across the sky, the breaks showing the periods of obscured sun. Three grooves are provided to receive the cards, one each for winter and summer, and one for autumn and spring.

The Campbell-Stokes sunshine recorder is the simplest possible instrument, and is widely used throughout the world, but it provides no measure of the intensity of sunshine. For this it is necessary to use more elaborate instruments, such as photoelectric cells used in conjunction with sensitive electrical recording devices.

Sunshine State, see FLORIDA.

Sunspots, see SUN, *Sunspots*.

Sunstroke, or heatstroke, a condition of prostration or fever brought about by excessive exposure to the sun's rays, or to a high temperature, e.g. in stokeholds. The primary cause is probably the disturbance of the temperature-regulating centre in the brain. The body temperature rises, and there are disturbances in the respiratory and circulatory processes akin to those seen in SHOCK. The extent and form of these disturbances determine the various types of the disorder. Thus, fainting may be the predominant symptom; the patient is sick and giddy, and has a very weak pulse before he faints. He should be placed in a recumbent position. Besides the well-defined types of sunstroke, there are numerous varieties in which different forms of respiratory or circulatory disability are manifested. The treatment should be symptomatic. The form of sunstroke known as heat cramps, or miner's cramps, is caused by shortage of salt due to the loss of salt in sweating.

Suntan, and sunburn, are changes in the skin due to exposure to sunlight. The body gets most of its vitamin D from sunlight, hence moderate exposure is beneficial. Exposure causes production of melanin in the basal layers of the epidermis and this darkens the skin, forming the suntan. The tan protects the skin from harmful radiation emanating from the sun. However, overexposure will damage the skin and burn it. In severe sunburn, the skin is covered with large watery blisters and is extremely painful when touched. The victim should stay out of the sun and apply calamine lotion or cold cream or see a doctor if the burn is extensive. There is evidence that excessive exposure to sunlight over a lifetime is an important factor in the production of certain types of skin cancers (epitheliomas). There are many preparations on the market which can be used to produce a tan. These either contain suitable dyes in a cream or lotion base or chemicals which increase the production of melanin.

Suomenlinna, see SVEABORG.

Super-ego, see EGO.

Super Tax, see INCOME TAX.

Supercharger, see INTERNAL COMBUSTION ENGINE.

Superconductivity. The electrical conductance of most metals increases as the temperature is lowered, i.e., their resistances are lower at lower temperatures. For certain metals and alloys the remarkable phenomenon of superconductivity begins abruptly at well-established temperatures a few degrees above absolute zero, i.e., some 270 °C below the freezing-point of water. The resistance of the specimen below the transition temperature is zero and currents less than a critical value can flow indefinitely without generating any heat. Application of a magnetic field can destroy superconductivity and for some time there has been a search for so-called 'hard superconductors' that retain their superconductivity even in the presence of magnetic fields of tens or hundreds of thousands of gauss. Such materials are now available and enable electromagnets to be built to produce exceptionally high fields over useful volumes with the minimum dissipation of electric power. These 'superconducting magnets' must, however, be operated at liquid helium temperatures. Typical transition temperatures are lead 7·22 K (−266 °C), tin 3·74 K, niobium 9·2 K, zirconium 0·55 K. One of the highest values is 15·5 K for niobium nitride.

Superfluidity. The viscosity of liquid HELIUM decreases by a very large factor and its thermal conductivity becomes extraordinarily large when its temperature is reduced below the so-called λ-point at 2·186 K (approximately −271 °C). The phenomenon has some interesting parallels to SUPERCONDUCTIVITY but has so far found no applications outside pure research. It occurs only for the ⁴He isotope, indicating that it is quantum statistical in origin. Liquid helium II, i.e., liquid helium below the λ-point, is believed to consist of two components, the superfluid with zero viscosity and the normal fluid, the fraction of the former increasing to unity at absolute zero. To observe the phenomenon, the velocity of flow must be less than a critical value, depending on the temperature. Helium II not only has a greater latent heat of vaporisation but also has a much lower density and surface tension than Helium I. Its thermal conductivity becomes about 200 times that of copper.

Superheater, see BOILER.

Superheterodyne, see RECEIVER, RADIO.

Superior, port and city in Wisconsin, USA. It forms the southern half of the urban area at the head of Lake Superior, lying in Wisconsin, across St Louis Bay from DULUTH, its counterpart in Minnesota. Together, these two cities serve as the head of navigation on the Great Lakes, and as the shipping point for western produce reaching the lakes, particularly grain. Superior is one of the largest grain-shipping ports in the world. It also shares with Duluth the shipment of iron ore from the Mesabi Range, 100 km to the north-west; it contains the world's largest ore dock. There are also mills and canning plants and a campus of Wisconsin State University. Population 32,237.

Superior and superiority. In Scots law the person who makes a grant of land or a *feu* to a grantee is called the *superior* or *feudal superior*, and the grantee is called the *vassal*. If the grantor is himself a vassal his grantee is sub-vassal and he himself mid-superior, while the mid-superior's superior is over-superior in relation to the sub-vassal. The interest retained by the superior in the feu is styled *superiority* or *dominium directum*, which interest was originally the ownership of the land subject to the more or less precarious right of the vassal; the interest acquired by the vassal is the *dominium utile*, the beneficial ownership, now virtually the freehold.

Superior, Lake, largest and most westerly of the five GREAT LAKES of North America, and the second largest freshwater body in the world. It is 616 km long (east–west), and 260 km at its widest; its maximum depth is 407 m. Area 82,100 km²—29,000 km² in Canada, the rest in the USA. Its chief tributary is the St Louis river, 260 km long, which enters at DULUTH, Minnesota. The lake discharges by way of St Mary's river (100 km long) at the south-east into Lake HURON.

There are many islands in the lake, including Isle Royale (a national park). The shores are well-wooded and the region has valuable iron-ore deposits. This results in an immensely important iron-ore traffic upon the lake, mainly from the ports of Duluth and Superior. Fishing, hunting, and tourism are important in the region's economy, as the lake and its environs remain relatively unpolluted. See also ATLAS 51.

Supernovae, see NOVAE.

Superposition. The principle of superposition of strata was one of the two basic principles of stratigraphical geology laid down by William SMITH (1769–1839). It states that if one series of rocks lies above another, then the upper series was formed after the lower, unless it can be shown that the beds have been inverted by tectonic action such as folding. A sequence of sedimentary beds is said to be conformable when it represents an uninterrupted period of deposition; the bedding planes between the separate beds will all lie parallel to one another in such a sequence.

Supersonic Flight, flight faster than the speed of sound. Knowledge of motion at supersonic speeds came originally from the study of the flight of such projectiles as bullets, shells, and rockets. Then, during the Second World War, piston-engined fighter aircraft began to encounter compressibility shock-wave effects caused by airflow over their wings approaching the speed of sound; this produced buffeting and many broke up in the air. The problems were aggravated by the advent of jet-propulsion, which made possible even higher speeds.

Not until October 1947 was the US aircraft Bell X-1, flown at supersonic speeds, and considerable research effort has since been applied to the problems of supersonic aircraft design.

The supersonic aircraft differs from a projectile in the following main particulars: (1) it will normally have a considerably longer duration of flight to fulfil its useful function; (2) it must carry its human cargo safely, and thus cannot be subjected to high accelerations in take-off and manoeuvre; and (3) it must be controllable at all speeds up to its maximum and must fly on an even keel. Although the human frame is not affected by speed, it is affected by high acceleration, and pilots of high-speed aircraft wear 'anti-g' (anti-gravity) suits to minimise the effect of the high acceleration forces.

The design of a supersonic aircraft is complicated because the aircraft has to be stable and controllable under three sets of conditions. It must take off, land, and perform the first and last parts of its flight in the subsonic range; it must pass through the transonic range; and must fly safely in the supersonic range. Of the three the problems of transonic flight are the most serious, as changes in air-flow characteristics are taking place rapidly and erratically. The most important difference between airflow at supersonic speed and subsonic speed is that at high speed irreversible phenomena, in the form of shock waves, are set up. These give rise to a very considerable increase in drag and thus power consumed, and fundamentally affect the air-flow over and the stability of the aircraft. For the subsonic range, aircraft of the conventional type with reasonable aspect ratio are preferred. For the transonic range considerable sweep-back on all surfaces, a low aspect ratio wing, or a combination of the two is desirable. For the supersonic range thin, razor-edged aerofoils and high fineness ratio fuselages show performance gains although they introduce structural design and manufacturing problems. Many designers consider that the most efficient way of combining conflicting requirements is with delta-wing aircraft. In plan form these aircraft look rather like an obtuse-angled isosceles triangle travelling apex first. The wing section is pointed, symmetrical, and thin, the body blending into the wing to reduce body-wing effects. Control of the aircraft is either by conventional controls or by combined aileron elevators, known as elevons, on the wing trailing edge when no tailplane is fitted. In most supersonic aircraft the controls are power boosted, to prevent undue force being required by the pilot.

Existing engines are of the compact gas turbine type, probably with after-burning, rocket, or ram-jet (see JET PROPULSION). The gas turbine is limited by the throughput of air, and reaches maximum efficiency when the air passing through the first stage of the compressor reaches the local speed of sound. Gas turbines cannot be used efficiently for speeds much greater than twice the speed of sound. The rocket has great power, and increases in efficiency with the speed of the aircraft. Its best use is as a booster to take the aircraft quickly through the transonic range and enable a ram-jet to take control. A ram-jet is not practical under speeds of about 1½ times the speed of sound, but increases in efficiency with increasing speed of flight. When travelling at high speeds air friction causes heating of outside surfaces of aircraft, thus affecting material strength, and refrigeration is necessary. In addition, new materials such as titanium and K-monel are used to ensure greater strength at high temperature. Such aircraft are, of course, fully pressurised, as they fly at great heights.

The Olympus turbo-jet using reheat, which powers *Concorde*, has a high jet-exit velocity at take-off. This accounts for its increase in noise over most other aircraft. Future developments may lead to a variable-cycle engine which has lower jet velocity at take-off but which retains its capability in achieving good cruise performance. Aircraft speeds are often represented by the MACH NUMBER, which is the ratio of the speed of the aircraft to the speed of sound. Thus a Mach number less than 1 represents a subsonic speed, and a Mach number greater than 1 a supersonic speed.

See also SONIC BOOM.

Supersonics, see SOUND, *Ultrasonics*.

Superstition is a term often used to dismiss beliefs and practices one does not agree with. However, it can only reasonably be employed when such beliefs and practices contradict the weight of evidence and conception of reasonableness present in a given society.
Bibliography: G. Jahoda, *The Psychology of Superstition*, 1970.

Supervieille, Jules (1884–1960), French writer, born in Montevideo, Uruguay. He began by writing Parnassian poetry (see PARNASSIANS, THE), but sounded a more personal note in his *Gravitations*, 1925. His later poetry includes *Le Forçat innocent*, 1930, *Les Amis inconnus*, 1934, *La Fable du monde*, 1938, *Le Corps tragique*, 1959, and the beautiful wartime poems written in South America, *Poèmes de la France malheureuse*, 1941. Supervieille was also successful with his short-story collections, *L'Enfant de la haute mer*, 1930, *L'Arche de Noé*, 1938, and *Le Petit bois*, 1942. His work is marked by tenderness and simplicity, and a sincere, unsophisticated humanity.
Bibliography: R. Vivier, *Lire Supervieille*, 1972.

Supetar, see BRAČ.

Suppé, Franz von (1819–95), Austrian composer of Belgian descent, born at Spalato (Split), studied under Cigalla, Ferrari and others. He settled in Vienna, where he conducted at the Theater an der Wien (1845–62) and the Carltheater (1865–82). His best-known works are the *Poet and Peasant* and *Light Cavalry* overtures. He wrote five operas, 25 operettas and a mass of other music for the theatre.

Supply, grant of money provided in order to meet the expenses of government by the representatives of the people. In England the principle that the redress of grievances should be a return for supplies granted by Parliament gained recognition at the revolution of 1688, when the necessity for annual supplies ended the necessity legally to enact that Parliament should meet every year. The power of voting supplies is vested in the Commons. The power of the Lords in this respect was curtailed by the Parliament Acts of 1911 and 1949. A money bill, or bill of supply, must, however, receive the consent of Lords and sovereign.

In economics supply means the quantity of a commodity (or service) offered and sold at a given price. See PRICE; SUPPLY AND DEMAND.

Supply, Commissioners of. The Scots commissioners of supply, first appointed by the Act of Convention 1667, were for over a century, before county councils were instituted in 1889, the leading local authority. Their special or primary function was to levy the land tax. In 1857 by the County Police Act they were given the duty through a police committee of providing a county police force. The qualification to act as a commissioner has since 1854 been either a property or an *ex-officio* one, and the surviving duties are few.

Supply and Demand. According to orthodox microeconomic theory, bargaining between individuals in the market for goods and services produces a pattern of supply and demand which determines which goods are produced and what their relative prices will be. The demand for commodities provides the payments for the services of the factors used in making them, which in turn provide the incomes of their owners, the spending of which constitutes the demand for commodities. Market equilibrium is thus established by a circular system of relationships. The law of supply and demand states that a market will be brought into equilibrium if when a commodity is in excess supply its price is lowered and when there is excess demand for it its price is raised. Such a model can describe only the equilibrium corresponding to given initial conditions; it cannot be used to analyse processes going on through time.
Bibliography: H. D. Henderson, *Supply and Demand*, 1940; P. Samuelson, *An Introduction to Economics*, 1965.

Supporters, see HERALDRY, *Supporters*.

Suppuration, medical term for the formation of pus. See INFLAMMATION.

Suprarenal Gland, see ADRENAL GLANDS.

Supremacy, Royal, exercise of supreme ecclesiastical authority by the Crown. In the medieval Church authority descended from pope to bishops, but in practice kings exercised a good deal of power and influence. Royal supremacy was first enforced in England by Henry VIII in 1534. Repealed by Mary, it was reimposed under Elizabeth in 1559, and acceptance was enforced by an oath of supremacy. In 1689 the Convention Parliament required all holders of office in Church and state to take 'the oath of supremacy', but in a form that merely denied the papal supremacy; it contained no positive statement of the royal supremacy. By an Act passed in 1791 it was provided that no person should be liable to be summoned to take the oath of supremacy, or prosecuted for not obeying such summons. Roman Catholics, upon taking an oath in which the civil and temporal authority of the pope is abjured, could hold office without taking the oath of supremacy.

Suprematism, Russian abstract art movement c. 1914; related to CUBISM and led by Kasimir MALEVICH.

Supreme Council, see PEACE CONFERENCE (1919).

Supreme Court of Judicature. The Judicature Act 1873 united the then existing courts of CHANCERY, QUEEN'S BENCH, COMMON PLEAS, EXCHEQUER, the High Court of Admiralty, the Probate Court, and the Court for Divorce and Matrimonial Causes into one Supreme Court of Justice in England and Wales. These seven courts became five divisions of the new High Court of Justice: the Chancery, Queen's Bench, Common Pleas, Exchequer and Probate, Divorce and Admiralty Divisions. In 1880 these were reduced to three: Chancery, Queen's Bench, and Probate, Divorce and Admiralty Divisions. The old London Court of Bankruptcy remained a separate court until 1884, when it became consolidated with the Supreme Court of Justice by the Bankruptcy Act 1883.

The Supreme Court now consists of the Court of Appeal (see APPEAL, COURT OF) and the present HIGH COURT OF JUSTICE, which consists of Chancery, Queen's Bench, and Family Divisions.

Sur, see TYRE.

Surabaya, second largest city in Indonesia, located in north-eastern Java at the mouth of the Kali Mas river, opposite Madura Island. It has Indonesia's second largest port (Tanjung Perak), and, after being the main naval base of the Dutch fleet, is now headquarters of the Indonesian Fleet Command, the navy's main operating base with Indonesia's largest naval shipyard, associated with a modern shipbuilding industry. Surabaya is a manufacturing centre (second to Jakarta), with most activity in terms of value concentrated on shipbuilding and repair, some motor assembly, and rubber processing. There is a university and a major institute of technology, as well as an important railway terminus and an airport.

During the 13th and 14th centuries, Surabaya was a powerful port-kingdom thriving on the Moluccan spice trade and its strategic role in the Majapahit empire's expansion from Java. Then, during the 16th and 17th centuries, the walled city resisted attack by the Mataram kingdom until it was subjugated in 1625. It was the centre of considerable opposition to the Dutch until the Dutch conquest in 1707. After the end of the Second World War, Surabaya was the site of the Indonesian republic's first major battle in late 1945 against British forces holding Indonesia for the Dutch. Attacked from the sea and heavily bombed, civilian evacuation was necessary; after a seaborne British invasion Surabaya was subdued within

a month, before the Dutch returned to continue the war against Sukarno's nationalist army. Estimated 1975 population 1·8 million.

Suraj-ud-Daula, see SIRAJ-UD-DAULA.

Surakarta, formerly Solo, city in Central Java province, Indonesia, on the River Solo. Surakarta is a key railway centre and trade centre for the rich agricultural area of the Surakarta basin, where intensive wet rice, sugar, tobacco, and coffee are grown. It also manufactures leather, plastic, textile, and BATIK products. Historically, Surakarta is best known as the capital of one of the two residual *vorstenlanden* (or princely states) into which the Mataram empire was divided in 1755; the other was YOGYAKARTA. Surakarta claimed direct descent from the Majapahits, and for long remained loyal to the Dutch, unlike Yogyakarta. The town is a *kraton*, or court, town built around a large, ornate royal *kraton* nucleus. It remained relatively unchanged by Dutch rule, and retains its Javanese character for the most part with an overgrown village appearance beyond the immediate palace nucleus. Unlike Yogyakarta, its separate administrative status ended after the Second World War. Population (1975) 497,000.

Surat, city of GUJARAT state, India, on the Tapti river 25 km from its mouth. It was the chief port of the Moghul empire in the 16th and 17th centuries. The first British trading post was established here in 1612 and until 1687 was the East India Company's headquarters. The town, once with 800,000 people, declined still further until the cotton boom of the 1860s and its railway junctions made it more important. The town centre is fortified with surrounding narrow and twisting streets enclosed by a wall. No longer a port, newer industrial suburbs based on textiles have grown up to the east. Population (1971) 493,000.

Surbiton, suburb in the London Borough of KINGSTON-UPON-THAMES. Population of Surbiton Hill ward in 1971 was 5860.

Surcouf, Robert (1773–1827), French corsair, born at St Malo. He joined the French merchant navy in 1789 and arrived in Port Louis, Mauritius, from which he raided enemy commerce in the Indian Ocean. He secured numerous captures from Portuguese and British shipping, the most important being the East Indiaman *Kent*, which he boarded in the Bay of Bengal and captured after a fight against odds of three to one. Known as 'King of the Corsairs', he added a spirit of chivalry to great physical courage and admirable seamanship. He returned to France in 1809, and retired from the sea.

Surd. If a and n are integers then the RADICAL $a^{1/n}$ is either an integer or an irrational number (see NUMBERS). A surd is an expression that contains one or more irrational radicals. A surd is said to be in simplified form when all the radicals in it are in simplified form.

Suretyship, Contract of, see GUARANTEE.

Surf, see SEA WAVES AND SWELL.

Surf-bird, *Aphriza virgata*, a bird of family Charadriidae, order Charadriiformes, closely related to the turnstone. Its plumage is brown with white markings, and it occurs on the Pacific coast of America.

Surface, in geometry, a figure with two dimensions (see CURVE). See also CONE; CONIC SURFACE; CYLINDER; CYLINDRICAL SURFACE; ELLIPSOID; HYPERBOLOID; PARABOLOID; SPHERE; SPHEROID.

Surface Resistivity, the ratio (potential gradient parallel to the direction of the current flow along the surface of the material) ÷ (current per unit width of surface). This term is used in describing the properties of dielectrics and insulators, and its value for any material depends on several factors such as amount and type of surface contamination, environment, and the measuring technique used.

Bibliography: British Standards Institution, *4618 Section 2.4: 1975 Surface resistivity*.

Surface Soil, the soil moved by ploughing or cultivation, i.e. the uppermost 10 to 20 cm. It can be used with reference to SOIL EROSION AND CONSERVATION to denote the amount of soil lost, e.g. 50 per cent of the original surface soil was lost by erosion.

Surface Tension. Many phenomena show that LIQUIDS behave as though they were enclosed in a stretched membrane. The shapes of drops slowly forming at the end of a water tap may be imitated approximately by pouring water into a hoop across which is stretched a thin sheet of rubber, showing that the real drops of water behave as if enclosed in an elastic membrane. The shape assumed by a given volume of liquid, minimising its surface area, is a sphere. Small drops of mercury spilled on a table likewise assume the spherical form under the influence of surface tension, though large drops deviate from this shape because of the distorting effect of gravity on them. The spherical shape adopted by soap bubbles, where weight plays a negligible part, is also due to surface tension. The effect of surface tension is due to the different conditions that obtain at the surface of a liquid as opposed to those within the main bulk of it. At any point in the interior of the liquid a molecule is attracted by neighbouring molecules, such attractions being on the whole equal in every direction. A molecule near the surface, however, is subjected to downward attractions by the molecules below it, which are much greater than any attractions due to gaseous molecules above it. The surface film exists only in this sense: that the molecular attractions cause the liquid to behave as though it were enclosed by a membrane. The CAPILLARITY of liquids (an essential for the life of plants and trees) is due to surface tension, which is quantitatively different for different liquids. Petrol spreads rapidly on the surface of water because its surface tension is less than that of water. Thus it can form a film covering a pool, a fact of great practical significance in destroying mosquito larvae which hang from the surface of clean water in order to breathe but cannot do so from an oil surface.

Bibliography: C. V. Boys, *Soap Bubbles*, 1960; D. C. S. White, *Biological Physics*, 1974.

Surfing. This exciting and exhilarating sport which was popularised in Hawaii and Australia, is now firmly established in Europe, South America, South Africa, Japan, and many other parts of the world. It can be enjoyed wherever a long rolling sea breaks upon sandy shores. Thanks to the modern wet suit, now extensively used in many water sports, surfing is carried out off the north of Scotland in mid-winter as well as in the warm waters of the tropics. Apart from the wet suit, the basic requirement is for a surfboard (Malibu) around 1·8 m to 1·28 m in length and about 45 cm wide, made of polyurethane foam covered in glass fibre. The art of the sport is to paddle out, select a suitable wave and ride it as long as feasible, standing upright on the board.

Surfing countries hold their own national surfing contests, usually annually, and send teams to international championships and the European and world contests, which usually take place every two years. World contests have been held in Australia, California, Hawaii, etc., and in the future will be held in Europe and other parts of the world. In Great Britain the governing body for the sport is the British Surfing Association, 16–18 Bournemouth Road, Parkstone, Poole, Dorset BH14 0ES.

Surge Impedance, for electrical power transmission lines, is a measure of the opposition to the flow of current due to the voltage induced on a line by lightning discharges or switching effects.

When lightning strikes or occurs near a transmission line a disturbing voltage wave is imposed on the line causing current to flow, and the effect (called the surge) passes along the line to the ends and may be reflected backwards and forwards until the energy is absorbed by the resistances in the network. If, however, it is assumed that the resistance is negligible the velocity of propagation of the surge can be shown to be $1/\sqrt{(LC)}$ metres per second, where L and C are the inductance and capacitance respectively per unit length of the line.

The ratio of the voltage to current of the travelling wave is called the surge impedance Z_0 and can be shown to be equal to $\sqrt{(L/C)}$ ohms.

Surges may also be produced by faults on the line (e.g., short circuits or sudden breakages of the circuit), and are due to the necessity to dissipate the energy stored in the magnetic and electric fields around the conductor.

For two parallel conductors of radius r spaced a metres apart in air, the external inductance and capacitance per unit length are given by

$$L = (\mu_0/\pi)\log_e(a/r),$$
$$C = \pi\epsilon_0/\log_e(a/r),$$

and Z_0, the surge impedance, is $120\log_e(a/r)$ ohms.

Surgery, that branch of medicine which treats diseases, wholly or in part, by manual and operative procedures. Strictly speaking, the science of medicine involves only those methods of procedure consisting of the administration of substances which, by becoming incorporated into the bodily system, are expected to induce such changes as will lead to the diminution or cure of the disease. The practice of surgery, however, involves actual manipulation of the part, either with the hand or with instruments. The term medicine is usually applied to the whole science and art of healing, together with contributory sciences. In practice, the only measures that are popularly regarded as surgical are those involving the removal of diseased parts and substances foreign to the normal organism. Although modern practice in medicine and surgery has many inter-connecting features, the two arts have a separate history, and there has at times been a hostile relationship between practitioners of the kindred methods.

The early civilisations of Egypt, Greece, Mesopotamia, India and China found a place for the surgeon in their social organisation, and such operations as incisions for the removal of dropsical fluids, amputations with subsequent treatment of the stump with boiling oil or pitch, the removal of stones from the bladder, and trepanning of the skull, seem to have been practised at a very early period. The science of surgery was transmitted to Europe by Byzantine writers, and somewhat later by practitioners who followed the Arabian tradition. The Early Christian era added little to the surgeon's art, which was confined to the monasteries, where collections of books of a scientific character enabled the clergy to minister to the needs of the population. As with medicine, however, monastic surgical science became impregnated with superstition. The lancet was the only instrument in common use, and the practice of bleeding for any and every complaint was controlled by the observation of the changes of the moon and such phenomena. In Britain, for some reason the monks were interdicted from the practice of surgery in 1139 and again in 1163, but the interdict was not wholly effective. In 1540 the two callings of barbery (see BARBER) and surgery, formerly practised by the same individuals, were separated, though the same guild controlled both. Throughout Tudor and Stuart times the surgeons shared in the prosperity of physicians, and were favoured with the confidence of the higher classes. The greater power of the physicians' organisation enabled them to restrict the practice of surgeons, and it was enacted that no major operations, i.e. an operation involving danger to life, should be attempted without the presence of a physician. In 1745 the surgeons seceded from the Barber-Surgeons Company and formed the Company of Surgeons, which established the Surgeons' Hall at the Old Bailey. In 1800 the old company became the ROYAL COLLEGE OF SURGEONS.

With the more efficient organisation and the improved methods of surgical education the profession improved considerably in status. In the 19th century progress in anatomical knowledge led to the tendency to specialise. The introduction of anaesthetics greatly enlarged the scope of surgery. Actual speed became of smaller importance, and the knowledge resulting from careful and methodical operations resulted in a wider range of surgical possibilities. The inauguration of antiseptic methods by Lord LISTER is generally acknowledged to be the most important item in the events of surgical history. The mortality due to operative infection diminished enormously, and surgical methods gained much wider confidence. As a result of Lister's work, the abdomen and later the thorax and the brain came within the province of the surgeon. Joints, even the knee joint, which was formerly notorious for its liability to infection, began to be opened with impunity, whilst fractures were reduced by the 'open' method.

With the increasing knowledge of the nature of infection and the identification of many specific organisms by pathologists at the end of the last century (see BACTERIA; PATHOLOGY), it was but a short step from Lister's antiseptic methods to those of the practice of aseptic surgery. Here the aim was, and still is, to prevent the access of pathogenic bacteria to the field of operation by sterilising beforehand everything which would be introduced into or come in contact with the wound. The success of aseptic methods in reducing the incidence of surgical infections gave surgeons confidence to carry their procedures into tissues and organs hitherto denied them. It might be said that the only restrictions on the achievements of surgery from its advance at the beginning of this century were the amount of anaesthesia which could be administered safely and the amount of damage which the patient's body could endure without fatal consequences. Another problem had to be overcome, however. Asepsis prevents the introduction of infection from external sources, but is powerless to affect those septic conditions which are already present in the parts of the body which surgeons are called to operate on. To sum up, one may say that the science of surgery depends for its success on: (1) operative skill; (2) asepsis; (3) safe anaesthesia; and (4) maintenance of the patient's wellbeing during and after the operation. It is interesting to note that the great advances made in surgery during the last 50 years have resulted mostly from the application of the fruits of scientific research to the second, third and fourth of these factors.

Advances in these matters furnish an excellent example of the truth that the practice of medicine is indivisible and not that of distinct specialists. The discovery of the sulphonamides and the antibiotics largely solved the problem of the septic surgical field and the post-operative complications that so often ensued from it. Pharmacological research has developed a wide range of anaesthetics, relaxant drugs, and drugs for treating or preventing shock; physics and physiology have taught us how to maintain a proper gaseous exchange in the lungs under artificial conditions; and the ingenuity of the surgical-instrument maker has provided the apparatus to make these procedures mechanically possible. Lastly, pathologists have shown the way to combat shock and blood loss by blood and plasma transfusion. With the progress of the surgical art, specialisation within the fields of surgery has occurred. Thus there are the specialities of neuro-surgery, thoracic surgery, plastic surgery, abdominal surgery, urogenital surgery, orthopaedics, otolaryngology and ophthalmology. In addition, surgical physiologists have developed ways to maintain or correct the balance of water and chemicals in the tissues of the body by infusing fluid into the veins. In the same way intravenous drips can be used to nourish the body for weeks at a time, using solutions of carbohydrate, fat and amino acids. Lastly, IMMUNOLOGY is beginning to solve some of the problems of homograft and even heterograft transplants.

Recent Advances in Surgical Fields. In thoracic surgery correction of congenital heart defects in babies and complete replacement of an adult's heart are now possible with some success. In orthopaedic surgery the replacement of the moving parts of joints, especially the knee and hip, are now routine procedures. The operating microscope has opened up a new field of microsurgery in the ear in the last 25 years. In plastic surgery, the microscope now allows tiny blood vessels to be sewn together in the technique of 'free skin grafting'. This means that a piece of full-thickness skin, with its blood supply, can be removed from one part of the body and placed on another; its blood vessels are plugged in to the vessels in the new region. One of the most important developments in surgery in the future will be a better understanding of the body's immunology, thus making transplantation a safer and more effective procedure.

See also AMPUTATION; CATHETER; CAUTERY; GASTREC-TOMY; ORTHOPAEDIC SURGERY; TRACHEOSTOMY; TRANS-PLANT; TREPANNING.

Bibliography: D. Guthrie, *History of Medicine*, 2nd ed. 1958; S. Taylor and L. Cotton, *A Short Textbook of Surgery*, 3rd ed. 1973; J. L. Wilson, *Handbook of Surgery*, 5th ed. 1973; S. Taylor, *Recent Advances in Surgery*, 8th ed. 1973; *Year Book of Surgery*.

Suricate, see MEERKAT.

Surigao del Norte, province of north-east MINDANAO in the Philippines, facing Leyte across the Surigao Strait. Timber, farming (coconuts, hemp, rice), and fishing are the main economic activities. Its mineral deposits of iron-ore, manganese, and nickel still have to be developed fully. Area 2739 km². Population (1970) 238,823.

Surigao del Sur, coastal province of eastern MINDANAO in the Philippines. Inland routes are non-existent so the sea is the main transport route; all the major settlements are coastal. Iron ore in the mountains awaits exploitation. Timber and coconuts are the two major industries although farming is the main occupation. Area 4552 km². Population (1970) 261,487.

Surinam, formerly Netherlands Guiana, a republic on the north coast of South America between latitude 2° and 6°N and longitude 53° and 58°E, having an area of 163,265 km². It is bounded on the east by the River Maroni (or *Marowijne*) which separates it from French Guiana, on the west by the Courantyne (Dutch *Corantijn*), which divides it from Guyana, and on the south by dense forests bordering on Brazil. The general direction of the rivers in the interior is from south to north, but near the coast, most flow in a westerly direction, because the ocean currents sweeping west from the Amazon have deposited silt at their mouths and thereby considerably enlarged the original land area. A few kilometres from the coast there is a narrow zone of savannas, and beyond, drained in part by the upper reaches of the Maroni and the Nickerie, a region of thick rain forest and jungle stretching to the frontier of Brazil. It has a subtropical climate with a heavy rainfall; temperatures range from 21° to 30°C. Its population was estimated to be 405,000 in 1974. See also ATLAS 58.

Economy. In 1973 Surinam had a per capita income of $700, well above that of most Latin-American nations. Its prosperity depends largely on two products, bauxite and aluminium.

The country contains very large deposits of bauxite and was the third largest producer in the world in 1973 after Australia and Jamaica. In the late 1960s production rose but levelled off during the 70s; in 1975 it was 6·9 million t. Most of the bauxite is exported directly but the world's first mining, refining, and smelting complex was opened in 1966 in Paranam. This plant has a refining capacity of 800,000 t and a smelting capacity of 60,000 t. In 1974, 57,000 t of aluminium were produced. The long-term aim of the government is to increase the production of aluminium and aluminium products.

Rice is the principal agricultural export, the main food staple, and occupies three-quarters of the cultivated land.

The farms are mainly owner-occupied and by Latin American standards the land distribution is not a major problem. There are large areas of empty land but most require irrigation before they can be used for rice. Sugar cane and citrus fruits are also important products. The country also contains large timber reserves and exports considerable quantities of wood and wood products.

Electricity capacity was 260 MW in 1972 most of which was concentrated in the Afobaka hydro-electric power station (180 MW).

The currency in use is the *florin*.

Government. After 308 years of Dutch rule, Surinam became independent on 25 November 1975. The two major parties drew up the constitution which provides for a president and vice-president, both elected by parliament, and a parliament of 39 members elected by universal suffrage. Executive power is in the hands of a council of ministers responsible to parliament.

Parliamentary stability is delicately balanced with the two main parties representing the two major ethnic groups (Creole and Indian) having widely differing views.

Education and *Welfare.* Compulsory education for children between the ages of 6 and 12 has existed since 1876 and is given in government and denominational schools. Education is free up to and including higher education, provided by the University of Surinam. There is a modern medical service, financed by Dutch and EEC funds, but social welfare remains largely dependent on the various racial communities.

Religion. A wide variety of religions are practised; the most numerous groupings being Hindu, Roman Catholic, Muslim, Moravian Brethren, and Dutch Reformed.

Official Language. Dutch, although a wide range of other languages are also spoken and pidgin English is the native dialect.

National Flag. Five horizontal stripes: a broad central red band bearing a yellow star, edged with white, between bands of green.

History. The first attempt at the settlement of this area was made in 1630 by an Englishman, Capt. Marshall. In 1644 some Dutch and Portuguese Jews from Brazil introduced sugar cultivation; but it was not until 1650 that a permanent settlement was effected by Francis, Lord Willoughby of Parham. In 1666 the colony capitulated to the Dutch, and, by the Peace of Breda in 1667, it was ceded to the Netherlands in exchange for New Amsterdam, now New York, which thus became a British possession. Thereafter Surinam was twice in the possession of Britain, from 1799 to 1802, and from 1804 to 1816, when it was finally handed back to the Dutch. Until 1848 the governor of Surinam was also governor of the Netherlands Antilles (Curaçao and Aruba). He was assisted by a consultative council whose members were named for life. Surinam was late in abolishing slavery (1863); escaped slaves took refuge in British Guiana, which had declared abolition in 1838. Surinam remained a poor colony with a population hardly exceeding 60,000 and an economy that depended on exports of sugar-cane and cacao until, after 1870, the Dutch government decided to follow the example of British Guiana in sponsoring Asiatic immigration. Cacao production was hit by disease after 1900, and was gradually replaced by coffee. Sugar-cane was displaced by rice and tobacco. From 1945 bauxite was developed on such a scale as to make Surinam the world's third largest producer. In 1948 the Netherlands yielded control of internal affairs to a locally elected government while retaining responsibility for diplomacy and defence.

In 1950 Surinam obtained some measure of autonomy, and in 1954 became a self-governing part of the Netherlands until independence in 1975. The Creole-dominated government began to agitate for independence in 1973, although the opposition Hindu party wanted to delay such a major move. The Dutch government, with extreme haste, entered into negotiations in 1975 and agreed to a ten- to 15-year 'golden handshake' of development aid. The year 1975 also saw the emigration of 40,000 Surinamers to the Netherlands in order not to lose their Dutch nationality after independence, and for their own security. However this created a shortage of skilled labour in Surinam.

Bibliography: M. Devèze, *Les Guyanes*, 1968; A. Gastmann, *The Politics of Surinam and the Netherlands Antilles*, 1968.

Surrealism. *Time Transfixed* by Magritte, 1939. *(Courtesy of the Art Institute of Chicago)*

Surinam Toad, see PIPA PIPA.

Surkhandarya, *oblast* in the south-east of UZBEK SSR, USSR, with the Tadzhik SSR on the east and Afghanistan to the south, where the AMU DARYA forms the frontier. Most of the territory is mountainous. The main industries are oil extraction, coal-mining, metal processing, cotton-ginning, foodstuffs, and building materials. The main crop is cotton. TERMEZ is the capital. Area 20,800 km²; population (1970) 662,000 (16 per cent urban).

Surplice (Latin *superpelliceum*, above the fur dress), loose white linen garment with wide sleeves, worn over the cassock by clergy and laity in choir or when serving in the sanctuary, etc. The surplice reaches to the knees, is pleated from the yoke, and made with simple sleeves. It was once worn over furs by priests when conducting service in cold churches. A shortened surplice with a square neck, sometimes edged with lace, is called a cotta.

Surplus, in classical (and Marxian) economics, is the volume of commodities produced in excess of those needed to support the workers who produced them. Such a surplus exists in all societies, except the most primitive, but it is extracted from the production process in different ways. In a system where workers are paid wages, for instance, a higher wage means that the surplus must be reduced correspondingly.

Karl MARX held that the characteristics of the capitalist system were determined by the way in which the surplus was extracted during production, and that CAPITALISM could be understood only be analysing the origin of surplus, not only in technological terms, but also in the political and social conditions of society, which underlie the surface phenomena of wages and prices.

Surrealism, art movement expressed largely in painting, though possessing much influence in sculpture and literature. Its main tendency consists in the relation of forms and symbols, seldom found together in everyday life, producing dreamlike sensations or an expression of the subconscious. Charles Madge has called it 'a method of dealing with the irrational without sacrificing a rational point of view'. Surrealism owed something to the iconoclastic outburst of Dadaism towards the end of the First World War, but is an essentially romantic movement, reaching full fruition c. 1930–35, when it was a revolt against the purely aesthetic and abstract values that were then dominant in the advanced circles of art. There were two main trends, one towards pure fantasy using collage and frottage and juxtaposing unlikely objects to produce surprising relationships. The other consisted of elaborate, highly-detailed paintings of hallucinatory clarity expressing the complexity of the subconscious. It can claim roots as far back as the fantasy and symbolism of BOSCH and BRUEGHEL, and affinities in the last century with Henry FUSELI and later Gustave MOREAU and Odilon REDON. Among the precursors of Surrealism in the present century was Giorgio di CHIRICO. Paul KLEE and Marc CHAGALL are sometimes regarded as Surrealist, but more representative are Max ERNST, Joan MIRO, Yves TANGUY, René MAGRITTE, and Salvador DALI. For a time PICASSO also worked along surrealistic lines.

Bibliography: D. Gascoyne, *A Short Survey of Surrealism*, 1935; A. H. Barr, *Fantastic Art*, 1936; W. Fowlie, *Age of*

Surrender

Surrealism, 1953; W. Gaunt, *The Surrealists*, 1973; F. Šmejkal, *Surrealist Drawings*, 1974.

Surrender, see CAPITULATION.

Surrey, Henry Howard, Earl of (1517–47), English poet, the son of Lord Thomas HOWARD, afterwards Duke of Norfolk. He was earl marshal at Anne BOLEYN's trial in 1536, and the same year accompanied his father against the Yorkshire rebels. Imprisoned on a charge of treasonably quartering royal arms (these were the mythical Arms of the Confessor), he was executed on Tower Hill.

Surrey seems to have been a disciple of WYATT, but was more influenced by the Petrarchan convention (see PETRARCH). His poetry lacks the strength and urgency of Wyatt's, but is more graceful and courtly. For the sonnet on the Italian model cultivated by Wyatt, Surrey substituted the less elaborate and easier English form, which Shakespeare afterwards adopted, of three quatrains with different rhymes, ending with a couplet. He introduced blank verse, of five iambic feet, into English in his translation of the second and fourth books of the *Aeneid*. Surrey, like Wyatt, was ahead of his time, and a whole generation passed before his lead was followed. His *Description and Praise of his Love Geraldine*, together with 40 other poems, was printed in Tottel's *Songes and Sonettes*, 1557 (edited by H. E. Rollins, second edition 1965).

Bibliography: E. Jones (Ed.), *Poems*, 1964; E. Casady, *Henry Howard, Earl of Surrey*, 1938; G. Bullett (Ed.), *Silver Poets of the Sixteenth Century*, 1947; J. W. Lever, *The Elizabethan Love Sonnet*, 1956; H. W. Chapman, *Two Tudor Portraits*, 1960.

Surrey, Thomas Howard, Earl of, and 3rd Duke of Norfolk (1473–1554), English soldier. He took part in the battle of Flodden in 1513, and as warden-general of the Marches devastated the Scottish border and forced Albany to retreat in 1523. Having already held the position of lord-lieutenant of Ireland in 1520–21 and lord treasurer in 1522, he was made earl marshal in 1533. He was, however, ousted from favour by Hertford, and condemned to death; but Henry VIII's death prevented his execution, and on Mary's accession he was released and restored to his former positions.

Surrey, south-eastern county of ENGLAND, bounded by Greater London, East and West Sussex, Hampshire,

Surrey. View from Newlands Corner, near Guildford. *(Barnaby's Picture Library)*

Kent, Berkshire, and a small area of Buckinghamshire. It is about 65 km from east to west and about 48 km from north to south at its broadest. Historically, the northern boundary was the THAMES, but Surrey had no other natural boundaries and no natural centre, its principal settlements being GUILDFORD to the west and CROYDON to the east, and the Thames settlements at KINGSTON-UPON-THAMES and Southwark. Administrative changes mean that of these four towns only Guildford now remains in Surrey. Boundary changes in 1974 meant the loss of Gatwick to West Sussex, but major changes resulting from the previous (1888) reshaping affected the northern part of the county with losses to the former London County Council (e.g. Battersea, Camberwell) and the Greater London Council (Kingston, Croydon), although there have been more recent gains from Middlesex to the north of the Thames (e.g. STAINES).

Geologically, Surrey forms the northern counterpart of Sussex. In the south-east there are Hastings Beds on the Sussex–Kent border and the main strata, repeating those of Sussex in the reverse direction, are from south to north: WEALD clay; Lower Greensand widening in the west to include HINDHEAD and HASLEMERE; narrow belts of Gault and Upper Greensand; chalk forming the North Downs and passing through the centre of the county along the line Reigate, Dorking, Guildford, Farnham; and London Clay and Bagshot Beds in the north-west, largely used for military purposes. For further details see CRETACEOUS SYSTEM.

The main rivers are the Mole, Thames, and WEY. The county contains many well-known landmarks and beauty spots; on the chalk, Newlands Corner (164 m) near Guildford and BOX HILL (183 m) near Dorking; and on the Lower Greensand, the Devil's Punch Bowl at Hindhead, beneath Gibbet Hill (277 m), Hascombe and Holmbury Hills, both pre-Roman earthworks, and LEITH HILL (299 m), 5 km south of Dorking and the highest hill in South-East England. There are large areas of heath and common land, especially in the west; market gardening is carried on extensively in the Thames Valley, elsewhere there is mixed agriculture, with hops cultivated until recently in the Farnham district. Sheep are reared on the Downs. Fullers Earth is found near Reigate, and there are extensive sand and gravel pits in various parts of the county. All the larger towns have industries, greatly increased recently, but the chief concentration is within the limits of Greater London.

Archaeologically, Surrey is of national importance for the palaeolithic flints from Farnham and mesolithic finds from the Thames gravels and western sandy heaths. The Romano-British period is represented by many prosperous villas, such as those at Titsey, Farnham, Ashtead, and Rapsley, near Ewhurst. There are cemeteries—the remains of considerable Saxon settlement—along the River Wandle, but population was still comparatively sparse, and the most spectacular event was, after the Norman conquest, the signing of the Magna Carta at RUNNYMEDE in 1215 by King John. A royal castle had previously been established at Guildford after the conquest, and there were others at Abinger, Farnham, Reigate, and Bletchingley. Farnham Castle, now a college, is the only inhabited survivor of the many royal and ecclesiastical palaces such as Esher Place, Oatlands, and Nonsuch. There are also major religious sites such as Waverley

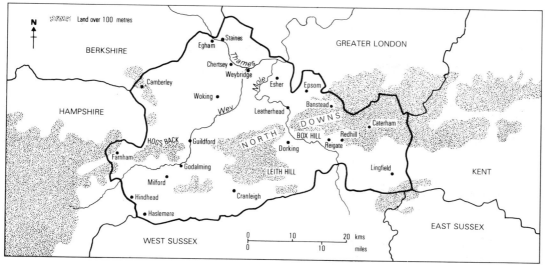

Surrey.

Abbey near Farnham, the first Cistercian foundation in this country, while successful excavations have been carried out at Merton Abbey and the Dominican friary site at Guildford. With the Tudor period, Surrey became the country home of many London professional and business men: Sutton Place, Great Tangley Manor, and Losely Park, all near Guildford, are examples of their building. Other great houses of later date are Clandon Park (1731), Hatchlands (1759), and Peper Harrow House (1775), but there are many fine examples of humbler dwellings from the typical Surrey 17th-century cottage, tile-hung and timber-framed, to the dignified Georgian brick of FARNHAM. After the coming of the railway, Surrey became increasingly residential, with many houses by well-known architects, e.g. Goldwyns near Dorking (by Lutyens).

One of the smaller counties, Surrey is now densely populated, particularly in the north-east and along the main commuter road and rail links to London. The rural areas are mainly south of the Downs and most of the county is now protected from further urban encroachment by designation as 'open space', or NATIONAL TRUST land, or common land, or areas of outstanding natural beauty, or metropolitan green belt. In total about 14,500 ha is open to the public and includes the important North Downs long distance footpath from Farnham eastwards. Administratively, Surrey is still divided between Guildford, the county town, and Kingston-upon-Thames, which has county hall and many administrative departments, but the former has become increasingly the focus, and with redevelopment in its old centre, and with the new cathedral and university on Stag Hill, Surrey is now looking to a nucleus never before possessed, being divided for so long between the countryside and the growing pull of London. Population (1971) 1,002,889.

Bibliography: Victoria County Histories of Surrey (4 vols), 1902–14; D. Whimster, *Archaeology of Surrey*, 1931; S. W. Wooldridge and F. Goldring, *The Weald*, 1953; I. Nairn and N. Pevsner, *The Buildings of England: Surrey*, 1971; J. Salmon, *The Surrey Countryside*, 1975.

Surrey Regiment, The East, see EAST SURREY REGIMENT, THE.

Surrey, University of, formerly Battersea College of Advanced Technology, incorporated by royal charter in 1966, and situated at Guildford. It provides courses and research facilities for degrees in the faculties of engineering, mathematical and physical sciences, biological and chemical sciences, and human studies. There are 3150 students.

Surrogate, in the Church of England, one appointed by the chancellor and the archdeacon in a diocese to act as their deputies in granting marriage licences. He is also empowered to take affidavits in matters within the jurisdiction of these principals, and to perform any other judicial business which may be specially deputed by them. According to Canon 128, a surrogate must be 'either a grave minister and a graduate, or a licensed public preacher, and a beneficed man near the place where the courts are kept, or a bachelor of law or master of arts at least, who hath some skill in the civil and ecclesiastical law, and is a favourer of true religion, and a man of modest and honest conversation', and any chancellor, commissary, or other ecclesiastical judge who appoints a non-qualified person as his surrogate is liable by the same canon to suspension and censure.

Surtees, John (1934–), British racing motorcyclist and racing driver, born in Tatsfield, Surrey. Surtees took up motorcycle racing in 1951, and won seven World Championships before transferring to cars in 1960. Riding for the Italian MV company, his last major victory came in the Isle of Man TT in 1960. Surtees was equally successful in cars, becoming a member of the Ferrari team in 1963, and winning the World Championship for them the following year. He is the only man ever to win World

Surtees, Robert Smith

Championships on two and four wheels. In 1968, Surtees founded his own company to build racing cars. Although he retired from active driving at the end of 1971, his cars still participate in Grand Prix competition.

Surtees, Robert Smith (1803–64), English novelist, born at Durham. Educated at the grammar school there, he inherited enough money to be able to devote himself to the life of a sporting gentleman with journalistic and literary tastes. He founded the *New Sporting Magazine* in 1831, and in it he published the sporting career of Jorrocks, a character who achieved lasting fame. Episodes appeared in book form in 1838 as *Jorrocks's Jaunts and Jollities*, and Jorrocks figured also in *Handley Cross*, 1843. Surtees's spirited writings combine humour, realism, and fancy, not unlike the Dickens of *Pickwick*. His other works include *Mr Sponge's Sporting Tour*, 1853, and *Mr Facey Romford's Hounds*, 1865.

> **Bibliography:** Study by F. Watson, 1933.

Surtsey, island to the south of the VESTMANNÆYJAR in Iceland, created by volcanic eruption in 1963. It has been the subject of intense scientific study, especially of its colonisation by flora and fauna. Landing is strictly controlled.

Survey, Courts of, courts created in England and Wales by the Merchant Shipping Act 1876 (see MERCHANT SHIPPING ACTS) to prevent unseaworthy or overloaded ships from going to sea.

The Merchant Shipping Act 1894 which replaces the above act, provides for the constitution, powers, and procedure of courts of survey. By these provisions a court of survey for a port or district is to consist of a judge with two assessors. The functions of the court are to act as a court of appeal from the decision of the secretary of state for Trade as to the seaworthiness of any particular ship. The court also acts as a court of appeal from the refusal of a certificate for clearance of an emigrant ship and in other matters relating to safety at sea. Every case must be heard in open court. Where the secretary of state for Trade thinks that an appeal involves a question of construction or design, or of scientific difficulty or important principle, he may refer the matter to scientific referees approved by a secretary of state, and such referees will act instead of, and have the powers of, a court of survey.

Surveying. The object of surveying is to determine the relative positions of points on the earth's surface and to portray this information in an ordered form, graphically as in a map or numerically as in a list of co-ordinates. With

Surveying. Linear measurement methods.

Direct linear comparison methods	Accuracy/length
Chain 20–30 m long, used on ground	1/1000
Steel tape 30–100 m long, used on ground	1/5000
Steel tape 100 m long, in catenary	1/200,000
Invar tape 30 m long, in catenary	1/200,000
Optical methods (up to 200 m)	
Theodolite, vertical staff tacheometry	1/30,000
Split-wedge tacheometer	1/5000
Theodolite and subtense bar	1/5000
Electronic distance measurement	
Microwave type range 70 km	±0·15m ± 1/100,000
Light-beam type range 2 km	±0·005m ± 1/200,000

most methods, the determination of horizontal position and the determination of vertical height above a datum surface, normally taken as mean sea-level, are treated separately, the latter by the method of LEVELLING.

Relative position may be defined by measured angles and measured distances. Since small measurement errors tend to accumulate as successive measurements are summed, it follows that an area of a given size should be surveyed with the minimum number of measurements of a given quality. This gives rise to the maxim of 'working from the whole to the part', i.e. first covering the survey area with a control framework of fixed lines, from which the individual ground details may be measured. The framework may be obtained by TRIANGULATION, in which the length of one or more BASE LINES is first measured to a high accuracy. Therefore only angles are measured and the position of new points is calculated by the solution of each triangle. Alternatively, if no angles are used and the lengths of each triangle side measured instead, the process is called TRILATERATION. An economical combination is to use successive angles and distances; this is termed traversing. The purposes for which the survey is intended dictate the methods and the accuracy required.

Geodetic surveys establish national and international control frameworks with triangulation points some 50 km apart (minimum 10 km and maximum 100 km), situated on prominent hill-tops for maximum visibility. Since the development of electronic distance measurement equipment in 1957, triangulation methods are being supplanted by traversing and, more recently, precise intercontinental connections have been made using an earth satellite as an intermediate and commonly visible station. The satellite may either be photographed against a background of stars, so defining its angular position from the terminal stations, or the distance to it may be measured as a function of the döppler shift of a transmitted radio frequency as the satellite passes overhead.

Topographic surveys, at map scales of 1/20,000 to 1/100,000 are normally produced by AERIAL SURVEYING. A number of ground control points, whose image may be precisely recognised on the photographs, are fixed from the geodetic framework and enable the photographs to be related in position, scale, and orientation to the ground co-ordinate system. After the photogrammetric plotting is complete, the sheets are taken into the field for checking, adding detail hidden from the air, and the recording of place names before being prepared for printing.

Cadastral surveys are necessary in those countries where the legal title to land depends not on any physical boundaries as may be described in the title, but on an original survey of the property. Boundary stones are erected at each change in direction of the boundary and their positions surveyed. In the event of loss or suspected movement, their positions may be relocated by survey techniques. The correct relation of adjacent properties is ensured by basing all work on the national framework, and the precision of fixation is varied according to the cost of the land involved. The work is restricted to professionally qualified surveyors.

Large-scale engineering surveys are undertaken to provide a basis for the planning of services or construction and may be at scales of 1/100 to 1/2500. For extensive projects, it will be necessary to connect the work to the national framework, but in most cases this will not be important, and very often it is assumed that the earth is flat over the area of the survey, so that no projection system need be used. Aerial survey is again employed for sites greater than say 10 ha, at scales no larger than 1/500, and the co-ordinate measuring system of the plotting machine may be used to provide a three-dimensional grid (or digital ground model), the values of which may be automatically recorded on punched paper tape and may be fed directly to a computer for calculation of earth volumes. By ground methods, a control framework is first established by traversing, triangulation, or chain survey-ing (a trilateration method), and then ground detail is positioned from the framework by individual angle/distance combinations.

The basic instrument for the measurement of horizontal and vertical angles is the THEODOLITE which may read directly from 1″ of arc (1/3600 of a degree) to 10′ of arc (1/6 of a degree). It is used either on a tripod or on a pillar and is accurately levelled to ensure that the angles are truly in the horizontal plane.

For hydrographic work, where levelling and steadiness is impossible, the SEXTANT is used since the angle sub-tended by the two simultaneously-viewed distant stations remains constant despite a motion of the instrument, which is hand-held.

Linear measurement methods are summarised in the figure. The ground measurement methods require that the lines are free from obstacles and of even slope. The chain/tape is aligned by eye between ranging poles, stretched taut, and each full tape-length marked with a steel arrow. The number of arrows collected by the second man can thus be a check on the number of whole tape-lengths. The inclination of each section of even slope is measured by CLINOMETER or by levelling, so that all distances may be reduced to their horizontal equival-ent.

Holding the tape suspended between tripod heads (in catenery) permits a higher accuracy, though to realise this, it is necessary to control the tension applied, to measure the ambient temperature and apply corrections for this, to frequently compare the tape against a known length standard, to correct each length for the amount of sag, in addition to measuring and correcting for slope. The optical methods are essentially short-range but are useful when the ground is rough or in measuring in and across thoroughfares.

The many makes of electronic distance measurement equipment fall into two groups; those employing micro-wave frequencies and those using visible or near-visible frequencies. The former, such as the Tellurometer MRA 101, have a longer range, but a low resolution, and the velocity of the transmitted wave is more affected by the meteorological conditions, which must be measured so that a correction may be applied. They involve two similar instruments, one at either end of the line, and incorporate a duplex radio telephone system for communication.

The latter, such as the Hewlett Packard 3800, project a beam of light to a prism reflector at the opposite end of the line, and receive the reflection. The higher frequency permits a high resolution (down to 1 mm) but suffers greater attenuation by the atmosphere, so restricting the range. Meteorological effects are smaller, but are applied for maximum accuracy. Both types are readily portable, are mounted on a tripod for measurement and run from 12 volt batteries. Use of them is widespread and gives a rapid and precise means of measurement.

Bibliography: HMSO, *Textbook of Topographic Surveying,* 1965; W. Curtin and R. Lane, *Concise Practical Surveying* (2nd ed.), 1970; A. L. Higgins, *Elementary Surveying,* 1970; K. Royer, *Applied Field Surveying,* 1970; D. Clark, *Plane and Geodetic Surveying,* 1971, and *Surveying for Engineers,* 1973; R. Spier, *Surveying and Mapping,* 1971; K. M. Hart and M. P. M. Hart, *Practical Surveying,* 1973.

Surveyors, skilled inspectors employed by governments, insurance companies, classification societies, and prospec-tive home purchasers, whose duty it is to ensure that certain rigid standards of construction and maintenance required by the respective bodies and by careful home buyers are complied with. In maritime matters, the Department of the Environment and LLOYD'S REGISTER OF SHIPPING are the leading employers of surveyors.

Surya, in Hindu mythology, the sun. He is represented as the son of Dyaus and the husband of Ushas the Dawn, and he moves in a car drawn by fiery horses. He is the preserver of all things stationary and moving, the source of life, and beholds the good and bad deeds of mortals.

'Sūrya Siddhānta' (Solution of the Sun), Indian text on astronomy written in the 6th century BC in 500 rhyming couplets. It includes the earliest known table of sines (see TRIGONOMETRY).

Sus, or Sous, river of MOROCCO, rising in the Atlas Mountains and flowing west to the Atlantic, which it reaches 8 km south of Agadir. Length 180 km.

Susa, ancient city of Persia, situated in south-east Dizfūl (Khuzistan). The site was settled from c. 4000 BC on, and was one of the main centres of the various Elamite dynasties from about the middle of the third millennium BC; destroyed by Ashurbanipal, c. 645–40 BC. It was incorporated into the old Persian Empire by CYRUS II THE GREAT, and used by him and subsequent Achae-menid rulers as a winter residence; it was here that a large portion of the Achaemenid treasury was stored (Herodo-tus v. 49). After its capture by ALEXANDER the Great, it was granted Greek city status by the Seleucidae, and continued a relatively prosperous existence under the Parthians and Sassanidae. Systematic excavations by the French have been in progress on the site since 1897.

See also PERSIA, *Art and Architecture.*

Bibliography: Mémoires de la Délégation en Perse (vol. I), 1900– .

Susanna, History of, one of the additions to the Book of Daniel (see DANIEL, BOOK OF) which forms chapter xiii in the Roman Catholic Bible and part of the Apocry-pha in the English Bible (see BEL AND THE DRAGON). The story of the woman tempted and falsely accused, and then vindicated by the clever young Daniel, is an edifying example of God's vindication of the innocent and of his punishment of the wicked. It has been a favourite motif of artists.

Susceptance, a measure of how easily a coil, capacitor, or other 'lossless' electrical component conducts alternat-ing current. It is the reactive component of the admit-tance. If the impedance of a circuit is $Z = R + jX$, the admittance is $1/Z = 1/(R + jX) = \{1/(R + jX)\}(R - jX)/(R - jX) = R/(R^2 + X^2)$

Susiana

$-jX/(R^2 + X^2) = G - jB$, where the susceptance is B, and G is the conductance. See ADMITTANCE; IMPEDANCE; REACTANCE.

Bibliography: B. F. Gray, *Electrical Engineering Principles*, 1970.

Susiana, see KHUZESTAN.

Suspension Bridge, see BRIDGE.

Susquehanna, river of Pennsylvania, USA, the main branch of which rises in Otsego Lake, and has a length of 708 km. The other branch rises in the Allegheny Mountains, and, after a circuitous course of 322 km, joins the main or eastern branch at Sudbury, Pennsylvania. The united stream then flows south-east past Harrisburg and Columbia, and enters CHESAPEAKE BAY at Havre de Grace. The Susquehanna was formerly much used for navigation, and parts of it were semi-canalised to form part of an intended canal joining eastern and western Pennsylvania across the APPALACHIAN MOUNTAINS. In 1972 it caused enormous flood damage to cities in its valley, e.g. Harrisburg and Wilkes-Barre.

Sussex, East, maritime south-east county of ENGLAND, fronting the ENGLISH CHANNEL and bounded by West Sussex, Surrey, and Kent. Both historical events and antiquities are numerous and there are castles at HASTINGS, LEWES, HERSTMONCEUX, PEVENSEY, and BODIAM (National Trust); abbeys at Bayham and BATTLE, and many other ancient buildings, both religious and secular. The South DOWNS in particular boast many prehistoric earthworks and Roman villas, as for example at Mount Caburn near Lewes. Noted events include the Battles of Hastings (1066) and Lewes (1264), and the exploits of Jack Cade (1450). Literary associations include the Sackvilles of Buckhurst; Kipling at Batemans in Burwash (National Trust); and the Woolfs at Rodmell. The University of Sussex (see below) was opened, sited to the east of Brighton, in 1961.

Sussex derives much of its character and charm from

East Sussex. The River Ouse. *(Camera Press/Jon Blau)*

the combination of WEALD, downland, marsh, and sea. In the east the coastline is generally unbroken, with the BEACHY HEAD promontory providing the eastern terminus of the South Downs which lie generally within 15 km of the sea. The South Downs Way is open for walkers from Beachy Head through East and West Sussex to the Hampshire border, giving grand views from vantage points such as DITCHLING BEACON at 248 m. The rivers OUSE and Cuckmere break through the Downs at Lewes and just east of Seaford, while the eastern Rother flows south-eastwards to reach the sea near Rye on the borders of ROMNEY MARSH. Here the former ports of RYE and WINCHELSEA are now inland towns and today, while there is a fishing industry at Hastings, the harbours are generally not good; however, there is a thriving cross-channel ferry service from NEWHAVEN. Noted seaside resorts include BRIGHTON, HASTINGS, BEXHILL-ON-SEA, SEAFORD, and St Leonards; while inland are small charming villages, nestling in the Downs and in the still-wooded Weald. East Sussex is in fact still one of the most wooded

East Sussex.

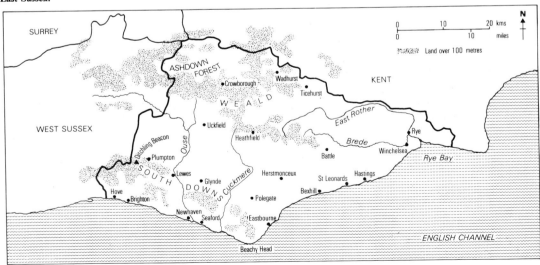

counties in England. The Weald is now a dairy farming area with scenic but agriculturally difficult small fields and dissected landscapes. ASHDOWN FOREST is a popular tourist attraction—originally a Norman hunting forest which has defied reclamation attempts because of its sterile soils. The Wealden iron industry was nationally important before the 17th century. Population (1971) 747,974.

Bibliography: Victoria County Histories of Sussex; I. Nairn and N. Pevsner, *The Buildings of England: Sussex*, 1965; J. R. Armstrong, *History of Sussex*, 1971; P. F. Brandon, *The Sussex Landscape*, 1974.

Sussex Regiment, The Royal, a British regiment, formerly the 35th and 107th Regiments. The 35th was raised in 1701 at Belfast and served in the defence of Gibraltar in 1704. It had a distinguished career in North America and the West Indies, and at Quebec under Wolfe gained its badge of the Rousillon plume, having defeated the French Royal Regiment of Rousillon. It was in the American War of Independence and the Indian Mutiny. It was made a royal regiment in 1832. The 107th was raised in 1854 in India as the 3rd Bengal European Regiment. This regiment was employed in various parts of Bengal during the Indian Mutiny. In 1861 it transferred as the 107th. In 1881 the two regiments were linked to form the present regiment. During the First World War 23 battalions were raised, which served in France, Flanders, Italy, Gallipoli, Egypt, Palestine, the North-West Frontier of India, and northern Russia. The regiment fought in France, East Africa, and Burma in the Second World War. Units were part of the famous 4th Indian Division which played a leading part at Sidi Barrani in the first great victory won by the British army in the war. On 31 December 1966 the regiment became part of the newly formed Queen's Regiment. This regiment then combined with the Royal Regiment of Fusiliers and the Royal Anglian Regiment to form the Queen's Division.

Bibliography: G. D. Martineau, *History of the Royal Sussex Regiment*, 1955.

Sussex Spaniel, see SPANIEL.

Sussex, University of, created by royal charter in 1961, the first of the new universities, sited on the South Downs near Brighton. It awards degrees in arts and social studies, science, and education. In 1975/76 there were over 3100 undergraduate and 1000 postgraduate students.

Sussex, West, a somewhat enlarged county due to 1974 reorganisation which took in parts of East Sussex and Surrey. Hampshire bounds it to the west. The familiar Sussex landscapes of WEALD, DOWNS, coast, and marsh are all present, together with the wide and fertile coastal plain stretching westwards from WORTHING, and the intricate channels of the CHICHESTER harbour area.

In the 1974 reorganisation, inland towns such as Haywards Heath, Burgess Hill, Cuckfield, and East Grinstead were gained, which, with HORLEY, CRAWLEY, and HORSHAM, constitute the larger inland centres of the Weald. However, there are also large tracts of Lower Greensand country, at places such as Blackdown, with magnificent views. The Downs are more wooded than in East Sussex, with beeches predominant in the Goodwood–Charlston area, while the coastal plain, much given over to market gardening, meets the sea in beaches as at LITTLEHAMPTON or BOGNOR REGIS, or as shallow inlets as at Pagham and Chichester harbours.

There is also a wealth of historical associations, from the castles at ARUNDEL and BRAMBER, to the city of Chichester with its cathedral; from the Roman villa at Fishbourne to the reputed landing place of the South Saxons near Selsey in 447. The large houses and grounds of PETWORTH, UPPARK, and GOODWOOD, with their reminders of past splendour, can be compared with the modern architecture of the new town—as at Crawley—and the motorway, such as the important M23 north–south route, or the shopping precinct as at Burgess Hill,

West Sussex.

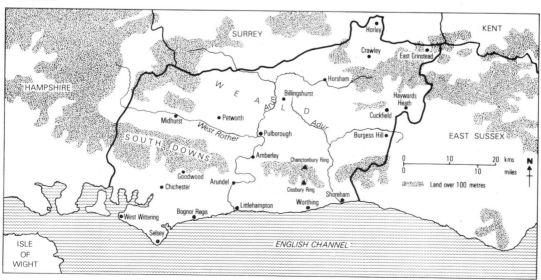

467

West Sussex. The valley of the Arun river near Arundel. *(Topham/Scowen)*

or the modern church architecture of the Mormons to the north of East Grinstead. There are many flourishing coastal resorts, as well as the busy port of Shoreham. Agriculturally the county is very dependent upon cereals, especially wheat and barley, dairying, market gardens, and fruit. Population (1971) 492,495.

Bibliography: see SUSSEX, EAST.

Susten Pass, Swiss pass connecting the REUSS valley in canton Uri with the AAR valley in canton Bern. A new motor road was opened in 1946. The pass commands a magnificent view of the snow-covered Swiss Alps.

Sustentation Fund, see FREE CHURCH OF SCOTLAND.

Sutcliffe, Frank Meadow (1859–1940), British photographer, born at Headingley, Leeds. He was an early professional photographer of scenes and inhabitants of Whitby, Yorkshire, which he recorded with great skill and sensitivity.

Bibliography: M. Hiley, *Frank Sutcliffe, Photographer of Whitby,* 1974.

Sutcliffe, Herbert (1894–1978), English cricketer, born at Summerbridge, Yorkshire. He first played for Yorkshire in 1919, and quickly established himself as an opening batsman. With his great Yorkshire partner P. Holmes he established the world record opening stand of 555 v. Essex, 1932, which stood until 1977. Their partnerships exceeded 100 74 times; 23 times they exceeded 200. In 1924–25 Sutcliffe joined Jack Hobbs as regular opener for England. In 54 tests he made 4555 runs; his career aggregate was 50,135 (highest score 313). He made over 1000 in a season 24 times; over 2000 12 times and over 3000 three times. His autobiography, *For England and Yorkshire,* was published in 1948.

Sutherland, Graham Vivian (1903–), British painter, born in London. He studied at Goldsmiths' School of Art. An etcher and engraver to begin with, he made a dramatic new start as a painter in 1935, and was official war artist in 1940. His semi-abstract landscapes, studies of inanimate objects, fine series of war paintings and heavy industry, and later imaginative works, have brought him international prominence. His works include a Crucifixion, 1946, for the church of St Matthew, Northampton,

portraits of Somerset Maugham and Lord Beaverbrook, and the design of the tapestry in Coventry Cathedral.

Bibliography: 'Graham Sutherland' in *Penguin Modern Painters,* 1943: and Studies by R. Melville, 1950, and Douglas Cooper, 1961.

Sutherland, Joan (1926–), Australian soprano, born in Sydney. She went to London to study with Clive Carey, and made her Covent Garden debut in 1952 as First Lady in *The Magic Flute.* She sang many roles with the company until 1959, when her performance of *Lucia di Lammermoor* turned her into a celebrity overnight. She then appeared at La Scala, Milan, the Metropolitan, New York, and every major opera house in the world, specialising in the coloratura roles of Handel, Rossini, Bellini, Donizetti and other composers. In 1954 she married the conductor Richard Bonynge.

Sutherland, Robert G., see GARIOCH, ROBERT.

Sutherland District, one of eight districts of HIGHLAND REGION, Scotland. It is mainly mountainous and is characterised by extremely low population densities. It coincides partly but not wholly with the former county of Sutherland. GOLSPIE is the administrative centre. Area 444,700 ha. Population (1971) 12,000.

Sutlej, river of India and Pakistan, rising in Tibet, crossing the Himalayas to flow east to south-west across the PUNJAB plain, receiving the Beas, and ending, with the Chenab, in the INDUS after almost 1500 km. Since the 1960 Indus Waters Agreement, India has utilised its waters: first, with dams at Bhakra and Nangal to irrigate via 1050 km of canals some 1,400,000 ha in the Punjab, Haryana, and Rajasthan, and to generate 604,000 kW at Bhakra; secondly, the Sutlej is integrated with the Ravi and Beas schemes.

Sūtra, see SUTTA.

Sutro, Alfred (1863–1933), English dramatist, born in London. Educated at the City of London School and in Brussels, Sutro turned to writing plays after a successful career in business, and was the author of about 30 plays on social themes, none of which are now remembered. His autobiography, *Celebrities and Simple Souls,* was published in 1933.

Sutta (Pāli) or Sūtra (Sanskrit), a discourse or sermon of the Buddha. See BUDDHISM; TIPITAKA.

Suttee, or Sati, Sanskrit word meaning 'a virtuous wife', applies to a practice once prevalent among the Brahmins of India. On the death of her husband a Brahmin or high-caste widow would proclaim herself *sati,* and at the cremation throw herself over her husband's body on the funeral pyre, having first distributed her jewels among the assembled mourners. The act was regarded as a voluntary one, but public opinion forced it upon a widow of good birth, and any woman who having proclaimed herself *sati* afterwards shrank from self-immolation was disgraced for life. Mothers of unborn babies and of children still minors were not allowed to become *sati.* The custom, frowned upon by enlightened sections of Indian opinion, was prohibited in 1829 by Lord William BENTINCK. A related primitive custom of providing women and slaves for service in the afterlife was widely practised in Bronze Age Britain, in Europe, Malaysia and North America, and in Black Africa.

Sutton, Sir Richard, see BRASENOSE COLLEGE.

Sutton, Thomas (1532–1611), English business man, born at Knaith, Lincolnshire, who amassed a great fortune and is best known for having founded and endowed a school and hospital at the CHARTERHOUSE.

Sutton, a London borough created on 1 April 1965, comprising the former municipal boroughs of Beddington and Wallington, Sutton and Cheam, and the urban district of Carshalton. Sutton's estimated population in 1974 was 167,200.

Settlement in the area dates from the Stone Age; a camp of this period has been excavated at Queen Mary's Hospital, Carshalton, and Roman remains have been found in many parts of the borough. Beddington consisted of two manors in Domesday, one of the manor houses still survives, its great hall dating from the 15th century; it is now Carew Manor Special School. One owner of the house was Sir Francis Carew, the famous horticulturalist. Elizabeth I came twice to visit his gardens, where he grew plants brought back by Sir Walter Raleigh from the New World. The 13th-century church contains many memorials to the Carew family.

Cheam was given by King Athelstan to Christchurch monastery at Canterbury. In 1018 Archbishop Lanfranc appropriated half the manor and at the Reformation both parts passed into secular hands. Between Cheam and Ewell was the site of Nonsuch Palace, built by Henry VIII to outrival the palaces of Francis I of France. Elizabeth I used it often, but subsequent sovereigns did not, and it was demolished in the 1680s. The site was excavated in 1959–60. Cheam School, attended by Prince Charles, seems to have originated in a school removed from London at the time of the 1665 plague, but the present buildings are modern. Sutton was held by Chertsey Abbey from the 7th century until 1537. Wallington too had medieval origins. These were all small agriculturally based communities until the mid-19th century when the advent of railways led to their rapid development as residential suburbs of London. The area is still being extended; Sutton, together with CROYDON, is developing the former Croydon aerodrome as a housing estate.

There are various industries based in the borough, especially engineering, building, electronics and the manufacture of plastics, vinyls, perfumes, chemicals, audio-visual equipment, and cricket bats.

Sutton Bridge, river port in Lincolnshire, England, on the River Nene near the Wash, 11 km north of Wisbech. It is in a potato-growing district, and trades in corn and timber. Nearby is the village of Long Sutton, noted for its old and beautiful church. Ruins of the old dock are still visible. Population (1971) 3300.

Sutton Coldfield, borough of West Midlands county, England, 11 km north-east of Birmingham, and a residential town, incorporated in the city of BIRMINGHAM in 1974. Sutton Park is a large open space including woodland, lakes, and heathland given to the townspeople in the 16th century. Population (1971) 83,630.

Sutton-in-Ashfield, industrial town in NOTTINGHAM-SHIRE, England, 22 km from Nottingham. The church

of St Mary Magdalene was built in the 12th century and restored in the 19th. Sutton-in-Ashfield has collieries, and manufactures cotton, hosiery, thread, light engineering products, plastics, tin, cardboard boxes, and precision tools. Population (1971) 40,700.

Suture, term in surgery and anatomy. In surgery: (1) a verb meaning to join tissue using stitches, as in closing a wound; (2) a noun meaning the material (catgut, silk, wire, nylon, etc.) used in stitching tissues together. In anatomy: a special kind of joint or articulation found only in the skull, by which the separate bones of the skull are joined together.

Suva, capital of the Fiji Islands, on the south-east coast of the island of Viti Levu, chief port of Fiji and seat of government. It is a commercial and light industrial centre; industries include coconut-oil processing, soap manufacture, biscuit making, small boat building, and the manufacture of cigarettes. Regular cargo, passenger, and mail services connect Suva with Britain, New Zealand, and other Pacific islands. Suva is linked by road and aeroplane with the international airport at Nadi, in the north-west of Viti Levu. Local government is an elected city council. The University of the South Pacific was founded here in 1968. Population 60,000.

Suvorov, Aleksandr Vasilievich, Count (1730–1800), Russian soldier. He distinguished himself in the Seven Years' War and in the Russo-Turkish wars, and commanded the Russian forces in Poland in 1768 and 1794. When Emperor Paul I joined the anti-French coalition in 1798 Suvorov was given the task of halting the French advance in Italy; in a series of brilliant attacks he defeated the French and conquered northern Italy. Transferred to Switzerland, he was surrounded by the French because of the confusion in the Allied command, but avoided disaster by one of the most daring feats in military history—he marched through the St Gotthard pass.

Suwannee, river of the USA. It rises in Georgia, flows south, and enters the Gulf of Mexico. It is navigable as far as White Springs. It is the 'Swannee River', mentioned in the well-known song. Length 400 km.

Suwarrow Nut, see BUTTERNUT.

Suzdal, small town in the VLADIMIR *oblast* of the RSFSR, USSR, 30 km north of Vladimir. It is a treasury of church architecture of the 13th–17th centuries and has been known since the 11th century. It was the capital of Central Russia 1095–1157, of Suzdal principality from 1238, and part of MUSCOVY from the mid-15th century. It is a popular tourist centre.

Suzerainty, the relationship between a feudal lord and his vassals. In international law distinctions have been drawn between dependent states under suzerainty and those under protection (see PROTECTORATE). A state under suzerainty is one which has acquired a degree of independence from the suzerain, of which it is properly part; a protected state is one which has given up part of its sovereignty to the protecting power. After the dissolution of the Holy Roman Empire in 1806, the chief instances of suzerainty were almost confined to states under the suzerainty of the PORTE, e.g. Moldavia, Wallachia, and Serbia, which had, however, definitely shaken off the Turkish yoke before being recognised, in 1878, as independent states. There does not appear to be any extant unarguable example of a relationship of suzerainty, although, in Europe, Andorra, San Marino, and Monaco may still correctly be termed protectorates.

Svalbard, see SPITSBERGEN.

Sveaborg, or Suomenlinna, fortress on the Gulf of Finland, occupying several islands 5 km south of Helsinki; it has been called 'the Gibraltar of the North'. It was fortified in 1749 by the Swedes. Until 1918 Sveaborg was called Viapori.

Svealand, central region of SWEDEN, historically the 'mother province' of the country.

Svedberg, Theodor (1884–1971), Swedish chemist, born at Valbo. He was educated at Uppsala University, where he became lecturer in chemistry in 1907, and where he was professor in physical chemistry (1912–49). Svedberg was visiting lecturer in colloid chemistry at the University of Wisconsin in 1923. In 1926 he was awarded the Nobel Prize in chemistry 'for his work on disperse systems'. In 1949 he became director of the Institute for Physical Chemistry. He published *Colloidal Chemistry*, 1923.

Svendborg, seaport in Svendborg Sound, Denmark, 140 km south-west of Copenhagen. It has one of the best harbours on FYN island and is an outlet for the island's agricultural produce. There are tanneries, shipbuilding yards, and foundries here also. Population 23,150.

Svendsen, Johan Severin (1840–1911), Norwegian composer, born in Oslo. He was conductor of the Musical Society in Oslo from 1872 to 1883 (apart from 1877 to 1880) and of the Royal Opera at Copenhagen from 1883 to 1908. His works include four Norwegian rhapsodies, two symphonies and other orchestral and chamber compositions and songs.

Sverdlov, Yakov Mikhailovich (1885–1919), Russian politician. He joined the Russian Social Democratic Workers' party in 1901, and worked, 1902–17, as a professional revolutionary in the Bolshevik organisations, always strictly following Lenin's policy. In 1913 he was co-opted onto the Bolshevik Central Committee. After the FEBRUARY REVOLUTION in 1917 Sverdlov became the party's main organiser. Soon after the seizure of power by the Bolsheviks (see OCTOBER REVOLUTION) he succeeded Kamenev as chairman of the All-Russian Central Executive Committee of the Soviets, and was thus titular head of the state. For a time in 1918–19 Sverdlov, together with Stalin, was Lenin's closest collaborator.

Sverdlovsk, *oblast* of the RSFSR, USSR, situated on the eastern slopes of the URALS and the adjacent part of the western Siberian lowland; largely covered with coniferous forests. There are rich iron-ore, copper, bauxite, asbestos, gold, platinum, and other mineral deposits. The province has the biggest industrial development in the Urals (engineering, iron and steel, non-ferrous metallurgical—notably the complex near NIZHNI TAGIL, chemical, timber, and paper-processing industries). Grain, potatoes, and vegetables are grown, and there is some dairy-farming (Tagil breed). The area was annexed by Russia in the 16th

century as part of the SIBERIAN KHANATE. Industrial development dates from the early 18th century. The main cities are Sverdlovsk (see below), Nizhni Tagil, SEROV, and KAMENSK-URALSKI. Area 194,800 km². Population (1975) 4,383,000 (84 per cent urban).

Sverdlovsk (formerly *Ekaterinburg* or *Yekaterinburg*), capital city of Sverdlovsk *oblast* (see above) and one of the major economic and cultural centres of the USSR, situated in the central URALS. It has large heavy engineering industries (metallurgy, electrical equipment), also chemical and diverse light and food industries. It is the centre of Uralmash, the largest machine-building plant in the USSR, and is also an important transportation centre (seven railway lines, an airport). Sverdlovsk is the seat of the Urals branch of the USSR Academy of Sciences (founded 1932), a university (founded 1920), a polytechnic institute (founded 1925), a mining institute (1914), and several other higher educational establishments. The city was founded in 1723 as a metal-works and fortress, and was the administrative centre of the Urals mining industry and a cultural centre of the Urals. In the late 19th and early 20th centuries it was also a flour-milling and commercial centre (trading in western Siberian grain, lard, cattle and iron). Tsar NICHOLAS II and his family were shot by the Bolsheviks here in 1918. From 1923 to 1934 it was the capital of the Urals. Population (1976) 1,171,000.

Sverdrup, Otto (1855–1930), Norwegian explorer, born at Bindal. He joined NANSEN's expedition of 1888, which crossed the GREENLAND icecap. Nansen, in 1893, offered him the command of the *Fram*, and in 1895 the ship was left in the pack-ice while Nansen made his attempt to reach the North Pole. The manner in which Sverdrup navigated the *Fram* home through the sea ice was warmly praised in Nansen's *Farthest North*. From 1898 to 1902 he attempted to circumnavigate Greenland via Baffin Bay. When he found that the way was blocked he turned his attention to exploring Ellesmere Island, to the west of Greenland. Among the islands he discovered to the west of Ellesmere Island were Axel Heiberg and the Ringnes Islands. These have been known as the Sverdrup Islands, since Canadian sovereignty was recognised in 1931. In 1914–15 Sverdrup had charge of an expedition to the Kara Sea for the relief of the Russian explorer Brusilov, and in 1920 he went to the rescue of the Russian icebreaker *Solovei*, which was icebound in the Kara Sea.
Bibliography: T. C. Fairley, *Sverdrup's Arctic Adventures*, 1959.

Sverre (1151–1202), King of Norway, native of the Faeroe Islands. He was proclaimed king in 1177, having been adopted as leader by the BIRKEBEINAR. He was a military genius, and having defeated Magnus (who was slain) at Fimreite (1184), built up a powerful monarchy in spite of opposition from the Church.

Svevo, Italo, pseudonym of Ettore Schmitz (1861–1928), Italian novelist, born at Trieste. The subject-matter of his work is the inner reality of the human conscience, which he explored in *Una vita*, 1892 (*A Life*, 1963), and *Senilità*, 1898 (*As a Man Grows Older*, 1962), through narrative techniques derived from the French school of Naturalism. With *La coscienza di Zeno*, 1923 (*Confessions of Zeno*, 1962), he gave Italy its first psychoanalytical novel. It was acclaimed abroad and established Svevo as one of Europe's major writers. He also wrote several plays and short stories.

Bibliography: A. Leone de Castris, *Italo Svevo*, 1959; B. Moloney, *Italo Svevo: a Critical Introduction*, 1974.

Svishtov, or Sistova, town of northern Bulgaria on the right bank of the River Danube, 61 km north-east of Pleven. Under the Turks (15th–19th centuries) it was an important trading town. In 1878 the town was sacked by the Russians. Svishtov is the centre of a fertile agricultural district, and there are fisheries on Svishtov lake, 8 km to the west. Population 22,000.

Swabia (German *Schwaben*). The name comes from the SUEVI, the original inhabitants of the area. A medieval German duchy, whose territory is now largely included in the *Länder* of Baden-Württemberg, Hessen, and Bavaria, it occupied an important strategic position between the Rhine and the Danube. After the fall of the Carlovingians it came into the hands of the Hohenstaufen. During the reign of the Emperor Charles IV the Swabian cities were leagued together and involved in the so-called 'war of the cities' in opposition to Charles's favourite, Everard II of Württemberg. Everard finally defeated the league in 1388, but a second Swabian League was formed in 1488 and, with the support of the dukes of Bavaria, the cities regained their territory from Ulric of Württemberg in 1519. This league came to an end in 1534. The name Swabia is still generally applied to the region of the former duchy. Its chief cities were AUGSBURG, ULM, Freiburg, and Konstanz.

Swadlincote, town in DERBYSHIRE, England, 20 km from Derby and 6 km from Burton-on-Trent. There are earthenware and fireclay manufactures, and coal-mines. The town has absorbed the villages of Church Gresley and Newhall. Population (1971) 21,060.

Swaffer, Hannen (1879–1962), British journalist, born at Lindfield, Sussex. Educated at Stroud Green, he started in journalism as an apprentice reporter at Folkestone and had further experience in provincial journalism before joining the *Daily Mail* in 1902. For the next 17 years he worked on newspapers controlled by Lord NORTHCLIFFE (who always referred to him as 'The Pope'), becoming editor of the *Weekly Dispatch* for a short period. However, his best work was done for the *Daily Mirror* which, helped by Swaffer's flair for knowing what the public wanted, Northcliffe transformed into a most successful picture paper.

In 1913, Swaffer started the first regular gossip column in the *Daily Sketch*, and next joined the *Daily Graphic* where his 'Mr London' page became a leading feature. In 1924 he was appointed editor of *The People*, but left in 1926 to become dramatic critic of the *Daily Express* and *Sunday Express*. A famous Fleet Street character, he championed many causes from socialism to spiritualism, and was, perhaps, the founder of the modern gossip column, while his dramatic criticism expressed forthright opinions. His name was commemorated in an annual award for the best in popular journalism.

Swaffham, market town in NORFOLK, England, 24 km south-east of King's Lynn. It has a fine church with a carved roof, a grammar school, a market cross, and the Swaffham Pedlar sign. There is a considerable agricultural trade, a fruit-canning industry, and a fireworks factory. Population (1971) 4160.

Swag, in architecture, a FESTOON.

Swahili, farming people inhabiting the coastal region of East Africa and Tanzania. They are of Bantu origin, but have mingled freely with the Arabs, who have greatly influenced their customs, language, and religion. Most are Muslims, and their language, Kiswahili (or Ki-Swahili), i.e. 'language of the coast', usually in a debased form, is used as the *lingua franca* of East Africa. The Swahili number about 1 million. See also AFRICAN LANGUAGES.

Swakopmund, formerly a port, now a seaside resort in South-West Africa (Namibia), north of Walvis Bay, with a railway to Windhoek. Until 1914 it was the chief harbour of German South-West Africa, but became sanded up. The administration moves to Swakopmund from Windhoek during December–January. Population 5681, of whom 2404 are whites.

Swale, river of North YORKSHIRE, England, rising in the mountains on the border of Cumbria, and flowing east and south-east to the Ure, which it joins to form the OUSE. It is 97 km long and is noted for its fishing.

Swaledale, dale in North YORKSHIRE, England, is 32 km in length from Keld to RICHMOND. It is the narrowest and grandest of the north-west dales, and is a well-known beauty spot. Up to 1880 lead mining supported a larger population in the dale than today's agriculture. Swaledale gives its name to an important breed of horned sheep. The spectacular Buttertubs Pass (526 m) connects Swaledale and Wensleydale. Arkengarthdale, a branch dale, starts from Reeth, the largest village, once a market town, and leads to Tan Hill Inn, England's highest inn (527 m). Below Reeth are the ruined nunneries of Marrick and Ellerton.

Bibliography: E. Cooper, *History of Swaledale*, 1973.

Swallow, *Hirundo rustica*, a well-known bird of family Hirundinidae, order Passeriformes, that is widely distributed throughout Europe during the summer, but winters in Africa and tropical Asia. Its back and wings are blue-black; the throat and forehead chestnut; and the breast pale buff or pinkish. Its two outside tail feathers are elongated into a graceful fork, which is more pronounced in the male. Its nest, somewhat like a flattened cup, is made of mud, straw, hair and feathers, and is usually attached to the rafters of barns. Swallows feed entirely on winged insects, capturing them with their mouth, which is lined with bristles made viscid by a salivary secretion. They are therefore of great economic value to man. Other species include the red-rumped swallow, *Cecropsis daurica*, of the eastern Mediterranean, and the martins. *Delichon urbica*, the house martin, is smaller than the swallows and also differs in having feathered feet and a pure white under-surface; its tail is less sharply forked and its wings are shorter. *Riparia riparia* is the sand martin. See also SWIFT.

Swallow-holes, see KARST; SINK-HOLE.

Swallowing, a complex co-ordinated reflex that is initiated voluntarily, mainly by tongue movements, and completed by the involuntary contractions of the oesophageal musculature. The contraction of the tongue muscles pushes the food on the tongue backwards to the fauces. The soft palate is then raised by reflex action to prevent the food entering the nasal cavity, and the larynx is also protected by reflex closures. The constrictor muscles of the pharynx then urge the food into the gullet, where it is impelled towards the stomach by peristaltic action. Swallowing is assisted by the secretion of saliva.

Swammerdam, Jan (1637–80), Dutch naturalist, born in Amsterdam, the son of an apothecary and naturalist. He took his doctor's degree at Leiden in 1667. He used the microscope as an instrument of continuous biological research. He was the first to describe (in 1658) the red blood corpuscles, and in addition studied the movements of the heart, lungs, and muscles. He also studied the life histories and structure of insects and published observations on tadpoles, including their cells, in *Biblia Naturae*. Included in this work is his discovery that the queen bee possesses ovaries and has a number of common features with the workers.

Swan, Sir Joseph Wilson (1824–1914), British inventor, born in Sunderland. The carbon process of printing in photography, the development of the 'rapid' photographic plate and many improvements in the processes of electro-reproduction are due to him. He is best known, however, for the incandescent-filament electric lamp, 1879, which was the first successful lamp of its kind. He also invented a miner's electric safety lamp. He became FRS in 1894 and a knight in 1904.

Swan, *Cygnus,* a genus of birds in order Anseriformes, with an elongated body and neck and short feet. The base of the bill is fleshy and naked, and the sexes are similar in plumage. About six species are known, of which three have been known to visit Britain in the wild state. The mute swan, *C. olor,* supposed to have been brought to England from the Crusades by Richard I to England from the Crusades, is the semi-domesticated bird of rivers and ornamental waters. The front part of the bill is orange. Its young are greyish-brown, while those of the smaller Polish swan, a sub-species, are white. Closely related to the mute swan are the Australian black swan, *C. atratus,* and the South American black-necked swan, *C. melanocorphyrus,* both of which are commonly kept as ornamental wildfowl on lakes.

The remaining species of swans have a somewhat complicated taxonomy but can be considered in two groups of two. All are northern species breeding in or near the arctic regions of Eurasia and North America. In Europe there are the whooper swan, *C. cygnus cygnus,* and Bewick swan, *C. columbianus bewicki,* both with yellow in different proportions on their otherwise black bills. In North America their equivalent subspecies are the trumpeter swan, *C. cygnus buccinator,* and the whistling swan, *C. columbianus columbianus.* These two have all black bills.

There is a further species not included in the genus *Cygnus, Coscoroba coscoroba.* It is an aberrant form from southern South America, which may or may not be a true swan.

Swan, The, constellation, see CYGNUS.

Swanage, holiday resort on the coast of Dorset, England,

flanked by hills. Purbeck stone is quarried nearby. Population (1971) 8556.

Swannee River, see SUWANNEE.

Swanscombe, town in Dartford District of Kent, England, set amidst chalk workings and the cement industry. In 1935 the Swanscombe Skull was discovered and further palaeolithic finds have made this area very important to British archaeology. Population (1971) 9145.

Swansea (Welsh *Abertawe*), seaport and city of West GLAMORGAN, South Wales, the county's administrative centre and also a district, 70 km west of Cardiff, at the mouth of the River TAWE, on a bay at the landward end of the GOWER Peninsula. The industrial and maritime activities of Swansea are carried on to the east of the High Street, the works and wharves being in the valleys beyond and down at the mouth of the Tawe. The residential parts of Swansea are well built, with wide streets and many parks, and have spread along the bay and over the hills behind. MUMBLES is 8 km to the south-west.

Swansea grew up around a Norman castle, and received its first charter in 1210. The old guildhall or town hall, near the docks, built in 1847, is in the Italian style. The new civic building, with its lofty central tower, in Victoria Park, embraces the new guildhall, law courts, and Brangwyn Hall. Other notable buildings are the Royal Institution of South Wales, with a museum and a library; the public library, which includes the corporation art gallery; the Glynn Vivian Art Gallery; and the Exchange Buildings or Chamber of Commerce. The University College of Swansea, a constituent college of the University of Wales, was established in 1920. Other educational institutions have been combined into a West Glamorgan Institute of Higher Education.

The port is the natural centre of the town's commercial importance. Many industries have grown up round it, and there are numerous collieries within a radius of 30 km. Long recognised as the chief metal port of Great Britain, Swansea is now also a large oil port, while remaining the leading centre of the tinplate trade. The largest docks are the Queen's, opened in 1920 (61 ha), and the King's (29 ha), the former used for the oil trade. Exports handled at the port are coal and coke, steel rails and iron work, tinplate, oil, merchandise, grain and flour, and cement; the imports include oil, merchandise, pitwood and mining timber, grain and flour, copper ores, and iron and steel. There is also a municipal dry dock for vessels up to 2000 t and a number of privately owned dry docks. In addition to its coal (the industry began in 1200) and oil (the oil refinery is at Llandarcy), Swansea District has natural resources in limestone, silica, brick earth, shales, and sand, and has for many years been the centre of one of the main steel-producing areas in the British Isles; most of the Welsh steel sheet and tinplate works are situated within a radius of 15 km of the city. Swansea's metallurgical importance was founded on copper ore, and copper works multiplied from the early 18th century. The scientific process of refining the ore was initiated in the Swansea region. The oil-refining industry yields a wide range of products. Other industries are paint, batteries, brewing, bricks, building and structural engineering, chemicals, concrete, electrical fittings, machinery, ship-repairing, zinc, and sulphuric acid manufacture. Swansea received a new charter in 1655, and it was made a city in 1970. It suffered greatly from air raids in 1941 and much of the town centre has been rebuilt. Area (district) 245 km². Population (city) 173,413; (district) 190,500.

Bibliography: W. G. V. Balchin (Ed.), *Swansea and its Region*, 1971; N. L. Thomas and D. G. Bowden, *Swansea Old and New*, 1974.

Swastika (from Sanskrit *su*, well, and *as*, to be, all be well), a very ancient and widespread decorative motive; it is also known as *fylfot* (perhaps from 'fill-foot', i.e. a pattern 'filling the foot' of a painted window), or *fylfot cross* or *crosse cramponnée*. In form the swastika is a Greek cross, the arms of which are like elbow-joints, all bent at right angles. It is to be found on early Elamite ceramics of the 4th millennium BC, as well as on ceramics of the 2nd and 1st millennia BC from Troy, Greece, Cyprus, India, Tibet, China, Japan, etc. It is also found in Christian inscriptions from the 2nd century onwards, as well as among the Amerindians. It was often used as a charm against 'the evil eye', and was used as a religious symbol by the Buddhists and Jains. Its origin is uncertain, but it may be a sun symbol, representing the movement of the sun. Adopted in 1910 by some German groups as the symbol of the 'Aryan race', it later became the official symbol of the Nazis (the female form).

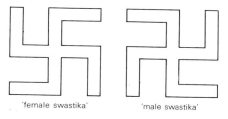
'female swastika'　　　'male swastika'

Swatow (Chinese *Shan-t'ou*), port in KWANGTUNG province of south-east China, and one of the first treaty ports to be opened to trade with the West in the 1850s. As a port, it serves the Han river basin but is of little more than local and regional significance. Population (1970) 400,000.

Swazi, BANTU farming people numbering over 1 million. The Swazi live in Swaziland and adjacent parts of South Africa. Until the end of the 19th century, the Swazi, under their king, were organised into age regiments which fought in the eastern part of South Africa. Today this structure remains but it has been neutralised by the South African government. Political and religious power is divided between the king and the queen mother, and the power of the ancestors is respected.

The Swazi 'homeland' (see HOMELANDS) in South Africa is situated in the eastern Transvaal, bordering SWAZILAND in the south. The homeland will eventually consist of contiguous territory, according to the 1973 consolidation proposals, but this will involve the removal of about 60,000 Swazi from an area east of the White river and Nelspruit. The capital is Schoemansdal. Area 2087 km²; population 117,845.

Bibliography: H. Kuper, *An African Aristocracy*, 1961.

Swaziland, kingdom of southern Africa, bounded on the north, west, and south by Transvaal, South Africa, and separated from Natal, South Africa, and Mozambique by

Swaziland. Plantations near the mining town of Havelock. *(Camera Press)*

the Lubombo Mountains. It is a former British protectorate and belongs to the Commonwealth. Area 17,185 km².

Geography. Relief. The country can be divided into four topographical regions running north-south: the mountainous Highveld (1250 m) in the west; the Middleveld (600 m); the Lowveld or Bushveld (300 m); and the Lubombo Mountains in the east. See ATLAS 46.

Climate. The whole of Swaziland has adequate rainfall. The Highveld receives 1000–2250 mm annually, the Middleveld and Lubombo Mountains 750–900 mm, and the Lowveld 500–750 mm. The rain falls mainly during the summer (November–March), when it is hot, especially in the Lowveld. The mean annual temperature is 23 °C.

Population. In 1974 the population of Swaziland was estimated at 494,400, including 32,218 absentees and 8000 whites. The SWAZI people are a branch of the Bantu-speaking group. The main towns are MBABANE (the capital) and MANZINI.

Economy. Agriculture. About 44 per cent of the land is held on freehold terms, largely by whites. This area includes estates producing sugar and citrus fruit under irrigation, commercial ranches, and large areas of commercial pine forest. The remainder is Swazi Nation land, on which plots are allocated by chiefs. Yields remain low, and techniques primitive; serious overstocking of communal grazing causes soil erosion. Attempts to improve peasant agriculture in rural development areas have been relatively unsuccessful, partly because of resistance from traditional authorities, but Commonwealth Development Corporation settlement schemes, e.g. Vuvulane in the Lowveld, have demonstrated that Swazis can become successful commercial farmers. Maize is the main subsistence crop.

Industry. Sugar and wood-pulp milling account for 80 per cent of manufacturing income. Light industries, including craft industries, are increasing in number, mainly in Matsapa and Mbabane. The HAVELOCK asbestos mine, opened in 1939, has an estimated further life of 20 years. The Ngwenya iron-ore mine, opened in 1964, is unlikely to remain open beyond 1978. Coal production in the Lowveld is growing, and a thermal power station exporting power to South Africa is a possibility.

Swaziland. Chinese teaching Africans rice culture. *(Camera Press/Jan Kopec)*

Communications. There are 1450 km of main roads, mostly untarred, and 1600 km of feeder roads; a comprehensive bitumenised system is planned at a cost of R9 million. The railway opened in 1964 to export iron-ore through Lourenço Marques may become uneconomic with this traffic, and at present it seems uneconomic to link it with the South African network for coal export. Matsapa Airport, near Manzini, has services to Lourenço Marques (renamed Maputo in 1976), Johannesburg, and Durban.

Trade. Exports (1973) totalled £46·2 million (wood pulp £9·4 million, sugar £8·3 million, iron ore £4·9 million, asbestos £4·1 million). Imports cost £41.7 million.

Bibliography: D. Fair et al., *Development in Swaziland: a Regional Analysis*, 1969.

Government. Constitution and *Legislature*. Following a short period of internal self-government, Swaziland became independent in September 1968. The King of Swaziland (King Sobhuza II, born in 1899) is head of state (*Ngwenyama*). Under the pre-independence constitution of 1967 his traditional authority was limited and power was vested in an elected legislature. The House of Assembly consisted of 24 members elected by universal adult suffrage and six nominees of the King. The Senate comprised 12 members, six elected and six nominated by the King. In the 1967 elections the King's party, the Gmbokodvo National Movement, gained all the Assembly seats. Following elections in 1972 when the opposition parties gained some seats, the King repealed the constitution in 1973 and assumed supreme legislative, judicial, and executive powers, ruling Swaziland by decree, advised by a council.

On 31 March 1976 Col. Maphevu Dlamini, commander of the Swaziland army, became prime minister in succession to Prince Makhosini Dlamini, who had resigned after being the head of government since 1967.

Justice. Romano-Dutch law is the common law, but in civil matters Swazi law and custom may be followed. The King appoints all judges.

Armed Forces. In April 1973 the King announced the establishment of an 800-strong army to be drawn from two ceremonial age-grade regiments. There is also a paramilitary police force.

Education. In 1975 there were 412 primary and 67 secondary schools catering for 89,000 and over 16,000 pupils respectively. There were 2363 primary and 739 secondary school teachers. Most education is undertaken in government or government-aided mission schools. The former University of Botswana, Lesotho and Swaziland was at Roma in Lesotho, until 'nationalised' by Chief Jonathan in 1975.

Welfare. The country has 52 doctors and 1414 hospital beds (1970). Health expenditure is under 8 per cent of the total budget.

Official Languages. English and Siswati.

National Flag. Blue with a yellow-edged horizontal crimson stripe in the centre, and a central black and white Swazi shield superimposed on two spears and a staff.

History. The SWAZI are of Bantu origin; they migrated southwards from central Africa in the 15th to 16th centuries and finally settled in Swaziland about the beginning of the 19th century. Often in conflict with the Zulus, they appealed to Sir Theophilus SHEPSTONE in 1840 for British protection. In the 1860s the South African Republic tried to annex Swaziland so as to obtain an outlet to the sea, but was stopped by the British and Portuguese governments.

Troubles over concessions to Boers and Britons resulted in 1890 in the first Swaziland Convention, under which dual control over Swaziland was agreed by the South African Republic and the British government. It was not successful and, after the Anglo-Boer War and Britain's annexation of the Transvaal, Swaziland came under British administration and in 1906–07 became a protectorate. The South Africa Act of 1909 provided for the possible transfer of the administration of Swaziland to South Africa but the Swazi rejected this proposal and in 1954 the British government made it clear that such a transfer would not be contemplated. In 1963 the South African prime minister stated that South Africa had no ambitions over Swaziland and the other protectorates of Bechuanaland (Botswana) and Basutoland (Lesotho). Following consultations with the European Advisory Council and the *Ngwenyama* the British government in 1960 set up a Swaziland Constitutional Committee. As a result of its report a new constitution was granted in 1963, consisting of an executive and legislative council. This was superseded a few years later by a new constitution on which independence was granted in 1968.

Following the repeal of the constitution, a commission was set up in 1975 to work out a new Western-type constitution; but in March 1977 the king announced that he was abandoning this attempt and would resort to government based on traditional tribal communities, known as *Tikhundla*, which would help him to govern.

Bibliography: H. Kuper, *An African Aristocracy*, 1947; *The Swazi, a South African Kingdom*, 1963; D. Barker, *Swaziland*, 1965; R. P. Stevens, *Lesotho, Botswana and Swaziland*, 1967; Central Office of Information pamphlet, *Swaziland*, 1968.

Sweating, see DIAPHORETICS; SKIN.

Sweating Sickness, a curious malady first observed in England in 1485: subsequent epidemics occurred in 1508,

1517, 1528 and 1551. It also occurred in Germany in 1529; and in France (Picardy sweat) in 1718 and later. The onset was sudden, and was heralded by profuse, often foetid, sweating: malaise, fever, headache, abdominal pain, and cerebral symptoms were common. A rash appeared in a few days. The disease was often fatal. It may have been a form of RELAPSING FEVER.

Sweating System. The sweating system of labour arose at the beginning of the 19th century, and was caused primarily by the practice of contractors placing the labour involved with sub-contractors. The system became known as the 'contract system', and operated principally in the clothing trade. It became a social scandal. It made possible the employment of impoverished unskilled workers, often women and children, at starvation wages, the work being done mainly in their own homes, or in overcrowded and insanitary workrooms. The evil attracted the attention of Charles KINGSLEY, who wrote a widely-read pamphlet under the pseudonym of 'Parson Lot' called *Cheap Clothes and Nasty*, and Thomas HOOD, whose *Song of the Shirt* made an impression equally deep. Kingsley and Hood attacked the system upon humanitarian grounds, but authorities like Seligman wrote of it from the standpoint of sociological study. The effect of these exposures, and of the findings of a House of Lords committee of 1888, was an agitation against the system at the end of the century. The increase in the immigration of poor foreigners round the turn of the century, attracted by prospects of employment at rates of pay higher than those in their own country, increased the evil. It was difficult for the sweated workers to organise themselves against exploitation, because their work was for the most part temporary, depending upon the fluctuation of the business. The establishment of trade boards which prescribed a minimum wage, the development of collective bargaining, and of modern mass production, and general social and economic progress caused the elimination of the system.

Sweden (Swedish *Sverige*), country of northern Europe comprising the eastern portion of the Scandinavian peninsula; it is bounded on the north-west by Norway, on the east by Finland, the Gulf of Bothnia, and the Baltic Sea, on the south by the Baltic Sea, and on the west by the KATTEGAT. Its area (449,800 km²) includes the great lakes of VÄNERN, VÄTTERN, Mälaren, and Hjälmaren.

Geography. Relief. The north-west part of the country is mountainous, the highest peak, Kebnekaise, reaching about 2100 m; the remainder is flatter, sloping to the east and divided by many rivers, notably the DAL, Indal, Ångerman, and Skellefte. These rivers are often linked by finger lakes made by morainic dams, and often have falls in their courses which are used for hydro-electric power generation. The whole landscape shows both erosional and depositional glaciation features (see GLACIATION). Physically, the country is traditionally divided into the three regions of Norrland, Svealand, and Götaland.

Norrland is the most northerly, a region of high mountains and dramatic scenery. This relatively wild and unspoilt landscape contains some national parks and is popular with tourists during the spring and summer. Svealand covers the lower slopes of the highlands and the central lowlands studded with lakes. A characteristic of the region is the gravel ridges deposited by the retreating ice, formerly used as highways. South of Svealand lies Götaland, a region of hills and plains. The Skåne plains at the southern tip of the country are the most fertile and thus the most densely populated region. The Swedish coastline is typified by hundreds of small offshore islands, wooded and rounded by the action of the icesheet. See ATLAS 28.

Climate. In spite of its northerly position, Sweden has a relatively mild climate, owing to the influence of the North Atlantic Drift. Climatic variations are, however, considerable; the average temperature in the south is 7 °C, and in the north (where summer lasts only two months) it is 2 °C. The rainfall varies in different parts of the country, the average being 80–240 mm per year. Due to its proximity to the Arctic Circle, the country has long hours of daylight in the summer, ranging from 17 in the south to 23 in the north: the 'Midnight Sun' phenomenon.

Population. In 1975 the population totalled 8,208,442. Over the last 100 years there has been a marked shift of population from the rural districts to the towns and from the outlying remote districts to the central counties. Nearly 90 per cent of Sweden's population, small in relation to its land area, live in the southern half of the country and about 80 per cent live in towns or urban areas, the most important being STOCKHOLM (the capital), GÖTEBORG, MALMÖ, UPPSALA, VÄSTERÅS, and NORRKÖPING.

Economy. Agriculture and Forestry. Swedish agriculture is concentrated in the fertile south of the country; most of the output consists of cereals, potatoes, and dairy products (30 per cent of the farming output). Sweden's forests provide the materials for paper, rayon, and other industries. Half the country is covered with productive forests. Only a quarter of a million people in total are employed in agriculture, forestry, and fishing.

Industry. Sweden has long been famous for her mineral resources, and especially iron ore which accounts for 5 per cent of world production. The major fields are at Kiruna and Malmberget, north of the Arctic Circle. Formerly mined by open-cast methods, now there are mostly underground workings (1974 production was 36 million t). The ore forms the basis of the country's heavy industry and supplies the industrial markets of Western Europe. About

Sweden. The Fallforsen Falls on the Umeå river. (*Camera Press/Gullers*)

Sweden

one-quarter of the working population are engaged in manufacturing industry. Other minerals include zinc, lead, tungsten, manganese, and copper. There are important metalworking, engineering, electronic, textile, and chemical industries.

Energy. Sweden is dependent on imported oil for supplying her thermal power stations, but water power supplies much of her electricity, in fact, 75 per cent of the 74,280 million kWh produced. Because of her many rivers having large waterfalls, Sweden has almost totally developed her hydro-electric power potential; any falls now undeveloped will remain so because of the desire to preserve the natural environment. Thermal power complements hydroelectricity and produces about 20 per cent of the energy total. Nuclear power stations have been built but have proved very controversial and the new government (1976) is committed to a running down of the country's nuclear programme.

Communications. There are 11,360 km of state railway track (7000 km are electrified) and 98,000 km of roads. Ferry services link Sweden with Denmark and East Germany. Swedish airlines are part of the Scandinavian airline system (SAS). Current communications policy maintains that each transport service should be self-supporting; this has hit railways especially hard. The private car accounts for over 80 per cent of all passenger traffic. There are at least nine ports heavily engaged in foreign trade and the Swedish merchant fleet has a gross tonnage of about 7.5 million.

Trade. Sweden's economy is exceptionally strong, with a long-standing balance of payments surplus. Though a founder member of EFTA, the country has refused to join the EEC but has favourable agreements with it. Sweden is dependent on foreign trade for its economic growth and development. Mining and mineral products and forestry make up 75 per cent of its exports. Its main trading partners are West Germany, Great Britain, the USA, and the other Scandinavian states.

Planning. There is a strong socialist element in Sweden's economy, many businesses and industries being wholly or partly nationalised. Taxes are high, supporting a very advanced welfare system (see below).

Labour. There is a labour force of about 4 million, of whom 1,120,000 are employed in manufacturing. The standard of living is one of the highest in the world. The Swedish Trade Union Confederation has 25 affiliated unions with 1,771,000 members, and there are three independent unions with a total of over a million more members.

Finance. In Swedish currency 100 *öre* = 1 *krona*. At the 1977 rate of exchange 7·5 *kronor* = £1 sterling. The 1975–76 budget estimated government revenue at 82,000 million and expenditure at 87,000 million *kronor*.

Bibliography: M. Schnitzer, *Economy of Sweden*, 1970; Nagel Guides, *Sweden*, 1973; OECD, *Agricultural Policy in Sweden*, 1975.

Government. Constitution and *Legislature*. Sweden is a constitutional monarchy, but under the constitution that came into effect on 1 January 1975 the king has no political power: he does not sign government decisions and he does not select the prime minister, which is the job of the speaker of the parliament. Parliament, the *Riksdag*, consists of one chamber of 349 members, elected every three years by a system of proportional representation. There is universal adult suffrage, the minimum voting age being 18. A peculiar feature of the Swedish constitution is that government and administration are two separate functions. The central administrative agencies execute government decisions without interference from ministers. Another feature of the constitution is that official documents and the files of any administrative office are,

Sweden. The Gruvön pulp mills on Lake Vänern. *(Camera Press)*

Sweden. Modern urban growth in the Stockholm suburb of Farstar. *(Camera Press/Gullers)*

unless specifically marked secret, open for inspection to any member of the public.

Until 1976, the Social Democratic party had been in power almost continuously since 1932, sometimes in coalition with other groups. The government formed following elections held on 19 September 1976 is a Centre-Liberal-Conservative Moderate coalition, with Thorbjörn Fälldin (Centre) as prime minister. Other political parties are the Christian Democrats and two Communist parties.

The historical divisions of Sweden are Svealand, Götaland, and Norrland. The two former represent an ancient division which, in turn, represents a difference of race and tradition. Svealand may be regarded as the 'mother province' of Sweden. For administrative purposes, the country is divided into counties (*län*) as follows: STOCK-HOLM, UPPSALA, SÖDERMANLAND, ÖSTERGÖTLAND, JÖN-KÖPING, KRONOBERG, KALMAR, GOTLAND, BLEKINGE, KRISTIANSTAD, MALMÖHUS, HALLAND, GÖTEBORG and BOHUS, ÄLVSBORG, SKARABORG, VÄRMLAND, ÖREBRO, VÄSTMANLAND, KOPPARBERG, GÄVLEBORG, VÄSTER-NORRLAND, JÄMTLAND, VÄSTERBOTTEN, and NORRBOT-TEN. The counties are headed by a governor (*landshövding*), who is appointed by the government. There are elected county councils (*landsting*). The counties are subdivided into 278 communes. County councils are responsible for health services.

Justice. Judicial administration is not dependent on the government. Its administration is supervised by the attorney-general, appointed by the *Riksdag*. Sweden has a supreme court, high courts, and district courts that can deal with both civil and criminal cases. The *Justitie Ombudsmän* (Parliamentary Commissioners) investigate maladministration of the law. Swedish law has developed from domestic traditions; there is close co-operation with other Scandinavian countries (see NORDIC COUNCIL).

Education. Since 1842 elementary education has been compulsory and free. There is ten-year comprehensive primary schooling. For those entering employment immediately on leaving these schools, courses in continuation schools are available. In secondary education the standard of technical education is particularly high. There are several universities and university branches. The oldest are in Uppsala (founded 1477) and Lund (founded 1666).

Welfare. Sweden is advanced in the field of social welfare. Government spending on this is heavy even by Scandinavian standards: in the 1976 budget, 26,000 million *kronor* out of a total expenditure of 87,000 million. Different kinds of insurance form the basis for the welfare system: the national retirement pension, compulsory health insurance (in which a maternity grant is included), insurance against industrial injury, and voluntary unemployment insurance. In addition to this, there are a number of family welfare benefits: a general family allowance for every child under 16, free health supervision of children up to school age, free school meals, free school books, free holidays for housewives with at least two children, etc. Since the beginning of the 20th century,

477

Sweden

Swedish municipalities and other public bodies have built many modern residential estates, comprising flats and houses, in town and country areas to replace former slum areas or undeveloped hamlets, and many Swedish building projects have served as models for similar schemes all over Western Europe.

Armed Forces. Sweden has adopted a policy of non-alignment, with a strong defence force. Its peacetime strength is about 68,000, of which 18,000 are long service regulars and 50,000 conscripts. The Home Guard numbers more than 100,000. On mobilisation the army would expand to about 750,000. The Swedish army is organised into wartime field units, local defence units, and Home Guard units. British Centurion tanks (mounting 105 mm guns) are in service in armoured and infantry divisions. The Swedish navy comprises eight destroyers, 22 submarines, 33 motor torpedo-boats, and about 120 minor war vessels. The coast artillery forms part of the navy, and is responsible for the defence of naval bases and important ports.

The Swedish air force is highly efficient and equipped with modern aircraft, which, unlike those of most smaller countries, are manufactured in Sweden. There are about 40 squadrons, most of them all-weather fighter and attack units. Types of aircraft include the Draken (Dragon), an all-weather fighter and reconnaissance aircraft. Armament includes Sidewinder and Falcon air-to-air missiles, Bloodhound surface-to-air missiles, and a Swedish air-to-surface missile. The build-up of a still more advanced air defence system, based on a new aircraft, the Viggen, was announced in 1962, and the first planes were delivered in 1971.

Sweden has made civil defence compulsory. About 300,000 persons are enrolled in civil defence organisations, where they receive special training. Shelters against nuclear bombs are built underground, including subterranean hangers, naval bases, hospitals, and factories.

Religion. There is complete religious freedom in Sweden, though more than 95 per cent of the population adhere to the state church, which is the Evangelical Lutheran church.

Language. The official language of Sweden is Swedish; some Lappish and Finnish are spoken in the north, and there are large groups of immigrants with their native languages—Finns, Yugoslavs, Greeks, and Turks.

National Anthem. The national anthem is *Du gamla, du fria* (Thou old, thou free).

National Flag. The Swedish flag consists of a yellow cross on a light blue field.

Bibliography: T. Husen and G. Boalt, *Case of Sweden: Educational Research and Change*, 1968; J. B. Board, *Government and Politics of Sweden*, 1971; W. Fleisher, *Sweden: The Welfare State*, 1973; D. M. Hancock, *Sweden: The Politics of Post-industrial Change*, 1973; L. Hufford, *Sweden: The Myth of Socialism*, 1973.

Prehistory. The earliest traces of man c. 10,000 BC have been found at Segebro near Malmö, and a small population of hunters probably inhabited the southern part. The Maglemosian culture c. 6000 BC found all over Scandinavia is represented at sites such as Lilla Loshult Mosse and round Ringsjö. Pottery appears first on sites of the Ertebølle culture c. 4000 BC. Invasions of Neolithic people have been found in settlements in Skäne, Blekinge, etc. with the first traces of agriculture, and at Östia Viå and Mogetorp in Sodermanland remains of houses as well as pottery and stone tools of the Viå culture. Later neolithic immigrants brought a megalithic culture. In the middle of the 2nd millennium bronze weapons and tools were imported and made locally in the Lake Mälaren area. Burial mounds and cairns of the Bronze Age are common in south Sweden. The transition from the Bronze to the Iron Age (600–400 BC) is poorly represented. The change of climate may have caused general emigration and Sweden seems to have remained outside the general development. In the Middle or Roman Iron Age the return of an equable climate brought about an expansion of culture and the many Roman imports denote a higher standard of living. The Migration period (c. AD 400–550) shows a marked increase in prosperity and is one of the great periods of Swedish art. Important gold hoards have been found at Timboholm and near Tureholm. The goldsmiths' work is of fine quality, e.g. collars from Ålleberg and Möne.

See also VIKINGS; VIKING ART.

Bibliography: H. Shetelig and H. Falle, *Scandinavian Archaeology*, 1937; M. Stenberger, *Sweden*, 1962.

History. The early history of Sweden is contained in legend and saga. The country appears to have been inhabited by two separate but closely related races, the Swedes and the Goths. These played some part in the great Viking expansion (see VIKINGS), although their

Sweden. The town of Kiruna and its iron-ore mines. *(Camera Press)*

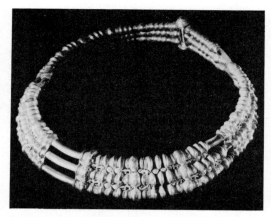

Sweden. Gold three-ringed collar from the Migration period, 6th century AD, decorated with filigree granulation and carved figures. Found at Ålleberg, Västergotland, it is now in the Statens Historiska Museum, Stockholm. *(Werner Forman Archive)*

penetration of the Baltic and Russia was more important. The old mythology of the North, or debased forms of it, remained the religion of many of the people until the 12th century, although Christianity was introduced at a much earlier period. It failed, however, to assimilate the whole of the country until later. By about the end of the 13th century Finland had been incorporated in the Swedish kingdom. The Middle Ages in Sweden are marked by a centralisation of power in the country, but also by clashes between rival claimants to the throne and between the king and the nobility. A notable event was the Union of Kalmar in 1397, when the kingdoms of Denmark, Norway, and Sweden came under the common regency of MARGARET of Denmark. Margaret's successors were not, however, always able to assert their authority in Sweden. A popular revolt was raised in 1434 under Engelbrekt Engelbrektsson, and during several periods Swedish noblemen were in effective control of Sweden. The union finally came to an end in the reign of Christian II, after his brutal treatment of the leaders of a rebellion (the Stockholm Bloodbath, 1520). Gustavus Vasa, a Swedish noble, started a revolt in Dalarna in 1521 and with help from Lübeck made Sweden independent of Denmark-Norway. He was elected king as GUSTAVUS I by the *Riksdag* in 1523 and survived a series of revolts to leave Sweden a financially and politically stable country on his death in 1560. He exploited the arrival of Lutheranism in Sweden to destroy the power of the Roman Catholic Church and to appropriate its possessions in 1527, but Lutheran services only gradually replaced Catholic ceremonies in Sweden. His son Eric XIV (king 1560–68) embarked on a campaign of expansion in the southern Baltic and took Estonia under Swedish protection in 1561, but otherwise had little success in an enervating seven years' war with Denmark. His half-brother, John III (king 1568–92), continued the Baltic campaign. Married to a Polish princess, he brought up his son Sigismund as a Roman Catholic and had him elected king of Poland in 1587. Sigismund's religion, however, proved a serious handicap on his accession to the Swedish throne in 1592, and he was opposed by his

ruthless and ambitious uncle Charles, who finally had Sigismund deposed and himself hailed as king by the *Riksdag* in 1600. As Charles IX he too fought in the Baltic states with little success, and on his death in 1611 he left his 16-year-old son GUSTAVUS II (Gustavus Adolphus) a country at war with Denmark, Poland, and Russia.

Sweden in 1611 was lacking in population, internal communications, and material resources, and its geographical position was unfavourable for the expansion of its trade, since its way to the open sea was controlled by Denmark. Gustavus Adolphus continued the policy of turning the Baltic into a 'Swedish lake'. He ended the war with Denmark, recovering territory lost by his father. War with Russia gave Sweden control of what is now the Baltic coast of Russia, whilst war with Poland ended in a truce (1629), which confirmed Sweden in possession of Livonia and gave it a grip on the mainland of Germany. Gustavus Adolphus now appeared as the Protestant champion of Europe. In 1631 and 1632 he won a series of spectacular triumphs; the Catholic League was defeated, the Catholic general, Tilly, out-manoeuvred and finally killed, and Gustavus Adolphus was able to penetrate to the south. He was recalled by the attacks of Wallenstein in Saxony, and fell at the battle of Lützen in 1632. He was the real founder of the greatness of Sweden. He made it a strong power by his domestic and financial reforms, and he won for it a great place in the councils of Europe. The government was centralised and strong; the army was reformed; and Sweden for the next century was one of the great powers in Europe. In fact, its resources were always strained to the utmost to maintain this position; and its Baltic possessions were to embroil it in a series of wars which it could not afford but without which it could not hope to keep them.

Gustavus Adolphus was succeeded by his daughter CHRISTINA, whose minority was made famous by the statecraft of the Chancellor, Axel OXENSTIERNA. The success of Sweden was seen in the Treaty of Westphalia, which marked the zenith of Swedish power. It became the controlling power of Germany, the Protestant champion of Europe, and the greatest power of the North. In 1645 Denmark was forced to give up its right to tolls in the Sound and ceded Gotland, Jämtland, Härjedalen, and, temporarily, Halland to Sweden. In 1654 Christina

Sweden. Early Bronze Age rock carvings with ships, animals, and human figures carrying weapons. *(Werner Forman Archive)*

Sweden

became a Catholic and abdicated in favour of her cousin Charles X. He continued the work of Gustavus Adolphus. He attacked Denmark and incorporated the provinces of Skåne, Blekinge, Halland, and Bohuslän into Sweden, thus establishing Sweden's natural frontiers along the western and southern coasts. Charles X died in 1660 and was succeeded by his son, CHARLES XI, who was only four years old. Charles XI proved to have inherited the military genius of the Vasas. When he assumed the crown he fought a series of wars by which he was able to preserve intact the territories of Sweden, and then turned his attention to domestic reform. He curbed the power of the nobility, and left Sweden reformed and restored at his death in 1697.

CHARLES XII (1682–1718), the wonder of Europe, succeeded. He spent the 20 years of his reign in almost constant warfare, and it was at this stage that the strain of maintaining a scattered empire, harassed by ambitious countries with large populations and resources, began to tell on a country which had only a small population. Charles astonished Europe by his enterprise and dash, and won many brilliant victories, penetrating, on one occasion, deep into Russia. But he had against him a formidable coalition of powers, and his schemes were too grandiose to be possible of fulfilment even by a military genius of his calibre. In the end he was clearly defeated, and his death probably alone saved Sweden from utter disaster. The Swedish empire was dismembered in a series of treaties, 1719–21. Most of the German provinces were ceded to Britain, Hanover, and Prussia, while Russia was confirmed in possession of Estonia, Livonia, and Ingermanland. On Charles XII's death the Swedish monarchy lost its absolute power, and under Frederick I (king 1720–51) and Adolphus Frederick (king 1751–71) a form of parliamentary government prevailed. This system, with its bitter party quarrels between the 'Hats' and the 'Caps', was brought to an end after a coup d'état by the young GUSTAVUS III in 1772, though this theatrical king proved ultimately more successful in his cultural than in his political ventures. He was assassinated at a masked ball in 1792.

His son, Gustavus IV, was an implacable opponent of Napoleon. After entering into alliance with France, Russia invaded and occupied Finland, and in 1809 this part of the Swedish kingdom had to be ceded to the tsar. Shortly before this Gustavus IV was deposed. His uncle, who succeeded as CHARLES XIII, was infirm, and to secure the goodwill of Napoleon the Riksdag accepted Napoleon's marshal, Bernadotte, as Crown Prince Charles John (see CHARLES XIV). He took over the government, but did not further Napoleon's ambitions against Britain and Russia. He became a truly national Swedish king. He made war on Denmark to secure Norway as recompense for the loss of Finland, and then later invaded Norway, whose union with Sweden was confirmed by the great powers in 1814.

In 1818 Charles XIII died and Bernadotte succeeded as Charles XIV, initiating the dynasty which still rules Sweden. His son Oscar I, who reigned from 1844 to 1859, introduced many democratic reforms. In the reign of Oscar II (1872–1907) Norway seceded from Sweden (1905), a peaceful settlement being made at Karlstad. Oscar II was succeeded by his son Gustavus V (1907–50), during whose reign democracy was further extended, social services introduced or expanded, and a universal franchise introduced. The acknowledgment of the growth of party politics dates from the dissolution of the union with Norway. Industrialisation had encouraged the growth of socialism, which, however, has always been of a very moderate nature in Sweden. During the First World War Sweden was neutral; it entered the League of Nations in 1920. In the 1920s party politics were irritated by the prohibition question, which completely split the Liberals and divided many of the left-wing sympathisers. There was a series of different governments. The problem of unemployment helped to increase the prestige of the Social Democrats. Total prohibition was rejected in 1922 and a liquor control system enforced which had some success in the rural districts, but was finally abolished in 1955.

Sweden was neutral during the Second World War, though when Russia invaded Finland Sweden showed its sympathy by opening its frontiers to Finnish refugees and enrolling volunteers. When the Germans made a demand for transit facilities for troops and supplies through Sweden in 1940 the Riksdag complied, but Sweden really had no choice in the matter. The Swedish prime minister, however, rejected Germany's invitation to Sweden to join its 'New Order'. Throughout 1943 Sweden continued to remain on friendly terms with all the belligerents, though public opinion had been largely pro-British, since the occupation of Norway and Denmark by Germany in 1940. In 1943 the government obtained Germany's consent to the cancellation of the transit agreement and transport of German material and military personnel through Sweden ceased. In September 1944 the Swedish government announced that all Swedish Baltic ports and waters would be closed to foreign shipping, owing to the new situation in the Baltic produced by the Russo-Finnish armistice of that year. This meant virtually the stoppage of Swedish-German trade for the duration of the war.

After the Second World War, Sweden took part in the relief work and reconstruction of the war-ravaged countries. It joined the United Nations in 1946 and has played an important part in the work of the organisation. Dag HAMMARSKJÖLD was secretary-general 1953–61, and Sweden has regularly contributed troops to UN peace-keeping forces—in the Middle East, the Congo, and Cyprus. Sweden promoted the UN conference on environmental protection in Stockholm, 1972. Sweden has maintained its neutrality, refusing to follow Norway and Denmark in joining the North Atlantic Treaty Organisation. It was a founder member of the NORDIC COUNCIL in 1952 and of the EUROPEAN FREE TRADE ASSOCIATION in 1959, but because of its neutrality has not sought membership of the European Economic Community. In home affairs, the Social Democrats remained in power after the war until 1976, under prime ministers Tage ERLANDER (1946–69) and Olof PALME (1969–76), but as a minority party for most of the post-war period, they were either in coalition with, or relied on, the support of other parties. A coalition of the Centre, Conservative, and Liberal parties, with Thorbjörn Fälldin as prime minister, took office in 1976, ending 44 years of Social Democratic rule. The government has operated a mixed economy in close co-operation with private industry, and central wage negotiations between employers and trade unions have produced almost unbroken industrial peace. The standard of living is probably the highest in Europe. A national health service was introduced in 1955 and a generous state pension scheme in 1959. An important constitutional reform was the replacement of the bicameral parliament by a one-chamber assembly in 1971. The rights of the king were also curtailed after the death of GUSTAVUS VI ADOLPHUS, who was king from 1950 to 1973; the present king, CHARLES XVI GUSTAVUS, has only a symbolic function.

Bibliography: I. Anderson, *A History of Sweden*, 1956; S. Oakley, *The Story of Sweden*, 1966; I. Scobbie, *Sweden*, 1972.

Architecture, see SCANDINAVIAN ARCHITECTURE.

Art. As with Norway and Denmark, the first outstanding Swedish artists appeared in the 18th century when, under the patronage of Gustavus III, national art and architecture as a whole flourished (see also SCANDINAVIAN ARCHITECTURE). The first Swedish painter to achieve European acclaim was the ex-patriot Michael Dahl (1659–1743) who had an enormous reputation in London as a portraitist, ranking with Kneller. Carl Gustav Pilo (1711–93) spent the years 1740–77 in Copenhagen where he became the leading artist of his kind: he painted somewhat austere portraits but his most outstanding work, though unfinished, is *The Coronation of Gustavus III*, 1782. Alexander Roslin (1718–93), who settled in Paris in 1757, was another portraitist who was specially famed for his rendering of draperies and costumes, while Carl Fredrik von Breda (1759–1818) was a pupil of Reynolds in England and is best known for his portrait of Gainsborough. Lafrensen (1737–1807), painter of *fêtes-galantes*, was also esteemed in Paris as was Peter Adolf Hall (1739–93), a miniaturist, who was elected to the Académie in 1769. The outstanding sculptor of the period was Johann Tobias Sergel (1740–1814), whose most important commission was a bronze statue of Gustavus III.

A further flowering of Swedish art occurred towards the end of the 19th century when the Konstnärsförbundet (Artists Association) had a strong influence. Its members were French-inspired and opposed to the academic tradition of art represented by the Stockholm Academy of Fine Arts. The most important painters of this generation included Ernst Josephson (1851–1906), a portraitist and painter of genre and realistic scenes who is particularly noted for his striking, intense use of colour; and Carl Fredrik Hill (1849–1911), a landscape-painter inspired particularly by Corot and the Barbizon school. Others included Karl Nordström (1855–1923), recognised as leader of the group; Anders Zorn (1860–1920), also a prominent etcher, who travelled widely, proving himself an exceptional water-colourist in England and devoting himself to oils about the time he went to Paris; he became successful as a portraitist, particularly in America. Carl Larsson (1853–1919) was also in Paris but returned to Sweden in 1889 to devote himself to a light decorative style, depicting his home and surrounding countryside and achieving continued popularity. Painters of the present century have again been influenced by France, and especially by Matisse, Cézanne and Gauguin. Karl Isakson (1878–1922), painter of still-lifes and landscapes, was influenced by Cubism, but was active mainly in Denmark. In sculpture, Carl Milles (1875–1955) gained a European reputation for his open-air fountains and monuments, ranging from the exuberant *Solglitter* to the more mystical *Orpheus Fountain*.

It is in the area of applied art that Sweden has achieved most international renown, especially for the very high standards of, for example, furniture and glass-making.

Bibliography: W. Nisser, *Michael Dahl and the contemporary Swedish school of painting in England*, 1927; J. Roosval, *Swedish Art*, 1940.

Art Museums. The National Museum in Stockholm began with the opening in 1794 of an art gallery in the royal palace in memory of Gustavus III, one of the earliest public art galleries in northern Europe. A large part of the present collections were amassed by Carl Gustav Tessin, Sweden's ambassador to France in the early 19th century. Besides French masters, Dutch and Flemish are also well represented, and the Museum also contains the country's largest collection of Swedish paintings.

The Modern Art Museum on Skeppsholmen Island, formerly part of Stockholm naval station, opened in 1954 and is widely representative of international modern art.

Language. Swedish is an important member of the group of SCANDINAVIAN LANGUAGES, which up until the medieval period could be described as NORSE LANGUAGES. With the exception of about 200,000 Finns, about 5000 Lapps (inhabiting the extreme north of the country), and some thousand speakers of other languages, the population of Sweden, numbering over 8,000,000, speaks Swedish. Moreover, this language is also spoken in western and southern Finland and the Åland islands (by about 375,000 people), by Swedish immigrants in Norway, Denmark, and other European countries, in the United States, in Canada, and in some other countries. It was formerly spoken in various Baltic provinces (Estonia, Livonia, Courland, etc.), and in parts of Russia. See also DENMARK, *Language*; ICELAND, *Language*; NORWAY, *Language*.

Sweden. The poet Carl Michael Bellman. *(Popperfoto)*

Sweden

Literature. There are four periods in the history of Swedish language and literature: archaic or common Scandinavian, 800–1225 (before Swedish emerged as a separate language), including mainly oral literature; classic, 1225–1375, which includes the earliest surviving document, a fragment of *Västgötalag*, a legal document, about 1250; middle Swedish, 1375–1525, producing mainly religious literature; and modern Swedish, which begins with the Lutheran translation of the New Testament in 1526, and other writings of Olaus PETRI. The most important early work written in modern Swedish is the Bible of Gustavus I, 1541.

Swedish literature was comparatively late in developing. The RUNES preserved on many stone monuments dating from the early Middle Ages have great historic and archaeological interest, but cannot be regarded as literature. The greatest medieval figure of Swedish religious and literary history is St Birgitta or BRIDGET, whose 14th-century mystical visions, *Revelationes*, were written in Latin. However, the virtual beginnings of its literature can be traced to the period when Sweden began to take active part in the politics of Europe. During the Reformation, the translation of the Bible into the vernacular by, among others, Olaus Petri, one of the masters of the Swedish language and author of religious works, dramas, and the first critical historical writings, and his brother Laurentius Petri (1499–1573), the first Lutheran bishop, fixed the Swedish language for centuries.

In the 17th century, Georg STIERNHIELM, the most important writer of the time and a versatile, learned man, was the first Swedish author to use classical verse metres. During the first half of the 18th century the influence of English authors such as STEELE, ADDISON, DEFOE, SWIFT, and POPE, was very strong, as was Addison's *Spectator* which was imitated, notably by Olof von DALIN in his *Den Svenska Argus*. A unique place in 18th-century literature is held by the great mystic Emanuel SWEDENBORG. About the mid-18th century a group of poets was active, among them Hedwig Charlotta Nordenflycht (1718–63), Gustaf Philip Creutz (1731–85), Gustaf Fredrik Gyllenborg (1731–1808), and, a little later, John Gabriel Oxenstierna (1750–1818). At the end of the century, French influence increased in Sweden, as in the rest of Europe, and is shown in the works of poets such as Johan Henrik KELLGREN, editor of the widely read *Stockholms posten* and the most influential literary figure of the time, Carl Gustaf af Leopold (1756–1829), and many others. The period has been seen as the Golden Age of Swedish literature, largely because of the patronage of King Gustav III. A special position is held by the poet Carl Michael BELLMAN, whose songs with Stockholm motifs are characterised by an incomparable vividness and directness, and are still popular. Thomas Thorild (1759–1808) was an interesting personality who projected some original philosophical concepts, and was opposed to the influence of French classicism.

About the beginning of the 19th century the ROMANTIC MOVEMENT was very strong as a result of influence both from England and Germany and prominent among the Romantics was Per Daniel Amadeus ATTERBOM, with his long verse dramas. The foremost poet of the period was the mystic Erik Johan Stagnelius (1793–1823), one of the greatest masters of the Swedish language. A reaction against the more metaphysical trends of the Romantic movement came from authors belonging to the so-called Gothic Union (Götiska Förbundet), whose purpose was the revival of historical traditions and national spirit after the loss of Finland to Russia. Members of this union were Esaias TEGNÉR, one of the greatest personalities in Swedish cultural history; and Erik Gustaf GEIJER, poet, thinker, and historian, an intellectual leader of his time. Swedish literature in Finland in the middle of the 19th century had a great poet, Johan Ludvig RUNEBERG, whose influence was considerable, and whose epic works, such as *Fänrik Ståls Sägner* (1848, 1860), about the Swedish-Russian war, 1808–09, became a national treasure in Finland.

The novel developed towards the middle of the 19th century in all its aspects, historical, social, and romantic, owing a great deal to the English influence of SCOTT and DICKENS. Carl Jonas Love ALMQVIST was an early master of the novel. Another well-known novelist, remembered also as the pioneer of the Swedish feminist movement, was Fredrika BREMER. A certain neo-Romanticism in poetry appeared in the 1860s, exemplified by Carl Snoilsky (1841–1903), with his *Svenska Bilder*, 1886, a collection of historical poems, and his songs from Italy. A central position in the cultural life of the time was held by Abraham Viktor RYDBERG, novelist, poet, and an advocate of liberal idealism and modern Bible criticism. Naturalism was less pronounced in Sweden than in France, the most outstanding representative of the movement being August STRINDBERG, the greatest genius of Swedish literature, and one of the creators of the modern theatre. A reaction against naturalism occurred about 1890 with a group of authors ('the nineties'), among them Verner von HEIDENSTAM, poet and author of historical and romantic novels; and Oscar LEVERTIN, who had great influence as a critic. To the group belonged two of Sweden's finest poets, Gustav FRÖDING and Erik Axel KARLFELDT. Also contemporary was Selma LAGERLÖF, with romantic novels, children's stories and tales, such as *Gösta Berlings Saga*, 1891.

During the first decade of the 20th century appeared many writers of the modern realistic novel. The foremost is Hjalmar SÖDERBERG, ironical sceptic and a fine stylist. Others include Sigfrid Siwertz (1882–1970), also active as a dramatist; Gustaf Hellström (1882–1953), journalist

Sweden. Erik Axel Karlfeldt, Swedish writer and the first to be awarded the Nobel Prize posthumously. *(Popperfoto)*

and author of partially autobiographical novels; and Elin Wägner (1882–1949), the leading woman author. Typically Swedish was the humorist Albert Engström (1869–1940), important both as author and artist. Another prominent figure is Hjalmar BERGMAN, whose novels are characterised by a bizarre fantasy and profound psychology. Of the succeeding generation, Pär LAGER-KVIST was a novelist, poet, and dramatist of great significance. Among 20th-century poets are Bo Bergman (1869–1967), Vilhelm Ekelund (1880–1949), Anders Österling (1884–), Birger Sjöberg (1885–1929), Hjalmar Gullberg (1898–1961), Karin Boye (1900–41), Gunnar EKELÖF (1907–68), Artur Lundkvist (1906–), and Harry MARTINSON (1904–78).

Martinson, also important as a prose writer, belongs to the large group of modern Swedish writers who come from the working class and are self-taught. Other leading representatives of this group are Eyvind JOHNSON, Jan Fridegård (1897–1968), Ivar Lo-Johansson (1901–), and Vilhelm MOBERG. In contrast, Agnes von Krusenstjerna (1894–1940) deals in her great novel series *Tony*, 1922–26, *Von Pahlen*, 1930–35, *Fattigadel*, 1935–38, with higher circles of society. Special positions in pre-war literature are held by Frans G. Bengtsson (1894–1955), author of humorous novels and a biography of Charles XII, and a master of the essay in its classic English form, and also by Tage Aurell (1895–), who is important for his stylistically impressive short novels.

Swedish literature of the 1940s is preoccupied, in the aftermath of war, with horror at man's situation, both in historical terms and in a metaphysical, Existentialist (see EXISTENTIALISM) sense. Apart from the poets Karl Vennberg (1910–) and Erik Lindegren (1910–68), the most important figure of the 1940s is Stig Dagerman (1923–54), whose works are permeated by anguish and guilt: for example, the short stories of *Nattens lekar*, 1947 (*The Games of Night*, 1959). Lars Gyllensten (1922–), a thoroughly intellectual writer, attempted to salvage something from an ideologically bankrupt world in *Moderna myter*, 1949, by preaching the value of scepticism, and continued this in *Kains memoarer*, 1963 (*The Testament of Cain*, 1967). Sara Lidman (1923–) and Per Olof Sundman (1922–) began their literary careers with studies of people in the rural north of Sweden, the former with great poetic intensity in *Regnspiran*, 1958 (*The Rain Bird*, 1963), the latter with a reporter's objectivity in *Undersökningen*, 1958. Sundman is one of several modern authors who have written documentary novels (a form intermediate between history and fiction), most successfully in *Ingenjör Andrées luftfärd*, 1967 (*The Flight of the Eagle*, 1970). Another is Per-Olov Enquist (1934–), with his novel about Baltic refugees, *Legionärerna*, 1968 (*The Legionnaires*, 1974). A writer who preferred to reflect society in highly imaginative ALLEGORY and satire is Per Christian Jersild (1935–); the equally impressive imagination of Sven Delblanc (1931–) is more burlesque, for example in *Homunculus*, 1965 (translated into English, 1969).

Among contemporary Swedish poets the best known are the boisterous Lars Forssell (1928–) and the restrained Tomas Tranströmer (1931–). Maj Sjöwall (1935–) and Per Wahlöö (1926–75) had great international success with their series of detective novels, realistic descriptions of police-work, beginning with

Roseanna, 1965. Another genre in which Swedish authors have won an international reputation is children's literature. Most famous are Astrid Lindgren (1907–), creator of Pippi Longstocking, and the Swedish-speaking Finn, Tove Jansson (1914–), with her Moomintroll books.
See also FINLAND, *Literature*.
Bibliography: A. Gustafson, *A History of Swedish Literature*, 1961.

Swedenborg, Emanuel (1688–1772), Swedish scientist, philosopher, and theologian, born at Stockholm, eldest son of Jesper Swedberg, Lutheran bishop of Skara. The family was ennobled in 1719 and assumed the name Swedenborg in accordance with custom. Swedenborg is so generally known as a theologian of heterodox views which have found acceptance by the New Church, sometimes called 'Swedenborgian', that it is seldom appreciated that he was one of the foremost scientific minds of his day and had gained a European reputation for science and philosophy before he ever turned to theology. Some of his conclusions have a surprisingly modern sound, and the wide range of his mind over all the known branches of science is comparable only with that of Leonardo da Vinci.

As a young man he was employed by Charles XII in civil and military engineering works, and was appointed assessor of the Royal College of Mines, in which office he gave valuable service to the metal industries of Sweden for 30 years. He declined a professorship of mathematics on the ground that his interests were in the practical applications of science. With the publication in 1734 of his *Opera philosophica et mineralia*, and in the same year of a smaller work on *The Infinite, and the Final Cause of Creation*, his reputation as a philosopher of the first rank was established throughout Europe. At about this time he began his researches into the nature of the soul, and

Emanuel Swedenborg. (*Mansell Collection*)

applied himself to anatomy and physiology, in which field he is considered the first to point out that the motion of the brain synchronises with that of the lungs rather than that of the heart. His chief publications in this period were *Oeconomia regni animalis*, 1740–41, and *Regnum animale*, 1744–45. About this time, however, Swedenborg turned away from the active pursuit of scientific interests and began to write in what was, for him, the new field of theology, believing himself to have received a direct revelation. In 1749 he published the first volume of *Arcana Caelestia*, and from then until 1771, when the *True Christian Religion*, a volume of systematised theology, was published, his pen was busy with divine themes.

His system of theology presents Christ not as the second person of the Trinity, but as the one God, the whole Trinity being in Him as soul, embodiment, and operation. Redemption consisted in the conquest, in the human, of temptations from all the hells and the subsequent control of the hells by the divine human. Swedenborg asserts that the word of God has an internal or spiritual meaning throughout, and the *Arcana Caelestia* consists of a detailed exposition of the 'spiritual sense' of Genesis and Exodus, and incidentally of many other parts of Scripture. The *Apocalypse Revealed*, 1766, and the posthumously published *Apocalypse Explained* deal similarly with the Book of Revelation. In the former work he declares that the Holy City, New Jerusalem, signifies a new 'Church' or dispensation of truth then being effected through these revelations. One of his first critics was KANT who directed *Träume eines Geistersehers*, 1766, against him.

Bibliography: R. L. Tafel (Ed. and Trans.), *Documents Concerning the Life and Character of Emanuel Swedenborg*, 1875–77; G. Trobridge, *A Life of Emanuel Swedenborg*, 1912; E. A. Sutton, *The Happy Isles*, 1938; S. Toskvig, *Emanuel Swedenborg: Scientist and Mystic*, 1949; C. O. Sigtedt, *The Swedenborg Epic*, 1952.

Swedenborg Society, in London, has as its main objects to print, publish, sell, and distribute the theological works of Emanuel SWEDENBORG in the original Latin and translated into English and other languages. The society maintains reference and lending libraries where all the principal works are available; the reference library also contains photo-reproductions of all the Swedenborg manuscripts extant, and the archives are a valuable collection of some 1600 items.

Swedenborgians, term sometimes, but inaccurately, applied to the members of the organisation known as the New Jerusalem Church, or New Church, who believe that the theological works of Emanuel SWEDENBORG are a divine revelation containing the doctrines of the New Church signified by the New Jerusalem in the Apocalypse. There are two branches of the New Church in Great Britain, the General Conference of the New Church and the General Church of the New Jerusalem. The first public association of New Church people took place in 1788 in Great Eastcheap, London. At the present time there are about 3500 New Church people in Great Britain and 50 places of worship.

Swedish Architecture, see SCANDINAVIAN ARCHITECTURE.

Sweelinck, Jan Pieterszoon (1562–1621), Dutch organist, harpsichordist and composer; studied under his father, Pieter, who became organist at the Old Church, Amsterdam, in 1566, and others. Jan succeeded to his father's post between 1577 and 1580 (the latter died in 1573), and held it until his death. Some of his famous pupils came from foreign countries. His works include four books of psalms for four to eight voices, *Cantiones Sacrae* for several voices; organ fantasias, toccatas and chorale variations; harpsichord pieces, etc.

Sweepstake, gaming transaction, in which one person wins (sweeps) the stakes of himself and others; or a prize in a horse race made out of any number of stakes. Sweepstakes as prizes in horse races are legal; they are illegal only when they are definitely lotteries.

Seè also BETTING AND BOOKMAKING; GAMBLING; HORSE RACING; LOTTERIES.

Sweet, Henry (1845–1912), British phonetician and philologist, born in London. Bernard Shaw partly based his character of Professor Higgins (*Pygmalion*) on Sweet. He became reader in phonetics at the University of Oxford (he declined the offers of chairs in the United States, Germany, and Scandinavia, being somewhat hostile to the German-dominated emphasis on studies abroad, where, however, he was better appreciated). Among his many publications are *A History of English Sounds*, 1874, *An Anglo-Saxon Reader*, 1876, 13th edition, revised by C. T. ONIONS, 1954, *An Anglo-Saxon Primer*, 1882, 9th edition, revised by N. Davis, 1953, *An Icelandic Primer*, 1886, *A Primer of Phonetics*, 1892, *A New English Grammar*, 1892–98, *The History of Language*, 1900, *The Sounds of English*, 1908, *The Students' Dictionary of Anglo-Saxon*, 1911, and *The Collected Papers of Henry Sweet*, 1913 (arranged by H. C. WYLD).

Sweet devised two types of phonetic alphabet: an 'organic notation', a revised version of A. M. Bell's 'Visible Speech', which used completely new characters; and a 'Romic notation', using the Latin alphabet augmented by additional characters, which was based on A. J. Ellis and Isaac PITMAN's 'Phonotypes' and which itself became the basis of the International Phonetic Alphabet (1888, with later revisions). Sweet must also be credited with awareness of the notion of the 'phoneme' (the term being introduced independently by B. de Courtenay). He also produced, at the request of the (London) Philological Society, a scheme for a limited reform of English orthography (see SIMPLIFIED SPELLING), and, like PASSY, was interested in the teaching applications of PHONETICS (*The Practical Study of Languages*, 1899).

Bibliography: T. A. Sebeok, *Portraits of Linguists* (vol. 1), 1966.

Sweet Bay, see BAY; LAUREL.

Sweet Brier, see ROSE.

Sweet Cicely, see MYRRHIS.

Sweet Corn, see MAIZE.

Sweet Fern, see COMPTONIA ASPLENIFOLIA.

Sweet Gale, see BOG MYRTLE.

Sweet Marjoram, see ORIGANUM.

Sweet Pea, *Lathyrus odoratus*, a popular annual garden plant. It is a typical member of the subfamily Papilionoideae of family Leguminosae. The large petal at the back is the standard, the two wings are lateral, and in front is the keel, formed from two petals which adhere along their lower edges. There are ten stamens, nine fused and one separate. The carpel is single, with a row of ovules. The species lends itself exceptionally to hybridisation, and indeed it and the edible pea were the subject of Mendel's invaluable experiments (see MENDELISM; GENETICS). Its original habitat was Sicily. Its numerous varieties cover a very extensive range of colour, though deep blue and most shades of yellow were unknown before 1913. The ground should be well prepared for plants by deep digging, and the seed can be either sown where the plants are to bloom or preferably under glass early in the year, the seedlings being planted out with a good ball of soil and roots about mid-April. Support by means of tall sticks or strings should be given early, and, when flowering starts, liberal supplies of water and liquid manure or other quick-acting fertiliser, and regular picking of the flowers, will prolong the blooming period and increase the beauty of the blooms.

Sweet Potato, *Ipomoea batatas*, a species of the family Convolvulaceae, allied to the morning glory, that has tuberous, edible roots. It is grown in tropical and subtropical regions as it needs four to five months of warm weather to mature. It has heart-shaped leaves on climbing stems and mauve-pink flowers. The sweet potato is eaten cooked in similar ways to the potato and yam, which are unrelated plants. The potato belongs to the genus *Solanum* in family Solanaceae, and the yam to genus *Dioscorea* in family Dioscoreaceae.

Sweet William, *Dianthus barbatus*, a perennial herb of the Caryophyllaceae (campion family). It is a native of eastern and southern Europe, often grown in British gardens as a biennial on account of its bright flowers and scent. See CATCHFLY.

Sweetbread, name given to certain glands of animals used as food. The pancreas of the ox or calf is most generally used, as it is palatable and digestible, when gently cooked, with seasoning to enhance the subtle flavour. It is particularly nutritious, as the flesh is mainly protein and is a store of iron and vitamins A and D. See also MEAT.

Swellendam, town in Cape Province, South Africa, near the Breede River, 48 km west of Heidelberg. The first South African republic was established here in 1795. Cereals, oranges, and wool are produced in the district. Population (1970) 7820, of which 2498 are whites.

Sweyn I (d. 1014), surnamed Forkbeard, King of Denmark, the son of HAROLD BLUETOOTH and the father of CANUTE THE GREAT, King of England. Sweyn himself led numerous invasions against England, but his wars were carried on more with a view to extort money from the English than with the idea of attempting any colonisation. Sweyn ruled at a juncture in the history of Denmark when the old Northern paganism was softening under the influence of Christianity, but he himself remained aggressively pagan.

Swidden Agriculture, also called 'slash-and-burn' agriculture, is a method of land-use in which a portion of forest is cut down and burnt for growing crops (swiddens) fertilised by the wood ash. Dry rice, millet, taro, yams, and maize are frequently grown in this way in the tropics and sub-tropics. The only basic implements necessary are the axe or adze, and the hoe or digging stick. Generally, yields decline after the second or third year, and the clearing is abandoned to allow the forest to reconstitute itself, for some ten or twenty years, depending on the soil type, forest type, and other ecological factors. The cultivators meanwhile move to a new area, repeating the process.

Swiddening is usually found in societies whose structures differ markedly from those with a PLOUGH AGRICULTURE, which are generally sedentary. Since the colonial and post-colonial periods, central governments in countries where swiddening is practised have often discouraged or forbidden its continued use. The basic problem for swidden agriculturalists occurs when the population density increases and the fallow period has to be cut. The primary forest is no longer able to reconstitute itself, different types of flora begin to dominate, and the ecology is irrevocably altered, with severe consequences for crop yields. Water drainage is particularly affected by excessive burning of the forest: the cleared soil lacks the intricate number of roots which retain soil; on mountain slopes rain runs off in a shorter time, carrying with it larger portions of the topsoil, which in turn affects the floral regrowth (see SOIL EROSION AND CONSERVATION). New techniques and strategies have to be found to deal with the situation, such as the use of animal dung as fertiliser (this requires that a herd be kept, and that grazing areas be allotted, with further effects on the ecology); or terracing and irrigation (both of which require a degree of sedentarisation, and alterations in the forms of land-ownership and co-operative labour). In some areas the most labour-consuming task is fence-building to keep out wild and domestic animals. The new techniques ultimately affect the whole social structure, bringing about extensive social changes. It is believed that it is in this manner that the early 'Asiatic' states of India, China, and South-east Asia developed. It is also thought that the savannah areas of Africa, both above and below the equator, are primarily due to swiddening.

See also LAND-TENURE IN NON-WESTERN SOCIETIES.

Bibliography: F. J. Ormeling, *The Timor Problem*, 1956; J. E. Spencer, *Shifting Cultivation in South East Asia*, 1966; C. Geertz, *Agricultural Involution: Process of Ecological Change in Indonesia*, 1969; D. B. Grigg, *Agricultural Systems of the World*, 1974; J. Friedman, *Tribes, States and Transformations* in R. Firth (Ed.), *Marxist Anthropology*, 1975.

Swidnica (German *Schweidnitz*), town of Poland, in Wrocław province, on the Bystrzyca River, 48 km south-west of Wrocław. It stands at the north-east edge of the SUDETEN MOUNTAINS, and was in Lower Silesia until 1945. The capital of a principality 1278–1386, it came under the Hapsburgs in 1526. In 1642 it was taken by Sweden. It was several times under siege in the Seven Years' War. There are textile, chemical, foodstuff, and engineering industries. Population 48,000.

Swietenia mahagoni, see MAHOGANY.

Swift, Jonathan (1667–1745), the greatest English satirist, born in Dublin, Ireland, of English parents. Born after his father's death into a poor family, he was sent to school at Kilkenny, where William CONGREVE was a fellow pupil, and afterwards went to Trinity College, Dublin, where he obtained a degree only by 'special grace'.

Swift, Jonathan

After James II's abdication and the disturbances after the Revolution of 1688, he left Ireland to join his mother, then at Leicester. He was admitted to the household of Sir William TEMPLE at Moor Park. Here he acted as secretary, had access to a well-stocked library, and wrote pindaric odes, one of which is said to have provoked DRYDEN to remark, 'Cousin Swift, you will never be a poet'. At Moor Park also he met Esther Johnson (Stella) who was afterwards to enter so largely into his life and whose precise relationship with Swift is still far from clear. Apparently dissatisfied that Temple did not do more for him, Swift left his service in 1694 and returned to Ireland where he took holy orders, and obtained the small living of Kilroot, near Belfast. In 1698 he threw up his living at Temple's request and returned to Moor Park. During this time he wrote *A Tale of a Tub*, one of his best works, a satire on 'corruptions in religion and learning', and *The Battle of the Books*, describing in mock-heroic style a contest between ANCIENTS AND MODERNS, in which Swift defended Temple's views, and *A Discourse Concerning the Mechanical Operation of the Spirit*. All three pieces were published in a single volume in 1704.

After Temple's death in 1699, Swift published, by request, his works and then returned to Ireland as chaplain to the Lord Deputy, the Earl of Berkeley, from whom he obtained some small preferments, including the vicarage of Laracor and a prebend of St Patrick's Cathedral. About this time he made frequent visits to London, and made friends with ADDISON, STEELE, Congreve, and other Whig writers. He also wrote various pamphlets, chiefly on ecclesiastical subjects. In 1708, under the pseudonym Isaac Bickerstaff, he parodied the almanac-maker John Partridge. Disgusted with the Whigs' neglect both of himself and of the claims of his Church, he abandoned them in 1710 and attached himself to the

Jonathan Swift.

Tories Robert HARLEY and Viscount Bolingbroke. The next few years were filled with political controversy. He attacked the Whigs in papers in the *Examiner* in 1710, and in his celebrated pamphlets, *The Conduct of the Allies*, 1712, *The Barrier Treaty*, 1713, and *The Public Spirit of the Whigs*, 1714. In 1713 he was made Dean of St Patrick's; it was the last patronage he received. The hostility of Queen Anne, partly provoked by *A Tale of a Tub*, proved an insurmountable obstacle to his further advancement. On the destruction of his hopes Swift returned to Ireland, where he spent the rest of his life. The series of letters which form the *Journal to Stella* sheds much light on Swift's character and on the political and social context of his life at this time. It was now also that the final rupture with Esther Vanhomrigh (Vanessa), who had been in love with him, took place. Swift had maintained a lengthy correspondence with her and addressed to her his poem *Cadenus and Vanessa*, 1726.

Though Swift disliked the Irish and considered residence in Ireland as banishment, he interested himself in Irish affairs, and gained extraordinary popularity there with his *Drapier's Letters*, 1724, directed against English policy in Ireland. In 1726 he visited England, arranged for the publication of *Gulliver's Travels* through intermediaries, and joined with POPE and ARBUTHNOT in publishing *Miscellanies*, 1727.

Gulliver's Travels is Swift's most widely and permanently popular work; a bitter satire, it has by a curious irony become, in expurgated form, a favourite children's book. In common with his other works it reveals Swift's anger that men's actions should fall so far below those of which they are capable as creatures of reason. Swift's last visit to England took place in 1727, and in the following year his beloved 'Stella' died. Though he had a circle of friends in Dublin and was, owing to his championing of the people against their grievances, a popular idol, age, sickness, and the fear of insanity pressed more and more upon him. He became increasingly morose, a direct result of the debilitating effects of MÉNIÈRE'S DISEASE (labyrinthine vertigo), and though there was a period of recovery during which he produced some of his most brilliant work—the *Rhapsody on Poetry*, *Verses on the Death of Dr Swift*, and *A Modest Proposal* (a horrible but masterly piece of irony)—he gradually sank into almost total loss of his faculties. He was buried beside 'Stella' in St Patrick's Cathedral.

The Prose Works of Jonathan Swift were edited by H. Davis (14 volumes), 1939–68; *The Poems of Jonathan Swift* (second edition) by H. Williams, 1958; and *The Correspondence of Jonathan Swift* (five volumes) by H. Williams, 1963–65.

See also SATIRE.

Bibliography: J. M. Bullitt, *Jonathan Swift and the Anatomy of Satire*, 1953; W. B. Ewald, *The Masks of Jonathan Swift*, 1954; I. Ehrenpreis, *The Personality of Jonathan Swift*, 1958, and *Swift: The Man, his Works and the Age*, 1962; P. Harth, *Swift and Anglican Rationalism*, 1961; E. J. Rosenheim, *Swift and the Satirist's Art*, 1963; M. Voigt, *Swift and the Twentieth Century*, 1964; J. J. Stathis, *A Bibliography of Swift Studies, 1945–1965*, 1967; C. Rawson, *Gulliver and the Gentle Reader*, 1973.

Swift, members of the family Micropodidae in order Apodiformes, closely related to the humming-birds, but not to the swallow, which they resemble superficially. The only British species, *Apus apus*, arrives in Britain in May, leaving in August for its winter quarters in Africa. It feeds entirely on small winged insects and in its search for them exhibits remarkable powers of flight. It nests in holes in tall buildings, laying two or three large white eggs. The adult bird is about 18 cm long. The plumage is blackish brown, except for a small greyish white patch under the chin. The tail is long and forked. An occasional visitor to Britain is the white-bellied or Alpine swift, *A. melba*. Close relatives of these two species are the edible-nest swiftlet, *Callocalia* species, the nests of which are used to make soup in China and other far-eastern countries. See NESTS, EDIBLE.

Swilly, Lough, inlet of County DONEGAL, Republic of Ireland, entering from the Atlantic between Fanad Point and Dunaff Head (6 km in width) and extending inland for 40 km.

Swimbladder, or airbladder, a structure found in some fishes which is filled with gas and serves as an organ of flotation. It occurs in the position occupied in air-breathers by the lungs, and is now believed to have derived from primitive lungs during the course of evolution. It may be connected to the gut by an open tube, the physostomatous condition, or completely cut off, the physoclystous. In either case its function is hydrostatic, being of negligible respiratory value. It acts to keep the density of the fish the same as that of the water at the level where the fish wishes to swim. Thus if a fish wishes to remain at the bottom of a deep pool, having previously been at the surface, it must increase its density, or it will tend to float back up to the surface again. To do this a physostomatous fish will expel a bubble of air from the swimbladder into the gut and out of the mouth. A physoclystous fish must reabsorb some gas into the blood, and lose it across the gills into the water in solution. To reverse the operation, the physostome will come to the surface and swallow air, the physoclyst will secrete it from the blood into the bladder by means of a gas gland.

The swimbladder is absent in all elasmobranchs, such as sharks; they left the rivers to become sea dwellers before the first lungs had been evolved in fish. They must keep swimming to maintain their level. The bladder is also missing from some permanently bottom-living forms, and also some deep-sea fish.

In some cases the bladder has become modified for other purposes, such as sound production (e.g. catfish) or hearing (e.g. some herrings and catfish).

Swimming, the art of propulsion in water without artificial assistance. Although the human body is slightly less dense than water, the margin is so small that the techniques of swimming have to be learned and involve some muscular effort. As an exercise it has considerable recreational qualities, and the virtues of swimming as a therapeutic exercise in cases of severe disablement (paralysis, amputation, spasticity, etc.) have been widely recognised. The utility of swimming techniques in life saving and in personal survival is of enormous importance, and the Royal Life Saving Society and the various national swimming associations actively promote these aspects of swimming as well as competitions.

Men have doubtless always been able to swim, for pleasure or out of necessity. Competitive swimming (for speed) was organised in 36 BC in Japan, and it is recorded that swimming became compulsory in schools there in 1603. In Europe fears of infection caused a decline in the practice during the Middle Ages, and it was not until the late 19th century that bathing again became sufficiently widespread for competitive swimming to become organised as we know it today.

The first 'modern' competitive races were held in Australia in the 1840s, and the idea of racing for speed rather than bathing for pleasure soon spread to Europe. The world's oldest swimming organisation, the direct ancestor of the present English Amateur Swimming Association (ASA), was formed as a result of this enthusiasm in 1869. England soon became the world's swimming centre, and in the absence of international competitions the ASA's championships were virtually world championships until the outbreak of the First World War. As the sport became organised it also became confined to amateurs, and professional performers have never been significant in the subsequent history of speed swimming.

In the early days the first widespread technique was the *breaststroke*, in which the body and limbs remain submerged in a prone position, propulsion being obtained by simultaneous and virtually symmetrical movements of the limbs. From the breaststroke developed the *sidestroke*, the *overarm sidestroke* (in which one arm recovered—i.e. came forward to start its propulsive pull—above the water), and the *trudgen* (so called after its first exponent, John Trudgen), in which the arms recovered above the water alternately, while the legs performed a breaststroke kick. It was only a short step from such leg-dominated strokes to the *crawl* in which the arms recover alternately above the water and also pull backwards alternately, while the legs make a balancing flutter kick (usually six, but often two and sometimes four kicks to each arm cycle). The crawl (and its variations) has been the world's fastest stroke for over 70 years.

It should not be assumed that swimming techniques developed only in Europe or Australia. Some improvements, notably the development of the crawl from the trudgen, were the result of observations made of the swimming habits of natives in Colombo.

Swimming on the back was at first a trick, and the first *backstroke* races were swum using a sort of inverted breaststroke. But the alternating back crawl stroke soon proved faster and the 'Old English backstroke', with its breaststroke movements, has been, since the 1920s, almost totally confined to life-saving. Both backstroke and breaststroke had their débuts as separate ASA championships in 1903.

The *butterfly* developed from the breaststroke in the 1930s when ambitious breaststrokers exploited a loophole in the rules and began to recover their arms over the water. So in 1952 the butterfly was recognised as a distinct stroke and, at the same time, the traditional breaststroke was rehabilitated. Butterfly swimmers soon abandoned the breaststroke kick and adopted a vertical 'dolphin' kick to such good effect that butterfly is, after the crawl, the second fastest stroke.

Freestyle swimming has never been defined: it has always been simply the fastest stroke, and for many years this has been the front crawl. Of the crawl's many antecedents in freestyle events, only the breaststroke is preserved in competition.

Swimming

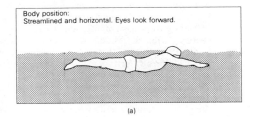

Body position:
Streamlined and horizontal. Eyes look forward.

(a)

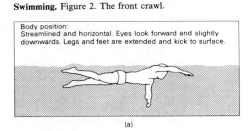

From an extended position arms pull sideways, backwards and downwards. Hands remain in front of shoulders. Breathe in.

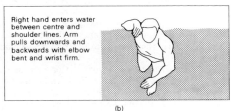

Movements of arms, and legs, must be simultaneous throughout stroke.

(b)

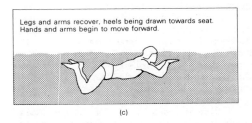

Legs and arms recover, heels being drawn towards seat. Hands and arms begin to move forward.

(c)

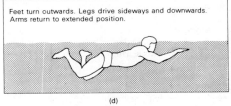

Feet turn outwards. Legs drive sideways and downwards. Arms return to extended position.

(d)

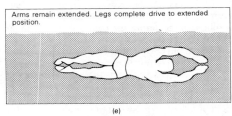

Arms remain extended. Legs complete drive to extended position.

(e)

Swimming. Figure 1. The breaststroke.

Swimming. Figure 2. The front crawl.

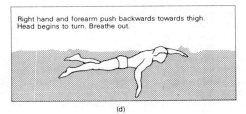

Body position:
Streamlined and horizontal. Eyes look forward and slightly downwards. Legs and feet are extended and kick to surface.

(a)

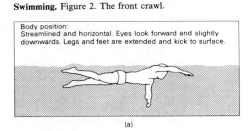

Right hand enters water between centre and shoulder lines. Arm pulls downwards and backwards with elbow bent and wrist firm.

(b)

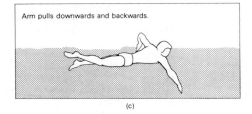

Arm pulls downwards and backwards.

(c)

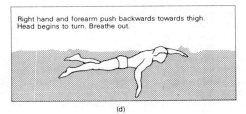

Right hand and forearm push backwards towards thigh. Head begins to turn. Breathe out.

(d)

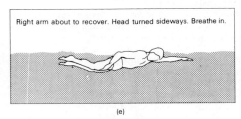

Right arm about to recover. Head turned sideways. Breathe in.

(e)

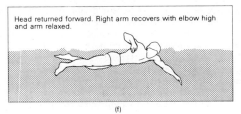

Head returned forward. Right arm recovers with elbow high and arm relaxed.

(f)

Body position:
Streamlined and horizontal. Eyes look upwards.
Legs and feet extended, kick to surface.

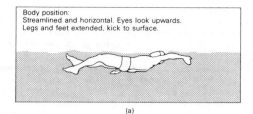

(a)

Left hand enters water above head, little finger leads, arm
straight. Right arm starts to recover.

(b)

Left arm pulls sideways and backwards. Depth of pull about,
12 inches. Right arm recovers.

(c)

The stroke is continuous and rhythmic. There are six leg kicks
to the cycle. Breathe in as one arm recovers. Breathe out as

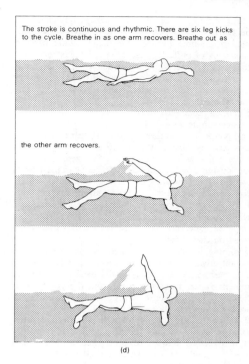

the other arm recovers.

(d)

Swimming. Figure 3. The backstroke.

Swimming. Figure 4. The butterfly.

Body position:
Streamlined and horizontal. Eyes look downwards. Legs and
feet extended and remain together throughout.

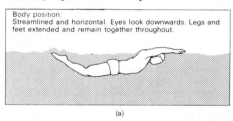

(a)

Arms begin pull. Head kept low. First down beat of leg kick
complete.

(b)

Arms pull to shoulders. Legs begin next downbeat. Head
begins to lift. Breathe out.

(c)

Arms bent under
shoulders, elbows high.

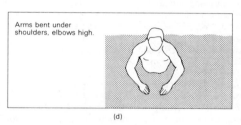

(d)

Arms push through to thighs. Head raised. Breathe in.
Second downbeat of leg kick complete.

(e)

Arms swing sideways and forwards above surface towards
entry position. Movements of arms, and legs, must be
simultaneous throughout stroke.

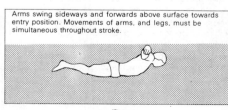

(f)

Swimming

A fifth 'style' of swimming, the *medley*, was pioneered in the USA in the 1930s and is now part of the international programme. Individual medley races are made up of equal legs of butterfly, backstroke, breaststroke, and another stroke (freestyle). The order for team events is backstroke, breaststroke, butterfly, and freestyle. Medley team events were first included in the 1960 Olympics, and individual medleys in 1964.

Swimming competitions can take two basic forms. There are simple head-to-head contests between teams scoring points in a number of events. Internationally the highest manifestation of this is the Europa Cup contest held biennially between teams from European countries. Championship events, ranging from the Olympic Games and world championships down to local events, usually involve eliminating heats. The fastest swimmers on a time basis go through to a final, though in some instances, especially at low levels of competition or where there is a shortage of time, no finals are held and winners are declared on their heat time.

Swimming in the 1970s ranked as the second most important Olympic sport and gained its popularity by its relative cheapness, the absence of a need for expensive equipment (apart from the pool), and the youth of its participants. The international programme centres on the Olympic Games and the world championships (first held 1973 and biennially thereafter). Other important international occasions include the European championships (first held 1926), the British Commonwealth Games (first held 1930), and the Pan-American Games (first held 1951). These are held at the height of the summer season, but less important competitions take place all through the year. Each country has its own national championships run along similar lines, and the basic international list of events recognised for world records is as follows:
freestyle: 100, 200, 400, 800, 1500 metres; 4 × 100, 4 × 200 m relay;
breaststroke, butterfly and *backstroke:* 100 and 200 m;
medley: 200 and 400 m; 4 × 100 m relay.

In the Olympic Games the following races are omitted: 800 m and 4 × 100 m freestyle for men; 1500 m and 4 × 200 m freestyle for women; 200 m medley for both.

The world governing body for swimming (and diving, water polo and synchronised swimming) is the Fédération Internationale de Natation Amateur (FINA), founded in 1908. This body regulates swimming throughout the world, and over a hundred countries are affiliated to it. The Olympic swimming events, world championships and world records list are all organised by FINA. Swimming in the British Isles is administered by the English, Scottish, and Welsh ASAs, with an Irish ASA taking in the whole of Ireland. The basic unit of organisation is the club, which exists in most areas.

The swimming season in most countries is customarily divided into two. A spring season of competition lasts from March to May in England, and the summer season— after a break for school and university examinations— from July to September. In England the foci of these periods are the national short course championships (pools less than 50 m long) and national long course championships (held in a 50-m pool, the standard international length).

An outstanding feature of swimming is age grouping, a system which matches children of the same age against each other. International age-group meets are now held, and although the world's top swimmers tend to be outside the age groups (the standard FINA ages are 10 and under, 11–12, 13–14, and 15–17), almost all have passed through the ranks.

It is not an exaggeration to state that American swimmers have dominated world swimming since the first decade of the 20th century. Other nations have played a major part, however, notably Australia in the 1920s, the late 1950s, and the early 1960s, Great Britain between 1900 and 1920, Japan in the 1930s, and East Germany in the 1970s. The American hegemony is the result of two factors: age-group swimming, pioneered in the USA, and the college system. Age grouping, practised on a large scale in the USA, provides a ready supply of hardened competitors. University and college swimming, for men at least, ensures a livelihood and training facilities for theoretically amateur swimmers. Most countries have now adopted age-group swimming and through the institution of grants in aid (as in Canada) or sinecures (as in Eastern Europe) have tried to mirror the college system with varying degrees of success.

Synchronised swimming, though not included in the Olympic Games, was recognised by the FINA in 1952 and forms part of the world championship programme. Synchronised swimming, or 'synchro', is essentially a water ballet and developed from individual displays of graceful or ornamental swimming. As a competitive event it almost always features only women and, like an ice-skating contest, is held in two parts—set stunts followed by a free-routine section.

There are five stunt groups: ballet leg (in which at some stage of the movement a leg is lifted vertically above the hip); dolphin head first (an open backward circle from a supine position); dolphin feet first; somersault; diverse (a miscellaneous group). The free routine, which is done to music and may include up to 20 seconds of 'land' movements, lasts five minutes. Judges mark on a 1 to 10 scale (tariffs are used in the stunt section) according to grace, rhythm, poise, and definition of movement. A plain black or navy costume is worn for the stunts, but there is considerable freedom in dress style for the free routine.

Three synchro events are recognised: solo, duet and team (four or more members). Additional marks are awarded to teams with more than four members (0·5 per addition), but such teams have much more difficulty with coordination.

See also CHANNEL SWIMMING; DIVING; WATER POLO.

Bibliography: F. Carlile, *On Swimming*, 1963; J. E. Counsilman, *The Science of Swimming*, 1968; F. Oppenheim, *The History of Swimming*, 1970; P. Besford, *Encyclopaedia of Swimming*, 1971; J.M. Hogg, *Land Conditioning for Competitive Swimming*, 1972. Periodicals: *Swimming World* (ed. A. Schoenfield; monthly); *FINA Handbook* (quarterly); *ASA Handbook* (annual); *Swimming World Swimmers' Annual*.

Swinburne, Algernon Charles (1837–1909), English poet, born in London. He was educated at Eton and Balliol College, Oxford, where he remained until 1860. He left without a degree, although in 1858 he won the Taylorian Prize for French and Italian. At Oxford he met D. G. ROSSETTI, to whom he dedicated his first published poetical drama *The Queen-Mother*, 1860. This, with a similar work, *Rosamond*, was inspired by Shakespeare, and neither succeeded. In 1865 Swinburne published two

Algernon Charles Swinburne, water-colour by Carlo Pellegrini ('Ape') drawn for *Vanity Fair*, 1874. *(National Portrait Gallery, London)*

much more successful poetic dramas, *Atalanta in Calydon* and *Chastelard*.

In 1866 his *Poems and Ballads* provoked scandal and a storm of abuse from the critics who were repelled by the sensuality which they declared characterised its pages. Their effects were gained by his powerful use of language and rhythm, producing unusual patterns of sound to express mood and feeling. However, Swinburne had made his name as a writer, and from then on produced a great number of poems and poetic dramas, and also several critical essays, the best of which include *William Blake*, 1868, *Essays and Studies*, 1875, *A Study of Shakespeare*, 1880, *Victor Hugo*, 1886, *Studies in Prose and Poetry*, 1894, and *The Age of Shakespeare*, 1909.

He identified himself with the PRE-RAPHAELITE BROTHERHOOD, and enthusiastically upheld the cause of Italian independence. His dissipated life caused a breakdown in health and in 1879 he moved to Putney, where he lived under the care of Theodore WATTS-DUNTON, until his death. *The Swinburne Letters* were edited by C. Y. Lang (six volumes), 1959–62.

Bibliography: E. Gosse and T. S. Wise, *Complete Works* (20 vols), 1925–27; E. Thomas, *Swinburne*, 1912; E. Gosse, *Life*, 1917; J. O. Fuller, *Swinburne: A Critical Biography*, 1968.

Swindon, town in WILTSHIRE, England, 123 km west of London, on the main railway line to Bristol and South Wales. An industrial town grew around the workshops of the former Great Western Railway, which was established in 1841. Swindon was approved as suitable for expansion under the Town Development Act 1952 and subsequently the whole town has been transformed into a modern shopping centre, with industrial and housing estates. There is an excellent railway museum in Swindon. Population (1971) 91,033.

Swine, see PIG.

Swinemünde, see ŚWINOUJŚCIE.

Swinford, market town in County MAYO, Republic of Ireland. Population 1105.

Swing, Raymond (1887–1968), US journalist and broadcaster, born at Cortland, New York; educated at Oberlin College, he started newspaper work in Cleveland, Ohio, in 1906. From 1913 until 1917 he was Berlin correspondent of the *Chicago Daily News*, and then, successively, Berlin correspondent of the *New York Herald*, foreign service director of the *Wall Street Journal*, London bureau chief of the *Philadelphia Public Ledger*, and of the *New York Evening Post*. However, it was as a broadcaster that he achieved an international reputation when from 1935 until 1945 he interpreted American affairs for the BBC. His autobiography, *Good Evening!*, was published in 1965.

Swinnerton, Frank Arthur (1884–), English novelist and critic, born in London, the son of an engraver. Starting work at an early age, he was for a time on the staff of the *Manchester Guardian*, and later was a publisher's reader. His most successful novels were *Nocturne*, 1917, *September*, 1919, *Young Felix*, 1923, and *Harvest Comedy*, 1937. Others are *Coquette*, 1921, *Sketch of a Sinner*, 1929, *The Two Wives*, 1939, *Thankless Child*, 1942, *A Woman in Sunshine*, 1944, *A Flower for Catharine*, 1951, *A Month in Gordon Square*, 1953, *The Woman from Sicily*, 1957, *The Grace Divorce*, 1960, *Quadrille*, 1965, *Rosalind Passes*, 1973, and *Some Achieve Greatness*, 1976. *The Georgian Literary Scene*, 1935, is a contemporary literary panorama. *Tokefield Papers*, 1927, and *A London Bookman*, 1928, are collections of essays, while *Swinnerton*, 1937, is an autobiography.

Świnoujście (German *Swinemünde*), town of Poland, in Szczecin province, 56 km north of Szczecin. It is on the eastern shore of USEDOM ISLAND, and was part of POMERANIA until 1945. It is a fishing port, spa, and seaside resort. Population 29,000.

Swinton, former urban district of South YORKSHIRE, England, 16 km north-east of Sheffield. It has railway works, and manufactures pottery, glass, steel, and electrical goods. Population (1971) 14,905.

Swinton and Pendlebury, town in the Salford borough of the Greater Manchester Metropolitan County, England, lying to the north-west of Manchester. It is an industrial area with some coal-mining. Population (1971) 40,167.

Swiss Guards, regiment of Swiss mercenaries, forming the French royal bodyguard constituted in 1616. They were conspicuous for their bravery in the defence of the Tuileries (1792), which was commemorated in 1821 by the great lion outside one of the gates of Lucerne. Swiss

Switch

Guards also form part of the Papal forces. They are recruited from every Swiss canton.

Switch, in electrical engineering, a mechanism for making or breaking a circuit, or for transferring a current from one conductor to another.

Switchback, originally a term applied to a railway which modified the steepness of a declivity by progressing alternately in each lateral direction as well as in the vertical direction up the slope. The railway, which was used for carrying coal, and on which trucks were carried down inclines by their own weight and assisted up the inclines by a stationary engine, was afterwards called a switchback railway. Still later the name was given to the elevated railways at exhibitions and fairs, in which the cars are hauled up to a height by a cable and then descend by a series of sharp ascents and descents. 'Switchback' is still used in this sense, although such names as 'scenic' or 'mountain' railways are more popular.

Switchgear, collective name for all the controlling and protective electrical apparatus in power stations, transmission networks, and large industrial premises connected with the operation and control of the network, machines, and buildings, and the safety of personnel. Large distribution networks are divided into sections, each provided with fuse (see FUSE, ELECTRIC) and CIRCUIT-BREAKER, which isolate the section in case of fault. All motors are controlled by starters, either hand- or push-button operated. In case of overload the overcurrent release trips the starter. Large motors also have their fuse or circuit-breaker as protection against short circuit. Transformers and alternators may be protected on the Merz-Price system (see RELAY). In factories and workshops earth-leakage protection is obligatory. In traction systems, starters, speed control, and braking require complicated switchgear. In coal mines all switchgear is steel-clad, enclosed in steel cabinets; flameproof motors and switchgear are used in all underground service. A large number of British Standard specifications give detailed information and rules for the design of switchgear.

Swithin, Saint, also Swithun (d. 862), born in Wessex, and educated at the Old Abbey at Winchester, though it is not certain that he ever became a monk. He was ordained and became chaplain to Egbert, King of the West Saxons, and tutor to his son Ethelwulf, who made him bishop of Winchester on his accession (852). The origin of the popular legend that if it rains on his day (15 July) it will do so for 40 succeeding days is uncertain.

Switzerland (French *Suisse*; German *Schweiz*; Italian *Svizzera*; Latin *Helvetia*), republic of central Western Europe, consisting of a confederation of 22 self-governing CANTONS (three of them subdivided), bounded on the north by West Germany, on the west by France, on the east by Austria and Liechtenstein, and to the south by Italy. It is 355 km in length from east to west and about 220 km from north to south. Its area is 41,290 km² (half the size of Scotland). While the official language of the cantons is High German, the German-speaking Swiss retain the local forms of Swiss German, which differ in each canton. The cantons are AARGAU, APPENZELL, BASEL, and BERN (all German-speaking), FRIBOURG (French- and German-speaking), GENEVA (French-

Switzerland. A typical mountain village scene. *(Topham/Fotogram)*

speaking), GLARUS (German-speaking), GRAUBÜNDEN (German, Italian, and Romansh are all spoken), JURA (French-speaking), LUCERNE (German-speaking), NEUCHÂTEL (French-speaking), ST GALLEN, SCHAFFHAUSEN, SCHWYZ, SOLOTHURN, and THURGAU (all German-speaking), TICINO (Italian-speaking), URI and UNTERWALDEN (both German-speaking), VALAIS and VAUD (French- and German-speaking), ZUG and ZÜRICH (German-speaking).

Geography. Relief. Switzerland is a land-locked state with a rich diversity of scenery including snow-capped mountains, extensive snowfields and glaciers contrasting with the green valleys, forested slopes, and a limited amount of cultivated land. It has many beautiful lakes. Cattle are reared on the summer Alpine pastures while ibex and chamois roam the rocky crags and forests.

The country is divided into three main regions: the JURA Mountains, extending along the north-western boundary, the Swiss Plateau (*Mittelland*), and the ALPS. The chief physical feature is the vast Alpine system, known by various names in different localities, e.g. the Rhaetian Alps cross the eastern frontier into the TIROL; the Bernese Alps or Oberland occupy the south-central part of the country; the Valais Alps lie on the south-west border; the Lepontine Alps, the Rheinwald Alps, and Glarner Alps are situated in the south-east; while the Urner Alps are in the centre of the country. The highest peak is Monte Rosa, on the Italian frontier, which is 4638 m above sea-level.

The main passes over the Alps are the Great St Bernard, leading from the canton of Valais to the Val d'Aosta; the Simplon, crossing Mount Simplon and leading into Lombardy; and the St Gotthard, leading to the southern canton of Ticino. There are several railway tunnels piercing the Alps, the main ones being the Simplon, the St Gotthard, and the Lötschberg (see under entries on individual passes). Light railways ascend many of the peaks, the JUNGFRAU railway running nearly to the Jungfraujoch (3457 m), starting from a height of 2063 m.

There are upwards of 1000 glaciers in Switzerland, the largest being the Aletsch in the Bernese Oberland, 19 km in extent, which descends from the slopes of the ALETSCHHORN (4182 m) to about 1676 m. Of the many beautiful lakes within, or partly within, the limits of the country, the following are the most important: Geneva (583 km²), Constance (538 km²), Neuchâtel (238 km²), Maggiore (217 km²), Lucerne (214 km²), Zürich (88 km²), Lugano, Thun, Bienne (Biel), Zug, Brienz, and Morat, the last six being under 51 km² in extent. The main rivers flowing through Switzerland are the RHINE, RHÔNE, INN, AAR, Reuss, Limmat, and Thur; the Aar being the most important entirely within Swiss territory. The first three rivers have their sources in Alpine glaciers; the Rhine flows north and north-west, the Rhône takes a westerly and then a southerly course, while the Inn flows north-east to join the Danube. Among the valleys may be mentioned the Val de Travers in the Jura and the valley of the Inn (or Engadine). There are large waterfalls, e.g. the Staubbach at Lauterbrunnen in the Bernese Oberland, which drops 298 m, and the Rheinfall, near Schaffhausen, where the river drops over 30 m in three sets of falls. Forests cover 24 per cent of the country.

See also ALPS; ATLAS 20.

Climate. Switzerland as a whole combines the four European climates into a single transitional climate with the Alps forming the dividing line. The climate is generally temperate but is marked by wide and sudden variations caused by differences in altitude, aspect, and gradient. The prevailing winds are from the west, but local winds are a characteristic of an alpine climate. Rainfall increases in direct proportion to altitude; the average annual precipitation over three-quarters of the country exceeds 1000 mm, varying proportions of which fall as snow. Above 3500 m all precipitation falls as snow; the snowline varies from 2760 m in the northern Alps to 3350 m in the Valais. In the mountains, distinct rain-shadow areas exist. The rarified air of the high-altitude towns of Davos and Arosa produces a perfect climate for medical cures. Temperature inversions are commonplace. Avalanches are mainly caused in spring by the gradual melting of the snows; some 10,000 occur annually. Forests are planted to block their path.

Population. Switzerland shows distinct regional variations in settlement patterns and styles. The valleys in the main are the residential areas with villages extending along the bases of the slopes. The 'commune' is an important settlement unit, its settlement boundaries often extending from one mountain crest to another. Location in relation to the traffic pattern has played an important part in the pattern of urban settlement. Foreign workers (*Gastarbeiter*) have been steadily growing more numerous since the end of the Second World War; they numbered over a million in 1974. About 100 communities with more than 10,000 inhabitants are classed as cities; the largest of which are ZÜRICH, BASEL, GENEVA, BERN (the capital), LAUSANNE, WINTERTHUR, ST GALLEN, and LUCERNE. The estimated population in 1976 was 6,333,200 (at the 1970 census it was 6,270,000).

Economy. Agriculture and *Industry.* Switzerland, although basically an agricultural country, cannot grow enough crops to support its population, so that wheat, vegetables, and fodder crops are imported. The productive land is owned mainly by farmers who grow wheat, barley, maize, and potatoes, and also make cheese and milk products. Much stock is raised, mainly cattle, sheep, goats, and horses (mainly in the Jura). Fruit is grown, and there are some 20,230 ha of vines. About 7·6 per cent of the workforce is employed in farming. Salt is mined at

Rheinfelden and Bex; a little iron ore is mined at Frick and Gonzen; asphalt is found in the Val de Travers.

With an increasingly urban population Switzerland thrives by importing raw materials and exporting costly finished products. The lack of coal and oil has hampered industrial development, but this has been offset by the use of hydro-electric power, and now nuclear energy. The manufacture of machinery is very important. Other industries include dairy products, the manufacture of silk and cotton goods, clocks and watches (in Geneva, Neuchâtel, La Chaux-de-Fonds, and Le Locle), optical and scientific instruments, chemicals, aniline dyes, aluminium, chocolate, cheese, lace, embroidery, and footwear. In pharmaceutical products, precision work, and the making of optical equipment and apparatus, the Swiss are exceptionally skilled.

Energy. Hydro-electric power is the main power source for the Swiss economy. With 400 plants in operation, some 95 per cent of the total harnessable power is utilised. The Alps have been the scene of major technical advances in building subterranean powerhouses and channels for such plants. The highest dams in Europe, Mauvoisin (237 m) and Grand Dixence (284 m) are to be found in the Valais. Switzerland has, in addition, both thermal and nuclear power plants.

Communications. Switzerland's control of the important Alpine passes and European trade routes has given the country a key rôle in Europe's traffic system. The national motorway network is a relatively recent achievement; some 18,000 km will have been completed by 1980. The main railway lines were nationalised from 1900 onwards. Their total length is 9400 km, including some 600 tunnels (the 20 km long Simplon Tunnel is the longest in the world). The whole of the Swiss Federal Railway system (3000 km) is electrified, and also the few remaining private railways. Swissair operates a few internal services and carried 180,000 passengers in 1973, but its main services are international. Major airports are near Zürich (Kloten), Geneva (Cointrin), and Basel (Mulhouse). A merchant marine was established in 1941, registered at Basel, an important inland port on the Rhine, and had 27 ocean-going vessels in 1974 totalling 200,000 t. There are three main, and a few local, broadcasting stations, as well as television stations, each linguistic region having its own channel.

The Federal Post Office operates, in addition to the usual postal services, the telegraph and telephone system, provides and maintains all wireless and television installations of a technical nature while granting relevant concessions to programme-organising companies. Its postal bus service itineraries cover about 6450 km including the Alpine passes kept open in winter by snow ploughs. Inhabitants of Alpine areas can travel on the buses at a reduced rate.

Tourism. This growth part of the economy employs almost as many people as farming does. Its attraction lasts throughout the year. Former spas and mountain sanatoria are now busy resorts. In 1951 16·8 million foreign tourists made overnight stays in the country; by 1976 this figure had more than doubled. About 40 per cent of the tourists are from other European countries.

Labour. Although state intervention in the free market economy goes against Swiss economic policy, the labour market is where the central government has had to inter-

493

vene. The influx of foreign workers had created such internal tensions in Swiss society that the government was forced to restrict the inflow.

Finance. The unit of currency is the Swiss franc of 100 rappen or centimes. The Federal Bank has the sole privilege of issuing bank-notes. The country has been protected from world inflation by the strength of the franc; in 1976 it was some 50 per cent above its 1971 level. Switzerland's central location has helped it to become one of the world's main financial centres contributing greatly to its invisible earnings.

Bibliography: J. O. Talbot, *Central Switzerland*, 1969; O. Bär, *Geographie der Schweiz*, 1971; D. Cowie, *Switzerland: The Land and People*, 1972; M. Ikle, *Switzerland: An International Banking and Finance Center*, 1972; W. Sorell, *The Swiss: Cultural Panorama of Switzerland*, 1973; H. Rees, *Switzerland, Austria and Italy*, 1974; C. J. Hughes, *Switzerland*, 1975.

Government. Constitution and Legislature. Switzerland is a federal republic with legislative and executive authority vested in the Federal Assembly, consisting of a National Council (200 directly elected members) and a Council of State (44 members—two from each canton). Women are not allowed to vote in some cantons. Executive power is vested in a Federal Council of seven members, presided over by the president, which sits at Bern, members being elected for four years by the Federal Assembly. Members of the Federal Council head administrative departments—foreign affairs, interior, justice and police, military, finance, public economy, transport and communications and power.

The referendum and the initiative are essential features of Swiss democracy. Every constitutional amendment requires ratification by a popular and a cantonal majority; a referendum on any law can be demanded by 30,000 voters or eight cantons; 50,000 voters can require the submission of any desired law to the usual legislative

Switzerland. Livestock are grazed on Alpine pastures while the valley bottoms are intensively cultivated. (*Topham/Fotogram*)

process. Recent referenda were called on the ratification of the EEC trade agreement and to annul the articles barring Jesuits. In three cantons direct democracy exists, the citizens of Appenzell, Glarus, and Unterwalden meeting annually in the open air (*Landsgemeinde*) to elect cantonal officials and pass laws. Every Swiss citizen has three allegiances: communal (local), cantonal, and national. Each canton has its own written constitution, government, and assembly. In 1973 a commission was set up to revise the constitution which dates back to 1848.

Justice. Each canton possesses its own judicial system of civil and criminal procedure; the high court, called the *Bundesgericht* or Federal Tribunal, sits at Lausanne, and is the supreme court and final court of appeal. It consists of 26–28 members elected by the Federal Assembly for six years, who are eligible for re-election. In 1942 a new federal penal code replaced the separate cantonal codes.

Education. Swiss reformers, including Rousseau and Pestalozzi, have played a large part in the evolution of modern educational theories in Western Europe. In all the Swiss cantons education is compulsory and free. In addition to primary and secondary schools, there are a wide range of further education colleges. The educational system used varies from canton to canton. There are a large number of private schools and many foreign children receive their education here. Switzerland has eight universities and two technical colleges, modelled on those of West Germany, governed by a rector and a senate. The number of students in higher education is over 48,000. There is also a Swiss Federal Institute of Technology at Zürich, maintained by the government. In 1927 a university institute for international studies was opened at Geneva.

Welfare. Switzerland has a comprehensive system of social security, regulated at federal and cantonal level, which explains the regional variations of social security administration. Swiss social security covers all the usual areas, such as old age pensions, invalids' pensions, health insurance (including maternity benefit), unemployment pay, and family allowance. It also covers some areas that are more peculiar to Swiss society, such as military insurance and compensation for loss of earnings paid to people on military service. Whether the benefits for all these are administered centrally or not, all these services have standard contributions. The Swiss welfare state is supported by many private social institutions which explains why the benefits of public schemes are smaller than in other countries.

Religion. In Switzerland there is full liberty of conscience. The churches are self-supporting. The Jesuits are barred as is the establishment of new orders and convents. The Protestants (48 per cent of the population) are in the majority in 12 of the cantons including Zürich, Bern, Basel, Schaffhausen, Vaud, and Neuchâtel, while Catholics (49 per cent) predominate in 10 cantons including Lucerne, Fribourg, Valais, and Ticino.

Armed Forces. Switzerland does not maintain a standing army but trains every citizen in the use of arms. Initial basic training in the army is for four months followed by refresher courses during the periods of 12 years in the 1st Reserve and 18 years in the 2nd Reserve. The total strength of the army is nearly 625,000 (including reservists who can be mobilised within 48 hours). The army is organised into four corps—one for the defence of the Alps, consisting of three mountain divisions; the other three are for the defence of the plain. There is a small but modern air force.

Official Languages. The Swiss official languages are German, French, Italian, and Romansh. Most Swiss are German-speaking (65 per cent), and the most important towns (Zürich, Bern, Lucerne, and Basel) are in the German area. French is spoken in Geneva, the Vaud, and along the western slopes of the Jura Mountains. Italian is spoken in the province of Ticino, south of the St Gotthard Pass. Romansh, derived from Latin, is spoken by small communities in remote Alpine villages.

National Anthem. Trittst im Morgenrot daher, written by L. Widmer and the tune composed by Josef Zwyssig in 1841.

National Flag. A symmetrical white cross on a red background.

Bibliography: A. Gretler and P. E. Mandi, *Values, Trends and Alternatives in Swiss Society*, 1973; H. H. Kerr, *Switzerland: Social Cleavages and Partisan Conflict*, 1974; J. Steiner, *Conflict Resolution in Switzerland*, 1974.

Early History. Switzerland, especially the southern provinces, was a centre of the LA TÈNE culture of the Early Iron Age. Settlements and forts have been excavated in the canton of Ticino. In the Bonaduz district (Grisons) a settlement was occupied by the Rhaetians until the Roman period. The original inhabitants of Switzerland were the Helvetii in the north-west and the Rhaetians in the south-east. The Roman conquest of these tribes began as early as 107 BC, when they were defeated in southern Gaul. Their subjection dates from 58 BC, when Julius Caesar defeated them at Col d'Armecy. The ancestors of the modern Swiss are the Germanic tribes who overran the Roman Empire: the Alemanni east of the Aar about 406, and the Burgundians in the south-west in 443. They became Christian about 600–650, but the Helvetii were not converted until later.

Between 700 and 1200 the country was under the influence successively of the descendants of Charlemagne, the German emperors, and the Zähringen dynasty. Charlemagne (768–814) included Switzerland in his territory. At his death this realm fell into confusion, and, in the subsequent partition of his lands, half of modern Switzerland was allotted to the Eastern Frankish kingdom and half to Lorraine. In 888 Rudolph of the Guelphic family founded the Kingdom of Burgundy, of which west Switzerland formed a part, while the German regions fell to the Duchy of Swabia in 917. In the 9th and 10th centuries several dynasties rose to power, such as the houses of Zähringen (1097–1218), of Lenzburg, Kyburg, and Savoy. The cities of Fribourg (1178) and Bern (1191) were founded by the Zähringen to secure their supremacy against the attacks of the rural nobility.

A period of chaos ensued, until in 1273 Rudolf of Hapsburg became emperor, with control of what is now German Switzerland. The extension of his power caused alarm and resistance in the regions round the Lake of Lucerne, and a few days after Rudolf's death, in 1291, the first Perpetual League of the three Forest States (Uri, Schwyz, Unterwalden) was formed, which, in 1315, defeated the Austrian forces at Morgarten. In 1332 Lucerne, in 1351 Zurich, in 1352 Zug and Glarus, in 1353 Bern joined the League, following on a war with Austria, which was defeated at Sempach and Näfels. As a result, the League extended its influence and lands. From this period dates the rise of Swiss education, art, and industry.

Modern History. From 1474 to 1477 the confederation was at war with Charles the Bold of Burgundy, defeating him at Grandson and Morat, 1476. In 1481 Fribourg and Solothurn came into the confederation. In 1499 Maximilian attempted to bring Rhaetia, which as the Grey League (Grisons or Graubünden) had asserted its independence, again under the Empire, but he was defeated at

Switzerland. *The Battle at Näfels*, tempera painting on paper by Ferdinand Hodler, 1896–97. *(Kunstmuseum, Basel)*

Switzerland

Calven. Later, during the Reformation, Austria was more successful, but the leaguers retained their independence until they at last joined the confederation in 1803. The recognition of Switzerland's independence dates from the victory over the Empire at Dornach in 1499, by which the confederation was released from the Imperial tax.

Switzerland became a centre of the Reformation which led to internal dissension, as the north generally followed the reformist teachings of ZWINGLI, while the Forest States remained Roman Catholic. In the hostilities that resulted the Catholic troops were victorious, Zwingli was slain (1531), and a truce was arranged, whereby each canton was left free to determine its own religion. A few years later a French theologian, Jean CALVIN, came to Geneva. He established a college of pastors there. After a long battle with some members of the Geneva urban patriciate, Calvin turned the city into a theocratic republic which had such influence that it became known as the 'Protestant Rome'. The city was visited by John Knox and other English and Scots theologians. Calvin was succeeded by Theodore Beza. Calvin's doctrines were far less compromising than Zwingli's, and the Calvinists brooked no opposition, either from Catholics or from dissident Protestants within their territory. So while Zwingli introduced Protestantism into the country and by his struggle and death ensured its survival, Calvin's doctrines reaped much of the benefit of his efforts.

In 1536 Bern took the Vaud from the dukes of Savoy. During the early-16th century Swiss mercenaries were widely employed in Europe, and fighting for foreign kings became a flourishing trade. In the peace treaty of Westphalia, 1648, the political separation of Switzerland from the German Empire was recognised by the powers. The history of the 17th and 18th centuries is mainly one of a patriciate in Bern, Fribourg, Solothurn, and Lucerne, and of civil oligarchies in Zürich, Basel, and Schaffhausen. During the whole of this period the peasantry were much oppressed, and their attempt in 1653 to secure better conditions was crushed. During the French Revolution Switzerland was seized by France, which made it the Helvetic Republic (1789), 'one and indivisible', strictly subordinated to the former. This centralisation did not conform to the Swiss tradition of local self-government; nevertheless, it created for the first time a national unity, though imposed from outside. The Helvetic Republic introduced a uniform Swiss monetary system, using Latin inscription, so as not to conflict with any of the various language-groups. This device is still being used. In the Act of Mediation (1802–03), Napoleon recognised the sovereignty of the cantons, but only in 1815 was Switzerland's independence restored, and its permanent neutrality guaranteed by the powers at the Congress of Vienna.

During the 19th century religious differences led to bitter controversy and to blows. In 1847 a savage war broke out between Protestants and the Seven Roman Catholic cantons, the latter having formed a separatist league or Sonderbund, as a result of the suppression of various monasteries by the Liberals in the canton of Aargau. After a short campaign, G. H. Dufour, at the head of the Federal army, defeated the Catholics. In 1848 a new federal constitution was adopted, and peace signed, giving the Protestants nearly all they had fought for. Switzerland was then transformed from a confederation of independent states into one federal state. In 1874 a revision of the federal constitution was carried, giving wider powers to the state, especially in military matters.

Surrounded by belligerent countries during the First World War, Switzerland nevertheless retained its neutrality, though the French Swiss and German Swiss naturally differed in their sympathies. In a non-military capacity Switzerland rendered assistance to both sides in organising Red Cross units, tracing the missing, and permitting

Switzerland. Geneva in 1551. *(Mansell Collection)*

Switzerland. *The Miraculous Draught of Fishes*, by Konrad Witz, 1444. Tempera on wood, in St Peter's Cathedral, Geneva. *(Musée d'Art et d'Histoire, Geneva)*

incapacitated prisoners of war to be interned within its frontiers. In 1920 Switzerland entered the League of Nations, which made its permanent head-quarters at Geneva. For the next 19 years Switzerland was, therefore, at the centre of international politics.

The outbreak of the Second World War found Switzerland well prepared, though the conquest of France by Germany made Switzerland economically entirely dependent upon the latter, and on 11 August 1940 a new trade agreement between the two was signed. In 1940 the Federal Council dissolved the Swiss Nationalist movement, a totalitarian organisation connected with the Nazis, and soon afterwards they dissolved the Communist party. When the war spread to Russia and the Balkans the trade agreement Switzerland had made with the USSR earlier in 1941 became worthless. Germany then brought pressure on Switzerland to enter into closest possible economic association, and, as a reprisal against this second agreement, Great Britain intensified its blockade against Switzerland. The country's position was no doubt hazardous, especially as it also had to protect itself against attempts to disintegrate it from within, through the machinations of the highly organised German Nazi party in Switzerland itself. After the German invasion of the USSR Germany demanded of Switzerland a participation in the 'fight for Europe' and adhesion to the 'New

Order'. Only very few Swiss fought in the Wehrmacht, and these were condemned *in contumaciam* by the military courts for serving with a foreign power.

Switzerland did not become a member of the United Nations, but joined UNESCO and other international organisations and took part in the Marshall Plan. Switzerland's economic development has been peaceful and prosperous since the end of the Second World War, although not unaffected by the unsteadiness of the capitalist world market. This has caused some problems, especially in relation to migrant workers, who comprise about one-sixth of the country's labour force. A referendum was held in 1975 by which the Swiss electorate rejected the idea of repatriation of migrant workers upon the advice of the federal government. Tourism has been a growth industry in Switzerland, bringing in large amounts of foreign currency. The Swiss landscape has given the country many natural advantages in this industry, but the influx of so many foreign tourists has not been without its side effects on the Swiss society and economy. Switzerland is a member of the EUROPEAN FREE TRADE ASSOCIATION, and not of the European Economic Community.

The formation of a new canton (Jura) along the Franco-German linguistic frontier has caused some friction between the two communities; these clashes have been of a quite serious nature. This is the first outbreak of

Switzerland

communal strife for many years and has disturbed the calm of the otherwise well-integrated community.

Bibliography: D. Cowie, *Switzerland: The Land and the People*, 1972; W. Sorell, *The Swiss: A Cultural Panorama of Switzerland*, 1973.

Art. Switzerland is early distinguished among the German-speaking lands by the art of Konrad WITZ, whose work survives in famous altar panels, now at Basel and Geneva. Urs Graf of Solothurn (1484–1528), painter and engraver, Nicolas Manuel DEUTSCH, painter, and Hans Leu (1490–1531) all specialised in designs for stained glass panels. Jost AMMAN was famous for his wood-engravings. Stained glass painting, a predominantly Swiss art since the Middle Ages, was raised to a pitch of perfection by Conrad Meyer and Christoph Maurer. The latter was also a noted draughtsman, as were Daniel Lindtmayer (1552–1607), Tobias Stimmer (1539–84), and Ludwig Ringler (1535–1605). Johann Heinrich FUSELI, painter of the famous *Nightmare*, became a Royal Academician in England. Among landscape-painters of the 18th and 19th centuries are Adrian Zingg (1734–1816), Wilhelm Gmelin (1745–1821), Johann

Switzerland. Bronze sculpture by Alberto Giacometti, *Head of Diego*, 1955. (*Tate Gallery, London*)

Switzerland. *Twittering Machine*, by Paul Klee, 1922. (*Collection, The Museum of Modern Art, New York*)

Hartmann (1753–1830) and Johann Bidermann (1762–1828). Angelica KAUFFMANN and Samuel Grimm, the topographical draughtsman, like Fuseli, worked mainly in England. Landscape and water-colour painters known in Europe are Wolfgang Toepffer (1766–1847), Johann Wetzel (1781–1834), Rudolph Toepffer (1794–1846), the caricaturist, Sigmund Freudenberger (1745–1801) and Arnold BÖCKLIN, the last-named famous for his *Great Pan* and *Isle of the Dead*, and other landscapes with mythological figures. The works of Franz Koenig (1760–1832) were an outstanding example of the tinted engravings which were a big industry in his time. Rudolf Koller (1828–1905) was a fine animal painter. Ferdinand HODLER is a great national figure in painting, known for his landscapes and historical scenes. Among modern painters are Félix Vallotton (1865–1925), associated with the Paris School, and the internationally famous expressionist Paul KLEE. During the Second World War Switzerland became a centre of beautiful book production and illustration.

In sculpture Jakob Russ was one of the best-known religious sculptors of the Middle Ages. Sixteenth-century sculptors of note were Jakob de Malacridis and Hans Geiler, an example of whose work may be seen in the Justice Fountain in Bern. Eminent modern Swiss sculptors are Hermann Haller (1880–1950) and Alberto GIACOMETTI.

Important in architecture was Carlo Maderno (1556–1629), who was born at Bissone and worked in Rome, designing the façade of St Peter's there, and who taught Francesco BORROMINI. Notable in the 17th century are the names of Jakob Khurer, the architect of Lucerne Cathedral, Niklaus Geissler the sculptor and Caspar Mosbrugger, who rebuilt the Benedictine monastery of Einseideln. Leaders of architecture in the 19th and early 20th centuries were Karl Moser, who built Zürich University and Congress House, and Paul Bodmer, the fresco painter. An outstanding leader in modern architecture has been LE CORBUSIER.

Bibliography: F. Fosca, *Histoire de la peinture en Suisse*, 1945; G. Gysin, *Swiss Medieval Tapestries*, 1947; A. Crivelli, *L'art renaissant en Suisse*, 1947; G. Jedlicka, *Zur schweiz, Malerei der Gegenwart*, 1947; P. Wescher, *Die Romantik in der schweiz. Malerei*, 1947; H. Reinhardt, *Kirchliche Baukunst in der Schweiz*, 1947, and *Swiss Stained Glass of the XIV Century*, 1950.

Language. German (spoken by about two-thirds of the population), French (by about one-fifth), and Italian (rather more than one-tenth) are national and official languages in Switzerland. The status of ROMANSH as a national language is also guaranteed by the constitution. With only some 50,000 speakers, in a total population of more than 6,000,000, it is, however, not an official language except for local affairs. A large proportion of the Swiss are fluent in two or more languages. See also FRANCE, *Language*; GERMAN LANGUAGE; ITALY, *Language*.

Literature. Swiss literature derives from a number of cultures with little essential connection in origin or history and can hardly be regarded as an entity before the 19th century. The first prominent figure in Swiss literary history is Balbulus Notker (c. 840–912), whose *Sequences* were an important contribution to the development of church music. Another early work is Ekkehard's *Waltarilied* (c. 940), a Latin poem in hexameters about Walter of Aquitaine. During the medieval period French and German courtly ROMANCES were written, as were German lyrics, French translations of the Bible, French miracle and MORALITY plays, and such compilations as Oton de Grandson's *Mireour de Monde*. *Edelstein*, by the fabulist Ulrich Bonner, dates from 1349; it was to be the first work printed in the German language. Johann von Kaisersberg Geiler (1445–1530) was accounted the greatest preacher of his day, and François Bonnivard (1496–1570), the hero of BYRON's *Prisoner of Chillon*, was a noted historian. Of the many popular heroic ballads the most influential was *Wilhelm Tell*.

Swiss writers of the Reformation period, several of whom were refugees from France and Germany, were mainly able classical scholars, but their vernacular writings contributed significantly to the development of French and German style. Such writers included ZWINGLI who translated the Bible into German, and CALVIN whose French prose was clear and incisive. Other scholars were J. SCALIGER and Conrad GESNER, while Nicolas Manuel (1484–1530) was an effective satirist. Théodore de

BÈZE (Beza), Calvin's successor in Geneva, was influential as a biblical scholar; he presented the *Codex D* to the University of Cambridge in 1581. Aegidius TSCHUDI, author of *Chronicon helveticum* (SCHILLER's source for *Wilhelm Tell*), was an authority on Swiss history from 1000 to 1470. Among German chroniclers of this period were Stumpf (1500–76) and BULLINGER. Thomas ERASTUS, physician and theologian, wrote on excommunication and his work was translated into English as the *Nullity of Church Censures*.

For a while during the 17th century Swiss literature declined, but the 18th century brought a reawakening and signs of the new spirit are found in the works of Crouaz and Ruchert, and Muralt's *Lettres sur les Anglais et les Français*. The philosopher Albrecht von HALLER was much influenced by the writings of Francis BACON and in 1732 published, in German, an *Essay on Swiss Poetry*. His own poems are full of grace and tenderness. Johann BODMER and Johann BREITINGER were Swiss leaders of the revolt against classicism in German literature in the 18th century. Bodmer wrote learned works on

Switzerland. Portrait of Conrad Meyer, the poet and novelist, drawn in 1887. *(Bildarchiv Preussischer Kulturbesitz)*

Switzerland

poetry and literature generally, and translated Milton's *Paradise Lost* in 1732. Gottlieb Emmanuel von Haller (1755–86), son of Albrecht, wrote the indispensable *Bibliothek der Schweizergeschichte*, and Emeric de Vattel (1714–67), a French-Swiss, produced *The Law of Nations* (1758), one of the fundamental works of international law. The widely read *Histoire des Républiques italiennes* was written by Léonard Sismondi (1773–1842) and Besenval's memoirs on the French Revolution are still useful for students of that period. Other significant writers of the time were the historian Johannes von MÜLLER; J. Georg Sulzer, author of a *General Theory of Beauty in Art*; Philippe BRIDEL; Mme de CHARRIÈRE; Benjamin CONSTANT, author of *Adolphe*; the theologian Alexandre Vinet (1797–1847), whose works (in French) are marked by an incisive, pure style; Johann WYSS, who wrote the Swiss national anthem, and, with his father, *The Swiss Family Robinson*; and Johann L. Burchardt (1784–1817), orientalist and ethnographer. Among the early 19th-century Swiss authors in German is Jeremias Gotthelf (pseudonym of Albert BITZIUS).

Probably no Swiss writer has been as influential as Jean-Jacques ROUSSEAU, and also famous as a great educational reformer was his follower, H. J. PESTALOZZI. However, among other Swiss writers of importance are Johann Kaspar BLUNTSCHLI, politician and jurist, who produced a work on contracts which has served as a model for contracts throughout the world; Eduard Zeller (1814–1908), historian and philosopher; and J. J. Bachofen (1815–87), who exerted great influence on ethnology by his work *Das Mutterrecht*, 1861. J. H. Merle d'AUBIGNÉ, historian of the Reformation, and Jean Gré-

Switzerland. The writer and influential critic, Johann Breitinger; portrait from an engraving. *(Mary Evans Picture Library)*

maud (1823–97), historian of Valais, are also notable.

Leading figures in 19th-century Swiss literature include the novelist and poet, Gottfried KELLER, one of the greatest of Swiss humorists, and Conrad Ferdinand MEYER, perhaps the greatest poet Switzerland has produced. Jakob BURCKHARDT made significant contributions to art history with his works on Constantine the Great, the Italian Renaissance, and Italian art, while the cosmopolitan novel in France was created by V. Chebruliez (1829–90). Carl SPITTELER was awarded the Nobel Prize for literature in 1920 for his epic *Olympian Spring*, and another novelist, the Catholic Heinrich Federer (1866–1928), wrote about the people of the mountain districts. Stories by the famous children's writer, Johanna SPYRI, especially *Heidi*, are still popular.

Among early 20th-century poets was Ernst Zahn, whose numerous novels were successful despite their rather flamboyant style. Jakob Schaffner (1875–1944) was a master of the short story and author of *Die goldene Fratze*, 1912, *A History of Switzerland*, 1915, and *Johannes*, 1922. John Knittel wrote novels on Arab countries. Joseph Widman (1842–1911), poet, dramatist, and critic; Arnold Ott, dramatist; Isabella Kaiser, author of *Mein Herz*, who wrote in German and French; Gottfried Strasser; Marc Monnier; Tissot; Combe; and Rannez were all prominent, as were the poets Tazan, Cougnard, and Dalcroze, all of whom wrote in French, and Paul Ilg, an epic poet, and author of *Menschlein Matthias*. An outstanding poet of the inter-war period was Albin ZOLLINGER. Charles Ferdinand RAMUZ, a great novelist of French-speaking Switzerland, wrote vivid books which, although dealing with the landscape and the people of his native region, made him known far beyond. Blaise CENDRARS, a more cosmopolitan figure, is also highly rated.

Among Swiss dramatists of the early 20th century, Caesar von Arx (1895–1949) became famous throughout Europe. Robert WALSER made a complete break with traditional Swiss literature, criticising the pompous and complacent middle-class life of his time in his ironical novels, and in so doing had a considerable influence on Franz KAFKA. Robert FAESI wrote, in the aristocratic tradition, artistic poems and dramas, and a series of novels dealing with the history of Zürich. Kurt Guggenheim's skilful novels on the cosmopolitan and urban life in Zürich from 1900 until 1950 (*Alles in Allem*, four volumes, 1952–54) won him the city's literary prize. Another historical novelist, Emanuel Stickelberger, wrote in the spirit of humanism and the Reformation (*Zwingli, Calvin, Holbein, Das Wunder von Leyden*). Felix Moeschlin produced vigorous novels, and Albert Welti is popular for his imaginative works, while Regina Ullmann's poetic stories reveal her attachment to RILKE. The works of the novelist and playwright R. J. Humm are distinguished by their capricious individuality and humour. Arnold Kübler is particularly known for his trilogy of autobiographical stories (*Oeppi*), and Meinrad Inglin (1893–1971), who became known by his *Schweizerspiegel*, an outstanding account of life in Switzerland before and during the First World War, is a prose writer in the conservative realistic tradition. Religious and metaphysical abstraction is the theme of Albert Steffen's poems, and among lyrical poets are Hermann Hiltbrunner, Albert Ehrismann, and Silja Walter. Marxist views are expressed in the dramas and novels of Jakob Bührer.

Outstanding dramatists of the mid-20th century are Max FRISCH and Friedrich DÜRRENMATT. Both attacking conservative traditionalism and devoting themselves to the contemporary problems of the individual in an absurd world, their reputations are international. Of modern prose writers, Peter BICHSEL, Walter DIGGELMANN, Hugo LOETSCHER, and Adolf MUSCHG have made a considerable impact.

Dialect literature flourishes particularly in the German-speaking part of Switzerland, where remarkable lyric poems and short novels have been written in local dialects, above all by Bernese writers.

Valuable contributions to Swiss literature from Italian-speaking writers have come from Francesco Chiesa, Giuseppe Zoppi (1896–1952), and Felice Filippini (1917–).

Bibliography: V. Rossel and E. Jenny, *Histoire de la littérature suisse* (2 vols), 1910; J. Nadler, *Literaturgeschichte der deutschen Schweiz,* 1932; C. Clerc, *Panorama des littératures contemporaines en Suisse,* 1938; H. Löhrer, *Die Schweiz im Spiegel der englischen Literatur von 1849–1875,* 1952; A. Bettex, *Spiegelungen der Schweiz in der deutschen Literatur 1870–1950,* 1954; H. Trümpy, *Schweizerdeutsche Sprache und Literatur im 17. und 18. Jahrhundert,* 1955; A. Nathan (Ed.), *Swiss Men of Letters,* 1970; A. Berchtold, *La Suisse romande...XXe siècle,* 1970.

Music. Switzerland has a strong tradition of folk-song, which is kept alive by the YODEL choirs today. Affiliations with Germany have led to a high standard of performance of classical music among the Swiss people, though with a few outstanding exceptions, such as Arthur HONEGGER, Othmar Schoeck (1886–1957), and Frank Martin (1890–1975), Swiss composers have had little influence outside their own country. Ernest Ansermet (1883–1969) has won world renown as the conductor of the Geneva symphonic concerts. Other composers of distinction are Hans Huber (1852–1921), Hermann Suter (1870–1926), Albert Moeschinger (1897–), Conrad Beck (1901–), Heinrich Sutermeister (1910–) and Rolf Liebermann (1910–).

Bibliography: Swiss Composers' League, *40 Contemporary Swiss Composers,* 1956.

Sword, a weapon with a long metal blade, either straight or curved, and usually sharpened along the edge or edges. The Bronze Age sword developed from the shorter dagger of copper, and was leaf-shaped and two-edged, with a point for thrusting. The sword of the Iron Age was not tempered, and so was easily bent. The Romans had two swords, the short straight *gladius* and the longer *spartha.* Carbonisation forming steel came with the Vikings. The Viking sword was straight, two-edged with a crossbar or quillons, and a pommel as a counterpoise. The medieval sword developed from the Viking sword and was usually cruciform in shape, two-edged and for thrusting.

The curved sword, with a single edge for cutting and less adapted for thrusting, was a favourite in the East. It is found in Europe in the Middle Ages in the form of the cleaver-like falchion. With the growing disuse of armour early in the 16th century the hilts of swords became more complicated, and bars were used to protect the hand, which had formerly been covered by a gauntlet. The principal components of the hilt were the knuckle-guard, the *pas d'âne* or branches, and the quillons.

The rapier, a long thrusting sword, became fashionable for civilian wear in the late 16th century and early 17th century, and was adopted for duelling. In the late 17th century the rapier was shortened and simplified to form the short or court sword. It is at this time that fencing schools were set up in most capital cities. Cavalry in the 17th century used the BROADSWORD, generally straight and with a single, or sometimes double, edge. Its place was taken in the 18th century by the sabre, which derived from the Persian *shamshir.* This was single-edged, curved, but not so curved that it could not be used with the point.

Varieties of swords are countless. The curved riding sword or hanger became the naval cutlass. In Asia one finds the curved SCIMITAR, the progenitor of the sabre, which became the European cavalry sword, principally a cutting sword, but which could be used with the point also. In Japan the making of sword blades was carried out with maximum skill, and swords by famous makers were handed down in the aristocracy and were objects of veneration. Most countries have their distinctive swords; the Arab *Kantar,* the Indian *Tulwar,* and the Japanese *Daisho.* The executioner's or heading sword was straight, two-edged, and with a blunt point. Swords have been a symbol of justice and of knighthood, and are still worn by officers of all services on ceremonial occasions.

See also ARMOUR; FENCING.

Sword Lily, see GLADIOLUS.

Swordfish, *Xiphias gladius,* the single species of the mackerel-like family Xiphiidae in order Perciformes. Its distribution is practically universal and it occasionally occurs round the British Isles. The average size of the fish is 2 m, but in some cases it attains a length of nearly 6 m. It is peculiar in possessing an elongated, sword-shaped snout formed from the upper jaw that is strong enough to pass through the planks of boats. It feeds on small fishes, sometimes slashing at them with the 'sword'.

Swords, village in County DUBLIN, Republic of Ireland, 20 km north of Dublin, noted for the remains of St Colmcille's foundation here, and Swords Castle (13th century). Population 4133.

Swordsmanship, see FENCING, *History of Swordsmanship.*

Sybaris, ancient Greek town in Lucania, Italy, near the Gulf of Tarentum. Founded 720 by Achaeans and Troezenians it quickly rose to great prosperity, and the word 'sybarite' was used as synonymous with 'voluptuary'. In 510 BC Sybaris was attacked and destroyed by the Crotonians, who diverted the River Crathis over its ruins. The site was identified by means of electronic instruments in 1963.

Sybel, Heinrich von (1817–95), Prussian historian, born at Düsseldorf. A pupil of RANKE, he became professor at Bonn, Marburg, and Munich. He founded the *Historische Zeitschrift,* soon the most important of German historical journals, and later director of the Prussian state archives. With TREITSCHKE Sybel was the most influential interpreter of 19th-century German history, moving from initial dislike of Bismarck to enthusiastic approval, especially for the Kulturkampf.

Sycamore

Sycamore, *Acer pseudoplatanus*, seeds, called samaras, and leaves. (LEFT *Topham/Coleman;* RIGHT *Topham/Markham*)

Sycamore (from Greek *sȳkon*, fig; *moron*, mulberry), name originally given to the European FIG tree, now used in North America for *Platanus* species (see PLANE), and in England for *Acer pseudoplatanus*, a handsome spreading tree (family Aceraceae), introduced into Britain during medieval times and now thoroughly naturalised. It bears large five-lobed serrated leaves in opposite pairs and pendulous racemes of green flowers, followed by reddish-green winged fruits (samaras). The wood is white and fine-grained, and is much used by turners. The tree is often planted on account of its rapid growth to form a screen for valuable fruit trees. See FORESTRY.

Sycophant (Greek *sukophantēs*, informer; from *sukon*, fig, *phainein*, to show). The Athenians had a law which punished by death those who stripped the figs from the fig-trees consecrated to Athena, while people who informed on such malefactors were rewarded. It became the custom for evil-doers to steal these figs themselves and then accuse those whom they wished to injure. Hence, by a figure of speech, the term sycophant grew to mean anyone guilty of a hypocritical or blackmailing offence, and, since an informer has to curry favour with those in authority, a sycophant today is regarded as a flatterer and parasite of his superiors.

Sydenham, Thomas (1624–89), British physician, born in Dorset, who was the founder of clinical medicine, and one of the first to recognise the importance of diet in resistance to disease. He was admitted a commoner of Magdalen Hall, Oxford, in 1642 and about 1648 obtained a fellowship of All Souls College. Subsequently he left Oxford, and having taken the degree of doctor of medicine at Cambridge (1676), settled in London. In 1666 Sydenham published his first work, a treatise on fevers. An enlarged edition of this appeared under a new name in 1675. Remarks on the epidemic diseases of London from 1675 to 1680, a treatise on dropsy and on the gout,

and a tract on the rise of a new fever were his other principal publications.

Bibliography: K. Dewhurst, *Dr Thomas Sydenham, 1624–89,* 1966.

Sydenham, see LEWISHAM.

Sydney, Algernon, see SIDNEY, ALGERNON.

Sydney, chief port of Australia, and capital of New South Wales, situated on PORT JACKSON inlet. Sydney was founded by Captain Arthur Phillip, who had been sent to Australia to establish a penal colony. He landed at Botany Bay in 1788, but finding it unsuitable for settlement, he proceeded to Port Jackson. The harbour at Sydney has a safe entrance and is regarded as one of the most beautiful and perfect harbours in the world. The area of the harbour is 54 km², of which approximately half has a depth of over 9 m at low water; the foreshores, which are irregular, extend over 142 km and afford facilities for extensive wharfage. Sydney carries practically all the overseas trade of New South Wales, and nearly half that of Australia. The southern shores are indented by numerous bays, whose waters are filled with shipping from all parts of the world. Over 34 million t of shipping entered and cleared the port in 1973–74. The harbour is crossed, in one span of 503 m, by a steel arch bridge, the Sydney Harbour Bridge, opened in 1932, carrying a roadway, two footways, and four railway lines. Sydney's impressive opera house was opened in 1973. Sydney University, founded in 1850, was attended in 1975 by 17,500 students. The University of New South Wales, also in Sydney, had 15,600 students in 1974. Macquarie University opened in 1966 and now has 5000 students. The city has many parks, and beautiful surfing beaches like Manly and Bondi. Boating and sailing in the harbour are popular sports. The mean seasonal range of temperature is only 9 °C from 21 °C in summer to 12 °C in winter; and the normal annual rainfall is 1194 mm. Sydney is the chief centre and terminus of the New South Wales railway system, and is served internally by a network of railways, buses, and ferries. Kingsford-Smith Airport at Sydney is an international air terminus, and also handles a considerable volume of domestic traffic. Sydney is the manufacturing as well as the commercial centre of New South Wales, and most types of products, except basic iron and steel, are produced there. Population (1975) 2,922,760.

Bibliography: R. Park, *Sydney*, 1974.

Sydney, seaport of Cape Breton Island, Nova Scotia, Canada. It is the centre of a coal-mining region which produces some 2,000,000 t of coal a year. The Dominion steel company established a plant there in 1890 making use of local coal and iron ore imported from Newfoundland. Increased competition from steel plants in central Canada resulted in the proposed closure of the mill in 1967, but because of the great importance of the industry to the economy of the area the plant was taken over by the provincial government. The main products are iron ingots and blooms, wire, and rails. Metal fabricating plants have been attracted to the area by the availability of iron and steel. Population 33,230.

'Sydney Daily Telegraph', Australian newspaper, established in 1879, and published in Sydney. A progressive paper with a strong editorial policy, it covers Austral-

ian and international affairs with additional features and a comprehensive sports report. Associated papers are the *Sydney Sunday Telegraph*, *Australian Women's Weekly*, *The Bulletin*, and *Everybody's*.

'Sydney Morning Herald', Australia's oldest newspaper, established in 1831 and published in Sydney. It gives wide local and overseas news cover, and special attention to politics and international affairs. It carries the largest volume of classified advertising in New South Wales. Associated newspapers are the *Sun*, *Sun-Herald*, and *Australian Financial Review*.

Sydney, University of, New South Wales, Australia, the oldest university in Australasia, founded in 1850 and granted a royal charter in 1858. Teaching and research is conducted in agriculture, architecture, arts, dentistry, divinity, economics, education, engineering, law, medicine, music, science, social work, and veterinary science. The library holds 2 million volumes. There are about 1200 academic staff members and student enrolment numbers 17,500. The University is financed principally by the Commonwealth government together with some private donations and bequests.

Syene, ancient name for ASWĀN.

Syenite, a coarse-grained igneous rock composed of alkali feldspar and up to 20 per cent ferro-magnesian

Sydney. *(Camera Press)*

minerals (usually biotite). Syenites occur as minor intrusions in alkaline rock complexes and are the coarse-grained equivalent of the lava TRACHYTE.

Syktyvkar (formerly *Ust Sysolsk*), town in the northeast European RSFSR, USSR, the capital and cultural centre of the KOMI ASSR. It has a large timber industry, and has been known since the late 16th century. During the 17th and 18th centuries it had a flourishing grain and fur trade. Population (1975) 152,000.

Sylhet, town and district in north-eastern BANGLADESH, the centre of the Surma Valley area where much tea is grown. The 13th century saw a great influx of settlers here from Central Asia; the Moguls took the town in 1612. Sylhet was formerly included in ASSAM, but the area became part of East Pakistan after a plebiscite. Natural gas at Manpur, with reserves estimated at 566,350 m³ a day for the next 35 years, supplies the fuel for the fertiliser factory at Fenchuganj. Cement is produced at nearby Chhatak. Cane for furniture is the main cottage industry. Shell is undertaking an oil search in the area. Population (1974) 45,000.

Syllabus, Papal, two lists of heresies and errors condemned by papal authority. The better known is the syllabus of Pius IX (1864), which condemned no less than 80 errors dealing with almost every department of modern thought. The syllabus of Pius X, the decree *Lamentabili sane exitu*, was issued in 1907, and condemns the chief tenets of MODERNISM in 65 theses. This syllabus is supplemented by the oath against modernism imposed in 1910.

Syllepsis (Greek *sun*, together; *lambanein*, to take), figure of speech in which one word acts in a sentence with two or more others; it applies properly to each of the other words, but the sense differs in each case. An example taken from Dickens is 'Miss Bolo went home in a flood of tears and a sedan chair'; one from Pope is 'This general is a great taker of snuff as well as of towns'.

Syllepsis differs from the allied figure ZEUGMA, with which it is often identified, by being grammatically correct, while in zeugma the single word actually fails to make sense with one of the two to which it is applied. See also FIGURE OF SPEECH.

Syllogism (Greek *sun*, together, and *logos*, thought; i.e. the joining together in thought of two propositions), in LOGIC 'the act of thought by which from two given propositions we proceed to a third proposition, the truth of which necessarily follows from the truth of these given propositions' (Jevons). The first two propositions in the syllogism are called the premisses and the last the conclusion, e.g. mercury is not solid; mercury is a metal; therefore some metal is not solid. The three propositions of a syllogism are made up of three ideas or terms, called the major, the minor, and the middle. The subject of the conclusion, which necessarily follows from the premisses, is called the minor term; its predicate is the major term, and the middle term is that which shows the connection between the major and minor terms in the conclusion. Syllogisms are sometimes divided into single, complex, conjunctive, etc., and sometimes into categorical, hypothetical, conditional, etc. The special rules of the syllogism are: (1) Every syllogism has three, and only

three, terms. (2) Every syllogism contains three, and only three, propositions. (3) The middle term must be distributed (i.e. taken universally) once at least, and must not be ambiguous. (4) No term must be distributed in the conclusion which was not distributed in one of the premisses. (5) From negative premisses nothing can be inferred. (6) If one premiss be negative, the conclusion must be negative; and vice versa, to prove a negative conclusion one of the premisses must be negative; and as corollaries from the above, the following two special rules. (7) From two particular premisses no conclusion can be drawn. (8) If one premiss be particular, the conclusion must be particular (Jevons). A bad syllogism, with one of the premisses implied only, is the first source of fallacy.

Sylphs, see ELEMENTAL SPIRITS.

Sylt, largest of the North Frisian Islands, forming part of the *Land* of SCHLESWIG-HOLSTEIN, West Germany. It has an area of 98 km² and is connected to the mainland at Klanxbüll by the Hindenburg dam. Its chief town is Westerland (population 12,500) on the western coast, a popular resort. Island population 24,000.

Sylva, Carmen, see ELIZABETH (Queen of Romania).

Sylvester I, Saint, Pope (bishop of Rome), 314–35, born in Rome, successor of St Melchaides. It was during his pontificate that Constantine the Great legalised the Christian religion and terminated the age of persecution. Sylvester founded the Roman basilicas of St John Lateran, St Peter, and St Paul. He was buried in a church built over the catacomb of Priscilla; his feast is on 31 December.

Sylvester II, Gerbert d'Aurillac, Pope, 999–1003, Benedictine monk and scholar who succeeded Gregory V. He obtained letters from the emperor recognising the temporal authority of the Holy See.

Sylvester, Joshua (1563–1618), English poet and translator, born in Kent. He is best known for his translation from the French of du BARTAS's *Divine Weekes and Workes* (first complete edition, 1608), an epic on the early sections of the Bible which was very popular in the first half of the 17th century, was safely orthodox on matters of natural science and theology, and may have influenced Shakespeare and Milton, among others. Sylvester was appointed groom of the Chamber to Prince Henry, 1606.

Bibliography: G. C. Taylor, *Milton's Use of Du Bartas*, 1934; L. B. Campbell, *Divine Poetry and Drama in 16th Century England*, 1959.

Sylviculture, see SILVICULTURE.

Sylvine, or sylvite, naturally occurring form of potassium chloride (KCl). It crystallises in the cubic system, is white in colour, and soluble in water (hardness 2; specific gravity 1·9). It occurs in bedded salt deposits. Deposits of DEVONIAN age are mined in New Mexico and Texas, and most is used as a fertiliser.

Symbiosis (Latin, living together), a constant intimate relationship between separate and dissimilar organisms. Symbiosis includes many types of associations which are often further specified as: *Mutualism*, a bilaterally advantageous symbiotic association; *Commensalism*, a situation in which only one of the partners profits. It is also applied to situations characterised by no obvious advantages or disadvantages; *Parasitism*, an association in which there is overt exploitation of one partner by the other, leading ultimately to severe injury or death; *Parasymbiosis* is a living together of organisms without either mutual harm or benefit. The term is also used to indicate symbioses in which there is no physical contact, e.g., in certain associations of bacteria where a useful or necessary compound (often a vitamin or other growth substance) made by one may diffuse from the donor to the recipient.

Examples of symbioses are LICHENS, where the separate partners or *bionts* are fungi and algae; MYCORRHIZA, which are fungi living in association with higher plants; ROOT NODULES containing symbiotic nitrogen-fixing *Rhizobia*; and endozoic algae known as *Zoochlorellae* or *Zooxanthellae*. The most well known endozoic alga is *Zoochlorella*, found in the gut of the coelenterate sea-animal *Hydra*. Unicellular algae form symbiotic associations with a wide range of invertebrates, primarily marine species, and are found in protozoa to protochordates. Insects also have symbiotic bacteria and fungi in their guts, and the protozoa that are in the mammalian gut probably have a similar function, assisting in the breakdown of foodstuffs and in the provision of certain vitamins. Very frequently symbiosis is an association of an autotrophic species (capable of synthesising food from air, water and sunlight), and heterotrophic species (feeding on organic matter) where the synthetic ability of the autotroph is used by the heterotroph in exchange for its providing a suitable environment for growth.

Symbolism, the representation, particularly in religion or art, of an idea or an emotion by a natural or material image. For example, the lion occurs frequently as a symbol of courage, while the lamb is one of meekness. Symbols include types, enigmas, parables, fables, allegories, emblems, and hieroglyphics. Some readily suggest what they represent; others often seem in no way related, the connection in some cases perhaps being due to a long-forgotten association of ideas.

From earliest times men have sought to express through symbols the mysteries of their experience. The world's religions are rich in poetic images of divine truth, motifs, allegories, icons, and symbols; their forms of ritual, as well as the fabric and architecture of their buildings, demonstrate how symbols are inextricably linked with religious faith and worship. The sacraments of the Christian religion are themselves, for example, the outward symbols of inward spiritual grace.

Ancient and often universal symbols are frequently embodied in oral tradition, folk tales, and mythology, and the relationships between such symbols and religious belief were investigated by the psychologists FREUD and JUNG. While Freud concluded that religion derived from fundamental sexual and family images, Jung proposed that there are certain recurring images, or archetypes, common to all cultures and which exist in what he termed the 'collective unconscious'. Symbols found in many ancient myths include the fountain, the underworld, the tree of life, the circle, the sun, and the moon.

Symbolism, so deeply rooted in human consciousness, has long been important in art, either overtly or implicitly. The use of symbols to convey meaning in words is apparent in ancient Hebrew, Greek, and Roman literature, while the parables of the New Testament can be seen as spontaneous symbols. Carrying greater intensity of meaning and allusion than METAPHOR, symbolism is the artist's attempt to perceive unity in diversity, or to draw together seemingly unrelated experiences. In such a way, the poetry and pictures of William BLAKE, who uses simple-seeming symbols to convey complicated and universal theories of truth, are a fascinating example. Old English literature is noted for its use of impressive and sometimes enigmatic symbols; religious symbols, as well as those derived from the unconscious, also occur in 13th-century metrical romances, as they do in later chivalric poetry and prose. The rose, a much-used medieval symbol, is the focus for the ROMAN DE LA ROSE, an example of ALLEGORY, or extended symbolism. Such use of symbolism appears throughout the history of literature and art in works as disparate as Swift's *Gulliver's Travels* and Botticelli's *Primavera*. It is a particular feature of poetic imagery, in verse or prose, often acting on a subconscious level; famous literary examples include Shakespeare's use of the storm in *King Lear* and Dickens's of the fog in *Bleak House*.

In 19th-century France there arose the Symbolist movement in poetry, a deliberate protest against naturalism and realism (see SYMBOLISTE, L'ÉCOLE). In seeking more suggestive, allusive, and subtle images, the Symbolists took Romantic theory a step forward (see ROMANTIC MOVEMENT). Symbolism was an intellectual approach, stressing the absolute significance of words as keys with which to unlock the doors of perception. They sought inspiration in music and adopted in particular the *leitmotif* of WAGNER as an example in music of what they strove to achieve in literature.

The French Symbolists introduced the concept of *modernismo* to Spanish and Portuguese literature, and influenced both T. S. ELIOT and W. B. YEATS. Eliot's regard for the neglected METAPHYSICAL POETS sprang from recognition that their 'obscure' imagery was in fact attempting to convey elusive experience directly in words. Symbolism also influenced Russian literature, and the work and ideas of Ezra POUND and the IMAGISTS, RILKE, and Paul VALÉRY, while painters attempted to emulate Symbolist poets by conveying emotion directly on to canvas. Poets and novelists of the late 19th and 20th centuries made much more conscious use of symbolism, constructing large novels, for example, around related groups of symbols, as did D. H. LAWRENCE in *The Rainbow* and *Women in Love*.

The new light shed on symbolism by psychologists working on the interpretation of dreams has sometimes encouraged critics to seek out symbols which are not always there. Symbolism is now widely used in poetry, novels, films, and plays; the danger in its too-eager use lies in allowing the symbols to obscure, rather than illuminate, the work.

See also ALLEGORY; ALPHABET; FABLE; PARABLE.

Bibliography: A. Symons, *The Symbolist Movement in Literature*, 1899; H. Bayley, *The Lost Language of Symbolism*, 1912; A. N. Whitehead, *Symbolism*, 1928; W. Empson, *Seven Types of Ambiguity*, 1930; E. Wilson, *Axel's Castle*, 1931; E. Bevan, *Symbolism and Belief*, 1937; A. Farrar, *A Rebirth of Images*, 1949; J. Chiari, *Symbolism from Poe to Mallarmé*, 1957; C. Chadwick, *Symbolism*, 1971.

Symbolist Movement, The, in painting, evolved from the literary movement in France c. 1886 and likewise had its roots in 19th-century Romanticism. An idealistic reaction against the scientific objectivity of IMPRESSIONISM and REALISM, it rejected naturalistic representation in favour of painting from memory and exercising the imagination to distil the 'idea' of a subject and transcend physical appearance. Synthesism and Cloisonnisme are synonymous with Symbolism. In 1889 GAUGUIN and other Pont-Aven artists exhibited 'Synthesist' paintings which expressed subjective mood and emotion and were executed in bright areas of colour separated by black lines. The simplified, decorative features of Symbolism are found in Gauguin and Van GOGH and in Maurice DENIS and the NABIS. The more literary side of the style is expressed by Gustave MOREAU, Puvis de CHAVANNES, and Odilon REDON with whom the Symbolists claimed kinship. The group held 12 exhibitions at Le Barc de Boutteville Gallery between 1891 and 1896.

Bibliography: J. Milner, *Symbolists and Decadents*, 1971; E. Lucie-Smith, *Symbolist Art*, 1972; P. Jullian, *The Symbolists*, 1974.

Symboliste, L'École, French literary movement representing a reaction against the objective, impersonal poetry of the Parnassians (see PARNASSIANS, THE). Their aim was to write poetry that was not 'plastic' and descriptive like that of the Parnassians, but 'fluid', suggestive and evocative, expressing the poet's innermost feelings and impressions and the depths of his soul by means of symbols.

They sought to go even further than the Romantics (see ROMANTIC MOVEMENT) in breaking away from the rigid traditional French versification and so they introduced *vers libéré* (which employed new metres and made innovations in the use of the traditional 12-syllabled alexandrine, but still depended on syllabic patterns and rhyme) and the even more revolutionary *verse libre* (which dispensed both with metrical regularity and with rhyme). The ideals of the movement are admirably expressed in VERLAINE's poem 'L'art poétique', and its beginnings may be dated around 1884. Among the best known Symbolist poets are MALLARMÉ, Verlaine, RIMBAUD, LAFORGUE, Henri de RÉGNIER, MORÉAS, Tristan Corbière, VILLIERS DE L'ISLE-ADAM, SAMAIN, and KAHN. BAUDELAIRE, who is sometimes grouped with the Symbolists, is better described as a precursor.

Symbolism also influenced the theatre, in particular the plays of MAETERLINCK and CLAUDEL. The Symbolists founded a number of periodicals, foremost among them the *Mercure de France* which became their official journal.

Bibliography: G. Kahn, *Symbolistes et décadents*, 1902, and *Les Origines du symbolisme*, 1936; S. Johansen, *Le Symbolisme*, 1945; A. M. Schmidt, *La Littérature symboliste*, 1942; G. Michaud, *Le Message poétique du symbolisme* (4 vols), 1947; P. Martino, *Parnasse et symbolisme*, rev. ed. 1964; J. R. Lawler, *The Language of French Symbolism*, 1969.

Symbols. A symbol is a conventional sign employed to convey a meaning, and is to be distinguished from impromptu, unintentional, or accidental signs. Objects and even gestures are sometimes employed as symbols, e.g., a bishop's crosier, a salute. Civilised man characteris-

The Symbolist Movement. *April* by Maurice Denis, 1892. *(Rijksmuseum Kröller-Müller, Otterloo)*

tically employs graphic or written symbols, of which an enormous number and variety are in common use. Examples are afforded by the letters of any alphabet, which are symbols standing for uttered sounds. Special subjects of study, such as the sciences and music, have their own codes of symbols, and these are usually internationally recognised. Some of them—the 'letter' symbols—are borrowed from alphabets and endowed with special meanings, but others have unique forms. Examples of both forms are given in the tables.

Chemistry and Alchemy. A capital letter symbol in chemistry usually means one atom of an element. Thus, O means one atom of oxygen. O_2 means one molecule of oxygen, consisting of two atoms. O_3 means one molecule of triatomic oxygen or ozone. Some symbols are derived from the Latin or Greek names of the elements, such as Fe (*ferrum*), iron; Au (*aurum*), gold; Hg (*hydrargyrum*), mercury. Such symbols are used in constructing chemical formulae, such as H_2O, which means one molecule of water, consisting of two atoms of hydrogen and one of oxygen. These symbols, introduced by Berzelius in 1818, superseded those of John Dalton (1803), who used circles enclosing either letters or distinguishing marks.

⨀	zinc	⊙	nitrogen
⊙	hydrogen	⊕	phosphorus
⊕	sulphur		

The earlier alchemists employed multifarious symbols for their four 'elements' and other substances. These varied from age to age and country to country. Examples are shown in table 2.

For meteorology symbols, see WEATHER FORECAST.

Bibliography: British Standards Institution, *3939: Graphical symbols for electrical power, telecommunications and electronics diagrams*, 1966 onwards, and *British Standard 1991: Part 1: 1967: Letter symbols, signs and abbreviations;* Symbols Committee of the Royal Society, *Quantities, Units, and Symbols*, 1971; H. Dreyfuss and R. Buckminster Fuller (Eds), *Symbol Sourcebook*, 1972.

Syme, James (1799–1870), British surgeon, born in Edinburgh. He studied anatomy under his cousin, Robert LISTON. At the age of 18 he discovered a method of making waterproof cloth, but C. Macintosh of Glasgow took out a patent for it and made a fortune from the 'macintosh'. Syme became a fellow of the College of Surgeons in 1823. He soon gained a great reputation as a surgeon. In 1829 he opened a surgical hospital at Minto House, which soon rivalled the Royal Infirmary in reputation. This small hospital has been immortalised by John Brown in his essay *Rab and his Friends*. In 1833 Syme was appointed to the chair of clinical surgery at Edinburgh and surgeon to the Royal Infirmary. In 1848 he accepted a similar chair at University College, London, but remained there for only a few months and returned to Edinburgh, being reinstated in his old professorship, which he retained until 1869. He was succeeded by Lister, who had been his house surgeon and who married his daughter. Many of his operations have become classics of

Symbols. Table 1.

Aeronautics

γ	dihedral angle	ϵ	angle of downwash	λ	damping coefficient
α	angle of attack	θ	angle of pitch	η	propeller efficiency
ψ	angle of yaw	ϕ	angle of roll or bank	Ω	torque

Astronomy and Astrology

☌	conjunction	☊	ascending node	♂	Mars
☍	opposition	☋	descending node	♃	Jupiter
◻	quadrature	i	inclination of orbit to ecliptic	♄	Saturn
●	new moon	α	right ascension	⛢ } Uranus	
☽	first quarter	δ	declination		
☾	last quarter	☿	Mercury	♆	Neptune
○	full moon	♀	Venus	♇	Pluto
☉	sun	⊕	Earth, solar halo		
▽	lunar halo				
▽	lunar corona	For the signs of the Zodiac, see ZODIAC.			
◐	solar corona				

Botany

ᚎ	tree	♀	female	∞	indefinite number of parts
♂ ♂ } male		☿	hermaphrodite, monoclinous	⊕	regular, actinomorphic
		✕	hybrid	↓ ·↓· } irregular zygomorphic	

Alchemy

▽	earth	♂	gold	△	sulphur
△	air	♄	lead	⚇	arsenic
△	fire	☿	mercury	⊖	salt
▽	water	♂	iron	☿	the hypothetical
☽	silver	♀	copper		'philosopher's stone'

Electricity and Magnetism

E	electromotive force	ϵ	permittivity	▱	modulator, demodulator or discriminator
V	potential	μ	permeability		
I	current	μ_0	permeability of a vacuum	—	direct current
J	current density			~	alternating current
G	conductance	Ψ	electric flux	÷	earth
B	susceptance	Φ	magnetic flux	⊣⊢	cell of battery or accumulator (long line represents positive pole, short line negative pole)
X	reactance	k or X_m	magnetic susceptibility		
Y	admittance				
Z	impedance	ϕ	phase displacement		
Q	charge	$+$	positive		battery of cells
L	inductance	$-$	negative	⊏⊐ or ⏦	resistance
C	capacitance	⌢	bell		inductor
⊗	signal lamp	▷ or ▷	amplifier	⊏⊐ or ⊙⊙	fuse
				⊣⊢	condenser, capacitor

Mathematics

$+$	(plus), addition	$\sqrt{}$	root, square root
$-$	(minus), subtraction	$|a|$	absolute value of a
$\pm$	plus or minus	$\parallel$	is parallel to
$\times$	multiplication	∦	is not parallel to
$\div$	division	$\perp$	is perpendicular to
$=$	is equal to	$\propto$	is proportional to
$\neq$	is not equal to	:	ratio, is to
$\approx$	is approximately equal to	∞	infinity
$>$	is greater than	$!$	factorial
$<$	is less than	Σ	sum
$\not>$	is not greater than	$\int$	integral
$\not<$	is not less than	Δ	finite difference
$\ll$	is much less than	Π	product
$\gg$	is much greater than	e	$\approx 2\cdot7182818$ (see Exponential
$\equiv$	is identically equal to, is congruent to (in geometry)		Function)
$\therefore$	therefore	i	square root of minus one
$\because$	because	r	radius
$\angle$	angle	π	(pi) ratio of circumference to diameter of circle
$\llcorner$	right angle		
Δ	triangle	$\cup$	union of two sets
$\in$	is a member of	$\cap$	intersection of two sets
$\subset$	is a subset of	$\varnothing$	empty set
D, d	differential	°	degrees of arc
∂	partial differentiation	'	see Prime
δ	increment, variation		

Pharmacy

℞	take	ss	half	O	pint
ℨ	drachm	āā	of each	ℳ	mix
℥	fluid ounce	C	gallon	♏	minimum or drop
℈	scruple				

Physics and Mechanics

μ	coefficient of friction; reduced mass $= \dfrac{m_1 m_2}{(m_1 + m_2)}$	λ	wavelength
		L or N_A	Avogadro's number
		Z	atomic number
γ	surface tension	h	Planck's constant
ρ	density, radius of curvature	$\hbar$	$h/2\pi$
p	pressure	G	universal gravitational constant
E	Young's Modulus	g	gravitational acceleration
ω	angular velocity	a	acceleration
α	fine structure constant $\mu_0 e^2 c/2h$	u	initial velocity
e	elementary charge (of proton)	v	final velocity
m_e	(rest) mass of electron	c	speed of light (or electromagnetic waves) in vacuo
k	Boltzmann's constant		
R	gas constant	d, s	distance
σ	standard deviation; Stefan-Boltzmann constant	n	principal quantum number; refractive index
A	relative atomic mass ('atomic weight')	L, l	orbital angular momentum quantum number
E	total energy	S	spin angular momentum quantum number
		M	magnetic quantum number
		T	kinetic energy

Symbols. Table 2.

surgery. He was a bold, resourceful, skilful surgeon, 'the Napoleon of surgery', one of the first to adopt ether anaesthesia and a champion of Lister's antiseptic method. Syme made many contributions to surgical literature, among them *Treatise on the Excision of Diseased Joints*, 1831, and *Principles of Surgery*, 1831.

Bibliography: J. A. Shepherd, *Simpson and Syme of Edinburgh*, 1969.

Symmetry. In geometry, the points P and P' are symmetric with respect to a third point C (called the centre of symmetry) if C is the mid-point of the line segment PP'. Points P and P' are symmetric with respect to a line L (called the axis of symmetry) if L is the perpendicular bisector of PP'. Points P and P' are symmetric with respect to a plane π (called the plane of symmetry) if π is the perpendicular bisector of PP'.

A geometric figure is symmetric with respect to a point, a line, or a plane if it consists of pairs of points which are symmetric about the point, line, or plane. If a plane figure is symmetric about an axis, or a surface or solid is symmetric about a plane, then the axis or plane divides the figure into two parts each of which is the reflection of the other in the axis or plane.

A symmetric FUNCTION is a function of two or more variables whose values are unchanged by the interchange of pairs of variables. For example, the function $f: \mathbf{R}^3 \rightarrow \mathbf{R}$, given by

$$f(x, y, z) = xyz + x^2 + y^2 + z^2,$$

is symmetric.

A relation Φ in a set A is symmetric if $\Phi = \Phi^{-1}$, that is, if $y \in \Phi(x)$ if and only if $x \in \Phi(y)$. The relation 'is a brother of' in the set of human beings is symmetric. The relation $=$ ('is equal to') in any set is symmetric. A relation Θ is antisymmetric if $x \in \Theta(y)$ and $y \in \Theta(x)$ imply $x = y$. The relation $\leqslant$ ('is less than or equal to') in the set of real numbers is antisymmetric.

Symmetry is used more loosely to describe crystalline repetitive similarity, for bilateral and radial symmetry in zoology, for botanic structures, and in art and material objects generally.

Symmetry Principles, see CONSERVATION LAWS OF PHYSICS.

Symonds, John Addington (1840–93), English poet and critic, born in Bristol; educated at Harrow and Balliol College, Oxford. He wrote good critical lives of SHELLEY, 1878, Sir Philip SIDNEY, 1886, and MICHELANGELO, 1893, and his *Autobiography of Benvenuto Cellini*, 1888, and his versions of the sonnets of Michelangelo and CAMPANELLA, show his flair for translation. Other works are his *History of the Italian Renaissance* (seven volumes), 1875–86, *Studies of the Greek Poets*, 1873–76, and *Shakespeare's Predecessors in the English Drama*, 1884. His *Letters* were edited by H. M. Schneller and R. L. Peter, 1968.

Bibliography: M. Symonds, *Last Days of J. A. Symonds*, 1906, and *Out of the Past*, 1925; P. Grosskurth, *John Addington Symonds*, 1964.

Symons, Arthur (1865–1945), Welsh poet and critic. Influenced by the French Symbolists (see SYMBOLISTE, L'ÉCOLE), in 1889 he published a book of verses, *Days and Nights*. His next two volumes of poetry, *Silhouettes*,

1892, and *London Nights*, 1895, showed the influence of VERLAINE, but the decisive influence upon his work was the aesthetic doctrine of Walter PATER. Though Symons never succeeded in constructing a system of aesthetics, he deserves to be remembered as a critic for such works as *Introduction to the Study of Browning*, 1886, *Studies in Two Literatures*, 1897, *Aubrey Beardsley*, 1898, *The Symbolist Movement in Literature*, 1899, a pioneer work in which he introduced to England the French poets of the later 19th century, *Studies in Seven Arts*, 1906, and his *Confessions: a Study in Pathology*, 1930, in which he analysed his own mental collapses of 1908.

Among his later works were *The Romantic Movement in English Poetry*, 1909, and *Studies in the Elizabethan Drama*, 1919. He also wrote books on Blake, 1907, Hardy, 1927, Wilde, 1930, and Pater, 1932.

Bibliography: A. Waugh, *Tradition and Change*, 1919; W. B. Yeats, *Autobiographies*, 1926; R. Lhombreaud, *Arthur Symons*, 1963.

Sympathetic Inks, see INK.

Symphonic Poem, or 'tone-poem', an orchestral form finding its inspiration in an extra-musical work such as a painting, poem, or perhaps folk-legends. A distinction can be made between the narrative tone-poem, such as Strauss's *Till Eulenspiegel*, the character piece, such as Elgar's *Falstaff*, and the atmospheric tone-poem which does not attempt to portray characters or events. A great variety of orchestral pieces have been produced in this genre, ranging from the macabre effects of Musorgski's *Night on the Bare Mountain* to the luxurious *Prélude à l'Après-midi d'un Faune* by Debussy.

Symphony, musical composition for orchestra, generally on a large scale, and possessing more architectural complexity and organic unity than the other orchestral forms. It evolved partly in Italy from the operatic overture and partly in the works of the Mannheim school of composers. In the classical period it became one of the most important genres allied to SONATA form and achieved its first definitive form in the hands of Haydn and Mozart: that of a generally four-movement work, the first movement (and sometimes others) in sonata-form, the second being slow and the third dance-like. Beethoven substituted the more robust scherzo for the minuet-type of third movement, and in his nine symphonies (the Ninth with solo voices and chorus in a vastly expanded finale) raised the form to heights of expressive and philosophical power which set a standard few later composers have approached. Schubert impressed his own personality on the purely classical form, and a classical ideal of formal perfection, tinged with increasingly strong Romantic elements, can be traced in the symphonies of Mendelssohn, Schumann and Brahms. Meanwhile Berlioz and Liszt introduced programmatic elements and the principle of themes appearing (sometimes metamorphosed) in different movements. Wagner's extended sense of time-scale affected the mighty, almost neo-Baroque symphonies of Bruckner; nationalist elements made themselves felt in those of Dvořák, Borodin and Tchaikovsky. At the turn of the century, hyper-expressive, almost confessional, elements were represented in the work of Mahler, who said that the symphony must contain the world; while Sibelius stood for the ideal of its perfection of form and organic unity of material. Between these antipodes the 20th-century symphony has charted a wavering course. The form has assumed many strange guises (single-movement structures becoming quite common), and has often been declared 'dead'; but it continues to represent the largest kind of public statement that a composer can make in purely musical terms, and so to demand the most sustained exercise of his creative powers. Notable symphonists of this century have been Elgar, Nielsen, Vaughan Williams, Martinů, Roberto Gerhard and Shostakovich among others.

Bibliography: R. Simpson (Ed.), *The Symphony*, 1967.

Symphyla, a class of phylum ARTHROPODA that contains 120 species of tiny centipede-like animals that live in the soil and in leaf mould. They are 2–10 mm long. The head has two long antennae, and the body has 12 segments, each bearing two legs, and a tail segment. They are found throughout the world except in very cold regions. Since they are so small, live in the soil and eat decayed vegetation, they are rarely noticed except for one species that may attack living plants.

Symphytum, see COMFREY.

Sympodium, see MONOPODIUM.

Symposium (Greek *sumposion*, a drinking party). The title was used by both Plato and Xenophon for books describing the conversations of Socrates and others, and the term has therefore come to mean a conference or general discussion. It is also used to signify a collection of opinions on a given subject by various contributors.

Symptom, any change that an individual notices himself when suffering from an illness. The term originally meant the disease itself, but with increasing knowledge about the unseen causes of disease (e.g. bacteria or biochemical changes) it has come to mean a way in which a disease shows itself to the patient, for example by pain, loss of appetite, weakness, loss of sensation, or a change in bowel habit. See also CLINICAL SIGNS; DIAGNOSIS.

Synagogue (Greek *sunagōgē*, an assembly), Jewish place of worship. The date of origin is uncertain. At Jerusalem, an inscription records the existence of a synagogue in the 1st century BC. The best preserved among a few ruined examples is at Capernaum, Galilee (late 2nd century AD), which is oriented southwards in the form of a basilica. The synagogue at Dura-Europos (3rd century AD) is remarkable for its frescoes. Persecution during the Middle Ages accounts for the scarcity of European examples, but at Worms there is a Romanesque synagogue and at Prague a Gothic synagogue. Two examples in Spain have been converted into Christian churches. Poland had a distinctive style of synagogue architecture, the construction being of timber and very picturesque. In the West, a Moorish style was adopted. There are important Renaissance examples at Amsterdam (1675) and Bevis Marks, London (1710). The plan of a synagogue is normally rectangular, with seats downstairs for men and a gallery for women. There is a curtained niche for the Ark opposite the entrance, with a rostrum or pulpit (*bimah*) in front of it.

In Jewish tradition, the synagogue has functioned as the *bet ha-tefilah* (house of prayer), *bet ha-midrash* (house of study), and *bet ha-knesset* (house of assembly). Its

importance from ancient times rests in its democratisation of worship, removing religion from the monopoly of priests and placing the authority on the community, thus creating patterns later adopted by the Christian church. The destruction of the temple in AD 70 marked the emergence of the synagogue as a preserving centre of Jewish life to modern times.

Synaptase, see EMULSIN.

Synchrocyclotron, or frequency-modulated cyclotron, machine to accelerate atomic particles to energies greater than those obtainable with a conventional CYCLOTRON. The principle was suggested independently by Veksler in the USSR, and E. M. McMillan in the USA in 1945. The construction is similar to that of the cyclotron, but instead of a fixed-frequency electric field between the 'dees' there is a changing frequency. As the particle attains higher energies it suffers a relativistic increase of mass and takes longer to traverse the half-circle within the dee. The frequency of the applied electric field is therefore reduced steadily to keep in step with the particle, and a synchronising action takes place which allows much higher energies to be attained. When a certain minimum frequency is reached, a pulse of protons is extracted from the machine by a subsidiary device. The frequency is then increased to the value appropriate to the speed of the injected protons and the cycle repeated. The path of the proton during its acceleration is a spiral. The first machine to be built was the modified 467-cm cyclotron in Berkeley, California, completed in 1946. It produced 350-MeV protons (see ELECTRON VOLT) with a variation of the frequency of the oscillator between 23 and 15·9 MHz with about 60 pulses per second. For yet higher energies the SYNCHROTRON is used.

Synchromesh Gears, see MOTOR-CARS, *Transmission*.

Synchronised Swimming, see SWIMMING.

Synchroniser, relay-operated automatic switch for connecting an alternator to the busbars when it has been run up to the speed, phase, and voltage of other alternators on the same busbars. It is used in telecontrol of power stations. For manual operation a synchroscope is used.

Synchroscope, instrument indicating when two alternators are running at the same speed and phase. When an alternator is to be connected to busbars which are already connected to one or more other alternators it is necessary that the speed, phase, and voltage of the incoming machine should be the same as those of the busbars. The synchroscope is an instrument for indicating the speed and phase differences. A rotor carrying a pointer and coils energised by the incoming machine is free to rotate inside fixed coils which are energised from the busbars. The rotor rotates at a speed equal to the frequency difference between the incoming machine and the busbars. The direction of rotation depends upon which source has the higher frequency and the displacement of the pointer from its zero position is a measure of the instantaneous phase difference. The correct moment for connection is when the pointer is stationary, or almost so, at the zero position.

Synchrotron, or proton synchrotron, machine designed to accelerate protons to energies greater than those obtainable with the CYCLOTRON and SYNCHROCYCLOTRON. The

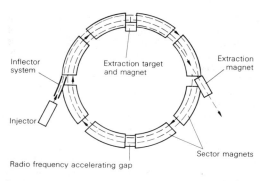

Inflector system

Extraction target and magnet

Extraction magnet

Injector

Sector magnets

Radio frequency accelerating gap

Synchrotron.

principle of action is an extension of those described for the lower-energy machines mentioned. By the simultaneous application of an increasing magnetic field and a high frequency electric field of decreasing frequency it is possible to keep the proton in a stable orbit of fixed size whilst gradually increasing its energy. The size and cost of magnets is greatly reduced because of the fixed size orbit, so that above 1000 MeV (1 GeV) proton synchrotrons are more economic than synchrocyclotrons.

The first machine was constructed at Birmingham, England, and produced 1-GeV protons. Proton synchrotrons operating include ones of 28 GeV at CERN, Geneva, 76 GeV at Serpukhov, USSR, and 500 GeV at Illinois, USA. A 300-GeV machine, which took eight years to build, was completed at CERN in 1976, and reached 400 GeV. It has a diameter of 2·4 km, and involves a 7-kilometre circumference underground tunnel for the beam.

Intersecting rings of circulating proton beams (storage rings) have been constructed at CERN using two proton beams of 28 GeV from the accelerator. Head-on collisions between these beams are equivalent to collisions of protons of greater than 1000 GeV with stationary proton targets.

See ACCELERATOR, PARTICLE.

Syncline, see FOLD.

Synchrotron. A section of the 7-GeV proton synchrotron 'Nimrod'. *(Science Research Council, Rutherford Laboratory)*

Syncopation, displacement of the musical accent to the weak beats or off-beats in the bar, the effect being that of a syncope or missing heart-beat. Syncopation is a universal musical technique, not the sole property of jazz.

Syncope (Greek *sungkopē*, cutting short), grammatical term denoting the elision or non-pronunciation of a letter in the middle of a word, as, for example, of the second 'e' in 'heav'n' and of the 'v' in 'e'er'.

Syncope, see FAINTING.

Syncrude, see SHALE OIL.

Syndicalism. The word is derived from the French *syndicat*. In France, where syndicalism originated, a syndicate did not mean, as in English, a trading company, but an organisation of working men. The fundamental difference between syndicalism and SOCIALISM lies in their attitude to the state and in the purpose for which industry is to be organised. The syndicalist, like the anarchist (see ANARCHISM), is in active hostility towards the state, which he repudiates. He sees social organisation as purely industrial and aims at organising all the workers in a trade into one union, and then to federate these unions into a national, and eventually into an international, organisation. Syndicalism organises industry in the interests of the workers in it. In theory, if not always in practice, socialism organises industry in the interests of the community as a whole.

Syndicalism made its appearance in Britain towards the end of the first decade of this century, but the general public was first made aware of its existence by the series of widespread strikes in the year 1911 (see LABOUR DISPUTE; INDUSTRIAL RELATIONS). Tom Mann, Guy Bowman, and Gaylord Wilshire were leading British syndicalists. The first international syndicalist conference was held in London in the autumn of 1913.

The intellectuals of the syndicalist movement in France were Sorel, Berth, and Lagardelle, and other chief exponents were the Italians, Labriola, Leone, and Malatesta, the Spaniard Durutti, and Leon of the USA.

The progress of syndicalism was stopped by the First World War, and many syndicalists transferred their allegiance to the Communists. Syndicalist ideas, however, have had some influence on the conception of the corporate state (see CORPORATIVE STATE) and on many modern Labour movements.

See also TRADE UNION.

Bibliography: W. A. McConacher, *Development of the Labour Movement in Great Britain, France and Germany*, 1942; F. F. Ridley, *Revolutionary Syndicalism in France: Direct Action in its Time*, 1971.

Syndicate, economic partnership of persons or companies formed to carry out a financial or industrial project. The legal basis of the partnership may vary, but usually, in the absence of express stipulation to the contrary, the partnership legally continues to the end of the venture. The formation of a syndicate is a common method of floating a company; and a syndicate is generally itself an incorporated company which, having acquired an undertaking, sells it to another company at a profit, taking either cash or shares or both in exchange, the directors and promoters of the preliminary company or syndicate, as a rule, becoming large shareholders and directors of the new company. One of the most important kinds of syndicate is that of LLOYDS. These syndicates are not usually partnerships; each name takes only his share of the risk.

A newspaper syndicate is one through which articles, stories, and cartoons are distributed among a large number of newspapers over a wide area.

Syndicate, The, see MAFIA.

Syndrome, a collection of features that taken together imply that a patient has a specific disease. Since the features may not obviously be related to each other, many syndromes are only recognised for the first time by exceptional perception or luck and are therefore named after the doctor who first described them. Occasionally a syndrome is described once, only to be forgotten, then rediscovered and published as a new observation by its new discoverer. This has led to bitter arguments about whose name the syndrome should carry. Many syndromes carry different eponyms in different countries which is confusing for doctors as well as patients.

Synecdoche (Greek *sun*, together; *ek*, out; *dechesthai*, to receive), figure of speech in which a part is used as a substitute for the whole; or the whole as a substitute for a part. Thus one term is substituted for another of more or less related meaning. An example of using a part for the whole is 'A fleet of fifty sail', and the whole for a part, 'England all out for 343'.

The figure differs from METONYMY in the closer association of the substituted word with the one it replaces, but the term metonymy is often used to cover both figures. See also FIGURE OF SPEECH.

Syngas, or SNG, synthetic gas to replace NATURAL GAS as the latter becomes less readily available. Processes based on COAL, OIL SHALE, and TAR SANDS are under investigation. Some of the gases are similar to COAL GAS.

Synge, John Millington (1871–1909), Irish dramatist, born at Rathfarnham, near Dublin, son of a barrister. Educated at Trinity College, Dublin, he studied music in Germany (1893) and literary criticism in Paris (1895), where he was 'discovered' by Yeats (1899) and persuaded to identify himself with the so-called 'Celtic Renaissance' movement. On Yeats's advice, he spent several summers in the Aran Islands, where he studied peasant customs and language, and found plots for his plays in the islanders' stories. His first play, *In the Shadow of the Glen*, 1903, was attacked by Irish critics for its portrayal of the peasantry, but that and *Riders to the Sea*, 1904, a one-act tragedy, were well-received when performed in London. When the ABBEY THEATRE became the home of the Irish dramatic revival Synge's plays entered its repertory, and he became its literary adviser and then a director. His masterpiece, *The Playboy of the Western World*, 1907, provoked riots when it was performed in Dublin, because patriotic audiences refused to believe that Irish peasants would protect a self-proclaimed murderer. It is now regarded as one of the classics of Irish theatre. His unfinished *Deirdre of the Sorrows* reverts to a legendary theme, and suggests that his talent would have developed even more impressively. The chief qualities of his work are his insight into the ordinary life of the Irish peasantry, and his lyrical feeling for their language, which he makes into a rich dramatic prose.

Other works are *The Aran Islands*, 1907; *In Wicklow, West Kerry and Connemara*, 1911; and *Poems and Translations*, 1909.

Bibliography: R. Skelton (Ed.), *Collected Works*, 1962; T. R. Henn (Ed.), *The Plays and Poems*, 1963; Study by W. B. Yeats, 1911; D. H. Greene and E. M. Stephens, *John Millington Synge, 1871–1909*, 1959; A. Price, *Synge and Anglo-Irish Drama*, 1961; R. Skelton, *The Writings of J. M. Synge*, 1971.

Synonym (Greek *sun*, together; *onoma*, word), in its narrowest sense a word which in all contexts has identical meaning to another word in the same language. Perfect synonyms barely exist, so in practice the term is used for words that are approximately equivalent. For example, *snuff it* and *decease* differ in formality, *lake* and *mere* in literary feeling, *cat* and *moggie* in regional dialect, *low* and *moo* in onomatopoeic overtones, *house* and *home* in emotive associations, *rob* and *steal* in grammatical construction following them; *kill* and *murder* are not even quite the same in their cognitive meaning (see SEMANTICS), apart from the more associative connotations of the other examples. Even with this wider interpretation, it often happens that words which are synonyms in one context fail to be interchangeable in another. For example, 'try' and 'endeavour' are usually close synonyms, but it cannot be said of a Rugby player that he scored a brilliant endeavour.

Bibliography: P. M. Roget, *International Thesaurus*, 1963, and *Thesaurus of English Words and Phrases*, 1972; *Webster's New Dictionary of Synonyms*, 1968.

Synoptic Problem, concerns the literary relationship which scholars detect between the first three (or synoptic) gospels. Which was written first, and who copied which and in what order? The phenomena to be explained are these:

(1) Some 90 per cent of Mark's 661 verses are found, very often *ipsis verbis*, in either Matthew or Luke or in both (over 600 of them in Matthew, and c. 350 in Luke).

(2) The order of Mark's narrative is reproduced similarly, either in Matthew or Luke or both.

(3) Where the wording differs at all, in a passage present in all three, Matthew and Luke very rarely agree together against Mark; one or the other usually supports him.

(4) Where there is no parallel passage in Mark (and this is chiefly in discourses) Matthew and Luke (in about 200 verses) closely resemble each other.

Practically all non-Roman Catholic scholars from C. Lachmann (1835) to the middle of the 20th century accepted as an established theory the Two-Document Hypothesis and that of Markan Priority. In other words, they maintain that Mark was written first, and was used by Matthew and Luke; and that the fourth peculiarity noted above is to be explained by their use of a second source (German *Quelle*, and so Q) which contained chiefly an account of the teaching of Christ.

The nature and the existence of the lost and hypothetical document Q has, however, been disputed, not least by Roman Catholic scholars who argue for the priority of Matthew (B. C. Butler, *The Originality of St Matthew*, 1951). An early version of the third Gospel (*Proto-Luke*) has been suggested by B. H. Streeter (*The Four Gospels*, 1924) and V. Taylor (*Behind the Third Gospel*, 1926). See MATTHEW; MARK; LUKE.

Bibliography: N. B. Stonehouse, *Origins of the Synoptic Gospels*, 1964.

Synoptic Reporting Stations, see METEOROLOGY.

Synovial Membrane, the membrane covering the articular extremities of bones and the inner surface of ligaments entering into the formation of a joint. It secretes a clear lubricating fluid with an alkaline reaction. Synovitis is inflammation of the synovial membrane. See JOINTS.

Synthetic Crude Oil, see BOGHEAD COAL; COAL, HYDROGENATION OF; SHALE OIL.

Synthetic Fibres, see FIBRES AND FIBROUS SUBSTANCES.

Synthetic Materials are materials that have been built up from simple chemical substances, and which simulate a natural product. See FIBRES AND FIBROUS SUBSTANCES; PLASTICS; RUBBER; SYNTHETIC RESINS.

Synthetic Resins, man-made polymers of many types used in a variety of ways: (1) as a film-forming emulsion, with water as the continuous phase—polyvinyl acetate, polyvinyl alcohol, and many synthetic RUBBERS, also polystyrene; (2) as a solution in a volatile solvent—all types of synthetic resins; (3) as a heat-sensitive or pressure-sensitive film—polyvinyl alcohol, urea formaldehyde, and phenol formaldehyde; and (4) as two separate components, a low polymer and a polymer catalyst, which when mixed shortly before use, react together in the joint to form a higher solid polymer—urea formaldehyde, phenol formaldehyde, and polyester resins.

Synthetic resin adhesives, developed by the modern plastics industry, set on being heated, cannot be resoftened by heat, and are water-resistant; they are being increasingly used in the manufacture of plywood and other composite timber products. See ADHESIVE; GLUE; PLASTICS.

Syntipas, see SEVEN WISE MASTERS.

Syphilis, a VENEREAL DISEASE due to infection by the bacterial organism *Treponema pallidum*. The name was created by Fracastoro of Verona in 1530, in a poem; Edwin Klebs saw the spirochaete in syphilitic material in 1875; Haensell in 1881 produced eye lesions in rabbits by inoculation of syphilitic material, and finally the role of the *Treponema* in creating syphilis was proved by transferring syphilis to primates.

The disease occurs in three stages: primary, secondary and tertiary. The primary stage usually (but not essentially) consists of a small nodule which breaks down to become an ulcerative sore (chancre), most often on the genitalia, but also occurring in some cases on the lip, tongue, anus, and other areas of the skin, depending on the site of contact. This primary manifestation then recedes and gives way to the secondary during the next one or two months: the chancre heals, and a rash appears distributed over the trunk, palms, face and legs. This eruption is very pleomorphic and mistaken diagnoses are sometimes made based on appearances alone. A moderate constitutional upset occurs during this phase, consisting of a sore throat

and raised temperature. This resolves also during the ensuing months, and often treatment is not sought owing to a mistaken belief that the disease has resolved spontaneously. The tertiary stage occurs with extreme variability, but usually appears some years after the secondary stage, presenting with destructive lesions of bone and soft tissues (gumma) and serious damage to the central nervous system and heart.

The principal lesions of the central nervous system include *tabes dorsalis* or locomotor ataxia, and general paralysis of the insane (GPI). Tabes is due to degeneration of the dorsal columns of the spinal cord, leading to inability to co-ordinate movements, eye defects and disturbances of special senses. Limb pains (lightning pains) are a feature, and errors of judgment occur. In GPI, which may appear many years after the initial infection, like tabes, the principal characteristics are psychological disturbances, such as delusions of grandeur, muscular weakness, imbalance and inco-ordination.

The investigations usually undertaken to diagnose the disease consist of recognition of *T. pallidum* in exudates from chancres, during the primary stage, and serum studies in other stages. These consist of tests performed by combining the patient's serum with known *T. pallidum* cultures and observing the effects when compared with serum from normal uninfected individuals, and non-specific tests using unrelated biological substances, which are less reliable but still in use because of the familiarity to laboratory workers and their reliability for evaluating case progress. Treatment is by penicillin, but serious reactions may occur to this series of injections and other antibiotics, such as minocycline, are now in use. The disease occurs worldwide, and man is the only known reservoir, although other mammals, for example rabbits, have venereal transmission of other strains of *Treponema*.

Congenital syphilis is syphilis caused by transmission of the organisms from the mother to infect the foetus during pregnancy, usually resulting in a stillborn infant or an abortion. A viable infant with congenital syphilis shows skin rashes, evidence of a generalised infection, and fails to thrive. The teeth are characteristically deformed, and central nervous system defects become apparent during puberty.

Non-Venereal syphilis or bejel is an acute infectious disease also due to the *T. pallidum*, but not showing the presence of a primary chancre, and only rarely progressing to serious tertiary central nervous system and cardiac disorder. It is not fatal. The disease is most common in poor living conditions, and foci exist in Eastern Europe and the Middle East. The principal manifestations of the illness are skin lesions of varying kinds such as rashes, painful fissures of the palms and soles, and pigment changes. Transmission is by contact with an infectious site, including indirect contact as in drinking from shared cups. The disease is curable, as is venereal syphilis, by antibiotics.

Syr Darya, *oblast* in UZBEK SSR, USSR; formed in 1963 from parts of Samarkand and Tashkent *oblasti*, with a few regions of the KAZAKH SSR. Most of the *oblast* is in the Betpak-Dala desert, traversed by the Syr Darya. It is an important new cotton-producing region of the USSR.

Syr Darya

Capital, Gulistan. Area 20,900 km²; population (1970) 575,000 (23 per cent urban).

Syr Darya (ancient *Jaxartes*), river of Soviet Central Asia, rises in the TIEN SHAN range and flows north-west 2212 km through the Kirgiz, Uzbek, and Kazakh SSRs into the Aral Sea. Its tributaries are used for irrigation and the river flows through the very fertile FERGANA VALLEY. The Amu and Syr Darya rivers are both important as they supply water to over half of the cultivated land of the central Asiatic republics of the USSR.

Syracuse (Italian *Siracusa*), province of Italy, in southeast SICILY. Area 2110 km². Population (1974) 365,000.

Syracuse (Italian *Siracusa*), seaport in SICILY, capital of the above province on the south-east coast, 200 km southeast of Palermo. In ancient times it was the richest and most populous city in Sicily. It was founded c.734 BC by settlers from Corinth led by Archias the Corinthian. It was at first an aristocracy, and later a democracy, until GELON made himself tyrant of Syracuse in 485 BC. Under the rule of Gelon and that of his brother, Hieron I, the city was raised to wealth and power. Hieron was succeeded by his brother, Thrasybulus, in 467, but the cruelty and rapacity of the new tyrant led to a revolt and the establishment of a democracy. The dominance of Syracuse in Sicily led to a war with Athens and in 413 BC the Athenian fleet and army were defeated. In 405 BC DIONYSIUS the Elder became tyrant of Syracuse, and in 397 BC he was victorious over the Carthaginians. In 263 BC Hieron II of Syracuse allied himself with Rome in the wars against Carthage. His successor Hieronymus (king in 216 BC) supported Carthage, and in 213 the city was besieged by MARCELLUS. When the city fell, ARCHIMEDES was among those put to death by the Romans. From this time, Syracuse became a city of the Roman province of Sicily, and its importance declined. In AD 878, the SARACENS captured and looted the city, afterwards burning it. In 1085 it was taken by the Normans, and later by Pisa, and Genoa. Syracuse forms an archbishopric with RAGUSA. Its cathedral (rebuilt 17th–18th centuries) was founded in 640 on the ruins of a temple of Minerva. Among the remarkable ancient remains are a fortress built by Dionysius, an immense Greek theatre, a Roman gymnasium, temples, aqueducts, and quarries now turned into gardens. There are 2nd–3rd century Christian catacombs, and the church of St Lucy has the saint's tomb. It is a centre in conjunction with AUGUSTA of chemical and petrochemical industries. Population (1974) 116,700.

Syracuse, city in New York state, USA. Originally an Indian settlement, it owed its early growth to the coming of the ERIE CANAL, which passed through the site. The canal was in due course followed by the New York Central Railroad's main New York–Chicago line and by the New York State Thruway, assuring Syracuse of a strategic position from which to tap for its industries the flow of freight between the Great Lakes in the west and the Hudson Valley and New York to the east. Twenty-six per cent of the workforce of the metropolitan area is engaged in manufacturing, with electrical machinery as the most important group, followed by non-electrical machines, food, and paper products. The city is the seat of Syracuse University. Population 197,208.

Syria, Republic of, an Arab state bounded to the west by the Mediterranean, the Lebanon, and by Israel, to the north by Turkey, to the east by Iraq, and to the south by Jordan. Modern Syria was formed from the Aleppo, Beirut, Damascus, Zor, and Jezira provinces of the OTTOMAN EMPIRE in the aftermath of the First World War. It achieved independence from the French Mandate in 1946. The total area is 185,000 km².

Geography. Relief and Climate. The physiography of Syria may be divided into four sections, which correspond also with climatic variations. The first is a narrow coastal zone backed by the Jebel Ansarieh, a range of mountains running from north to south at an average height of 1200 m. The range is bounded on the east side by the Ghab, a lowland rift valley 80 km by 150 km occupied by the Middle ORONTES river; east of the Ghab is the open irregular plateau around HAMA and Idlib. Climatic conditions alter rapidly away from the coast, where winters are mild and the annual rainfall is about 700 mm. Further east, in the mountain range of Ansarieh, and the Anti-Lebanon, which divides Syria from Lebanon, winters are cold; snow is of regular occurrence, the total annual precipitation being about 1300 mm. The mountains close much of inland Syria from any Mediterranean influence, so that further inland precipitation decreases and becomes less reliable to the south and east. Temperatures also are more extreme inland: Aleppo's coldest month, January, has an average of 6 °C, with the warmest month August, 32 °C. In the interior, partly true desert and partly STEPPE, is the Badiet es Sham, a mainly upland region with rainfall varying from 50 to 150 mm, very low humidity and very high summer daytime temperatures. Because of its openness of topography and relatively narrow extent this desert has from ancient times been a channel of routeways. Many passed through PALMYRA, now called Tadmor, an oasis that was formerly a trading centre. See also ATLAS 30.

Population. The physical environment greatly influences the distribution of population in Syria. A basic feature is the contrast between the arid central and eastern parts of the country inhabited only by numbers of nomadic pastoralists and with a small settled population along the EUPHRATES valley, and the closely settled parts of the west which contains nearly all the cropped land and 95 per cent of the total population. The highest rural densities are found in the intensively farmed valleys and basins of the western mountains. A number of towns and villages however lie along the transitional zone of steppe between the western mountains and the inner deserts of Arabia. Chief of these is DAMASCUS. The total population was given in 1970 as 6,924,000, with an annual growth rate of 3·3 per cent, and by 1976 it was estimated at 7,585,000 of which 46 per cent were living in urban areas. The largest towns are Damascus (837,000) and ALEPPO, which together contained one-fifth of the total population. According to the 1970 census 'Syrian Arabs' constitute 92 per cent of the population, but this included 300,000 Kurds living mostly in the north and east of the country, together with approximately 180,000 Armenians and 50,000 Circassians. Three religious groups are distinguished by the census: Muslims, comprising 87 per cent of the total settled population; Christians, 8 per cent; and Jews 0·1 per cent. It is likely that Sunni Muslims are

Syria. ABOVE The modern oil port of Tartus. BELOW Bedouin encampment in the Syrian Desert. *(Camera Press)*

Syria, Republic of

predominant, forming perhaps 75 per cent of the total population.

Bibliography: N. A. Ziadeh, *Syria and Lebanon*, 1968; T. Petras, *Syria*, 1972.

Economy. *Agriculture.* East of a line from Aleppo to Damascus, there is mainly desert and the inhabitants are nomads, dependent upon camels, goats, and sheep, but taking the country as a whole, more than 50 per cent of the people are peasants, and very few own their own land. Most of them worked under a scheme by which they cultivated crops and paid half the return to absentee landlords. Living standards were low as a consequence. Successive land reform laws, passed in 1958, 1963, and 1966, have changed the situation however. The largest holding permitted is 300 ha of arable land and 80 ha of irrigated land, which has enabled over 187,000 ha to be distributed to the landless.

Cotton is the main crop, and Syria is the third largest producer in the Arab world after Egypt and the Sudan. Along the alluvial plains of the Euphrates valley growing conditions are ideal, especially for the 'Carolina Queen' variety of cotton. Grain production is much less profitable than cotton, and yields are low, which forces the country to import to meet local consumption requirements. The completion of the first stage of the massive Euphrates Dam project in 1973 has boosted grain production, although the full effects have yet to be felt. Over 1 million ha will be irrigated under the scheme, which will almost double Syria's irrigated land area. An additional 180,000 agricultural jobs will be created, mostly in cattle breeding, and in the cultivation of vegetables, fruit, and maize.

Industry. Syria's growing industrial sector contributed almost one-third of the GNP by 1975. Textiles are the longest established and most important industrial activity. There are textile mills at Damascus, Aleppo, and Hama, and further mills are planned for Deir ez Zohr, Idleb, and Latakia. Although most are involved in spinning and weaving of cotton, a new factory at Damascus handles synthetics, including crimplene. Modern clothing factories are being built at Damascus, Aleppo, and Homs which will use these locally manufactured materials. Syria's other industries include a sugar refinery, a number of food processing factories, and a nitrogenous fertiliser plant. A steel rolling mill is under construction. The main extractive industries are oil and phosphates, but petroleum reserves have proved disappointing, although around 9·5 million t are produced annually, providing Syria's leading export.

Communications. In recent years the Syrian government has spent over one-tenth of its budget on improving communications, and as a consequence there is now a good road system connecting Damascus with Aleppo, with a link road to the main ports of Latakia and Tartus. Although only built in 1952, Latakia has become one of the major ports in the Eastern Mediterranean, with two large dry docks, cold storage capacity, and fully mechanised silos capable of holding 45,000 t of cereals. Development work costing £50 million was completed in 1976 at the port of Tartus, which now also has a new dry dock, and large deep-water quays.

Trade. Raw cotton is Syria's main export, accounting for around one-third of total foreign exchange earnings, while petroleum is the next most important item. Syria's oil exports are modest, but the royalties from the oil pipelines passing through the country from Iraq and Saudi Arabia amount to over £80 million annually. These earnings helped to cover Syria's large trade deficit which reached £280 million in 1974, when imports rose to over £900 million. Syria's main trading partners are Italy, the Soviet Union, and West Germany, though in recent years trade with other members of the Arab Common Market has been increasing, especially with Jordan, Iraq, and the Gulf states.

Bibliography: K. A. Shan, *Planning for a Middle Eastern Economy: A Model for Syria*, 1966; E. Y. Astour, *Syria: Development and Monetary Policy*, 1969.

Government. *Constitution.* The 1973 constitution defines Syria as democratic, republican, popular, and socialist. It provides for a seven-yearly elected President, a four-yearly elected People's Assembly, and a Council of Ministers. Supreme power resides with the President in conjunction with the Ba'ath party, the principles of which are written into the constitution where it is defined as the 'vanguard of the national progressive front of democratic organisations'. Equality before the law, freedom of religious belief, and private property are guaranteed within the general objective of a planned socialist economy. The President of the Republic is required to be Muslim, and Islamic law is recognised as a principal source of legislation.

The controlling party in government is the Syrian Regional Command of the Arab Socialist Ba'ath party. The Syrian Arab Socialist Union, the Arab Socialist party, and the Communist party of Syria combined with the Ba'ath in 1972 to form the National Progressive Front which has since held a clear majority of People's Assembly and Council of Ministers seats. Other politicians operate informally as independents or opposition, and some represent the corporate popular organisations of trade unionists, peasants, students, women, and youth.

Lt.-Gen. Hafez ASSAD is President of the Republic, commander-in-chief of the armed forces, secretary-general of the Syrian Ba'ath party, and president of the National Progressive Front. He and the core of his support belong to the Alawite sect of north-west Syria (see ALAWITES, TERRITORY OF THE). The régime is therefore based on Alawite loyalty, the sympathy of certain other minority groups, and the strength of both in the army, the

Syria. Salt pans near Tripoli. (*Barnaby's Picture Library/ Hubertus Kanus*)

police, the country-wide cells of the Ba'ath party, and the popular organisations. Within this strictly controlled framework Assad has broadened his régime by bringing into it other socialist parties and apolitical technocrats, and by infusing its socialist ideology with pragmatism. The régime dates from 1970, and has lasted longer than any other since-independence (1943–46).

Justice. The main judicial system is based on the French pattern: 75 conciliation courts constitute the lowest level, 41 courts of first instance the next level, and 30 appeal courts the next. These courts sit in local administrative centres, while the court of cassation, the supreme court, sits in Damascus. Special courts deal with minors, military cases, and constitutional law, and 20 religious courts, administering the law or custom of particular religions or sects, try personal status cases.

Armed Forces. The armed forces also have French traditions, but recently Soviet ideas, training, and weaponry have been superimposed. Expenditure on national security accounted for 22–25 per cent of the total state budgets of 1975 and 1976. Military service is compulsory for 30 months in the regular arms. Total active strength in 1975 was 177,500 or 2·4 per cent of the total population. Reserve forces numbered 102,500. Para-military forces numbered 8000 gendarmerie and 1500 desert guards. Chronic political instability since independence has politicised and factionalised the security forces. The security forces have become the object of successive political purges, and have become an instrument finely attuned to the prevailing political and social mood. Drawn largely from the old lower middle classes and traditional disadvantaged groups in society, the forces now provide the new social élite firmly tied to the government by ideological conviction, good pay, and high pensions.

Education. Education has been state-controlled since 1967 and great attention is being paid to the modernisation and expansion of the whole system. Greatest emphasis is on literacy (only 41 per cent in 1968) and on technical education. The primary level (six years) is free and theoretically compulsory: 1971 enrolment amounted to 63 per cent of the primary age group. The top level consists of the three universities of Damascus, Aleppo, and Latakia whose total staff strength in 1973–74 was 1175 and student enrolment 53,369. Expenditure on education, culture, and information accounted for 9–10 per cent of the total national budgets of 1975 and 1976.

Health and Welfare. While the endemic killer diseases have been virtually eliminated, the overall provision of modern health care, preventive or curative, is low. There is no universal health insurance, although some occupational schemes exist, and the very poor may be able to obtain free state medical care. The average life expectancy is 53 years. The average number of persons per doctor in 1973 was 2906, per dentist 12,282, per pharmacist 6781, per hospital bed 1032. The social and geographical distribution of all these elements is uneven.

Average population density is only 37 persons per square kilometre, but urban drift has produced a 50 per cent urban society with attendant social problems. The most pressing welfare needs in both urban and rural areas are improved housing, sanitation, and basic hygiene and nutrition education. Expenditure on social welfare including health accounted for 1 per cent of the total national budgets of 1975 and 1976, although part of the

9–12 per cent assigned to public utilities and works could probably also be included under this heading.

Religion. More than 90 per cent of the population is Muslim, mainly Sunni, with Shiite, Ismaili, Druse, Alawite, and Yazidi minorities. Less than 10 per cent is Christian, divided among Greek, Armenian, and Syrian persuasions of both Orthodox and Catholic kinds, and Maronites. A tiny fraction is Jewish. The traditional, conservative Sunni establishment has bitterly opposed the secularist Ba'ath party and the heterodox Alawite political and military domination of recent Ba'ath régimes. Assad's government has tried to inject an element of religious tact and toleration into Syrian affairs.

Official Language. Arabic is the official language. The Kurdish, Turkish, Armenian, Assyrian, Circassian, and Jewish minorities may speak their own languages as well.

National Anthem. The national anthem was adopted in about 1928 and consists of a two-verse text by Khalil Mardam Bey, set to music by Ahmad and Mohammed Flayfel.

National Flag. The national flag is a horizontal tricolour, red over white over black, the white bearing three five-pointed green stars. It is distinguishable from the Iraqi flag only by its horizontal:vertical proportion of 2:1 compared with the Iraqi 3:2.

Bibliography: A. Hourani, *Syria and Lebanon*, 1946; P. Seale, *The Struggle for Syria*, 1965; T. Petran, *Syria*, 1972; I. Rabinovich, *Syria under the Ba'ath 1963–6*, 1972.

History. Since the earliest times Syria's strategic geographical position has made it the gathering point for successive waves of immigrants; at one time or another the Canaanites, the Phoenicians, the Hebrews, the Arameans, and tribes from the Arabian peninsula swept over it. Before the Roman invasion in the 1st century BC came the Egyptians and Assyrians and subsequently the Hittites, Persians, Macedonian Greeks, and Byzantines.

Syria fell to the Muslims as they expanded out of Arabia in the 7th century and the Ummayad Caliphate ruled its vast empire between 661 and 750 from Damascus, and thereafter local and externally-supported dynasties disputed control. In the 11th–13th centuries Syria was part of the Crusaders' battleground. With the fall of Acre in 1291 the last Crusader foothold was removed by the Mamelukes, who ruled until 1517. The period spent within the Ottoman Empire was one of slow decay. Egypt conquered Syria between 1831 and 1840. Nevertheless Syria became a centre for the revival of Arab culture and of the drive for Arab self-determination.

Arab nationalists were disappointed at the end of the First World War when, instead of obtaining independence, they were pawns of Big Four diplomatic bargaining. Under the terms of the Sykes-Picot agreement of 1916, Syria (and Lebanon) were assigned to the French area of influence. The San Remo conference of April 1920 conferred the mandate of Greater Syria to France, which carried out considerable modernisation in the main population centres. But severe nationalist-inspired uprisings made clear the Syrians' feeling of betrayal. Some progress was made towards self-government, but attempts by France to reorganise Syria politically by according special administrative status to the various sections of the population met with hostility.

In September 1936 the principle of Syrian independence

was acknowledged in a treaty which was never ratified, and real moves towards independence were disrupted by the Second World War. French and British troops invaded Syria in order to drive out a commander loyal to the Vichy government. Independence was granted in theory in September 1941, but it was not until elections had been held in August 1943 (as a result of which Shukri Kuwatli became president) that it arrived in fact—in April 1946. Instability has been the hallmark of Syrian politics since. Syria has been caught in the cross currents of its internal divisions along tribal, ethnic, and religious lines; the frequent intervention of the military; a militant attitude towards the Arab-Israeli conflict; acutely differing concepts of pan-Arabism, particularly as protested by Ba'athism (see BA'ATH PARTY); and periods of stress alternating with others in which attempts were made at union with Egypt and Iraq.

Syrian forces took part in the 1948–49 war with Israel, and the country shared the sense of Arab disillusionment at the outcome. Col. Husni Zaim seized power briefly in March 1949, but internal and external pressure led to his overthrow and Col. Adib Shishakli took over in December and remained until 1954. Several economic projects were initiated in the comparative political tranquillity. Kuwatli was returned after an army insurrection, and the Soviet Union increased its influence, as did pressure for union with Egypt and identification with Nasser's policies.

The union came into being, under the name of the United Arab Republic, in February 1958, but growing discontent at Egyptian domination led to a military coup in September 1961, and separation. The secessionists were in turn ousted by Ba'athist officers in March 1963, led by Gen. Amin Hafez, who became president. Socialist policies were enacted, indicated by nationalisations and a foreign policy orientated towards the Communist countries. But the Ba'athists themselves were divided and the circle of coup and counter-coup was unbroken. The radical wing staged a military coup in February 1966, and the government survived a disastrous involvement in the 1967 war with Israel. This followed a long history of border incidents and resulted in the loss of territory on the Golan Heights, from which, prior to 1967, Syrian soldiers frequently shot at the Israeli farmers below. Nevertheless Syria remained among the militants in the Arab world, refusing negotiations, and backing the claims of the Palestinians.

Involvement in the 1970 war in Jordan exacerbated divisions in the Ba'ath party and resulted in Gen. ASSAD taking over in November, and being elected president. The more pragmatic, but still Ba'athist-dominated, régime that followed gave Syria its most stable period of government since independence. In September 1971 an agreement was signed to form, with Egypt and Libya, the Federation of Arab Republics, which has remained largely a loose union in name only. Syria's military performance was improved in the 1973 war with Israel, even though more land was lost. But honour had been sufficiently satisfied to permit the signing of an American-negotiated interim agreement in May 1974 which resulted in a partial withdrawal from the Golan Heights. Syria did not abandon its hard line on the Palestinians' claims and on a total Israeli withdrawal. Distinct strains emerged with Egypt because of its second interim agreement with Israel in Sinai, and with Iraq because of a dispute over the

headwaters of the Euphrates. Syria became deeply involved in 1975-76 in Lebanon's civil war, at first as a mediating influence and then on the side of the right-wing Christians against the Muslims and Palestinians. Its aim was to create an area of influence consisting of Lebanon, Syria, and Jordan (with which close relations were established) approximating to a modern form of Greater Syria.

Bibliography: A. H. Hourani, *Syria and Lebanon: A Political Study*, 1946; P. K. Hitti, *Syria: A Short History*, 1959; G. H. Torrey, *Syrian Politics and the Military 1945–58*, 1964; P. Seale, *The Struggle for Syria*, 1965; J. B. Glubb, *Syria, Lebanon, Jordan*, 1967; S. H. Longrigg, *Syria and Lebanon under French Mandate*, 1968; N. Ziadeh, *Syria and Lebanon*, 1968; A. L. Tibawi, *A Modern History of Greater Syria including Lebanon and Palestine*, 1969; M. H. Kerr, *The Arab Cold War 1958–70*, 1972; T. Petram, *Syria*, 1972.

Syria, Literature, see ARABIC LITERATURE.

Syriac Language. Syria and Syrians were the Greek terms for biblical ARAM and Aramaeans. Syriac is Aramaic in its later stage, as spoken by the Christian population of Syria (see SEMITES; SEMITIC-HAMITIC LANGUAGES). Syriac was then the language and script of the extensive Syriac literature, which is a Christian literature in a very special sense, all original documents dealing exclusively with Christian matter. Syriac script was an offshoot of a cursive Aramaic writing, perhaps of the Palmyrene cursive in its early stage (see ALPHABET).

The grammar of Syriac is in general fairly simple. Its syntax resembles that of Hebrew (see HEBREW LANGUAGE). As regards phonology, Syriac tends to shorten Hebrew long vowels and to substitute dentals for sibilants.

Edessa (in Syriac Ur-hai, now named Urfa), in northwest Mesopotamia, was the only centre of the early Christian period where the language of the Christian community was other than Greek. Christianity was preached there in the 2nd century; the city became the Christian metropolis of eastern Syria, and from here the Christian faith spread to Persia where it adopted the Edessan Syriac as the language of the Church, of literature, and of cultural intercourse. The same dialect was also adopted in the valley of Euphrates as a *lingua franca*, was used far and wide, and became after Greek the most important language in the Eastern Roman Empire. One of the earliest translations of the Bible, the *Peshito* or *Pĕshitiā* (pure, simple) was made in Syriac from about AD 200 onwards; it has come down in four recensions, Nestorian, Jacobite, Melchite, and Maronite.

From the 7th century onwards, Arabic everywhere put a speedy end to Syriac, which, however, has remained in use for liturgical purposes, and until recently was still spoken in a few villages near Damascus and in Lebanon, as well as near Lake Urmia (Persian Azerbaijan). In the 13th century Bar-Hebraeus tried to revive the Syriac language.

About 1840, American Protestant missionaries, using the old Nestorian script, reduced to writing the Eastern Syriac or neo-Aramaic dialect of Urmia, where they founded the first neo-Syrian printing press. Some 50 years ago two Catholic missions (of the Lazarists and of the Dominicans) reduced to writing the Syriac dialects still spoken in the plain of Salamas and of Mosul. Still more recently a periodical paper in 'Assyrian' was published in Tiflis.

Syriac Literature. The 2nd-century gnostic philosopher BARDESANES, born at Edessa on the Daisan, may be considered to be the first great Syriac writer. He wrote polemical dialogues, apologies, an Armenian Church history, and a book of 150 psalms or hymns, none of which have survived, but they are mentioned in later literature. Aphrahat or Aphraates (fl. 336–45), a great theologian of Persian origin, wrote numerous *memre* or dogmatic and theological homilies, but the greatest of the early Syriac fathers was St Aphrēm (Ephraim), known as Ephraem Syrus (306–72), a voluminous writer of commentaries, homilies, and poetical treatises of various sorts. According to Syriac tradition, he wrote more than 1000 Syriac works, but only very few have been preserved, some in 5th- or 6th-century Syriac manuscripts, some in Armenian translations. In the 5th century, vernacular Syriac historical literature began, and at about the same time the pure Syriac language began to import Greek loan-words, while Hebraisms also began to creep in. A large number of works, all of a religious tendency, and also much verse, are attributed to Isaac the Great of Antioch, a writer of the early Syriac Church, who lived in the 5th century. In the same period, two or three other Isaacs were producing Syriac literature, and there is much confusion in attributing the various works. According to Jacob of Edessa, there were three Isaacs, two 'orthodox' and one a Chalcedonian 'heretic'; two of them apparently were of Edessa. According to others, there were only two Isaacs, one of Amida, an orthodox disciple of St Ephraem, and the other of a slightly later period, Isaac of Antioch. To make things

more complicated, a St Isaac, refugee in Italy from the Syriac Monophysites in the early 6th century, also wrote some works, and some works by Isaac of Antioch are also attributed to him. According to Gennadius (*De vir. ill.,* *66*) 'Isaac of Antioch' visited Rome in the period of Arcadius (395–408) and died in 461; he wrote poems on secular games (404), on the conquest of Rome by Alaric (410), and many other works. The contemporaneous Bālay also wrote hymns and other poems, probably including 12 on Joseph, son of Jacob, which are sometimes attributed to St Ephraem. Cyrillōnā, another contemporary Syriac writer, composed various hymns, of which six are known. He also wrote a poem on the invasion of the Huns in 395. St Simeon Stylites, the Older (c. 390–459), is also remembered.

From the 5th century onwards the Syriac Church was torn with internal conflicts, which are reflected in the writings of the 6th and 7th centuries. Rabbūlā and Hibbā or Ibas (bishops of Edessa), Bābhōy or Barsawmā, Narsay and his disciple Joseph Hūzāyā, of Nisibis, the *catholicos* Mār *A* bhā (d. 552), Jacob of Serūgh, Filoxenus of Mabbūgh, Joshua Stylites, Sergius of Ras'ain (fl. 6th century), John of Asia (b. c. 505), and Jacob Baradaeus of Edessa (b. c. 640), the Monophysite, are important names of the great age of Syriac literature. But with the great schism in the 7th century between the Nestorians and the Jacobites a separation took place, followed by a break of tradition in the literature produced by the two sects. Ishō'yahbh II, Ishō'yahbh III (d. 657), Simeon of Rēwardāshīr, Ishō'bōkht of Rēwardāshīr, the monastic historian, and Thomas of Margā, however, deserve mention. But Syriac literature never regained its former glory.

See also SYRIAC LANGUAGE.

Syriam, township and town in Burma on the east bank of the Rangoon river opposite Rangoon, with important oil-refineries, being the terminus of a 500-km pipeline from the main oil-fields. Township: area 371 km²; population 90,300.

Syringa, the botanical name of LILAC but sometimes used also as a common name for PHILADELPHUS, the mock orange bush.

Syros (Greek *Síros*), island of Greece in the Aegean Sea, belonging to the CYCLADES group. It is barren and has little natural vegetation, but olives, figs, cereals, and vines are cultivated. Its position and importance in coastal trade have made it the most prosperous and densely populated of the island group. Its capital is HERMOUPOLIS. Area 85 km²; population 13,500.

Syrup (from Arabic *sharab*, drink) indicates primarily a saturated solution of SUGAR. For fruit syrup see FOOD PRESERVATION.

System Theory, in linguistics, see HALLIDAY, MICHAEL.

Systole (Greek *systole*, contraction), the phase in the sequence of a HEART beat, when the heart chambers contract and pump out the blood which collected in the previous DIASTOLE. First the atria contract (see ATRIUM), followed by the VENTRICLES. See also HEART.

Syzran, city in KUIBYSHEV *oblast* of the RSFSR, USSR,

Syriac Literature. Syriac manuscript of the 13th century illustrating Christ's entry into Jerusalem; from a Jacobite gospel lectionary. *(British Library, London)*

on the Middle VOLGA, 130 km west of Kuibyshev. It is an important industrial (engineering, oil extraction and processing, food industries) and transportation centre (port, five railway lines). It was founded in 1683. Population (1974) 181,000.

Syzygy (Greek *suzugia*, a yoking together), astronomical term denoting either of the two positions of the Moon when it is in line with the Sun and Earth, i.e., the new or the full moon.

Szabadka, see SUBOTICA.

Szabolcs-Szatmár, see NYÍREGYHÁZA.

Szálasi, Ferenc (1897–1946), Hungarian politician, leader of the Hungarian Arrow-Cross movement; he headed the puppet government imposed on the country by Hitler in October 1944. He was tried and executed as a war criminal in Budapest in 1946.

Szarvas, town of Hungary, near the River Körös, 45 km north-west of Békéscsaba. It is an agricultural centre in the ALFÖLD and its agricultural school, founded by Samuel Tessedik in 1779, is one of the oldest in Europe. Population 19,500.

Szatmár-Németi, see SATU-MARE.

Szczecin, province of North-West POLAND, bordered on the north by the Baltic Sea, on the east by Koszalin, on the south by Zielona Góra, and on the west by East Germany. It is low-lying, mainly agricultural, and drained by the River Oder. Until 1945 it was part of Germany (see POMERANIA). Area 12,754 km²; population 908,000.

Szczecin (German *Stettin*), city of Poland, capital of the province of Szczecin and formerly the capital of POMERANIA, 450 km west of Warsaw. It is on the River Oder, 25 km above the entrance of the river to the Baltic Sea by way of the ZALEW SZCZECIŃSKI. From 1278 a member of the HANSEATIC LEAGUE, Szczecin was held by Sweden from 1648 to 1720, when it became Prussian. In 1945 it passed to Poland. It is a very important port in Baltic trade, owing to its central position, and to its rich hinterland, served by rail, the navigable Oder, and Szczecin is connected by the Oder and the Hohenzollern canal with

Szczecin. (Centralna Agencja Fotograficzna)

the River Havel and Berlin, and is also connected with the Spree and Vistula rivers. Its industries include shipbuilding, engineering, and the manufacture of chemicals, textiles, paper, soap, cement, and sugar. Population (1974) 363,744.

Szczecinek (German *Neustettin*), town of Poland, in the province of Koszalin, 64 km south-east of Koszalin. Until 1945 it was in POMERANIA. There are timber and foodstuff industries. Population 30,000.

Széchenyi, Count István (1791–1860), the father of the Hungarian national movement. He was a wealthy landowner and aristocrat whose advocacy of national and social reform had great impact on his country. An opponent of the more radical Lajos KOSSUTH, Széchenyi served in the government of Lajos BATTHYÁNY in 1848 as minister of transport; he was deeply distressed by the upsurge of revolutionary radicalism and retired to a mental clinic for treatment in September 1848. He re-emerged as a merciless critic of the Austrian government and later took his life to escape from police vexations.

Szechwan, or Szechuan, one of the most important provinces of CHINA, both in size and in population. It is located in western China, being essentially an elevated basin between high ranges of mountains. The western and northern parts of the province are mountainous but the centre and the east of Szechwan consist of a broad and fertile plateau at a general height of about 500 m. The name Szechwan means 'four rivers'. These are generally considered to be the YANGTZE Kiang, which runs through the province from west to east, and three of its principal tributaries, the Min, the To, and the Chia-ling Kiang. The Yangtze runs through the province as a broad navigable stream but at Wanhsien it leaves Szechwan through a series of narrow and spectacular gorges.

Before the Second World War the political situation in Szechwan was very unstable and it was the scene of a great deal of fighting between rival warlords. However, during the SINO-JAPANESE WAR the Chinese government withdrew to a new western capital at Chungking within the province. Many industries were also transferred to the province from the coastal cities at this time. More recently, the Communist government has continued to emphasise the economic development of Szechwan and this has been aided by the construction of railways. CH'ENG-TU, the capital of the province, was linked to Paoki in Shensi province in 1956 and thus Szechwan became connected with the main Chinese rail network. An extension of this line has also been built from Ch'eng-tu to CHUNGKING, the largest city of Szechwan, and in addition the line now reaches further south from Ch'eng-tu to Kunming, the capital of Yunnan province. In 1955 the former SIKANG province was added to Szechwan. This territory in the west of Szechwan province is, however, very rugged and thinly populated.

Because it is protected from climatic extremes by the encircling mountains, the Szechwan basin has a generally mild climate which is very favourable for agriculture. The growing season extends for 11 months of the year over most of the province and for all of the year in the south. Winter temperatures are mild and the summers are hot and humid. Most of the rainfall comes in the summer months. Wherever topographically possible, cultivation is extremely intensive and rural population densities are some of the highest in China. Rice, wheat, and maize are the principal grain crops but the variety of agricultural products is very great and other crops of importance include sugar, tea, oranges, and tobacco. The rivers are used for irrigation, the principal irrigated area being the large alluvial fan formed by the Min river near Ch'eng-tu which has been irrigated since the 3rd century BC. The Yangtze is an important artery of commerce to other parts of China and in recent years considerable efforts have been made to clear it of natural obstructions in order to develop still further the river trade. Szechwan is richly endowed with mineral resources. Coal underlies much of the province and is mined at Peh-pei north of Chungking. A more recent coal-mining centre is Chungliangshan, west of Chungking. There is some production of petroleum and also natural gas at Lungnusze; this field came into production in 1958. Iron-ore, copper, asbestos, mica, and salt are also mined. Szechwan is China's main producer of asbestos. Area 56,000 km². Population (1972) 75,000,000.

Szeged, town of Hungary, near the Yugoslav border, 24 km south-west of Hódmezővásárhely. It stands at the confluence of the rivers Tisza and Mureşul and has been a river port since the 9th century; its prosperity then depended on the salt trade from TRANSYLVANIA. The Hungarian Diet of 1849 met in the town, which has also other associations with KOSSUTH. In 1879 Szeged was devastated by a flood, and was afterwards rebuilt; a Byzantine-style church (1924) commemorates the flood victims. There is a university (1921), a medical college, and an airport. Szeged has a large trade in cereals, poultry, paprika, and fruit from the ALFÖLD, and there are textile and river-fishing industries. Population (1975) 167,220.

Székesfehérvár (German *Stuhlweissenburg*), town of western Hungary, capital of the county of Fejér, 58 km south of Budapest. It was the Roman *Alba Regia*. In the Middle Ages it was, with Esztergom, one of the two centres of government, and 36 Hungarian kings were crowned in its cathedral. The present Baroque cathedral dates from the 18th century. There are several other Baroque buildings of note, including the town hall, and a Franciscan friary. There are aluminium, textile, and distilling industries and there is a trade in agricultural produce, tobacco, and wine. Population (1975) 91,737.

Szent-Györgyi, Albert (1893–), Hungarian biochemist, born in Budapest. From 1930 he was professor at the University of Szeged, and he has lived in the USA since 1947. He discovered vitamin C in paprika and received the 1937 Nobel Prize for chemistry for his discoveries on the role of organic compounds, especially vitamin C, in cell oxidative processes. His work on the organic acids of living cells led directly to Krebs' elucidation of the TRICARBOXYLIC ACID CYCLE. His next work was devoted to the biochemistry of MUSCLE; he discovered actin and showed the need for ADENOSINE TRIPHOSPHATE in muscle contraction. Since his emigration to the USA he has continued to supervise work on muscle biochemistry, but has turned his main attention to the factors underlying cell division and their relevance to cancer.

Szepes, see SPIŠ.

Szigeti, Joseph (1892–1973), Hungarian violinist, born in Budapest, studied under Hubay, and made his debut at the age of 13. He settled in the USA in 1926. He published an autobiography, *With Strings Attached*, 1947.

Szolnok, town of eastern Hungary, capital of Szolnok county, on the River Tisza, 93 km east of Budapest. In Roman times it was a crossing between DACIA and PANNONIA. It is a railway centre, and has cellulose, flour, alcohol, and sugar industries. Population (1974) 69,090.

Szombathely (German *Steinamanger*), town of western Hungary, capital of the county of Vas, near the Austrian border, 185 km west of Budapest. An important road junction in Roman times (*Sabaria*), it was once the capital of PANNONIA. There are Roman remains, and the cathedral and bishop's palace are fine examples of Baroque architecture. The principal industries are tanning and textiles. There is an airport here. Population (1975) 74,470.

Szymanowski, Karol (1882–1937), Polish composer, born in Timoshovka, Ukraine. He studied privately in Warsaw, where he returned as director of the Conservatoire (1927–29) having previously spent many years abroad. He is regarded as the most distinguished Polish composer after Chopin. At first influenced by Debussy, he arrived at a mastery which showed itself in skill of form and clarity as well as in his love of folk-music. He wrote three symphonies, two violin concertos, the operas *Hagith* (composed 1913, performed 1922) and *King Roger* (composed 1918–24, performed 1926), incidental music, many songs and piano works.
Bibliography: T. Chylińska, *Szymanowski*, 1973.

T

T, twentieth letter of the English alphabet and the nineteenth letter of the Greek and Latin alphabets. It was the twenty-second and last letter of the North Semitic (including Phoenician) alphabets, as it is in modern Hebrew. It stands for a voiceless dental or alveolar plosive. English spelling also uses the digraph *th* for the voiceless and voiced dental fricatives. The earliest form of the letter was ✕ or +, and its Semitic name is *taw*, mark, or sign. In early Greek manuscripts it is written +, which came to be written T.

See also ALPHABET; PHONETICS; PHONOLOGY.

Taaffe, Eduard, Count (1833–95), Austrian politician. Descended from an Irish family settled in Austria since the 17th century; he was a close friend of Emperor FRANCIS JOSEPH and held various governmental posts. From 1879 he was prime minister in a multinational Cabinet which attempted, by generally conservative policies tempered with timely concessions, to keep a balance between the country's conflicting national and social groups. Though often criticised as merely 'muddling along', his régime lasted for 14 years, the longest and most settled in Austrian history, before it disintegrated over the Czech-German antagonism in Bohemia and Taaffe was abruptly dismissed.

Bibliography: W. A. Jenks, *Austria under the Iron Ring,* 1963.

Taal, town in the province of BATANGAS on Luzon in the Philippines, on the strip of land between Lake Taal and the Gulf of Balayan. Lake Taal is a volcanic crater 24 km wide with a new and active volcano in its centre; it last erupted in 1965. The town is the centre for an agricultural region. Population (1970) 31,400.

Tabanidae, a family of the order Diptera, class Insecta. These are the horse flies or (genus *Chrysops*, USA) deer flies. There are usually eight to nine larval stages, which may develop over several years, the larva entering a resting phase (diapause) during winter. Some tropical species have two or three generations per year. The larvae are found in water, mud, swamp and marsh-land, rotting leaves, logs, and tree-holes. Most are predacious upon other insect larvae, or feed on decaying plant material. In all but a few more primitive, tropical genera the females are blood-feeding; the males always feed on nectar, honey-dew and plant sap.

The females of three genera: *Chrysops, Haematopota,* and *Tabanus,* commonly attack man and livestock sucking blood, and causing severe annoyance by their painful bites. The presence of these flies in very large swarms around cattle can cause the loss of so much blood that there is a large drop in the milk yield and a deterioration in their condition. Tabanids rarely attempt to engorge from any one feed, but seem to prefer to take frequent sips, often from different animals. This habit of interrupted feeding enables them to transmit a large number of diseases mechanically, that is the disease organisms do not develop within the fly, but are carried by it (e.g. on the mouthparts). The disease organisms of anaplasmosis, anthrax, tularemia, trypanosomiasis, swamp fever of horses, and vesicular stomatitis are known to be mechanically transmitted in this way by tabanids. There is now good evidence that in the case of TRYPANOSOMIASIS there is development of the trypanosomes in the tabanid vectors, such development being necessary for disease transmission. *Chrysops* species are also the vectors of *Loa loa* to man and monkeys in West and Central Africa. This filarial worm undergoes part of its development within the fly, which is therefore called its vector, as opposed to being a mechanical carrier.

See also HORSE-FLY.

Tabard, a loose surcoat, originally worn by peasants, but which superseded the jupon in the 15th century as the garment worn by knights over their armour and on which armorial bearings were displayed (whence the term 'coat of arms'). Today tabards of the Royal Arms are the distinctive garb of the heralds.

Tabari, or abu-ja'far Muhammad ibn-Jarir al-Tabari (c. 839–923), Persian writer, born near the Caspian Sea, who wrote in Arabic. Tabari travelled widely in search of learning before he settled in Baghdad. He composed the first history of the world in Arabic, which is most important for the early history of Islam, and compiled a vast commentary on the KORAN. He also wrote a book on law, most of which is lost. He broke away from the school of Shafi'i (see IMAM) and tried to found one of his own, but failed.

Tabasco, southern state of MEXICO, bounded on the north by the Gulf of Mexico, on the east by Campeche and Guatemala, on the south by Chiapas, and on the west by Veracruz. The surface is flat and the soil fertile, largely covered with semi-tropical forest, but yielding cacao, sugar, coffee, tobacco, rice, and fruit. Livestock raising is of major importance. Oil and natural gas are leading products. The chief towns are Villahermosa (the capital) and its port of Frontera (population 15,000). Area 24,661 km²; population (1975) 1,007,500.

Tabernacle (Latin *tabernaculum*, diminutive of *taberna*, booth, hut, temporary dwelling, etc.), term generally applied in the scriptures to the portable sanctuary of the Jews, which was erected by Moses, and which is described fully in Exod. xxv–xxvii and xxxvi–xxxviii. The specifications are for a tent constructed with extraordinary magnificence in every part, to measure c. 50 by 25 m. It contained an outer court, the Holy Place, and the HOLY OF HOLIES. This last contained the ARK OF THE COVENANT and the mercy seat. The altar of incense, the table of shewbread, and the golden candlestick stood in the Holy Place. An altar of burnt offerings and a laver for ceremonial washing stood in the outer court. Similar portable shrines are now known to have been used in Egypt before the time of Moses. In the New Testament the Epistle to the Hebrews treats the tabernacle as symbolic of heavenly things (Heb. viii. 5, ix. 9, 24).

Later in England the term tabernacle was applied to places of worship not dignified by the name of 'church', e.g. (1) temporary churches erected by Wren in London after the Great Fire, 1666; (2) certain Nonconformist chapels of the 18th–19th centuries, however substantial ('Spurgeon's Tabernacle' in south London holding 5000 persons); (3) temporary galvanised iron churches, 'tin tabernacles', erected by all denominations in the 19th century.
Bibliography: J. D. Douglas, *New Bible Dictionary*, 1962.

Tabernacles, Feast of (Hebrew *Sukkoth*, huts, or *hag ha'asiph*, feast of Ingathering), Jewish festival, celebrated from 15 to 23 TISHRI and commemorating the dwelling of the Israelites in the wilderness. All meals for eight days are eaten in an outdoor booth with a roof of branches.

Tabernaemontana, a genus of 100 tropical, evergreen trees or shrubs, of the Apocynaceae (periwinkle family). *T. coronaria* (Adam's apple, crape jasmine, Nero's crown) with white flowers, scented at night, and *T. dichotoma* (forbidden fruit, Eve's apple) with orange-yellow, half-round fruit, resembling a half-eaten apple, are grown in hothouses.

Tabes Dorsalis, see SYPHILIS.

Tabla, dissimilar pair of kettle-drums of north Indian classical music. Both drums are braced with leather thongs, but only the right-hand drum, which has a wooden body, has cylindrical wooden blocks under the thongs with which the drum can be tuned to the *Sa*, or keynote, of the music being played. The left-hand drum, the shell of which is today usually made of metal, is not tuned; the player can alter the tension of the skin, and hence its pitch, by pressure with the heel of the hand while playing. Both drums are played with the fingers, employing complex rhythmic and quasi-melodic patterns. The tabla are the most important accompanying instruments in north Indian music, a performance by SITAR and tabla being the Indian equivalent of a recital by violin and piano in our culture.

Tablature, various old systems of writing down music, especially for organ and for lute, without notes, but by means of letters, numbers or other signs. Only the ukelele

and similar guitar types still use a tablature notation, though the tonic sol-fa notation may be said to be a kind of tablature.

Table, see FURNITURE.

Table Bay, inlet of the Atlantic Ocean on the south-west coast of the Cape of Good Hope, on the south side of which CAPE TOWN is situated; it was discovered by Antonio de Saldanha (1503). The massacre of a Portuguese party on the shore of Table Bay (1510) probably accounts for the Portuguese not having settled here as they did to the east and later up the west coast of Africa.

Table Mountain, or Tafelberg, mountain of the Cape peninsula, South Africa, overlooking CAPE TOWN and Table Bay. The level top gives it the appearance of a table, and it is often covered with a dense white cloud called the 'Tablecloth'. There is a cableway to the summit; the highest point is Maclear's Beacon (1113 m).

Table Tennis, indoor game played on a regulation-sized table with bat and ball. The standard table measures 274 cm by 152·5 cm, with a 15·25 cm high net. The bats may be of any size, shape or weight, but each side must be uniformly dark-coloured and matt; rubber-covered or rubber and cellular rubber covered wood is generally used. The balls weigh between 2·4 g and 2·53 g and are of celluloid or similar plastic. The game is for two or four players, each serving five times successively, and no volleying is allowed. The game is played up to 21 points when a lead of at least two points must be obtained before the game is completed and won. The score is always called by stating the server's score first. Called 'ping-pong', the game was very popular from 1899 to 1904, and was revived in 1927; in 1975 over 8000 clubs were in membership. National and international championships are held annually; the International Federation (headquarters at Hastings, Sussex) has 121 associations in membership. The 1975 World Championships were held in Calcutta, India, and those of 1977 in Birmingham, England.

Tableland, see PLATEAU.

Tabley, Baron de, see DE TABLEY, JOHN BYRNE, LEICESTER WARREN, BARON.

Taboo, or tabu, from the Maori *tapu*, signifying a kind of fellowship between certain objects or living beings; it has the propensity to influence other entities with which it comes into contact. Broadly-speaking, it is associated by the Maori with male spiritual forces and raw food, and counteracted by female forces and cooked food. In particular, the act of sexual union is tapu.

Similar ideas have been found all over the world. The breach of a taboo is believed to be particularly dangerous and polluting in a supernatural sense, and the effects may have to be offset by a specific ritual. Sickness is frequently thought to be caused by a breach of a taboo. Birth, initiation, marriage, and sexual practice are brought under taboos to protect them from hostile influences. A commonly found taboo is that enforced on menstruating women and pregnancy. Sigmund FREUD demonstrated how taboos operate in Western societies, although frequently unrecognised as such: the INCEST taboo is a forceful example. Recently anthropologists have shown

Tábor

how taboos operate in our lives on a much more mundane level, as, for instance, with swear words, bad manners, or wearing the wrong kind of clothes for particular occasions.

See also TOTEMISM; WITCHCRAFT.

Bibliography: J. G. Frazer, *The Golden Bough*, 1936; S. Freud, *Totem and Taboo*, 1950; F. Steiner, *Taboo*, 1956; M. Douglas, *Purity and Danger*, 1970.

Tábor, town of Czechoslovakia, in South Bohemia on the River Lužnice. It was founded by the Hussites in 1420, and gave its name to the Taborites (see HUSSITES). There are textile and tobacco industries. Population 22,000.

Tabor (Old French *tabour*), DRUM used to accompany a pipe from the 13th century onwards. The size of the drum varied according to place and period, ranging from 7·5 cm diameter and depth to 40 cm diameter by 80 cm deep. The tabor was slung from the player's wrist or shoulder and the pipe played with the same hand; the other hand held the tabor beater. The tabor was always snared on the struck head.

Bibliography: J. Blades and J. Montagu, *Early Percussion Instruments*, 1975; J. Montagu, *Making Early Percussion Instruments*, 1975.

Tabor (Har Tavor), mountain in GALILEE, 11 km east of Nazareth, a dome-shaped mass rising abruptly from the Plain of ESDRAELON. It is the traditional scene of the Transfiguration. The summit has Orthodox and Franciscan churches, with convent buildings, and, in the latter case, a hospice. The fine modern Franciscan basilica, on the site of a medieval church, was designed in the 6th-century north Syrian style by the builder of the Franciscan basilica in Gethsemane. The Orthodox church is said to be on the site of the Cave of Melchizedek, the mysterious priest-king of Genesis xiv. Height 560 m.

Tabora, town and region in the centre of Tanzania, founded by Arabs about 1820 and was formerly a great centre of trade in slaves and ivory; today it is important as a trade centre and regional administrative headquarters. From Tabora a branch line from the Dar es Salaam–Kigoma railway runs to Mwanza, the chief southern port on Lake Victoria. Population 21,000.

Taborites, see HUSSITES, WAR OF THE.

Tabriz, ancient city, capital of the Iranian province of East AZERBAIJAN, and a commercial centre of IRAN. It is situated on a small river called Aji Chay running into Lake REZA'IYEH. Tabriz is one of the main industrial centres of Iran. The carpets manufactured here are of fine designs and quality, and are well known all over the world. Tabriz is connected by rail to Julfa (140 km) on the Russian border, and to Tehran. A university was established here in 1948. During the Perso-Turkish wars of the 16th and 17th centuries it frequently changed hands. The Arg, or citadel, and the Blue Mosque are of architectural interest. It was occupied by Russian forces in both world wars. Earthquakes have ruined the city several times. It was the capital of Iran in the time of Shah Ismail I and Ghazan Khan. Population (1974) 560,000.

Tabu, see TABOO.

Tabulata, an extinct Palaeozoic group of compound CORALS characterised by strongly tabulate corallites.

Tabulating Machine, see ACCOUNTING MACHINE.

Tacca, a genus of 30 tropical, rhizomatous herbs, in the family Taccaceae, mostly grown as greenhouse foliage plants. *T. leontopetaloides* is one of the sources of arrowroot, an edible starch.

Tacheometry, or tachymetry, survey by a tacheometer, which is generally a theodolite adapted to measure distance. In rugged country the tacheometer may be used to make subtense measurements. At one end of the ray to be measured two poles about 50 m apart are placed at right angles to the ray, their distance apart being accurately measured. These are observed through the theodolite and the angle subtended measured; representing the angle by 2τ, and the distance between the poles by $2s$, then the length of the ray $= s \tan \tau$. Another method for shorter rays is to use a theodolite with two wires at fixed distances apart on the field, and observe, along the ray, a graduated staff. The wires always give a fixed angle which will enclose more or fewer graduations on the staff, the farther or the nearer it is respectively. The stadia marks, as the wires are called, are so arranged that the graduations have only to be multiplied by a factor to give the distance of the staff from the observer. This factor varies with the distance of the wires from the optical centre of the objective, which is changed in altering the focus for different distances. The correction for this is small and variable, but is made by adding to the computed distance the distance from the centre of motion of the instrument to a point on the axis, beyond the objective, at a distance equal to the focal length from the optical centre. The tacheometer is an instrument which, by the introduction of a third lens in the telescope, the anallatic lens, eliminates the correction and gives the reading at once. The instrument is useful for small surveys and military work, but not for extended surveys. When used on the slope, if the graduated bar is horizontal, the computed distance must be multiplied by the cosine of the slope to give the horizontal distance; if vertical the multiplier is the square of the cosine. See also SURVEYING; LEVELLING.

Táchira, mountainous, inland state of VENEZUELA, bordering Colombia to the west. The Uribante river rises in and flows through the state. Agricultural products include coffee (of which it is the country's main producer) and cocoa. Silver, iron, and coal are mined on a small scale. SAN CRISTÓBAL is the capital. Area 11,138 km²; population (1975) 564,800.

Tachisme (French *tache*, stain, blot), name given to the method used by some contemporary French artists of exploiting the quality of freely flowing oil-paint for its own sake; one aspect of a tendency to seek new effects in paint substance and colour without representation or formal design, pursued both in Europe and America. See also ABSTRACT EXPRESSIONISM.

Tachometer, instrument for measuring the speed of rotation of a shaft, such as an engine crankshaft. Mechanical tachometers are similar in principle to a governor; the centrifugal force produced by rotating weights moves a pointer against the action of a spring. Electrical tachometers use a small generator, either coupled to a voltmeter which is calibrated in revolutions per minute or driving a motor which in turn drives a magnetic drag cup indicator.

Tachycardia (Greek *tachys*, swift, *kardia*, heart), medical term used to denote an excessively rapid heart beat, usually of more than 100 beats per minute. Tachycardia can be a normal, temporary response to exercise or emotional excitement. It can also be a sign of disease of the heart of other organs, e.g. the thyroid gland, if it occurs either transiently for no apparent reason or continues even at rest. It is classified as one of the ARRHYTHMIAS. When the tachycardia is due to heart disease, treatment is usually directed towards the causative disease itself. Certain medications can help in these cases and the elimination of tea, coffee and other stimulants' is desirable.

Tachygraphy, see SHORTHAND.

Tachylite, or basaltic glass; the basic rock equivalent to OBSIDIAN. It occurs as small interstitial patches in some basaltic rocks, also at the rapidly chilled margins of basalt lava flows and intrusions, and as glass threads (Pelées Hair) caused by lava spraying out of small fissures under pressure.

Tacitus, Marcus Claudius, Roman Emperor, 25 September AD 275–March 276. He succeeded Aurelian, much against his will, at the age of 70. His short reign was notable for improvements at home and victories abroad. He died at Tyana in Cappadocia.

Tacitus, Publius Cornelius (c. AD 55–c. 120), Roman historian. In 78 he married the daughter of AGRICOLA, who in the same year became governor of Britain. Tacitus was praetor in 88, and assisted as one of the *quindecemviri* at the *ludi saeculares* (see LUDI); he was consul suffectus in 97–98, and proconsul of Asia in 112–13. He was an intimate friend of PLINY.

The extant works of Tacitus are as follows: *Dialogus de Oratoribus*, a treatise on the decline of rhetoric; *Agricola* (98), a portrait of his father-in-law; *Germania*, a valuable ethnographical work; *Historiae*, a history of the empire from Galba to Domitian (69–96) in 12 or 14 books of which only iv and part of v remain; and *Annales* (115–17), a history of the empire from the death of Augustus to that of Nero, of which books vii–x and parts of v, xi and xvi are lost.

Though Tacitus did not, perhaps, quite attain his ideal of writing without prejudice, he remains the most reliable witness for the period covered by his works. His style is unique in ancient literature—rapid and condensed, combining great force with biting epigram. His moral dignity is impressed upon his work, which often rises to unsurpassed heights of sonority and splendour. His power derives largely from his knowledge of the human mind and its motives; and for this study he found abundant material in the history of the emperors. The best edition of Tacitus is that of C. D. Fisher and H. Furneaux (Oxford Classical Texts).

Bibliography: R. Syme, *Tacitus*, 1958; B. Walker, *Annals of Tacitus*, 1960; T. A. Dorey, *Tacitus*, 1969; R. Syme, *Ten Studies in Tacitus*, 1970.

Tack, in shipping, rope or wire used to secure the windward clews or corners of the courses to the ship's side, and the windward lower end of a fore-and-aft sail amidships. The term tack is also used for the lower forward corner of a fore-and-aft sail or the weather clew of a course. A ship sailing to windward is said to be on the port or starboard tack according to the side of the vessel towards which the wind is blowing. A ship is said to tack when she changes direction, passing head-to-wind, so as to bring the wind on the opposite side from which it was before she went about. See STAYS.

Tacloban, capital of LEYTE province in the Philippines. It is the largest city and distribution centre for the eastern islands, and has a deepwater port that handles bulk petroleum. It also exports hemp, copra, and timber, and was a temporary capital during the Second World War until Manila was liberated. Population (1970) 74,100.

Tacna, southernmost department of PERU, in the angle between the Pacific coast and the Chilean frontier. The coastal part is desert, interspersed with irrigated valleys; the Andean province of Tarata is a high, cold, grassy plateau region, as in western Bolivia. Cotton, vines, fruit, maize, and potatoes are grown. The great copper mine of Toquepala is near the border with the department of Moquegua. Tacna was under Chilean control from 1880 to 1929. Area 14,766 km². Population 95,623.

Tacna, capital of the above department in Peru, it is linked with ARICA in Chile, 60 km away, by a railway. There are plans to turn Tacna into an important industrial centre. Altitude 558 m. Population 42,000.

Tacoma, city of the state of Washington, USA. It is situated near the head of Puget Sound, and is an excellent port although 250 km from the open sea. The first settlement consisted of a few sawmills but the city was selected as the Pacific coast terminus of the first transcontinental railway to the north-west (the Northern Pacific) in 1883, and its future was thus assured. Although overshadowed today by Seattle, further to the north, Tacoma is an important industrial city; it is deeply involved in the north-west's lumber and paper industries, and has many plants serving each of these. In addition, it has two smelters of national importance, one producing aluminium and the other mainly copper. Population 154,581.

Tacsonia, see PASSION FLOWER.

Tactics, see STRATEGY AND TACTICS.

Tacuarembo, town and department of northern URUGUAY, bordered on the south by the Río Negro and Lake Río Negro from which the great hydro-electric plant at Rincón del Bonete draws its power. Cattle and sheep raising are the main economic activities. The town of Tacuarembo, also the departmental capital, is mainly a cattle and agricultural centre specialising in wool, hides, and skins, 350 km north of Montevideo. Area 15,873 km². Population (town) 30,000.

Tadcaster (Roman *Calcaria*), town in SELBY District, North YORKSHIRE, England, on the River Wharfe, 15 km south-west of York, on the site of a Roman encampment. There are building-stone quarries nearby, and Tadcaster is noted for brewing. About 3 km away is the battlefield of Towton. Population (1971) 5268.

Taddeo di Bartolo

Taddeo di Bartolo (active 1386, d. 1422), Italian painter, born in Siena. He was principally a fresco painter. Some of his best work, dating from 1414, is to be found in the municipal palace of Siena, continuing the Sienese tradition of civic commissions, exemplified in the work of Simone MARTINI and Ambrogio LORENZETTI. His nephew, Domenico Bartoli, was his pupil.

Tadema, see ALMA-TADEMA.

Tadmor, see PALMYRA.

Tadpole, see FROGS.

Tadzhik Soviet Socialist Republic, or Tadzhikistan (also known as Tajik SSR or Tajikistan), constituent republic of the USSR bordering on Afghanistan in the south and on China in the east. It was formed as an autonomous republic in 1924 and acquired the status of a union republic in 1929. The republic includes the GORNO-BADAKHSHAN Autonomous Oblast. It is mainly mountainous and includes the whole of the PAMIRS, and the Turkestan, Zeravshan, and Gissar ranges. Lowlands are located in the north-west along the SYR DARYA river, at the entrance to the FERGANA VALLEY, and in the south-west along the Kafirnigan and Vakhsh rivers. See ATLAS 28.

The economy is mainly concerned with the growing (Vakhsh valley) and processing of cotton. Food grains (wheat, barley, and millet) are grown in the south-east, and oil grains (flowering flax) in the south-west. There is a considerable cattle breeding industry. Lead and zinc are mined. Other industries include silk weaving (LENINA-BAD), textile weaving (Dushanbe), and fruit canning. There is a large carpet factory at Kayrakkum. In its hydro-electric resources the republic occupies second place in the USSR (after the RSFSR). A large hydro-electric station is under construction on the River Vakhsh near Nurek with a planned total power of 2,700,000 kW (the third of nine generators came into operation in 1973).

The administration is the standard one for Union republics (see KAZAKH SSR). There is a university and a branch of the Academy of Sciences at DUSHANBE, the capital. Area 143,100 km². Population (1976) 3,490,000; mainly Tadzhiks (56 per cent), Uzbeks (23 per cent), and Russians (11 per cent).

Tae-kwon-do, a fighting sport from Korea, meaning literally 'foot fist way'. It is a form of KARATE and is an amalgamation of a number of other Korean fighting styles, notably *tang-soo-do*, *kong-soo-do*, *tae-soo-do* and *soo-bak-do*. As in karate and JUDO, degrees of excellence (Dan) are awarded once the Black Belt has been gained, different belt colours indicating the competitors' levels of attainment. Tae-kwon-do has lacked the widespread popularity of karate, but a number of its exponents have been successful in American karate tournaments. A distinguishing feature of tae-kwon-do is the spectacular high kicks which are practised more frequently than in karate.

Taegu (Japanese *Taikyu*), one of the main cities of SOUTH KOREA, about 90 km north-west of Pusan. Important historically as far back as the 8th century AD, its textile industry contributes 30 per cent of the country's total output. Population (1970) 1,082,750.

Tael, or liang, east Asian, particularly Chinese, measure of weight, 1⅓ oz avoirdupois (37·8 g).

Taenia, see CESTODA.

Taewon'gun, the title by which Yi Ha-ung (1820–98), regent in Korea 1864–73, is usually known. Although descended from kings, he lived his early life in poverty and degradation. However when his son was chosen to be king in 1864 he was able to wield the actual power. He attempted reforms of Korea's antiquated court, administration, educational system, and economy, and attempted to re-assert Korea's rights as an independent kingdom. He was brought down by an alliance of conservative families in 1873, fought back unsuccessfully for some years, and was exiled to China from 1881 to 1885. In his remaining years he tended towards the pro-Japanese progressives and so died in disgrace, but he also contributed to the modernisation process in this period as patron of the arts.

Taf, river of Dyfed, Wales, rising on the eastern side of the Preseli Hills and flowing through south-east Dyfed to Carmarthen Bay. Length 40 km.

Tafelberg, see TABLE MOUNTAIN.

Taff (Welsh *Tâf*), river of Wales rising in the BRECON BEACONS. It flows through Mid and South Glamorgan and enters the Bristol Channel at Cardiff. The valley has considerable industrial importance. Its main tributary is the RHONDDA. MERTHYR TYDFIL is located where it enters Mid Glamorgan and PONTYPRIDD at its confluence with the Rhondda. Length 64 km.

Taff-Ely, new district of the county of Mid GLAMORGAN, South Wales. Area 168 km²; population (1975) 89,600.

Taff Vale Judgment, see TRADE UNION.

Taffeta, or taffety (Persian *tafta*), plain weave silk fabric introduced into England in the 14th century. It is woven so that warp and weft threads are evenly interlaced. Taffeta is either yarn-dyed, which gives a crisp taffeta used sometimes for academic hood linings, or dyed in the piece, which makes the fabric more pliable and it can be used for dress lining. 'Shot taffeta' has warp and weft of different colours which means that the fabric apparently changes colour with the fall of light on its surface.

Tafilalt, or Tafilet, oasis on the south-east of the ATLAS MOUNTAINS, Morocco, noted for its dates and leather. In contains some 300 villages, and is a caravan centre. It is the home of the reigning Moroccan dynasty.

Taft, Robert Alphonso (1889–1953), US politician, born at Cincinnati, the son of W. H. TAFT; educated at Harvard and Yale universities. He became a Republican member of the Senate in 1939 serving until his death. Taft's policy was traditionalist and isolationist. He campaigned for the Republican nomination as president on several occasions. In 1952 his rejection in favour of Eisenhower was interpreted as the end of an era in American Republicanism. After Eisenhower's election he became Senate majority leader.

Taft, William Howard (1857–1930), 27th President of the USA and chief justice, born at Cincinnati, Ohio. He graduated from Yale University in 1878, and from Cincin-

W. H. Taft photographed in 1906. *(Library of Congress)*

nati Law School in 1880. In 1887 he was a judge of the superior court of Ohio, and in 1890 was appointed solicitor-general of the USA, and in 1892 became a federal circuit court judge. In 1900 President McKinley made him president of the Philippines Commission, and in 1901 appointed him civil governor; Taft did much to pacify the islands. As secretary of war (1904–08) he took an important part in Latin American affairs. He was nominated and elected president by a large majority in 1908. Taft improved the financial position of the country, and sought peace agreements with several foreign powers. Though nominated by Theodore Roosevelt, Taft did not, however, carry on his predecessor's policy to the satisfaction of its originator, and the 1910 Tariff Acts were particularly unpopular. Roosevelt accused Taft of suffering the party to slip back again into the pockets of the trusts, and in 1912 stood once more as presidential candidate. Largely by the hostility to Roosevelt of the bosses and trusts Taft was chosen, but the resultant split in the party permitted the return of the Democratic Woodrow Wilson. Taft then became a law professor at Yale. From 1921 to 1930 he was chief justice, his real ambition achieved. He proved to be a conservative on the Court, and an important reformer of the Court's procedures. His published works include *Popular Government*, 1913, *The Anti-Trust Act and the Supreme Court*, 1914, and *Our Chief Magistrate and His Powers*, 1916.

Bibliography: A. E. Ragan, *Chief Justice Taft*, 1938; H. F. Pringle, *The Life and Times of William Howard Taft*, 2 vols, 1939; D. F. Anderson, *William Howard Taft: A Conservative's Conception of the Presidency*, 1973.

Taganrog, seaport city in the ROSTOV *oblast* of the RSFSR, USSR, on the Sea of AZOV, 75 km west of Rostov-on-Don. It is an important industrial centre: iron and steel (since 1897), engineering (combine-harvesters, boilers, machine-tools, aircraft), leather, and food industries. It was founded by Peter the Great in 1698, destroyed after the Pruth Treaty with Turkey in 1712, and rebuilt 1769–74; it was occupied by the Germans in 1918 and 1941–43. It is the birthplace of Anton CHEKHOV. Population (1974) 272,000.

Tagetes, see MARIGOLD.

Tagliamento, Italian river which rises in the Carnic Alps and flows south through Friuli-Venezia Giulia to the Gulf of Venice. There was heavy fighting on its banks during the First World War after the Italian defeat at Caporetto. Length 165 km.

Taglioni, Marie (1804–84), Italian ballet dancer, born in Stockholm, where her father, Filippo Taglioni (1778–1871), was *maître de ballet*. She was trained by her father, and he composed the ballet, *La Réception d'une jeune nymphe à la cour de Terpsichore*, in which she made her debut in Vienna (1822). In 1827 she first danced at the Paris Opéra, where she created the title role in *La Sylphide*, 1832, which marks one of the peaks of the Romantic renaissance of ballet. She danced also in St Petersburg, Milan and London, in the last city appearing in the *Pas de Quatre*, 1845. She retired as a dancer in 1847, but resumed her career as teacher and choreographer at the Paris Opéra from 1859 to 1870, staging *La Papillon* to an original Offenbach score in 1860 for Emma Livry. Her marriage to Comte Gilbert de Voisins (1832) was a failure. She later taught dancing and deportment in London. As a dancer she brought to her art a poetic quality which elevated it to a level unattained before her time.

Tagore, Rabindranath (1861–1941), Indian poet and author, born in Calcutta, the son of Maharshi Debendra Nath Tagore. In his youth he wrote verse in imitation of the old Vaishnava poets of Bengal, and first produced original work when he was 18. He visited England in 1877 to study law.

After his marriage in 1883 he spent 17 years managing the family estate at Śilāidaha, gaining insight into the life and needs of the Bengali villagers, whose legends and customs inspired so much of his writing. Between 1900

Rabindranath Tagore. *(Bisonte)*

and 1901 he established a self-governing, experimental school at Śantiniketan, which flourished and expanded in spite of financial difficulties, so that 20 years later he was able to found an international university, Viśvabhāratī, and realise his belief that men of different races and civilisations should study together in an atmosphere of peace, brotherhood, and joy in life and work.

As the result of a visit to England in 1912, a volume called *Gītānjali* (Song-Offerings) was published, translated by Tagore. He was the first Indian to be awarded the Nobel Prize for literature (1913) and accepted a knighthood two years later, which he disowned in 1919 as a protest against an incident in which British troops were ordered to fire on Punjab rioters. He travelled widely, lecturing in many countries in the world; after 1930 he took up painting and exhibited in New York and several European cities.

Some 35 volumes of Tagore's poems, plays, essays, novels, and short stories have been translated into English, many by the author. He set 300 of his poems to music. His poem *Conscience of the People* was chosen in 1950 (with music by Herbert Murrill) as the national anthem of India. Tagore brought new life to Indian literature by turning for inspiration to Bengali folklore and everyday life. He had interested himself in the Indian national movement, especially its social reforms, and believed that India's task was to show the world the way to peace by setting an example of brotherly co-operation between its various races and creeds. The core of his philosophy was an intense faith in the power of love as the key to man's fulfilment and freedom. His works include *Gītānjali*, 1912, *The Gardener*, 1913, *Chitra*, 1913, *The Post Office*, 1914, *My Reminiscences*, 1917, *The Home and the World*, 1919, *Gora*, 1924, *Red Oleander*, 1924, and *Collected Poems and Plays*, 1936.

Bibliography: Lives by M. Sykes, 1943, E. Thompson, 1949; K. Kripalani, *Rabindranath Tagore*, 1962.

Tagua, a name of Araucan origin for a palm-tree (*Phytelephas macrocarpa*) also known as the corozo. The seed of the tree has a hard, white, opaque endosperm that can be polished and carved, and is known as 'vegetable ivory'. There are groves of tagua palms in the lowlands of the coast of Colombia, and on the banks of the Magdalena and other rivers.

Tagus (Spanish *Tajo*; Portuguese *Tejo*), chief river of Spain and Portugal, which rises in the Sierra de Albarracín on the border between CUENCA and TERUEL. It flows past TOLEDO, and after Alcántara, forms the Spanish-Portuguese frontier for 50 km. It then crosses Portugal to its large estuary on the Atlantic Ocean at LISBON. In 1966 the Salazar Bridge was opened over the Tagus, spanning Alcántara (Lisbon) to Almada. It is navigable for 200 km from the sea. Length 1005 km.

Tahaa, island in the Society Group, adjacent to Raiatea.

Taharqa (Biblical Tirhakah), third king, c. 688–663 BC, of Egypt's 25th Dynasty. During his reign, ASHURBANIPAL occupied Egypt.

Tahiti, main island of the Windward Islands of the Society group and contains Papeete, the administrative centre of French Polynesia. It has a mountainous interior surrounded by a fertile alluvial belt; high rainfall and equable climate. Indigenous Polynesians are now mixed with Chinese and Europeans. The island exports copra, phosphates, pearl shell, and vanilla. Discovered in 1606 by Quiros, visited by Bougainville 1768, and Cook 1769. French protectorate 1847, ceded to France 1880 and became an overseas territory in 1958. Area 1040 km²; population (1967) 61,519.

T'ai Shan, a sacred mountain in Chinese mythology, located in Shantung Province; the greatest of five similar mountains, all closely associated with religious observances. It is said that Confucius climbed it and viewed the whole empire; that 72 legendary Emperors performed rites of worship there; and that the founders of the three earliest dynasties (Yu, 2205 BC; Ch'eng t'ang, 1741 BC; and Wu, 1117 BC) all paid their respects to the spirit of the mountain. An ancient stone stairway ascends the slopes and beside it have been built many small temples and shrines commemorating visits of august personages.

T'ai-yüan, walled capital city of SHANSI province in northern China, on the FEN HO. It lies in a rich coal- and iron-mining district, and is at present the most important centre of heavy industry, especially heavy-machine factories, in northern China (excluding MANCHURIA). It is the site of the Shansi University and many colleges. The city has experienced rapid industrial growth in recent years due to the Communist government's policy of industrial dispersal. It is now also one of China's most important iron and steel centres. Population (1970) 1,250,000.

T'ai-yueh-ta-ti, see EASTERN PEAK EMPEROR.

Taif, town in western Saudi Arabia, 65 km south-east of Mecca. It lies at 1550 m and is the centre of a fruit growing district. It was an important town in the time of Mohammed. Population c. 55,000.

Taiga, sub-Arctic coniferous forest zone, lying south of the TUNDRA and north of the STEPPE. Spruce, firs, pine, and larch are the chief trees. The taiga exists in North America, Europe, and Asia, and forms about one-third of the area of the USSR. It contains many swampy low-lying areas, and during the spring thaw is often flooded by northward-flowing rivers whose outlets are still frozen over.

Tailhade, Laurent (1854–1919), French writer, born at Tarbes. His work includes the poems, *Le Jardin des rêves*, 1880, and *Vitraux*, 1892, with two selections which were republished with others in 1907 under the title *Poèmes élégiaques*. He also wrote *Au pays du mufle*, 1891, and *A travers les grouins*, 1899, two volumes of invective verse published with others in 1904 as *Poèmes aristophanesques*, as well as essays, *Terre latine*, 1898, *Le Troupeau d'Aristée*, 1908, and *Un Monde qui finit*, 1910.

Taillefer (d. 1066), Norman *jongleur* who was killed fighting for William the Conqueror at the battle of Hastings. Wace, in the *Roman de Rou*, says that he led the Norman troops, inspiring them with his songs of Roland, of Charlemagne, and of the heroes of Roncesvalles.

Tailleferre, Germaine (1892–), French composer, born near Paris; the only woman member of the LES SIX group. Her works, though never attaining the popularity of her colleagues', include the opera *Il était un petit navire*, the ballet *Le Marchand d'oiseaux*, and several instrumental works.

Tailor-bird, *Orthotomus sutorius*, a small bird, of family Muscicapidae, order Passeriformes, native to India and other parts of Asia, where it feeds on ants and other insects. It is about 15 cm long and olive-green, with markings of other tints. Its nest is a dainty structure of leaves stitched together with silk, wool, hair and vegetable fibre, and contains three or four varicoloured eggs.

Tailoring (Old French *taillour*), cutting and making of clothes. Tailors originally made garments for both men and women, as well as the padding and lining of armour, for which reason the earliest charter of the Merchant Taylors Company was made out to the 'Taylors and Linen Armourers'. 'Bespoke' means simply that the garment is made to order for an individual customer. The key man in a bespoke tailor's business is the cutter. He is responsible for seeing that the garments fit the customers and satisfy them, so he must have wide technical experience. His first job is to advise the customer on the most suitable style and cloth and to take measurements. These are taken in great detail; in addition, he notes any unusual points about the customer's figure or way of standing. The cutter makes allowances for these peculiarities when marking out the cloth. Measurements are written down in an order book, together with notes about the cloth and style to be used. The cutter then drafts a pattern for the suit on stiff paper, working on a grid of basic measurements. On this grid he sketches in the outline of the various parts of the suit or garment. The cloth is then placed on the cutting board, doubled, so that the cutting is done through two thicknesses. In this way, one only needs patterns for half of each garment, but when the cloth is cut there will be enough pieces for both sides. The cutter takes great care to match any checks or stripes and at the same time, to waste as little material as possible. He passes the cut pieces to an assitant known as a trimmer, who cuts lengths of suitable lining material, canvas interlining, and tape. The trimmer then bundles everything together and sends it through to the tailoring workroom.

The tailor uses the main pieces of the cut cloth as a guide to cut the lining. The odd bits of cloth are used for cutting facings (the parts which form the lapel in a jacket) and pocket flaps. Much of the sewing is done by hand and the skill of a tailor or tailoress is shown largely by the neatness and strength of their stitching. A number of machines are now used to do the more repetitive work. The garment is at first 'basted' together, i.e., the seams are not fully sewn but joined with loose stitches that can easily be pulled out. It is now ready for the first fitting and is sent back to the cutter.

When the customer comes in for the fitting, the cutter checks the hang of the sleeves, the fit of the shoulders and collar, the balance of the jacket, and the general appearance of the garment. If any major alterations are needed, a further fitting is arranged; otherwise the garment goes back to the workroom for the final making-up.

Social and economic changes are contributing to a decline in bespoke tailoring, with the consequent strengthening of the market in the middle and lower ranges, from firms like Aquascutum and Austin Reed to the large multiples like C & A, Hepworths, Marks & Spencer, etc.; also, since the 1960s, the development of fashion conscious groups like Take 6 and Lord John, which are taking a larger share of the 'young' tailored market. The majority of young men now no longer buy a 'good' suit to last years, and want more variety and change. In the past two decades men's wear has become much more fashion conscious; this has affected the tailoring trade and made many firms with a conservative approach change their line of thinking and introduce a stronger style and fashion element. The general trend in tailoring is now moving towards an un-structured type of manufacture.

Bibliography: H. Carr, *The Clothing Factory*, Clothing Institute Management Handbook No. 1, 1972.

Tailteann Games, Irish national games of great antiquity, held in memory of Queen Tailta and continued for many centuries. Competitions were held in athletic events and also in poetry, drama and prose, art, music and dancing. They were temporarily revived in 1924 and 1928, following the Olympic Games.

Tailzie, in Scots law, is the usual form of entail. Tailzie is either simple or strict, although the latter can no longer be used.

Taimyr National Okrug, district in KRASNOYARSK *krai* of the RSFSR, USSR, comprising the Taimyr Peninsula with the adjacent mainland and islands. It includes Cape Chelyuskin, the northernmost point of Asia. Nickel, copper, uranium, and coal are mined; other activities include fishing, reindeer breeding, and fur trapping. The *okrug* was formed in 1930; capital, Dudinka. Area 862,100 km². Population (1975) 42,000 (62 per cent urban); mostly Nentsy people, a group of SAMOYEDS.

Tain, small town of Ross and Cromarty District, Highland Region, Scotland, on Dornoch Firth, 40 km northeast of Dingwall. Tain has a collegiate church (founded 1471, restored 1871–76); it is a local service centre with a distilling industry. Population 1942.

Tainan, city on the south-west coast of TAIWAN, the old capital and oldest city on the island. Here are the old Dutch city, and the temples of Confucius and Koxinga. It is the industrial centre of southern Taiwan, and is the seat of Chengkung University (engineering). Population (1972 estimate) 490,000.

Taine, Hippolyte Adolphe (1828–93), French philosopher and critic, born at Vouziers. He was awarded his doctorate for an important thesis on La Fontaine (1853). In 1856 he began a series of articles on English literature, published in 1864. In 1858 appeared a first collection of *Essais de critique et d'histoire*. The originality of his critical theories, as first expressed in the preface to his *Histoire de la littérature anglaise*, 1863, lies in the application of the scientific and naturalistic method to literature. In fact he makes too little allowance for the individual's deviations from type and tends to regard literary genius simplistically, as the mechanical outcome of known and defined productive forces. Taine became professor of aesthetics and the history of art at the École des Beaux Arts in 1864, a post he held for 20 years. *L'Intelligence*,

Taipei

1870, was a return to philosophy. His later years were mostly devoted to the series on *Les Origines de la France contemporaine*, 1875–94. Taine was a follower of Hegel and, more indirectly, of Spinoza. His determinist and materialist outlook had a great influence upon contemporaries, and especially on the novelist Zola.

Bibliography: S. J. Kahn, *Science and aesthetic judgment: a study in Taine's critical method*, 1953; D. G. Charlton, *Secular Religions in France 1815–1870*, 1963.

Taipei, principal city and capital of the island of TAIWAN in the China Sea. Since 1949 it has been the capital of the Nationalist government of China in exile. Taipei occupies a basin site surrounded by mountains in the north of the island. It is 36 km from the sea, its outport being Chilung. Since 1949 its population has been greatly swollen by refugees from mainland China, about 40 per cent being relative newcomers. In 1946 the population was 367,000; by 1974 it had risen to over 2 million. An important centre for overseas trade as well as being predominant in administrative functions within Taiwan, it was declared a special municipality in 1967 and given the status of a province. Manufacturing industry has become important in recent years, including textiles, electrical goods, canning of foodstuffs, and plastics industries.

Taipings, followers of Hung Hsiu-ch'üan, a Chinese peasant Christian leader, who rose against the Manchu emperor in 1851. By 1853 the rebels occupied all southern China, and their leader proclaimed himself emperor in Nanking. In 1860 the war with France and Britain came to an end, and the two powers assisted in the suppression of the rebels, partly owing to the threat posed to their interests in Shanghai.

Tait, Archibald Campbell (1811–82), Archbishop of Canterbury, born in Edinburgh. He was educated at Glasgow University and Balliol College, Oxford. In 1842 he succeeded Dr Arnold as headmaster of Rugby; in 1849 he became dean of Carlisle. In 1856 he was made bishop of London, and 12 years later was raised to the primacy. As archbishop he had to deal with the increasingly bitter conflicts between Ritualists and Low Churchmen. He was largely responsible for the Public Worship Regulation Act 1874; but many of the provisions which were to make it abortive were the result of amendments with which he disagreed.

Tait, Peter Guthrie (1831–1901), British mathematician and physicist, born at Dalkeith, Midlothian, and educated at Edinburgh Academy, Edinburgh University, and Peterhouse, Cambridge. In 1854 he was appointed to the professorship of mathematics at Queen's College (now Queen's University), Belfast, and removed to Edinburgh in 1860 to occupy the chair of natural philosophy. In mathematics he developed Hamilton's theory of quaternions and contributed to mathematical physics, especially in the *Treatise on Natural Philosophy*, 1867, written in collaboration with Professor W. Thomson (Lord Kelvin). His physical researches and experiments were mainly in connection with thermodynamics and thermoelectricity. He collaborated with Balfour Stewart in writing *The Unseen Universe, or Physical Speculation on a Future State*, 1875, and *Paradoxical Philosophy*, 1878.

Taiwan (formerly *Formosa*) is a large island off the

Taiwan. View across the Taipei valley. *(Camera Press/Nick de Morgoli)*

south-eastern coast of CHINA, separated from the mainland by the shallow Taiwan Strait about 150 km wide. It is one of the great series of islands which fringe the Western Pacific as part of an extensive system of folds. Taiwan stands on the edge of the continental shelf; immediately to the east, the PACIFIC OCEAN reaches great depths. Geologically, the island has been subject to intense folding, with the result that it now forms a contorted and tilted block, dominated by mountains which occupy most of the interior and run in a north-north-east to south-south-west direction. The highest peaks reach almost 4000 m and the east coast of the island has steep cliffs. Taiwan extends 320 km from its most northerly to its most southerly point and its total area is 36,000 km². Off the west coast are the P'enghu or PESCADORES islands. In addition, the Chinese Nationalist government, which controls Taiwan, also still has possession of two small islands near the Chinese mainland coast, Matsu and Kinmen (or Quemoy).

Geography. Relief. The principal effect of the lines of folding is to divide the island into a series of five longitudinal physical regions. In the central part of the east coast between Hualien and Taitung, are the Taitung Mountains, which are so steep and rugged as to make communication along the coast virtually impossible as they fall to the sea in a series of spectacular cliffs. Immediately west of these mountains is a deep rift valley, known as the Taitung valley, which is about 160 km long by 8 km wide. A motor road which encircles the whole island runs through this valley. The flat valley floor is intensively cultivated in parts. West of the Taitung valley lies the rugged mountainous backbone of Taiwan. The mountains occupy a large proportion of the island and consist of three major ranges, the Changyang Mountains, the Yu Shan, and Ali Shan. In general, this area is heavily forested and rather remote. Population is sparse, the most remote parts being inhabited only by scattered aboriginal tribes who are not Chinese and whose settlement in Taiwan pre-dates the Chinese colonisation of the island. Nearer to the west coast, the mountains are succeeded by a broad piedmont area. This consists of undulating and hilly land which is terraced for agriculture at the lower levels and interspersed with wide valleys where both agriculture and settlement are intensive. Along the coast itself lies an alluvial plain which in places may be as much as 45 km wide. However in the north it is much narrower and absent in many places. This is the main area for agriculture and settlement. See ATLAS 37.

Climate. Taiwan lies astride the Tropic of Cancer and its climate is dominated by the monsoons. The normal rainfall pattern consists of summer rain and winter drought. However in winter, cold air flowing out from the Siberian high pressure area passes over the Taiwan Strait, picking up moisture before it reaches the island. Thus the north-east of Taiwan does receive substantial rainfall in winter, a time when the rest of the island is suffering from a shortage. During the summer months Taiwan is under the influence of the south-west monsoon which brings substantial rainfall, particularly to the south of the island and to the western coastal plain. Typhoons are also usual at this season, perhaps as many as three a year. They bring widespread destruction to the crops because of the high winds. Summers are generally hot and humid, with daytime temperatures around 30 °C, while winters are warm and generally dry.

Economy. Since 1949, the Nationalist government, with the assistance of massive US economic aid, has rapidly developed Taiwan's resources. About one-quarter of the land surface can be used for agriculture, the main agricultural area being the western coastal plain. Rice is the principal farm crop, two crops a year being possible everywhere, and even three crops in the south-west of the island provided there is water for irrigation. In those parts where it is not possible to grow rice, sweet potatoes are the staple item of the diet. Vegetables are grown around all the villages, while major non-subsistence crops are sugar cane, tea, and pineapples. The forests contain important resources of camphor wood and Taiwan is the leading world producer of camphor. Agriculture has been greatly intensified in recent years and particular attention has been paid to increasing fertiliser production. During the early 1950s the government also carried out an extensive land reform programme which limited the size of farms and placed agricultural land in the hands of the peasant farmers. As a result, 70 per cent of the farms are now owner-occupied.

Because of the refugee immigration from China and their relatively high rates of natural increase, the population of Taiwan has now exceeded 16 million. To meet this challenge, the Nationalist government has adopted policies of industrialisation. In recent years machinery and electrical industries have grown rapidly as has the manufacture of textiles. Taiwan is now also producing a wide variety of manufactured consumer goods, such as rubber footwear, clothing, and plastic toys, for export to overseas markets. Its principal cities, TAIPEI, KAOHSIUNG, and TAINAN, have become industrial centres. The previous pattern of extreme reliance upon Japan for trade has now weakened considerably. The United States has become an important trading partner and industrial goods from Taiwan are also sold in many European markets. The future of Taiwan's economy remains in considerable doubt, however, despite its large measure of economic progress. Much will depend upon the attitude of the Peking government towards the eventual reincorporation of the island into the political system of the mainland.

Bibliography: The China Year Book, annually; C. M. Hsieh,

Taiwan-Ilha Formosa, 1964; A. Y. C. Koo, *Role of Land Reform in Economic Development: Case Study of Taiwan*, 1969; C. Y. Lin, *Industrialisation in Taiwan 1946–72*, 1974.

Government. The KUOMINTANG government moved to Taiwan after the Communist victory on the mainland in 1949. In Kuomintang eyes, Taiwan is both the provisional seat of the central government of the People's Republic of China and a province of that republic. The Communist government in Peking also regards Taiwan as a province of China. Since 1969 the municipality of Taipei has been directly under central government control. The structure of the central government is based on the constitution of December 1947. The president, who has supreme power, appoints the chairmen of the five *yuans* or councils (namely executive, legislative, judicial, control, and examination). In November 1971 the United Nations General Assembly voted to expel the Republic of China and offer the seat to the People's Republic of China. The province of Taiwan is divided into four municipalities and 16 counties. Taiwan has trade unions, but no collective bargaining in the Western sense.

Education and Welfare. Taiwan has approximately 13,000 doctors and 1·8 hospital beds per 1000. Public health measures have almost eradicated epidemics of communicable diseases. In 1968 free education was raised from six to nine years; elementary education is almost universal. In 1975, 275,000 students were attending a university, college, or advanced educational institute.

Bibliography: D. Mendel, *Politics of Formosan Nationalism*, 1970; G. Barclay, *Colonial Development and Population in Taiwan*, 1972; H. Chiu (Ed.), *China and the Question of Taiwan*, 1973.

History. From the 5th to the 6th centuries Taiwan was known as Ryukyu; the name 'Taiwan' occurred in Chinese history in the 16th century. In 1624 Dutch settlers occupied a port on the island, and encouraged the growing of sugar cane on the coastal plain. Two years later a Spanish naval force landed at its northern tip, Chi-lung, and christened the island 'Formosa' ('beautiful'). The Spanish were soon driven off by the Dutch, and, in 1661, the Chinese general, Cheng Ch'eng-kung, completely defeated the Dutch force and recovered the whole island with its archipelagoes. It was not until 1684 that the Manchu government was able to establish its administration on the island, which formed a prefecture of Fukien province. During the 18th and 19th centuries Chinese immigration increased significantly as population pressure in relation to the available cultivated land mounted in the nearby mainland provinces. In 1863 Taiwan was made a district of the Chinese province of FUKIEN. In spite of the 1871 Sino-Japanese treaty of amity, Japan invaded the island in 1874, but soon withdrew through the good offices of Sir Thomas Wade, the British minister to Peking. It was then made a separate province in 1886. In the 1894–95 Sino-Japanese War Japan again occupied the P'eng-hu archipelagoes, and by the Shimonoseki Treaty China ceded Taiwan to Japan. The people on the island, however, refused to be separated from their motherland, and the Japanese had to take it by force after three months of bitter fighting. In the following ten years no less than 13 major uprisings against the Japanese took place on the island, with hundreds of thousands of Chinese sacrificing their lives for the reunion of the island with China. After the Second World War Taiwan was returned to China in accordance with the Three-Power Cairo Declaration of 1 December 1943. When, in 1949, CHIANG KAI-SHEK was defeated in China he fled to Taiwan and set up a refugee government there under the protection of the US 7th Fleet.

In September 1954 the KUOMINTANG (KMT) government in Taiwan was forced to give up the Ta-ch'en islands after bombardment from the mainland. In December 1954 Taiwan and the USA signed a bilateral defence agreement. In 1958 bombardment of Quemoy resumed, and has continued at intervals ever since. The KMT continued to hope for an anti-Communist uprising on the mainland. Since 1949, anti-KMT Taiwanese independence movements have grown up, based in Japan or the USA. In 1971 Taiwan's 'Republic of China' lost its place in the UNO to Peking, causing a crisis in its foreign relations. In 1975 Chiang Kai-shek died and was succeeded as leader by his son, Chiang Ching-Kuo. He was re-elected chairman of the KMT party at its congress in November 1976.

Taizé Community, interdenominational monastic order established at Taizé in southern France since 1944. The Rule of Taizé (1952) is similar to that of other orders, with much emphasis on co-operative work, but members wear ordinary lay clothing. The community has played a positive role in Franco-German reconciliation and in the ecumenical movement.

Ta'izz, town in the highlands of the YEMEN ARAB REPUBLIC, 50 km east of Mocha, one of its largest urban centres and a former capital. It lies at an altitude of 1400 m and is the centre of a coffee-growing district. There are several notable mosques and government buildings in the town. Population (1970) 84,000.

Taj Mahal, mausoleum at AGRA, Uttar Pradesh State, India, in which lie the bodies of SHAH JAHAN, Moghul emperor (1627–58) and his favourite wife, Mumtaz Mahal, who married the emperor in 1612 and died in childbirth in 1631. The Taj Mahal is one of the great sights of the world. Splendidly situated above the River Yamuna, it is built mainly of white marble, beautifully carved in open traceries and designs, and largely inlaid with semi-precious stones, many of which have been stolen. The proportions and balance of the main structure, together with the four supporting minarets, show Moghul architecture at its peak. The whole building took 22 years to complete.

Tajik, or Tadjik, or Tadzhik, term originally used to describe the Iranian peoples of central Asia. Today it is applied to Iranian-speaking peoples living in northern Afghanistan and in Soviet central Asia, in Tadzhikistan and Uzbekistan. There are also 15,000 living in north-west China. Traditionally they are sedentary agriculturalists. From Persia their culture diffused to China. They linked Persia, India, and China by trade. They fought the UZBEKS when the Mongols moved west. They are mainly Sunni Muslims, but there are also some Shiites and some followers of the Aga Khan (see ISLAM).

Tajikistan, see TADZHIK SOVIET SOCIALIST REPUBLIC.

Tajo, see TAGUS.

Takahe, Notornis mantelli, flightless bird of New Zealand. It is a species of moorhen belonging to the Grui-

formes, weighs just over 2 kg and is about 46 cm high. The tail and back are bronze-green, the head and breast bluish-black, and the bill red and short. Its fossil remains were found in the 1840s and it was thought to be extinct, but living specimens were later caught, and specimens have been observed and photographed. It is now protected.

Takamatsu, city of Kagawa-ken, SHIKOKU, Japan, on the Inland Sea. A castle town of the Tokugawas (1642–1868). A railway ferry to Honshū has operated from here since 1910 and the island's economic traffic is centred on the city. Its primary function is as a seaport with shipbuilding and warehousing facilities. Population (1974) 294,000.

Takatsuki, city of Ōsaka-fu, Japan, located in the Yodogawa valley between Ōsaka and Kyōto. Takatsuki is partly a satellite city of Ōsaka, and partly a manufacturing centre. Industries include pharmaceutical goods and electric batteries and components. Population (1974) 320,000.

Takin, Budorcas taxicolor, a heavily built, goat-like mammal with the horns thickened at the base and growing outwards. It ranges from Bhutan in the Himalaya to Central China. Its only close relation is the MUSK OX.

Takizawa Bakin, see JAPAN, Literature.

Takla Makan, desert of the TARIM Basin in the SINKIANG UIGHUR autonomous region of China, and forming part of the GOBI Desert. It is bounded on the east by LOP NOR, on the west and north by the Yarkand Daria (River Tarim), and on the south by the Kunlun Mountains. It extends east–west for 970 km and north–south for 325 km.

Takoradi, see SEKONDI-TAKORADI.

Takutea, uninhabited island in the South Cook Group.

Tal (music), see INDIA, Music.

Tal, Mikhail (1936–), Soviet world chess champion, 1960–61. He became a national master at 16 and in 1957 an international grandmaster. Three years later he defeated BOTVINNIK and became world champion. In 1961 he lost the crown to his old rival and though he has played regularly for the USSR since then, ill health has affected his play.

Talavera de la Reina, town of Spain in the province of Toledo, on the River Tagus. Wellington here defeated the French on the 27 and 28 July 1809 (see PENINSULAR WAR). Talavera is in a wine-producing district, has Roman, Moorish, and Gothic remains, and is known for its ceramics. Population 32,000.

Talbot, Charles, see SHREWSBURY, CHARLES TALBOT, 12TH EARL AND ONLY DUKE OF.

Talbot, John, see SHREWSBURY, JOHN TALBOT, 1ST EARL OF.

Talbot, Richard, see TYRCONNEL, RICHARD TALBOT, EARL OF.

Talbot, William Henry Fox (1800–1877), English gentleman and pioneer photographer, born at Melbury Hall, Wiltshire. Educated at Harrow and Trinity College,

Cambridge, Talbot was a botanist, chemist, mathematician and physicist, and one of the first translators of the Assyrian CUNEIFORM inscriptions. He is best remembered for his invention in 1834 of the photogenic drawing process, an early form of photography, and for a subsequent improvement on it, the CALOTYPE, or Talbotype, process in 1840. The negative-positive principle which these methods incorporated is the basis of modern photography. From 1844 to 1846 he published *The Pencil of Nature*, in six parts, illustrated with original calotype prints, and the first publication to be illustrated with photographs. Among his later achievements was the invention of the first successful method of photoengraving in 1851. His life and work are commemorated in a museum at his ancestral home in Lacock, Wiltshire.

Talc, $Mg_6Si_8O_{20}(OH)_4$, hydrous bisilicate of magnesia, which crystallises in the rhombic system (hardness 1, relative density 2·8). Crystals are rare, and the massive form 'steatite' or 'soapstone' is more common. French chalk, potstone, and figure-stone are all varieties of talc. It is used as a filter for paints and paper, a toilet powder, for insulation and acid resistance, in soap as a lubricant, and for making ornaments.

Talca, province of central CHILE. Wheat, wine, and cattle are produced. It is one of the most agriculturally productive provinces of Chile. Area 10,140 km²; population (1974) 262,500.

Talca, capital of the above province in Chile, 240 km south of Santiago. It was founded in 1692 and completely rebuilt after the 1928 earthquake. At the centre of a rich agricultural area, it is also an important trading and manufacturing town and a railway junction. Its manufactures include matches (it has the largest match factory in Chile), shoes, paper, tobacco, flour, and biscuits; there are also several distilleries and foundries. Population 103,000.

Talcahuano, city in Concepción province, Chile, lying to the north-east of the city of CONCEPCIÓN for which it serves as a port. It is the Chilean fleet's main port and is also a major commercial, fishing, and industrial centre. Lumber, hides, wool, and coal are exported from here, and it also has an oil refinery. In the harbour is moored an old Peruvian iron warship captured in the War of the Pacific in 1879. Population (1970) 115,568.

Talent (Latin *talentum*, Greek *talanton* from verbal root *tla*-, to bear), unit of weight in use among the ancient Greeks. It was probably based on the Babylonian unit (called *gun* in Sumerian and *biltu* in Accadian). According to Herodotus, the talent was divided into 70 Euboic *minae*. The Attic talent weighed 26·20 kg, and was divided into 60 *minae* (of 436·6 g) or 6000 *drachmae*. The Egyptian *kerker* (of 300 *kitae*) of the Ptolemaic age corresponded to the Greek talent, but in later times various talents were current in Egypt. The Hebrew *kikkar* of the Hellenistic period corresponded to 10,000 Attic *drachmae* = 125 Roman lb. = 43·6 kg, but the weight of the pre-Hellenistic *kikkar* is uncertain. As gold and silver were not coined before the 7th century BC, the use of the balance for weighing out precious metals led to the employment of the unit of weight as a unit of value. Hence the term talent persisted as applied to money throughout

the east Mediterranean districts. Its use to denote intellectual gift is derived from the Biblical parable of the talents (Matthew xxv).

Ta-lien, see DAIREN.

Taliesin (fl. 550), Welsh poet, possibly a mythical figure, famed as the leading BARD of his day and said to have been a court poet in the kingdom of Rheged, in southern Scotland. His odes were written in praise of the victories of his patrons, Urien, King of Rheged, Cynan, King of Powis, and Gwallawg.

Taliesin is first mentioned in the *Historia Brittonum* of NENNIUS. The *Book of Taliesin* was not composed until the 14th century and contains work from different periods and by different authors. However, some dozen verses have been directly attributed to Taliesin. A village in Dyfed, reputedly the place of his death, is named after him.

Talisman, object allegedly having magical powers acquired from the influences of the planets and the celestial bodies operating at the time it is made. It is usually worn like an AMULET.

Tall al-Kabir, village in north-east Egypt, on the Freshwater Canal. It owes its fame to the fact that it was the scene of Wolseley's great victory over ARABI PASHA, 13 September 1882.

See also WOLSELEY, GARNET JOSEPH WOLSELEY, VISCOUNT.

Tallage, tax of the Anglo-Norman and Plantagenet periods, imposed on the royal towns, boroughs, and demesne lands. By the statute *de tallagio non concedendo*, 1297 (an unconfirmed draft of the *Confirmatio Cartarum*, which makes no mention of tallage), it was provided that no tallage should be taken without the consent of the Commons. Notwithstanding the strict legality of imposition, the levy was resisted until Parliament abolished the tax in 1340.

Tallahassee, city of Florida, USA. It was founded in 1823 to serve as state capital, the site chosen because it was more or less equidistant from the existing settlements of East and West Florida, around the Spanish towns of St Augustine and Pensacola. Its main business is government, but it is also the seat of two state universities and it serves as a market centre for the surrounding agricultural areas. Population 71,879.

Tallemant des Réaux, Gédéon (1619–92), French author, born at La Rochelle. His chief work is *Historiettes* (completed about 1659) composed of portraits of contemporaries; it remained unpublished until 1834–35, and is now recognised as an important, accurate, and full historical record of the period.

Bibliography: E. Magne, *La Joyeuse jeunesse de Tallemant des Réaux*, 1921.

Tallensi, a people living in northern Ghana, with a strong and elaborate clan system. Government is in the hands of chiefs and earth priests, who are ritually independent, and who represent two diverse stocks, said to have been the ancestral stock of the people.

Bibliography: M. Fortes, *Dynamics of Clanship among the Tallensi*, 1945; *The Web of Kinship among the Tallensi*, 1948.

Talleyrand-Périgord, Charles Maurice de (1754–1838), French statesman, born in Paris. He was sent to the Collège d'Harcourt, and thence to the seminary of St Sulpice and to the Sorbonne. In 1780 he was appointed general agent of the clergy of France. In 1788 he was appointed Bishop of Autun, became a member of the States-General convoked in 1789, and having accepted the civil constitution of the clergy, was excommunicated in 1791. In 1792 he went on a mission to England, and in 1794 was banned from France for supposed dealings with Louis XVI. He spent two years in England and America, returning to Paris in 1796. Talleyrand was appointed foreign minister by the Directory in 1797. He supported the foreign and domestic policy of Napoleon until he grew convinced that this policy could only lead to disaster for France, and at Erfurt, and afterwards, worked against the Emperor and for the restoration of the Bourbons in the name of 'legitimacy'. He became foreign minister to Louis XVIII in 1814.

At the Congress of Vienna Talleyrand played a leading part, obtaining favourable terms for France, and securing its readmission to the concert of European powers, by playing off the victorious allies against each other. He supported Louis Philippe in 1830, and until 1834 was envoy in London where he played an important part in the creation of a neutral Belgium, and concluded the Quadruple Alliance of 1830 with Britain, Spain, and Portugal. A man of considerable ability and intellect, his services to France under a succession of rulers were very great. His *Mémoires* were edited by the Duc de Broglie, 1892.

Bibliography: A. Duff Cooper, *Talleyrand*, 1932; J. Orieux (trans. P. Wolf), *Talleyrand: The Art of Survival*, 1974.

Tallien, Jean Lambert (1767–1820), French revolutionary, born in Paris. In 1791 he became famous as the author of the Jacobin sheet, *L'Ami des Citoyens*, *journal fraternel*, placarded twice weekly on the walls of Paris. He proved himself a fanatical terrorist as commissioner of the Convention, but later led the Thermidorian attack on Robespierre. From 1795 to 1798 he was one of the Council of Five Hundred.

His wife, Madame Tallien (1773–1835), later Princesse de Chimay, was instrumental in popularising Grecian-style costumes under the Directory.

Tallinn (formerly *Revel*; German *Reval*), capital of the ESTONIAN SSR, USSR, and a major port on the Gulf of Finland opposite HELSINKI. The leading industries are engineering and machine building (electrical equipment, excavators, oil industry equipment), with paper, textile, food, and furniture factories. It is a major cultural centre with the Estonian Academy of Sciences, and a number of polytechnic, arts, and other institutes. Tallinn is known from the 12th century and has many historical buildings, including the Vyshgorod castle (13th–14th centuries), town hall (14th–15th century), and Oleviste church (known from 12th century). Originally a Danish fortress town, it became Russian in 1710. Population (1976) 408,000.

Tallis, Thomas (c. 1505–85), English composer of church music, born probably in Leicestershire, was organist at Waltham Abbey until 1540, and from c. 1542 gentleman of the Chapel Royal, besides being with his pupil, BYRD, joint organist there. In 1575 they were

granted the monopoly of music publishing and produced, jointly, the *Cantiones Sacrae*. This monopoly lasted for 21 years. The second Prayer Book of Edward VI, issued in 1552, created the demand for new church music, which Tallis was one of the chief to supply, a notable work being the service in the Dorian mode, published in 1641. Other works by Tallis are the motet *Spem in alium* in 40 parts, c. 50 Latin motets, and c. 30 English anthems.

Bibliography: P. Doe, *Tallis*, 1968.

Tallow, substance composed chiefly of the triglycerides of palmitic, stearic, and oleic acids, derived mainly from beef and mutton suet. The fat is separated by steaming under pressure in steel cylinders. The top layer is drawn off and allowed to solidify. The quality depends on skill in rendering and the part of animal used. Best quality tallow is edible; other grades are used for soap manufacture, fatty acid manufacture, and lubricants. Tallow is now little used for candles.

Tallow Tree, *Sapium sebiferum*, a Chinese tree of the Euphorbiaceae (spurge family), which bears yellow flowers followed by small fruits; the seeds yield a wax used for making candles. An oil can be expressed from the seeds. The wood of the tree is very hard and is used in making blocks for printing. Another tree, *Pentadesma butyracea*, of the family Guttiferae, also called the butter tree, bears large red flowers followed by edible berries. A thick, yellow, greasy juice exudes from the tree when cut, and the seeds yield a greasy juice used as a butter substitute.

Tallinn. 17th-century architecture in the walled town. *(Barnaby's Picture Library)*

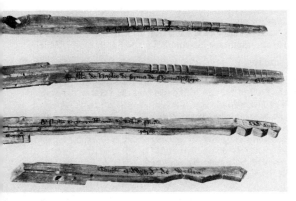

Tally. Exchequer tallies dating from the 13th century. *(Public Record Office)*

Tally (French *tailler*, to cut), stick or rod of well-seasoned hazel, willow, box, or other suitable wood, squared with a knife, and marked on one side with transverse notches of different size. The notched stick, a primitive mnemonic device or memory aid for recording numbers, was employed by some early peoples of Australia, North America, West Africa, and Asia and as an aid in conveying messages (see WRITING). It was used also in many European countries to express numbers. In England exchequer tallies for recording payment made by the Crown or government were introduced shortly after the Norman conquest; they had the advantage of providing a perfect check for both parties, and of being understood by illiterate people. The amount of the transaction (loan to the sovereign or tax, 'tallage') was cut (*taillé*) by the 'tallator', who also split the tally into two unequal parts: the chamberlain retained the smaller part (leaf, foil, or tally), the larger part (stalk, counterfoil, or counter-tally) being held by the other party. Tallies were used officially (notwithstanding Burke's act for their abolition, 1782) until the death of the last chamberlain of the Exchequer in 1826. The verb 'to tally', i.e. to agree, derives from the tally.

Talma, François Joseph (1763–1826), French actor, born in Paris; educated in London, where he hoped to appear at one of the patent theatres; but his father sent him back to Paris. He made his debut at the Comédie Française in 1787. During the French Revolution he became head of the Théâtre de la République (the present Comédie Française), where he played a number of classic roles, and several of Shakespeare's tragic heroes, in translation by Ducis. He was the favourite actor of Napoleon who took him to Erfurt in 1803 to play before five crowned heads and also consulted him over the new administrative code for the Comédie Française. Talma made many useful reforms in the theatre, particularly in costume, and continued to act until shortly before his death.

Talmud, The (Study), collection of Jewish books containing traditions, laws, rules, and institutions, by which, in addition to the Hebrew Bible, the conduct of Jewry is regulated. The fall of Jerusalem, the destruction of the temple, the dissolution of the Jewish state, and the disper-sion of its inhabitants (see JEWS) did not annihilate Judaism. The *Torah* (see PENTATEUCH), the 'Written Law' then came to be augmented by the 'Oral Law', the rabbinic interpretations recorded in the academies which became the Talmud.

During the exile, the teachers of the *Torah* were known as *sopherim* (scribes), but in later times they were called *tannaïm* (teachers). Hillel, born in Babylonia, is considered to be the first author of the arrangement of the *Mishna* (see below), although it was not yet reduced to writing. After the fall of Jerusalem in AD 70, Jochanan ben Zaccai, a disciple of Hillel, reorganised a Jewish academy at Jabneh or Jamnia. Akiba ben Joseph, a martyr in the Bar Cocheba war (AD 132–135) was a great expositor and *tanna* of the *Torah*, as well as systematiser of the multitude of rules and precepts which had accumulated down to his time, and reduced them to order. The great achievement of the compilation of the *Mishna* was accomplished by Jehuda ha-Nasi, 'the Prince' (died c. AD 219), the official leader of the Jewish community in Palestine. The *Mishna* (from the root *shanah*, 'to repeat', or 'to learn by heart') contains nearly 4000 rules, divided into six sections, called *sedarim* (orders), of agricultural regulations, festivals, marital laws, injuries (civil and criminal law), sacred things (sacrificial laws), and laws of cleanliness; each order consists of a number of *massich-toth* (tractates), the total being 63; each tractate is divided into chapters (523 in all; later another chapter was added), which were subdivided into paragraphs. Seven *massichtoth* were afterwards added to the Babylonian *Talmud* (see below), and four small tractates were added later. The language of the *Mishna* is Hebrew, known as *Mishnaic* Hebrew, which is of a more recent and more colloquial form than Biblical Hebrew. The *Mishna* became the standard text-book for the study of the *Torah*, and was adopted throughout the Jewish academies in Palestine and Babylonia.

The *Mishna* in its turn became the subject of study and explanation in the academies of Palestine and Babylonia. The main object of such study was to verify the *halachah* by establishing its connection with *Torah*, elucidating its meaning, and, in certain respects bringing it up to date by showing how it was to be applied to the circumstances of the time. Thus, the *Gemara* (from the root *gamar*, 'to complete'), or 'completion' was formed. The *Mishna*, together with its *Gemara*, makes up the *Talmud*. There is only one *Mishna*, but there are two *Talmuds* known as the Palestinian (or Jerusalem) and the Babylonian respectively, from the countries where the *Gemara* was completed. The Palestinian *Talmud* proceeded from the academy of Tiberias; it is attributed to Jochanan ben Nappacha (199–279), but it was probably completed in the late 4th century. The Babylonian *Talmud* was compiled by R. Ashi (died 427), and completed by Rabina and R. Jose in 499. Neither *Talmud* has a complete *Gemara*; the Palestinian *Gemara* covers 39 tractates; the Babylonian *Gemara* only 37, but the Babylonian *Talmud* is seven to eight times the size of the other.

The *Talmud* is the product of Rabbinic Judaism, by Jews, who have always valued it highly. Taken as a whole, it presents the appearance of a conglomerate of the most heterogeneous material, relating to religion, ethics, history, legend, folklore, astronomy, mathematics, law, physical life, botany, etc. The material of the *Talmud* may

Talysh

be divided into two main categories, the *halachah* and the *Aggadah* ('narration'). The latter word, originally applied to all the results of the interpretation of scripture, later (when the *halachah* was recognised and studied as a special department) denoted the non-*halachic* sections of the *Talmud*, i.e. the interpretation of the *Torah* for edification and not directly for the regulation of conduct. The Talmud has moulded the Jews' spiritual and religious life, promoting their intellectual activity, and regulating their conduct: in short, it has helped to preserve the existence of Jewry.

The Babylonian *Talmud* was first published by Daniel Bomberg in Venice (1520–23) in 12 folio volumes, and has been frequently reprinted. The Palestinian (Jerusalem) *Talmud* was first published by Daniel Bomberg (c. 1523–24) in folio volume then reprinted at Cracow (1609), at Krotoshin (1866), at Piortków (1898–1902), and at Wilno (1922). The first unabridged and authoritative English version, in 34 volumes was completed and published in 1949 (edited by Dr. I. Epstein). A comprehensive selection of the *Talmud* has been made by Dr. A. Cohen (*Everyman's Talmud*, 1932, 1949). An English version of the *Mishna* has been published by Canon Dr. H. Danby, Regius professor of Hebrew at Oxford, 1933. See also *The Living Talmud*, New American Library, 1957.

Talysh, Iranian-speaking people living in the USSR and Iran, on the south-west shores of the Caspian Sea, numbering about 150,000 (around 80,000 of these in Soviet Azerbaijan). They are mostly cattle-breeding peasants, mainly Sunni Muslims, although some are Shi'ite Muslims (see ISLAM). In Soviet Azerbaijan most of the Talysh are bilingual and are being assimilated by Azerbaijanis. Talysh Khanate, semi-independent from Persia, was formed in the 18th century; it became Russian in 1813, and was abolished in 1826.

Tam-tam, see GONG.

Tamale, town of northern Ghana, now only 50 km from the northern tip of Lake Volta. It is the administrative, communications, and service centre for much of the north of the country. Population 90,000.

Tamar, river of England, the boundary between the counties of Devon and Cornwall, which forms the estuary of the Hamoaze at Devonport and flows into Plymouth Sound. The river is 96 km long.

Tamarind, *Tamarindus indica*, a leguminous evergreen tree cultivated in India and other tropical countries for its hard, close-grained, heavy wood. It bears pinnate leaves and racemes of yellow, red-streaked flowers followed by legumes. The pulp of the fruit is a gentle laxative.

Tamarisk, *Tamarix*, a genus of 90 shrubs in the family Tamaricaceae. They are native to India, the Middle East and southern Europe. The common tamarisk, *T. anglica*, has become naturalised on the southern and eastern coasts of Britain, where it has been extensively planted to bind and cover sand-dunes. It is evergreen, having bright green, minute, scale-like leaves and spikes of rose-pink flowers. *T. pentandra* flowers in August and September, *T. gallica* in late summer, and both thrive by the sea. *T. mannifera* exudes manna when punctured by the scale insect *Trabutina mannipara*.

Tamatave, port of MADAGASCAR, on the Indian Ocean, 225 km north-east of Tananarive, with which it is connected by rail. CORAL reefs nearly encircle the harbour. It has an important airport. Population (1972) 59,500.

Tamate, see MELANESIA.

Tamaulipas, maritime state of north-east MEXICO, with the Gulf of Mexico to the east and the USA to the north. The Sierra Madre Oriental crosses the south-west part of the state and elsewhere, other than the coastal plain, there are several smaller mountain ranges. The 430 km long coastline is sandy or gravelly and has many lagoons and clusters of small islands. In the east the climate is tropical but high temperatures are moderated by sea breezes, and the annual rainfall varies between 500 and 1000 mm. In the higher altitudes of the west, the climate is temperate but dry. The numerous rivers run west to east into the Gulf of Mexico, and many are harnessed for power and irrigation. The chief crops are cotton (in the north), maize, beans, sugar cane, sisal, and fruits; cattle raising is also important. Timber is exploited, particularly pine, oak, and cedar. Fishing is a significant economic activity. There are oil-fields in the south but other minerals have not been exploited on a large scale. Oil production and refining are the chief industries, followed by vegetable oil processing, soap, flour milling, fish processing and preserving, sugar refining, and sisal. The capital is Ciudad Victoria (70,000 population) and other towns are the port of Tampico (222,000), Ciudad Madero (90,000), NUEVO LAREDO (193,000), Matamoros (172,000), and Reynosa (193,000). Area 79,829 km²; population (1975) 1,828,400.

Tambour, see EMBROIDERY.

Tambourine, percussion instrument consisting of a vellum head over a circular wooden frame in which 'jingles', i.e. small cymbals loosely working on a centre pin, are inserted. It is played by rapping or rubbing with the thumb, or by shaking.

Tambourine.

Tambov, *oblast* of the RSFSR, USSR, south-east of Moscow, situated on the Oka-Don plain in the black earth belt. About 10 per cent is covered with mixed forests, and there are peat deposits. Grain, potatoes, sunflowers, and sugar-beet are grown, and cattle, pigs, sheep, and horses are bred. There are also food, chemical, and textile (coarse cloth) industries. The chief cities are Tambov (see below) and MICHURINSK. Area 34,300 km². Population (1975) 1,419,000 (39 per cent urban).

Tambov, capital city, economic and cultural centre of Tambov *oblast* (see above), USSR, south-east of Moscow.

There are engineering (chemical apparatus, spare parts for agricultural machinery), food, and chemical industries, and it is an important railway junction. It was founded in 1636 as a fortress in the Muscovite southern defence lines, and became a provincial capital in 1779; prior to 1917 it was a centre of trade in grain and cattle. Population (1974) 252,000.

Tamerlane, or Timur (1335–1405), Sultan of Samarkand, born at Kesk, of Mongol origin, a direct descendant of GENGHIS KHAN. He assisted and then attacked Husein, Khan of North Khorasan and Jagatai, finally supplanting him in 1369. He made Samarkand his capital and rapidly made himself master of the whole of Turkestan and part of Siberia. He next attacked northeastern Persia. After a series of bloody and cruel conflicts, the whole of Persia, Georgia, Armenia, and the neighbouring states accepted him as suzerain. Tamerlane then turned his arms towards the north and overran Kiptshak. He then declared war against India, and in 1398 defeated the Indian army near Delhi. He later came into conflict with Europeans, when he attacked and took Smyrna, the property of the Knights of St John. He died at Otra on the Jaxartes as he was marching to attack China.

His name, Tamerlane, is a European corruption of Timûr-lenk (Timur the Lame). He figures as the hero of Christopher Marlowe's great drama, *Tamburlaine*.

Tameside, see MANCHESTER METROPOLITAN COUNTY, GREATER.

Tamil, a Dravidian language, the official language and script of the state of Tamil Nadu (Madras), India. It is the mother tongue of over 30,000,000 people (1961) in India, 2,000,000 in Sri Lanka, and of many more in South-East Asia and Africa. Inscriptions date from the 2nd century BC, and classical Tamil literature is attested from the early centuries AD onwards. A modern literature begins in the 19th century. See also INDIA, *Language*; INDIA, *Literature*.

Tamil Nadu, state of southern INDIA containing most Tamil-speaking areas, and bounded on the north by Karnataka and Andhra Pradesh, Kerala on the west, and facing the Bay of Bengal and Indian Ocean on the east and south. Tamil Nadu's 130,066 km² consists mainly of coastal plains, including the CAUVERY delta and the hilly hinterland of the NILGIRI HILLS and extensions of the Western GHATS. Rainfall is unreliable, derived mainly from the north-east monsoon (October to December), averaging 1270 mm for Madras, but with much less inland. As a result, multiple cropping of land for several rice crops, or rice-millet-groundnuts combination, is frequently dependent on tank and well irrigation as well as natural rainfall and large canal irrigation schemes. Sugarcane, cotton, coconuts, and pepper are important cash crops, with tea and coffee grown on plantations in the interior hills. The state is self-sufficient in food, and with wider use of fertilisers and a declining birth rate, should remain a food surplus area. Hydro-electric power has increased significantly, especially from the Mettur and Moyar schemes. Thermal stations at Ennore and at Neyveli using the latter's lignite deposits (production is 5 million t a year) are important in raising the industrial capacity of a rural state. Cars, motors, chemicals, oil

refining, fertilisers, cement, sugar, and cotton mills are in large-scale production, together with significant consumer industries including a big film industry and cycle works. Most industry is concentrated in and around MADRAS, the capital, with COIMBATORE, SALEM, and TIRUCHIRAPPALLI as lesser centres. Home-spun cottons remain significant for the majority of the rural population. There is a strong relationship between extreme poverty and former low caste groups. Generally living standards are below the national average. Literacy is 40 per cent, and cholera and malaria still recur. Of the population of 41,200,000, 90 per cent are Hindu, mostly Tamil-speaking, although Telugu is spoken by 10 per cent and English remains a widespread second language, especially for further education. Its peculiar Tamil-Hindu culture is exemplified by the temples of MADURAI, Bharata Natyam dancing, and Vedic scholarship; that it remains alive and thriving is evidenced by Tamil literature and films. The government is based at Madras. The legislature is of two houses with 235 and 63 members.

History. In the pre-Christian era, this part of India, as yet untouched by the Aryan invasion, was ruled by the powerful dynasties of the Cholas, Palavas, Pandyas, and Cheras. Its people sailed to distant lands and carried its culture to Ceylon (Sri Lanka), Indo-China, Malaya, Java, and Bali, just as in recent times Tamils have been the most numerous among the Indian communities in Malaya, South Africa, and the Caribbean islands. The VIJAYANA-

Tamerlane sacking a fortress. From an early 16th-century Persian manuscript of the *Life of Timur*. (*Victoria and Albert Museum, London*)

Tammany Hall and Society

Tamil Nadu. Terraced rice paddy fields. *(Barnaby's Picture Library)*

GAR empire included all of modern Tamil Nadu in the 14th–16th centuries, after which petty chiefs set up their own states, and later a Muslim overlord, the nawab of Carnatic, ruled. The British trading post at Madras (Fort St George), was their most important factory before the conquest of Bengal. The 18th-century wars between the British and the French and their respective Indian allies led to the British governing the Carnatic. The British presidency of Madras included much of what is now KERALA and ANDHRA PRADESH. Demands for linguistic divisions and more conveniently-sized administrative units led to the reduction of the state to its present extent to cover primarily Tamilnad (land of the Tamils). After the reorganisation of the constituent states in 1956, and again in 1960, parts of the then Madras state were lost to Kerala and Karnataka, but parts of Travancore-Cochin were gained. The state was renamed Tamil Nadu in 1968.

Tammany Hall and Society, New York party organisation established in 1789 as the Columbian Society, soon after Washington's installation as president, by an Irish-American, William Mooney, for social and charitable purposes. In 1805 it adopted the title of Tammany Society (apparently from the name of an Indian chief, Tammanena). Twenty-five years after its foundation it entered politics, and allied itself with the Democratic party of New York, and from 1834 established its nominees in the New York mayoral office in the majority of cases. Tammany Hall became an instrument of corruption in public life. Its later history is associated mainly with the names of Richard Croker, one-time keeper of a liquor saloon, and Charles F. Murphy. Croker held no civic office, but as chairman of the Tammany sub-committee controlled all the city officials, and inspired the city legislative proposals at Albany. Tammany Hall, much purged, continued to control New York politics until 1934, when LA GUARDIA stood for the mayorship on an anti-Tammany Hall platform and was elected. It still retained great influence in Democratic quarters, however, but again suffered a blow in 1964 when John LINDSAY was elected mayor.

Bibliography: G. Myers, *History of Tammany Hall,* 1972.

Tammuz, or Thammuz, Babylonian and Assyrian god, possibly to be identified with the Greek Adonis and the Egyptian Osiris. He represents the decay and growth of natural life, descending part of the year into the nether world, and being rescued from there by his sister, the heaven goddess, Innini (Innana) or ISHTAR, the Phoenician Astarte. In the myth Ishtar apparently descended into the nether world to rescue her dead husband. The fourth month of the Babylonian and Hebrew year was named after him.

Tampa, city of Florida, USA, and the focus of the metropolitan area of Tampa-St Petersburg. It is situated at the head of Tampa Bay, on Florida's west coast, 40 km from the open sea, and is a major port on the US coast of the Gulf of Mexico: in 1970 it handled over 13 million t of foreign trade and coastwise cargo of 16·5 million t. The metropolitan area employs over 50,000 workers in manufacturing industries; among its chief products are cigars, chemicals and fertilisers (Florida's phosphate mining has its focus just east of the city), food products, and paints. The bay's shrimp fishing fleet is famous. The best-known feature of the metropolitan area is its attraction as a place of retirement for the elderly. In 1970 20·3 per cent of its population was over 65; this proportion was the highest for any metropolitan area in the USA. For the city of St Petersburg alone the figure was as high as 35 per cent. The mild climate and high incidence of sunshine (an average of 360 days a year) are the principal attractions, but much has been done to beautify the cities and justify their high reputation as residential areas. For the younger section of the population there are five universities or senior colleges. Population (city) 277,767; (metropolitan area) 1,276,594.

Tampere (Swedish *Tammerfors*), town in FINLAND, 164 km north-west of Helsinki, on both sides of the Tammerkoski, whose rapids were originally utilised for the textile industry. It is the chief industrial town of Finland, and manufactures textiles, engineering products, timber, paper, and footwear. Its open-air theatre has a revolving auditorium. Population (1974) 165,300.

Tampico, port in the state of TAMAULIPAS, Mexico, on the Gulf of Mexico. It is the largest city in the state; one of Mexico's chief ports, its main industries are oil shipping and refining. It is connected by rail with MONTERREY. It is also an important fishing port, and fish processing and preserving forms a leading industry. The climate is hot, particularly in the summer when the rainfall is heavy. The town has played a prominent part in the development of the Mexican oil industry ever since an American refinery was installed here in 1898. Population (1975) 222,000.

Tamworth, borough and market town in STAFFORDSHIRE, England, at the junction of the Tame and Anker rivers, 24 km north-east of Birmingham. Tamworth, once the capital of Mercia, was one of the places where King Athelstan held his councils. The castle mound was built by Ethelfleda, daughter of Alfred; the castle is largely Saxon and Norman work. There is a 14th-century parish church; the town hall was built (1701) by Thomas GUY, founder of Guy's Hospital, who was educated at Tamworth, and in front of it is a statue of Peel, who represented Tamworth in Parliament from 1830 until his death in 1850. Industries include engineering, paper-making, and the manufacture of asbestos goods, sanitary ware, clothing, and small wares. In the vicinity are large market gardens and the North Warwickshire coalfield. In recent years there has been extensive development of industry and housing for the Birmingham overspill. Population (1971) 48,900.

Tamworth, town of New South Wales, Australia, on the River Peel, 454 km north of Sydney. It stands in an agricultural and sheep-rearing district and is a regional centre for New England. Population 24,440.

Tan Waste, spent bark from tan pits, which used to be used in gardening for making hotbeds, and as a material in which pots are plunged, and was also used on riding-tracks.

Tana, river of Kenya some 800 km long. It enters the Indian Ocean at Kipini. After leaving the highlands it flows through an arid area, and its irrigation potential is being developed.

Tana, river of FINNMARK, Norway, formed by the junction of the Anar and the Karas rivers. Its course is winding and generally north-east, and it enters the Arctic Ocean by Tana Fjord. It is the Finnish-Norwegian border for most of its length. Salmon are caught. Length 400 km.

Tana (Tsana), Lake, in northern ETHIOPIA, some 75 km long and 70 km wide. It is the source of the Blue NILE some 1800 m above sea-level. James Bruce reached its shores in 1770. The Blue Nile leaves the lake by way of the Tisisat Falls (40 m high), harnessed for hydro-electric power. Area 3673 km².

Tanacetum, see TANSY.

Tananarive market-place. (Camera Press/Richard Harrington)

Tanager, name for about 200 species of the bird family Emberizidae in order Passeriformes. They are natives of the Americas and nearly all of them have very brilliant plumage. One of the finest is the superb *Tangara chilensis;* its plumage has a remarkable metallic lustre; the head is sea-green in colour, the breast is violet, and there is a flame-coloured patch on the lower part of the back. It feeds on fruit and insects, and is sometimes kept in indoor aviaries. *Piranga olivacea,* the scarlet tanager or summer red bird, has brilliant scarlet plumage in the male with black wings and tail. In autumn its plumage changes to a dull green, like that of the female bird.

Tanagra, ancient town of Boeotia. Situated near the Attic border, it was exposed to attack by the Athenians, but the latter were themselves defeated here (457 BC) by a Spartan force on its way back from Doris (Thucydides, i. 107–8). The statuettes found on the site of Tanagra are characteristic of the best Greek work in terracotta; they date from c. 350 to 200 BC.

Tanais, see DON.

Tananarive, the capital of MADAGASCAR, situated in the interior of the island. It is built on the summit and slopes of a large V-shaped ridge over 200 m above the encircling paddy fields, which themselves are more than 1200 m above sea-level. This ridge, 5 km long, is very narrow, and most of the houses are built on artificial terraces rising tier on tier like the seats in an amphitheatre. Up to 1895, when it was bombarded by the French, Tananarive was a town of wood or rush dwellings, and a few timber palaces. Today it contains numerous public buildings—an observatory, a cathedral, a royal palace, government buildings, several brick and stone churches, hospitals, schools, a technical college, schools of law and medicine, a university, and law courts; also hundreds of substantially built dwellings and good if narrow roads. Tananarive is connected by rail with the seaport of TAMATAVE and is served by two airports. Industries include tobacco and food processing, leather goods, and clothing. Population (1972) 366,530.

Tanaro, Italian river draining southern PIEDMONT. It rises in the Ligurian Alps close to the French border and flows north and north-east past Asti and Alessandria to join the PO 16 km north-east of Alessandria. Length 274 km.

Tancred (1076–1112), leader of the First Crusade, nephew of Bohemond and a grandson of Robert Guiscard. He accompanied his uncle to Constantinople in 1096 and after the capture of Nicaea took service with the Emperor Alexis. He took Tarsus, but was evicted by Baldwin of Lorraine. He played a prominent part in the sieges of Antioch and Jerusalem, and became Prince of Galilee in 1099. When Baldwin became King of Jerusalem, Tancred took over the regency of Antioch (1100–03), and later became Prince of Edessa and Antioch. He fought chiefly against the rulers of northern Syria.

Bibliography: S. Runciman, *A History of the Crusades,* vol. 1, 1971.

Tandragee, market town of County Armagh, Northern Ireland, situated on the Cusher, 8 km south of Portadown. It manufactures textiles and potato crisps. Population (1971) 1722.

Tandy, James Napper

Tandy, James Napper (1740–1803), Irish patriot, born in Dublin, the first secretary of the Society of UNITED IRISHMEN. He established an armed force on the pattern of the Paris National Guard but his movement failed and he was obliged to take refuge in America. In 1798 he went to Paris, and in conjunction with Wolfe, Tone and others planned an invasion of Ireland, aided by the French. They landed in Ireland in September 1798 but the rising was unsuccessful. Tandy fled to Hamburg where he was arrested and taken to Ireland. He was convicted of treason but reprieved through the intervention of the French. Tandy is the hero of *The Wearing of the Green*.

Taney, Roger Brooke (1777–1864), US lawyer, born in County Calvert, Maryland; and educated at Dickinson College, Carlisle, Pennsylvania. He was admitted to the Bar in 1799, and immediately entered political life. In 1812 Taney transferred his adherence from the Federalists to the Republican party under Jackson on account of the Federalist opposition to the war of 1812, but the break did not become permanent until 1824. He was elected to the Maryland Senate, 1816; attorney general of the USA, 1831, and secretary of the Treasury, 1833. He was appointed chief justice of the Supreme Court in 1836.

Taneyev, Sergey Ivanovich (1856–1915), Russian composer, born at Vladimir-on-Klyazma, studied at the Moscow Conservatory, where Tchaikovsky was among his teachers. He toured much as a pianist before 1885, when he became director of the Conservatory. His works include the operatic trilogy *The Oresteia*, 1895, cantatas and unaccompanied choral works, four symphonies, six string quartets and other chamber music, about 50 songs, etc.

Tanga, bay and seaport of Tanzania, north-east of Zanzibar, 119 km north from Mombasa by sea. Tanga, with an excellent harbour but no deep-water quays, is the coastal terminus of the railway to Moshi and ARUSHA and has several large factories including a fertiliser plant. Population 61,000.

Tanganyika, Lake, lake of east-central Africa, situated in the Great Rift Valley. It forms the border between Tanzania and Zaire and is also shared by Burundi in the north and Zambia in the south. It is about 725 km in length (the longest lake in the world), with an average breadth of from 50 to 70 km, and an area of 32,893 km². With the exception of Lake Baikal, it is the deepest freshwater lake in the world, soundings of 1436 m having been taken. It is 766 m above sea-level. Discovered by BURTON and SPEKE in 1858, it provides valuable fisheries and is used for local and international transport. See also ATLAS 45.

Tanganyika Territory, see TANZANIA.

Tange, Kenzo (1913–), Japanese architect, born at Imabari City; educated at Tokyo University. Tange was deeply influenced by the INTERNATIONAL STYLE, and in particular by the architecture of LE CORBUSIER, but he sought to reinterpret it within the Japanese tradition. His important buildings include the Peace Centre, Hiroshima (1946–56), the Kagawa Prefectural Office (1955–58), and gymnasia for the 1964 Olympic Games. He was also responsible for the Skopje City Centre Reconstruction Project and the master plan for Expo 70, Osaka.

Tangent. The tangent at a point on a CIRCLE is the straight line which goes through that point and has no other point in common with the circle; it is perpendicular to the radius at that point. The same definition can be applied to other simple curves such as ellipses, but in order to define a tangent at a point *P* of any curve *L* a different viewpoint must be adopted. The tangent at *P* is defined as the straight line which most closely approximates the curve in the neighbourhood of *P*. This means that the tangent must go through *P* and must be as near as possible to the curve on both sides of *P*. The definition is only concerned with what happens in the immediate neighbourhood of *P*. A line may be a tangent at one point of a curve although it intersects the curve at other points (see figure). In analytical geometry the equation of a tangent may be determined by DIFFERENTIATION. See also TRIGONOMETRY.

Tangerine, see CITRUS FRUITS.

Tangier, or Tangiers, seaport of MOROCCO, on a bay on the Strait of Gibraltar, 58 km south-west of Gibraltar. Lying on a picturesque bank overlooking the Atlantic, the city is surrounded by old walls and dominated by a *kasbah* (fort). The 'Great Souk' (market place) is the end of the Saharan and Sudan caravan routes. Cigarette manufacturing is the most important industry, and there are

Tangent.

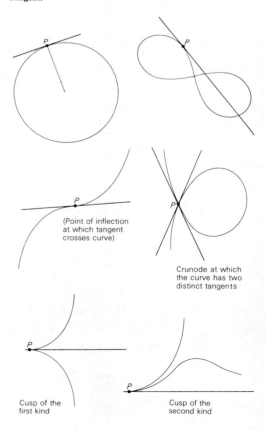

(Point of inflection at which tangent crosses curve)

Crunode at which the curve has two distinct tangents

Cusp of the first kind

Cusp of the second kind

Tangier. *(Topham/Fotogram)*

fisheries, market gardens, and preserving industries. Tangier is the northern terminus of the Tangier–Fez railway. Population (1971) 187,874.

History. Tangier was the capital of the Roman province of Mauretania Tingitana. It was taken by the Portuguese in 1471, and held by England, to whom it came as the dowry of Catherine of Braganza, from 1661 to 1684. It then came into the possession of the Moors. By the Treaty of Fez (November 1912) it was to become the centre of an international zone. Until 1923 the status of Tangier was undetermined; but in that year Britain and France drew up a statute, to which Spain added its signature in 1924. This statute remained in force until 1940. All the countries that had acceded to the Algeciras Act of 1906 were invited to accept the 1923–24 statute, and with the exception of Italy and the USA did so. (The USSR was not invited.) The Algeciras Act recognised Tangier and the surrounding territory (583 km²) as an international zone in the widest sense. Both France and Spain, sometimes separately, and at other times in conjunction, attempted to obtain complete control; but these attempts were frustrated until June 1940, following the collapse of France and Italy's entry into the war.

On 14 June 1940 Spanish troops occupied Tangier and in November Tangier was incorporated into the Spanish zone of Morocco. Under pressure, Spain formally undertook to keep the zone demilitarised. In 1945, Spain agreed to withdraw its troops from Tangier; the Mendoub was restored; and a general settlement reached regarding the future international status.

On 2 March 1956 France agreed to the abrogation of the Treaty of Fez, and recognised the independence of Morocco. Following a meeting of the interested powers in Rabat in July, a nine-power conference on the future of Tangier signed a declaration in October, abolishing the international régime as from 1 January 1957, when Tangier became an integral part of Morocco.

See MOROCCO, *History.*

Tango, Spanish solo and ballroom dance. The Spanish version was thought to have Arabic origins and was popularised and developed in Cadiz, the home of much Flamenco music. The music is in either 2-2 or 2-4 time and is rhythmically quite unlike the popular ballroom dance. Tientos and tanguillo are dances which have developed from the tango. The ballroom version is thought to have originated in South America and developed from rhythms brought there by African slaves and blended with those of the Spanish tango. The music and dance were adapted and returned to Europe in a very different form.

Tangshan, city in eastern HOPEH province, China, 160 km south-east of Peking. The site of China's first railway in 1882; it carried coal to Tientsin. Rapid development and modernisation of the city's coal, iron and steel, and cement industries began after 1949. In 1964 it was designated the centre of an experimental economic region designed to integrate all aspects of commercial life. In 1976 the city and surrounding area were devastated by two violent earthquakes. The city is probably to be rebuilt on a new site. Population (1970) around 1,100,000.

Tangus, a Mongolian people living in parts of Kansu, in China, and the Kuku-Nor and Khan districts in northeastern Tibet. Their way of life was nomadic but, by controlling the trade routes between central Asia and the West, they established the Hsi Hsia empire from the 11th to the 13th centuries. They were overrun by Genghis Khan in 1227. Buddhism was the state religion.

Tanguy, Yves (1900–55), French painter, born in Paris. Self-taught, he was directed towards imaginative painting through seeing the work of de CHIRICO and became a member of the Surrealist group in 1926. Smoothly finished painting of embryonic forms set in long perspectives are typical. See SURREALISM.

Tanis, ancient city in east delta of Egypt, modern San, 21 km south-west of Port Said, the biblical Zoan; founded in the Ramesside period as a new suburb or port for the capital Pi-Ramessu (modern El-Khatana and Qantir) which was once the HYKSOS Avaris. Although Middle Kingdom Egyptian statues usurped by the Hyksos were found at Tanis, there is a complete lack of archaeological strata before the 21st Dynasty. It became the new capital and residence of the 21st and 22nd Dynasties, Montet having recently found the royal cemetery there. Taharqa (25th Dynasty) resided there, in view of the threat from Assyria.

Tanistry, Pictish (see PICTS) law of succession.

Tanizaki Jun'ichiro, see JAPAN, *Literature*.

Tanker, a cargo boat designed to carry liquids, especially oil or oil products. When oil first entered into international trade its transport by sea was effected in specially made containers. At first wooden barrels were used, but these were subsequently replaced by large iron tanks fitted into the hull of the ship. As the economics of bulk transport became evident the idea was conceived of using the hull of the vessel itself as a container. The *Gluckauf* (2307 gross tons), built on the Tyne in 1885, is regarded as being the forerunner of the tanker of today, with machinery aft, and the hull divided into separate tanks by transverse and longitudinal bulkheads. At this time the hull was transversely framed, but in 1908 longi-

Yves Tanguy. *The Invisibles*, 1951. *(Tate Gallery, London)*

tudinal framing, giving a stronger but lighter hull, was introduced. Today most tankers are divided by two longitudinal bulkheads, giving an arrangement of three tanks across the ship and also a number of athwartship bulkheads. The total number of tanks depends on the trade of the ship. Oil tankers are loaded using shore pumps and discharged using the ship's pumps carried in a pump-room aft. Tankers are normally arranged in three main classes:

1. Crude oil tankers. The very large ships are known as ULCC (Ultra Large Crude Carrier). These include the largest ship in the world, the *Nissei Maru*, 484,377 t deadweight, 378.85 m long, which was built at a cost of £25 million, and can carry enough oil to meet Japan's demands for one day. It is powered by a 45,000-horsepower (33,500-kilowatt) steam turbine and has a speed of 14.3 knots (26.5 km/h). The very large crude carrier (VLCC) of around 250,000 t deadweight is only slightly smaller. These enormous tankers are able to carry oil cheaply between the Persian Gulf and Japan or Europe but because of their great size are limited in the number of ports that they can enter. These ships are not able to pass through the Suez Canal between Europe and the Persian Gulf or the Malacca Straits between Malaysia, Singapore and Japan. So the economics of scale must be offset by a longer distance. The tanker of between 40,000 and 150,000 t deadweight has the advantage of being able to enter a much wider range of ports while the smaller amount of cargo is adequate for many refineries with limited storage facilities.

2. Product tankers, designed to carry refined petroleum from the refineries to the areas where the oil is to be marketed. These ships are very much smaller than the crude oil tankers because the trade consists of many smaller parcels, and the ship is able to visit a very large range of ports. Today a typical product tanker displaces about 30,000 t deadweight. Product tankers differ from crude oil tankers in that they have to carry a variety of products, and it is essential that no mixing is allowed to occur. This means that their tank layout pipelines and pumping arrangements are more complicated than those of the crude oil carrier where the only cargo is crude oil. The stated intention of the oil-producing countries is to refine some of the oil themselves. This will mean refined products being shipped over longer distances than previously and product tankers may develop into ships of 100,000 t deadweight or more.

3. Parcel tankers, used to carry a range of chemical products, some of which are extremely dangerous, and must be carried in specially designed ships. These ships have double bottoms and sides to prevent leakage in the case of collision or stranding, separate pumps and pipes for each set of tanks to prevent accidental mixing of cargo, and arrangements to prevent the cargo from overflowing while it is being loaded. This type of tanker is more expensive than the product tanker and is slightly smaller, about 20,000 t deadweight on average. As well as carrying chemicals, many of these tankers are used to carry vegetable oils, palm oil, groundnut oil, and molasses.

Tankersley, parish of South YORKSHIRE, England, 7 km south of Barnsley, and a coal-mining district. The parish church dates from the 15th century, and the area was

Tanker. The *World Azalea*, dead weight c. 300,000 t. (*Barnaby's Picture Library*)

formerly an extensive deer park on the Rockingham estate.

Tanks, see ANTI-TANK WEAPONS; ARMOURED FIGHTING VEHICLES.

Tannahill, Robert (1774–1810), Scottish poet, born at Paisley. His *Poems and Songs*, 1807, had considerable success, and won the admiration of James HOGG. Disappointed in his plans for a new edition, Tannahill drowned himself in a fit of depression. His songs, such as 'The Bonnie Wood o' Craigieea' and 'The Lass o' Arrenteenie', are still popular in Scotland.

Tannenberg, Battle of, fought in 1410, between the TEUTONIC KNIGHTS of Prussia on one side, and the Poles and Lithuanians on the other. It resulted in a great victory for the latter, marking the emergence of Poland as a great power.

Tannenberg, Battle of (1914), see WORLD WAR, FIRST, *The Eastern Front 1914*.

Tannhäuser, legendary German knight, identical in name to a 13th-century minnesinger (see MINNESINGERS) and crusader whose poetry, which is sometimes parodistic and sometimes of an arcadian sensuality, may have made him appear suitable as the subject of the ballad. Its story is of a man who, wearying of the pleasures in the mountain of Lady Venus (Venusberg), travels to Rome to make his penance. Pope Urban IV, however, says that the staff in his hand could no more blossom than Tannhäuser find forgiveness. Dejected, Tannhäuser leaves Rome and when, three days later, the pope's staff begins to sprout shoots, he can no longer be found. He has returned to the mountain of Venus, and the unforgiving pope must be eternally damned.

Wagner's opera conflates this ballad with traditions deriving from the Singers' Contest in the Wartburg, where the poet at odds with his fellows is Heinrich von Ofterdingen for singing the praises of the Austrian Duke, whereas the others praise the Thuringian Landgrave Hermann (died 1217).

Bibliography: H. de Boor and R. Newald, *Geschichte der deutschen Literatur* (vols 2 and 3).

Tannin, or tannic acid, occurs in gall nuts and all kinds of bark. It is extracted by boiling water and is an almost colourless substance readily soluble in water, and difficult to purify and crystallise. Its solutions possess a very astringent taste, and with ferric chloride give a dark blue solution, and hence tannin is used in the manufacture of inks. Tannin is a glucoside of gallic acid and is converted into this acid and glucose by boiling with dilute sulphuric acid. Owing to its property of forming insoluble coloured compounds with many dyes, tannin is used largely as a mordant and is also extensively employed in 'tanning' (see LEATHER). In medicine tannin is employed in cases of diarrhoea and haemorrhage. Tannin is actually the name of a large class of related substances, the chief being Turkish tannin, Chinese tannin, and Hamameli tannin. Recently some synthetic tannins have been obtained.

Tanning, see LEATHER.

Tannu-Tuva, see MONGOLIA, *History*; TUVA ASSR.

Tansy, *Tanacetum*, a genus of perennial herbaceous plants of the Compositae (daisy family), with much-divided leaves and yellow flower-heads usually in flat-topped groups. The only British species is the common tansy, *T. vulgare*, which is often abundant in waste places. *T. leucophyllum*, a garden variety, has silvery leaves. Tansy is bitter and aromatic, and was employed as an anthelmintic and used in cooking and herb teas or tisanes.

Tanta, capital of GHARBIYA province, Egypt, 80 km north of Cairo. It is a major transport focus and is noted

Tantalite

for its fairs and its festivals, and has a branch of El-Azhar University. It is also a market centre for cotton and sugar. Population (1970) 253,600.

Tantalite, see TANTALUM; COLUMBITE.

Tantallon Castle, impressive ruin on the north coast of East Lothian District, Lothian Region, Scotland, 5 km east of North Berwick, on a high cliff fronting the BASS ROCK. It was the stronghold of the Earls of Douglas but was destroyed by Cromwell's army in 1651.

Tantalum, metallic chemical element, symbol Ta, atomic number 73, atomic weight 180·9479. It occurs associated with niobium in the minerals tantalite and columbite. Both are the tantalates and niobates of iron, the former richer in tantalum, the latter richer in niobium. Tantalum is white in colour, has a relative density of 16·8, and can be drawn into wire of great tenacity and high melting point (2850 °C). It was formerly used in constructing the filaments of electric lamps, but has now been replaced for this purpose by TUNGSTEN. It is, however, used in the manufacture of acid-resisting chemical apparatus, and in electrical rectifiers. The pentoxide is obtained when the metal is burned in air. Two oxides, however, are known, TaO_2 and Ta_2O_5. The latter gives rise to the tantalates, corresponding to the nitrates and metaphosphates. A characteristic salt is potassium fluotantalate, the potassium salt of hydrofluotantalic acid (H_2TaF_7), the latter being readily formed by solution of the pentoxide in hydrofluoric acid. Tantalum has been prepared from this by reduction with hydrogen followed by fusion *in vacuo*. Tantalum carbide is used for high-speed cutting tools, as it is very hard.

Tantalus, legendary son of Zeus, father of PELOPS and NIOBE, who divulged secrets entrusted to him by Zeus, and in Hades was afflicted with raging thirst and hunger, while standing in a lake which ebbed away when he stooped to drink it. Meanwhile above his head hung fruits which swung out of his reach when he tried to grasp them. Hence to 'tantalise'. For the fruit, Euripides (*Orestes*, v.) substitutes a rock, which was ever ready to fall and crush him.

Tantalus, a spirit case in which decanters are visible, but are held in position by a wooden collar that is secured by a lock. They were current in the mid-19th century.

Tantric Buddhism, a complicated system of meditation and yoga practice, evolving within MAHĀYĀNA Buddhism and based on the Tantras—religious works dating from about the 5th century in India. Two types of Tantricism developed: Buddhist and Hindu.

Although to a limited extent, Tantric Buddhism can be seen as a development from earlier modes of thought within the Mahāyāna, the methods it employs in its teaching are somewhat unique in the field of Buddhism. These methods involve a wide variety of esoteric practices, including the use of ritual gestures (MUDRĀS), sounds having spiritual significance (MANTRAS), and symbolical diagrams (MANDALAS). The highly cryptic nature of Tantricism makes it difficult to assess to what extent its ritual elements are to be interpreted symbolically, and to what extent literally.

There is a complex cosmological system in which Ultimate Reality is represented as Adi-Buddha. From Adi-Buddha emanate various Dhyāni-Buddhas and Bodhisattvas, representing different aspects of Reality, or different stages along the Path to Enlightenment. These are associated with particular elements, *mantras*, *mudrās*, colours, etc., as well as with particular parts of the body. The body is thus emphasised as the means to Enlightenment, and yoga and ritual are aimed at transforming consciousness through the integration of energies within the body. Furthermore, Enlightenment has two aspects: the passive or feminine Wisdom element (*Prajñā*), and the active male Compassion element (*Upāya*—literally, device), frequently personified as the male and female counterparts of the Transcendental Forms, or Buddhas and Bodhisattvas, locked together in sexual embrace. The Tantric focus on sexual union as a method of gaining spirituality has led to a great deal of condemnation from outside observers, but scholars differ as to what extent it is to be taken literally, and to what extent metaphorically.

Tantric doctrines spread from India to Tibet as the Vajrayāna School, and to China as the Mantra School. From China, Tantricism was carried to Japan and gave rise to the Shingon School.

Bibliography: A. Bharati, *The Tantric Tradition*, 1965.

Tantric Yoga, in Hinduism, the path of transformation. This yoga worships the Divine as two principles, male and female, Being and Becoming. ŚIVA, the masculine, is eternal Being, pure perfection and timeless wis-

Tantric Yoga. The six chakras of the subtle body, watercolour drawing from the Punjab hills, India, late 19th-century. (*Victoria and Albert Museum, London*)

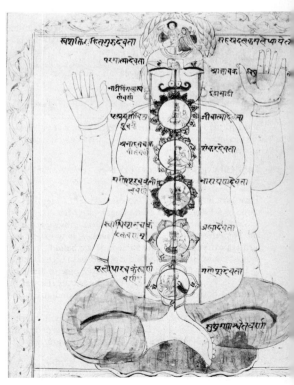

dom. ŚAKTI, the supreme Mother, is the creative power of Becoming, the origin of created form, and the cause of time. She mediates between the Absolute and the relative, between eternity and the flow of events in time. Thus it is to her that men turn when practising this yoga, for help and guidance in their journey towards perfection. It is believed that the power of Śakti is present in all living things giving them movement and life. Śiva is Mind, but Śakti is the vitalising creative power in matter and she dwells in man in the form of dynamic energy at the base of the spine (KUNDALINI). It is the aim of those who follow Tantric Yoga to awaken the pent-up Kundalini energy which will then travel up the spine to the brain where it unites with Śiva, the Mind, in an embrace of love which is often portrayed sexually. It is represented as a supreme marriage between Being and Becoming and this integration is said to give rise to a flood of joy throughout the body and mind.

Tantric followers believe that it is through fulfilment and not through austerity that man finds Reality. Self-mortification is regarded as an insult to Śakti and it is believed that natural desires should be fulfilled intelligently and attentively. The repression of desire leads to endless trouble and if a man listens to the wisdom of Śakti in his heart, his impulses will gradually become higher and more noble. Tantra bids men to enjoy the pleasures of the world, but at the same time begin to discover in themselves the presence of God. Tantric Yoga teaches certain practices and mystical rites which, if followed with pure motives, gradually transform the desires of the senses into love of God. Hence, the sexual act as such is never condemned, for it is believed that it will be its own remedy and will bring its practitioners into union with supreme Consciousness.

Tantra believes that there are six centres in the body which Kundalini energises. The intricate details of these centres have formed the basis of many books. They are called CHAKRAS. They are: *ājnā*, between the eyebrows; *vishuddha*, at the throat; *anāhata*, at the heart; *manipūraka*, at the navel; *swadisthāna*, at the genitals; *mūlādhāra*, at the base of the spine. The *chakras* are sometimes called the lotus centres, each *chakra* visualised as a lotus whose petals become erect as Kundalini enters them. In each lotus is a letter symbolising a sacred sound. Tantra has ascribed various deities as resident in the *chakras*. These deities are never regarded as real, but as a sort of symbolic language through which the ordinary man can become aware of his centres in a way that is superior to words.

Bibliography: A. Daniélou, *Hindu Polytheism*, 1964; H. Chaudhuri, *Integral Yoga*, 1965; J. Marquès Rivière, *Tantric Yoga*, 1970; E. Wood, *Yoga*, 1970; N. Douglas, *Tantra Yoga*, 1971.

Tantung (formerly *Antung*), city in LIAONING province, China, and one of the chief ports of MANCHURIA, near the mouth of the YALU river. It is a junction of the railway from Mukden and the North Korean railway. Its industries include lumber milling, paper and match manufacturing, chemicals, non-ferrous metal refining, cotton and silk weaving, and agricultural processing. It also has ship repair yards. Population (1970) 450,000.

Tanzam, or Tanzanian-Zambian, Railway, in East Africa. At 1860 km it is the longest built since the Second World War and represents the largest capital project undertaken by the Chinese outside of China. It was opened in October 1975 and after an initial running-in period was handed over to the respective governments although Chinese officials will aid in its running for some time to come. It runs from DAR ES SALAAM in Tanzania on the East African coast to Kapiri Mposhi in the Zambian Copperbelt; it is eventually hoped to extend it to LUSAKA, a further 200 km. It is mostly single-track and is meant to open up Tanzania's fertile southern highlands and to provide an export route for Zambian copper.

Tanzania, republic of East Africa, bounded on the north by Kenya, Lake Victoria, and Uganda; on the west by Rwanda, Burundi, Lake Tanganyika, Zambia, and Lake Malawi; on the south by Mozambique; and on the east by the Indian Ocean. The republic was created in 1964 by the union of Tanganyika, which became independent in 1961 after successive periods of German and British rule, and ZANZIBAR, which gained independence from Britain in 1963. It is a member of the Commonwealth. Area 937,000 km².

Geography. Relief. Along the coast lies a plain, varying in width from 15 to 65 km, behind which the country rises gradually to a plateau constituting the greater part of the hinterland. This plateau falls sharply from a general level of 1225 m to the level of lakes Tanganyika (765 m) and Malawi (490 m), which mark the Great Rift Valley, and is also broken by the extensive basin of the RUFIJI river. The highest points are in the north-east, where there are extinct volcanoes, KILIMANJARO (6010 m) and Mount MERU (4560 m). In the south-west are the Livingstone, or Kipengere, Mountains, where the highest peak is over 2743 m. See ATLAS 45.

Climate. The rainfall, generally speaking, is low for a tropical country and sometimes there are great droughts. Most of the plateau has a mean annual rainfall of 600 to 1000 mm, but a zone across the centre has only 400 to 600 mm. In the north there are two distinct wet seasons, in March–May and November–December, but to the south these merge into a single wet season in December–April. Temperatures at the coast average 26 to 28 °C, but are 3–4 °C lower over the plateau. Most areas have a savanna woodland vegetation, while the fauna is still

Tanzania. Kilimanjaro and the international airport. (*Camera Press*)

Tanzania

rich in large mammals in several areas now scheduled as game reserves. Diseases such as malaria remain a major problem.

Population. Tanzania contains many diverse ethnic groups, many from outside Africa. There remain small numbers of BUSHMEN who first entered the territory during the Stone Age. Later people from further north, including Ethiopia, migrated south, and these are represented in the highlands and the rift valley region. These movements were followed by BANTU-speakers coming in from the south and south-west, the present-day NGUNI and other tribes. The MASAI and LUO are members of the Nilotic group. In addition there are substantial minorities of Asians—Sikhs, Panjabis, Jains, Goanese, and Arabs—and Europeans. The total population (1975) is 15,155,000, and the main towns are DAR ES SALAAM (the capital, but a new one is planned at DODOMA), TANGA, MWANZA, and ZANZIBAR.

Bibliography: J. P. Moffet, *Handbook of Tanganyika*, 1958; L. Berry, *Tanzania in Maps*, 1971; W. T. W. Morgan, *East Africa*, 1973.

Economy. Tanzania is an extremely poor country, with a national income of only about US $100 per capita. Subsistence production is still very important, accounting for 30 per cent of this figure, and only 3 per cent of the population is in paid employment.

Agriculture. Almost 90 per cent of Tanzanians depend largely on the land for their livelihood. The traditional economy is based on shifting cultivation of millet and sorghum, increasingly supplemented by maize and cassava, and giving way to more intensive cultivation of bananas and sweet potatoes as staple foods in some well-watered areas. Most farmers keep some cattle, and there is some animal husbandry in the north. Some farmers obtain cash mainly from food crop or cattle sales, but

Tanzania. Coffee plants being pruned. (*Camera Press/Alexandra Lawrence*)

coffee, cotton, and cashew nuts are grown for sale by most people in specific regions. Plantation agriculture is also important, sisal (a fibre plant which grows on land too dry and infertile for most crops) dominating the country's exports until prices fell steeply in the 1960s. While sisal production has recently stagnated, that of tea (for export) and sugar (for local use) has expanded. Cloves form the main cash crop of Zanzibar, and especially Pemba. Another important element in the rural economy is small-scale fishing along the sea and lake shores.

In 1970 the government began an extensive rural settlement scheme, encouraging farmers to form communal *ujamaa* villages. The aim was to co-ordinate rural development, raise living standards, improve crop production, and develop agro-industries. The disruption that this caused to traditional agriculture coupled with serious droughts has meant a serious decline in crop production ever since; emergency food imports have been necessary.

Industry. Mining is largely confined to the working of one diamond deposit, where reserves are shrinking fast, although other minerals exist, including both coal and iron ore, which may form the basis for a future steel industry. Meanwhile the manufacturing sector is small, though rapidly expanding since independence. A policy of import substitution has attracted breweries, textile and clothing mills, a cement plant, and an oil refinery, while small-scale industries are developing steadily. Electricity needs have been met initially by thermal plant, and by hydro-electric stations first on the Pangani river and now on the Ruaha river.

Communications. Tanzania's great size and the wide scatter of its population heighten the importance of communications. Railways were built by the Germans leading inland from Dar es Salaam to Kigoma (with later branches to Mwanza and Mpanda), and from Tanga to Arusha. For many years the Tanga line has been connected to the Kenya–Uganda system, and Lake Victoria steamer services have linked Mwanza, Musoma, and Bukoba to Kenya and Uganda: recently greater integration of the network has been achieved with a new railway joining the Tanga and Central lines, and the introduction of train ferries on Lake Victoria. Whereas these services all form part of East African Railways, a separate administration controls the TANZAN railway built south-westwards from Dar es Salaam to Zambia and completed in 1975. The road network is extensive but skeletal, many communities being linked to it only by paths; there are still under 100,000 vehicles in use. While the process of national integration is steadily enhancing the importance of road transport, Tanzania remains heavily dependent on overseas trade and thus on its ports. Dar es Salaam is dominant among these, but Tanga, Mtwara, and Zanzibar are also important. In addition, 18 airlines serve Dar es Salaam, and East African Airways serves most regional headquarters.

Trade. The pattern of trade is dominated by exports of primary products and imports of manufactures and fuel, the two normally being roughly in balance. Exports are more diverse than in most African countries with coffee, cotton, cashew nuts, cloves, sisal, and diamonds each accounting for between 8 and 15 per cent of the total. Britain is still the leading trading partner, while Kenya is the second source of imports. Trade with China has

Tanzania. Inside a cotton ginnery. *(Camera Press/Sam Turner)*

increased in the 1970s.

Planning. Government planning of the economy is more comprehensive than in most African countries, assisted by national ownership of most large enterprises and planning mechanisms operating in the regions and districts as well as at the centre. Emphasis has been laid not on maximising economic growth, but on equalising its benefits both socially and spatially within the country.

Finance. The unit of currency is the shilling, of 100 cents.

Foreign Aid. The most significant contribution to the Tanzanian economy has been Chinese financing of the TANZAM (Tanzania–Zambia) railway.

Bibliography: A. M. O'Connor, *Economic Geography of East Africa*, 1971; J. Rweyamanu, *Underdevelopment and Industrialisation in Tanzania*, 1974.

Government. *Constitution.* The country of present-day Tanzania was formed in 1964 when the former United Nations Trusteeship Territory of Tanganyika, under British administration until it became independent in 1961, and the island of Zanzibar, a British protectorate before becoming independent in 1963, joined together as the United Republic of Tanzania.

The interim constitution of 1965 made provisional constitutional arrangements for the new republic, and in June 1965 the National Assembly approved the Interim Constitution Amendment Bill which embodied the principles of socialism and self-sufficiency in the constitution, as well as confirming the Tanganyika African National Union (TANU) as the only official political party on the mainland, and on Zanzibar, the Afro-Shirazi party. Thus

the constitution gave the respective parties virtually complete control over the political process. On 5 February 1977 the two parties were merged under the name of the Chama Cha Mapinduzi (CCM or Revolutionary Party), of which President Nyerere was unanimously elected chairman, and First Vice-President Aboud Jumbe (the president of the Afro-Shirazi Party) vice-chairman. Although the National Assembly is nominally the legislative body, the uncontested power and influence of the national executive of the CCM confirms it as the paramount policy-making body; it is the duty of the National Assembly simply to convert policy decisions into practical programmes.

At the executive level, the President is elected by direct universal suffrage after first being approved as the sole candidate by an electoral convention of the CCM. The President appoints two vice-presidents, from among the elected members of the National Assembly, and the first vice-president is also the President of Zanzibar.

Legislature. The National Assembly, although subordinate to the political will of the CCM, consists of 214 members selected as follows: 96 members elected from mainland constituencies, 46 appointees from Zanzibar, 20 regional party secretaries, eight presidential nominees, nine members appointed by the East African Legislative Assembly, and 35 members selected by the assembly itself from regional and national bodies. Internal matters in Zanzibar are dealt with by the Revolutionary Council of Zanzibar.

On mainland Tanzania the procedure for electing members of the National Assembly is that each of the 107 constituencies into which the country is divided has two candidates, and the electorate then chooses between these two.

For administrative purposes, the Tanzanian mainland is divided into 20 regions, each under the authority of a commissioner; traditional authority has been undermined to the extent that chiefs wishing to enter the administration must relinquish their traditional offices.

Justice. The people of mainland Tanzania have the right to appeal to the court of appeal for East Africa, whereas this is denied to those people living on Zanzibar. On the mainland, the internal legal structure is supervised by a permanent commission of enquiry, located in Dar es Salaam, and consists of a high court, district courts, and primary courts. The last two are presided over by magistrates, and there is a right of appeal to the high court. In 1969 chiefs were forbidden to exercise their traditional judicial authority under customary law. As for Zanzibar, a system of people's courts has been in operation since 1970, under the jurisdiction of magistrates who are elected by the people.

Armed Forces. The strength of the army in 1975 was of the order of 13,000 men, while the navy had 600, and the air force 1000. The citizen's militia, the main paramilitary force, numbered 35,000 and there is also a police marine unit. All the armed forces go under the umbrella-title of the Tanzania People's Defence Forces (TPDF), and the TPDF have re-affirmed publicly their willingness to serve the national cause, and to direct their energies outward, against Tanzania's enemies. The TPDF have also participated in the agricultural development programme, really an 'act of faith' to demonstrate the commitment of the armed forces to socialism.

Education. The literacy rate is between 10 and 15 per cent of the population for Swahili; less for English. There are not enough schools in the country as yet to implement universal primary education, and only 60 per cent of eligible children attend primary school. Although most of the existing schools are state-financed, the remainder are organised by missions and other voluntary agencies. In 1973 there were over 1,100,000 pupils in primary education and 35,000 in general education. The 1970 figure for secondary education was 37,000. The University College of Dar es Salaam is part of the University of East Africa.

Welfare. There is a rural development division which aims primarily at improving labour conditions and education and health facilities in small communities, but the ideology of self-reliance, beginning with the *Ujamaa* village principle and evolving hopefully into the true *Ujamaa* or socialist community, puts welfare firmly in the hands of the people themselves in the long run. The state has the bulk of the responsibility for the provision of medical facilities, although Christian missions are active to a lesser extent. In 1973 the number of hospitals and major health centres totalled 236 and less significant health centres 1555, giving a combined total of 26,409 hospital beds. The 1972 figures for medical personnel show that there were

Tanzania. Literacy classes. *(Topham/Fotogram)*

634 doctors, 45 pharmacists, 29 dentists, 2100 midwives, and 5600 nurses.

Religion. Slightly the majority of the population follow traditional beliefs, with the remainder divided into Christian, Hindu, and Muslim communities.

Language. The official languages are Swahili and English, but the tribal languages retain their importance.

National Flag. The Tanzanian flag is green at the top and blue at the bottom, the two colours separated by a diagonal stripe, brown with yellow edges, which runs from bottom left to top right.

Bibliography: G. A. Maguire, *Towards Uhuru in Tanzania,* 1969; J. Cameron and W. A. Dodd, *Society, Schools and Progress in Tanzania,* 1970; R. F. Hopkins, *Tanzania's First Decade,* 1971; C. R. Ingle, *From Village to State in Tanzania,* 1973; J. R. Nellis, *Tanzanian Example: Theory of Ideology,* 1973; UNESCO, *Cultural Policy of Tanzania,* 1975.

History. Arab traders visited the Tanganyika area in medieval times and later opened up the great slave route from Bangamoyo on the Indian Ocean to Ujiji on Lake Tanganyika. The British explorer, Richard Burton, first entered the territory in 1856, and was soon followed by Speke, Livingstone, and Stanley. The territory was visited in 1884 by Karl Peters, who concluded several treaties with the local chiefs and so paved the way for the establishment of a German protectorate. There were African revolts in 1889 and 1905; the latter, known as the Maji Maji rebellion, was crushed with cruelty and difficulty and African casualties were enormous. After the First World War virtually the whole of German Tanganyika was mandated to Britain.

From then onwards, constitutional progress was continuous as, initially, the British found they could rule through an African petty bureaucracy, although this led to the formation of the Tanganyika African Association (TAA), a political movement composed of Africans enjoying an early political experience compared to those in other parts of East Africa. To counter this, an abortive effort at indirect rule through chiefs was attempted. Economic problems for the African peasant, and the resentment of the privilege accorded to a minority of white settlers, encouraged, in 1954, the formation of the Tanganyikan African National Union (TANU) led by Julius NYERERE. Responsible government, with an elected majority was attained in September 1960. In December 1961 Tanganyika became an independent state within the Commonwealth, with Julius Nyerere as premier. It became a republic within the Commonwealth in December 1962 and Nyerere was the first president. There were Communist-inspired army mutinies in January 1964 but these were quelled with British assistance. In April 1964 ZANZIBAR united with Tanganyika and in October 1964 the composite state changed its name to Tanzania.

Tanzania's move towards a policy of development from within, i.e. a socialist strategy of development based on the Ujamaa village (the co-operative socialist community), as set out in TANU's Arusha Declaration of 1967, owed a great deal to external influences as well as to Nyerere's aim of reducing income differentials by involving the majority of the people, the peasant farmers, in the development effort. In the mid-1960s Tanzania found itself cut off from the stream of development aid, a situation arrived at partly by the sensitivity of the United States and West Germany to the Zanzibar problem, and also Tanzanian adherence to the resolution of the Organisation of African Unity that Britain should crush the Smith régime in Rhodesia.

Until 1972 a maximum of 12 per cent of the total population lived in Ujamaa villages, and there were also severe food problems in the country. Nyerere repeated the need for villagisation, only the first stage of Ujamaa, and appealed also for 'good leadership' at the community level. This, combined with careful efforts on the part of TANU to improve the quality of its leadership, even at the local branch level, saw a positive popular response, and by the end of the year nearly eight million people were living in Ujaama villages.

In external affairs, Tanzania has been very conscious of the rôle it can and must play in southern Africa. Tanzania was the foremost supporter of the liberation movement in Mozambique, and also provided assistance for Zambia in so far as it allowed, and co-operated in the building of the tarmac road, the pipeline, and the railway. Tanzania had, initially, a very uneasy relationship with Uganda following the attempted overthrow of President Amin in 1972 by supporters of ex-President Obote based in Tanzania; and Amin continues to accuse Tanzania of threatening invasion. Outside Africa, there has been a gradual restoration of the relationship with Britain, to the extent that substantial British development aid began to flow to Tanzania again in 1975.

Bibliography: W. H. Ingrams, *Zanzibar: Its History and People,* 1931; G. S. P. Freeman-Grenville, *The Medieval History of the Coast of Tanganyika, With Special Reference to Recent Archaeological Discoveries,* 1962; J. M. Gray, *History of Zanzibar from the Middle Ages to 1856,* 1962; J. C. Taylor, *The Political Development of Tanganyika,* 1963; J. Listowel, *The Making of Tanganyika,* 1965; H. J. Bienen, *Tanzania: Party Transformation and Economic Development,* 1967; L. Cliffe (Ed.), *One Party Democracy: the 1965 Tanzania General Elections,* 1967; M. F. Lofchie, *Zanzibar: Background to Revolution,* 1967; W. Tordoff, *Government and Politics in Tanzania: A Collection of Essays covering the period from September 1960 to July 1966,* 1967; H. W. Stephens, *The Political Transformation of Tanganyika, 1920–1967,* 1968; J. K. Nyerere, *Freedom and Unity—Uhuru Na Umoja: Essays on Socialism,* 1969; *Freedom and Unity: A Selection from Writings and Speeches, 1952–65,* 1971.

Tao Te Ching, see CHINESE LITERATURE.

Taoiseach, see DÁIL ÉIREANN.

Taoism (Chinese *tao,* way, path), a religious path practised in China up to 1949 and still having some scattered followers both in China and other parts of the world. The Way is the way of life itself and is to be discovered intuitively rather than intellectually; it is revealed in actual living, in the seeing of the Way in each moment of life. Thus Taoism has no dogma, for the ever-changing flow and growth of life itself cannot be bound by man-made categories. Life, when it is stripped to its bare essence, is free, unknowable and undifferentiated. It is One, the Tao, whole and unbound. Its power becomes manifest as all its myriad forms, each one unique; and each man must find his own relationship to the Tao, his own understanding of the truth, the fulfilment of the Way within his own life.

Taoism

Taoism was first given form in the 6th century BC by
LAO TZU, the first recorded Taoist sage, who wrote the
Tao Te Ching, the *Book of the Virtuous Way*. Second
only to the Bible in the numbers printed each year, the *Tao
Te Ching* has been translated into almost every living
language. It describes the Way as a perfect inner balance
arising when man's heart responds to life with spontaneous harmony and virtue, a state which Lao Tzu considered man to have lost. For although *'Te'* is usually
translated as 'virtue', the message of the *Tao Te Ching* is
that conventional virtue as we understand it already
belongs to a corrupt society. True untainted virtue arises
when man interacts so harmoniously with his surroundings that he is without thought of virtue.

> When people lost sight of the way to live
> Came codes of love and honesty,
> Learning came, charity came,
> Hypocrisy took charge. (*Tao Te Ching*)

There is no doctrine of sin in Taoism (and indeed no
word for it equivalent to the Western concept). Bad

Taoism. Shou-hsing, the Chinese god of longevity. Reverse side of
a jade plaque, believed to be Ming Dynasty, 1368–1644. (*Victoria
and Albert Museum, London*)

Taoism. Taoist temple in Hong Kong with the incense burners
which are the central objects in the temple and essential to every
Taoist rite. (*Barnaby's Picture Library*)

behaviour was regarded as stupidity and ignorance, for
no one would knowingly violate the natural Way.

Two of the major concepts of Taoism are stillness
within movement and strength within gentleness. As the
centre of a wheel is still while the spokes turn, so the Way
is the dynamic stillness at the heart of the phenomenal
world; and as the reed will bend under snow where the
thistle would snap, so manifestation of the Way involves
the exercise of power without the use of force and without undue interference with the surrounding environment.

Taoism is symbolised pictorially by the YANG AND YIN
diagram; by its subtle landscapes of lakes, mountains and
rivers, in which space is as important a component as
form; and by its depictions of sages, the two most famous
of whom were Lao Tzu and Chuang Tzu. In literature it
is expressed in the *Tao Te Ching*, *The Way of Chuang
Tzu*, and the *Book of Lieh-Tzu*.

The penetrating profundity of Taoism always existed
side by side with, and was eventually largely taken over
by, more superficial beliefs in magical heavens where
reigned the IMMORTALS; in Blessed Isles of the West where
the drug of immortality grew; in supernatural powers
gained through yoga; and in magic of all kinds. When
Buddhism came to China the essential Way of Taoism—
spontaneous action springing from inner harmony—came
to be one of the great influences in Ch'an (Zen) Buddhism. In the 4th and 5th centuries AD, however, Buddhism separated itself from Taoism, and the actual practices of Taoism came to be more and more identified
with their superficial aspects. It became associated with
secret societies, for which China is famous, and its original
pure teaching was expounded only by the monks of
mountain monasteries. These continued to exist, however,
until well into this century, but their present existence is
doubtful.

Bibliography: B. Watson, *The Complete Works of Chuang Tzu*,
1968; J. C. Cooper, *Taoism: the Way of the Mystic*, 1972; J.
Blofeld, *The Secret and Sublime*, 1973; A. Bancroft, *Religions of*

the East, 1974; A. Watts, *Tao: the Watercourse Way*, 1976.

Taormina (ancient *Tauromenium*), town and winter resort in SICILY, 40 km south-west of Messina. It stands near the coast, and is famous for its beauty. It was founded by the Greeks (c. 398 BC), and subsequently fell into Roman, Saracen, and Norman hands. It has a medieval cathedral, a ruined Greek theatre, and several Roman buildings. The town is within sight of Mount ETNA and has hot springs. Population (1974) 8700.

Tap Root, see ROOT.

Tapachula, town in CHIAPAS state, Mexico. Situated in the Pacific coastal lowlands at an altitude of 135 m, it is a few kilometres from the Guatemalan frontier, and is on the railway line running from Hidalgo (on the Guatemalan border) to Veracruz on the Gulf of Mexico. It is the commercial centre of a region producing cacao, coffee, and bananas. There are handicraft industries and aguardiente is distilled. Population 50,000.

Tape Recorder, an instrument for recording and reproducing sound on magnetic tape, as distinct from the grooved disc used in the RECORD PLAYER.

The tape recorder consists of a tape transport system, which sends the tape at a constant speed, usually 3·75 or 7·5 in/s (9·525 or 19·05 mm/s), although some machines, notably cassette recorders, use a tape speed of 1·875 in/s (4·7625 mm/s) and some best quality reel-to-reel recorders use 15 or 30 in/s (38·1 or 76·2 mm/s), past three tape heads. The first two are used in the recording process, and are driven by the recording amplifier: one is known as the 'erase head', and wipes off any signal already on the tape,

Taoism. Bronze incense burner in the form of Lao-Tzu riding the back of an ox, Japanese, c. 1800. (*Victoria and Albert Museum, London*)

while the second, the 'record head', puts the new sound onto the tape. The third is the 'playback head', which reproduces the sound on the tape. Some sophisticated tape recorders allow the playback head to be used during recording, to 'monitor' the recorded signal. The signal from the playback head is taken through a playback amplifier, which makes it larger and feeds it to a LOUD-SPEAKER. Some tape recorders use an external amplifier for playback, and are usually termed 'tape decks'.

Nowadays, all original recordings are made on magnetic tape. Tape has definite advantages over disc for recording purposes, and has ousted the latter in studios. From the original tape, it is possible to mix a master tape, tailoring the original sound in various ways (by cutting or boosting certain frequencies, adding echo, phasing, etc.) to suit the desires and needs of the producer. From the master tape it is possible both to make tape copies and, by a somewhat complex process, to make disc matrices from which records can be pressed. In addition, tape lends itself readily to editing, has less inherent distortion, and has a wider frequency response. The only real disadvantage of tape is 'tape hiss' (a random high-frequency sound produced by the tape passing over the heads). Tape hiss can, to a large extent, be removed by special filtering units, usually using a system developed by the Dolby Laboratories.

Tape is a far more manageable recording medium than disc. By making the actual contact between recording and reproducer electrical (tape-to-head), rather than mechanical (stylus-to-groove), the physical impossibility of making a point track with perfect accuracy in a modulated groove is obviated. Separation of stereophonic signals is better achieved on tape (see STEREOPHONY). In addition to tracking and tracing distortion involved in pickup-to-disc reproduction, there is no wear on tapes, although tape heads require regular replacement according to use. Unlike a worn stylus, however, a worn tape head does not damage the record material. In 1955 came a further advance, with the introduction by EMI (Electric and Musical Industries) of stereophonic tape records. The initial presentation of the tape record on a single reel, which involved the user in a relatively difficult handling operation compared to a disc, has been changed. The advent of the tape cartridge, using an endless loop running at 3·75 in/s (9·525 mm/s) enclosed in a plastic case, and of the musicassette, enclosing two reels, has solved the handling problem as both units are loaded into reproducing machines without touching the tapes. Quadraphonic tapes have also become available (see QUADRAPHONY).

In the field of amateur recording, tape has made notable progress. Both as a hobby, and in many varieties of professional work, the tape recorder has advanced in recent years to the position where it is as ubiquitous as the camera. Amateur tape recording ranges from the simple recording of private messages and samples of family life to ambitious recordings of professional quality (many of the finest recordings of bird-song, for example, have been made by amateur recordists). The many tape clubs which now exist all over the world are extremely active, and there is widespread interchange of tapes and information, often called 'tapesponding'.

Bibliography: W. S. Sharps, *Tape Recorder Manual*, 1960; H. G. Spratt, *Magnetic Tape Recording*, 1964; J. Aldred, *Manual of Sound Recording*, 1971.

Tapestry (French *tapis*, carpet or tablecloth; Latin *tapetum*, carpet), textile wall-hanging in which a design, often of a pictorial character, is woven on a loom by the use of different coloured threads in the woof. The distinction between high-warp and low-warp tapestry depends on whether the warp is set vertically or horizontally. The weaver works from a full-scale cartoon. The word tapestry is sometimes used incorrectly to describe an embroidery such as the BAYEUX TAPESTRY. The work is also sometimes used of coverings of furniture or carpets, and wool embroidery known generally as canvaswork or 'needlepoint' (see EMBROIDERY).

In antiquity woven and embroidered wall-hangings were widely used both in the Eastern kingdoms and in the Greek and Roman world, and are frequently mentioned in classical literature. Fragments of tapestries of the Hellenistic and Roman imperial periods have been found in Egypt. In the Middle Ages tapestries were widely used to decorate domestic and ecclesiastical buildings, and the art of weaving them is specially associated with France. The oldest surviving French tapestries are the series of scenes from Book of Revelation from the cathedral at Angers, woven at the end of the 14th century at Paris. Later the centre of manufacture shifted north to Arras,

Tapestry. LEFT Early 16th-century tapestry woven from precious metals showing the beheading of St John the Baptist. BELOW Plate from the *Dictionnaire des Sciences* of Diderot showing tapestry technique at the famous Gobelins factory. FACING PAGE *The Hunt of the Unicorn* is a series of seven Franco-Flemish tapestries dating from the late 15th century. This, the last of the series, shows the unicorn brought to captivity. Of wool and silk with metal threads, it was probably woven to celebrate the marriage of Anne of Brittany to King Louis XII. (*LEFT Museo di Santa del Fiore, Florence/Bisonte;* BELOW *Victoria and Albert Museum, London;* FACING PAGE *The Metropolitan Museum of Art, The Cloisters Collection, Gift of John D. Rockefeller, Jr. 1937, New York.*)

Tapeworm

which became so famous for this work as to give its name to the product. In the 16th century the main centre shifted north again, out of France to Flanders, and the famous Vatican tapestries of the lives of St Peter and St Paul were woven in Brussels between 1516 and 1519 after cartoons by Raphael, which are now in the Victoria and Albert Museum, London. In the 17th century France again became an important centre with the establishment of the state factory of the Hôtel Royal des Gobelins by Louis XIV in 1662, extended to become Manufacture Royale des Meubles de la Couronne in 1667. Charles Lebrun (1619–90) was the first director. The institution closed during the French crises of 1694–97. Many notable names have been connected with Gobelins: J.-P. Oudry (1686–1755) who is credited with the first 'woven paintings' and F. Boucher (1703–70), who drew designs for tapestries and became an inspector for Gobelins. Another French tapestry area was Aubusson, its manufactory being established in 1665. It specialised in low-warp loom tapestries (see WEAVING) under its director, J. de Mons (1731–55). Aubusson tapestries are distinguished by subdued colouring and complex designs. Both Gobelins and Aubusson maintained their high standard of hand-woven manufacture until modern times. In 1954–57 the Aubusson factory executed the Coventry Cathedral hanging, *Christ in Glory*, designed by Graham SUTHERLAND.

England was not famous for early tapestries, although its embroidery was supreme. In the 16th century tapestries were woven at Sheldon. In 1619 the Royal Manufactory was established at Mortlake. It employed 50 Flemish weavers under the direction of P. de Maecht. The zenith of Mortlake tapestries was 1625–35. Tapestries were woven from designs by van Dyck, Rubens and other artists. Increased foreign competition and home economic difficulties forced the factory's eventual closure in 1703.

Foremost in the names of 19th-century English tapestry designers are Sir Edward BURNE-JONES and William MORRIS. Today tapestries are again being recognised as decorative hangings and works of art; one of the most famous designers is Victor VASARELY. Modern tapestries are displayed in art galleries in many capital cities in the West, and they are incorporated by architects and interior decorators as part of their overall projects. LE CORBUSIER not only used them in his interiors but also designed them.

Bibliography: J. J. Guiffrey, *La Tapisserie*, 1905; A. L. Hunter, *Tapestries, their Origin, History and Renaissance*, 1912; H. C. Caudle, *The Tapestry Book*, 1913; A. H. Christie, *Embroidery and Tapestry Weaving*, 1924; F. Salet, *La Tapisserie française du moyen-âge à nos jours*, 1946; M. E. Jones, *British and American Tapestries*, 1952; J.-P. Asselberghs, *De Geschiedenis van Jakob*, 1972.

Tapeworm, see CESTODA.

Tàpies, Antonio (1923–), Spanish painter and sculptor, born in Barcelona. Self-taught during the Civil War period, he arrived at a style of abstract painting which presented objects, rather than pictures, for sensuous enjoyment, his work associating the sense of touch with that of sight. His sculpture is equally unconventional, using material such as straw and towelling combined with ready-made pieces of furniture.

Bibliography: J. Teixidos, *Antonio Tàpies*, 1965; B. Boret, *Antonio Tàpies*, 1969.

Tapioca, see CASSAVA.

Tapir, any member of the family Tapiridae in suborder Ceratomorpha (tapirs and rhinoceroses) of the order Perissodactyla, which also includes the horse. They have a short, movable trunk, four front toes, and no horns, and form one of the oldest mammalian types. The skin is hairy and very thick, and the tail is rudimentary. Tapirs frequent forests and are nocturnal in habit, living chiefly on vegetable matter, though probably omnivorous. Of the four living species, *Tapirus indicus*, the largest, is Malayan. The rest occur in Central and South America. These are black when adult although the young are striped yellow and white. Tapirs are strong but shy and inoffensive and are easily tamed.

Tapping, in surgery, an operation for the purpose of drawing off an accumulation of fluid in a body cavity. A puncture is made through the overlying tissues and a small tube is inserted. The fluid then releases itself by its own pressure, or may be withdrawn by suction.

Tar, see COAL TAR.

Tar Heel State, see NORTH CAROLINA.

Tar Sands, or bituminous sands, sandy or clayey material impregnated with PETROLEUM-type materials, with similar origins to petroleum. The most outstanding example is the Athabasca deposits of North Alberta in Canada, which may have reserves equal to all known petroleum reserves in the world. Extraction of the oil is difficult, but much experimental work has been done and the extraction should eventually be feasible.

Tara, village of County MEATH, Republic of Ireland, on the Boyne, 10 km south of Navan. The Hill of Tara (154 m) was in ancient times the religious, political, and cultural capital of Ireland; upon its summit was the coronation stone of the ancient kings, and a statue of St Patrick. It was a royal residence until 640 and national assemblies were held here. Important excavations began in 1952, but were suspended until Tara becomes a national park.

Tara Fern, *Pteridium aquilinum* variety *esculentum*, a variety of common bracken, native to the southern hemisphere. Its root stock is eaten by pigs, and when roasted is a favourite food of the aborigines.

Taranaki, province in the south-west of North Island, New Zealand, with an area of 9712 km². Formerly forest-clad, most of the ground has now been cleared and is used for sheep rearing and dairy farming and meat, wool, butter, and cheese are produced. NEW PLYMOUTH is the capital and port. There is a small oil-field in operation and the Kapuni natural gas field is nearby. Population 101,200.

Tarantella, lively courtship dance from southern Italy in 6-8 time. It is danced by couples, the movement having a sharp and neat quality, and the steps are performed at a quick tempo. One theory for the origin of its name is that a dance taken at this speed would allow a victim bitten by a tarantula spider to sweat the poison out of the body. The bite was thought to cause a disease known as tarantism (a type of CHOREA or St Vitus's dance). This superstition was used as a subject for a ballet of the romantic period, 'La Tarentule'. The name of the dance may also have derived from the town of Taranto, where it is supposed to have originated. In Naples the dance passed through the hands of dancing masters who gave it a precise and more theatrical quality. In Sicily and other areas a fairly simple but lively form is still danced. Tambourines and castanets are often played during the dance.

Tarantism, see TARANTELLA.

Taranto, province of Italy, in eastern APULIA. Area 2440 km². Population (1974) 512,000.

Taranto (ancient *Tarentum*), Italian seaport and capital of the above province in Apulia, on the Gulf of Taranto, 80 km south-east of Bari. It was taken by the Normans in 1063, and became a feudal principality subject to the Kingdom of NAPLES. Taranto has an archiepiscopal cathedral (11th–18th centuries) and an ancient castle. It is one of Italy's four naval bases where much of the Italian fleet was destroyed in 1940–41. The large iron and steel works is one of the most ambitious projects of the government's regional policy. It also has chemical, oil refining, and oyster and mussel fishing industries. Population (1975) 241,410.

Bibliography: D. Newton and A. C. Hampshire, *Taranto*, 1974.

Taranto, Gulf of, inlet of the IONIAN SEA, separating the 'toe' and 'heel' of Italy. It is bordered by Calabria, Basilicata, and Apulia. The main town on the gulf is Taranto (see above).

Tarantula, name originally applied to the wolf-spider *Lycosa tarentula* (family Lycosidae), of southern Europe, but now used for any member of the family Theraphosidae found in Europe and America. Theraphosids are large spiders, *Aphonopelma* reaching a body length of 5 cm and a leg span of 12.5 cm. They are no more poisonous than other spiders of similar size. They burrow in the ground and catch their prey by pouncing on it and not by means of a web.

Tarapacá, northernmost province of CHILE bordering on Peru and Bolivia. The whole province is a hot, arid, virtually rainless desert, with some scattered oases which are cultivated. Along with the other two northern provinces it is Chile's main source of sodium nitrate. The capital and main port is IQUIQUE; ARICA is also an important port. Area 58,073 km²; population (1976) 216,000.

Tarawa, see GILBERT ISLANDS AND TUVALU.

Taraxacum, a genus of herbaceous perennials, of the Compositae (daisy family); there are many species, of which *T. officinale* is the dandelion, and *T. bicorne* is grown as a source of rubber in Russia. The dried roots, when roasted, make a coffee substitute (see CHICORY).

Taraz, see DZHAMBUL.

Tarbert, fishing village in Argyll and Bute District, Strathclyde Region, Scotland, 59 km north-east of Campbeltown. The village lies on an isthmus between eastern Loch Tarbert (inlet of Loch FYNE, 1.5 km long) and western Loch Tarbert which cuts almost completely

across the KINTYRE peninsula. The ancient castle here was erected by Robert Bruce. There is a good harbour and boat-building industry. Population 1391.

Tarbes, French town, capital of the *département* of Hautes-Pyrénées, on the River Adour. It was the capital of Bigorre, and in the 16th and 17th centuries was a Huguenot stronghold. In 1814 Wellington defeated the French here. Tarbes has a 12th-century cathedral. It is noted for its horses and has a school of artillery, armament works and manufactures shoes, furniture, electrical apparatus, machinery, and pottery. GAUTIER and FOCH were born here. Population 59,400.

Tarbolton, village of Kyle and Carrick District, Strathclyde Region, Scotland, on Fail Water, 10 km north-east of Ayr. Coilsfield Castle and Bachelor's Club are here; it also has associations with Burns. Population 2224.

Tardieu, André Pierre Gabriel Amedée (1876–1945), French politician, born in Paris. He became a diplomat, but then took up journalism and became foreign editor of the *Temps* and editor of the *Revue des deux mondes*. He became a deputy in 1914. At the peace conference, 1919–20, he was a colleague of Clemenceau, with whom he later founded the *Echo national*, and strenuously opposed any revision of the Versailles Treaty. Tardieu was premier three times, and from 1936 was a strong critic of the Third Republic.

Tardigrada, or water bears, are microscopic animals up to 0.5 mm long with stumpy bodies carrying four pairs of claw-like legs. They feed on plant-cell contents. A few marine species are found among sand grains, but most live in the water films on terrestrial mosses and lichens.

Tare. The hairy tare is *Vicia hirsuta*, the slender tare, *Vicia tenuissima*; both are leguminous trailing annuals native to Britain. The tares of the parable (Matt. xii) are probably darnel (see RYE GRASS).

Tarentum (Greek *Taras*; modern TARANTO), ancient Greek colony in Italy, on the west coast of the peninsula of Calabria. Its greatness dates from 708 BC when the original inhabitants were expelled by a body of Lacedaemonian Partheniae under the leadership of Phalanthus. Tarentum remained autonomous, though with varying fortune, until 272 BC, when it was captured by the Romans. It revolted during the second Punic War, but was retaken in 209 BC, and was subsequently an ally and (in 123) a colony of Rome. It was taken by the Saracens in 830.

Target, or targe, a round SHIELD.

Target, the object at which archers and riflemen aim. In archery a target is a circular frame of straw, painted with concentric rings of 122-millimetre width; there are five rings, counting respectively 1, 3, 5, 7, or 9 points. For some time 'match' targets of rectangular shape were solely used by soldiers; the 'bull' counted 4 points, the inner ring 3, a 'magpie' (a shot in the second of the target's rings) 2 points, and an 'outer' (outside any of the rings) 1 point. In most armies this type of target is used only for recruits or elementary training. Advanced training is carried out with more practical targets, those in the British army consisting of the head and shoulders of a man and others of a similar realistic type, including 'figure target' used in battle practices.

Târgovişte, see TÎRGOVIŞTE.

Tarifa, town in the province of Cádiz, Spain, on the Strait of Gibraltar. It has harbours on both the Mediterranean and the Atlantic, and the isthmus on which it stands is joined by a causeway to the Isla de las Palomas and the Punta Marroquí, the most southerly point in Spain. The town is Arab in appearance, and has anchovy and tunny fisheries. Population 7800.

Tariffs, taxes paid on imports or exports for PROTECTION or revenue purposes. Although the UK abolished protective tariffs in the 19th century, in favour of FREE TRADE, a number of tariffs were retained for purely revenue purposes (for example, those on tea, coffee, wine, and spirits), excise duties being imposed as necessary to offset any protective effect. Tariffs may be levied on weight or value, percentage duties on value being known as *ad valorem* duties.

In the USA the first Congress, in 1789, enacted a tariff which served to provide both revenue and protection simultaneously—an unusual and difficult feat. After the 1812–15 war with Great Britain, tariffs were raised to stem the flood of British goods, with further measures of protection up to early in the 1830s, when a tendency towards lower tariffs prevailed generally up to the Civil War of 1861–65. After the war the Republicans passed a number of high-duty tariffs up to and including the Fordney-McCumber tariff of 1922 and the Hawley-Smoot tariff of 1930, interrupted from time to time by lower tariffs, such as the Wilson-Underwood tariff of 1913, promoted by the Democrats. The 1930 act was weakened through amendment in 1934 by the Reciprocal Trade Agreements Act empowering the president to reduce duties by 50 per cent. By 1939 agreements had been made with 21 countries. Further powers were given later, and further reductions negotiated at Geneva in 1947 under the GENERAL AGREEMENT ON TARIFFS AND TRADE (GATT) and again at Annecy in 1949 and Torquay in 1951.

The Trade Expansion Act was passed by the US Congress in 1962. This empowered the government to negotiate reciprocal tariffs on certain classes of goods and reciprocal reductions between the European Economic Community (EEC) and the USA. The act also empowered the US government to aid firms particularly hard hit by foreign competition and to take retaliatory action against unreasonable restrictions imposed by foreign countries.

The sixth round of negotiations under GATT was the most ambitious international attempt ever undertaken to lower the barriers to world trade. In all some 50 countries, accounting for about 75 per cent of total world trade, took part in the negotiations which opened on 4 May 1964 and concluded on 30 June 1967. The duty reductions agreed by the four major participants, the USA, the EEC, Japan and the UK, averaged nearly 40 per cent overall and were in many cases as high as 50 per cent. The agreed duty reductions were implemented in a series of instalments between 1968 and 1972 and it was estimated that the concessions affected trade (in 1964) valued at some $40,000 million.

Bibliography: H. G. Johnson, *Aspects of the Theory of Tariffs,* 1971.

Tarija, department of BOLIVIA, with Paraguay on the east and Argentina to the south. Whilst the eastern districts are part of the Gran Chaco, the rest of the department consists of high valleys which are rich in vegetation. The climate is of a semi-arid Mediterranean type. Wheat, maize, barley, grapes, tobacco, and groundnuts are produced in quantity. There is a small wine industry. Cattle are reared, and there are extensive forests. Area 24,882 km²; population (1975) 236,000.

Tarija, capital of the above department and one of the oldest settlements in Bolivia. Bad communications—no railway and only one good major road, though there is an airport—isolate the town. There is a university. Altitude 1875 m. Population 26,000.

Tarim, important river of SINKIANG UIGHUR autonomous region in China, formed by the junction of the Yarkand Daria and the Khotan Daria. The Tarim is a sluggish stream, shallow and tortuous, and after flowing along the edge of the TAKLA MAKAN, and through the oases of Yarkand, Kashgar, and Aksu, it dies away in the marsh of LOP NOR, after a course of 1600 km. The basin area is 893,550 km², over half of which consists of arid desert. The region was first explored by Sven Hedin and Sir Aurel Stein, who discovered the ancient civilisation of the basin.

Tariqa, or Tarika, see SUFISM.

Tarkington, (Newton) Booth (1869–1946), US dramatist, novelist and essayist, born at Indianapolis, Indiana. Educated at Purdue and Princeton universities, he was a member of the Indiana House of Representatives in 1902–03, but then gave up politics to devote himself to writing. He was successful with his first book, *The Gentleman from Indiana,* 1899, the model for further realistic novels of Middle West life. He twice won the Pulitzer Prize for novels with *The Magnificent Ambersons,* 1918, the chronicle of the decline of an Indiana family, and *Alice Adams,* 1921, the story of a girl whose love affair with a man of higher social standing is ended when he meets her mediocre family. Among others were *The Two Van Revels,* 1902, *The Conquest of Canaan,* 1905, and *The Plutocrat,* 1927.

In another vein were his stories of young people, *Penrod,* 1914, its sequels, and *Seventeen,* 1916, which won a new success for him. Standing apart in his work is the romance *Monsieur Beaucaire,* 1900. Tarkington dramatised it, and the play had much success in the United States and as the libretto of a popular opera in England. His many other plays include *Clarence,* 1919, and some comedies (with H. L. Wilson and J. Street). His reminiscences, *The World Does Move,* appeared in 1928. In 1942 he was awarded the Roosevelt Distinguished Service Medal, and in 1945 the Howells Medal of the American Academy of Arts and Letters.

Bibliography: Life by A. D. Dickinson, 1926; J. Woodress, *Booth Tarkington, Gentleman from Indiana,* 1955.

Tarlac, province of LUZON in the Philippines. An agricultural province of the central plain, its chief products are coconuts, rice, and sugar. Area 3053 km². Population (1970) 558,700.

Tarlac, capital of the above province in the Philippines. It is an important trade and transport centre situated 100 km north-west of Manila. Population (1970) 134,800.

Tarlatan, gauze-like muslin used for ladies' dresses, etc., originally produced in India.

Tarlton, Richard (d. 1588), English entertainer, born in Shropshire. The most famous of Elizabethan clowns, and a favourite of the Queen herself, he was probably the original of Hamlet's 'poor Yorick'. A drawing of him, preserved in the British Museum, and reproduced on the title page of the posthumous *Tarlton's Jests*, shows him as short and stout, with a large, flat face, curly hair, a wavy moustache, and a small beard. A second portrait, discovered in 1920, shows him with a flat nose and a squint. It is probable that the richly comic parts in Shakespeare—Launce, Bottom, Dogberry, the gravedigger—owe much to Tarlton, who also excelled in the Elizabethan jig. His own plays (among them the farcical *Seven Deadly Sinns, or Five Plays in One*, performed at Court, 1585) have not survived.

Tarn, *département* of southern France, formed from part of the old province of Languedoc. It is drained by the River Tarn and its tributary the Agout. In the east and south-east are the high plateaus of the Sidobre, in the west there is a fertile plain, and in the rest of the *département* there are small, wooded uplands. Cereals, vines, and vegetables are produced, and livestock is raised. There are metallurgical, textile, leather, glass, and paper industries. The principal towns are ALBI (the capital), and CASTRES. Area 5751 km²; population (1975) 335,000.

Tarn, river of France, rising in the CÉVENNES and flowing into the GARONNE. The chief towns on its banks are ALBI and MONTAUBAN. Length 375 km.

Tarn-et-Garonne, *département* of southern France, formed from parts of the old provinces of Guyenne, Gascony, and Languedoc. It is an alluvial plain formed by the confluence of the rivers Garonne, Tarn, and Aveyron. There are some hills and the region is generally wooded. Cereals, fruit trees, vines, and truffles are produced, and sheep are raised. There is little industrial development. The principal towns are MONTAUBAN (the capital) and Castelsarrasin. Area 3716 km²; population (1975) 183,400.

Tarnopol, see TERNOPOL.

Tarnowskie Góry, town of Poland, in Katowice province, 24 km north of Katowice. It was transferred from Germany to Poland in 1921. There are coal and iron-ore mines. Population (1974) 94,555.

Taro, or eddo, *Colocasia antiquorum* and its variety *esculenta*, tropical species of the Araceae (arum lily family). It is often used as a foliage plant. Its rhizomes (underground stems) are poisonous when raw, but once boiled form a nutritious starchy food.

Tarot, a pack of cards thought to be of ancient origin and used as a method of divination. Its exact beginnings are uncertain although theories have linked it with Egypt and India. On the whole, its conception appears to be principally medieval and Western, but many Tarot scholars hold to the view that at least the trump and pip cards date

Richard Tarlton playing the pipe and tabor, portrayed in an ornamental letter T, from a work published soon after his death. *(Mansell Collection)*

back to antiquity, and that the symbolism has evolved from an ancient occult tradition which contains a deeply profound significance.

The pack consists of 78 cards divided into the Greater Arcana and the Lesser Arcana. The Greater Arcana comprise 22 trump cards (or tarots) considered the 'keys' of the pack. They are named according to the picture symbols they display, such as the Juggler, the High Priestess, and the Wheel of Fortune. They are said to correspond with the 22 letters of the Hebrew alphabet, each letter having an occult significance in the Kabbalah tradition (see NUMEROLOGY). The remaining 56 cards (the Lesser Arcana) are similar to the ordinary playing cards pack except that they display pictures as well as numbers. There are four suits: rods or wands, cups, swords, and shekels or pentacles, corresponding to the clubs, hearts, spades and diamonds of the modern pack. As well as a king, queen and knave, each suit also has a knight.

See also DIVINATION; KABBALAH; CARDS, PLAYING.

Bibliography: A. E. Waite, *The Pictorial Key to the Tarot*, 1959; C. A. Pushong, *The Tarot of the Magi*, 1970.

Tarpaulin, coarse cloth, usually of jute, covered with tar to produce a waterproof material, used for roofing, etc.

Tarpeia, in Roman legend, daughter of Spurius Tarpeius, commander of the Capitol during the war that followed the rape of the Sabine women (see SABINES). Tarpeia offered to betray the Capitol to its besiegers if they would give her what they wore on their left arms, meaning their bracelets. The agreement was made, and Tarpeia opened one of the gates. But the Sabines obeyed the letter of their undertaking by crushing her to death with their shields. The Tarpeian rock was a place for the execution of traitors; but it is unlikely that the tradition (whcih contradicts the original story of the rape and its sequel) arose to account for this fact. More probably Tarpeia was a local deity in whose cult a heap of shields played some part and suggested the manner of her death, which in turn gave rise to the story of her crime.

Tarpon, *Megalops atlanticus*, in order Anguilliformes, a giant herring-like fish plentiful in warm American seas and off West African coasts. It grows to a length of 2 m or more, and to a weight of over 135 kg; the scales, which are tough like thin horn and are made into ornaments, are sometimes as much as 12 cm in diameter.

Tarquinia, Italian town in LAZIO, 100 km north-west of Viterbo. It stands near the mouth of the Marta, and in the late Middle Ages was a busy port. Nearby is the site of Tarquinii, one of the cities of the Etruscan Confederation (see ETRURIA); an Etruscan necropolis, with frescoed tombs dating from the 6th to the 2nd centuries BC, still exists. Population (1974) 10,300.

Tarquinius, name of an Etruscan family in early Roman history, to which the fifth and seventh legendary kings of Rome belonged.
Lucius Tarquinius Priscus, fifth king of Rome, 616–579 BC, in succession to ANCUS MARCIUS, defeated the Latins and Sabines. He is reputed to have modified the constitution and to have begun the building of the sewers and the Circus Maximus. He was murdered after a reign of 38 years.
Lucius Tarquinius Superbus, the seventh and last king of Rome, 534–510 BC, succeeded SERVIUS TULLIUS. Though a tyrant at home, he enhanced the power and prosperity of Rome, defeating the Volscians and taking Gabii. Following the rape of LUCRETIA in which his son was involved, Tarquinius Superbus and his family were exiled in 510 BC. The people of Tarquinia and VEII took up his cause and marched against Rome, but they were unsuccessful. Tarquinius next obtained the help of Lars PORSENA, king of Clusium, who marched against Rome, but was induced to make peace with the Romans. Thereupon Tarquinius took refuge with his son-in-law, Octavius Mamilius, who induced the Latin states to declare war against Rome, but they were defeated at the battle of Lake Regillus. Tarquinius then fled to Aristobulus at Cumae, where he died.

Tarracina, see TERRACINA.

Tarragon, *Artemisia dracunculus*, an aromatic perennial plant belonging to the Compositae (daisy family), the green or dried leaves of which are used for flavouring vinegar, for cooking and salads.

Tarragona, province of Spain, in CATALONIA, with a coastline on the Mediterranean. It is mountainous, and has a temperate coastal plain containing the mouth of the EBRO river. There is much forest, and the valleys are fertile. Wine, fruit, olive oil, silk, hemp, and cereals are produced. Copper, lead, silver, limestone, and marble are mined or quarried. Area 6490 km²; population 465,770.

Tarragona, city, capital of the province of Tarragona, Spain, on the Mediterranean coast at the mouth of the River Francolí. In Roman times it became the capital of Hither Spain, and afterwards of *Hispania Tarraconensis*

(see SPAIN, *History*). The Visigoths sacked it in 467, and the Moors in 714. ALFONSO I of Aragón took it from the Moors in 1120. In 1811 it was sacked by the French, and later the town was replanned. The older part of Tarragona stands on a high rock and has remarkable walls, portions of which date back to about the 6th century BC. The Romanesque and Gothic archiepiscopal cathedral stands on the site of a temple of Jupiter. In the town and in its vicinity are numerous Roman remains, including an amphitheatre and an aqueduct; in some cases the remains of Roman buildings have been incorporated into more modern structures. The modernised port of Tarragona has a trade in the produce of the Ebro valley, including wine, and a petrochemicals industry has been created. Population 78,236.

Tarrasa, town in the province of Barcelona, Spain. It is an important industrial centre, with cotton and woollen mills, and has a trade in agricultural produce, oil, and wine. Population 138,697.

Tarshish, in biblical geography, a far-distant locality, rich in silver, iron, tin and lead (Ezek. xxvii. 12). The largest ships of those days were called 'ships of Tarshish' (Ezek. xxvii. 25). It is commonly identified with the ancient Tartessus, situated in the south of Spain, which in the 8th and 7th centuries BC was under Phoenician hegemony. Less probable is the identification of Tarshish with Tarsus.

Tarsier, *Tarsius spectrum*, a small primate intermediate between lemurs and monkeys, a native of the East Indies. They are about the size of a small rat, have very large eyes, very long ankle bones, and sucker-like disks on the fingers and toes. The tarsier lives in trees, is nocturnal in habit and feeds mainly on insects. Its skull closely resembles that of the ape.

Tarsus, city of Cilicia in Asia Minor, on the River Cydnus, about 32 km west south-west of Adana. It was the birthplace of St Paul and, from AD 72, capital of the Roman province of Cilicia.

Tartaglia, Niccolò, real name Fontana (c. 1500–57), Italian scientist and mathematician, born at Brescia. When he was 12 he was wounded in the jaw and was nicknamed *Tartaglia*, or 'stammerer', which he adopted

Tarsier. *Tarsius spectrum*. (*Popperfoto*)

as a surname. He was mainly interested in the scientific and mathematical problems of gunnery and the art of warfare, particularly in projectiles. In 1521 he was a teacher of mathematics in Verona. He discovered a method of solving cubic equations of the form $x^3 + ax = b$, where a and b are both positive, and was involved in bitter arguments with Girolamo CARDANO over priority. His chief works are *Nova scientia* (A new science), 1537, on the theory and practice of gunnery, and *Trattato di numero e misuri* (Treatise on number and measures), 1556, 1560, dealing with arithmetic, algebra as far as quadratic equations, geometry, and mensuration. He published the first Italian translation of Euclid, 1543, and the earliest version of some of the principal works of Archimedes, 1543.

Tartan (from French *tiretaine*, a linsey-woolsey cloth). The word has come to mean the distinctive woollen cloth in which coloured threads are woven into both weft and warp at intervals to give a checkered or cross-striped effect, some patterns being so closely associated with certain highland Scottish families or clans as to be regarded as their exclusive property. In this modern sense tartans probably date from the upsurge of nationalism which eventually led to the Scottish rebellion of 1745, after the failure of which they were proscribed for 35 years. The rescinding of the proscription led to a new enthusiasm for tartans, but speaking generally new sets of designs were adopted by the qualifying families which did not correspond to those appearing in earlier family portraits. The use of tartans of different patterns or setts as a clan or family distinction is a feature of the Scottish social system of clanship in which the essential link is a theory of kinship between the chief and the people of the clan, though in large clans subdivisions into chieftains and septs have arisen for historical reasons.

The theory that distinctive clan or family tartans date from a period earlier than the 17th century cannot be supported by evidence. The use of checkered and striped cloths by primitive peoples is natural; the wool of the black sheep woven in a pattern of stripes or squares into the wool of the white sheep is the simplest form of decorative weaving, and it is this effect that is known as 'shepherd's plaid'. In the later Middle Ages cheap striped woollen cloth, which had been imported from North Africa and was the usual wear of Carmelite monks, was forbidden by the Pope because by that time it brought ridicule on the order. This cloth has remained a part of the general wear of some North African Arabs. Striped materials have often formed a part of European fashion, but it is only in Scotland that the systematic weaving of checkered cloths has taken on a special significance, and from surviving pieces it can be seen that the earliest tartans were often very elaborate in the arrangement of their colours. They were also, since only vegetable dyes were used, quite different in colour from modern tartans, though not necessarily less bright. Some families and clans have more than one tartan, a separate design being used, for instance, as a 'hunting' tartan. At the end of the 18th century certain 'loyal' regiments having Scottish associations were ordered to adopt their own regimental tartans from which kilts or trews and plaids were made. Although most clans have various tartans for different occasions, they usually today wear only one

tartan. It is rare for newcomers to Scotland to be accorded their personal tartan.

See also HIGHLAND DRESS.

Bibliography: Sir T. Innes of Learney, *Tartans of the Clans and Families of Scotland*, 6th ed. 1958; S. Maxwell and R. Hutchinson, *Scottish Costume 1550–1850*, 1958; *The Scottish Clans and their Tartans*, 41st ed. 1968.

Tartar Emetic (antimony potassium tartrate), a drug prepared by boiling potassium hydrogen tartrate with antimony oxide and water. It is readily soluble in water, and is used in dyeing as a mordant, and in medicine as an emetic. Given intravenously, it was first used in 1912 in the treatment of LEISHMANIASIS (kala-azar), caused by a parasite which is transmitted to humans by the sand-fly. It is also used in the treatment of SCHISTOSOMIASIS (bilharzia) caused by blood flukes. Antimony sodium tartrate is more soluble and less irritant and is now more commonly used than the potassium salt. All antimony compounds produce undesirable side-effects, and continuous treatment may lead to the development of toxic symptoms.

Tartaric Acid, otherwise dihydroxysuccinic acid, $(CH(OH)\cdot COOH)_2$, commonly occurring vegetable acid, contained in grapes and other fruits. During the later stages of the fermentation of grape-juice, impure potassium hydrogen tartrate or argol is deposited. From this salt the commercial acid is prepared. The crude argol is partially purified by recrystallisation from hot water, and it is then boiled in solution with chalk. Calcium tartrate is deposited, and the tartaric acid is set free from this by treating with dilute sulphuric acid. The acid forms large transparent crystals, is readily soluble in water and alcohol, but insoluble in ether (melting point 167 °C). Like other dicarboxylic acids, it forms both hydrogen and normal salts. The acid potassium salt is 'cream of tartar' and the potassium sodium salt is 'Rochelle salt'. Tartaric acid is used in the preparation of effervescing drinks and in baking powders. There are four optical isomers of the acid (see STEREOCHEMISTRY), viz. (+)-tartaric, (–)-tartaric, meso-tartaric (inactive), and RACEMIC ACID (inactive).

Tartars, see TATARS.

Tartarus, in Homer, a place of punishment reserved for the rebel TITANS, as far below HADES as heaven is above the earth. Later poets use the name as synonymous with Hades.

Tartini, Giuseppe (1692–1770), Italian composer and violinist, born at Pirano. As a result of a clandestine marriage he had to flee to Assisi but eventually returned to Padua. In 1728 he started a violin school of European fame. His compositions for violin comprise about 150 sonatas (including the famous 'Devil's Trill'), 50 trios and about 140 concertos. Tartini made several improvements in the technique and construction of the bow.

Tartu (Russian *Yurev*; German *Dorpat*), city and cultural centre of the ESTONIAN SSR, USSR, 160 km south-east of Tallinn. It has food, engineering, and metal-working industries. There is a university founded in 1632 by Gustavus Adolphus of Sweden, closed in 1710, and re-opened in 1802 by Alexander I (the language of instruction was German till 1895, Russian till 1918, and

559

Tashkent. The city at night. *(Novosti Press Agency)*

has been Estonian ever since), a university library (1802, largest in the Baltic republics), a botanical garden (1803), and an observatory (1809). Tartu was founded by the Russians in 1030 on the site of the Estonian village of Tarpatu, and belonged variously to the Livonian Order, Muscovy, Poland, and Sweden; it was Russian from 1704, and was occupied by the Germans in 1918 and 1941–44. The peace treaties were signed here by the Soviet Union with Estonia and Finland in 1920. Population (1970) 90,000.

Tarvisium, see TREVISO.

Tascher de la Pagerie, Joséphine, see JOSÉPHINE, MARIE ROSE.

Tashauz, *oblast* in TURKMEN SSR, USSR, only formed in 1970. Industry is mainly concentrated in the capital, Tashauz, and consists of cotton-ginning and food packing. Irrigated agriculture is practised in the AMU DARYA valley. Area 75,400 km²; population (1970) 411,000.

Tashkent, *oblast* in UZBEK SSR, USSR. Cotton and fruit are extensively cultivated, and the *oblast* has several important industries, including coal-mining, engineering, and textiles. There are several hydro-electric power stations in the region. Area 15,600 km²; population (1970) 2,865,000.

Tashkent, capital of Tashkent *oblast* (see above), and of the UZBEK SSR. It is the largest city in Soviet Asia and the fourth largest in the Soviet Union. Situated in the valley of the River Chirchik, it is an important rail and air passenger transport centre. It has textile and mining machinery works, and a large number of light industries. It is the terminus of the Dzharkak-Bukhara-Tashkent gas pipeline. A severe earthquake in 1966 caused extensive damage but rebuilding was rapid. There is a branch of the Academy of Sciences and a university, and it is the centre of Uzbek culture. Population (1976) 1,643,000.

Tashkurghan, town in BALKH province of Afghanistan. Some 6 km to the south lies the ancient ruined town of Khulm. Founded in 1750 it became an important trade centre between India and Bukhara.

Tashlin, Frank (1913–72), US film director and cartoonist. He worked as an animator for Warner Brothers'

560

Merrie Melodies and Looney Tunes during the 1930s; started the syndicated comic strip *Van Boring* in 1934, and then went to the Walt Disney studios as a story director for the *Mickey Mouse* and *Donald Duck* series (1939–45). In the late forties he began writing feature scripts, and in 1950 directed *The Lemon-Drop Kid*, since when he has worked with comedians such as Bob Hope, Robert Cummings, the Dean Martin-Jerry Lewis team, and Jerry Lewis on his own. As a director of comedy and satire he was the best of his time: *Artists and Models* (1955), *Hollywood or Bust* (1956), *The Lieutenant Wore Skirts* (1956), *The Girl Can't Help It* (1956), *Will Success Spoil Rock Hunter* (1957), *Bachelor Flat* (1962), *Who's Minding the Store* (1963), *The Disorderly Orderly* (1964), *The Alphabet Murders* (1965). He also wrote several books of cartoons.

Tashmetum, see NABU.

Tasman, Abel Janszoon (1603–59), Dutch navigator and explorer, born at Lutjegast. After journeys in China and India, he was sent by the Dutch East India Company to investigate the extent of Australia. On his second voyage, 1642–43, he discovered TASMANIA (which he named VAN DIEMEN's Land), NEW ZEALAND, FIJI, and TONGA. In 1644, he explored the Gulf of CARPENTARIA.

Tasman Glacier, in the south of the South Island, New Zealand, discovered in 1862 by Julius von Haast. It is 29 km long and 2 km wide.

Tasmania, one of the six states of Australia, an island once joined to the mainland but now separated by Bass Strait, which is c. 225 km wide. It is the smallest of the Australian states with an area of 67,800 km².

Over 50 islands are administered by Tasmania: the Furneaux group, at the eastern end of Bass Strait, and those off the north-east corner of Tasmania including Flinders islands, Cape Barren islands, and Clarke islands; besides these are Chapell islands and the Kent group.

Geography. Tasmania has two mountain chains which are continuations of the Dividing Range of the mainland. The eastern range has an average height of 1150 m and runs parallel with the east coast. The highest peaks are Mount Barrow, 1400 m, and Ben Lomond, 1573 m. The

Abel Tasman, after a portrait by Van der Helst. *(Mansell Collection)*

Tasmania. Hopfields in the Derwent river valley. *(Camera Press/Richard Harrington)*

western chain is an elevated tableland in the centre of the island averaging 915 m in height; it contains large lakes. The highest peaks here are Barn Bluff (1560 m), Mount Field West (1430 m), Cradle Mountain (1540 m), and Mount Ossa (1617 m). In the south is Mount Wellington (1260 m), at the foot of which stands HOBART.

The island has a well-developed drainage system. The main rivers are the Derwent, about 210 km long (on the estuary of which lies Hobart, with a deep and sheltered harbour), and which issues from Lake St Clair, the Huon, about 160 km in length, and the Arthur river—these last two draining into the Southern Ocean. On the north of the island, flowing into Bass Strait, are the Mersey and the Tamar (the last-named being navigable up to Launceston 64 km from its mouth). The rivers Gordon and King on the west coast are of remarkable beauty.

The west coast of Tasmania is bold, rocky, and inhospitable, but there are several accessible ports. The chief harbours are: on the west coast, Port Davey (formerly used by whaling vessels), Pieman river, and Macquarie Harbour: on the north coast, Stanley; and on the east coast, George's Bay, Oyster Bay, Prosser Bay, Spring Bay, and Fortescue Bay. The south and south-east of the island is studded with safe bays and harbours, the main ones being Storm Bay and D'Entrecasteaux Channel.

There are numerous extensive fresh-water lakes on the elevated tablelands, the largest being the Great Lake (1160 m above sea-level), covering an area of 104 km²; Lake Sorell about 52 km²; Lake St Clair; Arthur Lake, and Lake Echo. These lakes form the headwaters of the main rivers flowing south, west, and north.

In terms of landscape, Tasmania is a succession of peaks, hills, and valleys of varying height and depth, which presents a pleasing variety of scenery, with snow-capped mountains, glassy lakes, wild shores, green valleys, and extensive sheeplands, studded with homesteads, surrounded by fields, and highly cultivated gardens and orchards.

In temperature and rainfall Tasmania resembles Britain, although warmer and sunnier. Hot winds are almost

unknown, and the summer heat is tempered by sea breezes and mountain air. The average temperature of Hobart in the hottest month is 16 °C. The winter is cold enough to produce thin ice in the lowlands and snow in the mountains and plateaus. The average in the coldest month is 8 °C. The mean temperature for the year is 12 °C. The average rainfall is about 745 mm, but there is much variation in different districts, rainfall in the west sometimes reaching 4318 mm a year. Its population in 1975 was 410,222. See also ATLAS 61.

Economy. Tasmania, like all parts of Australia has undergone radical developments since the second world war. Its manufacturing and mining economies have been particularly stimulated.

Of the total 67,800 km² of land, only 160,000 ha are cultivated. The chief land-use is sown and natural pastures which are used for dairy cattle. From the 900,000 dairy cattle on the islands, 13 million kg of butter and 7 million kg of cheese are produced each year. The island's 4,200,000 sheep produce about 18 million kg of wool. The mild, moist climate of Tasmania is highly suitable for fruit and vegetable growing yet unsuitable for large-scale cereal growing. The area under wheat is negligible. Apples (108·8 million kg produced yearly) are the most important fruit crop followed by pears, raspberries, and blackcurrants. The chief vegetables are peas, beans, and potatoes. Crops of lesser importance are barley, oats, and hops.

Tasmania has a higher percentage of land under forest than any other Australian state. Forty-six per cent (or 3 million ha) are forested. The main species are *Eucalyptus* and *Pinus*. The forests have influenced the development of one of the most important parts of Tasmania's industries—pulp, paper, and newsprint.

The state has a well-developed mining sector although it is on a much smaller scale than Western Australia and Queensland. It has very important deposits of silver, lead, and zinc at Rosebery; tin at Renison and Cleveland; copper and pyrites at Mount Lyell (near QUEENSTOWN); and iron ore in the Savage river area. These centres are in the rugged western half of the state where most of the mining takes place. Outside this region there is tungsten and tin at Rossarden and mineral sands and tungsten on KING ISLAND. Tasmania lacks commercial deposits of coal, oil, and natural gas.

Mining has stimulated one of the major sectors of the manufacturing sector, mineral refining and smelting. Iron ore from the Savage river area is refined into pellets at Port Latta and exported to Japan; copper and pyrites are refined at Queenstown; zinc and lead at Rosebery; and alumina from Queensland is smelted into aluminium at Bell Bay, 50 km north of Launceston. Bell Bay also has an alumina refinery and a plant producing high-carbon ferro-manganese. Risdon (near Hobart) has the largest electrolytic zinc plant in the world. Because of the large timber stands newsprint is produced at Boyer (annual capacity 200,000 t) and Burnie; pulp and paper at Wesley Vale and Port Huon (near Hobart); and wood chips at Long Reach. Of growing importance are industrial gases (liquid oxygen and nitrogen) which are manufactured at Hobart, Launceston, and Burnie. At Devonport and Ulverstone vegetables are frozen and canned. As well as these main industries Tasmania has a wide variety of metal-working and food-processing industries.

Tasmanian Devil

One of the reasons for the development of electrolytic refineries and smelters in Tasmania is the availability of abundant electricity. The high precipitation and mountainous terrain of much of the island is ideal for hydro-electric power generation which supplies all of the island's electricity requirements, 6977 kWh annually. Future extension of the network is planned on the Gordon and the Pieman rivers (to be completed by 1985). Diversification of power sources occurred with the completion of two oil-fired thermal power stations at Bell Bay which have an annual capacity of 240,000 kWh.

Government. Tasmania has an upper house (Legislative Council) and a lower house (House of Assembly) with 19 and 35 members respectively. Power of government is vested in the Governor, the Cabinet (10 members), and the two houses. The state has 10 members in the Commonwealth Senate and five in the House of Representatives.

History. Tasmania was originally called Van Diemen's Land and was discovered by TASMAN on 24 November 1642. In 1777 it was visited by Cook, who thought it formed part of the mainland. Lieutenant William Bligh planted English fruit trees at Adventure Bay on 17 August 1788, on the outward voyage of the *Bounty* to Pitcairn Island. It was proved an island by circumnavigation by Bass and Flinders in 1798. The earliest settlement, mostly of convicts, was established under Lieutenant Bowen at Risdon, on the River Derwent, by Governor King of New South Wales, in 1803. The island was mainly used as a penal settlement, and increasing numbers of convicts were sent there after transportation to Australia had ended. This system ceased in 1853. In 1825 the island which had previously formed part of New South Wales, was proclaimed a separate colony, and in 1856 the name of Van Diemen's Land was changed to Tasmania and responsible government granted. In 1901 Tasmania united with the states of the mainland in establishing the Commonwealth of Australia.

Bibliography: M. Sharland, *Tasmanian Wild Life*, 1963; J. West, *History of Tasmania*, 1972; S. W. Jackman, *Tasmania*, 1974; *Tasmanian Year Book* (annual).

Tasmanian Devil, *Sarcophilus*, a small, bearlike mammal of the family Dasyuridae, order MARSUPIALIA. It has a compact body with a large head, brownish-black fur with a white breastmark, and resembles a bear, although

Tasmania. The Clark Dam. *(Camera Press/Hedda Morrison)*

Tasmanian Devil. *(Barnaby's Picture Library)*

it is only around 65 cm long and has a bushy tail of about 25 cm. It has strong teeth and is irritable. It has recently become extinct in Australia, but still occurs in remote parts of Tasmania.

Tass (Russian abbreviation for Telegraphic Agency of the Soviet Union), official Soviet Russian news agency attached to the USSR Council of Ministers. It was established in 1925. Tass is the only agency in the USSR for both internal and foreign news, serving 3600 Soviet newspapers and 300 foreign press agencies in 76 countries. In its work it is subordinated to the Propaganda Department of the Central Committee of the Communist Party of the Soviet Union.

Tassie, James (1735–99), gem-engraver and modeller, born at Pollokshaws, Scotland. With Henry Quin, Tassie invented the 'white enamel composition' which he used for his medallion portraits and cast reproduction of gems. The *Descriptive Catalogue*, 1791, of Raspe enumerates 16,000 pieces from his hands, but before his death this had reached 20,000. His nephew, William Tassie (1777–1860), was also an engraver and modeller.

Tassigny, Jean de Lattre de, see LATTRE DE TAS-SIGNY, JEAN MARIE GABRIEL DE.

Tasso, Bernardo (1493–1569), Italian poet, born in Venice; of high contemporary standing, he is now remembered as the father of Torquato TASSO. His works include the narrative poem *Amadigi*, 1560, and some lyrics.

Tasso, Torquato (1544–95), Italian poet, born at Sorrento, the son of Bernardo TASSO. In 1560 he was sent to Padua to study law, but, influenced by the literary environment of his early years at Rome and Venice, devoted himself to literature and philosophy.

In 1562 he produced *Rinaldo*, a romantic poem dedicated to Cardinal Luigi d'Este, who later became his patron. In 1572 he entered the service of Duke Alfonso at Ferrara. For the court theatre he wrote his pastoral play *Aminta*, 1573. It was in 1576 that he first showed signs of mental derangement, but he escaped from his place of confinement to Ferrara, wandered through the chief cities of Italy, and, in 1579, again returned to the court of the Duke of Ferrara. The Duke, however, received him coldly and Tasso, wounded by some real or fancied insult, hurled denunciations at the whole ducal household, with the result that he was confined as insane by the Duke from 1578 to 1586. During his confinement he produced much admirable verse, a number of philosophical dialogues, and an *Apologia* for *La Gerusalemme Liberata*, which had been completed by 1575 and published without his consent and with many errors.

The grotesque contrast between his fate and the rising fame of his masterpiece had roused public interest in him, and he was consequently released in 1586 on the intervention of Prince Vincenzo Gonzaga.

La Gerusalemme Liberata had been submitted to several critics, and on his release Tasso went to Mantua as the protégé of Prince Gonzaga, and here he rewrote his great epic in the light of his critics' suggestions. The result, *La Gerusalemme Conquistata*, 1592, was a pedantic effusion, in which he expurgated many of the passages that were to make the *Gerusalemme Liberata* for long the most popular work in Italian literature. Broken in health, he resumed his restless wanderings, spending, however, much of these later years between Naples and Rome, helped and protected by many friends and patrons. In 1595 he was summoned by the Pope to be crowned poet laureate, but he died on his arrival in Rome at the convent of Sant' Onofrio, without receiving the honour.

Tasso's poetry was an attempt to reconcile classic form with a deeper note of individual sentiment. His *Gerusalemme*, an idealisation of the first crusade, is a typical literary product of his age, its unquestioning acceptance of classic forms in marked conflict with newly revived theological interests. His other works include a comedy; a tragedy, *Discorsi*, elucidating his attitude to his own poetry; and religious poems.

Bibliography: W. Boulting, *Tasso and his Times*, 1907; E. Donadoni, *Torquato Tasso*, 1920; G. Getto, *Interpretazione del Tasso*, 1951; C. P. Brand, *Torquato Tasso*, 1965.

Tassoni, Alessandro (1565–1635), Italian poet, born at Modena. His principal works are *La Secchia Rapita*, 1622, a burlesque epic, *Considerazioni sopra il Petrarca*, 1609, and *Pensieri Diversi*, 1612.

Taste, see TONGUE.

Tata, Jamsetji Nasarwanji (1839–1904), Indian Parsi

Torquato Tasso reading his *Gerusalemme Liberata* before the Duke of Ferrara, from a painting by the French artist Montagny, 1815. *(Victoria and Albert Museum, London)*

merchant and philanthropist, born in Nosari in Baroda. He introduced a silk industry based on Japanese methods into Mysore, and endowed a research institute at Bangalore. His son, Sir Dorabji Jamestji Tata (1859–1932), discovered iron ore in Orissa, established an iron and steel works at Jamshedput, and developed hydro-electric power in the Western Ghats. Today the Tata family is one of the most powerful industrialist families in India.

Tatabánya, town of northern Hungary, capital of the county of Komárom, 48 km west of Budapest. It is an important modern lignite-mining centre. At the neighbouring spa of Tata there is a fine ESTERHAZY mansion. Population (1975) 70,000.

Tatar Autonomous Soviet Socialist Republic, formed in 1920 and lies in East European RSFSR, USSR, occupying a lowland area crossed by the Middle VOLGA and Lower KAMA. The northern part is in the mixed (mainly deciduous) forest belt, and the south is wooded steppe with black earth soils. There are extensive oil deposits and oil-extraction (largest in USSR), engineering, chemical, woodworking, and fur industries. Grain, sunflowers, and potatoes are grown, and horticulture and dairy-farming are widespread. The main urban centres are KAZAN (the capital), CHISTOPOL, NABEREZHNIYE CHELNY, ALMETYEVSK, and BUGULMA. For its early history see VOLGA BULGARIANS. Area 68,000 km². Population (1976) 3,328,000 (52 per cent urban); mostly Tatars and Russians.

Tatars (often, but wrongly, written 'Tartars'), peoples of mixed ethnic, linguistic, and cultural origin, nowadays speaking Turkic languages. They were dispersed over the steppes of eastern European Russia, central Asia, and Siberia. In the 8th century the word 'Tatar' was used in the ORKHON INSCRIPTIONS to denote the Mongolian-speaking peoples of the northern China frontier regions. It was later applied to Genghis Khan's Mongols, and particularly to Turkic peoples, such as the Bulgars, Qïpchägs, Turkomans, and others, who preceded and followed the Mongolian invasion of Europe. From the 14th century the name 'Tatary' was applied in western European languages to a vast area (corresponding partly to southern Russia and central Asia) that was inhabited by Tatars.

Today Tatars farm, fish, and breed horses. They are Sunni Muslims (see ISLAM), but retain shamanist (see SHAMANISM) practices. Traditionally many were teachers, traders, Islamic missionaries, and craftsmen. They now number between five and six million and many are urbanised.

Tatary, see TATARS.

Tate, Sir Henry (1819–99), British merchant and art patron, born at Chorley, Lancashire. He was a sugar merchant, and patented machinery for making sugar cubes. His firm of Henry Tate & Sons later became Tate & Lyle. He was instrumental in founding the TATE GALLERY in 1897, and was created baronet in 1898.

Tate, John Orley Allen (1899–), US poet and critic, born at Winchester, Kentucky. Educated at Vanderbilt University, he was on the English staff at the University of North Carolina and at Columbia; then from 1939 to 1942 he was fellow in creative writing at Princeton, from 1944 to 1950 fellow in American letters of the Library of Congress, and in 1951 became professor of English at the University of Minnesota. He was a founder member of the Fugitives group, with John Crowe RANSOM, and an advocate of the New Criticism.

In 1936 he published *Reactionary Essays in Poetry and Ideas*, and in 1941 *Reason in Madness*, which marked him as one of the leading critics of his time. Later essays are *On the Limits of Poetry*, 1948, *The Hovering Fly*, 1949, and *The Forlorn Demon*, 1953. His poetry, which shows the influence of Donne and T. S. Eliot, includes *The Winter Sea*, 1945, and *Poems 1922–1947*, 1948. He also published *Stonewall Jackson—The Good Soldier*, 1928, and *Jefferson Davis—His Rise and Fall*, 1929, and a novel, *The Fathers*, 1938.

Tate, Nahum (1652–1715), English poet, born in Dublin, the son of a clergyman named Faithful Teate. Educated at Trinity College, Dublin, he settled in London in 1672, and in 1677 published *Poems on Several Occasions*. He also wrote some indifferent plays, including an adaptation of Shakespeare's *King Lear* which was defended by Dr Johnson and was performed well into the 19th century. In 1682 he wrote, with DRYDEN's assistance, a second part to the poet's satire *Absalom and Achitophel*. In 1692 he was appointed poet laureate in succession to SHADWELL, as a result of which Pope pilloried him in the *Dunciad*; and in 1702 he was made Historiographer Royal. His chief original poem was *Panacea or a Poem on Tea*, 1700, but he is remembered mainly for the metrical version of the Psalms in which he collaborated with Nicholas BRADY; published in 1696, it gradually superseded the earlier version by Sternhold and Hopkins.

Tate & Lyle Limited is an English company established in 1921 from the amalgamation of two sugar-refining companies, Henry Tate & Sons Limited, and Abram Lyle and Sons Limited. It acquired United Molasses Company in 1965. Principal activities of the group now are the production and marketing of refined sugar; molasses, sugar, and other commodity trading; shipping, storage, and road transport; the manufacture of machinery and consultancy services for sugar and agricultural industries; and the manufacture of plastic and aluminium products for the construction industry. The group operates worldwide with principal subsidiaries in the UK, Canada, the USA, Belize, Jamaica, Nigeria, Norway, and Rhodesia, and associates in Zambia and South Africa. The company mounted a successful public relations campaign to prevent its nationalisation immediately after the Second World War, employing 'Mr Cube', an anthropomorphic sugar lump. The company has since been a noted publicist of private enterprise.

Tate Gallery, Millbank, London, contains the national collection of British painting from the 16th century to the present day, modern foreign painting from approximately 1880, and modern sculpture. The Tate Gallery has unique collections of the work of Turner and Blake, also one of the best collections of Pre-Raphaelite painting. More recently the Tate Gallery has begun to form a major collection of modern British prints and an archive of modern British art.

Sir Henry TATE financed the building of the gallery on the site of Jeremy Bentham's 'Model' Penitentiary, and it

was opened by King Edward VII as Prince of Wales in 1897. This housed the Tate gift of 65 British paintings, the collection purchased under the terms of the Chantrey Bequest, the Vernon Collection, bequeathed in 1847, and the Watts gift. Sir Henry Tate made possible the addition, in 1899, of eight further galleries, and in 1910, through the generosity of Sir Joseph Duveen senior, the wing to house the Turner bequest of 1856, which had been in the possession of the National Gallery, was opened, while his son Lord Duveen, gave additional galleries in 1926 and an immense sculpture hall, opened in 1937. In 1977 a new extension opened making available 50 per cent more space for showing the permanent collections, and includes a large and well-equipped conservation department.

The nucleus of the collection of modern foreign art was established by the bequest of Sir Hugh LANE in 1915, and the endowment by Samuel COURTAULD in 1923. The Tate Gallery's collections have been greatly enriched by many other bequests and gifts, and an effort has been made since the war, in spite of limitations of finance and space, to clarify and extend its two separate functions as the National Collection of Modern Art and National Collection of Historical British Painting. A series of important exhibitions have been held since 1946, including the following in recent years: The Age of Charles I, Constable, The Elizabethan Image, Caspar David Friedrich, Fuseli, Richard Hamilton, Barbara Hepworth, Hogarth, Landscape in Britain, Henry Moore, Paul Nash, Picasso, and Andy Warhol.

Tati, Jacques (1908–), French film actor and director; real name J. Tatischeff. He was a music-hall player before appearing in films. *Jour de fête*, *Monsieur Hulot's Holiday*, *Mon Oncle* and *Playtime* achieved great popularity and won awards; they depend on Tati's imagination as a director and exploitation of his long, thin figure and bird-like mannerisms. A later film was *Traffic*, 1971.

Tati, district of Botswana, formerly known as the Tati Concession, notably a gold-mining district but over the years its yield of gold has not been great. The mineral rights are now vested in the Anglo-American De Beers group and large-scale prospecting has been organised. Area 5180 km^2.

Tatian (fl. c. 160), early Christian apologist, born in Assyria and learned in Greek. He was converted to Christianity at Rome and became a disciple of Justin Martyr. He wrote a number of works of which *The Discourse to the Greeks* survives. More important is the *Diatessaron*, a harmony of the Four Gospels, written in Greek or in Syriac, which has been largely reconstructed from fragments and quotations.

Bibliography: T. Zahn, *Tatian's Diatessaron*, 1881; G. Bardy, 'Tatien', in *Dictionnaire de Théologie Catholique* (Vacant-Mangenot), Vol. xv. 1946.

Tatius, Achilles, see ACHILLES TATIUS.

'Tatler, The', journal founded by Sir Richard STEELE, and published twice weekly in London between April 1707 and January 1711. At first, Steele wrote all the contributions, but at the 18th issue Joseph ADDISON began writing essays for the periodical. It aimed to entertain the reader, while discussing society's faults and postulating its ideal behaviour. After the *Tatler* ceased publication, Addison and Steele founded the *Spectator* (see 'SPECTATOR, THE'). See also MAGAZINES.

Tatlin, Vladimir (1885–1953), Russian sculptor and painter, born at Kharkov, died in Moscow. He visited Paris in 1913 where he was impressed by the constructions of PICASSO. On his return to Moscow, he made abstract constructions in wire and sheet metal. After the Revolution he became head of the Moscow section of the Department of Fine Art and advocated a utalitarian approach to art. In 1920 he designed the *Monument to the Third International*, an iron spiral framework with a sloping core which would operate as an information centre. From 1929–32 he was engaged on the design of the *Letatlin*, a man-powered aeroplane. Although today most of his work is known only in photographs, he is acknowledged as an important pioneer of CONSTRUCTIVISM.

Tatra Mountains, see CARPATHIANS, *Geography*.

Tattersall's, name of the firm established in 1766 by Richard Tattersall for the purpose of selling horses by public auction. Today it holds large bloodstock auctions at Park Paddocks, Newmarket, at fixed times annually.

Tattersall's Committee is in no way related to the above; it is an authority set up to settle questions relating to bets, wagers or gaming transactions on horse racing. It has the power to report defaulters to the Jockey Club. The Jockey Club take no cognisance of any disputes or claims with respect to bets, but if any defaulter is reported to them by Tattersall's, the defaulter is warned off by the Jockey Club until the report is withdrawn.

Tattershall, village in Lincolnshire, England, 13 km south of Horncastle. Its first charter was granted in 1201; its famous castle, built in 1440 by Ralph, Lord Cromwell, is one of the finest and earliest examples of East Anglian brickwork in England. It was restored and bequeathed to the National Trust in 1926 by Lord Curzon. The parish church, formerly a collegiate church, was begun by Ralph, Lord Cromwell, and completed by William of Waynfleet.

Tatting (French *frivolité*), a lace worked with a small hand-held shuttle and thread which is knotted at frequent intervals to produce the required formation. Tatting was known in England and Europe in the Middle Ages but its high point was in the 17th century. It is today enjoying a noticeable revival.

Tatting is generally worked today with embroidery or crochet threads, stranded cotton or wool. Modern tatting

Tatting. Figure 1. Tatting shuttle: (a) side view of a modern lightweight shuttle, flexible and easy to handle; (b) the thread wound round the shuttle's shaft.

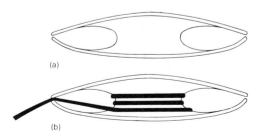

Tatting. Border of thread tatting, made at Ardee, Ireland, c. 1880. *(Victoria and Albert Museum, London)*

shuttles are usually plastic. Old shuttles, now popular collectors' items, included those of silver, mother-of-pearl, bone and tortoiseshell.

(a)   (b)

Tatting. Figure 2. Using a hand-held tatting shuttle, the main thread is knotted around a core thread known as a 'running line' (1); a series of knots is then joined together to form a basic ring (b).

Tatting instructions are clearly printed like knitting and crochet patterns. Technical terms include the basic ring (a loop of thread composed of tatted knots). See also MACRAMÉ.

Bibliography: Lady K. Hoare, *The Art of Tatting*, 1910; E. Nicholls, *Tatting*, 1962; *The Basic Book of Macramé and Tatting*, 1973; I. Waller, *Tatting*, 1974.

Tatton Park, mansion 5 km north of Knutsford, Cheshire. Originally built in the 17th century, Tatton Park was rebuilt from 1780 to 1813 by Samuel and Lewis Wyatt. The house, furniture, silver and paintings, as well as a 22-hectare garden, were bequeathed to the National Trust by the 4th Lord Egerton of Tatton, and the 800-hectare estate came to the Trust through the Treasury in 1960. Humphry REPTON designed the park and garden.

Tattoo (Dutch *tap toe*, literally 'tap shut', meaning the time of closing public-houses) is the signal, by drum-beat or bugle, for soldiers to return to their quarters at night, just before 'lights out'. The word is also applied to a kind of military pageant consisting of spectacular evolutions with musical accompaniment, performed at night by artificial light. In some garrison towns, such as Aldershot and York, tattoos have been held on an annual or periodic basis during the summer months, as a form of public entertainment, the profits being given to military charities. The Tattoo is a highlight of the annual Edinburgh Festival.

Tattooing

Tattooing, custom of marking the skin with incisions which are filled with colouring matter to produce an indelible stain. Tattooing has been widely practised since the Palaeolithic period. Among the Thracians it was a sign of rank. Caesar mentions the painted bodies of the Britons, and the Picts may have received their name from the practice of painting or tattooing.

In later periods it was used mostly for identifying convicts and slaves. In the British army, until 1876, the letters BC (for 'bad conduct') and D (for 'deserter'), were still tattooed on soldiers. In modern Western society it survives only among certain sections of the population as ornament, but it can be used to disguise birth-marks, or even to remove them, a neutral-coloured pigment being injected to obliterate any discoloration of the skin.

In many non-Western societies tattooing is a necessary indication of adult status (see AINUS; MAORI) and, especially in East Africa, may be performed during puberty initiation rites. Some peoples tattoo only on the face, others on the back, chest, arms, and thighs also. In Polynesia it has been brought to a fine art. It is done with a sharp bone with the end cut into teeth, which is dipped in a solution of charcoal or cinnabar to produce black or red markings respectively.

Bibliography: R. Scutt and C. Gotch, *Skin Deep: The Mystery of Tattooing*, 1974.

Tatung, see SHANSI.

Tauber, Richard, real name Ernst Seiffert (1892–1948), Austrian-born tenor, conductor and composer, from Linz. He studied at Freiburg and made his operatic debut in 1913 at Chemnitz, as Tamino in *The Magic Flute*, becoming an unrivalled interpreter of Mozart's tenor roles. Later he turned to operetta, appearing in many works written for him by Lehar, including *The Land of Smiles*, which he sang in London in 1931. He became a British subject in 1940.

Tauchnitz, Christian Bernhard Freiherr von (1816–95), German publisher, born at Schleinitz, nephew of Karl Christoph Traugott TAUCHNITZ. He founded in 1837 a printing and publishing house in Leipzig, which became more famous than that belonging to the senior branch of the family. In 1841, Tauchnitz began a library of British and American authors; in 1868 he began the collection of German authors and in 1886 the Student's Tauchnitz editions appeared.

Tauchnitz, Karl Christoph Traugott (1761–1836), German printer and publisher, born near Grimma, Saxony; he established a printing business in Leipzig in 1796 and a publishing house in 1798. His special publications were stereotyped editions of the Greek and Roman classics, but he also printed Bibles and dictionaries. His son, Karl Christian Philipp Tauchnitz (1798–1884), carried on the business, and left money for philanthropic purposes.

Tauler, Johann (c. 1300–61), German Dominican friar and mystic, born at Strasbourg. He came under the pietistic influence of Master ECKHART of Cologne, and showed the devotional fervour of the 'Rhine mystics' at its purest and most perfect. A popular man, he became famous as a preacher and for his care of the sick during the Black Death. His *Sermons*, full of mystical devotion and practical piety, highly esteemed by LUTHER, were printed at Leipzig in 1498. There is a modern edition by E. Hugueny and L. A. Corier (Paris), 1928–35.

Bibliography: J. M. Clark, *The Great German Mystic*, 1949.

Taunton, the county town of SOMERSET, England, 50 km north-east of Exeter, 70 km south-west of Bristol. It is situated in the heart of the fertile valley of Taunton Deane, and is sheltered on the north and south by the Quantock and Blackdown Hills. The M5 motorway runs to the east of the town. St Mary Magdalene parish church is a stately perpendicular 15th-century building, noted for its double aisles and monuments and for its fine tower. Other buildings of note are: a 12th–13th-century lazar house or leper hospital; Priory Barn, sole relic of an important 12th-century Augustinian priory; and Gray's Almshouses (1635). Taunton Castle is a Norman and Edwardian building and stands on the site of a Saxon fort. It contains the Great Hall in which Judge JEFFREYS held his 'Bloody Assize'. Part of the municipal buildings originally housed the 16th-century grammar school, now known as King's College; there are several other large schools in the town. Taunton is an agricultural, educational, and administrative centre, and an Army headquarters. It is the chief marketing centre for west Somerset and east Devon. Local industries include textile and leather goods; gloves; aeronautical instruments; agricultural, mining, and other machinery, and cider-making. The Admiralty Hydrographic Establishment is here. It is the seat of a suffragan bishop. Taunton existed in Saxon times, and had a market before the Conquest, receiving its first charter in the reign of Stephen, though its last charter of incorporation was not granted until 1877. During the Civil War Taunton was held for Parliament, and later in the same century it witnessed the proclamation of Monmouth as king, and the brutalities of Judge Jeffreys and Kirke's 'lambs' (it was from the signboard of the White Hart Inn, now a shop, that Colonel Kirke hanged Monmouth's rebels). Population (1971) 37,444.

Tattooing. A colourful example showing the possibilities of the tattooist's art. *(Barnaby's Picture Library)*

Taunus Mountains, range in HESSEN, West Germany, lying between the Rhine, Main, and Lahn rivers. The chief summits are the Grosser Feldberg (880 m) and the Kleiner Feldberg (827 m). They are well wooded, and the southern lower slopes (Rheingau) are particularly fertile; the vineyards produce such famous wines as Rüdesheimer and Hochheimer. The Rhein-Taunus Nature Park (650 km²) was designated in 1968. There are well-known spas, including Homburg, Wiesbaden, and Nauheim in the region.

Taupo, lake of North Island, New Zealand, situated in the centre of the island, 357 m above sea-level. Area 600 km², maximum depth 159 m, drained by the Waikato river.

Tauranga, town of North Island, New Zealand, on the Bay of Plenty. Its chief industries are tourism and farming. Population 29,500.

Taurine, $H_2NCH_2CH_2SO_3H$, amino-ethylsulphonic acid, a crystalline substance produced in the decomposition of bile.

Tauromenium, see TAORMINA.

Taurus, 'the Bull', the second sign of the ZODIAC and a conspicuous northern CONSTELLATION. In the conventional constellation figure Taurus represents only the forepart of a bull. The V-shaped HYADES cluster forms the head with the bright red ALDEBARAN (Alpha Tauri) as the fiery eye. The PLEIADES, the best known of all star clusters, are in the shoulder. The tips of the horns are marked by Beta and Zeta Tauri. BAYER regarded Beta Tauri as belonging also to AURIGA and as such called it Gamma Aurigae. Close to Zeta Tauri are the remnants of the supernova of AD 1054 now known as 'the CRAB NEBULA'. Visible as gaseous nebulosity it is also a strong radio and X-ray source and the location of one of the first PULSARS to be discovered. T Tauri is the prototype of a class of VARIABLE STARS thought to represent an early stage of stellar formation.

Taurus Mountains (Turkish *Toros Dağları*), range in the south of Asiatic Turkey, extending from the River EUPHRATES to the Aegean Sea. Portions of the range are known by different names as Ala Dağları, Bolkar Dağları and Bey Dağları. Heights exceed 3000 m in several places.

Tautology (Greek *tauto*, the same), figure of speech employing superfluous words that are in the same grammatical relation; in this way it differs from PLEONASM. Needless repetition is seen in phrases such as 'free, gratis, and for nothing', 'the shortest and nearest way'. Sometimes, however, what appears to be tautology expresses different shades of meaning, as in Pope's lines:

Oh happiness! our being's end and aim!
Good, pleasure, ease, content, whate'er thy name.

See also FIGURE OF SPEECH.

Tautomerism, in chemistry, the phenomenon whereby some chemicals exist in more than one chemical form. Such substances are usually present as equilibrium mixtures of the interconvertible forms, and show the chemical properties of both forms, depending on the reaction condition. For example, keto-esters, such as ethyl aceto-acetate, sometimes behave as if they had a ketonic carbonyl group (see KETONES):

$$CH_3 \cdot \overset{\overset{\displaystyle O}{\|}}{C} \cdot CH_2 \cdot CO \cdot O \cdot C_2H_5 \,,$$

and sometimes as if they had an enolic hydroxyl group:

$$CH_3 \cdot \overset{\overset{\displaystyle OH}{|}}{C} = CH \cdot CO \cdot O \cdot C_2H_5 \,.$$

Although the ketone form predominates, both structures are present. This phenomenon explains many otherwise unexpected reactions.

Tavener, John (1944–), British composer, born in London; studied at the Royal Academy of Music under Berkeley, and later with David Lumsdaine. His dramatic cantata *The Whale* (1966) delighted critics when it appeared in 1968; both it and *A Celtic Requiem* (1968–69) stamp Tavener as the most spirited English exponent of avant-garde collage.

Tavern (Latin *taberna*, booth, hut, from the same root as *table*), a house where wines and other alcoholic liquors are sold and where accommodation is given to travellers or parties. Taverns existed in England as early as the 13th century. By an Act of 1284 they were ordered to be closed at curfew. In Edward III's reign only three were allowed in London: in 'Chepe', 'Walbrok' and Lombard Street. By Edward VI (1552–53) 40 were allowed in London, eight in York, six in Bristol, four each in Cambridge, Canterbury, Chester, Exeter, Gloucester, Hull, Newcastle upon Tyne and Norwich; and three each in Colchester, Hereford, Ipswich, Lincoln, Oxford, Salisbury, Shrewsbury, Southampton, Westminster, Winchester and Worcester. Among famous taverns are the Chequers Inn, Canterbury; the 'Bear and Billet', Chester; the Bull Inn, later called the George Inn (pulled down in 1808), York; the 15th-century Maid's Head Hotel, Norwich; the 'Great White Horse', the 'Coach and Horses' and many others in Ipswich; the Lion Hotel and the now vanished Talbot Hotel, Shrewsbury; the Old George Hotel mentioned by Pepys, Salisbury; the 'Saracen's Head', Lincoln; the Mermaid Tavern, which formerly stood in Cheapside; the Tabard Inn, Southwark, from which Chaucer started his pilgrims; and 'Ye Olde Cheshire Cheese' (or 'Chop House') in Fleet Street, London. Some premises are still called taverns, mainly for historic reasons.

Taverner, John (c. 1495–1545), English composer, born at Tattershall or Boston, Lincolnshire. In 1526 he vacated a benefice in the collegiate church of Tattershall to become choirmaster at Cardinal College, Oxford (later Christ Church). He was imprisoned for heresy in 1528 and left Oxford about 1530. The rest of his life was spent at Boston, where he died. His works include eight masses, of which *The Westerne Wynde* is the best known, though the *Missa sine nomine* is probably finer. Especially important is his mass *Gloria tibi Trinitas* which began the history of the instrumental IN NOMINE. He also wrote motets, services, etc.

Bibliography: E. H. Fellowes, *Tudor Church Music: Appendix,* 1948.

Tavernier, Jean Baptiste, Baron d'Aubonne (1605–89), French traveller, born in Paris. He began his career as a traveller in 1631, when he went to Turkey and Persia (Iran). During succeeding years he travelled much in the East, visiting Persia, Syria, India, and Batavia. He published his famous *Six Voyages* in 1676.

Tavistock, market town in DEVON, England, 24 km north of Plymouth, on the River Tavy. It forms one of the gateways to DARTMOOR. It is connected with the Tamar by canal. Known as the 'Gothic Town of the West', it has several fine buildings, chief amongst which are the parish church of St Eustachius (14th century) and the guild-hall. There are also the remains of an abbey, founded in the 10th century, which was granted to the Russell family at the time of the dissolution by Henry VIII. Part of this now constitutes a public library. Tavistock is an agricultural centre. An annual 'Goose Fair' is held under royal charter granted by Henry I in 1105. Population (1971) 7620.

Tavistock Institute of Medical Psychology was founded in 1920 (incorporated 1929) under the name of the Tavistock Clinic to provide out-patient treatment for those suffering from psychoneurotic illness. From the outset research and training were carried on alongside treatment of patients. When the National Health Service was introduced in 1948 the Clinic became part of it, whilst the Institute remained independent so as to maintain and develop pioneer services as well as the research and training which had grown up around the Clinic.

Bibliography: H. V. Dicks, *Fifty Years of the Tavistock Clinic,* 1970.

Tavoliere, see FOGGIA.

Tavoy, township and town in Tenasserim division, Burma. The town lies 48 km from the mouth of the Tavoy river. It is a small port used for coastal trade and is the divisional capital. The township produces mainly rice, and tin, wolfram, and iron ore are mined nearby. Township: area 6748 km^2; population 101,500.

Tavy, river of Devon, England, rising on DARTMOOR and flowing into the TAMAR.

Taw, river of Devon, England, rising on DARTMOOR and flowing into Bideford Bay. It is 80 km in length.

Tawe, river of Wales rising in the BLACK MOUNTAIN in south Powys. It flows through West Glamorgan and enters the Bristol Channel at Swansea. Length 58 km.

Tawfiq al-Hakim, see HAKIM, TAWFIQ AL-.

Tawney, Richard Henry (1880–1962), British historian, born in Calcutta, and educated at Rugby and Balliol College, Oxford, where he was a fellow from 1918–1921. He was professor of economic history at London University, 1931–49. Tawney was a member of the executive of the Workers' Educational Association, 1905–47, and its president, 1928–44. His *Religion and the Rise of Capitalism,* 1926, established him as the spokesman of a new school of thought on the growth of modern capitalist society. His other publications include: *The Agrarian Problem in the Sixteenth Century,* 1912; *The Acquisitive Society,* 1920; *Land and Labour in China,* 1931; *Beatrice Webb,* 1945; *Tudor Economic Documents* (with Eileen Power), 1951; *The Attack,* 1953; and *Lionel Cranfield as Merchant and Minister,* 1958.

Bibliography: R. Terrill, *R. H. Tawney and his times: Socialism as fellowship,* 1974.

Taxales, a monotypic order of GYMNOSPERMAE containing the YEW family Taxaceae.

Taxation, the method of raising the revenue required for public services through compulsory levies.

General Principles of Taxation. There have been three schools of thought on the purpose of taxation. The first was that taxation should be designed solely to raise the revenue required by the expenditure authorised in the Budget. The second was that taxation should also be used to promote social justice and equality. In Britain, Lloyd George was the first major user of taxation as an instrument of social reform. The two world wars, with the necessity for raising higher revenue and need for 'equality of sacrifice' by the whole population, left no other choice but to design taxation in conformity with the prevailing ideas of social equality. The Second World War, especially, brought a redistribution of incomes, and through INCOME TAX and surtax extinguished very high incomes considered as antisocial. With the increase of public expenditure (and the consequent need for permanent high taxation) the third school emerged. This is that taxation should be used as an instrument of general economic policy in order to contribute to general stability (in addition to the traditional means of monetary policy) or to achieve specific aims. Examples are maintenance of high rates of income and CORPORATION TAX at periods when inflation is threatened and the former levying of higher rates of PURCHASE TAX on goods which would be particularly suitable for exports.

The functions of taxation at the present time may be summarised as: (1) to control the allocation of resources amongst various goods and services (including those supplied by the government); (2) to control the distribution of incomes; (3) to influence the level of total output (i.e. the level of GROSS NATIONAL PRODUCT—via the supply of resources, the demand for goods, and growth in capacity and productivity).

Economists are still discussing the four canons set out by Adam Smith on the standards by which the quality of a tax should be judged. These are: (1) equality—the subjects of the state should contribute to the support of the state as nearly as possible according to their ability; (2) certainty, not arbitrariness; (3) convenience of payment; (4) economy of collection. In considering the first principle of equality Adam Smith himself recognised that a progressive tax system is more equitable than a proportional one.

Classification of Taxation. Taxes can be classified according to a number of different principles, e.g. the tax base (income tax, etc.), the regularity of levy (income tax to be paid annually), and taxes arising on specific events such as estate duty and capital gains tax. The distinction between direct and indirect taxes (e.g. between income tax and VALUE ADDED TAX) relates in practice rather to the method of collection than to incidence.

The question of *incidence* is an important problem in the theory of taxation. If the government collects a tax on cigarettes from the manufacturer, the amount of the tax can, to an extent depending on the 'elasticity' of demand, be passed on to the consumer. This *shifting* of the tax may take place from the original payer to someone else either once (e.g. with the rates from the landlord to the tenant of a dwelling), or through a whole chain of economic relationships (from the tobacco manufacturer to the wholesaler to the retailer to.the consumer). The *incidence* of a tax is on that group which cannot shift it farther. Taxes which are levied on large classes of the population, e.g. income tax, cannot be shifted.

Licence revenue obtained as the result of an annual tax on the right to use a certain commodity (e.g. a television set) may be classed as a direct tax, whereas a tax on enjoyment or consumption will be classed as indirect if the (initial) impact and the (final) incidence fall on different parties. Taxes such as excise duties fall in this second class, but there is no distinction in kind between a periodical tax on the continued enjoyment of a commodity while it remains in use and a tax on its enjoyment in the form of a once-for-all tax paid at the time of its purchase. Modern economists therefore make a truer distinction between income and capital taxes on the one hand, and expenditure taxes on the other. Taxation in the first category includes: (a) taxes on net incomes which are progressive as they allow liability to be adjusted in accordance with ability to pay; (b) taxes on profits; (c) CAPITAL GAINS TAX; and (d) CAPITAL TRANSFER TAXES. The second category—expenditure taxes—comprises taxes on commodities and services. An expenditure tax is a tax on consumption assessed either on the value of the commodity or in the form of a licence. When assessed on the value of the goods the tax is either *ad valorem*, i.e. related to the selling price, or specific, i.e. reckoned in accordance with quantity.

Taxation in post-Second World War Britain, as a proportion of the national income, is often believed to be very high, but the proportion of national income taken in all forms of taxation is about the same as that in other Western industrial countries, although the breakdown of the total between the different forms of taxation varies considerably. Public expenditure (central and local government and national insurance funds) reached 40 per cent of the national product after the war and has since remained at a similarly high level.

A further problem is the economic effect of taxation. Too high corporation and income tax may act as a discouragement to enterprise. Similarly, too high rates of income tax on wages, or a sudden steep rise after a certain amount of income, may act as a discouragement to the worker, who does not feel it worthwhile to work overtime if he has to pay to the state a large part of his additional earnings. The 1955 Royal Commission on taxation arrived at the opinion that high tax on the salaries and incomes of professional and business men did not have much effect on their normal activities, although it might either reduce or increase their willingness to undertake additional work. It admitted, however, that it was too soon to reach a conclusion. The fact that high taxation has been accompanied by economic expansion and enterprise in the postwar world is no evidence that it does not deter effort. The postwar generation grew up with certain habits of work, but there is no certainty that these habits will not change under the impact of high taxation. At some point the new generation is likely to prefer leisure to highly taxed income which produces only a few pence out of each additional pound earned. Also the tendency for young people to emigrate could indicate that lower taxation in other countries exerts a powerful attraction.

See also CUSTOMS AND EXCISE DUTIES; LOCAL GOVERNMENT; PUBLIC REVENUE; STAMP DUTY.

Bibliography: R. A. Musgrove, *Theory of Public Finance, a study in Public Economy*, 1959; W. J. Blum and H. Kalvin, *The Uneasy Case for Progressive Taxation*, 1963; C. G. Clark, *Taxmanship, Principles and Proposals for the Reform of Taxation*, 2nd ed., 1970.

Taxation of Costs, see COSTS; TAXING MASTER.

Taxco, town in the state of GUERRERO, Mexico. An Aztec community before the Spanish conquered it in 1531, Taxco is now a national monument. One of the most attractive towns in Mexico, it has many beautiful churches and colonial period buildings. Owing its fame to the great production of silver in the 18th century, it is today the leading centre of silverware craftsmanship in the country. Silver is still mined and so are copper, zinc, and lead; particularly important are the fluorite mines a few kilometres outside the town. The parish church of Santa Prisca is one of the best examples of Baroque architecture in Mexico. Its altitude is 1728 m with mountain peaks towering above it. Population 28,000.

Taxicab, see CAB; HACKNEY CARRIAGE.

Taxidermy, the art of preparing the skins of vertebrate animals so as to give them the appearance of life and preserve their characteristics as nearly as possible. The art began to be practised in the 16th century, and the Sloane collection, which formed the nucleus of the natural history collection at the British Museum, was made in the early 18th century. Skinning must be done with great care, for if the skin is flayed off there is great difficulty in restoring its proper proportions. A bird is opened under the wing. If opened on the breast, the bowels may be cut into, and a white breast spoiled. After the body is removed measurements are taken. While the skin is inside-out it is painted with a preservative soap. In making a skin, the head is filled with tow before being turned through the neck, and with this material a false body is then constructed by wrapping the tow round a piece of wire. This is put into the skin, and while drying any irregularity is corrected. 'Setting up' may be done by wiring and filling in with fine wood wool. Another method is to retain the skeleton and, after freeing it from flesh and washing it with carbolic acid, to work over it with tow or clay to produce a shape like that of the body. With larger birds and most mammals an alternative method is to prepare a mould of plaster by arranging the hardened carcase in a suitable attitude. When the mould is dry paper casts are made by pressing a series of layers of paper into the mould, so that when the model is properly mounted and prepared the skin can be drawn over it. After setting up, the specimen is painted over with a solution of bichloride of mercury in methylated spirit as a protection against the ravages of insects. With the exception of grasses, mosses and dried leaves, real natural objects should be excluded from the 'mounting', as they are almost certain to harbour insects. The highest art of the taxidermist fails with fishes, for shrinking and shrivelling of the skin cannot be avoided. A more satisfactory method is to take a cast as soon as possible after capture, and make an exact model in plaster.

Today smaller animals and plants can be preserved by freeze-drying. This involves drying the specimen under vacuum and at a low temperature. It can take a few days to complete, depending on the size of the subject, but the results are permanent and include the internal organs.

Bibliography: L. Pray, *Taxidermy*, 1967; G. J. Grantz, *Home Book of Taxidermy and Tanning*, 1973.

Taximeter, instrument for use in a hired vehicle, as a motor cab, for automatically showing the fare due. Grüner of Magdeburg invented the modern taximeter in 1895. The name 'taxi' for a motor cab is derived from this apparatus. It is operated from the gear-box of the vehicle by a flexible cable, and comprises in its essentials a clock-winder, a gear-box, and, attached to the latter, a meter which registers the time and distance.

Taxing Master, in England and Wales, an official of the High Court who assesses the amount of COSTS payable by the loser to the winner of litigation in that court.

Taxodium, a small genus of three deciduous coniferous trees in the family Taxodiaceae, native to the south-eastern United States and Mexico. *T. distichum*, the swamp cypress, is a tall tree often grown in Britain, bearing cones about the size of a walnut; the trunk is usually very thick and the base is often swollen, while knees or hollow protuberances rise from the roots when the tree grows in swampy soil. The timber is of considerable value. Other species include *T. heterophyllum*, the Chinese water pine, and *T. mucronatum*.

Taxonomy, the science of biological classification, involving the division of living organisms into taxa (biological categories, e.g. species and subspecies). In botany and zoology such categories are embodied, or in process of becoming so, in International Codes of Botanical and Zoological Nomenclature. Traditionally, taxonomy has been based on the morphological and anatomical similarities and differences between groups. The human brain is adept at assimilating and comparing large numbers of visual characters, and an expert in a particular animal or plant group is usually able to classify an unknown species simply by looking at it and comparing it with specimens or drawings of known species. Sometimes this is insufficient, however, and techniques have therefore been developed to provide a more objective basis for classification.

The new methods are collectively known as 'experimental taxonomy' and the most important are chemotaxonomy, cytotaxonomy and numerical taxonomy. In chemotaxonomy, certain chemical constituents are extracted from items under investigation and the number of constituents which these items have in common is used as an aid to their classification. Various chemical constituents may be used, including proteins, pigments and aromatic oils. The method of extraction depends on the nature of the chemical being isolated and it is not necessary to identify the chemicals. Thus, one plant species may contain pigments A, B, C and D whilst another species contains A and B and one other pigment, E, but not C or D. Cytotaxonomy is the use of microscopic characters in classification, particularly the number and structure of the CHROMOSOMES. Each species has a characteristic chromosome number, e.g. man has 46, the chimpanzee 48, the gibbon 44, and the shape and size of the chromosomes is also characteristic in each species. The development of the scanning electron microscope has also enabled minute details of structure, such as surface sculpturing on pollen grains, to be used as taxonomic characters. Finally, numerical taxonomy involves the use of computers to compare taxa in respect of large numbers of characters and produce a statistically based classification. Computer techniques are particularly valuable when a large number of taxa is being compared, or when chemical and microscopic characters are being assessed along with gross morphological ones, since it is difficult to make an objective evaluation of characters which differ greatly in nature.

Besides its use in identifying individual species, taxonomic classification is used to arrange organisms into higher categories that reflect their similarities and differences; that is, to define their degree of relatedness. Ideally this would be determined from their evolutionary relationship, but many organisms have left no fossil record. The only natural category is the SPECIES; the classification groupings above this: GENUS, family, order, class, phylum or division, and KINGDOM, are theoretical. Classification groups are proposed by biologists for their convenience, and as more is learned about the organisms, groups are split up or lumped together in new patterns. At any one time, although the organism's specific name is accepted by most biologists, its higher classification will be subject to opinion, and it will be classified differently by those who tend to emphasise differences, the splitters, and those who give more weight to similarities, the lumpers. Living organisms show so much variety in their structures and habits that the assignment of organisms to certain taxa must be considered only as a useful index and not a definitive description of the relationships in the natural world.

See also CLASSIFICATION OF ANIMALS; CLASSIFICATION OF PLANTS; BINOMIAL SYSTEM OF NOMENCLATURE; CELL.

Taxus, see YEW.

Tay, river and firth of SCOTLAND. It rises in the Central Highlands, and flows first of all in a north-easterly direction and then at the confluence of the TUMMEL, in a south-easterly direction. It flows through Tayside Region and its estuary forms the divide between Tayside and Fife Regions. Its chief tributaries are the Tummel, the Braan, the Almond, and the Earn. The Earn joins it at its estuary. The total length of the river, including the firth, is 184 km. It is crossed at Dundee by the famous Tay Bridge. Part of the first bridge, opened in 1878, was blown, together with a train passing over it, into the river in 1879. The bridge was rebuilt by 1887. A road bridge, Newport to Dundee, was completed in 1966. The chief port is DUNDEE, but the river is navigable as far as the town of PERTH. The total area of the Tay basin is nearly 6400 km². It is the longest river in Scotland. The drainage basin of the Tay and its tributaries forms one of the most fully integrated hydro-electric developments of the North of Scotland Board.

Tay, Loch, lake (24 km long and 1·5 km wide) in Perth and Kinross District, Tayside Region, Scotland, one of several found in the course of the River TAY, and not very far from its source before it joins the TUMMEL. There is good fishing in the loch.

Tay Ninh, capital of the province of the same name in VIETNAM, situated 90 km north-west of Saigon. Known chiefly as the 'holy see' of CAODAISM and for its architecturally remarkable Caodaist cathedral and statuary. Provincial population (1971) 387,000.

Tay-Son, name of a rebellion in VIETNAM in the 1770s, and of the dynasty which grew out of it and survived until 1802. The revolt began in the southern part of Vietnam about 1773, and was directed against the NGUYEN family which had ruled that area since the 16th century. By 1775, the rebel brothers controlled a significant part of the country and the last Nguyen survivor fled to the far south, and for a time even to Siam. In 1787, after a series of unrelated revolts in northern Vietnam, the Tay-Son brothers intervened there and in 1789 one of them established himself as emperor with the title Quang Trung. He resisted a Chinese invasion, and consequently is recognised as a Vietnamese national hero. But after his death in 1793 the country again collapsed into disunity, and the Nguyen supporters were eventually able to recover control of the whole country. In 1802, as a result of this complex period of civil war, the present Vietnam was for the first time united under a single central government.

Tayabas, see QUEZON.

Taylor, A(lan) J(ohn) P(ercivale) (1906–), British historian and journalist, born at Birkdale, Lancashire, and educated at Bootham School and Oriel College, Oxford. As fellow and tutor of modern history at Magdalen College, Taylor became known for his authoritative studies of German and Austrian 19th- and 20th-century constitutional history. He is also known from his broadcast and television appearances. His publications include: *The Hapsburg Monarchy, 1815–1918,* 1941; *The Course of German History,* 1945; *The Struggle for Mastery in Europe,* 1954; *Bismarck,* 1955; *The Origins of the Second World War,* 1961; *History of the First World War,* 1963; *English History 1914–45,* 1965; *From Sarajevo to Potsdam,* 1966; *Europe: Grandeur and Decline,* 1967; *War by Timetable,* 1969; *Beaverbrook,* 1971; *The Second World War: an illustrated history,* 1975; and *Essays in English History,* 1976.

Taylor, Ann, see TAYLOR, JANE.

Taylor, Bayard (1825–78), US author, born in Pennsylvania. He was apprenticed to a printer, but spent much of his life in travel, visiting, among other countries, Mexico, Egypt, India, China, Japan and Scandinavia, and writing about them in *Views Afoot,* 1846, and *El Dorado,* 1850. He published several novels, of which the best is *Hannah Thurston,* 1863, some poems and plays, and a translation of Goethe's *Faust,* 1871, one of the best attempts of its kind.
Bibliography: Study by R. C. Beatty, 1936.

Taylor, Brook (1685–1731), British mathematician,

born at Edmonton, Middlesex, entered St John's College, Cambridge, in 1701. He became a Fellow of the Royal Society in 1712, and its secretary in 1714. In 1716 he went to Paris and had an enthusiastic reception from the French savants. He returned to England in 1717, and resumed his studies, but was forced by declining health to resign his secretaryship in 1719. His *Methodus incrementorum* (Methods of incrementation) and a *Treatise on Linear Perspective* were published in 1715. The former contains the proof of TAYLOR'S THEOREM.

Taylor, Edward (1642–1729), American Puritan divine and poet, born in England. Taylor graduated from Harvard and became minister at Westfield, Massachusetts. A vigorous scholar and theologian, he produced volumes of sermons and meditations, but gradually moved toward verse expression. After a *Metrical History of Christianity* he undertook a complex sequence, *God's Meditations Touching His Elect,* and a 217-poem sequence called *Preparatory Meditations,* 1682–1725; a debt to DONNE and the English METAPHYSICAL POETS is apparent, especially in some of his more fugitive verses, like 'Upon a Spider Catching a Fly'.

Taylor sought to suppress his poetry, but it was deposited at Yale and recovered in 1937; *The Poetical Works of Edward Taylor,* edited by Thomas H. Johnson, appeared in 1939, and Donald Stanford re-edited his poems in 1960.
Bibliography: N. Grabo, *Edward Taylor,* 1961.

Taylor, Elizabeth (1932–), British film actress who became famous for her film appearances while still a child. These included parts in *Lassie Come Home, National Velvet* and *Little Women.* Latterly she has excelled in sultry roles, and her films include: *Raintree County, Cat on a Hot Tin Roof, Cleopatra* and *Who's Afraid of Virginia Woolf?* Her husbands have included Michael Wilding, Mike Todd and Richard BURTON.

Taylor, Jane (1783–1824), English poet, born in London, the daughter of an engraver. In 1804 she collaborated with her sister Ann (1782–1866) in *Original Poems for Infant Minds,* which went through 50 editions. *Rhymes for the Nursery* followed in 1806, and in 1808 *Hymns for Infant Minds,* which went through 100 editions. Among Ann's most famous pieces are 'My Mother' and 'Meddlesome Matty', while Jane is best remembered as the author of 'Twinkle, Twinkle, Little Star'.
Bibliography: Mrs H. C. Knight, *Life and Letters of Jane Taylor,* 1880.

Taylor, Jeremy (1613–67), English prelate, born in Cambridge, educated at Gonville and Caius College, Cambridge, and University College, Oxford. He took holy orders in 1634. His sermons attracted the attention of Laud, who sent him to Oxford, where he was elected to a fellowship at All Souls in 1636. He became chaplain to Laud and shortly afterwards was appointed one of the king's chaplains. In 1643 he was made rector of Overstone, and two years later was taken prisoner by the Parliamentary forces at Cardigan Castle. He settled in Golden Grove, Carmarthenshire, and wrote his well-known works, *The Liberty of Prophesying,* 1646 (a noble and comprehensive plea for toleration), *The Rule and Exercises of Holy Living,* 1650, and *The Rule and Exercises of Holy Dying,* 1651. His more formal treatises include *An Apology for Authorised and Set Forms of Liturgy*, 1646, *The Worthy Communicant*, 1660, *The Rite of Confirmation*, 1663, and *Ductor Dubitantium, or the Rule of Conscience*, 1660, the subtlest of his works, and intended as a handbook of Christian casuistry. After the Restoration he was appointed Bishop of Down and Connor and made vice-chancellor of Dublin University, and was also made 'administrator' of the diocese of Dromore; but his desire for an English bishopric was never gratified, though his claims for such preferment were incontestable. Taylor was also appointed a member of the Irish Privy Council. His tenure of the Irish bishopric was apparently unhappy; his strict episcopalianism and extremely High Church views made him unpopular among his clergy and his Irish Protestant congregations.

Taylor was one of the most literary of churchmen, and his books are still regarded as among the masterpieces of theological literature. His prose style has a nobility and passion which invites comparison with that of BOSSUET. He was a brilliant scholar of the late Renaissance period, but his writing is distinguished not only by its logic, but also by its imagination, purity, and complete sincerity. His works were first collected by Bishop Reginald Heber in 1822, and these were revised by C. P. Eden, 1847–52. The *Poems and Verse Translations* were edited by A. B. Grosart, 1870.

Bibliography: Lives by E. Gosse, 1904, W. J. Brown, 1925, and E. J. Stroaks, 1952; H. T. Hughes, *The Piety of Jeremy Taylor*, 1960.

Taylor, John (1580–1653), English poet, commonly called the 'Water-Poet', born at Gloucester. He became a waterman and achieved notoriety by a number of eccentric journeys, notably the voyage from London to Queenborough, Kent, in a paper boat, described in *The Praise of Hempseed*, 1620, and the journey from London to Edinburgh on foot told in his *Penniless Pilgrimage*, 1618. His *Works* were reprinted by the Spenser Society (1868–78).

Bibliography: W. Notestein, *Four Worthies*, 1956.

Taylor, Sir Robert (1714–88), British architect, apprenticed as a stone-mason. His father sent him to Rome to study sculpture, but he changed to architecture on returning home. He became surveyor to the Crown, the Bank of England, HM Customs, Lincoln's Inn and Greenwich Hospital. His work included Asgill House, Richmond (1758–67); additions to the Bank of England (now replaced); and Stone Buildings, Lincoln's Inn, London (1775–80). He left his fortune (£180,000) to found the Taylor Institution, Oxford.

Taylor, Rowland (d. 1555), English Protestant martyr, born at Rothbury, Northumberland. He became chaplain to Cranmer in 1540, incumbent of Hadleigh, Suffolk, in 1544, and archdeacon of Exeter in 1552. He was one of the first to suffer martyrdom in Mary's reign, and was celebrated as the ideal of a Protestant parish priest.

Taylor, Tom (1817–80), English dramatist, born in Sunderland. Educated at Glasgow and Cambridge, he was professor of English literature at London University from 1845 to 1847. From 1854 to 1871 he was secretary to the Local Government Board. He was the author of about one hundred dramatic pieces, original and adapted, including *Still Waters Run Deep*, 1855, *Our American Cousin*, 1858, and *Lady Clancarty*, 1871. He was also a contributor to *Punch*, which he edited from 1874 till his death.

Taylor, Zachary (1784–1850), 12th President of the USA, born in Orange County, Virginia. He entered the army in 1808, and distinguished himself in several engagements against the Indians. After the annexation of Texas he resisted the Mexican invasion, winning the battles of Palo Alto and Resaca de la Palma, and seizing Matamoros and Monterey, and later gained the memorable victory over Santa Anna at Buena Vista in 1847. On his return he was elected president (1848) as a Whig (see WHIG PARTY), just at the time when the struggle over the extension of slavery had begun, but he died during the negotiations for the Compromise of 1850.

Taylor Woodrow Group, founded in 1921, with headquarters in Southall, Greater London, is one of the world's largest building, and civil and mechanical engineering groups, consisting of over 160 associated or subsidiary companies operating in five continents. The group's projects range from nuclear power stations, harbours, and offshore oil to factories, housing estates, motorways, and airports.

Taylor's Theorem. If *f* is a function mapping a subset of **R** into **R** and the value of *f* at a point *a* is known, then Taylor's theorem provides an approximation to the value of *f* at a nearby point $x + h$. The theorem states that

$$f(x + h) = f(x) + hf'(a) + \frac{h^2}{2!}f''(a)$$

$$+ \dots + \frac{h^n}{n!}f^{(n)}(a) + \frac{h^{n+1}}{(n+1)!}f^{(n+1)}(x + c)$$

where $0 < c < h$. The theorem is true if *f* and the first *n* derived functions exist and are continuous in the closed interval $[x, x + h]$ and the $(n + 1)$th derived function exists in the open interval $(x, x + h)$. See also ANALYTIC FUNCTION.

Tayport, or Ferry-Port-on-Craig, burgh in North-East Fife District, Fife Region, Scotland, on the shore of the Firth of Tay, 5 km south-east of Dundee. It has foundries, engine works, and timber yards, and linen and jute are manufactured. Population 2897.

Tayra, *Eira barbara*, a relation of badgers and weasels in family Mustelidae of order Carnivora, which is found in South America. The tayra is about 1 m long with dark brown fur marked on the throat with an orange patch. They are more sociable than their relations. They eat fruit as well as meat.

Tayside Region, in SCOTLAND; an amalgamation of the former county of Angus and parts of the counties of Perthshire and Kinross-shire. This region is subdivided into three districts—ANGUS, PERTH AND KINROSS, and the City District of DUNDEE—the boundaries of which are clearly defined on the regional map. Topography varies between that of the GRAMPIANS in the north and west, rising to 1214 m at Ben Lawers; the lower range of the SIDLAW HILLS, parallel to the Firth of Tay, which forms the southern perimeter of the region; and several low-lying

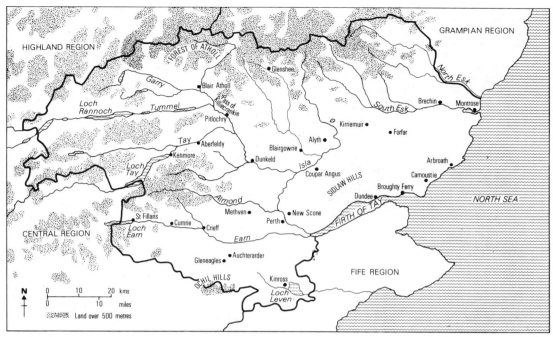

Tayside Region.

fertile areas such as the wide Vale of STRATHMORE, the CARSE OF GOWRIE, and Strathearn. The area is drained by the River TAY which forms the central axis, and the rivers Earn, Isla, and North and South Esk. The city of DUNDEE is the largest urban centre, but there are several other large towns within the Tayside Region, notably PERTH, ARBROATH, FORFAR, MONTROSE, BRECHIN, CARNOUSTIE, CRIEFF, and BLAIRGOWRIE AND RATTRAY. Area 750,305 ha. Population (1971) 327,123.

Bibliography: Scottish Development Department, *Tayside—Potential for Development*, 1970.

Tbilisi, or Tiflis, capital city of the GEORGIAN SSR, USSR, and a major industrial and cultural centre situated on both banks of the River KURA. It has diverse engineering (machine-tools, equipment for food and textile industries, radio and telegraph equipment, etc), food, and light industries, and is an important transportation centre (four railway lines, airport, Georgian Military Road to ORDZHONIKIDZE). It is the seat of the Georgian Academy of Sciences (founded 1935 as the Georgian branch of the USSR Academy of Sciences), a university (founded 1918), a conservatoire (founded 1917), an arts academy (founded 1875 as a school of painting) and several other higher educational establishments. It also has a public library (1850), a Georgian museum (1867), and an opera and ballet theatre (1851). There are many treasures of Georgian architecture, including 5th–7th century churches (St David's and Anchiskhat churches, and Zion cathedral), Lurdzhi monastery church (12th century), Metekhi Castle (1278–89), and Anchiskhat bell-tower (1675). Known since the 4th century AD, it has been the capital of Georgia or East Georgia since the 11th century. It became Russian in 1801 and was the seat of the Viceroy

of Caucasus until 1882. It was the capital of the anti-Bolshevik TRANSCAUCASIAN FEDERATION (1917–18), of independent Georgia (1918–20), of the Transcaucasian Federal Republic within the USSR (1922–36), and of Tbilisi *oblast* within the Georgian SSR (1951–53). It is an old centre of Georgian culture (printing press in 1709, philosophical seminary in 1755, theatre in the 1790s, first newspaper in 1819); in the 19th and early 20th centuries it was the cultural centre of the whole of TRANSCAUCASIA. Politically it was one of the strongholds of Social Democracy in Russia. It is also a spa; its name derived from the presence of several hot sulphur springs nearby (Georgian *tbili*, warm). Population (1976) 1,029,000.

Tchad, see CHAD.

Tchaikovsky, Pëtr Ilich (1840–93), Russian composer, born in Kamsko-Vokinsk. He was taught music early at home, but in 1850 entered the School of Jurisprudence in St Petersburg, and in 1859 became a clerk in the Ministry of Justice. He studied harmony with Zaremba, and in 1862 entered the Conservatoire, where he also studied composition with Anton Rubinstein from 1863. In 1865 he was appointed a professor at the Moscow Conservatoire. He met Balakirev in 1868 and accepted his advice, but did not join his circle or subscribe to its exclusive nationalist attitude: technically his music remained cosmopolitan, although it often has a distinctly Russian flavour. His early operas, the first two symphonies and the piano Concerto in B flat minor had won him recognition by 1875, and the following year a wealthy widow, Nadezhda von Meck, offered him financial support on condition that they should never meet. In 1877 he married Antonina Milyukova, who had sent him a declaration of love, but his homosexuality prevented him from returning her feelings. He had a serious breakdown and left her within a month of the wedding. After some months in Switzerland and Italy he resigned his post and settled in a country house. In 1888 he made his first international tour, in 1891 he visited the USA, and in 1893 paid a second visit to England. After a performance of the 'Pathetic' Symphony in St Petersburg he drank a glass of unboiled water and died there of cholera.

Of his 11 operas *Eugene Onegin*, 1879, and *The Queen of Spades*, 1890, both based on Pushkin, have remained in the world repertory, and so have the ballets *Swan Lake*, 1877, *The Sleeping Beauty*, 1890, and *The Nutcracker*, 1892. Three of the six symphonies and the first of the three piano concertos are also permanent favourites, but there is much else that remains characteristic and valuable, such as the symphonic poems *Romeo and Juliet*, *Francesca da Rimini*, and *Hamlet*, the *Capriccio italien* and *1812 Overture*, the violin Concerto and the Piano Trio. Among his other music are church and secular choral works, many attractive songs and there is much that deserves to be remembered among his many piano pieces.

Bibliography: G. Abraham (Ed.), *Tchaikovsky: a Symposium*, 1946; E. Garden, *Tchaikovsky*, 1973; J. Warrack, *Tchaikovsky*, 1973.

Tcheka, see CHEKA.

Tcherkesses, see CIRCASSIANS.

Tchernichowski, Saul (1875–1943), Hebrew poet, born in the Crimea. His upbringing was less strictly Jewish than many others of his time in Eastern Europe, and this is reflected in his work, which has a secularity reinforced by his love of ancient Greek culture. He left Russia in 1899, going first to Germany and then Switzerland, before returning to Russia, where he served as a doctor during the First World War. In 1930 he settled in Palestine.

Very different from other Hebrew work, Tchernichowski's poetry has a sensuousness, especially when describing nature, which has often been described as pagan. A brilliant translator, he wrote Hebrew versions of many classics, including the *Iliad* and *Odyssey*.

Tchitcherin, see CHICHERIN, GEORGI VASILIEVICH.

Tchuvashes, see CHUVASHES.

Tczew (German *Dirschau*), town of Poland, in Gdańsk province, on the River Vistula, 32 km south of Gdańsk. It is an important river port and has a trade in timber and cereals, and manufactures bricks, agricultural machinery, and beer. Population 42,000.

Te Anau, lake in Otago, South Island, New Zealand, in the Southern Alps. Maximum length 61 km, width 10 km, and area 142 km². It is used as a reservoir for hydro-electricity schemes.

Te Deum Laudamus ('We praise thee, O God'), well-known non-metrical Latin hymn, found in the Roman breviary at the end of Matins, and also used on occasions of rejoicing. There has been much discussion of its origin, and modern scholars have shown that it consists largely of borrowings from older sources. Its present form is probably due to Niceta, Bishop of Remesiana (d. c. 414). It occurs, in English, in Anglican matins.

Tea, beverage used since a remote period in China, but unknown in England until 1657. Though it at once attracted great interest, it was obtainable only by wealthy people until about 1750. At first it was infused and kept in barrels, being drawn like beer, and warmed for use. In 1660 a tax of 1s. 6d. was imposed per gallon of liquid tea (c. 1½ p/l), but in 1680 a tax of 5s. per lb (c. 55 p/kg) was substituted. The tax has since been altered and repealed from time to time, and in 1976 stood at 4 per cent on imports weighing less than 3 kg from countries outside the European Economic Community (tax-free inside the Community). No tax is levied on imports of more than 3 kg, and no value added tax is imposed on the sale of any quantity of tea within the United Kingdom (unless consumed on the premises when 8 per cent tax is imposed). (See also BOSTON TEA PARTY.) The first shipment of Indian tea was made from Assam in 1839. Tea is derived from *Camellia sinensis*, which is indigenous to Assam and China. The young leaves and shoots (the 'flush') are picked from the bushes by women. After gathering they are taken to the factory, spread thinly over wire or bamboo trays, and placed on wire or hessian racks to wither, after which they can be rolled without breaking. The length of time required for withering depends on climatic conditions, the shortest time being about 12 hours, and the average 24 hours. During the wet seasons, and in specially humid areas, the leaves are withered by artificial heat. The next process, that of rolling, is done entirely by machine so far as general commercial production is concerned. It causes the juice to be exuded, and it imparts to the leaf the twist characteristic of its manufactured state. The leaf is then spread out thinly in the fermenting room, where the air is kept moist, and there in a few hours it changes from green to copper colour. It is then 'fired' by being spread on trays which pass through a hot-air chamber. After being sorted or classified, a process carried on in modern factories by machinery, the tea is packed for export.

More than one-third of the tea exported from tea-producing countries is consumed in Great Britain and Northern Ireland. In relation to imports the next largest consumers—outside the producing countries—are the USA, Australia, and Canada. In the past tea was always made by pouring water over loose tea-leaves, but nowadays tea-leaves are often contained in tea-bags in Western countries.

Some fortune tellers claim that they can foretell the future from the pattern of leaves left in a cup after the tea has been drunk.

In Japan traditional tea-drinking ceremonies are sometimes held.

See also COOKERY, *Beverages*; MATÉ.

Bibliography: C. R. Harler, *The Culture and Marketing of Tea*, 1956, *Tea Manufacture*, 1963, and *Tea Growing*, 1966; T. Eden, *Tea*, 2nd ed. 1965; Sir P. Griffiths, *History of Indian Tea Industry*, 1967; E. Bramah, *Tea and Coffee: Three Hundred Years of Tradition*, 1972; D. R. MacGregor, *Tea Clippers*, rev. ed. 1972; G. K. Sarkar, *World Tea Economy*, 1972; D. M. Forrest, *Tea for the British: The Social and Economic History of a Famous Trade*, 1973; H. Sandon, *Coffee Pots and Tea Pots*, 1973; S. Tanaka, *Tea Ceremony* (trans. P. Reich), 1974.

Tea Rose, see ROSE.

Tea Seed Oil is commercially produced in China from *Thea sasanqua*, cultivated for its seed. Tea plants, *T.*

sinensis and *T. japonica* are cultivated for their leaves at the expense of the seed, and yield less than 10 per cent of the commercial tea seed oil. The seed kernel of *T. sasanqua* contains 56–60 per cent of oil, which is yellow to brown and may have a very biting, unpleasant taste. It refines to a pale yellow oil with very little taste and odour, resembles olive oil in both chemical and physical characteristics, and is used mainly as a salad and frying oil. Only low-grade oil is used for making soap. Component fatty acids of the oil are: saturated, total 6–12 per cent; unsaturated, oleic (74–87 per cent) and linoleic (2–15 per cent). The cake remaining after extraction of the oil has astringent properties: it has limited use as an insecticide.

Teaching, see EDUCATION.

Teak, timber tree indigenous to India, Sri Lanka, Burma, Thailand, and Indonesia, particularly Java. It is produced from *Tectona grandis* of the Verbenaceae family, and is one of the most useful timbers on account of its many valuable properties, notably durability, good strength to moderate weight, and small movement when used in fluctuating atmospheres. The usual colour of the wood is golden brown, sometimes figured with dark markings. The best Burma teak is straight-grained, and uniform in colour with few markings. Indian teak, particularly from the Malabar Coast, is of more handsome appearance but tends to be rather hard. Teak has a variety of uses, especially in shipbuilding, and is used extensively in garden furniture, doors, window frames, furniture, veneer, and constructional work. Its resistance to a variety of chemical reagents makes it especially valuable for many uses in industrial chemical plants and laboratories. Teak weighs about 640 kg/m³ when seasoned.

Teal, *Anas crecca*, small freshwater duck, order Anseriformes. The male is dusky grey; its tail-feathers ashy grey; the crown of its head deep cinnamon or chestnut; its eye is surrounded by a black band, glossed with green or purple, which unites on the nape; its wing markings are black and white; and its bill is black and resembles that of the widgeon. The female is mottled brown. The total length is about 35 cm.

Teallach, An (The Forge or Hearth), in HIGHLAND REGION, Scotland. A mountain of 14 TORRIDONIAN sandstone tops. So named for three reasons: its smoke-like mists, the reflected glow sometimes seen after sunset below the main pyramid, and the horizontally bedded sandstone strata. The summit is Bidein a'Ghlas Thuill, 1062 m.

Tear Gas, a lachrymatory irritant used as a riot control agent and as a harassing agent in warfare. The main tear gases are CA gas or Camite (brombenzylcyanide), CN gas or CAP (chloracetophenone), and CS gas (orthochlorbenzalmalononitrile). CA gas and CN gas were first developed in the First World War and CS gas in 1928. They are used in the form of grenades that explode to give a spray or smoke containing the gas. The gases cause a burning sensation in the eyes and tears, and difficulty in breathing. They may also produce nausea and vomiting. Although tear gases are often described as non-lethal, they are in fact lethal substances and casualties have been caused by their use. They have an incapacitating effect if inhaled in high concentrations, as can occur when tear gas is used in a closed space, and damage may be caused if the eyes are rubbed. CS gas is now widely used by the police and armies for the dispersal of rioters. It was also used by the US army in Vietnam, and several sources have claimed that deaths resulted. The Geneva Protocol (1925), an international treaty for the restriction of chemical and biological warfare that has been ratified by many nations, prohibits the use of asphyxiating and poisonous gases in warfare. The United States claimed that the tear gases used in Vietnam were not asphyxiating or poisonous.

Bibliography: J. Cookson and J. Nottingham, *Survey of Chemical and Biochemical Warfare*, 1969.

Tears, secretion of the lachrymal gland. See EYE.

Teasdale, Sara (1884–1933), US poet, born in St Louis, Missouri. She excelled in lyric verse, her earliest influence being Christina ROSSETTI with whom she has been compared. Books of her poetry include *Sonnets to Duse*, 1907, *Helen of Troy*, 1911, *Rivers to the Sea*, 1915, *Love Songs*, 1917, which was awarded the Columbia University Prize, *Flame and Shadow*, 1920, *Dark of the Moon*, 1926, and *Strange Victory*, 1933. Her *Collected Poems* were published in 1937.

Teasel, *Dipsacus*, in the family Dipsacaceae, a genus of prickly biennial herbs, native to Europe, Asia and Northern Africa. *D. fullonum* has two subspecies, *sylvestris*, the wild teasel, and *fullonum*, Fuller's teasel, still grown as a crop for its persistent seed heads which are used for raising nap on certain cloths. They and *D. pilosus*, the small teasel, are all found in Britain. A rosette of basal leaves forms during the first year, then the plants throw up prickly, angled stems, with blunt, conical purplish flower-heads, held erect.

Teate, see CHIETI.

Tebaldi, Renata (1922–), Italian operatic soprano, born at Pesaro. She studied at Parma and made her debut at Rovigo in 1944; by the 1950s she was recognised as one of the world's leading singers. Her powerful lyricism was particularly suited to Puccini and Verdi operas.

Tébessa (ancient *Theveste*), town in ALGERIA, in the department of Constantine, famous for its Roman ruins. It is the place where St Crispin suffered martyrdom and, situated at the junction of the roads to Carthage (near TUNIS), Cirta (modern, CONSTANTINE), Lambessa (now Tazoult), and Tacape (modern, Gabes), it soon became a place of primary importance, both as a military and commercial centre. Tébessa is assumed to have been founded about AD 71, just after the Jewish war. It was probably one of the first towns to adopt Christianity after its introduction into Carthage, AD 150, and many famous bishops ruled over the church there. Its period of greatest splendour was the beginning of the 2nd century and from that time there began the construction of its finest monuments. Later it was razed by the Vandals and disappeared from history until its restoration by the Byzantine armies, Solomon being its second founder. The modern town, which is contained within the walls of the Byzantine citadel, is 18 km from the Tunisian frontier and north of the mountains of Bon Rouman. One of the most interesting of its Roman ruins is that of the great basilica, originally a temple of Minerva. There is also an enormous circus and a triumphal arch. Near Tébessa are some important phosphate quarries. Population 40,521.

Technetium, originally masurium, chemical element, symbol Tc, atomic number 43. Noddack and Tacke, after an examination of certain platinum ores and of the mineral columbite, in 1925 claimed to have obtained definite evidence of a new element which fitted in with the requirements of MENDELÉEV's predicted eka-manganese. They relied largely on observations of X-ray spectra, and named the new element masurium. All the isotopes of this element, now called technetium (Greek *technetos*, artificial), are known to be radioactive and to exist in nature only as fission products of uranium. The first radioisotope was produced by Perrier and Segré in 1937 by bombarding molybdenum with deuterons; this has since been shown to give at least five active isotopes of atomic number 43. The longest-lived isotope is ^{99}Tc, which has a half-life of 2·1 million years.

Technical Education, term used to describe courses of instruction, in a variety of institutions, in subjects directly applicable to the purposes of agriculture, industry, trade, or commercial life. A distinction is sometimes made between technical education and COMMERCIAL EDUCATION. In its limited sense technical education is provided for three categories of personnel. Technologists, who make a scientific study of the practical or industrial arts, have a university degree or some comparable qualification, are usually eligible for membership of one of the professional institutions, and are expected, in their careers, to accept a high degree of responsibility and initiate advances in their own field. Technicians, while specialists by virtue of their theoretical and practical training, usually require a good knowledge of the mathematics and science related to their speciality. They work under the general direction of technologists, and in the factory would occupy such positions as assistant designers, or junior managerial positions, for example, in industrial workshops. Craftsmen represent the skilled labour of manufacturing industry, and account for a high proportion of its manpower. Each category has its appropriate qualifying examinations—degrees, technical diplomas, and certificates. In the UK these awards are made by a variety of bodies—universities, technical colleges, the City and Guilds of the London Institute, Regional Examining Unions, and other professional and trade organisations.

Since technical education in the UK developed piecemeal, courses are offered in a great variety of institutions. Apart from the universities there are over 700 technical or commercial establishments in England and Wales. These include polytechnics, technical colleges, technical institutes, colleges of technology, art and commerce, colleges of commerce, colleges of further education, the seven National Colleges of technology—Horology, Foundry, Rubber Technology, Heating and Ventilating, Leather, Food Technology, Aeronautics—and the Royal College of Art. Nearly three-quarters of the students attend evening courses; most of the rest are released by their employers to attend courses under the day-release scheme; a few are in full-time attendance. Industry co-operates in technical education through 'sandwich' courses—substantial periods of full-time study are alternated with periods of industrial training.

Within the secondary school system in England and Wales there are a number of technical schools which provide a general secondary education with an increasing technical bias in the later years of the course. It is probable that these schools will send on an increasing number of their pupils to further technological training. The demand for technically trained personnel has been emphasised ´in a series of government reports since the Second World War (e.g. the Barlow Report 1944, the Percy Report 1945, and Technical Education Report 1956), and the number of technically trained personnel in the UK compares unfavourably with other countries, particularly the USA and USSR. The ROBBINS REPORT proposed that several Colleges of Advanced Technology should be up-graded to technological universities.

See also EDUCATION; UNIVERSITIES.

Bibliography: P. F. R. Venables, *Technical Education*, 1955; S. Cotgrove, *Technical Education and Social Change*, 1958; and G. L. Payne, *Britain's Scientific and Technological Manpower*, 1960; P. F. R. Venables, *Changing Pattern of Technical and Higher Education*, 1970.

Technicolor, leading colour process employed in modern CINEMATOGRAPHY. The first technicolor film was made in 1921: a special lens and filters were used to obtain a two colour image, which was based upon the principles known as the additive process. This was later abandoned when the two colour subtractive process was introduced, which was followed in 1935 (*Becky Sharp*) by the three colour subtractive process, the system now employed. The technicolor three-colour camera photographs the three primary aspects of a scene (red, green and blue) upon three separate film strips, without fringe or parallax, in balance, and in proper register with each other. These separate strips are developed to negatives of equal contrast and are always considered and handled as a group. From these colour-separation negatives, printing is carried out by projection through the celluloid upon a specially prepared stock, which is then developed and processed to produce positive relief images in hardened gelatin. These three reliefs are then used as printing matrices which absorb dye. The dye is then transferred by imbibition printing to another film strip, which, when it has received all three transfers, becomes the completed print ready for projection. This process is designed to reproduce whatever is placed in front of the camera, not only as to colour, but also as to light and shade.

The technicolor process reproduces a full scale of contrasts and effects of light and shade, and consequently the designer of settings has to bear in mind the cameraman's problem of achieving the necessary light-levels with a minimum number of sources of illumination. Technicolor adds few complications to sound recording, but the 'whistle' from the arcs caused by high-frequency ripples in the electric current coming from the commutators of direct-current generators must be eliminated. This is done by the combination of an alternating-current filter at the generator and additional choke-coils at the individual arc units. Modern film production, American and British has proved that, used imaginatively, colour heightens dramatic effect.

Bibliography: J. Huntley, *British Technicolor Films*, 1949.

Teck, German family whose name was taken from a castle of Württemberg. Francis, a prince of Württemberg, who became duke of Teck, married Mary Adelaide, daughter of the Duke of Cambridge, and settled in Britain. He died in 1900 and his wife in 1897. Their daughter, Mary, married King George V. Of their three sons, Adolphus, Duke of Teck (1868–1927), married a daughter of the 1st Duke of Westminster and was created marquess of Cambridge in 1917; Francis died in 1910; and Alexander was created earl of Athlone in 1917. In the latter year the family name was changed to Cambridge, when that of the royal family was changed to Windsor.

Tecton, distinguished firm of British architects, established by Bernhold Lubetkin (1901–); Denys LASDUN was at one time a partner. They designed the Penguin Pool and Gorilla House at London Zoo, 1934–38, two blocks at Highpoint and North Hill flats at Highgate, 1936–38, Finsbury Health Centre, 1938–39, and flats in Roseberry Avenue, 1946–49.

Tedder of Glenguin, Arthur William Tedder, 1st Baron (1890–1967), British airman, Marshal of the RAF, educated at Whitgift School and Magdalene College, Cambridge. He entered the colonial service in 1914. Commissioned in 1914 in the Dorset Regiment, he went to France in 1914 and was seconded to the Royal Flying Corps in 1916. He was given a permanent commission in the RAF in 1919. He held several important posts and became air officer, commander-in-chief Middle East, 1941–43, and air commander-in-chief, Mediterranean air command, in 1943. Tedder, appointed deputy supreme commander under Gen. Eisenhower for the Anglo-American expeditionary force, was the first British airman to assume so important a military post. He was a specialist in strategy, moulding to his own shape the current ideas on air co-operation with armies. Appointed chief of the air staff in 1945 he retired in 1950 at his own request. He was knighted in 1942 and created a peer in 1946.
Bibliography: R. Owen, *Tedder*, 1965.

Teddington, see RICHMOND-UPON-THAMES.

Tees, river of England, rising in Cross Fell, CUMBRIA, and flowing south-east and then north-east for 112 km, entering the estuary called Tees Mouth to join the North Sea. It is navigable to MIDDLESBROUGH, and has a port trade of 25 million t, including oil and iron ore. The river valley, known as Teesdale, includes Mickle Fell (790 m), the highest point in Yorkshire, and the great waterfall of High Force; among the fells near the river's source are found Alpine flowers.

Teesdale, district of County DURHAM, England, occupying an area of 843 km², comprising the Tees valley above Darlington and rising to 790 m on Mickle Fell. Mixed and cattle farming extend upwards to a height of 300 m, with the urban centres at Barnard Castle (population in 1971, 5800) and MIDDLETON-IN-TEESDALE. There are new reservoirs to supply Cleveland, and at HIGH FORCE the Tees crosses the Whin Sill in a 21-metre waterfall. Population (1971) 23,900.

Teesside, industrial conurbation in CLEVELAND, England, on either side of the TEES estuary including STOCKTON-ON-TEES, MIDDLESBROUGH, BILLINGHAM, and REDCAR. From 1969 to 1974 Teesside formed a county borough in the North Riding of Yorkshire. Population (1971) 395,000.

Teeth, calcareous structures occupying the alveolar arch (bony ridge with sockets for the teeth) of the upper and lower jaw, and serving to tear, cut or grind food.

In man there are 32 permanent teeth, 16 in each jaw. They are divided as follows: two incisors, one canine, two premolars or bicuspids, and three molars, in the lateral half of each jaw. The incisors have chisel-shaped crowns and are therefore adapted for dividing food by cutting. In the upper jaw the incisor teeth develop in the premaxillary bone. The canine teeth are conical in shape and are adapted for piercing. In carnivorous animals the canines are often greatly developed; they may be very long (e.g. walrus's tusks) and serve to hold and tear the prey. The length of these teeth can be very great; in the sabre-tooth tiger the development of these teeth led to the downfall of the animal because their unnecessary length became a liability to the animal, preventing normal activities.

All the other teeth are found in the maxillary bones of the upper jaw and the mandible of the lower jaw. The upper first premolar usually has two roots although occasionally it has one like the lower premolars and upper second premolars, which are almost always single-rooted. The molars are the teeth at the back of the mouth and in man are the largest teeth, being adapted to grinding and chewing. The upper molars normally have four cusps

Teeth. The development of the permanent teeth. (*Peter Walker, Partnerplan Ltd, National Dental Health Action Campaign*)

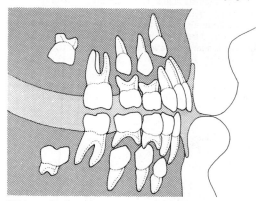

Child-age six. Several permanent teeth have already erupted.

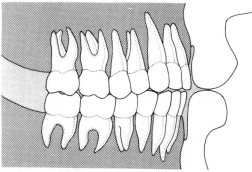

Age fourteen. All permanent teeth (excepting 'wisdom' teeth) have erupted.

Teeth

and three roots, while the lower molars have four or five cusps and two roots. The last molar is known as the 'wisdom' tooth. Herbivorous animals have greatly enlarged molar teeth with ridges across them to provide a grinding surface, a special adaptation to the chewing of coarse plant food. Animals have greatly differing numbers and kinds of teeth which correspond to their diets, ranging from a large number of continually replaced teeth in the shark to no teeth in the scaly anteater.

In mammals the arrangement and number of teeth is given by a 'dental formula', which in man is 2123/2123. This indicates that in each half of each jaw there are two incisors, one canine, two premolars, and three molars. The first permanent teeth erupt at around the age of six, and the last molar, the wisdom tooth, erupts at around 18–20 years. The permanent dentition is preceded by a deciduous dentition of 'milk' teeth which erupt during the first 2½ years of life and are shed between the ages of six and twelve years. The deciduous teeth are smaller, whiter, bulbous, and with more divergent roots than their permanent successors. There are 20 deciduous teeth in man, represented by the formula 2102/2102. The structure of all the teeth is basically the same (see diagram). The outer layer of the crown is enamel. This is the hardest biological tissue, consisting of a small amount of organic matrix and water and approximately 96 per cent mineral salts which are mainly calcium hydroxy-apatite, with small amounts of calcium and magnesium carbonate, phosphate, fluoride, and trace elements. The inner layer is dentine which consists of similar constituents but the organic matrix and water account for approximately 30 per cent of this tissue. It is not as hard as enamel and is resilient. The dentine consists of a large number of tubes connecting the pulp to the rest of the tooth by extensions (processes) of the pulp

Teeth. The internal structure of a tooth. *(Peter Walker Partnerplan Ltd, National Dental Health Action Campaign)*

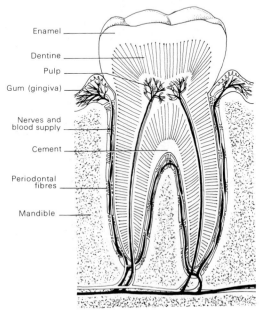

- Enamel
- Dentine
- Pulp
- Gum (gingiva)
- Nerves and blood supply
- Cement
- Periodontal fibres
- Mandible

cells which traverse the dentine through these tubes. These processes are responsible for the sensitivity of the tooth, as they transmit stimuli to the pulp where they are recorded as pain sensations. Toothache is normally associated with stimulation of the pulp through these processes by hot or cold foods, or by the breakdown products of dental caries (decay) which, if untreated, will lead to death of the pulp and abscess formation. The pulp, which is surrounded by dentine, contains blood vessels, nerves, and other cells and communicates with the rest of the body at the apex of the root. The root of the tooth has no enamel but is covered by a layer of cementum which resembles bone and attaches the tooth to the surrounding bone via the fibres of the periodontal membrane.

Dental caries is the most widespread and commonest disease affecting the civilised human race. It is caused by the presence of a dental plaque on the surface of the enamel. This plaque is formed by the accumulation of food debris, saliva, bacteria, and other substances. It is particularly associated with a high intake of refined carbohydrate. The plaque produces acid which causes demineralisation of the enamel and this in turn allows ingress of the acid and bacteria into the dentine. There the attack is much more rapid because of the lower mineral content and the presence of tubes which allow easy spread of the lesion and breakdown of tooth substance leading to cavity formation. The pulp is affected at this stage by inflammatory changes which will progress to pulp death if untreated. Once the teeth have developed cavities the only remedy is to resort to dental surgery to repair the damage with a 'filling' or to extract the diseased tooth. Both dental caries and PYORRHOEA can have harmful effects on the general health of the individual.

Prevention of dental caries can be attained by plaque control, dietary control, or by increasing the resistance of the teeth by fluoride (see FLUORIDATION) or coating the teeth with an acid-resistant coat. The latter method is still in the experimental stages. Plaque control can be achieved by correct and regular tooth brushing and the use of dental floss to clean between teeth after each meal. A careful diet, confined to mealtimes and with a minimum of refined carbohydrate, is also a great help in preventing dental disease.

See also DENTISTRY.

Bibliography: J. H. Scott and N. B. B. Symons, *Introduction to Dental Anatomy*, 7th ed. 1974; The British Dental Health Foundation, *Home Mouth Care Manual*, 1976.

Tegea, town of Arcadia in ancient Greece, named after its reputed founder, Tegeates, son of Lycaon. It was long subject to the hegemony of Sparta, but became independent after the Theban victory at Leuctra (371 BC). Tegea was famous for its temple of Pallas Athene (394 BC). Extensive excavations have been made on its site.

Tegernsee, Alpine lake, and village on its eastern shore, in BAVARIA, West Germany, 44 km south-east of Munich. It is a popular tourist resort and sporting centre. Length of lake 6 km; width 2 km; the village has a castle (once a Benedictine abbey) belonging to the Duke of Bavaria. Population 4600.

Tegnér, Esaias (1782–1846), Swedish poet, born at By, Värmland. He studied at Lund University, where in 1802 he became lecturer in philosophy. In 1811 he published a

Tehran. The suburb of Shemran. *(Camera Press/William MacQuitty)*

patriotic ode, *Svea*, and was awarded a prize by the Swedish Academy, of which he became a member in 1818. In 1820 he published *Nattvardsbarnen* (translated by H. W. LONGFELLOW as *The Children of the Lord's Supper*), in 1822 *Axel*, and in 1825 *Frithiofs Saga*, a paraphrase of an Icelandic SAGA. He was also a critic of considerable ability. Tegnér had been ordained in 1812 and in 1824 was made bishop of Växjö.

Tegnér is regarded as one of Sweden's greatest poets. Although in the classical tradition, he was much influenced by the Romanticism of SCHILLER. His finest pieces, whether inspired by love, patriotism, politics, or philosophy, display great originality of thought, and a blending of the new Romantic style with the Scandinavian saga heritage. Among his best poems, besides those mentioned, are *Song to the Sun*, 1817, and *Degree Day at Lund*, 1820.

Bibliography: M. Gravier, *Tegnér et la France*, 1942; F. Böök, *E. Tegnér* (2 vols), 1946–47.

Tegucigalpa, capital of the Central American republic of
HONDURAS. The city is situated at an altitude of 975 m in an intermontane basin ringed on three sides by mountains, of which one is the extinct volcano El Picacho at the foot of which the city is built. The city is separated from the town of Comayagüela by the River Choluteca spanned by three bridges. Each town has its own municipal council but is administratively unified as the Central District. There is a markedly dry season from December to May when the temperature rises from 10 °C to 32 °C but during the rainy season the climate is temperate. Founded in the 16th century by the Spaniards, the city has escaped earthquake or fire damage and remains basically unchanged apart from considerable modernisation. Notable buildings are the cathedral of San Miguel, the palace of the central district, the presidential palace, the legislative palace, and the central bank. Silver and gold are mined nearby (as they have been since the 16th century)

and there is considerable industrial development. The main industries include cotton textile manufacture, clothing, construction materials, food processing, beverages, and soap. Tegucigalpa is one of the few capitals in the world without a railway. However air services are good, Toncontin airport being 6 km outside the city. Road communications are also relatively good, Tegucigalpa being 352 km by road from PUERTO CORTÉS, Honduras's chief port in the north, and 120 km from AMAPALA on the Pacific. The national university has been transferred to a new university city in Comayagüela. Population 210,000.

Tehran, or Teheran, city and capital of IRAN. The city is built at an average altitude of 1220 m, on a gentle slope running south from the ELBURZ MOUNTAINS. The climate has marked seasonal contrasts with a short mild spring and autumn separating a long severely cold winter and a hot dry summer. Formerly a suburb of REY, Tehran became the capital in 1785 under the Qajar dynasty and expanded steadily in the 19th century. After the accession of Riza Shah Pahlavi (1925–41) the city was replanned and largely rebuilt, the walls demolished, and new avenues cut through residential quarters. The public buildings of the time, such as the university (founded 1935), employed Achaemenian or Sassanian styles for their exteriors. Modern Tehran exhibits marked internal differences; the southernmost part, the poorest, is a reception area for migrants from all over Iran and is socially the most conservative; further north, upslope, are the bazaar and many of the ministry buildings while further north still the former 19th-century upper-class suburbs, with leafy avenues and older buildings, have most of the foreign embassies. The modern central business district is now centred on Takhte Jamshid and Firdausi avenues. Since the Second World War however there has been rapid residential expansion north from here towards SHEMIRAN, much of it in the form of four-storey apartment blocks.

On the lower foothills of Tochal, the 3800-metre peak that dominates the northern skyline, are the new national university, the Hilton Hotel, and the Sheraton Towers block, all in modern style. Places of interest include the Sepahsolar Mosque and library, the Gulistan Palace, and the Iran Bastan Museum. The modern functions of the city are varied; as the capital and largest city, Tehran is the seat of all the ministries, and much of Iran's industrial development is concentrated here. The city acts also as capital of the Central province. The growth of modern Tehran has been to some extent at the expense of other Iranian cities. Population (1975) 3,400,000; Greater Tehran 4,171,000.

Tehuacán, town of MEXICO, in the state of PUEBLA and 104 km south-east of Puebla city, at an altitude of 1650 m. It is noted for its mineral springs and has an equable climate. Founded in 1540, it is now a modern city with the manufacture of agricultural products, flour milling, tanning, textiles, and chemicals. It is the junction of the Mexico City–Veracruz and Mexico City–Oaxaca railways. Population 45,000.

Tehuantepec, Isthmus of, situated in the south of MEXICO with the Atlantic (Gulf of Mexico) to the north and Pacific to the south, the land at the narrowest point being about 208 km between the oceans. The small port of Salina Cruz on the Pacific is connected by road and rail with the port of Coatzacoalcos on the Gulf. Near the latter are important oil-fields and refineries.

Tehuantepec, Santo Domingo de, town of Mexico, in OAXACA state, 19 km up the Rio Tehuantepec from Salina Cruz on the Pacific coast. It gives its name to the Isthmus of Tehuantepec. It is inhabited mainly by the indigenous Zapotec tribe. Population 25,000.

Tehuantepec Winds, see WIND.

Teifi, or Teivy, river of Wales, rising in Llyn Teifi in north Dyfed. It flows south and then west to enter Cardigan Bay in a wide estuary. It is 85 km long.

Teign, river of Devon, England, rising in DARTMOOR, above Chagford; after flowing for 48 km it enters the English Channel at Teignmouth. Its estuary is over a kilometre across.

Teignmouth, John Shore, 1st Baron (1751–1834), British Governor-General of India. He entered the service of the East India Company as a cadet at the age of 18. A man of great personal integrity and devotion to duty, he rose rapidly, and by 1787 was a member of the Supreme Council. In 1793 he succeeded Cornwallis as governor-general. He retired from this office in 1797 and received a barony. Shore was an evangelical, closely connected with the CLAPHAM SECT, and became first president of the British and Foreign Bible Society.

Teignmouth, seaport and holiday resort in DEVON, England, at the mouth of the River Teign, with a sea-wall 3 km long. Teignmouth is built partly on a tongue of land between the Teign and the sea, and partly on rising wooded ground enclosing the valley which rises to the high moors below Haytor. The commercial netting of

salmon is practised in the Teign. Population (1971) 12,575.

Teilhard de Chardin, Pierre (1881–1955), French theologian, philosopher, and scientist, born at Sarcenat near Clermont-en-Auvergne and died in New York. He was educated at the Jesuit College of Mongré and entered the Society of Jesus in 1899. He spent three years in Cairo (1905–08) teaching physics, and returned to Europe in 1908 to begin his course of theology. Ordained priest in 1911, he served throughout the First World War as a stretcher-bearer in the French army, his activities earning him a military medal and the Legion of Honour. He then resumed the study of palaeontology and in 1919 was made professor of geology at the Institut Catholique in Paris. In 1923 he went to China, the first of several visits to that country, where he studied in detail its rich palaeontological remains. After the Second World War (which he spent in China) he returned to Europe, and in 1951 was attached to the Wenner-Gren Foundation for anthropological research, making trips to South Africa in 1951 and 1953.

The fruit of all these journeys and labours is to be found in the stream of papers and articles which he published in various learned journals between 1913 and his death. His major work Le Phénomène Humain, 1955 (English translation The Phenomenon of Man, 1959) is a study of the process by which man has developed to his present condition and which looks forward to a future where man, now controlling the evolutionary process, will achieve his final fulfilment. Owing to the fears of ecclesiastic authority about the orthodoxy of some of his views, the work (which was finished in 1939) was not published until after his death. Taken in conjunction with his more directly theological study Le Milieu Divin, 1957 (English translation 1960), it has, however, proved a fruitful source of inspiration to many Christians.

Teilhard remains an extremely controversial figure, regarded by his admirers as the major modern Christian thinker but dismissed by many scientists as lacking in rigour in his presentation of argument and evidence.

Among Teilhard's works which have appeared in English are The Phenomenon of Man, 1959, Letters from a Traveller, 1962, The Future of Man, 1964, The Appearance of Man, 1965, The Making of a Mind, 1965.

Bibliography: C. Cuénot, Teilhard de Chardin (includes bibliography), 1958; de Lubac, The Faith of Teilhard de Chardin, 1965; R. Speaight, The Life of Teilhard de Chardin, 1967; A. Hanson (Ed.), Teilhard Reassessed, 1970.

Teinds. The teinds of a Scottish parish, like the TITHES of English law, are that proportion of rents or goods which goes to the maintenance of the clergy. The clergy, however, have now no right to teinds beyond a suitable provision or stipend.

Teith, river of Scotland, rising 26 km north-east of Inveraray, and flowing east to join the Forth 3 km from Stirling. Length 53 km.

Teixeira de Pascoaes, pseudonym of Joaqium Pereira Teixeira de Vasconcellos (1879–1952), Portuguese poet and essayist, born at Gatão. His early work was lyrical in character, but later, particularly in his prose writings, he concentrated more on a metaphysical discussion of the problem of good and evil and the progress of humanity.

His published works include *Jesus e Pan*, 1903, *Regresso ao Paraíso*, 1912, *Santo Paulo*, 1934, and *Santo Agostinho*, 1945.

Tejo, see TAGUS.

Tejuco, see DIAMANTINA.

Tel al Amarna, see TELL EL-AMARNA.

Tel Aviv (Hebrew, Hill of Spring), largest city of ISRAEL, situated on the coast of Sharon Plain, 77 km north-west of Jerusalem. Founded in 1909, on bare sand-dunes to the north of JAFFA, it was intended only as a suburb of the latter. It became a municipality in its own right in 1921, and absorbed its smaller neighbour in 1950. Tel Aviv was the capital of Israel from the state's declaration of independence until 1950.

Beginning with 60 small villas, the municipal area of Tel Aviv has rapidly grown to its present municipal area, and now houses almost one in four of the country's inhabitants. By 1930 it had become Israel's leading economic centre, its activities including chemicals, pharmaceuticals, confectionery, textiles, banking, and almost all of the country's book, newspaper, and magazine publishing. Tel Aviv is also the seat of the national theatres (English and Hebrew), the state ballet, the Israel Philharmonic Orchestra, which is of international renown, a municipally-run university, and the Bar Ilan religious university. There is a famous museum of ancient glass ('ha Aretz'), and the art gallery is deservedly well known. In the European modernity of its buildings and way of life, Tel Aviv provides a strong contrast to the orientalism of

Jaffa. The building of the city's light port was forced upon it by the destruction of the harbour facilities of Jaffa during the disturbances of 1936; its present traffic is not heavy, but an extension is planned. ASHDOD acts as the main port. Population of Tel-Aviv–Jaffa (1976) 353,800.

Bibliography: M. Kohansky, *Tel-Aviv and Environs*, 1974.

Telamon, brother of PELEUS, who with him killed Phocus their half-brother. Telamon fled from Aegina to Salamis, where he married the daughter of the king and ultimately succeeded to the throne. He was one of the Calydonian hunters and an ARGONAUT. He also helped HERACLES to take Troy. Telamon was the father of AJAX by his second wife, Periboea.

Telecommunications, science of communication by electrical means. See RADIOCOMMUNICATION; TELEGRAPHY; TELEPHONY; TELEVISION.

Telecontrol, Electric, the starting, stopping, and regulation of machines, and operation of switchgear from a distance, sometimes of many kilometres, by electric current signals in a telecommunication system. The operation of a section of an interconnected network, including generating stations and distributing substations, is controlled at a central control room.

Telegonus, in Greek legend, son of ODYSSEUS and CIRCE. Sent by her to find Odysseus, he landed in Ithaca, but was attacked by his father and Telemachus, who imagined him a pirate. He killed Odysseus, not knowing who he was, then conveyed the body to Circe for burial and later married PENELOPE.

Tel Aviv. *(Camera Press/Werner Braun)*

Telegraphy

Telegraphy, system for conveying information between two points. The first serviceable telegraphic device, invented by Chappe (France) in 1792, was a form of SEMAPHORE. In 1816 Ronald (Britain) produced his pith-ball telegraph, where an electric current to line caused two pith-balls to diverge, and their movement indicated a character. In 1819 Oersted discovered that an electric current deflected a neighbouring magnetic needle, the direction of movement depending on the direction of current flow. Cooke and Wheatstone, applying this principle, produced the first practical electric telegraph system in 1837. Their first system was a five-needle telegraph requiring five lines. This was followed by the double-needle and then the single-needle system. Fig. 1 shows the system in its simplest form. When a message is to be transmitted from A to B, the key is depressed as shown and line current flows through the recorder at B to earth and deflects the recorder needle.

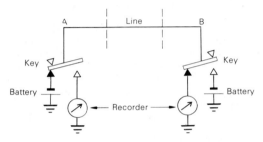

Telegraphy. Figure 1. Principle of Cooke and Wheatstone electric telegraph.

Karl Steinheil (1836) devised an acoustic telegraph with two gongs of different notes. Line current deflected one or two needles depending on the current direction. Attachments to these needles struck the gongs, and thus gave a code of audible signals. In 1837 Morse produced his electromagnetic telegraph. The Morse code consists of two distinct signals in groups to define the various characters. One signal is a 'dot' and the other a 'dash', the dash being three times the duration of the dot. There are intervals between the letters and a longer interval between words (fig. 2). In the elementary Morse system the recorder at each end (fig. 1) is replaced by a sounder (fig. 3). It consists of a U-shaped electromagnet M and a soft iron bar A attached to a brass bar B. The brass bar is pivoted; its free end is normally kept up by a spring S. When the signal current flows through the electromagnet the iron bar A is attracted, the brass bar is pulled down and the screw C strikes the frame. When the current ceases, the spring pulls the bar up again and its end strikes the screw D. The receiving operator hears the two taps; if the interval between them is short the signal is a dot; if long, a dash. Later a number of systems were produced where the dots and dashes were ink recorded on a paper tape. Galvanometers are included at each direct-sounder station to enable the operator to verify that the key operation is actually causing current to flow to line.

The direct-sounder system can be used only over short lines. On longer lines the sounder is replaced by a relay which requires a much smaller operating current. The

A	.—	S	...
B	—...	T	—
C	—.—.	U	..—
D	—..	V	...—
E	.	W	.——
F	..—.	X	—..—
G	——.	Y	—.——
H	....	Z	——..
I	..	1	.————
J	.———	2	..———
K	—.—	3	...——
L	.—..	4	....—
M	——	5	.....
N	—.	6	—....
O	———	7	——...
P	.——.	8	———..
Q	——.—	9	————.
R	.—.	0	—————

Telegraphy. Figure 2. The Morse code.

relay contacts complete a local circuit to operate the sounder.

The single-current working so far described involves signal distortion and requires a slow signalling speed to prevent interference. In double-current working the interval between the signal (mark) currents is filled by currents (space) flowing in the reverse direction. The effect is to accelerate the discharge of the line (fig. 4). This method is used extensively on long submarine cables. The cable code is similar to the Morse code, except that the dots and dashes are distinguished by direction of current flow. They appear as punched holes in a paper tape, and the two signals are readily distinguished by their relative positions on the tape. This method permits a greater signalling speed.

In simplex working (fig. 5) operation is only possible in one direction at a time. To increase the traffic-carrying capacity of circuits, duplex working is used. This permits the simultaneous transmission of signals in both directions on the one line. Two simplex circuits, one in each direction, may be combined to give duplex facilities (two-way simplex).

The Bridge duplex (fig. 6), used on submarine cables, is based on the principle of the Wheatstone Bridge, and depends for its action upon the balance of potentials across

Telegraphy. Figure 3. Morse sounder.

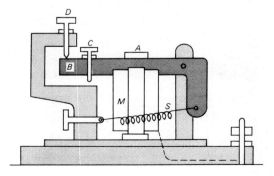

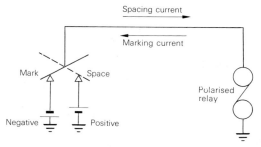

Telegraphy. Figure 4. Double-current working.

a relay connected in the diagonal of the bridge. The line-signal conditions give potential balance and unbalance conditions to operate the relay.

An extension of the duplex principle gives quadruplex working, a duplex system in which simultaneous transmission of two messages in each direction is possible over a single circuit. One message is given by the direction of current flow and the other by the actual current value.

High-speed Automatic Systems. The Baudot system (1874) was a multiplex printing system worked double-current. It used a five-unit code in which each character was made up of a combination of five currents, each current being positive or negative. A multiplex system is a multiple-way arrangement of sending two or more messages over the same line by the allocation of the exclusive use of the line in rapid succession. A number of operators are given the exclusive use of the line for a time sufficient to transmit one character (time-division multiplex).

Signals are transmitted and received by means of segmented distributors with contacting brushes rotated in synchronism at each end of the line. The distributors enable up to six operators to use the line during one revolution of the brushes around the distributors. Assuming six operators, the distributor periphery is divided into six sections, each serving one operator. Each section is further subdivided into five segments. The rotating brushes make contact with the corresponding segments in the respective sections at the same time. Each successive segment at each end is thus in circuit with the line for the short time the brushes rest on them and, during this time,

information may be passed between the two segments.

Stop-Start Teleprinter Working. Modern inland telegraphic communication is now carried out by teleprinters. The teleprinter consists of (1) the transmitter, and (2) the receiver, which are mounted upon one base and are driven by a small electric motor. The transmitter consists of a keyboard, and a transmitting unit, controlled by the keyboard, which transmits signals in the form of electrical impulses. The receiver part consists of an electromagnet, operated by the line signals, and a mechanism which causes the character corresponding to the signals to be printed on a moving paper tape.

Modern teleprinter working uses the Murray five-unit signal code (fig. 7). Here the signal time for each character is the same. Five electrical impulses of equal duration are transmitted for each character. Various formations of these impulses make up the different characters. In double-current working, space signals are positive battery and the mark negative battery. The maximum number of different characters that can be obtained is 32, and since it is necessary to transmit numerals as well as the alphabet, the machine is arranged to use the same combinations for figures as for letters. Start and stop pulses accompany every character combination. The motors run continuously, but when no signals are passing the transmitting and receiving mechanisms are at rest. When a key is depressed, both mechanisms make one revolution, during which time the start pulse, character combination, and stop pulse are sent. At the receiving end the start pulse sets the receiving mechanism in motion for one revolution. The character combination is received while the mechanism is in motion and finally the stop pulse is received. The start and stop signals obviate maintaining continuously correct phase relationship between the teleprinters at each end of the line such as is required in multiplex systems. The time for one revolution is approximately 150 ms and the system is capable of working at approximately 66 words per minute.

Where the traffic is too heavy for direct keyboard operation, automatic tape transmission may be used. The operator prepares the message, to the five-unit code, on perforated tape. This is fed through an automatic tape transmitter which transmits the signals to line.

Repeaters. With direct current (d.c.) signalling the speed at which long circuits, having large values of capacitance and resistance, can be worked is limited. A

Telegraphy. Figure 5. Simplex working.

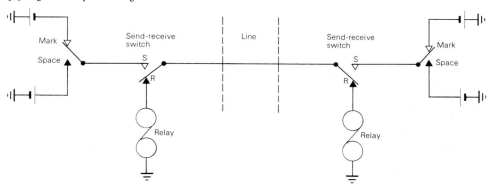

repeater inserted in the line permits a greater speed, as the repeater effectively breaks the line up into a number of shorter links. The simple type consists of a relay receiving and retransmitting the signal to the receiving station. A regenerative repeater is one which accepts distorted signals and retransmits them free from distortion. This type has application in repeating signals to enable long submarine cable circuits to be extended via land lines.

Telegraph Signalling. DC signals are subject to distortion. On inland networks the modern method is to signal by alternating current (a.c.) in the voice-frequency range. Such signals can be passed over standard telephone trunk lines, and amplified by thermionic valve or transistor amplifiers. AC signals retain their shape in transmission with sufficient accuracy almost without distance limit.

The British Post Office uses a multichannel voice-frequency signalling method for inland networks. In this system 24 channels are obtained on one line. Each channel has its own signalling frequency, which is transmitted within a narrow frequency band. The frequency bands are at 420, 540, 660 Hz, etc., at every 120 Hz interval up to 3180 Hz. This is a form of frequency division multiplex and the 24 channels are thus accommodated within the frequency band of a normal telephone circuit.

Facsimile, or picture telegraphy, transmitting still pictures, or printed matter, over an electrical circuit, is now finding increasing application, particularly for press work. A typical technique incorporates a sender, which is arranged to scan the picture in a regular manner by means of a light spot. The variations in tone of the picture are interpreted into variations in amplitude of a.c. passed to line to a receiver. Here a light from a constant source is arranged to fall on a piece of photographic material and scan this at exactly the same rate as the sender light spot. The variation of incoming current from the line operates a light valve, which controls the intensity of the light falling on the photographic material to reproduce the original picture.

See CABLES, ELECTRIC; POST OFFICE; SIGNALS AND SIGNALLING.

Bibliography: E. H. Jolley, *Introduction to Telephony and*

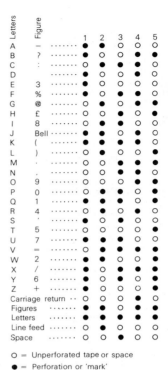

Letters	Figure	1	2	3	4	5
A	—	●	●	O	O	O
B	?	●	O	O	●	●
C	:	O	●	●	●	O
D		●	O	O	●	O
E	3	●	O	O	O	O
F	%	●	O	●	●	O
G	@	O	●	O	●	●
H	£	O	O	●	O	●
I	8	O	●	●	O	O
J	Bell	●	●	O	●	O
K	(	●	●	●	●	O
L	)	O	●	O	O	●
M	.	O	O	●	●	●
N	,	O	O	●	●	O
O	9	O	O	O	●	●
P	0	O	●	●	O	●
Q	1	●	●	●	O	●
R	4	O	●	O	●	O
S	'	●	O	●	O	O
T	5	O	O	O	O	●
U	7	●	●	●	O	O
V	=	O	●	●	●	●
W	2	●	●	O	O	●
X	/	●	O	●	●	●
Y	6	●	O	●	O	●
Z	+	●	O	O	O	●
Carriage return		O	O	O	●	O
Figures		●	●	O	●	●
Letters		●	●	●	●	●
Line feed		O	●	O	O	O
Space		O	O	●	O	O

O = Unperforated tape or space

● = Perforation or 'mark'

Telegraphy. Figure 7. Murray five-unit signal code.

Telegraphy, 1968; D. Roddy, *Radio and Line Transmission* (vols 1–2), 1968–72; S. F. Smith, *Telephony and Telegraphy: Introduction to Telephone and Telegraph Instruments and Exchanges,* 1969; W. Fraser, *Telecommunications,* 3rd ed. 1970.

Telegraphy, Wireless, see WIRELESS TELEGRAPHY.

Teleki, name of a Hungarian family of Transylvania dating back to the early 15th century.

Telegraphy. Figure 6. Bridge duplex.

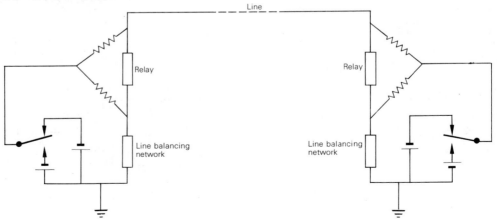

Mihály Teleki (1634–90), was chancellor of Transylvania and received the title 'Count' from Emperor Leopold in 1685.

Count László Teleki (1811–61), was Hungarian government envoy in Paris in 1848; he worked for reconciliation between the Slavs, Romanians, and the Hungarians. He was arrested in Dresden in 1860, was extradited to Austria, and was set free on condition that he kept out of politics. Later when he found himself at the head of a radical party that emerged at the Diet in 1861 he took his life, thus opening the way to DEÁK's more moderate policies.

Count Paul Teleki (1879–1941), was Hungarian premier between July 1920 and April 1921 and again after February 1939. His government signed a friendship treaty with Yugoslavia in December 1940 but then, under pressure from Hitler, decided to attack Yugoslavia together with Germany. Count Paul took his life on 3 April 1941, ashamed at having broken the treaty.

Telekinesis, the movement of objects by a person without that person having any physical contact with them. It is a common feature of physical phenomena in SPIRITUALISM. See also PSYCHOKINESIS.

Telemachus, in Greek legend, son of ODYSSEUS and PENELOPE, a child when his father set out for Troy. After about 20 years he set sail in search of news of him, visiting Pylos and Sparta, and returning to Ithaca in time to help his father in the famous fight with the suitors.

Telemann, Georg Philipp (1681–1767), German composer, born at Magdeburg. He studied languages and law at Leipzig University and was mainly self-taught in music, but in 1704 secured the appointment of organist at the New Church there and founded a students' music society, the Collegium Musicum, which was later to be conducted by J. S. Bach. After various appointments at Sorau, Eisenach, Frankfurt and Bayreuth, he became music director of the Johanneum at Hamburg in 1721 and organist at the five principal churches. Telemann was one of the most prolific and facile composers of the late Baroque period. His works include much occasional music, but also many pieces of lasting value. In style they are transitional, mixing Baroque procedures with the new, lighter 'rococo' manner, particularly under French influence. He wrote several operas and oratorios, chamber and church music, and achieved great popularity in his own time—far more so than his contemporary, Bach—although Telemann's music has only recently been revalued after a long period of disfavour.

Bibliography: Life by E. Valentin, 1931.

Telemark, county of NORWAY, on the south coast. It is a mountainous region, with vast reserves of timber. Skien, birthplace of Ibsen (his *Peer Gynt* has its setting in Telemark), is the capital. Industries include timber, paper, and chemicals. Telemark contains some of Norway's wildest and most picturesque scenery. Of particular interest is Rjukan (126 m), one of Europe's finest waterfalls, providing power for chemical works. Area 15,320 km²; population (1975) 158,000.

Telemeter, see RANGEFINDER.

Telemetering, measurement of physical quantities such as pressure, speed, current, temperature, and voltage, on meters placed at a distance from where the phenomena occur that are measured. For example, the operating characteristics of boiler plant, turbines, generators, and transformers in a power station are indicated on meters in the control room. The practice has become highly devel-

Telemachus, Penelope and Laërtes's never completed shroud, from an Attic red-figure skyphos, c. 450 BC. *(Mansell Collection)*

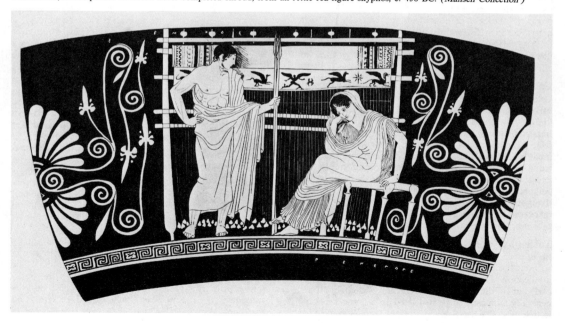

Teleostei. Among the huge range of forms are the seahorses, family Syngnathidae. *(Topham/Fox)*

oped in research using artificial satellites, with miniaturisation of detectors and transmitters.

Teleology, in philosophy, is the theory that things are determined by the ends towards which they strive. This notion was central to ARISTOTLE's metaphysics and his theory of causality. For example, on a teleological view of falling bodies one might say that bodies fall because they seek the centre. Vestiges of this way of talking survive in science. Aristotle developed this view from his interests in biology, where it has some semblance of plausibility. Certainly one can speak of ends as having causal power in the case of human affairs, where a goal can determine the efforts of the person who strives to attain it. In natural science, the teleological notion of final cause has been totally superseded by what Aristotle called the efficient cause.

Teleostei, the largest group of FISH, in class OSTEICHTHYES, the bony fishes. This is the largest group of living vertebrate animals; more than 20,000 species are known. There are 30–40 orders of Teleostei. Some of the important ones are: Elopiformes, the tarpons and bonefish; Anguilliformes, the eels; Clupeiformes, which includes herring and anchovies; Salmoniformes, salmon, trout, whitefish, smelts and pikes; Cypriniformes, carp and some electric eels; Siluriformes, catfish; Gadiformes, cod, hakes; Lophiiformes, anglerfishes; Atheriniformes, flying fishes, swordtail; Perciformes, perch, swordfish, mackerel; Gasterosteiformes, sea horses; Pleuronectiformes, flat-fishes.

Telepathy, name given by F. W. H. MYERS to the transference of knowledge from one mind to another without the use of any normal sensory channel of communication. The reality of this power was proved in the early days of the Society for Psychical Research, but it was generally supposed to be restricted to a few exceptional individuals. The more recent work of Dr J. B. RHINE has shown that it is much more widespread than was at first supposed, and that the paranormal acquisition of knowledge is not restricted to what is in another person's mind, since a fact not known to any other person may also be known without the use of any normal sense channel. Telepathy is thus only one example of a more general paranormal power of obtaining knowledge, often now referred to as EXTRASENSORY PERCEPTION (or the *psi* capacity). Experimental work in extrasensory perception is commonly done by a method of guessing the order of a pack of 25 cards containing five each of five symbols, and performing a statistical analysis of the results to discover whether more have been guessed right than can be accounted for by chance. Explanations of telepathy by unknown radiations acting on an unknown sense organ are now generally rejected. It seems necessary to make a more radical reorientation of the theory of the way in which knowledge is obtained. See also PSYCHICAL RESEARCH.

Bibliography: R. H. Ashby, *The Guidebook for the Study of Psychical Research*, 1973; J. B. Rhine, *New Frontiers of the Mind: The Story of the Duke Experiments*, 1973.

Telephony, system of reproducing sounds at a distance. Credit for the production of the first practical telephone is due to Alexander Graham BELL. In Bell's original electromagnetic telephone, the receiver and transmitter both consisted of an electromagnet with a pivoted armature connected to the centre of a flexible diaphragm. The two instruments were then connected together with a battery in circuit. The current in the electromagnet windings produced a magnetic flux (see INDUCTION, ELECTROMAGNETIC) dependent on the RELUCTANCE of the AIR GAP between the end of the electromagnet and the armature. Sound waves created by speech vibrated the diaphragm, varying the reluctance. The fluctuations in the induced electromotive force (e.m.f.) (see CURRENT ELECTRICITY, *Electromotive Force and Resistance*) resulted in fluctuating current in the circuit, and thus in fluctuating excitation of the receiver electromagnet.

In the modern transmitter (fig. 1) two carbon electrodes, connected to a direct current (d.c.) source, are immersed in a chamber filled with carbon granules. The rear electrode is fixed and the front electrode attached to the centre of a light cone-shaped duralumin diaphragm clamped around its periphery. Vibration of the diaphragm due to speech moves the front electrode, thus varying the resistance of the granules (normally about 60 Ω) and hence the current. Fig. 2a shows the older type of receiver in which varying alternating currents through the coil alternately aid and oppose the magnetic flux of the permanent magnet, thus varying the attraction of the iron diaphragm. The modern 'rocking armature' receiver is shown in fig. 2b. In this a current which increases the flux through the upper limb of the yoke will decrease the flux through the lower limb, thus causing the armature to rotate slightly about its central pivot. This motion is conveyed to a conical diaphragm via the drive pin.

In early telephone systems (fig. 3) local batteries supply current to each transmitter, the transformers preventing the battery current from flowing in the external line. The a.c. components of the fluctuating current in the transformer primary (*P*) induce an alternating e.m.f. into the secondary (*S*) circuit, which includes both receivers and the line. Manual telephone exchanges are becoming

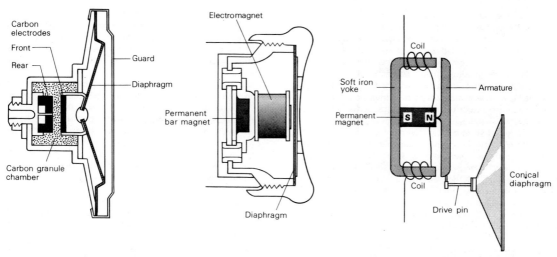

Telephony. ABOVE LEFT Figure 1. Modern inset transmitter. ABOVE CENTRE Figure 2(a). Diaphragm inset receiver. ABOVE RIGHT Figure 2(b). Rocking armature receiver.

increasingly rare and will therefore not be described here.

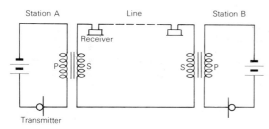

Telephony. Figure 3. Local battery telephone circuit.

Automatic Telephone Exchanges. In automatic working, machine equipment at the exchange completes the call without the aid of an operator. The subscriber controls the exchange equipment by the operation of a dial which is part of the telephone instrument, although a certain number of operators are still required to assist a subscriber in case of difficulty, and for those international calls which cannot be dialled directly. All automatic systems are based on the central battery system, in which a central battery at the exchange supplies current for both speech and signalling, the signalling being automatic. In 1912 the first public automatic exchange in Great Britain was opened at Epsom. This exchange was based on the Strowger step-by-step principle, and this is still the most widely used system.

Step-by-step (Strowger) System. The exchange equipment consists of: (1) line switches, (2) group selectors, and (3) final selectors. The operation is controlled by the subscriber's dial, which interrupts the current from the exchange at regular intervals, depending on the digit dialled. These electrical impulses operate the group and final selectors which seek out the called line and connect the calling line to it. The selector switch used in step-by-

step systems is a two-motion type in that it is actuated first vertically and then horizontally. The switch consists of three main units: (1) relays, (2) contact bank, and (3) switching mechanism, including wipers, shaft, and controlling magnets. Fig. 4 shows a typical telephone relay. The magnetic circuit consists of the coil core, the heelpiece, and the armature, all of which are made of magnetic material. When a current flows in the coil the armature pivots on the knife-edge, and is attracted to the core face. The spring assembly is actuated by the armature and is arranged, by the making or breaking of the contacts, to provide the desired electrical circuit conditions.

The two-motion switch bank consists of two banks (private and line) mounted at the bottom of the mechanism. The top (private) bank consists of 100 contacts arranged in 10 horizontal rows of 10 contacts each, arranged in a semicylindrical form so that a pair of wiper springs on the selector shaft may make connection with any contact in the 100 group. The shaft raises the wipers to the horizontal level and then rotates the wipers over the

Telephony. Figure 4. Modern telephone relay.

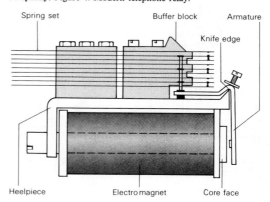

level to the desired contact. The lower (line) bank contains 200 contacts arranged in 10 horizontal levels, each having 10 sets of two contacts each. In some cases the selector has 200, instead of 100, circuits wired to the bank, and there are three banks, one private and two line.

The corresponding bank contacts of a group of Strowger switches are multiplied together to provide the same basic arrangement found in manual multiple switchboards. The subscriber's line is thus accessible from a number of switches.

The basic two-motion switch mechanism consists of an electromagnetic device that is capable of raising, rotating, and releasing a wiper-carrying shaft. The Strowger two-motion selector consists of a central shaft carrying flexible spring wipers at the lower end. These springs make contact with the required bank contact by wiping over the level to which the shaft is raised—hence the name 'wipers'. Two notched ratchets, the vertical and rotary ratchets, are attached to the shaft. Two electromagnets, the vertical and rotary magnets, by attracting their respective armatures, control the motion of the wiper-carrying shaft. When the vertical magnet is impulsed a pawl engages with the vertical ratchet, and the shaft (and wipers) is stepped vertically to the bank level corresponding to the digit dialled. When the rotary magnet is impulsed a pawl engages with the rotary ratchet and the wipers are rotated horizontally over the level to the desired contact. To release the selector the rotary action is continued until the wipers disengage from the bank. In this position the shaft falls, and when clear of the bank it is turned back to its normal position by a spring.

The line-switch mechanism is self-actuated and is independent of dialled impulses. The wipers move round a bank of contacts in one direction only, and for this reason

the switch is called a uniselector. It searches for a subsequent switch wired to its contact bank. This subscriber's uniselector automatically connects the calling line, wired to its wipers, to an idle two-motion selector wired to its bank, when a call is initiated and before the subscriber commences to dial.

Exchange Trunking. A feature of the step-by-step system is the straightforward decimal selection. The number of selector stages required depends on the number of subscribers on the exchange. Fig. 5 shows the trunking of a 100-line exchange. As all the subscribers on the exchange can appear on the bank of a two-motion switch, only one selector stage, the final selector, is required. A number of selectors are multiplied together, the actual number depending on the traffic. The first (tens) dialled digit steps the final selector vertically, and the second (units) digit makes the rotary step to the called line. The capacity of the exchange may be extended by additional switching stages known as group selectors, and fig. 6 shows the trunking of a 1000-line exchange, which is regarded as consisting of ten 100-line groups. Access to a group is obtained by an additional switching stage, and three digits are dialled by the subscriber. The additional stage (first group selector) steps vertically to the first (hundreds) dialled digit, and then hunts automatically over the level to find a free final selector in the particular hundreds groups. The final selector responds vertically to the second (tens) dialled digit and rotary to the (units) digit. If 10 similar arrangements of the group and final selectors shown in fig. 6 are provided, and a rank of first group selectors added so that the first group selectors in fig. 6 now become second group selectors, the capacity of the exchange is 10,000 lines. The size of automatic exchanges is usually limited to 10,000 lines. Extension

Telephony. Figure 5. LEFT Trunking diagram for a 100-line exchange. Figure 6. RIGHT Trunking diagram for a 1000-line exchange.

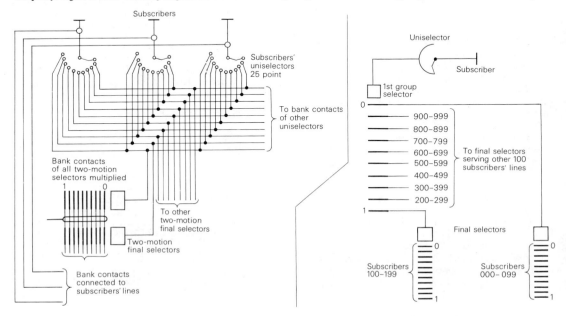

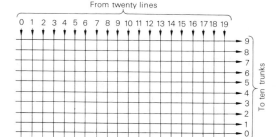

Telephony. Figure 7. Principle of the crossbar switch.

of this selector-switch stage principle permits calls to be routed from exchange to exchange, and the ultimate objective of telephone administrations is to permit any subscriber, national or international, to be called by a system of long-distance dialling.

Basic Working. When the receiver is removed the subscriber's uniselector searches for and connects a first group selector to the calling subscriber's line. A dial tone is now transmitted to the subscriber, informing him that he may now dial. The dialled digits route the call through the several switching stages, and the wipers of the final selector stage are set on contacts to which the called line is connected. If the line is engaged, a 'busy' tone is returned to the calling subscriber. If the line is free, the bell is rung by ringing current applied to the required subscriber's line from the final selector. At the same time a 'ring' tone is transmitted to the calling subscriber to inform him that the required number is being rung. When the call is answered ring and ring tone are ceased, the call is automatically metered against the caller, and a speaking circuit is completed by the exchange equipment. The connection is held under the control of the calling party.

Multi-exchange Areas. In an area where the total number of subscribers does not exceed 10,000, and these are served by a number of exchanges, the traffic can be routed to the various exchanges from the first group selector levels.

Step-by-step System. The director method of working is used for the large cities in Great Britain, in a number of areas in the USA, and in other countries. In such areas 'tandem' working is adopted. Each exchange must be obtained by dialling a fixed code to permit a common director to be used throughout the area. This involves the use of equipment which will automatically change the dialled code digits into other digits appropriate to the particular routings (translation). Each exchange must have a dialling code containing the same number of digits. A subscriber dials a total of seven digits, the first three being the exchange code. Director equipment is provided at each exchange in a director area, and the equipment is used to direct the call to the required exchange. The director receives all the digits dialled by the subscriber, translates the three code digits into 2–6 digits as necessary to route the call to the required exchange, and transmits these digits followed by the four non-translated numerical digits. Director equipment is required only during the setting up of a call; it releases after the numerical digits have been sent and becomes available for other calls.

The Crossbar Automatic Telephone System. The Bell Laboratories developed the crossbar system to supersede the panel system (not described here). The crossbar system makes use of a sender. It consists wholly of relay type crossbar switches and multi-contact relays. Connections between the subscriber's lines are accomplished by the operation, controlled by senders and markers, of the crossbar units.

The system has a sender-marker method of control which permits apparatus, common to all the subscribers, to be used to set up the call to the required subscriber, then released prior to the speech period.

The crossbar switch consists of: (1) typically 20 separate vertical circuit paths; (2) 10 separate horizontal circuit paths; and (3) a mechanical means for connecting any one of the 20 vertical paths to any one of the 10 horizontal paths by the operation of electromagnets.

Fig. 7 shows the schematic arrangement of the switch; 10 simultaneous connections can be established, one on each horizontal path. The number of lines that can be connected to the same 10 trunks may be increased by adding other switches wired to different groups of 20 lines and connecting the horizontal contacts in multiple to other switches. The assembly of switches is called a link frame.

Frequency Division Multiplex. Between exchanges it is usual for many separate conversations to be carried over a single line, and this is usually done by 'carrier working' in which the different conversations are transposed to

Telephony. Figure 8. Three waveforms *A*, *B*, and *C*.

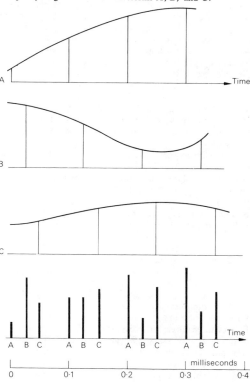

Telephony

different carrier frequencies. Although speech contains a very wide range of frequencies, its intelligibility is not appreciably reduced if the frequency range is only from 300 to 3400 Hz. The speech waveform is used to modulate a carrier wave whose frequency is well above this range, and the carrier and the upper sideband are then suppressed giving single sideband MODULATION. A 64-kHz carrier modulated in this way will give a band of from $(64 - 0.3)$ kHz down to $(64 - 3.4)$ kHz; this speech now occupies a bandwidth of 60.6 to 63.7 kHz. A second speech input when used to modulate a 68-kHz carrier in the same way will give a bandwidth from 64.6 to 67.7 kHz, and a third modulating 72 kHz will give frequencies from 68.6 to 71.7 kHz. In the usual system, the basic 'group' of 12 channels occupy from 60 to 108 kHz, each channel being 4 kHz wide. Five such groups are stacked to give a 'supergroup' of 60 channels occupying a bandwidth of 312 to 552 kHz. Sixteen of the supergroups can be combined to give a total of 960 channels in a band from 60 kHz to 4.028 MHz. This wide band of frequencies is transmitted by a single coaxial cable, and at intervals of about 10 km wideband AMPLIFIERS or 'repeaters' are inserted to compensate for the attenuation of the cable.

At the receiving end the various groups are separated by frequency selective filters, and, with the aid of further filters and demodulators, the whole 960 separate conversations are obtained. Since telephone communication must be two-way, with a 'GO' and a 'RETURN' path, two separate sets of equipment are needed, each with its own modulators, filters, coaxial cable, and amplifiers. Although much of the traffic between major cities is transmitted in this way, the tendency is for the coaxial cable to be replaced by a microwave link, the whole composite wideband signal being used to modulate a carrier wave at a frequency of several thousand megaherz. At these extremely high frequencies, radio waves can be focused by parabolic reflectors into a narrow beam and directed from the transmitter towards the receiving station; so low power operation is sufficient. As it is essential that the transmitting and receiving stations be in a direct 'line-of-sight' path, high towers spaced at roughly 50 to 80 km intervals are constructed to act as intermediate amplifying and relaying stations (see POST OFFICE TOWER).

Time Division Multiplex. In recent years the advent of cheap and reliable TRANSISTORS and INTEGRATED CIRCUITS has lead to this form of transmission of several channels over a single line. In fig. 8, A, B, and C represent three waveforms at the start of the time scale the output is taken from A, and the height of the pulse in the multiplexed waveform is equal to that of A at this instant. About 25 μs later (in fig. 8) the amplitude of B is sampled, and then C. Although only three such waveforms are multiplexed in fig. 8, in practice up to 100 separate waveforms can be 'interleaved' in this way, and sent along a single line. The basic idea of this 'time-division-multiplex' method is illustrated in fig. 9 by a rotating commutator connecting the line distinctive signal for synchronisation. The receiver will then know that the first channel after the reception of this 'sync' signal is channel A, the second B, and so on. This system of transmitting samples of the waveforms showing their amplitudes at the instants of sampling is called 'time division multiplex, pulse amplitude modulation' (TDM,

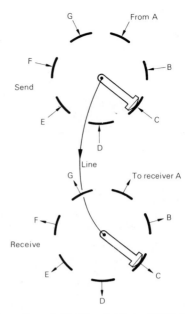

Telephony. Figure 9. The 'time-division-multiplex' method.

PAM), and although it has been used in a few instances, it has been discarded in favour of the more efficient TDM, pulse code modulation (TDM,PCM) system.

Pulse Code Modulation was conceived in 1928 by A. H. Reeves of the Standard Telephone Company. The advantages of this system in giving virtually noise-free communication over a noisy channel were immediately obvious, but the system was completely uneconomic until the advent of cheap and reliable digital circuits. Transistors made PCM possible and integrated circuits have made its use very common. Two fundamental processes are involved, 'sampling' and 'quantisation'. In all pulse modulation methods, the transmitted pulse or pulses represent the 'sampled' signal waveform, and if this signal contains no component above a frequency of F, it is sufficient for the waveform to be sampled at a frequency a little above $2F$. The highest frequency used in telephony for the transmission of speech is 3.4 kHz, and the usual sampling frequency for this is 8 kHz.

Suppose that the sampled pulse can have any value between 0 and 16 V; there is an infinite number of possible levels for the signal amplitude. When a signal is 'quantised', only a finite number of levels are recognised, and the one nearest to that of the sampled signal is chosen. If it were decided that there should be 32 possible levels for the signal, then they could be equally spaced and separated by 0.5 V. A signal at, say, 11.7 V would be quantised to the nearest permissible level, which would be 11.5 V, and since this is the 23rd level, a series of pulses would be sent to indicate 'level number 23'. If a simple binary code were used, then 10111 would be sent. Thus quantisation gives an approximation of the precise voltage, but if a large number of quantisation levels are possible in a system, then the approximation becomes very close. The British Post Office uses 128 levels, which requires a train of seven binary digits to specify a particular level, since $2^7 = 128$.

Unless the noise in the line (or the radio channel) is so severe that a transmitted 1 is received as a 0, or vice versa, no noise will be added by the channel. Provided that at no stage has the signal degenerated so much that 0 and 1 are confused, then a PCM signal can be amplified and relayed again and again by repeater stations without any noise at all being added. There is no need for the levels to be equally spaced in voltage, and a logarithmic scale with a closer spacing at low amplitudes and wider spacing at high amplitudes is preferable. This nonlinear spacing is most easily obtained by 'compressing' the signal before quantisation, and expanding it at the receiver.

PCM, like all pulse communication systems, is very suited to multiplexing on a time-division basis, and it is this feature which has led to its adoption by telephone companies in many countries. A single pair of wires originally intended for a single telephone channel can now carry 24 channels using PCM and time division multiplex. This represents an increase in traffic by a factor of 12. (The original wires carried signals in both directions, but with PCM a separate pair of wires is required for the 'GO' and for the 'RETURN' directions.) A typical system might be of 24 channels, each quantised into 128 levels, and although only seven digits are necessary, an additional digit is often added for synchronising and signalling purposes. The sampling frequency is typically 8 kHz, and so each of the 24 channels must be sampled 8000 times per second, each sample requiring an eight-digit train of pulses. Therefore

$$8000 \times 24 \times 8 = 1,536,000 \text{ pulses}$$

must be sent each second, i.e., the 'bit frequency' will be 1·536 MHz. Typically the pulses are of about 3 V amplitude and their width 0·3 μs. High fidelity speech and music, and even television waveforms, can be transmitted by PCM but for these the sampling rate must be much higher than 8 kHz, and they should be quantised into more levels, and so a far higher 'bit frequency' would be needed.

Bibliography: J. Atkinson, *Telephony: Telephone Exchange Systems of the British Post Office* (vols 1–2), 1968; E. H. Jolley, *Introduction to Telephony and Telegraphy*, 1968; D. Roddy, *Radio and Line Transmission* (vols 1–2), 1968–72; S. F. Smith, *Telephony and Telegraphy: Introduction to Telephone and Telegraph Instruments and Exchanges*, 1969; K. W. Cattermole, *Principles of Pulse Code Modulation*, 1970.

Teleprinters, see TELEGRAPHY.

Telescope, an optical instrument for examining distant objects. A Dutchman, Jan Lippershey, is usually given the credit for constructing the first telescope in 1608. Hearing of the invention in 1609, Galileo quickly constructed one for himself and went on to produce a succession of such instruments which he used from 1610 onwards for astronomical observations. His telescope consisted of a weak convex lens, focal length F, as objective and a stronger concave lens, focal length f, as eye-piece (fig. 1). The length of the instrument was $F - f$, objects appeared the right way up, and the magnification, i.e., the ratio of the angle subtended by the distant object when viewed through the instrument to the angle when viewed with the naked eye, was F/f. Galileo's arrangement has the merits of simplicity and compactness but the disadvantage of a small field of view if large magnifications are used. It is

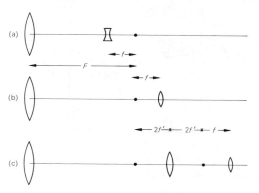

Telescope. Figure 1. Some basic forms of refractor. (a) Galilean (b) Keplerian or astronomical; (c) terrestrial with erecting lens used at unit magnification. Focal lengths: objective, F; eye-piece, f; erecting lens, f.

an ideal arrangement for opera glasses for which the magnification is usually only $2 \times$ or $3 \times$.

Another simple telescopic system, sometimes attributed to Kepler, is that in which Galileo's concave eye-piece is replaced by a convex one of focal length f. The magnification is still F/f, but the object appears upside-down and the length of the instrument is $F + f$. On the other hand the field of view is larger and a reticule or cross wires can be fitted at the common focus of the eye-piece and objective making the telescope a very useful measuring or pointing device. This is the usual form of the astronomical refractor and of many of the reading telescopes used in laboratories. For normal terrestrial applications an extra lens, the 'erector', can be inserted in front of the eye-piece to make the object appear the right way up. Alternatively the field can be reversed by two crossed reflections either by a suitably designed roof prism just in front of the eye-piece or by the Porro system of crossed right-angle prisms. This latter arrangement, which is used in prismatic binoculars, enables the optical system to be folded on itself and thus gives a very compact instrument. In practice the objective usually consists of a crown-glass convex lens cemented to a weaker concave lens of flint glass, the combination being so calculated that the lens as a whole is achromatic. Less frequently the eye lens and the erector lens (if any) are similarly treated, but this is

Telescope. Figure 2. Simple eye-pieces: (a) Huygenian; (b) Ramsden. F, focal point of objective; E, position of exit pupil or Ramsden disk.

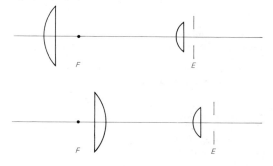

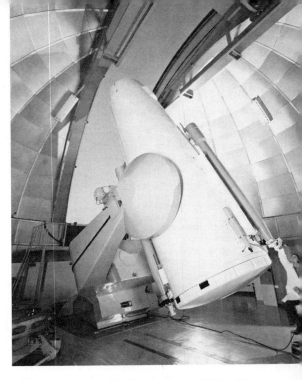

Telescope. ABOVE LEFT The 40-inch refractor of Yerkes Observatory, USA. ABOVE The 48-inch Schmidt telescope at Siding Spring, Australia. LEFT Royal Greenwich Observatory, Herstmonceux Castle. (*ABOVE LEFT Yerkes Observatory;* ABOVE *Royal Observatory, Edinburgh;* LEFT *Royal Greenwich Observatory*)

not so necessary since it is possible to replace these single lenses by pairs of lenses so positioned that the combination gives a wider and clearer field of view that is effectively achromatic. The two simplest combinations in common use as eye-pieces are the Huygens and Ramsden (fig. 2). The Huygens, which is used when no cross wires are required, consists of two plano-convex, or nearly plano-convex, lenses with the ratio of their focal lengths varying from 3:1 to 1·5:1 according to the type of correction required and separated by a distance equal to one-half of the sum of their focal lengths, the lenses having their curved sides facing the objective.

In measuring instruments the more usual form of eye-piece is the Ramsden consisting of two equal plano-convex lenses placed with their curved sides facing each other and separated by approximately two-thirds of their common focal length. The back lens of a compound eye-piece is usually known as the eye lens and the front one as the field lens since its size determines that of the field of view.

All the light that enters the telescope objective must pass through the image of the objective formed by the eye-piece system. In a Galilean instrument this is a virtual image inside the telescope; in a Keplerian or 'astronomical' telescope the image is usually just outside the eye-piece and can be seen as a bright circle of light on a piece of paper held near the eye-piece when the telescope is pointed to the sky. This image is known as the Ramsden disk and marks the place where the eye should be placed if the telescope is to be used most efficiently. The size of the disk is Df/F or D/M, where D is the diameter of the

objective and M the effective magnification of the telescope. If all the light entering the telescope is to reach the observer's eye, the Ramsden disk must not be larger than the pupil of his eye, while if it is smaller the surface brightness of an object seen through the telescope will be less than when it is viewed directly. If the average size of the pupil of the eye be taken as 5 mm (it varies from about 2 to 8 mm according to the brightness of illumination), a telescope giving a magnification of 20 diameters should have an objective of at least $5 \times 20 = 100$ mm diameter if the view it gives is not to be unduly faint.

Similar considerations apply to astronomical telescopes when these are used, as is now rather unusual, for direct visual observation. As stars are virtually self luminous points their brightness as viewed through a telescope depends only on the size of the objective since magnification cannot alter their apparent size or brightness. In practice the degree of magnification that can be used is limited by the seeing or, if that is very good, by the resolving power of the objective. Because of the wave nature of light the image of a bright point such as a star formed by an optically perfect circular objective is a small central disk of light surrounded by alternate dark and bright diffraction rings. The larger the objective the smaller the angular radii of the central disk and of the rings surrounding it. Two points can just be recognised as separate if the central bright disk of the image of the first lies on the first dark ring of the image of the second. This is the case if the angle subtended by the two points is $1\cdot22\lambda/D$ radians or 206,265 times this if the angle is expressed in seconds of arc, λ being the wavelength of the light in question and D the diameter of the objective, both measured in the same unit of length. Thus for an optical telescope, the resolving power is approximately $11 \cdot 3/D$ seconds of arc, D being expressed in centimetres. As the limit of resolution of the normal eye is about one minute of arc, a magnification of $60/(11 \cdot 3/D)$, i.e., approximately $5 \cdot 3D$, is required to get the maximum resolution from an objective. The empirical rule for astronomers using small telescopes is never to use a power of more than $20D$ and that only in the very finest conditions. The seeing disk at even the very best ground-based sites is rarely as small as a quarter of a second of arc and is more usually of the order of one or two seconds. Thus, as far as resolution is concerned, there is little reason to increase the aperture of the telescope beyond 45 cm and the magnification much beyond 250 diameters, or, at the very most, 1000 diameters.

However nowadays astronomers rarely use telescopes for direct visual observations. For them a telescope is either a convenient method of collecting light from a celestial source to feed into some subsidiary apparatus such as a spectrograph, or it is a very large camera. In the former case only a sharp, highly concentrated image on the axis is required, but in the latter case as large a field as possible in good definition is required.

A mirror with a parabolic surface makes an ideal flux

Telescope. Figure 3. Some common arrangements of the parabolic reflector: (a) prime focus; (b) Newtonian; (c) Cassegrain; (d) coudé. F is position of effective focus.

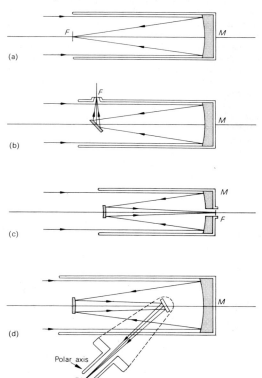

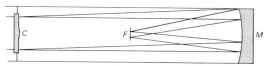

Telescope. Figure 4. Schmidt camera. M is a spherical concave mirror with its centre of curvature at C, the middle of the aspherical corrector plate. The focal surface F is spherical, concentric with the surface of the mirror and of half its radius.

collector since all rays parallel to its axis are reflected back through its focus where the light receiver can be mounted. If this is not convenient, or if a longer effective focal length is required, subsidiary mirrors can be introduced to deflect the light where it is wanted. Some of the more usual of these arrangements are shown in fig. 3; not shown, because it is now rarely used, is that in which the secondary is a concave mirror placed beyond the prime focus. This was the scheme proposed by James Gregory in 1663, some five years before Newton made his first telescope.

Unfortunately the field of good definition of a parabolic mirror is comparatively small, especially if its focal ratio, i.e., the ratio of its focal length to its diameter, is small. This is usually the case for the primary mirror since its focal length is made as small as is practicable to keep down the size and cost of the mechanical mounting. The field at the prime focus can be improved by inserting a specially designed lens system but the improvement is obtained at some expense to the on-axis images and the sacrifice of the achromatic properties of an all-reflecting system. When it is desired to take photographs with an instrument having a small focal ratio it is better to use a Schmidt camera, the principle of which is shown in fig. 4.

Basically what SCHMIDT pointed out was that a spherical mirror, unlike a paraboloid, has no particular axis and is thus automatically free from many of the aberrations that plague the conventional reflector. It does, however, suffer from spherical aberration, but he demonstrated that this could be corrected by a properly shaped correcting plate placed at the centre of curvature. In fig. 4 the thickness and curvatures of the correcting plate are greatly exaggerated to show its form more clearly. In practice its surface contours are barely detectable but as it acts by refraction it only functions perfectly for one chosen colour. The fall off in performance for other colours is not usually serious, but separate correcting plates should be used if observations are required in widely different wavelengths. Schmidt-type cameras have been built in many different forms and sizes and for widely varying purposes. One of the more useful variations, which has also been adapted for visual telescopes, is shown in fig. 5. This was devised independently by a Russian and a Dutchman and arose from their realisation that it was possible to correct the spherical aberration of the main mirror by using a negative meniscus lens. By suitably choosing the curvatures of the surfaces of this lens, the combination can be made free from both spherical and chromatic aberrations. Moreover the tube length required is considerably shorter than that of the equivalent Schmidt.

Another optical system which is becoming increasingly popular for general-purpose telescopes is the Ritchey-Chrétien which has a hyperbolic primary mirror and an ellipsoidal secondary used in a Cassegrain configuration.

Telescopium

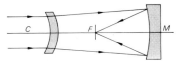

Telescope. Figure 5. Maksutov-Bowers camera. It resembles the Schmidt camera but a meniscus lens replaces the nearly flat corrector plate and gives a more compact system.

If the focal ratio is not smaller than 6 it gives a moderately-sized field in good definition without the use of refracting materials.

See ASTRONOMY; HALE OBSERVATORIES; OBSERVATORY; RADIO ASTRONOMY.

Bibliography: H. C. King, *The History of the Telescope*, 1955; G. R. Miczaika and W. M. Sinton, *Tools of the Astronomer*, 1961; N. E. Howard, *Handbook for Telescope Making*, 1962.

Telescopium, 'the Telescope', an inconspicuous southern CONSTELLATION.

Television is the transmission and visible reproduction of pictures or scenes by line or RADIOCOMMUNICATION.

History. The earliest practical demonstration of television was given by J. L. BAIRD before the Royal Institution in 1926. In 1928 the British Broadcasting Corporation (BBC) experimented with the transmission of still pictures, using the 'fultograph', and in the same year Baird transmitted a low-definition picture by radio to the USA. In 1929 Baird commenced an experimental low-definition service from the Crystal Palace, and in August 1932 the BBC conducted tests in conjunction with the Baird Company, using a 30-line system radiated from the Brookman's Park station. The Postmaster-General appointed a Television Advisory Committee in 1934 to determine which system should be followed for a public service. They recommended the abandoning of low-definition television and accordingly, in September 1935, the BBC transmissions ceased. The first high-definition television service in the world began in November 1936 with the opening of the BBC's station at Alexandra Palace. See BRITISH BROADCASTING CORPORATION (BBC); INDEPENDENT BROADCASTING AUTHORITY.

Scanning. The subject matter to be 'televised' is scanned electrically, the resulting signals being transmitted for subsequent reconstitution at the receiver into an image. The scanning process takes place: (1) at the TRANSMITTER, where the image is broken down, and (2) at the receiver, where the cycle follows that at the transmitter and is synchronised with it by means of synchronising signals transmitted with the picture. Fig. 1 shows the stages between transmission and reception.

Scanning for Transmission. The scene to be transmitted is focused by a lens system on the flat 'target plate' of the camera tube, which in the modern 'videcon' is made of photoconductive material. The resistance of this is high, but in the illuminated areas it falls to a low value. An electron beam (similar to that in the CATHODE-RAY TUBE of a television receiver) is deflected by TIME BASES so that it scans the whole surface of the plate. The complicated action may be summarised by saying that the current flowing to the target depends on the resistance of the small area of the target being scanned at that time, and therefore on the level of the light on that part of the target. In this way the output from the camera tube is an electrically varying current which represents, line by line, and frame by frame, the make-up of light and shade in the picture.

Scanning at the Receiver. This is carried out by the moving electron beam in the cathode-ray tube, which is deflected in synchronism with that in the camera tube. Two time bases are used, a horizontal ('line time base') and one causing vertical deflection ('the frame time base'). These operate in the same manner as those in an OSCILLOSCOPE. In the British television system 625 lines are transmitted in 0·04 s, thus the line frequency is 15·625 kHz. (For the obsolescent 405-line system the line frequency is 10·125 kHz.) While these lines are being transmitted the frame time base applies its deflecting voltage at right angles to the horizontal lines drawn on the tube by the line time base. The frequency of the frame time base is 50 Hz, so that during one complete oscillation the line time base completes only 312½ lines. At the centre of the 313th line the downward motion of the beam ceases and the frame time base cycle starts again, so that a further 312½ lines are completed, but interlaced with the first 312½. This gives a completed picture of 625 lines in 0·04 s (fig. 2). The full frame is made up of two interlaced halves. This reduces the flicker of the repeating frames. The completed rectangle so reproduced on the face of the cathode-ray tube is called the raster.

The BBC Television Waveform. Both line and frame synchronising signals are essential to ensure that the receiver time bases are in step with those of the camera tube. The actual picture signal accompanying these must be capable of transmitting all the details of light and shade present in the camera, and frequencies up to 5·5 MHz must be transmitted to give good definition in the horizontal and vertical directions. Negative MODULATION is used such that peak 'white' in the picture is represented by 30 per cent modulation of the carrier, 'black' by 76 per cent, with the intermediate shades in between. From 76 to 100 per cent modulation is used for transmitting the synchronising signals (often called synch pulses) which do not appear on the raster. At the receiver the line and the frame time bases must keep in time with those in the camera, and for this purpose line and frame synchronising pulses are sent from the transmitter at the correct instants. At the receiver these are separated and used to trigger the appropriate time base.

Television. Figure 2.

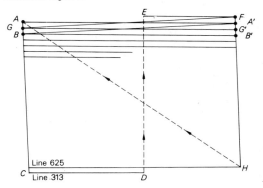

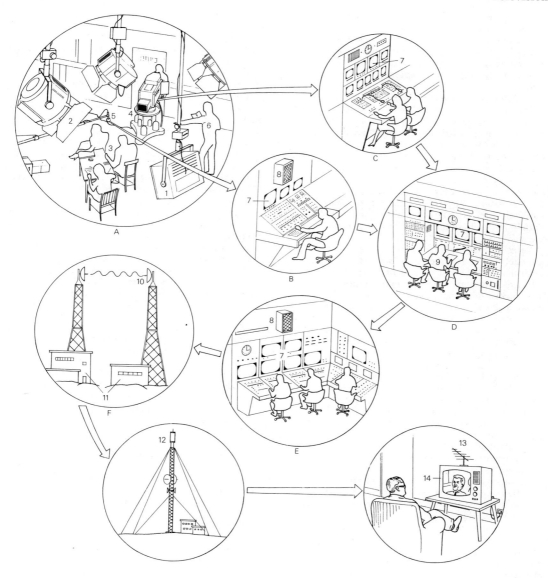

A Studio
B Sound control room
C Lighting and vision control room
D Production control room
E Central control room
F National network

1 2-kw lighting
2 Spotlight
3 Performers
4 Camera on hydraulic pedestal
5 Microphone

6 Studio director
7 Bank of monitor screens
8 Loudspeaker
9 Producer directing cameras and choosing picture to be transmitted

10 Directional aerial
11 Microwave relay station
12 Transmitting aerial
13 Receiving aerial
14 Television

Television. Figure 1.

Film Scanners. Increasing use of cinematograph film is being made in compiling television programmes. Modern film scanners have been developed especially for television transmission in which the film moves through the 'gate' at a constant speed, and scanning is accomplished by means of a 'flying spot' scanner. The latter, in its

Television

simplest form, produces a raster on the screen of a special cathode-ray tube operated to give a very bright image. Nothing except the lines of the raster appear on the tube screen, but these are focused on the film in the gate behind which a photocell picks up the light passing through the film as the flying spot on the scanning tube builds up the raster.

Reception. Receiving Aerials. Because the wavelength of any television station is short a resonant AERIAL becomes possible, and this usually consists of a half-wave aerial made of light alloy or steel tube, and fed at the centre with low-impedance coaxial or balanced cable. Greater gain is obtained if a reflector element is added, and quite complicated arrays are used in areas of weak signal strength (see BEAM RADIO). These aerials are mounted either vertically or horizontally to conform with the polarisation of the transmitting aerials. Tubing is used for the elements, since an aerial made of wire would be too sharply resonant, with resulting loss of bandwidth, and therefore poor picture definition.

Receivers. Receivers used for broadcast reception are invariably of the 'superhet' type (see RECEIVER, RADIO). Their main characteristics are that they should have sufficient sensitivity; the bandwidth accepted should be wide enough to reproduce all the picture detail; the time bases should lock easily and not respond to impulsive interference; both vision and sound channels should also discriminate against such interference; and, finally, the picture should be sharply focused and bright, with correct grading of half-tones.

In a superhet receiver the first stage is a tuned radio frequency (RF) amplifier accepting both sound and vision channels. This is followed by a frequency changer stage which converts the RF into the intermediate frequency (IF). Then follow stages of IF amplification. The vision (or 'video') signal is detected, amplified, and passed to the electrode of the cathode-ray tube which controls the intensity of the beam, and hence the light and shade of the picture. At the same time, the process of 'synch separation' is performed. The synch separator removes the synchronising signals from the video signal existing after detection discriminating between line and frame signals, and passing them to their respective time bases. In addition to the normal voltages common to other valves in the receiver, a source of 'extra high tension' is necessary, which may be up to 25 kV in a colour receiver. Some receivers employ 'line flyback' making use of the fact that, on the horizontal return stroke of the beam, a very rapid change of current takes place in the winding of the line transformer which, possessing appreciable inductance,

opposes this change so that a high-voltage pulse appears across it. This pulse can be rectified, voltage doubled or trebled, smoothed and used for the final anode of the cathode-ray tube. Another system employs a separate RF oscillator having a sinusoidal waveform, which after amplification is passed through a peak rectifier, and thus the necessary extra high tension is obtained.

Colour Television. J. L. Baird was an early pioneer in this direction, and one of the first techniques developed employed a system whereby the normal frame frequency was increased by a factor of 3, each successive frame containing the material for one primary colour. The receiver used revolving colour disks in front of the viewing screen, synchronised with the correct frame colours at the camera. A similar system replaced the colour disks by three superimposed projected pictures corresponding to the three primary colours.

A colour television system must be compatible, that is, it must give a good picture on a black and white television receiver. The Radio Corporation of America produced such a system in 1949, and this method was adopted by the US National Television Systems Committee (NTSC). Colour television using this NTSC system started in the USA in 1953, and this system is now used throughout the American continents and in Japan. In Europe there are two different systems, SECAM (sequential colour with memory), developed in France, and used there, in the USSR, Eastern Europe, and North Africa; and PAL (phase alternate line) developed by the Telefunken company at their Hanover laboratories, and used in many European countries, including the German Federal Republic and the UK. Both SECAM and PAL are fundamentally the NTSC system, but each incorporates its own method for keeping the colour rendering at the receiver constant: under unfavourable reception conditions this is liable to vary.

Principles of Colour Television. Light of any colour, including white, can be made from red, green, and blue light, added together in the correct proportions. (This is different from the 'subtractive' mixing of paints, where the primary colours are red, yellow, and blue.) Behind the lens in a colour television camera there is an assembly of prisms or mirrors which splits the light into three paths as shown in fig. 3. Each path leads to a camera tube similar to that used in black and white television, but in front of each tube there is a coloured glass filter, so that one tube receives only red light, a second tube only green light, and the third blue light. The outputs from the three camera tubes go to an 'encoding unit' from which the 'luminance' (brightness) and the 'chrominance' (colour

Television. Figure 3.

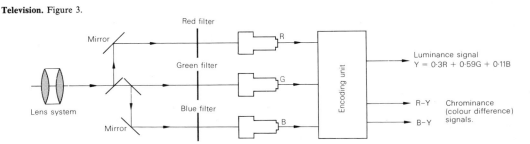

Red filter — Mirror — R — Encoding unit — Luminance signal $Y = 0.3R + 0.59G + 0.11B$

Green filter — G

Lens system — Blue filter — B — R−Y / B−Y Chrominance (colour difference) signals.

Mirror

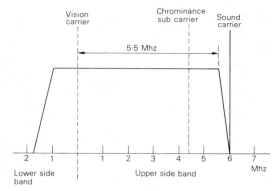

Vision carrier | Chrominance sub carrier | Sound carrier

5·5 Mhz

Lower side band

Upper side band

Mhz

Television. Figure 4.

or hue) signals are obtained. The luminance signal, usually denoted by Y, is made from the tube outputs thus:

$$Y = 0\cdot3R + 0\cdot59G + 0\cdot11B,$$

where R, G, and B are the outputs from the red, green, and blue tubes. This signal is used to modulate the vision carrier as in black and white television; the numbers in the above expression were chosen to give an acceptable variation of grey tones when a scene is viewed in black and white. The chrominance information is conveyed by only two signals $(R - Y)$ and $(B - Y)$, since Y includes information about the green light G. These two chrominance signals modulate a sine wave whose frequency in British television is 4·43361875 MHz: this is called the 'colour sub-carrier'. (In order that two separate signals can modulate one carrier, double sideband suppressed carrier modulation is used, the two signals being in phase quadrature.) The vision signals are transmitted as asymmetrical sideband modulation in which frequencies greater than 1 MHz are attenuated in the lower sideband: sound is transmitted by frequency modulating a carrier 6 MHz above the vision carrier. The whole spectrum is shown in fig. 4, and occupies a bandwidth of 8 MHz.

The cathode-ray tube in a colour receiver has three separate electron guns, and its screen is composed of over a million dots, one-third of which emit red, one-third green, and one-third blue light when struck by an electron beam. Between the three guns and the screen is a 'shadow mask' made from a metal sheet containing a very large number of tiny holes precisely positioned so that the electron beam from a particular gun strikes the dots of one colour only (fig. 5). Since the dot structure of the screen is too fine to be discerned by the unaided eye, simultaneous emissions of electrons from the 'red' and 'green' guns will give the screen a yellow appearance, and any colour including white can by synthesised by controlling the relative strengths of the three electron beams.

In black and white receivers the brightness of the spot is varied as it travels along the line by changing the cathode potential of the electron gun: in colour television, separate signals are needed for the three guns, and this extra information on the colour is obtained by demodulating the chrominance signal. To do this it is essential that the receiver produces an oscillation of exactly the

4·43361875 MHz of the chrominance sub-carrier. This accuracy is achieved by the television transmitter sending out a short 'colour burst' of 10 cycles of this chrominance sub-carrier frequency just before the start of each line. This enables the receiver oscillator to 'lock on' to this frequency, and so in effect its frequency is corrected 15,625 times each second. Errors in the phase of this reconstructed sine wave and in that of the received chrominance signals will cause incorrect colour rendering, and it was to minimise these phase problems that SECAM and PAL were devised. In the PAL system the phase of the colour signals is reversed in alternate lines, and this has the effect of cancelling out most of the phase errors, leading to a more consistently accurate colour rendering.

See also BROADCASTING, *Recent Technical Developments*; SATELLITE COMMUNICATIONS.

Bibliography: P. S. Carnt and G. B. Townsend, *Colour Television* (vols 1–2), 1969; G. J. King, *Beginner's Guide to Colour Television*, 2nd ed. 1973.

Telford, Thomas (1757–1834), British civil engineer, born at Westerkirk, Dumfriesshire, son of an Eskdale shepherd, and apprenticed to a local stone-mason when 14 years old. He went to Edinburgh in 1780, and to London and Portsmouth in 1784. Telford built the Severn bridges at Montford and Buildwas, 1793–96; the Ellesmere Canal, 1796–1801; the Caledonian Canal, 1801–23; and in the same period over 1600 km of road and 120 bridges throughout Scotland. His greatest achievement was the improvement of the London–Holyhead road (A5) with the building of the Menai suspension bridge. He also did much harbour work in Scotland; he built St Katherine Dock, London; the Gotha Canal, Sweden; and designed the Warsaw frontier road for Tsar Alexander. A man of talent, wholly self-educated, Telford often gave his services gratuitously. He was one of the founders of the Institution of Civil Engineers (1818), and was its first president. He is buried in Westminster Abbey. His autobiography was published in 1838.

Telford New Town, in SALOP, England, 15 km west of

Television. Figure 5.

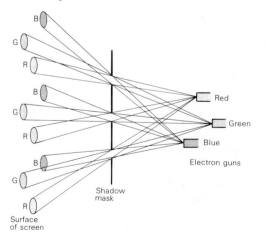

Red

Green

Blue

Electron guns

Shadow mask

Surface of screen

Tell, William

the Wolverhampton–Birmingham urban complex, which the New Town is intended to relieve, drawing off population and industry. Telford was originally (1963) Dawley New Town, but was extended and renamed in 1968. It is expected to reach a population of 250,000 by the year 2001.

Tell, William, romantic national hero of Switzerland. Although the form in which his story first appears, in a Swiss chronicle written between 1467 and 1476, is legendary, it is suggested by several Swiss authorities that Tell really did live, and that his history has been obscured by romantic tales and folklore. His part in the uprising of the Forest Cantons against the oppression of the Austrian Hapsburgs seems to have been much exaggerated.

The main source of the life and deeds of William Tell is the *Chronicon Helveticum* of Aegidus Tschudi (1505–72), which contains further embellishments. The story of William Tell and the apple has been popularised in the masterpiece by the German playwright, Friedrich Schiller, which was published in 1804. It is a patriotic play, reminding people of resistance to foreign oppressors in past times. The story centres on the struggle for independence of the cantons of Uri, Schwyz, and Unterwalden, and is as follows: Tell, having refused to do homage to the ducal hat which Gessler, the Austrian governor, set up for the purpose in the market-place of Altdorf, was taken prisoner, and on being brought before the landgrave was promised his liberty if he could shoot an apple in two, placed on his son's head, at the distance of 80 paces. He accomplished the task, but confessed on compulsion that the other arrow in his hand was meant for Gessler's heart had he killed his son, whereupon he was again seized and taken on the lake, bound for Küsnacht Castle. But a storm having arisen, Tell was asked to steer the ship, and while doing so effected his escape. He sprang ashore, pushing the boat back from the shore by his spring, an incident which has given its name to a place, the Tellsprung. He afterwards killed the landgrave, and his actions became symbolic of the courage of the Inner Cantons in their struggle against the Hapsburgs.
Bibliography: J. C. F. von Schiller (trans. J. Prudhoe), *Wilhelm Tell*, 1970.

Tell el-Amarna, modern name of ancient site on the east bank of the Nile about 290 km south of Cairo. The ruins are those of Akhetaton, the capital of Akhnaton, who built it c. 1375 BC to replace Thebes when he abandoned the worship of Amun for Aton. After his death the city was abandoned and has since been uninhabited. In 1887 peasants found there about 400 clay tablets, consisting of letters mostly in cuneiform from Asiatic potentates and Egyptian vassals in Palestine and Syria to Akhnaton and his father, which are of great historical importance. Most are now in Berlin and the British and Cairo Museums. Excavations by PETRIE disclosed inlaid coloured pavements and important evidence for the early manufacture of glass. In the hills east of the city were cut tombs for Akhnaton's courtiers, containing scenes typical of the art of the period, and hymns to the Aton. Later excavations have uncovered palaces, villas and a huge Aton temple.

Tell-el-Kebir, see TALL AL-KABIR.

Teller, Edward (1908–), Hungarian-US physicist, born in Budapest; educated at the Karlsruhe Institute of Tech-

William Tell shooting the apple from his son's head. From a woodcut in Henry Petri's edition of Munster's *Cosmography*, published in 1554. *(Mansell Collection)*

nology and the universities of Leipzig and Munich. He did research at the universities of Leipzig and Göttingen but left Germany in 1933 when the Nazis came to power. He lectured at the University of London for a year and then became professor of physics at George Washington University, Washington, DC, until 1941 when he became professor at Columbia University. In 1942 he began his long association with nuclear weapons. He supported the development of the hydrogen bomb and was assistant director of the Los Alamos Scientific Laboratory from 1949 to 1952. Teller is known as the 'father of the H-bomb'. From 1946 to 1952 he was also professor at the University of Chicago. Since 1953 he has been a professor at the University of California and since 1954 has been director of the university's Lawrence Radiation Laboratory.

His publications include *Our Nuclear Future*, 1958; *The Legacy of Hiroshima* (with A. Brown), 1962; *The Reluctant Revolutionary*, 1964; *Constructive Uses of Nuclear Explosives*, 1968; and *Great Men of Physics*, 1969.

Tellers of the Exchequer, see TALLY.

Téllez, Gabriel, see TIRSO DE MOLINA.

Tellurium, chemical element, symbol Te, atomic number 52, atomic weight 127·6; it occurs in the free state in nature, but is chiefly obtained in combination with other elements, as in tellurite (TeO_2) and tetradymite (Bi_2Te_3). With SELENIUM, it is found in the 'anode mud' resulting from electrolytic copper refining, from which it is isolated by reduction with coke. This is the principal source of tellurium. It is a bluish-white solid with a metallic lustre (melting point 452 °C; relative density 6·26), and burns in air to form a dioxide, TeO_2. Although unaffected by non-oxidising acids, such as hydrochloric acid, it is oxidised by nitric and sulphuric acids. It forms tellurides with hydrogen and the metals, corresponding to the sulphides. Two oxides, the dioxide and trioxide, are known, which give rise respectively to the two acids, tellurous acid and telluric acid. The salts of tellurium, known as tellurates, resemble selenium salts (sellenates) in chemical behaviour, but, unlike them, they are not isomorphous (i.e., of the same crystalline form) with the sulphates, nor do they form double salts, or ALUMS.

Telpher, see MONORAIL.

Telugu, a Dravidian language, the official language and script of the state of Andhra Pradesh, India. It is the mother tongue of nearly 38,000,000 people (1961). Telugu literature is attested since the 11th century. See also INDIA, *Language*.

Tembuland, region in the TRANSKEI, Cape Province, South Africa, situated near the coast to the south-west of Griqualand East. UMTATA is the capital. The main inhabitants are the Tembu, one of the Cape NGUNI peoples. Area 8786 km².

Temenos (Greek from *temnein*, to cut), in Greek architecture, a sacred enclosure often surrounding a temple.

Temesvár, see TIMIŞOARA.

Temirtau, town in Karaganda *oblast*, KAZAKH SSR, USSR, 30 km north-west of KARAGANDA. It has iron and steel and chemical (synthetic rubber) industries. The Karaganda metallurgical complex, one of the largest in the USSR, was formed here in 1970 on the site of the former Karaganda metallurgical plant (on-stream 1960). Population (1974) 192,000.

Tempe, valley of northern Thessaly, famous for its beautiful scenery, to which there are many references in ancient literature. It was the traditional scene of APOLLO's purification after the killing of PYTHON, and of DAPHNE's metamorphosis.

Tempera, painting medium consisting of: (1) Pure *Egg-Tempera*, where well-ground inorganic pigments mixed on a white palette with egg-yolk and water are applied to a slightly absorbent gesso panel. (The yellow of egg-yolk bleaches out, whereas white of egg may turn brown.) In early Italian painting, the initial lay-in of a design was often done with *terra-verde*, hence the term *verdaccio*. Colours are first applied in a mixture with flake or zinc white, and then strengthened and modelled with glazes or hatches of pure transparent colour. (2) *Tempera-emulsion* uses for its medium a well-fused mixture of egg-yolk and stand-oil, which permits of dilution with water. It dries hard sooner and, being more flexible, can be used on canvas prepared with a water-ground, i.e. with size and gesso. The early Italian procedure is delightfully described by a pupil of Giotto, Cennino CENNINI.

A variant of egg-tempera is *casein*, where the medium is fresh white curd and a little slaked lime, diluted with water.

See also PAINTING TECHNIQUES.

Temperament, in music, is connected with the intonation of the notes in a scale, on the one hand, and the tuning of instruments, on the other. In vocal, and to a great extent in instrumental, music the intervals of a scale are flexible, even if we disregard the ever-present danger of singing and playing out of tune. A singer or string player with a keen ear, especially if unaccompanied by a tempered instrument, such as the piano, will instinctively or consciously make a slight difference between A flat and G sharp, which on the piano or the organ are played by one and the same mechanism. The tuning of keyboard instruments had thus always to be slightly adjusted, and until equal temperament came into universal use for the tuning, some notes, and therefore some keys, were more noticeably out of tune than others. Thus B flat on a harpsichord was purer than A sharp, and F sharp purer than G flat, with the result that the extreme sharp and flat keys were considerably out of tune and therefore rarely used. Equal temperament, on the other hand, adjusted all the intervals so that there was exactly the same difference in the ratio of vibrations between all of them, with the result that the black-key notes remained the same whether sharp or flat, at the cost of very slightly distorting many of the intervals within the scale. Bach, by writing 48 preludes and fugues in all the major and minor keys in his *Well-tempered Clavier*, proved that the distortion is too small to disturb even a musician with so fine an ear as his and that keyboard instruments could henceforth be regarded as capable of dealing satisfactorily enough with any key. The revolution of equal temperament has had a subtle but all-pervasive effect on European musical history ever since; it would be true to say that the pace of technical and stylistic development has since been dictated by instrumental and orchestral forms, and not, as previously, by vocal or choral ones.

Temperance Movement, a series of campaigns that have tried to persuade people to reduce or to abstain from the intake of alcoholic beverages. Social, educational and legislative means have been employed, and women have been very active in the movement. It has also been closely connected with the Christian churches. The temperance movement started in the USA early in the 19th century. The Ulster Temperance Society was founded in 1829, the Church of England Temperance Society in 1862, and others were started around this time in several European countries. The International Prohibition Federation was founded at a conference in London in 1909.

Legislation has included PROHIBITION of the buying or selling of intoxicating liquors for a time in the USA, Canada, and a few other countries; state ownership of shops for the sale of alcoholic beverages; rationing; and various licensing laws that regulate who may sell alcoholic beverages and during what hours. Many countries now have laws making it illegal to drive a car after drinking (see MOTOR LAW).

Alcoholics Anonymous has been among the most active social and educational organisations in the campaign against ALCOHOLISM.

Temperature (meteorology). A fundamental element in the study of weather and climate is the measurement and forecast of temperature at the ground surface and of the air at all levels of the ATMOSPHERE. The source of heat is the SUN, and temperature is modified by solar radiation (or insolation), of which about 45 per cent reaches the earth's surface; this heat is released back into the atmosphere by terrestrial radiation, the most important aspect for meteorology. Heat is also transferred between the earth and the air, and within the atmosphere (see AIR MASS) by conduction and convection.

Upper Air Temperature. Overall, temperature decreases with height; this decrease is the lapse rate and is measured in °C/km. It is, however, quite possible for layers of the atmosphere to have a constant temperature in spite of height increase (called an isothermal layer), or

Temperature

for the temperature to rise absolutely (called a temperature inversion). Isothermal layers have negative rates and inversion layers negative lapse rates. Within the troposphere, where almost all weather processes take place, there is a positive lapse rate (see CLOUD; PRECIPITATION; WIND). There are in the upper atmosphere (above the tropopause) two layers, the ionosphere and the ozonosphere, warmed by absorption of the sun's ultraviolet radiation.

Lower Air Temperature. The amount of insolation that reaches the surface is governed by cloud cover (which allows only limited insolation to pass through but re-radiates terrestrial radiation) and latitude (high latitudes in all SEASONS and mid-latitudes for six months of the year receive only indirect insolation). The amount of heat absorbed by the earth, and therefore the amount given out from it, varies according to the surface material: land gains and loses heat more rapidly than water. Temperature changes over any 24-hour period (diurnal variation) when the surface is first absorbing heat and then emitting it, are of great consequence in meteorology. For example, coastal areas experience a complete reversal of their daytime wind pattern because of the heat transmission differential of the land and the neighbouring water surface (see WIND); also, cloudless skies at night allow a greater amount of terrestrial radiation to be lost into the atmosphere than if there were cloud cover, often resulting in FROST. Temperature changes may also be effected by the replacement of air which has been subject to one set of conditions in its development by another quite different air mass.

Temperature Measurement. See METEOROLOGY.

Temperature. The temperature of the body varies with the different forms of life. In man it lies between 36·9 ° and 37·4 °C in a state of health, varying slightly with the time of day, exercise, ingestion of food, and the temperature of the surrounding atmosphere. The temperatures of cold-blooded animals have a wider range and are much lower than in the warm-blooded ones. Thus the temperature of the frog may vary from 17·2 ° to 8·8 °C, according to circumstances, and that of the python, about 24·4 °C, may be higher when the female is coiled around her eggs. It is not always easy to draw a hard-and-fast line between the cold-blooded and warm-blooded animals: hibernating animals like the dormouse, hedgehog, and others resemble cold-blooded animals during their winter sleep. Some of the mammals that are born naked and blind, like rabbits and rats, have low temperatures similar to those of cold-blooded animals.

There are small fluctuations in the temperature of human beings during the day; it reaches its maximum during the afternoon and evening, from about 4 p.m. to 9 p.m., and a minimum in the morning, from about 1 a.m. to 7 a.m. The source of animal heat is due to the oxidation within the tissues of the body (see RESPIRATION, INTERNAL), and different foods have different values as heat producers. The almost uniform temperature of the body is maintained by a process of adjustment controlled by a heat-regulating centre in the brain. When the body is too hot, more blood flows near the skin, giving off its heat to the surrounding air. Sweat increases the dispersion of heat, and some is given off through the lungs. When the body becomes cool, the blood vessels near the skin constrict, so that less heat is lost through the skin. The process of heat regulation in warm-blooded animals is very delicate, as the temperature must be kept within narrow limits for all the chemical reactions that make up the processes of life to be able to proceed.

Temperature, in physics, the degree of hotness of a body, the condition determining the power of a body to transfer or receive heat from another body. A body X is said to be at a higher temperature than a body Y if heat flows from X to Y when the two bodies are placed in contact. Any property of a body which depends on temperature, e.g., its length or electrical resistance, can be used to define a scale of temperature. It is necessary first to assign temperatures to two 'fixed points', e.g., the melting point of ice and the boiling-point of water under specified conditions. The particular property considered, e.g., the length of a column of mercury in a glass capillary, is measured at these two fixed points and a relation is assumed to exist between the change in the property (length) and the change of temperature. In the simplest case the relation assumed is a linear one, i.e., change of length is proportional to change of temperature. The CENTIGRADE scale takes the ice point to be 0 °C and the steam point to be 100 °C. If L_0 is the length of the mercury column at 0 °C and L_{100} that at 100 °C, the temperature T °C corresponding to a length L_T is given by

$$T = (L_T - L_0)100/(L_{100} - L_0) \text{ °C}.$$

The FAHRENHEIT scale defines 32 °F and 212 °F as the ice and steam points. Scales of temperature defined in terms of the properties of various thermometric substances are not exactly the same. KELVIN defined an absolute scale of temperature (see THERMODYNAMICS) and showed that it was the same as the perfect gas scale. This can be closely approximated to in practice, and other scales can be corrected by comparison for more precise measurements. See GAS; METROLOGY; PYROMETER; THERMOMETERS AND THERMOMETRY.

Bibliography: D. K. C. Macdonald, *Near Zero*, 1962; J. A. Hall, *Measurement of Temperature*, 1966.

Tempering, heat-treatment process for relieving certain stresses that may occur in hardened steels, and for recovering to specific limits the toughness and ductility essential to hardened steels. This process usually follows hardening of a steel by quenching from above its upper critical temperature into cold water or oil. Quench hardening produces MARTENSITE, which is commonly too hard and brittle for general engineering use and must be softened by tempering. The process consists of reheating the steel to a selected temperature in the range 200–650 °C and then cooling in oil, water, or air. This causes the martensite to decompose into a tough form of steel consisting of a fine dispersion of iron carbide particles in iron. The hardness of the tempered steel decreases with increase in the tempering temperature. This temperature is therefore chosen according to the purpose for which the steel will be used. The oldest method of determining temperature is one of observing the surface oxide colour tints that occur whilst the steel is being reheated. These tints indicate with some measure of accuracy the temperatures reached. This method is not capable of close control of temperature, and is not now often used. The methods used for heating steels to tempering temperatures are:

1. By the use of hot cast-iron plates, upon which the parts to be tempered are placed. As soon as the required tempering colour appears the parts are removed from the heat.

2. The parts to be tempered are placed in a box or tray of clean dry sand and heated upon a fire, hearth, or forge.

3. Baths containing oil, lead or salt are heated and maintained at exact temperatures. The parts to be tempered are placed in a suitable basket or cradle and suspended in, or passed through, the hot liquid.

4. Lastly, there are various types of electrically heated and air-controlled furnaces in which the parts to be tempered are heated.

The trend in modern methods of tempering is to use liquid baths for reheating, and towards the use of pyrometer and thermo-electric control for accurate measuring of tempering temperatures.

Temperley, Harold William Vazeille (1879–1939), British historian, born at Cambridge, and educated at Sherborne School and at King's College and Peterhouse, Cambridge. He became a fellow of Peterhouse in 1904. From 1920 to 1924 he edited the *History of the Peace Conference of Paris*. Temperley was recognised as one of the leading modern historians by his work on the *Foreign Policy of Canning*, 1925. He collaborated in the production of the *Cambridge Modern History*. With G. P. GOOCH he was given the task of editing the British documents relating to the origins of the First World War, which were produced in 11 volumes, 1926–38, as *British Documents on the Origins of the War*. From 1931 he was professor of modern history in the University of Cambridge. From 1938 until his death he was master of Peterhouse.

Tempest, Dame Marie, real name Mary Susan Etherington (1864–1942), British actress, born in London. Educated at a convent in Belgium, she studied music in Paris and London, and made her first appearances on the London stage in light opera. From 1895 to 1900 she drew large audiences to Daly's to see her in *The Geisha, San Toy* and other musical comedies, and then gave up music for straight comedy. She was seen in such romantic parts as Nell Gwynn and Peg Woffington, and made a great success in *The Marriage of Kitty*, in which she toured all over the world. She had a brittle but extremely competent technique which in her later years served her admirably in such parts as Olivia in *Mr Pim Passes By*, the title role in *The First Mrs Fraser*, and Fanny in *Theatre Royal*. She was created DBE in 1937.

Templars, or Knights Templars, military order founded in 1118 by nine French knights, led by Hugh de Payns. They received their rule in 1128 from Saint Bernard. Their original vow was simply to maintain free passage for the pilgrims who should visit the Holy Land. The name that they first took was the Poor Soldiers (*Pauperes Commilitones*) of the Holy City, and they professed to have no source of subsistence but the alms of the faithful. Pope Honorius II confirmed their rule and assigned a white mantle as their badge. Pope Eugenius III added a red cross on the left breast to the mantle. The ancient banner of the Templars, *Beauseant* (Old French, a black and white horse), was party per pale argent and sable, and *Beauseant*

was the famous war-cry of the order. Their motto was *Non nobis, Domine, non nobis, sed Nomini tuo da gloriam*; and their seal showed two knights riding on one horse.

The constitution of the Knights Templars was simple. At the head was the grand master, who was elected by the general body of the knights. Under him was his seneschal or lieutenant; among other high officers were the marshal and the treasurer. The countries in Asia and Europe in which the order had possessions were called 'provinces' and each of them was presided over by a resident chief, called a grand prior, grand preceptor, or provincial master. Under the provincial masters were the priors, otherwise called bailiffs or masters, who each had charge of one of the districts into which the province was divided; and finally, under the priors, were the preceptors, each of whom presided over a single house or establishment, hence called a preceptory.

For more than 170 years the Soldiers of the Temple formed the most renowned portion of the Christian troops. By 1300 the order had 15,000 members, and its property included 9000 castles and manors. The destroyer of the Templars was Philippe le Bel of France. He compelled the Pope to summon the grand master, Jacques de MOLAY to Europe. In 1307, whilst Molay was at Paris, two individuals of notoriously evil character made certain revelations accusing the Templars of heresy, idolatry, unbelief, and a number of foul practices. As a result, the order was suppressed at the Council of Vienne in 1312, many of its members executed, and its property confiscated. It was revived, however, in Portugal, where it took the new name of the Order of Christ. The name survives in the Temple, London, and the Temple, Paris, and a number of their churches, built in the round style peculiar to the order, still exist. The London Temple Church survived the Second World War with severe damage, but has since been restored.

Bibliography: R. Rudorff, *The Knights and their world*, 1974.

Temple, Frederick (1821–1902), English prelate, educated at Blundell's School, Tiverton, and Balliol College, Oxford. Temple was ordained priest in 1847. In 1857 he became headmaster of Rugby, where he continued the work of Arnold, though he laid more stress than the latter on the place of orthodox religion in school life. His friendship with Gladstone, whose Liberal views he shared, led to his being appointed in 1869 to the see of Exeter, where he won popularity by his sincerity and humanity. He was appointed bishop of London in 1885, and in 1896 archbishop of Canterbury. He worked hard to prevent the influence of the OXFORD MOVEMENT from resulting in a split within the fabric of Anglicanism.

Bibliography: Lives by W. F. Aitken, 1903, and E. G. Sandford (Ed.), 1906.

Temple, Henry John, see PALMERSTON, HENRY JOHN TEMPLE, 3RD VISCOUNT.

Temple, Shirley Jane (1929–), US child actress, born at Santa Monica, California. She made her screen debut in 1932 in *Red Haired Alibi*. She was a leading figure in the *Baby Burlesque* series. Her appearance in *Stand Up and Cheer* (1934) resulted in a highly successful career; she is probably the best-known child star ever to appear

Temple, Sir William

in films. Her pictures include *Baby Takes a Bow, Bright Eyes, The Little Colonel, Our Little Girl, Curly Top, The Littlest Rebel, Poor Little Rich Girl, Heidi, Rebecca of Sunnybrook Farm, The Little Princess, Susannah of the Mounties* and *The Blue Bird*. With the passing of childhood her popularity faded, although she made a number of later films and in recent years has appeared on television. As Shirley Temple-Black she has latterly played a part in Republican politics.

Temple, Sir William (1628–99), English statesman and man of letters, born in London. Educated at Emmanuel College, Cambridge, he travelled in his youth, and in 1655 married Dorothy OSBORNE. In 1666 he was created baronet, and appointed envoy at Brussels. He was largely responsible for carrying through the triple alliance formed against Spain in 1668 between England, Holland, and Sweden. He was later ambassador at The Hague, but was recalled in 1670. Four years later he returned to The Hague to arrange the marriage between Princess Mary of England and William of Orange. He was offered a secretaryship of state in 1677 and 1679 but declined.

When he moved to Moor Park he engaged SWIFT as his secretary, and was assisted by him in the composition of his *Memoirs*. His *Miscellanea* were published in 1680 and two more series in 1692 and 1701. Temple's essays and reflections are polished and graceful; his originality lies in his economic theories, and his ideas on labour and trade were of particular importance. His essay *Of Ancient and Modern Learning* provoked the ANCIENTS AND MODERNS literary controversy, to which Swift contributed with *The Battle of the Books*. His *Essays* were edited by G. Nicklin, 1903; and *Five Miscellaneous Essays*, by S. H. Monk, 1963.

Bibliography: H. E. Woodbridge, *Temple: the Man and His Work*, 1940; D. C. Douglas, *English Scholars 1660–1730*, rev. ed. 1951.

Temple, William (1881–1944), English prelate, archbishop of Canterbury, 1942–44, born at Exeter, son of Frederick TEMPLE, educated at Rugby and Balliol College, Oxford. He was fellow and lecturer in philosophy at Queen's College, Oxford, 1904–10. He was ordained priest in 1909, and was chaplain to the archbishop of Canterbury, 1910–21, headmaster of Repton School, 1910–14, rector of St James's, Piccadilly, 1914–18, and canon of Westminster, 1919–21. He was bishop of Manchester, 1921–29, and was appointed archbishop of York and a privy councillor in 1929. In 1942 he became archbishop of Canterbury.

As a writer, his reputation rests chiefly on his essays in philosophy and on his application of that philosophy to social and economic problems. The two volumes of his *Readings in the Gospel of St John*, 1939, show his deep devotion. His Gifford Lectures, delivered at Glasgow University and collected as *Nature, Man and God*, 1934, were an outstanding contribution to theology. His other works include *The Kingdom of God*, 1912, *Plato and Christianity*, 1916, *Mens Creatrix*, 1917, *Faith and Modern Thought*, 1921, *Christus Veritas*, 1924, *Christianity and the State*, 1928, *Christianity and the Social Order*, 1932, *Citizen and Churchman*, 1941, and *The Resources and Influence of English Literature*, 1943. Temple led the Life and Liberty Movement which resulted in the Enabling Act, 1919, and the setting up of the

CHURCH ASSEMBLY. To Temple the unity of the Church was an urgent and practical necessity, not merely a pious hope or an intellectually necessary end to the Christian interpretation of history. But he made his greatest impact on the public by his pronouncements on Christian social theory, having started out as a Christian Socialist.

Bibliography: F. A. Iremonger, *William Temple*, 1948; F. S. Temple (Ed.), *Some Lambeth Letters*, 1963; R. Craig, *Social Concern in the Thought of William Temple*, 1963.

Temple, English earldom, held from the 18th century by the Grenville family together with the dukedom of Buckingham and Chandos. The first earl was Richard Grenville (1711–79), eldest son of Richard Grenville (1678–1727) and Hester Temple, afterwards Countess Temple; he succeeded to his mother's peerage in 1752 and took the name of Grenville-Temple.

George Nugent-Temple-Grenville (1753–1813), second son of George GRENVILLE and nephew of the 1st Earl Temple, succeeded his uncle as 2nd Earl Temple in 1779. He was created Marquess of Buckingham in 1784 and was a lord-lieutenant of Ireland.

Richard Temple Nugent Brydges Chandos Grenville (1776–1839), the son of the 2nd Earl Temple, became 1st Duke of Buckingham and Chandos and Earl Temple of Stowe in 1822.

Richard Plantagenet Temple Nugent Brydges Chandos Grenville (1797–1861), son of the 1st Duke, was 2nd Duke of BUCKINGHAM AND CHANDOS. His successor, Richard, the 3rd Duke (1823–99) was colonial secretary, 1866–68. On his death the dukedom became extinct. His titles of Earl Temple and Viscount Cobham passed to relatives. The 7th Earl Temple of Stowe was born in 1910 and succeeded to the title in 1966.

Temple, London, see INNS OF COURT.

Temple, structure designed for the worship of a deity or deities. The first *templum* of the Romans was simply the space of earth and sky marked off by an augur for divination. The ancient Egyptians built enormous temples by degrees over a long period; ancient India is noted for cave temples hewn out of the solid rock; Hindu temples always include the shrine in front of which it is customary to remove one's shoes. In the Far East and in South-East Asia the temple is known as *pagoda*, while the ancient Mexican temple was known as *teocalli*. In France Protestant churches are known as temples as also are some Jewish synagogues and Masonic halls. The most celebrated temples of antiquity were those of the Ancient Greeks. See TEMPLE, CLASSICAL.

See also AZTEC; EGYPT, ANCIENT; INDIA, *Architecture*; JAPAN, *Architecture*; SOUTH AMERICA, *Archaeology and Ancient Civilisation*; MAYA; OLYMPIA; PARTHENON; THEBES; UR; ZIMBABWE.

Other famous temples are:

1. *The First Temple.* The sacred edifice of the ancient Hebrews was erected in Jerusalem on Mount Moriah, one of the hills of Mount Zion, where Abraham is reputed to have attempted to sacrifice Isaac. The idea of building the temple was suggested to David, but it was Solomon, his son and successor, who commenced the work. The rock-altar (see below) is the only remains still preserved. The site of the temple lies today within the sacred enclosure of the Muslims known as the Haram esh-Sherif ('The

Noble Sanctuary'). The most striking natural feature of the Haram is the ancient rock-altar (a great outcropping of rock), known as es-Sakhra ('sacred rock'), and covered by the Kubbet es-Sakhra ('Dome of the Rock'). One can still trace on this rock the channels which conducted the blood to an opening which in turn conducted it to a sacred cave underneath.

2. *The Second Temple*, built on the same site, by Zerubbabel, was completed in 516 BC, 70 years after the first temple was destroyed. It was probably without ornaments, and was as nothing in the eyes of those who had seen the temple in its former glory.

3. *The Herodian Temple* (described by Josephus, *Jewish Antiquities* xv, xi, and *Jewish Wars* v, v, and in the Babylonian Talmud, *Qodashim*, *Middoth*) was begun in 20–19 BC and was finished in AD 64, six years before it was finally destroyed. According to Tacitus, it was 'a temple of immense wealth'. The 'Western' or 'WAILING WALL' belongs to the remains of the enclosure-walls of the Herodian temple.

Temple, Classical. The essential room in a Greek temple was the *cella* or *naos*, containing the cult statue. In small temples it might simply have a porch (*pronaos*) in front, the façade formed either by columns (usually two) between the extended side walls (*in antis*) or by columns standing in front of the extended walls (*prostyle*). In major temples there was a matching false porch (*opisthodomos*) at the rear of the cella and a colonnade round the whole building (*peripteral*), while colossal temples might have two surrounding colonnades (*dipteral*). Roman temples usually had a deep porch of free-standing columns in front of the cella, with half-columns attached to the side and rear walls (pseudoperipteral). For the treatment of the columns see ORDERS OF ARCHITECTURE. The façades were always crowned by a low-pitched gable (*pediment*), which was often filled with sculpture, and a free-standing figure or other decoration (*akroterion*) might also be placed at its apex and lower angles. The roof was tiled, with decorative *antefixes* terminating the rows of cover tiles. The portico and pediment motif, derived from the temple, was a favourite one with Renaissance and later architects.

Temple Bar, formerly a gateway marking the boundary between the cities of London and Westminster. A barrier existed here in medieval times after the City of London extended beyond the old wall. It was removed in 1669, and in 1670–72 a new archway was erected to Wren's designs. Soon after there began the practice (discontinued

Classical Temple. LEFT General plan of a Greek temple. RIGHT BELOW Façade of the Megarian Treasury, Olympia, c. 510 BC (Doric). RIGHT ABOVE Façade of the temple of Artemis Leukophryene, Magnesia, 2nd century BC (Ionic).

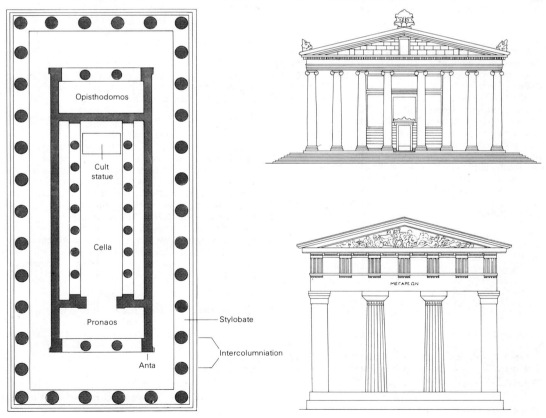

in 1772) of exhibiting the heads of executed criminals and rebels. It was removed in 1878 and later re-erected at Theobald's Park, near Cheshunt, Hertfordshire, and the site is marked by the Temple Bar Memorial, which was erected in 1880. In former times the sovereign sought permission of the lord mayor at Temple Bar before entering the City of London, and the act continues to be symbolically performed.

Templemore, market town of County TIPPERARY, Republic of Ireland, 55 km north of Clonmel, at the foot of Devil's Bit Mountain (480 m). Loughmoe Castle and Barna Castle are nearby. The police training centre for Ireland is located here. Population 2174.

Templer, Sir Gerald (Walter Robert) (1898–), British soldier, educated at Wellington and Royal Military College. He joined the Royal Irish Fusiliers in 1916, and served in France and Belgium. Between the wars he served in Iran, Iraq, and Palestine and was a lieutenant-colonel at the outbreak of the Second World War, in France. Two years later he was a lieutenant-general. Subsequently in that war he commanded the 1st and 56th divisions and the 6th Armoured Division. After the war he was serving as GOC, Eastern Command, when the need arose for a 'strong man' in Malaya, where a Communist terror campaign was disrupting the life of the country. He was sent as high commissioner, with broad military powers, and soon his vigorous and original measures proved successful. From 1955 to 1958 Templer was chief of the Imperial General Staff. He was promoted field marshal in 1956 and KG in 1963.

Templewood of Chelsea, Samuel John Gurney Hoare, 1st Viscount (1880–1959), British statesman and diplomat, educated at Harrow and at New College, Oxford. From 1910 until 1944 he was Conservative MP for Chelsea. He was secretary of state for air from 1922 to 1924, and from November 1924 to 1929, and secretary of state for India from 1931 to 1935. He then became foreign secretary, but resigned, owing to the violent criticism evoked by the HOARE-LAVAL PACT. Later, he held successively the posts of home secretary and secretary for air, and from 1940 to 1944 was ambassador in Spain. In 1944 he was created a viscount. Templewood was deeply interested in penal reform. His publications include *The Shadow of the Gallows*, 1951; and *Nine Troubled Years*, 1954.

Tempo (Italian, time), musical pace. The speed of any musical composition is determined, not by the note-values used by the composer, which are relative, but by the directions set above the stave at the opening of a piece or section (e.g. *allegro*, *andante*, *adagio*, etc.). These words cannot fix the exact pace required by the composer; this can be done only by means of metronome marks (e.g. ♩ = 96, i.e. 96 crotchets to the minute, etc.).

Temporal bone, part of the base and lateral walls of the skull. It has squamous, tympanic and petrous parts, the last including the mastoid process behind the external ear. The petrous portion has important nerves and vessels running through it and contains the middle and inner ear.

Temporary Rank, see RANK.

Temuco, city of southern Chile, capital of the province of Cautín, 688 km south of Santiago and the fourth largest city in Chile. Cereals, timber, and apples are the main products. Temuco is a cathedral city at the gateway to the Chilean Lake District. It has grown rapidly in the last decade. Population 150,000.

Temujin, see GENGHIS KHAN.

Ten, Council of, secret committee of the Venetian senate, created after the defeat of Tiepolo's revolution in 1310, and vested with executive authority to cope with extraordinary crises. Its institution marked the final overthrow of the democratic constitution in favour of a system of close oligarchies of hereditary aristocrats. Eventually the Council of Ten, though theoretically outside the constitution, became the most powerful organ of government. It was not abolished until 1797, the date of the fall of the republic.

Ten Commandments, see DECALOGUE.

Ten Thousand, Expedition of the, an army originally composed partly of large levies of native troops in the Persian satrapies of Asia Minor, but mainly of Greek mercenaries collected by CYRUS, younger son of King Darius II of Persia, who hoped to win the crown from his elder brother Artaxerxes II. At the battle of Cunaxa (401 BC) the Greeks routed their opponents, but Cyrus was killed. The native levies at once dispersed, and the Greek mercenaries found themselves isolated in Mesopotamia. Their officers were killed by a trick of the enemy. The Greeks chose new officers, among them XENOPHON, the historian of the expedition, and fought their way north into the Armenian mountains. Ultimately they reached the Euxine at Trapezus (Trebizond). The journey caused a great sensation throughout the Greek world, and, by revealing the weakness of Persia, did much to pave the way for Alexander the Great (see ALEXANDER III).

Tenacity, see ELASTICITY; MATERIALS, STRENGTH OF.

Tenancy in Common. Where two or more persons hold land in distinct equal or unequal shares, so that each is able to devise his share by will, they hold the land as tenants in common. This is distinguished, in English law, from a JOINT TENANCY in that in the latter there is no ability to devise individual shares. On the death of one joint tenant his share accrues to the survivors: there is a right of survivorship. Since 1926 a tenancy in common can only exist in equity behind a trust for sale; the legal estate in the land must be held by trustees as joint tenants (see LAND LAWS). A tenancy in common arises where co-owners of land as joint tenants sever the joint tenancy so as to defeat the right of survivorship.

Tenant, see LANDLORD AND TENANT.

Tenasserim, division of BURMA, consisting of a narrow strip of land lying to the east of the Bay of Bengal and bordering Thailand on the east. The rainfall in the region is heavy, and where cultivation is possible, rice is grown. Some tin is mined. The capital is TAVOY. There is also a town and river of the same name in the division. Area 42,838 km²; population 717,607.

Tenby, Gwilym Lloyd George, 1st Viscount (1894–1967), British politician, son of David LLOYD

GEORGE, educated at Eastbourne College and Jesus College, Cambridge. He entered Parliament as a Liberal in 1922 and, after holding a number of minor offices, was minister of food, 1941–42, and minister of fuel and power, 1942–45. In 1951 he was returned as a Liberal and Conservative MP and joined the Conservative government as minister of food, 1951–54. From 1954 until 1957, when he was created a viscount, he was home secretary and minister of Welsh Affairs. He was appointed chairman of the Council on Tribunals in 1961.

Tenby, seaside resort of the South Pembrokeshire District of DYFED, Wales, 15 km east of Pembroke. It is situated on a narrow promontory jutting out into Carmarthen Bay. Tenby has a long history, and by the late 15th century was a prosperous little port. Part of the castle and most of the town walls still exist. Population 4994.

Tench, *Tinca tinca*, order Cypriniformes, a European freshwater fish with exceedingly small scales, a slimy skin, and a short barbel at each angle of the mouth. It is rich olive green in colour, shading into light grey on the belly. It spawns in early summer, the greenish ova numbering about 250,000. Like the carp, to whose family it belongs, it feeds on both animal and vegetable substances. It attains a length of c. 45 cm and a weight of 2 kg.

Tender, in English law, offer of money in payment of a debt. To be valid it must be: (1) Unconditional; but a tender will not be invalid merely because it is made under protest. (2) Of the whole debt; though if the creditor's claim is made up of separate items the debtor may validly make a tender of payment of any one item provided he makes it clear in respect of which item it is made. (3) In the current coin of the realm. All English bank-notes are legal tender in England and Wales and all bank-notes of less than £5 in Scotland and Northern Ireland. Coins which are made by the Mint in accordance with the Coinage Act 1971 are legal tender as follows: (a) if gold, up to any amount; (b) if silver or cupro-nickel of denominations of more than 10 p, up to £10; (c) if silver or cupro-nickel of other denominations, up to £5; (d) if bronze up to 10 p; (e) other coins up to any amount (not over £10) as may be declared by proclamation.

A valid tender does not extinguish the debt, but a plea of tender, if sustained by the debtor, will result in the plaintiff having to pay the costs of the action. The other effects of tender are that it stops the further accrual of interest, and extinguishes any right of LIEN the creditor may have.

A tender in commerce is a written offer of terms for executing a specific piece of work or for supplying a certain consignment of merchandise.

Tendon, immensely strong connective tissue composed of bundles of parallel collagen fibres. Tendons are attached at one end to the sarcolemma or connective tissue around muscle fibres, and at the other end to the periosteum, the connective tissue surrounding bone. Tendon can stand a stress of 500 kg/sq cm before snapping; this is about eight times the force which can be exerted by one square centimetre of muscle and therefore the transmission of force by tendons greatly reduces the bulk of structures such as the hand. Tendons have a relatively poor blood supply and if they are torn, healing is slow.

Tendon of Achilles, tendon attaching the muscles of the calf of the leg to the heel-bone. It is capable of resisting a great tensional strain, and yet is sometimes ruptured by the contraction of the muscles in sudden extension of the foot. Ancient surgeons regarded wounds in this tendon as fatal, probably because of the legend of Achilles, which relates how the mother of the hero Achilles dipped him when an infant into the Styx, so that he became invulnerable except for the heel by which she held him.

Tendril, in botany, a thread-like growth by which some plants climb. Tendrils may be modified terminal shoots, as in vines, leaves as in peas, leaf-stalks as in clematis, or branch stems as in white bryony; they are sensitive to contact and react by twining around supports.

Tenebrae (Latin *tenebrae*, darkness), solemn recitation of the canonical hours of Matins and Lauds during the last three days of Holy Week, timed so as to finish as it is growing dark. Distinctive features were the extinction of a candle at the end of each psalm, and the making of a slight noise at the end of Lauds, typifying the earthquake felt on the death of Christ (Matt. xxvii. 51). Liturgical changes have removed this service, in favour of the more solemn eucharistic rites of these days.

Tenebrionidae, one of the largest families of beetles, in order Coleoptera, numbering some 20,000 species, which exhibit a wide range of variations. A number of the species are agricultural pests. In North America the beetles are known as darkling beetles, from the nocturnal habits and the generally black or brown colour. Many species greatly resemble GROUND BEETLES, and in many respects tenebrionids fill in arid areas the ecological niche of the latter. However, tenebrionids are not normally predaceous, but feed typically on plant material and other matter already subjected to some bacterial breakdown. The family is most successful in terms of numbers and species in tropical forest (e.g. equatorial Africa) and desert (e.g. Central Asia, Namib Desert). Tenebrionids are also commonly found in caves, though not showing any particular adaptations. Certain species, e.g. of *Eleodes*, show characteristic head-standing, with emission of evil-smelling fluid, as a defence mechanism.

Three species of flour beetles belonging to the genus *Tribolium* are almost universally distributed: *T. confusum*, *T. castaneus* and *T. destructor*. They are major pests of stored agricultural products, such as flour, and abound in granaries and stores where both the adult beetles and the larvae feed on damaged grain or flour. Neither adults nor larvae can eat intact grains.

The genus *Tenebrio* includes species that are minor pests of stored products. Both *T. molitor* and *T. obscurus* are cosmopolitan and abound in storehouses where there are farinaceous products. All stages (eggs, larvae and adults) of the life-history are to be found in flour. Both species can survive on whole grain. (See also MEALWORM.)

The British fauna is small, with only some 35 species.

Tenerife, largest of the CANARY ISLANDS, in the province of Santa Cruz de Tenerife. It is divided in two by a mountain chain. The volcanic Pico de Teide rises to 3712 m. The flora is very varied, and the island is known for early fruits and vegetables, and also for bananas. It is a popular tourist and health resort. The capital is Santa Cruz de Tenerife. Area 2020 km²; population 473,971.

Teng Hsiao-p'ing (1902–), general-secretary of the Chinese Communist party (CCP) and member of the seven-man standing committee of the Politburo between 1956 and 1967, born at Chiating, Szechwan. The details of his early life are obscure. It is known he went to France in 1920 under a work-study scheme, and joined the Paris branch of the CCP in the winter of 1921–22. He left France for Moscow in 1925, returning to China the next year. He became a political instructor at a military school in Sanyuan, Shensi province, set up by the warlord Feng Yü-hsiang, who was at that time in league with the Nationalists. In July 1929 he was sent to work in Kwangsi province, where he helped to organise the Red Seventh Army. He remained as CCP representative in the unit. For five years his unit was based in Kiangsi, then with the main body of Communist forces they made the Long March to the north-east of China. In 1937 Teng was appointed political commissar for the 129th Division of the Eighth Route army, commanded by Liu Po-ch'eng, which worked behind Japanese lines in occupied China. At the end of the war he was elected to the central committee of the CCP. In 1946 he joined up again with Liu Po-ch'eng in the Second Field Army to fight the Nationalists. When victory was won he stayed on in the Second Army's theatre of war as first secretary of the South-West Bureau of the CCP.

Transferred to Peking in 1952, Teng became a vice-premier, and subsequently held several high government posts. His proper sphere of activity, however, was party organisation: he became general secretary in 1956. In later years he became prominent as a spokesman in Sino-Soviet doctrinal disputes.

During the Cultural Revolution he was denounced as 'No 2 capitalist-roader' and deprived of all posts. He was sensationally rehabilitated in 1973 and appointed a vice-premier. After the 4th National People's Congress in January 1975 he was promoted to one of the vice-chairmen of the CCP, 1st vice-premier of the State Council, and chief-of-staff of the PLA. He was dismissed from all his posts, after an inner-party struggle, in April 1976. Following the 11th Communist Party Congress held in August 1977, Teng was again rehabilitated and named as one of the five members of the Politburo standing committee. He had previously been renamed chief of staff of the armed forces.

See also CHINA, *Modern History*.

Tengri Khan, see KHAN-TENGRI.

Teniers, David, the Elder (1582–1649), Flemish painter, born at Antwerp. He studied painting under RUBENS and Adam ELSHEIMER at Rome. His subjects were mainly religious; as a painter of Flemish life he was eclipsed by his son and pupil, Teniers the Younger.

Teniers, David, the Younger (1610–90), Flemish painter, born in Antwerp, the son of David Teniers the Elder, from whom he received his principal instruction. He was a master in the Antwerp Guild (1632–3). He was appointed court painter to Archduke Leopold and keeper of his pictures. His work was a development of his father's style influenced also by BROUWER, and was extremely popular. He was happiest in his portrayals of small figures

in landscape or rustic interiors. His best picture, *Meeting of the Civic Guards*, 1642, is at Leningrad, while his *Village Fête*, 1643, and many other works are in the National Gallery, London. He continued the Flemish tradition of secular rustic scenes, epitomised in BRUEGHEL.

Tenison, Thomas (1636–1715), English prelate, born at Cottenham, Cambridgeshire, and educated at the Grammar School, Norwich, and at Corpus Christi College, Cambridge. In 1680 he was presented to the living of St Martin-in-the Fields, London. In 1689 he was made archdeacon of London, in 1691 became bishop of Lincoln, and in 1694 archbishop of Canterbury. In St Martin-in-the-Fields he endowed a free school and founded a library. Tenison was strongly Whig and Protestant in sympathy. As such he secured favour under William III, and was never popular with Anne, or with his High Church Convocation. He worked zealously to improve the quality of parochial Anglicanism, and was a supporter of missionary endeavour.

Bibliography: Life by E. Carpenter, 1949.

Tennant, Emma, see OXFORD AND ASQUITH, EMMA ALICE MARGARET, COUNTESS OF.

Tennant, Kylie (1912–), Australian novelist, born at Manly, New South Wales. Educated at Sydney University, she married Lewis C. Rodd in 1932. Her first novel, *Tiburon*, 1935, and *The Battlers*, 1941, were both set in a country town during the Australian Depression, and both won the Prior Memorial prize. The latter was also awarded the gold medal of the Australian Literary Society. *Ride On, Stranger*, 1943, ardently resented by some left-wing groups because of its satiric treatment of their tactics, nonetheless represents her strong socialist sympathies in a convincing urban setting. Others of her novels are *Foveaux*, 1939, *Time Enough Later*, 1943, *Lost Haven*, 1946, and the outstanding *The Honey Flow*, 1956. *Tell Morning This*, 1967, is the full text of the abridged *The Joyful Condemned*, 1953. In these novels she depicts with irony and gusto the life of the Australian poor. She also edited two collections of *Summer's Tales*, 1964 and 1965, and published her own short stories in *Ma Jones and the Little White Cannibals*, 1967.

Bibliography: M. Dick, *The Novels of Kylie Tennant*, 1966.

Tennessee (Volunteer State), central-southern state of the USA, having an area of 109,417 km². Its boundaries on the north are Kentucky and Virginia; on the east North Carolina; on the south Georgia, Alabama, and Mississippi; and the Mississippi river on the west separates it from Arkansas and Missouri. Along the eastern boundaries rise the Unaka and Great Smoky Mountains, with peaks over 1830 m; between these highlands and the Cumberland Plateau, the mean elevation of which is 550 m, is the valley of east Tennessee, part of the great valley of the APPALACHIAN MOUNTAINS. The Cumberland river, affluent of the Ohio, drains a fertile valley west of the Cumberland Mountains in the north of the state. There are wide level tracts in the west between the Mississippi and the lower Tennessee. The climate ranges with the topography from warm temperate in the Mississippi lowlands to montane in the Great Smokies; at Memphis, in the extreme south-west, the January daily mean is 5·7 °C and that for July 27·1, while Bristol in the

Tennessee. Watts Bar Dam on the Tennessee river. *(Library of Congress)*

north-east has 1·5 and 23·5 respectively. Precipitation over the state averages 1250 mm and reaches 2000 mm in the eastern mountains. There are 5·2 million ha of commercial forests, the greater part made up of valuable hardwoods, and industries like paper making, which are based on the forest products, are everywhere important. Agriculture is varied; there are 6·1 million ha of farmland, 1·6 million of them under crops; these include some 200,000 ha under cotton in the western end of the state, and an important tobacco crop. The major sources of farm income, however, are livestock and dairy products, for which the Nashville Basin, in particular, is famous. It is noteworthy, however, that of the state's 120,000 farms in 1969, no less than 75,000 had sales of produce of less than $2500; that is, they were hardly to be regarded as serious commercial enterprises. It was the poor condition of Tennessee's farms which lay behind the creation in 1933 of the TENNESSEE VALLEY AUTHORITY (TVA), as one of the measures known collectively as the NEW DEAL of President Franklin Roosevelt. Soil erosion had stripped soil from the hillsides, and the small farmers were in a desperate plight, caught between ignorance, poverty, and world depression. The TVA was created to control floods on the Tennessee river and, to this end, to build dams and arrest erosion; as a by-product, electricity was generated at the dams, and the state's present capacity is about 2 million kW. The TVA, although strongly challenged in its early years, has survived to prove highly successful, not only materially but also psychologically to the region, by showing how poverty can be combatted. The availability of power has attracted industry—so much industry that the Tennessee valley now relies far more heavily on thermal power stations than on the hydroelectricity which was the initial attraction. Although the TVA has nowhere else been duplicated within the USA, it has served as a model for planners in numerous other parts of the world. Today there are over 5000 industrial plants in the state, employing 450,000 workers. Mineral resources are varied; Tennessee is the leading US producer of zinc, ranks third for phosphates, and produces 8–9 million t of coal a year. Nevertheless, the average standard of living remains low: among the 50 states, Tennessee ranks 43rd in personal income per capita.

There are 110,000 km of roads outside the cities, but the road network is sparse in the eastern mountains, where there is a heavy tourist traffic. The population of the state in 1974 was 4,129,000, an increase of 10 per cent in the previous decade. It is 16 per cent black and 59 per cent urban. The capital is NASHVILLE. The state was first settled from North Carolina in the 1750s, and was admitted to the Union in 1796. It fought on the side of the Confederacy (the South) in the Civil War, and was the scene of heavy fighting, especially in the area round CHATTANOOGA.

Bibliography: S. Folmsbe and others, *Tennessee: A Short History,* 1969.

Tennessee, tributary of the Ohio river, USA. The Holston and French Broad, which unite near Knoxville, Tennessee, are its headstreams. The river winds through eastern Tennessee, Alabama, western Tennessee, and Kentucky and finally reaches the Ohio at Paducah. It is now navigable from its mouth 1005 km upstream. Length 1050 km. See TENNESSEE VALLEY AUTHORITY.

Tennessee Valley Authority, created by the Tennessee Valley Act in 1933, one of the acts initiated by Franklin D. Roosevelt's administration as part of the NEW DEAL. The authority initiated regional planning on a scale never previously attempted. Among the reasons why the Tennessee valley was selected as the site of this great experiment was the existence of a large government-built nitrate plant, the Muscle Shoals works at the Wilson Dam, built during the First World War. Proper control of the Tennessee river was also crucial for the prevention of disastrous floods on the lower Mississippi river. There was further the consideration that flood control could be readily related to improved navigation and to the profitable generation of electric power; and the needs of this backward region could be alleviated by cheap electric power. The Tennessee valley used to be known as one of the most depressed areas of the USA, affecting parts of the states of Alabama, Kentucky, Tennessee, Virginia, Georgia, and North Carolina. Its disastrous state was due to reckless exploitation by early settlers: the soils were eroded and the woods had been cut down, and the rivers frequently flooded. Under the Tennessee Valley Authority water control was begun. Co-ordinated research plans were undertaken throughout the entire area, which is approximately 116,550 km². Soil regeneration, afforestation, malaria control, and similar measures were scientifically applied. National parks were laid out, tourist facilities organised, and cultural and educational activities promoted. The whole project affords a valuable lesson in the possibilities of judiciously applied regional planning, though it was opposed by numbers of influential interests. There was particular opposition to the idea that the federal government should sell electricity in competition with private companies, but over the years these sales have enabled the Tennessee Valley Authority to repay to the government the capital sums originally invested, and this source of income has been one of the key factors in the authority's success. Its impact on the region has been twofold: it has created a fresh and optimistic atmosphere in a region formerly depressed, and it has provided power which, in turn, has attracted industry. So large has the demand for power become that it far exceeds the capacity of the hydro-electric generators at the dams, and has required the construction of a number of thermal

Sir John Tenniel. Alice arming Tweedledum and Tweedledee, an illustration for *Through the Looking Glass, and What Alice Found There* by Lewis Carroll, 1872. *(Victoria and Albert Museum, London)*

power stations, from which the bulk of the power supply is now derived.

Tenniel, Sir John (1820–1914), British cartoonist and illustrator, born in London. Tenniel studied at the Royal Academy schools. In 1850 Mark Lemon invited him to succeed Richard Doyle as joint cartoonist with John Leech in *Punch*, his illustrations to Aesop's *Fables* having attracted much attention. Some 2300 cartoons and many smaller drawings were executed by Tenniel before he severed his connection with *Punch* in January 1901. In them can be traced a political history of the period. His illustrations for Lewis Carroll's *Alice in Wonderland*, 1865, and *Through the Looking-Glass*, 1872, have delighted children of all ages and are his greatest claim to fame. He was knighted in 1893.

Bibliography: C. Monkhouse, *The Life and Works of Sir John Tenniel*, 1901; F. Sarzano, *Tenniel*, 1948.

Tennis, Lawn, see LAWN TENNIS.

Tennis, Real, one of the oldest ball games in existence played by two or four players; called 'real' tennis (USA 'court tennis'; Australia 'royal tennis') to distinguish it from LAWN TENNIS which developed from it around 1860. Even in 1100 the game is known to have resembled closely the game still played today.

The royal tennis court at Hampton Court is the oldest place in the world where this racket and ball game is still played. It was built in 1529 by Henry VIII and served as

a model for all later courts erected in England. Among other courts in active use are those at Lord's and Queen's Club London, and at Manchester, Leamington, Oxford, Cambridge, Moreton, and Murrel, in all totalling around 15. The game was ousted in general popularity by lawn tennis and squash owing to the expense of building and maintaining a court. However, a resurgence occurred in the 1970s and the game became popular in the USA. It is played in Australia and also France, where it retains the ancient name *jeu de paume*. There are governing bodies for the game in the UK, the USA and France.

Regulation courts measure 29·3 m (32 yd) by 9·8 m (10 yd). Round the two ends and along one of the side walls runs the penthouse, a sloping roof over the dedans, gallery and grille. This roof is 2·1 m (7 ft) wide and is 2·14 m (7 ft 3 in) high at the side of the court and 3·2 m (10 ft 6 in) at the farther edge. Across the middle of the court is stretched a net 1·52 m (5 ft) high at the sides and 914 cm (3 ft) in the centre. In the back wall on the service side is a rectangular opening—the dedans. On the back wall of the hazard side is a small square opening—the grille. A ball struck so that it enters the dedans, the grille or the gallery on the hazard side farthest from the net, known as the winning gallery, wins the point outright. On the main wall, near the grille, is a projection known as the tambour. The winner of the toss has choice of ends and usually takes the service side. A service to be good must strike the penthouse at least once on the hazard side of the court and drop into a prescribed area on the floor. The striker-out may volley the service or return it at first bounce.

Basically the scoring is as in lawn tennis except for a great number of variations; e.g. if the server fails to touch the ball with his racket when it is returned, the marker watches where the ball falls on its second bounce, and calls the chase, the floor being marked with chase lines for this purpose. That point is held in abeyance, and when two chases have been made the players cross over, and the one who is now striker-out must make a better, i.e. shorter, chase in order to win the point. If he makes the same chase, the score remains unaltered, and the marker calls 'chase off'. If either player is at game point, they cross over if one chase is made.

A short chase is made by playing the tennis 'stroke', i.e. a heavily cut stroke that comes down sharply off the wall below the dedans. There are also chases on the hazard side. A set is the best of 11 games. The balls are solid, and are approximately 64 mm in diameter. They should weigh not less than 71 g and not more than 78 g. There are no restrictions as to size or shape of rackets.

Bibliography: C. G. Heathcote, *Tennis, Lawn Tennis, Rackets, Fives*, 1903; M. D. Whitman, *Tennis Origins and Mysteries*, 1952; Lord Aberdare (Ed.), *Rackets, Squash Rackets, Tennis, Fives and Badminton*, 1933.

Tennyson, Alfred, 1st Baron (1809–92), English poet, born at Somersby, Lincolnshire, son of the rector of Somersby, and younger brother of Charles Tennyson TURNER and Frederick TENNYSON who were both poets. He was educated at Louth Grammar School and at Trinity College, Cambridge. An unhappy childhood and youth may account for Tennyson's remarkable sensitivity and melancholia in later years. In 1827 he published with his brother Charles a volume called *Poems by Two Brothers*, to which Frederick also contributed. At Cambridge Tennyson won the chancellor's medal for

Alfred, Lord Tennyson. *(Mansell Collection)*

English verse in 1829 with a poem on 'Timbuctoo', and the next year produced a volume of *Poems chiefly Lyrical*, containing some verse of great promise. In the same year he toured the Continent with Arthur Henry HALLAM, and the impressions he gained inspired many of his works.

In 1833 he published *Poems*, including 'The Lady of Shalott', 'The Lotus Eaters', and 'A Dream of Fair Women'; the volume was generally liked and acclaimed by Tennyson's friends, but was virulently attacked in the *Edinburgh Quarterly*. In the same year Arthur Hallam died suddenly in Vienna and Tennyson began his brilliant elegy, *In Memoriam*, which grew over the years into a record of spiritual conflict and a confession of faith. It was published anonymously in 1850 as *In Memoriam A. H. H.* In 1842 he published *Poems*, containing 'Locksley Hall' and 'Ulysses' and in 1847 *The Princess*, a serio-comic epic containing some of his finest lyrical poems. This was his first popular success, running through five editions in six years. After the publication of *In Memoriam* Tennyson earned enough money to allow him to marry Emily Sellwood after a seven year engagement. On Wordsworth's death in 1850, Tennyson accepted the poet laureateship.

The 'Ode on the Death of the Duke of Wellington' appeared in 1852 and was followed by 'The Charge of the Light Brigade', showing the jingoistic aspect of Tennyson's work. They were published in the volume *Maud and other Poems*, 1855, which contained a number of fine pieces. 'Maud', an extraordinary study of murderous instincts and insanity, has passages of power and contains some beautiful lyrics. In 1859 *Idylls of the King*, variations in poetic form on the Arthurian romances, were published. These contain some of Tennyson's most telling descriptive passages and have a musical quality, but lack the vigour and fire of MALORY's interpretation of the legends. His later poems included *Enoch Arden, and Other Poems*, 1864, *Tiresias*, 1885, *Locksley Hall, Sixty Years After*, 1886, *Demeter and Other Poems*, 1889, including 'Crossing the Bar', and *The Death of Oenone*, 1892. From 1853 to 1869 Tennyson had lived in the Isle of Wight; he then built a house at Aldworth, near Haslemere, which was his home until his death. In 1884 he was raised to the peerage. He died in his eighty-fourth year and received a public funeral.

Tennyson's poetry is characterised by wide interests, by intense sympathy with the deepest feelings and aspirations of humanity and awareness of the problems of life and thought, an exquisite sense of beauty, and a marvellous power of vivid and minute description, often achieved by a single phrase, and heightened by the perfect matching of sense and sound. Few poets have excelled him in precision and delicacy of language. As a lyrist he ranks with the highest in English poetry.

Bibliography: C. Ricks (Ed.), *Poems*, 1968, and *Tennyson*, 1972; E. F. Shannon, Jr, *Tennyson and the Reviewers: a study of his literary reputation and of the influence of the critics upon his poetry, 1827–1851*, 1952; J. Killham, *Tennyson and 'The Princess'*, 1958; J. Richardson, *The Pre-eminent Victorian; a study of Tennyson*, 1962; R. W. Rader, *Tennyson's Maud*, 1963; D. J. Palmer (Ed.), *Tennyson*, 1973.

Tennyson, Charles, see TURNER, CHARLES TENNYSON.

Tennyson, Frederick (1807–98), English poet, born at

Tenochtitlán

Louth, Lincolnshire, eldest brother of Alfred, Lord TENNYSON. Educated at Eton and Cambridge, he spent most of his life in Italy and Jersey. He contributed four pieces to the *Poems by Two Brothers*, 1827, and published *Days and Hours*, 1854, *The Isles of Greece*, 1890, *Daphne*, 1891, and *Poems of the Day and Year*, 1895.

Bibliography: H. Nicolson, *Tennyson's Two Brothers*, 1947.

Tenochtitlán, see AZTEC.

Tenon, see JOINERY.

Tenor, term in music denoting: (1) the highest natural adult male voice, the compass being from tenor C to about treble B, i.e. an octave below soprano. It is so called because in polyphony it was the tenor part which 'held' the CANTUS FIRMUS (if any), around which the other parts were woven. (2) It also denotes a musical instrument playing the part between bass and alto. With wind instruments in particular there is considerable confusion and overlapping between alto and tenor in America and Britain. English tenor is often the same as American alto (but note that the British treble RECORDER is the American alto). (3) The largest bell of a ring or set is known as the tenor (see CAMPANOLOGY).

Tenor Oboe, see COR ANGLAIS.

Tenpin Bowling, indoor game played on a bowling lane with balls made of hard rubber or plastic. Though played in Germany and the Low Countries from the 14th century, it attained its greatest popularity in the USA where it was introduced by Dutch immigrants. Up to 1840 the Dutch population of New York played the game on the green, and the bowlers' square north of the Battery is still called Bowling Green.

The first covered lanes were of hardened clay or slate, but they are now of maple pine strips of a width of 2·54 cm set on edge, fastened together and to the bed of the alley. The maple strips are placed in the areas likely to receive the greatest wear, that is the approach (the first 5 m of the pin deck area). The alley itself is 105 cm wide and 24·38 m long, while on each side is a gutter of 23 cm to catch 'wides', and at the back a heavy curtain.

The game is played with ten pins, or skittles (the tenth having been added to evade the law against the game of ninepins), which are set up in front of a triangle with the apex to the front. The ball may not exceed 68·5 cm in circumference and 8·6 kg in weight; it has three holes for the thumb, middle and forefinger.

While there is no limit to the number of players, five is usual for league play. The object of the game is to knock the pins down, each player rolling two balls (a frame), ten frames making a game. A mode of scoring by strikes and spares is used.

Variations in the size, number or disposition of the pins, the size of the balls and the mode of scoring constitute the games of 'cocked hat', 'quitet', 'four back', 'duck pin', 'head pin', etc.

During the 1960s tenpin bowling achieved a good deal of popularity in Britain, alleys often being built on old cinema and theatre sites. There are many thousands of bowling clubs throughout the world, with 53 nations affiliated to the Fédération Internationale des Quillers.

See also SKITTLES.

Tenrec (tenerec or tanrac), small mammals of order Insectivora. The 23 species are placed in the family Tenrecidae, confined to Madagascar and the Comoro Islands. The common tenrec is *Tenrec ecaudatus*, a tailless animal about 40 cm long, which is one of the largest insectivores. It has a brownish coat with spines along the top of the head and neck. Tenrecs usually have rounded bodies and large heads with a long snout. They eat insects, worms, other small animals and fruit, live in burrows and are nocturnal. The female gives birth to up to 21 young at a time, more than any other mammal.

Tense, in grammar, involves the expression of time; either the time sense expressed by the verb in a sentence, or the relation between time as expressed in the sentence and the time that the sentence is made. Three tenses, past, present, and future, are common to many languages. Differences of tense are indicated mainly by the use of INFLECTIONS, and AUXILIARY VERBS. See also GRAMMAR; MOOD.

Tension, in physics, a force of stretching or pulling. Newton's third law states that action and reaction are always equal and opposite. Where the action and reaction of two bodies tend to keep them apart, these constitute a thrust, but where they tend to keep two bodies together they constitute a tension. A good illustration is a tug of war, the tension in the rope being the same everywhere. Tension is measured in the same way as other forces.

Tent, moveable dwelling or shelter made of cloth, skins, or tree bark supported by poles and secured by ropes and pegs. Tents have been used by nomadic peoples since the dawn of history. Those used by the Bedouin Arabs are made of strips of woven goat's hair and have changed little over the centuries. The *tepi* of the North American Indian is a conical-shaped tent made generally of skins or tree bark stretched over a tripod of poles. Probably the most luxurious tent used by nomadic peoples is the Mongol *yurt*, a felt-covered dwelling with walls of latticed hurdles; richly embroidered felt curtains line the interior and form partitions. Tents have long been recognised as a means of housing troops in active service areas. Modern tents vary in size from the smallest one-man sleeping shelter to the very large marquees, but have in common the fact that they are generally made of canvas suspended on a minimum framework of poles—sometimes

Tent. Nomads' tents in Kabul, Afghanistan. *(Popperfoto)*

only by a single pole—and are held secure by adjustable guy-lines of cord or rope attached to pegs in the ground.

Tenterden, town in Ashford District of Kent, England, with a wide variety of Georgian architecture in a broad tree-lined High Street. St Mildred's church is basically 13th-century, its magnificent tower giving wide views over the WEALD. Tenterden was originally a swine pasture for Thanet but later became a member of the CINQUE PORTS Confederation as a 'limb' of Rye. Population (1971) 5700.

Tenth, the tenth part of the annual income of an ecclesiastical living which formerly went to the pope, but at the Reformation was transferred to the Crown. Afterwards small benefices were exempted from payment of tenths altogether. See also QUEEN ANNE'S BOUNTY; TITHE.

Tenths, in music, the octave plus a third; an interval comprehending nine conjoint degrees, or ten sounds, diatonically divided.

Tentyra, or Tentyris, see DENDERA.

Tenure, Feudal. The theory that all land was held mediately or immediately of the sovereign in return for either free or base services is now generally considered a Norman innovation brought into England and adapted by William I from European feudal institutions. In return for his loan of land the feudal tenant was bound to perform either free or base services. From these services were developed respectively FREEHOLD tenure and COPYHOLD through tenure in villeinage.

Since the Law of Property Act 1922 (which took effect on 1 January 1926), all land has been held in freehold tenure, or free and common socage, which is not however, to be confused with the popular term 'freehold', which corresponds with an estate in FEE SIMPLE.

See also LAND LAWS.

Tenzing Norgay (1914–), Sherpa mountaineer who reached the summit of EVEREST (8850 m) with Edmund HILLARY on 29th May 1953. Born at Tsa-chu, near Makalu, and bred in the village of Thami (3660 m) in Solo Khombu, at 18 years of age he ran away from home to Darjeeling and became a mountain porter. Between 1935 and 1953 he took part in 19 expeditions to all parts of the Himalayas. He made several first attempts and became a distinguished sirdar ('Sherpa leader') and climber. He received the George Medal in 1953. He has for some time been a director of the Himalayan Institute of Mountaineering, a school of mountain training centred at Darjeeling, and is author of two autobiographies, *Man of Everest*, 1955 (as told to and written by J. R. Ullman), and *After Everest*, 1977 (as told to and written by M. Barnes).

Teotihuacán (Abode of the Gods), remains of an ancient Toltec (see TOLTECS) city, 39 km north-east of Mexico City. It is famous for its pyramids, which form the largest artificial tumuli on the American continent. The Pyramid of the Sun (709 m) has terraced sides and wide stairs leading to the top; the Pyramid of the Moon is 459 m high. There are also the remains of temples to Aztec gods. The remains cover an area of about 21 km².

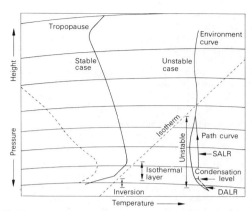

Tephigram. *(Source: R.G. Barry and R.J. Chorley, Atmosphere, Weather and Climate, 1976.)*

Bibliography: W. Bray, *Ancient Mesoamerica: Pre-Columbian Mexican and Maya Art*, 1970.

Tephigram (*T φ*-gram), a thermodynamic diagram used in METEOROLOGY to complete in a vertical direction the weather analysis achieved horizontally in a weather map. It was devised by Sir Napier Shaw, its name being derived from the main co-ordinates, temperature (*T*) and entropy (*φ*). The diagram consists of five lines: Dry Adiabatic Lapse Rate (parallel lines from bottom right to top left); Saturated Adiabatic Lapse Rate (curved lines sloping up from right to left); constant temperature, an isotherm (parallel lines from bottom left to top right); constant pressure (slightly curved nearly horizontal lines); and saturation mixing ratio (lines at a slight angle to the isotherms).

Tephilin, see PHYLACTERIES.

Tepic, capital of the state of NAYARIT, Mexico. Situated at an altitude of 2700 m in the Valley of Tepic, it is close to the volcano Sanganguey. It is the commercial centre of an agricultural and cattle-raising region, and its industries include cotton spinning and weaving, sugar refining, and distilleries. It is on the Southern Pacific railway and the Pacific Highway. Founded in 1531, it still retains, despite extensive modernisation, some fine period buildings. Population 111,300.

Teplice-Šanov (German *Teplitz-Schönau*), town of Czechoslovakia, in northern Bohemia, in the Biela valley at the foot of the ERZGEBIRGE. It is a popular spa. The district has coal-mines, and the town has several industries, including paper, glass, and pottery. Population 51,000.

Teramo, province of Italy, in north-east ABRUZZI. Area 1948 km². Population (1974) 257,00.

Teramo, Italian town and capital of the above province, situated on the Tordino, 40 km north-east of L'Aquila. It has a cathedral with a remarkable 14th-century Gothic portal, and there are Roman remains. Textiles and ceramics are manufactured, and there is a trade in agricultural produce (grain) and wine. Population (1974) 31,200; municipality (1971) 47,000.

Teraphim

Teraphim, biblical term of uncertain etymology, probably indicating small portable images (Gen. xxxi. 19, 35) such as have often been dug up in the course of excavation. They were household deities, and may have constituted a sort of legal title of ownership for the house. They have often been compared to the Roman *lares* and *penates*. The teraphim were closely associated with the practice of divination (1 Sam. xv. 23; Zech. x. 2); they would drive away evil spirits and plague demons (1 Sam. xix. 13).

Terbium, metallic chemical element, symbol Tb, atomic number 65, atomic weight 158·9254. It is a member of the group of LANTHANIDES.

Ter Borch, Gerard, also Terborch or Terburg (1617–81), Dutch painter, born at Zwolle. He studied under his father, Gerard the Elder, and later in Haarlem under Pieter de Molyn, and was very precocious. He was one of the most distinguished of Dutch genre painters, his small intimate works being characterised by a beautiful, cool tonality and an exquisite ability to render the texture of rich materials. His portraits, often painted on copper, are marked by a similar restraint and delicacy. Unlike most of his Dutch contemporaries, he travelled widely in Europe.

Terbrugghen, Hendrik (1588–1629), Dutch genre painter, born at Deventer. A prominent member of the Utrecht School, he was one of the first northern followers of CARAVAGGIO (with whom he may have been in direct contact in Rome), adopting the latter's CHIAROSCURO but developing a clearer, silvery light which anticipates the Delft School and VERMEER.

Terce, in Scots law, was a real right whereby a widow who had not accepted any special provision was entitled to a LIFERENT of one-third of the heritage owned by her husband at the date of his death. The corresponding right of a widower to a liferent of his wife's heritage was called *courtesy*. Both rights were abolished by the Succession (Scotland) Act 1964. See also SUCCESSION, INTESTATE.

Terebene, colourless liquid consisting of terpene and other hydrocarbons. It is prepared by treating turpentine with successive quantities of sulphuric acid and distilling the produce. The smell of terebene resembles thyme or pinewood; it is used as an antiseptic and deodoriser.

Terebinth, see PISTACIA.

Teredo, the ship worm or woodworm, a genus of bivalve molluscs with a long worm-like body clothed in a thin shelly sheath. The shell is small and occurs at the thicker end where it protects the various organs. At the more slender end are two tubes, one of which conveys water to the gills and the other expels it with excavated matter. With its shell valves it bores into timber, and is very destructive to ships, piers and submarine cables. Francis Drake's *Golden Hind* was destroyed by *Teredo*.

Terek, river in the North Caucasus, USSR, rising on the southern slopes of Mount KAZBEK. It traverses the main Caucasian range through DARYAL gorge, and flows into the Caspian Sea. Length 623 km.

Terence (Publius Terentius Afer) (c. 195–159 BC), Roman comic poet, born at Carthage, probably of Libyan stock. Brought to Rome as a slave by P. Terentius Lucanus, he received a good education and was afterwards manumitted. Six of his plays are extant: *Andria*, 166, *Hecyra*, 165, *Heauton Timoroumenus*, 163, *Eunuchus*, 162, *Phormio*, 162, and *Adelphi*, which was first performed at the funeral games of L. Aemilius Paulus, 160. Four of these are adaptations from Menander, two from Apollodorus. Supreme both in point of style and dramatic skill, Terence influenced many later writers, including Molière. Even more than PLAUTUS's plays, Terence's comedies supplied the model for the modern comedy of manners. The best edition is that of R. Kauer and W. M. Lindsay, 1926.

Bibliography: G. Norwood, *Terence*, 1923; W. Beare, *The Roman Stage*, 1950.

Terengganu, state of MALAYSIA, with a total area of 13,000 km². On the east coast of PENINSULAR MALAYSIA, Terengganu is bounded by Kelantan to the north and north-west and Pahang to the south and southwest. Its inland boundaries follow the watersheds of its largest rivers, the Besut, Terengganu, and Kemaman, in the hills of the north–south aligned East Coast Range. The Terengganu Highlands (average height 762 m) occupy most of the western half of the state, falling to a narrow coastal plain (25 to 50 km wide) marked on the seaward edge by *permatang*, or parallel sandy ridges alternating with swampland, a characteristic east coast landform. The interior is sparsely inhabited and the population is concentrated along the rivers and coast, especially in the delta area of Kuala Terengganu. Wet-rice and fishing are by far the main components of an economy geared largely to local Malay needs: the 36,000 ha of wet paddy land consist mainly of holdings under 1·5 ha; coastal fishing in small boats provides the basic protein in the east coast Malay diet, and in Terengganu employs 11,000 men. Both paddy-farming and fishing are marked by high rates of underemployment, and rural poverty is a serious problem. Export agriculture has developed considerably since 1965 with some 73,000 ha of rubber and 24,600 ha of oil-palm. Iron mining was important until 1970, when Malaysia's largest iron-ore mine, at Bukit Besi, closed. Terengganu's roads are mainly of gravel and subject to flooding, and there is no railway. The ports are all small fishing ports, although in 1955, with a population of 12,000, Dungun handled a greater tonnage of cargo than Port Kelang (almost wholly iron-ore for export to Japan).

Population (1970) 405,539 (Malays 94 per cent, Chinese 5·3 per cent). Terengganu, in population, is the most 'Malay' state of all 13 states of Malaysia; and one of the most rural and conservative in culture. The Sultan's residence, at the state capital of Kuala Terengganu (population 53,320), remains on the site of one of the older river-mouth *kampongs*, or villages.

The early history of Terengganu is obscure. A Chinese source notes it as subject to the Sumatran Palembang kingdom during the 6th century; it came under Javanese control in the 7th century, was a tributary of the Javanese Majapahit Empire in the 14th century, and was under the Kingdom of Melaka's influence in the 15th century. Siamese influence became strong, and in the 18th century Terengganu came under Siamese suzerainty until Siam transferred suzerainty to Britain by treaty in 1909. Terengganu remained outside the Federated Malay States and a British Adviser was appointed in 1919. In 1948 it became part of the Federation of Malaya and later of Malaysia.

Terephthalic Acid, $C_6H_4(CO_2H)_2$, is prepared by the oxidation of *para*-xylene. Terephthalic acid is used as one starting material in the production of artificial polyester fibres.

Teresa of Avila, Saint, or Theresa (1515–82), Spanish nun and monastic reformer, born as Teresa Cepeda de Ahumada, at Avila. She entered a Carmelite convent in her native town in 1533 but was not fully converted to her life of perfection till 1555. Soon afterwards she received her first ecstasy and an intellectual vision of Christ. Seeing the relaxation of discipline within the religious orders, she determined on reform and set about founding a house in which all the original rules of the Carmelite order would be observed. She met with strong opposition from clerical and lay authorities, but having obtained permission from the pope, she established (1562) the ancient Carmelite rule at a small house in Avila which she dedicated to St Joseph. Here the sisters (at first only four in number) lived according to the primitive rule. After a time the number was increased to 13, and Teresa herself took up her abode with them spending, as she says, the five happiest years of her life. Her energy and administrative ability were exceptional; between 1562 and her death she founded 15 new houses directly, and 17 through others. With the help of St JOHN OF THE CROSS she established her reform among the Carmelite friars. It is estimated that her work did much to prevent the spread of Protestantism to Spain. It inspired the leaders of the COUNTER-REFORMATION all over Europe. Teresa combined practical common sense and industry with extraordinary mystical graces, which are described in her writings. These latter are among the classics of Spanish literature and masterpieces of mystical theology. She was canonised in 1622; her feast is on 15 October. She was declared a a doctor of the Church in 1970. Her works include *The Way of Perfection*, *The Castle of the Soul*, and *The Book of the Foundations*, all translated into English by E. A. Peers, 1946.

Bibliography: V. Sackville-West, *The Eagle and the Dove*, 1943; E. W. T. Dicken, *The Crucible of Love*, 1963.

Tereshkova, Valentina Vladimirovna (1937–), Soviet cosmonaut, a former mill-worker, born at Masleyanikovo, USSR. She joined the Soviet space programme in 1962, and in 1963 made a flight of 48 orbits of the earth in *Vostok 6*, being the first woman to enter space. She subsequently (1963) married Major Anchien Nikolayev, another Soviet cosmonaut, and they have a daughter.

Teresina, capital of the state of PIAUÍ, Brazil. It is situated about 400 km inland on the Rio Parnaiba. It is the commercial centre of an agricultural and cattle-raising area. Its main lines of communication with the coast are either by river to the port of Parnaiba at the mouth of the Rio Parnaiba or by rail to São Luís in the neighbouring state of Mahanhão. Population (1975) 290,000.

Tereus, in Greek legend, son of King Ares of Daulis in Phocis. He married Procne, daughter of Pandion, King of Athens, who bore him a son named Itys. Wishing to marry her sister Philomela also, he hid Procne in the country and

told Philomela she was dead; then, having married Philomela, he cut out her tongue. But Philomela soon learned the truth about Procne, to whom she made known her own fate by means of a few words woven into a garment. Procne at once killed Itys and served up his flesh. The sisters fled, pursued by Tereus. Before they were overtaken they appealed to the gods for help, and their prayer was heard: Procne became a nightingale, Philomela a swallow, Tereus a hoopoe (crested bird). Ovid (*Metamorphoses* vi. 565) reverses the roles of Procne and Philomela; some writers make Procne the swallow, Philomela the nightingale.

Tergeste, see TRIESTE.

Term, or terminal figure, in classical architecture, representation of the upper half of a human figure, springing from a pedestal or pillar.

Termez, town in UZBEK SSR, USSR, and capital of Surkhandarya *oblast*, on the Amu Darya river, the Bukhara-Dushanbe railway, and the frontier with Afghanistan. It is the centre of an area growing fine-fibre cotton. Population (1970) 35,000.

Terminable Annuities, see PUBLIC DEBT.

Terminal Velocity. If a body moves under the influence of a continuous force in a resisting medium, e.g., the atmosphere, the resistance increasing with the velocity of the body, there is a limit to the velocity that it can attain. The terminal velocity is small for snowflakes, greater for drops of rain, and greater still for hailstones, and it depends largely on the size, shape, and density of the falling body, in addition to the weather conditions, which involve variations in the humidity and density of the air. See also VISCOSITY.

Terminator, the line which divides the dark from the illuminated portion of the disk of the MOON or of a planet.

Termini Imerese (ancient *Thermae Himerenses*), fishing port and tourist resort in SICILY, on the northern coast, 35 km south-east of Palermo. It has a beautiful 16th-century cathedral and Roman remains. The Greek city of Himera (founded 648 BC) was razed in 408 BC by the Carthaginians, who built a new town on the opposite bank of the river. It was the birthplace (361 BC) of Agathocles, tyrant of Syracuse from 317 to 289 BC. Hot mineral springs are found in the vicinity. The town has a trade in agricultural produce, olive oil, and fish. Population (1974) 24,100.

Terminus, Roman god of boundaries and frontiers. His cult was supposed to have been introduced by Numa, who made everyone mark the boundaries of his land with stones consecrated to Jupiter, and offer yearly sacrifices at these stones. This festival was the Terminalia held on 23 February.

Termite, or white ant, an insect in the order ISOPTERA. There are about 2000 species. Most of these insects are to be found in the tropics although some species are found in Europe; e.g. *Kalotermes flavicollis* and *Reticulitermes lucifugus*.

Termites are grouped into five families: (1) Mastotermitidae, e.g. *Mastotermes darwiniensis* from North

Termite

Australia; (2) Kalotermitidae, e.g. *Kalotermes* and *Neotermes*; no workers are present in the community; (3) Hodotermitidae, e.g. genus *Hodotermes*; workers may or may not be found; (4) Rhinotermitidae; workers are present and almost all members are subterranean, e.g. *Rhinotermes*; (5) Termitidae, the largest family, which includes about two-thirds of all the species recorded; workers are present; representative genera include *Termes*, *Microtermes*, and *Nasutitermes*.

The name 'white ant' is wrong as termites are far removed from the true ants, but the worker nymphs of some species are opaque white and superficially bear some resemblance to ants. Like ants they are social insects exhibiting caste systems.

The social organisation of termites is complex and fascinating. Although differences are found from one species to the next, and some species lack workers, the organisational hierarchy in general includes primary reproductive types that develop into winged fertile males and winged fertile females. These forms leave the original colony, swarm and form pairs. After pairing, both male and female shed their wings and build a nuptial chamber, in which they copulate and become established as the king and queen of a new colony. The female's rate of egg-laying is initially low; about 15–50 eggs are laid in the first season. Thereafter the queen becomes an egg-laying machine, laying several thousand eggs per day. Three castes are produced: workers, soldiers and supplementary reproductives.

1. *Workers:* these include sterile male and female forms. Compound eyes may or may not be present; the mandibles are strong and adapted for gnawing wood and other plant tissue. They do not participate in defence of the colony

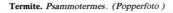

Termite. *Psammotermes.* *(Popperfoto)*

Termite nests. *(Popperfoto)*

and do not reproduce, but perform all other routine jobs essential for the survival of the colony: caring for and feeding young reproductives; caring for, feeding, and attending the queen; where a 'fungus-garden' is present, cultivating this; foraging for food; building and expanding the colony; repairing and other maintenance work. Sometimes workers may be divided into 'major' and 'minor' forms. In this case the minor forms resemble the major forms, but are smaller and have smaller heads and mandibles.

2. *Soldiers:* these are sterile forms, including males and females, who participate in the defence of the colony. Basically two morphologically different types of soldiers are distinguished according to their mode of defence. (1) The *mandibulate type* has a very large head and powerful mandibles. Such types are found when defence involves seizing and bodily removing intruders. (2) The *nasute type* carries out its defence role by emitting a repellent fluid from a frontal pore located on the head. In such types the mandibles are often degenerate and the head is drawn out anteriorly into a rostrum. Soldiers also escort foraging workers on their food gathering trips, which often go some distance from the colony.

3. *Supplementary Reproductives:* these include males and females. They are usually produced after the worker and soldier forms have appeared in the colony, and in any case some weeks after the initial colony has been established. They act as 'stand-bys', ready to replace the founder male or female (king or queen) should they die.

Colonies may be fairly simple in structure or they may be complex and involve a series of corridors, galleries and antechambers, all of which lead up to the royal chamber. They may be subterranean or they may be built above the ground, and some Australian species, e.g. *N. triodiae*, build steeple-like structures which attain a height of almost 7 m (basal diameter 3·6 m). These termitaria are constructed from soil particles that are bound together firmly by means of a sticky fluid secreted by the workers (usually saliva or saliva plus regurgitated matter). In theory such colonies are everlasting, and some Termitidae have colonies estimated to be 40–100 years old.

Bibliography: P. E. Howse, *Termites*, 1970; A. D. Imms, *Textbook of Entomology*, 1970; E. O. Wilson, *The Insect Societies*, 1971.

Terms, in English law, the portions of the year during which the High Court sits. There are four: Michaelmas (1 October to 21 December); Hilary (11 January to the Wednesday after Easter Sunday); Easter (Second Tuesday after Easter Sunday to the Friday before the Spring bank holiday); Trinity (Second Tuesday after the Spring bank holiday to 31 July). The Inns of Court terms, which are about three weeks long within the Law Terms and are called by the same names, are the 'dining terms' for students, who in the process of qualifying for call to the Bar fulfil the requirement of residence by eating dinners during term time.

Terms, in universities and colleges, the time during which instruction is regularly given to students. Schools have adopted the same system. In the UK there are usually three terms. The academic year starts in September/October, and there are breaks at Christmas, Easter, and during the summer months. Many colleges and universities in the USA operate on a two-term (nine months) academic year and hold summer sessions during June, July, and August.

Terms, in formal logic, the expression in language of the notion obtained in an act of apprehension. Terms are divided into simple, singular, universal, common, univocal, equivocal, abstract, concrete, etc.

See also SYLLOGISM.

Tern, river of Salop, England, which joins the Severn at Atcham. Length 51 km.

Tern, or sea swallow, *Sterna*, a genus of birds in order Charadriiformes. They resemble the gulls, to which they are related, but are smaller and slender, with a forked tail. They are extensively distributed, especially in temperate climates. Though poor walkers and swimmers, they are very active on the wing, skimming the surface of the sea from sunrise to sunset in search of small fish and other marine animals. A number of species occur in Britain, notably the common tern, *S. hirundo*, with grey plumage. The others are the Arctic tern, *S. paradisea*, the Sandwich tern, *S. sandvicensis*, the little tern, *S. albifrons*, and the roseate tern, *S. dougallii*. The Arctic tern is remarkable for the range of its migration, from Greenland, North America and northern Europe as far south as the Antarctic. The black tern and other similar species known as marsh terns are now placed in the genus *Chlidonias*. They are distinguished by their shorter bills, short and slightly forked tails, and less fully webbed feet.

Ternate and Tidore, islands in the province of Maluku, Indonesia, best known as two of the major spice islands of the Moluccas, the region of earliest and most intense European imperial rivalry in Asia. These two small islands were powerful Muslim sultanates after the arrival of Islam in the Moluccas in the late 15th century. They played a crucial role in the history of Portuguese, Spanish, English, and Dutch imperial expansion during the 16th and 17th centuries, determining much of the nature and direction of European activity in Asia during this time, solely on account of Europe's heavy demand for spices and the two islands' monopoly of world production of clove and nutmeg.

Portuguese traders obtained cloves from the sultans of Ternate and Tidore in 1513, and established factories on both islands. Ferdinand MAGELLAN arrived for the Spanish in 1521, Spanish-Portuguese conflict ensued, with each claiming the islands and each aligned with one of the two rival sultans (the Spanish with the sultan of Tidore, the Portuguese with the sultan of Ternate). Then, under the Treaty of Saragossa (1529), Spain relinquished its tenuous claim to the Moluccas, but continued to be a major force in the region, especially after the union of Spain and Portugal in 1580, from its Filipino base. Portuguese treachery and Christian proselytising alienated the sultanate of Ternate and by 1574 the Portuguese presence there was eliminated. The Portuguese gained permission from the sultan of Tidore to build a new fort on the neighbouring island, but in 1579 Francis DRAKE's arrival in Ternate enhanced English interest in the Spice Islands, and by 1600 the Dutch had arrived. After conflict between the Hispano-Portuguese and Dutch forces, a truce was achieved in 1609. Henceforth the Dutch gradually consolidated their power over the sultanates, against Spanish and English competition, until the sultan of Tidore accepted Dutch sovereignty in 1667. The sultanate of Ternate, the dominant power in the eastern archipelago during the 16th and 17th centuries, accepted Dutch control in 1683. Under the Dutch spice monopoly, production of cloves and nutmeg was forbidden in the two islands (being confined to the BANDA ISLANDS and AMBON). Once prosperous centres of a thriving spice trade, Ternate and Tidore were reduced to poverty, their hereditary rulers to meek pensioned compliance.

Both are volcanic islands: Ternate's 106 km² are little more than the triple-crater volcano of the 1715-m Gama Gama, and Tidore's 116 km² are dominated by a symmetrical volcanic cone in the south of the island. Ternate is densely forested, and exports timber, copra, and spices, but Tidore is more open, with fertile soil producing cotton, maize, fruits, and spices. Estimated 1975 population (Ternate) 20,000; (Tidore) 27,000.

Terneuzen, port in the province of Zeeland, Netherlands, situated on an arm of the River Scheldt, 45 km north-west of Antwerp, Belgium. It is at the end of the 32 km long Ghent-Terneuzen Canal, on which are located iron and steel works and other major industries. Population 32,900.

Terni, province of Italy, in south UMBRIA. Area 2121 km². Population (1974) 223,000.

Terni (ancient *Interamna Nahars* or *Interamna Umbrica*), Italian town and capital of the above province, situated on the edge of a rich well-watered basin 80 km from Rome. Its site is believed to have been occupied since 1000 BC, and the town has Roman remains and early Christian tombs. The cathedral (13th–17th centuries) has a 10th-century crypt. It has steelworks (stainless steel is a major product), iron foundries, fertiliser, plastics, engineering, and textile works. It is also a centre of hydroelectric power production from the rivers Nera and Velino, particularly at the Marmore waterfall nearby. It is thought to have been the birthplace of TACITUS. Population (1974) 111,043.

Ternopol, *oblast* in western UKRAINIAN SSR, USSR, on the Volhynia-Podolia upland north of the River DNIESTER, in the black earth belt with wooded steppe vegetation. There are lignite and peat deposits. Wheat, maize, and sugar-beet are grown, and cattle and pigs are raised. There are also varied food industries. For the province's history, see GALICIA. Area 13,800 km². Population (1970) 1,153,000 (23 per cent urban).

Ternopol, or Tarnopol, capital city of Ternopol *oblast* (see above), USSR, on the River Seret south-east of Lvov. It is a major railway junction (five lines), with food and light industries. Founded in 1540 as a fortress, it later became an important trading centre; it has been a provincial capital since 1921. Fierce fighting took place here in 1944. Population (1970) 85,000, before the Second World War half Jewish.

Terpander (7th century BC), Greek musician and poet, born at Antissa in Lesbos. He has been called the father of Greek lyric poetry, but no genuine fragment of his work survives.

Terpenes, general name given to hydrocarbons which occur in essential oils and have a molecular formula $(C_5H_8)_n$. They can be classified as mono- ($n = 2$, e.g. p-cymene), sesqui- ($n = 3$), di- ($n = 4$) and tri-terpenes ($n = 6$). They are all volatile and unsaturated compounds, the most important being limonene, camphene and PINENE, many of them being derivatives of p-cumene (p-methyl *iso-* propyl benzene). There are also useful derivatives of terpenes such as alcohols (e.g. terpineol, menthol), terpene ketones (e.g. carvone, camphors, menthone), terpene ethers (e.g. cineole) and acyclic members (e.g. geraniol, citral and myrcene).

Terpsichore, muse of choral dance and song. See MUSES.

Terra Australis Incognita, vast unknown continent which was commonly believed to lie beyond the ocean of the southern hemisphere as a counterpart to the land masses of Europe, Asia, and Africa. The belief was held by the geographers of antiquity and the Middle Ages and was only finally exploded by Capt. James Cook in the late 18th century. Terra Australis Incognita was believed to stretch in a solid mass as far north as Tierra del Fuego as late as the 16th century. Discoveries by MAGELLAN, DRAKE, TORRES, TASMAN, and other explorers gradually brought about a realisation that this supposed land mass did not exist; finally, COOK ascertained the limits of Australia and of the Antarctic continent and proved the original theory entirely false. See also ANTARCTIC EXPLORATION.

Terra Cotta (Italian, baked earth, Latin *terra cocta*), hard, unglazed pottery, used for bricks, tiles and architectural ornaments, as well as for tombs and coffins, vases and statues. It may be left with its natural brownish red

surface, painted as was customary among the Greeks, or covered with enamel.
Bibliography: R. A. Higgins, *Catalogue of Terracottas* (vol. 1) British Museum, 1954.

Terra di Lavoro, see CASERTA.

Terra Japonica, see CATECHU.

Terra Rossa Soils, see RENDZINA AND TERRA ROSSA SOILS.

Terra Sigillata, see SAMIAN WARE.

Terrace, bench in a river valley profile denoting a former level of the valley floor or floodplain. More or less constant in height, they are separated from each other and the present valley by low bluffs or scarps. Two types of terraces are generally recognised: erosional and depositional. The first are carved out of bedrock or an earlier accumulation of stream deposits, and the second results from the building up of the valley floor by the deposition of ALLUVIUM. Terraces which correspond in height on opposite sides of the valley are termed 'paired' in distinction to 'unpaired' terraces which are staggered or single in occurrence. Paired terraces usually result from sudden rapid incision (rejuvenation) of a valley previously displaying extensive lateral erosion. Unpaired terraces, on the other hand, imply slower discontinuous incision with continued lateral erosion. Some paired terraces merely reflect the presence of horizontal hard layers of rock. See also BEACH, RAISED.
Bibliography: G. H. Dury, *Rivers and River Terraces*, 1970.

Terracina, or Tarracina, Italian seaport and resort in LAZIO, on the Tyrrhenian Sea coast 35 km south-east of Latina, at the southern extremity of the PONTINE MARSHES. Originally a town of the VOLSCI, under the name of ANXUR, it became in time a Roman colony. The cathedral (11th–17th centuries) stands on the site of an ancient temple; a Roman aqueduct remains, and overlooking the town is a ruined temple of Jupiter. The muscatel wine of the region is well known. Population (1974) 24,100.

Terramare (from Italian *terra*, earth, and *marna*, marl), natural fertiliser found in the valley of the River Po, Italy, in flat-topped mounds which were villages of peoples of a BRONZE AGE culture. The settlements, which were built on pile foundations but which were nevertheless on land, have taken generally the name of the fertiliser.
Bibliography: R. Munro, *Palaeolithic Man and Terramara settlements in Europe*, 1912; L. Barfield, *Northern Italy before Rome*, 1971.

Terranova di Sicilia, see GELA.

Terranova Pausania, see OLBIA.

Terrapin, various TORTOISES of the families Testudinidae and Dermatemydidae of the order CHELONIA. Some of them, especially the diamondback terrapin, *Malaclemys terrapin*, found in the salt marshes on the eastern shores of North America, are highly valued as food. Among the most important are the yellow-bellied, the red-bellied, the chicken, and the salt-water terrapins. They are all active swimmers, their clawed digits being united by a web. They are almost omnivorous, but feed chiefly on aquatic animals. In North America and Australia they are commonly kept and fattened in captivity.

Terre Adélie, French sector of the continent of ANTARCTICA, between longitudes 136° and 142°E. It was first visited by Dumont d'Urville in 1840 and named by him for his wife. French expeditions, *Expéditions Polaires Françaises*, led by P.-E. Victor have explored and mapped much unknown land here since 1948.

Terre Haute, city and county seat of Vigo county, Indiana, USA, on the Wabash river, 109 km south-west of Indianapolis in an agricultural and coal-mining region. It manufactures bricks, tiles, chemicals, metal products, and glass. It has a state university and the Rose Polytechnic Institute. Population 70,286.

Terres Australes et Antarctiques Françaises, French Antarctic possessions, established by law No. 55–1052 and previously administered (from 1924) as dependencies of Madagascar. They consist of Île St Paul, Île Amsterdam, Îles Crozet (CROZET ARCHIPELAGO), Îles de Kerguelen (KERGUELEN ISLANDS), and Terre Adélie.

Terrestrial Magnetism, see GEOMAGNETISM; MAGNETISM.

Terrier, term originally applied to dogs which pursue rabbits and other game into their burrows. The following are true terriers: Airedale, Australian, Bedlington, Border, Bull, Cairn, Dandie Dinmont, Fox, Irish, Kerry Blue, Lakeland, Manchester, Norfolk, Norwich, Scottish, Sealyham, Skye, Staffordshire Bull, Welsh, and Welsh Highland White. But the word is also now applied to a number of breeds of foreign origin, for example Boston and Tibetan terriers.

Terriss, William, real name William Charles James Lewin, (1847-97), British actor, born in London He was very popular as a hero of melodrama, playing for years at the Adelphi Theatre, at the stage door of which he was assassinated by a mad and obscure unsuccessful actor. His daughter Ellaline married Sir Seymour HICKS.

Territorial Army.
History. When the British infantry was territorialised under Lord Cardwell's scheme of 1881, volunteer rifle corps were linked with regular and militia units to form the regimental district. For this reason most Territorial Army infantry units carried the title of a line regiment (e.g. Green Howards) with a battalion number 4 or above. There are exceptions to this, of the following order: 'expatriate' units with titles like 'London Scottish'; battalions from counties which did not support a regular regiment, such as Monmouthshire; numerous London Light Infantry units with roots in the 1859 Volunteer Movement such as the Artists' Rifles, Queen's Westminster; and the unique Honourable Artillery Company, which was formed before the regular regiments existed. Nevertheless, every Territorial Army unit was affiliated to some regular unit whether it shared its name or not. After the passing of the Territorial and Reserve Forces Act of 1907 and Lord Haldane's administration of it, liaison between regular and TA units became a reality. Under this act county associations were formed which raised and administered (but did not command) the new territorial force.

The territorial force was intended at first for home service only, but provision was made for individuals to volunteer for overseas service. In 1914 so many of the 11,900 officers and 302,000 other ranks did so volunteer that war units were mobilised in their entirety and brigaded in the 15 territorial (and yeomanry) divisions which took part in the First World War. The 14 mounted brigades which completed the force up to 1914 were not employed as such, but the 53 regiments of which they were composed went to reinforce other armies or to form the 74th Division, where units came from all parts of the UK. The other 14 divisions were at first known only by their regimental designation, and the numbers were not allotted until May 1915.

Up to 1914 the defence forces by land consisted of: first line, regular army; second line, special reserve; third line, territorial force. In 1920 a reorganisation promoted the territorial from third to second line and renamed them the Territorial Army; the special reserve reverted to its old name of MILITIA, but in practice no militia was raised intil 1938. The 1920 establishment provided for the same 14 infantry divisions (but only two brigades of cavalry), some army troops, and a coast defence and an anti-aircraft (AA) component. The obligation to serve overseas was placed on all members. A small proportion of the cavalry was mechanised. About 150,000 men were recruited, and numbers remained at about this figure until 1938. In 1935 a new establishment was drawn up and partly put into effect: 46 and 47 Divisions were disbanded and went to fill the ranks of five AA divisions; the field force was now to consist of nine infantry, three motorised, and one armoured division. Now for the first time old promises were implemented: some brigades and a few divisions were commanded by TA officers, and the deputy director general was also a TA officer. In 1938 numbers rose to 204,000, and between then and the outbreak of war almost doubled. But of these 405,000 some 107,000 belonged to air-defence units, so that approximately the same numbers were available for the field force as in 1918. During the war the TA ceased to exist as a separate force, and recruiting for it ceased. But the fusion of regular TA and conscript elements in the air-defence force, which then retained only men of certain medical categories, had the effect of releasing enough fit men to form a further seven divisions, largely composed of territorials, for the field force.

As in 1920, so on 1 January 1947, the TA was re-established. There were besides the field force some independent brigades and a much higher proportion than before of corps, army, and GHQ troops, drawn principally from regions where the field force division had been disbanded. National servicemen, on completion of full-time service with the regular army, up to 1957 undertook a further 3½ years' part-time service in the TA; they were required by law to complete a total of 45 days' training with the TA during these 3½ years. In 1956 a further reorganisation took place. Provision was made for ten infantry divisions, two being earmarked for NATO.

On 31 March, 1967, the TA was disbanded and the following day the Territorial and Army Volunteer Reserve (TAVR) was formed. The establishment of the new force was to be 50,000 against the 183,000 of the TA.

Territorial Army

All Division, Armoured, and Infantry Brigade head-quarters disappeared. Apart from two Engineer Brigades and three Signal Groups, no Formations headquarters were retained. The units making up the NATO part of the force were mainly logistic, although a few of the old units survived. The Army Emergency Reserve also disappeared and its units became an integral part of the TAVR. The force was divided into four categories. TAVR, the Ever-readies, consisted of some units and individuals who had volunteered for a call-out liability requiring them to reinforce the Regular Army when required for a period of up to six months. TAVR II, mostly logistic units, were liable for call-out in support of the Regular Army in NATO when warlike operations were in progress or preparation. TAVR III consisted of 87 infantry type units and was paid for from the Home Office vote for the Home Service only, mainly in aid of the civil authority. TAVR IV was made up of a number of other units, such as OTCs, bands, and units which did not have a rôle under the other categories.

In 1968 it was announced that TAVR III was to be disbanded. For nine months the men in these units carried on without pay and allowances and without any official financial support. On 1 January 1969, the 87 units were reduced to cadre form, each with an establishment of three officers and five soldiers. Their main rôle was to form a basis for any future expansion. They maintained the traditions and property of the old TA units, from whom they were directly descended and whose names in most cases they bore. On the formation of the TAVR, there had been 84 Territorial Auxiliary Force Associations covering the whole country, most of them based on one county. In 1968 these were reduced to 14 by amalgamation of TAFAs in each region.

In 1970 plans were announced for an immediate expansion of the TAVR, mainly to fill the lack of any uncommitted reserve capable of undertaking unexpected military tasks, but particularly the defence of the UK base. The additional units were formed on 1 April 1971 and consisted of one additional Armoured Car Regiment with a NATO rôle (there are now two) and 20 infantry type units made up of 77 sub-units, most of which were formed from the cadres. The new units were given the same overseas liability as the old units, but they were initially earmarked for tasks in the UK. All category numbers were discarded and the TAVR is now one force.

The TAVR currently numbers approximately 54,000 men and women against an establishment of 74,044 and its strength is distributed as follows: 44 per cent logistic, 38 per cent combat, and 18 per cent engineer and signal units. The majority of recruits are raised locally and they take part in a training programme spanning the whole year. With certain exceptions all TAVR members must spend 15 days at annual camp. The period of additional out-of-camp training is set at 16 days for first year recruits, 12 days for units committed to NATO, and 6 days for units with a United Kingdom rôle. A tax free bounty of £10–25 is paid for annual training and there is a taxable bounty of £60 for accepting liability for service. During training days volunteers receive the same pay and allowances as regular soldiers and their travelling expenses from home to place of training are paid. Both officers and men of the TAVR can volunteer for full-time service with the Regular Army. Soldiers under 30 years of age serve for one year, while officers may volunteer for six to eighteen months' service with the option of an extension to a maximum of two years.

Territorial Waters. Most modern states recognise the sovereignty of every other state over its own territorial waters. The limit was generally fixed at one marine league (c. 3 miles, 4·8 km) from the shore, measured from low-water mark. This distance of permissible appropriation is the subject of much criticism by writers on INTERNATIONAL LAW, because it was in its origin suggested by the supposed range of a gun; the tremendous range of modern artillery has made the distance meaningless. Three miles (4·8 km) at low-water mark, however, remains the minimum claim by a coastal state to sovereign control of the seas. A more extensive jurisdiction to the waters surrounding their coasts is claimed by a great many states, though this extended claim may be restricted to certain specific purposes, for example fishing.

The acquittal, for want of jurisdiction, of a German prisoner charged at the Central Criminal Court with manslaughter through the running down of the *Strathclyde* by the *Franconia* (in the trial of *R.* v. *Keyn*, 1876) 3.2 km off Dover led to the passing of the Territorial Waters Jurisdiction Act 1878. By that act the English courts have jurisdiction to arrest and try persons, whether British subjects or not, for offences committed on the seas within the territorial waters of the Crown, i.e. within one marine league from the coast.

A conference on the law of the sea at Geneva in 1958 failed to agree to the demand of Iceland and other countries that the limit of territorial waters should be extended to 12 miles (19·3 km). A second conference took place at Geneva in 1960, at which the US-Canadian proposal to extend the limit of territorial waters to 6 miles (9·6 km), with a contiguous zone of a further 6 miles (9·6 km) in which coastal states would enjoy exclusive fishing rights, failed to obtain the necessary majority. At the international conferences at Caracas and Geneva in 1974/5 again no agreement was reached, though the movement towards a consensus continued. The general trend in thinking seems to be towards a 12-mile (19·3 km) territorial sea and a 200-mile (321·9 km) economic zone. In Europe, the situation came to a head in the 'Cod Wars' of 1972/3, and 1975/6 involving Iceland, the UK, and West Germany.

Although no international negotiations have been successful, bilateral agreements have been reached between interested parties over fishing rights.

See also SOVEREIGNTY OF THE SEA.

Terror, Reign of, see FRANCE, *Modern History*.

Terrorism, Urban, the name given to the activities of the urban guerrilla, criminal acts undertaken by small groups of criminals or political dissidents as a means of securing funds, obtaining publicity, or seeking to blackmail governments into meeting their demands. The prefix 'urban' is used because the attackers employ the anonymity and obscurity of the modern city and all the resources of modern society against its rulers, and to contrast them with the brigands and guerrillas of the past, essentially part of rural society (see GUERRILLAS).

The western world in the 1960s and 1970s realised just

how vulnerable it was to attack by urban guerrillas. Some earlier, mainly anti-colonial, movements had employed tactics akin to those of the urban guerrilla, notably the Jewish Stern Gang and Arab terrorists who attacked the British Mandatory régime in Palestine. It is ironic, therefore, that it is the Arab opposition to the Israeli régime that has been the most publicised exponent of urban terrorism; many of the most spectacular HIJACKINGS and other acts of terrorism are the work of the Palestine Liberation Organisation or other opponents of Israel. For example, in May 1972 three Japanese, acting on behalf of the Palestinians, machine-gunned 24 people at Lod airport, and, in September 1972, 11 members of the Israeli team at the Munich Olympics were kidnapped and eventually murdered by the PLO.

The Arab-Israeli conflict is not, of course, the only source of terrorism. The Tupamaro movement in Uruguay conducts an urban guerrilla campaign against the established government of that country. The movement began, in 1963, with 20 people and carried out bank raids; by 1971 it claimed a strength of 3000. It partially succeeded in its aims and, in 1973, army action ended the parliamentary régime; but the strengthened forces of law and order virtually stamped out the Tupamaros.

In the neighbouring country of Argentina the use of kidnapping, for mercenary and political motives, has had considerable success. In 1973 over £1 million was paid for the release of one businessman, and in 1974 terrorists killed an average of one person a day and kidnapped over 500 in the year, receiving ransoms totalling over £25 million.

Even the British police force has had to adapt to new conditions and use firearms to a greater extent than hitherto. In February 1973 two young men who attacked the Indian High Commission offices in London were shot dead by police, and in June 1973 an armed policeman returning from embassy guard duty returned the fire of an armed bank raider and killed his assailant. Army and police have taken part in exercises to practise defence against hijackers of aircraft. In 1975 two 'sieges' in London featured armed men holding hostages and themselves surrounded by armed police. In both cases the police, by patience and determination, were able to persuade the gunmen to surrender. Similar tactics were used by the Irish police and, with minor concessions, the Dutch authorities faced with the hijacking of trains: but the Austrian authorities immediately acceded to the demands of terrorists who, in 1975, had seized the OPEC oil ministers in Vienna.

Bibliography: R. Clutterbuck, *Protest and the Urban Guerrilla*, 1973; L. Macfarlane, *Violence and the State*, 1974; P. Wilkinson, *Political Terrorism*, 1974; L. A. Sobel (Ed.), *Political Terrorism*, 1975.

Terry, family of illustrious English actors and actresses, of whom the parents, Benjamin (1818–96) and Sarah (Ballard) (1819–92) were well-known in the provinces, and later appeared in London with Macready and Charles KEAN. Their eldest child Kate (1844–1924) was a successful actress until she retired on her marriage in 1867. Kate's daughter, Mabel Gwynedd Terry-Lewis (1872–1957) was a well-known actress, while another daughter (also Kate) was the mother of Val and John GIELGUD. Two other daughters of Benjamin and Sarah went on the stage: Marion (1852–1930), who was the first Mrs Erlynne in *Lady Windermere's Fan*; and Florence (1854–96). The youngest child, Fred (1863-1933), was a successful romantic lead, who often played opposite his wife, Julia NEILSON. Their children, Phyllis (1892–) and Dennis (1895–1932) were both on the stage, and it was under Phyllis's management that John Gielgud made his first professional appearance. Fred's elder brothers, Charles and George, were theatre administrators, and

Terry Family. Benjamin and Sarah Terry, seated, with (left to right) Tom, Florence, Ellen, Kate, Charles, and Marion; photograph taken by the Rev. C. L. Dodgson (Lewis Carroll). *(Victoria and Albert Museum, London)*

Terry, Sir Richard Runciman

Charles's daughters, Beatrice and Minnie, were actresses. The most eminent member of the Terry family, however, was Benjamin and Sarah's second child, Dame Ellen Alicia Terry (1847–1928), who was leading-lady to Sir Henry IRVING at the Lyceum between 1878 and 1902. Together, they played numerous Shakespearean and modern roles. Dame Ellen later appeared under her own management at the Imperial Theatre, and in 1906 celebrated her stage jubilee at Drury Lane with a matinee in which 23 members of her family appeared with the leading theatrical figures of the day. As an actress, she is said to have had a fresh and lively technique, though without much talent for the weightier tragic roles. She was several times married and one of her children was Edward Gordon CRAIG. She published her autobiography in 1908, and was created DBE in 1925.

Bibliography: M. Steen, *A Pride of Terrys*, 1962.

Terry, Sir Richard Runciman (1865–1938), British musicologist, born at Ellington, Northumberland. After various appointments he became organist and choirmaster at Downside Abbey in 1896 and at Westminster Cathedral in 1901, where he remained until 1924. He did great work there accompanying the mass and divine office according to the highest musical standards and traditions, and he wrote on and edited much church music. He had a specialist's knowledge of sea shanties and carols. He was knighted in 1922.

Tertian Fever, see MALARIA.

Tertiaries, see FRANCISCANS.

Tertiary System, occurs above the CRETACEOUS and below the QUATERNARY SYSTEMS. It began about 64 million years ago and ended two million years ago. Tertiary rocks in Britain occur as two widely differing FACIES; shallow-water sediments in south-east England, and volcanic rocks of lower Tertiary age in western Scotland, northern England, and north-east Ireland. The Tertiary System is divided into a number of series, the lowest of which is the Palaeocene series; this is followed by the Eocene, Oligocene, Miocene, and Pliocene series. Prior to the deposition of the Tertiary sediments, the Cretaceous strata of southern England were uplifted, tilted, and eroded, and the succeeding Tertiary period saw a total change in the fauna from the dominant reptiles of the Jurassic and Cretaceous to the coming of the mammals. The flora also changed radically, with modern forms such as grasses appearing for the first time in the Tertiary.

In southern England Tertiary sediments are found in two areas, the London and Hampshire Basins, where they lie in synclinal basins floored by chalk. While the sediments were being deposited the two areas were joined and were part of a much larger Anglo-Gallic Basin extending over northern France and Belgium. To the north-west lay a continental land mass supplying sediment by means of large rivers. All the sediments show an east–west variation from continental to marine deposition, and were laid down in successive cycles, each showing a marine incursion at the base, passing up into continental conditions. There is therefore great lateral variation in beds of the same age.

The base of the Palaeocene is marked by a transgression of the sea over the eastern part of the London Basin; glauconitic sands, known as the Thanet Sands, were deposited over much of Kent, with a maximum thickness of 30 m. They contain marine molluscs and fish remains. The overlying Woolwich and Reading Beds mark a more widespread incursion of the sea at the base, but this was followed by the deposition of continental sands and clays in the west of the London Basin (the so-called Reading Beds); these represent sediments laid down by an enormous river delta. In places the sands have been cemented together by silica, and the Hertfordshire Pudding Stone is a distinctive hard conglomerate formed by the cementation of a flint-pebble bed. Further east the continental Reading Beds pass laterally into the Woolwich Beds, fossiliferous sands, clays, and pebble beds laid down in a lagoonal environment. Further east they pass into marine glauconitic sandstones.

In the London Basin the Blackheath or Oldhaven Beds occur at the base of the Eocene in the eastern part of the basin. They are composed of pebble beds and sandstones and represent a marine incursion; towards the south they overlap the underlying Palaeocene to rest directly on the chalk of the North DOWNS. To the north and west they disappear completely and the overlying London clay rests directly on Palaeocene deposits. The basal beds of the London clay in these areas are sandy, but pass up into a uniform blue-grey clay which weathers to yellow-brown on the surface. This is the typical London clay found over the whole of the London Basin. Septarian nodules (large cementstone concretions) occur at several horizons and yield most of the fossils found in the London clay. These include many different shells, fish, starfish, lobsters, crabs, turtles, crocodiles, birds, mammals, and plant remains. The latter include *Nipa* (the stemless palm), oak, almond, magnolia, and laurel, indicating a warmer climate than at present. The London clay passes up into the Claygate Beds, which consist of thin sands and clays, which in turn pass up into the Bagshot Beds. These are fluviatile, current-bedded sands, pale in colour and unfossiliferous, containing thin seams of pipeclay.

In the Hampshire Basin the London clay rests directly on the Palaeocene, and is composed of silty clays and fine sands, thinning westwards and indicating deposition in much shallower water than that of the London Basin. The fossils are also very different. The overlying Bagshot Beds are of marine facies in the east and fluviatile in the west of the basin. Around Bournemouth they contain rich seams of pipeclay, the source material for the potteries at Poole.

No Eocene sediments occur above the Bagshot Beds in much of the London Basin, but in the Hampshire Basin they are succeeded by the Bracklesham Beds which are sandy clays, locally rich in fossils. The foraminifera *Nummulites* is found in these beds and different species are used in correlating different horizons throughout the Anglo-Gallic Basin. At Alum Bay on the Isle of Wight the Bracklesham Beds occur as vertically inclined strata of finely laminated sand of varying colours, often collected or sold as souvenirs. Towards the east they become clay-rich and glauconitic and contain marine shellbands. The highest Eocene strata are the Barton Beds, which overlie the Bracklesham Beds and consist of clays at the base, passing up into sand; they are highly fossiliferous, containing gasteropods and lamellibranchs similar to forms found at present in seas around Australia and Japan.

By the end of the Eocene the whole Anglo-Gallic Basin had become silted up, and the open sea lay to the east over Germany and Russia. Deposits above the Eocene are all continental in character. Only the Lower Oligocene is represented in Britain; it occurs as the Headon Beds, found only in the north of the Isle of Wight and the adjacent mainland. These beds consist of marls, sandy clays, and occasional limestone bands, containing a variety of fossils including freshwater snails, water lilies, palms, birds, mammals, and reptiles. The overlying Osborne Beds are also freshwater marls and clays with limestones such as the Bembridge limestone. In the overlying Bembridge marls is an insect bed which has yielded 20 different species of fossil insect. The highest Oligocene strata are the Hamstead Beds which consist of shales and sands. Much further west, beds of Oligocene age are preserved in the Bovey Tracey Basin; they are the remains of a large lake and contain valuable pipeclay deposits.

During the Miocene and Pliocene periods the sea withdrew further east, and there are no sediments of Miocene age in Britain. Pliocene beds occur in eastern England, where they rest on a surface of folded Tertiary and Cretaceous strata, evidence of the ALPINE OROGENY which was taking place in continental Europe during the Miocene. Britain lay on the margin of the Alpine orogenic belts, and so although folding and faulting occurred there was no metamorphism associated with the movements. The folding was strongest in the Isle of Wight and the Isle of Purbeck.

The Pliocene strata consist mainly of thick deposits of crag in East Anglia, together with the Lenham Beds found overlying the chalk in East Kent, and as beach deposits in the CHILTERN HILLS. The crag succession is Coralline crag at the base, followed by Red crag and Icenian crag. They are all shelly sands deposited in very shallow water. The Coralline crag contains polyzoa and molluscs of warm-water origin, while the Red crag shows a gradual influx of colder-water molluscs, many of which are still found in Arctic waters. The Icenian crag was deposited from a large delta flowing north from the Ardennes, and again shows an increase in cold-water molluscs. The crag succession is overlain in Norfolk by the Cromer Forest bed series; peats, loams, and sands with a very mixed fauna. Above this again is the Arctic freshwater bed of peaty loams containing Arctic willow and birch. The whole of the Pliocene in Britain shows evidence of continuing climatic changes resulting in a drop in temperature, and the extinction of many groups of mammals. This climatic change led eventually to the Pleistocene GLACIAL PERIOD.

To the north, in the western part of Scotland, rocks of Palaeocene to Eocene age are represented by the vast lava fields and igneous intrusive centres of the Brito-Arctic or Thulean volcanic province. Volcanic rocks of the same age occur in Ireland, the Faeroe Islands, Rockall, East Greenland, and on the island of Lundy in the Bristol Channel. The volcanic activity was initiated and was most widespread in the Palaeocene, but it continued in places in the form of dyke intrusions (found in Scotland and northern England) and small plutonic centres well into the Eocene. The lavas are mainly basaltic in composition, and were produced by a number of large volcanoes. These volcanoes have since been deeply eroded and the underlying plutonic rocks are now well-exposed. These are predominantly gabbros and granites, together with many other minor intrusive rock types, showing a long history of intrusion at each plutonic centre.

Bibliography: J. E. Richey, *Tertiary Volcanic Districts*, 1961; A. M. and C. M. Davies, *Tertiary Faunas*, 1971–75.

Tertis, Lionel (1876–1975), British viola-player, born at West Hartlepool. He studied music at Leipzig and in London, and became a brilliant viola player and great teacher, in addition to arranging much music for the viola. He wrote an autobiography, *My Viola and I*, 1974.

Tertullian, Quintus Septimius Florens (c. 160–230), early Christian apologist, born probably at Carthage, attained some eminence as an advocate or rhetorician. At Carthage, probably, he was converted to Christianity, around 190, and at once ordained priest. He speaks of having been at Rome, and he could write Greek. About the end of the 2nd century he became a Montanist (see MONTANISM). According to Jerome, this was because of the envy and insults of the Roman clergy, but a more adequate and probable reason lies in the character of Tertullian himself. He was a rigorist and violently opposed to the restoration to communion of penitent adulterers and fornicators, a concession made by Agrippinus, Bishop of Carthage.

Tertullian holds one of the first places among the Latin fathers for learning and intellectual power. His writings are apologetic, practical, and doctrinal. The *Apology* written at Carthage, probably in the reign of Severus, contributed largely to the better understanding of Christianity and the mitigation of persecution.

Bibliography: J. Morgan, *The Importance of Tertullian in the Development of Christian Dogma*, 1928; R. A. Norris, *God and the World*, 1966; T. P. O'Malley, *Tertullian and the Bible*, 1967; T. D. Barnes, *Tertullian: A Historical and Literary Study*, 1971.

Tertz, Avram, see SINYAVSKI, ANDREI DONATEVICH.

Teruel, province of Spain in ARAGÓN. It is very mountainous, the highest point being in the Sierra de Jabalambre (2002 m), and has several large rivers including the GUADALAVIAR, the Guadalôpe and the Jiloca. The TAGUS has its source on the border between Teruel and Cuenca. Teruel has deposits of iron and lignite and produces cereals, fruit, oil, and wine. Area 14,820 km²; population 162,000.

Teruel, capital of the province of Teruel, Spain, on the River Guadalaviar. Portions of its old walls remain, and the town has a Gothic cathedral, badly restored, fine old houses, several *mudéjar* towers, and a 16th-century aqueduct. It was severely damaged in the civil war of 1936–39. Population 23,000.

Terylene, see POLYESTER.

Terza Rima, verse form consisting of three-line stanzas, the middle line of each stanza rhyming with the first and last lines of the succeeding stanza: *aba bcb cdc ded*. Terza rima originated in Italy in the 13th century and the most famous example of its use is DANTE's *Divina Commedia*. At the time of the Renaissance it was introduced into English by Sir Thomas WYATT, in his satires, and by SURREY, and also into French.

Among 19th-century English poets who used terza rima

are Shelley (*Prince Athenase* and *Triumph of Life*), Byron (*Prophecy of Dante*), and Elizabeth Barrett Browning (*Casa Guidi Windows*). Dante used an 11-syllabled line; the line used in English terza rima is the iambic pentameter and in French the 12-syllabled alexandrine. Terza rima has also been used in other languages, including German.

See also METRE.

Teschen, ancient town and duchy in SILESIA, on the Olsa. In 1625 it became an apanage of the Bohemian court, and in 1723 passed to Austria. In 1920 it was divided, along the line of the river, between Poland and Czechoslovakia, forming two towns: Těšín in Czechoslovakia, and Cieszyn in Poland. In 1938, after the MUNICH PACT, Poland seized Těšín, but it was restored to Czechoslovakia in 1945.

Teschenite, a basic intrusive igneous rock composed of basic plagioclase (near to labradorite), clinopyroxene (usually titanaugite), and analcite. Teschenites form large intrusions, for example Salisbury Crag in Edinburgh, and although usually of medium-grain size may on rare occasions be very coarse-grained.

Teso, or Iteso, or Itesot, a Nilo-Hamitic people of Uganda, now settled in the low country north of Lake Kioga. They grow cotton and number over 500,000, being the second largest people in Uganda.

Tesseræ, small cubes of natural stone, pottery, marble or glass used in the construction of mosaic floors and other surface decoration. The Roman and Byzantine mosaics were especially notable.

Tessin, see TICINO.

Test, river of Hampshire, England, which rises near Ashe. It is 48 km long and is famous for its trout fishing. Stockbridge and Romsey are the largest places on its banks.

Test Act. By the Test Act 1673 all office-holders of the English Crown, civil and military, were obliged within six months after appointment to make a declaration against transubstantiation, take the sacrament in accordance with the ceremony of the Church of England, and take the oaths of allegiance and supremacy. This act was usually conjoined with the Corporation Act of 1661, which compelled all holders of municipal offices to take the sacrament, a provision aimed at both Presbyterians and Roman Catholics. Lord John Russell in 1828 carried a motion for their repeal, but both by then were ineffective. The Test Act of 1678, passed after the Popish Plot, excluded all Roman Catholics except the Duke of York from both houses of Parliament.

Test Matches, see CRICKET.

Test-papers, paper slips impregnated with some chemical reagent. Litmus papers are used for testing for acids and alkalis, acids turning the blue variety to a red colour, and alkalis turning the red papers to a blue. Paper containing lead acetate is used as a test for hydrogen sulphide, which turns it brown. Oxidising agents, such as chlorine, and ozone are tested for with papers containing potassium iodide and starch, which are turned blue by their presence. Turmeric paper, yellow in colour, is used as a test for alkalis and boric acid, which cause it to become reddish-brown.

Testa, see SEED.

Testament, see BIBLE.

Testament, see COVENANT; WILLS AND TESTAMENTS.

Testamentum Domini, an early Christian Church order, originally written in Greek probably in Asia Minor between 350 and 550. Based on the *Apostolic Tradition* of HIPPOLYTUS, it was valued by the Monophysite Churches.
Bibliography: J. Cooper and A. J. Maclean, *The Testament of our Lord*, 1902.

Testi, Fulvio (1593–1646), Italian poet, born at Ferrara, notable mainly for his *canzoni* in the classical style relating to contemporary events (see CANZONE).

Testicle, see TESTIS.

Testimony, see DECLARATIONS OF DECEASED PERSONS.

Testing Clause, in Scots law, technical name for the clause in a written deed or other formal legal instrument which authenticates the document according to the forms of law. It contains a record of the number of folios of which the document consists, the names and designations of the witnesses to the writer's signature and the date and place of execution.

Testis (testicle), the reproductive organ of the male animal, in which the reproductive cells (spermatozoa or sperm) that fertilise the egg (ovum) are produced. There is usually one pair of testes in each individual. In the human foetus the testes develop on the posterior abdominal wall, slowly descending as the foetus grows, until by the end of the eighth month of pregnancy they reach the scrotum. Occasionally for some reason a testis becomes halted in its descent and is not in the scrotum at birth, a condition known as 'undescended testis'. Unless it descends in the few months following birth, a simple

Testis. The human testis.

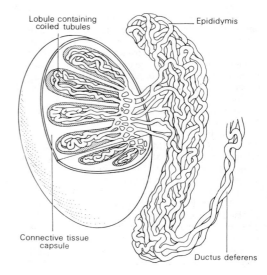

Lobule containing coiled tubules

Epididymis

Connective tissue capsule

Ductus deferens

operation is usually performed before the onset of puberty to bring the testis into the scrotum. The testes are the main source of the male sex-hormone testosterone.

Testudo, see TORTOISE.

Tetanus, a disease caused by *Clostridium tetani*, a bacterium capable of living and reproducing in the absence of oxygen and showing a predilection for wounds contaminated by debris and dirt. The presence of dirt tends to alter the redox potential, i.e. the degree of effective aerobic conditions in the tissues, thus creating favourable conditions for the germination of the *Clostridium* spores. A toxin that is secreted by the multiplying bacteria causes the main symptom of the disease, painful muscular spasms (hence the old name lockjaw), that may lead to respiratory failure and death. The microbe is widespread, being detectable in the faeces of most mammals, but no harm results from its presence in the gut. In the past, clinical descriptions of the various forms of tetanus were regarded as separate diseases, but now it is known to be associated with even very minor forms of injury, especially among gardeners. Burns also may be contaminated with *Clostridium* spores, as may the newborn's umbilicus.

Prevention is the aim, an effective vaccine being available in the form of the toxin (prepared from growing cultures in the laboratory), which is made harmless by treatment with chemicals. In this form, the immunisation is often given with diphtheria and whooping-cough vaccines (known as triple immunisation) during infancy, with booster doses every five to eight years. Once the disease has developed to the spasm stage, recovery occurs in only 70 per cent of cases or less.

Tetbury, market town in Gloucestershire, England, 16 km south-west of Cirencester and 16 km from Stroud. It is a centre for agriculture. Population (1971) 3461.

Tete, town in MOZAMBIQUE, an important trading centre on the banks of the Zambezi, founded by the Portuguese in 1531, on the main road between Rhodesia and Malawi. The cathedral built in 1563 still survives. There are important coal mines near Tete, at Moatize. Before work started on the CABORA BASSA DAM, the population was about 40,000; it is increasing rapidly, and the town should grow in importance with the irrigation and industrialisation of the lower Zambezi basin.

Tethys, in Greek mythology, daughter of Uranus and Gē, and wife of OCEANUS, by whom she was the mother of the Oceanides and the river gods. She was also the teacher of Hera. Tethys is also the name of the third satellite of Saturn.

Tethys Sea, the name given to an ancient ocean which covered much of southern Europe, the Mediterranean, North Africa, Iran, the Himalayas, and South-East Asia in the MESOZOIC era. Thick deposits of sedimentary rocks were laid down, and it later became the site of the Alpine orogenic belt in Tertiary times. The ALPINE OROGENY was caused by the gradual moving together and collision of rigid plates in the earth's crust. As the African and European continents converged, the sediments of the old ocean floor were crushed and folded together with rocks of the continental margins to form the Alpine fold mountain chain, which consists not only of the Alps but also the Himalayas and a whole range of mountains running from Spain to China.

Tetiaroa, one of the SOCIETY ISLANDS, formerly owned by the Tahitian royal family, 41 km north of Tahiti. It is an uninhabited atoll, visited by labourers for copra-making.

Tetouan, or Tetuán, city of MOROCCO, on the Mediterranean, 65 km south-east of Tangier, and a few kilometres south of the Strait of Gibraltar. The town is surrounded by walls and includes a citadel. The chief industries are textiles and building materials. The port ships livestock and agricultural products. Tetouan was the headquarters of the former Spanish Zone in Morocco. Population (1971) 139,105.

Tetracyclines, a group of ANTIBIOTIC drugs with a wide spectrum of antimicrobial activity. They include tetracycline, chlortetracycline, oxytetracycline, and dimethylchlortetracycline.

Tetraethyl Lead (TEL), $Pb(C_2H_5)_4$, first prepared in 1859, was found to be an extremely efficient anti-knock additive for PETROL in 1921. Very small amounts (e.g., 0.06 per cent by volume) will increase the OCTANE NUMBER of a fuel considerably (e.g., by 5 to 10 octane numbers). TEL is manufactured by heating an alloy of lead and sodium with ethyl chloride in a closed vessel at 60–80 °C. It is a poisonous, colourless, stable liquid, immiscible with water. When used as an anti-knock it is mixed with ethylene dibromide, which prevents lead deposition in the engine by formation of volatile lead-bromine compounds which are exhausted along with the combustion products.

Recent concern over the effect of lead on the environment has led to legislation in many countries reducing the maximum permitted concentration of lead in petrol (e.g., 0.15 g/l in West Germany in 1976). In the USA many cars must use lead-free petrol because lead poisons the catalysts used to reduce carbon monoxide and hydrocarbon exhaust emissions. See also KNOCKING.

Tetrafluoroethylene, $CF_2:CF_2$, prepared by the high-temperature condensation of difluorochloromethane, and used as the monomer in the manufacture of polytetrafluoroethylene (see PLASTICS).

$$2CHClF_2 \xrightarrow{800°C} CF_2{=}CF_2 + 2HCl$$

Tetrahedron, a POLYHEDRON with four faces.

Tetrameter (Greek, four measure), in verse, a line containing four feet, usually iambs (see IAMBUS) or trochees. After iambic PENTAMETER, iambic tetrameter is the most commonly used metre in English poetry. See also METRE.

Tetrarch, Roman term for a ruler over the fourth part of a country. The term was borrowed by the Romans from the Greeks. On the death of Herod the Great, his dominions were divided among Archelaus, Herod Antipas, and Herod Philip. Part remained under the direct rule of a Roman procurator.

Tetras, see CHARACIN.

Tetrazene

Tetrazene, an initiating explosive (see DETONATOR; EXPLOSIVES), discovered in 1910.

$$
\begin{array}{c}
\text{N} \longrightarrow \text{N} \\
\ \ \| \qquad\quad \diagdown \\
\qquad\qquad\ \ \text{C} \longrightarrow \text{N} = \text{N} \longrightarrow \text{NH} \longrightarrow \text{NH} \longrightarrow \text{C} \\
\ \ \| \qquad\quad \diagup \qquad\qquad\qquad\qquad\qquad\qquad\ \ \diagdown \\
\text{N} \longrightarrow \text{NH}
\end{array}
\quad
\begin{array}{c}
\text{NH}_2 \\
\\
\text{NH} \cdot \text{H}_2\text{O}
\end{array}
$$

Tetrazzini, Luisa (1871–1940), Italian soprano, born in Florence. She studied with her sister Eva, and with Ceccherini at Florence, where she made her debut in 1895. Later she toured Europe, Mexico and South America. She appeared in London at Covent Garden in 1907, as Violetta in *La Traviata*. With brilliant coloratura technique she achieved particular successes in the title role of *Lucia di Lammermoor*, and as Amina in *La Sonnambula*. In 1921 she published her reminiscences, *My Life of Song*.

Tetricus, Gaius Esuvius, last of the pretenders who ruled Gaul during its separation from the Roman Empire. He reigned from AD 270 to 274, when he was defeated by Aurelian at Châlons.

Tetryl, high explosive, $C_7H_5O_8N_5$, consisting of pale yellow crystals with a melting-point of 129·1 °C. Obtained by nitrating pure dimethylaniline with nitric and sulphuric acids, it is sensitive and detonates on striking. It is mainly used as a booster. See EXPLOSIVES.

Tetschen, see DĚČIN.

Tettenhall, town in West Midlands county, England, 3 km from and now part of WOLVERHAMPTON. Wightwick Manor is nearby, with William Morris furnishings, pre-Raphaelite paintings, and tiles by William De Morgan.

Tetuan, Duke of, see O'DONNELL, LEOPOLDO, DUKE OF TETUAN.

Tetzcoco, see TEXCOCO.

Tetzel, Johann (c. 1465–1519), German Dominican friar, born at Leipzig. By the scandalous manner in which he carried on the traffic in indulgences, Tetzel roused Luther to precipitate the German Reformation in 1517 wth the issue of his Ninety-Five Theses. Tetzel was later discredited and retired to a monastery.

Teutoburger Wald, range of hills in Lower Saxony and NORTH RHINE-WESTPHALIA, running north-west from Detmold. It stretches for some 97 km and is heavily wooded. The highest peak is Volmerstod (463 m). It is reputed to be the scene of the battle in which Arminius and the German tribes defeated the Roman legions under Quintilius Varus (AD 9). The northern section is part of a large nature park covering 1092 km².

Teutonic Knights, one of the great semi-religious orders of knights founded during the period of the crusades. It originated in a brotherhood formed by certain German merchants of Bremen and Lübeck to alleviate the sufferings of the attacking troops during the siege of Acre in 1190. A hospital was started, and as a result the Teutonic Knights of the Hospital of St Mary of Jerusalem were founded. The new order, distinguished by a white mantle with a black cross, was formed on the model of the KNIGHTS HOSPITALLERS and its members were also pledged to tend the sick, to protect the Church, and to wage war against the heathen. In 1198 the hospital was turned into an order of knighthood. The Teutonic Knights conquered Lithuania and the Baltic regions of Prussia during the 13th and 14th centuries. For a century their headquarters were at Acre (1191–1291), but the seat of the order was transferred to Marienburg in 1308. Their defeat at the hands of the Poles and Lithuanians at Tannenburg (1410) struck a great blow at their prestige and the order declined rapidly. It had already departed from its original moral standards.

In 1525 the 'high master', Albert of Brandenburg, secularised the order in Prussia, but it survived in Catholic Germany with a new headquarters at Bad Mergentheim until suppressed by Napoleon in 1809. An Austrian branch survives in attenuated form to this day as a purely religious community.

See also PRUSSIA, *History*.
Bibliography: M. Tumler, *Der Deutsche Order*, 1955.

Teutons, or Teutones, a German people, first mentioned by the Greek navigator PYTHEAS as living on the coast of what was later called Holstein. They migrated and wandered with the CIMBRI between 120 and 102 BC and, becoming a threat to northern Italy, were annihilated in battle by the consul Marius at Aix-en-Provence in 102 BC. The name 'Teutons' later became a synonym for Germans.

Tevere, see TIBER.

Teviot, river of Borders Region, Scotland, joining the TWEED at Kelso. It has good salmon and trout fishing. The valley it drains is called Teviotdale. Length 60 km.

Tew, Great, village of Oxfordshire, England, 8 km east of Chipping Norton. Most of the houses, of mellow local stone, were built during the 17th century and Great Tew is one of the earliest existing examples of a planned village. The subsequent replanning of the estate on landscape and ecological principles in the early 18th century suggests that it was carried out by John LOUDON. Population (1971) 210.

Tewkesbury, market town in GLOUCESTERSHIRE, England. It is situated on the Avon, close to the point where that river joins the Severn, 16 km north-east of Gloucester. The 'Bloody Meadow' on the southern side of the town was the site of the fiercest combat of the Battle of Tewkesbury, 4 May 1471, one of the most bitter battles of the Wars of the Roses, in which the Lancastrians were routed. Tewkesbury was settled in Roman times and in 1087 was a borough and market. Its most magnificent building is its abbey church, all that is left of a great Benedictine abbey erected in the 12th century on a Saxon foundation. Monuments include the Beauchamp Chantry (1422) and the tomb of Hugh Despenser (d. 1349). Prince Edward, son of Henry VI, is reputed to be buried under the tower.

Tewkesbury has a 16th-century grammar school and several old timbered houses. In Tudor times it was famous for mustard making; now it is an agricultural centre. Mrs Craik's *John Halifax, Gentleman* is set in Tewkesbury. The M5 motorway passes close by the town. Population (1971) 8749.

Tex, universal system of describing the linear density of textile fibres and yarns as well as cordage. It is defined as the number of grams per kilometre. For fibres and yarns the decitex (dtex), grams per 10 kilometres, is often more convenient and for heavy cordage, etc., the kilotex (ktex), the number of kilograms per kilometre, is also used.

Texarkana, dual city of Bowie county, north-east Texas, and capital of Miller county, north-west Arkansas, USA, astride the state line near Red river. Texarkana has two municipal governments. It is a railway, distributive, processing and manufacturing centre for a livestock, dairying, and agricultural region (cotton). Population 52,185; 30,500 in Texas, 21,685 in Arkansas.

Texas (Lone Star State), the southernmost of the central states of the USA and the largest (682,835 km²) in the Union before the admission of Alaska, with a coastline along the Gulf of Mexico stretching for 595 km from Mexico north-east to Louisiana. Its extreme length is 1223 km and extreme breadth 1000 km. It is separated from Mexico, on the south-west, by the Rio Grande; New Mexico and Oklahoma border it on the north, and Arkansas and Louisiana on the east. The general relief slopes from north-west to south-east. The Llano Estacado is a barren plateau in the west with a mean elevation of 915 to 1525 m. The descent to the coastal plain at a height of 300 m is swift, and then come fertile tracts of rolling prairie crossed by plentiful forests of yellow pine in the east, and with rich pastures alternating with corn lands—tracts which extend terrace-like to the fertile lowlands and barren swamps of the coastal belt. Behind Padre Island, which hugs the shore for over 160 km northward from the mouth of the Rio Grande to that of the Nueces, is a region of white sands, known as 'the desert'. With the exception of the Red and Canadian, which carry their waters eastward to the Mississippi, all the rivers, including the Brazos, Colorado, and Trinity, drain south-east to the Gulf of Mexico. Texas is too large to enjoy a uniform climate, and it has extremes ranging from temperate to sub-tropical, and from the humid coast to the dry plains of the west.

The wide climatic range is reflected in the state's agricultural production. In 1969 there were 214,000 farms covering 58 million ha, and this area in farms had shown no tendency to decline, as in so many other states. The largest share of the farm income is derived from livestock products: in the early 1970s there were 12·5 million cattle and 4 million sheep in Texas, and the state produced 170–180 million broiler fowls a year. Cattle and sheep dominate western Texas, where some of the largest ranches in the USA are to be found. Among field crops, the largest area is under cotton (1·8–1·9 million ha), and Texas is the leading US producer. Grain sorghum takes second place but Texas is better known nationally for such fruit and vegetable specialities as cabbages, onions, citrus fruit, and watermelons, most of them grown under irrigation and many of them in the so-called 'winter garden' between Uvalde and Laredo or in the lower Rio Grande valley. There are 5·2 million ha of commercial forests, and coastal fisheries are valuable to the ports of the Gulf coast.

Mineral production is of greater value to the state, which leads all others in this respect. Petroleum is the most valuable mineral product, representing more than one-third of US total output. Texas is the leading US producer (150 to 163 million t a year), as it is also of natural gas, asphalts, and pyrites; in the production of helium, clays, magnesium, sulphur, and gypsum it is second. Manufacturing employs over 700,000 workers; the original agricultural processing industries have been augmented by petroleum-based industries and later by regional steel production, aircraft manufacture, and vehicle assembly for the rich Texan market.

Texas has 300,000 km of roads, apart from municipal streets, and more airports than any other state—over 1100, but 860 of them are private. Its ports handle over 100 million t of goods annually, and the Intracoastal Waterway runs parallel to the long coastline all the way from Brownsville to Port Arthur.

The Spanish explorers de Vaca and Coronado were the first to explore the region now known as Texas (the name was that of an Indian tribe), but the first permanent

Texas oil wells. *(Topham/Fotogram)*

Texas City

settlement was made by LA SALLE in 1685 at Fort St Louis. Texas was surrendered in 1713 by France to Spain, which founded many religious missions. When Mexico revolted and became independent in 1821, Coahuila and Texas formed one state. Texas was colonised to a large extent by Americans and British, and when trouble broke out with the Mexican government, Texas was constituted an independent republic in 1836. In 1845 it sought and gained admission as a state of the USA. After the Mexican War, which was precipitated by this admission, Texas prospered. In 1861 it seceded with the Southern states.

In 1974 Texas ranked fourth in population among the states, with 12,050,000 people. This gave an average density of 17·6 per km²; rather surprisingly in view of the popular image of Texans, the population is 80 per cent urban. Some 12·5 per cent of the population is Black. Texas is a state of rapid growth, the wealth generated by oil production having been channelled into the construction of spectacular cities and homes. The capital is AUSTIN, but its three largest cities are HOUSTON, DALLAS, and SAN ANTONIO.

Bibliography: W. T. Chambers and L. Kennamer, *Texans and Their Land*, 1963; D. W. Meinig, *Imperial Texas*, 1969; H. Hansen (Ed.), *Texas: A Guide to the Lone Star State*, 1969; R. L. Martin, *Economic and Industrial Growth in Central West Texas*, 1970; W. R. Hogan, *Texas Republic: A Social and Economic History*, 1973.

Texas City, port of Texas, USA, on the Bay of Galveston, 8 km north-west of Galveston city. In 1970 it handled 6·5 million t of cargo. A severe explosion on board a ship in Texas City harbour in 1947 killed over 600 people and destroyed much of the city. Population 38,908.

Texcoco, or Tetzcoco, ancient capital of the AZTECS in MÉXICO state on the central plateau of Mexico, with many archaeological remains in the district. It is now a prosperous agricultural and cattle raising centre. Population 49,000.

Texel, largest of the West Frisian islands in the province of North Holland, Netherlands, covering 183 km². It is separated from the mainland by the 4 km wide Marsdiep channel and is reached by boat from DEN HELDER. The northern part of the island is called Eierland (Egg Land) due to its bird observatory, where thousands of birds belonging to more than a hundred species breed every year. The inhabitants of Texel live by sheep-breeding, agriculture, and fishing. Texel ewe-cheese is famous as a Dutch export. The farmhouses have a peculiarly square shape, with tall pyramidal roofs (*stolpen*). Population 11,800.

Textile Finishing, a series of processes applied to textile goods in their final state (e.g., cloth, yarns for sewing, embroidery, or knitting) to produce an improved product. The dyeing and printing processes can be considered as part of the finishing operations, but being so specialised are invariably described as processes in their own right.

Yarns for sewing, usually called threads, have their frictional properties improved by such processes as singeing, mercerising, impregnation with suitable lubricating agents, and polishing.

For cloth, machinery requirements and processes depend very greatly on the material, which can range from very wide carpet to narrow silk braids, from heavy over-coatings to delicate silks, from firm to very stretchy cloths, and include all fibres and mixtures of fibres. The finishing processes are also determined by the end use to which the material is put. It is convenient to classify according to the nature of the fabric, knitted or woven, and according to fibre type: (1) wool and the hairs; (2) cotton, viscose, and the vegetable fibres; (3) man-made fibres.

1. Wool and the hairs. Cloth finishing processes can range between two extremes: one which conceals all the character of the weave by a compact mass of fibre, and one in which the weave is made clearly visible. Woven woollen cloths are typical of the first type and are first scoured to remove the oils, etc., incorporated as spinning or weaving assistants; at the same time or in the next process the cloth is given a fulling or milling treatment, often in warm soapy water which felts up the fibres and produces a more compact cloth. The cloth is dried and the surface is broken up or raised with either wire bristles or the spiky seed pods of a plant called teasel. Raising produces a pile on the cloth which may be left in a definite direction, as for simulated furs, or randomly, as in the case of a blanket. Finally the cloth is dried by passing through a machine called a tenter or stenter in which the selvage of the cloth is gripped by a series of sharp spikes and the cloth is pulled out to the required width and weight. Care is taken that the weave is straight, i.e., warp and weft are at right angles.

The relative amounts of milling and raising vary greatly according to the end use, the nature of the wool fibre, the presence of other fibres, the spinning and weaving processes also having a great effect on the final cloth.

Other processes incorporated are moth- or mould-resistance, shrink-resist, and many others.

Woven worsted wool cloths are first lightly scoured, care being taken to prevent felting, and then wound very tightly and with great care round a perforated metal core which is lowered into boiling water. This process, known as potting, sets the fabric in a flat crease-free state, confers a high degree of shrink resistance, and prevents any distortion of the weave. The cloth is sheared or cropped by passing through a machine where protruding hairs are cut away, and the cloth is pressed to produce a

Textile Finishing. A stenting machine which grips the selvages of the cloth, so stretching it to the correct width. (*Mather and Platt*)

very compact fabric. The cloth is finally passed through a stenter to ensure it is the correct width.

2. Cotton, viscose, and the vegetable fibres are finished in a great variety of ways but the following processes are the most typical. The woven cotton is first cleaned by treatment with very hot alkali in large vessels called kiers, followed by bleaching. Bleaching is accomplished by the use of chemicals which can liberate chlorine, such as sodium hypochlorite, $NaClO$, by hydrogen peroxide, H_2O_2, or by sodium chlorite, $NaClO_2$. Sodium hypochlorite is cheap and is used for batch production of pure cotton; hydrogen peroxide is useful when other fibres are present which would be damaged by chlorine. Sodium chlorite is used in continuous processes as it is very fast-acting, but being extremely corrosive the equipment in which it is used must be either glass-lined or made of pure titanium.

The cloth is singed or gassed by passing over a red-hot plate or through a gas flame to remove surface hairs. Present trends are to combine all these preliminary processes in a complex series of machines so that the cloth passes continuously through all the processes and emerges ready for the next operation.

Much cotton cloth is mercerised, a process which improves the strength and lustre of the cloth. The cotton is treated with cold, very strong caustic soda solution and whilst tightly tensioned the caustic soda is rinsed away.

Some cotton is treated with resins, which are absorbed into the cotton fibres and render the fibre plastic in heat whilst still retaining the attractive handle and water absorption of the original cotton. The cotton may easily be damaged and feel harsh if the resin process is not very closely controlled, yet if the resin is not properly fixed it is removed in laundering. The resins used were originally urea-formaldehyde condensation products but it was found these products absorbed chlorine from domestic bleach, which was subsequently changed into hydrochloric acid and damaged the cotton. More sophisticated resins are now used which are not able to absorb chlorine, which are easier to control in processing, and provide better final properties.

The fabric is sometimes too open and too rough for its end use, so is closed up and smoothed by a beating treatment called beetling. A series of hammers fall under their own weight onto the cloth and thus produce the desired finish needed for dress goods, especially linen fabrics.

Many cloths are calendered by passing between nips formed by rotating cylinders, one surface of heated metal and another of hard paper. The cylinders are often mounted one above the other so that the fabric passes through several nips. The cloth becomes smoother and more compact as the gaps in the weave structure are closed.

Friction calendering is a process for increasing the lustre in which the cloth passes between two heated rollers. The upper metal roller rotates faster than the cloth giving a skidding effect. This finish is useful for curtains and chintz cloths. In another process the cloth passes into a nip composed of a hot metal roller and a very yielding rubber surface so that the cloth is gripped by the rubber surface and is compressed lengthwise as it runs into the nip. The stretch which may have been created by

tension in previous processing is reduced or eliminated; this process is used for special applications such as shirt collars under names such as Rigmel. Seersucker effects can be produced by the use of fluted rollers so that only lengthwise strips of the cloth are compacted, the remainder bulging out to produce the seersucker style.

If the calender and compacting effects are carried out on resinated cloth a finish resistant to laundering is produced and the cloth is resistant to shrinking during domestic laundering. Resinating is usually carried out after dyeing and printing. The resin is normally cured during the final stenter process.

3. The finishing of woven synthetic fibres and their blends with wool and cotton is usually similar to one or other of the above processes but the exact conditions and methods must be modified to allow for the nature of the synthetic fibre. The final stentering is important as this operation determines the width and weight per square metre and stability of the cloth.

Knitted fabric finishing methods are similar to those for woven cloths but the machinery is usually more sophisticated to prevent lengthwise tension which would distort the knitted fabric. Double jersey wool cloths are finished in a manner similar to worsted cloths.

For all products the final feel of the cloth may be modified either to a harsh or to a slippery feel by a treatment with a variety of products, of which the most important are the softeners, used for the man-made fibres. By reducing the friction between fibres they may improve bulkiness but excessive amounts of softener may increase dirt retention. Correct softener application is important if sewing performance of the cloth is critical.

Bibliography: J. T. Marsh, *Introduction to Textile Bleaching*, 1951; H. Spibey (Ed.), *British Wool Manual*, 2nd ed. 1970.

Textile History. As one of the essential requirements of mankind, textile processing was established many thousands of years ago and textiles have had a great influence on the wealth and social structure of many nations. Spinning was developed by the use of the whorl several thousand years ago. The operator makes a heavy plate rotate, then feeds fibre by hand so that fibre is twisted to a yarn. The loom was brought to a recognisable form by the Egyptians, who processed cotton and flax; jute, probably the sackcloth mentioned in the Bible, and the animal fibres were also known to the civilisations of the Near East. In China and India silk and cotton were woven into very high-quality cloths by 1500 BC and India continued the highest quality cloths up to the 16th century AD, some Indian cotton cloths being so fine that 140 m^2 weigh only 1 kg. Cotton was known and grown in the Greek and Roman empires and the technology was preserved by the Moors, being reintroduced via Genoa and Venice at the time of the Crusades.

European textiles were dominated by wool during the Middle Ages. The spinning wheel was invented in the 13th century and worsted and woollen spinning, weaving, dyeing, and finishing were developed, Britain being an important wool producer. The supply of wool was greatly limited until the great wool producing nations of the Southern Hemisphere were discovered and developed in the early 19th century, so the tremendous technical activity of the 18th century was concerned almost solely with cotton. In the 16th and 17th centuries cotton technology had been learnt by the flax workers of Germany and the Low Countries, but as Britain began to dominate trade with India and as religious persecution forced the skilled workers into the UK they brought cotton-processing skills with them.

The British established cotton growing in the West Indies and the southern part of what is now the USA. It was to operate the cotton farms that slaves were imported from Africa into these parts of America. By 1800 the import of cotton to Britain had exceeded 10 million kg per annum and the old laws which protected the wool industry and forbade cotton processing had been largely repealed.

The mechanisation of cotton spinning was accomplished in the 18th century. In 1738 Lewis Paul invented the drawing machine, an essential part of the spinning processes. Between 1764 and 1767 James Hargreaves invented the spinning jenny and Arkwright improved on Paul's machine. Finally between 1774 and 1779 Samuel Crompton combined the drawing machine and the water-driven jenny to produce the mule, which lasted in Britain for nearly 200 years. The weaving process was made suitable for mechanisation by John Kay in 1737 when a method of propelling the shuttle carrying the weft was discovered—the 'flying shuttle'. The basic movements of the loom were mechanised first by Cartwright, by Horrocks in 1813, and Roberts in the 1820s. Although carpet weaving was one of the last processes to be mechanised, this was achieved by the 1850s and such complex fabrics as velvets were being woven on power looms by the 1880s.

The various finishing processes were made suitable for bulk production although many new methods were introduced as a result of the developments in chemistry that took place in the 18th century, in particular the production of sulphuric acid by Tennants, and Berthollet's and Scheele's work which led to chlorine-based bleaches. In the latter part of the 19th century the work, originally by Perkin and others in the UK, but taken over by Bayer and others in Germany, laid the foundations of the modern synthetic dye industry.

The wool industry tended to follow closely on the improvements of the cotton industry but the demand by the industry for greater wool production was partly responsible for the 'clearances' of the Scottish Highlands after the 1745 Rebellion and the rapid build-up of the Dutch colony in South Africa and the British colonies in Australia, both of which introduced sheep in the 1790s.

The spinning, weaving, and finishing industries had been the subject of much legislation and tradition, and before the factory system could operate many obstacles had to be overcome. Resistance was often strong and the Luddite riots are the most well-known of the protest movements where skilled workers in the cloth shearing process protested against the use of machinery.

The wool-combing process was one of the last to be mechanised. Although Cartwright had produced a machine it was Noble and Lister (later Lord Masham) who finally produced workable machines.

Bibliography: T. Ellison, *The Cotton Trade of Great Britain, 1886*, 1968; T. K. Derry and T. I. Williams, *Short History of Technology from the Earliest Times to A.D. 1900*, new ed. 1970.

Textile Printing, the application of colour to specific areas of textile material. Printing was practised by the Egyptians using very sophisticated dyeing techniques (mordant processes), and in India, from where the art was brought first by the Dutch to Holland and then to England in about 1676. London and the Lea Valley area were at one time important cloth-printing centres before the cotton textile trade became dominated by Lancashire. The colour application stage of printing can be performed by four main processes: block, roller, screen, and transfer.

Block Printing. The block is covered with a liquid consisting of dyestuff and a thickener (such as a natural, modified, or an artificial starch) and such chemicals as are necessary to fix the dye onto the fibre. The block is placed on the cloth, its position being fixed by two projecting pins which touch the cloth and form the 'register' mark to be seen on most block-printed cloth. The block is hammered onto the cloth to ensure proper contact and removed. Many colours can be applied by this method and the setting-up cost for preparing the blocks is relatively low, but the process is slow and is now only used on expensive cloths printed in short runs to 'exclusive' designs.

Roller Printing. For roller printing the design is first engraved upon a soft steel roller, which is hardened and made to impress the design in relief on a second steel cylinder. This cylinder is hardened in its turn and finally transfers the original design to a copper roller, which is then electroplated with a hard-wearing metal such as nickel. Each individual colour to be printed demands a separate roller, so that machines carrying as many as 20 copper cylinders may be employed. Each printing cylinder is mounted so as to press against a large central roller, around which the cloth to be printed passes. The colour is supplied to each copper cylinder by a colour-box in which a small roller, covered in bristles, presses against the copper cylinder.

The 'colour doctor', a thin steel blade fitting against the surface of the copper cylinder before contact with the cloth, removes excess colouring matter. Print paste therefore remains in the depth of the engravings and, as the cloth supported on a soft rubber 'blanket' is pressed onto the engraved roller, the colour paste is deposited onto the cloth.

Textile Printing. Diagram of a printing roller.

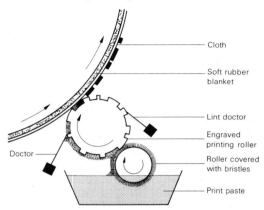

- Cloth
- Soft rubber blanket
- Lint doctor
- Engraved printing roller
- Roller covered with bristles
- Print paste
- Doctor

Another steel blade called the 'lint doctor' is similarly fitted after the printing cylinder leaves the cloth to remove, to waste, all impurities such as short fibre and previously applied print pastes which have been transferred onto the roller from the cloth.

In Duplex printing both sides of the cloth are printed in one operation.

Screen Printing. In screen printing a very finely woven fabric or screen, formerly of silk but now nylon or metal, is processed so that in certain areas the holes between the weave are blocked. For short sample runs this can be done by sticking paper or a plastic film, suitably cut, onto the screen, but commercially the design is usually made by photographic processes and the screen treated with varnishes so that the blocked-out areas are permanently sealed.

The screen is placed on the cloth in the correct position and print paste pressed across and through the screen by the action of a flexible rubber blade called a squeegee, so that the paste runs onto the cloth only in those areas in which the screen is still open. Many colours may be applied consecutively and there is a possibility of producing a gradation of colours if the screen is made with certain areas partially blocked (half-tone printing).

This process is still carried out by hand for expensive cloths and short production runs usually of exclusive designs, but the process has been automated by using flat screens and more recently using rotary or cylindrically shaped screens. The number of colours applied is usually up to eight for automatic machines, but for hand printing many more colours are used; if the half-tone techniques are used the effect is of a great number of different colours. This process may be used for all types of cloth and recently rotary screen printing of tufted carpets has become popular.

Transfer Printing has been developed since about 1965; paper is printed using textile dyes which are then transferred to fabric in dry heat by pressing the cloth onto the paper at temperatures of 160–210 °C. The present limitations of dyes confine the original process to polyester if a high standard of washing fastness is required, but for many uses where washability is not so important nylon, triacetate, and acrylics are being printed. The advantage of the process is that skilled printing operatives are not required in the textile factory, that there are no problems of water supply and effluent, and that with a stock of the specially printed paper the textile printer can very quickly execute customer orders in smaller batches than would be economical by roller or screen methods.

The high temperatures and pressures used produce a polishing effect on the cloth, which is not always required, but machines in which the transferring is done in a vacuum and without pressure on the cloth were introduced in 1974. Using these machines no pressure need be applied to the cloth and the dyes may even penetrate thick fabrics such as simulated furs, velvets, and carpets. In 1975 a transfer process for wool, cotton, and other fibres was introduced in which the dyes on the paper transfer to wet cloth.

Other Processes. A method of coloration by allowing drips or streams of dye to drop onto cloth was introduced in 1972. This method can produce designs without having to make screens or rollers. The process is now being used commercially.

Textile Printing. A roller machine for printing in six colours. *(Mather and Platt)*

Other forms of textile goods may be printed. Yarn in the form of a warp is printed using a roller-printing technique and the yarns are very carefully handled so that they may be woven into cloth and produce the right design. This process was used for finishing fabrics, tapestry, printed Wilton carpets, and was reintroduced in 1974 for tufted carpets.

Yarn may also be printed by rollers to produce a random colour effect for many types of fancy cloths, both knitted and woven, and fancy yarns can be produced by knitting to a very simple tube of cloth, printing, and unravelling the knitting.

Fibre may also be printed. The melange printing of wool or polyester sliver using a simple roller method leads to the production of a very uniform colour mixture. Thus if the print is, as is usual, black, then very uniform greys are produced in the final cloth, whereas if black and white fibres are mixed the final cloth has a speckled appearance.

Most goods can be printed directly with dyestuffs which are fixed in position in subsequent treatment usually by steam or sometimes by dry heat. Care must be taken to choose the correct dyestuffs and to have the correct chemicals present to ensure good fixation onto the cloth. After fixation the cloth is thoroughly washed to remove unfixed dyestuff and the cloth is dried.

The use of different chemical techniques gives rise to a series of printing styles. 'Burn-out' styles are printed cloths containing two or more fibres in which a print paste is used which will destroy one fibre. A lace-like fabric is produced. The destruction of the cotton component by acid print pastes in a cotton/polyester blended fabric is the most usual application of the process but there are many other possibilities. Discharge styles are useful where large areas of background colour are required. Printing large areas of colour would be likely to give unacceptable variations of colour, so the cloth is evenly dyed and then printed with a chemical which destroys the dye to produce a white area, or to destroy the original dye and replace it with another dye in the so-called illuminated discharge style. This style can usually be detected as the chemical which destroys the background shade spreads further than the new colour and a white 'halo' is produced.

Textiles

Bibliography: R. S. Horsfall and L. G. Lawrie, *Dyeing of Textile Fibres*, 2nd ed. 1949; W. Clarke, *Introduction to Textile Printing*, 4th ed. 1974.

Textiles, see COTTON; FABRICS, TEXTILE; FIBRES AND FIBROUS SUBSTANCES; SILK AND SERICULTURE; SPINNING; TEXTILE FINISHING; TEXTILE HISTORY; TEXTILE PRINTING; WEAVING; WOOL.

Teyte, Dame Maggie (1888–1976), English soprano, born in Wolverhampton. She studied in London and Paris, made her debut at Monte Carlo in 1907 and then appeared at the Paris Opéra-Comique. In 1908 Debussy chose her to sing the heroine in his *Pelléas et Mélisande* at the theatre. She also sang at Covent Garden, in Chicago, Boston and New York. In later years she excelled as an interpreter of songs, especially French. She was created DBE in 1958. She published her autobiography, *Star on the Door*, in 1958.

Teziutlán, town in the state of PUEBLA, Mexico. There is agricultural production and processing, and copper is mined nearby. Altitude 1980 m. Population 26,000.

Thackeray, William Makepeace (1811–63), English novelist and essayist, born in Calcutta, where his father, Richmond Thackeray, was in the service of the East India Company. He died in 1815, leaving his son an inheritance of nearly £20,000. Thackeray was sent to England in 1817, and was educated at Charterhouse and at Trinity College, Cambridge, where he was a friend of FITZGERALD and TENNYSON. He left the university after almost two years and travelled in Germany. In 1832 he entered the Middle Temple, and studied law for a while. He spent much of the following year in Paris, and in 1833 became part owner of a weekly paper, the *National Standard*. When the paper came to an end in the following year, its losses were borne by Thackeray, and the remainder of his inheritance disappeared with the failure of an Indian bank in 1833.

At this time he was in Paris studying art as he now hoped to earn his living as an illustrator, and in 1836 published *Flore et Zephyr—Ballet Mythologique*, a set of nine plates. In August he married Isabella Shawe, and

William Makepeace Thackeray. *(Bisonte)*

shortly afterwards became Paris correspondent of a daily newspaper, the *Constitutional*. This also failed, and in 1837 he returned to London, where his daughter Anne Isabella, later Lady RITCHIE, the eldest of his three children, was born. To this period belong his contributions to *Fraser's Magazine*, including the *Yellowplush Correspondence*, 1837–38, and *Catherine*, 1839–40. From this time onwards Thackeray's life was permanently clouded by his wife's insanity. The *Paris Sketch Book* followed *Catherine* in 1840. In 1841 *Comic Tales and Sketches* was published, a collection of his periodical writings under his two pseudonyms 'Yellowplush' and 'Michael Angelo Titmarsh'. The *Irish Sketch-Book* appeared in 1843. His friendship with Mrs Brookfield, begun in 1842, marked by a correspondence extending over many years, was one of the major influences of his life.

The *Great Hoggarty Diamond* appeared serially in *Fraser's*, 1841, as did the brilliant *Barry Lyndon* in 1844. Since 1842 he had contributed regularly to *Punch* and increased his reputation with *The Book of Snobs*, which appeared there, 1846–47. *Mrs Perkins' Ball*, 1847, a 'Christmas Book', brought him further popularity, but he did not become really famous until the publication of *Vanity Fair*, which was brought out in monthly parts from January 1847 to July 1848. This is Thackeray's masterpiece; one of the greatest social satires in English, it demonstrates the ambivalence of human motive and the hypocrisy of society through the story of the passive Amelia Sedley and the brilliant, vivacious, unscrupulous Becky Sharp. The first edition, in one volume, was published in 1848 and its success was slow at first. As soon as it was finished he began work on *Pendennis*, and the first of 24 monthly parts appeared in November 1848. These two satirical works placed him in the forefront of contemporary novelists.

In 1851 he resigned from the *Punch* staff in order to write *The History of Henry Esmond*, which was published in 1852. In October he sailed to America, where his lectures on *The English Humorists of the Eighteenth Century* were very successful. *The Newcomes* was published in monthly parts from October 1853 to August 1855. While it was appearing, *The Rose and the Ring*, a delightful extravaganza, was produced in 1854. In 1855 Thackeray repeated his American success, travelling and lecturing on *The Four Georges*. In 1857 he contested Oxford for parliament as a Liberal, but was unsuccessful. *The Virginians* was published serially, 1857–59, and in 1860 Thackeray became first editor of the highly successful *Cornhill Magazine*, to which he contributed *Lovel the Widower*, 1860, *The Adventures of Philip*, 1861–62, and the *Roundabout Papers*, 1860–63, before resigning as editor in 1862. At the time of his death he was writing *Denis Duval*, a fragment of which was published in 1864. Thackeray's *Letters and Private Papers* were edited in four volumes, 1945–46.

Bibliography: Works (17 vols), 1908; G. N. Ray, *The Buried Life*, 1952, *Thackeray: The Uses of Adversity, 1811–1846*, 1955, and *Thackeray: The Age of Wisdom, 1847–1863*, 1958; G. Tillotson, *Thackeray the Novelist*, 1954; B. Hardy, *The Exposure of Luxury*, 1972; J. A. Sutherland, *Thackeray at Work*, 1974.

Thai Boxing, a form of combat sport practised principally in Thailand, where it originated. Unlike KARATE and TAE-KWON-DO which have suffered as sports because the need to avoid serious injury demands that blows must be

Thailand. Sunset near Chiengmai. (*Camera Press/Alexandra Lawrence*)

'pulled', Thai boxing has never been limited by such restriction. Competitors wear gloves, a groin protector and an anklet and are permitted to punch, kick, knee and elbow each other. Inside and outside leg throws are also permitted. Fights take place in a ring which is similar to that used in Western-style boxing, to which the weight divisions also approximate (see BOXING).

Thailand (formerly *Siam*), a country of mainland South-East Asia, bordered on the north by Burma and Laos, on the east by Laos and Kampuchea (Cambodia), and on the west by Burma. Thailand extends southward as a peninsula with the Gulf of Thailand to its east and the Indian Ocean to its west. In the south of the peninsula, it borders Malaysia.

Geography. Relief. The total area is 514,000 km² which can be divided broadly into four major natural regions: the northern valleys, the central plain, the north-east plateau, and the peninsula. The central plain is drained by the CHAO PHRAYA river, whose four major tributaries rise in the extreme north of the country and flow through small basins in the north before coming together at the head of the central plain and flowing in a series of tributaries to the sea in the Gulf of Thailand. The valleys of the northern region are separated by high, forest-covered ridges and these extend southward as a line of mountains which form the eastern border of the country and constitute the backbone of the southern peninsula. A distinctly separate region is the low plateau of Khorat, the scarp of which overlooks the central plain in the east and which drains eastward and northward to the MEKONG river which forms most of the boundary with Laos. The edge of this north-east plateau also shows a distinct scarp to the basin of Kampuchea to the south.

Climate. Thailand's climate is basically monsoonal, with a rainy season from May to October, followed by a

Thailand

long dry season during which temperatures increase gradually to a maximum of about 30 °C in March–April. In areas like the southern peninsula, most exposed to the effects of the monsoon, rainfall averages over 2000 mm per annum, but relief provides rain-shadows and in the north-central plain, the northern valleys, and parts of the north-east, this annual total falls to under 1000 mm. In the north-east region the effect of the rain is reduced by the permeable sandy subsoil. As a result, the natural vegetation cover in this area is dry deciduous forest, found also in small areas in other regions. This contrasts with the tropical monsoonal forests in the mountainous areas of the north and west, famous for their teak stands, and similar luxuriant vegetation in the southern peninsula. The central plain, fringed by mangroves on the coast, is almost wholly under rice fields.

Population. The population at the 1970 census was 34·39 million and was estimated to be growing at 2·7 per cent per annum. At present the population is certainly over 42 million (1977), approximately 95 per cent of whom profess the Theravada form of Buddhism.

Thailand is perhaps the most ethnically homogeneous country of South-East Asia. The dominant Thai group are a Sinic people related to a wider group which includes the Chuangs of China, the Shans of Burma, and the Lao peoples. In fact the majority of the population of the north-east region of Khorat are culturally and linguistically Lao, a significant sub-group about 10 million strong. Apart from the Lao, the minority peoples in the country are small in number. The northern and western hills are populated by various hill-peoples, notably the Karen in the west and the Meo, Lisu, and Muser in the north. In the southern border provinces, there is a significant Malay-speaking, Muslim minority, whose isolation from Bangkok has led to recent calls for independence. Over the last two centuries, a substantial Chinese community has entered Thailand in pursuit of economic opportunity. Estimates of the size of the community vary and are made difficult by considerable intermarriage with the Thai population. Government policy has encouraged integration, most Chinese are Thai-speaking and have Thai names and only occasionally does economic pressure cause minor incidents.

Most of the Thai population continue to live in the countryside, although the BANGKOK conurbation has grown to be one of the largest cities in the Orient. By comparison other cities in Thailand are small. In the north is CHIENGMAI, in the south, HAAD YAI, and in the north-east, NAKHON RATCHASIMA, Udorn Thani, and Ubol Ratchathani. Until recently swelled by the presence of US air bases, each have populations of about 100,000. The rural population is mainly in nucleated villages. The concentrations are greatest in areas of good rice land, i.e. in the northern valleys, in the heart of the central plain, and in the valleys of the north-east. In the central plain, villages are to be found strung out along the irrigation and drainage canals. In recent years, land has become scarce in the plains, particularly in the north, and large numbers of people have moved to areas more suited to upland cultivation, especially along major routeways. This movement has given rise to more scattered settlements, frequently on rather steep slopes.

Economy. Agriculture. Still the basis of the Thai economy, it employs 70 per cent of the total labour force

631

Thailand

of 17 million. The sector is equally dominated by rice production. There has been a steady expansion of the rice area since the mid-19th century, keeping pace with population growth and allowing a major export trade. Area planted in rice now totals 8.04 million ha (1973–74). Throughout most of the country age-old practices of cultivation are followed, utilising the labour of water buffaloes and the farm household, but mechanisation is now commoner in the central plain. The growth in planted area is now slowing, but the introduction of new rice varieties, increased use of chemical fertilisers, and improvements in water control due to the construction of storage dams on the headwaters of the Chao Phraya and north-eastern rivers have brought substantial increases in yield. Yields are now up to 1900 kg per ha nationally and annual production has topped 14 million t. Thus exports have been maintained and usually total over one million t of rice per annum. In the post-war period, Thai agriculture has seen considerable diversification. New cash crops have been introduced and widely adopted; the export base has been widened. Of the new crops, maize is grown chiefly in the north central plain, cassava in the south-east, sugar cane in the west central plain, and kenaf in the north-east. In the southern peninsula, smallholder rubber cultivation remains an important enterprise (see Table 1).

Industry. Despite improvements in communications, Thai industry remains concentrated in the Bangkok metropolitan region. Manufacturing, employing 10 per cent of the working population, is mainly oriented towards import substitution of consumer goods, with food processing and textiles the most important sectors of employment. The need to import basic raw materials emphasises the concentration on Bangkok. The main oil

Table 1

Crop	Area planted (hectares)	1973–1974 Production (000s tonnes)
Maize	1,094,000	2,343
Kenaf	434,000	469
Cassava	427,000	6,301
Sugar cane	258,000	13,339
Mung bean	233,000	192
Soya bean	142,000	152
Peanut	118,000	153
Rubber	892,000	368

refineries are on the coast nearby. Up country the main industries are rice-milling and saw-milling, although some other processing of agricultural raw materials is carried out, such as sugar refining and fruit canning. In the extractive sector, although limestone quarrying and lignite and fluorite mining are significant, the tin and tungsten mining industry of the peninsula is still most important. Tin mining is carried out by hydraulicking, and by dredging both onshore and offshore; a tin-smelter has been built at Phuket. Production in 1974 was 28,000 t. The vast salt and phosphate deposits underlying the north-east plateau have not yet been exploited, nor have possible petroleum supplies been explored in the Gulf of Thailand, although concessions have been granted for preliminary exploration by several oil companies.

Energy. Overall the country is short of energy and the small Fang oil-field cannot reduce the heavy reliance on imported petroleum. Lignite-fired power stations make some contribution to electricity supplies, but the major source is the great Phumiphol dam and other smaller hydro-electric schemes in the north and north-east. There

Thailand. Vegetable crops need protection from the sun. *(Camera Press)*

are plans for a nuclear plant on the coast near Bangkok.

Communications. Much of the recent development of new crops has taken place in upland areas newly opened up by improved transport links. The easy navigability of the Chao Phraya and its tributaries assisted the early development of the rice trade and a railway system centred on Bangkok supplemented this with lines to Chiengmai, Nongkhai, Ubol Ratchathani, and linking with the Malayan railway system at Haad Yai. The whole system now has 3765 km of track. The main modern achievement has been in the construction of roads. Partly connected with ensuring the security of outlying areas, these have nevertheless greatly improved access. Notable have been the 'Friendship' highway into the north-east region and its extensions to Nongkhai and Nakhon Phanom, and various parts of the Asian highway from Lampang in the north, across the central plain and down the peninsula. Thailand also has an extensive internal airline network, Thai Airways, which flies mainly Fokker Friendships, and there are two international airlines, the state-controlled Thai International and the private Air Siam.

Trade. Increasing import requirements have left Thailand with a long-term external trade deficit, particularly since 1966. Imports are mainly manufactures and industrial raw materials, exports chiefly agricultural produce. The structure of this trade and the chief trading partners are shown in Table 2 below.

Planning. Government planning policies accept the budget deficit situation and all three development plans to date have anticipated substantial foreign investment. The first and second plans, 1961–66 and 1967–71, concentrated mainly on the creation of infrastructure; in the third plan . emphasis has turned towards social services. Although the government entered into industrial promotion in the 1950s, it has since left this sector to private enterprise.

Finance. The Thai currency is the baht (100 satangs = 1 baht), which is tied to the US dollar (US $1 = 20·9 baht in 1976).

Bibliography: T. H. Silcock, *Economic Development of Thai Agriculture*, 1970; G. A. Marzouk, *Case Study of Thailand: Economic Development and Policies*, 1972; E. V. Roy, *Economic Systems of Northern Thailand: Structure and Change*, 1972; J. W. Watson, *Thailand: Rice Bowl of Asia*, 1973; M. Caldwell, *American Economic Aid to Thailand*, 1974.

Government. *Constitution.* Since 1932 Thailand has had several constitutions and the present one was promulgated on 22 October 1976. It provides for the continuation of the monarchy. It has established an elected chamber (the National Administrative Reform Assembly) of 300–400 members. Members are appointed for a four-year term by the king, and there are no political parties.

Legislature. Legislative power effectively lies with the prime minister, the cabinet and the Advisory Council. Administration in Thailand is highly centralised and appointments of top central and provincial civil servants are often political. In the central government structure, below the minister and his deputy, who are responsible to the assembly, each ministry is divided into departments each run by a director-general. Administrators at the provincial level are directly responsible to these departments rather than to the head of the provincial administra-

Table 2

Exports 1974

Category	Value (million baht)
Rice	9,792
Maize	6,047
Rubber	5,036
Tapioca	3,836
Sugar	3,757
Tin	3,071
Kenaf	838
Shrimps	608

Imports 1974

Non-electrical Machinery	10,978
Crude Oil	10,382
Chemicals	5,893
Iron and Steel	4,322
Vehicles	4,182
Base Metals	2,400
Textile Fibres	1,878

Exports 1974

Destination	Value (million baht)
Japan	12,853
Netherlands	4,328
Singapore	4,142
USA	3,985
Hong Kong	3,577
Taiwan	3,316
Malaysia	2,433

Imports 1974

Source	
Japan	20,102
USA	8,642
W. Germany	4,676
Saudi Arabia	3,062
United Kingdom	2,970
Australia	1,904

tration, the governor. Governors and district officers of the next lowest administrative unit are appointed within the framework of the Ministry of the Interior, not elected locally. The country is divided into 71 provinces.

Justice. One of the country's main problems is law and order. Despite a large police force, the annual total of murders and gang robberies is high. The country retains the death penalty and laws relating to labour organisations are strict, trade unions having only just been legalised. Divorce is common and relatively informal.

Armed Forces. Thailand's armed forces have long been linked with the presence of US troops. In 1975 the army numbered 135,000, including 11 artillery battalions and three tank battalions wth a force of 280 light tanks; it also has Hawk missiles. The navy of 27,000 men included 6000 marines, and is mainly equipped for coastal defence with 28 patrol vessels, but it also has four frigates. The air

Thailand

force, 42,000 strong, has a substantial counter-insurgency capability, but only a small force of 32 fighter-bombers.

Education. Thailand adopted the principle of universal primary education in 1904 as a means of building national unity. At present all children receive at least four years of primary education and this is steadily being increased to seven years as expansion at the commune level progresses. Basic literacy is extremely high and education services are supported by regional radio and television networks. Over 5 million children are receiving primary education, but the secondary sector is relatively underdeveloped. State secondary schools are present in most district centres and these are supplemented by private schools in Bangkok and other larger towns. About 1·5 million pupils are currently in secondary education, but the service is not free and thus restricts the opportunity for children of poorer families. The tertiary sector consists of three elements: vocational schools, concentrating on technical skills (notably agriculture), which have an intake of over 100,000; teacher training colleges numbering 33 in 1971 with 75,000 students; while the population of the 15 regular universities and institutes, including military academies, was 56,000. Until recently these were concentrated in Bangkok, where the largest colleges were Thammasat and Chulalongkorn Universities and Prasanmitr College of Education and Science. New foundations have now been made in the provinces, notably at Khon Kaen and Mahasarakham, and Prince of Songkhla University in the south. Another new venture is the 'open' Rama Khamheng University in Bangkok.

Welfare. Thailand's health and other social services are progressing rapidly, although treatment is not free except in Bangkok. All provincial centres have general hospitals and many villages boast clinics. The country has 17 doctors and 43 nurses per 100,000 people. Mahidol University graduates 600 doctors and dentists each year. Other services are confined chiefly to Bangkok, where a public housing programme has begun and where students and schoolchildren have free travel facilities. Rice is subsidised by the government and a minimum industrial wage has been instituted, 25 baht per day in Bangkok.

Official Language. Thai.

National Anthem. The king's anthem, which is normally played on official occasions, was composed by the king (Rama IX) himself, an accomplished musician of international standing.

National Flag. Known as the 'Trairanga Flag', it has a horizontal pattern of five red, white, and blue stripes; the top and bottom being red, the second and fourth white, and the broad central stripe, white.

Bibliography: W. G. Skinner, *Leadership and Power in the Chinese Community in Thailand*, 1958; D. E. Nuechterlein, *Thailand and the Struggle for South-East Asia*, 1966; D. A. Wilson, *Politics in Thailand*, 1967; D. K. Wyatt, *Politics of Reform in Thailand: Education in the Reign of King Chulalongkorn*, 1970; Institute for the Study of Conflict, *Thailand: The Dual Threat to Stability*, 1974.

History. Ancient. Recent archaeological discoveries have suggested that the area of modern Thailand was the centre of a significant neolithic culture as early as 3500 BC and of iron-working as early as 2000 BC. The Thai peoples were relatively late arrivals in the area. The earliest historical evidence suggests that the area was mostly under the control of the FUNAN Empire,

Thailand. Ruins of a Buddhist temple at Wat Phra Sri Sanpet. *(Barnaby's Picture Library)*

centred on Cambodia, in the 5th century, although by the 7th century, various kingdoms of MON peoples had been established in the Chao Phraya valley. The north-east region on the other hand remained in the hands of the Khmer empires which followed Funan, notably that of ANGKOR after the 8th century.

The Thais themselves began to move into their present territory in the 8th and 9th centuries from the kingdom of Nan Chao in the Yunnan area of China. Small states were established in the 11th century and in 1238 the first major kingdom was founded at SUKHOTHAI. Mongol invasions of Nan Chao forced greater migrations, and under King Rama Khamheng Sukhothai expanded to overcome the Mon kingdoms of the lower Chao Phraya valley and extend its rule down the southern peninsula. The Sukhothai kingdom was, however, short-lived and by 1350 power had passed to the south where another prince, Ramatipadi, founded Ayuthya. From this capital, Thailand was involved in a protracted power struggle with first Cambodia and then Burma. The contest with Burma was particularly long and after successes on both sides, it led in 1767 to the destruction of Ayuthya. Order in Thailand was subsequently restored and in 1782 the present Chakri dynasty came to power in the new capital of Bangkok.

Modern. Siam (which was the name of the country until 1939) first came into contact with European powers in South-East Asia in the early 17th century, when trading rivalries between the Dutch, British, and French developed rapidly. France was particularly active and sought domination in Siam, which brought a wary Siamese reaction to European power. This circumspection continued into the 19th century and it was only with the accession of King MONGKUT (Rama IV) in 1851 that Siamese attitudes changed. In 1855 a treaty was signed with Britain and similar arrangements with other powers followed. King Mongkut and his successor, King CHULALONGKORN, employed Western advisers to assist in the modernisation of the country's administration and commerce and managed to maintain Siam's independence by playing off the British interests to the west and south against those of the French to the east. Some territorial concessions were made in this cause with the Laotian territories east of the Mekong going to France along with the Cambodian provinces of Battambang and Siem Reap. In 1909 rights to four Malay states of southern Siam were transferred to British Malaya. Siam remained a British sphere of influence in the early 20th century, becoming Britain's wartime ally in 1917. Major financial difficulties hit the country in the 1930s and these precipitated a political coup in 1932. The coup created a constitutional monarchy and parliamentary government, but throughout the 1930s politics were marked by considerable unrest and by increasing nationalism. This was used by the invading Japanese in 1940–41, who signed a treaty with the government of Phibun Songkhram and later encouraged annexation of the French Indochinese territories lost in 1893 and 1907. By 1942 Thailand had declared war on the West.

After the war Thailand restored the French territories and signed treaties with her enemies, but another period of unstable government followed, particularly as a result of the mysterious death of Rama VIII in 1946. The year 1947 saw another military coup by Phibun Songkhram, since when the country has been controlled mainly by a succession of military governments under Phibun, Sarit Thanarat, and Thanom Kittikachorn. Thailand has followed a steady anti-Communist line under the influence of its alliance with the United States, and was a founder member of SEATO.

From time to time experiments at liberalisation have been made, by Phibun in 1955 and by Thanom in 1968, but results have been fractious and further military coups have resulted. Thanom ruled through a National Executive Council until 1973, when growing unrest over lack of basic freedom and foreign policy led to student riots in Bangkok culminating in the fall of the government. Again there has been a further attempt at constitutional government, but this too has been characterised by party factionalism, and again in 1976 the army was forced to take over, led by Admiral Chaloryoo, Thanin Kraivichien becoming prime minister. Martial law was declared. The government has, however, succeeded in re-orienting the country's foreign policy in the aftermath of the VIETNAM WAR. The United States has withdrawn all its substantial military presence in Thailand; diplomatic relations have been opened with China, North Korea, and the new government of Kampuchea (Cambodia). Disputes with Laos and with Vietnam have yet to be solved, however, and Thailand remains firmly within the non-Communist Association of South-East Asian Nations.

Bibliography: Sir J. Bowring, *Kingdom and People of Siam*, 1970; E. Nagel, *Thailand and Angkor*, 1971.

Architecture, see SOUTH-EAST ASIAN ARCHITECTURE.

Literature, see SOUTH-EAST ASIAN LITERATURE.

Thākurs, see RAJPUT.

Thalassaemia, see ANAEMIA.

Thaler, the popular name of a German and Austrian silver coin which had a wide currency from the 16th to 19th century. The name is the abbreviation for the Joachimsthaler, a silver coin of c. 28 g, struck at Joachimsthal in Bohemia by Count Stephen von Schlick (1505–26); coins of this issue were very numerous and popular and their name was therefore applied to other similar coins of the same value. The denomination was also popular outside Germany, hence the Italian *tallero* and English and American DOLLAR.

Thales (c. 636–c. 546 BC), Greek philosopher, first of the SEVEN SAGES, born at Miletus. He taught that water or moisture was the one element from which all things evolved. He appears to have owed much to the astronomy of the Egyptians and the civilisation of Mesopotamia. He is regarded as the founder of abstract geometry, of the strict deductive form as shown in Euclid's collections; he is said to have shown how to calculate the distance of a ship at sea and the heights of objects. In astronomy he was credited by the ancients with the prediction of the total solar eclipse identified by Airy, Zech, and Hind as occurring on 28 May 585 BC. Thales is also said to have noted the 'Lesser Bear' and to have shown its superiority for the purposes of navigation.

Bibliography: W. K. C. Guthrie, *A History of Greek Philosophy* (vol. 1), 1967.

Thalia, muse of comedy and idyllic poetry. See MUSES.

Thalia, one of the CHARITES.

Thaliacea, a class of invertebrate marine animals in subphylum TUNICATA of phylum CHORDATA. They are free-swimming and barrel-shaped, and take in water through a siphon at the front end, extract food and oxygen from it, then squirt it out of another siphon at the hind end, with sufficient force to propel the animal through the sea.

Thalidomide (alpha-phthalimidoglutarimide) is a hypnotic (sleep-inducing) and sedative drug synthesised in Germany in 1953 and introduced in Britain in 1958. The harm caused to the foetus when it was administered to women during the early stages of pregnancy was realised in 1961 and the drug was withdrawn from the British market in December of that year. Children born to women who took it had phocomelia (seal extremities), in which the long bones of the limbs were defective, but the hands and feet were normal.

Thallium, metallic chemical element, symbol Tl, atomic number 81, atomic weight 204·37. It was discovered in 1861 by Crookes in the seleniferous deposits from sulphuric acid manufacture. It occurs in small quantities in iron pyrites, and also occurs associated with copper, silver, and selenium in the mineral 'crookesite'. The metal is prepared by displacement from its solutions by means of zinc. Thallium compounds give a bright green line in the spectrum (hence the name, from Greek *thallos*, a green shoot); some of them find a use in the manufacture of optical glass.

Thallus, term used of the plant body of an alga or fungus, where there is no differentiation into root, stem or leaf.

Thälmann, Ernst (1886–1944), German Communist politician, born at Hamburg. He was a member of the Reichstag, 1924–33, leader of the German Communist party, and stood as Communist candidate for the presidency in 1932. A close associate of Stalin, he maintained a narrowly pro-Soviet stance. After Hitler came to power Thälmann was sent to a concentration camp and was probably executed at Buchenwald in August 1944.

Thame, market town of OXFORDSHIRE, England. It is

Thames

situated on the River Thame, 21 km from Oxford and 72 km from London. Its most important building is the church of St Mary the Virgin, which is an exceptionally large church in mainly Early English and Perpendicular styles, containing some interesting brasses. Thame has a 16th-century grammar school and a famous inn known as the 'Spread Eagle'. The river has its source in the Chiltern Hills and flows past Thame to the THAMES, which it joins near Dorchester; it is 56 km long. Population (1971) 5948.

Thames, river of ENGLAND, which rises near Cirencester in the COTSWOLD HILLS and follows a course of 330 km to the NORE, where it debouches into the North Sea. It is England's largest and most important river. At GRAVESEND, the head of the estuary, it has a width of a kilometre, gradually increasing thence to 16 km at the Nore. Tidal waters reach Teddington, 100 km from its mouth, where the first lock from the sea (except for the tidal lock at Richmond) is located. There are in all 47 locks, St John's Lock, Lechlade, being nearest the source. The normal rise and fall of the tide is from 4·5 to 7 m at London Bridge and from 4 to 6 m at Tilbury. Until Tower Bridge was built, London Bridge was the lowest in the course; the reach between these two bridges is known as the 'Pool of London'. Lying some 5 km south-west of the Nore is the mouth of the MEDWAY estuary, at the head of which lie CHATHAM with important naval dockyards, GILLINGHAM, and ROCHESTER. Gravesend on the south bank of the river, some 40 km from the Nore, has developed at a point where vessels formerly awaited the turn of the tide. TILBURY, FORT AND DOCKS, important as the main London container terminal, lies opposite Gravesend on the northern bank. At WOOLWICH, some 30 km above Tilbury, is the arsenal; GREENWICH, a little farther upriver, has the Royal Naval College. Between Tilbury and

Thames. The river at Marlow, Buckinghamshire. *(Topham/Scowen)*

London Bridge (some 40 km upstream) stretches the London dock system and many wharves. The embankments of the Thames in London were the work of Sir Joseph BAZALGETTE (1819–91), chief engineer of the Metropolitan Board of Works. The Albert Embankment on the south side was completed in 1869, the Victoria Embankment from Westminster to Blackfriars in 1870, and the Chelsea Embankment from the Royal Hospital to Battersea Bridge in 1874. In January 1949 work was started on a new embankment, designed by J. Rawlinson, chief engineer of the former LCC, on the south side from County Hall to Waterloo Bridge. These embankments were raised after 1974 and it is planned to build a tidal barrier below London to reduce the danger of flooding by tidal surges. The river is spanned by over 50 bridges, including Tower Bridge (a bascule bridge), and suspension bridges at Hammersmith and Marlow. The chief tunnels under the Thames are the Thames Tunnel, completed by Brunel in 1841, now used by railways only; the Blackwall Tunnel (1897) from East India Dock Road to East Greenwich, and now dual carriageway, the Rotherhithe Tunnel (1918) from Shadwell to Rotherhithe, and the Dartford tunnel completed in 1963. In 1948 a scheme was put in motion for the maintenance of the tow-paths from Teddington to Cricklade as a riverside walk. The PORT OF LONDON AUTHORITY is responsible for the control and conservation of the river below Teddington; above Teddington the Thames Conservancy is the responsible authority.

Steamers ply regularly from Kingston to Folly Bridge, Oxford, during the summer. The scenery along this part of the river is pleasant, varied, and in some places beautiful, e.g. at Cliveden, Cookham, Sonning, and Pangbourne. There are fine bridges at Richmond, Hampton Court, Chertsey, Maidenhead, and Shillingford. Henley, Wallingford, Dorchester, and Abingdon are pretty places, and Eton and Windsor are famous. Along the 80 km from its source beneath a tree in 'Trewsbury Mead' to Oxford, the Thames glides through tranquil meadows, its course interrupted only by the small towns of Lechlade and Cricklade and the charming stone-built hamlets of Kelmscott and Ashton Keynes. In these upper reaches there are two picturesque medieval bridges—New Bridge and Radcot Bridge. Motor launches can reach Lechlade; beyond that point it is possible to canoe up to Cricklade, but the final 16 km to the source of the Thames is best traversed on foot, through great meadows filled in spring with cowslips and fritillaries. It is a peaceful and most attractive walk. The other particularly attractive section is the steep-sided valley through the chalk hills between Goring and Reading, known as the Goring Gap.

Until the 19th century the London Thames was an important means of transport for passengers; the names of 'stairs' are traces of the great passenger barge traffic. Since the Second World War passenger traffic on the Thames has been revived by 'water buses' and hydrofoils. The Thames has been frozen over at various times, the earliest recorded occasion being AD 1150. The Thames is of great importance to the water supply of London, partly because the many springs in the chalk usually maintain a steady flow in summer.

Bibliography: J. H. B. Peel, *Portrait of the Thames*, 1967; F. Martin, *Thames Valley*, 1973; J. R. L. Anderson, *Upper Thames*,

1974; P. Atterbury and A. Darwin (Eds), *Guide to the Thames*, 1974; Tourist Board, *Thames and Chilterns*, 1976.

Thames Ditton, residential district of Surrey, England, in Elmbridge District. The Swan and Angel Hotels are 16th-century foundations, and there are almshouses built around 1720. Population (1971) 10,600.

Thames Water Authority is one of ten regional water authorities set up in England and Wales under the Water Act 1973. On 1 April 1974 the Authority took over responsibility for managing the entire water cycle throughout the Thames Basin area. This includes water resources, water supply, sewerage, sewage treatment and disposal, rivers, pollution control, amenity, and recreation. The Thames Region stretches from the Cotswolds in the west to Gravesend in the east; Banbury and Luton in the north to the southern limit formed by the North Downs, Hampshire Downs, and Marlborough Downs. The region is 13,100 km² in area and serves a population of almost 12 million. This area was previously administered by 200 different undertakings, including the Metropolitan Water Board, Thames Conservancy, and the Greater London Council Main Drainage service. Seven independent water companies supply water within the Thames Water area and local sewerage work is carried out for the Authority by local authorities acting as agents.

Thane, or thegn, an Anglo-Saxon word, meaning 'one who serves', seems to have been applied to the personal followers of the king or a great man. They had a duty to serve both in peace and war and, although including men of varying degrees of wealth ranging right down to men little different from CEORLS, their high status is confirmed by the fact that men of this class had a WERGILD of 1200 shillings. The king's thegns had particular importance in local administration, served at court, and attended the WITENAGEMOT.
Bibliography: F. M. Stenton, *Anglo-Saxon England*, 3rd ed. 1971.

Thanet, Isle of, extreme eastern part of KENT, formerly separated from the mainland by the River Wantsum which remained in part navigable up to the end of the 15th century. Ebbsfleet was the landing place of the Saxons in AD 449, and in the same area St AUGUSTINE and the Christian missionaries made their landfall in 597. Traditionally a cereal growing area, it has now become noted for its extensive vegetable production, especially green vegetables and potatoes. MARGATE, BROADSTAIRS, and RAMSGATE are well-known resorts. Manston, originally a USAF base, is now a civil airport.

Thanet Sands, see TERTIARY SYSTEM.

Thanh Hoa, capital of a province of the same name in northern-central VIETNAM, situated 25 km from the sea. There is a citadel and a Roman Catholic cathedral. The province produces large quantities of rice, and pottery is manufactured. Provincial population (1971) 1,598,300.

Thanjavur, town in Tamil Nadu state, India, 273 km south of Madras. It has an 11th-century Hindu temple, an old palace of the rajas, and the remains of a fort. Thanjavur stands at the head of the CAUVERY delta which is heavily irrigated, densely populated, and very fertile. Rice is the main crop. The town is a Brahmin centre and a

U Thant. *(Popperfoto)*

noted political, literary, and educational focus, with four colleges affiliated to the University of Madras. Population (1971) 140,500.

Thanksgiving Day, annual festival of thanksgiving in the USA, celebrated as a national holiday, according to the choice of President Lincoln in 1864, on the last Thursday in November. In 1941 President Roosevelt further defined the date of celebration as the fourth Thursday in November. It is in essence a national harvest celebration, and was first observed by the Pilgrim Fathers at Plymouth in 1621 after their first harvest.

Thant, U (1909–74), Burmese administrator and UNITED NATIONS official, educated at Rangoon University. Originally a teacher, he was secretary to the Burmese premier in 1953, and Burma's permanent representative at the UN, 1957–61. After Dag HAMMARSKJÖLD's death, Thant, a compromise candidate, was acting secretary-general of the UN from November 1961 to November 1962, when he was confirmed as secretary-general. Thant showed skill in holding the UN organisation together at a difficult period in its history and remained as secretary-general until 1971. His peace initiatives included his invitation to the Pope to address the UN in New York in 1965. In 1973 Thant became president of the World Federation of UN Associations. His publications include: *League of Nations*, 1933; *Democracy in Schools*, 1952; *History of Post-War Burma*, 2 vols, 1961.

Thapsus, ancient city of north Africa, 48 km south-east of Susa. In 46 BC Julius CAESAR here routed the Pompeians under CATO, METELLUS SCIPIO, and JUBA II.

Thasos (Greek *Thásos*), island of Greece in the north of the Aegean Sea, off the coast of Macedonia. Today it is part of the department of Kavalla. It was early on occupied by Phoenicians, on account of its gold mines. Thasos was afterwards colonised by the Parians in 708 BC, and among the colonists was the poet Archilochus. The Thasians once possessed a considerable territory on the coast of Thrace, and were one of the richest and most powerful peoples in the northern Aegean. After subjugation by Persia, they regained their independence in 479 BC and joined the DELIAN LEAGUE, from which they twice revolted (465 and 411 BC). The island was finally restored to Athens in 409 BC. The island was ruled successively by Romans, Byzantines, and Turks before it was finally ceded to Greece in 1913. Area 378 km²; population 16,000.

Thatcher, Margaret Hilda (1925–), British politician, became leader of the Conservative party in 1975, educated at Kesteven and Grantham Girls' Grammar School and Somerville College, Oxford. She began her career as a research chemist, but became a barrister before being elected as Conservative MP for Finchley in 1959. From 1961 to 1964 she was parliamentary secretary, Ministry of Pensions and National Insurance. She served as an Opposition spokesman between 1964 and 1970 and entered the Cabinet as secretary of state for Education and Science in 1970, a post she held until the Conservative defeat of 1974. In February 1975 Mrs Thatcher successfully challenged Edward HEATH for the leadership of the Conservative party and thus became the first woman to lead a political party in Britain.

Thatching, art of roofing houses or protecting stacks of hay or grain with a covering of reeds, rushes, straw, etc. Thatch should be at least 30 cm in thickness and laid to a pitch of 45 degrees. Best or true Norfolk reed is used in thatching. Norfolk reed with an admixture of lesser reed mace lasts longer, besides being less expensive

Margaret Thatcher. *(Camera Press/J. Blau)*

than best reed. Wheat or rye straw is considerably cheaper than reed, but may require renewal after 20 years, whereas reed thatch should last about 75 years. Heather also provides a durable thatch but in exposed places is liable to strip. Thatching is now a dying art and is seldom used except for renovations. Thatching is usually covered with wire wefts to prevent birds from building nests.

Thaumaturgy, healing by means of some supernormal ability not yet usually verifiable by science. It includes faith healing (healing which is said to be effected by the patient's faith in divine power); spirit healing (healing which is claimed to be due to spirit doctors working through mediums); and contact healing (described as a transmission of healing energy from healer to patient through bodily contact of some sort). Many different religions and mystical philosophies believe in thaumaturgy, and over the years there have been innumerable accounts of miraculous recoveries having occured as a result of it. See also MIRACLE.
Bibliography: H. Edwards, *Spirit Healing*, 1963; A. Guirdham, *The Nature of Healing*, 1964; R. H. Ashby, *The Guidebook for the Study of Psychical Research*, 1973.

Thaxted, town in ESSEX, England, 11 km north of Great Dunmow. It was important in medieval times for its cutlery industry, and was formerly a borough, incorporated by charter of Philip of Spain and Mary I. It is famous for its massive Perpendicular church, which has a fine crotcheted spire (55 m) and is one of the finest in Essex. The guildhall in Town Street is a picturesque three-storeyed timber-framed building of mid-15th century date, and is one of the few remaining medieval guildhalls in England. Horham Hall is in the parish. Population (1971) 2100.

Thayet-myo, township and town of Magwe division, Burma. The town, on the west bank of the Irrawaddy river, manufactures cement. The surrounding district produces rice, cotton, and groundnuts. Township: area 1175 km²; population 77,331.

Theatines, Roman Catholic religious order of priests, marked by its extreme observance of poverty. It was founded in 1524 by Gaetano dei Conti (1480–1547), canonised in 1671, and Giovanni Caraffa, afterwards Pope Paul IV, with the object of restoring the standard of clerical life and recalling the laity to the practice of virtue. Theatines are mainly found today in Italy. There are also Theatine nuns, founded by Ursula Benincasa in 1583.

Theatre, building or area specially designated for the presentation of a performance by an actor or actors in front of an audience; also, all the physical elements which make up the presentation.
  The basic physical requirements of any organised drama are an area which the actor(s) can enter, perform in and exit from without impediment, and an area, normally with some kind of controlled entry, in which the spectators can stand or sit. Everything else—scenery, props, costumes, technical effects, a changing room for the actors and space to store accessories—may be regarded as more or less refinements, however important they may be in practice. In the course of its development the drama has witnessed numerous changes in the physical conditions and relationship of these two basic requirements, the

Theatre. The amphitheatre at Epidaurus, one of the better preserved Greek theatres. *(Topham/Fotogram)*

stage and the auditorium, not to mention the remarkable variety of styles in scenery, costume, and the other elements of spectacle. Although these features have been isolated for discussion here, they cannot ultimately be divorced from the historical development of the substance of the DRAMA, or from the wider social and cultural factors which generate both the drama and its physical presentation.

Greece and Rome. The religious origins of Greek drama led to the first known theatres being built on sacred sites in close proximity to the temples. At first, plays were performed in theatres consisting of wooden stands or seats on a slope with an open playing area which was clearly visible to the large crowd of spectators. By the mid-5th century a wooden *skene* (scene building), probably of two storeys and with three entrance doors, was being temporarily erected as a background to the performance, and its front painted to suggest a particuar location. In the *skene* the actors could dress and wait for their cues, while its roof could support rudimentary machinery, such as that required for the customary descent of the god at the end of the play. Around 425 BC the *skene* became more elaborate, so that it consisted of a long front wall with projecting wings (*paraskenia*) at the sides. In front of the *skene* was the columned *proskenion* (whence proscenium) where the actors performed, while the chorus occupied the circular *orchestra*, in the middle of which stood an altar. By 330 BC in Athens (earlier in Syracuse) the *orchestra* and auditorium were constructed of stone. The audience could enter the auditorium through gateways at ground level on either side of the theatre, and walk

round the edge of the *orchestra* to reach the seats on the surrounding slope.

The changes in the Greek theatre which took place over several centuries ran parallel with the decreasing importance of the chorus. At first comprised of 50 persons, and acting only in the *orchestra*, it gradually dwindled to a few performers. The actors, who had gradually become detached from the chorus, thus grew increasingly prominent, so that in the newer theatres of the Hellenistic period the focus of attention ceased to be the *orchestra* and became the stage on which the actors played. The latter was now raised and supported by a row of columns. The *skene* was made much larger, and its front, which was now ample, was fitted with large openings (*thyromata*) into which large painted panels (probably more 'realistically' painted than previously) could be set. In general, there was also a movement towards greater architectural, as well as scenic, elaboration.

In addition to the official drama there is some literary and pictorial evidence of private shows put on by the travelling players of BURLESQUE and FARCES, often in the houses of the wealthy. These performances took place on simple wooden raised stages, the front of the stage perhaps being decorated with a painted panel or drape. Scenic decoraton was at a minimum, as were props.

Around the end of the 2nd century BC the stage of the official drama was further enlarged so that it encroached on the *orchestra* (which now became only slightly more than a semi-circle), the scenic background was enlarged and embellished, and the acting platform itself became much deeper. The Hellenistic colonists built stone theatres, and when the first was constructed in Rome in 55 BC (soon followed by two others) important new features were displayed. The auditorium (*cavea*) was now strictly semi-circular, as was the *orchestra*, which in some theatres was used for extra seating or gladiatorial contests, and the theatres themselves were now normally built on level ground. The stage, which was lower and deeper, was backed by a highly embellished *frons scaenae* (the front of the scene building). The *proskenion* (now Latinised as the *proscaenium*) was decorated with columns and other architectural refinements, and a front curtain was added, which could be lowered into a trench in the *orchestra*, while other curtains were used to cover parts of the *frons scaenae*. The building was enclosed with high walls, also often architecturally elaborate. Finally, the bringing together of the architectural elements into a single entity resulted in the top of the *frons scaenae* being level with the top of the auditorium, so that the entire theatre could be covered with a large awning (*velum*).

Playhouses of this sort, and of increasing splendour, were built in many Roman towns and cities. Ironically, little of any dramatic merit was ever performed in them and they were largely given over to various kinds of spectacle. Equally ironically, Roman actors had, for the most part, none of the dignified status of the Greek actor. With the advent of organised Christianity and the collapse of the Roman empire the regular theatre disappeared, the only survivors being the MIMES and PANTOMIMES, who continued a very early Greek theatrical tradition. Although we know little of their activities, there is no doubt that they continued to perform, presumably on the most rudimentary stages, when opportunity allowed. The tradition which they represent re-emerges, though still obscurely, in the high Middle Ages, in occasional references to entertainers variously described as *mimes*, *scurri* and *histriones*.

The Middle Ages. The staging of the liturgical plays of the medieval Church was governed by the physical conditions of the church or cathedral and by the devotional purposes of the music-drama. These purposes could be adequately served by the use of visual symbols which were easily identifiable by the audience. It was unnecessary—and undesirable—to use properties with some claim to visual realism: the clergy was not interested in presenting the Christmas crib or Easter sepulchre as authentic reproductions of the real historical objects, but as visual signals to the enduring spiritual significance of the crib or sepulchre. However, the expansion of the liturgical narrative into anything more complicated than the most simple of actions entailed the presentation of several different, easily identifiable locations. To achieve this it was necessary to provide a multiplicity of visual symbols, often drawn from everyday contemporary life, which were then used to direct attention to the most exalted of spiritual meanings.

The area in which the visual symbol of place was set was known as the *locus*, and if this *locus* was a place where someone lived, it could also be known as a *domus* or 'mansion'. It might be either a simple chair (*sedes*), or a chair supplemented by a curtain or gate. When the dramatic narrative was expanded and it became necessary to provide several symbols, the extension was lengthwise, down the nave. By the end of the 12th century the full length of the church could be taken up with the multiple

loca and the open and unlocalised acting-area adjacent to them, the *platea*. The spectators may have been placed in the side aisles, though a better view of the action and an improved acoustic probably resulted from the audience occupying the triforium and clerestory.

The belief—severely questioned in recent years—that the cycle-plays developed directly out of liturgical music-drama has tended to distract attention away from the possible influence of popular performance techniques on the vernacular religious drama. The 12th century Anglo-Norman plays, *Mystère d'Adam* and *La Seinte Resureccion*, as well as the plays of the Arras poet-dramatists, Jean Bodel and ADAM DE LA HALLE, certainly incorporate popular elements. The English *Interludium de Clerico et Puella* and the French *Le Garçon et l'Aveugle*, both of them simple farces, survive as indications of the fare offered by itinerant secular actors. These were performed on rudimentary booth stages, probably consisting of a stage of planks and a curtain behind which the actors could prepare and await their cues. It is perhaps due to the influence of such a popular acting tradition that even in the earliest vernacular religious plays vigorous and informal conventions are adopted, including the scurrying of 'devils' around the acting area and into the audience.

The vernacular religious plays—whether MIRACLE PLAY cycles, moralities (see MORALITY), or SAINTS' PLAYS—conformed in general to the *loca* and *platea* convention of staging already described. It is certain, though, that there were two basic variations on this pattern: the station-to-station form, in which moveable pageant wagons were used for performances at different

Theatre. A 16th-century perspective stage set at the Teatro Olympico, Vicenza, constructed by Scamozzi to a design by Palladio. *(Mansell Collection)*

Theatre. A performance by the 17th-century troupe of Gille le Niais, after an engraving by Abraham Bosse. *(Raymond Mander and Joe Mitchenson Theatre Collection)*

locations in the town; and the stationary place-and-scaffold structures representing separate locations. The latter was the usual method of staging in medieval France and many of the German-speaking countries, while in England both types were used for cycle and non-cycle plays. If the pageant stages were but one manifestation of a great deal of pagantry for state and civic occasions, as they almost certainly were, evidence of their structure and scenic decoration can be gleaned. They were impressive, being brightly coloured and using sophisticated machinery such as windlasses, and furnished with an array of richly decorated scenic emblems such as hills, fountains, forests, 'heavens' and 'hell-mouths'.

The Renaissance. The Italian rediscovery of classical dramatists, especially PLAUTUS and TERENCE, in the 15th century led to attempts in schools and academies to reconstruct the physical conditions of their original performance. The emphasis was firmly placed on ancient Roman practice, not only because there was much more interest in Roman comedy than in Greek drama but also because interest in classical staging centred on the rediscovered works of the Roman Vitruvius, whose *De Architectura* was published in Latin in 1486 and in Italian in 1521. The great monument, still surviving, to the antiquarian pursuit of a reconstructed classical theatre is the *Teatro Olimpico*, which was designed and built by Palladio and Scamozzi at Vicenza in 1585. Although the intention, according to a contemporary observer, was to 'construct a theatre according to the ancient use of the Greeks and Romans', the visitor will recognise the remarkable similarity of the *Teatro Olimpico* to the Roman theatres, with their splendid *frons scaenae*, rather than to any surviving Greek theatres.

The growing interest in the 16th century in perspective scenery, however, displaced to a large extent the original scholarly interest in staging classical plays or their imitations in the original manner. We know that a perspective setting was used in Ferrara in 1508, though this was probably a painted backcloth; but by 1531 Peruzzi was designing scenes which showed a perspective street in a three-dimensional set. The main debt to Vitruvius was now restricted to his classification of the scene into three categories—comic, tragic and satyric—and his use of *periaktoi*—triangular revolving prisms on each side of the stage, each side being painted to indicate a separate locality. In 1545 Sebastiano SERLIO published an influential work which helped disseminate further the idea of perspective scenery, and in 1589 Bernardo Buontalenti staged a play in which Serlian frame-and-canvas angled houses were included in a perspective which comprised views of three streets. The scenery was changed for each of the six *intermezzi* (spectacular items between the acts proper) in this play, though it is not clear if this was done by means of *periaktoi* or through early use of sliding flat wings. To stage these spectacular *intermezzi* a sophisticated range of machinery was developed. The truly revolutionary scenic discovery of the early 17th century, however—which was to dominate European theatre for the next three centuries—was that of painted side wings, which could not only offer interesting perspective

641

scenes but could be easily changed to reveal a number of different scenes in the course of a play or opera.

In the course of the 17th century the conception of spectacle, which originated and was developed in Italy, spread throughout Europe as a result of the efforts of such designers as Bernini, Torelli and Inigo JONES. Perspective scenery, the use of elaborate stage machinery to achieve spectacular effects, and the proscenium-arched stage were absorbed by all the European countries, though in the process the Italianate style of staging developed unique national features as it encountered native traditions in specific historical circumstances. In France, the later drawings of Mahelot show an increasingly unified perspective effect. In England, it was Inigo Jones, who had trained as a designer in Italy, who introduced and experimented with Italian innovations in his designs for MASQUES and plays presented at Court. Jones developed a system of flats moving in grooves in and above the stage, the backcloth being formed of two shutters which could open to reveal another elaborate scene behind. In Italy, the need for quick scene-changes in opera led to the development of elaborate machinery to remove the flat wings with their profiled edges (which 'receded' through the simple expedient of the decreasing size of the flats upstage), and replace them with other wings comprising another perspective vista. The most common methods of doing so were the 'chariot-and-pole' and the 'drum-and-shaft' techniques. In the former, the wings were hung on a pole so that they just cleared the floor, and the poles were fixed through slits in the stage to wheeled carriages running on rails in the cellar; the system was duplicated at each wing position and all were connected to a central shaft in such a way that one wing could move off-stage as another moved on. A similar effect was achieved by attaching ropes from all the flats to be moved to a revolving drum under the stage, which then worked on the lever principle.

Italianate stage practice spread from the court theatres of the 17th and 18th centuries to the public theatres. The tragedies of CORNEILLE and RACINE were played in a neutral palace setting derived from Italian precedent and the formal concern with the Unity of Place (see DRAMATIC UNITIES). The reopening of the English theatres at the Restoration signalled the triumph of the perspective and proscenium stage, though at first a traditional apron stage protruded in front of the proscenium arch, and two pairs of doors were fitted to allow the actors easy access to the main acting area. Gradually, however, the doors were replaced by boxes and the apron further and further curtailed, though it was not until 1843 that the apron stage entirely disappeared from British theatres. In general, however, late 17th century theatres were conservative in that scenery was conceived of as a background accompanying the development of the action rather than as scenic environment in which action was understood to be taking place.

While momentous developments were occurring in Italy in the late 15th and 16th centuries, popular medieval traditions of staging flourished throughout the rest of Europe. The religious plays continued to be staged regularly in England until the final quarter of the 16th century, and the professional itinerant actors performed their INTERLUDES on stages erected against the hall-screens of Tudor halls and on curtained booth stages wherever

Theatre. Playbill for Vanbrugh's comedy, *The Provok'd Wife*, 1774. (*Victoria and Albert Museum, London*)

they could find an audience.

The COMMEDIA DELL' ARTE, which emerged in Italy in the 16th century, quickly won widespread popularity in European courts and villages. It is largely in this native medieval tradition that English and Spanish theatres and staging conventions of the late 16th and early 17th centuries are to be understood, and the same is true for those of the German-speaking countries of the period, and even, to some degree, for those of France.

The most important piece of pictorial evidence relating to English stage conditions of the Elizabethan period is the copy by Van Buchell of de Witt's drawing of the interior of the Swan Playhouse. This shows a large platform stage supported by what appear to be wooden trestles, and a back wall with two large doors, above which is a balcony occupied by several people (who might be either spectators or actors). Above the stage is a sloping roof supported by two large and ornate pillars, which de Witt recorded as being wooden and painted to give the appearance of marble. Above the sloping roof is the 'hut', with its flag to signal that a performance would be given that day and with a trumpeter. The stage and dressing room area appear to constitute an architectural entity, more or less distinct from the frame of the building. Spectators could be accommodated in the three tiers overlooking the arena, access to which was by stairways marked in the drawing by the word *ingressus*, or around the three sides of the stage. The area labelled *orchestra* (with its corresponding area on the other side of the stage) accommodated those gentlemen who were prepared to pay considerably more than the rest to sit near the stage. Presumably, the balcony above the stage would be used solely by actors if the play required scenes to be played 'above', or by spectators if this was not the case. The entrance to the playhouse was through a main door directly beneath where de Witt was sitting when he drew the sketch.

Since there is no good reason to doubt the essential reliability of the de Witt sketch we must assume that it accurately depicts the physical conditions of one Elizabethan playhouse. At the same time, we may expect considerable variations in detail among playhouses of this period, even while a basic architectural and stage form predominates. Evidence for both beliefs is forthcoming from a number of documentary sources, including the surviving contracts for the building of the Fortune Theatre (1600) and the Hope Theatre (1613), panoramic maps which include illustrations of playhouses, evidence from plays and contemporary literature, and such relevant foreign evidence as the woodcuts of the Nuremberg Fechthaus (1627). These sources indicate that the acting platform was in general very large, for the Fortune contract specifies a stage 43 ft (13·1 m) wide and between 30 ft (9·1 m) and 40 ft (12·2 m) deep. The 'heavens' supported on pillars were apparently normal in playhouses built between 1590 and 1610, but were probably not a permanent feature of the earliest theatres. The 'heavens' was so named because the ceiling was painted with a Zodiac on a blue background, thus serving as a symbol of the celestial world. A trapdoor in this ceiling allowed the descents of characters or scenic units like thrones from the loft. There is no evidence of the so-called 'inner-stage', allegedly set into the back wall; it is likely that 'discovery' or other 'interior' scenes were presented in a curtained area immediately behind one of the stage-doors, or in a

moveable structure set against the back wall. Finally, playhouses of the Elizabethan or Jacobean periods could be circular, octagonal, or square in shape, and—if de Witt's evidence is correct—they could accommodate a large number of spectators, for he claims that the Swan could hold 3000 people.

The notion that the Elizabethan and Jacobean stages had little or no scenery has recently been strongly questioned. It must be remembered that the company with which Shakespeare was associated (the King's Men) regularly performed in places other than the Globe; in the indoor Blackfriars, from 1608; in the banqueting halls of the royal palaces; and in the provinces, when plague was rife in London. It seems certain that there was a basic similarity between the staging conventions normally employed at the Globe and those regularly employed at these other locations. If this is so, it is incredible that the actors performed with little or no scenery at the Globe, for there is ample evidence of the use of a wide variety of scenic units such as castles, battlements, palaces, cities, tombs and caves in Tudor interludes and entertainments at Court. That such units were also employed on the stages of the public playhouses is confirmed by the list of properties (dated 1598) which survives in the papers of Philip HENSLOWE, a leading theatrical entrepreneur of the time. It would, in any case, be remarkable if the kind of staging common during the late Middle Ages and that employed during the Restoration—both of which offered plenty of scenic effects—was interrupted by an almost complete absence of scenery during the Elizabethan and Jacobean period. The idea that Shakespeare's theatre was characterised physically by almost bare stages in small, soberly timbered playhouses must be put aside, and replaced by the image of sumptuously decorated and coloured architecture, and stages occupied by the same utilitarian but impressive scenic emblems that were used

Theatre. Engraving after a painting by Zoffany of a scene from *The Provok'd Wife*, with David Garrick in the role of Sir John Brute. *(Victoria and Albert Museum, London)*

in Court entertainments and religious and civic pageantry.

On the Continent, Spanish playhouses of this period had much in common with the London playhouses. The first permanent Spanish playhouse was built only three years after the first London one, and although there were differences in physical conditions, the Spanish *corrales* resembled their counterparts in London in being open-air, with stages equipped with a balcony, trapdoors and doors fitted into the back wall, and spectators congregating in the yard or sitting in the surrounding three tiers. Scenic units similar to those in use in England were also employed. In France, there had been a continuous tradition of indoor performance from the late 14th century, and in 1548 the *Confrérie de la Passion* had converted a hall in the *Hôtel de Bourgogne* into a theatre for the performance of secular plays. The evidence to be gleaned from the surviving detailed sketches and notes (most of them by the designer Mahelot) for productions between 1633 and 1678 indicates that French staging continued to owe much to the simultaneous staging of the medieval period. The various scenic units needed to identify locations in a play were all on stage throughout, just as they were in performances of the *mystères*. In Mahelot's sketches, however, Italian influence is apparent in the way the units are placed in receding rows, to obtain a perspective effect, and in the Serlian designs of the wood and canvas houses. For farce, which was a popular attraction at the *Hôtel de Bourgogne*, the style of staging was influenced by the traditional *commedia dell'arte* scene, with its two side houses.

The 18th and 19th Centuries. The history of theatre architecture and scenery in these centuries consists to a large extent in the elaboration of developments already apparent in the late 17th century. In Europe generally, the 18th century was the age of the opera houses, with their sumptuously decorated horseshoe auditoria round the proscenium-arched stage, and their galleries divided into boxes providing excellent acoustics but not always a good view. Towards the end of the century, especially in England, there developed a movement towards greater historical realism in costume, and later in scenery. William Capon made a number of designs for painted backcloths in the final decade of the century which incorporated careful antiquarian research into the portrayal of ancient buildings and street scenes. In the last quarter of the century Phillipe Jacques de Loutherbourg made romantic landscape designs for plays and non-dramatic shows which were based on careful observations of real landscape, and experimented with lighting techniques designed to simulate natural light and shade.

The movement towards greater historical accuracy continued apace throughout Europe in the 19th century. This tendency was not, of course, the result solely of dedicated antiquarianism, for it also allowed theatres to attract large audiences with the prospect of wings and painted backcloths offering impressive pageantry and spectacle. In England, this type of staging was associated especially with the Shakespearean productions of Charles KEAN in the 1850s. Spectacle was also the keynote of the popular MELODRAMA of the 19th century, and elaborate machinery was invented to reproduce, with maximum effect, such sensational events as train crashes, horse races and ships in storm-tossed seas. The box set, an arrangement of painted flats joined together to form three walls, with realistic doors, windows, fireplaces and so forth contained in them, was introduced by T. W. ROBERTSON in his domestic melodramas of the 1860s; and mechanical devices such as elevator platforms, sliding stages and revolving platforms were developed to effect easy transformations of three-dimensional sets. Most significant of all, however, were the advances in stage lighting; by 1830 gas

Theatre. Painting of the banquet scene in *Macbeth*, Act 3 Scene 4, as a record of the production by Charles Kean. (*Victoria and Albert Museum, London*)

Theatre. Vittorio Gassman as Hamlet at the Arts Theatre in Rome, 1952–53. *(Raymond Mander and Joe Mitchenson Theatre Collection)*

lighting was being used in London, and first limelight and then electric lighting were introduced during the second half of the century. As a result, the darkened auditorium and the illuminated and realistically decorated stage became entirely separated, the front curtain became increasingly vital, and behind the proscenium arch ever more naturalistic settings were sought.

Naturalism in scenery, costume and acting was the logical culmination of the lengthy movement towards a more convincing illusion of actuality in photographic terms which originated with Italian scenic experiments of the 16th and 17th centuries. In Paris, André Antoine founded his *Théâtre Libre* in 1887 so that serious naturalistic plays could be produced in an appropriate manner. Similar theatres, like J. T. Grein's Independent Theatre in London and, more importantly, Stanislavsky's Moscow Art Theatre were also established in the final decade of the 19th century. Curiously, however, Naturalism was hardly established as the new scenic orthodoxy in Europe and the USA before the more creative designers and directors were experimenting with new styles and conventions.

The 20th Century. The 20th-century theatre has until now been a place of experiment and innovation, as much in staging methods as in artistic and intellectual terms, in which numerous styles have existed side by side. Even at the Moscow Art Theatre, which is usually associated with naturalistic productions, highly experimental non-naturalistic methods were in evidence at the turn of the century. Early reaction against photographic naturalism in stage design is linked with the names of two designers whose ideas had much in common, Adolphe APPIA and Edward Gordon CRAIG, who were part of a general movement called 'Theatricalism'. Appia's most significant contribution was his working-out of a complete theory of electrical stage lighting, which he advocated should be used in conjunction with abstract, non-representational settings. Craig's ideas constitute a complete antithesis to the naturalistic theatre's concern with precise historical detail; like Appia, he rejected illusionism and advocated a theatre of romantic 'mood', in which dance and mime would be prominent.

In France, the reaction against elaborate effects and naturalistic detail is evident in the work of Jacques COPEAU during and after the First World War. Copeau insisted that the art of the theatre is the art of acting, and in some of his productions used only lighting and a few key props to establish the setting. This emphasis on the actor and acting has been evident in France ever since, especially in the theories of Antonin ARTAUD, who was greatly influenced by Oriental conventions of performance (see ORIENTAL DRAMA), as well as in the work of such directors as Jean-Louis BARRAULT and Peter BROOK (much of whose work has been done in France).

Experimental work was also done in the Russian theatre at the beginning of the century, especially in the period immediately following the Revolution. Two former students of Stanislavsky were particularly prominent: Evgeny VAKHTANGOV and Vsevolod MEYERHOLD. The latter is chiefly famous for his theory of Biomechanics, aimed at developing acrobatic skill and emotional discipline in actors. During the 1920s Meyerhold dispensed entirely with traditional staging methods, filling his acting area with machinery and elaborate abstract arrangements of scaffolding. In Germany, the Expressionist movement developed a form of presentation in which states of mind were evoked by stylisation of the décor and acting, and by the elaborate use of lighting effects. Aspects of previous experiment in several styles were incorporated into the Epic theatre of Erwin PISCATOR and Bertolt BRECHT, who sought to 'distance' the spectators from the stage spectacle so that they could think more critically about what they saw.

In one form or another, the contemporary experimental

Theatre. Moscow Arts Theatre production of Chekhov's *The Cherry Orchard.* *(Novosti Press Agency)*

theatres continue to explore and develop the implications of all the major influences of this century. In recent years, the work of such companies as the American Living Theatre, the Polish Laboratory Theatre (see Jerzy GROTOWSKI) and Peter Brook's International Centre for Theatre Research (as well as his productions for the Royal Shakespeare Company) have excited much interest and some controversy. In the commercial theatre in Europe and the USA staging conventions which were once regarded as experimental are now regularly employed in a suitably adapted form, though traditional naturalistic settings are still much in evidence. And while many existing theatres are of 19th-century design, and cannot be satisfactorily modified to accommodate modern theories of staging, numerous theatres have been built in recent years which dispense with the proscenium arch and combine features associated with medieval and Elizabethan stages together with the facilities offered by modern technology.

Bibliography: R. Southern, *Changeable Scenery*, 1952; S. W. Cheney, *The Theatre*, 1959; A. M. Nagler, *A Source Book in Theatrical History*, 1959; S. Selden and H. D. Sellman, *Stage Scenery and Lighting*, 1959; H. Hunt, *The Live Theatre*, 1962; R. Southern, *The Seven Ages of the Theatre*, 1962; A. Nicoll, *The Development of the Theatre*, 1966; B. Gascoigne, *World Theatre*, 1968.

Théâtre, Libre, see ANTOINE, ANDRÉ; FRANCE, *Literature*.

Theatre of the Absurd, a term coined to describe those modern plays which dramatise some aspect of the philosophical belief that, since there is no God, there is therefore no essential meaning to human existence.

Among the major recent dramatists whose work has been critically included within this category are Eugene IONESCO, Samuel GENET and Harold PINTER, though there is doubt as to what extent some of these playwrights would accept the ascription, at least for some of their work: Beckett, for example, has insisted that he is not an Absurdist. As a critical term, it has the merit of indicating the underlying common preoccupations and attitudes of much modern thought and drama, even if these assume widely varying treatments in the hands of individual dramatists.

Bibliography: A. P. Hinchcliffe, *The Absurd*, 1969; M. Esslin, *Theatre of the Absurd*, 1970.

Theatre Royal. In London DRURY LANE THEATRE, the HAYMARKET THEATRE and the Royal Opera House, Covent Garden (see COVENT GARDEN THEATRE), are permitted to use this title. The title of Theatre Royal in respect of the Haymarket was granted only for the lifetime of Samuel FOOTE. Many provincial theatres were similarly named after being granted licenses (e.g. Bristol, Norwich).

Theatre Royal Bristol, which opened in 1766 is England's only surviving example of the larger town theatre of the 18th century and is the oldest theatre in the country which has, with a few short breaks, been continuously used for performances. Architecturally the auditorium owes much to the DRURY LANE THEATRE, 1674, but is believed to be the first in England constructed in a horseshoe shape. Its history, and its association with great actors and actresses both of the past and present, give it a position unequalled among provincial playhouses. The theatre has been the home of the Bristol Old Vic Company since 1946; it reopened in January 1972 after 20 months rebuilding which has put the unaltered auditorium at the heart of a large complex of buildings, including a new and much enlarged stage and flytower, new workshops, dressing rooms, rehearsal rooms and wardrobe facilities. In the space previously occupied by the old theatre entrance there is a small experimental Studio Theatre which with its flexible seating and staging is in every respect complementary to the 18th century Theatre Royal.

Thebaine ($C_{19}H_{21}NO_3$), one of the alkaloids present to a small extent in OPIUM. It is very poisonous, causing severe convulsions.

Theban Legend. Polydorus, son of CADMUS, succeeded his brother-in-law PENTHEUS as third king of Thebes. His son Laius, who succeeded him, married Jocasta, great-granddaughter of Pentheus and sister of Creon. They had only one son.

Immediately after his birth, the child was exposed on Mount Cithaeron with his feet pierced and tied together,

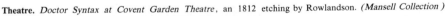

Theatre. *Doctor Syntax at Covent Garden Theatre*, an 1812 etching by Rowlandson. *(Mansell Collection)*

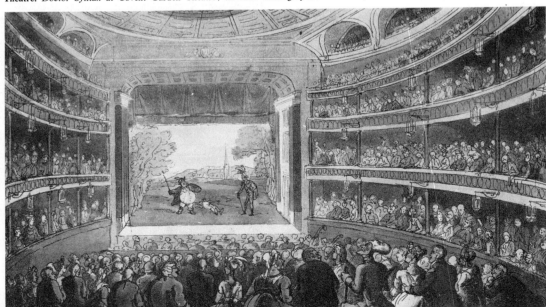

Thebes. The colossal statues of the Memnon. *(Popperfoto/D. McLeish)*

because Laius had learned from an oracle that he would die by the hand of his own son. The baby was found by a shepherd in the employ of King Polybus of Corinth, and called Oedipus because of his swollen feet. Polybus brought him up as his own son; but when Oedipus grew up, he was told by the oracle at Delphi that he would kill his father and marry his mother. Thinking that Polybus was his father, he would not return to Corinth; but on the road between Delphi and Daulis, he met Laius, whom he killed in a scuffle.

Meanwhile the Sphinx had appeared in the neighbourhood of Thebes. Seated on a cliff, she put a riddle to every passer-by: 'What goes on four feet in the morning, on two at noon, and on three in the evening?' None could answer, and all were consequently put to death by the monster. The Thebans swore that anyone who could deliver the country from the Sphinx would obtain the kingdom, with Jocasta as his wife.

Oedipus solved the riddle, the answer being man, who crawls on all fours in infancy, walks on two feet in his prime, and in old age is supported by a staff. The Sphinx at once threw herself from the cliff; Oedipus was hailed as king of Thebes, and married Jocasta, his own mother, who bore him two sons, Eteocles and Polynices, and two daughters, Antigone and Ismene. Thebes was then visited by a plague. The oracle directed that the murderer of Laius should be expelled, and the seer Tiresias pronounced Oedipus the guilty man. Jocasta hanged herself; Oedipus tore out his own eyes, and wandered from Thebes, accompanied by his daughter Antigone. At last he found refuge at Colonus in Attica, where the EUMENIDES removed him from the earth (Sophocles, *Oedipus the King* and *Oedipus at Colonus*). Antigone returned to Thebes.

After the departure of Oedipus, his sons Eteocles and Polynices succeeded as joint sovereigns; but disputes arose between them, and it was agreed that they should rule for alternate years, the one who was not in office withdrawing from Thebes. Polynices accordingly withdrew, but when Eteocles's first year of kingship ended, he would not allow his brother to return. Polynices appealed to Adrastus, King of Argos. Adrastus organised the expedition known as the 'Seven against Thebes', although his brother-in-law AMPHIARAÜS had foretold it would end disastrously.

Eteocles and Polynices killed one another in single combat, and five of the other chiefs were killed. Adrastus alone escaped (Aeschylus, *Seven against Thebes*).

Creon now succeeded to the throne of Thebes. His first act was to forbid the burial of Polynices, and he sentenced Antigone to death for disobeying this order. She was walled up in a cave, where she took her own life, together with her lover Haemon, Creon's son (Sophocles, *Antigone*).

Ten years after these events, Adrastus persuaded the descendants of the Seven to undertake another expedition against Thebes. In this war, Thebes was captured and destroyed. The only one of the expedition to be killed was Aegialeus, son of Adrastus. His father died of grief and was buried at Megara on his way home to Argos.

Theban Legion, The, traditionally a legion which consisted of Christians recruited in Upper Egypt and massacred in 287 when its members refused to take part in the pagan sacrifices prepared by the Emperor Maximian at Agaunum (St Maurice-en-Valois), Switzerland, before engaging in battle. The names of some of the martyrs are known. A basilica was built at Agaunum in the 4th century to enshrine the martyrs' relics. Historic martyrdoms were doubtless magnified in legend. The feast of St Maurice and his companions is celebrated on 22 September.

Thebes (Greek *Thebai*; Egyptian *Wast*, later Niut, the city, sometimes Niut-Amen, hence biblical No-Amon, the city of Amun), name of ancient city of Upper Egypt, known latterly as Thebais. It survives today in the magnificent ruins of Karnak and Luxor, which mostly date from the New Kingdom, when it was the capital. It rose into prominence under the princes, who in the 11th Dynasty reunited Egypt. One of these princes, Mentuhotep II, has left a fine funerary temple at Deir el-Bahri on the west bank of Thebes which was particularly developed by the 18th Dynasty. He also enriched the whole area with monuments and began the long series of royal tombs in the Valley of the Kings behind Deir el-Bahri, where Hatshepsut built her graceful funerary temple alongside that of Mentuhotep II, and Amenhotep III built his farther south, of which only the Colossi of Memnon survive; at Medinet Habu, farther south still, he constructed a palace and great lake for his queen Tiy.

Thebes was the centre of worship of Amen-Ra, with his consort Mut, the vulture mother-goddess, and their son Khons. Each king added to the great temple of Amun at Karnak, and the priests of Amun became excessively rich and powerful. They suffered a temporary setback under AKHNATON but under the 19th Dynasty the architectural magnificence of Thebes increased. Seti I and Rameses II built great additions to the temples of Karnak and funerary temples on the west bank. Rameses III built a temple and tower at Medinet Habu. The 25th Dynasty made Thebes their capital, but under them it was sacked by the Assyrians. Homer describes Thebes as 'hundred-gated', referring to the monuments.

Under the Ptolemies it ceased to be the capital of Upper Egypt, but as always it was liable to be the centre of nationalist movements. It was severely punished after a rising in 86 BC by Ptolemy IX and destroyed in the reign of Augustus for another rising.

See EGYPT, *History*.

Thebes

Thebes, chief city of Boeotia in ancient Greece and the birthplace of PINDAR. Its position was well defended, since it was situated in a plain surrounded by mountains. No place is more celebrated in Greek legend. Here the alphabet was introduced from Phoenicia; here was the birthplace of DIONYSUS and HERACLES; here too lived Tiresias the soothsayer and Amphion the musician. It was also the scene of the THEBAN LEGEND. The first historical trace of the city dates from Boeotian (Dorian) conquest, c. 1100 BC. Thebes then became the chief city of a confederation. She became the closest ally of the Spartans, and during the Peloponnesian War was Athens's bitterest foe. In 394 BC, however, she allied with Athens against Sparta. In 382 the citadel was occupied by Spartan troops, and its recovery by Theban exiles in 378 led to war with Sparta. After the battle of Leuctra (371 BC) for a short time she became, under EPAMINONDAS, the most powerful state in Greece; but with the death of Epaminondas at the battle of Mantinea, 362, Thebes lost her hegemony. In 338 BC she shared the Greek defeat at Chaeronea. Three years later she defied Alexander and was largely destroyed. The city was rebuilt by Cassander and the Athenians in 316 BC. In 290 it was taken by Demetrius Poliorcetes, and thereafter declined rapidly. The final blow was administered by SULLA, who gave half its territory to Delphi.

Thecla, Saint (fl. 1st century AD), Greek saint. The *Acts of Paul and Thecla*, which was written in the 2nd century and is often untrustworthy, describes her as a member of a noble family in Iconium, in Lycaonia, who was converted by the preaching of St Paul. She is said to have followed him, dressed in boy's clothes, to have suffered much for her faith, and to have died in Seleucia. Though the story seems to have a factual basis, it has become much embellished. Her feast day, formerly 23 September, was suppressed in the Roman Catholic Church in 1969.

Thecodonts, small, lizard-like, bipedal Triassic reptiles with sharp teeth set in sockets, which were probably the ancestors of the more advanced archosaurs or ruling reptiles (DINOSAURS, pterosaurs, and crocodiles).

Theft is defined, in English law, by the Theft Act 1968 as the dishonest appropriation of property belonging to another with the intention of permanently depriving the other of it. The offence of theft replaces the old offences of larceny, embezzlement, and fraudulent conversion. Property is widely defined to include money, real property, personal property, and intangible property, except that land cannot usually be stolen. The definition of property excludes wild mushrooms, flowers, fruit, and foliage except when taken for a commercial purpose; and wild animals cannot be stolen unless they have previously been reduced into possession. Theft is punishable by a maximum sentence of imprisonment for ten years.

The intention of permanent deprivation is defined to cover the situation where a person appropriates property without intending the owner to lose it forever but effectively to deprive him of his enjoyment of the property. Thus the return of a wasting asset, e.g. a season ticket, after is has expired does not prevent the original taking from being theft; and the appropriation of property which is later sold back to the owner is theft. It seems clear that the wide definition of theft involves an overlap between theft and obtaining property by deception. Under the old law a distinction was drawn between the passing of possession and of actual ownership, even though induced by fraud. This distinction has not been preserved by the Theft Act.

See also BURGLARY; DECEPTION, OBTAINING PROPERTY BY, AND OBTAINING A PECUNIARY ADVANTAGE BY.

Bibliography: E. Griew, *The Theft Act 1968*, 2nd ed., 1974.

Thegn, see THANE.

Thebes. Temple built by Amenhotep III at Luxor, dedicated to Amen, Mut, and Khons, 1408–1300 BC. *(Werner Forman Archive)*

Theism, see DEISM; MONOTHEISM; PANTHEISM; POLYTHEISM; RELIGION; THEOLOGY.

Theiss, see TISZA.

Thellusson, Peter (1737–97), British merchant, born in Paris; he settled in London and became naturalised. He amassed a great fortune, and his son, Peter Isaac Thellusson, was created Baron Rendlesham in 1806. His name is remembered for his eccentric will, the harsh provisions of which led to the passing of what is known as the Thellusson Act (1800). By his will Thellusson directed the income of his property to be accumulated during the lives of all his children, grandchildren and great-grandchildren who were living at the time of his death, for the benefit of some future descendants to be living at the decease of the survivor, thus keeping within the common law rule which allowed ACCUMULATION within any life in being at the date of the direction. The accumulation was upheld but the weakness of the common law was thereby exposed and the Thellusson Act was passed to cut down the maximum period of accumulation. Sir William Holdsworth in his *History of English Law* recounts that the accumulation could have resulted in a fund of £100 million at the date of its distribution, but that, in fact, poor management and dissipation of the fund in litigation produced only a relatively small sum.

Theme, in music, principal melodic feature in a composition, differing from a subject by greater length and more self-contained completeness, a subject being usually susceptible to development, e.g. in a fugue or sonata-form work, whereas a theme may be said more often to undergo restatement or decorative elaboration, especially in varied form. Sets of variations are usually based on a theme.

Themistocles (c. 528–c. 460 BC), Athenian soldier and statesman. He was appointed archon of Athens in 493 and instigated the construction of harbours in the bays of Piraeus. In 483 he helped to secure the ostracism of Aristides. Then, foreseeing the likelihood of another Persian attack (see PERSIAN WARS), he persuaded the Athenians to employ the revenues from their silver mines at Laurium in building 100 triremes, and to move the naval base from Phalerum to Piraeus.

When XERXES began his invasion (480), Themistocles was appointed commander of the Athenian fleet, in which capacity he was responsible for the victory of Salamis. He next induced his fellow citizens to build the Long Walls, and to abolish the *metoikon*, a tax on aliens, removal of which encouraged many foreign traders and craftsmen to settle in Athens. But his arrogance soon resulted in a decline of his popularity; he was accused (perhaps justly) of peculation and ostracised in 471 (see OSTRACISM). He settled at Argos, but not long afterwards evidence was found that seemed to implicate him in the conspiracy of PAUSANIAS, and envoys were sent from Athens to arrest him (468). Themistocles, however, learning what was afoot, escaped first to Corcyra, then to Epirus, whence he made his way to the coast of Asia Minor. Having spent a year learning the Persian language and customs, he was welcomed by Artaxerxes I, who provided him with a handsome maintenance. He took up residence at Magnesia, promising to do the king good service, but died before he could fulfil that undertaking.

Theobald (d. 1161), archbishop, born near Thièvceville, Normandy, studied law under Lanfranc at Bec. In 1138 he was nominated archbishop of Canterbury by Stephen. It was probably at his instigation that the pope refused to give his permission to Theobald to crown Stephen's son Eustace as king of England (1152). Under Theobald the Church became more powerful; though he had crowned Stephen, he was ready to resist him whenever he felt the power of the Church threatened. He was one of a select body of experienced English advisers who were appointed by Henry II soon after his coronation as justiciars, and introduced the study of civil law into England.

Theobald's Park, estate in HERTFORDSHIRE, England, near Cheshunt, 20 km from London. The park takes its name from Theobald's Palace, built by Lord Burleigh in the 16th century; James I lived for a time in the palace, and died there in 1625. The house was pulled down c. 1765 and a second one built. TEMPLE BAR, moved from Fleet Street, London, in 1878, stands in the park. The house, formerly the property of the Meux family, is now a secondary school.

Theobromine ($C_7H_8N_4O_2$; 3,7-dimethylxanthine), a xanthine derivative, found in cocoa, which has actions similar to those of caffeine and theophylline, but which has a much weaker stimulatory action on the central nervous system. It has been used as a DIURETIC, heart stimulant, and in ANGINA PECTORIS to dilate the arteries of the heart. The diuretic action is due to theobromine inhibiting reabsorption in the kidney tubules.

Theocracy (Greek *theokratia*, government by God), a term applied to the constitution of the Israelite government as established by Moses, because it was under the direct control of Jehovah. This constitution underwent modification with the election of Saul as king; and with the subsequent choice of David, the king 'after God's own heart', Israel became a theocratic monarchy: the king was considered as mediator between God and his people (2 Sam. xxiv. 17). In the books of the Maccabees the concept of God's personal government is less apparent (see 1 Macc. iv. 20).

Theocritus (c. 310–250 BC), Greek pastoral poet, born at Syracuse. Having studied under Philetas in Cos, he visited Alexandria and obtained the patronage of PTOLEMY Philadelphus, in whose praise he wrote the 14th, 15th, and 17th idylls. Theocritus was the creator of bucolic (see BUCOLICS) poetry; his idylls, of which 30 survive, are of a dramatic and mimetic character, and are pictures of the ordinary life of the common people of Sicily.

Bibliography: U. von Wilamowitz-Moellendorff, *Bucolici Graeci*, 1910; A. S. F. Gow (Ed.), *Theocritus*, 2nd ed. 1952; T. G. Rosenmeyer, *Green Cabinet: Theocritus and the European Pastoral Lyric*, 1973.

Theodicy (Greek *theoudiké*), etymologically the justice of god. Our present application of the term is due to LEIBNIZ, who published in 1710 his *Essai de Theodicée sur la Conté de Dieu, la liberté de l'homme et l'origine du mal*, a defence of the justice of God and investigation of the problem of evil. A sub-division of NATURAL THEOLOGY, it follows logically from the treatise on the existence and nature of God.

Theodolite

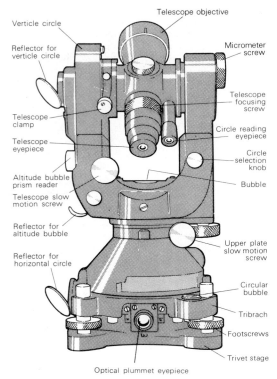

Theodolite.

Theodolite, an instrument used extensively in surveying for measuring angles in horizontal and vertical planes. It consists essentially of a small sighting telescope mounted ALTAZIMUTHly and fitted with graduated circles so that the amount of motion about both the horizontal and vertical axes can be recorded. Clamps and slow-motion screws allow the telescope to be quickly and accurately pointed. In a modern theodolite, such as that illustrated, the graduated circles are etched on glass, are totally enclosed, and can be read from a position close to the telescope eye-piece. The optical train for doing this incorporates a micrometer device and views both ends of a diameter of the relevant circle. The base carrying the vertical axis is fitted with foot screws and an appropriate series of bubbles to allow the instrument to be accurately levelled when placed either on a tripod or concrete pillar such as are used to mark Ordnance Survey triangulation stations. The vertical axis can be set immediately over a reference mark by the optical plummet which replaces the plumb-line formerly used. An automatic levelling arrangement is incorporated into the reading system of the vertical circle so that altitude readings are not critically dependent on the precise levelling of the instrument.

Many theodolites have horizontal 'stadia' lines ruled on the reticule in the telescope in addition to the usual cross. These allow the theodolite to be used as a tacheometer, i.e., in conjunction with a levelling staff to measure distances quickly. Thus if the interval between the stadia lines is arranged to be such that it subtends an angle of 34′ 22·6″ at the optical centre of the telescope lens, the distance to the staff will be 100 times the length on the staff seen between the stadia lines.

Bibliography: M. A. R. Cooper, *Modern Theodolites and Levels*, 1971.

Theodora (c. 500–48), wife of the Byzantine Emperor JUSTINIAN I, notorious before her marriage as an actress and dancer of ill-repute, was proclaimed empress in 527. She showed great courage in the Nika insurrection (532), and was an able counsellor in all matters of state. Her character suffered no taint after her marriage, and indeed posterity might have known nothing derogatory to her but for the *Secret History* of PROCOPIUS, whose other writings extolled Justinian and his empress.

Bibliography: R. Browning, *Justinian and Theodora*, 1971.

Theodore I Lascaris (c. 1175–1222), Byzantine Emperor, son-in-law of Alexius III. After the Crusaders' conquest of Constantinople (1204), he created a Byzantine Empire in exile in western Asia Minor, based at Nicea (1208), repelling attacks by the Latins and Seljuk Turks. See also BYZANTINE EMPIRE.

Theodore, name of three Russian tsars, see FĒDOR.

Theodore of Mopsuestia (c. 350–428), Christian bishop, born at Antioch, a friend of St John CHRYSOSTOM, who converted him to the ascetic life. Ordained in 383, he was a great preacher and scholar, and became bishop of Mopsuestia in Cilicia around 392. He was a prolific writer, and opposed St Augustine's teaching on original sin. He was attacked after his death for encouraging, by his writing, the heresies of PELAGIUS and NESTORIUS, and some of his works were condemned at the fifth synod of Constantinople, in 553, with the reluctant assent later of Pope Vigilius.

Bibliography: L. Patterson, *Theodore of Mopsuestia and Modern Thought*, 1926; Studies by R. A. Greer, 1961, and R. A. Norris, 1963.

Theodore of Tarsus, Saint (c. 602–690), Archbishop of Canterbury, born in Tarsus, Cilicia. He spent some time at Athens and became a monk at Rome. At the age of 66 he was appointed by Pope St Vitalian to the see of Canterbury at the suggestion of the African St Adrian, who accompanied him to England and acted as his adviser. Theodore has been rightly called the second founder of the see of Canterbury and the first primate of the English church. He travelled extensively over the country, promoted learning, opened schools, consolidated or re-established dioceses and held the first national council in 673 at Hertford. His activities involved him in disputes with St Chad and St Wilfrid on questions of jurisdiction, but these controversies were amicably settled.

Bibliography: E. Carpenter, *Cantuar: Archbishops in Their Office*, 1971.

Theodoret of Cyrrhus (c. 393–457), Syrian bishop and theologian. Trained by THEODORE OF MOPSUESTIA and St John CHRYSOSTOM, he became a deacon at Antioch, and in 423 bishop of Cyrrhus. He was so successful against the heretic Marcionites (see MARCION) that he claimed to have baptised 10,000 of them. He protested against the condemnation of NESTORIUS, a friend of his student days, by the Council of Ephesus (432), and was deposed and retired to a monastery (449). But at the Council of Chalcedon (451) he submitted and was reinstated. Theodoretus wrote an immense number of works though only a small number have come down to us, among them a *History of the Church*, a continuation of EUSEBIUS' work to the year 428; *Graecarum Affectionum Curatio*, one of the finest Christian apologies; and a concise *History of Heresies*. His life was written by Marcel Richard, 1934.

Theodoric I (d.451), King of the Visigoths (418–51), and son of Alaric I. He succeeded Wallia, and fought the Romans from 425 to 440, defeating them at Toulouse (439), soon afterwards concluding peace with them. Then, joining with Aetius, the Roman general, against Attila the Hun (450), he was killed in the battle of Châlons (451). Theodoric II, his second son, became king of the Visigoths (452–66), after murdering the elder, Thorismond, and ruled over most of Spain and Gaul. He was assassinated by his brother, Euric.

Bibliography: H. St L. B. Moss, *The Birth of the Middle Ages 395–814*, 1935.

Theodoric the Great (c. 445–526), founder of the Ostrogothic monarchy in Italy, born in Pannonia. As a child he was sent as a hostage to Constantinople, and soon after his return to his father, Theodemir, attacked the King of the Sarmatians and captured Singidunum (Belgrade). Theodemir and his son then successfully invaded Moesia and Macedonia, and on Theodemir's death (c.

474), Theodoric, after some raids against the Emperor Zeno and a rival Gothic chieftain, set out to win Italy from ODOACER, whom he defeated at Verona and then besieged in Ravenna. After the capitulation, Theodoric violated the terms by killing Odoacer (493). Theodoric's 33-years reign was a period of peace and prosperity for Italy such as it had not known for centuries. He maintained his traditional Arian creed, but was tolerant in religious matters. His closing years were sullied with the judicial murders of BOETHIUS and the latter's father-in-law, Symmachus. Theodoric figures in the *Nibelungenlied*, being known to the Germans as Dietrich of Bern (Verona).

Bibliography: H. St L. B. Moss, *The Birth of the Middle Ages 395–814*, 1935; A. H. M. Jones, *The Later Roman Empire, 284–602*, 1964.

Theodorus Studita (759–826), Byzantine monk and abbot of the Studios monastery. He is famous for his uncompromising opposition to the reintroduction of Iconoclasm (see ICONOCLASTS) by the Emperor LEO V, for which he was exiled (815). He also fought obstinately for the independence of the church from the state and its well-being in all contexts. Thus he campaigned for reform in monasteries, and promoted the idea of communal living for which he wrote a rule. The school of disciples he left proved as fanatical as himself, and a most disruptive force in Byzantine life.

Theodosia, see FEODOSIYA.

Theodora makes a religious offering, from a 6th-century mosaic in the Chiesa di S. Vitale, Ravenna. (*Photo Anderson*)

Theodosius I

Theodosius I, or Flavius Theodosius, known as the Great (347–395), Byzantine Emperor, son of Theodosius, general of Valentinian I. He was proclaimed emperor of the East by Gratian in 379. Theodosius warred successfully against the Goths, and by skilful diplomacy enlisted them as his allies (382). In 388 he defeated the usurper Maximus at Aquileia, and secured the Western throne for Valentinian II, brother of Gratian. After Valentinian's death (392) Theodosius defeated another usurper, Eugenius (394), and became sole emperor. A few months later, however, he died, and the Empire was divided between his two sons, Arcadius in the East, and Honorius in the West. Theodosius's most important acts were the adoption of the Nicene definition of Christianity as the state religion, and the prohibition of other heretical doctrines and paganism (380, 391). He was also responsible for the bloody massacre at Thessalonica for which St Ambrose made him do public penance (390).

Theodosius II (401–50), Eastern Roman Emperor, 408–50, grandson of Theodosius the Great and son of ARCADIUS, whom he succeeded at the age of seven. His sister Pulcheria and the praetorian prefect, Anthemius, ruled during his minority. Wars with the Persians (421 and 441) and the Huns under Attila (441–48) were among the chief events of his reign. The *Codex Theodosianus*, a codification of laws in 16 books, was published in 438.
Bibliography: J. B. Bury, *A History of the Later Roman Empire*, 1923.

Theognis of Megara (late 6th century BC), Greek elegiac poet (see ELEGY), and reputed author of a collection of political verses strongly aristocratic in temper.
Bibliography: C. M. Bowra, *Early Greek Elegists*, 1938.

Theology (Greek *theos*, god; *logos*, science), science of religion, dealing therefore with God, and man in his relations to God. Systematic theology deals with the specific doctrines, principles, and characteristics, for example of Christianity. Theology is treated under two main headings, Natural and Revealed Theology; but various causes, especially the application of the theory of evolution to religion and theology, gave rise to a Broad or Modernist school of thought, which sought to do away with hard-and-fast divisions.

Catholic theology of all ages, takes its stand upon a divine revelation from without the human mind, though insisting that certain revealed truths, such as the existence of God, are also within the reach of natural reason and so form part of natural as well as revealed theology. Revealed theology may be analysed according either to its matter or to its method. The division according to its matter gives us the two branches of *Fundamental* and of *Dogmatic Theology*: the former is concerned with the grounds upon which Revealed theology and religion rest, the Fact of Revelation, the Founts of Revelation and the way in which it is received; the latter, dealing with the truths so revealed falls into two branches, theoretical (see DOGMATIC THEOLOGY) and practical (see MORAL THEOLOGY). The division according to method gives us *Positive* and *Speculative Theology*. *Positive Theology* seeks to establish, expound, and prove the truths of theology; it is further divided into *Biblical Theology* (if it is concerned only with Scriptual sources and proofs), *Patristic Theology* (if it draws only upon the Fathers), and *Symbolic Theology* (which confines its scope to the creeds and formularies of the Church). Akin to these (as also to Fundamental Theology) are *Polemic* or *Apologetic Theology*, which seek to defend and to commend theological doctrine in a hostile, sceptical world. *Speculative Theology* makes use of philosophy and other rational inquiries to probe more fully into the nature and implications of the truths of religion.

Essential to the study of theology is exegesis, the submission of the Scriptures to the Lower and Higher Criticism and from this follows *Historical Theology*, the study of Christian doctrine as it has manifested itself in the history of the Church from the formative or Patristic period to the present day. The philosophy of religion, with which Natural Theology is now identified, concerns itself with the study of the idea of God, the freedom of God and the operation of Grace, and finally with the nature of immortality, which is also the subject of ESCHATOLOGY. The philosophy of religion, which also embraces comparative religion and the psychology of religion, has reached its modern scientific forms only since the Renaissance. It has divided into two main streams: the traditional, founded on revelation as it exists in the Scriptures, and the empirical, which, though recognising the Scriptures as the source of doctrine, argues the existence of God from the nature of man. In the 19th century, mainly through the influence of HEGEL, SCHLEIERMACHER, and Otto, this view of theology held sway among Protestants. In more recent times they have shown a marked swing away from traditional and rationalistic views, and towards a theology based on religious experience and the 'super historical' fact of Jesus's life and Passion. This movement is associated particularly with the 'theology of crisis' of Karl Barth.

See also BIBLE; FAITH; RELIGION.
Bibliography: N. Smart, *Philosophers and Religious Truth*, 1969; T. F. Torrance, *Theology in Reconstruction*, 1965; F. G. Healey (Ed.), *Prospect for Theology*, 1966.

Theophrastus (c. 370–c. 286 BC), Greek philosopher, born at Eresos in Lesbos. Though he had begun to study at Athens before the death of Plato (347 BC), he soon afterwards joined ARISTOTLE at Assos and Mitylene. He became Aristotle's most able pupil and succeeded him as head of the Peripatetic school in 322 BC. From that time until his death he laboured to consolidate and expand the work of his master, a task which he fulfilled with great success. A close follower of Aristotle's thought and method, he gave particular attention to natural science and botany. His surviving works include *The History of Plants* and *The Causes of Plants* (2 vols, Loeb Library, 1916), *From the Metaphysics*, and a very readable book called *Ethical Characters*, a collection of typical 'bad hats' (Loeb Library, 1929).
Bibliography: A. H. Armstrong (Ed), *Later Greek and Earlier Medieval Philosophy*, 1967.

Theophylline ($C_7H_8N_4O_2$, 1,3 dimethylxanthine), a substance found in tea, with actions similar to those of caffeine, but with a weaker stimulant action on the central nervous system and a stronger DIURETIC action; it is sometimes given with another diuretic, e.g. mersalyl. It is used in the more soluble form aminophylline for its muscle relaxant properties in bronchial asthma, in oedema due to heart, lung or kidney failure, and as a heart stimulant in congestive heart failure. Aminophylline can be administered intravenously, intramuscularly or as a suppository.

Theorbo, bass lute with a long neck, shorter than that of the CHITARRONE, bearing two pegboxes. The lower carries the strings which run over the fingerboard; the higher, which is cranked to one side, carries bass strings which run beside the fingerboard and so cannot be stopped to vary their length or pitch. The theorbo is said to have been invented in Padua in the 16th century and was widely used for continuo parts into the 18th century. There were usually from six to ten double courses over the fingerboard and up to seven double open bass courses.

Theorem (Greek *theōrēma*, something to be looked at or seen), in mathematics, a statement which has been proved to be true. The word is often reserved for particularly important statements.

Theory, the presentation of a set of facts as a connected account consisting of interdependent statements. The term literally means a sight-seeing, which is the source of the contrast made later between theory and practice, the latter indicating the doing of things. The function of theory is to account for the observed facts; it must 'save the appearances', to use Plato's phrase. The object of scientific research is to provide ever wider and more comprehensive as well as more accurate accounts of the world, i.e. to create increasingly satisfactory theories. The aim of a theory is to articulate the facts concerned in a logical order, starting from general principles and proceeding by deductive steps, on the model of Euclid's *Elements*. In philosophy the term theory is sometimes used less strictly to refer to some general proposition defining a concept in some special way.

Theosophy (Greek *theos*, god; *sophia*, wisdom) is a term which in a general sense can be applied to those forms of religion which are pantheistic and which often claim esoteric knowledge. It is usually used in a more restricted sense to apply to the late-Victorian religious movement founded by Madame Blavatsky. As such, it may be defined as a syncretistic religion professing to afford a higher knowledge or more immediate approach to God than is offered by any single religion based on revelation or reason.

Theosophists claim to include in their ranks Paracelsus, Boehme and the Rosicrucians, and to be of ancient oriental origin; the Sanskrit equivalent of theosophy being *Brahma-Vidyä*, or divine knowledge. It is based to some extent on oriental mysticism, believes in one absolute, incomprehensible and supreme deity, who is the root of all nature, and of all that is visible and invisible, and in man's eternal nature, which, being a radiation of the universal soul, is of an identical essence with it, teaching that by returning to the purity of nature, one can gain certain occult powers.

Helena Petrovna BLAVATSKY, a Russian princess, who it is claimed was initiated in Tibet, is the recognised founder of the two great branches of today. Theosophy is supposed to be preserved by initiates scattered over the world who have attained spiritual perfection, but elect to watch over religion, which they hope to unify under one system of ethics. A group of these Arhats, MAHATMAS or Masters, it is said, led Helena Blavatsky to found the Theosophical Society in 1875. Its teachings in general may be said to be founded on the two great principles of 'KARMA' and REINCARNATION, or the belief that man must undergo a series of lives until he has assimilated all the soul-experiences and can attain to NIRVANA. The terminology and the thoughts are derived from HINDUISM and BUDDHISM, but theosophy claims to be distinct from either. After Helena Blavatsky died, W. G. Judge, of America, became the leader, and upon his death the society split into two sections, one following Katherine Tingley, and the other Annie Besant.

See also KRISHNAMURTI.

Bibliography: H. Blavatsky, *Isis Unveiled*, 1877, *The Secret Doctrine*, 1888, and *The Key to Theosophy*, 1889; A. Besant, *Theosophy and the New Psychology*, 1904.

Theotokopoulos, Domenikos, see EL GRECO.

Thera, see THÍRA.

Therapnae, town in Laconia, on the Eurotas, near Sparta, celebrated in Greek mythology as the birthplace of Castor and Pollux (see DIOSCURI). Menelaus and HELEN were said to be buried here.

Therapsids, mammal-like reptiles of Permo-Triassic age from the Karroo beds of South Africa. They display radiation into several varied groups, and gave rise to the mammals.

Therapy or therapeutics, that branch of medicine that deals with the treatment of disease and the application of remedies. Some types of therapy used today include occupational therapy, physiotherapy, psychotherapy, radiotherapy, and chemotherapy.

Theravāda (Teaching of the Elders), one of the two main forms of Buddhism, the other being MAHĀYĀNA

Theravāda. Worship in a temple at Bangkok. *(Fotogram/Topham)*

Theravāda

(Great Vehicle). The designation Hīnayāna (Small Vehicle) is no longer generally used, as Theravādins consider it to have derogatory implications—it was originated by the Mahāyānists to distinguish what they claimed was a teaching too rigid to suit the majority from their own more liberally interpretative approach. Often called the Southern School, its canon is recorded in the PĀLI language and was first written down on ola leaves in c. 80 BC, at a special council held for that purpose in Ceylon (see TIPITAKA). Before that, the scriptures had been handed down orally; the Buddha himself wrote nothing.

The differences between the Theravāda and the various Mahāyāna schools are mainly of emphasis; on the fundamental doctrines of Buddhist philosophy such as The Four Noble Truths and The Noble Eightfold Path (see BUDDHISM), there is no disagreement. Although there have been instances through the centuries when local conditions and influences have led to rivalry between the two forms, they have on the whole co-existed peacefully, and Theravādins and Mahāyānists have even been known to share the same monastery.

Buddhism in Sri Lanka (Ceylon). There is certain evidence to suggest that Sri Lanka was the first country to receive Buddhism from India. During the 3rd century BC, the Indian emperor, Aśoka, sent Buddhist ambassadors to various parts of the then known world. To Sri Lanka, he sent his son (or younger brother), Mahinda, and his daughter, Saṅghamitta. The latter took with her a cutting from the Bo or Bodhi tree at Buddha Gaya (Bodh Gaya). A pipal tree is still growing in the ruins of the old capital, Anuradhapura, and is believed to be the growth of this original cutting, making it the oldest tree in existence. Brother and sister were warmly welcomed by the king, who gave them a grant of land for a monastery. The Buddhism they introduced into Sri Lanka was of the original orthodox form; this later came to be known as the School of Theravāda, and has remained the dominant type of Buddhism in the country. In the 1st century BC, a special council of monks was held in Sri Lanka to record the teaching of the Buddha, which had been handed down orally since his death 400 years previously. The result was the Tipitaka, a gigantic work in Pāli embodying the Canon of the Theravāda. Commentaries have been added through the centuries but little of the original text has been altered. The 5th-century Buddhist scholar, Buddhaghosa, who went to Sri Lanka to translate Sinhalese Commentaries into Pāli (which had been losing ground to Sanskrit as the language of Buddhism in India), is highly venerated for restoring the prestige of Pāli learning and literature. Over the centuries, Sinhalese Buddhism suffered various setbacks such as Tamil invasions from south India and European colonisation, but the Theravāda teachings remained unpolluted, and Sri Lanka enjoys the distinction of being the country with the longest unbroken record of Buddhist tradition and practice.

Buddhism in Burma. Both Theravāda and Mahāyāna doctrines were to be found in the country by the first few centuries AD. However, a king of north Burma, Anawrahta, was converted to Theravāda in the 11th century, and as a result of his efforts, this school soon became generally dominant; Mahāyāna surviving only to the extent that it influenced the mixture of indigenous nature worship (*nat*) and Buddhist beliefs and practices—which remains, to a significant degree, the Burmese Buddhism of the lay majority. Anawrahta built hundreds of Buddhist temples during his reign, thus initiating a pattern that has made Burma into an Asian 'pagodaland'. The famous Shwe Dagon or Golden Pagoda in Rangoon draws Buddhist pilgrims from all over South-East Asia and is a world centre of Buddhism. A Mongol invasion in the 13th century disrupted Burma and it was not until the 16th century that it once again became united as a Buddhist kingdom. British colonial rule followed with not too harmful an effect on monastic establishments, and today there are many monasteries continuing to exert a strong moral influence on the country. If the Sinhalese Saṅgha may be said to be the greatest authority on the section of the Tipitaka known as the *Sutta Pitaka* (Teachings of the Buddha), and the Thai on the *Vinaya Pitaka* ('Discipline' or 'Rules'), then the Burmese community of monks is equally famous for its study of the *Abhidhamma* (the division of the Pāli Canon dealing with Scriptural Commentaries and mind-training, including psychology and metaphysics). At present, the Burmese Saṅgha also provides the majority of meditation teachers, many of whom are living in Thailand and Sri Lanka.

Buddhism in Thailand. Buddhism was probably being practised in Thailand from the 2nd century AD, although it is difficult to define the early origins of the religion in the country with any accuracy. However, during the ensuing centuries, both Theravāda and Mahāyāna were in evidence to a greater or lesser extent. By 1200, the Thai people—who had probably known Buddhism in their native China—were moving south, and a century later, the reigning king invited the Sinhalese Theravāda School to establish a Saṅgha in Thailand. Since then, Theravāda has been the predominant form of Buddhism in the country. An important figure in later history is the 19th-century king, Rama IV or Mongkut, who lived as a Buddhist monk for many years before ascending the throne. He introduced new reforms into the Order and founded a reform school, the Dhammayutika. For the past 600 years there has been a close relationship between the royal house and the Saṅgha, and the Thai monks play a large role in the life of the people.

Buddhism in the Khmer Republic (Cambodia), Laos and Vietnam. Although all three countries were traditionally Buddhist for many centuries prior to French colonisation in the latter half of the 19th century, it is difficult to assess the extent of pure Buddhist influence today—at least in the case of Laos and Vietnam. Nevertheless, Laos is generally described as a predominantly Theravāda country, having close monastic ties with Thailand. Before war broke out in the 1960s in Vietnam, both Mahāyāna and Theravāda were enjoying a revival in the country. In the case of the Khmer Republic, Theravāda has been predominant since the 14th century as a result of Thai influence dating from that time.

Bibliography: W. Rahula, *History of Buddhism in Ceylon*, 1956; E. Conze, *Buddhism: Its Essence and Development*, 1959; K. E. Wells, *Thai Buddhism: Its Rites and Activities*, 1960; M. E. Spiro, *Buddhism and Society: A Great Tradition and Its Burmese Vicissitudes*, 1970; C. Humphreys, *Buddhism*, 1975.

Theresa of Avila, Saint, see TERESA OF AVILA, SAINT.

Thérèse of Lisieux, Saint (1873–97), 'The Little

Flower', French Carmelite nun, born at Alençon, the ninth child of Louis and Zélie Martin. The family moved to Lisieux and at 15 she became Sister Teresa of the Child Jesus in the Carmelite convent there, where she remained until she died of tuberculosis.

Her autobiography, *Histoire d'une âme* (*The Story of a Soul*, translated by R. A. Knox, 1958) was written at the command of her superiors, 1894–97, and was not seen outside the convent until after her death. Its publication evoked a world-wide wave of acclamation, and the shower of miracles immediately following her death led to her canonisation in 1925 (commemorated 3 October). Her 'little way', lived under ever-increasing suffering, teaches the way of 'spiritual childhood'. She appealed especially to ordinary people by showing that a state of sanctity was possible by continual renunciation in small matters and not only through extreme mortification. She is the patroness of all priests, especially in the mission field, in their vocation of winning souls for Christ.

Bibliography: H. Petitot, *Saint Teresa of Lisieux: A Spiritual Renascence*, 1948; M. M. Philipon, *The Message of Thérèse of Lisieux*, 1950.

Therm, British statutory unit of heat. It is equal to 100,000 British Thermal Units (BThU), and the latter unit is defined as the amount of heat required to raise the temperature of 1 lb of water through 1 °F (from 60 to 61 °F), and equals 251·9 calories (1055 J). See PHYSICAL CONSTANTS.

Thermae, Roman public bath buildings comprising not only baths of various kinds but often also libraries, gymnasia, theatres, etc. The bathing suite consisted of a dressing-room (*apodyterium*), a cold room (*frigidarium*), a warm room (*tepidarium*), a hot room (*caldarium*), and often an open air swimming pool (*natatio*). The procedure was similar to a Turkish bath, and the rooms were heated as required by hot air from a furnace passing under the floor and up flues within the walls.

The principal surviving ruins of thermae in Rome were built by Caracalla, c. AD 215, and by Diocletian, AD 306 (converted by MICHELANGELO into the church of Santa Maria degli Angeli). Others were erected by Agrippa, 25–12 BC, and by the emperors Nero, AD 62, Titus c. 80, Trajan, c. 115, etc. Provincial cities also had numerous thermae, e.g. at Pompeii, Lepcis Magna (Libya), Trier (Germany), and in England at Bath, Wroxeter, and the Chesters fort on Hadrian's wall.

Thermae Himerenses, see TERMINI IMERESE.

Thermal Insulation can be considered as the means whereby the transfer of heat is retarded. Heat transfer through a building structure will occur when a temperature difference exists between one side of the structure and the other. This heat can flow in three ways, i.e., by conduction, by convection, and by radiation.

Insulation materials can be divided into two main groups, *conductive* and *reflective*. The former rely on their thermal conductivity property to reduce the conducted heat flow. Examples of such materials are granulated cork, polyurethane foam, and glass-fibre quilt. These materials have a low conducting power or conductivity and are used in composite floor, wall, or roof construction. Reflective insulation materials depend on low emissivity and absorptivity surface characteristics for their effectiveness. Aluminium foil is commonly used in building construction to reduce the heat flow across an air space. Some 60 to 65 per cent of the total heat transfer across a cavity wall or roof/ceiling air space is by radiation and a considerable reduction can be effected by using reflective insulation on one or both sides of the space.

Requirements concerning the maximum permitted thermal transmittance coefficients of the various parts of

Thermae. Ruins of the thermae built by Caracalla at Rome. *(Mansell Collection)*

Thermal Unit

a building are laid down in building regulations.

See also CONDUCTION OF HEAT; HEAT; HEATING.

Bibliography: British Standards Institution, CP 3: Chapter II: 1970 *Thermal insulation in relation to the control of environment.*

Thermal Unit, see CALORIE; ELECTRICITY AND MAGNETISM; HEAT; THERM.

Thermidor, the eleventh month of the year in the French Revolutionary CALENDAR.

Thermionic Emission. The heating of a solid may give some loosely bound electrons in the solid sufficient energy to be emitted from the surface. This is called thermionic emission, and may be considered as an evaporation of electrons from the surface. The temperature required depends on the *work function* of the metal, which is the energy that must be given to an electron for it to escape from the attractive forces holding it in the solid. Unfortunately, most metals with low work functions melt at quite low temperatures, but certain rare-earth or alkaline-earth ELEMENTS have low work functions, and so are used to coat the electron-emitting hot CATHODES in electronic VALVES, which utilise the effect. The evaporation depends on the nature of the surrounding gas, but O. W. Richardson found that in a highly evacuated atmosphere the formula

$$n = AT^2 \exp(-b/T)$$

is a fairly accurate representation of the phenomenon. n is the number of electrons emitted per square centimetre of the surface of the body per second, T is its absolute temperature, and A and b are constants, typical of the body. Further investigation by Langmuir led to the discovery that the evaporated electrons form a 'cloud' surrounding the heated body, and that ultimately equilibrium is established between the rate of evaporation and the rate of condensation, i.e., the return of the electrons under the electrical repulsion of the electron cloud or 'space-charges'.

The application of the results of Richardson's and Langmuir's researches led to the discovery and subsequent development of modern wireless technique, which depends for its success on the thermionic valve.

Thermit, or thermite, a mixture of powdered aluminium and a metal oxide, most commonly iron oxide. When this mixture is ignited there is a strongly exothermic (heat-producing) reaction in which the aluminium combines with the oxygen from the metal oxide which is reduced to the metallic state. The heat evolved is sufficient to melt most metals. Red thermit contains the red oxide of iron (Fe_2O_3) and black thermit contains the black oxide of iron (Fe_3O_4).

The thermite process, also known as the Goldschmidt process, is the use of the thermite reaction to reduce the oxides of metals which have high melting points and are difficult or impossible to reduce with carbon, e.g., chromium, manganese, molybdenum, vanadium, and tungsten. This method is particularly convenient for making ferro-alloys such as ferro-chrome and ferro-tungsten when the mixed oxides of iron and chromium oxides are simultaneously reduced by aluminium powder in a refractory lined crucible.

In thermit welding, a mould is built around the parts to be joined. Thermit mixture is ignited in a crucible and the molten iron produced is poured into the mould. The superheat in the iron is sufficient to form a fusion weld.

Thermochemistry, science founded on the law of the conservation of energy, which deals with the thermal effects accompanying chemical actions. Reactions in which heat is evolved are called 'exothermic', and where heat is absorbed they are termed 'endothermic'. Measurements of the heat of formation of substances, the heat of solution, of combustion, and of the neutralisation of acids and bases, have been made; also the heat of hydration, the heat of combustion, the heat of ionisation, the heat of dilution, etc. The amount of heat liberated in chemical reaction is determined by allowing it to warm a known quantity of liquid (generally water) whose specific heat is known, and measuring the rise of temperature by means of an accurate thermometer. The water calorimeter generally employed for this purpose consists of an inner platinum vessel surrounded by water contained in an outer vessel of silver, which is protected by poorly conducting material so as to diminish the loss of heat by radiation. The reacting substances, either in the pure state or in solution, are brought to the same temperature and introduced into the inner vessel. The temperature of the water is taken before and after the reaction, and from the rise of temperature, the quantity of water present, and its specific heat (and knowing the water equivalent of the calorimeter) the amount of heat liberated is determined. In order that a reaction may be studied thermochemically it must take place at ordinary temperatures and must proceed rapidly to the end. Many reactions which do not fulfil these conditions, such as many processes of combustion, can be made to fulfil them. This is done by causing the substance to be burnt, in the presence of oxygen under increased pressure, in a steel bomb lined with platinum or enamel. Only in a comparatively few cases has it been possible to make direct determinations of the heat value of chemical changes. Thermal values which cannot be determined directly can be calculated indirectly by methods depending on the fundamental principle of thermochemistry which was propounded by Hess (see HESS'S LAW). The heat change is dependent only on the initial and final stages of the reaction or system of reaction. Thus the heat of formation of methane cannot be determined directly, but a value may be arrived at by subtracting the heat evolved when methane is burnt from that evolved when the corresponding weights of free carbon and hydrogen are burnt. The unit of heat used in thermochemical measurements is the joule, J, or sometimes more appropriately the kilojoule, kJ. The results of measurements are expressed by symbols, which refer to 1 mole of the substances which react. Thus $H_2 + O = H_2O$ ($\Delta H = -285.84$ kJ) means that 285.84 kJ of heat are liberated when 2 g of hydrogen and 16 g of oxygen unite at ordinary temperature to form 18 g of water. If the reacting substances are in solution, the presence of a large quantity of water is denoted by the symbol aq. Thus: KOH aq + HCl aq = KCl aq ($\Delta H = -54.85$ kJ).

As well as being of theoretical importance, thermochemistry has been found of great value in determining the heating power of fuels for commercial purposes and energy values of foodstuffs.

Thermodynamics

Bibliography: B. H. Mahan, *Elementary Chemical Thermodynamics,* 1964.

Thermodynamics, the science of HEAT in relation to other forms of energy. The early caloric theory of heat was widely accepted until its falsification by the researches of Mayer and Joule in 1849. Joule's experiment is described in the article on heat, and it showed very clearly that a definite amount of work was needed to produce a given amount of heat. In 1847 Helmholtz read a paper to the Physical Society of Berlin, *Ueber die Erhaltung der Kraft* (On the Conservation of Force), and he is regarded as one of the founders of the law of the Conservation of Energy which was propounded the same year by Joule in a lecture in Manchester, in which he gave 'the first full and clear exposition of the universal conservation of that principle now called energy'. His ideas met with a hostile reception, not only in Manchester, but also from the British Association itself at its meeting in Oxford that year.

Fortunately the attempt made to stifle the discussion of the paper by the illustrious chairman was frustrated by the enthusiasm of a young man in the audience, William Thomson, afterwards Lord KELVIN, and from that date the real importance of the principle began to be realised. Expressed in simple terms, the First Law of Thermodynamics states that work and heat are equivalent energy forms. Refined experiments, notably by Callendar and Barnes, and by Reynolds and Moody, confirmed Joule's conclusions, and the accepted quantitative relation between heat and work is 1 calorie = 4·186 joules. The First Law of Thermodynamics is a *sine qua non* of the Kinetic Theory of Matter that regards heat as the kinetic and potential energy of the particles of a substance. Further, it was of importance in leading to the recognition that heat, light, electricity, and sound are all forms of energy.

Thermodynamics, however, had its origin in an attempt by Carnot 'to determine mathematically how much work can be gotten out of a steam-engine'. Carnot's researches were published in 1824, when he still held to the caloric theory. His theories were subsequently modified by Kelvin to accord with the dynamical theory of heat as expressed in the First Law of Thermodynamics. Carnot began by considering an ideal heat engine, performing in a manner that enabled him to deduce the relation between the work done by the engine and the heat taken in from the furnace. A modern statement of his principles is as

Thermodynamics. Figure 1.

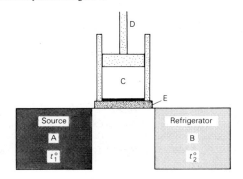

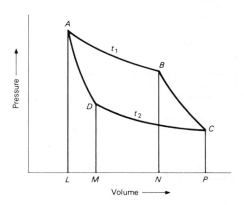

Thermodynamics. Figure 2.

follows: Carnot's engine (fig. 1) is a cylinder C fitted with a frictionless and air-tight piston D. The piston and the sides of the cylinder are supposed to be perfect non-conductors of heat, while the base is a perfect conductor of heat. The cylinder C can be placed either on a non-conducting slab E, or in contact with the source of heat A at $t_1°$ or with the 'refrigerator', or, as we should say, condenser, receiver, or 'sink', B at $t_2°$. The cylinder may contain air or any other working substance under pressure. Fig. 2 is the pressure-volume diagram of the Carnot cycle of operations performed by the engine. The cycle consists of parts of two isothermals (lines through points at the same temperature) AB, CD, corresponding to the temperatures $t_1°$, $t_2°$, and parts of two ADIABATICS AD, BC. The four stages corresponding to the parts AB, BC, CD, DA, of a complete cycle are as follows: (1) The cylinder is placed in contact with the hot source at $t_1°$ and the piston is allowed to rise slowly so that while the working substance expands it takes up heat from the source, so that its temperature remains constant at $t_1°$. This isothermal expansion is represented by AB on the indicator diagram. (2) The cylinder is now placed on the non-conducting slab E and the piston is allowed to rise still farther. The expansion is adiabatic, i.e., no heat is communicated to or abstracted from the working substance during this expansion, in which the temperature falls from $t_1°$ to $t_2°$: the expansion is represented by BC on the indicator diagram. (3) The cylinder is now placed in contact with the condenser at temperature $t_2°$ and the piston is slowly driven inwards, so that while the working substance is compressed it gives up heat to the condenser, and its temperature and that of the condenser remain constant at $t_2°$. The isothermal compression is represented by CD in the indicator diagram. (4) The final stage is an adiabatic compression. The cylinder is placed on the non-conducting slab and compressed so that its temperature rises from $t_2°$ to $t_1°$. The adiabatic compression is represented by DA in the indicator diagram and the cycle of operations is now complete.

We can deduce the efficiency of this engine in the following way. Let Q_1 be the heat absorbed by the working substance while in contact with the hot source during the isothermal expansion AB; let Q_2 be the heat rejected by the working substance to the condenser during the isothermal compression, CD. The mechanical work done by the engine during one complete cycle is then represented by the area

$ABNLA + BCPNB - DCPMD - ADMLA$
$= $ area $ABCD$.

By the First Law of Thermodynamics this work $W = $ net heat converted into work. Hence $W = Q_1 - Q_2$, since no heat is transferred to or from the substance during the adiabatic changes. The *efficiency* of an engine being defined as the ratio of the mechanical work done to the heat taken in at the source, the efficiency of the Carnot engine is W/Q_1 or $(Q_1 - Q_2)/Q_1$.

Reversible Engines. Carnot's engine is an ideal one, but it gives us a start in the development of the subject of thermodynamics. A reversible engine is not merely one that will work in the reverse direction, in the sense that the cycle is performed backwards and work is converted into heat, but one that works backwards so that at each stage of the process the heat taken up (or rejected) is exactly equal to the heat rejected (or taken up) in the forward process. Furthermore, the work done by the engine in the reversed process must be exactly equal to the work done by the engine at the corresponding stage of the forward process. The conditions for reversibility in this sense include: (1) complete absence of frictional forces causing a dissipation of mechanical work; (2) that no conduction of heat shall take place; (2) that pressure differences between the working substance and the external atmosphere shall always be so small that 'free' expansion does not take place at any stage. It is clear that no real engine would be reversible. Nevertheless, in accordance with the usual practice of discussing the mathematical physics of ideal processes in order to develop the underlying theory of engineering processes, the study of reversible engines leads to valuable results. Carnot's engine is a reversible engine, and from a study of its performance we are led to the conclusion known as *Carnot's Principle*, viz. no heat engine working between two given temperatures as source and condenser, respectively, can be more efficient than a reversible one. The formal proof of this principle depends on *The Second Law of Thermodynamics*. Two equivalent statements of this law are as follows: 'It is impossible for a self-acting machine, unaided by any external agency to convey heat from one body to another at a higher temperature' (Clausius). In other words, heat cannot of itself pass from one body to a hotter body. Kelvin's statement of this law reads: 'It is impossible by means of inanimate material agency to derive mechanical effect by cooling a body below the temperature of the coldest of the surrounding bodies.' In other words, work cannot be obtained by using up the heat of the coldest body of a system.

The Second Law applies only to complete cyclical processes; there is no direct proof of this law. Our confidence in it depends on the fact that it accords with our practical experience, and no objection to it has yet been upheld. The meaning of the law may be realised from the approximate statement that an engine must work by drawing heat from a furnace and rejecting heat to a condenser. If the condenser is at the same temperature as the furnace, the engine will not work; further, the engine will not work by using up the heat of the condenser and rejecting heat to the furnace.

Proof of Carnot's Principle. Let A be a reversible engine, and let B be an engine working between the same source and condenser as A. Then it follows that the efficiency of B cannot be greater than that of A. For suppose it is; let the two engines be coupled together so that B working forwards drives A working backwards, and let B take up a quantity of heat Q from the source, while the amount of working substance in engine A is adjusted so that it delivers Q to the source when working backwards. If B rejects a quantity of heat Q_B to the condenser while A takes up a quantity of heat Q_A from it, then the efficiency of B is $(Q - Q_B)/Q$, while that of A is $(Q - Q_A)/Q$. Since the former is supposed to be greater than the latter, $Q - Q_B > Q - Q_A$, therefore $Q_A > Q_B$. The work done by B is $Q - Q_B$; that done by A is $Q - Q_A$. Hence the compound engine can do an amount $Q_B - Q_A$ of work in an external system. Now the net loss of heat from the source is zero, while the net loss of heat from the condenser is $Q_A - Q_B$. Hence this compound engine does work by using up the heat of the condenser. This violates the Second Law of Thermodynamics. Hence $(Q - Q_B)/Q$ cannot be greater than $(Q - Q_A)/Q$, i.e., no engine can be more efficient than the reversible one working between the same source and condenser. Similarly, it may be proved for all reversible engines working between the same source and condenser. It is interesting to note that the most efficient heat engines, the steam turbines, actually used today have an efficiency of about 33 per cent, and the efficiency of Diesel engines may be as high as 38 per cent.

The whole science of thermodynamics is based on the two laws stated. From this juncture, however, the science developed along two main lines: (1) its applications to heat engines; (2) pure thermodynamics, a powerful method of analysis in deriving a variety of important physical and chemical results. The theory of heat engines derives much from the theory of pure thermodynamics.

Kelvin's Absolute Scale of Temperature. The definition of a scale of temperature is given under THERMOMETERS AND THERMOMETRY. Kelvin's absolute scale of temperature is independent of the properties of any thermometric substance, and it is 'absolute' in this sense. It is derived as follows: Let Q_1 be the heat taken in at temperature $t_1°$ by a reversible engine, and let Q_2 be the heat it rejects to the condenser at temperature $t_2°$. $(Q_1 - Q_2)/Q_2$ is its efficiency and by Carnot's Principle this is the efficiency of all reversible engines working between the source and condenser. Hence $(Q_1 - Q_2)/Q_1$ or $1 - (Q_2/Q_1)$ depends only on t_1 and t_2, or mathematically,

$$Q_1/Q_2 = f(t_1, t_2)$$

where f is an unknown function. Suppose two reversible engines, one working between t_1 and t_2 and the other between t_2 and t_3, adjusted so that the first absorbs Q_1 from the source and rejects Q_2 to the condenser, while the second absorbs Q_2 from its source and rejects Q_3 to its condenser. Then

$$Q_1/Q_2 = f(t_1, t_2) \text{ and } Q_2/Q_3 = f(t_2, t_3).$$

If these engines are coupled together they will act as a compound reversible engine absorbing Q_1 at the source t_1 and rejecting Q_3 to the condenser at t_3.

Hence $Q_1/Q_3 = f(t_1, t_3)$.

But $Q_1/Q_3 = (Q_1/Q_2)(Q_2/Q_3)$.
Hence $f(t_1, t_3) = f(t_1, t_2)f(t_2, t_3)$.
Therefore $f(t_1, t_2) = f(t_1, t_3)/f(t_2, t_3)$.

Suppose, now, t_3 is some standard temperature whereas t_1 and t_2 are variable. The $f(t_1, t_3)$ may be written as $\phi(t_1)$, where ϕ is some different function, and

$f(t_2, t_3) = \phi(t_2)$.
Hence $f(t_1, t_2) = \phi(t_1)/\phi(t_2)$,

and therefore

$Q_1/Q_2 = \phi(t_1)/\phi(t_2)$.

Kelvin therefore adopted a scale of temperature on which $\phi(t_1) = T_1$; $\phi(t_2) = T_2$. Hence $Q_1/Q_2 = T_1/T_2$. In other words, on the Kelvin scale of temperature the ratio of two temperatures is defined as the ratio of the heat absorbed at the source to the heat rejected to the condenser by a reversible engine working between those two temperatures. In view of Carnot's principle the ratio T_1/T_2 is the same whatever be the working substance in the engine, i.e., this scale is independent of the peculiar properties of any thermometric substance, and it is therefore 'absolute'.

A thermodynamic thermometer is a theoretical entity consisting of a series of reversible engines each doing the same amount of work W in a cycle. The first takes in Q_1 at temperature T_1 and rejects Q_2 at temperature T_2; the second takes in Q_2 at temperature T_2 and rejects Q_3 at temperature T_3; etc. But

$W = Q_1 - Q_2 = Q_2 - Q_3 = ...,$

and from above,

$Q_1/T_1 = Q_2/T_2 = Q_3/T_3 = ...$

Therefore

$T_1 - T_2 = T_2 - T_3 = ...$

Thus equal intervals of temperature are indicated on the absolute scale of temperature. When we reach the temperature 0° on this scale usually written 0 K, the above equations show that the heat rejected to the condenser is zero, i.e., the condenser at that temperature cannot give up any heat to an engine using it as source. This is therefore the lowest possible temperature, and the zero of the absolute scale of temperature is the absolute zero of temperature. The Kelvin scale is, of course, an ideal scale, but the scale of a perfect gas thermometer can be shown to coincide with its indications. Now although there is no gas that is perfect, it is possible to reduce the readings of a gas thermometer, such as the hydrogen thermometer, to those of the ideal perfect gas thermometer. Hence all thermometer readings can be referred to the absolute scale of temperature thus avoiding the 'idiosyncrasies' of the different thermometric substances.

Entropy. If a substance undergoing a reversible change takes in a quantity of heat dQ at temperature T, dQ/T is called the increase of entropy of the substance. All natural processes are irreversible, and it can be shown that there is always an increase of entropy in such processes. Increase of entropy is accompanied by a loss of available energy in a system. Hence it follows that the processes of radiation, convection, conduction, etc., that involve an increase of entropy of the material universe also involve a loss of available energy in the universe. The entropy of the universe tends to a maximum that will be reached when all temperature differences have disappeared. The available energy in the universe will then be exhausted (Second Law of Thermodynamics) and the universe will suffer, what Jeans termed a 'Heat-death'. Entropy, like potential energy, has an arbitrary zero. Only changes of entropy are significant, indicating the change of state of a system.

Bibliography: J. K. Roberts and A. R. Miller, *Heat and Thermodynamics,* 1951; J. L. Fuick, *Thermodynamics from the Classic and Generalized Standpoints,* 1955; A. D. Buckingham, *The Laws and Applications of Thermodynamics,* 1964; J. F. Sandfort, *Heat Engines,* 1964; P. A. H. Wyatt, *Energy and Entropy in Chemistry,* 1967; M. W. Zemansky, *Heat and Thermodynamics: An Intermediate Textbook,* 5th ed. 1968; M. N. Saha and B. N. Srivastava, *A Treatise on Heat,* 5th ed. 1973.

Thermoelectric Pyrometer, see PYROMETER.

Thermoelectricity. Seebeck found in 1821 that if a circuit consisting of two dissimilar metals be taken and the junctions kept at different temperatures, a steady current will flow in the circuit. The two metals are said to form a *thermocouple,* and this *Seebeck effect* is now widely used for the measurement of temperature. In 1834, Peltier found that when a current was passed across a junction of two dissimilar metals reversible heating effects occur. Heat is evolved when the current passes one way across the junction and absorbed when it passes in the opposite way. This is called the *Peltier effect.* From thermodynamic reasoning, if a circuit were made of two dissimilar metals and one junction were kept at a constant temperature, the electromotive force in the circuit should increase as the temperature of the other junction is increased. It is found, however, that as the temperature of the second junction is gradually raised, the electromotive force increases to a certain limit, then decreases again and is finally reversed. Lord Kelvin predicted in 1851 and later observed that when a current flows along a wire the temperature of which varies from point to point, heat is liberated at a given point in the wire when the current is flowing in one direction, and absorbed when the current is flowing in the opposite direction. This reversible heating effect is known as the *Thomson effect.*

Thermograph, automatically recording thermometer. There are three main types, bimetallic, mercury-in-steel, and electrical-resistance. The bimetallic thermograph (a standard meteorological instrument) works by the coiling and uncoiling of a strip formed by welding together two metals with different coefficients of thermal expansion, the movement being magnified, and transmitted to a pen working on a drum, by levers. The mercury-in-steel type, in which changes in pressure caused by expansion and contraction of the mercury in a metallic bulb are transmitted to the recorder by a narrow-bore steel tube, is specially suitable for remote recording. The electrical resistance thermometer (also suitable for remote recording) depends on the fact that the electrical resistance of a wire (usually platinum or nickel) varies with its temperatures. The record is usually made by a recording potentiometer. See THERMOMETERS AND THERMOMETRY.

Thermoluminescence Dating, see DATING IN ARCHAEOLOGY.

Thermometers and Thermometry

Thermometers and Thermometry. A thermometer is an instrument that measures the variations of sensible HEAT or TEMPERATURE. The commonest form of thermometer utilises the change with temperature of the volume of a liquid in a container, e.g., mercury in glass. Two temperatures are taken as points of reference: that of melting ice and that of steam given off by water boiling under normal atmospheric pressure. This is essential, as the boiling-point is affected by atmospheric pressure. Many other precautions and refinements are necessary in the manufacture of thermometers, and for these details readers are referred to any standard work on heat. Three thermometer scales are in general use, the CENTIGRADE (or Celsius) (the centesimal scale was adopted by Celsius in 1742), the FAHRENHEIT, and the Réaumur. The relations between these scales are shown in fig. 1. The Réaumur scale is sometimes used in Europe for medical and domestic purposes. Clinical thermometers in many countries, including Britain, are graduated in degrees Fahrenheit (°F). The Celsius or Centigrade scale (°C) is the commonest scale in scientific research, and the Kelvin or absolute scale (K) is based on the same number of degrees (100) between the upper and lower fixed points (see ABSOLUTE TEMPERATURE; THERMODYNAMICS). Mercury as a thermometric liquid has many advantages over other liquids, among which may be noticed its wide range (−40 to 356 °C, and up to 570 °C under pressure) in the liquid state; its regular expansion, which is very nearly, though not quite, proportional to changes of absolute temperature; its utility in fine capillary tubes, which it does not 'wet'; and the expeditious way of obtaining it in a very pure form. On the other hand, alcohol has a lower range (to −80 °C) while pentane can be used as low as −200 °C.

Maximum and minimum thermometers for recording the highest and lowest temperatures vary in construction. Rutherford's maximum self-registering thermometer consists of an ordinary mercury thermometer placed in a horizontal position, and having a small piece of steel inside the tube *beyond* the mercury. As the mercury expands with increase of temperature it pushes the steel before it, and as it contracts it leaves the steel in the farthest position to which it has been driven. The end of the steel nearest the surface of the mercury marks the highest temperature attained since it was last set. The instrument can be reset for further observation by means of a magnet. The minimum thermometer contains alcohol instead of mercury, and *inside* the alcohol contained in the tube there is a small index of glass, with the farthest end touching the surface of the alcohol. This tube is also placed horizontally. As the alcohol contracts it carries the glass index with it, but when it expands the index is left behind. Thus the end of the index nearest the surface of the spirit shows the lowest temperature. The two actions are commonly combined in a single 'maximum-minimum' thermometer.

In addition to the usual thermometer in which mercury, alcohol, etc., indicate the changes in temperature there are other types, such as the metallic thermometer, the platinum resistance thermometer, the thermocouple thermometer, and the gas thermometer. The metallic thermometer depends on the principle that if two strips of different metals with unequal coefficients of expansion be firmly fixed (e.g., riveted) together and wound into a spiral with the more expansible metal inside, a rise of temperature causes the spiral to unwind. This is due to the greater expansion of the inner strip, and similarly, a fall of temperature causes the spiral to wind up. A needle deflected in the process of winding or unwinding indicates temperature variation. In the platinum resistance thermometer use is made of the fact that the electrical resistance of most metals varies with temperature. Variations of the Wheatstone bridge allow very small changes in resistance to be detected, and hence the small changes in temperature can be determined. The thermocouple thermometer is based on the thermoelectric effect—that electric currents can be produced by applying heat or cold to one of the junctions in a circuit composed of two different metals. If a very sensitive galvanometer is used to measure the current temperatures up to 1500 °C can be measured with great accuracy in this way. The colour and brightness of an electrically heated filament depend on its temperature, and by matching the filament to a furnace the temperature of the latter can be measured in terms of the current through the filament. This is the basis of the radiation PYROMETER. A gas thermometer is much more sensitive than ordinary types of thermometers, owing to the relatively large coefficient of expansion of gas. It suffers from the defect that it is cumbersome, and also requires a large amount of the fluid whose temperature is to be found.

Fig. 2 shows essential parts of a simple gas thermometer—the constant-volume air thermometer. The large bulb A and the connecting wide capillary tube contain a gas or air, while the tubes BDC form a simple manometer. With volume A at the temperature to be measured, C is raised or lowered until the mercury level in the other tube coincides with a graduation mark at B. The height difference between the two mercury levels plus the barometric height is proportional to the pressure p on the gas in A. If p_0 and p_{100} are the values when the bulb A is in melting

Thermometers and Thermometry. Figure 1.

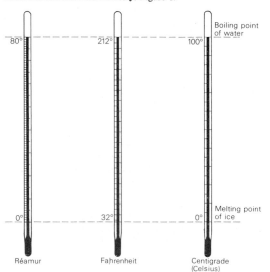

Réaumur	Fahrenheit	Centigrade (Celsius)	
80°	212°	100°	Boiling point of water
0°	32°	0°	Melting point of ice

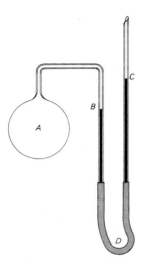

Thermometers and Thermometry. Figure 2.

ice and in steam respectively, then the temperature for the pressure p is given by $100(p - p_0)/(p_{100} - p_0)$ °C.

Bibliography: A. J. Hall, *Fundamentals of Thermometry*, 1953, and *Practical Thermometry*, 1953; C. M. Herzfeld (Ed.), *Temperature: Its Measurement and Control in Science and Industry* (parts 1, 2, and 3), 1963, 1962, and 1963; W. E. K. Middleton, *Invention of the Meteorological Instruments*, 1969; C. R. Barber (Ed.), *Calibration of Thermometers*, 1971.

Thermonuclear Reaction, a reaction caused by an extremely high local temperature (e.g., 10 million degrees) which causes high velocity collisions between atomic nulcei. The reaction can lead to the FUSION of two nuclei of low atomic weight to form a single nucleus, the mass of which is less than the sum of the masses of the two original nuclei. The excess mass appears as a relatively large amount of energy. This in turn can cause more light nuclei to react, and produce yet more energy, and a chain reaction can result. More complex nuclear reactions can also take place, but the ones of particular interest are those in which energy is produced by the transmutation of the mass of the original particles (see MASS ENERGY). A device designed on this principle can therefore explode, or may be controlled to act as a new source of nuclear power (see FUSION REACTOR). This has been realised in the HYDROGEN BOMB or H-bomb, which is many times more powerful than the conventional ATOMIC BOMB, which works by FISSION, i.e., the splitting, of heavy nuclei. The main difficulty is to produce a sufficiently high temperature for the thermonuclear reaction to be initiated. In the H-bomb the source of heat is an atomic fission bomb embedded inside the light elements, and a jacket of fissionable material is usually added to increase the efficiency.

Thermoplastics, see PLASTICS.

Thermopylae, often called simply Pylae, celebrated pass leading from Thessaly into Locris. The pass of Thermopylae is especially celebrated on account of its heroic defence by LEONIDAS against the Persians in 480 BC.

Thermos Flask, see VACUUM FLASK.

Thermosetting, see PLASTICS.

Thermostat, device for maintaining an appliance set at a preset temperature. All thermostats comprise essentially an element extremely sensitive to temperature changes and a switch or lever. Use is made of one or other of the following properties: the expansion of metals, the increase in volume of a liquid, and the increase in pressure of a fluid.

Thermostats that depend upon the expansion of metals are known as the bimetallic type and consist of a composite strip of two metals with widely different coefficients of expansion. This strip may be used flat or formed into a coil, one end being free and the other fixed. When the temperature alters, the unequal expansion of the two metals causes distortion, and an appreciable movement is produced at the free end, which in turn moves the switch or lever. A magnet is sometimes used so that the completion of the closing operation is positive and quick; this is useful in the control of an electrical device to prevent any sparking which might be caused by a poor contact. The two metals usually employed are brass, which has a large expansion, and a steel alloy with a negligible expansion. For liquid heating control the composite strip is in a brass tube inserted in the medium. Bimetallic thermostats are used for many types of temperature control, among which may be mentioned the regulation of boilers, immersion heaters, cookers, and space heating.

The second type of thermostat consists of a cylindrical bulb, a capillary tube, and a metallic bellows. The system is completely filled with liquid and sealed, so that the only way in which the liquid can expand when the temperature rises is by exerting pressure on the bellows. Attached to the latter is a rod with spring adjustment which moves the

Thermostat. (a) Bimetallic strip; (b) liquid/bellows.

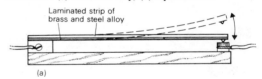

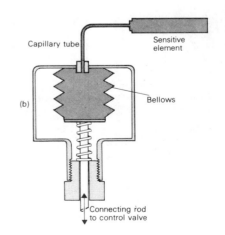

Thesaurus

device attached to it. The bellows type is often used where it is necessary or desirable for the sensitive element to be at a distance from the switch or lever. It is used in most refrigerators and in some air-conditioning plants. In space-heating the sensitive bulb is mounted directly on the bellows.

The third or vapour-pressure type thermostat is similar to the second except that the system is only partially filled with a volatile fluid of a low boiling-point, leaving a vapour space. As the pressure of the vapour will vary according to the temperature movement will again be produced by the bellows.

See also FIRE BRIGADES AND FIRE FIGHTING.

Bibliography: R. Griffiths, *Thermostats and Temperature-Regulating Instruments*, 3rd ed. 1951; C. M. Herzfeld (Ed.), *Temperature: Its Measurement and Control in Science and Industry* (parts 1, 2, and 3), 1963, 1962, and 1963.

Thesaurus, see DICTIONARY.

Theseus, legendary hero of Attica, son of Aegeus, King of Athens, and Aethra, daughter of King Pittheus of Troezen. Brought up by his mother at her father's court, when he reached maturity he took his father's sword and sandals, and went to Athens. The Cretan Bull, released by HERACLES, had wandered into Attica and was ravaging the plain of Marathon. Theseus killed it, and was acknowledged by Aegeus as his heir. Next he went of his own accord as one of the seven youths and seven girls the

Theseus slaying the Minotaur, from an Attic black figure amphora, about 560–550 BC. *(Ashmolean Museum, Oxford)*

Athenians were obliged to send every year to Crete, to be devoured by the MINOTAUR. On his arrival, Ariadne, daughter of King MINOS, fell in love with Theseus and gave him a sword and a length of thread, with which respectively he killed the Minotaur and found his way out of the labyrinth in which the monster was kept. Theseus then sailed away, taking Ariadne whom he soon afterwards abandoned in the island of Naxos. Approaching Athens, he forgot to hoist the white sail (black was used on those mournful voyages) which was to have been the signal of his success; Aegeus, watching, thought his son had perished and threw himself into the sea. Theseus was now king of Athens. He fought the Amazons and carried off their queen, Hippolyte (or Antiope), who bore him a son HIPPOLYTUS. He was also one of the ARGONAUTS, hunted the Calydonian boar (see MELEAGER), helped Adrastus to recover the bodies of those killed at Thebes (see THEBAN LEGEND), abducted Helen from Sparta and hid her at Aphidnae, whence she was rescued by the Dioscuri. For this last episode and the attempted abduction of Persephone from Hades see PIRITHOUS. During Theseus's absence, the Athenians had been roused against him, and Theseus, unable to re-establish his authority, retired to Scyros, where he was treacherously hurled to death from a cliff by King Lycomedes. In historical times Theseus was said to have appeared at Marathon and assisted the Athenians (490 BC).

Thesiger, Frederic Augustus, see CHELMSFORD, FREDERIC AUGUSTUS THESIGER, 2ND BARON.

Thesiger, Frederic John Napier, see CHELMSFORD, FREDERIC JOHN NAPIER THESIGER, 1ST VISCOUNT AND 3RD BARON.

Thesmophoria, annual Greek festival in honour of DEMETER. In most parts of Greece it lasted for three days, but at Athens it lasted for five days in the month Pyanepsion (early November), only women of Attic birth and stainless character taking part. It was a corn festival, and the occasion of a rather unpleasant rite. At the festival of Schirophoria, four months earlier, or at the Thesmophoria in previous years, pigs were hurled into subterranean caves, their rotting remains were brought out at the Thesmophoria and mixed with seed-corn on an altar. This practice was believed to ensure a good corn crop.

Thespiae, ancient Greek city near the foot of Mount Helicon in Boeotia. The neighbouring and more powerful city of Thebes dismantled its walls in 423 BC, captured it in 372, and razed it to the ground. A famous statue of Eros by PRAXITELES was preserved here.

Thespis (fl. 6th century BC), called the father of Greek tragedy, born at Icarus, one of the Attic demes. He was the first to introduce an actor into what had been hitherto a merely choral performance. This individual took various parts in the same piece under the several disguises provided by linen masks.

Bibliography: A. W. Pickard-Cambridge, *Dithyramb, Tragedy and Comedy*, 1927.

Thesprotía, department of north-west Greece, in Epirus. It is bordered by Albania on the north. Its chief town is Hegoumenitsa (*Igoumenítsa*). Area 1515 km²; population 40,700.

Thessalonians, Epistles to the, written by St Paul probably from Corinth, when he was working there with Silvanus and TIMOTHY (Acts xviii. 5) between AD 51 and 53. They are, therefore, among the earliest of St Paul's epistles, and their genuineness is universally acknowledged. Acts xvii describes St Paul's visit to Thessalonica, and the bad reception he received from the Jews. The Greeks and devout women, however, showed much eagerness, and to them he turned. The epistles, which followed each other closely, were addressed to a Gentile audience. The immediate occasion of the first epistle is the good news brought by Timothy of the steadiness of the Thessalonians in the faith in spite of persecution by their countrymen. From it we learn what had been St Paul's message and appeal when he was himself in Thessalonica. He had appealed to the primary feelings of the human heart and then passed on to speak of Jesus, 'who delivereth us from the wrath to come' (i. 10). This particular insistence on the Judgement and the second advent had led to much questioning, and in the latter part of the letter, St Paul deals with this. His letter, however, did not settle all difficulties, though the news which he later received from Thessalonica was in many aspects encouraging. The expectation of the second coming of the Lord still caused great excitement and the neglect of the duties of daily life. The second epistle is intended to correct this. See commentaries by L. Morris, 1959; E. Best, 1972.

Thessaloníki, see SALONIKA.

Thessaly, largest division of ancient Greece. Thessaly proper is a large plain, drained by the River Peneus and its affluents. About 113 km across, it is shut in on every side by mountain barriers, broken only at the north-east corner by the valley and defile of Tempe, which separates Ossa from Olympus. There were two other districts included under the general name of Thessaly; one, called Magnesia, being a long narrow strip of country extending along the coast of the Aegean Sea from Tempe to the Pagasaean Gulf, and the other a long narrow vale at the extreme south of the country, lying between Mounts Othrys and Oeta.

Thessaly proper was divided in very early times into four districts or tetrarchies, a division which we still find subsisting in the Peloponnesian War. These districts were: (1) Hestiaeotis, in the north-west; (2) Pelasgiotis, in the east; (3) Thessaliotis, in the south-west; and (4) Phthiotis, in the east. It is in this district that Homer places Phthia and Hellas proper, and the dominions of Achilles. Besides these there were four other districts, viz.: (5) Magnesia; (6) Dolopia, a small district bounded on the east by Phthiotis, on the north by Thessaliotis, on the west by Athamania, and on the south by Oetaea; (7) Oetaea, a district in the upper valley of the Spercheus; and (8) Malis. The Thessalians were a Thesprotian tribe, and invaded the western part of the country, afterwards called Thessaliotis, whence they subsequently spread over the other parts of the country. The government in the separate cities became oligarchical, the power being chiefly in the hands of a few great families descended from the ancient kings. Of these, two of the most powerful were the Aleuadae and the Scopadae. The Thessalians never became of much importance in Greek history. In 344 BC Philip completely subjected Thessaly to Macedonia. The victory of Titus Quinctius Flamininus at Cynoscephalae,

in 197, again gave the Thessalians a semblance of independence under the Romans.

The area of modern Thessaly is 22,530 km² and its population (1971) is 659,243. Excavations were made there by the British School of Archaeology in Athens. Mineral deposits exploited include iron-pyrites, copper, zinc, bitumen, and marble.

Bibliography: H. D. Westlake, *Thessaly in the Fourth Century B.C.,* 1935; J. A. O. Larsen, *Greek Federal States,* 1968.

Thetford, market town in NORFOLK, England, situated on the borders of the great state forest of Thetford Chase and the Breckland. The rivers Thet and Little Ouse unite just above the town bridge. Thetford was once the capital of the kingdom of East Anglia. The earthworks of Castle Hill date from the Iron Age and were later occupied by the Normans. The site of the Saxon town has been excavated by the Ministry of Works, and many interesting objects can be seen in the Ancient House Museum. The ruins of the Cluniac priory (founded c. 1103) stand on the banks of the Little Ouse. There are remains of the Benedictine nunnery of St George and of the monastery of the Canons of the Holy Sepulchre. Since 1960 the town has been greatly expanded by means of an agreement with the Greater London Council. Thousands of new houses have been built and major industrial development has been attracted to the town. The central shopping area has been rebuilt and greatly extended to accommodate this growth. Population (1971) over 15,000.

Thetis, Greek sea-goddess, daughter of Nereus and Doris, and mother of ACHILLES. Poseidon and Zeus sued for her hand; but when Themis declared that Thetis's son would outshine his father, both gods withdrew. Others said Thetis rejected Zeus because she had been reared by Hera and the god, in revenge, decreed that she should marry a mortal. At length she was married against her will to PELEUS.

Thiard, Pontus de, also Thyard, or Tyard (1521–1605), French poet, born at Bissy, near Chalon-sur-Saône. He was a member of the PLÉIADE. His works, notable for their Platonism, include three volumes of *Erreurs amoureuses* (sonnets), 1549–55, and various prose *Discours philosophiques,* published between 1552 and 1558 (*Discours des muses ou de la fureur poétique* and *Discours de la musique,* for example). He became bishop of Chalon in 1578.

Thibaud, Jacques (1880–1953), French violinist, born in Bordeaux. He studied under Marsick at the Paris Conservatoire, and his rise to fame as a virtuoso dates from 1898. He represented the technique of the great classical school passed down to him through Marsick and Ysaÿe. From 1905 he was especially associated in a trio with CORTOT and CASALS. He was killed in an air crash.

Thibaudet, Albert (1874–1936), French literary historian, born at Tournus. Among his works are *La Poésie de Mallarmé,* 1912, *Flaubert,* 1922, *Intérieurs,* 1924, *La République des professeurs,* 1927, *Mistral,* 1930, *Physiologie de la critique,* 1930, *Stendhal,* 1931, *Histoire de la littérature française de 1789 à nos jours,* 1936.

Bibliography: J. C. Davies, *L'Œuvre critique d'Albert Thibaudet,* 1955.

Thibault, Jacques-Anatole

Thibault, Jacques-Anatole, see FRANCE, ANATOLE.

Thierry, Jacques Nicolas Augustin (1795–1856), French historian, born at Blois. On leaving school he became secretary to Saint-Simon, at whose suggestion he published his first work, *De la réorganisation de la société européenne*, 1814. He became blind in 1826, but continued his historical studies. His *Histoire de la Conquête de L'Angleterre par les Normands* was published in 1825. His other works include *Lettres sur l'histoire de France*, 1820; *Dix ans d'études historiques*, 1834; *Récits des temps mérovingiens*, and *Recueil des Monuments inédits de l'histoire du Tiers État*, 1850–70. Thierry belongs to the now unfashionable school of Romantic historians, but his accurate scholarship makes his work of lasting value in spite of its somewhat florid style.

Thiers, Louis Adolphe (1797–1877), French statesman and historian, born at Marseilles and studied law at Aix. In 1821 he began writing for the *Constitutionnel*, and next collaborated with Félix Bodin in the production of *Histoire de la révolution française*, 1823–27. In 1830 with Carrel, he founded the *National*, which helped to provoke the revolution later that year. After Louis Philippe became king, Thiers was rewarded for his publicist services by being nominated a councillor of state and given a post in the Treasury. Later he became under-secretary of state to the Treasury (1831), supporting the peace policy of Casimir Périer. Thiers was minister of the interior in Soult's Cabinet of 1832 during some difficult months. Four years later he was placed at the head of the Cabinet, and adopted aggressive foreign policies. In 1840 he became president of the council and foreign secretary. He supported Mehemet Ali against Turkey with the object of assuring to the latter the retention of Egypt. Later, after the conclusion of peace between Britain, Russia, Turkey, Prussia, and Austria, he prepared for war as a demonstration against the exclusion of France from the European concert, but his policy did not have the support of the King, Louis Philippe, and he was dismissed from office. He then devoted himself to writing historical works, and published his huge work, the *Histoire du Consulat et de l'Empire*, 1845–69. After the *coup d'état* of 1851 Thiers was arrested and exiled. He returned to France the following year, but did not re-enter political life until 1860. In 1863 he was nominated deputy for one of the divisions of Paris. On the fall of the Empire following upon the débâcle at Sedan, he was elected president of the Assembly, and shortly after became president of the executive government, and supported the Paris Commune of 1871. In 1873 he was defeated and resigned.

Bibliography: R. L. Dreyfus, *La République de M. Thiers, 1871–73,* 1930; R. Christophe, *Le Siècle de Monsieur Thiers,* 1966; J. M. S. Allison, *Thiers and the French Monarchy,* 1968.

Thiès, town in west SENEGAL, situated 70 km east of DAKAR. It is an important transportation centre on the Dakar–Niger railway. Its central position has made it into a light industry centre. Population (1974) 90,000.

Thigh, the part of the lower limb between the pelvis and the knee. The thigh-bone, or *femur*, is the longest bone in the human body, constituting about a quarter of the height

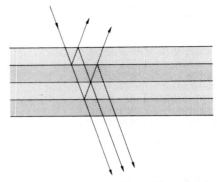

Thin-film Optics. Figure 1. A thin-film multilayer, showing a few of the many possible reflections producing interference effects.

from sole to crown. It articulates with the hipbone above, and with the *tibia* (shinbone) below.

Thimphu, see BHUTAN.

Thin-film Optics, the study of the properties and applications of layers of transparent or absorbing materials, each of thickness of the order of magnitude of the wavelength of light. When light falls on a single thin film, say the surface of a soap bubble, the light is reflected at both surfaces and the two reflected beams interfere; the INTERFERENCE effects depend on the thickness of the film, on its REFRACTIVE INDEX, on the angle of incidence of the light, and on its wavelength and state of polarisation, so that even with a single film quite complicated and beautiful effects are seen. When several films are used together even more complex effects occur: fig. 1 shows four layers, each of which might be perhaps a quarter of a wavelength thick (the average wavelength of the spectral range to be used is implied here), and possibly all having different refractive indices. The properties of such a multilayer are in fact not calculated by tracing multiple reflections such as those indicated but rather by a special calculus developed for the purpose and based on the electromagnetic wave theory of light. The most striking kinds of multilayer are those in which all the materials used are transparent. These are the all-dielectric multilayers. High-reflecting mirrors consist of alternate films of high and low refractive index, each a quarter of a wavelength thick; they reflect more than 99 per cent of the incident light over a wavelength range of about 100 nm and they show a brilliant metallic lustre, in spite of containing no metal layers; they are used as end mirrors in LASERS, as reflecting coatings for Fabry-Perot etalons and many situations where a more highly reflecting surface than aluminium or silver is required. Polarising beamsplitters are shown in fig. 2; the reflected and transmitted beams are almost completely polarised in opposite senses. Colour separation filters, used in colour television cameras, reflect one portion of the spectrum and transmit another. INTERFERENCE FILTERS could really be any thin-film optical device, but the term has come to be used only for filters which transmit a very narrow spectral range; interference filters can be made to transmit a spectral band as narrow as 1–2 Å (0·1 to 0·2 nm), but the wavelength of maximum transmission changes if the filter is inclined to the beam of light, so that it is necessary to have a well collimated beam. Other thin-film devices include anti-reflection coatings, heat-reflecting coatings, and transparent protective layers for aluminium mirrors.

Thin-film materials include magnesium fluoride, used in a single layer as an antireflective coating, zinc sulphide, bismuth oxide, neodymium oxide, silicon monoxide and dioxide, titanium dioxide, and zirconium oxide. The films are usually deposited on a glass support or substrate by evaporating the material in vacuum and allowing it to condense on the substrate. Sometimes a metal film is evaporated and oxidised on the substrate.

See also BLOOMING OF LENSES.

Bibliography: H. A. Macleod, *Thin Film Optical Filters*, 1969.

Thiols, see MERCAPTANS.

Thionville (German *Diedenhofen*), French town in the *département* of Moselle, 25 km north of Metz, on the River Moselle. Imperial diets were held here in the 8th century. It has large iron and steel works, and manufactures chemicals. Population 136,500.

Thiopentone, see ANAESTHESIA; BARBITURATES.

Thiophene, C_4H_4S, a colourless liquid with boiling point 84 °C, discovered in 1883 by Victor Meyer as an impurity in benzene obtained from coal-tar. It gives a blue coloration with isatin dissolved in concentrated sulphuric acid. In its general properties thiophene closely resembles BENZENE, from which it may be removed by prolonged shaking with cold concentrated sulphuric acid.

Thiourea, $(NH_2)_2CS$, a derivative of urea, was first introduced for the treatment of exophthalmic GOITRE in 1943 to reduce the amount of excess thyroid hormone responsible for the condition. Thiouracil and other drugs, such as carbimazole and methimazole, are now used in preference to suppress the activity of the THYROID GLAND.

Thin-film Optics. Figure 2. Polarising beam splitter.

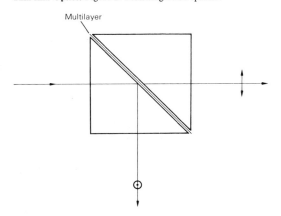

Multilayer

Thíra. *(Barnaby's Picture Library)*

Thíra, or Thera (formerly Santorini), island of Greece in the Aegean Sea, the most southerly of the CYCLADES group, lying about 95 km north of Crete. Its steep cliffs vary in height from 150 to 350 m. The northern half of the island is composed of lava, and from the earliest times the island has been a centre of volcanic activity; neighbouring islets are the remnants of a submerged volcano which last erupted in 1925–26. Thíra and the islet of Theresia have abundant archaeological evidence of occupation before 2000 BC. Some researchers have suggested that the destruction of this early civilisation by a volcanic eruption may have been the basis of the ATLANTIS myth. The villages on Thíra are built along the edge of the cliffs, which are black and deep red-coloured in places. The island produces some cereals, figs, and olives, but vines are the main crop. There is no fresh water on Thíra, except from rain collected in tanks. Area 75 km²; population 7750. See also CYRENE.

Bibliography: H. M. Denham, *The Aegean: A Sea-Guide to its Coasts and Islands*, 1963.

Third, in music, the interval comprising any three successive notes of a diatonic scale. Thirds can be major, minor, augmented or diminished. On keyboard instruments an augmented third, e.g. C–E sharp, is identical with a perfect fourth, and a diminished third e.g. C sharp–E flat, is identical with a major second.

Third Estate, that French social class which was represented in the states-general, as well as the clergy and nobility. If it was relatively easy to designate the clergy, or First Estate, or heterogeneous nobility of the Second Estate, the Third Estate contained everyone else and ranged from beggars to millionaires and those who were on the fringe of nobility. In general wealth was a means to social advancement in the different orders of French society rather than an end in itself.

Third International, see COMINTERN.

Third Party Insurance, see INSURANCE.

Third Reich, term applied to the German National Socialist régime, formally begun 1 February 1934, which viewed itself as direct successor to the Holy Roman Empire and to the German Empire of 1871–1918 (see GERMAN HISTORY).

Third Republic, in France, lasted from the fall of the Second Empire in 1870 to the surrender of the French government on 17 June 1940. It was a period of French history which started uncertainly, and few expected it to represent a stable form of government or a united society. But the Third Republic withstood the crises of Boulangism and of the Dreyfus Affair, and then survived the most terrible experience of the First World War. But after 1918 both the international and economic situations turned against France and the defeat of 1940 was complete.

Third World, The, a term used to refer to those countries which have neither fully developed capitalist nor planned socialist economies. Despite enormous differences in history, geography, social structure, and culture, they have the following characteristics in common: their modern industrial sectors are relatively undeveloped; they are mainly producers of primary commodities for the capitalist countries; their populations are poor and chiefly engaged in agriculture. Spokesmen for such countries are increasingly regarding them as a group which has been exploited in the past by the developed nations and has a right to catch up with them. The early 1970s saw the beginnings of attempts by Third World countries to act together in confronting the powerful industrialised countries over such matters as the level of prices of primary products.

Thirlage, in Scots law, the obligation under which possessors of certain lands were bound to have their grain ground at a particular mill—to which mill the lands were said to be 'astricted' or 'thirled'.

Thirlmere, lake in the Cumbrian LAKE DISTRICT, England, 6 km south-east of Keswick. It is 5 km long and 1 km wide. Having the HELVELLYN ridge to the east and lesser but impressive fells to the west, it is surrounded by forests planted when it became a reservoir for Manchester in 1894. The main road from Windermere to Keswick runs along its east side.

Thirlwall, Connop (1797–1875), British historian and bishop of St David's, born in London; educated at the Charterhouse and Trinity College, Cambridge. His principal work is a *History of Greece*, 8 vols, 1935–44.
Bibliography: J. C. Thirlwall, *Connop Thirlwall*, 1936.

Thirsk, market town in the Hambleton District, North YORKSHIRE, England, 37 km from York. It has a beautiful parish church. Its fairs and markets are noted, and a trade is carried on in livestock, corn, wool, timber, etc. With the parish of Sowerby, it forms one continuous built-up area. Population (1971: parish) 2884.

Thirst, the desire for drink, made known by sensations projected to the pharynx. The amount of water contained in the body is subject to great changes. It is always being lost by various organs, the amount lost varying greatly with the conditions of life. This loss directly affects the blood, but this is not lasting, as the blood draws upon the vast resources of the other body tissues for its supply of water; consequently the tissues require a new supply to restore them to their normal state. The sense of thirst then comes into play; we become thirsty and take into our bodies water in varying quantities according to our needs. The sensation of thirst is due to several factors, the most important being the sense organs in a special centre of the hypothalamus of the brain, which are stimulated if the concentration of the blood rises. Drying of the mucous membranes of the mouth also help to produce the sensation. Thirst is temporarily quenched partly by the subjective knowledge of having drunk, partly by the mouth being wetted and the stomach filled with liquid. However, unless the blood concentration is lowered, the sensation of thirst returns in a few minutes. ANGIOTENSIN also causes thirst via its action on the brain, both directly and indirectly.

Thirty-Nine Articles, articles of the Church of England described in their heading as 'agreed upon by the archbishops and bishops of both provinces and the whole clergy, in the Convocation holden at London in the year 1562, for the avoiding of diversities of opinions and for the establishing of consent touching true religion'. Their history, however, begins before this date. On the death of Henry VIII, the government of the country was left in the hands of a group of nobles, of whom almost all were in favour of the reformed doctrines (see REFORMATION), and the changes in the teaching and practice of the Church increased with great rapidity. The ancient landmarks were being removed, and it was desirable that fresh ones should be set up. In 1549 Parliament empowered the king to appoint a commission for the drawing up of ecclesiastical laws, and in accordance with this act a commission was appointed in 1551. The commission, which included Cranmer, Ridley, and Coverdale, began by drawing up a code of 42 articles which were published by royal authority in 1553. To these articles was prefixed Cranmer's *Catechism*.

In the same year Edward VI died, and the Convocation of the first year of the Catholic Queen Mary denied that the articles had received its consent, and entirely repudiated them. But on the accession of Elizabeth, a Protestant, a revised form of the original 42 articles was submitted to Convocation. These were reduced in number to 39 and were finally promulgated in 1571. In 1604 they were finally settled in the form in which they are now used. The Thirty-Nine Articles were adopted by the Convocation of the Irish Church in 1635, and by the Scottish Episcopal Church in 1804.

There has been, especially during the last century, much controversy as to the nature and meaning of the articles. The terms of clerical subscription were reduced to general assent in 1865, and in 1975 replaced by a statement of loyalty to the historic faith expressed in these and other documents.
Bibliography: W. H. G. Thomas, *The Principles of Theology, an Introduction to the Thirty-Nine Articles*, 1930.

Thirty Years' War. The siege and sacking of Magdeburg by Tilly on 20 May 1631. *(Mansell Collection)*

Thirty Tyrants, name in Greek history, sometimes simply 'the Thirty', of an oligarchical government of 30 members imposed on the Athenians after the occupation of their city by Lysander, 404 BC (see Aristotle, *Athenian Constitution* 35–38). They were succeeded by a government known as the Ten, who in turn were defeated later in the same year by the returning exiles under Thasybulus and deposed.

Thirty Tyrants, name given collectively to a succession of Roman generals who assumed the purple in various provinces of the Empire during the reigns of Valerian and Gallienus (AD 254–68).

Thirty Years' War, The. Practically it may be said that the Thirty Years' War was the result of the German Reformation and the Counter-Reformation. The war was begun in 1618 by the revolt of the Bohemians against their Hapsburg ruler, FERDINAND II, and the acceptance of their crown by the Calvinist Elector Palatine, FREDERICK V, son-in-law of James I of England and father of the princes Rupert and Maurice. The troops of the Emperor immediately entered Bohemian territory and drove out Frederick, depriving him also of his electorate of the Lower Palatinate, a task rendered more easy by the inactivity of James I of England and the Protestant princes of Germany. Catholic Austria, Spain, and Bavaria all profited from this situation in different ways.

The Hapsburgs now developed their policy on larger lines; Germany was to become an exclusive Hapsburg possession and the land lost to Catholicism by the Refor-

mation was to be regained. The Imperial generals, TILLY and WALLENSTEIN swept all before them; northern Germany and the Baltic ports seemed to lie at their mercy. Christian IV of Denmark came forward as the champion of German Protestantism, but was defeated and forced to make peace in 1629 at Lübeck. Wallenstein had established the Hapsburg supremacy in the north, but had failed to take Stralsund. In the following year GUSTAVUS II (ADOLPHUS) aided by French subsidies, took Christian's place as the champion of Protestantism, and with his appearance began the turn of the tide. Wallenstein had been dismissed at the Diet of Ratisbon; the German princes feared the man whom they regarded as a mere mercenary upstart. Gustavus Adolphus marched from victory to victory. Tilly was defeated at Breitenfeld, and Gustavus marched to the south. In 1631 he again defeated, and killed, Tilly on the bank of the Lech, and then Wallenstein was recalled. Gustavus won the battle of Lützen (1632), but was killed, and much of his work was undone.

From this point the religious motives of the war entirely disappear. France, anxious to break the power of the Hapsburgs, gave support to the Swedes and German Protestant princes. Richelieu played his hand well; enemies to the Hapsburgs were raised up in Germany, Italy, and Spain; the Dutch were given support in their struggle against Spanish power; and the power of the Hapsburgs, both Austrian and Spanish, began to decline. The policy of Richelieu was continued after his death by Mazarin, and the French generals Condé and Turenne won brilliant victories over the Imperialists. Finally the end came in 1648, when the Emperor, suffering from defeats in Germany at the hands of the Swedes and the French, agreed to terms of peace. The Treaty of Westphalia (see WEST-PHALIA, TREATY OF) was signed in October 1648. The territorial gains of France and Sweden, and the independence of the German princes, were recognised. The attempted revival of the power of Catholicism by the sword had failed, and the Imperial power became nominal except in Austria. The independence of Switzerland and the United Provinces (Holland) were also recognised by this treaty. The terrible devastation which the war caused in Germany had political and social consequences of long duration, although not all areas suffered in equal measure.

See also GERMAN HISTORY.

Bibliography: C. V. Wedgwood, *Thirty Years War*, 1938; S. H. Steinberg, *Thirty Years War*, 1966; G. Pages (trans. D. Maland and J. Hooper), *Thirty Years War, 1618–48*, 1971; J. Polišenský (trans. R. Evans), *The Thirty Years War*, 1971.

Thisbe, see PYRAMUS AND THISBE.

Thistle, the general name for a number of spiny plants, especially certain members of the Compositae (daisy family), with characteristically-shaped flower-heads consisting of tubular florets, usually purplish but sometimes yellowish or white in colour. Most British species belong to the genera *Carduus* and *Cirsium*; the most important economically is the creeping thistle, *Cirsium arvense*, a persistent weed. Thistles of related genera include Scotch thistle, *Onopordum acanthium*—actually commonest in south-east England—a tall plant with woolly white hairs among its spines; also holy thistle, *Silybum marianum*, with edible roots and young leaves; the scented musk-thistle, *Carduus nutans*; and carline thistle, *Carlina*. Globe thistle, *Echinops*, often grown in gardens, has spherical heads of complex compound structure. Sow-thistles (milk-thistles) with white juice and yellow, dandelion-like flower heads, belong to the genus SONCHUS. Hedgehog thistle is a totally different plant, being a type of CACTUS, genus *Echinocactus*.

Thistle, Order of the, see ORDERS OF KNIGHTHOOD, *Great Britain and Ireland (2)*.

Thistlewood, Arthur (1772–1820), British conspirator, born at Tupholme, Lincolnshire. He served in the army, and having absorbed revolutionary ideas in America and France, became a reformer and sought to achieve his ends by the use of violence. His project in 1820 to assassinate the entire Cabinet when gathered together at dinner at Lord Harrowby's house in Grosvenor Square, failed owing to the presence of a spy among the conspirators. Thistlewood and his associates were caught in a loft in Cato Street, London, and the attempt became known as the CATO STREET CONSPIRACY. Thistlewood was tried for high treason and hanged.

Bibliography: J. Stanhope, *Cato Street Conspiracy*, 1962.

Tholed Assize, in Scots criminal law, the term to indicate that the accused has stood trial for an offence and cannot, therefore, be re-tried for it.

Tholos (Greek), in Greek architecture, either: (1) a prehistoric circular tomb with corbelled roof; or (2) a circular building surrounded by columns.

Thomas, Saint, one of the 12 apostles, called also Didymus (John xi. 6), i.e. 'the twin'. All the information about him in scripture is given in the fourth gospel. Later tradition says that he evangelised southern India and Parthia, dying at Edessa.

Thomas, Christians of Saint, see NESTORIUS.

Thomas, Ambroise (1811–96), French composer, born at Metz, son of a musician. He studied music at the Paris Conservatoire, 1828–32, winning the Prix de Rome at 21. The opera by which he is chiefly remembered is *Mignon*, 1866. Other famous operas are *Raymond*, 1851, and *Hamlet*, 1868. Thomas also wrote numerous cantatas, part-songs and choral pieces. He became a member of the Institute in 1851, professor of composition at the Conservatoire in 1852, and director in 1871.

Thomas, Arthur Goring (1850–92), British composer, born at Ratton Park, Sussex. Educated at Haileybury College, he studied music in Paris and at the Royal Academy, London, under Prout and Sullivan. The success of his *The Light of the Harem* in 1879 led to the Carl Rosa Company's invitation to write the opera *Esmeralda*, which was successfully produced at Drury Lane (1883). His best opera is *Nadeshda*, 1885, libretto by J. Sturgis. He also composed the cantatas *The Sun Worshippers* and *The Swan and the Skylark*, and some songs.

Thomas, Bertram Sydney (1892–1950), British explorer and orientalist. His crossing of the Rub' al-Khali, the great desert of southern Arabia, in the winter of 1930–31 was a great feat of endurance; Thomas went with a camel caravan. Previously, in 1927–28, he had made a 970-kilometre journey through the southern borderlands from the south-east toe of Arabia to Dhofar, and in 1929–30 he explored 320 km to the north of Dhofar, right to the edge of the sands. He published *Alarms and Excursions in Arabia*, 1931; *Arabia Infelix*, 1932.

Thomas, Dylan Marlais (1914–53), Welsh poet, born in Swansea and educated there at the grammar school where his father was senior English master. Thomas was a reporter for a time on the *South Wales Evening Post*, and had a number of poems printed in the *Sunday Referee*. His first book, *Eighteen Poems*, 1934, containing some surrealist verse, was praised by Dame Edith Sitwell. In 1936 he published *Twenty-Five Poems*, and in 1938 won a prize offered by the Chicago magazine *Poetry*. *The Map of Love*, a collection of stories and verse, appeared in 1939.

Rejected for service in the Second World War, Thomas worked for the BBC. In 1940 he published *Portrait of the Artist as a Young Dog*, a series of humorous autobiographical sketches. *Deaths and Entrances*, 1946, and *In Country Sleep*, 1951, are considered the finest volumes of his poetry, which has affinities with the works of BLAKE and Gerard Manley HOPKINS. *Collected Poems 1934–52* was published in 1966, and *The Notebooks of Dylan Thomas*, which contains many previously unpublished poems, in 1968. Regarded by some as the most outstanding poet of his generation, his heavy drinking contributed to his early death during a lecture tour of the USA.

Under Milk Wood, 'a play for voices', was written for radio and first broadcast in 1954. The play was published in London and New York in the same year, and a stage

Dylan Thomas. *(Camera Press/Jane Bown)*

version was produced at the Edinburgh Festival, 1956, and was later seen in London. Posthumously published prose works are *Quite Early One Morning*, 1954, *Adventures in the Skin Trade*, 1955, and *A Prospect of the Sea*, 1955. His *Letters to Vernon Watkins* were edited by the latter in 1957; *Selected Letters* appeared in 1966.

Bibliography: J. M. Brinnin, *Dylan Thomas in America*, 1956; R. Maud, *Dylan Thomas in Print: A Bibliographical History*, 1968; W. Davies, *Dylan Thomas: New Critical Essays*, 1972; P. Ferris, *Dylan Thomas*, 1977; D. Jones, *My Friend Dylan Thomas*, 1977.

Thomas, George Henry (1816–70), US general, born in Southampton County, Virginia, and educated at West Point Military Academy. He served in the Seminole War and the Mexican War, and was instructor at West Point from 1851 to 1854. At the outbreak of the Civil War he adhered to the Northern cause; he was appointed colonel, and later brigadier-general of volunteers. In 1862 he gained the victory of Mill Springs, and distinguished himself at Perryville, Murfreesboro, and Chickamauga. From the last of those actions he gained his sobriquet 'The Rock of Chickamauga'. He was made commander of the army at Cumberland, and fought the battle of Chattanooga in 1863. In 1864 he defeated Hood at Nashville.

Thomas, Hugh Owen (1834–91), British manipulative surgeon, born in Bodedern, Anglesey. He came of a family famous for generations as bone-setters. His father was unqualified, but gave Hugh the benefit of a medical training at Edinburgh and University College, London. He qualified MRCS in 1857, and in the following year

practised with his father and brother in Liverpool, but in 1859 set up on his own. The methods he introduced for the treatment of orthopaedic conditions make him the true founder of orthopaedic surgery in Britain. He wrote little, and it was left to his nephew and apprentice (Sir) Robert Jones, afterwards an eminent orthopaedic surgeon, to preach Thomas's principles and make them, after many years, acceptable to the medical profession. He wrote *Diseases of the Hip, Knee and Ankle Joints*, 1875, in which he described the Thomas splint, and *Contributions to Surgery and Medicine*, 1883–90.

Bibliography: Life by T. P. McMurray, 1935; R. Roberts, *Doctor Thomas: His Life and Work*, 1954.

Thomas, James Henry (1874–1949), British Labour politician, born at Newport, Monmouthshire (Gwent), son of a labourer. As an engine-driver he was elected to the Swindon town council, and in 1904 became president of the Amalgamated Society of Railway Servants. Thomas was Labour MP for Derby from 1910 to 1936. In the First World War he was a member of Balfour's mission to the USA. Thomas was appointed secretary of state for the colonies in the first Labour government, 1924, and lord privy seal and minister of employment in the second Labour government, 1929–30. In June 1930 he became secretary of state for dominion affairs, being transferred to the Colonial Office in 1935. In 1936 he resigned both from office and from Parliament as a result of the report of a tribunal set up to consider unauthorised disclosures relating to the Budget. Thomas was author of *When Labour Rules*, 1920; *The Red Light on Railways*, 1921; and *My Story*, 1937.

Bibliography: G. Blaxland, *J. H. Thomas: a life for unity*, 1964.

Thomas, (Philip) Edward (1878–1917), English poet and essayist, born in London of Welsh parents; educated at St Paul's and Lincoln College, Oxford. His first book, *The Woodland Life*, appeared in 1897, and two years later, while still an undergraduate, he married Helen Noble. They lived in poverty in various parts of Kent while he tried to make a living by his books and by hack journalism. On the outbreak of the First World War he enlisted as a private, and had received his commission as a second lieutenant when he was killed at Arras.

An intense love of the country is shown in his works, which include *Oxford*, 1903, *The Heart of England*, 1906, *The Country*, 1913, and *A Literary Pilgrim in England*, 1917. Thomas wrote no poetry until 1912, when he used the pseudonym Edward Eastaway; his *Collected Poems*, 1920, in a style limpid and fastidious, were praised by Walter de la Mare. *The Happy-Go-Lucky Morgans*, 1913, is a novel.

Bibliography: H. Thomas, *As It Was*, 1926, and *World Without End*, 1931; H. Coombes, *Edward Thomas*, 1973.

Thomas, R(onald) S(tuart) (1913–), Welsh poet, born in Cardiff; educated at University College, Bangor, and St Michael's College, Llandaff. He was ordained a priest in 1937. Though he writes in English, his verse is close to Welsh traditions in its concern for the threatened values and existence of the rural Welsh communities in which he has lived, and his respect for his parishioners. *Selected Poems, 1946–1968* was published in 1974. He has also edited several works, including *A Book of Country Verse*, 1961.

Thomas, (Thomas) George

Thomas, (Thomas) George (1909–), British politician, educated at a state secondary school and the University of Southampton. A teacher, he was elected Labour MP for Cardiff Central in 1945 and has been MP for Cardiff West since 1950. From 1951 to 1964 he was a member of the Chairmen's Panel of the House of Commons and between 1964 and 1968 he was successively parliamentary under secretary at the Home Office, minister of state at the Welsh Office, and minister of state at the Commonwealth Office. He entered the Cabinet in 1968 as secretary of state for Wales, a post he held until Labour's defeat in 1970. In 1974 he became chairman of Ways and Means and deputy speaker of the House of Commons and in 1976 he became only the second Labour MP to become Speaker of the House of Commons.

Thomas à Kempis (c. 1380–1471), Augustinian canon and religious writer, called after his birthplace Kempen, near Düsseldorf. His real surname was Hammerken, and he came of a peasant family. He was educated at the school of the BRETHREN OF THE COMMON LIFE at Deventer. In 1399 he joined the Augustinians of Mount St Agnes at Zwolle and was professed in 1406. Here he remained almost continually for the rest of his life, copying manuscripts, writing, and directing novices. By far the most celebrated of his numerous treatises (though his authorship is sometimes denied) is the *Imitatio Christi* (Imitation of Christ), which has been translated into more languages than any other book except the Bible. An edition of Kempis's complete works was edited by M. J. Pohl (1902–22).
Bibliography: Lives by J. C. Montmorency, 1906; J. Williams, 1910; A. Klockner, 1921.

Thomas Aquinas, see AQUINAS, THOMAS, SAINT.

Thomas Becket, see BECKET, THOMAS.

Thomas of Celano (c. 1190–1260), Italian Franciscan monk and poet. According to an uncertain tradition he wrote the words of the long 13th-century hymn or sequence *Dies irae, dies illa* which forms the Sequence in the *Requiem* or *Mass for the Dead*. Celano wrote biographies of St Francis much admired at the time though their historicity has been questioned since, and also of St Clare. See also DIES IRAE.

Thomas of Woodstock, see GLOUCESTER, DUKES AND EARLS OF.

Thomasius, Christian (1655–1728), German jurist, born at Leipzig, where he began to lecture on law in 1684. In 1687 he took the daring step of lecturing in German instead of Latin, and in the following year sided with the PIETISTS in their controversy with the orthodox. He removed to the University of Halle on its foundation in 1694. Thomasius was a leading proponent of natural law and an opponent of superstition and intolerance.

Thompson, Alice, see MEYNELL, ALICE CHRISTIANA GERTRUDE.

Thompson, Sir Benjamin, Count Rumford (1753–1814), Anglo-American scientist and administrator, born at Woburn, Massachusetts, his family having settled in New England. At an early age he made chemical and mechanical experiments and, by turns, studied medicine and took up school teaching. At 19 he married the well-to-do widow of a Colonel Rolfe, and daughter of a minister who had settled at Rumford, now called Concord. This marriage was the foundation of his success, though within a few years he left his wife to settle in Europe. During the war of American Independence his sympathies were opposed to the American cause, and in 1776 he was therefore chosen by Governor Wentworth of New Hampshire to bear dispatches to London and later became an under-secretary of state. His official duties, however, did not preclude scientific pursuits, and in 1779 he was elected a fellow of the Royal Society. Among the subjects of which he made special study were ballistic experiments, a differential thermometer and lighthouse improvements; but he is chiefly noted for his researches in HEAT, the caloric notion of which was rejected when he noticed that the metal chips from the boring of a cannon were very hot. A few years later he was introduced to Karl Theodor, elector of Bavaria, and entered the service of that state as minister of war, grand chamberlain and principal adviser to the elector. He was knighted by George III in 1784 shortly before his departure for Bavaria. In 1791 he was created a count of the Holy Roman Empire, choosing his title of Rumford from his American associations. In 1795 he again visited England, devoting himself to the problems of smoke abatement. In 1799 he co-operated with Sir Joseph Banks in projecting the establishment of the Royal Institution. Thompson himself selected Sir Humphry Davy as the first scientific lecturer there. He was the founder and first recipient of the Rumford Medal of the Society.
Bibliography: E. Larsen, *An American in Europe: The Life of Benjamin Thompson, Count Rumford*, 1953.

Thompson, Edward Herbert (1856–1935), US explorer. In 1885 he was sent as US consul to Yucatan, Mexico, and inspired by the early Spanish writings and by native legends, he explored the ruined Maya cities. His most notable achievement was the excavation of the temples and the sacred well of the ancient Maya capital of Chichen Itza. Using a derrick and dredging equipment, and diving himself, he recovered from the bottom of the well jewellery and other objects in jade, gold, and copal, textiles, and human skeletons, which confirmed the old stories that it had been a centre for sacrificial rites. His adventures are described in his *People of the Serpent*, 1933.

Thompson, Flora (1877–1948), English novelist, born at Juniper Hill, Oxfordshire. She is best known for her autobiographical novels *Lark Rise*, 1939, *Over to Candleford*, 1941, and *Candleford Green*, 1943, forming a trilogy later published as *Lark Rise to Candleford*, 1945, which lovingly describe rural life at the turn of the 19th century. Other works are *Bog Myrtle and Peat*, 1921, a volume of verse, and *Still Glides the Stream*, 1948.

Thompson, Francis (1859–1907), English poet, born at Preston, Lancashire. A Roman Catholic, he was educated at Ushaw College, near Durham, and afterwards studied medicine at Owens College, Manchester. Failing to take a degree, he went to London. Here he worked in various occupations, until in 1888 he sent two poems to the magazine *Merry England*. These were recognised by Wilfrid MEYNELL as works of merit. Meynell rescued Thompson from poverty and opium addiction and helped him to publish his first volume of *Poems*, 1893, which was praised by Coventry PATMORE in the *Fortnightly Review*. *Sister Songs*, 1895, and *New Poems*, 1897, both gained him recognition as a poet. He also gained a reputation as a prose writer, and published *Health and Holiness*, 1905, dealing with the ascetic life; *Essay on Shelley*, 1909; and lives of St Ignatius Loyola, 1909, and John Baptiste de la Salle, 1911. His most famous poem is 'The Hound of Heaven'.

Bibliography: The Works of Francis Thompson (3 vols), 1913; J. Thompson, *Francis Thompson, Poet and Mystic*, 1923; E. Meynell, *The Life of Francis Thompson*, 1926; R. L. Mégroz, *Francis Thompson, Poet of Earth in Heaven*, 1927; T. L. Connolly (Ed.), *Poems*, 1941, and *Literary Criticisms*, 1948; P. H. Butter, *Francis Thompson*, 1961.

Thoms, William John (1803–85), British antiquary and miscellaneous writer, born at Westminster. He was founder in 1849 of *Notes and Queries*, which for some years he also edited. He introduced the word 'folklore' into the language.

Thomsen, Christian Jürgensen (1788–1865), Danish archaeologist, reputed to have been the first to have devised the three-age system, whereby prehistory was divided into the three successive ages of Stone, Bronze, and Iron. In 1816 he became the first curator of the National Museum of Denmark, and used this system, which was, until recently, the framework for European prehistoric chronology, as a means for classifying the collections. His guide to the museum (1836) was translated into English as *A Guide to Northern Antiquities*, 1848.

Bibliography: G. Daniel, *The Three Ages*, 1943, and *150 Years of Archaeology*, 1975.

Thomsen, Grímur (1820–96), Icelandic diplomat, politician, and poet. Many of his subjects are taken from the SAGAS, as, for example, in his series of poems *Búarímur*. His satire *Á Glæsisvöllum* and his translations of the Greek dramatists are also important.

Thomson, Sir Charles Wyville (1830–82), British zoologist, born at Bonnyside, West Lothian; educated at Edinburgh University, he became professor of zoology at Cork, and, from 1870, at Edinburgh. He is chiefly remembered as director of the scientific staff in the *Challenger* Expedition (1872–76). This appointment he owed to his important studies of biological conditions in the depths of the sea made in two expeditions in HMS *Lightning* and *Porcupine* with Dr W. B. Carpenter in 1868–69. He was knighted in 1876. He wrote *The Depths of the Sea*, 1872, *The Voyage of the Challenger*, 1877.

Thomson, Elihu (1853–1937), US inventor, born in Manchester, England, and moved to the USA with his parents while a child. He was educated at the Central High School in Philadelphia, and was professor of mechanics and chemistry at this institution from 1875 to 1880. From 1880 he was chief electrician for the Thomson-Houston Company and the General Electric Company which, due to his inventions, operate more than 600 patents. Besides numerous inventions in electric lighting and generator design, he discovered incandescent electric welding. He was the first to utilise a magnetic field to deflect an electric arc, made the first high-frequency alternator, invented a watt-hour meter, and was the first to make stereoscopic X-ray pictures.

Thomson, Sir George Paget (1892–), British physicist, born at Cambridge, son of Sir J. J. THOMSON. Elected a fellow of Corpus Christi College, Cambridge, in 1914, he served in France 1914–15, and worked on aerodynamical problems from then until 1919, when he returned to Cambridge. From 1922 to 1930 he held the chair of natural philosophy at Aberdeen, and in 1930 was appointed professor of physics at the Imperial College of Science and Technology, South Kensington. He was Master of Corpus Christi College, Cambridge, 1952–62.

De Broglie's view that electrons possess not merely the properties of discrete particles but also have many of the attributes of wave motion was strongly supported by experiments performed by Thomson, for which he shared the 1937 Nobel Prize for physics with C. J. DAVISSON. He was elected FRS in 1930. He was a member of the Aeronautical Research Committee 1937–41, and in 1943–44 acted as scientific adviser to the Air Ministry. He was knighted in 1943. From 1946 to 1947 Thomson was scientific adviser to the British delegation to the Atomic Energy Commission of the UN.

His publications include *Applied Aerodynamics*, 1920; *The Wave Mechanics of Free Electrons*, 1930; *Electron Diffraction*, (with W. Cochrane), 1939; *The Foreseeable Future*, 2nd ed. 1960; *The Atom*, 6th ed. 1962; and *J. J. Thomson and the Cavendish Laboratory*, 1964.

Thomson, James (1700–48), English poet, born at Ednam in Roxburghshire, Scotland. He was educated at Edinburgh University, where he wrote great quantities of verse, and had three poems published in the *Edinburgh Miscellany* of 1720. He had originally some intention of entering the ministry, but he abandoned all thought of this, and in 1725 went to London to pursue a literary career.

He became tutor to Thomas Hamilton (afterwards 7th Earl of Haddington), and made the acquaintance of many of the leading men of letters. He published in 1726 *Winter*, which was highly praised, and this he followed in the next year with *Summer*. *Spring* appeared in 1728, and two years later he republished these three poems, adding to them *Autumn*, under the title of *The Seasons*. He subsequently carefully revised this work, but it was not brought out in its amended form until 1744. It was the first lengthy nature poem in English and foreshadowed the work of the Romantics (see ROMANTIC MOVEMENT) in its treatment of natural surroundings and their effects on the poet and, through his descriptions, on the reader.

In 1730 Thomson's play *Sophonisba* was produced at Drury Lane, but in spite of its many merits it was not successful. In 1731 he accompanied the son of Lord Chancellor Talbot on the 'grand tour'. This inspired the poem *Liberty*, 1734. *Agamemnon*, 1738, was his next work, and in 1740, in collaboration with David MALLET, he wrote *The Masque of Alfred*, which is famous because in it first appeared the ode 'Rule Britannia' and it is virtually certain that Thomson was its author. Since 1738 Thomson had received a pension from Frederick, Prince of Wales, and in 1744 he was given the sinecure office of surveyor-general of the Leeward Islands.

His later works include the plays *Edward and Eleonora*,

1739, *Tancred and Sigismunda*, 1745, in which GARRICK played Tancred, and *Coriolanus*, 1748. *The Castle of Indolence*, 1748, an allegorical poem in the Spenserian stanza, is often reckoned his finest work.

When Thomson began to write, English poetry was dominated by artificiality, and POPE was the principal living poet; but Thomson employed a true, simple, romantic treatment of nature, and his influence on his contemporaries, as on his successors, was considerable. Thomson's *Works* were first collected in 1763. The poetical works were edited by J. L. Robertson, 1908; *The Castle of Indolence and other Poems* (two volumes) by H. D. Roberts and E. Gosse, 1906; and *Letters and Documents* by A. D. McKillop, 1958.

Bibliography: P. M. Spacks, *The Varied God: a critical study of Thomson's 'The Seasons'*, 1959; R. Cohen, *The Art of Discrimination*, 1964, and *The Unfolding of the Seasons*, 1970.

Thomson, James (1822–92), British physicist, born in Belfast, brother of Lord KELVIN OF LARGS; he was also an engineer, inventor, and geologist. He was professor of civil engineering at Queen's College, Belfast (1857–73) and Glasgow University (1873–89), and was the first to demonstrate the possibility of lowering the freezing point of water, etc., by pressure. He was elected FRS in 1877.

Thomson, James (1834–82), Scottish poet, born at Port Glasgow. Educated at the Royal Caledonian Asylum and the Military Asylum, Chelsea, he became a schoolmaster in Ireland and then an army teacher in Dublin, Aldershot, and Portsmouth, but was discharged in 1862 for a breach of discipline.

Moving to London, he worked as clerk and journalist, writing under the initials B. V. for Bysshe Vanolis, a combination of SHELLEY's middle name with an anagram of NOVALIS, the German poet. His other influences were Dante and LEOPARDI. In 1874 he contributed to the *National Reformer* his best-known poem, 'The City of Dreadful Night', which made him famous as a poet of pessimism and despair. It was published with other pieces in 1880, and in 1881 a second volume of verse and a collection of essays appeared. His *Poems and Some Letters* were edited by A. Ridler, 1963.

Bibliography: I. Walker, *James Thomson: A Critical Study*, 1950; W. D. Schaefer (Ed.), *James Thomson (B. V.)*, 1966.

Thomson, Sir John Arthur (1861–1933), British naturalist, born in East Lothian; educated at the universities of Edinburgh, Jena, and Berlin. Sometime lecturer in zoology and biology in the School of Medicine, Edinburgh, he was also regius professor of natural history, Aberdeen, 1899–1920. Author of: *Study of Animal Life*, 1892 (revised 1917), *Herbert Spencer*, 1906, *Darwinism and Human Life*, 1910 (revised 1916), *Biology of Birds*, 1923, *Science and Religion*, 1925, *Outline of Biology*, 1930, *Biology for Everyman*, 1934. He was knighted in 1930.

Thomson, Sir Joseph John (1856–1940), British physicist, born near Manchester; educated at Owens College and Trinity College, Cambridge. He was a lecturer at Trinity College, 1883, Master of Trinity College and professor of physics, his association with Cambridge lasting throughout his life. In 1884 he succeeded Lord Rayleigh as Cavendish Professor of Experimental Physics (1884–1918). To Thomson belongs, by general consent, the credit for the discovery of the electron. His book, *Application of Dynamics to Physics and Chemistry*, 1888, was to a great extent the foundation stone on which the study of physical chemistry was built. This was followed by numerous papers on electrical theory and experiments on gases. After Röntgen had demonstrated the existence of X-rays produced by substances struck by cathode rays, Thomson (assisted by Rutherford, then a young research student from New Zealand) adapted the discovery to his own use and used the X-rays for producing more controllable ionised gas. Through his researches in this field he concluded that all matter is composed of electrically charged particles and that electricity is atomic in nature. His subsequent researches into the nature of electricity resulted in the development of the study of atomic physics, in which Thomson, as a pioneer, gained international recognition from the scientific world, and in 1906 he was awarded the Nobel Prize for physics. He was knighted in 1908. In 1912 he was made a member of the Order of Merit and was president of the Royal Society from 1916 to 1920.

His publications include *A Treatise on the Motion of Vortex Rings*, 1883; *Applications of Dynamics to Physics and Chemistry*, 1888; *The Discharge of Electricity through Gases*, 1898; *Corpuscular Theory of Matter*, 1907; *Elements of the Mathematical Theory of Electricity and Magnetism*, 5th ed. 1921; *The Electron in Chemistry*, 1923; and *The Conduction of Electricity Through Gases* (2 vols), 3rd ed. 1928–33.

Bibliography: R. J. Strutt, *The Life of Sir J. J. Thomson*, 1942; Sir G. P. Thomson, *J. J. Thomson and the Cavendish Laboratory in His Day*, 1964.

Thomson, Virgil (1896–), US composer and music critic, born at Kansas City. He studied with Boulanger in Paris and with Scalero in New York. Influenced by SATIE and 'LES SIX' he developed a deadpan style, often based on American folk material. His works include the operas *Four Saints in Three Acts*, *The Mother of us all* and *Lord Byron*, the first two having texts by Gertrude Stein, orchestral pieces, choral music, piano music, film scores, etc. Among his books are *Virgil Thomson*, 1966, *American Music since 1910*, 1971, and several volumes of collected criticism.

Thomson, William, see KELVIN OF LARGS, WILLIAM THOMSON, 1ST BARON.

Thomson Effect, or Kelvin effect, see THERMOELECTRICITY.

Thomson of Dundee, George Morgan Thomson, Baron (1921–), British politician, educated at Grove Academy, Dundee. After war service he became a journalist and was elected Labour MP for Dundee East in 1952. Between 1964 and 1967 he held office as minister of state at the Foreign Office and as chancellor of the Duchy of Lancaster. In 1967 he entered the Cabinet as secretary of state for Commonwealth Affairs and then became minister without portfolio in 1968 and chancellor of the Duchy of Lancaster again in 1969. Strongly in favour of British membership of the European Economic Community, he was responsible for negotiations for British entry between 1968 and 1970. In 1972–73 he was chairman of the Labour Committee for Europe and in 1973 he became one of Britain's two nominees on the Commission of the European Communities, with special responsibility for regional policy. His term of office expired in 1977.

Thomson of Fleet, Roy Herbert Thomson, 1st Baron (1894–1976), British newspaper proprietor, born in Toronto, Canada; educated at Jarvis Collegiate, Toronto. He left school at 14 and was successively clerk, salesman, farmer, and book-keeper. In 1929 he established a small, successful local radio station. Subsequently he took over a weekly newspaper in payment of a bad debt, and within ten years owned a chain of provincial Canadian newspapers and three radio stations. By 1953 he was a millionaire.

Thomson then turned his attention to Britain, acquired control of the *Scotsman* group of newspapers, and secured the independent television licence for Scottish television. In 1959 he took over KEMSLEY Newspapers Ltd, and in 1967 acquired *The Times* and its subsidiaries. His worldwide organisation grew until it owned over 140 newspapers and 150 magazines, as well as book-publishing companies and printing firms. He became a British citizen in 1963 and was created a baron the following year.

See also NEWSPAPERS.

Thor, Teutonic god of thunder, identified by the Romans with JUPITER, or Jove, hence Thursday for *Jovis dies*, French *jeudi*. See also MYTHOLOGY, *Teutonic*.

Thoracic Duct, the duct which conveys the greater part of the lymph and chyle into the blood (see LYMPHATIC SYSTEM). It is the common lymph trunk of the body except for the right upper arm, right side of the head, neck and thorax, right lung, right side of the heart and the convex side of the liver. It does not, as its name would seem to imply, lie wholly within the thoracic cavity, but begins in the abdomen, on the front of the body of the second lumbar vertebra, by a dilation known as the *receptaculum chyli*. It reaches the thorax by passing through the aortic openings in the diaphragm, passes upwards to the root of the neck, and then takes a curved course outwards and downwards, emptying into the left subclavian vein at its junction with the left internal jugular vein. The duct is, in the adult, between 37·5 and 50 cm long.

Thorax, the part of the body which is above, or in front of, the abdomen and below, or behind, the head. The lowest animals do not have their bodies divided in this way. In insects, the thorax includes the three segments to which the legs and wings are attached. In crustaceans, such as lobsters, it is often fused with the head, forming the cephalothorax. In vertebrate animals, it contains the heart and lungs, which are enclosed within the protective rib cage. In mammals, the division between the thorax and abdomen is the muscular diaphragm.

In man, the thorax or chest is shaped like a truncated cone with the diaphragm as its base. The bony thoracic cage, on which the musculature is hung, is formed by the vertebral column behind and the twelve pairs of ribs which run round to the costal cartilages and sternum (breastbone) anteriorly. The thoracic inlet is small, slopes downwards and forwards and contains the oesophagus (gullet) and trachea (windpipe), and those arteries and veins leading from and to the heart through the neck, together with certain nerves. The thoracic outlet is larger, slopes

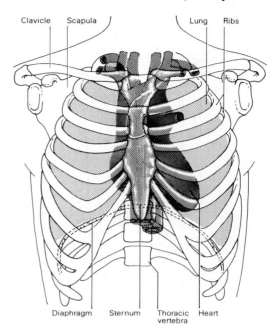

Thorax. A diagrammatic representation of the human thorax showing the heart, lungs, diaphragm, and bones.

downwards and backwards and is filled by the diaphragm, which is convex above.

The intercostal spaces between adjacent ribs are sealed by three layers of intercostal muscles. During inspiration these muscles lift the ribs and the diaphragm flattens, causing an increase in all dimensions of the thorax. The lungs expand to fill this extra space with a consequent drawing in of air. Conversely, in expiration the relaxation of the intercostal muscles and diaphragm, combined with the elastic recoil of the lungs, forces air out of the lungs.

Thórdarson, Thorbergur (1889–1974), Icelandic author known chiefly for his essays, which in his early period were coloured by his study of Eastern mysticism but which later reflected his enthusiasm for socialism. He also published autobiographical works and poetry.

Thoreau, Henry David (1817–62), US writer, born at Concord, Massachusetts. Educated at Concord Academy and Harvard, he published his first book, *A Week on the Concord and Merrimack River*, in 1849. Through EMERSON he came to know Hawthorne and Channing and was drawn to TRANSCENDENTALISM. In 1845 he built a cabin on Emerson's land and lived there near Walden Pond for two years in an attempt to rediscover the essentials of life. *Walden, or Life in the Woods* was published in 1854.

Thoreau's influential essay on 'Civil Disobedience' appeared in 1849. This work was much admired by Gandhi and, through him, by Martin Luther King. His other works include *Excursions*, 1863, *The Maine Woods*, 1864, *Cape Cod*, 1865, and *A Yankee in Canada*, 1866. He was also a poet, a collection of his nature poems

Henry David Thoreau.

appearing in 1895.

Bibliography: Riverside edition (10 vols), 1894–95; H. S. Canby (Ed.), *The Works of Thoreau*, 1947; W. Harding, *The Days of Henry Thoreau*, 1965; (Ed.), *Thoreau Centennial Papers*, 1973; J. W. Krutch, *Henry David Thoreau*, new ed. 1973.

Thorez, Maurice (1900–64), French politician, born at Noyelles Godault, Pas de Calais, adopted son of a coal miner. He joined the Communist party in 1920, and was its leader from 1933. When war broke out Thorez was conscripted, but deserted and made his way to Moscow, returning to France in 1944 to become a member of the consultative assembly and a minister of state under de Gaulle. He held various Cabinet offices until 1947, when Auriol removed Communist ministers after they had opposed the government of which they were a part. Thorez subsequently led French Communist opposition to alliances, military or economic, with other West European countries, and was bitterly opposed to de Gaulle and to the negotiations which led to an Algerian settlement. A semi-invalid from 1950, Thorez became president of the French Communist party in May 1964, being succeeded as secretary-general by Waldeck Rochet.

Thorium, metallic chemical element, symbol Th, atomic number 90, atomic weight 232·0381; one of the ACTINIDES. It was discovered by BERZELIUS in 1818, and its identity confirmed ten years later. It is present in several complex silicate ores (thorite, gadolinite, and orangeite) found in Sweden and Norway, and also in the monazite sand of Brazil and the USA. It is extracted by treating the sand with concentrated sulphuric acid, and neutralising the resulting solution with alkali. Thorium phosphate is precipitated out, from which the thorium is extracted as the dioxide, thoria (ThO_2), which is used in the manufacture of incandescent gas mantles. Metallic thorium is difficult to isolate, owing to its chemical activity, but it

has been prepared pure by reduction of the oxide and by electrolysis. It is a white metal, melting at 1842 °C. When heated in air or oxygen it burns brilliantly. Thorium is radioactive and, under neutron bombardment in a nuclear reactor, the common isotope thorium-232 forms the fissile isotope uranium-233, which is a valuable nuclear fuel.

Thorláksson, Gudbrandur (1542–1627), Icelandic prelate and translator of the Bible, which he published in 1584, the first complete Icelandic edition. He was bishop of the North see (Hólar) for 56 years and established the Lutheran reformation in Iceland on a secure basis. He is one of the great names in the history of Iceland.

Thorn, see TORUŃ.

Thorn, name of the Old English letter þ, pronounced *th* as in *th* in. Its form gradually became the same as *y*, which appears in antique spelling of the definite article as 'ye', often mistakenly pronounced like the old plural form of 'you' in pseudo-antique phrases like 'Ye olde tea shoppe'.

Thorn, of a plant, see HAIRS IN PLANTS.

Thorn Apple, see DATURA.

Thornaby-on-Tees, town in the STOCKTON-ON-TEES District of CLEVELAND, England, on the Tees, south-west of MIDDLESBROUGH. The borough's principal industries are engineering, bridge-building, iron founding, sugar refining, and wire-rope manufacture. Population (1971) 25,000.

Thorndike, Dame Sybil (1882–1976), British actress, born at Gainsborough, Lincolnshire, educated at Rochester High School. She joined Ben Greet's company, her first professional appearance being in 1904 at Cambridge. After touring in America for four years, she was with Miss Horniman's Manchester Company, 1908–09. She married in 1908 the actor and producer Sir Lewis Thomas Casson (1875–1969), with whom she often appeared. She joined the Charles Frohman repertory, 1910, and made an American tour with John Drew, 1910–11. From 1914 to 1918 she played leading roles at the Old Vic, and at the Little Theatre from 1920 to 1922. Her creation of the title role in Shaw's *St Joan* in 1924 gained her wide recognition. Her range and quality were shown in the classical parts of Lady Macbeth, Medea and Lady Teazle, Aase (in *Peer Gynt*) and in such modern plays as *The Corn is Green* and *The Linden Tree*. To celebrate her golden

Dame Sybil Thorndike as St Joan. (*Raymond Mander and Joe Mitchenson Theatre Collection*)

wedding she appeared with Sir Lewis in *Eighty in the Shade*, specially written for them by Clemence Dane, and they both appeared at the first Chichester Festival (1962) in *Uncle Vanya*. She was created DBE in 1931 and CH in 1970.

Bibliography: J. Casson, *Lewis and Sybil: A Memoir*, 1972.

Thorne, market town and rural district of South YORK-SHIRE, England, on the River Don, with shipbuilding, engineering, textile industries, and formerly a colliery working one of the most productive coalfields in England. Population (1971: town) 16,694; (rural district) 39,650.

Thornhill, Sir James (1676–1734), British painter, born at Melcombe Regis, Dorset; studied under High-more. He was much employed by Queen Anne, who commissioned him to paint the interior of the dome of St Paul's, and the princesses' apartments at Hampton Court. Thornhill's other decorative works include the great hall at Greenwich Hospital, the hall at Blenheim, and paintings in Kensington Palace. He also painted altarpieces for All Souls' and Queen's College chapels, Oxford, and portraits of Sir Isaac Newton and Steele. He founded a school of art in Covent Garden, attended by Hogarth, who became his son-in-law. Thornhill (long undervalued) was a very able practitioner of the 'baroque' style of decorative painting.

Bibliography: E. K. Waterhouse, *Painting in Britain, 1530–1790*, 2nd ed. 1962.

Thornhill, picturesque village in Nithsdale District, Dumfries and Galloway Region of Scotland, 24 km north of Dumfries. Near it are Drumlanrig Castle, a seat of the Duke of Buccleuch and Queensberry, and Maxwelton House, birthplace of Annie Laurie. Population 1510.

Thornton Cleveleys. Thornton, a village on the River Wyre away from the sea, joined with Cleveleys on the Fylde coast to form this urban district; it lies to the north of Blackpool and is part of the 25-kilometres-long urban coastal area of the Fylde from FLEETWOOD to LYTHAM ST ANNE'S. It is in the new Wyre borough of LANC-ASHIRE, England. Population (1971) 26,837.

Thornycroft, Sir John Isaac (1843–1928), British naval architect, born in Rome, eldest son of Thomas and Mary Thornycroft, sculptors. A draughtsman in Palmer's shipbuilding yard in Glasgow, he studied under Lord Kelvin and Macquorn Rankine at the university and later worked for John Elder, marine engineer. He established at Chiswick (1866) a yard for launches and torpedo-craft and built the first torpedo-boat of the Royal Navy in 1877. In 1906 he moved his boatyard to Woolston, South-ampton. He supplied the Admiralty with coastal motor boats during the First World War; in 1893 he became a Fellow of the Royal Society, and was knighted in 1902.

Thoroddsen, Jón (1818–68), Icelandic writer, born at Barðastrandarsýsla; he has rightly been called 'the father of the modern Icelandic novel'. His *Piltur og stúlka*, 1850 (*Lad and Lass*, 1890), is a story of young love, while *Maður og kona*, 1876 (*Man and Wife*), also has a romantic plot but is more mature and humorous.

Thorough-Bass (actually the old spelling of through-bass), system of shorthand notation used by composers for keyboard instruments during the early part of the 17th century and persisting until about the middle of the 18th, after which time it was normally used only in church music. Composers, instead of writing out the full harmony they required, often contented themselves with setting out only the chief melodic parts over a single bass-line, under which they wrote figures indicating what the harmony above that bass was to be, but not how it was to be spaced or distributed, much less giving any indication as to how it might be broken up into figuration or made more interesting by such devices as passing-notes, all of which was left to the ingenuity of the player at the harpsichord or organ, who was expected to improvise an interesting part to amplify the music with a background of texture and harmony. The Italian for thorough-bass was *basso continuo*, frequently shortened to *continuo*.

Thoroughbred, see HORSE; HORSE RACING.

Thorow-wax, see BUPLEURUM.

Thorpe, Jim, properly James Francis (1888–1953), great US Indian all-round athlete, born in Oklahoma. He won the pentathlon and the decathlon at the 1912 Olympic Games. Later it was revealed that in 1909 he had played professional baseball and he was deprived of his amateur status following an investigation, his name being struck off the list of Olympic champions. Thorpe played professional football until he was over 40, being voted the greatest football player of the half century.

Thorpe, (John) Jeremy (1929–), British politician, born in London, educated at Eton and Trinity College, Oxford. He was called to the Bar in 1954 and was elected a Liberal MP for North Devon in 1959. Thorpe succeeded Jo GRIMOND as leader of the Liberal party after Grimond's resignation in January 1967. During his leadership the Liberal party enjoyed a considerable revival, culminating in the winning of over six million votes, nearly one-fifth of those cast, in February 1974 and securing the election of 14 MPs. The election of October 1974 was disappointing for the Liberals and Thorpe came under increasing criticism, eventually leading to his resignation in 1976. He was succeeded by David STEEL. His publications include: *To all who are interested in Democracy*, 1951, and (jointly) *Europe: the case for going in*, 1971.

Thorshavn, capital of the FAEROE ISLANDS, situated on the south-east coast of Strømø. It is the island's main harbour and the centre of a thriving fishing industry. Population 10,000.

Thorwaldsen, Bertel (1770–1844), Danish sculptor, born in Copenhagen, son of a poor wood-carver. He studied for a while in the school of art in his birthplace and subsequently went to Italy, where he was influenced by CANOVA, and where he remained for 23 years. Soon after his death a permanent exhibition of his work was formed at Copenhagen, while his statue of Byron is now at Trinity College, Cambridge. The Lion of Luzern is also his work. Thorwaldsen established an international reputation during his lifetime, and examples of his monumental sculpture may be seen on buildings and in churches all over Europe. His art was dominated by classical Greek and Roman sculpture, and his artistic achievement is one of successful imitation and of skill rather than creative vision.

Bibliography: Lives and Studies by J. M. Thiele, 1852–56; A. Rosenberg, 2nd ed. 1901; E. E. Douglas, 1933.

Thoth, early Egyptian deity of wisdom and magic. He invented writing, and was the patron of scribes. Thoth was represented by a baboon or that persistent searcher, the ibis, and associated with the moon, whose phases were used for reckoning. Hermopolis (Ashmunein) was the centre of the cult. With HORUS, Thoth was chief lustrator of OSIRIS. He accompanied the sun god, Ra, in his boat and recorded the result of the weighing of the hearts of the dead.

Thothmes, Tuthmosis or Tehutmes, name of four kings of ancient Egypt, who belong to the 18th Dynasty; *Thothmes I* (c. 1525 BC) finally subdued Kush or Nubia, fixed the boundary of his kingdom at the fifth cataract, and made successful campaigns as far as the Euphrates. He enlarged the Theban temple of Amun at THEBES, which eventually became the largest temple in the world. He was the first king to be interred in the valley of the tombs of the kings at Thebes. *Thothmes II*, his son, reigned less than 10 years. *Thothmes III*, the son of Thothmes II, did little till the death of his step-mother, the despotic Queen Hatshepsut. He fought successful campaigns during the rebellion in Syria, secured the Phoenician ports and received annual tribute from Nubia, Crete, Cyprus, and the Aegean Islands. He built a large number of temples, including the great hall at Karnak, and set up several magnificent obelisks. His conquests enriched the country, and he proved an efficient administrator. His total reign lasted 54 years. *Thothmes IV* was a grandson of Thothmes III; he married a Mitanni princess, and ruled till about 1417 BC.

Thou, Jacques Augusta de (1553–1617), French historian, born in Paris. He helped to draft the Edict of Nantes (1598). He wrote a *Historia sui temporis*, 1604–08, which has considerable historical value.

Thousand and One Nights, see ARABIAN NIGHTS.

Thrace, or Thracia (Modern Greek *Thráki*; Turkish *Trakya*), was the name of the vast tract of country bounded on the north by the Danube, on the south by the Propontis and the Aegean, on the east by the Pontus Euxinus (Black Sea), and on the west by the River Strymon and the easternmost of the Illyrian peoples. It was divided into two parts by Mount Haemus (the Balkans) running from west to east and separating the plain of the lower Danube from the rivers which fall into the Aegean. At a later time the name Thrace was applied to a more limited area. Thrace, in its widest extent, was inhabited in the 5th century BC by different peoples. The earliest Greek poets and other cultural pioneers are represented as coming from Thrace, which received Greek colonies at an early date. The first really historical fact in respect of the Thracians is their subjugation by Megabazus, Darius's general. After the Persians had been driven out of Europe by the Greeks, the Thracians recovered their independence; and at the beginning of the Peloponnesian War almost all the Thracian peoples were united under the dominion of Sitalces, King of the Odrysae, whose kingdom extended from Abdera to the Euxine and

the mouth of the Danube. Sitalces fell in battle against the Triballi in 424, and was succeeded by his nephew, Seuthes, who raised his kingdom to a height of power and prosperity which it had never previously attained. Philip, the father of Alexander the Great, reduced the greater part of Thrace; and after the death of Alexander the country fell to the share of Lysimachus. It subsequently formed a part of the Macedonian dominions.

Thrace was the centre of disturbances in more modern times. It was one of the theatres of war in the Balkan War of 1912 (see BALKAN WARS, THE), when the Bulgarians entered it and defeated the Turks. With help of the Serbs, Bulgaria took Adrianople, and nearly all Thrace was given to Bulgaria by the Treaty of London, which was signed in 1913. However, quarrels with its allies about the division of the conquered territories led to the second Balkan War in 1913, when the Turks recaptured Adrianople and reoccupied Thrace. The treaty of 1913 gave Bulgaria its outlet to the Aegean Sea through Thrace. In 1919, after the First World War, the boundary was again changed, and the sea coast given to Greece, which obtained most of Thrace by 1920. In 1923 the Treaty of Lausanne provided for the relinquishing to Turkey of eastern Thrace as far as the Maritsa, and western Thrace, except Karagach, was given to Greece.

Thrace in Greece has an area of 8586 km² and is divided into three *nomes*—Evros, Rhodope, and Xanthi. Total population 356,000. Eastern Thrace, Trakya, or Turkey-in-Europe, has an area of 23,732 km² and includes the cities of Istanbul and Edirne (formerly Adrianople). Population, 3,210,792.

Thrale, Hester Lynch, see PIOZZI, HESTER LYNCH.

Thrasybulus (d. 388 BC), son of Lycus, an Athenian. He took an active part in overthrowing the Four Hundred in 411 BC, was banished by the THIRTY TYRANTS, but returned to expel them and restore the Athenian democracy in 403. In 390 Thrasybulus commanded the Athenian fleet in the Aegean, and recovered much territory for Athens before his murder by the inhabitants of Aspendus in Pamphylia, 388 BC.

Thread, in textile terms, a continuous cord made by twisting fibres of such natural substances as cotton, wool, silk and flax or those of a man-made fibre such as nylon or polyester. The slightly twisted yarns used for weaving are strictly called threads, but the term is more commonly applied to the stronger and more highly finished cords used for hand or machine sewing.

The cotton or other material is first twisted into yarn, which is doubled upon itself and twisted in the opposite direction to the original twist. The product is then two-ply thread. To make a stronger thread, e.g. six-cord thread, a number of two-ply yarns are twisted by the winding machine again in the opposite direction to the previous twist.

See also EMBROIDERY; FIBRES AND FIBROUS SUBSTANCES; SEWING-MACHINE.

Thread (of screws), see SCREWS, BOLTS, AND NUTS.

Thread Cell, see NEMATOCYST.

Threadneedle Street, in the City of London, running eastward from the BANK OF ENGLAND. At the east end where Threadneedle Street joins Old Broad Street is the new STOCK EXCHANGE Building. The name of the street probably indicates that the property once belonged to the Needlemakers Company, whose sign is three needles in fesse argent. The nickname 'The Old Lady of Threadneedle Street' as applied to the Bank of England was used by Richard Brinsley Sheridan.

Threadworm, see NEMATODA.

Threats are frequently crimes and so punishable by the English courts. A threat with a view to gaining property or money may be BLACKMAIL; it is defined as any unwarranted demand with menaces. The demand is unwarranted unless the person believes he has reasonable grounds for making the demand, and that the use of menaces is a proper means. It is punishable by up to 14 years in jail. A physical threat to injure someone may be an ASSAULT, if he fears immediate personal violence (even if the assailant does not in fact touch him), and threats may open the way to a charge of RAPE. A written threat to murder someone is similarly an offence, and a threat to a witness or juror before or after a trial is punishable as CONTEMPT OF COURT. Threats may be sufficient to enable a defendant to plead duress to a charge that he has committed a crime. It is not clear how serious the threats must be to afford this defence but the seriousness will probably vary with the nature of the charge. Threats may also form the basis of the TORT of intimidation or the tort of inducing a breach of contract.

Three Chapters, Controversy of the, a theological dispute of the 6th century AD which gave rise to the Second Council of Constantinople (553). In the reign of Justinian I, the Monophysites sometimes protested that they could not accept the decrees of Chalcedon which, they alleged, had virtually approved three writers tainted with Nestorianism: Theodore of Mopsuestia, Theodoret, and Ibas, Bishop of Edessa. Justinian therefore issued an edict denouncing the writings concerned, and called upon the bishops of both East and West to subscribe it. The four eastern patriarchs obeyed; but in the West there was strong resistance. After long disputes and negotiations, Justinian summoned the fifth ecumenical council (Constantinople II). Its decrees were accepted in the East, but in the western Church resulted in a schism lasting over a century in north Italy.

Three Choirs Festival, music festival established in 1724. It is held annually, in September, alternately in the cathedrals of Hereford, Gloucester and Worcester. New works from eminent contemporary composers have always been a feature of the festival, the works of Parry, Elgar and Vaughan Williams having especially been promoted there. Orchestral and chamber concerts are also included.

Three-colour Process, see PHOTOENGRAVING.

Three Kings, Feast of, see EPIPHANY.

Three-Mile Limit, see TERRITORIAL WATERS.

Three-phase System, electric supply system to which are connected three alternating electromotive forces of equal peak values of the same frequency but displaced in time phase by one-third of a cycle (120 electrical degrees). In three-phase generators and transformers the ends of each of the three-phase windings may be so connected internally as to make necessary only three external conductors for carrying the current over transmission lines or distribution networks (see ELECTRICAL MACHINES; TRANSMISSION OF ELECTRIC POWER). A fourth conductor is usually added in distribution networks, connected to the 'star' point (neutral) and to earth. If the voltage between the lines of a distribution network is 415 V the voltage between any one of the lines and the fourth conductor (neutral) is $415/\sqrt{3} = 240$ V (see STAR/DELTA). In a three-phase system the power in watts is $V \times I \times \sqrt{3}$, where V and I are line values of voltage and current respectively. It is important to maintain a 'balanced' load in a three-phase four-wire network by loading phases equally as far as possible; the supply authority adopts the necessary measures to arrange this system balance. Three-phase alternating current supply systems are standard over most of the world and in order to ensure correct connection of apparatus such as transformers, the lines are distinguished by labelling and colouring bus-bars and terminals. In the UK the practice is to designate the three phases as 'red', 'yellow', 'blue' and wiring diagrams have the three phases labelled R, Y, B. Phase rotation or sequence, the order in which the three-phase voltages attain maximum value, can be R, Y, B or B, Y, R.

Threnody (Greek *thrēnos*, wailing, and *ōdē*, ode), song of lamentation, especially on a person's death; the term originates in Greek choral odes, but has been applied to a wide variety of poetic forms. Gaelic literature supplies examples in the typical 'keens'. See also DIRGE; ELEGY; GAELIC LANGUAGE.

Thresher Shark, *Alopias vulpes*, a common species of SHARK belonging to the family Alopiidae, suborder Galeoidei. It is found in the Mediterranean and the Atlantic and in most subtropical and temperate seas. Its chief characteristic is a very long tail which is nearly half the total length of about 6 m. The thresher shark follows the shoals of small fish, such as herrings or pilchards, driving them together by lashing its tail.

Threshing, separation of the grain from the straw, or the seed from the haulm. Formerly the operation was performed by the flail, and this laborious but effective implement is still occasionally used by seed growers and on small holdings. The first workable threshing machine was invented by Andrew Meikel about 1786; the modern machine, besides effectively sorting out the products of the sheaf, delivers the straw unbroken and ready for trussing. The machine was at first worked by hand, then by portable steam-engines which were drawn from farm to farm by horses, until they were superseded by self-propelled steam-engines. These, in turn, were followed by tractors, those with Diesel engines appearing to be the most suitable. Water power and even horse gears are occasionally employed, more especially with fixed machines. The corn is passed by hand or self-feeder into the drum mouth and is threshed out by beaters. The straw is passed out after the grain has been shaken away by means of riddles, an air blast from a fan, and rotary screens which grade the corn. The most common of the threshing machine's auxiliaries are the chaff cutter, for cutting oats or barley straw into short lengths for cattle feed; the straw tier, which produces bundles or trusses of straw; the straw baler, which compresses the straw into wire-bound bales; and the huller, which is used for threshing very small seeds. The combine harvester cuts and threshes in one operation and has a threshing mechanism similar to that of a stationary thresher. However, it is not always possible to produce clean grain, because of the quantities of green weeds cut close to the ground which tend to clog the sieves in the machinery, and thus small pieces become included in the threshed grain; for this reason it may be necessary to pass the grain through a separate dressing machine. Since the grain is cut and threshed at the same time, and has no opportunity to dry naturally in the stook and stack, the moisture content may remain high (see REAPING). Unless the grain is then dried artificially in plant installed in the farm buildings for that purpose it may heat or ferment when stored. The straw left by the combine tends to be much broken, but if wanted for litter or fodder it can be collected by a pick-up baler or swept up to a stationary baler or stack. Otherwise it is left to be ploughed in or burnt.

Thrift, sea pink, *Armeria maritima*, a summer-flowering perennial plant of the family Plumbaginaceae. It has slender, stiff, grass-like leaves growing in bundles from the woody branches of the rootstock. The globular heads of soft, funnel-shaped, rosy flowers rise on slender hairy stems from the tufts of leaves. Thrift grows wild on cliffs and rocks in seaside places, and also in mountain districts. *A. plantaginea* is the Jersey thrift.

Thring, Edward (1821–87), British educationist, born in Somerset and educated at Eton and King's College, Cambridge. He was influential in the formation of the Headmasters' Conference (1869), but is perhaps best known for his work as headmaster of Uppingham from 1853 to his death. In the face of prevailing practice he argued in favour of small classes (no more than 30 in a class) and, in boarding schools, small houses. He thought that 400 pupils were the maximum any headmaster could know personally, and hence wished to restrict the size of schools to this number. He insisted that a school should have a variety of studies and occupations. His book, *The Theory and Practice of Teaching*, 1883, was for long regarded as necessary reading for intending teachers.
Bibliography: G. Hoyland, *The Man Who Made a School*, 1946.

Thrips, insect belonging to the order THYSANOPTERA. Thripses are minute, dark-coloured insects, measuring no more than 2–3 mm long. Because of their size they are seldom noticed, or they may be mistaken for a speck of soot or a dust particle. They are abundant during the summer months, when they are found on plants such as primroses and legumes. They are capable of inflicting irritating bites on the human skin. A number of species are pests of flowers, greenhouses and field crops such as onions, pears, cotton and citrus fruits.

Throat, the front of the neck; or the upper part of the respiratory passages in the neck. See LARYNX; PHARYNX; TONSILS.

Thrombin, an ENZYME which plays a crucial role in BLOOD CLOTTING. It is formed only as a result of a complex series of reactions involving a number of plasma proteins and calcium ions. As this sequence normally occurs only at the site of a wound, thrombin (clotting factor IIa) is not present as such, but in the form of its inactive precursor, prothrombin (factor II). For coagulation to occur, thromboplastin (factor III) accelerates the conversion of prothrombin to thrombin, which then in turn catalyses the formation of fibrin (factor Ia) from fibrinogen (factor I). Thrombin is active enough to produce a quantity of fibrin a million times its own weight. The production of prothrombin, and hence of thrombin, is dependent upon a sufficiency of vitamin K; thus a deficiency of this relatively abundant vitamin causes a depletion of this and some other clotting factors.

The clotting mechanism is disturbed in the conditions of (1) THROMBOSIS, when it takes place within the blood vessels, and (2) HAEMOPHILIA, an inherited disease in which the blood continues to flow for a long period even from a small wound. A mucopolysaccharide known as *heparin*, which occurs in many tissues, but most abundantly in the liver, when injected into the bloodstream prevents coagulation by stopping the conversion of prothrombin into thrombin. It is used therapeutically in cases of thrombosis, particularly coronary thrombosis.

Thrombosis, formation of a clot (thrombus) of blood, within a blood vessel or inside a heart chamber. The thrombus is usually attached to the inner lining (intima) of the vessel and obstructs the flow of blood through it. Among the various factors encouraging the process of thrombosis are: (1) damage to the intimal lining of the affected vessel, (2) an increase in the clotting properties of the blood, and (3) stagnation of blood in the vessel affected. The intimal thrombosis can start as a very small lump attached to the damaged part of the intima. Its presence encourages further thrombosis to occur, and has the effect of causing a slow-down of blood flow by reducing the inner diameter of the vessel. Further slowing and extension of the thrombosis occur, encouraging growth of the initially small thrombus, and often leading to almost total blockage of the affected blood vessel. If thrombosis takes place in one of the ARTERIES, the tissues supplied by that artery may be deprived of oxygen and nutrition, causing damage or death of the tissue (gangrene). The severity of the damage depends upon the position and size of the thrombosis, the speed at which it grows and whether the affected area has only one artery or is supplied by an ANASTOMOSIS of blood vessels. If the vessel to a vital organ is affected, e.g. the heart (see CORONARY THROMBOSIS) or the brain (see CEREBRAL HAEMORRHAGE), the person may be severely crippled or killed.

Sometimes a thrombus may contain infective organisms such as bacteria, and 'septic thrombosis' may occur, with the formation of pus and infection of the surrounding tissues.

As the flow of blood is usually much slower in the VEINS than in the arteries, thrombosis occurs more often in veins. It usually occurs in the deeper veins of the legs, sometimes following surgery. Often this only produces an ache, swelling and slight CONGESTION of the affected area, and may heal spontaneously. Sometimes a part of the clot breaks off and circulates in the blood. This is called an embolus (see EMBOLISM). It will soon lodge in a vessel that is too small to allow it to pass, usually in the LUNGS, causing a pulmonary embolus.

Various drugs are used in the treatment of thrombosis

and drugs which break down the clots are currently being tested.

Throtmanni, see DORTMUND.

Throwing events in athletics generally consist of discus, hammer and javelin throwing and putting the shot (or weight). A Scottish variation is 'tossing the caber' (see HIGHLAND GAMES).

Throwing the discus was an event first held in Ancient Greece, though there the discus was thrown from an elevated stand. Discoi were of many different sizes and style of throw rather than distance was an important consideration. The discus is now thrown from a circle 2·50 m in diameter. The discus must land within a 45° sector and, as in the shot and hammer, the thrower must not leave the circle before the implement has landed, and only then from the rear half. This is to prevent following through. The men's modern discus weighs 2 kg, with an outer diameter of 219 mm. The women's discus weighs 1 kg, with a diameter of 180 mm to 182 mm. World records for the men's event: 1925—47·89 m; 1950—56·97 m; 1975—69·10 m. World records for the women's event: 1950—53·25 m; 1975—70·20 m.

Throwing the hammer, possibly originated as an event for blacksmiths, certainly a wooden handle was used; it remains a men's event, unlike discus, javelin and the shot. The modern hammer weighs 7·26 kg; the head, having a diameter of 10·2 cm to 12·0 cm, must be completely spherical in shape. The handle is made of spring steel wire which must not stretch appreciably when the hammer is being thrown. The length of the hammer measured from the inside of the grip must be between 117·5 cm and 121·5 cm. The rules are similar to the discus and shot. A wire cage surrounds the playing area to protect all onlookers. World records: 1925—66·62 m; 1950—78·70 m; 1975—94·08 m.

Throwing the javelin, an event also practised in Ancient Greece, though the construction of the javelin and the method of throw were different. In the Middle Ages the sport consisted of accurately bombarding a target rather than throwing for distance. The javelin was first introduced into the Olympic Games in 1908 though it did not feature in the Amateur Athletic Association Championships until 1914.

The men's javelin weighs 800 g and must be between 260 and 270 cm long. The women's weighs 600 g, length 220 to 230 cm. There is a cord grip at the centre about 15 cm long, by which the javelin must be held during the throw. The throw is made from behind a scratch line which is in fact part of the arc of a circle constructed at the end of a runway 36 m long and 4 m wide. The throw is not a good one unless the tip of the javelin strikes the ground first and the thrower remains behind the arc and within the run-up as he throws. He must not cross the scratch line before the throw has been measured. World records for men: 1925—66·62 m; 1950—78·70 m; 1976—95·48 m. World records for women: 1950—53·41 m; 1975—67·22 m.

Putting the shot (or weight). This event, using large stones, is of great antiquity; the modern event uses a round implement weighing 7·26 kg (for women, 4 kg) which probably owes its size and weight to cannonballs. The shot is made of iron, brass, or any metal not softer than brass, or a shell of such metal filled with lead or other material.

It must be spherical with a diameter between 110 mm and 130 mm (for women, 95 to 110 mm). The surface must be smooth. The shot is put from a circle 2·13 m in diameter, the rules being as for the discus. The shot must be put from the shoulder with one hand only, and must not be brought behind the line of the shoulder. World records for men: 1925—15·54 m; 1950—19·95 m; 1975—21·82 m. World records for women: 1950—15·02 m; 1976—21·89 m.

Thrush, about 300 species of the bird family Muscicapidae, order Passeriformes, with very extensive distribution and of omnivorous diet. The typical genus *Turdus* includes several British species, such as the blackbird, ring ouzel, redwing and fieldfare, to which the name thrush is not commonly applied. The SONG THRUSH, or mavis, is one of the best-known British song-birds. The mistle thrush or holm thrush, *T. viscivorus*, is a larger bird with a slightly forked tail.

Thrush, see CANDIDIASIS; MYCOSIS.

Thucydides (c. 455–c. 401 BC), Greek historian, born at Halimus in Attica. He is said to have been instructed in oratory by Antiphon, and in philosophy by Anaxagoras. He possessed gold mines in that part of Thrace which is opposite the island of Thasos, and there he was a person of the greatest consequence. In the Peloponnesian War he caught the plague, but recovered, and commanded an Athenian squadron of seven ships at Thasos (424). Failing in his attempt to save Amphipolis, he was exiled, and retired to Thrace. He spent 20 years in exile, returning in 404 BC, when a general amnesty was granted on the restoration of the democracy. According to some accounts, he was assassinated at Athens or possibly in Thrace; according to others, he died at Thasos, and his remains were carried to Athens. At all events, his death cannot be placed later than 401. He must be distinguished from his near contemporary, the Athenian statesman Thucydides, who led the opposition against Pericles, and was ostracised in 443 BC.

The Peloponnesian War forms the subject of the history of Thucydides. Though he was engaged in collecting material during the whole of the war, he continued rewriting his history throughout, since he alludes in many parts of it to the conclusion of the war (i. 13; v. 26). He did not, however, live to complete it: the eighth book ends abruptly in the middle of the year 411 BC, seven years before the termination of the war.

The object of the history was to give such a faithful representation of the past as would serve as a guide for the future (i. 22). His observation of human character was profound, and his painstaking accuracy and careful attention to chronology are remarkable. His strict impartiality is another feature of his work. His style is marked by great strength and energy, but he is often obscure, particularly in the speeches.

The Oxford Text, *Thucydides Historia* (Ed. H. Stuart-Jones 1898–1902) was edited with critical additions by J. E. Powell (1942). The translation by Jowett is used in Trevor-Roper (Ed.), *The Great Histories*, 1963.

Bibliography: A. W. Gomme, *A Historical Commentary on Thucydides*, 1945; G. B. Grundy, *Thucydides and the History of his Age*, 1948; F. E. Adcock, *Thucydides and his History*, 1963; H. D. Westlake, *Individuals in Thucydides*, 1968, and *Essays on*

Thucydides

Greek Historians, 1969; A. G. Woodhead, Thucydides on the Nature of Power, 1970.

Thucydides (c. 485–c. 425 BC), son of Melesias, Athenian politician. He was connected by marriage with Cimon, and on Cimon's death in 449 BC he took over the leadership of the opposition to PERICLES. The aggressive, imperialist policy of the Athenian democracy was unpopular with landowners and farmers, who had most to lose in the event of war, and an invasion of Attica by Sparta. These classes therefore formed the nucleus of Thucydides' support, but politically they were at a disadvantage, as most of them lived some distance from the city, and Thucydides was ostracised (see OSTRACISM) in 443 BC, leaving Pericles with no serious rival in Athenian public life. Thucydides may have been the maternal grandfather of the historian Thucydides.

Thugs, roving bands of fanatical murderers and robbers who used to infest parts of central and northern India. Thuggery, as their system was called, had a religious basis; the murdered persons and a certain part of their belongings were regarded by the Thugs as sacrifices to the goddess Kali. The systematic suppression of the Thugs was begun about 1830 by Capt. W. H. Sleeman, Bengal Army (afterwards Maj.-Gen. Sir William Sleeman), and continued for many years afterwards; indeed, the department for the suppression of Thagi and Dakaiti ended only in the 20th century.

Thuja, a genus of six conifers in family Cupressaceae, native to China, Formosa, Japan and North America. They are pyramidal in habit, with scale-like leaves on flattened branchlets. *T. occidentalis* is the American arbor-vitae or white cedar; *T. orientalis*, Chinese arbor-vitae; and *T. plicata*, western arbor-vitae or western red cedar. All are hardy in British gardens.

Thule, name given by the ancient Greeks to the most northerly part of Europe known to them. Pliny said it was an island in the northern ocean discovered by the navigator PYTHEAS of Massilia, six days' sail from the Orcades. Müllenhoff plausibly identifies it with the Shetlands. Procopius and others use the name for Scandinavia. It appears to be a Greek form of the Gothic *Tiel* or *Tiule*, meaning 'remotest land'. See also GREENLAND.

Thulium, metallic chemical element, symbol Tm, atomic number 69, atomic weight 168·9342, belonging to the group of LANTHANIDES. It was discovered in 1879 by Cleve, but was first prepared pure by James in 1911. Its salts are pale green in colour. Thulium is extracted from the minerals gadolinite, euxenite, etc.

Thumbscrew, iron instrument of torture for compressing or breaking the thumbs. It was used by the Spanish Inquisition and in the persecutions of the Covenanters in Scotland, where its last recorded use was towards the end of the 17th century.

Thun, town in the canton of BERN, Switzerland, 23 km south-east of Bern, on the River AAR just below its exit from the Lake of Thun. It is a castle town and has a tourist industry (centre for the Bernese Oberland). The lake is 19 km long and has an area of some 48 km²; maximum depth 217 m. Population (1974) 36,800; mainly German-speaking Protestants.

Thun, lake in the canton of Bern, Switzerland, formed by an expansion of the River AAR. Length 16 km; average width 3 km; greatest depth 215 m; altitude 560 m.

Thunder Bay, city of Ontario, Canada, created in 1970 by the amalgamation of Fort William and Port Arthur. It is situated on the north-west coast of Lake SUPERIOR and is the lakehead terminus of the Canadian National Railway. It is a major wheat exporting port with the biggest number of grain elevators in the world. Its other industries include shipbuilding, timber and wood-working plants, paper and pulp mills. The city's importance has been increased by the ST LAWRENCE SEAWAY, of which it is virtually the terminus. In the vicinity there are deposits of iron pyrites, molybdenum, feldspar for potash, silica for glass, silver, lead, copper, zinc, and gold mines and the largest haematite iron-ore mine in Canada. Lakehead University was founded in 1965. In 1870 Lord Wolseley disembarked troops here from eastern Canada, on the way to quell an Indian rebellion, and named the spot Prince Arthur's Landing, after the Duke of Connaught, later governor-general of Canada. The town of Prince Arthur was incorporated in 1884. Population (city) 107,800; (metropolitan area) 151,500.

Thunderbolt, or thunderstone, common name for objects once thought to have been formed by thunder and lightning, the belief being that thunder somehow sent out a destructive bolt or dart (such as ZEUS's bolts in Greek mythology).

A so-called thunderbolt is really a discharge of lightning from one part of the sky to another, and especially one which strikes the earth, causing damage. Lightning in certain cases does leave behind it a vitrified tube, called a FULGURITE, which is created by vitrification or fusing on the spot where it is found.

The term thunderstone is used especially for objects having more or less a dart or arrow shape, for belemnites, meteorites, and the pyritous nodules to be found in cretaceous rocks.

The thunderbolt myth recurs in many lands and the Sioux consider that lightning enters the ground and scatters there in all directions thunder-bolt stones (flints, etc.), their reason being that these siliceous stones produce a flash when struck. In the traditions of the Finns concerning purification by fire, it became expedient to find a substitute, and hence the healing virtues of the thunderbolt were embodied in the *Keraunia* or thunderstones. The 'holy stones' of the Anglo-Saxons, or 'holed stones', arrow heads, flint knives, and the like worked by prehistoric men were popularly believed to be stones which, falling from heaven, possessed heavenly virtues, which were of great use in all sorts of diseases.

Thunderstorm, a rain, snow, or hail storm with thunder and lightning. LIGHTNING is an electrical discharge which causes rapid expansion and contraction of the air, producing the sound of thunder. The light from a stroke travels at 299,000 km/s, but thunder at only 335 m/s, so that, although both occur simultaneously, thunder is heard some time later, 5 seconds for every 1·6 km away. Since different parts of the lightning flash are at different distances and heights, and the speed of sound decreases with height, the thunder is not normally heard as a single crack but as a succession of rolling sounds. As a rule thunder can be heard only at distances up to 16 km, but this varies with the conditions, and thunder has on occasion been heard up to 300 seconds after the lightning flash—from 96 km away.

Observations in the United States by a close network of ground stations and specially-equipped fighter aircraft have shown that a thunderstorm consists of several convective cells, each up to 24 km in diameter, starting with an up-current extending up to more than 6000 m and often attaining more than 96 km/h. As this air rises, its temperature soon falls to the dew point (see CLOUD) and below, and water droplets condense, forming cloud and eventually raindrops in great quantities. The maximum raindrop size is 5·5 mm diameter, with a maximum falling velocity through the air of 29 km/h; after any further growth the raindrops are deformed and broken (see PRECIPITATION), so that they are carried up into the top parts of the cloud. From there, and even lower levels if the up-current is slanting, the rain can fall into surrounding, initially drier, air into which it begins to evaporate. This air then becomes colder and heavier than its surroundings and generates a down-current which appears at the surface as a cold gust or squall. Although much of the rain is evaporated in maintaining the saturation of the down-current, most reaches the surface, and the heaviest rainfall is observed in this region of cold air. When the down-current reaches the surface it must spread out and can extend as far as 19 km in advance of the thunderstorm. It acts as a cold wedge, and may give the initial upthrust to start new convection cells. Eventually the up-current in the older convection cell fades from the base upwards, and the whole cell then consists of a down-current before dying away completely.

A thundercloud (cumulonimbus) is essentially a gigantic electricity generator which works, like all generators, by separating positive and negative charges. It is now generally agreed that almost all thunderclouds have a preponderance of positive charge at the top and negative charge at the base, but the mechanism by which this distribution is brought about is still a matter of debate. It is clear, however, that the violent up-and-down air currents within the cloud supply the energy necessary to effect the separation of charge. Many theories have been put forward, but, according to accepted recent research, the charge separation is a thermo-electric effect arising when supercooled droplets of water freeze suddenly and disrupt. In a very short period of time the outer shell of a frozen droplet becomes colder than the inner liquid core and is positively charged owing to the greater mobility of the positive (hydrogen) ions. See also ATMOSPHERE; ELECTRICITY, ATMOSPHERIC; LIGHTNING.

Bibliography: L. J. Battan, *The Thunderstorm*, 1964.

Thurber, James Grover (1894–1961), US humorist, born at Columbus, Ohio. Educated at Ohio University, he worked as a journalist and artist, and in 1926 became a leading member of the staff of the *New Yorker* (see NEW YORKER).

In his first book, *Is Sex Necessary?*, 1929, he collaborated with E. B. White. His other works, illustrated with his own drawings, include *The Owl in the Attic*, 1931, *The Seal in the Bedroom*, 1932, *The Middle-Aged Man on the Flying Trapeze*, 1935, *Let Your Mind Alone*, 1937, *The Last Flower*, 1939, *Fables for Our Times*, 1940,

Men, Women, and Dogs, 1943, *The Great Quillow*, 1944, *The Beast in Me and Other Animals*, 1948, *The Thirteen Clocks*, 1950 (a fantasy for children, as is *The Wonderful O*, 1957), *The Thurber Album*, 1952, and *The Thurber Country*, 1953. Together with Elliot Nugent he wrote a successful stage play, *The Male Animal*, 1940. Perhaps Thurber's best known story is 'The Secret Life of Walter Mitty', the tale of an escaper into fantasy. *My Life and Hard Times*, 1933, is autobiographical. His work has been described as a mixture of absurdity, inconsequence, and irony. *The Thurber Carnival*, 1945, is a collection of some of his writings and drawings.

Thurgau (French *Thurgovie*), canton of north-east SWITZERLAND, having Lake Constance and the Rhine to the north and north-east respectively. It is drained by the Thur, Sitter, and Murg. The canton is a prosperous agricultural area famous for its fruit and viticulture. Embroidery, printing, and textiles are the chief industries. The capital is FRAUENFELD. Area 1009 km². Population (1974) 187,800; mostly German-speaking and two-thirds Protestant.

Thurifer (Latin *thus*, incense; *fero*, I bear), the server who bears the incense in Catholic worship.

Thurii, more rarely Thurium (*Terra Nuova*), Greek city in Lucania, founded in 443 BC near the site of the ancient Sybaris. It was founded by colonists from all parts of Greece, among whom were the historian Herodotus and the orator Lysias. The new city rapidly became one of the most important Greek towns in the south of Italy.

Thuringia (German *Thüringen*), name given to a region of central Germany. The region comprised mainly the duchies and principalities which derived from the country allotted to the Ernestine branch of the WETTIN family at the division of the possessions of the house in 1485. The chief states referred to as Thuringia were: Saxe-Weimar, Saxe-Coburg-Gotha, Saxe-Meiningen, Saxe-Altenburg, Schwarzburg-Rudolstadt, Schwarzburg-Sondershausen and the two Reuss principalities (see SAXON DUCHIES). In 1919 the Reuss principalities were merged into one People's State of Reuss, and Coburg elected to merge with BAVARIA. In the same year the seven Thuringian states were amalgamated to form the province of Thuringia. In 1945 Thuringia became a *Land* of East Germany, but in 1952 it was divided into the *Bezirke* of Erfurt, Gera, and Suhl. The most important town in Thuringia was WEIMAR.

Thuringian Forest (German *Thüringer Wald*), range of wooded hills in East Germany, extending for about 130 km south-east to north-west, from the River Werra near Eisenach to the Saale. The highest point is the Grosse Beerberg (980 m) in the north-west.

Thurles, market town of County TIPPERARY, Republic of Ireland, on the River Suir. It is on the main Dublin–Cork road and rail routes. The Catholic Cathedral (1857) was built on the site of the Carmelite foundation (1300). St Patrick's Diocesan College was established in 1837. There are turf workings and coal-mines nearby, and Thurles produces sugar-beet and has wool spinning, food processing and packaging, and mineral water factories. Population 7087.

Thurloe, John (1616–68), English politician, son of an Essex clergyman. He was appointed secretary of the Council of State in 1652, and, effectively, all the principal civil business of the Commonwealth, foreign and domestic, passed through his hands during the next eight years. He organised an intelligence network to uncover the plots of the enemies of the administration. He sat in Parliament (1654–56) and in Cromwell's second council (1657), and was appointed governor of the Charterhouse (1657), and chancellor of Glasgow University (1658). His life was spared at the Restoration and he remained in England although declining to serve Charles II. The *Thurloe Papers* are one of the major original sources for the history of the Protectorate.

Bibliography: D. Underdown, *Royalist Conspiracy in England 1649–1660*, 1960.

Thurlow, Edward Thurlow, 1st Baron (1732–1806), English lawyer, born at Bracon-Ash, Norfolk. Educated at Canterbury Grammar School and at Caius College, Cambridge, he was sent down for insubordination in 1751, without a degree. Called to the Bar, 1754, he took silk in 1762. In 1768 he became Tory MP for Tavistock, and his speech in the same year in the Douglas Peerage case greatly enhanced his reputation. As a zealous supporter of Lord North he became solicitor-general in 1770 and attorney-general the following year, supporting the government's stand against the rights of juries in cases of libel and the liberty of the press. He won over George III by upholding his American policy and sharing the King's hostility towards the North American colonies. In 1778 he became lord chancellor and was raised to the peerage. While retaining office under the Rockingham government he opposed all its measures in a spirit of violent factiousness. Under Fox and North, however, he was forced to resign, but returned to the Woolsack under Pitt, when he once more began to undermine the influence of his colleagues. Eventually, when he openly attacked Pitt's National Debt Redemption Scheme, the King agreed to Thurlow's removal (1792). He was the patron of Dr Johnson and of George Crabbe.

Thurmayr, Johann, see AVENTINUS.

Thurn and Taxis, a powerful south German and Bohemian family, whose most famous member, Count Matthias, commanded the Bohemian forces at the outbreak of the Thirty Years' War, and later served Denmark and Sweden. The princes (after 1695) of Thurn and Taxis claimed a hereditary right over the administration of postal affairs in Central Europe, having established posts as early as 1460. The last vestige of these rights disappeared in 1866 with their purchase by the North German Federation.

Thurrock, town in ESSEX, England, created as an urban district in 1936 by the amalgamation of the former urban districts of Grays, Thurrock, Tilbury, and Purfleet, and the rural district of Orsett. Industries include the manufacture of cement, soaps, footwear, detergents, and margarine, oil refining and storage, and the excavation of sand and gravel. A portion of Roman tesselated pavement and other antiquities have been found at Grays. In Hangman's Wood, Little Thurrock, are a celebrated group of dene holes. A road tunnel connects Thurrock and Dartford on the south bank of the Thames. Population (1971: district) 125,000.

See also TILBURY FORT AND DOCKS.

Thursday, fifth day of the week. It is named after Thor, the Scandinavian god of thunder. In the Roman calendar the fifth day was Jupiter's Day, *dies Jovis*.

Thursday Island, lies 40 km off the northern tip of Cape York Peninsula, Queensland, Australia; it is the centre of the Torres Straits pearling industry. Area 3·8 km^2. Population 2350, most of which is Aboriginal.

Thursley (from Thor's lea), village in Waverley District of Surrey, England, near Hindhead, with a picturesque common, parish church with Saxon elements, and good vernacular architecture. Population (1971) 620.

Thurso, small town of Caithness District, Highland Region, Scotland. It stands on the north coast of Scotland, 140 km north-east of Inverness. Thurso was once the centre of Norse power on the mainland in the early 11th century and afterwards until the Battle of Largs. The town houses workers from the Dounreay nuclear station. Its former industry of quarrying and exporting Caithness flagstones has declined. Population 9087.

Thylacine, or Tasmanian wolf, *Thylacinus cynocephalus*, a carnivorous mammal of order MARSUPIALIA, found in Tasmania. It somewhat resembles a wolf. The fur, however, is close and short, and the tail long and tapering; its fur is grey-brown and striped with black. The four young are carried in the pouch until they outgrow it. The species is probably extinct now.

Thyme, *Thymus*, a genus of small-leaved aromatic plants in family Labiatae (deadnettle family), with rose-coloured, white or heliotrope flowers. The two British species are *T. pulegioides* and the creeping wild thyme, *T. serpyllum*, of which the lemon-scented thyme of gardens is a variety. The thyme used for seasoning and flavouring is *T. vulgaris*, a native of southern Europe.

Thymus Gland, a roughly triangular lymphoid organ which lies in the chest immediately behind the upper part of the breastbone. It reaches its greatest size in relation to the rest of the body at two years of age and thereafter only grows slowly. After puberty the thymus ceases to grow and gradually becomes smaller. The rôle of the thymus is still not completely understood.

The thymus is the first LYMPHOID TISSUE to develop, appearing in the human embryo during the eighth week of pregnancy. It has long been associated with the production of LYMPHOCYTES both pre- and post-natally, although there is some dispute as to whether the lymphocytes actually originate in the thymus. There is clear evidence that, in post-natal animals at least, there are primitive cells which develop in the bone marrow and then circulate to the thymus where they develop into 'T-lymphocytes'. Some of these T-lymphocytes then migrate to 'thymus-dependent' zones of lymph nodes and the spleen.

The explosion of research in this field resulted from the finding in 1961 that if the thymus is removed from a newborn animal, its blood and lymphoid tissue later contained fewer lymphocytes than normal. Furthermore, the thymectomised animals showed impaired immunological development, particularly in their ability to reject transplanted skin. Before 1961, the thymus had only been removed from more mature animals, without any serious consequences. It was generally assumed that the impaired immunological reactions of animals thymectomised at birth resulted directly from their reduced lymphocyte population. However, a series of experiments by Osoba and Miller has suggested that this may not be the complete explanation. They have proposed that the thymus releases a hormone that influences the immunological development of other lymphoid tissue during the first few weeks of life.

Children born without a thymus gland have Di George's syndrome and do not develop CELL-MEDIATED IMMUNITY; they are thus more susceptible to fungal and viral diseases.

Thyroid Gland. One of the ENDOCRINE GLANDS, the thyroid is situated in the front of the neck; it consists of two lobes and is applied to the front of the larynx. It also (in the case of man) contains two to six PARATHYROID GLANDS whose role is quite separate. The most important activity of the gland is to manufacture the two thyroid hormones: tri-iodothyronine and tetra-iodothyronine (thyroxine).

1.
$$HO-\!\!\bigcirc\!\!-O-\!\!\bigcirc\!\!-CH_2\,CH\,(NH_2)\,COOH$$
3, 5, 3'-tri-iodothyronine (T_3)

2.
$$HO-\!\!\bigcirc\!\!-O-\!\!\bigcirc\!\!-CH_2\,CH\,(NH_2)\,COOH$$
3, 5, 3', 5',-tetra-iodothyronine (T_4)

Since both of these hormones require iodine for their synthesis, the thyroid is very dependent on the availability of iodine in the diet. Iodine (see MINERALS IN FOOD) is present in particularly high concentrations in sea food. After being absorbed by the intestine, the iodine passes into the blood stream and is 'trapped' by the thyroid gland, and is then incorporated into the molecules of the thyroid hormones (T_3 and T_4). Unlike most endocrine glands, the hormones are stored within the substance of the gland, contained in the interstices of a storage colloid called thyroglobulin. T_3 and T_4 are released from thyroglobulin under the influence of a hormone produced by the anterior pituitary gland, thyroid stimulating hormone (TSH). The system is one of negative feedback, and is described in more detail under HORMONE, HYPOTHALAMUS, and HYPOTHYROIDISM.

The effects of T_3 and T_4 on the body are very profound. The two hormones speed up almost every biochemical process, and are essential for normal growth. The two hormones seem to be universally distributed throughout the animal kingdom, and one of the first of their activities to be described was their rôle in the metamorphosis of tadpoles into frogs.

Thyrotoxicosis, see HYPERTHYROIDISM.

Thysanoptera, an order of the class Insecta, subclass PTERYGOTA. These are the thripses. They are small insects measuring 0·5 mm to 0·8 mm in length with short antennae of six to ten segments, and asymmetrical, piercing mouthparts. The two pairs of wings, when present, are very narrow with fringed margins giving a hairy appearance. The wings are interlocked by several hooked spines on the hindwing, or may be reduced or absent. Metamorphosis is complete, with one or two pupal stages.

Yellow, brown or black in colour, they are found on many types of vegetation feeding on plant sap. Several species are important as vectors of plant viruses, others are destructive to many crops of importance to man. Still others are predacious on other insects, feeding on their body fluids and will sometimes probe other animals with which they come in contact, including man, although this is accidental. The nymphs resemble the adults, but pass through at least one, sometimes two, quiescent pupal stages.

Thysanura, the three-pronged bristletails, an order of the class Insecta, subclass APTERYGOTA. They are wingless insects with mandibulate (chewing) mouthparts. The eyes may be present or absent. There are paired appendages on the abdomen, which terminate in a pair of cerci composed of many segments, and a segmented median process, giving the three-pronged appearance. This order contains the most primitive insects.

Recent research has shown that the order as viewed earlier in fact consists of two distinct lineages, now distinguished as the orders Microcoryphia (with large compound eyes and long processes on abdomen and legs; families Machilidae and Meinertellidae) and Thysanura (with small or no compound eyes, and small processes on abdomen only; silverfish, firebrats and familiar bristletails—families Lepismatidae and Nicoletiidae). Members of the two orders range from minute to moderately large, the maximum size being 2 cm. They are widely distributed, living under stones, dead wood, and leaves. There are approximately 350 species, three of which are domestic pests mainly of nuisance value, although they can cause damage to books and paper. They are the common silver-fish, *Lepisma saccharina* and *Ctenolepisma longicaudata*, which are usually found in cool moist situations, and the fire-brat, *Thermobia domestica*, which, preferring warmer situations, is a pest of bakehouses and kitchens.

See also DIPLURA.

Thyssen, Fritz (1873–1951), German industrialist, born at Mülheim, Ruhr, son of August Thyssen (1842–1926), one of the founders of the German steel industry. His father left him a 26 per cent interest in the vast Vereinigte Stahlwerke, or German steel cartel, and he became its chairman of directors after 1926. He was among the first German industrialists to aid Hitler's rise to power, and after Hitler became chancellor Thyssen was rewarded by the reorganisation of his virtually bankrupt company at the expense of the Reich, becoming, in effect, economic dictator of the Ruhr industrial region. From 1936, however, he began to disagree with Hitler's policies, and at the outbreak of war in September 1939 he fled abroad. After the war a denazification tribunal deprived him of part of his property, and Thyssen died in Buenos Aires. He wrote *I Paid Hitler*, 1941.

Tiara, jewelled head ornament (for which see below), and specifically the papal triple crown, which is a symbol of sovereign power (not sacred like the mitre), a high cap

Tiber. The river flowing through Rome. *(Topham/Fotogram)*

of gold cloth or metal, encircled by three coronets and surmounted by a gold cross.

In a general sense a tiara is a jewelled head ornament, usually of precious metal or diamonds, worn on the forepart of the head. It often begins in a foliage or scroll design at the sides of the head, rising to a higher central group. Diadems of flat bands of gold links were found in the ruins of Troy, and elaborate gold head-dresses of great magnificence, dating from 3500 BC, were found in the tombs of the Chaldean kings. The modern gem-set tiara dates from a Napoleonic court fashion. It is worn on full-dress occasions.

Tiaret, town and department of north-central ALGERIA, extending from the Tell to the Saharan Atlas. The town is situated in the Tell Atlas and has therefore a cooler climate. It is a major agricultural centre for the Sersou plain mainly trading in cereals and livestock but Arabian horses are also bred. Area (department) 25,660 km². Population (town) 37,060; (department) 404,000.

Tiber (Italian *Tevere*; Latin *Tiberis*), third longest river of ITALY, rising in the APENNINES on the eastern borders of TUSCANY and flowing generally south past Perugia and ROME to the Tyrrhenian Sea near Lido di Roma (see OSTIA). It is joined near Narni by the Nera, its most important tributary; other tributaries are the Aniene, the Chiani, and Paglia. The Tiber empties into the sea via two channels: the southern one (*Fiumara*) is silted up; the other (*Fiumicino*) is canalised. On the latter branch, close to the international airport, is the hexagonal port built by Trajan. The land mass between the channels was once known as the Sacred Island, or the Isle of Venus. Small ships can sail up river as far as Rome. Length 400 km.

Tiberias, capital of Galilee; town on the west shore of the Sea of Galilee, Israel, 207 km below sea-level. It was founded by Herod Antipas, AD 26, and named in honour of the Roman Emperor Tiberius. After the destruction of Jerusalem in AD 70, many Jewish scholars and rabbis settled in the town and a large proportion of the Jerusalem TALMUD was written there. The city fell to the Arabs in 687, and later to the crusaders who fortified it and built a church, but they lost the place in 1187. Almost the whole of the old city, with its girdle of walls, is built of black basalt. The modern residential quarter stands on

the hills to the west of Tiberias. To the south are the renowned hot baths, famous from Roman times and praised by Pliny; they have curative properties for cases of rheumatism and skin infections. Near the baths are the tombs of the famous rabbis, Jochanan B. Zakkai, Maimonides, Me'ir Baal ha-Ness, and Akiba. In 1968 the population was 23,600. At the north end of the Lake are the traditional sites of the Sermon on the Mount and the excavated and restored synagogue of Capernaum.

Tiberine Republic, see ITALY, *Modern History*.

Tiberius, full name Tiberius Claudius Nero Caesar (42 BC–AD 37), Roman Emperor, AD 14–37, son of Tiberius Claudius Nero and Livia, afterwards wife of AUGUSTUS. Tiberius was born 16 November 42 BC; he was carefully educated and became well acquainted with both Greek and Latin literature. At the age of 22 he was sent by Augustus on a diplomatic mission to Armenia, and in 13 BC he was consul with P. Quinctilius Varus. Three years before this, Tiberius with his brother, Nero Claudius Drusus, had been entrusted with the defence of the northern frontiers, and during the years 12–9 BC he fought successful campaigns against the Dalmatians and Pannonians. After the death of Drusus in the latter year, Tiberius took command in Germany, and remained there until 6 BC, when he was granted the *tribunicia potestas* for five years and retired with the emperor's permission to Rhodes. This sudden withdrawal from public affairs at the age of 36 was dictated by domestic unhappiness. Tiberius was married to Vipsania Agrippina, to whom he was deeply attached and who had borne him a son, Drusus. But in c. 12 BC Augustus compelled him to divorce Vipsania and marry the emperor's own daughter Julia. In AD 4 he was adopted by Augustus and given command of the armies in northern Germany. Except for occasional brief visits to the capital he remained there for seven years. On the death of Augustus (AD 14) he returned home, and the skilful management of his mother Livia secured the throne for him without opposition.

Tiberius was a suspicious character, and he began his reign by putting to death Postumus Agrippa, the surviving grandson of Augustus. Then he proceeded to make his rule absolute. He governed with justice and moderation from AD 14 to 23 (Tacitus, *Annals*, i–iii), and in 26 left Rome, never to return. He went first to Campania on the pretext of dedicating temples, but in the next year he moved to the island of Capri off the Campanian coast. Meanwhile his minister SEJANUS, in whose hands the government of the state had long rested, was plotting to obtain for himself the imperial throne. Tiberius realised the situation in AD 31, and had him put to death.

In the last six years of his life, his mind was almost certainly unbalanced, and in AD 37 he was found dead, smothered, it was said, by order of Macro, the praetorian prefect. The character of Tiberius has been much disputed. Tacitus and Suetonius paint it in the darkest colours, but it has been defended by many historians from Merivale onwards.

Bibliography: R. S. Rogers, *Studies in the Reign of Tiberius*, 1972; C. E. Smith, *Tiberius and the Roman Empire*, 1972.

Tibesti Mountains, range of the central SAHARA, on the borders of Libya, Niger, and Chad. They are some 500 km long and 300 km wide and their highest peak (3415 m) is the highest point in the Sahara. The mountains are a block of volcanic rocks that have forced their way through the surrounding sandstone plateau and now form a residual mass. Dry watercourses in the region would appear to indicate that the climate was formerly less arid.

Tibet (Chinese *Sitsang*), autonomous region of the People's Republic of CHINA, formerly a dependency of China. It is bounded by the KUNLUN MOUNTAINS on the north, separating it from the SINKIANG UIGHUR Autonomous Region, and bounded by Tsinghai and Szechwan provinces to the east, by the Himalayas to the south, and by Kashmir on the west. The boundaries are, in some cases, ill defined, e.g. with Bhutan where the bamboo forests are regarded as the frontier.

Tibet may be divided into three major physical regions: (*a*) the Northern Plains (Ch'iang T'ang), a region of plains and valleys, averaging over 4880 m and rising several hundred metres higher in its peaks and ridges, the most important of which are the Nien-chen-tang-la and the Hlunpo-Gangri ranges. This region is bounded on the north by the Kunlun and the steppes of TSAIDAM, and extends south to the valley of the upper Brahmaputra. (*b*) South Tibet consists of the valleys of the upper INDUS and SUTLEJ in the west and the great valley of the BRAHMAPUTRA (or Tsangpo) in the south and east. The three great rivers all have their source in the same region, near the

Tibet. Page from a Tibetan Bible. (*British and Foreign Bible Society*)

sacred Lake Manasarowar. (*c*) East Tibet comprises the mountains and valleys lying between the Ch'iang T'ang and the Chinese frontier. On the eastern slopes rise the great rivers of South-East Asia, the SALWEEN, MEKONG and YANGTZE KIANG; somewhat to the north rises the Hwang Ho. The Northern Plains are treeless owing to the great elevation; vegetation is scanty grass, but sufficient to graze large numbers of yaks, asses, goats, sheep, and other animals. Because of the rigours of the climate this region, which covers almost two-thirds of Tibet, is very thinly populated. South Tibet is Tibet proper, and here are found the chief towns, LHASA (the capital), SHIGATSE, and GYANGTSE. East Tibet is a land of considerable natural resources; grazing is abundant, agriculture is possible, and mineral wealth is known to be considerable. See also ATLAS 36.

Gold is found in Tibet, but amounts extracted are now small. Iron pyrites is found and lapis-lazuli and mercury in small quantities, also salt and borax among the lakes of the north. The climate varies considerably, though for the most part it is cold and dry. It is influenced by the south-west monsoon, and high winds are frequent. In certain districts the rainfall is very high, and in parts extremes of cold and heat are felt. Sheep and cattle are reared, also goats, pigs, and poultry; horses, mules, and donkeys are used. There are innumerable species of wild animals.

Trade is carried on principally with Szechwan, Sinkiang, Tsinghai, Inner Mongolia, Nepal, India, and Indochina. The Tibetans are keen traders, and the country is well supplied with trade routes. There is the Srinagar–Leh–Shigatse route, which is joined at Leh by the 'Hindustan–Tibet' road via Simla. But the most important route from India is from Kalimpong (Darjeeling district) across the Dzelep La via the CHUMBI VALLEY to Phari and thence by motor road to Lhasa. From Lhasa two motorways were built in 1955: one strikes north, passing the Tsaidam basin to join the railway junction at Lanchow in Kansu; the other goes due east via Chamdo and Tatsienlu (Kang-ting) to Ch'eng-tu, the railway centre in Szechwan. Tatsienlu is an important entrepôt of trade and lies on the ethnographic frontier between Tibet and China. Here the wool of Tibetan sheep is exchanged for Chinese tea, which the Tibetans prefer to Indian. A third highway was built in the late 1950s from Pulan Dzang in West Tibet to Karghalik in Sinkiang. This is the road which passes through disputed territory in Aksai Chin. Motor cars and lorries are becoming more frequent, and the price of industrial goods from other parts of China has consequently been greatly reduced. An air service between Lhasa and Peking and Lhasa and India was inaugurated in 1956, and both the Dalai Lama and the Panchen Lama visited India in that year by flying over the Himalayas. In recent years, however, the Lhasa–India service has been suspended.

The chief imports are silk, carpets, gold lace, tea, porcelain, leather, cotton goods, horses, and sheep, and the chief exports are wool and woollen goods, salt, rugs, furs, drugs, borax, and some gold and silver.

Since the late 1950s there have been considerable efforts made to develop agriculture in South Tibet. Some new settlements have been established, tea has been introduced into the crop system, and the production of such crops as barley, wheat, and rye increased. A good deal of prospect-

Tibet

ing for minerals has also been carried out. Area 1,221,700 km². Population (estimated 1971) 1,300,000. The population mainly lives in the districts between Lhasa and the Chinese border.

Bibliography: G. Tucci, *Tibet: Land of Snows*, 1967; C. Bell, *Religion of Tibet*, 1969; B. H. Hodgson, *Essays on the Languages, Literatures and Religions of Tibet and Nepal*, 1972; D. Norbu, *Red Star over Tibet*, 1974.

Archaeology. Prior to China's annexation of Tibet, archaeological investigations were prohibited by religious custom, and our knowledge of the subject is therefore based on reports of travellers in the area. The only exception is provided by Aufschnaiter's excavation of Neolithic tombs in the Lhasa area. These were of a complex structure containing human remains and pottery. Similar tombs exist throughout the country, identifiable by stone circles on the surface. Other stone circles, containing standing monoliths in their centre, are thought to have had a ritual purpose. Their shape is later echoed by the apparently circular design of the pre-Buddhist temples of the Bon tradition. It would appear that Tibet's megalithic proto-culture evolved out of neolithic traditions which had moved from the Kokonor region into central Tibet and into Kashmir and Spiti. Research into the subject, however, has been so negligible as to preclude firm conclusions. Surface finds include small metal objects bearing motifs that link them to the art of the Central Asian steppes. Metal-forging itself existed in Tibet at an early date. Such objects and the stone axeheads that are turned up in fields are regarded locally as powerful talismans. The greatest archaeological site of Tibet's historical period is undoubtedly that of the royal tombs at Yarlung. The largest is the 'Red Tomb' of King Songtsen Gampo (d. 649) around which are grouped those of his successors. Elaborate funeral cults involving human and animal sacrifices are attested to in the early records. Despite the activity of tomb robbers, proper investigations should eventually reveal a great deal concerning their structure and content.

Architecture. Tibetan architecture of all periods, whether domestic, military or religious, is characterised by massive, inward sloping walls. This distinctive feature, combined with the Tibetans' fine instinct for the siting of their buildings, taking every advantage of the lie of the land, gives them the appearance of growing spontaneously out of the ground. The most famous example of this is the Potala Palace, residence of the Dalai Lamas, completed in 1694. The decorative features of this magnificent building, such as its 'pagoda roof', derive ultimately from Indian, Nepalese and Chinese models. The oldest temples in Tibet, up to the 7th century AD, were of much less ambitious proportions though the most revered of these, the Jo-khang of Lhasa, was later enlarged and restored many times. During Trisong Detsen's reign (740–c. 798) the first monastery, Samyé, was built under the direction of an Indian teacher, Śāntarakshita, and is said to have been modelled on the Indian Buddhist monastery of Odantapuri in Bihar. Its ground plan consisting of a central building (its three stories constructed in Indian, Chinese and Tibetan styles) with its four sides aligned to the four quarters follows the arrangement of a *mandala* ('sacred circle'). During this early period the STUPA was introduced together with its rich and varying symbolism. Known as *chöten* in Tibetan,

these beautiful edifices that everywhere enhance the Tibetan landscape serve to represent to the traveller and pilgrim the ultimate spiritual essence of the Buddha. The later religious architecture is typified by spectacular temples built on high cliffs and greatly expanded monastic complexes, such as those of the 'universities' of Sera, Ganden and Drepung, near Lhasa.

Art. Tibetan art is basically religious in inspiration and serves as a ritual and meditational aid, its scope and subject matter therefore reflecting all the complexities of Tantric Buddhism. Although certain lamas are known to have composed *thangkas* (painted wall hangings) on the basis of divine dreams and visions, even these conform strictly to a carefully prescribed iconographic code as received from Indian traditions. Tibetan scholars themselves recognise the existence of at least six major styles of painting which have at different times shown influences drawn variously from India, China, Nepal, Kashmir and Khotan. This fusion of styles produced an art which in the end remains distinctly Tibetan in all its expressions. The great STUPA at Gyantse known as the Kumbum, completed in 1427, is considered the finest example of Tibetan art, its magnificent frescoes harmonising all the influences hitherto adopted. The first source of inspiration for the plastic arts, in particular for the metal casting of Buddhist images, seems to have been provided by the Newari artisans of Nepal. During the MING dynasty close diplomatic relations and a frequent exchange of images took place between Tibet and China that led to a special Sino-Tibetan style in bronze statuary. Painted clay images, some of enormous dimensions, are also met with in Tibet. Among the applied arts, weaving was practised throughout the country to produce carpets whose techniques of manufacture were derived from the Iranian world and whose motifs were adapted from those used on Chinese carpets. The mobile arts of music, dancing and drama are perhaps the one sphere in which the

Tibet. A water flask of iron encrusted with silver, brass, and copper. From Chamdo, East Tibet, 19th century. (*Victoria and Albert Museum, London*)

Tibet. ABOVE The Potala, the former winter palace of the Dalai Lamas in Lhasa, now a museum of Tibetan culture and religion. BELOW Sheep on the northern plains; the shepherds live in summer tents. *(Camera Press)*

Tibet. A 'tangka', or painted wall hanging, for a temple. This one dates from the 17th or 18th century, and depicts Vajrabhairava. *(Victoria and Albert Museum, London)*

Tibetans retained indigenous traditional forms intact with little apparent influence drawn from outside.

Language. As one of the principal Tibeto-Burman languages, Tibetan forms part of the broad Sino-Tibetan family. Basically mono-syllabic, it is spoken not only by the inhabitants of Tibet itself but also by many peoples beyond its political boundaries. Although considerable differences exist between the regional dialects (to the extent, in some cases, of mutual incomprehensibility) the official Lhasa tongue became at an early date the *lingua franca* among educated classes. The Tibetan script, an 8th-century adaptation of a northern form of the Indian Gupta alphabet, has 30 letters and 4 vowel signs. Tibetan orthography has changed very little since it was first devised and as such preserves many obsolete consonants no longer pronounced except in the peripheral areas of Ladakh and Amdo.

Literature. Almost exclusively religious, Tibetan literature can be conveniently divided into two categories, indigenous and non-indigenous. Foremost in the latter stand the *Kanjur* (the Translated Words of the Buddha) and the *Tenjur* (the Translated Commentaries), comprising some 4569 translations from SANSKRIT. Alongside the scholastic and ritual works which the Tibetans themselves composed, drawing heavily on Indian inspiration, there exists a rich fund of historical and biographical writings and of oral literature, such as the epic of Gesar. The discovery of ancient Tibetan documents at Tun-Huang has added greatly to our knowledge of the early literature. Following the Chinese annexation of Tibet, there has been rapid growth of a modern literary style and the re-emergence of many rare works brought out by refugees.

Tibetan History. Little is known of the early history of Tibet, except what can be gleaned from a study of the T'ang Annals and the cache of ancient Tibetan documents discovered at Tun-huang. In 639 Songsten Gampo founded Lha-ldan, which later became Lhasa, and also introduced Buddhism into the country. In 641 Songsten married Princess Wen Cheng of the T'ang Imperial House; her statue is still kept in the Potala in Lhasa. Tribute was paid to the Chinese court as late as 672; but from 676 onwards Tibet made successive raids on the north-west border of China, gradually encroaching further and further into the territory of the T'ang Empire until it controlled almost the whole of Kansu and the greater portion of Szechwan and Yunnan. China was eventually forced to pay an annual tribute of 50,000 rolls of silk to Tibet. In 821 a peace treaty between China and Tibet was agreed, the terms of which were inscribed on a huge stone pillar in Lhasa. Chinese annals record that Tibet declined in 866, probably due to constant warfare with its western neighbours.

From the 5th to the 9th century Tibet was a monarchy, which eventually disintegrated owing to opposition among the nobles to the increase of temporal power among the priesthood. The period of disunion lasted from the 9th to the 13th century. Atisha, the Indian Buddhist, came to Tibet in 1042 and is credited with a great revitalising of Tibetan Buddhism. In 1253 all the eastern part of the country was conquered by KUBLAI KHAN, and it was he who first placed the government in the hands of the LAMAS. The first priest-king was the abbot of

the Sakya lamasery, who had converted Kublai. After the decline of Sakya power in Tibet there followed a period of loose hegemonies during which the Phamodrupa, Ringpung, and Tsangpa princes succeeded each other in their control of the country. The degeneration of some of the ancient so-called 'Red-Hat' sects led to the formation of the strict 'Yellow-Hat' sect founded by Tsong-kha-pa (b. 1359), who built the Ganden monastery in the early 15th century. Tsong-kha-pa's disciple, Gentun Drupa, was the first Dalai Lama incarnation; but it was only the fifth Dalai Lama, Ngawang Lobsang Gyamtso, abbot of Drepung monastery, who achieved complete religious and political ascendancy in Tibet, in the 17th century, with the help of Mongol armies. It was not until 1720 that the country was finally brought under the influence of the Manchu Dynasty.

In 1774 Warren Hastings made amicable contacts with the Panchen Lama, then the regent of Tibet. But these came to nothing of a permanent nature owing to Tibetan suspicion that the British had fomented a Nepalese invasion of Tibet in 1792, and throughout the 19th century it proved impossible to come to any sort of agreement at all. India had always been anxious to open up trade with Tibet, and between 1872 and 1886 three different missions were organised, but were abandoned. In 1888 the Chinese invaded Sikkim and a military expedition was sent to drive them out, which resulted in a treaty (1890–93). It appeared to the British authorities that the lamas, taking offence at not having been consulted in the matter, revenged themselves by trying to bring about a treaty with Russia. In fact no such treaty was envisaged. Further inroads were made into Sikkim, and Lord Curzon, then viceroy of India, came to the conclusion that strong measures were necessary. Col. (afterwards Sir) F. Younghusband was sent with an escort to see if he could come to terms, but he was unable to do anything. It was then decided to send an armed expedition, and in December 1903 Col. Younghusband, with Gen. Ronald Macdonald in command of the troops, set out, and after some severe fighting they reached Lhasa in August 1904, and the Dalai Lama fled. Peace was concluded by a treaty which provided against further incursions into Sikkim and established British trade markets, and also prevented any foreign power receiving concessions in the country; the Tibetans also had to pay an indemnity. A treaty with Russia was concluded in 1907, in which it was agreed that no concessions should be sought by either power, and no expeditions dispatched without the consent of both countries, for a term of three years, and Chinese suzerainty over Tibet was recognised.

In 1909 the Dalai Lama returned to Lhasa but fled to British protection in India after the Chinese invaded Tibet with a force that they claimed was intended to 'police the trade marts'. In his absence the Dalai Lama was declared deposed. After the Chinese revolution of 1911 the Chinese agreed (1912) to leave the country and the Dalai Lama returned. In July 1912 the Chinese government sent out another expedition with the object of reconquering Tibet, but in consequence of a memorandum sent to China by the British government, drawing attention to the Anglo-Chinese treaty of 1906, it was withdrawn. A conference was held at Simla, 1913–14, between Britain, China, and Tibet, but the convention which was then drawn up assuring autonomy to Tibet was not ratified by China.

Tibetan Book of the Dead

Further trouble arose between Tibet and China in 1917, and in 1920 the British representative in Tibet was invited to negotiate for peace at Lhasa. No final settlement was reached. Despite its inability to gain international recognition of its sovereignty, Tibet demonstrated from 1913 to 1950 the conditions of statehood as generally accepted under international law, and clearly enjoyed at the very least a *de facto* independence.

In 1933 the 13th Dalai Lama died and a regent assumed control. In 1939 a new and very youthful Dalai Lama was discovered and installed with the customary ceremony. The Tibetan government admitted to Lhasa a Chinese mission of condolence on the death of the 13th Dalai Lama, and from 1939 the Republic of China had a commissioner at Lhasa. The regent, who acted on behalf of the minor Dalai Lama, the temporal and spiritual head of the country, was assisted by a council (*Kashag*) of four ministers (*Shapes*). There was also a national assembly (*Tsongdu*), an advisory body containing most of the monastic and lay officials. Tibet had its own national defence force, issued its own postage currency, and passports and had direct trade relations with its neighbours.

In 1950 the Peking government sent an army from Szechwan to Tibet, but halted it at the border. The Panchen Lama pleged his loyalty to the new government and went to Peking via Tsinghai. The Dalai Lama was urged to send his representatives to Peking for negotiation, and an agreement was reached in May 1951, in which *inter alia*, the Peking government granted the Tibetans the right of national regional autonomy within China. Peking, though, retained control of defence and foreign affairs. In 1954 both Dalai Lama and Panchen Lama went to Peking as Tibetan representatives in the National People's Congress, and were elected vice-chairmen of the Congress. In March 1959 smouldering discontent with the Chinese burst into large-scale revolt, particularly serious in eastern Tibet, during which the Dalai Lama fled to India. After the revolt was suppressed the Chinese imposed direct control. Approximately 80,000 Tibetan refugees are now settled in India, and the Himalayan states of Nepal, Sikkim, and Bhutan.

See also TIBET.

Bibliography: C. Bell, *Tibet Past and Present*, 1924; H. E. Richardson, *A Short History of Tibet*, 1962; W. D. Shakabpa, *Tibet: A Political History*, 1967; G. Tucci, *Tibet, Land of Snows*, 1967; D. L. Snellgrove and H. E. Richardson, *A Cultural History of Tibet*, 1968; R. A. Stein, *Tibetan Civilization*, 1972; M. Pallis, *Peaks and Lamas*, 3rd ed. 1974.

Tibetan Book of the Dead, English rendering of the Tibetan *Bardo Thödol*, meaning 'Liberation by Hearing on the After-Death Plane'. The *Bardo Thödol* is a Tantric work (see TANTRIC BUDDHISM) of the Nyingmapa School of Buddhism (see MAHĀYĀNA, *Buddhist Schools of Tibet*), and consists of advice about after-death experience.

Tibetan Mastiff, ancient breed of dog, used in Tibet as a watch-dog; it is a very powerful animal with a long coat. Mentioned in old Chinese literature and by Marco Polo, the Tibetan mastiff is regarded as the ancestor of many present breeds. Its height is about 71 cm and its weight 60 kg. Its colour is black or black and tan.

Tibetan Spaniel, see SPANIEL.

Tibetan Terrier, resembles a small old English sheepdog in appearance, and despite its name has no relationship to the terriers. The profuse coat completely covers the whole head, body and limbs. The eyes are dark and large though obscured by the long hair on the head. The ears are pendant and the tail, which is left undocked, is carried in a loose curl over the back. The colour is white, golden, cream, grey, black, tricolour or particolour. Its height is from 35 to 41 cm.

Tibia, the larger of the two bones in the lower part of the leg, popularly called the shinbone. It articulates with the femur above to form the knee joint, the fibula externally at its upper and lower ends, and with the talus below, forming the ankle-joint.

Tibullus, Albius (c. 54–19 BC), Roman elegiac poet (see ELEGY). In 28 BC he accompanied his patron, Messala, as governor of Aquitania, and later started for the East; but he was taken ill at Corcyra and had to return. Tibullus's poetry addressed to two mistresses, Delia and Nemesis, has little ardour, but is notable for its quiet tenderness and spirit of self-denial. His bucolic elegies (see BUCOLICS), on the other hand, are among the most charming pieces in the whole range of Latin poetry.

Bibliography: J. P. Postgate (Ed.), *Works*, 2nd ed. 1914; P. J. Dunlop (Trans.), *Poems*, 1972.

Tibur, see TIVOLI.

Tic Douloureux, see CRANIAL NERVES.

Tichborne Case, famous English criminal trial. The prisoner, Thomas Castro, otherwise 'Bullocky Orton', a butcher from Wapping, was tried and convicted of perjury in putting forward a bogus claim to the Tichborne title and estates in 1872. Not only did Orton, in posing as Sir Roger Tichborne, son of Sir J. F. Doughty Tichborne, who had died in 1862, answer with astonishing skill every question put to him in the civil actions, but even the real Tichborne's mother at first 'identified' him as her missing son. The whole proceedings cost the Tichborne family some £70,000 in legal expenses. In 1874 Castro was sentenced on two counts to two cumulative terms of seven years' penal servitude each.

Ticino, or Tessin, canton of southern SWITZERLAND, lying on the southern slopes of the ALPS. In the south it

Ticino. Lake Lugano. *(Barnaby's Picture Library)*

Tichborne Case. The Tichborne Claimant, drawn by 'Ape' in 1874. *(Mary Evans Picture Library)*

merges into the LOMBARDY Plain. It is drained by the Ticino and its tributaries. It has no mineral resources but has abundant hydro-electric power. It also contains lakes Lugano and Maggiore. Cereals, tobacco, fruit, chestnuts, and vines are cultivated. It was taken by the Swiss from Italy in 1512 and joined the confederation in 1803. Hannibal won a victory here in 218 BC. Its capital is BELLINZONA, but its largest tourist resorts are LUGANO and LOCARNO. Area 2811 km². Population (1974) 267,500; Italian-speaking and mainly Roman Catholics.

Ticino, river of Switzerland and northern Italy, which rises in the canton of Ticino on the ST GOTTHARD Pass, flows through Lake MAGGIORE between Piedmont and Lombardy, and joins the PO 6 km south-east of Pavia. Length 246 km.

Ticinum, see PAVIA.

Tickell, Thomas (1686–1740), English poet, born at Bridekirk, Cumberland. Educated at Oxford, he was appointed professor of poetry there in 1731. His complimentary verse *Rosamund* brought him to the notice of ADDISON, who, on becoming secretary of state in 1717, made Tickell his under-secretary. He wrote much minor verse, his longest work being *Kensington Gardens*, 1722,

his most popular *Lucy and Colin*, 1725, and his finest the elegy prefixed to his edition of Addison's works, 1721.

Bibliography: R. E. Tickell, *Thomas Tickell and the Eighteenth-century Poets, 1685–1740*, 1931.

Tickhill, former urban district of South Yorkshire, England, 10 km south of DONCASTER. There are ruins of a Norman castle, an Augustinian priory, a 13th-century hospital of St Leonard, and a 14th-century church. Population (1971) 3262.

Ticks, animals of the families Argasidae (the soft ticks) and, more commonly, Ixodidae (the hard ticks) of the order Acarina (ticks and mites), in the class ARACHNIDA of phylum ARTHROPODA. They have flat bodies protected by horny shields. During part of their existence they are blood-sucking parasites on animals and birds, for which they have developed a rostrum or beak composed of two barbed harpoons above and a dart below. Their eggs are laid on rough herbage and hatch into white six-legged larvae, which climb up the legs of passing animals and in some species complete their life history on the animal's skin, but in others return to the grass for a period. Ticks cause irritation and anaemia, but their chief danger to their hosts is in the introduction of the numerous diseases of veterinary and medical importance they transmit, such as ROCKY MOUNTAIN SPOTTED FEVER.

Ticonderoga, village of New York, USA, in Essex county, situated north-west of Lake George. During the French war Ticonderoga was unsuccessfully attacked by General Abercrombie, and General Howe was killed here in 1758. It was taken by Amherst in 1759. In the War of Independence it was taken by Americans under Ethan Allen in 1775. It was retaken by General Burgoyne, on whose surrender it was abandoned, but reoccupied by the British in 1780.

Ticunas, American Indians of the Upper Amazon of

Ticks. *(Popperfoto)*

Tiddley-winks

Peru and Brazil. They are farmers and grow manioc and maize.

Tiddley-winks, game of flicking counters into a receptacle. Each player has six discs and flicks one in turn. If he flicks it into the cup he has another go; if not, the next flick must be taken from the place where the disc lies. If one player's disc is covered by that of another, he cannot flick it until he has put all his free discs into the cup. If the covered disc is his only remaining one he must miss a turn before flicking it.

Tidelands Oil, for years the ownership of off-shore resources along the US coast-line has been a subject of controversy. The coastal states have maintained that the submerged lands and the resources which they contain, lying within the three-mile (4·8-kilometre) limit controlled by the states under international law, are the property of the state concerned. The US Supreme Court has taken the position that such lands and resources are Federal property. In 1945 the submerged lands and their resources were declared a naval petroleum reserve by President Truman. In 1953 President Eisenhower passed a bill which gave the coastal states title to all submerged lands which lay within their historic boundaries, with rights to develop whatever resources lay therein. In May 1960 the Supreme Court ruled that the off-shore rights of Louisiana, Alabama, and Mississippi be limited to three miles, but that those of Florida and Texas were exercisable up to nine sea miles. In the case of Florida the ruling only applies to the waters of the Gulf of Mexico.

Tides, regular disturbances of the fluids on the earth's surface produced by the action of gravitational forces of the moon and sun. There is some evidence of tidal action in the ATMOSPHERE. This is greatest at the tropics, but even there it produces differences in barometric pressure of less than 0·1 mb. The oceanic waters, however, are considerably disturbed.

Tide Generating Forces. Consider the earth and moon in motion about their common centre of gravity (fig. 1). If the centres of the earth and moon are A and B, then the distance AB is such that, if the masses of the earth and moon were concentrated at A and B, the gravitational attractive force between the bodies is just the centrifugal force required to keep the bodies in their orbits around each other. The attractive gravitational force between two

bodies is inversely proportional to the square of the distance between them. Thus, at any place on the earth's surface in the hemisphere facing the moon (e.g. P), such that the distance PB is less than AB, then the attractive gravitational force between P and the moon will be larger than the centrifugal force needed to keep the bodies in their orbit. Thus the resultant force between the point P and the moon will be along the line PB towards the moon as indicated on fig. 1. Similarly, for any point on the hemisphere of the earth facing away from the moon (e.g. R), where RB is larger than AB, the centrifugal force will be larger than the gravitational attraction between R and the moon, so that the resultant force will be in the direction BR as shown on fig. 1. If the distance AB is much larger than the radius of the earth AF, then there will be zero force acting at the points C and D. The outward acting forces at P and R can be resolved into their normal components, PO and RT, and their tangential components, PQ and RS. The magnitude of the normal components, PO and RT, is about one in nine million compared to gravity and can therefore be ignored. The tangential forces, PQ and RS, are the tide generating forces. They can be shown to be zero at the points C, D, E, and F and are largest at the points 1, 2, 3, and 4. In the hemisphere facing the moon the tide generating forces are acting to produce high water at F, whereas in the hemisphere facing away from the moon they are acting to produce high water at E.

Let E and F be points on the equator of the earth with F on 0° longitude and E on 180° longitude. The plane CEDF can cut the earth at any angle so that C and D need not necessarily be the North and South Poles, but can be any points on opposite sides of the earth along the lines of longitude 90°W and 90°E. It now follows (fig. 2) that if F and E are the points on the equator with 0° and 180° longitude, then the tide generating forces produce the maximum high tide at the two points E and F, whereas the maximum low tide is at all points along the lines of longitude 90°W and 90°E. In fig. 2, the shaded regions will have the water level above the average level, and it will be below average in the unshaded regions. Thus as the earth spins once on its axis, the water level at any point on the earth, except the two poles, will rise and fall twice. The maximum tide amplitude will be along the equator and is zero at the poles. In fact, the moon rotates about the earth once every 28 days in the same direction as the earth's

Tides. Figure 1.

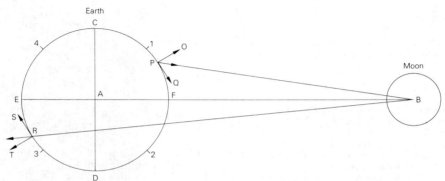

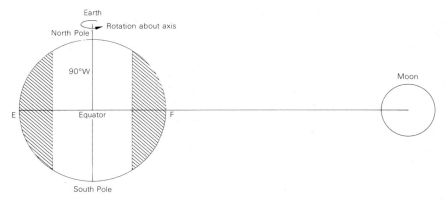

Tides. Figure 2.

spin, so that the time taken for the point F to be exactly opposite to the moon again will be just longer than one day; about $(1 + \frac{1}{28})$ days. Thus the moon tides rise and fall twice in a period of 24 hours 51 minutes.

The tides caused by the sun are produced in exactly the same way. The sun is much more massive than the moon (1 : 27 million), but is 390 times farther away so that the sun's tide generating forces are in the ratio 27 million to 390^3 or 1 : 2·17 compared with those of the moon. Since the earth orbits the sun once every 365¼ days, the time for two tides due to the sun is $(1 + \frac{1}{365})$ days or 24 hours 4 minutes. When the sun, moon, and earth are in a straight line, at a new or full moon, the tides due to the sun and moon reinforce each other and the resulting high tides are called spring tides. Similarly if the sun and moon are 90° out of alignment, at half moon, then the resulting tides are smaller and are called neap tides. Spring and neap tides occur twice every 29½ days—the time interval between successive occasions when the moon is between the earth and sun.

Another factor affecting the magnitude of the tides is declination (fig. 3). The angle between the earth's equatorial axis and the direction of the moon or sun is known as the declination, and it varies monthly and annually respectively. Figs 1 and 2 were drawn with zero declination which produces the largest tides, whereas if the declination is non-zero the tides are smaller. The sun's declination is almost constant at 23° while the moon's declination varies between 18° and 29° over a period of 19 years.

The moon's orbit around the earth and the earth's orbit around the sun are ellipses not circles. Since the gravitational attraction depends upon the distance between two bodies, the moon tides will be larger when the moon is closest to the earth, called its perigee, and they will be smaller when the moon is farthest away from the earth, called its apogee. Similarly the sun's tide is larger and smaller when the earth is closest and farthest away from the sun, at the December and June solstices respectively.

The discussion so far has assumed that the earth is entirely covered with ocean, whereas in practice the tides vary enormously with location upon the earth. For instance, there is very little tide in an enclosed sea such as the Caspian; only a small tide is generated in each basin of the Mediterranean because the Straits of Gibraltar are too narrow to allow the ingress and egress of the tidal wave from the Atlantic. Tides are generally uniform along the open coast bounding an ocean such as the Atlantic, but they are subject to great changes in bays and gulfs, e.g. the Bay of Fundy, where the tidal range is 18 m. High tides can also occur where the tidal waves from two different oceans meet. The theoretical problem of tidal behaviour in the oceans themselves has not yet been solved. Terrestial conditions are not alone responsible for the variations in the behaviour of the tidal wave, which is influenced by the gyroscopic effect of the rotation of the earth (see GYROSCOPE). Generally there is a lag in time between the exertion of the tide generating forces and the response of the water on which it acts and which varies from place to place. Moreover the response does not always correspond to the magnitude of the force to which it is subject. For example the solar tide generating forces are only about 46 per cent of the lunar, yet in some parts of the world the ratio of the former to the latter is 100 : 6.

Although, as we have seen in theory the highest tides, spring tides, should occur at the time of new and full moons, in Europe they lag some two to three days behind this event and in other parts of the world they precede it. When the lag in the solar response is greater than that in the lunar one, they occur later, and hence it is only when

Tides. Figure 3.

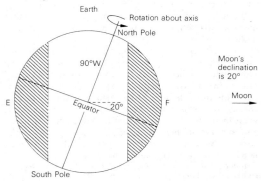

Tides

moonrise occurs after sunrise that the two combine to exert their maximum effect. At places where the lag of the lunar response is greater than that of the sun, spring tides occur before new and full moons.

In order to predict tidal behaviour at any place, it is necessary to analyse the component forces operating there to determine the tide's magnitude as well as the amount of lag. This system can give a sufficiently accurate prediction for ordinary purposes, although for scientific evaluations as many as 30 are used. The four referred to are: (1) M2, the average semi-diurnal tide generating forces; (2) K1, the average diurnal tide generating forces; (3) S2, the variation in the solar semi-diurnal tide generating forces; and (4) 01, the variation in the diurnal tide generating forces caused by the moon's changing declination.

Tides and Practical Navigation. Table 7 of the Admiralty Tide Tables, *Tide and Tidal Streams of the Atlantic and Indian Oceans, and the Pacific Ocean and Adjacent Seas*, contains astronomical data for the prediction of tidal information at ports throughout the world. Full instructions regarding the use of this information are contained in the *Admiralty Tidal Prediction Form HD 289*. At certain well-known ports throughout the world, called standard ports, tidal predictions are tabulated in Part I of the Admiralty Tide Tables for every day in the year. These predictions can generally be relied upon to give the times of high and low water within a few minutes and the heights within a few centimetres; times and heights at secondary ports, found by means of the tidal differences given in Part II, are considerably less exact than those predicted in the tables for standard ports; times and heights found from the tidal constants may be considerably in error, and caution is advised, particularly in waters where diurnal inequality is great.

The data used on the charts of different nations vary considerably. By international agreement chart datum should be on a plane so low that the tide will seldom fall below it. That adopted for the Admiralty charts founded on surveys carried out by the surveying vessels of the British Royal Navy is an amount below mean low water springs depending on the diurnal inequality in the area. As a very long series of tidal observations is required before either of these levels can be definitely determined and as the chart datum depends, in most cases, on a few weeks' observation only, the datum adopted must always be considered as approximate, and differs considerably in some cases from the theoretical datum. Where Admiralty charts are founded on the charts of other nations, the datum is that used by the original authority.

It has to be remembered by navigators that the tide may fall below datum, except in cases where the lowest possible low water has been used as datum. In waters where diurnal inequality is small the lowest tides usually occur when the moon is near perigee and near the equator at springs, or at the equinoxes; where diurnal inequality is great the lowest tides usually occur when both the moon and sun are in high declination at springs or at the solstices. Wind or a high barometer may also reduce the height of the tide and cause it to fall below datum.

Bibliography: H. Lamb, *Hydrodynamics*, 1932; A. T. Doodson and H. D. Warburg, *Admiralty Manual of Tides* (HMSO), 1941; *Admiralty Tidal Handbook* (nos 1–3), 1954, 1960, 1964; A.

Defant, *Physical Oceanography*, 1961; R. Gordon Pirie (Ed.), *Oceanography*, 1973; G. L. Pickard, *Descriptive Physical Oceanography*. 1975.

Tideswell, town in Derbyshire, England, 9 km east of Buxton, in the Peak District. It has a 14th-century church. There are lead-mines in the area. Population (1971) 1850.

Tidore, see TERNATE AND TIDORE.

Tieck, Johann Ludwig (1773–1853), German writer, born in Berlin; he studied literature at Erlangen and Göttingen. Tieck was drawn to the Romantic school (see ROMANTIC MOVEMENT) by the brothers SCHLEGEL. He tried his hand in many fields: critical writings (*Dramatische Blätter*); poetry (*Romantische Dichtungen*, two volumes, 1799–1800); drama (*Blaubart*, 1797, *Der gestiefelte Kater*, 1797, *Kaiser Oktavianus*, 1804); but he was especially successful as a writer of short stories. His *Phantasus*, 1812–17, is a collection of old tales and legends. In later years he freed himself from the Romantic, and wrote many *Novellen*, which rank amongst his best work, for example, *Das Dichterleben* and *Der Tod des Dichters*. The novel *Der Aufruhr in den Cevennen*, 1826, remained incomplete. He made his own translations of Shakespeare and also helped in the great translation by August Schlegel.

Bibliography: R. Minder, *Ludwig Tieck*, 1936.

Tiel, town in the province of Gelderland, Netherlands, on the River Waal. It is the centre of a fruit-growing district and has a large jam factory. In the Middle Ages Tiel was a member of the HANSEATIC LEAGUE. Population 22,900.

T'ien Hou, the Empress of Heaven in Chinese legend. Once she was a girl on the holy island of Mei-Chou, but one day, while her four sailor brothers were at sea, she fell into a faint and was thought dead. Powerful stimulants revived her, but she complained that she had been brought round too soon. Three of her brothers later came home and told of a violent storm from which they were saved by the appearance of their sister. The fourth brother had drowned, however, for the girl had been revived too soon to help him.

She herself died soon afterwards and her spirit became constantly active in saving sailors from storms or pirates. She was designated Empress of Heaven by the Emperor Yung Lo of the Ming Dynasty and her image usually adorns all water-craft.

Tienen (French *Tirlemont*), town of Brabant, Belgium, 40 km east of Brussels, situated on the River Gette. The town is probably of Roman origin. It was a busy market in the early Middle Ages. It has an important sugar industry (based on locally-grown beet) and other industries. Population 22,600.

Tien Shan (Russian *Tyan-Shan*, from the Chinese, celestial mountains), mountain chain of Central Asia, forming part of the boundary between the USSR and China (Sinkiang Uighur), and extending north-east from the PAMIRS to the western fringe of the GOBI desert. Folding occurred in Hercynian (see VARISCAN OROGENY) and earlier periods; subsequent reneplanation was followed by late Tertiary and Quaternary uplifting, which with glaci-

Tien Shan. The Khan-Tengri peak has a classic pyramidal form. *(Novosti Press Agency)*

ation and rapid dissection is largely responsible for the present relief. The main ranges form the border ridge of the high plateau of East Asia. In this chain are the chief peaks, POBEDA PEAK (7439 m), KHAN-TENGRI (6995 m), and the largest glaciers, and it is crossed by passes at 3000–4000 m. Forest occurs from 1200 to 3000 m. The chief lakes of the region are the ISSYK-KUL (6236 km²), Sonkël, and Chatyrkël. Non-ferrous and rare metals are found here, together with coal, oil, and rock-salt.

Tientsin, municipality and port in CHINA, at the junction of the Pai Ho with the GRAND CANAL, 120 km southeast of Peking. Administratively, it is independent of the province of HOPEH in which it is located. It is the main trading centre for north China. Its industrial development began after it was made a treaty port in 1860. It was bombed and occupied by the Japanese in 1937. Since 1950 it has become a centre of heavy and light industry in China and major new port developments have also been undertaken. Area 3900 km². Population (1970) 4,500,000.

Tiepolo, Giovanni Battista (1696–1770), Italian painter, born in Venice. He was the last great Italian decorative painter in the tradition which had begun in the 13th century with Giotto, and was arguably the greatest painter of the 18th century. He trained under Lazzarini and soon rose, almost from his earliest works (painted in the style of Piazzetta), to a position of peerless eminence which he held for half a century. He was constantly sought after and his output was prodigious: he did a great deal of work on the huge ceilings and walls of the villas and palaces of Venice and its environs and worked in various other parts of Italy, as well as in Germany and Spain. He brought new freedom and lightness to the fresco medium in which he principally worked, but although his clear, bright colours and airy sense of space are Rococo in feeling, the monumental grandeur of his figures and his firmness of design are Baroque. He revived the glories of

16th-century Venetian painting—Veronese was a particular influence—and enriched his work with new perspective techniques. His son, Giandomenico (1727–1804), was a faithful follower and in 1757 worked with his father on the decoration of the Villa Valmarana near Vicenza, perhaps his greatest masterpiece.
Bibliography: Life by A. Morassi, 1955, and also catalogue of works, 1962.

Tierra del Fuego, group of islands separated from the southern extremity of Chile by the Strait of Magellan (see MAGELLAN, STRAIT OF). It consists of several large islands, the main ones being called Tierra del Fuego or Isla Grande (area 48,100 km²), Navarin, Hoste, Clarence, and Santa Inez. Tierra del Fuego was discovered by Magellan in 1520. Half of Tierra del Fuego Islands, and the islands west of it, belong to Chile, the rest forms an Argentinian territory (its capital is at Ushuaia), with an area of 20,800 km² and a population of 7000. PUNTA ARENAS is the major settlement of the Chilean part, where sheep farming is a major industry, there being over 3 million sheep. Oil-fields were discovered in the 1940s and have been rapidly developed. Storms and strong winds are the main climatic features and during the winter months most of the islands is snow covered. See also ATLAS 59.
Bibliography: E. Shipton, *Tierra del Fuego: the Fatal Lodestone*, 1973.

Tiers État, see THIRD ESTATE.

Tiflis, see TBILISI.

Tigellinus (d. AD 69), son of a native of Agrigentum, praetorian prefect, minister to NERO's worst passions, and of all his favourites the most obnoxious to the Roman people. On the accession of OTHO, Tigellinus committed suicide (Tacitus, *Annals* xiv, xv; *Histories* i).

Tiger, *Leo tigris*, a large and powerful mammal of the cat family, Felidae, in order CARNIVORA. They live in Asia, from Siberia south to Sumatra. The Indian tiger rarely exceeds 3 m in length, and the female averages about 2.6 m. Fine males weigh 170–230 kg. Young animals, which

Tientsin. The city's temple. *(Barnaby's Picture Library)*

Tiger Beetle

are characterised by their canine teeth being hollow throughout, are handsomer than older ones, the tawny orange colour being richer and the stripes darker and closer together. Tigers are monogamous, though there is no reason to suppose that they pair for life. The period of gestation is 14 or 15 weeks, and from one to six cubs are born, though no more than two are usually reared. They will eat carrion, but generally kill for themselves. Their food consists principally of deer, antelopes and smaller animals, but they sometimes kill wild boar.

The tiger has been crossed experimentally with the lion; the resulting hybrid, the *tigon*, is faintly striped; it is sterile. Tigers are now in grave danger of extinction in the wild, due to over-hunting and the high prices paid for the pelt. All types of tiger (Siberian, Amoy, Sumatran and Javan) are classified as rare by the International Union for the Conservation of Nature and National Resources, with the exception of the Indian tiger, but the numbers of even this tiger had been reduced from 40,000 in 1930 to 2000 in 1972.

Tiger Beetle, any member of the family Cicindelidae in the order COLEOPTERA. Some 2000 species have been recorded, mostly in the tropics. Tiger beetles are typically found on sand or dry soils. The main genus is *Cicindela*, which includes four British species. Most adult tiger beetles are brightly coloured in shades of blue, bronze or green, with yellow or white markings. They generally have long legs and antennae. The most striking feature is the large eyes. The adults move rapidly and fly readily. The larvae live in burrows in the soil, where they lie in wait with their powerful mandibles ready to grab any insect that passes by. *C. silvatica* is the British forest tiger beetle. It is about 17 mm long, dark brown, and lives in coniferous forests. The common tiger beetle, *C. hybrida*, is found on the edges of British forests. It is also about 17 mm long, and has copper-coloured wing cases.

Tiger-cat, see OCELOT.

Tiger Flower, see TIGRIDIA.

Tiger Lily, see LILY.

Tiger. (*Topham/Coleman*)

Tiglath-pileser III. Limestone slab, from Nimrud, carved in relief with a scene of the king capturing the city of Astartu in Palestine. (*British Museum, London*)

Tighina, see BENDERY.

Tighnabruaich, village in Argyll and Bute District, Strathclyde Region, Scotland, a popular holiday resort and sailing centre situated on the KYLES OF BUTE. Population 181.

Tightrope Walker, see ACROBAT.

Tiglath-pileser I, King of ASSYRIA (c. 1115–1060 BC). He restored his country's declining power by a series of campaigns which re-established control as far west as the Mediterranean.

Tiglath-pileser II, Assyrian king (see ASSYRIA). He reigned from c. 956 to 934 BC.

Tiglath-pileser III, or Pul, Assyrian king, 745–727 BC. In a series of extensive wars, he initiated a system of provinces owing direct allegiance to his court and enforced by the deportation of recalcitrant populations. There are records of his actions on behalf of Ahaz (Jehoahaz) of Judah, and against Israel and Damascus. Sculpture from his palace at NIMRUD is in the British Museum. See ASSYRIA.

Tigranes, or Dikran, name of several kings of ancient Armenia, one of whom flourished as early as 550 BC, and was a friend of CYRUS II the Great, helping to overthrow the Median Empire. The best-known bearer of the name (c. 121–55 BC) was the son-in-law of Mithridates the Great. He was king of Armenia (c. 96–55 BC), and master of the Syrian Empire from the Euphrates to the sea (83), founding the city of Tigranocerta. Tigranes at first supported Mithridates against the Romans (76), but was defeated by Lucullus (69–68) and by Pompey (66).

Tigre, province of northern ETHIOPIA. It is a major source of hides and skins for export and also an important producer of grain, beeswax, and wool. Potash and sulphur deposits occur in economic quantities. The towns of Axum, ADOWA, and Adigrat are historically famous. The

Tigreans are a Semitic race. Area 65,900 km²; population density 27·8 per km²; population (1972) 1,828,900.

Tigridia, tiger flower, a genus of bulbous plants in the family Iridaceae, natives of tropical America. They are grown in the cool greenhouse and also in warm borders, with winter protection. *T. pavonia* and its varieties are particularly beautiful but the flowers only last a few hours.

Tigris, one of the two large rivers of IRAQ, the other being the EUPHRATES. It rises in Turkey on the southern slopes of the Taurus range, and flows east across Turkey through Diyarbakir, entering Iraq east of Nusaybin. Then it flows south-east to Mosul and Samarra and then south through Baghdad. It is joined by the Euphrates 80 km north-west of Basra to form the Shatt-al-Arab, which flows into the Persian Gulf. Length 1850 km. It is navigable to within 50 km of Mosul. See ATLAS 41.

Tihwa, see URUMCHI.

Tijuana, city in BAJA CALIFORNIA (NORTE) state, Mexico, on the US border near the Pacific coast and a popular tourist centre. It has developed as a border resort, particularly for Californians. Irrigation has opened up vast areas of surrounding farmland growing wheat, barley, and grapes. Population (1975) 386,800.

Tikopia, a small island in Melanesia, but whose inhabitants have a Polynesian culture. They have sacred chiefs and, although under 1500 in number, a highly complex social organisation based on patrilineal clans.
Bibliography: R. Firth, *We, the Tikopia*, 1936.

Tilak, Bal Gangadhar (1856–1920), a Brahmin from Maharashtra, the first Indian nationalist to unite religious and cultural sentiment with positive political action. He was western-educated and supported the moderates in Bombay, and later produced a newspaper to increase support for them. Through the paper, he sponsored two festivals, one to the Hindu god, Ganesh, and the other to the Maratha hero, Sivaji. He interpreted British government action as a threat to Hinduism. His militant action led to imprisonment. He called for *swarej,* complete independence. The division of Bengal in 1905, seen as a humiliation by his followers, was an excuse for a wave of violent action. Until Ghandi appeared, Tilak was seen as the leader of Indian nationalism.
Bibliography: S. A. Wolpert, *Tilak and Gokhale,* 1962.

Tilander, Artur Gunnar (1894–), Swedish Romance philologist. His many publications relating to French, Spanish, Portuguese, and other languages deal primarily with the Roman de Renard, medieval Spanish laws or *fueros,* and the etymological investigation of the vocabulary of hunting in various languages.

Tilburg, town in the province of North Brabant, Netherlands, 24 km south-west of 's Hertogenbosch. It is a great industrial centre, manufacturing cloth, woollens and soap. There is a Catholic economic university (1927). Population (1975) 152,100.

Tilbury Fort and Docks, fortification in ESSEX, England, on the Thames opposite Gravesend, enclosed by a moat. Originally built by Henry VIII, it was enlarged by Charles II. The troops raised in anticipation of a Spanish invasion were reviewed here (1588). The docks (205 ha), which lie 366 m above Tilbury Ness, opposite GRAVESEND, 42 km below London Bridge and about the same distance from the Nore, were opened in 1886, and formerly belonged to the London and East India Dock Company, but are now under the control of the Port of London Authority. The great development of trade since 1886 has rendered frequent changes necessary. From 1917 to 1928–29 the Port of London Authority extended the main dock 442 m at a cost of £2,500,000, enabling London to compete for the large ocean-liner traffic. They comprise a new entrance dock, 300 m by 34 m with a depth of 14 m, a floating structure, a dry dock 229 m by 34 m, and a passenger landing stage 348 m in length, at which vessels can be dealt with at any state of tide, day and night. The dry dock is so constructed that it can be extended when necessary, without interference with its use, to a total length of 305 m. Further major extensions have been built since 1960 as the London docks upstream have declined and containers have come to dominate cargo movements. Tilbury is now the major dock complex of the Port of London Authority. Population (1971) 11,360.
See also THURROCK.

Tilden, Samuel Jones (1814–86), US lawyer and statesman, born at New Lebanon, New York. In 1874 he became governor of New York. He was Democratic candidate for president (1877), and was believed elected, but a special commission decided that the disputed votes of Florida, South Carolina, and Louisiana should go to R. B. HAYES, his Republican opponent, who was thereupon declared president.

Tilden, William, usually known as Bill (1893–1953), US tennis player, born in Philadelphia. Though he did not win a major title until he was 27, he was the first US citizen to win Wimbledon, which he won twice thereafter, and also won the US Championship seven times. He won 11 Davis Cup Challenge Round singles in succession.

Tilden, Sir William Augustus (1842–1926), British chemist, born in London. He taught chemistry at Clifton College, 1873–80, and was made professor of chemistry at Birmingham in 1880. He was called to the Royal College of Science, London, in 1894, and was elected a fellow of the Royal Society. His chemical work dealt mainly with the constitution of the TERPENES, and he showed that ISOPRENE, which is one of the compounds produced when they decompose, would polymerise to form synthetic rubber. Tilden was knighted in 1909.

Tile, thin plate of various materials, e.g., earthenware, porcelain, marble, and glass, used for roofing, flooring, walls, and fireplaces. Roofing tiles of marble-coloured clay were used in ancient Greece and Rome; coloured glazed roofing tiles were known in ancient China and Japan; and unglazed red earthenware roofing tiles were used in medieval Europe. During the 16th to 18th centuries glazed roofing tiles, especially those intended as finials, e.g., for the apex of a gable, were often fashioned in fantastically elaborate, tall forms. Floor tiles of medieval Europe, as much a branch of brick-making as of ceramics, were made of red earthenware often with a lead-glaze and slip decoration (see SLIPWARE). Large pavements of these tiles were mosaic in form. The use of earthenware tiles for wall decoration is of Near-Eastern origin, as early as Darius

I, c. 500 BC. Painted specimens from Samaria (Mesopotamia) are of 9th century origin, and dated examples from Persia go back to the 13th century BC. The mosaic type of tile work, cutting to shape from slabs of tin-glazed earthenware, spread from North Africa to Spain under the Moors. Spanish tiles with coloured glazes, lustred, stamped in relief and painted, were made at Seville, Valencia, in Catalonia, and elsewhere. The imported Spanish tiles led the Italians to imitate them and to create MAIOLICA tiles for flooring. But in the Netherlands the maiolica technique was extended to pictorial representations extending over many tiles for wall and fireplace decoration, and the great Dutch tile manufacturers of the 17th century favoured blue-and-white designs. These were copied in northern France, Germany, and Britain, where, in about 1756 at Liverpool, transfer-printed decoration was used. Painted porcelain tiles were made at Meissen and Fürstenberg.

During the 19th century after the invention of the process by which ceramic tiles were pressed from clay dust, many manufacturers established factories, particularly in Staffordshire and Shropshire (Salop). Technical invention and innovation over the last fifty years includes the automatic pressing of tiles, firing by tunnel kiln, automatic glazing, and decorating. Ceramic tiles are also manufactured in most countries of the world, particularly Germany, Italy, and Spain.

See also MOSAIC; ROOF.

Bibliography: E. A. Lane, *Guide to Collection of Tiles*, 1960; A. Berendsen, *Tiles: A General History*, 1967; E. S. Eames, *Mediaeval Tiles: A Handbook*, 1968; C. H. De Jonge, *Dutch Tiles*, 1971 (trans. from the Dutch); J. Bernard, *Victorian Ceramic Tiles*, 1972.

Till, see BOULDER CLAY.

Tillage, see CULTIVATION.

Tillandsia, a genus of the Bromeliaceae (pineapple family) including 500 species of herbaceous plants, natives of tropical and subtropical America, usually epiphytic. *T. usneoides* is Spanish moss or old man's beard, which hangs from trees in the tropics and resembles the lichen *Usnea*. *T. utriculata*, the wild pine of Jamaica, has leaves with expanded bases, retaining water as if in a bottle. Several species are cultivated as pot plants or epiphytes in a warm greenhouse; most of these have a rosette of rather tough, parallel-veined leaves.

Tillett, Benjamin (1860–1943), British labour leader and politician, born in Bristol, began his career in a brickworks, later joining the Royal Navy. Subsequently he organised the Dockers' Union of which he became general secretary. Tillett played the principal part in organising the dock strike of 1889. He shared responsibility for the developments which placed the general labour unions in an equal position with the organisations of skilled craftsmen inside the Trade Union Congress. He was Labour MP for North Salford (1917–24 and 1929–31), and president of the TUC (1929). Tillet published his *Memories and Reflections* in 1931.

Tilley, Edgar Cecil (1894–1973), Australian geologist, born in Adelaide, and educated at the universities of Adelaide and Sydney. He moved to Cambridge in 1920, becoming professor of the newly-created department of mineralogy and petrology in 1931; he remained there until his retirement in 1961. He is well-known for his work in PETROLOGY, initially in metamorphic rocks and later in volcanic rocks, particularly those of Hawaii, also on the genesis of basaltic MAGMA and the origin of the Alkali Rocks. He received many honours; he was president of the Geological Society, 1949, president of the Mineralogical Society, 1948–51, was elected a Fellow of the Royal Society in 1938, and was a vice-president in 1949–50.

Tilley, Vesta, real name Matilda Alice Powles (1864–1952), British music-hall performer, born in Worcester, best remembered for her male impersonations: her father was a music-hall chairman under the name of Harry Ball, and she made her first appearance with him in Nottingham at the age of three. In 1873 she first appeared in London, playing three halls a night. Among the songs she made famous were 'The Piccadilly Johnny', 'The Girl who Loves a Soldier' and 'Six Days' Leave'. She retired at the height of her popularity in 1920.

Tillich, Paul (1886–1965), German theologian, born at Starzeddal. He studied at the universities of Berlin, Tübingen, and Halle and was ordained as a Lutheran minister (1912). His sympathy with socialism led to his emigration to the USA after the Nazis took power; he taught at the Union Theological Seminary, New York (1934–55), at Harvard (1955–62), and at Chicago University (1962–65). Tillich's insistence on a contemporary and relevant form of Christian belief appears in *The Shaking of the Foundations*, 1948, *The Courage to Be*, 1952, *Love, Power and Justice*, 1954, *The Eternal Now*, 1963, and above all his three-volume *Systematic Theology*, 1950–63.

Tillicoultry, burgh in Clackmannan District, Central Region of Scotland, 7 km from Alloa, situated at the foot of the OCHIL HILLS. Industries are paper coatings, textiles, and colour printing. Population 4026.

Tillotson, John Robert (1630–94), Archbishop of Canterbury, born at Halifax; educated at Cambridge. He was at first a Presbyterian, but was ordained in 1660 or 1661, accepted the Act of Uniformity, and became chaplain to Charles II (1666). In 1672 he became dean of Canterbury, in 1675 canon of St Paul's, in 1689 dean of St Paul's, and in 1691 archbishop of Canterbury. He was strongly anti-Catholic, and published *Rule of Faith*, 1666, and four lectures on the Socinian controversy, 1693. His sermons are famous for their prose style, and are among the best examples of the pulpit oratory of his time.

Bibliography: J. Moffat (Ed.), *The Golden Book of Tillotson*, 1926; L. G. Locke, *Tillotson. A Study in Seventeenth Century Literature*, 1954.

Tilly, Johan Tserclaes, Count von (1559–1632), German soldier, born at Tilly in Brabant and brought up by Jesuits. He served in the Spanish army in the Netherlands. Later he left the Spanish service for Austria, and in 1607 became general of the Bavarian army and Catholic League, greatly distinguishing himself during the Thirty Years' War. He won the great battle of the White Mountain, near Prague, in 1620, and was also victorious at Wimpfen, Stadtlohn, Wiesloch, Hochst, and Lutter. In 1620 Tilly was appointed commander-in-chief of the Imperial forces, and besieged and took Magdeburg after a fierce struggle. Four months later, however, he was defeated by Gustavus Adolphus at Breitenfeld, and, shortly afterwards, on the banks of the Lech, where he was mortally wounded.

Tillyard, E(ustace) M(andeville) W(etenhall) (1889–1962), English scholar, born at Cambridge; educated at Perse School and Jesus College, Cambridge. He was one of the leading figures in the school of English at Cambridge from soon after its foundation until 1954. His publications include *Milton*, 1930, *The Elizabethan World Picture*, 1943, and studies of Shakespeare.

Tilsit, see SOVETSK.

Timaeus (c. 345–c. 250 BC), Greek historian, the son of Andromachus, tyrant of Tauromenium in Sicily. He was banished from Sicily by Agathocles, and passed his exile at Athens, where he had been living for 50 years when he wrote the thirty-fourth book of his History. This, his greatest work, was a history of Sicily from the earliest times to 264 BC, of which fragments are extant.
Bibliography: T. S. Brown, *Timaeus of Tauromenium*, 1958.

Timaru, seaport of South Island, New Zealand, on the east coast between Christchurch and Dunedin, and the chief town of the southern Canterbury district. Industries include the manufacture of woollen goods, flour, and allied products. Population 28,600.

Timber, term for wood, other than fuelwood, that is either sawn or prepared in some way; it is also used to denote a group of trees from which timber may be obtained (hence, 'standing timber'), or for wood used in heavy construction, for example shipbuilding.

Timber is described as either 'softwood' or 'hardwood', depending on whether it originates from coniferous or broadleaved trees. These terms are widely used, although many 'hardwoods' are soft, for instance the balsa (*Ochroma lagopus*), and some 'softwoods' are quite hard; the yew (*Taxus baccata*) for instance, is almost as hard as oak. However, the terms are also used literally to denote the actual hardness of the timber.

There are many more species of hardwood (broadleaved trees) than of softwood (conifers). The main source of softwood timber is the north temperate zone: for instance, the great pine forests of northern USSR, Finland, and Scandinavia, and of Canada and the USA. Softwoods also occur in Central America, south and south-east Asia in mountainous areas, and they are widely grown in PLANTATIONS. Hardwoods occur throughout the forested regions of the world, and very large numbers of different species are found in the tropical high forests and savannahs. Many of these are difficult to utilise commercially though advances in the technology of wood utilisation are continually being made. Many of the most valuable hardwoods are difficult to regenerate after felling, whether the remaining forest is manipulated, or whether planting is carried out, and where this is the case, as in many parts of the tropics, plantations of other hardwoods or softwoods are created in order to maintain production. Hardwood was sold by the cubic foot, and softwood by the standard of 165 cubic feet, but the metric measure now in use for both is the cubic metre (m^3), equivalent to 35·32 cubic feet. Timber is Britain's third largest import, after food and oil.

The weight, or density, of timber, was formerly measured in lb per ft^3, and is now recorded either as kg per m^3 (water = 1000 kg per m^3) or in terms of specific gravity (water = 1·0). Hardwoods vary greatly in density, from about 110 kg per m^3 for balsa, to 960 kg per m^3 for lignum vitae (*Guaiacum officinale*) from Guyana. Most hardwoods have values in the range 500 to 1000; for instance mahogany, teak, and oak have values of about 700 kg per m^3. Softwoods are less variable and generally have values of about 500 kg per m^3. Hardwoods are more variable than softwoods in other properties, too. The most important properties include: durability, hardness, toughness, stability under conditions of varying moisture content, working properties, and, of course, appearance. A larger number of hardwood than softwood species is therefore in use in Britain. Six or seven softwoods account for the bulk of the wood used, and include European redwood and whitewood, Douglas fir, western hemlock, western red cedar, and other species of pines and spruces. The principal uses of timber are in house building and other constructional work, boxes and packing cases, railway sleepers, mining timber, marine use, telegraph and transmission poles, joinery, flooring, furniture, cooling towers, vats and barrels, tool handles, and many other domestic and agricultural purposes.

The versatility of wood has been increased by the development of new production methods. Especially in combination with synthetic resins, wood products can be made that are more easily moulded into special shapes than ordinary boards, and that have improved qualities over ordinary wood, such as resistance to fire, insects, fungi, and moisture, or greater strength. An object made of strong but ugly wood may be covered with a thin *veneer*, a very thin layer of more attractive wood. *Plywood* is made up of several layers of wood, with the grain running in different directions, glued together. This gives it greater strength and stability.

Particles and fibres of wood, often the residue of other wood-using industries or from poor-quality trees, are now used to make boards and sheets of material with special properties, that are often cheaper than panels of whole wood. These include *fibreboard*, a sheet material made under heat and pressure from the fibres of woody tissue, often with the addition of bonding agents. Hardboard is a thin fibreboard with a density of over 0·5 g per cm^3. Many hardboards are specially treated to increase their strength or waterproof qualities, and are widely used in building. Softboard is a fibreboard with a density of less than 0·4 g per cm^3, and is used in insulation. *Particleboard*, including chipboard, is a sheet material made from woody particles bonded together with synthetic resin or another binder under pressure and heat. It is a cheap, strong material, often used for furniture and shelves, in which case it is covered with an attractive veneer.

See also AFFORESTATION; FOREST; FORESTRY; LUMBER AND LUMBERING; WOOD.
Bibliography: F. D. Silvester, *Timber: Its Mechanical Properties and Factors Affecting its Structural Use*, 1967; G. Tsoumis, *Wood as a Raw Material*, 1968; F. W. Jane, *The Structure of Wood*, 2nd ed. 1970; B. J. Rendle, *The Growth and Structure of Wood* (FPR Bulletin 56; rev. by J. D. Brazier), 1971; R. H. Farmer, *Handbook of Hardwoods*, 2nd ed. 1972; 'Materials and Technology' (vol. 6), *Wood Fibres, Plastics and Photography*, 1973; US Department of Agriculture, *Wood Handbook* (USDA Agriculture Handbook No. 72), 1974.

Timber

Timber, in the English law of real property, means oak, ash, and elm by general custom, and various other trees by local custom. It becomes important to consider what 'timber' denotes when construing the powers of a tenant-for-life under a settlement. See also WASTE.

Timbrel (Old French *timbre*; Middle English *tymbre*), 16th-century name for the TAMBOURINE, used in the authorised version of the Bible to translate the Hebrew *tof*.

Timbuktu, see TOMBOUCTOU.

Time. We are subjectively aware of the passage of time, which can be measured objectively by counting the cycles of a recurring phenomenon. Experience has gradually made us familiar with the concept of *uniform time* which is probably best defined as the independent variable in the accepted dynamical equations of motion. Its present practical expression is the system of *Co-ordinated Universal Time* (UTC), which is based on a series of extremely accurate electronic clocks maintained at various institutions round the world and regularly compared with each other (see *Universal Time* below). Its second is defined as the duration of 9,192,631,770 periods of the radiation corresponding to the transition between the two hyperfine levels of the ground state of the caesium-133 atom. The UTC day, which consists of $24 \times 60 \times 60$ of these seconds is intended to be a close representation of the former unit of time, the *mean solar day* as represented by UT2 and found from astronomical observation. To keep UTC in step with the observed rotation of the Earth, leap seconds are introduced when the discrepancy is approaching 0·7 seconds, the adjustment being made to the last second of a month, preferably on 31 December and/or 30 June.

Man's first practical measures of time, such as those made with a sundial, were of *apparent solar time*. Its unit is the *apparent solar day* defined as the interval between successive meridian transits of the actual Sun. This interval is made up of the time it takes the Earth to revolve once on its axis relative to a fixed direction plus the time it takes to turn through the angle that the Earth has moved round the Sun during the interval. This latter time varies partly because the Earth's orbit is elliptical and the Earth, in accordance with Kepler's Second Law, moves more quickly round the Sun in January when it is near perihelion than it does at aphelion in July, and partly because the plane of the ecliptic in which the orbit lies is inclined at 23½° to the plane of the equator. This means that equal distances along the orbit subtend greater angles about the Earth's axis at the time of the solstices than they do at the equinoxes.

This variation in the length of the apparent solar day was of no practical importance until the 17th century when the introduction of pendulum clocks so improved the standard of time-keeping that it became intolerable. The difficulty was overcome by use of a mathematical fiction called the *mean sun*, which is regarded as moving uniformly round the equator at such a speed that it completes a circuit of the heavens, i.e., a year, in exactly the same period as does the actual Sun. It is the hour angle of this fictitious body that defines *mean solar time*, just as the hour angle of the true Sun measures apparent solar time. The difference between the two is called the *equation of time* and this varies from 14·3 minutes in mid-February when the sundial is slow by mean time to 16·4 minutes at the beginning of November when the sundial is fast. The equation vanishes, i.e., the two times coincide, on about 16 April, 14 June, 2 September, and 25 December.

Since the mean sun is a hypothetical entity it cannot be directly observed. Mean solar time has therefore to be calculated from *sidereal time* which is found by observing stars of known right ascension (see CELESTIAL SPHERE). Sidereal time is defined as the western hour angle of the First Point of Aries, i.e., the position of the Sun at the moment of the March equinox. It is directly related to mean solar time by the fact that there is exactly one more sidereal than solar days in a year. Hence one mean sidereal day = 23 h 56 min 4·09054 s of mean solar time, and one mean solar day = 24 h 3 min 56·55536 s of mean sidereal time.

Standard Time. All three times that have so far been defined are *local* and refer only to the place of observation. At any given instant the local times as measured at two places differ, that at the more westerly place being $4L$ minutes slow on the other, where $L°$ is their difference in longitude (1° = 4 minutes, 15° = 1 hour, 360° = 24 hours). Up to the middle of the 19th century each place kept its own local time, but with the coming of the railways and the electric telegraph, it began to be very inconvenient that every station along the line was using a different time. 'Railway time' was introduced but was gradually replaced by *standard time*, which was the local mean solar time on a chosen standard meridian. In the UK the passing of the Statutes (Definition of Time) Act in 1880 made *Greenwich Mean Time* the standard for the whole country. An international conference held at Washington in 1884 selected the meridian of Greenwich as longitude zero, and suggested that the meridians selected as standard for time-keeping should be those whose longitudes were a whole number of hours or half hours. The use of half hours has been gradually discontinued and the world is now divided into 24 time zones, each forming a belt of approximately 7½° on either side of its standard meridian, the exact boundaries being determined by political and geographical considerations. The United States is divided into seven standard time zones roughly centred along the 75°, 90°, 105°, 120°, 135°, 150°, and 165° meridians and named the Eastern(5), Central(6), Mountain(7), Pacific(8), Yukon(9), Alaska-Hawaii(10), and Bering(11) Time Zones, the number in parentheses indicating how many hours that zone is earlier than Greenwich mean solar time.

Universal Time. On account of NUTATION, the First Point of Aries does not move perfectly uniformly so that the sidereal time as previously defined, which should really have been called the apparent sidereal day, is not quite constant in length. The variations are small, however, and were tacitly ignored until clocks achieved a sustained accuracy of the order of 0·01 seconds per day as they did with the introduction of the Shortt free pendulum clocks in the 1920s. The quartz-crystal clocks of the 1930s did much better than this, and their successors controlled by caesium beam oscillators maintain rates that make a microsecond per day significant. Nutation must therefore be taken into account and use made of *mean sidereal time*, the analogue of mean solar time. The difference between mean and apparent sidereal time, which is the nutation in right ascension, is called the *equation of the equinoxes*. Its biggest component has a semi-amplitude of approximately 1·2 seconds in a period of 18·6 years, but there are also components with periods as short as 15 days and semi-amplitudes of the order of 0·02 seconds.

Mean sidereal time would be completely satisfactory for regulating clocks if the Earth revolved uniformly round an axis which remained fixed relatively to its surface. Neither of these conditions is strictly true. That the surface of the Earth does not move relatively to the axis of rotation was discovered from systematic variations in observed latitudes, and the implied motion of the pole has been carefully monitored since the 1890s. The corresponding variations in longitude, which in latitude 45° are of the order of 0·02 seconds of time, can be computed and time observations corrected accordingly. It had long been suspected that the Earth was being gradually slowed down by tidal friction, but it came as a surprise in the 1930s to find from similar discrepancies between the observed and computed positions of the Sun, Moon, Mercury, and Venus that the Earth was apt to change its rate of rotation by small and sudden amounts. It was later found that there are also fairly regular seasonal variations in the rate of rotation whose integrated effect over a year is to make the actually observed time differ from the mean time by as much as 0·025 seconds.

As the railways produced a need for standard time, so the airways and the world-wide use of radio produced a need for a time that would be the same all over the world at the same instant. The first form of this *universal time* (UT0), was computed by an agreed formula from the mean sidereal time as observed at Greenwich. It was a refined version of Greenwich mean solar time with 12 hours added to make the UT day begin at midnight. UT0 (UT nought) was then improved to UT1 by applying a correction to remove the effect of longitude variation, and later to UT2 by correcting for the regular seasonal variation in the Earth's rate of rotation.

Ephemeris Time. UT2 would be a good approximation to uniform time if it were not for sudden and, as yet, unpredictable changes in the Earth's rate of rotation. The recognition of this fact led to the introduction of *ephemeris time*, which was conceived as a measure of the uniform time inherent in Newtonian gravitational theory. Although convenient for celestial mechanics this time is not suitable for everyday use since it can only be determined by fairly complicated calculations from the observed motions of the solar system and of the Moon in particular. This lack of practicability is reflected in the formal definition of its unit, the ephemeris second, as being $1/(31,556,925\cdot974)$ of the length of the tropical year in 1900. In 1975 its difference from mean solar time, with which by definition it coincided in 1900, was 45·6 seconds.

Atomic Time. The ephemeris second was adopted as the unit of time by the Comité International des Poids et Mesures in 1956 and was carefully evaluated in terms of the frequency of caesium which in 1967 was used to define the international second which was adopted as standard. *International Atomic Time* (TAI) is the accumulation of atomic seconds from 00 hours on 1 January 1958 when, by definition, TAI and UT2 were coincident.

The Earth ceased to be regarded as the standard time-keeper on 1 January 1972. From that date Co-ordinated Universal Time (UTC) has been used. This is essentially atomic time kept in step with UT2 by the insertion of leap seconds as required. Approximately 30 national laboratories and observatories collaborate in the maintenance of TAI and UTC, each having a series of quartz-crystal clocks whose rates are constantly monitored by caesium beam standards. Regular comparisons among the various institutions are made through the series of radio time and standard frequency signals each controls, but to avoid uncertainties produced by variations in radio travel times, the clocks in key institutions have been synchronised to about 0·1 microseconds by special clocks transported by air from one laboratory to another. Responsibility for TAI, UTC, and the final synthesis of all this work is vested in the Bureau International de l'Heure which was established in Paris in 1913. The link with the rotation of the Earth depends mainly on observations of UT1 made regularly at a score of national observatories, usually with either a photographic zenith tube or a Danjon prismatic ASTROLABE. For the benefit of navigators, surveyors and others who need UT1 its difference from UTC is given to 0·1 seconds in a Morse addendum to the regular standard time signals.

See also RELATIVITY.

Bibliography: S. T. Butler and H. Messel, *Time: Selected Lectures*, 1965; T. Gold and D. L. Schumacher (Ed.), *Nature of Time*, 1968; S. Goudsmit and R. Claiborne, *Time*, 1968; E. B. Magrab and D. S. Blomquist, *Measurement of Time-varying Phenomena: Fundamentals and Applications*, 1971; J. Zeman, *Time in Science and Philosophy: An International Study of Some Current Problems*, 1971; K. F. Welch, *Time Measurement: An Introductory History*, 1972; G. W. Dorling, *Time*, 1973; J. R. Lucas, *Treatise on Time and Space*, 1973; G. J. Whitrow, *Nature of Time*, new ed. 1975; I. Zelkind and J. Sprug, *Time Research: 1172 Studies*, 1975.

'Time', US magazine founded in New York in 1923 by Henry R. LUCE and Briton Hadden. Described by its subtitle as a 'weekly newsmagazine', it issues editions circulated overseas, as well as American and Canadian editions. See also MAGAZINES.

'Time and Tide', British weekly magazine containing political and literary articles, with editorial comment. *Time and Tide* was founded in 1920 by Viscountess Rhondda as an independent, non-party, strongly anti-totalitarian review. In 1962, after several changes of ownership and corresponding variations in policy, it took over *John O'London's*, which was established in 1919 as *John O'London's Weekly*, ceased publication in 1954 and reappeared in 1959, before merging with *Business World* in 1976.

Time Base, device for generating a voltage of saw-tooth waveform applied to the deflecting plates of an OSCILLO-SCOPE, producing an adjustable horizontal deflection of the spot with a quick fly-back at the end. It usually consists of a capacitor whose charge and discharge is controlled by electronic circuits.

Time Constant, τ, is the time required to reach the final steady-rate value for a quantity following the laws of exponential rise and fall with respect of time, if the

Time Constant

initial rate of increase or decrease were maintained (see figure).

Under transient conditions, certain physical quantities follow the laws of exponential growth and decay, and it can be shown that

$$x = X\{1 - \exp(-t/\tau)\}$$

for exponential growth, where exp is the base of natural logarithms, x is the magnitude of the quantity at any time t, X is the final steady value of the quantity (i.e., when t becomes infinite) and τ is the time constant for the system considered. Putting $t = \tau$ gives $x = 0.632X$. For exponential decay,

$$x = X\exp(-t/\tau),$$

and here X is the initial value of the quantity (i.e., at $t = 0$) and τ is the time constant of the system. Putting $t = \tau$ gives $x = 0.368X$.

Examples: Electrical. 1. Voltage V applied suddenly to a circuit having resistance R and inductance L. The magnitude of the circuit current at any time t following the application of the voltage is given by

$$i = (V/R\{1 - \exp(t/\tau)\},$$

in which $\tau = L/R$.

2. Decay of current in a resistive-inductive circuit.

$$i = (V/R)\exp(-t/\tau),$$

where $\tau = L/R$.

3. Voltage V applied suddenly to a series circuit having resistance R and capacitance C. The voltage across the capacitor at any time t following the application of the voltage is

$$v_c = V\{(1 - \exp(-t/\tau)\},$$

in which $\tau = CR$.

4. Discharge of a capacitor (C) through resistor (R). The circuit current at any time t following the connection of the capacitor across the resistor is

$$i = (V_c/R)\exp(-t/\tau),$$

in which $\tau = CR$ and V_c is the initial capacitor voltage, i.e., at $t = 0$.

Thermal. 1. If heat energy is supplied to a homogeneous mass at a constant rate P watt then the average temperature rise of the body, above ambient, at any time t after the commencement of the supply of that energy is

$$\theta = \theta_s\{1 - \exp(-t/\tau)\},$$

in which θ_s is the final steady state average temperature

Time Constant.

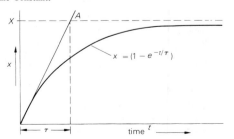

rise, and τ is the thermal time constant; $\tau = ms/kA$, where m is the mass of the body, s is its specific heat, A is the cooling surface area, and k is the emmissivity of the cooling surface.

2. If the supply of heat energy ceases when the body has reached a temperature rise of θ_r, then the equation of the cooling curve is

$$\theta = \theta_r\exp(-t/\tau).$$

Time of Troubles, see TROUBLES, TIME OF.

Time Series, see STATISTICS.

Timentel, Eleonora, see FONSECA, MARCHESA DE.

Timer, see CHRONOGRAPH.

'Times, The', British daily newspaper, founded in 1785 as the *Daily Universal Register*. John WALTER, the publisher, hoped only to establish himself as a book publisher by promoting a more economic method of type-setting, using units of words or groups of letters as well as single letters. The 'logographic' invention was a failure, but the news-sheet printed as an advertisement was a success, and on 1 January 1788 it was re-titled *The Times*. In 1803 the management, and in 1812 the proprietorship, passed to his second son, John Walter, under whom the paper maintained its independence and secured a paramount position. In 1817 Thomas BARNES was appointed editor. He became the outstanding journalist of the century, and, as the champion of middle-class opinion, won for *The Times* the nickname of 'The Thunderer'. The third John Walter succeeded his father as proprietor in 1847. His editor, John DELANE, claimed for the press a responsibility in national affairs that was conspicuously demonstrated by the newspaper's successful agitation for the proper equipment and care of troops in the Crimea. The competition of cheaper journals after the repeal of the Stamp Act of 1855 was severe, but John Walter refused to imperil the independence or inclusiveness of the paper.

During the editorship of G. E. BUCKLE, *The Times* suffered a catastrophic reverse when it indicted J. S. PARNELL on the basis of a letter secured in good faith, but found by the Parnell Commission (1889) to be forged. The reputation of the paper was damaged and its resources crippled. Arthur Fraser Walter, chief proprietor, 1894–1908, and chairman, 1908–10, appointed as acting manager C. F. Moberly BELL, who worked to retrieve solvency. Nevertheless, family disputes made necessary the public sale of *The Times* in 1908. Though the Walter interest was retained, the paper came under the control of Lord NORTHCLIFFE. His first editor, Geoffrey Dawson (1912–19), directed the paper's demands for a vigorous prosecution of the First World War, and under H. Wickham STEED *The Times* contributed, in particular, to the success of the Washington Conference and the Irish settlement.

On Northcliffe's death in 1922 control was acquired by Major the Hon. J. J. Astor (later Lord Astor of Hever), in association with the fourth John Walter. Dawson returned to conduct the paper until 1941, to be followed until 1948 by R. M. Barrington-Ward. His successor, W. F. Casey, retired in 1952, when Sir William HALEY became editor. In 1966, in an attempt to increase circulation, *The Times* modernised its layout and news replaced classified advertisements on the front page. But modernisation failed to overcome the paper's financial difficulties and in 1967 *The Times* was taken over by Lord THOMSON of Fleet who brought it under the control of Times Newspapers Limited, part of the Thomson organisation. Sir William Haley was made chairman of the company, and William Rees-Mogg became editor of the paper.

Closely connected with *The Times* are *The Times Educational Supplement*, founded in 1910 as a monthly insert in *The Times* and published as a separate weekly in 1916, and the *Higher Education Supplement*, published separately in 1972. Covering education and teaching, their advertisements act as national notice boards for educational appointments. As departments of *The Times*, their editors are subject to its editor.

The Times Literary Supplement, founded in 1902, began to be published by Times Newspapers Limited in 1967. One of the leading literary weeklies in Britain, it owes its position to its comprehensive coverage of literature and its scholarly criticism. Besides book reviews, it carries occasional articles on literary and allied subjects.

Bibliography: The History of the Times: vol. 1, *The Thunderer in the Making*, 1935; vol. 2, *The Tradition Established*, 1939; vol. 3, *The Twentieth Century Test*, 1947; *House of Commons Paper No. 273* (HMSO) Dec. 1966.

'Times of India', see 'HINDU, THE'.

Timgad, ancient Roman city of Algeria in the department of Constantine, founded by TRAJAN in AD 100. Since the visit of James Bruce in 1765, Timgad has proved to be of great archaeological interest and importance. Extensive excavations have been carried out.

Timişoara (Hungarian *Temesvár*), town of Romania, on the River Bega, capital of the province of Timiş, near the Yugoslav border. The Turks captured it in 1552 and held it till 1716. In 1920, by the Treaty of Trianon, it passed from Hungary to Romania. It has a fine cathedral and castle. Industries include brewing and distilling, chemicals, engineering, and leather goods. Population (1974) 225,600.

Timmins, town of Ontario, Canada, 740 km north of Toronto. It is the centre of the Porcupine gold-mining area of northern Ontario, but zinc, silver, and tin have become important since the discovery of large new deposits in 1964. It has an additional source of future prosperity in the adjoining great clay belt of fertile agricultural land estimated at 60,000 km², where settlement has only just begun. Besides the large gold mines, there are saw and planing mills. Population 28,550.

Timoleon (4th century BC), Corinthian patriot. He spent his life in the cause of liberty, and as a youth murdered his own brother Timophanes, who was trying to establish a tyranny. In 346 BC the Greek cities of Sicily applied to Corinth for aid against the Carthaginians, and Timoleon was sent with a small force. He took Syracuse, and set about the establishment of democratic government in all the Sicilian colonies. Meanwhile the Carthaginians landed at Lilybaeum. Timoleon was not able to collect more than 12,000 men, but with these he won a victory on the Crimissus (341). A treaty was concluded in the next year, and Timoleon continued his work of democratisation, though he himself was *de facto* ruler of the island.

The flourishing state of Sicily at the time of his death shows how beneficial was his influence. See Holden's introduction to Plutarch's *Life of Timoleon*, 1889.

Bibliography: H. D. Westlake, *Timoleon and his relations with Tyrants*, 1952; R. J. A. Talbert, *Timoleon and the Revival of Greek Sicily*, 1975.

Timon the Misanthrope (late 5th century BC), Athenian who lived at the time of the Peloponnesian War. On account of ingratitude and disappointments which he believed himself to have suffered, he secluded himself from the society of all but his friend Alcibiades. He is the central figure of Shakespeare's *Timon of Athens*.

Timor, largest and most easterly island of the Lesser Sunda Islands, partitioned until 1976 between Indonesian West Timor (14,931 km²) and (formerly Portuguese) East Timor (18,982 km² including the western Oé-Cusse enclave in Indonesian territory). The island is the driest of all in the Indonesian archipelago, being strongly affected by the south-east monsoon. Consequently, the soil is dry and relatively infertile, and vegetation is scrub-like with tropical deciduous forest stands. In flora and fauna, Timor belongs to the 'Australian' biogeographical realm (see WALLACE LINE). Throughout, the island has a dissected mountainous landscape, rising to over 3000 m in both west and east. Not markedly volcanic, there is evidence of recent or dying vulcanicity. See ATLAS 61.

Out of a total population of 1·2 million (estimated 1975), 658,000 live in West Timor. The coastal peoples, of mainly Deutero-Malay stock, include the Belunese and Atonis stock, and are predominantly Muslim in the western half of the island and largely Christian in the east. The interior peoples, of Australoid and Melanesian stock, are animist-Christian in religion. There is considerable intermingling between the two groups. In East Timor, there are small Chinese, Eurasian, and European minorities. The main towns of the two territories are Kupang (population 25,000) in West Timor and Dili (about 27,000) in East Timor. Reflecting a marked lack of economic and social development, the illiteracy rate is about 90 per cent.

The local economy is based on shifting cultivation and both wet and dry settled rice farming, with cash crops of coffee, cocoa, coconut, and sandalwood, and some cattle and specialised pony rearing. The staple food crop, in the predominant shifting cultivation system, is sago. While most cash cropping in West Timor is done by smallholders, Portuguese colonial plantations traditionally produced most coffee in East Timor (in 1974, coffee earned US $5·8 million of East Timor's US $6·8 million export receipts). There are about 4000 km of roads on the whole island. Timor suffers from generally poor communications, with a single main road traversing the interior of West Timor from Kupang in the west to Atambua in the east, and a coastal road linking Dili in East Timor with the island's eastern tip (of the latter's 1900 km of road, only a few miles around Dili are surfaced, and communications with the interior are rudimentary, often mere tracks). There are indications of oil and gas around Timor, but the deposits are as yet undeveloped.

History. By virtue of a fortified post there, Timor was part of the Portuguese 'garrison empire' in Asia from the

15th century. The island was divided between Portugal and Holland by treaty in 1859, with boundaries settled by arbitration in 1914. After western Timor became part of independent Indonesia in 1949, the Portuguese sector remained a colony. By 1975, the latter was still severely underdeveloped. Its economy depended on one export crop, it had one high school and a literacy rate of 7 per cent, and its budget was two-thirds subsidised by Portugal. Portugal also made up a persistent trade deficit, and a small group of Portuguese together with 7000 Chinese dominated the economy.

The colony was scheduled to become independent in October 1978, but civil war broke out in 1975. The moderate-left Revolutionary Front for the Independence of East Timor (FRETILIN), with the support of about 60 per cent of the population, wanted immediate independence; the right-wing Democratic Union of Timor (UDT), with minority support of the wealthier Timorese, the middle civil servants and Chinese, wanted gradual independence with continuing close links with Portugal; and the Popular Democratic Association of Timor (APODETI), with about 5 per cent popular support, wanted integration with Indonesia, citing the historical boundary of the Javanese Majapahit empire, under whose influence Timor fell for a period during the 14th century. Indonesian fears of a left-wing victory, and Indonesian intervention during 1975, led to annexation by Indonesia in 1976 with subsequent continuation of guerrilla warfare.

Timoshenko, Semën Konstantinovich (1895–1970), Soviet marshal, born at Furmanka, on the old Russo-Romanian frontier. Called up for military service in 1915, he fought in the First World War. Early in 1918 he was with the Black Sea Partisan detachment, a cavalry force, fighting in the Crimea and against Kaledin's Don Cossacks. He later joined Budënny's First Cavalry Army and rose to the rank of general. In 1920 he was in the Russo-Polish campaign, and after the defeat near Warsaw he returned to the Crimea, where, at Perekop, he was defeated by Wrangel's troops and wounded for the fourth time. At the Frunze Military Academy, which he entered in 1922, he qualified for high command after study both there and at the Military and Political Academy for commanders and commissars, which he joined in 1930. It was Timoshenko who retrieved the Russian military position in the Russo-Finnish War of 1939–40. When the Germans invaded Russia, Timoshenko, who, as defence commissar, had reorganised the Red Army and introduced many reforms, was entrusted with the defence of Moscow. After he had repulsed the Germans, Stalin sent him to stem the enemy's advance in the Ukraine in November 1941. From 1939 to 1952 he was a member of the Central Committee of the Communist Party and was subsequently a candidate member.

Timotheus of Miletus (446–357 BC), Greek lyric poet. He added an 11th string to the lyre (or cithara) and so incurred the displeasure of Athens and Sparta. EURIPIDES wrote a prologue to his lyric nome, the *Persea*, of which fragments were discovered in 1902.

Bibliography: E. Diehl, *Anthologia Lyrica Graeca*, 1949.

Timothy, Saint (d. AD 97), young friend and fellow-labourer of St Paul. He was a native of Lystra, his mother Eunice being a Jewess and his father a Greek. He accompanied St Paul on the second missionary journey, and the lives of the two are henceforward closely connected. Timothy was left as the apostle's representative at Ephesus, where he received two epistles from him. Eusebius says that he met his death there in a popular riot, after denouncing the worship of Artemis.

Timothy, Epistles to, form with the Epistle to Titus the group known since 1703 (after D. N. Berdot) as the Pastoral Epistles, which give detailed instructions for the appointment of officers and the pastoral care of the Christian churches. They were for centuries believed to have been written by St Paul, but many Protestant scholars consider that they are later in date. The Pastorals are strongly doctrinal. The Christian life must show no incongruity between creed and practice, and Christianity must be translated into ethical and spiritual terms. The Christian is to fight a good fight and expect suffering, and his swan song will be a song of victory. Other points are the unity of God; the inspiration of scripture; and the danger of riches. There are commentaries on the Pastoral Epistles by D. Guthrie, 1957; J. N. D. Kelly, 1964; R. A. Ward, 1975.

Timothy Grass, common name of *Phleum pratense*, a perennial grass native to Britain, and often grown as fodder for livestock.

Timpani, the orchestral kettle-drums. Imported from the Turkish armies through Hungary at the end of the 15th century, they were adopted as royal instruments in all the courts of Europe. They were introduced into the orchestra in the 17th century and were commonly associated with the trumpets. Because the body is a closed vessel they can be accurately tuned to precise pitches by varying the tension of the skin with tuning handles. Modern instruments can be tuned instantaneously by a pedal which acts on all the tuning handles simultaneously. A set of timpani, from two to six, each of a different size and so producing a different range of pitches, are used in the orchestra, the basic pair being 63·5 cm and 71 cm in diameter, producing a range of C–high F and low G–C respectively. Timpani are normally played with felt-headed sticks though other materials are used for special effects; a player carries a variety of pairs of sticks, each of which will produce a different sonority.

Bibliography: P. R. Kirby, *The Kettle-Drums*, 1930; J. Blades, *Percussion Instruments and their History*, 1975.

Timrod, Henry (1828–67), US poet, born at Charleston, South Carolina. Educated at Franklin College, he studied law, but gave that up and became a schoolmaster. In 1860 he published a volume of verse, and many of his war poems, such as 'A Cry to Arms' and 'Carolina', were such an inspiration to the South in the Civil War that he was termed 'the laureate of the Confederacy'. The war ruined him in both fortunes and health.

Bibliography: G. A. Wauchope, *Henry Timrod, Man and Poet*, 1915; V. P. Clare, *Harp of the South*, 1936.

Tin, metallic chemical element, symbol Sn, atomic number 50, atomic weight 118·69; one of the seven metals of the ancients. It occurs free in nature in scattered deposits, but the oxide—tinstone or cassiterite—found in Cornwall, Australia, Malaysia, Nigeria, and South

America, is the only commercial source. Although it is widely used, it is not an abundant metal, being, for example, less common than titanium. The metal is prepared from the ore by roasting to remove arsenic and sulphur followed by heating in a reverberatory furnace with anthracite. The tin so formed is remelted and allowed to flow from the higher-melting impurities; some tin is purified by electrolysis. Tin melts at 232 °C. There are at least two allotropic forms: grey tin (relative density 5·8) exists below 13 °C; above this temperature, white tin (relative density 7·3) is stable. White tin is crystalline in structure and when bent emits a curious crackling sound called the 'cry of tin'. Tin is not acted upon by the air, and is therefore used for tinning iron. Tin readily dissolves in hydrochloric acid with evolution of hydrogen and the formation of stannous chloride ($SnCl_2$). It is not acted upon by dilute sulphuric acid but dissolves in the concentrated acid. Stannic oxide is formed by the action of nitric acid on the metal, while chlorine acting on the metal forms the tetrachloride ($SnCl_4$). Tin forms two series of salts, the stannous, in which it is bivalent, and the stannic, in which it is quadrivalent. The stannic salts correspond with similar compounds of carbon and silicon, the oxide (SnO_2) is acidic, and the tetrachloride is a fuming liquid. The stannous salts are strong reducing agents. The oxide (SnO) is basic but also acts as an acid-forming oxide towards strong bases. The alloys of tin are of great value, and include gunmetal (copper 88, tin 10, zinc 2 per cent), bronze (copper and tin), phosphor bronze (0·5 per cent phosphorus), pewter (tin 80, lead 20 per cent), modern pewter (tin, antimony, copper, with a little bismuth), solder, bell metal, as well as a large number of alloys with other metals such as gold, iron, and bismuth. The most important tin compound is stannous chloride, which is used as a mordant and as a reducing agent.

Tin-plate and Sheet, basis of low-carbon unalloyed mild steel coated by hot-dipping or electrodeposition with pure tin. It is used chiefly for the manufacture of cans and boxes. See IRON AND STEEL; METALLURGY.

Tinamou, any game bird of the family Tinamidae, inhabiting the forests of tropical and South America and placed in a separate order, Tinamiformes. They resemble partridges in appearance, but have little or no tail. However, this resemblance is only superficial, for the tinamous have a number of anatomical features in common with the flightless RATITES.

Despite their large flight muscles, they are not good flyers, being slow and clumsy. They generally escape predators by standing still, or by stealing away through dense cover. The coloration of the plumage is highly protective and they are well camouflaged. They feed largely on vegetable matter supplemented by insects. Polygamy appears to predominate; often several females lay eggs in one nest; one hen may also lay eggs in nests guarded by different males. The males build the nests and incubate the eggs.

Tincture, see HERALDRY, *Tinctures*.

Tindal, Matthew (c. 1656–1733), English deist, born at Bere Ferrers, Devon, and educated at Lincoln College, Oxford, becoming fellow of All Souls (1678). After having been received into the Roman Catholic Church (1685) he returned to the Church of England (1688), and

later wrote controversial pamphlets, which all met with vehement opposition from the High Church party. He aroused fierce controversy with the publication of *The Rights of the Christian Church Against all Romish and Other Priests*, 1706. But his famous work was his *Christianity as Old as the Creation*, 1730, popularly known as 'The Deist's Bible', which had for its purpose the 'stripping of religion of the additions which policy, mistakes and the circumstances of the times have made to it'.

Bibliography: E. Curll, *Memoirs of the Life and Writings of Matthew Tindal*, 1734; J. Hunt, *Religious Thought in England*, ii, 431, 1896.

Tindale, William, see TYNDALE, WILLIAM.

Tindemans, Leo (1922–), Prime Minister of Belgium. Born at Zwijndrecht, a Flemish community in the north of Brabant, he was educated at the State University of Ghent and at the Catholic University of Louvain. He entered the Chamber of Deputies in 1961 as a member for the Christian Socialist party. He immediately attracted the attention of senior members of his party and received rapid promotion. In 1972 he was appointed deputy prime minister and was given responsibility for the Budget in the Cabinet. In 1973, after a governmental crisis, the King called upon him to form a government. In 1974 he became secretary general of the European Union of Christian Democrats. He is an expert on constitutional and international problems and has published several books upon these subjects.

Tinea, see RINGWORM.

Tinned Meat, see CANNING; FOOD PRESERVATION.

Tinnitus, ringing in the ears. It is a frequent symptom of EAR disease and may be described by the patient as a buzzing, humming, hissing, whistling, crackling, jangling or roaring sound. Tinnitus is a purely subjective phenomenon resulting from some disorder of the auditory system and is not due to sound waves from the outside being received by the ear. It may be due to trivial conditions in the external or middle ear such as a plug of wax or a blocked Eustachian tube. Disorders of the middle ear which give rise to tinnitus are otosclerosis and OTITIS media. (See DEAFNESS.) The causes of tinnitus in the inner ear are not known, but it is a constant feature of MENIÈRE'S DISEASE and often accompanies presbycusis, the senorineural deafness of old age. Diseases of the auditory nerve or the higher auditory centre in the temporal lobe of the brain also cause tinnitus. People show wide variation in their tolerance of tinnitus, and nervous or tense people may become profoundly depressed by the constant annoyance. Unfortunately for these sufferers, there is no medical or surgical treatment for tinnitus, although it may fade of its own accord or following treatment of the underlying condition.

Tinsel, in Scots law, is the process open to the SUPERIOR if the vassal fails for two consecutive years to pay the feu-duty (see FEU AND FEU-DUTY). The effect of the tinsel is to reduce the entire feu-contract, and the land reverts to the superior.

Tintagel, coastal village and parish on the north coast of CORNWALL, England. The correct name of the village proper is Trevena, which merges with Bossiney. Tintagel

Tintern Abbey

is a celebrated holiday resort with good bathing beaches. On Tintagel Head, a promontory 91 m high on the Atlantic coast, are the ruins of a castle, famous in the Arthurian romances. Some affirm that King ARTHUR was born here and held his court at Tintagel. In other versions Tintagel is the impregnable retreat of King Mark. In 1685 a borough charter was granted to Tintagel, Trevena, and Bossiney. Population (1971) of parish, including Trevena and Bossiney, 1372.

Tintern Abbey, famous ruins at Tintern village beautifully situated on the WYE river, north of Chepstow, Gwent. They date from 1131, when Walter de Clare founded a Cistercian house which became one of the wealthiest foundations in England. The building was mainly erected between 1269 and 1287 by Roger Bigod, Earl of Norfolk, but work continued until 1320. The chief remains are the ruins of the magnificent cruciform church, the chapter-house and refectory. The great west window is one of the finest examples of curvilinear tracery. Tintern has been considered one of the most picturesque and romantic spots in Britain since the 18th century, and has often been celebrated in water-colour and verse. The site was purchased by the Crown in 1901.

Tínto, Río, see RÍO TÍNTO.

Tintoretto, Jacopo Robusti (1518–94), chief painter of the later Venetian school, born in Venice. He studied under Titian, and was considerably influenced by Michelangelo, writing on the wall of his studio the precept 'Michelangelo's drawing, Titian's colour'. His paintings show never-failing imagination, broad and dramatic composition, fine draughtsmanship and a superb use of colour. His industrious life was spent almost entirely in Venice where he had a workshop which included his sons Domenico (c. 1560–1635), Marco (d. 1637) and daughter Marietta (c.1556–90?). There he painted his great *Miracle of St Mark*, 1548, his decorations for the Scuola di San Rocco (including the vast *Christ before Pilate* and *Last Supper*), and the *Paradise* for the Doge's Palace, 1588. The *St George and the Dragon* (National Gallery, London) demonstrates his characteristic originality in depicting figures in rushing movement, and *The Origin of the Milky Way* (National Gallery) is one of the most

Tintern Abbey. *(National Monuments Record)*

Tintoretto. *The Origin of the Milky Way* (finished 1578). Jupiter holds the infant Hercules to the breast of Juno; milk spills upwards to form the Milky Way and downwards to form lilies. *(National Gallery, London)*

beautiful allegories. His oeuvre includes a large number of portraits, e.g. *Vincenzo Morosini* (National Gallery).

Bibliography: Lives by E. M. Philips, 1911, L. Coletti, 1944, H. Tietze, 1948, E. Newton, 1952; J. S. Schulz, *Venetian Painted Ceilings of the Renaissance*, 1968.

Tintype, see FERROTYPE.

Tipitaka (Sanskrit *Tripitaka*) or Triple Basket, the canonical writings in Pāli of THERAVĀDA Buddhism. The name derives from the containers in which the scrolls were originally stored. These scriptures, otherwise known as the Pāli Canon, were first written down (on ola leaves) at a special council held in Sri Lanka (Ceylon) in c. 80 BC, and are among the earliest existing record of the *Buddha Dhamma* (Teaching of the Buddha). Until then, the *Dhamma* had been passed down orally by the Elders of the SAṄGHA. Many times longer than the Christian Bible, the Tipitaka is divided into three sections: the *Vinaya Pitaka* ('Discipline' or 'Rules for the Order'); the *Sutta Pitaka* ('Discourses' or 'Sermons'); and the *Abhidhamma Pitaka* ('Special Teaching'—commentaries and a collection of material dealing with mind-development). Over the years, commentaries have been added to the Tipitaka, but little of the original text has been altered.

See BUDDHISM; PĀLI.

Tipperary, inland county of the province of Munster, Republic of IRELAND, bounded by Galway and Offaly in the north, Cork and Waterford to the south, Laois and Kilkenny to the east, and Clare and Limerick to the west. The county is one of those supposed to have been made by King John in 1210. It was granted to the Earls of Ormonde in 1328, and was the last of the Irish palatine counties. In 1848 it was the scene of the Young Ireland rising, an abortive rebellion. To the north and west lies a mountainous region with Keeper Hill (672 m), and in the south are the Galtee Mountains with Galtymore (920 m), the Knockmealdown Mountains and, farther east, the Slieveardagh Hills. The Bog of ALLEN adjoins Kilkenny, while in the south-west lies the Golden Vale, one of the most fertile regions in all Ireland. The principal rivers are the SHANNON in the north-west, Little Brosna, and Nenagh, and the Suir in the centre; Lough Derg on the north-west boundary is the only lake of any size. Agriculture is the chief industry; barley and oats are the main crops, and potatoes and turnips are also grown; but most of the area is under pasture, and cattle are reared in large numbers. Dairy farming flourishes, and there are a number of butter factories. There are also flour and meal mills. Coal, copper, lead, and zinc are mined, also slate and limestone, and peat production is being extended. There are many interesting castles and ecclesiastical buildings in various parts of the county, notably at Cashel, where there is a round tower at Ardfinnan, at Athassel (an Augustinian priory), at Holycross (Cistercian abbey), and at Fethard and Roscrea (abbeys). Moor Abbey stands at the head of the Glen of Aherlow. The county is divided into a north and south riding. The county town is CLONMEL; other towns are Tipperary, Carrick-on-Suir, Nenagh, Thurles, Cashel, and Templemore. Area 4296 km²; population 123,565.

Tipperary, market town of County TIPPERARY, Republic of Ireland, at the foot of the Slievenamuck Hills. In the fertile plain known as the Golden Vale, it is famous for its butter making, and there are also condensed and powdered-milk factories and lino and glove manufacturers. Some 6 km from the town is the Glen of Aherlow, and just outside the town is New Tipperary, the village built by William O'Brien in 1890 for the tenants of Smith-Barry who gave up their holdings on account of a Land League dispute. Charles Kickham, the patriot poet and novelist, was born in Tipperary. Population 4717.

Tippett, Sir Michael (1905–), British composer, born in London of Cornish stock; studied at the Royal College of Music under Charles Wood and later under R. O. Morris. Most of his early works were withdrawn. His humanitarian views first found significant expression in *A Child of Our Time*, a war-time oratorio (1941). Shortly afterwards Tippett was imprisoned for violating the terms of his exemption from military service as a conscientious objector. From 1940 to 1951 he was musical director of Morley College; otherwise he has spent all his time composing. Tippett is very deliberate and highly self-critical, so that works appear in slow succession, but always show closely concentrated craftsmanship and great originality. He owes nothing to current systems, much less to fashions, but his work is distinctly modern in a very personal way. It includes three symphonies, a Concerto for double string orchestra, a Fantasy on a Theme by Handel, a Concerto for piano and orchestra, a Concerto for orchestra, three string quartets, three piano sonatas, two sets of songs, *Boyhood's End* (W. H. Hudson) and *The Heart's Assurance*, the operas *The Midsummer Marriage* (1955), *King Priam* (1962), *The Knot Garden* (1970), and *The Ice Break* (1977), and the oratorio *The Vision of Saint Augustine*, 1966. He was made a CBE in

1959; Hon D Mus Cantab, in 1964. He was knighted in 1966.
Bibliography: J. Kemp (Ed.), *Michael Tippett: a Symposium*, 1965.

Tippoo Sultan, see TIPU SAHIB.

Tipstaff, in England and Wales, an officer of the High Court whose function it is to arrest and take to prison any person committed by the court. The name is often extended to any constable, sheriff's officer, court crier, or usher, and is connected with the staff tipped with metal or a small crown which was formerly his badge of office.

Tipton, town formerly in Staffordshire; now part of DUDLEY, in West Midlands county, England. Its parish registers, beginning in 1513, are the oldest in England.

Tiptree, village in Essex, England, 74 km from London. It is noted for fruit and seed growing, and for its jam factory. Population (1971) 6160.

Tipu Sahib (1749–99), son of HAIDER ALI, succeeded his father as Sultan of Mysore in 1782. He had previously distinguished himself in the Maratha War, 1775–79, and in the first Mysore War had defeated the British in 1782. As sultan he concluded a treaty with the British in 1784, but in spite of this invaded the protected state of Travancore in 1789. War followed, and in 1792 he was obliged to resign half of his dominions. He continued his intrigues, urging the French to stir up war with Britain, the result of which was the storming of his capital, Seringapatam, by the British, during which action Tipu was killed.
Bibliography: M. H. Khan, *History of Tipu Sultan*, 1952; D. Forrest, *Tiger of Mysore, the life and death of Tipu Sultan*, 1970.

Tiraboschi, Gerolamo (1731–94), Italian scholar, born at Bergamo. He was a Jesuit and professor of rhetoric in the University of Milan, 1755. Among his works are *Vetera Humiliatorum Monumenta*, 1766, and *Storia della Letteratura Italiana* (13 volumes), 1772–81, the latter being his most famous accomplishment.

Tiranë, capital of ALBANIA and of Tiranë district, 27 km from the Adriatic Sea, on the River Ishm, situated in a fertile plain. The town was founded in the 17th century as Teheran by a Turkish governor when Albania was within the Ottoman Empire. It was chosen as the capital in 1920 and in the 1930s King Zog commissioned Italian architects to replan the existing town. Districts of the old town and several old mosques are preserved. Tiranë is the country's industrial and commercial, as well as administrative, centre and its industries include metallurgy, textiles, cigarettes, foodstuffs, and timber. There is an airport and rail links to Elbasan and DURRËS which serves as Tiranë's port. Population (town) 182,500; (district) 272,000.

Tiraspol, city in the MOLDAVIAN SSR, USSR, on the Dniester north-west of Odessa. It is an important industrial centre, especially of food products (tinned goods, fruit and vegetables, wines and spirits). It was founded in 1792 and was capital of the Moldavian Autonomous Republic 1924–40. Population (1970) 105,000.

Tiratana, or Triratna, see TRIPLE-GEM.

Tiree

Tiree, small island in the Inner HEBRIDES, Scotland, 21 km west of MULL and 2 km south-west of COLL. Apart from the western part of the island, it is very flat and low. Seventy-five per cent of its area of 7700 ha lies below the 20 m contour and 33·5 per cent is composed of sand dunes and fertile MACHAIR. With one of the highest sunshine totals in Britain and a dry climate, Tiree has had a reputation for rich fodder crops and excellent cattle stock. It is also an important tourist area, with good air services to Glasgow from Reef airfield. The main village is Scarinish, with boat services to Coll, Mull, and Oban. Population 875.

Tiresias, legendary blind soothsayer of Thebes (see THEBAN LEGEND). After the defeat of Thebes, he fled with other refugees—or, according to another version, was carried off captive—but on the road he drank from the spring Tilphusa, and died. He was believed to retain his powers as a seer in the underworld (Odyssey xi. 90–150).

Tîrgovişte, town and capital of Dîmboviţa province, Romania, 70 km north-west of Bucharest. There is a 16th-century Orthodox church and ruins of a 14th-century castle. From 1383 to 1698 Tîrgovişte was capital of WALLACHIA. Population 64,000.

Tîrgu Jiu, town in south-western Romania, the capital of Gorj province some 80 km north-west of Craiova. It has rapidly developed as an industrial centre since 1945 with important coal-mines and oil-fields in the vicinity. Population 43,000.

Tîrgu-Mureş (Hungarian *Maros-Vásárhely*; German *Neudorf*), town of TRANSYLVANIA, Romania, capital of Mureş province, 80 km east of Cluj, on the left bank of the River Mureş. There is an old fortress with a Gothic church, and a palace with a library of 90,000 volumes. Sugar, textiles, leather, spirits, and furniture are among the articles made, and there is a trade in grain and wool. Population (1974) 139,375.

Tiridates, name of several Parthian and Armenian kings. The two best known are Tiridates I and II.

Tiridates I conquered Armenia with the assistance of his brother, Vologaeses I of Parthia. In AD 63 he was obliged by the victories of Corbulo to abdicate and accept his crown anew at the hands of Nero.

Tiridates II, who had been educated at Rome, was placed on the throne of Armenia by Diocletian in 286. He was constantly at war with the Persians, and died a Christian in 314.

Tirlemont, see TIENEN.

Tiro, Marcus Tullius, freedman, secretary and friend of CICERO. He was himself an author of no mean reputation, and notices of his works have been preserved by ancient writers. After Cicero's death (43 BC) Tiro bought a farm in the neighbourhood of Puteoli, and is said to have died at the age of over 100. He is commonly believed to have invented the first system of Latin SHORTHAND.

Tirol, or Tyrol, former crown land of the Austro-Hungarian Empire, now part of a province of AUSTRIA (see below). In Roman times it was part of Rhaetia. It was later ruled by the bishops of Brixen and Trent, and came into the possession of the house of HAPSBURG in 1363. It

was ceded to Bavaria in 1805 (see also HOFER, ANDREAS), but was returned to Austria by the Congress of VIENNA in 1814. By the Treaty of ST GERMAIN-EN-LAYE in 1919, it was divided, the part north of the BRENNER PASS becoming a province of the new Austrian republic, and the part south of the pass being ceded to Italy. Italian *Tirolo*—the Trentino and the upper ADIGE—was the subject of bitter contention between Austria and Italy (1919–39). (For the history of this question, see under AUSTRIA, *History*.) After the Second World War it was decided, despite Austrian demands to the contrary, that South Tirol should remain Italian. An Austro-Italian agreement relating to the region was incorporated into the peace treaty of 1947. Under the agreement, German- and Italian-speaking people have equal rights, and the region has a degree of legislative and administrative autonomy, but Austrian dissatisfaction with the settlement remains, and since 1947 there have been many sabotage incidents in the region, perpetrated by pro-Austrian elements.

Tirol, or Tyrol, Alpine province of western AUSTRIA, and the northern half of the former crown land (see above). It is bounded on the north by Bavaria and on the south by Italy. East Tirol, the part south of the Hohe Tauern, is detached from the rest of the province. The main part of the province contains the valleys of the INN and the LECH—both trending south-west to north-east. The Alpine ranges separating these valleys are broken up by many small rivers flowing south–north. Grossglockner (3798 m), the highest peak in Austria, is at the junction of the borders of East Tirol, Salzburg, and Styria. The valley of the upper Drau crosses East Tirol. The province is heavily forested. The chief occupations are dairy-farming, stock-raising, and forestry. Lignite, nickel, lead, and other minerals are found; there are textile and chemi-

Tirol. The tropical park at Merano lies within sight of the Otztaler Alps. *(Camera Press/Carl Pospesch)*

cal industries, and there are several hydro-electric installations. Tourism is a major source of revenue. The capital is ĪNNSBRUCK. Area 12,650 km². Population (1971) 540,771.

Tirpitz, Alfred Peter Friedrich von (1849–1930), German grand-admiral, born at Küstrin. He attended the Realschule at Frankfurt am Main, passed into the Prussian navy in 1865, and for 30 years was almost continuously at sea. In the 1870s Tirpitz, a lieutenant-commander, prepared memoranda on torpedoes, which led to the creation of a torpedo-section in 1885. In 1892 he was appointed to the naval staff at Berlin. He was made a rear-admiral in 1895, and in 1896 he was appointed to command the Asiatic Cruiser Squadron; under his direction Tsingtao became a German naval base. On returning home in 1897 he became secretary of state for the navy. In 1898 he presented to the Reichstag his first Navy Bill, the beginning of the serious growth of the German navy. His second bill, brought in in 1900, started the naval armament race which was much influenced by the astute propaganda for his view that a strong fleet was the essential guarantee of Germany's position as a great power. He was made admiral in 1903, and grand-admiral in 1911. At the beginning of the First World War he was still secretary of state for the navy; but he was on bad terms with his naval colleagues and did not succeed in his purpose of making full use of the navy from the beginning. He resigned on 15 March 1916, and was a Nationalist member of the Reichstag from 1924 to 1928, and then retired to private life. He wrote *My Memoirs*, 1919, and *Der Aufbau der deutschen Weltmacht*, 1924.

Bibliography: J. Steinberg, *Yesterday's Deterrent*, 1967; V. R. Berghahn, *Der Tirpitz-Plan*, 1971.

Tirso de Molina, pseudonym of Gabrile Téllez (c. 1584–1648), Spanish dramatist, born in Madrid. He was a very prolific writer, and wrote three hundred comedies. His best-known play is *El Burlador de Sevilla*, introducing the figure of Don Juan. He also excelled in historical plays, such as *La Prudencia en la Mujer*, and biblical dramas, like *La Venganza de Tamar*. His work combines an ironical approach to human problems, especially those connected with free will and grace, with a frequently violent or melodramatic stage-action.

Bibliography: I. L. MacClelland, *Tirso de Molina; Studies in Dramatic Realism*, 1948; A. H. Bushee, *Three Centuries of Tirso de Molina*, 1939.

Tiruchirappalli, or Trichinopoly, town of TAMIL NADU state, India. It is an important rail centre at the head of the CAUVERY river delta with textile, cement, as well as railway goods manufacturing at Golden Rock. The town is dominated by an isolated hill with a fort and temple, and was the scene of much fighting between British and French forces until annexed by Britain in 1801. Population (1971) 464,625.

Tiryns, ancient city of Argolis, traditionally founded by Proetus, who was said to have built the walls with the aid of the Cyclopes. Tiryns existed in the 3rd millennium BC; its earliest fortifications were erected about 1000 years later, and rebuilt at least twice. The city was finally destroyed by the people of Argos in 468 BC. Excavations made between 1884 and 1927 have revealed many interesting structures, including the remains of two palaces dating from about 1400 BC. See also AEGEAN CULTURE.

Tisa, see TISZA.

Tisarana, see TRIPLE-GEM.

Tischendorf, Konstantin von (1815–74), German biblical scholar, born at Legenfeld in Saxony. He made a special study of New Testament criticism at the University of Leipzig, and in 1845 became professor there. He discovered the 4th-century Sinaitic Codex (see SINAITICUS, CODEX), at the monastery on Mount Sinai. His works include editions of the Sinaitic Codex, 1862–63, *Editio VIII* of the New Testament, 1864–72, the *Monumenta Sacra Inedita*, 1846–71, *Reise in den Orient*, 1846, and *Aus dem Heiligen Lande*, 1862, which describe his journeys.

Tiselius, Arne Wilhelm Kaurin (1902–71), Swedish biochemist, born in Stockholm. In 1931 he took a DPhil at Uppsala, where he worked on chemistry, electrophoresis, and absorption analysis, and made discoveries on the nature of serum proteins. He received the Nobel Prize for chemistry in 1948.

Tishri, the seventh month of the ecclesiastical but the first month of the civil Jewish CALENDAR. It corresponds to parts of September and October. The Jewish New Year begins on 1 Tishri, and is followed by the DAY OF ATONEMENT (10 Tishri) and the festival of Tabernacles (15–22 Tishri). See ROSH HA-SHANAH; TABERNACLES, FEAST OF.

Tisio da Garofalo, see GAROFALO.

Tisiphone, see ERINYES.

Tissa, see TISZA.

Tissaphernes, Persian satrap of Asia Minor (414 BC). During the Peloponnesian War he pretended to support the Spartans; but his real aim was the exhaustion of both sides through the continuance of hostilities. At the battle of Cunaxa (401 BC) Tissaphernes was one of the four generals commanding the army of Artaxerxes, and his troops were the only part of the left wing not routed by the Greeks. When the TEN THOUSAND began their retreat Tissaphernes offered to conduct them to safety, but he had their generals arrested and put to death. As a reward for his services he was invested by Artaxerxes with the territories formerly governed by CYRUS THE YOUNGER, who had given the Spartans effective aid. The result was war with Sparta; Tissaphernes was defeated by Agesilaus II near Sardis, and was put to death (395 BC) through the influence of the queen-mother, Parysatis.

Tisserand, François Félix (1845–96), French astronomer, born at Nuits-Saint-Georges, Côte d'Or. He was director of the observatories of Toulouse (1873) and Paris (1892). His work included many branches of celestial mechanics, especially the orbits of comets; he founded the *Bulletin Astronomique*, 1884, and published *Traité de Mécanique céleste* (vols 1–4), 1889–96.

Tissington, village in Derbyshire, England, 13 km southwest of Wirksworth, noted for the well-dressing ceremonies carried out on Ascension Day, when five wells, which were of benefit to the inhabitants during the Black Death, are decorated with pictures made from flower

Tissot, James Joseph Jacques

petals, leaves, and mosses set in damp clay, and visited in procession.

Tissot, James Joseph Jacques (1836–1902), French painter, born at Nantes. Initially he was influenced by DEGAS and shared his interest in Japanese prints. He settled in England after 1870 where he did illustrations for London journals. He also illustrated the life of Christ, spending ten years in Palestine, but is better-known for charming pictures of late-Victorian life, for example *The Picnic* and *The Ball on Shipboard* (both in the Tate Gallery). He was also an accomplished etcher.

Bibliography: J. Laver, *Vulgar Society: the romantic career of James Tissot*, 1936.

Tissue, a collection of associated cells having in common form, function, and/or other characteristics. In animals there is frequently dead, non-cellular material (matrix) deposited between the cells, as for instance in bone and cartilage. The study of tissues is HISTOLOGY. Tissues may be named according to the types of cells composing them, e.g. muscular and nervous tissues of animals, and parenchymatous, prosenchymatous and sclerenchymatous tissues of plants; or according to their function, e.g. connective tissues of animals, vascular and storage tissues of plants; or according to their position, e.g. epithelial tissue of animals and dermal tissues, such as cork and bark, of plants. The discovery of nutritional media in which living tissues may be cultivated *in vitro* (see TISSUE CULTURE) has added much to the knowledge of cell division and differentiation and of the behaviour of strains of cancer cells. See also DEVELOPMENTAL BIOLOGY; EMBRYOLOGY.

Tissue Culture, a technique of cutting out small portions of living tissues and placing them in conditions where the cells can grow and develop autonomously. The conditions required are: nutritive elements suitable for cell growth and division, an oxygen supply, a suitable temperature near that of the organism from which the tissue was taken, removal of excretory products or the reculturing of the cells in fresh media, and aseptic conditions.

The first attempts at tissue culture were performed by Ross Harrison in 1907 when he developed the hanging drop method, a technique still used. For this, cells are placed in a drop of culture medium on a coverslip (a small thin glass slide). This is inverted and placed over a hollow cavity in a thick glass slide, and the edges are sealed. The cells can be observed in the liquid drop through the coverslip, using a microscope. Natural culture media may be used, such as plasma or embryonic fluid, when the nutrients present are not exactly known. In 1946 White developed synthetic solutions of known composition for culturing cells and this trend has continued, allowing the control of the external environment of living cells in culture. With this degree of control, experiments regarding nutrient requirements for growth and differentiation, for instance, can be carried out by varying one nutrient in the culture medium at a time. Other experiments that can be carried out using specific culture media include the effects of hormones on growth, tumour development, cell adhesion, cell motility, and cell behaviour in general. By growing cells outside of the living body, a vast amount of knowledge can be gained.

Bibliography: J. Paul, *Cell and Tissue Culture*, 4th ed. 1970.

Tissue Paper, see PAPER.

Tisza (German *Theiss*; Serbo-Croatian *Tisa*), river of the Ukraine, .Hungary, and Yugoslavia. It rises in two headstreams in the CARPATHIANS and flows across the ALFÖLD, generally parallel with the DANUBE, which it joins at NOVI SAD. In its lower reaches in Yugoslavia it is also connected with the Danube by canal. At Tiszalök, south of TOKAJ, there is an important hydroelectric station and a scheme for irrigating part of the HORTOBÁGY *puszta*. The principal tributaries are the Körös and the Mureşul. Length 1350 km.

Tisza of Borosjenö and Szeged, István, Count (1861–1918), Hungarian statesman, born in Budapest, son of Kálmán Tisza, a former Liberal prime minister of Hungary. He was prime minister from 1903 to 1905 and again from 1913. A staunch supporter of Hungary's links with Austria, Tisza kept the franchise narrow and refused to make concessions to the national demands of Slav and Romanian politicians. On the death of the Emperor Francis Joseph in 1916, Tisza's influence began to wane. The Emperor Charles favoured a policy of conciliation towards the Slavs and also a democratisation of the franchise. Tisza resigned in May 1917, and was assassinated by soldiers on 31 October 1918.

Tit, or titmouse, birds of the family Paridae in order Passeriformes. Six species, all insect-eaters, are common in Britain and one occurs occasionally. The crested tit, *Parus cristatus*, occurs only in parts of Scotland though it sometimes visits England. The blue tit, or tomtit, *P. caeruleus*, is the commonest one; its prevailing colour is blue, with green above, and a black throat. The coal tit, *P. ater*, has a black head, with a white patch on the nape. The great tit, *P. major*, is about 15 cm long and is yellow on the back, breast and sides, with grey wings and tail, and black head and throat. The marsh tit, *P. palustris*, and the willow tit, *P. montanus*, resemble the coal tit except for the latter's white nape and white spots on the wings. The long-tailed tit, *Aegithalos caudatus*, is about 13 cm long, and has prolonged, graduated black tail feathers. The bearded tit, *Panurus biarmicus*, is not a true tit and is more correctly called the bearded reedling. It is found mainly in Norfolk and the male is about 15 cm long, light red, with a tuft of black feathers on either side of its head. In North America tits are called chickadees.

Tit-lark, see PIPIT.

Titan, sixth and largest satellite of SATURN.

'Titanic' Disaster, caused when the White Star liner *Titanic*, then the largest vessel afloat, collided with an iceberg on the night of 14 April 1912, while on her maiden voyage to New York. She sank within three hours of impact and of her 2206 passengers, only 703 were saved. After an inquiry into the disaster, improvements in life-saving equipment were introduced and boat-drill for passengers made obligatory.

Bibliography: L. H. Beesley, *The Sinking of the Titanic*, 1912; W. Lord, *A Night to Remember*, 1956; W. J. Oldham, *The Ismay Line*, 1961.

Titanium, metallic chemical element, symbol Ti, atomic number 22, atomic weight 47·9. Titanium ranks ninth in abundance amongst the elements in the earth's crust, but owing to its reactivity at high temperatures its extraction from its ores, anatase, ilmanite, rutile, brookite, and aeschinite is particularly difficult. The element was first discovered in England by Gregor in 1790, but did not receive its name until Klaproth found it in Hungary in 1795 and named it after the mythological first sons of the earth, the Titans. Neither Gregor nor Klaproth succeeded in isolating elemental titanium, but isolated its oxide. It was in 1910 that Hunter succeeded in preparing the metal by the reduction of titanium tetrachloride with sodium in a sealed steel vessel. It was not until 1946, however, that Kroll first produced the metal on a pilot-plant scale by reducing the tetrachloride with magnesium; this method is now being generally used commercially, although sodium is sometimes used instead of magnesium. The du Pont Company became the first producers of metallic titanium for general sale in 1948. Since the molten metal (melting point 1660 °C) reacts with every known refractory sufficiently to produce serious contamination, special methods have had to be devised to melt and cast the pure metal. To overcome contamination a water-cooled metal crucible, usually copper, is used. The charge of titanium sponge obtained by the magnesium reduction of the tetrachloride is melted by a direct-current arc in an inert atmosphere of argon or helium. Additional sponge or titanium scrap is added and an ingot is built up layer by layer. The electrode assembly of tungsten is also water cooled. The metal does not wet or react with the water-cooled metal crucible. Continuous operation is maintained by slowly lowering the base of the crucible. Round ingots weighing 2000 kg have been produced by this method.

Titanium is a white, lustrous metal of low density (relative density 4·5) and high strength, and is resistant to corrosion. It is used in aircraft manufacture, in the manufacture of propeller shafts and other marine parts, and in surgery, because it is resistant to corrosion and is physiologically inert. Titanium dioxide (TiO_2) is an important white pigment, particularly useful in that it is non-toxic and does not discolour with age.

Titanotheres, extinct mammals of order Perissodactyla (horses) that lived in Eocene and early Oligocene times. They were of considerable size, and had large horn-like processes on the front of the skull. The teeth were primitive and the animals probably lived on soft vegetation.

Titans, fabulous beings in Greek mythology. Uranus and Gē (Heaven and Earth) had 18 children: (1) the three Hecatoncheires (hundred-handed monsters), named Aegaeon or Briareus, Gyas or Gyges, and Cottus; (2) the three Cyclopes, named Arges, Steropes, and Brontes; (3) six sons and six daughters called Titans, the most important of whom were CRONUS and RHEA.

Uranus cast the Hecatoncheires and Cyclopes into Tartarus, and Rhea, indignant, persuaded the Titans to rebel against their father. She gave Cronus a sickle, with which he emasculated Uranus and threw his genitals into the sea. From the blood that fell on the earth sprang the Gigantes, and (according to post-Homeric poets) from the foam thus generated in the sea rose APHRODITE. The Titans then deposed Uranus, freed their brothers and made Cronus their king.

Cronus flung the Hecatoncheires and Cyclops back into Tartarus and married his sister Rhea. But he had been warned by his parents that one of his own children

would dethrone him; so he swallowed each of them at birth: Hestia, Demeter, Hera, Pluto, and Poseidon. Rhea therefore, when carrying ZEUS went to Crete, bore her child in the Dictaean cave, left him in the charge of the CURETES and gave Cronus a stone wrapped in a cloth, which he swallowed believing it to be his son.

When Zeus grew up he employed Metis to give Cronus a potion which caused him to vomit up the children he had swallowed. Together with his brothers and sisters Zeus then began his struggle with the ruling Titans. It lasted ten years, until Gē promised victory to Zeus if he would deliver the Hecatoncheires and Cyclopes from Tartarus. He did so, and overcame the Titans with the help of the Cyclopes. The Titans were then thrust into Tartarus and the Hecatoncheires set to guard them.

Titchener, Edward Bradford (1867–1927), British experimental psychologist, born in Chichester. He graduated from Oxford 1890 and took a PhD at Leipzig 1892, following Wundt's ideas. Later he moved to Cornell University where he became a world recognised figure in experimental psychology. His important works include *Experimental Psychology—A Manual of Laboratory Practice* (2 vols) 1927.

Tite, Sir William (1798–1873), British architect, born in London. In 1824 he won competitions for the Presbyterian Church, Regent Square, and for the new buildings of Mill Hill School; and in 1840 for the Royal Exchange, London. He also built many railway stations in England and France including Edinburgh (1847) and Perth (1848).

Tithe, the 'tenth part of the increase yearly arising from the profits of lands, stocks upon lands, and the industry of the parishioners, payable for the maintenance of the parish priest, by everyone who had things titheable, if he cannot show a special exemption' (Thomas Wood's *Institute of the Laws of England*). Tithes were payable before the Christian era, but in the Christian Church tithes were first given by the faithful as spontaneous offerings in kind, e.g. wool, corn, or other agricultural or farm produce. Canon law later enjoined payment as a legal obligation in accordance with the divine law of the Old Testament (see TEINDS). Tithes were either *praedial*, *personal*, or *mixed*: praedial being the produce of the soil (e.g. corn, wood); personal, the produce of labour and industry; and mixed, the produce of animals, also including eggs. Before the Lateran Council (1215), it was a common practice to pay tithe payment to the parsons of parishes. In consequence most tithes belonged as of common right to the parish incumbents, though sometimes laymen could show a right to a portion of tithes based upon a prior voluntary grant to some spiritual corporation. Again, rectorial tithes, after the dissolution of the monasteries, frequently found their way into lay hands.

The only lands exempt from tithes were barren heath, waste forest, or glebe, old monastic lands held prior to the dissolution exempt from tithes, Crown lands, or lands held by a spiritual corporation, which had never been known to pay tithes, and lands in respect of which was payable a modus or composition real, an agreement between parson ordinary and landowners and patron, whereby the land-owners agreed to pay a perpetual sum

Tithe

in lieu of tithe. The Tithe Commutation Act 1836 and amending acts commuted all the tithes of England and Wales into tithe rentcharge and fixed the total amount of the rentcharge for which the tithes of each parish were to be commuted.

Provision was made by the Tithe Act 1918 for the compulsory redemption of rent charges exceeding 20s., the consideration money for redemption being the amount agreed between the owners of the land and of the rent-charge. Provision for the apportionment of annuities created by the redemption of tithe rentcharge was made by an act passed in 1921. The Tithe Act 1925 still further amended the law on tithe rentcharges, rents, etc., in lieu of tithe, and the payment of rates on rentcharge, etc. By this act any tithe rentcharge which before 31 March 1927 was attached to a benefice or to an ecclesiastical corpor-ation was transferred to be vested in the Governors of Queen Anne's Bounty and held in trust for the incumbent or corporation.

Notwithstanding much legislation, rentcharge gave rise to agitation and remained a vexed question which was settled only by another act, the Tithe Act of 1936, which at last ended a system containing ineradicable difficulties. This act extinguishes both rentcharge and extraordinary rentcharge, and makes provision through a Tithe Redemption Commission for compulsory redemption and for the compensation of persons interested, by the issue of 'redemption stock' charged on the Consolidated Fund. In other words, the rentcharge, previously payable to the Church, the Ecclesiastical Commissioners, Queen Anne's Bounty, and some lay owners, is replaced by 'redemption annuities' payable to the Crown, and the Crown issued government stock to the tithe-owners. Thus for the first time in its long history tithe was divorced from the Church. The annuities will be payable until 1996, when they should cease and all tithe (with a few minor exceptions, such as corn rent) will be abolished. A capital loss estimated at £17·75 million resulted to the Church of England from the act of 1936, a situation which called for every possible adjustment by the Ecclesiastical Com-missioners and Queen Anne's Bounty (now amalgamated as the Church Commissioners).

Tithonus, in Greek mythology, son of Laomedon, brother of Priam, loved for his beauty by Eos, who secured from Zeus for him the gift of immortality. Not, however, having eternal youth, he grew hideously old, and Eos turned him into a grasshopper.

Titian, otherwise called Tiziano Vecelli (c.1487/90–1576), Italian painter of the Venetian school, born at Pieve, in Cadore. He first studied under Zuccati, a mosaicist at Venice, afterwards becoming a

Titian. *Concert Champêtre.* It is generally believed that Titian completed this work after Giorgione's death. *(Louvre, Paris/Giraudon)*

Lake Titicaca. Harpoon fishing. *(Topham/Fotogram)*

pupil of Giovanni BELLINI and working with GIORGIONE. He emulated the latter's style so successfully that their contributions are inseparable in works which Titian completed after Giorgione's death in 1510. These include the Dresden *Venus* and the *Concert Champêtre* in Paris. He is reputed to have assisted Giorgione on the exterior fresco decorations of the Fondaco dei Tedeschi, Venice, which have since disappeared. His *Assumption of the Virgin* altarpiece in the Frari secured his reputation in Venice and was an important innovatory development in Venetian painting. His *Christ and the Tribute Money* (Dresden Gallery) was spoken of by Vasari as something stupendous and miraculous. In 1516 he was made official painter to the council in Venice. In 1522 he went to Ferrara, and executed amongst other works the glorious masterpiece *Bacchus and Ariadne* (National Gallery, London). In 1532 the Emperor Charles V commissioned a portrait of himself and rewarded Titian by making him a Count Palatine and a Knight of the Golden Spur. He was now of European eminence. He was with the Emperor at Milan in 1541, and in 1545 went to Rome where he painted portraits of Pope Paul III as well as *Danaë*, now in the Naples Museum. In 1548 he crossed the Alps to join Charles V at Augsburg, and painted the well-known portraits of Philip of Spain. From this time he was chiefly occupied in working at Venice where his large workshop included his son, Orazio. He died of plague in 1576. Titian's works are remarkable for their magnificent colouring and technical skill. He painted religious pictures, mythological, poetical and allegorical subjects and excelled as a portrait painter.

Bibliography: J. A. Crowe and G. B. Cavalcaselle, *Life and Times of Titian*, 1887; Studies by D. von Hadeln, 1927, R. F. Heath, 1930, H. Tietze, 1950, D. Cecchi (trans. N. Wydenbruck), 1957, C. Gould, 1969; H. Wethey, *The Religious Paintings*, 1969 and *The Portraits*, 1971.

Titicaca, Lake, mountain lake in the ANDES, half in Bolivia and half in Peru, between the main Andean range and the Cordillera Real. It is 3750 m above sea-level and claims to be the highest navigated lake in the world. Its area is about 9100 km² (including its 36 islands) and its maximum depth is about 450 m. The water is fresh, being supplied by 25 streams from the snow on the mountains surrounding the lake, and provides a significant amount of edible fish. There is a steamer service between the port of Guaqi in Bolivia and Puno in Peru forming an important commercial link between the two countries. Many Inca legends are associated with the lake.

Title Deeds, documents showing title to interests in land (for example, a conveyance, a lease, and a mortgage).

Titles, additions to a person's name, indicative of some honour, office, or dignity, e.g. emperor, prince, chancellor, primate, duke, mayor. Some titles are held *virtute officii*, as for instance 'king'; others, like the titles of the five orders of nobility, and baronets in Britain, are hereditary, while others still, like that of knight, are conferred for life.

See also ADDRESS, FORMS OF; NAMES; NOBILITY; ORDERS OF KNIGHTHOOD.

Titmouse, see TIT.

Titmuss, Richard Morris (1907–73), British sociologist. After work in industry and commerce, 1922–42, he became historian at the Cabinet Office, 1942–49, working on social policy development in the war. He became the first professor of social science and administration at the London School of Economics. He was largely responsible for the creation of social administration (the study of social needs and provision to meet them) as a separate academic discipline. His key works include *The Social Division of Welfare*, which questions normal definitions of welfare services, and *The Gift Relationship*, 1970, which opens up many questions concerning the place of altruism in social policy. He was made CBE in 1966 and FBA in 1972.

Tito

Tito, originally Josip Broz (1890–), Yugoslav soldier and statesman, born at Kumrovec near Zagreb. He came of peasant stock, and worked as a farm-labourer for a time. After the First World War he became a Communist, and spent some time in Moscow. In the winter of 1928–29 he was arrested in Zagreb. After a short time in the Zagreb prison Tito returned to Moscow and attended the Lenin school for two years. In 1934 he became a member of the Yugoslav Politburo, and in 1937, general secretary of the Yugoslav Communist party. Tito dissolved it and ordered a re-registration, thus ensuring that he was surrounded by loyal adherents. Unlike most of the other Communist leaders of Europe, who remained safely in Moscow during the Second World War, Tito was in his own country organising resistance to the Nazis. His antagonists included, besides the Nazis, the Mihajlović (see MIHAJLO-VIĆ, DRAŽA) partisans, and the NKVD observers in his own Politburo. By welding peasants, factory workers, and intellectuals into a victorious guerrilla partisan army he felt he had contributed not only a new Communist experience but something novel in Stalinist doctrine. His independent attitude and popular national following did not suit Moscow.

In mid-1948 the Cominform expelled Tito and urged the Yugoslav people to turn him out of office if he did not change his policy. The quarrel with Soviet Russia made serious political and economic difficulties for Yugoslavia; but there was no doubt that Tito was still genuinely popular with supporters from all classes of the people and all parts of the country; for the idea that Moscow should try to control Yugoslav internal affairs, or limit its industrial expansion, roused their national pride and rallied many Yugoslavs hitherto hostile to his government round Tito. As a consequence of this quarrel the Cominform countries decided to impose economic sanctions, and therefore stopped sending to Yugoslavia any capital

Tito photographed in 1943 after receiving a hand wound during a bombing operation. (Bisonte)

equipment, hoping that unemployment and food shortage would eventually bring about the wholesale collapse of the Yugoslav economy; but Tito, adhering to his five-year plan, made trade treaties with over a score of countries, many of them in Western Europe, and received economic aid from Britain, France, and the USA. After Stalin's death he resumed relations with USSR, though maintaining his country's independence of the Soviet bloc. When the Yugoslav constitution was revised in 1953 Tito became president, being re-elected in 1954, 1958, 1963, 1967, and 1971. In 1974 he was made president for life.

See also EASTERN FRONT IN THE SECOND WORLD WAR; YUGOSLAVIA, *History*.

Bibliography: H. F. Armstrong, *Tito and Goliath*, 1951; V. Dedijer, *Tito Speaks*, 1953; F. Maclean, *Disputed Barricade*, 1957; F. W. Neal, *Titoism in Action*, 1958; E. Halperin, *The Triumphant Heretic*, 1957; F. Maclean, *Eastern Approaches*, 1966; P. Auty, *Tito: A Biography*, 1970.

Titograd (formerly *Podgorica* or *Podgoritza*), town in Yugoslavia, the capital of the republic of MONTENEGRO. It is at the confluence of the rivers Ribnica and Morača. It was seriously damaged in the Second World War, but has been rebuilt as a fine modern city with many facilities including a university. It was renamed in 1946 in honour of the Yugoslav leader, Marshal TITO. Its commercial and industrial importance is growing. Population (1971) 98,800.

Titration, method of quantitative chemical analysis. The weight of a substance in a definite volume of solution is determined by causing it to react with a solution of another reagent of known strength. This reagent is contained in a burette and run out into the other solution till reaction is complete, as shown by change of colour of an indicator such as litmus, methyl orange, phenolphthalein, or by cessation of effervescence, etc. The volume is noted, and the weight of reagent contained is thus known. From the chemical equation and the atomic weights, the weight of the other solute can then be calculated. Titration methods are quick and, under suitable conditions, accurate. They have therefore largely displaced the older gravimetric methods, though these are still employed when even greater accuracy is required. Titration was introduced by GAY-LUSSAC early in the 19th century.

Titus, Saint, friend and companion of St Paul who consecrated him bishop of Crete. All we know of him is learned from the canonical epistle addressed to him by St Paul. Eusebius says that Titus remained unmarried and died in old age.

Bibliography: J. N. D. Kelly, *The Pastoral Epistles*, 1964.

Titus, full name Titus Flavius Sabinus Vespasianus (c. AD 40–81), Roman Emperor, 79–81, son of VESPASIAN. As a young man he served as military tribune in Britain and Germany; later he commanded a legion and served under his father in the Jewish war. In July 69, when Vespasian went to take possession of the imperial throne, Titus was left in command of operations in Palestine; he captured Jerusalem in the following year. In 71 he returned to Rome, celebrated a TRIUMPH with his father and was given the title Caesar. He succeeded to the Empire in 79, and one of his first acts was to put away

Titus. *(Vatican Museum/Photo Anderson)*

BERENICE, sister of Agrippa, his attachment to whom had made him unpopular. The first year of Titus's reign was memorable for the eruption of Vesuvius and a great fire at Rome. He completed the Colosseum and built the baths named after him. His death was greatly mourned by the Romans, especially after the accession of his brother Domitian.

Tiv, a people living in the Benue province of Central Nigeria. Originally they were subsistence farmers growing yams and millet; today they produce cash crops of soya beans. In the traditional system there was no centralised political authority but their markets served as forums for debate on public issues. Their social organisation is based on a system of segmentary lineages and their religion, or a belief of the power of forces (*akombo*), is manifested in emblems and fetishes. The Tiv number about 1·5 million.

    Bibliography: L. and P. Bohannan, *The Tiv of Central Nigeria*, 1953.

Tiverton, town in DEVON, England, on the Exe, 22 km north-east of Exeter. The chief building of interest is the church of St Peter. Textile manufacture is the chief industry. Blundell's School is in Tiverton. Population (1971) 15,566.

Tivoli (ancient *Tibur*), Italian town in LAZIO, 25 km north-east of Rome. It stands on the Aniene, at the point where the river forms a series of falls down to the CAMPAGNA DI ROMA; these cascades have been celebrated

for their beauty since classical times, and now they produce electric power for Rome. In Horace's day Tivoli was the resort of wealthy Romans; the ruins still exist of fine Roman villas, in particular a magnificent villa built by Hadrian, and of mausolea, aqueducts, and a temple of Vesta. The modern town has a cathedral, interesting churches, and villas, the gardens of which (notably those of the 16th-century Villa d'Este) are extremely beautiful. The local wine is well-known. Vast quantities of travertine used as a decorative building stone, are quarried in the vicinity. Population (1974) 28,400; municipality (1971) 41,000.

Tizard, Sir Henry Thomas (1885–1959), British scientist, educated at Westminster School and at Magdalen College, Oxford. One of the leading British aeronautical scientists, he made many important contributions to scientific development in the RAF before and during the Second World War. His appointments included those of rector of the Imperial College of Science and Technology, 1929–42; chairman of the Aeronautical Research Committee, 1933–43; member of the Air Council, chief scientific adviser to the Ministry of Aircraft production, 1939–45; and chairman of the Advisory Council on Scientific Policy and Defence Research Policy Committee, 1946–52.

Tizi-Ouzou, town and department of north-central ALGERIA, lying between the Mediterranean and the Djurdjura Mountains. The town lies in a deep valley and is a regional trade centre for olives, figs, and grapes. Area (department) 5720 km². Population (town) 53,291; (department) 936,000.

Tlaxcala, smallest state of MEXICO. Extremely mountainous, it is traversed north to south by the Sierra Madre Oriental and east to west by the Cordillera Neovolcánica and varies in altitude from 2107 m to 4389 m—the height of the volcano La Malinche. The climate depends on altitude but the chief feature is the daily great variation from hot to cold. Essentially an agricultural and cattle-raising state, agriculture is heavily dependent on artificial irrigation. The chief crops are maize, barley, wheat, potatoes, beans, alfalfa, and fruits. The considerable forests have been exploited to such an extent as to present problems of soil erosion. The main industries include cotton and woollen textile manufacturing, flour milling, foodstuff processing, and cement. The ancient ruins, the buildings of the colonial period, and local handicrafts have attracted a substantial tourist industry. The capital is Tlaxcala and other sizeable towns are Apizaco (population 23,000), Santa Inés Zacateleo (21,000), and Vicente Guerrero (19,000). Area 3914 km²; population (1975) 490,000.

Tlaxcala, capital of the above state in Mexico, its full name being Tlaxcala de Xicotencati. Situated at an altitude of 2240 m at the foot of the north-west slope of the La Malinche volcano, it has a temperate climate with rainfall only in the summer and autumn. The commercial centre of an agricultural and cattle-raising district, its chief industries are cotton and woollen textile manufacturing. It is one of the most ancient cities in Mexico and in and near it are many buildings and features of historical interest, including the oldest church in North America. Population 13,000.

Tlemçen

Tlemçen, province of north-western Algeria. Area 8120 km²; population (1970) 500,000.

Tlemçen, capital of the above department in ALGERIA, 130 km south-west of Oran. Formerly the Roman town of *Pomaria*, it was later the Moorish capital. Much of the old town still remains. It fell to the French in 1842. It has synagogues, mosques, and a museum of antiquities. It exports blankets, olive oil, and alfalfa, and manufactures leather work and native carpets. Most of its European population left for France after Algerian independence in 1962. Population (1966) 96,072.

Tmesis (Greek *temnein*, to cut), figure of speech involving the separation of parts of a word by inserting one or more words. It is rarely used in English, but appears in jocular expressions like 'abso-bally-lutely'. Kipling uses 'If there be trouble to herward', and Gerard Manley Hopkins writes 'brim in a flash full'. See also FIGURE OF SPEECH.

Toad, common name for frog-like, tailless, rough-skinned, hopping members of order ANURA, class AMPHIBIA. The name is used loosely, but the true toads belong to the family Bufonidae, with about 300 species, and especially the genus *Bufo* with over 200 species. They differ from FROGS chiefly by the total absence of teeth, and in certain other anatomical features. In British toads, a large gland, called the parotid, occurs, but this is absent from frogs. The gland provides a noxious substance when its secretion is mixed with the toad's blood, through an abrasion or other means, and thus affords some protection to the animal when attacked. The skin of the toad is drier and more warty than that of the frog. The two British toads are the natterjack (*Bufo calamita*) and the common toad (*Bufo vulgaris*). The latter is generally distributed over Great Britain, though absent from Ireland. It has longer hind limbs than the other and is able to hop. Its eyes are more lateral and the irises reddish-copper colour. The females are usually larger than the males. The natterjack, which is local in England, cannot hop, as the hind limbs are too short, but it is able to run and is often called the running toad. Its eyes are more prominent and the irises greenish-yellow; a thin yellow line runs along the middle of the back. During the breeding season the males croak loudly and the eggs are laid in strings. The value of

toads to the farmer and gardener cannot be exaggerated, as they feed entirely on insects, millipedes, woodlice, slugs and snails. They are quite harmless to man.

European toads range in size from about 2 to 25 cm. They live mostly on land, are active at night and hibernate in burrows during the winter. Breeding takes place in winter and the eggs are laid in water in the spring. The animals migrate large distances (up to 1·5 km) from their land quarters to suitable breeding waters. The eggs are laid in two long strings, not in a mass as in frogs.

Toadflax, *Linaria*, a genus of 150 species of the Scrophulariaceae (foxglove family); the flowers resemble small snapdragons (see ANTIRRHINUM) with a spur at the base of the petal tube. Among the natives of Britain, the yellow toadflax (*L. vulgaris*) is commonest. Purple toadflax (*L. purpurea*) and other species are grown in gardens and sometimes escape. BASTARD TOADFLAX belongs to the family SANTALACEAE.

Toadstool, common name for the fruiting-body of a fungus in subdivision Basidiomycotina that resembles a mushroom but is inedible. See FUNGI; POISONOUS PLANTS AND FUNGI.

Tobacco, plant of the genus *Nicotiana* in family Solanaceae, from which are manufactured smoking and chewing tobacco, cigarettes, cigars, and snuff. There are over 50 varieties of the plant, many of which are cultivated in gardens, but only a few varieties are used for smoking purposes. The varieties of most importance to smokers are *N. tabacum* and *N. rustica*. The former, a native of the West Indies, bears pink or rose-coloured flowers and grows from 1 to 3 m high. The bulk of tobacco used in the trade of most countries of the world is produced from this variety. The latter, a native of Mexico, bears greenish-yellow flowers, and is a much smaller plant than *N. tabacum*. *N. rustica* was cultivated by the ancient Mexicans and by the North American Indians, but early in the 17th century it was largely superseded by *N. tabacum*.

Growth and Cultivation. Tobacco seedlings are grown in sheltered level ground containing loamy, mellow soil. The crops need a lot of potassium fertiliser and very little nitrogen fertiliser. Sowing takes place in the early spring. The seed is minute. After sowing, the bed may be covered with cheesecloth or grass to protect the plant in the early stages of growth. When the plants are about 15 cm high they are transplanted by hand into fields which have been thoroughly broken up by repeated harrowings. In land that does not drain easily they are usually set in ridges. About 1800 plants are set to the hectare. Very careful cultivation is essential. 'Topping', the cutting away of the stalk carrying the top leaves and the flower bud, is necessary to prevent seeding and to put more strength in the remaining leaves, usually 10–16 in number. Harvesting takes place in the hottest part of the year. Leaves may be picked individually as they ripen (known as 'priming'), or by the whole-plant method, after which they are conveyed to barns for curing.

Curing. Curing is an operation requiring skill and experience. There are four methods: flue-curing, firing, air-curing, and sun-curing. Flue-curing barns are heated by iron flues and the leaves are hung above the flues. No smoke comes into contact with the tobacco. Flue-curing is done in three stages: yellowing the leaf, fixing the

Toad. *(Topham/Coleman)*

Tobacco. Tobacco harvesting in Africa. *(Camera Press)*

colour, and drying out the stem; the whole operation takes four to five days. In fire-curing the tobacco is hung in the barns over wood fires lit in trenches in the floors, and the smoke comes into direct contact with the tobacco. The length of the process varies from about one to six weeks; generally speaking, the longer and more gradual the process, the better the result. For air-curing the tobacco is hung in the barns, protected from the rain but exposed to the passage of air, and the curing is a natural process extending over about two months. Sun-curing is a similar process except that in the early stages the leaf is exposed in the open to the sun's rays.

Production and Types of Tobacco. The production of tobacco is world-wide, extending as far north as Sweden and as far south as New Zealand. In some countries, China for example, the production is almost entirely for domestic use, and in others, England, for example, because of unsuitable climatic conditions, only tobacco of low yield and poor smoking quality can be produced commercially. The principal types of tobacco and the main exporting countries are as follows:

1. Flue-cured tobaccos, brights, and semi-brights: USA (North and South Carolina, Georgia, Virginia), eastern Canada, Malawi, Rhodesia, some parts of India, and Brazil. This is the type of tobacco most used in the UK, where most cigarettes are made from it, and it is also extensively used in pipe tobacco. It is grown on light, sandy soil and obtains its nourishment from applications of chemical fertilisers. It has a characteristic bright colour.

2. Burley tobacco and other air-cured tobaccos: USA (Kentucky, Tennessee, Maryland), eastern Canada, parts of India, and Malawi. This type is used in very large quantities in the USA both for cigarettes and pipe tobacco. It is used to a lesser extent in the UK for pipe tobacco only. It is grown from distinctive kinds of seeds, and its reddish-brown colour is obtained by air-curing.

3. Dark fired tobacco: USA (Kentucky, Tennessee, Virginia), eastern Canada, Malawi, and Rhodesia. This type of tobacco is used for the manufacture of roll and shag tobacco and produces a strong smoke. It is a large heavy type of leaf grown on richer soil than the flue-cured variety.

4. Latakia and Latakia-type tobacco: Syria and Cyprus. Latakia tobacco has a flavour peculiar to itself and is used

in the UK entirely in pipe-smoking mixtures. It is the smallest of all the tobacco plants, and its leaves are barely 5 cm in length. The whole plant is cured by heavy firing, which gives the characteristic black appearance and distinctive flavour.

5. Oriental tobacco: Turkey, Greece, Bulgaria, and the borders of the Black Sea. Oriental tobacco has a highly distinctive aromatic flavour. It is used in oriental and 'blended' brands of cigarettes. The Oriental tobacco plant is of small growth, producing a delicate type of leaf.

6. Cigar tobaccos, see CIGAR.

History. Tobacco was used by American Indians from time immemorial. Its first mention in Europe was in the writings of Friar Romano Pane, who accompanied Columbus on his second voyage to the Americas. It was used medicinally and in religious ceremonies. In 1526 Gonzalo Fernandez de Oviedo described how natives burned the leaf and inhaled the smoke through a hollow cane called tobacco; this was the name Spaniards gave the plant and its products. It was first brought to Europe in 1559 by physician Francisco Hernandez de Toledo, who had been sent to Mexico by Philip II of Spain to investigate Mexico's products. In 1560 it was introduced to France by Jean Nicot, ambassador to Portugal, who gave the plant its botanical name, Nicotiana. Its use spread rapidly and tobacco was prized for its medicinal and pleasurable qualities. Smoked in clay pipes, the poor used nutshells and reed stems. Despite efforts to stamp out smoking, or 'drinking' smoke as it was then termed, with taxes, laws, and even threats of excommunication, it became general in most parts of the civilised world. Developments in usage came first with snuff, ground tobacco, made popular in the 18th century with upper classes; cigars in the first part of the 19th century; cigarettes in the latter half. Then cigarettes were made by hand with experienced operators producing over 1500 a day. In 1881 an American, James Bonsack, patented a machine for making cigarettes at 200 per minute, which revolutionised the industry. Mass production led to wider use and was the basis of the modern world-wide industry. In the 1950s development started of man-made cellulose-based tobacco substitutes. The product is in use in a few cigarettes on the Continent, but natural tobacco is still supreme. It is one of the few world crops traded entirely on a leaf basis and is the most widely grown non-food plant.

Tobacco in Britain. Tobacco came to Britain about the time of Hawkins and Drake and was made popular with courtiers by Sir Walter Raleigh. By the end of Elizabeth I's reign smoking was general and so also was tax on tobacco. James I, first of the anti-smokers with his dislike of tobacco, was quick to realise its duty potential. He boosted tax to 34p a pound at a time when imports totalled over 16,000 pounds. He also granted a charter to the company of tobacco pipe makers, later to incorporate blenders. Subsequently, to protect trade with new colonies in America, growing was prohibited in Britain by Cromwell and Charles II. In the Georgian period snuff taking became very fashionable. Cigars started to be smoked in quantity after the Napoleonic wars and soldiers returning from the Crimea popularised cigarettes. These achieved mass appeal following the introduction of American machinery. Following the report of the Royal College of Physicians the unofficial and government anti-smoking campaigns have been stepped up, with resultant restrictions on advertising. Consumption in the UK has ceased to grow, but revenue has not. Tax on tobacco produces around £1770 million a year against £11 million in 1900. The average British smoker consumes 3000 cigarettes a year compared with 2500 in Germany and 1800 in France. The British market is dominated by the Imperial Group, formed by the threat posed by an American 'invasion' of the market before the 1914–18 war.

Tobago, island of the WEST INDIES, about 121 km south-east of Grenada and 34 km north-east of Trinidad. The island is 42 km long and 12 km wide and has an area of 301 km². Tobago is mountainous in the centre and at the north-east end, and undulating and flat in the south and west. The highest peak is 641 m. Deep fertile valleys run down from either side of the main ridge. The principal river is the Courland, named after the Viking duke who in the 17th century ruled the island almost as a sovereign. Scarborough on the south coast, formerly called Port Louis, is the capital. The only other major town is Roxborough. The climate is most agreeable; the mean temperature is 27 °C, but owing to the long seaboard the heat is generally tempered by a cool sea breeze. In the central and windward districts the rainfall varies from 2160 to 2410 mm and in the north may exceed 2540 mm. At a distance of 2 km from the north-east end of Tobago, opposite the village of Speyside (40 km from Scarborough), is the island of Little Tobago or Bird of Paradise Island, the only place in the Western hemisphere where these birds are found in their wild state. The rocks between it and Tobago are known collectively as Goat Island. Population (1970) of Tobago 39,000.

Cocoa, coconuts, and limes have taken the place of sugar which was the staple industry before being ruined by foreign sugar bounties. Tobago is linked to Trinidad by two ships and a domestic airline; Crown Point airport is so far used only for inter-island travel. There is a government radio station and telephone system on the island.

Tobago is known to many people by its nickname, Robinson Crusoe's Island. For though the actual story of Crusoe's life on his island of Juan Fernández was based largely on Alexander Selkirk's adventures there, there can be no doubt that Defoe, in describing his mythical island, had Tobago in mind, and it may safely be assumed that 'Robinson Crusoe Cave', near Scarborough, is well named. The history of Tobago shows that it changed hands a dozen times during a period of less than two centuries; the reason being that it was an attractive fertile island lying near enough to the Guiana coast to be a jumping-off ground for those anxious to explore the ORINOCO, and also because its sheltered bays gave a safe anchorage with deep soundings.

History. Columbus discovered Tobago in 1498 and named it 'Tabago', from a notion that it resembled in shape the Carib tobacco pipe. Sir Robert Dudley, natural son of the Earl of Leicester, is believed to have visited Tobago and hoisted the English flag in 1580. Nearly 36 years later British colonists from Barbados effected the first settlement, but no successful settlement was made for nearly a century and a half after the discovery of the island. For the ensuing 40 years the island's history was a struggle between Dutch colonists and some Baltic settlers from Courland, varied by French and British inva-

sions. After that and for the next 20 years the island was declared neutral but, nonetheless, alternated between French and British possession until, in 1814, it was finally ceded to Britain. It became part of the independent Commonwealth state of Trinidad and Tobago in August 1962.

See also TRINIDAD AND TOBAGO.

Tobata, see KITAKYŪSHŪ.

Tobermory, important small harbour, service, and tourist centre on the north-east coast of MULL, Scotland, 48 km from Oban. In 1588, following the scattering of the Spanish Armada, a Spanish galleon sank in Tobermory Bay with, it was believed, a large cargo of treasure. In 1912 Colonel Foss recovered some coins and silver goblets, and the search is being continued. Population 641.

Tobey, Mark (1890–), US painter, born at Centerville, Wisconsin. He studied art in Europe and the Far East and afterwards lived at Seattle. Regarded as the leader of the 'West Coast' School in the USA, he is noted for his calligraphic use of the brush derived from the East, which he called 'white writing', and his elaborately patterned abstract paintings.

Bibliography: W. E. Seitz, *Mark Tobey*, 1962; W. Schmied (Ed.), *Mark Tobey*, 1966.

Tobit, Book of, in the Apocrypha but included in the Roman Catholic Bible as deutero-canonical (see BIBLE). It is a Haggadic version of a popular adventure and love story, embodying a series of moral and religious lessons. Its date is c. 190–170 BC. Versions appear in Greek, Latin, Syriac, Hebrew, and Ethiopic. Fragments in Hebrew and Aramaic were found among the DEAD SEA SCROLLS. In the Middle Ages Christian couples were advised to follow the example of Tobias and Sarah in the tale and give the first three nights after marriage to prayer. The characters in Tobit provided a favourite subject for Renaissance artists.

Tobogganing, descending an ice track on a vehicle comprising a platform resting on runners, developed from primitive forms of transport used before 3000 BC in the European Alps. From it evolved three modern sports, BOBSLEDDING, luge tobogganing and Cresta Run skeleton tobogganing.

Luge tobogganing (or lugeing) originated in 1879 at Davos, Switzerland. World championships began in 1955. The International Luge Federation was formed in 1957 and Olympic status was gained in 1964. For single riders or crews of two, the sport has been most popular in Austria, East and West Germany, Poland and Italy. Two East Germans, Thomas Köhler and Otrun Enderlein, have been outstanding respectively in men's and women's events.

The luge is made of wood with twin metal runners and is steered by the feet, a handrope and weight transference, the rider adopting a backward-leaning sitting posture. The absence of any mechanical means of steering or braking is a clear distinction from bobsledding. The single-seater is limited to 1·5 m in length, 44 cm in width, 15 cm in height and 20 kg in weight. The double-seater, although longer, has the same weight restriction. A rider wears a crash helmet, goggles and padded clothing, also spikes and rakes on the boots to assist braking, steering and pushing off. Senior courses, banked and usually steeper than for bobsledding, are about 1000 m long with at least 12 bends. Speeds of 130 kmph are possible. Championships are determined, as in bobsledding, by the aggregate times of four descents. Flexibility of the sled is possible because the front runners can be moved independently by leg pressure.

Cresta Run skeleton tobogganing, uniquely characterised by riding prone and head first, takes place on only one course, the Cresta Run at St Moritz, Switzerland. The track was built in 1884 by an Englishman, Major W. H. Bulpetts. With steeply banked bends, including the notorious Stream Corner, the course from Top is 1213 m long, with an elevation of 156·7 m. The fastest descents have exceeded an average speed of 80 kmph. From a lower start, Junction, a shortened course measures 887·9 m.

Although internationally supported, there are no world championships, but the sport was twice included in the Winter Olympics, when held at St Moritz in 1928 and 1948. The foremost annual classic races are the Grand National from Top and the Curzon Cup from Junction. Nino Bibbia (Italy) has won each eight times.

The skeleton toboggan comprises a flat wooden platform on steel runners. Since 1901 a sliding body support has been incorporated. There is no restriction as to weight, size or design. Mechanical steering-gear or brakes are not permitted. Events are normally decided by the aggregate times of three descents by each rider.

Tobol, navigable tributary of the River Irtysh in south-west Siberia, USSR. It rises in the foothills of the Urals and flows north-east through a fertile region with rich mineral resources now being rapidly cultivated and industrialised. Length 1591 km.

Tobolsk, city in Tyumen *oblast* of the RSFSR, USSR, in West Siberia, on the River Irtysh, the centre of a lumbering and dairy-farming area and supply point for the northern part of the *oblast*. There is some industry, and an old bone-carving craft is still carried on. It is an important local cultural centre (a theatre was founded here in 1705). The city was founded by Russian Cossacks in 1587 near the old capital of the Siberian Khanate; it was capital of Siberia, 1596–1824, and provincial capital until 1923. It was formerly a place of banishment, including that of Nicholas II (1917–18). Until the second half of the 18th century the Moscow–Siberian highway passed through here, and it was a major trading centre. Population (1970) 48,000.

Tobruk, seaport of Libya, North Africa. It has an excellent harbour, and was occupied by Italy in 1912. It was the scene of much fighting in the Libyan campaign of the Second World War. It was captured by the British from the Italians in January 1941; unsuccessfully besieged by Axis forces for eight months in 1941; relieved by the British in December 1941; captured by the Axis in June 1942, and finally recaptured by the British in November 1942. See also Africa, North, Second World War, Campaigns in. The town now has a modern oil refinery linked by a 560-kilometre pipeline to the Spirit oil-field. Population (1970) 28,000.

Toc H, a movement to bring together into interdenominational Christian fellowship men and women of every class and opinion for the purpose of social service of all kinds, with groups and branches throughout the world. The name Toc H comes from the army signallers' designation of the initials TH, which stood for Talbot House, opened in December 1915 at Poperinghe in Flanders as a chapel and club for soldiers. It was a memorial to Gilbert Talbot, who was killed in July 1915, and was founded by his brother, Neville Talbot, later Bishop of Pretoria, and the Rev. P. B. ('Tubby') Clayton. In 1920 Clayton formed a small Toc H group in London, and in 1922 Toc H was incorporated by royal charter. The *Toc H Journal* is published monthly.

Tocantins, river of northern Brazil, rising in the state of Goiás and flowing north into the Amazon delta. Its largest tributary is the Araguaia. Its course, which is much interrupted by rapids, is navigable only in some parts. Its economic value rests in the babaçu palms watered by its upper reaches. Length 2560 km.

Toccata (from Italian *toccare*, literally, to touch; figuratively, to play), originally, in the 17th century, simply 'a thing to play' as distinct from *cantata*, 'a thing to sing'. But it soon acquired a sense of touching a keyboard instrument, for the purpose of trying or testing it, which meant that it usually contained scales, shakes and other brilliant figuration, often interspersed with slow chordal passages. Modern toccatas usually lay stress on brilliance and rapid execution alone, and are often more or less uniform in figuration throughout. Well-known examples are found in the works of Bach, Schumann, Debussy, Ravel and Prokofiev.

Tocopilla, town and port of Antofagasta province, northern Chile. Main exports include nitrate, iodine, and copper ore. Tocopilla supplies power to the important copper mine of Chuquicamata. Population 27,000.

Tocqueville, Alexis Charles Henri Maurice Clérel de (1805–59), French historian, born at Verneuil, Seine-et-Oise. He went to America to study prisons in 1831, and took the opportunity to collect materials for his *De la Démocratie en Amérique*, 1835–40, a work of peculiar interest as the first reasoned and more or less unbiased exposition of popular government in that country. A moderate Liberal in politics, he was elected vice-president of the Assembly in 1849, was dismissed when Louis Napoleon became emperor, and met with an enthusiastic reception from John Stuart Mill and other prominent Whigs when he visited England. He published *Ancien Régime*, 1856. His *Souvenirs*, first published in 1893, and edited and translated with an introduction by J. P. Mayer in 1948, relate to the years 1848–49 and are interesting for their account of the political upheavals of that time.

Bibliography: A. de Tocqueville (ed. H. S. Commager, trans. Reeve), *Democracy in America*, 1961; A. de Tocqueville (trans. S. Gilbert), *Ancien Regime and the French Revolution*, 1966; R. Herr, *Tocqueville and the Old Regime*, 1966; H. Brogan, *Tocqueville*, 1973.

Todas, see Badaga.

Todd, Reginald Stephen Garfield (1908–), New Zealand-born Rhodesian politician, educated at Otago University and Witwatersrand University. Later he became a missionary in Rhodesia. Todd entered politics and was MP for Shabani, 1946–58; he formed the United

Rhodesia party and was returned to power as premier of Southern Rhodesia, 1953–58, but lost office when his progressive policies were rejected by the electorate in favour of the more conservative programme of WHITE-HEAD's United Federal party. In 1965, after his outspoken criticism of the SMITH government, he was placed under restriction and was not released until 1976.

Todd, Ruthven (1914–), Scottish poet, essayist, and novelist, born in Edinburgh. He was educated at Fettes College and the College of Art, Edinburgh. A leading authority on William BLAKE, he produced a modern edition of Gilchrist's *Life of Blake*. A collection of essays *Tracks in the Snow*, 1946, deals with the mythology of the 18th century in its effects upon Blake, John MARTIN, and Henry FUSELI, and with the influence of science on the artists and writers of the period. He wrote the life of DUMAS in *The Laughing Mulatto*, 1939. He published four books of poems, including *The Planet in My Hand*, 1946, and *In Other Worlds*, 1950. His first novel, *Over the Mountain*, 1939, an allegorical fantasy, was followed by *The Lost Traveller*, 1943, and *The Ruins of Time*, 1950.

Toddy, in cold and temperate countries, usually a drink of spirits, sugar, and hot water with a slice of lemon; in tropical countries, beverages fermented from the sap of various palms.

Todhunter, Isaac (1820–84), British mathematician, born at Rye. At St John's College, Cambridge, he was a scholar, fellow, and lecturer in turn, heading the degree list as Senior Wrangler and gaining the mathematical blue riband, Smith's Prize. He was a member of the council of the Royal Society, of which he was elected a Fellow in 1862. His edition of EUCLID's *Elements* and his text-books on algebra, trigonometry, and calculus attained a world-wide circulation. He also wrote on the history of 19th-century mathematics.

Todmorden, municipal borough until 1974, now in CAL-DERDALE District, West Yorkshire, England, 17 km west of HALIFAX. It has cotton weaving and spinning factories, foundries and machine shops, and manufactures clothes, venetian blinds, tubular steel furniture, and sanitary pipes and fittings. Population (1971: municipal borough) 15,163.

Todt, Fritz (1891–1942), German engineer, born in Baden, the constructor of the German West Wall and the *Autobahnen* (motorways) in Germany. He became Inspector-General of Reich Roads in 1933. He was made major-general in 1939 in recognition of his work in the western anti-aircraft defensive zone, and was Reich Minister of Arms and Munitions from March 1940 until he died in an air crash.

The construction of the 'Atlantic Wall' was carried out at great speed because of the tense political situation, and for this purpose Todt created his 'Todt Organisation', which completed the task with almost incredible speed. Todt was also largely responsible for the very efficient road-transport of supplies, upon which the Nazi *Blitzkrieg* mainly depended.

Tofua, uninhabited volcanic island in the Haapai group, Tonga.

Toga, the formal dress of a Roman citizen obligatory on public occasions. It was made of white wool. Laid flat, it resembled a semicircle with the straight side bent outwards to form an obtuse angle. The toga measured lengthwise about three times, in width about twice, the wearer's height. The method of donning a toga was as follows. It was formed into thick folds lengthwise and cast over the left shoulder so that one-third of the total length hung down in front; the remainder was passed behind, under the left arm, and thence over the left shoulder. The left arm being now almost covered, the part lying across the back was spread to cover the right shoulder, and the front was arranged in a series of folds, forming a pocket (sinus). Curule magistrates and boys wore the *toga praetexta*, with a purple border; on attaining manhood the *toga virilis*, without the border, was assumed. The *toga picta* (embroidered) was worn by generals at their triumph; the *toga pulla* (of dark stuff) by mourners and persons impeached. After Augustus, the emperors commonly wore a purple toga.

Togliatti, Palmiro (1893–1964), Italian Communist politician, formerly a journalist. He lived in exile in the USSR during the Mussolini régime, and became a prominent member of the Comintern. He fought in the Spanish Civil War and returned to Italy in 1944. In a speech made in Salerno in that year he announced that the Italian Communist party was prepared to collaborate with all other democratic parties, so laying the basis for strategy in the post-war years. He was vice-premier from 1944 to 1945 and minister of justice from 1945 to 1946. With the onset of the cold war the PCI (the Italian Communist party) was excluded from the government, and Togliatti retained leadership in opposition. His influence acted to liberalise the Party, and he supported the notions of 'polycentrism' and 'gradualism'. He died in the USSR.

Togo, Heihachiro (1847–1934), Japanese admiral, born at Kagoshima. He studied at the Royal Naval College, Greenwich. Promoted to admiral in 1904 he was commander-in-chief of the Japanese navy on the outbreak of the RUSSO-JAPANESE WAR and succeeded in destroying the Russian fleet at Port Arthur and later in defeating that of Adm. Rozhdestvensky at the battle of Tsushima in 1905.

Admiral Togo. (*Bisonte*)

Togo, Republic of, small republic in WEST AFRICA, sandwiched between GHANA on the west and BENIN on the east; the country is barely 100 km wide at any point but extends inland to a northern border with UPPER VOLTA, a distance of 560 km (area 56,000 km²). Formerly Togoland, a German colony, the present republic was administered by the French until independence in 1960 (the western half of Togoland, administered by the British, is now part of Ghana).

Geography. Relief. The sand-bar coast gives way to sheltered lagoons, backed by a coastal plain developed on soft sedimentary rocks, and forming a productive farming area called the 'Terre-de-Barre', extending into neighbouring Benin. Inland a range of quartzitic hills traverse the country obliquely from the south-west (the Togo Mountains reach 850 m) towards the north-east where they pass into Benin as the Atacora Mountains (700 m). Granitic rocks form broken country in the far north. See ATLAS 40.

Climate. The coastal zone from southern Ghana into Togo is unusually dry for West Africa and rainfall is only around 1000 mm, falling mainly from May to July and in October. At Lomé daytime temperatures range from 27 °C (August/September) to 32 °C (March), and fall to around 23 °C at night. In the north the range is greater, and maximum temperatures increase to 36 °C or more in March and April.

Vegetation and Soils. True rain forest does not occur in this part of West Africa and most of the country is covered by forms of savanna grassland or woodland, much modified by farming especially in the south. The Togo–Atacora Mountains, however, are well wooded and carry good crops of coffee and cocoa. The better soils occur on the Terre-de-Barre in the south and on the slopes of the hills; rather poor, sandy soils occur in the north.

Population. Only 15 per cent of the population are classified as urban; LOMÉ, the largest urban centre, is widely spread along the coast. The population densities decrease northwards from the coast. The total population in 1977 was an estimated 2,312,000.

Economy. Agriculture. This is the leading sector of the economy. It occupies 90 per cent of the working population and provides over 40 per cent of the Gross Domestic Product. The chief crops are yams, millet, cassava, and maize; the chief cash crops are coffee, cocoa, cotton, groundnuts, and palm kernels. In recent years both crop sectors production has been very low. Livestock breeding and fishing also contribute to the internal economy. Forests, which cover 10 per cent of the country's area, are a source of tropical hardwoods.

Industry. This sector is small but growing, mainly processing agricultural products and producing consumer goods. The most important current projects are the construction of an oil refinery and a cement plant due to begin production in 1978. Phosphates have long been the country's leading export; with the tripling of world prices in 1974 this importance has been accentuated. The state nationalised the mining sector in 1974. Limestone and marble are also quarried.

Communications. There are 500 km of railways, including three lines inland from Lomé and a coastal rail link with its neighbours. There are 7000 km of roads, about 25 per cent are all-weather. Lomé is the major port, although phosphates are exported through Kpémé. The three railways each deal with a specialist cash crop (cocoa, copra, and cotton) exclusively.

Trade. The rise in phosphate prices provided the first trade independence for Togo. Coffee, cocoa, and phosphates form the bulk of the exports, which mainly go to EEC countries. Imports come mainly from Japan and France. There is a smuggling problem, particularly with cocoa.

Bibliography: R. J. Harrison Church, *West Africa,* 1974.

Government. Constitution. This former United Nations Trust Territory, administered by France, received its independence in 1960, and promulgated its first constitution in May 1963; this constitution was suspended in January 1967 following an army coup d'état, led by Lieutenant-Colonel Étienne Gnassing de Eyadéma. The National Assembly was abolished, as were all political parties, and in April 1967, Eyadéma vested executive power in himself as President, although assisted by a cabinet. In October 1967, a constitutional committee began the work of drafting a new constitution, but although the preliminary work was completed in 1969, no constitution has yet been promulgated. Following a reorganisation of the government in January 1977, Eyadema is now the sole representative of the military, all other portfolios being entrusted to civilians. The Togolese People's Rally (*Rassemblement du peuple togolais*) is the sole political party.

Legislature. The National Assembly, established under the 1963 constitution, was effectively abolished after the military take-over in January 1967, and fresh elections, which it was promised would be held within three months, have never taken place. Since 1968, however, an economic and social council has been functioning in an advisory capacity, its 25 members including five representatives of each of trade unionists, industry and commerce, agriculture, technologists, and economists and sociologists. For the purposes of local government, the country is divided into four regions, governed by an appointed inspector and an elected council. The regions are sub-divided into 19 administrative divisions, having a divisional council elected by universal suffrage, and a chief of division, nominated by the President.

Justice. The formal law structure is headed by a Supreme Court of four chambers. Criminal justice is administered by a court of appeal, four courts of summary jurisdiction (i.e. able to impose penalties of up to five years' imprisonment), and eight police courts (i.e. able to impose penalties of up to five days' imprisonment). Civil and commercial law is enforced by a court of appeal, four courts applying modern law, and eight courts operating according to customary law. Since November 1974, the emphasis has been on the 'authenticity' i.e. its applicability to the country, and this has resulted in attempts to find a code of law which is a synthesis between customary law and that introduced by the French.

Armed Forces. All services are grouped under the army and total 2250. The army proper includes one infantry battalion and one reconnaissance squadron. There is also a paratroop battalion, a small air force (four aircraft), and a small naval force. Under the terms of an agreement with France, the Togolese armed forces are given equipment and training. Para-military forces number 1200.

Education. About half the schools provide free education, and 50 per cent of children of primary school age

Togo, Republic of

attend primary school. Mission schools continue to make an important contribution, educating half of those attending school. In 1972–73 there were 300,000 primary school pupils being taught by 5238 teachers, in secondary education 31,000 pupils and 1455 teachers, and 28,000 pupils sought technical instruction from 405 teachers. There is a university at Lomé, with 1385 students in 1972.

Welfare. In 1972 there were six hospitals, eight medical centres, 30 infirmaries, three dispensaries with beds, 92 conventional dispensaries, and 17 maternity clinics. Medical personnel in 1973 consisted of 61 doctors, nine pharmacists, two dentists, 156 midwives, and 613 nurses. There were a total of 3010 hospital beds available.

Religion. Nearly 50 per cent of the population follow traditional animist beliefs; 40 per cent are Christian (with Catholics being 20 per cent of the total population); and the Muslim community forms 10 per cent of the population.

Official Language. French.

National Anthem. Title: *Land of our Ancestors*.

National Flag. Five stripes of green and yellow, with a square red canton, containing a five-pointed white star, in the upper hoist.

History. The Ewe, who form the largest ethnic group in present-day Togo, migrated to that country from the area of the Niger from the 14th to the 16th centuries. During the 17th century a number of peoples migrated to Togo from the Gold Coast: these included the Mina, Ga-Adangme, Kepelle, Awyana, Chakossi, and Dagomba peoples. From the north, the most important group to infiltrate into this area were the Mossi. The first Europeans to establish coastal trading stations were the Portuguese, and very often these settlements were operated by Portuguese of Brazilian birth. The area of present-day Togo suffered a fairly heavy population loss—about 23 per cent—during the period of the Atlantic Slave Trade, largely as a result of Portuguese shipments of slaves to work on Brazilian plantations.

The export trade in slaves gave way during the 19th century to legitimate commerce, mainly the export of palm oil. The Danes sold their fort at Keta to the British in 1852, and later in the century the Portuguese and Spaniards wound up their trading operations on the coast. But, in 1884, the Germans made a number of treaties with chiefs in Togo, and had visions of extending their influence to the Niger hinterland. The Germans attempted to create a model colony in Togo, but, despite the provision of material benefits for the country and the people, there was popular resentment against German systems of forced labour and heavy taxation. In 1914 Togo was the scene of the first Allied victory in the First World War, as British and French troops forced a German surrender. German Togo was divided into British and French spheres, a division formalised by the 1922 decision of the League of Nations that Britain and France were to hold the Togolese mandate. The British administered the western part of Togo in much the same way as the Gold Coast, that is, ruling indirectly through the chiefs and delegating some measure of administrative responsibility to elected native authorities in the villages and districts. For their part, the French were consistent in that they applied the system of direct rule through the colonial officials.

Although the Ewe chiefs had demanded national unity in the inter-war period, it was only under the Trusteeship System of the United Nations, established in 1946, that the movement for unification of the two Togos gained momentum, led this time not by the chiefs, but by modern political elements, the intellectuals, who made use of the press and formed national political parties. But there were separatist movements also, and plebiscites in British Togo showed a majority in favour of union with the Gold Coast.

In 1955 French Togo had been granted a considerable degree of political and administrative autonomy, and in 1958 the elections for the legislative assembly saw the majority victory of the Committee of Togolese Unity (CUT) led by Sylvanus Olympio, who became prime minister in 1958 and president of the newly independent republic in 1960. Despite a creditable trade performance which enabled Togo to become independent of the French subsidy, Olympio's government became increasingly unpopular, especially amongst ex-servicemen unable to find employment, and on 13 January 1963 Olympio was killed in the course of the military coup which overthrew his government.

The leading opposition leader, Nicolas Grunitzky, formed a coalition government, but was unable to convince the CUT supporters to support the new government, and eventually Grunitzky and the vice-president, Antoine Meatchi assumed full powers. By November 1966 civil war was imminent, and it was to prevent this course of events that the army, led by Col. Étienne Eyadéma, seized power in the coup of 13 January 1967.

Eyadéma has proclaimed his duty as being to unite the nation, and in 1968 he founded a new political party, the Movement of the Togolese National Rally, overtly a party of national unity. Ninety-nine per cent of the population approved of Eyadéma's position as president in the referendum of January 1972.

Bibliography: V. Thompson and R. Adloff, *French West Africa*, 1958; J. D. Hargreaves, *West Africa: The Former French States*, 1967.

Tojo, Hideki (1884–1948), Japanese politician and general, born in Tokyo; came into office with the expansionist elements in the army and navy. In 1940, when Prince Konoye founded his new National party, Tojo, as war minister, was one of the two leading figures in the Cabinet formed by Konoye, whom he succeeded as prime minister.

Hideki Tojo photographed during his trial in Tokyo in 1948. *(Popperfoto)*

722

It was Tojo who ordered soon afterwards the attack on PEARL HARBOR. Tojo assured his position at home in 1942 by dissolving the Diet and appointing a National Service Political Council to control the Diet in the interests of the government. In 1944 Tojo reorganised the High Command by combining, and himself taking, the posts of war minister and army chief of staff and combining the posts of navy minister, and navy chief of staff. When Saipan fell, Tojo resigned and was succeeded by Gen. Koiso. After the Japanese collapse Tojo was tried in Tokyo (1947–48) and hanged.

Tokaj (English *Tokay*), town of Hungary, in Borsod-Abaúj-Zemplén county, near the junction of the rivers Tisza and Bodrog, 45 km east of Miskolc. The town is at the foot of Mount Tokaj (515 m), which gives its name to the celebrated wine produced on its slopes and in the surrounding hilly district of Hegyalja. Population 5000.

Tokat, town and capital of Tokat province, Asiatic Turkey, situated on the Yeşilırmak river, 75 km north of Sivas. It manufactures copper and leather ware. Population (town) 44,110; (province) 540,900.

Tokay, see HUNGARIAN WINES.

Tokay, see TOKAJ.

Tokelau Islands, formerly Union Islands, group of islands, central Pacific Ocean, about 434 km due north of Apia, Western Samoa. They comprise three atolls, Atafu, Nukunono, and Fakaofu. In 1925 New Zealand agreed to administer the islands and in 1948 they were included in the territorial boundaries of New Zealand. The office of the Tokelau Islands administration is based in Apia. Total area of the islands, 1012 ha. The main export is copra; handicrafts are also exported. Population 1603.

Token (money), coin of higher nominal than intrinsic value; or a stamped piece of metal issued as a limited medium of exchange, as for bus fares, and at a nominal value much greater than its commodity value; or anything of only nominal value similarly used, as a piece of paper currency. See TRADESMEN'S TOKENS.

Tokharian, Tocharian, or Tocharish, one of the INDO-EUROPEAN LANGUAGES, which exists in the form of a number of texts, for example, translations of parts of Buddhist religious works, letters, merchants' accounts, and caravan passes, discovered in two areas, near Turfan and Kucha in Chinese Turkestan, between 1903 and 1909, some of them going back probably to the 7th century. Owing to the existence of Buddhist texts which could be compared with a SANSKRIT version, it was not difficult to interpret the language. The extant documents contain specimens of two different dialects of Tokharian, usually referred to as Tokharian A and Tokharian B and sometimes, though perhaps not entirely accurately, considered to represent eastern and western dialects respectively.

Bibliography: E. Sieg and W. Siegling, *Tocharische Sprachreste*, 1921, and (with W. Schulzer), *Tocharische Grammatik*, 1931; H. Pedersen, *Tocharisch vom Gesichtspunkt der indoeuropäischen Sprachvergleichung*, 1941; E. Schwentrer, *Tocharische Bibliographie*, 1959.

Tokitaro, Ando, see HIROSHIGE.

Tokyo (formerly Edo or Yedo), capital of JAPAN, sited in south-east Honshū, on the north-west shore of Tokyo

Tokyo. *(Bisonte)*

Bay, on the delta of the Sumida river, which separates the city proper on the west bank from the Kōto on the east. It was founded in 1457 by Ota Dokan, who built his castle here, and received its present name when the court moved from KYŌTO in 1868; the following year, it was opened to foreigners. The magnificent palace, in a blend of Japanese and European styles, stands in the Fukiage park, not far from the ancient castle. To the east of the palace lies the commercial and industrial part of the city, while the northern part is mainly educational and contains many universities, colleges, and beautiful temples. In the west and south-west are the foreign embassies and legations. Tokyo has its own seaport, YOKOHAMA, 30 km away, and Haneda airport is 16 km to the south of the city.

Tokyo has suffered frequently from fire (many of the houses were, and still are, built of wood), storms, earthquakes, and epidemics. The municipal buildings had to be rebuilt after the fire of 1891. In September 1923 great portions of the city were destroyed by a disastrous earthquake and the ensuing fire. Nearly 100,000 people were killed, and nearly a million migrated after the disaster. Reconstruction work was begun at once and completed by March 1930. Tokyo was frequently and heavily bombed during the Second World War, and according to official estimates, more than 80 per cent of the houses were completely destroyed.

Tokyo city consists of 23 wards, and is the capital of a prefecture (Tokyo-to) which includes 22 other cities. Tokyo contains a large number of universities and colleges. The city is served by eight television channels and eight radio stations, and is the headquarters for the national newspaper companies, and for nearly all the leading national commercial and industrial companies, located especially in the Ginza and Marunouchi districts. The latter district also contains many large department stores, cinemas, and theatres. There is an extensive network of underground railways and an urban motorway system. Over 1·5 million commuters travel to work in central Tokyo each day from the suburbs and from surrounding cities.

As well as being by far the leading centre of political and cultural affairs in Japan, Tokyo also functions as the nucleus of Japan's largest industrial region, and is the centre of a bay-head zone of factories which produce over 30 per cent of the value of Japan's output of manufactured goods. Although heavy industries are concentrated in neighbouring cities such as KAWASAKI, Yokohama, and CHIBA, Tokyo is nevertheless important as a manufacturing centre in its own right. A high proportion of its factories are small-scale enterprises, and many of them manufacture components which are assembled in plants outside the city boundaries. Industries include food and beverages, printing and publishing, chemicals, textiles, electrical machinery, cameras, optical goods, precision instruments, and rubber. Industrial development has brought about serious problems of atmospheric pollution and the city also suffers from traffic congestion and many other problems associated with acute shortage of land. In recent years, the population of Tokyo has declined slightly, the decrease being especially conspicuous in the central wards of the city. The population of the city (as distinct from the wider area of Tokyo-to) amounts to 8,642,000 (1975).

Bibliography: S. Miyas and F. Dunbar, *Tokyo: Past and Present*, 1973.

Tokyo Trials, see JAPANESE (WAR CRIMINALS) TRIAL.

Tolbert, William Richard (1913–), Liberian politician and 19th President of Liberia, born at Bensonville and educated at Liberia College, now the University of Liberia, from which he graduated in 1934. He entered the Liberian Treasury in 1935 and served as disbursing officer from 1936 to 1943. Over the period 1943 to 1951 he was the elected member for Montsenado in the House of Representatives. He was TUBMAN's vice-president for 20 years, 1951–71, before becoming president in 1971, on Tubman's death. In 1965 he had become president of the Baptist World Alliance.

Tolbukhin (formerly *Dobrich*), town of north-eastern Bulgaria, capital of Tolbukhin province, 42 km north of Varna. It belonged to Turkey until 1878, and was part of

Romania 1913–40. It is the centre of the Bulgarian DOBRUJA region. It has textile, metal, and foodstuff industries, and has a trade in agricultural produce. Population 67,000.

Toledo, province of Spain, in Castilla la Nueva, lying in the Tagus basin south of Madrid. In the north is a rocky plateau, and in the south are the Montes de Toledo. Livestock, including fighting bulls, are raised, and there are silk, cutlery, wine, oil, and pottery manufactures. Area 15,348 km²; population 444,000.

Toledo, city of Spain, capital of the province of Toledo, built on a rock above the River Tagus. Important under the Romans (as *Toletum*), it became the capital of the Visigoths (see GOTHS) in 418. In 711 it was taken by the MOORS, and in 1085 it became a capital of CASTILE, and later, of Spain. The town centre is the Plaza de Zocodover, once the scene of *autos-da-fé*, masquerades, and bullfights. To the south is the ruined *alcázar*, and to the west the great five-aisled Gothic cathedral (13th–17th centuries) of the primate of Spain. There are many curious old streets and mansions. Several churches preserve paintings by EL GRECO, once a resident. Toledo sword blades were long famous, and fine knives are still manufactured, as well as silks, ceramics, and objects of church art. Population 44,434.

Toledo, city and county seat of Lucas county, Ohio, USA, on Maumee Bay of Lake Erie, 153 km west of

Toledo. The city, cathedral, and River Tagus. (*Topham/Fotogram*)

Cleveland. It is a railway centre and oil pipeline terminus, and a principal Great Lakes port, ranking high among world ports for the shipment of coal (24 million t shipped in 1970). Important for shipbuilding and oil refining, it also manufactures glass, automobiles, electrical equipment, and steel. Toledo has the city manager plan of government with proportional representation, and maintains a large public library, a noted museum of art, and the University of Toledo. Population (city) 383,318; (metropolitan area) 782,000; the latter is an increase of 13 per cent on the 1970 figure.

Toleration, doctrine that a citizen may adopt or discard any religion without state interference. Toleration became practically universal during the 19th century; but the rise of fascism and communism tended to restrict it in many countries, though most governments still claim to support it. Toleration is not a direct offspring of the Reformation, which accepted the principle 'Cuius regio, eius religio', i.e. a man should follow the religion of his king. But in effect this principle implied a theoretical equality of religions, and so paved the way for toleration. Modern indifference to religion also contributed to the development of toleration. Where it exists, it extends only to matters of doctrine; the State still exercises certain (diminishing) rights as a guardian of morality.
Bibliography: W. K. Jordan, *Development of Religious Toleration*, 1932–38.

Toleration, Act of, see ACT OF TOLERATION.

Tolima, department of COLOMBIA, lying in the valley of the Río Magdalena between the Central and Eastern Cordilleras. It is a rich agricultural district with coffee as the main crop; stock raising is also important. Capital is IBAGUÉ. Area 22,464 km². Population (1973) 900,000.

Tolkien, J(ohn) R(ouald) R(evel) (1892–1973), English writer, born at Bloemfontein, South Africa, but brought up in England. He taught English at Leeds University, 1920–25, was professor of Anglo-Saxon at Oxford, 1925–45, and then Merton professor of English language and literature until his retirement in 1959. He published studies and editions of Anglo-Saxon and Middle English works, but is best known for his unique and vastly popular imaginative writings, especially the *Lord of the Rings* trilogy (*The Fellowship of the Ring*, 1954, *The Two Towers*, 1954, *The Return of the King*, 1955). These expand the adventures of dwarfs, hobbits, monsters, and other creatures first created in *The Hobbit*, 1937, into a complete and self-contained world with its own history and geography, reminiscent of Norse myth. Tolkien's other books include *Farmer Giles of Ham*, 1949, *The Adventures of Tom Bombadil*, 1962, *Smith of Wootton Major*, 1967, *The Silmarillion*, 1977, and (with Donald Swann) a collection of songs *The Road Goes Ever On*, 1968.
Bibliography: H. Carpenter, *J. R. R. Tolkien: A Biography*, 1977.

Toll and Team, incidents of private jurisdiction in England, dating from before the Norman Conquest. Toll gave the lord power to exact payment on sales of livestock, goods, etc., within his estate, and team the power to hold a court to determine the proper possession of such goods.

Toller, Ernst (1893–1939), German poet and playwright, born at Samotschin (Posen), son of a Jewish merchant. He fought in the First World War as a volunteer and, being a socialist, he was prominent in the struggle for power in Bavaria, 1919, and suffered imprisonment. A refugee from the National Socialists, he committed suicide in New York. His expressionist drama has communistic and pacifist tendencies. His plays, many of which were translated into English, include: *Masse Mensch*, 1921, *Maschinenstürmer*, 1922, *Hinkemann*, 1924, *Tag des Proletariats*, 1926, *Hoppla, wir leben*, 1927; autobiography, *Eine Jugend in Deutschland*, 1933; verse, *Gedichte der Gefangenen*, 1921, and *Das Schwalbenbuch*, 1924.
Bibliography: W. A. Willibrand, *Ernst Toller and his Ideology*, 1945.

Tolls, taxes imposed in consideration of some privilege. In the feudal system it meant the right to tollage villeins. Later it became the distinguishing mark of a turnpike road, i.e. a road with toll-gates or bars on it, called 'turns'. These 'turns' appear to have been first constructed about the middle of the 18th century, when certain interested persons subscribed among themselves for the repair of various roads, and exacted a toll for the privilege of using the roads so repaired. The popular resistance to these exactions led to the passing of acts to regulate tolls.

Where a claim to demand tolls is made, there is a distinction between a *toll thorough* (through) and a *toll traverse* (across); the former being granted in consideration of the performance of a continuing beneficial service, such as the repair of a road or the maintenance of a bridge or ferry; the latter, of permitting the general public to pass over the land of the grantee of the toll. Military vehicles are exempt from payment. Other kinds of tolls are *port-tolls*, or charges on goods carried into a port; and *turn tolls*, or charges on cattle driven to market and returned unsold. Most road tunnels under rivers and ferries impose a toll, as do motorways in Italy and the USA.

Tolly, Mikhail Barclay de, see BARCLAY DE TOLLY, MIKHAIL.

Tolpuddle Martyrs, six farm labourers of Tolpuddle, 11 km from Dorchester, Dorset, who in 1834 formed an association to resist wage reductions. They were sentenced to seven years' transportation on the charge of administering illegal oaths but after widespread protests were reprieved two years later. Theirs is perhaps the best known case in the early history of trade unionism.

Tolstoi, Count Aleksei Nikolaevich (1883–1945), Soviet novelist and playwright, an outstanding representative of NATIONAL BOLSHEVISM. He established a name as a Neo-Realist before the 1917 Revolution, was with the Whites during the Civil War, emigrated, but in 1923 returned to Russia. At first he was treated by Communists with suspicion as a FELLOW TRAVELLER, but from the middle 1930s he enjoyed a privileged position as a pillar of Stalinism and directly contributed to the Stalin cult with *Bread*, 1937 (translated by S. Garry, 1938). His best works are the trilogy *The Road to Calvary*, 1921–41 (translated by E. Bone, 1946), on the life of the Russian intelligentsia, 1914–21, and the unfinished novel *Peter the Great*, 1929–45 (translated by T. Shebunina, 1959).

Tolstoi, Count Lev Nikolaevich

Tolstoi, Count Lev Nikolaevich (1828–1910), Russian novelist and social reformer, born into an old aristocratic family on their estate, Yasnaya Polyana, in the Tula province, where he spent most of his life. He became an orphan at nine and was brought up by a distant cousin, studied at Kazan University, but left it before graduating and gave himself up to pleasure for some years. In 1851 he joined the Russian forces in the Caucasus, and on the outbreak of the Crimean War was at his own request transferred to the Danube army and then to Sevastopol, taking part as an artillery officer in its heroic defence. While in the Caucasus he wrote the autobiographical works *Childhood*, 1852, and *Boyhood*, 1854, and a number of war stories which revealed what were to be the main features of Tolstoi's literary work; acute observation and perception, and a moral sincerity. In 1855 when he arrived in St Petersburg, he was received with admiration in the literary circles of the capital—by GONCHAROV, OSTROVSKY, CHERNYSHEVSKI, TURGENEV, NEKRASOV, among others—as a new star of Russian letters.

The first works were followed by the *Tales of Sevastopol*, 1855, which debunked romantic ideas of martial bravery, and *Youth*, the third part of the autobiographical trilogy, 1857. In 1857 and 1860 he travelled widely in western Europe, experiencing disgust at its materialism. The second journey was largely devoted to the study of educational methods. In the 1860s and 1870s Tolstoi devoted much of his time and energy to educational activities, running a school on his estate, publishing a special magazine, and writing textbooks, as one of the pioneers of 'free education'. The 1860s and 1870s were also the period of his most intensive literary work. For over six years, 1863–69, Tolstoi worked on *War and*

Lev Tolstoi. BELOW Tolstoi working at his home estate of Yasnaya Polyana, 1910. RIGHT A page from the manuscript of *Youth*. *(Novosti Press Agency)*

Peace, often called the greatest novel in world literature, a panorama of Russian society on the eve of, and during, the war of 1812 against Napoleon. In it Tolstoi expressed the view that history is made not by great men like Napoleon, but by the countless unconscious actions of individuals. Thus his wise characters are those who spontaneously accept life as it comes, listening only to their consciences. Tolstoi's own search for a way to live is reflected in *War and Peace* and still more strongly in *Anna Karenina*, 1873–77, in which the ethics of marriage and broader questions of life and death are examined. Both novels reveal his amazingly subtle appreciation of his characters' inner worlds and his eye for the tiny but revealing detail.

By the time he finished *Anna Karenina* Tolstoi had approached a spiritual crisis, which in the following years was resolved by his working out a new religious and social teaching based on the conviction that the whole message of Christ was contained in the words 'that ye resist not evil'. Renunciation of violence, wealth, and sex, a need for inner self-improvement and love for all living things are the main tenets of Tolstoian Christianity and can be found in *What I Believe In*, 1883, *A Confession*, 1884, and *What Are We To Do?*, 1886.

In *What is Art?*, 1896, Tolstoi argued that art should be simple and universally comprehensible, as well as morally uplifting, and rejected the 'superfluous detail' of his great realistic creations. The imaginative works of Tolstoi's later years, the long stories *The Death of Ivan*

Ilich, 1884, *The Kreutzer Sonata*, 1889, *Master and Man*, 1895, *Hadji-Murad*, 1896–1904; the novel *Resurrection*, 1889–99; the plays *The Power of Darkness*, 1886, *The Fruits of Enlightenment*, 1890, and *The Living Corpse*, 1900; and many popular stories, all to a greater or lesser extent serve to illustrate and propagate his new philosophy. His rejection of Church and State brought him excommunication and government hostility. The fame of his teaching soon crossed the frontiers of Russia, and during the last 15 or 20 years of his life Tolstoi was probably the most venerated man in the world.

While Yasnaya Polyana became a place of pilgrimage, Tolstoi himself felt increasingly estranged from it and from his family, who did not share his views. Unable to reconcile his ideal of simple life with the atmosphere of his family estate, he secretly left Yasnaya Polyana and ten days later died of pneumonia at a small railway station. Tolstoi the artist has had much influence on subsequent literature. Tolstoi the thinker has proved much less influential, and his only great disciple was GANDHI. His collected works were published in Russia in 90 volumes.

Bibliography: L. and A. Maude (Trans.), *Collected Works* (21 vols), 1928–37; I. Berlin, *The Hedgehog and the Fox*, 1954; G. Steiner, *Tolstoy or Dostoyevsky?*, 1960; J. Bayley, *Tolstoy and the Novel*, 1968; R. F. Christian, *Tolstoy. A Critical Introduction*, 1969.

Toltecs, semi-legendary people of Mexico and Central America, to whom the AZTECS and MAYAS ascribed many cities, monuments, and arts. Though their certain origin is not known, they were the reputed conquerors of the Mayas. They are said to have migrated southward along the Mexican plateau from the north. In the basin of Mexico they subdued the peoples already settled on the land and founded their own capital, calling the land Anáhuac, 'edge of the water', on account of its many lakes. It is thought their main centre was at Tula (Tollán). They reached the zenith of their power between 700 and 1100, conquering many neighbouring peoples, and in time the confines of their empire extended as far north as the Tropic of Cancer and as far south as the southern border of Guatemala. Their name means 'builder', and they are famous for the great pyramids of TEOTIHUACÁN. The legendary Toltec leader, Quetzalcoatl or Kukulcán (Feathered Serpent), who is said to have died in 895, forced the Maya city states to cease their internecine warfare and accept his rule, but when the power of the Toltecs declined the Mayas resumed their mutual strife, which resulted in their abandonment of the towns of north-west Yucatán.

Toluca, town of MEXICO, capital of the state of México, 60 km south-west of Mexico City. It is the centre of an agricultural and stock-farming region. To reach Toluca from Mexico City, it is necessary to climb by road above 3000 m over the intervening mountain range. The centre of the region, known as the basin of Toluca, is swampy; but maize, wheat, beans, and alfalfa are grown. The chief industries comprise cotton and woollen textile manufacturing and the processing of agricultural products. Population (1975) 142,000.

Toluene, or methyl benzene, $C_6H_5CH_3$, mobile liquid (boiling point 110 °C) which resembles BENZENE in most respects. It is prepared from the 90 per cent benzol obtained from coal-tar and from the cracking of petroleum, and is used in the preparation of aniline dyes, explosives and many other AROMATIC COMPOUNDS.

Tolyatti (formerly *Stavropol*), town in the KUIBYSHEV *oblast* of the RSFSR, USSR, which also functions as a port on the Kuibyshev Reservoir (part of the Volga system), north-west of Kuibyshev. An important industrial centre with synthetic rubber, chemical, nitro-fertiliser, electro-technical, and cement works, and ship-repair yards. The Volga car works began production in 1970. It was renamed in honour of the Italian Communist leader Palmiro Togliatti. Population (1974) 403,000 and growing rapidly (1970, 251,000).

Tom Thumb, see DWARF.

Tomar, town of Portugal, in Santarém district. It was the seat of the Order of Christ between the 14th and 16th centuries, and it was here that PHILIP II of Spain was proclaimed king of Portugal. The town has a splendid convent-castle of the KNIGHTS TEMPLARS. Population 8100.

Tomášek, Václav (1774–1850), Czech composer and teacher, born in Prague. Although almost self-taught he became the most important Czech composition and piano teacher of his age. He wrote songs, piano and chamber music, three symphonies, church music and three operas. His keyboard works pioneer the type of short lyric piano pieces of the Romantic era. His 13 volumes in this genre were popular all over Europe and directly influenced Schubert. His memoirs provide much information about the musical life of his time.

Tomasi, Giuseppe, Prince of Lampedusa, see LAMPEDUSA, GIUSEPPE TOMASI, PRINCE OF.

Tomaso de Vio, see CAJETAN, JACOPO.

Tomaszów Mazowiecki, town of Poland, in Łódź province, on the River Pilica, 47 km south of Łódź. It has woollen textile industries. Population 56,000.

Tomato, *Lycopersicum esculentum*, an annual plant in the family Solanaceae, bearing globose or ovoid red or yellow fruit. Round fruits are generally grown in Britain; imported tinned tomatoes are often ovoid. Formerly it was known as 'love apple'. It was introduced into England in 1596 from America, but has only become popular in Britain since 1900. Its production is now an important world-wide industry. In Britain the tomato is grown chiefly under glass, for except in sheltered and especially favoured situations, and when the season is sunny, the culture of the fruit out of doors is unsatisfactory. The plants are raised from seed early in the year in a warm place. They are confined to a single stem, shoots at the axils of the leaves being regularly pinched out. Liberal watering and manuring are necessary while the fruit is setting. Late fruit may be ripened in the dark in a temperature of 10 °C.

Tomb (Greek *tumbos*), properly signifies a mass of masonry raised over a grave or vault used for interment; but it is applied, in a wider sense, to any sepulchral structure. Of primitive sepulchres there are two classes, one subterraneous, the other of raised mounds or tumuli. Monuments of the first kind are numerous in Egypt; the pyramids had no doubt a common origin with the tumulus. At some places in Etruria the tombs are hewn out on the sides of rocks and hills, and their entrances present an architectural façade. Sepulchral edifices are numerous throughout Latium and Magna Graecia, many being remarkable for the architectural decoration bestowed on them. The tombs of the Middle Ages within buildings (churches, chantries, cloisters, etc.) exhibit a variety of form and enrichment, from the primitive stone coffin to the lavishly decorated canopied monuments. Another class consists of altar or table tombs. The next in order is the effigy tomb, first introduced in the 13th century, with a recumbent figure of the deceased upon it, extended, the hands slightly raised and joined in the attitude of prayer. Altar and effigy tombs were usually placed between the piers of an arch, or within a recess in a wall, and the whole tomb was frequently covered by an arch forming a sort of canopy over it as in that of Aymer de Valence in Westminster Abbey. See FUNERAL RITES AND BURIAL CUSTOMS; MASTABA; MAUSOLEUM; PYRAMID; SARCOPHAGUS.

Tombolo, see SPIT.

Tombouctou, or Timbuktu, town of MALI, West Africa, situated near the most northerly point on the NIGER river. Its position made it a focus of caravan routes between North and West Africa, and it flourished as a trade centre in the 12th century. European influence reoriented trade towards the coast during the 20th century, and the town's population has fallen from a peak of 50,000 to about 9000 today.

Tomis (modern Kustendje or Constanta), town of Thrace on the west shore of the Euxine, often but inaccurately called Tomi (later Tomiswar, or Jegni Pangola). Once the capital of Scythia Minor, it was colonised by Greeks from Miletus (c. 600 BC), and is famous as the place to which Ovid was banished.

Tomlinson, Charles (1927–), English poet, born at Stoke-on-Trent; educated at Cambridge, where he studied with Donald DAVIE, and London. He became reader in English poetry at the University of Bristol. Tomlinson is also a painter and his poetry is usually concerned with seeing, attempting to extend our sensual perception of the world around us. His verse often achieves a refreshing rhetorical simplicity and great metrical beauty. Among his volumes of poetry are *Seeing is Believing*, 1960, *America West Southwest*, 1969, and *Written on Water*, 1972. He has also translated several volumes with Henry Gifford, including *Castilian Ilexes: Versions from Machado*, 1963.

Tomlinson, Henry Major (1873–1958), English novelist and travel writer, born in London. At the age of 12 he became a clerk in a shipping company, but disliked the work and turned to writing. In 1904 he joined the staff of the *Morning Leader*, and in 1912 made a voyage up the Amazon, of which he wrote in *The Sea and the Jungle*. During the First World War he was a war correspondent, then was literary editor of the *Nation* from 1917 to 1923. His novels include *Gallions Reach*, 1927, *All Our Yesterdays*, 1930, *The Snows on Helicon*, 1933, *All Hands*, 1937, and *Morning Light*, 1946. He is best known for his travel books, *Old Junk*, 1918, *London River*, 1921, *Under the Red Ensign*, 1926, *Out of Soundings*, 1931,

The Wind is Rising, 1941, *Turn of the Tide*, 1945, and *Malay Waters*, 1950. *A Mingled Yarn*, 1953, is a book of autobiographical essays.

Tommaso di Stefano, see GIOTTINO.

Tommy Atkins, slang name for the British private soldier; more shortly 'Tommy' as in the opening poem of Kipling's *Barrack Room Ballads*, 1892. Originally the suppositious name used in a specimen form in an official handbook issued by the War Office after the Napoleonic wars, it was afterwards generally applied to describe the British regular soldier. The vogue of the name, which is used in a friendly rather than in any derogatory sense, was due largely to Kipling. There seems to be no convincing evidence that the name was that of an identifiable individual, though the theory has been advanced that a soldier called Tommy Atkins was killed while serving with Wellington in Holland, and that many years later the Duke, when secretary of state, adopted the name in the army form. The Scots equivalent is 'Jock'.

'Tommy Gun', see SUBMACHINE-GUN.

Tompion, Thomas (1638–1713), British watchmaker, born at Northill, Bedfordshire. Throughout his career he was closely associated with some of the leading mathematicians and philosophers of the time. The theories of Robert HOOKE and Edward Barlow would, in all probability, never have been put into practice but for Tompion's skilful execution of them. Early in his career he became a leading watchmaker to the court of King Charles II, and was everywhere welcomed as a craftsman of exceptional ability. Tompion was closely associated with the Worshipful Co. of Clockmakers, being elected a brother in 1671, a freeman in 1674, and master in 1704. He is buried in Westminster Abbey. See also WATCH.

Tomsk, *oblast* of the RSFSR, USSR, in West SIBERIA, traversed by the River OB, and consisting largely of flat lowland with moraines and glacial lakes. Thirty-five per cent of the area is swampy; 54 per cent is covered with forests (mainly coniferous), the main resource. There are also peat, iron ore, oil, and natural gas deposits. There are lumbering, wood processing, metal-working, and food industries, fur trapping, grain and flax growing, and dairy-farming. It was formerly an area of banishment and labour camps. Tomsk (see below) is the only major city. Area 316,900 km². Population (1975) 824,000 (59 per cent urban).

Tomsk, capital city and economic centre of Tomsk *oblast* (see above), USSR; an important rail and river tranship-ment centre (sited on the River Tom, a tributary of the Ob), and a major cultural centre of SIBERIA. There are engineering, chemical, and woodworking industries. It has a university (the oldest in Siberia; founded 1888) and a polytechnic institute (founded 1900). It was founded in 1604 as a fortress town and played an important part in the Russian advance into Siberia, as a trade and transportation focus, though its rôle declined after it was bypassed by the TRANS-SIBERIAN RAILWAY. It was a provincial capital (1782–1925) and the administrative centre of a gold-mining area from the 1830s; industrial development has taken place since the 1930s, and particularly since the Second World War. Population (1974) 386,000.

Tomtit, see TIT.

Ton, see METROLOGY.

Tonalite, type of quartz diorite found in the Adamello Alps. Plagioclase quartz, hornblende, and biotite are its dominant minerals, with magnetite and zircon as accessories. The granite diorites of the USA are of this type, which is also found among the Scottish plutonic rocks.

Tonality, in music, a synonym for key, but with the more specific implication of the feeling of a definite key suggested by a composition or passage. It might be viewed as the art of HARMONY projected onto the largest scale and affecting a composition as a whole. It is thus one of the most powerful determining factors in musical structure, operating through the establishment of, and rate of change in, dominating harmonies, by the agency of modulation and the sense of CADENCE. In Baroque and Classical music it was usual for a composition or movement to end in the same key in which it began (see, for example, SONATA). In later times it became permissible to end in a different key (as in the 'progressive tonality' of Nielsen); and the adoption by Schoenberg and others of totally-chromatic harmony introduced, for expressive purposes, much greater ambiguity into the area of key—although in fact the tonal relationships do not cease to operate, and a key-sense is definitely discernible in many of their works. The would-be antithetical term 'atonality' is therefore inadmissible, and 'polytonality' (the idea that music can be written in three or more keys simultaneously) is equally so, as the individual lines in fact present themselves to the ear as elements of a single highly chromaticised vertical harmony. Schoenberg held that, theoretically, each piece of music possesses only *one* tonality, all other key-areas being subordinate or tributary 'regions' for exploration during the course of the composition.

Tonbridge, town in Tonbridge and Malling District of KENT, England. It lies on the River MEDWAY with a castle originally guarding the ford, of 12th and 13th century origin. On Castle Hill there was an Iron Age hill-fort. Tonbridge School was founded in 1553 by Sir Andrew Judd who placed it in the care of Skinners' company. The Reverend George Austen, Jane's father, was a master here. Today the town is a market centre with printing, bricks, plasters, tanning, and distilling industries. The Medway is navigable up to here for pleasure craft. Population (1971) 30,325.

Tønder, former county in south-west JUTLAND, Denmark. The soil is mainly marshy, but there is some agriculture. From 1864 until the plebiscite of 1920 the district was part of West Germany. Area 1386 km². Population 42,000. The capital is Tønder (population 8000).

Tone, (Theobald) Wolfe (1763–98), Irish rebel and patriot, born in Dublin and educated at Trinity College there. He was called to the Irish Bar in 1789, but devoted himself to politics and printed articles attacking the government. With Thomas Russell and James TANDY he founded the Society of UNITED IRISHMEN in 1791 and in the same year was elected secretary to the Catholic Committee. In 1795 he went to the USA and in the following year was in Paris consolidating his plans for a French invasion of Ireland. In the resultant expedition Tone was given a command under HOCHE but the French failed to effect a landing. In 1798 there was a rebellion in Ireland to which the Directory sent meagre support in the form of small expeditions to various points on the coast. Tone was captured off Lough Sully, tried by court-martial, and sentenced to be hanged for treason. He cut his own throat in prison.

Bibliography: T. Pakenham, *The Year of Liberty,* 1969.

Tone, in music: (1) The interval of a major second. In the natural scale of C the interval C–D is a major tone (8 : 9), D–E is a minor tone (9 : 10).

(2) In American usage = note; in England used in this sense only of a 'pure tone', i.e. a note which has no overtones.

(3) The quality of a musical sound, especially with reference to performance.

(4) In plainsong the name of one of the eight melodic formulas used for chanting the psalms.

Tone (in painting). Just as colour is a quality of light, so tone is an amount of light. The range of tone becomes 'tonality' when it provides proportionable ratios just as form and colour do. Striking decorative effects can be obtained from well-planned areas of light, middle-tone and dark, which is the basis of CHIAROSCURO.

Another pictorial means of expression derives from what physicists call 'percentage reflectivity'. This means that if the illuminated side of a form reflects a certain percentage of the light falling upon it, and its shadow side the same percentage but only of scattered light, then any other forms, different in intrinsic tone but lit under the same conditions, will preserve the same percentage ratio between their lighted and shadowed sides. Thus the percentage will be constant but the amount of difference will be considerable, thus producing a 'variety in unity', which is the essence of art. The reason why the paintings of a master like VERMEER seem so ineffable is that he gets his tonal ratios right, and so founds his harmonies on those of the universal laws of Nature.

Tone-poem, see SYMPHONIC POEM.

Tones, Partial, see HARMONICS.

Tonga, or Friendly Islands, kingdom formerly under British protection in the west Pacific, to the south-east of Fiji, between 15° and 23° latitude. Since 1970 it has been an independent state. Of about 200 small islands making up the group 36 are inhabited; estimated area, including inland water, 699 km². The population in 1975 was estimated at 100,105, nearly all Tongans. The islands on the east side are of coral formation, the chain on the west is volcanic; there are four volcanoes, and the islands are subject to hurricanes. The Tongans are Polynesians, allied to the Maori and Samoans. See also ATLAS 64.

Economy. The majority of the islands have an inherently fertile soil and the economy is based on agriculture. The two chief crops are coconuts and bananas. Agriculture employs about three-quarters of the working population. Prospecting for offshore oil began in 1975. The country's two development plans so far have aimed at stimulating the coconut industry and tourism and at improving communications.

Trade. The soil is fertile, yielding coconuts, bananas,

Tonga

and a variety of other fruits and vegetables; the principal exports are copra (shipped to UK) and bananas (shipped to New Zealand). Imports are mainly of textiles, foodstuffs, and fuels. Exports in 1974–75 were valued at $T4,613,210 and imports at $T12,970,000. The Tongan dollar is equivalent to about 70p sterling. The main source of revenue is customs duties.

Communications. There is a good airfield on Tongatapu and limited seaplane facilities at Nukualofa and airstrips at Vavau and Haapai. Fiji Airways operate five flights a week beteen Fiji and Tongatapu. Passenger and cargo shipping services call regularly and the Tongan Shipping Agency operates scheduled inter-islands services and a four-weekly service to Fiji. There are telephone services in Nukualofa and Vavau and a broadcasting service was opened in 1961.

Government. The government consists of the sovereign, a privy council, and cabinet, a legislative assembly and the judiciary. The sovereign presides over the privy council, which consists of the premier, the ministers (who are also heads of government departments) and the governors of Vavau and Haapai. The constitution of the cabinet is similar, except that the premier presides. The legislative assembly consists of the members of the cabinet, seven representatives of the people elected triennially, every Tongan who has reached the age of 21, pays taxes and can read and write being entitled to vote. The courts consist of a supreme court, a magistrate's court, and a land court.

Education is free and compulsory between the ages of 6 and 14; 151 primary and 28 post-primary schools comprise both state and mission schools. The largest of three public hospitals is at Nukualofa, the capital.

History. Tonga was discovered by Tasman in 1643 and visited in 1773 by Cook, who called the islands the Friendly Islands on account of the friendliness of the people. The first Europeans to visit any part of the group were the Dutchmen Cornelis Schouten and Jacob le Maire in 1616. Tasman landed in 1643. The first Englishman to visit Tonga was Captain Wallis, who in 1767 gave the name of Keppel to the northern island of Niuatoputapu. Captain Cook paid several visits between 1773 and 1777 and gave a full account of the islands and the people on his return home. In the early 19th century Tonga was torn by civil wars between rival dynasties, from which it was rescued by a member of the 19th Tui Kanokubolu, or 3rd dynasty, Taufa'ahau Tupou, an able warrior and administrator who had been converted to Christianity in 1831. At their baptism he and his wife took the names of George and Salote (i.e. Charlotte) in honour of George III and his consort, and those names have persisted in the Tupou dynasty to this day. By 1845 King George Tupou I had brought the whole kingdom under his control and when he died in 1893, aged 96, he had given the people a land system, a constitution, and the beginnings of parliamentary government. In 1900 Tonga became by treaty a British protected state; a revised treaty was signed in 1958 and another in 1967, giving Tonga increasing control over its affairs. On June 4, 1970 it became fully independent, joining the Commonwealth on the same date. The islands are ruled by King Tupou who succeeded his mother Queen Salote in 1965. The people are Christian, mostly Wesleyans, the first Wesleyan missionaries having landed in 1826.

Bibliography: Sir H. Luke, *Queen Salote and her Kingdom*, 1954.

Tongaland, or Amatongaland, region of NATAL, South Africa, situated on the east coast north of Zululand and south of Mozambique. The inhabitants are chiefly Tongas. Tongaland was annexed to Natal in 1897, and was previously part of Zululand. Prior to that time it was ruled by an hereditary dynasty under British supervision. Area 1500 km².

Tongareva, see PENRHYN.

Tongariro, volcanic peak (1968 m) in Tongariro National Park, in the northern part of the North Island of New Zealand, 32 km south-west of Lake Taupo. The northern plateau, to which the name is confined, has eight craters.

Tongatapu, principal island of TONGA.

Tongeren (French *Tongres*), town in the province of Limbourg, Belgium, 19 km south-east of Hasselt, generally considered to be the oldest town of Belgium. It was called *Civitas Tongrorum* under the Romans. Part of the Roman defensive wall can still be seen. It has a 15th-century basilican church of Notre-Dame, a convent, and the Moerepoort, an interesting remnant of the fortification of the 14th century. Tongeren has an important cattle market. Population 20,400.

Tongking, see TONKIN.

Tongue, village and parish on the north coast of Sutherland District, Highland Region, Scotland, on the east shore of the Kyle of Tongue. To the west of the Kyle are the impressive cliffs of Kennageall or Whiten Head.

Tongue, the movable muscular organ attached to the floor of the mouth that is concerned in the operations of mastication, deglutition (swallowing), speaking, and tasting. The base is attached to the HYOID BONE; the upper surface, or dorsum, is free as are the edges and the anterior portion of the lower surface. The substance of the tongue is striped MUSCLE, and is innervated by the hypoglossal nerve. The dorsum of the tongue is subdivided by a V-shaped groove, the sulcus terminalis, into an anterior palatine part and a posterior pharyngeal part. The anterior portion of the tongue receives its sensory supply from the lingual nerve and taste fibres from the chorda tympani (Vth and VIIth cranial nerves respectively). The glossopharyngeal nerve (IX) subserves taste and common sensation for the pharyngeal part. Immediately in front of the sulcus terminalis lie a row of vallate papillae which bear many·taste buds. Small salivary glands are also scattered over the dorsum of the tongue. The tongue undergoes alterations during disease. The easily recognised phenomenon of furring may indicate a raised temperature (from any cause) but is generally of little medical significance. Deficiency of the B group of vitamins, especially nicotinic acid, riboflavin, folic acid, and cyanocobalamin, can produce a bald tongue as can iron deficiency anaemia. Ulcers of the tongue may be caused by ill-fitting dentures, or broken teeth, or be associated with infective conditions of the mouth. Long lasting ulceration may be caused by cancer of the tongue. Leucoplakia, the chronic presence of white, firm, smooth patches on the tongue, is probably caused by chronic infection and may turn into cancer in some cases. Another cause of white patches on the tongue is the fungus *Candida albicans* or thrush. Black tongue may result from administration of antibiotics or it may have no apparent cause.

Tongue Worm, see PENTASTOMIDA.

Tonic, in music, the fundamental keynote of a scale. See also MUSIC.

Tonic, an old-fashioned medical concept; a tonic was considered to be an agent which re-established the proper performance of the body. Tonics differ from stimulants in that the latter produce a transient effect rapidly, while the former theoretically gradually build up a permanent effect. Tonics are used medically when the reasons for a patient's weakness and lack of enthusiasm for life cannot be attributed to any disease for which there is a remedy. They often stimulate the appetite; this is due to the presence of aromatic bitters which stimulate the nerve endings in the mouth. Examples of tonics are gentian, nux vomica (containing strychnine), and cinchona (containing quinine). Their value depends on suggestion and they are ineffective in children.

Tonic Sol-fa, see SOLMISATION.

Tonic Sol-fa College, see CURWEN, JOHN.

Tonic Water, see SOFT DRINKS.

Tonka, see DIPTERYX.

Tonkin, or Tongking, the northern region of VIETNAM and the part which has been longest under Vietnamese rule. It was governed as a separate protectorate by the French from 1883 till 1945, and since 1954 has been part of the Democratic Republic of Vietnam. Its capital is HANOI.

Tonkin, Gulf of, an arm of the South China Sea, between TONKIN and the island of HAINAN. In August 1964 it was the scene of a minor engagement between American destroyers and vessels of the Democratic Republic of VIETNAM, which greatly increased tension between the two countries, and was used by President Johnson as the basis for a major congressional resolution, which he later claimed as authority for his actions throughout the VIETNAM WAR (until 1968).

Tonle Sap, large tidal lake in north-west CAMBODIA, fed by the River MEKONG. It is the centre of Cambodia's fishing industry and the source of irrigation for a large region of the country.

Tonnage. A ship's capacity is measured in four different ways depending on what is required. The word 'ton' came from a tun of wine, which was a barrel holding 252 gallons (1145·6 l), and was the first measure of a ship's carrying capacity. The *gross tonnage* of a ship is the volume of all the enclosed spaces measured at 2·83 cubic metres to the ton less certain exemptions. *Register tonnage* (net tonnage) is the tonnage arrived at after certain spaces are deducted from the gross tonnage. Net tonnage is basically the space available in a ship for carrying cargo and it is on this that port and canal dues are levied. Thames measurement is an older form of measurement, now used only for yachts. *Deadweight tonnage* is the maximum weight of cargo, fuel, and stores that a ship can carry, and is a useful measurement for tankers and bulk carriers which are normally limited by the weight of cargo they can carry. The general cargo ship is limited by the space available for carrying cargo and so net tonnage is the most useful measurement. *Displacement tonnage* is used for warships and is the weight of the ship which is equal to the amount of water displaced, 1 m^3 of sea-water weighing 1·025 t.

Bibliography: P. M. Alderton, *Sea Transport: Operation and Economics,* 1973.

Tonnage and Poundage. Tonnage, a tax levied on each tun of wine or liquor imported into or exported from the UK, seems first to have appeared in the 12th century; poundage, a similar tax on every pound of dry goods, was first levied in the 13th century. From 1350 they were granted together as a subsidy and from 1415 allowed to sovereigns for life. Charles I's insistence on levying tonnage and poundage without parliamentary consent became a major political issue: Parliament protested its right to control taxation and John HAMPDEN's resistance to the collection of the tax expressed the widespread discontent over the question which contributed to the outbreak of the Civil War. In 1660 the tax was granted to Charles II, made perpetual under Anne, and abolished on the reorganisation of customs and excise in 1787.

Tonnage Dues, rates levied on the TONNAGE of ships entering ports or navigable public waters. The dues are devoted to the upkeep of harbours, wharves, the maintenance of buoys, moorings, river channels, and docks. Light dues are generally paid separately for upkeep of lights. Pilotage dues are often paid on tonnage, and all ships passing through the Suez, Panama, and other such canals pay tonnage dues.

Tönnies, Ferdinand (1855–1936), German sociologist, born in northern Germany; he taught at Kiel University until the Nazis removed him. His most famous work, *Gemeinschaft und Gesellschaft,* was published in 1887 (English edition 1955). It is concerned with a distinction between the social relationships pertaining to a real, interacting community and those of individualistic, atomistic society. This work has become a classic and is often used as a starting point for discussions of community.

Tonquin Bean, see DIPTERYX.

Tonsillitis, an acute inflammation of the tonsils causing difficulty in swallowing, usually associated with fever and painful enlargement of the regional lymph nodes. Commonly infection is viral, but in patients with severe symptoms, it may be due to haemolytic streptococci, glandular fever (infectious mononucleosis) or diphtheria. Only bacterial cases respond to treatment with antibiotics.

Tonsils, a pair of almond-shaped bodies situated in the fossa between the pillars of the fauces (at the soft palate near the uvula) in the pharyngeal cavity. Each consists of a mass of lymphoid tissue plentifully supplied with blood vessels, and is covered with mucous membrane which dips into depressions called crypts. The tonsils form part of a ring of LYMPHOID TISSUE guarding the common entrance of the alimentary and respiratory tracts. Thus they function as a first line of immunological defence against infective agents. Because of their exposed position, they are a frequent site of inflammation from septic infection. Tonsillitis, as this inflammation is called, may be acute or chronic. Acute tonsillitis is most often due to infection with the streptococcus, and may be the starting point of generalised streptococcal infections such as RHEU-MATIC FEVER and SCARLET FEVER. The treatment of acute tonsillitis consists of the administration of the appropriate antibiotic, but mild cases dissolve in a few days without specific treatment. Chronic tonsillitis, as its name implies, is a state of chronic inflammation resulting from one or more attacks of acute tonsillitis. It is invariably accompanied by overgrowth of the adenoids in the nasal pharynx. The treatment is usually surgical removal of the tonsils and adenoids. *Quinsy* is the term given to an acute suppurative tonsillitis with abscess formation in and around the tonsils.

Tonson, Jacob (c. 1656–1736), British publisher. He was apprenticed to a stationer and having been admitted a freeman of the Stationers' Company in 1677, began business on his own account. Tonson purchased DRY-DEN's *Troilus and Cressida* in 1679, and in 1681 acquired the valuable half-share in the rights of MILTON's *Paradise Lost*; he bought the other half in 1690. Tonson was secretary of the KIT-CAT CLUB, and became associated as publisher with the principal men of letters of his day, including STEELE, POPE, ADDISON, CONGREVE, and WYCHERLEY. He was also printer of parliamentary votes. See also BOOKSELLING.

Tonsure, the cutting of the hair in a certain form as a symbol of self-dedication to the monastic life. The custom first appears at the end of the 4th or beginning of the 5th century. In the ancient Celtic Church all the head was shaved in front of a line drawn from ear to ear. In the Roman Catholic Church the 'coronal of St Peter' has always been used. In this tonsure the crown of the head is shaved to leave a fringe of hair all round. In Italy a small shaven area, about the size of a large coin, is a mark of holy orders.

Tontine, form of mutual life insurance in which a number of people invest a sum of money in the purchase of a property. They share the income, and as each dies the shares become proportionately larger per survivor, until all the property eventually devolves on one. It owes its name to an Italian banker, Lorenzo Tonti, whose idea it was. In France and Great Britain in the 18th century, the state raised money by this means.

Tooke, John Horne (1736–1812), British politician and philologist, born in London and educated at Westminster, Eton, and St John's College, Cambridge. He was ordained in 1759, but resigned his living in 1773. He at first supported John Wilkes, but quarrelled with him in 1771. His support for the American colonists and for the French Revolution brought him political notoriety. In 1801 he was elected to Parliament, but immediately after this an act excluding the Anglican clergy from membership was passed, which disqualified him. He wrote an important work on philology: *Epea Pteroenta, or the Diversions of Purley*, 1786–1805.

Toole, John Laurence (1830–1906), British actor, born in London, educated at the City of London School. After several years in the provinces, in 1856 he established himself in London. He was at the Adelphi for nine years,

in roles such as Bob Cratchit and Caleb Plummer. He took over the Charing Cross Theatre in 1882, giving it his own name, and in 1892 produced Sir James Barrie's first play, a farce entitled *Walker, London*. He retired in 1895, the last of the old-style 'low comedians'.

Tools, Machine. All machine tools must provide for relative motion between the cutting tool and the workpiece in two directions at right angles, to give a cutting movement and a feeding movement. Each may be obtained by moving either the tool or the workpiece. On the LATHE the workpiece is rotated about a horizontal axis to give the cutting motion, its surface moving past the tool which is fed parallel to the axis. On the milling machine the cutter rotates and has teeth round its periphery; the workpiece is clamped to a horizontal table which is fed past the cutter. On the *drilling machine* the work is held stationary, both cutting and feeding motions being given to the tool. The work is also stationary on the *shaping machine*; the tool is moved backwards and forwards across it and is given an intermittent feeding movement between cutting strokes. The *planing machine* is similar in principle except that the work moves to and fro past the tool (see PLANE).

At one time machine tools were driven by long belts from overhead shafting, a number of machines being powered by a water-wheel, steam engine, or an electric motor. Several pulley combinations were provided, to enable changes of speed to be made; often the auxiliary drive for the feed motion was also by belts. Nowadays each machine has its own individual motor with gearboxes providing a range of cutting and feeding speeds. The frames of early machine tools were invariably cast but in recent years welded construction has become widely used. It is most important that the structure of the machine should be rigid to avoid distortion and vibration, which would lead to inaccuracy and a poor surface finish for the work.

The growing demand, especially in the motor industry, for the mass-production of large quantities of identical components has led to the development of machine tools which will carry out a number of operations in sequence; in many cases the change from one operation to the next is carried out automatically so that all the operator has to do is to load and unload the machine. A further development is the use of transfer machines; several machines carrying out successive operations on a component are linked together and the work is automatically transferred from one to the next by a conveyor. Where necessary, the work may be rotated or turned upside down between machines. Arrangements are made to ensure that the work is correctly located on each machine before it is clamped down and cutting begins, and a system of automatic inspection causes the machine to stop if any errors occur in the components. Tape- or computer-controlled machine tools, in achieving greater utilisation of the tools with great flexibility and accuracy, are becoming popular and economic for short production runs.

In *ultrasonic machining* the workpiece is subjected to repeated blows from a tool which is given a very small movement (about 0·025 mm) at a high frequency (approximately 10 kHz). The process is especially useful for piercing intricate shapes in hard, brittle materials such as tool steels, glass, and ceramics.

Toombs, Robert (1810–85), US statesman, born in Georgia and educated at the universities of Georgia and Virginia. After a number of terms in the House of Representatives of his state he was a congressman from Georgia from 1845 to 1853, and US senator from Georgia from 1853 to 1861. When the Southern Confederacy was formed and Jefferson DAVIS was named president, the latter appointed a Cabinet whose only strong men were Toombs as secretary of state and Judah P. BENJAMIN as attorney-general. When the grave question of attacking FORT SUMTER, at the entrance to the harbour of Charleston, South Carolina, was discussed, Toombs counselled caution, but was overruled. Later he quarrelled with Davis and left the Cabinet to become inspector-general of the Georgia troops. When the war was lost he remained in exile in Europe until 1867, when he returned to his native state.

Toorop, Jan Theodoor (1858–1928), Dutch Symbolist painter, born in Java; also known for his poster and stained-glass designs and illustrations. The influence of Jean MOREAU can be seen in his early work together with that of Javanese motifs; he also adopted Neo-Impressionism for a time, but is best-known for his paintings which employ stylised, flowing linear patterns. He met William Morris in England and exerted particular influence on Dutch Art Nouveau; he also influenced C. R. MACKINTOSH of the Glasgow School.

Tooth, see TEETH.

Toothwort, *Lathraea*, a genus of plants of the Orobanchaceae (broomrape family), parasitic and lacking chlorophyll. *L. squamaria*, the only British species, has a fleshy branched rhizome clothed with tooth-like scales and bearing a raceme of drooping, dull, whitish pink flowers, parasitic on hazel, beech and woody plants. *L. clandestina* is parasitic on willows and poplars. It has single, bright purple flowers rising from buds at ground level.

Tooting, see WANDSWORTH.

Toowoomba, second largest town in Queensland, Australia, in the centre of the rich DARLING DOWNS, 162 km west of Brisbane. It serves vast farming and dairying areas, where meat, wheat, and wool are produced. Population 57,578.

Topaz, mineral crystallising in the orthorhombic system, with cleavage parallel to the basal face, a fluosilicate of aluminium, $Al_2[SiO_4](OH,F)_2$. The colour range includes colourless, yellow (pale to brown), and blue. Hardness 8; specific gravity 3·5. The pink topaz seen in jewellery is produced by heating brownish-yellow stones which change colour on cooling. Topaz is abundantly found in Brazil, Siberia, Sri Lanka, Mexico, Japan, and Tasmania. The true topaz should not be confused with the yellow quartz known as citrine (hardness 7, specific gravity 2·65).

Topeka, capital of Kansas, USA, and county seat of Shawnee county, on the Kansas river, 85 km west of Kansas City. It is a distributional and manufacturing centre, serving eastern Kansas, with processing industries for farm produce. It is the seat of Washburn University, and has the Mid-American fairgrounds. Population 125,011.

Topelius, Zachris (1818–98), Finnish novelist and poet who wrote in Swedish, born at Kuddnäs. He entered journalism and for 20 years edited a newspaper in Helsinki. In 1854 he was appointed professor extraordinary of Finnish history at the University of Helsinki and nine years later professor of Finnish, Russian, and Scandinavian history. From 1875 to 1878 he was rector of the University.

Topelius was the author of several volumes of descriptive and lyrical poems, but his fame rests on a series of historical novels, grouped under the title of *Fältskärns berättelser*, 1859–67 (*The Surgeon's Stories*, 1872, 1883), describing Finnish life over three centuries. Their historical background is well described and the stories finely imagined. Topelius also compiled a notable collection of children's stories, *Läsning för barn*, 1865–96.
Bibliography: S. Lagerlöf, *Zachris Topelius*, 1921; P. B. Nyberg, *Zachris Topelius*, 1949.

Tophet(h), 'fire-place', south of Jerusalem, at the junction of the valley of the Sons of Hinnom (Ge-bene-Hinnom, Jer. xix. 2—shortened to Ge-Hinnom, 2 Kings xxiii. 10), the modern Wadi er-Rababi, and the Kidron valley. Child sacrifices were offered there to MOLECH, god of the Ammonites, whose worship Solomon introduced (1 Kings xi. 7). AHAZ offered up his son there (2 Kings xvi. 3), and the practice was common later (Jer. vii. 31). The evil place was later defiled and made the refuse dump of the city. See GEHENNA.

Topiary, the training and clipping of trees and shrubs into ornamental shapes. The art was most greatly developed in Tudor times, and was a definite feature of old-world gardens: some of the more ambitious examples still exist at Elvaston Castle, Derby, and Leven's Hall, Westmorland. Evergreens are most popular for topiary work, though hawthorn stands up to clipping well and is often used. The two best species, being long-lived and able to withstand severe and constant clipping, are yew, *Taxus baccata*, and box, *Buxus sempervirens*. Holly, *Ilex aquifolium*, and its variegated varieties, and evergreen oak, *Quercus ilex*, are often used, and the larger-leaved sweet bay, *Laurus nobilis*, and Portugal laurel, *Prunus lusitanica*, may be trained in simple formal shapes.
Bibliography: M. Hadfield, *Topiary and Ornamental Hedges*, 1971.

Toplady, Augustus Montague (1740–78), English Anglican divine and hymn-writer, born at Farnham, Surrey, and educated at Westminster and Trinity College, Dublin. He was ordained in 1762, and became vicar of Harpford (1766) and Broad Hembury (1768). In 1775 he became minister at the French Calvinist Chapel in London. He is remembered for his hymn, 'Rock of Ages'.
Bibliography: Life by T. Wright, 1911.

Topography is the general form and configuration of the earth's surface resulting from the geological agencies of erosion and deposition. Individual topographic features are known as landforms, and the science of landforms is termed geomorphology. The surface features of the earth result from three main controlling factors, 'process, structure and stage' (W. M. Davis). Geology controls the

Topography

initial large-scale landforms (structure), but the reworking and detailed sculpturing of these forms into their present configuration is achieved by different processes operating for varying periods of time (stage). Structure not only denotes the attitude and stratigraphy of the bedrock, but also their constituent properties such as permeability, porosity, and hardness. The term process covers the different agencies of weathering and erosion, i.e. water (rivers, coasts), ice (glaciers), and gravity (mass movement). The stage at which a given landform evolves reflects its position within the 'geographical cycle' or 'cycle of erosion', a term also introduced by the American geomorphologist, W. M. Davis, at the end of the 19th century.

According to this cyclic concept landforms evolve through a series of stages (fig. 1). Following uplift of the land-mass the phase of youth, typified by rapid incision into the newly-emergent flat plain, gives way to maturity, characterised by further dissection and the establishment of a drainage system and maximum relief. Ultimately the whole land-mass is nearly reduced to sea-level at the old-age stage, marked by the emergence of a peneplain, a gently undulating almost featureless plain. Interruption of the cycle caused by additional uplift results in a return to youth; such a phase is termed rejuvenation. A wide range of landforms are encompassed within the cyclic scheme, e.g. valleys, slopes, and stream patterns. In its initial form the cycle was termed the normal cycle of erosion. Other cycles representing the evolution of the landscape under other climatic régimes and processes have been developed by Davis and his followers, e.g. the cycle of shoreline development, the cycle of glacial erosion, and the karstic cycle.

Recently the theory of the cycle of erosion has been

Topography. Figure 1. Stages in the cycle of land mass denudation in a humid climate. *(Source: A.N. Strahler, Physical Geography, 1975)*

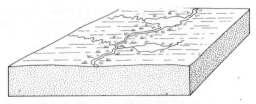

1 In the initial stage, relief is slight, drainage poor.

4 In maturity, the region consists of valley slopes and narrow divides.

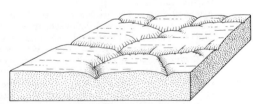

2 In early youth, stream valleys are narrow, uplands broad and flat.

5 In late maturity, relief is subdued, valley floors broad.

3 In late youth, valley slopes predominate but some interstream uplands remain.

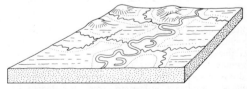

6 In the old stage, a peneplain with monadnocks is formed.

7 Uplift of the region brings on a rejuvenation, or second cycle of denudation, shown here to have reached early maturity.

Constructional		Destructional		
Processes	Forms	Reduction Forms	Residual Forms	Processes
Diastrophic	Plains and plateaus, grabens, fault mountains, down-warped basins, dome mountains, fold and complex	?	?	Diastrophic
Volcanic	Lava plains and plateaus, volcanoes	Calderas?	?	Volcanic
Weathering and soil movements	Talus, rock glaciers, landslide accumulations	Landslide scars	Exfoliation domes	Weathering and soil movements
Depositional — Fluvial	Plains and plateaus, fans, cones, deltas, floodplains, precipitation forms	Valleys, straths, peneplains	Monadnocks	Fluvial — *Erosional*
Glacial	Moraines, drumlins, outwash plains	Troughs, cirques	Arêtes, horns	Glacial
Eolian	Loess plains, dunes	Deflation hollows	Yardangs	Eolian
Littoral	Offshore bars, beaches, embankments	Sea cliffs, wave-cut terraces	Sea stacks	Littoral
Lacustrine	Lake plains, precipitation forms	?	?	Lacustrine
Terraqueous	Cones, terraces	Sinks	Natural bridges (in part)	Terraqueous
Impact	?	Meteor scars	?	Impact
Organic	Coral reefs	?	?	Organic

Topography. Figure 2.

seriously challenged on the ground that certain landforms achieve a state of dynamic equilibrium and undergo no further change of form through time. This occurs if the rate of weathering and erosion is sufficient to cause the height of the landform to be reduced commensurate with the amount of concurrent uplift. Thus the morphology of the landscape remains constant and the erosive processes are in equilibrium with tectonic activity and climate.

Many different classifications of landforms have been attempted using such criteria as gross topography, geological structure, superficial shape, micro-relief, size, active processes, and inherited features. The one adopted below (based on that derived by Howard and Spock) has the merit of being simple, logical, and all-inclusive, although it is better applied to minor rather than major landform types (fig. 2). The first basis for classification is the distinction between constructional and destructional landforms. The former are those landforms produced by accumulation of sediment or by diastrophism (uplift of the earth's surface by tectonic forces). Included under the heading of constructional processes are volcanism, deposition, soil movement, and the various components of diatrophic activity. Destructional landforms are those which result from the removal of matter from the initial land surface. A second basis for classification is the nature of the processes involved and whether depositional or erosive forces are dominant. The diverse régimes noted by fig. 2 predominantly reflect climatic controls (glacial, fluvial, arid, and semi-arid), the nature of the bedrock (karstic/limestone or granitic landforms), and the processes operative at the land/sea margin.

See also COAST; DESERT; GLACIATION; KARST; LANDFORMS, STRUCTURAL; RIVER; VOLCANO.

Bibliography: W. D. Thornbury, *Principles of Geomorphology*, 1954; G. H. Dury, *The Face of the Earth*, 1960; A. Holmes, *Principles of Physical Geology*, 1965; A. L. Bloom, *The Surface of the Earth*, 1969; R. J. Small, *The Study of Landforms*, 1970; B. W. Sparks, *Geomorphology*, 1972; A. N. Strahler, *Physical Geography*, 1975.

Topology is the branch of mathematics that deals with the properties of certain kinds of FUNCTIONS, which are called continuous functions. It originated as a generalisation of geometry when it was noted that certain simple characteristics of geometric figures are unaltered by quite drastic changes in their shape, size, and orientation. An example is the 'Euler characteristic'.

If a closed network is drawn on a surface then the number

$V - E + F$, where
V = number of vertices in the network
E = number of edges in the network
F = number of areas enclosed by the edges,

is called the Euler characteristic of the network. If the network is one plane polygon then

$$V - E + F = 1$$

because the polygon encloses 1 area ($F = 1$) while the numbers of vertices and edges must always be equal ($V = E$). Draw a plane polygon divided up in any way into smaller polygons (in other words, a closed network) (fig. 1). Then $V - E + F$ is still 1. To prove that, take one outer edge and delete it. That means that there is 1

Topology

(and only 1) less enclosed area in the network and 1 less edge; both F and E have been reduced by 1 so $V - E + F$ for the network is unchanged. That deletion may have left an edge that is no longer part of a closed polygon: delete it and the vertex at the end that was not joined to another edge; that means both E and V have been decreased by 1 but $V - E + F$ is unchanged. Continue the deletion process, always leaving $V - E + F$ unchanged, until there is only one polygon left; then $V - E + F = 1$ as already proved. It does not matter whether the network has straight sides. In fact $V - E + F = 1$ for any network which is drawn on a surface that can be transformed into a disk (a circle and its interior) by a process of bending and stretching without tearing (a circle by itself is 1 edge which meets itself at 1 vertex enclosing 1 area).

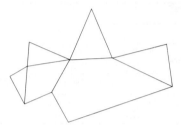

Topology. Figure 1.

Now consider a polyhedron (fig. 2). It is a closed network made up of vertices, edges and areas enclosed by the edges. The only way in which it can be transformed into a plane network is to make a hole in one enclosed area and then flatten out the polyhedron. Thus one enclosed area is lost and the result must have the 'circle' Euler characteristic of 1. That is

$$V - E + (F - 1) = 1;$$
$$V - E + F = 2.$$

In this case, the Euler characteristic of 2 is possessed by any network drawn on any size or shape of surface that can be transformed into a *sphere* by stretching and bending without cutting or puncturing.

It seems that geometrical figures can be put into mutually exclusive categories. All figures with the same Euler characteristic are in the same category. A figure in one category can be transformed, by a process of bending and stretching without tearing or puncturing, into any

Topology. Figure 2.

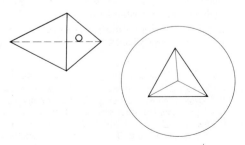

other figure in the same category, but cannot be transformed in that way into a figure in a different category. It is the object of topology to give a more precise description of the 'allowable' transformations and to study the nature of the properties that these transformations leave invariant. The properties studied in topology are fundamental to large areas of mathematics (especially the area traditionally called ANALYSIS) and topological methods are now used to supply very general statements of basic theorems.

A more precise description of the transformations that preserve such topological invariants as the Euler characteristic can be given by first noting that a transformation of one figure into another is simply a FUNCTION mapping the points of the first figure into the points of the other. A function that enables one to identify two figures as equivalent must have an inverse (because it should not matter which figure one starts with in the transformation process) and must therefore be a 1–1 correspondence. The 'no tearing or puncturing' condition is interpreted as a requirement for the function to have 'continuity' in the sense that points which are nearby in one figure must be transformed into points that are nearby in the other figure and not 'torn apart'. The idea of continuity is given a very general formulation in topology. The idea is to impose on a set the minimum amount of structuring necessary to make the idea of continuity meaningful. (Saying that a set is domain or codomain of a function says nothing at all about the structure of the set, so the idea of a function is obviously very general in character; it would be useful if the idea of a continuous function could be made just as general.) The structure that is given to a set is called a 'topology' and it consists of a collection of selected subsets of the set. Take any set E and a collection $\mathcal{T}$ of subsets of E with the property that (1) if T_1 and T_2 are in $\mathcal{T}$ then so is $T_1 \cap T_2$; (2) if $T_1, T_2, \ldots$ is any collection of sets that are all in $\mathcal{T}$ then

$$T_1 \cup T_2 \cup \ldots$$

is also in $\mathcal{T}$. The second condition means that the union X of all the sets in $\mathcal{T}$ is also in $\mathcal{T}$. $(X, \mathcal{T})$ is called a *topological space*; X is the space; $\mathcal{T}$ is the topology, and the elements of $\mathcal{T}$ are called the *open sets* of $(X, \mathcal{T})$. A single space X can have many different topologies, but if X is structured in some other way (for example, if there is an order relationship between the elements of X, or if the distance between pairs of elements has been defined) then there may be a 'natural' topology for X based on that structure.

If $x \in X$ then a subset N of X which contains x is called a *neighbourhood* of x if, and only if, N is contained in an open set. If $(X_1, \mathcal{T}_1)$ and $(X_2, \mathcal{T}_2)$ are topological spaces and f maps X_1 into X_2, then f is said to be *continuous* at $x \in X_1$ if, and only if, whenever V is a neighbourhood of $f(x)$ then $f^{-1}(V)$ is a neighbourhood of x. In other words, the condition for continuity is that every neighbourhood of $f(x)$ contains the image of some neighbourhood of x, which ensures that neighbourhoods of x are not split up by f. If f is a 1–1 correspondence between X_1 and X_2 and both f and f^{-1} are continuous for all points in X_1 and X_2 then f is called a *homeomorphism*. Any property of a topological space that is preserved by all homeomorphisms is called a *topological property*. Being an open set is a topological property for if $(X_1, \mathscr{T}_1)$, $(X_2, \mathscr{T}_2)$ are topological spaces and $f: X_1 \to X_2$ is a homeomorphism and $T_1 \in \mathscr{T}_1$ then $f(T_1) \in \mathscr{T}_2$ (this fact is sometimes used as a definition of continuity).

The number of open sets in a topology is usually very large and it is often more convenient to describe only a 'base' for a topology, which is a collection of sets $\mathscr{B}$ with the property that any open set in the topology consists of the union of some sets from $\mathscr{B}$.

In the set of real numbers **R**, all sets of the type

$$I = \{ x \in \mathbf{R} \| x - a | < b \}$$

form a base for a topology of **R** (called the 'usual' topology for **R**). This shows the origin of the terminology 'open'. I has no end-points or 'boundary' points. In the set of complex numbers the usual topology has a base formed by the open disks of the type

$$D = \{ z \in \mathbf{C} | z - a | < c \}.$$

In a topological space $(X, \mathscr{T})$ the following definitions are used. If T is an open set then its complement in X is a closed set. If E is a subset of X then $x \in X$ is a limit point of E if, and only if, whenever

$x \in G \in \mathscr{T}$ then
$E \cap G - \{ x \} \neq \varnothing;$

in other words, x is as near as possible to E but is not necessarily an element of E. A closed set contains all its limit points; if any set K is combined with its own limit points the result is a closed set called the closure of K. A set $E \subset X$ is said to be connected if, and only if, it is impossible to divide it up into two non-empty, disjoint sets A and B such that $A \cup B = E$, $A \cap B = \varnothing$, A contains no limit points of B, and B contains no limit points of A. Thus connectedness corresponds to the intuitive idea of a set 'being in one piece'. Connectedness is preserved by homeomorphisms. The only connected sets in **R** (with the 'usual' topology) are intervals.

Bibliography: J. L. Kelley, *General Topology*, 1955; E. M. Patterson, *Topology*, 2nd ed. 1959; B. H. Arnold, *Intuitive Concepts in Elementary Topology*, 1962; W. J. Pervin, *Foundations of General Topology*, 1964; B. Mendelson, *Introduction to Topology*, 2nd ed. 1968.

Topsail, see SAILS AND RIGGING.

Topsoil, a popular term used in a variety of senses to describe variously (1) the surface layer which is ploughed (the Ap horizon); (2) the A1 horizon which varies in depth with different natural soils; (3) the total group of A horizons which, like (2) above, varies from soil to soil in the uncultivated state; and (4) soil material used for top dressing by gardeners. It is normally envisaged as the upper 20 cm which is dark in colour owing to the presence of organic matter and is characterised as the major zone of organic matter accumulation. Topsoil is the soil normally moved in tillage practices and is the major zone of root development carrying many of the nutrients and supplying much of the water available to plants. It is possible by management practices such as ploughing, digging, and cultivation to manipulate and modify the characteristics of this part of the soil. Thus it can be drained, and organic and chemical nutrients added to it and hence the productivity can be raised, lowered, or stabilised. Topsoil contains approximately 45 per cent

mineral matter, 5 per cent organic matter, 25 per cent air, and 25 per cent water, but air and water vary constantly (see SOIL MOISTURE).

Tor, see INSELBERG.

Tor Bay, on the south coast of Devon, England, the landing place of William of Orange (1688). On its shores are the towns of TORQUAY, PAIGNTON, and BRIXHAM.

Torbanite, see BOGHEAD COAL.

Torbay, county borough in DEVON, England, which was formed in 1968 and includes Brixham, Churston Ferrers, Cockington, Goodrington, Maidencombe, Paignton, Shiphay, and Torquay. Population (1971) 109,257.

Torc, see TORQUE.

Torch-thistle, see CEREUS.

Torez (until 1964, *Chistyakovo*), town in the DONETSK *oblast* of the Ukrainian SSR, USSR, 60 km east of Donetsk. Coal is mined and there are electro-technical and ferro-concrete works, the latter providing roof-supports for the coal-mines. Renamed in honour of Maurice Thorez, the French Communist leader. Population (1970) 93,000.

Torfaen, new district of the county of GWENT, South Wales. Area 127 km²; population (1975) 89,870.

Torga, Miguel, pseudonym of Adolfo Rocha (1907–), Portuguese poet, novelist, dramatist, and short-story writer. An independent and staunch individualist among literary circles, he pursues a long-drawn speculation on the relationship between the material and the spiritual, mingling a deep sensuousness with an all-embracing love for every living form in the universe. His works include *Criação do Mundo* (3 volumes), 1937–38, *Bichos*, 1940, *Diário*, 1941–49, *Mar*, 1941, and *Sinfonia*, 1947.

Torgau, town of East Germany, in the district of Leipzig, on the River Elbe, 48 km north-east of Leipzig. In 1526 the Torgau League (of Protestant princes) was formed here. It was the first meeting place of US and Soviet troops in the advance through Germany on 27 April 1945. There is a Gothic church containing the grave of LUTHER's wife. Chemicals and machinery are manufactured. Population 19,800.

Torhout (French *Thourhout*), town in the province of West Flanders, Belgium, 19 km south-west of Bruges. Near Torhout lies the beautiful castle of Wijnendale, built in the 11th century. In 1940 King Leopold III had his headquarters at Torhout and capitulated here on 28 May. The town is considered to be the oldest place in Flanders and was once the chief cloth market of the country. It has linen manufactures and is an important horse market. Population 15,500.

Torino, see TURIN.

Tormentil, *Potentilla erecta*, a perennial herb in the family Rosaceae, native to Britain and also found in the Azores, Siberia and Europe. The leaves are divided into three, sometimes five, leaflets; the flowers, which are yellow, have four, rarely five, petals. The rootstock was used in tanning, having an astringent quality.

Tornado, see CYCLONE.

Toronto

Toronto, capital of the province of ONTARIO, Canada, 2900 km west of the Atlantic Ocean on a bay on the north shore of Lake Ontario, 535 km south-west of Montreal and 383 km east of Detroit. The crossroads of trade since Indian times, Toronto's strategic position was fought for by French, Americans, and English.

The site of the present city was chosen by Lord Dorchester, governor of Canada, as the seat of government for the newly created province of Upper Canada in May 1793. Sir John Graves Simcoe, first lieutenant-governor, named the new town York. It was occupied by US forces in 1813 when legislative buildings and archives were burned and the mace carried away, to be returned by President Roosevelt at the centennial celebrations in 1934. Self-government was granted to the town of York in 1817, and it was incorporated as a city under the name of Toronto in 1834. Its name, of Huron Indian origin, means 'a place of meeting'.

The site is good for government, business, and industry alike located as it is on a large low-lying plain opposite the great hooked spit which protects the harbour. The Humber and the Don valleys carry roads and railways inland. These valleys along with the lake shore have emerged as areas of industrial development. Inland the beach ridge formed around old Lake Iroquois has emerged as the main area of suburban residential development. Capitalising on its focal position Toronto emerged at an early date as the major manufacturing, service, and financial focus for southern Ontario, and with the coming of the railway era, and later car transport, extended its sphere of influence to encompass the entire country. At the present time the largest single source of employment continues to be manufacturing (30 per cent of the metropolitan labour force) but its predominance is declining slowly. Secondary production which includes both manufacturing and construction now account for 33 per cent as compared with 43 per cent in 1951. This change reflects the growth in the tertiary sector, a response to a diversification of the city's employment structure. Prominence in finance is the hallmark of metropolitan dominance, and the Toronto stock exchange accounts for about two-thirds of the value of Canadian sales of stocks. Over 37 per cent of all life assurance assets are in Toronto-based companies, more than half the fire and casualty firms have head offices in the city, 45 per cent of Canada's bank assets, and Toronto's share of bank clearings in Canada amounts to over 37 per cent. This gives some idea of the measure of the importance of its tertiary activities, and when taken in conjunction with the city's important retailing and wholesaling functions accounts for the growth in tertiary employment. The chief industries are metal founding and machine shops, shipbuilding, and agricultural implements; together with meat packing, flour milling, and canning; textiles, automobiles, furnishings, and clothing; paper products, printing and publishing—a range of industries drawing raw materials from all over Canada. Between 1953 and 1973 metropolitan Toronto and the province spent over $(Can)1200 million on the development of a rapid transit rail system and an urban motorway network which is the envy of most large cities in North America.

In an attempt to find a solution for many of the problems facing large urban areas, the new municipality of metropolitan Toronto was created in 1954. It encompasses the city and 12 adjacent municipalities. This experiment in metropolitan government has a council of 24, 12 members from the city and one from each of the 12 suburban municipalities. The success of this experiment has led many other cities in North America to consider implementing similar schemes. Population (city) 712,790; (metropolitan area) 2,741,100.

Bibliography: J. E. Middleton, *The Municipality of Toronto: A History* (3 vols), 1923; D. Kerr and J. Spelt, *The Changing Face of Toronto*, 1965; G. P. de T. Glazebrook, *Story of Toronto*, 1972; A. Rose, *Governing Metropolitan Toronto*, 1973; E. Arthur, *Toronto: No Mean City*, 1975.

'Toronto Star', Canadian newspaper, an evening daily, established in 1892. It circulates throughout the province of Ontario and includes full coverage of world and home news. Associated with it is the *Star Weekly*, established in 1910, which has a national circulation.

Torpedo, self-propelled submarine explosive device. Early 'torpedoes' (not necessarily self-propelled) were of many different forms: one type was towed across the bows of enemy vessels by small torpedo-boats; another was the 'spar' torpedo, which was carried at the end of a spar at the bows of a launch. The spar was arranged to lower the torpedo below the water-line just before striking, later models being fired electrically. Defensive measures eventually rendered ineffective this form of attack. Meanwhile efforts were concentrated upon the development of a self-propelled type. In 1866 Robert WHITEHEAD succeeded, where many previous inventors had failed, in producing a satisfactory torpedo. The secret of his success lay in the hydrostatic valve which he linked to the horizontal rudders and later to a pendulum and which overcame the depth-keeping problem. In 1871 the manufacturing rights were purchased by the British government after successful trials, in 1876 the servo-motor was added by Whitehead, and in 1895 he put the finishing touch to his invention by the addition of a gyroscope, which solved the problem of straight running. These principles form the basis of all torpedoes in use today.

The shape of the modern torpedo resembles a cigar with a rounded or blunt nose. It is constructed of special steel, and divided into a number of compartments: the explosive head, compressed-air chamber, balance chamber, engine room, and buoyancy chamber. Although in most navies torpedoes with a diameter of 53 cm carrying a warhead with 270 kg of explosive are standard, during the Second World War the Japanese developed a 69-centimetre diam-

Torpedo.

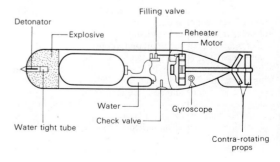

eter torpedo known as *Long Lance*, which carried a 454-kilogram charge. It was 9·1 m long compared with 7·0 m for the standard pattern. The warhead of a torpedo is detonated by a pistol actuated either by contact with the hull of the target ship or by the latter's magnetic field as it passes under it. For peace-time practice, special heads are fitted containing water and cork. The head is bolted on to the compressed-air chamber, which is forged from high-tensile steel and contains air at a pressure of over 15 MN/m^2 supplied from air compressors on board the warship. Next follows the balance chamber containing the mechanism for controlling the depth the torpedo will run at, as well as, in the later types, vessels containing fuel, water, and a special heater apparatus. Depth control is effected by a swinging weight of pendulum which, being affected by any alteration in tilt, sets in motion a servo-motor, contained in the engine-room, which provides the necessary power to actuate the horizontal rudders which correct the vertical deflection of the torpedo from its proper depth. A hydrostatic valve is fitted to ensure that the torpedo attains the correct depth. The engines, placed abaft the balance chamber, are of the four-cylinder, single-acting, *Brotherhood* type. The *Ikara* and other types of missile are directed by the parent ship to carry the torpedo to a launching position, where the torpedo is lowered to the sea by parachute, and it then acts as a homing torpedo.

Torpedoes are normally housed in tubes, which may be either above water or submerged, from which they are discharged either by compressed air or by the ignition of a cartridge of coarse grained powder. During the Second World War they were carried by aircraft slung under the fuselage and proved a very effective weapon. Today they have been superseded by rocket weapons for anti-ship work, but special anti-submarine torpedoes have been designed for use by helicopters.

'Human torpedoes' or 'chariots' were successfully used in the Second World War, first by the Italians and later by the British, Germans, and Japanese. 'Human torpedoes' are normally larger than the ordinary torpedo, and are driven by electric batteries. They are manned by a crew of two, who wear diving-suits and sit astride the weapon. A charge similar to the warhead of the ordinary torpedo is attached to the nose. The torpedo is manoeuvred at slow speed towards its target and dives under it. The charge is then detached and fixed to the bottom of the enemy ship; the fuse is set and the vessel is driven away to be clear of the target area before the charge detonates. The Japanese version known as *Kaiten* was 16·5 m long and carried a 1360-kilogram warhead. It had a one-man crew who, like the pilot of the *kamikaze* aircraft, perished when the charge exploded. The Germans developed no fewer than six types of midget submarines, and one long-range torpedo known as *Dackel* with a running range of 56 km.

Torpedo, or electric ray, a member of the elasmobranch family Torpedinidae in order BATOIDEI. Torpedos are characterised by the possession of ELECTRIC ORGANS which are present between the head and the pectoral fins. The shock which they are capable of producing is from 20 to 30 volts in *T. marmorata*. The largest species may be up to 180 cm in length.

Torpedo-boat, warship which is now obsolete, having

been replaced by the DESTROYER and motor torpedo-boat, now classified, together with motor gunboats, as fast patrol-boats. The first torpedo-boat was built by Thornycroft for the Norwegian government in 1873, for the 'towing' type of torpedo. In 1879 the same firm built the *Lightning*, 27 t, with a speed of 19 knots (25 km/h), for the Admiralty. She was fitted with a bow torpedo tube for launching a Whitehead torpedo. As these vessels grew in size and speed, it became necessary to evolve some means of protecting battleships from the threat of their attack. At first quick-firing guns and nets seemed to provide the answer, but eventually the torpedo-boat gave way to the torpedo-boat destroyer, in which the functions of both torpedo-boat and anti-torpedo-boat were combined. See also GUNBOAT.

Torpedo-boat Destroyer, see DESTROYER.

Torphichen, parish and village of West Lothian District, Lothian Region, Scotland. Torphichen Preceptory was the headquarters of the KNIGHTS HOSPITALLERS of St John of Jerusalem in Scotland. Population 401. Nearby, in the Bathgate Hills, lies Cairnpapple Hill, a complex prehistoric burial and ritual monument.

Torquatus, name of a patrician family of Rome of the *gens* Manlia (see MANLIUS, MARCUS). The members were:

Titus Manlius Imperiosus, statesman, who fought against the Gauls (361 BC), winning his name Torquatus by taking the necklace (*torques*) from the body of a Gaul slain by him in single combat. He was dictator in 353 and 349, and consul in 347, 344, and 340. On the last of these occasions he and his colleague P. Decius Mus defeated the Latins at the foot of Vesuvius.

Titus Manlius, conqueror of the Sardinians, was consul in 235 and 224, and censor in 231 BC. He opposed the ransom of the Roman prisoners of Cannae (216). He was dictator in 210.

Lucius Manlius was consul with L. Aurelius Cotta (65 BC). He helped to suppress the Catiline conspiracy (see CATILINA, LUCIUS SERGIUS) (63), and supported CICERO in his exile (58).

Lucius Manlius, his son, was praetor 49 BC, and opposed CAESAR on the outbreak of civil war. Obliged to surrender Oricum, he was taken prisoner but released. He fought again in Africa, but was captured and slain after Thapsus (46).

A. Manlius, friend of Cicero, who presided at the trial of MILO (52 BC). He sided with Pompey (see POMPEIUS) in the civil war, and was an exile at Athens (45).

Torquay, administrative centre of TORBAY, seaport, and holiday resort in south DEVON, England, on Tor Bay, 41 km south of Exeter and 320 km from London. Its picturesque scenery and mild climate make it a favourite health resort. Terra cotta, clay, and marble are found in the neighbourhood of the town. The Domesday survey identifies part of the site of Torquay with the Norman period, recording that William I gave the manor of *Cockintone* (now Cockington) to a follower, Hostiarius. But by far the earliest link with the past is Kent's Cavern, in the Ilsham valley. A large and fine collection of the remains of extinct animals which once frequented the cave, and of the implements made by the men of the Old Stone Age, forms part of the exhibits at the Museum of the Torquay Natural History Society. In 1196 the PREMONSTRATENSIANS founded Torre Abbey, the ruins of which, together with the restored Monastic Barn and the Mansion House, dating in some parts from about the 15th century, are a conspicuous feature today on the seafront. The development of Torquay as a modern seaside resort dates back to the end of the 18th century when 'Tor Kay' or 'Tor Key' was no more than a cluster of fishermen's huts on the shore with the village of Tor (or Torre) about a kilometre inland. To deal with the threat of invasion by Napoleon, ships of the fleet constantly used Torbay as an anchorage, and houses were built on the shores of the bay for the accommodation of the wives and families of the officers. Of Torquay's total area (2527 ha) over 404 ha are occupied by parks, pleasure grounds, and public gardens, with tennis courts, bowling greens, etc. Torbay, which is notable for its regattas, provides one of the best yachting courses in Great Britain and has been the scene of AMERICA'S CUP trials: the yachting events of the 1948 Olympic Games were contested in the bay.

Torque, a dress ornament worn around the neck like a collar. They were common from the Bronze and Iron Ages in Britain, Ireland and north-west Europe, especially among Celtic peoples (see CELTIC ART). Gold was the usual material used. One of the torques found at Snettisham, Norfolk, weighed nearly 2 kg.

Torque Converter, a device which acts as infinitely variable gear. The most common form is the hydraulic torque converter which is used in motor-vehicle and locomotive transmissions and consists essentially of a pump driving a hydraulic turbine. A disadvantage of the hydraulic torque converter is that it only has a high efficiency over a limited range of speed ratios, and when the ratio approaches one to one the efficiency falls off considerably. Because of this, vehicle transmissions seldom rely entirely on a torque converter but incorporate a simple gearbox which provides at least two alternative ratios, so that the range covered by the torque converter is fairly small. In addition, provision is made for locking the torque converter to give a direct drive in top gear.

Torquemada, Tomás de (1420–98), Spanish Dominican friar and Grand Inquisitor, born at Valladolid, who in 1483 was entrusted by Queen Isabella with the establishment of the Spanish Inquisition. Ascetic in his private life, he was ruthless towards suspected or convicted heretics. Of 100,000 said to have been accused, about 2000 were put to death, others fined and penanced. He was one of the leading instigators of the conquest of Granada and of the expulsion of the Jews.
    Bibliography: Lives by H. G. de Saint Amand, 1910, and E. Lucka, 1926.

Torre, Duque de la, see SERRANO Y DOMÍNGUEZ, FRANCISCO, DUQUE DE LA TORRE.

Torre Annunziata, Italian seaport and resort in CAMPANIA, on the Bay of Naples, 20 km south-east of Naples. It manufactures macaroni and has a steel tube works, and fisheries. Population (1974) 57,500.

Torre del Greco, Italian resort and fishing port in CAMPANIA, on the Bay of Naples, 12 km south-east of Naples. It stands near the south-western foot of VESUVIUS,

which has frequently damaged the town by its eruptions. It has boatbuilding yards, and produces cameos and worked coral and lava. Population (1974) 84,800.

Torrence, Frederic Ridgely (1875–1950), US poet and playwright, born at Xenia, Ohio. He was educated at Miami University, for six years was a librarian in New York, then held various editorial posts, from 1920 to 1933 being literary editor of the *New Republic*.
    After making a tour of Europe with his friend William Vaughn MOODY, he began writing verse plays and composed *El Dorado*, 1903, and *Abelard and Heloise*, 1907. These were followed by his plays for a Negro theatre, *Granny Maumee*, *The Rider of Dreams* and *Simon the Cyrenian*, all produced in 1917. A pioneer in this type of production, he opened the way for others such as O'Neill's *Emperor Jones* and Connelly's *The Green Pastures*. Of his volumes of verse *Hesperides* appeared in 1925, *Poems*, which received the Shelley Memorial Prize, in 1941, and *Last Poems* in 1944.

Torrens, Lake, large salt lake of South Australia, discovered in 1840 by Eyre, 56 km north of Port Augusta. Its average width is 32 km, length 209 km. It becomes a salt marsh in dry weather.

Torreón, town in the state of COAHUILA, Mexico. With an altitude of 1116 m it has a hot and very dry climate with great seasonal variations in temperature. It is not only an important railway junction, but also lies at the centre of an oasis-like area called La Laguna which produces a substantial proportion of Mexico's cotton and wheat. The land has been settled by agricultural co-operative communities. The town has considerable industry including cotton gins, cotton-spinning and weaving mills, flour mills, smelting plants, oil-processing and meat-packing plants. Population (1975) 251,300.

Torres, Niceto Alcalá-Zamora y, see ALCALÁ-ZAMORA Y TORRES, NICETO.

Torres Strait, in the south Pacific Ocean, separating New Guinea and Australia by a channel 130 to 145 km wide.

Torres Vedras, town of Portugal, 43 km north of Lisbon. It was here that Wellington constructed the famous field-works called the 'Lines of Torres Vedras' during the PENINSULAR WAR, when he withdrew his forces, in face of Masséna's invasion of Portugal, for the winter of 1810. The triple line of fortifications, stretching 45 km to the River TAGUS, consisted of 100 forts joined together by entrenchments and watercourses, and Wellington successfully defended it until he was able to advance and drive the French back into Spain. Torres Vedras is the centre of a wine-producing region. Population 13,100.

'Torrey Canyon', a Liberian tanker of 120,000 t deadweight which was bound from Mina al Ahmadi in Kuwait to Milford Haven in Wales on 18 March 1967, and became grounded on the Seven Stones reef north-east of the Scilly Isles. At that time she was the largest ship to be involved in a marine disaster, and the resulting oil pollution led to anti-pollution legislation in a number of countries.

Torricelli, Evangelista (1608–47), Italian physicist, born at Faenza. He acted as secretary to Galileo during the last three months of Galileo's life, succeeded

Galileo as professor of mathematics at Florence and carried on Galileo's work in mechanics. In 1643, continuing Galileo's work on water pumps, Torricelli upended a half-closed tube of mercury in a dish of mercury. Some of the mercury in the tube flowed out; the remaining column varied slightly in height from day to day; above the column was apparently a vacuum. Like Galileo, Torricelli believed that a vacuum could not exist and he never adequately explained his experiment. Later Étienne PASCAL argued strongly that the space above the mercury column is a vacuum and the idea became acceptable. Torricelli believed that his most important work was in mathematics where he succeeded in deriving a formula for the area bounded by an arc of a CYCLOID. He also deduced the first quantitative law of hydrodynamics: the flow of a liquid through an orifice is proportional to the square root of the height of the liquid.

Torridge, river in Devon, England, rising 6 km southeast of Hartland Point, and joining the Taw estuary at Barnstaple Bay.

Torridon, hamlet and sea-loch on the west coast of Scotland, in Ross and Cromarty District, Highland Region, set amid magnificent mountain scenery (Liathach, 1053 m).

Torridonian, a series of unmetamorphosed sandstones, conglomerates, and siltstones of late PRE-CAMBRIAN age, outcropping in north-west Scotland and on several Hebridean islands. Most of the Torridonian sediments occur outside the Caledonian orogenic belt, the boundary of which is the Moine Thrust. They are thought to be the lateral equivalent of the metamorphosed MOINE SERIES which occurs within the Caledonian belt to the south-west.

The Stoer group at the base of the Torridonian consists of gneiss breccias and conglomerates with red sandstones and siltstones, all of which rest with strong unconformity on a strong topography cut into the LEWISIAN rocks below. The Stoer group is about 2000 m thick. The environment of deposition was probably one of playa-lake cycles of desiccation interrupting a fluvial red sandstone FACIES, deposited by west-flowing currents. The Stoer group is unconformably overlain by the Torridon group, which is regionally more extensive than the Stoer group and overlaps it onto the Lewisian; it is about 7300 m thick. The lowest division is the Diabaig formation, a series of breccias, sandstones, and siltstones; this is followed by the Applecross formation, consisting of cross-bedded red fluvial arkoses containing pebbles of a variety of metamorphic rock types. At the top of the Torridon group is the Aultbea formation, a series of grey shales overlain by cross-bedded red sandstones. The whole Torridon group was deposited by east-flowing currents. During the late Pre-Cambrian the Torridonian was tilted westwards and eroded before a marine transgression in Lower Cambrian times.

Torrigiano, Pietro, or Torrigiani (1470–1522), Florentine sculptor, said to have broken Michelangelo's nose in a quarrel. Torrigiano worked in Rome for Pope Alexander VI; he was also a hired soldier for a while in various states. He was invited to England to execute the tomb for Henry VII and his queen in Westminster Abbey, which he completed in 1519—a splendid work in the mature Renaissance style. A tomb for Henry VIII at Windsor was left unfinished and its bronze melted during the Commonwealth. Torrigiano died in Spain, where he was imprisoned by the Inquisition.

Torrington, George Byng, Viscount (1663–1733), English admiral, born at Wrotham, Kent; went to sea at the age of 15; was made captain by the Prince of Orange in 1688, and in 1703 became rear-admiral of the Red. In 1704 he served under Sir Cloudesley Shovell, distinguished himself at Gibraltar, and was knighted by Queen Anne for gallantry at Málaga. In 1708 he was made admiral of the Blue and defeated the French fleet of the Old Pretender. In 1715 he served against the French in the Downs and was made a baronet; in 1718 he dispersed the Spanish Fleet off Messina, and was appointed treasurer of the navy and rear-admiral of Great Britain. In 1721 he became a privy councillor, Baron Southhill, and Viscount Torrington; in 1725 a Knight of the Bath, and in 1727 first lord of the Admiralty.

Torrington, or Great Torrington, a market town on the River Torridge in Devon, England. Its Saxon name was *Toritone*. The Blue Coat School was established here in 1671. There is a milk-canning factory and gloves and glass are made. Population (1971) 3531.

Torsion, strain produced by a twisting motion, for example, by a couple acting in a plane at right angles to the axis of a prism, cylinder or other body. The distortion produced is a type of shearing stress. Resistance to torsion determines the rigidity of the bar, and resistance to permanent distortion depends upon its elasticity. The amount of 'torque' or twist required to produce torsion in cylindrical bars of the same material varies as the fourth power of their diameters. In bars of section other than circular the rigidity is lessened, so that in practical application cylindrical bars are best adapted to resist a twisting strain. See ELASTICITY.

Torsion Balance, Coulomb's, see ELECTROSTATICS.

Torstensson, Lennart (1603–51), Swedish soldier, born at Torstena. After serving under GUSTAVUS II (ADOLPHUS) he became a leader in the Thirty Years' War, becoming commander-in-chief in 1641. His greatest victory was at Breitenfeld in 1642, over the Imperialists. In 1643 he defeated the Danes, the Imperialists again in 1644, and threatened Vienna in 1645.

Tort, in a general sense, in English law, is the breach by act or omission of a duty imposed from the outside by law (as opposed to one assumed by the parties under a CONTRACT) which gives the injured party a right to DAMAGES. The word is also used in a narrower sense to mean the breach of a particular duty, such a breach being known as a tort: e.g. the tort of trespass, and the tort of nuisance. Thus the law of torts is itself made up of a number of individual torts which in nearly all cases have their historical origins in the old technical forms of action or writs which date from the 12th century.

The same act may sometimes be both a tort and a crime; but the essential difference is that a crime is something for which the law prescribes certain punishment, whereas a tort is something for which the injured party may recover compensation in the shape of damages. Again, the same act may be a tort and a breach of contract; here the essential difference is that in the case of a tort the duty broken is one imposed by the law, whereas in the case of a contract it is one that has been undertaken by agreement among the parties.

In general, a person is liable only if there is some fault on his part, either by doing something that he ought not to have done or by failing to do something he ought to have done. But sometimes he may be liable without any actual fault at all, in which case his liability is said to be 'strict'. The most important example of this is the rule that if a person brings on to his land something not naturally there which may cause damage if it escapes, he is liable for any damage caused by its escape regardless of whether he was in any way at fault, for he brings it on to his land at his peril. Thus where a man had a reservoir built on his land, and because of a fault in it, for which he was in no way responsible, water escaped and flooded a neighbour's property, he was liable. However, he is not liable if the escape was caused by an 'act of God' or interference by a stranger, or if, by bringing the substance on to his land, he was not making a 'non-natural user' of his land. What amounts to a non-natural user can be a difficult question, but installing normal domestic water supplies does not amount to such.

Many statutes impose obligations upon individuals and the question may arise whether or not a person who has sustained some loss because of a breach of that obligation may bring an action in tort. Each case depends upon its own facts, and the statute must be considered to see whether Parliament must be presumed to have intended an action in tort to be available. Even if that is established the plaintiff must still show that Parliament intended to protect him so that if, for example, the object of the statute was to protect other road users, a person injured in quite different circumstances, even though by breach of the same duty, cannot rely on it to found his action.

In general, a person is liable only for a tort committed by himself; but he may be vicariously liable for the wrongful acts of another person if that person is his employee in which case the employer may be sued as well as the employee. But the employer may only be sued if the employee committed the tort within the scope of his employment, by which is meant that the wrong is one done in the course of carrying out his duties and is necessarily incidental to them or occurs when he is doing something he is authorised to do, although in an unauthorised manner. The employer may still be liable in appropriate circumstances even if the employee's act was extremely stupid or careless or even deliberate. If, for example, a man is employed to drive from A to B, and while on the way he injures someone by careless driving, the employer is liable; but if the driver, for purposes of his own, has turned off the route to go to C, and injures the person while off the route, he is not acting within the scope of his employment.

But a man is not generally liable for the torts of his independent contractor. If, for example, a firm of builders is engaged to carry out repairs to a house, they are not agents but independent contractors, so that if one of them were to drop a hammer on to a passer-by, the owner of the house would not be liable. Broadly speaking, the test is whether or not the employer has the right to say not only what shall be done but also how it shall be done. If he has, then the relationship is one of employer and employee; if

not, then the other party is an independent contractor. However, a man may be liable for the torts of his independent contractors if the work the contractor is required to do is by its nature hazardous to other persons or property. If the contractor is incompetent, the employer may be liable, not directly for the contractor's negligence, but for his own negligence in selecting an incompetent contractor. Also, a person's liability may be strict, in which case he cannot discharge it by employing a competent independent contractor. Thus, if there is a lamp bracket projecting over the street from a house, and it falls and injures a passer-by, the owner is liable even if he employed a competent independent contractor to see that it was safe, and who negligently failed to do so, because his duty is a personal one to keep the bracket safe, and he cannot discharge it by delegating performance to another. Although very similar to vicarious liability, the true basis of the liability in these cases is the breach of a duty owed personally.

A number of situations in which liability in tort may arise, though by no means an exhaustive list, are mentioned here:

Liability for Animals. The general rule, that a person who commits a wrong through an innocent agent is himself liable for the wrong, applies equally in the case of animals, so that to set one's dog on another person is just as much an assault as actually to hit him, and to ride one's horse over another's land is as much trespass as to walk over it. The rules as to the liability of owners of animals for damage caused by their animals are now contained in the Animals Act 1971. Generally, the owner of an animal belonging to a dangerous species is liable for any damage caused by the animal, but the owner of an animal which does not belong to a dangerous species is not liable for damage caused by it, unless the animal was likely to cause damage unless restrained, the animal possessed characteristics not normally found in members of its species, and those characteristics were known to the owner. A dangerous species is defined in the act as a species not commonly domesticated in the British Isles and fully grown members of which are likely to cause damage unless restrained.

Assault and Battery. Strictly speaking an assault is any act which gives another person a reasonable apprehension that a battery will follow, and a battery is the intentional application of force to another person. So, if an assailant is restrained before he has actually hit the plaintiff, the assault is complete but no battery has been committed. Words alone cannot be an assault; there must be some physical gesture: to point a gun at another is an assault, even if it is unloaded, and so is the shaking of a fist. But words may prevent an otherwise threatening gesture from being an assault. Very little force is required to constitute a battery: 'the least touching of another in anger is a battery', as in spitting in a man's face, kissing a woman against her will, and, probably, flashing the sun into another's eyes with a mirror. But merely to stand passively in the way is no battery.

Children. Liability in respect of children may be that of a parent for the acts of his child or that for injury done to a child. Generally, a parent is not liable for torts committed by his child, though if he is in fact employing the child, he will be vicariously liable in the same way as any employer is for his employee. A parent will also be liable if the child's tort arises from the parent's negligent control, so that where, even after a child had smashed a window with an air rifle, the father still allowed him to use the air rifle without supervision, he was liable when the child later injured another. But if the father had forbidden the child to use the air rifle outside the cellar of the house, and in defiance of this the child did so, the father would not be liable for any resultant injury. A person is liable for a wrong done to a child in the same way as for wrongs to an adult; but in addition children may either be too young to appreciate a danger obvious to adults, or else their naturally inquisitive nature may lead them into danger, so that a person may be liable, as an occupier of land, for the injuries suffered by a child trespassing on his land where he would not be liable if an adult had been injured.

Conspiracy. Interference with Contract. Intimidation. If two or more persons join together with the sole or predominant motive of damaging the plaintiff in some legitimate interest of his, and the plaintiff suffers damage as a result, the tort of conspiracy is committed, whether or not the means actually employed were themselves lawful. The essence of the tort is the combination, so that it does not matter that a single person could quite lawfully have done what was done. But if the defendants had some lawful justification, e.g. they were a properly constituted disciplinary body, or their real object was to further their own legitimate trade interests, the tort is not committed. To interfere with a contract between other persons may be a tort. So if A, knowing that B has made a contract with C, without lawful justification interferes with that contract with the object of prejudicing the contractual relationship beween B and C, he commits a tort. The interference may be in the form of a conspiracy, a direct inducement to B or C to break his contract, a wrong against B or C with the object and effect of upsetting the contract, or procuring an agent of B or C to do something with that effect or a third party to do an unlawful act with that effect. The tort of intimidation is committed when someone makes unlawful threats which cause the plaintiff to act in a way damaging to himself, or when unlawful threats are made to a third party who acts in a way damaging to the plaintiff.

Conversion and Detinue. Conversion is any act in relation to the goods of a person which amounts to a wrongful denial of his right to them. To succeed in an action in conversion, the plaintiff must, at the time of the defendant's act, have the ownership or possession or immediate right to possession of the goods. An immediate right to possession of the goods in effect amounts to a legal right to demand that they be handed to him forthwith, so that if A agrees to let C hire his car for a month, and gives it to B to give to C, C has the immediate right to possession of the car. The defendant's act must be inconsistent with the plaintiff's right, and be done with the intention of denying that right: examples are misappropriation, wrongful detention (even if the defendant honestly thought he was entitled to detain the goods), wrongful delivery to another person, destruction, and unjustifiable sale. In general it is no defence to prove that some other person had a better right to the goods than the plaintiff, but where the plaintiff's claim is based solely on his having the immediate right to possession and not on his having been in actual possession of the goods at the time of the defendant's act, this plea of a *ius tertii* is a defence.

Good faith or honest but mistaken belief that one's conduct is right in law is not, however, a defence.

Detinue is very similar, but is restricted to the wrongful detention of an article. Here the plaintiff, even if he is in fact the owner, must have the immediate right to possession, and have demanded the goods from the defendant who had declined to give them up. If the defendant has at one time had the goods, he may still be liable even though he no longer has them—e.g. where he has delivered them to the wrong person by mistake. But if he has lost possession of the goods without any fault on his part, he will not be liable. The same act may be, but is not necessarily, both conversion and detinue; but conversion requires that the act amount to a denial of the plaintiff's title, whereas detinue does not. REPLEVIN is a third tort against chattels.

Liability for Dangerous Chattels. Although the classification of liability in certain cases as liability for dangerous chattels is convenient and often used, it has frequently been criticised and it is probable that the law knows no such thing as a dangerous chattel, but certain articles, either because of their nature, or because of the circumstances, require a person to exercise particular care and failure to do so is merely a particular example of negligence. The greater the danger, the higher is the standard of care required. So, if A allowed his ten-year old son, B, to have his loaded shotgun, and as a result C was injured, A would be liable to C because it was negligent of him to allow B to have the gun without close supervision. Often the relationship between the person injured and the person at fault will be that of buyer and seller, so that the liability there may well be regulated by contract. But where A hands the article to B who hands it to C who is injured, A may be liable to C in certain circumstances; e.g. if a man were to conceal a defect in a gun which made it dangerous to fire, and of which he knew, he would be liable to the person who was ultimately injured by firing it. Again, a person who sells an old car might be liable to a person injured by reason of a defect in the steering if the defect was one that the seller could have discovered by inspection. A manufacturer will be liable to anyone injured as a result of a defect in an article he produces if the defect was the result of negligence on his part, provided that the person injured could not be expected to examine the article first, or could not have discovered the defect had he done so, and provided that the manufacturer must have realised that lack of care on his part would result in injury to the ultimate user; and this principle applies also to a repairer. But if the manufacturer has given a warning of possible dangers, but the intermediary has failed to pass that warning on, the manufacturer probably escapes liability if the warning should have been sufficient to prevent injury.

Deceit. If A makes a statement of fact which he knows to be false, or which he does not believe to be true, intending that B shall act upon it, and B does so act and suffers damage, A is liable in deceit. There must be a representation of present or past fact by words or by conduct, but in appropriate circumstances a statement of intention may be a statement of fact: a statement of opinion may itself carry with it the implication that the person making it knows facts to support it, and by the same token a statement of law may involve a statement of fact. The statement must be false, and the person making

Tort

it must know of its falsity or else make it without caring whether it be true or false (see DEFAMATION). It need not be made specifically to the plaintiff, but it is enough that it should be intended that someone should act upon it, and the plaintiff actually did so to his detriment, whether financial or physical.

Employer's Liability. An employer's liability to his employees falls under two heads: that under the common law, which may itself be either in tort or in contract, since the same duties as the common law imposes upon the employer are themselves implied into the contract of employment; and that under statutes. At common law the employer is required to take care to provide a competent staff, so that if he employs an incompetent or unqualified person to do a particular job, and as a result another employee is injured, he is liable. He must take care to provide adequate and suitable plant and equipment for the job and to maintain it in proper condition. There is also a duty to provide a safe system of work, and in devising such a system, the employer must bear in mind the tendency of workmen to become careless and to cut corners as they become familiar with a job, and he must take reasonable care to see that his system is complied with. But there are limits to this, and he is not required to act as though he were a nursemaid. The employer must also take care to see that the place of work is reasonably safe, though naturally his duty is less stringent if the employer has no control over the place, e.g. where a contractor sends a workman to do work in a private house. In all cases, the employer's common law duty is only to take care to protect his employees, and although a high standard is required, his duty is not an absolute one: all the duties owed by him can be summed up as a single duty not to expose his employee to unnecessary risk, by which is meant a risk which can be foreseen and guarded against. But, while not absolute, the duty is personal to the employer so that he cannot escape liability by delegating his responsibility to another.

The most important statutes in this field are the Factories Acts and the Mines and Quarries Acts and the regulations made in them. Under the Factories Acts, provided that the premises are a factory as defined by the acts, there is a duty to fence dangerous machinery and transmission machinery, however difficult and inconvenient it may be to do so. In other parts of the acts, such as those dealing with safe means of access to a place of work, the duty is only to provide these so far as is reasonably practicable. The Mines and Quarries Acts also impose duties on the employer. In all cases, if the employer is in breach of his duty and a workman is injured, the employer is liable in damages (as well as in criminal proceedings) unless he can show that the accident would still have occurred even if he had not broken the duty.

Deprivation of Consortium. Broadly speaking, consortium is a general term covering the mutual right of a husband and wife to each other's companionship and services. A husband (but not a wife) may sue any person who does some wrongful act to his wife which had the result of depriving him of her consortium, e.g. a personal injury necessitating hospital treatment.

False Imprisonment. The unlawful bodily restraint of the plaintiff is termed 'false imprisonment'. The restraint must be complete, so that merely barring the way would not be false imprisonment. It is not, however, false imprisonment to prevent a person from leaving premises until he has satisfied a reasonable condition subject to which he entered the premises, nor was it false imprisonment when a miner, in the middle of a shift and with no valid reason, demanded to be brought to the surface, but the mine operator refused to do so until the end of the shift.

Malicious Prosecution. Where a person prosecutes or causes a prosecution to be brought against another person without reasonable and probable cause and with malice, then if the plaintiff is ultimately acquitted, even if only on appeal, the prosecutor is liable for malicious prosecution. The action is rare and the burden on the plaintiff is very heavy. Reasonable and probable cause requires that there must be sufficient grounds for 'thinking that the plaintiff was probably guilty of the crime imputed'. Malice is more difficult to define and broadly involves feelings which are directed personally against the plaintiff and not generally towards upholding the law. Absence of reasonable and probable cause is evidence of malice, though not necessarily conclusive evidence. The tort is aimed at, and an action will usually only succeed in, cases of trumped up charges.

Negligence is the breach of a duty of care imposed by the general law. One person owes a duty of care to another if that other is so closely affected by the act or omission of the first that the first ought reasonably to have the other in his contemplation when directing his mind to the act or omission in question. The duty is breached if an act is done which a reasonable man would not have done, or if an omission is made which a reasonable man would not have made, or if an act is done in a way in which a reasonable man would not have done it. Where there has been a breach of a duty of care, anybody to whom the duty was owed may recover damages from the person in breach for any loss, damage, or injury suffered which ought reasonably to have been foreseen by the latter. Negligence is now the most frequent cause of action in the law of tort. It is relied upon most commonly for actions involving personal injuries, and actions arising from motor accidents and from accidents at work. But there can be no action in negligence in the absence of damage suffered by the plaintiff.

Contributory negligence is a defence, usually only partial, to an action in negligence. In this context the meaning of negligence is not so technical. The plaintiff in an action for negligence will have the damages awarded to him reduced on account of his contributory negligence if he has not taken proper care and this has contributed to his injury, loss, or damage. The reduction will be made as a percentage of the damages that would have been awarded if the defendant had been held totally liable; the size of the percentage reduction will reflect the degree of fault on the part of the plaintiff.

Negligent Mis-statements should be clearly distinguished from fraudulent mis-statements in that the latter require an absence of honest belief in the truth of the statement, whereas a negligent mis-statement may be made with a genuine belief that it is true. There may be liability where only financial loss results, e.g. where a firm considering whether or not to grant credit to another seeks a banker's reference as to credit worthiness, and through the negligence of the banker a good report is given which is wholly at variance with the facts. There must be some special relationship between the person giving the information and the person acting on it. Clearly there can be no liability arising from information communicated in idle conversation. It must at least be foreseeable by the defendant that the plaintiff would rely upon his statement and it must be reasonable for the plaintiff to do so. Thus the informant must, it seems, be possessed of some special skill relating to the communicated material; it may be that the informant must also be in the business of giving the advice of the kind on which the action is based or at least hold himself out as being possessed of the necessary skill and as being prepared to exercise due diligence in giving reliable advice.

Nervous Shock. A person who, as a practical joke, falsely tells another, for example, that his wife has met with a serious accident, is liable to that person if he suffers nervous shock as a result. But when a person is injured by the defendant's negligence, and a relative suffers shock on being told, the defendant is not liable to that person for that alone. If, however, that person in fact witnessed the accident, and a normal person would have suffered shock from witnessing the accident, or if he was himself in a position in which he might have been injured, or his shock were due to a fear that he might be injured, then it seems that he may recover damages.

Nuisance. Nuisances are either public or private. Broadly speaking a public nuisance is something which materially affects the health and comfort of the public or a section of it, such as obstructing the highway, or selling food unfit for consumption. For this a private individual may not bring an action unless he can show that he has suffered some special damage not suffered by other members of the public: e.g. where a lamp bracket overhanging the highway falls on him as he passes by he may sue in nuisance. A private nuisance, however, is the unlawful interference with someone's use or enjoyment of his land or some right connected with it, and is thus a much narrower concept than the ordinary meaning of the word. The same act may be both a public and a private nuisance: e.g. an obstruction of the highway which also blocks the plaintiff's gateway is a public nuisance because it obstructs the right of the public to pass along the highway and a private nuisance because it interferes with the plaintiff's access to his land.

Almost anything may amount to a private nuisance: noise, smells, and vibration; the collapse of a garden wall, or water dripping on to a neighbour's land from a faulty gutter. But some noise is inevitable in modern life, so that a reasonable balance has to be struck, and whether or not a particular activity amounts to an actionable nuisance depends not upon the degree of sensitiveness of the plaintiff but upon the 'plain and sober and simple notions among the English people'. The test is whether an ordinary person of normal tolerance and reasonableness would find it a nuisance. But while reasonableness plays an important part in determining whether there is or is not a nuisance, it has no relevance to the question whether or not the defendant is liable; it does not matter that he has done his best to prevent his activity from being a nuisance if in fact it is one.

The area in which the activity complained of is carried on may also be relevant; e.g. to open a fish and chip shop, with its attendant smells of frying, would be a nuisance in a private residential area, but not in a high street where other similar businesses were conducted. And what would be a nuisance in one part of the country might not be a nuisance in another if the inhabitants of the latter area are so accustomed to the activity that they do not regard it as abnormal.

Because private nuisance is an interference with rights over land, only the person who has such rights may sue, and not, for example, his wife. Thus in nearly all cases the plaintiff will be the occupier of the land, whether as owner or tenant. But a non-occupying owner may sue if the nuisance is likely to cause a permanent injury, for he has an interest in the land, namely his right to recover possession when his tenant's lease expires. The defendant need have no interest in the land, since any person who creates a nuisance is liable. But where the nuisance originates from private land the occupier may well be liable even if not he, but some trespasser, created the nuisance, if after he knew or ought to have known of the nuisance he allowed it to continue or adopted it. He would also be liable if his family or, for example, persons he has allowed to camp on his land created the nuisance. A landlord may be liable for a nuisance originating on land he has let to his tenant if he knew or ought to have known of it before he let the land, or he is under a duty or has the right to enter and do repairs on the property.

Occupier's Liability. The liability of the occupier of land and other structures for injury to persons on their property caused by the defective state of the premises or by something done on them is governed by the Occupier's Liability Act 1957. By that act, the occupier owes a duty to all his lawful visitors to take such care as in all the circumstances of the case is reasonable to see that the visitor will be reasonably safe in using the premises for the purpose for which he is invited or permitted to be there. Visitors are those who have a lawful right to enter the premises including those who have implied permission to do so: e.g. tradesmen and other callers, though a 'No Hawkers' notice would probably exclude all but regular tradesmen. Persons who have been tacitly permitted to take a short cut across a field for some time are also visitors, but trespassers are not. No duty is usually owed to a trespasser, but once the occupier knows that there is a trespasser present, he must not do anything further which would endanger the trespasser, and a landowner may be held liable for injuries suffered by a child trespasser even though there would be no liability to an adult trespasser. The duty is to take care, but the act expressly lays down that the occupier must be prepared for children to be less careful for their own safety than adults, and also that the occupier may expect that a person in the exercise of his profession or calling will appreciate and guard against special risks attaching to it. Furthermore the act provides that the occupier only discharges his duty by warning his visitors of the danger if the warning is in all the circumstances sufficient to enable the visitor to be reasonably safe. The occupier may sometimes discharge his duty by entrusting work to an independent contractor so that he will not be liable even if the contractor, through negligence, leaves the premises in a dangerous state, but only if it was reasonable to entrust the work to an independent contractor, and he had taken all such steps as he reasonably ought, if any, to satisfy himself that the contractor was competent and had carried the work out properly.

The occupier may restrict or exclude his duty by suit-

Torticollis

able conditions which are brought to the notice of the visitor before he enters, but only 'in so far as he is free to do so'. Thus it is probable that where the visitor has right in law to enter, for example an official of the Electricity Board who has come to read the meter, the duty to him cannot be restricted. By the Defective Premises Act 1972, where premises are let under a tenancy and the tenancy puts an obligation on the landlord to keep the premises in repair, the landlord owes, not only to the tenant but also to all those who might reasonably be expected to be affected by his failure to repair, a duty to repair defects of which he has, or ought reasonably to have, knowledge.

Trespass. The unauthorised entry on to another person's land is trespass. It is not necessary for actual damage to be done (though that would be relevant to the size of any sum awarded as damages) or that the person should know that he is trespassing. The mere entry on to another person's land without actual or implied permission is technically trespass. A popular fallacy is that trespass is a crime; it is not, and notices to the effect that 'trespassers will be prosecuted' have been referred to as a 'wooden lie'. But trespassers may, of course, be sued for damages, though unless actual damage is done the damages awarded will be purely nominal.

Trespass is a wrong against possession, so that where land is let, it is the tenant who may sue and not the owner. But the owner will recover the land when the lease ends and therefore if the trespasser in some way permanently damages the land, e.g. by digging a hole, the owner may also sue because of the injury to his reversion. It is not necessary actually to enter land to commit a trespass: trespass may be committed by sending one's dog on to the land, or throwing a stone on to it; and to hang a sign from one's own house projecting out over another's land is trespass. By statute, aircraft flying at a reasonable height do not commit trespass. If a person has a right in law, as opposed to permission granted by the occupier, to enter land and to do something there, and he abuses this right, he commits *trespass ab initio* and is treated as a trespasser from the moment he set foot on the land.

The owner or occupier may use just so much force as is reasonably necessary to remove a trespasser from his land, but no more than that. Thus the trespasser must first be asked to leave, and then he may be taken by the arm in an attempt to lead him off. If he still declines to leave, more forcible measures may be adopted.

Trespass to land is the most common form of trespass, but there may also be trespass to the person and trespass to goods. These actions are now virtually obsolete, and the ground they once covered is now covered by other torts, for example, assault, battery, conversion, and detinue. Other torts include defamation and the tort of 'passing off', which is committed when one trader represents his goods or services to be those of another, even if the representation is entirely innocent (see TRADE-MARK).

Bibliography: J. W. Salmond, *The Law of Torts,* 16th ed. 1973.

Torticollis, contracture of the sternomastoid muscle in the neck, usually on one side, causing an abnormal posture of the head, or 'wryneck'. Torticollis may be present in infants from birth injury, and in longstanding cases the face and skull develop asymmetrically because of the abnormal pull of the sternomastoid muscle. Gentle man-

ual stretching may be effective in straightening the neck, but in established cases division of the sternomastoid muscle is necessary. Torticollis of acute onset occurs in childhood as a result of trauma to the neck or local inflammation, such as tonsillitis, producing muscle spasm. In adults the muscle spasm is most usually due to irritation of nerves by an abnormal cervical disc, and occasionally by pyogenic or tuberculous infection in the neck. Treatment consists of appropriate treatment of any underlying pathology and the wearing of a cervical collar.

Tortoise, land animals of the order CHELONIA. They are cold-blooded, four-footed reptiles, without teeth, and are protected by a large shell on top, called a carapace, with a thinner shell, the plastron, under the belly. All lay eggs, but otherwise there is wide diversity in their habits. They are of great geological age, and their tenacity of life has enabled them to survive where more recent animals of higher types have become extinct. The most familiar example of the land tortoises (Testudinidae) is the common tortoise (*Testudo graeca*), which occurs around the Mediterranean and is popular as a pet. It is entirely vegetarian in its diet, though frequently sold as an insect killer.

Among the most interesting kind of tortoises are the giant tortoises formerly found in great numbers in the Galápagos and Mascarene islands. When discovered, these islands were uninhabited; the tortoises therefore enjoyed perfect security, and this, as well as their extraordinary longevity, accounts for their great size (as much as 1·5 m in length) and numbers.

Tortoise Beetle, any member of the subfamily Cassidinae of family Chrysomelidae in order COLEOPTERA. The outer margins of the wing covers and the prothorax (shield) are drawn out and form a convex shield reminiscent of the outline of a tortoise, hence their more popular name of tortoise beetles. In general they are leaf-feeders in both adult and larval stages. They are often brilliantly coloured with a metallic sheen. The larvae generally have spiky outgrowths, and they cover themselves with excrement or cast skins as methods of camouflage. These beetles are usually found in the tropics; however *Cassida vibex* is found on the leaves of chickweed

Tortoise. *Testudo elegans,* the Indian star tortoise. *(Topham/Coleman)*

and tansy in the British Isles. It is bright green and about 7 mm long, and the larvae and pupae are also green.

Tortoise-shell, in commerce, is the horny plates of the hawksbill turtle (*Chelonia imbricata*). The largest of these plates are about 45 cm long by 15 cm broad, and rarely exceed 3 mm in thickness. Tortoise-shell is semi-transparent, and mottled with various shades of yellow and brownish-red. Its value depends on the brightness and form of the markings, and, if taken from the animal after death and decomposition, the colour of the shell becomes clouded and milky. Hence great cruelty has been exercised in removing the plates from living turtles, but the finest tortoise-shell is derived from shells immersed in boiling water immediately after the death of the animal. Numerous imitations and substitutes are made. Tortoise-shell probably first began to be used to decorate furniture in northern Europe around 1640. Its popularity may well have been due at first to its similarity to the more expensive amber much used by the Germans to decorate early 17th-century furniture. The vogue lasted until about 1680 when tortoise-shell began to be employed in France by Boulle in conjunction with brass inlay. During the 18th century the fashion for tortoise-shell on furniture died out, but the material continued to be used for small boxes, combs, and other *objets de vertu*, often with a silver inlay: this is called *piqué* work.

Torture, the application of bodily pain as a prelude to, or an accompaniment of, capital punishment, as an act of vengeance upon defeated enemies, or as a means of extracting confessions or other evidence from accused persons. It has taken a large variety of more or less atrocious forms and has been employed by peoples and states of varying degrees of political and social sophistication.

In England torture as punishment was virtually ended in 1640; in Scotland an act of 1709 was passed abolishing its use. Torture was used by both the Nazis and the Japanese during the Second World War, both to extort information from prisoners and as a form of punishment in concentration camps. There have been many proven instances of torture, and many more allegations of its use, in the period since the Second World War, both in conflicts where there has been open warfare and in those where opponents of the régime in power have been active in lesser forms of rebellion. In 1975 the United Nations adopted a Declaration against the use of torture.

Toruń (German *Thorn*), town of Poland, in Bydgoszcz province, on the River Vistula, 42 km east of Bydgoszcz. It was part of POMERANIA between 1793–1807, 1815–1918, and 1939–45. Treaties concluded here in 1411 and 1466 made the TEUTONIC KNIGHTS vassals of the Polish kings. COPERNICUS was born in Toruń. There are engineering, chemical, and textile industries. Population (1974) 143,872.

Tory, synonym, though historically inappropriate, for a Conservative. The word 'tory' is Irish, and signified, during the time of the wars in Ireland in the reign of Elizabeth I, a kind of bandit, who, being attached to neither army, preyed generally upon the country. They were especially prominent in the Protestant massacres of 1641. From this the term came to be applied to a body of men who, in 1680, appear to have ridiculed the Popish Plot and yet encouraged the Papists to revive it. Their political object was to banish the Duke of Monmouth and recall the Duke of York, and to further their end they endeavoured to thwart the Bill of Exclusion (from their abhorrence to which they were called 'abhorrers' and their opponents the 'petitioners'). Ultimately the 'abhorrers' and 'petitioners' became identified with the Tories and Whigs respectively.

Toscana, see TUSCANY.

Toscanini, Arturo (1867–1957), Italian conductor, born in Parma. He studied at the Parma Conservatory, where he gained his diploma in cello and composition in 1885, and began his career as a conductor in 1886 at Rio de Janeiro. His reputation rapidly gained ground. After several years at Turin he was appointed to La Scala, Milan, 1898, and in 1907 he was nominated conductor to the Metropolitan, New York. He was conductor of the Philharmonic Symphony Society of New York, 1926–36, and of the NBC Orchestra, 1937–54. His chief centres of activity were the opera-houses and concert halls of Milan and New York, but he was also guest conductor at Bayreuth, Vienna, Salzburg, Paris and elsewhere. He conducted at Covent Garden during the coronation celebrations of George VI, 1937. Many new Italian operas were presented by him.
    Bibliography: F. Sacchi, *Toscanini*, 1951.

Tosk, see ALBANIA, *Language*.

Tostig (d. 1066), Earl of Northumbria, son of Earl Godwin, and brother of HAROLD II. In 1065 he was banished from his realm because of his cruel, repressive measures and replaced by MORCAR. The following year he returned with Harold Haardraade, King of Norway, and was killed at the battle of Stamford Bridge.

Total Chromaticism, in music, the harmonic condition in which all 12 notes of the CHROMATIC SCALE occur with such frequency as to saturate—though not necessarily immobilise—the harmony. Most serial music (see SERIALISM) is totally-chromatic in its harmonic vocabulary, but not all totally-chromatic works use serial organisation (which is one of the ways of combating total chromaticism's extreme instability as a structural element—another is ruthless brevity of form). The outright use of total chromaticism first appeared in the works which Schoenberg composed in the period 1908–17, such as Five Orchestral Pieces and the monodrama *Erwartung*.

Totalisator, machine or apparatus, set up on racecourses for recording bets and payment of winnings on the principle that all money staked is pooled and shared (subject to a percentage deduction) by those who have backed winners. This system, known as the *pari-mutuel*, was invented in France by M. Oller in 1872. The first machine used to operate this system was set up at Christchurch, New Zealand, in 1880, and the first totalisator in Europe was operated at Longchamps, near Paris, in 1929. Totalisators were introduced into Britain in the same year, and by the end of 1930, 92 racecourses were provided with them. In the same year they were also installed at many greyhound tracks. A mechanised *pari-mutuel* system was operated in Maryland, USA, in 1930.

In Great Britain the control of totalisators on horse

racecourses is under the jurisdiction of the Horse Race Totalisator Board consisting of a Chairman and three members, all four appointed by the Home Secretary in accordance with the Betting, Gaming and Lotteries Act 1963. Under this Act, the Horse Race Betting Levy Board was constituted with power to collect monetary contributions from the Totalisator Board (besides bookmakers) in respect of any levy, with a view to benefiting the sport of horse racing, contributing to the advancement of veterinary science and making payments to certain charities. The income of the Horse Race Board is derived by deducting from the amount staked on the totalisator such percentage of that amount as may be determined from time to time by the Board. The amount staked with the totalisator on horse racing during the year 1974–75 was £45 million.

Approximately 80 greyhound racecourses in England, Wales and Scotland are equipped with totalisators which, under the Betting, Gaming and Lotteries Act 1963, must be mechanically or electrically operated installations complying with prescribed conditions. A percentage not exceeding 6 per cent may be deducted by the operator from the amounts staked. Between 1948 and 1964 the amount staked with the totalisator on greyhound racing was £1195 million.

On a fully mechanised totalisator of the type installed on greyhound racecourses, at the time of the issue of the tickets, each 10p unit is automatically added and recorded on a miniature indicator in the Totalisator Control Room and simultaneously indicated to the public on the main visual indicators. All payments from the pools are under the control of an accountant (appointed by the licensing authority) who must be present at each meeting. The price of a ticket on horse and greyhound racecourses varies from 10p to £10, and on some horse racecourses can be £100. Facilities also exist for 'off-the-course' betting on totalisators on horse racing and at totalisator odds on greyhound racing. Totalisator betting represents only a small proportion of off-course betting on horse and greyhound racing, whereas it represents a larger proportion of on-course betting. For discussion of totalisators and *parimutuel* systems, see BETTING.

Totalitarianism, social and political system involving the conscious political control of and intervention in all aspects of private and public life. As such it stands in ideological opposition to extreme 19th-century Liberalism. Although many régimes have in the past attempted to exercise such control there is a distinction between such autocracies and totalitarianism. The latter is essentially a modern phenomenon made possible through the existence of sophisticated means of control and manipulation. The organisation of control is invariably through the monopolisation of the organs of the state by a centrally directed party, this party usually subscribing to an ideology involving fundamental social reorganisation. It should be noted, however, that single-party rule does not always involve totalitarianism.

Bibliography: C. J. Friedrich and Z. Brzezinski, *Totalitarian Dictatorship and Autocracy*, 1965; H. Arendt, *The Origins of Totalitarianism*, 1967.

Totemism (Algonquin Indian *totem*, guardian spirit), belief of descent from an original ancestor who is also the ancestor of certain plants or animals; the term is extended to any belief that one shares some common essence with a plant or animal. Totemism has been found among many peoples of the world, and certainly existed at one time among Europeans. The belief is frequently accompanied by a prohibition to harm, kill, or eat the plant or animal with whom one shares a totemic ancestor, akin to a TABOO and should this occur accidentally, elaborate rituals may be necessary to offset the believed damaging spiritual consequences.

In some North American Indian peoples the totem is an individual concern: the totem is received in a dream after ritual consumption of a drug or in a vision whilst fasting alone away from the settlement. In Australia, parts of Africa and elsewhere, totems are a clan affair, and are passed on to the children by the father or the mother; in this case it is usually forbidden to marry someone who has the same totem (see EXOGAMY).

The phenomenon of totemism long puzzled anthropologists and psychologists alike, who attributed it to some kind of primitive mentality, inferior to Western rational thought. The problem was finally resolved by LEVI-STRAUSS who showed that what mattered was less the believed relationship between an individual or a clan and the totemic animal than the existing relationships between members of society. It is now clear that Europeans and Australian Aborigines alike tend to attribute qualities to natural creatures and impute relationships between them which are in fact the qualities of men and the relationships between human beings. Scientific thought alone tries to avoid this.

See also CLAN.

Bibliography: Sir J. G. Frazer, *Totemism and Exogamy*, 1910; S. Freud, *Totem and Taboo*, 1913; E. Durkheim, *The Elementary Forms of the Religious Life*, 1915; C. Levi-Strauss, *Totemism* 1964 and *The Savage Mind*, 1966.

Totila (d. 552), King of the Ostrogoths in Italy, was proclaimed in 541. He at once began the restoration of the Ostrogoth kingdom of Italy and gained a victory over the Romans near Faenza. He captured Rome in 546. In 547 BELISARIUS recovered possession and repulsed three assaults made by Totila, who did not succeed in retaking the city till 549. Owing to Totila's continued successes the Emperor Justinian sent a large army against him led by the eunuch NARSES, who encountered Totila at Tagina and killed him.

Bibliography: H. St L. B. Moss, *The Birth of the Middle Ages 395–814*, 1935.

Totnes (the *Toteneis* of Saxon times), an ancient market town in DEVON, England, on the River Dart, with boatbuilding, a bacon factory, a creamery, sawmills, and timber yards. The grammar school was founded in 1553. There is a Norman castle and the Guildhall also dates from 1553. Population (1971) 5772.

Tottenham, see HARINGEY.

Tottington, town to the north-west of Bury which now lies within the Bury borough of the new Greater Manchester Metropolitan County, England. It has varied textile industries and has grown recently through housing development. Population (1971) 9758.

Toucan, any bird of the genus *Ramphastos*. The name is often applied to the whole family Ramphastidae of the order Piciformes. They are all natives of tropical America and are characterised by their enormous brightly-coloured bill. In confinement they are almost omnivorous, but in the wild state they live chiefly on fruit, seeds and insects. In the true toucans the ground colour of the plumage is generally black; the throat, breast and rump are adorned with yellow, red and white; the body is short and thick; the tail is rounded or even and can be turned up over the back when the bird goes to roost. The largest are about 60 cm long.

Touch, sensation due to the stimuli of pressure and contact acting on the body. The peripheral nerves supplying the skin terminate either on or between epithelial cells, or in special corpuscles. Certain of these act as transducers which change the mechanical energy of pressure into a nervous signal. Like all other sensations, that of touch is perceived by the brain, and is conveyed to it by afferent nerves or fibres which travel in special tracts of the SPINAL CORD distinct from those conveying impulses of pain.

Touch-me-not, see IMPATIENS.

Toul, French town in the *département* of Meurthe-et-Moselle, on the River Moselle and the Marne–Rhine canal. Taken by the French from the Germans in 1552, it was finally ceded to France in 1648 (see WESTPHALIA, TREATY OF). The fine church of St-Étienne was built between 965 and 1496. Pottery is manufactured. Population 15,000.

Toulet, Paul-Jean (1867–1920), French writer, born in Paris. He published a number of novels, including *Monsieur de Paur, homme public*, 1898, *Le Mariage de Don Quichotte*, 1902, *Tendres ménages*, 1904, *Mon amie Nane*, 1905, and *La Jeune fille verte*, 1920. The short stories of *Béhanzigue* and a volume of poetry, *Les Contrerimes*, were published posthumously in 1920 and 1921, respectively.

Toulon, French seaport in the *département* of Var, on the Mediterranean, 46 km south-east of Marseilles. It became the seat of a bishopric in the 6th century. In 1793, at the beginning of the French Revolution, it was surrendered to the English by the royalists, but was retaken by the republicans in December of the same year; during this siege the young Bonaparte (see NAPOLEON I) first distinguished himself. In modern times Toulon has been an important naval station and is now one of the three naval headquarters in France (see BREST and CHERBOURG). In 1911 the battleship *Liberté* caught fire and blew up in the harbour; many ships nearby were damaged and some 200 persons perished. During the Second World War, in 1942, the bulk of the French fleet was scuttled in Toulon harbour to prevent it falling into German hands. Subsequent Allied bombing almost completely destroyed the harbour (by then a submarine base) and its installations. The town was taken by French troops in August 1944. There are marine engineering, armament, chemical, oil, and textile industries. Population 340,000.

Toulouse, Count of, see RAYMOND VI.

Toulouse, French town, capital of the *département* of Haute-Garonne, 200 km south-east of Bordeaux, on the River Garonne. It was the old capital of LANGUEDOC. A Celto-Ligurian settlement (see CELTS; LIGURIA), it was colonised by the Romans in 106 BC who called it *Tolosa*. In 419 it became the capital of the Visigoths (see GOTHS),

and in 506 became capital of AQUITAINE. Simon IV de MONTFORT was killed in 1218 while besieging the town during the campaign against the ALBIGENSES. The last action of the PENINSULAR WAR was fought here in 1814. Toulouse is the fourth city of France, a centre of communications and the seat of an archbishopric and of a university (founded 1229). The old abbey church of St Sernin is probably the finest Romanesque church in France. Other remarkable churches include the cathedral of St Étienne, which is partly 12th-century. There are museums, art galleries, and libraries, and the town is a publishing and banking centre. A 16th–17th century bridge joins it to the western suburb of St-Cyprien. The new city of Le Mirail will house 100,000. Toulouse has aircraft, armament, chemical, footwear, metallurgical, textile, and flour industries and a large trade in agricultural produce. Population 440,000.

Toulouse-Lautrec-Monfa, Count Henri Marie Raymond de (1864–1901), French painter, born at Albi. He broke both legs in boyhood and this prevented their normal growth. He turned, in compensation, from aristocratic country life to painting and the contemplation of the amusements and vices of Paris. His prolific period was between 1885 and 1899, two famous studies of the Moulin Rouge and its denizens belonging to 1892. He visited England in 1895. Strongly influenced by DEGAS, he is more of a social commentator than that master. He painted with verve, and excelled in graphic art, notably in

Toulouse. The Champs Élysées. *(Topham/Fotogram)*

the posters he himself lithographed in colour for various Parisian resorts, which show the influence of Japanese prints. His subject matter is intimately connected with the life he led; scenes in bars, dance-halls and brothels predominate.

Bibliography: Studies by G. Coquiot, 1921, M. Joyant (2 vols), 1926, 1927; D. Cooper, *Toulouse-Lautrec*, 1955; J. Adhémar, *Toulouse-Lautrec, Complete Lithographs and Drypoints*, 1965; F. Novotny, *Toulouse-Lautrec*, 1969.

Toungoo, township and town of Pegu division, Burma, situated on the west bank of the Sittang river, down which logs from the extensive forests are floated to the coast. The town is the former capital of a 14th–16th century kingdom and has among its monuments the fine Shwesandaw pagoda, the ruins of which are preserved. The surrounding district produces rice and rubber. Area 1697 km^2; population 143,838.

Touraco, or turaco, a beautiful African bird of the family Musophagidae or plantain-eaters in the order Cuculiformes. The touraco has a small high bill, notched and serrated mandibles, short rounded wings and a long rounded tail. It has an erectile crest on the head. Many of them are brilliantly coloured with glossy blue, red, violet and green plumage. There are about 18 species including the violet plantain eater, *Muscophaga violacea*, and the giant, or great blue, touraco, *Corythaeola cristata*.

Touraine, old province of France, now the *département* of Indre-et-Loire and a part of Vienne. Its capital was Tours and it was named from the local Gallic tribe of the Turones. With Anjou and Orléanais, it was a source of dispute between France and England. It came to England with Henry II in 1154, and was regained for France by Joan of Arc.

Tourane, see Da Nang.

Tourcoing, French town in the *département* of Nord, 13 km north-east of Lille. It was the scene of a French victory over the Austrians in 1794. It has an important textile industry, especially in woollens (dating from the 12th century), commercial activities, and forms part of the Tourcoing-Lille-Roubaix urban complex. Population 98,800.

Touré, Ahmed Sékou (1922–), Guinean politician, born at Faranah and educated at an Islamic school in Conakry, various Guinean primary schools, and at a professional school in Conakry. In 1941 he took up a position in the Post and Telecommunications Service, and by 1945 had become secretary-general of the Post and Telecommunications Workers' Union, as well as being a member of the Guinean Consultative Labour Committee, the Guinean Consultative Territorial Committee, and various other administrative committees. In 1946 he entered the Guinean Treasury department and soon held the post of secretary-general of the Union of Treasury Employees. He was a founder member of, then vice-president of, the African Democratic Rally (RDA), which was established in 1946. By 1948 he had widened the scope of his trade union activities to become secretary-general of the Territorial Union of the General Workers' Confederation (CGT—Confédération Générale du Travail) and in 1950 secretary-general of the Co-ordination Committee, for French West Africa and Togoland, of the

CGT. In 1952, he was appointed secretary-general of the Guinean Democratic party, and by 1956 was mayor of Conakry and a deputy to the French National Assembly. He was co-founder and secretary, then president, of the General Union of Workers of Black Africa (UGTAN) formed in 1957. On 14 May 1957 he became vice-president of the Government Council, and then president. After Guinea's declaration of independence he held the post of Head of State, becoming the first president of the Republic of Guinea on 27 January 1961. He was re-elected in 1963, 1968, and 1974.

Bibliography: L. Adamolekun, *Sékou Touré's Guinea*, 1976.

Tourguenieff, or Tourgueniev, see Turgenev, Ivan Sergeevich.

Tourism, travel as a leisure pursuit, for recreational as opposed to business purposes. The term is also taken to embrace collectively the many components of the vast and relatively youthful industry that has grown up around the modern, mass-oriented product, from government-created ministries of tourism downwards.

Although mass tourism is a phenomenon of fairly recent origin, travel purely for pleasure is as old as recorded history itself. Alexander the Great, Strabo, Herodotus, and St Paul may be said to have been business travellers; not so the Queen of Sheba who journeyed some 1900 km from one end of Arabia to the other simply to satisfy her curiosity about King Solomon's wisdom ('to prove him with hard questions'). The spectators who made their way to Greece from countries both near and far for the first (776 BC) and subsequent Olympic Games were tourists, and so were the ancient Romans who regularly repaired to their seaside villas—and, in the case of the richest ones, to foreign parts—during the summer months.

It was within the Roman Empire that the foundations of modern tourism were laid: the network of well-constructed and well-maintained roads, studded at appropriate intervals with hostelries where travellers could rest, and with smaller intervening establishments where their horses could be changed, was necessary for the business of policing, extending, and administering so large an empire. But it was also extensively used by ordinary citizens for private, leisure journeys. With the decline of the Roman Empire, these roads gradually became both unsound and unsafe and tourism, except in such specialised forms as pilgrimages, virtually ceased to exist for more than a thousand years after the fifth century AD.

Its revival was largely stimulated by two factors, both still important motivations in modern tourism: the quest for knowledge and the quest for health. From early medieval times there had been an increasing amount of movements by scholars between the monasteries and other seats of learning throughout Europe, and this was followed in about the 16th century by a renewal of interest in the curative properties of mineral springs that had been practically ignored since the Roman era. By this time, of course, hotels or posting-houses had either disappeared altogether or had seriously deteriorated, to be replaced by monastic or private hospitality. But with the resurgence of tourism, and especially following the advent, in the 17th century, of the stage-coach, accommodation began once again to be built all over Europe: along the main routes of communication, in the major cultural and social centres, and at the spas.

By the beginning of the 18th century both the spa holiday and, to a lesser extent, the grand tour, had become part of an accepted way of life among certain elements of the aristocratic moneyed classes. Inland spas and their close rivals, the seaside watering-places, which were to be found in many European countries, prospered chiefly upon domestic tourism, and continued to do well upon it for over a century; overseas travel, on the other hand, as represented by the European grand tour, was a costly, difficult, and often dangerous business and developed more slowly. The start of the 19th century, however, saw the end of the Napoleonic wars, bringing peace and more settled political conditions to Europe. This state of affairs was followed by the invention of the steam engine, which heralded the industrial age, and these factors between them spurred the birth of mass tourism as we know it today. Industrialisation not only generated greater wealth but also caused it to be more widely disseminated among the various social classes; steamships and railways facilitated mobility and brought down its cost; greater political stability removed some of the more hazardous aspects of travel. Only lack of knowledge—of foreign languages and customs and currencies—and lack of sophistication prevented the newly-affluent middle classes from partaking of the pleasures of tourism, and this was soon remedied by the advent of Thomas COOK, pioneer of mass tourism.

So timely was his appearance on the scene that only 14 years were to separate his first organised public excursion (Leicester to Loughborough, for a temperance meeting, in 1841) from his first overseas tour (Leicester to the Paris Exhibition of 1855), and the organisation he built up throughout Europe and the Levant had handled its millionth passenger less than ten years after that, by 1864. Tourism in Europe was coming within the reach of ordinary people. Mr Cook and his emulators, together with the railway companies and other private interests, engaged as they were in the building of hotels as well as in the transportation of passengers, provided the ways; industrial affluence provided the means, and the growing prevalence of the annual paid holiday provided working people with the time. Two world wars, each stimulating colossal technological advances, particularly in the development of air transport and methods of communication, accelerated the spread of mass tourism to the present point where its influence is apparent even to the most resolutely non-travelling European man-in-the-street, for he has become involved in it, however unwillingly, on the receiving end.

The history of tourism in other parts of the world has followed much the same pattern. Most of it dates, however, from more recent times: the early navigators and explorers were motivated primarily by considerations of conquest, or commerce and trade, and were thus strictly speaking business travellers rather than tourists. Even Marco Polo, the history of whose travels in the 13th century provided the first recorded accounts of life in China by a European, originally went there in the company of merchantmen: his father and uncle who had already established trading links with the extreme Orient. Not until the early 19th century did tourism reach measurable proportions in the New World. Intertribal warfare and religious impulses prompted the movements of the early peoples—Mayas, Mixtecs, Toltecs, Incas, Aztecs—of Central and South America and, when the European conquerors reached the western hemisphere, the hazards of travel there deterred all but the most determined prospectors, traders, and land-hungry settlers from penetrating it very thoroughly until the coming of steam locomotion. Thereafter, as the railway pushed westwards across the United States and Canada, and hotel building kept pace with its progress, tourism within the United States, especially, increased rapidly. In the other direction, the development of commercial transatlantic steamship services in the 1840s opened the way for the first waves of American tourists to Europe (by the First World War their numbers were to swell to about 150,000 a year), and also brought the earliest European tourists, such as Isabella Bird, to the New World.

Isabella Bird (later Isabella Bishop) was but one of the intrepid British Victorians who took immediate advantage of the increasing scope afforded in the 19th century by the new methods of transport to travel outside Europe, and were thus the forerunners of tourism in the Third World. The Blunts, the Burtons and Doughty in the Middle East, Bent and Butler in South and West Africa, Chalmers, Miss Gordon Cumming, Swettenham and Wallace in the Far East, Marianne North in the Caribbean and South America; and Pembroke and Kingsley in the South Pacific, all played through their writings a part in opening up new and distant vistas for tourists. Until the advent of relatively cheap air travel following the Second World War, however, such destinations were accessible only to the comparatively few, and the combination of its recent origins and very high rate of development has made the impact of tourism upon the Third World a more disruptive affair altogether than is the case elsewhere.

The effects of modern tourism upon host countries—and, indeed, on modern tourists themselves—is a subject that has only latterly begun to arouse the interest of uncommitted observers of the tourist scene. The momentum that propels the complex machinery of modern tourism is enormous, but comes from such a variety of sources and is stimulated by such a variety of motives that a coherent, dispassionate, and disinterested approach to its evaluation is seldom achieved. Likewise, the distinctions between today's tourists are infinitely more blurred than those of a century ago, between Mr Cook's excursionists and travellers like Mrs Bridges who made an independent, 30-month world tour in the mid-19th century. Youthful 'drop-outs' in search of eternal values are tourists, so are accompanying spouses at international business conventions, and together with the itinerant millions in all the intervening gradations they constitute so heterogenous a throng that to assess both the influences they absorb and those that they exert amounts to a formidable exercise.

In the early stages of tourism, its benefits were obvious and its disadvantages easily circumvented: villages where new posting-houses had been built immediately became more prosperous, and those villagers who did not want their children corrupted by casual wayfarers simply kept them away from the hostelry. Nowadays the pros and cons are harder to appraise. Tourism is on the one hand held to break down artificial barriers, overcome misconceptions, and promote greater understanding between nations. It is also accused, on the other hand, of threatening to destroy the very goals it pursues simply by reaching them, not merely by polluting beaches and rivers, but also by requiring certain facilities that are alien to the terminal environment, such as roads and hotels. Since it is cheaper and simpler to provide these amenities to a standard pattern, the argument runs, tourism may well be precipitating its own destruction through increasing uniformity. Already people are beginning to become aware of the similarity everywhere of airports and hotels, food and drink, souvenirs and entertainment; nor is it escaping notice that the inhabitants of formerly remote places are adopting Western dress and manners, intoning popular Western songs, and addressing foreign visitors in accents gleaned from those very visitors' own canned-entertainment exports. If this trend is not halted by international accord and action, some maintain that tourism will eventually cease to be worthwhile to the tourists themselves, and will accordingly wither away.

Even the supposed financial advantages of tourism to host countries—especially, but by no means invariably, in the Third World—are beginning to be questioned and sometimes failing to stand up to close scrutiny. With the growth of vast international finance corporations and linked transportation and accommodation organisations it is questionable how much of the money tourists spend actually remains in the host country, and whether it is sufficient to show a profit for that country. Superficially, tourism appears to be an easy revenue earner for non-industrial countries, but the ministries of tourism they find it necessary to create are not cheap to maintain, nor are the power plants, sewers, road systems, and other components of tourist infrastructure cheap to build and run, and if much of the necessary equipment and construction materials must be imported, then will tourist revenues recover that expenditure and more? Furthermore, how much food and drink and other commodity items will also need to continue being imported to keep tourists happy, and how badly will previously agrarian-based economies suffer from the drift of labour away from the land?

Mass tourism has now reached the point (well over 200 million tourist arrivals world wide in 1974, and the great majority of Russians, Indians, and Chinese have not yet started travelling) where these and a host of ancillary questions are beginning to be of importance. In some places, however, where the answers might well prove to be largely negative, the process of appraisal has been abandoned because it is already too late to remedy the situation, except by calling a halt to further development. In other places the questions have yet to be asked and there is still time; in only a very few others are positive steps being taken to exert some sort of control over the burgeoning tourist phenomenon.

See also CIVIL AVIATION; HOTEL; INN.

Bibliography: H. Van Thal (Ed.), *Victoria's Subjects Travelled*, 1951; Central Office of Information, *Britain and International Tourism*, 1972; G. Young, *Tourism: Blessing or Blight*, 1973; D. McEwen (Ed.), *European Tourist Markets*, 1975; L. Turner and J. Ash, *The Golden Hordes: International Tourism and the Pleasure Periphery*, 1975; D. MacCannell, *The Tourist*, 1976; H. Robinson, *Geography of Tourism*, 1976. Reports of: *Economist Intelligence Unit* (quarterly); *Organisation for Economic Cooperation and Development* (irregularly); *World Tourist Organisation* (annually).

Tourmaline, a complex aluminium silicate mineral. It crystallises in the hexagonal system as prismatic crystals, often triangular in section. It also occurs massive and compact and in radiate fibrous masses. It is generally black, more rarely green, blue, and red and, still more rarely, colourless. The black variety is termed schorl. The mineral is pyro- and piezo-electric. On account of its hardness (7·5; specific gravity 3), it is sometimes cut as a gem. Varieties of tourmaline are rubellite (red or pink), indicolite (indigo blue), Brazilian sapphire (Berlin blue and transparent), Brazilian emerald (green), and peridot of Sri Lanka (yellow). Tourmaline occurs in granite, granitic pegmatites, and metamorphic rocks; it is found in Cornwall and Devon, England, Brazil, the USSR, and the USA. Gem tourmalines come mainly from Brazil. Its piezo-electric properties are utilised in the construction of pressure gauges.

Tournai (Flemish *Doornik*), town in the province of Hainaut, Belgium, situated on the River Scheldt, 43 km north-east of Mons. It is an important railway junction. Tournai's fine Romanesque and Gothic cathedral was built from the 11th to the 14th centuries. The belfry is the oldest in the country. There are quarries of freestone and limestone, and the chief manufactures are Brussels carpets, pottery, and woollen and cotton goods. Population 33,400.

Tournament, also tourney or joust, a form of martial sport very popular in the Middle Ages. Combats took place between men of noble rank, and a prize was given by the lady of the tournament to the knight who had displayed the greatest prowess. The custom was introduced into England from France during the 11th century. Tournaments were regulated by very strict etiquette as well as definite rules. The weapons used, spears, lances, swords or daggers, had to be blunted. Each jouster was attended by his squire, who acted as his second. In spite of precautions, however, accidents and rough dealings were not infrequent. In its earlier form the tournament often took the form of a private war; it was more than once banned (though ineffectively) by the Church, for example at the Councils of Clermont (1130) and the Lateran (1179). It was in the tournament that spectacular conventions of staging, including elaborate scenic emblems and rich symbolic costuming, were developed. In modern times the term is sometimes used for a military display, preferably of a competitive nature, although not necessarily so. The best example of this use of the word is the Royal Tournament which takes place every summer at Earls Court, London, and in which the three fighting services participate.

Bibliography: F. H. Cripps-Day, *History of the Tournament*, 1918.

Tournefort, Joseph Pitton de (1656–1708), French botanist, born at Aix, Provence; professor of botany at the Jardin des Plantes in 1683. His *Eléments de Botanique*, 1694, embodies a systematic arrangement of some 8000 species of plants, classified, mainly, according to the corolla (petals), a system for long adopted on the Continent. His chief work was *Institutiones Rei Herbariae* (3 vols), 1700, which prepared the way for Linnaeus, whose system of classification eventually superseded that of Tournefort.

Tourneur, Cyril, also Turnour or Turner (c. 1575–1626), English poet and dramatist. Very little is known of his life. He was a soldier much of the time, served in the Low Countries, accompanied Sir Edward Cecil's expedition to Cadiz, and died on his return to Kinsale, Ireland. In the six years which he devoted to literature Tourneur was a prolific writer. He wrote *The Atheist's Tragedy*, 1611, a poem, *The Transformed Metamorphosis*, which was discovered only in 1872, and a lost play, *The Nobleman*. Tourneur's masterpiece (although his authorship has been contested, some considering it the work of Thomas MIDDLETON) is *The Revenger's Tragedy*, 1607. Having close affinities with the morality tradition, it is a revenge play which explores courtly corruption and evil. It combines sensation and horror with psychological intensity and, on occasion, poetry of lyrical beauty.

Bibliography: His works were edited by J. C. Collins in 1878 and by A. Nicholl, 1930; see also T. S. Eliot, *Elizabethan Essays*, 1934; U. M. Ellis-Fermor, *The Jacobean Drama*, 1936; F. T. Bowers, *Elizabethan Revenge Tragedy*, 1940; A. Kernan, *The Cankered Muse*, 1959; P. Murray, *A Study of Cyril Tourneur*, 1966.

Tourniquet, a BANDAGE or cuff which can be tightened around the upper end of the thigh or arm to close the arteries to the limb and thus stop the flow of blood. Tourniquets should not be used in the First Aid treatment of bleeding, since direct pressure over a bleeding area is usually enough to stop the haemorrhage. (Tourniquets are seldom applied tightly enough to stop bleeding from arteries and if left in place for more than an hour they may cause death of muscles and nerves in the limb). The commonest use of tourniquets is in the operating theatre, to prevent bleeding during operations on the arm or leg. Care must be taken to note the time when the tourniquet was put on the patient and to make certain that it is removed at the end of an operation.

Tours, French city, of the *département* of Indre-et-Loire, lying between the rivers Loire and Cher, south-west of Paris. It was formerly the capital of TOURAINE. Known to the Romans as *Caesarodonum*, the town passed to the Visigoths in the 5th century. It developed in importance after the time of St MARTIN, and it was here that St GREGORY founded the abbey which was later associated with the name of ALCUIN and which became one of the great centres of learning in the Middle Ages. Near Tours in 732 Charles MARTEL stopped the advance of the Saracens. A silk industry was established by Louis XI, but it declined after the revocation of the EDICT OF NANTES, since most of the craftsmen were Huguenots. During the siege of Paris in 1870, Tours was the seat of the French government, and it was again the seat of the government for four days in 1940. The archiepiscopal cathedral (13th–16th centuries) has fine glass and cloisters. There is an archiepiscopal palace (17th–18th centuries), now a museum, and there are some notable old houses. Machinery, textiles, electrical goods, and chemicals are manufactured, there is a publishing industry, and there is a trade in agricultural produce, fruit, wines, and spirits. Tours has a university and is an important railway centre. Population 201,550.

Tourville, Anne Hilarion de Cotentin, Comte de (1642–1701), French admiral and Marshal of France, born in Normandy, distinguished himself in the battle of Palermo against the combined fleets of the Dutch and Spaniards (1676). But his most famous victory was won in 1690 off Beachy Head against the Dutch and British. On 19 May 1692 Tourville was defeated by a British fleet under Russell at La Hogue.

Toussaint, Anna Louisa Geertruida, see BOSBOOM-TOUSSAINT, ANNA LOUISA GEERTRUIDA.

Toussaint L'Ouverture, Pierre Dominique (1743–1803), Negro liberator of HAITI. Born a slave (although the grandson of an African chieftain), he taught himself to read, and this, together with his personal experience of the inhuman treatment of slaves, caused him to interest himself in the question of social justice. The French Revolution of 1789 had great repercussions in Haiti, one of France's most lucrative colonies. The outlawing of slavery by France caused considerable disturbances and conflicts here. By 1791 Toussaint found himself the leader of the Negro population and for ten years he and his Negro army successfully fought off French, British, and

Pierre Toussaint L'Ouverture. *(Bisonte)*

Spanish efforts to suppress the freedom movement. In 1801 he appointed himself governor-general for life, an action which caused Napoleon Bonaparte to despatch a strong expeditionary force which finally forced Toussaint's surrender. He was sent to a French prison where he died. In 1804 Haiti achieved its independence.

Bibliography: P. Sannon, *Histoire de Toussaint L'Ouverture*, 1930; C. L. R. James, *The Black Jacobin*, 1938; R. Korngold, *Citizen Toussaint*, 1944; S. Alexis, *Black Liberator: The Life of Toussaint L'Ouverture*, 1949.

Tout, Thomas Frederick (1855–1929), British historian, born in London; educated at St Olave's School, Southwark, and Balliol College, Oxford. He was professor of history at St David's College, Lampeter, from 1881 to 1890 and at Manchester University from 1890 to 1925. He was president of the Royal Historical Society in 1925. His works include a number of successful textbooks and very valuable contributions to the administrative history of medieval England which was his particular interest: *The Place of the Reign of Edward II in English History*, 1914; and *Chapters in the Administrative History of Medieval England*, 6 vols, 1920–31.

Tovey, Sir Donald Francis (1875–1940), British composer, pianist and scholar, born at Eton. He was early associated with JOACHIM and later with Casals. From childhood his knowledge of the musical classics, his memory and his contrapuntal skill were prodigious. Tovey entered Balliol College, Oxford, in 1894, where he studied classics. From 1900 he gave concerts in London, Berlin and Vienna, and from 1914 was Reid Professor of Music at Edinburgh University. He conducted the Reid Orchestra, Edinburgh, founded in 1924. Tovey's music is classical in form and style; as a pianist he was for some time in the front rank with his interpretations of Bach, Beethoven and Brahms. As a teacher of music he was regarded with the greatest esteem. His *Essays in Musical Analysis* (six vols), 1935–38, were notes for performances by the Reid Orchestra. His *Essays and Lectures on Music* were edited by H. Foss, 1950. He was knighted in 1935.

Bibliography: Life by M. Grierson, 1952.

Tower Hamlets. Regents Canal Dock seen from the Grand Union Canal. *(London Borough of Tower Hamlets)*

Towcester, town in NORTHAMPTONSHIRE, England, 13 km south-west of Northampton, on Watling Street and known to the Romans as *Lactodorum*. Towcester has an ancient parish church at which Archdeacon William Sponne (d. 1449) was rector for 28 years, during which time he founded the grammar school. The chief industry is light engineering, and there is an agricultural trade. Some 6 km to the south-west is Silverstone, with a notable motor-race track, formerly an airfield. Population (1971) 2750.

Tower, lofty structure (other than a dome) rising above the general roof-level of a building, whether for defence or observation, or as a landmark. See also CAMPANILE; MINARET; PHAROS; SPIRE; STEEPLE.

Tower Bridge, the easternmost bridge over the River Thames, built in 1886–94. It was designed by Sir Horace Jones and Sir John Wolfe Barry and it cost the city corporation £1·5 million. It has two high Gothic towers 60·9 m apart, and is connected with either bank by single-span suspension bridges. The span between the towers in the centre of the river consists of a pair of drawbridges, which can be raised in 1·5 minutes, and thus permit the passage of vessels.

Tower Hamlets, a London borough created on 1 April 1965, comprising the former metropolitan boroughs of Bethnal Green, Poplar, and Stepney. The borough's estimated population in 1974 was 150,000.

Settlement in the area dates from the time of the Romans. Stepney was a London suburb as early as the composition of the Domesday Book, when it had a population of about 800. The Royal MINT and the TOWER OF LONDON both lay just outside the City of London and within the borough. Another early foundation was the Royal Hospital of St Katherine by the Tower, which, founded by Queen Matilda in 1148, has always had queens as its patrons. It was founded for the sick and elderly, and in the 1820s, when the site was used for St Katherine's Dock, it was moved to Regent's Park. In the 1950s it moved back to Stepney and is now located in Butcher Row, partly housed in an 18th-century merchant's house. The chapel still has medieval stalls and carvings. St Dunstan's church dates from the Middle Ages, and the manor house at Bromley from the 15th century. Ratcliff, a Stepney hamlet, has long been a dock area and it was from here in the 16th century that Frobisher and Willoughby sailed to Russia while searching for the northwest passage. Later this section of riverside became notorious for its rowdy public houses. Wapping, an adjacent hamlet, was the site of execution docks, where such men as Captain Kidd were executed for crimes on the high seas. The Thames tunnel, built between 1824 and 1843, links Wapping and Rotherhithe. Blackwall docks were built in 1612–14, followed by the West India Docks in 1799–1802, the East India Docks in 1803–06, and Milwall Docks in 1868. The area of the West India and Millwall docks is a peninsula known as the Isle of Dogs. Ships were built here, one of the most famous being the Great Eastern which was launched 1858, but this trade has now almost ceased. The construction of Limehouse Cut in 1770 linking the River Lea and the Thames, and the Regent's Canal between 1812 and 1820, helped further the progress of industrialisation. Limehouse, an area adjacent to the docks, received the name from the lime kilns which were in use from the Middle Ages until the 19th century; it was also known for its considerable Chinese population. In the 17th and 18th centuries many Huguenot refugees settled in the area and Spitalfields became a centre for silk-weaving; even today one of the main industries of the area is the clothing trade. Bow had a porcelain factory in the 18th century producing 'Bow China'. Bethnal Green was mostly farmland in the 18th century until, as did the rest of the area, it became largely residential.

Tower Hamlets is also an industrial area; its products include chemicals, matches, paints, glasswork, paper, foodstuffs, and engineering. Bells have been cast at Whitechapel Bell Foundry for over 400 years, and these hang in many famous churches including Westminster Abbey. The Liberty Bell, which was rung to mark the acceptance by the US Congress of the Declaration of Independence, was cast in Whitechapel in 1752. Although several of the docks are now closed the remainder provide employment for many local workers, and are continually modernised; a recent feature is the bulk wine terminal at the India and Millwall Docks which can now hold over 4·5 million litres.

Bibliography: V. Leff and G. H. Blunden, *The Story of Tower Hamlets*, 1967.

Tower Mills, see WINDMILL.

Tower of London, situated on the north bank of the Thames, the most historic building in London, connected intimately with the tragic side of English history because of the long roll of state prisoners lodged there, so many of whom were executed within or outside its walls. It was first built by William the Conqueror to protect and control the City. His building, the Great Tower or Keep, generally called the White Tower, is the oldest part of the Tower of London, and lay within the Roman walled city. Enlargement in the 12th century carried the buildings beyond the wall. Part of the Tower therefore lies outside the City, but it forms a Liberty in itself. Considerable successive additions and alterations have been made to the buildings, and they exhibit a variety of architectural styles from the 11th to the 20th centuries. The inner ward is defended by a wall flanked by 13 towers. The outer ward is defended by another wall, flanked by six towers on the south, or river side and by bastions on the north-west and north-east, the whole surrounded by a moat, now empty. At the south-west angle there were originally three drawbridges (none survives) and three towers (two survive) before entrance was gained to the outer ward.

The Tower of London has been a fortress, a palace, a prison, has housed the public records, the Royal Mint, the royal menagerie (from the 13th or 14th century until 1834, when it was removed to Regent's Park), the Royal Observatory (for a short time), and was for centuries the arsenal for small arms. It is now a museum of armour, in a limited sense a fortress (it has a military garrison), the repository of the Crown Jewels, and the greatest showpiece of London. As a palace (the palace buildings have not survived), it was used by all sovereigns down to James I. By custom each sovereign lodged in the Tower before coronation and then rode in procession to Westminster.

The White Tower houses the Armouries, and contains

the Chapel of St John, the earliest Norman building in London. In the north-western corner of the inner ward is the Chapel of St Peter ad Vincula, rebuilt in 1512 after a fire, where many famous people executed after incarceration in the Tower are buried, among them Anne Boleyn, Sir Thomas More, Lady Jane Grey, the Earl of Essex, and the Duke of Monmouth. The space south of the chapel, Tower Green, is where executions took place within the Tower. The Bloody Tower, built by Henry III, is believed to be the scene of the murder of the 'Princes in the Tower', Edward V and his brother, the Duke of York. Sir Walter Raleigh was in this tower for 13 years. Adjoining it is the Wakefield Tower, also built by Henry III, which houses the Crown Jewels. On its western side there formerly stood the Great Hall, pulled down during the Commonwealth, where Anne Boleyn was tried. The Beauchamp Tower, built probably in Henry III's reign, contains the inscriptions of many famous prisoners. The famous Traitors' Gate, under St Thomas' Tower, originally a useful river-entrance to the Tower, later became a convenient landing-place for prisoners tried at Westminster. On Tower Hill, north-west of the Tower, a permanent scaffold was erected in 1465, though the first recorded execution had taken place in 1388; and the last was that of Simon Fraser, Lord Lovat, in 1747.

See also YEOMEN OF THE GUARD.

Bibliography: C. Hibbert, *Tower of London*, 1972; A. L. Rowse, *The Tower of London in the History of the Nation*, 1972.

The Tower of London. *(Aerofilms)*

Town and Country Planning

Town and Country Planning. Many ancient and medieval towns, particularly colonial towns, were originally laid out on definite plans, often by powerful rulers for military reasons, e.g. the Greek cities (Priene, Ephesus), Roman towns (Chester) and the BASTIDES (Flint).

Most towns, however, grew organically. Even where there was originally a plan, there was no continuous control of changes in and extensions of towns, except in a few large estates developed by private landowners on a leasehold basis. In most countries land is held in parcels of varying sizes by many owners, and the siting and character of buildings have been matters of individual enterprise. Villages grew into towns and towns into great cities without any overall consideration of the total results. In Great Britain during the 18th and 19th centuries the industrial revolution led to a vastly increased concentration of production and wealth in cities. The opportunities for work in factories attracted large numbers of people into the cities from the countryside. The speed at which this occurred created low standards in housing for the new work force. Rows and rows of drab terraces were packed tightly together around the work places. They were populated at the highest possible densities and characterised by overcrowding and insanitary conditions. As conditions worsened and created health hazards, such as cholera epidemics, government action was demanded in the interests of social well-being. This took the form of public health legislation, e.g. in establishing minimum standards for control of street widths and heights and structure and layout of buildings. This legislation was extended to cover the whole town and was the forerunner of modern town planning.

A famous early example of a public health project occurred in Paris (1853–269) when HAUSSMAN prepared a comprehensive plan for drainage and roads. A similar scheme was carried out by Joseph Bazalgette in London (1848–65). The political leaders of France and England (Napoleon III and Disraeli) realised that this kind of project led to greater political stability.

Another approach to reducing the problems of the industrial town was that of the Utopian socialists. Robert Owen (1771–1858) attempted to put into practice his ideas for reorganising urban life in New Lanark and other towns. His new political and economic premises resulted in better pay, shorter working hours, better housing, increased education and leisure, and an improved design and layout of buildings. This experiment was followed by many others, e.g. SALTAIRE (1853), BOURNVILLE (1878), PORT SUNLIGHT (1887), which provided the foundation for the garden city movement popularised by Ebenezer Howard's book *Tomorrow: a Peaceful Path to Real Reform* (see GARDEN CITIES; HOWARD, SIR EBENEZER).

Interest in Howard's ideas led to the founding of the Garden City Association in 1899. This later expanded its aims to include the promotion of town planning, and changed its name to the Garden Cities and Town Planning Association.

The development of modern transport enabled the growth of vast suburban extensions to the cities, but the spacious surroundings of suburban life were offset by the long journeys between home and work, a continuing characteristic of cities today. Recognition that the problems caused by industrialisation and city growth make public control of the use of land necessary has come slowly. But it is now agreed in all countries, especially where rising standards are demanded for houses, schools, business and public buildings, roads, sports, entertainment and cultural facilities, and airfields, that the needs cannot be met without a considerable measure of planning control.

Hence the emergence of town and country planning as a new branch of government. Planning legislation in the modern sense came into vogue in the 1860s and 1870s, beginning in Italy, Sweden, Austria and Germany with laws to control the layout of suburban extensions, and gradually spreading to other countries. In Britain the Housing, Town Planning, etc., Act of 1909, while not a successful piece of legislation, was the first attempt to introduce some compulsion into the organisation of the city environment. It also reflected a new role played by the state in helping society to face rapid social and economic

Town and Country Planning. The bastide town of Aigues Mortes, built by Louis IX as the embarkation point for his two crusades. The walls and the medieval town plan remain. *(Popperfoto)*

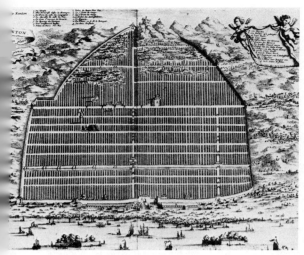

Town and Country Planning. Town plan of Canton, one of China's main commercial and trading centres and the first port to be regularly visited by European traders. From *L'Ambassade de la Compagnie Orientale*, 1662. *(Bisonte)*

1942, while accepting this general thesis, stressed the safeguarding of good agricultural land and countryside amenities; and that of the Uthwatt Committee on *Compensation and Betterment*, 1942, proposed stronger powers for public acquisition of land and a radical solution to the compensation problem. These three reports, and the problems created by war damage in many towns, led to an entirely new conception of national town and country planning.

In 1943 all land in Great Britain was brought under 'interim planning control', and in 1944 urban authorities were given positive powers to acquire, replan and rebuild areas of extensive war damage, bad layout or obsolete development.

These and previous Acts were replaced by the two Town and Country Planning Acts of 1947, for England and Wales and for Scotland, since consolidated by the Act of 1962. By these the town and country planning administration and procedure were revolutionised. Planning powers, previously exercised in England and Wales by district councils and all boroughs, were transferred to county councils and county borough councils, with permissive delegation of detailed administration to the smaller authorities; and in Scotland to the large burghs, the county councils and the two small burghs of St Andrews and Thurso. All planning authorities made a full survey of physical and other resources and existing development, and a series of plans, and revised these each five years. Development plans on 1 in (2·54 cm) and 6 in (15·24 cm) scales showed the allocations of land for particular uses for 20 years ahead. Where necessary there were also central development area (CDA) plans, often associated with compulsory purchase orders (CPO) for unifying ownerships for redevelopment schemes. All plans

change through town planning. The Act gave permissive powers to certain local authorities to make plans, subject to ministerial approval, for areas in course of or prospect of new development. These plans (few of which were completed) aimed at 'securing proper sanitary conditions, amenity and convenience'. The Act was therefore a logical extension of the public health legislation previously introduced. In 1919 such planning became obligatory on local authorities with populations of 20,000 or over. The 1919 Act introduced the principle of state subsidies for housing and began the widespread growth of council house estates. House-building was spurred on by a new political awareness of the need for an extensive programme of working-class housing under the post-war slogan, 'Homes for Heroes', and by rapid developments in transportation which opened up new areas for suburbanisation. In Acts of 1925 and 1932 the powers were extended to all county district and county borough councils, and to the parts of towns already built up. Useful control was exercised and experience gained, but all these Acts proved inadequate for the right placing of new development or for good redevelopment. Most planning areas were too small, and few authorities could meet the costs of compensation for desirable restrictions.

Realisation that more comprehensive measures were needed prompted the appointment in 1937 of the Royal Commission on the Distribution of Population, set up to inquire into the causes and effects of population distribution in Great Britain, to assess the directions of change, and to suggest remedial measures in the national interest. Its report (the Barlow Report) in 1940 recommended planned redevelopment of congested areas, the dispersal of part of their industry and population to garden cities and smaller towns, the promotion of a better balance of employment throughout the country, and a national authority to give effect to these proposals. The report of the Scott Committee on *Land Utilisation in Rural Areas*,

Town and Country Planning. Cumbernauld New Town, Scotland, founded in 1956. The first phase of the multi-storey town centre is shown in the background. *(Bisonte)*

were subject to approval, in England and Wales by the Ministry of Housing and Local Government, and in Scotland by the Department of Health for Scotland. Draft plans were made public and the ministers had to consider local objections. Plans were prepared in this way for most parts of the country. Pressures for change in planning legislation built up during the early 1960s, and led to the appointment by the government of the Planning Advisory Group (PAG) in 1964, charged with examining the deficiencies of the existing planning system and with making recommendations for a new system. The PAG reported the following year that existing development plans were inadequate to deal with the increased dimension of planning problems that now required a comprehensive approach (see BUCHANAN REPORT). Other problems identified were the slow and cumbersome administrative procedures required by the existing Act that did not match the current pace of change, and the need for greater involvement in planning decisions by the public. The PAG therefore recommended that there should be a two-tier system of development planning, separating strategic from local issues, that central government approval should only be required for strategic level plans, and that more publicity of plans at both levels was needed.

These recommendations were all incorporated into the 1968 Town and Country Planning Act for England and Wales (and into the 1969 Act for Scotland). These Acts were modified in 1971 and 1972 to incorporate the needs of local government reorganisation in 1972.

Structure Plans are concerned with broad, strategic issues and require the approval of the Secretary of State. A structure plan may be prepared for the whole of an administrative county, and separately for large urban areas within it, and may be prepared jointly by more than one authority. The plan is a written statement of the local authority's main long-term intentions for the area, and is concerned with 'the social, economic and physical systems of an area, so far as they are subject to planning control and influence'. They may be illustrated by maps which are not on an ordnance survey base.

Local Plans deal with detailed matters within the structure plan's framework, and only require 'adoption' by the local planning authority to come into operation. They are intended to express the authority's proposals in more detail, including the precise definition of land required for different uses. There are three kinds: (1) district plans for detailed planning of parts of the area covered by the structure plan; (2) action area plans for comprehensive planning of areas under immediate change and identified in the structure plan; (3) subject plans, dealing with single aspects, e.g. mineral extraction, tourism, etc.

With old-style development plans there was usually a public inquiry held to examine objections. This has been replaced by a new and more informal procedure, the 'examination in public', for which a code of practice was published in 1973.

In the reorganised local government system the county council prepare structure plans and the county or district council prepare local plans. The allocation of responsibility for the latter is decided in a Development Plan Scheme, agreed by both authorities.

Other important legislative changes and reports of recent years include:

Civic Amenities Act, 1967, which placed a duty on local authorities to identify areas of special architectural or historic interest, and to designate them as Conservation Areas in which more stringent controls are imposed.

The Skeffington Report (People and Planning). A committee was set up by government in 1968 to examine public participation in planning, and was reported in 1969. The report recommended, for example, that people be kept informed throughout the preparation of a structure and local plan for their area, and that the local authorities should consider continuously representations made by members of the public. In addition there should be 'set pauses' in the process of plan preparation when the public's views are positively sought. It also recommended that local authorities should set up community forums where members of organisations could discuss planning matters, as well as have community development officers to stimulate interest amongst the 'non-joiners'. Government expressed its views on these recommendations in Circular 52/72, rejecting the idea of community development officers, while remaining non-commital about community forums, but accepting the intentions of the report's other ideas.

Planning permission has to be sought for all proposed developments, including changes of use of land or premises and the construction or alteration of buildings, roads, etc.—with the exception of farm buildings and minor alterations under General Development Orders. There is a right of appeal to the Minister against local planning decisions, and in important cases public inquiries into objections are held. Some 13,000 appeals are submitted each year.

The Town and Country Planning Acts also empower public authorities to acquire and develop land, and to retain or lease it, and provide for government grants for these purposes. In some circumstances an owner can require the authority to purchase his land if planning proposals (e.g. a road widening which would obliterate his house) rendered it unsaleable at a reasonable price. Normally compensation at full market value is payable for land acquired, though there are complicated exceptions to this arising from the rule requiring the value to be assessed with regard to the provisions of the current development plan. Compensation for refusal of permission to develop land is in general limited to development value as it was in 1948 where building development is prohibited. No compensation at all is paid where restrictions (e.g. an intensity of development lower than the most profitable) are imposed, nor where development is prohibited because the land is liable to flood or subsidence, nor where permission is delayed because of current lack of an available water supply or sewerage. This was the situation which emerged after successive amendments to the financial provisions of the Town and Country Planning Act of 1947, in 1953, 1954, 1959 and 1961. It was further modified by the Land Commission Act, 1967, which imposed a 'betterment levy' of a percentage of the increased value caused by permitted changes of use on land acquired for development.

Other important provisions of the Town and Country Planning Acts are for the control of outdoor advertisements (see ADVERTISING), for preserving buildings of architectural or historic interest, and for preserving trees, woodland and countryside (see NATIONAL PARKS;

NATIONAL TRUST). Conditions for the restoration of land may be imposed where permission is given for mineral workings.

The Acts also provide that applications for consent for building factories or extensions in excess of certain limits and in certain areas must be supported by Department of Industry certificates that the proposals are 'consistent with the proper distribution of industry'. The Department also has powers of planning importance under the Local Employment and Industry Acts, 1945 and 1950, for assisting the establishing of factories in areas of unemployment and declining industry designated as development in intermediate areas (see INDUSTRIAL TRADING ESTATES). The same principle was extended to office premises in 1965.

The aim of British planning now is to balance the claims of agriculture, industry, housing, public services, military developments, mineral workings, etc., so that land is used in the best interests of the community with the least possible hardship to personal interests. The national policy is to check the growth of London and other over-large conurbations, to reduce their congestion, to promote development in less concentrated regions, to safeguard good agricultural land, to reserve green belts around towns and to disperse 'overspills' of persons and employment to new towns and smaller existing towns. Since 1956 there has been an increasing accent on slum clearance and large-scale reconstruction within the cities, with much debate as to how to provide adequately for the 'overspill' if the rebuilding is to be on satisfactory standards of housing density and open space, and as to how to deal with the growing problem of traffic congestion and car parking. More recently, with the decline in rate of economic and population growth, the emphasis has shifted towards policies of improvements to existing buildings, traffic management and more efficient use of existing resources. (See GREEN BELTS; NEW TOWNS; OPEN SPACES; OVERSPILL; TRANSPORT.)

Though the necessity of much dispersal is generally accepted, planning theorists differ as to its scale and as to the permissible density of housing redevelopment. Some follow the Swiss architect LE CORBUSIER in favouring very high blocks of flats, contending that high central density would reduce journeys to work and the need of dispersal, or that dispersal would absorb too much agricultural land. Others argue for terrace housing at high densities with very small gardens. Advocates of dispersal reply that flats are acceptable only to a small minority; that they are very costly and involve huge housing subsidies; and that the utmost compression of housing would economise a negligible percentage of farm land. Ultimately the resolution of these warring views depends upon effective public opinion. (See also FLAT.)

Regional Planning. In 1964–65 official regional studies

Town and Country Planning. Table of new towns.

Name	Date of designation	Existing population	Population at 31 Dec 1974	Ultimate proposed population	Estimated capital expenditure to 31 Dec 1974 £m
London Region					
Basildon	1949	5149	84900	134000	135·100
Bracknell	1949	9100	41300	55–60000	63·100
Crawley	1947	4500	71000	85000	51·120
Harlow	1947	8500	82250	undecided	92·000
Hatfield	1948	21000	26000	29000	14·585
Hemel Hempstead	1947	6700	73000	80000	49·226
Stevenage	1946	18500	74800	100–105000	63·460
Welwyn Garden City	1948		40000	50000	26·003
Rest of England		60			
Aycliffe	1947	235638	25000	45000	28·600
Central Lancashire	1970	15700	242500	420000*	22·500
Corby	1950	40000	53750	83000	32·108
Milton Keynes	1967	131120	64000	250000	92·817
Northampton	1968	81000	145400	260000	45·250
Peterborough	1967	200	98000	182000 **	56·174
Peterlee	1948	32000	26500	30000	30·280
Redditch	1964	28500	49730	90000	41·226
Runcorn	1964	10000	48200	100000	53·375
Skelmersdale	1961	70000	39000	80000	63·212
Telford	1968	122300	94200	250000	68·000
Warrington	1968	20000	133000	225000	16·000
Washington	1964		43000	80000	48·343
Wales		12000			
Cumbra	1949	5000	43000	55000	37·341
Mid-Wales (Newtown)	1967		6700	13000	7·810
Scotland		3000			
Cumbernauld	1955	2400	38500	100000	62·851
East Kilbride	1947	1100	71500	90000	86·300
Glenrothes	1948	34600	32500	70000	42·000
Irvine	1966	2000	50100	120000	22·703
Livingstone	1962	7250	22470	100000	47·674
Stonehouse	1973		7800	70000	2·020

* By 2001
**Without natural increase

Town and Country Planning

were published on social characteristics, population changes, employment, land use and communications, for central Scotland and for north-east, north-west, and south-east England and the Midlands, and the government announced a positive policy for the promotion of a better distribution of population and economic activity. An economic planning board of officials of the relevant government departments was appointed in each region, along with an economic planning council to advise on the formulation of a regional plan. The new set-up involved a close integration of town and country planning and economic planning both regionally and nationally. However, the plans produced were oriented towards helping central government to allocate resources to the regions. They have not provided the context in which local planning authorities can produce structure plans. There is no machinery for deciding on the distribution of resources within regions on the basis of a comprehensive strategy. This requires decisions concerning priorities between local authorities. This problem was considered in the Kilbrandon Report (or Royal Commission on the Constitution), 1974.

Planning Associations. The Town and Country Planning Association (17 Carlton House Terrace, London SW1), a voluntary society open to anyone interested, has since 1899 consistently advocated the policy of city decongestion, green belts and dispersal to new towns, etc. (see GARDEN CITIES). The National Housing and Town Planning Council (42 Devonshire Street, London W1) represents the local authorities concerned with these subjects. The Royal Town Planning Institute is the chief professional body granting qualifications for planning. Several universities, polytechnics and other professional institutions also grant degrees and qualifications. The

Town and Country Planning. The Arc de Triomphe de l'Étoile, Paris, with its grand boulevards connecting principal historic buildings and establishing prominent sites for monuments, became a model for urban planning in the 19th century. *(Mansell Collection)*

Councils for the Preservation of Rural England, Wales and Scotland, with their many county branches, maintain a close watch on developments in the countryside.

Town Planning Abroad. Most of the countries belonging to the Commonwealth adopted the planning laws and administration that were devised in this country after the Second World War. However, the more recent developments embodied in the 1968 Town and Country Planning Act and subsequent legislation have not necessarily been adopted. Town plans for many of the major cities in Commonwealth countries were prepared by British consultants during the 1950s (see CHANDIGARH). The less developed countries that belong to the Commonwealth are only just beginning to develop their own experts in town planning, and so most planning in these countries is still carried out by foreign experts under the auspices of the World Bank or the United Nations.

In the USA the system of planning law and administration is very different from that in Great Britain and involves far less control of development. It relies principally on zoning laws rather than comprehensive plans and policies, and the administration has no permanent structure. Planners are employed on fixed contracts to carry out particular projects or consultants are used. The laws and the extent of planning projects vary from state to state.

In the USSR and other Communist countries of Europe a very elaborate system of planning exists and the powers to implement these plans are very strong, as there is no free market system. Town plans must conform to a hierarchy of other plans, e.g. at the regional, republic and national levels. All policies have to conform to the national economic plan.

Other countries in Europe vary considerably in their town and country planning procedures. Some, such as Spain and Italy, have minimal sets of laws to control development, while others have systems that are similar in comprehensiveness to that of Britain, as with the Netherlands and Denmark. In Germany and Sweden extensive ownership of land by cities has facilitated planned development; in Germany also an age-old municipal control of building pre-dated planning in producing some harmony and order; yet the great cities exhibit the usual defects. The International Federation for Housing and Planning (offices at The Hague) holds world congresses of planners from all countries, and is an important means of exchange of experience and ideas. The United Nations agencies (ECOSOC and WHO) also contribute to such exchange. There is now a vast output of planning literature in all languages, and a constant flow of visiting experts between countries, and many come to Great Britain to study its recent developments in law and policy.

Bibliography: Sir R. Unwin, *Town Planning in Practice*, 1911; P. Geddes, *Cities in Evolution*, 1916; P. Abercrombie, *Town and Country Planning*, 1933; Le Corbusier, *Concerning Town Planning*, 1947; W. Ashworth, *The Genesis of Modern British Town Planning*, 1954; L. B. Keeble, *Principles and Practice of Town and Country Planning*, 1959; L. Mumford, *The City in History*, 1962; D. Heap, *Outline of Planning Law*, 1963; L. Benevolo, *The Origins of Modern Town Planning*, 1967; J. B. McLoughlin, *Urban and Regional Planning*, 1969; J. B. Cullingworth, *Town and Country Planning*, 1972; P. Hall and others, *The Containment of Urban England*, 1974; G. Cherry, *The Evolution of British Town Planning*, 1974. Also journals: *Town and Country Planning* (monthly), *The Planner* (monthly), but especially May 1974, Vol. 60; *Town Planning Review* (quarterly); also bibliographies for NATIONAL PARKS; NEW TOWNS; TRANSPORT.

Town Council, see BOROUGH; LOCAL GOVERNMENT.

Towneley Plays, The, see MIRACLE PLAY.

Townes, Charles Hard (1915–), US physicist, born at Greenville, South Carolina; educated at Furman University, Greenville, Duke University, and the California Institute of Technology. From 1939 to 1947 he was a member of the technical staff of Bell Telephone Laboratories where he worked on radar. In 1948 he joined the teaching staff of Columbia University. Townes wished to solve the problem of generating high-intensity microwaves (ELECTROMAGNETIC WAVES with a wavelength between 10 mm and 1 m). In 1951 (while sitting on a park bench) he conceived the idea of irradiating ammonia with low-intensity microwaves at the frequency at which the ammonia molecules naturally vibrated. Each molecule would then 'resonate' and emit its own microwave radiation which would affect other molecules in a chain reaction. This was the principle of the 'maser' (microwave amplification by stimulated emission of radiation). In 1953 Townes and his colleagues produced a working maser. In 1957 he proposed that the technique should be extended to amplification of visible light—the LASER— and in 1960 T. H. Maiman succeeded in constructing such a device. Townes was awarded the Nobel Prize for physics in 1964 jointly with the Soviet physicists N. G. Basov and A. M. Prokhorov, who had independently worked out the theory of the maser. From 1961 to 1967 Townes was professor of physics at Massachusetts Institute of Technology and since 1967 has been professor at the University of California, Berkeley. He has been prominent in the public use of science, including serving as chairman from 1964 to 1969 of NASA's scientific and technical advisory committee for manned space flight.

Townshend, Charles Townshend, 2nd Viscount (1674–1738), English statesman, born at Raynham Hall, Norfolk; educated at Eton and King's College, Cambridge. He was one of the commissioners for the Union with Scotland, was joint plenipotentiary with Marlborough at The Hague, and negotiated with Holland the Barrier Treaty. Dismissed in 1712 on the formation of the Harley ministry, he kept up a correspondence with the court of Hanover, secured the confidence of George I, and on the latter's accession was appointed secretary of state of the Northern Department. He lost favour in 1716, but in 1720 he was president of the council under Stanhope, and on Stanhope's death in 1721 became again secretary of state, a position he held until 1730, when he retired into private life. He took a considerable interest in agriculture, encouraged turnip growing, greatly improved the rotation of crops, and came to be known as 'Turnip Townshend'.

Townshend, George Townshend, 4th Viscount and 1st Marquess (1724–1807), British soldier, brother of Charles Townshend (1725–67). He took part in the battles of Dettingen (1743), Fontenoy (1745), Culloden (1746), and Laffeldt (1747). At Quebec he took command after the fall of Wolfe. From 1767 to 1772 he was lord lieutenant of Ireland, and from 1783 was master general of the ordnance. He was made field-marshal in 1796.

Township, or vill, originally probably a group of allodial (see ALLODIUM) proprietors united by community or agricultural interests, the chief officer of which was the town-reeve. The township is almost certainly one of the antecedents of the medieval borough. The term is not now in common use, but until recently meant legally a town containing more than one parishioner. In some areas of Scotland parishes are still termed townships. See also LOCAL GOVERNMENT.

Townsville, port of Queensland, Australia, 1339 km north of Brisbane. It is the chief commercial and administrative centre for a large section of northern Queensland, contains a large bulk sugar refinery, and is the chief port through which are exported sugar, wool, meat (chilled, frozen, and canned), meat by-products, sheep, cattle, minerals, coal, silver, lead, zinc concentrates, copper, nickel, and uranium. Population 68,591.

Towse, Sir Beachcroft (1864–1948), British soldier and president of the National Institute for the Blind. He went to Wellington College and, in 1885, was gazetted to the Gordon Highlanders, with whom he served in Egypt, Malta, and India. He was with the Chitral Relief Force, and was at the storming of the Malakand Pass. In 1899 he went with his regiment to South Africa, where he was awarded the Victoria Cross, was severely wounded, and lost his sight. In 1901 he joined the council of the National Institute for the Blind, of which he became chairman in 1921. His maxim was: 'Blindness can either master a man or a man can master blindness'. He converted his house at Goring into the first of the Institute's homes for the rehabilitation for the blind.

Towton, parish in the SELBY District, North Yorkshire, England, midway between LEEDS and YORK, the scene of the Yorkist victory of 1461. Population (1971) 105.

Towy (Welsh *Tywi*), river of Wales, rising in the hills between Dyfed and Powys. It flows south, passing Llandovery and Carmarthen, and enters Carmarthen Bay at Llanstephan. Length 106 km.

Towyn, seaside resort of Meirionydd District, GWYNEDD, North Wales, situated on Cardigan Bay. Its church of St Cadfan is the largest and most interesting example of Norman architecture (1150–1200) in Meirionydd. Within it is preserved an inscribed stone dating back to the 7th century and considered to be probably the most ancient source where the Welsh language is used. Population 3500.

Toxaemia, the presence of toxins (poisons) in the blood. The term is generally used to mean the presence of toxins due to absorption from a local infection. For toxaemia of pregnancy, see PREGNANCY.

Toxicology, the study of POISONS. Its main branches deal with the chemical nature of poisons, their origin and preparation; their physiological action and the tests by means of which their presence may be detected; the pathological changes due to their presence and the recognition of them by post-mortem evidence; and their chemical reactions with a view to the determination of the antidote and its physiological action. Poisons may act on

Toxin

various organs and systems of the body; for example, acids and alkalis are corrosive to the alimentary tract, carbon monoxide reduces the oxygen-carrying capacity of the blood by combining with haemoglobin; digitalis affects the heart, and strychnine affects the brain and spinal cord.

Toxin, any poisonous substance derived from a plant (particularly a fungus or bacterium), animal, or virus. See PASSIVE IMMUNISATION; POISONS.

Toxophily, see ARCHERY.

Toy-dogs, diminutive breeds usually developed purely as pets. See BRUSSELS GRIFFON; CHIHUAHUA; ENGLISH TOY TERRIER; ITALIAN GREYHOUND; KING CHARLES SPANIEL; MALTESE DOG; PAPILLON; PEKINGESE; POMERANIAN; PUG; YORKSHIRE TERRIER.

Toy Theatre, as opposed to three-dimensional PUPPETS, is a product of the 19th-century popular print trade in England and several European countries. Japan had its own version, dating from slightly earlier. Traditionally, European toy theatre consisted of printed paper scenery, characters and theatre proscenium to be pasted on card, cut out and mounted on a wooden structure with a stage, for model performances. Characters were moved by wires from above or the sides, with a slight agitation accompanying speech.

In England, prints were coloured by hand professionally or sold uncoloured for colouring at home, hence the phrase 'A Penny Plain and Twopence Coloured', made famous by Robert Louis Stevenson's essay of that title on English toy theatre. Prints could be bought singly, at first in printshops and later in small stationers and tobacconists. Called the 'Juvenile Drama', it originated in the theatrical souvenir portrait trade around 1811, developing by popular demand of children into complete plays with playbooks based on real London productions, which at that time were particularly suitable for boisterous reconstruction. The craze reached its peak in 1835, while generations of children revelled in cutting and colouring for family performances. Favourite among hundreds published was Pocock's 'The Miller and His Men'. Diaghilev produced a ballet based on English toy theatre called 'The Triumph of Neptune', with music by Lord Berners.

Foreign toy theatre, though often based on real plays or operas and provided with playbooks, is less actable than the English version, which supplies each character in

Toy Theatre. 'Pollock's Characters', sheet from a battle of Waterloo story.

762

many costumes and poses (e.g. fainting, dancing). In 'Der Trompeter von Säkkingen' the hero blows his trumpet throughout the play. Foreign prints are sometimes for setting up rather than acting, for example a farm or school scene. Whether actable or not, each publisher, at home and abroad, had his range of castles, forests, cottages, palaces, caves and landscapes—wild, rustic or exotic—with sets of characters for a particular play, or sheets of persons of every type set out in neat rows, Hamlet rubbing shoulders with the country doctor. The plays from real theatre on which prints were based were many, while the theatres themselves were modelled on real ones or invented. Popular sizes for backdrop scenes varied from 20 × 15 cm to 57 × 40 cm. A typical English character stood 6 to 7 cm high. Each country had its own variations: English character sheets are full of movement in the Rowlandson–Cruikshank tradition, the scenery is 'picturesque'; France produced stiff little woodcuts of Rococo salons, neat gardens, large scenes of a draper's shop, a Café de la Gare, or a Casino, besides numerous 'Napoleon' subjects. German sheets include Biedemeyer rooms with their buxom owners, haunted glens for 'Der Freischutz', knights' castles looking either romantically medieval or something like a gasworks. Austrian sets record splendid operas from Weber or Meyerbeer. Denmark issued a huge series of wholesome plays for children from Jules Verne, Hans Anderson and the Copenhagen theatres, requiring numerous fairy-tale settings, students' attics, open-air beer gardens. In the USA, English plays were reissued with new titles and an American slant by 'Seltz's American Boys' Theatre'. Quantities of such material was published from the 1830s; from about 1880 the fashion began to fade as the imaginative outlet provided by the plays became the prerogative of modern publishing methods and magazines. Today, 'out of date' has become 'period toy', and business continues in London and Copenhagen.

Toy theatre provides the collector with a unique record of 19th-century productions for which little other pictorial information survives. In addition, it presents a cavalcade of graphic techniques: etching and engraving, wood engraving, pen lithography, chromo-lithography and modern reproduction.

Bibliography: W. Röhler, *Grosse Liebe zu Kleinen Theatern*, 1963; G. Speaight, *The History of the English Toy Theatre*, rev. ed. 1969; G. Garde, *Theater-Geschichte im Spiegel der Kinder-Theater*, 1971.

Toynbee, Arnold (1889–1975), British historian, born in London, the nephew of Arnold and Paget Toynbee. He was educated at Winchester and Balliol College, Oxford, of which he later became fellow and tutor, 1912–15. After serving for a short time as professor of Byzantine and modern Greek at London University he became, in 1925, director of studies at the then newly founded ROYAL INSTITUTE OF INTERNATIONAL AFFAIRS (Chatham House), from which he retired in 1955. It is with this institution that his name is chiefly associated. There he wrote contemporary history in the annual *Survey of International Affairs*. The 12 volumes which comprise *A Study of History*, published between 1934 and 1961, form a standard work on the evolution of civilisations which reveals great erudition in the treatment of ancient and modern historical problems.

His other publications include: *Greek Historical Thought*, 1924; *Greek Civilisation and Character*, 1924; *The World After the Peace Conference*, 1925; *A Journey to China*, 1931; *Christianity and Civilisation*, 1940; *Civilisation on Trial*, 1948; *The World and the West*, 1953; *Hellenism*, 1959; *Comparing Notes: a Dialogue across a Generation*, 1963; *Between Niger and Nile*, 1965; *Hannibal's Legacy*, 1965; *Change and Habitat*, 1966; *Acquaintances*, 1967; *The Crucible of Christianity*, 1968; *Cities of Destiny*, 1969; *Some Problems of Greek History*, 1969; *Surviving the Future*, 1971; *A Study of History* (illustrated abridgement), 1972.

Toynbee, Joseph (1815–66), British otologist (ear specialist), born at Heckington, Lincolnshire. He studied particularly the pathology of the ear and published in 1860 his medical classic, *Diseases of the Ear*. He was appointed in 1857 aural surgeon to St Mary's Hospital, London, which was the first general hospital to establish an ear department. Toynbee died as a result of an experiment in which he inhaled chloroform and prussic acid to test its effect on tinnitus (noises) of the ear.

Toynbee, (Theodore) Philip (1916–), English novelist, born at Oxford, son of Arnold TOYNBEE; educated at Rugby and Christ Church. He was the first Communist president of the Oxford Union. Later he resigned from the Communists and supported Labour, and in 1950 he joined the staff of the *Observer*. He wrote several experimental novels, *The Savage Days*, 1937, *The Barricades*, 1943, and *Tea With Mrs Goodman*, 1947; and several others in verse, including *The Fearful Choice*, 1958, and *Two Brothers*, 1964. He is a frequent contributor to literary and other periodicals, such as the *New Statesman*, *Nation*, and *Horizon*.

Toynbee Hall, Whitechapel, London, the first English university settlement, founded by Canon Barnett, Rector of St Jude's, Whitechapel, and named after his friend, Arnold Toynbee (1852–83). See also SOCIAL SETTLEMENTS.

Toyohara, see YUZHNO-SAKHALINSK.

Toyonaka, city of Ōsaka-fu, Japan, located 12 km to the north of Ōsaka. Since 1955 Toyonaka has developed as a dormitory settlement for Ōsaka commuters. The growth rate of its population has been unusually high, even by Japanese standards. Ōsaka International Airport is located on the eastern fringe of the city. Population (1974) 381,000.

Trabzon (ancient *Trapezus*, formerly *Trebizond*), seaport on the Black Sea coast of Asiatic Turkey and capital of Trabzon province. The province is mountainous and heavily forested and is noted for the production of hazelnuts. Trabzon was formerly of great significance as an outlet for the wares of Kurdistan and Persia, but lost much of its transit trade when the Batumi–Tbilisi railway was opened. Since the Second World War, the port has been modernised and the road to Iran improved so that some of this traffic has returned. Trabzon was founded in 600 BC by Greek settlers from Sinope. In 1204 it became the capital of TREBIZOND, a kingdom founded by Alexius Comnenus which lasted until its capture by the Turks in 1462. It once had a large Armenian population but is now almost wholly Turkish. It was captured by the Russians

Trace Element

in 1916 but was retaken by the Turks in 1918. In addition to its important transit trade it exports the local agricultural products. Population (town) 80,800; (province) 659,120.

Trace Element, a chemical element present in minute quantities. Trace elements are important in the NUTRITION of both plants and animals. See also FERTILISERS; MINERALS IN FOOD.

Tracery, in architecture, occurs only in the Gothic period. At first it took the form of 'plate' tracery, in which a thin panel of stone or wood was inserted into the window frame, and this was pierced by circular and lancet-shaped openings. Later, only the upper part of the window above the lancets was made from a single pierced plate (see fig. 1). The next stage, first taken at Reims and then in England c. 1240, was to reduce the masonry between the various openings to narrow vertical moulded bars of stone (see MULLION) and to continue these moulded bars around the tops of the lancets and around the circular window, thus forming 'geometrical tracery' (fig. 2), so called because it consisted of regular geometrical shapes; it is characteristic of the period c. 1250–1300 in England. In the third stage (fig. 3), the masons introduced flowing curvilinear designs instead of regular geometric forms; these were introduced at the beginning of the 14th century in England and later became popular in France. Finally, the flowing designs gave way to nearly rectilinear 'lights' and, as the size of windows increased, both in width and height, horizontal transoms were introduced to strengthen the mullions (fig. 4). This 'rectilinear' or 'perpendicular' tracery, largely restricted to England, prevailed until the end of the true Gothic style in the middle of the 16th century.

See also ENGLISH ARCHITECTURE.

Trachea, or windpipe, the air tube which leads from the larynx to the bronchi. It is about 11 cm long and is made up of fibro-elastic membrane which is kept open by C-shaped cartilaginous rings about 1·6 cm in diameter. The incomplete portion of the C is at the back where the trachea is in contact with the oesophagus. The interior is lined with submucous tissue and ciliated epithelium. The trachea begins at the larynx and proceeds downwards in front of the oesophagus until it bifurcates into the two BRONCHI.

Tracheid, a conducting cell in the wood, particularly of ferns and gymnosperms. It is a long, dead narrow cell containing watery sap. Its walls are thickened with lignin, a complex carbohydrate. Tracheids differ from vessel elements of the xylem in being closed at upper and lower ends. Like them, however, tracheids conduct water and solutes from the roots to other parts of the plant.

Tracery. Diagram showing the development of English tracery.

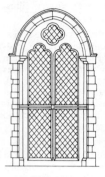

Plate tracery

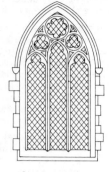

Geometrical tracery

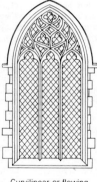

Curvilinear or flowing tracery

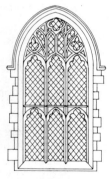

Penpendicular or rectilinear tracery, with transome